American Literature

CONCISE EDITION

American Literature
A Prentice Hall Anthology

EMORY ELLIOTT, General Editor
University of California, Riverside

LINDA K. KERBER
University of Iowa

A. WALTON LITZ
Princeton University

TERENCE MARTIN
Indiana University

PRENTICE HALL, ENGLEWOOD CLIFFS, NEW JERSEY 07632

Library of Congress Cataloging-in-Publication Data
American literature: a Prentice Hall anthology / Emory Elliott,
  general editor . . . [et al.]. — Concise ed.
      p. cm.
    Includes bibliographical references and index.
    ISBN 0-13-025750-8
    1. American literature.   I. Elliott, Emory (date).
PS507.A5757   1991
810.8--dc20   90-26101
                                                                   CIP

Acquisition editor: Kate Morgan
*Editorial/production supervision and
   interior design:* Hilda Tauber
Development editor: Karen S. Karlin
Prepress buyer: Herb Klein
Manufacturing buyer: Patrice Fraccio
Photo research: Barbara Schultz
Photo editor: Lorinda Morris-Nantz
Design director: Florence Dara Silverman
Art preparation: Maria Piper, Carol Hyland
Cover design: Lydia Gershey
Cover art: "Bird of Paradise" applique quilt-top, ca. 1858–1863 (detail).
Artist unknown. Poughkeepsie, N.Y. 87 × 71½". Museum of American Folk Art;
Gift of the Trustees. (Photograph courtesy George E. Schoellkopf Gallery)

© 1991 by Prentice-Hall, Inc.
A Simon & Schuster Company
Englewood Cliffs, New Jersey 07632

Printed in the United States of America
10 9 8 7 6 5 4 3 2 1

ISBN   0-13-025750-8

Prentice-Hall International (UK) Limited, *London*
Prentice-Hall of Australia Pty. Limited, *Sydney*
Prentice-Hall Canada Inc., *Toronto*
Prentice-Hall Hispanoamericana, S.A., *Mexico*
Prentice-Hall of India Private Limited, *New Delhi*
Prentice-Hall of Japan, Inc., *Tokyo*
Simon & Schuster Asia Pte. Ltd., *Singapore*
Editora Prentice-Hall do Brasil, Ltda., *Rio de Janeiro*

Contents

═ PART TWO ═

The Age of the Democratic Revolution: The Late 18th Century   **201**

LATE 18TH-CENTURY NONFICTION PROSE   *211*

PART THREE

Progress and Crisis: The Early to Middle 19th Century   333

PART FOUR

Expansion and National Redefinition: The Late 19th Century **993**

LATE 19TH-CENTURY POETRY *1001*

Emily Dickinson (1830–1886)   **1105**

Hilda Doolittle (H. D.) (1886–1961)   **1473**

Ezra Pound (1885–1972)   **1477**

Marianne Moore (1887–1972)   **1486**

T. S. Eliot (1888–1965)   **1497**

PART SIX

*Diversity, Technology, and Social Change: The Middle
to Late 20th Century*   **1685**

MIDDLE TO LATE 20TH-CENTURY DRAMA   *1694*

MIDDLE TO LATE 20TH-CENTURY POETRY   *1790*

MIDDLE TO LATE 20TH-CENTURY FICTION   *1953*

Preface

During the past twenty years, the field of American literature has been going through one of the most exciting periods in its development as a discipline. Of the many changes in literary theory and in critical methods, the most significant advance affecting the teaching of American writing—and thereby anthologies of American literature—has been the discovery and rediscovery of important works that had received little critical attention in the past. For the most part, these newly valued texts are by women writers and members of ethnic and racial minority groups whose works had been misunderstood, overlooked, or consciously rejected by the professors who were in positions to make such decisions, most of whom were themselves male and primarily interested in the English heritage of American literature. Thus, for example, anthologies always used to begin with the writings of the English Puritans who came to what was referred to as a "new world." One recent shift has been the recognition that long before the English arrived in the land now called America, that land had been inhabited for centuries by peoples who possessed rich and complex literary cultures that form part of American literature. Before the English arrived, explorers from Spain, Italy, and other parts of the world had also left a literary record of their encounters with this land and its peoples. Today's literature courses and anthologies present these earlier writings as more accurate beginnings of American literature.

Whereas the list of writers and texts in American literature has grown substantially as a result of these new attitudes, the number of weeks in each semester and the number of courses in college curricula allotted for the teaching of the subject have not expanded. Teachers in the field would like more time to do justice to the established writers such as Emerson, Melville, James, and Faulkner, whose works have long been studied. Concurrently, they want to introduce students to the many rewarding texts by writers such as Kate Chopin, Charlotte Perkins Gilman, Emma Lazarus, Charles W. Chesnutt, Paul Laurence Dunbar, Booker T. Washington, and W. E. B. Du Bois, to note a few examples from the 1880s and 1890s alone. To accommodate these desires, anthology editors have been producing longer and longer texts. Teachers lament that they are overwhelmed by the huge number of choices to be made and frustrated by the hundreds of pages to be covered in a given year. The large physical size of the books has even become an inconvenience, and in some cases the efforts of publishers to produce smaller books has led to the use of very thin paper and a reduced typeface that makes reading the texts difficult.

Balancing the Canon

Before beginning this anthology, Prentice Hall conducted an extensive survey of American literature teachers at a wide range of institutions of higher learning. The results demonstrated that most teachers want an anthology that is more concise and, at the same time, provides a balance of works by the long-established authors and by those receiving recognition and attention long overdue. Therefore, the editors of *American Literature: A Prentice Hall Anthology* have attempted to produce a text that is complete and contemporary in its inclusion of the widest representation of American writing and yet is more concise than other available texts. In every decision about the table of contents, the format, and the critical apparatus of this anthology, we have kept the needs of teachers and students in the forefront. By making the difficult decision to exclude some texts by established authors that are not frequently taught, we have been able to make room for ample selections by writers excluded in the past. We believe that this anthology provides teachers and students with a practical and useable text that fully reflects the cultural diversity of our national literature.

Indeed, teachers will find many authors and selections that either have not been included in previous anthologies or have only very recently been acknowledged as part of the canon. Phillis Wheatley and Olaudah Equiano are included with Philip Freneau and Joel Barlow to represent African-American authors in the late eighteenth century. Susanna Haswell Rowson is presented with Charles Brockden Brown to exemplify the important women novelists of the 1780s and 1790s. The Southwest humorist Thomas Bangs Thorpe appears with James Fenimore Cooper and Edgar Allan Poe to reflect the present attention being given to the regional writing of the early nineteenth century. Fanny Fern joins Lydia Maria Child, Margaret Fuller, Rebecca Harding Davis, and Frances E. W. Harper in the antebellum period, and the Declaration of Sentiments, issued at the Seneca Falls Women's Rights Convention, provides readers with a chorus of voices for women's rights in the 1840s. In the twentieth-century sections, Zora Neale Hurston, Alice Walker, Toni Morrison, Paula Gunn Allen, Simon J. Ortiz, and Louise Glück are included with T. S. Eliot, William Faulkner, and Flannery O'Connor. We offer the complete texts of "Benito Cereno," "Life in the Iron-Mills," *Nature,* the *Narrative of the Life of Frederick Douglass,* and "The Waste Land," as well as N. Scott Momaday's *The Way to Rainy Mountain.* These are only a few examples of the newly recognized and established authors and texts that readers will find here. The limited number of selections by Hemingway, Fitzgerald, and Faulkner are the result of restrictions their publishers have placed upon reprinting their works.

Placing Works in Contexts

This anthology focuses strongly upon the connections between American literature and its various contexts: historical, political, economic, religious, intellectual, and international. Because teachers report that students are often daunted by extremely long period introductions that attempt to cover too much history and literature at once, we have provided shorter introductory background segments and placed them closer to the appropriate texts. We have avoided overly long introductions and designed a combination of historical background essays by editor-historian Linda K. Kerber and essays on the various literary genres. This separation enables readers to perceive the literary matters in relation to—but separate from—the political and social contexts at the time of writing. The repeated juxtaposition of literary text with historical material reminds the readers of the connections between them as well. The historical introductions engage controversial issues of American history and examine the conflicts and failures as well as the victories of America's past. Genre introductions discuss the development and complexities of the literary forms and styles in relation to the intellectual movements of the time periods.

Along with the emphasis upon linking texts and contexts more closely, we have placed in each section several "Contexts" boxes, which present relevant historical and critical statements or examples of other pertinent literature. In some cases, the "Contexts" boxes present special developments: a series of boxes in the twentieth-century sections traces the chronological development of different schools of literary criticism and theory. Throughout the text, boxes help to define and illustrate key terms such as "neoclassicism," "romanticism," and "modernism." Significant nonliterary documents also appear, including portions of the "I Have a Dream" speech by Dr. Martin Luther King, Jr.

Adding the Visual Element

With the strong emphasis upon the visual in our society, it is surprising how few illustrations appear in literature anthologies. The Prentice Hall anthology has portraits of authors and additional illustrations that capture the feel of the historical periods, the action and events that surrounded the writing of the literature, and the associations between writing and other arts. For example, students using this text will be able to see the domes and columns of neoclassical architecture and thus better grasp the relationship between the balance and form of eighteenth-century writing and the style of neoclassical buildings. The illustrations add an exciting feature to the Prentice Hall anthology that distinguishes it sharply from others.

With the daily experiences of teachers and students in mind, we have sought to make an anthology that people will truly enjoy using. Avoiding overly long biographical essays, we have made the headnotes more concise. In addition to historical period introductions, we have provided illustrated, eye-catching time lines that integrate key historical and literary events and their dates. Readers will obtain a clear picture of the chronology and the interconnection of texts and contexts. A glossary at the end of the volume serves to underscore and define literary terms that arise in the historical and genre introductions and headnotes as well as those that naturally come up in classroom discussions. An appendix, "Writing About Literature," discusses the student's special problems involved in writing an essay about literature and outlines procedures for meeting the challenge successfully. We have tried to annotate the texts sensibly in order to provide in a concise form the essential information students need. Dates for the initial publication of works are listed at the end of each selection; when known, dates of composition precede the publication dates. Whenever possible, we have used the approved, definitive editions of the texts. For ease of reading we have modernized archaic punctuation and spelling of some works in the early period. Readers should note that within excerpts of works, three centered asterisks indicate an omission of a paragraph or more.

ACKNOWLEDGMENTS

Many scholars provided various forms of assistance in the preparation of this anthology. We are grateful to Anne Agee, Anne Arundel Community College; Steven Gould Axelrod, University of California, Riverside; David Arnold, University of California, Riverside; David Austin; Lea Baechler, Columbia University; Rosemarie Battaglia, Michigan State University; Ronald Bosco, State University of New York, Albany; Jack Branscomb, East Tennessee State University; Brian Bremen, University of Texas; Mark Busby, Texas A & M University; James Buzzard, Harvard University; Bruce Coad, Mountain View College; Joan Corcoran, Columbia University; Gwen Crane, Princeton University; Keith Cushman, University of North Carolina, Greensboro; Allan Emery, Bowling Green State University; Joseph Essid, Indiana University; Virginia Feury-Gagnon; Thomas Fick, Southeastern Louisiana University; Joan Frederick, James Madison University; Sam Girgus, Vanderbilt University; Sonja Froiland, Indiana University; Maureen Goldman, Bentley College; Consuela Golden; Janet Gray, Princeton University; Jennifer M. Ginn, North Carolina State University; June Chase Hankins, Southwest Texas State University; Joseph Heininger, University of Michigan; Wendy Hirsh, Columbia University; Anne Hiemstra, Columbia University; Michael J. Hoffman, University of California, Davis; Joonok Huh, Northern Colorado University; Mary Hunter, University of California, Riverside; Claudia Johnson, University of Alabama; Emory D. Jones, Northeast Mississippi Community College; Alan Kaufman, Bergen Community College; Margot Kelley, Indiana University; Katherine Kinney, University of California, Riverside; James A. Levernier, University of Arkansas, Little Rock; Ina Lipkowitz, Columbia University; Michael Lofaro, University of Tennessee; Mason Lowance, University of Massachusetts; Robert Lynch, University of Nebraska; John McCammon, Indiana University; John H. McElroy, University of Arizona; June J. McManus, San Antonio College; Marilyn Miller; Randall Moon, University of California, Riverside; Nancy A. Mower, University of Hawaii; Anne C. Myers, DeVry Institute of Technology, Phoenix; Louis Owens, University of New Mexico; Jay Parini, Middlebury College; Mark Patterson, University of Washington; Timothy Redman, Ohio State University; Mary Margaret Richards, University of Texas, Permian Basin; Judith M. Riggin, Northern Virginia Community College; Michael Robertson, Lafayette College; James K. Ruppert, University of Alaska; Ramón Saldivar, University of Texas, Austin; Rosalind Sackoff; William J. Scheick, University of Texas; James

Scrimgeour; Thomas E. Shields, East Carolina University; Frank Shuffelton, Rochester University; William Shurr, University of Tennessee; Nancy Craig Simmons, Virginia Polytechnic Institute and State University; Pat Skantze, Columbia University; Diane Stevens, Indiana University; Gordon Tapper, Columbia University; John Timmerman, Calvin College; David Van Leer, University of California, Davis; Edward Watts, Indiana University; Lori J. Williams, Indiana University; Ann Woodlief, Virginia Commonwealth University; and David Wyatt, University of Maryland. We also thank Josephine Koster Tarvers of Rutgers University, New Brunswick, for composing the essay "Writing About Literature."

Several students, secretaries, family members, and friends have provided various forms of editorial assistance. We wish to thank Deborah Barker, Sara Lynn Bowers, Marcia Hack, Bruce Hagood, Carla Latteri, Kandi Leonard, Barbara Burke Martin, Elizabeth Patton, Marsha Rosh, Maggi Schuman, Estelle Shapiro-Childers, and Holly Witten. The staffs of the following libraries have been quite helpful: the University of California, Riverside; the University of California, Los Angeles; the Huntington Library; Princeton University; the University of Iowa; and Indiana University, especially Anthony Shipps.

Finally, we wish to thank the following people at Prentice Hall who worked closely with us: our development editor, Karen Karlin, whose endurance, patience, and editorial skills have been remarkable; Hilda Tauber, our production editor and designer, for her imaginative work and flexible planning; and editor in chief Phil Miller and senior English editor Kate Morgan for directing the project with wisdom and good cheer. Others who contributed in important ways are supplements editor Ann Knitel, photo editor Lorinda Morris-Nantz, design director Florence Silverman, permissions researcher Mary Helen Fitzgerald, marketing managers Tracy Augustine and Gina Sluss, and assistants Fran Falk, Heidi Moore, Page Poore, and Kathy Hursch.

EMORY ELLIOTT
General Editor

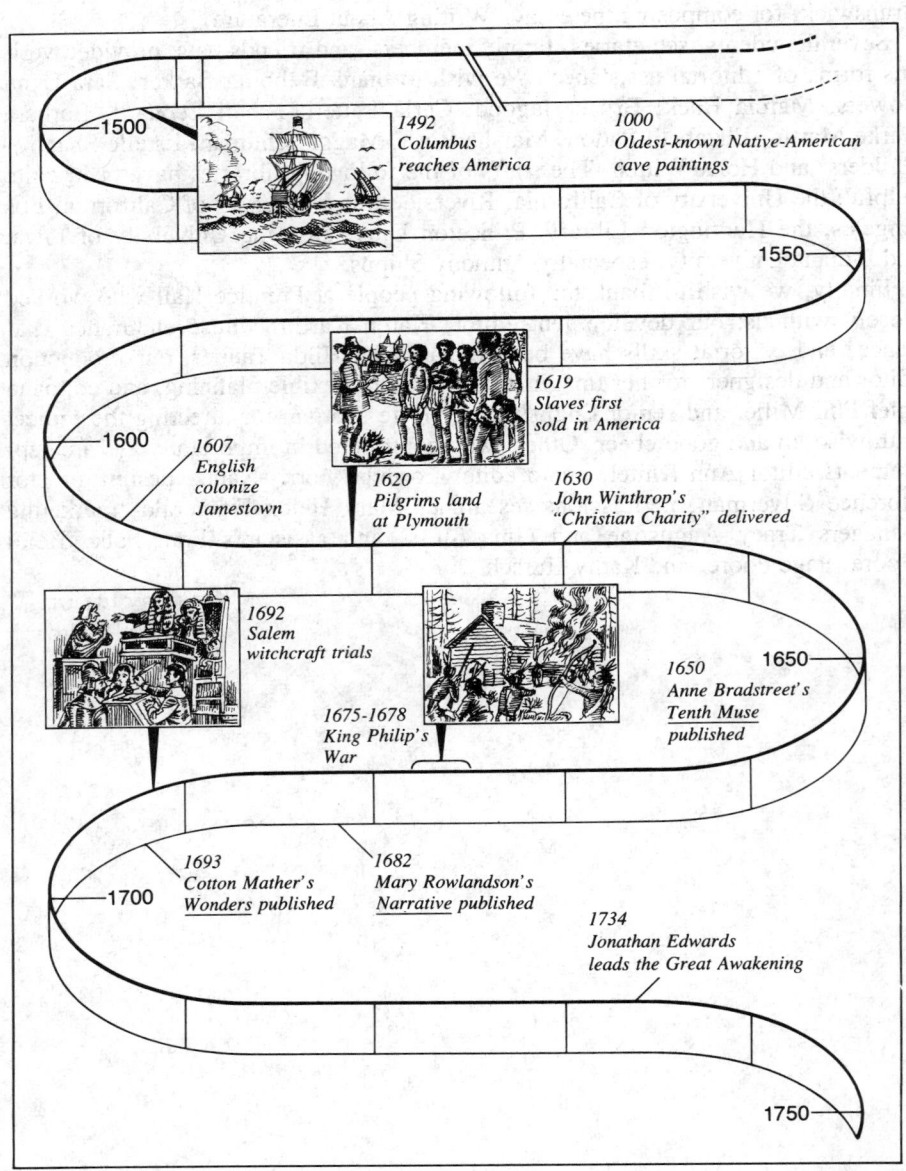

1000
Oldest-known Native-American
cave paintings

1492
Columbus
reaches America

1619
Slaves first
sold in America

1607
English
colonize
Jamestown

1620
Pilgrims land
at Plymouth

1630
John Winthrop's
"Christian Charity" delivered

1692
Salem
witchcraft trials

1675-1678
King Philip's
War

1650
Anne Bradstreet's
Tenth Muse
published

1693
Cotton Mather's
Wonders published

1682
Mary Rowlandson's
Narrative published

1734
Jonathan Edwards
leads the Great Awakening

1500

1550

1600

1650

1700

1750

The European Colonization of the Americas

Through the Middle 18th Century

> *Historians . . . believe that the meaning of an event is perpetually open to revision, that its meaning for successive generations will differ from its contemporary meaning or its causes.*
>
> —JAMES AXTELL, The European and the Indian, 1981

We are so used to the terms "Old World" and "New World" that we can easily fall into the habit of thinking that, somehow, the Western Hemisphere is literally new. As late as the eighteenth century, a French scientist explained that Florida is swampy because it had not quite dried out from the Flood. We inherit these terms from European explorers, who worked the concept of old and new into their rationalization for conquest and destruction. Their conquest myth—that America was virgin land, empty wilderness, inhabited by savages incapable of civilization—is still resonant in the twentieth century. This myth began in Columbus's own lifetime and received an early and powerful literary formulation in William Shakespeare's final play, *The Tempest* (1611). In that play European civilization is embodied in a wise philosopher/scientist who is shipwrecked with his beautiful daughter, Miranda, on an island in the "brave new world." There he uses his knowledge to subdue an evil witch, who is native to the island, and her crude and hostile son, Caliban.

The peoples of the Americas were not witches. They were descendants of the several hundred Asians who had moved across the now-submerged land bridge between Siberia and Alaska as early as twenty-five thousand years ago, over the course of hundreds of centuries. When Christopher Columbus stepped out on a gleaming beach of white coral on October 12, 1492, he in effect reconstituted the land bridge. The land he claimed was no empty wilderness; it was inhabited by some 100 million people speaking over 850 languages. The earliest Americans had developed a stunning range of societies. Many, such as the Algonquins of the Northeast, were hunting and gathering clans; others, including the Mayas and Aztecs of the central regions and the Incas of the South, had developed highly com-

1

plex, sophisticated societies characterized by major engineering feats, precise mathematical calculation, astronomy, and written languages.

Columbus came as explorer and scientist but also as conqueror. Historians traditionally distinguish between his expedition and those of the "conquistadores"—his successors, including Hernando Cortés and Francisco Pizarro, who came explicitly as military men and intended to conquer the region by means of military power. However, Columbus was commissioned by Queen Isabella of Spain as part of a great celebration of the defeat of the Muslim kings of Grenada in 1492, of the unification of the territories held by the crowns of Aragon and Castille, and of the expulsion from Spain of the last Moslems and of the Jews. His expedition celebrated the extirpation of a great multiracial, multicultural society. Columbus's expedition was delayed three days because the harbor at Cádiz, Spain, was blocked by the boats of desperate Jewish refugees. As the historian Samuel Eliot Morison wrote (*Admiral of the Ocean Sea*, 1942), Columbus could see weeping women and children on board.

The era of the invasion of America, from the fifteenth century through the eighteenth, was characterized from the start by a complex mixture of courage, scientific quest, and display of imperial power. The invasion was accompanied by major dislocations. First, Europeans disrupted Native-American societies on a scale that was truly genocidal. Second, Europeans who had already begun to subject black Africans to forced labor in the sugar plantations of the Azores developed an extensive transatlantic slave trade, which affected the African societies that sold captives and the communities to which captive labor was sold as well as the men and women forced into lifelong captivity. Third, the era of settlement was shaped by major dislocations within European society, notably the Protestant Reformation, both a religious and social revolution, and by the commercial revolution engendered by the importation of wealth from the Americas. Fourth and last, the encounter with the Americas posed an extraordinary intellectual challenge to Europeans, who struggled to understand the world they had encountered and to express this understanding in political theory, law, scientific description and prediction, and imaginative literature. All writing, however mundane, is an act of the imagination; nowhere is that principle easier to discern than in the fiction and nonfiction of the American colonies and early republic. In those genres, men and women struggled for words and narrative structures to describe experiences for which their contemporaries in Europe had no parallel, sometimes no appropriate words.

From the start, Columbus found the American lands strange and troubling. "The trees were as different from ours as day from night, and so the fruits, the herbage, the rocks, and all things," Columbus wrote (as quoted in Alfred W. Crosby, Jr., *The Columbian Exchange* [1972]). One sixteenth-century explorer in Brazil complained that he found only three familiar plants—purslane, basil, and a certain fern. Animals, too, were unfamiliar. Explorers noted that the animals tended to be smaller than their Asian and African counterparts: for example, the American jaguar was considerably smaller than the African lion. The explorers were amazed at the iguana, at electric eels, and at catfish (Crosby, 1972).

═CONTEXTS═

Impressions of the New World

The very first American literatures, oral narratives and poems of the Native American, may have been produced contemporaneously with similar expressions in Europe as early as 1000 B.C. A literary record written in stone dating about A.D. 1000 still exists in narrative cave paintings in what is now the southwestern United States. The written literature of the first 130 years after the arrival of Europeans in the Americas consist of travel narratives, personal accounts and letters, histories, and propaganda encouraging migration to the New World.

The journals and letters of Columbus, Giovanni da Verrazzano, Alvar Núñez Cabeza de Vaca, Amerigo Vespucci, Richard Hakluyt, Pedro de Casteñeda, Thomas Harriot, and Samuel de Champlain testify to the awe and confusion with which European minds confronted very different cultures and peoples. In Europe important Renaissance authors drew upon these accounts in creating influential images. William Shakespeare created a clearly negative image of the New World's natives through his grotesque character Caliban in *The Tempest*. In contrast, the Elizabethan poet Michael Drayton created a glowingly positive image of the New World's natural resources in his poem "To the Virginian Voyage" (1619). The poem was written in response to Richard Hakluyt's accounts of early explorations of the New World and in anticipation of the Virginia Company's expedition to colonize the land in 1607.

To the Virginian Voyage

> Virginia,
> Earth's only paradise,
>
> Where nature hath in store
> Fowl, venison, and fish,
>   And the fruitful'st soil
>   Without your toil
> Three harvests more,
> All greater than your wish.
>   Michael Drayton, 1606, 1619

The intellectual system brought by Columbus and his successors had no room for what they saw. Christians believed that the book of Genesis was definitive in that "there was one God, and there had been one Creation . . . . [But] if God had created all of the life forms in one week in one place and they had then spread out . . . over the whole world, then why are life forms in the eastern and western hemispheres so different?" (Crosby, 1972). Indeed, what could be made of the people found in America? They looked very different from any people Europeans had encountered. Europeans "knew" that individual possession was the "proper" way to handle property; what could they think of the Carib people, who shared what they possessed? Christians "knew" that heterosexual monogamy was the way to handle sex; what could they think when they encountered people happily practicing promiscuity, polygamy, and homosexuality (Francis Jennings, *The Invasion of America*, 1975)?

Faced with the challenge of the unknown and the inexplicable, Europeans could either invoke cultural toleration or condemn Native Americans as allies of the Devil. Virtually all Europeans did the latter. The Devil's true allies were the germs the European conquerors carried to the New World. Since antiquity, Asians, Africans, and Europeans were in contact through trade and had built up some immunity to each others' diseases. However, the peoples of America had been isolated from Europe. As descendants of the original inhabitants who had crossed the land bridge, they shared a limited gene pool that lessened the range of their resistance (Crosby, 1972).

The most deadly of the early epidemics were fevers—smallpox, measles, typhus. "Not even the most brutally depraved of the conquistadors was able purposely to slaughter Indians on the scale that the gentle priest unwittingly accomplished by going from his sickbed ministrations to lay his hands in blessing on his Indian converts" (Jennings, 1975). In an unvaccinated population, smallpox can infect virtually everyone, killing thirty percent of those infected. According to one Spanish historian, a million Native Americans lived in the Antilles when the Spanish arrived in 1492; by 1548 no more than five hundred were left. Virtually the entire Arawak people, the first to greet Columbus, died (Crosby, 1972). Central Mexico's population plummeted from 25 million to 2 million within less than a century.

The pattern was repeated in North America, where, well before the Pilgrims landed, English explorers and fishing parties brought typhus and smallpox. While the Pilgrims were buying their ships in Leiden, the Netherlands, in 1616 and 1617, a pestilence swept through New England, nearly exterminating the Massachuset Indians and depopulating the area. Years later Cotton Mather, a famous Puritan minister and historian, discerned the hand of God, who had cleared the land "of those pernicious creatures, to make room for better growth." The settlement of America was a resettlement; nearly every European settlement—Mexico City, Quebec, Montreal, Plymouth, Salem, Boston, New Amsterdam, Philadelphia, Detroit, Chicago—had previously been a Native-American town (Jennings, 1975).

The devastation of European illness had important imaginative effects as well as the obvious demographic ones. By undermining the natives' confidence in their gods, the destruction also undermined the natives' psychological resistance to European power. The ability of Europeans to survive when so many Native Americans were dying added to the myth of the Europeans' strength. Not understanding the physiology of immunity, they truly believed and told the natives that disease was sent as punishment and that the Europeans' ability to survive was a mark of divine favor (Crosby, 1972).

Thus, if the encounter between Europeans and Native Americans was a matter of empire and of demography, it was also a matter of understanding and imagination. This point was marked from the moment that Columbus, setting foot on the first island he encountered, undertook to name it rather than to learn the existing name from the inhabitants. This insistence that the lands were for Europeans to name and to define freely, without constraints set by the natives, permanently characterized the European encounter with the New World.

In general, most Europeans understood the Native Americans to be cruel savages, only marginally human, agents of the Devil, and best served by enforced acculturation in European plantations or townships. Others understood that they had encountered people who lived together harmoniously, their needs simple and their lives cooperative. The Americas seemed a golden world that had escaped expulsion from the Garden of Eden and had never known Original Sin. The concept that the lands in the West somehow had a special life-sustaining power has haunted the European imagination ever since and continues to be embedded in American political rhetoric. In the seventeenth century, when Europeans began to theorize about the origins of human society and of inequality, they found a point of departure in the conditions of "natural" equality and shared property that the first European adventurers had found.

European Forms on the American Land

The Europe from which Columbus sailed was rigidly hierarchical, not only in power relationships, but in the very concepts of self. There was, for example, strict division by gender: the nature of men and women was considered to be fundamentally different. "Male" was associated with heat and dryness and was symbolized by the sun. "Female" was associated with coolness and wetness and was symbolized by the moon, whose waxing and waning phases symbolized women's changeable, fluid nature. Conception was understood to involve a man implanting a miniature person in a woman's womb, implying that the source of life is male.

Deriving their status through fathers and husbands, women were placed in society differently than were men. Rituals of knighthood and institutions such as the courts and universities were strictly organized along gender lines. Among the upper classes, knowledge of Latin and of the written vernacular language was so generally confined to men that the two sexes literally used different languages. In a society in which perhaps one out of five men could read, the literacy of women hovered at half that of men, a relationship that continued through the eighteenth century, even as literacy of both sexes slowly improved. This gender system began to come under direct attack as being illogical and an inequitable ascription of power to one sex over the other.

Columbus's contemporaries, already living in a gendered hierarchy, also lived in a world rigidly divided by class. The political world was strictly divided into estates, each with its own hierarchical alignments. Thus, the "First Estate," the church, was ordered by popes, bishops, priests, abbots and monks, and abbesses and nuns. The "Second Estate," the nobility, was aligned from kings, to dukes and counts, to knights. Among the commoners, landowners and bourgeois (city-property owners) were superior to artisans, who in turn were superior to unskilled workers in the cities or peasants in the countryside, many of whom owed labor service to the large landowners. The hierarchical system was rigidly Christian.

The last European Moslems were expelled from southern Europe by Ferdinand and Isabella; Jews throughout Europe were strictly controlled as to where they could live and what work they could pursue (and typically what they could wear) both by law and by custom.

With few exceptions the Europeans who ventured to the Americas expected to replicate there the class hierarchies with which they were familiar. They commonly succeeded, especially in Central and South America, where the Spanish came with sufficient military strength to force Native Americans into service on plantations. In New England churches, pews were allocated by rank. However, the conditions that sustained hierarchy generally did not exist in North America. Moreover, some elements of traditional class structure were already breaking down within Europe. The rigidity of the church was shattered by the challenge of the Reformation. Only twenty-five years after Columbus's voyage, Martin Luther called for the priesthood of all believers and for the recognition that God could be served in any calling, not just a religious vocation. Luther demanded that all believers be literate enough to read the Bible. "A priesthood of all believers" eventually disrupted secular intellectual hierarchies as well as religious ones. People who learned to question their religious superiors could conceive of questioning their political superiors.

The Reformation also affected the relationships among the nations of Europe. In 1533, when the pope rejected Henry VIII's efforts to divorce his Spanish wife for not producing a male heir, the king broke with the Catholic church. In effect, he proclaimed his own reformation, creating a Protestant church of England. Those who came to England's North American colonies during the following century embodied elements of the religious upheavals at home: Anglicans moved to Virginia; a wide range of Protestant dissenters traveled to New England, New York, New Jersey, and Pennsylvania; and Catholic refugees fled to Maryland. Furthermore, the religious break with the church sealed an enmity between England and Spain when an already overextended Spanish empire sent its great armada against England in 1588, only to be defeated. The power to control North Atlantic shipping routes—and thus North America—passed to England.

New sources of wealth, American mines and trade with the Americas, recast European economies in the sixteenth and seventeenth centuries. The old hereditary nobilities were uprooted, engendering a capitalist revolution that encouraged commercial growth, wider markets, pride in personal profit, and greatly expanded credit facilities in the form of banks and joint-stock companies. Merchants and traders, not titled nobility, then led the various efforts to settle North America. The privileged nobility was always a minor element in North American society and was easily erased during the Revolution. Also, the economic revolution destabilized old peasant and artisan relationships. Working people who were insecure, even desperate, found the promise of North America appealing. Nearly one-half of all immigrants came as indentured servants, bound to work for the costs of their passage.

Over the course of two centuries, the English established and maintained some seventeen colonial settlements in America. The sugar produced in Jamaica and Barbados made those settlements by far the most profitable ones. As late as 1776, guide books published in London paid much more attention to West Indian possessions than to the mainland colonies, then on the brink of rebellion. Only hindsight draws historians of the United States to the mainland colonies.

British settlements sorted into three economic/cultural groups. A historical scenario in which three nations could have formed after the Revolution can easily be imagined: a racially divided nation stretching from Virginia to the West Indies; New England, which was ethnically English, religiously derived from Puritan sects, and marked by widespread land ownership and political participation; and the middle colonies, with an ethnically diverse society.

After a number of attempts by individual entrepreneurs to establish trading settlements in North America failed, those who wished to venture across the Atlantic experimented with joint-stock companies. These companies were chartered by the Crown and permitted to sell shares. The resources of a large number of small investors were pooled, thereby raising money and spreading the risk. This type of organization was used both by the Virginia Company that settled Jamestown in 1607 and the Virginia Company of London, which established the Massachusetts Bay Colony in 1620. The use of joint-stock companies as a method of settlement had crucial political implications. Men who brought their families and paid their own passage became stockholders of the company and could claim a voice in the settlement's affairs.

Landholders in Virginia were defined as "burgesses," equivalent to urban voters in England, and beginning in 1619 were permitted to elect representatives to a House of Burgesses. Within a few years of settlement, the freemen of the Massachusetts Bay Colony demanded to see their charter and deduced that they had the right to a representative assembly to determine the affairs of the corporation. Because the economic aspects of the corporation were impossible to disentangle from the political ones, those who had an economic relationship to the joint-stock com-

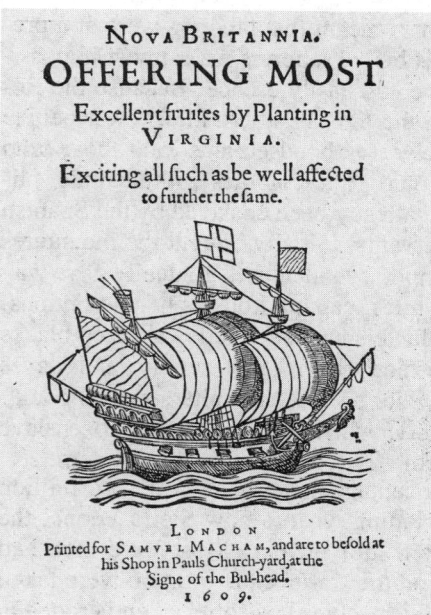

An advertisement to encourage immigration to the New World.

pany could also claim a political voice. Men who had not been able to vote in England because they would not meet high property requirements could easily meet traditional minimal property requirements in America, where land seemed "empty." Almost from the beginning, the settlements were the scene of an inadvertent but far-reaching political revolution.

The South

The Virginia Colony was the scene of a far-reaching social revolution as well. The earliest settlers were largely single men who had come, they thought, to make their fortunes; they were ill-prepared to deal with malaria and other fevers endemic to the swampy shores on which they found themselves. Starvation was prevalent throughout the first years, as wave after wave of adventurers met disaster. Only thirteen hundred of the first eight thousand are estimated to have survived. As tobacco became established as a reliable and profitable crop, the population stabilized, but deaths outnumbered births in the Chesapeake until well into the seventeenth century. Most who came were male indentured servants, who could form families only after they had worked out the terms of their bondage and who typically died young.

This demographic instability had important social implications. For example, in a society in which the death rate was high and men outnumbered women, even poor women seemed to have a wider range of marriage choices than they had in England. The control of fathers over daughters eroded; the father who came with his daughter to America or who, if she were born here, lived to see her to maturity, was rare. Workmen could fairly easily establish themselves on their own land after their indentures were complete. The appeal of the Chesapeake was that a person would not have to work for a master.

The very prosperity of the southern colonies meant that laborers were at a premium. Forcing Native Americans to work as bound laborers was almost impossible; they were familiar with the terrain and could easily escape. Because the English economy had improved (due in part to the transatlantic trade), fewer people were desperate enough to indenture themselves as bondservants, and those who did as the seventeenth century progressed could go to colonies with healthier climates than Virginia had. Black Africans had already been enslaved by the Spanish and Portuguese. Planters, who had white servants, initially bought the indentures of blacks for limited periods of time, but temporary indentures gradually gave way to permanent bondage. Unlike indentured whites, captured blacks had no options. They were not in a position to resist when planters changed the law to keep blacks in service for life. Slavery provided a constant, cheap labor supply, and slaves could not easily assimilate with the free, white society as white servants could. Ironically, the same market forces that made whites free conspired to enslave blacks: slavery and freedom developed together as a single economic system.

From the 1670s on, over the course of a century and a half, nearly 10 million Africans—largely from the West coast, including what is now Sierra Leone, the Ivory Coast, Benin, and Biafra—were taken into slavery. Most were men and were taken to South and Central America and the Caribbean; 300,000 were taken to the mainland colonies. Although English hierarchies had softened and eroded in the Americas, a new kind of hierarchy, based on race, was energetically invented and maintained. It came to infuse the culture of the American colonies and of the new republic.

The English culture in southern America produced a rich literature throughout the seventeenth and early eighteenth centuries. As in New England, the scope of religious literature was considerable, consisting of sermons, theological tracts, personal diaries, and spiritual autobiographies—such as Thomas Cradock's "Sermon on the Governance of Maryland's Established Church" (1753) and Samuel Davies' *The State of Religion Among the Protestant Dissenters in Virginia* (1751). The South supported a large body of secular writing as well. Produced mostly by aristocratic men of classical training, such texts as *The History of the Dividing Line* (first published in 1841) by Virginia's William Byrd II, are witty, sophisticated, and richly detailed accounts of life on southern plantations. Works of satire and comedy followed the classical and Renaissance English traditions. Robert Beverley's *The History of the Present State of Virginia* (1705) is a serious account of Virginia's exploration and settlement but contains satiric observations of social follies. Ebenezer Cook's comic poem *The Sot-Weed Factor* (1708) is a mock-epic satire of Maryland colonial life and the exchanges and conflicts between the new Americans and their English competitors in the marketplace.

New England

The early settlements of New England were established by people who, although Protestant, dissented from the Church of England and merged religious motives with economic ones for their departure from England. Pilgrims, who wished to separate completely from the Church of England, and Puritans, who planned to purify it from within, understood themselves to be founding a godly community in which religious leaders and secular leaders would be allies. Intensely committed to their faith and to examining their souls for evidence of salvation, they encouraged confessional diaries and journals detailing their experiences on the road to salvation. Especially in the early years of settlement, Puritans were particularly worried about dissent in a godly community; though they had left England to live their own way, they did not tolerate Quakers, Baptists, or atheists. Captain John Smith, one of the most important promotional writers of the early seventeenth century, whose *A Description of New England* (1616) helped entice the Puritans to America in 1630, had himself been turned down as an undesirable person in his offer to guide the Puritans to America.

In the South, people claimed their lands individually. In New England, land was granted first to a group of town leaders, who then allocated it to the original settlers, taking social position into account. Thus, ministers, lawyers, and men who had been elite in England received the largest and most central allotments. Compact towns were understood to nurture a godly community in which traditional leadership patterns could be maintained. The dream of "peaceable kingdoms" could not be sustained indefinitely, especially as seaport towns (including Boston and Newport, Rhode Island) became small metropolises into which international trade and thousands of immigrants poured annually.

In the 1630s the Puritans had little difficulty expelling religious dissenters, such as Roger Williams and Anne Hutchinson, from the Massachusetts Bay Colony. However, by the mid-eighteenth century Boston had itself become an urban center of some twenty thousand residents, the hub of a trade in which New England shippers sold fish, livestock, and lumber to the West Indies and fish, furs, and lumber to England. From the West Indies, ships returned with slaves for sale in the southern colonies and with molasses, to be distilled into rum, for sale in the northern colonies and in Africa, where the rum would be traded for more slaves. Thus, even the regions in which slavery was not a major source of labor were economically dependent on the institution of slavery, a pattern that persisted until the Civil War.

Puritan Writing. Puritan literature consisted mostly of various forms of religious writing: sermons, theological treatises, spiritual autobiographies, spiritualized histories, diaries, and religious poetry. Because the Puritans believed that the Bible should serve as the source of all knowledge and inspiration, they wondered whether the writings of human beings are not merely presumptuous efforts to compete with God's sacred words. Despite this reservation, the Puritans produced an extraordinary volume of writings while attempting to explain and understand the Scriptures and their plans, efforts, and failures.

During the two decades after the settlement of New England in 1630, ties between England and the American colonies remained strong: many Massachusetts Puritans planned to return to England if Puritans there gained control of the government. The learned continued to purchase books from abroad and studied the classics and Renaissance literature as well as the works of Puritan theologians. Because of their commitment to the pursuit of God's word, the Puritans put great stock in education and literacy. As soon as the basics for sustaining life were established, the leaders set about creating the first college in America, established in 1636 and named after John Harvard. Exhibiting the "plaine style" that was to appeal to reason and not to the emotions, Puritan writing is direct and highly controlled. Nevertheless, because the Puritan venture was dramatic and culturally important to America in subsequent years, many of these works remain engaging today.

As the century progressed, Puritan writers developed new genres and styles. The clergy of the second and third generations after settlement redefined or abandoned the plain style in favor of figurative language, classical references, and a liberalized use of biblical typology—a language system for drawing parallels between biblical history and Puritan experience. The Puritan imagination was characterized by two strong tendencies. One, the Puritans were much inclined to read meaning out of natural events, biblical passages, and history and always tried to discern the plan behind happenings that might to the untrained mind seem to be random. Two, to discover if they were saved or damned, the Puritans constantly searched their own minds and hearts, worrying that self-delusion might damn them as hypocrites who would be exposed on Judgment Day. Thus, Puritan writings are packed with emotion, as individual souls struggled through language for truths of immense importance and as writers of the communal experience tried to determine if God supported the Puritans in their errand into the wilderness.

Those themes run through the sermons and histories and make such poems as Michael Wigglesworth's *The Day of Doom* (1662) unmistakably Puritan. Still, even within what would seem to be a very limited literary frame, poets such as Anne Bradstreet and Edward Taylor composed moving expressions of universal human experiences. Samuel Sewall's eloquent description of Plum Island, from his *Phaenomena Quaedam Apocalyptica* (1697), and his impassioned repudiation of slavery, *The Selling of Joseph* (1700), put into perspective his fretting over theological fine points that appear in his *Diary* (1673–1729, first published 1878–1882).

By the beginning of the eighteenth century, many of the original doctrines and social controls of the first Puritans had eroded, and Anglicans, Quakers, and others had settled among the saints. Imposed by the English Crown, religious toleration drastically changed the character of Boston and other New England towns. The writings of such thinkers as John Locke, Sir Isaac Newton, and René

=CONTEXTS=

Anne Hutchinson's Puritan Challenge

An early challenge to the authority of the Puritan ministers and magistrates came from Anne Hutchinson. A devout parishioner of Rev. John Cotton in Boston, England, Hutchinson and her family followed Cotton to New England. There she raised twelve children and served the community as a midwife and nurse. An intelligent reader of the Scriptures, she regularly held meetings in her home for as many as eighty people to discuss theology. Her view, which she attributed to Cotton's sermons, that saved Christians could interpret the Bible without the help of clerics (a position called antinomianism) was controversial. For her beliefs she was tried for heresy and banished from Massachusetts in 1637. Even Cotton abandoned her cause. During her trial she defended herself with learning, grace, and courage that has made her a champion of independent thought. Below is an excerpt from the court record of her trial:

Mrs. H. [Hutchinson]. Now if you do condemn me for speaking what in my conscience I know to be truth I must commit myself unto the Lord.

Mr. Nowell [a magistrate]. How do you know that that was the spirit?

Mrs. H. How did Abraham know that it was God that bid him offer his son, being a breach of the sixth commandment?

Dep. Gov. [Deputy Governor]. By an immediate voice.

Mrs. H. So to me by an immediate revelation.

Dep. Gov. How! an immediate revelation.

Mrs. H. By the voice of his own spirit to my soul . . . I have been confident of what he hath revealed unto me . . . . I was then much troubled concerning the ministry under which I lived, and then that place in the 30th of Isaiah [Isaiah 30:20] was brought to my mind. "Though the Lord give thee bread of adversity and water of affliction yet shall not thy teachers be removed into corners any more, but thine eyes shall see thy teachers." The Lord giving me this promise and they being gone there was none then left that I was able to hear, and I could not be at rest but I must come hither. Yet that place of Isaiah did much follow me, though the Lord give thee the bread of adversity and water of affliction. This place lying I say upon me then this place in Daniel [Daniel 6:4–5] was brought unto me and did shew me that though I should meet with affliction yet I am the same God that delivered Daniel out of the lion's den, I will also deliver thee.

Court record of Anne Hutchinson's trial, 1637

The clothing in this anonymous 1674 portrait of Elizabeth Freake and her baby, Mary, shows that the Puritans appreciated rich adornment despite their religious purity and simplicity. The Puritans viewed children as small adults and dressed them as such. (Worcester Art Museum)

Descartes had begun to affect European thought in ways that would usher in the Enlightenment, with its stress on reason and science.

Before the demise of the Enlightenment, the American Puritan theologian Jonathan Edwards produced a major body of writing. Young Edwards observed the decline of the religion of his father and grandfathers and concurrently studied Newton and Locke. By his early twenties, Edwards was working to create a philosophical and theological synthesis of traditional Puritan doctrines regarding free will and God's sovereignty with the Enlightenment philosophy of Locke and of others. As Edwards labored at this stunning intellectual feat in the 1730s, he preached at a church in Northampton, Massachusetts. Beginning then and sweeping the colonies in the 1740s was a remarkable religious revival that became known as the first Great Awakening. The writings that Edwards produced during the next two decades, while he struggled to reconcile the Bible with philosophy and human experience, stand as eloquent expressions of a brilliant literary imagination.

The Middle Colonies

Historians are only now beginning to appreciate the continuities of the societies that were established in the region between New England and the Chesapeake, although that region is still known by the vague term "the middle colonies." With no established churches and a wide range of ethnic and religious groups, this region possessed less sense of community than New England had and less permanent class division than the Chesapeake had. The middle colonies set the model for the cultural pluralism that continues to characterize American life.

Dutch settlement of New Amsterdam (now Manhattan) was once understood by historians to be largely a failure: an expected fortune in the fur trade never materialized, the Dutch failed to establish lasting legislatures, and the English were easily able to capture the colony in 1664. Fewer of the Dutch were willing to migrate than were the English, thousands of whom were dislocated subjects with no other options. Yet, from another perspective, the Dutch experience is exemplary. While the English were deeply embroiled in civil war and were hesitant to tolerate dissenters, the Dutch, having recently concluded their civil and religious wars, had created a stable society at home and tolerated religious diversity (including the refugee Jews expelled by Ferdinand and Isabella).

In New Amsterdam, the Dutch were receptive to many cultures: eighteen languages are said to have been spoken there in the seventeenth century, and dissenters from the Massachusetts Bay Colony were welcome in Dutch settlements on Long Island. Dutch family law was much more concerned with women's and children's rights than was English law. For example, married women in their own right could inherit real estate. When New Netherland became New York, married women's property rights declined sharply.

William Penn was a Quaker who had managed to claim a charter from the Crown in 1681. He governed his colony (now Pennsylvania) as though he were a private proprietor with the right to design its government. Penn defined his colony as a refuge for Quakers and other victims of religious persecution. "Any government is free where the laws rule," he wrote in the introduction to the first Frame of Government (1682), "and the people are a party to those laws . . . . Governments, like clocks, go from the motion men give them, and as governments are made and moved by men, so by turn are they ruined too."

Migration to Pennsylvania in the 1680s was as phenomenal as the great migration to the Massachusetts Bay Colony in the 1630s had been. Within six years of its founding in 1682, Pennsylvania had twelve thousand settlers. The deep radicalism of English Quakers infused the early settlement. Custom respected the Quaker refusal to take oaths and to remove hats as a sign of deference and the Quaker insistence that all—men and women, rich and poor—could speak in meeting and achieve salvation. Penn's first Frame of Government explicitly guaranteed freedom of worship to all religious groups. All Christian men could vote and hold office. As pacifists the Quakers avoided warfare with Native Americans: Penn did not allocate land until he had first purchased it. In fact, no major Native-American war occurred in Pennsylvania until the 1750s. Quakers were skeptical of slavery, as were Mennonites, who published the first public protest against "Traffic in Men's Bodies" (1688).

Pennsylvania quickly became a magnet. Not long after settlement, representatives of a wide variety of religions were found in that colony: Quakers, Anglicans, Lutherans, Mennonites, Catholics, Moravians. Fertile lands meant rapid economic prosperity, and within a few years of settlement, Philadelphia became a seaport rivaling Boston. The Pennsylvania experience reveals the tensions of a political society composed of distinct ethnic and religious groups. By the mid-eighteenth century, Pennsylvania politics were sharply divided along ethnic/cultural lines, as politics continue to be in the United States.

In addition to being lively in social and political activity, Pennsylvania, especially Philadelphia, developed into the colonies' leading cultural center. Whereas the Puritan temper continued to impose restraint upon the development of imaginative literature in New England, the more liberal spirit of the city of Friends, as the Quakers were called, encouraged the arts. The leading literary figure of Philadelphia was Benjamin Franklin, who founded the first circulating library in 1831, among his many other accomplishments. With his graceful style and wit, Franklin typified the cosmopolitan ideal in both his life and his writing.

Whereas Franklin made a mark for American letters abroad by his verbal skills and personality, the Quaker author John Woolman combined the traditions of religious writing and a sophisticated Enlightenment style to preach, lecture, and write about the social ills in America. Woolman's *Some Considerations on the Keeping of Negroes* (1754) powerfully argues for the abolition of slavery. His *A Plea for the Poor or a Word of Remembrance and Caution to the Rich* (written in 1763 but not published until 1793) is directed to issues of class division and social injustice.

William Smith, the energetic provost of the College of Philadelphia (now the University of Pennsylvania), was himself an important writer. He inspired young authors such as Thomas Godfrey, whose *The Prince of Parthia* (1767) may have been the first play genuinely written by an American and produced in America. By the time of the American Revolution, Philadelphia was a major publishing center of the small literary world that was taking shape in the colonies.

Traditional Native-American Literary Expression

When European explorers began to visit the Americas, they found more than three hundred cultural groups speaking some two hundred languages from several major language families in North America alone. These tribes varied widely in political organization, economic structure, and cultural values, but they all had in common a rich oral literature, developed over centuries and perfectly responsive to cultural needs and social relations. However, the oral nature of traditional Native-American literary expression, the violent political struggle between the colonists and native tribes, and their differing social systems made it difficult for the colonists to appreciate native creativity.

There are significant differences between the written and oral modes of expression, even without considerations of translation or divergent cultural expectations. But all literature presents verbal creation rising from negotiations between individual talent and a supporting tradition regardless of the format. A vibrant oral tradition was central to most Native-American societies and continues to be so today. Through the oral tradition, people pass on their wisdom, their understanding of how to survive, their cultural values, and their sense of identity. Native-American societies clarify their relationship to the world around them, to both seen and unseen powers, as exemplified by the Trickster myth of Wisconsin's Winnebago tribe. They formally encode a world view and make sacred their paths through life in a way that requires the older generations to encourage and guide the younger ones. In the oral tradition communities are bound together, and individuals find their place in society. Over centuries, an expressive body of literature has matured. That literature may be divided into oral narratives, oratory, song/poetry, and religious expression. However, these categories are not exclusive and may overlap.

Europeans expressed fascination with the Native Americans in painting as well as in writing. John White painted this watercolor, The Flyer, *after arriving in Roanoke, Virginia, with Sir Walter Raleigh.*

Oral narratives might consist of sacred or secular stories. Most often they were told by an elder in a storytelling session with young people and adults in attendance, as were the myths of the Cherokees. Some narratives were told in religious circumstances as part of a larger ritual. Others deal with more historical material, as does the Tlingit tribe's story of their first contact with white people—and with the experience of one person or ancestor.

Native-American orators perfected their rhetorical skills during such events as council meetings, religious presentations, welcomings, petitions, and meetings with other tribes. The highly personal and transitory nature of this form has made it difficult to record, but some traditions have been documented by tribal and nontribal scholars. Many of the speeches of noted orators and chiefs, such as the Seneca chief known as Red-jacket, were recorded at official meetings between natives and whites.

Native-American song may also be of a religious or personal nature. Most often it has been written in English with the appearance of poetry, as have the war song of the Papagos of the Southeast and the transcribed hieroglyphs of the Mayas of Central America. The oral context of a song or chant makes it something quite different from poetry of the western tradition; the importance that poetry places on appreciating each word and pause is similar to the appreciation of Native-American song traditions. The reader must supply much of the music, gesture, and social context that informs the expression.

The forms of Native-American religious expression may vary from dance dramas staged as public ritual to personal vision songs, depending on the individual tribal tradition and religious activity. Religious expression may take the form of a highly formalized series of chants that take years to learn or a personal rite evoking an animal spirit protector. Expressions from any of the other categories might also be religious, but some literary works, such as Zuni prayers, fit most conveniently into this category.

Because oral literature is a performance literature, written texts of oral expression can present only one dimension of a multifaceted experience. In Native-American oral performance the audience plays a crucial role in shaping the total expression. An intense interactive context is built up, extending into a tradition of previous performances and a web of shared cultural expectations and references. In reading written translations of verbal acts, we may be unaware of aesthetic norms and cultural expectations unique to Native Americans or to a specific tribal group. Even the best of translations must struggle to give the reader of English some sense of the texture of the language used—which might include its formality, voice, word choice—and of the dramatic sense of performance and religious ramifications of the verbal event. But from these translations we gain deeper insight into the native peoples of the Americas and into the fascinating variety of literary expression illuminating the human experience.

Suggested Readings: W. Apes, *The Experiences of Five Christian Indians: Or, the Indian's Looking Glass for the White Men*, 1833. Sagoyewatha, *Biography and History of the Indians of North America*, ed. S. E. Drake, 1834. M. Austin, *The American Rhythm: Studies and Reexpressions of Amerindian Songs*, 1930. *Singing for Power*, ed. R. Underhill, 1938. Black Hawk, *Black Hawk: An Autobiography*, ed. D. Jackson, 1955. *The Trickster: A Study in American Indian Mythology*, ed. P. Radin, 1956. M. Astrov, ed., *The Winged Serpent: An Anthology of American Indian Prose and Poetry*, 1973. R. Slotkin, *Regeneration Through Violence: The Mythology of the American Frontier, 1600–1860*, 1973. M. Castro, *Interpreting the Indian: Twentieth-Century Poets and the Native American*, 1983. *Haa Shuka, Our Ancestors: Tlingit Oral Narratives*, ed. N. M. Dauenhauer and R. Dauenhauer, 1987. H. D. Brumble, *American Indian Autobiography*, 1988. J. M. Dent, *Savagism and Civilization: A Study of the Indian and the American Mind*, 1988. A. Krupat, *The Voice in the Margin: Native American Literature and the Canon*, 1989.

Texts Used: "How the World Was Made": *Nineteenth Annual Report of the Bureau of American Ethnology, 1897–1898*, Pt. I, ed. J. W. Powell, 1900. "They Came From the East": *The Book of Chilam Balam of Chumayel*, trans. R. L. Roys. 1967.

CHEROKEE MYTH

HOW THE WORLD WAS MADE*

The earth is a great island floating in a sea of water, and suspended at each of the four cardinal points by a cord hanging down from the sky vault, which is of solid rock. When the world grows old and worn out, the people will die and the cords will break and let the earth sink down into the ocean, and all will be water again. The Indians are afraid of this.

When all was water, the animals were above in Gălûñ′lătĭ,[1] beyond the arch; but it was very much crowded, and they were wanting more room. They wondered what was below the water, and at last Dâyuni′sĭ, "Beaver's Grandchild," the little Water-beetle, offered to go and see if it could learn. It darted in every direction over the surface of the water, but could find no firm place to rest. Then it dived to the bottom and came up with some soft mud, which began to grow and spread on every side until it became the island which we call the earth. It was afterward fastened to the sky with four cords, but no one remembers who did this.

At first the earth was flat and very soft and wet. The animals were anxious to get down, and sent out different birds to see if it was yet dry, but they found no place to alight and came back again to Gălûñ′lătĭ. At last it seemed to be time, and they sent out the Buzzard and told him to go and make ready for them. This was the Great Buzzard, the father of all the buzzards we see now. He flew all over the earth, low down near the ground, and it was still soft. When he reached the Cherokee country, he was very tired, and his wings began to flap and strike the ground, and wherever they struck the earth there was a valley, and where they turned up again there was a mountain. When the animals above saw this, they were afraid that the whole world would be mountains, so they called him back, but the Cherokee country remains full of mountains to this day.

When the earth was dry and the animals came down, it was still dark, so they got the sun and set it in a track to go every day across the island from east to west, just overhead. It was too hot this way, and Tsiska′gĭlĭ′, the Red Crawfish, had his shell scorched a bright red, so that his meat was spoiled: and the Cherokee do not eat it. The conjurers put the sun another hand-breadth higher in the air, but it was still too hot. They raised it another time, and another, until it was seven hand-breadths high and just under the sky arch. Then it was right, and they left it so. This is why the conjurers call the highest place Gûlkwâ′gine Di′gălûñ′lătiyûn′, "the seventh height," because it is seven hand-breadths above the earth. Every day the sun goes along under this arch, and returns at night on the upper side to the starting place.

There is another world under this, and it is like ours in everything—animals, plants, and people—save that the seasons are different. The streams that come down from the mountains are the trails by which we reach this underworld, and the springs at their heads are the doorways by which we enter it, but to do this one

---

* This Cherokee story was collected in North Carolina, where some Cherokee communities survived dissolution and removal. Such creation stories are told to explain the origin of the world, but more importantly they establish the nature of the processes that have influenced the world and continue to do so. This story reflects a type of Native-American creation story known as the "earthdiver motif," but it is only one of the many different creation stories of Native-American communities.

[1] The Cherokees believed the world consists of various levels: the earth, an underworld, a heaven, and this level between heaven and earth.

must fast and go to water and have one of the underground people for a guide. We know that the seasons in the underworld are different from ours, because the water in the springs is always warmer in winter and cooler in summer than the outer air.

When the animals and plants were first made—we do not know by whom—they were told to watch and keep awake for seven nights, just as young men now fast and keep awake when they pray to their medicine. They tried to do this, and nearly all were awake through the first night, but the next night several dropped off to sleep, and the third night others were asleep, and then others, until, on the seventh night, of all the animals only the owl, the panther, and one or two more were still awake. To these were given the power to see and to go about in the dark, and to make prey of the birds and animals which must sleep at night. Of the trees only the cedar, the pine, the spruce, the holly, and the laurel were awake to the end, and to them it was given to be always green and to be greatest for medicine, but to the others it was said: "Because you have not endured to the end you shall lose your hair every winter."

Men came after the animals and plants. At first there were only a brother and sister until he struck her with a fish and told her to multiply, and so it was. In seven days a child was born to her, and thereafter every seven days another, and they increased very fast until there was danger that the world could not keep them. Then it was made that a woman should have only one child in a year, and it has been so ever since.

1900

MAYAN HISTORICAL POETRY

They Came From the East*

They came from the east when they arrived.
Then Christianity also began.
The fulfillment of its prophecy is ascribed to the east . . .
Then with the true God, the true *Dios,*
came the beginning of our misery.
It was the beginning of tribute,
the beginning of church dues,
the beginning of strife with purse-snatching,
the beginning of strife with blow-guns;
the beginning of strife by trampling on people,   10
the beginning of robbery with violence,
the beginning of forced debts,
the beginning of debts enforced by false testimony,
the beginning of individual strife,
a beginning of vexation.

1542?, 1933

* This poem was transcribed from Mayan hieroglyphs shortly after the Spanish conquest of the Central American peoples in 1541. It was preserved in *The Book of Chilam Balam of Chumayel*, translated in 1933 by Ralph L. Roys.

The Literature of Exploration
(Late 15th–17th Centuries)

The literature of the early European explorers of North America is characterized by the conflicts between the explorers' preconceptions and the realities of the Western Hemisphere. The first Europeans to investigate what they perceived as a "new world"—including Christopher Columbus, an Italian whose voyages were financed by Spain—were initially convinced that they had reached Asia. This conclusion was based on classical calculations of the earth's size and on biblical prophecies; the Europeans were not aware that the North and South American continents existed. With the 1501 voyage to Brazil by Amerigo Vespucci, which he described in a letter after returning to Portugal in 1502, it was acknowledged that the continent we know as North America was a region previously unknown to Europeans. (That region was named for Vespucci, a Florentine navigator, at the suggestion of Martin Waldseemüller, a German geographer.) Although European interest in establishing trade routes to the Orient persisted through the sixteenth century, the immediate focus shifted to exploitation, and later to colonization, of the "newly discovered" continent.

Deeper exploration of the Americas bred further ambivalence. Early accounts, many designed to generate funding for further exploration, described the region as an earthly paradise, a fertile garden where food falls from the trees and fish leap from the oceans. European interest was also inflamed by reports of alleged "cities of gold" in South America and in what is now southwestern America. However, other tales of the harsh realities of existence in the Americas tempered the optimism engendered by these fabulous reports. One such sobering story is *The Narrative of the Expedition of Coronado* (1896), the account by Pedro de Casteñeda of Francisco Vásquez de Coronado's ill-fated search from 1540 to 1542 for the Seven Golden Cities of Cibola. Casteñeda, a native of northern Spain, was a colonist at San Miguel Culiacan in northwestern Mexico when Coronado's expedition moved through that area. Casteñeda joined the expedition as a private soldier. Though he admits that he is no great rhetorician, his narrative remains one of the most important documents of this expedition and vividly portrays the dangers and hardships attendant upon the pursuit of easy wealth in the Americas.

Europeans' struggles for survival gave shape to many early forms of exploration literature. Narratives of hardship, captivity, and survival stressed the kinds of traits and skills uniquely suited to life in the wilderness. Strength, endurance, a measure of cunning, and an understanding of nature became the prime elements of the literature of exploration. Works such as the *Relation of Núñez Cabeza de Vaca* (1542), by Alvar Núñez Cabeza de Vaca, in which four shipwrecked Europeans wander for eight years in the Gulf Coast region, emphasize the skills necessary for adaptation and survival. After his rescue in 1536 Cabeza de Vaca was appointed governor and captain-general of the South American province Paraguay, but political intrigue led to his arrest and return to Spain. Though he was eventually acquitted, he found it difficult to realign himself with European society, and his experiences can be seen as representative of the problems early explorers and colonists faced in reconciling a European set of intellectual paradigms with American realities.

Another narrative indicative of the conflicts Europeans encountered in their early investigations of the Americas is *Voyages of Samuel de Champlain, 1604–1618* (1907). A native of Brouage, a small French port on the Bay of Biscay, Samuel de Champlain displayed early in life an aptitude for sea travel and for administration. In 1608, on his third trip to Canada, he founded Quebec and explored the New England coast and the Great

Lakes region, documenting in the *Voyages* his disputes with the Iroquois Indians. Those disputes initiated long-standing hostility between the French and the Iroquois.

For Europeans the existence of two enormous continents between Europe and Asia was a cultural shock. When the transatlantic contact was first made, many Europeans had already begun to doubt the received authority of popes, kings, and traditionally educated scholars in all aspects of life. The explorers of the Americas provided new facts about the nature and shape of the world and thus fed a growing skepticism among European thinkers. This skepticism, which characterized the Renaissance and the Reformation, intensified the desire to investigate the American continents and report the facts—yet, every new account inflamed imaginations and produced new myths and mysteries. The ambivalence to the Americas expressed by the early explorers reflects the questioning nature of the Renaissance-era European mind, and their literature gives shape to the paradoxes of American experience that would become the foundation of classic American literature.

Suggested Readings: *Voyages of Samuel de Champlain: Original Narratives of Early American History: Voyages of Samuel de Champlain, 1604–1618*, ed. W. L. Grant, 1907. *Relations of Núñez Cabeza de Vaca: Original Narratives of Early American History: Spanish Explorers in the Southern United States, 1528–1543*, ed. J. F. Jameson, 1925. *The Journal of the First Voyage of Christopher Columbus: Journals and Other Documents on the Life and Voyages of Christopher Columbus*, ed. S. E. Morison, 1963. D. B. Quinn, ed., *North American Discovery, ca. 1000–1612*, 1971. W. P. Cumming, R. A. Eston, and D. B. Quinn, *The Discovery of North America*, 1972. F. Chiappelli, ed., *First Images of America*, 1976. D. B. Quinn, ed., *North America From Earliest Discovery to First Settlements: The Norse Voyages to 1612*, 1977. D. B. Quinn, ed., *New American World: A Documentary History of North America to 1612*, 5 vols., 1979. S. E. Morison, *Admiral of the Ocean Sea: A Life of Christopher Columbus*, 1983. F. W. Hodge and T. H. Lewis, *Spanish Explorers in the Southern United States*, 1528–1543, 1984. S. H. Palmer and D. Reinhartz, eds., *Essays on the History of North American Discovery and Exploration*, 1988.

Texts Used: Letter of Vespucci's First Brazilian Voyage: *The European Discovery of America: The Southern Voyages*, A.D. *1492–1616*, trans. S. E. Morison, 1974. *The Narrative of the Expedition of Coronado: Original Narratives of Early American History: Spanish Explorers in the Southern United States, 1528–1543*, ed. J. F. Jameson, 1925.

from   LETTER OF VESPUCCI'S FIRST BRAZILIAN VOYAGE*

by   AMERIGO VESPUCCI (1454–1512)

[*The "Reasoning Animals" of the New World*]

Now we come to the reasoning animals. We found all the earth inhabited by people completely nude, men as well as women, without covering their shame. They have bodies well proportioned, white in color with black hair, and little or no beard. I tried very hard to understand their life and customs because for 27 days I ate and slept with them, and that which I learned of them follows:

They have no laws or faith, and live according to nature. They do not recognize the immortality of the soul, they have among them no private property, because everything is common; they have no boundaries of kingdoms and provinces, and

---

* Vespucci wrote this letter, known as the "Bartolozzi Letter," to his former employer, Lorenzo di Pier Francesco de' Medici, after Vespucci had returned to Lisbon, Portugal, in September 1502 from his 1501 Brazilian voyage. The text was translated by Samuel E. Morison and Dr. Gino Corti.

no king! They obey nobody, each is lord unto himself; no justice, no gratitude, which to them is unnecessary because it is not part of their code. They live in common in houses made like very large cabins; and for people who have no iron or other metal, it is possible to say that their cabins are truly wonderful, for I have seen houses which are 200 *passi*[1] long and 30 wide and artfully made by craftsmen, and in one of these houses were 500 or perhaps 600 souls. They slept in nets[2] woven of cotton, exposed to the air without any other covering; they eat seated on the ground; their food is roots of herbs and many good fruits, an infinity of fish and great quantities of shellfish; crabs, oyster, lobster, crayfish, and many other things which the sea produces. The meat which they eat commonly is human flesh, as shall be told. When they can have other flesh of animals and birds they eat that too but they do not hunt for it much because they have no dogs and their land is very full of woods which are filled with fierce wild beasts, so they do not ordinarily enter the woods unless with a crowd of people.

1502, 1974

from THE NARRATIVE OF THE EXPEDITION OF CORONADO*

by PEDRO DE CASTEÑEDA (1510?–1570?)

Chapter 3: Of How They Killed the Negro Estevan[1] at Cibola, and Friar Marcos Returned in Flight

After Estevan had left the friars, he thought he could get all the reputation and honor himself, and that if he should discover those settlements with such famous high houses, alone, he would be considered bold and courageous. So he proceeded with the people who had followed him, and attempted to cross the wilderness which lies between the country he had passed through and Cibola. He was so far ahead of the friars that, when these reached Chichilticalli,[2] which is on the edge of the wilderness, he was already at Cibola, which is eighty leagues beyond. It is 220 leagues from Culican[3] to the edge of the wilderness, and eighty across the desert, which makes 300, or perhaps ten more or less. As I said, Estevan reached Cibola loaded with the large quantity of turquoises they had given him and some

---

[1] Portuguese measurements.   [2] Hammocks.

* Casteñeda was a member of the expeditions of Francisco Vasquez de Coronado (1510–1554), the governor of New Galicia, into what is now Arizona, New Mexico, Texas, Oklahoma, and Kansas. Friar Marcos de Niza (?–1558), or Marcos of Nice, returned from exploring land north of Mexico in 1539 with reports of vast riches in "Seven Golden Cities of Cibola," actually the Zuni Pueblos of present-day New Mexico. Coronado's expedition found such natural riches as the Grand Canyon but no gold. The narrative was started at least twenty years after the journey ended and was first translated into English in 1896 by George Parker Winship.

[1] A Moor who had followed his master, Andrés Dorante, to the New World from Spain on the unsuccessful expedition of Pánfilo de Narváez in 1528; Estevan was one of the four survivors, along with Alvar Núñez Cabeza de Vaca. Estevan led the scouting party of Friar Marcos.

[2] "Red House," as the Aztecs called this city, probably on or near the Río Gila in what is now southern Arizona.

[3] San Miguel Culiacan, in Sinaloa, northwestern Mexico.

beautiful women whom the Indians who followed him and carried his things were taking with them and had given him. These had followed him from all the settlements he had passed, believing that under his protection they could traverse the whole world without any danger. But as the people in this country were more intelligent than those who followed Estevan, they lodged him in a little hut they had outside their village, and the older men and the governors heard his story and took steps to find out the reason he had come to that country. For three days they made inquiries about him and held a council. The account which the negro gave them of two white men who were following him, sent by a great lord, who knew about the things in the sky, and how these were coming to instruct them in divine matters, made them think that he must be a spy or a guide from some nations who wished to come and conquer them, because it seemed to them unreasonable to say that the people were white in the country from which he came and that he was sent by them, he being black. Besides these other reasons, they thought it was hard of him to ask them for turquoises and women, and so they decided to kill him. They did this, but they did not kill any of those who went with him, although they kept some young fellows and let the others, about sixty persons, return freely to their own country. As these, who were badly scared, were returning in flight, they happened to come upon the friars in the desert sixty leagues from Cibola, and told them the sad news, which frightened them so much that they would not even trust these folks who had been with the negro, but opened the packs they were carrying and gave away everything they had except the holy vestments for saying mass. They returned from here by double marches, prepared for anything, without seeing any more of the country except what the Indians told them.

1565?–1596, 1896

Powhatan
(1550?–1618)

When Jamestown, Virginia, was founded in 1607, Wahunsonacock—or Powhatan, as the English called him, after his principal village, Powhatans—was the leader of the Algonquian confederacy of tidewater tribes dwelling near the English settlement. Powhatan, believed to have been born around 1550, appears to have lived in style: Captain John Smith first saw the "Emperour" bedecked with pearl necklaces, covered with raccoon skins and surrounded by attendants. Smith's account of that meeting, in *A True Relation of . . . Virginia* (1608), notes that Powhatan's will was law to his people, who revered their leader as "halfe a God."

With numbers far superior to those of the English and with a capacity for violence, Powhatan could have had the Jamestown Colony destroyed. He refrained from doing so, probably because he was confident that the feeble enterprise would soon extinguish itself and because he hoped to use the English as temporary allies against competing tribes. Meanwhile, the colonists desperately needed the food the Algonquians could provide. Thus, an uneasy accord developed. Powhatan and Smith tolerated each other partly because Pocahontas, Powhatan's favorite daughter, reportedly felt affection for Smith but mainly because they were concerned for their own interests. In 1608 Powhatan was given an elaborate coronation to ensure his subjection to the English, but the phony ceremony did not go smoothly. Powhatan refused to come to the English fort to be crowned, and when the ceremony was performed at one of his villages, he could not be persuaded to kneel. "At last," Smith reports, "he a little stooped, and . . . the Crowne [was placed] on his head."

Peace between Powhatan and the English temporarily ended in 1609, when Smith left Virginia. In 1612 the English kidnapped Pocahontas in an effort to control Powhatan. The Algonquian leader's refusal to negotiate might have ended in disaster for his daughter had she not charmed the Englishman John Rolfe, who married her in 1614. The ensuing peace lasted until the deaths of Pocahontas and Powhatan in 1617 and 1618, respectively. In 1622 Powhatan's successor, Opechancanough, attacked the James River settlements in force, killing over three hundred colonists. Henceforth, the English had no cause to continue the policy of restraint pursued by Smith, and the deliberate extermination of Native Americans began.

Powhatan's significance lies in his role as the first Native-American leader to deal extensively with English colonists. His interactions with them—marked by disdain and distrust on the Native-American side and fear and condescension on the colonial side—predicted the interactions to follow. Smith viewed Powhatan as a "subtile Salvage," whose greed and cruelty (as well as strength and intelligence) were unquestionable. Later observers more sympathetic to the Native-American position have portrayed Powhatan as a victim of white treachery. Some truth lies in both views. Powhatan seems to have been a powerful ruler whose primary motive in 1607 was to put the English presence in Virginia to personal use. Yet, the unequal nature (and eventual outcome) of the struggle between Native Americans and whites lends sympathy to the leader finally doomed—as later tribe leaders would be—to see his lands confiscated, his authority removed, and his culture obliterated. Powhatan's speech to Smith during a meeting in 1609 can be interpreted (as Smith interpreted it) as a ploy to persuade the colonists to disarm themselves. Regardless of Powhatan's motives, his illusory vision of a harmonious relationship between Native Americans and whites and his prophetic vision of Native-American life style characterized by anxiety and deprivation provide a poignant picture of what might have been, and a tragic depiction of what was to be, in America.

Suggested Readings: G. Nash, *Red, White, and Black: The Peoples of Early America*, 1974. F. Jennings, *The Invasion of America*, 1974. K. Kupperman, *Settling With the Indians*, 1980. B. Sheehan, *Savagism and Civility*, 1980. J. Smith, *Complete Works of Captain John Smith*, 3 vols., ed. P. L. Barbour, 1986.

Text Used: S. G. Drake, *Biography and History of the Indians of North America*, 1841.

SPEECH TO CAPTAIN JOHN SMITH

I am now grown old, and must soon die; and the succession must descend, in order, to my brothers, *Opitchapan, Opekankanough,* and *Catataugh,* and then to my two sisters, and their two daughters. I wish their experience was equal to mine; and that your love to us might not be less than ours to you. Why should you take by force that from us which you can have by love? Why should you destroy us, who have provided you with food? What can you get by war? We can hide our provisions, and fly into the woods; and then you must consequently famish by wronging your friends. What is the cause of your jealousy? You see us unarmed, and willing to supply your wants, if you will come in a friendly manner, and not with swords and guns, as to invade an enemy. I am not so simple, as not to know it is better to eat good meat, lie well, and sleep quietly with my women and children; to laugh and be merry with the English; and, being their friend, to have copper, hatchets, and whatever else I want, than to fly from all, to lie cold in the woods, feed upon acorns, roots, and such trash, and to be so hunted, that I cannot rest, eat, or sleep. In such circumstances, my men must watch, and if a twig should but break, all would cry out, *"Here comes Capt. Smith"*; and so, in this miserable manner, to end my miserable life; and, Capt. Smith, this *might* be soon your fate too, through your rashness and unadvisedness. I, therefore, exhort you to peaceable councils; and, above all, I insist that the guns and swords, the cause of all our jealousy and uneasiness, be removed and sent away.

1609, 1841

John Smith
(1580–1631)

By age twenty-five John Smith had lived the romantic life of an English mercenary and adventurer throughout Europe, or so he claimed in *The True Travels, Adventures, and Observations of Captaine John Smith* (1630). Smith always played the hero of his own narratives, but evidence suggests that his stories generally are based on fact. Born in 1580 in Lincolnshire, England, to a freeman farmer, George Smith, and his wife Ann, John Smith received his first taste of adventure at seventeen when he fought in the Netherlands against Spain. Soon came more adventure: sea battles and abandonment by shipmates, combat against the Turks in the Balkans (off the Mediterranean Sea), capture and enslavement by the Turks, and even rescue by beautiful maidens. By the time he returned to England in 1605, he was Captain John Smith, still eager for travel. He then looked to America for adventure.

In 1606 England's King James chartered the London Trading Company to explore and settle the American mainland, hoping to compete with successful Spanish explorations. Smith left for Virginia as one of the settlement's seven leaders in December 1606. The unpleasant four-month-long voyage was especially dangerous for Smith; he was arrested for mutiny and kept from the governing board until 1607. Thus began a continuing conflict between Smith and other colonists, brought on, he claimed, by their jealousy. Hoping to find rich deposits of gold and other precious metals, the colonists were unprepared for the harsh conditions of Virginia. The group arrived at Jamestown in April 1607, but by September half the group members were lost to disease or fights with the natives. By the next spring only 38 out of the original 105 colonists had survived.

Smith's experience in survival soon proved valuable to the starving colonists, and he led the colony from September 1608 to August 1609. During an early exploration, he was captured by Native Americans and condemned to death. His first account of his capture, *A*

A map of Virginia engraved by William Hole and used by John Smith.

True Relation of . . . Virginia (1608), made no mention of the Algonquian girl Pocahantas. His version sixteen years later, *The General History of Virginia, New England, and the Summer Isles* (1624), introduces the now-familiar story of his rescue by the Algonquian leader Powhatan's daughter. As is true of Smith's other writings, how much of the story is factual is unclear. However, it accurately depicts the uncertain, often violent relations with the natives. Smith was able to bargain with, even cajole, them for corn in order to keep the colonists from starving. Still, his severe rule did not win willing supporters. Seriously wounded in October 1609 by an accidental explosion of his gunpowder bag, Smith left for England to recover.

Although he never returned to Jamestown, Smith traveled in 1614 to the place he named "New England," what is now Maine and Massachusetts. After spending the winter, he returned to England, hoping to encourage others to settle in New England. He offered to lead the Pilgrims from the Netherlands, but they rejected his offer and later settled at Plymouth. Smith was never to travel to America again. Instead, he compiled travel narratives and wrote of his adventures. In *A Description of New England* (1616), *New England Trials* (1620), and especially *The General History of Virginia,* he provided a wealth of information and adventure stories for future colonists of America. He died in London in 1631.

Suggested Readings: E. Emerson, *Captain John Smith,* 1971. A. T. Vaughan, *American Genesis: Captain John Smith and the Founding of Virginia,* 1975.

Text Used: *The Travels and Works of Captaine John Smith,* 2 vols., ed. E. Arber, 1910 (some spelling and punctuation modernized).

from   THE DESCRIPTION OF NEW ENGLAND

[*Growing Wealthy in New England*]

I have not been so ill bred, but I have tasted of plenty and pleasure, as well as want and misery; nor does necessity yet, or occasion of discontent, force me to these endeavors; nor am I ignorant what small thanks I shall have for my pains, or that many would have the world imagine them to be of great judgement, that can but blemish these my designs,[1] by their witty objections and detractions. Yet (I hope) my reasons with my deeds will so prevail with some that I shall not want employment in these affairs, to make the most blind see his own senselessness and incredulity, hoping that gain will make them affect that which religion, charity, and the common good cannot. It were but a poor device in me to deceive myself, much more the King, State, my friends and country, with these inducements: which seeing His Majesty hath given permission, I wish all sorts of worthy, honest, industrious spirits would understand, and if they desire any further satisfaction, I will do my best to give it, not to persuade them to go only, but go with them; not leave them there, but live with them there.

I will not say, but by ill providing and undue managing, such courses may be taken [that] may make us miserable enough. But if I may have the execution of what I have projected; if they want to eat, let them eat or never digest[2] me. If I perform what I say, I desire but that reward out of the gains [which] may suit my pains, quality, and condition. And if I abuse you with my tongue, take my head for satisfaction. If any dislike at the year's end, defraying their charge, by my consent they should freely return. I fear not want of company sufficient, were it but known what I know of those countries; and by the proof of that wealth I hope yearly to return, if God please to bless me from such accidents as are beyond my power in reason to prevent. For I am not so simple to think that ever any other motive than wealth will ever erect there a commonwealth or draw company from their ease and humors[3] at home to stay in New England to effect my purposes.

And lest any should think the toil might be insupportable, though these things may be had by labor and diligence, I assure myself there are those who delight extremely in vain pleasure, that take much more pains in England to enjoy it than I should do here [New England] to gain wealth sufficient. And yet I think they should not have half such sweet content, for our pleasure here is still gains; in England charges and loss. Here nature and liberty afford us that freely which in England we want, or it costs us dearly. What pleasure can be more than (being tired with any occasion ashore, in planting vines, fruits, or herbs, in contriving their own grounds, to the pleasure of their own minds, their fields, gardens, or-

---

[1] His plans to form a colony in New England.   [2] Tolerate.   [3] Fancies.

chards, buildings, ships, and other works, etc.) to recreate themselves[4] before their own doors, in their own boats upon the sea, where man, woman, and child, with a small hook and line, by angling may take diverse sorts of excellent fish at their pleasures? And is it not pretty sport to pull up two pence, six pence, and twelve pence as fast as you can haul and veer[5] a line? He is a very bad fisher [that] cannot kill in one day with his hook and line one, two, or three hundred cods, which dressed and dried, if they be sold there for ten shillings the hundred [pounds], though in England they will give more than twenty, may not both the servant, the master, and merchant be well content with this gain? If a man works but three days in seven he may get more than he can spend, unless he will be excessive. Now that carpenter, mason, gardener, tailor, smith, sailor, forgers, or what other, may they not make this a pretty recreation, though they fish but an hour in the day, to take more than they eat in a week? Or if they will not eat it, because there is so much better choice, yet sell it or change it with the fishermen or merchants for anything they want. And what sport does yield a more pleasing content and less hurt or charge than angling with a hook and crossing the sweet air from isle to isle, over the silent streams of a calm sea? Wherein the most curious may find pleasure, profit, and content.

Thus, though all men be not fishers, yet all men, whatsoever, may in other matters do as well. For necessity does in these cases so rule a commonwealth, and each in their several functions, as their labors in their qualities, may be as profitable because there is a necessary mutual use of all.

For gentlemen, what exercise should more delight them than ranging daily those unknown parts, using fowling and fishing, for hunting and hawking? And yet you shall see the wild hawks give you some pleasure, in seeing them stoop[6] (six or seven after one another) an hour or two together at the schools of fish in the fair harbors, as those ashore [do] at a fowl, and never trouble nor torment yourselves with watching, mewing,[7] feeding, and attending them, nor kill a horse and man with running and crying "See you not a hawk?" For hunting also, the woods, lakes, and rivers afford not only chase sufficient for any that delight in that kind of toil or pleasure, but such beast to hunt that besides the delicacy of their bodies for food, their skins are so rich as may well recompense thy daily labor with a Captain's pay.

For laborers, if those [in England] that sow hemp, rape,[8] turnips, parsnips, carrots, cabbage, and such like, give twenty, thirty, forty, fifty shillings yearly for an acre of ground, and meat, drink, and wages to use it and yet grow rich, when better or at least as good ground may be had [in New England] and cost nothing but labor, it seems strange to me any such should there grow poor.

My purpose is not to persuade children from their parents, men from their wives, nor servants from their masters; only such as with free consent may be spared. But that each parish or village, in city or country, that will but apparel[9] their fatherless children of thirteen or fourteen years of age, or young married people that have small wealth to live on, here by their labor may live exceedingly well: provided always that first there be a sufficient power to command them, houses to receive them, means to defend them, and meet[10] provisions for them, for any place may be overlain,[11] and it is most necessary to have a fortress (ere

---

[4] To rest.   [5] Let out.   [6] Swoop.   [7] Caging.
[8] A plant whose leaves are used as fodder for sheep and hogs.   [9] Make ready.   [10] Appropriate.
[11] Overtaken.

this grow to practice) and sufficient masters (as carpenters, masons, fishers, fowlers, gardeners, husbandmen,[12] sawyers,[13] smiths, spinners, tailors, weavers, and such like) to take ten, twelve, or twenty, or as there is occasion, for apprentices. The masters by this may quickly grow rich; these [apprentices] may learn their trades themselves to do the like, to a general and an incredible benefit for king and country, master and servant.

1614, 1616

William Bradford
(1590–1657)

William Bradford, governor and principal historian of the Plymouth Colony, had probably intended to take over his father's small estate in Austerfield, Yorkshire, England, until Bradford heard the sermons of Richard Clyfton, a Nonconformist minister. That sermon moved Bradford, then age twelve, to join a Nonconformist congregation in nearby Scrooby. Born in Austerfield in 1590, Bradford had lost both his father and mother by 1597, leaving him to be raised locally by his grandparents and uncles. The Scrooby congregation became a spiritual home for young Bradford, against the wishes of his family. There Bradford acquired the dedicated spiritual piety that was to lead him from England to Holland and eventually to the New World.

By 1606 England's Reformation had reached such a pitch of self-purification that the Scrooby congregation, believing that even the Church of England was too corrupt to reform, decided to separate. Their decision to create a Separatist church was made in part out of fear that the recently crowned James I was sympathetic to the Catholic church. Believing Scripture to be a more trustworthy guide and authority than church hierarchy, the Scrooby congregation modeled the covenant made among its members on God's covenants with Adam and Abraham. Separation, however, was considered treason by the Crown, so in 1608 the group, including Bradford, traveled to Amsterdam and in 1609 to Leyden, the Netherlands, reportedly a haven for religious freedom. There Bradford bought a house and loom, went into business, and married Dorothy May in 1613—intending, like the others, to stay.

Making a living in the textile trade was difficult, and as time passed, the religious leaders discovered the younger members departing from the group. In *Of Plymouth Plantation* (not published until 1856), Bradford describes the decision in 1620 to travel to "those vast and unpeopled countries of America, which are fruitful and fit for habitation." The group, which Bradford called Pilgrims, successfully petitioned the Virginia Company of London for land in the Virginia Territory, which extended as far North as New York City today. But when the *Mayflower* was forced by storms to land at what is now Plymouth, Massachusetts, the winter weather and the immigrants' exhaustion convinced them to stay rather than continue southward.

Only about forty percent of the *Mayflower*'s passengers were part of the religious com-

---

[12] Farmers.   [13] A person who saws wood.

munity; the others (including Myles Standish) were "strangers," many of whom were sent by London merchants to represent the financial backers' economic interests. Out of fear that this diversity would invite dissension, Bradford and other Pilgrims drew up the May-flower Compact. That document legitimized a government to support the Pilgrims' desire for a religious society in Plymouth and provided the first quasidemocratic government in the New World. Upon the death of the Plymouth Colony's first governor, John Carver, Bradford was elected governor, a position he held thirty times between 1621 and 1656.

Having lost his first wife at the end of the voyage, Bradford married Alice Carpenter Southworth in 1623. In 1630 he began writing *Of Plymouth Plantation*, perhaps in re-sponse to the arrival of John Winthrop and the neighboring colonists of Massachusetts Bay. In fact, the arrival of the Puritans, part of the "Great Migration" of twenty thousand people between 1628 and 1642, opened a new market for the Plymouth Colony's food and goods. Reflecting the unique circumstances of the Pilgrims, Bradford's history is a very different document than Winthrop's *Journal* (begun in 1630 but published in 1790). *Of Plymouth Plantation* is more consciously crafted, shaped by Bradford's awareness that the Pilgrims' original goals and ideals were often diverted by human weaknesses or the machi-nations of Satan's henchmen. The portion written in 1630 begins with a prologue chroni-cling the "wars and oppositions" that "Satan hath raised, maintained and continued against the Saints," thus making the Pilgrims part of a universal battle between good and evil.

Essential to Bradford's history is its conscious parallel between the Pilgrims' migration and Old Testament accounts of the Israelites journeying out of captivity toward the Prom-ised Land. God's providence provides for the Scrooby community in its journey from England to Holland and then to America, just as God had supported the Israelites' exodus. The first part of Bradford's history ends optimistically with the Pilgrims erecting their first house in the New World.

In 1646, when Bradford began writing the second book of his history, social changes dampened his enthusiasm. An economic depression and internal problems created a new plot for his history. Although the Plymouth community's holy covenant with God remains of utmost importance, the history depicts the main villains to be corrupt humans rather than Satan. The community's problems are less universal and more tied to historical cir-cumstances. The conflicts themselves are in some cases morally ambiguous even to Bradford. For example, although tradition has depicted a harmonious relation between Pilgrims and Native Americans, Bradford's history reveals a dark side to the relationship. At first helped by a friendly alliance with the Wampanoag chief, Massasoit, the Pilgrims found themselves caught up in battles between the Narragansetts and the Mohegans. Dur-ing the Pequot War in 1637, the combined New England colonies and the Narragansetts attacked the Pequot fort at Mystic, Connecticut, killing four hundred Pequots who had been sleeping inside. In *Of Plymouth Plantation* Bradford, not present during the attack, simply praises "God, who had wrought so wonderfully for" the Pilgrims.

The spiritual certainty and communal unity with which the Pilgrims arrived dissipates in *Of Plymouth Plantation* as more treachery and evil occurs in the community. As noted in *Of Plymouth Plantation*, in preparation for their trip to America the Pilgrims had antici-pated John Winthrop's famous "Model of Christian Charity" sermon (given in 1630 but published in 1838) by declaring "We are knit together as a body in a most strict and sacred bond and covenant of the Lord." But at a much later date, in an aged hand Bradford added a footnote to this passage: "But (alas) that subtle serpent hath slyly wound in himself under fair pretences of necessity and the like, to untwist these sacred bonds and ties, and as it were insensibly by degrees to dissolve, or in a great measure to weaken, the same." De-spite his doubts Bradford remained an able governor and honest historian until his death in 1657. In 1692 the Plymouth Colony merged with the more successful Massachusetts Bay Colony, and together they became an increasingly diverse and secular society.

Suggested Readings: B. Smith, *Bradford of Plymouth*, 1951. S. E. Morison, *Builders of the Bay Colony*, 1958. P. Gay, *A Loss of Mastery: Puritan Historians in Colonial America*, 1966.

Text Used: *Of Plymouth Plantation*, ed. S. E. Morison, 1952.

from   OF PLYMOUTH PLANTATION

from   BOOK I

Chapter IV: Showing the Reasons and Causes of Their Removal

After they had lived in this city[1] about some eleven or twelve years (which is the more observable being the whole time of that famous truce between that state and the Spaniards)[2] and sundry of them were taken away by death and many others began to be well stricken in years (the grave mistress of Experience having taught them many things), those prudent governors with sundry of the sagest members began both deeply to apprehend their present dangers and wisely to foresee the future and think of timely remedy. In the agitation of their thoughts, and much discourse of things hereabout, at length they began to incline to this conclusion: of removal to some other place. Not out of any newfangledness or other such like giddy humor by which men are oftentimes transported to their great hurt and danger, but for sundry weighty and solid reasons, some of the chief of which I will here briefly touch.

And first, they saw and found by experience the hardness of the place and country to be such as few in comparison would come to them, and fewer that would bide it out and continue with them. For many that came to them, and many more that desired to be with them, could not endure that great labour and hard fare, with other inconveniences which they underwent and were contented with. But though they loved their persons, approved their cause and honoured their sufferings, yet they left them as it were weeping, as Orpah did her mother-in-law Naomi,[3] or as those Romans did Cato[4] in Utica who desired to be excused and borne with, though they could not all be Catos. For many, though they desired to enjoy the ordinances of God in their purity and the liberty of the gospel with them, yet (alas) they admitted of bondage with danger of conscience, rather than to endure these hardships. Yea, some preferred and chose the prisons in England rather than this liberty in Holland with these afflictions.[5] But it was thought that if a better and easier place of living could be had, it would draw many and take away these discouragements. Yea, their pastor would often say that many of those who both wrote and preached now against them, if they were in a place where they might have liberty and live comfortably, they would then practice as they did.

[1] Leyden, the Netherlands.

[2] The twelve years' truce (of the Dutch war for independence from Spain), signed in 1609, was due to end in 1621.

[3] In Ruth 1:14, Orpah weeps when she must leave her mother-in-law, Naomi.

[4] Marcus Porcius (95–46 B.C.), a Roman statesman and philosopher, known as Cato the Younger, who committed suicide rather than surrender to Julius Caesar.

[5] The Netherlands were overpopulated during Bradford's time, and the standard of living was low.

Secondly. They saw that though the people generally bore all these difficulties very cheerfully and with a resolute courage, being in the best and strength of their years; yet old age began to steal on many of them; and their great and continual labours, with other crosses and sorrows, hastened it before the time. So as it was not only probably thought, but apparently seen, that within a few years more they would be in danger to scatter, by necessities pressing them, or sink under their burdens, or both. And therefore according to the divine proverb, that a wise man seeth the plague when it cometh, and hideth himself, Proverbs xxii.3, so they like skillful and beaten[6] soldiers were fearful either to be entrapped or surrounded by their enemies so as they should neither be able to fight nor fly. And therefore thought it better to dislodge betimes to some place of better advantage and less danger, if any such could be found.

Thirdly. As necessity was a taskmaster over them so they were forced to be such, not only to their servants but in a sort to their dearest children, the which as it did not a little wound the tender hearts of many a loving father and mother, so it produced likewise sundry sad and sorrowful effects. For many of their children that were of best dispositions and gracious inclinations, having learned to bear the yoke in their youth[7] and willing to bear part of their parents' burden, were often-times so oppressed with their heavy labours that though their minds were free and willing, yet their bodies bowed under the weight of the same, and became decrepit in their early youth, the vigour of nature being consumed in the very bud as it were. But that which was more lamentable, and of all sorrows most heavy to be borne, was that many of their children, by these occasions and the great licentiousness of youth in that country,[8] and the manifold temptations of the place, were drawn away by evil examples into extravagant and dangerous courses, getting the reins off their necks and departing from their parents. Some became soldiers, others took upon them far voyages by sea, and others some worse courses tending to dissoluteness and the danger of their souls, to the great grief of their parents and dishonour of God. So that they saw their posterity would be in danger to degenerate and be corrupted.[9]

Lastly (and which was not least), a great hope and inward zeal they had of laying some good foundation, or at least to make some way thereunto, for the propagating and advancing the gospel of the kingdom of Christ in those remote parts of the world; yea, though they should be but even as stepping-stones unto others for the performing of so great a work.

These and some other like reasons moved them to undertake this resolution of their removal; the which they afterward prosecuted with so great difficulties, as by the sequel will appear.

The place they had thoughts on was some of those vast and unpeopled countries of America, which are fruitful and fit for habitation, being devoid of all civil inhabitants, where there are only savage and brutish men which range up and down, little otherwise than the wild beasts of the same. This proposition being made public and coming to the scanning of all, it raised many variable opinions amongst men and caused many fears and doubts amongst themselves. Some, from their reasons and hopes conceived, laboured to stir up and encourage the rest to

---

[6] Experienced.   [7] "It is good for a man that he bear the yoke in his youth," from Lamentations 3:27.

[8] Unlike the English, the Dutch (especially children) feasted and enjoyed themselves after attending church on Sundays.

[9] The Pilgrims feared that their children would be assimilated into the Dutch "melting pot."

undertake and prosecute the same; others again, out of their fears, objected against it and sought to divert from it; alleging many things, and those neither unreasonable nor unprobable; as that it was a great design and subject to many unconceivable perils and dangers; as, besides the casualties of the sea (which none can be freed from), the length of the voyage was such as the weak bodies of women and other persons worn out with age and travail (as many of them were) could never be able to endure. And yet if they should, the miseries of the land which they should be exposed unto, would be too hard to be borne and likely, some or all of them together, to consume and utterly to ruinate them. For there they should be liable to famine and nakedness and the want, in a manner, of all things. The change of air, diet and drinking of water[10] would infect their bodies with sore sicknesses and grievous diseases. And also those which should escape or overcome these difficulties should yet be in continual danger of the savage people, who are cruel, barbarous and most treacherous, being most furious in their rage and merciless where they overcome; not being content only to kill and take away life, but delight to torment men in the most bloody manner that may be; flaying some alive with the shells of fishes, cutting off the members and joints of others by piecemeal and broiling on the coals, eat the collops[11] of their flesh in their sight whilst they live, with other cruelties horrible to be related.[12]

And surely it could not be thought but the very hearing of these things could not but move the very bowels of men to grate within them and make the weak to quake and tremble. It was further objected that it would require greater sums of money to furnish such a voyage and to fit them with necessaries, than their consumed estates would amount to; and yet they must as well look to be seconded with supplies as presently to be transported. Also many precedents of ill success and lamentable miseries befallen others in the like designs were easy to be found, and not forgotten to be alleded; besides their own experience, in their former troubles and hardships in their removal into Holland, and how hard a thing it was for them to live in that strange place, though it was a neighbour country and a civil and rich commonwealth.

It was answered, that all great and honourable actions are accompanied with great difficulties and must be both enterprised and overcome with answerable courages. It was granted the dangers were great, but not desperate. The difficulties were many, but not invincible. For though there were many of them likely, yet they were not certain. It might be sundry of the things feared might never befall; others by provident care and the use of good means might in a great measure be prevented; and all of them, through the help of God, by fortitude and patience, might either be borne or overcome. True it was that such attempts were not to be made and undertaken without good ground and reason, not rashly or lightly as many have done for curiosity or hope of gain, etc. But their condition was not ordinary, their ends were good and honourable, their calling lawful and urgent; and therefore they might expect the blessing of God in their proceeding. Yea, though they should lose their lives in this action, yet might they have comfort in the same and their endeavours would be honourable. They lived here but as men in exile and in a poor condition, and as great miseries might possibly befall them in this place; for the twelve years of truce were now out and there was nothing but

---

[10] During Bradford's time, well water was typically contaminated.   [11] Fatty folds.
[12] The travel narratives of the time made the Pilgrims respect the Native Americans and find the Spaniards in the New World distasteful.

beating of drums and preparing for war, the events whereof are always uncertain. The Spaniard might prove as cruel as the savages of America, and the famine and pestilence as sore here as there, and their liberty less to look out for remedy.

After many other particular things answered and alleged on both sides, it was fully concluded by the major part to put this design in execution and to prosecute it by the best means they could.

Chapter IX: Of Their Voyage, and How They Passed the Sea; and of Their Safe Arrival at Cape Cod

September 6.[1] These troubles being blown over, and now all being compact together in one ship,[2] they put to sea again with a prosperous wind, which continued divers days together, which was some encouragement unto them; yet, according to the usual manner, many were afflicted with seasickness. And I may not omit here a special work of God's providence. There was a proud and very profane young man, one of the seamen, of a lusty,[3] able body, which made him the more haughty; he would alway be contemning the poor people in their sickness and cursing them daily with grievous execrations; and did not let[4] to tell them that he hoped to help to cast half of them overboard before they came to their journey's end, and to make merry with what they had; and if he were by any gently reproved, he would curse and swear most bitterly. But it pleased God before they came half seas over, to smite this young man with a grievous disease, of which he died in a desperate manner, and so was himself the first that was thrown overboard. Thus his curses light on his own head, and it was an astonishment to all his fellows for they noted it to be the just hand of God upon him.

After they had enjoyed fair winds and weather for a season, they were encountered many times with cross winds and met with many fierce storms with which the ship was shroudly[5] shaken, and her upper works made very leaky; and one of the main beams in the midships was bowed and cracked, which put them in some fear that the ship could not be able to perform the voyage. So some of the chief of the company, perceiving the mariners to fear the sufficiency of the ship as appeared by their mutterings, they entered into serious consultation with the master and other officers of the ship, to consider in time of the danger, and rather to return than to cast themselves into a desperate and inevitable peril. And truly there was great distraction and difference of opinion amongst the mariners themselves; fain would they do what could be done for their wages' sake (being now near half the seas over) and on the other hand they were loath to hazard their lives too desperately. But in examining of all opinions, the master and others affirmed they knew the ship to be strong and firm under water; and for the buckling of the main beam, there was a great iron screw the passengers brought out of Holland, which would raise the beam into his place; the which being done, the carpenter and master affirmed that with a post put under it, set firm in the lower deck and other-

---

[1] Bradford used the Julian, not the Gregorian calendar, so his dates are 10 days earlier than they would be in our system.
[2] One of the two ships on which the Separatists set sail from England, the *Speedwell,* was not fit to make the voyage. Its passengers and cargo were transferred to the *Mayflower* back in England; the *Mayflower* then departed for America.
[3] Hardy, spirited.   [4] Hesitate.   [5] Shrewdly, originally meaning "wickedly."

ways bound, he would make it sufficient. And as for the decks and upper works, they would caulk them as well as they could, and though with the working of the ship[6] they would not long keep staunch,[7] yet there would otherwise be no great danger, if they did not overpress her with sails. So they committed themselves to the will of God and resolved to proceed.

In sundry of these storms the winds were so fierce and the seas so high, as they could not bear a knot of sail, but were forced to hull[8] for diverse days together. And in one of them, as they thus lay at hull in a mighty storm, a lusty young man called John Howland, coming upon some occasion above the gratings[9] was, with a seele[10] of the ship, thrown into sea; but it pleased God that he caught hold of the topsail halyards which hung overboard and ran out at length. Yet he held his hold (though he was sundry fathoms under water) till he was hauled up by the same rope to the brim of the water, and then with a boat hook and other means got into the ship again and his life saved. And though he was something ill with it, yet he lived many years after and became a profitable member both in church and commonwealth. In all this voyage there died but one of the passengers, which was William Butten, a youth, servant to Samuel Fuller, when they drew near the coast.

But to omit other things (that I may be brief) after long beating at sea they fell with that land which is called Cape Cod;[11] the which being made and certainly known to be it, they were not a little joyful. After some deliberation had amongst themselves and with the master of the ship, they tacked about and resolved to stand for the southward (the wind and weather being fair) to find some place about Hudson's River for their habitation.[12] But after they had sailed that course about half the day, they fell amongst dangerous shoals and roaring breakers, and they were so far entangled therewith as they conceived themselves in great danger; and the wind shrinking upon them withal, they resolved to bear up again for the Cape and thought themselves happy to get out of those dangers before night overtook them, as by God's good providence they did. And the next day[13] they got into the Cape Harbor[14] where they rid in safety.

A word or two by the way of this cape. It was thus first named by Captain Gosnold and his company,[15] Anno 1602, and after by Captain Smith was called Cape James; but it retains the former name amongst seamen. Also, that point which first showed those dangerous shoals unto them they called Point Care, and Tucker's Terrour; but the French and Dutch to this day call it Malabar by reason of those perilous shoals and the losses they have suffered there.

Being thus arrived in a good harbor, and brought safe to land, they fell upon their knees and blessed the God of Heaven[16] who had brought them over the vast and furious ocean, and delivered them from all the perils and miseries thereof, again to set their feet on the firm and stable earth, their proper element. And no marvel if they were thus joyful, seeing wise Seneca[17] was so affected with sailing

---

[6] Twisting of the ship's planks, creating leaks in the hull.
[7] Watertight.   [8] Under short sail, to drift with the wind.   [9] Wooden crossbars on the deck.
[10] Roll or toss.
[11] At daybreak on November 19 (9, with Bradford's timeframe), 1620, the Pilgrims first sighted the Cape Cod highlands.
[12] The English did not honor the Dutch's claims to the area and hoped to be the first to colonize it.
[13] November 21 (11), 1620; the journey from England took sixty-five days.
[14] Provincetown Harbor, today.
[15] Bradford's note: "Because they took much of that fish there."   [16] Daniel 2:19.
[17] A Roman philosopher and statesman (4? B.C.–A.D. 65).

a few miles on the coast of his own Italy, as he affirmed, that he had rather remain twenty years on his way by land than pass by sea to any place in a short time, so tedious and dreadful was the same unto him.[18]

But here I cannot but stay and make a pause, and stand half amazed at this poor people's present condition; and so I think will the reader, too, when he well considers the same. Being thus passed the vast ocean, and a sea of troubles before in their preparation (as may be remembered by that which went before), they had now no friends to welcome them nor inns to entertain or refresh their weather-beaten bodies; no houses or much less towns to repair to, to seek for succour. It is recorded in Scripture[19] as a mercy to the Apostle and his shipwrecked company, that the barbarians showed them no small kindness in refreshing them, but these savage barbarians, when they met with them (as after will appear) were readier to fill their sides full of arrows than otherwise. And for the season it was winter, and they that know the winters of that country know them to be sharp and violent, and subject to cruel and fierce storms, dangerous to travel to known places, much more to search an unknown coast. Besides, what could they see but a hideous and desolate wilderness, full of wild beasts and wild men—and what multitudes there might be of them they knew not. Neither could they, as it were, go up to the top of Pisgah[20] to view from this wilderness a more goodly country to feed their hopes; for which way soever they turned their eyes (save upward to the heavens) they could have little solace or content in respect of any outward objects. For summer being done, all things stand upon them with a weatherbeaten face, and the whole country, full of woods and thickets, represented a wild and savage hue. If they looked behind them, there was the mighty ocean which they had passed and was now as a main bar and gulf to separate them from all the civil parts of the world. If it be said they had a ship to succour them, it is true; but what heard they daily from the master and company? But that with speed they should look out a place (with their shallop[21]) where they would be, at some near distance; for the season was such as he would not stir from thence till a safe harbor was discovered by them, where they would be, and he might go without danger; and that victuals consumed apace but he must and would keep sufficient for themselves and their return. Yea, it was muttered by some that if they got not a place in time, they would turn them and their goods ashore and leave them. Let it also be considered what weak hopes of supply and succour they left behind them, that might bear up their minds in this sad condition and trials they were under; and they could not but be very small. It is true, indeed, the affections and love of their brethren at Leyden was cordial and entire towards them, but they had little power to help them or themselves; and how the case stood between them and the merchants[22] at their coming away hath already been declared.

What could now sustain them but the Spirit of God and His grace? May not and ought not the children of these fathers rightly say: "Our fathers were Englishmen which came over this great ocean, and were ready to perish in this wilderness; but

---

[18] Bradford's note: "Epistle 53," referring to Seneca's *Epistles*.

[19] Bradford's note: "Acts xxviii," referring to Acts 28, verse 2, in which the shipwrecked Paul is helped by "barbarous people."

[20] The mountain on which Moses stood to view the Promised Land, in Deuteronomy 34:1–4.

[21] An open boat with at least one mast, used in shallow waters.

[22] Those who had financed the Pilgrims' voyage.

they cried unto the Lord, and He heard their voice and looked on their adversity,"[23] etc. "Let them therefore praise the Lord, because He is good: and His mercies endure forever." "Yea, let them which have been redeemed of the Lord, shew how He hath delivered them from the hand of the oppressor. When they wandered in the desert wilderness out of the way, and found no city to dwell in, both hungry and thirsty, their soul was overwhelmed in them. Let them confess before the Lord His lovingkindness and His wonderful works before the sons of men."[24]

Chapter X: Showing How They Sought out a Place of Habitation; and What Befell Them Thereabout

Being thus arrived at Cape Cod the 11th of November, and necessity calling them to look out a place for habitation (as well as the master's and mariners' importunity); they having brought a large shallop[1] with them out of England, stowed in quarters in the ship, they now got her out and set their carpenters to work to trim her up; but being much bruised and shattered in the ship with foul weather, they saw she would be long in mending. Whereupon a few of them tendered themselves to go by land and discover those nearest places, whilst the shallop was in mending; and the rather because as they went into that harbor there seemed to be an opening some two or three leagues off, which the master judged to be a river. It was conceived there might be some danger in the attempt, yet seeing them resolute, they were permitted to go, being sixteen of them well armed under the conduct of Captain Standish,[2] having such instructions given them as was thought meet.

They set forth the 15th of November; and when they had marched about the space of a mile by the seaside, they espied five or six persons with a dog coming towards them, who were savages; but they fled from them and ran up into the woods, and the English followed them, partly to see if they could speak with them, and partly to discover if there might not be more of them lying in ambush. But the Indians seeing themselves thus followed, they again forsook the woods and ran away on the sands as hard as they could, so as they could not come near them but followed them by the track of their feet sundry miles and saw that they had come the same way. So, night coming on, they made their rendezvous and set out their sentinels, and rested in quiet that night; and the next morning followed their track till they had headed a great creek and so left the sands, and turned another way into the woods. But they still followed them by guess, hoping to find their dwellings; but they soon lost both them and themselves, falling into such thickets as were ready to tear their clothes and armor in pieces; but were most distressed for want of drink. But at length they found water and refreshed themselves, being the first New England water they drunk of, and was now in great thirst as pleasant unto them as wine or beer had been in foretimes.

---

[23] Bradford's note: "Deuteronomy xxvi.5, 7," referring to the Israelites' deliverance from the bondage of Egypt.

[24] Bradford's note: "Psalms cvii, 1–5, 8."

[1] An open boat with at least one mast, used in shallow waters.

[2] Myles Standish (1584?–1656), a professional soldier, was not a Pilgrim. He was employed to aid the colonists in their military affairs, and became a loyal supporter.

Afterwards they directed their course to come to the other shore, for they knew it was a neck of land they were to cross over, and so at length got to the seaside and marched to this supposed river, and by the way found a pond[3] of clear, fresh water, and shortly after a good quantity of clear ground where the Indians had formerly set corn, and some of their graves. And proceeding further they saw new stubble where corn had been set the same year; also they found where lately a house had been, where some planks and a great kettle was remaining, and heaps of sand newly paddled with their hands. Which, they digging up, found in them divers fair Indian baskets filled with corn, and some in ears, fair and good, of divers colours, which seemed to them a very goodly sight (having never seen any such before). This was near the place of that supposed river they came to seek, unto which they went and found it to open itself into two arms with a high cliff of sand in the entrance[4] but more like to be creeks of salt water than any fresh, for aught they saw; and that there was good harborage for their shallop, leaving it further to be discovered by their shallop, when she was ready. So, their time limited them being expired, they returned to the ship lest they should be in fear of their safety; and took with them part of the corn and buried up the rest. And so, like the men from Eshcol, carried with them of the fruits of the land and showed their brethren;[5] of which, and their return, they were marvelously glad and their hearts encouraged.

After this, the shallop being got ready, they set out again for the better discovery of this place, and the master of the ship desired to go himself. So there went some thirty men but found it[6] to be no harbour for ships but only for boats. There was also found two of their houses covered with mats, and sundry of their implements in them, but the people were run away and could not be seen. Also there was found more of their corn and of their beans of various colours; the corn and beans they brought away, purposing to give them full satisfaction when they should meet with any of them as, about some six months afterward they did, to their good content.

And here is to be noted a special providence of God, and a great mercy to this poor people, that here they got seed to plant them corn the next year, or else they might have starved, for they had none nor any likelihood to get any till the season had been past, as the sequel did manifest. Neither is it likely they had had this, if the first voyage had not been made, for the ground was now all covered with snow and hard frozen; but the Lord is never wanting unto His in their greatest needs; let His holy name have all the praise.

The month of November being spent in these affairs, and much foul weather falling in, the 6th of December they sent out their shallop again with ten of their principal men and some seamen, upon further discovery, intending to circulate that deep bay of Cape Cod. The weather was very cold and it froze so hard as the spray of the sea lighting on their coats, they were as if they had been glazed. Yet that night betimes they got down into the bottom of the bay, and as they drew near the shore they saw some ten or twelve Indians[7] very busy about something. They landed about a league or two from them, and had much ado to put ashore any-

---

[3] The pond for which Pond Village, Truro (in Massachusetts) was named.

[4] The Pamet River, a salt creek.

[5] In Numbers 13:23–26, grapes from the Valley of Eshcol were so heavy that two of Moses' scouts were needed to carry them.

[6] The mouth of the Pamet River, now Cold Harbor.

[7] Near Eastham, Massachusetts, home of the Nauset Indians.

where—it lay so full of flats. Being landed, it grew late and they made themselves a barricado with logs and boughs as well as they could in the time, and set out their sentinel and betook them to rest, and saw the smoke of the fire the savages made that night. When morning was come they divided their company, some to coast along the shore in the boat, and the rest marched through the woods to see the land, if any fit place might be for their dwelling. They came also to the place where they saw the Indians the night before, and found they had been cutting up a great fish like a grampus,[8] being some two inches thick of fat like a hog, some pieces whereof they had left by the way. And the shallop found two more of these fishes dead on the sands, a thing usual after storms in that place, by reason of the great flats of sand that lie off.

So they ranged up and down all that day, but found no people, nor any place they liked. When the sun grew low, they hasted out of the woods to meet with their shallop, to whom they made signs to come to them into a creek hard by,[9] the which they did at high water; of which they were very glad, for they had not seen each other all that day since the morning. So they made them a barricado as usually they did every night, with logs, stakes and thick pine boughs, the height of a man, leaving it open to leeward, partly to shelter them from the cold and wind (making their fire in the middle and lying round about it) and partly to defend them from any sudden assaults of the savages, if they should surround them; so being very weary, they betook them to rest. But about midnight they heard a hideous and great cry, and their sentinel called "Arm! arm!" So they bestirred them and stood to their arms and shot off a couple of muskets, and then the noise ceased. They concluded it was a company of wolves or such like wild beasts, for one of the seamen told them he had often heard such a noise in Newfoundland.

So they rested till about five of the clock in the morning; for the tide, and their purpose to go from thence, made them be stirring betimes. So after prayer they prepared for breakfast, and it being day dawning it was thought best to be carrying things down to the boat. But some said it was not best to carry the arms down, others said they would be the readier, for they had lapped them up in their coats from the dew; but some three or four would not carry theirs till they went themselves. Yet as it fell out, the water being not high enough, they laid them down on the bank side and came up to breakfast.

But presently, all on the sudden, they heard a great and strange cry, which they knew to be the same voices they heard in the night, though they varied their notes; and one of their company being abroad came running in and cried, "Men, Indians! Indians!" And withal, their arrows came flying amongst them. Their men ran with all speed to recover their arms, as by the good providence of God they did. In the meantime, of those that were there ready, two muskets were discharged at them, and two more stood ready in the entrance of their rendezvous but were commanded not to shoot till they could take full aim at them. And the other two charged again with all speed, for there were only four had arms there, and defended the barricado, which was first assaulted. The cry of the Indians was dreadful, especially when they saw their men run out of the rendezvous toward the shallop to recover their arms, the Indians wheeling about upon them. But some running out with coats of mail on, and cutlasses in their hands, they soon got their arms and let fly amongst them and quickly stopped their violence. Yet there was a lusty man, and no less valiant, stood behind a tree within half a musket shot, and

---

[8] Most likely a blackfish.   [9] The mouth of Herring River in present-day Eastham.

let his arrows fly at them; he was seen [to] shoot three arrows, which were all avoided. He stood three shots of a musket, till one taking full aim at him and made the bark or splinters of the tree fly about his ears, after which he gave an extraordinary shriek and away they went, all of them. They[10] left some to keep the shallop and followed them about a quarter of a mile and shouted once or twice, and shot off two or three pieces, and so returned. This they did that they might conceive that they were not afraid of them or any way discouraged.

Thus it pleased God to vanquish their enemies and give them deliverance; and by His special providence so to dispose that not any one of them were either hurt or hit, though their arrows came close by them and on every side [of] them; and sundry of their coats, which hung up in the barricado, were shot through and through. Afterwards they gave God solemn thanks and praise for their deliverance, and gathered up a bundle of their arrows and sent them into England afterward by the master of the ship, and called that place the First Encounter.

From hence they departed and coasted all along but discerned no place likely for harbor; and therefore hasted to a place that their pilot (one Mr. Coppin who had been in the country before) did assure them was a good harbor, which he had been in, and they might fetch it before night; of which they were glad for it began to be foul weather.

After some hours' sailing it began to snow and rain, and about the middle of the afternoon the wind increased and the sea became very rough, and they broke their rudder, and it was as much as two men could do to steer her with a couple of oars. But their pilot bade them be of good cheer for he saw the harbor; but the storm increasing, and night drawing on, they bore what sail they could to get in, while they could see. But herewith they broke their mast in three pieces and their sail fell overboard in a very grown sea, so as they had like to have been cast away. Yet by God's mercy they recovered themselves, and having the flood[11] with them, struck into the harbor. But when it came to, the pilot was deceived in the place, and said the Lord be merciful unto them for his eyes never saw that place before; and he and the master's mate would have run her ashore in a cove full of breakers before the wind. But a lusty seaman which steered bade those which rowed, if they were men, about with her or else they were all cast away; the which they did with speed. So he bid them be of good cheer and row lustily, for there was a fair sound before them, and he doubted not but they should find one place or other where they might ride in safety. And though it was very dark and rained sore, yet in the end they got under the lee of a small island and remained there all that night in safety. But they knew not this to be an island till morning, but were divided in their minds; some would keep the boat for fear they might be amongst the Indians, other were so wet and cold they could not endure but got ashore, and with much ado got fire (all things being so wet); and the rest were glad to come to them, for after midnight the wind shifted to the northwest and it froze hard.

But though this had been a day and night of much trouble and danger unto them, yet God gave them a morning of comfort and refreshing (as usually He doth to His children) for the next day was a fair, sunshining day, and they found themselves to be on an island secure from the Indians, where they might dry their stuff, fix their pieces[12] and rest themselves; and gave God thanks for His mercies in their manifold deliverances. And this being the last day of the week, they prepared there to keep the Sabbath.

---

[10] The English.   [11] The flood tide, averaging 9 ft. there today.   [12] Armaments.

On Monday they sounded[13] the harbor and found it fit for shipping, and marched into the land and found divers cornfields and little running brooks, a place (as they supposed) fit for situation.[14] At least it was the best they could find, and the season and their present necessity made them glad to accept of it. So they returned to their ship again with this news to the rest of their people, which did much comfort their hearts.

On the 15th of December they weighed anchor to go to the place they had discovered, and came within two leagues of it, but were fain to bear up again; but the 16th day, the wind came fair, and they arrived safe in this harbor. And afterwards took better view of the place, and resolved where to pitch their dwelling; and the 25th day began to erect the first house for common use to receive them and their goods.

from   BOOK II

from   *Chapter XI: The Remainder of Anno 1620**
[The Mayflower Compact]

I shall a little return back, and begin with a combination[1] made by them before they came ashore; being the first foundation of their government in this place. Occasioned partly by the discontented and mutinous speeches that some of the strangers[2] amongst them had let fall from them in the ship: That when they came ashore they would use their own liberty, for none had power to command them, the patent they had being for Virginia and not for New England, which belonged to another government, with which the Virginia Company had nothing to do.[3] And partly that such an act by them done, this their condition considered, might be as firm as any patent,[4] and in some respects more sure.

The form was as followeth:[5]

IN THE NAME OF GOD, AMEN.

We whose names are underwritten, the loyal subjects of our dread Sovereign Lord King James, by the Grace of God of Great Britain, France, and Ireland King, Defender of the Faith, etc.

Having undertaken, for the Glory of God and advancement of the Christian Faith and Honour of our King and Country, a Voyage to plant the First Colony in the Northern Parts of Virginia,[6] do by these presents[7] solemnly and mutually in the presence of God and one of another, Covenant and Combine ourselves to-

---

[13] Measured the depth of.

[14] Morison's note: "Here is the only contemporary authority for the 'Landing of the Pilgrims on Plymouth Rock' on Monday 11 [21] Dec. 1620." The landing was made from the shallop while the *Mayflower* was in Provincetown Harbor; no women landed and no Native Americans greeted the landing party, which may not have landed on the boulder now called Plymouth Rock.

* Bradford numbered his manuscript only up to Chapter X; Morison uses these chapter numbers.

[1] An agreement.   [2] The Puritans' term for those outside their church.

[3] The Mayflower Compact, signed on November 21 (11), 1620, was drawn up to provide the Pilgrims with a document validating their colonization in New England, as their charter from the Virginia Company of London authorized colonization south of 41° N (as far north as New York City).

[4] A legal document signed by a sovereign to grant special privileges.

[5] Morison's note: "The original document has disappeared, so this may be regarded as the most authentic text of the Compact. It was first printed in *Mourt's Relation* (1622). . . . "

[6] New England.   [7] Provisions.

gether into a Civil Body Politic, for our[8] better ordering and preservation and furtherance of the ends aforesaid; and by virtue hereof to enact, constitute and frame such just and equal Laws, Ordinances, Acts, Constitutions and Offices, from time to time, as shall be thought most meet and convenient for the general good of the Colony, unto which we promise all due submission and obedience. In witness whereof we have hereunder subscribed our names at Cape Cod, the 11th of November, in the year of the reign of our Sovereign Lord King James, of England, France and Ireland the eighteenth, and of Scotland the fifty-fourth. Anno Domini 1620.

After this they chose, or rather confirmed, Mr. John Carver[9] (a man godly and well approved amongst them) their Governor for that year. And after they had provided a place for their goods, or common store (which were long in unlading[10] for want of boats, foulness of the winter weather and sickness of diverse)[11] and begun some small cottages for their habitation; as time would admit, they met and consulted of laws and orders, both for their civil and military government as the necessity of their condition did require, still adding thereunto as urgent occasion in several times, and as cases did require.

In these hard and difficult beginnings they found some discontents and murmurings arise amongst some, and mutinous speeches and carriages[12] in other; but they were soon quelled and overcome by the wisdom, patience, and just and equal carriage of things, by the Governor and better part, which clave[13] faithfully together in the main.

Chapter XXVIII: Anno Dom: *1637*
[*The Pequot War*]

In the fore part of this year, the Pequots[1] fell openly upon the English at Connecticut, in the lower parts of the river,[2] and slew sundry of them as they were at work in the fields, both men and women, to the great terrour of the rest, and went away in great pride and triumph, with many high threats. They also assaulted a fort at the river's mouth, though strong and well defended; and though they did not there prevail, yet it struck them with much fear and astonishment to see their bold attempts in the face of danger. Which made them in all places to stand upon their guard and to prepare for resistance, and earnestly to solicit their friends and confederates in the Bay of Massachusetts to send them speedy aid, for they looked for more forcible assaults. Mr. Vane,[3] being then Governor, writ from their General Court to them here to join with them in this war. To which they were cordially willing, but took opportunity to write to them about some former things, as well as present, considerable hereabout. The which will best appear in the Governor's answer, which he returned to the same, which I shall here insert.

---

[8] Bradford replaced "ye" with "our."

[9] John Carver (1575?–1621), a tradesman who had been appointed governor of the Pilgrim colony even before they set sail from England; his election after the compact was signed confirmed that appointment.

[10] Unloading.   [11] Various people.   [12] Conduct.   [13] Cleaved.

[1] An Algonquian Indian tribe of Connecticut; their disputes with the colonists ended in the Pequot War of 1637.

[2] The Connecticut River.

[3] Sir Henry Vane (1613–1662), then the Massachusetts Bay Colony's governor.

In the meantime, the Pequots, especially in the winter before, sought to make peace with the Narragansetts, and used very pernicious arguments to move them thereunto: as that the English were strangers and began to overspread their country, and would deprive them thereof in time, if they were suffered to grow and increase. And if the Narragansetts did assist the English to subdue them, they did but make way for their own overthrow, for if they were rooted out, the English would soon take occasion to subjugate them. And if they would hearken to them they should not need to fear the strength of the English, for they would not come to open battle with them but fire their houses, kill their cattle, and lie in ambush for them as they went abroad upon their occasions; and all this they might easily do without any or little danger to themselves. The which course being held, they well saw the English could not long subsist but they would either be starved with hunger or be forced to forsake the country. With many the like things; insomuch that the Narragansetts were once wavering and were half minded to have made peace with them, and joined against the English. But again, when they considered how much wrong they had received from the Pequots, and what an opportunity they now had by the help of the English to right themselves; revenge was so sweet unto them as it prevailed above all the rest, so as they resolved to join with the English against them, and did.

The Court here agreed forthwith to send fifty men at their own charge; and with as much speed as possibly they could, got them armed and had made them ready under sufficient leaders,[4] and provided a bark[5] to carry them provisions and tend upon them for all occasions. But when they were ready to march, with a supply from the Bay, they had word to stay; for the enemy was as good as vanquished and there would be no need.

I shall not take upon me exactly to describe their proceedings in these things, because I expect it will be fully done by themselves who best know the carriage and circumstances of things. I shall therefore but touch them in general. From Connecticut, who were most sensible of the hurt sustained and the present danger, they set out a party of men, and another party met them from the Bay, at Narragansetts', who were to join with them.[6] The Narragansetts were earnest to be gone before the English were well rested and refreshed, especially some of them which came last. It should seem their desire was to come upon the enemy suddenly and undiscovered. There was a bark of this place, newly put in there, which was come from Connecticut, who did encourage them to lay hold of the Indians' forwardness, and to show as great forwardness as they, for it would encourage them, and expedition might prove to their great advantage. So they went on and so ordered their march as the Indians brought them to a fort[7] of the enemy's (in which most of their chief men were) before day. They approached the same with great silence and surrounded it both with English and Indians, that they might not break out; and so assaulted them with great courage, shooting amongst them, and entered the fort with all speed. And those that first entered found sharp resistance from the

---

[4] Lieutenant William Holmes (?–1662); Thomas Prence (1600–1673), later a governor of the Plymouth Colony; and forty-two men.

[5] A sailing ship.

[6] The Connecticut party of ninety men was led by Captain John Mason (1588–1635), later a founder of the Dover Colony (New Hampshire); the Bay party of forty men was led by Captain John Underhill (1597?–1672), later a governor of the Dover Colony; one hundred more men were to follow.

[7] Mystic Fort, on the western bank of Connecticut's Mystic River.

enemy who both shot at and grappled with them; others ran into their houses and brought out fire and set them on fire, which soon took in their mat;[8] and standing close together, with the wind all was quickly on a flame, and thereby more were burnt to death than was otherwise slain; It burnt their bowstrings and made them unserviceable; those that scaped the fire were slain with the sword, some hewed to pieces, others run through with their rapiers, so as they were quickly dispatched and very few escaped. It was conceived they thus destroyed about 400 at this time. It was a fearful sight to see them thus frying in the fire and the streams of blood quenching the same, and horrible was the stink and scent thereof; but the victory seemed a sweet sacrifice,[9] and they gave the praise thereof to God, who had wrought so wonderfully for them, thus to enclose their enemies in their hands and give them so speedy a victory over so proud and insulting an enemy.

The Narragansett Indians all this while stood round about, but aloof from all danger and left the whole execution to the English, except it were the stopping of any that broke away. Insulting over their enemies in this their ruin and misery, when they saw them dancing in the flames, calling them by a word in their own language, signifying "O brave Pequots!" which they used familiarly among themselves in their own praise in songs of triumph after their victories. After this service was thus happily accomplished, they marched to the waterside where they met with some of their vessels, by which they had refreshing with victuals and other necessaries. But in their march the rest of the Pequots drew into a body and accosted them, thinking to have some advantage against them by reason of a neck of land. But when they saw the English prepare for them they kept aloof, so as they neither did hurt nor could receive any.

After their refreshing, and repair together for further counsel and directions, they resolved to pursue their victory and follow the war against the rest. But the Narragansett Indians, most of them, forsook them, and such of them as they had with them for guides or otherwise, they found them very cold and backward in the business, either out of envy, or that they saw the English would make more profit of the victory than they were willing they should; or else deprive them of such advantage as themselves desired, by having them become tributaries unto them, or the like.

For the rest of this business, I shall only relate the same as it is in a letter which came from Mr. Winthrop to the Governor here, as followeth.

That I may make an end of this matter, this Sassacus (the Pequots' chief sachem) being fled to the Mohawks, they cut off his head, with some other of the chief of them, whether to satisfy the English or rather the Narragansetts (who, as I have since heard, hired them to do it) or for their own advantage, I well know not; but thus this war took end. The rest of the Pequots were wholly driven from their place, and some of them submitted themselves to the Narragansetts and lived under them. Others of them betook themselves to the Mohegans under Uncas, their sachem, with the approbation of the English of Connecticut, under whose protection Uncas lived; and he and his men had been faithful to them in this war and done them very good service. But this did so vex the Narragansetts, that they had not the whole sway over them, as they have never ceased plotting and contriving how to bring them under; and because they cannot attain their ends, because of

---

[8] The wall and floor mats caught fire.
[9] In Leviticus 2:1–2, the priest's ceremonial burning was "a sweet savour unto the Lord."

the English who have protected them, they have sought to raise a general conspiracy against the English, as will appear in another place.

from   Chapter XXXVI: Anno Dom: 1646
[Winslow's Final Departure]

This year Mr. Edward Winslow[1] went into England, upon this occasion: some discontented persons under the government of the Massachusetts sought to trouble their peace and disturb, if not innovate,[2] their government by laying many scandals upon them, and intended to prosecute against them in England by petitioning and complaining to the Parliament.[3] Also, Samuel Gorton and his company made complaints against them.[4] So as they made choice of Mr. Winslow to be their agent to make their defense, and gave him commission and instructions for that end. In which he so carried himself as did well answer their ends and cleared them from any blame or dishonour, to the shame of their adversaries. But by reason of the great alterations in the State,[5] he was detained longer than was expected, and afterwards fell into other employments there; so as he hath now been absent this four years, which hath been much to the weakening of this government, without whose consent he took these employments upon him.

Anno 1647.   And Anno 1648.[6]

1630–1651, 1856

John Winthrop
(1588–1649)

Born in Edwardstone, England, into the Old World culture of Elizabethan England in 1588, the year the Spanish Armada was launched against England, John Winthrop played a major role in shaping the New World fortunes of Puritan New England. Winthrop was the son of Anne Browne and Adam Winthrop, the successful lord of Groton Manor. At age fourteen Winthrop entered Trinity College, Cambridge. There, during an illness, he experienced the religious conversion that brought him to the Puritans, the conservative and reformist wing of the Church of England.

[1] Edward Winslow (1595–1655), was the founder and a governor of the Plymouth Colony. An original *Mayflower* passenger, he returned to England in 1646 to defend the Massachusetts Bay Colony against depriving Church of England members of their civil and religious rights; once successful, Winslow remained in England.

[2] Disrupt.   [3] The Remonstrance and Petition to the General Court on May 6, 1646.

[4] Samuel Gorton (1592–1677), a notorious troublemaker in New England, was banished from four colonies and eventually founded Warwick, Rhode Island.

[5] The Puritan Revolution in England, in which King Charles was executed; Oliver Cromwell (1599–1658) was established as Lord Protector of the Commonwealth, now a Puritan republic.

[6] No entries follow this, completed in 1650. In 1651 Bradford added the names of the *Mayflower* passengers.

Winthrop's decision to immigrate to America resulted from the increasingly difficult economic and political conditions in England. A depression in the textile industry forced him into the practice of law in London, and in 1627 he was appointed attorney to the Court of Wards and Liveries. However, the new king, Charles I, was determined to keep the Puritans out of power. Winthrop eventually found himself out of a job. In 1629 Charles I dissolved Parliament, precipitating a crisis that eventually led to civil war. For Winthrop such events meant trouble. "I am veryly perswaded, God will bringe some heauye [heavy] Affliction vpon this lande," he wrote to his third wife (of four), Margaret Tyndal. But he added, "If the Lord seeth it wilbe good for vs, he will prouide a shelter and a hidinge place for vs and ours."

The shelter proved to be the Massachusetts Bay Company, a group of Puritans intent on colonizing America under royal charter. This charter, unlike most, did not require that the company hold meetings in England, so when Winthrop was elected governor of the company in 1629, the group found itself relatively independent. Even though the Puritans had not separated from the Church of England, as had the Pilgrims of Plymouth, they enjoyed a good deal of religious and political autonomy. When Winthrop left for New England on the *Arbella* in 1630, the ground was already prepared for the planting of seeds of a Puritan commonwealth based on strict religious principles.

In his famous 1630 sermon "A Model of Christian Charity" (not published until 1838), Winthrop articulated these underlying principles even as the *Arbella* sailed to New England. Foremost of these principles is "charity," or love, the force by which individual differences are overcome by a desire for connection to a larger body of people or to Christ himself. Using the metaphor of the body, Winthrop describes this company of Puritans as a single organic entity: "Christ and His church make one body . . . but when Christ comes and by His spirit and love knits all these parts to Himself and each to other, it is become the most perfect and best proportioned body in the world." Traveling from a deeply divided England under both a new charter and a new covenant with God, Winthrop hoped to protect the body politic from internal dissent and external danger. Whereas failure would mean that God might "withdraw his present help from us," the Puritans' success would insure that "The Lord will be our God, and delight to dwell among us as His own people."

Winthrop's sermon proved to be both a social blueprint and a warning of future problems for the young Massachusetts Bay Colony. Winthrop, serving as governor or deputy governor during most of the next two decades, faced several serious threats to the colony's unity and to his own authority. One of the first challenges was posed by Roger Williams, an iconoclastic religious radical who argued that Winthrop's colony should follow the Plymouth Colony's example and separate formally from the Church of England to achieve purity of religious doctrine. Winthrop rebutted him on this point, but Williams's later claim that the magistrate's power had come from the people and thus could not dictate religious matters, was too much for Winthrop, who believed his authority was derived from the colony's covenant with God. Williams fled to Rhode Island when he learned that Winthrop meant to send him back to England.

A more serious threat to the colony came from Anne Hutchinson and the "antinomian controversy" beginning in 1636. Hutchinson was "a woman of ready wit and bold spirit," according to Winthrop, but she attacked the colony's ministers for preaching the Old Covenant of works doctrine that "sanctification"—leading a righteous life and doing good works—is proof of salvation. Hutchinson believed that converts need look only for, and follow the indwelling of, the Holy Spirit in the New Covenant of faith, thus making ministers' sermons unnecessary for spiritual guidance. At her house (across the street from Winthrop's) Hutchinson began to hold meetings that grew to eighty women and men, including several influential merchants.

Nineteenth-century artists tended to paint romanticized visions of the early history of America and ignored the bitter hardships involved. This mural, Governor Winthrop Arrives at Salem on the Arbella—1630, *was painted by Charles Hoffbauer during the nineteenth century.*

The crisis came to head in her trial of 1637. With Winthrop as her chief questioner, Hutchinson fended the accusations off by arguing that her beliefs were within the realm of Puritan orthodoxy, and it appeared that the case against her might collapse. But when she claimed to have gained knowledge by an immediate revelation from God in God's own words, the court convicted her of heresy and banished her to Rhode Island in November 1637. (When Hutchinson suffered a miscarriage, Winthrop called it "proof" of God's displeasure with her.) Although this outcome insured the power of Winthrop and the clergy to control opinion and upheld the political model of government outlined in "A Model of Christian Charity," it also memorialized Hutchinson, on whose courage Nathaniel Hawthorne modeled Hester Prynne of *The Scarlet Letter* (1850), some two hundred years after Winthrop's death in 1649.

In his *Journal* (parts published in 1790; published in entirety as *The History of New England* [1825–1826]) Winthrop chronicled his conflicts with Anne Hutchinson as well as other matters—both serious and mundane—that occurred in the colony during its first nineteen years. Providing a day-to-day look at life in the New World, the *Journal* never loses its conviction that events and people are ultimately meaningful as expressions of God's will. In a ship's explosion, for example, Winthrop notes that "the judgment of God appeared, for the master and company were many of them profane scoffers at us, and at the ordinances of religion here." In describing the wars with the Pequot Indians, the disputes with Dutch settlers, and the punishments of internal troublemakers, Winthrop's *Journal* provides a revealing account of the Puritans' dedication and difficulties in establishing their "holy city on a hill."

Suggested Readings: *The History of New England*, 2 vols., ed. J. Savage, 1853, 1972. P. Miller, *The New England Mind: The Seventeenth Century*, 1939. E. S. Morgan, *The Puritan Dilemma*,

1958. D. Rutman, *Winthrop's Boston,* 1965. T. Welde, "A Short Story of the Rise, Reign, and Ruin of the Antinomians, Familiasts & Libertines" in *The Antinomian Controversy 1636–1638,* ed. D. Hall, 1968.

Text Used: *Winthrop Papers,* Vol. II, 1623–1630, ed. A. Forbes, 1931 (some spelling and punctuation modernized).

==CONTEXTS==

The Bay Psalm Book

The Whole Booke of Psalmes Faithfully Translated Into English Metre (1640) was the first book both written and printed in America. *The Bay Psalm Book,* as it is commonly known, was the product of as many as thirteen New England clergymen—including Richard Mather (1596–1669), a prominent preacher and grandfather of Cotton Mather—who sought to provide a plain translation of the Hebrew Psalms into English. The preface was written by the Puritan leader John Cotton (1584–1652). With the Bible and John Bunyan's *The Pilgrim's Progress* (1674), the *Bay Psalm Book* was for two centuries one of the most popular books in New England.

Psalm 1

O Blessed man, that in th' advice
  Of wicked doth not walk:
Nor stand in sinners' way, nor sit
  In chair of scornful folk.
But in the law of Jehovah
  Is his longing delight:
And in his law doth meditate,
  By day and eke by night.
And he shall be like to a tree
  Planted by water-rivers:
That in his season yields his fruit,
  And his leaf never withers.
And all he doth, shall prosper well,
  The wicked are not so:
But they are like unto the chaff,
  Which wind drives to and fro.
Therefore shall not ungodly men,
  Rise to stand in the doom,
Nor shall the sinners with the just,
  In their assembly come.
For of the righteous men, the Lord
  Acknowledgeth the way:
But the way of ungodly men,
  Shall utterly decay.

Various New England clergymen, 1640

from   A MODEL OF CHRISTIAN CHARITY*

Written on Boarde the Arbella, On the Atlantic Ocean. By the Honorable John Winthrop Esquire.

In His passage, (with the great Company of Religious people, of which Christian Tribes he was the Brave Leader and famous Governor;) from the Island of Great Britain, to New-England in the North America. Anno 1630.

CHRISTIAN CHARITY

A Model Hereof

God Almighty in his most holy and wise providence hath so disposed of the condition of mankind, as in all times some must be rich, some poor, some high and eminent in power and dignity; others mean and in subjection.

The Reason Hereof

1.REAS: First, to hold conformity with the rest of his works, being delighted to show forth the glory of his wisdom in the variety and difference of the creatures and the glory of his power, in ordering all these differences for the preservation and good of the whole; and the glory of his greatness, that as it is the glory of princes to have many officers, so this great King will have many stewards, counting himself more honored in dispensing his gifts to man by man than if he did it by his own immediate hand.

2.REAS: Secondly, that he might have the more occasion to manifest the work of his Spirit: first upon the wicked in moderating and restraining them, so that the rich and mighty should not eat up the poor, nor the poor and despised rise up against their superiors and shake off their yoke; secondly in the regenerate, in exercising his graces, in them, as in the great ones, their love, mercy, gentleness, temperance, etc.; in the poor and inferior sort, their faith patience, obedience, etc.

3.REAS: Thirdly, that every man might have need of other, and from hence they might be all knit more nearly together in the bond of brotherly affection. From hence it appears plainly that no man is made more honorable than another or more wealthy, etc., out of any particular and singular respect to himself, but for the glory of his Creator and the common good of the creature, man. Therefore God still reserves the property of these gifts to himself as [in] Ezekiel 16:17.[1] He there calls wealth his gold and his silver, etc. [In] Proverbs 3:9, he claims their service as his due, honor the Lord with thy riches, etc.[2] All men being thus (by divine

---

* This sermon was read by Winthrop on the *Arbella* during its journey to America in 1630. Although the original manuscript has been lost, copies were made and circulated in Winthrop's lifetime.

[1] "Thou hast also taken thy fair jewels of my gold and silver, which I had given thee, and madest to thyself images of men, and didst commit whoredom with them."

[2] "Honor the Lord with thy substance, and with the first fruits of all thine increase: so shall thy barns be filled with plenty, and thy presses burst out with new wine."

providence) ranked into two sorts, rich and poor; under the first are comprehended all such as are able to live comfortably by their own means duly improved; and all others are poor according to the former distribution. There are two rules whereby we are to walk one towards another: Justice and Mercy. These are always distinguished in their act and in their object, yet may they both concur in the same subject in each respect; as sometimes there may be an occasion of showing mercy to a rich man in some sudden danger of distress, and also doing of mere justice to a poor man in regard of some particular contract, etc. There is likewise a double law by which we are regulated in our conversation one towards another: in both the former respects, the law of nature and the law of grace, or the moral law or the law of the Gospel, to omit the rule of justice as not properly belonging to this purpose otherwise than it may fall into consideration in some particular cases. By the first of these laws man as he was enabled so withal [is] commanded to love his neighbor as himself.[3] Upon this ground stands all the precepts of the moral law, which concerns our dealings with men. To apply this to the works of mercy, this law requires two things: first, that every man afford his help to another in every want or distress; secondly, that he performed this out of the same affection which makes him careful of his own goods, according to that of our Savior. Math [7:12]:[4] "Whatsoever ye would that men should do to you." This was practiced by Abraham and Lot in entertaining the Angels and the old man of Gibeah.[5]

The law of grace or the Gospel hath some difference from the former, as in these respects: first, the law of nature was given to man in the estate of innocency; this of the Gospel in the estate of regeneracy.[6] Secondly, the former propounds one man to another, as the same flesh and image of God; this as a brother in Christ also, and in the communion of the same spirit, and so teacheth us to put a difference between Christians and others. Do good to all, especially to the household of faith:[7] Upon this ground the Israelites were to put a difference between the brethren of such as were strangers though not of the Canaanites.[8] Thirdly, the law of nature could give no rules for dealing with enemies, for all are to be considered as friends in the state of innocency, but the Gospel commands love to an enemy. Proof: "If thine Enemy hunger, feed him;"[9] "Love your Enemies, do good to them that hate you," Math 5:44.

This law of the Gospel propounds likewise a difference of seasons and occasions. There is a time when a Christian must sell all and give to the poor, as they did in the Apostles' times.[10] There is a time also when a Christian (though they give not all yet) must give beyond their ability, as they of Macedonia, Cor 2:6.[11] Likewise community of perils calls for extraordinary liberality, and so doth community in some special service for the Church. Lastly, when there is no other means whereby our Christian brother may be relieved in this distress, we must

---

[3] Matthew 5:43; 19:19.   [4] Matthew 7:12.

[5] In Genesis 18:1–2 Abraham entertains the angels; in Judges 19:16–21 an old man of Gibeah offers shelter to a traveling priest, a Levite, and defends him from enemies from a nearby city.

[6] "Man" is believed to have fallen to an unregenerate state after Adam and Eve sinned; Christ redeemed mankind through his suffering, and those who believe in him become saved or regenerate.

[7] Galatians 6:10.   [8] Those who live in Canaan, the Promised Land.

[9] Paraphrased from Proverbs 25:21.

[10] "Sell all that thou hast, and distribute unto the poor, and thou shalt have treasure in heaven," from Luke 18:22.

[11] 11 Corinthians 8[not 6]:1–4.

help him beyond our ability, rather than tempt God in putting him upon help by miraculous or extraordinary means.

* * *

It rests now to make some application of this discourse by the present design, which gave the occasion of writing of it. Herein are 4 things to be propounded: first, the persons; secondly, the work; thirdly, the end; fourthly, the means.

First, for the persons. We are a company professing ourselves fellow members of Christ, in which respect only though we were absent from each other many miles, and had our employments as far distant, yet we ought to account ourselves knit together by this bond of love, and live in the exercise of it, if we would have comfort of our being in Christ. This was notorious in the practice of the Christians in former times; as is testified of the Waldenses,[12] from the mouth of one of the adversaries Æneas Sylvius,[13] *"mutuo solent amare penè antequam norint,"* they used to love any of their own religion even before they were acquainted with them.

Secondly, for the work we have in hand. It is by a mutual consent, through a special overruling providence, and a more than an ordinary approbation of the Churches of Christ, to seek out a place of cohabitation and consortship under a due form of government both civil and ecclesiastical. In such cases as this, the care of the public must oversway[14] all private respects, by which, not only conscience, but mere civil policy, doth bind us. For it is a true rule that particular estates cannot subsist in the ruin of the public.

Thirdly, the end is to improve our lives to do more service to the Lord; the comfort and increase of the body of Christ whereof we are members; that ourselves and posterity may be the better preserved from the common corruptions of this evil world, to serve the Lord and work out our salvation under the power and purity of his holy ordinances.

Fourthly, for the means whereby this must be effected. They are twofold, a conformity with the work and end we aim at. These we see are extraordinary, therefore we must not content ourselves with usual ordinary means. Whatsoever we did or ought to have done when we lived in England, the same must we do, and more also, where we go. That which the most in their churches maintain as a truth in profession only, we must bring into familiar and constant practice, as in this duty of love. We must love brotherly without dissimulation;[15] we must love one another with a pure heart fervently.[16] We must bear one another's burdens.[17] We must not look only on our own things, but also on the things of our brethren, neither must we think that the Lord will bear with such failings at our hands as he doth from those among whom we have lived; and that for 3 reasons.

First, in regard of the more near bond of marriage between him and us, wherein he hath taken us to be his after a most strict and peculiar manner, which will make him the more jealous of our love and obedience. So he tells the people of Israel, you only have I known of all the families of the earth, therefore will I punish you for your transgressions.[18] Secondly, because the Lord will be sanctified in them that come near him. We know that there were many that corrupted the service of

---

[12] Followers of Pater Valdes (?–1217?), a French reformer who rejected the authority of the pope and believed the Bible to be the sole authority in religion.

[13] Pope Pius II, or Aeneas Sylvius Piccolomini (1405–1464), a scholar and historian who reigned as pope from 1458 to 1464.

[14] Outweigh.   [15] Paraphrased from Romans 12:9–10.   [16] Paraphrased from I Peter 1:22.

[17] Galatians 6:2.   [18] Amos 3:2.

the Lord, some setting up altars before his own, others offering both strange fire and strange sacrifices also; yet there came no fire from heaven, or other sudden judgment upon them, as did upon Nadab and Abihu,[19] who yet we may think did not sin presumptuously. Thirdly, when God gives a special commission, he looks to have it strictly observed in every article. When he gave Saul a commission to destroy Amalek,[20] he indented with him upon certain articles, and because he failed in one of the least, and that upon a fair pretense, it lost him the kingdom, which should have been his reward if he had observed his commission. Thus stands the cause between God and us. We are entered into covenant[21] with him for this work. We have taken out a commission, the Lord hath given us leave to draw our own articles. We have professed to enterprise[22] these actions, upon these and those ends, we have hereupon besought him of favour and blessing. Now if the Lord shall please to hear us, and bring us in peace to the place we desire, then hath he ratified this covenant and sealed our commission, [and] will expect a strict performance of the articles contained in it; but if we shall neglect the observation of these articles which are the ends we have propounded, and, dissembling with our God, shall fall to embrace this present world and prosecute our carnal intentions, seeking great things for ourselves and our posterity, the Lord will surely break out in wrath against us, be revenged of such a perjured people and make us know the price of the breach of such a covenant.

Now the only way to avoid this shipwreck and to provide for our posterity is to follow the counsel of Micah,[23] to do justly, to love mercy, to walk humbly with our God. For this end, we must be knit together in this work as one man. We must entertain each other in brotherly affection. We must be willing to abridge ourselves of our superfluities, for the supply of other's necessities. We must uphold a familiar commerce together in all meekness, gentleness, patience and liberality. We must delight in each other, make other's conditions our own, rejoice together, mourn together, labour and suffer together, always having before our eyes our commission and community in the work, our community as members of the same body. So shall we keep the unity of the spirit in the bond of peace.[24] The Lord will be our God and delight to dwell among us, as his own people, and will command a blessing upon us in all our ways, so that we shall see much more of his wisdom, power, goodness and truth than formerly we have been acquainted with. We shall find that the God of Israel is among us, when ten of us shall be able to resist a thousand of our enemies; when he shall make us a praise and glory that men shall say of succeeding plantations, "the Lord make it like that of New England." For we must consider that we shall be as a city upon a hill.[25] The eyes of all people are upon us, so that if we shall deal falsely with our God in this work we have undertaken, and so cause him to withdraw his present help from us, we shall be made a story and a by-word through the world. We shall open the mouths of enemies to

---

[19] In Leviticus 10:1–2 two sons of Aaron who were destroyed for their sin in making an unauthorized offering to God.

[20] In I Samuel 15:1–34 God ordered Saul to destroy the Amalekites and all they possessed, but Saul spared their sheep and oxen and so disobeyed God.

[21] A legal contract in which God offers protection to those who faithfully abide by His word.

[22] Undertake.

[23] A paraphrase of Micah 6:8, the words of the eighth-century B.C. prophet Micah: " . . . what doth the Lord require of thee, but to do justly, and to love mercy, and to walk humbly with thy God?"

[24] Ephesians 4:3.

[25] "Ye are the light of the world. A city that is set on a hill cannot be hid. Neither do men light a candle, and put it under a bushel, but on a candlestick; and it giveth light unto all that are in the house," from Matthew 5:14–15.

speak evil of the ways of God and all professors for God's sake. We shall shame the faces of many of God's worthy servants, and cause their prayers to be turned into curses upon us 'til we be consumed out of the good land whither we are going. And to shut up this discourse with that exhortation of Moses, that faithful servant of the Lord, in his last farewell to Israel, Deut 30.[26] Beloved, there is now set before us life and good, death and evil, in that we are commanded this day to love the Lord our God, and to love one another, to walk in his ways and to keep his commandments and his ordinance, and his laws, and the articles of our covenant with him, that we may live and be multiplied, and that the Lord our God may bless us in the land whither we go to possess it. But if our hearts shall turn away so that we will not obey, but shall be seduced, and worship other gods, our pleasures and profits, and serve them; it is propounded unto us this day, we shall surely perish out of the good land whither we pass over this vast sea to possess it.

> Therefore let us choose life,[27]
> that we and our seed
> may live by obeying his
> voice and cleaving to him,
> for he is our life and
> our prosperity.

1630, 1838

Anne Bradstreet
(1612?–1672)

Anne Bradstreet was colonial America's earliest published poet, its first woman poet, and one of its most admired. Born Anne Dudley in Northampton, England, around 1612, she was the second of the six children of Thomas Dudley and Dorothy Yorke. By age four Anne was living on the estate of the earl of Lincoln, where her father was the chief steward. Her religious training began early. In an undated letter "To my dear children," written shortly before her death, she recalled that when she was six or seven she was conscious of her capacity for sin and had begun a lifelong practice of taking "comfort from the Scriptures." She was nine years old when she met her husband-to-be, Simon Bradstreet, a twenty-one-year-old Cambridge University graduate, who joined the household in 1621 as

---

[26] "And it shall come to pass, when all these things are come upon thee, the blessing and the curse, which I have set before thee, and thou shalt call them to mind among all the nations, whither the Lord thy God hath driven thee, and shalt return unto the Lord thy God, and shalt obey his voice according to all that I command thee this day, thou and thy children, with all thine heart, and with all thy soul; that then the Lord thy God will turn thy captivity, and have compassion upon thee, and will return and gather thee from all the nations, whither the Lord thy God hath scattered thee," from Deuteronomy 30:1–3.

[27] " . . . I have set before you life and death, blessing and cursing: therefore, choose life, that both thou and thy. seed may live . . . ," from Deuteronomy 30:19.

an aide to Dudley. In 1624 the Dudleys moved to Boston, England. When she was sixteen she had smallpox, recovered, and married Simon Bradstreet. Although the marriage was probably arranged, it was by all accounts, especially Anne Bradstreet's, an extraordinarily happy one.

The Bradstreets and the Dudleys were among the Puritan dissenters in England who were the target of the anti-Puritan policies of King Charles I and Archbishop Laud. Possibly sensing their own danger after the earl of Lincoln was imprisoned for his refusal to pay a forced loan, the Bradstreets and Dudleys joined with other Puritans, notably John Winthrop and the preacher John Cotton, to form a "plantation" in the Massachusetts Bay. Carrying the charter for the settlement with them, these members of the Massachusetts Bay Company, of which Simon Bradstreet was secretary, set sail with eleven ships in April 1630. The Bradstreets and Dudleys were on the flagship, *Arbella,* which arrived in Salem harbor in late June. Conditions were much worse than they had expected. Remembering this experience, Anne Bradstreet wrote in the letter to her children, "I found a new world and new manners, at which my heart rose." Thomas Dudley was more explicit in a letter to the countess of Lincoln, writing that Salem was in unexpectedly poor condition with many who were "weak and sick" and the food hardly sufficient for "a fortnight." However, soon the two families had settled in Newtowne, now Cambridge, Massachusetts, and Anne Bradstreet yielded and joined the church at Boston.

From then until her death at age sixty in 1672, Bradstreet lived a harsh frontier existence and experienced a number of what she called "lingering sicknesses," one of which she explained in her first known poem, "Upon a Fit of Sickness, 1632." In this poem death seems like a relief from "care and strife." Her care included children; Bradstreet was no more than twenty-one when her first child, Simon, was born in 1633. Her last child, John, was born in 1642 when Bradstreet was forty. She writes in the poem "In Reference to Her Children" (1678), "I had eight birds hatched in one nest / Four Cocks there were, and Hens the rest."

For all its harshness and domestic care, Bradstreet's life was intellectually active, nurtured by her family and environment. Her father encouraged her to write poetry and sent her his own verses. When the Bradstreets moved to Ipswich, Massachusetts, in 1635, they were joined by some of the best-educated individuals in the Bay Colony, including John Winthrop, Jr., who possessed a fine library, and Nathaniel Ward, author of *The Simple Cobbler of Aggawam* (1646?). This accomplished group provided a ready audience for Bradstreet's work.

Moreover, unlike most women of the time, Bradstreet was educated and continued an active intellectual life in the New World. She read widely in history, science, and literature, especially the classics in translation. Her reading showed a particular interest in history, perhaps reflecting her realization that she was part of the Puritan "Great Migration" to a new Canaan, or Promised Land, in the wilderness. This migration, Puritans believed, was part of God's providential direction of history toward the millennium when evil would be banished from the earth and the righteous would remain. Her favorite reading of this time, Joshua Sylvester's translation of du Bartas's *Divine Weeks and Works* (1621), which contained du Bartas's long poem on the history of the Creation and Sir Walter Raleigh's *History of the World* (1614), provided her with material to support these views and with inspiration for her own writing.

Isolated though she was, Bradstreet followed the political developments in England but increasingly identified with the New World rather than the Old World. When in 1642 civil war broke out between the Puritans under the English revolutionary leader Oliver Cromwell and the Royalists under Charles I, Bradstreet viewed the situation as an episode in God's providential direction of history and responded with "A Dialogue Between Old

England and New" (1642). In this poem the relationship between Old England and New England is that of mother and daughter: there is love but also separation. Old England must root out internal corruption and popery, or Catholicism, and prepare for the day of redemption. Until then, New England, sympathetic but distant, bids "farewell." For New England, and for Bradstreet, the wilderness was now home.

Most of all, Bradstreet was a writer of both poetry and prose, and with her writing she tested the tolerance of the Puritan community. Puritan men believed that a women should be silent and modest and ought to leave intellectual pursuits (such as writing) to men, whose wits were supposedly stronger. Writing about politics or controversial subjects was especially outside a woman's domain. Although some carping about her work evidently occurred, as Bradstreet suggests in her poem "The Prologue" (1650), she had little patience with it. Those who doubted female wits should look to Queen Elizabeth, who, Bradstreet asserted in her elegy "In Honour of Queen Elizabeth" (1643), was "argument enough to make you mute."

Bradstreet's friends and relatives were proud of her work. Without her knowledge, John Woodbridge, her brother-in-law, carried to England a manuscript of thirteen of Bradstreet's poems and a number of commendatory verses written by her admirers. These were published by the printer Stephen Bowtell in 1650, under the title *The Tenth Muse Lately Sprung Up in America*. This volume contains a poem to her father; two long historical poems; elegies to the politician Sir Philip Sidney, the poet du Bartas, and Queen Elizabeth; the "Dialogue," a biblical paraphrase; and a poem on the "Vanity of All Worldy Creatures." The *Tenth Muse* was the first published book of English poetry written in America. Its publication was a surprise to the author, who was somewhat taken aback. In the poem "The Author to Her Book" (1678), Bradstreet recalls her concern at the appearance of her "ill-formed offspring," but, although apologetic for its faults, she immediately began to correct and polish her work.

Bradstreet continued to write poetry and prose, though nothing more was published in her lifetime. The then unpublished material is of a more private nature than the poems in *The Tenth Muse*. Whereas most of the poetry in *The Tenth Muse* concerns history, politics, and public figures and demonstrates the poet's learning, her private poems and prose give a picture of the poet's everyday concerns and of her relationship with her family. The private works also give a picture of her inner, spiritual life, the life that gave meaning to Bradstreet's, and to every Puritan's, existence in New England.

A number of these poems concern her husband, whose absences from home she frequently marked with a poem. Sometimes witty, anguished, or relieved, the poems reflect the depth of affection and confidence in this relationship and the physical as well as spiritual unity that characterized their marriage. Forthright, sincere, and assured in style and manner, these poems are much admired.

Some of these private poems and much of the prose deal with Bradstreet's family life, the subjects ranging from the fear of death in childbirth to the growth of her children into adulthood. A prose series, "Meditations Divine and Moral," which she began in 1664 for her son Simon reveals another dimension of her private life, demonstrating the moral wisdom and "spiritual advantage" she had gained in her maturity. Taken together with the domestic poems, the meditations complete a picture of Bradstreet's life—warm, spirited, and loving—certainly not the narrow, humorless life typically associated with Puritanism.

Most of all, the private poems and prose reveal Bradstreet's deeply spiritual nature and tell of her struggle to submit to God's will. The spiritual struggle is commonly discussed as a conflict between the attractions of this world and those of the next, a preoccupation suggesting to some readers that she had difficulty accepting the Puritan insistence that people may be in this world but not of it, and that she might have missed the rich life of the

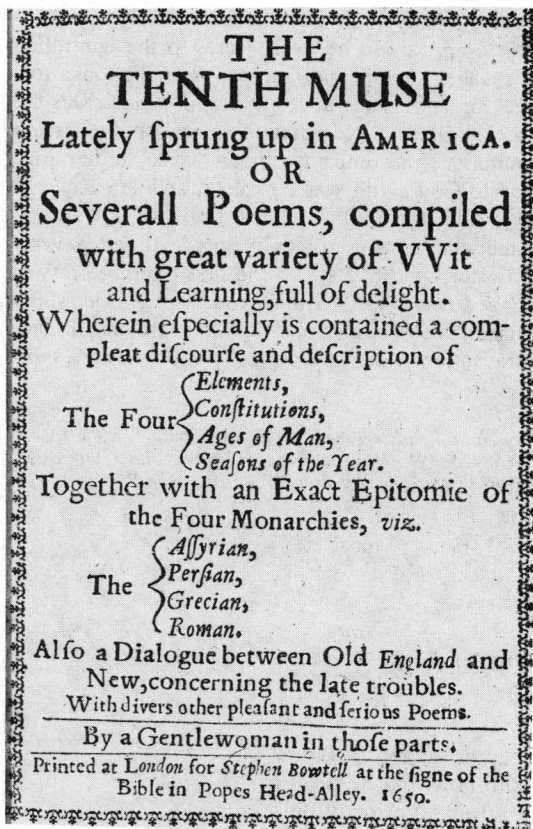

THE
TENTH MUSE
Lately fprung up in AMERICA.
OR
Severall Poems, compiled
with great variety of VVit
and Learning, full of delight.
Wherein efpecially is contained a com-
pleat difcourfe and defcription of

The Four {
Elements,
Conftitutions,
Ages of Man,
Seafons of the Year.

Together with an Exact Epitomie of
the Four Monarchies, viz.

The {
Affyrian,
Perfian,
Grecian,
Roman.

Alfo a Dialogue between Old England and
New, concerning the late troubles.
With divers other pleafant and ferious Poems.

By a Gentlewoman in thofe parts.

Printed at London for Stephen Bowtell at the figne of the
Bible in Popes Head-Alley. 1650.

The title page of Anne Bradstreet's The Tenth Muse Lately Sprung Up in America.

Old World when she accepted the hard life of the wilderness. In some poems, however, the poet appears to be at home in her New England environment and expresses an acceptance of human mortality. Such a poem is "Contemplations," probably written during the mid-1640s when the Bradstreet family had settled in the frontier town of Andover, Massachusetts. The first poem in the colonial New World to be inspired by the American landscape, "Contemplations" expresses an appreciation of nature as a manifestation of God's glory and an emblem of the eternal glory to come. The language, virtually free of classical allusions, is spare and direct, a good example of the Puritan plain style.

Most of the time Bradstreet's spiritual struggles were internal. As she wrote in the letter "To my dear children" (1867), she had "many times sinkings and droopings" in her spiritual pilgrimage. Yet, fits of sickness, concern for her absent children, or worry about her husband, who in 1662 was on a diplomatic mission in England, furnished the poet with occasions to consider "God's gracious dealings" with her. Moreover, she wrote in the letter, God never allowed her "long to sit loose" from Him and often chastised her with a sickness or a hardship that brought her to the recognition that her true life was "above." In her old age, Bradstreet's resignation to God's will underwent severe testing with the deaths of four of her eldest son's five children and his wife's death in childbirth. The elegies Bradstreet wrote for these children and their mother reveal a restrained and somber acceptance of God's power.

With Bradstreet's last known poem, "As Weary Pilgrim," written in 1669 and published in 1867, her struggle with the world appears to be over. Here, in the controlled voice of the mature poet, life offers the speaker "bryars and thornes," and she looks forward to throwing off her "corrupt carcass" for a "glorious body" in eternity. Such was the attitude that Bradstreet brought to her own last illness. According to an account by her son Simon, a minister, she suffered a "consumption," accompanied by an "issue" in her arm. Yet at this time in her life her submission to God's will was complete, and she accepted her suffering as a prerequisite to passage to salvation.

After Bradstreet's death the first American edition of her poems, entitled *Several Poems,* was published in 1678 by John Foster, who had set up the first printing press in Boston. In 1867 John Harvard Ellis published *The Works of Anne Bradstreet in Poetry and Prose,* which contains previously unpublished poems. Since that time, generations of readers have appreciated the work of Anne Bradstreet, which so eloquently expresses the spirit of Puritan life in New England.

Suggested Readings: *The Complete Works of Anne Bradstreet,* ed. J. R. McElrath, Jr., and A. P. Robb, 1981. J. K. Piercy, *Anne Bradstreet,* 1965. E. W. White, *Anne Bradstreet: The Tenth Muse,* 1971. A. Stratford, *Anne Bradstreet: The Worldy Puritan, an Introduction to Her Poetry,* 1974. W. Martin, *An American Triptych,* 1984.

Text Used: *The Works of Anne Bradstreet,* ed. J. Hensley, 1967.

THE PROLOGUE*

I

To sing of wars, of captains, and of kings,
Of cities founded, commonwealths begun,
For my mean[1] pen are too superior things:
Or how they all, or each their dates have run
Let poets and historians set these forth,
My obscure lines shall not so dim their worth.

2

But when my wond'ring eyes and envious heart
Great Bartas[2] sugared lines do but read o'er,
Fool I do grudge the Muses[3] did not part
'Twixt him and me that overfluent store;   10
A Bartas can do what a Bartas will
But simple I according to my skill.

3

From schoolboy's tongue no rhet'ric we expect,
Nor yet a sweet consort[4] from broken strings,

---

* "The Prologue," first published in *The Tenth Muse* (1650), prefaced Bradstreet's "Quaternions," a series of poems about the history of civilization.
[1] Humble.   [2] Guillaume du Bartas (1544–1590) a French poet much admired by the Puritans.
[3] According to Greek myth, the nine goddesses who preside over literature and the arts and sciences.
[4] Harmony.

Nor perfect beauty where's a main defect:
My foolish, broken, blemished Muse so sings,
And this to mend, alas, no art is able,
'Cause nature made it so irreparable.

4

Nor can I, like that fluent sweet tongued Greek[5]
Who lisped at first, in future times speak plain.   20
By art he gladly found what he did seek,
A full requital of his striving pain.
Art can do much, but this maxim's most sure:
A weak or wounded brain admits no cure.

5

I am obnoxious to each carping tongue
Who says my hand a needle better fits,
A poet's pen all scorn I should thus wrong,
For such despite they cast on female wits:
If what I do prove well, it won't advance,
They'll say it's stol'n, or else it was by chance.   30

6

But sure the antique Greeks were far more mild
Else of our sex, why feigned they those nine
And poesy made Calliope's[6] own child;
So 'mongst the rest they placed the arts divine:
But this weak knot they will full soon untie,
The Greeks did nought, but play the fools and lie.

7

Let Greeks be Greeks, and women what they are
Men have precedency and still excel,
It is but vain unjustly to wage war;
Men can do best, and women know it well.   40
Preeminence in all and each is yours;
Yet grant some small acknowledgement of ours.

8

And oh ye high flown quills[7] that soar the skies,
And ever with your prey still catch your praise,
If e'er you deign these lowly lines your eyes,
Give thyme or parsley wreath, I ask no bays;[8]
This mean and unrefined ore of mine
Will make your glist'ring gold but more to shine.

1643?, 1650

---

[5] Demosthenes (384–322 B.C.), an Athenian statesman and orator who overcame a speech defect.
[6] According to Greek myth, the Muse of epic poetry.
[7] Quill pens.   [8] Laurels used as a crown to adorn a poet's head.

AN EPITAPH ON MY DEAR AND EVER-HONOURED MOTHER MRS. DOROTHY DUDLEY, WHO DECEASED DECEMBER 27, 1643, AND OF HER AGE, 61

Here lies,
A worthy matron of unspotted life,
A loving mother and obedient wife,
A friendly neighbor, pitiful to poor,
Whom oft she fed and clothed with her store;
To servants wisely awful, but yet kind,
And as they did, so they reward did find.
A true instructor of her family,
The which she ordered with dexterity.
The public meetings ever did frequent,
And in her closet constant hours she spent;
Religious in all her words and ways,
Preparing still for death, till end of days:
Of all her children, children lived to see,
Then dying, left a blessed memory.

1643, 1678

CONTEMPLATIONS

[1]

Some time now past in the autumnal tide,
When Phoebus[1] wanted but one hour to bed,
The trees all richly clad, yet void of pride,
Where gilded o'er by his rich golden head.
Their leaves and fruits seemed painted, but was true,
Of green, of red, of yellow, mixed hue;
Rapt were my senses at this delectable view.

2

I wist[2] not what to wish, yet sure thought I,
If so much excellence abide below,
How excellent is He that dwells on high,   10
Whose power and beauty by his works we know?
Sure he is goodness, wisdom, glory, light,
That hath this under world so richly dight;[3]
More heaven than earth was here, no winter and no night.

3

Then on a stately oak I cast mine eye,
Whose ruffling top the clouds seemed to aspire;
How long since thou wast in thine infancy?

---

[1] According to Greek myth, the personification of the sun god, Apollo.   [2] Knew.   [3] Decorated.

Thy strength, and stature, more thy years admire,
Hath hundred winters past since thou wast born?
Or thousand since thou brakest thy shell of horn?[4]   20
If so, all these as nought, eternity doth scorn.

4

Then higher on the glistering Sun I gazed,
Whose beams was shaded by the leavie tree;
The more I looked, the more I grew amazed,
And softly said, "What glory's like to thee?"
Soul of this world, this universe's eye,
No wonder some made thee a deity;
Had I not better known, alas, the same had I.

5

Thou as a bridegroom from thy chamber rushes,
And as a strong man, joys to run a race;[5]   30
The morn doth usher thee with smiles and blushes;
The Earth reflects her glances in thy face.
Birds, insects, animals with vegative,[6]
Thy heat from death and dullness doth revive,
And in the darksome womb of fruitful nature dive.

6

Thy swift annual and diurnal course,
Thy daily straight and yearly oblique path,
Thy pleasing fervor and thy scorching force,
All mortals here the feeling knowledge hath.
Thy presence makes it day, thy absence night,   40
Quaternal[7] seasons caused by thy might:
Hail creature, full of sweetness, beauty, and delight.

7

Art thou so full of glory that no eye
Hath strength thy shining rays once to behold?
And is thy splendid throne erect so high,
As to approach it, can no earthly mould?
How full of glory then must thy Creator be,
Who gave this bright light luster unto thee?
Admired, adored for ever, be that Majesty.

8

Silent alone, where none or saw, or heard,   50
In pathless paths I lead my wand'ring feet,
My humble eyes to lofty skies I reared

---

[4] An acorn.

[5] ". . .the sun, which is as a bridegroom coming out of his chamber, and rejoiceth as a strong man to run a race," from Psalm 19:5.

[6] Plants.   [7] Four.

To sing some song, my mazed[8] Muse thought meet.[9]
My great Creator I would magnify,
That nature had thus decked liberally;
But Ah, and Ah, again, my imbecility.

9

I heard the merry grasshopper then sing.
The black-clad cricket bear a second part;
They kept one tune and played on the same string,
Seeming to glory in their little art.
Shall creatures abject thus their voices raise
And in their kind resound their Maker's praise,
Whilst I, as mute, can warble forth no higher lays?[10]

60

10

When present times look back to ages past,
And men in being fancy those are dead,
It makes things gone perpetually to last,
And calls back months and years that long since fled.
It makes a man more aged in conceit[11]
Than was Methuselah,[12] or's grandsire great,
While of their persons and their acts his mind doth treat.

70

11

Sometimes in Eden fair he seems to be,
Sees glorious Adam there made lord of all,
Fancies the apple, dangle on the tree,
That turned his sovereign to a naked thrall.[13]
Who like a miscreant's driven from that place,
To get his bread with pain and sweat of face,
A penalty imposed on his backsliding race.

12

Here sits our grandame[14] in retired place,
And in her lap her bloody Cain new-born;
The weeping imp oft looks her in the face,
Bewails his unknown hap[15] and fate forlorn;
His mother sighs to think of Paradise,
And how she lost her bliss to be more wise,
Believing him that was, and is, father of lies.[16]

80

13

Here Cain and Abel come to sacrifice,
Fruits of the earth and fatlings[17] each do bring,
On Abel's gift the fire descends from skies,

---

[8] Amazed.   [9] Proper.   [10] Songs.   [11] Thought.
[12] In Genesis 5:27, Methuselah lived 969 years.   [13] A slave.
[14] Eve, the mother of Cain and Abel (see Genesis).   [15] Circumstances.
[16] In Genesis 3, Eve lost paradise by believing in Satan, the "father of lies."
[17] Young animals fattened for slaughter.

But no such sign on false Cain's offering;
With sullen hateful looks he goes his ways,
Hath thousand thoughts to end his brother's days,   90
Upon whose blood his future good he hopes to raise.

14
There Abel keeps his sheep, no ill he thinks;
His brother comes, then acts his fratricide;
The virgin Earth of blood her first draught drinks,
But since that time she often hath been cloyed.
The wretch with ghastly face and dreadful mind
Thinks each he sees will serve him in his kind,
Though none on earth but kindred near then could he find.

15
Who fancies not his looks now at the bar,[18]
His face like death, his heart with horror fraught,   100
Nor malefactor ever felt like war,
When deep despair with wish of life hath fought,
Branded with guilt and crushed with treble woes,
A vagabond to Land of Nod[19] he goes.
A city builds, that walls might him secure from foes.

16
Who things not oft upon the father's ages,
Their long descent, how nephews' sons they saw,
The starry observations of those sages,
And how their precepts to their sons were law,
How Adam sighed to see his progeny,   110
Clothed all in his black sinful livery
Who neither guilt nor yet the punishment could fly.

17
Our life compare we with their length of days
Who to the tenth of theirs doth now arrive?
And though thus short, we shorten many ways,
Living so little while we are alive;
In eating, drinking, sleeping, vain delight
So unawares comes on perpetual night,
And puts all pleasures vain unto eternal flight.

18
When I behold the heavens as in their prime,   120
And then the earth (though old) still clad in green,
The stones and trees, insensible of time,
Nor age nor wrinkle on their front are seen;
If winter come and greenness then do fade,

---

[18] A place of judgment.
[19] In Genesis 4:16, a land east of Eden, where Cain resided after slaying Abel.

A spring returns, and they more youthful made;
But man grows old, lied down, remains where once he's laid.

19

By birth more noble than those creatures all,
Yet seems by nature and by custom cursed,
No sooner born, but grief and care makes fall
That state obliterate he had at first;   130
Nor youth, nor strength, nor wisdom spring again,
Nor habitations long their names retain,
But in oblivion to the final day remain.

20

Shall I then praise the heavens, the trees, the earth
Because their beauty and their strength last longer?
Shall I wish there, or never to had birth,
Because they're bigger, and their bodies stronger?
Nay, they shall darken, perish, fade and die,
And when unmade, so ever shall they lie,
But man was made for endless immortality.   140

21

Under the cooling shadow of a stately elm
Close sat I by a goodly river's side,
Where gliding streams the rocks did overwhelm,
A lonely place, with pleasures dignified.
I once that loved the shady woods so well,
Now thought the rivers did the trees excel,
And if the sun would ever shine, there would I dwell.

22

While on the stealing stream I fixt mine eye,
Which to the longed-for ocean held its course,
I marked, nor crooks, nor rubs[20] that there did lie   150
Could hinder ought,[21] but still augment its force.
"Oh happy flood," quoth I, "that holds thy race
Till thou arrive at thy beloved place,
Nor is it rocks or shoals that can obstruct thy pace,

23

Nor is't enough, that thou alone mayst slide,
But hundred brooks in thy clear waves do meet,
So hand in hand along with thee they glide
To Thetis' house,[22] where all embrace and greet.
Thou emblem true of what I count the best,
O could I lead my rivulets to rest,   160
So may we press to that vast mansion, ever blest."

---

[20] Neither bends nor obstacles.   [21] Anything.
[22] The sea; according to Greek myth, Thetis was a sea nymph.

24

Ye fish, which in this liquid region 'bide,
That for each season have your habitation,
Now salt, now fresh where you think best to glide
To unknown coasts to give a visitation,
In lakes and ponds you leave your numerous fry;[23]
So nature taught, and yet you know not why,
You wat'ry folk that know not your felicity.

25

Look how the wantons frisk to taste the air,
Then to the colder bottom straight they dive;   170
Eftsoon[24] to Neptune's glassy hall[25] repair
To see what trade they great ones there do drive,
Who forage o'er the spacious sea-green field,
And take the trembling prey before it yield,
Whose armour is their scales, their spreading fins their shield.

26

While musing thus with contemplation fed,
And thousand fancies buzzing in my brain,
The sweet-tongued Philomel[26] perched o'er my head
And chanted forth a most melodious strain
Which rapt me so with wonder and delight,   180
I judged my hearing better than my sight,
And wished me wings with her a while to take my flight.

27

"O merry Bird," said I, "that fears no snares,
That neither toils nor hoards up in thy barn,
Feels no sad thoughts nor cruciating[27] cares
To gain more good or shun what might thee harm.
Thy clothes ne'er wear, thy meat is everywhere,
Thy bed a bough, thy drink the water clear,
Reminds not what is past, nor what's to come dost fear."

28

"The dawning morn with songs thou dost prevent,[28]   190
Sets hundred notes unto thy feathered crew,
So each one tunes his pretty instrument,
And warbling out the old, begin anew,
And thus they pass their youth in summer season,
Then follow thee into a better region,
Where winter's never felt by that sweet airy legion."

---

[23] Young fish.
[24] Soon thereafter.   [25] The sea; according to Roman myth, Neptune was the sea god.
[26] The nightingale. According to Greek myth, Philomela, a princess of Athens, was turned into a nightingale after her brother-in-law raped her and tore out her tongue.
[27] Excruciating.   [28] Foresee.

29

Man at the best a creature frail and vain,
In knowledge ignorant, in strength but weak,
Subject to sorrows, losses, sickness, pain,
Each storm his state, his mind, his body break,   200
From some of these he never finds cessation,
But day or night, within, without, vexation,
Troubles from foes, from friends, from dearest, near'st relation.

30

And yet this sinful creature, frail and vain,
This lump of wretchedness, of sin and sorrow,
This weatherbeaten vessel wracked with pain,
Joys not in hope of an eternal morrow;
Nor all his losses, crosses, and vexation,
In weight, in frequency and long duration
Can make him deeply groan for that divine translation.[29]   210

31

The mariner that on smooth waves doth glide
Sings merrily and steers his bark with ease,
As if he had command of wind and tide,
And now become great master of the seas:
But suddenly a storm spoils all the sport,
And makes him long for a more quiet port,
Which 'gainst all adverse winds may serve for fort.

32

So he that saileth in this world of pleasure,
Feeding on sweets, that never bit of th' sour,
That's full of friends, of honour, and of treasure,   220
Fond fool, he takes this earth ev'n for heav'n's bower.
But sad affliction comes and makes him see
Here's neither honour, wealth, nor safety;
Only above is found all with security.

33

O Time the fatal wrack[30] of mortal things,
That draws oblivion's curtains over kings;
Their sumptuous monuments, men know them not,
Their names without a record are forgot,
Their parts, their ports, their pomp's[31] all laid in th' dust
Nor wit nor gold, nor buildings scape times rust;   230
But he whose name is graved in the white stone[32]
Shall last and shine when all of these are gone.

1666?, 1678

---

[29] Transformation.   [30] Destroyer.
[31] Their features, their shelters, their vanity.
[32] "To him that overcometh will I give . . . a white stone, and in the stone a new name written, which no man knoweth saving him that receiveth it," from Revelation 2:17.

THE FLESH AND THE SPIRIT

In secret place where once I stood
Close by the banks of Lacrim flood,[1]
I heard two sisters reason on
Things that are past and things to come;
One Flesh was called, who had her eye
On worldly wealth and vanity;
The other Spirit, who did rear
Her thoughts unto a higher sphere:
Sister, quoth Flesh, what liv'st thou on,
Nothing but meditation?   10
Doth contemplation feed thee so
Regardlessly to let earth go?
Can speculation satisfy
Notion without reality?
Dost dream of things beyond the moon,
And dost thou hope to dwell there soon?
Hast treasures there laid up in store
That all in th' world thou count'st but poor?
Art fancy sick, or turned a sot[2]
To catch at shadows which are not?   20
Come, come, I'll show unto thy sense,
Industry hath its recompense.
What canst desire, but thou may'st see
True substance in variety?
Dost honour like? Acquire the same,
As some to their immortal fame,
And trophies to thy name erect
Which wearing time shall ne'er deject.
For riches doth thou long full sore?
Behold enough of precious store.   30
Earth hath more silver, pearls, and gold,
Than eyes can see or hands can hold.
Affect's[3] thou pleasure? Take thy fill,
Earth hath enough of what you will.
Then let not go, what thou may'st find
For things unknown, only in mind
Spirit: be still thou unregenerate[4] part,
Disturb no more my settled heart,
For I have vowed (and so will do)
Thee as a foe still to pursue.   40
And combat with thee will and must,
Until I see thee laid in th' dust.
Sisters we are, yea, twins we be,
Yet deadly feud 'twixt thee and me;
For from one father are we not,

---

[1] The river of tears; *lacrima* is Latin for "tear."   [2] Turned a fool, or hallucinating.   [3] Seek.
[4] Unrepentant.

Thou by old Adam wast begot,
But my arise is from above,
Whence my dear Father I do love.
Thou speak'st me fair, but hat'st me sore,
Thy flatt'ring shows I'll trust no more.   50
How oft thy slave, hast thou me made,
When I believed what thou hast said,
And never had more cause of woe
Than when I did what thou bad'st do.
I'll stop mine ears at these thy charms.
And count them for my deadly harms.
Thy sinful pleasures I do hate,
Thy riches are to me no bait,
Thine honours do, nor will I love;
For my ambition lies above.   60
My greatest honour it shall be
When I am victor over thee,
And triumph shall with laurel head,[5]
When thou my captive shalt be led,
How I do live, thou need'st not scoff,
For I have meat thou know'st not of;[6]
The hidden manna[7] I do eat,
The word of life it is my meat.
My thoughts do yield me more content
Than can thy hours in pleasure spent.   70
Nor are they shadows which I catch,
Nor fancies vain at which I snatch,
But reach at things that are so high,
Beyond thy dull capacity;
Eternal substance I do see,
With which enriched I would be.
Mine eye doth pierce the heavens and see
What is invisible to thee.
My garments are not silk nor gold,
Nor such like trash which earth doth hold,   80
But royal robes I shall have on,
More glorious than the glist'ring sun;
My crown not diamonds, pearls, and gold,
But such as angels' heads enfold.
The city[8] where I hope to dwell,
There's none on earth can parallel;
The stately walls both high and strong,
Are made of precious jasper stone;
The gates of pearl, both rich and clear,
And angels are for porters there;   90
The streets thereof transparent gold,

[5] A crown of laurel, a symbol of victory.

[6] Paraphrasing Jesus' words to his disciples, "But he said unto them, I have meat to eat that ye know not of," from John 4:32.

[7] In Exodus 16:15, the spiritual food God sent to the Israelites in the wilderness.

[8] The description of this city follows that of the New Jerusalem in Revelation 21 and 22.

Such as no eye did e'er behold;
A crystal river there doth run,
Which doth proceed from the Lamb's throne.
Of life, there are the waters sure,
Which shall remain forever pure,
Nor sun, nor moon, they have no need,
For glory doth from God proceed.
No candle there, nor yet torchlight,
For there shall be no darksome night.   100
From sickness and infirmity
For evermore they shall be free;
Nor withering age shall e'er come there,
But beauty shall be bright and clear;
This city pure is not for thee,
For things unclean there shall not be.
If I of heaven may have my fill,
Take thou the world and all that will.

1666?, 1678

THE AUTHOR TO HER BOOK*

Thou ill-formed offspring of my feeble brain,
Who after birth didst by my side remain,
Till snatched from thence by friends, less wise than true,
Who thee abroad, exposed to public view,
Made thee in rags, halting to th' press to trudge,
Where errors were not lessened (all may judge).
At thy return my blushing was not small,
My rambling brat (in print) should mother call,
I cast thee by as one unfit for light,
Thy visage was so irksome in my sight;   10
Yet being mine own, at length affection would
Thy blemishes amend, if so I could:
I washed thy face, but more defects I saw,
And rubbing off a spot still made a flaw.
I stretched thy joints to make thee even feet,[1]
Yet still thou run'st more hobbling than is meet;[2]
In better dress to trim thee was my mind,
But nought save homespun cloth i' th' house I find.
In this array 'mongst vulgars[3] may'st thou roam.
In critic's hands beware thou dost not come,   20
And take thy way where yet thou art not known;
If for thy father asked, say thou hadst none;
And for thy mother, she alas is poor,
Which caused her thus to send thee out of door.

1650?, 1670

*The "book" is *The Tenth Muse* (1650), published without her knowledge; this poem appeared in its second edition.
[1] Metrical feet.   [2] Proper.   [3] Common people.

BEFORE THE BIRTH OF ONE OF HER CHILDREN

All things within this fading world hath end,
Adversity doth still our joys attend;
No ties so strong, no friends so dear and sweet,
But with death's parting blow is sure to meet.
The sentence past is most irrevocable,
A common thing, yet oh, inevitable.
How soon, my Dear, death may my steps attend,
How soon't may be thy lot to lose thy friend,
We both are ignorant, yet love bids me
These farewell lines to recommend to thee,   10
That when that knot's untied that made us one,
I may seem thine, who in effect am none.
And if I see not half my days that's due,
What nature would, God grant to yours and you;
The many faults that well you know I have
Let be interred in my oblivious grave;
If any worth or virtue were in me,
Let that live freshly in thy memory
And when thou feel'st no grief, as I no harms,
Yet love thy dead, who long lay in thine arms.   20
And when thy loss shall be repaid with gains
Look to my little babes, my dear remains.
And if thou love thyself, or loved'st me,
These O protect from step-dame's[1] injury.
And if chance to thine eyes shall bring this verse,
With some sad sighs honour my absent hearse;[2]
And kiss this paper for thy love's dear sake,
Who with salt tears this last farewell did take.

1640–1652?, 1678

TO MY DEAR AND LOVING HUSBAND

If ever two were one, then surely we.
If ever man were loved by wife, then thee;
If ever wife was happy in a man,
Compare with me, ye women, if you can.
I prize thy love more than whole mines of gold
Or all the riches that the East doth hold.
My love is such that rivers cannot quench,
Nor ought[1] but love from thee, give recompense.
Thy love is such I can no way repay,
The heavens reward thee manifold, I pray.   10
Then while we live, in love let's so persevere[2]
That when we live no more, we may live ever.

1641–1643?, 1678

---

[1] Stepmother's.   [2] Corpse.
[1] Anything.   [2] Then pronounced "pur-séver," i.e., rhymed with "ever."

A LETTER TO HER HUSBAND, ABSENT UPON PUBLIC EMPLOYMENT

My head, my heart, mine eyes, my life, nay, more,
My joy, my magazine[1] of earthly store,
If two be one, as surely thou and I,
How stayest thou there, whilst I at Ipswich[2] lie?
So many steps, head from the heart to sever,
If but a neck, soon should we be together.
I, like the Earth this season, mourn in black,
My Sun is gone so far in's zodiac,
Whom whilst I 'joyed, nor storms, nor frost I felt,
His warmth such frigid colds did cause to melt.   10
My chilled limbs now numbed lie forlorn;
Return, return, sweet Sol,[3] from Capricorn,[4]
In this dead time, alas, what can I more
Than view those fruits which through thy heat I bore?
Which sweet contentment yield me for a space,
True living pictures of their father's face.
O strange effect! now thou art southward gone,
I weary grow the tedious day so long;
But when thou northward to me shalt return,
I wish my Sun may never set, but burn   20
Within the Cancer[5] of my glowing breast,
The welcome house of him my dearest guest.
Where ever, ever stay, and go not thence,
Till nature's sad decree shall call thee hence;
Flesh of thy flesh, bone of thy bone,[6]
I here, thou there, yet both but one.

1641–1643?, 1678

ANOTHER

As loving hind[1] that (hartless)[2] wants her deer,
Scuds[3] through the woods and fern with hark'ning ear,
Perplext, in every bush and nook doth pry,
Her dearest deer, might answer ear or eye;
So doth my anxious soul, which now doth miss
A dearer dear (far dearer heart) than this.
Still wait with doubts, and hopes, and failing eye,
His voice to hear or person to descry.

---

[1] A warehouse.
[2] Ipswich, Massachusetts (north of Boston), where the Bradstreets lived from about 1635 to 1645.
[3] The sun.   [4] The zodiac's tenth sign, indicating winter.
[5] The zodiac's fourth sign, indicating summer.
[6] Adam, from whose rib Eve was made, states "This is now bone of my bones, and flesh of my flesh: she shall be called Woman because she was taken out of Man," from Genesis 2:23.
[1] A female deer.   [2] A male deer: a pun on "heart" and "hart."   [3] Runs.

Or as the pensive dove doth all alone
(On withered bough) most uncouthly bemoan   10
The absence of her love and loving mate,
Whose loss hath made her so unfortunate,
Ev'n thus do I, with many a deep sad groan,
Bewail my turtle[4] true, who now is gone,
His presence and his safe return still woos,
With thousand doleful sighs and mournful coos.
Or as the loving mullet, that true fish,
Her fellow lost, nor joy nor life do wish,
But launches on that shore, there for to die,
Where she her captive husband doth espy.   20
Mine being gone, I lead a joyless life,
I have a loving peer,[5] yet seem no wife;
But worst of all, to him can't steer my course,
I here, he there, alas, both kept by force.
Return my dear, my joy, my only love,
Unto thy hind, thy mullet, and thy dove,
Who neither joys in pasture, house, nor streams,
The substance gone, O me, these are but dreams.
Together at one tree, oh let us browse,
And like two turtles roost within one house,   30
And like the mullets in one river glide,
Let's still remain but one, till death divide.
      Thy loving love and dearest dear,
      At home, abroad, and everywhere.

1678

IN REFERENCE TO HER CHILDREN, 23 JUNE, 1659

I had eight birds hatched in one nest,
Four cocks there were, and hens the rest.
I nursed them up with pain and care,
Nor cost, nor labour did I spare,
Till at the last they felt their wing,
Mounted the trees, and learned to sing;
Chief of the brood then took his flight[1]
To regions far and left me quite.
My mournful chirps I after send,
Till he return, or I do end: 10
Leave not thy nest, thy dam and sire,
Fly back and sing amidst this choir.
My second bird did take her flight,[2]

---

[4] A turtledove.   [5] A mate.

[1] Her firstborn, Samuel, studied medicine in England from 1657 to 1661.

[2] Her daughter Dorothy married Rev. Seaborn Cotton in 1654 and moved first to Wethersfield, Connecticut, and then to Hampton, New Hampshire.

And with her mate flew out of sight;
Southward they both their course did bend,
And seasons twain they there did spend,
Till after blown by southern gales,
They norward steered with filled sails.
A prettier bird was no where seen,
Along the beach among the treen.[3]   20
I have a third[4] of colour white,
On whom I placed no small delight;
Coupled with mate loving and true,
Hath also bid her dam adieu;
And where Aurora[5] first appears,
She now hath perched to spend her years.
One to the academy flew[6]
To chat among that learned crew;
Ambition moves still in his breast
That he might chant above the rest,   30
Striving for more than to do well,
That nightingales he might excel.
My fifth, whose down is yet scarce gone,[7]
Is 'mongst the shrubs and bushes flown,
And as his wings increase in strength,
On higher boughs he'll perch at length.
My other three still with me nest,[8]
Until they're grown, then as the rest,
Or here or there they'll take their flight,
As is ordained, so shall they light.   40
If birds could weep, then would my tears
Let others know what are my fears
Lest this my brood some harm should catch,
And be surprised for want of watch,
Whilst pecking corn and void of care,
They fall un'wares in fowler's[9] snare,
Or whilst on trees they sit and sing,
Some untoward boy at them do fling,
Or whilst allured with bell and glass,
The net be spread, and caught, alas.   50
Or lest by lime-twigs they be foiled,[10]
Or by some greedy hawks be spoiled.
O would my young, ye saw my breast,
And knew what thoughts there sadly rest,
Great was my pain when I you bred,
Great was my care when I you fed,
Long did I keep you soft and warm,

---

[3] Trees.
[4] Her daughter Sarah, who married Richard Hubbard and moved to Ipswich, Massachusetts.
[5] According to Roman myth, the goddess of the dawn.   [6] Her son Simon went to Harvard College.
[7] Most likely a reference to her seventh child, Dudley (skipping daughters Hannah and Mercy).
[8] Her children Hannah, Mercy, and John were still living at home.   [9] A birdcatcher.
[10] Birdlime, a sticky substance, was smeared on branches to catch birds.

And with my wings kept off all harm,
My cares are more and fears than ever,
My throbs such now as 'fore were never.   60
Alas, my birds, you wisdom want,
Of perils you are ignorant;
Oft times in grass, on trees, in flight,
Sore accidents on you may light.
O to your safety have an eye,
So happy may you live and die.
Meanwhile my days in tunes I'll spend,
Till my weak lays[11] with me shall end.
In shady woods I'll sit and sing,
And things that past to mind I'll bring.   70
Once young and pleasant, as are you,
But former toys (no joys) adieu.
My age I will not once lament,
But sing, my time so near is spent.
And from the top bough take my flight
Into a country beyond sight,
Where old ones instantly grow young,
And there with seraphims[12] set song;
No seasons cold, nor storms they see;
But spring lasts to eternity.   80
When each of you shall in your nest
Among your young ones take your rest,
In chirping language, oft them tell,
You had a dam that loved you well,
That did what could be done for young,
And nursed you up till you were strong,
And 'fore she once would let you fly,
She showed you joy and misery;
Taught what was good, and what was ill,
What would save life, and what would kill.   90
Thus gone, amongst you I may live,
And dead, yet speak, and counsel give:
Farewell, my birds, farewell adieu,
I happy am, if well with you.

1659, 1678

IN MEMORY OF MY DEAR GRANDCHILD ELIZABETH BRADSTREET, WHO DECEASED AUGUST, 1665, BEING A YEAR AND HALF OLD

[1]

Farewell dear babe, my heart's too much content,
Farewell sweet babe, the pleasure of mine eye,
Farewell fair flower that for a space was lent,

[11] Songs.   [12] Angels.

Then ta'en away unto eternity.
Blest babe, why should I once bewail thy fate,
Or sigh thy days so soon were terminate,
Sith[1] thou art settled in an everlasting state.

2

By nature trees do rot when thy are grown,
And plums and apples thoroughly ripe do fall,
And corn and grass are in their season mown,   10
And time brings down what is both strong and tall.
And plants new set to be eradicate,
And buds new blown to have so short a date,
Is by His hand alone that guides nature and fate.

1665, 1678

HERE FOLLOWS SOME VERSES UPON THE BURNING OF OUR HOUSE JULY 10TH, 1666

COPIED OUT OF A LOOSE PAPER*

In silent night when rest I took
For sorrow near I did not look
I wakened was with thund'ring noise
And piteous shrieks of dreadful voice.
That fearful sound of "Fire!" and "Fire!"
Let no man know is my desire.
I, starting up, the light did spy,
And to my God my heart did cry
To strengthen me in my distress
And not to leave me succorless.   10
Then, coming out, beheld a space
The flame consume my dwelling place.
And when I could no longer look,
I blest His name that gave and took,[1]
That laid my goods now in the dust.
Yea, so it was, and so 'twas just.
It was His own, it was not mine,
Far be it that I should repine;
He might of all justly bereft
But yet sufficient for us left.   20
When by the ruins oft I past
My sorrowing eyes aside did cast,
And here and there the places spy
Where oft I sat and long did lie:

---

[1] Since.

* First published in *The Works of Anne Bradstreet* (ed. J. Ellis) in 1867, this poem was copied by Bradstreet's son Simon.

[1] "The Lord gave, and the Lord hath taken away; blessed be the name of the Lord," from Job 1:21.

Here stood that trunk, and there that chest,
There lay that store I counted best.
My pleasant things in ashes lie,
And them behold no more shall I.
Under thy roof no guest shall sit,
Nor at thy table eat a bit.   30
No pleasant tale shall e'er be told,
Nor things recounted done of old.
No candle e'er shall shine in thee,
Nor bridegroom's voice e'er heard shall be.
In silence ever shall thou lie,
Adieu, Adieu, all's vanity.[2]
Then straight I 'gin my heart to chide,
And did thy wealth on earth abide?
Didst fix thy hope on mold'ring dust?
The arm of flesh didst make thy trust?   40
Raise up thy thoughts above the sky
That dunghill mists away may fly.
Thou hast an house on high erect,
Framed by that mighty Architect,
With glory richly furnished,
Stands permanent though this be fled.
It's purchased and paid for too
By Him who hath enough to do.
A price so vast as is unknown
Yet by His gift is made thine own;   50
There's wealth enough, I need no more,
Farewell, my pelf,[3] farewell my store.
The world no longer let me love,
My hope and treasure lies above.

1666, 1867

AS WEARY PILGRIM

As weary pilgrim, now at rest,
    Hugs with delight his silent nest,
His wasted limbs now lie full soft
    That mirey steps have trodden oft,
Blesses himself to think upon
    His dangers past, and travails done.
The burning sun no more shall heat,
    Nor stormy rains on him shall beat.
The briars and thorns no more shall scratch,
    Nor hungry wolves at him shall catch.   10
He erring paths no more shall tread,
    Nor wild fruits eat instead of bread.
For waters cold he doth not long

[2] "Vanity of vanities, saith the Preacher, vanity of vanities; all is vanity," from Ecclesiastes 1:2.
[3] Wealth or riches.

For thirst no more shall parch his tongue.
No rugged stones his feet shall gall,[1]
Nor stumps nor rocks cause him to fall.
All cares and fears he bids farewell
   And means in safety now to dwell.
A pilgrim I, on earth perplexed
   With sins, with cares and sorrows vext,   20
By age and pains brought to decay,
   And my clay house[2] mold'ring away.
Oh, how I long to be at rest
   And soar on thigh among the blest.
This body shall in silence sleep,
   Mine eyes no more shall ever weep,
No fainting fits shall me assail,
   Nor grinding pains my body frail,
With cares and fears ne'er cumb'red be
   Nor losses know, nor sorrows see.   30
What though my flesh shall there consume,
   It is the bed Christ did perfume,
And when a few years shall be gone,
   This mortal shall be clothed upon.
A corrupt carcass down it lays,
   A glorious body it shall rise.
In weakness and dishonour sown,
   In power 'tis raised by Christ alone.
Then soul and body shall unite
   And of their maker have the sight.   40
Such lasting joys shall there behold
   As ear ne'er heard nor tongue e'er told.
Lord make me ready for that day.
   Then come, dear Bridegroom,[3] come away.

                   1669, 1867

Edward Taylor
(1642?–1729)

The scholar Thomas H. Johnson's late 1930s discovery and initial publication of Edward Taylor's poetry in 1939 is one of the twentieth century's monumental contributions to the history of early New England life and letters. Taylor was virtually unknown—except as a preacher and physician in the frontier town of Westfield, Massachusetts—before Johnson

[1] Make sore.   [2] Body.
[3] "And Jesus said unto them, can the children of the bridechamber fast, while the bridegroom is with them? as long as they have the bridegroom with them, they cannot fast," from Mark 2:29; Christ is considered the bridegroom of the soul.

found his manuscript poems in the Yale University Library. Whereas historians and literary critics of the nineteenth century typically measured the Puritan aesthetic by the poems of Anne Bradstreet and of Michael Wigglesworth and invariably found that aesthetic wanting, Taylor's work has offered more recent scholars a new and unexpected measure of Puritan influence on the quality of art in colonial America. Taylor, though every bit as much a Calvinist as his companion poets, eclipsed them as an artist. His religious convictions, personal humility, and love of God served as a moving inner source of poetic expression, not as an impediment to poetic expression, as some have argued is true for Bradstreet and Wigglesworth.

Because Taylor spent most of his life in frontier obscurity and because two centuries separate his death and the discovery of his poems, it is not surprising that details of Taylor's life are vague and largely conjectural. Born in Sketchley, England, around 1642, probably to dissenters, Taylor enjoyed a youth generally free of religious persecution. Although biographers have speculated that he began college studies at Cambridge University, no evidence has been found of his presence there before the Restoration—yet, after the Restoration his refusal to submit to the required loyalty oaths would have precluded his admission to study. By Taylor's own account, he taught school in the English countryside in the mid-1660s.

Eventually deciding to emigrate to the colonies, Taylor sailed for Massachusetts Bay in 1668 and, as did many Puritans before him, left home and family behind in search of religious freedom in the New World. Once in Massachusetts, he presented letters of introduction to Increase Mather, Master of the Mint John Hull, and others and began to study for the ministry at Harvard College. After graduating with a B.A. in 1671, he rode the one hundred miles to Westfield, where he had accepted a call as the town's only minister. He remained there for the next fifty-eight years, until his death in 1729. During those many years in Westfield, Taylor married twice (Elizabeth Fitch in 1674 and Ruth Wyllys in 1692) and fathered fourteen children, most of whom he survived. Though he was the correspondent and friend of persons such as Increase Mather and Samuel Sewall and a vigorous defender of the conservative wing of Puritanism, Taylor rarely came into the larger public view.

Given these few details and what we know of Taylor's theology, he would have been a likely candidate for the uncomplimentary treatment accorded Puritan poets by influential nineteenth-century literary critics such as Moses Coit Tyler. In *A History of American Literature, 1607–1765* (1878), Tyler summarizes the popular view of the relationship between Puritan faith and Puritan art in terms that targeted poets such as Bradstreet and Wigglesworth (and would have targeted Taylor, had his poetry been discovered): "the typical Puritan . . . believed that there was an inappeasable feud between religion and art; and hence, the duty of suppressing art was bound up in his soul with the master purpose of promoting religion. He cultivated the grim and the ugly . . . ." Our access to Taylor's poetry today allows us to reexamine the assumptions out of which such critics wrote and to examine the feeling, depth, and artistic sophistication in Puritan poetry.

Of all poets who wrote in America during the seventeenth and eighteenth centuries, Taylor is foremost for showing that Puritanism was not antithetical to art and that quite apart from "the grim and the ugly" the Puritan poets were said to have cultivated, they could cultivate opportunities for favoring images of the beautiful and the divine in their writings. In the work of Taylor (and by his example perhaps that of other Puritan poets as well) are found an appreciation of poetic precedent and a finely developed symbolic imagination. Among the precedents most often noticed, particularly in extravagant language and emotionalism of Taylor's meditational poems, is the influence of the English metaphysical and meditational verse traditions represented by Francis Quarles, John Donne, George Herbert, Richard Crashaw, and Andrew Marvell. Detectable in Taylor's poems, especially

*Edward Taylor's
gravestone in
Westfield,
Massachusetts.*

in his longer pieces, is an affinity for the dramatic representation of larger-than-life religious conflict, associated with poetic works such as John Milton's *Paradise Lost* (*1667*) and Wigglesworth's *The Day of Doom* (*1662*) and prose works such as John Bunyan's *The Holy War* (*1682*).

At the same time, staples unique to the American Puritan poetic tradition abound in Taylor's poetry. Vestiges of the early Puritans' "plaine style" are noticeable, especially in the range of homelike and natural images Taylor introduces into his poems. Also apparent is the Puritans' fondness for typology, or symbolism. Favored by Puritan preachers and historians as well as poets, typology was understood in two contexts, and both are developed in Taylor's poems. Through typological treatment of the Bible individuals, places, or events in the Old Testament (the type) were interpreted as foreshadowings of individuals, places, or events in the New Testament (the antitype). Thus, Old Testament Passover rites were thought to foreshadow the rituals associated with the "Lord's Supper" in the New Testament; similarly, Old Testament images of captivity and bondage were thought to foreshadow the bondage in sin of New Testament figures who failed to yield to the redemptive power of grace. Typology also offered Puritans a way of seeing the world as a physical or material representation of the divine will toward humans. In Taylor's poetry, development of commonplace realities—a spider catching a fly, for instance, or the ravages of a "Sweeping Flood"—signals the poet's desire to plumb the material world for examples of the divine mind expressing its truths to humankind.

Following the topical and chronological arrangement in Taylor's manuscripts, his poetry is usually separated into three groups. Poems of the first group are collected under Taylor's own heading: *God's Determinations touching his Elect*. Written during the late 1670s and early 1680s, the thirty-five poems that comprise *God's Determinations* attempt to trace the religious course of human history from Creation, through the Fall, to the point of man's opportunity for redemption through the suffering of Christ. Collectively, the poems present the prospect of a merciful God witnessing the battle between Christ and Satan for control of the elect (those chosen by God for salvation).

Emphasizing a God of mercy as opposed to the fire and brimstone God who dispenses justice in Wigglesworth's *The Day of Doom, God's Determinations* humanizes the Calvinists' typical portrait of the divine in a sometimes playful, but ultimately serious and affecting, manner. In "The Preface," for instance, Creator and Creation take on distinctly unorthodox characteristics: the Creator as sportsman in "this Bowling Alley" of a universe bowls the sun into place and as divine designer hangs the "Tapistry" of the world's landscape and decorates the sky with "twinckling Lanthorns" (lanterns). But throughout *God's Determinations*, lest the seriousness of his point be lost, Taylor repeatedly reminds the reader of the smallness of humans and of the need for divine support in the war between the forces of good and evil, a war in which humans would seem to be nothing more than unwitting pawns. But humans must fight, as well, against Satan's wiles and hoodwinks and against the doubts that compromise every Christian soldier's spirit when, as Taylor writes in "Some of Satan's Sophistry," the possibility of salvation through grace seems but a dim hope and sin looms so large as to seem unabsolvable. Yet, the reward for the enduring soldier—a ride heavenward in Christ's victory coach—justifies the struggle and is available for all who share Taylor's belief in God's final mercy toward the saints. That ride is assured in the refrain of "The Joy of Church Fellowship Rightly Attended": "in Christ's Coach they sweetly sing /As they to Glory ride therein."

The second group of Taylor's poems is the smallest of the three. Because the poems collected there use allegories based on natural events to demonstrate the poet coming to terms with necessity or to treat religious doctrine, they are intriguing and rewarding glimpses into the Puritan imagination. These occasional poems (poems for special occasions) were probably written in the 1680s. One, "Upon Wedlock, & Death of Children," is a particularly moving piece in which marital love, tried and strengthened by the loss of children, serves as a model for the poet's conversion of a trial of faith into a strengthening of his love for God and an expression of his willingness to accept the divine will. Marriage he calls a "Curious Knot," and by playing on the modern meaning of knot (the "True-Love Knot" that binds couples together) along with its archaic meaning (a garden), he reaffirms his love for his wife even as he surrenders the flowers of their love's labor to an untimely fate. The ultimate affirmation Taylor makes in the poem is to the will of God, and the poet pledges to "piecemeale pass" whatever additional flowers are required for God's glory.

Although none of Taylor's other occasional poems is quite so personal, most develop the symbolic content of events in a way that includes even the good Puritan preacher in their message. In "Upon the Sweeping Flood," for instance, Taylor interprets the ravages of rain and flood as heavenly "Excrements" sent to "drown [the] Carnal love" (that is, the worldliness) of a people incapable of crying over the effects of their sin. In "Upon a Spider Catching a Fly," the dance of death between spider, fly, and wasp symbolizes the spiritual dance of death between "Hell's Spider" (Satan), the unregenerate who court sin much as a "Silly Fly" might court death in a spider's web, and those born again in grace who, like a powerful wasp, have the ability to thwart all satanic "Stratigems."

Had they been all that survived, *God's Determinations* and the collection of occasional poems would have assured Taylor's reputation as a poet of rare merit. However, his enduring contribution to early-American letters will likely be *Preparatory Meditations*, his third group of poems. Composed between 1682 and 1725 and collected under the title *Prepara-*

tory Meditations Before My Approach to the Lord's Supper by Taylor, the nearly two hundred meditations are the most unusual poetic expressions known to have been written in colonial America. In part, the meditations are thoroughly Puritan: many are typological studies, and some appear to portray the human condition with all the darkness and depravity suggested by the unmodified Calvinist writings of Wigglesworth or of Jonathan Edwards. Yet, the meditations are distinctly non-Puritan, and it is for their exception to practically every rule of Puritan poetry that they are most highly prized.

Taylor composed the meditations to put himself in the proper frame of mind prior to administering communion to his congregation. Neither the formal title nor the occasion suggests the depth of personal feeling and the sheer weight of personality revealed in the poems. For Taylor these meditations constituted a spiritual autobiography or an extended record of the spiritual content of his journey through this world. No Puritan poems equal in intensity Taylor's poetic confessions of love for God or of belief—almost to the point of presumption—in God's love for humans, and no Puritan poet has expressed the ecstasy that Taylor cannot conceal when he meditates on the efficacy of grace. Because words often seem insufficient to him to express the boundless love, indeed, the passion, flowing between God and poet, Taylor resorts to elaborate conceits and bold exaggerations. At these times, God's love becomes "matchless . . . [,] filling Heaven to the brim!" Taylor is always poised to admit his unworthiness, to confess himself the sinner desperate for, but not deserving of, redemption.

The majority of Taylor's contemporaries never read Taylor's writings. The responses of any who actually knew his poems remain shrouded in the obscurity in which the poems themselves languished for two centuries. That Taylor found poetry a congenial and inspiring medium for expressing his love of God and writing out his own interpretation of church doctrine is clear from the number of poems he wrote and from the fact that he wrote throughout his adult life. Ironically, in Edward Taylor New England Puritanism speaks with its most powerful, vital, and unique poetic voice, a voice that it never had the pleasure of hearing.

Suggested Readings: *Edward Taylor's Christographia*, ed. N. S. Grabo, 1962. *The Diary of Edward Taylor*, ed. F. Murphy, 1964. *A Transcript of Edward Taylor's Metrical History of Christianity*, ed. D. E. Stanford, 1977. *The Unpublished Writings of Edward Taylor*, 3 vols., ed. T. M. Davis and V. L. Davis, 1981. N. S. Grabo, *Edward Taylor*, 1961. *Early American Literature*, special Taylor issue, 4 (Winter 1969–1970). W. J. Scheick, *The Will and the Word: The Poetry of Edward Taylor*, 1974. K. Keller, *The Example of Edward Taylor*, 1975. K. E. Rowe, *Saint and Singer: Edward Taylor's Typology and the Poetics of Meditation*, 1986. J. Gatta, *Gracious Laughter: The Meditative Wit of Edward Taylor*, 1989.

Text Used: *The Poems of Edward Taylor*, ed. D. E. Stanford, 1960 (some spelling and punctuation modernized).

from   GOD'S DETERMINATIONS*

THE PREFACE

Infinity, when all things it beheld
In nothing, and of nothing all did build,
Upon what base was fixed the lathe, wherein

---

* Taylor wrote *God's Determinations Touching His Elect: And the Elect's Combat in Their Conversion, and Coming up to God in Christ, Together With the Comfortable Effects Thereof*, a series of lyrics and sermons in verse, to celebrate God's power and to trace the progress made by human souls since Creation.

He turn'd this globe, and riggaled[1] it so trim?
Who blew the bellows of his furnace vast?
Or held the mold wherein the world was cast?
Who laid its corner stone?[2] Or whose command?
Where stand the pillars upon which it stands?
Who laced and filleted[3] the earth so fine,
With rivers like green ribbons smaragdine?[4]   10
Who made the sea's its selvage,[5] and its locks
Like a quilt ball[6] within a silver box?
Who spread its canopy? Or curtains spun?
Who in this bowling alley bowled the sun?
Who made it always when it rises set
To go at once both down, and up to get?
Who th'curtain rods made for this tapestry?
Who hung the twinkling lanthorns[7] in the sky?
Who? who did this? or who is he? Why, know
Its only might almighty this did do.   20
His hand hath made this noble worke which stands
His glorious handywork not made by hands.
Who spake all things from nothing; and with ease
Can speak all things to nothing, if he please.
Whose little finger at his pleasure can
Out mete[8] ten thousand worlds with half a span:
Whose might almighty can by half a looks
Root up the rocks and rock the hills by th'roots.
Can take this mighty world up in his hand,
And shake it like a squitchen[9] or a wand.   30
Whose single frown will make the heavens shake
Like as an aspen leaf the wind makes quake.
Oh! what a might is this whose single frown
Doth shake the world as it would shake it down?
Which all from nothing fet,[10] from nothing, all:
Hath all on nothing set, lets nothing fall.
Gave all to nothing man indeed, whereby
Through nothing man all might him glorify.
In nothing then imbossed the brightest gem
More precious than all preciousness in them.   40
But nothing man did throw down all by sin:
And darkened that lightsome gem in him.
      That now his brightest diamond is grown
      Darker by far than any coalpit stone.

1680?, 1939

[1] Grooved.
[2] "Where wast thou when I laid the foundations of the earth? . . . or who laid the cornerstone thereof: When the morning stars sang together, and all the sons of God shouted for joy?" from Job 38:4–8.
[3] Encircled with decoration.   [4] Emerald green.   [5] A border, as on a piece of cloth.
[6] A ball of yarn, which would unravel if not stored in a box.   [7] Lanterns.   [8] Outmeasure.
[9] A stick used for whipping.   [10] Made.

THE JOY OF CHURCH FELLOWSHIP RIGHTLY ATTENDED*

In Heaven soaring up, I dropped an ear
    On earth: and oh! sweet melody:
And listening, found it was the saints[1] who were
    Encoached for Heaven that sang for joy.
    For in Christ's coach[2] they sweetly sing;
    As they to glory ride therein.

Oh! joyous hearts! Enfired with holy flame!
    Is speech thus tassled[3] with praise?
Will not your inward fire of joy contain;
    That it in open flames doth blaze?   10
    For in Christ's coach saints sweetly sing,
    As they to glory ride therein.

And if a string[4] do slip, by chance, they soon
    Do screw it up again: whereby
They set it in a more melodious tune
    And a diviner harmony.
    For in Christ's coach they sweetly sing.
    As they to glory ride therein.

In all their acts, public, and private, nay
    And secret too, they praise impart.   20
But in their acts divine and worship, they
    With hymns do offer up their heart.
    Thus in Christ's coach they sweetly sing
    As they to glory ride therein.

Some few not in;[5] and some whose time, and place
    Block up this coach's way[6] do go
As travellers afoot, and so do trace
    The road that gives them right thereto
    While in this coach these sweetly sing
    As they to glory ride therein.   30

1680?, 1939

---

* The final poem in the *God's Determination* series.
[1] Those who, when alive, were church members—"visible saints."
[2] The church, the means by which the elect could rise to Heaven.
[3] Ornamented.   [4] A musical instrument's string; when it has slipped, it must be tightened.
[5] Those few who are saved but choose to remain outside the church.
[6] Those who are saved but live in non-Christian regions or preceded Christ.

from PREPARATORY MEDITATIONS*

THE REFLEXION

Lord, art thou at the table head above
　　Meat, med'cine, sweetness, sparkling beauties to
Enamor souls with flaming flakes of love,
　　And not my trencher,[1] nor my cup o'erflow?
　　Be n't I a bidden guest? Oh! sweat mine eye.
　　O'erflow with tears: Oh! draw thy fountains dry.

Shall I not smell thy sweet, oh! Sharon's rose?[2]
　　Shall not mine eye salute thy beauty? Why?
Shall thy sweet leaves their beautious sweets upclose?
　　As half ashamed my sight should on them lie?　　　　　10
　　Woe's me! for this my sighs shall be in grain[3]
　　Offer'd on sorrow's altar for the same.

Had not my soul's thy conduit, pipes stopped been
　　With mud, what ravishment would'st thou convey?
Let grace's golden spade dig till the spring
　　Of tears arise, and clear this filth away.
　　Lord, let thy spirit raise my sighings till
　　These pipes my soul do with thy sweetness fill.

Earth once was paradise of Heaven below
　　Till inkfac'd sin had it with poison stocked　　　　　20
And chased this paradise away into
　　Heav'n's upmost loft, and it in glory locked.
　　But thou, sweet Lord, hast with thy golden key
　　Unlocked the door, and made, a golden day.

Once at thy feast,[4] I saw thee pearl-like stand
　　'Tween Heaven, and earth where heaven's bright glory all
In streams fell on thee, as a floodgate and,
　　Like sunbeams through thee on the world to fall.
　　Oh! sugar sweet then! my dear sweet Lord, I see
　　Saints' Heavens-lost happiness restor'd by thee.　　　30

Shall Heaven, and earth's bright glory all up lie
　　Like sunbeams bundled in the sun, in thee?
Dost thou sit rose at table head, where I
　　Do sit, and carv'st no morsel sweet for me?

---

* Published as *Preparatory Meditations Before My Approach to the Lord's Supper: Chiefly Upon the Doctrine Preached Upon the Day of Administration* [of Holy Communion].
　[1] A wooden plate.
　[2] "I am a rose of Sharon, a lily of the valleys," from Song of Solomon 2:1. The Plain of Sharon in Palestine was well known as a fertile coastal plain.
　[3] Entirely.
　[4] The Eucharist, or Holy Communion, in which believers share in the blood and body of Christ.

So much before, so little now! Sprindge,[5] Lord,
Thy rosy leaves, and me their glee afford.

Shall not thy rose my garden fresh perfume?
Shall not thy beauty my dull heart assail?
Shall not thy golden gleams run through this gloom?
Shall my black velvet mask thy fair face veil?   40
Pass o'er my faults: shine forth, bright sun: arise
Enthrone thy rosy-self within mine eyes.

1683, 1939

MEDITATION 8 (FIRST SERIES)

John 6:51. *I am the living bread.*[1]

I kenning[2] through astronomy divine
  The world's bright battlement,[3] wherein I spy
A golden path my pencil cannot line,
  From that bright throne unto my threshold lie.
  And while my puzzled thoughts about it pour,
  I find the bread of life in't at my door.

When that this bird of paradise[4] put in
  This wicker cage (my corpse) to tweedle[5] praise
Had pecked the fruit forbade: and so did fling
  Away its food; and lost its golden days;   10
  It fell into celestial famine sore:
  And never could attain a morsel more.

Alas! alas! Poor bird, what wilt thou do?
  The creature's field[6] no food for souls e'er gave.
And if thou knock at angels doors they show
  An empty barrel: they no soul bread have.
  Alas! Poor bird, the world's white loaf is done.
  And cannot yield thee here the smallest crumb.

In this sad state, God's tender bowels[7] run
  Out streams of grace: and he to end all strife   20
The purest wheat in Heaven, his dear-dear Son
  Grinds, and kneads up into this bread of life.

---

[5] Spread.
[1] "I am the living bread which came down from heaven: if any man eat of this bread, he shall live for ever: and the bread that I will give is my flesh, which I will give for the life of the world," from John 6:51.
[2] Discerning.   [3] The towers of Heaven.   [4] The human soul.   [5] To sing.
[6] The world of humans.   [7] The inner body, thought to be the source of compassion.

Which bread of life from Heaven down came and stands
Dished on thy table up by angel's hands.

Did God mold up this bread in Heaven, and bake,
   Which from his table came, and to thine goeth?
Doth he bespeak thee thus, this soul bread take.
   Come eat thy fill of this thy God's white loaf?
   It's food too fine for angels, yet come, take
   And eat thy fill. It's Heaven's sugar cake.   30

What grace is this knead in this loaf? This thing
   Souls are but petty things it to admire.
Yee angels, help: This fill would to the brim
   Heav'n's whelm'd-down[8] crystal meal bowl, yea and higher.
   This bread of life dropped in thy mouth, doth cry.
   Eat, eat me, soul, and thou shalt never die.

1684, 1939

MEDITATION 39 (FIRST SERIES)

    1 John 2:1 *If any man sin, we have an advocate.*[1]

My sin! my sin, My God, these cursed dregs,
   Green, yellow, blue streaked poison hellish, rank,
Bubs[2] hatched in nature's nest on serpents' eggs,
   Yelp, chirp and cry; they set my soul acramp.
   I frown, chide, strike and fight them, mourn and cry
   To conquer them, but cannot them destroy.

I cannot kill nor coop them up: my curb
   'S less than a snaffle[3] in their mouth: my reins
They as a twine thread, snap: by hell they're spurred:
   And load my soul with swagging loads of pains.   10
   Black imps, young devils, snap, bite, drag to bring
   And pick me headlong hell's dread whirlpool in.

Lord, hold thy hand: for handle me thou may'st
   In wrath: but, oh, a twinkling ray of hope
Methinks I spy thou graciously display'st.
   There is an advocate: a door is ope.
   Sin's poison swell my heart would till it burst,
   Did not a hope hence creep in't thus, and nurse't.

Joy, joy, God's Son's the sinner's advocate
   Doth plead the sinner guiltless, and a saint.   20

[8] Inverted.
   [1] "And if any man sin, we have an advocate with the Father, Jesus Christ the righteous: And he is the propitiation for . . . the sins of the whole world," from I John 2:1–2.
   [2] Pustules.   [3] A bit on a horse's bridle.

But yet attorney's pleas spring from the state
   The case is in: if bad it's bad in plaint.[4]
My papers do contain no pleas that do
   Secure me from, but knock me down to, woe.

I have no plea mine advocate to give:
   What now? He'll anvil arguments great store
Out of his flesh and blood to make thee live.
   O dear bought arguments: Good pleas therefore.
   Nails made of heavenly steel, more choice than gold
   Drove home, well clenched, eternally will hold.   30

Oh! Dear bought plea, dear Lord, what buy't so dear?
   What with thy blood purchase thy plea for me?
Take argument out of thy grave t'appear
   And plead my case with, me from guilt to free.
   These maul both sins, and devils, and amaze
   Both saints, and angels; wreath their mouths with praise.

What shall I do, my Lord? what do, that I
   May have thee plead my case? I fee[5] thee will
With faith, repentance, and obediently
   Thy service gainst satanic sins fulfill.   40
   I'll fight thy fields while live I do, although
   I should be hacked in pieces by thy foe.

Make me thy friend, Lord, be my surety: I
   Will be thy client, be my advocate:
My sins make thine, thy pleas make mine hereby.
   Thou wilt me save, I will thee celebrate.
   Thou'lt kill my sins that cut my heart within:
   And my rough feet[6] shall thy smooth praises sing.

                        1684?, 1954

MEDITATION 7 (SECOND SERIES)

Psalms 105:17. *He sent a man before them, even Joseph, who was sold, etc.*[1]

All dull, my Lord, my spirits flat, and dead
   All water-soaked and sapless[2] to the skin.
Oh! Screw me up and make my spirit's bed
   Thy quickening virtue for my ink is dim,

---

[4] A written grievance.   [5] Pay.   [6] Metrical units of verse.
[1] "He sent a man before them, even Joseph, who was sold for a servant," from Psalm 105:17; Joseph, a son of Rachel and Jacob, was sold into slavery in Egypt by his jealous brothers but became a high-ranking official.
[2] Frail.

My pencil blunt. Doth Joseph type out thee?[3]
Heralds of angels sing out, bow the knee.

Is Joseph's glorious shine a type of thee?
How bright art thou? He envied was as well.
And so was thou. He's stripped, and picked, poor he,
Into the pit. And so was thou. They shell   10
Thee of thy kernel. He by Judas[4] sold
For twenty bits, thirty for thee he'd told.

Joseph was tempted by his mistress vile.
Thou by the Devil, but both shame the foe.
Joseph was cast into the jail awhile.
And so was thou. Sweet apples mellow so.
Joseph did from his jail to glory run.
Thou from death's pallet rose like morning sun.

Joseph lays in[5] against the famine, and
Thou dost prepare the bread of life for thine.   20
He bought with corn for pharaoh th'men and land.
Thou with thy bread mak'st such themselves consign
Over to thee, that eat it. Joseph makes
His brethren bow before him. Thine too quake.

Joseph constrains his brethren till their sins
Do gall their souls. Repentance babbles fresh.
Thou treatest sinners till repentance springs
Then with him sendst a Benjamin-like mess.[6]
Joseph doth cheer his humble brethren. Thou
Dost stud[7] with joy the mourning saints that bow.   30

Joseph's bright shine th'Eleven Tribes must preach.
And thine Apostles now eleven, thine.
They bear his presents to his friends: thine reach
Thine unto thine, thus now behold a shine.
How hast thou pencilled out, my Lord, most bright
Thy glorious image here, on Joseph's light.

This I bewail in me under this shine
To see so dull a color in my skin.
Lord, lay thy brightsome colors on me thine.
Scour thou my pipes then play thy tunes therein.   40

[3] Because of similarities between the events of Joseph's life and those of Jesus, Joseph has generally been considered to be a prefigurement, or type, of Jesus (see Genesis 37–50).

[4] In Matthew 26:14, 48, Judas Iscariot, the disciple who betrayed Jesus.   [5] Stores away goods.
[6] A special meal; in Genesis 35:18 Benjamin was the favorite son of Jacob and Rachel.
[7] To ornament.

I will not hang my harp in willows by,[8]
While thy sweet praise, my tunes doth glorify.

1694, 1939

MEDITATION 150 (SECOND SERIES)

Canticles 7:3. *Thy two breasts are like two young roes that are twins.*[1]

My Blessed Lord, how doth thy beautious spouse[2]
  In stately stature rise in comeliness?
With her two breasts like two little roes that browse
  Among the lilies in their shining dress
  Like stately milk pails ever full and flow
  With spiritual milk to make her babes to grow.

Celestial nectar wealthier far than wine
  Wrought in the spirit's brew house and up tunned[3]
Within these vessels which are trussed up fine
  Likened to two pretty, neat twin roes that run'd   10
  Most pleasantly by their dam's sides like cades[4]
  And suckle with their milk Christ's spiritual babes.

Lord put these nibbles then my mouth into
  And suckle me therewith I humbly pray,
Then with this milk thy spiritual babe I'dst grow,
  And these two milk pails shall themselves display
  Like to these pretty twins in pairs round neat
  And shall sing forth thy praise over this meat.[5]

1719, 1960

UPON A SPIDER CATCHING A FLY

Thou sorrow, venom elf.
  Is this thy play,
To spin a web out of thyself
  To catch a fly?
  For why?

---

[8] "By the rivers of Babylon, there we [the Israelites] sat down, yea, we wept, when we rememberd Zion. On the willows there we hung our lyres. . . . How shall we sing the Lord's song in a strange land?" from Psalm 137:1–4.
[1] The poems of the Song of Solomon, or Canticles, celebrate love and the union of marriage; roes are small deer.
[2] The bride is considered to be God's spouse.
[3] Stored in barrels.   [4] Pets.   [5] The host, or food, that symbolizes Christ's flesh.

I saw a pettish[1] wasp
    Fall foul therein.
Whom yet thy whorl pins[2] did not clasp
    Lest he should fling
        His sting.   10

But as afraid, remote
    Didst stand hereat
And with thy little fingers stroke
    And gently tap
        His back.

Thus gently him didst treat
    Lest he should pet,[3]
And in a froppish,[4] waspish heat
    Should greatly fret
        Thy net.   20

Whereas the silly fly,
    Caught by its leg
Thou by the throat tookst hastily
    And 'hind the head
        Bite dead.

This goes to pot, that not
    Nature doth call.[5]
Strive not above what strength hath got
    Lest in the brawl
        Thou fall.   30

This fray seems thus to us.
    Hell's spider gets
His intrails spun to whip cords[6] thus
    And wove to nets
        And sets.[7]

To tangle Adam's race
    In's stratigems
To their destructions, spoil'd, made base
    By venom things
        Damn'd sins.   40

But mighty, gracious Lord
    Communicate

---

[1] Angry.   [2] The pins that catch the thread on a spinning wheel.   [3] Grow angry.   [4] Irritable.
[5] Those who do not call upon nature—natural reason, or, to the Puritans, the ability to know God's truth—are destroyed.
[6] Strong cords.   [7] Snares.

Thy grace to break the cord, afford
   Us glory's gate
     And state.

We'll nightingale sing like
   When pearched on high
In glory's cage, thy glory, bright,
   And thankfully,
     For joy.   50

                   1680–1682?, 1939

UPON A WASP CHILLED WITH COLD*

The bear[1] that breaths the northern blast
Did numb, torpedo-like,[2] a wasp
Whose stiffened limbs encramped, lay bathing
In Sol's[3] warm breath and shine as saving,
Which with her hands she chafes and stands
Rubbing her legs, shanks, thighs, and hands.
Her petty toes, and fingers' ends
Nipped with this breath, she out extends
Unto the sun, in great desire
To warm her digits at that fire.   10
Doth hold her temples in this state
Where pulse doth beat, and head doth ache.
Doth turn, and stretch her body small,
Doth comb her velvet capital.[4]
As if her little brain pan were
A volume of choice precepts clear.
As if her satin jacket hot
Contained apothecary's shop
Of nature's receipts,[5] that prevails
To remedy all her sad ails,   20
As if her velvet helmet high
Did turret[6] rationality.
She fans her wing up to the wind
As if her petticoat were lined,
With reason's fleece, and hoists sails
And humming flies in thankful gales
Unto her dun curled[7] palace hall
Her warm thanks offering for all.

---

* Taylor's actual title was "Upon a Wasp Child With Cold."
[1] The Great Bear, the constellation Ursa Major; or the North wind.
[2] Like the torpedo fish, which stuns its victims by electric shock.   [3] The sun's.
[4] Head.   [5] Recipes.   [6] Enclose, contain.   [7] Dark curved.

Lord clear my misted sight that I
May hence view thy divinity.   30
Some sparks whereof thou up dost hasp[8]
Within this little downy wasp
In whose small corporation[9] we
A school and a schoolmaster see
Where we may learn, and easily find
A nimble spirit bravely mind
Her work in ev'ry limb: and lace
It up neat with a vital grace,
Acting each part though ne'er so small
Here of this fustian[10] animal.   40
Till I enravished climb into
The Godhead on this ladder do.
Where all my pipes inspired upraise
An heavenly music furred[11] with praise.

1674–1689?, 1943

HUSWIFERY*

Make me, O Lord, thy spinning wheel complete.
  Thy Holy Word my distaff[1] make for me.
Make mine affections thy swift flyers[2] neat
  And make my soul thy holy spool to be.
  My conversation make to be thy reel[3]
  And reel the yarn thereon spun of thy wheel.

Make me thy loom then, knit therein this twine:
  And make thy Holy Spirit, Lord, wind quills:[4]
Then weave the web thyself. The yarn is fine.
  Thine ordinances make my fulling mills.[5]   10
  Then dye the same in heavenly colors choice,
  All pinked[6] with varnished[7] flowers of paradise.

Then clothe therewith mine understanding, will,
  Affections, judgment, conscience, memory
My words, and actions, that their shine may fill
  My ways with glory and thee glorify.
  Then mine apparel shall display before ye
  That I am clothed in holy robes for glory.

1682–1683?, 1939

---

[8] Shut.   [9] Body.   [10] Coarse-clothed; fustian is a cloth similar to corduroy.   [11] Fur-trimmed.
* Housekeeping; here, specifically weaving.
[1] The part of a spinning wheel that holds the raw wool fibers.
[2] The revolving part of a spinning wheel that twists the fibers into yarn or thread.
[3] The spool of a spinning wheel on which yarn or thread is wound.   [4] Bobbins or spools.
[5] Mills where cloth is cleaned with soap, or fuller's earth.   [6] Adorned.   [7] Sparkling.

UPON WEDLOCK, AND DEATH OF CHILDREN

A curious knot[1] God made in paradise,
   And drew it out enameled neatly fresh.
It was the true-love knot, more sweet than spice
   And set with all the flowers of grace's dress.
   It's wedding's knot, that ne'er can be untied.
   No Alexander's sword can it divide.[2]

The slips[3] here planted, gay and glorious grow:
   Unless an hellish breath do singe their plumes.
Here primrose, cowslips, roses, lilies blow[4]
   With violets and pinks that void[5] perfumes.   10
   Whose beautious leaves o'erlaid with honey dew.
   And chanting birds chirp out sweet music true.

When in this knot I planted was, my stock[6]
   Soon knotted, and a manly flower[7] outbroke.
And after it my branch again did knot.
   Brought out another flower[8] its sweet breathed mate.
   One knot gave one t'other the t'other's place.
   Whence chuckling smiles fought in each other's face.

But oh! a glorious hand from glory came
   Guarded with angels, soon did crop this flower   20
Which almost tore the root up of the same
   At that unlooked for, dolesome, darksome hour.
   In prayer to Christ perfumed it did ascend,
   And angels bright did it to Heaven tend.

But pausing on't, this sweet perfum'd my thought,
   Christ would in glory have a flower, choice, prime,
And having choice, chose this my branch forth brought.
   Lord take't. I thank thee, thou takst ought of mine,
   It is my pledge in glory,[9] part of me
   Is now in it, Lord, glorified with thee.   30

But praying o'er my branch, my branch did sprout
   And bore another manly flower,[10] and gay
And after that another,[11] sweet broke out.
   The which the former hand soon got away.

[1] A flower bed as well as the marital bond.
[2] According to legend, Alexander the Great (356– 323 B.C.) cut the knot tied by King Gordius of Phrygia, a knot to be undone only by the future master of Asia; "to cut the Gordian knot" means to find a quick solution for a problem.
[3] Plant cuttings.   [4] Blossom.   [5] Give off.   [6] A plant's main stem or trunk.
[7] Taylor refers to four of his children, two of whom had died before the poem was written, as flowers. Here he means his son Samuel (1675–?)
[8] Taylor's daughter Elizabeth (1676–1677).   [9] The assurance of a resting place in Heaven.
[10] Taylor's son James (1678–?).   [11] Taylor's daughter Abigail (1681–1682).

But oh! the tortures, vomit, screechings, groans,
And six weeks' fever would pierce hearts like stones.

Grief o'er doth flow: and nature fault would find
    Were not thy Will, my spell, charm, joy, and gem:
That as I said, I say, take, Lord, they're thine.
    I piecemeal pass to glory bright in them.   40
    I joy, may I sweet flowers for glory breed,
    Whether thou getst them green, or lets them seed.

                         1682–1683?, 1939

THE EBB AND FLOW

When first thou on me Lord wrought'st thy sweet print,
    My heart was made thy tinderbox.[1]
My 'ffections were thy tinder in't.
    Where fell thy sparks by drops.
Those holy sparks of heavenly fire that came
Did ever catch and often out would flame.

But now my heart is made thy censear[2] trim,
    Full of thy golden altar's fire,
    To offer up sweet incense in
        Unto thyself entire: 10
I find my tinder scarce thy sparks can feel
That drop out from thy holy flint and steel.

Hence doubts out bud for fear thy fire in me
    'S a mocking ignis fatuus[3]
    Or lest thine altar's fire out be,
        Its hid in ashes thus.
Yet when the bellows of thy spirit blow
Away mine ashes, then thy fire doth glow.

                        1674–1689?, 1939

UPON THE SWEEPING FLOOD, AUG. 13–14, 1683

Oh! that I'd had a tear to've quenched that flame
    Which did dissolve the heavens above
    Into those liquid drops that came
        To drown our carnal[1] love.

---

[1] A box for holding tinder, flint, and steel for starting a fire.
[2] A receptacle used for burning incense.
[3] Foolish fire (Latin), a term used for natural phosphorescent lights over a swamp, which caused travelers to lose their way; a "will-o-the-wisp," or misleading influence.
[1] Earthly.

Our cheeks were dry and eyes refused to weep.
Tears bursting out ran down the sky's dark cheek.

Were th'heavens sick? must we their doctors be
  And physic² them with pills, our sin?
  To make them purge and vomit, see,
    And excrements out fling?   10
We've griev'd them by such physic that they shed
Their excrements upon our lofty heads.

1683, 1943

A FIG FOR THEE OH! DEATH*

Thou king of terrors with thy gastly eyes
With butter¹ teeth, bare bones, grim looks likewise.
And grizzly hide, and clawing talons, fell,²
Op'ning to sinners vile, trap door of Hell,
That on in sin impenitently trip
The downfall³ art of the infernal pit,
Thou struckst thy teeth deep in my Lord's bless'd side:
Who dashed it out, and all its venom 'stroyed
That now thy poundrill⁴ shall only dash
My flesh and bones to bits, and cask⁵ shall clash.   10
Thou'rt not so frightful now to me, thy knocks
Do crack my shell. Its heavenly kernel's box
Abides most safe. Thy blows do break its shell,
Thy teeth its nut. Cracks are that on it fell.
Thence out its kernel fair and nut, by worms
Once vitiated out, new formed forth turns
And on the wings of some bright angel flies
Out to bright glory of God's blissful joys.
Hence thou to me with all thy gastly face
Art not so dreadful unto me through grace.   20
I am resolved to fight thee, and ne'er yield,
Blood up to th'ears; and in the battlefield
Chasing thee hence: But not for this my flesh,
My body, my vile harlot, it's thy mess,⁶
Laboring to drown me into sin, disguise
By eating and by drinking such evil joys
Though grace preserv'd me that I ne'er have
Surprised been nor tumbled in such grave.⁷
Hence for my strumpet I'll ne'er draw my sword

---

² To dose with medicine.
* "Fig" here means a trifling amount, something of no value.
¹ Yellowed.   ² Deadly.   ³ Precipice.   ⁴ Pestle, or pounder.   ⁵ Body.   ⁶ Meal.
⁷ Lines 24–28 are clearer in an earlier version of this poem: "My harlot body, make thou it thy mess,/That oft ensnared me with its strumpet's guise/Of meat's and drink's dainty sensu-alities,/Yet grace ne'er suffer[ed] me to turn aside/As sinners oft fall in and do abide."

Nor thee restrain at all by iron curb[8]   30
Nor for her safety will I 'gainst thee strive
But let thy frozen grips take her captive
And her imprison in thy dungeon cave
And grind to powder in thy mill the grave,
Which powder in thy van[9] thou'st safely keep
Till she hath slept out quite her fatal sleep.
When the last cock shall crow the last day[10] in
And the archangel's trumpet's sound shall ring
Then th'eye omniscient seek shall all there round
Each dust death's mill had very finely ground,   40
Which in death's smoky furnace well refined
And each to'ts fellow hath exactly joined,
Is raised up anew and made all bright
And crystallized; all top full of delight.
And entertains its soul again in bliss
And holy angels waiting all on this,
The soul and body now, as two true lovers
E'ry night how do they hug and kiss each other.
And going hand in hand thus through the skies
Up to eternal glory glorious rise.   50
Is this the worst thy terrors then canst, why
Then should this grimace at me terrify?
Why cam'st thou then so slowly? Mend[11] thy pace.
Thy slowness me detains from Christ's bright face.
Although thy terrors rise to th'high'st degree,
I still am where I was, a fig for thee.

1960

Mary Rowlandson
(1637?–1711?)

We have few facts about the life of Mary Rowlandson, the author of *The Narrative of the Captivity and Restoration of Mrs. Mary Rowlandson* (1682), one of the most widely read literary works to come out of the colonial period. She was probably born Mary White in 1637 in England but grew up in Salem, Massachusetts. In the early 1650s her father, John White, a wealthy landowner, helped to establish the town of Lancaster, Massachusetts, about thirty miles West of Boston. There Mary settled with her husband, Joseph Rowlandson, the town's first minister. They had four children, one of whom died in infancy.

Mary Rowlandson lived on the frontier for a short but fierce period during the settlement of New England, called King Philip's War (1675?–1678). The war resulted from

---

[8] A restrainer such as a horse's bit.   [9] A winnowing basket; possibly, a tomb.
[10] Judgment Day.   [11] Improve.

tensions between the Puritans and Native Americans—tensions building since the death of Massasoit, chief of the Wampanoag Indians of southeastern Massachusetts and ally of the Puritans, in 1661. The new chief was Metacomet, son of Massasoit. Called "King Philip," by the English, Metacomet remembered his father's status as a great chief before the Puritan arrival and sought to preserve the Wampanoag's dignity as a sovereign entity. With settlements crowding the Native Americans and their survival threatened, conflict was predictable. It broke out after Plymouth authorities executed three Wampanoags in January 1675 for the alleged murder of an Englishman. For the next eighteen months Wampanoags and Puritans fought, and the battleground typically was a frontier town.

In February 1676 a four-hundred-man war party consisting of Wampanoag, Quabaug, Nashaway, Narraganset, and Nipmuck Indians attacked Lancaster. The town had feared the raid, and Joseph Rowlandson was in Boston at the time, arranging for military aid. The Native Americans wounded Mary Rowlandson and her six-year-old daughter and took Rowlandson and her three children captives. Rowlandson was separated from her two oldest children, and her wounded daughter died nine days later. Until her release, nearly twelve weeks after her capture, Rowlandson was placed in the service of Quanopin, a sagamore (secondary chief) and brother-in-law of Metacomet, and Quanopin's wife, Wetamoo, who treated her decently.

From this experience Rowlandson composed *The Narrative*. It begins with a vigorous and unsentimental description of the nightmarish attack on Lancaster, including the savage treatment of so many of Rowlandson's relatives and neighbors. Twenty "removes," or relocations, to various campsites followed for the next eleven weeks and five days as Rowlandson endured freezing cold, sickness, loneliness, and fear—in what was ultimately a test of endurance. Against the day to day events are moments of unexpected confrontations with terror and death, which serve as dramatic punctuation in this tale of perseverance.

The Narrative is very much a Puritan's story. Framed as a tale of woe, it warns that God will punish Rowlandson and her community until they correct their ways and realize their complete dependence on God's will. The Native Americans are depicted as instruments of the Devil and as God's scourges sent to "afflict" the settlers until they reform. However, God's providence is reassuring, and Rowlandson's faith armed this New England Puritan against the terrors of the "howling wilderness." As Rowlandson explains in *The Narrative,* she could endure the hardships of the captivity because "God was carrying me along and bearing up my spirit." She searched for analogies between her experiences and passages in the Bible, referring to the Bible more than sixty-five times. Her release, she was convinced, was evidence of God's providential direction of her life and of the life of the colony.

Although *The Narrative* is didactic, finding a moral in every event, it is also realistic, giving a rare picture of Native-American life in this period of conflict. Along with their captives, the natives must live on nuts and berries, sleep out in the freezing New England winter, and meet death through war and privation. Even so, many Wampanoags find the means to "refresh" the starving Rowlandson from their limited resources, and she is thankful.

Many of the Wampanoags emerge from *The Narrative* with distinctive personalities, no one more than Metacomet, whom Rowlandson met at various times. To the reader, if not to Rowlandson, as he tries to profit from his captive, the chief appears somewhat more human than the ferocious enemy of the Puritans he was reputed to be. He instructs Rowlandson to stand before what he perhaps humorously calls "the General Court" and recommends the price of her ransom. Shortly thereafter, she is ransomed, apparently for the price of two coats, twenty pounds, half a bushel of seed corn, and some tobacco.

Rowlandson's release occurred near the end of King Philip's War, in which the Wampanoags were completely defeated. Whereas the colonists lost six hundred lives, the na-

=CONTEXTS=

The New England Primer

For the Puritans, religion and learning were always linked. The Puritans believed that every Christian must be literate in order to read the Bible and other religious writing. This essential tie between learning and spiritual life was established for children through *The New England Primer*, first published in the Massachusetts Bay Colony before 1690. This book contains prayers, hymns, verse, and an illustrated alphabet accompanied by moral principles, so that the very act of learning to read became a religion lesson. Nearly every Puritan and Presbyterian household from the seventeenth through the mid-nineteenth century had a copy of the *Primer*, which was estimated to have sold over 5 million copies before 1850.

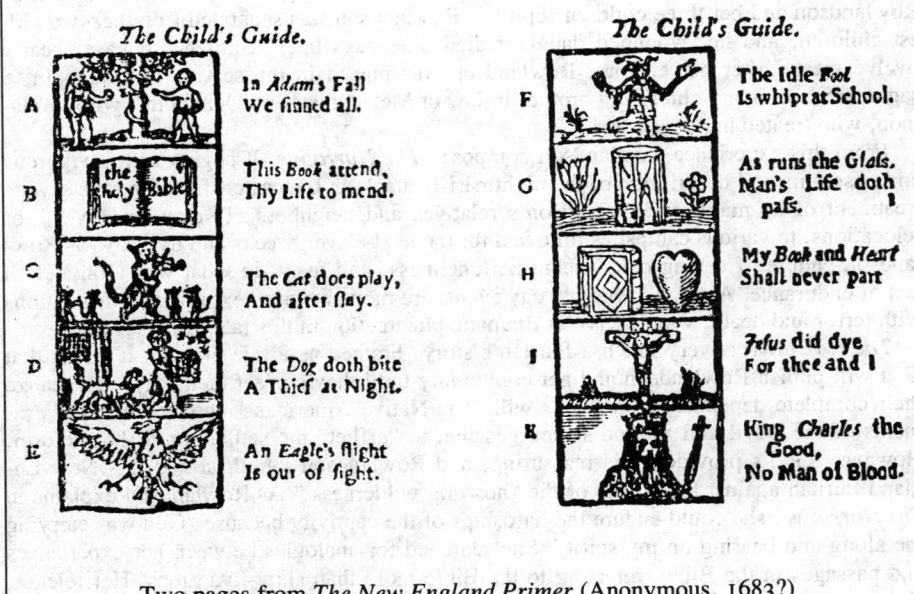

The Child's Guide.

A   In *Adam's* Fall
We finned all.

B   This *Book* attend,
Thy Life to mend.

C   The *Cat* does play,
And after flay.

D   The *Dog* doth bite
A Thief at Night.

E   An *Eagle's* flight
Is out of fight.

The Child's Guide.

F   The Idle *Fool*
Is whipt at School.

G   As runs the Glaſs.
Man's Life doth
paſs.

H   My *Book* and *Heart*
Shall never part

I   *Jeſus* did dye
For thee and I

K   King *Charles* the
Good,
No Man of Blood.

Two pages from *The New England Primer* (Anonymous, 1683?)

tives lost three thousand. Metacomet was killed, and his wife, children, and many other Native Americans were sold into slavery in the West Indies.

Once she and her children were freed, Rowlandson moved to Wethersfield, Connecticut, where her husband had accepted a ministry. When Rowlandson's husband died in 1678, the town gave her a pension for the remainder of her life. She is believed to have died in 1711.

Published in Boston in 1682, Rowlandson's *Narrative* was an immediate success, though her only known writing, and at least thirty editions of it have followed. It served as a model for other captivity narratives, commonly more sensational and sentimental than Rowlandson's. The captivity narrative entered American fiction in such stories about the Native American wars as James Fenimore Cooper's *The Last of the Mohicans* (1826). *The Narrative* remains important in its own right as a vigorous tale of frontier experience and for its heartfelt expression of a Puritan's deep religious experience. It is as well a powerful account of one of the Native American's many doomed attempts to halt colonial expansion.

Suggested Readings: *Narratives of the Indian Wars, 1675–1699*, ed. Charles H. Lincoln, 1913. *Held Captive by the Indians: Selected Narratives, 1642–1836*, ed. R. D. Van Der Beets, 1973. A. Keiser, *The Indian in American Literature*, 1933. R. H. Pearce, "The Significance of the Captivity Narrative" in *American Literature* XIX, 1947. R. Van Der Beets, *The Indian Captivity Narrative: An American Genre*, 1983. D. L. Greene, "New Light on Mary Rowlandson" in *Early American Literature* 20, 1985.

Text Used: *The Narrative of the Captivity and Restoration of Mrs. Mary Rowlandson*, 1930.

from THE NARRATIVE OF THE CAPTIVITY AND RESTORATION OF MRS. MARY ROWLANDSON*

On the tenth of February, 1675, [1] came the Indians in great numbers upon Lancaster.[2] Their first coming was about sun-rising. Hearing the noise of some guns, we looked out: several houses were burning, and the smoke ascending to heaven. There were five persons[3] taken in one house; the father, the mother, and a suckling child they knocked on the head; the other two they took and carried away alive. There were two others, who being out of their garrison[4] upon some occasion, were set upon; one was knocked on the head, the other escaped. Another there was, who, running along, was shot and wounded, and fell down; he begged of them his life, promising them money, (as they told me,) but they would not hearken to him, but knocked him in head, and stripped him naked, and split open his bowels. Another, seeing many of the Indians about his barn, ventured and went out, but was quickly shot down. There were three others belonging to the same garrison[5] who were killed; the Indians getting up upon the roof of the barn, had advantage to shoot down upon them over their fortification. Thus these murderous wretches went on burning and destroying [all] before them.

At length they came and beset our own house, and quickly it was the dolefulest day that ever mine eyes saw. The house stood upon the edge of a hill; some of the Indians got behind the hill, others into the barn, and others behind any thing that would shelter them; from all which places they shot against the house, so that the bullets seemed to fly like hail; and quickly they wounded one man among us, then another, and then a third. About two hours (according to my observation in that

---

* Rowlandson's full title is *The Sovereignty and Goodness of GOD, Together With the Faithfulness of His Promises Displayed; Being a Narrative of the Captivity and Restoration of Mrs. Mary Rowlandson, Commended by Her, to All That Desires to Know the Lord's Doings to, and Dealings With Her. Especially to Her Dear Children and Relations. The Second Addition Corrected and Amended. Written by Her Own Hand for Her Private Use, and Now Made Public at the Earnest Desire of Some Friends, and for the Benefit of the Afflicted.*

[1] Rowlandson used the Julian, not the Gregorian, calendar, so her dates are ten days earlier than they would be in our system, and February was considered the last month of the year: her February 10, 1675/76 corresponds to our February 20, 1676.

[2] Lancaster, Massachusetts, Rowlandson's hometown and the site of her capture.

[3] The family of John Ball (?–1676), a tailor.

[4] A fortified house where people assembled for defense.

[5] The garrison of Richard Wheeler (?–1676).

amazing time) they had been about the house before they prevailed to fire it (which they did with flax and hemp which they brought out of the barn, there being no defense about the house,[6] only two flankers[7] at two opposite corners, and one of them not finished). They fired it once, and one ventured out and quenched it, but they quickly fired it again, and that took. Now is the dreadful hour come, that I have often heard (in time of war, as was the case with others) but now mine eyes see it. Some in our house were fighting for their lives, others wallowing in their blood, the house on fire over our heads, and the bloody heathen ready to knock us on the head if we stirred out. Now might we hear mothers and children crying out for themselves, and one another, "Lord, what shall we do?" Then I took my children (and one of my sisters her's) to go forth and leave the house: but as soon as we came to the door, and appeared, the Indians shot so thick, that the bullets rattled against the house, as if one had taken an handful of stones and threw them, so that we were fain to give back. We had six stout dogs belonging to our garrison, but none of them would stir, though [at] another time, if an Indian had come to the door, they were ready to fly upon him and tear him down. The Lord hereby would make us the more to acknowledge his hand, and to see that our help is always in him. But out we must go, the fire increasing, and coming along behind us, roaring, and the Indians gaping before us with their guns, spears, and hatchets, to devour us. No sooner were we out of the house, but my brother-in-law[8] (being before wounded, in defending the house, in or near the throat) fell down dead, whereat the Indians scornfully shouted, and hallooed, and were presently upon him, stripping off his clothes. The bullets flying thick, one went through my side, and the same (as [it] would seem) through the bowels and hand of my dear child in my arms.[9] One of my elder sister's children, named William,[10] had then his leg broken, which the Indians perceiving, they knocked him on the head. Thus were we butchered by those merciless heathens, standing amazed, with the blood running down to our heels. My elder sister being yet in the house, and seeing those woeful sights, the infidels hauling mothers one way, and children another, and some wallowing in their blood, as her eldest son[11] telling her that her son William was dead, and myself was wounded, she said, And "Lord let me die with them": which was no sooner said, but she was struck with a bullet, and fell down dead over the threshold. I hope she is reaping the fruit of her good labors, being faithful to the service of God in her place. In her younger years she lay under much trouble upon spiritual accounts, till it pleased God to make that precious scripture take hold of her heart, 2 Corinthians xii:9. "And he said unto me, my grace is sufficient for thee." More than twenty years after, I have heard her tell how sweet and comfortable that place was to her. But to return: the Indians laid hold of us, pulling me one way, and the children another, and said, "Come, go along with us." I told them they would kill me. They answered, if I were willing to go along with them, they would not hurt me.

Oh! the doleful sight that now was to behold at this house! Come, behold the works of the Lord, what desolations he has made in the earth.[12] Of thirty-seven

---

[6] The Rowlandson house was not fortified and fell to the attackers.

[7] A projection for fortification.

[8] Ensign John Divoll (?–1676), commander of the garrison that day, was married to Rowlandson's youngest sister, Hannah.

[9] Rowlandson's daughter Sarah (1670–1676).

[10] William Kerley (1659–1676), son of Elizabeth and Lieut. Henry Kerley.

[11] Henry Kerley, Jr. (1657–?).   [12] Psalm 46:8.

persons[13] who were in this one house, none escaped either present death, or a bitter captivity, save only one,[14] who might say as in Job i:15: And I only am escaped to tell the news. There were twelve killed, some shot, some stabbed with their spears, some knocked down with their hatchets. When we are in prosperity, oh, the little that we think of such dreadful sights, and to see our dear friends and relations lie bleeding out their heart's blood upon the ground. There was one who was chopped into the head with a hatchet, and stripped naked, and yet was crawling up and down. It is a solemn sight to see so many Christians lying in their blood, some here, and some there, like a company of sheep torn by wolves. All of them stripped naked by a company of hell-hounds, roaring, singing, ranting, and insulting, as if they would have torn our very hearts out; yet the Lord by his almighty power preserved a number of us from death, for there were twenty-four of us taken alive and carried captive.

I had often before this said, that if the Indians should come, I should choose rather to be killed by them, than taken alive; but when it came to the trial, my mind changed; their glittering weapons so daunted my spirit, that I chose rather to go along with those (as I may say) ravenous bears, than that moment to end my days. And that I may the better declare what happened to me during that grievous captivity, I shall particularly speak of the several removes[15] we had up and down the wilderness.

THE FIRST REMOVE

Now away we must go with those barbarous creatures, with our bodies wounded and bleeding, and our hearts no less than our bodies. About a mile we went that night, up upon a hill[16] within sight of the town, where they intended to lodge. There was hard by a vacant house (deserted by the English before, for fear of the Indians). I asked them whether I might not lodge in the house that night, to which they made answer, what, will you love Englishmen still? This was the dolefulest night that ever my eyes saw. Oh the roaring and singing and dancing and yelling of those black creatures in the night, which made the place a lively resemblance of hell; and as miserable was the waste that was there made, of horses, cattle, sheep, swine, calves, lambs, roasting pigs, and fowl, (which they had plundered in the town,) some roasting, some lying and burning, and some boiling, to feed our merciless enemies, who were joyful enough, though we were disconsolate. To add to the dolefulness of the former day, and the dismalness of the present night, my thoughts ran upon my losses and sad bereaved condition. All was gone, my husband gone, (at least separated from me, he being in the Bay;[17] and to add to my grief, the Indians told me they would kill him as he came homeward;) my children gone, my relations and friends gone, our house and home and all our comforts within door and without, all was gone, except my life, and I knew not but the next

---

[13] Current historians give numbers ranging from thirty-seven to more than fifty-five.

[14] Ephraim Roper. Unbeknownst to Rowlandson, three children of Elizabeth and John Kettle escaped, too.

[15] Moves to different areas; after each, the group spent a few days in camp. The first remove was made on February 10, 1675/76 [20, 1676].

[16] George Hill, the highest elevation in Lancaster.

[17] Rev. Rowlandson had gone to Boston (on Massachusetts Bay) to get help in case of a Native-American attack on Lancaster but was too late.

moment that might go too. There remained nothing to me but one poor wounded babe, and it seemed at present worse than death, that it was in such a pitiful condition, bespeaking compassion, and I had no refreshing for it, nor suitable things to revive it. Little do many think what is the savageness and brutishness of this barbarous enemy, even those that seem to profess more than others among them, when the English have fallen into their hands.

Those seven that were killed at Lancaster the summer before upon a Sabbath day,[18] and the one that was afterwards killed upon a week day, were slain and mangled in a barbarous manner, by One-eyed John, and Marlborough "Praying Indians," which Captain Moseley brought to Boston, as the Indians told me.

1682

Cotton Mather
(1663–1728)

Few early Americans equaled Cotton Mather in his dramatic involvement in the spiritual and political affairs of late seventeenth-century and early eighteenth-century New England. In colonial Boston, a community that relished foreshadowings of providence's blessing upon its endeavors, Mather's birth in 1663 must have appeared to be a particularly auspicious event. The grandson of the eminent first-generation Puritan ministers Richard Mather and John Cotton and the son of Maria Cotton and Increase Mather, then a rapidly rising figure in New England ecclesiastic circles, Cotton Mather was born into a position of privilege and promise. His accomplishments as a child and young man all seemed to validate the community's high expectations. He spent his formative years mastering Latin, Greek, and other ancient languages and practicing homiletic form (the form of sermons), graduated at age fifteen from Harvard College, and finished an M.A. there at age eighteen. Ordained his father's colleague at Boston's prestigious North Church in 1685, Mather published his first book, *The Call of the Gospel,* the following year.

Over the next forty years Mather lived through a succession of professional and personal ecstasies and agonies that possibly only a colonial Puritan could appreciate. He quickly joined his father in the vanguard of New England's political and ecclesiastic elite. Although both Mathers realized that old-style Puritanism was being eroded by an increasingly cosmopolitan, secular, and scientific temperament, neither fully understood that their collective activities actually encouraged the proliferation of that temperament. Cotton Mather was caught between familial and communal pressures to preserve the idealistic vision of New England's founders and a personal disposition to engage in scientific speculation, to believe in spiritual evidence in the physical world, and to endorse religious libertarianism even as he preached out of a virtually unmodified Calvinism. Mather endures as the most prolific and eloquent defender of the religious convictions under which New Eng-

---

[18] August 22, 1675, when Lancaster was attacked by the Nashaway Indians, led by Monoco (?–1676), or One-eyed John, and Christianized Native Americans, or "Praying Indians," of Marlborough, Massachusetts (brought there by force by Captain Samuel Moseley).

land was settled and as the most gifted, persistent voice providing the terms with which to challenge those convictions.

In more than four hundred books and sermons published during his lifetime and in a score of unpublished historical and theological manuscripts, Mather writes out all the paradoxes of his professional life. In the *Magnalia Christi Americana* (1702), his most famous work, he interprets the history of New England's first seventy years of settlement as a religious experience of epic proportions. He tries to move his contemporaries to follow in the footsteps of their ancestors, seemingly not realizing that American Puritanism had already passed its moment of glory or that, as Ralph Waldo Emerson explained many years later, each generation has to establish its own particular relation to God and the universe.

If Mather's historical writings, such as the *Magnalia,* fail to mesh his brand of religion, the expectations of the age, and his own intellectual curiosity, his writings that combine his typically contradictory scientific, speculative, theological, and humanitarian interests hardly fare much better. In these nonhistorical writings Mather vacillates between genius and blind superstition, arrogance, and simplicity. His belief in the existence of witches as a divine judgment against a sinful people and his fervid defense of the Salem witchcraft trials oddly juxtapose with his explicit distrust of "spectral evidence," as expressed in *The Wonders of the Invisible World* (1693). Throughout his ministerial career Mather harangued his congregation with awesome visions of divine retribution and believed he heard God's voice in the fury of storms as well as in angelic apparitions. Yet, he was an uncommonly brilliant man whose extensive correspondence with foreign intellectuals merited his induction into the Royal Society of London in 1713. His writings on the necessity of doing good for one's fellows (especially the essay *Bonifacius* [1710]) exerted a profound and lasting influence on figures such as Benjamin Franklin. In 1721 Mather championed smallpox inoculation and then catalogued common maladies and their remedies in *The Angel of Bethesda* (1722), significantly advancing colonial medicine.

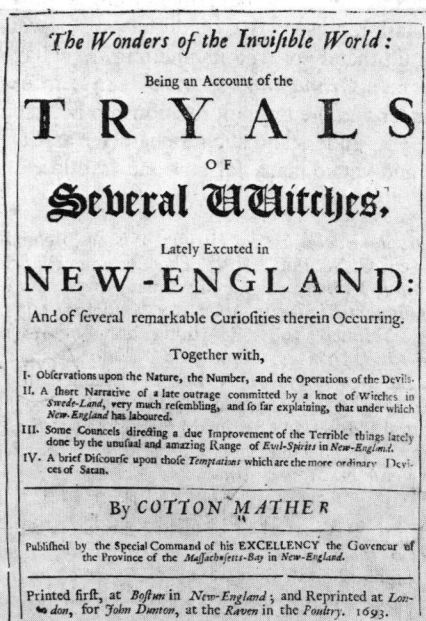

The title page of Cotton Mather's Wonders of the Invisible World.

The extent to which Mather felt the difficulty of reconciling aspects of his old-style orthodoxy with his forward-looking intellectual curiosity is unknown. But as the product of an age that believed in the symbolic importance of events and as a leading proponent of that belief, Mather likely appreciated the awkwardness of his own situation. In his seven-volume *Diary* and autobiography *Paterna* (not published until 1911–1912 and 1976, respectively), he tended to write out of a sense of frustration over the course of his professional life and represents that frustration as an extension of his sometimes tragic personal life as well as of the inability of contemporaries to appreciate the quality of his mind. In Mather's private writing, between large meditational passages typical of Puritan spiritual writing are the trials of his professional career reconstituted in terrible private suffering, so that the professional and the personal become indistinguishable. This holds true for his diary's and autobiography's implications of disappointment over Mather's failing to succeed his father as Harvard's president and of his anguish over what he perceived as his failure to perpetuate the "Mather dynasty" (his favored son, named Increase after Mather's father, turned out to be a rogue more prone to carousing through the night than to preparing for the ministry). Mather's life seemed to offer few compensations for such disappointment and anguish. Although he fathered fifteen children, only two survived him, neither possessing an intellect or an imagination equal to those of their father or of their grandfather. Even marriage proved a trial: after two happy marriages (to Abigail Phillips in 1686 and to Elizabeth Clark Hubbard in 1703) cut short by death, Mather's third wife (as of 1715), Lydia Lee George, wrecked him financially and eventually went insane. It is little wonder that under such circumstances Mather, a few months before his death in 1728, concluded *Paterna*, composed over many years for the edification of his children, by imagining his death as a literal repetition of Christ's own crucifixion.

Mather's biographers have struggled with the complexities of his character and its relation to his time and place. Even fiction writers such as Washington Irving and Nathaniel Hawthorne have incorporated images of Mather into their narratives in an effort to explain to later generations the intricacies and eccentricities of life in Puritan America. Most biographers and writers agree that Mather stands as a stark representative of all that was powerful in New England's Puritan spirit and of all that ultimately proved its undoing. Few have been more succinct than the narrator of Hawthorne's *Grandfather's Chair* (1841) in expressing the paradoxical nature of Mather's character and the implicit relationship between Mather and his time: "It is difficult . . . to make you understand such a character as Cotton Mather's, in whom there was so much good, and yet so many failings and frailties."

Suggested Readings: *Magnalia Christi Americana: Or, the Ecclesiastical History of New-England, Second Book,* 1853. *Diary of Cotton Mather,* 2 vols., ed. C. W. Ford, 1957. The Christian *Philosopher,* ed. J. K. Piercy, 1968. *Selected Letters of Cotton Mather,* ed. K. Silverman, 1971. O. T. Beall, Jr., and R. Shryock, *Cotton Mather: First Significant Figure in American Medicine,* 1954. B. Wendell, *Cotton Mather: The Puritan Priest,* ed. A. Heimert, 1963. R. Middlekauf, *The Mathers: Three Generations of Puritan Intellectuals, 1596–1728,* 1971. S. Bercovitch, "Cotton Mather" in *Major Writers of Early American Literature,* ed. E. Emerson, 1972. R. A. Bosco, "Editor's Introduction" in *Paterna: The Autobiography of Cotton Mather,* 1976. D. Levin, *Cotton Mather,* 1978. B. Levy, *Cotton Mather,* 1979. M. R. Breitwieser, *Cotton Mather and Benjamin Franklin: The Price of Representative Personality,* 1984. K. Silverman, *The Life and Times of Cotton Mather,* 1984. D. D. Knight, "Editor's Introduction" in *Cotton Mather's Verse in English,* 1989.

Texts Used: A People of God Settled in the Devil's Territories and "The Trial of Martha Carrier": *The Wonders of the Invisible World: Being an Account of the Trials of Several Witches Lately Executed in New-England,* 1862. "Relative to Home and Neighborhood": *Bonifacius: An Essay Upon the Good,* ed. D. Levin, 1966. (Some spelling and punctuation modernized.)

from THE WONDERS OF THE INVISIBLE WORLD*

[A *People of God Settled in the Devil's Territories*]

The New-Englanders are a people of God settled in those, which were once the Devil's territories; and it may easily be supposed that the Devil was exceedingly disturbed, when he perceived such a people here accomplishing the promise of old made unto our blessed Jesus, *That He should have the utmost parts of the earth for his possession.*[1] There was not a greater uproar among the Ephesians,[2] when the Gospel was first brought among them, than there was among the powers of the air (after whom those Ephesians walked) when first the silver trumpets of the Gospel here made the joyful sound. The Devil thus irritated immediately tried all sorts of methods to overturn this poor plantation: and so much of the church, as was fled into this wilderness, immediately found the serpent cast out of his mouth a flood for the carrying of it away.[3] I believe that never were more satanical devices used for the unsettling of any people under the sun, than what have been employed for the extirpation of the vine which God has here planted, casting out the heathen, and preparing a room before it, and causing it to take deep root, and fill the land, so that it sent its boughs unto the Atlantic Sea eastward, and its branches unto the Connecticut River westward, and the hills were covered with the shadow thereof.[4] But, all those attempts of Hell, have hitherto been abortive, many an Ebenezer[5] has been erected unto the praise of God, by his poor people here; and having obtained help from God, we continue to this day. Wherefore the Devil is now making one attempt more upon us; an attempt more difficult, more surprising, more snarl'd with unintelligible circumstances than any that we have hitherto encountred; an attempt so critical, that if we get well through, we shall soon enjoy halcyon days[6] with all the vultures of Hell trodden under our feet. He has wanted his incarnate legions to persecute us, as the people of God have in the other hemisphere[7] been persecuted: he has therefore drawn forth his more spiritual ones to make an attack upon us. We have been advised by some credible Christians yet alive that a malefactor, accused of witchcraft as well as murder, and executed in this place more than forty years ago, did then give notice of an horrible plot against the country by witchcraft, and a foundation of witchcraft then laid, which if it were not seasonably discovered, would probably blow up, and pull down all the churches in the country. And we have now with horror seen the discovery of such a witchcraft! An army of Devils is horribly broke in upon the place which is

---

* Mather wrote *The Wonders of the Invisible World: Being an Account of the Trials of Several Witches Lately Executed in New-England* at the request of the judges of the 1692 Salem, Massachusetts, witchcraft trials.

[1] Psalm 2:8.

[2] The people of Ephesus, a city in ancient Ionia, now part of Turkey. Missionaries tried to convert the Ephesians but riots broke out following the missionaries' sermons (see Acts 19:21–40).

[3] "And the serpent cast out of his mouth water as a flood after the woman, that he might cause her to be carried away of the flood," from Revelation 12:15.

[4] "Thou hast brought a vine out of Egypt: thou hast cast out the heathen, and planted it. Thou preparedst room before it, and didst cause it to take deep root, and it filled the land. The hills were covered with the shadow of it, and the boughs thereof were like the goodly cedars. She sent out her boughs unto the sea and her branches unto the river," from Psalm 80:8–11.

[5] A stone monument commemorating the Israelites' victory over the Philistines (I Samuel 7:12).

[6] Idyllic times gone by.   [7] The Old World.

the center, and after a sort, the first-born of our English settlements:[8] and the houses of the good people there are fill'd with the doleful shrieks of their children and servants, tormented by invisible hands, with tortures altogether preternatural. After the mischiefs there endeavored, and since in part conquered, the terrible plague of evil angels hath made its progress into some other places, where other persons have been in like manner diabolically handled. These our poor afflicted neighbors, quickly after they become infected and infested with these Dæmons, arrive to a capacity of discerning those which they conceive the shapes of their troublers; and notwithstanding the great and just suspicion, that the dæmons might impose the shapes of innocent persons in their spectral exhibitions upon the sufferers (which may perhaps prove no small part of the witch-plot in the issue), yet many of the persons thus represented, being examined, several of them have been convicted of a very damnable witchcraft: yea, more than one twenty have confessed, that they have signed unto a book, which the Devil show'd them, and engaged in his hellish design of bewitching and ruining our land. We know not, at least I know not, how far the delusions of Satan may be interwoven into some circumstances of the confessions; but one would think all the rules of understanding humane affairs are at an end, if after so many most voluntary harmonious confessions, made by intelligent persons of all ages, in sundry towns, at several times, we must not believe the main strokes wherein those confessions all agree: especially when we have a thousand preternatural things every day before our eyes, wherein the confessors do acknowledge their concernment, and give demonstration of their being so concerned. If the devils now can strike the minds of men with any poisons of so fine a composition and operation, that scores of innocent people shall unite in confessions of a Crime, which we see actually committed, it is a thing prodigious beyond the wonders of the former ages, and it threatens no less than a sort of a dissolution upon the world. Now, by these confessions 'tis agreed that the Devil has made a dreadful knot[9] of witches in the country, and by the help of witches has dreadfully increased that knot: that these witches have driven a trade of commissioning their confederate spirits to do all sorts of mischiefs to the neighbors, whereupon there have ensued such mischievous consequences upon the bodies and estates of the neighborhood as could not otherwise be accounted for: yea that at prodigious witch-meetings the wretches have proceeded so far as to concert and consult the methods of rooting out the Christian religion from this country, and setting up instead of it perhaps a more gross diabolism than ever the world saw before. And yet it will be a thing little short of miracle, if in so spread a business as this, the Devil should not get in some of his juggles[10] to confound the discovery of all the rest.

V: The Trial of Martha Carrier

At the Court of Oyer and Terminer,[11] Held by Adjournment at Salem, August 2, 1692

I. Martha Carrier was indicted for the bewitching certain persons, according to the form usual in such cases, pleading not guilty, to her indictment; there were first brought in a considerable number of the bewitched persons; who not only made

---

[8] Salem, the first settlement of the Massachusetts Bay Colony.   [9] Cluster or entanglement.
[10] Tricks.
[11] "To hear and to determine" (Middle English), a commission authorizing judges to hear and determine criminal cases.

the court sensible[12] of an horrid witchcraft committed upon them, but also deposed that it was Martha Carrier, or her shape, that grievously tormented them by biting, pricking, pinching and choking of them. It was further deposed that while this Carrier was on her examination before the magistrates, the poor people were so tortured that every one expected their death upon the very spot, but that upon the binding of Carrier they were eased. Moreover the look of Carrier then laid the afflicted people for dead; and her touch, if her eye at the same time were off them, raised them again: which things were also now seen upon her trial. And it was testified that upon the mention of some having their necks twisted almost round, by the shape of this Carrier, she replied, "It's no matter though their necks had been twisted quite off."

II. Before the trial of this prisoner, several of her own children had frankly and fully confessed not only that they were witches themselves, but that this their mother had made them so. This confession they made with great shows of repentance, and with much demonstration of truth. They related place, time, occasion; they gave an account of journeys, meetings and mischiefs by them performed, and were very credible in what they said. Nevertheless, this evidence was not produced against the prisoner at the bar,[13] inasmuch as there was other evidence enough to proceed upon.

III. Benjamin Abbot gave his testimony that last March was a twelvemonth, this Carrier was very angry with him, upon laying out some land near her husband's: her expressions in this anger were that she would stick as close to Abbot as the bark stuck to the tree; and that he should repent of it afore seven years came to an end, so as Doctor Prescot should never cure him. These words were heard by others besides Abbot himself, who also heard her say she would hold his nose as close to the grindstone as ever it was held since his name was Abbot. Presently after this, he was taken with a swelling in his foot, and then with a pain in his side, and exceedingly tormented. It bred into a sore, which was lanced by Doctor Prescot, and several gallons of corruption[14] ran out of it. For six weeks it continued very bad, and then another sore bred in the groin, which was also launced by Doctor Prescot. Another sore then bred in his groin, which was likewise cut, and put him to very great misery: He was brought unto death's door, and so remained until Carrier was taken, and carried away by the constable, from which very day he began to mend, and so grew better every day, and is well ever since.

Sarah Abbot also, his wife, testified that her husband was not only all this while afflicted in his body, but also that strange extraordinary and unaccountable calamities befel his cattle; their death being such as they could guess at no natural reason for.

IV. Allin Toothaker testified that Richard, the son of Martha Carrier, having some difference with him, pull'd him down by the hair of the head. When he rose again, he was going to strike at Richard Carrier but fell down flat on his back to the ground, and had not power to stir hand or foot, until he told Carrier he yielded; and then he saw the shape of Martha Carrier go off his breast.

This Toothaker had received a wound in the wars; and he now testified that Martha Carrier told him he should never be cured. Just afore the apprehending of Carrier, he could thrust a knitting needle into his wound, four inches deep; but presently after her being seized, he was thoroughly healed.

He further testified that when Carrier and he some times were at variance, she would clap her hands at him, and say he should get nothing by it; whereupon he

[12] Aware.   [13] In court.   [14] Pus.

several times lost his cattle by strange deaths, whereof no natural causes could be given.

V. John Rogger also testified that upon the threatening words of this malicious Carrier, his cattle would be strangely bewitched; as was more particularly then described.

VI. Samuel Preston testified that about two years ago, having some difference with Martha Carrier, he lost a cow in a strange preternatural unusual manner; and about a month after this, the said Carrier, having again some difference with him, she told him he had lately lost a cow, and it should not be long before he lost another; which accordingly came to pass; for he had a thriving and well-kept cow, which without any known cause quickly fell down and died.

VII. Phebe Chandler testified that about a fortnight before the apprehension of Martha Carrier, on a Lord's-day,[15] while the Psalm was singing in the church, this Carrier then took her by the shoulder and, shaking her, asked her where she lived: she made her no answer, although as Carrier, who lived next door to her father's house, could not in reason but know who she was. Quickly after this, as she was at several times crossing the fields, she heard a voice that she took to be Martha Carrier's, and it seemed as if it was over her head. The voice told her she should within two or three days be poisoned. Accordingly, within such a little time, one half of her right hand became greatly swollen, and very painful; as also part of her face: whereof she can give no account how it came. It continued very bad for some days; and several times since, she has had a great pain in her breast; and been so seized on her legs that she has hardly been able to go. She added that lately, going well to the house of God, Richard, the son of Martha Carrier, looked very earnestly upon her, and immediately her hand, which had formerly been poisoned, as is abovesaid, began to pain her greatly, and she had a strange burning at her stomach; but was then struck deaf, so that she could not hear any of the prayer, or singing, till the two or three last words of the Psalm.

VIII. One Foster, who confessed her own share in the witchcraft for which the prisoner stood indicted, affirmed that she had seen the prisoner at some of their witch-meetings, and that it was this Carrier who persuaded her to be a witch. She confessed that the Devil carried them on a pole to a witch-meeting; but the pole broke, and she hanging about Carrier's neck, they both fell down, and she then received an hurt by the fall, whereof she was not at this very time recovered.

IX. One Lacy, who likewise confessed her share in this witchcraft, now testified that she and the prisoner were once bodily present at a witch-meeting in Salem Village; and that she knew the prisoner to be a witch, and to have been at a diabolical sacrament, and that the prisoner was the undoing of her, and her children, by enticing them into the snare of the Devil.

X. Another Lacy, who also confessed her share in this witchcraft, now testified that the prisoner was at the witch-meeting in Salem Village, where they had bread and wine administred unto them.

XI. In the time of this prisoner's trial, one Susanna Sheldon in open court had her hands unaccountably tied together with a wheel-band,[16] so fast that without cutting, it could not be loosed: it was done by a specter; and the sufferer affirmed it was the prisoner's.

---

[15] Sunday.   [16] A strap that wraps around a wheel.

Memorandum. This rampant hag, Martha Carrier, was the person of whom the confessions of the witches, and of her own children among the rest, agreed that the Devil had promised her she should be Queen of Heb.[17]

1692, 1693

from BONIFACIUS: AN ESSAY UPON THE GOOD*

from [*Chapter Three: Relative to Home and Neighborhood*]

§11. The useful man may now with a very good grace, extend and enlarge the sphere of his consideration. My next proposal now shall be: Let every man consider the relation, wherein the Sovereign God has placed him, and let him devise what good he may do, that may render his relatives, the better for him. One great way to prove ourselves really good, is to be relatively good. By this, more than by anything in the world, it is, that we adorn the doctrine of God our Saviour. It would be an excellent wisdom in a man, to make the interest he has in the good opinion and affection of anyone, an advantage to do good service for God upon them: He that has a friend will show himself indeed friendly, if he thinks, "Such an one loves me, and will hearken to me; what good shall I take advantage hence to persuade him to?"

This will take place more particularly, where the endearing ties of natural relation do give us an interest. Let us call over our several relations, and let us have devices of something that may be called heroical goodness, in our discharging of them. Why should we not, at least once or twice in a week, make this relational goodness, the subject of our inquiries, and our purposes? Particularly, let us begin with our domestic relations, and provide for those of our own house, lest we deny some glorious rules and hopes of our Christian faith, in our negligence.

First, in the conjugal relation, how agreeably may the consorts[1] think on those words: "What knowest thou, O wife, whether thou shalt save thy husband?" Or, "How knowest thou, O man, whether thou shalt save thy wife?"

The husband will do well to think: "What shall I do, that my wife may have cause forever to bless God, for bringing her unto me?" And, "What shall I do that in my carriage[2] towards my wife, the kindness of the blessed Jesus towards His Church, may be followed and resembled?" That this question may be the more perfectly answered, Sir, sometimes ask her to help you in the answer; ask her to tell you, what she would have you to do.

But then, the wife also will do well to think: "Wherein may I be to my husband, a wife of that character: she will do him good, and not evil, all the days of his life?"

With my married people, I will particularly leave a good note, which I find in the memorials of Gervase Disney, Esq.[3] "Family passions, cloud faith, disturb

---

[17] Queen of Hebrews.

* Mather's subtitle is *An Essay Upon the Good, That Is to Be Devised and Designed, by Those Who Desire to Answer the Great End of Life, and to Do Good While They Live.*

[1] Marital partners.   [2] Behavior.

[3] A wealthy English landowner whose spiritual autobiography was published in 1692.

duty, darken comfort." You'll do the more good unto one another, the more this note is thought upon. When the husband and wife are always contriving to be blessings unto one another, I will say with Tertullian, *Unde sufficiam ad enarrandam faelicitatem ejus matrimonii!*[4] O happy marriage!

Parents, Oh! how much ought you to be continually devising, and even travailing, for the good of your children. Often devise: how to make them wise children; how to carry on a desirable education for them; an education that shall render them desirable; how to render them lovely, and polite creatures, and serviceable in their generation. Often devise, how to enrich their minds with valuable knowledge; how to instill generous, and gracious, and heavenly principles into their minds; how to restrain and rescue them from the paths of the Destroyer, and fortify them against their special temptations. There is a world of good, that you have to do for them. You are without bowels,[5] Oh! be not such monsters! if you are not in a continual agony to do for them all the good that ever you can. It was no mistake of Pacatus Drepanius in his panegyric to Theodosius: *Instituente natura plus fere filios quam nosmetipsos diligimus.*[6]

I will prosecute this matter, by transcribing a copy of parental resolutions, which I have somewhere met withal.[7]

I. "At the birth of my children, I would use all explicit solemnity in the baptismal dedication and consecration of them unto the Lord. I would present them to the baptism of the Lord, not as a mere formality; but wondering at the grace of the infinite God, who will accept my children as His, I would resolve to do all I can that they may be His. I would now actually give them up unto God; entreating, that the child may be a child of God the Father, a subject of God the Son, a temple of God the Spirit, and be rescued from the condition of a child of wrath, and be possessed and employed by the Lord as an everlasting instrument of His glory.

II. "My children are no sooner grown capable of minding the admonitions, but I would often, often admonish them to be sensible of the baptismal engagements to be the Lord's. Often tell them, of their baptism, and of what it binds 'em to: oftener far, and more times than there are drops of water, that were cast on the infant, upon that occasion!

"Often say to them, 'Child, you have been baptized; you were washed in the name of the great God; now you must not sin against Him; to sin is to do a dirty, a filthy thing.' Say, 'Child, you must every day cry to God that He would be your Father, and your Savior, and your Leader; in your baptism He promised that He would be so, if you sought unto Him.' Say, 'Child, you must renounce the service of Satan, you must not follow the vanities of this world, you must lead a life of serious religion; in your baptism you were bound unto the service of your only Savior.' Tell the child: 'What is your name; you must sooner forget this name, that was given you in your baptism, than forget that you are a servant of a glorious Christ whose name was put upon you in your baptism.'

III. "Let my prayers for my children be daily, with constancy, with fervency, with agony; yea, by name let me mention each one of them, every day before the Lord. I would importunately beg for all suitable blessings to be bestowed upon

---

[4] "How can I find words to express the happiness of their marriage!" (Latin); Tertullian (A.D. 160?–230?) was a theologian from Carthage.

[5] Tender emotions.

[6] "Nature teaches us to love our children as ourselves" (Latin); Latinius Pacatus Drepanius was a Roman orator who lauded the Roman emperor Theodosius I (A.D. 346?–395).

[7] These resolutions were set down, or met, in Mather's autobiography, *Paterna,* published in entirety in 1976.

them: that God would give them grace, and give them glory, and withhold no good thing from them; that God would smile on their education, and give His good angels the charge over them, and keep them from evil, that it may not grieve them; that when their father and mother shall forsake them, the Lord may take them up. With importunity I would plead that promise on their behalf: the Heavenly Father will give the Holy Spirit unto them that ask Him. Oh! happy children, if by asking I may obtain the Holy Spirit for them!

IV. "I would betimes entertain the children, with delightful stories out of the Bible. In the talk of the table, I would go through the Bible, when the olive-plants about my table[8] are capable of being so watered. But I would always conclude the stories with some lessons of piety, to be inferred from them.

V. "I would single out some Scriptural sentences of the greatest importance; and some also that have special antidotes in them against the common errors and vices of children. They shall quickly get those golden sayings by heart, and be rewarded with silver or gold, or some good thing, when they do it. Such as,

Psalm 111:10
The fear of the Lord, is the beginning of wisdom.
Matthew 16:26
What is a man profited, if he gain the whole world,
and lose his own soul.
I Timothy 1:15
Jesus Christ came into the world to save
sinners, of whom I am chief.
Matthew 6:6
Enter into thy closet, and when thou hast shut thy door,
pray to thy Father which is in secret.
Ecclesiastes 12:14
God shall bring every work into judgment, with every
secret thing.
Ephesians 5:25
Put away lying, speak everyone the truth.
Psalm 138:6
The Lord hath respect unto the lowly, but the proud
He knows afar off.
Romans 12:17, 19
Recompense to no one evil for evil. Dearly beloved,
avenge not yourselves.
Nehemiah 13:18
They bring wrath upon Israel, by profaning the
Sabbath.

A Jewish treatise quoted by Wagenseil[9] tells us, that among the Jews, when a child began to speak, the father was bound to teach him that verse: Deuteronomy 33:4, 'Moses commanded us a Law, even the inheritance of the Congregation of Jacob.' Oh! let me betimes make my children acquainted with the Law which our blessed Jesus has commanded us! 'Tis the best inheritance I can derive unto them.

---

[8] Mather's children.
[9] Johann Christoph Wagenseil (1633–1705), a Christian who studied the Jews' system of ethics and customs.

VI. "I would betimes cause my children to learn the Catechism.[10] In catechizing of them, I would break the answer into many lesser and proper questions; and by their answer to them, observe and quicken their understandings. I would bring every truth, into some duty and practice, and expect them to confess it, and consent unto it, and resolve upon it. As we go on in our catechizing, they shall, when they are able, turn to the proofs, and read them, and say to me, what they prove, and how. Then, I will take my times, to put nicer[11] and harder questions to them; and improve the times of conversation with my family (which every man ordinarily has or may have) for conferences on matters of religion.

VII. "Restless would I be, till I may be able to say of my children, 'Behold, they pray!' I would therefore teach them to pray. But after they have learned a form of prayer, I will press them, to proceed unto points which are not in their form. I will show them the state of their own souls; and on every stroke inquire of them, what they think ought now to be their prayer. I will direct them, that every morning they shall take one text or two out of the Sacred Scripture, and shape it into a desire, which they shall add unto their usual prayer. When they have heard a sermon, I will mention to them over again the main subject of it, and ask them thereupon what they have now to pray for. I will charge them, with all possible cogency, to pray in secret; and often call upon them, 'Child, I hope, you don't forget my charge to you, about secret prayer: your crime is very great, if you do!'

VIII. "I would betimes do what I can, to beget a temper of benignity in my children, both towards one another, and towards all other people. I will instruct them how ready they should be to communicate unto others, a part of what they have; and they shall see my encouragements when they discover a loving, a courteous, an helpful disposition. I will give them now and then a piece of money, for them with their own little hands to dispense unto the poor. Yea, if any one has hurt them, or vexed them, I will not only forbid them all revenge, but also oblige them to do a kindness as soon as may be to the vexatious person. All coarseness of language or carriage in them, I will discountenance it.

IX. "I would be solicitous to have my children expert not only at reading handsomely, but also at writing a fair hand. I will then assign them such books to read, as I may judge most agreeable and profitable: obliging them to give me some account of what they read; but keep a strict eye upon them, that they don't stumble on the Devil's library, and poison themselves with foolish romances, or novels, or plays, or songs, or jests that are not convenient.[12] I will set them also, to write out such things, as may be of the greatest benefit unto them; and they shall have their blank books, neatly kept on purpose, to enter such passages as I advise them to. I will particularly require them now and then, to write a prayer of their own composing, and bring it unto me; that so I may discern, what sense they have of their own everlasting interests.

X. "I wish that my children may as soon as may be, feel the principles of reason and honor working in them, and that I may carry on their education, very much upon those principles. Therefore, first, I will wholly avoid that harsh, fierce, crabbed[13] usage of the children that would make them tremble, and abhor to come into my presence. I will so use them that they shall fear to offend me, and yet mightily love to see me, and be glad of my coming home, if I have been abroad at any time. I would have it looked upon as a severe and awful punishment

[10] A formal set of questions and answers for teaching religious principles.
[11] Finely discriminating.   [12] Appropriate.   [13] Ill-tempered.

for a crime in the family, to be forbidden for awhile to come into my presence. I would raise in them an high opinion of their father's love to them, and of his being better able to judge what is good for them, than they are for themselves. I would bring them to believe, 'tis best for them to be and do as I would have them. Hereupon I would continually magnify the matter to them, what a brave thing 'tis to know the things that are excellent; and more brave to do the things that are virtuous. I would have them to propose it as a reward of their well-doing at any time, I will now go to my father, and he will teach me something that I was never taught before. I would have them afraid of doing any base thing, from an horror of the baseness in it. My first animadversion[14] on a lesser fault in them, shall be a surprise, a wonder, vehemently expressed before them, that ever they should be guilty of doing so foolishly; a vehement belief, that they will never do the like again; a weeping resolution in them, that they will not. I will never dispense a blow, except it be for an atrocious crime, or for a lesser fault obstinately persisted in; either for an enormity, or for an obstinacy. I would ever proportion chastisements unto miscarriages;[15] not smite bitterly for a very small piece of childishness, and only frown a little for some real wickedness. Nor shall my chastisements ever be dispensed in a passion and a fury; but with them, I will first show them the command of God, by transgressing whereof they have displeased me. The slavish, raving, fighting way of education too commonly used, I look upon it, as a considerable article in the wrath and curse of God, upon a miserable world.

XI. "As soon as we can, we'll get up to yet higher principles. I will often tell the children, what cause they have to love a glorious Christ, who has died for them. And, how much He will be well-pleased with their well-doing. And, what a noble thing, 'tis to follow His example; which example I will describe unto them. I will often tell them that the eye of God is upon them; the great God knows all they do, and hears all they speak. I will often tell them that there will be a time, when they must appear before the Judgment-Seat of the holy Lord; and they must now do nothing that may then be a grief and shame unto them. I will set before them the delights of that Heaven that is prepared for pious children; and the torments of that Hell that is prepared of old, for naughty ones. I will inform them, of the good offices[16] which the good angels do for little ones that have the fear of God, and are afraid of sin. And, how the devils tempt them to do ill things; how they hearken to the devils, and are like them, when they do such things; and what mischiefs the devils may get leave to do them in this world, and what a sad thing 'twill be, to be among the devils in the Place of Dragons.[17] I will cry to God, that He will make them feel the power of these principles.

XII. "When the children are of a fit age for it, I will sometimes closet[18] them; have them with me alone; talk with them about the state of their souls; their experiences, their proficiencies, their temptations; obtain their declared consent unto every stroke in the Covenant of Grace;[19] and then pray with them, and weep unto the Lord for His grace, to be bestowed upon them, and make them witnesses of the agony with which I am travailing to see the image of Christ formed in them. Certainly, they'll never forget such actions!

[14] An act of criticizing adversely.   [15] Failures.   [16] Services.
[17] Hell; Satan is known as the Old Serpent, an archaic form of "dragon."
[18] To shut up in a private room for discussion.
[19] The Puritans' New Covenant, or the agreement God made with Adam after he ate the forbidden fruit and fell from grace.

XIII. "I would be very watchful and cautious about the companions of my children. I will be very inquisitive what company they keep; if they are in hazard of being ensnared by any vicious company, I will earnestly pull them out of it, as brands out of the burning. I will find out, and procure, laudable companions for them.

XIV. "As in catechizing the children, so in the repetition of the public sermons, I would use this method. I will put every truth into a question to be answered still, with Yes, or No. By this method, I hope to awaken their attention as well as enlighten their understanding. And thus I shall have an opportunity to ask, 'Do you desire such or such a grace of God?' and the like. Yea, I may have opportunity to demand, and perhaps to obtain their early, and frequent, and why not sincere?, consent unto the glorious articles of the New Covenant. The spirit of grace may fall upon them in this action; and they may be seized by Him, and held as His temples, through eternal ages.

XV. "When a Day of Humiliation[20] arrives, I will make them know the meaning of the day. And after time given them to consider of it, I will order them to tell me: what special afflictions they have met withal? And, what good they hope to get by those afflictions? On a Day of Thanksgiving, they shall also be made to know the intent of the day. And after consideration, they shall tell me, what mercies of God unto them they take special notice of: And, what duties to God, they confess and resolve, under such obligations? Indeed, for something of this importance, to be pursued in my conversation with the children, I would not confine myself unto the solemn days, which may occur too seldom for it. Very particularly, when the birthdays of the children anniversarily arrive to any of them, I would then take them aside, and mind them of the age, which having obtained help from God they are come unto; how thankful they should be for the mercies of God, which they have hitherto lived upon; how fruitful they should be in all goodness, that so they may still enjoy their mercies. And I would inquire of them, whether they have ever yet begun to mind the work which God sent them into the world upon; how far they understand the work; and what good strokes they have struck at it; and, how they design to spend the rest of their time, if God still continue them in the world.

XVI. "When the children are in any trouble, as, if they be sick, or pained, I will take advantage therefrom to set before them the evil of sin, which brings all our trouble; and how fearful a thing it will be to be cast among the damned, who are in easeless and endless trouble. I will set before them the benefit of an interest in a Christ, by which their trouble will be sanctified unto them, and they will be prepared for death, and for fullness of joy in an happy eternity after death.

XVII. "I incline that among all the points of a polite education which I would endeavor for my children, they may each of them, the daughters as well as the sons, have so much insight into some skill, which lies in the way of gain (the limners',[21] or the scriveners',[22] or the apothecaries',[23] or some other mystery,[24] to which their own inclination may most carry them) that they may be able to subsist themselves, and get something of a livelihood, in case the providence of God should bring them into necessities. Why not they as well as Paul the Tent-Maker![25] The children of the best fashion, may have occasion to bless the parents,

---

[20] A day on which a child becomes aware of having offended God.
[21] Those who illustrate manuscripts.   [22] Scribes.   [23] Pharmacists.
[24] A special skill known only to a small group.
[25] In Acts 18:3 the Apostle Paul is a tent maker by trade.

that make such a provision for them! The Jews have a saying; 'tis worth my remembering it: Quicunque filium suum non docet opificium, perinde est ac si eum doceret latrocinium.[26]

XVIII. "As soon as ever I can, I would make my children apprehensive of the main end for which they are to live; that so they may as soon as may be, begin to live; and their youth not be nothing but vanity. I would show them, that their main end must be to acknowledge the great God, and His glorious Christ; and bring others to acknowledge Him: and that they are never wise nor well, but when they are doing so. I would show them, what the acknowledgments are, and how they are to be made. I would make them able to answer the grand question, why they live; and what is the end of the actions that fill their lives? Teach them, how their Creator and Redeemer is to be obeyed in everything; and, how everything is to be done in obedience to Him; teach them, how even their diversions, and their ornaments,[27] and the tasks of their education, must all be to fit them for the further service of Him, to whom I have devoted them; and how in these also, His commandments must be the rule of all they do. I would sometimes therefore surprise them with an inquiry, 'Child, what is this for? Give me a good account, why you do it?' How comfortably shall I see them walking in the light, if I may bring them wisely to answer this inquiry; and what children of the light?[28]

XIX. "I would oblige the children to retire sometimes, and ponder on that question: 'What shall I wish to have done, if I were now a-dying?' And report unto me, their own answer to the question; of which I would then take advantage, to inculcate the lessons of godliness upon them. I would also direct them and oblige them, at a proper time for it, seriously to realize their own appearance before the awful Judgment-Seat of the Lord Jesus Christ, and consider what they have to plead, that they may not be sent away into everlasting punishment; what they have to plead, that they may be admitted into the Holy City. I would instruct them, what plea to prepare; first, show them, how to get a part in the righteousness of Him that is to be their Judge; by receiving it with a thankful faith, as the gift of infinite grace unto the distressed and unworthy sinner: then, show them how to prove that their faith is not a counterfeit, by their continual endeavor to please Him in all things, who is to be their Judge, and to serve His Kingdom and interest in the world. And I would charge them, to make this preparation.

XX. "If I live to see the children marriageable, I would, before I consult with Heaven and earth for their best accommodation in the married state, endeavor the espousal of their souls unto their only Savior. I would as plainly, and as fully as I can, propose unto them the terms on which the glorious Redeemer would espouse them to Himself, in righteousness and judgment, and favor, and mercies forever; and solicit their consent unto His proposals and overtures. Then would I go on, to do what may be expected from a tender parent for them, in their temporal circumstances."

From these parental resolutions, how naturally, how reasonably may we pass on to say:

"Children, the Fifth Commandment[29] confirms all your other numberless and powerful obligations, often to devise, 'Wherein may I be a blessing to my parents?' Ingenuity would make this the very top of your ambition; to be a credit, and

---

[26] "He who does not teach his son a craft, teaches him theft" (Latin).   [27] Adornments, attire.

[28] ". . . for the children of this world are in their generation wiser than the children of light," from Luke 16:8.

[29] "Honor thy father and thy mother: that thy days may be long upon the land which the Lord thy God giveth thee," from Exodus 20:12.

a comfort of your parents; to sweeten, and if it may be, to lengthen the lives of those, from whom, under God, you have received your lives. And God the Rewarder usually gives it, even in this life, a most observable recompense. But it is possible, you may be the happy instruments of more than a little good unto the souls of your parents (will you think, how!); yea, though they should be pious parents, you may by some exquisite methods, be the instruments of the growth in piety, and in preparation for the Heavenly world. O thrice and four times happy children! Among the Arabians, a father sometimes takes his name from an eminent Son, as well as a son from his reputed father. A man is called with an Abu, as well as an Ebn. Verily, a son may be such a blessing to his father that the best surname for the glad father would be, the father of such an one."

Masters, yea, and mistresses too, must have their devices, how to do good unto their servants; how to make them the servants of Christ, and the children of God. God whom you must remember to be your Master in Heaven, has brought them, and put them into your hands. Who can tell what good He has brought them for? How if they should be the elect of God, fetched from Africa, or the Indies, and brought into your families, on purpose, that by the means of their being there, they may be brought home unto the Shepherd of Souls? Oh! that the souls of our slaves, were of more account with us! that we gave a better demonstration that we despise not our own souls, by doing what we can for the souls of our slaves, and not using them as if they had no souls! that the poor slaves and blacks, which live with us, may by our means be made the candidates of the heavenly life! How can we pretend unto Christianity, when we do no more to Christianize our slaves! Verily, you must give an account unto God, concerning them. If they be lost, through your negligence, what answer can you make unto God the Judge of all! Methinks, common principles of gratitude should incline you to study the happiness of those by whose obsequious labors your lives are so much accommodated. Certainly, they would be the better servants to you, the more faithful, the more honest, the more industrious, and submissive servants to you, for your bringing them into the service of your common Lord.

But if any servant of God, may be so honored by Him, as to be made the successful instrument, of obtaining from a British Parliament, an act for the Christianizing of the slaves in the plantations; then it may be hoped, something more may be done, than has yet been done, that the blood of souls may not be found in the skirts of our nation: a controversy of Heaven with our colonies may be removed, and prosperity may be restored; or, however [whoever?] the honorable instrument, will have unspeakable peace and joy in the remembrance of his endeavors. In the meantime, the slave-trade is a spectacle that shocks humanity.

> The harmless natives basely they trepan,[30]
> And barter baubles for the souls of men.
> The wretches they to Christian climes bring o'er
> To serve worse heathens than they did before.

I have somewhere met with a paper under this title, "The Resolution of a Master," which may here afford an agreeable paragraph and parenthesis.

I. "I would always remember that my servants are in some sort my children. In a care that they may want nothing that may be good for them, I would make them as my children. And, as far as the methods of instilling piety, which I use with my

---

[30] Trap or trick.

children, may be properly and prudently used with these, they shall be partakers in them. Nor will I leave them ignorant of anything, wherein I may instruct them to be useful in their generation.

II. "I will see that my servants be furnished with Bibles, and able and careful to read the lively oracles.[31] I will put both Bibles and other good and fit books into their hands; and allow them time to read, but assure myself that they don't misspend this time. If I can discover any wicked books in their hands, I will take away from them, those pestilential instruments of wickedness. They shall also write as well as read, if I can bring them to it. And I will set them now and then such things to write, as may be for their greatest advantage.

III. "I will have my servants present at the religious exercises of my family; and let fall either in the speeches, or in the prayers, of the daily sacrifice in the family, such passages, as may have a tendency to quicken a sense of religion in them.

IV. "The catechizing stroke as far as the age or state of the servants will permit, that it may be done with decency, shall extend unto them also. And they shall be concerned in the conferences, wherein the repetition of the public sermons, may engage me with my family. If any of them, when they come to me, have not learned the Catechism, I will see to it that they shall do it, and give them a reward when they have done it.

V. "I will be very inquisitive and solicitous about the company chosen by my servants; and with all possible cogency rescue them from the snares of evil company: forbid their being the companions of fools.

VI. "Such of my servants as may be employed for that purpose, I will employ to teach lessons of piety unto my children, and recompense them for doing so. But I would with a particular artifice contrive them to be such lessons, as may be for their own edification too.

VII. "I will sometimes call my servants alone; talk with them about the state of their souls; tell them how to close with their only Savior; charge them to do well, and lay hold on eternal life; and show them very particularly, how they may render all the service they do for me, a service to the glorious Lord; how they may do all from a principle of obedience to the Lord, and become entitled unto the reward of the heavenly inheritance."[32]

I make this appendix to these resolutions. I have read such a passage as this: "Age is well nigh sufficient with some masters to obliterate every letter and action, in the history of a meritorious life; and old services are generally buried under the ruins of an old carcass." And this passage, "It's a barbarous inhumanity in men towards their servants, to make their small failings to be a crime, without allowing their past services to have been a virtue. Good God, keep thy servant from such ingratitude! Worse than villainous ingratitude!"

But then, O servants, if you would arrive to the reward of the inheritance, you should set yourselves to devise: "How shall I approve myself such a servant, that the Lord may bless the house of my master, the more for my being in it?" Certainly, there are many ways, wherein servants may be blessings. Let your studies with your continual prayers for the welfare of the families to which you belong, and the example of your sober carriage, render you such. If you will remember but four words, and endeavor all that is comprised in them, obedience, honesty, industry, and piety, you will be the blessings and the Josephs[33] of the families to

---

[31] Divine announcements.   [32] Salvation.
[33] Joseph, though sold into slavery by his brothers, was a credit to his parents, Jacob and Rachel, as he became a high-ranking official in Egypt (see Genesis 32:22–24).

which you belong. Let those four heads be distinctly and frequently thought upon. And go cheerfully through all you have to do, upon this consideration: that it is an obedience to Heaven, and from thence will have a recompense. It was the observation even of a pagan that a master may receive a benefit from a servant. And, *Quod fit affectu amici, desinit esse ministerium.*[34] It is a friendship rather than a service, young man, if it be with the affection of a friend, that you do what you do for your master. Yea, even the maid-servants in the house may do an unknown service to it, by instructing the infants, and instilling the lessons of goodness into them. So, by Bilhah, and Zilpah,[35] may children be born again; the mistresses may by the travail of the maid-servants, have children, brought into the Kingdom of God.

I will go on. Humanity teaches us to take notice of all that are our kindred. Nature bespeaks that which we call a natural affection to all that are akin to us. To be without it, is a very bad character; 'tis a brand on the worst of men; on such as forfeit the name of men. But now, Christianity is to improve it. Our natural affection is to be improved into a religious intention. Sir, take a catalogue of all your more distant relatives. Consider them one after another; and make every one of them the subjects of your good devices. Think: "Wherein may I pursue the good of such a relative?" And, "By what means may I render such a relative the better for me?" It is possible, you may do something, that may give them cause to bless God, that ever you have been related unto them. Have they no calamity, under which you may give them some relief? Is there no temptation against which you may give them some caution? Is there no article of their prosperity, to which you may be subservient? At least; with your affectionate prayers, you may go over your catalogue; you may successively pray for every one of them all by name; and, if you can, why should you not also put agreeable books of piety into their hands, to be lasting remembrancers of their duties to God, and of your desires for them?

§ 12. Methinks, this excellent zeal should be carried into our neighborhood. Neighbors, you stand related unto one another; and you should be full of devices, that all the neighbors may have cause to be glad of your being in the neighborhood. We read, "The righteous is more excellent than his neighbor." But we shall scarce own him so, except he be more excellent as a neighbor. He must excel in the duties of good neighborhood. Let that man be better than his neighbor, who labors to be a better neighbor; to do most good unto his neighbor.

And here, first, the poor people that lie wounded, must have wine and oil poured into their wounds. It was a charming stroke in the character with [which?] a modern prince had given to him, to be in distress, is to deserve his favor. O good neighbor, put on that princely, that more than royal quality. See who in the neighborhood may deserve the favor. We are told, this is pure religion and undefiled (a jewel, that neither is a counterfeit, nor has any flaws in it): to visit the fatherless and widows in their affliction. The orphans and the widows, and so all the children of affliction in the neighborhood, must be visited, and relieved with all agreeable kindnesses.

Neighbors, be concerned, that the orphans and widows in your neighborhood, may be well provided for. They meet with grievous difficulties; with unknown

---

[34] "What is done with the affection of a friend is no longer the act of a mere servant" (Latin).

[35] In Genesis 29:29 Bilhah is the handmaid of Jacob's wife Rachel; in Genesis 29:24 Zilpah is the handmaid of Jacob's wife Leah.

temptations. While their next relatives were yet living, they were, perhaps, but meanly[36] provided for. What must they now be in their more solitary condition? Their condition should be considered: and the result of the consideration should be that: I delivered the orphan, that had no helper, and I caused the heart of the widow to sing for joy.[37]

By consequence, all the afflicted in the neighborhood are to be thought upon. Sirs, would it be too much for you, at least once in a week, to think, "What neighbor is reduced into a pinching and painful poverty? Or in any degree impoverished with heavy losses?" Think, "What neighbor is languishing with sickness; especially if sick with sore maladies, and of some continuance?" Think, "What neighbor is heartbroken with sad bereavements; bereaved of desirable relatives?" And think: "What neighbor has a soul buffeted, and buried with violent assaults of the Wicked one?"[38] But then think, "What shall be done for such neighbors?"

First, you will pity them. The evangelical precept is, have compassion one of another, be pitiful. It was of old, and ever will be, the just expectation, to him that is afflicted, pity should be shown. And let our pity to them, flame out in our prayer for them. It were a very lovely practice for you, in the daily prayer of your closet every evening, to think, "What miserable object have I seen today, that I may do well now to mention for the mercies of the Lord?"

But this is not all. 'Tis possible, 'tis probable, you may do well to visit them; and when you visit them, comfort them. Carry them some good word, which may raise a gladness, in an heart stooping with heaviness.

And lastly, Give them all the assistances that may answer their occasions: assist them with advice to them; assist them with address to others for them. And if it be needful, bestow your alms upon them; deal thy bread to the hungry; bring to thy house the poor that are cast out; when thou seest the naked, cover him.[39] At least, Nazianzen's[40] charity, I pray: Si nihil habes, da lacrymulam;[41] if you have nothing else to bestow upon the miserable, bestow a tear or two upon their miseries. This little, is better than nothing!

Would it be amiss for you, to have always lying by you, a list of the poor in your neighborhood, or of those whose calamities may call for the assistances of the neighborhood? Such a list would often furnish you with matter for an useful conversation, when you are talking with your friends, whom you may provoke to love and good works.

I will go on to say: Be glad of opportunities to do good in your neighborhood: yea, look out for them, lay hold on them, with a rapturous assiduity. Be sorry for all the bad circumstances of any neighbor, that bespeak your doing of good unto him. Yet, be glad, if any one tell you of them. Thank him who tells you, as having therein done you a very great civility. Let him know, that he could not by anything have more gratified you. Any civility that you can show, by lending, by watching, by—all the methods of courtesy; show it; and be glad you can show it. Show it, and give a pleasant countenance (cum munere vultum) in the showing of it. Let your wisdom cause your face always to shine; look, not with a cloudy but a serene and shining face, upon your neighbors; and shed the rays of your courtesy

---

[36] Poorly.   [37] Paraphrased from Job 29:12–13.   [38] Satan.

[39] Paraphrased from Matthew 25:37–38.

[40] Of Gregory Nazianzen (A.D. 325?–390?), or Saint Gregory of Nazianzus.

[41] "If you have nothing, give a tear" (Latin).

upon them, with such affability, that they may see they are welcome to all you can do for them. Yea, stay not until you are told of opportunities to do good. Inquire after them; let the inquiry be solicitous, be unwearied. The incomparable pleasure is worth an inquiry.

There was a generous pagan who counted a day lost if he had obliged nobody in the day. *Amici, diem perdidi!*[42] O Christian, let us try whether we can't attain to do something, for some neighbor or other, every day that comes over our head. Some do so; and with a better spirit than ever Titus Vespasian[43] was acted withal. Thrice in the Scriptures, we find the good angels rejoicing: 'tis always at the good of others. To rejoice in the good of others, and most of all in doing of good unto them, 'tis angelical goodness.

In moving for the devices of good neighborhood, a principal motion which I have to make is that you consult the spiritual interests of your neighborhood, as well as the temporal. Be concerned, lest the deceitfulness of sin undo any of the neighbors. If there by any idle persons among them, I beseech you, cure them of their idleness; don't nourish 'em and harden 'em in that; but find employment for them. Find 'em work; set 'em to work; keep 'em to work. Then, as much of your other bounty to them, as you please.

If any children in the neighborhood are under no education, don't allow 'em to continue so. Let care be taken, that they may be better educated; and be taught to read; and be taught their Catechism; and the truths and ways of their only Savior.

Once more. If any in the neighborhood, are taking to bad courses, lovingly and faithfully admonish them. If any in the neighborhood are enemies to their own welfare, or their families, prudently dispense your admonitions unto them. If there are any prayerless families, never leave off entreating and exhorting of them, till you have persuaded them, to set up the worship of God. If there be any service of God, or of His people, to which any one may need to be excited, give him a tender excitation. Whatever snare you see any one in, be so kind as to tell him of his danger to be ensnared, and save him from it. By putting of good books into the hands of your neighbors, and gaining of them a promise to read the books, who can tell what good you may do unto them! It is possible you may in this way, with ingenuity, and with efficacy, administer those reproofs, which you may owe unto such neighbors, as are to be reproved for their miscarriages. The books will balk nothing that is to be said on the subjects that you would have the neighbors advised upon.

Finally. If there be any base houses, which threaten to debauch, and poison, and confound the neighborhood, let your charity to your neighbors, make you do all you can, for the suppression of them.

That my proposal to do good in the neighborhood, and as a neighbor, may be more fully formed and followed; I will conclude it, with minding you, that a world of self-denial is to be exercised in the execution of it. You must be armed against selfishness, all selfish and squinting intentions, in your generous resolutions. You shall see how my demands will grow upon you.

1710

---

[42] "Friends, I have lost the day!" (Latin).
[43] Vespasian (A.D. 9–79) was a much loved emperor of Rome (69–79) and founder of the Flavian dynasty.

Sarah Kemble Knight
(1666–1727)

A third-generation American, Sarah Kemble was born in Boston in 1666 to Elizabeth Tre-rice and the merchant Thomas Kemble. Before 1689 Sarah Kemble married Captain Rich-ard Knight, a shipowner much older than herself. They had a daughter, Elizabeth, and Captain Knight died some time before 1706. Sarah Kemble Knight was a contemporary of another Bostonian, the indefatigable Puritan historiographer Cotton Mather. In the writing school she operated in Boston from 1706 to 1713, Madam Knight (as she was called in recognition of her writing and legal skills), is believed to have taught Mather's son Samuel and young Benjamin Franklin.

Knight's writing indicates that she was widely read in the standard literature of the time. Other than legal documents, the only surviving writing by the vigorous and quick-witted Knight is the journal of her journey by horse from Boston to New York City and back, between October 1704 and March 1705. First published in 1825, the slim volume *The Journal of Madam Knight* captures realities of colonial American life often lacking in Puritan literature: the rewards and hardships of travel, the variety of manners and charac-ters, the collision of wilderness and culture, along with a genuine sense of the author's personality as an intrepid traveler in a rugged frontier.

Knight's journey probably resulted from her activity in the field of law. In 1704, one of her boarders, a young widow, married Knight's cousin, Caleb Trowbridge of New Haven, Connecticut. Within two months, the affluent Trowbridge died. Three weeks later Knight

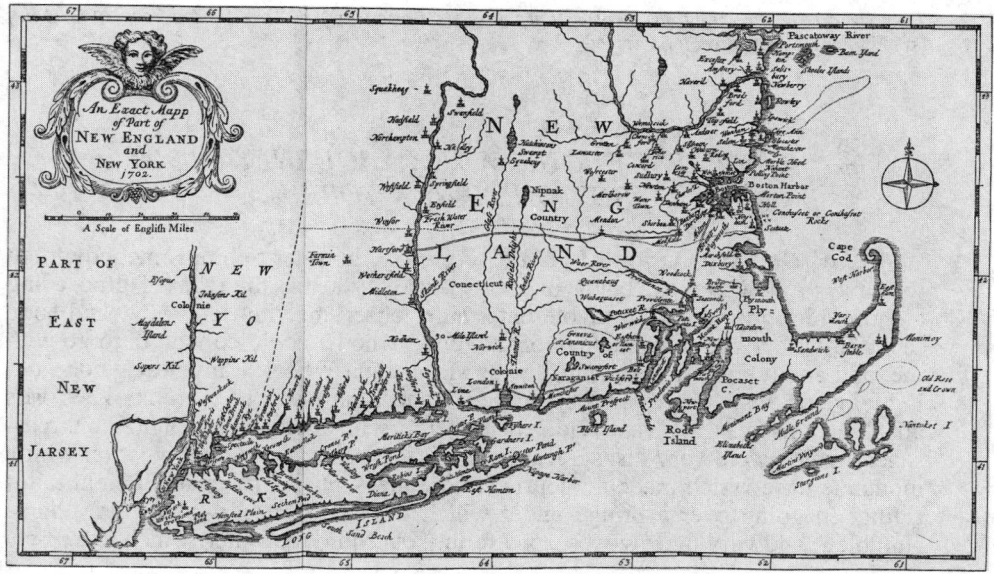

The 1702 map of Sarah Kemble Knight's journey through New England and New York.

left Elizabeth in her grandmother's care in Boston and headed for New Haven to help Trowbridge's widow. Knight's familiarity with legal documents is probably what enabled her to act as lawyer for her cousin's widow.

Knight arrived in New Haven (126 miles away on today's roads) after five grueling days of travel recorded in vivid detail in her journal, with a series of guides, through a wilderness with few roads, bridges, and lodgings. She remained there for two months, attending to business and informing herself about the local manners and customs. When kinsman Thomas Trowbridge (probably Caleb's father) planned to go to New York City, Knight decided to accompany him. Leaving New Haven in early December, they arrived in New York City three days later. Within two weeks they had concluded their business, while Knight again documented the local manners and customs. The trip from New York City back to New Haven took three days. The legal process continued slowly; Knight suspected the delays were intended to try her patience. Nevertheless, she persisted until she had achieved a happy settlement. Leaving New Haven in late February, Knight was back in Boston within a week and summed up this return trip quickly, without making separate entries for each day.

To be near her daughter, Knight moved to Connecticut in 1713. There Knight continued to prosper, buying farms and an inn. She died at age sixty-one in New London, Connecticut, leaving an estate valued at eighteen hundred pounds, more than one hundred times the wealth of the average person in 1727.

Suggested Readings: *The Journal of Madam Knight*, intro. G. P. Winship, pref. K. Silverman, 1970. A. Margolies, "The Editing and Publication of *The Journal of Madam Knight*" in *Papers of the Bibliographical Society of America* 1964, 58: 25–32. P. Thorpe, "Sarah Kemble Knight and the Picaresque Tradition" in *College Language Association Journal* 1966, 10: 114–121. R. D. Arner, "Sarah Kemble Knight" in *American Literature Before the 1800s*, ed. J. A. Levernier and D. R. Wilmes, 1983.

Text Used: *The Private Journal of a Journey From Boston to New York, in the Year 1704*, 1865 (spelling and punctuation modernized).

from THE PRIVATE JOURNAL OF A JOURNEY FROM BOSTON TO NEW YORK

Friday, Oct. Sixth [1704]. I got up very early, in order to hire somebody to go with me to New Haven, being in great perplexity at the thoughts of proceeding alone; which my most hospitable entertainer observing, himself went, and soon returned with a young gentleman of the town, who he could confide in to go with me; and about eight this morning, with Mr. Joshua Wheeler[1] my new guide, taking leave of this worthy gentleman, we advanced on toward Seabrook. The roads all along this way are very bad, encumbered with rocks and mountainous passages, which were very disagreeable to my tired carcass; but we went on with a moderate pace which made the journey more pleasant. But after about eight miles riding, in going over a bridge under which the river run very swift,[2] my horse stumbled, and very narrowly escaped falling over into the water; which extremely

---

[1] Wheeler (1681–?) the son of John Wheeler, a shipping merchant of New London, Connecticut.
[2] Most likely the Niantic River.

frightened me. But through God's goodness I met with no harm, and mounting again, in about half a mile's riding, come to an ordinary,[3] were well entertained by a woman of about seventy and vantage,[4] but of as sound intellectuals as one of seventeen. She entertained Mr. Wheeler with some passages of a wedding awhile ago at a place hard by, the bride's-groom being about her age or something above, saying his children was dreadfully against their father's marrying, which she condemned them extremely for.

From hence we went pretty briskly forward, and arrived at Saybrook ferry about two of the clock afternoon; and crossing it, we called at an inn to bait[5] (foreseeing we should not have such another opportunity 'til we come to Killingsworth). Landlady come in, with her hair about her ears, and hands at full pay[6] scratching. She told us she had some mutton which she would broil, which I was glad to hear; but I suppose forgot to wash her scratches; in a little time she brought it in; but it being pickled, and my guide said it smelled strong of head sauce,[7] we left it, and paid sixpence a piece for our dinners, which was only smell.

So we put forward with all speed, and about seven at night come to Killingsworth, and were tolerably well with travelers' fare, and lodged there that night.

Saturday, Oct. 7th [1704], we set out early in the morning, and being something unaquainted with the way, having asked it of some we met, they told us we must ride a mile or two and turn down a lane on the right hand; and by their direction we rode on, but not yet coming to the turning, we met a young fellow and asked him how far it was to the lane which turned down towards Guilford. He said we must ride a little further, and turn down by the corner of Uncle Sam's lot. My guide vented his spleen at the lubber;[8] and we soon after came into the road, and keeping still on, without any thing further remarkable, about two o'clock [in the] afternoon we arrived at New Haven, where I was received with all possible respects and civility. Here I discharged Mr. Wheeler with a reward to his satisfaction, and took some time to rest after so long and toilsome a journey; and informed myself of the manners and customs of the place, and at the same time employed myself in the affair I went there upon.

They are governed by the same laws as we in Boston (or little differing), throughout this whole colony of Connecticut, and much the same say of church government, and many of them good, sociable people, and I hope religious too. . . .

Dec. 6th [1704].

* * *

The city of New York is a pleasant, well-compacted place, situated on a commodious river which is a fine harbor for shipping. The buildings brick generally, very stately and high, though not altogether like ours in Boston. The bricks in some of the houses are of diverse colors and laid in checkers, being glazed look very agreeable. The inside of them are neat to admiration, the wooden work, for only the walls are plastered, and the summers and gist[9] are plained and kept very

---

[3] An inn.   [4] About age seventy or more.   [5] To rest.   [6] Busily.
[7] Cheese sauce.   [8] Expressed his anger at the lout.
[9] The main beams and parallel horizontal supporting beams, or joists.

white scowered as so is all the partitions if made of boards. The fireplaces have no jambs (as ours have) but the backs run flush with the walls, and the hearth is of tiles and is as far out into the room at the ends as before the fire, which is generally five foot in the lower rooms, and the piece over where the mantle tree should be is made as ours with joiners' work,[10] and as I suppose is fastened to iron rods inside. The house where the vendue[11] was had chimney corners like ours, and they and the hearths were laid with the finest tile that I ever see, and the staircases laid all with white tile which is ever clean,[12] and so are the walls of the kitchen which had a brick floor. They were making great preparations to receive their governor, Lord Cornbury[13] from the Jerseys, and for that end raised the militia to guard him on shore to the fort.

They are generally of the Church of England and have a New England gentleman[14] for their minister, and a very fine church set out with all customary requisites. There are also a Dutch and diverse conventicles[15] as they call them, *viz.* Baptist, Quakers, etc. They are not strict in keeping the sabbath as in Boston and other places where I had been, but seem to deal with great exactness as far as I see or deal with. They are sociable to one another and courteous and civil to strangers and fare well in their houses. The English go very fashionable in their dress. But the Dutch, especially the middling sort, differ from our women, in their habit go loose, wear French muchets which are like a cap and a headband in one, leaving their ears bare, which are set out with jewels of a large size and many in number. And their fingers hooped with rings, some with large stones in them of many colors as were their pendants in their ears, which you should see very old women wear as well as young.

They have vendues very frequently and make their earnings very well by them, for they treat with good liquor liberally, and the customers drink as liberally and generally for't as well, by paying for that which they bid up briskly for, after the sack[16] has gone plentifully about, though sometimes good penny worths are got there. Their diversions in the winter is riding sleighs about three or four miles out of town, where they have houses of entertainment at a place called the Bowery, and some go to friends' houses who handsomely treat them. Mr. Burroughs carried his spouse and daughter and myself out to one Madame Dowes, a gentlewoman that lived at a farm house, who gave us a handsome entertainment of five or six dishes and choice beer and metheglin,[17] cider, etc., all which she said was the produce of her farm. I believe we met 50 or 60 sleighs that day—they fly with great swiftness and some are so furious that they'll turn out of the path for none except a loaden cart. Nor do they spare for any diversion the place affords, and sociable to a degree, their tables being as free to their neighbors as to themselves.

Having here transacted the affair I went upon and some other that fell in the way, after about a fortnight's stay there I left New York with no little regret. . . .

1704–1705, 1825

---

[10] Similar to carpenter's work but more finely finished.   [11] Auction.
[12] Set into the wall, forming a continuous border one tile in width.
[13] Edward Hyde (1661–1723), the governor of New Jersey and New York from 1702 to 1708.
[14] William Vesey (1674–1746), the rector of New York's Trinity Church.
[15] Religious assemblies held illegally by Protestant sects that disputed the Church of England's authority.
[16] Dry white wine, generally imported from Spain or the Canary Islands.
[17] A spiced alcoholic drink.

William Byrd II
(1674–1744)

A premier example of southern colonial aristocracy, William Byrd II was born the first child of William Byrd and Mary Horsmanden in 1674 in what is now Richmond, Virginia. Designated his father's successor in business and politics, he was sent to school in Essex, England, in 1681; about 1690 he began to learn the world of business and trade, in Holland and then in London. He commenced the study of law at the Middle Temple, a London legal society, in 1692 and was subsequently admitted to the bar.

A polished gentleman trained to carry on his father's lucrative Native-American, colonial, and trans-Atlantic trade, Byrd joined Cotton Mather in 1696 as the only American members of London's Royal Society, the preeminent scientific body of its day. That year Byrd returned briefly to Virginia, was elected to the House of Burgesses there, and became the colony's representative before England's influential Board of Trade. In 1702 he lost that post by presenting directly to the king his constituents' protest against raising troops and taxes to defend New York's frontiers.

When Byrd journeyed to Westover, Virginia, to claim his inheritance in 1705, a year after his father's death, England was the home Byrd knew. He spent the next twenty-one years struggling to become a Virginian. His eighteenth-century English rearing, which emphasized classical education, balance, moderation, tolerance, and good taste, was fortunately compatible with his life as part of Virginia's ruling class. Byrd built a library of over thirty-six hundred volumes, second in size only to Cotton Mather's and second to none in its scope. But Westover was not London. Byrd's plantation was a retreat from city life and an anticipation of Jefferson's Monticello, just as Byrd, in the breadth of his humanistic and scientific concerns, anticipated Jefferson.

In 1706, as the newly appointed receiver general of Virginia, Byrd married Lucy Parke, whose father Daniel Parke was the only colonial to become a royal governor. Byrd's appointment in 1709 to the Council of Virginia marked a rise in political fortunes, but his underestimation and hasty assumption of his late father-in-law's debts in 1712, in return for Parke's estate, drained Bryd's resources almost until his death in 1744. Byrd became a Council leader, but spent years in London dealing with Parke's debts and, after Lucy's death in 1716, seeking a wealthy wife. After a year or two in Virginia, the council urged him back to England to try to preserve its powers. He married Maria Taylor in 1724, returned to Westover in 1726, and eventually expanded his father's 26,000 acres to 179,440 acres.

Byrd's role on the council enabled him to view himself first as a Virginian and second as an Englishman, a reconciliation echoed in his letters, in his "secret" diaries (written in a variation of shorthand), and in his major achievement, *The History of the Dividing Line* (first published in 1841). Based on Byrd's 1728 expeditions that set the boundary between Virginia and North Carolina, the work deemphasized the satire, sarcasm, and sexual humor of the previously written *Secret History* (first published in 1929) to reveal the expeditions as a myth-making process. That process captured the spirit of American frontier exploration and established the *History* as a prototype of discovery literature.

Suggested Readings: *The Secret History of the Line, in William Byrd's Histories of the Dividing Line Betwixt Virginia and North Carolina,* ed. W. K. Boyd, 1929. *The Secret Diary of William Byrd of Westover, 1709–1712,* ed. L. B. Wright and M. Tinling, 1941. A. Hatch, *The Byrds of Virginia,* 1969. R. C. Beatty, *William Byrd of Westover,* 1970. P. Marambaud, *William Byrd of Westover, 1674–1744,* 1971. K. A. Lockridge, *The Diary, and Life, of William Byrd II of Virginia, 1674–1744,* 1987. R. Turbet, *William Byrd: A Guide to Research,* 1987.

Text Used: *The Prose Works of William Byrd of Westover,* ed. L. B. Wright, 1966.

from   THE HISTORY OF THE DIVIDING LINE*

[*March 10, 1728*]

10. The Sabbath happened very opportunely, to give some ease to our jaded people, who rested religiously from every work but that of cooking the kettle. We observed very few cornfields in our walks and those very small, which seemed the stranger to us because we could see no other tokens of husbandry or improvement. But upon further inquiry we were given to understand people only made corn for themselves and not for their stocks, which know very well how to get their own living. Both cattle and hogs ramble into the neighboring marshes and swamps, where they maintain themselves the whole winter long and are not fetched home till the spring. Thus these indolent wretches during one half of the year lose the advantage of the milk of their cattle, as well as their dung, and many of the poor creatures perish in the mire, into the bargain, by this ill management. Some who pique themselves more upon industry than their neighbors will now and then, in compliment to their cattle, cut down a tree whose limbs are loaded with the moss afore-mentioned. The trouble would be too great to climb the tree in order to gather this provender, but the shortest way (which in this country is always counted the best) is to fell it, just like the lazy Indians, who do the same by such trees as bear fruit and so make one harvest for all. By this bad husbandry milk is so scarce in the winter season that were a big-bellied woman to long for it she would tax her longing. And, in truth I believe this is often the case and at the same time a very good reason why so many people in this province are marked with a custard complexion.

The only business here is raising of hogs, which is managed with the least trouble and affords the diet they are most fond of. The truth of it is, the inhabitants of North Carolina devour so much swine's flesh that it fills them full of gross humors. For want, too, of a constant supply of salt, they are commonly obliged to eat it fresh, and that begets the highest taint of scurvy. Thus, whenever a severe cold happens to constitutions thus vitiated, 'tis apt to improve into the yaws,[1] called there very justly the country distemper. This has all the symptoms of the pox, with this aggravation, that no preparation of mercury will touch it. First it seizes the throat, next the palate, and lastly shows its spite to the poor nose, of

---

* Byrd's *The History of the Dividing Line Betwixt Virginia and North Carolina* accounts the official survey to establish the boundary between the two states, begun on March 5, 1728.
[1] A skin disease.

which 'tis apt in a small time treacherously to undermine the foundation. This calamity is so common and familiar here that it ceases to be a scandal, and in the disputes that happen about beauty the noses have in some companies much ado to carry it. Nay, 'tis said that once, after three good pork years, a motion had like to have been made in the House of Burgesses that a man with a nose should be incapable of holding any place of profit in the province; which extraordinary motion could never have been intended without some hopes of a majority.

Thus, considering the foul and pernicious effects of eating swine's flesh in a hot country, it was wisely forbid and made an abomination to the Jews, who lived much in the same latitude with Carolina.

* * *

[March 25, 1728]

25. The air was chilled this morning with a smart Northwest wind, which favored the Dismalites[2] in their dirty march. They returned by the path they had made in coming out and with great industry arrived in the evening at the spot where the line had been discontinued. After so long and laborious a journey, they were glad to repose themselves on their couches of cypress bark, where their sleep was as sweet as it would have been on a bed of Finland down.

In the meantime, we who stayed behind had nothing to do but to make the best observations we could upon that part of the country. The soil of our landlord's plantation, though none of the best, seemed more fertile than any thereabouts, where the ground is near as sandy as the deserts of Africa and consequently barren. The road leading from thence to Edenton, being in distance about twenty-seven miles, lies upon a ridge called Sandy Ridge, which is so wretchedly poor that it will not bring potatoes. The pines in this part of the country are of a different species from those that grow in Virginia: their bearded leaves are much longer and their cones much larger. Each cell contains a seed of the size and figure of a black-eyed pea, which, shedding in November, is very good mast[3] for hogs and fattens them in a short time. The smallest of these pines are full of cones which are eight or nine inches long, and each affords commonly sixty or seventy seeds. This kind of mast has the advantage of all other by being more constant and less liable to be nipped by the frost or eaten by the caterpillars.

The trees also abound more with turpentine and consequently yield more tar than either the yellow or the white pine and for the same reason make more durable timber for building. The inhabitants hereabouts pick up knots of lightwood in abundance, which they burn into tar and then carry it to Norfolk or Nansemond[4] for a market. The tar made in this method is less valuable because it is said to burn the cordage, though it is full as good for all other uses as that made in Sweden and Muscovy.[5]

Surely there is no place in the world where the inhabitants live with less labor than in North Carolina. It approaches nearer to the description of Lubberland[6] than any other, by the great felicity of the climate, the easiness of raising provisions,

---

[2] Residents of the Dismal Swamp.   [3] Nuts used as feed for hogs.
[4] A region in southeastern Virginia.   [5] Russia.
[6] From thirteenth-century fable, a land of riches and leisure.

and the slothfulness of the people. Indian corn is of so great increase that a little pains will subsist a very large family with bread, and then they may have meat without any pains at all, by the help of the low grounds and the great variety of mast that grows on the high land. The men, for their parts, just like the Indians, impose all the work upon the poor women. They make their wives rise out of their beds early in the morning, at the same time that they lie and snore till the sun has risen one-third of his course and dispersed all the unwholesome damps.[7] Then, after stretching and yawning for half an hour, they light their pipes, and, under the protection of a cloud of smoke, venture out into the open air; though it if happen to be never so little cold they quickly return shivering into the chimney corner. When the weather is mild, they stand leaning with both their arms upon the cornfield fence and gravely consider whether they had best go and take a small heat at the hoe but generally find reasons to put it off till another time. Thus they loiter away their lives, like Solomon's sluggard,[8] with their arms across, and at the winding up of the year scarcely have bread to eat. To speak the truth, 'tis a thorough aversion to labor that makes people file off to North Carolina, where plenty and a warm sun confirm them in their disposition to laziness for their whole lives.

[March 26, 1728]

26. Since we were like to be confined to this place till the people returned out of the Dismal, 'twas agreed that our chaplain might safely take a turn to Edenton[9] to preach the Gospel to the infidels there and christen their children. He was accompanied thither by Mr. Little, one of the Carolina commissioners, who, to show his regard for the church, offered to treat him on the road with a fricassee of rum. They fried half a dozen rashers of very fat bacon in a pint of rum, both which being dished up together served the company at once both for meat and drink.

Most of the rum they get in this country comes from New England and is so bad and unwholesome that it is not improperly called "kill-devil." It is distilled there from foreign molasses, which, if skillfully managed, yields near gallon for gallon. Their molasses comes from the same country and has the name of "long sugar" in Carolina, I suppose from the ropiness of it, and serves all the purposes of sugar, both in their eating and drinking. When they entertain their friends bountifully, they fail not to set before them a capacious bowl of bombo, so called from the admiral of that name. This is a compound of rum and water in equal parts, made palatable with the said long sugar. As good humor begins to flow and the bowl to ebb they take care to replenish it with sheer rum, of which there always is a reserve under the table.

But such generous doings happen only when that balsam of life is plenty; for they have often such melancholy times that neither landgraves nor caciques[10] can procure one drop for their wives when they lie in or are troubled with the colic or vapors. Very few in this country have the industry to plant orchards, which, in a dearth of rum, might supply them with much better liquor. The truth is, there is one inconvenience that easily discourages lazy people from making this improve-

---

[7] Dampness.
[8] In Proverbs 6:6–11 the wise King Solomon warns against laziness, using the ant as an example of industriousness.
[9] A commercial center and, unofficially, North Carolina's capital.
[10] Princes nor Native-American chiefs.

ment: very often, in autumn, when the apples begin to ripen, they are visited with numerous flights of parakeets,[11] that bite all the fruit to pieces in a moment for the sake of the kernels. The havoc they make is sometimes so great that whole orchards are laid waste, in spite of all the noises that can be made or mawkins[12] that can be dressed up to fright 'em away. These ravenous birds visit North Carolina only during the warm season and so soon as the cold begins to come on retire back toward the sun. They rarely venture so far north as Virginia, except in a very hot summer, when they visit the most southern parts of it. They are very beautiful but, like some other pretty creatures, are apt to be loud and mischievous.

[*March 27, 1728*]

27. Betwixt this [plantation] and Edenton there are many huckleberry slashes,[13] which afford a convenient harbor for wolves and foxes. The first of these wild beasts is not so large and fierce as they are in other countries more northerly. He will not attack a man in the keenest of his hunger but run away from him, as from an animal more mischievous than himself. The foxes are much bolder and will sometimes not only make a stand but likewise assault anyone that would balk them of their prey. The inhabitants hereabouts take the trouble to dig abundance of wolf pits, so deep and perpendicular that when a wolf is once tempted into them he can no more scramble out again than a husband who has taken the leap can scramble out of matrimony.

Most of the houses in this part of the country are log houses, covered with pine or cypress shingles, three feet long and one broad. They are hung upon lathes with pegs, and their doors, too, turn upon wooden hinges and have wooden locks to secure them, so that the building is finished without nails or other ironwork. They also set up their pales[14] without any nails at all, and, indeed, more securely than those that are nailed. There are three rails mortised[15] into the posts, the lowest of which serves as a sill, with a groove in the middle big enough to receive the end of the pales; the middle part of the pale rests against the inside of the next rail, and the top of it is brought forward to the outside of the uppermost. Such wreathing of the pales in and out makes them stand firm and much harder to unfix than when nailed in the ordinary way.

Within three or four miles of Edenton the soil appears to be a little more fertile, though it is much cut with slashes, which seem all to have a tendency toward the Dismal. This town is situated on the north side of Albemarle Sound, which is there about five miles over. A dirty slash runs all along the back of it, which in the summer is a foul annoyance and furnishes abundance of that Carolina plague, mosquitoes. There may be forty or fifty houses, most of them small and built without expense. A citizen here is counted extravagant if he has ambition enough to aspire to a brick chimney. Justice herself is but indifferently lodged, the courthouse having much of the air of a common tobacco house. I believe this is the only metropolis in the Christian or Mahometan[16] world where there is neither church, chapel, mosque, synagogue, or any other place of public worship of any sect or religion whatsoever. What little devotion there may happen to be is much more private than their vices. The people seem easy without a minister as long as

---

[11] The Carolina parakeet, now extinct.   [12] Scarecrows.   [13] Swamps.
[14] Fenceposts.   [15] Fastened securely.   [16] Mohammedan.

they are exempted from paying him. Sometimes the Society for Propagating the Gospel has had the charity to send over missionaries to this country; but, unfortunately, the priest has been too lewd for the people, or, which oftener happens, they too lewd for the priest. For these reasons these reverend gentlemen have always left their flocks as arrant heathen as they found them. Thus much, however, may be said for the inhabitants of Edenton, that not a soul has the least taint of hypocrisy or superstition, acting very frankly and aboveboard in all their exercises.

Provisions here are extremely cheap and extremely good, so that people may live plentifully at a trifling expense. Nothing is dear but law, physic,[17] and strong drink, which are all bad in their kind, and the last they get with so much difficulty that they are never guilty of the sin of suffering it to sour upon their hands. Their vanity generally lies not so much in having a handsome dining room as a handsome house of office:[18] in this kind of structure they are really extravagant. They are rarely guilty of flattering or making any court to their governors but treat them with all the excesses of freedom and familarity. They are of opinion their rulers would be apt to grow insolent if they grew rich, and for that reason take care to keep them poorer and more dependent, if possible, than the saints in New England used to do their governors. They have very little coin, so they are forced to carry on their home traffic with paper money. This is the only cash that will tarry in the country, and for that reason the discount goes on increasing between that and real money and will do so to the end of the chapter.

* * *

[April 7, 1728]

7. The next day being Sunday, we ordered notice to be sent to all the neighborhood that there would be a sermon at this place an an opportunity of christening their children. But the likelihood of rain got the better of their devotion and, what perhaps might still be a stronger motive, of their curiosity. In the morning we dispatched a runner to the Nottoway[19] town to let the Indians know we intended them a visit that evening, and our honest landlord was so kind as to be our pilot thither, being about four miles from his house. Accordingly, in that afternoon we marched in good order to the town, where the female scouts, stationed on an eminence for that purpose, had no sooner spied us but they gave notice of our approach to their fellow citizens by continual whoops and cries, which could not possibly have been more dismal at the sight of their most implacable enemies. This signal assembled all their great men, who received us in a body and conducted us into the fort.

This fort was a square piece of ground, enclosed with substantial puncheons or strong palisades[20] about ten feet high and leaning a little outwards to make a scalade[21] more difficult. Each side of the square might be about a hundred yards long, with loopholes at proper distances through which they may fire upon the enemy. Within this enclosure we found bark cabins sufficient to lodge all their people in case they should be obliged to retire thither. These cabins are no other but close arbors made of saplings, arched at the top and covered so well with bark

---

[17] Medicine.   [18] A structure separate from the main house.
[19] A now-extinct Iroquoian people of southeastern Virginia (also "Nottaway").
[20] Wooden posts or stakes.   [21] Scaling of the walls.

as to be proof against all weather. The fire is made in the middle, according to the Hibernian[22] fashion, the smoke whereof finds no other vent but at the door and so keeps the whole family warm, at the expense both of their eyes and complexion. The Indians have no standing furniture in their cabins but hurdles[23] to repose their persons upon which they cover with mats or deerskins. We were conducted to the best apartments in the fort, which just before had been made ready for our reception and adorned with new mats that were very sweet and clean.

The young men had painted themselves in a hideous manner, not so much for ornament as terror. In that frightful equipage they entertained us with sundry war dances, wherein they endeavored to look as formidable as possible. The instrument they danced to was an Indian drum, that is, a large gourd with a skin braced taut over the mouth of it. The dancers all sang to this music keeping exact time with their feet while their head and arms were screwed into a thousand menacing postures.

Upon this occasion the ladies had arrayed themselves in all their finery. They were wrapped in their red and blue matchcoats,[24] thrown so negligently about them that their mahogany skins appeared in several parts, like the Lacedaemonian[25] damsels of old. Their hair was braided with white and blue peak and hung gracefully in a large roll upon their shoulders.

This peak consists of small cylinders cut out of a conch shell, drilled through and strung like beads. It serves them both for money and jewels, the blue being of much greater value than the white for the same reason that Ethiopian mistresses in France are dearer than French, because they are more scarce. The women wear necklaces and bracelets of these precious materials when they have a mind to appear lovely. Though their complexions be a little sad-colored, yet their shapes are very straight and well proportioned. Their faces are seldom handsome, yet they have an air of innocence and bashfulness that with a little less dirt would not fail to make them desirable. Such charms might have had their full effect upon men who had been so long deprived of female conversation but that the whole winter's soil was so crusted on the skins of those dark angels that it required a very strong appetite to approach them. The bear's oil with which they anoint their persons all over makes their skins soft and at the same time protects them from every species of vermin that use to be troublesome to other uncleanly people.

We were unluckily so many that they could not well make us the compliment of bedfellows according to the Indian rules of hospitality, though a grave matron whispered one of the commissioners very civilly in the ear that if her daughter had been but one year older she should have been at his devotion. It is by no means a loss of reputation among the Indians for damsels that are single to have intrigues with the men; on the contrary, they account it an argument of superior merit to be liked by a great number of gallants. However, like the ladies that game,[26] they are a little mercenary in their amours and seldom bestow their favors out of stark love and kindness. But after these women have once appropriated their charms by marriage, they are from thenceforth faithful to their vows and will hardly ever be tempted by an agreeable gallant or be provoked by a brutal or even by a fumbling husband to go astray.

The little work that is done among the Indians is done by the poor women, while the men are quite idle or at most employed only in the gentlemanly diversions of hunting and fishing. In this, as well as in their wars, they now use nothing

[22] Irish or Celtic.   [23] Frames made of interlaced twigs.   [24] Loose wraps.
[25] Of ancient Sparta.   [26] Engage in prostitution.

but firearms, which they purchase of the English for skins. Bows and arrows are grown into disuse, except only amongst their boys. Nor is it ill policy, but on the contrary very prudent, thus to furnish the Indians with firearms, because it makes them depend entirely upon the English, not only for their trade but even for their subsistence. Besides, they were really able to do more mischief while they made use of arrows, of which they would let silently fly several in a minute with wonderful dexterity, whereas now they hardly ever discharge their firelocks[27] more than once, which they insidiously do from behind a tree and then retire as nimbly as the Dutch horse used to do now and then formerly in Flanders.

We put the Indians to no expense but only of a little corn for our horses, for which in gratitude we cheered their hearts with what rum we had left, which they love better than they do their wives and children. Though these Indians dwell among the English and see in what plenty a little industry enables them to live, yet they choose to continue in their stupid idleness and to suffer all the inconveniences of dirt, cold, and want rather than disturb their heads with care or defile their hands with labor.

The whole number of people belonging to the Nottoway town, if you include women and children, amount to about two hundred. These are the only Indians of any consequence now remaining within the limits of Virginia. The rest are either removed or dwindled to a very inconsiderable number, either by destroying one another or else by the smallpox and other diseases. Though nothing has been so fatal to them as their ungovernable passion for rum, with which, I am sorry to say it, they have been but too liberally supplied by the English that live near them.

And here I must lament the bad success Mr. Boyle's[28] charity has hitherto had toward converting any of these poor heathens to Christianity. Many children of our neighboring Indians have been brought up in the College of William and Mary. They have been taught to read and write and been carefully instructed in the principles of the Christian religion till they came to be men. Yet after they returned home, instead of civilizing and converting the rest, they have immediately relapsed into infidelity and barbarism themselves.

And some of them, too, have made the worst use of the knowledge they acquired among the English by employing it against their benefactors. Besides, as they unhappily forget all the good they learn and remember the ill, they are apt to be more vicious and disorderly than the rest of their countrymen.

I ought not to quit this subject without doing justice to the great prudence of Colonel Spotswood[29] in this affair. That gentleman was Lieutenant Governor of Virginia when Carolina was engaged in a bloody war with the Indians. At that critical time it was thought expedient to keep a watchful eye upon our tributary savages, who we knew had nothing to keep them to their duty but their fears. Then it was that he demanded of each nation a competent number of their great men's children to be sent to the College, where they served as so many hostages for the good behavior of the rest and at the same time were themselves principled in the Christian religion. He also placed a schoolmaster among the Saponi Indians, at the salary of 50 pounds per annum, to instruct their children. The person that

---

[27] An early type of musket.

[28] Robert Boyle (1627–1691), an English philosopher-scientist who bequeathed money to be used to spread Christianity among the "heathen"; some of the money went to the College of William and Mary for the education of Native Americans.

[29] Alexander Spotswood (1676–1740), Virginia's lieutenant governor from 1710 to 1722, who encouraged better relations with the Native Americans.

undertook that charitable work was Mr. Charles Griffin, a man of a good family, who by the innocence of his life and the sweetness of his temper was perfectly well qualified for that pious undertaking. Besides, he had so much the secret of mixing pleasure with instruction that he had not a scholar who did not love him affectionately. Such talents must needs have been blessed with a proportionable success, had he not been unluckily removed to the College, by which he left the good work he had begun unfinished. In short, all the pains he had taken among the infidels had no other effect but to make them something cleanlier than other Indians are.

The care Colonel Spotswood took to tincture[30] the Indian children with Christianity produced the following epigram, which was not published during his administration for fear it might then have looked like flattery.

> Long has the furious priest assayed in vain,
> With sword and faggot, infidels to gain,
> But now the milder soldier wisely tries
> By gentler methods to unveil their eyes.
> Wonders apart, he knew 'twere vain t'engage
> The fixed preventions of misguided age.
> With fairer hopes he forms the Indian youth
> To early manners, probity, and truth.
> The lion's whelp thus, on the Libyan shore,
> Is tamed and gentled by the artful Moor,
> Not the grim sire, inured to blood before.

I am sorry I can't give a better account of the state of the poor Indians with respect to Christianity, although a great deal of pains has been and still continues to be taken with them. For my part, I must be of opinion, as I hinted before, that there is but one way of converting these poor infidels and reclaiming them from barbarity, and that is charitably to intermarry with them, according to the modern policy of the Most Christian King in Canada and Louisiana. Had the English done this at the first settlement of the colony, the infidelity of the Indians had been worn out at this day with their dark complexions, and the country had swarmed with people more than it does with insects. It was certainly an unreasonable nicety that prevented their entering into so good-natured an alliance. All nations of men have the same natural dignity, and we all know that very bright talents may be lodged under a very dark skin. The principal difference between one people and another proceeds only from the different opportunities of improvement. The Indians by no means want understanding and are in their figure tall and well proportioned. Even their copper-colored complexion would admit of blanching, if not in the first, at the farthest in the second, generation. I may safely venture to say, the Indian women would have made altogether as honest wives for the first planters as the damsels they used to purchase from aboard the ships. 'Tis strange, therefore, that any good Christian should have refused a wholesome, straight bedfellow, when he might have had so fair a portion with her as the merit of saving her soul.

1728, 1844

---

[30] To permeate.

The First Great Awakening

Beginning in the 1730s a series of religious revivals swept the American colonies. In New England the movement was led by Jonathan Edwards, who was both delighted and deeply troubled by the explosion of religious feeling. Because the revivals came at a time when religious devotion had been on the wane, the "Great Awakening," as they were called, seemed a blessing; but because Puritan doctrine had always stressed reason over emotionalism and sudden conversions, Edwards and other ministers were skeptical as well. The revival spread to the middle colonies and the South when the English Methodist preacher George Whitefield (1714–1770) toured America from 1739 to 1741. Doctrinal disputes in the Protestant churches over the role of emotion and immediate conversion led to a split of the clergy into two camps: "New Light" ministers, who favored the revival movement, and "Old Light" clergy, who rejected it. The College of New Jersey (now Princeton) was founded as a theological seminary for New Light ministers, and Jonathan Edwards was one of its first presidents.

Jonathan Edwards
(1703–1758)

Jonathan Edwards was born in East Windsor, Connecticut, in 1703 to the minister Timothy Edwards and Esther Stoddard. Her father, Solomon Stoddard, was one of the most powerful clergymen in New England; he became known as "Pope Stoddard" by those who feared and admired him. In 1727 Edwards married Sarah Pierpont of New Haven, Connecticut, a young woman of tremendous emotional fervor. The story of Jonathan Edwards is one of triumph and tragedy. Unlike some of his contemporaries, Edwards enjoyed an extremely happy marriage to a woman he loved deeply and whose support he enjoyed. At the same time, his ministry in Northampton, Massachusetts, was a failure. In 1750, twenty-one years after he had assumed the pulpit from Solomon Stoddard, the congregation overwhelmingly voted to dismiss Edwards as their minister. This defeat represented a rejection of a leading "New Light" minister, a spearheader of the Great Awakening of the 1730s and 1740s in New England.

Edwards was essentially exiled to Stockbridge, Massachusetts, where, with even less success than he had had in Northampton, he ministered to Native Americans. His world turned inward from the public meetings and mass gatherings of the preaching tour of New England he had made with Rev. George Whitefield at the beginning of the Awakening. From the early 1740s and the decline of Edwards's ministry in Northampton to the time of his appointment as the third president of the College of New Jersey (now Princeton University) in 1758, he wrote many of the theological treatises for which he is now remembered. Thus, his long exile was quite productive for the development of American philosophy. Jonathan Edwards and Benjamin Franklin remain the two most prominent thinkers and influential figures in eighteenth-century American culture.

Young Edwards was tutored at home, a custom for Puritan children in New England. At age thirteen Edwards entered Yale College, where he remained after graduating in 1720 to read theology. In 1722 he became a minister at a Presbyterian church in New York City but withdrew after only nine months. From 1724 to 1725 he tutored at Yale, until his teaching career was interrupted by illness. In 1726 Edwards became assistant minister to Solomon Stoddard. He was elected to succeed Solomon Stoddard as minister to the Northampton congregation in 1729. Edwards's success with the evangelical awakening of the next twenty years was paralleled by a decline of influence with his own congregation. He had extremely poor relations with his flock, which resulted in petty squabbles. In 1744 he publicly listed persons from Northampton who were involved in "immoral practices," such as using "foul language" and reading a book about midwifery. He proceeded to read from the pulpit a long list that included many of the town's more prominent children, without bothering to distinguish between those who were accused of immoral practices and the accusers themselves.

As in all congregational matters, Edwards's timing was dreadful. He attempted to state his case from the pulpit, but his parishioners refused to listen. Finally, he was reduced to publishing his views in *An Humble Inquiry Into the Rules of the Word of God* (1749). Few parishioners bothered even to cut the pages open, as many extant copies of this dull vol-

The Jonathan Edwards Memorial by Herbert Adams in the First Church of Northampton, Massachusetts.

ume clearly show. Edwards was finished as a minister long before he penned this defense. However, from a historical perspective, that he fully expressed his views is important. His reputation as a leading theologian rose dramatically because of his published works. Following his exile in Stockbridge, Edwards assumed the presidency of the College of New Jersey at Princeton. But soon he was inoculated with a primitive vaccine against smallpox; the inferior vaccine caused his death in 1758. Ironically, this inoculation, introduced into the colonies by Cotton Mather, was designed to preserve human life but ended the life of a man whose fifty-five years were spent showing others how to achieve eternal life.

In retrospect Edwards is now regarded as the most powerful thinker of colonial America, and Benjamin Franklin the most influential shaper of America's literary and philosophical discourse. Edwards and Franklin, both heirs to the Puritan ethic, perceived the world as spiritual and material and believed that man's first duty is to discover ways of comprehending the physical universe. For Franklin scientific investigation became the means to higher understanding; for Edwards nothing discovered in nature could contravene those truths revealed through the "word of God," Scripture. Since his youth Edwards had expressed a keen interest in the natural universe, writing descriptive pieces on spiders, lightning, and mathematics. The Connecticut Valley was very much frontier in the early eighteenth century. In 1715, at age twelve, Edwards composed his well-known dissertation on the spider, entitled "Of Insects." Edwards's interest in the natural world, unlike that of Franklin, was meant to reinforce the Bible's vision of Creation.

While at Yale Edwards read such works as Isaac Newton's *Principia Mathematica* (1687) and John Locke's *An Essay Concerning Human Understanding* (1690). These proponents of the "new science" profoundly influenced Edward's thinking and style of writing. Edwards emerged as a leading eighteenth-century philosopher and prominent American literary figure because of his concern to express his understanding of God's ideas in language that could be accommodated to reason and emotion. Following the attempts of his contemporaries to express things in ordered, rational forms, Edwards adopted a plain, direct style that employed images from the natural universe to communicate a vision of God that was frightening to the unregenerate and often comforting to the regenerate, or saved. The vehicle for his expression was the prose sermon and the essay or treatise. Edward's most influential sermon was *Sinners in the Hands of an Angry God* (1741); his most important philosophical essay was *A Treatise Concerning Religious Affections* (1746). The epistemology of the Great Awakening and the psychology of individual conversion are summarized in *Treatise*. Both documents reveal Edwards at his literary best, and each makes a peculiar contribution to the development of American literature.

Edwards was not unique in preaching a "born-again" theology, as Puritans had always stressed the value of transformation from a hardened heart of stone to the full measure of God's divine grace. But for Edwards this transforming experience was expressed in the language of sensory experience, as his *Personal Narrative* (written about 1740 but published in 1765) shows. His writings and preaching during the Great Awakening exhibit the power of God revealed in the beauty and perfection of the natural universe. His prose style is stimulating and powerful. Edwards's sermons reveal a conscious commitment to imagery, communicating God through the senses as well as through the language of Scripture. Edwards is best remembered for *Sinners in the Hands of an Angry God*. The sermon, first preached in 1741, is representative of Edwards as a literary stylist, but not because it shows him to be a "fire and brimstone" evangelist. Rather, this document shows careful craftsmanship, meticulous care in the arrangement of themes and images, and a close attention to the psychology of divine revelation. For Edwards the ultimate objective of the sermon's power was to bring about a wrenching conversion in his listener, a passage from terror and despair to the hope of salvation.

Edwards recorded many of his experiences in the *Personal Narrative,* less a chronology of his life's activities than a record of his inner life, that "habit of mind" by which the reader may eventually know Edwards as a thinker. In *Personal Narrative* he says that his own conversion led to a new way of perceiving the universe around him. Conversion and renewal bring about a heightened sense of the natural world, which in turn leads to further understanding of spiritual matters. Edwards makes it perfectly clear that this "new sense of things" is available only to the regenerate mind, that those not slated for election and regeneration would be like dumb animals in their efforts to comprehend God's natural manifestations. The new beginning or fresh start commonly associated with migration to America from Europe in the nineteenth century originated in the Puritan notion that conversion leads to a total transformation of an individual: each regenerated person would essentially have the opportunity to start over again, leaving the "old self" behind, just as the Old World had been abandoned in favor of the New World.

A History of the Work of Redemption, a series of sermons preached in 1739, was left in manuscript form at the time of Edwards's death and was not published until 1774. It gives the most complete summary of Edwards's orthodox and conservative approach to the eternal work of the Holy Spirit and contains a particularly illuminating section on the imagery of Scripture. His *A Faithful Narrative of the Surprising Work of God* (1737), *The Distinguishing Marks of a Work of the Spirit of God* (1741), and *Some Thoughts Concerning the Present Revival of Religion in New England* (1742) treat the revivalism of the Great Awakening and defend the work of the Holy Spirit in contemporary New England. Another important epistemological document is *Images or Shadows of Divine Things* (first published in 1948), a commonplace book in which Edwards recorded impressions and ideas in a journal format.

Edwards's perception of the natural world provided Christian theology with a new dimension. Edwards had entered nature organically, as American transcendentalists (such as Ralph Waldo Emerson and Henry David Thoreau) were to do a century later, his mind open to receive the impressions garnered through his experience, and the impressions themselves assisted his regenerate spirit in comprehending the mysteries of God's ways toward man. The effective communication of this comprehension through language and imagery constitutes Edwards's most significant contribution to American literature and culture.

Suggested Readings: *The Printed Writings of Jonathan Edwards, 1703–1758: A Bibliography,* ed. T. H. Johnson, 1940. *The Works of Jonathan Edwards,* 7 vols., ed. J. E. Smith, 1959. *The Great Awakening,* ed. C. C. Goen, 1972. *Jonathan Edwards: A Reference Guide,* ed. M. X. Lesser, 1981. P. Miller, *Jonathan Edwards: The Life of the Mind,* 1949. E. H. Davidson, *Jonathan Edwards: The Narrative of a Puritan Mind,* 1966. R. Delattre, *Beauty and Sensibility in the Thought of Jonathan Edwards,* 1968. D. Shea, "Jonathan Edwards, Historian of Consciousness," in *Major Writers of Early American Literature,* ed. E. Emerson, 1972. J. Wilson, "Jonathan Edwards as Historian," in *Church History,* March 1977. M. Lowance, *The Language of Canaan: Metaphor and Symbol in New England From the Puritans to the Transcendentalists,* 1980. N. Fiering, *Jonathan Edwards's Moral Thought and Its British Context,* 1981. P. Tracy, *Jonathan Edwards: Pastor,* 1981.

Texts Used: Sarah Pierpont and *Personal Narrative: The Life of President Edwards,* ed. S. E. Dwight, 1830. *Sinners in the Hands of an Angry God: The Works of President Edwards,* Vol. VII, ed. S. E. Dwight, 1829. (Some spelling and punctuation modernized.)

Sarah Pierpont*

They say there is a young lady in [New Haven] who is beloved of that Great Being, who made and rules the world, and that there are certain seasons in which this Great Being, in some way or other invisible, comes to her and fills her mind with exceeding sweet delight, and that she hardly cares for any thing, except to meditate on him—that she expects after a while to be received up where he is, to be raised up out of the world and caught up into heaven; being assured that he loves her too well to let her remain at a distance from him always. There she is to dwell with him, and to be ravished with his love and delight forever. Therefore, if you present all the world before her, with the richest of its treasures, she disregards it and cares not for it, and is unmindful of any pain or affliction. She has a strange sweetness in her mind, and singular purity in her affections; is most just and conscientious in all her conduct; and you could not persuade her to do any thing wrong or sinful, if you would give her all the world, lest she should offend this Great Being. She is of a wonderful sweetness, calmness and universal benevolence of mind; especially after this Great God has manifested himself to her mind. She will sometimes go about from place to place, singing sweetly; and seems to be always full of joy and pleasure; and no one knows for what. She loves to be alone, walking in the field and groves, and seems to have some one invisible always conversing with her.

1723, 1829

PERSONAL NARRATIVE†

I had a variety of concerns and exercises[1] about my soul from my childhood, but had two more remarkable seasons of awakening[2] before I met with that change by which I was brought to those new dispositions and that new sense of things that I have since had. The first time was when I was a boy, some years before I went to college, at a time of remarkable awakening in my father's congregation. I was then very much affected for many months and concerned about the things of religion and my soul's salvation and was abundant in duties. I used to pray five times a day in secret, and to spend much time in religious talk with other boys and used to meet with them to pray together. I experienced I know not what kind of delight in religion. My mind was much engaged in it, and had much self-righteous pleasure; and it was my delight to abound in religious duties. I, with some of my schoolmates, joined together and built a booth in a swamp, in a very secret and retired place, for a place of prayer. And besides, I had particular secret places of my own in the woods, where I used to retire by myself, and used to be from time to time much affected. My affections seemed to be lively and easily moved, and I

---

* Edwards wrote this tribute when he was twenty and Sarah Pierpont (1710–1758) was thirteen. They married in 1727.

   † Edwards's autobiography was published in 1765 in *The Life and Character of the Late Rev. Mr. Jonathan Edwards* by his friend Samuel Hopkins; it was titled "An Account of His Conversions, Experiences, and Religious Exercises, Given by Himself."

   [1] Religious activities.   [2] Religious arousing.

seemed to be in my element, when engaged in religious duties. And I am ready to think, many are deceived with such affections and such a kind of delight, as I then had in religion, and mistake it for grace.

But in process of time, my convictions and affections wore off; and I entirely lost all those affections and delights, and left off secret prayer, at least as to any constant performance of it, and returned like a dog to his vomit, and went on in ways of sin.[3]

Indeed, I was at some times very uneasy, especially towards the latter part of the time of my being at college. 'Til it pleased God, in my last year at college, at a time when I was in the midst of many uneasy thoughts about the state of my soul, to seize me with a pleurisy;[4] in which he brought me nigh to the grave, and shook me over the pit of hell.

But yet, it was not long after my recovery before I fell again into my old ways of sin. But God would not suffer me to go on with any quietness; but I had great and violent inward struggles: 'til after many conflicts with wicked inclinations and repeated resolutions and bonds that I laid myself under by a kind of vows to God, I was brought wholly to break off all former wicked ways and all ways of known outward sin, and to apply myself to seek my salvation and practice the duties of religion, but without that kind of affection and delight that I had formerly experienced. My concern now wrought more by inward struggles and conflicts and self-reflections. I made seeking my salvation the main business of my life. But yet it seems to me I sought after a miserable manner, which has made me sometimes since to question whether ever it issued in that which was saving,[5] being ready to doubt, whether such miserable seeking was ever succeeded. But yet I was brought to seek salvation in a manner that I never was before. I felt a spirit to part with all things in the world for an interest in Christ. My concern continued and prevailed, with many exercising thoughts and inward struggles; but yet it never seemed to be proper to express my concern that I had, by the name of terror.

From my childhood up, my mind had been wont to be full of objections against the doctrine of God's sovereignty, in choosing whom he would to eternal life and rejecting whom he pleased, leaving them eternally to perish and be everlastingly tormented in hell. It used to appear like a horrible doctrine to me. But I remember the time very well when I seemed to be convinced, and fully satisfied, as to this sovereignty of God and his justice in thus eternally disposing of men according to his sovereign pleasure. But never could give an account how or by what means I was thus convinced; not in the least imagining, in the time of it nor a long time after, that there was any extraordinary influence of God's spirit in it; but only that now I saw further, and my reason apprehended the justice and reasonableness of it. However, my mind rested in it; and it put an end to all those cavils and objections, that had 'til then abode with me, all the proceeding part of my life. And there has been a wonderful alteration in my mind, with respect to the doctrine of God's sovereignty, from that day to this; so that I scarce ever have found so much as the rising of an objection against God's sovereignty, in the most absolute sense, in showing mercy to whom he will show mercy and hardening and eternally damning whom he will.[6] God's absolute sovereignty and justice, with respect to

---

[3] "As a dog returneth to his vomit, so a fool returneth to his folly," from Proverb 26:11.

[4] A respiratory inflammation.   [5] Spiritually redeeming.

[6] "Therefore hath he mercy on whom he will have mercy, and whom he will be hardeneth," from Romans 9:18.

salvation and damnation, is what my mind seems to rest assured of, as much as of anything that I see with my eyes; at least it is so at times. But I have oftentimes since that first conviction had quite another kind of sense of God's sovereignty than I had then. I have often since not only had a conviction, but a delightful conviction. The doctrine of God's sovereignty has very often appeared an exceeding pleasant, bright and sweet doctrine to me; and absolute sovereignty is what I love to ascribe to God. By my first conviction was not with this.

The first that I remember that ever I found anything of that sort of inward, sweet delight in God and divine things, that I have lived much in since, was on reading those words, 1 Timothy 1:17, "Now unto the king eternal, immortal, invisible, the only wise God, be honor and glory for ever and ever, Amen." As I read the words, there came into my soul, and was as it were diffused through it, a sense of the glory of the Divine Being, a new sense, quite different from anything I ever experienced before. Never any words of scripture seemed to me as these words did. I thought with myself, how excellent a being that was, and how happy I should be if I might enjoy that God and be rapt[7] up to God in Heaven, and be as it were swallowed up in him. I kept saying, and as it were singing over these words of scripture to myself; and went to prayer to pray to God that I might enjoy him; and prayed in a manner quite different from what I used to do, with a new sort of affection. But it never came into my thought that there was anything spiritual or of a saving nature in this.

From about that time I began to have a new kind of apprehensions and ideas of Christ, and the work of redemption, and the glorious way of salvation by him. I had an inward, sweet sense of these things, that at times came into my heart; and my soul was led away in pleasant views and contemplations of them. And my mind was greatly engaged to spend my time in reading and meditating on Christ, and the beauty and excellency of his person, and the lovely way of salvation, by free grace in him. I found no books so delightful to me as those that treated of these subjects. Those words Canticles[8] 2:1, used to be abundantly with me: "I am the Rose of Sharon, the lily of the valleys." The words seemed to me, sweetly to represent the loveliness and beauty of Jesus Christ. And the whole book of Canticles used to be pleasant to me; and I used to be much in reading it, about that time. And found, from time to time, an inward sweetness that used, as it were, to carry me away in my contemplations, in what I know not how to express otherwise, than by a calm, sweet abstraction of soul from all the concerns of this world, and a kind of vision, or fixed ideas and imaginations, of being alone in the mountains or some solitary wilderness, far from all mankind, sweetly conversing with Christ, and rapt and swallowed up in God. The sense I had of divine things would often of a sudden as it were, kindle up a sweet burning in my heart, an ardor of my soul, that I know not how to express.

Not long after I first began to experience these things, I gave an account to my father of some things that had passed in my mind. I was pretty much affected by the discourse we had together. And when the discourse was ended, I walked abroad alone, in a solitary place in my father's pasture, for contemplation. And as I was walking there, and looked up on the sky and clouds; there came into my mind a sweet sense of the glorious majesty and grace of God that I know not how to express. I seemed to see them both in a sweet conjunction, majesty and meek-

---

[7] Lifted.   [8] Another name for the biblical Song of Solomon.

ness joined together. It was a sweet and gentle, and holy majesty; and also a majestic meekness; an awful sweetness; a high, and great, and holy gentleness.

After this my sense of divine things gradually increased, and became more and more lively, and had more of that inward sweetness. The appearance of everything was altered: there seemed to be, as it were, a calm, sweet cast, or appearance of divine glory, in almost everything. God's excellency, his wisdom, his purity and love, seemed to appear in everything: in the sun, moon and stars; in the clouds, and blue sky; in the grass, flowers, trees; in the water, and all nature; which used greatly to fix my mind. I often used to sit and view the moon for a long time, and so in the daytime spent much time in viewing the clouds and sky to behold the sweet glory of God in these things, in the meantime, singing forth with a low voice my contemplations of the Creator and Redeemer. And scarce anything, among all the works of nature, was so sweet to me as thunder and lightning. Formerly, nothing had been so terrible to me. I used to be a person uncommonly terrified with thunder, and it used to strike me with terror when I saw a thunderstorm rising. But now, on the contrary, it rejoiced me. I felt God at the first appearance of a thunderstorm. And used to take the opportunity at such times to fix myself to view the clouds, and see the lightnings play, and hear the majestic and awful voice of God's thunder, which often times was exceeding entertaining, leading me to sweet contemplations of my great and glorious God. And while I viewed, used to spend my time, as it always seemed natural to me, to sing or chant forth my meditations, to speak my thoughts in soliloquies, and speak with a singing voice.

I felt then a great satisfaction as to my good estate.[9] But that did not content me. I had vehement longings of soul after God and Christ, and after more holiness, wherewith my heart seemed to be full and ready to break: which often brought to mind the words of the psalmist, Psalm 119:28: "My soul breaketh for the longing it hath." I often felt a mourning and lamenting in my heart that I had not turned to God sooner, that I might have had more time to grow in grace. My mind was greatly fixed on divine things; I was almost perpetually in the contemplation of them. Spent most of my time in thinking of divine things, year after year. And used to spend abundance of my time in walking alone in the woods and solitary places for meditation, soliloquy and prayer, and converse with God. And it was always my manner, at such times, to sing forth my contemplations. And was almost constantly in ejaculatory prayer, wherever I was. Prayer seemed to be natural to me, as the breath by which the inward burnings of my heart had vent.

The delights which I now felt in things of religion were of an exceeding different kind from those forementioned, that I had when I was a boy. They were totally of another kind; and what I then had no more notion or idea of, than one born blind has of pleasant and beautiful colors. They were of a more inward, pure, soul-animating and refreshing nature. Those former delights never reached the heart, and did not arise from any sight of the divine excellency of the things of God or any taste of the soul-satisfying and life-giving good there is in them.

My sense of divine things seemed gradually to increase, 'til I went to preach at New York,[10] which was about a year and a half after they began. While I was

---

[9] Spiritual condition.

[10] From August 1722 to April 1723, Edwards assisted as pastor in a Presbyterian church in New York City.

there, I felt them, very sensibly,[11] in a much higher degree, than I had done before. My longings after God and holiness, were much increased. Pure and humble, holy and heavenly Christianity appeared exceeding amiable to me. I felt in me a burning desire to be in everything a complete Christian, and conformed to the blessed image of Christ, and that I might live in all things, according to the pure, sweet and blessed rules of the gospel. I had an eager thirsting after progress in these things. My longings after it put me upon pursuing and pressing after them. It was my continual strife day and night, and constant inquiry, how I should be more holy, and live more holily, and more becoming a child of God, and disciple of Christ. I sought an increase of grace and holiness, and that I might live an holy life with vastly more earnestness than ever I sought grace, before I had it. I used to be continually examining myself, and studying and contriving for likely ways and means how I should live holily with far greater diligence and earnestness than ever I pursued anything in my life; but with too great a dependence on my own strength, which afterwards proved a great damage to me. My experience had not then taught me, as it has done since, my extreme feebleness and impotence, every manner of way, and the innumerable and bottomless depths of secret corruption and deceit that there was in my heart. However, I went on with my eager pursuit after more holiness, and sweet conformity to Christ.

The Heaven I desired was a heaven of holiness, to be with God, and to spend my eternity in divine love, and holy communion with Christ. My mind was very much taken up with contemplations on heaven, and the enjoyments of those there, and living there in perfect holiness, humility and love. And it used at that time to appear a great part of the happiness of heaven that there the saints could express their love to Christ. It appeared to me a great clog and hindrance and burden to me that what I felt within I could not express to God and give vent to as I desired. The inward ardor of my soul seemed to be hindered and pent up, and could not freely flame out as it would. I used often to think how in heaven this sweet principle should freely and fully vent and express itself. Heaven appeared to me exceeding delightful as a world of love. It appeared to me that all happiness consisted in living in pure, humble, heavenly, divine love.

I remember the thoughts I used then to have of holiness. I remember I then said sometimes to myself, "I do certainly know that I love holiness such as the gospel prescribes." It appeared to me there was nothing in it but what was ravishingly lovely. It appeared to me to be the highest beauty and amiableness, above all other beauties, that it was a divine beauty, far purer than anything here upon earth; and that everything else, was like mire, filth and defilement in comparison of it.

Holiness, as I then wrote down some of my contemplations on it, appeared to me to be of a sweet, pleasant, charming, serene, calm nature. It seemed to me it brought an inexpressible purity, brightness, peacefulness and ravishment to the soul, and that it made the soul like a field or garden of God, with all manner of pleasant flowers; that is, all pleasant, delightful and undisturbed, enjoying a sweet calm, and the gently vivifying beams of the sun. The soul of a true Christian, as I then wrote my meditations, appeared like such a little white flower as we see in the spring of the year, low and humble on the ground, opening its bosom, to receive the pleasant beams of the sun's glory, rejoicing as it were, in a calm rapture, diffusing around a sweet fragrancy, standing peacefully and lovingly in the

[11] Perceptibly.

midst of other flowers round about, all in like manner opening their bosoms, to drink in the light of the sun.

There was no part of creature holiness that I then, and at other times, had so great a sense of the loveliness of, as humility, brokenness of heart and poverty of spirit, and there was nothing that I had such a spirit to long for. My heart, as it were, panted after this to lie low before God, and in the dust; that I might be nothing, and that God might be all; that I might become as a little child.[12]

While I was there at New York, I sometimes was much affected with reflections on my past life, considering how late it was, before I began to be truly religious and how wickedly I had lived 'til then; and once so as to weep abundantly, and for a considerable time together.

On January 12, [1723] I made a solemn dedication of myself to God, and wrote it down; giving up myself, and all that I had to God; to be for the future in no respect my own; to act as one that had no right to himself, in any respect. And solemnly vowed to take God for my whole portion and felicity, looking on nothing else as any part of my happiness, nor acting as if it were: and his law for the constant rule of my obedience, engaging to fight with all my might against the world, the flesh and the devil,[13] to the end of my life. But have reason to be infinitely humbled, when I consider, how much I have failed of answering my obligation.

I had then abundance of sweet religious conversation in the family where I lived, with Mr. John Smith, and his pious mother. My heart was knit in affection to those in whom were appearances of true piety, and I could bear the thoughts of no other companions but such as were holy, and the disciples of the blessed Jesus.

I had great longings for the advancement of Christ's kingdom in the world. My secret prayer used to be in great part taken up in praying for it. If I heard the least hint of anything that happened in any part of the world that appeared to me in some respect or other, to have a favorable aspect on the interest of Christ's kingdom, my soul eagerly catched at it; and it would much animate and refresh me. I used to be earnest to read public newsletters, mainly for that end, to see if I could not find some news favorable to the interest of religion in the world.

I very frequently used to retire into a solitary place, on the banks of Hudson's river, at some distance from the city, for contemplation on divine things and secret converse with God, and had many sweet hours there. Sometimes Mr. Smith and I walked there together to converse of the things of God, and our conversation used much to turn on the advancement of Christ's kingdom in the world, and the glorious things that God would accomplish for his church in the latter days.

I had then, and at other times, the greatest delight in the holy Scriptures, of any book whatsoever. Oftentimes in reading it, every word seemed to touch my heart. I felt an harmony between something in my heart, and those sweet and powerful words. I seemed often to see so much light exhibited by every sentence, and such a refreshing ravishing food communicated, that I could not get along in reading. Used oftentimes to dwell long on one sentence, to see the wonders contained in it; and yet almost every sentence seemed to be full of wonders.

---

[12] ". . .Whosoever shall not receive the kingdom of God as a little child, he shall not enter therein," from Mark 10:15.

[13] "Good Lord, deliver us, From all inordinate and sinful affections; and from all the deceits of the world, the flesh, and the devil," from "Litany," the Anglican Book of Common Prayer.

I came away from New York in the month of April, 1723, and had a most bitter parting with Madam Smith and her son. My heart seemed to sink within me, at leaving the family and city, where I had enjoyed so many sweet and pleasant days. I went from New York to Weathersfield[14] by water. As I sailed away, I kept sight of the city as long as I could; and when I was out of sight of it, it would affect me much to look that way, with a kind of melancholy mixed with sweetness. However, that night after this sorrowful parting, I was greatly comforted in God at Westchester,[15] where we went ashore to lodge, and had a pleasant time of it all the voyage to Saybrook.[16] It was sweet to me to think of meeting dear Christians in heaven, where we should never part more. At Saybrook we went ashore to lodge on Saturday, and there kept sabbath where I had a sweet and refreshing season, walking alone in the fields.

After I came home to Windsor,[17] remained much in a like frame of my mind as I had been in at New York, but only sometimes felt my heart ready to sink with the thoughts of my friends at New York. And my refuge and support was in contemplations on the heavenly state, as I find in my diary of May 1, 1723. It was my comfort to think of that state where there is fulness of joy; where reigns heavenly, sweet, calm and delightful love, without alloy; where there are continually the dearest expressions of this love; where is the enjoyment of the persons loved without ever parting; where these persons that appear so lovely in this world will really be inexpressibly more lovely, and full of love to us. And how sweetly will the mutual lovers join together to sing the praises of God and the Lamb![18] How full will it fill us with joy to think that this enjoyment, these sweet exercises will never cease or come to an end, but will last to all eternity!

Continued much in the same frame in the general that I had been in at New York, 'til I went to New Haven to live there as tutor of the college,[19] having some special seasons of uncommon sweetness; particularly once at Bolton[20] in a journey from Boston, walking out alone in the fields. After I went to New Haven, I sunk in religion, my mind being diverted from my eager and violent pursuits after holiness by some affairs that greatly perplexed and distracted my mind.

In September, 1725, was taken ill at New Haven, and endeavoring to go home to Windsor, was so ill at the North Village that I could go no further where I lay sick for about a quarter of a year. And in this sickness, God was pleased to visit me again with the sweet influences of his spirit. My mind was greatly engaged there on divine, pleasant contemplations and longings of soul. I observed that those who watched with me would often be looking out for the morning, and seemed to wish for it. Which brought to my mind those words of the psalmist, which my soul with sweetness made its own language: "My soul waitest for the Lord, more than they that watch for the morning, I say, more than they that watch for the morning."[21] And when the light of the morning came, and the beams of the sun came in at the windows, it refreshed my soul from one morning to another. It seemed to me to be some image of the sweet light of God's glory.

I remember, about that time, I used greatly to long for the conversion of some that I was concerned with. It seemed to me I could gladly honor them, and with delight be a servant to them, and lie at their feet, if they were but truly holy.

But sometime after this, I was again greatly diverted in my mind with some temporal concerns that exceedingly took up my thoughts, greatly to the wound-

---

[14] Wethersfield, Connecticut.   [15] Westchester, New York.   [16] Saybrook, Connecticut.
[17] Windsor, Connecticut.   [18] Christ.   [19] Yale College, in 1724.
[20] Bolton, Connecticut.   [21] Psalm 130:6.

ing of my soul, and went on through various exercises, that it would be tedious to relate, that gave me much more experience of my own heart than ever I had before.

Since I came to this town,[22] I have often had sweet complacency in God, in views of his glorious perfections and the excellency of Jesus Christ. God has appeared to me a glorious and lovely Being, chiefly on the account of his holiness. The holiness of God has always appeared to me the most lovely of all his attributes. The doctrines of God's absolute sovereignty and free grace in showing mercy to whom he would show mercy, and man's absolute dependence on the operations of God's Holy Spirit, have very often appeared to me as sweet and glorious doctrines. These doctrines have been much my delight. God's sovereignty has ever appeared to me as great part of his glory. It has often been sweet to me to go to God and adore him as a sovereign God, and ask sovereign mercy of him.

I have loved the doctrines of the gospel; they have been to my soul like green pastures. The gospel has seemed to me to be the richest treasure, the treasure that I have most desired and longed that it might dwell richly in me. The way of salvation by Christ has appeared in a general way glorious and excellent, and most pleasant and beautiful. It has often seemed to me that it would in a great measure spoil heaven to receive it in any other way. That text has often been affecting and delightful to me, Isaiah 32:2: "A man shall be an hiding place from the wind, and a covert from the tempest," etc.

It has often appeared sweet to me to be united to Christ; to have him for my head, and to be a member of his body; and also to have Christ for my teacher and prophet. I very often think with sweetness and longings and pantings of soul, of being a little child, taking hold of Christ, to be led by him through the wilderness of this world. That text, Matthew 18:3 at the beginning, has often been sweet to me, "Except ye be converted, and become as little children, etc." I love to think of coming to Christ, to receive salvation of him, poor in spirit, and quite empty of self; humbly exalting him alone; cut entirely off from my own root, and to grow into and out of Christ; to have God in Christ to be all in all; and to live by faith on the Son of God, a life of humble, unfeigned confidence in him. That Scripture has often been sweet to me, Psalm 115:1: "Not unto us, O Lord, not unto us, but unto Thy name give glory, for Thy mercy, and for Thy truth's sake." And those words of Christ, Luke 10:21: "In that hour Jesus rejoiced in spirit, and said, I thank thee, O Father, Lord of heaven and earth, that Thou hast hid these things from the wise and prudent, and hast revealed them unto babes: Even so Father, for so it seemed good in Thy sight." That sovereignty of God that Christ rejoiced in seemed to me to be worthy to be rejoiced in, and that rejoicing of Christ seemed to me to show the excellency of Christ, and the spirit that he was of.

Sometimes only mentioning a single word causes my heart to burn within me, or only seeing the name of Christ or the name of some attribute of God. And God has appeared glorious to me on account of the Trinity. It has made me have exalting thoughts of God, that he subsists in three persons: Father, Son, and Holy Ghost.

The sweetest joys and delights I have experienced have not been those that have arisen from a hope of my own good estate, but in a direct view of the glorious things of the gospel. When I enjoy this sweetness it seems to carry me above the

[22] Northampton, Massachusetts, in 1726; he was appointed minister there in 1727.

thoughts of my own safe estate. It seems at such times a loss that I cannot bear, to take off my eye from the glorious, pleasant object I behold without me, to turn my eye in upon myself, and my own good estate.

My heart has been much on the advancement of Christ's kingdom in the world. The histories of the past advancement of Christ's kingdom have been sweet to me. When I have read histories of past ages, the pleasantest thing in all my reading has been to read of the kingdom of Christ being promoted. And when I have expected in my reading to come to any such thing, I have lotted[23] upon it all the way as I read. And my mind has been much entertained and delighted with the Scripture promises and prophecies of the future glorious advancement of Christ's kingdom on earth.

I have sometimes had a sense of the excellent fullness of Christ, and his meetness and suitableness as a Savior; whereby he has appeared to me, far above all, the chief of ten thousands.[24] And His blood and atonement has appeared sweet, and His righteousness sweet; which is always accompanied with an ardency of spirit, and inward strugglings and breathings and groanings, that cannot be uttered, to be emptied of myself and swallowed up in Christ.

Once, as I rid out into the woods for my health, Anno 1737, and having lit from my horse in a retired place, as my manner commonly has been, to walk for divine contemplation and prayer, I had a view, that for me was extraordinary, of the glory of the Son of God, as mediator between God and man, and his wonderful, great, full, pure and sweet grace and love, and meek and gentle condescension. This grace, that appeared to me so calm and sweet, appeared great above the heavens. The person of Christ appeared ineffably excellent, with an excellency great enough to swallow up all thought and conception, which continued, as near as I can judge, about an hour, which kept me, the bigger part of the time, in a flood of tears, and weeping aloud. I felt withal an ardency of soul to be, what I know not otherwise how to express, than to be emptied and annihilated; to lie in the dust, and to be full of Christ alone; to love him with a holy and pure love; to trust in him; to live upon him; to serve and follow him, and to be totally wrapt up in the fullness of Christ; and to be perfectly sanctified and made pure with a divine and heavenly purity. I have several other times had views very much of the same nature and that have had the same effects.

I have many times had a sense of the glory of the third person in the Trinity in his office of sanctifier; in his holy operations communicating divine light and life to the soul. God in the communications of his Holy Spirit has appeared as an infinite fountain of divine glory and sweetness, being full and sufficient to fill and satisfy the soul, pouring forth itself in sweet communications, like the sun in its glory, sweetly and pleasantly diffusing light and life.

I have sometimes had an affecting sense of the excellency of the Word of God, as a word of life; as the light of life; a sweet, excellent, life-giving word, accompanied with a thirsting after that word, that it might dwell richly in my heart.

I have often, since I lived in this town, had very affecting views of my own sinfulness and vileness; very frequently so as to hold me in a kind of loud weeping, sometimes for a considerable time together, so that I have often been forced to shut myself up.[25] I have had a vastly greater sense of my wickedness, and the

---

[23] Delighted.
[24] "My beloved is . . . the chiefest among ten thousand," from Song of Solomon 5:10.
[25] To meditate alone in his study.

badness of my heart, since my conversion, than ever I had before. It has often appeared to me, that if God should mark iniquity against me, I should appear the very worst of all mankind, of all that have been since the beginning of the world of this time, and that I should have by far the lowest place in hell. When others that have come to talk with me about their soul concerns have expressed the sense they have had of their own wickedness by saying that it seemed to them that they were as bad as the devil himself, I thought their expressions seemed exceeding faint and feeble to represent my wickedness. I thought I should wonder that they should content themselves with such expressions as these, if I had any reason to imagine that their sin bore any proportion to mine. It seemed to me I should wonder at myself if I should express my wickedness in such feeble terms as they did.

My wickedness, as I am in myself, has long appeared to me perfectly ineffable and infinitely swallowing up all thought and imagination, like an infinite deluge or infinite mountains over my head. I know not how to express better what my sins appear to me to be than by heaping infinite upon infinite, and multiplying infinite by infinite. I go about very often, for this many years, with these expressions in my mind and in my mouth, "Infinite upon infinite. Infinite upon infinite!" When I look into my heart and take a view of my wickedness, it looks like an abyss infinitely deeper than hell. And it appears to me that were it not for free grace, exalted and raised up to the infinite height of all the fullness and glory of the great Jehovah,[26] and the arm of his power and grace stretched forth, in all the majesty of his power and in all the glory of his sovereignty, I should appear sunk down in my sins infinitely below hell itself, far beyond sight of everything but the piercing eye of God's grace, that can pierce even down to such a depth and to the bottom of such an abyss.

And yet I be not in the least inclined to think that I have a greater conviction of sin than ordinary. It seems to me my conviction of sin is exceeding small and faint. It appears to me enough to amaze me that I have no more sense of my sin. I know certainly that I have very little sense of my sinfulness. That my sins appear to me so great don't seem to me to be because I have so much more conviction of sin than other Christians, but because I am so much worse and have so much more wickedness to be convinced of. When I have had these turns of weeping and crying for my sins, I thought I knew in the time of it that my repentance was nothing to my sin.

I have greatly longed of late for a broken heart and to lie low before God. And when I ask for humility of God, I can't bear the thoughts of being no more humble than other Christians. It seems to me that though their degrees of humility may be suitable for them, yet it would be a vile self-exaltation in me not to be the lowest in humility of all mankind. Others speak of their longing to be humbled to the dust. Though that may be a proper expression for them I always think for myself that I ought to be humbled down below hell. 'Tis an expression that it has long been natural for me to use in prayer to God. I ought to lie infinitely low before God.

It is affecting to me to think how ignorant I was, when I was a young Christian, of the bottomless, infinite depths of wickedness, pride, hypocrisy and deceit left in my heart.

I have vastly a greater sense of my universal, exceeding dependence on God's grace and strength and mere good pleasure, of late, than I used formerly to have,

[26] In the Old Testament, the Hebrew God.

and have experienced more of an abhorrence of my own righteousness. The thought of any comfort or job, arising in me, on any consideration or reflection on my own amiableness, or any of my performances or experiences, or any goodness of heart or life is nauseous and detestable to me. And yet I am greatly afflicted with a proud and self-righteous spirit, much more sensibly than I used to be formerly. I see that serpent rising and putting forth its head, continually, everywhere, all around me.

Though it seems to me that in some respects I was a far better Christian for two or three years after my first conversion than I am now, and lived in a more constant delight and pleasure, yet of late years I have had a more full and constant sense of the absolute sovereignty of God and a delight in that sovereignty, and have had more of a sense of the glory of Christ as a mediator as revealed in the gospel. On one Saturday night in particular, had a particular discovery of the excellency of the gospel of Christ, above all other doctrines, so that I could not but say to myself, "This is my chosen light, my chosen doctrine," and of Christ, "This is my chosen prophet." It appeared to me to be sweet beyond all expression to follow Christ and to be taught and enlightened and instructed by him, to learn of him, and live to him.

Another Saturday night, January, [1739], had such a sense how sweet and blessed a thing it was to walk in the way of duty, to do that which was right and meet to be done and agreeable to the holy mind of God, that it caused me to break forth into a kind of a loud weeping, which held me some time, so that I was forced to shut myself up, and fasten the doors. I could not but as it were cry out, "How happy are they which do that which is right in the sight of God! They are blessed indeed, they are the happy ones!" I had at the same time, a very affecting sense how meet and suitable it was that God should govern the world, and order all things according to his own pleasure, and I rejoiced in it, and God reigned, and that his will was done.

1740, 1765

SINNERS IN THE HANDS OF AN ANGRY GOD*

DEUTERONOMY XXXII: 35

Their foot shall slide in due time.[1]

In this verse is threatened the vengeance of God on the wicked unbelieving Israelites, who were God's visible people, and who lived under the means of grace;[2] but who, nonwithstanding all God's wonderful works towards them, remained (as verse 28)[3] void of counsel, having no understanding in them. Under all

---

* Edwards preached this sermon on July 8, 1741, in Enfield, Connecticut.

[1] "To me belongeth vengeance, and recompense; their foot shall slide in due time: for the day of their calamity is at hand . . . ."

[2] By the laws of the Ten Commandments; in comparison, the Puritans' "means of grace" meant preaching God's word, and administering the sacraments of the Lord's supper and baptism.

[3] "They are a nation void of counsel, neither is there any understanding in them," from Deuteronomy 32:28.

the cultivations of heaven, they brought forth bitter and poisonous fruit; as in the two verses next preceding the text.[4]—The expression I have chosen for my text, Their foot shall slide in due time, seems to imply the following things, relating to the punishment and destruction to which these wicked Israelites were exposed.

1. That they were always exposed to destruction; as one that stands or walks in slippery places is always exposed to fall. This is implied in the manner of their destruction coming upon them, being represented by their foot sliding. The same is expressed, Psalm lxxiii: 18. "Surely thou didst set them in slippery places; thou castedst them down into destruction."

2. It implies, that they were always exposed to sudden unexpected destruction. As he that walks in slippery places is every moment liable to fall, he cannot foresee one moment whether he shall stand or fall the next; and when he does fall, he falls at once without warning: which is also expressed in Psalm lxxiii: 18, 19. "Surely thou didst set them in slippery places; thou castedst them down into destruction: How are they brought into desolation as in a moment!"

3. Another thing implied is, that they are liable to fall of themselves, without being thrown down by the hand of another; as he that stands or walks on slippery ground needs nothing but his own weight to throw him down.

4. That the reason why they are not fallen already, and do not fall now, is only that God's appointed time is not come. For it is said, that when that due time, or appointed time comes, their foot shall slide. Then they shall be left to fall, as they are inclined by their own weight. God will not hold them up in these slippery places any longer, but will let them go; and then, at that very instant, they shall fall into destruction; as he that stands on such slippery declining ground, on the edge of a pit, he cannot stand alone, when he is let go he immediately falls and is lost.

The observation from the words that I would now insist upon is this. "There is nothing that keeps wicked men at any one moment out of hell, but the mere pleasure of God." By the mere pleasure of God, I mean his sovereign pleasure, his arbitrary will, restrained by no obligation, hindered by no manner of difficulty, any more than if nothing else but God's mere will had in the least degree, or in any respect whatsoever, any hand in the preservation of wicked men one moment. The truth of this observation may appear by the following considerations.

1. There is no want of power in God to cast wicked men into hell at any moment. Men's hands cannot be strong when God rises up. The strongest have no power to resist him, nor can any deliver out of his hands. He is not only able to cast wicked men into hell, but he can most easily do it. Sometimes an earthly prince meets with a great deal of difficulty to subdue a rebel, who has found means to fortify himself, and has made himself strong by the numbers of his followers. But it is not so with God. There is no fortress that is any defense from the power of God. Though hand join in hand, and vast multitudes of God's enemies combine and associate themselves, they are easily broken in pieces. They are as great heaps of light chaff before the whirlwind; or large quantities of dry stubble before devouring flames. We find it easy to tread on and crush a worm that we see crawling on the earth; so it is easy for us to cut or singe a slender thread that any thing hangs by: thus easy is it for God, when he pleases, to cast his enemies down

---

[4] "For their vine is of the vine of Sodom, and fields of Gomorrah: their grapes are grapes of gall, their clusters are bitter: their wine is the poison of dragons, and the cruel venom of asps," from Deuteronomy 32:32–33; in Genesis 19:28 Sodom and Gomorrah were cities destroyed for their wickedness.

to hell. What are we, that we should think to stand before him, at whose rebuke the earth trembles, and before whom the rocks are thrown down?

2. They deserve to be cast into hell; so that divine justice never stands in the way, it makes no objection against God's using his power at any moment to destroy them. Yea, on the contrary, justice calls aloud for an infinite punishment of their sins. Divine justice says of the tree that brings forth such grapes of Sodom, "Cut it down, why cumbereth it the ground?" Luke xiii: 7. The sword of divine justice is every moment brandished over their heads, and it is nothing but the hand of arbitrary mercy, and God's mere will, that holds it back.

3. They are already under a sentence of condemnation to hell. They do not only justly deserve to be cast down thither, but the sentence of the law of God, that eternal and immutable rule of righteousness that God has fixed between him and mankind, is gone out against them, and stands against them; so that they are bound over already to hell. John iii: 18, "He that believeth not is condemned already." So that every unconverted man properly belongs to hell; that is his place; from thence he is, John viii: 23. "Ye are from beneath:" and thither he is bound; it is the place that justice, and God's word, and the sentence of his unchangeable law assign to him.

4. They are now the objects of that very same anger and wrath of God, that is expressed in the torments of hell. And the reason why they do not go down to hell at each moment, is not because God, in whose power they are, is not then very angry with them; as he is with many miserable creatures now tormented in hell, who there feel and bear the fierceness of his wrath. Yea, God is a great deal more angry with great numbers that are now on earth: yea, doubtless, with many that are now in this congregation, who it may be are at ease, than he is with many of those who are now in the flames of hell.

So that it is not because God is unmindful of their wickedness, and does not resent it, that he does not let loose his hand and cut them off. God is not altogether such an one as themselves, though they may imagine him to be so. The wrath of God burns against them, their damnation does not slumber; the pit is prepared, the fire is made ready, the furnace is now hot, ready to receive them; the flames do now rage and glow. The glittering sword is whet,[5] and held over them, and the pit hath opened its mouth under them.

5. The devil stands ready to fall upon them, and seize them as his own, at what moment God shall permit him. They belong to him; he has their souls in his possession, and under his dominion. The scripture represents them as his goods, Luke xi: 12.[6] The devils watch them; they are ever by them at their right hand; they stand waiting for them, like greedy hungry lions that see their prey, and expect to have it, but are for the present kept back. If God should withdraw his hand, by which they are restrained, they would in one moment fly upon their poor souls. The old serpent is gaping for them; hell opens its mouth wide to receive them; and if God should permit it, they would be hastily swallowed up and lost.

6. There are in the souls of wicked men those hellish principles reigning, that would presently kindle and flame out into hell fire, if it were not for God's restraints. There is laid in the very nature of carnal men, a foundation for the torments of hell. There are those corrupt principles, in reigning power in them, and in full possession of them, that are seeds of hell fire. These principles are active and powerful, exceeding violent in their nature, and if it were not for the restrain-

---

[5] Sharpened.   [6] "Or if he shall ask an egg, will he offer him a scorpion?"

ing hand of God upon them, they would soon break out, they would flame out after the same manner as the same corruptions, the same enmity does in the hearts of damned souls, and would beget the same torments as they do in them. The souls of the wicked are in scripture compared to the troubled seas, Isaiah lvii: 20.[7] For the present, God restrains their wickedness by his mighty power, as he does the raging waves of the troubled sea, saying, "Hitherto shalt thou come, but no further;"[8] but if God should withdraw that restraining power, it would soon carry all before it. Sin is the ruin and misery of the soul; it is destructive in its nature; and if God should leave it without restraint, there would need nothing else to make the soul perfectly miserable. The corruption of the heart of man is immoderate and boundless in its fury; and while wicked men live here, it is like fire pent up by God's restraints, whereas if it were let loose, it would set on fire the course of nature; and as the heart is now a sink of sin, so if sin was not restrained, it would immediately turn the soul into a fiery oven, or a furnace of fire and brimstone.

7. It is no security to wicked men for one moment, that there are no visible means of death at hand. It is no security to a natural man, that he is now in health, and that he does not see which way he should now immediately go out of the world by any accident, and that there is no visible danger in any respect in his circumstances. The manifold and continual experience of the world in all ages, shows this is no evidence, that a man is not on the very brink of eternity, and that the next step will not be into another world. The unseen, unthought-of ways and means of persons going suddenly out of the world are innumerable and inconceivable. Unconverted men walk over the pit of hell on a rotten covering, and there are innumerable places in this covering so weak that they will not bear their weight, and these places are not seen. The arrows of death fly unseen at noonday;[9] the sharpest sight cannot discern them. God has so many different unsearchable ways of taking wicked men out of the world and sending them to hell, that there is nothing to make it appear, that God had need to be at the expence of a miracle, or go out of the ordinary course of his providence, to destroy any wicked man, at any moment. All the means that there are of sinners going out of the world, are so in God's hands, and so universally and absolutely subject to his power and determination, that it does not depend at all the less on the mere will of God, whether sinners shall at any moment go to hell, than if means were never made use of, or at all concerned in the case.

8. Natural men's prudence and care to preserve their own lives, or the care of others to preserve them, do not secure them a moment. To this, divine providence and universal experience do also bear testimony. There is this clear evidence that men's own wisdom is no security to them from death; that if it were otherwise we should see some difference between the wise and politic men of the world, and others, with regard to their liableness to early and unexpected death: but how is it in fact? Ecclesiastes ii: 16. "How dieth the wise man? even as the fool."

9. All wicked men's pains and contrivance which they use to escape hell, while they continue to reject Christ, and so remain wicked men, do not secure them from hell one moment. Almost every natural[10] man that hears of hell, flatters himself that he shall escape it; he depends upon himself for his own security; he

---

[7] "But the wicked are like the troubled sea, when it cannot rest, whose waters cast up mire and dirt."

[8] Job 38:11.

[9] "Thou shalt not be afraid for the terror by night; nor for the arrow that flieth by day," from Psalm 91:5.

[10] Unsaved.

flatters himself in what he has done, in what he is now doing, or what he intends to do. Every one lays out matters in his own mind how he shall avoid damnation, and flatters himself that he contrives well for himself, and that his schemes will not fail. They hear indeed that there are but few saved, and that the greater part of men that have died heretofore are gone to hell; but each one imagines that he lays out matters better for his own escape than others have done. He does not intend to come to that place of torment; he says within himself, that he intends to take effectual care, and to order matters so for himself as not to fail.

But the foolish children of men miserably delude themselves in their own schemes, and in confidence in their own strength and wisdom; they trust to nothing but a shadow. The greater part of those who heretofore have lived under the same means of grace, and are now dead, are undoubtedly gone to hell; and it was not because they were not as wise as those who are now alive: it was not because they did not lay out matters as well for themselves to secure their own escape. If we could speak with them, and inquire of them, one by one, whether they expected, when alive, and when they used to hear about hell, ever to be the subjects of that misery: we doutless, should hear one and another reply, "No, I never intended to come here: I have laid out matters otherwise in my mind; I thought I should contrive well for myself: I thought my scheme good. I intended to take effectual care; but it came upon me unexpected; I did not look for it at that time, and in that manner; it came as a thief: Death outwitted me: God's wrath was too quick for me. Oh, my cursed foolishness! I was flattering myself, and pleasing myself with vain dreams of what I would do hereafter; and when I was saying, Peace and safety, then suddenly destruction came upon me."

10. God has laid himself under no obligation, by any promise to keep any natural man out of hell one moment. God certainly has made no promises either of eternal life, or of any deliverance or preservation from eternal death, but what are contained in the covenant of grace,[11] the promises that are given in Christ, in whom all the promises are yea and amen. But surely they have no interest in the promises of the covenant of grace who are not the children of the covenant, who do not believe in any of the promises, and have no interest in the Mediator of the covenant.[12]

So that, whatever some have imagined and pretended about promises made to natural men's earnest seeking and knocking,[13] it is plain and manifest, that whatever pains a natural man takes in religion, whatever prayers he makes, till he believes in Christ, God is under no manner of obligation to keep him a moment from eternal destruction.

So that, thus it is that natural men are held in the hand of God, over the pit of hell; they have deserved the fiery pit, and are already sentenced to it; and God is dreadfully provoked, his anger is as great towards them as to those that are actually suffering the executions of the fierceness of his wrath in hell, and they have done nothing in the least to appease or abate that anger, neither is God in the least bound by any promise to hold them up one moment; the devil is waiting for them, hell is gaping for them, the flames gather and flash about them, and would fain lay hold on them, and swallow them up; the fire bent up in their own hearts is struggling to break out: and they have no interest in any Mediator, there are no means

---

[11] The covenant by which God restored the possibility of salvation (due to Jesus' atonement), previously unattainable because of the Covenant of Works, made by God after the fall of Adam.
[12] Jesus.   [13] To gain salvation.

within reach that can be any security to them. In short, they have no refuge, nothing to take hold of; all that preserves them every moment is the mere arbitrary will, and uncovenanted, unobliged forbearance of an incensed God.

Application

The use of this awful[14] subject may be for awakening unconverted persons in this congregation. This that you have heard is the case of every one of you that are out of Christ. That world of misery, that lake of burning brimstone, is extended abroad under you. There is the dreadful pit of the glowing flames and of the wrath of God; there is hell's wide gaping mouth open; and you have nothing to stand upon, nor any thing to take hold of: there is nothing between you and hell but the air; it is only the power and mere pleasure of God that holds you up.

You probably are not sensible[15] of this; you find you are kept out of hell, but do not see the hand of God in it; but look at other things, as the good state of your bodily constitution, your care of your own life, and the means you use for your own preservation. But indeed these things are nothing; if God should withdraw his hand, they would avail no more to keep you from falling, than the thin air to hold up a person that is suspended in it.

Your wickedness makes you as it were heavy as lead, and to tend downwards with great weight and pressure towards hell; and if God should let you go, you would immediately sink and swiftly descend and plunge into the bottomless gulf, and your healthy constitution, and your own care and prudence, and best contrivance, and all your righteousness, would have no mere influence to uphold you and keep you out of hell, than a spider's web would have to stop a fallen rock. Were it not for the sovereign pleasure of God, the earth would not bear you one moment; for you are a burden to it; the creation groans with you; the creature[16] is made subject to the bondage of your corruption, not willingly; the sun does not willingly shine upon you to give you light to serve sin and Satan; the earth does not willingly yield her increase to satisfy your lusts; nor is it willingly a stage for your wickedness to be acted upon; the air does not willingly serve you for breath to maintain the flame of life in your vitals, while you spend your life in the service of God's enemies. God's creatures are good, and were made for men to serve God with, and do not willingly subserve to any other purpose, and groan when they are abused to purposes so directly contrary to their nature and end. And the world would spew you out, were it not for the sovereign hand of him who hath subjected it in hope. There are black clouds of God's wrath now hanging directly over your heads, full of the dreadful storm, and big with thunder; and were it not for the restraining hand of God, it would immediately burst forth upon you. The sovereign pleasure of God, for the present, stays his rough wind; otherwise it would come with fury, and your destruction would come like a whirlwind, and you would be like the chaff of the summer threshing floor.

The wrath of God is like great waters that are dammed for the present; they increase more and more, and rise higher and higher, till an outlet is given; and the longer the stream is stopped, the more rapid and mighty is its course, when once it is let loose. It is true, that judgment against your evil works has not been executed hitherto; the floods of God's vengeance have been withheld; but your guilt in the

---

[14] Awesome.   [15] Aware.   [16] Body.

mean time is constantly increasing, and you are every day treasuring up more wrath; the waters are constantly rising, and waxing more and more mighty; and there is nothing but the mere pleasure of God, that holds the waters back, that are unwilling to be stopped, and press hard to go forward. If God should only withdraw his hand from the flood-gate, it would immediately fly open, and the fiery floods of the fierceness and wrath of God, would rush forth with inconceivable fury, and would come upon you with omnipotent power; and if your strength were ten thousand times greater than it is, yea, ten thousand times greater than the strength of the stoutest, sturdiest devil in hell, it would be nothing to withstand or endure it.

The bow of God's wrath is bent, and the arrow made ready on the string, and justice bends the arrow at your heart, and strains the bow, and it is nothing but the mere pleasure of God, and that of an angry God, without any promise or obligation at all, that keeps the arrow one moment from being made drunk with your blood. Thus all you that never passed under a great change of heart, by the mighty power of the Spirit of God upon your souls; all you that were never born again, and made new creatures, and raised from being dead in sin, to a state of new, and before altogether unexperienced light and life, are in the hands of an angry God. However you may have reformed your life in many things, and may have had religious affections, and may keep up a form of religion in your families and closets,[17] and in the house of God, it is nothing but his mere pleasure that keeps you from being this moment swallowed up in everlasting destruction. However unconvinced you may now be of the truth of what you hear, by and by you will be fully convinced of it. Those that are gone from being in the like circumstances with you, see that it was so with them; for destruction came suddenly upon most of them; when they expected nothing of it, and while they were saying, peace and safety: now they see, that those things on which they depended for peace and safety, were nothing but thin air and empty shadows.

The God that holds you over the pit of hell, much as one holds a spider, or some loathsome insect over the fire, abhors you, and is dreadfully provoked: his wrath towards you burns like fire; he looks upon you as worthy of nothing else, but to be cast into the fire; he is of purer eyes than to bear to have you in his sight; you are ten thousand times more abominable in his eyes, than the most hateful venomous serpent is in ours. You have offended him infinitely more than ever a stubborn rebel did his prince; and yet it is nothing but his hand that holds you from falling into the fire every moment. It is to be ascribed to nothing else, that you did not go to hell the last night; that you was suffered to awake again in this world, after you closed your eyes to sleep. And there is no other reason to be given, why you have not dropped into hell since you arose in the morning, but that God's hand has held you up. There is no other reason to be given why you have not gone to hell, since you have sat here in the house of God, provoking his pure eyes by your sinful wicked manner of attending his solemn worship. Yea, there is nothing else that is to be given as a reason why you do not this very moment drop down into hell.

O sinner! Consider the fearful danger you are in: it is a great furnace of wrath, a wide and bottomless pit, full of the fire of wrath, that you are held over in the hand of that God, whose wrath is provoked and incensed as much against you, as against many of the damned in hell. You hang by a slender thread, with the flames

---

[17] Study rooms for meditation.

of divine wrath flashing about it, and ready every moment to singe it, and burn it asunder: and you have no interest in any Mediator, and nothing to lay hold of to save yourself, nothing to keep off the flames of wrath, nothing of your own, nothing that you ever have done, nothing that you can do, to induce God to spare you one moment.—And consider here more particularly,

1. Whose wrath it is: it is the wrath of the infinite God. If it were only the wrath of man, though it were of the most potent prince, it would be comparatively little to be regarded. The wrath of kings is very much dreaded, especially of absolute monarchs, who have the possessions and lives of their subjects wholly in their power, to be disposed of at their mere will. Proverbs xx: 2, "The fear of a king is as the roaring of a lion: Whoso provoketh him to anger, sinneth against his own soul." The subject that very much enrages an arbitrary prince, is liable to suffer the most extreme torments that human art can invent, or human power can inflict. But the greatest earthly potentates in their greatest majesty and strength, and when clothed in their greatest terrors, are but feeble, despicable worms of the dust, in comparison of the great and almighty Creator and King of heaven and earth. It is but little that they can do, when most enraged, and when they have exerted the utmost of their fury. All the kings of the earth, before God, are as grasshoppers; they are nothing, and less than nothing: both their love and their hatred is to be despised. The wrath of the great King of kings, is as much more terrible than theirs, as his majesty is greater. Luke xii: 4, 5, "And I say unto you, my friends, Be not afraid of them that kill the body, and after that, have no more that they can do. But I will forewarn you whom you shall fear: fear him, which after he hath killed, hath power to cast into hell; yea, I say unto you, Fear him."

2. It is the fierceness of his wrath that you are exposed to. We often read of the fury of God; as in Isaiah lix: 18. "According to their deeds, accordingly he will repay fury to his adversaries." So Isaiah lxvi: 15, "For behold, the Lord will come with fire, and with his chariots like a whirlwind, to render his anger with fury, and his rebuke with flames of fire." And in many other places. So, Revelation xix: 15, we read of "the wine press of the fierceness and wrath of Almighty God." The words are exceeding terrible. If it had only been said, "the wrath of God," the words would have implied that which is infinitely dreadful: but it is "the fierceness and wrath of God." The fury of God! the fierceness of Jehovah![18] Oh, how dreadful must that be! Who can utter or conceive what such expressions carry in them! But it is also "the fierceness and wrath of Almighty God." As though there would be a very great manifestation of his almighty power in what the fierceness of his wrath should inflict, as though omnipotence should be as it were enraged, and exerted, as men are wont to exert their strength in the fierceness of their wrath. Oh! then, what will be the consequence! What will become of the poor worms that shall suffer it! Whose hands can be strong? And whose heart can endure? To what a dreadful, inexpressible, inconceivable depth of misery must the poor creature be sunk who shall be the subject of this!

Consider this, you that are here present, that yet remain in an unregenerate state. That God will execute the fierceness of his anger, implies, that he will inflict wrath without any pity. When God beholds the ineffable extremity of your case, and sees your torment to be so vastly disproportioned to your strength, and sees how your poor soul is crushed, and sinks down, as it were, into an infinite gloom; he will have no compassion upon you, he will not forbear the executions of his

---

[18] In the Old Testament, The Hebrew God.

wrath, or in the least lighten his hand; there shall be no moderation or mercy, nor will God then at all stay his rough wind; he will have no regard to your welfare, nor be at all careful lest you should suffer too much in any other sense, than only that you not suffer beyond what strict justice requires. Nothing shall be withheld, because it is so hard for you to bear. Ezekiel viii: 18, "Therefore will I also deal in fury: mine eye shall not spare, neither will I have pity; and though they cry in mine ears with a loud voice, yet I will not hear them." Now God stands ready to pity you; this is a day of mercy; you may cry now with some encouragement of obtaining mercy. But when once the day of mercy is past, your most lamentable and dolorous cries and shrieks will be in vain; you will be wholly lost and thrown away of God, as to any regard to your welfare. God will have no other use to put you to, but to suffer misery; you shall be continued in being to no other end; for you will be a vessel of wrath fitted to destruction; and there will be no other use of this vessel, but to be filled full of wrath. God will be so far from pitying you when you cry to him, that it is said he will only "laugh and mock," Proverbs i: 25, 26,[19] etc.

How awful are those words, Isaiah lxiii: 3, which are the words of the great God. "I will tread them in mine anger, and will trample them in my fury, and their blood shall be sprinkled upon my garments, and I will stain all my raiment. It is perhaps impossible to conceive of words that carry in them greater manifestations of these three things, viz. contempt, and hatred, and fierceness of indignation. If you cry to God to pity you, he will be so far from pitying you in your doleful case, or showing you the least regard or favor, that instead of that, he will only tread you under foot. And though he will know that you cannot bear the weight of omnipotence treading upon you, yet he will not regard that, but he will crush you under his feet without mercy; he will crush out your blood, and make it fly, and it shall be sprinkled on his garments, so as to stain all his raiment. He will not only hate you, but he will have you, in the utmost contempt: no place shall be thought fit for you, but under his feet to be trodden down as the mire of the streets.

3. The misery you are exposed to is that which God will inflict to that end, that he might show what that wrath of Jehovah is. God hath had it on his heart to show to angels and men, both how excellent his love is, and also how terrible his wrath is. Sometimes earthly kings have a mind to show how terrible their wrath is, by the extreme punishments they would execute on those that would provoke them. Nebuchadnezzar, that mighty and haughty monarch of the Chaldean[20] empire, was willing to show his wrath when enraged with Shadrack, Meshech, and Abednego;[21] and accordingly gave orders that the burning fiery furnace should be heated seven times hotter than it was before; doubtless, it was raised to the utmost degree of fierceness that human art could raise it.[22] But the great God is also willing to show his wrath, and magnify his awful majesty and mighty power in the extreme sufferings of his enemies. Romans ix: 22, "What if God, willing to show his wrath, and to make his power known, endure with much long-suffering the vessels of wrath fitted to destruction?" And seeing this is his design, and what he has determined, even to show how terrible the unrestrained wrath, the fury and fierceness of Jehovah is, he will do it to effect. There will be something accom-

---

[19] "But ye have set at nought all my counsel, and would none of my reproof: I will also laugh at your calamity; I will mock you when your fear cometh."

[20] A Semitic people related to the Babylonians.

[21] In Daniel 3:12–27 three captives who emerged unharmed from a fiery furnace.

[22] Daniel 3:1–30.

plished and brought to pass that will be dreadful with a witness. When the great and angry God hath risen up and executed his awful vengeance on the poor sinner, and the wretch is actually suffering the infinite weight and power of his indignation, then will God call upon the whole universe to behold that awful majesty and mighty power that is to be seen in it. Isaiah xxxiii:12–14, "And the people shall be as the burnings of lime, as thorns cut up shall they be burnt in the fire. Hear ye that are far off, what I have done; and ye that are near, acknowledge my might. The sinners in Zion are afraid; fearfulness hath surprised the hypocrites," etc.

Thus it will be with you that are in an unconverted state, if you continue in it; the infinite might, and majesty, and terribleness of the omnipotent God shall be magnified upon you, in the ineffable strength of your torments. You shall be tormented in the presence of the holy angels, and in the presence of the Lamb;[23] and when you shall be in this state of suffering, the glorious inhabitants of heaven shall go forth and look on the awful spectacle, that they may see what the wrath and fierceness of the Almighty is; and when they have seen it, they will fall down and adore that great power and majesty. Isaiah lxvi: 23, 24, "And it shall come to pass, that from one new moon to another, and from one sabbath to another, shall all flesh come to worship before me, saith the Lord. And they shall go forth and look upon the carcasses of the men that have transgressed against me; for their worm[24] shall not die, neither shall their fire be quenched, and they shall be an abhorring unto all flesh."

4. It is everlasting wrath. It would be dreadful to suffer this fierceness and wrath of Almighty God one moment; but you must suffer it to all eternity. There will be no end to this exquisite horrible misery. When you look forward, you shall see a long for ever, a boundless duration before you, which will swallow up your thoughts, and amaze your soul; and you will absolutely despair of ever having any deliverance, any end, any mitigation, any rest at all. You will know certainly that you must wear out long ages, millions of millions of ages, in wrestling and conflicting with this almighty merciless vengeance; and then when you have so done, when so many ages have actually been spent by you in this manner, you will know that all is but a point to what remains. So that your punishment will indeed be infinite. Oh, who can express what the state of a soul in such circumstances is! All that we can possibly say about it, gives but a very feeble, faint representation of it; it is inexpressible and inconceivable: For "who knows the power of God's anger?"[25]

How dreadful is the state of those that are daily and hourly in the danger of this great wrath and infinite misery! But this is the dismal case of every soul in this congregation that has not been born again, however moral and strict, sober and religious, they may otherwise be. Oh that you would consider it, whether you be young or old! There is reason to think, that there are many in this congregation now hearing this discourse, that will actually be the subjects of this very misery to all eternity. We know not who they are, or in what seats they sit, or what thoughts they now have. It may be they are now at ease, and hear all these things without much disturbance, and are now flattering themselves that they are not the persons, promising themselves that they shall escape. If we knew that there was one person, and but one, in the whole congregation, that was to be the subject of this

---

[23] Jesus.   [24] The worm that gnaws at their carcasses.
[25] "Who knoweth the power of thine anger? even according to thy fear, so is thy wrath," from Psalm 90:11.

misery, what an awful thing would it be to think of! If we knew who it was, what an awful sight would it be to see such a person! How might all the rest of the congregation lift up a lamentable and bitter cry over him! But, alas! instead of one, how many is it likely will remember this discourse in hell? And it would be a wonder, if some that are now present should not be in hell in a very short time, even before this year is out. And it would be no wonder if some persons, that now sit here, in some seats of this meeting-house, in health, quiet and secure, should be there before to-morrow morning. Those of you that finally continue in a natural condition, that shall keep out of hell longest will be there in a little time! your damnation does not slumber; it will come swiftly, and, in all probability, very suddenly upon many of you. You have reason to wonder that you are not already in hell. It is doubtless the case of some whom you have seen and known, that never deserved hell more than you, and that heretofore appeared as likely to have been now alive as you. Their case is past all hope; they are crying in extreme misery and perfect despair; but here you are in the land of the living and in the house of God, and have an opportunity to obtain salvation. What would not those poor damned hopeless souls give for one day's opportunity such as you now enjoy!

And now you have an extraordinary opportunity, a day wherein Christ has thrown the door of mercy wide open, and stands in calling and crying with a loud voice to poor sinners; a day wherein many are flocking to him, and pressing into the kingdom of God. Many are daily coming from the east, west, north and south; many that were very lately in the same miserable condition that you are in, are now in a happy state, with their hearts filled with love to him who has loved them, and washed them from their sins in his own blood, and rejoicing in hope of the glory of God. How awful is it to be left behind at such a day! To see so many others feasting, while you are pining and perishing! To see so many rejoicing and singing for joy of heart, while you have cause to mourn for sorrow of heart, and howl for vexation of spirit! How can you rest one moment in such a condition? Are not your souls as precious as the souls of the people at Suffield,[26] where they are flocking from day to day to Christ?

Are there not many here who have lived long in the world, and are not to this day born again? and so are aliens from the commonwealth of Israel,[27] and have done nothing ever since they have lived, but treasure up wrath against the day of wrath? Oh, sirs, your case, in an especial manner, is extremely dangerous. Your guilt and hardness of heart is extremely great. Do you not see how generally persons of your years are passed over and left, in the present remarkable and wonderful dispensation of God's mercy? You had need to consider yourselves, and awake thoroughly out of sleep. You cannot bear the fierceness and wrath of the infinite God. And you, young men, and young women, will you neglect this precious season which you now enjoy, when so many others of your age are renouncing all youthful vanities, and flocking to Christ? You especially have now an extraordinary opportunity; but if you neglect it, it will soon be with you as with those persons who spent all the precious days of youth in sin, and are now come to such a dreadful pass in blindness and hardness. And you, children, who are unconverted, do not you know that you are going down to hell, to bear the dreadful wrath of that God, who is now angry with you every day and every night? Will

---

[26] Dwight's note: "A town in the neighborhood," in Connecticut.
[27] Are not among the Chosen, the elect.

you be content to be the children of the devil, when so many other children in the land are converted, and are become the holy and happy children of the King of kings?

And let every one that is yet of Christ, and hanging over the pit of hell, whether they be old men and women, or middle aged, or young people, or little children, now hearken to the loud calls of God's word and providence. This acceptable year of the Lord, a day of such great favors to some, will doubtless be a day of as remarkable vengeance to others. Men's hearts harden, and their guilt increases apace at such a day as this, if they neglect their souls; and never was there so great danger of such persons being given up to hardness of heart and blindness of mind. God seems now to be hastily gathering in his elect in all parts of the land; and probably the greater part of adult persons that ever shall be saved, will be brought in now in a little time, and that it will be as it was on the great out-pouring of the Spirit upon the Jews in the apostles' days;[28] the election will obtain, and the rest will be blinded. If this should be the case with you, you will eternally curse this day, and will curse the day that ever you was born, to see such a season of the pouring out of God's Spirit, and will wish that you had died and gone to hell before you had seen it. Now undoubtedly it is, as it was in the days of John the Baptist, the axe is in an extraordinary manner laid at the root of the trees, that every tree which brings not forth good fruit, may be hewn down and cast into the fire.[29]

Therefore, let every one that is out of Christ, now awake and fly from the wrath to come. The wrath of Almighty God is now undoubtedly hanging over a great part of this congregation: Let every one fly out of Sodom: "Haste and escape for your lives, look not behind you, escape to the mountain, lest you be consumed."[30]

1741

Benjamin Franklin
(1706–1790)

One of fifteen children, Benjamin Franklin was born in 1706 in Boston. His father, Josiah Franklin, a candle and soap maker, had come to America from England in 1682. Franklin's mother, Abiah Folger, was the daughter of a teacher, and the Franklins valued education highly, sending young Benjamin to the Boston Grammar School. Eventually unable to afford this luxury, Franklin was forced to return to work in the family business, which he disliked intensely. To provide him with a more stimulating occupation, Josiah Franklin apprenticed Benjamin at age twelve, to his older brother James, a printer. Under the pseudonym Silence Dogood, Benjamin Franklin, an eager student, published in his half-brother's newspaper; when James was imprisoned in 1722 for offending Massachusetts authorities, the paper was left in Ben's care, although he was only sixteen. The experience

---

[28] In Acts 2, Peter cautions a group to repent and to be converted.
[29] A paraphrase of Matthew 3:10.   [30] Genesis 19:17.

inspired Franklin's desire for independence, and one year later he abandoned his apprenticeship—a punishable offense—and left Boston for Philadelphia. There he flourished as a
printer, and by age twenty-four was the publisher of the *Pennsylvania Gazette* and had
commenced publication of *Poor Richard's Almanac* (1733–1758), issued under the pseudonym Richard Saunders. These immensely popular almanacs contain astronomical and
astrological information and aphoristic wisdom with an emphasis on frugality, such as "a
penny saved is a penny earned." The printing shop, the newspaper, and the almanacs made
Franklin very wealthy and able to retire at age forty-two from full-time business.

Franklin, whose image and life were popularized by the wide circulation of his *Autobiography* (1771–1790, published in entirety in 1867), came to represent the American
Dream realized and actualized. His father had not provided him rank and privilege, and
Franklin was able to rise from "rags to riches" in the New World during his lifetime. Not
only was he wealthy at a relatively early age, but he became one of the most significant
figures in the era of the American Revolution: a signer of the Declaration of Independence,
a framer of the Constitution, and a negotiator of the Treaty of Paris (by which the Revolutionary War was ended in 1783). Franklin was a skilled writer as well. The *Autobiography*
is his most significant contribution to the development of American literature and is one of
the most widely circulated American works ever printed. The *Autobiography* reader must
distinguish between real events of Franklin's life and the image of Franklin that appears in
that text. The real events of the *Autobiography* carry the reader only to Franklin at age
fifty-nine, though he lived to be eighty-four. Yet, the image of Franklin as perpetuated by
the *Autobiography* is immortal. In a scant sixty years the *Autobiography's* subject moves
from youthful apprenticeship to great wealth and prominence in public life. The image
developed in the *Autobiography* creates a formula for success in America, a diagram by
which a person may realize the secular American dream and enjoy its benefits while contributing to the community.

This image is as important as Franklin's life itself, for the *Autobiography* was translated
into many languages during the nineteenth century. The account gave the world some idea
of the type of new nation that was evolving under the highly experimental government,
which was called "Democracy in America" (1835–1840) by Alexis de Tocqueville, a
Frenchman who visited the United States in its infancy. As Ambassador to France for the
new nation, Franklin established himself as a representative American and was known as
being shrewd, politically tough, and extremely clever. That the *Autobiography* was initially published in French indicates just how completely immersed in European culture
Franklin's image had become by the 1790s, following his death. This account was further
popularized in America through translation and by the virtual resetting of the text by Parson Mason Weems, whose *Life of Benjamin Franklin* (1815) was one of a series of biographies Weems wrote and published to give the new nation an instant galaxy of heroes.
These biographies were credible in their authority to report the events of the early political
leaders' lives. However, much of what the accounts contain is image-making and the stuff
of mythology. In Weems's *The Life and Memorable Actions of George Washington*
(1800?), for example, we find for the only time in American literature the story of Washington cutting the cherry tree.

Franklin's own life story and satirical style are ideal material for Weems's mytholo-
gizing of the American hero. Together, both accounts of Franklin give the world a vision
that wonderfully represents his own approach to the writing of literature: speaking through
a mask, an invented persona, to an audience that is receptive to this process of image-
making more than it is concerned about fidelity to truth and accuracy of portraiture. For
example, in Franklin's essay "The Way to Wealth" (1758), the narrator, Richard Saunders, comes upon a group gathered in a public marketplace where an elderly man, Father

Abraham, is "preaching" in a sermon that develops a strategy for monetary success. The quoted maxims become the text for the sermon, and most are taken from *Poor Richard's Almanac*.

The *Autobiography* consists of four parts; Part I commences with "Dear Son," an address to posterity, as though Franklin were writing to a young man who, in moving from adolescence to adulthood, would benefit from the wisdom of his parent. These words were addressed to William Franklin, Franklin's illegitimate son, then forty-two years old and the governor of New Jersey. Part I moves forward in a conventional autobiographical style, one that idealizes the subject and was borrowed from the Puritans, from whom Franklin was descended. Part I discusses generations past, with fathers instructing sons concerning their ancestors and with each succeeding generation improving the life of the preceding one. In Part II Franklin shifts away from the persona of a parent instructing a child and expands his audience to include all his followers who wish to learn how to become virtuous, industrious, and successful. He lists thirteen "virtues" and includes a chart by which he measured his personal habits, a programmed approach to personal living that has been adapted by self-improvement advisors. This section of the narrative is the best known and the most often quoted.

Parts III and IV indicate how the author's moral behavior led not only to worldly success but also to an expanded role as a public figure. Franklin's significant achievements of the late eighteenth century, such as his role in the Continental Congress and his ambassadorship in Paris, are not recorded in the *Autobiography*. However, that Franklin turned his own personal success into a contribution to the public good is clear. The persona of Benjamin Franklin that emerges as an adult is less judgmental and self-righteous than the youthful figure who during his lunch breaks drinks water and reads by himself while his peers indulge themselves with stronger drink and lengthy conversation. Even Franklin's marriage in 1730 to Deborah Read, the daughter of his first landlady, is recorded as a useful match, ultimately part of a programmed scheme for self-improvement and personal development. At the time, Read was married to John Rogers, a debtor who had left her without a divorce; thus, Franklin's relationship to her was a common-law marriage. The common-law arrangement was apparently very satisfactory to both parties and lasted forty-four years, until Read died in 1774.

Throughout his life Franklin was obsessed with scientific experimentation, and he especially indulged this passion after retiring from the printing business in 1746. He is credited with having invented the Franklin stove (a cast-iron heating stove) and bifocal glasses, and he founded the college that became the University of Pennsylvania. Like Thomas Jefferson, whose brilliant and comprehensive mind ranged from ancient philosophy to architecture and astronomy, Franklin believed the empirical or scientific method for establishing truth to be essential to learning and human development and throughout his career fought against superstition and religious dogmatism. In his "Letter to Ezra Stiles," printed in the *Autobiography*, Franklin asserts his simple faith, deism, which acknowledges that a supreme being created the universe but does not intervene in its functioning. In the letter Franklin expresses his doubts about the divinity of Jesus Christ, " . . . though it is a question I do not dogmatize upon, having never studied it." This cautious approach and undogmatic rejection of commitment in the face of little evidence characterizes Franklin's reasoning process and shows how steady a scientist he would have made. However, political and civic duties attracted him equally, and he was responsible for organizing the first lending library (1731) and the first fire department in Philadelphia and founding the American Philosophical Society. His close association with the evolving sentiment for revolution against England, and the military and political events that consumed the colonies between 1760 and 1787, left Franklin little time for scientific investigation other than his lightning

Benjamin Franklin's snake device, published in the Pennsylvania Gazette *in 1754, came to symbolize the colonies' growing resistance to England.*

and kite experiments, published in *Experiments and Observations on Electricity* (1751–1753).

Franklin spent his later years as a diplomat, living for long periods in London and Paris as well as Philadelphia. The unsophisticated runaway was by now a thoroughly urbane and successful diplomat who had taught himself French, Spanish, Italian, and Latin, all important to his negotiations at court and to his social popularity throughout Europe. He always dressed plainly and kept a personal profile that contrasted with that of the European courtiers with whom he regularly associated. The diplomat Franklin was witty and charming, learned and well versed. He also fathered several illegitimate children. His public life was devoted to his emerging nation. More than any other American figure, including George Washington, Franklin stood for the character, integrity, freedom, and opportunity that the United States came to symbolize to the world. Important to Franklin's public life were diplomatic missions abroad, to England (1757–1762 and 1764–1785) and to France (1776–1785), during his "retirement." He also traveled in Germany and, with his son William, visited Holland and Belgium. In America Franklin had homes in Boston and Philadelphia, then the two most significant cultural centers in the New World.

Franklin's writings support the view that he was sophisticated and worldly, urbane and scholarly. His penchant for satire, one of the most difficult literary genres to craft successfully, is realized in such works as "The Speech of Polly Baker" (1747), a narrative about a pregnant defendant who is being tried for her social misconduct but cannot "conceive" what she has done wrong, and Franklin's favorite satire, "Rules by Which a Great Empire May Be Reduced to a Small One" (1773). In his "Father Abraham's Speech" (1758, 1774) the author's persona narrator stands in the audience while his own dogmas are thrust upon an admiring crowd of his peers by an elder statesman who resembles Franklin himself. This document contains some of Franklin's finest satire and rhetorical strategies.

Many of Franklin's themes were inherited from the Puritans who preceded and surrounded him. His *Autobiography* was written in a form very well developed by Puritan authors of spiritual autobiographies. Franklin adapted the form to a secular purpose and used as his spiritual "text" the wisdom of the ancients and the practical wisdom of *Poor Richard's Almanac*. The work ethic Franklin developed so fully in his *Autobiography* was an extension of the Protestant/Puritan ethic of European and English origins, whereby the most visible sign of sanctification and of being chosen by God is worldly success. (A sad corollary of this ethic placed the impoverished in league with the Devil.) Even his "Dogood Papers" (1722) were echoes of Cotton Mather's *Bonifacius: An Essay Upon the Good* (1710). If Franklin's rhetorical style commonly resembles that of the English essayists Joseph Addison and Richard Steele and the satirist Jonathan Swift, his content is typically the legacy of American Puritanism.

The *Autobiography*'s youthful runaway apprentice, who arrives in Philadelphia with a loaf of bread under his arm, may prefigure Huckleberry Finn as an archetypal American hero. However, this youth's development into an emergent American national figure, larger than life, signals a new purpose in the Franklin image-building process: the continuous extension of, rather than the denial of, the purposes of New England Puritanism. Franklin should be read in the context of America's gradual transition from the Puritan seventeenth century to the Age of Enlightenment, a philosophical movement marked by rationalism and the impetus toward empirical learning, in the eighteenth-century world of Thomas Paine and Thomas Jefferson. Franklin's secular humanism, which embraced the ethical morality of Puritanism and modernized it in the process, made it possible for generations of American readers to inherit the ethical legacy of Puritanism without having to embrace its spiritual tenets.

Franklin the man died in Philadelphia in 1790 shortly after signing a petition for Congress to abolish slavery. Over twenty thousand people attended his funeral, a massive public celebration of this genuine American hero. His image has endured, and his writings create and extend Franklin's influence well into modern times.

Suggested Readings: C. Van Doren, *Benjamin Franklin,* 1938. A. O. Aldridge, *Benjamin Franklin: Philosopher and Man,* 1965. M. Twain, "The Late Benjamin Franklin," in *Galaxy,* July 1870, 10:138–140. R. Amacher, *Benjamin Franklin,* 1962. D. Levin, "The *Autobiography* of Benjamin Franklin: The Puritan Experimenter in Life and Art," in *Yale Review,* December 1963, 43:258–275. B. I. Granger, *Benjamin Franklin: An American Man of Letters,* 1964. P. Miller, "Jonathan Edwards and Benjamin Franklin," in *Major Writers of America,* 1964. R. F. Sayre, *The Examined Self: Benjamin Franklin, Henry Adams, Henry James,* 1964. R. W. Ketcham, *Benjamin Franklin,* 1965. N. Fiering, "Benjamin Franklin and the Way to Virtue," in *American Quarterly,* Summer 1978. J. A. L. LeMay, "Benjamin Franklin: Universal Genius," in *The Renaissance Man in the Eighteenth Century,* 1978.

Texts Used: "The Way to Wealth": *The Papers of Benjamin Franklin,* Vol. 7, ed. L. W. Labaree, 1963. *The Autobiography of Benjamin Franklin,* ed. L. W. Labaree, R. L. Ketcham, H.C. Boatfield, and H. H. Fineman, 1964. All else: *The Writings of Benjamin Franklin,* Vols. VIII–XI, ed. A. H. Smyth, 1906. (Some spelling and punctuation modernized.)

from   *POOR RICHARD**

THE WAY TO WEALTH

Courteous Reader,

I have heard that nothing gives an author so great pleasure, as to find his works respectfully quoted by other learned authors. This pleasure I have seldom enjoyed; for tho' I have been, if I may say it without vanity, an eminent author of almanacs annually now a full quarter of a century, my brother authors in the same way, for what reason I know not, have ever been very sparing in their applauses; and no other author has taken the least notice of me, so that did not my writings produce me some solid pudding, the great deficiency of praise would have quite discouraged me.

---

* This essay was published as the preface to *Poor Richard Improved,* an expanded version of *Poor Richard's Almanac,* for the twenty-fifth anniversary edition. The essay was also known as "Father Abraham's Speech." Franklin fictionalized an old man addressing an auction and using many of the maxims in earlier editions of *Poor Richard.*

I concluded at length, that the people were the best judges of my merit; for they buy my works; and besides, in my rambles, where I am not personally known, I have frequently heard one or other of my adages repeated, with, as Poor Richard says, at the end on't; this gave me some satisfaction, as it showed not only that my instructions were regarded, but discovered[1] likewise some respect for my authority; and I own, that to encourage the practice of remembering and repeating those wise sentences, I have sometimes quoted myself with great gravity.

Judge then how much I must have been gratified by an incident I am going to relate to you. I stopped my horse lately where a great number of people were collected at a vendue[2] of merchant goods. The hour of sale not being come, they were conversing on the badness of the times, and one of the company called to a plain clean old man, with white locks, "Pray, Father Abraham, what think you of the times? Won't these heavy taxes quite ruin the country? How shall we be ever able to pay them? What would you advise us to?" Father Abraham stood up, and replied, "If you'd have my advice, I'll give it you in short, for a *word to the wise is enough, and many words won't fill a bushel, as Poor Richard says.*" They joined in desiring him to speak his mind, and gathering round him, he proceeded as follows:

"Friends, says he, and neighbors, the taxes are indeed very heavy, and if those laid on by the government were the only ones we had to pay, we might more easily discharge them; but we have many others, and much more grievous to some of us. We are taxed twice as much by our idleness, three times as much by our pride, and four times as much by our folly, and from these taxes the commissioners cannot ease or deliver us by allowing an abatement. However let us hearken to good advice, and something may be done for us; *God helps them that help themselves,* as Poor Richard says, in his almanac of 1733.[3]

"It would be thought a hard government that should tax its people one tenth part of their time, to be employed in its service. But idleness taxes many of us much more, if we reckon all that is spent in absolute sloth, or doing of nothing, with that which is spent in idle employments or amusements, that amount to nothing. Sloth, by bringing on diseases, absolutely shortens life. *Sloth, like rust, consumes faster than labor wears, while the used key is always bright,* as Poor Richard says. But *dost thou love life, then do not squander time, for that's the stuff life is made of,* as Poor Richard says. How much more than is necessary do we spend in sleep! forgetting that *the sleeping fox catches no poultry,* and that *there will be sleeping enough in the grave,* as Poor Richard says. If time be of all things the most precious, *wasting time* must be, as Poor Richard says, *the greatest prodigality,* since, as he elsewhere tells us, *lost time is never found again,* and what we call *time-enough, always proves little enough:* let us then be up and be doing, and doing to the purpose; so by diligence shall we do more with less perplexity. *Sloth makes all things difficult, but industry all easy,* as Poor Richard says; and *he that riseth late, must trot all day, and shall scarce overtake his business at night.* While *laziness travels so slowly, that poverty soon overtakes him,* as we read in Poor Richard, who adds, *drive thy business, let not that drive thee;* and *early to bed, and early to rise, makes a man healthy, wealthy and wise.*

"So what signifies wishing and hoping for better times. We may make these times better if we bestir ourselves. *Industry need not wish,* as Poor Richard says, and *he that lives upon hope will die fasting. There are no gains, without pains,*

---

[1] Showed.   [2] An auction.   [3] Actually, 1736.

then *help hands, for I have no lands,* or if I have, they are smartly taxed. And, as Poor Richard likewise observes, *he that hath a trade hath an estate,* and *he that hath a calling hath an office of profit and honor;* but then the trade must be worked at, and the calling well followed, or neither the estate, nor the office, will enable us to pay our taxes. If we are industrious we shall never starve; for, as Poor Richard says, *at the working man's house hunger looks in, but dares not enter.* Nor will the bailiff nor the constable enter, for *industry pays debts, while despair encreaseth them,* says Poor Richard. What though you have found no treasure, nor has any rich relation left you a legacy, *diligence is the mother of good luck,* as Poor Richard says, and *God gives all things to industry.* Then *plough deep, while sluggards sleep, and you shall have corn to sell and to keep,* says Poor Dick. Work while it is called today, for you know not how much you may be hindered tomorrow, which makes Poor Richard say, *one today is worth two tomorrows;* and farther, *have you somewhat to do tomorrow, do it today.* If you were a servant, would you not be ashamed that a good master should catch you idle? Are you then your own master, *be ashamed to catch yourself idle,* as Poor Dick says. When there is so much to be done for yourself, your family, your country, and your gracious king, be up by peep of day; *let not the sun look down and say, inglorious here he lies.* Handle your tools without mittens; remember that *the cat in gloves catches no mice,* as Poor Richard says. 'Tis true there is much to be done, and perhaps you are weak handed, but stick to it steadily, and you will see great effects, for *constant dropping wears away stones,* and by *diligence and patience the mouse ate in two the cable;* and *little strokes fell great oaks,* as Poor Richard says in his almanac, the year I cannot just now remember.

"Methinks I hear some of you say, must a man afford himself no leisure? I will tell thee, my friend, what Poor Richard says, *employ thy time well if thou meanest to gain leisure;* and, *since thou art not sure of a minute, throw not away an hour.* Leisure is time for doing something useful; this leisure the diligent man will obtain, but the lazy man never; so that, as Poor Richard says, a *life of leisure and a life of laziness are two things.* Do you imagine that sloth will afford you more comfort than labor? No, for as Poor Richard says, *trouble springs from idleness, and grievous toil from needless ease. Many without labor would live by their wits only, but they break for want of stock.*[4] Whereas industry gives comfort, and plenty, and respect: *fly*[5] *pleasures, and they'll follow you. The diligent spinner has a large shift,*[6] and *now I have a sheep and a cow, everybody bids me good morrow,* all which is well said by Poor Richard.

"But with our industry, we must likewise be steady, settled and careful, and oversee our own affairs with our own eyes, and not trust too much to others; for, as Poor Richard says,

> *I never saw an oft removed*[7] *tree,*
> *Nor yet an oft removed family,*
> *That throve so well as those that settled be.*

"And again, *three removes is as bad as a fire,* and again, *keep the shop, and thy shop will keep thee;* and again, *if you would have your business done, go; if not, send.* And again,

---

[4] For lack of a supply of wits.   [5] Avoid.   [6] Wardrobe.   [7] Moved.

> *He that by the plough would thrive,*
> *Himself must either hold or drive.*

"And again, *the eye of a master will do more work than both his hands;* and again, *want of care does us more damage than want of knowledge;* and again, *not to oversee workmen is to leave them your purse open.* Trusting too much to others' care is the ruin of many; for, as the almanac says, *in the affairs of this world men are saved not by faith, but by the want of it;* but a man's own care is profitable; for, saith Poor Dick, *learning is to the studious,* and *riches to the careful,* as well as *power to the bold,* and *Heaven to the virtuous.* And farther, *if you would have a faithful servant, and one that you like, serve yourself.* And again, he adviseth to circumspection and care, even in the smallest matters, because sometimes *a little neglect may breed great mischief;* adding, *for want of a nail the shoe was lost; for want of a shoe the horse was lost, and for want of a horse the rider was lost,* being overtaken and slain by the enemy, all for want of care about a horse-shoe nail.

"So much for industry, my friends, and attention to one's own business; but to these we must add frugality, if we would make our industry more certainly successful. A man may, if he knows not how to save as he gets, *keep his nose all his life to the grindstone, and die not worth a groat*[8] at last. *A fat kitchen makes a lean will,* as Poor Richard says; and,

> *Many estates are spent in the getting,*
> *Since women for tea forsook spinning and knitting,*
> *And men for punch forsook hewing and splitting.*

If you would be wealthy, says he, in another almanac, *think of saving as well as of getting: the Indies have not made Spain rich, because her outgoes are greater than her incomes.* Away then with your expensive follies, and you will not have so much cause to complain of hard times, heavy taxes, and chargeable families; for, as Poor Dick says,

> *Women and wine, game and deceit,*
> *Make the wealth small, and the wants great.*

And farther, *what maintains one vice, would bring up two children.* You may think perhaps that a little tea, or a little punch now and then, diet a little more costly, clothes a little finer, and a little entertainment now and then, can be no great Matter; but remember what Poor Richard says, *many* a little *makes a mickle,*[9] and farther, *beware of little expenses; a small leak will sink a great ship,* and again, *who dainties love, shall beggars prove,* and moreover, *fools make Feasts, and wise men eat them.*

"Here you are all got together at this vendue of fineries and knicknacks. You call them goods, but if you do not take care, they will prove evils to some of you. You expect they will be sold cheap, and perhaps they may for less than they cost; but if you have no occasion for them, they must be dear to you. Remember what Poor Richard says, *buy what thou hast no need of, and ere long thou shalt sell thy*

---

[8] A silver coin, roughly four pence.   [9] A lot.

necessaries. And again, *at a great pennyworth*[10] *pause a while:* he means, that perhaps the cheapness is apparent only, and not real; or the bargain, by straitning thee in thy business, may do thee more harm than good. For in another place he says, *many have been ruined by buying good pennyworths*. Again, Poor Richard says, *'tis foolish to lay our money in a purchase of repentance;* and yet this folly is practised every day at vendues, for want of minding the almanac. *Wise men,* as Poor Dick says, *learn by others' harms, fools scarcely by their own,* but, *felix quem faciunt aliena pericula cautum.*[11] Many a one, for the sake of finery on the back, have gone with a hungry belly, and half starved their families; *silks and satins, scarlet and velvets,* as Poor Richard says, *put out the kitchen fire.* These are not the necessaries of life; they can scarcely be called the conveniencies, and yet only because they look pretty, how many want to have them. The artificial wants of mankind thus become more numerous than the natural; and, as Poor Dick says, *for one* poor *person, there are an hundred* indigent. By these, and other extravagancies, the genteel are reduced to poverty, and forced to borrow of those whom they formerly despised, but who through industry and frugality have maintained their standing; in which case it appears plainly, that a *ploughman on his legs is higher than a gentleman on his knees,* as Poor Richard says. Perhaps they have had a small estate left them, which they knew not the getting of; they think *'tis day, and will never be night;* that a little to be spent out of so much, is not worth minding; (*a child and a fool,* as Poor Richard says, *imagine twenty shillings and twenty years can never be spent*) but, *always taking out of the meal-tub, and never putting in, soon comes to the bottom;* then, as Poor Dick says, *when the well's dry, they know the worth of water.* But this they might have known before, if they had taken his advice; *if you would know the value of money, go and try to borrow some,* for, *he that goes a borrowing goes a sorrowing,* and indeed so does he that lends to such people, when he goes to get it in again. Poor Dick farther advises, and says,

> *Fond pride of dress, is sure a very curse;*
> *E'er fancy you consult, consult your purse.*

And again, *pride is as loud a beggar as want, and a great deal more saucy.* When you have bought one fine thing you must buy ten more, that your appearance may be all of a piece; but Poor Dick says, *'tis easier to suppress the first desire than to satisfy all that follow it.* And 'tis as truly folly for the poor to ape the rich, as for the frog to swell, in order to equal the ox.

> *Great estates may venture more,*
> *But little boats should keep near shore.*

'Tis however a folly soon punished; for *pride that dines on vanity sups on contempt,* as Poor Richards says. And in another place, *pride breakfasted with plenty, dined with poverty, and supped with infamy.* And after all, of what use is this *pride of appearance,* for which so much is risked, so much is suffered? It cannot promote health; or ease pain; it makes no increase of merit in the person, it creates envy, it hastens misfortune.

---

[10] Bargain.
[11] "They are fortunate who have been made wary by the misfortunes of others" (Latin).

> *What is a butterfly? At best*
> *He's but a caterpillar dressed.*
> *The gaudy fop's his picture just,*

as Poor Richard says.

"But what madness must it be to run in debt for these superfluities! We are offered, by the terms of this vendue, six months' credit; and that perhaps has induced some of us to attend it, because we cannot spare the ready money, and hope now to be fine without it. But, ah, think what you do when you run in debt; *you give to another power over your liberty*. If you cannot pay at the time, you will be ashamed to see your creditor; you will be in fear when you speak to him, you will make poor pitiful sneaking excuses, and by degrees come to lose you veracity, and sink into base downright lying; for, as Poor Richard says, *the second vice is lying, the first is running in debt*. And again to the same purpose, *lying rides upon debt's back*. Whereas a freeborn Englishman ought not to be ashamed or afraid to see or speak to any man living. But poverty often deprives a man of all spirit and virtue: *'tis hard for an empty bag to stand upright,* as Poor Richard truly says. What would you think of that Prince, or that government, who should issue an edict forbidding you to dress like a gentleman or a gentlewoman, on pain of imprisonment or servitude? Would you not say, that you are free, have a right to dress as you please, and that such an edict would be a breach of your privileges, and such a government tyrannical? And yet you are about to put yourself under that tyranny when you run in debt for such dress! Your creditor has authority at his pleasure to deprive you of your liberty, by confining you in gaol[12] for life, or to sell you for a servant, if you should not be able to pay him! When you have got your bargain, you may, perhaps, think little of payment; but *creditors,* Poor Richard tells us, *have better memories than debtors,* and in another place says, *creditors are a superstitious sect, great observers of set days and times*. The day comes round before you are aware, and the demand is made before you are prepared to satisfy it. Or if you bear your debt in mind, the term which at first seemed so long, will, as it lessens, appear extreamly short. Time will seem to have added wings to his heels as well as shoulders. *Those have a short Lent,* saith Poor Richard, *who owe money to be paid at Easter*. Then since, as he says, *the borrower is a slave to the lender, and the debtor to the creditor,* disdain the chain, preserve your freedom; and maintain your independency: be industrious and free; be frugal and free. At present, perhaps, you may think yourself in thriving circumstances, and that you can bear a little extravagance without injury; but,

> *For age and want, save while you may;*
> *No morning sun lasts a whole day,*

as Poor Richard says. Gain may be temporary and uncertain, but ever while you live, expense is constant and certain; and *'tis easier to build two chimneys than to keep one in fuel,* as Poor Richard says. So *rather go to bed supperless than rise in debt*.

> *Get what you can, and what you get hold;*
> *'Tis the stone that will turn all your lead into gold,*

[12] Jail.

as Poor Richard says. And when you have got the philosopher's stone,[13] sure you will no longer complain of bad times, or the difficulty of paying taxes.

"This doctrine, my friends, is reason and wisdom; but after all, do not depend too much upon your own industry, and frugality, and prudence, though excellent things, for they may all be blasted without the blessing of heaven; and therefore ask that blessing humbly, and be not uncharitable to those that at present seem to want it, but comfort and help them. Remember Job[14] suffered, and was afterwards prosperous.

"And now to conclude, *experience keeps a dear*[15] *school, but fools will learn in no other, and scarce in that,* for it is true, *we may give advice, but we cannot give conduct,* as Poor Richard says: however, remember this, *they that won't be counseled, can't be helped,* as Poor Richard says: and farther, that *if you will not hear reason, she'll surely rap your knuckles.*"

Thus the old gentleman ended his harangue. The people heard it, and approved the doctrine, and immediately practiced the contrary, just as if it had been a common sermon; for the vendue opened, and they began to buy extravagantly, notwithstanding all his cautions, and their own fear of taxes. I found the good man had thoroughly studied my almanacs, and digested all I had dropped on those topics during the course of five-and-twenty years. The frequent mention he made of me must have tired any one else, but my vanity was wonderfully delighted with it, though I was conscious that not a tenth part of the wisdom was my own which he ascribed to me, but rather the gleanings I had made of the sense of all ages and nations. However, I resolved to be the better for the echo of it; and though I had at first determined to buy stuff for a new coat, I went away resolved to wear my old one a little longer. Reader, if thou wilt do the same, thy profit will be as great as mine. I am, as ever, thine to serve thee,

Richard Saunders.[16]

July 7, 1757.

1757, 1758

from INFORMATION TO THOSE WHO WOULD REMOVE TO AMERICA*

Many persons in Europe, having directly or by letters, expressed to the writer of this, who is well acquainted with North America, their desire of transporting and establishing themselves in that country; but who appear to have formed, through ignorance, mistaken ideas and expectations of what is to be obtained there; he thinks it may be useful, and prevent inconvenient, expensive, and fruitless removals and voyages of improper persons, if he gives some clearer and truer notions of that part of the world, than appear to have hitherto prevailed.

He finds it is imagined by numbers, that the inhabitants of North America are rich, capable of rewarding, and disposed to reward, all sorts of ingenuity; that

---

[13] In alchemy, a substance thought to convert base metals into gold.
[14] In the Old Testament a man who endured much suffering without losing faith.
[15] Expensive.   [16] The pseudonym Franklin used for *Poor Richard*.
* This title was used on an edition published in 1784 without Franklin's permission; he used the title *Advice to Such As Would Remove to America* on his own edition of the pamphlet later that year in Paris, where he was serving as U.S. minister to France.

they are at the same time ignorant of all the sciences, and, consequently, that strangers, possessing talents in the belles-lettres, fine arts, etc., must be highly esteemed, and so well paid, as to become easily rich themselves; that there are also abundance of profitable offices to be disposed of, which the natives are not qualified to fill; and that, having few persons of family among them, strangers of birth must be greatly respected, and of course easily obtain the best of those offices, which will make all their fortunes; that the governments too, to encourage emigrations from Europe, not only pay the expense of personal transportation, but give lands gratis to strangers, with Negroes to work for them, utensils of husbandry, and stocks of cattle. These are all wild imaginations; and those who go to America with expectations founded upon them will surely find themselves disappointed.

The truth is that though there are in that country few people so miserable as the poor of Europe, there are also very few that in Europe would be called rich; it is rather a general happy mediocrity that prevails. There are few great proprietors of the soil, and few tenants; most people cultivate their own lands, or follow some handicraft or merchandise; very few rich enough to live idly upon their rents or incomes, or to pay the high prices given in Europe for paintings, statues, architecture, and the other works of art, that are more curious than useful. Hence the natural geniuses that have arisen in America with such talents, have uniformly quitted that country for Europe, where they can be more suitably rewarded. It is true that letters and mathematical knowledge are in esteem there, but they are at the same time more common than is apprehended; there being already existing nine colleges or universities, viz. four in New England, and one in each of the provinces of New York, New Jersey, Pennsylvania, Maryland, and Virginia, all furnished with learned professors; besides a number of smaller academies; these educate many of the youth in the languages, and those sciences that qualify men for the professions of divinity, law, or physic.[1] Strangers indeed are by no means excluded from exercising those professions; and the quick increase of inhabitants everywhere gives them a chance of employ, which they have in common with the natives. Of civil offices, or employments, there are few; no superflous ones, as in Europe; and it is a rule established in some of the states that no office should be so profitable as to make it desirable. The 36th Article of the Constitution of Pennsylvania runs expressly in these words: "As every freeman, to preserve his independence (if he has not a sufficient estate) ought to have some profession, calling, trade, or farm, whereby he may honestly subsist, there can be no necessity for, nor use in, establishing offices of profit; the usual effects of which are dependance and servility, unbecoming freemen, in the possessors and expectants; faction, contention, corruption, and disorder among the people. Wherefore, whenever an office, through increase of fees or otherwise, becomes so profitable, as to occasion many to apply for it, the profits ought to be lessened by the legislature."

These ideas prevailing more or less in all the United States, it cannot be worth any man's while, who has a means of living at home, to expatriate himself, in hopes of obtaining a profitable civil office in America; and, as to military offices, they are at an end with the war,[2] the armies being disbanded. Much less is it adviseable for a person to go thither, who has no other quality to recommend him but his birth. In Europe it has indeed its value; but it is a commodity that cannot be carried to a worse market than that of America, where people do not inquire con-

---

[1] Medicine.   [2] The Revolutionary War.

cerning a stranger, "What is he?" but, "What can he do?" If he has any useful art, he is welcome; and if he exercises it, and behaves well, he will be respected by all that know him; but a mere man of quality, who, on that account, wants to live upon the public, buy some office or salary, will be despised and disregarded. The husbandman[3] is in honor there, and even the mechanic,[4] because their employments are useful. The people have a saying, that God Almighty is himself a mechanic, the greatest in the universe; and he is respected and admired more for the variety, ingenuity, and utility of his handyworks than for the antiquity of his family. They are pleased with the observation of a Negro, and frequently mention it, that *Boccarorra* (meaning the white men) *make de black man workee, make de horse workee, make de ox workee, make ebery ting workee; only de hog. He, de hog, no workee; he eat, he drink, he walk about, he go to sleep when he please, he libb like a gentleman.* According to these opinions of the Americans, one of them would think himself more obliged to a genealogist, who could prove for him that his ancestors and relations for ten generations had been ploughmen, smiths, carpenters, turners, weavers, tanners, or even shoemakers, and consequently that they were useful members of society; than if he could only prove that they were gentlemen, doing nothing of value, but living idly on the labor of others, mere *fruges consumere nati,*[5] and otherwise good for nothing, till by their death their estates, like the carcass of the Negro's gentleman-hog, come to be cut up.

With regard to encouragements for strangers from government, they are really only what are derived from good laws and liberty. Strangers are welcome, because there is room enough for them all, and therefore the old inhabitants are not jealous of them; the laws protect them sufficiently, so that they have no need of the patronage of great men; and every one will enjoy securely the profits of his industry. But, if he does not bring a fortune with him, he must work and be industrious to live. One or two years' residence gives him all the rights of a citizen; but the government does not at present, whatever it may have done in former times, hire people to become settlers, by paying their passages, giving land, Negroes, utensil, stock, or any other kind of emolument whatsoever. In short, America is the land of labor, and by no means what the English call *Lubberland,*[6] and the French *Pays de Cocagne,*[7] where the streets are said to be paved with half-peck loaves, the houses tiled with pancakes, and where the fowls fly about ready roasted, crying, "Come eat me!"

1782, 1784

REMARKS CONCERNING THE SAVAGES
OF NORTH AMERICA

Savages we call them because their manners differ from ours, which we think the perfection of civility; they think the same of theirs.

Perhaps, if we could examine the manners of different nations with impartiality; we should find no people so rude, as to be without any rules of politeness; nor any so polite, as not to have some remains of rudeness.

---

[3] Farmer.   [4] Manual laborer.
[5] Franklin's note: " '. . . born Merely to eat up the corn'—Watts."
[6] A land of slow, lazy people.   [7] Dreamland.

The Indian men, when young, are hunters and warriors; when old, counselors; for all their government is by counsel of the sages; there is no force, there are no prisons, no officers to compel obedience, or inflict punishment. Hence they generally study oratory, the best speaker having the most influence. The Indian women till the ground, dress the food, nurse and bring up the children, and preserve and hand down to posterity the memory of public transactions. These employments of men and women are accounted natural and honorable. Having few artificial wants, they have abundance of leisure for improvement by conversation. Our laborious manner of life, compared with theirs, they esteem slavish and base; and the learning, on which we value ourselves, they regard as frivolous and useless. An instance of this occurred at the Treaty of Lancaster, in Pennsylvania, Anno 1744, between the government of Virginia and the Six Nations.[1] After the principal business was settled, the commissioners from Virginia acquainted the Indians by a speech, that there was at Williamsburg a college, with a fund for educating Indian youth;[2] and that, if the Six Nations would send down half a dozen of their young lads to that college, the government would take care that they should be well provided for, and instructed in all the learning of the white people. It is one of the Indian rules of politeness not to answer a public proposition the same day that it is made; they think it would be treating it as a light matter, and that they show it respect by taking time to consider it, as of a matter important. They therefore deferred their answer till the day following; when their speaker began, by expressing their deep sense of the kindness of the Virginia government, in making them that offer; "for we know," says he, "that you highly esteem the kind of learning taught in those colleges, and that the maintenance of our young men, while with you, would be very expensive to you. We are convinced, therefore, that you mean to do us good by your proposal; and we thank you heartily. But you, who are wise, must know that different nations have different conceptions of things; and you will therefore not take it amiss, if our ideas of this kind of education happen not to be the same with yours. We have had some experience of it; several of our young people were formerly brought up at the colleges of the northern provinces; they were instructed in all your sciences; but, when they came back to us, they were bad runners, ignorant of every means of living in the woods, unable to bear either cold or hunger, knew neither how to build a cabin, take a deer, or kill an enemy, spoke our language imperfectly, were therefore neither fit for hunters, warriors, nor counselors; they were totally good for nothing. We are however not the less obliged by your kind offer, tho' we decline accepting it; and, to show our grateful sense of it, if the gentlemen of Virginia will send us a dozen of their sons, we will take great care of their education, instruct them in all we know, and make men of them."

Having frequent occasions to hold public councils, they have acquired great order and decency in conducting them. The old men sit in the foremost ranks, the warriors in the next, and the women and children in the hindmost. The business of the women is to take exact notice of what passes, imprint it in their memories (for they have no writing), and communicate it to their children. They are the records of the council, and they preserve traditions of the stipulations in treaties 100 years back; which, when we compare with our writings, we always find exact. He that would speak, rises. The rest observe a profound silence. When he has finished and

---

[1] A coalition of the Iroquois tribes Oneida, Onondaga, Mohawk, Seneca, Cayuga, and Tuscarora.

[2] Some of the money bequeathed by Robert Boyle (1627–1691), an English philosopher-scientist, to spread Christianity among the "heathen" went to the College of William and Mary for the education of Native Americans.

sits down, they leave him 5 or 6 minutes to recollect, that, if he has omitted any thing he intended to say, or has any thing to add, he may rise again and deliver it. To interrupt another, even in common conversation, is reckoned highly indecent. How different this is from the conduct of a polite British House of Commons, where scarce a day passes without some confusion, that makes the speaker hoarse in calling "to order;" and how different from the mode of conversation in many polite companies of Europe, where, if you do not deliver your sentence with great rapidity, you are cut off in the middle of it by the impatient loquacity of those you converse with, and never suffered to finish it!

The politeness of these savages in conversation is indeed carried to excess, since it does not permit them to contradict or deny the truth of what is asserted in their presence. By this means they indeed avoid disputes; but then it becomes difficult to know their minds, or what impression you make upon them. The missionaries who have attempted to convert them to Christianity all complain of this as one of the great difficulties of their mission. The Indians hear with patience the truths of the Gospel explained to them, and give their usual tokens of assent and approbation; you would think they were convinced. No such matter. It is mere civility.

A Swedish minister, having assembled the chiefs of the Susquehannah Indians,[3] made a sermon to them, acquainting them with the principal historical facts on which our religion is founded; such as the fall of our first parents by eating an apple,[4] the coming of Christ to repair the mischief, his miracles and suffering, etc. When he had finished, an Indian orator stood up to thank him. "What you have told us," says he, "is all very good. It is indeed bad to eat apples. It is better to make them all into cider. We are much obliged by your kindness in coming so far, to tell us these things which you have heard from your mothers. In return, I will tell you some of those we have heard from ours. In the beginning, our fathers had only the flesh of animals to subsist on; and if their hunting was unsuccessful, they were starving. Two of our young hunters, having killed a deer, made a fire in the woods to broil some part of it. When they were about to satisfy their hunger, they beheld a beautiful young woman descend from the clouds, and seat herself on that hill, which you see yonder among the blue mountains. They said to each other, it is a spirit that has smelt our broiling venison, and wishes to eat of it; let us offer some to her. They presented her with the tongue; she was pleased with the taste of it, and said, 'Your kindness shall be rewarded; come to this place after thirteen moons, and you shall find something that will be of great benefit in nourishing you and your children to the latest generations.' They did so, and, to their surprise, found plants they had never seen before; but which, from that ancient time, have been constantly cultivated among us, to our great advantage. Where her right hand had touched the ground, they found maize; where her left hand had touched it, they found kidney beans; and where her backside had sat on it, they found tobacco." The good missionary, disgusted with this idle tale, said, "What I delivered to you were sacred truths; but what you tell me is mere fable, fiction, and falsehood." The Indian, offended, replied, "My brother, it seems your friends have not done you justice in your education; they have not well instructed you in the rules of common civility. You saw that we, who understand and practise those rules, believed all your stories; why do you refuse to believe ours?"

---

[3] An Iroquois tribe in Pennsylvania.

[4] In the old Testament the Fall, or Original Sin, in which Adam yielded to temptation by eating the forbidden fruit and subsequently fell from grace; "our first parents" are Adam and Eve.

When any of them come into our towns, our people are apt to crowd round them, gaze upon them, and incommode them, where they desire to be private; this they esteem great rudeness, and the effect of the want of instruction in the rules of civility and good manners. "We have," say they, "as much curiosity as you, and when you come into our towns, we wish for opportunities of looking at you; but for this purpose we hide ourselves behind bushes, where you are to pass, and never intrude ourselves into your company."

Their manner of entering one another's village has likewise its rules. It is reckoned uncivil in traveling strangers to enter a village abruptly, without giving notice of their approach. Therefore, as soon as they arrive within hearing, they stop and hollow,[5] remaining there till invited to enter. Two old men usually come out to them, and lead them in. There is in every village a vacant dwelling, called the stranger's house. Here they are placed, while the old men go round from hut to hut, acquainting the inhabitants, that strangers are arrived, who are probably hungry and weary; and every one sends them what he can spare of victuals, and skins to repose on. When the strangers are refreshed, pipes and tobacco are brought; and then, but not before, conversation begins, with enquiries who they are, whither bound, what news, etc; and it usually ends with offers of service, if the strangers have occasion of guides, or any necessaries for continuing their journey; and nothing is exacted for the entertainment.

The same hospitality, esteemed among them as a principal virtue, is practiced by private persons; of which Conrad Weiser, our interpreter, gave me the following instance. He had been naturalized among the Six Nations, and spoke well the Mohawk language. In going through the Indian country, to carry a message from our governor to the council at Onondaga, he called at the habitation of Canassatego, an old acquaintance, who embraced him, spread furs for him to sit on, placed before him some boiled beans and venison, and mixed some rum and water for his drink. When he was well refreshed, and had lit his pipe, Canassatego began to converse with him; asked how he had fared the many years since they had seen each other; whence he then came; what occasioned the journey, etc. Conrad answered all his questions; and when the discourse began to flag, the Indian, to continue it, said, "Conrad, you have lived long among the white people, and know something of their customs; I have been sometimes at Albany, and have observed, that once in seven days they shut up their shops, and assemble all in the great house; tell me what it is for? What do they do there?" "They meet there," says Conrad, "to hear and learn 'good things.'" "I do not doubt," says the Indian, "that they tell you so; they have told me the same; but I doubt the truth of what they say, and I will tell you my reasons. I went lately to Albany to sell my skins and buy blankets, knives, powder, rum, etc. You know I used generally to deal with Hans Hanson; but I was a little inclined this time to try some other merchant. However, I called first upon Hans, and asked him what he would give for beaver. He said he could not give any more than four shillings a pound; 'but' says he, 'I cannot talk on business now; this is the day when we meet together to learn "good things," and I am going to the meeting.' So I thought to myself, 'Since we cannot do any business today, I may as well go to the meeting too,' and I went with him. There stood up a man in black, and began to talk to the people very angrily. I did not understand what he said; but, perceiving that he looked much at me and at Hanson, I imagined he was angry at seeing me there; so I went out, sat down near the house, struck fire, and lit my pipe, waiting till the meeting

---

[5] Cry out.

should break up. I thought too, that the man had mentioned something of beaver, and I suspected it might be the subject of their meeting. So, when they came out, I accosted my merchant. 'Well, Hans' says I, 'I hope you have agreed to give more than four shillings a pound.' 'No,' says he, 'I cannot give so much; I cannot give more than three shillings and sixpence.' I then spoke to several other dealers, but they all sung the same song—three and sixpence, three and sixpence. This made it clear to me that my suspicion was right; and, that whatever they pretended of meeting to learn "good things," the real purpose was to consult how to cheat Indians in the price of beaver. Consider but a little, Conrad, and you must be of my opinion. If they met so often to learn "good things," they would certainly have learned some before this time. But they are still ignorant. You know our practice. If a white man, in travelling through our country, enters one of our cabins, we all treat him as I treat you; we dry him if he is wet, we warm him if he is cold, we give him meat and drink, that he may allay his thirst and hunger; and we spread soft furs for him to rest and sleep on; we demand nothing in return. But, if I go into a white man's house at Albany, and ask for victuals and drink, they say, 'Get out, you Indian dog.' You see they have not yet learned those little "good things," that we need no meetings to be instructed in, because our mothers taught them to us when we were children; and therefore it is impossible their meetings should be, as they say, for any such purpose, or have any such effect; they are only to contrive the cheating of Indians in the price of beaver."[6]

1784

AN ADDRESS TO THE PUBLIC

FROM THE PENNSYLVANIA SOCIETY FOR PROMOTING
THE ABOLITION OF SLAVERY, AND THE RELIEF OF FREE NEGROES
UNLAWFULLY HELD IN BONDAGE

It is with peculiar satisfaction we assure the friends of humanity, that, in prosecuting the design of our association, our endeavors have proved successful, far beyond our most sanguine expectations.

Encouraged by this success, and by the daily progress of that luminous and benign spirit of liberty, which is diffusing itself throughout the world, and humbly hoping for the continuance of the divine blessing on our labors, we have ventured to make an important addition to our original plan, and do therefore earnestly solicit the support and assistance of all who can feel the tender emotions of sympathy and compassion, or relish the exalted pleasure of beneficence.

Slavery is such an atrocious debasement of human nature, that its very extirpation, if not performed with solicitous care, may sometimes open a source of serious evils.

The unhappy man, who has long been treated as a brute animal, too frequently sinks beneath the common standard of the human species. The galling chains that

---

[6] Franklin's note: "It is remarkable that in all ages and countries hospitality has been allowed as the virtue of those whom the civilized were pleased to call barbarians. The Greeks celebrated the Scythians for it. The Saracens possessed it eminently, and it is to this day the reigning virture of the wild Arabs. St. Paul, too, in the relation of his voyage and shipwreck on the Island of Melita says the barbarous people showed us no little kindness; for they kindled a fire, and received us every one, because of the present rain, and because of the cold."

bind his body, do also fetter his intellectual faculties, and impair the social affections of his heart. Accustomed to move like a mere machine, by the will of a master, reflection is suspended; he has not the power of choice; and reason and conscience have but little influence over his conduct, because he is chiefly governed by the passion of fear. He is poor and friendless; perhaps worn out by extreme labor, age, and disease.

Under such circumstances, freedom may often prove a misfortune to himself, and prejudicial to society.

Attention to emancipated black people, it is therefore to be hoped, will become a branch of our national policy; but, as far as we contribute to promote this emancipation, so far that attention is evidently a serious duty incumbent on us, and which we mean to discharge to the best of our judgment and abilities.

To instruct, to advise, to qualify those, who have been restored to freedom, for the exercise and enjoyment of civil liberty, to promote in them habits of industry, to furnish them with employments suited to their age, sex, talents, and other circumstances, and to procure their children an education calculated for their future situation in life; these are the great outlines of the annexed plan, which we have adopted, and which we conceive will essentially promote the public good, and the happiness of these our hitherto too much neglected fellow creatures.

A plan so extensive cannot be carried into execution without considerable pecuniary resources, beyond the present ordinary funds of the Society. We hope much from the generosity of enlightened and benevolent freemen, and will gratefully receive any donations or subscriptions for this pupose, which may be made to our treasurer, James Starr, or to James Pemberton, chairman of our committee of correspondence.

Signed, by order of the Society,

B. Franklin, President.

Philadelphia, 9th of
    November, 1789.

1789

from   THE AUTOBIOGRAPHY*

from   PART ONE

Twyford,[1] at the Bishop of St. Asaph's 1771.

Dear Son,

I have ever had a Pleasure in obtaining any little Anecdotes of my Ancestors. You may remember the Enquiries I made among the Remains of my Relations when you were with me in England; and the Journey I took for that purpose.[2] Now

---

* In 1771 at age sixty-five Franklin began writing his *Autobiography*, which he called "Memoirs," for his son William (1731–1813), then governor of New Jersey. Franklin wrote three more sections during the next nineteen years, until just before his death in 1790, although the account stops at 1758, before he had begun his work in international diplomacy and in public service. Franklin never published his *Autobiography;* the text here retains the original spelling and punctuation.

[1] The country home of Jonathan Shipley, bishop of St. Asaph and Franklin's friend; near Winchester, England. Franklin was vacationing there.

[2] Franklin and his son William visited Ecton and Banbury, both in Northamptonshire, England, in 1758 to visit the homes of their ancestors and their remaining family.

imagining it may be equally agreeable to you to know the Circumstances of *my* Life, many of which you are yet unacquainted with; and expecting a Weeks uninterrupted Leisure in my present Country Retirement, I sit down to write them for you. To which I have besides some other Inducements. Having emerg'd from the Poverty and Obscurity in which I was born and bred, to a State of Affluence and some Degree of Reputation in the World, and having gone so far thro' Life with a considerable Share of Felicity, the conducing Means I made use of, which, with the Blessing of God, so well succeeded, my Posterity may like to know, as they may find some of them suitable to their own Situations, and therefore fit to be imitated. That Felicity, when I reflected on it, has induc'd me sometimes to say, that were it offer'd to my Choice, I should have no Objection to a Repetition of the same Life from its Beginning, only asking the Advantage Authors have in a second Edition to correct some Faults of the first. So would I if I might, besides corr[ectin]g the Faults, change some sinister Accidents and Events of it for others more favourable, but tho' this were deny'd, I should still accept the Offer. However, since such a Repetition is not to be expected, the next Thing most like living one's Life over again, seems to be a *Recollection* of that Life; and to make that Recollection as durable as possible, the putting it down in Writing. Hereby, too, I shall indulge the Inclination so natural in old Men, to be talking of themselves and their own past Actions, and I shall indulge it, without being troublesome to others who thro' respect to Age might think themselves oblig'd to give me a Hearing, since this may be read or not as any one pleases. And lastly, (I may as well confess it, since my Denial of it will be believ'd by no body) perhaps I shall a good deal gratify my own *Vanity*. Indeed I scarce ever heard or saw the introductory Words, *Without Vanity I may say,* etc., but some vain thing immediately follow'd. Most People dislike Vanity in others whatever Share they have of it themselves, but I give it fair Quarter[3] wherever I meet with it, being persuaded that it is often productive of Good to the Possessor and to others that are within his Sphere of Action: And therefore in many Cases it would not be quite absurd if a Man were to thank God for his Vanity among the other Comforts of Life.

And now I speak of thanking God, I desire with all Humility to acknowledge, that I owe the mention'd Happiness of my past Life to his kind Providence, which led me to the Means I us'd and gave them Success. My Belief of this, induces me to *hope,* tho' I must not *presume,* that the same Goodness will still be exercis'd towards me in continuing that Happiness, or in enabling me to bear a fatal Reverse, which I may experience as others have done, the Complexion of my future Fortune being known to him only: and in whose Power it is to bless to us even our Afflictions.

The Notes one of my Uncles[4] (who had the same kind of Curiosity in collecting Family Anecdotes) once put into my Hands, furnish'd me with several Particulars relating to our Ancestors. From these Notes I learnt that the Family had liv'd in the same Village, Ecton in Northamptonshire, for 300 Years, and how much longer he knew not (perhaps from the Time when the Name *Franklin* that before was the Name of an Order of People,[5] was assum'd by them for a Surname, when others took Surnames all over the Kingdom). (Here a Note)[6] on a Freehold[7] of about 30 Acres, aided by the Smith's Business which had continued in the Family

---

[3] Consideration.   [4] Benjamin Franklin the Elder, or Uncle Benjamin.
[5] "Franklin" meant "freeholder" in medieval England—a landowner not of noble birth.
[6] Franklin never inserted the intended note.
[7] In feudal times, land free of other claims of ownership.

till his Time, the eldest Son being always bred to that Business. A Custom which he and my Father both followed as to their eldest Sons. When I search'd the Register at Ecton, I found an Account of their Births, Marriages and Burials, from the Year 1555 only, there being no Register kept in that Parish at any time preceding. By that Register I perceiv'd that I was the youngest Son of the youngest Son for 5 Generations back.

My Grandfather Thomas, who was born in 1598, lived at Ecton till he grew too old to follow Business longer, when he went to live with his Son John, a Dyer at Banbury in Oxfordshire, with whom my Father serv'd an Apprenticeship. There my Grandfather died and lies buried. We saw his Gravestone in 1758. His eldest Son Thomas liv'd in the House at Ecton, and left it with the Land to his only Child, a Daughter, who with her Husband, one Fisher of Wellingborough sold it to Mr. Isted, now Lord of the Manor there. My Grandfather had 4 Sons that grew up, viz. Thomas, John, Benjamin and Josiah. I will give you what Account I can of them at this distance from my Papers, and if they are not lost in my Absence, you will among them find many more Particulars. Thomas was bred a Smith under his Father, but being ingenious, and encourag'd in Learning (as all his Brothers like wise were) by an Esquire Palmer[8] then the principal Gentleman in that Parish, he qualify'd for the Business of Scrivener,[9] became a considerable Man in the County Affairs, was a chief Mover of all publick Spirited Undertakings, for the County, or Town of Northampton and his own Village, of which many Instances were told us at Ecton and he was much taken Notice of and patroniz'd by the then Lord Halifax. He died in 1702, Jan. 6, old Stile,[10] just 4 Years to a Day before I was born. The Account we receiv'd of his Life and Character from some old People at Ecton, I remember struck you, as something extraordinary from its Similarity to what you knew of mine. Had he died on the same Day, you said one might have suppos'd a Transmigration.[11]

John was bred a Dyer, I believe of Woollens. Benjamin, was bred a Silk Dyer, serving an Apprenticeship at London. He was an ingenious Man, I remember him well, for when I was a Boy he came over to my Father in Boston, and lived in the House with us some Years. He lived to a great Age. His Grandson Samuel Franklin now lives in Boston. He left behind him two Quarto[12] Volumes, M.S. of his own Poetry, consisting of little occasional Pieces address'd to his Friends and Relations, of which the following sent to me, is a Specimen. (Here insert it.)[13] He had form'd a Shorthand of his own, which he taught me, but never practising it I have now forgot it. I was nam'd after this Uncle, there being a particular Affection between him and my Father. He was very pious, a great Attender of Sermons of the best Preachers, which he took down in his Shorthand and had with him many Volumes of them. He was also much of a Politician, too much perhaps for his Station. There fell lately into my Hands in London a Collection he had made of all the principal Pamphlets relating to Publick Affairs from 1641 to 1717. Many of the Volumes are wanting, as appears by the Numbering, but there still remains 8 Vols. Folio, and 24 in 4to and 8vo.[14] A Dealer in old Books met with them, and

---

[8] John Palmer.   [9] A professional writer of legal documents.

[10] England changed over to the Gregorian, or "New Style," calendar in 1752 from the Julian, or "Old Style," calendar. Franklin's birthday in the New Style calendar was January 17.

[11] The soul's passage at death into another body.

[12] A book made from sheets with four pages printed on each side.

[13] Franklin made no insertion into the original manuscript.

[14] Book sizes ranging from large to small. A folio is made from sheets with two pages printed on each side; quarto ("4to"); and octavo ("8vo"), eight pages.

knowing me by my sometimes buying of him, he brought them to me. It seems my Uncle must have left them here when he went to America, which was above 50 Years since. There are many of his Notes in the Margins.

This obsure Family of ours was early in the Reformation, and continu'd Protestants thro' the Reign of Queen Mary,[15] when they were sometimes in Danger of Trouble on Account of their Zeal against Popery. They had got an English Bible, and to conceal and secure it,[16] it was fastned open with Tapes under and within the Frame of a Joint Stool.[17] When my Great Great Grandfather read in it to his Family, he turn'd up the Joint Stool upon his Knees, turning over the Leaves then under the Tapes. One of the Children stood at the Door to give Notice if he saw the Apparitor coming, who was an Officer of the Spiritual Court.[18] In that Case the Stool was turn'd down again upon its feet, when the Bible remain'd conceal'd under it as before. This Anecdote I had from my Uncle Benjamin. The Family continu'd all of the Church of England till about the End of Charles the 2ds[19] Reign, when some of the Ministers that had been outed for Nonconformity, holding Conventicles[20] in Northamptonshire, Benjamin and Josiah adher'd to them, and so continu'd all their Lives. The rest of the Family remain'd with the Episcopal Church.

Josiah, my Father, married young, and carried his Wife with three Children unto New England, about 1682.[21] The Conventicles having been forbidden by Law, and frequently disturbed, induced some considerable Men of his Acquaintance to remove to that Country, and he was prevail'd with to accompany them thither, where they expected to enjoy their Mode of Religion with Freedom. By the same Wife he had 4 Children more born there, and by a second Wife ten more, in all 17, of which I remember 13 sitting at one time at his Table, who all grew up to be Men and Women, and married. I was the youngest Son and the youngest Child but two, and was born in boston, N. England.

My Mother the 2d Wife was Abiah Folger, a Daughter of Peter Folger, one of the first Settlers of New England, of whom honourable mention is made by Cotton Mather, in his Church History of that Country, (entitled Magnalia Christi Americana)[22] as a *godly learned Englishman,* if I remember the words rightly. I have heard that he wrote sundry small occasional Pieces, but only one of them was printed[23] which I saw now many Years since. It was written in 1675, in the homespun Verse of that Time and People, and address'd to those then concern'd in the Government there. It was in favour of Liberty of Conscience, and in behalf of the Baptists, Quakers, and other Sectaries,[24] that had been under Persecution; ascribing the Indian Wars and other Distresses, that had befallen the Country to that Persecution, as so many Judgments of God, to punish so heinous an Offence; and exhorting a Repeal of those uncharitable Laws. The whole appear'd to me as written with a good deal of Decent Plainness and manly Freedom. The six last con-

---

[15] Mary I (1516–1558), or Mary Tudor, queen of England from 1553 to 1558. She earned the name "Bloody Mary" for persecuting Protestants, in an attempt to restore Roman Catholicism as the state church.

[16] Many Bibles were destroyed during Queen Mary's reign to eliminate Protestantism.

[17] A stool that is joined but not nailed together.

[18] An ecclesiastical court for the elimination of heresy.

[19] Charles II (1630–1685), king of England, Scotland, and Ireland from 1660 to 1685.

[20] Secret, illegal meetings of Nonconformists, who refused to follow the Church of England.

[21] Actually 1683; Josiah Franklin's first wife was Ann Child.   [22] Published in 1702.

[23] *A Looking Glass for the Times: Or, the Former Spirit of New England Revived in This Generation* (1676); Folger (1617–1690) was a pioneer of Nantucket.

[24] Members of a sect.

cluding Lines I remember, tho' I have forgotten the two first of the Stanza, but the Purport of them was that his Censures proceeded from *Goodwill,* and therefore he would be known as the Author,

> because to be a Libeller, (says he)
>   I hate it with my Heart.
> From Sherburne Town[25] where now I dwell,
>   My Name I do put here,
> Without Offence, your real Friend,
>   It is Peter Folgier.

My elder Brothers were all put Apprentices to different Trades. I was put to the Grammar School at Eight Years of Age, my Father intending to devote me as the Tithe[26] of his Sons to the Service of the Church. My early Readiness in learning to read (which must have been very early, as I do not remember when I could not read) and the Opinion of all his Friends that I should certainly make a good Scholar, encourage'd him in this Purpose of his. My Uncle Benjamin too approv'd of it, and propos'd to give me all his Shorthand Volumes of Sermons I suppose as a Stock to set up with, if I would learn his Character.[27] I continu'd however at the Grammar School not quite one Year, tho' in that time I had risen gradually from the Middle of the Class of that Year to be the Head of it, and farther was remov'd into the next Class above it, in order to go with that into the third at the End of the Year. But my Father in the mean time, from a View of the Expence of a College Education which, having so large a Family, he could not well afford, and the mean Living many so educated were afterwards able to obtain, Reasons that he gave to his Friends in my Hearing, altered his first Intention, took me from the Grammar School, and sent me to a school for Writing and Arithmetic kept by a then famous Man, Mr. Geo. Brownell, very successful in his Profession generally, and that by mild encouraging Methods. Under him I acquired fair Writing pretty soon, but I fail'd in the Arithmetic, and made no Progress in it.

At Ten Years old, I was taken home to assist my Father in his Business, which was that of a Tallow Chandler and Sope-Boiler.[28] A Business he was not bred to, but had assumed on his Arrival in New England and on finding his Dying Trade would not maintain his Family, being in little Request. Accordingly I was employed in cutting Wick for the Candles, filling the Dipping Mold, and the Molds for cast Candles, attending the Shop, going of Errands, etc. I dislik'd the trade and had a strong Inclination for the Sea; but my Father declar'd against it; however, living near the Water, I was much in and about it, learnt early to swim well, and to manage Boats, and when in a Boat or Canoe with other Boys I was commonly allow'd to govern,[29] especially in any case of Difficulty; and upon other Occasions I was generally a Leader among the Boys, and sometimes led them into Scrapes, of which I will mention one Instance, as it shows an early projecting public Spirit, tho' not then justly conducted. There was a Salt Marsh that bounded part of the Mill Pond, on the Edge of which at Highwater, we us'd to stand to fish for Minews.[30] By much Trampling, we had made it a mere Quagmire. My Pro-

---

[25] Franklin's note: "In the Island of Nantucket."
[26] One-tenth; literally a portion of income given to the church.   [27] Shorthand system.
[28] A maker of candles and soap.   [29] To steer.   [30] Minnows.

posal was to build a Wharf there fit for us to stand upon, and I show'd my Comrades a large Heap of Stones which were intended for a new House near the Marsh, and which would very well suit our Purpose. Accordingly in the Evening when the Workmen were gone, I assembled a Number of my Playfellows, and working with them diligently like so many Emmets,[31] sometimes two or three to a Stone, we brought them all away and built our little Wharff. The next Morning the Workmen were surpriz'd at Missing the Stones; which were found in our Wharff; Enquiry was made after the Removers; we were discovered and complain'd of; several of us were corrected by our Fathers; and tho' I pleaded the Usefulness of the Work, mine convinc'd me that nothing was useful which was not honest.

I think you may like to know Something of his Person and Character. He had an excellent Constitution of Body, was of middle Stature, but well set and very strong. He was ingenious, could draw prettily, was skill'd a little in Music and had a clear pleasing Voice, so that when he play'd Psalm Tunes on his Violin and sung withal as he sometimes did in an Evening after the Business of the Day was over, it was extreamly agreable to hear. He had a mechanical Genius too, and on occasion was very handy in the Use of other Tradesmen's Tools. But his great Excellence lay in a sound Understanding, and solid Judgment in prudential Matters, both in private and publick Affairs. In the latter indeed he was never employed, the numerous Family he had to educate and the straitness of his Circumstances, keeping him close to his Trade, but I remember well his being frequently visited by leading People, who consulted him for his Opinion in Affairs of the Town or of the Church he belong'd to and show'd a good deal of Respect for his Judgment and Advice. He was also much consulted by private Persons about their Affairs when any Difficulty occur'd, and frequently chosen an Arbitrator between contending Parties. At his Table he lik'd to have as often as he could, some sensible Friend or Neighbour, to converse with, and always took care to start some ingenious or useful Topic for Discourse, which might tend to improve the Minds of his Children. By this means he turn'd our Attention to what was good, just, and prudent in the Conduct of Life; and little or no Notice was ever taken of what related to the Victuals on the Table, whether it was well or ill drest, in or out of season, of good or bad flavour, preferable or inferior to this or that other thing of the kind; so that I was bro't up in such a perfect Inattention to those Matters as to be quite Indifferent what kind of Food was set before me; and so unobservant of it, that to this Day, if I am ask'd I can scarce tell, a few Hours after Dinner, what I din'd upon. This has been a Convenience to me in travelling, where my Companions have been sometimes very unhappy for want of a suitable Gratification of their more delicate because better instructed Tastes and Appetites.

My Mother had likewise an excellent Constitution. She suckled all her 10 Children. I never knew either my Father or Mother to have any Sickness but that of which they dy'd he at 89 and she at 85 Years of age. They lie buried together at Boston, where I some Years since plac'd a Marble stone over their Grave with this Inscription

Josiah Franklin
And Abiah his Wife
Lie here interred.
They lived lovingly together in Wedlock
Fifty-five Years.

---

[31] Ants.

Without an Estate or any gainful Employment,[32]
By constant labour and Industry,
With God's Blessing,
They maintained a large Family
Comfortably;
And brought up thirteen Children,
And seven Grand Children
Reputably.
From this Instance, Reader,
Be encouraged to Diligence in thy Calling,
And distrust not Providence.
He was a pious & prudent Man,
She a discreet and virtuous Woman.
Their youngest Son,
In filial Regard to their Memory,
Places this Stone.
J.F. born 1655—Died 1744. Ætat[33] 89
A.F. born 1667—died 1752———85

By my rambling Digressions I perceive my self to be grown old. I us'd to write more methodically. But one does not dress for private Company as for a publick Ball. 'Tis perhaps only Negligence.

To return. I continu'd thus employ'd in my Father's Business for two Years, that is till I was 12 Years old; and my Brother John,[34] who was bred to that Business having left my Father, married and set up for himself at Rhodeisland, there was all Appearance that I was destin'd to supply his Place and be a Tallow Chandler. But my Dislike to the Trade continuing, my Father was under Apprehensions that if he did not find one for me more agreable, I should break away and get to Sea, as his Son Josiah had done to his great Vexation. He therefore sometimes took me to walk with him, and see Joiners,[35] Bricklayers, Turners, Braziers,[36] etc. at their Work, that he might observe my Inclination, and endeavour to fix it on some Trade or other on Land. It has ever since been a Pleasure to me to see good Workmen handle their Tools; and it has been useful to me, having learnt so much by it, as to be able to do little Jobs my self in my House, when a Workman could not readily be got; and to construct little Machines for my Experiments while the Intention of making the Experiment was fresh and warm in my Mind. My Father at last fix'd upon the Cutler's Trade, and my Uncle Benjamin's Son Samuel who was bred to that Business in London being about that time establish'd in Boston, I was sent to be with him some time on liking. But his Expectations of a Fee with me displeasing my Father, I was taken home again.

From a Child I was fond of Reading, and all the little Money that came into my Hands was ever laid out in Books. Pleas'd with the Pilgrim's Progress, [37] my first Collection was of John Bunyan's Works, in separate little Volumes. I afterwards sold them to enable me to buy R. Burton's Historical Collections;[38] they were

---

[32] Without "privileged" employment, or an inheritance.   [33] "Aged" (Latin).
[34] John Franklin (1690–1756), Franklin's favorite brother; later, postmaster of Boston.
[35] Woodworkers.   [36] Latheworkers and brassworkers.
[37] *The Pilgrim's Progress* (1678), by the Puritan preacher John Bunyan (1628–1688).
[38] Nathaniel Crouch (1632?–1725?), popularizer of British history, wrote as Robert or Richard Burton.

small Chapmen's [39] Books and cheap, 40 or 50 in all. My Father's little Library consisted chiefly of Books in polemic Divinity, most of which I read, and have since often regretted, that at a time when I had such a Thirst for Knowledge, more proper Books had not fallen in my Way, since it was now resolv'd I should not be a Clergyman. Plutarch's Lives[40] there was, in which I read abundantly, and I still think that time spent to great Advantage. There was also a Book of Defoe's, called an Essay on Projects,[41] and another of Dr. Mather's, call'd Essays to do Good[42] which perhaps gave me a Turn of Thinking that had an Influence on some of the principal future Events of my Life.

This Bookish Inclination at length determin'd my Father to make me a Printer, tho' he had already one Son, (James)[43] of that Profession. In 1717 my Brother James return'd from England with a Press and Letters [44] to set up his Business in Boston. I lik'd it much better than that of my Father, but still had a Hankering for the Sea. To prevent the apprehended Effect of such an Inclination, my Father was impatient to have me bound[45] to my Brother. I stood out some time, but at last was persuaded and signed the Indentures, when I was yet but 12 Years old. I was to serve as an Apprentice till I was 21 Years of Age, only I was to be allow'd Journeyman's[46] Wages during the last Year. In a little time I made great Proficiency in the Business, and became a useful Hand to my Brother. I now had Access to better Books. An Acquaintance with the Apprentices of Booksellers, enabled me sometimes to borrow a small one, which I was careful to return soon and clean. Often I sat up in my Room reading the greatest Part of the Night, when the Book was borrow'd in the Evening and to be return'd early in the Morning lest it should be miss'd or wanted. And after some time an ingenious Tradesman Mr. Matthew Adams who had a pretty[47] Collection of Books, and who frequented our Printing House, took Notice of me, invited me to his Library, and very kindly lent me such Books as I chose to read. I now took a Fancy to Poetry, and made some little Pieces. My Brother, thinking it might turn to account encourag'd me, and put me on composing two occasional Ballads. One was called the *Light House Tragedy,* and contain'd an Account of the drowning of Capt. Worthilake with his Two Daughters; the other was a Sailor Song on the Taking of *Teach* or Blackbeard the Pirate.[48] They were wretched Stuff, in the Grubstreet Ballad Stile,[49] and when they were printed he sent me about the Town to sell them. The first sold wonderfully, the Event being recent, having made a great Noise. This flatter'd my Vanity. But my Father discourag'd me, by ridiculing my Performances, and telling me Verse-makers were generally Beggars; so I escap'd being a Poet, most probably a very bad one. But as Prose Writing has been of great Use to me in the Course of my Life, and was a principal Means of my Advancement, I shall tell you how in such a Situation I acquir'd what little Ability I have in that Way.

---

[39] Peddlar's.

[40] *Parallel Lives,* by the Greek writer Plutarch (A.D. 46–120), is a series of forty-six biographies of Greek and Roman notables.

[41] *Essay Upon Projects* (1697), by Daniel Defoe (1659?–1731), proposes schemes for civic and economic improvements.

[42] *Bonifacius: An Essay Upon the Good* (1710), by Cotton Mather, influenced Franklin's *Dogood Papers* (1722).

[43] James Franklin (1697–1735).   [44] Type.   [45] Apprenticed.   [46] Daily.   [47] Fine.

[48] The texts of the ballads are not known in entirety. George Worthylake, keeper of the Beacon Island light (in Boston Harbor), his wife, and a daughter drowned November 3, 1718; the pirate Edward Teach was attacked in North Carolina waters by forces from Virginia and killed November 22, 1718.

[49] London's Grub Street housed literary "hacks."

There was another Bookish Lad in the Town, John Collins by Name, with whom I was intimately acquainted. We sometimes disputed, and very fond we were of Argument, and very desirous of confuting one another. Which disputacious Turn, by the way, is apt to become a very bad Habit, making People often extreamly disagreable in Company, by the Contradiction that is necessary to bring it into Practice, and thence, besides souring and spoiling the Conversation, is productive of Disgusts and perhaps Enmities where you may have occasion for Friendship. I had caught it by reading my Father's Books of Dispute about Religion. Persons of good Sense, I have since observ'd, seldom fall into it, except Lawyers, University Men, and Men of all Sorts that have been bred at Edinborough. A Question was once some how or other started between Collins and me, of the Propriety of educating the Female Sex in Learning, and their Abilities for Study. He was of Opinion that it was improper; and that they were naturally unequal to it. I took the contrary Side, perhaps a little for Dispute sake. He was naturally more eloquent, had a ready Plenty of Words, and sometimes as I thought bore me down more by his Fluency than by the Strength of his Reasons. As we parted without settling the Point, and were not to see one another again for some time, I sat down to put my Arguments in writing, which I copied fair and sent to him. He answer'd and I reply'd. Three or four Letters of a Side had pass'd, when my Father happen'd to find my Papers, and read them. Without entring into the Discussion, he took occasion to talk to me about the Manner of my Writing, observ'd that tho' I had the Advantage of my Antagonist in correct Spelling and pointing[50] (which I ow'd to the Printing House) I fell far short in elegance of Expression, in Method and in Perspicuity, of which he convinc'd me by several Instances. I saw the Justice of his Remarks, and thence grew more attentive to the *Manner* in Writing, and determin'd to endeavour at Improvement.

About this time I met with an odd Volume of the Spectator.[51] It was the third. I had never before seen any of them. I bought it, read it over and over, and was much delighted with it. I thought the Writing excellent, and wish'd if possible to imitate it. With that View, I took some of the Papers, and making short Hints of the Sentiment in each Sentence, laid them by a few Days, and then without looking at the Book, try'd to compleat the Papers again, by expressing each hinted Sentiment at length and as fully as it had been express'd before, in any suitable Words, that should come to hand.

Then I compar'd my Spectator with the Original, discover'd some of my Faults and corrected them. But I found I wanted a Stock of Words or a Readiness in recollecting and using them, which I thought I should have acquir'd before that time, if I had gone on making Verses, since the continual Occasion for Words of the same Import but of different Length, to suit the Measure,[52] or of different Sound for the Rhyme, would have laid me under a constant Necessity of searching for Variety, and also have tended to fix that Variety in my Mind, and make me Master of it. Therefore I took some of the Tales and turn'd them into Verse: And after a time, when I had pretty well forgotten the Prose, turn'd them back again. I also sometimes jumbled my Collections of Hints into Confusion, and after some Weeks, endeavour'd to reduce them into the best Order, before I began to form the full Sentences, and compleat the Paper. This was to teach me Method in the Arrangement of Thoughts. By comparing my work afterwards with the original, I

---

[50] Punctuation, which, along with spelling, was not standardized at the time.
[51] A popular English daily paper, published from March 1, 1711, to December 6, 1712, covered literary topics and contained essays by Joseph Addison (1672–1719) and Richard Steel (1672–1729).
[52] Meter.

discover'd many faults and amended them; but I sometimes had the Pleasure of Fancying that in certain Particulars of small Import, I had been lucky enough to improve the Method or the Language and this encourag'd me to think I might possibly in time come to be a tolerable English Writer, of which I was extreamly ambitious.

My time for these Exercises and for Reading, was at Night, after Work or before Work began in the Morning; or on Sundays, when I contriv'd to be in the Printing House alone, evading as much as I could the common Attendance on publick Worship, which my Father used to exact of me when I was under his Care: And which indeed I still thought a Duty; tho' I could not, as it seemed to me, afford the Time to practise it.

When about 16 Years of Age, I happen'd to meet with a Book, written by one Tryon,[53] recommending a Vegetable Diet. I determined to go into it. My Brother being yet unmarried, did not keep House, but boarded himself and his Apprentices in another Family. My refusing to eat Flesh occasioned an Inconveniency, and I was frequently chid for my singularity. I made my self acquainted with Tryon's Manner of preparing some of his Dishes, such as Boiling Potatoes or Rice, making Hasty Pudding,[54] and a few others, and then propos'd to my Brother, that if he would give me Weekly half the Money he paid for my Board I would board my self. He instantly agreed to it, and I presently found that I could save half what he paid me. This was an additional Fund for buying Books: But I had another Advantage in it. My Brother and the rest going from the Printing House to their Meals, I remain'd there alone, and dispatching presently my light Repast, (which often was no more than a Bisket or a Slice of Bread, a Handful of Raisins or a Tart from the Pastry Cook's, and a Glass of Water) had the rest of the Time till their Return, for Study, in which I made the greater Progress from that greater Clearness of Head and quicker Apprehension which usually attend Temperance in Eating and Drinking. And now it was that being on some Occasion made asham'd of my Ignorance in Figures, which I had twice failed in learning when at School, I took Cocker's Book of Arithmetick,[55] and went thro' the whole by my self with great Ease. I also read Seller's and Sturmy's Books of Navigation, and became acquainted with the little Geometry they contain, but never proceeded far in that Science. And I read about this Time Locke on Human Understanding, and the Art of Thinking by Messrs. du Port Royal.[56]

While I was intent on improving my Language, I met with an English Grammar (I think it was Greenwood's)[57] at the End of which there were two little Sketches of the Arts of Rhetoric and Logic, the latter finishing with a Specimen of a Dispute in the Socratic Method. And soon after I procur'd Xenophon's Memorable Things of Socrates,[58] wherein there are many Instances of the same Method. I was charm'd with it, adopted it, dropt my abrupt Contradiction, and positive Argu-

[53] *The Way to Wealth, Long Life and Happiness: Or, a Discourse of Temperance* (1683), by Thomas Tryon.

[54] Boiled oatmeal or cornmeal mush.

[55] One of several books on arithmetic by Edward Cocker (1631–1675).

[56] *An Epitome of the Art of Navigation* (1681), by John Seller; *The Mariner's Magazine: Or, Sturmy's Mathematical and Practical Arts* (1669), by Samuel Sturmy; *Essays Concerning Human Understanding* (1690), by John Locke (1632–1704); and *Logic: Or, the Art of Thinking* (1687), by Antoine Arnauld (1560–1619) and Pierre Nicole (1625?–1695).

[57] James Greenwood's *An Essay Towards a Practical English Grammar* (1711).

[58] *The Memorable Things of Socrates*, translated in 1712 by Edward Bysshe; the Athenian philosopher Socrates (470?–399 B.C.) used a method of teaching that involved a series of questions and answers.

mentation, and put on the humble Enquirer and Doubter. And being then, from reading Shaftsbury and Collins,[59] become a real Doubter in many Points of our Religious Doctrine, I found this Method safest for my self and very embarassing to those against whom I used it, therefore I took a Delight in it, practis'd it continually and grew very artful and expert in drawing People even of superior Knowledge into Concessions the Consequences of which they did not foresee, entangling them in Difficulties out of which they could not extricate themselves, and so obtaining Victories that neither my self nor my Cause always deserved.

I continu'd this Method some few Years, but gradually left it, retaining only the Habit of expressing my self in Terms of modest Diffidence, never using when I advance any thing that may possibly be disputed, the Words, *Certainly, undoubtedly,* or any others that give the Air of Positiveness to an Opinion; but rather say, I conceive, or I apprehend a Thing to be so or so, It appears to me, or I should think it so or so for such and such Reasons, or I imagine it to be so, or it is so if I am not mistaken. This Habit I believe has been of great Advantage to me, when I have had occasion to inculcate my Opinions and persuade Men into Measures that I have been from time to time engag'd in promoting. And as the chief Ends of Conversation are to *inform,* or to be *informed,* to *please* or to *persuade,* I wish wellmeaning sensible Men would not lessen their Power of doing Good by a Positive assuming Manner that seldom fails to disgust, tends to create Opposition, and to defeat every one of those Purposes for which Speech was given us, to wit, giving or receiving Information, or Pleasure: For if you would *inform,* a positive dogmatical Manner in advancing your Sentiments, may provoke Contradiction and prevent a candid Attention. If you wish Information and Improvement from the Knowledge of others and yet at the same time express your self as firmly fix'd in your present Opinions, modest sensible Men, who do not love Disputation, will probably leave you undisturb'd in the Possession of your Error; and by such a Manner you can seldom hope to recommend your self in *pleasing* your Hearers, or to persuade those whose Concurrence you desire. Pope says, judiciously,

Men should be taught as if you taught them not,
And things unknown propos'd as things forgot,

farther recommending it to us,

To speak tho' sure, with seeming Diffidence.[60]

And he might have coupled with this Line that which he has coupled with another, I think less properly,

For Want of Modesty is Want of Sense.[61]

---

[59] *Characteristics of Men, Manners, Opinions, Times* (1711), by Anthony Ashley Cooper (1671–1713), third earl of Shaftesbury; and *A Discourse of Free Thinking* (1713), by Anthony Collins (1676–1729).

[60] From *Essay on Criticism* (1711), by Alexander Pope (1688–1744); actually the first line here (line 574) reads "Men *must* be taught. . . .," and the third line (line 577), "*And* speak tho' sure. . . . "

[61] From *Essay on Translated Verse* (1684), by Wentworth Dillon (1633?–1685), earl of Roscommon; actually this line (line 114) reads "For want of *decency.* . . . "

If you ask why, *less properly,* I must repeat the Lines;

> Immodest Words admit of *no* Defence;
> *For* Want of Modesty is Want of Sense.

Now is not *Want of Sense* (where a Man is so unfortunate as to want it) some Apology for his *Want of Modesty?* and would not the Lines stand more justly thus?

> Immodest words admit *but this* Defence,
> That Want of Modesty is Want of Sense.

My Brother had in 1720 or 21, begun to print a Newspaper. It was the second that appear'd in America, and was called *The New England Courant.*[62] The only one before it, was *the Boston News Letter.* I remember his being dissuaded by some of his Friends from the Undertaking, as not likely to succeed, one Newspaper being in their Judgment enough for America. At this time 1771 there are not less than five and twenty. He went on however with the Undertaking, and after having work'd in composing the Types and printing off the Sheets I was employ'd to carry the Papers thro' the Streets to the Customers. He had some ingenious Men among his Friends who amus'd themselves by writing little Pieces for this Paper, which gain'd it Credit, and made it more in Demand; and these Gentlemen often visited us. Hearing their Conversations, and their Accounts of the Approbation their Papers were receiv'd with, I was excited to try my Hand among them. But being still a Boy, and suspecting that my Brother would object to printing any Thing of mine in his Paper if he knew it to be mine, I contriv'd to disguise my Hand, and writing an anonymous Paper[63] I put it in at Night under the Door of the Printing House. It was found in the Morning and communicated to his Writing Friends when they call'd in as usual. They read it, commented on it in my Hearing, and I had the exquisite Pleasure, of finding it met with their Approbation, and that in their different Guesses at the Author none were named but Men of some Character among us for Learning and Ingenuity.

I suppose now that I was rather lucky in my Judges: And that perhaps they were not really so very good ones as I then esteem'd them. Encourag'd however by this, I wrote and convey'd in the same Way to the Press several more Papers, which were equally approv'd, and I kept my Secret till my small Fund of Sense for such Performances was pretty well exhausted, and then I discovered[64] it; when I began to be considered a little more by my Brother's Acquaintance, and in a manner that did not quite please him, as he thought, probably with reason, that it tended to make me too vain. And perhaps this might be one Occasion of the Differences that we frequently had about this Time. Tho' a Brother, he considered himself as my Master, and me as his Apprentice; and accordingly expected the same Services from me as he would from another; while I thought he demean'd

---

[62] Actually, James Franklin's *New England Courant,* begun on August 7, 1721, followed *Public Occurrences* (only one issue was published, on September 25, 1690), the *Boston News Letter,* the *Boston Gazette,* and the *American Weekly Mercury.*

[63] The first of fourteen *Silence Dogood Letters,* published in the *Courant* between April 12 and October 8, 1722; Franklin's earliest surviving writings and the first essay series published in America.

[64] Revealed.

me too much in some he requir'd of me, who from a Brother expected more Indulgence. Our Disputes were often brought before our Father, and I fancy I was either generally in the right, or else a better Pleader, because the Judgment was generally in my favour: But my Brother was passionate and had often beaten me, which I took extreamly amiss; and thinking my Apprenticeship very tedious, I was continually wishing for some Opportunity of shortening it, which at length offered in a manner unexpected.[65]

One of the Pieces in our News-Paper, on some political Point which I have now forgotten, gave Offence to the Assembly.[66] He was taken up, censur'd and imprison'd for a Month by the Speaker's Warrant, I suppose because he would not discover his Author. I too was taken up and examin'd before the Council; but tho' I did not give them any Satisfaction, they contented themselves with admonishing me, and dismiss'd me; considering me perhaps as an Apprentice who was bound to keep his Master's Secrets. During my Brother's Confinement, which I resented a good deal, notwithstanding our private Differences, I had the Management of the Paper, and I made bold to give our Rulers some Rubs[67] in it, which my Brother took very kindly, while others began to consider me in an unfavourable Light, as a young Genius that had a Turn for Libelling and Satyr.[68] My Brother's Discharge was accompany'd with an Order of the House, (a very odd one) *that James Franklin should no longer print the Paper called the New England Courant*. There was a Consultation held in our Printing House among his Friends what he should do in this Case. Some propos'd to evade the Order by changing the Name of the Paper; but my Brother seeing Inconveniences in that, it was finally concluded on as a better Way, to let it be printed for the future under the Name of *Benjamin Franklin*. And to avoid the Censure of the Assembly that might fall on him, as still printing it by his Apprentice, the Contrivance was, that my old Indenture should be return'd to me with a full Discharge on the Back of it, to be shown on Occasion; but to secure to him the Benefit of my Service I was to sign new Indentures for the Remainder of the Term, which were to be kept private. A very flimsy Scheme it was, but however it was immediately executed, and the Paper went on accordingly under my Name for several Months.[69] At length a fresh Difference arising between my Brother and me, I took upon me to assert my Freedom, presuming that he would not venture to produce the new Indentures. It was not fair in me to take this Advantage, and this I therefore reckon one of the first Errata[70] of my Life: But the Unfairness of it weigh'd little with me, when under the Impressions of Resentment, for the Blows his Passion too often urg'd him to bestow upon me. Tho' he was otherwise not an ill-natur'd Man: Perhaps I was too saucy and provoking.

When he found I would leave him, he took care to prevent my getting Employment in any other Printing-House of the Town, by going round and speaking to every Master, who accordingly refus'd to give me Work. I then thought of going to New York as the nearest Place where there was a Printer: and I was the rather inclin'd to leave Boston, when I reflected that I had already made myself a little

---

[65] Franklin's note: "I fancy his harsh and tyrannical Treatment of me, might be a means of impressing me with that Aversion to arbitrary Power that has stuck to me thro' my whole Life."

[66] The June 11, 1722, issue of the *Courant* insinuated that local authorities were in collusion with pirates raiding Boston Harbor; the Assembly, one house of the Massachusetts legislature, had James Franklin jailed for a month.

[67] Insults.   [68] Satire.

[69] Actually, the *Courant* continued to appear in Benjamin Franklin's name until at least June 25, 1726, nearly three years after he had left Boston.

[70] "Errors" (Latin).

obnoxious to the governing Party; and from the arbitrary Proceedings of the Assembly in my Brother's Case it was likely I might if I stay'd soon bring myself into Scrapes; and farther that my indiscrete Disputations about Religion began to make me pointed at with Horror by good People, as an Infidel or Atheist. I determin'd on the Point: but my Father now siding with my Brother, I was sensible that if I attempted to go openly, Means would be used to prevent me. My Friend Collins therefore undertook to manage a little for me. He agreed with the Captain of a New York Sloop for my Passage, under the Notion of my being a young Acquaintance of his that had got a naughty Girl with Child, whose Friends would compel me to marry her, and therefore I could not appear or come away publickly. So I sold some of my Books to raise a little Money, Was taken on board privately, and as we had a fair Wind in three Days I found my self in New York near 300 Miles from home, a Boy of but 17, without the least Recommendation to or Knowledge of any Person in the Place, and with very little Money in my Pocket.

My Inclinations for the Sea, were by this time worne out, or I might now have gratify'd them. But having a Trade, and supposing my self a pretty good Workman, I offer'd my Service to the Printer of the Place, old Mr. Wm. Bradford,[71] (who had been the first Printer in Pensilvania, but remov'd from thence upon the Quarrel of Geo. Keith).[72] He could give me no Employment, having little to do, and Help enough already: But, says he, my Son[73] at Philadelphia has lately lost his principal Hand, Aquila Rose,[74] by Death. If you go thither I believe he may employ you. Philadelphia was 100 Miles farther. I set out, however, in a Boat for Amboy,[75] leaving my Chest and Things to follow me round by Sea. In crossing the Bay we met with a Squall that tore our rotten Sails to pieces, prevented our getting into the Kill,[76] and drove us upon Long Island. In our Way a drunken Dutchman, who was a Passenger too, fell over board; when he was sinking I reach'd thro' the Water to his shock Pate[77] and drew him up so that we got him in again. His Ducking sober'd him a little, and he went to sleep, taking first out of his Pocket a Book which he desir'd I would dry for him. It prov'd to be my old favourite Author Bunyan's Pilgrim's Progress in Dutch, finely printed on good Paper with copper Cuts, a Dress better than I had ever seen it wear in its own Language. I have since found that it has been translated into most of the Languages of Europe, and suppose it has been more generally read than any other Book except perhaps the Bible. Honest John was the first that I know of who mix'd Narration and Dialogue, a Method of Writing very engaging to the Reader, who in the most interesting Parts finds himself as it were brought into the Company, and present at the Discourse. Defoe in his Cruso, his Moll Flanders, Religious Courtship, Family Instructor, and other Pieces, has imitated it with Success. And Richardson has done the same in his Pamela, etc.[78]

---

[71] William Bradford (1663–1752), a pioneer American printer.

[72] George Keith (1638?–1716), a controversial Quaker missionary.

[73] Andrew Bradford (1686–1742), founder of the *American Weekly Mercury* in 1719 and Franklin's principal competitor in printing.

[74] Rose (1695?–1723) was a poet and printer working for Andrew Bradford.

[75] Perth Amboy, New Jersey.

[76] The Kill van Kull or the Arthur Kill, narrow channels separating Staten Island from New Jersey.

[77] Bushy hair.

[78] *Robinson Crusoe* (1719), *Moll Flanders* (1722), *Religious Courtship* (1722), and *The Family Instructor* (1715–1718), by Daniel Defoe; and *Pamela: Or, Virtue Rewarded* (1740), by Samuel Richardson (1689–1761). Franklin's 1744 reprinting of *Pamela* was the first novel published in America.

When we drew near the Island we found it was at a Place where there could be no Landing, there being a great Surff on the stony Beach. So we dropt Anchor and swung round towards the Shore. Some People came down to the Water Edge and hallow'd to us, as we did to them. But the Wind was so high and the Surff so loud, that we could not hear so as to understand each other. There were Canoes on the Shore, and we made Signs and hallow'd that they should fetch us, but they either did not understand us, or thought it impracticable. So they went away, and Night coming on, we had no Remedy but to wait till the Wind should abate, and in the mean time the Boatman and I concluded to sleep if we could, and so crouded into the Scuttle[79] with the Dutchman who was still wet, and the Spray beating over the Head of our Boat, leak'd thro' to us, so that we were soon almost as wet as he. In this Manner we lay all Night with very little Rest. But the Wind abating the next Day, we made a Shift to reach Amboy before Night, having been 30 Hours on the Water without Victuals, or any Drink but a Bottle of filthy Rum: The Water we sail'd on being salt.

In the Evening I found my self very feverish, and went in to Bed. But having read somewhere that cold Water drank plentifully was good for a Fever, I follow'd the Prescription, sweat plentifully most of the Night, my Fever left me, and in the Morning crossing the Ferry, I proceeded on my Journey, on foot, having 50 Miles to Burlington[80] where I was told I should find Boats that would carry me the rest of the Way to Philadelphia.

It rain'd very hard all the Day, I was thoroughly soak'd and by Noon a good deal tir'd, so I stopt at a poor Inn, where I staid all Night, beginning now to wish I had never left home. I cut so miserable a Figure too, that I found by the Questions ask'd me I was suspected to be some runaway Servant, and in danger of being taken up on that Suspicion. However I proceeded the next Day, and got in the Evening to an Inn within 8 or 10 Miles of Burlington, kept by one Dr. Brown.[81]

He entred into Conversation with me while I took some Refreshment, and finnding I had read a little, became very sociable and friendly. Our Aquaintance continu'd as long as he liv'd. He had been, I imagine, an itinerant Doctor, for there was no Town in England, or Country in Europe, of which he could not give a very particular Account. He had some Letters,[82] and was ingenious, but much of an Unbeliever, and wickedly undertook some Years after to travesty the Bible in doggrel Verse as Cotton[83] had done Virgil. By this means he set many of the Facts in a very ridiculous Light, and might have hurt weak minds if his Work had been publish'd: but it never was. At his House I lay that Night, and the next Morning reach'd Burlington. But had the Mortification to find that the regular Boats were gone, a little before my coming, and no other expected to go till Tuesday, this being Saturday. Wherefore I return'd to an old Woman in the Town of whom I had bought Gingerbread to eat on the Water, and ask'd her Advice; she invited me to lodge at her house till a Passage by Water should offer: and being tired with my foot Travelling, I accepted the Invitation. She understanding I was a Printer, would have had me stay at that Town and follow my Business, being ignorant of the Stock necessary to begin with. She was very hospitable, gave me a Dinner of

---

[79] An opening in a ship's deck or hull, with a lid.
[80] Then the capital of West Jersey, about eighteen miles North of Philadelphia.
[81] John Browne (1667?–1737), a Burlington innkeeper, physician, and religious skeptic.
[82] Education.
[83] Charles Cotton (1630–1687), English poet who satirized the Roman poet Virgil (70–19 B.C.) in *Scarronides: Or, the First Book of Virgil Travestied* (1664).

Ox Cheek with great Goodwill, accepting only a Pot of Ale in return. And I tho't my self fix'd till Tuesday should come. However walking in the Evening by the Side of the River a Boat came by, which I found was going towards Philadelphia, with several People in her. They took me in, and as there was no Wind, we row'd all the Way; and about Midnight not having yet seen the City, some of the Company were confident we must have pass'd it, and would row no farther, the others knew not where we were, so we put towards the Shore, got into a Creek, landed near an old Fence with the Rails of which we made a Fire, the Night being cold, in October, and there we remain'd till Daylight. Then one of the Company knew the Place to be Cooper's Creek a little above Philadelphia, which we saw as soon as we got out of the Creek, and arriv'd there about 8 or 9 a Clock, on the Sunday morning,[84] and landed at the Market street Wharff.

I have been the more particular in this Description of my Journey, and shall be so of my first Entry into that City, that you may in your mind compare such unlikely Beginnings with the Figure I have since made there. I was in my Working Dress, my best Cloaths being to come round by Sea. I was dirty from my Journey; my Pockets were stuff'd out with Shirts and Stockings; I knew no Soul, nor where to look for Lodging. I was fatigu'd with Travelling, Rowing and Want of Rest. I was very hungry, and my whole Stock of Cash consisted of a Dutch Dollar and about a Shilling in Copper. The latter I gave the People of the Boat for my Passage, who at first refus'd it on Account of my Rowing; but I insisted on their taking it, a Man being sometimes more generous when he has but a little Money than when he has plenty, perhaps thro' Fear of being thought to have but little.

Then I walk'd up the Street, gazing about, till near the Market House I met a Boy with Bread. I had made many a Meal on Bread, and inquiring where he got it, I went immediately to the Baker's he directed me to in second Street; and ask'd for Bisket, intending such as we had in Boston, but they it seems were not made in Philadelphia, then I ask'd for a threepenny Loaf, and was told they had none such: so not considering or knowing the Difference of Money and the greater Cheapness nor the Names of his Bread, I bad him give me three penny worth of any sort. He gave me accordingly three great Puffy Rolls. I was surpriz'd at the Quantity, but took it, and having no room in my Pockets, walk'd off, with a Roll under each Arm, and eating the other. Thus I went up Market Street as far as fourth Street, passing by the Door of Mr. Read, my future Wife's[85] Father, when she standing at the Door saw me, and thought I made as I certainly did a most awkward ridiculous Appearance. Then I turn'd and went down Chestnut Street and part of Walnut Street, eating my Roll all the Way, and coming round found my self again at Market Street Wharff, near the Boat I came in, to which I went for a Draught of the River Water, and being fill'd with one of my Rolls, gave the other two to a Woman and her Child that came down the River in a Boat with us and were waiting to go farther. Thus refresh'd I walk'd again up the Street, which by this time had many clean dress'd People in it who were all walking the same Way; I join'd them, and thereby was led into the great Meeting house of the Quakers near the Market. I sat down among them, and after looking round a while and hearing nothing said, being very drowzy thro' Labour and want of Rest the preceding Night, I fell fast asleep, and continu'd so till the Meeting broke up, when one was kind enough to rouse me. This was therefore the first House I was in or slept in, in Philadelphia.

[84] A Sunday in October 1723.   [85] Deborah Read (?–1774), whom Franklin married in 1730.

Walking again down towards the River, and looking in the Faces of People, I met a young Quaker Man whose Countenance I lik'd, and accosting him requested he would tell me where a Stranger could get Lodging. We were then near the Sign of the Three Mariners. Here, says he, is one Place that entertains Strangers, but it is not a reputable House; if thee wilt walk with me, I'll show thee a better. He brought me to the Crooked Billet[86] in Water-Street. Here I got a Dinner. And while I was eating it, several sly Questions were ask'd me, as it seem'd to be suspected from my youth and Appearance, that I might be some Runaway. After Dinner my Sleepiness return'd: and being shown to a Bed, I lay down without undressing, and slept till Six in the Evening; was call'd to Supper; went to Bed again very early and slept soundly till the next Morning. Then I made my self as tidy as I could, and went to Andrew Bradford the Printer's. I found in the Shop the old Man his Father, whom I had seen at New York, and who travelling on horse back had got to Philadelphia before me. He introduc'd me to his Son, who receiv'd me civilly, gave me a Breakfast, but told me he did not at present want a Hand, being lately supply'd with one. But there was another Printer in town lately set up, one Keimer,[87] who perhaps might employ me; if not, I should be welcome to lodge at his House, and he would give me a little Work to do now and then till fuller Business should offer.

The old Gentleman said, he would go with me to the new Printer: And when we found him, Neighbour, says Bradford, I have brought to see you a young Man of your Business, perhaps you may want such a One. He ask'd me a few Questions, put a Composing Stick[88] in my Hand to see how I work'd, and then said he would employ me soon, tho' he had just then nothing for me to do. And taking old Bradford whom he had never seen before, to be one of the Towns People that had a Good Will for him, enter'd into a Conversation on his present Undertaking and Prospects; while Bradford not discovering that he was the other Printer's Father, on Keimer's saying he expected soon to get the greatest Part of the Business into his own Hands, drew him on by artful Questions and starting little Doubts, to explain all his Views, what Interest he rely'd on, and in what manner he intended to proceed. I who stood by and heard all, saw immediately that one of them was a crafty old Sophister,[89] and the other a mere Novice. Bradford left me with Keimer, who was greatly surpriz'd when I told him who the old Man was.

Keimer's Printing House I found, consisted of an old shatter'd Press, and one small worn-out Fount of English,[90] which he was then using himself, composing in it an Elegy on Aquila Rose beforementioned, an ingenious young Man of excellent Character much respected in the Town, Clerk of the Assembly, and a pretty Poet. Keimer made Verses, too, but very indifferently. He could not be said to write them, for his Manner was to compose them in the Types directly out of his Head; so there being no Copy, but one Pair of Cases,[91] and the Elegy likely to require all the Letter, no one could help him. I endeavour'd to put his Press (which he had not yet us'd, and of which he understood nothing) into Order fit to be work'd with; and promising to come and print off his Elegy as soon as he should have got it ready, I return'd to Bradford's who gave me a little Job to do for the present, and there I lodged and dieted.[92] A few Days after Keimer sent for

---

[86] A tavern.
[87] Samuel Keimer (1688?–1742), an English printer who had come Philadelphia the previous year; unsuccessful there, he left in 1730.
[88] An instrument for setting type.   [89] A trickster.   [90] An oversized font, or type.
[91] Trays containing uppercase and lowercase types.   [92] Boarded.

me to print off the Elegy.[93] And now he had got another Pair of Cases, and a Pamphlet to reprint, on which he set me to work.

These two Printers I found poorly qualified for their Business. Bradford had not been bred to it, and was very illiterate; and Keimer tho' something of a Scholar, was a mere Compositor, knowing nothing of Presswork. He had been one of the French Prophets[94] and could act their enthusiastic Agitations. At this time he did not profess any particular Religion, but something of all on occasion; was very ignorant of the World, and had, as I afterwards found, a good deal of the Knave in his Composition. He did not like my Lodging at Bradford's while I work'd with him. He had a House indeed, but without Furniture, so he could not lodge me: But he got me a Lodging at Mr. Read's before-mentioned, who was the Owner of his House. And my Chest and Clothes being come by this time, I made rather a more respectable Appearance in the Eyes of Miss Read, than I had done when she first happen'd to see me eating my Roll in the Street.

I began now to have some Acquaintance among the young People of the Town, that were Lovers of Reading with whom I spent my Evenings very pleasantly and gaining Money by my Industry and Frugality, I lived very agreably, forgetting Boston as much as I could, and not desiring that any there should know where I resided, except my Friend Collins who was in my Secret, and kept it when I wrote to him. At length an Incident happened that sent me back again much sooner than I had intended.

* * *

from PART TWO

Continuation of the Account of my Life

Begun at Passy[1] 1784

* * *

It was about this time that I conceiv'd the bold and arduous Project of arriving at moral Perfection. I wish'd to live without committing any Fault at any time; I would conquer all that either Natural Inclination, Custom, or Company might lead me into. As I knew, or thought I knew, what was right and wrong, I did not see why I might not *always* do the one and avoid the other. But I soon found I had undertaken a Task of more Difficulty than I had imagined. While my *Attention was taken up* in guarding against one Fault, I was often surpriz'd by another. Habit took the Advantage of Inattention. Inclination was sometimes too strong for Reason. I concluded at length, that the mere speculative Conviction that it was our Interest to be compleatly virtuous, was not sufficient to prevent our Slipping, and that the contrary Habits must be broken and good ones acquired and established, before we can have any Dependance on a steady uniform Rectitude of Conduct. For this purpose I therefore contriv'd the following Method.

---

[93] *An Elegy on the Much Lamented Death of the Ingenious and Well-Beloved Aquila Rose, Clerk to the Honourable Assembly at Philadelphia, Who Died the 24th of the 4th Month, 1723. Aged 28.*

[94] French Protestant refugees in England in 1706, given to trances.

[1] A Paris suburb; Franklin stayed at the Hotel de Valentois in Passy while he was negotiating the Treaty of Paris. Although the treaty was signed September 3, 1783, ending the Revolutionary War, Franklin remained in Paris as minister until July 1785.

In the various Enumerations of the moral Virtues I had met with in my Reading, I found the Catalogue more or less numerous, as different Writers included more or fewer Ideas under the same Name. Temperance, for Example, was by some confin'd to Eating and Drinking, while by others it was extended to mean the moderating every other Pleasure, Appetite, Inclination or Passion, bodily or mental, even to our Avarice and Ambition. I propos'd to myself, for the sake of Clearness, to use rather more Names with fewer Ideas annex'd to each, than a few Names with more Ideas; and I included under Thirteen Names of Virtues all that at that time occurr'd to me as necessary or desirable, and annex'd to each a short Precept, which fully express'd the Extent I gave to its Meaning.

These Names of Virtues with their Precepts were

1. TEMPERANCE.

Eat not to Dulness.
Drink not to Elevation.

2. SILENCE.

Speak not but what may benefit others or yourself. Avoid trifling Conversation.

3. ORDER.

Let all your Things have their Places. Let each Part of your Business have its Time.

4. RESOLUTION.

Resolve to perform what you ought. Perform without fail what you resolve.

5. FRUGALITY.

Make no Expence but to do good to others or yourself: i.e. Waste nothing.

6. INDUSTRY.

Lose no Time. Be always employ'd in something useful. Cut off all unnecessary Actions.

7. SINCERITY.

Use no hurtful Deceit.
Think innocently and justly; and, if you speak, speak accordingly.

8. JUSTICE.

Wrong none, by doing Injuries or omitting the Benefits that are your Duty.

9. MODERATION.

Avoid Extreams. Forbear resenting Injuries so much as you think they deserve.

10. CLEANLINESS.

Tolerate no Uncleanness in Body, Cloaths or Habitation.

11. TRANQUILITY.

Be not disturbed at Trifles, or at Accidents common or unavoidable.

12. CHASTITY.

Rarely use Venery but for Health or Offspring; Never to Dulness, Weakness, or the Injury of your own or another's Peace or Reputation.

13. HUMILITY.

Imitate Jesus and Socrates.

My Intention being to acquire the *Habitude* of all these Virtues, I judg'd it would be well not to distract my Attention by attempting the whole at once, but to fix it on one of them at a time, and when I should be Master of that, then to proceed to another, and so on till I should have gone thro' the thirteen. And as the previous Acquisition of some might facilitate the Acquisition of certain others, I arrang'd them with that View as they stand above. *Temperance* first, as it tends to procure that Coolness and Clearness of Head, which is so necessary where constant Vigilance was to be kept up, and Guard maintained, against the unremitting Attraction of ancient Habits, and the Force of perpetual Temptations. this being acquir'd and establish'd, *Silence* would be more easy, and my Desire being to gain Knowledge at the same time that I improv'd in Virtue, and considering that in Conversation it was obtain'd rather by the use of the Ears than of the Tongue, and therefore wishing to break a Habit I was getting into of Prattling, Punning and Joking, which only made me acceptable to trifling Company, I gave *Silence* the second Place. This, and the next, *Order,* I expected would allow me more Time for attending to my Project and my Studies; RESOLUTION, once become habitual, would keep me firm in my Endeavours to obtain all the subsequent Virtues; *Frugality* and *Industry,* by freeing me from my remaining Debt, and producing Affluence and Independance, would make more easy the Practice of *Sincerity* and *Justice,* etc., etc. Conceiving then that agreable to the Advice of Pythagoras[2] in his Golden Verses daily Examination would be necessary, I contriv'd the following Method for conducting that Examination.

Form of the Pages

Temperance.						
Eat not to Dulness. Drink not to Elevation.						
S	M	T	W	T	F	S
T						
S	••	•		•		•
O	•	•	•		•	•
R			•			•
F		•			•	
I			•	•		
S						
J						
M						
Cl.						
T						
Ch.						
H						

[2] Pythagoras (6th century B.C.) was a Greek mathematician and philosopher; his "Golden Verses" were translated in Franklin's note: "Let sleep not close your eyes till you have thrice examined the transactions of the day: where have I strayed, what have I done, what good have I omitted?"

I made a little Book in which I allotted a Page for each of the Virtues. I rul'd each Page with red Ink, so as to have seven Columns, one for each Day of the Week, marking each Column with a Letter for the Day. I cross'd these Columns with thirteen red Lines, marking the Beginning of each Line with the first Letter of one of the Virtues, on which Line and in its proper Column I might mark by a little black Spot every Fault I found upon Examination to have been committed respecting that Virtue upon that Day.

I determined to give a Week's strict Attention to each of the Virtues successively. Thus in the first Week my great Guard was to avoid every the least Offence against Temperance, leaving the other Virtues to their ordinary Chance, only marking every Evening the Faults of the Day. Thus if in the first Week I could keep my first Line marked T clear of Spots, I suppos'd the Habit of that Virtue so much strengthen'd and its opposite weaken'd, that I might venture extending my Attention to include the next, and for the following Week keep both Lines clear of Spots. Proceeding thus to the last, I could go thro' a Course compleat in Thirteen Weeks, and four Courses a Year. And like him who having a Garden to weed, does not attempt to eradicate all the bad Herbs at once, which would exceed his Reach and his Strength, but works on one of the Beds at a time, and having accomplish'd the first proceeds to a Second; so I should have, (I hoped) the encouraging Pleasure of seeing on my Pages the Progress I made in Virtue, by clearing successively my Lines of their Spots, till in the End by a Number of Courses, I should be happy in viewing a clean Book after thirteen Weeks daily Examination.

This my little Book had for its Motto these Lines from Addison's *Cato;*[3]

> Here will I hold: If there is a Pow'r above us,
> (And that there is, all Nature cries aloud
> Thro' all her Works) he must delight in Virtue,
> And that which he delights in must be happy.

Another from Cicero.[4]

> O Vitœ Philosophia Dux! O Virtutum indagatrix, expultrixque vitiorum! Unus dies bene, et ex preceptis tuis actus, peccanti immortalitati est anteponendus.

Another from the Proverbs of Solomon speaking of Wisdom or Virtue;

> Length of Days is in her right hand, and in her Left Hand Riches and Honours; Her Ways are Ways of Pleasantness, and all her Paths are Peace.
>
> III, 16, 17.

---

[3] Joseph Addison's *Cato, A Tragedy* (1713), V.i.15–18.

[4] Marcus Tullius Cicero (106–43 B.C.), a Roman philosopher, statesman, and orator. Several lines of his *Tusculan Disputations*, (V.ii.5), are missing after *vitiorum:* "Oh philosophy, guide of life! Oh searcher out of virtues and expeller of vices! . . . One day lived well and according to thy precepts is to be preferred to an eternity of sin."

And conceiving God to be the Fountain of Wisdom, I thought it right and necessary to solicit his Assistance for obtaining it; to this End I form'd the following little Prayer, which was prefix'd to my Tables of Examination; for daily Use.

O Powerful Goodness! bountiful Father! merciful Guide! Increase in me that Wisdom which discovers my truest Interests; Strengthen my Resolutions to perform what that Wisdom dictates. Accept my kind Offices to thy other Children, as the only Return in my Power for thy continual Favours to me.

I us'd also sometimes a little Prayer which I took from Thomson's Poems.[5] viz

> Father of Light and Life, thou Good supreme,
> O teach me what is good, teach me thy self!
> Save me from Folly, Vanity and Vice,
> From every low Pursuit, and fill my Soul
> With Knowledge, conscious Peace, and Virtue pure,
> Sacred, substantial, neverfading Bliss!

The Precept of *Order* requiring that *every Part of my Business should have its allotted Time,* one Page in my little Book contain'd the following Scheme of Employment for the Twenty-four Hours of a natural Day,

The Morning Question, What Good shall I do this Day?	5 6 7 8	Rise, wash, and address *Powerful Goodness;* Contrive Day's Business and take the Resolution of the Day; prosecute the present Study: and breakfast?
	9 10 11	Work.
	12 1	Read, or overlook my Accounts, and dine.
	2 3 4 5	Work.
	6 7 8 9	Put Things in their Places, Supper, Musick, or Diversion, or Conversation, Examination of the Day.
Evening Question, What Good have I done to day?	10 11 12	
	1 2 3 4	Sleep.

[5] From *The Seasons* (1726), by James Thomson (1700–1748), "Winter," lines 218–223.

I enter'd upon the Execution of this plan for Self Examination, and continu'd it with occasional Intermissions for some time. I was surpriz'd to find myself so much fuller of Faults than I had imagined, but I had the Satisfaction of seeing them diminish. To avoid the Trouble of renewing now and then my little Book, which by scraping out the Marks on the Paper of old Faults to make room for new Ones in a new Course, became full of Holes: I transferr'd my Tables and Precepts to the Ivory Leaves of a Memorandum Book, on which the Lines were drawn with red Ink that made a durable Stain, and on those Lines I mark'd my Faults with a black Lead Pencil, which Marks I could easily wipe out with a wet Sponge. After a while I went thro' one Course only in a Year, and afterwards only one in several Years, till at length I omitted them entirely, being employ'd in Voyages and Business abroad with a Multiplicity of Affairs, that interfered, but I always carried my little Book with me.

My Scheme of ORDER, gave me the most Trouble, and I found, that tho' it might be practicable where a Man's Business was such as to leave him the Disposition of his Time, that of a Journey-man Printer for instance, it was not possible to be exactly observ'd by a Master, who must mix with the World, and often receive People of Business at their own Hours. *Order* too, with regard to Places for Things, Papers, etc. I found extreamly difficult to acquire. I had not been early accustomed to *Method,* and having an exceeding good Memory, I was not so sensible of the Inconvenience attending Want of Method. This Article therefore cost me so much painful Attention and my Faults in it vex'd me so much, and I made so little Progress in Amendment, and had such frequent Relapses, that I was almost ready to give up the Attempt, and content my self with a faulty Character in that respect. Like the Man who in buying an Ax of a Smith my neighbour, desired to have the whole of its Surface as bright as the Edge; the Smith consented to grind it bright for him if he would turn the Wheel. He turn'd while the Smith press'd the broad Face of the Ax hard and heavily on the Stone, which made the Turning of it very fatiguing. The Man came every now and then from the Wheel to see how the Work went on; and at length would take his Ax as it was without farther Grinding. No, says the Smith, Turn on, turn on; we shall have it bright by and by; as yet 'tis only speckled. Yes, says the Man; but—*I think I like speckled Ax best.* And I believe this may have been the Case with many who having for want of some such Means as I employ'd found the Difficulty of obtaining good, and breaking bad Habits, in other Points of Vice and Virtue, have given up the Struggle, and concluded that *a speckled Ax was best.* For something that pretended to be Reason was every now and then suggesting to me, that such extream Nicety as I exacted of my self might be a kind of Foppery in Morals, which if it were known would make me ridiculous; that a perfect Character might be attended with the Inconvenience of being envied and hated; and that a benevolent Man should allow a few Faults in himself, to keep his Friends in Countenance.

In Truth I found myself incorrigible with respect to *Order;* and now I am grown old, and my Memory bad, I feel very sensibly the want of it. But on the whole, tho' I never arrived at the Perfection I had been so ambitious of obtaining, but fell far short of it, yet I was by the Endeavour a better and a happier Man than I otherwise should have been, if I had not attempted it; As those who aim at perfect Writing by imitating the engraved Copies, tho' they never reach the wish'd for Excellence of those Copies, their Hand is mended by the Endeavour, and is tolerable while it continues fair and legible.

And it may be well my Posterity should be informed, that to this little Artifice, with the Blessing of God, their Ancestor ow'd the constant Felicity of his Life down to his 79th Year in which this is written. What Reverses may attend the Remainder is in the Hand of Providence: But if they arrive the Reflection on past Happiness enjoy'd ought to help his Bearing them with more Resignation. To *Temperance* he ascribes his long-continu'd Health, and what is still left to him of a good Constitution. To *Industry* and *Frugality* the early Easiness of his Circumstances, and Acquisition of his Fortune, with all that Knowledge which enabled him to be an useful Citizen, and obtain'd for him some Degree of Reputation among the Learned. To *Sincerity* and *Justice* the Confidence of his Country, and the honourable Employs it conferr'd upon him. And to the joint Influence of the whole Mass of the Virtues, even in the imperfect State he was able to acquire them, all that Evenness of Temper, and that Chearfulness in Conversation which makes his Company still sought for, and agreable even to his younger Acquaintance. I hope therefore that some of my Descendants may follow the Example and reap the Benefit.

It will be remark'd that, tho' my Scheme was not wholly without Religion there was in it no Mark of any of the distinguishing Tenets of any particular Sect. I had purposely avoided them; for being fully persuaded of the Utility and Excellency of my Method, and that it might be serviceable to People in all Religions, and intending some time or other to publish it, I would not have any thing in it that should prejudice any one of any Sect against it. I purposed writing a little Comment on each Virtue, in which I would have shown the Advantages of possessing it, and the Mischiefs attending its opposite Vice; and I should have called my Book the ART *of Virtue,* because it would have shown the *Means* and *Manner* of obtaining Virtue, which would have distinguish'd it from the mere Exhortation to be good, that does not instruct and indicate the Means; but is like the Apostle's Man of verbal Charity, who only, without showing to the Naked and the Hungry *how* or where they might get Cloaths or Victuals, exhorted them to be fed and clothed. *James* II, 15, 16.[6]

But it so happened that my Intention of writing and publishing this Comment was never fulfilled. I did indeed, from time to time put down short Hints of the Sentiments, Reasonings, etc., to be made use of in it; some of which I have still by me: But the necessary close Attention to private Business in the earlier part of Life, and public Business since, have occasioned my postponing it. For it being connected in my Mind with a *great and extensive Project* that required the whole Man to execute, and which an unforeseen Succession of Employs prevented my attending to, it has hitherto remain'd unfinish'd.

In this Piece it was my Design to explain and enforce this Doctrine, that vicious Actions are not hurtful because they are forbidden, but forbidden because they are hurtful, the Nature of Man alone consider'd: That it was therefore every one's Interest to be virtuous, who wish'd to be happy even in this World. And I should from this Circumstance, there being always in the World a Number of rich Merchants, Nobility, States and Princes, who have need of honest Instruments for the

---

[6] "If a brother or sister be naked, and destitute of daily food, And one of you say unto them, Depart in peace, be ye warmed and filled; notwithstanding ye give them not those things which are needful to the body; what doth it profit?"

Management of their Affairs, and such being so rare have endeavoured to convince young Persons, that no Qualities were so likely to make a poor Man's Fortune as those of Probity and Integrity.

My List of Virtues contain'd at first but twelve: But a Quaker Friend having kindly inform'd me that I was generally thought proud; that my Pride show'd itself frequently in Conversation; that I was not content with being in the right when discussing any Point, but was overbearing and rather insolent; of which he convinc'd me by mentioning several Instances; I determined endeavouring to cure myself if I could of this Vice or Folly among the rest, and I add *Humility* to my List, giving an extensive Meaning to the Word. I cannot boast of much Success in acquiring the *Reality* of this Virtue; but I had a good deal with regard to the *Appearance* of it. I made it a Rule to forbear all direct Contradiction to the Sentiments of others, and all positive Assertion of my own. I even forbid myself agreable to the old Laws of our Junto,[7] the Use of every Word or Expression in the Language that imported[8] a fix'd Opinion; such as *certainly, undoubtedly,* etc., and I adopted instead of them, *I conceive, I apprehend,* or *I imagine* a thing to be so or so, or it so appears to me at present. When another asserted something, that I thought an Error, I deny'd my self the Pleasure of contradicting him abruptly, and of showing immediately some Absurdity in his Proposition; and in answering I began by observing that in certain Cases or Circumstances his Opinion would be right, but that in the present case there *appear'd* or *seem'd* to me some Difference, etc. I soon found the Advantage of this Change in my Manners. The Conversations I engag'd in went on more pleasantly. The modest way in which I propos'd my Opinions, procur'd them a readier Reception and less Contradiction; I had less Mortification when I was found to be in the wrong, and I more easily prevail'd with others to give up their Mistakes and join with me when I happen'd to be in the right. And this Mode, which I at first put on, with some violence to natural Inclination, became at length so easy and so habitual to me, that perhaps for these Fifty Years past no one has ever heard a dogmatical Expression escape me. And to this Habit (after my Character of Integrity) I think it principally owing, that I had early so much Weight with my Fellow Citizens, when I proposed new Institutions, or Alterations in the old; and so much Influence in public Councils when I became a Member. For I was but a bad Speaker, never eloquent, subject to much Hesitation in my choice of Words, hardly correct in Language, and yet I generally carried my Points.

In reality there is perhaps no one of our natural Passions so hard to subdue as *Pride.* Disguise it, struggle with it, beat it down, stifle it, mortify it as much as one pleases, it is still alive, and will every now and then peep out and show itself. You will see it perhaps often in this History. For even if I could conceive that I had compleatly overcome it, I should probably [be] proud of my Humility.

Thus far written at Passy 1784

1771–1790, 1791

---

[7] Spanish for "joined," a small secret group.
[8] Suggested.

Neoclassicism

The eighteenth century in Europe and America is commonly referred to as the Age of Reason or the Age of Enlightenment because of its renewed interest in science, empiricism, and philosophy. In literature and the arts the period was also characterized by a revival and imitation of the artistic principles of the ancient Greeks and Romans. Much of the poetry, painting, drama, and architecture of the eighteenth century exhibits the classical values of order, symmetry, elegance, and clarity. In American colleges, students adopted classical pseudonyms, such as Cicero and Augustus, as they imitated classical models in their poetry and essays. Another name for the period is the "Augustan Age." Public buildings and even farmhouses followed the Greco-Roman designs with classical colonnades and domes, a style that can still be viewed today in Washington, D.C., and throughout the South.

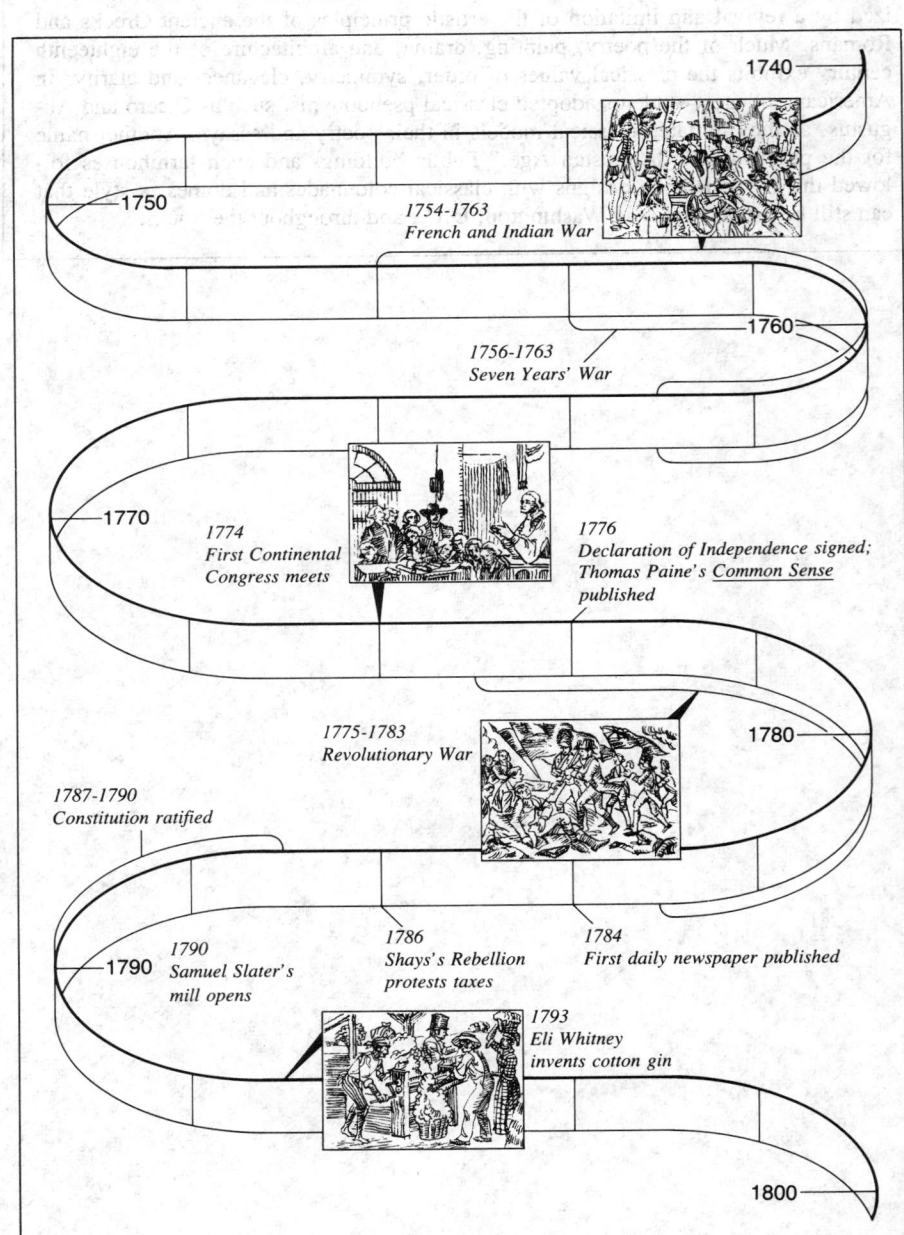

1740

1750

1754-1763
French and Indian War

1760

1756-1763
Seven Years' War

1770

1774
First Continental
Congress meets

1776
Declaration of Independence signed;
Thomas Paine's <u>Common Sense</u>
published

1775-1783
Revolutionary War

1780

1787-1790
Constitution ratified

1790
Samuel Slater's
mill opens

1786
Shays's Rebellion
protests taxes

1784
First daily newspaper published

1790

1793
Eli Whitney
invents cotton gin

1800

PART TWO

The Age of the Democratic Revolution
The Late 18th Century

In the latter half of the eighteenth century, Olaudah Equiano, an enslaved African, traveled through much of the British empire and keenly observed a wide range of societies from the British West Indies to South Carolina and Virginia to London. It was not obvious to him that mainland colonies were fated to be independent. However, during his lifetime the people of the mainland colonies came to feel distinctly different from other societies held by Britain and destined to separate from the British empire.

Over the course of a period historians have called "the long eighteenth century," 1689 to 1815, England and France were at war six times. These were trans-atlantic confrontations in which control of Atlantic commerce was at stake and in which the colonies of each nation were major suppliers of war material. English colonists and, during the American and French Revolutions, independent Americans fought in the armies and navies. The indigenous American peoples played complex roles as they sought to decrease European influence in America and also to use European presence to their own advantage.

The stakes steadily increased as did the European immigrant population in America, from 250,000 in 1700, to 1.15 million in 1750, to over 2 million by 1760. These immigrants were recruited from a wide range of countries—not only England, but various German principalities and Ireland (largely transplanted Scottish Protestants). As Parliament came to appreciate the formidable potential of the American colonies, it expanded its efforts to regulate their trade, particularly by taxing the highly profitable colonial trade with the French sugar islands. But taxes that seemed sensible to London legislators engaged in war with France seemed outrageous to colonists, who felt very distant from the European rivalries. An entire generation of colonial merchants and traders grew experienced at evading royal authority. Whereas the first three wars of the eighteenth century were fought largely at sea, the Seven Years' War (1756–1763) involved substantial confrontation on North American soil—deep in the West, as the French sought to exclude the English from the fur trade of the Ohio Valley, and in the Northeast, where major battles including colonial soldiers were fought for control of the fortresses guarding access to New France, in Nova Scotia. When peace was accomplished in 1763, the English had expelled France from North America.

Gratitude is not something to count on in international relations. Although the mainland colonies benefited from the removal of the French threat, colonists believed they had made major sacrifices in the venture. Nearly every working-class man in Boston had fought in the war, and many of them died; their impoverished widows and orphaned children were a painful legacy of the war. The proportion of poor people grew sharply in other cities as well. As the number of poor increased, the number of people with mixed feelings about the advantages of the British empire also swelled, and Americans' sense of dependence on their English mentors decreased. Legislators who had successfully struggled with colonial governors emerged with a new sense of competence.

However, the British Parliament understood the colonies to have been well served by the removal of the French threat. That removal had been expensive: the English national debt had doubled during the war. Americans were the least taxed people in the empire, indeed in the Atlantic world. There was now French-speaking Canada to support, peace to be maintained between Native Americans and settlers, and commerce to be managed, all requiring an enlarged British presence in the colonies and higher taxes to pay for that presence.

During the next ten years Parliament established a series of regulations intended to tighten and rationalize the administration of the colonies and a series of taxes generally calculated to be reasonable and mild. The strength and seriousness of colonial resistance to these measures and eventual defiance of British authority surprised not only Parliament but also colonial elites. Between 1764 and 1774 relations between the colonies and England were destabilized. In a series of now-famous crises many men and women took to the streets, sometimes violently, to express their resistance to English control. As they did so, internal political relationships within each colony were also destabilized. Group after group—lawyers objecting to stamp taxes on documents, merchants objecting to tight restrictions on shipping, consumers objecting to export and import taxes, artisans objecting to impressment into service in the British navy—rejected England's claims of benevolent rule, redefined themselves as deeply skeptical of the empire, and gradually claimed that their inheritance as free-born subjects entitled them to a final break with king and empire. These protests expressed an egalitarian ideology and a rejection of deference that infused American politics long after independence was accomplished.

The American Revolution

In each colony extralegal bodies bypassed official colonial governors and assemblies, trained militias, enforced boycotts of British goods, and obstructed British officials. Fighting broke out when the English General Thomas Gage sought to seize illegal stores of arms and ammunition in towns outside Boston. His detachment of men was met on the Lexington town common by seventy "minutemen." Eight Americans were killed, and the skirmish initiated both an undeclared war with England and a civil war between patriots and Loyalists. Americans could not

The Declaration of Independence *(1786) by John Trumbull. (Yale University Art Gallery)*

really explain what they were doing; successful rebellion of colonies against a powerful empire had not occurred since the Renaissance and not on so large a scale. Colonists were fighting for their traditional liberties as English subjects. It took fifteen months of public and private debate and the escalation of violence, during which Thomas Paine's extraordinary manifesto *Common Sense* (1776) was published, before the claim of independence could be articulated.

The war itself, as the historian John Shy wrote in *A People Numerous and Armed* (1976), was "a social process of political education." An estimated 250,000 men, eighty percent of adult males, served in the military at some point, and a higher percentage of the total population died than in any other American conflict except the Civil War. Men were held in the colonial army less by desperation and fear than by patriotism and commitment; to some extent this was also true of the British, with whom about 50,000 American Loyalists enlisted. The Revolution was one of the last wars in which women followed the armies of both sides, serving as an informal quartermaster corps—cooking food and laundering clothing for the soldiers.

The Revolutionary War stretched on for more than seven years; in American history, only the Vietnam War was longer. The British evacuated Boston shortly after the battle of Bunker Hill in 1776. The fighting then centered on the Middle Atlantic states, shifting to the South in 1778. General George Washington tried to avoid formal battles in which his vulnerable army was at risk, preferring harassment and skirmishing to wear down the British. In 1778 the Continental Congress negotiated a treaty of alliance with France, drawing French naval forces into the war on the American side—thus continuing the century-long Anglo-French hostility and eventually providing the margin of power that enabled the defeat of British forces in the battle of Yorktown in 1781. Even after the British surrender, skirmishing between American Loyalists and patriots continued, especially in the South, until the ratification of the Treaty of Paris ended the war in 1783. That treaty, brilliantly negotiated by John Adams, John Jay, and to a lesser extent Benjamin Franklin, defused French temptations to establish a peace between England and France that would have ignored American interests. The treaty recognized full independence, territorial claims to the Mississippi River, and American fishing rights off Nova Scotia's highly profitable Grand Banks.

The American Constitution

While the battles of the war for independence were being fought, Americans faced the challenge of institutionalizing the republic they had claimed. It was one thing to declare that they were no longer subjects of the king and that the people ought to rule themselves; it was quite another to invent the mechanism by which that could be done. Thomas Jefferson gave the claim to independence classic expression in 1776 in the Declaration of Independence. But several years passed before Americans identified themselves not as "inhabitants" of America or as "members" of their states but as "citizens." The concept of citizenship implies conscious choice: that people could become citizens of nations other than those into which they were born; that a citizen's primary obligation to the republic is loyalty. But citizenship was expressed in different modes for people of different sexes. By the example of the Roman republic of antiquity and the Italian republics of the Renaissance, only for men did citizenship include the obligation to bear arms in defense of the state and the right of property holders to vote for legislators. Furthermore, citizenship, as developed in America, was completely denied to slaves.

Each colony, using its long experience in colonial assemblies, declared itself to be a state, joined in a confederation of equals. Each created for itself a written constitution modeled on (but rarely duplicating) the old colonial charters given by the king to trading companies or proprietors. Into these new constitutions were embedded bills of rights, based on the British example but protecting citizen against state more broadly than the British model of protection of Parliament against king.

Post-Revolutionary America

After the Revolution American society was caught in major social transformations that shattered old rhythms of life. Could the new nation respond to political and social challenges in such a way as to confirm its republican assertions and to maintain its political integrity? The nation was populated with former soldiers, slaves who had learned the language of freedom and were making claims for their own, Native Americans who did not recognize England's peace treaty, and former Loyalists whose emotional connection to the new nation was tenuous. Could a people who had learned how to overthrow government be governed? In 1786 armed Massachusetts farmers led by war-veteran Daniel Shays demonstrated (in Shays' Rebellion) how intensely people might defy regressive taxes, deflationary monetary policies, and elite claims of political hegemony. Members of elites feared that Americans, having learned to sustain popular militancy, would make it the norm in the new republic. This fear reinforced other reasons for restlessness with the Articles of Confederation—America's first constitution, adopted in 1781—notably a confederation's weakness in dealing with matters of foreign policy and taxation, and strengthened those who called for a convention to revise the Articles of Confederation.

Fifty-five delegates from twelve states (all except Rhode Island) devised a strikingly new frame of government, sharply different from the Articles of Confederation they had set out to revise. The new government would have a national judiciary, a national Congress with the power to tax and to regulate foreign and interstate commerce, and a president. Members of the Senate were to be selected by state legislatures, the president by an electoral college. The new government was to have broad grants of power, such as authority to provide for the "general welfare of the United States."

Slavery was the most potentially explosive issue at the Constitutional Convention. Northern delegates who hoped for the natural erosion of the slave system settled for the avoidance of the term "slave" in the text and for the right to end the slave trade after 1808. Persons "held to service" were required to be "delivered up" to those who claimed them if they had fled across state lines. Most important, the Constitution provided that three-fifths of the slave population would be counted for purposes of representation (though not for the purposes of taxation, as originally proposed in the "Three-Fifth's Compromise"). Thus, slavery and sectional differences were inextricably bound in the new political order.

By including provision for amendment, the framers of the Constitution embedded in it the capacity for change. This resiliency was its salvation. Several states ratified it only on the understanding that it would quickly be amended to make explicit that Congress might not abridge freedom of speech, press, or religion; that it would protect individual rights to trial by "an impartial jury"; that citizens would not be "deprived of life, liberty, or property, without due process of law"; and that citizens would be "secure in their persons, houses, papers, and effects, against unreasonable searches and seizures." The ratification process, in which delegates especially elected for that purpose voted on the Constitution in special conventions in each state (1787–1790), was a dazzling political innovation that had already been developed for state constitutions during the war. The process clearly separated the statutory law of legislatures from the fundamental law of the Constitution; it was the mechanism by which "the people's" claims to sovereignty could be put into practice.

The combatants in the great political debates of the early republic—supporting or opposing a federal Constitution, subsequently opponents in the first party system of Federalists and Republicans—were locked in an uneasy dialectic made intense by the understanding that decisions once made were likely to set permanent precedents. The victors in a revolution typically define themselves as heirs of its principles and define their political opponents as counter-revolutionary. That happened in France in the 1790s, in many postcolonial African nations, and in the

Soviet Union, Eastern Europe, and China in the twentieth century. During the party battles of the 1790s Jeffersonians defined their opponents as "monarchists"; Federalists called their opponents "seditious." But the postwar consensus that established the federal Constitution did not unravel into a repeated cycle of revolutions. Instead of dividing into pro- and anti-Revolutionary factions, American political parties groped toward a theory of legitimate opposition and modern political parties well before it was expressed elsewhere. In 1800 Thomas Jefferson became the first postrevolutionary leader ever to be elected head of state by the votes of an opposition party. Among the revolutionary generation's most important contributions to political theory is the concept of the "loyal opposition."

===CONTEXTS===

From the early 1770s through 1790s African-American slaves petitioned the state of Massachusetts to recognize their legal right to freedom. The ideas and language of these petitions first anticipated and later echoed the Declaration of Independence. The following excerpt is from a petition to the Massachusetts Bay Colony's House of Representatives (original spelling retained).

[The Early Abolition Movement]

The petition of A Great Number of Blackes detained in a State of slavery in the Bowels of a free & Christian Country Humbly shuwith that your Petitioners apprehend that they have in Common with all other men a Natural and Unaliable Right to that freedom which the Grat Parent of the Unavers hath Bestowed equalley on all menkind and which they have Never forfuted by any Compact or agreement whatever—but thay wher Unjustly Dragged by the hand of cruel Power from their Derest friends and sum of them Even torn from the Embraces of their tender Parents—from A popolous Pleasant and plentiful contry and in violation of Laws of Nature and off Nations and in defiance of all the tender feelings of humanity Brough hear Either to Be sold Like Beast of Burthen & Like them Condemnd to Slavery for Life—Among A People Profesing the mild Religion of Jesus A people Not Insensible of the Secrets of Rationable Being Nor without spirit to Resent the unjust endeavours of others to Reduce them to a state of Bondage and Subjection your honouer Need not to be informed that A Life of Slavery Like that of your petioners Deprived of Every social privilege of Every thing Requiset to Render Life Tolable is far worse then Nonexistance.

Your petioners . . . therfor humble Beseech your honours to give this petion its due weight & consideration and cause an act of the Legislatur to be past Wherby they may Be Restored to the Enjoyments of that which is the Naturel Right of all men—and their Children who wher Born in this Land of Liberty may not be heald as Slaves after they arive at the age of Twenty one years so may the Inhabitance of thes Stats No longer chargeable with the inconsistancey of acting themselves the part which they condem and oppose in others Be prospered in their present Glorious struggle for Liberty and have those Blessing to them, &c.

Anonymous black slaves, 1777

The New Republic's Emerging Culture

The Revolution did not produce an egalitarian economic order. A commercial revolution and the early stages of industrial revolution undermined traditions of artisan production. Recent studies of major cities reveal stunning disparities of wealth both before and after the Revolution. In *Render Them Submissive* (1980) the historian John Alexander reports that less than one percent of Philadelphia's taxpayers owned more taxable property than did the bottom seventy-five percent in 1800. The earliest factories for mass production of textiles—beginning with Samuel Slater's mill in Pawtucket, Rhode Island, in 1790—employed a work force largely composed of women and children and signaled a major shift in employer/employee relations. Whites continued to be made indentured servants; one out of five Americans remained enslaved.

The era of the early republic was a paradoxical moment in the history of slavery. On the one hand, the defense of slavery was shaken in theory by the Revolution's egalitarian principle. "See your Declaration, Americans!!! Do you understand your own language?" demanded the freeborn African-American David Walker in his powerful pamphlet *Appeal to the Colored Citizens of the World* (1829). The institution of slavery was shaken in practice when African-Americans served in patriot armies or fled with the British and took advantage of the disruptions of war to shape their own communities. During the 1780s slavery lost its legal foundations in much of the North. The phrase "all men are born free and equal" was interpreted by the Massachusetts courts to outlaw slavery implicitly. Pennsylvania, Rhode Island, New York, and Connecticut adopted gradual-emancipation laws. The Northwest Ordinance, one of the last statutes of the Continental Congress, forbade slavery in the region that is now Ohio, Indiana, Illinois, and Michigan. On the other hand, Eli Whitney's invention of the cotton gin in 1793, the subsequent invigoration of the cotton economy, and the opening of the Old Southwest to settlement and of the Old South to the slave trade until 1808 resulted in an extraordinary expansion of slavery in the postwar period. The historian Allan Kulikoff in his essay "Uprooted Peoples" (in *Slavery and Freedom in the Age of the American Revolution* [1983, Ira Berlin and Ronald Hoffman, eds.]) estimates that at least 250,000 slaves were forcibly moved from the Old South to the frontier and at least another 100,000 new slaves were imported during the quarter-century after the Treaty of Paris was signed. The phrase "all men are born free and equal" was interpreted by Virginia courts *not* to outlaw slavery, and emancipation was severely constrained by law in most southern states. These developments heightened the social differences between northern society, where slavery was declining, and southern society, where technology and geographic expansion supported the region's "peculiar institution."

Despite an antimilitarist tradition and a rhetoric that proclaimed "no standing armies" and called for reliance on militia, the national government built a professional army. Within twenty-five years after the Revolution, the military establishment included 14 frontier forts, 13 frigates, and 6 arsenals. Struggle over how the national defense was to be managed became one of the distinguishing features of the debate between Federalists and Jeffersonians. In the end even the Jeffersonians conceded that to rely on the militia—egalitarian and democratic though it might be—risked anarchy and vulnerability. When Jefferson came to power, one of his first acts was to establish a military academy.

=CONTEXTS=

After the Revolution, occupation of Native-American lands had government sanction through treaties. Because the native tribes were separated by great distances, their members did not consult among themselves about their property rights. The famous Shawnee leader Tecumseh (1768–1813) traveled across the Midwest and South, urging the many tribes to unite into one resisting political force. Although his plan failed he became legendary for his effort, initiative, and oratory. This speech was addressed to the Osage tribe of the Ohio River Valley.

[Tecumseh Speaks]

Brothers—We all belong to one family; we are all children of the Great Spirit; we walk in the same path; slake our thirst at the same spring; and now affairs of the greatest concern lead us to smoke the pipe around the same council fire!

Brothers—We are friends; we must assist each other to bear our burdens. The blood of many of our fathers and brothers has run like water on the ground, to satisfy the avarice of the white men. We, ourselves, are threatened with a great evil; nothing will pacify them but the destruction of all the red men.

Brothers—When the white men first set foot on our grounds, they were hungry; they had no place on which to spread their blankets, or to kindle their fires. They were feeble; they could do nothing for themselves. Our fathers commiserated their distress, and shared freely with them whatever the Great Spirit had given his red children. They gave them food when hungry, medicine when sick, spread skins for them to sleep on, and gave them grounds, that they might hunt and raise corn.

Brothers—The white people are like poisonous serpents: when chilled, they are feeble, and harmless, but invigorate them with warmth, and they sting their benefactors to death.

* * *

Brothers—Our Great Father [King George III] over the great waters is angry with the white people, our enemies. He will send his brave warriors against them; he will send us rifles, and whatever else we want—he is our friend, and we are his children.

Brothers—Who are the white people that we should fear them? They cannot run fast, and are good marks to shoot at: they are only men; our fathers have killed many of them; we are not squaws, and we will stain the earth red with their blood.

Brothers—The Great Spirit is angry with our enemies; he speaks in thunder, and the earth swallows up villages, and drinks up the Mississippi. The great waters will cover their lowlands; their corn cannot grow; and the Great Spirit will sweep those who escape to the hills from the earth with his terrible breath.

Brothers—We must be united; we must smoke the same pipe; we must fight each other's battles; and more than all, we must love the Great Spirit; he is for us; he will destroy our enemies, and make his red children happy.

Tecumseh, 1810

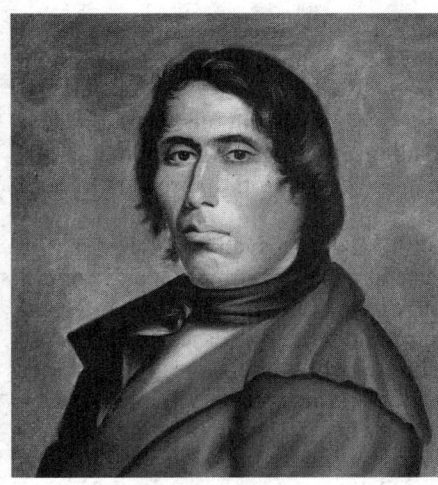

*Portrait of Tecumseh,
by an unknown artist.*

The army of the early republic was used mainly against Native Americans. Alliance with Britain and subsequent defeat had a profound impact on tribal cultures. New national policy offered native peoples the choice of forcible removal or complete disruption of their culture. Federal policy was shaped by ambivalence about the future place of indigenous peoples and by resentment of the ability of Native Americans to maintain control over substantial regions of the new nation, especially the Ohio Valley. Historians, once apt to assume that Native-American cultures were doomed to extinction before the inexorable pressures of "civilization," now tend to emphasize the dynamism of native cultures, the vigor of efforts of leaders such as Tecumseh to sustain the vitality of Native-American alliances, and the military force that was required to silence Native-American resistance.

The Revolutionary era was one of major cultural shifts. One of the most deeply radical choices made by the Revolutionary generation was the separation of church and state. So long as the Anglican church, headed by the king of England, was established by the government, political revolution against the king could not help but be a religious revolution also. Many individuals, by refusing to take communion in the established church, may well have become aware that there might be secular concerns, as well, over which the state had no right to dictate. The separation of church and state was expressed in Thomas Jefferson's "Bill for Establishing Religious Freedom" (1786): "Our civil rights have no dependence on our religious opinions . . . truth is great and will prevail if left to herself . . . ."

Literacy in Post-Revolutionary America

The early years of the republic were marked by a growth of literacy and by the transition to a print culture. Because the increasingly commercial economy relied on written accounts and contracts, more people needed to learn to write and to use arithmetic. Historians of literacy now argue that the availability of print materials was the most important factor in the spread of literacy in America and in Europe. It engendered a "need" to read, write, and compute in order to carry out work, interact with merchants and traders, and connect with society outside one's own family and community. The first newspaper to be produced daily, the *Pennsylvania Packet* in 1784, made fresh reading material available every day in Philadelphia. The establishment of schools followed rather than initiated the spread of literacy. The growing understanding of reading, writing, and arithmetic now seems to have been due primarily to a commercial revolution that rewarded holders of these skills.

In addition, individuals possessing these skills had the psychological advantage of being less dependent on social superiors as sources of information and control. Although women's literacy lagged behind that of men of their own race and class, a gradual growth in the ability of women to read and write decreased their intellectual dependence on local sources of information such as ministers, parents, perhaps husbands; a woman could read broadsides and newspapers for herself and subscribe to books and magazines published elsewhere. The literacy gap between white men and women, substantial in the 1790s, virtually closed by the national census of 1840, which showed nearly universal literacy among northern whites and no gender disparity. At least fifty percent of free black people could read, a stunning accomplishment considering that slaves were generally denied access to print and that the free blacks of 1850 were likely to belong to the first generation in their families to be literate. To the extent that later marriages, a decline of household production, and the increasing availability of consumer goods permit control of one's life, these factors appear to have fostered the demographic transition denoted by a substantial decline in average family size among whites in the new republic.

Increased access to information accompanied a new understanding of citizenship; the "private" roles of wife and mother came to have an important political dimension. When Abigail Adams demanded that the new code of laws "remember the ladies," she proceeded to the issue of domestic violence: "Put it out of the power of husbands to use us with impunity; remember all men would be tyrants if they could," she wrote to John Adams in 1776. She understood that public and private arrangements were inextricably linked. The republic relied on mothers, it was understood, because mothers would socialize the next generation of virtuous citizens. But the new republic made no space for women as formal participants in political decision-making.

Many of the first novels written in America, the literary critic Cathy Davidson observes in *Revolution and the Word* (1986), "emphasized the class, gender and racial inequities in the new land." Lacking the optimism of the essayist Michel-Guillaume Jean de Crèvecoeur and the poets Philip Freneau and Joel Barlow, female novelists such as Susannah Haswell Rowson and Hannah Webster Foster stressed the dangers awaiting women in the new society: women's vulnerability to seduction and disaster when acting on their inclinations for independence and self-fulfillment, which the ideology of the early republic prescribed for men. When Thomas Jefferson scorned fiction and denied it to his daughter, he was barring her from virtually the only category of literature in which women were portrayed as active agents in shaping their own lives.

"Early national America" was a postrevolutionary society with problems of instability not unlike those that face other societies emerging from profoundly disruptive struggles. It was a society caught in the later stages of a commercial revolution and in the early stages of industrialization: a society in the early stages of becoming what we now call modern. It was a society committed to maintaining slavery and deferential patterns of race relations. But it was also a society developing a radically new political system and at the same time adjusting to new modes of communication, new styles of consumption, new patterns of family relations, and newly negotiated gender relations.

LATE 18TH-CENTURY NONFICTION PROSE

Nonfiction prose in seventeenth-century America was predominantly religious in tone and European in audience. In the eighteenth century the growing economic and political interdependence within the colonies altered both these emphases. Changing patterns of literary production and distribution transformed the cultural geography of the nation. Early in the eighteenth century the publishing center for American texts began to shift from London to America, a shift not completed until the nineteenth century. Books had been published as early as 1639 in Massachusetts; by 1763 all thirteen colonies had successful printers. The growth of an indigenous publishing industry was affected by the availability of transportation routes to facilitate distribution. With its underdeveloped roads and rural economy, the South lagged behind New England and the Middle Atlantic states. Even in New England, which produced a large number of texts, circulation was relatively restricted. The difficulty of travel prevented Boston and other New England towns from having easy access to outlying regions, possible in the more centrally located cities farther south.

The center of publishing relocated from Boston to New York and especially to Philadelphia. This relocation was accompanied by a broadening of the audience. Given the high cost of books—roughly three to four times modern prices—readers increasingly turned to lending libraries. In addition to circulating libraries, where individual books were rented for a small charge, and to institutional libraries attached to colleges, social or subscription libraries had appeared in most towns by the end of the eighteenth century. Members of such libraries paid an annual fee for the privilege of unlimited borrowing.

Those readers who found books too expensive or time-consuming turned to newspapers. Starting in 1690 with the short-lived Boston *Publick Occurrences Both Forreign and Domestick,* by the publisher Benjamin Harris, most colonies had at least one weekly publication by mid-century. To supplement this periodical source of literature and politics, and as a partial outgrowth of it, printers issued pamphlets, almanacs, ballads, broadsides (large sheets of paper on which a political message or advertisement is printed), and other flimsily-bound publications sold individually at a low price. In the post-Revolutionary War period these mass-market issues were joined by somewhat more elitist magazines: the *Columbian Magazine*, the *American Museum*, the *Massachusetts Magazine*, and the *New York Magazine*.

The variety of these eighteenth-century publications and of their means of production challenges traditional assumptions about aesthetic value and even about "the book" as the primary object of literary study. These publications shared a common concern with the consolidation of the colonies into a political and cultural unit. Whereas seventeenth-century writers looked primarily to God for salvation and to England for population and approval, eighteenth-century writers characteristically looked homeward in an attempt to construct an independent cultural identity for America.

The shift in emphasis is clearest in descriptions of the land. Early accounts of America were highly rhetorical, overstating and at times mythicizing the country's charms to attract immigrants and income. By the end of the seventeenth century, writers had begun to study the landscape for its own sake. Samuel Sewall's 1697 Puritan celebration of the beauty of Plum Island foreshadows the rising concern with natural history and scientific observation. Subsequent thinkers such as Cotton Mather, Jonathan Edwards, and Benjamin Franklin were admired as much for their scientific endeavors as for their theology and politics. Travel narratives including the journal of Sarah Kemble Knight (first published in 1825) and nature descriptions, including botanist John Bartram's *Observations* (1751), marked the public's taste for realistic depictions of the countryside. This popular fascination with the picturesque quality of American geography culminated with Thomas Jefferson's masterful *Notes on the State of Virginia* (1785) and with *Travels* (1791) by William Bartram.

A similar realism infused the historical accounts of the period. The Puritan notion of history as providential, a progress report on God's ongoing plans for (and sometimes controversies with) His chosen people, continued in Cotton Mather's magisterial *Magnalia Christi Americana* (1702). But allegorical readings of the spiritual history of New England were overshadowed by more factual accounts of the colonies: Robert Beverley's *The History and Present State of Virginia* (1705); John Lawson's *A New Voyage to Carolina* (1709); Thomas Prince's *Chronological History of New England in the Form of Animals* (1736); Cadwallader Colden's *History of the Five Indian Nations* (1727); and especially William Byrd's *The History of the Dividing Line* (first published in 1841). In his official account of the surveying trip that drew the line between Virginia and North Carolina, the Virginian Byrd epitomized the cultured man of the world who was quickly replacing the Boston theologian as the prototypical American.

Like the histories of the colonies, the personal histories of individuals became more worldly. The Puritan tradition of the spiritual autobiography continued in the biographical sections of Mather's *Magnalia* and in Edwards's unpublished "Personal Narrative" (written in 1740?). But like regionalism, sectarianism was giving way to a more inclusive view of the variety of religious experience. This ecumenical approach was evident in the interest in conversions of other sects, especially in Quaker narratives such as the *Journals* of Thomas Chalkley (1747) and of John Woolman (1774) and the *Accounts* of Elizabeth Ashbridge (1774) and of John Churchman (1779).

Although the famous secular diaries of Byrd and Knight were not published during the eighteenth century, their viewpoint was central to that period's most

Many buildings from the eighteenth century, known as the neoclassical period, imitate ancient Greece and Rome architecturally. Thomas Jefferson's designs for his home, Monticello, helped promote a classical revival.

celebrated personal narrative—Franklin's *Autobiography* begun in 1771 but not published in entirety until 1867. Bostonian and Philadelphian, printer and writer, scientist and politician, entrepreneur and philanthropist, Franklin symbolized the transitional character of the late eighteenth century. By describing the purely secular pursuit of success with the spiritual intensity of the Puritans, Franklin completed the shift from piety to moralism already begun by Cotton Mather's brief moral handbook *Bonifacius* (1710). Adopting a falsely naïve narrative voice, Franklin defined a new American hero, one whose devotion to America was as religious as was the Puritans' devotion to the church.

Franklin's *Autobiography* was one of the stylistic jewels of its time and served as the model for an ongoing tradition of rags-to-riches success stories that includes the work of Horatio Alger, Mark Twain, Frederick Douglass, Louisa May Alcott, F. Scott Fitzgerald, Edna Ferber, and J. D. Salinger. Yet, the contradictions inherent in Franklin's celebration of individual ingenuity were faced more directly in the other new form of autobiography of the time—the slave narrative. Earlier narratives had depicted captivity by Native Americans as an emblem of the soul's enslavement to, and ultimate escape from, sin. The slave narrative found a parallel in the captivity not of individuals but of a whole race. Beginning in 1760 with Briton Hammon's *A Narrative of the Uncommon Sufferings, and Surprising Deliverance of Briton Hammon, a Negro Man,* free blacks or fugitives such as John Marrant, James Albert Ukawsaw Gronniosaw, Venture Smith, and Abraham Johnstone recounted their persecution to argue for the redemptive power of religion and for the need to abolish the slave trade. The early masterpiece in this genre, *The Interesting Narrative of the Life of Olaudah Equiano, or Gustavus Vassa, the African* (1789), embodied the contradictions of the tradition and of the white culture that fostered it. Equiano's international identity and his black sense of self called into question the very notions of "America" and "liberty" then being institutionalized at the Constitutional Convention in Philadelphia. Equiano's mixture of morality and economics suggested even more fully than did Franklin's complacency the antisocial bias of the individualism that sponsored upward mobility.

=CONTEXTS=

After the Revolution the nature of American versus "the King's" English was a subject of great controversy. In his essays, dictionaries, and schoolbooks, Noah Webster (1758–1843) led efforts to define a distinctive American language. The following excerpt is from his preface to *An American Dictionary of the English Language* (1828).

[American English]

It is not only important, but, in a degree necessary, that the people of this country, should have an *American Dictionary* of the English Language; for, although the body of the language is the same as in England, and it is desirable to perpetuate that sameness, yet some differences must exist. Language is the expression of idea; and if the people of one country cannot preserve an identity of ideas, they cannot retain an identity of language. Now an identity of ideas depends materially upon a sameness of things or objects with which the people of the two countries are conversant. But in no two portions of the earth, remote from each other, can such identity be found. Even physical objects must be different.

* * *

It has been my aim in this work, now offered to my fellow citizens, to ascertain the true principles of the language, in its orthography and structure; to purify it from some palpable errors, and reduce the number of its anomalies, thus giving it more regularity and consistency in its forms, both of words and sentences; and in this manner, to furnish a standard of our vernacular tongue, which we shall not be ashamed to bequeath to *three hundred millions of people,* who are destined to occupy, and I hope, to adorn the vast territory within our jurisdiction.

Noah Webster, 1828

The tension between individual advancement and group loyalty implicit throughout the secular biographies was explicit in the controversial publications of political pamphleteers. Like their English counterparts, Americans had always debated issues of general concern through pamphlet wars. The spiritual revivals of the 1730s, 1740s, and 1750s initiated an endless series of denunciations and vindications of the doctrine of original sin and of the role of religion in salvation. In the 1760s, however, the rising hostility to British colonialism combined with advances in printing technology to produce an unparalleled outpouring: nine thousand publications between 1763 and 1783, of which some two thousand were political pamphlets. Their rhetoric drew on established sermon techniques and on traditional English models of Joseph Addison, Richard Steele, Jonathan Swift, and Daniel Defoe. The theory in these pamphlets was equally eclectic—a mixture of Puritan theology, the views of John Locke and other Enlightenment philosophers, and the oppositional politics of the English Commonwealth and later English Whig-party republicans. These intellectual and rhetorical sources were turned against themselves thematically to cut the colonies' religious and political ties to Europe.

The value of many pamphlets—produced swiftly and anonymously, commonly as reprints from newspapers—lies more in their historical importance than in their literary sophistication. Yet, some writers wrote often enough to perfect their literary skills as well. James Otis's *The Rights of the British Colonies* (1764) and *A Vindication of the British Colonies* (1765) and especially John Dickinson's *Letters from a Farmer in Pennsylvania* (1768) address problems more universal than the local British injustices that occasioned the writings. The master of pamphlet rhetoric was Thomas Paine. The precise reasons for Paine's preeminence are unclear. His late entry into the debate may have heightened the originality of his voice; his English training may have given him a stylistic edge; that he was not a native American may have saved him from the regional envy that restricted the audience of the talented but very Yankee John Adams. Paine may simply have published *Common Sense* (1776), the first American call for immediate independence from England, at exactly the right moment. Whatever the reasons, that pamphlet quickly became an international bestseller, matched in popularity only by Paine's later defense of the French Revolution and attack on English aristocracy, *The Rights of Man* (1791–1792).

The paradoxical combination of universal truth and individualized voice generally characteristic of the pamphleteers informed the most important political documents of the period, The Declaration of Independence (1776) and the essays of *The Federalist* (1787–1788), which sought to ratify the Constitution. *The Federalist* interests modern readers less for its explanation (correct or not) of the theory of representative government than for its depiction of the confusion and uncertainties surrounding the Constitution's ratification. Via the split personality of "Publius," the pseudonym used by *The Federalist* authors, New Yorker Alexander Hamilton and Virginian James Madison acted out the compromises—between federalism and nationalism, elitism and populism, North and South—that characterized the uneasy unification of thirteen disparate colonies and cultures.

The diversity of the new republic's literature was perhaps best represented by the masterpiece that began the national tradition in American literature, Michel-Guillaume Jean de Crèvecoeur's *Letters From an American Farmer* (1782). The work and author were in every sense anomalies. Crèvecoeur was a French aristocrat who relocated to French Canada and subsequently became a naturalized British subject in upstate New York. Persecuted by both sides during the early years of the American Revolution, he fled to France in 1780 with his manuscript and subsequently published an account of these experiences. Crèvecoeur imitated the pamphleteer tradition through a discontinuous series of fictional "letters." The sentimental appreciation of the landscape, the close observation of nature, the value of travel, and the cultural differences throughout the Americas were all treated in turn. The account darkened with the approaching threat of war and with the twin problems of slavery and Indian hostility. Crèvecoeur's famous question "What is an American?" marked a turning point. For the first time American literature explicitly and directly confronted its own unique character. Yet, the answer was at best preliminary; Crèvecoeur's sense of America was limited by his perspective as a privileged white male.

Crèvecoeur's limitations and ambivalences summarize the contradictory thrust of his time. Despite Abigail Adams's famous warning to her husband, John, not to forget "the ladies," the Constitutional Convention neglected to include women as participants in the new government. The construction of an independent identity for America required the redefinition and exclusion of a wide range of cultural differences—in politics and theology as well as in race and gender. Just as the importance of the American Revolution has at times made it seem the sole event of the eighteenth century, so the political writings of the revolutionaries have obscured a wealth of other literature. Subsequent analyses of that burgeoning cultural identity have only further simplified the transition from colony to republic by isolating Jefferson's democratic philosophy from the slave society in which he practiced it, for example, or Crèvecoeur's hopeful predictions for America from the irony and despair in which his book and life ended. Only when we attend to the extraordinary range of voices within eighteenth-century American literature and to the full complexity of each individual voice can we truly understand the richness and depth of this eclectic period.

Thomas Jefferson
(1743–1826)

"I have sworn upon the altar of God, eternal hostility against every form of tyranny over the mind of man." When Thomas Jefferson wrote these words in a letter to the physician/educator Benjamin Rush in 1800, Jefferson was at the midpoint of an already illustrious public career and would soon become president. A product of the Enlightenment, Jefferson believed that the United States offered the best hope for establishing a society based upon mankind's natural, inalienable rights. His writings, such as The Declaration of Independence (1776; of which he wrote the first draft), were typically the finest expression of the ideals that came to define the American national character.

Much of Jefferson's practical republicanism was the direct outgrowth of his early training. He was born in 1743 in Albemarle County, Virginia, to Jane Randolph and Peter Jefferson and into a lineage that combined the blue blood of the Virginia aristocracy with that of the self-made man. Throughout his life he fought against inherited privilege and preferment and argued in favor of a natural aristocracy, one open to all men but predicated upon virtue, merit, and achievement rather than on birthright. At age nine Jefferson studied Latin, Greek, and French; at fourteen he entered the school of Rev. James Maury. There Jefferson learned other languages and acquired a love of classical literature and gained a lifelong admiration for Greek and Roman ethical thought and self-discipline. At the College of William and Mary he was influenced by Dr. William Small, a professor of mathematics and philosophy, who developed Jefferson's knowledge of science and inductive reasoning. However, Jefferson made sharp distinctions between the learning he thought appropriate for women and that for men. As his letter to Nathaniel Burwell shows, he emphasized the practical, thought women should not study the classical languages, and was skeptical of fiction.

After graduating in 1762 Jefferson began a five-year intensive study of the law, particularly its guarantees of liberty, under the famed attorney George Wythe. Soon after Jefferson opened his law practice, he was elected to represent Albemarle County in the House of Burgesses in 1769. That year he began to build his home, Monticello. He married Martha Wayles Skelton in 1772, the year after his reelection; she died only ten years later after giving birth to their sixth child.

With the onset of the Revolution Jefferson became extraordinarily active in American politics. He represented Virginia in the Second Continental Congress in 1775, revised that state's legal code, drafted a public education bill, and, returning to the House of Burgesses (1776–1779), wrote the Statute of Virginia for Religious Freedom (not accepted until 1786). He then served as governor of Virginia (1779–1781) and as a congressman (1783–1784) and assisted Benjamin Franklin and John Adams with treaty negotiations in Paris in 1784 before succeeding Franklin as minister to France (1785–1789). From 1789 to 1793 Jefferson served as the first secretary of state and often opposed the extreme Federalist policies of Alexander Hamilton, favoring strong rights at the state and local levels.

Narrowly defeated for the presidency in 1776 by John Adams, Jefferson became vice-president, as was then the custom. As president from 1801 to 1809, he continued to champion individuals' and states' rights; made the Louisiana Purchase, which more than doubled America's size in 1803 and provided the land for individual ownership (which Jefferson considered necessary for human happiness); sponsored the Lewis and Clark expedition (1804–1806); and in 1806 signed a bill prohibiting the importation of slaves. After his political career ended, Jefferson sold his library of more than ten thousand volumes to the new nation in 1814 to form the core collection of the Library of Congress and founded the University of Virginia in 1817.

No summary of offices and achievements can present a full portrait of a man as complex as Jefferson. Politician, statesman, scientist, philosopher, architect, environmental planner, agriculturalist, inventor, writer, and patron of education and learning, he epitomized the eighteenth-century gentleman who did all things well and with easy grace. Yet, he was a man of paradoxes. An aristocrat, he established the small landowner as the ideal citizen; he loved Paris but promulgated the benefits of agrarian life; an indifferent orator,

A draft of the Declaration of Independence in Thomas Jefferson's handwriting.

he was a master of prose; and although he kept a large number of slaves, he saw slavery as a moral evil.

More than any of his peers in the American Revolution, Jefferson captured the country's spirit in his writing. His stirring words were so apt that they became the foundation of the nation's civil religion. His statements in the Declaration of Independence were the natural outgrowths of his earlier highly influential work, *A Summary of the Rights of British America* (1774), and led to his bill establishing religious freedom in Virginia. But the literary Jefferson is best known from his only book, *Notes on the State of Virginia* (1785), and his correspondence. The *Notes* were Jefferson's responses to a series of questions put to him by François Marbois, the secretary to the French minister in Philadelphia. Jefferson's analyses and sweeping descriptions compensate for what the notes lack in formal unity. In answering Marbois's queries about America and particularly Virginia, Jefferson chose to present his view of the "state" of the new nation, its condition and governance. Jefferson used the *Notes* to justify the Declaration of Independence, to show that the United States would succeed, and to disprove the French naturalist Georges Buffon's theory that all species, including man, tended to degenerate in the New World.

After his second term as president Jefferson returned to Monticello and entered a very active retirement marked by an enormous increase in his correspondence. In many ways the letter was his ideal literary form; it showcased his wit, zest, and wisdom as he expounded his ideas on religion, ethics, language, education, politics, and American society. Jefferson honed his artfulness through practice; more than twenty-five thousand of his letters survive, and a definitive collected edition of his works would likely exceed sixty volumes. One highlight of his letter-writing skills was the series of letters he exchanged with John Adams from 1811 until just before their deaths on the same day, July 4, 1826, the fiftieth anniversary of the signing of the Declaration of Independence. Following the direct style that paced his letters, Jefferson ordered the following epitaph engraved on his tombstone to sum up his life: ". . .Author of the Declaration of American Independence, of the Statute of Virginia for Religious Freedom, and Father of the University of Virginia."

Suggested Readings: A. Koch, *The Philosophy of Thomas Jefferson*, 1943. D. Malone, *Jefferson and His Times*, 6 vols., 1948–1981. F. Brodie, *Thomas Jefferson: An Intimate History*, 1974. H. S. Commager, *Jefferson, Nationalism and the Enlightenment*, 1975. G. Wills, *Inventing America: Jefferson's Declaration of Independence*, 1978. C. A. Miller, *Jefferson and Nature: An Interpretation*, 1988.

Texts Used: The Declaration of Independence: *Old South Leaflets*, Gen. Series, No. 3, Vol. I, (n.d.). "Queries": *Notes on the State of Virginia*, ed. W. Peden, 1955. "To John Adams," Oct. 28, 1813: *The Writings of Thomas Jefferson*, 1807–1815, Vol. IX, ed. P. L. Ford, 1898. "To Nathaniel Burwell," March 14, 1818: *The Writings of Thomas Jefferson*, 1816–1826, Vol. X, ed. P. L. Ford, 1899.

THE DECLARATION OF INDEPENDENCE

The Unanimous Declaration of the Thirteen United States of America

In Congress, July 4, 1776.

When in the Course of human events, it becomes necessary for one people to dissolve the political bands which have connected them with another, and to assume among the Powers of the earth, the separate and equal station which the Laws of Nature and of Nature's God entitle them, a decent respect to the opinions of mankind requires that they should declare the causes which impel them to the separation.

We hold these truths to be self-evident, that all men are created equal, that they are endowed by their Creator with certain unalienable Rights, that among these are Life, Liberty and the pursuit of Happiness. That to secure these rights, Governments are instituted among Men, deriving their just powers from the consent of the governed, That whenever any Form of Government becomes destructive of these ends, it is the Right of the People to alter or to abolish it, and to institute new Government, laying its foundation on such principles and organizing its powers in such form, as to them shall seem most likely to effect their Safety and Happiness. Prudence, indeed, will dictate that Governments long established should not be changed for light and transient causes; and accordingly all experience hath shown, that mankind are more disposed to suffer, while evils are sufferable, than to right themselves by abolishing the forms to which they are accustomed. But when a long train of abuses and usurpations, pursuing invariably the same Object evinces a design to reduce them under absolute Despotism, it is their right, it is their duty, to throw off such Government, and to provide new Guards for their future security.—Such has been the patient sufferance of these Colonies; and such is now the necessity which constrains them to alter their former Systems of Government. The history of the present King of Great Britain is a history of repeated injuries and usurpations, all having in direct object the establishment of an absolute Tyranny over these States. To prove this, let Facts be submitted to a candid world.

He has refused his Assent to Laws, the most wholesome and necessary for the public good.

He has forbidden his Governors to pass Laws of immediate and pressing importance, unless suspended in their operation till his Assent should be obtained; and when so suspended, he has utterly neglected to attend to them.

He has refused to pass other Laws for the accommodation of large districts of people, unless those people would relinquish the right of Representation in the Legislature, a right inestimable to them and formidable to tyrants only.

He has called together legislative bodies at places unusual, uncomfortable, and distant from the depository of their Public Records, for the sole purpose of fatiguing them into compliance with his measures.

He has dissolved Representative Houses repeatedly, for opposing with manly firmness his invasions on the rights of the people.

He has refused for a long time, after such dissolutions, to cause others to be elected; whereby the Legislative Powers, incapable of Annihilation, have returned to the People at large for their exercise; the State remaining in the mean time exposed to all the dangers of invasion from without, and convulsions within.

He has endeavoured to prevent the population of these States; for that purpose obstructing the Laws for Naturalization of Foreigners; refusing to pass others to encourage their migration hither, and raising the conditions of new Appropriations of Lands.

He has obstructed the Administration of Justice, by refusing his Assent to Laws for establishing Judiciary Powers.

He has made Judges dependent on his Will alone, for the tenure of their offices, and the amount and payment of their salaries.

He has erected a multitude of New Offices, and sent hither swarms of Officers to harrass our People, and eat out their substance.

He has kept among us, in times of peace, Standing Armies without the Consent of our legislature.

He has affected to render the Military independent of and superior to the Civil Power.

He has combined with others to subject us to a jurisdiction foreign to our constitution, and unacknowledged by our laws; giving his Assent to their Acts of pretended Legislation:

For quartering large bodies of armed troops among us:

For protecting them, by a mock Trial, from Punishment for any Murders which they should commit on the Inhabitants of these States:

For cutting off our Trade with all parts of the world:

For imposing taxes on us without our Consent:

For depriving us in many cases, of the benefits of Trial by Jury:

For transporting us beyond Seas to be tried for pretended offences:

For abolishing the free System of English Laws in a neighbouring Province, establishing therein an Arbitrary government, and enlarging its Boundaries so as to render it at once an example and fit instrument for introducing the same absolute rule into these Colonies:

For taking away our Charters, abolishing our most valuable Laws, and altering fundamentally the Forms of our Governments:

For suspending our own Legislatures, and declaring themselves invested with Power to legislate for us in all cases whatsoever.

He has abdicated Government here, by declaring us out of his Protection and waging War against us.

He has plundered our seas, ravaged our Coasts, burnt our towns, and destroyed the lives of our people.

He is at this time transporting large armies of foreign mercenaries to compleat the works of death, desolation and tyranny, already begun with circumstances of Cruelty & perfidy scarcely paralleled in the most barbarous ages, and totally unworthy the Head of a civilized nation.

He has constrained our fellow Citizens taken Captive on the high Seas to bear Arms against their Country, to become the executioners of their friends and Brethren, or to fall themselves by their Hands.

He has excited domestic insurrections amongst us, and has endeavoured to bring on the inhabitants of our frontiers, the merciless Indian Savages, whose known rule of warfare, is an undistinguished destruction of all ages, sexes and conditions.

In every stage of these Oppressions We have Petitioned for Redress in the most humble terms: Our repeated Petitions have been answered only by repeated injury. A Prince, whose character is thus marked by every act which may define a Tyrant, is unfit to be the ruler of a free People.

Nor have We been wanting in attention to our Brittish brethren. We have warned them from time to time of attempts by their legislature to extend an unwarrantable jurisdiction over us. We have reminded them of the circumstances of our emigration and settlement here. We have appealed to their native justice and magnanimity, and we have conjured them by the ties of our common kindred to disavow these usurpations, which would inevitably interrupt our connections and correspondence. They too have been deaf to the voice of justice and of consanguinity. We must, therefore, acquiesce in the necessity, which denounces our Separation, and hold them, as we hold the rest of mankind, Enemies in War, in Peace Friends.

We, therefore, the Representatives of the united States of America, in General Congress, Assembled, appealing to the Supreme Judge of the world for the rectitude of our intentions, do, in the Name, and by Authority of the good People of these Colonies, solemnly publish and declare, That these United Colonies are, and of Right ought to be Free and Independent States; that they are Absolved from all Allegiance to the British Crown, and that all political connection between them and the State of Great Britain, is and ought to be totally dissolved; and that as Free and Independent States, they have full Power to levy War, conclude Peace, contract Alliances, establish Commerce, and to do all other Acts and Things which Independent States may of right do. And for the support of this Declaration, with a firm reliance on the Protection of Divine Providence, we mutually pledge to each other our Lives, our Fortunes and our sacred Honor.

1776

from *NOTES ON THE STATE OF VIRGINIA**

QUERY XVII: RELIGION

The first settlers in this country were emigrants from England, of the English church, just at a point of time when it was flushed with complete victory over the religious of all other persuasions. Possessed, as they became, of the powers of making, administering, and executing the laws, they shewed equal intolerance in this country with their Presbyterian brethren, who had emigrated to the northern government. The poor Quakers were flying from persecution in England. They cast their eyes on these new countries as asylums of civil and religious freedom; but they found them free only for the reigning sect. Several acts of the Virginia assembly of 1659, 1662, and 1693, had made it penal in parents to refuse to have their children baptized; had prohibited the unlawful assembling of Quakers; had made it penal for any master of a vessel to bring a Quaker into the state; had ordered those already here, and such as should come thereafter, to be imprisoned till they should abjure the country; provided a milder punishment for their first and second return, but death for their third; had inhibited all persons from suffering their meetings in or near their houses, entertaining them individually, or disposing of books which supported their tenets. If no capital execution took place here, as did in New-England, it was not owing to the moderation of the church, or spirit of the legislature, as may be inferred from the law itself; but to historical circumstances which have not been handed down to us. The Anglicans retained full possession of the country about a century. Other opinions began then to creep in, and the great care of the government to support their own church, having begotten an equal degree of indolence in its clergy, two-thirds of the people had become dissenters at the commencement of the present revolution. The laws indeed were still oppressive on them, but the spirit of the one party had subsided into moderation, and of the other had risen to a degree of determination which commanded respect.

The present state of our laws on the subject of religion is this. The convention of May 1776, in their declaration of rights, declared it to be a truth, and a natural right, that the exercise of religion should be free; but when they proceeded to form

---

* Jefferson wrote *Notes on the State of Virginia* in response to twenty-three queries by the French government, concerning Virginia's people, history, geography, and ecology.

on that declaration the ordinance of government, instead of taking up every principle declared in the bill of rights, and guarding it by legislative sanction, they passed over that which asserted our religious rights, leaving them as they found them. The same convention, however, when they met as a member of the general assembly in October 1776, repealed all *acts of parliament* which had rendered criminal the maintaining any opinions in matters of religion, the forbearing to repair to church, and the exercising any mode of worship; and suspended the laws giving salaries to the clergy, which suspension was made perpetual in October 1779. Statutory oppressions in religion being thus wiped away, we remain at present under those only imposed by the common law, or by our own acts of assembly. At the common law, *heresy* was a capital offence, punishable by burning. Its definition was left to the ecclesiastical judges, before whom the conviction was, till the statute of the 1 El. c. 1.[1] circumscribed it, by declaring, that nothing should be deemed heresy, but what had been so determined by authority of the canonical scriptures, or by one of the four first general councils, or by some other council having for the grounds of their declaration the express and plain words of the scriptures. Heresy, thus circumscribed, being an offence at the common law, our act of assembly of October 1777, c. 17. gives cognizance of it to the general court, by declaring, that the jurisdiction of that court shall be general in all matters at the common law. The execution is by the writ *De hæretico comburendo.*[2] By our own act of assembly of 1705, c. 30, if a person brought up in the Christian religion denies the being of a God, or the Trinity, or asserts there are more Gods than one, or denies the Christian religion to be true, or the scriptures to be of divine authority, he is punishable on the first offence by incapacity to hold any office or employment ecclesiastical, civil, or military; on the second by disability to sue, to take any gift or legacy, to be guardian, executor, or administrator, and by three years imprisonment, without bail. A father's right to the custody of his own children being founded in law on his right of guardianship, this being taken away, they may of course be severed from him, and put, by the authority of a court, into more orthodox hands. This is a summary view of that religious slavery, under which a people have been willing to remain, who have lavished their lives and fortunes for the establishment of their civil freedom.

The error seems not sufficiently eradicated, that the operations of the mind, as well as the acts of the body, are subject to the coercion of the laws.[3] But our rulers can have authority over such natural rights only as we have submitted to them. The rights of conscience we never submitted, we could not submit. We are answerable for them to our God. The legitimate powers of government extend to such acts only as are injurious to others. But it does me no injury for my neighbour to say there are twenty gods, or no god. It neither picks my pocket nor breaks my leg. If it be said, his testimony in a court of justice cannot be relied on, reject it then, and be the stigma on him. Constraint may make him worse by making him a hypocrite, but it will never make him a truer man. It may fix him obstinately in his errors, but will not cure them. Reason and free enquiry are the only effectual agents against error. Give a loose to them, they will support the true religion, by bringing every false one to their tribunal, to the test of their investigation. They are the natural enemies of error, and of error only. Had not the Roman govern-

---

[1] The first year of Queen Elizabeth's reign, 1558–1559.   [2] On the burning of a heretic (Latin).
[3] Jefferson's note: "Furneaux passim." Philip Furneaux (1726–1783) was an English minister and author.

ment permitted free enquiry, Christianity could never have been introduced. Had not free enquiry been indulged, at the æra of the reformation, the corruptions of Christianity could not have been purged away. If it be restrained now, the present corruptions will be protected, and new ones encouraged. Was the government to prescribe to us our medicine and diet, our bodies would be in such keeping as our souls are now. Thus in France the emetic was once forbidden as a medicine, and the potatoe as an article of food. Government is just as infallible too when it fixes systems in physics. Galileo was sent to the inquisition for affirming that the earth was a sphere: the government had declared it to be as flat as a trencher, and Galileo was obliged to abjure his error. This error however at length prevailed, the earth became a globe, and Descartes[4] declared it was whirled round its axis by a vortex. The government in which he lived was wise enough to see that this was no question of civil jurisdiction, or we should all have been involved by authority in vortices. In fact, the vortices have been exploded, and the Newtonian principle of gravitation is now more firmly established, on the basis of reason, than it would be were the government to step in, and to make it an article of necessary faith. Reason and experiment have been indulged, and error has fled before them. It is error alone which needs the support of government. Truth can stand by itself. Subject opinion to coercion: whom will you make your inquisitors? Fallible men; men governed by bad passions, by private as well as public reasons. And why subject it to coercion? To produce uniformity. But is uniformity of opinion desireable? No more than of face and stature. Introduce the bed of Procrustes[5] then, and as there is danger that the large men may beat the small, make us all of a size, by lopping the former and stretching the latter. Difference of opinion is advantageous in religion. The several sects perform the office of a Censor morum[6] over each other. Is uniformity attainable? Millions of innocent men, women, and children, since the introduction of Christianity, have been burnt, tortured, fined, imprisoned; yet we have not advanced one inch towards uniformity. What has been the effect of coercion? To make one half the world fools, and the other half hypocrites. To support roguery and error all over the earth. Let us reflect that it is inhabited by a thousand millions of people. That these profess probably a thousand different systems of religion. That ours is but one of that thousand. That if there be but one right, and ours that one, we should wish to see the 999 wandering sects gathered into the fold of truth. But against such a majority we cannot effect this by force. Reason and persuasion are the only practicable instruments. To make way for these, free enquiry must be indulged; and how can we wish others to indulge it while we refuse it ourselves. But every state, says an inquisitor, has established some religion. No two, say I, have established the same. Is this a proof of the infallibility of establishments? Our sister states of Pennsylvania and New York, however, have long subsisted without any establishment at all. The experiment was new and doubtful when they made it. It has answered beyond conception. They flourish infinitely. Religion is well supported; of various kinds, indeed, but all good enough; all sufficient to preserve peace and order: or if a sect arises, whose tenets would subvert morals, good sense has fair play, and reasons and laughs it out of doors, without suffering the state to be troubled with it. They do not hang more malefactors than we do. They are not more disturbed with reli-

---

[4] René Descartes (1596–1650), a French philosopher and scientist.
[5] In classical mythology Procrustes was a highwayman who, to fit his iron bed, cut off or stretched his captives' legs.
[6] A critic of morals (Latin).

gious dissensions. On the contrary, their harmony is unparalleled, and can be ascribed to nothing but their unbounded tolerance, because there is no other circumstance in which they differ from every nation on earth. They have made the happy discovery, that the way to silence religious disputes, is to take no notice of them. Let us too give this experiment fair play, and get rid, while we may, of those tyrannical laws. It is true, we are as yet secured against them by the spirit of the times. I doubt whether the people of this country would suffer an execution for heresy, or a three years imprisonment for not comprehending the mysteries of the Trinity. But is the spirit of the people an infallible, a permanent reliance? Is it government? Is this the kind of protection we receive in return for the rights we give up? Besides, the spirit of the times may alter, will alter. Our rulers will become corrupt, our people careless. A single zealot may commence persecutor, and better men be his victims. It can never be too often repeated, that the time for fixing every essential right on a legal basis is while our rulers are honest, and ourselves united. From the conclusion of this war we shall be going down hill. It will not then be necessary to resort every moment to the people for support. They will be forgotten, therefore, and their rights disregarded. They will forget themselves, but in the sole faculty of making money, and will never think of uniting to effect a due respect for their rights. The shackles, therefore, which shall not be knocked off at the conclusion of this war, will remain on us long, will be made heavier and heavier, till our rights shall revive or expire in a convulsion.

QUERY XVIII: MANNERS

It is difficult to determine on the standard by which the manners of a nation may be tried, whether *catholic,*[1] or *particular*. It is more difficult for a native to bring to that standard the manners of his own nation, familiarized to him by habit. There must doubtless be an unhappy influence on the manners of our people produced by the existence of slavery among us. The whole commerce between master and slave is a perpetual exercise of the most boisterous passions, the most unremitting despotism on the one part, and degrading submissions on the other. Our children see this, and learn to imitate it; for man is an imitative animal. This quality is the germ of all education in him. From his cradle to his grave he is learning to do what he sees others do. If a parent could find no motive either in his philanthropy or his self-love, for restraining the intemperance of passion towards his slave, it should always be a sufficient one that his child is present. But generally it is not sufficient. The parent storms, the child looks on, catches the lineaments of wrath, puts on the same airs in the circle of smaller slaves, gives a loose to his worst of passions, and thus nursed, educated, and daily exercised in tyranny, cannot but be stamped by it with odious peculiarities. The man must be a prodigy who can retain his manners and morals undepraved by such circumstances. And with what execration should the statesman be loaded, who permitting one half the citizens thus to trample on the rights of the other, transforms those into despots, and these into enemies, destroys the morals of the one part, and the amor patriæ[2] of the other. For if a slave can have a country in this world, it must be any other in preference to that in which he is born to live and labour for another: in which he must lock up the faculties of his nature, contribute as far as depends on his individual en-

[1] Universal.   [2] "Patriotism" (Latin).

deavours to the evanishment of the human race, or entail[3] his own miserable condition on the endless generations proceeding from him. With the morals of the people, their industry also is destroyed. For in a warm climate, no man will labour for himself who can make another labour for him. This is so true, that of the proprietors of slaves a very small proportion indeed are ever seen to labour. And can the liberties of a nation be thought secure when we have removed their only firm basis, a conviction in the minds of the people that these liberties are of the gift of God? That they are not to be violated but with his wrath? Indeed I tremble for my country when I reflect that God is just: that his justice cannot sleep for ever: that considering numbers, nature and natural means only, a revolution of the wheel of fortune, an exchange of situation, is among possible events: that it may become probable by supernatural interference! The Almighty has no attribute which can take side with us in such a contest.—But it is impossible to be temperate and to pursue this subject through the various considerations of policy, of morals, of history natural and civil. We must be contented to hope they will force their way into every one's mind. I think a change already perceptible, since the origin of the present revolution. The spirit of the master is abating, that of the slave rising from the dust, his condition mollifying, the way I hope preparing, under the auspices of heaven, for a total emancipation, and that this is disposed, in the order of events, to be with the consent of the masters, rather than by their extirpation.   *1781–1782, 1785*

LETTERS TO JOHN ADAMS

[*Natural Aristocracy*]

Monticello October 28, 1813.

DEAR SIR,—

* * *

For I agree with you that there is a natural aristocracy among men. The grounds of this are virtue and talents. Formerly, bodily powers gave place among the aristoi.[1] But since the invention of gunpowder has armed the weak as well as the strong with missile death, bodily strength, like beauty, good humor, politeness and other accomplishments, has become but an auxiliary ground for distinction. There is also an artificial aristocracy, founded on wealth and birth, without either virtue or talents; for with these it would belong to the first class. The natural aristocracy I consider as the most precious gift of nature, for the instruction, the trusts, and government of society. And indeed, it would have been inconsistent in creation to have formed man for the social state, and not to have provided virtue and wisdom enough to manage the concerns of the society. May we not even say, that that form of government is the best, which provides the most effectually for a pure selection of these natural aristoi into the offices of government? The artificial aristocracy is a mischievous ingredient in government, and provision should be made to prevent its ascendency. On the question, what is the best provision, you and I

---

[3] Impose.
[1] "Aristocrats" (Greek).

differ; but we differ as rational friends, using the free exercise of our own reason, and mutually indulging its errors. You think it is best to put the pseudo-aristoi into a separate chamber of legislation, where they may be hindered from doing mischief by their co-ordinate branches, and where, also, they may be a protection to wealth against the Agrarian and plundering enterprises of the majority of the people. I think that to give them power in order to prevent them from doing mischief, is arming them for it, and increasing instead of remedying the evil. For if the co-ordinate branches can arrest their action, so may they that of the co-ordinates. Mischief may be done negatively as well as positively. Of this, a cabal in the Senate of the United States has furnished many proofs. Nor do I believe them necessary to protect the wealthy; because enough of these will find their way into every branch of the legislation, to protect themselves. From fifteen to twenty legislatures of our own, in action for thirty years past, have proved that no fears of an equalization of property are to be apprehended from them. I think the best remedy is exactly that provided by all our constitutions, to leave to the citizens the free election and separation of the aristoi from the pseudo-aristoi, of the wheat from the chaff. In general they will elect the really good and wise. In some instances, wealth may corrupt, and birth blind them; but not in sufficient degree to endanger the society.

It is probable that our difference of opinion may, in some measure, be produced by a difference of character in those among whom we live. From what I have seen of Massachusetts and Connecticut myself, and still more from what I have heard, and the character given of the former by yourself,[2] who know them so much better, there seems to be in those two States a traditionary reverence for certain families, which has rendered the offices of the government nearly hereditary in those families. I presume that from an early period of your history, members of those families happening to possess virtue and talents, have honestly exercised them for the good of the people, and by their services have endeared their names to them. In coupling Connecticut with you, I mean it politically only, not morally. For having made the Bible the common law of their land, they seemed to have modeled their morality on the story of Jacob and Laban.[3] But although this hereditary succession to office with you, may, in some degree, be founded in real family merit, yet in a much higher degree, it has proceeded from your strict alliance of Church and State. These families are canonized in the eyes of the people on common principles, "you tickle me, and I will tickle you." In Virginia we have nothing of this. Our clergy, before the revolution, having been secured against rivalship by fixed salaries, did not give themselves the trouble of acquiring influence over the people. Of wealth, there were great accumulations in particular families handed down from generation to generation, under the English law of entails.[4] But the only object of ambition for the wealthy was a seat in the King's Council.[5] All their court then was paid to the crown and its creatures; and they Philipised[6] in all collisions between the King and the people. Hence they were unpopular; and that unpopularity continues attached to their names. A Randolph, a

---

[2] Jefferson's note: "Vol. 1, page 111." Jefferson is referring to Adams's *Defense of the Constitutions of Government of the United States* (1787).

[3] A dynastic family (see Genesis 24–31).

[4] Law by which an estate must pass via an established list of successors rather than via a written will.

[5] The Privy Council, an advisory council selected by the king.

[6] Fought against independence for the people.

Carter, or a Burwell[7] must have great personal superiority over a common competitor to be elected by the people even at this day. At the first session of our legislature after the Declaration of Independence, we passed a law abolishing entails. And this was followed by one abolishing the privilege of primogeniture,[8] and dividing the lands of intestates[9] equally among all their children, or other representatives. These laws, drawn by myself, laid the ax to the foot of pseudo-aristocracy. And had another which I prepared been adopted by the legislature, our work would have been complete. It was a bill for the more general diffusion of learning. This proposed to divide every county into wards of five or six miles square, like your townships; to establish in each ward a free school for reading, writing, and common arithmetic; to provide for the annual selection of the best subjects from these schools, who might receive, at the public expense, a higher degree of education at a district school; and from these district schools to select a certain number of the most promising subjects, to be completed at an University, where all the useful sciences should be taught. Worth and genius would thus have been sought out from every condition of life, and completely prepared by education for defeating the competition of wealth and birth for public trusts. My proposition had, for a further object, to impart to these wards those portions of self-government for which they are best qualified, by confiding to them the care of their poor, their roads, police, elections, the nomination of jurors, administration of justice in small cases, elementary exercises of militia; in short, to have made them little republics, with a warden at the head of each, for all those concerns which, being under their eye, they would better manage than the larger republics of the county or State. A general call of ward meetings by their wardens on the same day through the State, would at any time produce the genuine sense of the people on any required point, and would enable the State to act in mass, as your people have so often done, and with so much effect by their town meetings. The law for religious freedom, which made a part of this system, having put down the aristocracy of the clergy, and restored to the citizen the freedom of the mind, and those of entails and descents nurturing an equality of condition among them, this on education would have raised the mass of the people to the high ground of moral respectability necessary to their own safety, and to orderly government; and would have completed the great object of qualifying them to select the veritable aristoi, for the trusts of government, to the exclusion of the pseudalists; and the same Theognis[10] who has furnished the epigraphs of your two letters, assures us that "Ουδεμιαν πω, Κυρν,' αγαθοι πολιν ωλεσαν ανδρες."[11] Although this law has not yet been acted on but in a small and inefficient degree, it is still considered as before the legislature, with other bills of the revised code, not yet taken up, and I have great hope that some patriotic spirit will, at a favorable moment, call it up, and make it the key-stone of the arch of our government.

With respect to aristocracy, we should further consider, that before the establishment of the American States, nothing was known to history but the man of the old world, crowded within limits either small or overcharged, and steeped in the vices which that situation generates. A government adapted to such men would be one thing; but a very different one, that for the man of these States. Here every

---

[7] Virginian aristocrats John Randolph, Landon Carter, Lewis Burwell.
[8] An eldest son's right to his father's estates.
[9] Those who die without leaving a will.   [10] A Greek poet of the sixth century B.C.
[11] "Curnis, good men have never harmed any city" (Greek).

one may have land to labor for himself, if he chooses; or, preferring the exercise of any other industry, may exact for it such compensation as not only to afford a comfortable subsistence, but wherewith to provide for a cessation from labor in old age. Every one, by his property, or by his satisfactory situation, is interested in the support of law and order. And such men may safely and advantageously reserve to themselves a wholesome control over their public affairs, and a degree of freedom, which, in the hands of the *canaille*[12] of the cities of Europe, would be instantly perverted to the demolition and destruction of everything public and private. The history of the last twenty-five years of France,[13] and of the last forty years in America, nay of its last two hundred years, proves the truth of both parts of this observation.

But even in Europe a change has sensibly taken place in the mind of man. Science had liberated the ideas of those who read and reflect, and the American example had kindled feelings of right in the people. An insurrection has consequently begun, of science, talents, and courage, against rank and birth, which have fallen into contempt. It has failed in its first effort, because the mobs of the cities, the instrument used for its accomplishment, debased by ignorance, poverty and vice, could not be restrained to rational action. But the world will recover from the panic of this first catastrophe. Science is progressive, and talents and enterprise on the alert. Resort may be had to the people of the country, a more governable power from their principles and subordination; and rank, and birth, and tinsel-aristocracy will finally shrink into insignificance, even there. This, however, we have no right to meddle with. It suffices for us, if the moral and physical condition of our own citizens qualifies them to select the able and good for the direction of their government, with a recurrence of elections at such short periods as will enable them to displace an unfaithful servant, before the mischief he meditates may be irremediable.

I have thus stated my opinion on a point on which we differ, not with a view to controversy, for we are both too old to change opinions which are the result of a long life of inquiry and reflection; but on the suggestions of a former letter of yours, that we ought not to die before we have explained ourselves to each other. We acted in perfect harmony, through a long and perilous contest for our liberty and independence. A constitution has been acquired, which, though neither of us thinks perfect, yet both consider as competent to render our fellow citizens the happiest and the securest on whom the sun has ever shone. If we do not think exactly alike as to its imperfections, it matters little to our country, which, after devoting to it long lives of disinterested labor, we have delivered over to our successors in life, who will be able to take care of it and of themselves.

Of the pamphlet on aristocracy which has been sent to you, or who may be its author, I have heard nothing but through your letter. If the person you suspect, it may be known from the quaint, mystical, and hyperbolical ideas, involved in affected, new-fangled and pedantic terms which stamp his writings. Whatever it be, I hope your quiet is not to be affected at this day by the rudeness or intemperance of scribblers; but that you may continue in tranquillity to live and to rejoice in the prosperity of our country until it shall be your own wish to take your seat among the aristoi who have gone before you. Ever and affectionately yours.

1813, 1829

---

[12] "Mob" (French).   [13] Since the French Revolution, 1789.

LETTER TO NATHANIEL BURWELL

[On Female Education]

Monticello, March 14, 1818

DEAR SIR,—

Your letter of February 17th found me suffering under an attack of rheumatism, which has but now left me at sufficient ease to attend to the letters I have received. A plan of female education has never been a subject of systematic contemplation with me. It has occupied my attention so far only as the education of my own daughters occasionally required. Considering that they would be placed in a country situation, where little aid could be obtained from abroad, I thought it essential to give them a solid education, which might enable them, when become mothers, to educate their own daughters, and even to direct the course for sons, should their fathers be lost, or incapable, or inattentive. My surviving daughter accordingly, the mother of many daughters as well as sons, has made their education the object of her life, and being a better judge of the practical part than myself, it is with her aid and that of one of her élèves[1] that I shall subjoin a catalogue of the books for such a course of reading as we have practiced.

A great obstacle to good education is the inordinate passion prevalent for novels, and the time lost in that reading which should be instructively employed. When this poison infects the mind, it destroys its tone and revolts it against wholesome reading. Reason and fact, plain and unadorned, are rejected. Nothing can engage attention unless dressed in all the figments of fancy, and nothing so bedecked comes amiss. The result is a bloated imagination, sickly judgment, and disgust towards all the real businesses of life. This mass of trash, however, is not without some distinction; some few modelling their narratives, although fictitious, on the incidents of real life, have been able to make them interesting and useful vehicles of a sound morality. Such, I think, are Marmontel's[2] new moral tales, but not his old ones, which are really immoral. Such are the writings of Miss Edgeworth,[3] and some of those of Madame Genlis.[4] For a like reason, too, much poetry should not be indulged. Some is useful for forming style and taste. Pope, Dryden, Thompson, Shakespeare, and of the French, Molière, Racine, the Corneilles,[5] may be read with pleasure and improvement.

The French language, become that of the general intercourse of nations, and from their extraordinary advances, now the depository of all science, is an indispensable part of education for both sexes. In the subjoined catalogue, therefore, I have placed the books of both languages indifferently, according as the one or the other offers what is best.

---

[1] "Students" (French).

[2] Jean François Marmontel (1723–1799), a French dramatist and novelist who wrote *Moral Tales* (1781).

[3] Maria Edgeworth (1767–1849), an English novelist known for *Castle Rackrent* (1800).

[4] Stéphanie Félicité du Crest de Saint-Aubin, Comtesse de Genlis (1746–1830), a French novelist known for *Madame de Cleremont* (1802).

[5] Writers Alexander Pope (1688–1744), John Dryden (1631–1700), James Thompson (1700–1748), William Shakespeare (1564–1616), Molière (Jean Baptiste Poquelin, 1622–1673), Jean Baptiste Racine (1639–1699), and Pierre Corneille (1606–1684) and his brother Thomas (1625–1709).

The ornaments too, and the amusements of life, are entitled to their portion of attention. These, for a female, are dancing, drawing, and music. The first is a healthy exercise, elegant and very attractive for young people. Every affectionate parent would be pleased to see his daughter qualified to participate with her companions, and without awkwardness at least, in the circles of festivity, of which she occasionally becomes a part. It is a necessary accomplishment, therefore, although of short use, for the French rule is wise, that no lady dances after marriage. This is founded in solid physical reasons, gestation and nursing leaving little time to a married lady when this exercise can be either safe or innocent. Drawing is thought less of in this country than in Europe. It is an innocent and engaging amusement, often useful, and a qualification not to be neglected in one who is to become a mother and an instructor. Music is invaluable where a person has an ear. Where they have not, it should not be attempted. It furnishes a delightful recreation for the hours of respite from the cares of the day, and lasts us through life. The taste of this country, too, calls for this accomplishment more strongly than for either of the others.

I need say nothing of household economy, in which the mothers of our country are generally skilled, and generally careful to instruct their daughters. We all know its value, and that diligence and dexterity in all its processes are inestimable treasures. The order and economy of a house are as honorable to the mistress as those of a farm to the master, and if either be neglected, ruin follows, and children destitute of the means of living.

This, Sir, is offered as a summary sketch on a subject on which I have not thought much. It probably contains nothing but what has already occurred to yourself, and claims your acceptance on no other ground than as a testimony of my respect for your wishes, and of my great esteem and respect.

1818

Thomas Paine
(1737–1809)

"Independence is my happiness, and I view things as they are, without regard to place or purpose; my country is the world, and my religion is to do good." Although these words from Thomas Paine's *The Rights of Man* (1791–1792) did not produce the same passionate response as did his "These are the times that try men's souls" from *The American Crisis* (1776), they tell more of his central core of vision than do his many well-known quotations. The work of this inspired agitator had international ramifications and belonged to the Enlightenment in its broadest terms. Whether Paine sought wage and labor reform or the direct overthrow of a monarchy, his quest was for human dignity and independence, for the creation of democratic republics, and ultimately for world peace. Paine saw the United States as the key to completing what he called the "circle of civilization." If each state could come together for the common good, then so could nations.

This early promoter of a utopian global village was born to Joseph Paine and Frances Cocke in Thetford, England, in 1737. At age thirteen Paine apprenticed with his father as a corset maker but ran away three years later to become a sailor. He then commenced a series of unsuccessful careers as a corset maker, excise (tax) officer, teacher, tobacconist, and grocer. Between 1757 and 1774 he married twice. In 1768, Paine wrote his first known pamphlet, *The Case of the Officers of Excise* (1772), to organize the excise collectors to raise their salary, and solicited the aid of British writer Oliver Goldsmith to influence Parliament. Obstinate and argumentative, Paine identified with those whose lives were limited by social class, poverty, or a repressive government and fought to improve their lot. In 1774 he was discharged as an excise officer for neglecting his duties.

Thirty-seven years old, penniless, and with poor prospects for employment, Paine set sail for America, bringing little more with him than a modest statement of his abilities in a letter of introduction from his recent acquaintance Benjamin Franklin. Arriving in November 1774 Paine found himself in a unique moment in history. Within a year he became the editor of the *Pennsylvania Magazine* and tripled its circulation via his powerful essays, one of which, "A Serious Thought," anticipated much of the Declaration of Independence. Paine had studied the anti-British pamphlets written since 1760 and the proceedings of the First Continental Congress and kept abreast of the worsening relationship with the English government.

Common Sense, Paine's first master stroke in the American cause, was published anonymously in January 1776. The one hundred thousand copies circulated in the following months rallied immense support for the Revolution and proved Paine's genius as a propagandist. Late that year, when George Washington retreated across the Delaware at perhaps

COMMON SENSE;

ADDRESSED TO THE

INHABITANTS

OF

AMERICA,

On the following interesting

SUBJECTS.

I. Of the Origin and Design of Government in general,
with concise Remarks on the English Constitution.

II. Of Monarchy and Hereditary Succession.

III. Thoughts on the present State of American Affairs.

IV. Of the present Ability of America, with some miscellaneous Reflections.

Man knows no Master save creating HEAVEN,
Or those whom choice and common good ordain.
THOMSON.

PHILADELPHIA;
Printed, and Sold, by R. BELL, in Third-Street.
MDCCLXXVI.

The title page of Thomas Paine's Common Sense.

one of the darkest times of the war, Paine again rallied American resistance. His essay *The American Crisis* united the colonies into a force composed of far more than the "summer soldier and the sunshine patriot" and directly influenced the American victory at Trenton.

Employed by Congress and then the Pennsylvania Assembly, Paine wrote fifteen more Crisis papers over the next seven years. They formed a compelling record of the ebb and flow of American fortunes in the war. His poor finances at the end of the Revolution mirrored those of his country. Out of gratitude his countrymen provided him with $3,000 and a confiscated Tory estate in New Rochelle, New York, but no employment. The resourceful Paine turned to invention, creating a smokeless candle and a single-span iron bridge. He sailed for France in 1787 to follow the spirit of revolution as much as to patent and promote his bridge.

Well received in France and England, Paine was soon at work. *The Rights of Man*, his attack on Edmund Burke's *Reflections on the Revolution in France*, espoused mankind's natural rights and the overthrow of hereditary monarchy. Paine was indicted for treason in 1792 but escaped to France, where he was greeted enthusiastically, was elected a representative to the National Assembly, and became an honorary citizen. Too revolutionary for the British, Paine proved too moderate for the radical French. His opposition to France's Reign of Terror and to the execution of the king and queen resulted in his arrest in 1793 and confinement in Luxembourg prison for ten months. Escaping the guillotine by mere luck, he was finally freed through the efforts of James Monroe, then ambassador to France.

Just before his imprisonment Paine gave the first part of *The Age of Reason* (1794) to his friend Joel Barlow for publication. In it and in the second part (1795), Paine brings his arsenal of effective rhetoric, satire, ridicule, and emotional appeal to bear on the abuses of organized religion and on the Bible as a source of divine revelation. Although his belief in God is clearly stated in this work, Paine was condemned as an atheist. His former popularity was further undercut by his *Letter to George Washington* (1796), a series of scathing attacks that accused the president of betraying their friendship by allowing Paine to remain in prison.

Impoverished and in ill health, Paine was invited to return to the United States in 1802 by his old friend, President Thomas Jefferson. Paine's last years were far from happy. Forgotton by all but the orthodox Christians who reviled him, the Revolution's premier pamphleteer experienced an assassination attempt, was denied the right to vote, and was refused Quaker burial. Only a handful of people attended Paine's funeral on his farm in 1809.

Paine was not to rest easy even in death. William Cobbett, an enthusiastic admirer, illegally exhumed the casket in 1819 and shipped it to England to make it part of a monument he planned to erect in Paine's memory. The scheme failed and the remains were up for auction as part of Cobbett's estate in 1835. Morbidly, legend has kept track of the scattered parts of Paine's skeleton. The courageous revolutionary, the articulate exponent of liberal political thought and republican virtue, the humanitarian who tried to be the social conscience of an age, was never laid to rest; neither were the ideas to which he gave such eloquent voice.

Suggested Readings: *The American Crisis, The Writings of Thomas Paine, 1774–1779*, Vol. I, ed. M. D. Conway, 1894. P. Davidson, *Propaganda and the American Revolution, 1763–1783*, 1941. B. Bailyn, *The Ideological Origins of the American Revolution*, 1969. E. Foner, *Tom Paine and Revolutionary America*, 1976. A. O. Aldridge, *Thomas Paine's American Ideology*, 1984. I. Dyck, *Citizen of the World: Essays on Thomas Paine*, 1987. A. J. Ayer, *Thomas Paine*, 1988.

Texts Used: "Introduction" and "Thoughts on the Present State of American Affairs" from *Common Sense: The Writings of Thomas Paine*, 1774–1779, Vol. I, ed. M. D. Conway, 1894. *The Age of Reason*, Pt. I: *The Writings of Thomas Paine*, Vol. IV, ed. M. D. Conway, 1967.

from   COMMON SENSE*

INTRODUCTION

Perhaps the sentiments contained in the following pages, are not *yet* sufficiently fashionable to procure them general Favor; a long Habit of not thinking a Thing *wrong,* gives it a superficial appearance of being *right,* and raises at first a formidable outcry in defence of Custom. But the Tumult soon subsides. Time makes more Converts than Reason.

As a long and violent abuse of power is generally the means of calling the right of it in question, (and in matters too which might never have been thought of, had not the sufferers been aggravated into the inquiry,) and as the King of England hath undertaken in his *own right,* to support the Parliament in what he calls *Theirs,* and as the good People of this Country are grievously oppressed by the Combination, they have an undoubted privilege to enquire into the Pretensions of both, and equally to reject the Usurpation of *either.*

In the following Sheets, the Author hath studiously avoided every thing which is personal among ourselves. Compliments as well as censure to individuals make no part thereof. The wise and the worthy need not the triumph of a Pamphlet; and those whose sentiments are injudicious or unfriendly will cease of themselves, unless too much pains is bestowed upon their conversions.

The cause of America is in a great measure the cause of all mankind. Many circumstances have, and will arise, which are not local, but universal, and through which the principles of all lovers of mankind are affected, and in the event of which their affections are interested. The laying a country desolate with fire and sword, declaring war against the natural rights of all mankind, and extirpating the defenders thereof from the face of the earth, is the concern of every man to whom nature hath given the power of feeling; of which class, regardless of party censure, is

The Author.

Postscript to Preface in the third edition

P.S. The Publication of this new Edition hath been delayed, with a view of taking notice (had it been necessary) of any attempt to refute the Doctrine of Independence: As no answer hath yet appeared, it is now presumed that none will, the

---

* This pamphlet was published with the title COMMON SENSE: Addressed to the Inhabitants of America, on the following Interesting Subjects, viz.: I. Of the Origin and Design of Government in General; with Concise Remarks on the English Constitution.   II. Of Monarchy and Hereditary Succession.   III. Thoughts on the Present State of American Affairs.   IV. Of the Present Ability of America; with some Miscellaneous Reflections.

time needful for getting such a Performance ready for the Public being considerably past.

Who the Author of this Production is, is wholly unnecessary to the Public, as
the Object for Attention is the *Doctrine itself,* not the *Man.* Yet it may not be
unnecessary to say, That he is unconnected with any party, and under no sort of
Influence, public or private, but the influence of reason and principle.

Philadelphia, February 14, 1776.

THOUGHTS ON THE PRESENT STATE OF AMERICAN AFFAIRS

In the following pages I offer nothing more than simple facts, plain arguments,
and common sense: and have no other preliminaries to settle with the reader, than
that he will divest himself of prejudice and prepossession, and suffer his reason
and his feelings to determine for themselves: that he will put on, or rather that he
will not put off, the true character of a man, and generously enlarge his views
beyond the present day.

Volumes have been written on the subject of the struggle between England and
America. Men of all ranks have embarked in the controversy, from different motives, and with various designs; but all have been ineffectual, and the period of
debate is closed. Arms as the last resource decide the contest; the appeal was the
choice of the King, and the Continent has accepted the challenge.

It hath been reported of the late Mr. Pelham[1] (who tho' an able minister was
not without his faults) that on his being attacked in the House of Commons on the
score that his measures were only of a temporary kind, replied, *"they will last my
time."* Should a thought so fatal and unmanly possess the Colonies in the present
contest, the name of ancestors will be remembered by future generations with
detestation.

The Sun never shined on a cause of greater worth. 'Tis not the affair of a City,
a County, a Province, or a Kingdom; but of a Continent—of at least one eighth
part of the habitable Globe. 'Tis not the concern of a day, a year, or an age;
posterity are virtually involved in the contest, and will be more or less affected
even to the end of time, by the proceedings now. Now is the seed-time of Continental union, faith and honour. The least fracture now will be like a name engraved with the point of a pin on the tender rind of a young oak; the wound would
enlarge with the tree, and posterity read it in full grown characters.

By referring the matter from argument to arms, a new æra for politics is
struck—a new method of thinking hath arisen. All plans, proposals, &c. prior to
the nineteenth of April, *i.e.* to the commencement of hostilities,[2] are like the al-
manacks of the last year; which tho' proper then, are superceded and useless now.
Whatever was advanced by the advocates on either side of the question then, terminated in one and the same point, viz. a union with Great Britain; the only difference between the parties was the method of effecting it; the one proposing force,
the other friendship; but it hath so far happened that the first hath failed, and the
second hath withdrawn her influence.

[1] Henry Pelham, British prime minister from 1743 to 1754.
[2] The start of the American Revolution at Lexington, Massachusetts, where the "minutemen" defended their ammunitions against the English on April 19, 1775.

As much hath been said of the advantages of reconciliation, which, like an agreeable dream, hath passed away and left us as we were, it is but right that we should examine the contrary side of the argument, and enquire into some of the many material injuries which these Colonies sustain, and always will sustain, by being connected with and dependant on Great-Britain. To examine that connection and dependance, on the principles of nature and common sense, to see what we have to trust to, if separated, and what we are to expect, if dependant.

I have heard it asserted by some, that as America has flourished under her former connection with Great-Britain, the same connection is necessary towards her future happiness, and will always have the same effect. Nothing can be more fallacious than this kind of argument. We may as well assert that because a child has thrived upon milk, that it is never to have meat, or that the first twenty years of our lives is to become a precedent for the next twenty. But even this is admitting more than is true; for I answer roundly, that America would have flourished as much, and probably much more, had no European power taken any notice of her. The commerce by which she hath enriched herself are the necessaries of life, and will always have a market while eating is the custom of Europe.

But she has protected us, say some. That she hath engrossed us is true, and defended the Continent at our expense as well as her own, is admitted; and she would have defended Turkey from the same motive, *viz.* for the sake of trade and dominion.

Alas! we have been long led away by ancient prejudices and made large sacrifices to superstition. We have boasted the protection of Great Britain, without considering, that her motive was *interest* not *attachment;* and that she did not protect us from *our enemies* on *our account;* but from *her enemies* on *her own account,* from those who had no quarrel with us on any *other account,* and who will always be our enemies on the *same account.* Let Britain waive her pretensions to the Continent, or the Continent throw off the dependance, and we should be at peace with France and Spain, were they at war with Britain. The miseries of Hanover last war[3] ought to warn us against connections.

It hath lately been asserted in parliament, that the Colonies have no relation to each other but through the Parent Country, *i.e.* that Pennsylvania and the Jerseys,[4] and so on for the rest, are sister Colonies by the way of England; this is certainly a very roundabout way of proving relationship, but it is the nearest and only true way of proving enmity (or enemyship, if I may so call it.) France and Spain never were, nor perhaps ever will be, our enemies as *Americans,* but as our being the *subjects of Great Britain.*

But Britain is the parent country, say some. Then the more shame upon her conduct. Even brutes do not devour their young, nor savages make war upon their families; Wherefore, the assertion, if true, turns to her reproach; but it happens not to be true, or only partly so, and the phrase *parent* or *mother country* hath been jesuitically adopted by the King and his parasites, with a low papistical design of gaining an unfair bias on the credulous weakness of our minds. Europe, and not England, is the parent country of America. This new World hath been the asylum for the persecuted lovers of civil and religious liberty from *every part* of Europe. Hither have they fled, not from the tender embraces of the mother, but from the

---

[3] The Seven Years' War of 1756 to 1763. Britain's King George III descended from the Prussian House of Hanover.

[4] East and West Jersey, separated at that time.

cruelty of the monster, and it is so far true of England, that the same tyranny which drove the first emigrants from home, pursues their descendants still.

In this extensive quarter of the globe, we forget the narrow limits of three hundred and sixty miles (the extent of England) and carry our friendship on a larger scale; we claim brotherhood with every European Christian, and triumph in the generosity of the sentiment.

It is pleasant to observe by what regular gradations we surmount the force of local prejudices, as we enlarge our acquaintance with the World. A man born in any town in England divided into parishes, will naturally associate most with his fellow parishioners (because their interests in many cases will be common) and distinguish him by the name of *neighbour,* if he meet him but a few miles from home, he drops the narrow idea of a street, and salutes him by the name of *townsman;* if he travel out of the county and meet him in any other, he forgets the minor divisions of street and town, and calls him *countryman, i.e. countyman;* but if in their foreign excursions they should associate in France, or any other part of Europe, their local remembrance would be enlarged into that of *Englishmen.* And by a just parity of reasoning, all Europeans meeting in America, or any other quarter of the globe, are *countrymen;* for England, Holland, Germany, or Sweden, when compared with the whole, stand in the same places on the larger scale, which the divisions of street, town, and county do on the smaller ones; Distinctions too limited for Continental minds. Not one third of the inhabitants, even of this province, [Pennsylvania], are of English descent. Wherefore, I reprobate the phrase of Parent or Mother Country applied to England only, as being false, selfish, narrow and ungenerous.

But, admitting that we were all of English descent, what does it amount to? Nothing. Britain, being now an open enemy, extinguishes every other name and title: and to say that reconciliation is our duty, is truly farcical. The first king of England, of the present line (William the Conqueror) was a Frenchman, and half the peers of England are descendants from the same country; wherefore, by the same method of reasoning, England ought to be governed by France.

Much hath been said of the united strength of Britain and the Colonies, that in conjunction they might bid defiance to the world: But this is mere presumption; the fate of war is uncertain, neither do the expressions mean any thing; for this continent would never suffer itself to be drained of inhabitants, to support the British arms in either Asia, Africa, or Europe.

Besides, what have we to do with setting the world at defiance? Our plan is commerce, and that, well attended to, will secure us the peace and friendship of all Europe; because it is the interest of all Europe to have America a free port. Her trade will always be a protection, and her barrenness of gold and silver secure her from invaders.

I challenge the warmest advocate for reconciliation to show a single advantage that this continent can reap by being connected with Great Britain. I repeat the challenge; not a single advantage is derived. Our corn will fetch its price in any market in Europe, and our imported goods must be paid for buy them where we will.

But the injuries and disadvantages which we sustain by that connection, are without number; and our duty to mankind at large, as well as to ourselves, instruct us to renounce the alliance: because, any submission to, or dependance on, Great Britain, tends directly to involve this Continent in European wars and quarrels, and set us at variance with nations who would otherwise seek our friendship, and against whom we have neither anger nor complaint. As Europe is our market for trade, we ought to form no partial connection with any part of it. It is the true interest of America to steer clear of European contentions, which she never can do, while, by her dependance on Britain, she is made the make-weight in the scale of British politics.

Europe is too thickly planted with Kingdoms to be long at peace, and whenever a war breaks out between England and any foreign power, the trade of America goes to ruin, *because of her connection with Britain.* The next war may not turn out like the last,[5] and should it not, the advocates for reconciliation now will be wishing for separation then, because neutrality in the case would be a safer convoy than a man of war. Everything that is right or reasonable pleads for separation. The blood of the slain, the weeping voice of nature cries, 'TIS TIME TO PART. Even the distance at which the Almighty hath placed England and America is a strong and natural proof that the authority of the one over the other, was never the design of Heaven. The time likewise at which the Continent was discovered, adds weight to the argument, and the manner in which it was peopled, encreases the force of it. The Reformation was preceded by the discovery of America: As if the Almighty graciously meant to open a sanctuary to the persecuted in future years, when home should afford neither friendship nor safety.

The authority of Great Britain over this continent, is a form of government, which sooner or later must have an end: And a serious mind can draw no true pleasure by looking forward, under the painful and positive conviction that what he calls "the present constitution" is merely temporary. As parents, we can have no joy, knowing that this government is not sufficiently lasting to ensure any thing which we may bequeath to posterity: And by a plain method of argument, as we are running the next generation into debt, we ought to do the work of it, otherwise we use them meanly and pitifully. In order to discover the line of our duty rightly, we should take our children in our hand, and fix our station a few years farther into life; that eminence will present a prospect which a few present fears and prejudices conceal from our sight.

Though I would carefully avoid giving unnecessary offence, yet I am inclined to believe, that all those who espouse the doctrine of reconciliation, may be included within the following descriptions.

Interested men, who are not to be trusted, weak men who *cannot* see, prejudiced men who will not see, and a certain set of moderate men who think better of the European world than it deserves; and this last class, by an ill-judged deliberation, will be the cause of more calamities to this Continent than all the other three.

It is the good fortune of many to live distant from the scene of present sorrow; the evil is not sufficiently brought to their doors to make them feel the precariousness with which all American property is possessed. But let our imaginations transport us a few moments to Boston; that seat of wretchedness will teach us wisdom, and instruct us for ever to renounce a power in whom we can have no trust.[6] The inhabitants of that unfortunate city who but a few months ago were in ease and affluence, have now no other alternative than to stay and starve, or turn out to beg. Endangered by the fire of their friends if they continue within the city, and plundered by the soldiery if they leave it, in their present situation they are

---

[5] When the Seven Years' War had ended, all French territory in North America was handed over to Britain by the Treaty of Paris in 1763.

[6] For six months Boston was barricaded under British military control.

prisoners without the hope of redemption, and in a general attack for their relief they would be exposed to the fury of both armies.

Men of passive tempers look somewhat lightly over the offences of Great Britain, and, still hoping for the best, are apt to call out, *Come, come, we shall be friends again for all this*. But examine the passions and feelings of mankind: bring the doctrine of reconciliation to the touchstone of nature and then tell me whether you can hereafter love, honour, and faithfully serve the power that hath carried fire and sword into your land? If you cannot do all these, then are you only deceiving yourselves, and by your delay bringing ruin upon posterity. Your future connection with Britain, whom you can neither love nor honour, will be forced and unnatural, and being formed only on the plan of present convenience, will in a little time fall into a relapse more wretched than the first. But if you say, you can still pass the violations over, then I ask, hath your house been burnt? Hath your property been destroyed before your face? Are your wife and children destitute of a bed to lie on, or bread to live on? Have you lost a parent or a child by their hands, and yourself the ruined and wretched survivor? If you have not, then are you not a judge of those who have. But if you have, and can still shake hands with the murderers, then are you unworthy the name of husband, father, friend, or lover, and whatever may be your rank or title in life, you have the heart of a coward, and the spirit of a sycophant.

This is not inflaming or exaggerating matters, but trying them by those feelings and affections which nature justifies, and without which we should be incapable of discharging the social duties of life, or enjoying the felicities of it. I mean not to exhibit horror for the purpose of provoking revenge, but to awaken us from fatal and unmanly slumbers, that we may pursue determinately some fixed object. 'Tis not in the power of Britain or of Europe to conquer America, if she doth not conquer herself by delay and timidity. The present winter is worth an age if rightly employed, but if lost or neglected the whole Continent will partake of the misfortune; and there is no punishment which that man doth not deserve, be he who, or what, or where he will, that may be the means of sacrificing a season so precious and useful.

'Tis repugnant to reason, to the universal order of things, to all examples from former ages, to suppose that this Continent can long remain subject to any external power. The most sanguine in Britain doth not think so. The utmost stretch of human wisdom cannot, at this time, compass a plan, short of separation, which can promise the continent even a year's security. Reconciliation is *now* a fallacious dream. Nature hath deserted the connection, and art cannot supply her place. For, as Milton wisely expresses, "never can true reconcilement grow where wounds of deadly hate have pierced so deep."[7]

Every quiet method for peace hath been ineffectual. Our prayers have been rejected with disdain; and hath tended to convince us that nothing flatters vanity or confirms obstinacy in Kings more than repeated petitioning—and nothing hath contributed more than that very measure to make the Kings of Europe absolute. Witness Denmark and Sweden.[8] Wherefore, since nothing but blows will do, for God's sake let us come to a final separation, and not leave the next generation to be cutting throats under the violated unmeaning names of parent and child.

To say they will never attempt it again is idle and visionary; we thought so at

[7] From John Milton's *Paradise Lost* (1674, IV. 98–99).
[8] Both recently threatened by absolute monarchies.

the repeal of the stamp act, yet a year or two undeceived us; as well may we suppose that nations which have been once defeated will never renew the quarrel.

As to government matters, 'tis not in the power of Britain to do this continent justice: the business of it will soon be too weighty and intricate to be managed with any tolerable degree of convenience, by a power so distant from us, and so very ignorant of us; for if they cannot conquer us, they cannot govern us. To be always running three or four thousand miles with a tale or a petition, waiting four of five months for an answer, which, when obtained, requires five or six more to explain it in, will in a few years be looked upon as folly and childishness. There was a time when it was proper, and there is a proper time for it to cease.

Small islands not capable of protecting themselves are the proper objects for government to take under their care; but there is something absurd, in supposing a Continent to be perpetually governed by an island. In no instance hath nature made the satellite larger than its primary planet; and as England and America, with respect to each other, reverse the common order of nature, it is evident that they belong to different systems. England to Europe: America to itself.

I am not induced by motives of pride, party, or resentment to espouse the doctrine of separation and independence; I am clearly, positively, and conscientiously persuaded that it is the true interest of this Continent to be so; that everything short of *that* is mere patchwork, that it can afford no lasting felicity,—that it is leaving the sword to our children, and shrinking back at a time when a little more, a little further, would have rendered this Continent the glory of the earth.

As Britain hath not manifested the least inclination towards a compromise, we may be assured that no terms can be obtained worthy the acceptance of the Continent, or any ways equal to the expence of blood and treasure we have been already put to.

The object contended for, ought always to bear some just proportion to the expense. The removal of North,[9] or the whole detestable junto, is a matter unworthy the millions we have expended. A temporary stoppage of trade was an inconvenience , which would have sufficiently ballanced the repeal of all the acts complained of, had such repeals been obtained; but if the whole Continent must take up arms, if every man must be a soldier, 'tis scarcely worth our while to fight against a contemptible ministry only. Dearly, dearly do we pay for the repeal of the acts, if that is all we fight for; for, in a just estimation 'tis as great a folly to pay a Bunker-hill price[10] for law as for land. As I have always considered the independancy of this continent, as an event which sooner or later must arrive, so from the late rapid progress of the Continent to maturity, the event cannot be far off. Wherefore, on the breaking out of hostilities, it was not worth the while to have disputed a matter which time would have finally redressed, unless we meant to be in earnest: otherwise it is like wasting an estate on a suit at law, to regulate the trespasses of a tenant whose lease is just expiring. No man was a warmer wisher for a reconciliation than myself, before the fatal nineteenth of April, 1775,[11] but the moment the event of that day was made known, I rejected the hardened, sullen-tempered Pharaoh of England[12] for ever; and disdain the wretch, that with the pretended title of FATHER OF HIS PEOPLE can unfeelingly hear of their slaughter, and composedly sleep with their blood upon his soul.

[9] Frederick North, earl of Guilford and British prime minister from 1770 to 1782, who was blamed for exploiting the colonies via taxation.

[10] The high price of extensive casualties at the Battle of Bunker Hill, June 17, 1775.

[11] Date of the battles of Lexington and Concord.   [12] King George III.

But admitting that matters were now made up, what would be the event? I answer, the ruin of the Continent. And that for several reasons.

First. The powers of governing still remaining in the hands of the king, he will have a negative over the whole legislation of this Continent. And as he hath shown himself such an inveterate enemy to liberty, and discovered such a thirst for arbitrary power, is he, or is he not, a proper person to say to these colonies, *You shall make no laws but what I please!?* And is there any inhabitant of America so ignorant as not to know, that according to what is called the *present constitution,* this Continent can make no laws but what the king gives leave to; and is there any man so unwise as not to see, that (considering what has happened) he will suffer no law to be made here but such as suits *his* purpose? We may be as effectually enslaved by the want of laws in America, as by submitting to laws made for us in England. After matters are made up (as it is called) can there be any doubt, but the whole power of the crown will be exerted to keep this continent as low and humble as possible? Instead of going forward we shall go backward, or be perpetually quarrelling, or ridiculously petitioning. We are already greater than the King wishes us to be, and will he not hereafter endeavor to make us less? To bring the matter to one point, Is the Power who is jealous of our prosperity, a proper power to govern us? Whoever says *No,* to this question, is an Independant for independency means no more than this, whether we shall make our own laws or, whether the King, the greatest enemy this continent hath, or can have, shall tell us *there shall be no laws but such as I like.*

But the King, you will say, has a negative in England; the people there can make no laws without his consent. In point of right and good order, it is something very ridiculous that a youth of twenty-one (which hath often happened) shall say to several millions of people older and wiser than himself, "I forbid this or that act of yours to be law." But in this place I decline this sort of reply, though I will never cease to expose the absurdity of it, and only answer that England being the King's residence, and America not so, makes quite another case. The King's negative here is ten times more dangerous and fatal than it can be in England; for there he will scarcely refuse his consent to a bill for putting England into as strong a state of defense as possible, and in America he would never suffer such a bill to be passed.

America is only a secondary object in the system of British politics. England consults the good of this country no further than it answers her own purpose. Wherefore, her own interest leads her to suppress the growth of ours in every case which doth not promote her advantage, or in the least interferes with it. A pretty state we should soon be in under such a second hand government, considering what has happened! Men do not change from enemies to friends by the alteration of a name: And in order to show that reconciliation now is a dangerous doctrine, I affirm, *that it would be policy in the King at this time to repeal the acts, for the sake of reinstating himself in the government of the provinces;* In order that HE MAY ACCOMPLISH BY CRAFT AND SUBTLETY, IN THE LONG RUN, WHAT HE CANNOT DO BY FORCE AND VIOLENCE IN THE SHORT ONE. Reconciliation and ruin are nearly related.

Secondly. That as even the best terms which we can expect to obtain can amount to no more than a temporary expedient, or a kind of government by guardianship, which can last no longer than till the Colonies come of age, so the general face and state of things in the interim will be unsettled and unpromising. Emigrants of property will not choose to come to a country whose form of government hangs but by a thread, and who is every day tottering on the brink of commotion and disturbance; and numbers of the present inhabitants would lay hold of the interval to dispose of their effects, and quit the Continent.

But the most powerful of all arguments is, that nothing but independance, *i.e.* a Continental form of government, can keep the peace of the Continent and preserve it inviolate from civil wars. I dread the event of a reconciliation with Britain now, as it is more than probable that it will be followed by a revolt some where or other, the consequences of which may be far more fatal than all the malice of Britain.

Thousands are already ruined by British barbarity; (thousands more will probably suffer the same fate.) Those men have other feelings than us who have nothing suffered. All they now possess is liberty; what they before enjoyed is sacrificed to its service, and having nothing more to lose they disdain submission. Besides, the general temper of the Colonies, towards a British government will be like that of a youth who is nearly out of his time; they will care very little about her: And a government which cannot preserve the peace is no government at all, and in that case we pay our money for nothing; and pray what is it that Britain can do, whose power will be wholly on paper, should a civil tumult break out the very day after reconciliation? I have heard some men say, many of whom I believe spoke without thinking, that they dreaded an independance, fearing that it would produce civil wars: It is but seldom that our first thoughts are truly correct, and that is the case here; for there is ten times more to dread from a patched up connection than from independance. I make the sufferer's case my own, and I protest, that were I driven from house and home, my property destroyed, and my circumstances ruined, that as a man, sensible of injuries, I could never relish the doctrine of reconciliation, or consider myself bound thereby.

The Colonies have manifested such a spirit of good order and obedience to Continental government, as is sufficient to make every reasonable person easy and happy on that head. No man can assign the least pretence for his fears, on any other grounds, than such as are truly childish and ridiculous, viz., that one colony will be striving for superiority over another.

Where there are no distinctions there can be no superiority; perfect equality affords no temptation. The Republics of Europe are all (and we may say always) in peace. Holland and Switzerland are without wars, foreign or domestic: Monarchical governments, it is true, are never long at rest: the crown itself is a temptation to enterprising ruffians at home; and that degree of pride and insolence ever attendant on regal authority, swells into a rupture with foreign powers in instances where a republican government, by being formed on more natural principles, would negociate the mistake.

If there is any true cause of fear respecting independance, it is because no plan is yet laid down. Men do not see their way out. Wherefore, as an opening into that business I offer the following hints; at the same time modestly affirming, that I have no other opinion of them myself, than that they may be the means of giving rise to something better. Could the straggling thoughts of individuals be collected, they would frequently form materials for wise and able men to improve into useful matter.

Let the assemblies be annual, with a president only. The representation more equal, their business wholly domestic, and subject to the authority of a Continental Congress.

Let each Colony be divided into six, eight, or ten, convenient districts, each district to send a proper number of Delegates to Congress, so that each Colony send at least thirty. The whole number in Congress will be at least 390. Each congress to sit and to choose a President by the following method. When the Delegates are met, let a Colony be taken from the whole thirteen Colonies by lot, after which let the Congress choose (by ballot) a president from out of the Delegates of that Province. In the next Congress, let a Colony be taken by lot from twelve only, omitting that Colony from which the president was taken in the former Congress, and so proceeding on till the whole thirteen shall have had their proper rotation. And in order that nothing may pass into a law but what is satisfactorily just, not less than three fifths of the Congress to be called a majority. He that will promote discord, under a government so equally formed as this, would have joined Lucifer in his revolt.

But as there is a peculiar delicacy from whom, or in what manner, this business must first arise, and as it seems most agreeable and consistent that it should come from some intermediate body between the governed and the governors, that is, between the Congress and the People, let a Continental Conference be held in the following manner, and for the following purpose,

A Committee of twenty six members of congress, *viz.* Two for each Colony. Two Members from each House of Assembly, or Provincial Convention; and five Representatives of the people at large, to be chosen in the capital city or town of each Province, for, and in behalf of the whole Province, by as many qualified voters as shall think proper to attend from all parts of the Province for that purpose; or, if more convenient, the Representatives may be chosen in two or three of the most populous parts thereof. In this conference, thus assembled, will be united the two grand principles of business, *knowledge* and *power*. The Members of Congress, Assemblies, or Conventions, by having had experience in national concerns, will be able and useful counsellors, and the whole, being impowered by the people, will have a truly legal authority.

The conferring members being met, let their business be to frame a Continental Charter, or Charter of the United Colonies; (answering to what is called the Magna Charta of England) fixing the number and manner of choosing Members of Congress, Members of Assembly, with their date of sitting; and drawing the line of business and jurisdiction between them: Always remembering, that our strength is Continental, not Provincial. Securing freedom and property to all men, and above all things, the free exercise of religion, according to the dictates of conscience; with such other matter as it is necessary for a charter to contain. Immediately after which, the said conference to dissolve, and the bodies which shall be chosen conformable to the said charter, to be the Legislators and Governors of this Continent for the time being: Whose pease and happiness, may GOD preserve. AMEN.

Should any body of men be hereafter delegated for this or some similar purpose, I offer them the following extracts from that wise observer on Governments, Dragonetti. "The science," says he, "of the Politician consists in fixing the true point of happiness and freedom. Those men would deserve the gratitude of ages, who should discover a mode of government that contained the greatest sum of individual happiness, with the least national expense." (Dragonetti on "Virtues and Reward.")[13]

But where, say some, is the King of America? I'll tell you, friend, he reigns above, and doth not make havoc of mankind like the Royal Brute of Great Britain. Yet that we may not appear to be defective even in earthly honours, let a day be

---

[13] *Le Virtù ed i Premi* (1767), by Giacinto Dragonetti.

solemnly set apart for proclaiming the Charter; let it be brought forth placed on the Divine Law, the Word of God; let a crown be placed thereon, by which the world may know, that so far as we approve of monarchy, that in America the law is king. For as in absolute governments the King is law, so in free countries the law ought to be king; and there ought to be no other. But lest any ill use should afterwards arise, let the Crown at the conclusion of the ceremony be demolished, and scattered among the people whose right it is.

A government of our own is our natural right: and when a man seriously reflects on the precariousness of human affairs, he will become convinced that it is infinitely wiser and safer, to form a constitution of our own in a cool deliberate manner, while we have it in our power, than to trust such an interesting event to time and chance. If we omit it now, some Massanello[14] may hereafter arise, who, laying hold of popular disquietudes, may collect together the desperate and the discontented, and by assuming to themselves the powers of government, finally sweep away the liberties of the Continent like a deluge. Should the government of America return again into the hands of Britain, the tottering situation of things will be a temptation for some desperate adventurer to try his fortune; and in such a case, what relief can Britain give? Ere she could hear the news, the fatal business might be done; and ourselves suffering like the wretched Britons under the oppression of the Conqueror. Ye that oppose independance now, ye know not what ye do: ye are opening a door to eternal tyranny, by keeping vacant the seat of government. There are thousands and tens of thousands, who would think it glorious to expel from the Continent, that barbarous and hellish power, which hath stirred up the Indians and the Negroes to destroy us; the cruelty hath a double guilt, it is dealing brutally by us, and treacherously by them.

To talk of friendship with those in whom our reason forbids us to have faith, and our affections wounded thro' a thousand pores instruct us to detest, is madness and folly. Every day wears out the little remains of kindred between us and them; and can there be any reason to hope, that as the relationship expires, the affection will encrease, or that we shall agree better when we have ten times more and greater concerns to quarrel over than ever?

Ye that tell us of harmony and reconciliation, can ye restore to us the time that is past? Can ye give to prostitution its former innocence? neither can ye reconcile Britain and America. The last cord now is broken, the people of England are presenting addresses against us. There are injuries which nature cannot forgive; she would cease to be nature if she did. As well can the lover forgive the ravisher of his mistress, as the Continent forgive the murders of Britain. The Almighty hath implanted in us these unextinguishable feelings for good and wise purposes. They are the Guardians of his Image in our hearts. They distinguish us from the herd of common animals. The social compact would dissolve, and justice be extirpated from the earth, or have only a casual existence were we callous to the touches of affection. The robber and the murderer would often escape unpunished, did not the injuries which our tempers sustain, provoke us into justice.

O! ye that love mankind! Ye that dare oppose not only the tyranny but the tyrant, stand forth! Every spot of the old world is overrun with oppression. Freedom hath been hunted round the Globe. Asia and Africa have long expelled her.

---

[14] Paine's note: "Thomas Anello, otherwise Massanello, a fisherman of Naples, who after spiriting up his countrymen in the public marketplace, against the oppression of the Spaniards, to whom the place was then subject, prompted them to revolt, and in the space of a day became King."

Europe regards her like a stranger, and England hath given her warning to depart. O! receive the fugitive, and prepare in time an asylum for mankind.

1776

from *THE AGE OF REASON*

CHAPTER I. THE AUTHOR'S PROFESSION OF FAITH

It has been my intention, for several years past, to publish my thoughts upon religion; I am well aware of the difficulties that attend the subject, and from that consideration, had reserved it to a more advanced period of life. I intended it to be the last offering I should make to my fellow-citizens of all nations, and that at a time when the purity of the motive that induced me to it could not admit of a question, even by those who might disapprove the work.

The circumstance that has now taken place in France,[1] of the total abolition of the whole national order of priesthood, and of everything appertaining to compulsive systems of religion, and compulsive articles of faith, has not only precipitated my intention, but rendered a work of this kind exceedingly necessary, lest, in the general wreck of superstition, of false systems of government, and false theology, we lose sight of morality, of humanity, and of the theology that is true.

As several of my colleagues, and others of my fellow-citizens of France, have given me the example of making their voluntary and individual profession of faith, I also will make mine; and I do this with all that sincerity and frankness with which the mind of man communicates with itself.

I believe in one God, and no more; and I hope for happiness beyond this life.

I believe the equality of man, and I believe that religious duties consist in doing justice, loving mercy, and endeavouring to make our fellow-creatures happy.

But, lest it should be supposed that I believe many other things in addition to these, I shall, in the progress of this work, declare the things I do not believe, and my reasons for not believing them.

I do not believe in the creed professed by the Jewish church, by the Roman church, by the Greek church, by the Turkish church, by the Protestant church, nor by any church that I know of. My own mind is my own church.

All national institutions of churches, whether Jewish, Christian, or Turkish, appear to me no other than human inventions set up to terrify and enslave mankind, and monopolize power and profit.

I do not mean by this declaration to condemn those who believe otherwise; they have the same right to their belief as I have to mine. But it is necessary to the happiness of man, that he be mentally faithful to himself. Infidelity does not consist in believing, or in disbelieving; it consists in professing to believe what he does not believe.

It is impossible to calculate the moral mischief, if I may so express it, that mental lying has produced in society. When a man has so far corrupted and prostituted the chastity of his mind, as to subscribe his professional belief to things he

---

[1] By 1792 the Catholic church in France had been dissolved by the French Revolution's leaders, and churches had closed.

does not believe, he has prepared himself for the commission of every other crime. He takes up the trade of a priest for the sake of gain, and, in order to qualify himself for that trade, he begins with a perjury. Can we conceive anything more destructive to morality than this?

Soon after I had published the pamphlet COMMON SENSE, in America, I saw the exceeding probability that a revolution in the system of government would be followed by a revolution in the system of religion. The adulterous connection of church and state, wherever it had taken place, whether Jewish, Christian, or Turkish, had so effectually prohibited, by pains and penalties, every discussion upon established creeds, and upon first principles of religion, that until the system of government should be changed, those subjects could not be brought fairly and openly before the world; but that whenever this should be done, a revolution in the system of religion would follow. Human inventions and priest-craft would be detected; and man would return to the pure, unmixed, and unadulterated belief of one God, and no more.   *1793, 1794*

William Bartram
(1739–1823)

William Bartram's *Travels*, published in Philadelphia in 1791, began as a diary or journal made by Bartram during a four-year-long journey that started with the preparations for an extensive foray into the southern colonies in autumn 1772. From this diary, itself an extensive document, Bartram wrote his *Travels* for publication some twenty years later, in much the same way that Henry David Thoreau recapitulated in *Walden* (1850) his experience of two years spent at Walden Pond. Like Thoreau, Bartram was a keen observer of nature whose scientific investigations of the New World gave readers in England a clear sense of the natural beauty and power of America. A writer of considerable merit, Bartram shaped a document that was successful not only as an exploration of natural phenomena but as a work of literature.

Born in Philadelphia in 1739, Bartram was the son of Quaker John Bartram, now regarded to be the first American-born botanist. Both in England and America the eighteenth century was a period of intense interest in the natural universe. The Bartram family maintained a botanical garden at Kingseesing, on the Schuylkill River near Philadelphia, where father and son experimented with plant development. By 1772 William Bartram was exceptionally well prepared for the extensive journey and for the composition of the journal that became the foundation for his *Travels* narrative. He had already traveled with his father, who authored *Observations . . . From Pensilvania to Lake Ontario* (1751) and *A Description of Florida* (1769). Like these accounts, William Bartram's *Travels* includes long passages in which nature is observed in technical detail at close range, so that the reader is given an accurate, even scientific, picture of the writer's observations. Credibility and veracity were important to both Bartrams, even if their observations may, by modern scientific standards of data gathering and observation, appear to be amateurish.

Bartram's *Travels* goes beyond his father's work by attempting, like Thomas Jefferson's *Notes on the State of Virginia* (1785), to present a cultural and anthropological portrait of the inhabitants of North America, together with some observations about their customs and manners. The anthropological commentary and the philosophical excursions based on natural observations give *Travels* its unique quality and render it a fit transition piece between the purely descriptive accounts of the New World, which date back to the earliest explorations—with travel narratives written largely to justify the exploration to a partron or sponsor—and the type of personal, literary account Thoreau provided in *Walden*. Unlike *Walden*, which was revised by the author several times, *Travels* remains a large-scale canvas, one in which all elements of the experience are communicated to the reader as separate parts with less of the cohesive, pervasively metaphorical structure of Thoreau's work.

William Bartram enjoyed the sponsorship of Dr. John Fothergill, a British botanist who advised Bartram to keep a journal of the local soil types, flora, and fauna. But Bartram's finished product goes far beyond this challenge. It is an anthropological return to the Garden of Eden and a literary work that gives mythic proportion to the vast wilderness of America. That Bartram's *Travels* influenced writers such as Samuel Coleridge, William Wordsworth, and Thomas Jefferson is commonly acknowledged, and scholars attribute the inclusion of engravings in Benjamin Barton's *Elements of Botany* (1808) to the drawings of William Bartram. *Travels* was translated into several languages soon after its publication—a clear sign of its influence and success. For modern readers the formal language and long sentences may appear to be complex; however, by considering the historical con-

William Bartram's 1788 drawing of Franklinia alatamaha, *the flowering tree he and his father saved from extinction by planting its seeds in their garden; it was last seen growing wild in 1803.*

text, *Travels* provides an understanding and perception unavailable before Bartram made his arduous journey through the southern colonies.

Suggested Readings: *The Travels of William Bartram,* ed. M. Van Doren, 1940. *Travels in Georgia and Florida, 1773-1774: A Report to Dr. John Fothergill,* ed. F. Harper, 1944. N. B. Fagin, *William Bartram: Interpreter of the American Landscape,* 1933. *John and William Bartram's America: Selections From the Writings,* ed. H. G. Cruikshank, 1957.

Text Used: *The Travels of William Bartram,* ed. F. Harper, 1958.

from TRAVELS*

from CHAPTER VII

A Journey From Spalding's Lower Trading House to Talahasochte or White King's Town, on the River Little St. Juan, Thirty Miles Above Fort St. Marks in the Bay of Apalatche

On my return to the trading house, from my journey to the great savanna, I found the trading company for Little St. Juan's,[1] were preparing for that post.

My mind yet elate with the various scenes of rural nature, which as a lively animated picture, had been presented to my view; the deeply engraven impression, a pleasing flattering contemplation, gave strength and agility to my steps, anxiously to press forward to the delightful fields and groves of Apalatche.

The trading company for Talahasochte being now in readiness to proceed for that quarter, under the direction of our chief trader, in the cool of the morning we set off, each of us having a good horse to ride, besides having in our caravan several pack horses laden with provisions, camp equipage and other necessaries; a young man from St. Augustine, in the service of the governor of East Florida accompanied us, commissioned to purchase of the Indians and traders, some Siminole horses. They are the most beautiful and sprightly species of that noble creature, perhaps any where to be seen; but are of a small breed, and as delicately formed as the American roe buck. A horse in the Creek or Muscogulge tongue is echoclucco, that is the great deer, (echo is a deer and clucco is big:) the Siminole horses are said to descend originally from the Andalusian breed, brought here by the Spaniards when they first established the colony of East Florida. From the forehead to their nose is a little arched or aquiline, and so are the fine Chactaw horses among the Upper Creeks, which are said to have been brought thither from New-Mexico across Mississippi, by those nations of Indians who emigrated from the West, beyond the river. These horses are every way like the Siminole breed, only being larger, and perhaps not so lively and capricious. It is a matter of conjecture and enquiry, whether or not the different soil and situation of the country,

---

* The full title is *Travels Through North and South Carolina, Georgia, East and West Florida, the Cherokee Country, the Extensive Territories of the Muscogulges, or Creek Confederacy, and the Country of the Chactaws, Containing an Account of the Soil and Natural Productions of Those Regions, Together With Observations on the Manners of the Indians,* from Pt. II.

[1] The Saint John's River, which runs northward through Florida.

may have contributed in some measure, in forming and establishing the difference in size and other qualities betwixt them. I have observed the horses and other animals in the high hilly country of Carolina, Georgia, Virginia and all along our shores, are of a much larger and stronger make, than those which are bred in the flat country next the sea coast; a buck-skin of the Upper Creeks and Cherokees will weigh twice as heavy as those of the Siminoles or Lower Creeks, and those bred in the low flat country of Carolina.

Our first days journey was along the Alachua roads, twenty-five miles to the Half-way Pond, where we encamped, the musquitoes were excessively troublesome the whole night.

Decamped early next morning, still pursuing the road to Alachua, until within a few miles of Cuscowilla, when the road dividing, one for the town and the other for the great savanna; here our company separated, one party chose to pass through the town, having some concerns there; I kept with the party that went through the savanna, it being the best road, leading over a part of the savanna, when entering the groves on its borders, we travelled several miles over these fertile eminences and delightful, shady, fragrant forests, then again entered upon the savanna, and crossed a charming extensive green cove or bay of it, covered with a vivid green grassy turf, when we again ascended the woodland hills, through fruitful Orange groves and under shadowy Palms and Magnolias. Now the Pine forests opened to view, we left the magnificent savanna and its delightful groves, passing through a level, open, airy Pine forest, the stately trees scatteringly planted by nature, arising strait and erect from the green carpet, embellished with various grasses and flowering plants, and gradually ascending the sand hills soon came into the trading path to Talahasochte; which is generally, excepting a few deviations, the old Spanish highway to St. Mark's. At about five miles distance beyond the great savanna, we came to camp late in the evening, under a little grove of Live Oaks just by a group of shelly rocks, on the banks of a beautiful little lake, partly environed by meadows. The rocks as usual in these regions partly encircled a spacious sink or grotto, which communicates with the waters of the lake; the waters of the grotto are perfectly transparent, cool and pleasant, and well replenished with fish. Soon after our arrival here, our companions who passed through Cuscowilla joined us. A brisk cool wind during the night kept the persecuting musquitoes at a distance.

The morning pleasant, we decamped early, proceeding on, rising gently for several miles, over sandy, gravelly ridges, we find ourselves in an elevated, high, open, airy region, somewhat rocky, on the backs of the ridges, and presents to view on every side, the most dreary, solitary, desart waste I had ever beheld; groups of bare rocks emerging out of the naked gravel and drifts of white sand; the grass thinly scattered and but few trees; the Pines, Oaks, Olives and Sideroxilons,[2] poor, misshapen and tattered; scarce an animal to be seen or noise heard, save the symphony of the Western breeze, through the bristly Pine leaves, or solitary sand crickets screech, or at best the more social converse of the frogs, in solemn chorus with the swift breezes, brought from distant fens and forests. Next we joyfully enter the borders of the level Pine forest and savannas, which continued for many miles, never out of sight of little lakes or ponds, environed with illumined meadows, the clear waters sparkling through the tall Pines.

[2] Buckthorn.

Having a good spirited horse under me, I generally kept a-head of my companions, which I often chose to do, as circumstances offered or invited, for the sake of retirement and observation.

The high road being here open and spacious, at a good distance before me, I observed a large hawk on the ground, in the middle of the road; he seemed to be in distress, endeavouring to rise; when, coming up near him, I found him closely bound up by a very long coach-whip snake, that had wreathed himself several times round the hawk's body, who had but one of his wings at liberty; beholding their struggles a while, I alighted off my horse with an intention of parting them; when, on coming up, they mutually agreed to separate themselves, each one seeking his own safety, probably considering me as their common enemy. The bird rose aloft and fled away as soon as he recovered his liberty, and the snake as eagerly made off, I soon overtook him but could not perceive that he was wounded.

I suppose the hawk had been the aggressor, and fell upon the snake with an intention of making a prey of him, and that the snake dexterously and luckily threw himself in coils round his body, and girded him so close as to save himself from destruction.

The coach-whip snake is a beautiful creature; when full grown they are six and seven feet in length, and the largest part of their body not so thick as a cane or common walking stick; their head not larger than the end of a man's finger; their neck is very slender, and from the abdomen tapers away in the manner of a small switch or coach-whip; the top of the head and neck, for three or four inches, is as black and shining as a raven; the throat and belly as white as snow; and the upper side of their body of a chocolate colour, excepting the tail part, almost from the abdomen to the extremity, which is black: it may be proper to observe, however, that they vary in respect to the colour of the body; some I have seen almost white or cream colour, others of a pale chocolate or clay colour, but in all the head and neck is black, and the tail dark brown or black. They are extremely swift, seeming almost to fly over the surface of the ground, and that which is very singular, they can run swiftly on only their tail part, carrying their head and body upright: one very fine one accompanied me along the road side, at a little distance, raising himself erect, now and then looking me in the face, although I proceeded on a good round trot on purpose to observe how fast they could proceed in that position. His object seemed mere curiosity or observation; with respect to venom they are as innocent as a worm, and seem to be familiar with man. They seem a particular inhabitant of East Florida, though I have seen some of them in the maritime parts of Carolina and Georgia, but in these regions they are neither so large or beautiful.

We rise again, passing over sand ridges of gentle elevation, savannas and open Pine forests. Masses or groups of rocks present to view on every side, as before mentioned, and with difficulty we escaped the circular infundibuliform[3] cavities or sinks in the surface of the earth; generally a group of rocks, shaded by Palms, Live Oaks and Magnolias, is situated on their limb: some are partly filled up with earth, whilst others and the greater number of them are partly filled with transparent cool water, which discover the well or perforation through the rocks in the center. This day being remarkably sultry, we came to camp early, having chosen our situation under some stately Pines, near the verge of a spacious savanna.

---

[3] Funnel-shaped.

After some refreshment, our hunters went out into the forest, and returned towards evening; amongst other game, they brought with them a savanna crane which they shot in the adjoining meadows. This stately bird is above six feet in length from the toes to the extremity of the beak when extended, and the wings expand eight or nine feet; they are above five feet high when standing erect; the tail is remarkably short, but the flag or pendant feathers which fall down off the rump on each side, are very long and sharp pointed, of a delicate texture, and silky softness; the beak is very long, strait and sharp pointed; the crown of the head bare of feathers, of a reddish rose colour, thinly barbed with short, stiff, black hair; the legs and thighs are very long, and bare of feathers a great space above the knees; the plumage of this bird is generally of a pale ash colour, with shades or clouds of pale brown and sky blue, the brown prevails on the shoulders and back; the barrels of the prime quill-feathers are long and of a large diameter, leaving a large cavity when extracted from the wing: all the bones of this bird have a thin shell, and consequently a large cavity or medullary receptacle. When these birds move their wings in flight, their strokes are slow, moderate and regular, and even when at a considerable distance or high above us, we plainly hear the quill-feathers, their shafts and webs upon one another, creak as the joints or working of a vessel in a tempestuous sea.

We had this fowl dressed for supper and it made excellent soup; nevertheless as long as I can get any other necessary food I shall prefer his seraphic music in the etherial skies, and my eyes and understanding gratified in observing their economy and social communities, in the expansive green savannas of Florida.

Next morning we arose early, and proceeding, gradually descended again, and continued many miles along a flat, level country, over delightful green savannas, decorated with hommocks[4] or islets of dark groves, consisting of Magnolia grandiflora, Morus, tilia, Zanthoxilon, Laurus Borbonia, Sideroxilon, Quercus sempervirens, Halesia diptera, Callicarpa, Corypha palma, &c. there are always groups of whitish testaceous[5] rocks and sinks where these hommocks are. We next crossed a wet savanna, which is the beginning of a region still lower than we had traversed; here we crossed a rapid rivulet of exceeding cool, pleasant water, where we halted to refresh ourselves. But it must be remarked here, that this rivulet, though lively and rapid at this time, is not a permanent stream, but was formed by a heavy rain that fell the day before, as was apparent from its bed, besides it is at best but a jet or mere phantom of a brook, as the land around is rocky and hollow, abounding with wells and cavities. Soon after leaving the brook we passed off to the left hand, along the verge of an extensive savanna, and meadows many miles in circumference, edged on one border with detached groves and pompous Palms, and embellished with a beautiful sparkling lake; its verges decorated with tall, waving grass and floriferous plants; the pellucid[6] waters gently rolling on to a dark shaded grotto, just under a semicircular, swelling, turfy ascent or bank, skirted by groves of Magnolias, Oaks, Laurels and Palms. In these expansive and delightful meadows, were feeding and roving troops of the fleet Siminole horse. We halted a while at this grotto, and after refreshing ourselves we mounted horse and proceeded across a charming lawn, part of the savanna, entering on it through a dark grove. In this extensive lawn were several troops of horse, and our company had the satisfaction of observing several belonging to themselves. One occurrence, remarkable here, was a troop of horse under the control and care of a single black

[4] Hummocks, or low, rounded hills. [5] Shell-like. [6] Transparent.

dog, which seemed to differ in no respect from the wolf of Florida, except his being able to bark as the common dog. He was very careful and industrious in keeping them together, and if any one strolled from the rest at too great a distance, the dog would spring up, head the horse and bring him back to the company. The proprietor of these horses is an Indian in Talahasochte, about ten miles distance from this place, who, out of humour and experiment, trained his dog up from a puppy to this business; he follows his master's horses only, keeping them in a separate company where they range, and when he is hungry or wants to see his master, in the evening he returns to town, but never stays at home a night.

The region we had journeyed through, since we decamped this morning, is of a far better soil and quality than we had yet seen since we left Alachua; generally a dark greyish, and sometimes brown and black loam, on a foundation of whitish marl, chalk and testaceous limestone rocks, and ridges of a loose, coarse, reddish sand, producing stately Pines in the plains, and Live Oak, Mulberry, Magnolia, Palm, Zanthoxilon, etc. in the hommocks, and also in great plenty the perennial Indigo; it grows here five, six and seven feet high, and as thick together as if it had been planted and cultivated. The higher ridges of hills afford great quantities of a species of iron ore, of that kind found in New-Jersey and Pennsylvania, and there called bog ore; it appears on the surface of the ground in large detached masses and smaller fragments; it is ponderous and seemed rich of that most useful metal; but one property remarkable in these terrigenous stones is, they appeared to be blistered, somewhat resembling cinders, or as if they had suffered a violent action of fire.

Leaving the charming savanna and fields of Capola, we passed several miles through delightful plains and meadows, little differing from the environs of Capola, diversified with rocky islets or hommocks of dark woodland.

We next entered a vast forest of the most stately Pine trees that can be imagined, planted by nature at a moderate distance, on a level, grassy plain, enamelled with a variety of flowering shrubs, viz. Viola, Ruellia infundibuliformea, Amaryllis atamasco, Mimosa sensitiva, Mimosa intsia and many others new to me. This sublime forest continued five or six miles, when we came to dark groves of Oaks, Magnolias, Red bays, Mulberrys, &c. through which proceeding near a mile, we entered open fields and arrived at the town of Talahasochte, on the banks of Little St. Juan.

The river Little St. Juan may, with singular propriety, be termed the pellucid river. The waters are the clearest and purest of any river I ever saw, transmitting distinctly the natural form and appearance of the objects moving in the transparent floods, or reposing on the silvery bed, with the finny inhabitants sporting in its gently flowing stream.

The river at the town is about two hundred yards over, and fifteen or twenty feet in depth. The great swamp and lake Oaquaphenogaw[7] is said to be its source, which is about one hundred miles by land North of this place, which would give the river a course of near two hundred miles from its source to the sea, to follow its meanders; as in general our rivers, that run any considerable distance through the country to the sea, by their windings and roving about to find a passage through the ridges and heights, at least double their distance.

The Indians and traders say that this river has no branches or collateral brooks or rivers tributary to it, but that it is fed or augmented by great springs which

[7] The Okenfenokee Swamp in southeast Georgia.

break out through the banks. From the accounts given by them, and my own observations on the country round about, it seems a probable assertion, for there was not a creek or rivulet, to be seen, running on the surface of the ground, from the great Alachua Savanna to this river, a distance of about seventy miles; yet, perhaps, no part of the earth affords a greater plenty of pure, salubrious waters. The unparalleled transparency of these waters furnishes an argument for such a conjecture, that amounts at least to a probability, were it not confirmed by ocular demonstration; for in all the flat countries of Carolina and Florida, except this isthmus, the waters of the rivers are, in some degree, turgid, and have a dark hue, owing to the annual firing of the forests and plains, and afterwards the heavy rains washing the light surface of the burnt earth into rivulets, and these rivulets running rapidly over the surface of the earth, flow into the rivers, and tinge the waters the colour of lye or beer, almost down to the tide near the sea coast. But here behold how different the appearance, and how manifest the cause; for although the surface of the ground produces the same vegetable substances, the soil the same, and suffers in like manner a general conflagration, and the rains, in impetuous showers, as liberally descend upon the parched surface of the ground; but the earth being so hollow and porous, these superabundant waters cannot constitute a rivulet or brook to continue any distance on its surface, before they are arrested in their course and swallowed up, thence descending, are filtered through the sands and other strata of earth, to the horizontal beds of porous rocks, which being composed of thin separable laminae,[8] lying generally in obliquely horizontal directions over each other, admit these waters to pass on by gradual but constant percolation; which collecting and associating, augment and form little rills, brooks and even subterraneous rivers, which wander in darkness beneath the surface of the earth, by innumerable doublings, windings and secret labyrinths; no doubt in some places forming vast reservoirs and subterranean lakes, inhabited by multitudes of fish and aquatic animals: and possibly, when collected into large rapid brooks, meeting irresistible obstructions in their course, they suddenly break through these perforated fluted rocks, in high, perpendicular jets, nearly to their former level, flooding large districts of land: thus by means of those subterranean courses, the waters are purified and finally carried to the banks of great rivers, where they emerge and present themselves to open day-light, with their troops of finny inhabitants, in those surprising vast fountains near the banks of this river; and likewise on and near the shores of Great St. Juan, on the East coast of the isthmus, some of which I have already given an account of.

On our arrival at Talahasochte, in the evening we repaired to the trading house formerly belonging to our chief, where were a family of Indians, who immediately and complaisantly moved out to accommodate us. The White King with most of the male inhabitants were out hunting or tending their Corn plantations.

The town is delightfully situated on the elevated East banks of the river, the ground level to near the river, when it descends suddenly to the water; I suppose the perpendicular elevation of the ground may be twenty or thirty feet. There are near thirty habitations constructed after the mode of Cuscowilla; but here is a more spacious and neat council-house.

These Indians have large handsome canoes, which they form out of the trunks of Cypress trees (Cupressus disticha) some of them commodious enough to accomodate twenty or thirty warriors. In these large canoes they descend the river on

[8] Layers.

trading and hunting expeditions on the sea coast, neighbouring islands and keys, quite to the point of Florida, and sometimes cross the gulph, extending their navigations to the Bahama islands and even to Cuba: a crew of these adventurers had just arrived, having returned from Cuba but a few days before our arrival, with a cargo of spirituous liquors, Coffee, Sugar and Tobacco. One of them politely presented me with a choice piece of Tobacco, which he told me he had received from the governor of Cuba.

They deal in the way of barter, carrying with them deer skins, furs, dry fish, bees-wax, honey, bear's oil and some other articles. They say the Spaniards receive them very friendly, and treat them with the best spirituous liquors.

* * *

We came up to this vast plain where the ancient Spanish high way crosses it to Pensacola; there yet remain plain vestiges of the grand causeway, which is open like a magnificent avenue, and the Indians have a bad road or pathway on it. The ground or soil of the plain is a perfectly black, rich soapy earth, like a stiff clay or marle, wet and boggy near shore, but, further in, firm and hard enough in the summer season, but wet and in some places under water during the winter.

This vast plain together with the forests contiguous to it, if permitted (by the Siminoles who are sovereigns of these realms) to be in possession and under the culture of industrious planters and mechanicks, would in a little time exhibit other scenes than it does at present, delightful as it is; for by the arts of agriculture and commerce, almost every desirable thing in life might be produced and made plentiful here, and thereby establish a rich, populous and delightful region; as this soil and climate appear to be of a nature favourable for the production of almost all the fruits of the earth, as Corn, Rice, Indigo, Sugar-cane, Flax, Cotton, Silk, Cochineal and all the varieties of esculent [9] vegetables; and I suppose no part of the earth affords such endless range and exuberant pasture for cattle, deer, sheep, &c. the waters every where, even in the holes in the earth abound with varieties of excellent fish; and the forests and native meadows with wild game, as bear, deer, turkeys, quail, and in the winter season geese, ducks and other fowl; and lying contiguous to one of the most beautiful navigable rivers in the world; and not more than thirty miles from St. Marks on the great bay of Mexico; is most conveniently situated for the West-India trade and the commerce of all the world.

After indulging my imagination in the contemplation of these grand diversified scenes, we turned to the right hand, riding over the charming green terrace dividing the forests from the plains, and then entering the groves again, continued eight or nine miles up the river, four or five miles distance from its banks; having continually in view on one side or other, expansive green fields, groves and high forests; the meadows glittering with distant lakes and ponds, alive with cattle, deer and turkeys, and frequently present to view remains of ancient Spanish plantations. At length, towards evening, we turned about and came within sight of the river, where falling on the Indian trading path, we continued along it to the landing-place opposite the town, when hallooing and discharging our pieces, an Indian with a canoe came presently over and conducted us to the town before dark.

On our arrival at the trading house, our chief was visited by the head men of the town, when instantly the White King's arrival in town was announced; a messenger had before been sent in to prepare a feast, the king and his retinue having

[9] Edible.

killed several bears. A fire is now kindled in the area of the public square; the royal standard is displayed, and the drum beats to give notice to the town of the royal feast.

The ribs and the choice pieces of the three great fat bears already well barbecued or broiled, are brought to the banqueting house in the square, with hot bread; and honeyed water for drink.

When the feast was over in the square, (where only the chiefs and warriors were admitted, with the white people) the chief priest, attended by slaves, came with baskets and carried off the remainder of the victuals etc. which was distributed amongst the families of the town; the king then withdrew, repairing to the council house in the square, whither the chiefs and warriors, old and young, and such of the whites as chose, repaired also; the king, war-chief and several ancient chiefs and warriors were seated on the royal cabins, the rest of the head men and warriors, old and young, sat on the cabins on the right hand of the king's, and the cabins of seats on the left, and on the same elevation are always assigned for the white people, Indians of other towns, and such of their own people as chose.

Our chief, with the rest of the white people in town, took their seats according to order; Tobacco and pipes are brought, the calumet[10] is lighted and smoaked, circulating according to the usual forms and ceremony, and afterwards black drink concluded the feast. The king conversed, drank Cassine[11] and associated familiarly with his people and with us.

After the public entertainment was over, the young people began their music and dancing in the square, whither the young of both sexes repaired, as well as the old and middle aged; this frolick continued all night.

The White King of Talahasochte is a middle aged man, of moderate stature, and though of a lofty and majestic countenance and deportment, yet I am convinced this dignity which really seems graceful, is not the effect of vain supercilious pride, for his smiling countenance and his cheerful familiarity bespeak magnanimity and benignity.

Next a council and treaty was held, they requested to have a trading house again established in the town, assuring us that every possible means should constantly be pursued to prevent any disturbance in future on their part; they informed us that the murderers of M'Gee[12] and his associates, were to be put to death, that two of them were already shot, and they were in pursuit of the other.

Our chief trader in answer, informed them that the re-establishment of friendship and trade was the chief object of his visit, and that he was happy to find his old friends of Talahasochte in the same good disposition, as they ever were towards him and the white people, that it was his wish to trade with them, and that he was now come to collect his pack-horses to bring them goods. The king and the chiefs having been already acquainted with my business and pursuits amongst them, received me very kindly; the king in particular complimented me, saying that I was as one of his own children or people, and should be protected accordingly, while I remained with them, adding, "Our whole country is before you, where you may range about at pleasure, gather physic plants and flowers, and every other production;" thus the treaty terminated friendly and peaceably.

Next day early in the morning we left the town and the river, in order to fix our encampment in the forests about twelve miles from the river, our companions with the pack-horses went a head to the place of rendezvous, and our chief conducted

---

[10] A ceremonial pipe, a "peace pipe."   [11] A drink made from the holly tree's leaves.
[12] The leader of a Georgia family whose camp was attacked by predatory Indians.

me another way to shew me a very curious place, called the Alligator-Hole, which was lately formed by an extraordinary eruption or jet of water; it is one of those vast circular sinks, which we behold almost every where about us as we traversed these forests, after we left the Alachua savanna: this remarkable one is on the verge of a spacious meadow, the surface of the ground round about uneven by means of gentle rising knolls; some detached groups of rocks and large spreading Live-Oaks shade it on every side; it is about sixty yards over, and the surface of the water six or seven feet below the rim of the funnel or bason; the water is transparent, cool and pleasant to drink, and well stored with fish; a very large alligator at present is lord or chief; many have been killed here, but the throne is never long vacant, the vast neighbouring ponds so abound with them.

The account that this gentleman, who was an eye-witness of the last eruption, gave me of its first appearance; being very wonderful, I proceed to relate what he told me whilst we were in town, which was confirmed by the Indians, and one or more of our companions, who also saw its progress, as well as my own observations after I came to the ground.

This trader being near the place (before it had any visible existence in its present appearance) about three years ago (as he was looking for some horses which he expected to find in these parts) when, on a sudden, he was astonished by an inexpressible rushing noise, like a mighty hurricane or thunder storm, and looking around, he saw the earth overflowed by torrents of water, which came, wave after wave, rushing down a vale or plain very near him, which it filled with water, and soon began to overwhelm the higher grounds, attended with a terrific noise and tremor of the earth; recovering from his first surprise, he immediately resolved to proceed for the place from whence the noise seemed to come, and soon came in sight of the incomparable fountain, and saw, with amazement, the floods rushing upwards many feet high, and the expanding waters, which prevailed every way, spreading themselves far and near: he at length concluded (he said) that the fountains of the deep were again broken up, and that an universal deluge had commenced, and instantly turned about and fled to alarm the town, about nine miles distance, but before he could reach it he met several of the inhabitants, who, already alarmed by the unusual noise, were hurrying on towards the place, upon which he returned with the Indians, taking their stand on an eminence to watch its progress and the event: it continued to jet and flow in this manner for several days, forming a large, rapid creek or river, descending and following the various courses and windings of the valley, for the distance of seven or eight miles, emptying itself into a vast savanna, where was a lake and sink which received and gave vent to its waters.

The fountain, however, gradually ceased to overflow, and finally withdrew itself beneath the common surface of the earth, leaving this capacious bason of waters, which, though continually near full, hath never since overflowed. There yet remains, and will, I suppose, remain for ages, the dry bed of the river or canal, generally four, five and six feet below the natural surface of the land; the perpendicular, ragged banks of which, on each side, shew the different strata of the earth, and at places, where ridges or a swelling bank crossed and opposed its course and fury, are vast heaps of fragments of rocks, white chalk, stones and pebbles, which were collected and thrown into the lateral valleys, until the main stream prevailed over and forced them aside, overflowing the levels and meadows, for some miles distance from the principal stream, on either side. We continued down the great vale, along its banks, quite to the savanna and lake where it vented itself, while its ancient subterranean channel was gradually opening, which, I imagine, from some hidden event or cause had been choaked up, and which, we may suppose, was the immediate cause of the eruption.

In the evening having gained our encampment, on a grassy knoll or eminence, under the cover of spreading Oaks, just by the grotto or sink of the lake, which lay as a sparkling gem on the flowery bosom of the ample savanna; our roving associates soon came in from ranging the forests; we continued our encampment at this place for several days, ranging around the delightful country to a great distance, every days excursion presenting new scenes of wonder and delight.

Early in the morning our chief invited me with him on a visit to the town, to take a final leave of the White King. We were graciously received, and treated with the utmost civility and hospitality; there was a noble entertaintment and repast provided against our arrival, consisting of bears ribs, venison, varieties of fish, roasted turkeys (which they call the white man's dish) hot corn cakes, and a very agreeable, cooling sort of jelly, which they call conte; this is prepared from the root of the China brier.

* * *

About midnight, having fallen asleep, I was awakened and greatly surprised at finding most of my companions up in arms, and furiously engaged with a large alligator but a few yards from me. One of our company, it seems, awoke in the night, and perceived the monster within a few paces of the camp, who giving the alarm to the rest, they readily came to his assistance, for it was a rare piece of sport; some took fire-brands and cast them at his head, whilst others formed javelins of saplins, pointed and hardened with fire; these they thrust down his throat into his bowels, which caused the monster to roar and bellow hideously, but his strength and fury was so great that he easily wrenched or twisted them out of their hands, which he wielded and brandished about and kept his enemies at distance for a time; some were for putting an end to his life and sufferings with a rifle ball, but the majority thought this would too soon deprive them of the diversion and pleasure of exercising their various inventions of torture; they at length however grew tired, and agreed in one opinion, that he had suffered sufficiently, and put an end to his existence. This crocodile was about twelve feet in length: we supposed that he had been allured by the fishy scent of our birds, and encouraged to undertake and pursue this hazardous adventure which cost him his life; this, with other instances already recited, may be sufficient to prove the intrepidity and subtilty of those voracious, formidable animals.

We set off early next morning, and soon after falling into the trading path, accomplished about twenty miles of our journey, and in the evening encamped as usual, near the banks of savannas and ponds, for the benefit of water and accommodations of pasture for our creatures. Next day we passed over part of the great and beautiful Alachua Savanna, whose exuberant green meadows, with the fertile hills which immediately encircle it, would if peopled and cultivated after the manner of the civilized countries of Europe, without crouding or incommoding families, at a moderate estimation, accommodate in the happiest manner, above one hundred thousand human inhabitants, besides millions of domestic animals; and I make no doubt this place will at some future day be one of the most populous and delightful seats on earth.

We came to camp in the evening, on the banks of a creek but a few miles distance from Cuscowilla, and two days more moderate travelling brought us safe back again to the lower trading-house, on St. Juan, having been blessed with health and a prosperous journey.

On my arrival at the stores, I was happy to find all well as we had left them, and our bringing with us friendly talks from the Siminole towns, and the Nation likewise, compleated the hopes and wishes of the trading company, with respect to their commercial concerns with the Indians, which, as the chearing light of the sun-beams after a dark, tempestuous night, diffused joy and conviviality throughout the little community, where were a number of men with their families, who had been put out of employment and subsistence, anxiously waiting the happy event.

1772-1776, 1791

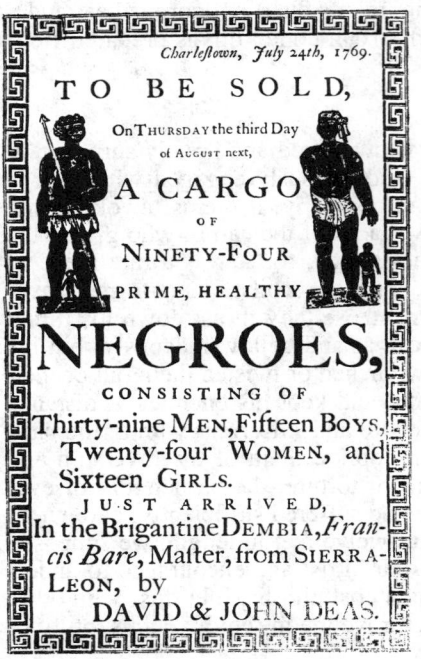

A broadside advertising a sale of slaves in South Carolina.

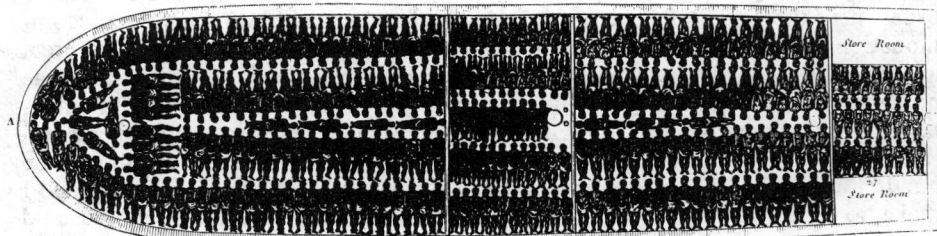

The slave ship Brookes *out of Liverpool was able to hold a "cargo" of 454 slaves, according to an act of 1788; the hold was only 22 inches high.*

Olaudah Equiano (Gustavus Vassa)
(1745?–1801?)

Born in 1745 in what is now Nigeria, Olaudah Equiano was kidnapped at age eleven by African slave traders. Carried to Africa's western coast, he was sold to white traders and transported to Barbados. During the Atlantic crossing and after being bought and shipped to a Virginia plantation, he experienced the horrors of slavery. Yet, his circumstances improved somewhat when he was purchased by Michael Henry Pascal, a British naval lieutenant, who brought Equiano to England, treated him well, and renamed him Gustavus Vassa, after a Swedish king.

During the Seven Years' War between England and France (1756 to 1763), Equiano, assuming that he would be freed after the war, bravely served his master in several important naval engagements. Instead, he was transported to the Caribbean isle of Montserrat and purchased by a Quaker merchant, Philadelphian Robert King. King also treated Equiano well, allowing the slave to become a sailor on merchant vessels in the Caribbean and encouraging him to earn a tiny income through small trading ventures. However, Equiano continued to experience slavery's emotional abuses and to long for freedom.

His loyalty to his master and his efficient and responsible service were rewarded when Equiano was freed in 1766. In 1767 he returned to London and became a valet for a physician, Charles Irving. In summer 1773, he and Irving joined an Arctic expedition, becoming trapped in the Greenland ice and narrowly escaping. On voyages to Turkey, Portugal, and Italy and return trips to the West Indies, Equiano discovered that free blacks were everywhere vulnerable to abuse, prejudice, and reenslavement.

In 1774 Equiano underwent a powerful conversion experience and joined the Methodist church. That move led him to travel with Irving the next year to what is now Nicaragua, where Equiano hoped not only to further Irving's mercantile interests but also to convert the local natives. After barely avoiding being resold into slavery, he returned to England in 1777. During the 1780s, when abolitionist sentiment ran high in England, Equiano brought cases of slave abuse before the public, lectured on slavery, worked to organize an African resettlement effort, and published *The Interesting Narrative of the Life of Olaudah Equiano, or Gustavus Vassa, the African, Written by Himself* (1789). This book was exceedingly popular. In 1792 Equiano married Susanna Cullen. Their only child died less than three months after her father, around 1801.

Equiano's *Narrative* is the most important predecessor of nineteenth-century slave narratives, which provided materials for white abolitionist authors, such as Harriet Beecher Stowe, and helped create a literary genre that influenced many African-American authors, including Booker T. Washington, Richard Wright, Ralph Ellison, and Toni Morrison. Widening the range of American literature, the slave narrative and its recent fictional offspring have promoted black self-expression, demonstrated black creativity, and built black self-respect. Yet, with its memorable accounts of African, Caribbean, American, and European cultures, of Equiano's adventures, and of slave suffering and religious decision, the *Narrative* is important in its own right. With its emphasis on moral improvement and financial progress à la Benjamin Franklin, its emphasis on religious conversion à la Jon-

athan Edwards, and its emphasis on the evils of oppression à la Thomas Jefferson, Equiano's *Narrative* is an unforgettable portrait of an interestingly American mind.

Suggested Readings: *The Interesting Narrative,* ed. P. Edwards, 1969. *Great Slave Narratives,* ed.
A. Bontemps, 1969. M. Starkey, *Striving to Make It My Home,* 1964. F. D. Adams and B. Sanders,
Three Black Writers in Eighteenth-Century England, 1971. V. Smith, *Self-Discovery and Authority
in Afro-American Narrative,* 1987.

Text Used: *The Interesting Narrative of the Life of Olaudah Equiano, or Gustavus Vassa, the African,* 1814, in *The Classic Slave Narratives,* ed. H. L. Gates, Jr., 1987.

from THE INTERESTING NARRATIVE OF THE LIFE OF OLAUDAH EQUIANO

CHAPTER II

I. I hope the reader will not think I have trespassed on his patience, in introducing myself to him with some account of the manners and customs of my country.
They had been implanted in me with great care, and made an impression on my
mind, which time could not erase, and which all adversity and variety of fortune I
have since experienced, served only to rivet and record; for, whether the love of
one's country be real or imaginary, a lesson of reason or an instinct of nature, I
still look back with pleasure on the first scenes of my life, though that pleasure has
been for the most part mingled with sorrow.

I have already acquainted the reader with the time and place of my birth. My
father, besides many slaves, had a numerous family, of which seven lived to grow
up, including myself and a sister, who was the only daughter. As I was the youngest of the sons, I became, of course, the greatest favourite with my mother, and
was always with her, and she used to take particular pains to form my mind. I was
trained up from my earliest years in the art of war: my daily exercise was shooting
and throwing javelins; and my mother adorned me with emblems, after the manner of our greatest warriors. In this way I grew up till I was turned the age of
eleven, when an end was put to my happiness in the following manner:—When
the grown people in the neighbourhood were gone far in the fields to labour, the
children generally assembled together in some of the neighbours' premises to
play; and some of us often used to get up into a tree to look out for any assailant,
or kidnapper, that might come upon us. For they sometimes took those opportunities of our parents' absence, to attack and carry off as many as they could seize.
One day, as I was watching at the top of a tree in our yard, I saw one of those
people come into the yard of our next neighbour but one, to kidnap, there being
many stout young people in it. Immediately on this I gave the alarm of the rogue,
and he was surrounded by the stoutest of them, who entangled him with cords, so
that he could not escape till some of the grown people came and secured him.

II. But alas! ere long it was my fate to be thus attacked, and to be carried off,
when none of the grown people were nigh. One day, when all our people were
gone out to their work as usual, and only I and my sister were left to mind the
house, two men and a woman got over our walls, and in a moment seized us both;
and without giving us time to cry out, or to make any resistance, they stopped our
mouths and ran off with us into the nearest wood. Here they tied our hands, and

continued to carry us as far as they could, till night came on, when we reached a small house, where the robbers halted for refreshment and spent the night. We were then unbound, but were unable to take any food; and being quite overpowered by fatigue and grief, our only relief was some sleep, which allayed our misfortune for a short time. The next morning we left the house, and continued travelling all the day. For a long time we had kept the woods, but at last we came into a road which I believed I knew. I had now some hopes of being delivered; for we had advanced but a little way before I discovered some people at a distance, on which I began to cry out for their assistance; but my cries had no other effect than to make them tie me faster and stop my mouth; they then put me into a large sack. They also stopped my sister's mouth, and tied her hands; and in this manner we proceeded till we were out of sight of these people.

When we went to rest the following night, they offered us some victuals; but we refused it; and the only comfort we had was in being in one another's arms all that night, and bathing each other with tears. But alas! we were soon deprived of even the small comfort of weeping together. The next day proved one of greater sorrow than I had yet experienced; for my sister and I were then separated, while we lay clasped in each other's arms. It was in vain that we besought them not to part us; she was torn from me, and immediately carried away, while I was left in a state of distraction not to be described. I cried and grieved continually; and for several days did not eat any thing but what they forced into my mouth. At length, after many days' travelling, during which I had often changed masters, I got into the hands of a chieftain, in a pleasant country. This man had two wives and some children; and they all used me extremely well, and did all they could to comfort me; particularly the first wife, who was something like my mother. Although I was a great many days' journey from my father's house, yet these people spoke exactly the same language with us. This first master of mine, as I may call him, was a smith,[1] and my principal employment was working his bellows, which were the same kind as I had seen in my vicinity. They were in some respects not unlike the stoves here in gentlemen's kitchens; and were covered over with leather, and in the middle of that leather a stick was fixed, and a person stood up and worked it, in the same manner as is done to pump water out of a cask with a hand pump. I believe it was gold he worked, for it was of a lovely bright yellow colour, and was worn by the women on their wrists and ankles.

I was there, I suppose, about a month, and they at length used to trust me some little distance from the house. I employed this liberty in embracing every opportunity to inquire the way to my own home: and I also sometimes, for the same purpose, went with the maidens, in the cool of the evenings, to bring pitchers of water from the springs for the use of the house. I had also remarked where the sun rose in the morning, and set in the evening, as I had travelled along: and had observed that my father's house was towards the rising of the sun. I therefore determined to seize the first opportunity of making my escape, and to shape my course for that quarter; for I was quite oppressed and weighed down by grief after my mother and friends; and my love of liberty, ever great, was strengthened by the mortifying circumstance of not daring to eat with the free-born children, although I was mostly their companion.

III. While I was projecting my escape, one day an unlucky event happened, which quite disconcerted my plan, and put an end to my hopes. I used to be sometimes employed in assisting an elderly woman slave to cook and take care of

---

[1] A goldsmith.

the poultry: and one morning, while I was feeding some chickens, I happened to toss a small pebble at one of them, which hit in on the middle, and directly killed it. The old slave having soon after missed the chicken, inquired after it; and on my relating the accident (for I told her the truth, because my mother would never suffer me to tell a lie) she flew into a violent passion, threatened that I should suffer for it; and, my master being out, she immediately went and told her mistress what I had done. This alarmed me very much, and I expected an instant flogging, which to me was uncommonly dreadful; for I had seldom been beaten at home. I therefore resolved to fly; and accordingly I ran into a thicket that was hard by, and hid myself in the bushes. Soon afterwards my mistress and the slave returned, and, not seeing me, they searched all the house, but not finding me, and I not making answer when they called me, they thought I had run away, and the whole neighbourhood was raised in the pursuit of me.

In that part of the country, as well as in ours, the houses and villages were skirted with woods, or shrubberies, and the bushes were so thick that a man could readily conceal himself in them, so as to elude the strictest search. The neighbours continued the whole day looking for me, and several times many of them came within a few yards of the place where I lay hid. I expected every moment, when I heard a rustling among the trees, to be found out, and punished by my master. But they never discovered me, though they often were so near that I even heard their conjectures, as they were looking about for me; and I now learned from them, that any attempt to return home would be hopeless. Most of them supposed I had fled towards home; but the distance was so great, and the way so intricate, that they thought I could never reach it, and that I should be lost in the woods. When I heard this I was seized with a violent panic, and abandoned myself to despair. Night too began to approach, and aggravated all my fears. I had before entertained hopes of getting home and had determined when it should be dark to make the attempt; but I was now convinced it was fruitless, and began to consider that, if possibly I could escape all other animals, I could not those of the human kind; and that, not knowing the way, I must perish in the woods. Thus was I like the hunted deer:

> Ev'ry leaf, and ev'ry whisp'ring breath
> Convey'd a foe, and ev'ry foe a death.

I heard frequent rustlings among the leaves, and being pretty sure they were snakes, I expected every instant to be stung by them. This increased my anguish, and the horror of my situation became now quite insupportable. I at length quitted the thicket, very faint and hungry, for I had not eaten nor drunk any thing all the day. I crept to my master's kitchen, from whence I set out at first, which was an open shed, and laid myself down in the ashes with an anxious wish for death to relieve me from all my pains. I was scarcely awake in the morning, when the old woman slave, who was the first up, came to light the fire, and saw me in the fire place. She was very much surprised to see me, and could scarcely believe her own eyes. She now promised to intercede for me, and went for her master, who soon after came, and, having slightly reprimanded me, ordered me to be taken care of, and not ill treated.

IV. Soon after this my master's only daughter and child by his first wife, sickened and died, which affected him so much that for some time he was almost frantic, and really would have killed himself, had he not been watched and prevented. However, in a small time afterwards he recovered, and I was again sold. I was now carried to the left of the sun's rising, through many dreary wastes and dismal woods, amidst the hideous roaring of wild beasts. The people I was sold to used to carry me very often, when I was tired, either on their shoulders or on their backs. I saw many convenient well-built sheds along the road, at proper distances, to accommodate the merchants and travellers. They lie in those buildings along with their wives, who often accompany them: and they always go well armed.

From the time I left my own nation I always found somebody that understood me till I came to the sea coast. The languages of different nations did not totally differ, nor were they so copious as those of the Europeans, particularly the English. They were therefore easily learned; and, while I was journeying thus through Africa, I acquired two or three different tongues. In this manner I had been travelling for a considerable time, when one evening, to my great surprise, whom should I see brought to the house where I was, but my dear sister? As soon as she saw me she gave a loud shriek, and ran into my arms. I was quite overpowered: neither of us could speak; but for a considerable time, clung to each other in mutual embraces, unable to do any thing but weep. Our meeting affected all who saw us; and indeed I must acknowledge, in honour of those sable destroyers of human rights, that I never met with any ill treatment, or saw any offered to their slaves, except tying them, when necessary, to keep them running away.

When these people knew we were brother and sister, they indulged us to be together; and the man, to whom I supposed we belonged, lay with us, he in the middle, while she and I held one another by the hands across his breast all night; and thus for a while we forgot our misfortunes in the joy of being together. But even this small comfort was soon to have an end, for scarcely had the fatal morning appeared, when she was again torn from me for ever! I was now more miserable, if possible, than before. The small relief which her presence gave me from pain was gone, and the wretchedness of my situation was redoubled by my anxiety after her fate, and my apprehensions lest her sufferings should be greater than mine, when I could not be with her to alleviate them.

Yes, dear partner of all my childish sports! Sharer of my joys and sorrows; happy should I have ever esteemed myself to encounter every misery for you, and to procure your freedom by the sacrifice of my own! Though you were early forced from my arms, your image has been always rivetted in my heart, from which neither time nor fortune has been able to remove it: so that, while the thoughts of your sufferings have damped my prosperity, they have mingled with adversity and increased its bitterness. To that Heaven, which protects the weak from the strong, I commit the care of your innocence and virtues, if they have not already received their full reward, and if your youth and delicacy have not long since fallen victims to the violence of the African trader, the pestilential stench of a Guinea ship, the seasoning in the European colonies, or the lash and lust of a brutal and unrelenting overseer.

I did not long remain after my sister. I was again sold, and carried through a number of places, till, after travelling a considerable time, I came to a town called Tinmah, in the most beautiful country I had yet seen in Africa: It was extremely rich, and there were many rivulets which flowed through it, and supplied a large pond in the centre of the town, where the people washed. Here I first saw and tasted cocoa nuts, which I thought superior to any nuts I had ever tasted before; and the trees which were loaded, were also interspersed among the houses, which had commodious shades adjoining, and were in the same manner as ours, the insides being neatly plastered and whitewashed. Here I also saw and tasted, for the first time, sugar-cane. Their money consisted of little white shells, the size of the fingernail. I was sold for one hundred and seventy-two of these, by a merchant who lived at this place. I had been about two or three days at his house, when a wealthy widow, a neighbour of his came there one evening, and brought with her an only son, a young gentleman about my own age and size. Here they saw me; and, having taken a fancy to me, I was bought of the merchant, and went home with them. Her house and premises were situated close to one of those rivulets I have mentioned, and were the finest I ever saw in Africa: they were very extensive, and she had a number of slaves to attend her. The next day I was washed and perfumed, and when meal-time came, I was led into the presence of my mistress, and ate and drank before her with her son. This filled me with astonishment; and I could scarcely avoid expressing my surprise that the young gentleman should suffer me, who was bound, to eat with him who was free; and not only so, but that he would not at any time either eat or drink till I had taken first, because I was the eldest, which was agreeable to our custom. Indeed every thing here, and their treatment of me, made me forget that I was a slave. The language of these people resembled ours so nearly, that we understood each other perfectly. They had also the very same customs as we. There were likewise slaves daily to attend us, while my young master and I, with other boys, sported with our darts, and bows and arrows, as I had been used to do at home. In this resemblance to my former happy state, I passed about two months; and now I began to think I was to be adopted into the family, and was beginning to be reconciled to my situation, and to forget by degrees my misfortunes, when all at once the delusion vanished; for, without the least previous knowledge, one morning, early, while my dear master and companion was still asleep, I was awakened out of my reverie to fresh sorrow, and hurried away even amongst the uncircumcised.[2]

Thus, at the very moment I dreamed of the greatest happiness, I found myself most miserable; and it seemed as if fortune wished to give me this taste of joy only to render the reverse more poignant. The change I now experienced was as painful as it was sudden and unexpected. It was a change indeed from a state of bliss to a scene which is inexpressible by me, as it discovered to me an element I had never before beheld, and of which till then had no idea; and wherein such instances of hardship and cruelty continually occurred, as I can never reflect on but with horror.

V. All the nations and people I had hitherto passed through resembled our own in their manners, customs, and language: but I came at length to a country, the inhabitants of which differed from us in all these particulars. I was very much struck with this difference, especially when I came among a people who did not circumcise, and who ate without washing their hands. They cooked their provisions also in iron pots, and had European cutlasses and cross bows, which were unknown to us; and fought with their fists among themselves. Their women were not so modest as ours, for they ate, drank, and slept with their men. But, above all, I was amazed to see no sacrifices or offerings among them. In some of those places the people ornamented themselves with scars, and likewise filed their teeth very sharp. They sometimes wanted to ornament me in the same manner, but I would not suffer them; hoping that I might sometime be among a people who did not thus disfigure themselves, as I thought they did. At last I came to the banks of

---

[2] Treated like a heathen.

a large river, covered with canoes, in which the people appeared to live, with their household utensils, and provisions of all kinds. I was beyond measure astonished at this, as I had never before seen any water larger than a pond or a rivulet: and my surprise was mingled with no small fear when I was put into one of these canoes, and we began to paddle and move along the river. We continued going on thus till night; and when we came to land, and made fires on the banks, each family by themselves, some dragged their canoes on shore, others cooked in theirs, and laid in them all night. Those on the land had mats, of which they made tents, some in the shape of little houses: in these we slept: and after the morning meal, we embarked again, and proceeded as before. I was often very much astonished to see some of the women as well as the men, jump into the water, dive to the bottom, come up again, and swim about. Thus I continued to travel, both by land and by water, through different countries and various nations, till at the end of six or seven months after I had been kidnapped, I arrived at the sea coast.

It would be tedious and uninteresting to relate all the incidents which befell me during this journey, and which I have not yet forgotten, or to mention the various lands I passed through, and the manners and customs of the different people among whom I lived: I shall therefore only observe, that in all the places where I was, the soil was exceedingly rich; the pomkins, aedas,[3] plantains, yams, &c. &c. were in great abundance, and of incredible size. There were also large quantities of different gums, though not used for any purpose; and every where a great deal of tobacco. The cotton even grew quite wild; and there was plenty of red wood. I saw no mechanics whatever in all the way, except such as I have mentioned. The chief employment in all these countries was agriculture, and both the males and females, as with us, were brought up to it, and trained in the arts of war.

The first object that saluted my eyes when I arrived on the coast was the sea, and a slave ship, which was then riding at anchor, and waiting for its cargo. These filled me with astonishment, that was soon converted into terror, which I am yet at a loss to describe, and much more the then feelings of my mind when I was carried on board. I was immediately handled and tossed up to see if I was sound, by some of the crew; and I was now persuaded that I had got into a world of bad spirits, and that they were going to kill me. Their complexions too, differing so much from ours, their long hair, and the language they spoke, which was very different from any I had ever heard, united to confirm me in this belief. Indeed such were the horrors of my views and fears at the moment, that if ten thousand worlds had been my own, I would have freely parted with them all to have exchanged my condition with the meanest slave in my own country. When I looked round the ship too, and saw a large furnace or copper boiling and a multitude of black people, of every description, chained together, every one of their countenances expressing dejection and sorrow, I no longer doubted of my fate; and, quite overpowered with horror and anguish, I fell motionless on the deck, and fainted. When I recovered a little, I found some black people about me, who I believed were some of those who brought me on board, and had been receiving their pay: they talked to me in order to cheer me, but all in vain. I asked them if we were not to be eaten by those white men with horrible looks, red faces, and long hair. They told me I was not: and one of the crew brought me a small portion of spirituous liquor in a wine glass; but, being afraid of him, I would not take it out of his hand. One of the blacks therefore took it from him and gave it to me,

---

[3] Pumpkins; eddoes (edible tropical roots).

and I took a little down my palate, which, instead of reviving me, as they thought it would, threw me into the greatest consternation at the strange feeling it produced, having never tasted any such liquor before.

Soon after this the blacks who brought me on board went off, and left me abandoned to despair. I now saw myself deprived of all chance of returning to my native country, or even the least glimpse of gaining the shore, which I now considered as friendly; and I even wished for my former slavery, in preference to my present situation, which was filled with horrors of every kind, still heightened by my ignorance of what I was to undergo. I was not long suffered to indulge my grief. I was soon put down under the decks, and there I received such a salutation in my nostrils as I had never experienced in my life: so that, with the loathsomeness of the stench, and with my crying together, I became so sick and low that I was not able to eat, nor had I the least desire to taste any thing. I now wished for the last friend, death, to relieve me; but soon, to my grief, two of the white men offered me eatables; and, on my refusing to eat, one of them held me fast by the hands, and laid me across, I think, the windlass, and tied my feet, while the other flogged me severely. I had never experienced any thing of this kind before, and although, not being used to the water, I naturally feared that element the first time I saw it, yet nevertheless, could I have got over the nettings, I would have jumped over the side, but I could not; and besides the crew used to watch us very closely, who were not chained down to the decks, lest we should leap into the water. I have seen some of these poor African prisoners most severely cut for attempting to do so, and hourly whipped for not eating. This indeed was often the case with myself. In a little time after, amongst the poor chained men, I found some of my own nation, which in a small degree gave ease to my mind. I inquired of these what was to be done with us. They gave me to understand we were to be carried to these white people's country to work for them. I was then a little revived, and thought if it were no worse than working, my situation was not so desperate. But still I feared I should be put to death, the white people looked and acted, as I thought, in so savage a manner; for I had never seen among any people such instances of brutal cruelty: and this is not only shewn towards us blacks, but also to some of the whites themselves. One white man in particular I saw, when we were permitted to be on deck, flogged so unmercifully with a large rope near the foremast, that he died in consequence of it; and they tossed him over the side as they would have done a brute. This made me fear these people the more; and I expected nothing less than to be treated in the same manner. I could not help expressing my fearful apprehensions to some of my countrymen; I asked them if these people had no country, but lived in this hollow place, the ship. They told me they did not, but came from a distant one. 'Then,' said I, 'how comes it, that in all our country we never heard of them?' They told me, because they lived so very far off. I then asked, where their women were: had they any like themselves. I was told they had. 'And why,' said I, 'do we not see them?' They answered, because they were left behind. I asked how the vessel could go. They told me they could not tell; but that there was cloth put upon the masts by the help of the ropes I saw, and then the vessel went on; and the white men had some spell or magic they put in the water, when they liked, in order to stop the vessel. I was exceedingly amazed at this account, and really thought they were spirits. I therefore wished much to be from amongst them, for I expected they would sacrifice me; but my wishes were in vain, for we were so quartered that it was impossible for any of us to make our escape.

VI. While we stayed on the coast I was mostly on deck; and one day, to my great astonishment, I saw one of these vessels coming in with the sails up. As soon as the whites saw it, they gave a great shout, at which we were amazed; and the more so as the vessel appeared larger by approaching nearer. At last she came to an anchor in my sight, and when the anchor was let go, I and my countrymen who saw it, were lost in astonishment to observe the vessel stop, and were now convinced it was done by magic. Soon after this the other ship got her boats out, and they came on board of us, and the people of both ships seemed very glad to see each other. Several of the strangers also shook hands with us black people, and made motions with their hands, signifying, I suppose, we were to go to their country; but we did not understand them. At last, when the ship, in which we were, had got in all her cargo, they made ready with many fearful noises, and we were all put under deck, so that we could not see how they managed the vessel.

But this disappointment was the least of my grief. The stench of the hold, while we were on the coast, was so intolerably loathsome, that it was dangerous to remain there for any time, and some of us had been permitted to stay on the deck for the fresh air; but now that the whole ship's cargo were confined together, it became absolutely pestilential. The closeness of the place, and the heat of the climate, added to the number in the ship, being so crowded that each had scarcely room to turn himself, almost suffocated us. This produced copious perspirations, so that the air soon became unfit for respiration, from a variety of loathsome smells, and brought on a sickness among the slaves, of which many died, thus falling victims to the improvident avarice, as I may call it, of their purchasers. This deplorable situation was again aggravated by the galling of the chains, now become insupportable; and the filth of necessary tubs, into which the children often fell, and were almost suffocated. The shrieks of the women, and the groans of the dying, rendered it a scene of horror almost inconceivable. Happily, perhaps, for myself, I was soon reduced so low here that it was thought necessary to keep me almost continually on deck; and from my extreme youth, I was not put in fetters. In this situation I expected every hour to share the fate of my companions, some of whom were almost daily brought upon deck at the point of death, and I began to hope that death would soon put an end to my miseries. Often did I think many of the inhabitants of the deep much more happy than myself; I envied them the freedom they enjoyed, and as often wished I could change my condition for theirs. Every circumstance I met with served only to render my state more painful, and heighten my apprehensions and my opinion of the cruelty of the whites. One day they had taken a number of fishes; and when they had killed and satisfied themselves with as many as they thought fit, to our astonishment who were on deck, rather than give any of them to us to eat, as we expected, they tossed the remaining fish into the sea again, although we begged and prayed for some as well as we could, but in vain; and some of my countrymen, being pressed by hunger, took an opportunity, when they thought no one saw them, of trying to get a little privately; but were discovered, and the attempt procured for them some very severe floggings.

One day, when we had a smooth sea and moderate wind, two of my wearied countrymen, who were chained together, (I was near them at the time) preferring death to such a life of misery, somehow made through the nettings and jumped into the sea: immediately another quite dejected fellow, who on account of his illness was suffered to be out of irons also followed their example; and I believe many more would very soon have done the same, if they had not been prevented by the ship's crew, who were instantly alarmed. Those of us who were the most active were in a moment put down under the deck; and there was such a noise and confusion amongst the people of the ship as I never heard before, to stop her and get the boat out to go after the slaves. However, two of the wretches were drowned; but they got the other, and afterward flogged him unmercifully, for thus attempting to prefer death to slavery. In this manner we continued to undergo more hardships than I can now relate, hardships which are inseparable from this accursed trade. Many a time we were near suffocation from the want of fresh air, being deprived thereof for days together. This, and the stench of the necessary tubs, carried off many.

VII. During our passage I first saw flying fishes, which surprised me very much: they used frequently to fly across the ship, and many of them fell on the deck. I also now first saw the use of the quadrant. I had often with astonishment seen the mariners make observations with it, and I could not think what it meant. They at last took notice of my surprise: and one of them, willing to increase it, as well as to gratify my curiosity, made me one day look through it. The clouds appeared to me to be land, which disappeared as they passed along. This heightened my wonder; and I was now more persuaded than ever that I was in another world, and that every thing about me was magic. At last we came in sight of the island of Barbadoes, at which the whites on board gave a great shout, and made many signs of joy to us. We did not know what to think of this, but as the vessel drew nearer we plainly saw the harbour, and other ships of different kinds and sizes; and we soon anchored amongst them off Bridge Town. Many merchants and planters now came on board, though it was in the evening. They put us in separate parcels, and examined us attentively. They also made us jump, and pointed to the land, signifying we were to go there. We thought by this we should be beaten by these ugly men, as they appeared to us; and, when soon after we were all put down under the deck again, there was much dread and trembling among us, and nothing but bitter cries to be heard all the night from these apprehensions, insomuch that at last the white people got some old slaves from the land to pacify us. They told us we were not to be eaten, but to work, and were soon to go on land, where we should see many of our country people. This report eased us much; and, sure enough, soon after we landed, there came to us Africans of all languages.

We were conducted immediately to the merchant's yard, where we were all pent up together like so many sheep in a fold, without regard to sex or age. As every object was new to me, every thing I saw filled me with surprise. What struck me first was that the houses were built with bricks in stories,[4] and were in every other respect different from those I had seen in Africa; but I was still more astonished at seeing people on horseback. I did not know what this could mean; and indeed I thought these people full of nothing but magical arts. While I was in this astonishment one of my fellow prisoners spoke to a countryman of his about the horses, who said they were the same kind they had in their country. I understood them, though they were from a distant part of Africa, and I thought it odd I had not seen any horses there; but afterwards, when I came to converse with different Africans, I found they had many horses amongst them, and much larger than those I then saw.

[4] The houses had two stories.

We were not many days in the merchants' custody before we were sold after the usual manner, which is this:—On a signal given, such as the beat of a drum, the buyers rush at once into the yard where the slaves are confined, and make choice of that parcel they like best. The noise and clamour with which this is attended, and the eagerness visible in the countenances of the buyers, serve not a little to increase the apprehensions of the terrified Africans, who may well be supposed to consider them the ministers of that destruction to which they think themselves devoted. In this manner, without scruple, are relations and friends separated, most of them never to see each other again. I remember in the vessel in which I was brought over in, in the man's apartment, there were several brothers, who, in the sale, were sold in different lots; and it was very moving on this occasion to see their distress and hear their cries at parting. O, ye nominal[5] Christians! might not an African ask you, "learned you this from your God, who says unto you, Do unto all men as you would men should do unto you? Is it not enough that we are torn from our country and friends, to toil for your luxury and lust of gain? Must every tender feeling be likewise sacrificed to your avarice? Are the dearest friends and relations now rendered more dear by their separation from the rest of their kindred, still to be parted from each other, and thus prevented from cheering the gloom of slavery, with the small comfort of being together, and mingling their sufferings and sorrows? Why are parents to lose their children, brothers their sisters, or husbands their wives? Surely this is a new refinement in cruelty, which, while it has no advantage to atone for it, thus aggravates distress, and adds fresh horrors even to the wretchedness of slavery."

1789

The Federalist
(1787–1788)

The drafters of the Articles of Confederation (America's first constitution), approved in 1776 by thirteen colonies determined to wage a successful war for independence against Britain, were hardly eager to create a strong central government for America, one that could substitute a republican tyranny for a monarchical one. Thus, they created only one institution—the Continental Congress—and denied this body the ability to control commerce or levy taxes, a prohibition that seriously undermined the war effort. After peace came in 1783, further problems arose as states placed tariffs on imports from other states, seized the ships of their neighbors, argued over boundaries, printed their own money, and otherwise behaved as tiny uncooperative nations. Conversely, the Continental Congress successfully concluded the war, negotiated a favorable peace treaty, and permitted the states a wide range of options in enacting a republican government.

In early 1787, after four years of discord, the Continental Congress endorsed the idea of

---

[5] In name only.

a convention for the purpose of revising the Articles. Yet, the delegates who met in Philadelphia the following summer did more than revise. They drafted a constitution that entirely replaced the Articles, calling for a two-chambered national legislature with the power to levy taxes, regulate commerce, and raise and support an army; a chief magistrate who could veto Congressional laws, make treaties, and command the army; and federal judges, appointed for life by the president. On September 20 the Continental Congress voted to send the Constitution to the states for ratification. Although the approval of only nine states was required, the refusal of any state to ratify would have greatly weakened the new nation.

Because New York City was then the nation's capital and a major commercial center, the vote in New York state was particularly important. One New York delegate to the Constitutional Convention and strong supporter of the Constitution, Alexander Hamilton, decided to influence its outcome. Born in the West Indies in 1757, Hamilton had come to America at age sixteen, studied at King's College (now Columbia University), and risen from the ranks to become Washington's aide-de-camp during the Revolution. In 1782, Hamilton was elected to Congress. A strong defender of vigorous, powerful, and even "splendid" government, Hamilton wanted to model America's political system after Britain's (with a president and senators serving for life, an executive with absolute veto, and the near elimination of state governments) but was willing to support the new Constitution as an improvement over the status quo.

An effective writer, Hamilton decided to promote the Constitution in New York City newspapers, enlisting the help of James Madison and John Jay. Born into an influential Virginia family in 1751, graduated from Princeton University, and elected to Congress in 1780, Madison was the most influential delegate at the Constitutional Convention. Less impressed with the idea of a glorious America than was Hamilton, Madison saw a strong national government as merely necessary to protect rights and ensure justice but agreed with Hamilton on the need for a new Constitution. Jay, a New Yorker born in 1745 and a King's College graduate, served as president of Congress in 1778 and helped to negotiate the peace treaty with Britain. Planning to participate fully in Hamilton's propaganda offensive, Jay was forced to withdraw from the project almost entirely because of illness.

Hamilton's first essay, "The Federalist No. 1," appeared in the *Independent Journal* in October 1787. Eighty-four more essays followed over the next ten months, printed two or three a week in up to four newspapers. All eighty-five were published as *The Federalist* in 1788. Hamilton wrote 51; Madison, 29; and Jay, 5. All three authors signed their essays 'Publius' to hide their identities, to present a united front, and to link their government-building enterprise with that of Publius Valerius, a consul who established a stable republic in Rome after the last Roman king was overthrown.

The "anti-Federalists," or opponents of the Constitution, believed in participatory democracy, preferred small nations of like-minded citizens, and opposed large governments with complex systems of representation. Conversely, the Federalists were committed to a "republican" system in which representatives rather than the people themselves governed. Federalists preferred leaders who were superior to their constituents in education and in status. They admired large nations in which governments arbitrated the diverse interests of heterogeneous populations. The Federalists made certain unflattering assumptions about human nature. In *The Federalist* No. 1 Hamilton insists that people are prone to "angry and malignant passions," particularly in times of political crisis. In Nos. 10 and 54, Madison views self-interested behavior—in individuals, political groups, and states—as equally inevitable. According to both writers, government's primary aim is to keep these negative human traits from threatening the public welfare.

The Federalist papers were hailed by Thomas Jefferson, and some later commentators

T H E

FEDERALIST:

A COLLECTION

O F

E   S   S   A   Y   S,

WRITTEN IN FAVOUR OF THE

NEW CONSTITUTION,

AS AGREED UPON BY THE FEDERAL CONVENTION,
SEPTEMBER 17, 1787.

IN TWO VOLUMES.

V O L. I.

N E W - Y O R K:

PRINTED AND SOLD BY J. AND A. M'LEAN,
No. 41, HANOVER-SQUARE,
M,DCC,LXXXVIII.

The title page of
The Federalist.

have similarly placed them among the classics of political theory. Critics have found them vague, self-contradictory, and unenlightened in their acceptance of the notion of slaves as subhuman. Clearly, the essays are historically important as the plainest and fullest expression of the founding fathers' interpretation of America's most basic political document. The essays also have obvious literary value. Through the learnedness, reasonableness, and civility of their discourse, *The Federalist* authors invented a new literary genre, raising the standards for journalistic political debate, lifting it above the name-calling and vituperation of earlier political writing. Through the vividness of their account of a balanced government, smoothly functioning within a complex society of happily competitive persons, *The Federalist* authors also prove that political writing can be as imaginative as other forms of literature.

Thanks in part to the power and persuasiveness of *The Federalist,* the eventual vote in the New York convention was 30 to 27 in favor of ratification. Hamilton, Madison, and Jay later became secretary of the treasury, president, and chief justice, respectively, of the nation they helped to create. Partly because of the *Federalist* authors' willingness to build into their political system a capacity for change, that nation has continued to function— much as they imagined—for more than two hundred years.

Suggested Readings: *The Federalist,* ed. I. Kramnick, 1987. G. Wood, *The Creation of the American Republic, 1776-1787,* 1972. H. J. Storing, *What the Anti-Federalists Were For,* 1981. A. Furtwangler, *The Authority of Publius,* 1984.

Text Used: *The Federalist,* ed. B. F. Wright, 1961.

from THE FEDERALIST

NUMBER 10: THE SIZE AND VARIETY OF THE UNION AS A CHECK ON FACTION

[by James Madison]

To the People of the State of New York:

Among the numerous advantages promised by a well-constructed Union, none deserves to be more accurately developed than its tendency to break and control the violence of faction. The friend of popular governments never finds himself so much alarmed for their character and fate, as when he contemplates their propensity to this dangerous vice. He will not fail, therefore, to set a due value on any plan which, without violating the principles to which he is attached, provides a proper cure for it. The instability, injustice, and confusion introduced into the public councils, have, in truth, been the mortal diseases under which popular governments have everywhere perished; as they continue to be the favorite and fruitful topics from which the adversaries to liberty derive their most specious declamations. The valuable improvements made by the American constitutions on the popular models, both ancient and modern, cannot certainly be too much admired; but it would be an unwarrantable partiality, to contend that they have as effectually obviated the danger on this side, as was wished and expected. Complaints are everywhere heard from our most considerate and virtuous citizens, equally the friends of public and private faith, and of public and personal liberty, that our governments are too unstable, that the public good is disregarded in the conflicts of rival parties, and that measures are too often decided, not according to the rules of justice and the rights of the minor party, but by the superior force of an interested and overbearing majority. However anxiously we may wish that these complaints had no foundation, the evidence of known facts will not permit us to deny that they are in some degree true. It will be found, indeed, on a candid review of our situation, that some of the distresses under which we labor have been erroneously charged on the operation of our governments; but it will be found, at the same time, that other causes will not alone account for many of our heaviest misfortunes; and, particularly, for that prevailing and increasing distrust of public engagements, and alarm for private rights, which are echoed from one end of the continent to the other. These must be chiefly, if not wholly, effects of the unsteadiness and injustice with which a factious spirit has tainted our public administrations.

By a faction, I understand a number of citizens, whether amounting to a majority or minority of the whole, who are united and actuated by some common impulse of passion, or of interest, adverse to the rights of other citizens, or to the permanent and aggregate interests of the community.

There are two methods of curing the mischiefs of faction: the one, by removing its causes; the other, by controlling its effects.

There are again two methods of removing the causes of faction: the one, by destroying the liberty which is essential to its existence; the other, by giving to every citizen the same opinions, the same passions, and the same interests.

It could never be more truly said than of the first remedy, that it was worse than the disease. Liberty is to faction what air is to fire, an aliment[1] without which it instantly expires. But it could not be less folly to abolish liberty, which is essential to political life, because it nourishes faction, than it would be to wish the annihilation of air, which is essential to animal life, because it imparts to fire its destructive agency.

The second expedient is as impracticable as the first would be unwise. As long as the reason of man continues fallible, and he is at liberty to exercise it, different opinions will be formed. As long as the connection subsists between his reason and his self-love, his opinions and his passions will have a reciprocal influence on each other: and the former will be objects to which the latter will attach themselves. The diversity in the faculties of men, from which the rights of property originate, is not less an insuperable obstacle to a uniformity of interests. The protection of these faculties is the first object of government. From the protection of different and unequal faculties of acquiring property, the possession of different degrees and kinds of property immediately results; and from the influence of these on the sentiments and views of the respective proprietors, ensues a division of the society into different interests and parties.

The latent causes of faction are thus sown in the nature of man; and we see them everywhere brought into different degrees of activity, according to the different circumstances of civil society. A zeal for different opinions concerning religion, concerning government, and many other points, as well of speculation as of practice; an attachment to different leaders ambitiously contending for pre-eminence and power; or to persons of other descriptions whose fortunes have been interesting to the human passions, have, in turn, divided mankind into parties, inflamed them with mutual animosity, and rendered them much more disposed to vex and oppress each other than to co-operate for their common good. So strong is this propensity of mankind to fall into mutual animosities, that where no substantial occasion presents itself, the most frivolous and fanciful distinctions have been sufficient to kindle their unfriendly passions and excite their most violent conflicts. But the most common and durable source of factions has been the various and unequal distribution of property. Those who hold and those who are without property have ever formed distinct interests in society. Those who are creditors, and those who are debtors, fall under a like discrimination. A landed interest, a manufacturing interest, a mercantile interest, a moneyed interest, with many lesser interests, grow up of necessity in civilized nations, and divide them into different classes, actuated by different sentiments and views. The regulation of these various and interfering interests forms the principal task of modern legislation, and involves the spirit of party and faction in the necessary and ordinary operations of the government.

No man is allowed to be a judge in his own cause, because his interest would certainly bias his judgment, and, not improbably, corrupt his integrity. With equal, nay with greater reason, a body of men are unfit to be both judges and parties at the same time; yet what are many of the most important acts of legislation, but so many judicial determinations, not indeed concerning the rights of single persons, but concerning the rights of large bodies of citizens? And what are the different classes of legislators but advocates and parties to the causes which they

[1] Nutriment.

determine? Is a law proposed concerning private debts? It is a question to which the creditors are parties on one side and the debtors on the other. Justice ought to hold the balance between them. Yet the parties are, and must be, themselves the judges; and the most numerous party, or, in other words, the most powerful faction must be expected to prevail. Shall domestic manufactures be encouraged, and in what degree, by restrictions on foreign manufactures? are questions which would be differently decided by the landed and the manufacturing classes, and probably by neither with a sole regard to justice and the public good. The apportionment of taxes on the various descriptions of property is an act which seems to require the most exact impartiality; yet there is, perhaps, no legislative act in which greater opportunity and temptation are given to a predominant party to trample on the rules of justice. Every shilling with which they overburden the inferior number, is a shilling saved to their own pockets.

It is in vain to say that enlightened statesmen will be able to adjust these clashing interests, and render them all subservient to the public good. Enlightened statesmen will not always be at the helm. Nor, in many cases, can such an adjustment be made at all without taking into view indirect and remote considerations, which will rarely prevail over the immediate interest which one party may find in disregarding the rights of another or the good of the whole.

The inference to which we are brought is, that the *causes* of faction cannot be removed, and that relief is only to be sought in the means of controlling its *effects*.

If a faction consists of less than a majority, relief is supplied by the republican principle, which enables the majority to defeat its sinister views by regular vote. It may clog the administration, it may convulse the society; but it will be unable to execute and mask its violence under the forms of the Constitution. When a majority is included in a faction, the form of popular government, on the other hand, enables it to sacrifice to its ruling passion or interest both the public good and the rights of other citizens. To secure the public good and private rights against the danger of such a faction, and at the same time to preserve the spirit and the form of popular government, is then the great object to which our inquiries are directed. Let me add that it is the great desideratum[2] by which this form of government can be rescued from the opprobrium under which it has so long labored, and be recommended to the esteem and adoption of mankind.

By what means is this object attainable? Evidently by one of two only. Either the existence of the same passion or interest in a majority at the same time must be prevented, or the majority, having such coexistent passion or interest, must be rendered, by their number and local situation, unable to concert and carry into effect schemes of oppression. If the impulse and the opportunity be suffered to coincide, we well know that neither moral nor religious motives can be relied on as an adequate control. They are not found to be such on the injustice and violence of individuals, and lose their efficacy in proportion to the number combined together, that is, in proportion as their efficacy becomes needful.

From this view of the subject it may be concluded that a pure democracy, by which I mean a society consisting of a small number of citizens, who assemble and administer the government in person, can admit of no cure for the mischiefs of faction. A common passion or interest will, in almost every case, be felt by a majority of the whole; a communication and concert result from the form of gov-

[2] That which is desired or thought to be necessary.

ernment itself; and there is nothing to check the inducements to sacrifice the weaker party or an obnoxious individual. Hence it is that such democracies have ever been spectacles of turbulence and contention; have ever been found incompatible with personal security or the rights of property; and have in general been as short in their lives as they have been violent in their deaths. Theoretic politicians, who have patronized this species of government, have erroneously supposed that by reducing mankind to a perfect equality in their political rights, they would, at the same time, be perfectly equalized and assimilated in their possessions, their opinions, and their passions.

A republic, by which I mean a government in which the scheme of representation takes place, opens a different prospect, and promises the cure for which we are seeking. Let us examine the points in which it varies from pure democracy, and we shall comprehend both the nature of the cure and the efficacy which it must derive from the Union.

The two great points of difference between a democracy and a republic are: first, the delegation of the government, in the latter, to a small number of citizens elected by the rest; secondly, the greater number of citizens, and greater sphere of country, over which the latter may be extended.

The effect of the first difference is, on the one hand, to refine and enlarge the public views, by passing them through the medium of a chosen body of citizens, whose wisdom may best discern the true interest of their country, and whose patriotism and love of justice will be least likely to sacrifice it to temporary or partial considerations. Under such a regulation, it may well happen that the public voice, pronounced by the representatives of the people, will be more consonant to the public good than if pronounced by the people themselves, convened for the purpose. On the other hand, the effect may be inverted. Men of factious tempers, of local prejudices, or of sinister designs, may, by intrigue, by corruption, or by other means, first obtain the suffrages,[3] and then betray the interests, of the people. The question resulting is, whether small or extensive republics are more favorable to the election of proper guardians of the public weal;[4] and it is clearly decided in favor of the latter by two obvious considerations:

In the first place, it is to be remarked that, however small the republic may be, the representatives must be raised to a certain number, in order to guard against the cabals[5] of a few; and that, however large it may be, they must be limited to a certain number, in order to guard against the confusion of a multitude. Hence, the number of representatives in the two cases not being in proportion to that of the two constituents, and being proportionally greater in the small republic, it follows that, if the proportion of fit characters be not less in the large than in the small republic, the former will present a greater option, and consequently a greater probability of a fit choice.

In the next place, as each representative will be chosen by a greater number of citizens in the large than in the small republic, it will be more difficult for unworthy candidates to practise with success the vicious arts by which elections are too often carried; and the suffrages of the people being more free, will be more likely to centre in men who possess the most attractive merit and the most diffusive and established characters.

It must be confessed that in this, as in most other cases, there is a mean, on

---

[3] Votes.   [4] Well-being.   [5] Plots.

both sides of which inconveniences will be found to lie. By enlarging too much the number of electors, you render the representative too little acquainted with all their local circumstances and lesser interests; as by reducing it too much, you render him unduly attached to these, and too little fit to comprehend and pursue great and national objects. The federal Constitution forms a happy combination in this respect; the great and aggregate interests being referred to the national, the local and particular to the State legislatures.

The other point of difference is, the greater number of citizens and extent of territory which may be brought within the compass of republican than of democratic government; and it is this circumstance principally which renders factious combinations less to be dreaded in the former than in the latter. The smaller the society, the fewer probably will be the distinct parties and interests composing it; the fewer the distinct parties and interests, the more frequently will a majority be found of the same party; and the smaller the number of individuals composing a majority, and the smaller the compass within which they are placed, the most easily will they concert and execute their plans of oppression. Extend the sphere, and you take in a greater variety of parties and interests; you make it less probable that a majority of the whole will have a common motive to invade the rights of other citizens; or if such a common motive exists, it will be more difficult for all who feel it to discover their won strength, and to act in unison with each other. Besides other impediments, it may be remarked that, where there is a consciousness of unjust or dishonorable purposes, communication is always checked by distrust in proportion to the number whose concurrence is necessary.

Hence, it clearly appears, that the same advantage which a republic has over a democracy, in controlling the effects of faction, is enjoyed by a large over a small republic, — is enjoyed by the Union over the States composing it. Does the advantage consist in the substitution of representatives whose enlightened views and virtuous sentiments render them superior to local prejudices and to schemes of injustice? It will not be denied that the representation of the Union will be most likely to possess these requisite endowments. Does it consist in the greater security afforded by a greater variety of parties, against the event of any one party being able to outnumber and oppress the rest? In an equal degree does the increased variety of parties comprised within the Union, increase this security? Does it, in fine,[6] consist in the greater obstacles opposed to the concert and accomplishment of the secret wishes of an unjust and interested majority? Here, again, the extent of the Union gives it the most palpable advantage.

The influence of factious leaders may kindle a flame within their particular States, but will be unable to spread a general conflagration through the other states. A religious sect may degenerate into a political faction in a part of the Confederacy; but the variety of sects dispersed over the entire face of it must secure the national councils against any danger from that source. A rage for paper money, for an abolition of debts, for an equal division of property, or for any other improper or wicked project, will be less apt to pervade the whole body of the Union than a particular member of it; in the same proportion as such a malady is more likely to taint a particular county or district, than an entire State.

In the extent and proper structure of the Union, therefore, we behold a republican remedy for the diseases most incident to republican government. And accord-

---

[6] In the end.

ing to the degree of pleasure and pride we feel in being republicans, ought to be our zeal in cherishing the spirit and supporting the character of Federalists.

PUBLIUS

LATE 18TH-CENTURY POETRY

In Royall Tyler's play *The Contrast* (1787), the unlearned bumpkin Jonathan admits to his would-be love that he cannot woo her with high-flown verses; the only poems he knows are the Psalms and "Yankee Doodle." We tend to assume that Jonathan's ignorance represents a widespread disinterest in poetry in eighteenth-century America. Yet, poetry was then a highly respected form of literature. Not only was poetry an accepted genre in which to argue philosophical, theological, and political points, versification was an essential skill of the educated, required of all college students. However crude Jonathan's poetic recitations were, *The Contrast* began, in the accepted mode of eighteenth-century drama, with an elegant prologue in heroic couplets (rhymed pairs of lines), delivered by the actor who played the unversed Jonathan.

The importance of poetry in the Revolutionary period is disguised in part by our modern desire to differentiate poetry from prose. In the eighteenth century such distinctions were less important, and many works now labeled prose include poetic passages. Theater dialogue regularly incorporated verse. Comedies typically alternated scenes of poetry and of prose, whereas heroic dramas such as those of Mercy Otis Warren and William Dunlap, modeled on the great Elizabethan tragedies, were written entirely in blank verse. Similarly, most of the novels of Revolutionary time contained poetry, either as chapter epigraphs or within the narrative itself. And though much of the novels' verse was drawn from English sources, some was American. For example, the title page of Susanna Rowson's *Charlotte Temple* (1794) quotes one of Rowson's earlier ballads. William Hill Brown's *The Power of Sympathy* (1789) includes not only numerous passages of original poetry but an extended defense of the way in which poetry "enlarges and strengthens the mind, refines the taste and improves the judgment," especially of "ladies."

Nonfiction prose incorporated poetry as regularly as did fiction. Even so prosaic a soul as Benjamin Franklin felt the need to versify. When Franklin was only sixteen, his character Silence Dogood attacked the Puritan tradition of writing elegies by producing her own satirical versions of their funeral poetry. Dogood's satire was directed against the content, not the form, of Puritan poetry. Franklin's later persona, Poor Richard, employed the balanced cadences of poetry. Most of his sayings—such as the celebrated "Early to bed and early to rise . . ."—were constructed explicitly as poetic couplets or triplets.

There was no lack of verse in the eighteenth century. The conceptual difficulty began when poetry began to be separated from prose as an independent genre. The very popularity of poetry made it a less profitable form of writing than prose; with so much verse available, poets, unlike prose writers, were rarely paid for newspaper publication of their work. Moreover, a poet's market tended to be very localized and class-specific. Such writers as Joel Barlow and Robert Treat Paine, Jr., who were able to realize some profits on their poetry, did so largely through pre-selling the work on subscription to a small circle of highly supportive friends. Unintentionally, such narrow marketing fostered an elitism at odds with the generally democratic thrust of the poets' messages.

The necessary limitations surrounding distribution were compounded by the more subtle limitations of the literary form itself. The reigning poetic genres in this so-called neoclassical period were the epic, the satire, the pastoral (a poem about rural life), and the prospect poem (combining naturalistic description and nationalistic prophecy). The preferred meter was the "closed" heroic couplet, two lines of rhyming iambic pentameter (five bisyllabic metrical units per line) generally expressing a single idea. The preeminent masters of these forms were the English writers Alexander Pope and Samuel Johnson. However, the rhetorical symmetry and metrical regularity most admired in their aristocratic, neoclassical poetry was not always appropriate for the anti-establishment sentiments of the American Revolution. Pope's preference for rules over inspiration did not answer well the poetic needs of a youthful nation searching for identity.

Some American poetry of the Revolutionary period resolved this tension between aristocratic form and democratic content conservatively by ridiculing the limitations of American culture. These satires from a loosely interconnected group of poets known as the Connecticut Wits culminated in the collaborative *The Anarchiad* (1786–1787), a multifaceted critique of the postwar period, patterned on Pope's angry *The Dunciad* (1728). But the conservative thrust of the Wits was most clearly (and successfully) represented in the burlesques of John Trumbull. Trumbull's *The Progress of Dulness* (1772–1773) exposed the inadequacies of American education. His later *M'Fingal* (1782) presented itself as a political account of the conflict with England. Yet, apart from mildly ridiculing Tory rhetoric, Trumbull's tone was far from the incendiarism of Thomas Paine's *Common Sense* (1776) and genial enough to please both sides in the Revolution.

The conservative irony of American satires masked more progressive elements in their social vision. If in his burlesques Trumbull minimized the achievements of the new nation, fellow Wits Timothy Dwight and Joel Barlow expressed both support for the age's political programs and faith in literature's ability to accelerate social change. Dwight's Calvinism, a legacy from his grandfather Jonathan Edwards, occasionally seemed old-fashioned, even gloomy. In Dwight's *The Triumph of Infidelity* (1788) Satan reviews in placid heroic couplets the westward progress not of civilization but of ignorance and irreligion. Dwight's religious rhetoric generally serves more positively as a bridge between America's Puritan past and its republican future. In *The Conquest of Canaan* (1785) Dwight retells the Biblical story of Joshua's military victory as an allegory of the American Revolution, suggesting both the promise of America and its potential for backsliding and failure. In *Greenfield Hill* (1794) Dwight, finding in America a natural fecun-

John Singleton Copley's Watson and the Shark *(1778) displays the grandiose manner and balanced neoclassical composition that characterize the efforts of poets such as Joel Barlow to create American epics. (Museum of Fine Arts, Boston)*

dity absent in the "deserted" English villages, prophesies an economic and spiritual utopia, revising his skeptical predictions from the Satanic "Triumph."

The epic visions of Joel Barlow similarly combine optimistic prophecy and social critique without resolving the tensions between the two. Barlow's major poetic work, *The Vision of Columbus* (1787), revised as *The Columbiad* (1807), is an account of contemporary American culture. *Vision* relates an angel's prophecy to an imprisoned Columbus. The poem's contradictory mixture of Puritan imagery and social activism marks Barlow's youthful attraction to religion and politics. His return to these issues after his conversion from piety to the secular philosophies of the Enlightenment eliminates the narrative contradictions without improving the poetry. Although structurally more complex than *Vision,* the expanded *Columbiad* courted a cosmopolitan readership only by sacrificing the symbolic richness of the provincial version. The aesthetic failure of this revision suggests the difficulty with which Barlow imagined his audience. He knew his American readers to be in some senses "vulgar" and understood his own share in that vulgarity as both a source of power and something to be overcome. Barlow never resolved these dilemmas of audience or narrative voice; only in his brief mock-epic *The Hasty Pudding* (1796) was he able to combine successfully the sophisticated diction of Enlightenment rhetoric and a truly American celebration.

In their elevation of science and lawfulness, Enlightenment thinkers typically dismissed poetic imagination as mere "fancy" and saw the mind as a passive processor of sensations. Even the Scottish common sense philosophers, who saw imagination as more than delusion, described the operation of imagination via a mechanistic rhetoric. Such a mechanistic theory of knowledge handicapped even the most imaginative American poet of the generation, Philip Freneau. More technically adept and politically engaged than the Wits, Freneau experimented with a wide variety of poetic forms and topics. His gentle lyrics in such poems as "The Wild Honey Suckle" (1786) anticipate romantic nature poetry. Equally powerful are his topical works such as the antislavery address "To Sir Toby" (1792) or the sea allegory *The Hurricane* (1786), in which a realistic description of a storm images widespread social problems. Even his explicitly propagandistic works of the late 1790s and 1800s display poetic invention and typically caustic wit, as in "To a New England Poet" (1832), a cutting attack on Washington Irving's Anglophilia. Though able to reconcile the poet's private and public roles more skillfully than the Wits, Freneau was, like them, unable to believe in the creative power of literature. In "To an Author" (1788) Freneau complains of the bleakness of American culture, in which reason overpowers "lovely Fancy." Yet, his own failure to attribute to poetry any more forceful characteristic than "loveliness" insured that imagination as "fancy" would remain subordinate to reason.

The sole Revolutionary poet to suspect that poetry's persuasive power rests as fully in its form as in its argument was ironically the one who profited least from the Revolution's liberating power—the black female poet Phillis Wheatley. African-American poetry did not begin with Wheatley. She was preceded in the eighteenth century by the public poets Lucy Terry and Jupiter Hammons; and the anonymous poetry of folk tales and spirituals was fairly extensive when Wheatley began writing in the 1760s. Her importance rests instead in her subtle intertwining of the themes of political liberation, racial and sexual subordination, and aesthetic creativity. Required to adapt her beliefs for an audience sensitive to the needs of neither women nor blacks, Wheatley's protests were carefully muted. Yet, in such poems as "America" (1768, unpublished) or "To the Right Honorable William, Earl of Dartmouth" (1773), Wheatley's comparison of political liberty to her own youth in Africa implies that England's mistreatment of the colonies was not the only tyranny.

In striking anticipation of romanticism, Wheatley's poem "On Imagination" (1773), unlike Freneau's "The Power of Fancy" (1770), acknowledges the creative potential of the mind. For Wheatley imagination was itself divine. Like all Revolutionary poets, she was limited by her environment—by discriminatory presuppositions about race and gender and more generally about the social role of poets. In her ability to stretch these bounds, Wheatley epitomized the weaknesses and strengths of eighteenth-century poetry in America. The poets of the American

Revolution sought to express through traditional forms an antitraditional message: to offer in aristocratic diction a call to liberation, and in symbolic discourse a practical social influence. Even the most successful of these poets realized their goals only partly and sporadically. In their failure as fully as in their triumphs, these founders of our national poetic tradition capture the transitional character of this initial stage of American writing.

Phillis Wheatley
(1753–1784)

In her short life, Phillis Wheatley, the first published African-American poet, received both national and international recognition. As a frail child of about seven, Phillis arrived in Boston from Africa in 1761, wrapped, so the story goes, in dirty carpet, missing her front teeth, and speaking not a word of English. According to one account she was purchased "for a trifle" by Susannah Wheatley, the wife of the prosperous tailor John Wheatley. The Wheatleys were part of a trans-Atlantic Methodist reform movement that was deeply skeptical of slavery. Some sixteen months after her arrival, Phillis (the name given to her by the Wheatleys) had learned to read and write English, was reading the Bible and English literature, and had begun to study Latin—all at a time when most white women were unable to read or write.

Provided with a fire and a candle in her room so that she could compose her thoughts even at night, Phillis concentrated on writing poetry. Fostering her talent, the Wheatleys gave her light domestic duties and encouraged her to read her work to their circle of acquaintances. Boston society soon recognized her as a phenomenon, a child prodigy, a slave with extraordinary creativity and intellectual gifts.

In 1770, at age seventeen, Wheatley published the elegy "On the Death of Mr. George Whitefield," about the noted Methodist minister who had earned international fame for his fiery preaching. The poem appeared in numerous editions both in the colonies and in London. It attracted the attention of the countess of Huntingdon, leader of the Methodists in London and patron of Rev. Whitefield. It was through her influence that Olaudah Equiano was able to purchase his freedom. By invitation of the countess, Wheatley traveled to London in June 1773. There she came to be known as the "Sable Muse" and was among such notables as Benjamin Franklin and the lord mayor of London, who gave her a volume of John Milton's *Paradise Lost* (1667). At age twenty Wheatley published *Poems on Various Subjects, Religious and Moral* (1773) in London. This collection of her poems was prefaced by an attestation from eighteen leaders of Massachusetts, including Governor Thomas Hutchinson and John Hancock, that this was indeed the work of a female slave who but a few years earlier had been "an uncultivated barbarian from Africa."

Wheatley returned to the colonies in July 1773 to find Susannah Wheatley dying and the people of Boston preparing for revolution. At the request of the poet's "friends" in England, John Wheatley freed her. Soon Boston was under siege, and the patriot army, led

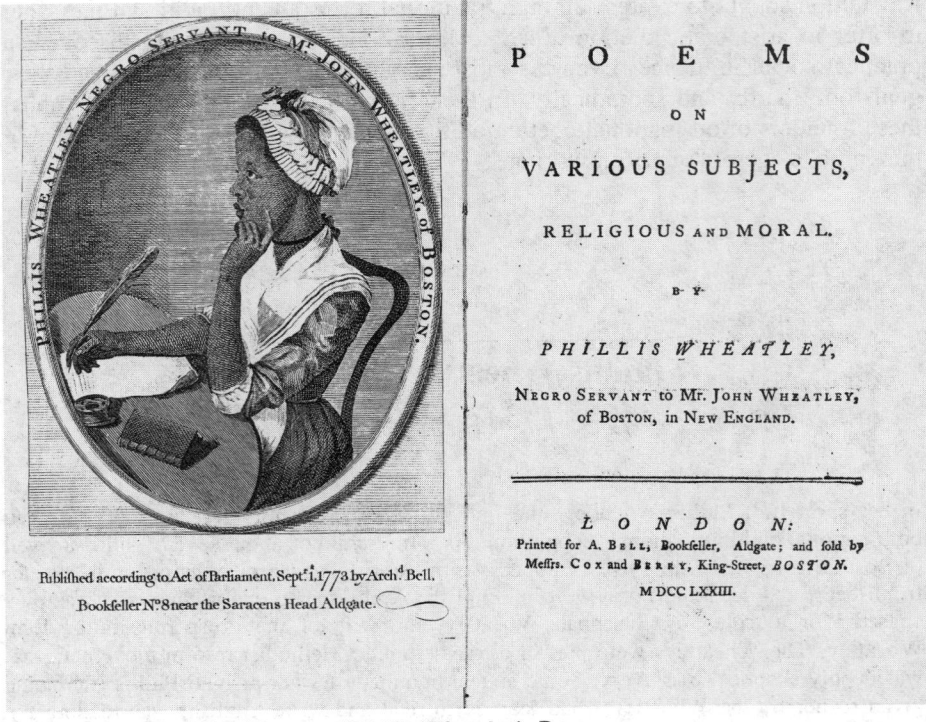

The frontispiece and title page of Phillis Wheatley's Poems.

by General George Washington, had camped at Cambridge. Firmly on the patriot side, Phillis Wheatley sent Washington the laudatory poem "To His Excellency General Washington" in late 1775. After a few months, the twenty-three-year-old poet was invited to his headquarters, where she received the "polite attention" of the general and of other officers.

Her career as a prodigy soon came to an end. The country, turning its attention to war, had little interest in poetry. With the death of John Wheatley in 1778 and of his daughter shortly thereafter, the poet was left very much on her own. Her life changed abruptly and for the worse. In April of 1778, Phillis married John Peters, a freed man about whom little is known for certain, except that he and Phillis lived in poverty. In 1779 Phillis Wheatley Peters tried to publish a second volume of verse but did not succeed. Meanwhile, she bore two children who died in infancy and tried to run a small school. When that failed, she had to earn her own living (Peters had been imprisoned for nonpayment of debts) in a boarding house for African Americans. With her third child, a mortally ill infant, at her side, Wheatley died at age thirty-one in 1784. An unknown observer recorded that she "was carried to her last earthly resting-place, without one of the friends of her prosperity to follow her, and without a stone to mark her grave." Her prized volume of *Paradise Lost* was sold to pay John Peters's debts and is now in the possession of Harvard University.

Within her lifetime Phillis Wheatley had published one book of verse, over fifty other pieces of poetry, and some prose in broadsides, pamphlets, and newspapers in America and abroad. Most of her poems are elegies to well-known contemporaries or personal acquaintances, philosophical poems, translations and biblical paraphrases, and poems on subjects taken from the Bible. They are neoclassical in form and express the poet's deep piety. Unavailable immediately after her death, her work was reprinted by abolitionists in the 1830s. Since then, her *Poems* has been reprinted more than two dozen times, and her poetry is regularly anthologized.

While acknowledging her achievement as remarkable, many critics have observed that much of Wheatley's poetry is conventional and derived from other sources, reflecting the middle-class values of the Wheatleys. For many, her work is evidence of unfulfilled potential; this female African-American slave in Revolutionary Boston, writing for a predominantly white audience, may not have had a chance to reach the full measure of her abilities.

Yet, Wheatley's work has much to offer. It commonly questions the assumptions of her society, especially in regard to slavery. In this respect she belongs with other colonial writers, such as Philip Freneau, who questioned the established order even as they used conventional neoclassical forms. Although she wrote that her own experience with slavery, having introduced her to Christianity, was fortunate, Wheatley consistently opposed the institution of slavery and the attitudes that made it possible. She was a nineteen-year-old slave when she addressed a poem published in 1773 to the earl of Dartmouth, urging freedom for America on the basis of a slave's own knowledge of "tyrannic sway." Her poem "On the Death of General Wooster" wondered aloud why God should help the Americans win freedom while they "hold in bondage Afric's blameless race." Once free, Wheatley continued to publish her views on the evil of slavery, most notably in a strong antislavery letter published in a number of New England newspapers in 1774. In the letter, she points out the "universal Love of Freedom . . . , impatient of oppression," of which she says "I humbly think it does not require the penetration of a philosopher to determine."

As writing by African-American women is increasingly becoming available, the recognition of Phillis Wheatley as a pioneer and a significant poet during the American Revolution grows. Readers find a consistent poetic voice, from her earliest work to her latest. That voice is pious and humble yet firm in its conviction of self worth and its concern with freedom.

Suggested Readings: *The Collected Works of Phillis Wheatley,* ed. J. C. Shields, 1988. M. A. Richmond, *Bid the Vassal Soar: Interpretive Essays on the Life and Poetry of Phillis Wheatley and George Moses Horton,* 1974. W. H. Robinson, *Phillis Wheatley and Her Writings,* 1984. D. Grimsted, "Anglo-American Racism and Phillis Wheatley's 'Sable Veil,' 'Knitted Heart,' " in R. Hoffmann, ed., *Women in the Age of the American Revolution,* 1989.

Text Used: *The Poems of Phillis Wheatley,* ed. J. Mason, Jr., 1966.

ON BEING BROUGHT FROM AFRICA TO AMERICA

> 'Twas mercy brought me from my *Pagan* land,
> Taught my benighted soul to understand
> That there's a God, that there's a *Saviour* too:
> Once I redemption neither sought nor knew.
> Some view our sable race with scornful eye,
> "Their colour is a diabolic die."
> Remember, *Christians, Negros,* black as *Cain,*
> May be refin'd, and join th' angelic train.

1773

TO THE UNIVERSITY OF CAMBRIDGE,[1]
IN NEW-ENGLAND

While an intrinsic ardor prompts to write,
The muses promise to assist my pen;
'Twas not long since I left my native shore
The land of errors,[2] and *Egyptian* gloom:
Father of mercy, 'twas thy gracious hand
Brought me in safety from those dark abodes.

    Students, to you 'tis giv'n to scan the heights
Above, to traverse the ethereal space,
And mark the systems of revolving worlds.
Still more, ye sons of science[3] ye receive   10
The blissful news by messengers from heav'n,
How *Jesus'* blood for your redemption flows.
See him with hands out-stretcht upon the cross;
Immense compassion in his bosom glows;
He hears revilers, nor resents their scorn:
What matchless mercy in the Son of God!
When the whole human race by sin had fall'n,
He deign'd to die that they might rise again,
And share with him in the sublimest skies,
Life without death, and glory without end.   20

    Improve your privileges while they stay,
Ye pupils, and each hour redeem, that bears
Or good or bad report of you to heav'n.
Let sin, that baneful evil to the soul,
By you be shunn'd, nor once remit your guard;
Suppress the deadly serpent in its egg.
Ye blooming plants of human race devine,
An *Ethiop*[4] tells you 'tis your greatest foe;
Its transient sweetness turns to endless pain,
And in immense perdition sinks the soul.   30

1767, 1773

ON THE DEATH OF THE REV. MR. GEORGE
WHITEFIELD[1] 1770

Hail, happy saint, on thine immortal throne,
Possest of glory, life and bliss unknown;
We hear no more the music of thy tongue,

---

[1] Harvard University.
[2] Africa, land of "theological errors" because its people had not been converted to Christianity.
[3] Knowledge.   [4] Ethiopian.
[1] George Whitefield (1714–1770), an English follower of John Wesley (founder of Methodism) and a well-known revivalist, who died in Newburyport, Massachusetts.

Thy wonted[2] auditories cease to throng.
Thy sermons in unequall'd accents flow'd,
And ev'ry bosom with devotion glow'd;
Thou didst in strains of eloquence refin'd
Inflame the heart, and captivate the mind.
Unhappy we the setting sun deplore,
So glorious once, but ah! it shines no more.   10

Behold the prophet in his tow'ring flight!
He leaves the earth for heav'n's unmeasur'd height,
And worlds unknown receive him from our sight.
There *Whitefield* wings with rapid course his way,
And sails to *Zion*[3] through vast seas of day.
Thy pray'rs, great saint, and thine incessant cries
Have pierc'd the bosom of thy native skies.
Thou moon hast seen, and all the stars of light,
How he has wrestled with his God by night.
He pray'd that grace in ev'ry heart might dwell,   20
He long'd to see *America* excel;
He charg'd its youth that ev'ry grace divine
Should with full lustre in their conduct shine;
That Saviour, which his soul did first receive,
The greatest gift that ev'n a God can give,
He freely offer'd to the num'rous throng,
That on his lips with list'ning pleasure hung.

   "Take him, ye wretched, for your only good,
"Take him ye starving sinners, for your food;
"Ye thirsty, come to this life-giving stream,   30
"Ye preachers, take him for your joyful theme;
"Take him my dear *Americans*, he said,
"Be your complaints on this kind bosom laid:
"Take him, ye *Africans,* he longs for you,
"*Impartial Saviour* is his title due:
"Wash'd in the fountain of redeeming blood,
"You shall be sons, and kings, and priests to God."

   Great *Countess,*[4] we *Americans* revere
Thy name, and mingle in thy grief sincere;
New England deeply feels, the *Orphans* mourn,   40
Their more than father will no more return.

   But, though arrested by the hand of death,
Whitefield no more exerts his lab'ring breath,
Yet let us view him in th' eternal skies,
Let ev'ry heart to this bright vision rise;

---

[2] Accustomed.   [3] The city of God.
[4] The countess of Huntingdon, Selina Shirley Hastings (1707–1791), a supporter of her chaplain, Whitefield.

> While the tomb safe retains its sacred trust,
> Till life divine re-animates his dust.

1770

ON IMAGINATION

Thy various works, imperial queen, we see,
How bright their forms! how deck'd with pomp by thee!
Thy wond'rous acts in beauteous order stand,
And all attest how potent is thine hand.

From *Helicon's*[1] refulgent heights attend,
Ye sacred choir, and my attempts befriend:
To tell her glories with a faithful tongue,
Ye blooming graces, triumph in my song.

Now here, now there, the roving *Fancy* flies,
Till some lov'd objects strikes her wand'ring eyes,   10
Whose silken fetters all the senses bind,
And soft captivity involves the mind.

Imagination! who can sing thy force?
Or who describe the swiftness of thy course?
Soaring through air to find the bright abode,
Th' empyreal palace of the thund'ring God,
We on thy pinions[2] can surpass the wind,
And leave the rolling universe behind:
From star to star the mental optics rove,
Measure the skies, and range the realms above.   20
There in one view we grasp the mighty whole,
Or with new worlds amaze th' unbounded soul.

Though *Winter* frowns to *Fancy's* raptur'd eyes
The fields may flourish, and gay scenes arise;
The frozen deeps may break their iron bands,
And bid their waters murmur o'er the sands.
Fair *Flora*[3] may resume her fragrant reign,
And with her flow'ry riches deck the plain;
Sylvanus[4] may diffuse his honours round,
And all the forest may with leaves be crown'd: 30
Show'rs may descend, and dews their gems disclose,
And nectar sparkle on the blooming rose.

---

[1] According to Greek myth, Mount Helicon is home to the Muses, the nine goddesses presiding over literature, art, and music.
[2] Wings.   [3] The Roman goddess of flowers.   [4] The Roman god of the forest.

Such is thy pow'r, nor are thine orders vain,
O thou the leader of the mental train:
In full perfection all thy works are wrought,
And thine the sceptre o'er the realms of thought.
Before thy throne the subject-passions bow,
Of subject-passions sov'reign ruler Thou,
At thy command joy rushes on the heart,
And through the glowing veins the spirits dart.   40

 Fancy might now her silken pinions try
To rise from earth, and sweep th' expanse on high;
From *Tithon's* bed now might *Aurora*[5] rise,
Her cheeks all glowing with celestial dies,
While a pure stream of light o'erflows the skies.
The monarch of the day I might behold,
And all the mountains tipt with radiant gold,
But I reluctant leave the pleasing views,
Which *Fancy* dresses to delight the *Muse;*
Winter austere forbids me to aspire,   50
And northern tempests damp the rising fire;
They chill the tides of *Fancy's* flowing sea,
Cease then, my song, cease the unequal lay.[6]

         1767?–1773, 1773

THOUGHTS ON THE WORKS OF PROVIDENCE

Arise, my soul, on wings enraptur'd, rise
To praise the monarch of the earth and skies,
Whose goodness and beneficence appear
As round its centre moves the rolling year,
Or when the morning glows with rosy charms,
Or the sun slumbers in the ocean's arms:
Of light divine be a rich portion lent
To guide my soul, and favour my intent.
Celestial muse, my arduous flight sustain,
And raise my mind to a seraphic[1] strain!   10

 Ador'd for ever be the God unseen,
Which round the sun revolves this vast machine,
Though to his eye its mass a point appears:
Ador'd the God that whirls surrounding spheres,
Which first ordain'd that mighty *Sol*[2] should reign
The peerless monarch of th' ethereal train:
Of miles twice forty millions is his height,

---

[5] The Roman goddess of the dawn, equivalent to the Greek Eos, who loved Tithonus.
[6] Ballad.
[1] Angelic. [2] The sun.

And yet his radiance dazzles mortal sight
So far beneath—from him th' extended earth
Vigour derives, and ev'ry flow'ry birth: 20
Vast through her orb she moves with easy grace
Around her *Phœbus*[3] in unbounded space;
True to her course th' impetuous storm derides,
Triumphant o'er the winds, and surging tides.

Almighty, in these wond'rous works of thine,
What *Pow'r,* what *Wisdom,* and what *Goodness* shine?
And are thy wonders, Lord, by men explor'd,
And yet creating glory unador'd!

Creation smiles in various beauty gay,
While day to night, and night succeeds to day: 30
That *Wisdom,* which attends *Jehovah's* ways,
Shines most conspicuous in the solar rays:
Without them, destitute of heat and light,
This world would be the reign of endless night:
In their excess how would our race complain,
Abhorring life! how hate its length'ned chain!
From air adust what num'rous ills would rise?
What dire contagion taint the burning skies?
What pestilential vapours, fraught with death,
Would rise, and overspread the lands beneath?   40

Hail, smiling morn, that from the orient main[4]
Ascending dost adorn the heav'nly plain!
So rich, so various are thy beauteous dies,
That spread through all the circuit of the skies,
That, full of thee, my soul in rapture soars,
And thy great God, the cause of all adores.

O'er beings infinite his love extends,
His *Wisdom* rules them, and his *Pow'r* defends.
When tasks diurnal[5] tire the human frame,
The spirits faint, and dim the vital flame,   50
Then too that ever active bounty shines,
Which not infinity of space confines.
The sable veil, and *Night* in silence draws,
Conceals effects, but shes th' *Almighty Cause;*
Night seals in sleep the wide creation fair,
And all is peaceful but the brow of care.
Again, gay *Phœbus,* as the day before,
Wakes ev'ry eye, but what shall wake no more;
Again the face of nature is renew'd,

---

[3] The Greek sun god, Apollo.   [4] Eastern ocean.   [5] Daily.

Which still appears harmonious, fair, and good.   60
May grateful strains salute the smiling morn,
Before its beams the eastern hills adorn!

    Shall day to day, and night to night conspire
To show the goodness of the Almighty Sire?
This mental voice shall man regardless hear,
And never, never raise the filial pray'r?
To-day, O hearken, nor your folly mourn
For time mispent, that never will return.

    But see the sons of vegetation rise,
And spread their leafy banners to the skies.   70
All-wise Almighty providence we trace
In trees, and plants, and all the flow'ry race;
As clear as in the nobler frame of man,
All lovely copies of the Maker's plan.
The pow'r the same that forms a ray of light,
That call'd creation from eternal night.
"Let there be light,"[6] he said: from his profound
Old *Chaos* heard, and trembled at the sound:
Swift as the word, inspir'd by pow'r divine,
Behold the light around its maker shine,   80
The first fair product of th' omnific God,
And now through all his works diffus'd abroad.

    As reason's pow'rs by day our God disclose,
So we may trace him in the night's repose:
Say what is sleep? and dreams how passing strange!
When action ceases, and ideas range
Licentious and unbounded o'er the plains,
Where *Fancy's*[7] queen in giddy triumph reigns.
Here in soft strains the dreaming lover sigh
To a kind fair, or rave in jealousy;   90
On pleasure now, and now on vengeance bent,
The lab'ring passions struggle for a vent.
What pow'r, Oh man! thy *reason* then restores,
So long suspended in nocturnal hours?
What secret hand returns the mental train,
And gives improv'd thine active pow'rs again?
From thee, O man, what gratitude should rise!
And, when from balmy sleep thou op'st thine eyes,
Let first thoughts be praises to the skies.
How merciful our God who thus imparts   100
O'erflowing tides of joy to human hearts,
When wants and woes might be our righteous lot,
Our God forgetting, by our God forgot!

[6] From Genesis 1.3.   [7] Imagination's.

Among the mental pow'rs a question rose,
"What must the image of th' Eternal shows?"
When thus to *Reason* (so let *Fancy* rove)
Her great companion spoke immortal *Love*.

"Say, mighty pow'r, how long shall strife prevail,
"And with its murmurs load the whisp'ring gale?
"Refer the cause to *Recollection's* shrine,   110
"Who loud proclaims my origin divine,
"The cause whence heav'n and earth began to be,
"And is not man immortaliz'd by me?
"*Reason* let this most causeless strife subside."
Thus *Love* pronounc'd, and *Reason* thus reply'd.

"Thy birth, celestial queen! 'tis mine to own,
"In thee resplendent is the Godhead shown;
"Thy words persuade, my soul enraptur'd feels
"Resistless beauty which thy smile reveals."
Ardent she spoke, and, kindling at her charms,   120
She clasp'd the blooming goddess in her arms.

Infinite *Love* wher'er we turn our eyes
Appears: this ev'ry creature's wants supplies;
This most is heard in *Nature's* constant voice,
This makes the morn, and this the eve rejoice;
This bids the fost'ring rains and dews descend
To nourish all, to serve one gen'ral end,
The good of man; yet man ungrateful pays
But little homage, and but little praise.
To him, whose works array'd with mercy shine,   130
What songs should rise, how constant, how divine!
                                    1767?–1773, 1773

TO S. M.,[1] A YOUNG AFRICAN PAINTER, ON SEEING HIS WORKS

To show the lab'ring bosom's deep intent,
And thought in living characters to paint,
When first thy pencil did those beauties give,
And breathing figures learnt from thee to live,
How did those prospects give my soul delight,
A new creation rushing on my sight?

[1] Identified by Benjamin Brawley in *The Negro in Literature and Art* (1934) as Scipio Moorhead, "a young man who exhibited some talent for drawing and who was a servant of the Rev. John Moorhead of Boston."

Still, wond'rous youth! each noble path pursue,
On deathless glories fix thine ardent view:
Still may the painter's and the poet's fire
To aid thy pencil, and thy verse conspire!   10
And may the charms of each seraphic[2] theme
Conduct thy footsteps to immortal fame!
High to the blissful wonders of the skies
Elate thy soul, and raise thy wishful eyes.
Thrice happy, when exalted to survey
That splendid city, crown'd with endless day,
Whose twice six gates[3] on radiant hinges ring:
Celestial *Salem*[4] blooms in endless spring.

Calm and serene thy moments glide along,
And may the muse inspire each future song!   20
Sill, with the sweets of contemplation bless'd,
May peace with balmy winds your soul invest!
But when these shades of time are chas'd away,
And darkness ends in everlasting day,
On what seraphic pinions[5] shall we move,
And view the landscapes in the realms above?
There shall thy tongue in heav'nly murmurs flow,
And there my muse with heav'nly transport glow:
No more to tell of *Damon's*[6] tender sighs,
Or rising radiance of *Aurora's*[7] eyes,   30
For nobler themes demand a nobler strain,
And purer language on th' ethereal plain.
Cease, gentle muse! the solemn gloom of night
Now seals the fair creation from my sight.

1767?–1773, 1773

TO HIS EXCELLENCY GENERAL WASHINGTON*

SIR,

I have taken the freedom to address your Excellency in the enclosed poem, and entreat your acceptance, though I am not insensible of its inaccuracies. Your being appointed by the Grand Continental Congress to be Generalissimo of the armies of North America, together with the fame of your virtues, excite sensations not easy to suppress. Your generosity, therefore, I presume, will pardon the attempt. Wish-

---

[2] Angelic.   [3] The twelve gates of Heaven.   [4] "Jerusalem" or Heaven.   [5] Angelic wings.
[6] According to classical myth, Damon pledged his life for his friend Pythias.
[7] The Roman goddess of the dawn.
* First printed in *The Pennsylvania Magazine* 2:93 (April 1776), while Thomas Paine was editor.

ing your Excellency all possible success in the great cause you are so generously engaged in. I am,

Your Excellency's most obedient humble servant,
PHILLIS WHEATLEY.

Providence, Oct. 26, 1775.
His Excellency Gen. Washington.

Celestial choir! enthron'd in realms of light,
Columbia's[1] scenes of glorious toils I write.
While freedom's cause her anxious breast alarms,
She flashes dreadful in refulgent arms.
See mother earth her offspring's fate bemoan,
And nations gaze at scenes before unknown!
See the bright beams of heaven's revolving light
Involved in sorrows and the veil of night!
The goddess comes, she moves divinely fair,
Olive and laurel[2] binds her golden hair: 10
Wherever shines this native of the skies,
Unnumber'd charms and recent graces rise.
Muse! bow propitious while my pen relates
How pour her armies through a thousand gates:
As when Eolus[3] heaven's fair face deforms,
Enwrapp'd in tempest and a night of storms;
Astonish'd ocean feels the wild uproar,
The refluent surges beat the sounding shore;
Or thick as leaves in Autumn's golden reign,
Such and so many, moves the warrior's train.   20
In bright array they seek the work of war,
Where high unfurl'd the ensign waves in air.
Shall I to Washington their praise recite?
Enough thou know'st them in the fields of fight.
Thee, first in peace and honours,—we demand
The grace and glory of thy martial band.
Fam'd for thy valour, for thy virtues more,
Hear every tongue thy guardian aid implore!
One century scarce perform'd its destined round,
When Gallic[4] powers Columbia's fury found;   30
And so may you, whoever dares disgrace
The land of freedom's heaven-defended race!
Fix'd are the eyes of nations on the scales,
For in their hopes Columbia's arm prevails.
Anon Britannia droops the pensive head,
While round increase the rising hills of dead.
Ah! cruel blindness to Columbia's state!

---

[1] America's.   [2] Signs of victory.   [3] Roman god of the winds.
[4] The French and Indian Wars (1689–1763), thought to have begun with King William's War (1689–1697), included four wars between France and England.

Lament thy thirst of boundless power too late.
   Proceed, great chief, with virtue on thy side,
Thy ev'ry action let the goddess guide.   40
A crown, a mansion, and a throne that shine,
With gold unfading, WASHINGTON! be thine.

1775, 1776

Philip Freneau
(1752–1832)

Born in New York City in 1752, Philip Freneau was the son of a prosperous wine merchant of French descent and a well-to-do New Jersey farmer's daughter. The Freneaus reared their children according to the doctrines of orthodox Calvinism. Following his father's death in 1767, Freneau entered the College of New Jersey (now Princeton University), expecting to become a minister. There, however, along with his classmates James Madison and Hugh Henry Brackenridge, he became involved in the patriotic ferment that preceded the Revolutionary War. Discovering in himself a literary bent, Freneau began to produce poems. The most important of these, "The Rising Glory of America," was co-written with Brackenridge, who read the poem at their class commencement ceremony in 1771. The poem celebrates the promising future of an America seen in its dedication to liberty rather than to gold, as morally superior to the colonies of Spain.

In 1775 Freneau traveled to New York and again jumped into the political fray, contributing anti-British and pro-American odes, satires, and other verses to local magazines and newspapers. By 1780 he had earned the title "Poet of the Revolution." Exhausted by political strife, he abandoned New York in 1776 and sailed to Santa Cruz in the Caribbean. There he enjoyed the beauties of the isles, noted the horrors of slavery, and likely had an affair with an island belle. In 1778, however, he returned to America, enlisted in the New Jersey militia, and saw action on blockade runners. Two years later, Freneau's ship, the *Aurora*, was captured by a British vessel. Freneau spent six grueling weeks on a British prison ship and, after becoming ill, six worse weeks on a British hospital ship moored in New York City's East River. Sick and exhausted, he was freed in July 1780, having enhanced his hatred of the British.

After recuperating at his mother's home in Mt. Pleasant, New Jersey (to which he regularly returned throughout his life), Freneau went to Philadelphia. There, in the *Freeman's Journal* he continued to vilify the British and their American sympathizers. After the Revolutionary War ended in 1783, he briefly returned to the Caribbean. On the way, he encountered the worst hurricane to hit the region in decades; he describes the experience in his popular poem "The Hurricane" (1785). From 1785 to 1789 he served as captain on merchant vessels shuttling between New Jersey and South Carolina. Perhaps depressed by the war ending, by his hurricane experience, or (most likely) by a woman's rejection, Freneau began to write more personal poems, such as "The Wild Honey Suckle" (1786) and "The Indian Burying Ground" (1788), marked by an emphasis on life's transience. In

1788 he published *The Miscellaneous Works of Philip Freneau*, which contains not only poetry from his dark period but lighter prose essays previously contributed to magazines, under various pseudonyms.

Freneau married the wealthy and beautiful Eleanor Forman in 1790, whereupon his poetry immediately lost much of its gloom. He soon returned to public affairs, contributing republican, anti-Federalist rhetoric to the *National Gazette,* which he edited. Freneau's staunch republicanism led Thomas Jefferson to insist that Freneau had kept the country from "galloping into monarchy" during the 1790s. Yet, Freneau's continual characterization of George Washington as the "monarchical" successor to England's King George III led Washington to dub him a "rascal." Though publication of the *National Gazette* ended in 1793, Freneau was henceforth remembered as a partisan debater, an image that overshadowed his reputation as a poet.

From 1795 to 1798 Freneau edited a country newspaper (in which he published essays under the pseudonym Tomo-Cheeki, an imaginary Creek Indian chief supposedly living in Philadelphia) and a literary magazine. Between 1798 and 1815 he managed the family farm in New Jersey and served again as a merchant captain. He also published more essays under the pseudonym Robert Slender, a cobbler who pretended humility and naïveté while attacking federalism and Britain and defending republicanism and France. Collections of Freneau's poetry appeared in 1795, 1809, and 1815. During his later years, Freneau's verse expressed a deistic confidence in a benevolent nature wholly absent from his poetry of the 1780s. Yet, as an old man Freneau experienced poverty and professional neglect, seeing his lands sold at auction and his poems pass out of print. He died near his home in 1832 after losing his way in a snowstorm.

Freneau's writings—like his life—manifest considerable variety, ranging from political propaganda to philosophical speculation, from urbane essay to lyric effusion, from pious optimism to atheistical despair. Moreover, Freneau seems to alternate between eighteenth-century neoclassicism, with its regard for reason and its imitative theory of literature, and nineteenth-century romanticism, with its emphasis on emotion and its redefinition of literature as the expression of the writer's feelings. Despite his fluctuations, Freneau is consistent in his preromantic preference for traditional verse forms, his belief in the natural goodness of human beings, his determination to see corrupting social and political institutions abolished, and his loyalty to the themes of liberty and the ability to change. Whether describing the cruelties of slavery or the tyrannies of George III, the beaches of Santa Cruz or the freedoms available in a "glorious" America, Freneau was convinced that liberty is essential to the happiness of every human being. And whether describing the destructive power of a hurricane, or the brief lifetime of a honeysuckle, or the poignant doom of the last apple on a tree, he likewise was aware that, even if life goes on, individual lives must end.

Freneau's work has continuing importance. Having composed two dozen memorable poems and a number of valuable essays, Freneau is something other than a study in failure, as has been suggested, and something more than a precursor of Edgar Allan Poe and Ralph Waldo Emerson, as has been argued also. Freneau's vision of America may now seem naïve, his patriotic tone shrill, and his fear of federalism slightly paranoid, but his public writings will continue to inspire so long as freedom remains important. And though Freneau's emphasis on death and decay may now seem quaint or morbid, his best private writings will likewise be widely read so long as people continue to love life enough to mourn its loss.

Suggested Readings: *The Last Poems of Philip Freneau*, ed. L. Leary, 1945. *The Prose of Philip Freneau*, ed. P. M. Marsh, 1955. L. Leary, *That Rascal Freneau*, 1941. R. C. Vitzhum, *Land and Sea*, 1978.

Texts Used: "To Sir Toby": *Poems of Philip Freneau*, Vol. II, ed. F. L. Pattee, 1902–1907. All others: *The Poems of Philip Freneau*, No. 19, ed. H. H. Clark, 1929.

TO SIR TOBY*

A SUGAR PLANTER IN THE INTERIOR PARTS OF JAMAICA, NEAR THE CITY OF
SAN JAGO DE LA VEGA (SPANISH TOWN), 1784

> "*The motions of his spirit are black as night,*
> *And his affections dark as Erebus.*" [1]
> —SHAKESPEARE. [2]

If there exists a hell—the case is clear—
Sir Toby's slaves enjoy that portion here:
Here are no blazing brimstone lakes—'tis true;
But kindled Rum too often burns as blue;
In which some fiend, whom nature must detest,
Steeps Toby's brand, and marks poor Cudjoe's breast. [3]
Here whips on whips excite perpetual fears,
And mingled howlings vibrate on my ears:
Here nature's plagues abound, to fret and teaze,
Snakes, scorpions, despots, lizards, centipees—   10
No art, no care escapes the busy lash;
All have their dues—and all are paid in cash—
The eternal driver keeps a steady eye
On a black herd, who would his vengeance fly,
But chained, imprisoned, on a burning soil,
For the mean avarice of a tyrant, toil!
The lengthy cart-whip guards this monster's reign—
And cracks, like pistols, from the fields of cane.
    Ye powers! who formed these wretched tribes, relate,
What had they done, to merit such a fate!   20
Why were they brought from Eboe's[4] sultry waste,
To see that plenty which they must not taste—
Food, which they cannot buy, and dare not steal;
Yams and potatoes—many a scanty meal!—
    One, with a gibbet[5] wakes his negro's fears,
One to the windmill nails him by the ears;
One keeps his slave in darkened dens, unfed,
One puts the wretch in pickle ere he's dead:

---

* From the edition of 1809 (lines 13-16 added then); first published in the *National Gazette*, July 21, 1792, as "The Island Field Hand."

[1] According to Greek myth, the region through which the dead pass from the earth to Hades.

[2] From *The Merchant of Venice*, V.i.79. Freneau substituted "black as night" for "dull as night."

[3] Freneau's note: "This passage has a reference to the West India custom (sanctioned by law) of branding a newly imported slave on the breast, with a red hot iron, as an evidence of the purchaser's property."

[4] Freneau's note: "A small negro kingdom near the river Senegal."   [5] Gallows.

This, from a tree suspends him by the thumbs,
That, from his table grudges even the crumbs!   30
   O'er yond' rough hills a tribe of females go,
Each with her gourd, her infant, and her hoe;
Scorched by a sun that has no mercy here,
Driven by a devil, whom men call overseer—
In chains, twelve wretches to their labours haste;
Twice twelve I saw, with iron collars graced!—
   Are such the fruits that spring from vast domains?
Is wealth, thus got, Sir Toby, worth your pains!—
Who would your wealth on terms, like these, possess,
Where all we see is pregnant with distress—   40
Angola's[6] natives scourged by ruffian hands,
And toil's hard product shipp'd to foreign lands.
   Talk not of blossoms, and your endless spring;
What joy, what smile, can scenes of misery bring?—
Though Nature, here, has every blessing spread,
Poor is the labourer—and how meanly fed!—
   Here Stygian[7] paintings light and shade renew,
Pictures of hell, that Virgil's[8] pencil drew:
Here, surly Charons[9] make their annual trip,
And ghosts arrive in every Guinea ship,[10]   50
To find what beasts these western isles afford,
Plutonian[11] scourges, and despotic lords:—
   Here, they, of stuff determined to be free,
Must climb the rude cliffs of the Liguanee;[12]
Beyond the clouds, in sculking haste repair,
And hardly safe from brother traitors[13] there.—

1784, 1792

THE WILD HONEY SUCKLE

Fair flower, that dost so comely grow,
Hid in this silent, dull retreat,
Untouched thy honied blossoms blow,[1]
Unseen thy little branches greet:
   No roving foot shall crush thee here,
   No busy hand provoke a tear.

---

[6] A Portuguese colony in West Africa.   [7] Hell-like.
[8] Freneau's note: "See Eneid, Book 6th.—and Fenelon's Telemachus, Book 18." Virgil (70–19 B.C.), a Latin poet, wrote the *Aeniad* (30–19 B.C.), in which Aeneas reaches the underworld; François de Salignac de la Mothe-Fénelon (1651–1715), a theologian, wrote *Télémaque* (1699), about Ulysses and his son.
[9] According to Greek myth, the ferryman who carried the dead over the river Styx to Hades.
[10] Ship carrying slaves from West Africa.   [11] Reference to the Greek underworld god, Pluto.
[12] Freneau's note: "The mountains northward of Kingston."
[13] Freneau's note: "Alluding to the *Independent* negroes in the blue mountains, who for a stipulated reward, deliver up every fugitive that falls into their hands, to the English Government."
[1] Bloom.

By Nature's self in white arrayed,
She bade thee shun the vulgar[2] eye,
And planted here the guardian shade,
And sent soft waters murmuring by;   10
    Thus quietly thy summer goes,
    Thy days declining to repose.

Smit with those charms, that must decay,
I grieve to see your future doom;
They died—nor were those flowers more gay,
The flowers that did in Eden bloom;
    Unpitying frosts, and Autumn's power
    Shall leave no vestige of this flower.

From morning suns and evening dews
At first thy little being came:
If nothing once, you nothing lose,   20
For when you die you are the same;
    The space between, is but an hour,
    The frail duration of a flower.

1786

THE INDIAN BURYING GROUND

In spite of all the learned have said,
I still my old opinion keep;
'The *posture*, that *we* give the dead,
Points out the soul's eternal sleep.

Not so the ancients of these lands—
The Indian, when from life released,
Again is seated with his friends,
And shares again the joyous feast.[1]

His imaged birds, and painted bowl,
And venison, for a journey dressed.   10
Bespeak the nature of the soul,
ACTIVITY, that knows no rest.

His bow, for action ready bent,
And arrows, with a head of stone,
Can only mean that life is spent,
And not the old ideas gone.

---

[2] Common.
[1] Freneau's note: "The North American Indians bury their dead in a sitting posture; decorating the corpse with wampum, the images of birds, quadrupeds, etc: And (if that of a warrior) with bows, arrows, tomhawks and other military weapons."

Thou, stranger, that shalt come this way,
No fraud upon the dead commit—
Observe the swelling turf, and say
They do not *lie*, but here they *sit*.   20

Here still a lofty rock remains,
On which the curious eye may trace
(Now wasted, half, by wearing rains)
The fancies of a ruder race.

Here still an aged elm aspires,
Beneath whose far-projecting shade
(And which the shepherd still admires)
The children of the forest played!

There oft a restless Indian queen
(Pale *Shebah*,[2] with her braided hair)   30
And many a barbarous form is seen
To chide the man that lingers there.

By midnight moons, o'er moistening dews,
In habit for the chase arrayed,
The hunter still the deer pursues,
The hunter and the deer, a shade![3]

And long shall timorous fancy see
The painted chief, and pointed spear,
And Reason's self shall bow the knee
To shadows and delusions here.   40

                                                    1787

TO AN AUTHOR

Your leaves bound up compact and fair,
In neat array at length prepare,
To pass their hour on learning's stage,
To meet the surly critic's rage;
The statesman's slight, the smatterer's sneer—
Were these, indeed, your only fear,
You might be tranquil and resigned:
What most should touch your fluttering mind;
Is that, few critics will be found
To sift your works, and deal the wound.   10

Thus, when one fleeting year is past
On some bye-shelf *your* book is cast—

---

[2] The Queen of Shebah, known for her wisdom and beauty (I Kings 10.1–10.13).   [3] A ghost.

Another comes; with *something new,*
And drives you fairly out of view:
With some to praise, *but more to blame,*
The mind returns to—whence it came;
And some alive, who *scarce could read*
Will publish satires on the dead.

Thrice happy Dryden,[1] who could meet
Some rival bard in every street!   20
When all were bent on writing well
It was some credit to excel:—

Thrice happy Dryden, who could find
A *Milbourne*[2] for his sport designed—
And *Pope,*[3] who saw the harmless rage
Of *Dennis*[4] bursting o'er his page
Might justly spurn the *critic's aim,*
Who only helped to swell his fame.

On these bleak climes by Fortune thrown,
Where rigid *Reason* reigns alone,   30
Where lovely *Fancy* has no sway,
Nor magic forms about us play—
Nor nature takes her summer hue
Tell me, what has the muse to do?—

An age employed in edging steel
Can no poetic raptures feel;
No solitude's attracting power,
No leisure of the noon day hour,
No shaded stream, no quiet grove
Can this fantastic century move;   40

The muse of love in no request—
Go—try your fortune with the rest,
One of the nine you should engage,
To meet the follies of the age:—
On *one,* we fear, your choice must fall—
The least engaging of them all—
Her visage stern—an angry style—
A clouded brow—malicious smile—
A mind on *murdered victims* placed—
She, only she, can please the taste!   50

1787?, 1788

---

[1] Freneau's note: "See Johnson's lives of the English Poets." In *Lives of the Poets* (1779–1781) Samuel Johnson (1709–1784) discusses John Dryden (1631–1700), an English poet.
[2] English poet (1649–1720) whom Dryden considered "the worst poet of the age."
[3] Alexander Pope (1688–1744), an English poet.
[4] John Dennis (1657–1734), a writer satirized by Pope as being pompous.

ON THE RELIGION OF NATURE

The power, that gives with liberal hand
  The blessings man enjoys, while here,
And scatters through a smiling land
  Abundant products of the year;
    That power of nature, ever bless'd,
    Bestow'd religion with the rest.

Born with ourselves, her early sway
  Inclines the tender mind to take
The path of right, fair virtue's way
  Its own felicity to make.   10
    This universally extends
    And leads to no mysterious ends.

Religion, such as nature taught,
  With all divine perfection suits;
Had all mankind this system sought
  Sophists[1] would cease their vain disputes,
    And from this source would nations know
    All that can make their heaven below.

This deals not curses on mankind,
  Or dooms them to perpetual grief,   20
If from its aid no joys they find,
  It damns them not for unbelief;
    Upon a more exalted plan
    Creatress nature dealt with man—

Joy to the day, when all agree
  On such grand systems to proceed,
From fraud, design, and error free,
  And which to truth and goodness lead:
    The persecution will retreat
    And man's religion be complete.   30

1815

Joel Barlow
(1754–1812)

Born in 1754, Joel Barlow spent the first nineteen years of his life on his family's farm in Redding, Connecticut. There he tended crops and livestock and became familiar with rural tasks and customs. In 1774 he entered Yale College, but his education was disrupted by

---

[1] Teachers of philosophy.

the Revolutionary War. When the governor of Connecticut called for volunteers to defend New York City in 1776, Barlow joined the Revolutionary Army for a summer, returning to Yale only after the Battle of Long Island had been lost. At his graduation in 1778 Barlow, named class poet, read "The Prospect of Peace," the first of his several poetical envisionings of an ideal postrevolutionary America.

After graduation, Barlow moved to Hartford, Connecticut, where he married Ruth Baldwin and, over the next ten years, held the jobs of newspaper editor, bookseller, teacher, and lawyer. From 1780 to 1782 he served as chaplain of a Revolutionary War brigade quartered in New Jersey. Having heard Barlow's patriotic sermons praised, George Washington invited the youthful chaplain to dinner.

In the mid-1780s Barlow joined other Hartford writers to produce a series of satiric newspaper articles describing *The Anarchiad* (1786–1787), a fictitious serial poem celebrating the triumph of political chaos. Calling themselves the Connecticut Wits, Barlow and his friends used their commentary on *The Anarchiad* to decry the leveling tendencies then observable in American politics and to encourage the conservative political reaction that culminated in the Constitutional Convention of 1787. In that year Barlow completed and published *The Vision of Columbus*. Written in heroic couplets (rhymed pairs of lines), this long poem describes the settling of America, the Revolutionary War, an American future marked by scientific progress, the end of language differences and political hostilities in the Western Hemisphere, and the unification of all Western peoples under the American banner of democracy. Popular with an audience eager to hear America praised, *The Vision of Columbus* became a bestseller after the Revolutionary War.

In 1788 Barlow left for Europe, having accepted a position to sell parcels of American farmland to potential immigrants. By 1790, however, he had become deeply involved in European politics, associating with Thomas Paine, Mary Wollstonecraft, and other major critics of monarchical government, and abandoning the political conservatism of his own Hartford years. When Edmund Burke's *Reflections on the Revolution in France* appeared in 1790, Barlow expedited the publication of Paine's *The Rights of Man* (1791–1792), the most influential reply to Burke, and published his own reply, *Advice to the Privileged Orders* (1792). In *Advice* Barlow lodges careful complaints against such institutions as kings, established churches, and standing armies; praises the libertarian reforms of France's new French government; and cites the positive steps taken in America during and after its own revolution.

Barlow argues in *Advice* that Burke's defense of authoritarian social and political structures was based on the faulty assumption that human beings are unable to recognize or promote their own best interests—and thus need to be led by political and religious "superiors." Barlow suggests that although people have been manipulated into believing that such is the case, a state of equality is the only natural state for human beings. This will inevitably occur, Barlow predicts, when people lose their "superstitious" regard for oppressive institutions. The reasonableness of Barlow's tone was not sufficient to disguise the radicalness of his argument: following the publication of his book, he was forced to leave London.

More popular in Paris, Barlow was made an honorary French citizen in 1793 and sought election (in vain) to the French National Assembly that year. While campaigning in Savoy, France, he received from his friends a dish of hasty pudding, the cornmeal mush he had enjoyed as a boy. In the guise of a mock-epic tribute to this familiar food, Barlow produced *The Hasty Pudding* (1796), a defense of American folk rituals and critique of European traditions. Despite France's Reign of Terror, in which many citizens were executed, Barlow retained his confidence in the ultimate success of the French Revolution. In 1793 he launched a business shipping goods to France, eventually amassing a considerable fortune. In the late 1790s Barlow expressed in a letter his fear that the Federalists in Washington would provoke a confrontation between the United States and France. Published without authorization, the letter caused some Americans to view Barlow as disloyal to his country. However, upon the ascension of his friend Thomas Jefferson to the presidency in 1800, Barlow's reputation was restored. In 1805, after an absence of seventeen years, he and his wife returned to America and bought an expensive home in Washington, D.C.

Barlow's last major work was *The Columbiad* (1807), a reworking of *The Vision of Columbus*. As before, an angelic spirit visits a dejected Columbus in prison and reveals to him the glorious future of the lands he discovered. New to the poem is a critique of American slavery, portrayed as incongruous in a libertarian America. In 1811 Barlow was appointed minister to France by President James Madison and sent to negotiate a treaty with Napoleon. Barlow journeyed to the Russian front, where feelings of revulsion inspired him to compose "Advice to a Raven in Russian" (published in 1843). In the midst of Napoleon's retreat from Russia in 1812, Barlow died of pneumonia in Poland.

Barlow's literary significance lies partly in his conviction that America is a prime subject for epic poetry and that the serious American poet is obliged to tackle this subject. Barlow was the first in a line of poets, including Walt Whitman, Hart Crane, William Carlos Williams, and Allen Ginsberg, to view themselves as America's bards. Barlow is important, too, for his vision of America as a place where persons of all races could for the first time in human history achieve a society characterized by social equality, political freedom, and perpetual peace. Although America has never achieved perfect equality, peace, and freedom, Barlow's vision remains valuable. Through his poems and equally powerful prose, Barlow suggests that just as the most troubling social and political problems—racism, tyranny, war—stem from the fears and misconceptions of the human mind, so do solutions to these problems become possible when people are able to change their attitudes and to throw off their mental shackles. With his heroic couplets, hasty pudding, and old-fashioned revolutionary optimism, Barlow implies that cynicism is itself a manacle of the mind, a limiting habit of thought.

Suggested Readings: *Advice to the Privileged Orders.* 1956. *The Hasty Pudding*, J. Woodress, *A Yankee's Odyssey: The Life of Joel Barlow*, 1958. *Writings of Joel Barlow*, 2 vols., ed. W. K. Bottorff and A. L. Ford, 1970. L. Howard, *The Connecticut Wits*, 1943. L. Lemay, "The Contexts and Themes of 'The Hasty-Pudding,' " in *Early American Literature* 17 (1982)."

Texts Used: L. Howard, "Joel Barlow and Napoleon," in *The Huntington Library Quarterly* 2:1, October 1938 (some spelling and punctuation modernized).

ADVICE TO A RAVEN IN RUSSIA

DECEMBER, 1812

Black fool, why winter here? These frozen skies,
Worn by your wings and deafen'd by your cries,
Should warn you hence, where milder suns invite,
And day alternates with his mother night.
    You fear perhaps your food will fail you there,
Your human carnage, that delicious fare
That lured you hither, following still your friend
The great Napoleon to the world's bleak end.
You fear, because the southern climes pour'd forth

Their clustering nations to infest the north,   10
Bavarians, Austrians, those who Drink the Po[1]
And those who skirt the Tuscan seas below,
With all Germania, Neustria, Belgia, Gaul,[2]
Doom'd here to wade thro slaughter to their fall,
You fear he left behind no wars, to feed
His feather'd canibals and nurse the breed.
  Fear not, my screamer, call your greedy train,
Sweep over Europe, hurry back to Spain,
You'll find his legions there; the valliant crew
Please best their master when they toil for you.   20
Abundant there they spread the country o'er
And taint the breeze with every nation's gore,
Iberian, Lusian,[3] British widely strown,
But still more wide and copious flows their own.
  Go where you will; Calabria,[4] Malta, Greece,
Egypt and Syria still his fame increase,
Domingo's[5] fatten'd isle and India's plains
Glow deep with purple drawn from Gallic veins.
No Raven's wing can stretch the flight so far
As the torn bandrols[6] of Napoleon's war.   30
Choose then your climate, fix your best abode,
He'll make you deserts and he'll bring you blood.
  How could you fear a dearth? have not mankind,
Tho slain by millions, millions left behind?
Has not CONSCRIPTION still the power to weild
Her annual faulchion[7] o'er the human field?
A faithful harvester! or if a man
Escape that gleaner, shall he scape the ban?[8]
The triple BAN, that like the hound of hell[9]
Gripes with three joles,[10] to hold his victim well.   40
  Fear nothing then, hatch fast your ravenous brood,
Teach them to cry to Bonaparte for food;
They'll be like you, of all his suppliant train,
The only class that never cries in vain.
For see what mutual benefits you lend!
(The surest way to fix the mutual friend)
While on his slaughter'd troops your tribes are fed,
You cleanse his camp and carry off his dead.
Imperial Scavenger! but now you know
Your work is vain amid these hills of snow.   50
His tentless troops are marbled thro with frost
And change to crystal when the breath is lost.
Mere trunks of ice, tho limb'd like human frames

---

[1] A river in Italy that runs from the Alps to the Adriatic Sea.
[2] Germany, northern France, the Netherlands, France.
[3] Lusitania, roughly equivalent to Portugal today.   [4] In southern Italy.
[5] Of the West Indies.   [6] Flags carried in war.   [7] Sword.   [8] Curse.
[9] According to Greek myth, Cerberus, the three-headed dog who guards the gates of Hades.
[10] Jaws.

And lately warm'd with life's endearing flames,
They cannot taint the air, the world impest,[11]
Nor can you tear one fiber from their breast.
No! from their visual sockets, as they lie,
With beak and claws you cannot pluck an eye.
The frozen orb, preserving still its form,
Defies your talons as it braves the storm,   60
But stands and stares to God, as if to know
In what curst hands he leaves his world below.
    Fly then, or starve; tho all the dreadful road
From Minsk to Moskow with their bodies strow'd
May count some Myriads, yet they can't suffice
To feed you more beneath these dreary skies.
Go back, and winter in the wilds of Spain;
Feast there awhile, and in the next campaign
Rejoin your master; for you'll find him then,
With his new million of the race of men,   70
Clothed in his thunders, all his flags unfurl'd,
Raging and storming o'er the prostrate world.
    War after war his hungry soul requires,
State after State shall sink beneath his fires,
Yet other Spains in victim smoke shall rise
And other Moskows suffocate the skies,
Each land lie reeking with its people's slain
And not a stream run bloodless to the main.
Till men resume their souls, and dare to shed
Earth's total vengeance on the monster's head,   80
Hurl from his blood-built throne this king of woes,
Dash him to dust, and let the world repose.

1812, 1843

LATE 18TH-CENTURY DRAMA

In eighteenth-century American art and letters, the issues of political independence and cultural self-definition emerge as supremely important, dominating all others—the former culminating in the American Revolution, the latter in a peculiarly nationalistic, or "American," view of art. This twin theme of national emergence pervades and in fact inspired the bourgeoning drama of the period, whether written as entertainment or propaganda. A sense of striking historical immediacy gives that drama, sparse and uneven as it is, charm and interest as well as significance today. Both the form and the sociopolitical overtones of American drama may be attributed to its simultaneous emergence with the national consciousness and the spirit of revolution. As discontent with England began to rise, American drama began to sustain momentum.

[11] Infect.

The Federal Street Theater, designed by Charles Bulfinch and built in 1794, was New England's first theater.

The early eighteenth century was a time when a stern tradition of Puritan and Quaker opposition to all things theatrical pervaded the New England colonies. That view was intensified by the influence of the Great Awakening at mid-century, when a new sense of religious urgency spread throughout America. In the Cavalier areas of the South, where the Church of England held sway, theater was tolerated; in some areas, such as Charleston, it even flourished. North of Virginia, though, theater was discouraged; not until 1794 did New England have its first site for the production of plays, Boston's Federal Street Theater. Discouragement commonly took the form of law. Typical perhaps is the fate of *Ye Bare and Ye Cubb* (1665), the first play written for performance in America. Whether it ever reached the stage is not clear because the author, William Darby, was arrested merely for having proposed its performance. For having agreed to act in it, two performers were jailed for immorality.

Theater remained under a cloud of suspicion for two more centuries in religious America. Even the troops under George Washington, himself an avid theater-goer, were forbidden by the Continental Congress from frequenting professional theaters, such as Philadelphia's Southwark. Yet, while official disapproval of the-ater continued in the eighteenth century, American drama began to emerge. With the English Restoration of 1660 came a brilliant revival of theater, previously

---

==CONTEXTS==

The early Puritan rejection of drama as sinful continued to influence attitudes in post-Revolutionary America. While plays were produced, moralists such as John Witherspoon (1723–1794), president of Princeton University and a Declaration of Independence signer, condemned the stage. The following excerpt is from Witherspoon's sermon "A Serious Inquiry Into the Nature and Effects of the Stage."

[Debate Over Drama]

It is very plain, that were men but seriously disposed, and without prejudice desiring the knowledge of their duty, it would not be necessary, in order to show the unlawfulness of the stage, as it now is, to combat it in its imaginary reformed state. Such a reformation, were not men by the prevalence of vicious and corrupt affections, in love with it, even in its present condition, would have been long ago given up as a hopeless and visionary project, and the whole trade or employment detested, on account of the abuses that had always adhered to it. But since all advocates for the stage have and do still defend it in this manner, by forming an idea of it separate from its evil qualities; since they defend it so far with success, that many who would otherwise abstain, do, upon this very account, allow themselves in attending the theatre sometimes, to their own hurt and that of others; and, as I am convinced on the most mature deliberation, that the reason why there never was a well regulated stage, in fact, is because it cannot be, the nature of the thing not admitting of it. I will endeavor to shew, that PUBLIC THEATRICAL REPRESENTATIONS, either tragedy or comedy, are, in their general nature or in their best possible state, unlawful, contrary to the purity of our religion: and that writing, acting, or attending them, is inconsistent with the character of a Christian.

John Witherspoon, 1757

---

banished from Puritan England, and increased toleration of theater in the American colonies. Furthermore, at the same time in America, power began to shift from the Puritan patriarchs to the royal governors, who were appointed by the Crown. Wherever the Crown stationed British troops before and during the Revolution—in Boston, Philadephia, Albany, New York City—drama was in special demand. To some extent, the great influence of the British aristocracy neutralized religious opposition to the theater, allowing that art form to grow. Ironically, the very first plays by American writers, made possible by the tone set by the British aristocracy, were attacks on the British Crown and its colonial appointees. For their own amusement British officers, trapped in an alien wilderness far from home, satirized the locals; local Patriots, emulating the British, satirized the Crown.

Thus, even though American theater is said to have begun in the revolutionary years, not all that is classified as "American" drama in that period is either stageable or American, except in the loosest possible sense of having been written in America. One Tory playwright living in America was Jonathan Sewall, whose *The Americans Roused, in a Cure for the Spleen* was first performed for British troops in 1774. Another was the legendary British general John Burgoyne, who added his own efforts to the tradition of a time in which soldiers amused themselves by writing, staging, and acting in plays typically about themselves.

Most of the patriotic dramas of the day were essentially dialogues without conventional plot structure and with scant potential for stage success. Into this category fall the works of Hugh Henry Brackenridge and of America's foremost patriotic, dramatic propagandist, Mercy Otis Warren. Written before independence was declared, two of Warren's plays satirized Boston politics. *The Adulateur* (1773) ridicules Massachusetts governor Thomas Hutchinson; *The Group* (1775) attacks powerful politicians who remained loyal to George III even after the Crown repeatedly broke agreements. Other timely political dramas, including *The Blockheads* (1776) and *The Motley Assembly* (1779), have been attributed to Warren, and she continued to write after the war ended. Critics of drama, however, have found more literary merit in Hugh Henry Brackenridge's two long dramatic poems of patriotism, which were never intended for performance: *The Battle of Bunker Hill* (1776) and *The Death of General Montgomery, at the Siege of Quebec* (1777).

To find eighteenth-century political dramas indisputably intended for stage production, historians must turn to playwrights other than Warren and Brackenridge. One such playwright was New York's Governor Robert Hunter whose *Androboros* appeared in 1714; another reputedly was John Leacock, whose chronicle play *The Fall of British Tyranny* appeared in 1776. *Androboros,* thought to be the first play published in America, anticipates the slapstick and ribaldry of the nineteenth-century minstrel show. Aimed at New York politicians named in the list of characters, the play is enlivened by raucous and effective tricks of broad comedy, including dialects, malapropisms, nonsense legislative parlance, and scatology. The title character, General Francis Nicholson, is pushed into a collapsing chair, soaked with a bucket of sludge, sprayed with a mouthful of ale, belched on, and has snuff thrown in his eyes. The interplay of dramatic action and contemporary historical action takes an interesting turn in this play when Hunter includes himself as a character.

The revolutionary period was an extraordinary time in the history of drama because of this intersection of history and drama. Commonly, only a few hours lapsed between the events being played out in real life and the same events being presented on stage, actually blurring the lines between historical and dramatic events. Throughout the century this immediacy was underscored by the close relationship between the military and the theater. Plays about military engagements were written and performed by soldiers, usually for audiences of soldiers. One of the most dramatic examples is *The Blockade of Boston* (1776) by General John Burgoyne: While satirizing Americans, a cast of British soldiers on stage in Faneuil Hall received word that the Americans were attacking British forces a few miles away at Bunker Hill—a bulletin that caused the soldier–actors to run hastily for cover. This episode then became the subject of Mercy Otis Warren's satire *The Blockheads*. Warren's *The Group* was supposedly published in 1775 on the day before the battles of Lexington and Concord were fought.

Some other dramas written in the eighteenth century about eighteenth-century events are less political and more retrospective. *Ponteach* (1766), by Major

Robert Rogers, reputedly is the first serious dramatic treatment of Native Americans. William Dunlap's *André* (1798), about an event in the Revolutionary War, was written by America's first professional playwright and first theater historian. These highly playable works best exemplify the eighteenth-century and nineteenth-century popularity of the drama of American history, and both illustrate character types popular for over a century: the noble Native American and George Washington. Even in these two retrospective plays, however, the element of immediacy is striking. For example, after an illustrious career fighting Native Americans, Rogers turned his hand to a drama about a conflict that he knew intimately. Unpredictably, the hero of *Ponteach* is a Native American rather than a white man, and the murderous seducers of innocence come from the Christian civilization for which the playwright had spent his career fighting.

Events touching Dunlap's *André* illustrate the same extraordinary intersections of eighteenth-century American history and theater. Both Major André, a famous Revolutionary War figure, and playwright Dunlap were at different times soldiers, actors, and painters in America and performed or wrote about their lives. According to legend, Dunlap in his youth had seen the soldier André on stage, and in Dunlap's theatrical prime, while backstage in Philadelphia years after the first production of *André,* he had stumbled upon a theatrical scene painted by the protagonist of his successful play.

Dunlap's play illustrates how far the revolutionary drama had come by the end of the century. Removed from the heat of the subject, the play, unlike its episodic precursors, observes the three unities: unity of time, setting, and plot. It has a modest cast of characters, including George Washington, who was then and continued to be a popular character type. *André,* a sophisticated study of a complex situation into which the human element has been introduced, is essentially without villainous characters. André, the condemned spy, and his adversary, George Washington, are heroic figures in their own way. André's personal courage and humanity emerge in contradiction to the nature of his military mission; Washington reveals ambivalent complexity despite his heroism, condemning to death two basically good men who acted from conscience. In fact, Washington, though always regarded as the play's hero, comes very close to petty and bureaucratic inflexibility. With *André,* the play about the American Revolution came of age.

Other plays, still American in sentiment but distinctly British in form and style, were written in the eighteenth century by Americans. Two of the few extant dramas in this vein, one a tragedy and one a comedy, are *The Prince of Parthia* (published in 1765 and produced in 1767) by Thomas Godfrey and *The Contrast* (1787) by Royall Tyler. The attitude of *The Prince of Parthia* is fundamentally American despite the play's heavy debt to five or six Shakespearean tragedies and histories and its first-century B.C. setting. Like Rogers's *Ponteach,* Godfrey's play celebrates a noble-blooded hero who belongs to a disintegrating golden age. The heroes of both plays are warriors who must battle with enemies outside the tribe and within the family, the characters in effect reenacting the enmity between Cain and Abel on the outskirts of Paradise. Although *The Prince of Parthia,* thought to be the first professionally produced play written by an American, is classified in the tradition of the drama of America's noble savage, the play anticipates George

Henry Boker's *Francesca Da Rimini* (1855), the major romantic tragedy of the nineteenth-century American stage.

Tyler's *The Contrast,* sometimes cited as the first indigenous American comedy, reflects the English comedy of manners. Its theme is the contrast between slaves to a shallow European fashion and an independent-minded American hero who is unpretentious, down-to-earth, and solid. In short, the play is a cultural contrast between appearance and substance. That Tyler used Richard Sheridan's *School for Scandal* (1777) as a model for his American theme is telegraphed to the audience by the rustic Jonathan, the prototype of many rural stage Yankees to follow. Jonathan, having seen Sheridan's play on stage and mistaking it for an actual occurrence, gives his own comic interpretation of that play. Tyler's smooth, quick-paced comedy reads and plays extremely well, as though it emerged from the pen of a seasoned theatrical professional instead of an attorney with very little stage or drama experience.

Considered as a group, the plays of the eighteenth century are distinctly American. More than any other artistic genre of the period, they reinforce values that we associate with the "Party of Nature," as Emerson called it, laying some of the groundwork for the romanticism that flowered in all literary genres of the nineteenth-century American Renaissance. The values that emerge from these plays— simplicity, natural nobility, action, courage, truthfulness, rusticity—are clearly opposed to those of eighteenth-century and Restoration drama in England, which stressed style, elegance, and cultivation and studied wit and grace. Long before Emerson, Poe, and other nineteenth-century figures philosophically expressed the problem of America's artistic subservience to Britain and Europe, the battle for cultural independence was being waged in dramatic fashion on the stages of America.

Royall Tyler
(1757–1826)

Royall Tyler is best known as the author of the first successful American comedy produced on stage in the United States. *The Contrast: A Comedy in Five Acts,* a sophisticated comedy of manners, was first staged in New York City on April 16, 1787. This play introduced into American legend the characters of the homespun Jonathan, the typical Yankee; the practical, noble Colonel Manly, veteran of the Revolution; and the bourgeois father, with an eye on the "main chance." Despite its reliance on English models, *The Contrast* is a very American story that reveals the social, political, and legal limitations on freedom in the new nation, especially as they applied to women. Tyler claimed he wrote the play in three weeks, immediately before its first staging. After several performances in various cities, the play was printed in 1790. By the middle of the nineteenth century, however, it had disappeared. In 1876 a Vermont book collector spotted *The Contrast* in a list of

George Washington's books to be auctioned in Philadelphia and bought the signed copy for a few dollars. (In 1919 it sold for $2800.) Since that time the play has been reprinted and performed frequently.

America's first successful playwright spent most of his professional life as a Vermont lawyer and judge. Born into a prominent Anglican family in Boston in 1757, he was baptized William Clark Tyler. When his father, a wealthy merchant, died, the fourteen-year-old boy legally changed his first name to Royall. The elder Royall Tyler had been a Boston representative and king's councillor and a member of the Sons of Liberty, supporting the colonists in their opposition to the British. The younger Tyler received a strong classical education at Boston Latin School and Harvard College, where he graduated in 1776 with a reputation for his wit. Remaining in Cambridge, Massachusetts, to study law, Tyler served briefly in 1778 in the American Army during an unsuccessful attack on the British at Newport, Rhode Island. He returned to Harvard and received an M.A. in 1779.

With a sizable inheritance from his father, Tyler during his Harvard years led a dissipated social life of an affluent young man: drinking, carousing, and discussing literature, painting, and politics. He left Massachusetts to practice law in Maine in 1780 but moved in 1782 to Braintree (now Quincy), Massachusetts, where he fell in love with and proposed to seventeen-year-old Abigail (Nabby) Adams, daughter of future president John Adams. Her father, however, ordered Nabby to join him in Europe in 1784, not wanting a dissipated poet for a son-in-law.

Tyler slowly recovered from this rejection and set up a law practice in Boston in 1785. Boarding with the Palmer family, he met Mary Palmer, still a young girl. Ten years later, in May 1794, they secretly married. Eleven children were born to the couple, who appear to have had a very strong marriage. Mary's journal and reminiscences provide information about their life and attest to her singular devotion throughout her husband's periods of depression, political and literary triumphs, and last years of pain and sickness.

In the decade before his marriage, Tyler had matured as lawyer, diplomat, and writer, with a strong Federalist bent. In January 1787 he helped to quell Shays' Rebellion at Springfield, Massachusetts. Leading a state militia troop, Tyler helped convince the farmers, angered by the unstable postwar economy, to end their rebellion. His next mission was to convince the governor of Vermont not to grant political asylum to David Shays, who had escaped capture and fled to Vermont. Tyler was sent to New York City to negotiate for militia support against the rebels. At this time *The Contrast* was presented on stage in New York. The play can be considered Tyler's personal response to those deeply dissatisfied with what the American Revolution had wrought. On May 19, one month after the opening of *The Contrast*, New Yorkers were treated to a second Tyler play, the musical *May Day in Town*.

In 1791 Tyler reestablished his law practice in the remote village of Guilford, Vermont. From 1794 to 1801 he served as a state's attorney and wrote a newspaper column with Joseph Dennie, an editor and early champion of American literature. In the first piece, the pair advertised themselves as "Mess. COLON & SPONDEE [types of metrical units in poetry], WHOLESALE DEALERS IN VERSE, PROSE, & MUSIC." Over the years they published hundreds of columns in numerous newspapers, combining light satirical essays (by Dennie as "Colon") and verse (by Tyler as "Spondee") on politics, manners, religion, and literature. When Tyler was elected to the Vermont Supreme Court in 1801, he stopped contributing to the columns. In 1802 he was named a trustee of the University of Vermont, where he became professor of jurisprudence in 1811. From 1807 to 1813 he served as chief justice of the Vermont Supreme Court. His bid for election to the U.S. Senate in 1812 was unsuccessful, and in 1813 he lost his place on the court.

The frontispiece of Royall Tyler's The Contrast, *engraved by P. R. Maverick from a drawing by William Dunlap.*

Throughout these years Tyler continued to write, although sometimes hastily or superficially. In 1795 he reported he was working on another comedy, an opera, and a book of poetry. At this time he was also beginning his longest published work, *The Algerine Captive* (1797), a hybrid novel following the adventures of the narrator, Dr. Updike Underhill, whose education in the classics ill prepared him for life in the new republic. Underhill, born into an impoverished New Hampshire family, reaches the age of twenty-one in 1783, the year the colonies achieved independence. He thus represents the United States in its coming of age. *The Algerine Captive* begins as a picaresque adventure tracing the narrator's education and early career, revealing the limitations of American democracy. The book's second volume becomes a captivity narrative in which Underhill's experience as a slave in Algiers reflects on the question of slavery in a nation where all men are defined as equally endowed with "certain inalienable rights."

The end of Tyler's life was marked by the pain of cancer and the poverty that followed his failure to be recalled to the Supreme Court. During these years he completed four plays and a long poem and attempted to turn *The Algerine Captive* into an autobiographical novel, *The Bay Boy*. Tyler died in 1826, exactly a half-century following the beginning of the Revolution that had transformed America. His death, like the deaths of John Adams and Thomas Jefferson, signaled an end to the early republic Tyler had chronicled.

Suggested Readings: *The Algerine Captive: Or, the Life and Adventures of Doctor Updike Underhill, Six Years a Prisoner Among the Algerines*, ed. J.B. Moore, 1967. *The Verse of Royall Tyler*, ed.

M.B. Péladeau, 1968. *The Prose of Royall Tyler*, ed. M. B. Péladeau, 1972. G. T. Tanselle, *Royall Tyler*, 1967.

Text Used: *The Contrast: A Comedy in Five Acts*, ed. J. B. Wilbur, 1970.

from   THE CONTRAST

A COMEDY IN FIVE ACTS

PROLOGUE

WRITTEN BY A YOUNG GENTLEMAN OF NEW-YORK,
AND SPOKEN BY MR. WIGNELL[1]

EXULT, each patriot heart!—this night is shewn
A piece, which we may fairly call our own;
Where the proud titles of "My Lord! Your Grace!"
To humble *Mr*. and plain *Sir* give place.
Our Author pictures not from foreign climes
The fashions or the follies of the times;
But has confin'd the subject of his work
To the gay scenes—the circles of New-York.
On native themes his Muse displays her pow'rs;
If ours the faults, the virtues too are ours.
Why should our thoughts to distant countries roam,
When each refinement may be found at home?
Who travels now to ape the rich or great,
To deck an equipage and roll in state;
To court the graces, or to dance with ease,
Or by hypocrisy to strive to please?
Our free-born ancestors such arts despis'd;
Genuine sincerity alone they priz'd;
Their minds, with honest emulation fir'd;
To solid good—not ornament—aspir'd;
Or, if ambition rous'd a bolder flame,
Stern virtue throve, where indolence was shame.

    But modern youths, with imitative sense,
Deem taste in dress the proof of excellence;
And spurn the meanness of your homespun arts,
Since homespun habits would obscure their parts;
Whilst all, which aims at splendour and parade,
Must come from Europe, *and be ready made*.
Strange! we should thus our native worth disclaim,

---

[1] Thomas Wignell (1753–1803), a comic actor who first played the character Jonathan in *The Contrast*.

And check the progress of our rising fame.
Yet *one*, whilst imitation bears the sway,
Aspires to nobler heights, and points the way.
Be rous'd, my friends! his bold example view;
Let your own Bards be proud to copy *you!*
Should rigid critics reprobate our play,
At least the patriotic heart will say,
"Glorious our fall, since in a noble cause.
"The bold *attempt alone* demands applause."
Still may the wisdom of the Comic Muse
Exalt your merits, or your faults accuse.
But think not, 't is her aim to be severe;—
We all are mortals, and as mortals err.
If candour pleases, we are truly blest;
Vice trembles, when compell'd to stand confess'd.
Let not light Censure on your faults offend,
Which aims not to expose them, but amend.
Thus does our Author to your candour trust;
Conscious, the *free* are generous, as just.

1787, 1790

LATE 18TH-CENTURY FICTION

Is it not a little hard . . . that not one gentleman's daughter in a thousand should be
brought to read or understand her own natural tongue, or be the judge of the easiest
books that are written in it? . . . I hope you will recommend the study of Mr.
[Noah] *Webster's* Grammatical Institute, as the best work in our language to facilitate the knowledge of Grammar. I cannot but think Mr. *Webster* intended his valuable book for the benefit of his countrywomen; for while he delivers his *rules* in a
pure, precise, and elegant style, he *explains* his meaning by *examples* which are
calculated to inspire the female mind with a thirst for emulation, and a desire for
virtue.

Although this epigraph may seem to be part of an early-American sermon or
advice book, it actually appears in *The Power of Sympathy* (1789) by William Hill
Brown, then a twenty-three-year-old clockmaker's son. Both the factuality and
the highly sensationalized plot (involving adultery and incest) of *The Power of
Sympathy*, now widely accepted as the first American novel, set the tone for many
subsequent novels. Even the novel's frontispiece exploits one of postrevolu-
tionary-Boston's most notorious scandals, the story of Fanny Apthorp. Fanny
committed suicide after her illicit liaison with her sister's husband, a Harvard University graduate and Patriot, Perez Morton, was publicly disclosed. Fanny's
neighbor, Brown sympathizes with her in *The Power of Sympathy* and even names
her "Ophelia," after Shakespeare's tragic heroine. Morton, however, was a genuine seducer/villain. He becomes "Martin" in the novel, a maneuver clearly designed to expose the guilty.

That Brown would interrupt his plot for a digression on the best way to improve women's illiteracy may strike the contemporary reader as particularly strange, given the novel's lurid aspects. Yet, somewhere in their plots, virtually all early-American novels advocated greater literacy, education, and practical wisdom for the young female reader. The preface to *The Power of Sympathy* explicitly promises that the "dangerous Consequences of SEDUCTION are exposed, and the Advantages of FEMALE EDUCATION set forth and recommended." The implicit equation here and in many other novels of the period is that education can better prepare a woman for life: that, more explicitly, a woman's intellectual and sexual well being are directly related. For example, allegories of education and seduction appear in the two bestselling novels of the era, Susanna Haswell Rowson's *Charlotte Temple* (1791) and Hannah Webster Foster's *The Coquette* (1797). Charlotte Temple is misled by a handsome young soldier, her own naïveté, and a conniving French schoolmistress. The heroine of *The Coquette,* Eliza Wharton, is both older and better educated than Charlotte but nonetheless has received the kind of genteel female education typical of the period, an education that in no way prepares Eliza to support herself or to be sensible about the unequal gender politics of matrimony. For different reasons, and with differing degrees of self-awareness, both Charlotte and Eliza fall prey to seducing men, and each meets a grim death during childbirth.

Conversely, Judith Sargent Murray's indomitable Margaretta Melworth of *The Story of Margaretta* (1798) receives a superior education in traditionally male subjects, ranging from accounting to geography, as well as in the traditionally feminine curriculum of painting, needlepoint, piano playing, and French. Because she had a sound education, Margaretta is not fooled by the ominously named Sinisterus Courtland and instead rationally assesses and then chooses the admirable Edward Hamilton. The plots by Brown, Rowson, Foster, and Murray illustrated for American readers the ways in which a woman's intellect had to be improved in order for her to cope with a social situation in which her income, social identity, and even physical well-being were determined by her husband.

Much fiction of the new republic is explicitly or implicitly directed to the female reader, who by eighteenth-century American law and custom had few rights of her own. She could not vote (except, in New Jersey, briefly) or serve on a jury and even had few rights to her own body. Inheriting property was difficult, if not illegal, for her; in general, her personal wealth or income simply became her husband's. Given these restrictions, the question of matrimony loomed large in the advice books of the time and equally large in the early novel. Behind much fiction of the new republic is the insistent message that precisely because women continued to be relatively powerless within the postrevolutionary economy, they had to be especially shrewd in their marital choices. They literally could not afford to make a mistake.

Although not all early-American novels were addressed to the female reader, the novel tradition was so commonly associated with women that Hugh Henry Brackenridge overtly and explicitly explains in the preface to *Modern Chivalry* (1792–1815), that he is addressing a male readership. Education is an issue, even in *Modern Chivalry* because, as Brackenridge shows, a democracy cannot survive an uneducated voting population. Brackenridge confronts issues of class, race, nationality, religion and, in a few instances, gender. This is perhaps the most important point: whether addressed explicitly to a female readership or a male readership, the late eighteenth-century American novel took social responsibilities seriously. Different novelists responded to social issues in dramatically different ways (and not always in ways that twentieth-century readers would find admirable), but virtually all early-American novelists realized they were reshaping a European form to the specific political, economic, and social problems of a new nation.

Yet, for all its social consciousness, the novel did not receive universal approval, partly because some novels championed causes that many social authorities found to be disruptive to the broad fabric of America. Three U.S. presidents, myriad lesser elected officials, critics, college teachers, and ministers debated the nature and merits of the genre. Whether approved or despised (or, as Thomas Jefferson thought, fine for gentlemen but potentially dangerous for young women and lower-class workers), the novel was considered significant enough for its social effects as well as its literary merits to be debated. Newspapers and magazines of the day were filled with commentaries, including such hyperbolically negative

---

=CONTEXTS=

The teaching of literature in American colleges during the late eighteenth century was strongly influenced by thinkers of the Scottish Common-sense School of philosophy. A subject of much critical debate was the potential moral harm or benefit of novels (sometimes called "fictional histories"). Whereas many condemned fiction outright, the moderate views of Rev. Hugh Blair (1718–1800), a professor at Edinburgh University, were quite influential. The following excerpt is from his *Lectures on Rhetoric and Belles Lettres* (1783), a standard college text.

[Debate Over Fiction]

There remains to be treated of, another species of Composition in prose, which comprehends a very numerous, though, in general, a very insignificant class of Writings, known by the name of Romances and Novels. These may, at first view, seem too insignificant, to deserve that any particular notice should be taken of them. But I cannot be of this opinion. . . . For any kind of Writing, how trifling soever in appearance, that obtains a general currency, and especially that early preoccupies the imagination of the youth of both sexes, must demand particular attention. Its influence is likely to be considerable, both on the morals, and taste of a nation.

In fact, fictitious histories might be employed for very useful purposes. They furnish one of the best channels for conveying instruction, for painting human life and manners, for showing the errors into which we are betrayed by our passions, for rendering virtue amiable and vice odious. The effect of well contrived stories, towards accomplishing these purposes, is stronger than any effect that can be produced by simple and naked instruction. . . .

Rev. Hugh Blair, 1783

essays as "Novel Reading, a Cause of Female Depravity"(1802, anonymous) about the novel as a genre. No matter what the critics had to say, they all acknowledged that by the 1790s the "whole land" was filled with "modern travels and novels almost as incredible," as Royall Tyler notes in the preface to his novel *The Algerine Captive* (1797).

Many reasons for the popularity of novels in late eighteenth-century America can be postulated, but the most important economic factor contributing to the prevalence of the form was the concurrent establishment of lending libraries. Buying a novel was prohibitively expensive for most Americans. A typical early-American novel cost between seventy-five cents and a dollar at the time when that was a full day's wages for a laborer in Massachusetts or a week's salary for a serving girl. Especially in poor, rural areas, a female schoolteacher might have earned as little as seventy-five cents or a dollar a week (plus free room and board with a local family). For the price of an average novel, an upper-middle-class gentleman could have spent a night at the theater, or his wife could have purchased a season's supply of fashionable Parisian ribbons. A less wealthy woman could have purchased enough homespun to make dresses for herself and two or three of her daughters, or a family lower on the social ladder could have bought a substantial portion of their monthly diet—a bushel of potatoes and a half-bushel of corn.

Clearly, buying a novel was a luxury. Yet, lending libraries made novels available to all but the very lowest, most impoverished class of Americans. For as little as three to six dollars a year, payable in installments, a reader could borrow up to three novels a day from libraries such as Hocquet Caritat's Circulating Library in New York City, which stocked nearly fifteen hundred novels. According to diaries of the time, readers typically shared their borrowed novels with friends. In group tasks such as quilting, one person was commonly designated as "the reader" and would read aloud while others worked. A laborer in Philadelphia; a serving girl in Pelham, Massachusetts; a mechanic in New Haven; a farmhand in the small village of Harwinton, Connecticut; and even a pioneer in the frontier outpost of Belpre, Ohio, all had access to lending libraries. There, unaffordable novels were borrowed and anyone could read about a wide range of characters, including itinerants, factory girls, beggar maids, orphans, the illegitimate, and others deemed social outcasts by genteel society.

Despite the widespread popularity of fiction, no American novelist before James Fenimore Cooper was able to support herself or himself solely by writing fiction. Susanna Rowson comes closest to having been America's first professional novelist, but she wrote plays, songs, advice books, and textbooks as well as novels (and later turned her attention to running a progressive school for young women in order to support herself and her family). As expensive as buying a novel was, printing and publishing one during the early years of the republic was even more expensive. Books had to be set by hand; paper was handmade from expensive (and typically scarce) rags; and bindings, even of cheap books, were hand sewn. No writer got rich from an early-American novel, and no printer did, either. In fact, printing was generally a cottage industry, in which every family

SECOND STREET. North from Market S.ᵗ ᵗᵒ CHRIST CHURCH.
PHILADELPHIA.

During the eighteenth century, Philadelphia was a major publishing center (and also the U.S. capital from 1790 to 1800). W. Birch & Son's engraving shows Second Street in 1799.

member (female as well as male, child as well as adult) participated, and rarely yielded an affluent life style. Significantly, out of the hundreds of colonial and postcolonial American publishers, only one establishment (that of Mathew Carey) managed to survive into the middle of the nineteenth century.

Beside the cost of producing books before mechanization was the matter of authors' royalties. The absence of national and international copyright laws worsened the economics of authorship. Little in early-American law favored books written by Americans and published in the new United States. On the contrary, the Tariff Act of 1789, in which Congress placed sliding taxes on imported goods in order to aid American manufacturers, neglected to mention books or the book trade.

Because London had a large, concentrated population, publishing books was significantly cheaper in England than in the United States. American publishers simply waited to see what English novels did well on the English market and then had buyers purchase large quantities of these books, typically at a discounted price, and ship them to America. Otherwise, American importers bought remaindered books (books that did not sell) at bargain-basement prices in England and essentially dumped the books in America, where fewer literary choices were available. These cheap imports flooded the American market and threatened to destroy the early-American novel just as it was getting started.

Similarly, the absence of copyright laws enabled a publisher to reproduce with impunity a popular book on his (or rarely, her) own press. After 1790 and the passage of the first national copyright regulations, the reprinting of English novels was still possible. Thus, Rowson's *Charlotte Temple,* which was first published in England but became a bestseller only in America, apparently earned Rowson no royalties. In letters to Rowson, Mathew Carey praises her on the excellent sales of her book but never mentions profits that she could receive from her novel's various reprintings. Not until 1830, when the first international copyright laws were passed, did the pirating of foreign imprints (without due payment to the original author or publisher) become illegal.

Economics fostered a taste for British fiction and to a lesser extent French fiction, also. Americans certainly suffered the insecurities of cultural imperialism experienced in many postcolonial societies, then as now. In fashion, anything French was esteemed over clothing tailored at home; in literature, books from England had more status than did the local product. Although a war with England had been fought and won, many Americans insisted that England was still the intellectual and cultural fountainhead of America. As if to legitimate their own creative attempts, a number of new republic novelists defensively allude to English writers—Henry Fielding, Samuel Richardson, and Lawrence Sterne. However, rather than these highly praised (and now canonical) writers, the English writers most often sought by late eighteenth-century booksellers, lending libraries, and readers were Robert Bage, "Monk" Lewis, and Ann Radcliffe. Henry Brooke's *The Fool of Quality* (1766–1770), a popular English title now as obscure as most early American ones, was the novel most likely to be found in American bookshops or libraries.

For the most part, American writers did not ape their British counterparts. Hannah Webster Foster mentioned English novelists to disparage their morals as much as to praise their skill. Whereas American writers read British authors, British writers read American authors, too. Charles Brockden Brown read virtually everything by feminist philosopher Mary Wollstonecraft and her husband, William Godwin. In the preface to *Mandeville* (1817), Godwin returned the compliment by acknowledging his debt to Brown. A generation later, novelist Mary Godwin Shelley, the daughter of Wollstonecraft and Godwin, and Mary's husband, poet Percy Bysshe Shelley, were inspired by Brown. A persisting postcolonial inferiority complex may have deemphasized such a linkage, so that Mary Shelley's *Frankenstein* (1818) is rarely considered in the same breath as Brown's earlier tales of misguided intellect wreaking havoc on the unsuspecting.

Only recently has American fiction before Washington Irving and James Fenimore Cooper been given the attention it deserves. Against almost impossible odds, a curious band of women and men tried to reshape an evolving European narrative tradition into a genre that addressed the social and political conditions of the new republic. These authors produced a remarkably diverse body of work. The early-American novel took many forms and, in a very real way, fictionalized the aspirations of the new republic and voiced a profound critique of American society in its formative moments.

Susanna Haswell Rowson
(1762–1824)

Feisty, independent, determined, a woman of wit, talent, and sensitivity, Susanna Haswell Rowson achieved fame and professional success as an actress, dramatist, poet, novelist, and teacher. She was America's first bestselling novelist. Rowson demonstrated resourcefulness and independence in a period of history that encouraged female docility.

Susanna Haswell was born in Portsmouth, England, in 1762. Her mother died soon afterwards, and her father, a British naval officer, traveled to New England as a revenue collector, leaving his young daughter in the care of relatives. When she was five years old, she sailed from England to rejoin her father, by then remarried and settled at Nantasket, near Boston. The stormy crossing ended in shipwreck: she later used this experience in several of her novels. The Haswells settled into a comfortably genteel life at Nantasket, and by the time she was twelve Susanna gained a reputation for learning.

As English Loyalists, the Haswells suffered during the American Revolution: Their property was confiscated, Haswell was declared a prisoner of war, and for over two years, the family moved frequently, living in poverty and humiliation. In 1778 Haswell and his family were returned to London as part of a prisoner exchange. Susanna Haswell began working as a governess for the family of the duchess of Devonshire (and later dedicated her first novel, *Victoria* [1786] to the duchess). As a member of this aristocratic household, she met the prince of Wales, obtained a pension for her father, and toured Europe, gaining insights into the lives of the wealthy and powerful.

In 1786 Susanna married William Rowson. Charming but irresponsible, unreliable, and excessively fond of drink, he was equally unsuccessful as a hardware merchant, musician, and actor. The couple remained in London until William's hardware business failed in 1792. During that period Susanna Rowson published two volumes of poetry, including *A Trip to Parnassus* (1788), a long dramatic poem; four more novels, including *Charlotte Temple* (1794), her most well-known work; and a collection of moralistic letters and stories, *Mentoria; Or, the Young Lady's Friend* (1791), which includes an essay on women's education.

Charlotte Temple, the first American bestseller, has been called a literary classic, a book that barely rises above literacy's lower limits, the epitome of the seduction novel, an allegory of early America's changing sociopolitical conditions, and a powerful work that provides sisterly, affectionate "counsel" to girls who feel alone because they have no identity of their own, legally or politically. It tells the story of the seduction of a fifteen-year-old English schoolgirl and her abandonment in New York by a British officer, Montraville, during the American Revolution. Other characters include the conniving Mademoiselle La Rue and the villainous Belcour. Both sexes conspire, Rowson shows, to ensnare a helpless young girl like Charlotte.

SLAVES in ALGIERS;

OR, A

STRUGGLE for FREEDOM:

A PLAY,

INTERSPERSED WITH SONGS,

IN THREE ACTS.

By Mrs. ROWSON.

AS PERFORMED

AT THE

𝔑𝔢𝔴 𝔗𝔥𝔢𝔞𝔱𝔯𝔢𝔰,

IN

PHILADELPHIA and BALTIMORE.

PHILADELPHIA:

PRINTED FOR THE AUTHOR, BY WRIGLEY AND
BERKIMAN, N° 149, CHESNUT-STREET.

M,DCC,XCIV

*The title page of the
first American edition
of Susannah Haswell
Rowson's* Slaves in
Algiers.

Published in England in 1791 as *Charlotte: A Tale of Truth,* the first American edition came out in 1794, and during Rowson's lifetime forty more editions appeared. By the end of the nineteenth century more than two hundred editions had been printed, and Charlotte had become an important figure in American legend. For many readers, this was indeed a tale of truth. Over the years thousands wept at a tombstone marked "Charlotte Temple" at Trinity Church in New York City, where she supposedly was buried. The tradition that the story is based on the actual elopement of Rowson's cousin John Montresor and Charlotte Stanley is generally considered apocryphal today.

William Rowson's business went bankrupt, and the couple took theater jobs at Edinburgh, where the actor Thomas Wignell (who had played the lead in Royall Tyler's *The Contrast* in New York in 1787) persuaded them to join a new theater company in Philadelphia in 1793. Thus, Susanna Rowson lived the second half of her life in the United States, where she continued her theater career, singing, dancing, playing instruments, and composing songs, librettos, and plays, as well as acting in Annapolis and Philadelphia. She joined Boston's Federal Street Theater in 1796. The most successful of Rowson's seven plays is *Slaves in Algiers* (1794), which combines an attack on slavery with a feminist message.

In 1797 Rowson left the theater and opened a highly regarded academy for young ladies in Boston, remaining there until her retirement in 1822. She was innovative in providing a far more rigorous and varied education than was commonly available for girls, adding mathematics, science, geography, and history to the usual diet of needlework, music, and dancing. She was also a popular public lecturer and for many years headed Boston's charitable society for widows and orphans. She died at age sixty-three in 1824.

Rowson's professional life demonstrates the energy that characterized the early republic from 1793 to 1824. She saw young women as her primary audience and, through her writings and her example, tried to teach them resourcefulness and independence. Despite her declining health, she continued to write: plays, three more novels, poetry, biographies of famous women, a spelling dictionary, magazine pieces, songs, and textbooks in geography, Bible and church history, and history. Moreover, she was the main provider in a family that included not only the shiftless William but an adopted daughter, William's sister and her children, and William's illegitimate son. At the end of her life Rowson was working on a sequel called *Charlotte's Daughter: Or, The Three Orphans* (later retitled *Lucy Temple*), published four years after her death.

Suggested Readings: *Trials of the Human Heart,* 1795. *Sarah: Or, The Exemplary Wife,* 1813. D. Weil, *In Defense of Women: Susanna Rowson (1762–1824),* 1976. P. L. Parker, *Susanna Rowson,* 1986.

Texts Used: *Charlotte Temple,* Vol. I, ed. C. N. Davidson, 1986.

from CHARLOTTE TEMPLE

PREFACE

For the perusal of the young and thoughtless of the fair sex, this Tale of Truth is designed; and I could wish my fair readers to consider it as not merely the effusion of Fancy, but as a reality. The circumstances on which I have founded this novel were related to me some little time since by an old lady who had personally known Charlotte, though she concealed the real names of the characters, and likewise the place where the unfortunate scenes were acted: yet as it was impossible to offer a relation to the public in such an imperfect state, I have thrown over the whole a slight veil of fiction, and substituted names and places according to my own fancy. The principal characters in this little tale are now consigned to the silent tomb: it can therefore hurt the feelings of no one; and may, I flatter myself, be of service to some who are so unfortunate as to have neither friends to advise, or understanding to direct them, through the various and unexpected evils that attend a young and unprotected woman in her first entrance into life.

While the tear of compassion still trembled in my eye for the fate of the unhappy Charlotte, I may have children of my own, said I, to whom this recital may be of use, and if to your own children, said Benevolence, why not to the many daughters of Misfortune who, deprived of natural friends, or spoilt by a mistaken education, are thrown on an unfeeling world without the least power to defend themselves from the snares not only of the other sex, but from the more dangerous arts of the profligate of their own.

Sensible as I am that a novel writer, at a time when such a variety of works are ushered into the world under that name, stands but a poor chance for fame in the annals of literature, but conscious that I wrote with a mind anxious for the happiness of that sex whose morals and conduct have so powerful an influence on mankind in general; and convinced that I have not wrote a line that conveys a wrong idea to the head or a corrupt wish to the heart, I shall rest satisfied in the purity of my own intentions, and if I merit not applause, I feel that I dread not censure.

If the following tale should save one hapless fair one from the errors which ruined poor Charlotte, or rescue from impending misery the heart of one anxious parent, I shall feel a much higher gratification in reflecting on this trifling performance, than could possibly result from the applause which might attend the most elegant finished piece of literature whose tendency might deprave the heart or mislead the understanding.   *1791*

Charles Brockden Brown
(1771–1810)

Charles Brockden Brown, America's first professional novelist, was born in Philadelphia in 1771. His Quaker parents instilled in their son both a distaste for the tenets of Calvinism and a preoccupation with individual morality, which greatly influenced his later writings. After attending a Quaker school from 1781 to 1787, Brown was apprenticed to a lawyer but abandoned legal study in 1793 because of his moral reservations about the legal profession and his growing literary interests: in 1789 his first essays had been published in a local magazine. Upon leaving the law Brown moved to New York City and joined the Friendly Society. This group of freethinkers was enchanted with the radical ideas of novelists Mary Wollstonecraft, who in *Vindication of the Rights of Woman* (1792) calls for equal education for women, and her husband William Godwin, who in *Political Justice* (1793) argues for human perfectibility and against society's corrupting influences.

In 1798 the period of Brown's greatest literary productivity began. Living in New York that year with bachelor friends—the closest being the poet and physician Elihu Smith—Brown published the fictional *Alcuin: A Dialogue*, lamenting the situation of women within the constraints of marriage, and *Wieland*, his first and perhaps greatest novel. In 1799 yellow fever struck New York and killed Smith, who had charitably shared his apartment with a fellow physician afflicted with the disease; Brown was himself temporarily afflicted. Yet, during 1799 Brown produced three more novels (*Ormond*, Part I of *Arthur Mervyn*, and *Edgar Huntly*), apparently by working on more than one at a time. From 1799 to 1800, he also edited the *Monthly Magazine and Literary Review*, in which he regularly called for the creation of an indigenous American literature. After publishing Part II of *Arthur Mervyn* in 1800, Brown returned to Philadelphia and entered the family importing business, having failed to earn a secure income as an author despite his hard work.

Distant from the literary circles of New York and involved in business affairs, Brown nevertheless continued to pursue literary interests. He produced two more novels, *Clara Howard* and *Jane Talbot* in 1801, edited two magazines between 1803 and 1809, and added to his "History of the Carrils," a fictional family chronicle never published in its entirety. During these years Brown also pursued interests in politics and geography, publishing pamphlets in 1803 and 1809 urging the forcible annexation of the Louisiana Territories to the United States and calling for an end to Thomas Jefferson's embargo on

American trade with England and France. Brown struggled as well to complete a lengthy "Topographical, Statistical, and Descriptive Survey of the Earth." Over the objections of his Quaker parents, Brown married Elizabeth Linn, the daughter of a Presbyterian minister, in 1804. Together they lived happily until he died of tuberculosis in 1810.

Despite his attempts to enhance the literary reputation of his nation, Brown's works received little American notice during his lifetime: only one of his novels, *Edgar Huntly*, sold well enough to deserve reprinting. Ironically, however, his novels were praised by English reviewers, by his English mentor, William Godwin, and by the English poets John Keats and Percy Bysshe Shelley. Some years after Brown's death, his novels were also praised by Edgar Allan Poe and Nathaniel Hawthorne—and by the critic and writer Margaret Fuller, who appreciated Brown's support for women's issues. The appearance of an American edition of Brown's *Collected Novels* in 1827 attests to the American reading public's increasing interest in his work.

Today, a quartet of Brown's novels—*Wieland, Ormond, Edgar Huntly,* and *Arthur Mervyn*—form the primary basis of his literary reputation. To some extent, these novels all rely on Gothic melodrama and horror: on depraved and powerful villains, on virginal damsels in distress, on darkness, mystery, and motifs of enclosure and burial. Yet, as Brown notes in his preface to *Edgar Huntly*, they eschew much of the paraphernalia of European Gothicism, replacing barons and castles with middle-class American characters and ordinary American locales. Tending to substitute the psychological for the supernatural, all four novels also reveal Brown's paramount concern with the human mind, particularly under extreme physical, sexual, moral, or financial stress. Despite Brown's later interest in national affairs, his novels pay little attention to the world beyond the mind, rarely alluding to the social and political issues that confronted America in the late 1790s and early 1800s. Their similarities and their contemporaneity notwithstanding, Brown's four major novels are, however, valuably different: throughout his literary career Brown continued to try new techniques and explore new subjects. Based on a real episode in New York history, *Wieland* is the story of a young man who comes to believe God has ordered him to kill his wife and children. In addition to the dangers of religious obsession, the novel underscores the perils of mistaken perception. *Wieland*'s title character is wrongly convinced that he has heard God's voice, and the novel's narrator, Wieland's sister Clara, is likewise continually misled by her senses—and thus continually mistaken in both her assessments of physical reality and her judgments of people. The novel's villain, a dark stranger named Carwin, derives power from his ability (as a ventriloquist) to mislead people such as Clara. Nevertheless, *Wieland* is optimistic in its suggestion that human reason and moral firmness can protect at least some individuals from being destroyed by perceptual error: Clara's rationality and morality finally save her from the tragedy that befalls her brother. Brown's inclusion of this temporarily baffled but ultimately triumphant character demonstrates both his feminist respect for the intellectual and moral capacities of women and his Godwinian confidence in the fundamental resources of human nature.

Though it contains another strong female character, Constantia Dudley, Brown's *Ormond* raises very different issues. As the novel begins, Constantia's wealthy, artistic, and self-indulgent father suffers financial reverses, leaving her to cope more or less single-handedly with poverty, illness, and social isolation. Whenever her father's spirits flag (and they often do), Constantia is true to her name, remaining optimistic and courageous. She must display other virtues once she encounters the novel's title character. Ormond is a man who speaks his mind no matter how impolite the truth might be and who has arrogantly decided that his own reason is superior to everyone else's. He makes another young woman his mistress (rather than his wife) because he finds her mental attributes less appealing than her physical ones. He is attracted to Constantia (because she possesses a good mind and the virtues he lacks), and he attempts to rape her. By way of the highly intelligent but utterly selfish character Ormond, the novel calls into question the eighteenth-century conflation of morality and reason. Thus, differing from *Wieland* in theme, *Ormond* differs as well in technique: unlike Clara Wieland, *Ormond*'s narrator, Constantia's friend Sophia Westwyn is only tangentially involved in the action and provides a generally knowledgeable and even omniscient point of view. More panoramic than *Wieland*, *Ormond* is also less horrific.

Very different from *Ormond* and *Wieland*, *Edgar Huntly* is set in a wild region full of mountains, caves, panthers, and Native Americans, far from civilization. Curious about a guilty-looking young man named Clithero, who wanders nightly in the recesses of rural Pennsylvania, the novel's narrator/title character, is drawn into strange wanderings of his own. Waking up in a pitch-black cave and having no idea how he got there, Huntly must battle hunger, thirst, physical exhaustion, cruel savages, and especially his own tendency to lose hope, all in order to make his way back to civilization. His discovery that his adventures have resulted from sleepwalking (as had the nocturnal excursions of Clithero), helps to explain the significance of these adventures. Afflicted by mental tensions resembling Clithero's, Huntly has relieved these tensions through his wanderings. Signaling Brown's movement in new directions, *Edgar Huntly* points not only toward James Fenimore Cooper's work with its wilderness setting and Native-American episodes but also toward the work of Poe and Hawthorne with its use of psychological landscape and brilliant analysis of neurotic behavior.

In some ways *Arthur Mervyn: Or, Memoirs of the Year 1793* is a combination of *Ormond* and *Wieland*. Part I describes the triumph of the apparently virtuous title character over many of the adversities that beset Constantia Dudley; Part II casts serious doubt on the principles of Mervyn, again raising the issue of appearance and reality. Yet, *Arthur Mervyn* moves beyond *Ormond* and *Wieland* by focusing on the moral development of a single character. In Part I the youthful Mervyn, having recently arrived in the city, comes under the influence of an evil schemer named Welbeck, who quickly involves Mervyn in criminal activities and from whom Mervyn must eventually detach himself. As Part I ends, Mervyn seems determined only to clear his name and to rescue other victims of Welbeck's frauds and manipulations. Part II greatly alters the reader's attitude toward Mervyn. Rumors arise suggesting that the life story Mervyn told to the novel's kindly narrator in Part I was a veil of half-truths, disguising unpleasant aspects of Mervyn's character. Moreover, having won the love of the charming Eliza Hadwin, whose father befriended him during the crises of Part I, Mervyn first concludes that he cannot marry her, then, when she appears to have become an heiress, decides he can. However, he marries someone else when Eliza's fortune proves illusory. Possessing characteristics of Welbeck, the mature Mervyn may represent Brown's ironic commentary on the notions of success as promoted by writers such as Benjamin Franklin and those prevalent in America in the 1790s.

Brown's greatest liability as a writer is his penchant for unrealistic manipulation of events. Unlikely coincidences abound in his novels, and his endings are rather contrived. Some coincidences in Brown's novels (such as the character doublings in *Edgar Huntly*) may be strategic rather than accidental, designed to underscore Brown's subtle psychological themes; and his narrative idiosyncrasies (including his contrived endings) may be attributable not to his incompetence as a writer but to his desire to characterize his narrators through the unsatisfactoriness of their narratives. Nevertheless, all the problems with Brown's plots are not likely to be transformable into virtues. Brown was simply a writer with great talents—and a few rather obvious limitations.

Brown has been called "the first man of letters in America," but with his career a brief and unprosperous one, with Philip Freneau writing before him, and with no "first woman of letters" having been named, both the title and Brown's nomination seem suspect. Brown cannot be accurately called "the father of American fiction." Although some of his themes anticipate those of later American authors, evidence that Brown had a major direct influence on these authors is lacking. Moreover, if Brown's themes have proved popular with later authors, other themes have proved equally popular: Brown can be given credit for introducing only a few significant strands into the fabric of American fiction. Brown continues, however, to seem more creative and original than other early American novelists, including Susanna Haswell Rowson and Hugh Henry Brackenridge, who treat traditional subjects in traditional ways. The works of these authors are less diverse than Brown's, less engrossing as narratives, and less thematically complex. Thus, whereas Brown's other designations have rightly been stripped from him, the title of "America's premier early novelist" is likely to remain his—derived from four innovative and powerful novels, which after nearly two hundred years are still easy to admire and difficult to forget.

Suggested Readings: *Charles Brockden Brown's Novels,* 1963. N. Grabo, *The Coincidental Art of Charles Brockden Brown,* 1981. *Critical Essays on Charles Brockden Brown,* ed. B. Rosenthal, 1981. A. Axelrod, *Charles Brockden Brown: An American Tale,* 1983.

Texts Used: *Arthur Mervyn: Or, Memoirs of the Year 1793: The Novels and Related Works of Charles Brockden Brown,* Pt. I, ed. S. J. Krause, S. W. Reid, N. S. Grabo, and M. L. Williams, Jr., 1980. *Wieland: Or, The Transformation: The Novels and Related Works of Charles Brockden Brown,* ed. S. J. Krausse, S. W. Reid, and A. Cowie, 1977.

from ARTHUR MERVYN

from CHAPTER XV[1]

These meditations did not enfeeble my resolution, or slacken my pace. In proportion as I drew near the city, the tokens of its calamitous condition became more apparent. Every farm-house was filled with supernumerary tenants; fugitives from home, and haunting the skirts of the road, eager to detain every passsenger with inquiries after news. The passengers were numerous; for the tide of emigration was by no means exhausted. Some were on foot, bearing in their countenances the tokens of their recent terror, and filled with mournful reflections on the forlornness of their state. Few had secured to themselves an asylum; some were without the means of paying for victuals or lodging for the coming night; others, who were not thus destitute, yet knew not whither to apply for entertainment, every house being already over-stocked with inhabitants, or barring its inhospitable doors at their approach.

Families of weeping mothers, and dismayed children, attended with a few pieces of indispensable furniture, were carried in vehicles of every form. The parent or husband had perished; and the price of some moveable, or the pittance handed forth by public charity, had been expended to purchase the means of retiring from this theatre of disasters; though uncertain and hopeless of accommodation in the neighbouring districts.

[1] During the summer of 1793 Philadelphia suffered a yellow fever epidemic that left thousands dead. In this scene Arthur Mervyn enters the city as families who have lost loved ones and left everything behind are fleeing for their lives.

Between these and the fugitives whom curiosity had led to the road, dialogues frequently took place, to which I was suffered to listen. From every mouth the tale of sorrow was repeated with new aggravations. Pictures of their own distress, or of that of their neighbours, were exhibited in all the hues which imagination can annex to pestilence and poverty.

My preconceptions of the evil now appeared to have fallen short of the truth. The dangers into which I was rushing, seemed more numerous and imminent than I had previously imagined. I wavered not in my purpose. A panick crept to my heart, which more vehement exertions were necessary to subdue or control; but I harboured not a momentary doubt that the course which I had taken was prescribed by duty. There was no difficulty or reluctance in proceeding. All for which my efforts were demanded, was to walk in this path without tumult or alarm.

Various circumstances had hindered me from setting out upon this journey as early as was proper. My frequent pauses to listen to the narratives of travellers, contributed likewise to procrastination. The sun had nearly set before I reached the precincts of the city. I pursued the track which I had formerly taken, and entered High-street after nightfall. Instead of equipages[2] and a throng of passengers, the voice of levity and glee, which I had formerly observed, and which the mildness of the season would, at other times, have produced, I found nothing but a dreary solitude.

The market-place, and each side of this magnificent avenue were illuminated, as before, by lamps; but between the verge of Schuylkill[3] and the heart of the city, I met not more than a dozen figures; and these were ghost-like, wrapt in cloaks, from behind which they cast upon me glances of wonder and suspicion; and, as I approached, changed their course, to avoid touching me. Their clothes were sprinkled with vinegar; and their nostrils defended from contagion by some powerful perfume.

I cast a look upon the houses, which I recollected to have formerly been, at this hour, brilliant with lights, resounding with lively voices, and thronged with busy faces. Now they were closed, above and below; dark, and without tokens of being inhabited. From the upper windows of some, a gleam sometimes fell upon the pavement I was traversing, and shewed that their tenants had not fled, but were secluded or disabled.

These tokens were new, and awakened all my panicks. Death seemed to hover over this scene, and I dreaded that the floating pestilence had already lighted on my frame. I had scarcely overcome these tremors, when I approached an house, the door of which was open, and before which stood a vehicle, which I presently recognized to be an *hearse*.

The driver was seated on it. I stood still to mark his visage, and to observe the course which he proposed to take. Presently a coffin, bourne by two men, issued from the house. The driver was a negro, but his companions were white. Their features were marked by ferocious indifference to danger or pity. One of them as he asssisted in thrusting the coffin into the cavity provided for it, said, I'll be damned if I think the poor dog was quite dead. It wasn't the *fever* that ailed him, but the sight of the girl and her mother on the floor. I wonder how they all got into that room. What carried them there?

---

[2] Carriages.   [3] The Schuylkill River.

The other surlily muttered, Their legs to be sure.

But what should they hug together in one room for?

To save us trouble to be sure.

And I thank them with all my heart; but damn it, it wasn't right to put him in his coffin before the breath was fairly gone. I thought the last look he gave me, told me to stay a few minutes.

Pshaw! He could not live. The sooner dead the better for him; as well as for us. Did you mark how he eyed us, when we carried away his wife and daughter? I never cried in my life, since I was knee-high, but curse me if I ever felt in better tune for the business than just then. Hey! continued he, looking up, and observing me standing a few paces distant, and listening to their discourse, What's wanted? Any body dead?

1798–1799, 1799

from　*WIELAND*

Chapter XVII[1]

I had no inclination nor power to move from this spot. For more than an hour, my faculties and limbs seemed to be deprived of all activity. The door below creaked on its hinges, and steps ascended the stairs. My wandering and confused thoughts were instantly recalled by these sounds, and dropping the curtain of the bed, I moved to a part of the room where any one who entered should be visible; such are the vibrations of sentiment, that notwithstanding the seeming fulfilment of my fears, and increase of my danger, I was conscious, on this occasion, to no turbulence but that of curiosity.

At length he entered the apartment, and I recognized my brother. It was the same Wieland whom I had ever seen. Yet his features were pervaded by a new expression. I supposed him unacquainted with the fate of his wife, and his appearance confirmed this persuasion. A brow expanding into exultation I had hitherto never seen in him, yet such a brow did he now wear. Not only was he unapprized of the disaster that had happened, but some joyous occurrence had betided. What a reverse was preparing to annihilate his transitory bliss! No husband ever doated more fondly, for no wife ever claimed so boundless a devotion. I was not uncertain as to the effects to flow from the discovery of her fate. I confided not at all in the efforts of his reason or his piety. There were few evils which his modes of thinking would not disarm or their sting; but here, all opiates to grief, and all compellers of patience were vain. This spectacle would be unavoidably followed by the outrages of desperation, and a rushing to death.

---

[1] As the scene opens Clara, the speaker and Wieland's sister, has just discovered the body of her sister-in-law, murdered in Clara's bed. Not yet suspecting her brother to be the killer, she greets her "transformed" brother.

For the present, I neglected to ask myself what motive brought him hither. I was only fearful of the effects to flow from the sight of the dead. Yet could it be long concealed from him? Some time and speedily he would obtain this knowledge. No stratagems could considerably or usefully prolong his ignorance. All that could be sought was to take away the abruptness of the change, and shut out the confusion of despair, and the inroads of madness: but I knew my brother, and knew that all exertions to console him would be fruitless.

What could I say? I was mute, and poured forth those tears on his account, which my own unhappiness had been unable to extort. In the midst of my tears, I was not unobservant of his motions. These were of a nature to rouse some other sentiment than grief, or, at least, to mix with it a portion of astonishment.

His countenance suddenly became troubled. His hands were clasped with a force that left the print of his nails in his flesh. His eyes were fixed on my feet. His brain seemed to swell beyond its continent. He did not cease to breathe, but his breath was stifled into groans. I had never witnessed the hurricane of human passions. My element had, till lately, been all sunshine and calm. I was unconversant with the altitudes and energies of sentiment, and was transfixed with inexplicable horror by the symptoms which I now beheld.

After a silence and a conflict which I could not interpret, he lifted his eyes to heaven, and in broken accents exclaimed,"This is too much! Any victim but this, and thy will be done. Have I not sufficiently attested my faith and my obedience? She that is gone, they that have perished, were linked with my soul by ties which only thy command would have broken; but here is sanctity and excellence surpassing human. This workmanship is thine, and it cannot be thy will to heap it into ruins."

Here suddenly unclasping his hands, he struck one of them against his forehead, and continued—"Wretch! who made thee quicksighted in the councils of thy Maker? Deliverance from mortal fetters is awarded to this being, and thou art the minister of this decree."

So saying, Wieland advanced towards me. His words and his motions were without meaning, except on one supposition. The death of Catharine was already known to him, and that knowledge, as might have been suspected, had destroyed his reason. I had feared nothing less; but now that I beheld the extinction of a mind the most luminous and penetrating that ever dignified the human form, my sensations were fraught with new and insupportable anguish.

I had not time to reflect in what way my own safety would be affected by this revolution, or what I had to dread from the wild conceptions of a mad-man. He advanced towards me. Some hollow noises were wafted by the breeze. Confused clamours were succeeded by many feet traversing the grass, and then crowding into the piazza.

These sounds suspended my brother's purpose, and he stood to listen. The signals multiplied and grew louder; perceiving this, he turned from me, and hurried out of my sight. All about me was pregnant with motives to astonishment. My sister's corpse, Wieland's frantic demeanour, and, at length, this crowd of visitants so little accorded with my foresight, that my mental progress was stopped. The impulse had ceased which was accustomed to give motion and order to my thoughts.

Footsteps thronged upon the stairs, and presently many faces shewed[2] them-

---

[2] Showed.

selves within the door of my apartment. These looks were full of alarm and watch-fulness. They pryed into corners as if in search of some fugitive; next their gaze was fixed upon me, and betokened all the vehemence of terror and pity. For a time I questioned whether these were not shapes and faces like that which I had seen at the bottom of the stairs, creatures of my fancy or airy existences.

My eye wandered from one to another, till at length it fell on a countenance which I well knew. It was that of Mr. Hallet. This man was a distant kinsman of my mother, venerable for his age, his uprightness, and sagacity. He had long discharged the functions of a magistrate and good citizen. If any terrors remained, his presence was sufficient to dispel them.

He approached, took my hand with a compassionate air, and said in a low voice, "Where, my dear Clara, are your brother and sister?" I made no answer, but pointed to the bed. His attendants drew aside the curtain, and while their eyes glared with horror at the spectacle which they beheld, those of Mr. Hallet over-flowed with tears.

After considerable pause, he once more turned to me. "My dear girl, this sight is not for you. Can you confide in my care, and that of Mrs. Baynton's? We will see performed all that circumstances require."

I made strenuous opposition to this request. I insisted on remaining near her till she were interred. His remonstrances, however, and my own feelings, shewed me the propriety of a temporary dereliction. Louisa stood in need of a comforter, and my brother's children of a nurse. My unhappy brother was himself an object of solicitude and care. At length, I consented to relinquish the corpse, and go to my brother's, whose house, I said, would need a mistress, and his children a parent.

During this discourse, my venerable friend struggled with his tears, but my last intimation called them forth with fresh violence. Meanwhile, his attendants stood round in mournful silence, gazing on me and at each other. I repeated my resolu-tion, and rose to execute it; but he took my hand to detain me. His countenance betrayed irresolution and reluctance. I requested him to state the reason of his opposition to this measure. I entreated him to be explicit. I told him that my brother had just been there, and that I knew his condition. This misfortune had driven him to madness, and his offspring must not want a protector. If he chose, I would resign Wieland to his care; but his innocent and helpless babes stood in instant need of nurse and mother, and these offices I would by no means allow another to perform while I had life.

Every word that I uttered seemed to augment his perplexity and distress. At last he said, "I think, Clara, I have entitled myself to some regard from you. You have professed your willingness to oblige me. Now I call upon you to confer upon me the highest obligation in your power. Permit Mrs. Baynton to have the man-agement of your brother's house for two or three days; then it shall be yours to act in it as you please. No matter what are my motives in making this request; perhaps I think your age, your sex, or the distress which this disaster must occasion, inca-pacitates you for the office. Surely you have no doubt of Mrs. Baynton's tender-ness or discretion."

New ideas now rushed into my mind. I fixed my eyes stedfastly on Mr. Hallet. "Are they well?"said I. "Is Louisa well? Are Benjamin, and William, and Con-stantine, and Little Clara, are they safe? Tell me truly, I beseech you!"

"They are well," he replied; "they are perfectly safe."

"Fear no effeminate weakness in me: I can bear to hear the truth. Tell me truly, are they well?"

He again assured me that they were well.

"What then," resumed I, "do you fear? Is it possible for any calamity to dis-qualify me for performing my duty to these helpless innocents? I am willing to divide the care of them with Mrs. Baynton; I shall be grateful for her sympathy and aid; but what should I be to desert them at an hour like this!"

I will cut short this distressful dialogue. I still persisted in my purpose, and he still persisted in his opposition. This excited my suspicions anew; but these were removed by solemn declarations of their safety. I could not explain this conduct in my friend; but at length consented to go to the city, provided I should see them for a few minutes at present, and should return on the morrow.

Even this arrangement was objected to. At length he told me they were re-moved to the city. Why were they removed, I asked, and whither? My importuni-ties would not now be eluded. My suspicions were roused, and no evasion or artifice was sufficient to allay them. Many of the audience began to give vent to their emotions in tears. Mr. Hallet himself seemed as if the conflict were too hard to be longer sustained. Something whispered to my heart that havoc had been wider than I now witnessed. I suspected this concealment to arise from apprehen-sions of the effects which a knowledge of the truth would produce in me. I once more entreated him to inform me truly of their state. To enforce my entreaties, I put on an air of insensibility. "I can guess," said I, "what has happened—They are indeed beyond the reach of injury, for they are dead! Is it not so?" My voice faltered in spite of my courageous efforts.

"Yes," said he, "they are dead! Dead by the same fate, and by the same hand, with their mother!"

"Dead!" replied I; "what, all?"

"All!" replied he: "he spared *not one!*"

Allow me, my friends, to close my eyes upon the afterscene. Why should I protract a tale which I already begin to feel is too long? Over this scene at least let me pass lightly. Here, indeed, my narrative would be imperfect. All was tempes-tuous commotion in my heart and in my brain. I have no memory for ought but unconscious transitions and rueful sights. I was ingenious and indefatigable in the invention of torments. I would not dispense with any spectacle adapted to exasper-ate my grief. Each pale and mangled form I crushed to my bosom. Louisa, whom I loved with so ineffable a passion, was denied to me at first, but my obstinacy conquered their reluctance.

They led the way into a darkened hall. A lamp pendant from the ceiling was uncovered, and they pointed to a table. The assassin had defrauded me of my last and miserable consolation. I sought not in her visage, for the tinge of the morning, and lustre of heaven. These had vanished with life; but I hoped for liberty to print a last kiss upon her lips. This was denied me; for such had been the merciless blow that destroyed her, that *not a lineament*[3] *remained!*

I was carried hence to the city. Mrs. Hallet was my companion and my nurse. Why should I dwell upon the rage of fever, and the effusions of delirium? Carwin was the phantom that pursued my dreams, the giant oppressor under whose arm I was for ever on the point of being crushed. Strenuous muscles were required to hinder my flight, and hearts of steel to withstand the eloquence of my fears. In vain I called upon them to look upward, to mark his sparkling rage and scowling

---

[3] A facial feature.

contempt. All I sought was to fly from the stroke that was lifted. Then I heaped upon my guards the most vehement reproaches, or betook myself to wailing on the haplessness of my condition.

This malady, at length, declined, and my weeping friends began to look for my restoration. Slowly, and with intermitted beams, memory revisited me. The scenes that I had witnessed were revived, became the theme of deliberation and deduction, and called forth the effusions of more rational sorrow.

1798

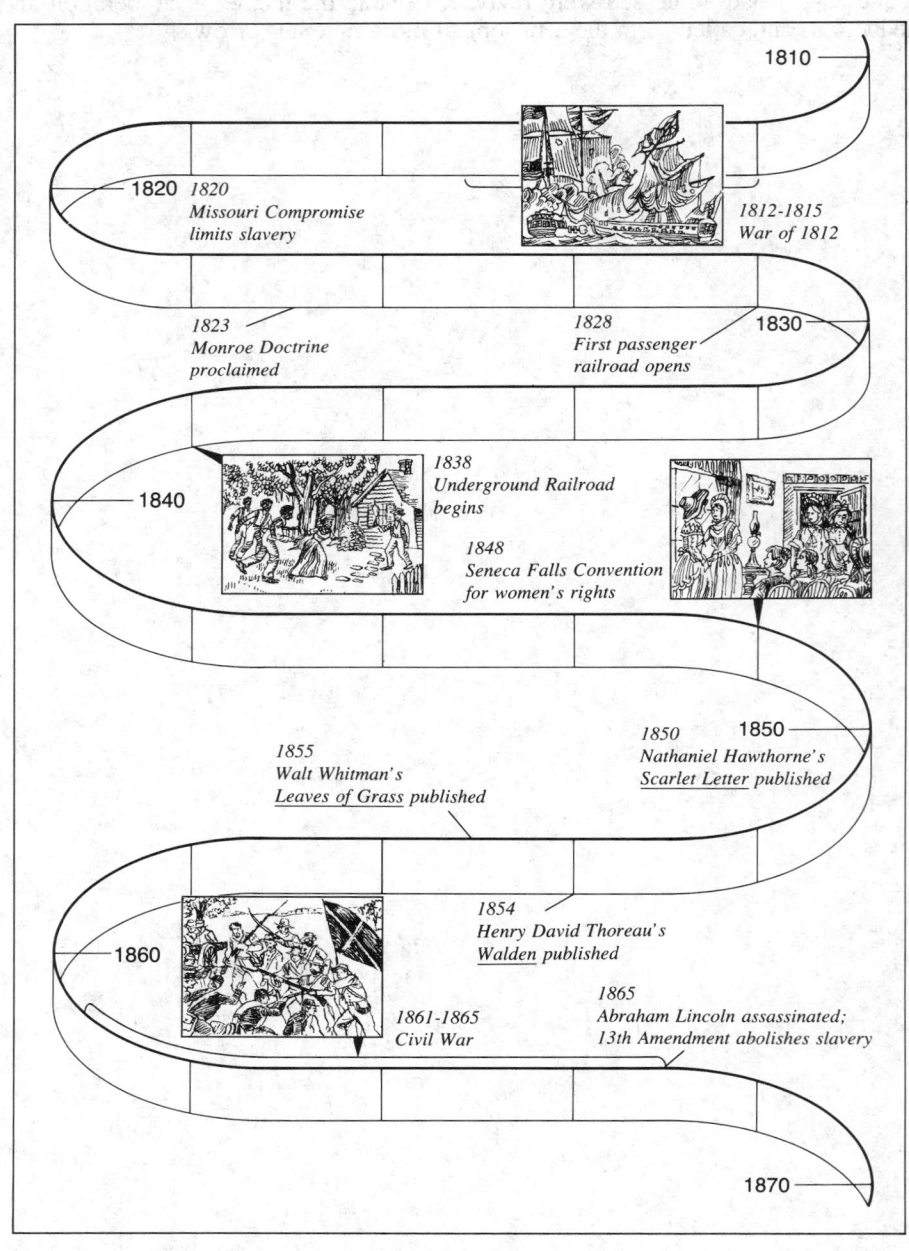

1810

1820
1820
Missouri Compromise
limits slavery

1812-1815
War of 1812

1823
Monroe Doctrine
proclaimed

1828
First passenger
railroad opens

1830

1840
1838
Underground Railroad
begins

1848
Seneca Falls Convention
for women's rights

1850
Nathaniel Hawthorne's
Scarlet Letter published

1850

1855
Walt Whitman's
Leaves of Grass published

1854
Henry David Thoreau's
Walden published

1860

1861-1865
Civil War

1865
Abraham Lincoln assassinated;
13th Amendment abolishes slavery

1870

PART THREE

Progress and Crisis
The Early to Middle 19th Century

The years from the founding of the republic to the outbreak of civil war were short enough to encompass a single life span. Washington Irving, for example, was born in 1783, the year the Treaty of Paris ended the Revolutionary War. He died in 1859; Abraham Lincoln was elected to the presidency the following year. James Fenimore Cooper was born in 1789, the year of George Washington's first inauguration. Lydia Maria Child was born two years into the nineteenth century; she died in 1880, after Reconstruction had come to an end. Ralph Waldo Emerson was a year younger than Child and outlived her by two years.

Their generation experienced an astonishing political and economic transformation. America once again faced England in war—the War of 1812, which arose over the British impressment of American seamen into naval service. (Before the British retreated at the Battle of New Orleans two and a half years after the war began, Washington, D.C., was in partial ruins.) Many problems we still face—in race relations, in the management of technological innovation, in the roles of men and women in an industrializing society—developed in the first half of the nineteenth century, and the ways in which they were understood still infuse our language. While this generation was alive, the physical size of the nation tripled: in 1783 the western boundary had been the Mississippi River; by 1860 it stretched to the Pacific. The Northwest Ordinance of 1787 provided the pattern by which new territory could be integrated into the political community, avoiding colonial status; the Missouri Compromise of 1820 determined which regions, new or extant, could maintain slaves. By mid-century the original thirteen states had increased to twenty-nine. The population size doubled nearly every twenty years, from 4 million people in 1790 to 30 million in 1860, although the average family size decreased sharply. A white woman in 1860 on average bore five children, compared to seven in 1800. The population growth came largely from foreign immigration in the 1840s and 1850s, a factor that changed the composition of the population; before 1840 an overwhelming majority of the population had been born in the United States.

Industrialization and Expansion

Postrevolutionary America was largely an agricultural nation. From North or South, slave or free, most Americans lived in the countryside and grew crops for market. As late as 1870, seventy percent of the population was defined as rural. In fact, the census bureau did not make a distinction between rural and urban populations until 1870, when a town with only eight thousand people was considered a city.

Nevertheless, the postrevolutionary generation experienced an extraordinary industrial transformation, which affected rural as well as urban life. Masters became capitalists; artisans became employees. The use of steam power to drive gears—resulting in steampowered boats, railroads, and textile machinery—restructured economic life. Despite a rhetoric of *laissez faire* and free trade, state support for the development of America's industrial capacity was widespread. States issued bonds in the 1820s and 1830s for building canals and in the 1840s and thereafter for building railroads, culminating in major federal land grants of the 1860s. Mill towns—Lowell, Massachusetts, was perhaps the most famous—embodied a new relationship between owners, employees, and technology. At its formation in the 1820s, Lowell attracted young, unmarried women who saw structured toil in factories as an improvement over unremitting toil on marginal New England family farms. Some found independence in the cash they received, but they came to resent a system in which they worked twelve hours a day, six days a week. Discrimination by gender and class was locked into the American factory system from the beginning; women could never earn wages comparable to men, who held all supervisory roles. The Lowell mill "girls" staged one of the nation's earliest industrial strikes in 1834. In the 1840s they were innovative in making demands not only of employers but of the state government: they demanded a ten-hour work day and the first state legislative hearing on industrial working conditions.

The growth America experienced in the first half of the nineteenth century depended on the clearing of land for homesteads, as in this woodcut by J. A. Ayres.

The major cities—Boston, New York, Philadelphia, and Charleston—were also transformed in the early nineteenth century. They became centers for national finance and communications, commerce, publishing, and small scale manufactures. The opening of the first passenger railroad in 1828 enabled business to be carried on over a wider region than was easily possible previously. Commercial development heightened inequities of wealth and power: in 1848 the poorest eighty percent of Boston's population owned only four percent of the city's wealth, while the richest one percent controlled thirty-seven percent of the city's wealth (E. Pessen, *Wealth Class, and Power Before the Civil War*, 1973).

The world of the farmer was rapidly transformed by technological innovation. Westward expansion provided cheap land; by 1840 5 million people, one-third of the U.S. population, lived west of the Appalachians. Inventions such as John Deere's steel plow and Cyrus McCormick's harvester made it possible to harvest larger crops, and steam-powered transportation on rivers and railroads made it possible to get the food to market faster so it could be sold more cheaply. The availability of inexpensive agricultural products in the cities resulted in cheap food for industrial workers and improved the ability of Americans to compete effectively in international markets.

In Europe industrialization forced massive disruption to rural populations, but in the United States it led to vibrant rural expansion. This expansion was not simply a matter of "manifest destiny"; it was the result of clear political choice and an insistence that there be no political limitations on westward movement—including no interference from Europe, as proclaimed by President James Monroe in 1823, in what became known as the Monroe Doctrine. By setting cheap prices for federal land, Congress encouraged farmers to move West. Congress supported white settlers' pressure for the repeated removal of native populations from desirable lands, even when, as in the case of the Cherokees in Georgia, the Native Americans had a sophisticated political system, a substantial number of English-speaking members, and a profitable economy. In 1837 federal troops forced the southeastern Cherokees across the Mississippi to what is now Oklahoma and Missouri; one out of four Cherokees died along the way. Other federal troops were used in guerrilla warfare against Seminoles in Florida and Sauks and Foxes in Illinois and Wisconsin.

The claim of manifest destiny was used also to rationalize American annexation of part of northern Mexico. During the 1830s slaveholding American settlers entered Mexico, which did not recognize slavery. In 1835 the slaveholders organized a revolt that the Mexican government resisted but lacked the force to squelch. When the independent republic of Texas appealed to Congress for annexation, Congress accepted, even though it meant war with Mexico; the Mexican War began in 1846. The resulting victory in 1848 brought under American control 500,000 square miles, including what is now California, Nevada, Utah, and most of New Mexico and Arizona. With this land came millions of Native-American and Hispanic inhabitants.

Slavery and the Economy. Slavery, which had developed in part as a response to a need for cheap labor, was now enlarged and strengthened. Although the slave plantation appeared to be a rural, agricultural enterprise, it, too, was embedded in a system of capitalist industrial production. The invention of the cotton gin and the development of large-scale textile mills in the Northeast and in Great Britain contributed to a virtually insatiable demand for cotton produced on new lands in the Southwest, including Texas. Cotton production soared from less than 500,000 bales in 1817 to 3 million bales in 1850. The British bought whatever northern mills did not; textile manufacturing was the single most important industry in America.

The profitability of textile production energized slavery, giving more white Americans, both northerners and southerners, a stake in its continuation and expansion. Although the foreign slave trade was ended in 1808, the internal slave trade remained a multimillion dollar "industry." At least 300,000 Virginia slaves were transported South between 1830 and 1850, and the number of slaves in America increased from 1.5 million in 1820 to 4 million by the eve of the Civil War. Slavery was profitable: just prior to the Civil War, a plantation slave produced on average about $80 in cotton earnings per year for the master, who spent less than half that much to provide the slave with marginal nutrition, clothing, and housing. Prices for slaves, which tripled between 1840 and 1860, reflected this profitability.

The profitability of slavery locked the South into economic underdevelopment in other ways as well. There was little industry and a far less developed railroad system than in the North. Less than one-third of white families owned slaves, and most of those owned very few. The majority of the rural white population consisted of marginal yeoman farmers whose opportunities for prosperity were far more limited than those of their northern counterparts.

African-American resentment of slavery occasionally exploded in violence. In 1831 Nat Turner, whose father had escaped slavery and whose African-born mother had brought him up to resist it, led an uprising in Southampton County, Virginia. Driven by rage, Turner and his associates killed some sixty white men, women, and children; in the aftermath about two hundred blacks were murdered by white vigilantes or executed in accordance with the law. After the rebellion slavery was placed under stricter legal controls throughout the South, and slave resistance took forms compatible with survival—notably running away and sabotage. Masters' fear of slave rebellion contributed to a political rigidity that not only inhibited manumission but pervaded much of southern political life and sharpened the distinctions between North and South.

Cultural Effects of Industrialization. The industrial revolution in America had important psychological dimensions. Faster, cheaper printing led to a virtual flood of printed materials—newspapers, pamphlets, books—after 1830. The availability of printed materials fostered literacy. The census of 1840 was the first to ask whether respondents could read and write. It established that the literacy gap between white men and white women in the North had virtually closed; in the south the ratio of literate white men to literate white women was five to four. Railroads allowed for faster, more reliable, and cheaper mail; coupled with inexpensive printing, a wider-ranging intellectual community was formed. Special-interest newspapers and pamphlets—such as William Lloyd Garrison's abolitionist newspaper, *The Liberator,* and Lydia Maria Child's abolitionist pamphlets—could be sent quickly and cheaply throughout the country. Subscribers, perhaps the lone abolitionist or temperance advocate in their own small towns, knew that they were not alone. Because it was easier and safer for women to travel by train than by stagecoach, railroads made a major change in what might be called the political culture of travel. Elizabeth Cady Stanton and other women's rights advocates have testified to the psychological freedom that rail travel brought women, and abolitionist organizations sent women as well as men on speaking tours. But perhaps the most stunning psychological impact of the industrial revolution was the invisible revolution generated by clocks. As clocks became less costly and more pervasive in the 1830s and 1840s, they transformed the rhythms by which people allocated time and organized their lives. The agricultural workday proceeded from sunrise to sunset, so that the workday was shorter in the winter than in the summer, but the factory workday was marked by the clock, which rang out twelve hours in both winter and summer and marked short lunch and dinner breaks as well. Railroads ran on rigid schedules. By mid-century, efficiency in the use of time was an essential ingredient of a "modern" way of life.

Political Growth and Polarization

During the first half of the nineteenth century, mass political parties developed in America. Property requirements for white male voters moved steadily downward and by mid-century had generally been eliminated. Voter participation was widely encouraged in rallies, parades, and conventions. While restrictions based on class were eliminated, and in some states (notably in New England) suffrage restrictions based on race also eroded, restrictions based on gender intensified. However, white women were part of the political community, and they organized themselves in groups that addressed a wide range of reform issues, particularly temperance and abolition. The difficulty of addressing such issues without the right to vote—and the persistence of the old rules of coverture, laws that denied married women control over their own property—led to a demand for the vote and for the right of married women to control property and to exercise the primary rights of citizenship.

Political parties raised money, selected and promoted candidates, and encouraged voter turnout. National parties linked vastly different regions and bridged the gap between the two political cultures of free workers and slaveowners. But the link between the two political economies had been brittle since the negotiation of the Three-fifths Compromise at the Constitutional Convention, and after the Mexican War it was subjected to strains it could not withstand. The territory acquired in the war was rich agricultural land. Northern farmers who wanted to move West did not want to compete with slave labor. Many among them were against slavery and wanted it excluded from the new territory. Southerners saw no reason why slaveowners should not take advantage of opportunity for profit. Political decisions had to be made about this new territory. In the course of the argument, issues of free speech (should northern abolitionists have the right to proselytize

=CONTEXTS=

The Fugitive Slave Act

In summer 1850 the controversies over the admission of California into the Union and the extension of slavery into the territories led to talk of secession among certain groups of southerners. The only concession Congress made to the South in the ensuing Compromise of 1850 was to pass a stricter fugitive slave law, requiring that northerners aid the capture of runaway slaves. The constitutionality of the Fugitive Slave Act, intended to hamper the operation of the Underground Railroad, was soon being debated by some of the most prominent lawyers in the country. James Russell Lowell, John Greenleaf Whittier, and Henry David Thoreau were among the prominent literary figures who raised their pens against the passage of this act. At the same time, American's mainstream clergy, businessmen, and industrialists in the cities and politicians in Congress were working hard to convince the public that opposition to the law's enforcement would lead to disruption of the Union.

William Still (1821–1902), corresponding secretary of the Underground Railroad's Vigilance Committee, kept records that describe the divisive effect the Fugitive Slave Act had on America. By writing and preserving these records during the 1850s, Still risked heavy fines and long imprisonment under the penalties of the Fugitive Slave Act. Still published his account in *The Underground Railroad* in 1871.

The Slave-Hunting Tragedy in Lancaster County, in September, 1851

. . . The deepest feelings of loathing, contempt and opposition were manifested by the opponents of Slavery on every hand. Anti-slavery papers, lecturers, preachers, etc., arrayed themselves boldly against [the Fugitive Slave Act] on the ground of its inhumanity and violation of the laws of God.

On the other hand, the slave-holders South, and their pro-slavery adherents in the North demanded the most abject obedience from all parties, regardless of conscience or obligation to God. In order to compel such obedience, as well as to prove the practicability of the law, unbounded zeal daily marked the attempt on the part of the slave-holders and slave-catchers to refasten the fetters on the limbs of fugitives in different parts of the North, whither they had escaped.

In this dark hour, when colored men's rights were so insecure, as a matter of self-defence, they felt called upon to arm themselves and resist all kidnapping intruders, although clothed with the authority of wicked law. . . .

William Still, 1871

freely in the South?), of free press (could abolitionist newspapers circulate freely?), of the right to petition (might Congress table abolitionist petitions and refuse even to read them?), of women's rights (should abolitionist organizations exclude women so as not to alienate men who would otherwise support the anti-slavery cause?), and of the Fugitive Slave Act of 1850 (did free people have a moral obligation to return fugitive slaves?) polarized people who did not care much about slavery but did care about civil liberties. The politics of the 1850s were poisoned by the debate over slavery in the new territories, resulting in civil disobedience, guerilla warfare in Kansas and Nebraska, and the breakdown of national churches into regional ones and national political parties into regionally based parties. The two sides were polarized between those insisting that the principles of local autonomy and majority rule gave local majorities the right to install slavery in at least part of the new territories, and those insisting on the moral primacy of freedom and maintaining that there are things that even majorities may not do. When Abraham Lincoln was elected president in 1860, it was with a pledge not to interfere with slavery as it existed in the South. Although he won overwhelmingly in the North, he received no support from southern states, which announced that the Constitution they had signed in 1787 was violated. As states, they reclaimed their right to withdraw from the Union they had made.

The Civil War

The Civil War remains the greatest national trauma of American life. One-third of all American men served in one of the armies. Nearly one-fifth of those who served died: 360,000 northern men and 260,000 southern men were killed, and more than 500,000 men were maimed permanently. The losses of the Civil War were greater than the combined losses of all other American wars, including Vietnam. The South was devastated: it is estimated that more than forty percent of its wealth (excluding that invested in slaves) was destroyed, and major cities, including Atlanta and Richmond, were burned to the ground. The cheerful assumptions with which most men on both sides had marched to battle in 1861—that courage, self-confidence, and heroism would overcome all obstacles—gave way to irony and depression. A war that began with violence limited to the battlefield (picnickers from Washington, D.C., went out to observe the first Battle of Bull Run in July 1861) ended with Union General William Tecumseh Sherman's March to the Sea, a conscious effort to demoralize civilians and a model of the total war, which would be characteristic of World War I, World War II, and Vietnam. By the end of 1864 the desertion rate in the Army of the Confederacy was fifty percent.

At the outset the advantage appeared to lie with the South, which was self-sufficient in food production and fighting on familiar ground, and which had a strong military tradition. All the South had to do was to maintain a separate army and make the war too expensive for the North to fight. But as time went on the balance shifted, partly because Lincoln defined his powers as a wartime president aggressively and partly because the advantages of the North's industrial base, eight times greater than that of the South, became more important with time. The North mobilized human and economic resources on a scale America had never experienced before—by selling treasury bonds and imposing substantial new taxes (including the first federal income tax) and high tariffs. In the process, the North improved its capacity to wage war: it increased its industrial capacity, adding an additional five thousand miles of railroad track, and tied the interests of business classes to the success of the Union. The South did not have a comparable war capacity, partly because it lacked the resources and partly because, having left the Union to ensure the right of states to dissent, the Confederate government was not in a position to assert claims to centralized power. Also, the South, always an industrially underdeveloped region, lost most of what limited industrial capacity it had.

Most significantly, the war destabilized and then ended slavery. Lincoln's early pledge not to interfere with slavery where it existed made it possible to keep border states—Maryland, Kentucky, Delaware, and Missouri—in the Union. But Lincoln was slowly and inexorably driven to define the war as one to end slavery. In 1861 Union General Benjamin Franklin Butler refused to return any slave who escaped behind Union lines. They were "contraband of war," he said, thus avoiding argument over whether they were or were not property, and he gave them sanctuary. As the war progressed, sentiment for abolition in the North strengthened, and in 1863 Lincoln issued the Emancipation Proclamation, which freed those slaves who were not in the border states nor at that moment under the control of federal armies. The Emancipation Proclamation transformed the Civil War into a revolutionary struggle. It encouraged the enlistment of African Americans in the Union Army, and thousands responded to the challenge. "By the war's end," writes Eric Foner, "180,000 blacks had served in the Union Army—over one-fifth of the nation's adult male black population under age forty-five" (*Reconstruction*, 1989). They served as soldiers, laborers, and sailors. Uncounted numbers of African-American women served in military camps as cooks and laundresses. In effect what occurred was a great slave rebellion, although it was not perceived as such because whites believed that a slave rebellion consisted of race riots and massacres. When the war was over, 3 million slaves were free, and a constitutional amendment, the thirteenth, guaranteed that freedom.

The assassination of Abraham Lincoln only five days after General Robert E. Lee's surrender in Appomattox Court House, Virginia, in 1865 was an eerie precursor of the violence and profound disruption that continued to characterize American life even after the Civil War had officially ended. The meaning of the Civil War remained contested. To many northerners the war had increasingly come to have a moral component, and victory seemed to validate the increased power of the central government, which had directed the war, and also to commit the nation to a revolution in race relations. For many white southerners, defeat in war signified simply an end to claims of southern independence and to the system of slavery. Many thought they could return to life as it had been before the guns fired on Fort Sumter in Charleston: that is, to a system of race relations in which whites were dominant and blacks were submissive, and to a political system in which the white men who had controlled politics would resume their seats in Congress and in state legislatures as though nothing had happened.

EARLY TO MIDDLE 19TH-CENTURY FICTION

American fiction of the first half of the nineteenth century is an original and diverse body of work that ranges from the comic fables of Washington Irving to the Gothic tales of Edgar Allan Poe, from the frontier adventures of James Fenimore Cooper to the grotesque yarns of Southwest Humorists, from the psychological romances of Nathaniel Hawthorne to the social realism of Rebecca Harding Davis, from the narrative quests of Herman Melville to the moral protests of Harriet Beecher Stowe. The lack of an international copyright law prior to 1830 posed a burden to all these writers. Publishers pirated the work of well-known British authors rather than pay royalties to aspiring Americans. But strategies of publishing simultaneously in England and the United States (with copyright protection in each country), together with a growing audience for writing that focused on American subjects, helped to foster the development of a uniquely American body of fiction by the middle of the nineteenth century. The wide popularity of Irving's *Sketch-Book* (1819–1820), containing such stories as "Rip Van Winkle" and "The Legend of Sleepy Hollow," and of Cooper's early novels, among them *The Spy* (1821) and *The Pioneers* (1823), demonstrated that there was an international market for American fiction that could find its way to publication.

The legacies of Cooper and Irving are demonstrably vital to the development of American literature. Cooper's sagas of the frontier spawned hundreds of imitations throughout the nineteenth century and resulted in the genre we call the "western." Irving's work contributed to the creation of a new literary genre, the short story, which Americans would continue to adapt to their own purposes. In three stories recounting the activities of the criminologist C. Auguste Dupin (a Sherlock Holmes-type sleuth who appeared more than fifty years before Holmes), Edgar Allan Poe invented the modern detective story. During this time Nathaniel Hawthorne explored new directions for the short story in such narratives as "My Kinsman, Major Molineux" (1832) and "The Birth-Mark" (1843). And in later years writers as different as O. Henry (William Sydney Porter), Flannery O'Connor, and Ann Beattie have continued to find the short story congenial to their own form of literary art.

During the decades in which American writers conceived and perfected the short story, another type of short fiction, earthy and vibrant, came into existence. Beginning with the various tellings of the adventures of the real Tennessee frontiersman-turned-politician, Davy Crockett, a group of writers from the Old Southwest (Georgia, Alabama, Louisiana, and Arkansas) transformed the traditions of the tall tale and the resources of regional dialect into fiction. Whereas the short story is distinguished by unity and compression and by an emphasis on character and moral nuance, the tall tale is marked by exaggeration, orality, and the conflict between gentility and unrefined comedy.

With their unromantic views of human relations, their coarse depictions of backwoods life, and their relentless use of vernacular speech, Southwest Humorists such as George Washington Harris and Thomas Bangs Thorpe made a unique contribution to the development of prose fiction in America. To examine Thorpe's "Big Bear of Arkansas" (1841) is to see that the interaction of social classes, the speech patterns, and the sheer exuberance of the fiction prefigures the later and more accomplished work of Mark Twain and of William Faulkner. Moreover, the humor and hyperbole of Thorpe's tale, and of the tall tale as a subgenre, would prove influential beyond the boundaries of prose fiction. Abraham Lincoln's political style, which evolved throughout the 1840s in small midwestern and southern towns, owed much to the defining characteristics of the tall tale.

The distinction between the tall tale and the short story rests fundamentally on a difference in treatment or representation, a difference between caricature and a more realistic depiction of event and character. And in much of the long fiction of this period, a similar distinction can be observed. Both Nathaniel Hawthorne and the southern writer William Gilmore Simms distinguished between the novel and the romance, Hawthorne in his preface to *The House of the Seven Gables* (1851), Simms in a preface to the 1850 edition of *The Yemassee* (1835). The novel, according to Hawthorne, "is presumed to aim at a very minute fidelity" to the "probable and ordinary course" of human experience, whereas the romance has "a certain latitude" of choice and presentation. The novel, according to Simms, derives from the newspaper story and recent events, whereas the romance traces its lineage to the fairy tale. Clearly, both writers think of the novel as more realistic than the romance, more social in subject and manner. The appeal of the romance is that it can fashion a world of its own and feature exaggerations of action and of character.

Late in the eighteenth century Charles Brockden Brown adapted the British-born Gothic romance—devised by Horace Walpole in *The Castle of Otranto* (1765) and popularly exemplified by Mary Shelley's *Frankenstein* (1818)—to American settings in such works as *Wieland* (1798) and *Arthur Mervyn* (1799). And in the mid-nineteenth century such writers as Poe, Hawthorne, and Melville infused their work with the mystery and extravagance of Gothic fiction. No longer did they employ the trappings of Gothicism—dark castles, haunted passageways, ghosts in armor; instead, they internalized the spirit of Gothicism, made it a feature of minds obsessed with a desire for wealth or revenge or truth. In temperament and imagination these three writers were drawn to the Gothic strain in fiction and not to the realism that developed out of the sentimental novels of Samuel Richardson in England and reached an apotheosis at the turn of the nineteenth century in the domestic novels of Jane Austen. Their concern with evil and abnormality—whether in Poe's *Narrative of Arthur Gordon Pym* (1838), Hawthorne's *Scarlet Letter* (1850), or Melville's *Moby-Dick* (1851)—stems from a central focus on the self rather than on society and on the elaborate web of social entanglements that characterize the more realistic form of the novel.

The romance and the novel, however, have never been mutually exclusive forms. Elements of social realism are present in such works as *The Scarlet Letter* and *The House of the Seven Gables* and even in *Moby-Dick* (when Captains Bildad and Peleg sign on the crew of the *Pequod* and, more importantly, when Chief Mate Starbuck says he came on the voyage to hunt whales, not his commander's vengeance). And Gothic interludes can be found even in such straightforward novels as Henry James's *The American* (1877). Moreover, even in the first half of the nineteenth century many people used the term "novel" to describe all long forms of fictional narrative, as we do now. But a definable Gothicism remains a vital force in American fiction, in the novels of William Faulkner and Robert Penn Warren, for example, and in the work of contemporary writers such as Joyce Carol Oates and Stephen King.

Until recently, literary historians have considered such late nineteenth-century novelists as William Dean Howells, Mark Twain, and Henry James as America's original realists. Their theories of the novel developed, as Howells argued in his

═CONTEXTS═════════════════════════════════

The Second Great Awakening

The reform movements from about 1800 to 1840—concerning everything from slavery to temperance to impovements in education—were a hallmark of American romanticism. At roughly the same time, a renewed interest in religion, known as the Second Great Awakening, swept the United States. Historians credit James McGready (1758?–1817), a preacher from North Carolina, with starting the custom of camp meetings, the first of which was held in Logan County, Kentucky, about 1800. At these meetings people were encouraged to pray and sing as much and as loud as they pleased. The traditional "welcome" extended to everyone, no matter what age, sex, race, or denomination—children and blacks as well as Native-American converts to Protestantism preached and reproved sin in equal voice with white women and men. The emphasis on the individual in the services agreed with the character of frontier society (although conservatives considered immoral the revivalist practice of men and women praying together in public). A typical camp meeting is described in the following excerpt from the eyewitness account of Dr. Richard Furman of Charleston:

[Camp Meetings]

. . . The numbers which assembled from various parts of the country, formed a very large congregation, the amount of which has been variously estimated; to me there appeared to be 3000 or perhaps 4000 persons; but some supposed there were 7000 or 8000. . . . The encampment was laid out in an oblong form, extending from the top of a hill down the south side of it, toward a stream of water. . . . Lines of tents were erected on every side of this space; and between them, and behind, were the waggons and riding carriages placed; the space itself being reserved for the assembling of the congregation. . . . Two stands were fixed on for this purpose: at the one a stage was erected under some lofty trees, which afforded an ample shade; at the other, which was not so well provided with shade, a waggon was placed for the rostrum. . . . Several persons suffered at this meeting those bodily affections, which have been experienced at Kentucky, North Carolina, and at other places, where the extraordinary revivals in religion within this year or two have taken place. Some of them fell instantaneously, as though struck with lightning, and continued insensible for a length of time; other were more mildly affected, and soon recovered their bodily strength, with a proper command of their mental powers. . . . These general meetings have a great tendency to excite the attention, and engage it to religion. . . .

Dr. Richard Furman, 1802

critical essays, from French and Russian models. We have come to understand of late, however, that the achievement of these realists was preceded by the earlier accomplishments of a number of American women novelists, some of whom found a model in the work of Jane Austen. These writers understood the tastes of their audience, wrote novels that sold far better than did the works of their male counterparts, and were able to support themselves with their pens.

The audience for fiction in the early and middle nineteenth century was for the most part made up of women, and their taste was less for metaphysical quests and characters isolated by obsession than for domestic fiction—novels about the trials, strength, and perseverance of women characters and the place of women in a male-dominated society. In critical circles the work of female novelists was accorded little status: to critics, they took refuge in formulas and consequently produced bestsellers. In an 1855 letter to his publisher Hawthorne himself commented (doubtless with more than a tinge of jealousy) on the "d——d mob of scribbling women" whose novels consistently outsold his. We now recognize that the best of the fiction written by these women has a dramatic eloquence that transcends formula and brings us to understand the issues of power and compliance at stake in the domestic world. Such novels as Susan Warner's *The Wide, Wide World* (1850), the first literary work by an American to sell over a million copies; Fanny Fern's *Ruth Hall* (1855), praised even by Hawthorne; E. D. E. N. Southworth's *The Hidden Hand* (1859), whose protagonist, Capitola the Madcap, is in some ways a female precursor of Huckleberry Finn; Rebecca Harding Davis's "Life in the Iron-Mills" (1861), a pioneer work of American realism; and Harriet Beecher Stowe's classic *Uncle Tom's Cabin* (1852) have taken their place in the canon of work that defines the achievement of American literature. They also provide a context in which to gain a fresh understanding of the darker symbolic romances of Hawthorne and of Melville.

As is true of any body of work that shares similarities and is eventually grouped together, the novels written by women in the middle nineteenth century were not nearly so monolithic as easy categorizing suggests. Although some of these books dealt with little beyond their domestic contexts, others were driven by social concerns. Davis's story "Life in the Iron-Mills" explores in achingly realistic detail

The Lowell Offering, *begun in 1842 by Harriet Farley, was a literary magazine containing the writings of female mill workers in Lowell, Massachusetts.*

the terrible working and living conditions of industrial workers in America's rapidly growing cities. *Uncle Tom's Cabin* depicts with startling moral fervor the evils of slavery. For Stowe this blatantly abolitionist novel was pointedly and consciously intended to appeal to the emotions of readers as it doggedly emphasized the cruelty and hypocrisy of southern slaveholders who thought of themselves as good Christians.

Social criticism was certainly not new to American writing nor to nineteenth-century fiction. Irving and Cooper were often pronounced in their criticisms of human conformity and the sometimes stultifying nature of civilization in America. Hawthorne and Melville could be severe in their criticisms of Ralph Waldo Emerson and the transcendentalists. Indeed, close examination suggests that fiction in the first half of the nineteenth century was contending with nonfiction as the principal vehicle in America for social commentary. And with its diversity, originality, and vitality, fiction was also replacing nonfiction prose as our dominant literary genre—a position that fiction, primarily in the form of the novel, continues to occupy. It is the power and diversity of fiction that accounts more than anything else for its influence in America, and that power and diversity is found in abundance in American fiction of the early to middle nineteenth century.

Washington Irving
(1783–1859)

Although Washington Irving no longer presides as the "Father of American Letters," the particular "firsts" of his literary career assure his place in American social and cultural history. He was the first American to succeed as a writer of "high" literature for commercial sale and the first American to win a reputation both at home and abroad for such writing. During his lifetime international acclaim for his work appeased nationalistic yearnings for an American literary culture; after his death his reputation as a founder promoted the status of American literature as a legitimate field of study. But early and perhaps excessive praise inevitably diminished. Much twentieth-century Irving scholarship pursues the problem formulated by Edgar Allan Poe in an 1838 letter to Nathan C. Brooks, that of distinguishing "between what is due to the pioneer solely, and what to the writer." Praise of the pioneer has generally outpaced praise of the writer; yet, a handful of Irving's works continue to command attention on their own merit.

Irving was born in New York City in 1783. He was the youngest of eleven children of an English mother and a Scottish father, a prosperous merchant. He attended private schools and went on to study law but, though an apt learner when interested, was generally a desultory student. Some of the things that did interest Irving are evident in his first work, "The Letters of Jonathan Oldstyle, Gent." (1802–1803), which satirizes New York theater and society life and was published in the *Morning Chronicle,* edited by his brother Peter. Following a tour of Europe from 1804 to 1806, Irving returned to New York and the law. He soon turned to writing again, collaborating with his brothers William and Peter and

William's brother-in-law James Kirke Paulding on a series of satirical sketches called *Salmagundi: Or, the Whim-Whams and Opinions of Launcelot Langstaff, Esq., and Others* (1807–1808), which brought local celebrity to its authors. Conservative in attitude and sportive in manner, these sketches established the tone and stance Irving would cultivate throughout his career. His next work featured the creation of Diedrich Knickerbocker as the antiquarian narrator of *A History of New-York From the Beginning of the World to the End of the Dutch Dynasty, by Diedrich Knickerbocker* (1809). At once a burlesque of the "heroic" mode of history-writing, a lampoon of the city and its founders, and a satire of Jeffersonian republicanism, *A History of New-York* brought Irving immediate fame and two thousand dollars.

This triumph was followed by ten years of near silence. During the completion of *A History of New-York* in 1809, Irving was devastated by the death of his fiancée, Matilda Hoffman, from consumption; the loss affected both his life and his work, and he never married. During these years he lobbied in Washington, D.C., on trade issues, published Thomas Campbell's poetry, and edited the *Analectic Magazine,* among other occupations. In 1815, "weary of everything," he sailed for Europe with a plan to study and write, only to become further dispirited by the protracted failure of the family business and the death of his mother.

Irving extricated himself from grief and financial necessity with the personal, commercial, and literary success of *The Sketch Book of Geoffrey Crayon, Gent.* (1819–1820),

The Return of Rip Van Winkle *(1849?), by John Quidor, inspired by the Washington Irving story, demonstrates the continuing link between literature and art.*

which includes "Rip Van Winkle" and "The Legend of Sleepy Hollow." The writing itself marked the onset of *vocation* in Irving's work, and his tales and sketches, bound together by the persona of Geoffrey Crayon, were well received upon their serial publication in New York. To protect his work against pirating, Irving arranged with the help of the Scottish poet and novelist Sir Walter Scott to publish a London edition, which was also very successful. Irving's next work, *Bracebridge Hall* (1822), a loosely plotted collection of sketches centered on an old English country estate, interestingly casts light on the success of *The Sketch Book*. With *Bracebridge Hall* Irving refined his commercial technique, securing his copyright with near-simultaneous publication in England and America. He also reflected in *Bracebridge Hall* that one source of his earlier success had been that an American could write "tolerable English." Finally, the centrality of *The Sketch Book* to Irving's image as a writer can be inferred by the fact that *Bracebridge Hall* came to be called the "English *Sketch Book*."

Bracebridge Hall sold well but did not receive resounding critical praise. And Irving's next collection, *Tales of a Traveller* (1824), drew bad reviews outright. At this point Irving's career, which had already shifted from youthful satires to genial sketches, took a successful turn into history and biography, genres that had been lampooned in Knickerbocker's *History of New-York*. Joining the American legation in Madrid, Irving seized the opportunity to reshape historical documents and Spanish works into the *Life and Voyages of Christopher Columbus* (1828). This he followed with *Chronicle of the Conquest of Granada* (1829), *Voyages and Discoveries of the Companions of Columbus* (1831), and another popular collection of sketches, *The Alhambra* (1832), later called the "Spanish *Sketch Book*." These Spanish works secured Irving's reputation, although he had already left Spain to join the American legation in London. In 1831 he received an honorary degree from Oxford University, and in 1832, after seventeen years' absence, he returned to his native land.

Perhaps sensitive to critical doubts about his Americanness, Irving immediately avowed his love for his country and set about demonstrating it in works about the American West. He traveled to the Oklahoma frontier and drew on that experience for *A Tour on the Prairies* (1835). Two other western books came by way of the library: *Astoria* (1836) and *Adventures of Captain Bonneville* (1837) are second-hand celebrations of American expansion. Settling at Sunnyside, his home near Tarrytown, New York (by Sleepy Hollow Valley), Irving composed no major works between 1837 and 1842. He then resumed government service, first as U.S. minister to Spain and later, in London, as an American publicist on the Oregon Question (a disagreement over who had the rights to the Oregon Territory— America or England). Two major projects dominated his later years. The fifteen-volume Author's Revised Edition (1848–1851) of his histories and fiction offered him an occasion to smooth some of the remaining edges in his earlier works. But the greatest achievement of the final years—and, to Irving's mind, of his career—was the five-volume *Life of Washington* (1855–1859), a biography of his namesake, George Washington. Conceived in 1825, begun in the 1840s, and completed only months before his death in 1859, *Life of Washington* crowned Irving's work by reforging the link between "the Father of His Country" and the author who was popularly understood to be his literary counterpart.

Suggested Readings: *The Complete Works of Washington Irving,* 19 of 27 vols. completed, ed. R. D. Rust, 1960– . S. T. Williams, *The Life of Washington Irving,* 2 vols., 1935. W. L. Hedges, *Washington Irving: An America Study,* 1965. H. Springer, *Washington Irving: A Reference Guide,* 1976. M. Roth, *Comedy and America: The Lost World of Washington Irving,* 1976. A. B. Myers, ed., *A Century of Commentary on the Works of Washington Irving,* 1976. M. W. Bowden, *Washington Irving,* 1981. S. Browdin, ed., *The Old and New World Romanticism of Washington Irving,*

1986. J. Rubin-Dorsky, *Adrift in the Old World: The Psychological Pilgrimage of Washington Irving*, 1988.

Text Used: *The Sketch Book of Geoffrey Crayon, Gent.*, ed. H. Springer, from *The Complete Works of Washington Irving*, Vol. VIII, 1978.

from **THE SKETCH BOOK OF GEOFFREY CRAYON, GENT.***

THE AUTHOR'S ACCOUNT OF HIMSELF

> *I am of this mind with Homer, that as the snaile that crept out of her shel was turned eftsoones into a Toad, and thereby was forced to make a stoole to sit on; so the traveller that stragleth from his owne country is in a short time transformed into so monstrous a shape that he is faine to alter his mansion with his manners and to live where he can, not where he would.*
>
> LYLY'S EUPHUES[1]

I was always fond of visiting new scenes and observing strange characters and manners. Even when a mere child I began my travels and made many tours of discovery into foreign parts and unknown regions of my native city; to the frequent alarm of my parents and the emolument of the town cryer.[2] As I grew into boyhood I extended the range of my observations. My holyday afternoons were spent in rambles about the surrounding country. I made myself familiar with all its places famous in history or fable. I knew every spot where a murder or robbery had been committed or a ghost seen. I visited the neighbouring villages and added greatly to my stock of knowledge, by noting their habits and customs, and conversing with their sages and great men. I even journeyed one long summer's day to the summit of the most distant hill, from whence I stretched my eye over many a mile of terra incognita,[3] and was astonished to find how vast a globe I inhabited.

This rambling propensity strengthened with my years. Books of voyages and travels became my passion, and in devouring their contents I neglected the regular exercises of the school. How wistfully would I wander about the pier heads in fine weather, and watch the parting ships, bound to distant climes. With what longing eyes would I gaze after their lessening sails, and waft myself in imagination to the ends of the earth.

Further reading and thinking, though they brought this vague inclination into more reasonable bounds, only served to make it more decided. I visited various parts of my own country, and had I been merely a lover of fine scenery, I should have felt little desire to seek elsewhere its gratification, for on no country have the

---

* Written under the pseudonym of Geoffrey Crayon, Gent., *The Sketch Book* was published serially in the United States in 1819 and 1820 and in England in 1820. This first version includes "The Author's Account of Himself" and "Rip Van Winkle." Irving later expanded *The Sketch Book* to a total of thirty-two tales and sketches.

[1] From *Euphues and His England* (1580), by John Lyly (1554?–1606). The epigraph serves as a mock warning about travel to the confirmed traveler, Geoffrey Crayon.

[2] Here the "town cryer" was paid to announce that a child was lost.

[3] "Unknown land" (Latin); frequently used on early maps.

charms of nature been more prodigally lavished. Her mighty lakes, like oceans of liquid silver; her mountains with their bright aerial tints; her valleys teeming with wild fertility; her tremendous cataracts thundering in their solitudes; her boundless plains waving with spontaneous verdure; her broad deep rivers, rolling in solemn silence to the ocean; her trackless forests, where vegetation puts forth all its magnificence; her skies kindling with the magic of summer clouds and glorious sunshine—no, never need an American look beyond his own country for the sublime and beautiful of natural scenery.

But Europe held forth the charms of storied and poetical association. There were to be seen the masterpieces of art, the refinements of highly cultivated society, the quaint peculiarities of ancient and local custom. My native country was full of youthful promise; Europe was rich in the accumulated treasures of age. Her very ruins told the history of times gone by, and every mouldering stone was a chronicle. I longed to wander over the scenes of renowned achievement—to tread as it were in the footsteps of antiquity—to loiter about the ruined castle—to meditate on the falling tower—to escape in short, from the commonplace realities of the present, and lose myself among the shadowy grandeurs of the past.

I had, beside all this, an earnest desire to see the great men of the earth. We have, it is true, our great men in America—not a city but has an ample share of them. I have mingled among them in my time, and been almost withered by the shade into which they cast me; for there is nothing so baleful to a small man as the shade of a great one, particularly the great man of a city. But I was anxious to see the great men of Europe; for I had read in the works of various philosophers, that all animals degenerated in America, and man among the number.[4] A great man of Europe, thought I, must therefore be as superior to a great man of America, as a peak of the Alps to a highland of the Hudson; and in this idea I was confirmed by observing the comparative importance and swelling magnitude of many English travellers among us; who, I was assured, were very little people in their own country.—I will visit this land of wonders, thought I, and see the gigantic race from which I am degenerated.

It has been either my good or evil lot to have my roving passion gratified. I have wandered through different countries and witnessed many of the shifting scenes of life. I cannot say that I have studied them with the eye of a philosopher, but rather with the sauntering gaze with which humble lovers of the picturesque stroll from the window of one print shop to another; caught sometimes by the delineations of beauty, sometimes by the distortions of caricature and sometimes by the loveliness of landscape. As it is the fashion for modern tourists to travel pencil in hand, and bring home their portfolios filled with sketches, I am disposed to get up a few for the entertainment of my friends. When I look over, however, the hints and memorandums I have taken down for the purpose, my heart almost fails me at finding how my idle humour has led me aside from the great objects studied by every regular traveller who would make a book. I fear I shall give equal disappointment with an unlucky landscape painter, who had travelled on the continent, but following the bent of his vagrant inclination, had sketched in nooks and

---

[4] In his influential *Natural History* (44 vols., 1749–1788), the French scientist George Louis Leclerc de Buffon (1707–1788) maintained that the environment in America would cause animals and humans to degenerate. After Thomas Jefferson sent him a panther skin, the skeleton of a moose, and a copy of Jefferson's *Notes on the State of Virginia* (1785), Buffon changed his view.

corners and bye places. His sketch book was accordingly crowded with cottages, and landscapes, and obscure ruins; but he had neglected to paint St. Peter's or the Coliseum; the cascade of Terni[5] or the Bay of Naples; and had not a single Glacier or Volcano in his whole collection.

1819

RIP VAN WINKLE

The following Tale was found among the papers of the late Diedrich Knicker-bocker, an old gentleman of New York, who was very curious in the Dutch history of the province, and the manners of the descendants from its primitive settlers. His historical researches, however, did not lie so much among books, as among men; for the former are lamentably scanty on his favourite topics; whereas he found the old burghers,[1] and still more, their wives, rich in that legendary lore so invaluable to true history. Whenever, therefore, he happened upon a genuine Dutch family, snugly shut up in its low roofed farm house, under a spreading sycamore, he looked upon it as a little clasped volume of black letter,[2] and studied it with the zeal of a bookworm.

The result of all these researches was a history of the province, during the reign of the Dutch governors, which he published some years since. There have been various opinions as to the literary character of his work and, to tell the truth, it is not a whit better than it should be. Its chief merit is its scrupulous accuracy, which indeed was a little questioned on its first appearance, but has since been completely established; and it is now admitted into all historical collections as a book of unquestionable authority.[3]

The old gentleman died shortly after the publication of his work, and now that he is dead and gone, it cannot do much harm to his memory to say that his time might have been much better employed in weightier labours. He, however, was apt to ride his hobby his own way; and though it did now and then kick up the dust a little in the eyes of his neighbours, and grieve the spirit of some friends for whom he felt the truest deference and affection; yet his errors and follies are remembered "more in sorrow than in anger,"[4] and it begins to be suspected that he never intended to injure or offend. But however his memory may be appreciated by criticks, it is still held dear by many folk whose good opinion is well worth having; particularly by certain biscuit bakers, who have gone so far as to imprint his likeness on their new year cakes, and have thus given him a chance for immor-

---

[5] St Peter's Cathedral in Rome is the largest church in the world; the Coliseum, an amphitheater in Rome, is a famous ruin dating from the first century A.D.; the cascade of Terni is a waterfall in northern Italy.

[1] Inhabitants of boroughs or towns.

[2] A typeface used in early printed books, now called Gothic or Old English. Some of these books had clasps so they could be snapped shut.

[3] Irving refers to his comic *History of New-York* (1809), "written" by his earlier persona, Diedrich Knickerbocker, whose extravagant pedantry is comic but hardly accurate.

[4] From Shakespeare's *Hamlet*, (I.1.232).

tality, almost equal to being stamped on a Waterloo medal, or a Queen Anne's farthing.[5]

Rip Van Winkle[6]

A POSTHUMOUS WRITING OF DIEDRICH KNICKERBOCKER

> By Woden,[7] God of Saxons,
> From whence comes Wensday, that is Wodensday,
> Truth is a thing that ever I will keep
> Unto thylke[8] day in which I creep into
> My sepulchre—
>
> CARTWRIGHT [9]

Whoever has made a voyage up the Hudson must remember the Kaatskill mountains.[10] They are a dismembered branch of the great Appalachian family, and are seen away to the west of the river swelling up to noble height and lording it over the surrounding country. Every change of season, every change of weather, indeed every hour of the day, produces some change in the magical hues and shapes of these mountains, and they are regarded by all the good wives far and near as perfect barometers. When the weather is fair and settled they are clothed in blue and purple, and print their bold outlines on the clear evening sky; but sometimes, when the rest of the landscape is cloudless, they will gather a hood of grey vapours about their summits, which, in the last rays of the setting sun, will glow and light up like a crown of glory.

At the foot of these fairy mountains the voyager may have descried the light smoke curling up from a village, whose shingle roofs gleam among the trees, just where the blue tints of the upland melt away into the fresh green of the nearer landscape. It is a little village of great antiquity, having been founded by some of the Dutch colonists in the early times of the province, just about the beginning of the government of the good Peter Stuyvesant,[11] (may he rest in peace!) and there were some of the houses of the original settlers standing within a few years; built of small yellow bricks brought from Holland, having latticed windows and gable fronts, surmounted with weathercocks.

---

[5] Waterloo medals, commemorating the British victory over Napoleon in 1815, were issued to everyone who took part in the historic battle; Queen Anne's farthings were small, supposedly rare coins minted during the reign of Queen Anne (1702–1714).

[6] In both "Rip Van Winkle" and "The Legend of Sleepy Hollow," Irving adapted German folk legends to American settings. His immediate source for "Rip" is J. C. C. N. Otmar's "Peter Klaus" (1800), in which the protagonist sleeps for twenty years. Irving brings the tale to America and has Rip Van Winkle sleep through the American Revolution.

[7] According to Norse myth, the supreme god and creator.   [8] "The" or "that".

[9] From the play *The Ordinary* (1651) (III.1. 1050–1054), by William Cartwright (1611–1643), an English clergyman, poet, and dramatist.

[10] The Catskill Mountains in southeastern New York.

[11] Stuyvesant (1592–1672) served as the last governor of New Netherlands from 1647 to 1664. In 1655 he led the Dutch forces to victory over Swedish colonists at Fort Christina, near what is now Wilmington, Delaware, as described in mock-epic terms in Knickerbocker's *History of New-York*.

In that same village, and in one of these very houses (which to tell the precise truth was sadly time worn and weather beaten) there lived many years since, while the country was yet a province of Great Britain, a simple good natured fellow of the name of Rip Van Winkle. He was a descendant of the Van Winkles who figured so gallantly in the chivalrous days of Peter Stuyvesant, and accompanied him to the siege of Fort Christina. He inherited, however, but little of the martial character of his ancestors. I have observed that he was a simple good natured man; he was moreover a kind neighbour, and an obedient, henpecked husband. Indeed to the latter circumstance might be owing that meekness of spirit which gained him such universal popularity; for those men are most apt to be obsequious and conciliating abroad, who are under the discipline of shrews at home. Their tempers doubtless are rendered pliant and malleable in the fiery furnace of domestic tribulation, and a curtain lecture[12] is worth all the sermons in the world for teaching the virtues of patience and long suffering. A termagant wife may therefore in some respects be considered a tolerable blessing—and if so, Rip Van Winkle was thrice blessed.

Certain it is that he was a great favourite among all the good wives of the village, who as usual with the amiable sex, took his part in all family squabbles, and never failed, whenever they talked those matters over in their evening gossippings, to lay all the blame on Dame Van Winkle. The children of the village too would shout with joy whenever he approached. He assisted at their sports, made their play things, taught them to fly kites and shoot marbles, and told them long stories of ghosts, witches and Indians. Whenever he went dodging about the village he was surrounded by a troop of them hanging on his skirts, clambering on his back and playing a thousand tricks on him with impunity; and not a dog would bark at him throughout the neighbourhood.

The great error in Rip's composition was an insuperable aversion to all kinds of profitable labour. It could not be from the want of assiduity or perseverance; for he would sit on a wet rock, with a rod as long and heavy as a Tartar's lance, and fish all day without a murmur, even though he should not be encouraged by a single nibble. He would carry a fowling piece on his shoulder for hours together, trudging through woods, and swamps and up hill and down dale, to shoot a few squirrels or wild pigeons; he would never refuse to assist a neighbour even in the roughest toil, and was a foremost man at all country frolicks for husking Indian corn, or building stone fences; the women of the village too used to employ him to run their errands and to do such little odd jobs as their less obliging husbands would not do for them—in a word Rip was ready to attend to any body's business but his own; but as to doing family duty, and keeping his farm in order, he found it impossible.

In fact he declared it was of no use to work on his farm; it was the most pestilent little piece of ground in the whole country; everything about it went wrong and would go wrong in spite of him. His fences were continually falling to pieces; his cow would either go astray or get among the cabbages, weeds were sure to grow quicker in his fields than any where else; the rain always made a point of setting in just as he had some outdoor work to do. So that though his patrimonial estate had dwindled away under his management, acre by acre until there was little more left than a mere patch of Indian corn and potatoes, yet it was the worst conditioned farm in the neighbourhood.

---

[12] A scolding of a husband by his wife after the bed curtains have been drawn.

His children too were as ragged and wild as if they belonged to nobody. His son Rip, an urchin begotten in his own likeness, promised to inherit the habits with the old clothes of his father. He was generally seen trooping like a colt at his mother's heels, equipped in a pair of his father's cast off galligaskins,[13] which he had much ado to hold up with one hand, as a fine lady does her train in bad weather.

Rip Van Winkle, however, was one of those happy mortals of foolish, well oiled dispositions, who take the world easy, eat white bread or brown, whichever can be got with least thought or trouble, and would rather starve on a penny than work for a pound. If left to himself, he would have whistled life away in perfect contentment, but his wife kept continually dinning in his ears about his idleness, his carelessness and the ruin he was bringing on his family. Morning noon and night her tongue was incessantly going, and every thing he said or did was sure to produce a torrent of household eloquence. Rip had but one way of replying to all lectures of the kind, and that by frequent use had grown into a habit. He shrugged his shoulders, shook his head, cast up his eyes, but said nothing. This, however, always provoked a fresh volley from his wife, so that he was fain to draw off his forces and take to the outside of the house—the only side which in truth belongs to a henpecked husband.

Rip's sole domestic adherent was his dog Wolf who was as much henpecked as his master, for Dame Van Winkle regarded them as companions in idleness, and even looked upon Wolf with an evil eye as the cause of his master's going so often astray. True it is, in all points of spirit befitting an honourable dog, he was as courageous an animal as ever scoured the woods—but what courage can withstand the ever during and all besetting terrors of a woman's tongue? The moment Wolf entered the house his crest fell, his tail drooped to the ground or curled between his legs, he sneaked about with a gallows air, casting many a sidelong glance at Dame Van Winkle, and at the least flourish of a broomstick or ladle he would fly to the door with yelping precipitation.

Times grew worse and worse with Rip Van Winkle as years of matrimony rolled on; a tart temper never mellows with age, and a sharp tongue is the only edged tool that grows keener with constant use. For a long while he used to console himself when driven from home, by frequenting a kind of perpetual club of the sages, philosophers and other idle personages of the village which held its sessions on a bench before a small inn, designated by a rubicund portrait of his majesty George the Third. Here they used to sit in the shade, through a long lazy summer's day, talking listlessly over village gossip, or telling endless sleepy stories about nothing. But it would have been worth any statesman's money to have heard the profound discussions that sometimes took place, when by chance an old newspaper fell into their hands from some passing traveller. How solemnly they would listen to the contents as drawled out by Derrick Van Bummel the schoolmaster, a dapper, learned little man, who was not to be daunted by the most gigantic word in the dictionary; and how sagely they would deliberate upon public events some months after they had taken place.

The opinions of this junto[14] were completely controlled by Nicholaus Vedder, a patriarch of the village, and landlord of the inn, at the door of which he took his seat from morning till night, just moving sufficiently to avoid the sun and keep in

---

[13] Loose breeches or pants.

[14] A committee; "a club of the sages," as Irving describes these men with mild irony.

the shade of a large tree; so that the neighbours could tell the hour by his movements as accurately as by a sun dial. It is true he was rarely heard to speak, but smoked his pipe incessantly. His adherents, however (for every great man has his adherents), perfectly understood him and knew how to gather his opinions. When any thing that was read or related displeased him, he was observed to smoke his pipe vehemently and to send forth short, frequent and angry puffs; but when pleased he would inhale the smoke slowly and tranquilly and emit it in light and placid clouds, and sometimes taking the pipe from his mouth and letting the fragrant vapour curl about his nose, would gravely nod his head in token of perfect approbation.

From even this strong hold the unlucky Rip was at length routed by his termagant wife who would suddenly break in upon the tranquility of the assemblage and call the members all to naught; nor was that august personage Nicholaus Vedder himself sacred from the daring tongue of this terrible virago, who charged him outright with encouraging her husband in habits of idleness.

Poor Rip was at last reduced almost to despair; and his only alternative to escape from the labour of the farm and the clamour of his wife, was to take gun in hand and stroll away into the woods. Here he would sometimes seat himself at the foot of a tree and share the contents of his wallet[15] with Wolf, with whom he sympathised as a fellow sufferer in persecution. "Poor Wolf," he would say, "thy mistress leads thee a dog's life of it, but never mind my lad, whilst I live thou shalt never want a friend to stand by thee!" Wolf would wag his tail, look wistfully in his master's face, and if dogs can feel pity I verily believe he reciprocated the sentiment with all his heart.

In a long ramble of the kind on a fine autumnal day, Rip had unconsciously scrambled to one of the highest parts of the Kaatskill mountains. He was after his favourite sport of squirrel shooting and the still solitudes had echoed and re-echoed with the reports of his gun. Panting and fatigued he threw himself, late in the afternoon, on a green knoll, covered with mountain herbage, that crowned the brow of a precipice. From an opening between the trees he could overlook all the lower country for many a mile of rich woodland. He saw at a distance the lordly Hudson, far, far below him, moving on its silent but majestic course, with the reflection of a purple cloud, or the sail of a lagging bark here and there sleeping on its glassy bosom, and at last losing itself in the blue highlands.

On the other side he looked down into a deep mountain glen, wild, lonely and shagged, the bottom filled with fragments from the impending cliffs and scarcely lighted by the reflected rays of the setting sun. For some time Rip lay musing on this scene, evening was gradually advancing, the mountains began to throw their long blue shadows over the valleys, he saw that it would be dark, long before he could reach the village, and he heaved a heavy sigh when he thought of encountering the terrors of Dame Van Winkle.

As he was about to descend he heard a voice from a distance hallooing "Rip Van Winkle! Rip Van Winkle!" He looked around, but could see nothing but a crow winging its solitary flight across the mountain. He thought his fancy must have deceived him and turned again to descend, which he heard the same cry ring through the still evening air: "Rip Van Winkle! Rip Van Winkle!"—at the same time Wolf bristled up his back and giving a low growl, skulked to his master's side, looking fearfully down into the glen. Rip now felt a vague apprehension

---

[15] A pouch or knapsack.

stealing over him; he looked anxiously in the same direction and perceived a strange figure slowly toiling up the rocks and bending under the weight of something he carried on his back. He was surprised to see any human being in this lonely and unfrequented place, but supposing it to be some one of the neighbourhood in need of his assistance he hastened down to yield it.

On nearer approach he was still more surprised at the singularity of the stranger's appearance. He was a short, square built old fellow, with thick bushy hair and a grizzled beard. His dress was of the antique Dutch fashion, a cloth jerkin[16] strapped round the waist, several pair of breeches, the outer one of ample volume decorated with rows of buttons down the sides and bunches at the knees. He bore on his shoulder a stout keg that seemed full of liquor, and made signs for Rip to approach and assist him with the load. Though rather shy and distrustful of this new acquaintance Rip complied with his usual alacrity, and mutually relieving each other they clambered up a narrow gully apparently the dry bed of a mountain torrent. As they ascended Rip every now and then heard long rolling peals like distant thunder, that seemed to issue out of a deep ravine or rather cleft between lofty rocks, toward which their rugged path conducted. He paused for an instant, but supposing it to be the muttering of one of those transient thunder showers which often take place in mountain heights, he proceeded. Passing through the ravine they came to a hollow like a small amphitheatre, surrounded by perpendicular precipices, over the brinks of which impending trees shot their branches, so that you only caught glimpses of the azure sky and the bright evening cloud. During the whole time Rip and his companion had laboured on in silence, for though the former marvelled greatly what could be the object of carrying a keg of liquor up this wild mountain, yet there was something strange and incomprehensible about the unknown, that inspired awe and checked familiarity.

On entering the amphitheatre new objects of wonder presented themselves. On a level spot in the centre was a company of odd looking personages playing at ninepins. They were dressed in a quaint outlandish fashion—some wore short doublets,[17] others jerkins with long knives in their belts and most of them had enormous breeches of similar style with that of the guide's. Their visages too were peculiar. One had a large head, broad face and small piggish eyes. The face of another seemed to consist entirely of nose, and was surmounted by a white sugarloaf hat, set off with a little red cock's tail. They all had beards of various shapes and colours. There was one who seemed to be the Commander. He was a stout old gentleman, with a weatherbeaten countenance. He wore a laced doublet, broad belt and hanger,[18] high crowned hat and feather, red stockings and high heel'd shoes with roses in them. The whole group reminded Rip of the figures in an old Flemish painting, in the parlour of Dominie[19] Van Schaick the village parson, and which had been brought over from Holland at the time of the settlement.

What seemed particularly odd to Rip was, that though these folks were evidently amusing themselves, yet they maintained the gravest faces, the most mysterious silence, and were, withal, the most melancholy party of pleasure he had ever witnessed. Nothing interrupted the stillness of the scene, but the noise of the balls, which, whenever they were rolled, echoed along the mountains like rumbling peals of thunder.

[16] A jacket or short coat, generally armless.   [17] A close-fitting, commonly elaborate jacket.
[18] A short sword, originally hung from the belt.   [19] Pastor.

As Rip and his companion approached them they suddenly desisted from their play and stared at him with such fixed statue like gaze, and such strange uncouth, lack lustre countenances, that his heart turned within him, and his knees smote together. His companion now emptied the contents of the keg into large flagons and made signs to him to wait upon the company. He obeyed with fear and trembling; they quaffed the liquor in profound silence and then returned to their game.

By degrees Rip's awe and apprehension subsided. He even ventured, when no eye was fixed upon him, to taste the beverage, which he found had much of the flavour of excellent hollands.[20] He was naturally a thirsty soul and was soon tempted to repeat the draught. One taste provoked another, and he reiterated his visits to the flagon so often that at length his senses were overpowered, his eyes swam in his head—his head gradually declined and he fell into a deep sleep.

On awaking he found himself on the green knoll from whence he had first seen the old man of the glen. He rubbed his eyes—it was a bright, sunny morning. The birds were hopping and twittering among the bushes, and the eagle was wheeling aloft and breasting the pure mountain breeze. "Surely," thought Rip, "I have not slept here all night." He recalled the occurrences before he fell asleep. The strange man with a keg of liquor—the mountain ravine—the wild retreat among the rocks—the woe begone party at ninepins—the flagon—"ah! that flagon! that wicked flagon!" thought Rip—"what excuse shall I make to Dame Van Winkle?"

He looked round for his gun, but in place of the clean well oiled fowling piece he found an old firelock lying by him, the barrel encrusted with rust; the lock falling off and the stock worm eaten. He now suspected that the grave roysters of the mountain had put a trick upon him, and having dosed him with liquor, had robbed him of his gun. Wolf too had disappeared, but he might have strayed away after a squirrel or partridge. He whistled after him and shouted his name—but all in vain; the echoes repeated his whistle and shout, but no dog was to be seen.

He determined to revisit the scene of the last evening's gambol, and if he met with any of the party, to demand his dog and gun. As he arose to walk he found himself stiff in the joints and wanting in his usual activity. "These mountain beds do not agree with me," thought Rip, "and if this frolick should lay me up with a fit of the rheumatism, I shall have a blessed time with Dame Van Winkle." With some difficulty he got down into the glen; he found the gully up which he and his companion had ascended the preceding evening, but to his astonishment a mountain stream was now foaming down it; leaping from rock to rock, and filling the glen with babbling murmurs. He, however, made shift to scramble up its sides working his toilsome way through thickets of birch, sassafras and witch hazel, and sometimes tripped up or entangled by the wild grape vines that twisted their coils and tendrils from tree to tree, and spread a kind of net work in his path.

At length he reached to where the ravine had opened through the cliffs, to the amphitheatre—but no traces of such opening remained. The rocks presented a high impenetrable wall over which the torrent came tumbling in a sheet of feathery foam, and fell into a broad deep basin black from the shadows of the surrounding forest. Here then poor Rip was brought to a stand. He again called and whistled after his dog—he was only answered by the cawing of a flock of idle crows, sporting high in air about a dry tree that overhung a sunny precipice; and who, secure in their elevation seemed to look down and scoff at the poor man's perplexities.

---

[20] Dutch gin.

What was to be done? The morning was passing away and Rip felt famished for want of his breakfast. He grieved to give up his dog and gun; he dreaded to meet his wife; but it would not do to starve among the mountains. He shook his head, shouldered the rusty fire lock and with a heart full of trouble and anxiety, turned his steps homeward.

As he approached the village he met a number of people, but none whom he knew, which somewhat surprised him, for he had thought himself acquainted with every one in the country round. Their dress too was of a different fashion from that to which he was accustomed. They all stared at him with equal marks of surprise, and whenever they cast their eyes upon him, invariably stroked their chins. The constant recurrence of this gesture induced Rip involuntarily to do the same, when to his astonishment he found his beard had grown a foot long!

He had now entered the skirts of the village. A troop of strange children ran at his heels, hooting after him and pointing at his grey beard. The dogs too, not one of which he recognized for an old acquaintance, barked at him as he passed. The very village was altered—it was larger and more populous. There were rows of houses which he had never seen before, and those which had been his familiar haunts had disappeared. Strange names were over the doors—strange faces at the windows—every thing was strange. His mind now misgave him; he began to doubt whether both he and the world around him were not bewitched. Surely this was his native village which he had left but the day before. There stood the Kaatskill mountains—there ran the silver Hudson at a distance—there was every hill and dale precisely as it had always been—Rip was sorely perplexed—"That flagon last night," thought he, —"has addled my poor head sadly!"

It was with some difficulty that he found the way to his own house, which he approached with silent awe, expecting every moment to hear the shrill voice of Dame Van Winkle. He found the house gone to decay—the roof fallen in, the windows shattered and the doors off the hinges. A half starved dog that looked like Wolf was skulking about it. Rip called him by name but the cur snarled, shewed his teeth and passed on. This was an unkind cut indeed—"My very dog," sighed poor Rip, "has forgotten me!"

He entered the house, which, to tell the truth, Dame Van Winkle had always kept in neat order. It was empty, forlorn and apparently abandoned. This desolateness overcame all his connubial fears—he called loudly for his wife and children—the lonely chambers rung for a moment with his voice, and then all again was silence.

He now hurried forth and hastened to his old resort, the village inn—but it too was gone. A large, ricketty wooden building stood in its place, with great gaping windows, some of them broken, and mended with old hats and petticoats, and over the door was printed "The Union Hotel, by Jonathan Doolittle." Instead of the great tree, that used to shelter the quiet little Dutch inn of yore, there now was reared a tall naked pole with something on top that looked like a red night cap,[21] and from it was fluttering a flag on which was a singular assemblage of stars and stripes—all this was strange and incomprehensible. He recognized on the sign, however, the ruby face of King George under which he had smoked so many a peaceful pipe, but even this was singularly metamorphosed. The red coat was

---

[21] A liberty pole and liberty cap, or Phrygian cap worn by slaves freed by the Romans, symbols of the American and French Revolutions.

changed for one of blue and buff;[22] a sword was held in the hand instead of a sceptre; the head was decorated with a cocked hat, and underneath was printed in large characters GENERAL WASHINGTON.

There was as usual a crowd of folk about the door; but none that Rip recollected. The very character of the people seemed changed. There was a busy, bustling disputatious tone about it, instead of the accustomed phlegm and drowsy tranquility. He looked in vain for the sage Nicholaus Vedder with his broad face, double chin and fair long pipe, uttering clouds of tobacco smoke instead of idle speeches. Or Van Bummel the schoolmaster doling forth the contents of an ancient newspaper. In place of these a lean bilious looking fellow with his pockets full of hand bills, was haranguing vehemently about rights of citizens—elections—members of Congress—liberty—Bunker's hill—heroes of seventy six—and other words which were a perfect babylonish jargon[23] to the bewildered Van Winkle.

The appearance of Rip with his long grizzled beard, his rusty fowling piece,[24] his uncouth dress and an army of women and children at his heels soon attracted the attention of the tavern politicians. They crowded around him eying him from head to foot, with great curiosity. The orator bustled up to him, and drawing him partly aside, enquired "on which side he voted?"—Rip stared in vacant stupidity. Another short but busy little fellow, pulled him by the arm and rising on tiptoe, enquired in his ear "whether he was Federal or Democrat?"[25]—Rip was equally at a loss to comprehend the question—when a knowing, self important old gentleman, in a sharp cocked hat, made his way through the crowd, putting them to the right and left with his elbows as he passed, and planting himself before Van Winkle, with one arm akimbo, the other resting on his cane, his keen eyes and sharp hat penetrating as it were into his very soul, demanded in an austere tone—"what brought him to the election with a gun on his shoulder and a mob at his heels, and whether he meant to breed a riot in the village?"—"Alas gentlemen," cried Rip, somewhat dismayed, "I am a poor quiet man, a native of the place, and a loyal subject of the King—God bless him!"

Here a general shout burst from the byestanders—"A tory! a tory! a spy! a Refugee! hustle him! away with him!"—It was with great difficulty that the self important man in the cocked hat restored order; and having assumed a ten fold austerity of brow demanded again of the unknown culprit, what he came there for and whom he was seeking. The poor man humbly assured him that he meant no harm; but merely came there in search of some of his neighbours, who used to keep about the tavern.

"—Well—who are they?—name them."

Rip bethought himself a moment and enquired, "Where's Nicholaus Vedder?"

There was a silence for a little while, when an old man replied, in a thin, piping voice, "Nicholaus Vedder? why he is dead and gone these eighteen years! There was a wooden tombstone in the church yard that used to tell all about him, but that's rotted and gone too."

"Where's Brom Dutcher?"

[22] Colors of Revolutionary Army uniforms.
[23] A puzzle; in Genesis 11:1–9 the "Confusion of Tongues" occurs at the Tower of Babel (Babel is apparently confused with Babylon).
[24] A shotgun for killing fowl.
[25] Political parties that grew during George Washington's administration: the first conservative, the second liberal.

"Oh he went off to the army in the beginning of the war; some say he was killed at the storming of Stoney Point—others say he was drowned in a squall at the foot of Antony's Nose[26]—I don't know—he never came back again."

"Where's Van Bummel the schoolmaster?"

"He went off to the wars too—was a great militia general, and is now in Congress."

Rip's heart died away at hearing of these sad changes in his home and friends, and finding himself thus alone in the world—every answer puzzled him too by treating of such enormous lapses of time and of matters which he could not understand—war—Congress, Stoney Point—he had no courage to ask after any more friends, but cried out in despair, "Does nobody here know Rip Van Winkle?"

"Oh. Rip Van Winkle?" exclaimed two or three—oh to be sure!—that's Rip Van Winkle—yonder—leaning against the tree."

Rip looked and beheld a precise counterpart of himself, as he went up the mountain: apparently as lazy and certainly as ragged! The poor fellow was now completely confounded. He doubted his own identity, and whether he was himself or another man. In the midst of his bewilderment the man in the cocked hat demanded who he was,—what was his name?

"God knows," exclaimed he, at his wit's end. "I'm not myself.—I'm somebody else—that's me yonder—no—that's somebody else got into my shoes—I was myself last night; but I fell asleep on the mountain—and they've changed my gun—and every thing's changed—and I'm changed—and I can't tell what's my name, or who I am!"

The byestanders began now to look at each other, nod, wink significantly and tap their fingers against their foreheads. There was a whisper also about securing the gun, and keeping the old fellow from doing mischief—at the very suggestion of which, the self important man in the cocked hat retired with some precipitation. At this critical moment a fresh likely looking woman pressed through the throng to get a peep at the greybearded man. She had a chubby child in her arms, which frightened at his looks began to cry. "Hush Rip," cried she, "hush you little fool, the old man won't hurt you." The name of the child, the air of the mother, the tone of her voice all awakened a train of recollections in his mind. "What is your name my good woman?" asked he.

"Judith Gardenier."

"And your father's name?"

"Ah, poor man, Rip Van Winkle was his name, but it's twenty years since he went away from home with his gun and never has been heard of since—his dog came home without him—but whether he shot himself, or was carried away by the Indians no body can tell. I was then but a little girl."

Rip had but one question more to ask, but he put it with a faltering voice—

"Where's your mother?"

Oh she too had died but a short time since—she broke a blood vessel in a fit of passion at a New England pedlar.—

There was a drop of comfort at least in this intelligence. The honest man could contain himself no longer—he caught his daughter and her child in his arms.—"I am your father!" cried he—"Young Rip Van Winkle once—old Rip Van Winkle now!—does nobody know poor Rip Van Winkle!"

[26] In July 1779 General Anthony Wayne (1745–1796) captured the British fort at Stony Point, on the Hudson River; Antony's Nose is a promontory on the Hudson, near West Point.

All stood amazed, until an old woman tottering out from among the crowd put her hand to her brow and peering under it in his face for a moment exclaimed— "Sure enough!—it is Rip Van Winkle—it is himself—welcome home again old neighbour—why, where have you been these twenty long years?"

Rip's story was soon told, for the whole twenty years had been to him but as one night. The neighbours stared when they heard it; some were seen to wink at each other and put their tongues in their cheeks, and the self important man in the cocked hat, who when the alarm was over had returned to the field, screwed down the corners of his mouth and shook his head—upon which there was a general shaking of the head throughout the assemblage.

It was determined, however, to take the opinion of old Peter Vanderdonk, who was seen slowly advancing up the road. He was a descendant of the historian of that name,[27] who wrote one of the earliest accounts of the province. Peter was the most ancient inhabitant of the village and well versed in all the wonderful events and traditions of the neighbourhood. He recollected Rip at once, and corroborated his story in the most satisfactory manner. He assured the company that it was a fact handed down from his ancestor the historian, that the Kaatskill mountains had always been haunted by strange beings. That it was affirmed that the great Hendrick Hudson,[28] the first discoverer of the river and country, kept a kind of vigil there every twenty years, with his crew of the Half Moon—being permitted in this way to revisit the scenes of his enterprize and keep a guardian eye upon the river and the great city called by his name. That his father had once seen them in their old Dutch dresses playing at nine pins in a hollow of the mountain; and that he himself had heard one summer afternoon the sound of their balls, like distant peals of thunder.

To make a long story short—the company broke up, and returned to the more important concerns of the election. Rip's daughter took him home to live with her; she had a snug well furnished house, and a stout cheery farmer for a husband whom Rip recollected for one of the urchins that used to climb upon his back. As to Rip's son and heir, who was the ditto of himself seen leaning against the tree; he was employed to work on the farm; but evinced an hereditary disposition to attend to any thing else but his business.

Rip now resumed his old walks and habits; he soon found many of his former cronies, though all rather the worse for the wear and tear of time; and preferred making friends among the rising generation, with whom he soon grew into great favour. Having nothing to do at home, and being arrived at that happy age when a man can be idle, with impunity, he took his place once more on the bench at the inn door and was reverenced as one of the patriarchs of the village and a chronicle of the old times "before the war." It was some time before he could get into the regular track of gossip, or could be made to comprehend the strange events that had taken place during his torpor. How that there had been a revolutionary war— that the country had thrown off the yoke of Old England and that instead of being a subject of his majesty George the Third, he was now a free citizen of the United States. Rip in fact was no politician; the changes of states and empires made but little impression on him; but there was one species of despotism under which he

---

[27] Adriaen Van der Donck (1620?–1655), a Dutchman who wrote a history of New Netherland, published in Amsterdam in 1655 and (in an English translation) in New Netherland in 1656.

[28] Henry Hudson (?–1611), an English navigator employed by the Dutch to explore what is now call the Hudson River; Irving uses a Dutch form of the name Henry. The "great city called by his name" is Hudson, New York, on the East bank of the river.

had long groaned and that was petticoat government. Happily that was at an end—
he had got his neck out of the yoke of matrimony, and could go in and out whenever he pleased without dreading the tyranny of Dame Van Winkle. Whenever her
name was mentioned, however, he shook his head, shrugged his shoulders and
cast up his eyes; which might pass either for an expression of resignation to his
fate or joy at his deliverance.

He used to tell his story to every stranger that arrived at Mr. Doolittle's Hotel.
He was observed at first to vary on some points, every time he told it, which was
doubtless owing to his having so recently awaked. It at last settled down precisely
to the tale I have related and not a man woman or child in the neighbourhood but
knew it by heart. Some always pretended to doubt the reality of it, and insisted
that Rip had been out of his head, and that this was one point on which he always
remained flighty. The old Dutch inhabitants, however, almost universally gave it
full credit—Even to this day they never hear a thunder storm of a summer afternoon about the Kaatskill, but they say Hendrick Hudson and his crew are at their
game of nine pins; and it is a common wish of all henpecked husbands in the
neighbourhood, when life hangs heavy on their hands, that they might have a
quieting draught out of Rip Van Winkle's flagon.

NOTE

The foregoing tale one would suspect had been suggested to Mr. Knickerbocker
by a little German superstition about the emperor Frederick *der Rothbart* and the
Kypphauser Mountain;[29] the subjoined note, however, which he had appended to
the tale, shews that it is an absolute fact, narrated with his usual fidelity.—

"The story of Rip Van Winkle may seem incredible to many, but nevertheless I
give it my full belief, for I know the vicinity of our old Dutch settlements to have
been very subject to marvellous events and appearances. Indeed I have heard
many stranger stories than this, in the villages along the Hudson; all of which were
too well authenticated to admit of a doubt. I have even talked with Rip Van Winkle myself, who when last I saw him was a very venerable old man and so perfectly rational and consistent on every other point, that I think no conscientious
person could refuse to take this into the bargain—nay I have seen a certificate on
the subject taken before a country justice and signed with a cross in the justice's
own hand writing. The story therefore is beyond the possibility of doubt. D.K."

POSTSCRIPT

The following are travelling notes from a memorandum book of Mr. Knickerbocker.[30]

The Kaatsberg or Catskill mountains have always been a region full of fable.
The Indians considered them the abode of spirits who influenced the weather,
spreading sunshine or clouds over the landscape and sending good or bad hunting

---

[29] The "superstition" of Frederick Barbarossa, the Holy Roman Emperor Frederick I (1123?–1190),
asleep at a table in the Kyffhaüser Mountain of Germany: when his red beard (the translation of
Barbarossa [Latin] and *Rothbart* [German]) circles the table three times, he will awaken and lead
Germany to world preeminence.

[30] This postscript takes Irving's fiction back from post-Revolutionary days and the clutter of Dutch
colonial times to a region of peace ruled by Native-American legends. It traces a path to a mythic
source that flows into history and the present day, thus linking fable and fact.

seasons. They were ruled by an old squaw spirit, said to be their mother. She dwelt on the highest peak of the Catskills and had charge of the doors of day and night to open and shut them at the proper hour. She hung up the new moons in the skies and cut up the old ones into stars. In times of drought, if properly propitiated, she would spin light summer clouds out of cobwebs and morning dew, and send them off, from the crest of the mountain, flake after flake, like flakes of carded cotton to float in the air: until, dissolved by the heat of the sun, they would fall in gentle showers, causing the grass to spring, the fruits to ripen and the corn to grow an inch an hour. If displeased, however, she would brew up clouds black as ink, sitting in the midst of them like a bottle bellied spider in the midst of its web; and when these clouds broke—woe betide the valleys!

In old times say the Indian traditions, there was a kind of Manitou or Spirit, who kept about the wildest recesses of the Catskill mountains, and took a mischievous pleasure in wreaking all kinds of evils and vexations upon the red men. Sometimes he would assume the form of a bear a panther or a deer, lead the bewildered hunter a weary chace through tangled forests and among rugged rocks; and then spring off with a loud ho! ho! leaving him aghast on the brink of a beetling precipice or raging torrent.

The favorite abode of this Manitou is still shewn. It is a great rock or cliff in the loneliest part of the mountains, and, from the flowering vines which clamber about it, and the wild flowers which abound in its neighborhood, is known by the name of the Garden Rock. Near the foot of it is a small lake the haunt of the solitary bittern, with water snakes basking in the sun on the leaves of the pond lillies which lie on the surface. This place was held in great awe by the Indians, insomuch that the boldest hunter would not pursue his game within its precincts. Once upon a time, however, a hunter who had lost his way, penetrated to the garden rock where he beheld a number of gourds placed in the crotches of trees. One of these he seized and made off with it, but in the hurry of his retreat he let it fall among the rocks, when a great stream gushed forth which washed him away and swept him down precipices where he was dashed to pieces, and the stream made its way to the Hudson and continues to flow to the present day: being the identical stream known by the name of the Kaaters-kill.

1819

James Fenimore Cooper
(1789–1851)

A year after James Cooper's birth in Burlington, New Jersey, in 1789, his parents Elizabeth Fenimore and Judge William Cooper moved their family to what would become the family estate in a town that was later named for them, Cooperstown, New York. The novelist's imposing father had acquired vast tracts of land in the area of Lake Otsego after the American Revolution. After a period of private tutoring, at age fourteen Cooper entered Yale University but was expelled in 1806 for committing a series of pranks and for unruly behavior. His father then sent him to sea, where Cooper served first on a merchant ship and later as a midshipman in the U.S. Navy from 1808 to 1811. Following his departure from the navy, Cooper married Susan De Lancy, daughter of a wealthy New York family. Soon afterward the death of his father left him an inheritance of more than $50,000, which allowed him to live as a country gentleman in Cooperstown and Scarsdale, New York. He lived well; by 1819 his inheritance had not only dwindled, but he had incurred heavy debts and he already had five children to care for (two more were yet to come).

According to his daughter Susan in her journal *Rural Hours* (1850), Cooper began writing by chance when his wife laughed at his claim that he could improve on the "newly imported novel" he was reading aloud to her. Thus, the man "who disliked writing even a letter" undertook *Precaution* (1820), an imitative drawing-room novel set in England, and began a prodigious career that encompassed thirty-two novels; four volumes of comments on Europe, *Gleanings in Europe* (1837–1838); a history of the American Navy (1839); and several books of social criticism. Dissatisfied with his efforts in *Precaution*, Cooper turned to the subject of the Revolutionary War for *The Spy* (1821), a novel praised both in the United States and in Europe. Next came *The Pilot* (1823), the first of Cooper's eleven sea novels, written to show that his knowledge of the sea surpassed that of Sir Walter Scott in *The Pirate* (1822). In the same year Cooper finished *The Pioneers* (1823), in which he relied on his memories of Lake Otsego and Cooperstown. It was the first of the five "Leather-Stocking Tales," the novels for which Cooper is best known, and it introduced (as an aging hunter) the figure of Natty Bumppo, or Leather-Stocking, who moves West to get away from society because he is "made for the wilderness." In the popular *Last of the Mohicans* (1826), Cooper made Natty younger, taking him back to the colonial wars of the 1750s as an intrepid scout who witnesses the death of the heroic Uncas—and thus the symbolic extinction of a Native-American tribe. In *The Prairie*, published in 1827, an aged Leather-Stocking dies, succumbing not simply to his infirmities but to the destructive thrust of civilization. At this point (as his letters show), Cooper saw *The Prairie* as the final novel in the Leather-Stocking series.

Once again financially secure, James Fenimore Cooper (he added his mother's maiden name at this time) took his family abroad in 1826 and toured several countries in Europe, but he spent most of his seven-year sojourn in Lyons, France. As a reply to English critics of American society, he published the fictional letters *Notions of the Americans* in 1828. Cooper continued writing fiction, notably the provocative *Wept of Wish-ton-Wish* in 1829 but also a trilogy—consisting of *The Bravo* (1831), *The Heidenmauer* (1832), and *The Headsman* (1833)—that undercuts the glamor of a feudal past and suggests the moral superiority of democracy.

When Cooper returned to the United States in 1833, he did not find the country he had remembered—or had imagined as its spokesman. What he did find from his evolving conservative perspective was a society leveled by mediocrity and democratic excess, manifestations of Jacksonian America that troubled his patrician spirit. Cooper's writing in these years expressed the depth of his disappointment and alienated a public that had once applauded his work: the homiletic tone of *A Letter to His Countrymen* (1834), the crude satire of *The Monikins* (1835), and the lofty assurance of *The American Democrat* (1838) spell out his differences with American society. The novels *Homeward Bound* (1838) and *Home As Found* (1838) cast the same strictures into narrative form. When a character in *Home As Found* laments "that the days of the Leather-Stocking are over," we sense Coo-

Leatherstocking Meets the Law *(1832), by John Quidor.*

per's frustration with the present as well as his nostalgia for a time and a vision that had brought him confidence and success.

Cooper resurrected Leather-Stocking, first in *The Pathfinder* (1840), then in the final novel of the series, *The Deerslayer* (1841), which presents Natty Bumppo at his youngest and most innocent. The setting of *The Deerslayer* is once again Lake Otsego (here called Lake Glimmerglass)—but years before the burgeoning village of Templeton in *The Pioneers* comes to occupy and transform the same locale. An undefiled wilderness provides the mood of the novel. Cooper is dreaming back to origins in *The Deerslayer*, putting Natty in a time prior to the civilization he can no longer escape by going West.

In the 1840s Cooper was once again at odds with critics and with society: arguing, bickering, engaged in an astonishing number of lawsuits. Yet, he continued to produce novels during this decade, among them the disturbing *Wyandotte* (1843), which deals with the outbreak of the Revolutionary War in upstate New York, and the trilogy that follows three generations of the Littlepage family to the "Anti-Rent War" of the 1840s—*Satanstoe* (1845), *The Chainbearer* (1845), and *The Redskins* (1846). He died in Cooperstown in 1851 and was eulogized by William Cullen Bryant.

His letters suggest that Cooper was both ambitious as a writer and at times strangely unaware of the significance of his work. The man who thought of naming the final novel of the Leather-Stocking series "Judith and Hetty: Or, the Girls of the Glimmerglass" rather than *The Deerslayer* could hardly have seen the meaning of that narrative in the way we have come to see it. Still, with a ponderousness that made him an easy target for Mark

Twain in "Fenimore Cooper's Literary Offences" (1895), Cooper wrote novels that engaged American history, sea narratives that commanded the respect of such writers as Herman Melville and Joseph Conrad, and, above all, the Leather-Stocking Tales, at once prophetic and nostalgic, which tell us of the world we had before we made it into the world we have.

Suggested Readings: *Notions of the Americans: Picked Up by a Travelling Bachelor,* 1828. *The Letters and Journals of James Fenimore Cooper,* 6 vols., ed. J. F. Beard, 1969–1968. *The Writings of James Fenimore Cooper,* ed. J. F. Beard et al., 1980– . H. N. Smith, *Virgin Land: The American West as Symbol and Myth,* 1950. J. P. McWilliams, Jr., *Political Justice in a Republic,* 1972. B. Nevius, *Cooper's Landscapes: An Essay on the Picturesque Vision,* 1976. H. D. Peck, *A World by Itself,* 1977. S. Railton, *Fenimore Cooper: A Study of His Life and Imagination,* 1981. W. Franklin, *The New World of James Fenimore Cooper,* 1982. W. P. Kelly, *Plotting America's Past: Fenimore Cooper and the Leather-Stocking Tales,* 1983. J. D. Wallace, *Early Cooper and His Audience,* 1986.

Texts Used: *The Deerslayer: Or, the First War-Path* (Darley edition), 1870.

PREFACE TO THE LEATHER-STOCKING TALES*

This series of Stories, which has obtained the name of "The Leather-Stocking Tales," has been written in a very desultory and inartificial manner. The order in which the several books appeared was essentially different from that in which they would have been presented to the world, had the regular course of their incidents been consulted. In the Pioneers, the first of the series written, the Leather-Stocking is represented as already old, and driven from his early haunts in the forest, by the sound of the axe, and the smoke of the settler. "The Last of the Mohicans," the next book in the order of publication, carried the readers back to a much earlier period in the history of our hero, representing him as middle-aged, and in the fullest vigor of manhood. In the Prairie, his career terminates, and he is laid in his grave. There, it was originally the intention to leave him, in the expectation that, as in the case of the human mass, he would soon be forgotten. But a latent regard for this character induced the author to resuscitate him in "The Pathfinder," a book that was not long after succeeded by "The Deerslayer," thus completing the series as it now exists.

While the five books that have been written were originally published in the order just mentioned, that of the incidents, insomuch as they are connected with the career of their principal character, is, as has been stated, very different. Taking the life of the Leather-Stocking as a guide, "The Deerslayer" should have been the opening book, for in that work he is seen just emerging into manhood; to be succeeded by "The Last of the Mohicans," "The Pathfinder," "The Pioneers," and "The Prairie." This arrangement embraces the order of events, though far from being that in which the books at first appeared. "The Pioneers" was published in 1822;[1] "The Deerslayer" in 1841; making the interval between them nineteen years. Whether these progressive years have had a tendency to lessen the value of the last-named book, by lessening the native fire of its author, or of adding some-

---

* This preface was written in 1850 for an edition of the five "Leather-Stocking Tales," which were published between 1823 and 1841, about the life of Leather-Stocking (or Natty Bumppo or Deerslayer).

[1] Actually, February 1823.

what in the way of improved taste and a more matured judgment, is for others to decide.

If anything from the pen of the writer of these romances is at all to outlive himself, it is, unquestionably, the series of "The Leather-Stocking Tales." To say this, is not to predict a very lasting reputation for the series itself, but simply to express the belief it will outlast any, or all, of the works from the same hand.

It is undeniable that the desultory manner in which "The Leather-Stocking Tales" were written, has, in a measure, impaired their harmony, and otherwise lessened their interest. This is proved by the fate of the two books last published, though probably the two most worthy an enlightened and cultivated reader's notice. If the facts could be ascertained, it is probable the result would show that of all those (in America, in particular) who have read the three first books of the series, not one in ten has a knowledge of the existence even of the two last. Several causes have tended to produce this result. The long interval of time between the appearance of "The Prairie" and that of "The Pathfinder," was itself a reason why the later books of the series should be overlooked. There was no longer novelty to attract attention, and the interest was materially impaired by the manner in which events were necessarily anticipated, in laying the last of the series first before the world. With the generation that is now coming on the stage this fault will be partially removed by the edition contained in the present work, in which the several tales will be arranged solely in reference to their connexion with each other.

The author has often been asked if he had any original in his mind, for the character of Leather-Stocking. In a physical sense, different individuals known to the writer in early life, certainly presented themselves as models, through his recollections; but in a moral sense this man of the forest is purely a creation. The idea of delineating a character that possessed little of civilization but its highest principles as they are exhibited in the uneducated, and all of savage life that is not incompatible with these great rules of conduct, is perhaps natural to the situation in which Natty was placed. He is too proud of his origin to sink into the condition of the wild Indian, and too much a man of the woods not to imbibe as much as was at all desirable, from his friends and companions. In a moral point of view it was the intention to illustrate the effect of seed scattered by the way side. To use his own language, his "gifts" were "white gifts," and he was not disposed to bring on them discredit. On the other hand, removed from nearly all the temptations of civilized life, placed in the best associations of that which is deemed savage, and favorably disposed by nature to improve such advantages, it appeared to the writer that his hero was a fit subject to represent the better qualities of both conditions, without pushing either to extremes.

There was no violent stretch of the imagination, perhaps, in supposing one of civilized associations in childhood, retaining many of his earliest lessons amid the scenes of the forest. Had these early impressions, however, not been sustained by continued, though casual connexion with men of his own color, if not of his own caste, all our information goes to show he would soon have lost every trace of his origin. It is believed that sufficient attention was paid to the particular circumstances in which this individual was placed, to justify the picture of his qualities that has been drawn. The Delawares early attracted the attention of the missionaries, and were a tribe unusually influenced by their precepts and example. In many instances they became Christians, and cases occurred in which their subsequent lives gave proof of the efficacy of the great moral changes that had taken place within them.

A leading character in a work of fiction has a fair right to the aid which can be obtained from a poetical view of the subject. It is in this view, rather than in one more strictly circumstantial, that Leather-Stocking has been drawn. The imagination has no great task in portraying to itself a being removed from the every-day inducements to err, which abound in civilized life, while he retains the best and simplest of his early impressions; who sees God in the forest; hears him in the winds; bows to him in the firmament that o'ercanopies all; submits to his sway in a humble belief of his justice and mercy; in a word, a being who finds the impress of the Deity in all the works of nature, without any of the blots produced by the expedients, and passion, and mistakes of man. This is the most that has been attempted in the character of Leather-Stocking. Had this been done without any of the drawbacks of humanity, the picture would have been, in all probability, more pleasing than just. In order to preserve the *vrai-semblable*,[2] therefore, traits derived from the prejudices, tastes, and even the weaknesses of his youth, have been mixed up with these higher qualities and longings, in a way, it is hoped, to represent a reasonable picture of human nature, without offering to the spectator a "monster of goodness."

It has been objected to these books that they give a more favorable picture of the red man than he deserves. The writer apprehends that much of this objection arises from the habits of those who have made it. One of his critics, on the appearance of the first work in which Indian character was portrayed, objected that its "characters were Indians of the school of Heckewelder,[3] rather than of the school of nature." These words quite probably contain the substance of the true answer to the objection. Heckewelder was an ardent, benevolent missionary, bent on the good of the red man, and seeing in him one who had the soul, reason, and characteristics of a fellow-being. The critic is understood to have been a distinguished agent of the government, one very familiar with Indians, as they are seen at the councils to treat for the sale of their lands, where little or none of their domestic qualities come in play, and where, indeed, their evil passions are known to have the fullest scope. As just would it be to draw conclusions of the general state of American society from the scenes of the capital, as to suppose that the negotiating of one of these treaties is a fair picture of Indian life.

It is the privilege of all writers of fiction, more particularly when their works aspire to the elevation of romances, to present the *beau-idéal*[4] of their characters to the reader. This it is which constitutes poetry, and to suppose that the red man is to be represented only in the squalid misery or in the degraded moral state that certainly more or less belongs to his condition, is, we apprehend, taking a very narrow view of an author's privileges. Such criticism would have deprived the world of even Homer.

1850

[2] "True semblance" (French): verisimilitude or realism.

[3] John Gottlieb Heckewelder (1743–1823), an early Moravian missionary among the Native Americans of Ohio; Cooper's information about Native-American customs came primarily from Heckewelder's *Account of the History, Manners, and Customs of the Indian Nations Who Once Inhabited Pennsylvania and the Neighboring States* (1819). Cooper quotes Lewis Cass (1782–1866), a governor of the Michigan territory; Cass's assessment of Cooper appeared in the *North American Review*, January 1826.

[4] "Ideal of beauty" (French).

from   THE DEERSLAYER*

from   CHAPTER VII

[Deerslayer Is Named Hawkeye by His Dying Foe]

When about a hundred yards from the shore,[1] Deerslayer rose in the canoe, gave three or four vigorous strokes with the paddle, sufficient of themselves to impel the bark to land, and then quickly laying aside the instrument of labor, he seized that of war. He was in the very act of raising the rifle, when a sharp report was followed by the buzz of a bullet that passed so near his body, as to cause him involuntarily to start. The next instant Deerslayer staggered, and fell his whole length in the bottom of the canoe. A yell—it came from a single voice—followed, and an Indian leaped from the bushes upon the open area of the point, bounding towards the canoe. This was the moment the young man desired. He rose on the instant, and levelled his own rifle at his uncovered foe; but his finger hesitated about pulling the trigger on one whom he held at such a disadvantage. This little delay, probably, saved the life of the Indian, who bounded back into the cover as swiftly as he had broken out of it. In the meantime Deerslayer had been swiftly approaching the land, and his own canoe reached the point just as his enemy disappeared. As its movements had not been directed, it touched the shore a few yards from the other boat;[2] and though the rifle of his foe had to be loaded, there was not time to secure his prize, and to carry it beyond danger, before he would be exposed to another shot. Under the circumstances, therefore, he did not pause an instant, but dashed into the woods and sought a cover.

On the immediate point there was a small open area, partly in native grass, and partly beach, but a dense fringe of bushes lined its upper side. This narrow belt of dwarf vegetation passed, one issued immediately into the high and gloomy vaults of the forest. The land was tolerably level for a few hundred feet, and then it rose precipitously in a mountain-side. The trees were tall, large, and so free from under-brush, that they resembled vast columns, irregularly scattered, upholding a dome of leaves. Although they stood tolerably close together, for their ages and size, the eye could penetrate to considerable distances; and bodies of men, even, might have engaged beneath their cover, with concert and intelligence.

Deerslayer knew that his adversary must be employed in re-loading, unless he had fled. The former proved to be the case, for the young man had no sooner placed himself behind a tree, than he caught a glimpse of the arm of the Indian, his body being concealed by an oak, in the very act of forcing the leathered bullet

---

* The title of *The Deerslayer* (1841) refers to Cooper's frontiersman and skilled hunter Nathaniel or Natty Bumppo, often called Leather-Stocking because of his characteristic apparel in the forest. Here the youthful Deerslayer is fired upon by a Native-American enemy during a colonial war between England and France, engages in one-to-one combat, and is named "Hawkeye" by the foe he conquers—the first human being he has killed. Cooper's frontiersman is called Hawkeye throughout the *The Last of the Mohicans*, published fifteen years earlier. In *The Deerslayer* Cooper goes back in time, presenting a very young Natty Bumppo.

[1] Deerslayer is guiding his canoe across Lake Glimmerglass (Lake Otsego, near what is now Cooperstown, New York). Although the novel is set in the mid-1750s, Cooper manages to suggest a pristine locale, "a world by itself."

[2] This "other boat" belongs to Deerslayer's acquaintances.

home. Nothing would have been easier than to spring forward, and decide the affair by a close assault on his unprepared foe; but every feeling of Deerslayer revolted at such a step, although his own life had just been attempted from a cover. He was yet unpractised in the ruthless expedients of savage warfare, of which he knew nothing except by tradition and theory, and it struck him as an unfair advantage to assail an unarmed foe. His color had heightened, his eye frowned, his lips were compressed, and all his energies were collected and ready; but, instead of advancing to fire, he dropped his rifle to the usual position of a sportsman in readiness to catch his aim, and muttered to himself, unconscious that he was speaking—

"No, no—that may be red-skin warfare, but it's not a Christian's gifts.[3] Let the miscreant charge, and then we'll take it out like men; for the canoe he *must* not, and *shall* not have. No, no; let him have time to load, and God will take care of the right!"

All this time the Indian had been so intent on his own movements, that he was even ignorant that his enemy was in the wood. His only apprehension was, that the canoe would be recovered and carried away before he might be in readiness to prevent it. He had sought the cover from habit, but was within a few feet of the fringe of bushes, and could be at the margin of the forest in readiness to fire in a moment. The distance between him and his enemy was about fifty yards, and the trees were so arranged by nature that the line of sight was not interrupted, except by the particular trees behind which each party stood.

His rifle was no sooner loaded, than the savage glanced around him, and advanced incautiously as regarded the real, but stealthily as respected the fancied position of his enemy, until he was fairly exposed. Then Deerslayer stepped from behind his own cover, and hailed him.

"This-a-way, red-skin; this-a-way, if you're looking for me," he called out. "I'm young in war, but not so young as to stand on an open beach to be shot down like an owl, by daylight. It rests on yourself whether it's peace or war atween us; for my gifts are white gifts, and I'm not one of them that thinks it valiant to slay human mortals, singly, in the woods."

The savage was a good deal startled by this sudden discovery of the danger he ran. He had a little knowledge of English, however, and caught the drift of the other's meaning. He was also too well schooled to betray alarm, but, dropping the butt of his rifle to the earth, with an air of confidence, he made a gesture of lofty courtesy. All this was done with the ease and self-possession of one accustomed to consider no man his superior. In the midst of this consummate acting, however, the volcano that raged within caused his eyes to glare, and his nostrils to dilate, like those of some wild beast that is suddenly prevented from taking the fatal leap.

"Two canoe," he said, in the deep guttural tones of his race, holding up the number of fingers he mentioned, by way of preventing mistakes; "one for you— one for me."

"No, no, Mingo,[4] that will never do. You own neither; and neither shall you have, as long as I can prevent it. I know it's war atween your people and mine, but that's no reason why human mortals should slay each other, like savage creatur's that meet in the woods; go your way, then, and leave me to go mine. The

---

[3] Throughout the five Leather-Stocking novels Natty Bumppo distinguishes between red and white "gifts" or codes of ethics and of warfare. (White codes are assumed to be Christian.) Thus, a Native American may scalp a conquered foe but a white man may not.

[4] An Iroquois or Sioux brave.

world is large enough for us both; and when we meet fairly in battle, why, the Lord will order the fate of each of us."

"Good!" exclaimed the Indian; "my brother missionary—great talk; all about Manitou."[5]

"Not so—not so, warrior. I'm not good enough for the Moravians,[6] and am too good for most of the other vagabonds that preach about in the woods. No, no, I'm only a hunter, as yet, though afore the peace is made, 'tis like enough there'll be occasion to strike a blow at some of your people. Still, I wish it to be done in fair fight, and not in a quarrel about the ownership of a miserable canoe."

"Good! My brother very young—but he very wise. Little warrior—great talker. Chief, sometimes, in council."

"I don't know this, nor do I say it, Injin," returned Deerslayer, coloring a little at the ill-concealed sarcasm of the other's manner; "I look forward to a life in the woods, and I only hope it may be a peaceable one. All young men must go on the war-path, when there's occasion, but war isn't needfully massacre. I've seen enough of the last, this very night, to know that Providence frowns on it; and I now invite you to go your own way, while I go mine; and hope that we may part fri'nds."

"Good! My brother has two scalp—grey hair under t'other. Old wisdom—young tongue."

Here the savage advanced with confidence, his hand extended, his face smiling, and his whole bearing denoting amity and respect. Deerslayer met his offered friendship in a proper spirit, and they shook hands cordially, each endeavoring to assure the other of his sincerity and desire to be at peace.

"All have his own," said the Indian; "my canoe, mine; your canoe, your'n. Go look; if your'n, you keep; if mine, I keep."

"That's just, red-skin; though you must be wrong in thinking the canoe your property. Howsever, seein' is believin', and we'll go down to the shore, where you may look with your own eyes; for it's likely you'll object to trustin' altogether to mine."

The Indian uttered his favorite exclamation of "good!" and then they walked side by side, towards the shore. There was no apparent distrust in the manner of either, the Indian moving in advance, as if he wished to show his companion that he did not fear turning his back to him. As they reached the open ground, the former pointed towards Deerslayer's boat, and said emphatically—

"No mine—pale-face canoe. *This* red-man's. No want other man's canoe—want his own."

"You're wrong, red-skin, you're altogether wrong. This canoe was left in old Hutter's keeping, and is his'n according to all law, red or white, till its owner comes to claim it. Here's the seats and the stitching of the bark to speak for themselves. No man ever know'd an Injin to turn off such work."

"Good! My brother little ole—big wisdom. Injin no made him. White man's work."

"I'm glad you think so, for holding out to the contrary might have made ill blood atween us; every one having a right to take possession of his own. I'll just

---

[5] Among various native tribes, an august power or deity that controls the forces of nature, synonomous with "God."

[6] A Protestant sect of missionaries who preached to Native Americans; Natty Bumppo learned Christian principles from them.

shove the canoe out of reach of dispute at once, as the quickest way of settling difficulties."

While Deerslayer was speaking, he put a foot against the end of the light boat, and giving a vigorous shove, he sent it out into the lake a hundred feet or more, where, taking the true current, it would necessarily float past the point, and be in no further danger of coming ashore. The savage started at this ready and decided expedient, and his companion saw that he cast a hurried and fierce glance at his own canoe, or that which contained the paddles. The change of manner, however, was but momentary, and then the Iroquois resumed his air of friendliness, and a smile of satisfaction.

"Good!" he repeated, with stronger emphasis than ever. "Young head, old mind. Know how to settle quarrel. Farewell, brother. He go to house in water— muskrat house[7]—Injin go to camp; tell chiefs no find canoe."

Deerslayer was not sorry to hear this proposal, for he felt anxious to join the females, and he took the offered hand of the Indian very willingly. The parting words were friendly, and, while the red-man walked calmly towards the wood, with the rifle in the hollow of his arm, without once looking back in uneasiness or distrust, the white man moved towards the remaining canoe, carrying his piece in the same pacific manner, it is true, but keeping his eyes fastened on the movements of the other. This distrust, however, seemed to be altogether uncalled for, and, as if ashamed to have entertained it, the young man averted his look, and stepped carelessly up to his boat. Here he began to push the canoe from the shore, and to make his other preparations for departing. He might have been thus employed a minute, when, happening to turn his face towards the land, his quick and certain eye told him, at a glance, the imminent jeopardy in which his life was placed. The black, ferocious eyes of the savage were glancing on him, like those of the crouching tiger, through a small opening in the bushes, and the muzzle of his rifle seemed already to be opening in a line with his own body.

Then, indeed, the long practice of Deerslayer, as a hunter, did him good service. Accustomed to fire with the deer on the bound, and often when the precise position of the animal's body had in a manner to be guessed at, he used the same expedients here. To cock and poise his rifle were the acts of a single moment and a single motion; then, aiming almost without sighting, he fired into the bushes where he knew a body ought to be, in order to sustain the appalling countenance which alone was visible. There was not time to raise the piece any higher, or to take a more deliberate aim. So rapid were his movements, that both parties discharged their pieces at the same instant, the concussions mingling in one report. The mountains, indeed, gave back but a single echo. Deerslayer dropped his piece, and stood, with head erect, steady as one of the pines in the calm of a June morning, watching the result; while the savage gave the yell that has become historical for its appalling influence, leaped through the bushes and came bounding across the open ground, flourishing a tomahawk. Still Deerslayer moved not, but stood with his unloaded rifle fallen against his shoulders, while, with a hunter's habits, his hands were mechanically feeling for the powder-horn and charger. When about forty feet from his enemy, the savage hurled his keen weapon; but it was with an eye so vacant, and a hand so unsteady and feeble, that the young man

---

[7] The houseboat of Floating Tom Hutter, a muskrat trapper who lives with his daughters, Hetty and Judith, in the middle of the lake.

caught it by the handle as it was flying past him. At that instant the Indian staggered and fell his whole length on the ground.

"I know'd it—I know'd it!" exclaimed Deerslayer, who was already preparing to force a fresh bullet into his rifle; "I know'd it must come to this, as soon as I had got the range from the creatur's eyes. A man sights suddenly, and fires quick when his own life's in danger; yes, I know'd it would come to this. I was about the hundredth part of a second too quick for him, or it might have been bad for me! The riptyle's bullet has just grazed my side—but, say what you will for or ag'in em, a red-skin is by no means as sartain with powder and ball as a white man. Their gifts don't seem to lie that-a-way. Even Chingachgook,[8] great as he is in other matters, isn't downright deadly with the rifle."

By this time the piece was reloaded, and Deerslayer, after tossing the tomahawk into the canoe, advanced to his victim, and stood over him, leaning on his rifle, in melancholy attention. It was the first instance in which he had seen a man fall in battle—it was the first fellow-creature against whom he had ever seriously raised his own hand. The sensations were novel; and regret, with the freshness of our better feelings, mingled with his triumph. The Indian was not dead, though shot directly through the body. He lay on his back motionless, but his eyes, now full of consciousness, watched each action of his victor—as the fallen bird regards the fowler—jealous of every movement. The man probably expected the fatal blow which was to precede the loss of his scalp; or perhaps he anticipated that this latter act of cruelty would precede his death. Deerslayer read his thoughts; and he found a melancholy satisfaction in relieving the apprehensions of the helpless savage.

"No, no, red-skin," he said; "you've nothing more to fear from me. I am of a Christian stock, and scalping is not of my gifts. I'll just make sartain of your rifle, and then come back and do you what sarvice I can. Though here I can't stay much longer, as the crack of three rifles will be apt to bring some of your devils down upon me."

The close of this was said in a sort of a soliloquy, as the young man went in quest of the fallen rifle. The piece was found where its owner had dropped it, and was immediately put into the canoe. Laying his own rifle at its side, Deerslayer then returned and stood over the Indian again.

"All inmity atween you and me's at an ind, red-skin," he said; "and you may set your heart at rest on the score of the scalp, or any further injury. My gifts are white, as I've told you; and I hope my conduct will be white also!"

Could looks have conveyed all they meant, it is probable Deerslayer's innocent vanity on the subject of color would have been rebuked a little; but he comprehended the gratitude that was expressed in the eyes of the dying savage, without in the least detecting the bitter sarcasm that struggled with the better feeling.

"Water!" ejaculated the thirsty and unfortunate creature; "give poor Injin water."

"Aye, water you shall have, if you drink the lake dry. I'll just carry you down to it, that you may take your fill. This is the way, they tell me, with all wounded people—water is their greatest comfort and delight."

So saying, Deerslayer raised the Indian in his arms, and carried him to the lake. Here he first helped him to take an attitude in which he could appease his burning

---

[8] Natty Bumppo's lifelong companion, a Mohican chief; he dies at an advancaed age in *The Pioneers* (1823).

thirst; after which he seated himself on a stone, and took the head of his wounded adversary in his own lap, and endeavored to soothe his anguish in the best manner he could.

* * *

. . . With the high innate courtesy that so often distinguishes the Indian warrior before he becomes corrupted by too much intercourse with the worst class of the white men, he endeavored to express his thankfulness for the other's good intentions, and to let him understand that they were appreciated.

"Good!" he repeated, for this was an English word much used by the savages— "good—young head; young *heart,* too, *Old* heart tough; no shed tear. Hear Indian when he die, and no want to lie—what he call him?"

"Deerslayer is the name I bear now, though the Delawares[9] have said that when I get back from this war-path, I shall have a more manly title, provided I can 'arn one."

"That good name for boy—poor name for warrior. He get better quick. No fear *there*"—the savage had strength sufficient, under the strong excitement he felt, to raise a hand and tap the young man on his breast—"eye sartain—finger lightning—aim, death—great warrior soon. No Deerslayer—Hawkeye—Hawkeye—Hawkeye. Shake hand."

Deerslayer—or Hawkeye, as the youth was then first named, for in after years he bore the appellation throughout all that region—Deerslayer took the hand of the savage, whose last breath was drawn in that attitude, gazing in admiration at the countenance of a stranger, who had shown so much readiness, skill, and firmness, in a scene that was equally trying and novel. . . .

1841

Edgar Allan Poe
(1809–1849)

Edgar Allan Poe's inventive brilliance, commitment to craft, and genius at transforming gothic formulas into surreal structures of the imagination are well-known aspects of his achievement as a writer. Yet, any such catalogue of praise yields only a partial portrait of this embattled virtuoso, whose chronic instability and self-destructive behavior consistently threatened to overshadow his literary achievement. Poe was and remains a complex figure, best understood by the very contradictions that made his life and career so difficult.

Edgar Poe was born in Boston to traveling actors in 1809, and his earliest years prefigured the lack of moorings in his later life: not long after Poe's birth his father, David Poe, Jr., deserted the family, and in 1811 his mother, Elizabeth Arnold Hopkins, died while on tour in Richmond, Virginia. Poe was taken in by the family of Frances and John Allan, a

---

[9] The Delaware Indians fought with the British in the colonial wars, the Iroquois with the French. The Mohicans were part of the large Delaware nation.

prosperous Richmond merchant, and eventually baptized Edgar Allan Poe by the man he then regarded as his benefactor. When Poe was seventeen he entered the University of Virginia and did well in his study of French and Latin. His fellow students knew him as an aspiring poet and a heavy drinker. He also had a reputation for gambling—not well, apparently, for he ran up gambling debts to the total of $2000. When John Allan refused to pay these debts, Poe left Virginia in anger, went to Boston, and enlisted in the army as Edgar A. Perry. In 1827, during his army service, he arranged for the publication of his first slender volume of verse, *Tamerlane and Other Poems*. Two years later, following his release from the army, he published a second volume, *Al Aaraaf, Tamerlane, and Minor Poems*.

Poe's complaints that Allan would not help him in times of distress have led many to see Allan as an insensitive and mean-spirited man of wealth who would not lend support to a foster child and aspiring artist. To read Poe's letters, however, is to see how the writer might have alienated Allan (or anyone) with his whining, self-dramatic, and condemnatory appeals for money. Repeatedly, Poe promises that he will never again ask for money; repeatedly he does ask, spends with astonishing speed what money may have been sent him, and says that Allan will be responsible for his destruction and death if further funds are not forthcoming. There is no doubt that throughout much of his life Poe was in need of money and that Allan refused to give it. But Allan's role in Poe's life must have been exasperating. It is no doubt easier to appreciate Poe from the distance of a century and a half.

The 1830s introduced Poe to a dizzying array of jobs and events. After a temporary reconciliation in 1830, Allan helped him secure an appointment to West Point. But during Poe's eight months at the academy it became clear that the man and the institution were not made for each other. A series of minor infractions brought about his dismissal from the academy in 1831. Undaunted by his severance, Poe turned to the writing of fiction and in 1832 published five stories in the Philadelphia *Saturday Courier*. The following year his story "MS. Found in a Bottle" won the $100 first prize in a short-story contest run by a Baltimore magazine. Also in 1833 he was named editor of the *Southern Literary Messenger* in Richmond, a magazine in which he published poems, stories, and over eighty reviews. Three years later, when he was twenty-seven, he married his thirteen-year-old cousin Virginia Clemm. Shortly after they married Poe left the *Southern Literary Messenger*, having had one of his many bitter arguments with magazine publishers over his drinking, his authoritarian editorial style, and the hatchetlike quality of his reviews.

During the 1830s and early 1840s Poe also published much fiction, including *The Narrative of Arthur Gordon Pym* (1838), "Ligeia" (1838), "The Fall of the House of Usher" (1839), and a collection of stories, *Tales of the Grotesque and Arabesque* (1840). Yet, Poe earned little money from these works we have come to prize (his collection of stories sold fewer than 750 copies). Despite a developing pattern of difficult behavior, he was able to obtain positions of responsibility on magazines: he became co-editor of *Burton's Gentleman's Magazine* in 1839, only to be discharged after several months because of arguments with the publisher over his reviews and his drinking. Soon afterward he became the editor of *Graham's Magazine* and wrote such tales as "A Descent Into the Maelstrom" (1841) and "The Masque of the Red Death" (1842) while he held that position.

Although Poe continued to write throughout the 1840s, he remained deeply in the grasp of poverty. Not even the popularity of "The Raven" (1844) and an increasing reputation as a writer could bring him financial security. In 1845 he became the editor of the *Broadway Journal* and wrote a series of articles suggesting that Henry Wadsworth Longfellow (already revered in New England) was a plagiarist—perhaps to enhance the circulation of the *Journal,* perhaps also because of an evolving paranoia that led Poe to wonder (quite incorrectly) if Nathaniel Hawthorne had not plagiarized from Poe's work. But the *Broadway Journal* failed in 1846, Poe's young wife died of tuberculosis in 1847, and Poe found it difficult to maintain professional or personal equilibrium after that time—although his provocative effort in cosmology, *Eureka: A Prose Poem* (1848), displays a strange combination of elation, erudition, and comedy. Toward the end of his life Poe returned to Richmond and became engaged to Elmira Royster Shelton, a widow who had been a neighbor of the Allans and the sweetheart of Poe's early years. During two tranquil months in Richmond he wrote "Annabel Lee" (posthumously published in 1849), gave readings of his poetry, and joined the Sons of Temperance in a final effort to change his habits. On his way to Philadelphia to receive payment for some freelance editing he had done, however, he stopped in Baltimore, disappeared mysteriously for several days, and was found unconscious on the street. Four days later, on October 7, 1849, he died.

There is no doubt that Poe's life presents a melodramatic and vexed scenario. He seemed to court literary feuds and to resent the prominence and assurance of the New England literary establishment. In a review he sneered, for example, at the "so-called poetry of the so-called Transcendentalists" and attacked numerous writers as literary hacks. In return, he was called "the jingle man" by Emerson because of the sing-song quality of his poetry and was described memorably by James Russell Lowell in "A Fable for Critics" (1848) as "three-fifths . . . genius and two-fifths sheer fudge."

The range and quality of Poe's achievement is undeniable. Not only did he perfect the modern form of the short story, but also he established many of the conventions of the modern detective story with his character C. Auguste Dupin—shrewd, logical, eccentric—who appears in "The Murders in the Rue Morgue" (1841), "The Mystery of Marie Roget" (1842–1843), and "The Purloined Letter" (1845). Additionally, in the midst of an emerging American romanticism to which he contributed both manner and substance, Poe advocated the idea of the poet as craftsman, one who constructs and shapes a poem and for

A portrait of Elmira Royster Shelton, Edgar Allen Poe's childhood sweetheart, reportedly sketched by Poe.

whom the form is integral to the meaning. That idea recommended Poe to the French symbolists and anticipated the disciplined poetics of some modernist poets in the twentieth century. More idiosyncratic was Poe's assertion that to preserve a necessary unity of effect a poem should be capable of being read at one sitting. The logical consequence, as Poe took pains to say, is that there is no such thing as a long poem. No matter the traditional praise heaped upon epic poems: Homer's *Iliad*, Poe boldly contended, proceeds from an imperfect sense of poetry; John Milton's *Paradise Lost* (1667) is a series of short poems with what is essentially prose sandwiched between them.

Poe's fiction thrives on wordplay, puzzles, and anagrams. The secret of "The Gold-Bug" (a prize-winning story first published in 1843 in a Philadelphia magazine) depends on a cryptograph and reflects an interest in deciphering codes, which brought Poe to write the essay "Cryptography," published in *Graham's Magazine* in 1841. "The Balloon Hoax," written as a news story in the New York *Sun* in 1844, details the supposed journey of a "Steering Balloon" from England to South Carolina. Even "The Philosophy of Composition" (1846), which purports to explain how Poe wrote "The Raven," may well be an after-the-fact parade of gamesmanship. A more bizarre type of playing can be seen in Poe's tales that defy consequences: the narrator of "Loss of Breath" (1835), for example, suffers a fractured skull and a hanging, yet relates his misadventures in the tone of one who is having a bad day. In "A Predicament" (1838) the case is even more extreme—the narrator has her head cut off by the minute hand of a clock and goes on talking with studied nonchalance. What Poe gives us in these tales is not the unreliable narrator we have come to know and mistrust but the indestructible narrator, a creature alien to our expectations yet confidential and even presumptuous in disclosure.

In a society that prized the domestic and valued the didactic for its moral utility, Poe became militantly antididactic, mischievously antidomestic. The narrator of "The Black Cat" (1843) presents the garish violence of his tale as "a series of mere household events." Fortunato in "The Cask of Amontillado" (1846) exults in the memory of revenge taken fifty years before—although some readers, uneasy at the amoral calisthenics of this tale, see the narrative as confessional and not celebratory. The point is that Poe was part of the society in which he wrote: he knew its values and pieties and inverted them for the complex purposes of his fiction.

Perhaps most importantly, in some of his best-known work Poe explores the intricate and baffling nature of the perverse. Characteristically, he uses first-person narrators who bid us watch as they destroy the "I"—the "self" that is glorified in the work of Ralph Waldo Emerson, of Henry David Thoreau, and of Walt Whitman, the *self* that is driven in Poe's fiction by the "unfathomable longing of the soul *to vex itself*—to offer violence to its own nature" (as we read in "The Black Cat"). The narrator of "The Tell-Tale Heart" (1843) is obsessed by the "eye" of the victim in that tale; without passion or object, he decides "to take the life of the old man, and thus rid myself of the eye forever." Given Poe's fondness for puns, it is an easy move to substitute an "eye" for an "I" in this context. Given Poe's addiction to anagrams it is tempting to see that the letters of "perverse" can also spell "preserve" and thereby understand the profound interrelationship between perversity and preservation in the world of Poe's fiction.

Poe's choice of Rufus Wilmot Griswold, a prominent journalist and editor, as his literary executor is a curious one. Griswold wrote the first biography of Poe, a malicious and distorted portrait that left the study of Poe's life in disarray for more than a century. As twentieth-century scholars have discovered, Griswold also changed the text of some Poe letters that had been left in his charge. Clearly, Griswold felt a deep antipathy of which Poe seems to have been unaware. Yet, the consequence suggests a reprise on the relationship between perversity and preservation: if it was (unconsciously) perverse for Poe to name Griswold as his literary executor, the act has helped to preserve his reputation at the expense of Griswold's. If Griswold is known at all, he is known as the biographer who falsified the facts and the documents of Poe's life. The dimensions of Poe's achievement, however, have become secure. Unstable and histrionic as he may have been as an editor, erratic as he may have become as a writer, Poe nonetheless produced haunted narratives that are triumphs of psychological exploration, mood poems that yearn beyond the boundaries of the finite world, and critical ideas that proclaim the enduring importance of form in the creation of art.

Suggested Readings: *The Complete Works of Edgar Allan Poe*, 17 vols., ed. J. A. Harrison, 1902. *The Letters of Edgar Allan Poe*, 2 vols., ed. J. W. Ostrom, 1966. *Collected Works*, 3 vols., ed. T. O. Mabbott et al., 1969–1978. *The Short Fiction of Edgar Allan Poe: An Annotated Edition*, ed. S. Levine and S. Levine, 1976. C. Baudelaire, *Baudelaire on Poe*, 1852. A. H. Quinn, *Edgar Allan Poe: A Critical Biography*, 1966. M. L. Allen, *Poe and the British Magazine Tradition*, 1969. D. Hoffman, *Poe, Poe, Poe, Poe, Poe, Poe, Poe*, 1973. G. R. Thompson, *Poe's Fiction: Romantic Irony in the Gothic Tales*, 1973. J. Dayan, *Fables of Mind: An Inquiry into Poe's Fiction*, 1987. J. G. Kennedy, *Poe, Death, and the Life of Writing*, 1987. D. Thomas and D. K. Jackson, eds., *The Poe Log: A Documentary Life of Edgar Allan Poe, 1809–1849*, 1987. J. P. Muller and W. J. Richardson, eds., *The Purloined Poe: Lacan, Derrida, and Psychoanalytic Reading*, 1988. M. J. S. Williams, *A World of Words: Language and Displacement in the Fiction of Edgar Allan Poe*, 1988.

Texts Used: "Ligeia": *The Complete Works*, Vol. I. "The Fall of the House of Usher": *The Complete Works*, Vol. III. "The Tell-Tale Heart" and "The Black Cat": *The Complete Works*, Vol. V. "The Cask of Amontillado": *The Complete Works*, Vol. VI. All poems: *The Complete Works*, Vol. VII. "The Philosophy of Composition": *The Complete Works*, Vol. XIV.

LIGEIA*

And the will therein lieth, which dieth not. Who knoweth the mysteries of the will, with its vigor? For God is but a great will pervading all things by nature of its intentness. Man doth not yield himself to the angels, nor unto death utterly, save only through the weakness of his feeble will.

JOSEPH GLANVILL[1]

I cannot, for my soul, remember how, when, or even precisely where, I first became acquainted with the lady Ligeia. Long years have since elapsed, and my memory is feeble through much suffering. Or, perhaps, I cannot *now* bring these points to mind, because, in truth, the character of my beloved, her rare learning, her singular yet placid cast of beauty, and the thrilling and enthralling eloquence of her low musical language, made their way into my heart by paces so steadily and stealthily progressive that they have been unnoticed and unknown. Yet I believe that I met her first and most frequently in some large, old, decaying city near the Rhine. Of her family—I have surely heard her speak. That it is of a remotely ancient date cannot be doubted. Ligeia! Ligeia! Buried in studies of a nature more than all else adapted to deaden impressions of the outward world, it is by that

---

* First published in *The American Museum* in 1838. Poe may have found the name "Ligeia" in Book IV of Virgil's *Georgics* (37?–30? B.C.), which is concerned with beekeeping, or in John Milton's *Comus* (1634), a masque, or theatrical entertainment.

[1] No such statement can be found in the work of Joseph Glanvill (1638–1680), a Cambridge Platonist, or seventeenth-century English religious philosopher. Poe probably made up the quotation for the purposes of his story.

sweet word alone—by Ligeia—that I bring before mine eyes in fancy the image of her who is no more. And now, while I write, a recollection flashes upon me that I have *never known* the paternal name of her who was my friend and my betrothed, and who became the partner of my studies, and finally the wife of my bosom. Was it a playful charge on the part of my Ligeia? or was it a test of my strength of affection, that I should institute no inquiries upon this point ? or was it rather a caprice of my own—a wildly romantic offering on the shrine of the most passionate devotion? I but indistinctly recall the fact itself—what wonder that I have utterly forgotten the circumstances which originated or attended it? And, indeed, if ever that spirit which is entitled *Romance*—if ever she, the wan and the misty-winged *Ashtophet*[2] of idolatrous Egypt, presided, as they tell, over marriages ill-omened, then most surely she presided over mine.

There is one dear topic, however, on which my memory fails me not. It is the *person* of Ligeia. In stature she was tall, somewhat slender, and, in her latter days, even emaciated. I would in vain attempt to portray the majesty, the quiet ease, of her demeanor, or the incomprehensible lightness and elasticity of her footfall. She came and departed as a shadow. I was never made aware of her entrance into my closed study save by the dear music of her low sweet voice, as she placed her marble hand upon my shoulder. In beauty of face no maiden ever equalled her. It was the radiance of an opium-dream—an airy and spirit-lifting vision more wildly divine than the phantasies which hovered about the slumbering souls of the daughters of Delos.[3] Yet her features were not of that regular mould which we have been falsely taught to worship in the classical labors of the heathen. "There is no exquisite beauty," says Bacon, Lord Verulam, speaking truly of all the forms and *genera* of beauty, "without some *strangeness* in the proportion."[4] Yet, although I saw that the features of Ligeia were not of a classic regularity—although I perceived that her loveliness was indeed "exquisite," and felt that there was much of "strangeness" pervading it, yet I have tried in vain to detect the irregularity and to trace home my own perception of "the strange." I examined the contour of the lofty and pale forehead—it was faultless—how cold indeed that word when applied to a majesty so divine!—the skin rivalling the purest ivory, the commanding extent and repose, the gentle prominence of the regions above the temples; and then the raven-black, the glossy, the luxuriant and naturally-curling tresses, setting forth the full force of the Homeric epithet, "hyacinthine!"[5] I looked at the delicate outlines of the nose—and nowhere but in the graceful medallions of the Hebrews had I beheld a similar perfection. There were the same luxurious smoothness of surface, the same scarcely perceptible tendency to the aquiline,[6] the same harmoniously curved nostrils speaking the free spirit. I regarded the sweet mouth. Here was indeed the triumph of all things heavenly—the magnificent turn of the short upper lip—the soft, voluptuous slumber of the under—the dimples which sported, and the color which spoke—the teeth glancing back, with a brilliancy almost startling, every ray of the holy light which fell upon them in her serene and placid, yet most exultingly radiant of all smiles. I scrutinized the formation of the chin—and here, too, I found the gentleness of breadth, the softness

---

[2] Ashtoreth, a Phoenecian goddess of fertility.

[3] A small island in the Aegean Sea; according to Greek myth, the birthplace of Apollo, the god of music and the arts, and of Artemis, goddess of the hunt; and the site of great festivals in their honor.

[4] From the essay "Of Beauty" (1625) by Francis Bacon (1561–1626), Baron Verulam; Poe uses "exquisite" in place of Bacon's "excellent."

[5] In Homer's *Odyssey*, Book VI, the curly hair of Odysseus is likened to a hyacinth.   [6] Curved.

and the majesty, the fullness and the spirituality, of the Greek—the contour which the god Apollo revealed but in a dream, to Cleomenes,[7] the son of the Athenian. And then I peered into the large eyes of Ligeia.

For eyes we have no models in the remotely antique. It might have been, too, that in these eyes of my beloved lay the secret to which Lord Verulam alludes. They were, I must believe, far larger than the ordinary eyes of our own race. They were even fuller than the fullest of the gazelle eyes of the tribe of the valley of Nourjahad.[8] Yet it was only at intervals—in moments of intense excitement—that this peculiarity became more than slightly noticeable in Ligeia. And at such moments was her beauty—in my heated fancy thus it appeared perhaps—the beauty of beings either above or apart from the earth—the beauty of the fabulous Houri of the Turk.[9] The hue of the orbs was the most brilliant of black, and, far over them, hung jetty lashes of great length. The brows, slightly irregular in outline, had the same tint. The "strangeness," however, which I found in the eyes, was of a nature distinct from the formation, or the color, or the brilliancy of the features, and must, after all, be referred to the *expression*. Ah, word of no meaning! behind whose vast latitude of mere sound we intrench our ignorance of so much of the spiritual. The expression of the eyes of Ligeia! How for long hours have I pondered upon it! How have I, through the whole of a midsummer night, struggled to fathom it! What was it—that something more profound than the well of Democritus[10]—which lay far within the pupils of my beloved? What *was* it? I was possessed with a passion to discover. Those eyes! those large, those shining, those divine orbs! they became to me twin stars of Leda,[11] and I to them devoutest of astrologers.

There is no point, among the many incomprehensible anomalies of the science of mind, more thrillingly exciting than the fact—never, I believe, noticed in the schools—that, in our endeavors to recall to memory something long forgotten, we often find ourselves *upon the very verge* of remembrance, without being able, in the end, to remember. And thus how frequently, in my intense scrutiny of Ligeia's eyes, have I felt approaching the full knowledge of their expression—felt it approaching—yet not quite be mine—and so at length entirely depart! And (strange, oh strangest mystery of all!) I found, in the commonest objects of the universe, a circle of analogies to that expression. I mean to say that, subsequently to the period when Ligeia's beauty passed into my spirit, there dwelling as in a shrine, I derived, from many existences in the material world, a sentiment such as I felt always aroused within me by her large and luminous orbs. Yet not the more could I define that sentiment, or analyze, or even steadily view it. I recognized it, let me repeat, sometimes in the survey of a rapidly-growing vine—in the contemplation of a moth, a butterfly, a chrysalis, a stream of running water. I have felt it in the ocean; in the falling of a meteor. I have felt it in the glances of unusually aged people. And there are one or two stars in heaven—(one especially, a star of the

---

[7] An Athenian artist who reputedly sculpted the original statue of the Venus de Medici in the third century B.C.

[8] From *The History of Nourjahad* (1767), an Oriental romance by the English writer Frances Sheridan (1724–1766).

[9] Beautiful maidens who wait in Paradise for deserving Mohammedans, from *The History of Nourjahad*.

[10] A fifth century B.C. Greek philosopher who characteristically laughed at the follies of mankind (according to the Roman satirist Juvenal), and said that "Truth lies at the bottom of a well."

[11] According to Greek myth, the rape of Leda by Zeus resulted in twin sons, Castor and Pollux, who were eventually reincarnated as stars in the constellation Gemini.

sixth magnitude, double and changeable, to be found near the large star in Lyra[12]) in a telescopic scrutiny of which I have been made aware of the feeling. I have been filled with it by certain sounds from stringed instruments, and not unfrequently by passages from books. Among innumerable other instances, I well remember something in a volume of Joseph Glanvill, which (perhaps merely from its quaintness—who shall say?) never failed to inspire me with the sentiment;— "And the will therein lieth, which dieth not. Who knoweth the mysteries of the will, with its vigor? For God is but a great will pervading all things by nature of its intentness. Man doth not yield him to the angels, nor unto death utterly, save only through the weakness of his feeble will."

Length of years, and subsequent reflection, have enabled me to trace, indeed, some remote connection between this passage in the English moralist and a portion of the character of Ligeia. An *intensity* in thought, action, or speech, was possibly, in her, a result, or at least an index, of that gigantic volition which, during our long intercourse, failed to give other and more immediate evidence of its existence. Of all the women whom I have ever known, she, the outwardly calm, the ever-placid Ligeia, was the most violently a prey to the tumultuous vultures of stern passion. And of such passion I could form no estimate, save by the miraculous expansion of those eyes which at once so delighted and appalled me—by the almost magical melody, modulation, distinctness and placidity of her very low voice—and by the fierce energy (rendered doubly effective by contrast with her manner of utterance) of the wild words which she habitually uttered.

I have spoken of the learning of Ligeia: it was immense—such as I have never known in woman. In the classical tongues was she deeply proficient, and as far as my own acquaintance extended in regard to the modern dialects of Europe, I have never known her at fault. Indeed upon any theme of the most admired, because simply the most abstruse of the boasted erudition of the academy, have I *ever* found Ligeia at fault? How singularly—how thrillingly, this one point in the nature of my wife has forced itself, at this late period only, upon my attention! I said her knowledge was such as I have never known in woman—but where breathes the man who has traversed, and successfully, *all* the wide areas of moral, physical, and mathematical science? I saw not then what I now clearly perceive, that the acquisitions of Ligeia were gigantic, were astounding; yet I was sufficiently aware of her infinite supremacy to resign myself, with a child-like confidence, to her guidance through the chaotic world of metaphysical investigation at which I was most busily occupied during the earlier years of our marriage. With how vast a triumph—with how vivid a delight—with how much of all that is ethereal in hope—did I *feel*, as she bent over me in studies but little sought—but less known—that delicious vista by slow degrees expanding before me, down whose long, gorgeous, and all untrodden path, I might at length pass onward to the goal of a wisdom too divinely precious not to be forbidden!

How poignant, then, must have been the grief with which, after some years, I beheld my well-grounded expectations take wings to themselves and fly away! Without Ligeia I was but as a child groping benighted. Her presence, her readings alone, rendered vividly luminous the many mysteries of the transcendentalism in which we were immersed. Wanting the radiant lustre of her eyes, letters, lambent and golden, grew duller than Saturnian lead.[13] And now those eyes shone less and

---

[12] The "large star" in the constellation Lyra is Vega, or Alpha Lyrae.

[13] In alchemy Saturn is the term for lead; to astrologers, the planet Saturn causes gloominess and sluggishness.

less frequently upon the pages over which I pored. Ligeia grew ill. The wild eyes blazed with a too—too glorious effulgence; the pale fingers became of the transparent waxen hue of the grave, and the blue veins upon the lofty forehead swelled and sank impetuously with the tides of the most gentle emotion. I saw that she must die—and I struggled desperately in spirit with the grim Azrael.[14] And the struggles of the passionate wife were, to my astonishment, even more energetic than my own. There had been much in her stern nature to impress me with the belief that, to her, death would have come without its terrors;—but not so. Words are impotent to convey any just idea of the fierceness of resistance with which she wrestled with the Shadow.[15] I groaned in anguish at the pitiable spectacle. I would have soothed—I would have reasoned; but, in the intensity of her wild desire for life,—for life—*but* for life—solace and reason were alike the uttermost of folly. Yet not until the last instance, amid the most convulsive writhings of her fierce spirit, was shaken the external placidity of her demeanor. Her voice grew more gentle—grew more low—yet I would not wish to dwell upon the wild meaning of the quietly uttered words. My brain reeled as I hearkened, entranced, to a melody more than mortal—to assumptions and aspirations which mortality had never before known.

That she loved me I should not have doubted; and I might have been easily aware that, in a bosom such as hers, love would have reigned no ordinary passion. But in death only, was I fully impressed with the strength of her affection. For long hours, detaining my hand, would she pour out before me the overflowing of a heart whose more than passionate devotion amounted to idolatry. How had I deserved to be so blessed by such confessions?—how had I deserved to be so cursed with the removal of my beloved in the hour of her making them? But upon this subject I cannot bear to dilate. Let me say only, that in Ligeia's more than womanly abandonment to a love, alas! all unmerited, all unworthily bestowed, I at length recognized the principle of her longing with so wildly earnest a desire for the life which was now fleeing so rapidly away. It is this wild longing—it is this eager vehemence of desire for life—*but* for life—that I have no power to portray—no utterance capable of expressing.

At high noon of the night in which she departed, beckoning me, peremptorily, to her side, she bade me repeat certain verses composed by herself not many days before. I obeyed her.—They were these:

> Lo! 't is a gala night
>   Within the lonesome latter years!
> An angel throng, bewinged, bedight[16]
>   In veils, and drowned in tears,
> Sit in a theatre, to see
>   A play of hopes and fears,
> While the orchestra breathes fitfully
>   The music of the spheres.[17]
>
> Mimes, in the form of God on high,
>   Mutter and mumble low,
> And hither and thither fly—
>   Mere puppets they, who come and go

[14] The Angel of Death in both Jewish and Moslem legend.   [15] Death.   [16] Adorned, arrayed.
[17] Melodies produced by the revolution of stars and planets, according to ancient astronomers.

At bidding of vast formless things
   That shift the scenery to and fro,
Flapping from out their Condor wings
   Invisible Wo!

That motley drama!—oh, be sure
   It shall not be forgot!
With its Phantom chased forever more,
   By a crowd that seize it not,
Through a circle that ever returneth in
   To the self-same spot,
And much of Madness and more of Sin,
   And Horror the soul of the plot.

But see, amid the mimic rout,
   A crawling shape intrude!
A blood-red thing that writes from out
   The scenic solitude!
It writhes!—it writhes!—with mortal pangs
   The mimes become its food,
And the seraphs sob at vermin fangs
   In human gore imbued.

Out—out are the lights—out all!
   And over each quivering form,
The curtain, a funeral pall,
   Comes down with the rush of a storm,
And the angels, all pallid and wan,
   Uprising, unveiling, affirm
That the play is the tragedy, "Man,"
   And its hero the Conqueror Worm.[18]

"O God!" half shrieked Ligeia, leaping to her feet and extending her arms aloft with a spasmodic movement, as I made an end of these lines—"O God! O Divine Father!—shall these things be undeviatingly so?—shall this Conqueror be not once conquered? Are we not part and parcel in Thee? Who—who knoweth the mysteries of the will with its vigor? Man doth not yield him to the angels, *nor unto death utterly,* save only through the weakness of his feeble will."

And now, as if exhausted with emotion, she suffered her white arms to fall, and returned solemnly to her bed of death. And as she breathed her last sighs, there came mingled with them a low murmur from her lips. I bent to them my ear and distinguished, again, the concluding words of the passage in Glanvill—*"Man doth not yield him to the angels, nor unto death utterly, save only through the weakness of his feeble will."*

She died;—and I, crushed into the very dust with sorrow, could no longer endure the lonely desolation of my dwelling in the dim and decaying city by the Rhine. I had no lack of what the world calls wealth. Ligeia had brought me far more, very far more than ordinarily falls to the lot of mortals. After a few months,

[18] This poem was first published as "The Conqueror Worm" in *Graham's Magazine* in January 1843 and was incorporated into "Ligeia" in 1845.

therefore, of weary and aimless wandering, I purchased, and put in some repair, an abbey, which I shall not name, in one of the wildest and least frequented portions of fair England. The gloomy and dreary grandeur of the building, the almost savage aspect of the domain, the many melancholy and time-honored memories connected with both, had much in unison with the feelings of utter abandonment which had driven me into that remote and unsocial region of the country. Yet although the external abbey, with its verdant decay hanging about it, suffered but little alteration, I gave way, with a child-like perversity, and perchance with a faint hope of alleviating my sorrows, to a display of more than regal magnificence within.—For such follies, even in childhood, I had imbibed a taste and now they came back to me as if in the dotage of grief. Alas, I feel how much even of incipient madness might have been discovered in the gorgeous and fantastic draperies, in the solemn carvings of Egypt, in the wild cornices and furniture, in the Bedlam[19] patterns of the carpets of tufted gold! I had become a bounden slave in the trammels[20] of opium, and my labors and my orders had taken a coloring from my dreams. But these absurdities I must not pause to detail. Let me speak only of that one chamber, ever accursed, whither in a moment of mental alienation, I led from the altar as my bride—as the successor of the unforgotten Ligeia—the fair-haired and blue-eyed Lady Rowena Trevanion, of Tremaine.

There is no individual portion of the architecture and decoration of that bridal chamber which is not now visibly before me. Where were the souls of the haughty family of the bride, when, through thirst of gold, they permitted to pass the threshold of an apartment *so* bedecked, a maiden and a daughter so beloved? I have said that I minutely remember the details of the chamber—yet I am sadly forgetful on topics of deep moment—and here there was no system, no keeping, in the fantastic display, to take hold upon the memory. The room lay in a high turret of the castellated abbey, was pentagonal in shape, and of capacious size. Occupying the whole southern face of the pentagon was the sole window—an immense sheet of unbroken glass from Venice—a single pane, and tinted of a leaden hue, so that the rays of either the sun or moon, passing through it, fell with a ghastly lustre on the objects within. Over the upper portion of this huge window, extended the trellice-work of an aged vine, which clambered up the massy walls of the turret. The ceiling, of gloomy-looking oak, was excessively lofty, vaulted, and elaborately fretted[21] with the wildest and most grotesque specimens of a semi-Gothic, semi-Druidical[22] device. From out the most central recess of this melancholy vaulting, depended, by a single chain of gold with long links, a huge censer of the same metal, Saracenic in pattern,[23] and with many perforations so contrived that there writhed in and out of them, as if endued with a serpent vitality, a continual succession of parti-colored fires.

Some few ottomans and golden candelabra, of Eastern figure, were in various stations about—and there was the couch, too—the bridal couch—of an Indian model, and low, and sculptured of solid ebony, with a pall-like canopy above. In each of the angles of the chamber stood on end a gigantic sarcophagus[24] of black granite, from the tombs of the kings over against Luxor,[25] with their aged lids full

---

[19] Insane, crazy. "Bedlam" is short for "Bethlehem Hospital," a London asylum for the mentally deranged.
[20] Restraints.   [21] Ornamented with intersecting patterns.
[22] The Druids were a mysterious priestly class in ancient Britain and Ireland.
[23] A container (of gold) for burning incense, with an Arabian design.   [24] A coffin.
[25] A city in ancient Egypt and site of famous ruins.

of immemorial sculpture. But in the draping of the apartment lay, alas! the chief phantasy of all. The lofty walls, gigantic in height—even unproportionably so—were hung from summit to foot, in vast folds, with a heavy and massive-looking tapestry—tapestry of a material which was found alike as a carpet on the floor, as a covering for the ottomans and the ebony bed, as a canopy for the bed, and as the gorgeous volutes[26] of the curtains which partially shaded the window. The material was the richest cloth of gold. It was spotted all over, at irregular intervals, with arabesque[27] figures, about a foot in diameter, and wrought upon the cloth in patterns of the most jetty black. But these figures partook of the true character of the arabesque only when regarded from a single point of view. By a contrivance now common, and indeed traceable to a very remote period of antiquity, they were made changeable in aspect. To one entering the room, they bore the appearance of simple monstrosities; but upon a farther advance, this appearance gradually departed; and step by step, as the visiter moved his station in the chamber, he saw himself surrounded by an endless succession of the ghastly forms which belong to the superstition of the Norman,[28] or arise in the guilty slumbers of the monk. The phantasmagoric effect was vastly heightened by the artificial introduction of a strong continual current of wind behind the draperies—giving a hideous and uneasy animation to the whole.

In halls such as these—in a bridal chamber such as this—I passed, with the Lady of Tremaine, the unhallowed hours of the first month of our marriage—passed them with but little disquietude. That my wife dreaded the fierce moodiness of my temper—that she shunned me and loved me but little—I could not help perceiving; but it gave me rather pleasure than otherwise. I loathed her with a hatred belonging more to demon than to man. My memory flew back, (oh, with what intensity of regret!) to Ligeia, the beloved, the august, the beautiful, the entombed. I revelled in recollections of her purity, of her wisdom, of her lofty, her ethereal nature, of her passionate, her idolatrous love. Now, then, did my spirit fully and freely burn with more than all the fires of her own. In the excitement of my opium dreams (for I was habitually fettered in the shackles of the drug) I would call aloud upon her name, during the silence of the night, or among the sheltered recesses of the glens by day, as if, through the wild eagerness, the solemn passion, the consuming ardor of my longing for the departed, I could restore her to the pathway she had abandoned—ah, *could* it be forever?—upon the earth.

About the commencement of the second month of the marriage, the Lady Rowena was attacked with sudden illness, from which her recovery was slow. The fever which consumed her rendered her nights uneasy; and in her perturbed state of half-slumber, she spoke of sounds, and of motions, in and about the chamber of the turret, which I concluded had no origin save in the distemper of her fancy, or perhaps in the phantasmagoric influences of the chamber itself. She became at length convalescent—finally well. Yet but a brief period elapsed, ere a second more violent disorder again threw her upon a bed of suffering; and from this attack her frame, at all times feeble, never altogether recovered. Her illnesses were, after

[26] Spiral or scroll-like designs.

[27] Intricate designs of flowers and fruit interlaced with figures of humans and animals. Poe called his first collection of tales, including "Ligeia," *Tales of the Grotesque and Arabesque* (1840).

[28] The Normans (or "Northmen," the term Poe used in *The American Museum* in 1838) were the Vikings who conquered the section of France known as Normandy; their art is known for its intricate designs.

this epoch, of alarming character, and of more alarming recurrence, defying alike the knowledge and the great exertions of her physicians. With the increase of the chronic disease which had thus, apparently, taken too sure hold upon her constitution to be eradicated by human means, I could not fail to observe a similar increase in the nervous irritation of her temperament, and in her excitability by trivial causes of fear. She spoke again, and now more frequently and pertinaciously, of the sounds—of the slight sounds—and of the unusual motions among the tapestries, to which she had formerly alluded.

One night, near the closing in of September, she pressed this distressing subject with more than usual emphasis upon my attention. She had just awakened from an unquiet slumber, and I had been watching, with feelings half of anxiety, half of vague terror, the workings of her emaciated countenance. I sat by the side of her ebony bed, upon one of the ottomans of India. She partly arose, and spoke, in an earnest low whisper, of sounds which she *then* heard, but which I could not hear—of motions which she *then* saw, but which I could not perceive. The wind was rushing hurriedly behind the tapestries, and I wished to show her (what, let me confess it, I could not *all* believe) that those almost inarticulate breathings, and those very gentle variations of the figures upon the wall, were but the natural effects of that customary rushing of the wind. But a deadly pallor, overspreading her face, had proved to me that my exertions to reassure her would be fruitless. She appeared to be fainting, and no attendants were within call. I remembered where was deposited a decanter of light wine which had been ordered by her physicians, and hastened across the chamber to procure it. But, as I stepped beneath the light of the censer, two circumstances of a startling nature attracted my attention. I had felt that some palpable although invisible object had passed lightly by my person; and I saw that there lay upon the golden carpet, in the very middle of the rich lustre thrown from the censer, a shadow—a faint, indefinite shadow of angelic aspect—such as might be fancied for the shadow of a shade. But I was wild with the excitement of an immoderate dose of opium, and heeded these things but little, nor spoke of them to Rowena. Having found the wine, I recrossed the chamber, and poured out a goblet-ful, which I held to the lips of the fainting lady. She had now partially recovered, however, and took the vessel herself, while I sank upon an ottoman near me, with my eyes fastened upon her person. It was then that I became distinctly aware of a gentle foot-fall upon the carpet, and near the couch; and in a second thereafter, as Rowena was in the act of raising the wine to her lips, I saw, or may have dreamed that I saw, fall within the goblet, as if from some invisible spring in the atmosphere of the room, three or four large drops of a brilliant and ruby colored fluid. If this I saw—not so Rowena. She swallowed the wine unhesitatingly, and I forbore to speak to her of a circumstance which must, after all, I considered, have been but the suggestion of a vivid imagination, rendered morbidly active by the terror of the lady, by the opium, and by the hour.

Yet I cannot conceal it from my own perception that, immediately subsequent to the fall of the ruby-drops, a rapid change for the worse took place in the disorder of my wife; so that, on the third subsequent night, the hands of her menials prepared her for the tomb, and on the fourth, I sat alone, with her shrouded body, in that fantastic chamber which had received her as my bride.—Wild visions, opium-engendered, flitted, shadow-like, before me. I gazed with unquiet eye upon the sarcophagi in the angles of the room, upon the varying figures of the drapery, and upon the writhing of the parti-colored fires in the censer overhead.

My eyes then fell, as I called to mind the circumstances of a former night, to the spot beneath the glare of the censer where I had seen the faint traces of the shadow. It was there, however, no longer; and breathing with greater freedom, I turned my glances to the pallid and rigid figure upon the bed. Then rushed upon me a thousand memories of Ligeia—and then came back upon my heart, with the turbulent violence of a flood, the whole of that unutterable wo with which I had regarded *her* thus enshrouded. The night waned; and still, with a bosom full of bitter thoughts of the one only and supremely beloved, I remained gazing upon the body of Rowena.

It might have been midnight, or perhaps earlier, or later, for I had taken no note of time, when a sob, low, gentle, but very distinct, startled me from my revery.— I *felt* that it came from the bed of ebony—the bed of death. I listened in an agony of superstitious terror—but there was no repetition of the sound. I strained my vision to detect any motion in the corpse—but there was not the slightest perceptible. Yet I could not have been deceived. I *had* heard the noise, however faint, and my soul was awakened within me. I resolutely and perseveringly kept my attention riveted upon the body. Many minutes elapsed before any circumstance occurred tending to throw light upon the mystery. At length it became evident that a slight, a very feeble, and barely noticeable tinge of color had flushed up within the cheeks, and along the sunken small veins of the eyelids. Through a species of unutterable horror and awe, for which the language of mortality has no sufficiently energetic expression, I felt my heart cease to beat, my limbs grow rigid where I sat. Yet a sense of duty finally operated to restore my self-possession. I could no longer doubt that we had been precipitate in our preparations—that Rowena still lived. It was necessary that some immediate exertion be made; yet the turret was altogether apart from the portion of the abbey tenanted by the servants—there were none within call—I had no means of summoning them to my aid without leaving the room for many minutes—and this I could not venture to do. I therefore struggled alone in my endeavors to call back the spirit still hovering. In a short period it was certain, however, that a relapse had taken place; the color disappeared from both eyelid and cheek, leaving a wanness even more than that of marble; the lips became doubly shrivelled and pinched up in the ghastly expression of death; a repulsive clamminess and coldness overspread rapidly the surface of the body; and all the usual rigorous stiffness immediately supervened. I fell back with a shudder upon the couch from which I had been so startlingly aroused, and again gave myself up to passionate waking visions of Ligeia.

An hour thus elapsed when (could it be possible?) I was a second time aware of some vague sound issuing from the region of the bed. I listened—in extremity of horror. The sound came again—it was a sigh. Rushing to the corpse, I saw— distinctly saw—a tremor upon the lips. In a minute afterward they relaxed, disclosing a bright line of the pearly teeth. Amazement now struggled in my bosom with the profound awe which had hitherto reigned there alone. I felt that my vision grew dim, that my reason wandered; and it was only by a violent effort that I at length succeeded in nerving myself to the task which duty thus once more had pointed out. There was now a partial glow upon the forehead and upon the cheek and throat; a perceptible warmth pervaded the whole frame; there was even a slight pulsation at the heart. The lady *lived*; and with redoubled ardor I betook myself to the task of restoration. I chafed and bathed the temples and the hands, and used every exertion which experience, and no little medical reading, could suggest. But in vain. Suddenly, the color fled, the pulsation ceased, the lips resumed the expression of the dead, and, in an instant afterward, the whole body took upon itself the icy chilliness, the livid hue, the intense rigidity, the sunken outline, and all the loathsome peculiarities of that which has been, for many days, a tenant of the tomb.

And again I sunk into visions of Ligeia—and again, (what marvel that I shudder while I write?) *again* there reached my ears a low sob from the region of the ebony bed. But why shall I minutely detail the unspeakable horrors of that night? Why shall I pause to relate how, time after time, until near the period of the gray dawn, this hideous drama of revivification was repeated; how each terrific relapse was only into a sterner and apparently more irredeemable death; how each agony wore the aspect of a struggle with some invisible foe; and how each struggle was succeeded by I know not what of wild change in the personal appearance of the corpse? Let me hurry to a conclusion.

The greater part of the fearful night had worn away, and she who had been dead, once again stirred—and now more vigorously than hitherto, although arousing from a dissolution more appalling in its utter hopelessness than any. I had long ceased to struggle or to move, and remained sitting rigidly upon the ottoman, a helpless prey to a whirl of violent emotions, of which extreme awe was perhaps the least terrible, the least consuming. The corpse, I repeat, stirred, and now more vigorously than before. The hues of life flushed up with unwonted energy into the countenance—the limbs relaxed—and, save that the eyelids were yet pressed heavily together, and that the bandages and draperies of the grave still imparted their charnel[29] character to the figure, I might have dreamed that Rowena had indeed shaken off, utterly, the fetters of Death. But if this idea was not, even then, altogether adopted, I could at least doubt no longer, when, arising from the bed, tottering, with feeble steps, with closed eyes, and with the manner of one bewildered in a dream, the thing that was enshrouded advanced boldly and palpably into the middle of the apartment.

I trembled not—I stirred not—for a crowd of unutterable fancies connected with the air, the stature, the demeanor of the figure, rushing hurriedly through my brain, had paralyzed—had chilled me into stone. I stirred not—but gazed upon the apparition. There was a mad disorder in my thoughts—a tumult unappeasable. Could it, indeed, be the *living* Rowena who confronted me? Could it indeed be Rowena at all—the fair-haired, the blue-eyed Lady Rowena Trevanion of Tremaine? Why, *why* should I doubt it? The bandage lay heavily about the mouth—but then might it not be the mouth of the breathing Lady of Tremaine? And the cheeks—there were the roses as in her noon of life—yes, these might indeed be the fair cheeks of the living Lady of Tremaine. And the chin, with its dimples, as in health, might it not be hers?—but *had she then grown taller since her malady?* What inexpressible madness seized me with that thought? One bound, and I had reached her feet! Shrinking from my touch, she let fall from her head, unloosened, the ghastly cerements[30] which had confined it, and there streamed forth, into the rushing atmosphere of the chamber, huge masses of long and dishevelled hair; *it was blacker than the raven wings of the midnight!* And now slowly opened *the eyes* of the figure which stood before me. "Here then, at least," I shrieked aloud, "can I never—can I never be mistaken—these are the full, and the black, and the wild eyes—of my lost love—of the lady—of the LADY LIGEIA."

1838

---

[29] Gravelike.   [30] Shrouds.

THE FALL OF THE HOUSE OF USHER*

Son cœur est un luth suspendu;
Sitôt qu'on le touche il résonne.
DE BÉRANGER[1]

During the whole of a dull, dark, and soundless day in the autumn of the year, when the clouds hung oppressively low in the heavens, I had been passing alone, on horseback, through a singularly dreary tract of country; and at length found myself, as the shades of the evening drew on, within view of the melancholy House of Usher. I know not how it was—but, with the first glimpse of the building, a sense of insufferable gloom pervaded my spirit. I say insufferable; for the feeling was unrelieved by any of that half-pleasurable, because poetic, sentiment, with which the mind usually receives even the sternest natural images of the desolate or terrible. I looked upon the scene before me—upon the mere house, and the simple landscape features of the domain—upon the bleak walls—upon the vacant eye-like windows—upon a few rank sedges—and upon a few white trunks of decayed trees—with an utter depression of soul which I can compare to no earthly sensation more properly than to the after-dream of the reveller upon opium—the bitter lapse into everyday life—the hideous dropping off of the veil. There was an iciness, a sinking, a sickening of the heart—an unredeemed dreariness of thought which no goading of the imagination could torture into aught of the sublime. What was it—I paused to think—what was it that so unnerved me in the contemplation of the House of Usher? It was a mystery all insoluble; nor could I grapple with the shadowy fancies that crowded upon me as I pondered. I was forced to fall back upon the unsatisfactory conclusion, that while, beyond doubt, there *are* combinations of very simple natural objects which have the power of thus affecting us, still the analysis of this power lies among considerations beyond our depth. It was possible, I reflected, that a mere different arrangement of the particulars of the scene, of the details of the picture, would be sufficient to modify, or perhaps to annihilate its capacity for sorrowful impression; and, acting upon this idea, I reined my horse to the precipitous brink of a black and lurid tarn[2] that lay in unruffled lustre by the dwelling, and gazed down—but with a shudder even more thrilling than before—upon the remodelled and inverted images of the gray sedge, and the ghastly tree-stems, and the vacant and eye-like windows.

Nevertheless, in this mansion of gloom I now proposed to myself a sojourn of some weeks. Its proprietor, Roderick Usher, had been one of my boon companions in boyhood; but many years had elapsed since our last meeting. A letter, however, had lately reached me in a distant part of the country—a letter from him—which, in its wildly importunate nature, had admitted of no other than a personal reply. The MS. gave evidence of nervous agitation. The writer spoke of acute bodily illness—of a mental disorder which oppressed him—and of an earnest desire to see me, as his best, and indeed his only personal friend, with a view of attempting, by the cheerfulness of my society, some alleviation of his malady.

---

* First published in *Burton's Gentleman's Magazine* in 1839 and collected in *Tales of the Grotesque and Arabesque* (1840).

[1] "His heart is a lute strung tight; / As soon as one touches it, it resounds," from the poem "Le Refus" (1831) by Pierre-Jean de Béranger (1780–1857); Poe changed "My heart" to "His heart."

[2] A small mountain lake.

It was the manner in which all this, and much more, was said—it was the apparent *heart* that went with his request—which allowed me no room for hesitation; and I accordingly obeyed forthwith what I still considered a very singular summons.

Although, as boys, we had been even intimate associates, yet I really knew little of my friend. His reserve had been always excessive and habitual. I was aware, however, that his very ancient family had been noted, time out of mind, for a peculiar sensibility of temperament, displaying itself, through long ages, in many works of exalted art, and manifested, of late, in repeated deeds of munificent yet unobtrusive charity, as well as in a passionate devotion to the intricacies, perhaps even more than to the orthodox and easily recognisable beauties, of musical science. I had learned, too, the very remarkable fact, that the stem of the Usher race, all time-honoured as it was, had put forth, at no period, any enduring branch; in other words, that the entire family lay in the direct line of descent, and had always, with very trifling and very temporary variation, so lain. It was this deficiency, I considered, while running over in thought the perfect keeping of the character of the premises with the accredited character of the people, and while speculating upon the possible influence which the one, in the long lapse of centuries, might have exercised upon the other—it was this deficiency, perhaps, of collateral issue, and the consequent undeviating transmission, from sire to son, of the patrimony with the name, which had, at length, so identified the two as to merge the original title of the estate in the quaint and equivocal appellation of the "House of Usher"—an appellation which seemed to include, in the minds of the peasantry who used it, both the family and the family mansion.

I have said that the sole effect of my somewhat childish experiment—that of looking down within the tarn—had been to deepen the first singular impression. There can be no doubt that the consciousness of the rapid increase of my superstition—for why should I not so term it?—served mainly to accelerate the increase itself. Such, I have long known, is the paradoxical law of all sentiments having terror as a basis. And it might have been for this reason only, that, when I again uplifted my eyes to the house itself, from its image in the pool, there grew in my mind a strange fancy—a fancy so ridiculous, indeed, that I but mention it to show the vivid force of the sensations which oppressed me. I had so worked upon my imagination as really to believe that about the whole mansion and domain there hung an atmosphere peculiar to themselves and their immediate vicinity—an atmosphere which had no affinity with the air of heaven, but which had reeked up from the decayed trees, and the gray wall, and the silent tarn—a pestilent and mystic vapour, dull, sluggish, faintly discernible, and leaden-hued.

Shaking off from my spirit what *must* have been a dream, I scanned more narrowly the real aspect of the building. Its principal feature seemed to be that of an excessive antiquity. The discoloration of ages had been great. Minute fungi overspread the whole exterior, hanging in a fine tangled web-work from the eaves. Yet all this was apart from any extraordinary dilapidation. No portion of the masonry had fallen; and there appeared to be a wild inconsistency between its still perfect adaptation of parts, and the crumbling condition of the individual stones. In this there was much that reminded me of the specious totality of old wood-work which has rotted for long years in some neglected vault, with no disturbance from the breath of the external air. Beyond this indication of extensive decay, however, the fabric gave little token of instability. Perhaps the eye of a scrutinising observer might have discovered a barely perceptible fissure, which, extending from the roof of the building in front, made its way down the wall in a zigzag direction, until it became lost in the sullen waters of the tarn.

Noticing these things, I rode over a short causeway to the house. A servant in waiting took my horse, and I entered the Gothic archway of the hall. A valet, of stealthy step, thence conducted me, in silence, through many dark and intricate passages in my progress to the *studio* of his master. Much that I encountered on the way contributed, I know not how, to heighten the vague sentiments of which I have already spoken. While the objects around me—while the carvings of the ceilings, the sombre tapestries of the walls, the ebon blackness of the floors, and the phantasmagoric armorial trophies which rattled as I strode, were but matters to which, or to such as which, I had been accustomed from my infancy—while I hesitated not to acknowledge how familiar was all this—I still wondered to find how unfamiliar were the fancies which ordinary images were stirring up. On one of the staircases, I met the physician of the family. His countenance, I thought, wore a mingled expression of low cunning and perplexity. He accosted me with trepidation and passed on. The valet now threw open a door and ushered me into the presence of his master.

The room in which I found myself was very large and lofty. The windows were long, narrow, and pointed, and at so vast a distance from the black oaken floor as to be altogether inaccessible from within. Feeble gleams of encrimsoned light made their way through the trellised panes, and served to render sufficiently distinct the more prominent objects around; the eye, however, struggled in vain to reach the remoter angles of the chamber, or the recesses of the vaulted and fretted ceiling. Dark draperies hung upon the walls. The general furniture was profuse, comfortless, antique, and tattered. Many books and musical instruments lay scattered about, but failed to give any vitality to the scene. I felt that I breathed an atmosphere of sorrow. An air of stern, deep, and irredeemable gloom hung over and pervaded all.[3]

Upon my entrance, Usher arose from a sofa on which he had been lying at full length, and greeted me with a vivacious warmth which had much in it, I at first thought, of an overdone cordiality—of the constrained effort of the *ennuyé*[4] man of the world. A glance, however, at his countenance, convinced me of his perfect sincerity. We sat down; and for some moments, while he spoke not, I gazed upon him with a feeling half of pity, half of awe. Surely, man had never before so terribly altered, in so brief a period, as had Roderick Usher! It was with difficulty that I could bring myself to admit the identity of the wan being before me with the companion of my early boyhood. Yet the character of his face had been at all times remarkable. A cadaverousness of complexion; an eye large, liquid, and luminous beyond comparison; lips somewhat thin and very pallid, but of a surpassingly beautiful curve; a nose of a delicate Hebrew model, but with a breadth of nostril unusual in similar formations; a finely moulded chin, speaking, in its want of prominence, of a want of moral energy; hair of a more than web-like softness and tenuity; these features, with an inordinate expansion above the regions of the temple, made up altogether a countenance not easily to be forgotten. And now in the mere exaggeration of the prevailing character of these features, and of the expression they were wont to convey, lay so much of change that I doubted to whom I spoke. The now ghastly pallor of the skin, and the now miraculous lustre of the eye, above all things startled and even awed me. The silken

---

[3] The poet Richard Wilbur has observed that the interior of the house is an analogue of Usher's "visionary Mind" (*The Recognition of Poe*, ed. E. Carlson, 1966).

[4] "Bored" (French).

hair, too, had been suffered to grow all unheeded, and as, in its wild gossamer texture, it floated rather than fell about the face, I could not, even with effort, connect its Arabesque[5] expression with any idea of simple humanity.

In the manner of my friend I was at once struck with an incoherence—an inconsistency; and I soon found this to arise from a series of feeble and futile struggles to overcome an habitual trepidancy—an excessive nervous agitation. For something of this nature I had indeed been prepared, no less by his letter, than by reminiscences of certain boyish traits, and by conclusions deduced from his peculiar physical conformation and temperament. His action was alternately vivacious and sullen. His voice varied rapidly from a tremulous indecision (when the animal spirits seemed utterly in abeyance) to that species of energetic concision—that abrupt, weighty, unhurried, and hollow-sounding enunciation—that leaden, self-balanced and perfectly modulated guttural utterance, which may be observed in the lost drunkard, or the irreclaimable eater of opium, during the periods of his most intense excitement.

It was thus that he spoke of the object of my visit, of his earnest desire to see me, and of the solace he expected me to afford him. He entered, at some length, into what he conceived to be the nature of his malady. It was, he said, a constitutional and a family evil, and one for which he despaired to find a remedy—a mere nervous affection, he immediately added, which would undoubtedly soon pass off. It displayed itself in a host of unnatural sensations. Some of these, as he detailed them, interested and bewildered me; although, perhaps, the terms, and the general manner of the narration had their weight. He suffered much from a morbid acuteness of the senses; the most insipid food was alone endurable; he could wear only garments of certain texture; the odours of all flowers were oppressive; his eyes were tortured by even a faint light; and there were but peculiar sounds, and these from stringed instruments, which did not inspire him with horror.

To an anomalous species of terror I found him a bounden slave. "I shall perish," said he, "I *must* perish in this deplorable folly. Thus, thus, and not otherwise, shall I be lost. I dread the events of the future, not in themselves, but in their results. I shudder at the thought of any, even the most trivial, incident, which may operate upon this intolerable agitation of soul. I have, indeed, no abhorrence of danger, except in its absolute effect—in terror. In this unnerved—in this pitiable condition—I feel that the period will sooner or later arrive when I must abandon life and reason together, in some struggle with the grim phantasm, FEAR."

I learned, moreover, at intervals, and through broken and equivocal hints, another singular feature of his mental condition. He was enchained by certain superstitious impressions in regard to the dwelling which he tenanted, and whence, for many years, he had never ventured forth—in regard to an influence whose supposititious force was conveyed in terms too shadowy here to be re-stated—an influence which some peculiarities in the mere form and substance of his family mansion, had, by dint of long sufferance, he said, obtained over his spirit—an effect which the *physique* of the gray walls and turrets, and of the dim tarn into which they all looked down, had, at length, brought about upon the *morale* of his existence.

He admitted, however, although with hesitation, that much of the peculiar gloom which thus afflicted him could be traced to a more natural and far more

---

[5] Here, complex or unfamiliar.

palpable origin—to the severe and long-continued illness—indeed to the evidently approaching dissolution—of a tenderly beloved sister—his sole companion for long years—his last and only relative on earth. "Her decease," he said, with a bitterness which I can never forget, "would leave him (him the hopeless and the frail) the last of the ancient race of the Ushers." While he spoke, the lady Madeline (for so was she called) passed slowly through a remote portion of the apartment, and, without having noticed my presence, disappeared. I regarded her with an utter astonishment not unmingled with dread—and yet I found it impossible to account for such feelings. A sensation of stupor oppressed me, as my eyes followed her retreating steps. When a door, at length, closed upon her, my glance sought instinctively and eagerly the countenance of the brother—but he had buried his face in his hands, and I could only perceive that a far more than ordinary wanness had overspread the emaciated fingers through which trickled many passionate tears.

The disease of the lady Madeline had long baffled the skill of her physicians. A settled apathy, a gradual wasting away of the person, and frequent although transient affections of a partially cataleptical[6] character, were the unusual diagnosis. Hitherto she had steadily borne up against the pressure of her malady, and had not betaken herself finally to bed; but, on the closing in of the evening of my arrival at the house, she succumbed (as her brother told me at night with inexpressible agitation) to the prostrating power of the destroyer; and I learned that the glimpse I had obtained of her person would thus probably be the last I should obtain—that the lady, at least while living, would be seen by me no more.

For several days ensuing, her name was unmentioned by either Usher or myself: and during this period I was busied in earnest endeavours to alleviate the melancholoy of my friend. We painted and read together; or I listened, as if in a dream, to the wild improvisations of his speaking guitar. And thus, as a closer and still closer intimacy admitted me more unreservedly into the recesses of his spirit, the more bitterly did I perceive the futility of all attempt at cheering a mind from which darkness, as if an inherent positive quality, poured forth upon all objects of the moral and physical universe, in one unceasing radiation of gloom.

I shall ever bear about me a memory of the many solemn hours I thus spent alone with the master of the House of Usher. Yet I should fail in any attempt to convey an idea of the exact character of the studies, or of the occupations, in which he involved me, or led me the way. An excited and highly distempered ideality threw a sulphureous lustre over all. His long improvised dirges will ring forever in my ears. Among other things, I hold painfully in mind a certain singular perversion and amplification of the wild air of the last waltz of Von Weber.[7] From the paintings over which his elaborate fancy brooded, and which grew, touch by touch, into vaguenesses at which I shuddered the more thrillingly, because I shuddered knowing not why;—from these paintings (vivid as their images now are before me) I would in vain endeavour to educe more than a small portion which should lie within the compass of merely written words. By the utter simplicity, by the nakedness of his designs, he arrested and overawed attention. If ever mortal painted an idea, that mortal was Roderick Usher. For me at least—in the circumstances then surrounding me—there arose out of the pure abstractions which the

---

[6] Without complete consciousness.

[7] "The Last Waltz of Von Weber," by Karl Gottlieb Reissiger (1798–1859), is a tribute to Karl Maria Von Weber (1786–1826), renowned creator of German romantic opera. In his edition of Poe's tales, Thomas O. Mabbott suggests that Usher is playing a dirge for himself at this point.

hypochondriac contrived to throw upon his canvas, an intensity of intolerable awe, no shadow of which felt I ever yet in the contemplation of the certainly glowing yet too concrete reveries of Fuseli.[8]

One of the phantasmagoric conceptions of my friend, partaking not so rigidly of the spirit of abstraction, may be shadowed forth, although feebly, in words. A small picture presented the interior of an immensely long and rectangular vault or tunnel, with low walls, smooth, white, and without interruption or device. Certain accessory points of the design served well to convey the idea that this excavation lay at an exceeding depth below the surface of the earth. No outlet was observed in any portion of its vast extent, and no torch, or other artificial source of light was discernible; yet a flood of intense rays rolled throughout, and bathed the whole in a ghastly and inappropriate splendour.

I have just spoken of that morbid condition of the auditory nerve which rendered all music intolerable to the sufferer, with the exception of certain effects of stringed instruments. It was, perhaps, the narrow limits to which he thus confined himself upon the guitar, which gave birth, in great measure, to the fantastic character of his performances. But the fervid *facility* of his *impromptus* could not be so accounted for. They must have been, and were, in the notes, as well as in the words of his wild fantasias (for he not unfrequently accompanied himself with rhymed verbal improvisations), the result of that intense mental collectedness and concentration to which I have previously alluded as observable only in particular moments of the highest artificial excitement. The words of one of these rhapsodies I have easily remembered. I was, perhaps, the more forcibly impressed with it, as he gave it, because, in the under or mystic current of its meaning, I fancied that I perceived, and for the first time, a full consciousness on the part of Usher, of the tottering of his lofty reason upon her throne. The verses, which were entitled "The Haunted Palace,"[9] ran very nearly, if not accurately, thus:

I

In the greenest of our valleys,
　By good angels tenanted,
Once a fair and stately palace—
　Radiant palace—reared its head.
In the monarch Thought's dominion—
　It stood there!
Never seraph spread a pinion
　Over fabric half so fair.

II

Banners yellow, glorious, golden,
　On its roof did float and flow;
(This—all this—was in the olden
　Time long ago)
And every gentle air that dallied,
　In that sweet day,
Along the ramparts plumed and pallid,
　A winged odour went away.

---

[8] Henry Fuseli (1741–1825), a Swiss-born painter whose career flourished in London, largely due to his interest in the supernatural and the terrifying.

[9] This poem was published separately in the *American Museum of Science, Literature, and the Arts,* in April 1839, five months before the publication of "The Fall of the House of Usher."

III

Wanderers in that happy valley
   Through two luminous windows saw
Spirits moving musically
   To a lute's well-tunèd law,
Round about a throne, where sitting
   (Porphyrogene![10])
In state his glory well befitting,
   The ruler of the realm was seen.

IV

And all with pearl and ruby glowing
   Was the fair palace door,
Through which came flowing, flowing, flowing,
   And sparkling evermore,
A troop of Echoes whose sweet duty
   Was but to sing,
In voices of surpassing beauty,
   The wit and wisdom of their king.

V

But evil things, in robes of sorrow,
   Assailed the monarch's high estate;
(Ah, let us mourn, for never morrow
   Shall dawn upon him, desolate!)
And, round about his home, the glory
   That blushed and bloomed
Is but a dim-remembered story
   Of the old time entombed.

VI

And travellers now within that valley,
   Through the red-litten[11] windows, see
Vast forms that move fantastically
   To a discordant melody;
While, like a rapid ghastly river,
   Through the pale door,
A hideous throng rush out forever,
   And laugh—but smile no more.

    I well remember that suggestions arising from this ballad led us into a train of thought wherein there became manifest an opinion of Usher's which I mention not so much on account of its novelty, (for other men[12] have thought thus,) as on

[10] Born to the purple, of royal birth; Poe assembled this word from Greek roots.   [11] Red-lighted.
[12] Poe's note: "Watson, Dr. Percival, Spallanzani, and especially the Bishop of Landaff.—See 'Chemical Essays,' vol. v." Richard Watson (1737–1816), Bishop of Llandaff, wrote *Chemical Essays,* 5 vols. (1781 and 1787); Thomas Percival (1740–1804), an English scientist, published an article on the sensory perceptions of vegetables in 1785; and the Abbe Lazzaro Spallanzani (1739–1799), an Italian researcher, wrote *Dissertations Relative to the Natural History of Animals and Vegetables* (trans. 1784). Usher's ultimate suggestion is that all matter is sentient, or able to sense.

account of the pertinacity with which he maintained it. This opinion, in its general form, was that of the sentience of all vegetable things. But, in his disordered fancy, the idea had assumed a more daring character, and trespassed, under certain conditions, upon the kingdom of inorganization. I lack words to express the full extent, or the earnest *abandon* of his persuasion. The belief, however, was connected (as I have previously hinted) with the gray stones of the home of his forefathers. The conditions of the sentience had been here, he imagined, fulfilled in the method of collocation of these stones—in the order of their arrangement, as well as in that of the many *fungi* which overspread them, and of the decayed trees which stood around—above all, in the long undisturbed endurance of this arrangement, and in its reduplication in the still waters of the tarn. Its evidence—the evidence of the sentience—was to be seen, he said, (and I here started as he spoke,) in the gradual yet certain condensation of an atmosphere of their own about the waters and the walls. The result was discoverable, he added, in that silent, yet importunate and terrible influence which for centuries had moulded the destinies of his family, and which made *him* what I now saw him—what he was. Such opinions need no comment, and I will make none.

Our books—the books which, for years, had formed no small portion of the mental existence of the invalid—were, as might be supposed, in strict keeping with this character of phantasm. We pored together over such works as the Ververt et Chartreuse of Gresset;[13] the Belphegor of Machiavelli; the Heaven and Hell of Swedenborg; the Subterranean Voyage of Nicholas Klimm by Holberg; the Chiromancy of Robert Flud, of Jean D'Indaginé, and of De la Chambre; the Journey into the Blue Distance of Tieck; and the City of the Sun of Campanella. One favourite volume was a small octavo edition of the *Directorium Inquisitorum,* by the Dominican Eymeric de Gironne; and there were passages in Pomponius Mela, about the old African Satyrs and Ægipans,[14] over which Usher would sit dreaming for hours. His chief delight, however, was found in the perusal of an exceedingly rare and curious book in quarto Gothic—the manual of a forgotten church—the *Vigiliæ Mortuorum secundum Chorum Ecclesiæ Maguntinæ.*[15]

I could not help thinking of the wild ritual of this work, and of its probable influence upon the hypochondriac, when, one evening, having informed me abruptly that the lady Madeline was no more, he stated his intention of preserving her corpse for a fortnight, (previously to its final interment,) in one of the numerous vaults within the main walls of the building. The worldly reason, however, assigned for this singular proceeding, was one which I did not feel at liberty

---

[13] The books are real, and most deal with the supernatural, demonism, and persecution: Jean Baptiste Louis Gresset (1709–1777), a French anticleric; Niccolo Macchiavelli (1469–1527), author of *Belphegor* (1553), in which a devil arrives on earth to prove that women lure men to Hell; Emanuel Swedenborg (1688–1772), a Swedish mystic and author of *Heaven and Hell* (1758); Ludwig Holberg (1684–1754), the apocalyptic Danish author of *Niels Klim's Underground Journey* (1741); Robert Fludd (1574–1637), Jean D'Indaginé (early 16th century), and Martin Cureau de la Chambre (1594–1669), investigators of chiromancy, or palm reading; Ludwig Tieck (1773–1853), author of *Blue Distance,* a narrative of a journey to another world; Tommaso Campanella (1568–1639), author of the utopian *City of the Sun* (1623); Nicholas Eymerico (1320–1399), Spain's grand inquisitor from 1356 to 1399 and author of *Directorium Inquisitorium* (1503), which chronicles the torture of heretics during the Inquisition; Pomponius Mela (A.D. 1st century), a Roman geographer who describes strange beasts in his *De Situ Orbis* (A.D. 43?).

[14] According to Greek myth, creatures that are half-goat, half-man.

[15] "*Vigils for the Dead According to the Church-Choir of Mayence*" (Latin), an anonymous book of requiem rituals printed in Switzerland around 1500.

to dispute. The brother had been led to his resolution (so he told me) by considerations of the unusual character of the malady of the deceased, of certain obtrusive and eager inquiries on the part of her medical men, and of the remote and exposed situation of the burial-ground of the family. I will not deny that when I called to mind the sinister countenance of the person whom I met upon the staircase, on the day of my arrival at the house, I had no desire to oppose what I regarded as at best but a harmless, and by no means an unnatural, precaution.[16]

At the request of Usher, I personally aided him in the arrangements for the temporary entombment. The body having been encoffined, we two alone bore it to its rest. The vault in which we placed it (and which had been so long unopened that our torches, half smothered in its oppressive atmosphere, gave us little opportunity for investigation) was small, damp, and entirely without means of admission for light; lying, at great depth, immediately beneath that portion of the building in which was my own sleeping apartment. It had been used, apparently, in remote feudal times, for the worst purposes of a donjon-keep,[17] and, in later days, as a place of deposit for powder, or some other highly combustible substance, as a portion of its floor, and the whole interior of a long archway through which we reached it, were carefully sheathed with copper. The door, of massive iron, had been, also, similarly protected. Its immense weight caused an unusually sharp grating sound, as it moved upon its hinges.

Having deposited our mournful burden upon tressels within this region of horror, we partially turned aside the yet unscrewed lid of the coffin, and looked upon the face of the tenant. A striking similitude between the brother and sister now first arrested my attention; and Usher, divining, perhaps, my thoughts, murmured out some few words from which I learned that the deceased and himself had been twins, and that sympathies of a scarcely intelligible nature had always existed between them. Our glances, however, rested not long upon the dead—for we could not regard her unawed. The disease which had thus entombed the lady in the maturity of youth, had left, as usual in all maladies of a strictly cataleptical character, the mockery of a faint blush upon the bosom and the face, and that suspiciously lingering smile upon the lip which is so terrible in death. We replaced and screwed down the lid, and, having secured the door of iron, made our way, with toil, into the scarcely less gloomy apartments of the upper portion of the house.

And now, some days of bitter grief having elapsed, an observable change came over the features of the mental disorder of my friend. His ordinary manner had vanished. His ordinary occupations were neglected or forgotten. He roamed from chamber to chamber with hurried, unequal, and objectless step. The pallor of his countenance had assumed, if possible, a more ghastly hue—but the luminousness of his eye had utterly gone out. The once occasional huskiness of his tone was heard no more; and a tremulous quaver, as if of extreme terror, habitually characterized his utterance. There were times, indeed, when I thought his unceasingly agitated mind was labouring with some oppressive secret, to divulge which he struggled for the necessary courage. At times, again, I was obliged to resolve all into the mere inexplicable vagaries of madness, for I beheld him gazing upon vacancy for long hours, in an attitude of the profoundest attention, as if listening to some imaginary sound. It was no wonder that his condition terrified—that it

---

[16] A precaution against Madeline's body being stolen from the grave and sold to medical students and doctors needing cadavers for dissection.

[17] A dungeon.

infected me. I felt creeping upon me, by slow yet certain degrees, the wild influences of his own fantastic yet impressive superstitions.

It was, especially, upon retiring to bed late in the night of the seventh or eighth day after the placing of the lady Madeline within the donjon, that I experienced the full power of such feelings. Sleep came not near my couch—while the hours waned and waned away. I struggled to reason off the nervousness which had dominion over me. I endeavoured to believe that much, if not all of what I felt, was due to the bewildering influence of the gloomy furniture of the room—of the dark and tattered draperies, which, tortured into motion by the breath of a rising tempest, swayed fitfully to and fro upon the walls, and rustled uneasily about the decorations of the bed. But my efforts were fruitless. An irrepressible tremour gradually pervaded my frame; and, at length, there sat upon my very heart an incubus[18] of utterly causeless alarm. Shaking this off with a gasp and a struggle, I uplifted myself upon the pillows, and, peering earnestly within the intense darkness of the chamber, hearkened—I know not why, except that an instinctive spirit prompted me—to certain low and indefinite sounds which came, through the pauses of the storm, at long intervals, I knew not whence. Overpowered by an intense sentiment of horror, unaccountable yet unendurable, I threw on my clothes with haste (for I felt that I should sleep no more during the night), and endeavoured to arouse myself from the pitiable condition into which I had fallen, by pacing rapidly to and fro through the apartment.

I had taken but few turns in this manner, when a light step on an adjoining staircase arrested my attention. I presently recognised it as that of Usher. In an instant afterward he rapped, with a gentle touch, at my door, and entered, bearing a lamp. His countenance was, as usual, cadaverously wan—but, moreover, there was a species of mad hilarity in his eyes—an evidently restrained *hysteria* in his whole demeanour. His air appalled me—but anything was preferable to the solitude which I had so long endured, and I even welcomed his presence as a relief.

"And you have not seen it?" he said abruptly, after having stared about him for some moments in silence—"you have not then seen it?—but, stay! you shall." Thus speaking, and having carefully shaded his lamp, he hurried to one of the casements, and threw it freely open to the storm.

The impetuous fury of the entering gust nearly lifted us from our feet. It was, indeed, a tempestuous yet sternly beautiful night, and one wildly singular in its terror and its beauty. A whirlwind had apparently collected its force in our vicinity; for there were frequent and violent alterations in the direction of the wind; and the exceeding density of the clouds (which hung so low as to press upon the turrets of the house) did not prevent our perceiving the life-like velocity with which they flew careering from all points against each other, without passing away into the distance. I say that even their exceeding density did not prevent our perceiving this—yet we had no glimpse of the moon or stars—nor was there any flashing forth of the lightning. But the under surfaces of the huge masses of agitated vapour, as well as all terrestrial objects immediately around us, were glowing in the unnatural light of a faintly luminous and distinctly visible gaseous exhalation which hung about and enshrouded the mansion.

"You must not—you shall not behold this!" said I, shudderingly, to Usher, as I led him, with a gentle violence, from the window to a seat. "These appearances, which bewilder you, are merely electrical phenomena not uncommon—or it may

[18] An evil spirit; here, an oppressive burden.

be that they have their ghastly origin in the rank miasma of the tarn. Let us close this casement;—the air is chilling and dangerous to your frame. Here is one of your favourite romances. I will read, and you shall listen;—and so we will pass away this terrible night together."

The antique volume which I had taken up was the "Mad Trist" of Sir Launcelot Canning;[19] but I had called it a favourite of Usher's more in sad jest than in earnest; for, in truth, there is little in its uncouth and unimaginative prolixity which could have had interest for the lofty and spiritual ideality of my friend. It was, however, the only book immediately at hand; and I indulged a vague hope that the excitement which now agitated the hypochondriac, might find relief (for the history of mental disorder is full of similar anomalies) even in the extremeness of the folly which I should read. Could I have judged, indeed, by the wild overstrained air of vivacity with which he hearkened, or apparently hearkened, to the words of the tale, I might well have congratulated myself upon the success of my design.

I had arrived at the well-known portion of the story where Ethelred, the hero of the Trist, having sought in vain for peaceable admission into the dwelling of the hermit, proceeds to make good an entrance by force. Here, it will be remembered, the words of the narrative run thus:

"And Ethelred, who was by nature of a doughty heart, and who was now mighty withal, on account of the powerfulness of the wine which he had drunken, waited no longer to hold parley with the hermit, who, in sooth, was of an obstinate and maliceful turn, but, feeling the rain upon his shoulders, and fearing the rising of the tempest, uplifted his mace outright, and, with blows, made quickly room in the plankings of the door for his gauntleted hand; and now pulling therewith sturdily, he so cracked, and ripped, and tore all asunder, that the noise of the dry and hollow-sounding wood alarmed and reverberated throughout the forest."

At the termination of this sentence I started, and for a moment, paused; for it appeared to me (although I at once concluded that my excited fancy had deceived me)—it appeared to me that, from some very remote portion of the mansion, there came, indistinctly, to my ears, what might have been, in its exact similarity of character, the echo (but a stifled and dull one certainly) of the very cracking and ripping sound which Sir Launcelot had so particularly described. It was, beyond doubt, the coincidence alone which had arrested my attention; for, amid the rattling of the sashes of the casements, and the ordinary commingled noises of the still increasing storm, the sound, in itself, had nothing, surely, which should have interested or disturbed me. I continued the story:

"But the good champion Ethelred, now entering within the door, was sore enraged and amazed to perceive no signal of the maliceful hermit; but, in the stead thereof, a dragon of a scaly and prodigious demeanour, and of a fiery tongue, which sate in guard before a palace of gold, with a floor of silver; and upon the wall there hung a shield of shining brass with this legend enwritten—

Who entereth herein, a conqueror hath bin;
Who slayeth the dragon, the shield he shall win;

And Ethelred uplifted his mace, and struck upon the head of the dragon, which fell before him, and gave up his pesty breath, with a shriek so horrid and harsh,

---

[19] A volume and author invented by Poe. "Trist" signifies a fated meeting or encounter.

and withal so piercing, that Ethelred had fain to close his ears with his hands against the dreadful noise of it, the like whereof was never before heard."

Here again I paused abruptly, and now with a feeling of wild amazement—for there could be no doubt whatever that, in this instance, I did actually hear (although from what direction it proceeded I found it impossible to say) a low and apparently distant, but harsh, protracted, and most unusual screaming or grating sound—the exact counterpart of what my fancy had already conjured up for the dragon's unnatural shriek as described by the romancer.

Oppressed, as I certainly was, upon the occurrence of the second and most extraordinary coincidence, by a thousand conflicting sensations, in which wonder and extreme terror were predominant, I still retained sufficient presence of mind to avoid exciting, by any observation, the sensitive nervousness of my companion. I was by no means certain that he had noticed the sounds in question; although, assuredly, a strange alteration had, during the last few minutes, taken place in his demeanour. From a position fronting my own, he had gradually brought round his chair, so as to sit with his face to the door of the chamber; and thus I could but partially perceive his features, although I saw that his lips trembled as if he were murmuring inaudibly. His head had dropped upon his breast—yet I knew that he was not asleep, from the wide and rigid opening of the eye as I caught a glance of it in profile. The motion of his body, too, was at variance with this idea—for he rocked from side to side with a gentle yet constant and uniform sway. Having rapidly taken notice of all this, I resumed the narrative of Sir Launcelot, which thus proceeded:

"And now, the champion, having escaped from the terrible fury of the dragon, bethinking himself of the brazen shield, and of the breaking up of the enchantment which was upon it, removed the carcass from out of the way before him, and approached valorously over the silver pavement of the castle to where the shield was upon the wall; which in sooth tarried not for his full coming, but fell down at his feet upon the silver floor, with a mighty great and terrible ringing sound."

No sooner had these syllables passed my lips, than—as if a shield of brass had indeed, at the moment, fallen heavily upon a floor of silver—I became aware of a distinct, hollow, metallic, and clangorous, yet apparently muffled reverberation. Completely unnerved, I leaped to my feet; but the measured rocking movement of Usher was undisturbed. I rushed to the chair in which he sat. His eyes were bent fixedly before him, and throughout his whole countenance there reigned a stony rigidity. But, as I placed my hand upon his shoulder, there came a strong shudder over his whole person; a sickly smile quivered about his lips; and I saw that he spoke in a low, hurried, and gibbering murmur, as if unconscious of my presence. Bending closely over him, I at length drank in the hideous import of his words.

"Not hear it?—yes, I hear it, and *have* heard it. Long—long—long—many minutes, many hours, many days, have I heard it—yet I dared not—oh, pity me, miserable wretch that I am!—I dared not—I *dared* not speak! *We have put her living in the tomb!* Said I not that my senses were acute? I *now* tell you that I heard her first feeble movements in the hollow coffin. I heard them—many, many days ago—yet I dared not—*I dared not speak!* And now—to-night—Ethelred—ha! ha!—the breaking of the hermit's door, and the death-cry of the dragon, and the clangour of the shield!—say, rather, the rending of her coffin, and the grating of the iron hinges of her prison, and her struggles within the coppered archway of the vault! Oh whither shall I fly? Will she not be here anon? Is she not hurrying to upbraid me for my haste? Have I not heard her footstep on the stair? Do I not distinguish that heavy and horrible beating of her heart? MADMAN!" here he sprang furiously to his feet, and shrieked out his syllables, as if in the effort he were giving up his soul—"MADMAN! I TELL YOU THAT SHE NOW STANDS WITHOUT THE DOOR!"

As if in the superhuman energy of his utterance there had been found the potency of a spell—the huge antique panels to which the speaker pointed, threw slowly back, upon the instant, their ponderous and ebony jaws. It was the work of the rushing gust—but then without those doors there DID stand the lofty and enshrouded figure of the lady Madeline of Usher. There was blood upon her white robes, and the evidence of some bitter struggle upon every portion of her emaciated frame. For a moment she remained trembling and reeling to and fro upon the threshold, then, with a low moaning cry, fell heavily inward upon the person of her brother, and in her violent and now final death-agonies, bore him to the floor a corpse, and a victim to the terrors he had anticipated.

From that chamber, and from that mansion, I fled aghast. The storm was still abroad in all its wrath as I found myself crossing the old causeway. Suddenly there shot along the path a wild light, and I turned to see whence a gleam so unusual could have issued; for the vast house and its shadows were alone behind me. The radiance was that of the full, setting, and blood-red moon which now shone vividly through that once barely-discernible fissure of which I have before spoken as extending from the roof of the building, in a zigzag direction, to the base. While I gazed, this fissure rapidly widened—there came a fierce breath of the whirlwind—the entire orb of the satellite burst at once upon my sight—my brain reeled as I saw the mighty walls rushing asunder—there was a long tumultuous shouting sound like the voice of a thousand waters—and the deep and dank tarn at my feet closed sullenly and silently over the fragments of the "HOUSE OF USHER."

1839

THE TELL-TALE HEART*

True!—nervous—very, very dreadfully nervous I had been and am; but why *will* you say that I am mad? The disease had sharpened my senses—not destroyed—not dulled them. Above all was the sense of hearing acute. I heard all things in the heaven and in the earth. I heard many things in hell. How, then, am I mad? Hearken! and observe how healthily—how calmly I can tell you the whole story.

It is impossible to say how first the idea entered my brain; but once conceived, it haunted me day and night. Object there was none. Passion there was none. I loved the old man. He had never wronged me. He had never given me insult. For his gold I had no desire. I think it was his eye! yes, it was this! He had the eye of a vulture—a pale blue eye, with a film over it. Whenever it fell upon me, my blood ran cold; and so by degrees—very gradually—I made up my mind to take the life of the old man, and thus rid myself of the eye forever.[1]

---

* First published in *The Pioneer* in 1843.
[1] Poe, who relished word games, seems to imply that the murderer identifies with his victim and in some way he is attacking himself: the narrator, the "I," determined to rid himself of the "eye" forever.

Now this is the point. You fancy me mad. Madmen know nothing. But you should have seen *me*. You should have seen how wisely I proceeded—with what caution—with what foresight—with what dissimulation I went to work! I was never kinder to the old man than during the whole week before I killed him. And every night, about midnight, I turned the latch of his door and opened it—oh so gently! And then, when I had made an opening sufficient for my head, I put in a dark lantern,[2] all closed, closed, so that no light shone out, and then I thrust in my head. Oh, you would have laughed to see how cunningly I thrust it in! I moved it slowly—very, very slowly, so that I might not disturb the old man's sleep. It took me an hour to place my whole head within the opening so far that I could see him as he lay upon his bed. Ha!—would a madman have been so wise as this? And then, when my head was well in the room, I undid the lantern cautiously—oh, so cautiously—cautiously (for the hinges creaked)—I undid it just so much that a single thin ray fell upon the vulture eye. And this I did for seven long nights—every night just at midnight—but I found the eye always closed; and so it was impossible to do the work; for it was not the old man who vexed me, but his Evil Eye. And every morning, when the day broke, I went boldly into the chamber, and spoke courageously to him, calling him by name in a hearty tone, and inquiring how he had passed the night. So you see he would have been a very profound old man, indeed, to suspect that every night, just at twelve, I looked in upon him while he slept.

Upon the eighth night I was more than usually cautious in opening the door. A watch's minute hand moves more quickly than did mine. Never before that night, had I *felt* the extent of my own powers—of my sagacity. I could scarcely contain *perception* my feelings of triumph. To think that there I was, opening the door, little by little, and he not even to dream of my secret deeds or thoughts. I fairly chuckled at the idea; and perhaps he heard me; for he moved on the bed suddenly, as if startled. Now you may think that I drew back—but no. His room was as black as pitch with the thick darkness, (for the shutters were close fastened, through fear of robbers,) and so I knew that he could not see the opening of the door, and I kept pushing it on steadily, steadily.

I had my head in, and was about to open the lantern, when my thumb slipped upon the tin fastening, and the old man sprang up in bed, crying out—"Who's there?"

I kept quite still and said nothing. For a whole hour I did not move a muscle, and in the meantime I did not hear him lie down. He was still sitting up in the bed listening;—just as I have done, night after night, hearkening to the death watches[3] in the wall.

Presently I heard a slight groan, and I knew it was the groan of mortal terror. It was not a groan of pain or of grief—oh, no!—it was the low stifled sound that arises from the bottom of the soul when overcharged with awe. I knew the sound well. Many a night, just at midnight, when all the world slept, it has welled up from my own bosom, deepening, with its dreadful echo, the terrors that distracted me. I say I knew it well. I knew what the old man felt, and pitied him, although I chuckled at heart. I knew that he had been lying awake ever since the first slight noise, when he had turned in the bed. His fears had been ever since growing upon

---

[2] A lantern with shutters to block the light.
[3] Small insects (such as beetles) that make a ticking sound superstitiously thought to predict death. Note the analogy made between the old man and the narrator.

him. He had been trying to fancy them causeless, but could not. He had been saying to himself—"It is nothing but the wind in the chimney—it is only a mouse crossing the floor," or "it is merely a cricket which has made a single chirp." Yes, he had been trying to comfort himself with these suppositions: but he had found all in vain. *All in vain;* because Death, in approaching him had stalked with his black shadow before him, and enveloped the victim. And it was the mournful influence of the unperceived shadow that caused him to feel—although he neither saw nor heard—to *feel* the presence of my head within the room.

When I had waited a long time, very patiently, without hearing him lie down, I resolved to open a little—a very, very little crevice in the lantern. So I opened it—you cannot imagine how stealthily, stealthily—until, at length a simple dim ray, like the thread of the spider, shot from out the crevice and fell full upon the vulture eye.

It was open—wide, wide open—and I grew furious as I gazed upon it. I saw it with perfect distinctness—all a dull blue, with a hideous veil over it that chilled the very marrow in my bones; but I could see nothing else of the old man's face or person: for I had directed the ray as if by instinct, precisely upon the damned spot.

And have I not told you that what you mistake for madness is but over acuteness of the senses?—now, I say, there came to my ears a low, dull, quick sound, such as a watch makes when enveloped in cotton. I knew *that* sound well, too. It was the beating of the old man's heart. It increased my fury, as the beating of a drum stimulates the soldier into courage.

But even yet I refrained and kept still. I scarcely breathed. I held the lantern motionless. I tried how steadily I could maintain the ray upon the eye. Meantime the hellish tattoo of the heart increased. It grew quicker and quicker, and louder and louder every instant. The old man's terror *must* have been extreme! It grew louder, I say, louder every moment!—do you mark me well? I have told you that I am nervous: so I am. And now at the dead hour of the night, amid the dreadful silence of that old house, so strange a noise as this excited me to uncontrollable terror. Yet, for some minutes longer I refrained and stood still. But the beating grew louder, louder! I thought the heart must burst. And now a new anxiety seized me—the sound would be heard by a neighbour! The old man's hour had come! With a loud yell, I threw open the lantern and leaped into the room. He shrieked once—once only. In an instant I dragged him to the floor, and pulled the heavy bed[4] over him. I then smiled gaily, to find the deed so far done. But, for many minutes, the heart beat on with a muffled sound. This, however, did not vex me; it would not be heard through the wall. At length it ceased. The old man was dead. I removed the bed and examined the corpse. Yes, he was stone, stone dead. I placed my hand upon the heart and held it there many minutes. There was no pulsation. He was stone dead. His eye would trouble me no more.

If still you think me mad, you will think so no longer when I describe the wise precautions I took for the concealment of the body. The night waned, and I worked hastily, but in silence. First of all I dismembered the corpse. I cut off the head and the arms and the legs.

I then took up three planks from the flooring of the chamber, and deposited all between the scantlings.[5] I then replaced the boards so cleverly, so cunningly, that

---

[4] Bedclothes or heavy comforter.   [5] Beams that support floor boards.

no human eye—not even *his*—could have detected any thing wrong. There was nothing to wash out—no stain of any kind—no blood-spot whatever. I had been too wary for that. A tub had caught all—ha! ha!

When I had made an end of these labors, it was four o'clock—still dark as midnight. As the bell sounded the hour, there came a knocking at the street door. I went down to open it with a light heart,—for what had I *now* to fear? There entered three men, who introduced themselves, with perfect suavity, as officers of the police. A shriek had been heard by a neighbour during the night; suspicion of foul play had been aroused; information had been lodged at the police office, and they (the officers) had been deputed to search the premises.

I smiled,—for *what* had I to fear? I bade the gentlemen welcome. The shriek, I said, was my own in a dream. The old man, I mentioned, was absent in the country. I took my visitors all over the house. I bade them search—search *well*. I led them, at length, to *his* chamber. I showed them his treasures, secure, undisturbed. In the enthusiasm of my confidence, I brought chairs into the room, and desired them *here* to rest from their fatigues, while I myself, in the wild audacity of my perfect triumph, placed my own seat upon the very spot beneath which reposed the corpse of the victim.

The officers were satisfied. My *manner* had convinced them. I was singularly at ease. They sat, and while I answered cheerily, they chatted of familiar things. But, ere long, I felt myself getting pale and wished them gone. My head ached, and I fancied a ringing in my ears: but still they sat and still chatted. The ringing became more distinct:—it continued and became more distinct: I talked more freely to get rid of the feeling: but it continued and gained definiteness—until, at length, I found that the noise was *not* within my ears.

No doubt I now grew *very* pale;—but I talked more fluently, and with a heightened voice. Yet the sound increased—and what could I do? It was *a low, dull, quick sound—much such a sound as a watch makes when enveloped in cotton.*[6] I gasped for breath—and yet the officers heard it not. I talked more quickly—more vehemently; but the noise steadily increased. I arose and argued about trifles, in a high key and with violent gesticulations; but the noise steadily increased. Why *would* they not be gone? I paced the floor to and fro with heavy strides, as if excited to fury by the observations of the men—but the noise steadily increased. Oh God! what *could* I do? I foamed—I raved—I swore! I swung the chair upon which I had been sitting, and grated it upon the boards, but the noise arose over all and continually increased. It grew louder—louder—*louder!* And still the men chatted pleasantly, and smiled. Was it possible they heard not? Almighty God!—no, no! They heard!—they suspected!—they *knew!*—they were making a mockery of my horror!—this I thought, and this I think. But anything was better than this agony! Anything was more tolerable than this derision! I could bear those hypocritical smiles no longer! I felt that I must scream or die! and now—again!—hark! louder! louder! louder! *louder!*

"Villains!" I shrieked, "dissemble no more! I admit the deed!—tear up the planks! here, here!—it is the beating of his hideous heart!"

1843

---

[6] The sound is a ticking, an echo of the death-watch ticking the narrator has heard before.

THE BLACK CAT*

For the most wild, yet most homely narrative which I am about to pen, I neither expect nor solicit belief. Mad indeed would I be to expect it, in a case where my very senses reject their own evidence. Yet, mad am I not—and very surely do I not dream. But tomorrow I die, and to-day I would unburthen my soul. My immediate purpose is to place before the world, plainly, succinctly, and without comment, a series of mere household events.[1] In their consequences, these events have terrified—have tortured—have destroyed me. Yet I will not attempt to expound them. To me, they have presented little but Horror—to many they will seem less terrible than *baroques*.[2] Hereafter, perhaps, some intellect may be found which will reduce my phantasm to the common-place—some intellect more calm, more logical, and far less excitable than my own, which will perceive, in the circumstances I detail with awe, nothing more than an ordinary succession of very natural causes and effects.

From my infancy I was noted for the docility and humanity of my disposition. My tenderness of heart was even so conspicuous as to make me the jest of my companions. I was especially fond of animals, and was indulged by my parents with a great variety of pets. With these I spent most of my time, and never was so happy as when feeding and caressing them. This peculiarity of character grew with my growth, and, in my manhood, I derived from it one of my principal sources of pleasure. To those who have cherished an affection for a faithful and sagacious dog, I need hardly be at the trouble of explaining the nature or the intensity of the gratification thus derivable. There is something in the unselfish and self-sacrificing love of a brute, which goes directly to the heart of him who has had frequent occasion to test the paltry friendship and gossamer fidelity of mere *Man*.

I married early, and was happy to find in my wife a disposition not uncongenial with my own. Observing my partiality for domestic pets, she lost no opportunity of procuring those of the most agreeable kind. We had birds, gold fish, a fine dog, rabbits, a small monkey, and *a cat*.

This latter was a remarkably large and beautiful animal, entirely black, and sagacious to an astonishing degree. In speaking of his intelligence, my wife, who at heart was not a little tinctured with superstition, made frequent allusion to the ancient popular notion, which regarded all black cats as witches in disguise. Not that she was ever *serious* upon this point—and I mention the matter at all for no better reason than that it happens, just now, to be remembered.

Pluto[3]—this was the cat's name—was my favorite pet and playmate. I alone fed him, and he attended me wherever I went about the house. It was even with difficulty that I could prevent him from following me through the streets.

Our friendship lasted, in this manner, for several years, during which my general temperament and character—through the instrumentality of the Fiend Intemperance—had (I blush to confess it) experienced a radical alteration for the worse. I grew, day by day, more moody, more irritable, more regardless of the feelings of others. I suffered myself to use intemperate language to my wife. At length, I

---

* First published in the *United States Saturday Post,* a Philadelphia weekly paper, in 1843.
  [1] Among nineteenth-century American writers, only Poe would present the lurid events of this tale as "a series of mere household events." "The Black Cat" is a prime example of mock-domestic fiction.
  [2] Bizarre, weird.   [3] According to Roman myth, the god of the dead and ruler of the underworld.

even offered her personal violence. My pets, of course, were made to feel the change in my disposition. I not only neglected, but ill-used them. For Pluto, however, I still retained sufficient regard to restrain me from maltreating him, as I made no scruple of maltreating the rabbits, the monkey, or even the dog, when by accident, or through affection, they came in my way. But my disease grew upon me—for what disease is like Alcohol!—and at length even Pluto, who was now becoming old, and consequently somewhat peevish—even Pluto began to experi- ence the effects of my ill temper.

One night, returning home, much intoxicated, from one of my haunts about town, I fancied that the cat avoided my presence. I seized him; when, in his fright at my violence, he inflicted a slight wound upon my hand with his teeth. The fury of a demon instantly possessed me. I knew myself no longer. My original soul seemed, at once, to take its flight from my body; and a more than fiendish malev- olence, gin-nurtured, thrilled every fibre of my frame. I took from my waistcoat- pocket a pen-knife, opened it, grasped the poor beast by the throat, and deliber- ately cut one of its eyes from the socket! I blush, I burn, I shudder, while I pen the damnable atrocity.

When reason returned with the morning—when I had slept off the fumes of the night's debauch—I experienced a sentiment half of horror, half of remorse, for the crime of which I had been guilty; but it was, at best, a feeble and equivocal feeling, and the soul remained untouched. I again plunged into excess, and soon drowned in wine all memory of the deed.

In the meantime the cat slowly recovered. The socket of the lost eye presented, it is true, a frightful appearance, but he no longer appeared to suffer any pain. He went about the house as usual, but, as might be expected, fled in extreme terror at my approach. I had so much of my old heart left, as to be at first grieved by this evident dislike on the part of a creature which had once so loved me. But this feeling soon gave place to irritation. And then came, as if to my final and irrevo- cable overthrow, the spirit of PERVERSENESS. Of this spirit philosophy takes no account. Yet I am not more sure that my soul lives, than I am that perverseness is one of the primitive impulses of the human heart—one of the indivisible primary faculties, or sentiments, which give direction to the character of Man. Who has not, a hundred times, found himself committing a vile or a silly action, for no other reason than because he knows he should *not?* Have we not a perpetual incli- nation, in the teeth of our best judgment, to violate that which is *Law,* merely because we understand it to be such? This spirit of perverseness, I say, came to my final overthrow. It was this unfathomable longing of the soul *to vex itself*—to offer violence to its own nature—to do wrong for the wrong's sake only[4]—that urged me to continue and finally to consummate the injury I had inflicted upon the unoffending brute. One morning, in cool blood, I slipped a noose about its neck and hung it to the limb of a tree;—hung it with the tears streaming from my eyes, and with the bitterest remorse at my heart;—hung it *because* I knew that it had loved me, and *because* I felt it had given me no reason of offence;—hung it *be- cause* I knew that in so doing I was committing a sin—a deadly sin that would so jeopardize my immortal soul as to place it—if such a thing were possible—even beyond the reach of the infinite mercy of the Most Merciful and Most Terrible God.

---

[4] This definition of "perverseness" is the most concise to be found in Poe's fiction, even more dra- matic in its clarity than the explanation given in "The Imp of the Perverse" (1845).

On the night of the day on which this cruel deed was done, I was aroused from sleep by the cry of fire. The curtains of my bed were in flames. The whole house was blazing. It was with great difficulty that my wife, a servant, and myself, made our escape from the conflagration. The destruction was complete. My entire worldly wealth was swallowed up, and I resigned myself thenceforward to despair.

I am above the weakness of seeking to establish a sequence of cause and effect, between the disaster and the atrocity. But I am detailing a chain of facts—and wish not to leave even a possible link imperfect. On the day succeeding the fire, I visited the ruins. The walls, with one exception, had fallen in. This exception was found in a compartment wall, not very thick, which stood about the middle of the house, and against which had rested the head of my bed. The plastering had here, in great measure, resisted the action of the fire—a fact which I attributed to its having been recently spread. About this wall a dense crowd were collected, and many persons seemed to be examining a particular portion of it with very minute and eager attention. The words "strange!" "singular!" and other similar expressions, excited my curiosity. I approached and saw, as if graven in *bas relief*[5] upon the white surface, the figure of a gigantic *cat*. The impression was given with an accuracy truly marvellous. There was a rope about the animal's neck.

When I first beheld this apparition—for I could scarcely regard it as less—my wonder and my terror were extreme. But at length reflection came to my aid. The cat, I remembered, had been hung in a garden adjacent to the house. Upon the alarm of fire, this garden had been immediately filled by the crowd—by some one of whom the animal must have been cut from the tree and thrown, through an open window, into my chamber. This had probably been done with the view of arousing me from sleep. The falling of other walls had compressed the victim of my cruelty into the substance of the freshly-spread plaster; the line of which, with the flames, and the *ammonia* from the carcass, had then accomplished the portraiture as I saw it.

Although I thus readily accounted to my reason, if not altogether to my conscience, for the startling fact just detailed, it did not the less fail to make a deep impression upon my fancy. For months I could not rid myself of the phantasm of the cat; and, during this period, there came back into my spirit a half-sentiment that seemed, but was not, remorse. I went so far as to regret the loss of the animal, and to look about me, among the vile haunts which I now habitually frequented, for another pet of the same species, and of somewhat similar appearance, with which to supply its place.

One night as I sat, half stupified, in a den of more than infamy, my attention was suddenly drawn to some black object, reposing upon the head of one of the immense hogsheads[6] of Gin, or of Rum, which constituted the chief furniture of the apartment. I had been looking steadily at the top of this hogshead for some minutes, and what now caused me surprise was the fact that I had not sooner perceived the object thereupon. I approached it, and touched it with my hand. It was a black cat—a very large one—fully as large as Pluto, and closely resembling him in every respect but one. Pluto had not a white hair upon any portion of his body; but this cat had a large, although indefinite splotch of white, covering nearly the whole region of the breast.

---

[5] Low relief; in sculpture, the slight (or low) projection of a figure from a flat background.
[6] Large casks containing up to 140 gallons.

Upon my touching him, he immediately arose, purred loudly, rubbed against my hand, and appeared delighted with my notice. This, then, was the very creature of which I was in search. I at once offered to purchase it of the landlord; but this person made no claim to it—knew nothing of it—had never seen it before.

I continued my caresses, and, when I prepared to go home, the animal evinced a disposition to accompany me. I permitted it to do so; occasionally stooping and patting it as I proceeded. When it reached the house it domesticated itself at once, and became immediately a great favorite with my wife.

For my own part, I soon found a dislike to it arising within me. This was just the reverse of what I had anticipated; but I know not how or why it was—its evident fondness for myself rather disgusted and annoyed. By slow degrees, these feelings of disgust and annoyance rose into the bitterness of hatred. I avoided the creature; a certain sense of shame, and the remembrance of my former deed of cruelty, preventing me from physically abusing it. I did not, for some weeks, strike, or otherwise violently ill use it; but gradually—very gradually—I came to look upon it with unutterable loathing, and to flee silently from its odious presence, as from the breath of a pestilence.

What added, no doubt, to my hatred of the beast, was the discovery, on the morning after I brought it home, that, like Pluto, it also had been deprived of one of its eyes. This circumstance, however, only endeared it to my wife, who, as I have already said, possessed, in a high degree, that humanity of feeling which had once been my distinguishing trait, and the source of many of my simplest and purest pleasures.

With my aversion to this cat, however, its partiality for myself seemed to increase. It followed my footsteps with a pertinacity which it would be difficult to make the reader comprehend. Whenever I sat, it would crouch beneath my chair, or spring upon my knees, covering me with its loathsome caresses. If I arose to walk it would get between my feet and thus nearly throw me down, or, fastening its long and sharp claws in my dress, clamber, in this manner, to my breast. At such times, although I longed to destroy it with a blow, I was yet withheld from so doing, partly by a memory of my former crime, but chiefly—let me confess it at once—by absolute *dread* of the beast.

This dread was not exactly a dread of physical evil—and yet I should be at a loss how otherwise to define it. I am almost ashamed to own—yes, even in this felon's cell, I am almost ashamed to own—that the terror and horror with which the animal inspired me, had been heightened by one of the merest chimæras[7] it would be possible to conceive. My wife had called my attention, more than once, to the character of the mark of white hair, of which I have spoken, and which constituted the sole visible difference between the strange beast and the one I had destroyed. The reader will remember that this mark, although large, had been originally very indefinite; but, by slow degrees—degrees nearly imperceptible, and which for a long time my Reason struggled to reject as fanciful—it had, at length, assumed a rigorous distinctness of outline. It was now the representation of an object that I shudder to name—and for this, above all, I loathed, and dreaded, and would have rid myself of the monster *had I dared*—it was now, I say, the image of a hideous—of a ghastly thing—of the Gallows!—oh, mournful and terrible engine of Horror and of Crime—of Agony and of Death!

---

[7] Frightening and incredible fancies.

And now was I indeed wretched beyond the wretchedness of mere Humanity. And *a brute beast*—whose fellow I had contemptuously destroyed—*a brute beast* to work out for *me*—for me a man, fashioned in the image of the High God—so much of insufferable wo! Alas! neither by day nor by night knew I the blessing of Rest any more! During the former the creature left me no moment alone; and, in the latter, I started, hourly, from dreams of unutterable fear, to find the hot breath of *the thing* upon my face, and its vast weight—an incarnate Night-Mare that I had no power to shake off—incumbent eternally upon my *heart!*

Beneath the pressure of torments such as these, the feeble remnant of the good within me succumbed. Evil thoughts became my sole intimates—the darkest and most evil of thoughts. The moodiness of my usual temper increased to hatred of all things and of all mankind; while, from the sudden, frequent, and ungovernable outbursts of a fury to which I now blindly abandoned myself, my uncomplaining wife, alas! was the most usual and the most patient of sufferers.

One day she accompanied me, upon some household errand, into the cellar of the old building which our poverty compelled us to inhabit. The cat followed me down the steep stairs, and, nearly throwing me headlong, exasperated me to madness. Uplifting an axe, and forgetting, in my wrath, the childish dread which had hitherto stayed my hand, I aimed a blow at the animal which, of course, would have proved instantly fatal had it descended as I wished. But this blow was arrested by the hand of my wife. Goaded, by the interference, into a rage more than demoniacal, I withdrew my arm from her grasp and buried the axe in her brain. She fell dead upon the spot, without a groan.

This hideous murder accomplished, I set myself forthwith, and with entire deliberation, to the task of concealing the body. I knew that I could not remove it from the house, either by day or by night, without the risk of being observed by the neighbors. Many projects entered my mind. At one period I thought of cutting the corpse into minute fragments, and destroying them by fire. At another, I resolved to dig a grave for it in the floor of the cellar. Again, I deliberated about casting it in the well in the yard—about packing it in a box, as if merchandize, with the usual arrangements, and so getting a porter to take it from the house. Finally I hit upon what I considered a far better expedient than either of these. I determined to wall it up in the cellar—as the monks of the middle ages are recorded to have walled up their victims.

For a purpose such as this the cellar was well adapted. Its walls were loosely constructed, and had lately been plastered throughout with a rough plaster, which the dampness of the atmosphere had prevented from hardening. Moreover, in one of the walls was a projection, caused by a false chimney, or fireplace, that had been filled up, and made to resemble the rest of the cellar. I made no doubt that I could readily displace the bricks at this point, insert the corpse, and wall the whole up as before, so that no eye could detect anything suspicious.

And in this calculation I was not deceived. By means of a crow-bar I easily dislodged the bricks, and, having carefully deposited the body against the inner wall, I propped it in that position, while, with little trouble, I re-laid the whole structure as it originally stood. Having procured mortar, sand, and hair, with every possible precaution, I prepared a plaster which could not be distinguished from the old, and with this I very carefully went over the new brick-work. When I had finished, I felt satisfied that all was right. The wall did not present the slightest appearance of having been disturbed. The rubbish on the floor was picked up with the minutest care. I looked around triumphantly, and said to myself—"Here at least, then, my labor has not been in vain."

My next step was to look for the beast which had been the cause of so much wretchedness; for I had, at length, firmly resolved to put it to death. Had I been able to meet with it, at the moment, there could have been no doubt of its fate; but it appeared that the crafty animal had been alarmed at the violence of my previous anger, and forebore to present itself in my present mood. It is impossible to describe, or to imagine, the deep, the blissful sense of relief which the absence of the detested creature occasioned in my bosom. It did not make its appearance during the night—and thus for one night at least, since its introduction into the house, I soundly and tranquilly slept; aye, *slept* even with the burden of murder upon my soul!

The second and the third day passed, and still my tormentor came not. Once again I breathed as a free-man. The monster, in terror, had fled the premises forever! I should behold it no more! My happiness was supreme! The guilt of my dark deed disturbed me but little. Some few inquiries had been made, but these had been readily answered. Even a search had been instituted—but of course nothing was to be discovered. I looked upon my future felicity as secured.

Upon the fourth day of the assassination, a party of the police came, very unexpectedly, into the house, and proceeded again to make rigorous investigation of the premises. Secure, however, in the inscrutability of my place of concealment, I felt no embarrassment whatever. The officers bade me accompany them in their search. They left no nook or corner unexplored. At length, for the third of fourth time, they descended into the cellar. I quivered not in a muscle. My heart beat calmly as that of one who slumbers in innocence. I walked the cellar from end to end. I folded my arms upon my bosom, and roamed easily to and fro. The police were thoroughly satisfied and prepared to depart. The glee at my heart was too strong to be restrained. I burned to say if but one word, by way of triumph, and to render doubly sure their assurance of my guiltlessness.

"Gentlemen," I said at last, as the party ascended the steps, "I delight to have allayed your suspicions. I wish you all health, and a little more courtesy. By the bye, gentlemen, this—this is a very well constructed house." [In the rabid desire to say something easily, I scarcely knew what I uttered at all.]—"I may say an *excellently* well constructed house. These walls—are you going, gentlemen?—these walls are solidly put together;" and here, through the mere phrenzy of bravado, I rapped heavily, with a cane which I held in my hand, upon that very portion of the brick-work behind which stood the corpse of the wife of my bosom.

But may God shield and deliver me from the fangs of the Arch-Fiend! No sooner had the reverberation of my blows sunk into silence, than I was answered by a voice from within the tomb!—by a cry, at first muffled and broken, like the sobbing of a child, and then quickly swelling into one long, loud, and continuous scream, utterly anomalous and inhuman—a howl—a wailing shriek, half of horror and half of triumph, such as might have arisen only out of hell, conjointly from the throats of the damned in their agony and of the demons that exult in the damnation.

Of my own thoughts it is folly to speak. Swooning, I staggered to the opposite wall. For one instant the party upon the stairs remained motionless, through extremity of terror and of awe. In the next, a dozen stout arms were toiling at the wall. It fell bodily. The corpse, already greatly decayed and clotted with gore, stood erect before the eyes of the spectators. Upon its head, with red extended mouth and solitary eye of fire, sat the hideous beast whose craft had seduced me into murder, and whose informing voice had consigned me to the hangman. I had walled the monster up within the tomb!

1843

THE CASK OF AMONTILLADO*

The thousand injuries of Fortunato I had borne as I best could, but when he ventured upon insult I vowed revenge. You, who so well know the nature of my soul, will not suppose, however, that I gave utterance to a threat. *At length* I would be avenged; this was a point definitely settled—but the very definitiveness with which it was resolved precluded the idea of risk. I must not only punish but punish with impunity. A wrong is unredressed when retribution overtakes its redresser. It is equally unredressed when the avenger fails to make himself felt as such to him who has done the wrong.[1]

It must be understood that neither by word nor deed had I given Fortunato cause to doubt my good will. I continued, as was my wont, to smile in his face, and he did not perceive that my smile *now* was at the thought of his immolation.

He had a weak point—this Fortunato—although in other regards he was a man to be respected and even feared. He prided himself on his connoisseurship in wine. Few Italians have the true virtuoso spirit. For the most part their enthusiasm is adopted to suit the time and opportunity, to practise imposture upon the British and Austrian *millionaires*. In painting and gemmary,[2] Fortunato, like his countrymen, was a quack, but in the matter of old wines he was sincere. In this respect I did not differ from him materially;—I was skilful in the Italian vintages myself,[3] and bought largely whenever I could.

It was about dusk, one evening during the supreme madness of the carnival season, that I encountered my friend. He accosted me with excessive warmth, for he had been drinking much. The man wore motley.[4] He had on a tight-fitting parti-striped dress, and his head was surmounted by the conical cap and bells. I was so pleased to see him that I thought I should never have done wringing his hand.

I said to him—"My dear Fortunato, you are luckily met. How remarkably well you are looking to-day. But I have received a pipe[5] of what passes for Amontillado, and I have my doubts."

"How?" said he. "Amontillado? A pipe? Impossible! And in the middle of the carnival!"

"I have my doubts," I replied; "and I was silly enough to pay the full Amontillado price without consulting you in the matter. You were not to be found, and I was fearful of losing a bargain."

---

* First published in *Godey's Lady's Book* in 1846. Amontillado is a pale, dry Spanish sherry.

[1] The narrator's conditions for revenge are: you must not get caught, and you must perform the act of vengeance yourself.

[2] Knowledge of gems and jewels.

[3] A curious remark, as no Italian wines are mentioned in the story.

[4] A multicolored costume worn by clowns and jesters. "Fortunato" means "lucky."

[5] An immense cask holding from 150 to 250 gallons.

"Amontillado!"

"I have my doubts."

"Amontillado!"

"And I must satisfy them."

"Amontillado!"

"As you are engaged, I am on my way to Luchresi. If any one has a critical turn it is he. He will tell me—"

"Luchresi cannot tell Amontillado from Sherry."[6]

"And yet some fools will have it that his taste is a match for his own."

"Come, let us go."

"Whither?"

"To your vaults."

"My friend, no; I will not impose upon your good nature. I perceive you have an engagement. Luchresi—"

"I have no engagement;—come."

"My friend, no. It is not the engagement, but the severe cold with which I perceive you are afflicted. The vaults are insufferably damp. They are encrusted with nitre."[7]

"Let us go, nevertheless. The cold is merely nothing. Amontillado! You have been imposed upon. And as for Luchresi, he cannot distinguish Sherry from Amontillado."

Thus speaking, Fortunato possessed himself of my arm; and putting on a mask of black silk and drawing a *roquelaire*[8] closely about my person, I suffered him to hurry me to my palazzo.[9]

There were no attendants at home; they had absconded to make merry in honour of the time. I had told them that I should not return until the morning, and had given them explicit orders not to stir from the house. These orders were sufficient, I well knew, to insure their immediate disappearance, one and all, as soon as my back was turned.

I took from their sconces two flambeaux,[10] and giving one to Fortunato, bowed him through several suites of rooms to the archway that led into the vaults. I passed down a long and winding staircase, requesting him to be cautious as he followed. We came at length to the foot of the descent, and stood together upon the damp ground of the catacombs of the Montresors.

The gait of my friend was unsteady, and the bells upon his cap jingled as he strode.

"The pipe," he said.

"It is farther on," said I; "but observe the white web-work which gleams from these cavern walls."

He turned towards me, and looked into my eyes with two filmy orbs that distilled the rheum of intoxication.

"Nitre?" he asked, at length.

"Nitre," I replied, "How long have you had that cough?"

"Ugh! ugh! ugh!—ugh! ugh! ugh!—ugh! ugh! ugh!—ugh! ugh! ugh!—ugh! ugh! ugh!"

---

[6] He cannot tell fine sherry from ordinary sherry.

[7] Potassium nitrate, a whitish mineral deposited in water.   [8] A cloak.

[9] "Palace" (Italian), or large home.

[10] Flaming torches, taken from holders (sconces) fixed to the wall.

My poor friend found it impossible to reply for many minutes.

"It is nothing," he said, at last.

"Come," I said, with decision, "we will go back; your health is precious. You are rich, respected, admired, beloved; you are happy, as once I was. You are a man to be missed. For me it is no matter. We will go back; you will be ill, and I cannot be responsible. Besides, there is Luchresi—"

"Enough," he said; "the cough is a mere nothing; it will not kill me. I shall not die of a cough."

"True—true," I replied; "and, indeed, I had no intention of alarming you unnecessarily—but you should use all proper caution. A draught of this Medoc[11] will defend us from the damps."

Here I knocked off the neck of a bottle which I drew from a long row of its fellows that lay upon the mould.

"Drink," I said, presenting him the wine.

He raised it to his lips with a leer. He paused and nodded to me familiarly, while his bells jingled.

"I drink," he said, "to the buried that repose around us."

"And I to your long life."

He again took my arm, and we proceeded.

"These vaults," he said, "are extensive."

"The Montresors," I replied, "were a great and numerous family."

"I forget your arms."[12]

"A huge human foot d'or, in a field azure;[13] the foot crushes a serpent rampant whose fangs are imbedded in the heel."

"And the motto?"

"*Nemo me impune lacessit.*"[14]

"Good!" he said.

The wine sparkled in his eyes and the bells jingled. My own fancy grew warm with the Medoc. We had passed through long walls of piled skeletons, with casks and puncheons[15] intermingling, into the inmost recesses of the catacombs. I paused again, and this time I made bold to seize Fortunato by an arm above the elbow.

"The nitre!" I said; "see, it increases. It hangs like moss upon the vaults. We are below the river's bed. The drops of moisture trickle among the bones. Come, we will go back ere it is too late. Your cough—"

"It is nothing," he said; "let us go on. But first, another draught of the Medoc."

I broke and reached him a flagon of De Grâve.[16] He emptied it at a breath. His eyes flashed with a fierce light. He laughed and threw the bottle upwards with a gesticulation I did not understand.

I looked at him in surprise. He repeated the movement—a grotesque one.

"You do not comprehend?" he said.

"Not I," I replied.

---

[11] A red wine from the Bordeaux region of France.

[12] The family's coat of arms; that Fortunato cannot recall the coat of arms of the narrator's "great and numerous" family is an insult to the name of Montresor.

[13] Foot of gold in a field of blue.

[14] "No one insults me with impunity" (Latin); or "No one insults me and gets away with it."

[15] Large casks.

[16] A large bottle of white wine from the Bordeaux region of France, the name used perhaps as a foreboding.

"Then you are not of the brotherhood."

"How?"

"You are not of the masons."[17]

"Yes, yes," I said; "yes, yes."

"You? Impossible! A mason?"

"A mason," I replied.

"A sign," he said, "a sign."

"It is this," I answered, producing from beneath the folds of my *roquelaire* a trowel.

"You jest," he exclaimed, recoiling a few paces. "But let us proceed to the Amontillado."

"Be it so," I said, replacing the tool beneath the cloak and again offering him my arm. He leaned upon it heavily. We continued our route in search of the Amontillado. We passed through a range of low arches, descended, passed on, and descending again, arrived at a deep crypt, in which the foulness of the air caused our flambeaux rather to glow than flame.

At the most remote end of the crypt there appeared another less spacious. Its walls had been lined with human remains, piled to the vault overhead, in the fashion of the great catacombs of Paris. Three sides of this interior crypt were still ornamented in this manner. From the fourth side the bones had been thrown down, and lay promiscuously upon the earth, forming at one point a mound of some size. Within the wall thus exposed by the displacing of the bones, we perceived a still interior crypt or recess, in depth about four feet, in width three, in height six or seven. It seemed to have been constructed for no especial use within itself, but formed merely the interval between two of the colossal supports of the roof of the catacombs, and was backed by one of their circumscribing walls of solid granite.

It was in vain that Fortunato, uplifting his dull torch, endeavoured to pry into the depth of the recess. Its termination the feeble light did not enable us to see.

"Proceed," I said; "herein is the Amontillado. As for Luchresi—" *the lure*

"He is an ignoramus," interrupted my friend, as he stepped unsteadily forward, while I followed immediately at his heels. In an instant he had reached the extremity of the niche, and finding his progress arrested by the rock, stood stupidly bewildered. A moment more and I had fettered him to the granite. In its surface were two iron staples, distant from each other about two feet, horizontally. From one of these depended a short chain, from the other a padlock. Throwing the links about his waist, it was but the work of a few seconds to secure it. He was too much astounded to resist. Withdrawing the key I stepped back from the recess.

"Pass your hand," I said, "over the wall; you cannot help feeling the nitre. Indeed, it is *very* damp. Once more let me *implore* you to return. No? Then I must positively leave you. But I must first render you all the little attentions in my power."

"The Amontillado!" ejaculated my friend, not yet recovered from his astonishment.

"True," I replied; "the Amontillado."

As I said these words I busied myself among the pile of bones of which I have before spoken. Throwing them aside, I soon uncovered a quantity of building

[17] The Freemasons, an international organization with secret signs and symbols. Fortunato again slights the narrator by saying it is "impossible" that he could be a mason; when asked for a sign to prove his membership, the narrator produces a trowel.

stone and mortar. With these materials and with the aid of my trowel, I began vigorously to wall up the entrance of the niche.

I had scarcely laid the first tier of the masonry when I discovered that the intoxication of Fortunato had in a great measure worn off. The earliest indication I had of this was a low moaning cry from the depth of the recess. It was *not* the cry of a drunken man. There was then a long and obstinate silence. I laid the second tier, and the third, and the fourth; and then I heard the furious vibrations of the chain. The noise lasted for several minutes, during which, that I might hearken to it with the more satisfaction, I ceased my labours and sat down upon the bones. When at last the clanking subsided, I resumed the trowel, and finished without interruption the fifth, the sixth, and the seventh tier. The wall was now nearly upon a level with my breast. I again paused, and holding the flambeaux over the mason-work, threw a few feeble rays upon the figure within.

A succession of loud and shrill screams, bursting suddenly from the throat of the chained form, seemed to thrust me violently back. For a brief moment I hesitated, I trembled. Unsheathing my rapier, I began to grope with it about the recess; but the thought of an instant reassured me. I placed my hand upon the solid fabric of the catacombs, and felt satisfied. I reapproached the wall; I replied to the yells of him who clamoured. I re-echoed, I aided, I surpassed them in volume and in strength. I did this, and the clamourer grew still.

It was now midnight, and my task was drawing to a close. I had completed the eighth, the ninth and the tenth tier. I had finished a portion of the last and the eleventh; there remained but a single stone to be fitted and plastered in. I struggled with its weight; I placed it partially in its destined position. But now there came from out the niche a low laugh that erected the hairs on my head. It was succeeded by a sad voice, which I had difficulty in recognizing as that of the noble Fortunato. The voice said—

"Ha! ha! ha!—he! he! he!—a very good joke, indeed—an excellent jest. We will have many a rich laugh about it at the palazzo—he! he! he!—over our wine—he! he! he!"

"The Amontillado!" I said.

"He! he! he!—he! he! he!—yes, the Amontillado. But is it not getting late? Will not they be awaiting us at the palazzo, the Lady Fortunato and the rest? Let us be gone."

"Yes," I said, "let us be gone."

"*For the love of God, Montresor!*"

"Yes," I said, "for the love of God!"

But to these words I hearkened in vain for a reply. I grew impatient. I called aloud—

"Fortunato!"

No answer. I called again—

"Fortunato!"

No answer still. I thrust a torch through the remaining aperture and let it fall within. There came forth in return only a jingling of the bells. My heart grew sick; it was the dampness of the catacombs that made it so. I hastened to make an end of my labour. I forced the last stone into its position; I plastered it up. Against the new masonry I re-erected the old rampart of bones. For the half of a century no mortal has disturbed them. *In pace requiescat!*[18]

1846

---

[18] "Rest in peace!" (Latin).

SONNET—TO SCIENCE*

Science! true daughter of Old Time thou art!
　Who alterest all things with thy peering eyes.
Why preyest thou thus upon the poet's heart,
　Vulture, whose wings are dull realities?
How should he love thee? or how deem thee wise,
　Who wouldst not leave him in his wandering
To seek for treasure in the jewelled skies,
　Albeit he soared with an undaunted wing?
Hast thou not dragged Diana[1] from her car?
　And driven the Hamadryad[2] from the wood   10
To seek a shelter in some happier star?
　Hast thou not torn the Naiad[3] from her flood,
The Elfin from the green grass, and from me
The summer dream beneath the tamarind tree?[4]

1829

TO HELEN†

Helen, thy beauty is to me
　Like those Nicéan barks[1] of yore,
That gently, o'er a perfumed sea,
　The weary, way-worn wanderer bore
　　To his own native shore.

On desperate seas long wont to roam,
　Thy hyacinth[2] hair, thy classic face,
Thy Naiad[3] airs have brought me home
　To the glory that was Greece,
　　And the grandeur that was Rome.   10

---

* First printed in *Al Aaraaf, Tamerlane, and Minor Poems,* in 1829. In this sonnet, science is the adversary of the imagination and of poetry.
　[1] According to Roman myth, the moon-goddess who drives through the sky in her chariot or "car."
　[2] According to Greek myth, a nymph who lives as a spirit within a tree and perishes when her tree dies.
　[3] A female spirit who lives in fountains and streams.　[4] A brightly colored tropical tree.
　† First published in *Poems* in 1831, then revised and reworked at various times in the next twelve years; this version was included in *The Raven and Other Poems* (1845). In its public dimension the poem honors Helen of Troy, according to Greek myth the beautiful daughter of the chief god Zeus; she was the fabled cause of the Trojan war. As Poe admitted privately in an 1848 letter to Sarah Helen Whitman, the poem was inspired by the "first, purely ideal love of my soul," Mrs. Jane Stith Stanard, mother of Poe's schoolmate Robert Stanard, in Richmond, Virginia.
　[1] Victorious (from the Greek *nike*) "victory" ships. Critics agree that the sound of "Nicéan," suggestive of a gentle homecoming in a classical world, contributes to the total effect of the poem.
　[2] Luxuriant and curling.
　[3] Nymphlike; according to Greek myth, Naiads are female spirits who inhabit fountains and streams.

Lo! in yon brilliant window-niche
　How statue-like I see thee stand,
The agate[4] lamp within thy hand!
　Ah, Psyche,[5] from the regions which
　Are Holy-Land!

1831

ISRAFEL*

In Heaven a spirit doth dwell
　"Whose heart-strings are a lute;"
None sing so wildly well
As the angel Israfel,[1]
And the giddy stars (so legends tell)
Ceasing their hymns, attend the spell
　Of his voice, all mute.

Tottering above
　In her highest noon,
　The enamoured moon
Blushes with love,
　While, to listen, the red levin[2]
　(With the rapid Pleiads,[3] even,
　Which were seven,)
Pauses in Heaven.

And they say (the starry choir
　And the other listening things)
That Israfeli's fire
Is owing to that lyre
　By which he sits and sings—
The trembling living wire
Of those unusual strings.

10

20

---

[4] This word first appeared in the final revision of the poem in 1843. According to Thomas O. Mabbott the agate "is named for 'fidus Acates,' the *faithful* friend of Aeneas" in Virgil's *Aenead*. Agate is a translucent variety of quartz, with a waxlike luster.

[5] "Soul" (Greek); according to Roman myth, Psyche was a damsel so beautiful that the goddess of love, Venus, was jealous of her. Thus, the poet's sign for this spiritualized beauty who comes from the "Holy-Land" of idealized love.

* First published in *Poems* in 1831, revised and reprinted in various journals in the 1830s and 1840s, and included in *The Raven and Other Poems* (1845). Poe added this note to the title: "And the angel Israfel, whose heart-strings are a lute, and who has the sweetest voice of all God's creatures.—KORAN," from the "Preliminary Discourse" to George Sale's translation of the Koran (1734).

[1] The source of Poe's idea for the "angel Israfel" is *Lalla Rookh* (1817), a series of Oriental tales by the Irish poet Thomas Moore (1779–1852), in which Israfel has an enchanting and wondrous voice.

[2] Lightning.

[3] According to Greek myth, the Pleiades were seven sisters pursued by the giant hunter Orion; both he and they were turned into heavenly constellations.

But the skies that angel trod,
  Where deep thoughts are a duty—
Where Love's a grown-up God[4]—
  Where the Houri[5] glances are
Imbued with all the beauty
  Which we worship in a star.

Therefore, thou art not wrong,
  Israfeli, who despisest   30
An unimpassioned song;
To thee the laurels belong,
  Best bard, because the wisest!
Merrily live, and long!

The ecstasies above
  With thy burning measures suit—
Thy grief, thy joy, thy hate, thy love,
  With the fervour of thy lute—
Well may the stars be mute!

Yes, Heaven is thine; but this   40
  Is a world of sweets and sours;
  Our flowers are merely—flowers,
And the shadow of thy perfect bliss
  Is the sunshine of ours.

If I could dwell
Where Israfel
  Hath dwelt, and he where I,
He might not sing so wildly well
  A mortal melody,
While a bolder note than this might swell   50
  From my lyre within the sky.

                              1831

THE RAVEN*

Once upon a midnight dreary, while I pondered, weak and weary,
Over many a quaint and curious volume of forgotten lore—
While I nodded, nearly napping, suddenly there came a tapping,

---

[4] According to Greek myth, the god of love, Eros, is a man.
[5] Dark-eyed nymphs of the Mohammedan paradise.
* First typeset for the February 1845 issue of the *American Review,* but before that issue appeared it was printed in the New York *Evening Mirror* on January 29, 1845. The poem was reprinted in other periodicals in that year and was included in *The Raven and Other Poems* (1845). Instantly popular, it has remained Poe's best-known poem.

As of some one gently rapping, rapping at my chamber door.
"'T is some visiter," I muttered, "tapping at my chamber door—
      Only this and nothing more."

Ah, distinctly I remember it was in the bleak December;
And each separate dying ember wrought its ghost upon the floor.
Eagerly I wished the morrow;—vainly I had sought to borrow
From my books surcease of sorrow—sorrow for the lost Lenore—   10
For the rare and radiant maiden whom the angels name Lenore—
      Nameless *here* for evermore.[1]

And the silken, sad, uncertain rustling of each purple curtain
Thrilled me—filled me with fantastic terrors never felt before;
So that now, to still the beating of my heart, I stood repeating
"'T is some visiter entreating entrance at my chamber door—
Some late visiter entreating entrance at my chamber door;—
      This it is and nothing more."

Presently my soul grew stronger; hesitating then no longer,
"Sir," said I, "or Madam, truly your forgiveness I implore;   20
But the fact is I was napping, and so gently you came rapping,
And so faintly you came tapping, tapping at my chamber door,
That I scarce was sure I heard you"—here I opened wide the door;———
      Darkness there and nothing more.

Deep into that darkness peering, long I stood there wondering, fearing,
Doubting, dreaming dreams no mortal ever dared to dream before;
But the silence was unbroken, and the stillness gave no token,
And the only word there spoken was the whispered word, "Lenore!"
This I whispered, and an echo murmured back the word "Lenore!"
      Merely this and nothing more.   30

Back into the chamber turning, all my soul within me burning,
Soon again I heard a tapping somewhat louder than before.
"Surely," said I, "surely that is something at my window lattice;
Let me see, then, what thereat is, and this mystery explore—
Let my heart be still a moment and this mystery explore;—
      'T is the wind and nothing more!"

Open here I flung the shutter, when, with many a flirt[2] and flutter
In there stepped a stately Raven of the saintly days of yore.
Not the least obeisance made he; not a minute stopped or stayed he;
But, with mien of lord or lady, perched above my chamber door—   40
Perched upon a bust of Pallas[3] just above my chamber door—
      Perched, and sat, and nothing more.

---

[1] Because Lenore has died, she will no longer be part of this world.   [2] A jerky movement.
[3] Pallas Athena: according to Greek myth, the goddess of wisdom.

Then this ebony bird beguiling my sad fancy into smiling,
By the grave and stern decorum of the countenance it wore,
"Though thy crest be shorn and shaven, thou," I said, "art sure no craven,[4]
Ghastly grim and ancient Raven wandering from the Nightly shore—
Tell me what thy lordly name is on the Night's Plutonian[5] shore!"
        Quoth the Raven, "Nevermore."

Much I marvelled this ungainly fowl to hear discourse so plainly,
Though its answer little meaning—little relevancy bore;   50
For we cannot help agreeing that no living human being
Ever yet was blessed with seeing bird above his chamber door—
Bird or beast upon the sculptured bust above his chamber door,
        With such name as "Nevermore."

But the Raven, sitting lonely on the placid bust, spoke only
That one word, as if his soul in that one word he did outpour.
Nothing farther then he uttered—not a feather then he fluttered—
Till I scarcely more than muttered "Other friends have flown before—
On the morrow *he* will leave me, as my hopes have flown before."
        Then the bird said "Nevermore."   60

Startled at the stillness broken by reply so aptly spoken,
"Doubtless," said I, "what it utters is its only stock and store
Caught from some unhappy master whom unmerciful Disaster
Followed fast and followed faster till his songs one burden bore—
Till the dirges of his Hope that melancholy burden bore
        Of 'Never—nevermore.'"

But the Raven still beguiling all my fancy into smiling,
Straight I wheeled a cushioned seat in front of bird, and bust and door;
Then, upon the velvet sinking, I betook myself to linking
Fancy unto fancy, thinking what this ominous bird of yore—   70
What this grim, ungainly, ghastly, gaunt, and ominous bird of yore
        Meant in croaking "Nevermore."

This I sat engaged in guessing, but no syllable expressing
To the fowl whose fiery eyes now burned into my bosom's core;
This and more I sat divining, with my head at ease reclining
On the cushion's velvet lining that the lamp-light gloated[6] o'er,
But whose velvet violet lining with the lamp-light gloating o'er,
        She shall press, ah, nevermore!

Then, methought, the air grew denser, perfumed from an unseen censer
Swung by Seraphim[7] whose foot-falls tinkled on the tufted floor.   80
    "Wretch," I cried, "thy God hath lent thee—by these angels he hath sent thee

---

[4] As Thomas O. Mabbott observes, a cowardly or craven knight sometimes had his head (crest) shaved. Mabbott also points out Poe's pun ("Nightly shore") in the following line.
[5] Black; according to Roman myth, Pluto is the ruler of the underworld of the dead.
[6] Glowed as well as shone down maliciously.
[7] Angels (with bells, or tinkling foot-falls, at their ankles).

Respite—respite and nepenthe[8] from thy memories of Lenore;
Quaff, oh quaff this kind nepenthe and forget this lost Lenore!"
        Quoth the Raven "Nevermore."

"Prophet!" said I, "thing of evil! prophet still, if bird or devil!—
Whether Tempter sent, or whether tempest tossed thee here ashore,
Desolate yet all undaunted, on this desert land enchanted—
On this home by Horror haunted—tell me truly, I implore—
Is there—*is* there balm in Gilead?[9]—tell me—tell me, I implore!"
        Quoth the Raven "Nevermore."   90

"Prophet!" said I, "thing of evil!—prophet still, if bird or devil!
By that Heaven that bends above us—by that God we both adore—
Tell this soul with sorrow laden if, within the distant Aidenn,[10]
It shall clasp a sainted maiden whom the angels name Lenore.—
Clasp a rare and radiant maiden whom the angels name Lenore."
        Quoth the Raven "Nevermore."

"Be that word our sign of parting, bird or fiend!" I shrieked, upstarting—
"Get thee back into the tempest and the Night's Plutonian shore!
Leave no black plume as a token of that lie thy soul hath spoken!
Leave my loneliness unbroken!—quit the bust above my door!   100
Take thy beak from out my heart, and take thy form from off my door!"
        Quoth the Raven "Nevermore."

And the Raven, never flitting, still is sitting, *still* is sitting
On the pallid bust of Pallas just above my chamber door;
And his eyes have all the seeming of a demon's that is dreaming,
And the lamp-light o'er him streaming throws his shadow on the floor;
And my soul from out that shadow that lies floating on the floor
        Shall be lifted—nevermore!

                                                                1845

ANNABEL LEE*

It was many and many a year ago,
    In a kingdom by the sea,
That a maiden there lived whom you may know

---

[8] A legendary drug that soothes and relieves anguish.
[9] "Is there no balm in Gilead?" from Jeremiah 8:22. Evergreens growing in Gilead, near the Sea of Galilee in Jordan, supplied a medicinal balm.
[10] Eden or Heaven, from the Arabic *Adn*.
* First published in the *New-York Tribune* on October 9, 1849, two days after Poe's death. In July 1849 Poe had sold the poem for publication to *Sartain's Union Magazine,* then given copies to several people who had helped him financially; some of them had the poem printed before *Sartain's* published it in January 1850.

By the name of ANNABEL LEE;
And this maiden she lived with no other thought
Than to love and be loved by me.

I was a child and *she* was a child,
In this kingdom by the sea,
But we loved with a love that was more than love—
I and my ANNABEL LEE—
With a love that the wingèd seraphs of heaven
Coveted her and me.

And this was the reason that, long ago,
In this kingdom by the sea,
A wind blew out of a cloud, chilling
My beautiful ANNABEL LEE;
So that her highborn kinsmen came
And bore her away from me,
To shut her up in a sepulchre
In this kingdom by the sea.

The angels, not half so happy in heaven,
Went envying her and me—
Yes!—that was the reason (as all men know,
In this kingdom by the sea)
That the wind came out of the cloud by night,
Chilling and killing my ANNABEL LEE.

But our love it was stronger by far than the love
Of those who were older than we—
Of many far wiser than we—
And neither the angels in heaven above,
Nor the demons down under the sea,
Can ever dissever my soul from the soul
Of the beautiful ANNABEL LEE:

For the moon never beams, without bringing me dreams
Of the beautiful ANNABEL LEE;
And the stars never rise, but I feel the bright eyes
Of the beautiful ANNABEL LEE:
And so, all the night-tide, I lie down by the side
Of my darling—my darling—my life and my bride,
In the sepulchre there by the sea—
In her tomb by the sounding sea.[1]

1849

---

[1] Early manuscript versions of the poem contain this final line, but in a late revision Poe altered it to read, "In her tomb by the side of the sea." Most critics prefer the earlier version.

THE PHILOSOPHY OF COMPOSITION*

Charles Dickens, in a note now lying before me, alluding to an examination I once made of the mechanism of "Barnaby Rudge,"[1] says—"By the way, are you aware that Godwin wrote his 'Caleb Williams' backwards?[2] He first involved his hero in a web of difficulties, forming the second volume, and then, for the first, cast about him for some mode of accounting for what had been done."

I cannot think this the *precise* mode of procedure on the part of Godwin—and indeed what he himself acknowledges, is not altogether in accordance with Mr. Dickens' idea—but the author of "Caleb Williams" was too good an artist not to perceive the advantage derivable from at least a somewhat similar process. Nothing is more clear than that every plot, worth the name, must be elaborated to its *dénouement*[3] before anything be attempted with the pen. It is only with the *dénouement* constantly in view that we can give a plot its indispensable air of consequence, or causation, by making the incidents, and especially the tone at all points, tend to the development of the intention.

There is a radical error, I think, in the usual mode of constructing a story. Either history affords a thesis—or one is suggested by an incident of the day—or, at best, the author sets himself to work in the combination of striking events to form merely the basis of his narrative—designing, generally, to fill in with description, dialogue, or authorial comment, whatever crevices of fact, or action, may, from page to page, render themselves apparent.

I prefer commencing with the consideration of an *effect*. Keeping originality *always* in view—for he is false to himself who ventures to dispense with so obvious and so easily attainable a source of interest—I say to myself, in the first place, "Of the innumerable effects, or impressions, of which the heart, the intellect, or (more generally) the soul is susceptible, what one shall I, on the present occasion, select?" Having chosen a novel, first, and secondly a vivid effect, I consider whether it can be best wrought by incident or tone—whether by ordinary incidents and peculiar tone, or the converse, or by peculiarity both of incident and tone—afterward looking about me (or rather within) for such combinations of event, or tone, as shall best aid me in the construction of the effect.

I have often thought how interesting a magazine paper[4] might be written by any author who would—that is to say who could—detail, step by step, the processes by which any one of his compositions attained its ultimate point of completion. Why such a paper has never been given to the world, I am much at a loss to say—but, perhaps, the autorial vanity has had more to do with the omission than any one other cause. Most writers—poets in especial—prefer having it understood that they compose by a species of fine frenzy—an ecstatic intuition—and would positively shudder at letting the public take a peep behind the scenes, at the elaborate and vacillating crudities of thought—at the true purposes seized only at the last moment—at the innumerable glimpses of idea that arrived not at the matu-

---

* First published in *Graham's Magazine* in 1846; in this famous essay Poe purports to explain step-by-step how he wrote "The Raven." Whether or not his explanation is serious, the idea of the artist as a deliberate craftsman is central to Poe's theory of art.
[1] While Dickens's novel *Barnaby Rudge* was being serialized in 1842, Poe wrote an analytical review predicting the conclusion and correctly identifying the murderer.
[2] In an 1832 preface to the novel *Caleb Williams* (1794), William Godwin (1756–1836) claims that he planned his novel from the ending to the beginning.
[3] The unraveling of the plot.   [4] Article.

rity of full view—at the fully matured fancies discarded in despair as unmanageable—at the cautious selections and rejections—at the painful erasures and interpolations—in a word, at the wheels and pinions—the tackle for scene-shifting—the step-ladders and demon-traps—the cock's feathers, the red paint and the black patches, which, in ninety-nine cases out of the hundred, constitute the properties of the literary *histrio*.[5]

I am aware, on the other hand, that the case is by no means common, in which an author is at all in condition to retrace the steps by which his conclusions have been attained. In general, suggestions, having arisen pell-mell, are pursued and forgotten in a similar manner.

For my own part, I have neither sympathy with the repugnance alluded to, nor, at any time the least difficulty in recalling to mind the progressive steps of any of my compositions; and, since the interest of an analysis, or reconstruction, such as I have considered a *desideratum*,[6] is quite independent of any real or fancied interest in the thing analyzed, it will not be regarded as a breach of decorum on my part to show the *modus operandi*[7] by which some one of my own works was put together. I select "The Raven," as most generally known. It is my design to render it manifest that no one point in its composition is referrible either to accident or intuition—that the work proceeded, step by step, to its completion with the precision and rigid consequence of a mathematical problem.

Let us dismiss, as irrelevant to the poem, *per se*, the circumstance—or say the necessity—which, in the first place, gave rise to the intention of composing *a* poem that should suit at once the popular and the critical taste.

We commence, then, with this intention.

The initial consideration was that of extent. If any literary work is too long to be read at one sitting, we must be content to dispense with the immensely important effect derivable from unity of impression—for, if two sittings be required, the affairs of the world interfere, and every thing like totality is at once destroyed. But since, *ceteris paribus*,[8] no poet can afford to dispense with *any thing* that may advance his design, it but remains to be seen whether there is, in extent, any advantage to counterbalance the loss of unity which attends it. Here I say no, at once. What we term a long poem is, in fact, merely a succession of brief ones—that is to say, of brief poetical effects. It is needless to demonstrate that a poem is such, only inasmuch as it intensely excites, by elevating, the soul; and all intense excitements are, through a psychal[9] necessity, brief. For this reason, at least one half of the "Paradise Lost"[10] is essentially prose—a succession of poetical excitements interspersed, *inevitably*, with corresponding depressions—the whole being deprived, through the extremeness of its length, of the vastly important artistic element, totality, or unity, of effect.

It appears evident, then, that there is a distinct limit, as regards length, to all works of literary art—the limit of a single sitting—and that, although in certain classes of prose composition, such as "Robinson Crusoe,"[11] (demanding no

---

[5] "Artist" or "performer" (Latin).   [6] "A thing to be desired" (Latin).

[7] "Mode of operation" (Latin).   [8] "Other things being equal" (Latin).   [9] Psychological.

[10] *Paradise Lost* (1667), an epic poem in twelve books by John Milton (1608–1674). In length, this ambitious poem about human disobedience and the loss of Paradise comes to more than 10,500 lines.

[11] *The Life and Strange Surprising Adventures of Robinson Crusoe* (1719), an episodic novel of shipwreck in the Caribbean Sea and the adventures following Crusoe's rescue, by Daniel Defoe (1660–1731).

unity,) this limit may be advantageously overpassed, it can never properly be overpassed in a poem. Within this limit, the extent of a poem may be made to bear mathematical relation to its merit—in other words, to the excitement or elevation—again in other words, to the degree of the true poetical effect which it is capable of inducing; for it is clear that the brevity must be in direct ratio of the intensity of the intended effect:—this, with one proviso—that a certain degree of duration is absolutely requisite for the production of any effect at all.

Holding in view these considerations, as well as that degree of excitement which I deemed not above the popular, while not below the critical, taste, I reached at once what I conceived the proper *length* for my intended poem—a length of about one hundred lines. It is, in fact, a hundred and eight.

My next thought concerned the choice of an impression, or effect, to be conveyed: and here I may as well observe that, throughout the construction, I kept steadily in view the design of rendering the work *universally* appreciable. I should be carried too far out of my immediate topic were I to demonstrate a point upon which I have repeatedly insisted, and which, with the poetical, stands not in the slightest need of demonstration—the point, I mean, that Beauty is the sole legitimate province of the poem. A few words, however, in elucidation of my real meaning, which some of my friends have evinced a disposition to misrepresent. That pleasure which is at once the most intense, the most elevating, and the most pure, is, I believe, found in the contemplation of the beautiful. When, indeed, men speak of Beauty, they mean, precisely, not a quality, as is supposed, but an effect—they refer, in short, just to that intense and pure elevation of *soul—not* of intellect, or of heart—upon which I have commented, and which is experienced in consequence of contemplating "the beautiful." Now I designate Beauty as the province of the poem, merely because it is an obvious rule of Art that effects should be made to spring from direct causes—that objects should be attained through means best adapted for their attainment—no one as yet having been weak enough to deny that the peculiar elevation alluded to is *most readily* attained in the poem. Now the object, Truth, or the satisfaction of the intellect, and the object Passion, or the excitement of the heart, are, although attainable, to a certain extent, in poetry, far more readily attainable in prose. Truth, in fact, demands a precision, and Passion a *homeliness* (the truly passionate will comprehend me) which are absolutely antagonistic to that Beauty which, I maintain, is the excitement, or pleasurable elevation, of the soul. It by no means follows from any thing here said, that passion, or even truth, may not be introduced, and even profitably introduced, into a poem—for they may serve in elucidation, or aid the general effect, as do discords in music, by contrast—but the true artist will always contrive, first, to tone them into proper subservience to the predominant aim, and, secondly, to enveil them, as far as possible, in that Beauty which is the atmosphere and the essence of the poem.

Regarding, then, Beauty as my province, my next question referred to the *tone* of its highest manifestation—and all experience has shown that this tone is one of *sadness*. Beauty of whatever kind, in its supreme development, invariably excites the sensitive soul to tears. Melancholy is thus the most legitimate of all the poetical tones.

The length, the province, and the tone, being thus determined, I betook myself to ordinary induction, with the view of obtaining some artistic piquancy which might serve me as a key-note in the construction of the poem—some pivot upon which the whole structure might turn. In carefully thinking over all the usual artistic effects—or more properly *points,* in the theatrical sense—I did not fail to perceive immediately that no one had been so universally employed as that of the *refrain*. The universality of its employment sufficed to assure me of its intrinsic value, and spared me the necessity of submitting it to analysis. I considered it, however, with regard to its susceptibility of improvement, and soon saw it to be in a primitive condition. As commonly used, the *refrain,* or burden, not only is limited to lyric verse, but depends for its impression upon the force of monotone—both in sound and thought. The pleasure is deduced solely from the sense of identity—of repetition. I resolved to diversify, and so heighten, the effect, by adhering, in general, to the monotone of sound, while I continually varied that of thought: that is to say, I determined to produce continuously novel effects, by the variation *of the application* of the *refrain*—the *refrain* itself remaining, for the most part, unvaried.

These points being settled, I next bethought me of the *nature* of my *refrain*. Since its application was to be repeatedly varied, it was clear that the *refrain* itself must be brief, for there would have been an insurmountable difficulty in frequent variations of application in any sentence of length. In proportion to the brevity of the sentence, would, of course, be the facility of the variation. This led me at once to a single word as the best *refrain*.

The question now arose as to the *character* of the word. Having made up my mind to a *refrain,* the division of the poem into stanzas was, of course, a corollary: the *refrain* forming the close of each stanza. That such a close, to have force, must be sonorous and susceptible of protracted emphasis, admitted no doubt: and these considerations inevitably led me to the long *o* as the most sonorous vowel, in connection with *r* as the most producible consonant.

The sound of the *refrain* being thus determined, it became necessary to select a word embodying this sound, and at the same time in the fullest possible keeping with that melancholy which I had predetermined as the tone of the poem. In such a search it would have been absolutely impossible to overlook the word "Nevermore." In fact, it was the very first which presented itself.

The next *desideratum* was a pretext for the continuous use of the one word "nevermore." In observing the difficulty which I at once found in inventing a sufficiently plausible reason for its continuous repetition, I did not fail to perceive that this difficulty arose solely from the pre-assumption that the word was to be so continuously or monotonously spoken by *a human* being—I did not fail to perceive, in short, that the difficulty lay in the reconciliation of this monotony with the exercise of reason on the part of the creature repeating the word. Here, then, immediately arose the idea of a *non*-reasoning creature capable of speech; and, very naturally, a parrot, in the first instance, suggested itself, but was superseded forthwith by a Raven, as equally capable of speech, and infinitely more in keeping with the intended *tone*.

I had now gone so far as the conception of a Raven—the bird of ill omen—monotonously repeating the one word, "Nevermore," at the conclusion of each stanza, in a poem of melancholy tone, and in length about one hundred lines. Now, never losing sight of the object *supremeness,* or perfection, at all points, I asked myself—"Of all melancholy topics, what, according to the *universal* understanding of mankind, is the *most* melancholy?" Death—was the obvious reply. "And when," I said, "is this most melancholy of topics most poetical?" From what I have already explained at some length, the answer, here also, is obvious—"When it most closely allies itself to *Beauty:* the death, then, of a beautiful woman is, unquestionably, the most poetical topic in the world—and equally is it beyond doubt that the lips best suited for such topic are those of a bereaved lover."

I had now to combine the two ideas, of a lover lamenting his deceased mistress and a Raven continuously repeating the word "Nevermore."—I had to combine these, bearing in mind my design of varying, at every turn, the *application* of the word repeated; but the only intelligible mode of such combination is that of imagining the Raven employing the word in answer to the queries of the lover. And here it was that I saw at once the opportunity afforded for the effect on which I had been depending—that is to say, the effect of the *variation of application*. I saw that I could make the first query propounded by the lover—the first query to which the Raven should reply "Nevermore"—that I could make this first query a commonplace one—the second less so—the third still less, and so on—until at length the lover, startled from his original *nonchalance* by the melancholy character of the word itself—by its frequent repetition—and by a consideration of the ominous reputation of the fowl that uttered it—is at length excited to superstition, and wildly propounds queries of a far different character—queries whose solution he has passionately at heart—propounds them half in superstition and half in that species of despair which delights in self-torture—propounds them not altogether because he believes in the prophetic or demoniac character of the bird (which, reason assures him, is merely repeating a lesson learned by rote) but because he experiences a phrenzied pleasure in so modeling his questions as to receive from the *expected* "Nevermore" the most delicious because the most intolerable of sorrow. Perceiving the opportunity thus afforded me—or, more strictly, thus forced upon me in the progress of the construction—I first established in mind the climax, or concluding query—that query to which "Nevermore" should be in the last place an answer—that in reply to which this word "Nevermore" should involve the utmost conceivable amount of sorrow and despair.

Here then the poem may be said to have its beginning—at the end, where all works of art should begin—for it was here, at this point of my preconsiderations, that I first put pen to paper in the composition of the stanza:

> "Prophet," said I, "thing of evil! prophet still if bird or devil!
> By that heaven that bends above us—by that God we both adore,
> Tell this soul with sorrow laden, if within the distant Aidenn,
> It shall clasp a sainted maiden whom the angels name Lenore—
> Clasp a rare and radiant maiden whom the angels name Lenore."
> Quoth the raven "Nevermore."

I composed this stanza, at this point, first that, by establishing the climax, I might the better vary and graduate, as regards seriousness and importance, the preceding queries of the lover—and, secondly, that I might definitely settle the rhythm, the metre, and the length and general arrangement of the stanza—as well as graduate the stanzas which were to precede, so that none of them might surpass this in rhythmical effect. Had I been able, in the subsequent composition, to construct more vigorous stanzas, I should, without scruple, have purposely enfeebled them, so as not to interfere with the climacteric[12] effect.

---

[12] Climactic.

And here I may as well say a few words of the versification. My first object (as usual) was originality. The extent to which this has been neglected, in versification, is one of the most unaccountable things in the world. Admitting that there is little possibility of variety in mere *rhythm,* it is still clear that the possible varieties of metre and stanza are absolutely infinite—and yet, *for centuries, no man, in verse, has ever done, or ever seemed to think of doing, an original thing.* The fact is, that originality (unless in minds of very unusual force) is by no means a matter, as some suppose, of impulse or intuition. In general, to be found, it must be elaborately sought, and although a positive merit of the highest class, demands in its attainment less of invention than negation.

Of course, I pretend to no originality in either the rhythm or metre of the "Raven." The former is trochaic—the latter is octameter acatalectic, alternating with heptameter catalectic[13] repeated in the *refrain* of the fifth verse, and terminating with tetrameter catalectic. Less pedantically—the feet employed throughout (trochees) consist of a long syllable followed by a short: the first line of the stanza consists of eight of these feet—the second of seven and a half (in effect two-thirds)—the third of eight—the fourth of seven and a half—the fifth the same—the sixth three and a half. Now each of these lines, taken individually, has been employed before, and what originality the "Raven" has, is in their *combination into stanza;* nothing even remotely approaching this combination has ever been attempted. The effect of this originality of combination is aided by other unusual, and some altogether novel effects, arising from an extension of the application of the principles of rhyme and alliteration.

The next point to be considered was the mode of bringing together the lover and the Raven—and the first branch of this consideration was the *locale.* For this the most natural suggestion might seem to be a forest, or the fields—but it has always appeared to me that a close *circumscription of space* is absolutely necessary to the effect of insulated incident:—it has the force of a frame to a picture. It has an indisputable moral power in keeping concentrated the attention, and, of course, must not be confounded with mere unity of place.

I determined, then, to place the lover in his chamber—in a chamber rendered sacred to him by memories of her who had frequented it. The room is represented as richly furnished—this in mere pursuance of the ideas I have already explained on the subject of Beauty, as the sole true poetical thesis.

The *locale* being thus determined, I had now to introduce the bird—and the thought of introducing him through the window, was inevitable. The idea of making the lover suppose, in the first instance, that the flapping of the wings of the bird against the shutter, is a "tapping" at the door, originated in a wish to increase, by prolonging, the reader's curiosity, and in a desire to admit the incidental effect arising from the lover's throwing open the door, finding all dark, and thence adopting the half-fancy that it was the spirit of his mistress that knocked.

I made the night tempestuous, first, to account for the Raven's seeking admission, and secondly, for the effect of contrast with the (physical) serenity within the chamber.

---

[13] The former composed of trochees, or metrical feet with one accented and one unaccented syllable; the latter is an eight-measure line of poetry with a complete syllable at the end, alternating with a five-measure line lacking a syllable at the end.

I made the bird alight on the bust of Pallas,[14] also for the effect of contrast between the marble and the plumage—it being understood that the bust was absolutely *suggested* by the bird—the bust of *Pallas* being chosen, first, as most in keeping with the scholarship of the lover, and, secondly, for the sonorousness of the word, Pallas, itself.

About the middle of the poem, also, I have availed myself of the force of contrast, with a view of deepening the ultimate impression. For example, an air of the fantastic—approaching as nearly to the ludicrous as was admissible—is given to the Raven's entrance. He comes in "with many a flirt and flutter."

> Not the *least obeisance made he*—not a moment stopped or stayed he,
> *But with mien of lord or lady,* perched above my chamber door.

In the two stanzas which follow, the design is more obviously carried out:—

> Then this ebony bird beguiling my sad fancy into smiling
> By the *grave and stern decorum of the countenance it wore,*
> "Though thy *crest be shorn and shaven* thou," I said, "art sure no craven,
> Ghastly grim and ancient Raven wandering from the nightly shore—
> Tell me what thy lordly name is on the Night's Plutonian shore?"
> Quoth the Raven "Nevermore."

> Much I marvelled *this ungainly fowl* to hear discourse so plainly
> Though its answer little meaning—little relevancy bore;
> For we cannot help agreeing that no living human being
> *Ever yet was blessed with seeing bird above his chamber door—*
> *Bird or beast upon the sculptured bust above his chamber door,*
> With such name as "Nevermore."

The effect of the *dénouement* being thus provided for, I immediately drop the fantastic for a tone of the most profound seriousness:—this tone commencing in the stanza directly following the one last quoted, with the line,

> But the Raven, sitting lonely on that placid bust, spoke only, etc.

From this epoch the lover no longer jests—no longer sees any thing even of the fantastic in the Raven's demeanor. He speaks of him as a "grim, ungainly, ghastly, gaunt, and ominous bird of yore," and feels the "fiery eyes" burning into his "bosom's core." This revolution of thought, or fancy, on the lover's part, is intended to induce a similar one on the part of the reader—to bring the mind into a proper frame for the *dénouement*—which is now brought about as rapidly and as *directly* as possible.

With the *dénouement* proper—with the Raven's reply, "Nevermore," to the lover's final demand if he shall meet his mistress in another world—the poem, in its obvious phase, that of a simple narrative, may be said to have its completion. So far, every thing is within the limits of the accountable—of the real. A raven, having escaped from the custody of its owner, is driven at midnight, through the violence of a storm, to seek admission at a window from which a light still

---

[14] Pallas Athena: according to Greek myth, the goddess of wisdom and art.

gleams—the chamber-window of a student, occupied half in poring over a volume, half in dreaming of a beloved mistress deceased. The casement being thrown open at the fluttering of the bird's wings, the bird itself perches on the most convenient seat out of the immediate reach of the student, who, amused by the incident and the oddity of the visitor's demeanor, demands of it, in jest and without looking for a reply, its name. The raven addressed, answers with its customary word, "Nevermore"—a word which finds immediate echo in the melancholy heart of the student, who, giving utterance aloud to certain thoughts suggested by the occasion, is again startled by the fowl's repetition of "Nevermore." The student now guesses the state of the case, but is impelled, as I have before explained, by the human thirst for self-torture, and in part by superstition, to propound such queries to the bird as will bring him, the lover, the most of the luxury of sorrow, through the anticipated answer "Nevermore." With the indulgence, to the extreme, of this self-torture, the narration, in what I have termed its first or obvious phase, has a natural termination, and so far there has been no overstepping of the limits of the real.

But in subjects so handled, however skilfully, or with however vivid an array of incident, there is always a certain hardness or nakedness, which repels the artistical eye. Two things are invariably required—first, some amount of complexity, or more properly, adaptation; and, secondly, some amount of suggestiveness—some under-current, however indefinite, of meaning. It is this latter, in especial, which imparts to a work of art so much of that *richness* (to borrow from colloquy a forcible term) which we are too fond of confounding with *the ideal*. It is the *excess* of the suggested meaning—it is the rendering this the upper instead of the under current of the theme—which turns into prose (and that of the very flattest kind) the so called poetry of the so called transcendentalists.

Holding these opinions, I added the two concluding stanzas of the poem—their suggestiveness being thus made to pervade all the narrative which has preceded them. The under-current of meaning is rendered first apparent in the lines—

> "Take thy beak from out *my heart*, and take thy form from off my door!"
> Quoth the Raven "Nevermore!"

It will be observed that the words, "from out my heart," involve the first metaphorical expression in the poem. They, with the answer, "Nevermore," dispose the mind to seek a moral in all that has been previously narrated. The reader begins now to regard the Raven as emblematical[15]—but it is not until the very last line of the very last stanza, that the intention of making him emblematical of *Mournful and Never-ending Remembrance* is permitted distinctly to be seen:

> And the Raven, never flitting, still is sitting, still is sitting,
> On the pallid bust of Pallas, just above my chamber door;
> And his eyes have all the seeming of a demon's that is dreaming,
> And the lamplight o'er him streaming throws his shadow on the floor;
> And my soul *from out that shadow* that lies floating on the floor
> Shall be lifted—nevermore.

1846

---

[15] Symbolic.

Thomas Bangs Thorpe
(1815–1878)

Born in 1815 in Westfield, Massachusetts, Thomas Bangs Thorpe spent his teen years in New York City, where he studied painting with John Quidor (known for his illustrations of Washington Irving). Despite Thorpe's talent, his artistic ambitions were frustrated by lack of funds. Unable to raise the money to study art in Europe, he enrolled at Wesleyan University in Connecticut in 1834. By 1836, however, he left Wesleyan, suffering from poor health and poor grades. Hoping for a more healthful climate and a chance to make money painting portraits, he moved to Baton Rouge, Louisiana. The move was the turning point of his career: rather than finding subjects for his portraits, Thorpe found ample subject matter for colorful tales about life on the southwestern frontier.

Thorpe's first tale, "Tom Owen, the Bee Hunter," was published in 1839 in William T. Porter's the *Spirit of the Times*, a journal that Thorpe later edited. Thorpe went on to publish many successful tales in the *Spirit*, among them his classic "Big Bear of Arkansas" in 1841 and others, which he collected in *The Mysteries of the Backwoods* (1846). From 1840 until his death in 1878 he wrote scores of articles, dealing with the fine arts, fishing, hunting, and the American landscape, which he published in magazines as diverse as *Harper's* and *Forest and Stream*. Today, however, Thorpe is remembered for his tall tales of southwestern life. Although his second collection of these stories, *The Hive of The Bee Hunter* (1854), established him as a major southern humorist, he never became completely southern in his sympathies. After serving as a colonel in the Mexican War, he returned to New York in 1853 and shortly afterward published *The Master's House: A Tale of Southern Life* (1854), a novel that attacks slavery. During the Civil War Thorpe served as a colonel with the Union forces that occupied New Orleans. In 1864 he again returned to New York, where he received a Customs House appointment, which he held until his death in 1878.

During his years in the Old Southwest, Thorpe observed the vanishing of the wilderness as a result of the progress of white settlers. He recorded the importation of outside refinements, such as a town's first piano in the story "A Piano in 'Arkansaw'." As his exuberant descriptions of the Arkansas backwoods demonstrate, he always retained his painter's sensitivity for landscape. "The Big Bear of Arkansas," for example, celebrates the incredible fertility of "the creation state" and records the passing of the frontier that makes such tall tales possible. Widely reprinted, Thorpe's story of an "unhuntable" bear is representative of the entire genre of Southwest Humor. As scholars agree, it stands as the beginning of the "Big Bear" tradition in American writing, which not only includes other bear stories in Southwest Humor but later fiction such as William Faulkner's "The Bear" (1942). "The Big Bear" contains a "ringtail roarer," a loud boaster, who speaks the dialect of the region, a fantastic "bar" hunt, and a vision of a fertile American wilderness that, like the big bear itself, seems ever beyond the pursuer's grasp.

Suggested Readings: *The Big Bear of Arkansas, and Other Sketches Illustrative of Characters and Incidents in the South and South-West*, ed. W. T. Porter, 1845. *The Mysteries of the Backwoods: Or, Sketches of the Southwest*, 1846. *The Master's House: A Tale of Southern Life*, 1854. N. W. Yates,

William T. Porter and "The Spirit of the Times" : A Study of the "Big Bear" School of Humor, 1957. M. Rickels, *Thomas Bangs Thorpe: Humorist of the Old Southwest*, 1962. E. Miles, *Southwest Humorists*, 1969.

Text Used: *Humor of the Old Southwest*, ed. H. Cohen and W. B. Dillingham, 1964.

THE BIG BEAR OF ARKANSAS*

A steamboat on the Mississippi, frequently, in making her regular trips, carries between places varying from one to two thousand miles apart; and, as these boats advertise to land passengers and freight at "all intermediate landings," the heterogeneous character of the passengers of one of these up-country boats can scarcely be imagined by one who has never seen it with his own eyes.

Starting from New Orleans in one of these boats, you will find yourself associated with men from every State in the Union, and from every portion of the globe; and a man of observation need not lack for amusement or instruction in such a crowd, if he will take the trouble to read the great book of character so favorably opened before him.

Here may be seen, jostling together, the wealthy Southern planter and the pedler of tin-ware from New England—the Northern merchant and the Southern jockey—a venerable bishop, and a desperate gambler—the land speculator, and the honest farmer—professional men of all creeds and characters—Wolvereens, Suckers, Hoosiers, Buckeyes, and Corncrackers,[1] beside a "plentiful sprinkling" of the half-horse and half-alligator species of men,[2] who are peculiar to "old Mississippi," and who appear to gain a livelihood by simply going up and down the river. In the pursuit of pleasure or business, I have frequently found myself in such a crowd.

On one occasion, when in New Orleans, I had occasion to take a trip of a few miles up the Mississippi, and I hurried on board the well-known "high-pressure-and-beat-every-thing" steamboat "Invincible," just as the last note of the last bell was sounding; and when the confusion and bustle that is natural to a boat's getting under way had subsided, I discovered that I was associated in as heterogeneous a crowd as was ever got together. As my trip was to be of a few hours' duration only, I made no endeavors to become acquainted with my fellow-passengers, most of whom would be together many days. Instead of this, I took out of my pocket the "latest paper," and more critically than usual examined its contents; my fellow-passengers, at the same time, disposed of themselves in little groups.

While I was thus busily employed in reading, and my companions were more busily still employed, in discussing such subjects as suited their humors best, we were most unexpectedly startled by a loud Indian whoop, uttered in the "social hall," that part of the cabin fitted off for a bar; then was to be heard a loud crowing, which would not have continued to interest us—such sounds being quite common in that *place of spirits*—had not the hero of these windy accomplish-

---

*First published in *The Spirit of the Times* in 1841; later included in the collection *The Hive of The Bee-Hunter* (1854).

[1] Nicknames for inhabitants of Michigan, Illinois, Indiana, Ohio, and Kentucky, respectively.

[2] Boastful, rowdy backwoodsmen from Kentucky and Tennessee and raftsmen on the Mississippi River.

ments stuck his head into the cabin, and hallooed out, "Hurra for the Big Bear of Arkansaw!"

Then might be heard a confused hum of voices, unintelligible, save in such broken sentences as "horse," "screamer," "lightning is slow," etc.

As might have been expected, this continued interruption, attracted the attention of every one in the cabin; all conversation ceased, and in the midst of this surprise, the "Big Bear" walked into the cabin, took a chair, put his feet on the stove, and looking back over his shoulder, passed the general and familiar salute—"Strangers, how are you?"

He then expressed himself as much at home as if he had been at "the Forks of Cypress," and "prehaps a little more so."

Some of the company at this familiarity looked a little angry, and some astonished; but in a moment every face was wreathed in a smile. There was something about the intruder that won the heart on sight. He appeared to be a man enjoying perfect health and contentment; his eyes were as sparkling as diamonds, and good-natured to simplicity. Then his perfect confidence in himself was irresistibly droll.

"Prehaps," said he, "gentlemen," running on without a person interrupting, "prehaps you have been to New Orleans often; I never made *the first visit before,* and I don't intend to make another in a crow's life. I am thrown away in that ar place, and useless, that ar a fact. Some of the gentlemen thar called me *green*— well, prehaps I am, said I, *but I arn't so at home;* and if I ain't off my trail much, the heads of them perlite chaps themselves wern't much the hardest; for according to my notion, they were *real know-nothings,* green as a pumpkin-vine—couldn't, in farming, I'll bet, raise a crop of turnips; and as for shooting, they'd miss a barn if the door was swinging, and that, too, with the best rifle in the country. And then they talked to me 'bout hunting, and laughed at my calling the principal game in Arkansaw poker, and high-low-jack.

"'Prehaps,' said I, 'you prefer checkers and roulette;' at this they laughed harder than ever, and asked me if I lived in the woods, and didn't know what *game* was?

"At this, I rather think *I* laughed.

"'Yes,' I roared, and says, I, 'Strangers, if you'd ask me *how we got our meat* in Arkansaw, I'd a told you at once, and given you a list of varmints that would make a caravan, beginning with the bar, and ending off with the cat; that's *meat* though, not game.

"Game, indeed,—that's what city folks call it; and with them it means chippen-birds and shite-pokes;[3] may be such trash live in my diggins, but I arn't noticed them yet: a bird anyway is too trifling. I never did shoot at but one, and I'd never forgiven myself for that, had it weighed less than forty pounds. I wouldn't draw a rifle on anything less heavy than that; and when I meet with another wild turkey of the same size, I will drap him."

"A wild turkey weighing forty pounds!" exclaimed twenty voices in the cabin at once.

"Yes, strangers, and wasn't it a whopper? You see, the thing was so fat that it couldn't fly far; and when he fell out of the tree, after I shot him, on striking the ground he bust open behind, and the way the pound gobs of tallow rolled out of the opening was perfectly beautiful."

"Where did all that happen?" asked a cynical-looking Hoosier.

---

[3] Chirping sparrows and green herons.

"Happen! happened in Arkansaw: where else could it have happened, but in the creation State, the finishing-up country—a State where the *sile* runs down to the centre of the 'arth, and government gives you a title to every inch of it? Then its airs—just breathe them, and they will make you snort like a horse. It's a State without a fault, it is."

"Excepting mosquitoes," cried the Hoosier.

"Well, stranger, except them; for it ar a fact that they are rather *enormous,* and do push themselves in somewhat troublesome. But, stranger, they never stick twice in the same place; and give them a fair chance for a few months, and you will get as much above noticing them as an alligator. They can't hurt my feelings, for they lay under the skin; and I never knew but one case of injury resulting from them, and that was to a Yankee: and they take worse to foreigners, any how, than they do to natives. But the way they used that fellow up! first they punched him until he swelled up and busted; then he sup-per-a-ted, as the doctor called it, until he was as raw as beef; then, owing to the warm weather, he tuck the ager,[4] and finally he tuck a steamboat and left the country. He was the only man that ever tuck mosquitoes at heart that I knowd of.

"But mosquitoes is natur, and I never find fault with her. If they ar large, Arkansaw is large, her varmints ar large, her trees ar large, her rivers ar large, and a small mosquito would be of no more use in Arkansaw than preaching in a cane-brake."

This knock-down argument in favor of big mosquitoes used the Hoosier up, and the logician started on a new track, to explain how numerous bear were in his "diggins," where he represented them to be "about as plenty as blackberries, and a little plentifuller."

Upon the utterance of this assertion, a timid little man near me inquired, if the bear in Arkansaw ever attacked the settlers in numbers.

"No," said our hero, warming with the subject, "no, stranger, for you see it ain't the natur of bear to go in droves; but the way they squander about in pairs and single ones is edifying.

"An then the way I hunt them—the old black rascals know the crack of my gun as well as they know a pig's squealing. They grow thin in our parts, it frightens them so, and they do take the noise dreadfully, poor things. That gun of mine is a perfect *epidemic among bear:* if not watched closely, it will go off as quick on a warm scent as my dog Bowieknife[5] will: and then that dog—whew! why the fellow thinks that the world is full of bear, he finds them so easy. It's lucky he don't talk as well as think; for with his natural modesty, if he should suddenly learn how much he is acknowledged to be ahead of all other dogs in the universe, he would be astonished to death in two minutes.

"Strangers, that dog knows a bear's way as well as a horse-jockey knows a woman's: he always barks at the right time, bites at the exact place, and whips without getting a scratch.

"I never could tell whether he was made expressly to hunt bear, or whether bear was made expressly for him to hunt; any way, I believe they were ordained to go together as naturally as Squire Jones says a man and woman is, when he moralizes in marrying a couple. In fact, Jones once said, said he, 'Marriage according to law

---

[4] Ague (chills and fever).
[5] The dog is named for the knife, which in turn is named for the frontiersman and soldier James Bowie (1799–1836), who died at the Alamo.

is a civil contract of divine origin; it's common to all countries as well as Arkansaw, and people take to it as naturally as Jim Doggett's Bowieknife takes to bear.'"

"What season of the year do your hunts take place?" inquired a gentlemanly foreigner, who, from some peculiarities of his baggage, I suspected to be an Englishman, on some hunting expedition, probably at the foot of the Rocky Mountains.

"The season for bear hunting, stranger," said the man of Arkansaw, "is generally all the year round, and the hunts take place about as regular. I read in history that varmints have their fat season, and their lean season. That is not the case in Arkansaw, feeding as they do upon the *spontenacious* productions of the sile, they have one continued fat season the year round; though in winter things in this way is rather more greasy than in summer, I must admit. For that reason bear with us run in warm weather, but in winter they only waddle.

"Fat, fat! its an enemy to speed; it tames every thing that has plenty of it. I have seen wild turkeys, from its influence, as gentle as chickens. Run a bear in this fat condition, and the way it improves the critter for eating is amazing; it sort of mixes the ile[6] up with the meat, until you can't tell t'other from which. I've done this often.

"I recollect one perty morning in particular, of putting an old he fellow on the stretch, and considering the weight he carried, he run well. But the dogs soon tired him down, and when I came up with him wasn't he in a beautiful sweat—I might say fever; and then to see his tongue sticking out of his mouth a feet,[7] and his sides sinking and opening like a bellows, and his cheeks so fat that he couldn't look cross. In this fix I blazed[8] at him, and pitch me naked into a briar patch, if the steam didn't come out of the bullet-hole ten foot in a straight line. The fellow, I reckon, was made on the high-pressure system, and the lead sort of bust his biler."[9]

"That column of steam was rather curious, or else the bear must have been very *warm*," observed the foreigner, with a laugh.

"Stranger, as you observe, that bear was WARM, and the blowing off of the steam show'd it, and also how hard the varmint had been run. I have no doubt if he had kept on two miles farther his insides would have been stewed; and I expect to meet with a varmint yet of extra bottom, that will run himself into a skinfull of bear's grease: it is possible; much onlikelier things have happened."

"Whereabouts are these bears so abundant?" inquired the foreigner, with increasing interest.

"Why, stranger, they inhabit the neighborhood of my settlement, one of the prettiest places on old Mississipp—a perfeet location, and no mistake; a place that had some defects until the river made the 'cut-off'[10] at 'Shirt-tail bend,' and that remedied the evil, as it brought my cabin on the edge of the river—a great advantage in wet weather, I assure you, as you can now roll a barrel of whiskey into my yard in high water from a boat, as easy as falling off a log. It's a great improvement, as toting it by land in a jug, as I used to do, *evaporated* it too fast, and it became expensive.

---

[6] Oil.   [7] Probably "foot."   [8] Fired shots rapidly.   [9] Boiler.

[10] A new channel made when a river cuts across a narrow bend, sometimes leaving towns miles from water; here, bringing a settlement to the river's edge.

"Just stop with me, stranger, a month or two, or a year, if you like, and you will appreciate my place. I can give you plenty to eat; for beside hog and hominy, you can have bear-ham, and bear-sausages, and a mattrass of bear-skins to sleep on, and a wildcat-skin, pulled off hull,[11] stuffed with corn-shucks, for a pillow. That bed would put you to sleep if you had the rheumatics in every joint in your body. I call that ar bed, a *quietus*.[12]

"Then look at my 'pre-emption'—the government ain't got another like it to dispose of. Such timber, and such bottom land,—why you can't preserve anything natural you plant in it unless you pick it young, things thar will grow out of shape so quick.

"I once planted in those diggins a few potatoes and beets; they took a fine start, and after that, an ox team couldn't have kept them from growing. About that time I went off to old Kaintuck on business, and did not hear from them things in three months, when I accidentally stumbled on a fellow who had drapped in at my place, with an idea of buying me out.

" 'How did you like things?' said I.

" 'Pretty well,' said he; 'the cabin is convenient, and the timber land is good; but that bottom land ain't worth the first red cent.' "

" 'Why?' said I.

" ''Cause,' said he.

" ''Cause what?' said I.

" ''Cause it's full of cedar stumps and Indian mounds, and *can't be cleared.*'

" 'Lord,' said I, 'them ar "cedar stumps" is beets, and them ar "Indian mounds" tater hills.'

"As I had expected, the crop was overgrown and useless: the sile is too rich, *and planting in Arkansaw is dangerous.*

"I had a good-sized sow killed in that same bottom land. The old thief stole an ear of corn, and took it down to eat where she slept at night. Well, she left a grain or two on the ground, and lay down on them: before morning the corn shot up, and the percussion killed her dead. I don't plant any more: natur intended Arkansaw for a hunting ground, and I go according to natur."

The questioner, who had thus elicited the description of our hero's settlement, seemed to be perfectly satisfied, and said no more; but the "Big Bear of Arkansaw" rambled on from one thing to another with a volubility perfectly astonishing, occasionally disputing with those around him, particularly with a "live Sucker" from Illinois, who had the daring to say that our Arkansaw friend's stories "smelt rather tall."

The evening was nearly spent by the incidents we have detailed; and conscious that my own association with so singular a personage would probably end before morning, I asked him if he would not give me a description of some particular bear hunt; adding, that I took great interest in such things, though I was no sportsman. The desire seemed to please him, and he squared himself round towards me, saying, that he could give me an idea of a bear hunt that was never beat in this world, or in any other. His manner was so singular, that half of his story consisted in his excellent way of telling it, the great peculiarity of which was, the happy manner he had of emphasizing the prominent parts of his conversation. As near as I can recollect, I have italicized the words, and given the story in his own way.

---

[11] Whole.   [12] An end, such as death or sleep.

"Stranger," said he, "in bear hunts *I am numerous,* and which particular one, as you say, I shall tell, puzzles me.

"There was the old she devil I shot at the Hurricane last fall—then there was the old hog thief I popped over at the Bloody Crossing, and then—Yes, I have it! I will give you an idea of a hunt, in which the greatest bear was killed that ever lived, *none excepted;* about an old fellow that I hunted, more or less, for two or three years; and if that ain't a *particular bear hunt,* I ain't got one to tell.

"But in the first place, stranger, let me say, I am pleased with you, because you ain't ashamed to gain information by asking and listening; and that's what I say to Countess's pups every day when I'm home; and I have got great hopes of them ar pups, because they are continually *nosing* about; and though they stick it sometimes in the wrong place, they gain experience any how, and may learn something useful to boot.

"Well, as I was saying about his big bear, you see when I and some more first settled in our region, we were drivin to hunting naturally; we soon liked it, and after that we found it an easy matter to make the thing our business. One old chap who had pioneered 'afore us, gave us to understand that we had settled in the right place. He dwelt upon its merits until it was affecting, and showed us, to prove his assertions, more scratches on the bark of the sassafras trees, than I ever saw chalk marks on a tavern door 'lection time.[13]

" 'Who keeps that ar reckoning?' said I.

" 'The bear,' said he.

" 'What for?' said I.

" 'Can't tell,' said he; 'but so it is: the bear bite the bark and wood too, at the highest point from the ground they can reach, and you can tell, by the marks,' said he, 'the length of the bear to an inch.'

" 'Enough,' said I; 'I've learned something here a'ready, and I'll put it in practice.'

"Well, stranger, just one month from that time I killed a bear, and told its exact length before I measured it, by those very marks; and when I did that, I swelled up considerably—I've been a prouder man ever since.

"So I went on, larning something every day, until I was reckoned a buster,[14] and allowed to be decidedly the best bear hunter in my district; and that is a reputation as much harder to earn than to be reckoned first man in Congress, as an iron ramrod is harder than a toadstool.

"Do the varmints grow over-cunning by being fooled with by greenhorn hunters, and by this means get troublesome, they send for me, as a matter of course; and thus I do my own hunting, and most of my neighbors'. I walk into the varmints though, and it has become about as much the same to me as drinking. It is told in two sentences—

"A bear is started, and he is killed.

"The thing is somewhat monotonous now—I know just how much they will run, where they will tire, how much they will growl, and what a thundering time I will have in getting their meat home. I could give you the history of the chase with all the particulars at the commencement, I know the signs so well—*Stranger, I'm certain.* Once I met with a match, though, and I will tell you about it; for a common hunt would not be worth relating.

[13] At election time, candidates often bought drinks for voters, and tavern keepers marked the reckoning on the doors.

[14] A record-buster.

"On a fine fall day, long time ago, I was trailing about for bear, and what should I see but fresh marks on the sassafras trees, about eight inches above any in the forests that I knew of. Says I, 'Them marks is a hoax, or it indicates the d——t bear that was ever grown.' In fact, stranger, I couldn't believe it was real, and I went on. Again I saw the same marks, at the same height, and *I knew the thing lived*. That conviction came home to my soul like an earthquake.

"Says I, 'Here is something a-purpose for me: that bear is mine, or I give up the hunting business.' The very next morning, what should I see but a number of buzzards hovering over my corn-field. 'The rascal has been there,' said I, 'for that sign is certain'; and, sure enough, on examining, I found the bones of what had been as beautiful a hog the day before, as was ever raised by a Buckeye. Then I tracked the critter out of the field to the woods, and all the marks he left behind, showed me that he was *the bear*.

"Well, stranger, the first fair chase I ever had with that big critter, I saw him no less than three distinct times at a distance; the dogs run him over eighteen miles and broke down, my horse gave out, and I was as nearly used up as a man can be, made on *my* principle, *which is patent*.[15]

"Before this adventure, such things were unknown to me as possible; but, strange as it was, that bear got me used to it before I was done with him; for he got so at last, that he would leave me on a long chase *quite easy*. How he did it, I never could understand.

"That a bear runs at all, is puzzling; but how this one could tire down and bust up a pack of hounds and a horse, that were used to overhauling everything they started after in no time, was past my understanding. Well, stranger, that bear finally got so sassy, that he used to help himself to a hog off my premises whenever he wanted one; the buzzards followed after what he left, and so, between *bear and buzzard,* I rather think I got *out of pork*.

"Well, missing that bear so often took hold of my vitals, and I wasted away. The thing had been carried too far, and it reduced me in flesh faster than an ager. I would see that bear in every thing I did: *he hunted me,* and that, too, like a devil, which I began to think he was.

"While in this shaky fix, I made preparations to give him a last brush, and be done with it. Having completed everything to my satisfaction, I started at sunrise, and to my great joy, I discovered from the way the dogs run, that they were near him. Finding his trail was nothing, for that had become as plain to the pack as a turnpike road.[16]

"On we went, and coming an an open country, what should I see but the bear very leisurely ascending a hill, and the dogs close at his heels, either a match for him this time in speed, or else he did not care to get out of their way—I don't know which. But wasn't he a beauty, though! I loved him like a brother.

"On he went, until he came to a tree, the limbs of which formed a crotch about six feet from the ground. Into this crotch he got and seated himself, the dogs yelling all around it; and there he sat eyeing them as quiet as a pond in low water.

"A greenhorn friend of mine, in company, reached shooting distance before me, and blazed away, hitting the critter in the centre of his forehead. The bear shook his head as the ball struck it, and then walked down from that tree, as gently as a lady would from a carriage.

---

[15] Clear, evident.   [16] A toll road.

"'Twas a beautiful sight to see him do that—he was in such a rage, that he seemed to be as little afraid of the dogs as if they had been sucking pigs; and the dogs warn't slow in making a ring around him at a respectful distance, I tell you; even Bowieknife himself, stood off. Then the way his eyes flashed!—why the fire of them would have singed a cat's hair; in fact, that bear was in a *wrath all over*. Only one pup came near him, and he was brushed out so totally with bear's left paw, that he entirely disappeared; and that made the old dogs more cautious still. In the mean time, I came up, and taking deliberate aim, as a man should do, at his side, just back of his foreleg, *if my gun did not snap,*[17] call me a coward, and I won't take it personal.

"Yes, stranger, *it snapped,* and I could not find a cap[18] about my person. While in this predicament, I turned round to my fool friend—'Bill,' says I, 'you're an ass—you're a fool—you might as well have tried to kill that bear by barking the tree[19] under his belly, as to have done it by hitting him in the head. Your shot has made a tiger of him; and blast me, if a dog gets killed or wounded when they come to blows, I will stick my knife into your liver, I will————.' My wrath was up. I had lost my caps, my gun had snapped, the fellow with me had fired at the bear's head, and I expected every moment to see him close in with the dogs and kill a dozen of them at least. In this thing I was mistaken; for the bear leaped over the ring formed by the dogs, and giving a fierce growl, was off—the pack, of course, in full cry after him. The run this time was short, for coming to the edge of a lake, the varmint jumped in, and swam to a little island in the lake, which it reached, just a moment before the dogs.

" 'I'll have him now,' said I, for I had found my caps in the *lining of my coat*—so, rolling a log into the lake, I paddled myself across to the island, just as the dogs had cornered the bear in a thicket. I rushed up and fired—at the same time the critter leaped over the dogs and came within three feet of me, running like mad; he jumped into the lake, and tried to mount the log I had just deserted, but every time he got half his body on it, it would roll over and send him under; the dogs, too, got around him, and pulled him about, and finally Bowieknife clenched with him, and they sunk into the lake together.

"Stranger, about this time I was excited, and I stripped off my coat, drew my knife, and intended to have taken a part with Bowieknife myself, when the bear rose to the surface. But the varmint staid under—Bowieknife came up alone, more dead than alive, and with the pack came ashore.

" 'Thank God!' said I, 'the old villain has got his deserts at last.'

"Determined to have the body, I cut a grape-vine for a rope, and dove down where I could see the bear in the water, fastened my rope to his leg, and fished him, with great difficulty, ashore. Stranger, may I be chawed to death by young alligators, if the thing I looked at wasn't a *she bear, and not the old critter after all*.

"The way matters got mixed on that island was onaccountably curious, and thinking of it made me more than ever convinced that I was hunting the devil himself. I went home that night and took to my bed—the thing was killing me. The entire team of Arkansaw in bear-hunting acknowledged himself used up, and the fact sunk into my feelings as a snagged boat will in the Mississippi. I grew as cross as a bear with two cubs and a sore tail. The thing got out 'mong my neighbors, and I was asked how come on that individ-u-al that never lost a bear when

[17] Misfire.   [18] A percussion cap, containing explosive powder.
[19] Shooting into the tree, creating splinters.

once started?[20] and if that same individ-u-al didn't wear telescopes when he turned a she-bear, of ordinary size, into an old he one, a little larger than a horse?

" 'Prehaps,' said I, 'friends'—getting wrathy—'prehaps you want to call somebody a liar?'

" 'Oh, no,' said they, 'we only heard of such things being *rather common* of late, but we don't believe one word of it; oh, no,'—and then they would ride off, and laugh like so many hyenas over a dead nigger.

"It was too much, and I determined to catch that bear, go to Texas, or die,— and I made my preparations accordin'.

"I had the pack shut up and rested. I took my rifle to pieces, and iled it.

"I put caps in every pocket about my person, *for fear of the lining*.

"I then told my neighbors, that on Monday morning—naming the day—I would start THAT BEAR, and bring him home with me, or they might divide my settlement among them, the owner having disappeared.

"Well, stranger, on the morning previous to the great day of my hunting expedition, I went into the woods near my house, taking my gun and Bowieknife along, just *from habit,* and there sitting down, also from habit,[21] what should I see, getting over my fence, but *the bear!* Yes, the old varmint was within a hundred yards of me, and the way he walked *over that fence*—stranger; he loomed up like a *black mist,* he seemed so large, and he walked right towards me.

"I raised myself, took deliberate aim, and fired. Instantly the varmint wheeled, gave a yell, and *walked through the fence,* as easy as a falling tree would through a cobweb.

"I started after, but was tripped up by my inexpressibles,[22] which, either from habit or the excitement of the moment, were about my heels, and before I had really gathered myself up, I heard the old varmint groaning, like a thousand sinners, in a thicket near by, and, by the time I reached him, he was a corpse.

"Stranger, it took five niggers and myself to put that carcass on a mule's back, and old long-ears waddled under his load, as if he was foundered[23] in every leg of his body; and with a common whopper of a bear, he would have trotted off, and enjoyed himself.

" 'Twould astonish you to know how big he was: I made a *bedspread of his skin,* and the way it used to cover my bear mattress, and leave several feet on each side to tuck up, would have delighted you. It was, in fact, a creation[24] bear, and if it had lived in Samson's[25] time, and had met him in a fair fight, he would have licked him in the twinkling of a dice-box.

"But, stranger, I never like the way I hunted him, *and missed him.* There is something curious about it, that I never could understand,—and I never was satisfied at his giving in *so easy at last.* Prehaps he had heard of my preparations to hunt him the next day, so he jist guv up, like Captain Scott's coon,[26] to save his wind to grunt with in dying; but that ain't likely. My private opinion is, that that bear was an *unhuntable bear, and died when his time come.*"[27]

---

[20] Flushed out of hiding.

[21] Having his habitual morning bowel movement.   [22] Underwear.   [23] Had gone lame.

[24] An original bear, dating from creation.

[25] In Judges 13–16, an Israelite hero famous for great strength.

[26] From a tall tale about the excellent marksman Captain Martin Scott, in which a raccoon (aware of Scott's prowess with the rifle) surrenders to him.

[27] The bear hunt episode here has many similarities with the final hunt for the bear Old Ben in William Faulkner's *Go Down, Moses* (1942). The notion that the bear dies only when his time has come is central to both works.

When this story was ended, our hero sat some minutes with his auditors, in a grave silence; I saw there was a mystery to him connected with the bear whose death he had just related, that had evidently made a strong impression on his mind. It was also evident that there was some superstitious awe connected with the affair,—a feeling common with all "children of the wood," when they meet with any thing out of their every-day experience.

He was the first one, however, to break the silence, and, jumping up, he asked all present to "liquor" before going to bed,—a thing which he did, with a number of companions, evidently to his heart's content.

Long before day, I was put ashore at my place of destination, and I can only follow with the reader, in imagination, our Arkansas friend, in his adventures at the "Forks of Cypress," on the Mississippi.

1841

Nineteenth-century writers and painters were awed by the beauty of the American West, such as that of California's giant redwoods, captured here by Albert Bierstadt.

Nathaniel Hawthorne
(1804–1864)

Born on the Fourth of July, 1804, in Salem, Massachusetts, Nathaniel Hawthorne was the descendant of determined Puritans. One of his Puritan ancestors, William Hathorne, came to Salem in 1630 and gained notoriety for persecuting Quakers; another, John Hathorne, was a judge at the Salem witchcraft trials in 1692. A keen sense of these two ancestors brought Hawthorne (the author himself added the "w" to his surname) to envision them in "The Custom–House" (1850) as stern men resolute in their intolerance, who would disapprove of him as a writer of storybooks. Following the death of his father, a sea captain, in Dutch Guiana in 1808, Hawthorne moved with his family to the home of relatives, the Mannings, in Raymond, Maine. In that rural setting he passed the years of his youth, reading extensively in the English classics and nursing the hope of becoming a writer.

Hawthorne entered Bowdoin College in Brunswick, Maine, in autumn 1821. Henry Wadsworth Longfellow and Horatio Bridge (later, a naval officer and an author) were members of Hawthorne's class; Franklin Pierce, the future president, was in the class ahead. Hawthorne joined the convivial Pot-8-o Club, demonstrated ability in Latin and English composition, and graduated eighteenth in a class of thirty-eight in September 1825. Clearly, he did not make a full commitment to academic success. During his years at Bowdoin he was distracted from formal study by his attempts to write fiction. The best evidence suggests that at this time he was working on the novel *Fanshawe* (1828) and "Seven Tales of My Native Land," which was never published. Following his graduation he returned to his mother's house. The family had moved back to Salem from Raymond in summer 1822, and thus Hawthorne went to Salem to live and write.

The years 1825 to 1837 have often been termed the years of solitude in Hawthorne's life. Although he was in no way a recluse, Hawthorne did cultivate habits of seclusion during this period to practice his craft as a writer. His claim of having been "the obscurest man of letters in America," prefacing his 1851 edition of *Twice-Told Tales,* refers not to any patterns of retirement, however, but to the fate of his early tales and sketches: for, because of editorial policies, all of Hawthorne's work before the initial publication of *Twice-Told Tales* in 1837 appeared anonymously or pseudonymously. In 1829 he wrote to the publisher Samuel G. Goodrich about a collection of his work to be called "Provincial Tales." Goodrich read the tales, as he said "with great pleasure." Rather than bring out the collection as a book, Goodrich chose to publish the tales individually in the *Token*—an annual that he edited. After putting four tales in the 1832 issue he explained in a letter to Hawthorne that because "they are anonymous, no objection arises from having so many pages by one author, particularly as they are as good, if not better, than anything else I get."

Throughout the early 1830s two, three, or four of Hawthorne's tales appeared in each issue of the *Token;* the 1837 issue contained no less than nine. And in 1835 the *New England Magazine* published eight of his tales and sketches. Hawthorne was publishing regularly but earning little money. To augment his income he edited the *American Magazine of Useful and Entertaining Knowledge* from March to August 1836. And despite a growing dissatisfaction with Goodrich, Hawthorne assembled—with assistance from his sister Elizabeth—*Peter Parley's Universal History* for Goodrich in 1836. The popular history was a financial success for the publisher but earned only $100 for the author.

The circumstances of periodical publication thus helped to keep Hawthorne anonymous. In 1836, harried by scrambling editorial work and having seen another collection of tales dismantled for magazine publication, he was understandably depressed about his career. To his rescue came Horatio Bridge, who had repeatedly urged Hawthorne to appear before the public under his own name. Without Hawthorne's knowledge Bridge arranged for the publication of a volume of his friend's tales and supplied $250 to guarantee the publishers against loss. Thus, *Twice-Told Tales,* containing eighteen of the thirty-six tales and sketches previously published in periodicals, appeared in 1837. Response to the volume was favorable, if not widespread. But the book sold well enough to enable the publisher to refund Bridge's money. After twelve years of writing in what he called his "dismal chamber," Hawthorne had achieved a literary reputation that went beyond the confines of editorial offices.

Hawthorne met Sophia Peabody in autumn 1838 and quickly came to see her as someone who had rescued him from a treacherous half-life, as a savior who made him whole, humanized by love. His letters to Sophia are eloquent testimonials to the enduring depth of his feeling. In January 1839 he was appointed measurer of salt and coal in the Boston Customhouse at an annual salary of $1500. With Sophia now his intended wife, he needed the security offered by a regular salary. From 1839 to 1840 he stayed in the Boston Customhouse, working hard, writing to Sophia of his "coal-begrimed visage and salt-befrosted locks." Early in 1841 he made a bold personal experiment: he invested $1000 in Brook Farm, George Ripley's utopian community near West Roxbury, Massachusetts, and went to live there. Several weeks after Hawthorne's arrival he wrote happily to his sister Louisa that he was "transformed into a complete farmer." He had loaded manure carts, planted potatoes and peas, and milked cows. But Hawthorne had not gone to Brook Farm out of transcendentalist convictions: he thought Brook Farm might afford an economical home for Sophia and himself after they married. When he came to believe that it would not, toward the end of 1841, he left the community in disenchantment.

After their marriage in 1842 Hawthorne and Sophia lived at the Old Manse in Concord, Massachusetts, the house in which Ralph Waldo Emerson had written *Nature* in 1836. The three years at the Old Manse were perhaps the happiest of Hawthorne's life, but the difficulty of earning a living was a nagging problem. "I did not come to see you," he wrote to Bridge in March 1843, "because I was very short of cash." Such difficulties "make me sigh for the regular monthly payments of the customhouse." During these years Hawthorne published almost two dozen tales and sketches. Most of them were included in *Mosses From an Old Manse,* which appeared in 1846 and contributed to a reputation that had been growing since the publication of *Twice-Told Tales.* But some readers preferred Hawthorne's first book. Edgar Allan Poe, for example, who had praised Hawthorne's genius in *Twice-Told Tales,* objected to the allegorical nature of *Mosses.* And Herman Melville, reading *Twice-Told Tales* after having lavished praise on *Mosses,* felt that the quality of the "earlier vintage" surpassed that of the later. Hawthorne himself announced that unless he could "do better" he would publish no more collections of tales. *Mosses,* however, contains some of Hawthorne's most respected work—including "Rappaccini's Daughter," "The Birth-Mark," and, perhaps most notably, "Young Goodman Brown," which Hawthorne had passed over for both the first and second editions of *Twice-Told Tales.*

In April 1846 Hawthorne secured an appointment as surveyor of the Salem Customhouse at an annual salary of $1200. Once again, however, working at a monotonous job meant abandoning the role of author. Though his duties were undemanding, Hawthorne wrote little during his three years in the customhouse. Dismissed in January 1849, he was somewhat frustrated and bitter; the machinations of small-time politics, he felt, had victimized him. But under Sophia's influence he turned to his writing, and by early February 1850 he had completed *The Scarlet Letter,* which was published one month later.

The Old Manse of Concord, Massachusets, built by Ralph Waldo Emerson's grandfather, was home to, and made famous by, Nathaniel Hawthorne.

The early 1850s was for Hawthorne a time of intense literary activity. *The Scarlet Letter* was followed by *The House of the Seven Gables* (1851) and by *The Blithedale Romance* (1852). And he found the energy for other work as well. *True Stories From History and Biography* (1851), *A Wonder-Book for Girls and Boys* (1852), *The Life of Franklin Pierce* (1852), and *Tanglewood Tales for Girls and Boys* (1853) evidence his ability to write for different markets. In 1852, with *Blithedale* completed, he announced his intention of beginning a new work "in a day or two." But the period of burgeoning literary activity was over. It was not until 1860 that Hawthorne published another romance—*The Marble Faun*, his last completed work of fiction.

From 1853 to 1857 Hawthorne served as U.S. consul at Liverpool, having been appointed by President Franklin Pierce. The financial advantage of the consular post (important now that he had three children to support), plus a desire to see England, encouraged Hawthorne to go abroad at this time. And see England he did, as his journal entries show. A record of his observations, he hoped, would prove useful for an English romance he planned to write. But that romance was never to be completed. A series of essays on England, first published in the *Atlantic Monthly* and then collected under the title *Our Old Home* in 1863, came instead from the penetrating sketches and observations in his journal—a charming but disappointing harvest from the rich soil of his recorded English experiences. In a studied and deeply personal act of gratitute Hawthorne dedicated *Our Old Home* to Franklin Pierce, the man who had made his years in England possible. Because Pierce had consistently advocated a moderate policy regarding slavery (in a vain hope of holding the Union together), many people regarded him as less a patriot than a temporizer. His popularity, never of magnitude in the North, had waned appreciably. By insisting that *Our Old Home* be dedicated to Pierce, Hawthorne thus made a point of his friendship with a man exceedingly out of fashion. Emerson was so irritated by Hawthorne's public thanks to Pierce that he ripped the dedicatory page from his copy of the book.

Hawthorne resigned his post in Liverpool in August 1857 and early in 1858 left for Italy. There during the final years of the decade he met artists and poets, visited cathedrals and museums, and assessed the mighty dimensions of the past. As his notebooks suggest, Italy challenged Hawthorne as no other experience in his life had done. All too often he could view the rich legacy of the Italian past only through the distracting lens of the Italian present. He could not ignore the dirt of Roman byways and even less the ever-present beggars, whose numbers exceeded the capacity of one man's charity. His daughter Una's illness in November 1858 cost him anxious weeks in an environment in which he felt himself to be essentially a stranger. Troubling and complex, Hawthorne's Italian experience was nonetheless rich in implication. For out of it came the idea for *The Marble Faun*, which he wrote in England after leaving Italy in 1859.

In 1860 Hawthorne returned to the United States and to his former home of Concord. During the final years of his life he began work on four romances—*Dr. Grimshawe's Secret*, *Septimius Felton*, *The Ancestral Footstep*, and *The Dolliver Romance*—none of which he could complete. In the context of the Civil War, his attempts to bring his kind of fiction into coherent form met with failure. He could not breathe vitality into the idea of a lost estate in England or of an elixir of life when the life of the nation was itself at stake. The effect of the Civil War does not fully explain Hawthorne's inability to complete these late romances: a loss of health also contributed to his difficulties. And perhaps he would have been unable to work successfully under the most favorable of circumstances. But his admission (in the preface to *Our Old Home*) that "the Present, the Immediate, the Actual, has proved too potent for me" suggests the way in which the war overpowered his imagination.

Shortly after Hawthorne's funeral in May 1864, Emerson wrote in his journal "I thought him a greater man than any of his works betray." The statement reveals Hawthorne's stature as a human being. But an artist is judged finally by the quality of his or her art. And in the best of his tales and romances Hawthorne created a literary art of enduring significance.

Suggested Readings: *The Centenary Edition of the Works of Nathaniel Hawthorne*, 20 vols., ed. W. Charvat et al., 1962–1988. *Hawthorne's Lost Notebooks, 1835-1841*, ed. B. Mouffe, 1978. H. James, *Hawthorne*, 1879. R. H. Pearce, ed., *Hawthorne Centenary Essays*, 1964. M. D. Bell, *Hawthorne and the Historical Romance of New England*, 1971. N. Baym, *The Shape of Hawthorne's Career*, 1976. E. Dryden, *Nathaniel Hawthorne: The Poetics of Enchantment*, 1977. A. Turner, *Nathaniel Hawthorne: A Biography*, 1980. J. R. Mellow, *Nathaniel Hawthorne in His Times*, 1980. T. Martin, *Nathaniel Hawthorne*, 1983. M. Colacurcio, *The Province of Piety: Moral History in Hawthorne's Early Tales*, 1984. L. S. Luedtke, *Hawthorne and the Romance of the Orient*, 1989.

Texts Used: "My Kinsman, Major Molineux," and "Ethan Brand": *The Snow-Image and Uncollected Tales*, in *The Centenary Edition*, Vol. XI, 1974. "Young Goodman Brown," "The Birth-Mark": *Mosses From an Old Manse*, in *The Centenary Edition*, Vol. X, 1974. "Wakefield": *Twice-Told Tales*, in *The Centenary Edition*, Vol. IX, 1974. Preface: *The House of the Seven Gables*, in *The Centenary Edition*, Vol. II, 1965. All else: *The American Notebooks*, in *The Centenary Edition*, Vol. VIII, 1973.

MY KINSMAN, MAJOR MOLINEUX*

After the kings of Great Britain had assumed the right of appointing the colonial governors, the measures of the latter seldom met with the ready and general approbation, which had been paid to those of their predecessors, under the original

* First published in *The Token* in 1832 and collected in *The Snow-Image, and Other Twice-Told Tales* (1851).

charters.[1] The people looked with most jealous scrutiny to the exercise of power, which did not emanate from themselves, and they usually rewarded the rulers with slender gratitude, for the compliances, by which, in softening their instructions from beyond the sea, they had incurred the reprehension of those who gave them. The annals of Massachusetts Bay will inform us, that of six governors, in the space of about forty years from the surrender of the old charter, under James II., two were imprisoned by a popular insurrection; a third, as Hutchinson[2] inclines to believe, was driven from the province by the whizzing of a musket ball; a fourth, in the opinion of the same historian, was hastened to his grave by continual bickerings with the House of Representatives; and the remaining two, as well as their successors, till the Revolution, were favored with few and brief intervals of peaceful sway. The inferior members of the court party,[3] in times of high political excitement, led scarcely a more desirable life. These remarks may serve as preface to the following adventures, which chanced upon a summer night, not far from a hundred years ago. The reader, in order to avoid a long and dry detail of colonial affairs, is requested to dispense with an account of the train of circumstances, that had caused much temporary inflammation of the popular mind.

It was near nine o'clock of a moonlight evening, when a boat crossed the ferry with a single passenger, who had obtained his conveyance, at that unusual hour, by the promise of an extra fare. While he stood on the landing-place, searching in either pocket for the means of fulfilling his agreement, the ferryman lifted a lantern, by the aid of which, and the newly risen moon, he took a very accurate survey of the stranger's figure. He was a youth of barely eighteen years, evidently country-bred, and now, as it should seem, upon his first visit to town. He was clad in a coarse grey coat, well worn, but in excellent repair; his under garments[4] were durably constructed of leather, and sat tight to a pair of serviceable and well-shaped limbs; his stockings of blue yarn, were the incontrovertible handiwork of a mother or a sister; and on his head was a three-cornered hat, which in its better days had perhaps sheltered the graver brow of the lad's father. Under his left arm was a heavy cudgel, formed of an oak sapling, and retaining a part of the hardened root; and his equipment was completed by a wallet,[5] not so abundantly stocked as to incommode the vigorous shoulders on which it hung. Brown, curly hair, well-shaped features, and bright cheerful eyes, were nature's gifts, and worth all that art could have done for his adornment.

The youth, one of whose names was Robin, finally drew from his pocket the half of a little province-bill[6] of five shillings, which, in the depreciation of that sort of currency, did but satisfy the ferryman's demand, with the surplus of a sexangular piece of parchment valued at three pence. He then walked forward into the town, with as light a step, as if his day's journey had not already exceeded thirty miles, and with as eager an eye, as if he were entering London city, instead of the little metropolis of a New England colony.[7] Before Robin had proceeded far, however, it occurred to him, that he knew not whither to direct his steps; so he paused, and looked up and down the narrow street, scrutinizing the small and mean wooden buildings, that were scattered on either side.

---

[1] King James II (1633–1701) of England appointed the first royal governor in 1685, after King Charles II (1630–1685) had rescinded the Massachusetts Charter in 1684.

[2] Thomas Hutchinson (1711–1780), the last royal governor of Massachusetts (1771–1774), who wrote *The History of the Colony and Province of Massachusetts-Bay* (1764, 1767).

[3] The Royalist party.   [4] The clothes on the lower half of his body.   [5] A knapsack.

[6] Paper money issued by a province or colony.   [7] Boston.

"This low hovel cannot be my kinsman's dwelling," thought he, "nor yonder old house, where the moonlight enters at the broken casement; and truly I see none hereabouts that might be worthy of him. It would have been wise to inquire my way of the ferryman, and doubtless he would have gone with me, and earned a shilling from the Major for his pains. But the next man I meet will do as well."

He resumed his walk, and was glad to perceive that the street now became wider, and the houses more respectable in their appearance. He soon discerned a figure moving on moderately in advance, and hastened his steps to overtake it. As Robin drew nigh, he saw that the passenger was a man in years, with a full periwig of grey hair, a wide-skirted coat of dark cloth, and silk stockings rolled about his knees. He carried a long and polished cane, which he struck down perpendicularly before him, at every step; and at regular intervals he uttered two successive hems, of a peculiarly solemn and sepulchral intonation. Having made these observations, Robin laid hold of the skirt of the old man's coat, just when the light from the open door and windows of a barber's shop, fell upon both their figures.

"Good evening to you, honored Sir," said he, making a low bow, and still retaining his hold of the skirt. "I pray you to tell me whereabouts is the dwelling of my kinsman, Major Molineux?"

The youth's question was uttered very loudly; and one of the barbers, whose razor was descending on a well-soaped chin, and another who was dressing a Ramillies wig,[8] left their occupations, and came to the door. The citizen, in the meantime, turned a long favored countenance[9] upon Robin, and answered him in a tone of excessive anger and annoyance. His two sepulchral hems, however, broke into the very centre of his rebuke, with most singular effect, like a thought of the cold grave obtruding among wrathful passions.

"Let go my garment, fellow! I tell you, I know not the man you speak of. What! I have authority, I have—hem, hem—authority; and if this be the respect you show your betters, your feet shall be brought acquainted with the stocks,[10] by daylight, tomorrow morning!"

Robin released the old man's skirt, and hastened away, pursued by an ill-mannered roar of laughter from the barber's shop. He was at first considerably surprised by the result of his question, but, being a shrewd youth, soon thought himself able to account for the mystery.

"This is some country representative," was his conclusion, "who has never seen the inside of my kinsman's door, and lacks the breeding to answer a stranger civilly. The man is old, or verily—I might be tempted to turn back and smite him on the nose. Ah, Robin, Robin! even the barber's boys laugh at you, for choosing such a guide! You will be wiser in time, friend Robin."

He now became entangled in a succession of crooked and narrow streets, which crossed each other, and meandered at no great distance from the water-side. The smell of tar was obvious to his nostrils, the masts of vessels pierced the moonlight above the tops of the buildings, and the numerous signs, which Robin paused to read, informed him that he was near the centre of business. But the streets were empty, the shops were closed, and lights were visible only in the second stories of a few dwelling-houses. At length, on the corner of a narrow lane, through which

[8] An ornate powdered wig with a braided tail, named for a British victory in Ramillies, Belgium, in 1706.

[9] A long face.

[10] A device for public punishment: a wooden frame with holes for locking in the feet and sometimes the hands.

he was passing, he beheld the broad countenance of a British hero swinging before the door of an inn,[11] whence proceeded the voices of many guests. The casement of one of the lower windows was thrown back, and a very thin curtain permitted Robin to distinguish a party at supper, round a well-furnished table. The fragrance of the good cheer steamed forth into the outer air, and the youth could not fail to recollect, that the last remnant of his travelling stock of provision had yielded to his morning appetite, and that noon had found, and left him, dinnerless.

"Oh, that a parchment three-penny might give me a right to sit down at yonder table," said Robin, with a sigh. "But the Major will make me welcome to the best of his victuals; so I will even step boldly in, and inquire my way to his dwelling."

He entered the tavern, and was guided by the murmur of voices, and fumes of tobacco, to the public room. It was a long and low apartment, with oaken walls, grown dark in the continual smoke, and a floor, which was thickly sanded, but of no immaculate purity. A number of persons, the larger part of whom appeared to be mariners, or in some way connected with the sea, occupied the wooden benches, or leather-bottomed chairs, conversing on various matters, and occasionally lending their attention to some topic of general interest. Three or four little groups were draining as many bowls of punch, which the great West India trade had long since made a familiar drink[12] in the colony. Others, who had the aspect of men who lived by regular and laborious handicraft, preferred the insulated bliss of an unshared potation, and became more taciturn under its influence. Nearly all, in short, evinced a predilection for the Good Creature[13] in some of its various shapes, for this is a vice, to which, as the Fast-day[14] sermons of a hundred years ago will testify, we have a long hereditary claim. The only guests to whom Robin's sympathies inclined him, were two or three sheepish countrymen, who were using the inn somewhat after the fashion of a Turkish Caravansary;[15] they had gotten themselves into the darkest corner of the room, and, heedless of the Nicotian[16] atmosphere, were supping on the bread of their own ovens, and the bacon cured in their own chimney-smoke. But though Robin felt a sort of brotherhood with these strangers, his eyes were attracted from them, to a person who stood near the door, holding whispered conversation with a group of ill-dressed associates. His features were separately striking almost to grotesqueness, and the whole face left a deep impression in the memory. The forehead bulged out into a double prominence, with a vale between; the nose came boldly forth in an irregular curve, and its bridge was of more than a finger's breadth; the eyebrows were deep and shaggy, and the eyes glowed beneath them like fire in a cave.

While Robin deliberated of whom to inquire respecting his kinsman's dwelling, he was accosted by the innkeeper, a little man in a stained white apron, who had come to pay his professional welcome to the stranger. Being in the second generation from a French Protestant,[17] he seemed to have inherited the courtesy of his parent nation; but no variety of circumstance was ever known to change his voice from the one shrill note in which he now addressed Robin.

---

[11] On a signboard.   [12] Punch made with rum.

[13] Alcoholic drinks; an allusion to I Timothy 4:4: "For every creature of God is good."

[14] Days designated for penance.   [15] An inn catering to those who travel in a caravan.

[16] Smoke-filled: "Nicotian" and "nicotine" come from Jean Nicot (1530?–1600), who brought tobacco to France in 1560 when he served as French ambassador to Portugal.

[17] Numerous French Protestants, or Huguenots, came to Massachusetts after 1685 when King Louis XIV issued the Edict of Nantes, which denied them religious liberty.

"From the country, I presume, Sir?" said he, with a profound bow. "Beg to congratulate you on your arrival, and trust you intend a long stay with us. Fine town here, Sir, beautiful buildings, and much that may interest a stranger. May I hope for the honor of your commands in respect to supper?"

"The man sees a family likeness! the rogue has guessed that I am related to the Major!" thought Robin, who had hitherto experienced little superfluous civility.

All eyes were now turned on the country lad, standing at the door, in his worn three-cornered hat, grey coat, leather breeches, and blue yarn stockings, leaning on an oaken cudgel, and bearing a wallet on his back.

Robin replied to the courteous innkeeper, with such an assumption of consequence, as befitted the Major's relative.

"My honest friend," he said, "I shall make it a point to patronize your house on some occasion, when—" here he could not help lowering his voice—"I may have more than a parchment three-pence in my pocket. My present business," continued he, speaking with lofty confidence, "is merely to inquire the way to the dwelling of my kinsman, Major Molineux."

There was a sudden and general movement in the room, which Robin interpreted as expressing the eagerness of each individual to become his guide. But the innkeeper turned his eyes to a written paper on the wall, which he read, or seemed to read, with occasional recurrences to the young man's figure.

"What have we here?" said he, breaking his speech into little dry fragments. " 'Left the house of the subscriber, bounden servant,[18] Hezekiah Mudge— had on, when he went away, grey coat, leather breeches, master's third best hat. One pound currency reward to whoever shall lodge him in any jail in the province.' Better trudge, boy, better trudge!"

Robin had begun to draw his hand towards the lighter end of the oak cudgel, but a strange hostility in every countenance, induced him to relinquish his purpose of breaking the courteous innkeeper's head. As he turned to leave the room, he encountered a sneering glance from the bold-featured personage whom he had before noticed; and no sooner was he beyond the door, than he heard a general laugh, in which the innkeeper's voice might be distinguished, like the dropping of small stones into a kettle.

"Now is it not strange," thought Robin, with his usual shrewdness, "is it not strange, that the confession of an empty pocket, should outweigh the name of my kinsman, Major Molineux? Oh, if I had one of these grinning rascals in the woods, where I and my oak sapling grew up together, I would teach him that my arm is heavy, though my purse be light!"

On turning the corner of the narrow lane, Robin found himself in a spacious street, with an unbroken line of lofty houses on each side, and a steepled building at the upper end, whence the ringing of a bell announced the hour of nine. The light of the moon, and the lamps from numerous shop windows, discovered people promenading on the pavement, and amongst them, Robin hoped to recognize his hitherto inscrutable relative. The result of his former inquiries made him unwilling to hazard another, in a scene of such publicity, and he determined to walk slowly and silently up the street, thrusting his face close to that of every elderly

---

[18] Someone indentured or "bound" as a paid servant, generally for a period of seven years, in exchange for transportation to the colonies. The innkeeper has checked a wanted sign to see if Robin is dressed like Hezekiah Mudge, who evidently left his employer, or "subscriber," before his term of indenture expired.

gentleman, in search of the Major's lineaments. In his progress, Robin encountered many gay and gallant figures. Embroidered garments, of showy colors, enormous periwigs, gold-laced hats, and silver hilted swords, glided past him and dazzled his optics. Travelled youths, imitators of the European fine gentlemen of the period, trod jauntily along, half-dancing to the fashionable tunes which they hummed, and making poor Robin ashamed of his quiet and natural gait. At length, after many pauses to examine the gorgeous display of goods in the shop windows, and after suffering some rebukes for the impertinence of his scrutiny into people's faces, the Major's kinsman found himself near the steepled building, still unsuccessful in his search. As yet, however, he had seen only one side of the thronged street; so Robin crossed, and continued the same sort of inquisition down the opposite pavement, with stronger hopes than the philosopher seeking an honest man,[19] but with no better fortune. He had arrived about midway towards the lower end, from which his course began, when he overheard the approach of some one, who struck down a cane on the flag-stones at every step, uttering, at regular intervals, two sepulchral hems.

"Mercy on us!" quoth Robin, recognizing the sound.

Turning a corner, which chanced to be close at his right hand, he hastened to pursue his researches, in some other part of the town. His patience was now wearing low, and he seemed to feel more fatigue from his rambles since he crossed the ferry, than from his journey of several days on the other side. Hunger also pleaded loudly within him, and Robin began to balance the propriety of demanding, violently and with lifted cudgel, the necessary guidance from the first solitary passenger, whom he should meet. While a resolution to this effect was gaining strength, he entered a street of mean appearance, on either side of which, a row of ill-built houses was straggling towards the harbor. The moonlight fell upon no passenger along the whole extent, but in the third domicile which Robin passed, there was a half-opened door, and his keen glance detected a woman's garment within.

"My luck may be better here," said he to himself.

Accordingly, he approached the door, and beheld it shut closer as he did so; yet an open space remained, sufficing for the fair occupant to observe the stranger, without a corresponding display on her part. All that Robin could discern was a strip of scarlet petticoat, and the occasional sparkle of an eye, as if the moonbeams were trembling on some bright thing.

"Pretty mistress,"—for I may call her so with a good conscience, thought the shrewd youth, since I know nothing to the contrary—"my sweet pretty mistress, will you be kind enough to tell me whereabouts I must seek the dwelling of my kinsman, Major Molineux?"

Robin's voice was plaintive and winning, and the female, seeing nothing to be shunned in the handsome country youth, thrust open the door, and came forth into the moonlight. She was a dainty little figure, with a white neck, round arms, and a slender waist, at the extremity of which her scarlet petticoat jutted out over a hoop, as if she were standing in a balloon. Moreover, her face was oval and pretty, her hair dark beneath the little cap, and her bright eyes possessed a sly freedom, which triumphed over those of Robin.

"Major Molineux dwells here," said this fair woman.

---

[19] The Greek philosopher Diogenes (412?–323 B.C.) supposedly roamed the world in search of an honest man.

Now her voice was the sweetest Robin had heard that night, the airy counterpart of a stream of melted silver; yet he could not help doubting whether that sweet voice spoke Gospel truth. He looked up and down the mean street, and then surveyed the house before which they stood. It was a small, dark edifice of two stories, the second of which projected over the lower floor; and the front apartment had the aspect of a shop for petty commodities.

"Now truly I am in luck," replied Robin, cunningly, "and so indeed is my kinsman, the Major, in having so pretty a housekeeper. But I prithee trouble him to step to the door; I will deliver him a message from his friends in the country, and then go back to my lodgings at the inn."

"Nay, the Major has been a-bed this hour or more," said the lady of the scarlet petticoat; "and it would be to little purpose to disturb him to-night, seeing his evening draught[20] was of the strongest. But he is a kind-hearted man, and it would be as much as my life's worth, to let a kinsman of his turn away from the door. You are the good old gentleman's very picture,[21] and I could swear that was his rainy-weather hat. Also, he has garments very much resembling those leather— But come in, I pray, for I bid you hearty welcome in his name."

So saying, the fair and hospitable dame took our hero by the hand; and though the touch was light, and the force was gentleness, and though Robin read in her eyes what he did not hear in her words, yet the slender waisted woman, in the scarlet petticoat, proved stronger than the athletic county youth. She had drawn his half-willing footsteps nearly to the threshold, when the opening of a door in the neighborhood, startled the Major's housekeeper, and, leaving the Major's kinsman, she vanished speedily into her own domicile. A heavy yawn preceded the appearance of a man, who, like the Moonshine of Pyramus and Thisbe,[22] carried a lantern, needlessly aiding his sister luminary in the heavens. As he walked sleepily up the street, he turned his broad, dull face on Robin, and displayed a long staff, spiked at the end.

"Home, vagabond, home!" said the watchman, in accents that seemed to fall asleep as soon as they were uttered. "Home, or we'll set you in the stocks by peep of day!"

"This is the second hint of the kind," thought Robin. "I wish they would end my difficulties, by setting me there to-night."

Nevertheless, the youth felt an instinctive antipathy towards the guardian of midnight order, which at first prevented him from asking his usual question. But just when the man was about to vanish behind the corner, Robin resolved not to lose the opportunity, and shouted lustily after him—

"I say, friend! will you guide me to the house of my kinsman, Major Molineux?"

The watchman made no reply, but turned the corner and was gone; yet Robin seemed to hear the sound of drowsy laughter stealing along the solitary street. At that moment, also, a pleasant titter saluted him from the open window above his head; he looked up, and caught the sparkle of a saucy eye; a round arm beckoned to him, and next he heard light footsteps descending the staircase within. But Robin, being of the household of a New England clergyman, was a good youth, as well as a shrewd one; so he resisted temptation, and fled away.

---

[20] Drink.   [21] You look just like the major.

[22] Moonshine appears in a comic rendition of the love story of Pyramus and Thisbe in Shakespeare's *A Midsummer Night's Dream* (III.i).

He now roamed desperately, and at random, through the town, almost ready to believe that a spell was on him, like that, by which a wizard of his country, had once kept three pursuers wandering, a whole winter night, within twenty paces of the cottage which they sought. The streets lay before him, strange and desolate, and the lights were extinguished in almost every house. Twice, however, little parties of men, among whom Robin distinguished individuals in outlandish attire, came hurrying along, but though on both occasions they paused to address him, such intercourse did not at all enlighten his perplexity. They did but utter a few words in some language of which Robin knew nothing, and perceiving his inability to answer, bestowed a curse upon him in plain English, and hastened away. Finally, the lad determined to knock at the door of every mansion that might appear worthy to be occupied by his kinsman, trusting that perseverance would overcome the fatality which had hitherto thwarted him. Firm in this resolve, he was passing beneath the walls of a church, which formed the corner of two streets, when, as he turned into the shade of its steeple, he encountered a bulky stranger, muffled in a cloak. The man was proceeding with the speed of earnest business, but Robin planted himself full before him, holding the oak cudgel with both hands across his body, as a bar to further passage.

"Halt, honest man, and answer me a question," said he, very resolutely. "Tell me, this instant, whereabouts is the dwelling of my kinsman, Major Molineux?"

"Keep your tongue between your teeth, fool, and let me pass," said a deep, gruff voice, which Robin partly remembered. "Let me pass, I say, or I'll strike you to the earth!"

"No, no, neighbor!" cried Robin, flourishing his cudgel, and then thrusting its larger end close to the man's muffled face. "No, no, I'm not the fool you take me for, nor do you pass, till I have an answer to my question. Whereabouts is the dwelling of my kinsman, Major Molineux?"

The stranger, instead of attempting to force his passage, stept back into the moonlight, unmuffled his own face and stared full into that of Robin.

"Watch here an hour, and Major Molineux will pass by," said he.

Robin gazed with dismay and astonishment, on the unprecedented physiognomy of the speaker. The forehead with its double prominence, the broad-hooked nose, the shaggy eyebrows, and fiery eyes, were those which he had noticed at the inn, but the man's complexion had undergone a singular, or, more properly, a two-fold change. One side of the face blazed of an intense red, while the other was black as midnight, the division line being in the broad bridge of the nose; and a mouth, which seemed to extend from ear to ear, was black or red, in contrast to the color of the cheek. The effect was as if two individual devils, a fiend of fire and a fiend of darkness, had united themselves to form this infernal visage. The stranger grinned in Robin's face, muffled his parti-colored features, and was out of sight in a moment.

"Strange things we travellers see!" ejaculated Robin.

He seated himself, however, upon the steps of the church-door, resolving to wait the appointed time for his kinsman's appearance. A few moments were consumed in philosophical speculations, upon the species of the *genus homo*, who had just left him, but having settled this point shrewdly, rationally, and satisfactorily, he was compelled to look elsewhere for amusement. And first he threw his eyes along the street; it was of more respectable appearance than most of those into which he had wandered, and the moon, "creating, like the imaginative power, a beautiful strangeness in familiar objects," gave something of romance to a scene, that might not have possessed it in the light of day. The irregular, and often quaint architecture of the houses, some of whose roofs were broken into numerous little peaks; while others ascended, steep and narrow, into a single point; and others again were square; the pure milk-white of some of their complexions, the aged darkness of others, and the thousand sparklings reflected from bright substances in the plastered walls of many; these matters engaged Robin's attention for awhile, and then began to grow wearisome. Next he endeavored to define the forms of distant objects, starting away with almost ghostly indistinctness, just as his eye appeared to grasp them; and finally he took a minute survey of an edifice, which stood on the opposite side of the street, directly in front of the church-door, where he was stationed. It was a large square mansion, distinguished from its neighbors by a balcony, which rested on tall pillars, and by an elaborate Gothic window, communicating therewith.

"Perhaps this is the very house I have been seeking," thought Robin.

Then he strove to speed away the time, by listening to a murmur, which swept continually along the street, yet was scarcely audible, except to an unaccustomed ear like his; it was a low, dull, dreamy sound, compounded of many noises, each of which was at too great a distance to be separately heard. Robin marvelled at this snore of a sleeping town, and marvelled more, whenever its continuity was broken, by now and then a distant shout, apparently loud where it originated. But altogether it was a sleep-inspiring sound, and to shake off its drowsy influence, Robin arose, and climbed a window-frame, that he might view the interior of the church. There the moonbeans came trembling in, and fell down upon the deserted pews, and extended along the quiet aisles. A fainter, yet more awful radiance, was hovering round the pulpit, and one solitary ray had dared to rest upon the opened page of the great Bible. Had Nature, in that deep hour, become a worshipper in the house, which man had builded? Or was that heavenly light the visible sanctity of the place, visible because no earthly and impure feet were within the walls? The scene made Robin's heart shiver with a sensation of loneliness, stronger than he had ever felt in the remotest depths of his native woods; so he turned away, and sat down again before the door. There were graves around the church, and now an uneasy thought obtruded into Robin's breast. What if the object of his search, which had been so often and so strangely thwarted, were all the time mouldering in his shroud? What if his kinsmen should glide through yonder gate, and nod and smile to him in passing dimly by?

"Oh, that any breathing thing were here with me!" said Robin.

Recalling his thoughts from this uncomfortable track, he sent them over forest, hill, and stream, and attempted to imagine how that evening of ambiguity and weariness, had been spent by his father's household. He pictured them assembled at the door, beneath the tree, the great old tree, which had been spared for its huge twisted trunk, and venerable shade, when a thousand leafy brethren fell. There, at the going down of the summer sun, it was his father's custom to perform domestic worship, that the neighbors might come and join with him like brothers of the family, and that the wayfaring man might pause to drink at that fountain, and keep his heart pure by freshening the memory of home. Robin distinguished the seat of every individual of the little audience; he saw the good man in the midst, holding the Scriptures in the golden light that shone from the western clouds; he beheld him close the book, and all rise up to pray. He heard the old thanksgivings for daily mercies, the old supplications for their continuance, to which he had so often listened in weariness, but which were now among his dear remembrances. He perceived the slight inequality of his father's voice when he came to speak of the

Absent One; he noted how his mother turned her face to the broad and knotted trunk; how his elder brother scorned, because the beard was rough upon his upper lip, to permit his features to be moved; how his younger sister drew down a low hanging branch before her eyes; and how the little one of all, whose sports had hitherto broken the decorum of the scene, understood the prayer for her playmate, and burst into clamorous grief. Then he saw them go in at the door; and when Robin would have entered also, the latch tinkled into its place, and he was excluded from his home.

"Am I here, or there?" cried Robin, starting; for all at once, when his thoughts had become visible and audible in a dream, the long, wide, solitary street shone out before him.

He aroused himself, and endeavored to fix his attention steadily upon the large edifice which he had surveyed before. But still his mind kept vibrating between fancy and reality; by turns, the pillars of the balcony lengthened into the tall, bare stems of pines, dwindled down to human figures, settled again in their true shape and size, and then commenced a new succession of changes. For a single moment, when he deemed himself awake, he could have sworn that a visage, one which he seemed to remember, yet could not absolutely name as his kinsman's, was looking towards him from the Gothic window. A deeper sleep wrestled with, and nearly overcame him, but fled at the sound of footsteps along the opposite pavement. Robin rubbed his eyes, discerned a man passing at the foot of the balcony, and addressed him in a loud, peevish, and lamentable cry.

"Halloo, friend! must I wait here all night for my kinsman, Major Molineux?"

The sleeping echoes awoke, and answered the voice; and the passenger, barely able to discern a figure sitting in the oblique shade of the steeple, traversed the street to obtain a nearer view. He was himself a gentleman in his prime, of open, intelligent, cheerful, and altogether prepossessing countenance. Perceiving a country youth, apparently homeless and without friends, he accosted him in a tone of real kindness, which had become strange to Robin's ears.

"Well, my good lad, why are you sitting here?" inquired he. "Can I be of service to you in any way?"

"I am afraid not, Sir," replied Robin, despondingly; "yet I shall take it kindly, if you'll answer me a single question. I've been searching half the night for one Major Molineux; now, Sir, is there really such a person in these parts, or am I dreaming?"

"Major Molineux! The name is not altogether strange to me," said the gentleman, smiling. "Have you any objection to telling me the nature of your business with him?"

Then Robin briefly related that his father was a clergyman, settled on a small salary, at a long distance back in the country, and that he and Major Molineux were brothers' children. The Major, having inherited riches, and acquired civil and military rank, had visited his cousin in great pomp a year or two before; had manifested much interest in Robin and an elder brother, and, being childless himself, had thrown out hints respecting the future establishment of one of them in life. The elder brother was destined to succeed to the farm, which his father cultivated, in the interval of sacred duties; it was therefore determined that Robin should profit by his kinsman's generous intentions, especially as he had seemed to be rather the favorite, and was thought to possess other necessary endowments.

"For I have the name of being a shrewd youth," observed Robin, in this part of his story.

"I doubt not you deserve it," replied his new friend, good naturedly; "but pray proceed."

"Well, Sir, being nearly eighteen years old, and well grown, as you see," continued Robin, raising himself to his full height, "I thought it high time to begin the world. So my mother and sister put me in handsome trim, and my father gave me half the remnant of his last year's salary, and five days ago I started for this place, to pay the Major a visit. But would you believe it, Sir? I crossed the ferry a little after dusk, and have yet found nobody that would show me the way to his dwelling; only an hour or two since, I was told to wait here, and Major Molineux would pass by."

"Can you describe the man who told you this?" inquired the gentleman.

"Oh, he was a very ill-favored fellow, Sir," replied Robin, "with two great bumps on his forehead, a hook nose, fiery eyes, and, what struck me as the strangest, his face was of two different colors. Do you happen to know such a man, Sir?"

"Not intimately," answered the stranger, "but I chanced to meet him a little time previous to your stopping me. I believe you may trust his word, and that the Major will very shortly pass through this street. In the mean time, as I have a singular curiosity to witness your meeting, I will sit down here upon the steps, and bear you company."

He seated himself accordingly, and soon engaged his companion in animated discourse. It was but of brief continuance, however, for a noise of shouting, which had long been remotely audible, drew so much nearer, that Robin inquired its cause.

"What may be the meaning of this uproar?" asked he. "Truly, if your town be always as noisy, I shall find little sleep, while I am an inhabitant."

"Why, indeed, friend Robin, there do appear to be three or four riotous fellows abroad to-night," replied the gentleman. "You must not expect all the stillness of your native woods, here in our streets. But the watch will shortly be at the heels of these lads, and—"

"Aye, and set them in the stocks by peep of day," interrupted Robin, recollecting his own encounter with the drowsy lantern-bearer. "But, dear Sir, if I may trust my ears, an army of watchmen would never make head against such a multitude of rioters. There were at least a thousand voices went to make up that one shout."

"May not one man have several voices, Robin, as well as two complexions?" said his friend.

"Perhaps a man may; but Heaven forbid that a woman should!" responded the shrewd youth, thinking of the seductive tones of the Major's housekeeper.

The sounds of a trumpet in some neighboring street now became so evident and continual, that Robin's curiosity was strongly excited. In addition to the shouts, he heard frequent bursts from many instruments of discord, and a wild and confused laughter filled up the intervals. Robin rose from the steps, and looked wistfully towards a point, whither several people seemed to be hastening.

"Surely some prodigious merrymaking is going on," exclaimed he. "I have laughed very little since I left home, Sir, and should be sorry to lose an opportunity. Shall we just step round the corner by that darkish house, and take our share of the fun?"

"Sit down again, sit down, good Robin," replied the gentleman, laying his hand on the skirt of the grey coat. "You forget that we must wait here for your kinsman; and there is reason to believe that he will pass by, in the course of a very few moments."

The near approach of the uproar had now disturbed the neighborhood; windows flew open on all sides; and many heads, in the attire of the pillow, and confused by sleep suddenly broken, were protruded to the gaze of whoever had leisure to observe them. Eager voices hailed each other from house to house, all demanding the explanation, which not a soul could give. Half-dressed men hurried towards the unknown commotion, stumbling as they went over the stone steps, that thrust themselves into the narrow foot-walk. The shouts, the laughter, and the tuneless bray, the antipodes of music, came onward with increasing din, till scattered individuals, and then denser bodies, began to appear round a corner, at the distance of a hundred yards.

"Will you recognize your kinsman, Robin, if he passes in this crowd?" inquired the gentleman.

"Indeed, I can't warrant it, Sir; but I'll take my stand here, and keep a bright look out," answered Robin, descending to the outer edge of the pavement.

A mighty stream of people now emptied into the street, and came rolling slowly towards the church. A single horseman wheeled the corner in the midst of them, and close behind him came a band of fearful wind-instruments, sending forth a fresher discord, now that no intervening buildings kept it from the ear. Then a redder light disturbed the moonbeams, and a dense multitude of torches shone along the street, concealing by their glare whatever object they illuminated. The single horseman, clad in a military dress, and bearing a drawn sword, rode onward as the leader, and, by his fierce and variegated countenance, appeared like war personified; the red of one cheek was an emblem of fire and sword; the blackness of the other betokened the mourning which attends them. In his train, were wild figures in the Indian dress, and many fantastic shapes without a model, giving the whole march a visionary air, as if a dream had broken forth from some feverish brain, and were sweeping visibly through the midnight streets. A mass of people, inactive, except as applauding spectators, hemmed the procession in, and several women ran along the sidewalks, piercing the confusion of heavier sounds, with their shrill voices of mirth or terror.

"The double-faced fellow has his eye upon me," muttered Robin, with an indefinite but uncomfortable idea, that he was himself to bear a part in the pageantry.

The leader turned himself in the saddle, and fixed his glance full upon the country youth, as the steed went slowly by. When Robin had freed his eyes from those fiery ones, the musicians were passing before him, and the torches were close at hand; but the unsteady brightness of the latter formed a veil which he could not penetrate. The rattling of wheels over the stones sometimes found its way to his ear, and confused traces of a human form appeared at intervals, and then melted into the vivid light. A moment more, and the leader thundered a command to halt; the trumpets vomited a horrid breath, and held their peace; the shouts and laughter of the people died away, and there remained only a universal hum, nearly allied to silence. Right before Robin's eyes was an uncovered cart. There the torches blazed the brightest, there the moon shone out like day, and there, in tar-and-feathery dignity, sat his kinsman, Major Molineux!

He was an elderly man, of large and majestic person, and strong, square features, betokening a steady soul; but steady as it was, his enemies had found the means to shake it. His face was pale as death, and far more ghastly; the broad forehead was contracted in his agony, so that his eyebrows formed one grizzled line; his eyes were red and wild, and the foam hung white upon his quivering lip. His whole frame was agitated by a quick, and continual tremor, which his pride strove to quell, even in those circumstances of overwhelming humiliation. But perhaps the bitterest pang of all was when his eyes met those of Robin; for he evidently knew him on the instant, as the youth stood witnessing the foul disgrace of a head that had grown grey in honor. They stared at each other in silence, and Robin's knees shook, and his hair bristled, with a mixture of pity and terror. Soon, however, a bewildering excitement began to seize upon his mind; the preceding adventures of the night, the unexpected appearance of the crowd, the torches, the confused din, and the hush that followed, the spectre of his kinsman reviled by that great multitude, all this, and more than all, a perception of tremendous ridicule in the whole scene, affected him with a sort of mental inebriety. At that moment a voice of sluggish merriment saluted Robin's ears; he turned instinctively, and just behind the corner of the church stood the lantern-bearer, rubbing his eyes, and drowsily enjoying the lad's amazement. Then he heard a peal of laughter like the ringing of silvery bells; a woman twitched his arm, a saucy eye met his, and he saw the lady of the scarlet petticoat. A sharp, dry cachinnation[23] appealed to his memory, and standing on tiptoe in the crowd, with his white apron over his head, he beheld the courteous little innkeeper. And lastly, there sailed over the heads of the multitude a great, broad laugh, broken in the midst by two sepulchral hems; thus—

"Haw, haw, haw—hem, hem—haw, haw, haw, haw!"

The sound proceeded from the balcony of the opposite edifice, and thither Robin turned his eyes. In front of the Gothic window stood the old citizen, wrapped in a wide gown, his grey periwig exchanged for a nightcap, which was thrust back from his forehead, and his silk stockings hanging down about his legs. He supported himself on his polished cane in a fit of convulsive merriment, which manifested itself on his solemn old features, like a funny inscription on a tombstone. Then Robin seemed to hear the voices of the barbers; of the guests of the inn; and of all who had made sport of him that night. The contagion was spreading among the multitude, when, all at once, it seized upon Robin, and he sent forth a shout of laughter that echoed through the street; every man shook his sides, every man emptied his lungs, but Robin's shout was the loudest there. The cloud-spirits peeped from their silvery islands, as the congregated mirth went roaring up the sky! The Man in the Moon heard the far bellow; "Oho," quoth he, "the old Earth is frolicsome to-night!"

When there was a momentary calm in that tempestuous sea of sound, the leader gave the sign, the procession resumed its march. On they went, like fiends that throng in mockery round some dead potentate, mighty no more, but majestic still in his agony. On they went, in counterfeited pomp, in senseless uproar, in frenzied merriment, trampling all on an old man's heart. On swept the tumult, and left a silent street behind.

"Well, Robin, are you dreaming?" inquired the gentleman, laying his hand on the youth's shoulder.

Robin started, and withdrew his arm from the stone post, to which he had instinctively clung, while the living stream rolled by him. His cheek was somewhat pale, and his eye not quite so lively as in the earlier part of the evening.

---

[23] Laugh.

"Will you be kind enough to show me the way to the ferry?" said he, after a moment's pause.

"You have then adopted a new subject of inquiry?" observed his companion, with a smile.

"Why, yes, Sir," replied Robin, rather dryly. "Thanks to you, and to my other friends, I have at last met my kinsman, and he will scarce desire to see my face again. I begin to grow weary of a town life, Sir. Will you show me the way to the ferry?"

"No, my good friend Robin, not to-night, at least," said the gentleman. "Some few days hence, if you continue to wish it, I will speed you on your journey. Or, if you prefer to remain with us, perhaps, as you are a shrewd youth, you may rise in the world, without the help of your kinsman, Major Molineux."

1832

WAKEFIELD*

In some old magazine or newspaper, I recollect a story, told as truth, of a man— let us call him Wakefield—who absented himself for a long time, from his wife. The fact, thus abstractedly stated, is not very uncommon, nor—without a proper distinction of circumstances—to be condemned either as naughty or nonsensical. Howbeit, this, though far from the most aggravated, is perhaps the strangest instance, on record, of marital delinquency; and, moreover, as remarkable a freak as may be found in the whole list of human oddities. The wedded couple lived in London. The man, under pretence of going a journey, took lodgings in the next street to his own house, and there, unheard of by his wife or friends, and without the shadow of a reason for such self-banishment, dwelt upwards of twenty years. During that period, he beheld his home every day, and frequently the forlorn Mrs. Wakefield. And after so great a gap in his matrimonial felicity—when his death was reckoned certain, his estate settled, his name dismissed from memory, and his wife, long, long ago, resigned to her autumnal widowhood—he entered the door one evening, quietly, as from a day's absence, and became a loving spouse till death.

This outline is all that I remember. But the incident, though of the purest originality, unexampled, and probably never to be repeated, is one, I think, which appeals to the general sympathies of mankind. We know, each for himself, that none of us would perpetrate such a folly, yet feel as if some other might. To my own contemplations, at least, it has often recurred, always exciting wonder, but with a sense that the story must be true, and a conception of its hero's character. Whenever any subject so forcibly affects the mind, time is well spent in thinking of it. If the reader choose, let him do his own meditation; or if he prefer to ramble with me through the twenty years of Wakefield's vagary, I bid him welcome; trusting that there will be a pervading spirit and a moral, even should we fail to find them, done up neatly, and condensed into the final sentence. Thought has always its efficacy, and every striking incident its moral.

* First published in *The New-England Magazine* in 1835 and included in *Twice-Told Tales* (1837).

What sort of a man was Wakefield? We are free to shape out our own idea, and call it by his name. He was now in the meridian[1] of life; his matrimonial affections, never violent, were sobered into a calm, habitual sentiment; of all husbands, he was likely to be the most constant, because a certain sluggishness would keep his heart at rest, wherever it might be placed. He was intellectual, but not actively so; his mind occupied itself in long and lazy musings, that tended to no purpose, or had not vigor to attain it; his thoughts were seldom so energetic as to seize hold of words. Imagination, in the proper meaning of the term, made no part of Wakefield's gifts. With a cold, but not depraved nor wandering heart, and a mind never feverish with riotous thoughts, nor perplexed with originality, who could have anticipated, that our friend would entitle himself to a foremost place among the doers of eccentric deeds? Had his acquaintances been asked, who was the man in London, the surest to perform nothing to-day which should be remembered on the morrow, they would have thought of Wakefield. Only the wife of his bosom might have hesitated. She, without having analyzed his character, was partly aware of a quiet selfishness, that had rusted into his inactive mind—of a peculiar sort of vanity, the most uneasy attribute about him—of a disposition to craft, which had seldom produced more positive effects than the keeping of petty secrets, hardly worth revealing—and, lastly, of what she called a little strangeness, sometimes, in the good man. This latter quality is indefinable, and perhaps nonexistent.

Let us now imagine Wakefield bidding adieu to his wife. It is the dusk of an October evening. His equipment is a drab great-coat, a hat covered with an oilcloth, top-boots, an umbrella in one hand and a small portmanteau[2] in the other. He has informed Mrs. Wakefield that he is to take the night-coach into the country. She would fain inquire the length of his journey, its object, and the probable time of his return; but, indulgent to his harmless love of mystery, interrogates him only by a look. He tells her not to expect him positively by the return coach, nor to be alarmed should he tarry three or four days; but, at all events, to look for him at supper on Friday evening. Wakefield himself, be it considered, has no suspicion of what is before him. He holds out his hand; she gives her own, and meets his parting kiss, in the matter-of-course way of a ten years' matrimony; and forth goes the middle-aged Mr. Wakefield, almost resolved to perplex his good lady by a whole week's absence. After the door has closed behind him, she perceives it thrust partly open, and a vision of her husband's face, through the aperture, smiling on her, and gone in a moment. For the time, this little incident is dismissed without a thought. But, long afterwards, when she has been more years a widow than a wife, that smile recurs, and flickers across all her reminiscences of Wakefield's visage. In her many musings, she surrounds the original smile with a multitude of fantasies, which make it strange and awful; as, for instance, if she imagines him in a coffin, that parting look is frozen on his pale features; or, if she dreams of him in Heaven, still his blessed spirit wears a quiet and crafty smile. Yet, for its sake, when all others have given him up for dead, she sometimes doubts whether she is a widow.

But, our business is with the husband. We must hurry after him, along the street, ere he loses his individuality, and melt into the great mass of London life. It would be vain searching for him there. Let us follow close at his heels, therefore, until, after several superfluous turns and doublings, we find him comfortably es-

---

[1] The mid-point.   [2] A large suitcase.

tablished by the fireside of a small apartment, previously bespoken. He is in the next street to his own, and at his journey's end. He can scarcely trust his good fortune, in having got thither unperceived—recollecting that, at one time, he was delayed by the throng, in the very focus of a lighted lantern; and, again, there were footsteps, that seemed to tread behind his own, distinct from the multitudinous tramp around him; and, anon, he heard a voice shouting afar, and fancied that it called his name. Doubtless, a dozen busy-bodies had been watching him, and told his wife the whole affair. Poor Wakefield! Little knowest thou thine own insignificance in this great world! No mortal eye but mine has traced thee. Go quietly to thy bed, foolish man; and, on the morrow, if thou wilt be wise, get thee home to good Mrs. Wakefield, and tell her the truth. Remove not thyself, even for a little week, from thy place in her chaste bosom. Were she, for a single moment, to deem thee dead, or lost, or lastingly divided from her, thou wouldst be woefully conscious of a change in thy true wife, forever after. It is perilous to make a chasm in human affections; not that they gape so long and wide—but so quickly close again!

Almost repenting of his frolic, or whatever it may be termed, Wakefield lies down betimes, and starting from his first nap, spreads forth his arms into the wide and solitary waste of the unaccustomed bed. "No"—thinks he, gathering the bed-clothes about him—"I will not sleep alone another night."

In the morning, he rises earlier than usual, and sets himself to consider what he really means to do. Such are his loose and rambling modes of thought, that he has taken this very singular step, with the consciousness of a purpose, indeed, but without being able to define it sufficiently for his own contemplation. The vagueness of the project, and the convulsive effort with which he plunges into the execution of it, are equally characteristic of a feeble-minded man. Wakefield sifts his ideas, however, as minutely as he may, and finds himself curious to know the progress of matters at home—how his exemplary wife will endure her widowhood, of a week; and, briefly, how the little sphere of creatures and circumstances, in which he was a central object, will be affected by his removal. A morbid vanity, therefore, lies nearest the bottom of the affair. But, how is he to attain his ends? Not, certainly, by keeping close in this comfortable lodging, where, though he slept and awoke in the next street to his home, he is as effectually abroad, as if the stage-coach had been whirling him away all night. Yet, should he reappear, the whole project is knocked in the head. His poor brains being hopelessly puzzled with this dilemma, he at length ventures out, partly resolving to cross the head of the street, and send one hasty glance towards his forsaken domicile. Habit—for he is a man of habits—takes him by the hand, and guides him, wholly unaware, to his own door, where, just at the critical moment, he is aroused by the scraping of his foot upon the step. Wakefield! whither are you going?

At that instant, his fate was turning on the pivot. Little dreaming of the doom to which his first backward step devotes him, he hurries away, breathless with agitation hitherto unfelt, and hardly dares turn his head, at the distant corner. Can it be, that nobody caught sight of him? Will not the whole household—the decent Mrs. Wakefield, the smart maid-servant, and the dirty little foot-boy—raise a hue-and-cry, through London streets, in pursuit of their fugitive lord and master? Wonderful escape! He gathers courage to pause and look homeward, but is perplexed with a sense of change about the familiar edifice, such as affects us all, when, after a separation of months or years, we again see some hill or lake, or work of art, with which we were friends, of old. In ordinary cases, this indescribable impression is caused by the comparison and contrast between our imperfect reminiscences and the reality. In Wakefield, the magic of a single night has wrought a similar transformation, because, in that brief period, a great moral change has been effected. But this is a secret from himself. Before leaving the spot, he catches a far and momentary glimpse of his wife, passing athwart the front window, with her face turned towards the head of the street. The crafty nincompoop takes to his heels, scared with the idea, that, among a thousand such atoms of mortality, her eye must have detected him. Right glad is his heart, though his brain be somewhat dizzy, when he finds himself by the coal-fire of his lodgings.

So much for the commencement of this long whim-wham.[3] After the initial conception, and the stirring up of the man's sluggish temperament to put it in practice, the whole matter evolves itself in a natural train. We may suppose him, as the result of deep deliberation, buying a new wig, of reddish hair, and selecting sundry garments, in a fashion unlike his customary suit of brown, from a Jew's old-clothes bag. It is accomplished. Wakefield is another man. The new system being now established, a retrograde movement to the old would be almost as difficult as the step that placed him in his unparalleled position. Furthermore, he is rendered obstinate by a sulkiness, occasionally incident to his temper, and brought on, at present, by the inadequate sensation which he conceives to have been produced in the bosom of Mrs. Wakefield. He will not go back until she be frightened half to death. Well, twice or thrice has she passed before his sight, each time with a heavier step, a paler cheek, and more anxious brow; and, in the third week of his non-appearance, he detects a portent of evil entering the house, in the guise of an apothecary.[4] Next day, the knocker is muffled. Towards night-fall, comes the chariot of a physician, and deposits its big-wigged and solemn burthen at Wakefield's door, whence, after a quarter of an hour's visit, he emerges, perchance the herald of a funeral. Dear woman! Will she die? By this time, Wakefield is excited to something like energy of feeling, but still lingers away from his wife's bedside, pleading with his conscience, that she must not be disturbed at such a juncture. If aught else restrains him, he does not know it. In the course of a few weeks, she gradually recovers; the crisis is over; her heart is sad, perhaps, but quiet; and, let him return soon or late, it will never be feverish for him again. Such ideas glimmer through the mist of Wakefield's mind, and render him indistinctly conscious, that an almost impassable gulf divides his hired apartment from his former home. "It is but in the next street!" he sometimes says. Fool! it is in another world. Hitherto, he has put off his return from one particular day to another; henceforward, he leaves the precise time undetermined. Not to-morrow—probably next week—pretty soon. Poor man! The dead have nearly as much chance of re-visiting their earthly homes, as the self-banished Wakefield.

Would that I had a folio to write, instead of an article of a dozen pages! Then might I exemplify how an influence, beyond our control, lays its strong hand on every deed which we do, and weaves its consequences into an iron tissue of necessity. Wakefield is spell-bound. We must leave him, for ten years or so, to haunt around his house, without once crossing the threshold, and to be faithful to his wife, with all the affection of which his heart is capable, while he is slowly fading out of hers. Long since, it must be remarked, he has lost the perception of singularity in his conduct.

---

[3] A fanciful notion or action based on a whim.

[4] One who prepares and sells drugs for medical purposes.

Now for a scene! Amid the throng of a London street, we distinguish a man, now waxing elderly, with few characteristics to attract careless observers, yet bearing, in his whole aspect, the hand-writing of no common fate, for such as have the skill to read it. He is meager; his low and narrow forehead is deeply wrinkled; his eyes, small and lustreless, sometimes wander apprehensively about him, but oftener seem to look inward. He bends his head, but moves with an indescribable obliquity of gait,[5] as if unwilling to display his full front to the world. Watch him, long enough to see what we have described, and you will allow, that circumstances—which often produce remarkable men from nature's ordinary handiwork—have produced one such here. Next, leaving him to sidle along the foot-walk, cast your eyes in the opposite direction, where a portly female, considerably in the wane of life, with a prayer-book in her hand, is proceeding to yonder church. She has the placid mien[6] of settled widowhood. Her regrets have either died away, or have become so essential to her heart, that they would be poorly exchanged for joy. Just as the lean man and well conditioned woman are passing, a slight obstruction occurs, and brings these two figures directly in contact. Their hands touch; the pressure of the crowd forces her bosom against his shoulder; they stand, face to face, staring into each other's eyes. After a ten years' separation, thus Wakefield meets his wife!

The throng eddies away, and carries them asunder. The sober widow, resuming her former pace, proceeds to church, but pauses in the portal, and throws a perplexed glance along the street. She passes in, however, opening her prayer-book as she goes. And the man? With so wild a face, that busy and selfish London stands to gaze after him, he hurries to his lodgings, bolts the door, and throws himself upon the bed. The latent feelings of years break out; his feeble mind acquires a brief energy from their strength; all the miserable strangeness of his life is revealed to him at a glance; and he cries out, passionately—"Wakefield! Wakefield! You are mad!"

Perhaps he was so. The singularity of his situation must have so moulded him to itself, that, considered in regard to his fellow-creatures and the business of life, he could not be said to possess his right mind. He had contrived, or rather he had happened, to dissever himself from the world—to vanish—to give up his place and privileges with living men, without being admitted among the dead. The life of a hermit is nowise parallel to his. He was in the bustle of the city, as of old; but the crowd swept by, and saw him not; he was, we may figuratively say, always beside his wife, and at his hearth, yet must never feel the warmth of the one, nor the affection of the other. It was Wakefield's unprecedented fate, to retain his original share of human sympathies, and to be still involved in human interests, while he had lost his reciprocal influence on them. It would be a most curious speculation, to trace out the effect of such circumstances on his heart and intellect, separately, and in unison. Yet, changed as he was, he would seldom be conscious of it, but deem himself the same man as ever; glimpses of the truth, indeed, would come, but only for the moment; and still he would keep saying—"I shall soon go back!"—nor reflect, that he had been saying so for twenty years.

I conceive, also, that these twenty years would appear, in the retrospect, scarcely longer than the week to which Wakefield had at first limited his absence. He would look on the affair as no more than an interlude in the main business of his life. When, after a little while more, he should deem it time to re-enter his

---

[5] Slightly sideways.   [6] Appearance.

parlor, his wife would clap her hands for joy, on beholding the middle-aged Mr. Wakefield. Alas, what a mistake! Would Time but await the close of our favorite follies, we should be young men, all of us, and till Doom's Day.

One evening, in the twentieth year since he vanished, Wakefield is taking his customary walk towards the dwelling which he still calls his own. It is a gusty night of autumn, with frequent showers, that patter down upon the pavement, and are gone, before a man can put up his umbrella. Pausing near the house, Wakefield discerns, through the parlor-windows of the second floor, the red glow, and the glimmer and fitful flash, of a comfortable fire. On the ceiling, appear a grotesque shadow of good Mrs. Wakefield. The cap, the nose and chin, and the broad waist, form an admirable caricature, which dances, moreover, with the up-flickering and down-sinking blaze, almost too merrily for the shade of an elderly widow. At this instant, a shower chances to fall, and is driven, by the unmannerly gust, full into Wakefield's face and bosom. He is quite penetrated with its autumnal chill. Shall he stand, wet and shivering here, when his own hearth has a good fire to warm him, and his own wife will run to fetch the gray coat and small-clothes,[7] which, doubtless, she has kept carefully in the closet of their bed-chamber? No! Wakefield is no such fool. He ascends the steps—heavily!—for twenty years have stiffened his legs, since he came down—but he knows it not. Stay, Wakefield! Would you go to the sole home that is left you? Then step into your grave! The door opens. As he passes in, we have a parting glimpse of his visage, and recognize the crafty smile, which was the precursor of the little joke, that he has ever since been playing off at his wife's expense. How unmercifully has he quizzed[8] the poor woman! Well; a good night's rest to Wakefield!

This happy event—supposing it to be such—could only have occurred at an unpremeditated moment. We will not follow our friend across the threshold. He has left us much food for thought, a portion of which shall lend its wisdom to a moral; and be shaped into a figure. Amid the seeming confusion of our mysterious world, individuals are so nicely adjusted to a system, and systems to one another, and to a whole, that, by stepping aside for a moment, a man exposes himself to a fearful risk of losing his place forever. Like Wakefield, he may become, as it were, the Outcast of the Universe.

1835

YOUNG GOODMAN BROWN*

Young Goodman Brown came forth, at sunset, into the street of Salem[1] village, but put his head back, after crossing the threshold, to exchange a parting kiss with his young wife. And Faith, as the wife was aptly named, thrust her own pretty head into the street, letting the wind play with the pink ribbons of her cap, while she called to Goodman Brown.

---

[7] Close-fitting knee britches.   [8] Played a practical joke on.

* First published in *The New-England Magazine* in 1835 and included in *Mosses From an Old Manse* (1846). "Goodman" is a polite form of address for a man of humble birth who headed a household. The common surname Brown suggests that Hawthorne's Goodman is an ordinary person.

[1] Salem, Massachusetts, the site of witchcraft trials and executions in 1692.

"Dearest heart," whispered she, softly and rather sadly, when her lips were close to his ear, "pr'y thee, put off your journey until sunrise, and sleep in your own bed to-night. A lone woman is troubled with such dreams and such thoughts, that she's afeard of herself, sometimes. Pray, tarry with me this night, dear husband, of all nights in the year!"

"My love and my Faith," replied young Goodman Brown, "of all nights in the year, this one night must I tarry away from thee. My journey, as thou callest it, forth and back again, must needs be done 'twixt now and sunrise. What, my sweet, pretty wife, dost thou doubt me already, and we but three months married!"

"Then, God bless you!" said Faith, with the pink ribbons, "and may you find all well, when you come back."

"Amen!" cried Goodman Brown, "Say thy prayers, dear Faith, and go to bed at dusk, and no harm will come to thee!"

So they parted; and the young man pursued his way, until, being about to turn the corner by the meeting-house, he looked back, and saw the head of Faith still peeping after him, with a melancholy air, in spite of her pink ribbons.

"Poor little Faith!" thought he, for his heart smote him. "What a wretch am I, to leave her on such an errand! She talks of dreams, too. Methought, as she spoke, there was trouble in her face, as if a dream had warned her what work is to be done to-night. But, no, no! 'twould kill her to think it. Well; she's a blessed angel on earth; and after this one night, I'll cling to her skirts and follow her to Heaven."

With this excellent resolve for the future, Goodman Brown felt himself justified in making more haste on his present evil purpose. He had taken a dreary road, darkened by all the gloomiest trees of the forest, which barely stood aside to let the narrow path creep through, and closed immediately behind. It was all as lonely as could be; and there is this peculiarity in such a solitude, that the traveller knows not who may be concealed by the innumerable trunks and the thick boughs overhead; so that, with lonely footsteps, he may yet be passing through an unseen multitude.

"There may be a devilish Indian behind every tree," said Goodman Brown, to himself; and he glanced fearfully behind him, as he added, "What if the devil himself should be at my very elbow!"

His head being turned back, he passed a crook of the road, and looking forward again, beheld a figure of a man, in grave and decent attire, seated at the foot of an old tree. He arose, at Goodman Brown's approach, and walked onward, side by side with him.

"You are late, Goodman Brown," said he. "The clock of the Old South[2] was striking as I came through Boston; and that is full fifteen minutes agone."

"Faith kept me back awhile," replied the young man, with a tremor in his voice, caused by the sudden appearance of his companion, though not wholly unexpected.

It was now deep dusk in the forest, and deepest in that part of it where these two were journeying. As nearly as could be discerned, the second traveller was about fifty years old, apparently in the same rank of life as Goodman Brown, and bearing a considerable resemblance to him, though perhaps more in expression than features. Still, they might have been taken for father and son. And yet,

---

[2] Boston's Old South Church, built in 1669. That this "figure" has come from Boston to Salem in just fifteen minutes signifies supernatural powers.

though the elder person was as simply clad as the younger, and as simple in manner too, he had an indescribable air of one who knew the world, and would not have felt abashed at the governor's dinner-table, or in King William's court,[3] were it possible that his affairs should call him thither. But the only thing about him, that could be fixed upon as remarkable, was his staff, which bore the likeness of a great black snake, so curiously wrought, that it might almost be seen to twist and wriggle itself, like a living serpent. This, of course, must have been an ocular deception, assisted by the uncertain light.

"Come, Goodman Brown!" cried his fellow-traveller, "this is a dull pace for the beginning of a journey. Take my staff, if you are so soon weary."

"Friend," said the other, exchanging his slow pace for a full stop, "having kept covenant by meeting thee here, it is my purpose now to return whence I came. I have scruples, touching the matter thou wot'st[4] of."

"Sayest thou so?" replied he of the serpent, smiling apart. "Let us walk on, nevertheless, reasoning as we go, and if I convince thee not, thou shalt turn back. We are but a little way in the forest, yet."

"Too far, too far!" exclaimed the goodman, unconsciously resuming his walk. "My father never went into the woods on such an errand, nor his father before him. We have been a race of honest men and good Christians, since the days of the martyrs.[5] And shall I be the first of the name of Brown, that ever took this path, and kept—"

"Such company, thou wouldst say," observed the elder person, interpreting his pause. "Well said, Goodman Brown! I have been as well acquainted with your family as with ever a one among the Puritans; and that's no trifle to say. I helped your grandfather, the constable, when he lashed the Quaker woman so smartly through the streets of Salem.[6] And it was I that brought your father a pitch-pine knot, kindled at my own hearth, to set fire to an Indian village, in King Philip's war.[7] They were my good friends, both; and many a pleasant walk have we had along this path, and returned merrily after midnight. I would fain be friends with you, for their sake."

"If it be as thou sayest," replied Goodman Brown, "I marvel they never spoke of these matters. Or, verily, I marvel not, seeing that the least rumor of the sort would have driven them from New-England. We are a people of prayer, and good works, to boot, and abide no such wickedness."

"Wickedness or not," said the traveller with the twisted staff, "I have a very general acquaintance here in New-England. The deacons of many a church have drunk the communion wine with me; the selectmen,[8] of divers towns, make me their chairman; and a majority of the Great and General Court[9] are firm supporters of my interest. The governor and I, too—but these are state-secrets."

"Can this be so!" cried Goodman Brown, with a stare of amazement at his undisturbed companion. "Howbeit, I have nothing to do with the governor and

---

[3] That of King William III (1650–1702), who ruled England from 1689 to 1702 with his wife, Queen Mary II (1662–1694), until her death.

[4] The matter you know.

[5] Protestants persecuted during the reign of Mary Tudor (1516–1558), queen of England from 1553 to 1558, called "Bloody Mary" because of her severity.

[6] A Puritan law passed in 1661 commanded that Quakers who broke the law be "whipped through the town."

[7] The war waged by the Wampanoag Indians against the colonists in 1675; King Philip is the name the English gave to Metacomet (?–1676), the Wampanoag chief.

[8] Village officials.   [9] The colony's legislature.

council; they have their own ways, and are no rule for a simple husbandman,[10] like me. But, were I to go on with thee, how should I meet the eye of that good old man, our minister, at Salem village? Oh, his voice would make me tremble, both Sabbath-day and lecture-day!"[11]

Thus far, the elder traveller had listened with due gravity, but now burst into a fit of irrepressible mirth, shaking himself so violently, that his snake-like staff actually seemed to wriggle in sympathy.

"Ha! ha! ha!" shouted he, again and again; then composing himself, "Well go on, Goodman Brown, go on; but pr'y thee, don't kill me with laughing!"

"Well, then, to end the matter at once," said Goodman Brown, considerably nettled, "there is my wife, Faith. It would break her dear little heart; and I'd rather break my own!"

"Nay, if that be the case," answered the other, "e'en go thy ways, Goodman Brown. I would not, for twenty old women like the one hobbling before us, that Faith should come to any harm."

As he spoke, he pointed his staff at a female figure on the path, in whom Goodman Brown recognized a very pious and exemplary dame, who had taught him his catechism, in youth, and was still his moral and spiritual adviser, jointly with the minister and Deacon Gookin.

"A marvel, truly, that Goody[12] Cloyse should be so far in the wilderness, at night-fall!" said he. "But, with your leave, friend, I shall take a cut through the woods, until we have left this Christian woman behind. Being a stranger to you, she might ask whom I was consorting with, and whither I was going."

"Be it so," said his fellow-traveller. "Betake you to the woods, and let me keep the path."

Accordingly, the young man turned aside, but took care to watch his companion, who advanced softly along the road, until he had come within a staff's length of the old dame. She, meanwhile, was making the best of her way, with singular speed for so aged a woman, and mumbling some indistinct words, a prayer, doubtless, as she went. The traveller put forth his staff, and touched her withered neck with what seemed the serpent's tail.

"The devil!" screamed the pious old lady.

"Then Goody Cloyse knows her old friend?" observed the traveller, confronting her, and leaning on his writhing stick.

"Ah, forsooth, and is it your worship, indeed?" cried the good dame. "Yea, truly is it, and in the very image of my old gossip, Goodman Brown, the grandfather of the silly fellow that now is. But—would your worship believe it?—my broomstick hath strangely disappeared, stolen, as I suspect, by the unhanged witch, Goody Cory, and that, too, when I was all anointed with the juice of smallage and cinque-foil and wolf's-bane—"[13]

"Mingled with fine wheat and the fat of a new-born babe," said the shape of old Goodman Brown.

---

[10] Ordinarily, a farmer; here, a man of modest status. Hawthorne plays on the word husbandman as he does on goodman.

[11] The midweek sermon day, generally Wednesday or Thursday.

[12] A contraction of "Goodwife," a polite term of address for a married woman of humble rank. Both Goody Cloyse and Goody Cory (later called an "unhanged witch") were sentenced to death at the Salem witchcraft trials.

[13] Plants associated with witchcraft.

"Ah, your worship knows the receipt," cried the old lady, cackling aloud. "So, as I was saying, being all ready for the meeting, and no horse to ride on, I made up my mind to foot it; for they tell me, there is a nice young man to be taken into communion to-night. But now your good worship will lend me your arm, and we shall be there in a twinkling."

"That can hardly be," answered her friend. "I may not spare you my arm, Goody Cloyse, but here is my staff, if you will."

So saying, he threw it down at her feet, where, perhaps, it assumed life, being one of the rods which its owner had formerly lent to the Egyptian Magi.[14] Of this fact, however, Goodman Brown could not take cognizance. He had cast up his eyes in astonishment, and looking down again, beheld neither Goody Cloyse nor the serpentine staff, but his fellow-traveller alone, who waited for him as calmly as if nothing had happened.

"That old woman taught me my catechism!" said the young man; and there was a world of meaning in this simple comment.

They continued to walk onward, while the elder traveller exhorted his companion to make good speed and persevere in the path, discoursing so aptly, that his arguments seemed rather to spring up in the bosom of his auditor, than to be suggested by himself. As they went, he plucked a branch of maple, to serve for a walking-stick, and began to strip it of the twigs and little boughs, which were wet with evening dew. The moment his fingers touched them, they became strangely withered and dried up, as with a week's sunshine. Thus the pair proceeded, at a good free pace, until suddenly, in a gloomy hollow of the road, Goodman Brown sat himself down on the stump of a tree, and refused to go any farther.

"Friend," said he, stubbornly, "my mind is made up. Not another step will I budge on this errand. What if a wretched old woman do choose to go to the devil, when I thought she was going to Heaven! Is that any reason why I should quit my dear Faith, and go after her?"

"You will think better of this, by-and-by," said his acquaintance, composedly. "Sit here and rest yourself awhile; and when you feel like moving again, there is my staff to help you along."

Without more words, he threw his companion the maple stick, and was as speedily out of sight, as if he had vanished into the deepening gloom. The young man sat a few moments, by the road-side, applauding himself greatly, and thinking with how a clear a conscience he should meet the minister, in his morning-walk, nor shrink from the eye of good old Deacon Gookin. And what calm sleep would be his, that very night, which was to have been spent so wickedly, but purely and sweetly now, in the arms of Faith! Amidst these pleasant and praise-worthy meditations, Goodman Brown heard the tramp of horses along the road, and deemed it advisable to conceal himself within the verge of the forest, conscious of the guilty purpose that had brought him thither, though now so happily turned from it.

On came the hoof-tramps and the voices of the riders, two grave old voices, conversing soberly as they drew near. These mingled sounds appeared to pass along the road, within a few yards of the young man's hiding-place; but owing, doubtless, to the depth of the gloom, at that particular spot, neither the travellers nor their steeds were visible. Though their figures brushed the small boughs by the way-side, it could not be seen that they intercepted, even for a moment, the faint

---

[14] Magicians; in Exodus 7:11 the magicians of Egypt turned their rods into serpents.

gleam from the strip of bright sky, athwart which they must have passed. Goodman Brown alternately crouched and stood on tip-toe, pulling aside the branches, and thrusting forth his head as far as he durst, without discerning so much as a shadow. It vexed him the more, because he could have sworn, were such a thing possible, that he recognized the voices of the minister and Deacon Gookin, jogging along quietly, as they were wont to do, when bound to some ordination or ecclesiastical council. While yet within hearing, one of the riders stopped to pluck a switch.

"Of the two, reverend Sir," said the voice like the deacon's, "I had rather miss an ordination-dinner[15] than to-night's meeting. They tell me that some of our community are to be here from Falmouth[16] and beyond, and others from Connecticut and Rhode-Island; besides several of the Indian powows,[17] who, after their fashion, know almost as much deviltry as the best of us. Moreover, there is a goodly young woman to be taken into communion."

"Mighty well, Deacon Gookin!" replied the solemn old tones of the minister. "Spur up, or we shall be late. Nothing can be done, you know, until I get on the ground."

The hoofs clattered again, and the voices, talking so strangely in the empty air, passed on through the forest, where no church had ever been gathered, nor solitary Christian prayed. Whither, then, could these holy men be journeying, so deep into the heathen wilderness? Young Goodman Brown caught hold of a tree, for support, being ready to sink down on the ground, faint and overburthened with the heavy sickness of his heart. He looked up to the sky, doubting whether there really was a Heaven above him. Yet, there was the blue arch, and the stars brightening in it.

"With Heaven above, and Faith below, I will yet stand firm against the devil!" cried Goodman Brown.

While he still gazed upward, into the deep arch of the firmament, and had lifted his hands to pray, a cloud, though no wind was stirring, hurried acros the zenith, and hid the brightening stars. The blue sky was still visible, except directly overhead, where this black mass of cloud was sweeping swiftly northward. Aloft in the air, as if from the depths of the cloud, came a confused and doubtful sound of voices. Once, the listener fancied that he could distinguish the accents of town's-people of his own, men and women, both pious and ungodly, many of whom he had met at the communion-table, and had seen others rioting at the tavern. The next moment, so indistinct were the sounds, he doubted whether he had heard aught but the murmur of the old forest, whispering without a wind. Then came a stronger swell of those familiar tones, heard daily in the sunshine, at Salem village, but never, until now, from a cloud of night. There was one voice, of a young woman, uttering lamentations, yet with an uncertain sorrow, and entreating for some favor, which, perhaps, it would grieve her to obtain. And all the unseen multitude, both saint and sinners, seemed to encourage her onward.

"Faith!" shouted Goodman Brown, in a voice of agony and desperation; and the echoes of the forest mocked him, crying—"Faith! Faith!" as if bewildered wretches were seeking her, all through the wilderness.

The cry of grief, rage, and terror, was yet piercing the night, when the unhappy husband held his breath for a response. There was a scream, drowned immediately

[15] A dinner to celebrate the ordination of a Puritan minister.
[16] Falmouth, Massachusetts, on Cape Cod.   [17] Medicine men.

in a louder murmur of voices, fading into far-off laughter, as the dark cloud swept away, leaving the clear and silent sky above Goodman Brown. But something fluttered lightly down through the air, and caught on the branch of a tree. The young man seized it, and beheld a pink ribbon.

"My Faith is gone!" cried he, after one stupefied moment. "There is no good on earth; and sin is but a name. Come, devil! for to thee is this world given."

And maddened with despair, so that he laughed loud and long, did Goodman Brown grasp his staff and set forth again, at such a rate, that he seemed to fly along the forest-path, rather than to walk or run. The road grew wilder and drearier, and more faintly traced, and vanished at length, leaving him in the heart of the dark wilderness, still rushing onward, with the instinct that guides mortal man to evil. The whole forest was peopled with frightful sounds; the creaking of the trees, the howling of wild beasts, and the yell of Indians; while, sometimes, the wind tolled like a distant church-bell, and sometimes gave a broad roar around the traveller, as if all Nature were laughing him to scorn. But he was himself the chief horror of the scene, and shrank not from its other horrors.

"Ha! ha! ha!" roared Goodman Brown, when the wind laughed at him. "Let us hear which will laugh loudest! Think not to frighten me with your deviltry! Come witch, come wizard, come Indian powow, come devil himself! and here comes Goodman Brown. You may as well fear him as he fear you!"

In truth, all through the haunted forest, there could be nothing more frightful than the figure of Goodman Brown. On he flew, among the black pines, brandishing his staff with frenzied gestures, now giving vent to an inspiration of horrid blasphemy, and now shouting forth such laughter, as set all the echoes of the forest laughing like demons around him. The fiend in his own shape is less hideous, than when he rages in the breast of man. Thus sped the demoniac on his course, until, quivering among the trees, he saw a red light before him, as when the felled trunks and branches of a clearing have been set on fire, and throw up their lurid blaze against the sky, at the hour of midnight. He paused, in a lull of the tempest that had driven him onward, and heard the swell of what seemed a hymn, rolling solemnly from a distance, with the weight of many voices. He knew the tune; it was a familiar one in the choir of the village meeting-house. The verse died heavily away, and was lengthened by a chorus, not of human voices, but of all the sounds of the benighted wilderness, pealing in awful harmony together. Goodman Brown cried out; and his cry was lost to his own ear, by its unison with the cry of the desert.

In the interval of silence, he stole forward, until the light glared full upon his eyes. At one extremity of an open space, hemmed in by the dark wall of the forest, arose a rock, bearing some rude, natural resemblance either to an altar or a pulpit, and surrounded by four blazing pines, their tops aflame, their stems untouched, like candles at an evening meeting. The mass of foliage, that had overgrown the summit of the rock, was all on fire, blazing high into the night, and fitfully illuminating the whole field. Each pendent twig and leafy festoon was in a blaze. As the red light arose and fell, a numerous congregation alternately shone forth, then disappeared in shadow, and again grew, as it were, out of the darkness, peopling the heart of the solitary woods at once.

"A grave and dark-clad company!" quoth Goodman Brown.

In truth, they were such. Among them, quivering to-and-fro, between gloom and splendor, appeared faces that would be seen, next day, at the council-board of the province, and others which, Sabbath after Sabbath, looked devoutly heaven-

ward, and benignantly over the crowded pews, from the holiest pulpits in the land.
Some affirm, that the lady of the governor[18] was there. At least, there were high
dames well known to her, and wives of honored husbands, and widows, a great
multitude, and ancient maidens, all of the excellent repute, and fair young girls,
who trembled, lest their mothers should espy them. Either the sudden gleams of
light, flashing over the obscure field, bedazzled Goodman Brown, or he recognized a score of the church-members of Salem village, famous for their especial
sanctity. Good old Deacon Gookin had arrived, and waited at the skirts of that
venerable saint, his revered pastor. But, irreverently consorting with these grave,
reputable, and pious people, these elders of the church, these chaste dames and
dewy virgins, there were men of dissolute lives and women of spotted fame,
wretches given over to all mean and filthy vice, and suspected even of horrid
crimes. It was strange to see, that the good shrank not from the wicked, nor were
the sinners abashed by the saints. Scattered, also, among their pale-faced enemies,
were the Indian priests, or powows, who had often scared their native forest with
more hideous incantations than any known to English witchcraft.

"But, where is Faith?" thought Goodman Brown; and, as hope came into his
heart, he trembled.

Another verse of the hymn arose, a slow and mournful strain, such as the pious
love, but joined to words which expressed all that our nature can conceive of sin,
and darkly hinted at far more. Unfathomable to mere mortals is the lore of fiends.
Verse after verse was sung, and still the chorus of the desert swelled between, like
the deepest tone of a mighty organ. And, with the final peal of that dreadful anthem, there came a sound, as if the roaring wind, the rushing streams, the howling
beasts, and every other voice of the unconverted wilderness, were mingling and
according with the voice of guilty man, in homage to the prince of all. The four
blazing pines threw up a loftier flame, and obscurely discovered shapes and visages of horror on the smoke-wreaths, above the impious assembly. At the same
moment, the fire on the rock shot redly forth, and formed a glowing arch above its
base, where now appeared a figure. With reverence be it spoken, the figure bore
no slight similitude, both in garb and manner, to some grave divine of the New-
England churches.

"Bring forth the converts!" cried a voice, that echoed through the field and
rolled into the forest.

At the word, Goodman Brown stept forth from the shadow of the trees, and
approached the congregation, with whom he felt a loathful brotherhood, by the
sympathy of all that was wicked in his heart. He could have well nigh sworn, that
the shape of his own dead father beckoned him to advance, looking downward
from a smoke-wreath, while a woman, with dim features of despair, threw out her
hand to warn him back. Was it his mother? But he had no power to retreat one
step, nor to resist, even in thought, when the minister and good old Deacon
Gookin seized his arms, and led him to the blazing rock. Thither came also the
slender form of a veiled female, led between Goody Cloyse, that pious teacher of
the catechism, and Martha Carrier,[19] who had received the devil's promise to be

---

[18] The wife of Sir William Phips (1651–1695), royal governor of Massachusetts from 1692 to 1694,
was accused but never tried for witchcraft in 1692.

[19] Carrier was hanged as a witch in Salem in 1692. During her trial she "confessed" that the Devil
promised that she would be queen of Hell.

queen of hell. A rampant hag was she! And there stood the proselytes,[20] beneath the canopy of fire.

"Welcome, my children," said the dark figure, "to the communion of your race! Ye have found, thus young, your nature and your destiny. My children, look behind you!"

They turned; and flashing forth, as it were, in a sheet of flame, the fiend-worshippers were seen; the smile of welcome gleamed darkly on every visage.

"There," resumed the sable[21] form, "are all whom ye have reverenced from youth. Ye deemed them holier than yourselves, and shrank from your own sin, contrasting it with their lives of righteousness, and prayerful aspirations heaven-ward. Yet, here are they all, in my worshipping assembly! This night it shall be granted to you to know their secret deeds; how hoary-bearded elders of the church have whispered wanton words to the young maids of their households; how many a woman, eager for widow's weeds, has given her husband a drink at bed-time, and let him sleep his last sleep in her bosom; how beardless youths have made haste to inherit their fathers' wealth; and how fair damsels—blush not, sweet ones!—have dug little graves in the garden, and bidden me, the sole guest, to an infant's funeral. By the sympathy of your human hearts for sin, ye shall scent out all the places—whether in church, bed-chamber, street, field, or forest—where crime has been committed, and shall exult to behold the whole earth one stain of guilt, one mighty blood-spot. Far more than this! It shall be yours to penetrate, in every bosom, the deep mystery of sin, the fountain of all wicked arts, and which inexhaustibly supplies more evil impulses than human power—than my power, at its utmost!—can make manifest in deeds. And now, my children, look upon each other."

They did so; and, by the blaze of the hell-kindled torches, the wretched man beheld his Faith, and the wife her husband, trembling before that unhallowed altar.

"Lo! there ye stand, my children," said the figure, in a deep and solemn tone, almost sad, with its despairing awfulness, as if his once angelic nature could yet mourn for our miserable race. "Depending upon one another's hearts, ye had still hoped, that virtue were not all a dream. Now are ye undeceived! Evil is the nature of mankind. Evil must be your only happiness. Welcome, again, my children, to the communion of your race!"

"Welcome!" repeated the fiend-worshippers, in one cry of despair and triumph.

And there they stood, the only pair, as it seemed, who were yet hesitating on the verge of wickedness, in this dark world. A basin was hollowed, naturally, in the rock. Did it contain water, reddened by the lurid light? or was it blood? or, perchance, a liquid flame? Herein did the Shape of Evil dip his hand, and prepare to lay the mark of baptism upon their foreheads, that they might be partakers of the mystery of sin, more conscious of the secret guilt of others, both in deed and thought, than they could now be of their own. The husband cast one look at his pale wife, and Faith at him. What polluted wretches would the next glance shew them to each other, shuddering alike at what they disclosed and what they saw!

"Faith! Faith!" cried the husband. "Look up to Heaven, and resist the Wicked One!"

Whether Faith obeyed, he knew not. Hardly had he spoken, when he found himself amid calm night and solitude, listening to a roar of the wind, which died

---

[20] New converts. [21] Black.

heavily away through the forest. He staggered against the rock and felt it chill and damp, while a hanging twig, that had been all on fire, besprinkled his cheek with the coldest dew.

The next morning, young Goodman Brown came slowly into the street of Salem village, staring around him like a bewildered man. The good old minister was taking a walk along the grave-yard, to get an appetite for breakfast and meditate his sermon, and bestowed a blessing, as he passed, on Goodman Brown. He shrank from the venerable saint, as if to avoid an anathema.[22] Old Deacon Gookin was at domestic worship, and the holy words of his prayer were heard through the open window. "What God doth the wizard pray to?" quoth Goodman Brown. Goody Cloyse, that excellent old Christian, stood in the early sunshine, at her own lattice, catechising a little girl, who had brought her a pint of morning's milk. Goodman Brown snatched away the child, as from the grasp of the fiend himself. Turning the corner by the meeting-house, he spied the head of Faith, with the pink ribbons, gazing anxiously forth, and bursting into such joy at sight of him, that she skipt along the street, and almost kissed her husband before the whole village. But, Goodman Brown looked sternly and sadly into her face, and passed on without a greeting.

Had Goodman Brown fallen asleep in the forest, and only dreamed a wild dream of a witch-meeting?

Be it so, if you will. But, alas! it was a dream of evil omen for young Goodman Brown. A stern, a sad, a darkly meditative, a distrustful, if not a desperate man, did he become, from the night of that fearful dream. On the Sabbath-day, when the congregation were singing a holy psalm, he could not listen, because an anthem of sin rushed loudly upon his ear, and drowned all the blessed strain. When the minister spoke from the pulpit, with power and fervid eloquence, and, with his hand on the open Bible, of the sacred truths of our religion, and of saint-like lives and triumphant deaths, and of future bliss or misery unutterable, then did Goodman Brown turn pale, dreading, lest the roof should thunder down upon the gray blasphemer and his hearers. Often, awakening suddenly at midnight, he shrank from the bosom of Faith, and at morning or eventide, when the family knelt down at prayer, he scowled, and muttered to himself, and gazed sternly at his wife, and turned away. And when he had lived long, and was borne to his grave, a hoary corpse, followed by Faith, an aged woman, and children and grandchildren, a goodly procession, besides neighbors, not a few, they carved no hopeful verse upon his tomb-stone; for his dying hour was gloom.

1835

THE BIRTH-MARK*

In the latter part of the last century, there lived a man of science—an eminent proficient in every branch of natural philosophy—who, not long before our story opens, had made experience of a spiritual affinity, more attractive than any chemical one. He had left his laboratory to the care of an assistant, cleared his fine

---

[22] A solemn curse.

* First published in the *Pioneer Magazine* in 1843 and included in *Mosses From an Old Manse* (1846).

countenance from the furnace-smoke, washed the stain of acids from his fingers, and persuaded a beautiful woman to become his wife. In those days, when the comparatively recent discovery of electricity, and other kindred mysteries of nature, seemed to open paths into the region of miracle, it was not unusual for the love of science to rival the love of woman, in its depth and absorbing energy. The higher intellect, the imagination, the spirit, and even the heart, might all find their congenial aliment in pursuits which, as some of their ardent votaries believed, would ascend from one step of powerful intelligence to another, until the philosopher should lay his hand on the secret of creative force, and perhaps make new worlds for himself. We know not whether Aylmer possessed this degree of faith in man's ultimate control over nature. He had devoted himself, however, too unreservedly to scientific studies, ever to be weaned from them by any second passion. His love for his young wife might prove the stronger of the two; but it could only be by intertwining itself with his love of science, and uniting the strength of the latter to its own.

Such a union accordingly took place, and was attended with truly remarkable consequences, and a deeply impressive moral. One day, very soon after their marriage, Aylmer sat gazing at his wife, with a trouble in his countenance that grew stronger, until he spoke.

"Georgiana," said he, "has it never occurred to you that the mark upon your cheek might be removed?"

"No, indeed," said she, smiling; but perceiving the seriousness of his manner, she blushed deeply. "To tell you the truth, it has been so often called a charm, that I was simple enough to imagine it might be so."

"Ah, upon another face, perhaps it might," replied her husband. "But never on yours! No, dearest Georgiana, you came so nearly perfect from the hand of Nature, that this slightest possible defect—which we hesitate whether to term a defect or a beauty—shocks me, as being the visible mark of earthly imperfection."

"Shocks you, my husband!" cried Georgiana, deeply hurt; at first reddening with momentary anger, but then bursting into tears. "Then why did you take me from my mother's side? You cannot love what shocks you!"

To explain this conversation, it must be mentioned, that, in the centre of Georgiana's left cheek, there was a singular mark, deeply interwoven, as it were, with the texture and substance of her face. In the usual state of her complexion,—a healthy, though delicate bloom,—the mark wore a tint of deeper crimson, which imperfectly defined its shape amid the surrounding rosiness. When she blushed, it gradually became more indistinct, and finally vanished amid the triumphant rush of blood, that bathed the whole cheek with its brilliant glow. But, if any shifting emotion caused her to turn pale, there was the mark again, a crimson stain upon the snow, in what Aylmer sometimes deemed an almost fearful distinctness. Its shape bore not a little similarity to the human hand, though of the smallest pigmy size. Georgiana's lovers were wont to say, that some fairy, at her birth-hour, had laid her tiny hand upon the infant's cheek, and left this impress there, in token of the magic endowments that were to give her such sway over all hearts. Many a desperate swain would have risked life for the privilege of pressing his lips to the mysterious hand. It must not be concealed, however, that the impression wrought by this fairy sign-manual varied exceedingly, according to the difference of temperament in the beholders. Some fastidious persons—but they were exclusively of her own sex—affirmed that the Bloody Hand, as they chose to call it, quite destroyed the effect of Georgiana's beauty, and rendered her countenance even hideous. But it would be as reasonable to say, that one of those small blue stains, which sometimes occur in the purest statuary marble, would convert the Eve of Powers[1] to a monster. Masculine observers, if the birth-mark did not heighten their admiration, contented themselves with wishing it away, that the world might possess one living specimen of ideal loveliness, without the semblance of a flaw. After his marriage—for he thought little or nothing of the matter before—Aylmer discovered that this was the case with himself.

Had she been less beautiful—if Envy's self could have found aught else to sneer at—he might have felt his affection heightened by the prettiness of this mimic hand, now vaguely portrayed, now lost, now stealing forth again, and glimmering to-and-fro with every pulse of emotion that throbbed within her heart. But, seeing her otherwise so perfect, he found this one defect grow more and more intolerable, with every moment of their united lives. It was the fatal flaw of humanity, which Nature, in one shape or another, stamps ineffaceably on all her productions, either to imply that they are temporary and finite, or that their perfection must be wrought by toil and pain. The Crimson Hand expressed the ineludible gripe, in which mortality clutches the highest and purest of earthly mould, degrading them into kindred with the lowest, and even with the very brutes, like whom their visible frames return to dust. In this manner, selecting it as the symbol of his wife's liability to sin, sorrow, decay, and death, Alymer's sombre imagination was not long in rendering the birth-mark a frightful object, causing him more trouble and horror than ever Georgiana's beauty, whether of soul or sense, had given him delight.

At all the seasons which should have been their happiest, he invariably, and without intending it—nay, in spite of a purpose to the contrary—reverted to this one disastrous topic. Trifling as it at first appeared, it so connected itself with innumerable trains of thought, and modes of feeling, that it became the central point of all. With the morning twilight, Aylmer opened his eyes upon his wife's face, and recognized the symbol of imperfection; and when they sat together at the evening hearth, his eyes wandered stealthily to her cheek, and beheld, flickering with the blaze of the wood fire, the spectral Hand that wrote mortality, where he would fain have worshipped. Georgiana soon learned to shudder at his gaze. It needed but a glance, with the peculiar expression that his face often wore, to change the roses of her cheek into a deathlike paleness, amid which the Crimson Hand was brought strongly out, like a bas-relief[2] of ruby on the whitest marble.

Late, one night, when the lights were growing dim, so as hardly to betray the stain on the poor wife's cheek, she herself, for the first time, voluntarily took up the subject.

"Do you remember, my dear Aylmer," said she, with a feeble attempt at a smile—"have you any recollection of a dream, last night, about this odious Hand?"

"None!—none whatever!" replied Aylmer, starting; but then he added in a dry, cold tone, affected for the sake of concealing the real depth of his emotion:—"I might well dream of it; for before I fell asleep, it had taken a pretty firm hold of my fancy."

---

[1] The marble statue *Eve Before the Fall* (1842?), produced by the American sculptor Hiram Powers (1805–1873) in Florence.

[2] "Low relief" (French); slightly raised.

"And you did dream of it," continued Georgiana, hastily; for she dreaded lest a gush of tears should interrupt what she had to say—"A terrible dream! I wonder that you can forget it. Is it possible to forget this one expression?—Reflect, my husband; for by all means I would have you recall that dream."

The mind is in a sad note, when Sleep, the all-involving, cannot confine her spectres within the dim region of her sway, but suffers them to break forth, affrighting this actual life with secrets that perchance belong to a deeper one. Aylmer now remembered his dream. He had fancied himself, with his servant Aminadab, attempting an operation for the removal of the birth-mark. But the deeper went the knife, the deeper sank the Hand, until at length its tiny grasp appeared to have caught hold of Georgiana's heart; whence, however, her husband was inexorably resolved to cut or wrench it away.

When the dream had shaped itself perfectly in his memory, Aylmer sat in his wife's presence with a guilty feeling. Truth often finds its way to the mind close-muffled in robes of sleep, and then speaks with uncompromising directness of matters in regard to which we practise an unconscious self-deception, during our waking moments. Until now, he had not been aware of the tyrannizing influence acquired by one idea over his mind, and of the lengths which he might find in his heart to go, for the sake of giving himself peace.

"Aylmer," resumed Georgiana, solemnly, "I know not what may be the cost to both of us, to rid me of this fatal birth-mark. Perhaps its removal may cause cureless deformity. Or, it may be, the stain goes as deep as life itself. Again, do we know that there is a possibility, on any terms, of unclasping the firm grip of this little Hand, which was laid upon me before I came into the world?"

"Dearest Georgiana, I have spent much thought upon the subject," hastily interrupted Aylmer—"I am convinced of the perfect practicability of its removal."

"If there be the remotest possibility of it," continued Georgiana, "let the attempt be made, at whatever risk. Danger is nothing to me; for life—while this hateful mark makes me the object of your horror and disgust—life is a burthen which I would fling down with joy. Either remove this dreadful Hand, or take my wretched life! You have deep science! All the world bears witness of it. You have achieved great wonders! Cannot you remove this little, little mark, which I cover with the tips of two small fingers? Is this beyond your power, for the sake of your own peace, and to save your poor wife from madness?"

"Noblest—dearest—tenderest wife!" cried Aylmer, rapturously. "Doubt not my power. I have already given this matter the deepest thought—thought which might almost have enlightened me to create a being less perfect than yourself. Georgiana, you have led me deeper than ever into the heart of science. I feel myself fully competent to render this dear cheek as faultless as its fellow; and then, most beloved, what will be my triumph, when I shall have corrected what Nature left imperfect, in her fairest work! Even Pygmalion,[3] when his sculptured woman assumed life, felt not greater ecstasy than mine will be."

"It is resolved, then," said Georgiana, faintly smiling,—"And, Aylmer, spare me not, though you should find the birth-mark take refuge in my heart at last."

Her husband tenderly kissed her cheek—her right cheek—not that which bore the impress of the Crimson Hand.

---

[3] According to Greek myth, a king of Cyprus who fell in love with a beautiful statue he had sculpted; Aphrodite, the goddess of love, brought the statue to life, and he married his creation.

The next day, Aylmer apprized his wife of a plan that he had formed, whereby he might have opportunity for the intense thought and constant watchfulness, which the proposed operation would require; while Georgiana, likewise, would enjoy the perfect repose essential to its success. They were to seclude themselves in the extensive apartments occupied by Aylmer as a laboratory, and where, during his toil-some youth, he had made discoveries in the elemental powers of nature, that had roused the admiration of all the learned societies in Europe. Seated calmly in this laboratory, the pale philosopher had investigated the secrets of the highest cloud-region, and of the profoundest mines; he had satisfied himself of the causes that kindled and kept alive the fires of the volcano; and had explained the mystery of fountains, and how it is that they gush forth, some so bright and pure, and others with such rich medicinal virtues, from the dark bosom of the earth. Here, too, at an earlier period, he had studied the wonders of the human frame, and attempted to fathom the very process by which Nature assimilates all her precious influences from earth and air, and from the spiritual world, to create and foster Man, her masterpiece. The latter pursuit, however, Aylmer had long laid aside, in unwilling recognition of the truth, against which all seekers sooner or later stumble, that our great creative Mother, while she amuses us with apparently working in the broadest sunshine, is yet severely careful to keep her own secrets, and, in spite of her pretended openness, shows us nothing but results. She permits us indeed, to mar, but seldom to mend, and, like a jealous patentee, on no account to make. Now, however, Aylmer resumed these half-forgotten investigations; not, of course, with such hopes or wishes as first suggested them; but because they involved much physiological truth, and lay in the path of his proposed scheme for the treatment of Georgiana.

As he led her over the threshold of the laboratory, Georgiana was cold and tremulous. Aylmer looked cheerfully into her face, with intent to reassure her, but was so startled with the intense glow of the birth-mark upon the whiteness of her cheek, that he could not restrain a strong convulsive shudder. His wife fainted.

"Aminadab! Aminadab!" shouted Aylmer, stamping violently on the floor.

Forthwith, there issued from an inner apartment a man of low stature, but bulky frame, with shaggy hair hanging about his visage, which was grimed with the vapors of the furnace. This personage had been Aylmer's under-worker during his whole scientific career, and was admirably fitted for that office by his great mechanical readiness, and the skill with which, while incapable of comprehending a single principle, he executed all the practical details of his master's experiments. With his vast strength, his shaggy hair, his smoky aspect, and the indescribable earthiness that incrusted him, he seemed to represent man's physical nature; while Aylmer's slender figure, and pale, intellectual face, were no less apt a type of the spiritual element.

"Throw open the door of the boudoir, Aminadab," said Aylmer, "and burn a pastille."[4]

"Yes, master," answered Aminadab, looking intently at the lifeless form of Georgiana; and then he muttered to himself:—"If she were my wife, I'd never part with that birth-mark."

When Georgiana recovered consciousness, she found herself breathing an atmosphere of penetrating fragrance, the gentle potency of which had recalled her from her deathlike faintness. The scene around her looked like enchantment.

[4] A pellet of aromatic paste-like incense.

Aylmer had converted those smoky, dingy, sombre rooms, where he had spent his brightest years in recondite pursuits, into a series of beautiful apartments, not unfit to be the secluded abode of a lovely woman. The walls were hung with gorgeous curtains, which imparted the combination of grandeur and grace, that no other species of adornment can achieve; and as they fell from the ceiling to the floor, their rich and ponderous folds, concealing all angles and straight lines, appeared to shut in the scene from infinite space. For aught Georgiana knew, it might be a pavilion among the clouds. And Aylmer, excluding the sunshine, which would have interfered with his chemical processes, had supplied its place with perfumed lamps, emitting flames of various hue, but all uniting in a soft, empurpled radiance. He now knelt by his wife's side, watching her earnestly, but without alarm; for he was confident in his science, and felt that he could draw a magic circle round her, within which no evil might intrude.

"Where am I?—Ah, I remember!" said Georgiana, faintly; and she placed her hand over her cheek, to hide the terrible mark from her husband's eyes.

"Fear not, dearest!" exclaimed he. "Do not shrink from me! Believe me, Georgiana, I even rejoice in this single imperfection, since it will be such rapture to remove it."

"Oh, spare me!" sadly replied his wife—"Pray do not look at it again. I never can forget that convulsive shudder."

In order to soothe Georgiana, and, as it were, to release her mind from the burthen of actual things, Aylmer now put in practice some of the light and playful secrets, which science had taught him among its profounder lore. Airy figures, absolutely bodiless ideas, and forms of unsubstantial beauty, came and danced before her, imprinting their momentary footsteps on beams of light. Though she had some indistinct idea of the method of these optical phenomena, still the illusion was almost perfect enough to warrant the belief, that her husband possessed sway over the spiritual world. Then again, when she felt a wish to look forth from her seclusion, immediately, as if her thoughts were answered, the procession of external existence flitted across a screen. The scenery and the figures of actual life were perfectly represented, but with that bewitching, yet indescribable difference, which always makes a picture, an image, or a shadow, so much more attractive than the original. When wearied of this, Aylmer bade her cast her eyes upon a vessel, containing a quantity of earth. She did so, with little interest at first, but was soon startled, to perceive the germ of a plant, shooting upward from the soil. Then came the slender stalk—the leaves gradually unfolded themselves—and amid them was a perfect and lovely flower.

"It is magical!" cried Georgiana, "I dare not touch it."

"Nay, pluck it," answered Aylmer, "pluck it, and inhale its brief perfume while you may. The flower will wither in a few moments, and leave nothing save its brown seed-vessels—but thence may be perpetuated a race as ephemeral as itself."

But Georgiana had no sooner touched the flower than the whole plant suffered a blight, its leaves turning coal-black, as if by the agency of fire.

"There was too powerful a stimulus," said Aylmer thoughtfully.

To make up for this abortive experiment, he proposed to take her portrait by a scientific process of his own invention. It was to be effected by rays of light striking upon a polished plate of metal.[5] Georgiana assented—but, on looking at the

---

[5] To accentuate Aylmer's inventive genius, Hawthorne has him anticipate the process of making a daguerreotype, an early photographic method introduced in 1839.

result, was affrighted to find the features of the portrait blurred and indefinable; while the minute figure of a hand appeared where the cheek should have been. Aylmer snatched the metallic plate, and threw it into a jar of corrosive acid.

Soon, however, he forgot these mortifying failures. In the intervals of study and chemical experiment, he came to her, flushed and exhausted, but seemed invigorated by her presence, and spoke in glowing language of the resources of his art. He gave a history of the long dynasty of the Alchemists, who spent so many ages in quest of the universal solvent, by which the Golden Principle might be elicted from all things vile and base. Aylmer appeared to believe, that, by the plainest scientific logic, it was altogether within the limits of possibility to discover this long-sought medium; but, he added, a philosopher who should go deep enough to acquire the power, would attain too lofty a wisdom to stoop to the exercise of it. Not less singular were his opinions in regard to the Elixir Vitæ.[6] He more than intimated, that it was his option to concoct a liquid that should prolong life for years—perhaps interminably—but that it would produce a discord in nature, which all the world, and chiefly the quaffer of the immortal nostrum, would find cause to curse.

"Aylmer, are you in earnest?" asked Georgiana, looking at him with amazement and fear; "it is terrible to possess such power, or even to dream of possessing it!"

"Oh, do not tremble, my love!" said her husband, "I would not wrong either you or myself by working such inharmonious effects upon our lives. But I would have you consider how trifling, in comparison, is the skill requisite to remove this little Hand."

At the mention of the birth-mark, Georgiana, as usual, shrank, as if a red-hot iron had touched her cheek.

Again Aylmer applied himself to his labors. She could hear his voice in the distant furnace-room, giving directions to Aminadab, whose harsh, uncouth, misshapen tones were audible in response, more like the grunt or growl of a brute than human speech. After hours of absence, Aylmer reappeared, and proposed that she should now examine his cabinets of chemical products, and natural treasures of the earth. Among the former he showed her a small vial, in which, he remarked, was contained a gentle yet most powerful fragrance, capable of impregnating all the breezes that blow across a kingdom. They were of inestimable value, the contents of that little vial; and, as he said so, he threw some of the perfume into the air, and filled the room with piercing and invigorating delight.

"And what is this?" asked Georgiana, pointing to a small crystal globe, containing a gold-colored liquid. "It is so beautiful to the eye, that I could imagine it the Elixir of Life."

"In one sense it is," replied Aylmer, "or rather the Elixir of Immortality. It is the most precious poison that ever was concocted in this world. By its aid, I could apportion the lifetime of any mortal at whom you might point your finger. The strength of the dose would determine whether he were to linger out years, or drop dead in the midst of a breath. No king, on his guarded throne, could keep his life, if I, in my private station, should deem that the welfare of millions justified me in depriving him of it."

"Why do you keep such a terrific drug?" inquired Georgiana in horror.

---

[6] "Elixir of life" (Latin): alchemists tried to turn base metal into gold, to discover the universal cure for diseases, and to develop an elixir that would prolong human life indefinitely.

"Do not mistrust me, dearest!" said her husband, smiling; "its virtuous potency is yet greater than its harmful one. But, see! here is a powerful cosmetic. With a few drops of this, in a vase of water, freckles may be washed away as easily as the hands are cleansed. A stronger infusion would take the blood out of the cheek, and leave the rosiest beauty a pale ghost."

"Is it with this lotion that you intend to bathe my cheek?"asked Georgiana anxiously.

"Oh, no!" hastily replied her husband—"this is merely superficial. Your case demands a remedy that shall go deeper."

In his interviews with Georgiana, Aylmer generally made minute inquiries as to her sensations, and whether the confinement of the rooms, and the temperature of the atmosphere, agreed with her. These questions had such a particular drift, that Georgiana began to conjecture that she was already subjected to certain physical influences, either breathed in with the fragrant air, or taken with her food. She fancied, likewise—but it might be altogether fancy—that there was a stirring up of her system,—a strange indefinite sensation creeping through her veins, and tingling, half painfully, half pleasurably, at her heart. Still, whenever she dared to look into the mirror, there she beheld herself, pale as a white rose, and with the crimson birth-mark stamped upon her cheek. Not even Aylmer now hated it so much as she.

To dispel the tedium of the hours which her husband found it necessary to devote to the processes of combination and analysis, Georgiana turned over the volumes of his scientific library. In many dark old tomes, she met with chapters full of romance and poetry. They were the works of the philosophers of the middle ages, such as Albertus Magnus, Cornelius Agrippa, Paracelsus, and the famous friar who created the prophetic Brazen Head.[7] All these antique naturalists stood in advance of their centuries, yet were imbued with some of their credulity, and therefore were believed, and perhaps imagined themselves, to have acquired from the investigation of nature a power above nature, and from physics a sway over the spiritual world. Hardly less curious and imaginative were the early volumes of the Transactions of the Royal Society,[8] in which the members, knowing little of the limits of natural possibility, were continually recording wonders, or proposing methods whereby wonders might be wrought.

But, to Georgiana, the most engrossing volume was a large folio from her husband's own hand, in which he had recorded every experiment of his scientific career, with its original aim, the methods adopted for its development, and its final success or failure, with the circumstances to which either event was attributable. The book, in truth, was both the history and emblem of his ardent, ambitious, imaginative, yet practical and laborious, life. He handled physical details, as if there were nothing beyond them; yet spiritualized them all, and redeemed himself from materialism, by his strong and eager aspiration towards the infinite. In his grasp, the veriest clod of earth assumed a soul. Georgiana, as she read, reverenced Aylmer, and loved him more profoundly than ever, but with a less entire dependence on his judgment than heretofore. Much as he had accomplished, she could not but observe that his most splendid successes were almost invariably failures, if compared with the ideal at which he aimed. His brightest

---

[7] Medieval and early Renaissance philosophers and scientists interested in alchemy and magic: Saint Albertus Magnus (1200?–1280); Agrippa (1486?–1535); Philippus Aureolus Paracelsus (1493?–1541); and Roger Bacon (1214–1294?), who fashioned a head made of brass to forecast such things as changes of climate and personal health.

[8] The Royal Society of London, established in 1660 to promote scientific discussion.

diamonds were the merest pebbles, and felt to be so by himself, in comparison with the inestimable gems which lay hidden beyond his reach. The volume, rich with achievements that had won renown for its author, was yet as melancholy a record as ever mortal hand had penned. It was the sad confession, and continual exemplification, of the short-comings of the composite man—the spirit burthened with clay and working in matter—and of the despair that assails the higher nature, at finding itself so miserably thwarted by the earthly part. Perhaps every man of genius, in whatever sphere, might recognize the image of his own experience in Aylmer's journal.

So deeply did these reflections affect Georgiana, that she laid her face upon the open volume, and burst into tears. In this situation she was found by her husband.

"It is dangerous to read in a sorcerer's books," said he, with a smile, though his countenance was uneasy and displeased. "Georgiana, there are pages in that volume, which I can scarcely glance over and keep my senses. Take heed lest it prove as detrimental to you!"

"It has made me worship you more than ever," said she.

"Ah! wait for this one success," rejoined he, "then worship me if you will. I shall deem myself hardly unworthy of it. But, come! I have sought you for the luxury of your voice. Sing to me, dearest!"

So she poured out the liquid music of her voice to quench the thirst of his spirit. He then took his leave, with a boyish exuberance of gaiety, assuring her that her seclusion would endure but a little longer, and that the result was already certain. Scarcely had he departed, when Georgiana felt irresistibly impelled to follow him. She had forgotten to inform Aylmer of a symptom, which, for two or three hours past, had begun to excite her attention. It was a sensation in the fatal birth-mark, not painful, but which induced a restlessness throughout her system. Hastening after her husband, she intruded, for the first time, into the laboratory.

The first thing that struck her eye was the furnace, that hot and feverish worker, with the intense glow of its fire, which, by the quantities of soot clustered above it, seemed to have been burning for ages. There was a distilling apparatus in full operation. Around the room were retorts, tubes, cylinders, crucibles, and other apparatus of chemical research. An electrical machine stood ready for immediate use. The atmosphere felt oppressively close, and was tainted with gaseous odors, which had been tormented forth by the process of science. The severe and homely simplicity of the apartment, with its naked walls and brick pavement, looked strange, accustomed as Georgiana had become to the fantastic elegance of her boudoir. But what chiefly, indeed almost solely, drew her attention, was the aspect of Aylmer himself.

He was pale as death, anxious, and absorbed, and hung over the furnace as if it depended upon his utmost watchfulness whether the liquid, which it was distilling, should be the draught of immortal happiness or misery. How different from the sanguine and joyous mien that he had assumed for Georgiana's encouragement!

"Carefully now, Aminadab! Carefully, thou human machine! Carefully, thou man of clay!" muttered Aylmer, more to himself than his assistant. "Now, if there be a thought too much or too little, it is all over!"

"Hoh! hoh!" mumbled Aminadab—"look, master, look!"

Aylmer raised his eyes hastily, and at first reddened, then grew paler than ever, on beholding Georgiana. He rushed towards her, and seized her arm with a gripe that left the print of his fingers upon it.

"Why did you come hither? Have you no trust in your husband?" cried he impetuously. "Would you throw the blight of that fatal birth-mark over my labors? It is not well done. Go, prying woman, go!"

"Nay, Aylmer," said Georgiana, with the firmness of which she possessed no stinted endowment, "it is not you that have a right to complain. You mistrust your wife! You have concealed the anxiety with which you watch the development of this experiment. Think not so unworthily of me, my husband! Tell me all the risk we run; and fear not that I shall shrink, for my share in it is far less than your own!"

"No, no, Georgiana!" said Aylmer impatiently, "it must not be."

"I submit," replied she calmly. "And, Aylmer, I shall quaff whatever draught you bring me; but it will be on the same principle that would induce me to take a dose of poison, if offered by your hand."

"My noble wife," said Aylmer, deeply moved, "I knew not the height and depth of your nature, until now. Nothing shall be concealed. Know, then, that this Crimson Hand, superficial as it seems, has clutched its grasp into your being, with a strength of which I had no previous conception. I have already administered agents powerful enough to do aught except to change your entire physical system. Only one thing remains to be tried. If that fail us, we are ruined!"

"Why did you hesitate to tell me this?" asked she.

"Because, Georgiana," said Aylmer, in a low voice, "there is danger!"

"Danger? There is but one danger—that this horrible stigma shall be left upon my cheek!" cried Georgiana. "Remove it! remove it!—whatever be the cost—or we shall both go mad!"

"Heaven knows, your words are too true," said Aylmer, sadly. "And now, dearest, return to your boudoir. In a little while, all will be tested."

He conducted her back, and took leave of her with a solemn tenderness, which spoke far more than his words how much was now at stake. After his departure, Georgiana became wrapt in musings. She considered the character of Aylmer, and did it completer justice than at any previous moment. Her heart exulted, while it trembled, at his honorable love, so pure and lofty that it would accept nothing less than perfection, nor miserably make itself contented with an earthlier nature than he had dreamed of. She felt how much more precious was such a sentiment, than that meaner kind which would have borne with the imperfection for her sake, and have been guilty of treason to holy love, by degrading its perfect idea to the level of the actual. And, with her whole spirit, she prayed, that, for a single moment, she might satisfy his highest and deepest conception. Longer than one moment, she well knew, it could not be; for his spirit was ever on the march—ever ascending—and each instant required something that was beyond the scope of the instant before.

The sound of her husband's footsteps aroused her. He bore a crystal goblet, containing a liquor colorless as water, but bright enough to be the draught of immortality. Aylmer was pale; but it seemed rather the consequence of a highly wrought state of mind, and tension of spirit, than of fear or doubt.

"The concoction of the draught has been perfect," said he, in answer to Georgiana's look. "Unless all my science have deceived me, it cannot fail."

"Save on your account, my dearest Aylmer," observed his wife, "I might wish to put off this birth-mark of mortality by relinquishing mortality itself, in preference to any other mode. Life is but a sad possession of those who have attained precisely the degree of moral advancement at which I stand. Were I weaker and blinder, it might be happiness. Were I stronger, it might be endured hopefully. But, being what I find myself, methinks I am of all mortals the most fit to die."

"You are fit for heaven without tasting death!" replied her husband. "But why do we speak of dying? The draught cannot fail. Behold its effect upon this plant!"

On the window-seat there stood a geranium, diseased with yellow blotches, which had overspread all its leaves. Aylmer poured a small quantity of the liquid upon the soil in which it grew. In a little time, when the roots of the plant had taken up the moisture, the unsightly blotches began to be extinguished in a living verdure.

"There needed no proof," said Georgiana, quietly. "Give me the goblet. I joyfully stake all upon your word."

"Drink then, thou lofty creature!" exclaimed Aylmer, with fervid admiration. "There is no taint of imperfection on thy spirit. Thy sensible frame, too, shall soon be all perfect!"

She quaffed the liquid, and returned the goblet to his hand.

"It is grateful," said she, with a placid smile. "Methinks it is like water from a heavenly fountain; for it contains I know not what of unobtrusive fragrance and deliciousness. It allays a feverish thirst, that had parched me for many days. Now, dearest, let me sleep. My earthly senses are closing over my spirit, like the leaves round the heart of a rose, at sunset."

She spoke the last words with a gentle reluctance, as if it required almost more energy than she could command to pronounce the faint and lingering syllables. Scarcely had they loitered through her lips, ere she was lost in slumber. Aylmer sat by her side, watching her aspect with the emotions proper to a man, the whole value of whose existence was involved in the process now to be tested. Mingled with this mood, however, was the philosophic investigation, characteristic of the man of science. Not the minutest symptom escaped him. A heightened flush of the cheek—a slight irregularity of breath—a quiver of the eyelid—a hardly perceptible tremor through the frame—such were the details which, as the moments passed, he wrote down in his folio volume. Intense thought had set its stamp upon every previous page of that volume; but the thoughts of years were all concentrated upon the last.

While thus employed, he failed not to gaze often at the fatal Hand, and not without a shudder. Yet once, by a strange and unaccountable impulse, he pressed it with his lips. His spirit recoiled, however, in the very act, and Georgiana, out of the midst of her deep sleep, moved uneasily and murmured, as if in remonstrance. Again, Aylmer resumed his watch. Nor was it without avail. The Crimson Hand, which at first had been strongly visible upon the marble paleness of Georgiana's cheek now grew more faintly outlined. She remained not less pale than ever; but the birth-mark, with every breath that came and went, lost somewhat of its former distinctness. Its presence had been awful; its departure was more awful still. Watch the stain of the rainbow fading out of the sky; and you will know how that mysterious symbol passed away.

"By Heaven, it is well nigh gone!" said Aylmer to himself, in almost irrepressible ecstasy. "I can scarcely trace it now. Success! Success! And now it is like the faintest rose-color. The slightest flush of blood across her cheek would overcome it. But she is so pale!"

He drew aside the window-curtain, and suffered the light of natural day to fall into the room, and rest upon her cheek. At the same time, he heard a gross, hoarse chuckle, which he had long known as his servant Aminadab's expression of delight.

"Ah clod! Ah, earthly mass!" cried Aylmer, laughing in a sort of frenzy. "You have served me well! Matter and Spirit—Earth and Heaven—have both done their part in this! Laugh, thing of senses! You have earned the right to laugh."

These exclamations broke Georgiana's sleep. She slowly unclosed her eyes, and gazed into the mirror, which her husband had arranged for that purpose. A faint smile flitted over her lips, when she recognized how barely perceptible was now that Crimson Hand, which had once blazed forth with such disastrous brilliancy as to scare away all their happiness. But then her eyes sought Aylmer's face, with a trouble and anxiety that he could by no means account for.

"My poor Aylmer!" murmured she.

"Poor? Nay, richest! Happiest! Most favored!" exclaimed he. "My peerless bride, it is successful! You are perfect!"

"My poor Aylmer!" she repeated, with a more than human tenderness. "You have aimed loftily!—you have done nobly! Do not repent, that, with so high and pure a feeling, you have rejected the best that earth could offer. Aylmer—dearest Aylmer—I am dying!"

Alas, it was too true! The fatal Hand had grappled with the mystery of life, and was the bond by which an angelic spirit kept itself in union with a mortal frame. As the last crimson tint of the birth-mark—that sole token of human imperfection—faded from her cheek, the parting breath of the now perfect woman passed into the atmosphere, and her soul, lingering a moment near her husband, took its heavenward flight. Then a hoarse, chuckling laugh was heard again! Thus ever does the gross Fatality of Earth exult in its invariable triumph over the immortal essence, which, in this dim sphere of half-development, demands the completeness of a higher state. Yet, had Aylmer reached a profounder wisdom, he need not thus have flung away the happiness, which would have woven his mortal life of the self-same texture with the celestial. The momentary circumstance was too strong for him; he failed to look beyond the shadowy scope of Time, and living once for all in Eternity, to find the perfect Future in the present.

1843

ETHAN BRAND*

A CHAPTER FROM AN ABORTIVE ROMANCE

Bartram, the lime-burner,[1] a rough, heavy-looking man, begrimed with charcoal, sat watching his kiln, at nightfall, while his little son played at building houses with the scattered fragments of marble; when, on the hill-side below them, they heard a roar of laughter, not mirthful, but slow, and even solemn, like a wind shaking the boughs of the forest.

---

* First published in the *Boston Weekly Museum* in 1850 and included in *The Snow-Image and Other Twice-Told Tales* (1851). As the subtitle and internal evidence suggest, Hawthorne may have intended this story to be part of a longer narrative.

[1] One who burns limestone to extract pure lime, which is used for cement.

"Father, what is that?" asked the little boy, leaving his play, and pressing betwixt his father's knees.

"Oh, some drunken man, I suppose," answered the lime-burner;—"some merry fellow from the bar-room in the village, who dared not laugh loud enough within doors, lest he should blow the roof of the house off. So here he is, shaking his jolly sides, at the foot of the Graylock."[2]

"But father," said the child, more sensitive than the obtuse, middle-aged clown, "he does not laugh like a man that is glad. So the noise frightens me!"

"Don't be a fool, child!" cried his father, gruffly. "You will never make a man, I do believe; there is too much of your mother in you. I have known the rustling of a leaf startle you. Hark! Here comes the merry fellow now. You shall see that there is no harm in him."

Bartram and his little son, while they were talking thus, sat watching the same lime-kiln[3] that had been the scene of Ethan Brand's solitary and meditative life, before he began his search for the Unpardonable Sin. Many years, as we have seen, had now elapsed, since that portentous night when the IDEA was first developed. The kiln, however, on the mountainside, stood unimpaired, and was in nothing changed, since he had thrown his dark thoughts into the intense glow of its furnace, and melted them, as it were, into the one thought that took possession of his life. It was a rude, round, towerlike structure, about twenty feet high, heavily built of rough stones, and with a hillock of earth heaped about the larger part of its circumference; so that blocks and fragments of marble might be drawn by cartloads, and thrown in at the top. There was an opening at the bottom of the tower, like an oven-mouth, but large enough to admit a man in a stooping posture, and provided with a massive iron door. With the smoke and jets of flame issuing from the chinks and crevices of this door, which seemed to give admittance into the hillside, it resembled nothing so much as the private entrance to the infernal regions, which the shepherds of the Delectable Mountains were accustomed to show to pilgrims.[4]

There are many such lime-kilns in that tract of country, for the purpose of burning the white marble which composes a large part of the substance of the hills. Some of them, built years ago, and long deserted, with weeds growing in the vacant round of the interior, which is open to the sky, and grass and wild flowers rooting themselves into the chinks of the stones, look already like relics of antiquity, and may yet be overspread with the lichens of centuries to come. Others, where the lime-burner still feeds his daily and night-long fire, afford points of interest to the wanderer among the hills, who seats himself on a log of wood or a fragment of marble, to hold chat with the solitary man. It is a lonesome, and when the character is inclined to thought, may be an intensely thoughtful occupation; as it proved in the case of Ethan Brand, who had mused to such strange purpose, in days gone by, while the fire in this very kiln was burning.

The man, who now watched the fire, was of a different order, and troubled himself with no thoughts save the very few that were requisite to his business. At frequent intervals he flung back the clashing weight of the iron door, and, turning

[2] The highest mountain in the Berkshires in western Massachusetts.

[3] The preferred pronunciation of the lime-burning furnace is "lime-kill," a foreboding detail in this story.

[4] In *Pilgrim's Progress* (1678, 1684), by John Bunyan (1628–1688), the pilgrims are taken to the top of the Delectable Mountains, from which point they can see the gates of the Celestial City (Heaven) and also the entrance to Hell.

his face from the insufferable glare, thrust in huge logs of oak, or stirred the immense brands with a long pole. Within the furnace, was seen the curling and riotous flames, and the burning marble, almost molten with the intensity of heat; while, without, the reflection of the fire quivered on the dark intricacy of the surrounding forest, and showed, in the foreground, a bright and ruddy little picture of the hut, the spring beside its door, the athletic and coal-begrimed figure of the lime-burner, and the half-frightened child, shrinking into the protection of his father's shadow. And when, again, the iron door was closed, then re-appeared the tender light of the half-full moon, which vainly strove to trace out the indistinct shapes of the neighboring mountains; and, in the upper sky, there was a flitting congregation of clouds, still faintly tinged with the rosy sunset, though, thus far down into the valley, the sunshine had vanished long and long ago.

The little boy now crept still closer to his father, as footsteps were heard ascending the hill-side, and a human form thrust aside the bushes that clustered beneath the trees.

"Halloo! who is it?" cried the lime-burner, vexed at his son's timidity, yet half-infected by it. "Come forward, and show yourself, like a man; or I'll fling this chunk of marble at your head!"

"You offer me a rough welcome," said a gloomy voice, as the unknown man drew nigh. "Yet I neither claim nor desire a kinder one, even at my own fireside."

To obtain a distincter view, Bartram threw open the iron door of the kiln, whence immediately issued a gush of fierce light, that smote full upon the stranger's face and figure. To a careless eye, there appeared nothing very remarkable in his aspect, which was that of a man in a coarse, brown, country-made suit of clothes, tall and thin, with the staff and heavy shoes of a wayfarer. As he advanced, he fixed his eyes, which were very bright, intently upon the brightness of the furnace, as if he beheld, or expected to behold, some object worthy of note within it.

"Good evening, stranger," said the lime-burner, "whence come you, so late in the day?"

"I come from my search," answered the wayfarer; "for, at last, it is finished."

"Drunk, or crazy!" muttered Bartram to himself. "I shall have trouble with the fellow. The sooner I drive him away, the better."

The little boy, all in a tremble, whispered to his father, and begged him to shut the door of the kiln, so that there might not be so much light; for that there was something in the man's face which he was afraid to look at, yet could not look away from. And, indeed, even the lime-burner's dull and torpid sense began to be impressed by an indescribable something in that thin, rugged, thoughtful visage, with the grizzled hair hanging wildly about it, and those deeply sunken eyes, which gleamed like fires within the entrance of a mysterious cavern. But, as he closed the door, the stranger turned towards him, and spoke in a quiet, familiar way, that made Bartram feel as if he were a sane and sensible man, after all.

"Your task draws to an end, I see," said he. "This marble has already been burning three days. A few hours more will convert the stone to lime."

"Why, who are you?" exclaimed the lime-burner. "You seem as well acquainted with my business as I myself."

"And well I may be," said the stranger, "for I followed the same craft, many a long year and here, too, on this very spot. But you are a new comer to these parts. Did you never hear of Ethan Brand?"

"The man that went in search of the Unpardonable Sin?" asked Bartram, with a laugh.

"The same," answered the stranger. "He has found what he sought, and therefore he comes back again."

"What! then you are Ethan Brand, himself?" cried the lime-burner in amazement. "I am a new comer here, as you say; and they call it eighteen years since you left the foot of Graylock. But, I can tell you, the good folks still talk about Ethan Brand, in the village yonder, and what a strange errand took him away from his lime-kiln. Well, and so you have found the Unpardonable Sin?"

"Even so!" said the stranger, calmly.

"If the question is a fair one," proceeded Bartram, "where might it be?"

Ethan Brand laid his finger on his own heart. "Here!" replied he.

And then, without mirth in his countenance, but as if moved by an involuntary recognition of the infinite absurdity of seeking throughout the world for what was the closest of all things to himself, and looking into every heart, save his own, for what was hidden in no other breast, he broke into a laugh of scorn. It was the same slow, heavy laugh, that had almost appalled the lime-burner, when it heralded the wayfarer's approach.

The solitary mountain-side was made dismal by it. Laughter, when out of place, mistimed, or bursting forth from a disordered state of feeling, may be the most terrible modulation of the human voice. The laughter of one asleep, even if it be a little child—the madman's laugh—the wild, screaming laugh of a born idiot, are sounds that we sometimes tremble to hear, and would always willingly forget. Poets have imagined no utterance of fiends or hobgoblins so fearfully appropriate as a laugh. And even the obtuse lime-burner felt his nerves shaken, as this strange man looked inward at his own heart, and burst into laughter that rolled away into the night, and was indistinctly reverberated among the hills.

"Joe," said he to his little son, "scamper down to the tavern in the village, and tell the jolly fellows there that Ethan Brand has come back, and that he has found the Unpardonable Sin!"

The boy darted away on his errand, to which Ethan Brand made no objection, nor seemed hardly to notice it. He sat on a log of wood, looking steadfastly at the iron door of the kiln. When the child was out of sight, and his swift and light footsteps ceased to be heard, treading first on the fallen leaves, and then on the rocky mountain-path, the lime-burner began to regret his departure. He felt that the little fellow's presence had been a barrier between his guest and himself, and that he must now deal, heart to heart, with a man who, on his own confession, had committed the only crime for which Heaven could afford no mercy. That crime, in its indistinct blackness, seemed to overshadow him. The lime-burner's own sins rose up within him, and made his memory riotous with a throng of evil shapes that asserted their kindred with the Master Sin, whatever it might be, which it was within the scope of man's corrupted nature to conceive and cherish. They were all of one family; they went to and fro between his breast and Ethan Brand's, and carried dark greetings from one to the other.

Then Bartram remembered the stories which had grown traditionary in reference to this strange man, who had come upon him like a shadow of the night, and was making himself at home in his old place, after so long absence that the dead people, dead and buried for years, would have had more right to be at home, in any familiar spot, than he. Ethan Brand, it was said, had conversed with Satan himself, in the lurid blaze of this very kiln. The legend had been matter of mirth heretofore, but looked grisly now. According to this tale, before Ethan Brand departed on his search, he had been accustomed to evoke a fiend from the hot furnace of the lime-kiln, night after night, in order to confer with him about the Unpardonable Sin; the Man and the Fiend each laboring to frame the image of some mode of guilt, which could neither be atoned for, nor forgiven. And, with the first gleam of light upon the mountain-top, the fiend crept in at the iron door, there to abide in the intensest element of fire, until again summoned forth to share in the dreadful task of extending man's possible guilt beyond the scope of Heaven's else infinite mercy.

While the lime-burner was struggling with the horror of these thoughts, Ethan Brand rose from the log and flung open the door of the kiln. The action was in such accordance with the idea in Bartram's mind, that he almost expected to see the Evil One issue forth, red-hot from the raging furnace.

"Hold, hold!" cried he, with a tremulous attempt to laugh; for he was ashamed of his fears, although they overmastered him. "Don't, for mercy's sake, bring out your devil now!"

"Man!" sternly replied Ethan Brand, "what need have I of the devil? I have left him behind me on my track. It is with such half-way sinners as you that he busies himself. Fear not, because I open the door. I do but act by old custom, and am going to trim your fire, like a lime-burner, as I was once."

He stirred the vast coals, thrust in more wood, and bent forward to gaze into the hollow prison-house of the fire, regardless of the fierce glow that reddened upon his face. The lime-burner sat watching him, and half suspected his strange guest of a purpose, if not to evoke a fiend, at least to plunge bodily into the flames, and thus vanish from the sight of man. Ethan Brand, however, drew quietly back, and closed the door of the kiln.

"I have looked," said he, "into many a human heart that was seven times hotter with sinful passions than yonder furnace is with fire. But I found not there what I sought. No; not the Unpardonable Sin!"

"What is the Unpardonable Sin?" asked the lime-burner; and then he shrank farther from his companion, trembling lest his question should be answered.

"It is a sin that grew within my own breast," replied Ethan Brand, standing erect, with the pride that distinguishes all enthusiasts of his stamp. "A sin that grew nowhere else! The sin of an intellect that triumphed over the sense of brotherhood with man, and reverence for God, and sacrificed everything to its own mighty claims! The only sin that deserves a recompense of immortal agony! Freely, were it to do again, would I incur the guilt. Unshrinkingly, I accept the retribution!"

"The man's head is turned," muttered the lime-burner to himself. "He may be a sinner, like the rest of us—nothing more likely—but I'll be sworn, he is a madman, too."

Nevertheless, he felt uncomfortable at his situation, alone with Ethan Brand on the wild mountain-side, and was right glad to hear the rough murmur of tongues, and the footsteps of what seemed a pretty numerous party, stumbling over the stones, and rustling through the underbrush. Soon appeared the whole lazy regiment that was wont to infest the village tavern, comprehending three or four individuals who had drunk flip[5] beside the bar-room fire, through all the winters, and

---

[5] A spicy, sweetened ale or beer.

smoked their pipes beneath the stoop, through all the summers since Ethan Brand's departure. Laughing boisterously, and mingling all their voices together in unceremonious talk, they now burst into the moonshine and narrow streaks of fire-light that illuminated the open space before the lime-kiln. Bartram set the door ajar again, flooding the spot with light, that the whole company might get a fair view of Ethan Brand, and he of them.

There, among other old acquaintances, was a once ubiquitous man, now almost extinct, but who we were formerly sure to encounter at the hotel of every thriving village throughout the country. It was the stage-agent. The present specimen of the genus was a wilted and smoke-dried man, wrinkled and red-nosed, in a smartly cut, brown, bob-tailed coat, with brass buttons, who, for a length of time unknown, had kept his desk and corner in the bar-room, and was still puffing what seemed to be the same cigar that he had lighted twenty years before. He had great fame as a dry joker, though, perhaps, less on account of any intrinsic humor, than from a certain flavor of brandy-toddy and tobacco-smoke, which impregnated all his ideas and expressions, as well as his person. Another well-remembered, though strangely-altered face was that of Lawyer Giles, as people still called him in courtesy; an elderly ragamuffin, in his soiled shirt-sleeves and tow-cloth[6] trowsers. This poor fellow had been an attorney, in what he called his better days, a sharp practitioner, and in great vogue among the village litigants; but flip, and sling, and toddy,[7] and cocktails, imbibed at all hours, morning, noon, and night, had caused him to slide from intellectual, to various kinds and degrees of bodily labor, till, at last, to adopt his own phrase, he slid into a soap-vat. In other words, Giles was now a soap-boiler, in a small way. He had come to be but the fragment of a human being, a part of one foot having been chopped off by an axe, and an entire hand torn away by the devilish gripe of a steam-engine. Yet, though the corporeal hand was gone, a spiritual member remained; for, stretching forth the stump, Giles steadfastly averred, that he felt an invisible thumb and fingers, with as vivid a sensation as before the real ones were amputated. A maimed and miserable wretch he was; but one, nevertheless, whom the world could not trample on, and had no right to scorn, either in this or any previous stage of his misfortunes, since he had still kept up the courage and spirit of a man, asked nothing in charity, and, with his one hand—and that the left one—fought a stern battle against want and hostile circumstances.

Among the throng, too, came another personage, who, with certain points of similarity to Lawyer Giles, had more of difference. It was the village Doctor, a man of some fifty years, whom, at an earlier period of his life, we should have introduced as paying a professional visit to Ethan Brand, during the latter's supposed insanity. He was now a purple-visaged, rude, and brutal, yet half-gentlemanly figure, with something wild, ruined, and desperate in his talk, and in all the details of his gesture and manners. Brandy possessed this man like an evil spirit, and made him as surly and savage as a wild beast, and as miserable as a lost soul; but there was supposed to be in him such wonderful skill, such native gifts of healing, beyond any which medical science could impart, that society caught hold of him, and would not let him sink out of its reach. So, swaying to and fro upon his horse, and grumbling thick accents at the bedside, he visited all the sick chambers for miles about among the mountain towns; and sometimes raised a dying man, as it were, by miracle, or, quite as often, no doubt, sent his patient to a grave

---

[6] Coarse cloth.   [7] Gin and water mixed with lemon and sugar; and rum and sweetened hot water.

that was dug many a year too soon. The Doctor had an everlasting pipe in his mouth, and, as somebody said, in allusion to his habit of swearing, it was always alight with hell-fire.

These three worthies pressed forward, and greeted Ethan Brand, each after his own fashion, earnestly inviting him to partake of the contents of a certain black bottle; in which, as they averred, he would find something far better worth seeking for, than the Unpardonable Sin. No mind, which has wrought itself, by intense and solitary meditation, into a high state of enthusiasm, can endure the kind of contact with low and vulgar modes of thought and feeling, to which Ethan Brand was now subjected. It made him doubt—and, strange to say, it was a painful doubt—whether he had indeed found the Unpardonable Sin, and found it within himself. The whole question on which he had exhausted life, and more than life, looked like a delusion.

"Leave me," he said bitterly, "ye brute beasts, that have made yourselves so, shrivelling up you souls with fiery liquors! I have done with you. Years and years ago, I groped into your hearts and found nothing there for my purpose. Get ye gone!"

"Why you uncivil scoundrel," cried the Fierce Doctor, "is that the way you respond to the kindness of your best friends? Then let me tell you the truth. You have no more found the Unpardonable Sin than yonder boy Joe has. You are but a crazy fellow, and the fit companion of old Humphrey, here!"

He pointed to an old man, shabbily dressed, with long white hair, thin visage, and unsteady eyes. For some years past, this aged person had been wandering about among the hills, inquiring of all travellers whom he met, for his daughter. The girl, it seemed, had gone off with a company of circus-performers; and, occasionally, tidings of her came to the village, and fine stories were told of her glittering appearance, as she rode on horseback in the ring, or performed marvellous feats on the tight-rope.

The white-haired father now approached Ethan Brand, and gazed unsteadily into his face.

"They tell me you have been all over the earth," said he, wringing his hands with earnestness. "You must have seen my daughter; for she makes a grand figure in the world, and everybody goes to see her. Did she send any word to her old father, or say when she is coming back?"

Ethan Brand's eye quailed beneath the old man's. That daughter, from whom he so earnestly desired a word of greeting, was the Esther of our tale;[8] the very girl whom, with such cold and remorseless purpose, Ethan Brand had made the subject of a psychological experiment, and wasted, absorbed, and perhaps annihilated her soul, in the process.

"Yes," murmured he, turning away from the hoary wanderer; "it is no delusion. There is an Unpardonable Sin!"

While these things were passing, a merry scene was going forward in the area of cheerful light, besides the spring and before the door of the hut. A number of the youth of the village, young men and girls, had hurried up the hill-side, impelled by curiosity to see Ethan Brand, the hero of so many a legend familiar to their childhood. Finding nothing, however, very remarkable in his aspect—nothing but a sunburnt wayfarer, in plain garb and dusty shoes, who sat looking into

---

[8] Because there is no Esther in this tale, this must be a loose end suggestive of Hawthorne's intention to tell a fuller story of Ethan Brand.

the fire, as if he fancied pictures among the coals—these young people speedily grew tired of observing him. As it happened, there was other amusement at hand. An old German Jew, travelling with a diorama[9] on his back, was passing down the mountain-road towards the village, just as the party turned aside from it; and, in hopes of eking out the profits of the day, the showman had kept them company to the lime-kiln.

"Come, old Dutchman," cried one of the young men, "let us see your pictures, if you can swear they are worth looking at!"

"Oh, yes, Captain," answered the Jew—whether as a matter of courtesy or craft, he styled everybody Captain—"I shall show you, indeed, some very superb pictures!"

So, placing his box in a proper position, he invited the young men and girls to look through the glass orifices of the machine, and proceeded to exhibit a series of the most outrageous scratchings and daubings, as specimens of the fine arts, that ever an itinerant showman had the face to impose upon his circle of spectators. The pictures were worn out, moreover, tattered, full of cracks and wrinkles, dingy with tobacco-smoke, and otherwise in most pitiable condition. Some purported to be cities, public edifices, and ruined castles, in Europe; others represented Napoleon's battles, and Nelson's[10] sea-fights; and in the midst of these would be seen a gigantic, brown, hairy hand—which might have been mistaken for the Hand of Destiny, though, in truth, it was only the showman's—pointing its forefinger to various scenes of the conflict, while its owner gave historical illustrations. When, with much merriment at its abominable deficiency of merit, the exhibition was concluded, the German bade little Joe put his head into the box. Viewed through the magnifying glasses, the boy's round, rosy visage assumed the strangest imaginable aspect of an immense, Titanic[11] child, the mouth grinning broadly, and the eyes, and every other feature, overflowing with fun at the joke. Suddenly, however, that merry face turned pale, and its expression changed to horror; for this easily impressed and excitable child had become sensible that the eye of Ethan Brand was fixed upon him through the glass.

"You make the little man to be afraid, Captain," said the German Jew, turning up the dark and strong outline of his visage, from his stooping posture. "But, look again; and, by chance, I shall cause you to see somewhat that is very fine, upon my word!"

Ethan Brand gazed into the box for an instant, and then starting back, looked fixedly at the German. What had he seen? Nothing, apparently; for a curious youth, who had peeped in, almost at the same moment, beheld only a vacant space of canvass.

"I remember you now," muttered Ethan Brand to the showman.

"Ah, Captain," whispered the Jew of Nuremberg, with a dark smile, "I find it to be a heavy matter in my show-box—this Unpardonable Sin! By my faith, Captain, it has wearied my shoulders, this long day, to carry it over the mountain."

"Peace!" answered Ethan Brand, sternly, "or get thee into the furnace yonder!"

The Jew's exhibition had scarcely concluded, when a great, elderly dog—who seemed to be his own master, as no person in the company laid claim to him—saw

---

[9] A box with a lens for viewing inserted pictures and paintings.
[10] Horatio Nelson (1758–1805), a British admiral whose greatest victory was a defeat over the combined fleets of France and Spain at Trafalgar in 1805.
[11] According to Greek myth, the Titans were a race of giant gods.

fit to render himself the object of public notice. Hitherto, he had shown himself a very quiet, well-disposed old dog, going round from one to another, and, by way of being sociable, offering his rough head to be patted by any kindly hand that would take so much trouble. But, now, all of a sudden, this grave and venerable quadruped, of his own mere notion, and without the slightest suggestion from anybody else, began to run round after his tail, which, to heighten the absurdity of the proceeding, was a great deal shorter than it should have been. Never was seen such headlong eagerness in pursuit of an object that could not possibly be attained; never was heard such a tremendous outbreak of growling, snarling, barking, and snapping—as if one end of the ridiculous brute's body were at deadly and most unforgivable enmity with the other. Faster and faster, roundabout went the cur; and faster and still faster fled the unapproachable brevity of his tail; and louder and fiercer grew his yells of rage and animosity; until, utterly exhausted, and as far from the goal as ever, the foolish old dog ceased his performance as suddenly as he had begun it. The next moment, he was as mild, quiet, sensible, and respectable in his deportment, as when he first scraped acquaintance with the company.

As may be supposed, the exhibition was greeted with universal laughter, clapping of hands, and shouts of encore; to which the canine performer responded by wagging all that there was to wag of his tail, but appeared totally unable to repeat his very successful effort to amuse the spectators.

Meanwhile, Ethan Brand had resumed his seat upon the log; and moved, it might be, by a perception of some remote analogy between his own case and that of this self-pursuing cur, he broke into the awful laugh, which, more than any other token, expressed the condition of his inward being. From that moment, the merriment of the party was at an end; they stood aghast, dreading lest the inauspicious sound should be reverberated around the horizon, and that mountain would thunder it to mountain, and so the horror be prolonged upon their ears. Then, whispering one to another, that it was late—that the moon was almost down—that the August night was growing chill—they hurried homeward, leaving the lime-burner and little Joe to deal as they might with their unwelcome guest. Save for these three human beings, the open space on the hill-side was a solitude, set in a vast gloom of forest. Beyond that darksome verge, the fire-light glimmered on the stately trunks and almost black foliage of pines, intermixed with the lighter verdure of sapling oaks, maples, and poplars, while, here and there, lay the gigantic corpses of dead trees, decaying on the leaf-strewn soil. And it seemed to little Joe—a timorous and imaginative child—that the silent forest was holding its breath, until some fearful thing should happen.

Ethan Brand thrust more wood into the fire, and closed the door of the kiln; then looking over his shoulder at the lime-burner and his son, he bade, rather than advised, them to retire to rest.

"For myself I cannot sleep," said he, "I have matters that it concerns me to meditate upon. I will watch the fire, as I used to do in the old time."

"And call the devil out of the furnace to keep you company, I suppose," muttered Bartram, who had been making intimate acquaintance with the black bottle above-mentioned. "But watch, if you like, and call as many devils as you like! For my part, I shall be all the better for a snooze. Come, Joe!"

As the boy followed his father into the hut, he looked back to the wayfarer, and the tears came into his eyes; for his tender spirit had an intuition of the bleak and terrible loneliness in which this man had enveloped himself.

When they had gone, Ethan Brand sat listening to the crackling of the kindled wood, and looking at the little spirts of fire that issued through the chinks of the door. These trifles, however, once so familiar, had but the slightest hold of his attention; while deep within his mind, he was reviewing the gradual, but marvellous change, that had been wrought upon him by the search to which he had devoted himself. He remembered how the night-dew had fallen upon him—how the dark forest had whispered to him—how the stars had gleamed upon him—a simple and loving man, watching his fire in the years gone by, and ever musing as it burned. He remembered with what tenderness, with what love and sympathy for mankind, and what pity for human guilt and woe, he had first begun to contemplate those ideas which afterwards became the inspiration of his life; with what reverence he had then looked into the heart of man, viewing it as a temple originally divine, and however desecrated, still to be held sacred by a brother; with what awful fear he had deprecated the success of his pursuit, and prayed that the Unpardonable Sin might never be revealed to him. Then ensued that vast intellectual development, which, in its progress, disturbed the counterpoise between his mind and heart. The Idea that possessed his life had operated as a means of education; it had gone on cultivating his powers to the highest point of which they were susceptible; it had raised him from the level of an unlettered laborer, to stand on a star-light eminence, whither the philosophers of the earth, laden with the lore of universities, might vainly strive to clamber after him. So much for the intellect! But where was the heart? That, indeed, had withered—had contracted—had hardened—had perished! It had ceased to partake of the universal throb. He had lost his hold of the magnetic chain of humanity. He was no longer a brother-man, opening the chambers or the dungeons of our common nature by the key of holy sympathy, which gave him a right to share in all its secrets; he was now a cold observer, looking on mankind as the subject of his experiment, and, at length, converting man and woman to be his puppets, and pulling the wires that moved them to such degrees of crime as were demanded for his study.

Thus Ethan Brand became a fiend. He began to be so from the moment that his moral nature had ceased to keep the pace of improvement with his intellect. And now, as his highest effort and inevitable development—as the bright and gorgeous flower, and rich, delicious fruit of his life's labor—he had produced the Unpardonable Sin!

"What more have I to seek? What more to achieve?" said Ethan Brand to himself. "My task is done, and well done!"

Starting from the log with a certain alacrity in his gait, and ascending the hillock of earth that was raised against the stone circumference of the lime-kiln, he thus reached the top of the structure. It was a space of perhaps ten feet across, from edge to edge, presenting a view of the upper surface of the immense mass of broken marble with which the kiln was heaped. All these innumerable blocks and fragments of marble were red-hot, and vividly on fire, sending up great spouts of blue flame, which quivered aloft and danced madly, as within a magic circle, and sank and rose again, with continual and multitudinous activity. As the lonely man bent forward over this terrible body of fire, the blasting heat smote up against his person with a breath that, it might be supposed, would have scorched and . shrivelled him up in a moment.

Ethan Brand stood erect and raised his arms on high. The blue flames played upon his face, and imparted the wild and ghastly light which alone could have suited its expression; it was that of a fiend on the verge of plunging into his gulf of intensest torment.

"Oh, Mother Earth," cried he, "who art no more my Mother, and into whose bosom this frame shall never be resolved! Oh, mankind, whose brotherhood I have cast off, and trampled thy great heart beneath my feet! Oh, stars of Heaven, that shone on me of old, as if to light me onward and upward!—farewell all, and forever! Come, deadly element of Fire—henceforth my familiar friend! Embrace me as I do thee!"

That night the sound of a fearful peal of laughter rolled heavily through the sleep of the lime-burner and his little son; dim shapes of horror and anguish haunted their dreams, and seemed still present in the rude hovel when they opened their eyes to the daylight.

"Up, boy, up!" cried the lime-burner, starting about him. "Thank Heaven, the night is gone at last; and rather than pass such another, I would watch my lime-kiln, wide awake, for a twelvemonth. This Ethan Brand, with his humbug of an Unpardonable Sin, has done me no such mighty favor in taking my place!"

He issued from the hut, followed by little Joe, who kept fast hold of his father's hand. The early sunshine was already pouring its gold upon the mountain-tops, and though the valleys were still in shadow, they smiled cheerfully in the promise of the bright day that was hastening onward. The village, completely shut in by hills, which swelled away gently about it, looked as if it had rested peacefully in the hollow the great hand of Providence. Every dwelling was distinctly visible; the little spires of the two churches pointed upward, and caught a fore-glimmering of brightness from the sun-gilt skies upon their gilded weathercocks. The tavern was astir, and the figure of the old, smoke-dried stage-agent, cigar in mouth, was seen beneath the stoop. Old Graylock was glorified with a golden cloud upon his head. Scattered, likewise, over the breasts of the surrounding mountains, there were heaps of hoary mist, in fantastic shapes, some of them far down into the valley, others high up towards the summits, and still others, of the same family of mist or cloud, hovering in the gold radiance of the upper atmosphere. Stepping from one to another of the clouds that rested on the hills, and thence to the loftier brotherhood that sailed in air, it seemed almost as if a mortal man might thus ascend into the heavenly regions. Earth was so mingled with sky that it was a day-dream to look at it.

To supply that charm of the familiar and homely, which Nature so readily adopts into a scene like this, the stagecoach was rattling down the mountain-road, and the driver sounded his horn; while echo[12] caught up the notes and intertwined them into a rich, and varied, and elaborate harmony, of which the original performer could lay claim to little share. The great hills played a concert among themselves, each contributing a strain of airy sweetness.

Little Joe's face brightened at once.

"Dear father," cried he, skipping cheerily to and fro, "that strange man is gone, and the sky and the mountains all seem glad of it!"

"Yes," growled the lime-burner with an oath, "but he has let the fire go down, and no thanks to him, if five hundred bushels of lime are not spoilt. If I catch the fellow hereabouts again I shall feel like tossing him into the furnace!"

---

[12] According to Greek myth, the nymph Echo was loved by Pan (the god of sheep and shepherds); when she fled from him she was changed into a voice that could only repeat the last words spoken to her.

With his long pole in his hand he ascended to the top of the kiln. After a moment's pause he called to his son.

"Come up here, Joe!" said he.

So little Joe ran up the hillock and stood by his father's side. The marble was all burnt into perfect, snow-white lime. But on its surface, in the midst of the circle—snow-white too, and thoroughly converted into lime—lay a human skeleton, in the attitude of a person who, after long toil, lies down to long repose. Within the ribs—strange to say—was the shape of a human heart.

"Was the fellow's heart made of marble?" cried Bartram, in some perplexity at this phenomenon. "At any rate, it is burnt into what looks like special good lime; and, taking all the bones together, my kiln is half a bushel the richer for him."

So saying, the rude lime-burner lifted his pole, and letting it fall upon the skeleton, the relics of Ethan Brand were crumbled into fragments.

1850

from *THE HOUSE OF THE SEVEN GABLES*

PREFACE*

When a writer calls his work a Romance, it need hardly be observed that he wishes to claim a certain latitude, both as to its fashion and material, which he would not have felt himself entitled to assume, had he professed to be writing a Novel. The latter form of composition is presumed to aim at a very minute fidelity, not merely to the possible, but to the probable and ordinary course of man's experience. The former—while, as a work of art, it must rigidly subject itself to laws, and while it sins unpardonably, so far as it may swerve aside from the truth of the human heart—has fairly a right to present that truth under circumstances, to a great extent, of the writer's own choosing or creation. If he think fit, also, he may so manage his atmospherical medium as to bring out or mellow the lights and deepen and enrich the shadows of the picture. He will be wise, no doubt, to make a very moderate use of the privileges here stated, and, especially, to mingle the Marvellous rather as a slight, delicate, and evanescent flavor, than as any portion of the actual substance of the dish offered to the Public. He can hardly be said, however, to commit a literary crime, even if he disregard this caution.

In the present work, the Author has proposed to himself (but with what success, fortunately, it is not for him to judge) to keep undeviatingly within his immunities. The point of view in which this Tale comes under the Romantic definition, lies in the attempt to connect a by-gone time with the very Present that is flitting away from us. It is a Legend, prolonging itself, from an epoch now gray in the distance, down into our own broad daylight, and bringing along with it some of its legendary mist, which the Reader, according to his pleasure, may either

---

* In his preface to *The House of the Seven Gables* (1851), Hawthorne makes a distinction between the "novel" and the "romance," which was common at the time. It amounts to a rationale for his type of fiction.

disregard, or allow it to float almost imperceptibly about the characters and events, for the sake of a picturesque effect. The narrative, it may be, is woven of so humble a texture as to require this advantage, and, at the same time, to render it the more difficult of attainment.

Many writers lay very great stress upon some definite moral purpose, at which they profess to aim their works. Not to be deficient, in this particular, the Author has provided himself with a moral;—the truth, namely, that the wrong-doing of one generation lives into the successive ones, and, divesting itself of every temporary advantage, becomes a pure and uncontrollable mischief;—and he would feel it a singular gratification, if this Romance might effectually convince mankind (or, indeed, any one man) of the folly of tumbling down an avalanche of ill-gotten gold, or real estate, on the heads of an unfortunate posterity, thereby to maim and crush them, until the accumulated mass shall be scattered abroad in its original atoms. In good faith, however, he is not sufficiently imaginative to flatter himself with the slightest hope of this kind. When romances do really teach anything, or produce any effective operation, it is usually through a far more subtle process than the ostensible one. The Author has considered it hardly worth his while, therefore, relentlessly to impale the story with its moral, as with an iron rod—or rather, as by sticking a pin through a butterfly—thus at once depriving it of life, and causing it to stiffen in an ungainly and unnatural attitude. A high truth, indeed, fairly, finely, and skilfully wrought out, brightening at every step, and crowning the final development of a work of fiction, may add an artistic glory, but is never any truer, and seldom any more evident, at the last page than at the first.

The Reader may perhaps choose to assign an actual locality to the imaginary events of this narrative. If permitted by the historical connection, (which, though slight, was essential to his plan,) the Author would very willingly have avoided anything of this nature. Not to speak of other objections, it exposes the Romance to an inflexible and exceedingly dangerous species of criticism, by bringing his fancy-pictures almost into positive contact with the realities of the moment. It has been no part of his object, however, to describe local manners, nor in any way to meddle with the characteristics of a community for whom he cherishes a proper respect and a natural regard. He trusts not to be considered as unpardonably offending, by laying out a street that infringes upon nobody's private rights, and appropriating a lot of land which had no visible owner, and building a house, of materials long in use for constructing castles in the air. The personages of the Tale—though they give themselves out to be of ancient stability and considerable prominence—are really of the Author's own making, or, at all events, of his own mixing; their virtues can shed no lustre, nor their defects redound, in the remotest degree, to the discredit of the venerable town[1] of which they profess to be inhabitants. He would be glad, therefore, if—especially in the quarter to which he alludes—the book may be read strictly as a Romance, having a great deal more to do with the clouds overhead, than with any portion of the actual soil of the County of Essex.

Lenox, January 27, 1851.

1851

---

[1] Salem, in Essex County, Massachusetts.

from THE AMERICAN NOTEBOOKS

[*Thoughts on Perfection: Toward "The Birth-Mark"**]

from   OCTOBER 25th, 1836

Those who are very difficult in choosing wives seem as if they would take none of Nature's ready-made works, but want a woman manufactured particularly to their order.

from   OCTOBER 16th, 1837

A person to be in possession of something as perfect as mortal man has a right to demand; he tries to make it better, and ruins it entirely.

A person to spend all his life and splendid talents in trying to achieve something naturally impossible,—as to make a conquest over Nature.

from   JANUARY 4th, 1839

A person to be the death of his beloved in trying to raise her to more than mortal perfection; yet this should be a comfort to him for having aimed so highly and holily.

Herman Melville
(1819–1891)

"Until I was twenty-five," Herman Melville wrote to his friend Nathaniel Hawthorne in 1850, "I had no development at all. From my twenty-fifth year I date my life." Melville had good reason to date his life from 1844, the year he returned without prospects or much formal education from a long stint as a common seaman on several whaling ships and an American man-of-war. During the next sixteen years he published five novels and established his reputation as a promising author; when he wrote to Hawthorne in 1850 Melville was working on his masterpiece, *Moby-Dick* (1851). But the curve of Melville's public career had peaked: *Moby-Dick* was not a popular success, his novel *Pierre* (1852) frustrated critics and public alike, and his obscure satire *The Confidence-Man* (1857) almost went unread. At his death in 1891 Melville was unknown beyond a small group of admirers; not until the Melville revival of the 1920s was his work given the attention it deserves. The shape of Melville's public career—early success, obscurity, posthumous vindica-

---

* Many of Hawthorne's notebook entries consist of ideas for stories. These entries from the 1830s contain his earliest thoughts on the theme of "The Birth-Mark" (1843).

tion—exercises a powerful fascination as a model of tragic authorship, but it is more than matched by the extraordinary drama of his inward development, which continued submerged but unabated through the years of public neglect.

Born in 1819 in New York City, Melville was the third of eight children of Maria Gansevoort and Allan Melvill (the "e" was added in the 1830s). Maria was the only daughter of General Peter Gansevoort, a Revolutionary War hero; Allan's father, Major Thomas Melvill, had taken part in the Boston Tea Party. This patrician ancestry helped shape Melville's life and work. As a child he was considered somewhat backward in development, especially in comparison with his more precocious brother Gansevoort, but his early years seem to have been happy. Melville was eleven when his father, a prosperous importer, was forced into bankruptcy in 1830. The family then moved to Albany, where for a short time their fortunes improved; but the business failed again, and Allan Melvill died in 1832 after suffering a mental and physical breakdown.

The trauma of his father's early death is reflected throughout Melville's fiction in the persistent concern with absent fathers; more immediately, however, it forced Melville to find a career. During the next few years he tried various professions—clerk, farmhand, bookkeeper, schoolmaster—with little pleasure or success. In 1839 he took the decisive step of working as a cabin boy on a packet ship bound for Liverpool; this first taste of a sailor's often brutal life provided material for his fourth novel, *Redburn* (1849). Back in the United States later that year, Melville briefly taught school and made a trip to Illinois, during which he took a steamboat excursion up the Mississippi River (the setting of *The Confidence-Man*). Returning East with no definite prospects, he left New Bedford, Massachusetts, in January 1841 on the *Acushnet,* a whaler bound for the South Pacific. Conditions on the ship proved intolerable: the captain was despotic, whales were scarce, and when the *Acushnet* reached the Marquesas Islands in July 1842, Melville and a shipmate, Richard Tobias Greene, jumped ship, intending to seek refuge with a friendly tribe. By error they made their way to the reputedly cannibalistic Taipis (Typees), with whom Melville remained for a month before escaping on an Australian whaler. Conditions on that ship were no better than those aboard the *Acushnet,* however, and Melville reluctantly joined a rebellion that landed him in a Tahitian prison. Soon released, he spent several months beachcombing before shipping out on the homeward-bound frigate *United States*. He was discharged from the navy in October 1844 with a valuable store of tales and a permanently altered perspective on western culture.

Encouraged by family and friends, Melville began writing about his South Pacific adventures, supplementing personal experience with information from secondary sources—a method of composition he used throughout his career. Published in England in 1846, *Typee: Or, a Peep at Polynesian Life* was an immediate success, although many readers were offended by Melville's critique of the hypocrisy and ethnocentric cruelty of Christian missionaries in the South Pacific. Reaction was so strong that to Melville's disgust an expurgated edition was published in the United States the following year. The novel *Omoo: A Narrative of Adventures in the South Seas* (1847) capitalized on *Typee*'s success by portraying Melville's adventures in Tahiti. By the time he began *Mardi* in 1848, however, Melville was beginning to feel the constraints of the picaresque travel narrative; because some critics had doubted the factual basis of his two novels, he proposed to write "a romance of Polynesian adventure." *Mardi* (1849) opens as a straightforward adventure tale but soon enters uncharted seas as the protagonist, Taji, voyages through an imaginary archipelago in search of an illusive maiden. At once allegory, satire, and philosophical speculation, *Mardi* reflects Melville's readings in Edmund Spenser, Dante, François Rabelais, and Thomas Browne and his own increasing interest in what he called "the great art of Telling the Truth."

A watercolor drawing of the whaling ship Acushnet, *on which Herman Melville sailed to the South Seas in 1841, by Henry Johnson (1847).*

Mardi was neither the critical success that Melville had expected nor the commercial success his circumstances demanded. In 1847 he had married Elizabeth Shaw, daughter of Lemuel Shaw (an influential judge who had been a good friend of Melville's father), and the first of their four children was born in 1849. To support his family Melville pushed himself to write two novels in rapid succession: *Redburn,* a tale of initiation based on his voyage to Liverpool, and *White-Jacket* (1850), about life on a man-of-war. Both offered nautical adventures of the sort Melville's audience had come to expect, and although they were popular successes Melville considered them hack work, written "to buy some tobacco with." This judgment is certainly too severe; both novels combine psychological observation and social commentary in ways that anticipate Melville's best work.

After Melville returned from a trip to England to arrange advantageous copyright terms for *White-Jacket,* he began a new book about the whaling industry. *Moby-Dick* bears the special impress of his readings in Thomas Carlyle, Johann Wolfgang von Goethe, the Bible, and William Shakespeare; the most formative influence, however, was exercised by Nathaniel Hawthorne. In August 1850 Melville published a buoyant nationalistic review of Hawthorne's *Mosses From an Old Manse* (1846) for the New York *Literary World,* touting the American writer as Shakespeare's equal and claiming him as a fellow traveler toward "the blackness of darkness beyond." The same month the two writers found themselves neighbors, Melville at Arrowhead, the 160-acre farm he had recently purchased near Pittsfield, Massachusetts, and Hawthorne in his little red house just outside nearby Lenox. They soon became friends, although the more demonstrative Melville noted in an 1851 letter to the editor Evert Duyckinck the lack of "plump sphericity" in Hawthorne and suggested a corrective diet of "roast-beef, done rare." Nevertheless, with Hawthorne, Melville could discourse freely about what he called "ontological heroics," and he found the support and inspiration needed to push *Moby-Dick* beyond its initially more conventional design. In his masterpiece Melville balances Captain Ahab's monomaniacal search for vengeance on the white whale with the narrator Ishmael's open-ended voyage for understanding his place as a cosmic orphan—a voyage the attentive reader must also make. Ballasted with facts about whales and whaling, *Moby-Dick* mixes sermons, drama, and dramatic monologues in a work whose dominant characteristics are its driving imaginative energy and linguistic exuberance. The book is dedicated to Hawthorne, "in token of my admiration for his genius."

Hawthorne responded knowingly to *Moby-Dick*, but many reviewers were confused by what an October 1851 London *Athenaeum* called "an ill-compounded mixture of romance and matter-of-fact." Once again, as Melville wrote Hawthorne in 1851, "what I feel most moved to write, that is banned—it will not pay. Yet, altogether, write the *other* way I cannot." Melville nevertheless determined to write his next novel "the other way"; it was going to be "a rural bowl of milk," as he explained to Hawthorne's wife, Sophia. But Melville could not refrain from extending pious formulas to parodic, and destructive, lengths. *Pierre: Or, the Ambiguities* is a disturbing psychological tale that follows the protagonist from gushy innocence to aggressive defiance and finally to death. With its own perverse brilliance, it is perhaps Melville's most personal work. The overwrought, subversive style, however, left many readers confused, offended at the spectacle of sentimental romance transformed to nightmare.

Profoundly disappointed by the reception of *Moby-Dick* and *Pierre,* Melville nevertheless continued to write. When he failed to receive an appointment as U.S. Consul to the Sandwich Islands (Hawaii), he turned to short fiction and published fourteen stories (among them "Bartleby the Scrivener" [1853]) between 1853 and 1856, mostly in *Putnam's* and *Harper's* magazines. The stories did little to reestablish Melville's reputation, even when some were collected in *The Piazza Tales* in 1856. Additionally, Melville wrote the restrained short novel *Israel Potter* about the life of a Revolutionary War soldier; serialized by *Putnam's,* it appeared in book form in 1855. During this period he began work on the last novel to be published during his lifetime, *The Confidence-Man: His Masquerade.* Set on a Mississippi River steamboat that begins its journey on April Fools' Day, this work is a picaresque philosophical and theological excursion that targets the optimistic philosophies of mid-century America. The ambivalent prose and mysterious cast of characters did not satisfy an audience expecting a more intelligible satire on American manners.

The years between 1850 and 1856 had taken a heavy toll on Melville, both physically and psychologically. In October 1856, after selling half his farm and accepting a loan from Judge Shaw, he set out on a voyage to Europe and the Near East in hope of regaining his health. In Liverpool he strolled with Hawthorne (then U.S. consul) and talked, as Hawthorne noted in his journal, "of Providence and futurity, and of everything that lies beyond human ken"—including their disbelief in "a temperance heaven." In mid-November Melville boarded a steamer for the Holy Land, which would provide the background for his long narrative poem *Clarel* (1876), and quickly toured Europe before returning to Liverpool. Back in the United States in May 1857, he tried lecturing on such topics as "Statues in Rome" and "The South Seas" but without much success, and after a voyage to San Francisco in 1860 he moved his family to New York City, where a legacy from Judge Shaw (who died in 1861) soon allowed them to live comfortably. In 1866, at age forty-seven, Melville began working as a customs inspector for the port of New York—a position that he held for almost twenty years. Although inheritances from several relatives eased the Melvilles' financial situation, personal tragedies continued: their oldest son, Malcolm, committed suicide in 1867; the second son, Stanwix, died almost twenty years later in San Francisco after years of unfocused wandering; and one daughter, Frances, felt so bitter toward her father because of his erratic and sometimes violent behavior that she would not speak to him.

The silence of Melville's last twenty-five years, however, is a matter of public rather than of private record: after *The Confidence-Man* Melville turned from prose fiction to the more private genre of poetry. In 1866 *Battle-Pieces*, a collection of poems about the Civil War, was published. In powerful but metrically irregular verse that found no critical acclaim, Melville probed the pain of war and conflated the healing of national wounds with hope for his own renewal. *Clarel*, a dense, eighteen thousand-line philosophical poem on faith and doubt that Melville had published with money provided by his uncle Peter Gansevoort, went virtually unnoticed. Undaunted, Melville published volumes of poetry at his own expense in 1888 and 1891 and at the time of his death had nearly completed *Billy Budd*, his only long prose fiction after *The Confidence-Man*. Although it was published in 1923, an authoritative text of *Billy Budd* was not available until 1962, and in some ways this tale of an innocent sailor's tragic confrontation with authority continues to resist definitive interpretation. Nevertheless, it shows Melville still questing for truth of character and action in a fallen world, still unwilling to rest in easy solutions. At the end of his career Melville remained an exemplary member of what he called the "corps of thought-divers, that have been diving & coming up again with bloodshot eyes since the world began," in an 1849 letter to Duyckinck.

Suggested Readings: *Billy Budd and Other Prose Pieces*, ed. R. W. Weaver, 1924. *Clarel*, ed. W. Bezanson, 1959. *Billy Budd*, ed. H. Hayford and M. M. Sealts, 1962. *Writings of Herman Melville*, 16 vols. projected (Northwestern-Newberry Edition), ed. H. Hayford, H. Parker, and G. T. Tanselle, 1968– . *The Melville Log: A Documentary Life of Herman Melville*, 2 vols., ed. J. Leyda, 1969. *The Collected Poems*, ed. H. P. Vincent, 1981. *Correspondence*, ed. L. Howth, 1990. C. Olson, *Call Me Ishmael*, 1958. H. Parker, ed., *The Recognition of Herman Melville: Selected Criticism Since 1846*, 1967. E. A. Dryden, *Melville's Thematics of Form: The Great Art of Telling the Truth*, 1969. J. Seelye, *Melville: The Ironic Diagram*, 1970. R. A. Sherrill, *The Prophetic Melville: Experience, Transcendence, and Tragedy*, 1979. T. W. Herbert, *Marquesan Encounters: Melville and the Meaning of Civilization*, 1980. C. L. Karcher, *Shadow Over the Promised Land: Slavery, Race, and Violence in Melville's America*, 1980. S. Cameron, *The Corporeal Self: Allegories of the Body in Melville and Hawthorne*, 1981. M. P. Rogin, *Subversive Geneology: The Politics and Art of Herman Melville*, 1985. W. B. Dillingham, *Melville's Later Novels*, 1986. M. Sealts, *Melville's Reading*, 1988. N. L. Tolchin, *Mourning, Gender, and Creativity in the Art of Herman Melville*, 1988. J. Samson, *White Lies: Melville's Narrative of Facts*, 1989.

Texts Used: "Bartleby the Scrivener" and "Benito Cereno": *The Piazza Tales*, 1856. Poetry: *Poems*, 1924.

BARTLEBY THE SCRIVENER*

A Story of Wall Street

I am a rather elderly man. The nature of my avocations, for the last thirty years, has brought me into more than ordinary contact with what would seem an interesting and somewhat singular set of men, of whom, as yet, nothing, that I know of, has ever been written—I mean, the law-copyists, or scriveners. I have known very many of them, professionally and privately, and, if I pleased, could relate

---

* First published in *Putnam's Monthly Magazine* in November and December 1853 and included in *The Piazza Tales* (1856), under the title "Bartleby." A scrivener is a writer (originally, "scribe").

divers histories, at which good-natured gentlemen might smile, and sentimental souls might weep. But I waive the biographies of all other scriveners, for a few passages in the life of Bartleby, who was a scrivener, the strangest I ever saw, or heard of. While, of other law-copyists, I might write the complete life, of Bartleby nothing of that sort can be done. I believe that no materials exist, for a full and satisfactory biography of this man. It is an irreparable loss to literature. Bartleby was one of those beings of whom nothing is ascertainable, except from the original sources, and, in his case, those are very small. What my own astonished eyes saw of Bartleby, *that* is all I know of him, except, indeed, one vague report, which will appear in the sequel.

Ere introducing the scrivener, as he first appeared to me, it is fit I make some mention of myself, my *employés,* my business, my chambers, and general surroundings; because some such description is indispensable to an adequate understanding of the chief character about to be presented. Imprimis:[1] I am a man who, from his youth upwards, has been filled with a profound conviction that the easiest way of life is the best. Hence, though I belong to a profession proverbially energetic and nervous, even to turbulence, at times, yet nothing of that sort have I ever suffered to invade my peace. I am one of those unambitious lawyers who never addresses a jury, or in any way draws down public applause; but, in the cool tranquillity of a snug retreat, do a snug business among rich men's bonds, and mortgages, and title-deeds. All who know me, consider me an eminently *safe* man. The late John Jacob Astor,[2] a personage little given to poetic enthusiasm, had no hesitation in pronouncing my first grand point to be prudence; my next, method. I do not speak it in vanity, but simply record the fact, that I was not unemployed in my profession by the late John Jacob Astor; a name which, I admit, I love to repeat; for it hath a rounded and orbicular sound to it, and rings like unto bullion. I will freely add, that I was not insensible to the late John Jacob Astor's good opinion.

Some time prior to the period at which this little history begins, my avocations had been largely increased. The good old office, now extinct in the State of New York, of a Master in Chancery,[3] had been conferred upon me. It was not a very arduous office, but very pleasantly remunerative. I seldom lose my temper; much more seldom indulge in dangerous indignation at wrongs and outrages; but, I must be permitted to be rash here, and declare, that I consider the sudden and violent abrogation of the office of Master in Chancery, by the new Constitution, as a —premature act; inasmuch as I had counted upon a life-lease of the profits, whereas I only received those of a few short years. But this is by the way.

My chambers were up stairs, at No. — Wall street. At one end, they looked upon the white wall of the interior of a spacious sky-light shaft, penetrating the building from top to bottom.

This view might have been considered rather tame than otherwise, deficient in what landscape painters call "life." But, if so, the view from the other end of my chambers offered, at least, a contrast, if nothing more. In that direction, my windows commanded an unobstructed view of a lofty brick wall, black by age and everlasting shade; which wall required no spy-glass to bring out its lurking beau-

---

[1] "In the first place" (Latin).

[2] Astor (1763–1848) was an American millionaire who made his fortune in the fur trade and in real-estate dealings.

[3] A new New York state constitution in 1846 had abolished the office of Master of Chancery as part of an outdated court system.

ties, but, for the benefit of all near-sighted spectators, was pushed up to within ten feet of my window panes. Owing to the great height of the surrounding buildings, and my chambers being on the second floor, the interval between this wall and mine not a little resembled a huge square cistern.

At the period just preceding the advent of Bartleby, I had two persons as copyists in my employment, and a promising lad as an office-boy. First, Turkey; second, Nippers; third, Ginger Nut. These may seem names, the like of which are not usually found in the Directory.[4] In truth, they were nicknames, mutually conferred upon each other by my three clerks, and were deemed expressive of their respective persons or characters. Turkey was a short, pursy[5] Englishman, of about my own age—that is, somewhere not far from sixty. In the morning, one might say, his face was of a fine florid hue, but after twelve o'clock, meridian[6]—his dinner hour—it blazed like a grate full of Christmas coals; and continued blazing—but, as it were, with a gradual wane—till six o'clock, P.M., or thereabouts; after which, I saw no more of the proprietor of the face, which, gaining its meridian with the sun, seemed to set with it, to rise, culminate, and decline the following day, with the like regularity and undiminished glory. There are many singular coincidences I have known in the course of my life, not the least among which was the fact, that, exactly when Turkey displayed his fullest beams from his red and radiant countenance, just then, too, at that critical moment, began the daily period when I considered his business capacities as seriously disturbed for the remainder of the twenty-four hours. Not that he was absolutely idle, or averse to business, then; far from it. The difficulty was, he was apt to be altogether too energetic. There was a strange, inflamed, flurried, flighty recklessness of activity about him. He would be incautious in dipping his pen into his inkstand. All his blots upon my documents were dropped there after twelve o'clock, meridian. Indeed, not only would he be reckless, and sadly given to making blots in the afternoon, but, some days, he went further, and was rather noisy. At such times, too, his face flamed with augmented blazonry, as if cannel coal had been heaped on anthracite.[7] He made an unpleasant racket with his chair; spilled his sand-box;[8] in mending his pens, impatiently split them all to pieces, and threw them on the floor in a sudden passion; stood up, and leaned over his table, boxing his papers about in a most indecorous manner, very sad to behold in an elderly man like him. Nevertheless, as he was in many ways a most valuable person to me, and all the time before twelve o'clock, meridian, was the quickest, steadiest creature, too, accomplishing a great deal of work in a style not easily to be matched—for these reasons, I was willing to overlook his eccentricities, though, indeed, occasionally, I remonstrated with him. I did this very gently, however, because, though the civilest, nay, the blandest and most reverential of men in the morning, yet, in the afternoon, he was disposed, upon provocation, to be slightly rash with his tongue—in fact, insolent. Now, valuing his morning services as I did, and resolved not to lose them—yet, at the same time, made uncomfortable by his inflamed ways after twelve o'clock—and being a man of peace, unwilling by my admonitions to call forth unseemly retorts from him, I took upon me, one Saturday noon (he was always worse on Saturdays) to hint to him, very kindly, that, perhaps, now that he was growing old, it might be well to abridge his labors; in

---

[4] The city directory of residents.   [5] Short-winded from being fat.   [6] Noon.
[7] Cannel coal (soft) burns quickly and brightly; anthracite (hard) burns more slowly and intensely.
[8] A box containing sand for blotting ink.

short, he need not come to my chambers after twelve o'clock, but, dinner over, had best go home to his lodgings, and rest himself till tea-time. But no; he insisted upon his afternoon devotions.[9] His countenance became intolerably fervid, as he oratorically assured me—gesticulating with a long ruler at the other end of the room—that if his services in the morning were useful, how indispensable, then, in the afternoon?

"With submission, sir," said Turkey, on this occasion, "I consider myself your right-hand man. In the morning I but marshal and deploy my columns; but in the afternoon I put myself at their head, and gallantly charge the foe, thus"—and he made a violent thrust with the ruler.

"But the blots, Turkey," intimated I.

"True; but, with submission, sir, behold these hairs! I am getting old. Surely, sir, a blot or two of a warm afternoon is not to be severely urged against gray hairs. Old age—even if it blot the page—is honorable. With submission, sir, we *both* are getting old."

This appeal to my fellow-feeling was hardly to be resisted. At all events, I saw that go he would not. So, I made up my mind to let him stay, resolving, nevertheless, to see to it that, during the afternoon, he had to do with my less important papers.

Nippers, the second on my list, was a whiskered, sallow, and, upon the whole, rather piratical-looking young man, of about five and twenty. I always deemed him the victim of two evil powers—ambition and indigestion. The ambition was evinced by a certain impatience of the duties of a mere copyist, an unwarrantable usurpation of strictly professional affairs, such as the original drawing up of legal documents. The indigestion seemed betokened in an occasional nervous testiness and grinning irritability, causing the teeth to audibly grind together over mistakes committed in copying; unnecessary maledictions, hissed, rather than spoken, in the heat of business; and especially by a continual discontent with the height of the table where he worked. Though of a very ingenious mechanical turn, Nippers could never get this table to suit him. He put chips under it, blocks of various sorts, bits of pasteboard, and at last went so far as to attempt an exquisite adjustment, by final pieces of folded blotting-paper. But no invention would answer. If, for the sake of easing his back, he brought the table lid at a sharp angle well up towards his chin, and wrote there like a man using the steep roof of a Dutch house for his desk, then he declared that it stopped the circulation in his arms. If now he lowered the table to his waistbands, and stooped over it in writing, then there was a sore aching in his back. In short, the truth of the matter was, Nippers knew not what he wanted. Or, if he wanted anything, it was to be rid of a scrivener's table altogether. Among the manifestations of his diseased ambition was a fondness he had for receiving visits from certain ambiguous-looking fellows in seedy coats, whom he called his clients. Indeed, I was aware that not only was he, at times, considerable of a ward-politician, but he occasionally did a little business at the Justices' courts, and was not unknown on the steps of the Tombs.[10] I have good reason to believe, however, that one individual who called upon him at my cham-

---

[9] He is devoted to his work. The religious overtones give this sentence a gentle irony.

[10] A New York City prison built in 1839, officially the Halls of Justice and House of Detention, the Tombs was named after the Egyptian Revival style of architecture that imitated Egyptian temples and tombs. Because Nippers is an ambitious "ward-politician," his presence at courts of law and on the steps of the city prison suggests to the narrator some questionable activities on his employee's part.

bers, and who, with a grand air, he insisted was his client, was no other than a dun,[11] and the alleged title-deed, a bill. But, with all his failings, and the annoyances he caused me, Nippers, like his compatriot Turkey, was a very useful man to me; wrote a neat, swift hand; and, when he chose, was not deficient in a gentlemanly sort of deportment. Added to this, he always dressed in a gentlemanly sort of way; and so, incidentally, reflected credit upon my chambers. Whereas, with respect to Turkey, I had much ado to keep him from being a reproach to me. His clothes were apt to look oily, and smell of eating-houses. He wore his pantaloons very loose and baggy in summer. His coats were execrable; his hat not to be handled. But while the hat was a thing of indifference to me, inasmuch as his natural civility and deference, as a dependent Englishman, always led him to doff it the moment he entered the room, yet his coat was another matter. Concerning his coats, I reasoned with him; but with no effect. The truth was, I suppose, that a man with so small an income could not afford to sport such a lustrous face and a lustrous coat at one and the same time. As Nippers once observed, Turkey's money went chiefly for red ink. One winter day, I presented Turkey with a highly respectable-looking coat of my own—a padded gray coat, of a most comfortable warmth, and which buttoned straight up from the knee to the neck. I thought Turkey would appreciate the favor, and abate his rashness and obstreperousness of afternoons. But no; I verily believe that buttoning himself up in so downy and blanket-like a coat had a pernicious effect upon him—upon the same principle that too much oats are bad for horses. In fact, precisely as a rash, restive horse is said to feel his oats, so Turkey felt his coat. It made him insolent. He was a man whom prosperity harmed.

Though, concerning the self-indulgent habits of Turkey, I had my own private surmises, yet, touching Nippers, I was well persuaded that, whatever might be his faults in other respects, he was, at least, a temperate young man. But, indeed, nature herself seemed to have been his vintner, and, at his birth, charged him so thoroughly with an irritable, brandy-like disposition, that all subsequent potations were needless. When I consider how, amid the stillness of my chambers, Nippers would sometimes impatiently rise from his seat, and stooping over his table, spread his arms wide apart, seize the whole desk, and move it, and jerk it, with a grim, grinding motion on the floor, as if the table were a perverse voluntary agent, intent on thwarting and vexing him, I plainly perceive that, for Nippers, brandy-and-water were altogether superfluous.

It was fortunate for me that, owing to its peculiar cause—indigestion—the irritability and consequent nervousness of Nippers were mainly observable in the morning, while in the afternoon he was comparatively mild. So that, Turkey's paroxysms only coming on about twelve o'clock, I never had to do with their eccentricities at one time. Their fits relieved each other, like guards. When Nippers's was on, Turkey's was off; and *vice versa*. This was a good natural arrangement, under the circumstances.

Ginger Nut, the third on my list, was a lad, some twelve years old. His father was a carman,[12] ambitious of seeing his son on the bench instead of a cart, before he died. So he sent him to my office, as student at law, errand-boy, cleaner and sweeper, at the rate of one dollar a week. He had a little desk to himself, but he did not use it much. Upon inspection, the drawer exhibited a great array of the shells of various sorts of nuts. Indeed, to this quick-witted youth, the whole noble

---

[11] A bill collector.   [12] A wagon driver.

science of the law was contained in a nut-shell. Not the least among the employ-ments of Ginger Nut, as well as one which he discharged with the most alacrity, was his duty as cake and apple purveyor for Turkey and Nippers. Copying law-papers being proverbially a dry, husky sort of business, my two scriveners were fain to moisten their mouths very often with Spitzenbergs,[13] to be had at the nu-merous stalls nigh the Custom House and Post Office. Also, they sent Ginger Nut very frequently for that peculiar cake—small, flat, round, and very spicy—after which he had been named by them. Of a cold morning, when business was but dull, Turkey would gobble up scores of these cakes, as if they were mere wa-fers—indeed, they sell them at the rate of six or eight for a penny—the scrape of his pen blending with the crunching of the crisp particles in his mouth. Of all the fiery afternoon blunders and flurried rashnesses of Turkey, was his once moisten-ing a ginger-cake between his lips, and clapping it on to a mortgage, for a seal. I came within an ace of dismissing him then. But he mollified me by making an oriental bow, and saying—

"With submission, sir, it was generous of me to find you in stationery on my own account."[14]

Now my original business—that of a conveyancer and title hunter, and drawer-up of recondite documents of all sorts[15]—was considerably increased by receiving the master's office. There was now great work for scriveners. Not only must I push the clerks already with me, but I must have additional help.

In answer to my advertisement, a motionless young man one morning stood upon my office threshold, the door being open, for it was summer. I can see that figure now—pallidly neat, pitiably respectable, incurably forlorn! It was Bartleby.

After a few words touching his qualifications, I engaged him, glad to have among my corps of copyists a man of so singularly sedate an aspect, which I thought might operate beneficially upon the flighty temper of Turkey, and the fiery one of Nippers.

I should have stated before that ground glass folding-doors divided my prem-ises into two parts, one of which was occupied by my scriveners, the other by myself. According to my humor, I threw open these doors, or closed them. I resolved to assign Bartleby a corner by the folding-doors, but on my side of them, so as to have this quiet man within easy call, in case any trifling thing was to be done. I placed his desk close up to a small side-window in that part of the room, a window which originally had afforded a lateral view of certain grimy backyards and bricks, but which, owing to subsequent erections, commanded at present no view at all, though it gave some light. Within three feet of the panes was a wall, and the light came down from far above, between two lofty buildings, as from a very small opening in a dome. Still further to a satisfactory arrangement, I pro-cured a high green folding screen, which might entirely isolate Bartleby from my sight, though not remove him from my voice. And thus, in a manner, privacy and society were conjoined.

At first, Bartleby did an extraordinary quantity of writing. As if long famishing for something to copy, he seemed to gorge himself on my documents. There was no pause for digestion. He ran a day and night line, copying by sun-light and by

---

[13] A type of apple.   [14] To supply you with stationery at my own expense.

[15] The narrator works on legal transfers of property, checks titles of ownership to be sure they are free and clear, and draws up complicated documents.

candle-light. I should have been quite delighted with his application, had he been cheerfully industrious. But he wrote on silently, palely, mechanically.

It is, of course, an indispensable part of a scrivener's business to verify the accuracy of his copy, word by word. Where there are two or more scriveners in an office, they assist each other in this examination, one reading from the copy, the other holding the original. It is a very dull, wearisome, and lethargic affair. I can readily imagine that, to some sanguine temperaments, it would be altogether intolerable. For example, I cannot credit that the mettlesome poet, Byron, would have contentedly sat down with Bartleby to examine a law document of, say five hundred pages, closely written in a crimpy hand.

Now and then, in the haste of business, it had been my habit to assist in comparing some brief document myself, calling Turkey or Nippers for this purpose. One object I had, in placing Bartleby so handy to me behind the screen, was, to avail myself of his services on such trivial occasions. It was on the third day, I think, of his being with me, and before any necessity had arisen for having his own writing examined, that, being much hurried to complete a small affair I had in hand, I abruptly called to Bartleby. In my haste and natural expectancy of instant compliance, I sat with my head bent over the original on my desk, and my right hand sideways, and somewhat nervously extended with the copy, so that, immediately upon emerging from his retreat, Bartleby might snatch it and proceed to business without the least delay.

In this very attitude did I sit when I called to him, rapidly stating what it was I wanted him to do—namely, to examine a small paper with me. Imagine my surprise, nay, my consternation, when, without moving from his privacy, Bartleby, in a singularly mild, firm voice, replied, "I would prefer not to."

I sat awhile in perfect silence, rallying my stunned faculties. Immediately it occurred to me that my ears had deceived me, or Bartleby had entirely misunderstood my meaning. I repeated my request in the clearest tone I could assume; but in quite as clear a one came the previous reply, "I would prefer not to."

"Prefer not to," echoed I, rising in high excitement, and crossing the room with a stride. "What do you mean? Are you moon-struck? I want you to help me compare this sheet here—take it," and I thrust it towards him.

"I would prefer not to," said he.

I looked at him steadfastly. His face was leanly composed; his gray eye dimly calm. Not a wrinkle of agitation rippled him. Had there been the least uneasiness, anger, impatience or impertinence in his manner; in other words, had there been any thing ordinarily human about him, doubtless I should have violently dismissed him from the premises. But as it was, I should have as soon thought of turning my pale plaster-of-paris bust of Cicero[16] out of doors. I stood gazing at him awhile, as he went on with his own writing, and then reseated myself at my desk. This is very strange, thought I. What had one best do? But my business hurried me. I concluded to forget the matter for the present, reserving it for my future leisure. So calling Nippers from the other room, the paper was speedily examined.

A few days after this, Bartleby concluded four lengthy documents, being quadruplicates of a week's testimony taken before me in my High Court of Chancery. It became necessary to examine them. It was an important suit, and great accuracy was imperative. Having all things arranged, I called Turkey, Nippers and Ginger

[16] Marcus Tullius Cicero (106–43 B.C.), a Roman philosopher, statesman, and orator.

Nut, from the next room, meaning to place the four copies in the hand of my four clerks, while I should read from the original. Accordingly, Turkey, Nippers, and Ginger Nut had taken their seats in a row, each with his document in his hand, when I called to Bartleby to join this interesting group.

"Bartleby! quick, I am waiting."

I heard a slow scrape of his chair legs on the uncarpeted floor, and soon he appeared standing at the entrance of his hermitage.

"What is wanted?" said he, mildly.

"The copies, the copies," said I, hurriedly. "We are going to examine them. There"—and I held towards him the fourth quadruplicate.

"I would prefer not to," he said, and gently disappeared behind the screen.

For a few moments I was turned into a pillar of salt,[17] standing at the head of my seated column of clerks. Recovering myself, I advanced towards the screen, and demanded the reason for such extraordinary conduct.

"*Why* do you refuse?"

"I would prefer not to."

With any other man I should have flown outright into a dreadful passion, scorned all further words, and thrust him ignominiously from my presence. But there was something about Bartleby that not only strangely disarmed me, but, in a wonderful manner, touched and disconcerted me. I began to reason with him.

"These are your own copies we are about to examine. It is làbor saving to you, because one examination will answer for your four papers. It is common usage. Every copyist is bound to help examine his copy. Is it not so? Will you not speak? Answer!"

"I would prefer not to," he replied in a flutelike tone. It seemed to me that, while I had been addressing him, he carefully revolved every statement that I made; fully comprehended the meaning; could not gainsay the irresistible conclusion; but, at the same time, some paramount consideration prevailed with him to reply as he did.

"You are decided, then, not to comply with my request—a request made according to common usage and common sense?"

He briefly gave me to understand, that on that point my judgment was sound. Yes: his decision was irreversible.

It is not seldom the case that, when a man is browbeaten in some unprecedented and violently unreasonable way, he begins to stagger in his own plainest faith. He begins, as it were, vaguely to surmise that, wonderful as it may be, all the justice and all the reason is on the other side. Accordingly, if any disinterested persons are present, he turns to them for some reinforcement for his own faltering mind.

"Turkey," said I, "what do you think of this? Am I not right?"

"With submission, sir," said Turkey, in his blandest tone, "I think that you are."

"Nippers," said I, "what do *you* think of it?"

"I think I should kick him out of the office."

(The reader, of nice[18] perceptions, will here perceive that, it being morning, Turkey's answer is couched in polite and tranquil terms, but Nippers replies in

---

[17] In Genesis 19:26, for her disobedience, Lot's wife is turned into a pillar of salt; here, the unoffending narrator suffers this fate metaphorically.

[18] Discriminative.

ill-tempered ones. Or, to repeat a previous sentence, Nippers's ugly mood was on duty, and Turkey's off.)

"Ginger Nut," said I, willing to enlist the smallest suffrage[19] in my behalf, "what do *you* think of it?"

"I think, sir, he's a little *luny*," replied Ginger Nut, with a grin.

"You hear what they say," said I, turning towards the screen, "come forth and do your duty."

But he vouchsafed no reply. I pondered a moment in sore perplexity. But once more business hurried me. I determined again to postpone the consideration of this dilemma to my future leisure. With a little trouble we made out to examine the papers without Bartleby, though at every page or two Turkey deferentially dropped his opinion, that this proceeding was quite out of the common; while Nippers, twitching in his chair with a dyspeptic nervousness, ground out, between his set teeth, occasional hissing maledictions against the stubborn oaf behind the screen. And for his (Nippers's) part, this was the first and the last time he would do another man's business without pay.

Meanwhile Bartleby sat in his hermitage, oblivious to everything but his own peculiar business there.

Some days passed, the scrivener being employed upon another lengthy work. His late remarkable conduct led me to regard his ways narrowly. I observed that he never went to dinner; indeed, that he never went anywhere. As yet I had never, of my personal knowledge, known him to be outside of my office. He was a perpetual sentry in the corner. At about eleven o'clock though, in the morning, I noticed that Ginger Nut would advance toward the opening in Bartleby's screen, as if silently beckoned thither by a gesture invisible to me where I sat. The boy would then leave the office, jingling a few pence, and reappear with a handful of ginger-nuts, which he delivered in the hermitage, receiving two of the cakes for his trouble.

He lives, then, on ginger-nuts, thought I; never eats a dinner, properly speaking; he must be a vegetarian, then, but no; he never eats even vegetables, he eats nothing but ginger-nuts. My mind then ran on in reveries concerning the probable effects upon the human constitution of living entirely on ginger-nuts. Ginger-nuts are so called, because they contain ginger as one of their peculiar constituents, and the final flavoring one. Now, what was ginger? A hot, spicy thing. Was Bartleby hot and spicy? Not at all. Ginger, then, had no effect upon Bartleby. Probably he preferred it should have none.

Nothing so aggravates an earnest person as a passive resistance. If the individual so resisted be of a not inhumane temper, and the resisting one perfectly harmless in his passivity, then, in the better moods of the former, he will endeavor charitably to construe to his imagination what proves impossible to be solved by his judgment. Even so, for the most part, I regarded Bartleby and his ways. Poor fellow! thought I, he means no mischief; it is plain he intends no insolence; his aspect sufficiently evinces that his eccentricities are involuntary. He is useful to me. I can get along with him. If I turn him away, the chances are he will fall in with some less-indulgent employer, and then he will be rudely treated, and perhaps driven forth miserably to starve. Yes. Here I can cheaply purchase a delicious self-approval. To befriend Bartleby; to humor him in his strange willfulness,

[19] Vote of support.

will cost me little or nothing, while I lay up in my soul what will eventually prove a sweet morsel for my conscience. But this mood was not invariable with me. The passiveness of Bartleby sometimes irritated me. I felt strangely goaded on to encounter him in new opposition—to elicit some angry spark from him answerable to my own. But, indeed, I might as well have essayed to strike fire with my knuckles against a bit of Windsor soap.[20] But one afternoon the evil impulse in me mastered me, and the following little scene ensued:

"Bartleby," said I, "when those papers are all copied, I will compare them with you."

"I would prefer not to."

"How? Surely you do not mean to persist in that mulish vagary?"

No answer.

I threw open the folding-doors near by, and, turning upon Turkey and Nippers, exclaimed:

"Bartleby a second time says, he won't examine his papers. What do you think of it, Turkey?"

It was afternoon, be it remembered. Turkey sat glowing like a brass boiler; his bald head steaming; his hands reeling among his blotted papers.

"Think of it?" roared Turkey; "I think I'll just step behind his screen, and black his eyes for him!"

So saying, Turkey rose to his feet and threw his arms into a pugilistic position. He was hurrying away to make good his promise, when I detained him, alarmed at the effect of incautiously rousing Turkey's combativeness after dinner.

"Sit down, Turkey," said I, "and hear what Nippers has to say. What do you think of it, Nippers? Would I not be justified in immediately dismissing Bartleby?"

"Excuse me, that is for you to decide, sir. I think his conduct quite unusual, and, indeed, unjust as regards Turkey and myself. But it may only be a passing whim."

"Ah," exclaimed I, "you have strangely changed your mind, then—you speak very gently of him now."

"All beer," cried Turkey; "gentleness is effects of beer—Nippers and I dined together to-day. You see how gentle *I* am, sir. Shall I go and black his eyes?"

"You refer to Bartleby, I suppose. No, not to-day, Turkey," I replied; "pray, put up your fists."

I closed the doors, and again advanced towards Bartleby. I felt additional incentives tempting me to my fate. I burned to be rebelled against again. I remembered that Bartleby never left the office.

"Bartleby," said I, "Ginger Nut is away; just step around to the Post Office, won't you? (it was but a three minutes' walk), and see if there is anything for me."

"I would prefer not to."

"You *will* not?"

"I *prefer* not."

I staggered to my desk, and sat there in a deep study. My blind inveteracy returned. Was there any other thing in which I could procure myself to be ignominiously repulsed by this lean, penniless wight?—my hired clerk? What added thing is there, perfectly reasonable, that he will be sure to refuse to do?

"Bartleby!"

No answer.

[20] A brand of hand soap.

"Bartleby," in a louder tone.

No answer.

"Bartleby," I roared.

Like a very ghost, agreeably to the laws of magical invocation, at the third summons, he appeared at the entrance of his hermitage.

"Go to the next room, and tell Nippers to come to me."

"I prefer not to," he respectfully and slowly said, and mildly disappeared.

"Very good, Bartleby," said I, in a quiet sort of serenely-severe self-possessed tone, intimating the unalterable purpose of some terrible retribution very close at hand. At the moment I half intended something of the kind. But upon the whole, as it was drawing towards my dinner-hour, I thought it best to put on my hat and walk home for the day, suffering much from perplexity and distress of mind.

Shall I acknowledge it? The conclusion of this whole business was, that it soon became a fixed fact of my chambers, that a pale young scrivener, by the name of Bartleby, had a desk there; that he copied for me at the usual rate of four cents a folio (one hundred words); but he was permanently exempt from examining the work done by him, that duty being transferred to Turkey and Nippers, out of compliment, doubtless, to their superior acuteness; moreover, said Bartleby was never, on any account, to be dispatched on the most trivial errand of any sort; and that even if entreated to take upon him such a matter, it was generally understood that he would "prefer not to"—in other words, that he would refuse point-blank.

As days passed on, I became considerably reconciled to Bartleby. His steadiness, his freedom from all dissipation, his incessant industry (except when he chose to throw himself into a standing revery behind his screen), his great stillness, his unalterableness of demeanor under all circumstances, made him a valuable acquisition. One prime thing was this—*he was always there*—first in the morning, continually through the day, and the last at night. I had a singular confidence in his honesty. I felt my most precious papers perfectly safe in his hands. Sometimes, to be sure, I could not, for the very soul of me, avoid falling into sudden spasmodic passions with him. For it was exceeding difficult to bear in mind all the time those strange peculiarities, privileges, and unheard of exemptions, forming the tacit stipulations on Bartleby's part under which he remained in my office. Now and then, in the eagerness of dispatching pressing business, I would inadvertently summon Bartleby, in a short, rapid tone, to put his finger, say, on the incipient tie of a bit of red tape with which I was about compressing some papers. Of course, from behind the screen the usual answer, "I prefer not to," was sure to come; and then, how could a human creature, with the common infirmities of our nature, refrain from bitterly exclaiming upon such perverseness—such unreasonableness. However, every added repulse of this sort which I received only tended to lessen the probability of my repeating the inadvertence.

Here it must be said, that according to the custom of most legal gentlemen occupying chambers in densely-populated law buildings, there were several keys to my door. One was kept by a woman residing in the attic, which person weekly scrubbed and daily swept and dusted my apartments. Another was kept by Turkey for convenience sake. The third I sometimes carried in my own pocket. The fourth I knew not who had.

Now, one Sunday morning I happened to go to Trinity Church,[21] to hear a celebrated preacher, and finding myself rather early on the ground I thought I would walk round to my chambers for a while. Luckily I had my key with me; but

---

[21] An Episcopal church in New York City's financial district (apparently near the narrator's office).

upon applying it to the lock, I found it resisted by something inserted from the inside. Quite surprised, I called out; when to my consternation a key was turned from within; and thrusting his lean visage at me, and holding the door ajar, the apparition of Bartleby appeared, in his shirt sleeves, and otherwise in a strangely tattered deshabille,[22] saying quietly that he was sorry, but he was deeply engaged just then, and—preferred not admitting me at present. In a brief word or two, he moreover added, that perhaps I had better walk round the block two or three times, and by that time he would probably have concluded his affairs.

Now, the utterly unsurmised appearance of Bartleby, tenanting my law-chambers of a Sunday morning, with his cadaverously gentlemanly *nonchalance,* yet withal firm and self-possessed, had such a strange effect upon me, that incontinently I slunk away from my own door, and did as desired. But not without sundry twinges of impotent rebellion against the mild effrontery of this unaccountable scrivener. Indeed, it was his wonderful mildness chiefly, which not only disarmed me, but unmanned me as it were. For I consider that one, for the time, is a sort of unmanned when he tranquilly permits his hired clerk to dictate to him, and order him away from his own premises. Furthermore, I was full of uneasiness as to what Bartleby could possibly be doing in my office in his shirt sleeves, and in an otherwise dismantled condition of a Sunday morning. Was anything amiss going on? Nay, that was out of the question. It was not to be thought of for a moment that Bartleby was an immoral person. But what could he be doing there?—copying? Nay again, whatever might be his eccentricities, Bartleby was an eminently decorous person. He would be the last man to sit down to his desk in any state approaching to nudity. Besides, it was Sunday; and there was something about Bartleby that forbade the supposition that he would by any secular occupation violate the proprieties of the day.

Nevertheless, my mind was not pacified; and full of a restless curiosity, at last I returned to the door. Without hindrance I inserted my key, opened it, and entered. Bartleby was not to be seen. I looked round anxiously, peeped behind his screen; but it was very plain that he was gone. Upon more closely examining the place, I surmised that for an indefinite period Bartleby must have ate, dressed, and slept in my office, and that, too without plate, mirror, or bed. The cushioned seat of a ricketty old sofa in one corner bore the faint impress of a lean, reclining form. Rolled away under his desk, I found a blanket; under the empty grate, a blacking box and brush; on a chair, a tin basin, with soap and a ragged towel; in a newspaper a few crumbs of ginger-nuts and a morsel of cheese. Yes, thought I, it is evident enough that Bartleby has been making his home here, keeping bachelor's hall all by himself. Immediately then the thought came sweeping across me, what miserable friendlessness and loneliness are here revealed! His poverty is great; but his solitude, how horrible! Think of it. Of a Sunday, Wall-street is deserted as Petra;[23] and every night of every day it is an emptiness. This building, too, which of week-days hums with industry and life, at nightfall echoes with sheer vacancy, and all through Sunday is forlorn. And here Bartleby makes his home; sole spectator of a solitude which he has seen all populous—a sort of innocent and transformed Marius[24] brooding among the ruins of Carthage!

---

[22] Dishabille, or clothing in disarray.

[23] An ancient city in what is now Jordan; its ruins were discovered in 1812.

[24] Gaius Marius (157?–86 B.C.), a Roman general and statesman who was exiled from Rome. Captured by his enemies, he finally escaped to Africa and, in a message to the Roman governor, said that he was sitting "amid the ruins of Carthage"—the man and the city having met similar fates. Marius became popularized in nineteenth-century American art and literature.

For the first time in my life a feeling of overpowering stinging melancholy seized me. Before, I had never experienced aught but a not unpleasing sadness. The bond of a common humanity now drew me irresistibly to gloom. A fraternal melancholy! For both I and Bartleby were sons of Adam. I remembered the bright silks and sparkling faces I had seen that day, in gala trim, swan-like sailing down the Mississippi of Broadway; and I contrasted them with the pallid copyist, and thought to myself, Ah, happiness courts the light, so we deem the world is gay; but misery hides aloof, so we deem that misery there is none. These sad fancyings—chimeras, doubtless, of a sick and silly brain—led on to other and more special thoughts, concerning the eccentricities of Bartleby. Presentiments of strange discoveries hovered round me. The scrivener's pale form appeared to me laid out, among uncaring strangers, in its shivering winding sheet.

Suddenly I was attracted by Bartleby's closed desk, the key in open sight left in the lock.

I mean no mischief, seek the gratification of no heartless curiosity, thought I; besides, the desk is mine, and its contents, too, so I will make bold to look within. Everything was methodically arranged, the papers smoothly placed. The pigeon holes were deep, and removing the files of documents, I groped into their recesses. Presently I felt something there, and dragged it out. It was an old bandanna handkerchief, heavy and knotted. I opened it, and saw it was a savings's [sic] bank.

I now recalled all the quiet mysteries which I had noted in the man. I remembered that he never spoke but to answer; that, though at intervals he had considerable time to himself, yet I had never seen him reading—no, not even a newspaper; that for long periods he would stand looking out, at his pale window behind the screen, upon the dead brick wall; I was quite sure he never visited any refectory or eating house; while his pale face clearly indicated that he never drank beer like Turkey, or tea and coffee even, like other men; that he never went anywhere in particular that I could learn; never went out for a walk, unless, indeed, that was the case at present; that he had declined telling who he was, or whence he came, or whether he had any relatives in the world; that though so thin and pale, he never complained of ill health. And more than all, I remembered a certain unconscious air of pallid—how shall I call it?—of pallid haughtiness, say, or rather an austere reserve about him, which had positively awed me into my tame compliance with his eccentricities, when I had feared to ask him to do the slightest incidental thing for me, even though I might know, from his long-continued motionlessness, that behind his screen he must be standing in one of those dead-wall reveries of his.

Revolving all these things, and coupling them with the recently discovered fact, that he made my office his constant abiding place and home, and not forgetful of his morbid moodiness; revolving all these things, a prudential feeling began to steal over me. My first emotions had been those of pure melancholy and sincerest pity; but just in proportion as the forlornness of Bartleby grew and grew to my imagination, did that same melancholy merge into fear, that pity into repulsion. So true it is, and so terrible, too, that up to a certain point the thought or sight of misery enlists our best affections; but, in certain special cases, beyond that point it does not. They err who would assert that invariably this is owing to the inherent selfishness of the human heart. It rather proceeds from a certain hopelessness of remedying excessive and organic ill. To a sensitive being, pity is not seldom pain. And when at last it is perceived that such pity cannot lead to effectual succor, common sense bids the soul be rid of it. What I saw that morning persuaded me that the scrivener was the victim of innate and incurable disorder. I might give alms to his body; but his body did not pain him; it was his soul that suffered, and his soul I could not reach.

I did not accomplish the purpose of going to Trinity Church that morning. Somehow, the things I had seen disqualified me for the time from church-going. I walked homeward, thinking what I would do with Bartleby. Finally, I resolved upon this—I would put certain calm questions to him the next morning, touching his history, etc., and if he declined to answer them openly and unreservedly (and I supposed he would prefer not), then to give him a twenty dollar bill over and above whatever I might owe him, and tell him his services were no longer required; but that if in any other way I could assist him, I would be happy to do so, especially if he desired to return to his native place, wherever that might be, I would willingly help to defray the expenses. Moreover, if, after reaching home, he found himself at any time in want of aid, a letter from him would be sure of a reply.

The next morning came.

"Bartleby," said I, gently calling to him behind his screen.

No reply.

"Bartleby," said I, in a still gentler tone, "come here; I am not going to ask you to do anything you would prefer not to do—I simply wish to speak to you."

Upon this he noiselessly slid into view.

"Will you tell me, Bartleby, where you were born?"

"I would prefer not to."

"Will you tell me *anything* about yourself?"

"I would prefer not to."

"But what reasonable objection can you have to speak to me? I feel friendly towards you."

He did not look at me while I spoke, but kept his glance fixed upon my bust of Cicero, which, as I then sat, was directly behind me, some six inches above my head.

"What is your answer, Bartleby," said I, after waiting a considerable time for a reply, during which his countenance remained immovable, only there was the faintest conceivable tremor of the white attenuated mouth.

"At present I prefer to give no answer," he said, and retired into his hermitage.

It was rather weak in me I confess, but his manner, on this occasion, nettled me. Not only did there seem to lurk in it a certain calm disdain, but his perverseness seemed ungrateful, considering the undeniable good usage and indulgence he had received from me.

Again I sat ruminating what I should do. Mortified as I was at his behavior, and resolved as I had been to dismiss him when I entered my office, nevertheless I strangely felt something superstitious knocking at my heart, and forbidding me to carry out my purpose, and denouncing me for a villain if I dared to breathe one bitter word against this forlornest of mankind. At last, familiarly drawing my chair behind his screen, I sat down and said: "Bartleby, never mind, then, about revealing your history; but let me entreat you, as a friend, to comply as far as may be with the usages of this office. Say now, you will help to examine papers to-morrow or next day: in short, say now, that in a day or two you will begin to be a little reasonable:—say so, Bartleby."

"At present I would prefer not to be a little reasonable," was his mildly cadaverous reply.

Just then the folding-doors opened, and Nippers approached. He seemed suffering from an unusually bad night's rest, induced by severer indigestion than common. He overheard those final words of Bartleby.

"*Prefer not*, eh?" gritted Nippers—"I'd *prefer* him, if I were you, sir," addressing me—"I'd *prefer* him; I'd give him preferences, the stubborn mule! What is it, sir, pray, that he *prefers* not to do now?"

Bartleby moved not a limb.

"Mr. Nippers," said I, "I'd prefer that you would withdraw for the present."

Somehow, of late, I had got into the way of involuntarily using this word "prefer" upon all sorts of not exactly suitable occasions. And I trembled to think that my contact with the scrivener had already and seriously affected me in a mental way. And what further and deeper aberration might it not yet produce? This apprehension had not been without efficacy in determining me to summary measures.

As Nippers, looking very sour and sulky, was departing, Turkey blandly and deferentially approached.

"With submission, sir," said he, "yesterday I was thinking about Bartleby here, and I think that if he would but prefer to take a quart of good ale every day, it would do much towards mending him, and enabling him to assist in examining his papers."

"So you have got the word, too," said I, slightly excited.

"With submission, what word, sir," asked Turkey, respectfully crowding himself into the contracted space behind the screen, and by so doing, making me jostle the scrivener. "What word, sir?"

"I would prefer to be left alone here," said Bartleby, as if offended at being mobbed in his privacy.

"*That's* the word, Turkey," said I—"*that's* it."

"Oh, *prefer?* oh yes—queer word. I never use it myself. But, sir, as I was saying, if he would but prefer—"

"Turkey," interrupted I, "you will please withdraw."

"Oh certainly, sir, if you prefer that I should."

As he opened the folding-door to retire, Nippers at his desk caught a glimpse of me, and asked whether I would prefer to have a certain paper copied on blue paper or white. He did not in the least roguishly accent the word prefer. It was plain that it involuntarily rolled from his tongue. I thought to myself, surely I must get rid of a demented man, who already has in some degree turned the tongues, if not the heads of myself and clerks. But I thought it prudent not to break the dismission at once.

The next day I noticed that Bartleby did nothing but stand at his window in his dead-wall revery. Upon asking him why he did not write, he said that he had decided upon doing no more writing.

"Why, how now? what next?" exclaimed I, "do no more writing?"

"No more."

"And what is the reason?"

"Do you not see the reason for yourself," he indifferently replied.

I looked steadfastly at him, and perceived that his eyes looked dull and glazed. Instantly it occurred to me, that his unexampled diligence in copying by his dim window for the first few weeks of his stay with me might have temporarily impaired his vision.

I was touched. I said something in condolence with him. I hinted that of course he did wisely in abstaining from writing for a while; and urged him to embrace that opportunity of taking wholesome exercise in the open air. This, however, he did not do. A few days after this, my other clerks being absent, and being in a great hurry to dispatch certain letters by the mail, I thought that, having nothing else earthly to do, Bartleby would surely be less inflexible than usual, and carry these letters to the post-office. But he blankly declined. So, much to my inconvenience, I went myself.

Still added days went by. Whether Bartleby's eyes improved or not, I could not say. To all appearance, I thought they did. But when I asked him if they did, he vouchsafed no answer. At all events, he would do no copying. At last, in reply to my urgings, he informed me that he had permanently given up copying.

"What!" exclaimed I; "suppose your eyes should get entirely well—better than ever before—would you not copy then?"

"I have given up copying," he answered, and slid aside.

He remained as ever, a fixture in my chamber. Nay—if that were possible—he became still more of a fixture than before. What was to be done? He would do nothing in the office; why should he stay there? In plain fact, he had now become a millstone to me, not only useless as a necklace, but afflictive to bear. Yet I was sorry for him. I speak less than truth when I say that, on his own account, he occasioned me uneasiness. If he would but have named a single relative or friend, I would instantly have written, and urged their taking the poor fellow away to some convenient retreat. But he seemed alone, absolutely alone in the universe. A bit of wreck in the mid Atlantic. At length, necessities connected with my business tyrannized over all other considerations. Decently as I could, I told Bartleby that in six days time he must unconditionally leave the office. I warned him to take measures, in the interval, for procuring some other abode. I offered to assist him in this endeavor, if he himself would but take the first step towards a removal. "And when you finally quit me, Bartleby," added I, "I shall see that you go not away entirely unprovided. Six days from this hour, remember."

At the expiration of that period, I peeped behind the screen, and lo! Bartleby was there.

I buttoned up my coat, balanced myself; advanced slowly towards him, touched his shoulder, and said, "The time has come; you must quit this place; I am sorry for you; here is money; but you must go."

"I would prefer not," he replied, with his back still towards me.

"You *must*."

He remained silent.

Now I had an unbounded confidence in this man's common honesty. He had frequently restored to me sixpences and shillings carelessly dropped upon the floor, for I am apt to be very reckless in such shirt-button[25] affairs. The proceeding, then, which followed will not be deemed extraordinary.

"Bartleby," said I, "I owe you twelve dollars on account; here are thirty-two; the odd twenty are yours—Will you take it?" and I handed the bills towards him.

But he made no motion.

"I will leave them here, then," putting them under a weight on the table. Then taking my hat and cane and going to the door, I tranquilly turned and added— "After you have removed your things from these offices, Bartleby, you will of course lock the door—since everyone is now gone for the day but you—and if you please, slip your key underneath the mat, so that I may have it in the morning. I shall not see you again; so good-by to you. If, hereafter, in your new place of

---

[25] Small or insignificant.

abode, I can be of any service to you, do not fail to advise me by letter. Good-by, Bartleby, and fare you well."

But he answered not a word; like the last column of some ruined temple, he remained standing mute and solitary in the middle of the otherwise deserted room.

As I walked home in a pensive mood, my vanity got the better of my pity. I could not but highly plume myself on my masterly management in getting rid of Bartleby. Masterly I call it, and such it must appear to any dispassionate thinker. The beauty of my procedure seemed to consist in its perfect quietness. There was no vulgar bullying, no bravado of any sort, no choleric hectoring, and striding to and fro across the apartment, jerking out vehement commands for Bartleby to bundle himself off with his beggarly traps. Nothing of the kind. Without loudly bidding Bartleby depart—as an inferior genius might have done—I *assumed* the ground that depart he must; and upon that assumption built all I had to say. The more I thought over my procedure, the more I was charmed with it. Nevertheless, next morning, upon awakening, I had my doubts—I had somehow slept off the fumes of vanity. One of the coolest and wisest hours a man has, is just after he awakes in the morning. My procedure seemed as sagacious as ever—but only in theory. How it would prove in practice—there was the rub. It was truly a beautiful thought to have assumed Bartleby's departure; but, after all, that assumption was simply my own, and none of Bartleby's. The great point was, not whether I had assumed that he would quit me, but whether he would prefer so to do. He was more a man of preferences than assumptions.

After breakfast, I walked down town, arguing the probabilities *pro* and *con*. One moment I thought it would prove a miserable failure, and Bartleby would be found all alive at my office as usual; the next moment it seemed certain that I should find his chair empty. And so I kept veering about. At the corner of Broadway and Canal street, I saw quite an excited group of people standing in earnest conversation.

"I'll take odds he doesn't," said a voice as I passed.

"Doesn't go?—done!" said I, "put up your money."

I was instinctively putting my hand in my pocket to produce my own, when I remembered that this was an election day. The words I had overheard bore no reference to Bartleby, but to the success or non-success of some candidate for the mayoralty. In my intent frame of mind, I had, as it were, imagined that all Broadway shared in my excitement, and were debating the same question with me. I passed on, very thankful that the uproar of the street screened my momentary absent-mindedness.

As I had intended, I was earlier than usual at my office door. I stood listening for a moment. All was still. He must be gone. I tried the knob. The door was locked. Yes, my procedure had worked to a charm; he indeed must be vanished. Yet a certain melancholy mixed with this: I was almost sorry for my brilliant success. I was fumbling under the door mat for the key, which Bartleby was to have left there for me, when accidentally my knee knocked against a panel, producing a summoning sound, and in response a voice came to me from within—"Not yet; I am occupied."

It was Bartleby.

I was thunderstruck. For an instant I stood like the man who, pipe in mouth, was killed one cloudless afternoon long ago in Virginia, by summer lightning; at his own warm open window he was killed, and remained leaning out there upon the dreamy afternoon, till some one touched him, when he fell.

"Not gone!" I murmured at last. But again obeying that wondrous ascendancy which the inscrutable scrivener had over me, and from which ascendancy, for all my chafing, I could not completely escape, I slowly went downstairs and out into the street, and while walking round the block, considered what I should next do in this unheard-of perplexity. Turn the man out by an actual thrusting I could not; to drive him away by calling him hard names would not do; calling in the police was an unpleasant idea; and yet, permit him to enjoy his cadaverous triumph over me—this, too, I could not think of. What was to be done? or, if nothing could be done, was there anything further that I could *assume* in the matter? Yes, as before I had prospectively assumed that Bartleby would depart, so now I might retrospectively assume that departed he was. In the legitimate carrying out of this assumption, I might enter my office in a great hurry, and pretending not to see Bartleby at all, walk straight against him as if he were air. Such a proceeding would in a singular degree have the appearance of a home-thrust.[26] It was hardly possible that Bartleby could withstand such an application of the doctrine of assumptions. But upon second thoughts the success of the plan seemed rather dubious. I resolved to argue the matter over with him again.

"Bartleby," said I, entering the office, with a quietly severe expression, "I am seriously displeased. I am pained, Bartleby. I had thought better of you. I had imagined you of such a gentlemanly organization, that in any delicate dilemma a slight hint would suffice—in sort, an assumption. But it appears I am deceived. Why," I added, unaffectedly starting, "you have not even touched that money yet," pointing to it, just where I had left it the evening previous.

He answered nothing.

"Will you, or will you not, quit me?" I now demanded in a sudden passion, advancing close to him.

"I would prefer *not* to quit you," he replied gently emphasizing the *not*.

"What earthly right have you to stay here? Do you pay any rent? Do you pay my taxes? Or is this property yours?"

He answered nothing.

"Are you ready to go on and write now? Are your eyes recovered? Could you copy a small paper for me this morning? or help examine a few lines? or step round to the post-office? In a word, will you do anything at all, to give a coloring to your refusal to depart the premises?"

He silently retired into his hermitage.

I was now in such a state of nervous resentment that I thought it but prudent to check myself at present from further demonstrations. Bartleby and I were alone. I remembered the tragedy of the unfortunate Adams[27] and the still more unfortunate Colt in the solitary office of the latter; and how poor Colt, being dreadfully incensed by Adams, and imprudently permitting himself to get wildly excited, was at unawares hurried into his fatal act—an act which certainly no man could possibly deplore more than the actor himself. Often it had occurred to me in my ponderings upon the subject, that had that altercation taken place in the public street, or at a private residence, it would not have terminated as it did. It was the circumstance of being alone in a solitary office, upstairs, of a building entirely unhal-

---

[26] A blow that hits home.

[27] The printer Samuel Adams, who was axe murdered by John C. Colt in 1841 when Adams tried to collect a debt. Prior to his arrest and conviction for murder, Colt apparently crated Adams's body for shipment to New Orleans. Shortly before his scheduled hanging, Colt married his mistress in his jail cell and was found stabbed to death soon afterward. Great material for a mini-series.

lowed by humanizing domestic associations—an uncarpeted office, doubtless, of a dusty, haggard sort of appearance—this it must have been, which greatly helped to enhance the irritable desperation of the hapless Colt.

But when this old Adam[28] of resentment rose in me and tempted me concerning Bartleby, I grappled him and threw him. How? Why, simply by recalling the divine injunction: "A new commandment give I unto you, that ye love one another."[29] Yes, this it was that saved me. Aside from higher considerations, charity often operates as a vastly wise and prudent principle—a great safeguard to its possessor. Men have committed murder for jealousy's sake, and anger's sake, and hatred's sake, and selfishness' sake, and spiritual pride's sake; but no man, that ever I heard of, ever committed a diabolical murder for sweet charity's sake. Mere self-interest, then, if no better motive can be enlisted, should, especially with high-tempered men, prompt all beings to charity and philanthropy. At any rate, upon the occasion in question, I strove to drown my exasperated feelings towards the scrivener by benevolently construing his conduct. Poor fellow, poor fellow! thought I, he don't mean anything; and besides, he has seen hard times, and ought to be indulged.

I endeavored, also, immediately to occupy myself, and at the same time to comfort my despondency. I tried to fancy, that in the course of the morning, at such time as might prove agreeable to him, Bartleby, of his own free accord, would emerge from his hermitage and take up some decided line of march in the direction of the door. But no. Half-past twelve o'clock came; Turkey began to glow in the face, overturn his inkstand, and become generally obstreperous; Nippers abated down into quietude and courtesy; Ginger Nut munched his noon apple; and Bartleby remained standing at his window in one of his profoundest dead-wall reveries. Will it be credited? Ought I to acknowledge it? That afternoon I left the office without saying one further word to him.

Some days now passed, during which, at leisure intervals I looked a little into "Edwards on the Will," and "Priestley on Necessity."[30] Under the circumstances, those books induced a salutary feeling. Gradually I slid into the persuasion that these troubles of mine, touching the scrivener, had been all predestinated from eternity, and Bartleby was billeted upon me for some mysterious purpose of an allwise Providence, which it was not for a mere mortal like me to fathom. Yes, Bartleby, stay there behind your screen, thought I; I shall persecute you no more; you are harmless and noiseless as any of these old chairs; in short, I never feel so private as when I know you are here. At last I see it, I feel it; I penetrate to the predestinated purpose of my life. I am content. Others may have loftier parts to enact; but my mission in this world, Bartleby, is to furnish you with office-room for such period as you may see fit to remain.

I believe that this wise and blessed frame of mind would have continued with me, had it not been for the unsolicited and uncharitable remarks obtruded upon me by my professional friends who visited the rooms. But thus it often is, that the constant friction of illiberal minds wears out at last the best resolves of the more generous. Though to be sure, when I reflected upon it, it was not strange that people entering my office should be struck by the peculiar aspect of the unac-

---

[28] The human tendency to sin.   [29] From John 13:34.

[30] *Freedom of the Will* (1754), by Jonathan Edwards (1703–1758), and *Doctrine of Philosophical Necessity Illustrated* (1777), by Joseph Priestley (1733–1804). The American clergyman Edwards and the English scientist Priestley both believed that the will is not free.

countable Bartleby, and so be tempted to throw out some sinister observations concerning him. Sometimes an attorney, having business with me, and calling at my office, and finding no one but the scrivener there, would undertake to obtain some sort of precise information from him touching my whereabouts; but without heeding his idle talk, Bartleby would remain standing immovable in the middle of the room. So after contemplating him in that position for a time, the attorney would depart, no wiser than he came.

Also, when a reference[31] was going on, and the room full of lawyers and witnesses, and business driving fast, some deeply-occupied legal gentleman present, seeing Bartleby wholly unemployed, would request him to run round to his (the legal gentleman's) office and fetch some papers for him. Thereupon, Bartleby would tranquilly decline, and yet remain idle as before. Then the lawyer would give a great stare, and turn to me. And what could I say? At last I was made aware that all through the circle of my professional acquaintance, a whisper of wonder was running round, having reference to the strange creature I kept at my office. This worried me very much. And as the idea came upon me of his possibly turning out a long-lived man, and keep occupying my chambers, and denying my authority; and perplexing my visitors; and scandalizing my professional reputation; and casting a general gloom over the premises; keeping soul and body together to the last upon his savings (for doubtless he spent but half a dime a day), and in the end perhaps outlive me, and claim possession of my office by right of his perpetual occupancy: as all these dark anticipations crowded upon me more and more, and my friends continually intruded their relentless remarks upon the apparition in my room; a great change was wrought in me. I resolved to gather all my faculties together, and forever rid me of this intolerable incubus.

Ere revolving any complicated project, however, adapted to this end, I first simply suggested to Bartleby the propriety of his permanent departure. In a calm and serious tone, I commended the idea to his careful and mature consideration. But, having taken three days to meditate upon it, he apprised me, that his original determination remained the same; in short, that he still preferred to abide with me.

What shall I do? I now said to myself, buttoning up my coat to the last button. What shall I do? what ought I to do? what does conscience say I *should* do with this man, or, rather, ghost. Rid myself of him, I must; go, he shall. But how? You will not thrust him, the poor, pale, passive mortal—you will not thrust such a helpless creature out of your door? you will not dishonor yourself by such cruelty? No, I will not, I cannot do that. Rather would I let him live and die here, and then mason up his remains in the wall. What, then, will you do? For all your coaxing, he will not budge. Bribes he leaves under your own paper-weight on your table; in short, it is quite plain that he prefers to cling to you.

Then something severe, something unusual must be done. What! surely you will not have him collared by a constable, and commit his innocent pallor to the common jail? And upon what ground could you procure such a thing to be done?—a vagrant, is he? What! he a vagrant, a wanderer, who refuses to budge? It is because he will *not* be a vagrant, then, that you seek to count him *as* a vagrant. That is too absurd. No visible means of support: there I have him. Wrong again: for indubitably he *does* support himself, and that is the only unanswerable proof that any man can show of his possessing the means so to do. No more, then. Since he will not quit me, I must quit him. I will change my offices; I will move

---

[31] A matter referred to a judge or referee.

elsewhere, and give him fair notice, that if I find him on my new premises I will then proceed against him as a common trespasser.

Acting accordingly, next day I thus addressed him: "I find these chambers too far from the City Hall; the air is unwholesome. In a word, I propose to remove my offices next week, and shall no longer require your services. I tell you this now, in order that you may seek another place."

He made no reply, and nothing more was said.

On the appointed day I engaged carts and men, proceeded to my chambers, and, having but little furniture, everything was removed in a few hours. Throughout, the scrivener remained standing behind the screen, which I directed to be removed the last thing. It was withdrawn; and, being folded up like a huge folio, left him the motionless occupant of a naked room. I stood in the entry watching him a moment, while something from within me upbraided me.

I re-entered, with my hand in my pocket—and—and my heart in my mouth.

"Good-by, Bartleby; I am going—good-by, and God some way bless you; and take that," slipping something in his hand. But it dropped upon the floor, and then—strange to say—I tore myself from him whom I had so longed to be rid of.

Established in my new quarters, for a day or two I kept the door locked, and started at every footfall in the passages. When I returned to my rooms, after any little absence, I would pause at the threshold for an instant, and attentively listen, ere applying my key. But these fears were needless. Bartleby never came nigh me.

I thought all was going well, when a perturbed-looking stranger visited me, inquiring whether I was the person who had recently occupied rooms at No.—Wall street.

Full of forebodings, I replied that I was.

"Then, sir," said the stranger, who proved a lawyer, "you are responsible for the man you left there. He refuses to do any copying; he refuses to do anything; he says he prefers not to; and he refuses to quit the premises."

"I am very sorry, sir," said I, with assumed tranquillity, but an inward tremor, "but, really, the man you allude to is nothing to me[32]—he is no relation or apprentice of mine, that you should hold me responsible for him."

"In mercy's name, who is he?"

"I certainly cannot inform you. I know nothing about him. Formerly I employed him as a copyist; but he has done nothing for me now for some time past."

"I shall settle him, then—good morning, sir."

Several days passed, and I heard nothing more; and, though I often felt a charitable prompting to call at the place and see poor Bartleby, yet a certain squeamishness, of I know not what, withheld me.

All is over with him, by this time, thought I, at last, when, through another week, no further intelligence reached me. But, coming to my room the day after, I found several persons waiting at my door in a high state of nervous excitement.

"That's the man—here he comes," cried the foremost one, whom I recognized as the lawyer who had previously called upon me alone.

"You must take him away, sir, at once," cried a portly person among them, advancing upon me, and whom I knew to be the landlord of No.— Wall street. "These gentlemen, my tenants, cannot stand it any longer; Mr. B—," pointing to the lawyer, "has turned him out of his room, and he now persists in haunting the

---

[32] An echo of Saint Peter's denial of Christ (see Mark 14:68, 70–71).

building generally, sitting upon the banisters of the stairs by day, and sleeping in the entry by night. Everybody is concerned; clients are leaving the offices; some fears are entertained of a mob; something you must do, and that without delay."

Aghast at this torrent, I fell back before it, and would fain have locked myself in my new quarters. In vain I persisted that Bartleby was nothing to me—no more than to any one else. In vain—I was the last person known to have anything to do with him, and they held me to the terrible account. Fearful, then, of being exposed in the papers (as one person present obscurely threatened), I considered the matter, and, at length, said, that if the lawyer would give me a confidential interview with the scrivener, in his (the lawyer's) own room, I would, that afternoon, strive my best to rid them of the nuisance they complained of.

Going up stairs to my old haunt, there was Bartleby silently sitting upon the banister at the landing.

"What are you doing here, Bartleby?" said I.

"Sitting upon the banister," he mildly replied.

I motioned him into the lawyer's room, who then left us.

"Bartleby" said I, "are you aware that you are the cause of great tribulation to me, by persisting in occupying the entry after being dismissed from the office?"

No answer.

"Now one of two things must take place. Either you must do something, or something must be done to you. Now what sort of business would you like to engage in? Would you like to re-engage in copying for some one?"

"No; I would prefer not to make any change."

"Would you like a clerkship in a dry-goods store?"

"There is too much confinement about that. No, I would not like a clerkship; but I am not particular."

"Too much confinement," I cried, "why you keep yourself confined all the time!"

"I would prefer not to take a clerkship," he rejoined, as if to settle that little item at once.

"How would a bar-tender's business suit you? There is no trying of the eye-sight in that."

"I would not like it at all; though, as I said before, I am not particular."

His unwonted wordiness inspirited me. I returned to the charge.

"Well, then, would you like to travel through the country collecting bills for the merchants? That would improve your health."

"No, I would prefer to be doing something else."

"How, then, would going as a companion to Europe, to entertain some young gentleman with your conversation—how would that suit you?"

"Not at all. It does not strike me that there is anything definite about that. I like to be stationary. But I am not particular."

"Stationary you shall be, then," I cried, now losing all patience, and, for the first time in all my exasperating connection with him, fairly flying into a passion. "If you do not go away from these premises before night, I shall feel bound—indeed, I *am* bound—to—to—to quit the premises myself!" I rather absurdly concluded, knowing not with what possible threat to try to frighten his immobility into compliance. Despairing of all further efforts, I was precipitately leaving him, when a final thought occurred to me—one which had not been wholly unindulged before.

"Bartleby," said I, in the kindest tone I could assume under such exciting circumstances, "will you go home with me now—not to my office, but my dwelling—and remain there till we can conclude upon some convenient arrangement for you at our leisure? Come, let us start now, right away."

"No: at present I would prefer not to make any change at all."

I answered nothing; but, effectually dodging every one by the suddenness and rapidity of my flight, rushed from the building, ran up Wall street towards Broadway, and, jumping into the first omnibus, was soon removed from pursuit. As soon as tranquillity returned, I distinctly perceived that I had now done all that I possibly could, both in respect to the demands of the landlord and his tenants, and with regard to my own desire and sense of duty, to benefit Bartleby, and shield him from rude persecution. I now strove to be entirely care-free and quiescent; and my conscience justified me in the attempt; though, indeed, it was not so successful as I could have wished. So fearful was I of being again hunted out by the incensed landlord and his exasperated tenants, that, surrendering my business to Nippers, for a few days, I drove about the upper part of the town and through the suburbs, in my rockaway;[33] crossed over to Jersey City and Hoboken, and paid fugitive visits to Manhattanville and Astoria.[34] In fact, I almost lived in my rockaway for the time.

When again I entered my office, lo, a note from the landlord lay upon the desk. I opened it with trembling hands. It informed me that the writer had sent to the police, and had Bartleby removed to the Tombs as a vagrant. Moreover, since I knew more about him than any one else, he wished me to appear at that place, and make a suitable statement of the facts. These tidings had a conflicting effect upon me. At first I was indignant; but, at last, almost approved. The landlord's energetic, summary disposition, had led him to adopt a procedure which I do not think I would have decided upon myself; and yet, as a last resort, under such peculiar circumstances, it seemed the only plan.

As I afterwards learned, the poor scrivener, when told that he must be conducted to the Tombs, offered not the slightest obstacle, but, in his pale, unmoving way, silently acquiesced.

Some of the compassionate and curious bystanders joined the party; and headed by one of the constables arm in arm with Bartleby, the silent procession filed its way through all the noise, and heat, and joy of the roaring thoroughfares at noon.

The same day I received the note, I went to the Tombs, or, to speak more properly, the Halls of Justice. Seeking the right officer, I stated the purpose of my call, and was informed that the individual I described was, indeed, within. I then assured the functionary that Bartleby was a perfectly honest man, and greatly to be compassionated, however unaccountably eccentric. I narrated all I knew, and closed by suggesting the idea of letting him remain in as indulgent confinement as possible, till something less harsh might be done—though, indeed, I hardly knew what. At all events, if nothing else could be decided upon, the alms-house must receive him. I then begged to have an interview.

Being under no disgraceful charge, and quite serene and harmless in all his ways, they had permitted him freely to wander about the prison, and, especially,

---

[33] A carriage with open sides and a top.

[34] Jersey City and Hoboken are in New Jersey; Manhattanville is on Manhattan Island, and Astoria, on Long Island.

in the inclosed grass-platted yards thereof. And so I found him there, standing all alone in the quietest of the yards, his face towards a high wall, while all around, from the narrow slits of the jail windows, I thought I saw peering out upon him the eyes of murderers and thieves.

"Bartleby!"

"I know you," he said, without looking round—"and I want nothing to say to you."

"It was not I that brought you here, Bartleby," said I, keenly pained at his implied suspicion. "And to you, this should not be so vile a place. Nothing reproachful attaches to you by being here. And see, it is not so sad a place as one might think. Look, there is the sky, and here is the grass."

"I know where I am," he replied, but would say nothing more, and so I left him.

As I entered the corridor again, a broad meat-like man, in an apron, accosted me, and, jerking his thumb over his shoulder, said—"Is that your friend?"

"Yes."

"Does he want to starve? If he does, let him live on the prison fare, that's all."

"Who are you?" asked I, not knowing what to make of such an unofficially speaking person in such a place.

"I am the grub-man. Such gentlemen as have friends here, hire me to provide them with something good to eat."

"Is this so?" said I, turning to the turnkey.

He said it was.

"Well, then," said I, slipping some silver into the grub-man's hands (for so they called him), "I want you to give particular attention to my friend there; let him have the best dinner you can get. And you must be as polite to him as possible."

"Introduce me, will you?" said the grub-man, looking at me with an expression which seemed to say he was all impatience for an opportunity to give a specimen of his breeding.

Thinking it would prove of benefit to the scrivener, I acquiesced; and, asking the grub-man his name, went up with him to Bartleby.

"Bartleby, this is a friend; you will find him very useful to you."

"Your sarvant, sir, your sarvant," said the grub-man, making a low salutation behind his apron. "Hope you find it pleasant here, sir; nice grounds—cool apartments—hope you'll stay with us some time—try to make it agreeable. What will you have for dinner to-day?"

"I prefer not to dine to-day," said Bartleby, turning away. "It would disagree with me; I am unused to dinners." So saying, he slowly moved to the other side of the inclosure, and took up a position fronting the dead-wall.

"How's this?" said the grub-man, addressing me with a stare of astonishment. "He's odd, ain't he?"

"I think he is a little deranged," said I, sadly.

"Deranged? deranged is it? Well, now, upon my word, I thought that friend of yourn was a gentleman forger; they are always pale and genteel-like, them forgers. I can't help pity 'em—can't help it, sir. Did you know Monroe Edwards?"[35]

---

[35] Edwards (1808–1847) was convicted in 1842 of defrauding two firms of $25,000 each, with forged letters of credit. First imprisoned in the Tombs, he was sent to Sing-Sing prison in Ossining, New York, where he died.

he added, touchingly, and paused. Then, laying his hand piteously on my shoulder, sighed, "he died of consumption at Sing-Sing. So you weren't acquainted with Monroe?"

"No, I was never socially acquainted with any forgers. But I cannot stop longer. Look to my friend yonder. You will not lose by it. I will see you again."

Some few days after this, I again obtained admission to the Tombs, and went through the corridors in quest of Bartleby; but without finding him.

"I saw him coming from his cell not long ago," said a turnkey, "may be he's gone to loiter in the yards."

So I went in that direction.

"Are you looking for the silent man?" said another turnkey, passing me. "Yonder he lies—sleeping in the yard there. 'Tis not twenty minutes since I saw him lie down."

The yard was entirely quiet. It was not accessible to the common prisoners. The surrounding walls, of amazing thickness, kept off all sounds behind them. The Egyptian character of the masonry weighed upon me with its gloom. But a soft imprisoned turf grew under foot. The heart of the eternal pyramids, it seemed, wherein, by some strange magic, through the clefts, grass-seed, dropped by birds, had sprung.

Strangely huddled at the base of the wall, his knees drawn up, and lying on his side, his head touching the cold stones, I saw the wasted Bartleby. But nothing stirred. I paused; then went close up to him; stooped over, and saw that his dim eyes were open; otherwise he seemed profoundly sleeping. Something prompted me to touch him. I felt his hand, when a tingling shiver ran up my arm and down my spine to my feet.

The round face of the grub-man peered upon me now. "His dinner is ready. Won't he dine to-day, either? Or does he live without dining?"

"Lives without dining," said I, and closed the eyes.

"Eh!—He's asleep, ain't he?"

"With kings and counselors," murmured I.[36]

There would seem little need for proceeding further in this history. Imagination will readily supply the meagre recital of poor Bartleby's interment. But, ere parting with the reader, let me say, that if this little narrative has sufficiently interested him, to awaken curiosity as to who Bartleby was, and what manner of life he led prior to the present narrator's making his acquaintance, I can only reply, that in such curiosity I fully share, but am wholly unable to gratify it. Yet here I hardly know whether I should divulge one little item of rumor, which came to my ear a few months after the scrivener's decease. Upon what basis it rested, I could never ascertain; and hence, how true it is I cannot now tell. But, inasmuch as this vague report has not been without a certain suggestive interest to me, however sad, it may prove the same with some others; and so I will briefly mention it. The report was this: that Bartleby had been a subordinate clerk in the Dead Letter Office at Washington, from which he had been suddenly removed by a change in the administration. When I think over this rumor, hardly can I express the emotions which seize me. Dead letters! does it not sound like dead men? Conceive a man by nature and misfortune prone to a pallid hopelessness, can any business seem more

---

[36] In his sufferings Job wishes he were " . . . at rest, With kings and counsellors of the earth which built desolate places for themselves," from Job 3:14.

fitted to heighten it than that of continually handling these dead letters, and assorting them for the flames? For by the cart-load they are annually burned. Sometimes from out the folded paper the pale clerk takes a ring—the finger it was meant for, perhaps, moulders in the grave; a bank-note sent in swiftest charity—he whom it would relieve, nor eats nor hungers any more; pardon for those who died despairing; hope for those who died unhoping; good tidings for those who died stifled by unrelieved calamities. On errands of life, these letters speed to death.

Ah, Bartleby! Ah, humanity!

1853

BENITO CERENO*

In the year 1799, Captain Amasa Delano,[1] of Duxbury, in Massachusetts, commanding a large sealer[2] and general trader, lay at anchor with a valuable cargo, in the harbor of St. Maria—a small, desert, uninhabited island toward the southern extremity of the long coast of Chili. There he had touched for water.

On the second day, not long after dawn, while lying in his berth, his mate came below, informing him that a strange sail was coming into the bay. Ships were then not so plenty in those waters as now. He rose, dressed, and went on deck.

The morning was one peculiar to that coast. Everything was mute and calm; everything gray. The sea, though undulated into long roods[3] of swells, seemed fixed, and was sleeked at the surface like waved lead that has cooled and set in the smelter's mould. The sky seemed a gray surtout.[4] Flights of troubled gray fowl, kith and kin with flights of troubled gray vapors among which they were mixed, skimmed low and fitfully over the waters, as swallows over meadows before storms. Shadows present, foreshadowing deeper shadows to come.

To Captain Delano's surprise, the stranger, viewed through the glass,[5] showed no colors; though to do so upon entering a haven, however uninhabited in its shores, where but a single other ship might be lying, was the custom among peaceful seamen of all nations. Considering the lawlessness and loneliness of the spot, and the sort of stories, at that day, associated with those seas, Captain Delano's surprise might have deepened into some uneasiness had he not been a person of a singularly undistrustful goodnature, not liable, except on extraordinary and repeated incentives, and hardly then, to indulge in personal alarms, any way involving the imputation of malign evil in man. Whether, in view of what humanity is capable, such a trait implies, along with a benevolent heart, more than ordinary quickness and accuracy of intellectual perception, may be left to the wise to determine.

But whatever misgivings might have obtruded on first seeing the stranger, would almost, in any seaman's mind, have been dissipated by observing that, the

---

* First published serially in *Putnam's Magazine* in October through December 1855 and was included in *Piazza Tales* (1856).

[1] Melville's plot is based on incidents related in Chapter 18 of Captain Amasa Delano's *Narrative of Voyages and Travels in the Northern and Southern Hemispheres* (1817). In adapting this *Narrative*, Melville moved the story from 1805 to 1799 and renamed the Spanish ship *Tryal* the *San Dominick* and the American ship *Perseverance* the *Bachelor's Delight*.

[2] A ship for seal hunting.   [3] Rods, units of linear measure.   [4] An overcoat.
[5] Spyglass, or telescope.

ship, in navigating into the harbor, was drawing too near the land; a sunken reef making out[6] off her bow. This seemed to prove her a stranger, indeed, not only to the sealer, but the island; consequently, she could be no wonted freebooter[7] on that ocean. With no small interest, Captain Delano continued to watch her—a proceeding not much facilitated by the vapors partly mantling the hull, through which the far matin[8] light from her cabin streamed equivocally enough; much like the sun—by this time hemisphered on the rim of the horizon, and, apparently, in company with the strange ship entering the harbor—which, wimpled[9] by the same low, creeping clouds, showed not unlike a Lima intriguante's one sinister eye peering across the Plaza from the Indian loop-hole of her dusk *saya-y-manta*.[10]

It might have been but a deception of the vapors, but, the longer the stranger was watched the more singular appeared her manœuvres. Ere long it seemed hard to decide whether she meant to come in or no—what she wanted, or what she was about. The wind, which had breezed up a little during the night, was now extremely light and baffling,[11] which the more increased the apparent uncertainty of her movements.

Surmising, at last, that it might be a ship in distress, Captain Delano ordered his whale-boat to be dropped, and, much to the wary opposition of his mate, prepared to board her, and, at the least, pilot her in. On the night previous, a fishing-party of the seamen had gone a long distance to some detached rocks out of sight from the sealer, and, an hour or two before daybreak, had returned, having met with no small success. Presuming that the stranger might have been long off soundings,[12] the good captain put several baskets of the fish, for presents, into his boat, and so pulled away. From her continuing too near the sunken reef, deeming her in danger, calling to his men, he made all haste to apprise those on board of their situation. But, some time ere the boat came up, the wind, light though it was, having shifted, had headed the vessel off, as well as partly broken the vapors from about her.

Upon gaining a less remote view, the ship, when made signally visible on the verge of the leaden-hued swells, with the shreds of fog here and there raggedly furring her, appeared like a white-washed monastery after a thunder-storm, seen perched upon some dun cliff among the Pyrenees.[13] But it was no purely fanciful resemblance which now, for a moment, almost led Captain Delano to think that nothing less than a ship-load of monks was before him. Peering over the bulwarks were what really seemed, in the hazy distance, throngs of dark cowls; while, fitfully revealed through the open port-holes, other dark moving figures were dimly descried, as of Black Friars[14] pacing the cloisters.

Upon a still nigher approach, this appearance was modified, and the true character of the vessel was plain—a Spanish merchantman of the first class, carrying negro slaves, amongst other valuable freight, from one colonial port to another. A very large, and, in its time, a very fine vessel, such as in those days were at intervals encountered along that main; sometimes superseded Acapulco treasure-

[6] Existing; the reef represents hidden danger.   [7] A pirate familiar with the waters.

[8] Early morning.   [9] Veiled.

[10] "Skirt and shawl" (Spanish); the shawl should cover the face so that only one eye of an intrigant, one involved in intrigue, would show.

[11] Uncertain.   [12] A long time away from shallow water.

[13] Mountains between France and Spain.

[14] Dominicans, an order of preaching friars who wore black hoods; Melville named the *San Dominick* after them.

ships, or retired frigates of the Spanish king's navy, which, like superannuated Italian palaces, still, under a decline of masters, preserved signs of former state.

As the whale-boat drew more and more nigh, the cause of the peculiar pipe-clayed[15] aspect of the stranger was seen in the slovenly neglect pervading her. The spars, ropes, and great part of the bulwarks, looked woolly, from long unacquaintance with the scraper, tar, and the brush. Her keel seemed laid, her ribs put together, and she launched, from Ezekiel's Valley of Dry Bones.[16]

In the present business in which she was engaged, the ship's general model and rig appeared to have undergone no material change from their original warlike and Froissart pattern.[17] However, no guns were seen.

The tops[18] were large, and were railed about with what had once been octagonal net-work, all now in sad disrepair. These tops hung overhead like three ruinous aviaries, in one of which was seen perched, on a ratlin, a white noddy,[19] a strange fowl, so called from its lethargic, somnambulistic character, being frequently caught by hand at sea. Battered and mouldy, the castellated forecastle[20] seemed some ancient turret, long ago taken by assault, and then left to decay. Toward the stern, two high-raised quarter galleries[21]—the balustrades here and there covered with dry, tindery sea-moss—opening out from the unoccupied state-cabin, whose dead-lights,[22] for all the mild weather, were hermetically closed and calked—these tenantless balconies hung over the sea as if it were the grand Venetian canal. But the principal relic of faded grandeur was the ample oval of the shield-like stern-piece, intricately carved with the arms of Castile and Leon,[23] medallioned about by groups of mythological or symbolical devices; uppermost and central of which was a dark satyr in a mask, holding his foot on the prostrate neck of a writhing figure, likewise masked.

Whether the ship had a figure-head, or only a plain beak, was not quite certain, owing to canvas wrapped about that part, either to protect it while undergoing a re-furbishing, or else decently to hide its decay. Rudely painted or chalked, as in a sailor freak,[24] along the forward side of a sort of pedestal below the canvas, was the sentence, *"Seguid vuestro jefe,"* (follow your leader); while upon the tarnished headboards, near by, appeared, in stately capitals, once gilt, the ship's name "SAN DOMINICK," each letter streakingly corroded with tricklings of copper-spike rust; while, like mourning weeds, dark festoons of sea-grass slimily swept to and fro over the name, with every hearse-like roll of the hull.

As, at last, the boat was hooked from the bow along toward the gangway amidship, its keel, while yet some inches separated from the hull, harshly grated as on a sunken coral reef. It proved a hugh bunch of conglobated[25] barnacles adhering below the water to the side like a wen[26]—a token of baffling airs and long calms passed somewhere in those seas.

---

[15] Whitened.

[16] "The Lord . . . set [Ezekiel] down in the midst of the valley which was full of bones," from Ezekiel 37:1.

[17] A medieval or ancient pattern; Jean Froissart (1333?–1400?) was a medieval French historian who wrote about the wars between France and England.

[18] Small platforms in the masts, used by lookouts.

[19] On the step of a rope ladder, a stout-bodied tern.

[20] The forward part of a ship's upper deck.   [21] Platforms on the side of a ship.

[22] Shutters that close over the port holes.

[23] Old kingdoms of Spain, united in 1230; the "shield-like stern-piece" displays a castle (Castile) and a lion (Leon). The other ornaments are ominous in nature.

[24] A joke.   [25] Ball-shaped.   [26] A cyst.

Climbing the side, the visitor was at once surrounded by a clamorous throng of whites and blacks, but the latter outnumbering the former more than could have been expected, negro transportation-ship as the stranger in port was. But, in one language, and as with one voice, all poured out a common tale of suffering; in which the negresses, of whom there were not a few, exceeded the others in their dolorous vehemence. The scurvy, together with the fever, had swept off a great part of their number, more especially the Spaniards. Off Cape Horn they had narrowly escaped shipwreck; then, for days together, they had lain tranced without wind; their provisions were low; their water next to none; their lips that moment were baked.

While Captain Delano was thus made the mark of all eager tongues, his one eager glance took in all faces, with every other object about him.

Always upon first boarding a large and populous ship at sea, especially a foreign one, with a nondescript crew such as Lascars or Manilla men,[27] the impression varies in a peculiar way from that produced by first entering a strange house with strange inmates in a strange land. Both house and ship—the one by its walls and blinds, the other by its high bulwarks like ramparts—hoard from view their interiors till the last moment: but in the case of the ship there is this addition; that the living spectacle it contains, upon its sudden and complete disclosure, has, in contrast with the blank ocean which zones it, something of the effect of enchantment. The ship seems unreal; these strange costumes, gestures, and faces, but a shadowy tableau just emerged from the deep, which directly must receive back what it gave.

Perhaps it was some such influence, as above is attempted to be described, which, in Captain Delano's mind, heightened whatever, upon a staid scrutiny, might have seemed unusual; especially the conspicuous figures of four elderly grizzled negroes, their heads like black, doddered[28] willow tops, who, in venerable contrast to the tumult below them, were couched, sphynx-like, one on the starboard cat-head,[29] another on the larboard, and the remaining pair face to face on the opposite bulwarks above the main-chains. They each had bits of unstranded old junk in their hands, and, with a sort of stoical self-content, were picking the junk into oakum,[30] a small heap of which lay by their sides. They accompanied the task with a continuous, low, monotonous chant; droning and druling[31] away like so many gray-headed bag-pipers playing a funeral march.

The quarter-deck rose into an ample elevated poop, upon the forward verge of which, lifted, like the oakum-pickers, some eight feet above the general throng, sat along in a row, separated by regular spaces, the cross-legged figures of six other blacks; each with a rusty hatchet in his hand, which, with a bit of brick and a rag, he was engaged like a scullion[32] in scouring; while between each two was a small stack of hatchets, their rusted edges turned forward awaiting a like operation. Though occasionally the four oakum-pickers would briefly address some person or persons in the crowd below, yet the six hatchet-polishers neither spoke to others, nor breathed a whisper among themselves, but sat intent upon their task, except at intervals, when, with the peculiar love in negroes of uniting industry with pastime, two and two they sideways clashed their hatchets together, like

---

[27] Sailors from East India or the Philippines.   [28] Without branches, due to age or decay.
[29] Projecting timber, near the bow, to which the anchor is secured.
[30] The worn-out rope into loose hemp fibers, used for caulking.
[31] Moaning.   [32] A kitchen worker.

cymbals, with a barbarous din. All six, unlike the generality, had the raw aspect of unsophisticated Africans.

But that first comprehensive glance which took in those ten figures, with scores less conspicuous, rested but an instant upon them, as, impatient of the hubbub of voices, the visitor turned in quest of whomsoever it might be that commanded the ship.

But as if not unwilling to let nature make known her own case among his suffering charge, or else in despair of restraining it for the time, the Spanish captain, a gentlemanly, reserved-looking, and rather young man to a stranger's eye, dressed with singular richness, but bearing plain traces of recent sleepless cares and disquietudes, stood passively by, leaning against the main-mast, at one moment casting a dreary, spiritless look upon his excited people, at the next an unhappy glance toward his visitor. By his side stood a black of small stature, in whose rude face, as occasionally, like a shepherd's dog, he mutely turned it up into the Spaniard's, sorrow and affection were equally blended.

Struggling through the throng, the American advanced to the Spaniard, assuring him of his sympathies, and offering to render whatever assistance might be in his power. To which the Spaniard returned for the present but grave and ceremonious acknowledgments, his national formality dusked by the saturnine mood of ill-health.

But losing no time in mere compliments, Captain Delano, returning to the gangway, had his basket of fish brought up; and as the wind still continued light, so that some hours at least must elapse ere the ship could be brought to the anchorage, he bade his men return to the sealer, and fetch back as much water as the whale-boat could carry, with whatever soft bread the steward might have, all the remaining pumpkins on board, with a box of sugar, and a dozen of his private bottles of cider.

Not many minutes after the boat's pushing off, to the vexation of all, the wind entirely died away, and the tide turning, began drifting back the ship helplessly seaward. But trusting this would not long last, Captain Delano sought, with good hopes, to cheer up the strangers, feeling no small satisfaction that, with persons in their condition, he could—thanks to his frequent voyages along the Spanish main[33]—converse with some freedom in their native tongue.

While left alone with them, he was not long in observing some things tending to heighten his first impressions; but surprise was lost in pity, both for the Spaniards and blacks, alike evidently reduced from scarcity of water and provisions; while long-continued suffering seemed to have brought out the less good-natured qualities of the negroes, besides, at the same time, impairing the Spaniard's authority over them. But, under the circumstances, precisely this condition of things was to have been anticipated. In armies, navies, cities, or families, in nature herself, nothing more relaxes good order than misery. Still, Captain Delano was not without the idea, that had Benito Cereno been a man of greater energy, misrule would hardly have come to the present pass. But the debility, constitutional or induced by hardships, bodily and mental, of the Spanish captain, was too obvious to be overlooked. A prey to settled dejection, as if long mocked with hope he would not now indulge it, even when it had ceased to be a mock, the prospect of that day, or evening at furthest, lying at anchor, with plenty of water for his people, and a brother captain to counsel and befriend, seemed in no perceptible de-

[33] The mainland coast of Spanish-owned South America.

gree to encourage him. His mind appeared unstrung, if not still more seriously affected. Shut up in these oaken walls, chained to one dull round of command, whose unconditionality cloyed him, like some hypochondriac abbot he moved slowly about, at times suddenly pausing, starting, or staring, biting his lip, biting his finger-nail, flushing, paling, twitching his beard, with other symptoms of an absent or moody mind. This distempered spirit was lodged, as before hinted, in as distempered a frame. He was rather tall, but seemed never to have been robust, and now with nervous suffering was almost worn to a skeleton. A tendency to some pulmonary complaint appeared to have been lately confirmed. His voice was like that of one with lungs half gone—hoarsely suppressed, a husky whisper. No wonder that, as in this state he tottered about, his private servant apprehensively followed him. Sometimes the negro gave his master his arm, or took his handkerchief out of his pocket for him; performing these and similar offices with that affectionate zeal which transmutes into something filial or fraternal acts in themselves but menial; and which has gained for the negro the repute of making the most pleasing body-servant in the world; one, too, whom a master need be on no stiffly superior terms with, but may treat with familiar trust; less a servant than a devoted companion.

Marking the noisy indocility of the blacks in general, as well as what seemed the sullen inefficiency of the whites it was not without humane satisfaction that Captain Delano witnessed the steady good conduct of Babo.

But the good conduct of Babo, hardly more than the ill-behavior of others, seemed to withdraw the half-lunatic Don[34] Benito from his cloudy languor. Not that such precisely was the impression made by the Spaniard on the mind of his visitor. The Spaniard's individual unrest was, for the present, but noted as a conspicuous feature in the ship's general affliction. Still, Captain Delano was not a little concerned at what he could not help taking for the time to be Don Benito's unfriendly indifference towards himself. The Spaniard's manner, too, conveyed a sort of sour and gloomy disdain, which he seemed at no pains to disguise. But this the American in charity ascribed to the harassing effects of sickness, since, in former instances, he had noted that there are peculiar natures on whom prolonged physical suffering seems to cancel every social instinct of kindness; as if, forced to black bread themselves, they deemed it but equity that each person coming nigh them should, indirectly, by some slight or affront, be made to partake of their fare.

But ere long Captain Delano bethought him that, indulgent as he was at the first, in judging the Spaniard, he might not, after all, have exercised charity enough. At bottom it was Don Benito's reserve which displeased him; but the same reserve was shown towards all but his faithful personal attendant. Even the formal reports which, according to sea-usage, were, at stated times, made to him by some petty underling, either a white, mulatto or black, he hardly had patience enough to listen to, without betraying contemptuous aversion. His manner upon such occasions was, in its degree, not unlike that which might be supposed to have been his imperial countryman's, Charles V.,[35] just previous to the anchoritish retirement of that monarch from the throne.

---

[34] A title (corresponding to "Sir") prefixed to the first name of a Spanish gentleman.

[35] Charles V (1500–1558), who became king of Spain in 1517 and Holy Roman Emperor in 1519. He began the passage of African slaves to the American colonies in 1517 and conducted wars with France, Germany, and Turkey. In 1556 he abdicated his titles and retired to a monastery.

This splenetic disrelish of his place was evinced in almost every function pertaining to it. Proud as he was moody, he condescended to no personal mandate. Whatever special orders were necessary, their delivery was delegated to his bodyservant, who in turn transferred them to their ultimate destination, through runners, alert Spanish boys or slave boys, like pages or pilot-fish[36] within easy call continually hovering round Don Benito. So that to have beheld this undemonstrative invalid gliding about, apathetic and mute, no landsman could have dreamed that in him was lodged a dictatorship beyond which, while at sea, there was no earthly appeal.

Thus, the Spaniard, regarded in his reserve, seemed the involuntary victim of mental disorder. But, in fact, his reserve might, in some degree, have proceeded from design. If so, then here was evinced the unhealthy climax of that icy though conscientious policy; more or less adopted by all commanders of large ships, which, except in signal emergencies, obliterates alike the manifestation of sway with every trace of sociality; transforming the man into a block, or rather into a loaded cannon, which, until there is call for thunder, has nothing to say.

Viewing him in this light, it seemed but a natural token of the perverse habit induced by a long course of such hard self-restraint, that, notwithstanding the present condition of his ship, the Spaniard should still persist in a demeanor, which, however harmless, or, it may be, appropriate, in a well-appointed vessel, such as the San Dominick might have been at the outset of the voyage, was anything but judicious now. But the Spaniard, perhaps, thought that it was with captains as with gods: reserve, under all events, must still be their cue. But probably this appearance of slumbering dominion might have been but an attempted disguise to conscious imbecility—not deep policy, but shallow device. But be all this as it might, whether Don Benito's manner was designed or not, the more Captain Delano noted its pervading reserve, the less he felt uneasiness at any particular manifestation of that reserve towards himself.

Neither were his thoughts taken up by the captain alone. Wonted to the quiet orderliness of the sealer's comfortable family of a crew, the noisy confusion of the San Dominick's suffering host repeatedly challenged his eye. Some prominent breaches, not only of discipline but of decency, were observed. These Captain Delano could not but ascribe, in the main, to the absence of those subordinate deck-officers to whom, along with higher duties, is intrusted what may be styled the police department of a populous ship. True, the old oakum-pickers appeared at times to act the part of monitorial constables to their countrymen, the blacks; but though occasionally succeeding in allaying trifling outbreaks now and then between man and man, they could do little or nothing toward establishing general quiet. The San Dominick was in the condition of a transatlantic emigrant ship, among whose multitude of living freight are some individuals, doubtless, as little troublesome as crates and bales; but the friendly remonstrances of such with their ruder companions are of not so much avail as the unfriendly arm of the mate. What the San Dominick wanted was, what the emigrant ship has, stern superior officers. But on these decks not so much as a fourth-mate was to be seen.

The visitor's curiosity was roused to learn the particulars of those mishaps which had brought about such absenteeism, with its consequences; because, though deriving some inkling of the voyage from the wails which at the first moment had greeted him, yet of the details no clear understanding had been had. The

---

[36] Small fish that swim near sharks and seem to escort them.

best account would, doubtless, be given by the captain. Yet at first the visitor was loth to ask it, unwilling to provoke some distant rebuff. But plucking up courage, he at last accosted Don Benito, renewing the expression of his benevolent interest, adding, that did he (Captain Delano) but know the particulars of the ship's misfortunes, he would, perhaps, be better able in the end to relieve them. Would Don Benito favor him with the whole story.

Don Benito faltered; then, like some somnambulist suddenly interfered with, vacantly stared at his visitor, and ended by looking down on the deck. He maintained this posture so long, that Captain Delano, almost equally disconcerted, and involuntarily almost as rude, turned suddenly from him, walking forward to accost one of the Spanish seamen for the desired information. But he had hardly gone five paces, when, with a sort of eagerness, Don Benito invited him back, regretting his momentary absence of mind, and professing readiness to gratify him.

While most part of the story was being given, the two captains stood on the after part of the main-deck, a privileged spot, no one being near but the servant.

"It is now a hundred and ninety days," began the Spaniard, in his husky whisper, "that this ship, well officered and well manned, with several cabin passengers—some fifty Spaniards in all—sailed from Buenos Ayres bound to Lima, with a general cargo, hardware, Paraguay tea and the like—and," pointing forward, "that parcel of negroes, now not more than a hundred and fifty, as you see, but then numbering over three hundred souls. Off Cape Horn we had heavy gales. In one moment, by night, three of my best officers, with fifteen sailors, were lost, with the main-yard; the spar snapping under them in the slings, as they sought, with heavers,[37] to beat down the icy sail. To lighten the hull, the heavier sacks of mata[38] were thrown into the sea, with most of the water-pipes[39] lashed on deck at the time. And this last necessity it was, combined with the prolonged detentions afterwards experienced, which eventually brought about our chief causes of suffering. When—"

Here there was a sudden fainting attack of his cough, brought on, no doubt, by his mental distress. His servant sustained him, and drawing a cordial[40] from his pocket placed it to his lips. He a little revived. But unwilling to leave him unsupported while yet imperfectly restored, the black with one arm still encircled his master, at the same time keeping his eye fixed on his face, as if to watch for the first sign of complete restoration, or relapse, as the event might prove.

The Spaniard proceeded, but brokenly and obscurely, as one in a dream.

—"Oh, my God! rather than pass through what I have, with joy I would have hailed the most terrible gales; but—"

His cough returned and with increased violence; this subsiding, with reddened lips and closed eyes he fell heavily against his supporter.

"His mind wanders. He was thinking of the plague that followed the gales," plaintively sighed the servant; "my poor, poor master!" wringing one hand, and with the other wiping the mouth. "But be patient, Señor," again turning to Captain Delano, "these fits do not last long; master will soon be himself."

Don Benito reviving, went on; but as this portion of the story was very brokenly delivered, the substance only will here be set down.

---

[37] In the ropes that attach yardarms to masts, as they sought to control the flapping sail, with bars used as levers.

[38] Mate, or Paraguay tea.   [39] Water casks.

[40] A medicine or liqueur that stimulates the heart.

It appeared that after the ship had been many days tossed in storms off the Cape, the scurvy broke out, carrying off numbers of the whites and blacks. When at last they had worked round into the Pacific, their spars and sails were so damaged, and so inadequately handled by the surviving mariners, most of whom were become invalids, that, unable to lay her northerly course by the wind, which was powerful, the unmanageable ship, for successive days and nights, was blown northwestward, where the breeze suddenly deserted her, in unknown waters, to sultry calms. The absence of the water-pipes now proved as fatal to life as before their presence had menaced it. Induced, or at least aggravated, by the more than scanty allowance of water, a malignant fever followed the scurvy; with the excessive heat of the lengthened calm, making such short work of it as to sweep away, as by billows, whole families of the Africans, and a yet larger number, proportionably, of the Spaniards, including, by a luckless fatality, every remaining officer on board. Consequently, in the smart west winds eventually following the calm, the already rent sails, having to be simply dropped, not furled, at need, had been gradually reduced to the beggars' rags they were now. To procure substitutes for his lost sailors, as well as supplies of water and sails, the captain, at the earliest opportunity, had made for Baldivia, the southernmost civilized port of Chili and South America; but upon nearing the coast the thick weather had prevented him from so much as sighting that harbor. Since which period, almost without a crew, and almost without canvas and almost without water, and, at intervals, giving its added dead to the sea, the San Dominick had been battle-dored[41] about by contrary winds, inveigled by currents, or grown weedy in calms. Like a man lost in woods, more than once she had doubled upon her own track.

"But throughout these calamities," huskily continued Don Benito, painfully turning in the half embrace of his servant, "I have to thank those negroes you see, who, though to your inexperienced eyes appearing unruly, have, indeed, conducted themselves with less of restlessness than even their owner could have thought possible under such circumstances."

Here he again fell faintly back. Again his mind wandered; but he rallied, and less obscurely proceeded.

"Yes, their owner was quite right in assuring me that no fetters would be needed with his blacks; so that while, as is wont in this transportation, those negroes have always remained upon deck—not thrust below, as in the Guinea-men[42]—they have, also, from the beginning, been freely permitted to range within given bounds at their pleasure."

Once more the faintness returned—his mind roved—but, recovering, he resumed:

"But it is Babo here to whom, under God, I owe not only my own preservation, but likewise to him, chiefly, the merit is due, of pacifying his more ignorant brethren, when at intervals tempted to murmurings."

"Ah, master," sighed the black, bowing his face, "don't speak of me; Babo is nothing; what Babo has done was but duty."

"Faithful fellow!" cried Captain Delano. "Don Benito, I envy you such a friend; slave I cannot call him."

As master and man stood before him, the black upholding the white, Captain Delano could not but bethink him of the beauty of that relationship which could

---

[41] Batted back and forth.   [42] Ships that carried slaves from Guinea, on the West coast of Africa.

present such a spectacle of fidelity on the one hand and confidence on the other. The scene was heightened by the contrast in dress, denoting their relative positions. The Spaniard wore a loose Chili jacket of dark velvet; white small-clothes and stockings, with silver buckles at the knee and instep; a high-crowned sombrero, of fine grass; a slender sword, silver mounted, hung from a knot in his sash—the last being an almost invariable adjunct, more for utility than ornament, of a South American gentlemen's dress to this hour. Excepting when his occasional nervous contortions brought about disarray, there was a certain precision in his attire curiously at variance with the unsightly disorder around; especially in the belittered Ghetto, forward of the main-mast, wholly occupied by the blacks.

The servant wore nothing but wide trowsers, apparently, from their coarseness and patches, made out of some old topsail; they were clean, and confined at the waist by a bit of unstranded rope, which, with his composed, deprecatory air at times, made him look something like a begging friar of St. Francis.

However unsuitable for the time and place, at least in the blunt-thinking American's eyes, and however strangely surviving in the midst of all his afflictions, the toilette of Don Benito might not, in fashion at least, have gone beyond the style of the day among South Americans of his class. Though on the present voyage sailing from Buenos Ayres, he had avowed himself a native and resident of Chili, whose inhabitants had not so generally adopted the plain coat and once plebeian pantaloons; but, with a becoming modification, adhered to their provincial costume, picturesque as any in the world. Still, relatively to the pale history of the voyage, and his own pale face, there seemed something so incongruous in the Spaniard's apparel, as almost to suggest the image of an invalid courtier tottering about London streets in the time of the plague.

The portion of the narrative which, perhaps, most excited interest, as well as some surprise, considering the latitudes in question, was the long calms spoken of, and more particularly the ship's so long drifting about. Without communicating the opinion, of course, the American could not but impute at least part of the detentions both to clumsy seamanship and faulty navigation. Eying Don Benito's small, yellow hands, he easily inferred that the young captain had not got into command at the hawse-hole,[43] but the cabin-window; and if so, why wonder at incompetence, in youth, sickness, and gentility united?

But drowning criticism in compassion, after a fresh repetition of his sympathies, Captain Delano, having heard out his story, not only engaged, as in the first place, to see Don Benito and his people supplied in their immediate bodily needs, but, also, now further promised to assist him in procuring a large permanent supply of water, as well as some sails and rigging; and, though it would involve no small embarrassment to himself, yet he would spare three of his best seamen for temporary deck officers; so that without delay the ship might proceed to Conception,[44] there fully to refit for Lima, her destined port.

Such generosity was not without its effect, even upon the invalid. His face lighted up; eager and hectic, he met the honest glance of his visitor. With gratitude he seemed overcome.

"This excitement is bad for master," whispered the servant, taking his arm, and with soothing words gently drawing him aside.

---

[43] A hole in a ship's bow, through which cables pass, implying that Don Benito has not worked his way up from the bottom but has come directly into authority.

[44] Concepción, Chile.

When Don Benito returned, the American was pained to observe that his hope-fulness, like the sudden kindling in his cheek, was but febrile and transient.

Ere long, with a joyless mien, looking up towards the poop, the host invited his guest to accompany him there, for the benefit of what little breath of wind might be stirring.

As, during the telling of the story, Captain Delano had once or twice started at the occasional cymballing of the hatchet-polishers, wondering why such an inter-ruption should be allowed, especially in that part of the ship, and in the ears of an invalid; and moreover, as the hatchets had anything but an attractive look, and the handlers of them still less so, it was, therefore, to tell the truth, not without some lurking reluctance, or even shrinking, it may be, that Captain Delano, with appar-ent complaisance, acquiesced in his host's invitation. The more so, since, with an untimely caprice of punctilio, rendered distressing by his cadaverous aspect, Don Benito, with Castilian[45] bows, solemnly insisted upon his guest's preceding him up the ladder leading to the elevation; where, one on each side of the last step, sat for armorial supporters and sentries two of the ominous file. Gingerly enough stepped good Captain Delano between them, and in the instant of leaving them behind, like one running the gauntlet, he felt an apprehensive twitch in the calves of his legs.

But when, facing about, he saw the whole file, like so many organ-grinders, still stupidly intent on their work, unmindful of everything beside, he could not but smile at his late fidgety panic.

Presently, while standing with his host, looking forward upon the decks below, he was struck by one of those instances of insubordination previously alluded to. Three black boys, with two Spanish boys, were sitting together on the hatches, scraping a rude wooden platter, in which some scanty mess had recently been cooked. Suddenly, one of the black boys, enraged at a word dropped by one of his white companions, seized a knife, and, though called to forbear by one of the oakum-pickers, struck the lad over the head, inflicting a gash from which blood flowed.

In amazement, Captain Delano inquired what this meant. To which the pale Don Benito dully muttered, that it was merely the sport of the lad.

"Pretty serious sport, truly," rejoined Captain Delano. "Had such a thing hap-pened on board the Bachelor's Delight, instant punishment would have followed."

At these words the Spaniard turned upon the American one of his sudden, star-ing, half-lunatic looks; then, relapsing into his torpor, answered, "Doubtless, doubtless, Señor."

Is it, thought Captain Delano, that this hapless man is one of those paper cap-tains I've known, who by policy wink at what by power they cannot put down? I know no sadder sight than a commander who has little of command but the name.

"I should think, Don Benito," he now said, glancing towards the oakum-picker who had sought to interfere with the boys, "that you would find it advantageous to keep all your blacks employed, especially the younger ones, no matter at what useless task, and no matter what happens to the ship. Why, even with my little band, I find such a course indispensable. I once kept a crew on my quarter-deck thrumming[46] mats for my cabin, when, for three days, I had given up my ship— mats, men, and all—for a speedy loss, owing to the violence of a gale, in which we could do nothing but helplessly drive before it."

---

[45] Courtly.   [46] Weaving with pieces of rope yarn and canvas.

"Doubtless, doubtless," muttered Don Benito.

"But," continued Captain Delano, again glancing upon the oakum-pickers and then at the hatchet-polishers, near by, "I see you keep some, at least, of your host employed."

"Yes," was again the vacant response.

"Those old men there, shaking their pows[47] from their pulpits," continued Captain Delano, pointing to the oakum-pickers, "seem to act the part of old dominies[48] to the rest, little heeded as their admonitions are at time. Is this voluntary on their part, Don Benito, or have you appointed them shepherds to your flock of black sheep?"

"What posts they fill, I appointed them," rejoined the Spaniard, in an acrid tone, as if resenting some supposed satiric reflection.

"And these others, these Ashantee[49] conjurors here," continued Captain Delano, rather uneasily eying the brandished steel of the hatchet-polishers, where, in spots, it had been brought to a shine, "this seems a curious business they are at, Don Benito?"

"In the gales we met," answered the Spaniard, "what of our general cargo was not thrown overboard was much damaged by the brine. Since coming into calm weather, I have had several cases of knives and hatchets daily brought up for overhauling and cleaning."

"A prudent idea, Don Benito. You are part owner of ship and cargo, I presume; but none of the slaves, perhaps?"

"I am owner of all you see," impatiently returned Don Benito, "except the main company of blacks, who belonged to my late friend, Alexandro Aranda."

As he mentioned this name, his air was heart-broken; his knees shook; his servant supported him.

Thinking he divined the cause of such unusual emotion, to confirm his surmise, Captain Delano, after a pause, said: "And may I ask, Don Benito, whether—since awhile ago you spoke of some cabin passengers—the friend, whose loss so afflicts you, at the outset of the voyage accompanied his blacks?"

"Yes."

"But died of the fever?"

"Died of the fever. Oh, could I but—"

Again quivering, the Spaniard paused.

"Pardon me," said Captain Delano, lowly, "but I think that, by a sympathetic experience, I conjecture, Don Benito, what it is that gives the keener edge to your grief. It was once my hard fortune to lose, at sea, a dear friend, my own brother, then supercargo.[50] Assured of the welfare of his spirit, its departure I could have borne like a man; but that honest eye, that honest hand—both of which had so often met mine—and that warm heart; all, all—like scraps to the dogs—to throw all to the sharks! It was then I vowed never to have for fellow-voyager a man I loved, unless, unbeknown to him, I had provided every requisite, in case of a fatality, for embalming his mortal part for interment on shore. Were your friend's remains now on board this ship, Don Benito, not thus strangely would the mention of his name affect you."

"On board this ship?" echoed the Spaniard. Then, with horrified gestures, as directed against some spectre, he unconsciously fell into the ready arms of his

---

[47] Heads.   [48] Schoolmasters or clergymen.   [49] Ashanti, a West African tribe.
[50] An officer in charge of the commercial concerns of a voyage.

attendant, who, with a silent appeal toward Captain Delano, seemed beseeching him not again to broach a theme so unspeakably distressing to his master.

This poor fellow now, thought the pained American, is the victim of that sad superstition which associates goblins with the deserted body of man, as ghosts with an abandoned house. How unlike are we made! What to me, in like case, would have been a solemn satisfaction, the bare suggestion, even, terrifies the Spaniard into this trance. Poor Alexandro Aranda! what would you say could you here see your friend—who, on former voyages, when you, for months, were left behind, has, I dare say, often longed, and longed, for one peep at you—now transported with terror at the least thought of having you anyway nigh him.

At this moment, with a dreary grave-yard toll, betokening a flaw, the ship's forecastle bell, smote by one of the grizzled oakum-pickers, proclaimed ten o'clock, through the leaden calm; when Captain Delano's attention was caught by the moving figure of a gigantic black, emerging from the general crowd below, and slowly advancing towards the elevated poop. An iron collar was about his neck, from which depended a chain, thrice wound round his body; the terminating links padlocked together at a broad band of iron, his girdle.

"How like a mute Atufal moves," murmured the servant.

The black mounted the steps of the poop, and, like a brave prisoner, brought up to receive sentence, stood in unquailing muteness before Don Benito, now recovered from his attack.

At the first glimpse of his approach, Don Benito had started, a resentful shadow swept over his face; and, as with the sudden memory of bootless[51] rage, his white lips glued together.

This is some mulish mutineer, thought Captain Delano, surveying, not without a mixture of admiration, the colossal form of the negro.

"See, he waits your question, master," said the servant.

Thus reminded, Don Benito, nervously averting his glance, as if shunning, by anticipation, some rebellious response, in a disconcerted voice, thus spoke:—

"Atufal, will you ask my pardon, now?"

The black was silent.

"Again, master," murmured the servant, with bitter upbraiding eyeing his countryman, "Again, master; he will bend to master yet."

"Answer," said Don Benito, still averting his glance, "say but the one word, *pardon,* and your chains shall be off."

Upon this, the black, slowly raising both arms, let them lifelessly fall, his links clanking, his head bowed; as much as to say, "no, I am content."

"Go," said Don Benito, with inkept and unknown emotion.

Deliberately as he had come, the black obeyed.

"Excuse me, Don Benito," said Captain Delano, "but this scene surprises me; what means it, pray?"

"It means that that negro alone, of all the band, has given me peculiar cause of offense. I have put him in chains; I—"

Here he paused; his hand to his head, as if there were a swimming there, or a sudden bewilderment of memory had come over him; but meeting his servant's kindly glance seemed reassured, and proceeded:—

"I could not scourge such a form. But I told him he must ask my pardon. As yet he has not. At my command, every two hours he stands before me."

---

[51] Useless, unavailing.

"And how long has this been?"

"Some sixty days."

"And obedient in all else? And respectful?"

"Yes."

"Upon my conscience, then," exclaimed Captain Delano, impulsively, "he has a royal spirit in him, this fellow."

"He may have some right to it," bitterly returned Don Benito, "he says he was king in his own land."

"Yes," said the servant, entering a word, "those slits in Atufal's ears once held wedges of gold; but poor Babo here, in his own land, was only a poor slave; a black man's slave was Babo, who now is the white's."

Somewhat annoyed by these conversational familiarities, Captain Delano turned curiously upon the attendant, then glanced inquiringly at his master; but, as if long wonted to these little informalities, neither master nor man seemed to understand him.

"What, pray, was Atufal's offense, Don Benito?" asked Captain Delano; "if it was not something very serious, take a fool's advice, and, in view of his general docility, as well as in some natural respect for his spirit, remit him his penalty."

"No, no, master never will do that," here murmured the servant to himself, "proud Atufal must first ask master's pardon. The slave there carries the padlock, but master here carries the key."

His attention thus directed, Captain Delano now noticed for the first, that, suspended by a slender silken cord, from Don Benito's neck, hung a key. At once, from the servant's muttered syllables, divining the key's purpose, he smiled and said:—"So, Don Benito—padlock and key—significant symbols, truly."

Biting his lip, Don Benito faltered.

Though the remark of Captain Delano, a man of such native simplicity as to be incapable of satire or irony, had been dropped in playful allusion to the Spaniard's singularly evidenced lordship over the black; yet the hypochondriac seemed some way to have taken it as a malicious reflection upon his confessed inability thus far to break down, at least, on a verbal summons, the entrenched will of the slave. Deploring this supposed misconception, yet despairing of correcting it, Captain Delano shifted the subject; but finding his companion more than ever withdrawn, as if still sourly digesting the lees[52] of the presumed affront above-mentioned, by-and-by Captain Delano likewise became less talkative, oppressed, against his own will, by what seemed the secret vindictiveness of the morbidly sensitive Spaniard. But the good sailor, himself of a quite contrary disposition, refrained, on his part, alike from the appearance as from the feeling of resentment, and if silent, was only so from contagion.

Presently the Spaniard, assisted by his servant somewhat discourteously crossed over from his guest; a procedure which, sensibly enough, might have been allowed to pass for idle caprice of ill-humor, had not master and man, lingering round the corner of the elevated skylight, began whispering together in low voices. This was unpleasing. And more; the moody air of the Spaniard, which at times had not been without a sort of valetudinarian[53] stateliness, now seemed anything but dignified; while the menial familiarity of the servant lost its original charm of simple-hearted attachment.

[52] Dregs.   [53] Infirm, sickly.

In his embarrassment, the visitor turned his face to the other side of the ship. By so doing, his glance accidentally fell on a young Spanish sailor, a coil of rope in his hand, just stepped from the deck to the first round of the mizzen-rigging.[54] Perhaps the man would not have been particularly noticed, were it not that, during his ascent to one of the yards, he, with a sort of covert intentness, kept his eye fixed on Captain Delano, from whom, presently, it passed, as if by a natural sequence, to the two whisperers.

His own attention thus redirected to that quarter, Captain Delano gave a slight start. From something in Don Benito's manner just then, it seemed as if the visitor had, at least partly, been the subject of the withdrawn consultation going on—a conjecture as little agreeable to the guest as it was little flattering to the host.

The singular alternations of courtesy and ill-breeding in the Spanish captain were unaccountable, except on one of two suppositions—innocent lunacy, or wicked imposture.

But the first idea, though it might naturally have occurred to an indifferent observer, and, in some respect, had not hitherto been wholly a stranger to Captain Delano's mind, yet, now that, in an incipient way, he began to regard the stranger's conduct something in the light of an intentional affront, of course the idea of lunacy was virtually vacated. But if not a lunatic, what then? Under the circumstances, would a gentleman, nay, any honest boor, act the part now acted by his host? The man was an impostor. Some low-born adventurer, masquerading as an oceanic grandee;[55] yet so ignorant of the first requisites of mere gentleman-hood as to be betrayed into the present remarkable indecorum. That strange cere-moniousness, too, at other times evinced, seemed not uncharacteristic of one play-ing a part above his real level. Benito Cereno—Don Benito Cereno—a sounding[56] name. One, too, at that period, not unknown, in the surname, to supercargoes and sea captains trading along the Spanish Main, as belonging to one of the most enterprising and extensive mercantile families in all those provinces; several mem-bers of it having titles; a sort of Castilian Rothschild,[57] with a noble brother, or cousin, in every great trading town of South America. The alleged Don Benito was in early manhood, about twenty-nine or thirty. To assume a sort of roving cadetship[58] in the maritime affairs of such a house, what more likely scheme for a young knave of talent and spirit? But the Spaniard was a pale invalid. Never mind. For even to the degree of simulating mortal disease, the craft of some tricksters had been known to attain. To think that, under the aspect of infantile weakness, the most savage energies might be couched—those velvets of the Spaniard but the silky paw to his fangs.

From no train of thought did these fancies come; not from within, but from without; suddenly, too, and in one throng, like hoar frost; yet as soon to vanish as the mild sun of Captain Delano's good-nature regained its meridian.

Glancing over once more towards his host—whose side-face, revealed above the skylight, was not turned towards him—he was struck by the profile, whose clearness of cut was refined by the thinness, incident to ill-health, as well as enno-bled about the chin by the beard. Away with suspicion. He was a true off-shoot of a true hidalgo[59] Cereno.

---

[54] The rigging on the mast near the stern.
[55] The highest rank of Spanish noblemen.   [56] High-sounding, bombastic.
[57] A famous German banking family with widespread European interests.
[58] An apprenticeship.   [59] A Spanish nobleman, below the rank of grandee.

Relieved by these and other better thoughts, the visitor, lightly humming a tune, now began indifferently pacing the poop, so as not to betray to Don Benito that he had at all mistrusted incivility, much less duplicity; for such mistrust would yet be proved illusory, and by the event; though, for the present, the circumstance which had provoked that distrust remained unexplained. But when that little mystery should have been cleared up, Captain Delano thought he might extremely regret it, did he allow Don Benito to become aware that he had indulged in ungenerous surmises. In short, to the Spaniard's black-letter text,[60] it was best, for awhile, to leave open margin.[61]

Presently, his pale face twitching and overcast, the Spaniard, still supported by his attendant, moved over towards his guest, when, with even more than his usual embarrassment, and a strange sort of intriguing intonation in his husky whisper, the following conversation began:—

"Señor, may I ask how long you have lain at this isle?"

"Oh, but a day or two, Don Benito."

"And from what port are you last?"

"Canton."[62]

"And there, Señor, you exchanged your sealskins for teas and silks, I think you said?"

"Yes. Silks, mostly."

"And the balance you took in specie,[63] perhaps?"

Captain Delano, fidgeting a little, answered—

"Yes; some silver; not a very great deal, though."

"Ah—well. May I ask how many men have you, Señor?"

Captain Delano slightly started, but answered—

"About five-and-twenty, all told."

"And at present, Señor, all on board, I suppose?"

"All on board, Don Benito," replied the Captain, now with satisfaction.

"And will be to-night, Señor?"

At this last question, following so many pertinacious ones, for the soul of him Captain Delano could not but look very earnestly at the questioner, who, instead of meeting the glance, with every token of craven discomposure dropped his eyes to the deck; presenting an unworthy contrast to his servant, who, just then, was kneeling at his feet, adjusting a loose shoe-buckle; his disengaged face meantime, with humble curiosity, turned openly up into his master's downcast one.

The Spaniard, still with a guilty shuffle, repeated his question:

"And—and will be to-night, Señor?"

"Yes, for aught I know," returned Captain Delano— "but nay," rallying himself into fearless truth, "some of them talked of going off on another fishing party about midnight."

"Your ships generally go—go more or less armed, I believe, Señor?"

"Oh, a six-pounder or two, in case of emergency," was the intrepidly indifferent reply, "with a small stock of muskets, sealing-spears, and cutlasses, you know."

As he thus responded, Captain Delano again glanced at Don Benito, but the latter's eyes were averted; while abruptly and awkwardly shifting the subject, he made some peevish allusion to the calm, and then, without apology, once more,

[60] A text printed in ornate script.   [61] To reserve judgment (with no marginal notes).
[62] A port in China.   [63] A coin of precious metal.

with his attendant, withdrew to the opposite bulwarks, where the whispering was resumed.

At this moment, and ere Captain Delano could cast a cool thought upon what had just passed, the young Spanish sailor, before mentioned, was seen descending from the rigging. In act of stooping over to spring inboard to the deck, his voluminous, unconfined frock, or shirt, of coarse woolen, much spotted with tar, opened out far down the chest, revealing a soiled under garment of what seemed the finest linen, edged, about the neck, with a narrow blue ribbon, sadly faded and worn. At this moment the young sailor's eye was again fixed on the whisperers, and Captain Delano thought he observed a lurking significance in it, as if silent signs, of some Freemason[64] sort, had that instant been interchanged.

This once more impelled his own glance in the direction of Don Benito, and, as before, he could not but infer that himself formed the subject of the conference. He paused. The sound of the hatchet-polishing fell on his ears. He cast another swift side-look at the two. They had the air of conspirators. In connection with the late questionings, and the incident of the young sailor, these things now begat such return of involuntary suspicion, that the singular guilelessness of the American could not endure it. Plucking up a gay and humorous expression, he crossed over to the two rapidly, saying:—"Ha, Don Benito, your black here seems high in your trust; a sort of privy-counselor, in fact."

Upon this, the servant looked up with a good-natured grin, but the master started as from a venomous bite. It was a moment or two before the Spaniard sufficiently recovered himself to reply; which he did, at last, with cold constraint:—"Yes, Señor, I have trust in Babo."

Here Babo, changing his previous grin of mere animal humor into an intelligent smile, not ungratefully eyed his master.

Finding that the Spaniard now stood silent and reserved, as if involuntarily, or purposely giving hint that his guest's proximity was inconvenient just then, Captain Delano, unwilling to appear uncivil even to incivility itself, made some trivial remark and moved off; again and again turning over in his mind the mysterious demeanor of Don Benito Cereno.

He had descended from the poop, and, wrapped in thought, was passing near a dark hatchway, leading down into the steerage, when, perceiving motion there, he looked to see what moved. The same instant there was a sparkle in the shadowy hatchway, and he saw one of the Spanish sailors, prowling there, hurriedly placing his hand in the bosom of his frock, as if hiding something. Before the man could have been certain who it was that was passing, he slunk below out of sight. But enough was seen of him to make it sure that he was the same young sailor before noticed in the rigging.

What was that which so sparkled? thought Captain Delano. It was no lamp—no match—no live coal. Could it have been a jewel? But how come sailors with jewels?—or with silk-trimmed under-shirts either? Has he been robbing the trunks of the dead cabin-passengers? But if so, he would hardly wear one of the stolen articles on board ship here. Ah, ah—if, now, that was, indeed, a secret sign I saw passing between this suspicious fellow and his captain awhile since; if I could only be certain that, in my uneasiness, my senses did not deceive me, then—

[64] A fraternal society of men, founded in the eighteenth century, that was secret and a political force in some countries. An active anti-Masonic movement influenced American politics in the 1820s and 1830s.

Here, passing from one suspicious thing to another, his mind revolved the strange questions put to him concerning his ship.

By a curious coincidence, as each point was recalled, the black wizards of Ashantee would strike up with their hatchets, as in ominous comment on the white stranger's thoughts. Pressed by such enigmas and portents, it would have been almost against nature, had not, even into the least distrustful heart, some ugly misgivings obtruded.

Observing the ship, now helplessly fallen into a current, with enchanted sails, drifting with increased rapidity seaward; and noting that, from a lately intercepted projection of the land, the sealer was hidden, the stout mariner began to quake at thoughts which he barely durst confess to himself. Above all, he began to feel a ghostly dread of Don Benito. And yet, when he roused himself, dilated his chest, felt himself strong on his legs, and coolly considered it—what did all these phantoms amount to?

Had the Spaniard any sinister scheme, it must have reference not so much to him (Captain Delano) as to his ship (the Bachelor's Delight). Hence the present drifting away of the one ship from the other, instead of favoring any such possible scheme, was, for the time, at least, opposed to it. Clearly any suspicion, combining such contradictions, must need be delusive. Beside, was it not absurd to think of a vessel in distress—a vessel by sickness almost dismanned of her crew—a vessel whose inmates were parched for water—was it not a thousand times absurd that such a craft should, at present, be of a piratical character; or her commander, either for himself or those under him, cherish any desire but for the speedy relief and refreshment? But then, might not general distress, and thirst in particular, be affected? And might not that same undiminished Spanish crew, alleged to have perished off to a remnant, be at that very moment lurking in the hold? On heartbroken pretense of entreating a cup of cold water, fiends in human form had got into lonely dwellings, nor retired until a dark deed had been done. And among the Malay pirates, it was no unusual thing to lure ships after them into their treacherous harbors, or entice boarders from a declared enemy at sea, by the spectacle of thinly manned or vacant decks, beneath which prowled a hundred spears with yellow arms ready to upthrust them through the mats. Not that Captain Delano had entirely credited such things. He had heard of them—and now, as stories, they recurred. The present destination of the ship was the anchorage. There she would be near his own vessel. Upon gaining that vicinity, might not the San Dominick, like a slumbering volcano, suddenly let loose energies now hid?

He recalled the Spaniard's manner while telling his story. There was a gloomy hesitancy and subterfuge about it. It was just the manner of one making up his tale for evil purposes, as he goes. But if that story was not true, what was the truth? That the ship had unlawfully come into the Spaniard's possession? But in many of its details, especially in reference to the more calamitous parts, such as the fatalities among the seamen, the consequent prolonged beating about, the past sufferings from obstinate calms, and still continued suffering from thirst; in all these points, as well as others, Don Benito's story had corroborated not only the wailing ejaculations of the indiscriminate multitude, white and black, but likewise—what seemed impossible to be counterfeit—by the very expression and play of every human feature, which Captain Delano saw. If Don Benito's story was, throughout, an invention, then every soul on board, down to the youngest negress, was his carefully drilled recruit in the plot: an incredible inference. And yet, if there was ground for mistrusting his veracity, that inference was a legitimate one.

But those questions of the Spaniard. There, indeed, one might pause. Did they not seem put with much the same object with which the burglar or assassin, by day-time, reconnoitres the walls of a house? But, with ill purposes, to solicit such information openly of the chief person endangered, and so, in effect, setting him on his guard; how unlikely a procedure was that? Absurd, then, to suppose that those questions had been prompted by evil designs. Thus, the same conduct, which, in this instance, had raised the alarm, served to dispel it. In short, scarce any suspicion or uneasiness, however apparently reasonable at the time, which was not now, with equal apparent reason, dismissed.

At last he began to laugh at his former forebodings; and laugh at the strange ship for, in its aspect, someway siding with them, as it were; and laugh, too, at the odd-looking blacks, particularly those old scissors-grinders, the Ashantees; and those bed-ridden old knitting women, the oakum-pickers; and almost at the dark Spaniard himself, the central hobgoblin of all.

For the rest, whatever in a serious way seemed enigmatical, was now good-naturedly explained away by the thought that, for the most part, the poor invalid scarcely knew what he was about; either sulking in black vapors, or putting idle questions without sense or object. Evidently, for the present, the man was not fit to be intrusted, with the ship. On some benevolent plea withdrawing the command from him, Captain Delano would yet have to send her to Conception, in charge of his second mate, a worthy person and good navigator—a plan not more convenient for the San Dominick than for Don Benito; for, relieved from all anxiety, keeping wholly to his cabin, the sick man, under the good nursing of his servant, would, probably, by the end of the passage, be in a measure restored to health, and with that he should also be restored to authority.

Such were the American's thoughts. They were tranquilizing. There was a difference between the idea of Don Benito's darkly pre-ordaining Captain Delano's fate, and Captain Delano's lightly arranging Don Benito's. Nevertheless, it was not without something of relief that the good seaman presently perceived his whale-boat in the distance. Its absence had been prolonged by unexpected detention at the sealer's side, as well as its returning trip lengthened by the continual recession of the goal.

The advancing speck was observed by the blacks. Their shouts attracted the attention of Don Benito, who, with a return of courtesy, approaching Captain Delano, expressed satisfaction at the coming of some supplies, slight and temporary as they must necessarily prove.

Captain Delano responded; but while doing so, his attention was drawn to something passing on the deck below: among the crowd climbing the landward bulwarks, anxiously watching the coming boat, two blacks, to all appearances accidentally incommoded by one of the sailors, violently pushed him aside, which the sailor someway resenting, they dashed him to the deck, despite the earnest cries of the oakum-pickers.

"Don Benito," said Captain Delano quickly, "do you see what is going on there? Look!"

But, seized by his cough, the Spaniard staggered, with both hands to his face, on the point of falling. Captain Delano would have supported him, but the servant was more alert, who, with one hand sustaining his master, with the other applied the cordial. Don Benito restored, the black withdrew his support, slipping aside a little, but dutifully remaining within call of a whisper. Such discretion was here evinced as quite wiped away, in the visitor's eyes, any blemish of impropriety which might have attached to the attendant, from the indecorous conferences before mentioned; showing, too, that if the servant were to blame, it might be more the master's fault than his own, since, when left to himself, he could conduct thus well.

His glance called away from the spectacle of disorder to the more pleasing one before him, Captain Delano could not avoid again congratulating his host upon possessing such a servant, who, though perhaps a little too forward now and then, must upon the whole be invaluable to one in the invalid's situation.

"Tell me, Don Benito," he added, with a smile—"I should like to have your man here, myself—what will you take for him? Would fifty doubloons[65] be any object?"

"Master wouldn't part with Babo for a thousand doubloons," murmured the black, overhearing the offer, and taking it in earnest, and, with the strange vanity of a faithful slave, appreciated by his master, scorning to hear so paltry a valuation put upon him by a stranger. But Don Benito, apparently hardly yet completely restored, and again interrupted by his cough, made but some broken reply.

Soon his physical distress became so great, affecting his mind, too, apparently, that, as if to screen the sad spectacle, the servant gently conducted his master below.

Left to himself, the American, to while away the time till his boat should arrive, would have pleasantly accosted some one of the few Spanish seamen he saw; but recalling something that Don Benito had said touching their ill conduct, he refrained; as a shipmaster indisposed to countenance cowardice or unfaithfulness in seamen.

While, with these thoughts, standing with eye directed forward towards that handful of sailors, suddenly he thought that one or two of them returned the glance and with a sort of meaning. He rubbed his eyes, and looked again; but again seemed to see the same thing. Under a new form, but more obscure than any previous one, the old suspicions recurred, but, in the absence of Don Benito, with less of panic than before. Despite the bad account given of the sailors, Captain Delano resolved forthwith to accost one of them. Descending the poop, he made his way through the blacks, his movement drawing a queer cry from the oakum-pickers, prompted by whom, the negroes, twitching each other aside, divided before him; but, as if curious to see what was the object of this deliberate visit to their Ghetto, closing in behind, in tolerable order, followed the white stranger up. His progress thus proclaimed as by mounted kings-at-arms,[66] and escorted as by a Caffre[67] guard of honor, Captain Delano, assuming a good-humored, off-handed air, continued to advance; now and then saying a blithe word to the negroes, and his eye curiously surveying the white faces, here and there sparsely mixed in with the blacks, like stray white pawns venturously involved in the ranks of the chessmen opposed.

While thinking which of them to select for his purpose, he chanced to observe a sailor seated on the deck engaged in tarring the strap of a large block, a circle of blacks squatted round him inquisitively eying the process.

The mean employment of the man was in contrast with something superior in his figure. His hand, black with continually thrusting it into the tar-pot held for him by a negro, seemed not naturally allied to his face, a face which would have

---

[65] Would you object to Spanish gold coins (equal to sixteen silver dollars each)?
[66] Heraldic officers.   [67] Kaffir, a Bantu tribe in South Africa, known for their height.

been a very fine one but for its haggardness. Whether this haggardness had aught to do with criminality, could not be determined; since, as intense heat and cold, though unlike, produce like sensations, so innocence and guilt, when, through casual association with mental pain, stamping any visible impress, use one seal—a hacked one.

Not again that this reflection occurred to Captain Delano at the time, charitable man as he was. Rather another idea. Because observing so singular a haggardness combined with a dark eye, averted as in trouble and shame, and then again recalling Don Benito's confessed ill opinion of his crew, insensibly he was operated upon by certain general notions which, while disconnecting pain and abashment from virtue, invariably link them with vice.

If, indeed, there be any wickedness on board this ship, thought Captain Delano, be sure that man there has fouled his hand in it, even as now he fouls it in the pitch. I don't like to accost him. I will speak to this other, this old Jack here on the windlass.[68]

He advanced to an old Barcelona tar, in ragged red breeches and dirty night-cap, cheeks trenched and bronzed, whiskers dense as thorn hedges. Seated between two sleepy-looking Africans, this mariner, like his younger shipmate, was employed upon some rigging—splicing a cable—the sleepy-looking blacks performing the inferior function of holding the outer parts of the ropes for him.

Upon Captain Delano's approach, the man at once hung his head below its previous level; the one necessary for business. It appeared as if he desired to be thought absorbed, with more than common fidelity, in his task. Being addressed, he glanced up, but with what seemed a furtive, diffident air, which sat strangely enough on his weather-beaten visage, much as if a grizzly bear, instead of growling and biting, should simper and cast sheep's eyes. He was asked several questions concerning the voyage—questions purposely referring to several particulars in Don Benito's narrative, not previously corroborated by those impulsive cries greeting the visitor on first coming on board. The questions were briefly answered, confirming all that remained to be confirmed of the story. The negroes about the windlass joined in with the old sailor; but, as they became talkative, he by degrees became mute, and at length quite glum, seemed morosely unwilling to answer more questions, and yet, all the while, this ursine[69] air was somehow mixed with his sheepish one.

Despairing of getting into unembarrassed talk with such a centaur,[70] Captain Delano, after glancing round for a more promising countenance, but seeing none, spoke pleasantly to the blacks to make way for him; and so, amid various grins and grimaces, returned to the poop, feeling a little strange at first, he could hardly tell why, but upon the whole with regained confidence in Benito Cereno.

How plainly, thought he, did that old whiskerando[71] yonder betray a consciousness of ill desert. No doubt, when he saw me coming, he dreaded lest I, apprised by his Captain of the crew's general misbehavior, came with sharp words for him, and so down with his head. And yet—and yet, now that I think of it, that very old fellow, if I err not, was one of those who seemed so earnestly eying me here awhile since. Ah, these currents spin one's head round almost as much as they do the ship. Ha, there now's a pleasant sort of sunny sight; quite sociable, too.

[68] This sailor here on the winch, or hoist.   [69] Bearlike.
[70] According to Greek myth, a half-man, half-horse.   [71] A bearded sailor.

His attention had been drawn to a slumbering negress, partly disclosed through the lacework of some rigging, lying, with youthful limbs carelessly disposed, under the lee of the bulwarks, like a doe in the shade of a woodland rock. Sprawling at her lapped breasts, was her wide-awake fawn, stark naked, its black little body half lifted from the deck, crosswise with its dam's; its hands, like two paws, clambering upon her; its mouth and nose ineffectually rooting to get at the mark; and meantime giving a vexatious half-grunt blending with the composed snore of the negress.

The uncommon vigor of the child at length roused the mother. She started up, at a distance facing Captain Delano. But as if not at all concerned at the attitude in which she had been caught, delightedly she caught the child up, with maternal transports, covering it with kisses.

There's naked nature, now; pure tenderness and love, thought Captain Delano, well pleased.

This incident prompted him to remark the other negresses more particuarly than before. He was gratified with their manners: like most uncivilized women, they seemed at once tender of heart and tough of constitution; equally ready to die for their infants or fight for them. Unsophisticated as leopardesses; loving as doves. Ah! thought Captain Delano, these, perhaps, are some of the very women whom Ledyard[72] saw in Africa, and gave such a noble account of.

These natural sights somehow insensibly deepened his confidence and ease. At last he looked to see how his boat was getting on; but it was still pretty remote. He turned to see if Don Benito had returned; but he had not.

To change the scene, as well as to please himself with a leisurely observation of the coming boat, stepping over into the mizzen-chains,[73] he clambered his way into the starboard quarter-gallery—one of those abandoned Venetian-looking water-balconies previously mentioned—retreats cut off from the deck. As his foot pressed the half-damp, half-dry sea-mosses matting the place, and a chance phantom catspaw[74]—an islet of breeze, unheralded, unfollowed—as this ghostly cats paw came fanning his cheek; as his glance fell upon the row of small, round dead-lights—all closed like coppered eyes of the coffined—and the state-cabin door, once connecting with the gallery, even as the dead-lights had once looked out upon it, but now calked fast like a sarcophagus lid; and to a purple-black tarred-over, panel, threshold, and post; and he bethought him of the time, when that state-cabin and this state-balcony had heard the voices of the Spanish king's officers, and the forms of the Lima viceroy's daughters had perhaps leaned where he stood—as these and other images flitted through his mind, as the cats-paw through the calm, gradually he felt rising a dreamy inquietude, like that of one who alone on the prairie feels unrest from the repose of the noon.

He leaned against the carved balustrade, again looking off toward his boat; but found his eye falling upon the ribbon grass, trailing along the ship's water-line, straight as a border of green box; and parterres[75] of sea-weed, broad ovals and crescents, floating nigh and far, with what seemed long formal alleys between,

---

[72] John Ledyard (1751–1789), an American traveler and writer, whose account of African woman, *Proceedings of the Association for Promoting the Discovery of the Interior Parts of Africa* (1790) was quoted by the famous Scottish explorer Mungo Park (1771–1806) in his *Travels in the Interior of Africa* (1799). Melville gave Park credit for the quotation in the *Putnam's Magazine* version of "Benito Cereno," then substituted Ledyard's name for Park's in *The Piazza Tales*.

[73] Supports for the mizzen rigging.   [74] A mild breeze (as light as a cat's paw).

[75] Ornamental gardens of flower beds.

crossing the terraces of swells, and sweeping round as if leading to the grottoes below. And overhanging all was the balustrade by his arm, which, partly stained with pitch and partly embossed with moss, seemed the charred ruin of some summer-house in a grand garden long running to waste.

Trying to break one charm, he was but becharmed anew. Though upon the wide sea, he seemed in some far inland country; prisoner in some deserted château, left to stare at empty grounds, and peer out at vague roads, where never wagon or wayfarer passed.

But these enchantments were a little disenchanted as his eye fell on the corroded mainchains.[76] Of an ancient style, massy and rusty in link, shackle and bolt, they seemed even more fit for the ship's present business than the one for which she had been built.

Presently he thought something moved nigh the chains. He rubbed his eyes, and looked hard. Groves of rigging were about the chains; and there, peering from behind a great stay,[77] like an Indian from behind a hemlock, a Spanish sailor, a marlingspike[78] in his hand, was seen, who made what seemed an imperfect gesture towards the balcony, but immediately, as if alarmed by some advancing step along the deck within, vanished into the recesses of the hempen forest, like a poacher.

What meant this? Something the man had sought to communicate, unbeknown to any one, even to his captain. Did the secret involve aught unfavorable to his captain? Were those previous misgivings of Captain Delano's about to be verified? Or, in his haunted mood at the moment, had some random, unintentional motion of the man, while busy with the stay, as if repairing it, been mistaken for a significant beckoning?

Not unbewildered, again he gazed off for his boat. But it was temporarily hidden by a rocky spur of the isle. As with some eagerness he bent forward, watching for the first shooting view of its beak, the balustrade gave way before him like charcoal. Had he not clutched an outreaching rope he would have fallen into the sea. The crash, though feeble, and the fall, though hollow, of the rotten fragments, must have been overheard. He glanced up. With sober curiosity peering down upon him was one of the old oakum-pickers, slipped from his perch to an outside boom;[79] while below the old negro, and, invisible to him, reconnoitering from a port-hole like a fox from the mouth of its den, crouched the Spanish sailor again. From something suddenly suggested by the man's air, the mad idea now darted into Captain Delano's mind, that Don Benito's plea of indisposition, in withdrawing below, was but a pretense: that he was engaged there maturing his plot, of which the sailor, by some means gaining an inkling, had a mind to warn the stranger against; incited, it may be, by gratitude for a kind word on first boarding the ship. Was it from foreseeing some possible interference like this, that Don Benito had, beforehand, given such a bad character[80] of his sailors, while praising the negroes; though, indeed, the former seemed as docile as the latter the contrary? The whites, too, by nature, were the shrewder race. A man with some evil design, would he not be likely to speak well of that stupidity which was blind to his depravity, and malign that intelligence from which it might not be hidden? Not unlikely, perhaps. But if the whites had dark secrets concerning Don Benito,

---

[76] Supports for the mainmast rigging.   [77] A strong rope used to support a mast.
[78] A pointed iron tool used in splicing.   [79] A spar extending from a mast to hold a sail.
[80] A reference.

could then Don Benito be any way in complicity with the blacks? But they were too stupid. Besides, who ever heard of a white so far a renegade as to apostatize[81] from his very species almost, by leaguing in against it with negroes? These difficulties recalled former ones. Lost in their mazes, Captain Delano, who had now regained the deck, was uneasily advancing along it, when he observed a new face; an aged sailor seated cross-legged near the main hatchway. His skin was shrunk up with wrinkles like a pelican's empty pouch; his hair frosted; his countenance grave and composed. His hands were full of ropes, which he was working into a large knot. Some blacks were about him obligingly dipping the strands for him, here and there, as the exigencies of the operation demanded.

Captain Delano crossed over to him, and stood in silence surveying the knot; his mind, by a not uncongenial transition, passing from its own entanglements to those of the hemp. For intricacy, such a knot he had never seen in an American ship, nor indeed any other. The old man looked like an Egyptian priest, making Gordian knots for the temple of Ammon.[82] The knot seemed a combination of double-bowline-knot, treble-crown-knot, back-handed-well-knot, knot-in-and-out-knot, and jamming-knot.

At last, puzzled to comprehend the meaning of such a knot, Captain Delano addressed the knotter:—

"What are you knotting there, my man?"

"The knot," was the brief reply, without looking up.

"So it seems; but what is it for?"

"For some one else to undo," muttered back the old man, plying his fingers harder than ever, the knot being now nearly completed.

While Captain Delano stood watching him, suddenly the old man threw the knot towards him, saying in broken English—the first heard in the ship—something to this effect: "Undo it, cut it, quick." It was said lowly, but with such condensation of rapidity, that the long, slow words in Spanish, which had preceded and followed, almost operated as covers to the brief English between.

For a moment, knot in hand, and knot in head, Captain Delano stood mute; while, without further heeding him, the old man was now intent upon other ropes. Presently there was a slight stir behind Captain Delano. Turning, he saw the chained negro, Atufal, standing quietly there. The next moment the old sailor rose, muttering, and, followed by his subordinate negroes, removed to the forward part of the ship, where in the crowd he disappeared.

An elderly negro, in a clout[83] like an infant's, and with a pepper and salt head, and a kind of attorney air, now approached Captain Delano. In tolerable Spanish, and with a good-natured, knowing wink, he informed him that the old knotter was simple-witted, but harmless; often playing his odd tricks. The negro concluded by begging the knot, for of course the stranger would not care to be troubled with it. Unconsciously, it was handed to him. With a sort of congé,[84] the negro received it, and, turning his back, ferreted into it like a detective custom-house officer after smuggled laces. Soon, with some African word, equivalent to pshaw, he tossed the knot overboard.

---

[81] To abandon a faith.

[82] The oracle at the temple of Ammon in Egypt prophesied that whoever untied King Gordius's intricate knot would become master of Asia. Alexander the Great simply cut the knot with his sword (and later defeated the Persian army).

[83] A patch of cloth.   [84] A low bow.

All this is very queer now, thought Captain Delano, with a qualmish sort of emotion; but, as one feeling incipient sea-sickness, he strove, by ignoring the symptoms, to get rid of the malady. Once more he looked off for his boat. To his delight, it was now again in view, leaving the rocky spur astern.

The sensation here experienced, after at first relieving his uneasiness, with unforeseen efficacy soon began to remove it. The less distant sight of that well-known boat—showing it, not as before, half blended with the haze, but with outline defined, so that its individuality, like a man's, was manifest; that boat, Rover by name, which, though now in strange seas, had often pressed the beach of Captain Delano's home, and, brought to its threshold for repairs, had familiarly lain there, as a Newfoundland dog; the sight of that household boat evoked a thousand trustful associations, which, contrasted with previous suspicions, filled him not only with lightsome confidence, but somehow with half humorous self-reproaches at his former lack of it.

"What, I, Amasa Delano—Jack of the Beach, as they called me when a lad—I, Amasa; the same that, duck-satchel in hand, used to paddle along the water-side to the school-house made from the old hulk—I, little Jack of the Beach, that used to go berrying with cousin Nat and the rest; I to be murdered here at the ends of the earth, on board a haunted pirate-ship by a horrible Spaniard? Too nonsensical to think of! Who would murder Amasa Delano? His conscience is clean. There is some one above. Fie, fie, Jack of the Beach! you are a child indeed; a child of the second childhood, old boy; you are beginning to dote and drule, I'm afraid."

Light of heart and foot, he stepped aft, and there was met by Don Benito's servant, who, with a pleasing expression, responsive to his own present feelings, informed him that his master has recovered from the effects of his coughing fit, and had just ordered him to go present his compliments to his good guest, Don Amasa, and say that he (Don Benito) would soon have the happiness to rejoin him.

There now, do you mark that? again thought Captain Delano, walking the poop. What a donkey I was. This kind gentleman who here sends me his kind compliments, he, but ten minutes ago, dark-lantern in hand, was dodging round some old grind-stone in the hold, sharpening a hatchet for me, I thought. Well, well; these long calms have a morbid effect on the mind, I've often heard, though I never believed it before. Ha! glancing towards the boat; there's Rover; good dog; a white bone in her mouth.[85] A pretty big bone though, seems to me.—What? Yes, she has fallen afoul of the bubbling tide-rip there. It sets her the other way, too, for the time. Patience.

It was now about noon, though, from the grayness of everything, it seemed to be getting towards dusk.

The calm was confirmed. In the far distance, away from the influence of land, the leaden ocean seemed laid out and leaded up, its course finished, soul gone, defunct. But the current from landward, where the ship was, increased; silently sweeping her further and further towards the tranced waters beyond.

Still, from his knowledge of those latitudes, cherishing hopes of a breeze, and a fair and fresh one, at any moment, Captain Delano, despite present prospects, buoyantly counted upon bringing the San Dominick safely to anchor ere night. The distance swept over was nothing; since, with a good wind, ten minutes' sailing would retrace more than sixty minutes, drifting. Meantime, one moment turn-

---

[85] A metaphor for a boat with sea foam under the bow.

ing to mark "Rover" fighting the tide-rip, and the next to see Don Benito approaching, he continued walking the poop.

Gradually he felt a vexation arising from the delay of his boat; this soon merged into uneasiness; and at last—his eye falling continually, as from a stage-box into the pit,[86] upon the strange crowd before and below him, and, by-and-by, recognizing there the face—now composed to indifference—of the Spanish sailor who had seemed to beckon from the main-chains—something of his old trepidations returned.

Ah, thought he—gravely enough—this is like the ague:[87] because it went off, it follows not that it won't come back.

Though ashamed of the relapse, he could not altogether subdue it; and so, exerting his good-nature to the utmost, insensibly he came to a compromise.

Yes, this is a strange craft; a strange history, too, and strange folks on board. But—nothing more.

By way of keeping his mind out of mischief till the boat should arrive, he tried to occupy it with turning over and over, in a purely speculative sort of way, some lesser peculiarities of the captain and crew. Among others, four curious points recurred:

First, the affair of the Spanish lad assailed with a knife by the slave boy; an act winked at by Don Benito. Second, the tyranny in Don Benito's treatment of Atufal, the black; as if a child should lead a bull of the Nile by the ring in his nose. Third, the trampling of the sailor by the two negroes; a piece of insolence passed over without so much as a reprimand. Fourth, the cringing submission to their master, of all the ship's underlings, mostly blacks; as if by the least inadvertence they feared to draw down his despotic displeasure.

Coupling these points, they seemed somewhat contradictory. But what then, thought Captain Delano, glancing towards his now nearing boat—what then? Why, Don Benito is a very capricious commander. But he is not the first of the sort I have seen; though it's true he rather exceeds any other. But as a nation—continued he in his reveries—these Spaniards are all an odd set; the very word Spaniard has a curious, conspirator, Guy-Fawkish[88] twang to it. And yet, I dare say, Spaniards in the main are as good folks as any in Duxbury, Massachusetts. Ah good! At last "Rover" has come.

As, with its welcome freight, the boat touched the side, the oakum-pickers, with venerable gestures, sought to restrain the blacks, who, at the sight of three gurried[89] water-casks in its bottom, and a pile of wilted pumpkins in its bow, hung over the bulwarks in disorderly raptures.

Don Benito, with his servant, now appeared; his coming, perhaps, hastened by hearing the noise. Of him Captain Delano sought permission to serve out the water, so that all might share alike, and none injure themselves by unfair excess. But sensible, and, on Don Benito's account, kind as this offer was, it was received with what seemed impatience; as if aware that he lacked energy as a commander, Don Benito, with the true jealousy of weakness, resented as an affront any interference. So, at least, Captain Delano inferred.

---

[86] An orchestra pit.   [87] Fever and chills.

[88] Guy Fawkes (1570–1606), a Catholic conspirator, was involved in the Gunpowder Plot to blow up the English Parliament building in 1605. Fawkes was executed, and Guy Fawkes Day became an occasion for anti-Catholic sentiment and suspicion.

[89] Slimy from fish entrails.

In another moment the casks were being hoisted in, when some of the eager negroes accidentally jostled Captain Delano, where he stood by the gangway; so that, unmindful of Don Benito, yielding to the impulse of the moment, with good-natured authority he bade the blacks stand back; to enforce his words making use of a half-mirthful, half-menacing gesture. Instantly the blacks paused, just where they were, each negro and negress suspended in his or her posture, exactly as the word had found them—for a few seconds continuing so—while, as between the responsive posts of a telegraph, an unknown syllable ran from man to man among the perched oakum-pickers. While the visitors attention was fixed by this scene, suddenly the hatchet-polishers half rose, and a rapid cry came from Don Benito.

Thinking that at the signal of the Spaniard he was about to be massacred, Captain Delano would have sprung for his boat, but paused, as the oakum-pickers, dropping down into the crowd with earnest exclamations, forced every white and every negro back, at the same moment, with gestures friendly and familiar, almost jocose, bidding him, in substance, not be a fool. Simultaneously the hatchet-polishers resumed their seats, quietly as so many tailors, and at once, as if nothing had happened, the work of hoisting in the casks was resumed, whites and blacks singing at the tackle.

Captain Delano glanced towards Don Benito. As he saw his meagre form in the act of recovering itself from reclining in the servant's arms, into which the agitated invalid had fallen, he could not but marvel at the panic by which himself had been surprised, on the darting supposition that such a commander, who, upon a legitimate occasion, so trivial, too, as it now appeared, could lose all self-command, was, with energetic iniquity, going to bring about his murder.

The casks being on deck, Captain Delano was handed a number of jars and cups by one of the steward's aids, who, in the name of his captain, entreated him to do as he had proposed—dole out the water. He complied, with republican impartiality as to this republican element, which always seeks one level, serving the oldest white no better than the youngest black; excepting, indeed, poor Don Benito, whose condition, if not rank, demanded an extra allowance. To him, in the first place, Captain Delano presented a fair pitcher of the fluid; but, thirsting as he was for it, the Spaniard quaffed not a drop until after several grave bows and salutes. A reciprocation of courtesies which the sight-loving Africans hailed with clapping of hands.

Two of the less wilted pumpkins being reserved for the cabin table, the residue were minced up on the spot for the general regalement. But the soft bread, sugar, and bottled cider, Captain Delano would have given the whites alone, and in chief Don Benito; but the latter objected; which disinterestedness not a little pleased the American; and so mouthfuls all around were given alike to whites and blacks; excepting one bottle of cider, which Babo insisted upon setting aside for his master.

Here it may be observed that as, on the first visit of the boat, the American had not permitted his men to board the ship, neither did he now; being unwilling to add to the confusion of the decks.

Not uninfluenced by the peculiar good-humor at present prevailing, and for the time oblivious of any but benevolent thoughts, Captain Delano, who, from recent indications, counted upon a breeze within an hour or two at furthest, dispatched the boat back to the sealer, with orders for all the hands that could be spared immediately to set about rafting casks to the watering-place and filling them. Likewise he bade word be carried to his chief officer, that if, against present expectation, the ship was not brought to anchor by sunset, he need be under no concern; for as there was to be a full moon that night, he (Captain Delano) would remain on board ready to play the pilot, come the wind soon or late.

As the two Captains stood together, observing the departing boat—the servant, as it happened, having just spied a spot on his master's velvet sleeve, and silently engaged rubbing it out—the American expressed his regrets that the San Dominick had no boats; none, at least, but the unseaworthy old hulk of the long-boat, which, warped as a camel's skeleton in the desert, and almost as bleached, lay pot-wise inverted amid-ships, one side a little tipped, furnishing a subterraneous sort of den for family groups of the blacks, mostly women and small children; who, squatting on old mats below, or perched above in the dark dome, on the elevated seats, were descried, some distance within, like a social circle of bats, sheltering in some friendly cave; at intervals, ebon flights of naked boys and girls, three or four years old, darting in and out of the den's mouth.

"Had you three or four boats now, Don Benito," said Captain Delano, "I think that, by tugging at the oars, your negroes here might help along matters some. Did you sail from port without boats, Don Benito?"

"They were stove in the gales, Señor."

"That was bad. Many men, too, you lost then. Boats and men. Those must have been hard gales, Don Benito."

"Past all speech," cringed the Spaniard.

"Tell me, Don Benito," continued his companion with increased interest, "tell me, were these gales immediately off the pitch[90] of Cape Horn?"

"Cape Horn?—who spoke of Cape Horn?"

"Yourself did, when giving me an account of your voyage," answered Captain Delano, with almost equal astonishment at this eating of his own words, even as he ever seemed eating his own heart, on the part of the Spaniard. "You yourself, Don Benito, spoke of Cape Horn," he emphatically repeated.

The Spaniard turned, in a sort of stooping posture, pausing an instant, as one about to make a plunging exchange of elements, as from air to water.

At this moment a messenger-boy, a white, hurried by, in the regular performance of his function carrying the last expired half hour[91] forward to the forecastle, from the cabin time-piece, to have it struck at the ship's large bell.

"Master," said the servant, discontinuing his work on the coat sleeve, and addressing the rapt Spaniard with a sort of timid apprehensiveness, as one charged with a duty, the discharge of which, it was foreseen, would prove irksome to the very person who had imposed it, and for whose benefit it was intended, "master told me never mind where he was, or how engaged, always to remind him, to a minute, when shaving-time comes. Miguel has gone to strike the half-hour afternoon. It is *now,* master. Will master go into the cuddy?"[92]

"Ah—yes," answered the Spaniard, starting, as from dreams into realities; then turning upon Captain Delano, he said that ere long he would resume the conversation.

"Then if master means to talk more to Don Amasa," said the servant, "why not let Don Amasa sit by master in the cuddy, and master can talk, and Don Amasa can listen, while Babo here lathers and strops."

---

[90] The point.

[91] The eighth half-hour in a ship's four-hour watch (one bell is struck for every half-hour in the watch). The messenger boy is going to strike eight bells, signaling the end of one four-hour watch and the beginning of another.

[92] A small cabin.

"Yes," said Captain Delano, not unpleased with this sociable plan, "yes, Don Benito, unless you had rather not, I will go with you."

"Be it so, Señor."

As the three passed aft, the American could not but think it another strange instance of his host's capriciousness, this being shaved with such uncommon punctuality in the middle of the day. But he deemed it more than likely that the servant's anxious fidelity had something to do with the matter; inasmuch as the timely interruption served to rally his master from the mood which had evidently been coming upon him.

The place called the cuddy was a light deck-cabin formed by the poop, a sort of attic to the large cabin below. Part of it had formerly been the quarters of the officers; but since their death all the partitionings had been thrown down, and the whole interior converted into one spacious and airy marine hall; for absence of fine furniture and picturesque disarray of odd appurtenances, somewhat answering to the wide, cluttered hall of some eccentric bachelor-squire in the country, who hangs his shooting-jacket and tobacco-pouch on deer antlers, and keeps his fishing-rod, tongs, and walking-stick in the same corner.

The similitude was heightened, if not originally suggested, by glimpses of the surrounding sea; since, in one aspect, the country and the ocean seem cousins-german.[93]

The floor of the cuddy was matted. Overhead, four or five old muskets were stuck into horizontal holes along the beams. On one side was a claw-footed old table lashed to the deck; a thumbed missal[94] on it, and over it a small, meagre crucifix attached to the bulk-head. Under the table lay a dented cutlass or two, with a hacked harpoon, among some melancholy old rigging, like a heap of poor friars' girdles.[95] There were also two long, sharp-ribbed settees of Malacca cane, black with age, and uncomfortable to look at as inquisitors' racks, with a large, misshapen arm-chair, which, furnished with a rude barber's crotch[96] at the back, working with a screw, seemed some grotesque engine of torment. A flag locker was in one corner, open, exposing various colored bunting, some rolled up, others half unrolled, still others tumbled. Opposite was a cumbrous washstand, of black mahogany, all of one block, with a pedestal, like a font, and over it a railed shelf, containing combs, brushes, and other implements of the toilet. A torn hammock of stained grass swung near; the sheets tossed, and the pillow wrinkled up like a brow, as if who ever slept here slept but illy, with alternate visitations of sad thoughts and bad dreams.

The further extremity of the cuddy, overhanging the ship's stern, was pierced with three openings, windows or port-holes, according as men or cannon might peer, socially or unsocially, out of them. At present neither men nor cannon were seen, though huge ring-bolts and other rusty iron fixtures of the wood-work hinted of twenty-four-pounders.

Glancing towards the hammock as he entered, Captain Delano said, "You sleep here, Don Benito?"

"Yes, Señor, since we got into mild weather."

"This seems a sort of dormitory, sitting-room, sail-loft, chapel, armory, and private closet all together, Don Benito," added Captain Delano, looking round.

"Yes, Señor; events have not been favorable to much order in my arrangements."

---

[93] First cousins.   [94] A prayer book.
[95] Rope belts worn by Franciscans and other religious orders.   [96] Headrest.

Here the servant, napkin on arm, made a motion as if waiting his master's good pleasure. Don Benito signified his readiness, when seating him in the Malacca arm-chair, and for the guest's convenience drawing opposite one of the settees, the servant commenced operations by throwing back his master's collar and loosening his cravat.

There is something in the negro which, in a peculiar way, fits him for avocations about one's person. Most negroes are natural valets and hair-dressers; taking to the comb and brush congenially as to the castinets, and flourishing them apparently with almost equal satisfaction. There is, too, a smooth tact about them in this employment, with a marvelous, noiseless, gliding briskness, not ungraceful in its way, singularly pleasing to behold, and still more so to be the manipulated subject of. And above all is the great gift of good-humor. Not the mere grin or laugh is here meant. Those were unsuitable. But a certain easy cheerfulness, harmonious in every glance and gesture; as though God had set the whole negro to some pleasant tune.

When to this is added the docility arising from the unaspiring contentment of a limited mind, and that susceptibility of blind attachment sometimes inhering in indisputable inferiors, one readily perceives why those hypochondriacs, Johnson and Byron—it may be, something like the hypochondriac Benito Cereno—took to their hearts, almost to the exclusion of the entire white race, their serving men, the negroes, Barber and Fletcher.[97] But if there be that in the negro which exempts him from the inflicted sourness of the morbid or cynical mind, how, in his most prepossessing aspects, must he appear to a benevolent one? When at ease with respect to exterior things, Captain Delano's nature was not only benign, but familiarly and humorously so. At home, he had often taken rare satisfaction in sitting in his door, watching some free man of color at his work or play. If on a voyage he chanced to have a black sailor, invariably he was on chatty and half-gamesome terms with him. In fact, like most men of good, blithe heart, Captain Delano took to negroes, not philanthropically, but genially, just as other men to Newfoundland dogs.

Hitherto, the circumstances in which he found the San Dominick had repressed the tendency. But in the cuddy, relieved from his former uneasiness, and, for various reasons, more sociably inclined than at any previous period of the day, and seeing the colored servant, napkin on arm, so debonair about his master, in a business so familiar as that of shaving, too, all his old weakness for negroes returned.

Among other things, he was amused with an odd instance of the African love of bright colors and fine shows, in the black's informally taking from the flag-locker a great piece of bunting of all hues, and lavishly tucking it under his master's chin for an apron.

The mode of shaving among the Spaniards is a little different from what it is with other nations. They have a basin, specifically called a barber's basin, which on one side is scooped out, so as accurately to receive the chin, against which it is closely held in lathering; which is done, not with a brush, but with soap dipped in the water of the basin and rubbed on the face.

In the present instance salt-water was used for lack of better; and the parts

---

[97] Francis Barber, the devoted black servant of Samuel Johnson (1709–1784) for thirty years, and William Fletcher, the white valet of Lord Byron (1788–1824). Melville apparently confused Fletcher with the black servant of Byron's friend Edward Trelawny.

lathered were only the upper lip, and low down under the throat, all the rest being cultivated beard.

The preliminaries being somewhat novel to Captain Delano, he sat curiously eying them, so that no conversation took place, nor, for the present, did Don Benito appear disposed to renew any.

Setting down his basin, the negro searched among the razors, as for the sharpest, and having found it, gave it an additional edge by expertly strapping it on the firm, smooth, oily skin of his open palm; he then made a gesture as if to begin, but midway stood suspended for an instant, one hand elevating the razor, the other professionally dabbling among the bubbling suds on the Spaniard's lank neck. Not unaffected by the close sight of the gleaming steel, Don Benito nervously shuddered; his usual ghastliness was heightened by the lather, which lather, again, was intensified in its hue by the contrasting sootiness of the negro's body. Altogether the scene was somewhat peculiar, at least to Captain Delano, nor, as he saw the two thus postured, could he resist the vagary, that in the black he saw a headsman, and in the white a man at the block.[98] But this was one of those antic conceits, appearing and vanishing in a breath, from which, perhaps, the best regulated mind is not always free.

Meantime the agitation of the Spaniard had a little loosened the bunting from around him, so that one broad fold swept curtain-like over the chair-arm to the floor, revealing, amid a profusion of armorial bars and ground-colors—black, blue, and yellow—a closed castle in a blood-red field diagonal with a lion rampant in a white.

"The castle and the lion," exclaimed Captain Delano—"why, Don Benito, this is the flag of Spain you use here. It's well it's only I, and not the King, that sees this," he added, with a smile, "but"—turning towards the black—"it's all one, I suppose, so the colors be gay;" which playful remark did not fail somewhat to tickle the negro.

"Now, master," he said, readjusting the flag, and pressing the head gently further back into the crotch of the chair; "now, master," and the steel glanced nigh the throat.

Again Don Benito faintly shuddered.

"You must not shake so, master. See, Don Amasa, master always shakes when I shave him. And yet master knows I never yet have drawn blood, though it's true, if master will shake so, I may some of these times. Now master," he continued. "And now, Don Amasa, please go on with your talk about the gale, and all that; master can hear, and, between times, master can answer."

"Ah yes, these gales," said Captain Delano; "but the more I think of your voyage, Don Benito, the more I wonder, not at the gales, terrible as they must have been, but at the disastrous interval following them. For here, by your account, have you been these two months and more getting from Cape Horn to St. Maria, a distance which I myself, with a good wind, have sailed in a few days. True, you had calms, and long ones, but to be becalmed for two months, that is, at least, unusual. Why, Don Benito, had almost any other gentleman told me such a story, I should have been half disposed to a little incredulity."

Here an involuntary expression came over the Spaniard, similar to that just before on the deck, and whether it was the start he gave, or a sudden gawky roll of

[98] An executioner, and in the white a man at the chopping block. Captain Delano repeatedly gets flashes of the true situation on the ship but reasons them away with his optimism and his tendency to stereotype blacks.

the hull in the calm, or a momentary unsteadiness of the servant's hand, however it was, just then the razor drew blood, spots of which stained the creamy lather under the throat: immediately the black barber drew back his steel, and, remaining in his professional attitude, back to Captain Delano, and face to Don Benito, held up the trickling razor, saying, with a sort of half humorous sorrow, "See, master—you shook so—here's Babo's first blood."

No sword drawn before James the First of England,[99] no assassination in that timid King's presence, could have produced a more terrified aspect than was now presented by Don Benito.

Poor fellow, thought Captain Delano, so nervous he can't even bear the sight of barber's blood; and this unstrung, sick man, is it credible that I should have imagined he meant to spill all my blood, who can't endure the sight of one little drop of his own? Surely, Amasa Delano, you have been beside yourself this day. Tell it not when you get home, sappy Amasa. Well, well, he looks like a murderer, doesn't he? More like as if himself were to be done for. Well, well, this day's experience shall be a good lesson.

Meantime, while these things were running through the honest seaman's mind, the servant had taken the napkin from his arm, and to Don Benito had said—"But answer Don Amasa, please, master, while I wipe this ugly stuff off the razor, and strop it again."

As he said the words, his face was turned half round, so as to be alike visible to the Spaniard and the American, and seemed, by its expression, to hint, that he was desirous, by getting his master to go on with the conversation, considerately to withdraw his attention from the recent annoying accident. As if glad to snatch the offered relief, Don Benito resumed, rehearsing to Captain Delano, that not only were the calms of unusual duration, but the ship had fallen in with obstinate currents; and other things he added, some of which were but repetitions of former statements, to explain how it came to pass that the passage from Cape Horn to St. Maria had been so exceedingly long; now and then mingling with his words, incidental praises, less qualified than before, to the blacks, for their general good conduct. These particulars were not given consecutively, the servant, at convenient times, using his razor, and so, between the intervals of shaving, the story and panegyric went on with more than usual huskiness.

To Captain Delano's imagination, now again not wholly at rest, there was something so hollow in the Spaniard's manner, with apparently some reciprocal hollowness in the servant's dusky comment of silence, that the idea flashed across him, that possibly master and man, for some unknown purpose, were acting out, both in word and deed, nay, to the very tremor of Don Benito's limbs, some juggling play before him. Neither did the suspicion of collusion lack apparent support, from the fact of those whispered conferences before mentioned. But then, what could be the object of enacting this play of the barber before him? At last, regarding the notion as a whimsy, insensibly suggested, perhaps, by the theatrical aspect of Don Benito in his harlequin ensign,[100] Captain Delano speedily banished it.

The shaving over, the servant bestirred himself with a small bottle of scented waters, pouring a few drops on the head, and then diligently rubbing; the vehemence of the exercise causing the muscles of his face to twitch rather strangely.

---

[99] James I (1566–1625), who reigned from 1604 to 1625, lived in fear of assassination by Catholics, especially after the Gunpowder Plot in 1605.

[100] The colorful Spanish flag.

His next operation was with comb, scissors, and brush; going round and round, smoothing a curl here, clipping an unruly whisker-hair there, giving a graceful sweep to the temple-lock, with other impromptu touches evincing the hand of a master; while, like any resigned gentleman in barber's hands, Don Benito bore all, much less uneasily, at least, than he had done the razoring; indeed, he sat so pale and rigid now, that the negro seemed a Nubian[101] sculptor finishing off a white statue-head.

All being over at last, the standard of Spain removed, tumbled up, and tossed back into the flag-locker, the negro's warm breath blowing away any stray hair which might have lodged down his master's neck; collar and cravat readjusted; a speck of lint whisked off the velvet lapel; all this being done; backing off a little space, and pausing with an expression of subdued self-complacency, the servant for a moment surveyed his master, as, in toilet at least, the creature of his own tasteful hands.

Captain Delano playfully complimented him upon his achievement; at the same time congratulating Don Benito.

But neither sweet waters, nor shampooing, nor fidelity, nor sociality, delighted the Spaniard. Seeing him relapsing into forbidding gloom, and still remaining seated, Captain Delano, thinking that his presence was undesired just then, withdrew, on the pretense of seeing whether, as he had prophesied, any signs of a breeze were visible.

Walking forward to the main-mast, he stood awhile thinking over the scene, and not without some undefined misgivings, when he heard a noise near the cuddy and turning, saw the negro, his hand to his cheek. Advancing, Captain Delano perceived that the cheek was bleeding. He was about to ask the cause, when the negro's wailing soliloquy enlightened him.

"Ah, when will master get better from his sickness; only the sour heart that sour sickness breeds made him serve Babo so; cutting Babo with the razor, because, only by accident, Babo had given master one little scratch; and for the first time in so many a day, too. Ah, ah, ah," holding his hand to his face.

Is it possible, thought Captain Delano; was it to wreak in private his Spanish spite against this poor friend of his, that Don Benito, by his sullen manner, impelled me to withdraw? Ah, this slavery breeds ugly passions in man.—Poor fellow!

He was about to speak in sympathy to the negro, but with a timid reluctance he now reentered the cuddy.

Presently master and man came forth; Don Benito leaning on his servant as if nothing had happened.

But a sort of love-quarrel, after all, thought Captain Delano.

He accosted Don Benito, and they slowly walked together. They had gone but a few paces, when the steward—a tall, rajah-looking mulatto, orientally set off with a pagoda turban formed by three or four Madras handkerchiefs[102] wound about his head, tier on tier—approaching with a salaam,[103] announced lunch in the cabin.

On their way thither, the two captains were preceded by the mulatto, who, turning round as he advanced, with continual smiles and bows, ushered them on, a

---

[101] A native of Nubia, now part of the Sudan.
[102] Colorful cotton handkerchiefs from Madras, India.
[103] "Health" (Arabic), a Moslem greeting.

display of elegance which quite completed the insignificance of the small bare-headed Babo, who, as if not unconscious of inferiority, eyed askance the graceful steward. But in part, Captain Delano imputed his jealous watchfulness to that peculiar feeling which the full-blooded African entertains for the adulterated one. As for the steward, his manner, if not bespeaking much dignity of self-respect, yet evidenced his extreme desire to please; which is doubly meritorious, as at once Christian and Chesterfieldian.[104]

Captain Delano observed with interest that while the complexion of the mulatto was hybrid, his physiognomy was European—classically so.

"Don Benito," whispered he, "I am glad to see this usher-of-the-golden-rod[105] of yours; the sight refutes an ugly remark once made to me by a Barbadoes planter; that when a mulatto has a regular European face, look out for him; he is a devil. But see, your steward here has features more regular than King George's of England; and yet there he nods, and bows, and smiles; a king, indeed—the king of kind hearts and polite fellows. What a pleasant voice he has, too?"

"He has, Señor."

"But tell me, has he not, so far as you have known him, always proved a good, worthy fellow?" said Captain Delano, pausing, while with a final genuflexion the steward disppeared into the cabin; "come, for the reason just mentioned, I am curious to know."

"Francesco is a good man," a sort of sluggishly responded Don Benito, like a phlegmatic appreciator, who would neither find fault nor flatter.

"Ah, I thought so. For it were strange, indeed, and not very creditable to us whiteskins, if a little of our blood mixed with the African's, should, far from improving the latter's quality, have the sad effect of pouring vitriolic acid into black broth; improving the hue, perhaps, but not the wholesomeness."

"Doubtless, doubtless, Señor, but"—glancing at Babo—"not to speak of ne-groes, your planter's remark I have heard applied to the Spanish and Indian inter-mixtures in our provinces. But I know nothing about the matter," he listlessly added.

And here they entered the cabin.

The lunch was a frugal one. Some of Captain Delano's fresh fish and pump-kins, biscuit and salt beef, the reserved bottle of cider, and the San Dominick's last bottle of Canary.[106]

As they entered, Francesco, with two or three colored aids, was hovering over the table giving the last adjustments. Upon perceiving their master they withdrew, Francesco making a smiling congé and the Spaniard, without condescending to notice it, fastidiously remarking to his companion that he relished not superfluous attendance.

Without companions, host and guest sat down, like a childless married couple, at opposite ends of the table, Don Benito waving Captain Delano to his place, and, weak as he was, insisting upon that gentleman being seated before himself.

The negro placed a rug under Don Benito's feet, and a cushion behind his back, and then stood behind, not his master's chair, but Captain Delano's. At

---

[104] Philip Dormer Stanhope (1694–1773), the fourth earl of Chesterfield, advocated a worldly code of conduct and ethics in letters to his illegitimate son, the opposite of that personified by Christ.

[105] Ushers walked formally before a person of rank; they were known by the color of the rod or staff they carried.

[106] Wine from the Canary Islands.

first, this a little surprised the latter. But it was soon evident that, in taking his position, the black was still true to his master; since by facing him he could the more readily anticipate his slightest want.

"This is an uncommonly intelligent fellow of yours, Don Benito," whispered Captain Delano across the table.

"You say true, Señor."

During the repast, the guest again reverted to parts of Don Benito's story, begging further particulars here and there. He inquired how it was that the scurvy and fever should have committed such wholesale havoc upon the whites, while destroying less than half of the blacks. As if this question reproduced the whole scene of plague before the Spaniard's eyes, miserably reminding him of his solitude in a cabin where before he had had so many friends and officers round him, his hand shook, his face became hueless, broken words escaped; but directly the sane memory of the past seemed replaced by insane terrors of the present. With starting eyes he stared before him at vacancy. For nothing was to be seen but the hand of his servant pushing the Canary over towards him. At length a few sips served partially to restore him. He made random reference to the different constitution of races, enabling one to offer more resistance to certain maladies than another. The thought was new to his companion.

Presently Captain Delano, intending to say something to his host concerning the pecuniary part of the business he had undertaken for him, especially—since he was strictly accountable to his owners—with reference to the new suit of sails, and other things of that sort; and naturally preferring to conduct such affairs in private, was desirous that the servant should withdraw; imagining that Don Benito for a few minutes could dispense with his attendance. He, however, waited awhile; thinking that, as the conversation proceeded, Don Benito, without being prompted, would perceive the propriety of the step.

But it was otherwise. At last catching his host's eye, Captain Delano, with a slight backward gesture of his thumb, whispered, "Don Benito, pardon me, but there is an interference with the full expression of what I have to say to you."

Upon this the Spaniard changed countenance; which was imputed to his resenting the hint, as in some way a reflection upon his servant. After a moment's pause, he assured his guest that the black's remaining with them could be of no disservice; because since losing his officers he had made Babo (whose original office, it now appeared, had been captain of the slaves) not only his constant attendant and companion, but in all things his confidant.

After this, nothing more could be said; though, indeed, Captain Delano could hardly avoid some little tinge of irritation upon being left ungratified in so inconsiderable a wish, by one, too, for whom he intended such solid services. But it is only his querulousness, thought he; and so filling his glass he proceeded to business.

The price of the sails and other matters was fixed upon. But while this was being done, the American observed that, though his original offer of assistance had been hailed with hectic animation, yet now when it was reduced to a business transaction, indifference and apathy were betrayed. Don Benito, in fact, appeared to submit to hearing the details more out of regard to common propriety, than from any impression that weighty benefit to himself and his voyage was involved.

Soon, his manner became still more reserved. The effort was vain to seek to draw him into social talk. Gnawed by his splenetic[107] mood, he sat twitching his

---

[107] Melancholy and peevish.

beard, while to little purpose the hand of his servant, mute as that on the wall, slowly pushed over the Canary.

Lunch being over, they sat down on the cushioned transom;[108] the servant placing a pillow behind his master. The long continuance of the calm had now affected the atmosphere. Don Benito sighed heavily, as if for breath.

"Why not adjourn to the cuddy," said Captain Delano; "there is more air there." But the host sat silent and motionless.

Meantime his servant knelt before him, with a large fan of feathers. And Francesco coming in on tiptoes, handed the negro a little cup of aromatic waters, with which at intervals he chafed his master's brow; smoothing the hair along the temples as a nurse does a child's. He spoke no word. He only rested his eye on his master's, as if, amid all Don Benito's distress, a little to refresh his spirit by the silent sight of fidelity.

Presently the ship's bell sounded two o'clock; and through the cabin windows a slight rippling of the sea was discerned; and from the desired direction.

"There," exclaimed Captain Delano, "I told you so, Don Benito, look!"

He had risen to his feet, speaking in a very animated tone, with a view the more to rouse his companion. But though the crimson curtain of the stern-window near him that moment fluttered against his pale cheek, Don Benito seemed to have even less welcome for the breeze than the calm.

Poor fellow, thought Captain Delano, bitter experience has taught him that one ripple does not make a wind, any more than one swallow a summer. But he is mistaken for once. I will get his ship in for him, and prove it.

Briefly alluding to his weak condition, he urged his host to remain quietly where he was, since he (Captain Delano) would with pleasure take upon himself the responsibility of making the best use of the wind.

Upon gaining the deck, Captain Delano started at the unexpected figure of Atufal, monumentally fixed at the threshold, like one of those sculptured porters of black marble guarding the porches of Egyptian tombs.

But this time the start was, perhaps, purely physical. Atufal's presence, singularly attesting docility even in sullenness, was contrasted with that of the hatchet-polishers, who in patience evinced their industry; while both spectacles showed, that lax as Don Benito's general authority might be, still, whenever he chose to exert it, no man so savage or colossal but must, more or less, bow.

Snatching a trumpet which hung from the bulwarks, with a free step Captain Delano advanced to the forward edge of the poop, issuing his orders in his best Spanish. The few sailors and many negroes, all equally pleased, obediently set about heading the ship towards the harbor.

While giving some directions about setting a lower stu'n'-sail,[109] suddenly Captain Delano heard a voice faithfully repeating his orders. Turning, he saw Babo, now for the time acting, under the pilot, his original part of captain of the slaves. This assistance proved valuable. Tattered sails and warped yards were soon brought into some trim. And no brace or halyard was pulled but to the blithe songs of the inspirited negroes.

Good fellows, thought Captain Delano, a little training would make fine sailors of them. Why see, the very women pull and sing too. These must be some of those Ashantee negresses that make such capital soldiers, I've heard. But who's at the helm. I must have a good hand there.

[108] A large crossbeam at a ship's stern.
[109] A studdingsail, an auxiliary sail set out in good weather.

He went to see.

The San Dominick steered with a cumbrous tiller, with large horizontal pullies attached. At each pully-end stood a subordinate black, and between them, at the tiller-head, the responsible post, a Spanish seaman, whose countenance evinced his due share in the general hopefulness and confidence at the coming of the breeze.

He proved the same man who had behaved with so shame-faced an air on the windlass.

"Ah,—it is you, my man," exclaimed Captain Delano—"well, no more sheep's-eyes now;—look straight forward and keep the ship so. Good hand, I trust? And want to get into the harbor, don't you?"

The man assented with an inward chuckle, grasping the tiller-head firmly. Upon this, unperceived by the American, the two blacks eyed the sailor intently.

Finding all right at the helm, the pilot went forward to the forecastle, to see how matters stood there.

The ship now had way enough to breast the current. With the approach of evening, the breeze would be sure to freshen.

Having done all that was needed for the present, Captain Delano, giving his last orders to the sailors, turned aft to report affairs to Don Benito in the cabin; perhaps additionally incited to rejoin him by the hope of snatching a moment's private chat while the servant was engaged upon deck.

From opposite sides, there were, beneath the poop, two approaches to the cabin; one further forward than the other, and consequently communicating with a longer passage. Marking the servant still above, Captain Delano, taking the nighest entrance—the one last named, and at whose porch Atufal still stood—hurried on his way, till, arrived at the cabin threshold, he paused an instant, a little to recover from his eagerness. Then, with the words of his intended business upon his lips, he entered. As he advanced toward the seated Spaniard, he heard another footstep, keeping time with his. From the opposite door, a salver in hand, the servant was likewise advancing.

"Confound the faithful fellow," thought Captain Delano; "what a vexatious coincidence."

Possibly, the vexation might have been something different, were it not for the brisk confidence inspired by the breeze. But even as it was, he felt a slight twinge, from a sudden indefinite association in his mind of Babo with Atufal.

"Don Benito," said he, "I give you joy; the breeze will hold, and will increase. By the way, your tall man and time-piece, Atufal, stands without. By your order, of course?"

Don Benito recoiled, as if at some bland satirical touch, delivered with such adroit garnish of apparent good breeding as to present no handle for retort.

He is like one flayed alive, thought Captain Delano; where may one touch him without causing a shrink?

The servant moved before his master, adjusting a cushion; recalled to civility, the Spaniard stiffly replied: "you are right. The slave appears where you saw him, according to my command; which is, that if at the given hour I am below, he must take his stand and abide my coming."

"Ah now, pardon me, but that is treating the poor fellow like an ex-king indeed. Ah, Don Benito," smiling, "for all the license you permit in some things, I fear lest, at bottom, you are a bitter hard master."

Again Don Benito shrank; and this time, as the good sailor thought, from a genuine twinge of his conscience.

Again conversation became constrained. In vain Captain Delano called attention to the now perceptible motion of the keel gently cleaving the sea; with lacklustre eye, Don Benito returned words few and reserved.

By-and-by, the wind having steadily risen, and still blowing right into the harbor, bore the San Dominick swiftly on. Rounding a point of land, the sealer at distance came into open view.

Meantime Captain Delano had again repaired to the deck, remaining there some time. Having at last altered the ship's course, so as to give the reef a wide berth, he returned for a few moments below.

I will cheer up my poor friend, this time, thought he.

"Better and better, Don Benito," he cried as he blithely re-entered: "there will soon be an end to your cares, at least for awhile. For when, after a long, sad voyage, you know, the anchor drops into the haven, all its vast weight seems lifted from the captain's heart. We are getting on famously, Don Benito. My ship is in sight. Look through this side-light here; there she is; all a-taunt-o![110] The Bachelor's Delight, my good friend. Ah, how this wind braces one up. Come, you must take a cup of coffee with me this evening. My old steward will give you as fine a cup as ever any sultan tasted. What say you, Don Benito, will you?"

At first, the Spaniard glanced feverishly up, casting a longing look towards the sealer, while with mute concern his servant gazed into his face. Suddenly the old ague of coldness returned, and dropping back to his cushions he was silent.

"You do not answer. Come, all day you have been my host; would you have hospitality all on one side?"

"I cannot go," was the response.

"What? it will not fatigue you. The ships will lie together as near as they can, without swinging foul. It will be little more than stepping from deck to deck; which is but as from room to room. Come, come, you must not refuse me."

"I cannot go," decisively and repulsively repeated Don Benito.

Renouncing all but the last appearance of courtesy, with a sort of cadaverous sullenness, and biting his thin nails to the quick, he glanced, almost glared, at his guest, as if impatient that a stranger's presence should interfere with the full indulgence of his morbid hour. Meantime the sound of the parted waters came more and more gurglingly and merrily at the windows; as reproaching him for his dark spleen, as telling him that, sulk as he might, and go mad with it, nature cared not a jot; since, whose fault was it, pray?

But the foul mood was now at its depth, as the fair wind at its height.

There was something in the man so far beyond any mere unsociality or sourness previously evinced, that even the forbearing good-nature of his guest could no longer endure it. Wholly at a loss to account for such demeanor, and deeming sickness with eccentricity, however extreme, no adequate excuse, well satisfied, too, that nothing in his own conduct could justify it, Captain Delano's pride began to be roused. Himself became reserved. But all seemed one to the Spaniard. Quitting him, therefore, Captain Delano once more went to the deck.

The ship was now within less than two miles of the sealer. The whale-boat was seen darting over the interval.

To be brief, the two vessels, thanks to the pilot's skill, ere long in neighborly style lay anchored together.

Before returning to his own vessel, Captain Delano had intended communicating to Don Benito the smaller details of the proposed services to be rendered. But,

[110] Fully rigged, looking fit.

as it was, unwilling anew to subject himself to rebuffs, he resolved, now that he had seen the San Dominick safely moored, immediately to quit her, without further allusion to hospitality or business. Indefinitely postponing his ulterior plans, he would regulate his future actions according to future circumstances. His boat was ready to receive him; but his host still tarried below. Well, thought Captain Delano, if he had little breeding, the more need to show mine. He descended to the cabin to bid a ceremonious, and, it may be, tacitly rebukeful adieu. But to his great satisfaction, Don Benito, as if he began to feel the weight of that treatment with which his slighted guest had, not indecorously, retaliated upon him, now supported by his servant, rose to his feet, and grasping Captain Delano's hand, stood tremulous; too much agitated to speak. But the good augury hence drawn was suddenly dashed, by his resuming all his previous reserve, with augmented gloom, as, with half-averted eyes, he silently reseated himself on his cushions. With a corresponding return of his own chilled feelings, Captain Delano bowed and withdrew.

He was hardly midway in the narrow corridor, dim as a tunnel, leading from the cabin to the stairs, when a sound, as of the tolling for execution in some jail-yard, fell on his ears. It was the echo of the ship's flawed bell, striking the hour, drearily reverberated in this subterranean vault. Instantly, by a fatality not to be withstood, his mind, responsive to the portent, swarmed with superstitious suspicions. He paused. In images far swifter than these sentences, the minutest details of all his former distrusts swept through him.

Hitherto, credulous good-nature had been too ready to furnish excuses for reasonable fears. Why was the Spaniard, so superfluously punctilious at times, now heedless of common propriety in not accompanying to the side his departing guest? Did indisposition forbid? Indisposition had not forbidden more irksome exertion that day. His last equivocal demeanor recurred. He had risen to his feet, grasped his guest's hand, motioned toward his hat; then, in an instant, all was eclipsed in sinister muteness and gloom. Did this imply one brief, repentant relenting at the final moment, from some iniquitous plot, followed by remorseless return to it? His last glance seemed to express a calamitous, yet acquiescent farewell to Captain Delano forever. Why decline the invitation to visit the sealer that evening? Or was the Spaniard less hardened than the Jew,[111] who refrained not from supping at the board of him whom the same night he meant to betray? What imported all those day-long enigmas and contradictions, except they were intended to mystify, preliminary to some stealthy blow? Atufal, the pretended rebel, but punctual shadow, that moment lurked by the threshold without. He seemed a sentry, and more. Who, by his own confession, had stationed him there? Was the negro now lying in wait?

The Spaniard behind—his creature before: to rush from darkness to light was the involuntary choice.

The next moment, with clenched jaw and hand, he passed Atufal, and stood unharmed in the light. As he saw his trim ship lying peacefully at anchor, and almost within ordinary call; as he saw his household boat, with familiar faces in it, patiently rising and falling on the short waves by the San Dominick's side; and then, glancing about the decks where he stood, saw the oakum-pickers still gravely plying their fingers; and heard the low, buzzing whistle and industrious hum of the hatchet-polishers, still bestirring themselves over their endless occupa-

[111] Judas Iscariot, who betrayed Christ after the Last Supper (see Matthew 26:20–25).

tion; and more than all, as he saw the benign aspect of nature, taking her innocent repose in the evening; the screened sun in the quiet camp of the west shining out like the mild light from Abraham's[112] tent; as charmed eye and ear took in all these, with the chained figure of the black, clenched jaw and hand relaxed. Once again he smiled at the phantoms which had mocked him, and felt something like a tinge of remorse, that, by harboring them even for a moment, he should, by implication, have betrayed an atheist doubt of the ever-watchful Providence above.

There was a few minutes' delay, while, in obedience to his orders, the boat was being hooked along to the gangway. During this interval, a sort of saddened satisfaction stole over Captain Delano, at thinking of the kindly offices he had that day discharged for a stranger. Ah, thought he, after good actions one's conscience is never ungrateful, however much so the benefited party may be.

Presently, his foot, in the first act of descent into the boat, pressed the first round of the side-ladder, his face presented inward upon the deck. In the same moment, he heard his name courteously sounded; and, to his pleased surprise, saw Don Benito advancing—an unwonted energy in his air, as if, at the last moment, intent upon making amends for his recent discourtesy. With instinctive good feeling, Captain Delano, withdrawing his foot, turned and reciprocally advanced. As he did so, the Spaniard's nervous eagerness increased, but his vital energy failed; so that, the better to support him, the servant, placing his master's hand on his naked shoulder, and gently holding it there, formed himself into a sort of crutch.

When the two captains met, the Spaniard again fervently took the hand of the American, at the same time casting an earnest glance into his eyes, but, as before, too much overcome to speak.

I have done him wrong, self-reproachfully thought Captain Delano; his apparent coldness has deceived me; in no instance has he meant to offend.

Meantime, as if fearful that the continuance of the scene might too much unstring his master, the servant seemed anxious to terminate it. And so, still presenting himself as a crutch, and walking between the two captains, he advanced with them towards the gangway; while still, as if full of kindly contrition, Don Benito would not let go the hand of Captain Delano, but retained it in his, across the black's body.

Soon they were standing by the side, looking over into the boat, whose crew turned up their curious eyes. Waiting a moment for the Spaniard to relinquish his hold, the now embarrassed Captain Delano lifted his foot, to overstep the threshold of the open gangway; but still Don Benito would not let go his hand. And yet, with an agitated tone, he said, "I can go no further; here I must bid you adieu. Adieu, my dear, dear Don Amasa. Go—go!" suddenly tearing his hand loose, "go, and God guard you better than me, my best friend."

Not unaffected, Captain Delano would now have lingered; but catching the meekly admonitory eye of the servant, with a hasty farewell he descended into his boat, followed by the continual adieus of Don Benito, standing rooted in the gangway.

Seating himself in the stern, Captain Delano, making a last salute, ordered the boat shoved off. The crew had their oars on end. The bowsmen pushed the boat a sufficient distance for the oars to be lengthwise dropped. The instant that was done, Don Benito sprang over the bulwarks, falling at the feet of Captain Delano; at the same time calling towards his ship, but in tones so frenzied, that none in the

---

[112] An Old Testament patriarch (see Genesis 18:1).

boat could understand him. But, as if not equally obtuse, three sailors, from three different and distant parts of the ship, splashed into the sea, swimming after their captain, as if intent upon his rescue.

The dismayed officer of the boat eagerly asked what this meant. To which, Captain Delano, turning a disdainful smile upon the unaccountable Spaniard, answered that, for his part, he neither knew nor cared; but it seemed as if Don Benito had taken it into his head to produce the impression among his people that the boat wanted to kidnap him. "Or else—give way[113] for your lives," he wildly added, starting at a clattering hubbub in the ship, above which rang the tocsin[114] of the hatchet-polishers; and seizing Don Benito by the throat he added, "this plotting pirate means murder!" Here, in apparent verification of the words, the servant, a dagger in his hand, was seen on the rail overhead, poised, in the act of leaping, as if with desperate fidelity to befriend his master to the last; while, seemingly to aid the black, the three white sailors were trying to clamber into the hampered bow. Meantime, the whole host of negroes, as if inflamed at the sight of their jeopardized captain, impended in one sooty avalanche over the bulwarks.

All this, with what preceded, and what followed, occurred with such involutions of rapidity, that past, present, and future seemed one.

Seeing the negro coming, Captain Delano had flung the Spaniard aside, almost in the very act of clutching him, and, by the unconscious recoil, shifting his place, with arms thrown up, so promptly grappled the servant in his descent, that with dagger presented at Captain Delano's heart, the black seemed of purpose to have leaped there as to his mark. But the weapon was wrenched away, and the assailant dashed down into the bottom of the boat, which now, with disentangled oars, began to speed through the sea.

At this juncture, the left hand of Captain Delano, on one side, again clutched the half-reclined Don Benito, heedless that he was in a speechless faint, while his right foot, on the other side, ground the prostrate negro; and his right arm pressed for added speed on the after oar, his eye bent forward, encouraging his men to their utmost.

But here, the officer of the boat, who had at last succeeded in beating off the towing sailors, and was now, with face turned aft, assisting the bowsman at his oar, suddenly called to Captain Delano, to see what the black was about; while a Portuguese oarsman shouted to him to give heed to what the Spaniard was saying.

Glancing down at his feet, Captain Delano saw the freed hand of the servant aiming with a second dagger—a small one, before concealed in his wool[115]—with this he was snakishly writhing up from the boat's bottom, at the heart of his master, his countenance lividly vindictive, expressing the centred purpose of his soul; while the Spaniard, half-choked, was vainly shrinking away, with husky words, incoherent to all but the Portuguese.

That moment, across the long-benighted mind of Captain Delano, a flash of revelation swept, illuminating, in unanticipated clearness, his host's whole mysterious demeanor, with every enigmatic event of the day, as well as the entire past voyage of the San Dominick. He smote Babo's hand down, but his own heart smote him harder. With infinite pity he withdrew his hold from Don Benito. Not Captain Delano, but Don Benito, the black, in leaping into the boat, had intended to stab.

---

[113] Row.   [114] An alarm bell.   [115] Hair.

Both the black's hands were held, as, glancing up towards the San Dominick, Captain Delano, now with scales dropped from his eyes, saw the negroes, not in misrule, not in tumult; not as if frantically concerned for Don Benito, but with mask torn away, flourishing hatchets and knives, in ferocious piratical revolt. Like delirious black dervishes,[116] the six Ashantees danced on the poop. Prevented by their foes from springing into the water, the Spanish boys were hurrying up to the topmost spars, while such of the few Spanish sailors, not already in the sea, less alert, were descried, helplessly mixed in, on deck, with the blacks.

Meantime Captain Delano hailed his own vessel, ordering the ports up, and the guns run out. But by this time the cable of the San Dominick had been cut; and the fag-end, in lashing out, whipped away the canvas shroud about the beak, suddenly revealing, as the bleached hull swung round towards the open ocean, death for the figure-head, in a human skeleton; chalky comment on the chalked words below, *"Follow your leader."*

At the sight, Don Benito, covering his face, wailed out: "'Tis he, Aranda! my murdered, unburied friend!"

Upon reaching the sealer, calling for ropes, Captain Delano bound the negro, who made no resistance, and had him hoisted to the deck. He would then have assisted the now almost helpless Don Benito up the side; but Don Benito, wan as he was, refused to move, or be moved, until the negro should have been first put below out of view. When, presently assured that it was done, he no more shrank from the ascent.

The boat was immediately dispatched back to pick up the three swimming sailors. Meantime, the guns were in readiness, though, owing to the San Dominick having glided somewhat astern of the sealer, only the aftermost one could be brought to bear. With this, they fired six times; thinking to cripple the fugitive ship by bringing down her spars. But only a few inconsiderable ropes were shot away. Soon the ship was beyond the gun's range, steering broad out of the bay; the blacks thickly clustering round the bowsprit,[117] one moment with taunting cries towards the whites, the next with upthrown gestures hailing the now dusky moors of ocean—cawing crows escaped from the hand of the fowler.

The first impulse was to slip the cables and give chase. But, upon second thoughts, to pursue with whale-boat and yawl seemed more promising.

Upon inquiring of Don Benito what firearms they had on board the San Dominick, Captain Delano was answered that they had none that could be used; because, in the earlier stages of the mutiny, a cabin-passenger, since dead, had secretly put out of order the locks of what few muskets there were. But with all his remaining strength, Don Benito entreated the American not to give chase, either with ship or boat; for the negroes had already proved themselves such desperadoes, that, in case of a present assault, nothing but a total massacre of the whites could be looked for. But, regarding this warning as coming from one whose spirit had been crushed by misery the American did not give up his design.

The boats were got ready and armed. Captain Delano ordered his men into them. He was going himself when Don Benito grasped his arm.

"What! have you saved my life, Señor, and are you now going to throw away your own?"

---

[116] Muslims who whirl as part of religious services.   [117] A large spar extending from a ship's bow.

The officers also, for reasons connected with their interests and those of the voyage, and a duty owing to the owners, strongly objected against their commander's going. Weighing their remonstrances a moment, Captain Delano felt bound to remain; appointing his chief mate—an athletic and resolute man, who had been a privateer's man[118]—to head the party. The more to encourage the sailors, they were told, that the Spanish captain considered his ship good as lost; that she and her cargo, including some gold and silver, were worth more than a thousand doubloons. Take her, and no small part should be theirs. The sailors replied with a shout.

The fugitives had now almost gained an offing.[119] It was nearly night; but the moon was rising. After hard, prolonged pulling, the boats came up on the ship's quarters, at a suitable distance laying upon their oars to discharge their muskets. Having no bullets to return; the negroes sent their yells. But, upon the second volley, Indian-like, they hurtled their hatchets. One took off a sailor's fingers. Another struck the whale-boat's bow, cutting off the rope there, and remaining stuck in the gunwale like a woodman's axe. Snatching it, quivering from it's lodgment, the mate hurled it back. The returned gauntlet now stuck in the ship's broken quarter-gallery, and so remained.

The negroes giving too hot a reception, the whites kept a more respectful distance. Hovering now just out of reach of the hurtling hatchets, they, with a view to the close encounter which must soon come, sought to decoy the blacks into entirely disarming themselves of their most murderous weapons in a hand-to-hand fight, by foolishly flinging them, as missiles, short of the mark, into the sea.

But, ere long, perceiving the stratagem, the negroes desisted, though not before many of them had to replace their lost hatchets with handspikes; an exchange which, as counted upon, proved, in the end, favorable to the assailants.

Meantime, with a strong wind, the ship still clove the water; the boats alternately falling behind, and pulling up, to discharge fresh volleys.

The fire was mostly directed towards the stern, since there, chiefly, the negroes, at present, were clustering. But to kill or maim the negroes was not the object. To take them, with the ship, was the object. To do it, the ship must be boarded; which could not be done by boats while she was sailing so fast.

A thought now struck the mate. Observing the Spanish boys still aloft, high as they could get, he called to them to descend to the yards, and cut adrift the sails. It was done. About this time, owing to causes hereafter to be shown, two Spaniards, in the dress of sailors, and conspicuously showing themselves, were killed; not by volleys, but by deliberate marksman's shots; while, as it afterwards appeared, by one of the general discharges, Atufal, the black, and the Spaniard at the helm likewise were killed. What now, with the loss of the sails, and loss of leaders, the ship became unmanageable to the negroes.

With creaking masts, she came heavily round to the wind; the prow slowly swinging into view of the boats, its skeleton gleaming in the horizontal moonlight, and casting a gigantic ribbed shadow upon the water. One extended arm of the ghost seemed beckoning the whites to avenge it.

"Follow your leader!" cried the mate; and, one on each bow, the boats boarded. Sealing-spears and cutlasses crossed hatchets and handspikes. Huddled upon the

---

[118] A private ship commissioned by a government to serve as a naval vessel to seize enemy ships; in *Putnam's Magazine* Melville added "and, as his enemies whispered, a pirate."
[119] Reached deep water.

long-boat amidships, the negresses raised a wailing chant, whose chorus was the clash of the steel.

For a time, the attack wavered; the negroes wedging themselves to beat it back; the half-repelled sailors, as yet unable to gain a footing, fighting as troopers in the saddle, one leg sideways flung over the bulwarks, and one without, plying their cutlasses like carters' whips. But in vain. They were almost overborne, when, rallying themselves into a squad as one man, with a huzza, they sprang inboard, where, entangled, they involuntarily separated again. For a few breaths' space, there was a vague, muffled, inner sound, as of submerged sword-fish rushing hither and thither through shoals of black-fish. Soon, in a reunited band, and joined by the Spanish seamen, the whites came to the surface, irresistibly driving the negroes toward the stern. But a barricade of casks and sacks, from side to side, had been thrown up by the mainmast. Here the negroes faced about, and though scorning peace or truce, yet fain would have had respite. But, without pause, overleaping the barrier, the unflagging sailors again closed. Exhausted, the blacks now fought in despair. Their red tongues lolled, wolf-like, from their black mouths. But the pale sailors' teeth were set; not a word was spoken; and, in five minutes more, the ship was won.

Nearly a score of the negroes were killed. Exclusive of those by the balls,[120] many were mangled; their wounds—mostly inflicted by the long-edged sealing-spears, resembling those shaven ones of the English at Preston Pans,[121] made by the poled scythes of the Highlanders. On the other side, none were killed, though several were wounded; some severely, including the mate. The surviving negroes were temporarily secured, and the ship, towed back into the harbor at midnight, once more lay anchored.

Omitting the incidents and arrangements ensuing, suffice it that, after two days spent in refitting, the ships sailed in company for Conception, in Chili, and thence for Lima, in Peru; where, before the vice-regal courts, the whole affair, from the beginning, underwent investigation.

Though, midway on the passage, the ill-fated Spaniard, relaxed from constraint, showed some signs of regaining health with free-will; yet, agreeably to his own foreboding, shortly before arriving at Lima, he relapsed, finally becoming so reduced as to be carried ashore in arms. Hearing of his story and plight, one of the many religious institutions of the City of Kings opened an hospitable refuge to him, where both physician and priest were his nurses, and a member of the order volunteered to be his one special guardian and consoler, by night and by day.

The following extracts, translated from one of the official Spanish documents, will, it is hoped, shed light on the preceding narrative, as well as, in the first place, reveal the true port of departure and true history of the San Dominick's voyage, down to the time of her touching at the island of St. Maria.

But, ere the extracts come, it may be well to preface them with a remark.

The document selected, from among many others, for partial translation, contains the deposition of Benito Cereno; the first taken in the case. Some disclosures therein were, at the time, held dubious for both learned and natural reasons. The tribunal inclined to the opinion that the deponent, not undisturbed in his mind by recent events, raved of some things which could never have happened. But subse-

---

[120] Those killed by musket balls.

[121] At the battle of Prestonpans, Scotland, in 1745, Scottish Highlanders armed with swords and with scythes fastened to poles defeated British forces.

quent depositions of the surviving sailors, bearing out the revelations of their captain in several of the strangest particulars, gave credence to the rest. So that the tribunal, in its final decision, rested its capital sentences upon statements which, had they lacked confirmation, it would have deemed it but duty to reject.

I, Don Jose de Abos and Padilla, His Majesty's Notary for the Royal Revenue, and Register of this Province, and Notary Public of the Holy Crusade of this Bishopric, etc.

Do certify and declare, as much as is requisite in law, that, in the criminal cause commenced the twenty-fourth of the month of September, in the year seventeen hundred and ninety-nine, against the negroes of the ship San Dominick, the following declaration before me was made:[122]

Declaration of the first witness, DON BENITO CERENO.

The same day, and month, and year, His Honor, Doctor Juan Martinez de Rozas, Councilor of the Royal Audience of this Kingdom, and learned in the law of this Intendency,[123] ordered the captain of the ship San Dominick, Don Benito Cereno, to appear; which he did in his litter,[124] attended by the monk Infelez; of whom he received the oath, which he took by God, our Lord, and a sign of the Cross; under which he promised to tell the truth of whatever he should know and should be asked;—and being interrogated agreeably to the tenor of the act commencing the process, he said, that on the twentieth of May last, he set sail with his ship from the port of Valparaiso, bound to that of Callao;[125] loaded with the produce of the country beside thirty cases of hardware and one hundred and sixty blacks, of both sexes, mostly belonging to Don Alexandro Aranda, gentleman, of the city of Mendoza;[126] that the crew of the ship consisted of thirty-six men, beside the persons who went as passengers; that the negroes were in part as follows:

[*Here, in the original, follows a list of some fifty names, descriptions, and ages, compiled from certain recovered documents of Aranda's, and also from recollections of the deponent, from which portions only are extracted.*]

—One, from about eighteen to nineteen years, named José, and this was the man that waited upon his master, Don Alexandro, and who speaks well the Spanish, having served him four or five years; * * * a mulatto, named Francesco, the cabin steward, of a good person and voice, having sung in the Valparaiso churches, native of the province of Buenos Ayres, aged about thirty-five years. * * * A smart negro, named Dago, who had been for many years a grave-digger among the Spaniards, aged forty-six years. * * * Four old negroes, born in Africa, from sixty to seventy, but sound, calkers by trade, whose names are as follows:—the first was named Muri, and he was killed (as was also his son named Diamelo); the second, Nacta; the third, Yola, likewise killed; the fourth, Ghofan; and six full-grown negroes, aged from thirty to forty-five, all raw, and born

---

[122] Melville edited and revised Delano's *Narrative*. He makes Babo more intelligent and subtle than he is in the official deposition of Benito Cereno; the Spanish captain's self-serving testimony is also more obvious. In the pages that follow, the brackets, italics, and ellipses are Melville's.

[123] A court district over which a provincial officer presides.

[124] A seat on which a person can be carried.

[125] Valparaiso, Chile; Callao, Peru.   [126] Mendoza, Argentina.

among the Ashantees—Matiluqui, Yan, Lecbe, Mapenda, Yambaio, Akim; four of whom were killed; * * * a powerful negro named Atufal, who being supposed to have been a chief in Africa, his owner set great store by him. * * * And a small negro of Senegal, but some years among the Spaniards, aged about thirty, which negro's name was Babo; * * * that he does not remember the names of the others, but that still expecting the residue of Don Alexandro's papers will be found, will then take due account of them all, and remit to the court; * * * and thirty-nine women and children of all ages.

[*The catalogue over, the deposition goes on*]

* * * That all the negroes slept upon deck, as is customary in this navigation, and none wore fetters, because the owner, his friend Aranda, told him that they were all tractable; * * * that on the seventh day after leaving port, at three o'clock in the morning, all the Spaniards being asleep except the two officers on the watch, who were the boatswain,[127] Juan Robles, and the carpenter, Juan Bautista Gayete, and the helmsman and his boy, the negroes revolted suddenly, wounded dangerously the boatswain and the carpenter, and successively killed eighteen men of those who were sleeping upon deck, some with hand-spikes and hatchets, and others by throwing them alive overboard, after tying them; that of the Spaniards upon deck, they left about seven, as he thinks, alive and tied, to manœuvre the ship, and three or four more, who hid themselves, remained also alive. Although in the act of revolt the negroes made themselves masters of the hatchway, six or seven wounded went through it to the cockpit,[128] without any hindrance on their part; that during the act of revolt, the mate and another person, whose name he does not recollect, attempted to come up through the hatchway, but being quickly wounded, were obliged to return to the cabin; that the deponent resolved at break of day to come up the companion-way, where the negro Babo was, being the ringleader, and Atufal, who assisted him, and having spoken to them, exhorted them to cease committing such atrocities, asking them, at the same time, what they wanted and intended to do, offering, himself, to obey their commands; that notwithstanding this, they threw, in his presence, three men, alive and tied, overboard; that they told the deponent to come up, and that they would not kill him; which having done, the negro Babo asked him whether there were in those seas any negro countries where they might be carried, and he answered them, No; that the negro Babo afterwards told him to carry them to Senegal, or to the neighboring islands of St. Nicholas; and he answered, that this was impossible, on account of the great distance, the necessity involved of rounding Cape Horn, the bad condition of the vessel, the want of provisions, sails, and water; but that the negro Babo replied to him he must carry them in any way; that they would do and conform themselves to everything the deponent should require as to eating and drinking; that after a long conference, being absolutely compelled to please them, for they threatened to kill all the whites if they were not, at all events, carried to Senegal, he told them that what was most wanting for the voyage was water; that they would go near the coast to take it; and thence they would proceed on their course; that the negro Babo agreed to it; and the deponent steered towards the intermediate ports, hoping to meet some Spanish or foreign vessel that would save them; that within ten or eleven days they saw the land, and continued their course

---

[127] A ship's officer in charge of the deck crew.   [128] Sleeping quarters for junior officers.

by it in the vicinity of Nasca;[129] that the deponent observed that the negroes were now restless and mutinous, because he did not effect the taking in of water, the negro Babo having required, with threats, that it should be done, without fail, the following day; he told him he saw plainly that the coast was steep, and the rivers designated in the maps were not to be found, with other reasons suitable to the circumstances; that the best way would be to go to the island of Santa Maria, where they might water easily, it being a solitary island, as the foreigners did; that the deponent did not go to Pisco,[130] that was near, nor make any other port of the coast, because the negro Babo had intimated to him several times, that he would kill all the whites the very moment he should perceive any city, town, or settlement of any kind on the shores to which they should be carried: that having determined to go to the island of Santa Maria, as the deponent had planned, for the purpose of trying whether, on the passage or near the island itself, they could find any vessel that should favor them, or whether he could escape from it in a boat to the neighboring coast of Arraco,[131] to adopt the necessary means he immediately changed his course, steering for the island; that the negroes Babo and Atufal held daily conferences, in which they discussed what was necessary for their design of returning to Senegal, whether they were to kill all the Spaniards, and particularly the deponent; that eight days after parting from the coast of Nasca, the deponent being on the watch a little after day-break, and soon after the negroes had their meeting, the negro Babo came to the place where the deponent was, and told him that he had determined to kill his master, Don Alexandro Aranda, both because he and his companions could not otherwise be sure of their liberty, and that to keep the seamen in subjection, he wanted to prepare a warning of what road they should be made to take did they or any of them oppose him; and that, by means of the death of Don Alexandro, that warning would best be given; but, that what this last meant, the deponent did not at the time comprehend, nor could not, further than that the death of Don Alexandro was intended; and moreover the negro Babo proposed to the deponent to call the mate Raneds, who was sleeping in the cabin, before the thing was done, for fear, as the deponent understood it, that the mate, who was a good navigator, should be killed with Don Alexandro and the rest; that the deponent, who was the friend, from youth, of Don Alexandro, prayed and conjured, but all was useless; for the negro Babo answered him that the thing could not be prevented, and that all the Spaniards risked their death if they should attempt to frustrate his will in this matter, or any other; that, in this conflict, the deponent called the mate, Raneds, who was forced to go apart, and immediately the negro Babo commanded the Ashantee Martinqui and the Ashantee Lecbe to go and commit the murder; that those two went down with hatchets to the berth of Don Alexandro; that, yet half alive and mangled, they dragged him on deck; that they were going to throw him overboard in that state, but the negro Babo stopped them, bidding the murder be completed on the deck before him, which was done, when, by his orders, the body was carried below, forward; that nothing more was seen of it by the deponent for three days; * * * that Don Alonzo Sidonia, an old man, long resident at Valparaiso, and lately appointed to a civil office in Peru, whither he had taken passage, was at the time sleeping in the berth opposite Don Alexandro's; that awakening at his cries, surprised by them, and at the sight of the negroes with their bloody hatchets in their hands, he threw himself into the sea

---

[129] Nasca, Peru.   [130] Pisco, Peru.   [131] Arraco, or Arica, Chile.

through a window which was near him, and was drowned, without it being in the power of the deponent to assist or take him up; * * * that a short time after killing Aranda, they brought upon deck his german-cousin, of middle-age, Don Francisco Masa, of Mendoza, and the young Don Joaquin, Marques de Aramboalaza, then lately from Spain, with his Spanish servant Ponce, and the three young clerks of Aranda, José Mozairi, Lorenzo Bargas, and Hermenegildo Gandix, all of Cadiz; that Don Joaquin and Hermenegildo Gandix, the negro Babo, for purposes hereafter to appear, preserved alive; but Don Francisco Masa, José Mozairi, and Lorenzo Bargas, with Ponce the servant, beside the boatswain, Juan Robles, the boatswain's mates, Manuel Viscaya and Roderigo Hurta, and four of the sailors, the negro Babo ordered to be thrown alive into the sea, although they made no resistance, nor begged for anything else but mercy; that the boatswain, Juan Robles, who knew how to swim, kept the longest above water, making acts of contrition, and, in the last words he uttered, charged this deponent to cause mass to be said for his soul to our Lady of Succor: * * * that, during the three days which followed, the deponent, uncertain what fate had befallen the remains of Don Alexandro, frequently asked the negro Babo where they were, and, if still on board, whether they were to be preserved for interment ashore, entreating him so to order it; that the negro Babo answered nothing till the fourth day, when at sunrise, the deponent coming on deck, the negro Babo showed him a skeleton, which had been substituted for the ship's proper figure-head—the image of Christopher Colon, the discoverer of the New World; that the negro Babo asked him whose skeleton that was, and whether, from its whiteness, he should not think it a white's; that, upon discovering his face, the negro Babo, coming close, said words to this effect: "Keep faith with the blacks from here to Senegal, or you shall in spirit, as now in body, follow your leader," pointing to the prow; * * * that the same morning the negro Babo took by succession each Spaniard forward, and asked him whose skeleton that was, and whether, from its whiteness, he should not think it a white's; that each Spaniard covered his face; that then to each the negro Babo repeated the words in the first place said to the deponent; * * * that they (the Spaniards) being then assembled aft, the negro Babo harangued them, saying that he had now done all; that the deponent (as navigator for the negroes) might pursue his course, warning him and all of them that they should, soul and body, go the way of Don Alexandro, if he saw them (the Spaniards) speak or plot anything against them (the negroes)—a threat which was repeated every day; that, before the events last mentioned, they had tied the cook to throw him overboard, for it is not known what thing they heard him speak, but finally the negro Babo spared his life, at the request of the deponent; that a few days after, the deponent, endeavoring not to omit any means to preserve the lives of the remaining whites, spoke to the negroes peace and tranquillity, and agreed to draw up a paper, signed by the deponent and the sailors who could write, as also by the negro Babo, for himself and all the blacks, in which the deponent obliged himself to carry them to Senegal, and they not to kill any more, and he formally to make over to them the ship, with the cargo, with which they were for that time satisfied and quieted.* * * But the next day, the more surely to guard against the sailors' escape, the negro Babo commanded all the boats to be destroyed but the long-boat, which was unseaworthy, and another, a cutter in good condition, which knowing it would yet be wanted for towing the water casks, he had it lowered down into the hold.

* * * * * * * * *

[*Various particulars of the prolonged and perplexed navigation ensuing here follow, with incidents of a calamitous calm, from which portion one passage is extracted, to wit:*]
—That on the fifth day of the calm, all on board suffering much from the heat, and want of water, and five having died in fits, and mad, the negroes became irritable, and for a chance gesture, which they deemed suspicious—though it was harmless—made by the mate, Raneds, to the deponent in the act of handing a quadrant,[132] they killed him; but that for this they afterwards were sorry, the mate being the only remaining navigator on board, except the deponent.

*   *   *   *   *   *   *   *   *

—That omitting other events, which daily happened, and which can only serve uselessly to recall past misfortunes and conflicts, after seventy-three days' navigation, reckoned from the time they sailed from Nasca, during which they navigated under a scanty allowance of water, and were afflicted with the calms before mentioned, they at last arrived at the island of Santa Maria, on the seventeenth of the month of August, at about six o'clock in the afternoon, at which hour they cast anchor very near the American ship, Bachelor's Delight, which lay in the same bay, commanded by the generous Captain Amasa Delano; but at six o'clock in the morning, they had already descried the port, and the negroes became uneasy, as soon as at distance they saw the ship, not having expected to see one there; that the negro Babo pacified them, assuring them that no fear need be had; that straightway he ordered the figure on the bow to be covered with canvas, as for repairs, and had the decks a little set in order; that for a time the negro Babo and the negro Atufal conferred; that the negro Atufal was for sailing away, but the negro Babo would not, and, by himself, cast about what to do; that at last he came to the deponent, proposing to him to say and do all that the deponent declares to have said and done to the American captain;

*   *   *   *   *   *   *   *   *

that the negro Babo warned him that if he varied in the least, or uttered any word, or gave any look that should give the least intimation of the past events or present state, he would instantly kill him, with all his companions, showing a dagger, which he carried hid, saying something which, as he understood it, meant that that dagger would be alert as his eye; that the negro Babo then announced the plan to all his companions, which pleased them; that he then, the better to disguise the truth, devised many expedients, in some of them uniting deceit and defense; that of this sort was the device of the six Ashantees before named, who were his bravoes;[133] that them he stationed on the break of the poop, as if to clean certain hatchets (in cases, which were part of the cargo), but in reality to use them, and distribute them at need, and at a given word he told them; that, among other devices, was the device of presenting Atufal, his right hand man, as chained, though in a moment the chains could be dropped; that in every particular he informed the deponent what part he was expected to enact in every device, and what story he was to tell on every occasion, always threatening him with instant death if he varied in the least: that, conscious that many of the negroes would be turbulent, the negro Babo appointed the four aged negroes, who were calkers, to keep what domestic order they could on the decks; that again and again he harangued the

---

[132] An instrument of navigation, used to determine latitude.
[133] Henchmen.

Spaniards and his companions, informing them of his intent, and of his devices, and of the invented story that this deponent was to tell; charging them lest any of them varied from that story; that these arrangements were made and matured during the interval of two or three hours, between their first sighting the ship and the arrival on board of Captain Amasa Delano; that this happened about half-past seven o'clock in the morning, Captain Amasa Delano coming in his boat, and all gladly receiving him; that the deponent, as well as he could force himself, acting then the part of principal owner, and a free captain of the ship, told Captain Amasa Delano, when called upon, that he came from Buenos Ayres, bound to Lima, with three hundred negroes; that off Cape Horn, and in a subsequent fever, many negroes had died; that also, by similar casualties, all the sea officers and the greatest part of the crew had died.

* * * * * * * *

[*And so the deposition goes on, circumstantially recounting the fictitious story dictated to the deponent by Babo, and through the deponent imposed upon Captain Delano; and also recounting the friendly offers of Captain Delano, with other things, but all of which is here omitted. After the fictitious story, etc. the deposition proceeds:*]

* * * * * * * *

—that the generous Captain Amasa Delano remained on board all the day, till he left the ship anchored at six o'clock in the evening, deponent speaking to him always of his pretended misfortunes, under the fore-mentioned principles, without having had it in his power to tell a single word, or give him the least hint, that he might know the truth and state of things; because the negro Babo, performing the office of an officious servant with all the appearance of submission of the humble slave, did not leave the deponent one moment; that this was in order to observe the deponent's actions and words, for the negro Babo understands well the Spanish; and besides, there were thereabout some others who were constantly on the watch, and likewise understood the Spanish;

* * * that upon one occasion, while deponent was standing on the deck conversing with Amasa Delano, by a secret sign the negro Babo drew him (the deponent) aside, the act appearing as if originating with the deponent; that then, he being drawn aside, the negro Babo proposed to him to gain from Amasa Delano full particulars about his ship, and crew, and arms; that the deponent asked "For what?" that the negro Babo answered he might conceive; that, grieved at the prospect of what might overtake the generous Captain Amasa Delano, the deponent at first refused to ask the desired questions, and used every argument to induce the negro Babo to give up this new design: that the negro Babo showed the point of his dagger; that, after the information had been obtained the negro Babo again drew him aside, telling him that that very night he (the deponent) would be captain of two ships, instead of one, for that, great part of the American's ship's crew being to be absent fishing, the six Ashantees, without any one else, would easily take it; that at this time he said other things to the same purpose; that no entreaties availed; that, before Amasa Delano's coming on board, no hint had been given touching the capture of the American ship: that to prevent this project the deponent was powerless; * * *—that in some things his memory is confused, he cannot distinctly recall every event; * * *—that as soon as they had cast anchor at six of the clock in the evening, as has before been stated, the American Captain took leave, to return to his vessel; that upon a sudden impulse, which the deponent believes to have come from God and his angels, he, after the farewell had been said, followed the generous Captain Amasa Delano as far as the gunwale,[134] where he stayed, under pretense of taking leave, until Amasa Delano should have been seated in his boat; that on shoving off, the deponent sprang from the gunwale into the boat, and fell into it, he knows not how, God guarding him; that—

* * * * * * * * *

[*Here, in the original, follows the account of what further happened at the escape, and how the San Dominick was retaken, and of the passage to the coast; including in the recital many expressions of "eternal gratitude" to the "generous Captain Amasa Delano." The deposition then proceeds with recapitulatory remarks, and a partial renumeration of the negroes, making record of their individual part in the past events, with a view to furnishing, according to command of the court, the data whereon to found the criminal sentences to be pronounced. From this portion is the following;*]

—That he believes that all the negroes, though not in the first place knowing to the design of revolt, when it was accomplished, approved it. * * * That the negro, José, eighteen years old, and in the personal service of Don Alexandro, was the one who communicated the information to the negro Babo, about the state of things in the cabin, before the revolt; that this is known, because, in the preceding midnight, he used to come from his berth, which was under his master's, in the cabin, to the deck where the ringleader and his associates were, and had secret conversations with the negro Babo, in which he was several times seen by the mate; that, one night, the mate drove him away twice; * * * that this same negro José was the one who, without being commanded to do so by the negro Babo, as Lecbe and Martinqui were, stabbed his master, Don Alexandro, after he had been dragged half-lifeless to the deck; * * * that the mulatto steward, Francesco, was of the first band of revolters, that he was, in all things, the creature and tool of the negro Babo; that, to make his court, he, just before a repast in the cabin, proposed, to the negro Babo, poisoning a dish for the generous Captain Amasa Delano; this is known and believed, because the negroes have said it; but that the negro Babo, having another design, forbade Francesco; * * * that the Ashantee Lecbe was one of the worst of them; for that, on the day the ship was retaken, he assisted in the defense of her, with a hatchet in each hand, with one of which he wounded, in the breast, the chief mate of Amasa Delano, in the first act of boarding; this all knew; that, in sight of the deponent, Lecbe struck, with a hatchet, Don Francisco Masa, when, by the negro Babo's orders, he was carrying him to throw him overboard, alive, beside participating in the murder, before mentioned, of Don Alexandro Aranda, and others of the cabin-passengers; that, owing to the fury with which the Ashantees fought in the engagement with the boats, but this Lecbe and Yan survived; that Yan was bad as Lecbe; that Yan was the man who, by Babo's command, willingly prepared the skeleton of Don Alexandro, in a way the negroes afterwards told the deponent, but which he, so long as reason is left him, can never divulge; that Yan and Lecbe were the two who, in a calm by night, riveted the skeleton to the bow; this also the negroes told him; that the negro Babo was he who traced the inscription below it; that the negro Babo was the plotter from first to last; he ordered every murder, and was the helm and keel of the revolt; that Atufal was his lieutenant in all; but Atufal, with his own hand, com-

---

[134] The upper edge of the side of a ship.

mitted no murder; nor did the negro Babo; * * that Atufal was shot, being killed in the fight with the boats, ere boarding, * * * that the negresses, of age, were knowing to the revolt, and testified themselves satisfied at the death of their master, Don Alexandro; that, had the negroes not restrained them, they would have tortured to death, instead of simply killing, the Spaniards slain by command of the negro Babo; that the negresses used their utmost influence to have the deponent made away with; that, in the various acts of murder, they sang songs and danced—not gaily, but solemnly; and before the engagement with the boats, as well as during the action, they sang melancholy songs to the negroes, and that this melancholy tone was more inflaming than a different one would have been, and was so intended; that all this is believed, because the negroes have said it.

—that of the thirty-six men of the crew, exclusive of the passengers (all of whom are now dead), which the deponent had knowledge of, six only remained alive, with four cabin-boys and ship-boys, not included with the crew; * * * —that the negroes broke an arm of one of the cabin-boys and gave him strokes with hatchets.

[*Then follow various random disclosures referring to various periods of time. The following are extracted;*]

—That during the presence of Captain Amasa Delano on board, some attempts were made by the sailors, and one by Hermenegildo Gandix, to convey hints to him of the true state of affairs; but that these attempts were ineffectual, owing to fear of incurring death, and, furthermore, owing to the devices which offered contradictions to the true state of affairs, as well as owing to the generosity and piety of Amasa Delano incapable of sounding such wickedness; * * * that Luys Galgo, a sailor about sixty years of age, and formerly of the king's navy, was one of those who sought to convey tokens to Captain Amasa Delano; but his intent, though undiscovered, being suspected, he was, on a pretense, made to retire out of sight, and at last into the hold, and there was made away with. This the negroes have since said; * * * that one of the ship-boys feeling, from Captain Amasa Delano's presence, some hopes of release, and not having enough prudence, dropped some chance-word respecting his expectations, which being overheard and understood by a slave-boy with whom he was eating at the time, the latter struck him on the head with a knife, inflicting a bad wound, but of which the boy is now healing; that likewise, not long before the ship was brought to anchor, one of the seamen, steering at the time, endangered himself by letting the blacks remark some expression in his countenance, arising from a cause similar to the above; but this sailor, by his heedful after conduct, escaped; * * * that these statements are made to show the court that from the beginning to the end of the revolt, it was impossible for the deponent and his men to act otherwise than they did; * * *—that the third clerk, Hermenegildo Gandix, who before had been forced to live among the seamen, wearing a seaman's habit, and in all respects appearing to be one for the time; he, Gandix, was killed by a musket ball fired through mistake from the boats before boarding; having in his fright run up the mizzen-rigging, calling to the boats—"don't board," lest upon their boarding the negroes should kill him; that his inducing the Americans to believe he some way favored the cause of the negroes, they fired two balls at him, so that he fell wounded from the rigging, and was drowned in the sea; * * *—that the young Don Joaquin, Marques de Aramboalaza, like Hermenegildo Gandix, the third clerk, was degraded to the office and appearance of a common seaman; that upon one occasion when Don Joaquin shrank, the negro Babo commanded the Ashantee Lecbe to take tar and heat it, and pour it upon Don Joaquin's hands; * * *—that Don Joaquin was killed owing to another mistake of the Americans, but one impossible to be avoided, as upon the approach of the boats, Don Joaquin, with a hatchet tied edge out and upright to his hand, was made by the negroes to appear on the bulwarks; whereupon, seen with arms in his hands and in a questionable attitude, he was shot for a renegade seaman; * * * —that on the person of Don Joaquin was found secreted a jewel, which, by papers that were discovered, proved to have been meant for the shrine of our Lady of Mercy in Lima; a votive offering, beforehand prepared and guarded, to attest his gratitude, when he should have landed in Peru, his last destination, for the safe conclusion of his entire voyage from Spain; * * * —that the jewel, with the other effects of the late Don Joaquin, is in the custody of the brethren of the Hospital de Sacerdotes, awaiting the disposition of the honorable court; * * * —that, owing to the condition of the deponent, as well as the haste in which the boats departed for the attack, the Americans were not forewarned that there were, among the apparent crew, a passenger and one of the clerks disguised by the negro Babo; * * * —that, beside the negroes killed in the action, some were killed after the capture and re-anchoring at night, when shackled to the ring-bolts on deck; that these deaths were committed by the sailors, ere they could be prevented. That so soon as informed of it, Captain Amasa Delano used all his authority, and, in particular with his own hand, struck down Martinez Gola, who, having found a razor in the pocket of an old jacket of his, which one of the shackled negroes had on, was aiming it at the negro's throat; that the noble Captain Amasa Delano also wrenched from the hand of Bartholomew Barlo a dagger, secreted at the time of the massacre of the whites, with which he was in the act of stabbing a shackled negro, who, the same day, with another negro, had thrown him down and jumped upon him; * * * —that, for all the events, befalling through so long a time, during which the ship was in the hands of the negro Babo, he cannot here give account; but that, what he has said is the most substantial of what occurs to him at present, and is the truth under the oath which he has taken; which declaration he affirmed and ratified, after hearing it read to him.

He said that he is twenty-nine years of age, and broken in body and mind; that when finally dismissed by the court, he shall not return home to Chili, but betake himself to the monastery on Mount Agonia without; and signed with his honor, and crossed himself, and, for the time, departed as he came, in his litter, with the monk Infelez, to the Hospital de Sacerdotes.   Benito Cereno.

Doctor Rozas.

If the Deposition have served as the key to fit into the lock of the complications which precede it, then, as a vault whose door has been flung back, the San Dominick's hull lies open today.

Hitherto the nature of this narrative, besides rendering the intricacies in the beginning unavoidable, has more or less required that many things, instead of being set down in the order of occurrence, should be retrospectively, or irregularly given; this last is the case with the following passages, which will conclude the account:

During the long, mild voyage to Lima, there was, as before hinted, a period during which the sufferer a little recovered his health, or, at least in some degree, his tranquillity. Ere the decided relapse which came, the two captains had many cordial conversations—their fraternal unreserve in singular contrast with former withdrawments.

Again and again it was repeated, how hard it had been to enact the part forced on the Spaniard by Babo.

"Ah, my dear friend," Don Benito once said, "at those very times when you thought me so morose and ungrateful, nay, when, as you now admit, you half thought me plotting your murder, at those very times my heart was frozen; I could not look at you, thinking of what, both on board this ship and your own, hung, from other hands, over my kind benefactor. And as God lives, Don Amasa, I know not whether desire for my own safety alone could have nerved me to that leap into your boat, had it not been for the thought that, did you, unenlightened, return to your ship, you, my best friend, with all who might be with you, stolen upon, that night, in your hammocks, would never in this world have wakened again. Do but think how you walked this deck, how you sat in this cabin, every inch of ground mined into honey-combs under you. Had I dropped the least hint, made the least advance towards an understanding between us, death, explosive death—yours as mine—would have ended the scene."

"True, true," cried Captain Delano, starting, "you have saved my life, Don Benito, more than I yours; saved it, too, against my knowledge and will."

"Nay, my friend," rejoined the Spaniard, courteous even to the point of religion, "God charmed your life, but you saved mine. To think of some things you did—those smilings and chattings, rash pointings and gesturings. For less than these, they slew my mate, Raneds; but you had the Prince of Heaven's safe-conduct through all ambuscades."

"Yes, all is owing to Providence, I know: but the temper of my mind that morning was more than commonly pleasant, while the sight of so much suffering, more apparent than real, added to my good-nature, compassion, and charity, happily interweaving the three. Had it been otherwise, doubtless, as you hint, some of my interferences might have ended unhappily enough. Besides, those feelings I spoke of enabled me to get the better of momentary distrust, at times when acuteness might have cost me my life, without saving another's. Only at the end did my suspicions get the better of me, and you know how wide of the mark they then proved."

"Wide, indeed," said Don Benito, sadly; "you were with me all day; stood with me, sat with me, talked with me, looked at me, ate with me, drank with me; and yet, your last act was to clutch for a monster, not only an innocent man, but the most pitiable of all men. To such degree may malign machinations and deceptions impose. So far may even the best man err, in judging the conduct of one with the recesses of whose condition he is not acquainted. But you were forced to it; and you were in time undeceived. Would that, in both respects, it was so ever, and with all men."

"You generalize, Don Benito; and mournfully enough. But the past is passed; why moralize on it? Forget it. See, yon bright sun has forgotten it all, and the blue sea, and the blue sky; these have turned over new leaves."

"Because they have no memory," he dejectedly replied; "because they are not human."

"But these mild trades[135] that now fan your cheek, do they not come with a human-like healing to you? Warm friends, steadfast friends are the trades."

---

[135] Trade winds.

"With their steadfastness they but waft me to my tomb, Señor," was the fore-boding response.

"You are saved," cried Captain Delano, more and more astonished and pained; "you are saved: what has cast such a shadow upon you?"

"The negro."

There was silence, while the moody man sat, slowly and unconsciously gathering his mantle about him, as if it were a pall.

There was no more conversation that day.

But if the Spaniard's melancholy sometimes ended in muteness upon topics like the above, there were others upon which he never spoke at all; on which, indeed, all his old reserves were piled. Pass over the worst, and, only to elucidate, let an item or two of these be cited. The dress, so precise and costly, worn by him on the day whose events have been narrated, had not willingly been put on. And that silver-mounted sword, apparent symbol of despotic command, was not, indeed, a sword, but the ghost of one. The scabbard, artificially stiffened, was empty.

As for the black—whose brain, not body, had schemed and led the revolt, with the plot—his slight frame, inadequate to that which it held, had at once yielded to the superior muscular strength of his captor, in the boat. Seeing all was over, he uttered no sound, and could not be forced to. His aspect seemed to say, since I cannot do deeds, I will not speak words. Put in irons in the hold, with the rest, he was carried to Lima. During the passage, Don Benito did not visit him. Nor then, nor at any time after, would he look at him. Before the tribunal he refused. When pressed by the judges he fainted. On the testimony of the sailors alone rested the legal identity of Babo.

Some months after, dragged to the gibbet at the tail of a mule, the black met his voiceless end. The body was burned to ashes; but for many days, the head, that hive of subtlety, fixed on a pole in the Plaza, met, unabashed, the gaze of the whites; and across the Plaza looked towards St. Bartholomew's church, in whose vaults slept then, as now, the recovered bones of Aranda: and across the Rimac bridge looked towards the monastery, on Mount Agonia without; where, three months after being dismissed by the court, Benito Cereno, borne on the bier, did, indeed, follow his leader.

1855

from *BATTLE-PIECES AND ASPECTS OF THE WAR*

THE PORTENT*

(1859)

Hanging from the beam,
  Slowly swaying (such the law),
Gaunt the shadow on your green,

---

* This poem, the first in *Battle-Pieces and Aspects of the War* (1866), presents the slave rebellion led by the abolitionist John Brown (1800–1859) at Harper's Ferry, then in Virginia, in October 1859 as a portent of the Civil War, which began in 1861.

Shenandoah![1]
The cut is on the crown[2]
  (Lo, John Brown),
And the stabs shall heal no more.

Hidden in the cap[3]
  Is the anguish none can draw
So your future veils its face,   10
    Shenandoah!
But the streaming beard is shown[4]
  (Weird[5] John Brown),
The meteor of the war.

1866

THE MARCH INTO VIRGINIA

Ending in the First Manassas*

(July 1861)

Did all the lets[1] and bars appear
  To every just or larger end,
Whence should come the trust and cheer?
  Youth must its ignorant impulse lend . . .
Age finds place in the rear.
  All wars are boyish, and are fought by boys,
The champions and enthusiasts of the state:
  Turbid ardours and vain joys
    Not barrenly abate . . .
Stimulants to the power mature,   10
    Preparatives of fate.
Who here forecasteth the event?
What heart but spurns at precedent
And warnings of the wise,
Contemned foreclosures of surprise?
The banners play, the bugles call,
The air is blue and prodigal.
  No berrying party, pleasure-wooed,

---

[1] Brown was hanged in the Shenandoah Valley, at Charlestown, Virginia (now Charles Town, West Virginia), in December 1859.
[2] Brown had received a head wound, when he was captured.
[3] The hood placed over the head of a condemned person.
[4] His beard can be seen beneath the cap.   [5] Uncanny, fantastic.

* On July 21, 1861, Confederate troops defeated Union forces at Bull Run, a stream near Manassas, Virginia. Melville portrays the Union soldiers as "boyish" and tragically light-hearted as they go into this first major battle of the Civil War.
[1] Obstacles.

No picnic party in the May,
Ever went less loth than they   20
   Into that leafy neighbourhood.
In Bacchic glee[2] they file toward Fate,
Moloch's[3] uninitiate;
Expectancy, and glad surmise
Of battle's unknown mysteries.

All they feel is this: 'tis glory,
A rapture sharp, though transitory,
Yet lasting in belaurelled story.
So they gaily go to fight,
Chatting left and laughing right.   30

But some who this blithe mood present,
   As on in lightsome files they fare,
Shall die experienced ere three days are spent . . .
   Perish, enlightened by the volleyed glare;
Or shame survive, and, like to adamant,[4]
   The throe of Second Manassas[5] share.

1866

SHILOH*

A Requiem

(April 1862)

Skimming lightly, wheeling still,
   The swallows fly low
Over the field in clouded days,
   The forest-field of Shiloh—
Over the field where April rain
Solaced the parched one stretched in pain
Through the pause of night
That followed the Sunday fight

---

[2] In revelry; Bacchus was the Roman god of wine.
[3] An ancient Semitic god of fire to whom children were offered in sacrifice.
[4] An imaginary stone of impenetrable hardness.
[5] In the Second Battle of Manassas, on August 30, 1862, Union forces met defeat by General Robert E. Lee and Thomas "Stonewall" Jackson's troops.
* This poem commemorates the soldiers (of both sides) who died during the Confederate victory at Shiloh, in western Tennessee, in early April 1862.

Around the church of Shiloh[1]—
The church so lone, the log-built one,   10
That echoed to many a parting groan
    And natural prayer
Of dying foemen mingled there—
Foemen at morn, but friends at eve—
    Fame or country least their care:
(What like a bullet can undeceive!)
    But now they lie low,
While over them the swallows skim
And all is hushed at Shiloh.

1866

THE COLLEGE COLONEL*

He rides at their head;
    A crutch by his saddle just slants in view,
One slung arm is in splints, you see,[1]
    Yet he guides his strong steed . . . how coldly too.
He brings his regiment home . . .
    Not as they filed two years before,
But a remnant half-tattered, and battered, and worn,
Like castaway sailors, who . . . stunned
        By the surf's loud roar,
    Their mates dragged back and seen no more . . .   10
Again and again breast the surge,
    And at last crawl, spent, to shore.

A still rigidity and pale . . .
    An Indian aloofness lones his brow;
He has lived a thousand years
Compressed in battle's pains and prayers,
    Marches and watches slow.

There are welcoming shouts, and flags;
    Old men off hat to the Boy,
Wreaths from gay balconies fall at his feet,   20
    But to *him* . . . there comes alloy.[2]

---

[1] Much of the fighting took place around the Shiloh Baptist church. Ironically, in this "Sunday fight" human beings were killing each other rather than worshiping in brotherhood.

* William Francis Bartlett, a Harvard University student who enlisted in the Union army and rose to the rank of colonel; Melville was living in Pittsfield, Massachusetts, when the town honored Colonel Bartlett with a homecoming celebration.

[1] In battle, Bartlett had lost a leg, and one of his arms was maimed.

[2] A private mood that cuts in on the public celebration.

It is not that a leg is lost,
  It is not that an arm is maimed,
It is not that the fever has racked . . .
  Self he has long disclaimed.

But all through the Seven Days' Fight,[3]
  And deep in the Wilderness[4] grim,
And in the field-hospital tent,
  And Petersburg crater,[5] and dim
Lean brooding in Libby,[6] there came . . .   30
  Ah heaven! . . . what *truth* to him.

1866

from *TIMOLEON*

MONODY*

To have known him, to have loved him
  After loneness long;
And then to be estranged in life,[1]
  And neither in the wrong;
And now for death to set his seal . . .
  Ease me, a little ease, my song!

By wintry hills his hermit-mound
  The sheeted snow-drifts drape,
And houseless there the snow-bird flits
  Beneath the fir-trees' crape:
Glazed now with ice the cloistral vine[2]   10
  That hid the shyest grape.

1891

---

[3] The Seven Days' Battle at Malvern Hill, Virginia, in July 1862.
[4] The Battle of the Wilderness in Virginia in May 1864.
[5] The siege of Petersburg, Virginia, which was followed by the Battle of the Crater in July 1864.
[6] Bartlett, captured in Petersburg, was incarcerated in the Confederate Libby Prison in Richmond, Virginia.
* A poem in which a single mourner laments, this monody is thought to be a lament for Nathaniel Hawthorne, who died in 1864.
[1] There is no evidence that Melville and Hawthorne were ever "estranged," although their lives went different ways in the early 1850s after they had been neighbors in western Massachusetts.
[2] In his book-length poem, *Clarel* (1876), Melville seems to have portrayed Vine, a shy character, from his memories of Hawthorne.

Harriet Beecher Stowe
(1811–1896)

One of the most popular writers in nineteenth-century America, Harriet Beecher Stowe produced a number of domestic works based on rural New England but is best known as the author of *Uncle Tom's Cabin* (1852). Rather than questing for self-realization, Stowe's female characters are notable for self-sacrifice in the service of a noble cause. Through such characters Stowe shared her concerns about a variety of social problems. She presented the evils of slavery through Little Eva in *Uncle Tom's Cabin,* for example, and challenged patriarchy through her idealized depictions of maternal life. Stowe's understanding of Calvinism led her to distinguish between God as stern father and God as loving mother. Ann Douglas, a critic, observes that Stowe identified religious institutions with male power; thus her female characters sometimes appear to wage a quasi-feminist battle against institutions of the church.

Harriet Beecher was born into a respected family of fifteen in Litchfield, Connecticut, in 1811. Her parents were Lyman Beecher, a prominent clergyman, and Roxana Foote; one of her brothers, Henry Ward, was a celebrated preacher; and her sister Catharine was a pioneer in women's education. In Hartford Catharine founded a women's seminary, which Harriet attended. In 1832 Harriet moved with her family to Cincinnati when her father became president of Lane Theological Seminary. Four years later she married Rev. Calvin Ellis Stowe, a professor of biblical literature there; the couple had seven children together. Her eighteen years in Cincinnati, directly across the Ohio River from Kentucky, gave her a close-up view of slavery.

Stowe moved to Brunswick, Maine, in 1850 when her husband was appointed to a post at Bowdoin College. The Fugitive Slave Act, announced the same year, inspired her to begin *Uncle Tom's Cabin: Or, Life Among the Lowly,* which was serialized in the *National Era* (1851–1852) and published shortly thereafter. The book brought her instant fame (350,000 copies were sold during the first year) and made a vital contribution to the abolitionist cause. Stowe claimed that it was not she, but God, who wrote the work. A year later she brought out *A Key to Uncle Tom's Cabin*—a compilation of facts drawn from court records, newspapers, and private letters—to defend herself against charges of inaccuracy. In 1853 she produced another antislavery novel, *Dred: A Tale of the Great Dismal Swamp,* which treats slavery's demoralizing influence upon whites. At the height of her fame in 1853, Stowe traveled through England and met several literary figures, including Charles Dickens, George Eliot, and Lady Byron, the poet's widow. Out of her friendship with Lady Byron came a controversial book, *Lady Byron Vindicated* (1870), which charged that Lord Byron had had incestuous relations with his sister. Rev. Stowe died in 1886, and despite the great fame she had achieved, Stowe spent her later years in virtual solitude and senility. She died in Hartford in 1896.

The phenomenal success of *Uncle Tom's Cabin* makes it easy to forget that Stowe wrote more than twenty-five novels, essays, poems, and stories, many set in her native

UNCLE TOM'S CABIN;

OR,

LIFE AMONG THE LOWLY.

BY

HARRIET BEECHER STOWE.

VOL. I.

BOSTON:
JOHN P. JEWETT & COMPANY.
CLEVELAND, OHIO:
JEWETT, PROCTOR & WORTHINGTON.
1852.

The title page of the first edition (in book form) of Harriet Beecher Stowe's Uncle Tom's Cabin.

New England. The novel *The Minister's Wooing* (1859) is a romance that attacks the injustice of Calvinism. *The Pearl of Orr's Island* (1862) and *Oldtown Folks* (1869) are local-color narratives: the former a depiction of rural Maine, the latter of domestic life in Massachusetts. In the fictional essays *My Wife and I* (1871) and *We and Our Neighbors* (1874), Stowe advocates women's rights and satirizes male sentimentalists. Although her romantic and local-color fiction never achieved wide popularity, it nevertheless had a positive influence on the work of emerging writers such as Sarah Orne Jewett and Mary E. Wilkins Freeman.

Suggested Readings: *The Writings of Harriet Beecher Stowe*, 16 vols., 1896. *Collected Poems*, ed. J. M. Moran, Jr., 1967. R. F. Wilson, *Crusader in Crinoline: The Life of Harriet Beecher Stowe*, 1941. C. H. Foster, *The Rungless Ladder: Harriet Beecher Stowe and New England Puritanism*, 1954. A. C. Crozier, *The Novels of Harriet Beecher Stowe*, 1969. E. Moers, *Harriet Beecher Stowe and American Literature*, 1978. E. Ammons, ed., *Critical Essays on Harriet Beecher Stowe*, 1980. G. Kimball, *The Religious Ideas of Harriet Beecher Stowe*, 1982. T. R. Hovet, *The Master Narrative: Harriet Beecher Stowe's Subversive Story of Slavery in "Uncle Tom's Cabin" and "Dred"*, 1989.

Text Used: *Novels and Stories by Harriet Beecher Stowe: Uncle Tom's Cabin: Or, Life Among the Lowly*, 1899.

from   UNCLE TOM'S CABIN: OR, LIFE AMONG THE LOWLY*

CHAPTER XXX: THE SLAVE WAREHOUSE[1]

A slave warehouse! Perhaps some of my readers conjure up horrible visions of such a place. They fancy some foul, obscure den, some horrible *Tartarus "informis, ingens, cui lumen ademptum."*[2] But no, innocent friend; in these days men have learned the art of sinning expertly and genteelly, so as not to shock the eyes and senses of respectable society. Human property is high in the market; and is, therefore, well fed, well cleaned, tended, and looked after, that it may come to sale sleek, and strong, and shining. A slave warehouse in New Orleans is a house externally not much unlike many others, kept with neatness; and where every day you may see arranged, under a sort of shed along the outside, rows of men and women, who stand there as a sign of the property sold within.

Then you shall be courteously entreated to call and examine, and shall find an abundance of husbands, wives, brothers, sisters, fathers, mothers, and young children, to be "sold separately, or in lots, to suit the convenience of the purchaser;" and that soul immortal, once bought with blood and anguish by the Son of God, when the earth shook, and the rocks were rent, and the graves were opened, can be sold, leased, mortgaged, exchanged for groceries or dry goods, to suit the phases of trade, or the fancy of the purchaser.

It was a day or two after the conversation between Marie and Miss Ophelia, that Tom, Adolph, and half a dozen others of the St. Clare estate, were turned over to the loving kindness of Mr. Skeggs, the keeper of a depot on ———— street, to await the auction next day.

Tom had with him quite a sizable trunk full of clothing, as had most others of them. They were ushered, for the night, into a long room, where many other men, of all ages, sizes, and shades of complexion, were assembled, and from which roars of laughter and unthinking merriment were proceeding.

"Ah, ha! that's right. Go it, boys,—go it!" said Mr. Skeggs, the keeper. "My people are always so merry! Sambo, I see!" he said, speaking approvingly to a burly negro who was performing tricks of low buffoonery, which occasioned the shouts which Tom had heard.

As might be imagined, Tom was in no humor to join these proceedings; and, therefore, setting his trunk as far as possible from the noisy group, he sat down on it, and leaned his face against the wall.

The dealers in the human article make scrupulous and systematic efforts to promote noisy mirth among them, as a means of drowning reflection, and rendering them insensible to their condition. The whole object of the training to which the negro is put, from the time he is sold in the northern market till he arrives south, is systematically directed towards making him callous, unthinking, and

---

* First published serially in the *National Era* from 1851 to 1852. Chapter XXX appeared in 1852.

[1] Primarily a set-piece, a dramatic essay on the inhumanity of large warehouses in which slaves were kept and sold regardless of family ties, this chapter also tells of Tom's sale to the infamous Simon Legree.

[2] Some horrible hell, "grotesque, vast, deprived of light" (Latin); according to Greek myth, Tartarus was an infernal abyss beneath Hades.

brutal. The slave-dealer collects his gang in Virginia or Kentucky, and drives them to some convenient, healthy place,—often a watering-place,—to be fattened.[3] Here they are fed full daily; and, because some incline to pine, a fiddle is kept commonly going among them, and they are made to dance daily; and he who refuses to be merry—in whose soul thoughts of wife, or child, or home, are too strong for him to be gay—is marked as sullen and dangerous, and subjected to all the evils which the ill-will of an utterly irresponsible and hardened man can inflict upon him. Briskness, alertness, and cheerfulness of appearance, especially before observers, are constantly enforced upon them, both by the hope of thereby getting a good master, and the fear of all that the driver may bring upon them, if they prove unsalable.

"What dat ar nigger doin' here?" said Sambo, coming up to Tom, after Mr. Skeggs had left the room. Sambo was a full black, of great size, very lively, voluble, and full of trick and grimace.

"What you doin' here?" said Sambo, coming up to Tom, and poking him facetiously in the side. "Meditatin', eh?"

"I am to be sold at the auction, to-morrow!" said Tom, quietly.

"Sold at auction,—haw! haw! boys, an't this yer fun? I wish't I was gwine that ar way!—tell ye, wouldn't I make 'em laugh? But how is it,—dis yer whole lot gwine to-morrow?" said Sambo, laying his hand freely on Adolph's shoulder.

"Please to let me alone!" said Adolph, fiercely, straightening himself up, with extreme disgust.

"Law, now, boys! dis yer's one o' yer white niggers,—kind o' cream-color, ye know, scented!" said he, coming up to Adolph and snuffing. "O Lor! he'd do for a tobaccer-shop; they could keep him to scent snuff! Lor, he'd keep a whole shop agwine,—he would!"

"I say, keep off, can't you?" said Adolph, enraged.

"Lor, now, how touchy we is,—we white niggers! Look at us, now!" and Sambo gave a ludicrous imitation of Adolph's manner; "here's de airs and graces. We's been in a good family, I specs."

"Yes," said Adolph; "I had a master that could have bought you all for old truck!"

"Laws, now, only think," said Sambo, "the gentlemens that we is!"

"I belonged to the St. Clare family," said Adolph, proudly.

"Lor, you did! Be hanged if they ar'n't lucky to get shet of ye. Spects they's gwine to trade ye off with a lot o' cracked teapots and sich like!" said Sambo, with a provoking grin.

Adolph, enraged at this taunt, flew furiously at his adversary, swearing and striking on every side of him. The rest laughed and shouted, and the uproar brought the keeper to the door.

"What now, boys? Order,—order!" he said, coming in and flourishing a large whip.

All fled in different directions, except Sambo, who, presuming on the favor which the keeper had to him as a licensed wag, stood his ground, ducking his head with a facetious grin, whenever the master made a dive at him.

"Lor, Mas'r, 't an't us,—we's reg'lar stiddy,—it's these yer new hands; they 's real aggravatin',—kinder pickin' at us all time!"

---

[3] Analogies with the treatment of cattle here emphasize that human beings are regarded as property.

The keeper, at this, turned upon Tom and Adolph, and distributing a few kicks and cuffs without much inquiry, and leaving general orders for all to be good boys and go to sleep, left the apartment.

While this scene was going on in the men's sleeping-room, the reader may be curious to take a peep at the corresponding apartment allotted to the women. Stretched out in various attitudes over the floor, he may see numberless sleeping forms of every shade of complexion, from the purest ebony to white, and of all years, from childhood to old age, lying now asleep. Here is a fine bright girl, of ten years, whose mother was sold out yesterday, and who to-night cried herself to sleep when nobody was looking at her. Here, a worn old negress, whose thin arms and callous fingers tell of hard toil, waiting to be sold to-morrow, as a cast-off article, for what can be got for her; and some forty or fifty others, with heads variously enveloped in blankets or articles of clothing, lie stretched around them. But, in a corner, sitting apart from the rest, are two females of a more interesting appearance than common. One of these is a respectably dressed mulatto woman between forty and fifty, with soft eyes and a gentle and pleasing physiognomy. She has on her head a high-raised turban, made of a gray red Madras handkerchief, of the first quality, and her dress is neatly fitted, and of good material, showing that she has been provided for with a careful hand. By her side, and nestling closely to her, is a young girl of fifteen,—her daughter. She is a quadroon,[4] as may be seen from her fairer complexion, though her likeness to her mother is quite discernible. She has the same soft, dark eye, with longer lashes, and her curling hair is of a luxuriant brown. She also is dressed with great neatness, and her white, delicate hands betray very little acquaintance with servile toil. These two are to be sold to-morrow, in the same lot with the St. Clare servants; and the gentleman to whom they belong, and to whom the money for their sale is to be transmitted, is a member of a Christian church in New York, who will receive the money, and go thereafter to the sacrament of his Lord and theirs, and think no more of it.

These two, whom we shall call Susan and Emmeline, had been the personal attendants of an amiable and pious lady of New Orleans, by whom they had been carefully and piously instructed and trained. They had been taught to read and write, diligently instructed in the truths of religion, and their lot had been as happy as one as in their condition it was possible to be. But the only son of their protectress had the management of her property; and, by carelessness and extravagance, involved it to a large amount, and at last failed. One of the largest creditors was the respectable firm of B. & Co., in New York. B. & Co. wrote to their lawyer in New Orleans, who attached the real estate (these two articles and a lot of plantation hands formed the most valuable part of it[5]), and wrote word to that effect to New York. Brother B., being, as we have said, a Christian man, and a resident in a free state, felt some uneasiness on the subject. He didn't like trading in slaves and souls of men,—of course, he didn't; but, then, there were thirty thousand dollars in the case, and that was rather too much money to be lost for a principle; and so, after much considering, and asking advice from those that he knew would advise to suit him, Brother B. wrote to his lawyer to dispose of the business in the way that seemed to him the most suitable, and remit the proceeds.

[4]A person with one black grandparent; therefore, the child of a mulatto and a white.
[5] Here, human beings are "real estate," to be bought and sold.

The day after the letter arrived in New Orleans, Susan and Emmeline were attached, and sent to the depot to await a general auction on the following morning; and as they glimmer faintly upon us in the moonlight which steals through the grated window, we may listen to their conversation. Both are weeping, but each quietly, that the other may not hear.

"Mother, just lay your head on my lap, and see if you can't sleep a little," says the girl, trying to appear calm.

"I haven't any heart to sleep, Em; I can't; it's the last night we may be together!"

"Oh, mother, don't say so! perhaps we shall get sold together,—who knows?"

"If 't was anybody's else case, I should say so, too, Em," said the woman; "but I'm so 'feard of losin' you that I don't see anything but the danger."

"Why, mother, the man said we were both likely, and would sell well."

Susan remembered the man's looks and words. With a deadly sickness at her heart, she remembered how he had looked at Emmeline's hands, and lifted up her curly hair, and pronounced her a first-rate article.[6] Susan had been trained as a Christian, brought up in the daily reading of the Bible, and had the same horror of her child's being sold to a life of shame that any other Christian mother might have; but she had no hope,—no protection.

"Mother, I think we might do first-rate, if you could get a place as cook, and I as chambermaid or seamstress, in some family. I dare say we shall. Let's both look as bright and lively as we can, and tell all we can do, and perhaps we shall," said Emmeline.

"I want you to brush your hair all back straight, to-morrow," said Susan.

"What for, mother? I don't look near so well, that way."

"Yes, but you'll sell better so."

"I don't see why!" said the child.

"Respectable families would be more apt to buy you, if they saw you looked plain and decent, as if you wasn't trying to look handsome. I know their ways better'n you do," said Susan.

"Well, mother, then I will."

"And, Emmeline, if we shouldn't ever see each other again, after to-morrow,—if I'm sold way up on a plantation somewhere, and you somewhere else,—always remember how you've been brought up, and all Missis has told you; take your Bible with you, and your hymn-book; and if you're faithful to the Lord, he'll be faithful to you."

So speaks the poor soul, in sore discouragement; for she knows that to-morrow any man, however vile and brutal, however godless and merciless, if he only has money to pay for her, may become owner of her daughter, body and soul; and then, how is the child to be faithful? She thinks of all this, as she holds her daughter in her arms, and wishes that she were not handsome and attractive. It seems almost an aggravation to her to remember how purely and piously, how much above the ordinary lot, she has been brought up. But she has no resort but to *pray;* and many such prayers to God have gone up from those same trim, neatly arranged, respectable slave-prisons,—prayers which God has not forgotten, as a coming day shall show; for it is written, "Whoso causeth one of these little ones to offend, it were better for him that a mill-stone were hanged about his neck, and that he were drowned in the depths of the sea."[7]

---

[6] Here, a young woman becomes an "article" for probable sexual exploitation.

[7] From Matthew 18:5–6.

The soft, earnest, quiet moonbeam looks in fixedly, marking the bars of the grated windows on the prostrate, sleeping forms. The mother and daughter are singing together a wild and melancholy dirge, common as a funeral hymn among the slaves:—

> "Oh, where is weeping Mary?
> Oh, where is weeping Mary?
>   'Rived in the goodly land.
> She is dead and gone to heaven;
> She is dead and gone to heaven;
>   'Rived in the goodly land."

These words, sung by voices of a peculiar and melancholy sweetness, in an air which seemed like the sighing of earthly despair after heavenly hope, floated through the dark prison-rooms with a pathetic cadence, as verse after verse was breathed out,—

> "Oh, where are Paul and Silas?
> Oh, where are Paul and Silas?
>   Gone to the goodly land.
> They are dead and gone to heaven;
> They are dead and gone to heaven;
>   'Rived in the goodly land."

Sing on, poor souls! The night is short, and the morning will part you forever!

But now it is morning, and everybody is astir; and the worthy Mr. Skeggs is busy and bright, for a lot of goods is to be fitted out for auction. There is a brisk lookout on the toilet; injunctions passed around to every one to put on their best face and be spry; and now all are arranged in a circle for a last review, before they are marched up to the Bourse.[8]

Mr. Skeggs, with his palmetto[9] on and his cigar in his mouth, walks around to put farewell touches on his wares.

"How's this?" he said, stepping in front of Susan and Emmeline. "Where's your curls, gal?"

The girl looked timidly at her mother, who, with the smooth adroitness common among her class, answers,—

"I was telling her, last night, to put up her hair smooth and neat, and not havin' it flying about in curls; looks more respectable so."

"Bother!" said the man, peremptorily, turning to the girl; "you go right along, and curl yourself real smart!" He added, giving a crack to a rattan[10] he held in his hand, "And be back in quick time, too!"

"You go and help her," he added, to the mother. "Them curls may make a hundred dollars difference in the sale of her."

Beneath a splendid dome were men of all nations, moving to and fro, over the marble pave. On every side of the circular area were little tribunes, or stations, for the use of speakers and auctioneers. Two of these, on opposite sides of the area,

---

[8] The Paris stock exchange; here, the "stock" is human.
[9] A stylish hat made of woven palm leaves.　　[10] A cane or switch.

were now occupied by brilliant and talented gentlemen, enthusiastically forcing up, in English and French commingled, the bids of connoisseurs in their various wares. A third one, on the other side, still unoccupied, was surrounded by a group, waiting the moment of sale to begin. And here we may recognize the St. Clare servants,—Tom, Adolph, and others; and there, too, Susan and Emmeline, awaiting their turn with anxious and dejected faces. Various spectators, intending to purchase, or not intending, as the case might be, gathered around the group, handling, examining, and commenting on their various points and faces with the same freedom that a set of jockeys discuss the merits of a horse.

"Hulloa, Alf! what brings you here?" said a young exquisite, slapping the shoulder of a sprucely dressed young man, who was examining Adolph through an eye-glass.

"Well, I was wanting a valet, and I heard that St. Clare's lot was going. I thought I'd just look at his"—

"Catch me ever buying any of St. Clare's people! Spoilt niggers, every one. Impudent as the devil!" said the other.

"Never fear that!" said the first. "If I get 'em, I'll soon have their airs out of them; they'll soon find that they've another kind of master to deal with than Monsieur St. Clare. 'Pon my word, I'll buy that fellow. I like the shape of him."

"You'll find it'll take all you've got to keep him. He's deucedly extravagant!"

"Yes, but my lord will find that he *can't* be extravagant with *me*. Just let him be sent to the calaboose[11] a few times, and thoroughly dressed down! I'll tell you if it don't bring him to a sense of his ways! Oh, I'll reform him, up hill and down,— you'll see. I buy him, that's flat!"

Tom had been standing wistfully examining the multitude of faces thronging around him, for one whom he would wish to call master. And if you should ever be under the necessity, sir, of selecting, out of two hundred men, one who was to become your absolute owner and disposer, you would, perhaps, realize, just as Tom did, how few there were that you would feel at all comfortable in being made over to. Tom saw abundance of men,—great, burly, gruff men; little, chirping, dried men; long-favored, lank, hard men; and every variety of stubbed-looking, commonplace men, who pick up their fellow-men as one picks up chips, putting them into the fire or a basket with equal unconcern, according to their convenience; but he saw no St. Clare.

A little before the sale commenced, a short, broad, muscular man, in a checked shirt considerably open at the bosom, and pantaloons much the worse for dirt and wear, elbowed his way through the crowd, like one who is going actively into a business; and, coming up to the group, began to examine them systematically. From the moment that Tom saw him approaching, he felt an immediate and revolting horror at him, that increased as he came near. He was evidently, though short, of gigantic strength. His round, bullet-head, large, light-gray eyes, with their shaggy, sandy eyebrows, and stiff, wiry, sunburned hair, were rather unprepossessing items, it is to be confessed; his large, coarse mouth was distended with tobacco, the juice of which, from time to time, he ejected from him with great decision and explosive force; his hands were immensely large, hairy, sunburned, freckled, and very dirty, and garnished with long nails, in a very foul condition. This man proceeded to a very free personal examination of the lot. He seized Tom

[11] Prison.

by the jaw, and pulled open his mouth to inspect his teeth; made him strip up his sleeve, to show his muscle; turned him round, made him jump and spring, to show his paces.

"Where was you raised?" he added, briefly, to these investigations.

"In Kintuck, Mas'r," said Tom, looking about, as if for deliverance.

"What have you done?"

"Had care of Mas'r's farm," said Tom.

"Likely story!" said the other, shortly, as he passed on. He paused a moment before Dolph; then spitting a discharge of tobacco-juice on his well-blacked boots, and giving a contemptuous umph, he walked on. Again he stopped before Susan and Emmeline. He put out his heavy, dirty hand, and drew the girl towards him; passed it over her neck and bust, felt her arms, looked at her teeth, and then pushed her back against her mother, whose patient face showed the suffering she had been going through at every motion of the hideous stranger.

The girl was frightened, and began to cry.

"Stop that, you minx!" said the salesman; "no whimpering here,—the sale is going to begin." And accordingly the sale began.

Adolph was knocked off, at a good sum, to the young gentleman who had previously stated his intention of buying him; and the other servants of the St. Clare lot went to various bidders.

"Now, up with you, boy! d'ye hear?" said the auctioneer to Tom.

Tom stepped upon the block, gave a few anxious looks round: all seemed mingled in a common, indistinct noise,—the clatter of the salesman crying off his qualifications in French and English, the quick fire of French and English bids; and almost in a moment came the final thump of the hammer, and the clear ring on the last syllable of the word *"dollars,"* as the auctioneer announced his price, and Tom was made over.—He had a master.

He was pushed from the block; the short, bullet-headed man, seizing him roughly by the shoulder, pushed him to one side, saying, in a harsh voice, "Stand there, *you!*"

Tom hardly realized anything; but still the bidding went on,—rattling, clattering, now French, now English. Down goes the hammer again,—Susan is sold! She goes down from the block, stops, looks wistfully back,—her daughter stretches her hands towards her. She looks with agony in the face of the man who has bought her,—a respectable, middle-aged man, of benevolent countenance.

"Oh, Mas'r, please do buy my daughter!"

"I'd like to, but I'm afraid I can't afford it!" said the gentleman, looking, with painful interest, as the young girl mounted the block, and looked around her with a frightened and timid glance.

The blood flushes painfully in her otherwise colorless cheek, her eye has a feverish fire, and her mother groans to see that she looks more beautiful than she ever saw her before. The auctioneer sees his advantage, and expatiates volubly in mingled French and English, and bids rise in rapid succession.

"I'll do anything in reason," said the benevolent-looking gentleman, pressing in and joining the bids. In a few moments they have run beyond his purse. He is silent; the auctioneer grows warmer; but bids gradually drop off. It lies now between an aristocratic old citizen and our bullet-headed acquaintance. The citizen bids for a few turns, contemptuously measuring his opponent; but the bullet-head has the advantage over him, both in obstinacy and concealed length of purse, and the controversy lasts but a moment; the hammer falls,—he has got the girl, body and soul, unless God help her.

Her master is Mr. Legree,[12] who owns a cotton plantation on the Red River. She is pushed along into the same lot with Tom and two other men, and goes off, weeping as she goes.

The benevolent gentleman is sorry; but, then, the thing happens every day! One sees girls and mothers crying, at these sales, *always!* it can't be helped, etc.; and he walks off, with his acquisition, in another direction.

Two days after, the lawyer of the Christian firm of B. & Co., New York, sent on their money to them. On the reverse of that draft, so obtained, let them write these words of the great Paymaster, to whom they shall make up their account in a future day; *"When he maketh inquisition for blood, he forgetteth not the cry of the humble!"*[13]

1851–1852

Mary Lyon, the founder of Mount Holyoke College (1837), the first women's college in the United States.

---

[12] Simon Legree, who later kills Tom—but never recovers from Tom's dying act of forgiveness.

[13] "When he maketh inquisition for blood, he remembereth them: he forgetteth not the cry of the humble," from Psalm 9:12.

Rebecca Harding Davis
(1831–1910)

Rebecca Harding Davis, one of America's earliest practitioners of realism, began her career as a sharp and shocking critic of American society. Her early works "Life in the Iron-Mills" (1861) and *Margaret Howth: A Story of Today* (1862) startled the reading public by displaying in a particularly harsh light some of the tragic consequences of industrialism. Later, however, Davis's writings lost their freshness and power and became didactic, domestic, and conventional.

Rebecca Blaine Harding was born in Washington, Pennsylvania, in 1831 but lived most of her early life in nearby Wheeling, Virginia (now West Virginia). The author Tillie Olsen writes in her edition of *Life in the Iron-Mills and Other Stories* (1973) that as a young woman Harding witnessed the ugly side of industrialization right across the street from her room. The pitiful individuals she saw through her windows were eventually fictionalized in "Life in the Iron-Mills," which appeared anonymously in the *Atlantic Monthly* in 1861. Her intent, Olsen writes, was "to dig into this commonplace, this vulgar American life," and see what was in it. What Harding found was so depressing that her editor, James T. Fields, requested that she make it less severe. Even though she softened the ending of "Iron-Mills" for publication, the story became a sensation because of its starkly realistic portrayal of the lives of industrial workers. Her second work, *Margaret Howth*, concerns the misfortunes of an African-American peddler girl who is barely recognized as a human being. The novel is also based on the life the author observed in Wheeling, which, because of its geographical location in a slave state sandwiched between the free states Pennsylvania and Ohio, exemplified the tragedies of a country divided by slavery.

The success of her first two works brought excitement into what Harding saw as her dull existence in Wheeling. Invited to Boston by Fields in 1862, she was introduced to a number of writers, including Ralph Waldo Emerson, Nathaniel Hawthorne, and Oliver Wendell Holmes. In Philadelphia, on her way home, she met L. Clarke Davis, a young apprentice lawyer four years her junior, who admired "Life in the Iron-Mills" and had asked Harding to meet him. They married the next year, but their life was not easy: Clarke's lack of regular employment forced the young couple to live with relatives in Philadelphia, and the ill health of Rebecca Davis's father required her to make frequent trips to Wheeling. The distress she felt at this time is evident in "The Wife's Story" (1864), which portrays the struggles of a married woman to resolve the conflicting claims of work and family. When the story appeared, Davis was already pregnant with the first of her three children (one of whom, Richard Harding Davis, became a well-known journalist).

Davis continued her exploration of contemporary issues in *Waiting for the Verdict* (1868), which deals with racial bias, and *John Andross* (1874), which discusses corruption in politics. However, family and home took precedence over her career. To raise necessary money, she wrote formula fiction for *Peterson's Magazine,* a popular journal for which her husband worked. In *Silhouettes of American Life* (1892) she showed flashes of her original brilliance along with a patterned sentimentality, but this volume of previously published stories did little to restore her reputation as a writer. Eventually, the uneven

An illustration from the first edition of Rebecca Davis's Waiting for the Verdict *(1868)*.

quality of such work reduced her following, and well before her death in 1910 Davis had lapsed into obscurity. Only recently has she regained some of her deserved reputation as a critic of nineteenth-century industrialism, racism, and politics.

Suggested Readings: *Margaret Howth: A Story of Today,* 1862. *Waiting for the Verdict,* 1868. *Life in the Iron-Mills and Other Stories,* 1985. W. Hesford, "Literary Contexts of 'Life in the Iron Mills,'" *American Literature,* 1977, 49:70–85. R. J. Strahl, "A Finessing of Form: The Sentimental and the Realistic in the Fiction of Rebecca Harding Davis, John DeForest, and William Dean Howells," Ph.D. diss., Indiana University, 1981. J. Fetterley, "Rebecca Harding Davis," in *Provisions: A Reader From 19th-Century American Women,* 1985. T. Olsen, "A Biographical Interpretation," in *Life in the Iron-Mills and Other Stories,* 1985.

Text Used: "Life in the Iron-Mills," *Atlantic Monthly,* VII:XLII, April 1861.

LIFE IN THE IRON-MILLS*

> *"Is this the end?*
> *O Life, as futile, then, as frail!*
> *What hope of answer or redress?"* [1]

A cloudy day: do you know what that is in a town[2] of iron-works? The sky sank down before dawn, muddy, flat, immovable. The air is thick, clammy with the breath of crowded human beings. It stifles me. I open the window, and, looking

* First published in the *Atlantic Monthly* in 1861.
[1] An adaptation of lines from Sections XII and LVI of *In Memoriam A. H. H.* (1850), by Alfred, Lord Tennyson (1809–1892).
[2] Harding does not name the town, but in atmosphere and setting it resembles her hometown of Wheeling, Virginia (now West Virginia).

out, can scarcely see through the rain the grocer's shop opposite, where a crowd of drunken Irishmen are puffing Lynchburg tobacco[3] in their pipes. I can detect the scent through all the foul smells ranging loose in the air.

The idiosyncrasy of this town is smoke. It rolls sullenly in slow folds from the great chimneys of the iron-foundries, and settles down in black, slimy pools on the muddy streets. Smoke on the wharves, smoke on the dingy boats, on the yellow river,—clinging in a coating of greasy soot to the house-front, the two faded poplars, the faces of the passers-by. The long train of mules, dragging masses of pig-iron[4] through the narrow street, have a foul vapor hanging to their reeking sides. Here, inside, is a little broken figure of an angel pointing upward from the mantel-shelf; but even its wings are covered with smoke, clotted and black. Smoke everywhere! A dirty canary chirps desolately in a cage beside me. Its dream of green fields and sunshine is a very old dream,—almost worn out, I think.

From the back-window I can see a narrow brick-yard sloping down to the riverside, strewed with rain-butts[5] and tubs. The river, dull and tawny-colored, (*la belle rivière!*[6]) drags itself sluggishly along, tired of the heavy weight of boats and coal-barges. What wonder? When I was a child, I used to fancy a look of weary, dumb appeal upon the face of the negro-like river slavishly bearing its burden day after day. Something of the same idle notion comes to me to-day, when from the street-window I look on the slow stream of human life creeping past, night and morning, to the great mills. Masses of men, with dull, besotted faces bent to the ground, sharpened here and there by pain or cunning; skin and muscle and flesh begrimed with smoke and ashes; stooping all night over boiling caldrons of metal, laired by day in dens of drunkenness and infamy; breathing from infancy to death an air saturated with fog and grease and soot, vileness for soul and body. What do you make of a case like that, amateur psychologist? You call it an altogether serious thing to be alive: to these men it is a drunken jest, a joke,—horrible to angels perhaps, to them commonplace enough. My fancy about the river was an idle one: it is no type of such a life. What if it be stagnant and slimy here? It knows that beyond there waits for it odorous sunlight,—quaint old gardens, dusky with soft, green foliage of apple-trees, and flushing crimson with roses,—air, and fields, and mountains. The future of the Welsh puddler[7] passing just now is not so pleasant. To be stowed away, after his grimy work is done, in a hole in the muddy graveyard, and after that,———*not* air, nor green fields, nor curious roses.

Can you see how foggy the day is? As I stand here, idly tapping the window-pane, and looking out through the rain at the dirty back-yard and the coalboats below, fragments of an old story float up before me,—a story of this old house into which I happened to come today. You may think it a tiresome story enough, as foggy as the day, sharpened by no sudden flashes of pain or pleasure.—I know: only the outline of a dull life, that long since, with thousands of dull lives like its

---

[3] Cheap tobacco from Lynchburg, Virginia.   [4] Crude iron directly from the blast furnace.
[5] Large wooden casks used to catch rainwater.
[6] "The beautiful river" (French); the phrase is used with a combination of irony and nostalgia for the Ohio river as seen by the early French fur traders.
[7] A worker who stirs oxides into molten pig-iron, turning it into wrought iron.

own, was vainly lived and lost: thousands of them,—massed, vile, slimy lives, like those of the torpid lizards in yonder stagnant water-butt.—Lost? There is a curious point for you to settle, my friend, who study psychology in a lazy, *dilettante*[8] way. Stop a moment. I am going to be honest. This is what I want you to do. I want you to hide your disgust, take no heed to your clean clothes, and come right down with me,—here, into the thickest of the fog and mud and foul effluvia. I want you to hear this story. There is a secret down here, in this nightmare fog, that has lain dumb for centuries: I want to make it a real thing to you. You, Egoist, or Pantheist, or Arminian,[9] busy in making straight paths for your feet on the hills, do not see it clearly,—this terrible question which men here have gone mad and died trying to answer. I dare not put this secret into words. I told you it was dumb. These men, going by with drunken faces and brains full of unawakened power,[10] do not ask it of Society or of God. Their lives ask it; their deaths ask it. There is no reply. I will tell you plainly that I have a great hope; and I bring it to you to be tested. It is this: that this terrible dumb question is its own reply; that it is not the sentence of death we think it, but, from the very extremity of its darkness, the most solemn prophecy which the world has known of the Hope to come. I dare make my meaning no clearer, but will only tell my story. It will, perhaps, seem to you as foul and dark as this thick vapor about us, and as pregnant with death; but if your eyes are free as mine are to look deeper, no perfume-tinted dawn will be so fair with promise of the day that shall surely come.

My story is very simple,—only what I remember of the life of one of these men,—a furnace-tender in one of Kirby & John's rolling-mills,—Hugh Wolfe. You know the mills? They took the great order for the Lower Virginia railroads there last winter; run usually with about a thousand men. I cannot tell why I choose the half-forgotten story of this Wolfe more than that of myriads of these furnace-hands. Perhaps because there is a secret underlying sympathy between that story and this day with its impure fog and thwarted sunshine,—or perhaps simply for the reason that this house is the one where the Wolfes lived. There were the father and son,—both hands, as I said, in one of Kirby & John's mills for making railroad-iron,—and Deborah, their cousin, a picker,[11] in some of the cotton-mills. The house was rented then to half a dozen families. The Wolfes had two of the cellar-rooms. The old man, like many of the puddlers and feeders[12] of the mills, was Welsh,—had spent half of his life in the Cornish[13] tin-mines. You may pick the Welsh emigrants, Cornish miners, out of the throng passing the windows, any day. They are a trifle more filthy; their muscles are not so brawny; they stoop more. When they are drunk, they neither yell, nor shout, nor stagger, but skulk along like beaten hounds. A pure, unmixed blood, I fancy: shows itself in the slight angular bodies and sharply-cut facial lines. It is nearly thirty years since the Wolfes lived here. Their lives were like those of their class: incessant

---

[8] A person who studies in a superficial way.

[9] Anyone who follows philosophical or theological abstractions and does not face the questions posed by real life: an Egoist is committed to self-interest as the most profitable way of living; a Pantheist believes that God and nature are one; an Arminian (following the ideas of the Dutch theologian Jacob Arminius [1560–1607]) opposes the Calvinistic doctrine of predestination.

[10] Throughout the story there is a sense of potential untapped, unawakened, going to waste.

[11] A worker who separates cotton fibers by machine in a cotton mill.

[12] A worker who feeds molten iron into casting forms, so that it will cool (without bubbles) into desired shapes.

[13] Of Cornwall, England.

labor, sleeping in kennel-like rooms, eating rank pork and molasses, drinking—God and the distillers only know what; with an occasional night in jail, to atone for some drunken excess. Is that all of their lives?—of the portion given to them and these their duplicates swarming the streets to-day?—nothing beneath?—all? So many a political reformer will tell you,—and many a private reformer, too, who has gone among them with a heart tender with Christ's charity, and come out outraged, hardened.

One rainy night, about eleven o'clock, a crowd of half-clothed women stopped outside of the cellar-door. They were going home from the cotton-mill.

"Good-night, Deb," said one, a mulatto, steadying herself against the gas-post. She needed the post to steady her. So did more than one of them.

"Dah 's a ball to Miss Potts' to-night. Ye 'd best come."

"Inteet, Deb, if hur 'll come, hur 'll hef fun," said a shrill Welsh voice in the crowd.

Two or three dirty hands were thrust out to catch the gown of the woman, who was groping for the latch of the door.

"No."

"No? Where 's Kit Small, then?"

"Begorra![14] on the spools. Alleys behint, though we helped her, we dud. An wid ye! Let Deb alone! It's ondacent[15] frettin' a quite body. Be the powers, an' we'll have a night of it! there'll be lashin's o' drink,—the Vargent[16] be blessed and praised for 't!"

They went on, the mulatto inclining for a moment to show fight, and drag the woman Wolfe off with them; but, being pacified, she staggered away.

Deborah groped her way into the cellar, and, after considerable stumbling, kindled a match, and lighted a tallow dip, that sent a yellow glimmer over the room. It was low, damp,—the earthen floor covered with a green, slimy moss,—a fetid air smothering the breath. Old Wolfe lay asleep on a heap of straw, wrapped in a torn horse-blanket. He was a pale, meek little man, with a white face and red rabbit-eyes. The woman Deborah was like him; only her face was even more ghastly, her lips bluer, her eyes more watery. She wore a faded cotton gown and a slouching bonnet. When she walked, one could see that she was deformed, almost a hunchback. She trod softly, so as not to waken him, and went through into the room beyond. There she found by the half-extinguished fire an iron saucepan filled with cold boiled potatoes, which she put upon a broken chair with a pint-cup of ale. Placing the old candlestick beside this dainty repast, she untied her bonnet, which hung limp and wet over her face, and prepared to eat her supper. It was the first food that had touched her lips since morning. There was enough of it, however: there is not always. She was hungry,—one could see that easily enough,—and not drunk, as most of her companions would have been found at this hour. She did not drink, this woman,—her face told that, too,—nothing stronger than ale. Perhaps the weak, flaccid wretch had some stimulant in her pale life to keep her up,—some love or hope, it might be, or urgent need. When that stimulant was gone, she would take to whiskey. Man cannot live by work alone. While she was skinning the potatoes, and munching them, a noise behind her made her stop.

"Janey!" she called, lifting the candle and peering into the darkness. "Janey, are you there?"

---

[14] An Irish expression equivalent of "by golly" or "by gosh" (mild forms of "by God").
[15] Indecent.   [16] The Virgin Mary.

A heap of ragged coats was heaved up, and the face of a young girl emerged, staring sleepily at the woman.

"Deborah," she said, at last, "I'm here the night."

"Yes, child. Hur 's welcome," she said, quietly eating on.

The girl's face was haggard and sickly; her eyes were heavy with sleep and hunger: real Milesian[17] eyes they were, dark, delicate blue, glooming out from black shadows with a pitiful fright.

"I was alone," she said, timidly.

"Where's the father?" asked Deborah, holding out a potato, which the girl greedily seized.

"He's beyant,—wid Haley,—in the stone house." (Did you ever hear the word *jail* from an Irish mouth?) "I came here. Hugh told me never to stay me-lone."

"Hugh?"

"Yes."

A vexed frown crossed her face. The girl saw it, and added quickly,—

"I have not seen Hugh the day, Deb. The old man says his watch[18] lasts till the mornin'."

The woman sprang up, and hastily began to arrange some bread and flitch[19] in a tin pail, and to pour her own measure of ale into a bottle. Tying on her bonnet, she blew out the candle.

"Lay ye down, Janey dear," she said, gently, covering her with the old rags. "Hur can eat the potatoes, if hur 's hungry."

"Where are ye goin', Deb? The rain 's sharp."

"To the mill, with Hugh's supper."

"Let him bide till th' morn. Sit ye down."

"No, no,"—sharply pushing her off. "The boy'll starve."

She hurried from the cellar, while the child wearily coiled herself up for sleep. The rain was falling heavily, as the woman, pail in hand, emerged from the mouth of the alley, and turned down the narrow street, that stretched out, long and black, miles before her. Here and there a flicker of gas lighted an uncertain space of muddy footwalk and gutter; the long rows of houses, except an occasional lager-bier shop, were closed; now and then she met a band of mill-hands skulking to or from their work.

Not many even of the inhabitants of a manufacturing town know the vast machinery of system by which the bodies of workmen are governed, that goes on unceasingly from year to year. The hands of each mill are divided into watches that relieve each other as regularly as the sentinels of an army. By night and day the work goes on, the unsleeping engines groan and shriek, the fiery pools of metal boil and surge. Only for a day in the week, in half-courtesy to public censure, the fires are partially veiled; but as soon as the clock strikes midnight, the great furnaces break forth with renewed fury, the clamor begins with fresh, breathless vigor, the engines sob and shriek like "gods in pain."

As Deborah hurried down through the heavy rain, the noise of these thousand engines sounded through the sleep and shadow of the city like far-off thunder. The mill to which she was going lay on the river a mile below the city-limits. It was

---

[17] Irish; the Milesians were the people of the legendary Spanish King Mil, whose ancestors supposedly invaded Ireland around 1300 B.C.

[18] Shift.   [19] A substandard grade of salt pork.

far, and she was weak, aching from standing twelve hours at the spools. Yet it was her almost nightly walk to take this man his supper, though at every square she sat down to rest, and she knew she should receive small word of thanks.

Perhaps, if she had possessed an artist's eye, the picturesque oddity of the scene might have made her step stagger less, and the path seem shorter; but to her the mills were only "summat deilish[20] to look at by night."

The road leading to the mills had been quarried from the solid rock, which rose abrupt and bare on one side of the cinder-covered road, while the river, sluggish and black, crept past on the other. The mills for rolling iron[21] are simply immense tent-like roofs, covering acres of ground, open on every side. Beneath these roofs Deborah looked in on a city of fires, that burned hot and fiercely in the night. Fire in every horrible form: pits of flame waving in the wind; liquid metal-flames writhing in tortuous streams through the sand; wide caldrons filled with boiling fire, over which bent ghastly wretches stirring the strange brewing; and through all, crowds of half-clad men, looking like revengeful ghosts in the red light, hurried, throwing masses of glittering fire. It was like a street in Hell. Even Deborah muttered, as she crept through, " 'T looks like t' Devil's place!" It did,—in more ways than one.

She found the man she was looking for, at last, heaping coal on a furnace. He had not time to eat his supper; so she went behind the furnace, and waited. Only a few men were with him, and they noticed her only by a "Hyur comes t' hunchback, Wolfe."

Deborah was stupid with sleep; her back pained her sharply; and her teeth chattered with cold, with the rain that soaked her clothes and dripped from her at every step. She stood, however, patiently holding the pail, and waiting.

"Hout, woman! ye look like a drowned cat. Come near to the fire,"—said one of the men, approaching to scrape away the ashes.

She shook her head. Wolfe had forgotten her. He turned, hearing the man, and came closer.

"I did no' think; gi' me my supper, woman."

She watched him eat with a painful eagerness. With a woman's quick instinct, she saw that he was not hungry,—was eating to please her. Her pale, watery eyes began to gather a strange light.

"Is 't good, Hugh? T' ale was a bit sour, I feared."

"No, good enough." He hesitated a moment. "Ye 're tired, poor lass! Bide here till I go. Lay down there on that heap of ash, and go to sleep."

He threw her an old coat for a pillow, and turned to his work. The heap was the refuse of the burnt iron, and was not a hard bed; the half-smothered warmth, too, penetrated her limbs, dulling their pain and cold shiver.

Miserable enough she looked, lying there on the ashes like a limp, dirty rag,—yet not an unfitting figure to crown the scene of hopeless discomfort and veiled crime: more fitting, if one looked deeper into the heart of things,—at her thwarted woman's form, her colorless life, her waking stupor that smothered pain and hunger,—even more fit to be a type of her class. Deeper yet if one could look, was there nothing worth reading in this wet, faded thing, half-covered with ashes? no story of a soul filled with groping passionate love, heroic unselfishness, fierce

---

[20] Somewhat devilish.   [21] Flattening iron ingots for industrial purposes.

jealousy? of years of weary trying to please the one human being whom she loved, to gain one look of real heart-kindness from him? If anything like this were hidden beneath the pale, bleared eyes, and dull, washed-out-looking face, no one had ever taken the trouble to read its faint signs: not the half-clothed furnace-tender, Wolfe, certainly. Yet he was kind to her: it was his nature to be kind, even to the very rats that swarmed in the cellar: kind to her in just the same way. She knew that. And it might be that very knowledge had given to her face its apathy and vacancy more than her low, torpid life. One sees that dead, vacant look steal sometimes over the rarest, finest of women's faces,—in the very midst, it may be, of their warmest summer's day; and then one can guess at the secret of intolerable solitude that lies hid beneath the delicate laces and brilliant smile. There was no warmth, no brilliancy, no summer for this woman; so the stupor and vacancy had time to gnaw into her face perpetually. She was young, too, though no one guessed it; so the gnawing was the fiercer.

She lay quiet in the dark corner, listening, through the monotonous din and uncertain glare of the works, to the dull plash of the rain in the far distance,—shrinking back whenever the man Wolfe happened to look towards her. She knew, in spite of all his kindness, that there was that in her face and form which made him loathe the sight of her. She felt by instinct, although she could not comprehend it, the finer nature of the man, which made him among his fellow-workmen something unique, set apart. She knew, that, down under all the vileness and coarseness of his life, there was a groping passion for whatever was beautiful and pure,—that his soul sickened with disgust at her deformity, even when his words were kindest. Through this dull consciousness, which never left her, came, like a sting, the recollection of the dark blue eyes and lithe figure of the little Irish girl she had left in the cellar. The recollection struck through even her stupid intellect with a vivid glow of beauty and of grace. Little Janey, timid, helpless, clinging to Hugh as her only friend: that was the sharp thought, the bitter thought, that drove into the glazed eyes a fierce light of pain. You laugh at it? Are pain and jealousy less savage realities down here in this place I am taking you to than in your own house or your own heart,—your heart, which they clutch at sometimes? The note is the same, I fancy, be the octave high or low.

If you could go into this mill where Deborah lay, and drag out from the hearts of these men the terrible tragedy of their lives, taking it as a symptom of the disease of their class, no ghost Horror would terrify you more. A reality of soul-starvation, of living death, that meets you every day under the besotted faces on the street,—I can paint nothing of this, only give you the outside outlines of a night, a crisis in the life of one man: whatever muddy depth of soul-history lies beneath you can read according to the eyes God has given you.

Wolfe, while Deborah watched him as a spaniel its master, bent over the furnace with his iron pole, unconscious of her scrutiny, only stopping to receive orders. Physically, Nature had promised the man but little. He had already lost the strength and instinct vigor of a man, his muscles were thin, his nerves weak, his face (a meek, woman's face) haggard, yellow with consumption. In the mill he was known as one of the girl-men: "Molly Wolfe" was his *sobriquet*.[22] He was never seen in the cockpit,[23] did not own a terrier, drank but seldom; when he did,

---

[22] Nickname.
[23] A pit in which fighting cocks with pointed spurs attached to their legs battle each other until one is disabled or dead; money goes to the victor's owner and to those who bet on the winner. Terriers were bred for hunting.

desperately. He fought sometimes, but was always thrashed, pommelled to a jelly. The man was game enough, when his blood was up: but he was no favorite in the mill; he had the taint of school-learning on him,—not to a dangerous extent, only a quarter or so in the free-school in fact, but enough to ruin him as a good hand in a fight.

For other reasons, too, he was not popular. Not one of themselves, they felt that, though outwardly as filthy and ash-covered; silent, with foreign thoughts and longings breaking out through his quietness in innumerable curious ways: this one, for instance. In the neighboring furnace-buildings lay great heaps of the refuse from the ore after the pig-metal is run. *Korl* we call it here: a light, porous substance, of a delicate, waxen, flesh-colored tinge. Out of the blocks of this korl, Wolfe, in his off-hours from the furnace, had a habit of chipping and moulding figures,—hideous, fantastic enough, but sometimes strangely beautiful: even the mill-men saw that, while they jeered at him. It was a curious fancy in the man, almost a passion. The few hours for rest he spent hewing and hacking with his blunt knife, never speaking, until his watch came again,—working at one figure for months, and, when it was finished, breaking it to pieces perhaps, in a fit of disappointment. A morbid, gloomy man, untaught, unled, left to feed his soul in grossness and crime, and hard, grinding labor.

I want you to come down and look at this Wolfe, standing there among the lowest of his kind, and see him just as he is, that you may judge him justly when you hear the story of this night. I want you to look back, as he does every day, at his birth in vice, his starved infancy; to remember the heavy years he has groped through as boy and man,—the slow, heavy years of constant, hot work. So long ago he began, that he thinks sometimes he has worked there for ages. There is no hope that it will ever end. Think that God put into this man's soul a fierce thirst for beauty,—to know it, to create it; to *be*—something, he knows not what,—other than he is. There are moments when a passing cloud, the sun glinting on the purple thistles, a kindly smile, a child's face, will rouse him to a passion of pain,—when his nature starts up with a mad cry of rage against God, man, whoever it is that has forced this vile, slimy life upon him. With all this groping, this mad desire, a great blind intellect stumbling through wrong, a loving poet's heart, the man was by habit only a coarse, vulgar laborer, familiar with sights and words you would blush to name. Be just: when I tell you about this night, see him as he is. Be just,—not like man's law, which seizes on one isolated fact, but like God's judging angel, whose clear, sad eye saw all the countless cankering days of this man's life, all the countless nights, when, sick with starving, his soul fainted in him, before it judged him for this night, the saddest of all.

I called this night the crisis of his life. If it was, it stole on him unawares. These great turning-days of life cast no shadow before, slip by unconsciously. Only a trifle, a little turn of the rudder, and the ship goes to heaven or hell.

Wolfe, while Deborah watched him, dug into the furnace of melting iron with his pole, dully thinking only how many rails the lump would yield. It was late,— nearly Sunday morning; another hour, and the heavy work would be done,—only the furnaces to replenish and cover for the next day. The workmen were growing more noisy, shouting, as they had to do, to be heard over the deep clamor of the mills. Suddenly they grew less boisterous,—at the far end, entirely silent. Something unusual had happened. After a moment, the silence came nearer; the men stopped their jeers and drunken choruses. Deborah, stupidly lifting up her head, saw the cause of the quiet. A group of five or six men were slowly approaching, stopping to examine each furnace as they came. Visitors often came to see the mills after night: except by growing less noisy, the men took no notice of them. The furnace where Wolfe worked was near the bounds of the works; they halted there hot and tired: a walk over one of these great foundries is no trifling task. The woman, drawing out of sight, turned over to sleep. Wolfe, seeing them stop, suddenly roused from his indifferent stupor, and watched them keenly. He knew some of them: the overseer, Clarke,—a son of Kirby, one of the mill-owners,— and a Doctor May, one of the town-physicians. The other two were strangers. Wolfe came closer. He seized eagerly every chance that brought him into contact with this mysterious class that shone down on him perpetually with the glamour of another order of being. What made the difference between them? That was the mystery of his life. He had a vague notion that perhaps to-night he could find it out. One of the strangers sat down on a pile of bricks, and beckoned young Kirby to his side.

"This *is* hot, with a vengeance. A match, please?"—lighting his cigar. "But the walk is worth the trouble. If it were not that you must have heard it so often, Kirby, I would tell you that your works look like Dante's Inferno."[24]

Kirby laughed.

"Yes. Yonder is Farinata[25] himself in the burning tomb,"—pointing to some figure in the shimmering shadows.

"Judging from some of the faces of your men," said the other, "they bid fair to try the reality of Dante's vision, some day."[26]

Young Kirby looked curiously around, as if seeing the faces of his hands for the first time.

"They 're bad enough, that's true. A desperate set, I fancy. Eh, Clarke?"

The overseer did not hear him. He was talking of net profits just then,—giving, in fact, a schedule of the annual business of the firm to a sharp peering little Yankee, who jotted down notes on a paper laid on the crown of his hat: a reporter for one of the city-papers, getting up a series of reviews of the leading manufactories. The other gentlemen had accompanied them merely for amusement. They were silent until the notes were finished, drying their feet at the furnaces, and sheltering their faces from the intolerable heat. At last the overseer concluded with—

"I believe that is a pretty fair estimate, Captain."

"Here, some of you men!" said Kirby, "bring up those boards. We may as well sit down, gentlemen, until the rain is over. It cannot last much longer at this rate."

"Pig-metal,"—mumbled the reporter,—"um!—coal facilities,—um!—hands employed, twelve hundred,—bitumen,[27]—um!—all right, I believe, Mr. Clarke;—sinking-fund,[28]—what did you say was your sinking-fund?"

"Twelve hundred hands?" said the stranger, the young man who had first spoken. "Do you control their votes, Kirby?"

"Control? No." The young man smiled complacently. "But my father brought seven hundred votes to the polls for his candidate last November. No force-work, you understand,—only a speech or two, a hint to form themselves into a society,

[24] The vision of Hell given in the first section of *The Divine Comedy*, by the Italian poet Dante Alighieri (1265–1321).

[25] In Canto 10 of Dante's *Inferno*, Farinata degli Uberti is immersed in a burning tomb as a punishment for heresy. Such an allusion differentiates the visitors from the workers: for the visitors, the scene before them is like an epic poem; for the workers, it is life.

[26] "They look as if they might be going to Hell, some day."

[27] A tarlike residue of coal distillation.   [28] Money set aside for future obligations.

and a bit of red and blue bunting to make them a flag. The Invincible Roughs,—I believe that is their name. I forget the motto: 'Our country's hope,' I think."

There was a laugh. The young man talking to Kirby sat, with an amused light in his cool gray eye, surveying critically the half-clothed figures of the puddlers, and the slow swing of their brawny muscles. He was a stranger in the city,—spending a couple of months in the borders of a Slave State,[29] to study the institutions of the South,—a brother-in-law of Kirby's—Mitchell. He was an amateur gymnast,—hence his anatomical eye; a patron, in a *blasé* way, of the prize-ring; a man who sucked the essence out of science or philosophy in an indifferent, gentlemanly way; who took Kant, Novalis, Humboldt,[30] for what they were worth in his own scales; accepting all, despising nothing, in heaven, earth, or hell, but one-idea men;[31] with a temper yielding and brilliant as summer water, until his Self was touched, when it was ice, though brilliant still. Such men are not rare in the States.

As he knocked the ashes from his cigar, Wolfe caught with a quick pleasure the contour of the white hand, the bloodglow of a red ring he wore. His voice, too, and that of Kirby's, touched him like music,—low, even, with chording cadences. About this man Mitchell hung the impalpable atmosphere belonging to the thorough-bred gentleman. Wolfe, scraping away the ashes beside him, was conscious of it, did obeisance to it with his artist sense, unconscious that he did so.

The rain did not cease. Clarke and the reporter left the mills; the others, comfortably seated near the furnace, lingered, smoking and talking in a desultory way. Greek would not have been more unintelligible to the furnace-tenders, whose presence they soon forgot entirely. Kirby drew out a newspaper from his pocket and read aloud some article, which they discussed eagerly. At every sentence, Wolfe listened more and more like a dumb, hopeless animal, with a duller, more stolid look creeping over his face, glancing now and then at Mitchell, marking acutely every smallest sign of refinement, then back to himself, seeing as in a mirror his filthy body, his more stained soul.

Never! He had no words for such a thought, but he knew now, in all the sharpness of the bitter certainty, that between them there was a great gulf[32] never to be passed. Never!

The bell of the mills rang for midnight. Sunday morning had dawned. Whatever hidden message lay in the tolling bells floated past these men unknown. Yet it was there. Veiled in the solemn music ushering the risen Saviour was a key-note to solve the darkest secrets of a world gone wrong,—even this social riddle which the brain of the grimy puddler grappled with madly to-night.

The men began to withdraw the metal from the caldrons. The mills were deserted on Sundays, except by the hands who fed the fires, and those who had no lodgings and slept usually on the ash-heaps. The three strangers sat still during the

---

[29] Set in the narrow finger of West Virginia that runs halfway up Ohio to the west, Wheeling in 1861 was in the slave state of Virginia, north of the Mason-Dixon line and west of the Appalachian Mountains. It would have been a dubious place to study southern institutions.

[30] Immanuel Kant (1724–1804), a German philosopher; Novalis: the pseudonym of Friedrich von Hardenberg (1772–1801), a German romantic writer; Alexander von Humboldt (1769–1859), a German scientist and explorer. Mitchell has chosen excellent people to study but seems less a scholar than a dabbler and dilettante.

[31] Men of one idea.

[32] "And beside all this, between us and you there is a great gulf fixed," from Luke 16:26, a parable about the beggar Lazarus, in Heaven, and a rich man, in Hell.

next hour, watching the men cover the furnaces, laughing now and then at some jest of Kirby's.

"Do you know," said Mitchell, "I like this view of the works better than when the glare was fiercest? These heavy shadows and the amphitheatre of smothered fires are ghostly, unreal. One could fancy these red smouldering lights to be the half-shut eyes of wild beasts, and the spectral figures their victims in the den."

Kirby laughed. "You are fanciful. Come, let us get out of the den. The spectral figures, as you call them, are a little too real for me to fancy a close proximity in the darkness,—unarmed, too."

The others rose, buttoning their overcoats, and lighting cigars.

"Raining, still," said Doctor May, "and hard. Where did we leave the coach, Mitchell?"

"At the other side of the works.—Kirby, what's that?"

Mitchell started back, half-frightened, as, suddenly turning a corner, the white figure of a woman faced him in the darkness,—a woman, white, of giant proportions, crouching on the ground, her arms flung out in some wild gesture of warning.

"Stop! Make that fire burn there!" cried Kirby, stopping short.

The flame burst out, flashing the gaunt figure into bold relief.

Mitchell drew a long breath.

"I thought it was alive," he said, going up curiously.

The others followed.

"Not marble, eh?" asked Kirby, touching it.

One of the lower overseers stopped.

"Korl, Sir."

"Who did it?"

"Can't say. Some of the hands; chipped it out in off-hours."

"Chipped to some purpose, I should say. What a flesh-tint the stuff has! Do you see, Mitchell?"

"I see."

He had stepped aside where the light fell boldest on the figure, looking at it in silence. There was not one line of beauty or grace in it: a nude woman's form, muscular, grown coarse with labor, the powerful limbs instinct with some one poignant longing. One idea: there it was in the tense, rigid muscles, the clutching hands, the wild, eager face, like that of a starving wolf's. Kirby and Doctor May walked around it, critical, curious. Mitchell stood aloof, silent. The figure touched him strangely.

"Not badly done," said Doctor May.

"Where did the fellow learn that sweep of the muscles in the arm and hand? Look at them! They are groping,—do you see?—clutching: the peculiar action of a man dying of thirst."

"They have ample facilities for studying anatomy," sneered Kirby, glancing at the half-naked figures.

"Look," continued the Doctor, "at this bony wrist, and the strained sinews of the instep! A working-woman,—the very type of her class."

"God forbid!" muttered Mitchell.

"Why?" demanded May. "What does the fellow intend by the figure? I cannot catch the meaning."

"Ask him," said the other, dryly. "There he stands,"—pointing to Wolfe, who stood with a group of men, leaning on his ash-rake.

The Doctor beckoned him with the affable smile which kind-hearted men put on, when talking to these people.

"Mr. Mitchell has picked you out as the man who did this,—I'm sure I don't know why. But what did you mean by it?"

"She be hungry."

Wolfe's eyes answered Mitchell, not the Doctor.

"Oh-h! But what a mistake you have made, my fine fellow! You have given no sign of starvation to the body. It is strong,—terribly strong. It has the mad, half-despairing gesture of drowning."

Wolfe stammered, glanced appealingly at Mitchell, who saw the soul of the thing, he knew. But the cool, probing eyes were turned on himself now,—mocking, cruel, relentless.

"Not hungry for meat," the furnace-tender said at last.

"What then? Whiskey?" jeered Kirby, with a coarse laugh.

Wolfe was silent a moment, thinking.

"I dunno," he said, with a bewildered look. "It mebbe. Summat to make her live, I think,—like you. Whiskey ull do it, in a way."

The young man laughed again. Mitchell flashed a look of disgust somewhere,—not at Wolfe.

"May," he broke out impatiently, "are you blind? Look at that woman's face! It asks questions of God, and says, 'I have a right to know.' Good God, how hungry it is!"

They looked a moment; then May turned to the mill-owner:—

"Have you many such hands as this? What are you going to do with them? Keep them at puddling iron?"

Kirby shrugged his shoulders. Mitchell's look had irritated him.

"Ce n'est pas mon affaire."[33] I have no fancy for nursing infant geniuses. I suppose there are some stray gleams of mind and soul among these wretches. The Lord will take care of his own; or else they can work out their own salvation. I have heard you call our American system a ladder which any man can scale. Do you doubt it? Or perhaps you want to banish all social ladders, and put us all on a flat table-land,—eh, May?"

The Doctor looked vexed, puzzled. Some terrible problem lay hid in this woman's face, and troubled these men. Kirby waited for an answer, and, receiving none, went on, warming with his subject.

"I tell you, there 's something wrong that no talk of '*Liberté*' or '*Egalité*'[34] will do away. If I had the making of men, these men who do the lowest part of the world's work should be machines,—nothing more,—hands. It would be kindness. God help them! What are taste, reason, to creatures who must live such lives as that?" He pointed to Deborah, sleeping on the ash-heap. "So many nerves to sting them to pain. What if God had put your brain, with all its agony of touch, into your fingers, and bid you work and strike with that?"

"You think you could govern the world better?" laughed the Doctor.

"I do not think at all."

---

[33] "It's not my affair" (French). Adding to the dimensions of the story are biblical overtones relating to Pontius Pilate, the Roman governor who condemned Christ to be crucified, and incidents in the life of Christ.

[34] *Liberté, Egalité,* and *Fraternité* ("Liberty," "Equality," and "Fraternity") were the rallying cries of the French Revolution.

"That is true philosophy. Drift with the stream, because you cannot dive deep enough to find bottom, eh?"

"Exactly," rejoined Kirby. "I do not think. I wash my hands of all social problems,—slavery, caste, white or black. My duty to my operatives[35] has a narrow limit,—the pay-hour on Saturday night. Outside of that, if they cut korl, or cut each other's throats, (the more popular amusement of the two,) I am not responsible."

The Doctor sighed,—a good honest sigh, from the depths of his stomach.

"God help us! Who is responsible?"

"Not I, I tell you," said Kirby, testily. "What has the man who pays them money to do with their souls' concerns, more than the grocer or butcher who takes it?"

"And yet," said Mitchell's cynical voice, "look at her! How hungry she is!"

Kirby tapped his boot with his cane. No one spoke. Only the dumb face of the rough image looking into their faces with the awful question, "What shall we do to be saved?"[36] Only Wolfe's face, with its heavy weight of brain, its weak, uncertain mouth, its desperate eyes, out of which looked the soul of his class,—only Wolfe's face turned towards Kirby's. Mitchell laughed,—a cool, musical laugh.

"Money has spoken!" he said, seating himself lightly on a stone with the air of an amused spectator at a play. "Are you answered?"—turning to Wolfe his clear, magnetic face.

Bright and deep and cold as Arctic air, the soul of the man lay tranquil beneath. He looked at the furnace-tender as he had looked at a rare mosaic in the morning; only the man was the more amusing study of the two.

"Are you answered? Why, May, look at him! '*De profundis clamavi.*'[37] Or, to quote in English, 'Hungry and thirsty, his soul faints in him.' And so Money sends back its answer into the depths through you, Kirby! Very clear the answer, too!—I think I remember reading the same words somewhere:—washing your hands in Eau de Cologne, and saying, 'I am innocent of the blood of this man. See ye to it!'"[38]

Kirby flushed angrily.

"You quote Scripture freely."

"Do I not quote correctly? I think I remember another line, which may amend my meaning: 'Inasmuch as ye did it unto one of the least of these, ye did it unto me.'[39] Deist? Bless you, man, I was raised on the milk of the Word.[40] Now, Doctor, the pocket of the world having uttered its voice, what has the heart to say? You are a philanthropist, in a small way,—*n'est ce pas?*[41] Here, boy, this gentleman can show you how to cut korl better,—or your destiny. Go on, May!"

"I think a mocking devil possesses you to-night," rejoined the Doctor, seriously.

---

[35] Workers.

[36] In Acts 16:30 the prison-keeper in Philippi asks, "What must I do to be saved?" after an earthquake had made it possible for the prisoners to escape.

[37] "Out of the depths have I cried unto thee," from the Latin text of Psalm 130:1.

[38] As Pontius Pilate washed his hands of responsibility for what was about to happen to Christ, he said "I am innocent of the blood of this just man: see ye to it," from Matthew 27:24.

[39] Christ's words in Matthew 25:40: "Verily I say unto you, Inasmuch as ye have done it unto one of the least of these my brethren, ye have done it unto me."

[40] A deist believes that God created the world but is not involved in its later workings; the "Milk of the Word" is the teachings of Christ.

[41] "Isn't that so?" (French).

He went to Wolfe and put his hand kindly on his arm. Something of a vague idea possessed the Doctor's brain that much good was to be done here by a friendly word or two; a latent genius to be warmed into life by a waited-for sunbeam. Here it was: he had brought it. So he went on complacently:—

"Do you know, boy, you have it in you to be a great sculptor, a great man?—do you understand?" (talking down to the capacity of his hearer: it is a way people have with children, and men like Wolfe,)—"to live a better, stronger life than I, or Mr. Kirby here? A man may make himself anything he chooses. God has given you stronger powers than many men,—me, for instance."

May stopped, heated, glowing with his own magnanimity. And it was magnanimous. The puddler had drunk in every word, looking through the Doctor's flurry, and generous heat, and self-approval, into his will, with those slow, absorbing eyes of his.

"Make yourself what you will. It is your right."

"I know," quietly. "Will you help me?"

Mitchell laughed again. The Doctor turned now, in a passion,—

"You know, Mitchell, I have not the means. You know, if I had, it is in my heart to take this boy and educate him for"—

"The glory of God, and the glory of John May."

May did not speak for a moment; then, controlled, he said,—

"Why should one be raised, when myriads are left?—I have not the money, boy," to Wolfe, shortly.

"Money?" He said it over slowly, as one repeats the guessed answer to a riddle, doubtfully. "That is it? Money?"

"Yes, money,—that is it," said Mitchell, rising, and drawing his furred coat about him. "You've found the cure for all the world's diseases.—Come, May, find your good-humor, and come home. This damp wind chills my very bones. Come and preach your Saint-Simonian[42] doctrines to-morrow to Kirby's hands. Let them have a clear idea of the rights of the soul, and I'll venture next week they'll strike for higher wages. That will be the end of it."

"Will you sent the coach-driver to this side of the mills?" asked Kirby, turning to Wolfe.

He spoke kindly: it was his habit to do so. Deborah, seeing the puddler go, crept after him. The three men waited outside. Doctor May walked up and down, chafed. Suddenly he stopped.

"Go back, Mitchell! You say the pocket and the heart of the world speak without meaning to these people. What has its head to say? Taste, culture, refinement? Go!"

Mitchell was leaning against a brick wall. He turned his head indolently, and looked into the mills. There hung about the place a thick, unclean odor. The slightest motion of his hand marked that he perceived it, and his insufferable disgust. That was all. May said nothing, only quickened his angry tramp.

"Besides," added Mitchell, giving a corollary to his answer, "it would be of no use. I am not one of them."

"You do not mean"—said May, facing him.

"Yes, I mean just that. Reform is born of need, not pity. No vital movement of the people's has worked down, for good or evil; fermented, instead, carried up the

[42] The Comte de Saint-Simon (1760–1825), whose works, including *The New Christianity* (1825), influenced socialist thought.

heaving, cloggy mass. Think back through history, and you will know it. What will this lowest deep—thieves, Magdalens,[43] negroes—do with the light filtered through ponderous Church creeds, Baconian theories, Goethe schemes?[44] Some day, out of their bitter need will be thrown up their own light-bringer,—their Jean Paul, their Cromwell,[45] their Messiah."

"Bah!" was the Doctor's inward criticism. However, in practice, he adopted the theory; for, when, night and morning, afterwards, he prayed that power might be given these degraded souls to rise, he glowed at heart, recognizing an accomplished duty.

Wolfe and the woman had stood in the shadow of the works as the coach drove off. The Doctor had held out his hand in a frank, generous way, telling him to "take care of himself, and to remember it was his right to rise." Mitchell had simply touched his hat, as an equal, with a quiet look of thorough recognition. Kirby had thrown Deborah some money, which she found, and clutched eagerly enough. They were gone now, all of them. The man sat down on the cinder-road, looking up into the murky sky.

"'T be late, Hugh. Wunnot hur come?"

He shook his head doggedly, and the woman crouched out of his sight against the wall. Do you remember rare moments when a sudden light flashed over yourself, your world, God? when you stood on a mountain-peak, seeing your life as it might have been, as it is? one quick instant, when custom lost its force and everyday usage? when your friend, wife, brother, stood in a new light? your soul was bared, and the grave,—a fore-taste of the nakedness of the Judgment-Day? So it came before him, his life, that night. The slow tides of pain he had borne gathered themselves up and surged against his soul. His squalid daily life, the brutal coarseness eating into his brain, as the ashes into his skin: before, these things had been a dull aching into his consciousness; to-night, they were reality. He gripped the filthy red shirt that clung, stiff with soot, about him, and tore it savagely from his arm. The flesh beneath was muddy with grease and ashes,—and the heart beneath that! And the soul? God knows.

Then flashed before his vivid poetic sense the man who had left him,—the pure face, the delicate, sinewy limbs, in harmony with all he knew of beauty or truth. In his cloudy fancy he had pictured a Something like this. He had found it in this Mitchell, even when he idly scoffed at his pain: a Man all-knowing, all-seeing, crowned by Nature, reigning,—the keen glance of his eye falling like a sceptre on other men. And yet his instinct taught him that he too———He! He looked at himself with sudden loathing, sick, wrung his hands with a cry, and then was silent. With all the phantoms of his heated, ignorant fancy, Wolfe had not been vague in his ambitions. They were practical, slowly built up before him out of his knowledge of what he could do. Through years he had day by day made this hope a real thing to himself,—a clear, projected figure of himself, as he might become.

Able to speak, to know what was best, to raise these men and women working at his side up with him: sometimes he forgot this defined hope in the frantic anguish to escape,—only to escape,—out of the wet, the pain, the ashes, some-

---

[43] Prostitutes (from the biblical Mary Magdalene).

[44] Truth coming from above, from theories such as those of the English essayist Francis Bacon (1561–1624) or the German writer Johann Wolfgang von Goethe (1749–1832), will not help the workers.

[45] Jean Paul Richter (1763–1825), a German novelist; Oliver Cromwell (1599–1658), a religious and political commander of England.

where, anywhere,—only for one moment of free air on a hill-side, to lie down and let his sick soul throb itself out in the sunshine. But to-night he panted for life. The savage strength of his nature was roused; his cry was fierce to God for justice.

"Look at me!" he said to Deborah, with a low, bitter laugh, striking his puny chest savagely. "What am I worth, Deb? Is it my fault that I am no better? My fault? My fault?"

He stopped, stung with a sudden remorse, seeing her hunchback shape writhing with sobs. For Deborah was crying thankless tears, according to the fashion of women.

"God forgi' me, woman! Things go harder wi' you nor me. It's a worse share."

He got up and helped her to rise; and they went doggedly down the muddy street, side by side.

"It's all wrong," he muttered, slowly,—"all wrong! I dunnot understan'. But it'll end some day."

"Come home, Hugh!" she said, coaxingly; for he had stopped, looking around bewildered.

"Home,—and back to the mill!" He went on saying this over to himself, as if he would mutter down every pain in this dull despair.

She followed him through the fog, her blue lips chattering with cold. They reached the cellar at last. Old Wolfe had been drinking since she went out, and had crept nearer the door. The girl Janey slept heavily in the corner. He went up to her, touching softly the worn white arm with his fingers. Some bitterer thought stung him, as he stood there. He wiped the drops from his forehead, and went into the room beyond, livid, trembling. A hope, trifling, perhaps, but very dear, had died just then out of the poor puddler's life, as he looked at the sleeping, innocent girl,—some plan for the future, in which she had borne a part. He gave it up that moment, then and forever. Only a trifle, perhaps, to us: his face grew a shade paler,—that was all. But, somehow, the man's soul, as God and the angels looked down on it, never was the same afterwards.

Deborah followed him into the inner room. She carried a candle, which she placed on the floor, closing the door after her. She had seen the look on his face, as he turned away: her own grew deadly. Yet, as she came up to him, her eyes glowed. He was seated on an old chest, quiet, holding his face in his hands.

"Hugh!" she said, softly.

He did not speak.

"Hugh, did hur hear what the man said,—him with the clear voice? Did hur hear? Money, money,—that it wud do all?"

He pushed her away,—gently, but he was worn out; her rasping tone fretted him.

"Hugh!"

The candle flared a pale yellow light over the cobwebbed brick walls, and the woman standing there. He looked at her. She was young, in deadly earnest; her faded eyes, and wet, ragged figure caught from their frantic eagerness a power akin to beauty.

"Hugh, it is true! Money ull do it! Oh, Hugh, boy, listen till me! He said it true! It is money!"

"I know. Go back! I do not want you here."

"Hugh, it is t' last time. I'll never worrit hur again."

There were tears in her voice now, but she choked them back.

"Hear till me only to-night! If one of t' witch people wud come, them we heard of t' home, and gif hur all hur wants, what then? Say, Hugh!"

"What do you mean?"

"I mean money."

Her whisper shrilled through his brain.

"If one of t' witch dwarfs wud come from t' lane moors to-night, and gif hur money, to go out,—*out,* I say,—out, lad, where t' sun shines, and t' heath grows, and t' ladies walk in silken gownds, and God stays all t' time,—where t' man lives that talked to us to-night,—Hugh knows,—Hugh could walk there like a king!"

He thought the woman mad, tried to check her, but she went on, fierce in her eager haste.

"If *I* were t' witch dwarf, if I had t' money, wud hur thank me? Wud hur take me out o' this place wid hur and Janey? I wud not come into the gran' house hur wud build, to vex hur wid t' hunch,—only at night, when t' shadows were dark, stand far off to see hur."

Mad? Yes! Are many of us mad in this way?

"Poor Deb! poor Deb!" he said, soothingly.

"It is here," she said, suddenly jerking into his hand a small roll. "I took it! I did it! Me, me!—not hur! I shall be hanged, I shall be burnt in hell, if anybody knows I took it! Out of his pocket, as he leaned against t' bricks. Hur knows?"

She thrust it into his hand, and then, her errand done, began to gather chips together to make a fire, choking down hysteric sobs.

"Has it come to this?"

T' at was all he said. The Welsh Wolfe blood was honest. The roll was a small green pocket-book containing one or two gold pieces, and a check for an incredible amount, as it seemed to the poor puddler. He laid it down, hiding his face again in his hands.

"Hugh, don't by angry wud me! It 's only poor Deb,—hur knows?"

He took the long skinny fingers kindly in his.

"Angry? God help me, no! Let me sleep. I am tired."

He threw himself heavily down on the wooden bench, stunned with pain and weariness. She brought some old rags to cover him.

It was late on Sunday evening before he awoke. I tell God's truth, when I say he had then no thought of keeping this money. Deborah had hid it in his pocket. He found it there. She watched him eagerly, as he took it out.

"I must gif it to him," he said, reading her face.

"Hur knows," she said with a bitter sigh of disappointment. "But it is hur right to keep it."

His right! The word struck him. Doctor May had used the same. He washed himself, and went out to find this man Mitchell. His right! Why did this chance word cling to him so obstinately? Do you hear the fierce devils whisper in his ear, as he went slowly down the darkening street?

The evening came on, slow and calm. He seated himself at the end of an alley leading into one of the larger streets. His brain was clear to-night, keen, intent, mastering. It would not start back, cowardly, from any hellish temptation, but meet it face to face. Therefore the great temptation of his life came to him veiled by no sophistry,[46] but bold, defiant, owning its own vile name, trusting to one bold blow for victory.

---

[46] Clever arguments.

He did not deceive himself. Theft! That was it. At first the word sickened him; then he grappled with it. Sitting there on a broken cart-wheel, the fading day, the noisy groups, the church-bells' tolling passed before him like a panorama,[47] while the sharp struggle went on within. This money! He took it out, and looked at it. If he gave it back, what then? He was going to be cool about it.

People going by to church saw only a sickly mill-boy watching them quietly at the alley's mouth. They did not know that he was mad, or they would not have gone by so quietly: mad with hunger; stretching out his hands to the world, that had given so much to them, for leave to live the life God meant him to live. His soul within him was smothering to death; he wanted so much, thought so much, and *knew*—nothing. There was nothing of which he was certain, except the mill and things there. Of God and heaven he had heard so little, that they were to him what fairy-land is to a child: something real, but not here; very far off. His brain, greedy, dwarfed, full of thwarted energy and unused powers, questioned these men and women going by, coldly, bitterly, that night. Was it not his right to live as they,—a pure life, a good, true-hearted life, full of beauty and kind words? He only wanted to know how to use the strength within him. His heart warmed as he thought of it. He suffered himself to think of it longer. If he took the money?

Then he saw himself as he might be, strong, helpful, kindly. The night crept on, as this one image slowly evolved itself from the crowd of other thoughts and stood triumphant. He looked at it. As he might be! What wonder, if it blinded him to delirium,—the madness that underlies all revolution, all progress, and all fall?

You laugh at the shallow temptation? You see the error underlying its argument so clearly,—that to him a true life was one of full development rather than self-restraint? that he was deaf to the higher tone in a cry of voluntary suffering for truth's sake than in the fullest flow of spontaneous harmony? I do not plead his cause. I only want to show you the mote[48] in my brother's eye: then you can see clearly to take it out.[49]

The money,—there it lay on his knee, a little blotted slip of paper, nothing in itself, used to raise him out of the pit; something straight from God's hand. A thief! Well, what was it to be a thief? He met the question at last, face to face, wiping the clammy drops of sweat from his forehead. God made this money—the fresh air, too—for his children's use. He never made the difference between poor and rich. The Something who looked down on him that moment through the cool gray sky had a kindly face, he knew,—loved his children alike. Oh, he knew that!

There were times when the soft floods of color in the crimson and purple flames, or the clear depth of amber in the water below the bridge, had somehow given him a glimpse of another world than this,—of an infinite depth of beauty and of quiet somewhere,—somewhere,—a depth of quiet and rest and love. Looking up now, it became strangely real. The sun had sunk quite below the hills, but his last rays struck upward, touching the zenith. The fog had risen, and the town and river were steeped in its thick, gray damp; but overhead, the sun-touched smoke-clouds opened like a cleft ocean,—shifting, rolling seas of crimson mist, waves of billowy silver veined with blood-scarlet, inner depths unfa-

---

[47] A continuous series of scenes painted on canvas and rolled before an audience.

[48] Speck of dust.

[49] From Christ's words in the Sermon on the Mount, "And why beholdest thou the mote that is in thy brother's eye, but considerest not the beam that is in thine own eye?" from Matthew 7:3–4 (here, a beam is a wooden roof-support).

thomable of glancing light. Wolfe's artist-eye grew drunk with color. The gates of that other world! Fading, flashing before him now! What, in that world of Beauty, Content, and Right, were the petty laws, the mine and thine, of mill-owners and mill-hands?

A consciousness of power stirred within him. He stood up. A man,—he thought, stretching out his hands,—free to work, to live, to love! Free! His right! He folded the scrap of paper in his hand. As his nervous fingers took it in, limp and blotted, so his soul took in the mean temptation, lapped it in fancied rights, in dreams of improved existences, drifting and endless as the cloud-seas of color. Clutching it, as if the tightness of his hold would strengthen his sense of possession, he went aimlessly down the street. It was his watch at the mill. He need not go, need never go again, thank God!—shaking off the thought with unspeakable loathing.

Shall I go over the history of the hours of that night? how the man wandered from one to another of his old haunts, with a half-consciousness of bidding them farewell,—lanes and alleys and backyards where the mill-hands lodged,—noting, with a new eagerness, the filth and drunkenness, the pig-pens, the ash-heaps covered with potato-skins, the bloated, pimpled women at the doors,—with a new disgust, a new sense of sudden triumph, and, under all, a new, vague dread, unknown before, smothered down, kept under, but still there? It left him but once during the night, when, for the second time in his life, he entered a church. It was a sombre Gothic pile, where the stained light lost itself in far-retreating arches; built to meet the requirements and sympathies of a far other class than Wolfe's. Yet it touched, moved him uncontrollably. The distances, the shadows, the still, marble figures, the mass of silent kneeling worshippers, the mysterious music, thrilled, lifted his soul with a wonderful pain. Wolfe forgot himself, forgot the new life he was going to live, the mean terror gnawing underneath. The voice of the speaker strengthened the charm; it was clear, feeling, full, strong. An old man, who had lived much, suffered much; whose brain was keenly alive, dominant; whose heart was summer-warm with charity. He taught it to-night. He held up Humanity in its grand total; showed the great world-cancer to his people. Who could show it better? He was a Christian reformer; he had studied the age thoroughly; his outlook at man had been free, world-wide, over all time. His faith stood sublime upon the Rock of Ages; his fiery zeal guided vast schemes by which the gospel was to be preached to all nations. How did he preach it to-night? In burning, light-laden words he painted the incarnate Life, Love, the universal Man: words that became reality in the lives of these people,—that lived again in beautiful words and actions, trifling, but heroic. Sin, as he defied it, was a real foe to them; their trials, temptations, were his. His words passed far over the furnace-tender's grasp, toned to suit another class of culture; they sounded in his ears a very pleasant song in an unknown tongue. He meant to cure this world-cancer with a steady eye that had never glared with hunger, and a hand that neither poverty nor strychnine-whiskey[50] had taught to shake. In this morbid, distorted heart of the Welsh puddler he had failed.

Wolfe rose at last, and turned from the church down the street. He looked up; the night had come on foggy, damp; the golden mists had vanished, and the sky lay dull and ash-colored. He wandered again aimlessly down the street, idly wondering what had become of the cloud-sea of crimson and scarlet. The trial-day of

---

[50] Cheap, impure whiskey that could cause nervous system damage or death.

this man's life was over, and he had lost the victory. What followed was mere drifting circumstance,—a quicker walking over the path,—that was all. Do you want to hear the end of it? You wish me to make a tragic story out of it? Why, in the police-reports of the morning paper you can find a dozen such tragedies: hints of shipwrecks unlike any that ever befell on the high seas; hints that here a power was lost to heaven,—that there a soul went down where no tide can ebb or flow. Commonplace enough the hints are,—jocose sometimes, done up in rhyme.

Doctor May, a month after the night I have told you of, was reading to his wife at breakfast from this fourth column of the morning-paper: an unusual thing,— these police-reports not being, in general, choice reading for ladies; but it was only one item he read.

"Oh, my dear! You remember that man I told you of, that we saw at Kirby's mill?—that was arrested for robbing Mitchell? Here he is; just listen:—'Circuit Court. Judge Day. Hugh Wolfe, operative in Kirby & John's Loudon Mills. Charge, grand larceny. Sentence, nineteen years hard labor in penitentiary.'— Scoundrel! Serves him right! After all our kindness that night! Picking Mitchell's pocket at the very time!"

His wife said something about the ingratitude of that kind of people, and then they began to talk of something else.

Nineteen years! How easy that was to read! What a simple word for Judge Day to utter! Nineteen years! Half a lifetime!

Hugh Wolfe sat on the window-ledge of his cell, looking out. His ankles were ironed. Not usual in such cases; but he had made two desperate efforts to escape. "Well," as Haley, the jailer, said, "small blame to him! Nineteen years' imprisonment was not a pleasant thing to look forward to." Haley was very good-natured about it, though Wolfe had fought him savagely.

"When he was first caught," the jailer said afterwards, in telling the story, "before the trial, the fellow was cut down at once,—laid there on that pallet like a dead man, with his hands over his eyes. Never saw a man so cut down in my life. Time of the trial, too, came the queerest dodge of any customer I ever had. Would choose no lawyer. Judge gave him one, of course. Gibson it was. He tried to prove the fellow crazy; but it wouldn't go. Thing was plain as daylight: money found on him. 'T was a hard sentence,—all the law allows; but it was for 'xample's sake. These mill-hands are gettin onbearable. When the sentence was read, he just looked up, and said the money was his by rights, and that all the world had gone wrong. That night, after the trial, a gentleman came to see him here, name of Mitchell,—him as he stole from. Talked to him for an hour. Thought he came for curiosity, like. After he was gone, thought Wolfe was remarkable quiet, and went into his cell. Found him very low; bed all bloody. Doctor said he had been bleeding at the lungs. He was as weak as a cat; yet, if ye 'll b'lieve me, he tried to get a-past me and get out. I just carried him like a baby, and threw him on the pallet. Three days after, he tried it again: that time reached the wall. Lord help you! he fought like a tiger,—giv' some terrible blows. Fightin' for life, you see; for he can't live long, shut up in the stone crib down yonder. Got a death-cough now. 'T took two of us to bring him down that day; so I just put the irons on his feet. There he sits, in there. Goin' to-morrow, with a batch more of 'em. That woman, hunchback, tried with him,—you remember?—she's only got three years. 'Complice. But *she's* a woman, you know. He 's been quiet ever since I put on irons: giv' up, I suppose. Looks white, sick-lookin'. It acts different on 'em, bein' sentenced. Most of 'em gets reckless, devilish-like. Some prays awful, and sings them vile songs of the mills, all in a breath. That woman, now, she 's des-per't'. Been beggin' to see Hugh, as she calls him, for three days. I'm a-goin' to let her in. She don't go with him. Here she is in this next cell. I'm a-goin' now to let her in."

He let her in. Wolfe did not see her. She crept into a corner of the cell, and stood watching him. He was scratching the iron bars of the window with a piece of tin which he had picked up, with an idle, uncertain, vacant stare, just as a child or idiot would do.

"Tryin' to get out, old boy?" laughed Haley. "Them irons will need a crowbar beside your tin, before you can open 'em."

Wolfe laughed, too, in a senseless way.

"I think I'll get out," he said.

"I believe his brain's touched," said Haley, when he came out.

The puddler scraped away with the tin for half an hour. Still Deborah did not speak. At last she ventured nearer, and touched his arm.

"Blood?" she said, looking at some spots on his coat with a shudder.

He looked up at her. "Why, Deb!" he said, smiling,—such a bright, boyish smile, that it went to poor Deborah's heart directly, and she sobbed and cried out loud.

"Oh, Hugh, lad! Hugh! dunnot look at me, when it wur my fault! To think I brought hur to it! And I loved hur so! Oh, lad, I dud!"

The confession, even in this wretch, came with the woman's blush through the sharp cry.

He did not seem to hear her,—scraping away diligently at the bars with the bit of tin.

Was he going mad? She peered closely into his face. Something she saw there made her draw suddenly back,—something which Haley had not seen, that lay beneath the pinched, vacant look it had caught since the trial, or the curious gray shadow that rested on it. That gray shadow,—yes, she knew what that meant. She had often seen it creeping over women's faces for months, who died at last of slow hunger or consumption. That meant death, distant, lingering: but this——Whatever it was the woman saw, or thought she saw, used as she was to crime and misery, seemed to make her sick with a new horror. Forgetting her fear of him, she caught his shoulders, and looked keenly, steadily, into his eyes.

"Hugh!" she cried, in a desperate whisper,—"oh, boy, not that! for God's sake, not *that!*"

The vacant laugh went off his face, and he answered her in a muttered word or two that drove her away. Yet the words were kindly enough. Sitting there on his pallet, she cried silently a hopeless sort of tears, but did not speak again. The man looked up furtively at her now and then. Whatever his own trouble was, her distress vexed him with a momentary sting.

It was market-day. The narrow window of the jail looked down directly on the carts and wagons drawn up in a long line, where they had unloaded. He could see, too, and hear distinctly the clink of money as it changed hands, the busy crowd of whites and blacks shoving, pushing one another, and the chaffering and swearing at the stalls. Somehow, the sound, more than anything else had done, wakened him up,—made the whole real to him. He was done with the world and the business of it. He let the tin fall, and looked out, pressing his face close to the rusty bars. How they crowded and pushed! And he,—he should never walk that pavement again! There came Neff Sanders, one of the feeders at the mill, with a basket on his arm. Sure enough, Neff was married the other week. He whistled, hoping he would look up; but he did not. He wondered if Neff remembered he was there,—if any of the boys thought of him up there, and thought that he never was to go down that old cinder-road again. Never again! He had not quite understood it before; but now he did. Not for days or years, but never!—that was it.

How clear the light fell on that stall in front of the market! and how like a picture it was, the dark-green heaps of corn, and the crimson beets, and golden melons! There was another with game: how the light flickered on that pheasant's breast, with the purplish blood dripping over the brown feathers! He could see the red shining of the drops, it was so near. In one minute he could be down there. It was just a step. So easy, as it seemed, so natural to go! Yet it could never be—not in all the thousands of years to come—that he should put his foot on that street again! He thought of himself with a sorrowful pity, as of some one else. There was a dog down in the market, walking after his master with such a stately, grave look!—only a dog, yet he could go backwards and forwards just as he pleased: he had good luck! Why, the very vilest cur, yelping there in the gutter, had not lived his life, had been free to act out whatever thought God had put into his brain; while he—No, he would not think of that! He tried to put the thought away, and to listen to a dispute between a countryman and a woman about some meat; but it would come back. He, what had he done to bear this?

Then came the sudden picture of what might have been, and now. He knew what it was to be in the penitentiary,—how it went with men there. He knew how in these long years he should slowly die, but not until soul and body had become corrupt and rotten,—how, when he came out, if he lived to come, even the lowest of the mill-hands would jeer him,—how his hands would be weak, and his brain senseless and stupid. He believed he was almost that now. He put his hand to his head, with a puzzled, weary look. It ached, his head, with thinking. He tried to quiet himself. It was only right, perhaps; he had done wrong. But was there right or wrong for such as he? What was right? And who had ever taught him? He thrust the whole matter away. A dark, cold quiet crept through his brain. It was all wrong; but let it be! It was nothing to him more than the others. Let it be!

The door grated, as Haley opened it.

"Come, my woman! Must lock up for t' night. Come, stir yerself!"

She went up and took Hugh's hand.

"Good-night, Deb," he said, carelessly.

She had not hoped he would say more; but the tired pain on her mouth just then was bitterer than death. She took his passive hand and kissed it.

"Hur 'll never see Deb again!" she ventured, her lips growing colder and more bloodless.

What did she say that for? Did he not know it? Yet he would not be impatient with poor old Deb. She had trouble of her own, as well as he.

"No, never again," he said, trying to be cheerful.

She stood just a moment, looking at him. Do you laugh at her, standing there, with her hunchback, her rags, her bleared, withered face, and the great despised love tugging at her heart?

"Come, you!" called Haley, impatiently.

She did not move.

"Hugh!" she whispered.

It was to be her last word. What was it?

"Hugh, boy, not THAT!"

He did not answer. She wrung her hands, trying to be silent, looking in his face in an agony of entreaty. He smiled again, kindly.

"It is best, Deb. I cannot bear to be hurted any more."

"Hur knows," she said, humbly.

"Tell my father good-bye; and—and kiss little Janey."

She nodded, saying nothing, looked in his face again, and went out of the door. As she went, she staggered.

"Drinkin' to-day?" broke out Haley, pushing her before him. "Where the Devil did you get it? Here, in with ye!" and he shoved her into her cell, next to Wolfe's, and shut the door.

Along the wall of her cell there was a crack low down by the floor, through which she could see the light from Wolfe's. She had discovered it days before. She hurried in now, and, kneeling down by it, listened, hoping to hear some sound. Nothing but the rasping of the tin on the bars. He was at his old amusement again. Something in the noise jarred on her ear, for she shivered as she heard it. Hugh rasped away at the bars. A dull old bit of tin, not fit to cut korl with.

He looked out of the window again. People were leaving the market now. A tall mulatto girl, following her mistress, her basket on her head, crossed the street just below, and looked up. She was laughing; but, when she caught sight of the haggard face peering out through the bars, suddenly grew grave, and hurried by. A free, firm step, a clear-cut olive face, with a scarlet turban tied on one side, dark, shining eyes, and on the head the basket poised, filled with fruit and flowers, under which the scarlet turban and bright eyes looked out half-shadowed. The picture caught his eye. It was good to see a face like that. He would try to-morrow, and cut one like it. *To-morrow!* He threw down the tin, trembling, and covered his face with his hands. When he looked up again, the daylight was gone.

Deborah, crouching near by on the other side of the wall, heard no noise. He sat on the side of the low pallet, thinking. Whatever was the mystery which the woman had seen on his face, it came out now slowly, in the dark there, and became fixed,—a something never seen on his face before. The evening was darkening fast. The market had been over for an hour; the rumbling of the carts over the pavement grew more infrequent: he listened to each, as it passed, because he thought it was to be for the last time. For the same reason, it was, I suppose, that he strained his eyes to catch a glimpse of each passer-by, wondering who they were, what kind of homes they were going to, if they had children,—listening eagerly to every chance word in the street, as if—(God be merciful to the man! what strange fancy was this?)—as if he never should hear human voices again.

It was quite dark at last. The street was a lonely one. The last passenger, he thought, was gone. No,—there was a quick step: Joe Hill, lighting the lamps. Joe was a good old chap; never passed a fellow without some joke or other. He remembered once seeing the place where he lived with his wife. "Granny Hill" the boys called her. Bedridden she was; but so kind as Joe was to her! kept the room so clean!—and the old woman, when he was there, was laughing at "some of t' lad's foolishness." The step was far down the street; but he could see him place the ladder, run up, and light the gas. A longing seized him to be spoken to once more.

"Joe!" he called, out of the grating. "Good-bye, Joe!"

The old man stopped a moment, listening uncertainly; then hurried on. The prisoner thrust his hand out of the window, and called again, louder; but Joe was too far down the street. It was a little thing; but it hurt him,—this disappointment.

"Good-bye Joe!" he called, sorrowfully enough.

"Be quiet!" said one of the jailers, passing the door, striking on it with his club. Oh, that was the last, was it?

There was an inexpressible bitterness on his face, as he lay down on the bed, taking the bit of tin, which he had rasped to a tolerable degree of sharpness, in his hand,—to play with, it may be. He bared his arms, looking intently at their corded veins and sinews. Deborah, listening in the next cell, heard a slight clicking sound, often repeated. She shut her lips tightly, that she might not scream; the cold drops of sweat broke over her, in her dumb agony.

"Hur knows best," she muttered at last, fiercely clutching the boards where she lay.

If she could have seen Wolfe, there was nothing about him to frighten her. He lay quite still, his arms outstretched, looking at the pearly stream of moonlight coming into the window. I think in that one hour that came then he lived back over all the years that had gone before. I think that all the low, vile life, all his wrongs, all his starved hopes, came then, and stung him with a farewell poison that made him sick unto death. He made neither moan nor cry, only turned his worn face now and then to the pure light, that seemed so far off, as one that said, "How long, O Lord? how long?"

The hour was over at last. The moon, passing over her nightly path, slowly came nearer, and threw the light across his bed on his feet. He watched it steadily, as it crept up, inch by inch, slowly. It seemed to him to carry with it a great silence. He had been so hot and tired there always in the mills! The years had been so fierce and cruel! There was coming now quiet and coolness and sleep. His tense limbs relaxed, and settled in a calm languor. The blood ran fainter and slow from his heart. He did not think now with a savage anger of what might be and was not; he was conscious only of deep stillness creeping over him. At first he saw a sea of faces: the mill-men,—women he had known, drunken and bloated,—Janeys timid and pitiful,—poor old Debs: then they floated together like a mist, and faded away, leaving only the clear, pearly moonlight.

Whether, as the pure light crept up the stretched-out figure, it brought with it calm and peace, who shall say? His dumb soul was alone with God in judgment. A Voice may have spoken for it from far-off Calvary, "Father, forgive them, for they know not what they do!"[51] Who dare say? Fainter and fainter the heart rose and fell, slower and slower the moon floated from behind a cloud, until, when at last its full tide of white splendor swept over the cell, it seemed to wrap and fold into a deeper stillness the dead figure that never should move again. Silence deeper than the Night! Nothing that moved, save the black, nauseous stream of blood dripping slowly from the pallet to the floor!

There was outcry and crowd enough in the cell the next day. The coroner and his jury, the local editors, Kirby himself, and boys with their hands thrust knowingly into their pockets and heads on one side, jammed into the corners. Coming and going all day. Only one woman. She came late, and outstayed them all. A Quaker, or Friend, as they call themselves. I think this woman was known by that name in heaven. A homely body, coarsely dressed in gray and white. Deborah (for Haley had let her in) took notice of her. She watched them all—sitting on the end of the pallet, holding his head in her arms—with the ferocity of a watch-dog,

[51] Christ's words from the cross: "Father, forgive them: for they know not what they do," from Luke 23:24; Calvary was the site of the crucifixion.

if any of them touched the body. There was no meekness, no sorrow, in her face; the stuff out of which murderers are made, instead. All the time Haley and the woman were laying straight the limbs and cleaning the cell, Deborah sat still, keenly watching the Quaker's face. Of all the crowd there that day, this woman alone had not spoken to her,—only once or twice had put some cordial to her lips. After they all were gone, the woman, in the same still, gentle way, brought a vase of wood-leaves and berries, and placed it by the pallet, then opened the narrow window. The fresh air blew in, and swept the woody fragrance over the dead face. Deborah looked up with a quick wonder.

"Did hur know my boy wud like it? Did hur know Hugh?"

"I know Hugh now."

The white fingers passed in a slow, pitiful way over the dead, worn face. There was a heavy shadow in the quiet eyes.

"Did hur know where they 'll bury Hugh?" said Deborah in a shrill tone, catching her arm.

This had been the question hanging on her lips all day.

"In t' town-yard? Under t' mud and ash? T' lad'll smother, woman! He wur born on t' lane moor, where t' air is frick[52] and strong. Take hur out, for God's sake, take hur out where t' air blows!"

The Quaker hesitated, but only for a moment. She put her strong arm around Deborah and led her to the window.

"Thee sees the hills, friend, over the river? Thee sees how the light lies warm there, and the winds of God blow all the day? I live there,—where the blue smoke is, by the trees. Look at me." She turned Deborah's face to her own, clear and earnest. "Thee will believe me? I will take Hugh and bury him there to-morrow."

Deborah did not doubt her. As the evening wore on, she leaned against the iron bars, looking at the hills that rose far off, through the thick sodden clouds, like a bright, unattainable calm. As she looked, a shadow of their solemn repose fell on her face: its fierce discontent faded into a pitiful, humble quiet. Slow, solemn tears gathered in her eyes: the poor weak eyes turned so hopelessly to the place where Hugh was to rest, the grave heights looking higher and brighter and more solemn than ever before. The Quaker watched her keenly. She came to her at last, and touched her arm.

"When thee comes back," she said, in a low, sorrowful tone, like one who speaks from a strong heart deeply moved with remorse or pity, "thee shall begin thy life again.—there on the hills. I came too late; but not for thee,—by God's help, it may be."

Not too late. Three years after, the Quaker began her work. I end my story here. At evening-time it was light. There is no need to tire you with the long years of sunshine, and fresh air, and slow, patient Christ-love, needed to make healthy and hopeful this impure body and soul. There is a homely pine house, on one of these hills, whose windows overlook broad, wooded slopes and clover-crimsoned meadows,—niched into the very place where the light is warmest, the air freest. It is the Friends' meeting-house.[53] Once a week they sit there, in their grave, earnest way, waiting for the Spirit of Love to speak, opening their simple hearts to receive His words. There is a woman, old, deformed, who takes a humble place among them: waiting like them: in her gray dress, her worn face, pure and meek, turned now and then to the sky. A woman much loved by these silent, restful people;

[52] Fresh.   [53] A Quaker place of worship.

more silent than they, more humble, more loving. Waiting: with her eyes turned to hills higher and purer than these on which she lives,—dim and far off now, but to be reached some day. There may be in her heart some latent hope to meet there the love denied her here,—that she shall find him whom she lost, and that then she will not be all-unworthy. Who blames her? Something is lost in the passage of every soul from one eternity to the other,—something pure and beautiful, which might have been and was not: a hope, a talent, a love, over which the soul mourns, like Esau deprived of his birthright.[54] What blame to the meek Quaker, if she took her lost hope to make the hills of heaven more fair?

Nothing remains to tell that the poor Welsh puddler once lived, but this figure of the mill-woman cut in korl. I have it here in a corner of my library. I keep it hid behind a curtain,—it is such a rough, ungainly thing. Yet there are about it touches, grand sweeps of outline, that show a master's hand. Sometimes,—to-night, for instance,—the curtain is accidentally drawn back, and I see a bare arm stretched out imploringly in the darkness, and an eager, wolfish face watching mine: a wan, woful face, through which the spirit of the dead korl-cutter looks out, with its thwarted life, its mighty hunger, its unfinished work. Its pale, vague lips seem to tremble with a terrible question. "Is this the End?" they say,—"nothing beyond?—no more?" Why, you tell me you have seen that look in the eyes of dumb brutes,—horses dying under the lash. I know.

The deep of the night is passing while I write. The gas-light wakens from the shadows here and there the objects which lie scattered through the room: only faintly, though; for they belong to the open sunlight. As I glance at them, they each recall some task or pleasure of the coming day. A half-moulded child's head; Aphrodite;[55] a bough of forest-leaves; music; work; homely fragments, in which lie the secrets of all eternal truth and beauty. Prophetic all! Only this dumb, woful face seems to belong to and end with the night. I turn to look at it. Has the power of its desperate need commanded the darkness away? While the room is yet steeped in heavy shadow, a cool, gray light suddenly touches its head like a blessing hand, and its groping arm points through the broken cloud to the far East, where, in the flickering, nebulous crimson, God has set the promise of the Dawn.

1861

EARLY TO MIDDLE 19TH-CENTURY NONFICTION PROSE

The emphasis of nonfiction prose in eighteenth-century America was, as would be expected, on political independence. The seminal piece of writing was the Declaration of Independence. Closely allied works were *The Federalist* papers (1787–1788) of Alexander Hamilton, James Madison, and John Jay; Thomas Paine's *Common Sense* (1776); and scores of political pamphlets. The writers of these works were attempting to carve out the ideas that would define a new nation. In the nineteenth century the concerns of writers of nonfiction prose broadened. Margaret Fuller, Elizabeth Cady Stanton, and other feminists wrote about women's rights. Frederick Douglass, Harriet Jacobs, and others produced accounts of their

---

[54] In Genesis 25: 27 Esau sold his birthright to his twin brother, Jacob.
[55] According to Greek myth, the goddess of love.

This early photograph shows how pioneers formed wagon trains, to protect against Native-American attacks and against the elements, as they proceeded in the great westward migration.

horrifying lives as slaves. Noah Webster published his two-volume *American Dictionary of the English Language* in 1828. Historians such as Francis Parkman, George Bancroft, and William Hickling Prescott began to write the history of the new country. And an untold number of men and women promoted abolitionism, advocated antiwar positions, and produced a vast amount of travel writing in the newspapers and magazines that proliferated in the early nineteenth century.

If, however, there is one central emphasis in nonfiction prose of the first half of the nineteenth-century, it is the unfolding of the self. The romanticism that developed in Europe at the beginning of the nineteenth century was fundamentally an assertion of the self. For the early romantics Johann Wolfgang von Goethe, Jean Jacques Rousseau, William Wordsworth, and Samuel Taylor Coleridge, personal autonomy and individual distinctiveness—perhaps best exemplified by Rousseau in *Confessions* (1781, 1788)—had become the cornerstones of human identity. And the romantics had a pronounced effect on America's writers. The Ralph Waldo Emerson who returned to the United States in 1833 after meeting Wordsworth, Coleridge, and Thomas Carlyle, among others, was fired with a romantic belief in the power of human intuition. Those nonfiction writers in America who argued on behalf of women's rights and abolitionism, who celebrated the natural beauty of native landscapes and bemoaned the corrupting influences of civilization, and who conceived of transcendentalism were inspired by the ideals of romanticism.

The transcendentalists are perhaps the most clearly romantic of American writers of nonfiction prose. Emerson says "trust thyself," and Henry David Thoreau encourages us to explore ourselves. Margaret Fuller, for two years editor of *The Dial,* the transcendentalist magazine, spent a career urging women to assert themselves. This expansion of the idea of self led naturally and logically to a conflict between the individual and society. We see it in Fuller's feminism. It is even more obvious in Thoreau's work, most notably in his essay "Resistance to Civil Government" (1849). That central document of American literature inspired the Indian nationalist Mahatma Gandhi and Martin Luther King, Jr., among others. "Resistance to Civil Government" was the result of Thoreau's being jailed overnight by Concord, Massachusetts, officials for his refusal to pay a poll tax to a government that tolerated slavery. He believed that an individual has, and must insist upon, the right to refuse to sanction a government if he or she strongly disagrees with the actions of that government. Private morality is, for Thoreau the principled romantic, a sacred area upon which government has no right to intrude.

The subject of slavery was, as we might imagine, central to mid-nineteenth-century discourse. Much of the nonfiction prose of the time—from newspaper articles to political oratory to the writings of abolitionists, including Thoreau, Lydia Maria Child, and the politician Wendell Phillips—engaged this heated subject. Even poets such as John Greenleaf Whittier attacked slavery. Slaves themselves, however, offered the most moving indictments of this demeaning institution. Beginning in the early eighteenth century, more than six thousand accounts of slaves' lives in captivity were produced. Unlike the earlier captivity narratives such as Mary Rowlandson's, which recount one white person's plight after abduction by a band of Native Americans and tend to end with an escape perceived as a triumph of the individual's religious faith, slave narratives are communal tales in which the captive stands for his or her collective race. Olaudah Equiano's *Narrative* (1789) was the prototype of this genre.

In the middle of the nineteenth century, two classic slave narratives appeared: Harriet Jacobs's *Incidents in the Life of a Slave Girl* (1861) and Frederick Douglass's *Narrative* (1845). Jacobs's harrowing autobiography tells a story of such brutality and degradation that its very credibility was questioned until the well-known abolitionist Lydia Maria Child agreed to "edit" and write a brief introduction to it. Douglass's *Narrative* was also introduced by a well-known white abolitionist, the newspaper editor William Lloyd Garrison. It is revealing of nineteenth-century attitudes toward blacks that these works had to be sanctioned by a white establishment figure in order to be fully accepted by a supposedly sympathetic audience.

Douglass's *Narrative* is a skillful literary document that appropriates both the artistic strategies and the language of the white middle class and of Christianity to indict the intertwined evils of racism and slavery. Douglass's search for his role in the world once he is a free man is recognizable as a romanticist's attempt to name, or identify, a self. Read this way, the *Narrative* is an exemplary tale that owes much not only to the genre that it epitomizes, but also to the larger historical moment during which its author lived. In other words, Douglass shares a literary relationship not only with Harriet Jacobs, but also with Emerson and Thoreau.

Moreover, this *Narrative* is a clear literary antecedent of such twentieth-century attempts to delineate an African-American self as Ralph Ellison's *Invisible Man* (1952).

After gaining his freedom Douglass devoted much of his energies to lecturing on what he called the "great work" of abolitionism. Doing so, he joined a lecture circuit that offered both a living and a testing ground for many of his contemporaries. Many of Emerson's essays were the revised products of orations that he gave during the winters he spent traveling America's burgeoning lecture circuit. Oratory was, in an age before the advent of the audio and video media, a popular communications medium. In the middle nineteenth century a large and eager audience might come out to hear Emerson exhort them to be self-reliant, to hear (and see) Douglass talk about the horrors of slave life, to see the latest English literary giant—Charles Dickens, for instance—read from his or her works, or to see and listen to political oratory of a vehemence and flamboyance that is all but lost.

=CONTEXTS=

The Emancipation Proclamation

In fighting the Civil War, President Abraham Lincoln's primary goal was to preserve the Union—with or without slavery. During the second year of fighting, he began to feel that an emancipation policy, which would take the collective strength of African Americans from the Confederacy and give it to the Union, might strengthen rather than weaken the Union cause. On September 22, 1862, Lincoln proclaimed emancipation as a war measure. As such, the policy could be applied only to Confederate states still in rebellion, not to border states loyal to the Union or to already conquered parts of the South. The provisions of the document, from which the excerpt below was taken, went into effect New Year's Day, 1863.

Final Proclamation of Emancipation

That on the 1st day of January, A.D. 1863, all persons held as slaves within any State or designated part of a State the people whereof shall then be in rebellion against the United States shall be then, thenceforward, and forever free; and the executive government of the United States including the military and naval authority thereof, will recognize and maintain the freedom of such persons and will do no act or acts to repress such persons, or any of them, in any efforts they may make for their actual freedom.

That the executive will on the 1st day of January aforesaid, by proclamation, designate the States and parts of States, if any, in which the people thereof, respectively, shall then be in rebellion against the United States; and the fact that any State or the people thereof shall on that day be in good faith represented in the Congress of the United States by members chosen thereto at elections wherein a majority of the qualified voters of such States shall have participated shall, in the absence of strong countervailing testimony, be deemed conclusive evidence that such State and the people thereof are not then in rebellion against the United States.

                                                            Abraham Lincoln, 1862

An especially memorable orator was Abraham Lincoln, who spoke simply and colloquially and whose humor owed much to the southwestern tall tale. The simplicity and clarity of Lincoln's nonfiction prose style (he used no speechwriter but wrote his own material) is evident in the Gettysburg Address (1863). Walt Whitman called Lincoln the writer an "idiomatic western genius."

The nonfiction prose produced by women in the early nineteenth century centered, as did the writings of slaves, around a potent social issue. Women such as Margaret Fuller, Fanny Fern, and Elizabeth Cady Stanton called attention to the inequality of women in a supposedly democratic society. Fern was the most popular of these authors, producing work that was often dismissed for sentimentality by the same readers who revered Charles Dickens's novels. Fuller and Stanton were more consciously militant writers. In her best-known work, *Woman in the Nineteenth Century* (1845), Fuller calls for equal opportunities for women as she castigates the hypocrisy of white males who championed freedom for blacks while restricting the rights of their own wives and daughters.

It was Stanton, however, who called the hypocrisy of white males's into clearest focus. In the 1848 Declaration of Sentiments she and her colleagues used the language of the Declaration of Independence itself to call for women's rights. The second paragraph of the Declaration of Sentiments begins "We hold these truths to be self-evident: that all men and women are created equal." The declaration commences a list of tyrannous "facts" with "The history of mankind is a history of repeated injustices and usurpations on the part of man toward woman."

In the militant writings of women and of slaves we recognize assertions of the self that are as powerful as the famous pronouncements of the transcendentalists. The central emphasis in the rich and varied accomplishments of America's early to middle nineteenth-century writers of nonfiction prose is a romantic call for the primacy of the self in the face of an increasingly conformist and intolerant society. America's nonfiction writers remind us—in their newspaper articles, orations, autobiographies, personal essays, and propaganda pieces—of the significance of the human "I" in a democracy.

Lydia Maria Child
(1802–1880)

In her forties Lydia Maria Child recalled that her childhood had been "cold, shaded, and uncongenial." She was born Lydia Maria Francis in Medford, Massachusetts, in 1802 to Susannah Rand and David Convers Francis. Her father disapproved of her reading, and when her mother died Lydia, age twelve, was sent to live with a sister in isolated Norridgewock, Maine. If her father hoped Lydia would give up her intellectual interests, he was disappointed: she continued to read widely and to correspond with her Harvard-educated brother, Convers, about Homer and John Milton. Out of the experience of patriarchal repression she wrote her first novel when she was twenty-two. Set in Puritan times and featuring the heroine's rebellious marriage to a Native American, *Hobomok* (1824) is both an attack on patriarchal authority and one of the first historical novels to make use of American materials.

During the next few years Lydia Francis pursued a busy literary career; she established the *Juvenile Miscellany* (the first successful children's magazine), wrote another historical novel (*The Rebels* [1825]), and compiled *The Frugal Housewife* (1829), a popular collection of household advice and traditional remedies. In 1828 she married David Lee Child—an idealistic lawyer and abolitionist but an incompetent provider—and, moving to a farm in Weyland, Massachusetts, undertook to support them with her writing. By 1832 she was a highly regarded author, one of only two women granted membership in the Boston Athenaeum. But her success was checked by the publication of the pamphlet *An Appeal in Favor of That Class of Americans Called Africans* (1833), which called for immediate emancipation and—most upsetting to conventional minds—argued against antimiscegenation laws, laws banning interracial marriage. Public reaction was swift and devastating: a Boston politician threw the *Appeal* out the window with tongs, the *Juvenile Miscellany* lost most of its subscribers, and Child's membership in the Boston Athenaeum was revoked.

Retracting nothing, Child continued to write essays and fiction for the abolitionist cause and on behalf of Native Americans. Moreover, she extended her concern to the plight of the elderly, Chinese immigrants, and the insane. In 1841 she moved to New York City, where she edited the abolitionist William Lloyd Garrison's newspaper *The National Anti-Slavery Standard*. Her wide-ranging newspaper sketches were collected as *Letters From New York* in 1843 and 1845. In 1861 she edited Harriet Jacobs's *Incidents in the Life of a Slave Girl*, and after the Civil War Child published *The Freedman's Book* (1865), a collection of essays directed to newly emancipated slaves. Never a radical feminist, she nonetheless worked for woment's rights with her biography of the writer Madame de Baronne de Staël, her novels *Philothea* (1836) and *A Romance of the Republic* (1867), and historical works such as *The History of the Condition of Women, in Various Ages and Nations* (1835), which documents the variety of women's roles in world history.

Although Child's *Philothea* can be considered one of the few transcendentalist novels, she had little sympathy for abstractions. For Child, as for Herman Melville, literature was concerned with "the great Art of Telling the Truth" (from Melville's "Hawthorne and His Mosses" [1850]), but her truths were practical, social, and political rather than transcendental. After receiving a copy of the just-published *Essays: Second Series* from her friend Ralph Waldo Emerson in 1844, she wrote to Augusta King that she objected to the idea that "everything is 'scene-painting and counterfeit'; . . . my being is so alive and earnest, that it resists and abhors these alluding spectres." Her writing powerfully attests to this vital and earnest concern.

Suggested Readings: *The Freedmen's Book*, 1865. *A Romance of the Republic*, 1867, 1969. *Selected Letters, 1817–1880*, ed. M. Meltzer, P. G. Holland, and F. Krasno, 1982. *Hobomok and Other Writings on Indians*, ed. C. L. Karcher, 1986. H. G. Baer, *The Heart Is Like Heaven: The Life of Lydia Maria Child*, 1964. M. Meltzer, *Tongue of Flame: The Life of Lydia Maria Child*, 1965. W. S. Osborne, *Lydia Maria Child*, 1980. J. F. Yellin, *Women and Sisters: The Antislavery Feminists in American Culture*, 1989.

Texts Used: *The American Frugal Housewife, Dedicated to Those Who Are Not Ashamed of Economy*, 1836.

from THE FRUGAL HOUSEWIFE*

GENERAL MAXIMS FOR HEALTH

Rise early. Eat simple food. Take plenty of exercise. Never fear a little fatigue. Let not children be dressed in tight clothes; it is necessary their limbs and muscles should have full play, if you wish for either health or beauty.

Avoid the necessity of a physician, if you can, by careful attention to your diet. Eat what best agrees with your system, and resolutely abstain from what hurts you, however well you may like it. A few days' abstinence, and cold water for a beverage, has driven off many an approaching disease.

If you find yourself really ill, send for a good physician. Have nothing to do with quacks; and do not tamper with quack medicines. You do not know what they are; and what security have you that they know what they are?

Wear shoes that are large enough. It not only produces corns, but makes the feet misshapen, to cramp them.

Wash very often, and rub the skin thoroughly with a hard brush.

Let those who love to be invalids drink strong green tea, eat pickles, preserves, and rich pastry. As far as possible, eat and sleep at regular hours.

Wash the eyes thoroughly in cold water every morning. Do not read or sew at twilight, or by too dazzling a light. If far-sighted, read with rather less light, and with the book somewhat nearer to the eye, than you desire. If near-sighted, read with a book as far as possible. Both these imperfections may be diminished in this way.

Clean teeth in pure water two or three times a day; but, above all, be sure to have them clean before you go to bed.[1]

Have your bed-chamber well aired; and have fresh bed linen every week. Never have the wind blowing directly upon you from open windows during the night. It is *not* healthy to sleep in heated rooms.

Let children have their bread and milk before they have been long up. Cold water and a run in the fresh air before breakfast.

Too frequent use of an ivory comb injures the hair. Thorough combing, washing in suds, or N. E. rum,[2] and thorough brushing, will keep it in order; and the washing does not injure the hair, as is generally supposed. Keep children's hair cut close until ten or twelve years old; it is better for health and the beauty of the hair. Do not sleep with hair frizzled, or braided. Do not make children cross-eyed, by having hair hang down about their foreheads, where they see it continually.

1829

---

* First published in 1829, this little volume of strikingly modern tips on health, housekeeping, cooking, and raising children was retitled *The American Frugal Housewife* and went through thirty-three American editions and twenty-one European editions.

[1] Dental hygiene was in its infancy at this time; tooth loss was common.

[2] Rum and water, a traditional drink in New England.

Education of Daughters

There is no subject so much connected with individual happiness and national prosperity as the education of daughters. It is a true, and therefore an old remark, that the situation and prospects of a country may be justly estimated by the character of its women; and we all know how hard it is to engraft upon a woman's character habits and principles to which she was unaccustomed in her girlish days. It is always extremely difficult, and sometimes utterly impossible. Is the present education of young ladies likely to contribute to their own ultimate happiness, or to the welfare of the country? There are many honorable exceptions; but we do think the general tone of female education is bad. The greatest and most universal error is, teaching girls to exaggerate the importance of getting married; and of course to place an undue importance upon the polite attentions of gentlemen. It was but a few days since, I heard a pretty and sensible girl say, "Did you ever see a man so ridiculously fond of his daughters as Mr.————? He is all the time with them. The other night, at the party, I went and took Anna away by mere force; for I knew she must feel dreadfully to have her father waiting upon her all the time, while the other girls were talking with the beaux." And another young friend of mine said, with an air most laughably serious, "I don't think Harriet and Julia enjoyed themselves at all last night. Don't you think, nobody but their *brother* offered to hand them to[1] the supper-room?"

That a mother should wish to see her daughters happily married, is natural and proper; that a young lady should be pleased with polite attentions is likewise natural and innocent; but this undue anxiety, this foolish excitement about showing off the attentions of somebody, no matter whom, is attended with consequences seriously injurious. It promotes envy and rivalship; it leads our young girls to spend their time between the public streets, the ball room, and the toilet; and, worst of all, it leads them to contract engagements, without any knowledge of their own hearts, merely for the sake of being married as soon as their companions. When married, they find themselves ignorant of the important duties of domestic life; and its quiet pleasures soon grow tiresome to minds worn out by frivolous excitements. If they remain unmarried, their disappointment and discontent are, of course, in proportion to their exaggerated idea of the eclat[2] attendant upon having a lover.[3] The evil increases in a startling ratio; for these girls, so injudiciously educated, will, nine times out of ten, make injudicious mothers, aunts, and friends; thus follies will be accumulated unto the third and fourth generation. Young ladies should be taught that usefulness is happiness, and that all other things are but incidental. With regard to matrimonial speculations, they should be taught nothing! Leave the affections to nature and to truth, and all will end well. How many can I at this moment recollect, who have made themselves unhappy by marrying for the sake of the *name* of being married! How many do I know, who have been instructed to such watchfulness in the game, that they have lost it by trumping their own tricks!

One great cause of the vanity, extravagance and idleness that are so fast growing upon our young ladies, is the absence of *domestic education*. By domestic education, I do not mean the sending daughters into the kitchen some half dozen

---

[1] Escort them into.　　[2] Acclaim.　　[3] A suitor.

times, to weary the patience of the cook, and to boast of it the next day in the parlor. I mean two or three years spent with a mother, assisting her in her duties, instructing brothers and sisters, and taking care of their own clothes. This is the way to make them happy, as well as good wives; for, being early accustomed to the duties of life, they will sit lightly as well as gracefully upon them.

But what time do modern girls have for the formation of quiet, domestic habits? Until sixteen they go to school; sometimes these years are judiciously spent, and sometimes they are half wasted; too often they are spent in acquiring the *elements* of a thousand sciences, without being thoroughly acquainted with any; or in a variety of accomplishments of very doubtful value to people of moderate fortune. As soon as they leave school, (and sometimes before,) they begin a round of balls and parties, and staying with gay young friends. Dress and flattery take up all their thoughts. What time have they to learn to be useful? What time have they to cultivate the still and gentle affections, which must, in every situation of life, have such an important effect on a woman's character and happiness?

As far as parents can judge what will be a daughter's station, education should be adapted to it; but it is well to remember that it is always easy to know how to spend riches, and always safe to know how to bear poverty.

A superficial acquaintance with such accomplishments as music and drawing is useless and undesirable. They should not be attempted unless there is taste, talent, and time enough to attain excellence. I have frequently heard young women of moderate fortune say, "I have not opened my piano these five years. I wish I had the money expended upon it. If I had employed as much time in learning useful things, I should have been better fitted for the cares of my family."

By these remarks I do not mean to discourage an attention to the graces of life. Gentility and taste are always lovely in all situations. But good things, carried to excess, are often productive of bad consequences. When accomplishments and dress interfere with the duties and permanent happiness of life, they are unjustifiable and displeasing; but where there is a solid foundation in mind and heart, all those elegancies are but becoming ornaments.

Some are likely to have more use for them than others; and they are justified in spending more time and money upon them. But no one should be taught to consider them valuable for mere parade and attraction. Making the education of girls such a series of "man-traps," makes the whole system unhealthy, by poisoning the motive.

1829

Ralph Waldo Emerson
(1803–1882)

Born in Boston, Massachusetts, in 1803, Ralph Waldo Emerson was the son of William Emerson, a descendant of a long line of New England clergymen, and Ruth Haskins, whose mercantile family had flourished in the distillery business. As Unitarian pastor of the First Church in Boston, William Emerson worked steadily at his sermons and at church business, never free from a concern about financial stability. His death when Ralph was eight years old left the family in straitened circumstances. The boy was raised by his mother, who went to work managing a series of boardinghouses, and his pious, sardonic, and talented Aunt Mary Moody Emerson. At the Boston Latin school Emerson received the kind of basic education that prepared him to enter Harvard College in 1817.

During these years the reigning philosophy at Harvard (and at most American colleges) was that of John Locke and the eighteenth-century Scottish "Common Sense" realists. Emerson dutifully studied the Scots under several professors, among them Levi Frisbie, who also came to Harvard in 1817 and began to expound theories on the development of the moral sense that he derived from the Common Sense philosophy of Thomas Reid and Dugald Stewart. In his senior year Emerson received a prize for his "Dissertation on the Present State of Ethical Philosophy," a thirty-four-page effort that emphasizes the importance of Reid and Stewart and shows little interest in the new German philosophical thought. Despite what this award might seem to signify, Emerson did not excel in his studies at Harvard. In 1821 he graduated in the middle of his class of fifty-nine students. But at Harvard he began the habit of keeping a journal, in which he recorded ideas, attitudes, and responses to books and authors. Over the years his journals, rich in concept and detail, became a register of the life of a mind; they provided the seeds and verbal patterns for many of Emerson's essays, lectures, and poems and served as a storehouse for the type of allusion that brought a characteristic texture to his oral and written work.

After his graduation Emerson taught intermittently and without commitment at his brother's Boston school for young ladies and lived for some months with his family near the Shaker village at Canterbury, New Hampshire. In 1825 he enrolled in the Harvard Divinity School. Although he showed no special zeal for the ministry even during his studies, he was approved to preach in October 1826 and made junior pastor at the Old Second Church in Boston, where such resolute Puritans as Increase Mather and Cotton Mather had once held office. Now it was Unitarian territory, and the liberal movement that rejected Calvinist orthodoxy and emphasized the individual's capacity for moral improvement became the context in which Emerson's doubts and convictions about personal and institutionalized faith came to fruition.

During the third year of his ministry, and with the unsolicited approval of his Aunt Mary (who was never reluctant to offer an opinion), Emerson married Ellen Tucker of Concord, New Hampshire. With this aspiring young poet he shared an all-too-brief period of happiness that temporarily subordinated the issue of religious doubt. But Ellen died of tuberculosis in 1831 when she was nineteen. A year later, with the feeling of being imprisoned in a diminishing faith, Emerson resigned his pastorate because he no longer believed in the validity of the Lord's Supper, the sacrament of communion. Such a move was inevitable: as a minister Emerson lacked the commitment of one whose faith was alive and ever-deepening; he was more interested in moral rectitude and virtuous living than in the revealed truths of the Bible. Indeed, the first inklings of an Emersonian emphasis on the "self" can be seen in his sermons. Increasingly, he felt it necessary to discern the origins of the self, to trace them to their source. When he concluded that the origins were in an Infinite Being, the foundation for his impressive work of the 1830s and 1840s was set.

On Christmas Day, 1832, Emerson sailed to Europe, where he visited Italy, France, and England. He saw the English writer and poet Walter Savage Landor in Florence and was deeply impressed by a tour of the Jardin des Plantes in Paris, which suggested to Emerson the concept of a unity among all living things. In England he visited Samuel Taylor Coleridge, whose ideas later helped him merge conceptually the philosophies of Neoplatonism and transcendental idealism. Emerson also called on Thomas Carlyle in

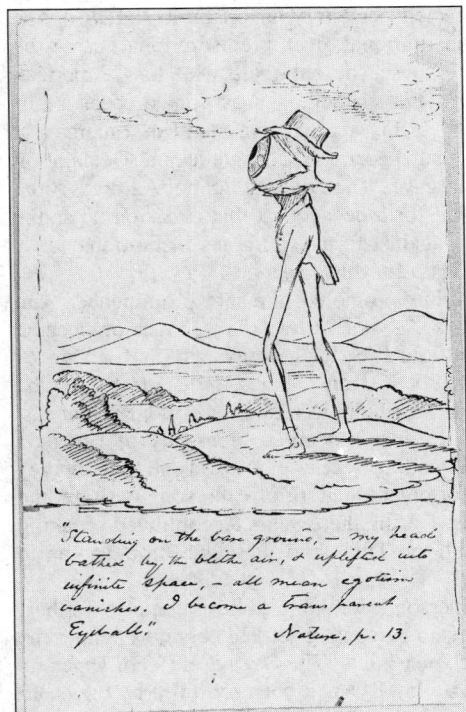

"Standing on the bare ground, — my head bathed by the blithe air, & uplifted into infinite space, — all mean egotism vanishes. I become a transparent Eyeball." *Nature, p. 13.*

Christopher Pearse Cranch's caricature of lines from Ralph Waldo Emerson's Nature.

Scotland at Craigenputtock and began a lasting friendship based on mutual perspectives and intellectual respect. Although Emerson made other trips to England and France between 1847 and 1848 and in 1872, this first visit released his thinking in a formative way.

Once back in the United States Emerson settled in Concord, Massachusetts. The following year, 1835, he married Lydia Jackson, who had heard him speak both in Boston and in her hometown of Plymouth, Massachusetts, and felt very much attuned to the developing tenor of his mind. With a legacy of $1,200 a year from his first wife and money earned by lecturing on the lyceum, or public lecture hall, circuit, Emerson and Lydian (as he called her) settled into a Concord life that provided generous opportunities for intellectual ferment. Beginning with the publication of *Nature* in 1836, Emerson established a reputation for originality of mind that expanded, not always to unqualified applause, over the next decade. Only two weeks after the publication of this eloquent manifesto, the Transcendental Club held the first of its informal meetings. With a membership that included the poet Jones Very, the abolitionist Theodore Parker, and the reformer George Ripley, who founded Brook Farm in 1841, as well as Emerson, this group of speculative thinkers (who called themselves the Symposium, in honor of Plato) met irregularly for more than six years, examining such matters as the basis of faith and the integrity of philosophical idealism. For Emerson the years marked a period of vibrant growth.

In *Nature* Emerson invokes the relation of the individual and the infinite, as he had done in his early sermons, but in this context to explain the possibility of creative human expression: defining "proper creation" as "the working of the Original Cause through the instruments he has already made," Emerson extends the miracle of Creation to the inspired words of poets and other transcendentally directed persons. Out of this belief in divine inspiration (by its very nature individual, noninstitutional, even preinstitutional) came the moral imperatives of Emerson's best-known essays. The nationalism of his "American Scholar" address delivered at Harvard in 1837 has an edge, an assurance, because of Emerson's commitment to the originating self. In his appreciative study of Emerson in 1885, Oliver Wendell Holmes looked back on that speech as "Our intellectual Declaration of Independence." At Harvard in 1838 Emerson gave "The Divinity School Ad-dress," the product of ideas that had percolated in his mind for a decade; on that occasion he spoke explicitly for intuitive spiritual experience and against formal religious institutions. As a result, he was not invited to speak at Harvard again for thirty years.

Emerson's life and work in the late 1830s thus promoted him into prominence. And with the publication of *Essays* (1841) and *Essays, Second Series* (1844), Emerson became a major force in American intellectual and cultural life. Such essays as "Self-Reliance" and "The Over-Soul" (from *Essays*) and "The Poet" (from *Second Series*) testify to the accumulating vitality of his ideas. There were those who objected to the non-Christian cast of Emerson's thought: as Ralph L. Rusk reports in his detailed biography of Emerson (1949), Mary Moody Emerson was not alone in calling "Self-Reliance" a "strange medley of atheism and false independence." But the formidable nature of Emerson's writing and lecturing was apparent to a variety of audiences. During these years he continued speaking on lyceum programs. And his involvement with the Transcendental Club brought him to serve as editor of *The Dial* from 1842 to 1844.

By the mid 1840s the radical thrust of Emerson's thinking could extend no farther. Even before that time the weight of experience and personal grief had begun to temper the buoyant perspective of such essays as "Self-Reliance" and "The Over-Soul." For Emerson was no stranger to loss: the death of his first wife in 1831 had been followed by the death of two brothers—Edward in 1834 (following seven years of mental instability) and Charles in 1836. And in 1842 the death of his son Waldo, not yet six years old, from scarlet fever affected him and Lydian deeply. Emerson's grief found expression both in the perplexed essay "Experience" (1844), where he confesses surprise at all he did not feel at this time of sorrow, and in the tender lines of the poem "Threnody" (1847), which portray Waldo as "the wondrous child," "the darling who shall not return." The reserved Emerson, who frequently expressed concern about his austerity of demeanor, is at his human best in this song of lamentation. In a marginal comment scrawled in his copy of the *Essays,* Herman Melville referred to "this Plato who talks thro' his nose" (with reference to Emerson's New England accent). In "Threnody," as Melville would have been the first to admit, Emerson is a father who writes from his heart.

With the publication of *Poems* in 1847, Emerson revealed a poetic impulse different in style and substance from that of such popular and accomplished writers as William Cullen Bryant and Henry Wadsworth Longfellow. Emerson was absorbed by a need to articulate. Elliptical in phasing, such poems as "The Problem" (1840) and "Ode, Inscribed to W. H. Channing" (1847) are demanding in argument, strikingly modern in line and image. The "Ode," particularly, shows an Emerson responsive to social issues of the day, just as his journals and letters testify to his deep moral concern over slavery, the Mexican War, and the removal of the Cherokee nation from the Southeast in the late 1830s. With their inability to be more than relentless efforts, Emerson's poems have an endearing vulnerability lacking in some of his more flinty prose.

In 1850 Emerson published *Representative Men,* a volume of seven essays based on lectures given in Boston in 1845 and 1846 and in England in 1847. Each of the essays is devoted to an individual who exemplifies, in Emerson's view, the best of humankind, who is an originator, a creator of possibility. Among these individuals are Plato, "the philosopher," Shakespeare, "the poet," and the Swedish theologian Emanuel Swedenborg, "the mystic." Six years later Emerson published *English Traits,* a series of incisive and perceptive observations derived from his lectures on England, given after his visit of 1847 to 1848. Two other volumes, *The Conduct of Life* (1860) and *Society and Solitude* (1870), register modifications in Emerson's attitude toward the individual in society. Based on materials from lyceum lectures, such essays as "Fate" and "Illusions" (in *Conduct*) offer a pessimistic and even sardonic view of human destiny, a view only partly offset by Emerson's refusal to be nihilistic. In the title essay "Society and Solitude," a more commonsense Emerson preaches the necessity for balance between the human need for solitude and that for social contact.

Contributing to the making of Emerson's ideas was an assortment of writers from different eras and nations, many of the important ones related by mystical tendencies and the romantic idea of organic form. Coleridge, Carlyle, and expounders of German idealism, for example, blended with Plato, Plotinus, and other Neoplatonic philosophers who sought to reconcile aspects of classical philosophy and Christianity; the ideas of Swedenborg and the experiences of the German mystic Jakob Böhme were linked in Emerson's mind and journals by the wisdom of sacred Eastern books such as the Hindu *Vedas* and the *Bhagavad-Gita.* The concern for the self no doubt came from the Puritan habit of inspecting the soul. But it was the forge of his own genius and temperament that took all these "influences" and produced Emerson's work.

In his later years Emerson suffered a gradual decline of his mental abilities. The writer who had lamented the manner in which we are enslaved by memory had finally no memory to encumber him. Gazing into the casket of his old friend Henry Wadsworth Longfellow in March 1882, Emerson asked who he was looking at, then retired in embarrassment when told. After almost a decade of senility, he died in April 1882 in Concord, the village in which his father had been born, and was buried in Sleepy Hollow Cemetary near the graves of Henry David Thoreau and Nathaniel Hawthorne.

Suggested Readings: *Lectures and Biographical Sketches,* 1904. *The Letters of Ralph Waldo Emerson,* ed. R. L. Rusk, 1939. *The Early Lectures of Ralph Waldo Emerson,* 3 vols., ed. S. Whicher, R. E. Spiller, and W.E. Williams, 1959–1972. *The Journals and Miscellaneous Notebooks of Ralph Waldo Emerson,* 16 vols., ed. W. Gilman et al., 1960–1986. *The Correspondence of Emerson and Carlyle,* ed. J. Slater, 1964. R. L. Rusk, *The Life of Ralph Waldo Emerson,* 1949. S. E. Whicher, *Freedom and Fate: An Inner Life of Ralph Waldo Emerson,* 1953. J. Porte, *Representative Man: Ralph Waldo Emerson in His Time,* 1979. J. Loving, *Emerson, Whitman, and the American Muse,* 1982. B. L. Packer, *Emerson's Fall: A New Interpretation of the Major Essays,* 1982. D. Van Leer, *Emerson's Epistemology: The Argument of the Essays,* 1986. M. Gonnaud, *An Uneasy Solitude: Individual and Society in the Work of Ralph Waldo Emerson,* 1987. M. K. Cayton, *Emerson's Emergence: Self and Society in the Transformation of New England, 1800–1845,* 1989. A. D. Holder, *Emerson's Rhetoric of Revelation: Nature, the Reader, and the Apocalypse Within,* 1989. J. Michael, *Emerson and Skepticism: The Cipher of the World,* 1989.

Texts Used: *Nature* and "The American Scholar": *The Collected Works of Ralph Waldo Emerson,* Vol. I, ed. A. R. Ferguson, 1971. "Self-Reliance": *The Collected Works,* Vol. II, ed. A. R. Ferguson and J. F. Carr, 1979. "The Poet": *The Collected Works,* Vol. III, ed. A. R. Ferguson, J. F. Carr, and D. E. Wilson, 1983. "Fate": *The Works of Ralph Waldo Emerson: The Conduct of Life,* 1888. Poems: *Poems,* 1918. Journal entry: *The Journals and Miscellaneous Notebooks of Ralph Waldo Emerson:* Vol. XV: 1860–1866, ed. L. Allardt, D. W. Hill, and R. H. Bennett, 1982. Emerson to Whitman, 1855: W. Whitman, *Leaves of Grass,* ed. H. W. Blodgett and S. Bradley, 1965.

NATURE*

A subtle chain of countless rings
The next unto the farthest brings;
The eye reads omens where it goes,
And speaks all languages the rose;
And, striving to be man, the worm
Mounts through all the spires of form.[1]

INTRODUCTION

Our age is retrospective. It builds the sepulchres of the fathers. It writes biographies, histories, and criticism. The foregoing generations beheld God and nature face to face; we, through their eyes. Why should not we also enjoy an original relation to the universe? Why should not we have a poetry and philosophy of insight and not of tradition, and a religion by revelation to us, and not the history of theirs? Embosomed for a season in nature, whose floods of life stream around and through us, and invite us by the powers they supply, to action proportioned to nature, why should we grope among the dry bones of the past, or put the living generation into masquerade out of its faded wardrobe? The sun shines to-day also. There is more wool and flax in the fields. There are new lands, new men, new thoughts. Let us demand our own works and laws and worship.

Undoubtedly we have no questions to ask which are unanswerable. We must trust the perfection of the creation so far, as to believe that whatever curiosity the order of things has awakened in our minds, the order of things can satisfy. Every man's condition is a solution in hieroglyphic to those inquiries he would put. He acts it as life, before he apprehends it as truth. In like manner, nature is already, in its forms and tendencies, describing its own design. Let us interrogate the great apparition, that shines so peacefully around us. Let us inquire, to what end is nature?

All science has one aim, namely, to find a theory of nature. We have theories of races and of functions, but scarcely yet a remote approach to an idea of creation. We are now so far from the road to truth, that religious teachers dispute and hate each other, and speculative men are esteemed unsound and frivolous. But to a sound judgment, the most abstract truth is the most practical. Whenever a true theory appears, it will be its own evidence. Its test is, that it will explain all phenomena. Now many are thought not only unexplained but inexplicable; as language, sleep, madness, dreams, beasts, sex.

Philosophically considered, the universe is composed of Nature and the Soul. Strictly speaking, therefore, all that is separate from us, all which Philosophy distinguishes as the NOT ME,[2] that is, both nature and art, all other men and my own body, must be ranked under this name, NATURE. In enumerating the values of

---

* First published anonymously in 1836 at Emerson's expense, *Nature* was a major statement of ideas fundamental to New England transcendentalism.

[1] The epigraph for the first edition was the quotation "Nature is but an image or imitation of wisdom, the last thing of the soul; nature being a thing which doth only do, but not know," from the Roman Neoplatonic philosopher Plotinus (A.D. 205?–270). In the 1849 edition Emerson substituted his own lines of poetry, here.

[2] A term used in *Sartor Resartus* (1833–1834), by Thomas Carlyle (1795–1881).

nature and casting up their sum, I shall use the word in both senses;—in its common and in its philosophical import. In inquiries so general as our present one, the inaccuracy is not material; no confusion of thought will occur. *Nature,* in the common sense, refers to essences unchanged by man; space, the air, the river, the leaf. *Art* is applied to the mixture of his will with the same things, as in a house, a canal, a statue, a picture. But his operations taken together are so insignificant, a little chipping, baking, patching, and washing, that in an impression so grand as that of the world on the human mind, they do not vary the result.

CHAPTER I: NATURE

To go into solitude, a man needs to retire as much from his chamber as from society. I am not solitary whilst I read and write, though nobody is with me. But if a man would be alone, let him look at the stars. The rays that come from those heavenly worlds, will separate between him and vulgar things. One might think the atmosphere was made transparent with this design, to give man, in the heavenly bodies, the perpetual presence of the sublime. Seen in the streets of cities, how great they are! If the stars should appear one night in a thousand years, how would men believe and adore; and preserve for many generations the remembrance of the city of God which had been shown! But every night come out these envoys of beauty, and light the universe with their admonishing smile.

The stars awaken a certain reverence, because though always present, they are always inaccessible; but all natural objects make a kindred impression, when the mind is open to their influence. Nature never wears a mean appearance. Neither does the wisest man extort all her secret, and lose his curiosity by finding out all her perfection. Nature never became a toy to a wise spirit. The flowers, the animals, the mountains, reflected all the wisdom of his best hour, as much as they had delighted the simplicity of his childhood.

When we speak of nature in this manner, we have a distinct but most poetical sense in the mind. We mean the integrity of impression made by manifold natural objects. It is this which distinguishes the stick of timber of the wood-cutter, from the tree of the poet. The charming landscape which I saw this morning, is indubitably made up of some twenty or thirty farms. Miller owns this field, Locke that, and Manning the woodland beyond. But none of them owns the landscape. There is a property in the horizon which no man has but he whose eye can integrate all the parts, that is, the poet. This is the best part of these men's farms, yet to this their warranty-deeds give no title.

To speak truly, few adult persons can see nature. Most persons do not see the sun. At least they have a very superficial seeing. The sun illuminates only the eye of the man, but shines into the eye and the heart of the child. The lover of nature is he whose inward and outward senses are still truly adjusted to each other; who has retained the spirit of infancy even into the era of manhood. His intercourse with heaven and earth, becomes part of his daily food. In the presence of nature, a wild delight runs through the man, in spite of real sorrows. Nature says,—he is my creature, and maugre[3] all his impertinent griefs, he shall be glad with me. Not the sun or the summer alone, but every hour and season yields its tribute of delight; for every hour and change corresponds to and authorizes a different state of the

---

[3] Despite.

mind, from breathless noon to grimmest midnight. Nature is a setting that fits equally well a comic or a mourning piece. In good health, the air is a cordial of incredibly virtue. Crossing a bare common, in snow puddles, at twilight, under a clouded sky, without having in my thoughts any occurrence of special good fortune, I have enjoyed a perfect exhilaration. Almost I fear to think how glad I am. In the woods too, a man casts off his years, as the snake his slough, and at what period soever of life, is always a child. In the woods, is perpetual youth. Within these plantations of God, a decorum and sanctity reign, a perennial festival is dressed, and the guest sees not how he should tire of them in a thousand years. In the woods, we return to reason and faith. There I feel that nothing can befal me in life,—no disgrace, no calamity, (leaving me my eyes,) which nature cannot repair. Standing on the bare ground,—my head bathed by the blithe air, and uplifted into infinite space,—all mean egotism vanishes. I become a transparent eye-ball. I am nothing. I see all. The currents of the Universal Being circulate through me; I am part or particle of God.[4] The name of the nearest friend sounds then foreign and accidental. To be brothers, to be acquaintances,—master or servant, is then a trifle and a disturbance. I am the lover of uncontained and immortal beauty. In the wilderness, I find something more dear and connate[5] than in streets or villages. In the tranquil landscape, and especially in the distant line of the horizon, man beholds somewhat as beautiful as his own nature.

The greatest delight which the fields and woods minister, is the suggestion of an occult relation between man and the vegetable. I am not alone and unacknowledged. They nod to me and I to them. The waving of the boughs in the storm, is new to me and old. It takes me by surprise, and yet is not unknown. Its effect is like that of a higher thought or a better emotion coming over me, when I deemed I was thinking justly or doing right.

Yet it is certain that the power to produce this delight, does not reside in nature, but in man, or in a harmony of both. It is necessary to use these pleasures with great temperance. For, nature is not always tricked[6] in holiday attire, but the same scene which yesterday breathed perfume and glittered as for the frolic of the nymphs, is overspread with melancholy today. Nature always wears the colors of the spirit. To a man laboring under calamity, the heat of his own fire hath sadness in it. Then, there is a kind of contempt of the landscape felt by him who has just lost by death a dear friend. The sky is less grand as it shuts down over less worth in the population.

Chapter II: Commodity[7]

Whoever considers the final cause[8] of the world, will discern a multitude of uses that enter as parts into that result. They all admit of being thrown into one of the following classes: Commodity; Beauty; Language; and Discipline.

Under the general name of Commodity, I rank all those advantages which our senses owe to nature. This, of course, is a benefit which is temporary and mediate,[9] not ultimate, like its service to the soul. Yet although low, it is perfect in its

---

[4] This famous "transparent eye-ball" passage ends on a mystical note, with the speaker not simply a creature of God but "part or particle of God." For Emerson, this sense of wholeness, oneness, is the very condition of spiritual health.
[5] Related, innate.
[6] Dressed.   [7] Usefulness.   [8] Purpose.
[9] In the middle (of our lives, experiences, daily affairs).

kind, and is the only use of nature which all men apprehend. The misery of man appears like childish petulance, when we explore the steady and prodigal provision that has been made for his support and delight on this green ball which floats him through the heavens. What angels invented these splendid ornaments, these rich conveniences, this ocean of air above, this ocean of water beneath, this firmament of earth between? this zodiac of lights, this tent of dropping clouds, this striped coat of climates, this fourfold year? Beasts, fire, water, stones, and corn serve him. The field is at once his floor, his work-yard, his play-ground, his garden, and his bed.

> "More servants wait on man
> Than he'll take notice of."———[10]

Nature, in its ministry to man, is not only the material, but is also the process and the result. All the parts incessantly work into each other's hands for the profit of man. The wind sows the seed; the sun evaporates the sea; the wind blows the vapor to the field; the ice, on the other side of the planet, condenses rain on this; the rain feeds the plant; the plant feeds the animal; and thus the endless circulations of the divine charity nourish man.

The useful arts are but reproductions or new combinations by the wit of man, of the same natural benefactors. He no longer waits for favoring gales, but by means of steam, he realizes the fable of Æolus's bag,[11] and carries the two and thirty winds in the boiler of his boat. To diminish friction, he paves the road with iron bars,[12] and, mounting a coach with a ship-load of men, animals, and merchandise behind him, he darts through the country, from town to town, like an eagle or a swallow through the air. By the aggregate of these aids, how is the face of the world changed, from the era of Noah to that of Napoleon! The private poor man hath cities, ships, canals, bridges, built for him. He goes to the post-office, and the human race run on his errands; to the book-shop, and the human race read and write of all that happens, for him; to the court-house, and nations repair his wrongs. He sets his house upon the road, and the human race go forth every morning, and shovel out the snow, and cut a path for him.

But there is no need of specifying particulars in this class of uses. The catalogue is endless, and the examples so obvious, that I shall leave them to the reader's reflection, with the general remark, that this mercenary benefit is one which has respect to a farther good. A man is fed, not that he may be fed, but that he may work.

Chapter III: Beauty

A nobler want of man is served by nature, namely, the love of Beauty.

The ancient Greeks called the world κόσμοδ,[13] beauty. Such is the constitution of all things, or such the plastic power of the human eye, that the primary forms, as the sky, the mountain, the tree, the animal, give us a delight *in and for themselves;* a pleasure arising from outline, color, motion, and grouping. This seems

---

[10] From "Man" (1633), by the English poet George Herbert (1593–1633). Emerson quotes from this poem at length in Chapter 8.

[11] In Book 10 of Homer's *Odyssey,* the Greek wind god Aeolus gives Odysseus a bag of winds to blow his ship homeward from Troy.

[12] Railroad tracks.   [13] "Cosmos": order, and hence the beauty of wholeness.

partly owing to the eye itself. The eye is the best of artists. By the mutual action of its structure and of the laws of light, perspective is produced, which integrates every mass of objects, of what character soever, into a well colored and shaded globe, so that where the particular objects are mean and unaffecting, the landscape which they compose, is round and symmetrical. And as the eye is the best composer, so light is the first of painters. There is no object so foul that intense light will not make beautiful. And the stimulus it affords to the sense, and a sort of infinitude which it hath, like space and time, make all matter gay. Even the corpse hath its own beauty. But beside this general grace diffused over nature, almost all the individual forms are agreeable to the eye, as is proved by our endless imitations of some of them, as the acorn, the grape, the pine-cone, the wheat-ear, the egg, the wings and forms of most birds, the lion's claw, the serpent, the butterfly, sea-shells, flames, clouds, buds, leaves, and the forms of many trees, as the palm.

For better consideration, we may distribute the aspects of Beauty in a threefold manner.

1. First, the simple perception of natural forms is a delight. The influence of the forms and actions in nature, is so needful to man, that, in its lowest functions, it seems to lie on the confines of commodity and beauty. To the body and mind which have been cramped by noxious work or company, nature is medicinal and restores their tone. The tradesman, the attorney comes out of the din and craft[14] of the street, and sees the sky and the woods, and is a man again. In their eternal calm, he finds himself. The health of the eye seems to demand a horizon. We are never tired, so long as we can see far enough.

But in other hours, Nature satisfies the soul purely by its loveliness, and without any mixture of corporeal benefit. I have seen the spectacle of morning from the hill-top over against my house, from day-break to sun-rise, with emotions which an angel might share. The long slender bars of cloud float like fishes in the sea of crimson light. From the earth, as a shore, I look out into that silent sea. I seem to partake its rapid transformations: the active enchantment reaches my dust, and I dilate and conspire[15] with the morning wind. How does Nature deify us with a few and cheap elements! Give me health and a day, and I will make the pomp of emperors ridiculous. The dawn is my Assyria;[16] the sun-set and moon-rise my Paphos,[17] and unimaginable realms of faerie; broad noon shall be my England of the senses and the understanding; the night shall be my Germany of mystic philosophy and dreams.[18]

Not less excellent, except for our less susceptibility in the afternoon, was the charm, last evening, of a January sunset. The western clouds divided and subdivided themselves into pink flakes modulated with tints of unspeakable softness; and the air had so much life and sweetness, that it was a pain to come within doors. What was it that nature would say? Was there no meaning in the live repose of the valley behind the mill, and which Homer or Shakespeare could not re-form for me in words? The leafless trees become spires of flame in the sunset, with the blue east for their background, and the stars of the dead calices[19] of flowers, and

---

[14] Craftiness, scheming.   [15] Breathe.

[16] An ancient Near Eastern empire legendary for its wealth.

[17] An ancient city on the island of Cyprus known for its worship of the Greek love goddess Aphrodite.

[18] The English philosophers Emerson read tended to be rational empiricists, whereas the German philosophers were idealists.

[19] Calyxes, the cuplike outer coverings at the base of flowers.

every withered stem and stubble rimed with frost, contribute something to the mute music.

The inhabitants of cities suppose that the country landscape is pleasant only half the year. I please myself with observing the graces of the winter scenery, and believe that we are as much touched by it as by the genial influences of summer. To the attentive eye, each moment of the year has its own beauty, and in the same field, it beholds, every hour, a picture which was never seen before, and which shall never be seen again. The heavens change every moment, and reflect their glory or gloom on the plains beneath. The state of the crop in the surrounding farms alters the expression of the earth from week to week. The succession of native plants in the pastures and road-sides, which make the silent clock by which time tells the summer hours, will make even the divisions of the day sensible to a keen observer. The tribes of birds and insects, like the plants punctual to their time, follow each other, and the year has room for all. By water-courses, the variety is greater. In July, the blue pontederia or pickerel-weed blooms in large beds in the shallow parts of our pleasant river,[20] and swarms with yellow butter-flies in continual motion. Art cannot rival this pomp of purple and gold. Indeed the river is a perpetual gala, and boasts each month a new ornament.

But this beauty of Nature which is seen and felt as beauty, is the least part. The shows of day, the dewy morning, the rainbow, mountains, orchards in blossom, stars, moonlight, shadows in still water, and the like, if too eagerly hunted, become shows merely, and mock us with their unreality. Go out of the house to see the moon, and 't is mere tinsel; it will not please as when its light shines upon your necessary journey. The beauty that shimmers in the yellow afternoons of October, who ever could clutch it? Go forth to find it, and it is gone: 't is only a mirage as you look from the windows of diligence.

2. The presence of a higher, namely, of the spiritual element is essential to its perfection. The high and divine beauty which can be loved without effeminacy, is that which is found in combination with the human will, and never separate. Beauty is the mark God sets upon virtue. Every natural action is graceful. Every heroic act is also decent,[21] and causes the place and the bystanders to shine. We are taught by great actions that the universe is the property of every individual in it. Every rational creature has all nature for his dowry and estate. It is his, if he will. He may divest himself of it; he may creep into a corner, and abdicate his kingdom, as most men do, but he is entitled to the world by his constitution. In proportion to the energy of thought and will, he takes up the world into himself. "All those things for which men plough, build, or sail, obey virtue;" said an ancient historian.[22] "The winds and waves," said Gibbon,[23] "are always on the side of the ablest navigators." So are the sun and moon and all the stars of heaven. When a noble act is done,—perchance in a scene of great natural beauty; when Leonidas[24] and his three hundred martyrs consume one day in dying, and the sun and moon come each and look at them once in the steep defile of Thermopylæ;

---

[20] The Concord River, near Emerson's home in Concord, Massachusetts.

[21] Honorable, suitably elegant.

[22] Gaius Sallustius Crispus, or Sallust (86–35 B.C.), a Roman historian; from one of Sallust's monographs, *The Conspiracy of Catiline*.

[23] Edward Gibbon (1737–1794), an English historian; from *The Decline and Fall of the Roman Empire* (1788).

[24] King Leonidas (?–480 B.C.) of Sparta, commander of the Greek forces at Thermopylae, who was killed while defending the pass against the Persian army led by Xerxes.

when Arnold Winkelried,[25] in the high Alps, under the shadow of the avalanche, gathers in his side a sheaf of Austrian spears to break the line for his comrades; are not these heroes entitled to add the beauty of the scene to the beauty of the deed? When the bark of Columbus nears the shore of America;—before it, the beach lined with savages, fleeing out of all their huts of cane; the sea behind; and the purple mountains of the Indian Archipelago around, can we separate the man from the living picture? Does not the New World clothe his form with her palm-groves and savannahs as fit drapery? Ever does natural beauty steal in like air, and envelope great actions. When Sir Harry Vane[26] was dragged up the Tower-hill, sitting on a sled, to suffer death, as the champion of the English laws, one of the multitude cried out to him, "You never sate on so glorious a seat." Charles II, to intimidate the citizens of London, caused the patriot Lord Russell[27] to be drawn in an open coach, through the principal streets of the city, on his way to the scaffold. "But," to use the simple narrative of his biographer, "the multitude imagined they saw liberty and virtue sitting by his side." In private places, among sordid objects, an act of truth or heroism seems at once to draw to itself the sky as its temple, the sun as its candle. Nature stretcheth out her arms to embrace man, only let his thoughts be of equal greatness. Willingly does she follow his steps with the rose and the violet, and bend her lines of grandeur and grace to the decoration of her darling child. Only let his thoughts be of equal scope, and the frame will suit the picture. A virtuous man is in unison with her works, and makes the central figure of the visible sphere. Homer, Pindar, Socrates, Phocion,[28] associate themselves fitly in our memory with the whole geography and climate of Greece. The visible heavens and earth sympathize with Jesus. And in common life, whosoever has seen a person of powerful character and happy genius, will have remarked how easily he took all things along with him,—the persons, the opinions, and the day, and nature became ancillary to a man.

3. There is still another aspect under which the beauty of the world may be viewed, namely, as it becomes an object of the intellect. Beside the relation of things to virtue, they have a relation to thought. The intellect searches out the absolute order of things as they stand in the mind of God, and without the colors of affection. The intellectual and the active powers seem to succeed each other in man, and the exclusive activity of the one, generates the exclusive activity of the other. There is something unfriendly in each to the other, but they are like the alternate periods of feeding and working in animals; each prepares and certainly will be followed by the other. Therefore does beauty, which, in relation to actions, as we have seen, comes unsought, and comes because it is unsought, remain for the apprehension and pursuit of the intellect; and then again, in its turn, of the active power. Nothing divine dies. All good is eternally reproductive. The beauty of nature reforms itself in the mind, and not for barren contemplation, but for new creation.

All men are in some degree impressed by the face of the world; some men even to delight. This love of beauty is Taste. Others have the same love in such excess,

---

[25] Winkelried (?–1386) was a Swiss hero killed in the Battle of Sempach against the Austrians.

[26] Vane (1613–1662), Puritan colonial governor of Massachusetts from 1636 to 1637, was executed for treason when Charles II was restored to the throne of England.

[27] William Russell (1639–1683), executed for plotting to overthrow Charles II.

[28] Homer was the eighth- or the ninth-century B.C. Greek epic poet who wrote *The Iliad* and *The Odyssey;* Pindar (522?–438? B.C.), a Greek lyric poet, was renowned for his odes; Socrates (469–399 B.C.) was the famed Athenian philosopher who was Plato's mentor; Phocion (402?–318 B.C.) was an Athenian general and statesman as well as a popular and effective orator.

that, not content with admiring, they seek to embody it in new forms. The creation of beauty is Art.

The production of a work of art throws a light upon the mystery of humanity. A work of art is an abstract or epitome of the world. It is the result or expression of nature, in miniature. For although the works of nature are innumerable and all different, the result or the expression of them all is similar and single. Nature is a sea of forms radically alike and even unique. A leaf, a sun-beam, a landscape, the ocean, make an analogous impression on the mind. What is common to them all,—that perfectness and harmony, is beauty. Therefore the standard of beauty is the entire circuit of natural forms,—the totality of nature; which the Italians expressed by defining beauty "il piu nell' uno."[29] Nothing is quite beautiful alone; nothing but is beautiful in the whole. A single object is only so far beautiful as it suggests this universal grace. The poet, the painter, the sculptor, the musician, the architect, seek each to concentrate this radiance of the world on one point, and each in his several work to satisfy the love of beauty which stimulates him to produce. Thus is Art, a nature passed through the alembic[30] of man. Thus in art, does nature work through the will of a man filled with the beauty of her first works.

The world thus exists to the soul to satisfy the desire of beauty. Extend this element to the uttermost, and I call it an ultimate end. No reason can be asked or given why the soul seeks beauty. Beauty, in its largest and profoundest sense, is one expression for the universe. God is the all-fair. Truth, and goodness, and beauty, are but different faces of the same All. But beauty in nature is not ultimate. It is the herald of inward and eternal beauty, and is not alone a solid and satisfactory good. It must therefore stand as a part and not as yet the last or highest expression of the final cause of Nature.

CHAPTER IV: LANGUAGE

A third use which Nature subserves to man is that of Language. Nature is the vehicle of thought, and in a simple, double, and three-fold degree.

1. Words are signs of natural facts.
2. Particular natural facts are symbols of particular spiritual facts.
3. Nature is the symbol of spirit.

1. Words are signs of natural facts. The use of natural history is to give us aid in supernatural history. The use of the outer creation is to give us language for the beings and changes of the inward creation. Every word which is used to express a moral or intellectual fact, if traced to its root, is found to be borrowed from some material appearance. *Right* originally means *straight; wrong* means *twisted. Spirit* primarily means *wind; transgression,* the crossing of a *line; supercilious,* the *raising of the eye-brow.* We say the *heart* to express emotion, the *head* to denote thought; and *thought* and *emotion* are, in their turn, words borrowed from sensible things, and now appropriated to spiritual nature. Most of the process by which this transformation is made, is hidden from us in the remote time when language was framed; but the same tendency may be daily observed in children. Children and

---

[29] "The many in one" (Italian). In his poem "Each and All" (1839), Emerson expresses this idea in the lines, "All are needed by each one; / Nothing is fair or good alone."
[30] An apparatus for distilling or refining.

savages use only nouns or names of things, which they continually convert into verbs, and apply to analogous mental acts.

2. But this origin of all words that convey a spiritual import,—so conspicuous a fact in the history of language,—is our least debt to nature. It is not words only that are emblematic; it is things which are emblematic. Every natural fact is a symbol of some spiritual fact. Every appearance in nature corresponds to some state of the mind, and that state of the mind can only be described by presenting that natural appearance as its picture. An enraged man is a lion, a cunning man is a fox, a firm man is a rock, a learned man is a torch. A lamb is innocence; a snake is subtle spite; flowers express to us the delicate affections. Light and darkness are our familiar expression for knowledge and ignorance; and heat for love. Visible distance behind and before us, is respectively our image of memory and hope.

Who looks upon a river in a meditative hour, and is not reminded of the flux of all things? Throw a stone into the stream, and the circles that propagate themselves are the beautiful type of all influence. Man is conscious of a universal soul within or behind his individual life, wherein, as in a firmament, the natures of Justice, Truth, Love. Freedom, arise and shine. This universal soul, he calls Reason:[31] it is not mine or thine or his, but we are its; we are its property and men. And the blue sky in which the private earth is buried, the sky with its eternal calm, and full of everlasting orbs, is the type of Reason. That which, intellectually considered, we call Reason, considered in relation to nature, we call Spirit. Spirit is the Creator. Spirit hath life in itself. And man in all ages and countries, embodies it in his language, as the FATHER.

It is easily seen that there is nothing lucky or capricious in these analogies, but that they are constant, and pervade nature. These are not the dreams of a few poets, here and there, but man is an analogist, and studies relations in all objects. He is placed in the centre of beings, and a ray of relation passes from every other being to him. And neither can man be understood without these objects, nor these objects without man. All the facts in natural history taken by themselves, have no value, but are barren like a single sex. But marry it to human history, and it is full of life. Whole Floras, all Linnæus' and Buffon's[32] volumes, are but dry catalogues of facts; but the most trivial of these facts, the habit of a plant, the organs, or work, or noise of an insect, applied to the illustration of a fact in intellectual philosophy, or, in any way associated to human nature, affects us in the most lively and agreeable manner. The seed of a plant,—to what affecting analogies in the nature of man, is that little fruit made use of, in all discourse, up to the voice of Paul, who calls the human corpse a seed,—"It is sown a natural body; it is raised a spiritual body."[33] The motion of the earth round its axis, and round the sun, makes the day, and the year. These are certain amounts of brute light and heat. But is there no intent of an analogy between man's life and the seasons? And do the seasons gain no grandeur or pathos from that analogy? The instincts of the ant are very unimportant considered as the ant's; but the moment a ray of relation is seen to extend from it to man, and the little drudge is seen to be a monitor, a little body with a mighty heart, then all its habits, even that said to be recently observed, that it never sleeps, become sublime.

[31] By "Reason" Emerson means an intuitive power within, which is bestowed by the "universal soul." He uses the term "Understanding" to signify the rational powers of the human being.

[32] Carolus Linnaeus, or Carl von Linné (1707–1778), a Swedish botanist and taxonomist; Comte de Buffon (1707–1788), a French naturalist. Both men devised elaborate classification schemes for plants ("Floras").

[33] The Apostle Paul, from I Corinthians 15:44.

Because of this radical[34] correspondence between visible things and human thoughts, savages, who have only what is necessary, converse in figures. As we go back in history, language becomes more picturesque, until its infancy, when it is all poetry; or, all spiritual facts are represented by natural symbols. The same symbols are found to make the original elements of all languages. It has moreover been observed, that the idioms of all languages approach each other in passages of the greatest eloquence and power. And as this is the first language, so is it the last. This immediate dependence of language upon nature, this conversion of an outward phenomenon into a type of somewhat in human life, never loses its power to affect us. It is this which gives that piquancy to the conversation of a strong-natured farmer or back-woodsman, which all men relish.

Thus is nature an interpreter, by whose means man converses with his fellow men. A man's power to connect his thought with its proper symbol, and so to utter it, depends on the simplicity of his character, that is, upon his love of truth and his desire to communicate it without loss. The corruption of man is followed by the corruption of langauge. When simplicity of character and the sovereignty of ideas is broken up by the prevalence of secondary desires, the desire of riches, the desire of pleasure, the desire of power, the desire of praise,—and duplicity and falsehood take place of simplicity and truth, the power over nature as an interpreter of the will, is in a degree lost; new imagery ceases to be created, and old words are perverted to stand for things which are not; a paper currency is employed when there is no bullion in the vaults. In due time, the fraud is manifest, and words lose all power to stimulate the understanding or the affections. Hundreds of writers may be found in every long-civilized nation, who for a short time believe, and make others believe, that they see and utter truths, who do not of themselves clothe one thought in its natural garment, but who feed unconsciously upon the language created by the primary writers of the country, those, namely, who hold primarily on nature.

But wise men pierce this rotten diction and fasten words again to visible things: so that picturesque language is at once a commanding certificate that he who employs it, is a man in alliance with truth and God. The moment our discourse rises above the ground line of familiar facts, and is inflamed with passion or exalted by thought, it clothes itself in images. A man conversing in earnest, if he watch his intellectual processes, will find that always a material image, more or less luminous, arises in his mind, cotemporaneous with every thought, which furnishes the vestment of the thought. Hence, good writing and brilliant discourse are perpetual allegories. This imagery is spontaneous. It is the blending of experience with the present action of the mind. It is proper creation. It is the working of the Original Cause through the instruments he has already made.

These facts may suggest the advantage which the country-life possesses for a powerful mind, over the artificial and curtailed life of cities. We know more from nature than we can at will communicate. Its light flows into the mind evermore, and we forget its presence. The poet, the orator, bred in the woods, whose senses have been nourished by their fair and appeasing changes, year after year, without design and without heed,—shall not lose their lesson altogether, in the roar of cities or the broil of politics. Long hereafter, amidst agitation and terror in national councils,—in the hour of revolution,—these solemn images shall reappear in their morning lustre, as fit symbols and words of the thoughts which the passing events

---

[34] Root.

shall awaken. At the call of a noble sentiment, again the woods wave, the pines murmur, the river rolls and shines, and the cattle low upon the mountains, as he saw and heard them in his infancy. And with these forms, the spells of persuasion, the keys of power are put into his hands.

3. We are thus assisted by natural objects in the expression of particular meanings. But how great a language to convey such peppercorn[35] informations! Did it need such noble races of creatures, this profusion of forms, this host of orbs in heaven, to furnish man with the dictionary and grammar of his municipal[36] speech? Whilst we use this grand cipher to expedite the affairs of our pot and kettle, we feel that we have not yet put it to its use, neither are able. We are like travellers using the cinders of a volcano to roast their eggs. Whilst we see that it always stands ready to clothe what we would say, we cannot avoid the question, whether the characters are not significant of themselves. Have mountains, and waves, and skies, no significance but what we consciously give them, when we employ them as emblems of our thoughts? The world is emblematic. Parts of speech are metaphors because the whole of nature is a metaphor of the human mind. The laws of moral nature answer to those of matter as face to face in a glass. "The visible world and the relation of its parts, is the dial plate of the invisible."[37] The axioms of physics translate the laws of ethics. Thus, "the whole is greater than its part;" "reaction is equal to action;" "the smallest weight may be made to lift the greatest, the difference of weight being compensated by time;" and many the like propositions, which have an ethical as well as physical sense. These propositions have a much more extensive and universal sense when applied to human life, than when confined to technical use.

In like manner, the memorable words of history, and the proverbs of nations, consist usually of a natural fact, selected as a picture or parable of a moral truth. Thus; A rolling stone gathers no moss; A bird in the hand is worth two in the bush; A cripple in the right way, will beat a racer in the wrong; Make hay whilst the sun shines; 'T is hard to carry a full cup even; Vinegar is the son of wine; The last ounce broke the camel's back; Long-lived trees make roots first;—and the like. In their primary sense these are trivial facts, but we repeat them for the value of their analogical import. What is true of proverbs, is true of all fables, parables, and allegories.

This relation between the mind and matter is not fancied by some poet, but stands in the will of God, and so is free to be known by all men. It appears to men, or it does not appear. When in fortunate hours we ponder this miracle, the wise man doubts, if, at all other times, he is not blind and deaf;

> ——"Can these things be,
> And overcome us like a summer's cloud,
> Without our special wonder?"[38]

for the universe becomes transparent, and the light of higher laws than its own, shines through it. It is the standing problem which has exercised the wonder and the study of every fine genius since the world began; from the era of the Egyptians

---

[35] Trifling.   [36] Local, ordinary.

[37] From the Swedish theologian and mystic Emanuel Swedenborg (1688–1772), whose ideas of correspondence between the spiritual and the natural world interested Emerson deeply.

[38] From Shakespeare's *Macbeth* (III. iv. 110–112), which actually reads, "Can *such* things be. . . . "

and the Brahmins,[39] to that of Pythagoras, of Plato, of Bacon, of Leibnitz,[40] of Swedenborg. There sits the Sphinx[41] at the road-side, and from age to age, as each prophet comes by, he tries his fortune at reading her riddle. There seems to be a necessity in spirit to manifest itself in material forms; and day and night, river and storm, beast and bird, acid and alkali, preëxist in necessary Ideas in the mind of God, and are what they are by virtue of preceding affections,[42] in the world of spirit. A Fact is the end or last issue of spirit. The visible creation is the terminus or the circumference of the invisible world. "Material objects," said a French philosopher,[43] "are necessarily kinds of *scoriæ* of the substantial thoughts of the Creator, which must always preserve an exact relation to their first origin; in other words, visible nature must have a spiritual and moral side."

This doctrine is abstruse, and though the images of "garment," "scoriæ," "mirror," may stimulate the fancy, we must summon the aid of subtler and more vital expositors to make it plain. "Every scripture is to be interpreted by the same spirit which gave it forth,"[44]—is the fundamental law of criticism. A life in harmony with nature, the love of truth and of virtue, will purge the eyes to understand her text. By degrees we may come to know the primitive sense of the permanent objects of nature, so that the world shall be to us an open book, and every form significant of its hidden life and final cause.

A new interest surprises us, whilst, under the view now suggested, we contemplate the fearful extent and multitude of objects; since "every object rightly seen, unlocks a new faculty of the soul."[45] That which was unconscious truth, becomes, when interpreted and defined in an object, a part of the domain of knowledge,—a new weapon in the magazine[46] of power.

CHAPTER V: DISCIPLINE

In view of this significance of nature, we arrive at once at a new fact, that nature is a discipline. This use of the world includes the preceding uses, as parts of itself.

Space, time, society, labor, climate, food, locomotion, the animals, the mechanical forces, give us sincerest lessons, day by day, whose meaning is unlimited. They educate both the Understanding and the Reason. Every property of matter is a school for the understanding,—its solidity or resistance, its inertia, its extension, its figure, its divisibility. The understanding adds, divides, combines,

---

[39] Brahmans, members of a priestly Hindu caste, named after Brahma, the supreme soul of the Hindu universe.

[40] Pythagoras was a sixth-century B.C. Greek philosopher who believed in the transmigration of souls and claimed he could remember his earlier incarnations; Plato (428–347 B.C.) was the most influential source of idealism in Western philosophical thought; Sir Francis Bacon (1561–1626) was an English statesman and philosopher who championed the inductive method; Gottfried Wilhelm Leibnitz (1646–1716) was a German mathematician and idealist philosopher and the founder of symbolic logic.

[41] According to Greek myth, a winged monster who killed all who failed to answer her riddle. (When Oedipus answered the riddle correctly, she killed herself.)

[42] All things preexist in the mind of God and exist in the world of spirit before they exist in the world of fact.

[43] Guillaume Oegger, in *The True Messiah* (1829); *scoriae* means slag or refuse from melting metals.

[44] From George Fox (1624–1691), an English mystic and founder of the Society of Friends (Quakers) in 1668.

[45] From *Aids to Reflection* (1825), by Samuel Taylor Coleridge (1772–1834).   [46] A storehouse.

measures, and finds everlasting nutriment and room for its activity in this worthy scene. Meantime, Reason transfers all these lessons into its own world of thought, by perceiving the analogy that marries Matter and Mind.

I. Nature is a discipline of the understanding in intellectual truths. Our dealing with sensible objects is a constant exercise in the necessary lessons of difference, of likeness, of order, of being and seeming, of progressive arrangement; of ascent from particular to general; of combination to one end of manifold forces. Proportioned to the importance of the organ to be formed, is the extreme care with which its tuition[47] is provided,—a care pretermitted[48] in no single case. What tedious training, day after day, year after year, never ending, to form the common sense; what continual reproduction of annoyances, inconveniences, dilemmas; what rejoicing over us of little men; what disputing of prices, what reckonings of interest,—and all to form the Hand of the mind;—to instruct us that "good thoughts are no better than good dreams, unless they be executed!"[49]

The same good office is performed by Property and its filial systems of debt and credit. Debt, grinding debt, whose iron face the widow, the orphan, and the sons of genius fear and hate;—debt, which consumes so much time, which so cripples and disheartens a great spirit with cares that seem so base, is a preceptor whose lessons cannot be foregone, and is needed most by those who suffer from it most. Moreover, property, which has been well compared to snow,—"if it fall level to-day, it will be blown into drifts to-morrow,"—is merely the surface action of internal machinery, like the index on the face of a clock. Whilst now it is the gymnastics of the understanding, it is hiving in the foresight of the spirit, experience in profounder laws.

The whole character and fortune of the individual are affected by the least inequalities in the culture of the understanding; for example, in the perception of differences. Therefore is Space, and therefore Time, that man may know that things are not huddled and lumped, but sundered and individual. A bell and a plough have each their use, and neither can do the office of the other. Water is good to drink, coal to burn, wool to wear; but wool cannot be drunk, nor water spun, nor coal eaten. The wise man shows his wisdom in separation, in gradation, and his scale of creatures and of merits, is as wide as nature. The foolish have no range in their scale, but suppose every man is as every other man. What is not good they call the worst, and what is not hateful, they call the best.

In like manner, what good heed, nature forms in us! She pardons no mistakes. Her yea is yea, and her nay, nay.

The first steps in Agriculture, Astronomy, Zoölogy, (those first steps which the farmer, the hunter, and the sailor take,) teach that nature's dice are always loaded; that in her heaps and rubbish are concealed sure and useful results.

How calmly and genially the mind apprehends one after another the laws of physics! What noble emotions dilate the mortal as he enters into the counsels of the creation, and feels by knowledge the privilege to BE! His insight refines him. The beauty of nature shines in his own breast. Man is greater that he can see this, and the universe less, because Time and Space relations vanish as laws are known.

Here again we are impressed and even daunted by the immense Universe to be

---

[47] Care, guardianship.   [48] Omitted, neglected.
[49] Paraphrased from the essay "Of Great Place" in Francis Bacon's *Essays* (1625).

explored. 'What we know, is a point to what we do not know.'[50] Open any recent journal of science, and weigh the problems suggested concerning Light, Heat, Electricity, Magnetism, Physiology, Geology, and judge whether the interest of natural science is likely to be soon exhausted.

Passing by many particulars of the discipline of nature we must not omit to specify two.

The exercise of the Will or the lesson of power is taught in every event. From the child's successive possession of his several senses up to the hour when he saith, "thy will be done!"[51] he is learning the secret, that he can reduce under his will, not only particular events, but great classes, nay the whole series of events, and so conform all facts to his character. Nature is thoroughly mediate. It is made to serve. It receives the dominion of man as meekly as the ass on which the Saviour rode.[52] It offers all its kingdoms to man as the raw material which he may mould into what is useful. Man is never weary of working it up. He forges the subtile and delicate air into wise and melodious words, and gives them wing as angles of persuasion and command. More and more, with every thought, does his kingdom stretch over things, until the world becomes, at last, only a realized will,—the double of the man.

2. Sensible objects conform to the premonitions of Reason and reflect the conscience. All things are moral; and in their boundless changes have an unceasing reference to spiritual nature. Therefore is nature glorious with form, color, and motion, that every globe in the remotest heaven; every chemical change from the rudest crystal up to the laws of life; every change of vegetation from the first principle of growth in the eye of a leaf, to the tropical forest and antediluvian[53] coal-mine; every animal function from the sponge up to Hercules,[54] shall hint or thunder to man the laws of right and wrong, and echo the Ten Commandments. Therefore is nature ever the ally of Religion: lends all her pomp and riches to the religious sentiment. Prophet and priest, David, Isaiah,[55] Jesus, have drawn deeply from this source.

This ethical character so penetrates the bone and marrow of nature, as to seem the end for which it was made. Whatever private purpose is answered by any member or part, this is its public and universal function, and is never omitted. Nothing in nature is exhausted in its first use. When a thing has served an end to the uttermost, it is wholly new for an ulterior service. In God, every end is converted into a new means. Thus the use of Commodity, regarded by itself, is mean and squalid. But it is to the mind an education in the great doctrine of Use, namely, that a thing is good only so far as it serves; that a conspiring of parts and efforts to the production of an end, is essential to any being. The first and gross manifestation of this truth, is our inevitable and hated training in values and wants, in corn and meat.

[50] An aphorism variously attrubuted to the English moralist Bishop Joseph Butler (1692–1752) in the British novel *Tremaine* (1825), by Robert P. Ward, and to the English mathematician and physicist Sir Isaac Newton (1642–1727). The idea has undoubtedly occurred to many other people.

[51] From the Lord's Prayer (Matthew 6:10, 26:42).

[52] "Behold, thy King cometh unto thee, meek, and sitting upon an ass," from Matthew 21:5.

[53] Before the biblical Flood, in Genesis 6:9 the Flood destroyed all creatures not on Noah's Ark.

[54] According to Greek myth, a hero renowned for feats of strength. Here Emerson is saying that ethics applies to life from the simplest animal to the most developed human being.

[55] The second king of Israel, and an Old Testament prophet.

It has already been illustrated, in treating of the significance of material things, that every natural process is but a version of a moral sentence. The moral law lies at the centre of nature and radiates to the circumference. It is the pith and marrow of every substance, every relation, and every process. All things with which we deal, preach to us. What is a farm but a mute gospel? The chaff and the wheat, weeds and plants, blight, rain, insects, sun,—it is a sacred emblem from the first furrow of spring to the last stack which the snow of winter overtakes in the fields. But the sailor, the shepherd, the miner, the merchant, in their several resorts, have each an experience precisely parallel and leading to the same conclusion: because all organizations are radically alike. Nor can it be doubted that this moral sentiment which thus scents the air, and grows in the grain, and impregnates the waters of the world, is caught by man and sinks into his soul. The moral influence of nature upon every individual is that amount of truth which it illustrates to him. Who can estimate this? Who can guess how much firmness the sea-beaten rock has taught the fisherman? how much tranquillity has been reflected to man from the azure sky, over whose unspotted deeps the winds forevermore drive flocks of stormy clouds, and leave no wrinkle or stain? how much industry and providence and affection we have caught from the pantomine of brutes? What a searching preacher of self-command is the varying phenomenon of Health!

Herein is especially apprehended the Unity of Nature,—the Unity in Variety,—which meets us everywhere. All the endless variety of things make a unique, an identical impression. Xenophanes[56] complained in his old age, that, look where he would, all things hastened back to Unity. He was weary of seeing the same entity in the tedious variety of forms. The fable of Proteus[57] has a cordial truth. Every particular in nature, a leaf, a drop, a crystal, a moment of time is related to the whole, and partakes of the perfection of the whole. Each particle is a microcosm, and faithfully renders the likeness of the world.

Not only resemblances exist in things whose analogy is obvious, as when we detect the type of the human hand in the flipper of the fossil saurus,[58] but also in objects wherein there is great superficial unlikeness. Thus architecture is called "frozen music," by De Stael and Goethe.[59] Vitruvius[60] thought an architect should be a musician. "A Gothic church," said Coleridge, "is a petrified religion."[61] Michael Angelo maintained, that, to an architect, a knowledge of anatomy is essential.[62] In Haydn's oratorios,[63] the notes present to the imagination not only motions, as, of the snake, the stag, and the elephant, but colors also; as the green grass. The law of harmonic sounds reappears in the harmonic colors. The granite is differenced in its laws only by the more or less of heat, from the river that wears it away. The river, as it flows, resembles the air that flows over it; the air resembles the light which traverses it with more subtile currents; the light resembles the

[56] Xenophanes (570–480 B.C.) was a Greek philosopher who taught that God is single and eternal.

[57] According to Greek myth, a sea god who could assume various shapes.

[58] Fossils of extinct reptiles.

[59] The French writer Anne Louise Germaine (1766–1817), or Mme. de Staël; the German poet and novelist Johann Wolfgang von Goethe (1749–1832).

[60] Vitruvius Pollio (50?–26 B.C.), a Roman writer on architecture.

[61] From Coleridge's "Lecture on the General Character of the Gothic Mind in the Middle Ages" (1836).

[62] In Volume V of his *Journals and Miscellaneous Notebooks* (1966), Emerson records this statement from the sketch of Michelangelo in *Lives of Eminent Persons* (1833), published in London under the auspices of the Society for the Diffusion of Useful Knowledge.

[63] Choral music of the Austrian composer Franz Joseph Haydn (1732–1809).

heat which rides with it through Space. Each creature is only a modification of the other; the likeness in them is more than the difference, and their radical law is one and the same. Hence it is, that a rule of one art, or a law of one organization, holds true throughout nature. So intimate is this Unity, that, it is easily seen, it lies under the undermost garment of nature, and betrays its source in universal Spirit. For, it pervades Thought also. Every universal truth which we express in words, implies or supposes every other truth. *Omne verum vero consonat.*[64] It is like a great circle on a sphere, comprising all possible circles; which, however, may be drawn, and comprise it, in like manner. Every such truth is the absolute Ens[65] seen from one side. But it has innumerable sides.

The same central Unity is still more conspicuous in actions. Words are finite organs of the infinite mind. They cannot cover the dimensions of what is in truth. They break, chop, and impoverish it. An action is the perfection and publication of thought. A right action seems to fill the eye, and to be related to all nature. "The wise man, in doing one thing, does all; or, in the one thing he does rightly, he sees the likeness of all which is done rightly."[66]

Words and actions are not the attributes of mute and brute nature. They introduce us to the human form, of which all other organizations appear to be degradations. When this organization appears among so many that surround it, the spirit prefers it to all others. It says, 'From such as this, have I drawn joy and knowledge. In such as this, have I found and beheld myself. I will speak to it. It can speak again. It can yield me thought already formed and alive.' In fact, the eye,— the mine,—is always accompanied by these forms, male and female; and these are incomparably the richest informations of the power and order that lie at the heart of things. Unfortunately, every one of them bears the marks as of some injury; is marred and superficially defective. Nevertheless, far different from the deaf and dumb nature around them, these all rest like fountain-pipes on the unfathomed sea of thought and virtue whereto they alone, of all organizations, are the entrances.

It were a pleasant inquiry to follow into detail their ministry to our education, but where would it stop? We are associated in adolescent and adult life with some friends, who, like skies and waters, are coextensive with our idea; who, answering each to a certain affection of the soul, satisfy our desire on that side; whom we lack power to put at such focal distance from us, that we can mend or even analayze them. We cannot chuse but love them. When much intercourse with a friend has supplied us with a standard of exellence, and has increased our respect for the resources of God who thus sends a real person to outgo our ideal; when he has, moreover, become an object of thought, and, whilst his character retains all its unconscious effect, is converted in the mind into solid and sweet wisdom,—it is a sign to us that his office is closing, and he is commonly withdrawn from our sight in a short time.

Chapter VI: Idealism

Thus is the unspeakable but intelligible and practicable meaning of the world conveyed to man, the immortal pupil, in every object of sense. To this one end of Discipline, all parts of nature conspire.

[64] "Every truth is consonant [agrees] with every other truth" (Latin).
[65] "Abstract being" (Latin).   [66] From Goethe's *Wilhelm Meister's Travels* (1821–1829).

A noble doubt perpetually suggests itself, whether this end be not the Final Cause of the Universe; and whether nature outwardly exists.[67] It is a sufficient account of that Appearance we call the World, that God will teach a human mind, and so makes it the receiver of a certain number of congruent sensations, which we call sun and moon, man and woman, house and trade. In my utter impotence to test the authenticity of the report of my senses, to know whether the impressions they make on me correspond with outlying objects, what difference does it make, whether Orion[68] is up there in heaven, or some god paints the image in the firmament of the soul? The relations of parts and the end of the whole remaining the same, what is the difference, whether land and sea interact, and worlds revolve and intermingle without number of end,—deep yawning under deep, and galaxy balancing galaxy, throughout absolute space, or, whether, without relations of time and space, the same appearances are inscribed in the constant faith of man? Whether nature enjoy a substantial existence without, or is only in the apocalypse[69] of the mind, it is alike useful and alike venerable to me. Be it what it may, it is ideal to me, so long as I cannot try the accuracy of my senses.

The frivolous make themselves merry with the Ideal theory, as if its consequences were burlesque; as if it affected the stability of nature. It surely does not. God never jests with us, and will not compromise the end of nature, by permitting any inconsequence in its procession. Any distrust of the permanence of laws, would paralyze the faculties of man. Their permanence is sacredly respected, and his faith therein is perfect. The wheels and springs of man are all set to the hypothesis of the permanence of nature. We are not built like a ship to be tossed, but like a house to stand. It is a natural consequence of this structure, that, so long as the active powers predominate over the reflective, we resist with indignation any hint that nature is more short-lived or mutable than spirit. The broker, the wheelwright, the carpenter, the toll-man, are much displeased at the intimation.

But whilst we acquiesce entirely in the permanence of natural laws, the question of the absolute existence of nature, still remains open. It is the uniform effect of culture on the human mind, not to shake our faith in the stability of particular phenomena, as of heat, water, azote;[70] but to lead us to regard nature as a phenomenon, not a substance; to attribute necessary existence to spirit; to esteem nature as an accident and an effect.

To the senses and the unrenewed understanding, belongs a sort of instinctive belief in the absolute existence of nature. In their view, man and nature are indissolubly joined. Things are ultimates, and they never look beyond their sphere. The presence of Reason mars this faith. The first effort of thought tends to relax this despotism of the senses, which binds us to nature as if we were a part of it, and shows us nature aloof, and, as it were, afloat. Until this higher agency intervened, the animal eye sees, with wonderful accuracy, sharp outlines and colored surfaces. When the eye of Reason opens, to outline and surface are at once added, grace and expression. These proceed from imagination and affection, and abate somewhat of the angular distinctness of objects. If the Reason be stimulated to more earnest vision, outlines and surfaces become transparent, and are no longer seen; causes and spirits are seen through them. The best, the happiest moments of life, are these delicious awakenings of the higher powers, and the reverential withdrawing of nature before its God.

---

[67] This is the crucial question of philosophical idealism (what Emerson calls "the Ideal theory" in his next paragraph).
[68] The hunter, a constellation seen near the equator.   [69] Revelation.   [70] Nitrogen.

Let us proceed to indicate the effects of culture. 1. Our first institution[71] in the Ideal philosophy is a hint from nature herself.

Nature is made to conspire with spirit to emancipate us. Certain mechanical changes, a small alteration in our local position apprizes us of a dualism. We are strangely affected by seeing the shore from a moving ship, from a balloon, or through the tints of an unusual sky. The least change in our point of view, gives the whole world a pictorial air. A man who seldom rides, needs only to get into a coach and traverse his own town, to turn the street into a puppetshow. The men, the women,—talking, running, bartering, fighting,—the earnest mechanic,[72] the lounger, the beggar, the boys, the dogs, are unrealized[73] at once, or, at least, wholly detached from all relation to the observer, and seen as apparent, not substantial beings. What new thoughts are suggested by seeing a face of country quite familiar, in the rapid movement of the rail-road car! Nay, the most wonted objects, (make a very slight change in the point of vision,) please us most. In a camera obscura,[74] the butcher's cart, and the figure of one of our own family amuse us. So a portrait of a well-known face gratifies us. Turn the eyes upside down, by looking at the landscape through your legs, and how agreeable is the picture, though you have seen it any time these twenty years!

In these cases, by mechanical means, is suggested the difference between the observer and the spectacle,—between man and nature. Hence arises a pleasure mixed with awe; I may say, a low degree of the sublime is felt from the fact, probably, that man is hereby apprized, that, whilst the world is a spectacle, something in himself is stable.

2. In a higher manner, the poet communicates the same pleasure. By a few strokes he delineates, as on air, the sun, the mountain, the camp, the city, the hero, the maiden, not different from what we know them, but only lifted from the ground and afloat before the eye. He unfixes the land and the sea, makes them revolve around the axis of his primary thought, and disposes them anew. Possessed himself by a heroic passion, he uses matter as symbols of it. The sensual man conforms thoughts to things; the poet conforms things to his thoughts. The one esteems nature as rooted and fast; the other, as fluid, and impresses his being thereon. To him, the refractory world is ductile and flexible; he invests dust and stones with humanity, and makes them the words of the Reason. The imagination may be defined to be, the use which the Reason makes of the material world. Shakespeare possesses the power of subordinating nature for the purposes of expression, beyond all poets. His imperial muse tosses the creation like a bauble from hand to hand, and uses it to embody any capricious shade of thought that is uppermost in his mind. The remotest spaces of nature are visited, and the farthest sundered things are brought together, by a subtile spiritual connexion. We are made aware that magnitude of material things is merely relative, and all objects shrink and expand to serve the passion of the poet. Thus, in his sonnets, the lays of birds, the scents and dyes of flowers, he finds to be the *shadow* of his beloved; time, which keeps her from him, is his *chest;* the suspicion she has awakened, is her *ornament;*[75]

> The ornament of beauty is Suspect,
> A crow which flies in heaven's sweetest air.[76]

---

[71] Lesson.   [72] Manual worker.   [73] No longer seen (realized) as what they are.
[74] A small chamber or box that reflects an image on a wall; an early version of the camera.
[75] Emerson refers to Shakespeare's Sonnets 98 and 65.   [76] From Shakespeare's Sonnet 70.

His passion is not the fruit of chance; it swells, as he speaks, to a city, or a state.

> No, it was builded far from accident;
> It suffers not in smiling pomp, nor falls
> Under the brow of thralling discontent;
> It fears not policy, that heretic,
> That works on leases of short numbered hours,
> But all alone stands hugely politic.[77]

In the strength of his constancy, the Pyramids seem to him recent and transitory.[78] And the freshness of youth and love dazzles him with its resemblance to morning.

> Take those lips away
> Which so sweetly were forsworn;
> And those eyes,—the break of day,
> Lights that do mislead the morn.[79]

The wild beauty of this hyperbole, I may say, in passing, it would not be easy to match in literature.

This transfiguration which all material objects undergo through the passion of the poet,—this power which he exerts, at any moment, to magnify the small, to micrify[80] the great,—might be illustrated by a thousand examples from his Plays. I have before me the Tempest, and will cite only these few lines.

> ARIEL. The strong based promontory
> Have I made shake, and by the spurs plucked up
> The pine and cedar.

Prospero calls for music to sooth the frantic Alonzo, and his companions;

> A solemn air, and the best comforter
> To an unsettled fancy, cure thy brains
> Now useless, boiled within thy skull.

Again;

> The charm dissolves apace
> And, as the morning steals upon the night,
> Melting the darkness, so their rising senses
> Begin to chase the ignorant fumes that mantle
> Their clearer reason.
> Their understanding

---

[77] From Shakespeare's Sonnet 124.

[78] "Thy pyramids built up with newer might / To me are nothing novel, nothing strange," from Shakespeare's Sonnet 123.

[79] From Shakespeare's *Measure for Measure* (IV. i. 1–4).   [80] To make small or insignificant.

> Begins to swell: and the approaching tide
> Will shortly fill the reasonable shores
> That now lie foul and muddy.[81]

The perception of real affinities between events, that is to say, of *ideal* affinities, for those only are real, enables the poet thus to make free with the most imposing forms and phenomena of the world, and to assert the predominance of the soul.

3. Whilst thus the poet delights us by animating nature like a creator, with his own thoughts, he differs from the philosopher only herein, that the one proposes Beauty as his main end; the other Truth. But, the philosopher, not less than the poet, postpones the apparent order and relations of things to the empire of thought. "The problem of philosophy," according to Plato, "is, for all that exists conditionally, to find a ground unconditioned and absolute."[82] It proceeds on the faith that a law determines all phenomena, which being known, the phenomena can be predicted. That law, when in the mind, is an idea. Its beauty is infinite. The true philosopher and the true poet are one, and a beauty, which is truth, and a truth, which is beauty, is the aim of both. Is not the charm of one of Plato's or Aristotle's definitions, strictly like that of the Antigone of Sophocles?[83] It is, in both cases, that a spiritual life has been imparted to nature; that the solid seeming block of matter has been pervaded and dissolved by a thought; that this feeble human being has penetrated the vast masses of nature with an informing soul, and recognised itself in their harmony, that is, seized their law. In physics, when this is attained, the memory disburthens itself of its cumbrous catalogues of particulars, and carries centuries of observation in a single formula.

Thus even in physics, the material is ever degraded before the spiritual. The astronomer, the geometer, rely on their irrefragable analysis, and disdain the results of observation. The sublime remark of Euler[84] on his law of arches, "This will be found contrary to all experience, yet is true;" had already transferred nature into the mind, and left matter like an outcast corpse.

4. Intellectual science has been observed to beget invariably a doubt of the existence of matter. Turgot[85] said, "He that has never doubted the existence of matter, may be assured he has no aptitude for metaphysical inquiries." It fastens the attention upon immortal necessary uncreated natures, that is, upon Ideas; and in their beautiful and majestic presence, we feel that our outward being is a dream and a shade. Whilst we wait in this Olympus of gods, we think of nature as an appendix to the soul. We ascend into their region, and know that these are the thoughts of the Supreme Being. "These are they who were set up from everlasting, from the beginning, or ever the earth was. When he prepared the heavens, they were there; when he established the clouds above, when he strengthened the fountains of the deep. Then they were by him, as one brought up with him. Of them took he counsel."[86]

---

[81] From Shakespeare's *The Tempest* (V. i. 46–48, 58–60, 64–68, 79–82). Lines 46–48 are spoken by Prospero, not by Ariel.

[82] From Plato's *Republic*, Book V; Emerson took the quotation from Coleridge's *The Friend* (1818).

[83] Aristotle (384–322 B.C.) was an eminent Greek philosopher and a student of Plato; Sophocles (496–406 B.C.) was a Greek dramatist: in his tragedy *Antigone* (441 B.C.), the heroine chooses death rather than compromise sacred principle.

[84] Leonhard Euler (1707–1783), a Swiss mathematician.

[85] Anne Robert Jacques Turgot (1727–1781), a French economist and statesman.

[86] A paraphrase of Proverbs 8:23–30.

Their influence is proportionate. As objects of science, they are accessible to few men. Yet all men are capable of being raised by piety or by passion, into their region. And no man touches these divine natures, without becoming, in some degree, himself divine. Like a new soul, they renew the body. We become physically nimble and lightsome; we tread on air; life is no longer irksome, and we think it will never be so. No man fears age or misfortune or death, in their serene company, for he is transported out of the district of change. Whilst we behold unveiled the nature of Justice and Truth, we learn the difference between the absolute and the conditional or relative. We apprehend the absolute. As it were, for the first time, *we exist*. We become immortal, for we learn that time and space are relations of matter; that, with a perception of truth, or a virtuous will, they have no affinity.

5. Finally, religion and ethics, which may be fitly called,—the practice of ideas, or the introduction of ideas into life,—have an analogous effect with all lower culture, in degrading nature and suggesting its dependence on spirit. Ethics and religion differ herein; that the one is the system of human duties commencing from man; the other, from God. Religion includes the personality of God; Ethics does not. They are one to our present design. They both put nature under foot. The first and last lesson of religion is, "The things that are seen, are temporal; the things that are unseen are eternal."[87] It puts an affront upon nature. It does that for the unschooled, which philosophy does for Berkeley and Viasa.[88] The uniform language that may be heard in the churches of the most ignorant sects, is,—'Contemn the unsubstantial shows of the world; they are vanities, dreams, shadows, unrealities; seek the realities of religion.' The devotee flouts nature. Some theosophists[89] have arrived at a certain hostility and indignation towards matter, as the Manichean[90] and Plotinus. They distrusted in themselves any looking back to these flesh-pots of Egypt.[91] Plotinus was ashamed of his body.[92] In short, they might all better say of matter, what Michael Angelo said of external beauty, "it is the frail and weary weed, in which God dresses the soul, which he has called into time."[93]

It appears that motion, poetry, physical and intellectual science, and religion, all tend to affect our convictions of the reality of the external world. But I own there is something ungrateful in expanding too curiously the particulars of the general proposition, that all culture tends to imbue us with idealism. I have no hostility to nature, but a child's love to it. I expand and live in the warm day like corn and melons. Let us speak her fair. I do not wish to fling stones at my beautiful mother, nor soil my gentle nest. I only wish to indicate the true position of nature in regard to man, wherein to establish man, all right education tends; as the ground which to attain is the object of human life, that is, of man's connexion with nature. Culture inverts the vulgar views of nature, and brings the mind to call that apparent, which it uses to call real, and that real, which it uses to call vision-

[87] From II Corinthians 4:18.

[88] Bishop George Berkeley (1685–1753), an English promoter of philosophical idealism; Vyāsa, a legendary Hindu philosopher and author of the Mahābhārata (200? B.C.).

[89] Those who claim direct mystical insight of a supreme being.

[90] A follower of Manes, a third-century Christian mystic who taught that there was a principle of good and a principle of evil in the universe.

[91] In Exodus 16:2–3 the Israelites in the wilderness yearned for the fleshpots, or luxuries, of Egypt.

[92] Plotinus expressed remorse that the eternal soul was trapped in a perishable body.

[93] From Michelangelo's Sonnet 51; here, "weed" means garment.

ary. Children, it is true, believe in the external world. The belief that it appears only, is an afterthought, but with culture, this faith will as surely arise on the mind as did the first.

The advantage of the ideal theory over the popular faith, is this, that it presents the world in precisely that view which is most desirable to the mind. It is, in fact, the view which Reason, both speculative and practical, that is, philosophy and virtue, take. For, seen in the light of thought, the world always is phenomenal; and virtue subordinates it to the mind. Idealism sees the world in God. It beholds the whole circle of persons and things, of actions and events, of country and religion, not as painfully accumulated, atom after atom, act after act, in an aged creeping Past, but as one vast picture, which God paints on the instant eternity, for the contemplation of the soul. Therefore the soul holds itself off from a too trivial and microscopic study of the universal tablet. It respects the end too much, to immerse itself in the means. It sees something more important in Christianity, than the scandals of ecclesiastical history or the niceties of criticism; and, very incurious concerning persons or miracles, and not at all disturbed by chasms of historical evidence, it accepts from God the phenomenon, as it finds it, as the pure and awful form of religion in the world. It is not hot and passionate at the appearance of what it calls its own good or bad fortune, at the union or opposition of other persons. No man is its enemy. It accepts whatsoever befals, as part of its lesson. It is a watcher more than a doer, and it is a doer, only that it may the better watch.

CHAPTER VII: SPIRIT

It is essential to a true theory of nature and of man, that it should contain somewhat[94] progressive. Uses that are exhausted or that may be, and facts that end in the statement, cannot be all that is true of this brave lodging wherein man is harbored, and wherein all his faculties find appropriate and endless exercise. And all the uses of nature admit of being summed in one, which yields the activity of man an infinite scope. Through all its kingdoms, to the suburbs and outskirts of things, it is faithful to the cause whence it had its origin. It always speaks of Spirit. It suggests the absolute. It is a perpetual effect. It is a great shadow pointing always to the sun behind us.

The aspect of nature is devout. Like the figure of Jesus, she stands with bended head, and hands folded upon the breast. The happiest man is he who learns from nature the lesson of worship.

Of that ineffable essence which we call Spirit, he that thinks most, will say least. We can foresee God in the course and, as it were, distant phenomena of matter; but when we try to define and describe himself, both language and thought desert us, and we are as helpless as fools and savages. That essence refuses to be recorded in propositions, but when man has worshipped him intellectually, the noblest ministry of nature is to stand as the apparition of God. It is the great organ through which the universal spirit speaks to the individual, and strives to lead back the individual to it.

When we consider Spirit, we see that the views already presented do not include the whole circumference of man. We must add some related thoughts.

---

[94] Something; Emerson regularly uses the older form "somewhat" for "something."

Three problems are put by nature to the mind; What is matter? Whence is it? and Whereto? The first of these questions only, the ideal theory answers. Idealism saith: matter is a phenomenon, not a substance. Idealism acquaints us with the total disparity between the evidence of our own being, and the evidence of the world's being. The one is perfect; the other, incapable of any assurance; the mind is a part of the nature of things; the world is a divine dream, from which we may presently awake to the glories and certainties of day. Idealism is a hypothesis to account for nature by other principles than those of carpentry and chemistry. Yet, if it only deny the existence of matter, it does not satisfy the demands of the spirit. It leaves God out of me. It leaves me in the splendid labyrinth of my perceptions, to wander without end. Then the heart resists it, because it baulks the affections in denying substantive being to men and women. Nature is so pervaded with human life, that there is something of humanity in all, and in every particular. But this theory makes nature foreign to me, and does not account for that consanguinity which we acknowledge to it.

Let it stand then, in the present state of our knowledge, merely as a useful introductory hypothesis, serving to apprize us of the eternal distinction between the soul and the world.

But when, following the invisible steps of thought, we come to inquire, Whence is matter? and Whereto? many truths arise to us out of the recesses of consciousness. We learn that the highest is present to the soul of man, that the dread universal essence, which is not wisdom, or love, or beauty, or power, but all in one, and each entirely, is that for which all things exist, and that by which they are; that spirit creates; that behind nature, throughout nature, spirit is present; that spirit is one and not compound; that spirit does not act upon us from without, that is, in space and time, but spiritually, or through ourselves. Therefore, that spirit, that is, the Supreme Being, does not build up nature around us, but puts it forth through us, as the life of the tree puts forth new branches and leaves through the pores of the old. As a plant upon the earth, so a man rests upon the bosom of God; he is nourished by unfailing fountains, and draws, at his need, inexhaustible power. Who can set bounds to the possibilities of man? Once inhale the upper air, being admitted to behold the absolute natures of justice and truth, and we learn that man has access to the entire mind of the Creator, is himself the creator in the finite. This view, which admonishes me where the sources of wisdom and power lie, and points to virtue as to

> "The golden key
> Which opes the palace of eternity,"[95]

carries upon its face the highest certificate of truth, because it animates me to create my own world through the purification of my soul.

The world proceeds from the same spirit as the body of man. It is a remoter and inferior incarnation of God, a projection of God in the unconscious. But it differs from the body in one important respect. It is not, like that, now subjected to the human will. Its serene order is inviolable by us. It is therefore, to us, the present expositor of the divine mind. It is a fixed point whereby we may measure our departure. As we degenerate, the contrast between us and our house is more evident. We are as much strangers in nature, as we are aliens from God. We do not

---

[95] From *Comus* (1634), lines 13–14, by John Milton (1608–1674).

understand the notes of birds. The fox and the deer run away from us; the bear and tiger rend us. We do not know the uses of more than a few plants, as corn and the apple, the potato and the vine. Is not the landscape, every glimpse of which hath a grandeur, a face of him? Yet this may show us what discord is between man and nature, for you cannot freely admire a noble landscape, if laborers are digging in the field hard by. The poet finds something ridiculous in his delight, until he is out of the sight of men.

CHAPTER VIII: PROSPECTS

In inquiries respecting the laws of the world and the frame of things, the highest reason is always the truest. That which seems faintly possible—it is so refined, is often faint and dim because it is deepest seated in the mind among the eternal verities. Empirical science is apt to cloud the sight, and, by the very knowledge of functions and processes, to bereave the student of the manly contemplation of the whole. The savant[96] becomes unpoetic. But the best read naturalist who lends an entire and devout attention to truth, will see that there remains much to learn of his relation to the world, and that it is not to be learned by any addition or subtraction or other comparison of known quantities, but is arrived at by untaught sallies of the spirit, by a continual self-recovery, and by entire humility. He will perceive that there are far more excellent qualities in the student than preciseness and infallibility; that a guess is often more fruitful than an indisputable affirmation, and that a dream may let us deeper into the secret of nature than a hundred concerted experiments.

For, the problems to be solved are precisely those which the physiologist and the naturalist omit to state. It is not so pertinent to man to know all the individuals of the animal kingdom, as it is to know whence and whereto is this tyrannizing unity in his constitution, which evermore separates and classifies things, endeavoring to reduce the most diverse to one form. When I behold a rich landscape, it is less to my purpose to recite correctly the order and superposition of the strata, than to know why all thought of multitude is lost in a tranquil sense of unity. I cannot greatly honor minuteness in details, so long as there is no hint to explain the relation between things and thoughts; no ray upon the *metaphysics* of conchology,[97] of botany, of the arts, to show the relation of the forms of flowers, shells, animals, architecture, to the mind, and build science upon ideas. In a cabinet of natural history,[98] we become sensible of a certain occult recognition and sympathy in regard to the most unwieldy and eccentric forms of beast, fish, and insect. The American who has been confined, in his own country, to the sight of buildings designed after foreign models, is surprised on entering York Minister or St. Peter's[99] at Rome, by the feeling that these structures are imitations also,—faint copies of an invisible archetype. Nor has science sufficient humanity, so long as the naturalist overlooks that wonderful congruity which subsists between man and the world; of which he is lord, not because he is the most subtile inhabitant, but because he is its head and heart, and finds something of himself in every great and small thing, in every mountain stratum, in every new law of color, fact of astron-

---

[96] Learned person.
[97] The study of seashells (conchs).   [98] A display case of specimens from nature.
[99] The cathedral at York, England, and St. Peter's Cathedral.

omy, or atmospheric influence which observation or analysis lay open. A perception of this mystery inspires the muse of George Herbert,[100] the beautiful psalmist of the seventeenth century. The following lines are part of his little poem on Man.

> "Man is all symmetry,
> Full of proportions, one limb to another,
> And to all the world besides.
> Each part may call the farthest, brother;
> For head with foot hath private amity,
> And both with moons and tides.

> "Nothing hath got so far
> But man hath caught and kept it as his prey;
> His eyes dismount the highest star;
> He is in little all the sphere.
> Herbs gladly cure our flesh, because that they
> Find their acquaintance there.

> "For us, the winds do blow,
> The earth doth rest, heaven move, and fountains flow;
> Nothing we see, but means our good,
> As our delight, or as our treasure;
> The whole is either our cupboard of food,
> Or cabinet of pleasure.

> "The stars have us to bed:
> Night draws the curtain; which the sun withdraws.
> Music and light attend our head.
> All things unto our flesh are kind,
> In their descent and being; to our mind,
> In their ascent and cause.

> "More servants wait on man
> Than he'll take notice of. In every path,
> He treads down that which doth befriend him
> When sickness makes him pale and wan.
> Oh mighty love! Man is one world, and hath
> Another to attend him."

The perception of this class of truths makes the eternal attraction which draws men to science, but the end is lost sight of in attention to the means. In view of this half-sight of science, we accept the sentence of Plato, that, "poetry comes nearer to vital truth than history." Every surmise and vaticination[101] of the mind is entitled to a certain respect, and we learn to prefer imperfect theories, and sentences, which contain glimpses of truth, to digested systems which have no one valuable suggestion. A wise writer will feel that the ends of study and composition

---

[100] Herbert (1593–1633) was an English metaphysical poet; Emerson quotes stanzas 1–4 and 6 of Herbert's poem "Man."
[101] Prophecy.

are best answered by announcing undiscovered regions of thought, and so communicating, through hope, new activity to the torpid spirit.

I shall therefore conclude this essay with some traditions of man and nature, which a certain poet[102] sang to me; and which, as they have always been in the world, and perhaps reappear to every bard, may be both history and prophecy.

'The foundations of man are not in matter, but in spirit. But the element of spirit is eternity. To it, therefore, the longest series of events, the oldest chronologies are young and recent. In the cycle of the universal man, from whom the known individuals proceed, centuries are points, and all history is but the epoch of one degradation.

'We distrust and deny inwardly our sympathy with nature. We own and disown our relation to it, by turns. We are, like Nebuchadnezzar,[103] dethroned, bereft of reason, and eating grass like an ox. But who can set limits to the remedial force of spirit?

'A man is a god in ruins. When men are innocent, life shall be longer, and shall pass into the immortal, as gently as we awake from dreams. Now, the world would be insane and rabid, if these disorganizations should last for hundreds of years. It is kept in check by death and infancy. Infancy is the perpetual Messiah, which comes into the arms of fallen men, and pleads with them to return to paradise.

'Man is the dwarf of himself. Once he was permeated and dissolved by spirit. He filled nature with his overflowing currents. Out from him sprang the sun and moon; from man, the sun; from woman, the moon. The laws of his mind, the periods of his actions externized themselves into day and night, into the year and the seasons. But, having made for himself this huge shell, his waters retired; he no longer fills the veins and veinlets; he is shrunk to a drop. He sees, that the structure still fits him, but fits him colossally. Say, rather, once it fitted him, now it corresponds to him from far and on high. He adores timidly his own work. Now is man the follower of the sun, and the woman the follower of the moon. Yet sometimes he starts in his slumber, and wonders at himself and his house, and muses strangely at the resemblance betwixt him and it. He perceives that if his law is still paramount, if still he have elemental power, "if his word is sterling yet in nature," it is not conscious power, it is not inferior but superior to his will. It is Instinct,' Thus my Orphic[104] poet sang.

At present, man applies to nature but half his force. He works on the world with his understanding alone. He lives in it, and masters it by a penny-wisdom; and he that works most in it, is but a half-man, and whilst his arms are strong and his digestion good, his mind is imbruted and he is a selfish savage. His relation to nature, his power over it, is through the understanding; as by manure; the economic use of fire, wind, water, and the mariner's needle; steam, coal, chemical agriculture; the repairs of the human body by the dentist and the surgeon. This is such a resumption of power, as if a banished king should buy his territories inch by inch, instead of vaulting at once into his throne. Meantime, in the thick darkness, there are not wanting gleams of a better light,—occasional examples of the

---

[102] Probably Emerson himself; most of the following passages come from his journals.

[103] Nebuchadnezzar (?–562 B.C.), a Babylonian king, lost his reason and "was driven from men, and did eat grass as oxen," from Daniel 4:33.

[104] Mystic or oracular after Orpheus, a mythical Greek poet; Emerson's most "orphic" friend was Bronson Alcott (1799–1888), a philosopher and education reformer who published *Orphic Sayings* in 1840. To apply the term "my Orphic poet" to Alcott, however, is to follow a false lead.

action of man upon nature with his entire force,—with reason as well as understanding. Such examples are; the traditions of miracles in the earliest antiquity of all nations; the history of Jesus Christ; the achievements of a principle, as in religious and political revolutions, and in the abolition of the Slave-trade; the miracles of enthusiasm,[105] as those reported of Swedenborg, Hohenlohe, and the Shakers;[106] many obscure and yet contested facts, now arranged under the name of Animal Magnetism;[107] prayer; eloquence; self-healing; and the wisdom of children. These are examples of Reason's momentary grasp of the sceptre; the exertions of a power which exists not in time or space, but an instantaneous in-streaming causing power. The difference between the actual and the ideal force of man is happily figured by the schoolmen,[108] in saying, that the knowledge of man is an evening knowledge, *vespertina cognitio,* but that of God is a morning knowledge, *matutina cognitio.*

The problem of restoring to the world original and eternal beauty, is solved by the redemption of the soul. The ruin or the blank, that we see when we look at nature, is in our own eye. The axis of vision is not coincident with the axis of things, and so they appear not transparent but opake. The reason why the world lacks unity, and lies broken and in heaps, is, because man is disunited with himself. He cannot be a naturalist, until he satisfies all the demands of the spirit. Love is as much its demand, as perception. Indeed, neither can be perfect without the other. In the uttermost meaning of the words, thought is devout, and devotion is thought. Deep calls unto deep.[109] But in actual life, the marriage is not celebrated. There are innocent men who worship God after the tradition of their fathers, but their sense of duty has not yet extended to the use of all their faculties. And there are patient naturalists, but they freeze their subject under the wintry light of the understanding. Is not prayer also a study of truth,—a sally of the soul into the unfound infinite? No man ever prayed heartily, without learning something. But when a faithful thinker, resolute to detach every object from personal relations, and see it in the light of thought, shall, at the same time, kindle science with the fire of the holiest affections, then will God go forth anew into the creation.

It will not need, when the mind is prepared for study, to search for objects. The invariable mark of wisdom is to see the miraculous in the common. What is a day? What is a year? What is summer? What is woman? What is a child? What is sleep? To our blindness, these things seem unaffecting. We make fables to hide the baldness of the fact and conform it, as we say, to the higher law of the mind. But when the fact is seen under the light of an idea, the gaudy fable fades and shrivels. We behold the real higher law. To the wise, therefore, a fact is true poetry, and the most beautiful of fables. These wonders are brought to our own door. You also are a man. Man and woman, and their social life, poverty, labor, sleep, fear, fortune, are known to you. Learn that none of these things is superficial, but that each phenomenon hath its roots in the faculties and affections of the mind. Whilst the abstract question occupies your intellect, nature brings it in the concrete to be

---

[105] Divine ecstacy.

[106] Leopold Franz Emmerich (1794–1849), a German Prince of Hohenlohe-Waldenberg-Schillingfurst, said to have been responsible for miracle cures; and members of the Millennial Church, founded in England in 1747, who were known for their ecstatic dancing and revelations.

[107] Hypnotism.

[108] Scholastic philosophers of the Middle Ages, chief among them Thomas Aquinas (1225–1274).

[109] "Deep calleth unto deep at the noise of thy waterspouts: all thy waves and thy billows are gone over me," from Psalm 42:7.

solved by your hands. It were a wise inquiry for the closet,[110] to compare, point by point, especially at remarkable crises in life, our daily history, with the rise and progress of ideas in the mind.

So shall we come to look at the world with new eyes. It shall answer the endless inquiry of the intellect,—What is truth? and of the affections,—What is good? by yielding itself passive to the educated Will. Then shall come to pass what my poet said; 'Nature is not fixed but fluid. Spirit alters, moulds, makes it. The immobility or bruteness of nature, is the absence of spirit; to pure spirit, it is fluid, it is volatile, it is obedient. Every spirit builds itself a house; and beyond its house, a world; and beyond its world, a heaven. Know then, that the world exists for you. For you is the phenomenon perfect. What we are, that only can we see. All that Adam had, all that Cæsar could, you have and can do. Adam called his house, heaven and earth; Cæsar called his house, Rome; you perhaps call yours, a cobler's trade; a hundred acres of ploughed land; or a scholar's garret. Yet line for line and point for point, your dominion is as great as theirs, though without fine names. Build, therefore, your own world. As fast as you conform your life to the pure idea in your mind, that will unfold its great proportions. A correspondent revolution in things will attend the influx of the spirit. So fast will disagreeable appearances, swine, spiders, snakes, pests, mad-houses, prisons, enemies, vanish; they are temporary and shall be no more seen. The sordor[111] and filths of nature, the sun shall dry up, and the wind exhale. As when the summer comes from the south, the snow-banks melt, and the face of the earth becomes green before it, so shall the advancing spirit create its ornaments along its path, and carry with it the beauty it visits, and the song which enchants it; it shall draw beautiful faces, and warm hearts, and wise discourse, and heroic acts, around its way, until evil is no more seen. The kingdom of man over nature, which cometh not with observation,[112]—a dominion such as now is beyond his dream of God,—he shall enter without more wonder than the blind man feels who is gradually restored to perfect sight.'

1836

THE AMERICAN SCHOLAR*

An Oration Delivered Before the Phi Beta Kappa Society, at Cambridge,
August 31, 1837

MR. PRESIDENT, AND GENTLEMEN,

I greet you on the re-commencement of our literary year.[1] Our anniversary is one of hope, and, perhaps, not enough of labor. We do not meet for games of strength or skill, for the recitaton of histories, tragedies and odes, like the ancient

---

[110] A small, private room; here, a study.   [111] Sordidness, squalor.
[112] "And when he was [asked] . . . , when the kingdom of God should come, he answered . . . , The kingdom of God cometh not with observation," from Luke 17:20.
* First published as a pamphlet in 1837, with the subtitle serving as the title. In *Nature, Addresses, and Lectures* (1849) Emerson changed the title to "The American Scholar," thereby addressing all persons devoted to independence of mind.
[1] The academic year, traditionally beginning in September.

Greeks; for parliaments of love and poesy, like the Troubadours;[2] nor for the advancement of science, like our contemporaries in the British and European capitals. Thus far, our holiday has been simply a friendly sign of the survival of the love of letters amongst a people too busy to give to letters any more. As such, it is precious as the sign of an indestructible instinct. Perhaps the time is already come, when it ought to be, and will be something else; when the sluggard intellect of this continent will look from under its iron lids and fill the postponed expectation of the world with something better than the exertions of mechanical skill. Our day of dependence, our long apprenticeship to the learning of other lands, draws to a close. The millions that around us are rushing into life, cannot always be fed on the sere remains of foreign harvests. Events, actions arise, that must be sung, that will sing themselves. Who can doubt that poetry will revive and lead in a new age, as the star in the constellation Harp[3] which now flames in our zenith, astronomers announce, shall one day be the pole-star[4] for a thousand years?

In the light of this hope, I accept the topic which not only usage, but the nature of our association, seem to prescribe to this day,—the AMERICAN SCHOLAR. Year by year, we come up hither to read one more chapter of his biography. Let us inquire what light new days and events have thrown on his character, his duties and his hopes.

It is one of those fables,[5] which out of an unknown antiquity, convey an unlooked-for wisdom, that the gods, in the beginning, divided Man into men, that he might be more helpful to himself; just as the hand was divided into fingers, the better to answer its end.

The old fable covers a doctrine ever new and sublime; that there is One Man,— present to all particular men only partially, or through one faculty; and that you must take the whole society to find the whole man. Man is not a farmer, or a professor, or an engineer, but he is all. Man is priest, and scholar, and statesman, and producer, and soldier. In the *divided* or social state, these functions are parcelled out to individuals, each of whom aims to do his stint of the joint work, whilst each other performs his. The fable implies that the individual to possess himself, must sometimes return from his own labor to embrace all the other laborers. But unfortunately, this original unit, this fountain of power, has been so distributed to multitudes, has been so minutely subdivided and peddled out, that it is spilled into drops, and cannot be gathered. The state of society is one in which the members have suffered amputation from the trunk, and strut about so many walking monsters,—a good finger, a neck, a stomach, an elbow, but never a man.

Man is thus metamorphosed into a thing, into many things. The planter, who is Man sent out into the field to gather food, is seldom cheered by any idea of the true dignity of his ministry. He sees his bushel and his cart, and nothing beyond, and sinks into the farmer, instead of Man on the farm. The tradesman scarcely ever gives an ideal worth to his work, but is ridden by the routine of his craft, and the soul is subject to dollars. The priest becomes a form; the attorney, a statute-book; the mechanic, a machine; the sailor, a rope of a ship.

In this distribution of functions, the scholar is the delegated intellect. In the right state, he is, *Man Thinking*. In degenerate state, when the victim of society,

---

[2] Eleventh-through thirteenth-century poets and musicians of southern France who celebrated courtly love.

[3] Vega, the bright star in the northern constellation Lyra (shaped like a lyre or harp.)

[4] The North Star, the star closest to the North celestial pole.

[5] *Symposium*, by the Greek philosopher Plato (427?–347? B.C.) includes a version of this fable.

he tends to become a mere thinker, or, still worse, the parrot of other men's thinking.

In this view of him, as Man Thinking, the whole theory of his office[6] is contained. Him nature solicits, with all her placid, all her monitory pictures. Him the past instructs. Him the future invites. Is not, indeed, every man a student, and do not all things exist for the student's behoof? And, finally, is not the true scholar the only true master? But, as the old oracle said, "All things have two handles. Beware of the wrong one."[7] In life, too often, the scholar errs with mankind and forfeits his privilege. Let us see him in his school, and consider him in reference to the main influences he receives.

I. The first in time and the first in importance of the influences upon the mind is that of nature. Every day, the sun; and, after sunset, night and her stars. Ever the winds blow; ever the grass grows. Every day, men and women, conversing, beholding and beholden. The scholar must needs stand wistful and admiring before this great spectacle. He must settle its value in his mind. What is nature to him? There is never a beginning, there is never an end to the inexpicable continuity of this web of God, but always circular power returning into itself. Therein it resembles his own spirit, whose beginning, whose ending he never can find—so entire, so boundless. Far, too, as her splendors shine, system on system shooting like rays, upward, downward, without centre, without circumference,—in the mass and in the particle nature hastens to render account of herself to the mind. Classification begins. To the young mind, every thing is individual, stands by itself. By and by, it finds how to join two things, and see in them one nature; then three, then three thousand; and so, tyrannized over by its own unifying instinct, it goes on tying things together, diminishing anomalies, discovering roots running under ground, whereby contrary and remote things cohere, and flower out from one stem. It presently learns, that, since the dawn of history, there has been a constant accumulation and classifying of facts. But what is classification but the perceiving that these objects are not chaotic, and are not foreign, but have a law which is also a law of the human mind? The astronomer discovers that geometry, a pure abstraction of the human mind, is the measure of planetary motion. The chemist finds proportions and intelligible method throughout matter: and science is nothing but the finding of analogy, identity in the most remote parts. The ambitious soul sits down before each refractory fact; one after another, reduces all strange constitutions, all new powers, to their class and their law, and goes on forever to animate the last fibre of organization, the outskirts of nature, by insight.

Thus to him, to this school-boy under the bending dome of day, is suggested, that he and it proceed from one root; one is leaf and one is flower; relation, sympathy, stirring in every vein. And what is that Root? Is not that the soul of his soul?—A thought too bold—a dream too wild. Yet when this spiritual light shall have revealed the law of more earthly natures,—when he has learned to worship the soul, and to see that the natural philosophy that now is, is only the first gropings of its gigantic hand, he shall look forward to an ever expanding knowledge as to a becoming creator. He shall see that nature is the opposite of the soul, answering to it part for part. One is seal, and one is print. Its beauty is the beauty of his own mind. Its laws are the laws of his own mind. Nature then becomes to him the measure of his attainments. So much of nature as he is ignorant of, so much of his

---

[6] Function, duty.   [7] From the Greek philosopher Epictetus (A. D. 50?–135?).

own mind does he not yet possess. And, in fine, the ancient precept, "Know thyself," and the modern precept, "Study nature," become at last one maxim.

II. The next great influence[8] into the spirit of the scholar, is, the mind of the Past,—in whatever form, whether of literature, of art, of institutions, that mind is inscribed. Books are the best type of the influence of the past, and perhaps we shall get at the truth—learn the amount of this influence more conveniently—by considering their value alone.

The theory of books is noble. The scholar of the first age received into him the world around; brooded thereon; gave it the new arrangement of his own mind, and uttered it again. It came into him—life; it went out from him—truth. It came to him—short-lived actions; it went out from him—immortal thoughts. It came to him—business; it went from him—poetry. It was—dead fact; now, it is quick[9] thought. It can stand, and it can go. It now endures, it now flies, it now inspires.[10] Precisely in proportion to the depth of mind from which it issued, so high does it soar, so long does it sing.

Or, I might say, it depends on how far the process had gone, of transmuting life into truth. In proportion to the completeness of the distillation, so will the purity and imperishableness of the product be. But none is quite perfect. As no air-pump can by any means make a perfect vacuum, so neither can any artist entirely exclude the conventional, the local, the perishable from his book, or write a book of pure thought that shall be as efficient, in all respects, to a remote posterity, as to cotemporaries, or rather to the second age. Each age, it is found, must write its own books; or rather, each generation for the next succeeding. The books of an older period will not fit this.

Yet hence arises a grave mischief. The sacredness which attaches to the act of creation,—the act of thought,—is instantly transferred to the record. The poet chanting, was felt to be a divine man. Henceforth the chant is divine also. The writer was a just and wise spirit. Henceforward it is settled, the book is perfect; as love of the hero corrupts into worship of his statue. Instantly, the book becomes noxious. The guide is a tyrant. We sought a brother, and lo, a governor. The sluggish and perverted mind of the multitude, always slow to open to the incursions of Reason, having once so opened, having once received this book, stands upon it, and makes an outcry, if it is disparaged. Colleges are built on it. Books are written on it by thinkers, not by Man Thinking; by men of talent, that is, who start wrong, who set out from accepted dogmas, not from their own sight of principles. Meek young men grow up in libraries, believing it their duty to accept the views which Cicero, which Locke, which Bacon[11] have given, forgetful that Cicero, Locke and Bacon were only young men in libraries when they wrote these books.

Hence, instead of Man Thinking, we have the bookworm. Hence, the book-learned class, who value books, as such; not as related to nature and the human constitution, but as making a sort of Third Estate[12] with the world and the soul.

---

[8] Inflowing.   [9] Living.   [10] Breathes in.

[11] The noted orator and Roman statesman Marcus Tullius Cicero (106–43 B.C.); the English philosopher and political theorist John Locke (1632–1704); the English statesman and philosopher Sir Francis Bacon (1561–1626), an early proponent of the inductive method.

[12] The three "estates," or classes, recognized by feudal Europe were the clergy, the nobility, and the commoners. Emerson's analogy criticizes those who value books as objects rather than as manifestations of the world and the spirit.

Hence, the restorers of readings, the emendators, the bibliomaniacs[13] of all degrees.

This is bad; this is worse than it seems. Books are the best of things, well used; abused, among the worst. What is the right use? What is the one end which all means go to effect? They are for nothing but to inspire. I had better never see a book than to be warped by its attraction clean out of my own orbit, and made a satellite instead of a system. The one thing in the world of value, is, the active soul,—the soul, free, sovereign, active. This every man is entitled to; this every man contains within him, although in almost all men, obstructed, and as yet unborn. The soul active sees absolute truth; and utters truth, or creates. In this action, it is genius; not the privilege of here and there a favorite, but the sound estate of every man. In its essence, it is progressive. The book, the college, the school of art, the institution of any kind, stop with some past utterance of genius. This is good, say they,—let us hold by this. They pin me down. They look backward and not forward. But genius always looks forward. The eyes of man are set in his forehead, not in his hindhead. Man hopes. Genius creates. To create,—to create,—is the proof of a divine presence. Whatever talents may be, if the man create not, the pure efflux[14] of the Diety is not his:—cinders and smoke, there may be, but not yet flame. There are creative manners, there are creative actions, and creative words; manners, actions, words, that is, indicative of no custom or authority, but springing spontaneous from the mind's own sense of good and fair.

On the other part, instead of being its own seer, let it receive always from another mind its truth, though it were in torrents of light, without periods of solitude, inquest and self-recovery, and a fatal disservice is done. Genius is always sufficiently the enemy of genius by over-influence. The literature of every nation bear me witness. The English dramatic poets have Shakspearized now for two hundred years.

Undoubtedly there is a right way of reading,—so it be sternly subordinated. Man Thinking must not be subdued by his instruments. Books are for the scholar's idle times. When he can read God directly, the hour is too precious to be wasted in other men's transcripts of their readings. But when the intervals of darkness come, as come they must,—when the soul seeth not, when the sun is hid, and the stars withdraw their shining,—we repair to the lamps which were kindled by their ray to guide our steps to the East again, where the dawn is. We hear that we may speak. The Arabian proverb says, "A fig tree looking on a fig tree, becometh fruitful."

It is remarkable, the character of the pleasure we derive from the best books. They impress us ever with the conviction that one nature wrote and the same reads. We read the verses of one of the great English poets, of Chaucer, of Marvell, of Dryden,[15] with the most modern joy,—with pleasure, I mean, which is in great part caused by the abstraction of all *time* from their verses. There is some awe mixed with the joy of our surprise, when this poet, who lived in some past world, two or three hundred years ago, says that which lies close to my own soul, that which I also had well-nigh thought and said. But for the evidence thence afforded to the philosophical doctrine of the identity of all minds, we should suppose some pre-established harmony, some foresight of souls that were to be, and

---

[13] Those who edit texts, and those obsessed with books.   [14] Outflowing, emanation.
[15] The English writers Geoffrey Chaucer (1340–1400), Andrew Marvell (1621–1678), and John Dryden (1631–1700).

some preparation of stores for their future wants, like the fact observed in insects, who lay up food before death for the young grub they shall never see.

I would not be hurried by any love of system, by any exaggeration of instincts, to underrate the Book. We all know, that as the human body can be nourished on any food, though it were boiled grass and the broth of shoes, so the human mind can be fed by any knowledge. And great and heroic men have existed, who had almost no other information than by the printed page. I only would say, that it needs a strong head to bear that diet. One must be an inventor to read well. As the proverb says, "He that would bring home the wealth of the Indies, must carry out the wealth of the Indies." There is then creative reading, as well as creative writing. When the mind is braced by labor and invention, the page of whatever book we read becomes luminous with manifold allusion. Every sentence is doubly significant, and the sense of our author is as broad as the world. We then see, what is always true, that as the seer's hour of vision is short and rare among heavy days and months, so is its record, perchance, the least part of his volume. The discerning will read in his Plato or Shakspeare, only that least part,—only the authentic utterances of the oracle,—and all the rest he rejects, were it never so many times Plato's and Shakspeare's.

Of course, there is a portion of reading quite indispensable to a wise man. History and exact science he must learn by laborious reading. Colleges, in like manner, have their indispensable office,—to teach elements. But they can only highly serve us, when they aim not to drill, but to create; when they gather from far every ray of various genius to their hospitable halls, and, by the concentrated fires, set the hearts of their youth on flame. Thought and knowledge are natures in which apparatus and pretension avail nothing. Gowns, and pecuniary foundations,[16] though of towns of gold, can never countervail the least sentence or syllable of wit.[17] Forget this, and our American colleges will recede in their public importance whilst they grow richer every year.

III. There goes in the world a notion that the scholar should be a recluse, a valetudinarian,[18]—as unfit for any handiwork or public labor, as a penknife for an axe. The so-called "practical men" sneer at speculative men, as if, because they speculate or *see,* they could do nothing. I have heard it said that the clergy,—who are always more universally than any other class, the scholars of their day,—are addressed as women: that the rough, spontaneous conversation of men they do not hear, but only a mincing and diluted speech. They are often virtually disfranchised; and, indeed, there are advocates for their celibacy. As far as this is true of the studious classes, it is not just and wise. Action is with the scholar subordinate, but it is essential. Without it, he is not yet man. Without it, thought can never ripen into truth. Whilst the world hangs before the eye as a cloud of beauty, we cannot even see its beauty. Inaction is cowardice, but there can be no scholar without the heroic mind. The preamble of thought, the transition through which it passes from the unconscious to the conscious, is action. Only so much do I know, as I have lived. Instantly we know whose words are loaded with life, and whose not.

The world,—this shadow of the soul, or *other me,* lies wide around. Its attractions are the keys which unlock my thoughts and make me acquainted with myself. I run eagerly into this resounding tumult. I grasp the hands of those next me, and take my place in the ring to suffer and to work, taught by an instinct that so

---

[16] Academic robes, and financial foundations.   [17] Intellectual quality.   [18] An invalid.

shall the dumb abyss be vocal with speech. I pierce its order; I dissipate its fear; I dispose of it within the circuit of my expanding life. So much only of life as I know by experience, so much of the wilderness have I vanquished and planted, or so far have I extended my being, my dominion. I do not see how any man can afford, for the sake of his nerves and his nap, to spare any action in which he can partake. It is pearls and rubies to his discourse. Drudgery, calamity, exasperation, want, are instructers in eloquence and wisdom. The true scholar grudges every opportunity of action past by, as a loss of power.

It is the raw material out of which the intellect moulds her splendid products. A strange process too, this, by which experience is converted into thought, as a mulberry leaf is converted into satin.[19] The manufacture goes forward at all hours.

The actions and events of our childhood and youth are now matters of calmest observation. They lie like fair pictures in the air. Not so with our recent actions,— with the business which we now have in hand. On this we are quite unable to speculate. Our affections as yet circulate through it. We no more feel or know it, than we feel the feet, or the hand, or the brain of our body. The new deed is yet part of life,—remains for a time immersed in our unconscious life. In some contemplative hour, it detaches itself from the life like a ripe fruit, to become a thought of the mind. Instantly, it is raised, transfigured; the corruptible has put on incorruption.[20] Always now it is an object of beauty, however base its origin and neighborhood. Observe, too, the impossibility of antedating this act. In its grub state, it cannot fly, it cannot shine,—it is a dull grub. But suddenly, without observation, the selfsame thing unfurls beautiful wings, and is an angel of wisdom. So is there no fact, no event, in our private history, which shall not, sooner or late, lose its adhesive inert form, and astonish us by soaring from our body into the empyrean.[21] Cradle and infancy, school and playground, the fear of boys, and dogs, and ferules,[22] the love of little maids and berries, and many another fact that once filled the whole sky, are gone already; friend and relative, profession and party, town and country, nation and world, must also soar and sing.

Of course, he who has put forth his total strength in fit actions, has the richest return of wisdom. I will not shut myself out of this globe of action and transplant an oak into a flower pot, there to hunger and pine; nor trust the revenue of some single faculty, and exhaust one vein of thought, much like those Savoyards,[23] who, getting their livelihood by carving shepherds, shepherdesses, and smoking Dutchmen,[24] for all Europe, went out one day to the mountain to find stock, and discovered that they had whittled up the last of their pine trees. Authors we have in numbers, who have written out their vein, and who, moved by a commendable prudence, sail for Greece or Palestine, follow the trapper into the prairie, or ramble round Algiers to replenish their merchantable stock.

If it were only for a vocabulary the scholar would be covetous of action. Life is our dictionary. Years are well spent in country labors; in town—in the insight into trades and manufactures; in frank intercourse with many men and women; in science; in art; to the one end of mastering in all their facts a language, by which to illustrate and embody our perceptions. I learn immediately from any speaker how

---

[19] Satin made from silk, which is produced by silkworms that feed on mulberry leaves.
[20] "For this corruptible must put on incorruption, and this mortal must put on immortality," from I Corinthians 15:53.
[21] The highest heaven.   [22] Rods or rulers for disciplining children.
[23] Inhabitants of Savoy, in the French Alps (then part of Italy).   [24] Pipes.

much he has already lived, through the poverty or the splendor of his speech. Life lies behind us as the quarry from whence we get tiles and copestones for the masonry of to-day. This is the way to learn grammar. Colleges and books only copy the language which the field and the work-yard made.

But the final value of action, like that of books, and better than books, is, that it is a resource. That great principle of Undulation in nature, that shows itself in the inspiring and expiring of the breath; in desire and satiety; in the ebb and flow of the sea, in day and night, in heat and cold, and as yet more deeply ingrained in every atom and every fluid, is known to us under the name of Polarity,—these "fits of easy transmission and reflection," as Newton[25] called them, are the law of nature because they are the law of spirit.

The mind now thinks; now acts; and each fit reproduces the other. When the artist has exhausted his materials, when the fancy no longer paints, when thoughts are no longer apprehended, and books are a weariness—he has always the resource to *live*. Character is higher than intellect. Thinking is the function. Living is the functionary. The stream retreats to its source. A great soul will be strong to live, as well as strong to think. Does he lack organ or medium to impart his truths? He can still fall back on this elemental force of living them. This is a total act. Thinking is a partial act. Let the grandeur of justice shine in his affairs. Let the beauty of affection cheer his lowly roof. Those "far from fame" who dwell and act with him will feel the force of his constitution in the doings and passages of the day better than it can be measured by any public and designed display. Time shall teach him that the scholar loses no hour which the man lives. Herein he unfolds the sacred germ of his instinct, screened from influence. What is lost in seemliness is gained in strength. Not out of those on whom systems of education have exhausted their culture, comes the helpful giant to destroy the old or to build the new, but out of unhandselled[26] savage nature, out of terrible Druids and Berserkirs, come at last Alfred and Shakspear[e].[27]

I hear therefore with joy whatever is beginning to be said of the dignity and necessity of labor to every citizen. There is virtue yet in the hoe and the spade, for learned as well as for unlearned hands. And labor is every where welcome; always we are invited to work; only be this limitation observed, that a man shall not for the sake of wider activity sacrifice any opinion to the popular judgments and modes of action.

I have now spoken of the education of the scholar by nature, by books, and by action. It remains to say somewhat of his duties.

They are such as become Man Thinking. They may all be comprised in self-trust. The office of the scholar is to cheer, to raise, and to guide men by showing them facts amidst appearances. He plies the slow, unhonored, and unpaid task of observation. Flamsteed and Herschel,[28] in their glazed observatories, may catalogue the stars with the praise of all men, and, the results being splendid and

---

[25] The English mathematician and natural philosopher Sir Issac Newton (1642–1727), in *Optics* (1704).

[26] Wild, primitive.

[27] The savage times of ancient pagan Celtic priests (Druids) and legendary Norse warriors who bit their shields and foamed at the mouth (Berserkers) finally gave way to the achievements of Alfred (849–901), king of the West Saxons (who established English laws and encouraged literacy).

[28] John Flamsteed (1646–1719), an astronomer who did pioneer work on mapping the Solar System; Sir William Herschel (1738–1822), an astronomer who discovered the planet Uranus in 1781 and conducted seminal research on nebulae and star clusters.

useful, honor is sure. But he, in his private observatory, cataloguing obscure and nebulous stars of the human mind, which as yet no man has thought of as such,— watching days and months, sometimes, for a few facts; correcting still his old records;—must relinquish display and immediate fame. In the long period of his preparation, he must betray often an ignorance and shiftlessness in popular arts, incurring the disdain of the able who shoulder him aside. Long he must stammer in his speech; often forego the living for the dead. Worse yet, he must accept— how often! poverty and solitude. For the ease and pleasure of treading the old road, accepting the fashions, the education, the religion of society, he takes the cross of making his own, and, of course, the self-accusation, the faint heart, the frequent uncertainty and loss of time which are the nettles and tangling vines in the way of the self-relying and self-directed; and the state of virtual hostility in which he seems to stand to society, and especially to educated society. For all this loss and scorn, what offset? He is to find consolation in exercising the highest functions of human nature. He is one who raises himself from private considerations, and breathes and lives on public and illustrious thoughts. He is the world's eye. He is the world's heart. He is to resist the vulgar prosperity that retrogrades ever to barbarism, by preserving and communicating heroic sentiments, noble biographies, melodious verse, and the conclusions of history. Whatsoever oracles the human heart in all emergencies, in all solemn hours has uttered as its commentary on the world of actions,—these shall receive and impart. And whatsoever new verdict Reason from her inviolable seat pronounces on the passing men and events of to-day,—this he shall hear and promulgate.

These being his functions, it becomes him to feel all confidence in himself, and to defer never to the popular cry. He and he only knows the world. The world of any moment is the merest appearance. Some great decorum, some fetish of a government, some ephemeral trade, or war, or man, is cried up by half mankind and cried down by the other half, as if all depended on this particular up or down. The odds are that the whole question is not worth the poorest thought which the scholar has lost in listening to the controversy. Let him not quit his belief that a popgun is a popgun, though the ancient and honorable of the earth affirm it to be the crack of doom. In silence, in steadiness, in severe abstraction, let him hold by himself; add observation to observation, patient of neglect, patient of reproach; and bide his own time,—happy enough if he can satisfy himself alone that this day he has seen something truly. Success treads on every right step. For the instinct is sure that prompts him to tell his brother what he thinks. He then learns that in going down into the secrets of his own mind, he has descended into the secrets of all minds. He learns that he who has mastered any law in his private thoughts, is master to that extent of all men whose language he speaks, and of all into whose language his own can be translated. The poet in utter solitude remembering his spontaneous thoughts and recording them, is found to have recorded that which men in crowded cities find true for them also. The orator distrusts at first the fitness of his frank confessions,—his want of knowledge of the persons he addresses,—until he finds that he is the complement of his hearers;—that they drink his words because he fulfils for them their own nature; the deeper he dives into his privatest secretest presentiment,—to his wonder he finds, this is the most acceptable, most public, and universally true. The people delight in it; the better part of every man feels. This is my music; this is myself.

In self-trust, all the virtues are comprehended. Free should the scholar be,— free and brave. Free even to the definition of freedom, "without any hindrance that does not arise out of his own constitution." Brave; for fear is a thing which a scholar by his very function puts behind him. Fear always springs from ignorance. It is a shame to him if his tranquillity, amid dangerous times, arise from the presumption that like children and women, his is a protected class; or if he seek a temporary peace by the diversion of his thoughts from politics or vexed questions, hiding his head like an ostrich in the flowering bushes, peeping into microscopes, and turning rhymes, as a boy whistles to keep his courage up. So is the danger a danger still: so is the fear worse. Manlike let him turn and face it. Let him look into its eye and search its nature, inspect its origin,—see the whelping of this lion,—which lies no great way back; he will then find in himself a perfect comprehension of its nature and extent; he will have made his hands meet on the other side, and can henceforth defy it, and pass on superior. The world is his who can see through its pretension. What deafness, what stone-blind custom, what overgrown error you behold, is there only by sufferance,—by your sufferance. See it to be a lie, and you have already dealt it its mortal blow.

Yes, we are the cowed,—we the trustless. It is a mischievous notion that we are come late into nature; that the world was finished a long time ago. As the world was plastic and fluid in the hands of God, so it is ever to so much of his attributes as we bring to it. To ignorance and sin, it is flint. They adapt themselves to it as they may; but in proportion as a man has anything in him divine, the firmament flows before him, and takes his signet[29] and form. Not he is great who can alter matter, but he who can alter my state of mind. They are the kings of the world who give the color of their present thought to all nature and all art, and persuade men by the cheerful serenity of their carrying the matter, that this thing which they do, is the apple which the ages have desired to pluck, now at last ripe, and inviting nations to the harvest. The great man makes the great thing. Wherever Macdonald sits, there is the head of the table.[30] Linnæus makes botany the most alluring of studies and wins it from the farmer and the herb-woman. Davy, chemistry: and Cuvier, fossils.[31] The day is always his, who works in it with serenity and great aims. The unstable estimates of men crowd to him whose mind is filled with a truth, as the heaped waves of the Atlantic follow the moon.

For this self-trust, the reason is deeper than can be fathomed,—darker than can be enlightened. I might not carry with me the feeling of my audience in stating my own belief. But I have already shown the ground of my hope, in adverting to the doctrine that man is one. I believe man has been wronged: he has wronged himself. He has almost lost the light that can lead him back to his prerogatives. Men are become of no account. Men in history, men in the world of to-day are bugs, are spawn, and are called "the mass" and "the herd." In a century, in a millenium, one or two men; that is to say—one or two approximations to the right state of every man. All the rest behold in the hero or the poet their own green and crude being—ripened; yes, and are content to be less, so *that* may attain to its full stature. What a testimony—full of grandeur, full of pity, is borne to the demands of his own nature, by the poor clansman, the poor partisan, who rejoices in the glory of his chief. The poor and the low find some amends to their immense moral capacity, for their acquiescence in a political and social inferiority. They are con-

---

[29] Seal, identifying stamp.   [30] From a Scottish proverb about a leader's authority.
[31] Carl von Linné (1707–1778), or Carolus Linnaeus, a Swedish botanist; Sir Humphrey Davy (1778–1829), an English chemist; Georges Cuvier (1769–1832), a French anatomist and paleontologist.

tent to be brushed like flies from the path of a great person, so that justice shall be done by him to that common nature which it is the dearest desire of all to see enlarged and glorified. They sun themselves in the great man's light, and feel it to be their own element. They cast the dignity of man from their downtrod selves upon the shoulders of a hero, and will perish to add one drop of blood to make that great heart beat, those giant sinews combat and conquer. He lives for us, and we live in him.

Men such as they are, very naturally seek money or power; and power because it is as good as money,—the "spoils," so called, "of office." And why not? for they aspire to the highest, and this, in their sleep-waking, they dream is highest. Wake them, and they shall quit the false good and leap to the true, and leave governments to clerks and desks. This revolution is to be wrought by the gradual domestication of the idea of Culture. The main enterprise of the world for splendor, for extent, is the upbuilding of a man. Here are the materials strown along the ground. The private life of one man shall be more an [word supplied] illustrious monarchy,—more formidable to its enemy, more sweet and serene in its influence to its friend, than any kingdom in history. For a man, rightly viewed, comprehendeth the particular natures of all men. Each philosopher, each bard, each actor, has only done for me, as by a delegate, what one day I can do for myself. The books which once we valued more than the apple of the eye, we have quite exhausted. What is that but saying that we have come up with the point of view which the universal mind took through the eyes of that one scribe; we have been that man, and have passed on. First, one; then, another; we drain all cisterns, and waxing greater by all these supplies, we crave a better and more abundant food. The man has never lived that can feed us ever. The human mind cannot be enshrined in a person who shall set a barrier on any one side to this unbounded, unboundable empire. It is one central fire which flaming now out of the lips of Etna, lightens the capes of Sicily; and now out of the throat of Vesuvius,[32] illuminates the towers and vineyards of Naples. It is one light which beams out of a thousand stars. It is one soul which animates all men.

But I have dwelt perhaps tediously upon this abstraction of the Scholar. I ought not to delay longer to add what I have to say, of nearer reference to the time and to this country.

Historically, there is thought to be a difference in the ideas which predominate over successive epochs, and there are data for marking the genius of the Classic, of the Romantic, and now of the Reflective or Philosophical age. With the views I have intimated of the oneness or the identity of the mind through all individuals, I do not much dwell on these differences. In fact, I believe each individual passes through all three. The boy is a Greek; the youth, romantic; the adult, reflective. I deny not, however, that a revolution in the leading idea may be distinctly enough traced.

Our age is bewailed as the age of Introversion. Must that needs be evil? We, it seems, are critical. We are embarrassed with second thoughts. We cannot enjoy any thing for hankering to know whereof the pleasure consists. We are lined with eyes. We see with our feet. The time is infected with Hamlet's unhappiness,—

"Sicklied o'er with the pale cast of thought."[33]

---

[32] Active volcanoes: Etna, on the East coast of Sicily; Vesuvius, near Naples, Italy.
[33] From Shakespeare's *Hamlet* (III.i.85).

Is it so bad then? Sight is the last thing to be pitied. Would we be blind? Do we fear lest we should outsee nature and God, and drink truth dry? I look upon the discontent of the literary class as a mere announcement of the fact that they find themselves not in the state of mind of their fathers, and regret the coming state as untried; as a boy dreads the water before he has learned that he can swim. If there is any period one would desire to be born in,—is it not the age of Revolution; when the old and the new stand side by side, and admit of being compared; when the energies of all men are searched by fear and by hope; when the historic glories of the old, can be compensated by the rich possibilities of the new era? This time, like all times, is a very good one, if we but know what to do with it.

I read with joy some of the auspicious signs of the coming days as they glimmer already through poetry and art, through philosophy and science, through church and state.

One of these signs is the fact that the same movement which effected the elevation of what was called the lowest class in the state, assumed in literature a very marked and as benign an aspect. Instead of the sublime and beautiful, the near, the low, the common, was explored and poetized. That which had been negligently trodden under foot by those who were harnessing and provisioning themselves for long journeys into far countries, is suddenly found to be richer than all foreign parts. The literature of the poor, the feelings of the child, the philosophy of the street, the meaning of household life, are the topics of the time. It is a great stride. It is a sign—is it not? of new vigor, when the extremities are made active, when currents of warm life run into the hands and the feet. I ask not for the great, the remote, the romantic; what is doing in Italy or Arabia; what is Greek art, or Provencal Ministrelsy;[34] I embrace the common, I explore and sit at the feet of the familiar, the low. Give me insight into to-day, and you may have the antique and future worlds. What would we really know the meaning of? The meal in the firkin;[35] the milk in the pan; the ballad in the street; the news of the boat; the glance of the eye; the form and the gait of the body:—show me the ultimate reason of these matters;—show me the sublime presence of the highest spiritual cause lurking, as always it does lurk, in these suburbs and extremities of nature; let me see every trifle bristling with the polarity that ranges it instantly on an eternal law; and the shop, the plough, and the le[d]ger, referred to the like cause by which light undulates and poets sing;—and the world lies no longer a dull miscellany and lumber room,[36] but has form and order; there is no trifle; there is no puzzle; but one design unites and animates the farthest pinnacle and the lowest trench.

This idea has inspired the genius of Goldsmith, Burns, Cowper, and, in a newer time, of Goethe, Wordsworth, and Carlyle.[37] This idea they have differently followed and with various success. In contrast with their writing, the style of Pope, of Johnson, of Gibbon,[38] looks cold and pedantic. This writing is blood-warm. Man is surprised to find that things near are not less beautiful and wondrous than things remote. The near explains the far. The drop is a small ocean. A man is related to all nature. This perception of the worth of the vulgar, is fruitful

---

[34] The musical entertainment of medieval troubadors, centered in Provence, in southeastern France.
[35] A small wooden tub.   [36] A storeroom.
[37] Preromantic writers Oliver Goldsmith (1730–1794), Robert Burns (1759–1796), and William Cowper (1731–1800); and romantic writers Johann Wolfgang von Goethe (1749–1832), William Wordsworth (1770–1850), and Thomas Carlyle (1795–1881).
[38] The eighteenth-century writers Alexander Pope (1688–1744), Samuel Johnson (1709–1784), and Edward Gibbon (1737–1794).

in discoveries. Goethe, in this very thing the most modern of the moderns, has shown us, as none ever did, the genius of the ancients.

There is one man of genius who has done much for this philosophy of life, whose literary value has never yet been rightly estimated;—I mean Emanuel Swedenborg.[39] The most imaginative of men, yet writing with the precision of a mathematician, he endeavored to engraft a purely philosophical Ethics on the popular Christianity of his time. Such an attempt, of course, must have difficulty which no genius could surmount. But he saw and showed the connexion between nature and the affections of the soul. He pierced the emblematic or spiritual character of the visible, audible, tangible world. Especially did his shade-loving muse hover over and interpret the lower parts of nature; he showed the mysterious bond that allies moral evil to the foul material forms, and has given in epical parables a theory of insanity, of beasts, of unclean and fearful things.

Another sign of our times, also marked by an analogous political movement is, the new importance given to the single person. Every thing that tends to insulate the individual,—to surround him with barriers of natural respect, so that each man shall feel the world is his, and man shall treat with man as a sovereign state with a sovereign state;—tends to true union as well as greatness. "I learned," said the melancholy Pestalozzi,[40] "that no man in God's wide earth is either willing or able to help any other man." Help must come from the bosom alone. The scholar is that man who must take up into himself all the ability of the time, all the contributions of the past, all the hopes of the future. He must be an university of knowledges. If there be one lesson more than another which should pierce his ear, it is, The world is nothing, the man is all; in yourself is the law of all nature, and you know not yet how a globule of sap ascends; in yourself slumbers the whole of Reason; it is for you to know all, it is for you to dare all. Mr. President and Gentlemen, this confidence in the unsearched might of man, belongs by all motives, by all prophecy, by all preparation, to the American Scholar. We have listened too long to the courtly muses of Europe. The spirit of the American freeman is already suspected to be timid, imitative, tame. Public and private avarice make the air we breathe thick and fat. The scholar is decent, indolent, complaisant.[41] See already the tragic consequence. The mind of this country taught to aim at low objects, eats upon itself. There is no work for any but decorous and the complaisant. Young men of the fairest promise, who begin life upon our shores, inflated by the mountain winds, shined upon by all the stars of God, find the earth below not in unison with these,—but are hindered from action by the disgust which the principles on which business is managed inspire, and turn drudges, or die of disgust,—some of them suicides. What is the remedy? They did not yet see, and thousands of young men as hopeful now crowding to the barriers for the career, do not yet see, that if the single man plant himself indomitably on his instincts, and there abide, the huge world will come round to him. Patience—patience;—with the shades of all the good and great for company; and for solace, the perspective of your own infinite life; and for work, the study and the communication of principles, the making those instincts prevalent, the conversion of the world. Is it not the chief disgrace in the world, not to be an unit;—not to be reckoned one char-

---

[39] Swedenborg (1688–1772) was a Swedish theologian and mystic whose idea of correspondence between the spiritual and the natural world virtually made Creation an allegory of the divine mind—a concept that intrigued Emerson.

[40] Johann Heinrich Pestalozzi (1746–1827), a Swiss educator.   [41] Willing to please.

acter;—not to yield that peculiar fruit which each man was created to bear, but to be reckoned in the gross, in the hundred, or the thousand, of the party, the section, to which we belong; and our opinion predicted geographically, as the north, or the south. Not so, brothers and friends,—please God, ours shall not be so. We will walk on our own feet; we will work with our own hands; we will speak our own minds. The study of letters shall be no longer a name for pity, for doubt, and for sensual indulgence. The dread of man and the love of man shall be a wall of defence and a wreath of joy around all. A nation of men will for the first time exist, because each believes himself inspired by the Divine Soul which also inspires all men.

1837

SELF-RELIANCE*

"Ne te quæsiveris extra."[1]

"Man is his own star; and the soul that can
Render an honest and a perfect man,
Commands all light, all influence, all fate;
Nothing to him falls early or too late.
Our acts our angels are, or good or ill,
Our fatal shadows that walk by us still."

Epilogue to Beaumont and Fletcher's *Honest Man's Fortune.*[2]

Cast the bantling[3] on the rocks,
Suckle him with the she-wolf's teat;
Wintered with the hawk and fox,
Power and speed be hands and feet.

I read the other day some verses written by an eminent painter[4] which were original and not conventional. The soul always hears an admonition in such lines, let the subject be what it may. The sentiment they instil is of more value than any thought they may contain. To believe your own thought, to believe that what is true for you in your private heart, is true for all men,—that is genius. Speak your latent conviction and it shall be the universal sense; for the inmost in due time becomes the outmost,—and our first thought is rendered back to us by the trumpets of the Last Judgment. Familiar as the voice of the mind is to each, the highest merit we ascribe to Moses, Plato, and Milton, is that they set at naught books and

---

* First published in *Essays* in 1841. Many of the ideas in this essay are taken from Emerson's journal entries, dating from 1832 to 1840.

[1] "Do not seek outside yourself" (Latin); from the first of six satires by Persius Flaccus (A. D. 34–62), a Roman Stoic writer.

[2] The Elizabethan dramatists Francis Beaumont (1584–1616) and John Fletcher (1579–1625); however, *The Honest Man's Fortune* (1647) is believed to have been written in 1613 by Fletcher and another dramatist, Philip Massinger (1583–1640).

[3] Infant. These four lines were composed by Emerson.

[4] Probably Washington Allston (1779–1843), an American painter and poet. Emerson praises a poem of Allston's in a journal entry for September 20, 1837.

traditions, and spoke not what men but what they thought. A man should learn to detect and watch that gleam of light which flashes across his mind from within, more than the lustre of the firmament of bards and sages. Yet he dismisses without notice his thought, because it is his. In every work of genius we recognize our own rejected thoughts: they come back to us with a certain alienated majesty. Great works of art have no more affecting lesson for us than this. They teach us to abide by our spontaneous impression with good-humored inflexibility then most when the whole cry of voices is on the other side. Else, tomorrow a stranger will say with masterly good sense precisely what we have thought and felt all the time, and we shall be forced to take with shame our own opinion from another.

There is a time in every man's education when he arrives at the conviction that envy is ignorance; that imitation is suicide; that he must take himself for better, for worse, as his portion; that though the wide universe is full of good, no kernel of nourishing corn can come to him but through his toil bestowed on that plot of ground which is given to him to till. The power which resides in him is new in nature, and none but he knows what that is which he can do, nor does he know until he has tried. Not for nothing one face, one character, one fact makes much impression on him, and another none. This sculpture in the memory is not without preëstablished harmony. The eye was placed where one ray should fall, that it might testify of that particular ray. We but half express ourselves, and are ashamed of that divine idea which each of us represents. It may be safely trusted as proportionate and of good issues, so it be faithfully imparted, but God will not have his work made manifest by cowards. A man is relieved and gay when he has put his heart into his work and done his best; but what he has said or done otherwise, shall give him no peace. It is a deliverance which does not deliver. In the attempt his genius deserts him; no muse befriends; no invention, no hope.

Trust thyself: every heart vibrates to that iron string. Accept the place the divine Providence has found for you; the society of your contemporaries, the connexion of events. Great men have always done so and confided themselves childlike to the genius of their age, betraying their perception that the absolutely trustworthy was seated at their heart, working through their hands, predominating in all their being. And we are now men, and must accept in the highest mind the same transcendent destiny; and not minors and invalids in a protected corner, not cowards fleeing before a revolution, but guides, redeemers, and benefactors, obeying the Almighty effort, and advancing on Chaos and the Dark.

What pretty oracles nature yields us on this text in the face and behavior of children, babes and even brutes. That divided and rebel mind, that distrust of a sentiment because our arithmetic has computed the strength and means opposed to our purpose, these have not. Their mind being whole, their eye is as yet unconquered, and when we look in their faces, we are disconcerted. Infancy conforms to nobody; all conform to it, so that one babe commonly makes four or five out of the adults who prattle and play to it. So God has armed youth and puberty and manhood no less with its own piquancy and charm, and made it enviable and gracious and its claims not to be put by, if it will stand by itself. Do not think the youth has no force because he cannot speak to you and me. Hark! in the next room his voice is sufficiently clear and emphatic. It seems he knows how to speak to his contemporaries. Bashful or bold, then, he will know how to make us seniors very unnecessary.

The nonchalance of boys who are sure of a dinner, and would disdain as much as a lord to do or say aught to conciliate one, is the healthy attitude of human nature. A boy is in the parlour what the pit[5] is in the playhouse; independent, irresponsible, looking out from his corner on such people and facts as pass by, he tries and sentences them on their merits, in the swift summary way of boys, as good, bad, interesting, silly, eloquent, troublesome. He cumbers himself never about consequences, about interests: he gives an independent, genuine verdict. You must court him: he does not court you. But the man is, as it were, clapped into jail by his consciousness. As soon as he has once acted or spoken with eclat,[6] he is a committed person, watched by the sympathy or the hatred of hundreds whose affections must now enter into his account. There is no Lethe[7] for this. Ah, that he could pass again into his neutrality! Who can thus avoid all pledges, and having observed, observe again from the same unaffected, unbiased, unbribable, unaffrighted innocence, must alway be formidable. He would utter opinions on all passing affairs, which being seen to be not private but necessary, would sink like darts into the ear of men, and put them in fear.

These are the voices which we hear in solitude, but they grow faint and inaudible as we enter into the world. Society everywhere is in conspiracy against the manhood of every one of its members. Society is a joint-stock company in which the members agree for the better securing of his bread to each shareholder, to surrender the liberty and culture of the eater. The virtue in most request is conformity. Self-reliance is its aversion. It loves not realities and creators, but names and customs.

Whoso would be a man must be a nonconformist. He who would gather immortal palms[8] must not be hindered by the name of goodness, but must explore if it be goodness. Nothing is at last sacred but the integrity of your own mind. Absolve you to yourself, and you shall have the suffrage of the world. I remember an answer which when quite young I was prompted to make to a valued adviser who was wont to importune me with the dear old doctrines of the church. On my saying, What have I to do with the sacredness of traditions, if I live wholly from within? my friend suggested—"But these impulses may be from below, not from above." I replied, "They do not seem to me to be such; but if I am the Devil's child, I will live then from the Devil." No law can be sacred to me but that of my nature. Good and bad are but names very readily transferable to that or this; the only right is what is after my constitution, the only wrong what is against it. A man is to carry himself in the presence of all opposition as if every thing were titular and ephemeral but he. I am ashamed to think how easily we capitulate to badges and names, to large societies and dead institutions. Every decent and well-spoken individual affects and sways me more than is right. I ought to go upright and vital, and speak the rude truth in all ways. If malice and vanity wear the coat of philanthropy, shall that pass? If an angry bigot assumes this bountiful cause of Abolition, and comes to me with his last news from Barbadoes,[9] why should I not say to him, 'Go love thy infant; love thy woodchopper: be good-natured and modest: have that grace; and never varnish your hard, uncharitable ambition with this incredible tenderness for black folk a thousand miles off. Thy love afar is spite at home.' Rough and graceless would be such greeting, but truth is handsomer than

---

[5] The cheapest seats in Elizabethan theaters, where the audience was not restrained by "proper" manners.
[6] "Brilliance of purpose" (French).
[7] According to Greek myth, the river of forgetfulness, in the underworld.   [8] Great honors.
[9] Slavery was abolished on this British West Indian island in 1834.

the affectation of love. Your goodness must have some edge to it—else it is none. The doctrine of hatred must be preached as the counteraction of the doctrine of love when that pules[10] and whines. I shun father and mother and wife and brother, when my genius calls me. I would write on the lintels[11] of the door-post, *Whim*. I hope it is somewhat better than whim at last, but we cannot spend the day in explanation. Expect me not to show cause why I seek or why I exclude company. Then, again, do not tell me, as a good man did to-day, of my obligation to put all poor men in good situations. Are they *my* poor? I tell thee, thou foolish philanthropist, that I grudge the dollar, the dime, the cent I give to such men as do not belong to me and to whom I do not belong. There is a class of persons to whom by all spiritual affinity I am bought and sold; for them I will go to prison, if need be; but your miscellaneous popular charities; the education at college of fools; the building of meeting-houses to the vain end to which many now stand; alms to sots; and the thousandfold Relief Societies;—though I confess with shame I sometimes succumb and give the dollar, it is a wicked dollar which by and by I shall have the manhood to withhold.

Virtues are in the popular estimate rather the exception than the rule. There is the man *and* his virtues. Men do what is called a good action, as some piece of courage or charity, much as they would pay a fine in expiation of daily non-appearance on parade. Their works are done as an apology or extenuation of their living in the world,—as invalids and the insane pay a high board. Their virtues are penances. I do not wish to expiate, but to live. My life is for itself and not for a spectacle. I much prefer that it should be of a lower strain, so it be genuine and equal, than that it should be glittering and unsteady. I wish it to be sound and sweet, and not to need diet and bleeding.[12] I ask primary evidence that you are a man, and refuse this appeal from the man to his actions. I know that for myself it makes no difference whether I do or forbear those actions which are reckoned excellent. I cannot consent to pay for a privilege where I have intrinsic right. Few and mean as my gifts may be, I actually am, and do not need for my own assurance or the assurance of my fellows any secondary testimony.

What I must do, is all that concerns me, not what the people think. This rule, equally arduous in actual and in intellectual life, may serve for the whole distinction between greatness and meanness. It is the harder, because you will always find those who think they know what is your duty better than you know it. It is easy in the world to live after the world's opinion; it is easy in solitude to live after our own; but the great man is he who in the midst of the crowd keeps with perfect sweetness the independence of solitude.

The objection to conforming to usages that have become dead to you, is, that it scatters your force. It loses your time and blurs the impression of your character. If you maintain a dead church, contribute to a dead Bible-Society, vote with a great party either for the Government or against it, spread your table like base housekeepers,—under all these screens, I have difficulty to detect the precise man you are. And, of course, so much force is withdrawn from your proper life. But do your work, and I shall know you. Do your work, and you shall reinforce your-

---

[10] Whimpers.

[11] Horizontal beams spanning doorways. Emerson equates the obligation to heed his "genius" with the biblical injunction to shun family in order to follow a divine command (see Matthew 10:34–37) and alludes to the Lord's instructions to Moses for marking with blood the doorposts of houses to be spared from punishment (see Exodus 12:21–23).

[12] Bloodletting, an old medical practice.

self. A man must consider what a blindman's-buff is this game of conformity. If I know your sect, I anticipate your argument. I hear a preacher announce for his text and topic the expediency of one of the institutions of his church. Do I not know beforehand that not possibly can he say a new and spontaneous word? Do I not know that with all this ostentation of examining the grounds of the institution, he will do no such thing? Do I not know that he is pledged to himself not to look but at one side,—the permitted side, not as a man, but as a parish minister? He is a retained attorney, and these airs of the bench are the emptiest affectation. Well, most men have bound their eyes with one or another handkerchief, and attached themselves to some one of these communities of opinion. This conformity makes them not false in a few particulars, authors of a few lies, but false in all particulars. Their every truth is not quite true. Their two is not the real two, their four not the real four; so that every word they say chagrins us, and we know not where to begin to set them right. Meantime nature is not slow to equip us in the prison-uniform of the party to which we adhere. We come to wear one cut of face and figure, and acquire by degrees the gentlest asinine expression. There is a mortifying experience in particular which does not fail to wreak itself also in the general history; I mean "the foolish face of praise,"[13] the forced smile which we put on in company where we do not feel at ease in answer to conversation which does not interest us. The muscles, not spontaneously moved, but moved by a low usurping wilfulness, grow tight about the outline of the face with the most disagreeable sensation.

For nonconformity the world whips you with its displeasure. And therefore a man must know how to estimate a sour face. The bystanders look askance on him in the public street or in the friend's parlor. If this aversation had its origin in contempt and resistance like his own, he might well go home with a sad countenance; but the sour faces of the multitude, like their sweet faces, have no deep cause, but are put on and off as the wind blows, and a newspaper directs. Yet is the discontent of the multitude more formidable than that of the senate and the college. It is easy enough for a firm man who knows the world to brook the rage of the cultivated classes. Their rage is decorous and prudent, for they are timid as being very vulnerable themselves. But when to their feminine rage the indignation of the people is added, when the ignorant and the poor are aroused, when the unintelligent brute force that lies at the bottom of society is made to growl and mow,[14] it needs the habit of magnanimity and religion to treat it godlike as a trifle of no concernment.

The other terror that scares us from self-trust is our consistency; a reverence for our past act or word, because the eyes of others have no other data for computing our orbit than our past acts, and we are loath to disappoint them.

But why should you keep your head over your shoulder? Why drag about this corpse of your memory, lest you contradict somewhat you have stated in this or that public place? Suppose you should contradict yourself; what then? It seems to be a rule of wisdom never to rely on your memory alone, scarcely even in acts of pure memory, but to bring the past for judgment into the thousand-eyed present, and live ever in a new day. In your metaphysics you have denied personality to the Deity; yet when the devout motions of the soul come, yield to them heart and life,

---

[13] From the ironic poem "Epistle to Dr. Arbuthnot" (1735), by Alexander Pope (1688–1744).
[14] To grimace or mock.

though they should clothe God with shape and color. Leave your theory as Joseph his coat in the hand of the harlot,[15] and flee.

A foolish consistency is the hobgoblin of little minds, adored by little statesmen and philosophers and divines. With consistency a great soul has simply nothing to do. He may as well concern himself with his shadow on the wall. Speak what you think now in hard words, and to-morrow speak what to-morrow thinks in hard words again, though it contradict every thing you said to-day.—'Ah, so you shall be sure to be misunderstood.'—Is it so bad then to be misunderstood? Pythagoras[16] was misunderstood, and Socrates, and Jesus, and Luther, and Copernicus, and Galileo, and Newton,[17] and every pure and wise spirit that ever took flesh. To be great is to be misunderstood.

I suppose no man can violate his nature. All the allies of his will are rounded in by the law of his being as the inequalities of Andes and Himmaleh[18] are insignificant in the curve of the sphere. Nor does it matter how you gauge and try him. A character is like an acrostic or Alexandrian stanza;[19]—read it forward, backward, or across, it still spells the same thing. In this pleasing contrite wood-life which God allows me, let me record day by day my honest thought without prospect or retrospect, and, I cannot doubt, it will be found symmetrical, though I mean it not, and see it not. My book should smell of pines and resound with the hum of insects. The swallow over my window should interweave that thread or straw he carries in his bill into my web also. We pass for what we are. Character teaches above our wills. Men imagine that they communicate their virtue or vice only by overt actions and do not see that virtue or vice emit a breath every moment.

There will be an agreement in whatever variety of actions, so they be each honest and natural in their hour. For of one will, the actions will be harmonious, however unlike they seem. These varieties are lost sight of at a little distance, at a little height of thought. One tendency unites them all. The voyage of the best ship is a zigzag line of a hundred tacks. See the line from a sufficient distance, and it straightens itself to the average tendency. Your genuine action will explain itself and will explain your other genuine actions. Your conformity explains nothing. Act singly, and what you have already done singly, will justify you now. Greatness apppeals to the future. If I can be firm enough to-day to do right and scorn eyes, I must have done so much right before, as to defend me now. Be it how it will, do right now. Always scorn appearances, and you always may. The force of character is cumulative. All the foregone days of virtue work their health into this. What makes the majesty of the heroes of the senate and the field, which so fills the imagination? The consciousness of a train of great days and victories behind. They shed an united light on the advancing actor. He is attended as by a visible escort of angels. That is it which throws thunder into Chatham's[20] voice, and

[15] In Genesis 39:12 when Potiphar's wife grabbed Joseph's coat and asked him to sleep with her, "he left his garment in her hand, and fled."

[16] A sixth-century B.C. Greek mathematician and philosopher.

[17] Martin Luther (1483–1546), the German leader of the Protestant Reformation; Nicolaus Copernicus (1473–1543), the Polish astronomer who determined the movements of the solar system; Galileo Galilei (1564–1642), the renowned Italian astronomer and physicist who supported Copernican theories rather than classical Ptolemaic ideas; Sir Issac Newton (1642–1727), the English mathematician and natural philosopher who formulated the laws of gravity and motion.

[18] The Himalaya Mountains.

[19] A palindrome, a word or phrase that reads the same forward or backward: "Madam, I'm Adam."

[20] William Pitt (1708–1778), the earl of Chatham, known as "the Great Commoner" for his eloquent insistence on constitutional rights.

dignity into Washington's port,[21] and America into Adams's[22] eye. Honor is venerable to us because it is no ephemeris. It is always ancient virtue. We worship it to-day, because it is not of to-day. We love it and pay it homage, because it is not a trap for our love and homage, but is self-dependent, self-derived, and therefore of an old immaculate pedigree, even if shown in a young person.

I hope in these days we have heard the last of conformity and consistency. Let the words be gazetted[23] and ridiculous henceforward. Instead of the gong for dinner, let us hear a whistle from the Spartan fife.[24] Let us never bow and apologize more. A great man is coming to eat at my house. I do not wish to please him: I wish that he should wish to please me. I will stand here for humanity, and though I would make it kind, I would make it true. Let us affront and reprimand the smooth mediocrity and squalid contentment of the times, and hurl in the face of custom, and trade, and office, the fact which is the upshot of all history, that there is a great responsible Thinker and Actor working wherever a man works; that a true man belongs to no other time or place, but is the centre of things. Where he is, there is nature. He measures you, and all men, and all events. Ordinarily every body in society reminds us of somewhat else or of some other person. Character, reality, reminds you of nothing else; it takes place of the whole creation. The man must be so much that he must make all circumstances indifferent. Every true man is a cause, a country, and an age; requires infinite spaces and numbers and time fully to accomplish his design;—and posterity seem to follow his steps as a train of clients. A man Cæsar is born, and for ages after, we have a Roman Empire. Christ is born, and millions of minds so grow and cleave to his genius, that he is confounded with virtue and the possible of man. An institution is the lengthened shadow of one man; as, Monachism, of the Hermit Antony;[25] the Reformation, of Luther; Quakerism, of Fox; Methodism, of Wesley; Abolition, of Clarkson.[26] Scipio,[27] Milton called "the height of Rome;" and all history resolves itself very easily into the biography of a few stout and earnest persons.

Let a man then know his worth, and keep things under his feet. Let him not peep or steal, or skulk up and down with the air of a charity-boy, a bastard, or an interloper, in the world which exists for him. But the man in the street finding no worth in himself which corresponds to the force which built a tower or sculptured a marble god, feels poor when he looks on these. To him a palace, a statue, or a costly book have an alien and forbidding air, much like a gay equipage, and seem to say like that, 'Who are you, sir?' Yet they are all his, suitors for his notice, petitioners to his faculties that they will come out and take possession. The picture waits for my verdict: it is not to command me, but I am to settle its claims to praise. That popular fable[28] of the sot who was picked up dead drunk in the street,

---

[21] George Washington's carriage or bearing.

[22] Samuel Adams (1722–1803), a spokesman for the Revolutionary movement in Massachusetts, or more likely Washington's contemporary John Adams (1735–1826), the second U.S. president, or John Quincy Adams (1767–1848), the sixth U.S. president.

[23] Put in a newspaper and made publicly ridiculous.

[24] The Spartans were known for their rigor and discipline; hence, sober music.

[25] St. Anthony (251?–350?), an Egyptian hermit known as the father of Christian monasticism ("Monachism").

[26] George Fox (1624–1691), founder of the Society of Friends (Quakers); John Wesley (1703–1791), founder of Methodism; Thomas Clarkson (1760–1846), an English abolitionist.

[27] Scipio Aemilianus (185?–129? B.C.), known as Scipio Africanus, Minor: the destroyer of Carthage (146 B.C.) and a patron of writers. John Milton (1608–1674) praises him in *Paradise Lost* (IX. 510).

[28] Known from the "Induction" to Shakespeare's *Taming of the Shrew*.

carried to the duke's house, washed and dressed and laid in the duke's bed, and, on his waking, treated with all obsequious ceremony like the duke, and assured that he had been insane, owes its popularity to the fact, that it symbolizes so well the state of man, who is in the world a sort of sot, but now and then wakes up, exercises his reason, and finds himself a true prince.

Our reading is mendicant and sycophantic.[29] In history, our imagination plays us false. Kingdom and lordship, power and estate are a gaudier vocabulary than private John and Edward in a small house and common day's work: but the things of life are the same to both: the sum total of both is the same. Why all this defer-ence to Alfred, and Scanderbeg, and Gustavus?[30] Suppose they were virtuous: did they wear out virtue? As great a stake depends on your private act to-day, as followed their public and renowned steps. When private men shall act with origi-nal views, the lustre will be transferred from the actions of kings to those of gen-tlemen.

The world has been instructed by its kings, who have so magnetized the eyes of nations. It has been taught by this colossal symbol the mutual reverence that is due from man to man. The joyful loyalty with which men have everywhere suffered the king, the noble, or the great proprietor to walk among them by a law of his own, make his own scale of men and things, and reverse theirs, pay for benefits not with money but with honor, and represent the Law in his person, was the hieroglyphic by which they obscurely signified their consciousness of their own right and comeliness, the right of every man.

The magnetism which all original action exerts is explained when we inquire the reason of self-trust. Who is the Trustee? What is the aboriginal Self on which a universal reliance may be grounded? What is the nature and power of that science-baffling star, without parallax,[31] without calculable elements, which shoots a ray of beauty even into trivial and impure actions, if the least mark of independence appear? The inquiry leads us to that source, at once the essence of genius, of virtue, and of life, which we call Spontaneity or Instinct. We denote this primary wisdom as Intuition, whilst all later teachings are tuitions. In that deep force, the last fact behind which analysis cannot go, all things find their common origin. For the sense of being which in calm hours rises, we know not how, in the soul, is not diverse from things, from space, from light, from time, from man, but one with them, and proceeds obviously from the same source whence their life and being also proceed. We first share the life by which things exist, and afterwards see them as appearances in nature, and forget that we have shared their cause. Here is the fountain of action and of thought. Here are the lungs of that inspiration which giveth man wisdom, and which cannot be denied without impiety and atheism. We lie in the lap of immense intelligence, which makes us receivers of its truth and organs of its activity. When we discern justice, when we discern truth, we do nothing of ourselves, but allow a passage to its beams. If we ask whence this comes, if we seek to pry into the soul that causes, all philosophy is at fault. Its presence or its absence is all we can affirm. Every man discriminates between the voluntary acts of his mind, and his involuntary perceptions, and knows that to his involuntary perceptions a perfect faith is due. He may err in the expression of

---

[29] Poverty-stricken and parasitical.
[30] King Alfred the Great (849–899) of England; George Castriota (1403?–1468), an Albanian chief-tain; King Gustavus Adolphus (1594–1632) of Sweden.
[31] Without an observable or measurable position.

them, but he knows that these things are so, like day and night, not to be disputed. My wilful actions and acquisitions are but roving;—the idlest reverie, the faintest native emotion, command my curiosity and respect. Thoughtless people contradict as readily the statement of perceptions as of opinions, or rather much more readily; for, they do not distinguish between perception and notion. They fancy that I choose to see this or that thing. But perception is not whimsical, but fatal. If I see a trait, my children will see it after me, and in course of time, all mankind,— although it may chance that no one has seen it before me. For my perception of it is as much a fact as the sun.

The relations of the soul to the divine spirit are so pure that it is profane to seek to interpose helps. It must be that when God speaketh, he should communicate not one thing, but all things; should fill the world with his voice; should scatter forth light, nature, time, souls, from the centre of the present thought; and new date and new create the whole. Whenever a mind is simple, and receives a divine wisdom, old things pass away,—means, teachers, texts, temples fall; it lives now and absorbs past and future into the present hour. All things are made sacred by relation to it,—one as much as another. All things are dissolved to their centre by their cause, and in the universal miracle petty and particular miracles disappear. If, therefore, a man claims to know and speak of God, and carries you backward to the phraseology of some old mouldered nation in another country, in another world, believe him not. Is the acorn better than the oak which is its fulness and completion? Is the parent better than the child into whom he has cast his ripened being? Whence then this worship of the past? The centuries are conspirators against the sanity and authority of the soul. Time and space are but physiological colors which the eye makes, but the soul is light; where it is, is day; where it was, is night; and history is an impertinence and an injury, if it be anything more than a cheerful apologue or parable of my being and becoming.

Man is timid and apologetic; he is not longer upright; he dares not say 'I think', 'I am,' but quotes some saint or sage. He is ashamed before the blade of grass or the blowing rose. These roses under my window make no reference to former roses or to better ones; they are for what they are; they exist with God to-day. There is no time to them. There is simply the rose; it is perfect in every moment of its existence. Before a leaf-bud has burst, its whole life acts; in the full-blown flower, there is no more; in the leafless root, there is no less. Its nature is satisfied, and it satisfies nature, in all moments alike. But man postpones or remembers; he does not live in the present, but with reverted eye laments the past, or, heedless of the riches that surround him, stands on tiptoe to foresee the future. He cannot be happy and strong until he too lives with nature in the present, above time.

This should be plain enough. Yet see what strong intellects dare not yet hear God himself, unless he speak the phraseology of I know not what David, or Jeremiah, or Paul.[32] We shall not always set so great a price on a few texts, on a few lives. We are like children who repeat by rote the sentences of grandames and tutors, and, as they grow older, of the men of talents and character they chance to see,—painfully recollecting the exact words they spoke; afterwards, when they come into the point of view which those had who uttered these sayings, they understand them, and are willing to let the words go; for, at any time, they can use words as good, when occasion comes. If we live truly, we shall see truly. It is as

---

[32] The second king of Israel, reputedly the author of the Book of Psalms; the Hebrew prophet who wrote the Book of Jeremiah; the Apostle known for his letters (New Testament Epistles).

easy for the strong man to be strong, as it is for the weak to be weak. When we have new perception, we shall gladly disburden the memory of its hoarded treasures as old rubbish. When a man lives with God, his voice shall be as sweet as the murmur of the brook and the rustle of the corn.

And now at last the highest truth on this subject remains unsaid; probably, cannot be said; for all that we say is the far off remembering of the intuition.[33] That thought, by what I can now nearest approach to say it, is this. When good is near you, when you have life in yourself, it is not by any known or accustomed way; you shall not discern the foot-prints of any other; you shall not see the face of man; you shall not hear any name;—the way, the thought, the good shall be wholly strange and new. It shall exclude example and experience. You take the way from man, not to man. All persons that ever existed are its forgotten ministers. Fear and hope are alike beneath it. There is somewhat low even in hope. In the hour of vision, there is nothing that can be called gratitude, nor properly joy. The soul raised over passion beholds identity and eternal causation, perceives the self-existence of Truth and Right, and calms itself with knowing that all things go well. Vast spaces of nature, the Atlantic Ocean, the South Sea,—long intervals of time, years, centuries,—are of no account. This which I think and feel underlay every former state of life and circumstances, as it does underlie my present, and what is called life, and what is called death.

Life only avails, not the having lived. Power ceases in the instant of repose; it resides in the moment of transition from a past to a new state, in the shooting of the gulf, in the darting to an aim. This one fact the world hates, that the soul *becomes;* for, that forever degrades the past, turns all riches to poverty, all reputation to a shame, confounds the saint with the rogue, shoves Jesus and Judas equally aside. Why then do we prate of self-reliance? Inasmuch as the soul is present, there will be power not confident but agent. To talk of reliance, is a poor external way of speaking. Speak rather of that which relies, because it works and is. Who has more obedience than I, masters me, though he should not raise his finger. Round him I must revolve by the gravitation of spirits. We fancy it rhetoric when we speak of eminent virtue. We do not yet see that virtue is Height, and that a man or a company of men plastic and permeable to priniciples, by the law of nature must overpower and ride all cities, nations, kings, rich men, poets, who are not.

This is the ultimate fact which we so quickly reach on this as on every topic, the resolution of all into the ever blessed ONE. Self-existence is the attribute of the Supreme Cause, and it constitutes the measure of good by the degree in which it enters into all lower forms. All things real are so by so much virtue as they contain. Commerce, husbandry, hunting, whaling, war, eloquence, personal weight, are somewhat, and engage my respect as examples of its presence and impure action. I see the same law working in nature for conservation and growth. Power is in nature the essential measure of right. Nature suffers nothing to remain in her kingdoms which cannot help itself. The genesis and maturation of a planet, its poise and orbit, the bended tree recovering itself from the strong wind, the vital resources of every animal and vegetable, are demonstrations of the self-sufficing, and therefore self-relying soul.

---

[33] For Emerson *in*tuition is knowledge that comes from within, directly from the Holy Spirit (which he later calls the Over-Soul); tuition is knowledge gained by experience or through the senses.

Thus all concentrates; let us not rove; let us sit at home with the cause. Let us stun and astonish the intruding rabble of men and books and institutions by a simple declaration of the divine fact. Bid the invaders take the shoes from off their feet, for God is here within.[34] Let our simplicity judge them, and our docility to our own law demonstrate the poverty of nature and fortune beside our native riches.

But now we are a mob. Man does not stand in awe of man, nor is his genius admonished to stay at home, to put itself in communication with the internal ocean, but it goes abroad to beg a cup of water of the urns of other men. We must go alone. I like the silent church before the service begins, better than any preaching. How far off, how cool, how chaste the persons look, begirt each one with a precinct or sanctuary. So let us always sit. Why should we assume the faults of our friend, or wife, or father, or child, because they sit around our hearth, or are said to have the same blood? All men have my blood, and I have all men's. Not for that will I adopt their petulance or folly, even to the extent of being ashamed of it. But your isolation must not be mechanical, but spiritual, that is, must be elevation. At times the whole world seems to be in conspiracy to importune you with emphatic trifles. Friend, client, child, sickness, fear, want, charity, all knock at once at thy closet door and say,—'Come out unto us.' But keep thy state; come not into their confusion. The power men possess to annoy me. I give them by a weak curiosity. No man can come near me but through my act. "What we love that we have, but by desire we bereave ourselves of the love."[35]

If we cannot at once rise to the sanctities of obedience and faith, let us at least resist our temptations; let us enter into the state of war, and wake Thor and Woden,[36] courage and constancy, in our Saxon breasts. This is to be done in our smooth times by speaking the truth. Check this lying hospitality and lying affection. Live no longer to the expectation of these deceived and deceiving people with whom we converse. Say to them, O father, O mother, O wife, O brother, O friend, I have lived with you after appearances hitherto. Henceforward I am the truth's. Be it known unto you that henceforward I obey no law less than the eternal law. I will have no covenants but proximities. I shall endeavor to nourish my parents, to support my family, to be the chaste husband of one wife,—but these relations I must fill after a new and unprecedented way. I appeal from your customs. I must be myself. I cannot break myself any longer for you, or you. If you can love me for what I am, we shall be the happier. If you cannot, I will seek to deserve that you should. I will not hide my tastes or aversions. I will so trust that what is deep is holy, that I will do strongly before the sun and moon whatever inly rejoices me, and the heart appoints. If you are noble, I will love you; if you are not, I will not hurt you and myself by hypocritical attentions. If you are true, but not in the same truth with me, cleave to your companions; I will seek my own. I do this not selfishly, but humbly and truly. It is alike your interest and mine and all men's, however long we have dwelt in lies, to live in truth. Does this sound harsh to-day? You will soon love what is dictated by your nature as well as mine, and if we follow the truth, it will bring us out safe at last.—But so you may give these friends pain. Yes, but I cannot sell my liberty and my power, to save their

[34] In Exodus 3:5 God tells Moses to "put off thy shoes from off they feet, for the place whereon thou standest is holy ground."

[35] From the German poet and dramatist Friedrich Schiller (1759–1805).

[36] According to Norse myth, the gods of thunder and of war.

sensibility. Besides, all persons have their moments of reason when they look out into the region of absolute truth; then will they justify me and do the same thing.

The populace think that your rejection of popular standards is a rejection of all standard, and mere antinomianism;[37] and the bold sensualist will use the name of philosophy to gild his crimes. But the law of consciousness abides. There are two confessionals, in one or the other of which we must be shriven. You may fulfil your round of duties by clearing yourself in the *direct,* or, in the *reflex* way. Consider whether you have satisfied your relations to father, mother, cousin, neighbor, town, cat, and dog; whether any of these can upbraid you. But I may also neglect this reflex standard, and absolve me to myself. I have my own stern claims and perfect circle. It denies the name of duty to many offices that are called duties. But if I can discharge its debts, it enables me to dispense with the popular code. If any one imagines that this law is lax, let him keep its commandment one day.

And truly it demands something godlike in him who has cast off the common motives of humanity, and has ventured to trust himself for a taskmaster. High be his heart, faithful his will, clear his sight, that he may in good earnest be doctrine, society, law to himself, that a simple purpose may be to him as strong as iron necessity is to others.

If any man consider the present aspects of what is called by distinction *society,* he will see the need of these ethics. The sinew and heart of man seem to be drawn out, and we are become timorous desponding whimperers. We are afraid of truth, afraid of fortune, afraid of death, and afraid of each other. Our age yields no great and perfect persons. We want men and women who shall renovate life and our social state, but we see that most natures are insolvent, cannot satisfy their own wants, have an ambition out of proportion to their practical force, and do lean and beg day and night continually. Our housekeeping is mendicant, our arts, our occupations, our marriages, our religion we have not chosen, but society has chosen for us. We are parlor soldiers. We shun the rugged battle of fate, where strength is born.

If our young men miscarry in their first enterprizes, they lose all heart. If the young merchant fails, men say he is *ruined.* If the finest genius studies at one of our colleges, and is not installed in an office within one year afterwards in the cities or suburbs of Boston or New York, it seems to his friends and to himself that he is right in being disheartened and in complaining the rest of his life. A sturdy lad from New Hampshire or Vermont, who in turn tries all the professions, who *teams it, farms it, peddles,* keeps a school, preaches, edits a newspaper, goes to Congress, buys a township, and so forth, in successive years, and always, like a cat, falls on his feet, is worth a hundred of these city dolls. He walks abreast with his days, and feels no shame in not 'studying a profession,' for he does not postpone his life, but lives already. He has not one chance, but a hundred chances. Let a Stoic[38] open the resources of man, and tell men they are not leaning willows, but can and must detach themselves; that with the exercise of self-trust, new powers shall appear; that a man is the word made flesh, born to shed healing to the nations,[39] that he should be ashamed of our compassion, and that the mo-

---

[37] Originally, the belief that faith alone, not obedience to the moral law, is needed for salvation; here, a rejection of moral duties and obligations.

[38] Stoic philosopher of Greece, from the fourth and third centuries B.C., who advocated detachment and independence from the world.

[39] "The Word was made flesh and dwelt among us . . . ," from John 1:14; "The leaves of the tree were for the healing of the nations," from Revelation 22:2.

ment he acts from himself, tossing the laws, the books, idolatries, and customs out of the window, we pity him no more but thank and revere him,—and that teacher shall restore the life of man to splendor, and make his name dear to all History.

It is easy to see that a greater self-reliance must work a revolution in all the offices and relations of men; in their religion; in their education; in their pursuits; their modes of living; their assocation; in their property; in their speculative views.

1. In what prayers do men allow themselves! That which they call a holy office, is not so much as brave and manly. Prayer looks abroad and asks for some foreign addition to come through some foreign virtue, and loses itself in endless mazes of natural and supernatural, and mediatorial and miraculous. Prayer that craves a particular commodity,—any thing less than all good,—is vicious. Prayer is the contemplation of the facts of life from the highest point of view. It is the soliloquy of a beholding and jubilant soul. It is the spirit of God pronouncing his works good.[40] But prayer as a means to effect a private end, is meanness and theft. It supposes dualism and not unity in nature and consciousness. As soon as the man is at one with God he will not beg. He will then see prayer in all action. The prayer of the farmer kneeling in his field to weed it, the prayer of the rower kneeling with the stroke of his oar, are true prayers heard throughout nature, though for cheap ends. Caratach, in Fletcher's Bonduca,[41] when admonished to inquire the mind of the god Audate, replies,—

> "His hidden meaning lies in our endeavors,
> Our valors are our best gods."

Another sort of false prayers are our regrets. Discontent is the want of self-reliance: it is infirmity of will. Regret calamities, if you can thereby help the sufferer; if not, attend your own work, and already the evil begins to be repaired. Our sympathy is just as base. We come to them who weep foolishly, and sit down and cry for company, instead of imparting to them truth and health in rough electric shock, putting them once more in communication with their own reason. The secret of fortune is joy in our hands. Welcome evermore to gods and men is the self-helping man. For him all doors are flung wide: him all tongues greet, all honors crown, all eyes follow with desire. Our love goes out to him and embraces him, because he did not need it. We solicitously and apologetically caress and celebrate him, because he held on his way and scorned our disapprobation. The gods love him because men hated him. "To the persevering mortal," said Zoroaster,[42] "the blessed Immortals are swift."

As men's prayers are a disease of the will, so are their creeds a disease of the intellect. They say with those foolish Israelites, 'Let not God speak to us, lest we die. Speak thou, speak any man with us, and we will obey.'[43] Everywhere I am hindered of meeting God in my brother, because he has shut his own temple doors, and recites fables merely of his brother's, or his brother's brother's God. Every new mind is a new classification. If it prove a mind of uncommon activity

---

[40] "And God saw everything that he had made, and behold, it was very good," from Genesis 1:31.

[41] A tragedy by John Fletcher, produced around 1614.

[42] A sixth- or seventh-century B.C. religious teacher and prophet in ancient Persia.

[43] A paraphrase of Exodus 20:19, words spoken by the Israelites to Moses after he brought them the Ten Commandments.

and power, a Locke, a Lavoisier, a Hutton, a Bentham, a Fourier,[44] it imposes its classification on other men, and lo! a new system. In proportion to the depth of the thought, and so to the number of the objects it touches and brings within reach of the pupil, is his complacency. But chiefly is this apparent in creeds and churches, which are also classifications of some powerful mind acting on the elemental thought of Duty, and man's relation to the Highest. Such is Calvinism, Quakerism, Swedenborgianism.[45] The pupil takes the same delight in subordinating every thing to the new terminology, as a girl who has just learned botany in seeing a new earth and new seasons thereby. It will happen for a time, that the pupil will find his intellectual power has grown by the study of his master's mind. But in all unbalanced minds, the classification is idolized, passes for the end, and not for a speedily exhaustible means, so that the walls of the system blend to their eye in the remote horizon with the walls of the universe; the luminaries of heaven seem to them hung on the arch their master built. They cannot imagine how you aliens have any right to see,—how you can see; 'It must be somehow that you stole the light from us.' They do not yet perceive, that light, unsystematic, indomitable, will break into any cabin, even into theirs. Let them chirp awhile and call it their own. If they are honest and do well, presently their neat new pinfold[46] will be too strait and low, will crack, will lean, will rot and vanish, and the immortal light, all young and joyful, million-orbed, million-colored, will beam over the universe as on the first morning.

2. It is for want of self-culture that the superstition of Travelling, whose idols are Italy, England, Egypt, retains its fascination for all educated Americans. They who made England, Italy, or Greece venerable in the imagination, did so by sticking fast where they were, like an axis of the earth. In manly hours, we feel that duty is our place. The soul is no traveller: the wise man stays at home, and when his necessities, his duties, on any occasion call him from his house, or into foreign lands, he is at home still, and shall make men sensible by the expression of his countenance, that he goes the missionary of wisdom and virtue, and visits cities and men like a sovereign, and not like an interloper or a valet.

I have no churlish objection to the circumnavigation of the globe, for the purposes of art, of study, and benevolence, so that the man is first domesticated, or does not go abroad with the hope of finding somewhat greater than he knows. He who travels to be amused, or to get somewhat which he does not carry, travels away from himself, and grows old even in youth among old things. In Thebes, in Palmyra,[47] his will and mind have become old and dilapidated as they. He carries ruins to ruins.

Travelling is a fool's paradise. Our first journeys discover to us the indifference of places. At home I dream that at Naples, at Rome, I can be intoxicated with beauty, and lose my sadness. I pack my trunk, embrace my friends, embark on the

---

[44] John Locke (1632–1704), an English philosopher who rejected Plato's doctrine of innate ideas; Antoine Laurent Lavoisier (1743–1794), the French chemist whose oxygen theory discredited a popular theory of combustion; James Hutton (1726–1797), a Scottish geologist who formulated controversial but currently accepted theories concerning geologic processes on earth; Jeremy Bentham (1748–1832), an English political scientist who helped reform criminal law and judicial procedures; François Marie Charles Fourier (1772–1837), the French social philosopher whose ideas on the "phalanx" influenced the founding of many utopian communities, including Brook Farm (1841–1847), near West Roxbury, Massachusetts.

[45] The religious doctrine of Emanuel Swedenborg (1688–1772), a Swedish theologian and mystic.   [46] An enclosure for animals.   [47] Ruins of ancient Egyptian and Syrian cities.

sea, and at last wake up in Naples, and there beside me is the stern Fact, the sad self, unrelenting, identical, that I fled from. I seek the Vatican, and the palaces. I affect to be intoxicated with sights and suggestions, but I am not intoxicated. My giant[48] goes with me wherever I go.

3. But the rage of travelling is a symptom of deeper unsoundness affecting the whole intellectual action. The intellect is vagabond, and our system of education fosters restlessness. Our minds travel when our bodies are forced to stay at home. We imitate; and what is imitation but the travelling of the mind? Our houses are built with foreign taste; our shelves are garnished with foreign ornaments; our opinions, our tastes, our faculties, lean, and follow the Past and the Distant. The soul created the arts wherever they have flourished. It was in his own mind that the artist sought his model. It was an application of his own thought to the thing to be done and the conditions to be observed. And why need we copy the Doric or the Gothic[49] model? Beauty, convenience, grandeur of thought, and quaint expression are as near to us as to any, and if the American artist will study with hope and love the precise thing to be done by him, considering the climate, the soil, the length of the day, the wants of the people, the habit and form of the government, he will create a house in which all these will find themselves fitted, and taste and sentiment will be satisfied also.

Insist on yourself; never imitate. Your own gift you can present every moment with the cumulative force of a whole life's cultivation; but of the adopted talent of another, you have only an extemporaneous, half possession. That which each can do best, none but his Maker can teach him. No man yet knows what it is, nor can, till that person has exhibited it. Where is the master who could have taught Shakspeare? Where is the master who could have instructed Franklin, or Washington, or Bacon,[50] or Newton? Every great man is a unique. The Scipionism of Scipio is precisely that part he could not borrow. Shakspeare will never be made by the study of Shakspeare. Do that which is assigned you, and you cannot hope too much or dare too much. There is at this moment for you an utterance brave and grand as that of the colossal chisel of Phidias,[51] or trowel of the Egyptians, or the pen of Moses, or Dante, but different from all these. Not possibly will the soul all rich, all eloquent, with thousand-cloven tongue, deign to repeat itself; but if you can hear what these patriarchs say, surely you can reply to them in the same pitch of voice: for the ear and the tongue are two organs of one nature. Abide in the simple and noble regions of thy life, obey thy heart, and thou shalt reproduce the Foreworld again.

4. As our Religion, our Education, our Art look abroad, so does our spirit of society. All men plume themselves on the improvement of society, and no man improves.

Society never advances. It recedes as fast on one side as it gains on the other. It undergoes continual changes: it is barbarous, it is civilized, it is christianized, it is rich, it is scientific; but this change is not amelioration. For every thing that is given, something is taken. Society acquires new arts and loses old instincts. What a contrast between the well-clad, reading, writing, thinking American, with a watch, a pencil, and a bill of exchange in his pocket, and the naked New Zealan-

---

[48] A person of extraordinary size and power lives within each of us.   [49] Classical or medieval.
[50] The English philosopher, essayist, and statesman Sir Francis Bacon (1561–1626).
[51] The fifth-century B.C. Greek sculptor who designed the frieze of the Parthenon and a statue of Zeus at Olympia.

der, whose property is a club, a spear, a mat, and an undivided twentieth of a shed to sleep under. But compare the health of the two men, and you shall see that the white man has lost his aboriginal strength. If the traveller tell us truly, strike the savage with a broad axe, and in a day or two the flesh shall unite and heal as if you struck the blow into soft pitch, and the same blow shall send the white to his grave.

The civilized man has built a coach, but has lost the use of his feet. He is supported on crutches, but lacks so much support of muscle. He has a fine Geneva watch, but he fails of the skill to tell the hour by the sun. A greenwich nautical almanac he has, and so being sure of the information when he wants it, the man in the street does not know a star in the sky. The solstice he does not observe; the equinox he knows as little; and the whole bright calendar of the year is without a dial in his mind. His note-books impair his memory; his libraries overload his wit; the insurance office increases the number of accidents; and it may be a question whether machinery does not encumber; whether we have not lost by refinement some energy, by a christianity entrenched in establishments and forms, some vigor of wild virtue. For every stoic was a stoic; but in Christendom where is the Christian?

There is no more deviation in the moral standard than in the standard of height or bulk. No greater men are now than ever were. A singular equality may be observed between the great men of the first and of the last ages; nor can all the science, art, religion and philosophy of the nineteenth century avail to educate greater men than Plutarch's heroes,[52] three or four and twenty centuries ago. Not in time is the race progressive. Phocion, Socrates, Anaxagora, Diogenes,[53] are great men, but they leave no class. He who is really of their class will not be called by their name, but will be his own man, and, in his turn the founder of a sect. The arts and inventions of each period are only its costume, and do not invigorate men. The harm of the improved machinery may compensate its good. Hudson and Behring accomplished so much in their fishing-boats, as to astonish Parry and Franklin,[54] whose equipment exhausted the resources of science and art. Galileo, with an opera-glass, discovered a more splendid series of celestial phenomena than any one since. Columbus found the New World in an undecked boat. It is curious to see the periodical disuse and perishing of means and machinery which were introduced with loud laudation, a few years or centuries before. The great genius returns to essential man. We reckoned the improvements of the art of war among the triumphs of science, and yet Napoleon conquered Europe by the Bivouac,[55] which consisted of falling back on naked valor, and disencumbering it of all aids. The Emperor held it impossible to make a perfect army, says Las Cases,[56] "without abolishing our arms, magazines, commissaries, and carriages,

---

[52] Plutarch (A. D. 46?–120?) wrote a series of biographies featuring the "parallel lives" of eminent Greeks and Romans.

[53] Phocion (402?–317? B. C.) was an Athenian statesman and general; Socrates (470?–399 B. C.), Anaxagoras (500?–428? B. C.), and Diogenes (412?–323? B. C.) were Greek philosophers.

[54] The findings of early navigators Henry Hudson (?–1611) and Vitus Bering (1680–1741) astounded the later and better-equipped William Edward Parry (1790–1855) and John Franklin (1786–1847), English Arctic explorers.

[55] A temporary encampment without tents or regular means of supply introduced by Napoleon in his victorious campaigns.

[56] Comte Emmanuel Augustin de Las Cases (1766–1842), the French historian who transcribed Napoleon's comments.

until in imitation of the Roman custom, the soldier should receive his supply of corn, grind it in his hand-mill, and bake his bread himself."

Society is a wave. The wave moves onward, but the water of which it is composed, does not. The same particle does not rise from the valley to the ridge. Its unity is only phenomenal. The persons who make up a nation to-day, next year die, and their experience with them.

And so the reliance on Property, including the reliance on governments which protect it, is the want of self-reliance. Men have looked away from themselves and at things so long, that they have come to esteem the religious, learned, and civil institutions, as guards of property, and they deprecate assaults on these, because they feel them to be assaults on property. They measure their esteem of each other, by what each has, and not by what each is. But a cultivated man becomes ashamed of his property, out of new respect for his nature. Especially he hates what he has, if he see that it is accidental,—came to him by inheritance, or gift, or crime; then he feels that it is not having; it does not belong to him, has not root in him, and merely lies there, because no revolution or no robber takes it away. But that which a man is, does always by necessity acquire, and what the man acquires is living property, which does not wait the beck of rulers, or mobs, or revolutions, or fire, or storm, or bankruptcies, but perpetually renews itself wherever the man breathes. "Thy lot or portion of life," said the Caliph Ali,[57] "is seeking after thee; therefore be at rest from seeking after it." Our dependence on these foreign goods leads us to our slavish respect for numbers. The political parties meet in numerous conventions; the greater the concourse, and with each new uproar of announcement, The delegation from Essex![58] The Democrats from New Hampshire! The Whigs of Maine! the young patriot feels himself stronger than before by a new thousand of eyes and arms. In like manner the reformers summon conventions, and vote and resolve in multitude. Not so, O friends! will the God deign to enter and inhabit you, but by a method precisely the reverse. It is only as a man puts off all foreign support, and stands alone, that I see him to be strong and to prevail. He is weaker by every recruit to his banner. Is not a man better than a town? Ask nothing of men, and in the endless mutation, thou only firm column must presently appear the upholder of all that surrounds thee. He who knows that power is inborn, that he is weak because he has looked for good out of him and elsewhere, and so perceiving throws himself unhesitatingly on his thought, instantly rights himself, stands in the erect postion, commands his limbs, works miracles; just as a man who stands on his feet is stronger than a man who stands on his head.

So use all that is called Fortune. Most men gamble with her, and gain all, and lose all, as her wheel rolls. But do thou leave as unlawful these winnings, and deal with Cause and Effect, the chancellors of God. In the Will work and acquire, and thou hast chained the wheel of Chance, and shalt sit hereafter out of fear from her rotations. A political victory, a rise of rents, the recovery of your sick, or the return of your absent friend, or some other favorable event, raises your spirits, and you think good days are preparing for you. Do not believe it. Nothing can bring you peace but yourself. Nothing can bring you peace but the triumph of principles.

1841

---

[57] Ali ibn-abi-Tālib, the fourth Moslem caliph of Mecca (A.D. 600?–661); Emerson knew this oracular statement from *History of the Saracens* (1708–1757), by Simon Ockley (1678–1720).
[58] Essex County, Massachusetts.

THE POET*

A moody child and wildly wise
Pursued the game with joyful eyes,
Which chose, like meteors, their way,
And rived the dark with private ray:
They overleapt the horizon's edge,
Searched with Apollo's privilege;
Through man, and woman, and sea, and star,
Saw the dance of nature forward far;
Through worlds, and races, and terms, and times,
Saw musical order, and pairing rhymes.[1]

Olympian bards who sung
  Divine ideas below,
Which always find us young,
  And always keep us so.[2]

Those who are esteemed umpires of taste, are often persons who have acquired some knowledge of admired pictures or sculptures, and have an inclination for whatever is elegant; but if you inquire whether they are beautiful souls, and whether their own acts are like fair pictures, you learn that they are selfish and sensual. Their cultivation is local, as if you should rub a log of dry wood in one spot to produce fire, all the rest remaining cold. Their knowledge of the fine arts is some study of rules and particulars, or some limited judgment of color or form, which is exercised for amusement or for show. It is a proof of the shallowness of the doctrine of beauty, as it lies in the minds of our amateurs, that men seem to have lost the perception of the instant dependence of form upon soul. There is no doctrine of forms in our philosophy. We were put into our bodies, as fire is put into a pan, to be carried about; but there is no accurate adjustment between the spirit and the organ, much less is the latter the germination of the former. So in regard to other forms, the intellectual men do not believe in any essential dependence of the material world on thought and volition. Theologians think it a pretty air-castle to talk of the spiritual meaning of a ship or a cloud, of a city or a contract, but they prefer to come again to the solid ground of historical evidence; and even the poets are contented with a civil and conformed manner of living, and to write poems from the fancy, at a safe distance from their own experience. But the highest minds of the world have never ceased to explore the double meaning, or, shall I say, the quadruple, or the centuple, or much more manifold meaning, of every sensuous fact: Orpheus, Empedocles, Heraclitus, Plato, Plutarch, Dante, Swedenborg,[3] and the masters of sculpture, picture, and poetry. For we are not pans and barrows, nor even porters of the fire and torch-bearers, but children of the fire, made of it, and only the same divinity transmuted, and at two or three

---

* First published in *Essays, Second Series* in 1844.
[1] These lines are from an unfinished poem by Emerson, published posthumously as "The Poet" (1883).
[2] These lines are from Emerson's "Ode to Beauty" (1843).
[3] A mythical Greek poet; Greek philosophers of the fifth and fifth to six centuries B.C., respectively; the renowned Greek philosopher Plato (427?–347? B.C.); Plutarch (46?–120? A.D.), a biographer of ancient Greeks and Romans; the medieval Italian poet Dante Alighieri (1265–1321); the theologian and mystic Emanuel Swedenborg (1688–1772).

removes, when we know least about it. And this hidden truth, that the fountains whence all this river of Time, and its creatures, floweth, are intrinsically ideal and beautiful, draws us to the consideration of the nature and functions of the Poet, or the man of Beauty, to the means and materials he uses, and to the general aspect of the art in the present time.

The breadth of the problem is great, for the poet is representative. He stands among partial men for the complete man, and apprises us not of his wealth, but of the commonwealth. The young man reveres men of genius, because, to speak truly, they are more himself than he is. They receive of the soul as he also receives, but they more. Nature enhances her beauty to the eye of loving men, from their belief that the poet is beholding her shows at the same time. He is isolated among his contemporaries, by truth and by his art, but with this consolation in his pursuits, that they will draw all men sooner or later. For all men live by truth, and stand in need of expression. In love, in art, in avarice, in politics, in labor, in games, we study to utter our painful secret. The man is only half himself, the other half is his expression.

Notwithstanding this necessity to be published, adequate expression is rare. I know not how it is that we need an interpreter; but the great majority of men seem to be minors, who have not yet come into possession of their own, or mutes, who cannot report the conversation they have had with nature. There is no man who does not anticipate a supersensual utility in the sun, and stars, earth, and water. These stand and wait to render him a peculiar service. But there is some obstruction, or some excess of phlegm[4] in our constitution, which does not suffer them to yield the due effect. Too feeble fall the impressions of nature on us to make us artists. Every touch should thrill. Every man should be so much an artist, that he could report in conversation what had befallen him. Yet, in our experience, the rays or appulses[5] have sufficient force to arrive at the senses, but not enough to reach the quick, and compel the reproduction of themselves in speech. The poet is the person in whom these powers are in balance, the man without impediment, who sees and handles that which others dream of, traverses the whole scale of experience, and is representative of man, in virtue of being the largest power to receive and to impart.

For the Universe has three children, born at one time, which reappear, under different names, in every system of thought, whether they be called cause, operation, and effect; or, more poetically, Jove, Pluto, Neptune;[6] or, theologically, the Father, the Spirit, and the Son; but which we will call here, the Knower, the Doer, and the Sayer. These stand respectively for the love of truth, for the love of good, and for the love of beauty. These three are equal. Each is that which he is essentially, so that he cannot be surmounted or analyzed, and each of these three has the power of the others latent in him, and his own patent.

The poet is the sayer, the namer, and represents beauty. He is a sovereign, and stands on the centre. For the world is not painted, or adorned, but is from the beginning beautiful; and God has not made some beautiful things, but Beauty is the creator of the universe. Therefore the poet is not any permissive potentate, but is emperor in his own right. Criticism is infested with a cant of materialism, which assumes that manual skill and activity is the first merit of all men, and disparages

---

[4] Sluggishness, apathy.   [5] Energies.

[6] According to Roman myth, the supreme god (Jupiter) and the gods of the underworld and of the sea.

such as say and do not, overlooking the fact, that some men, namely, poets, are natural sayers, sent into the world to the end of expression, and confounds them with those whose province is action, but who quit it to imitate the sayers. But Homer's words are as costly and admirable to Homer, as Agamemnon's victories are to Agamemnon.[7] The poet does not wait for the hero or the sage, but, as they act and think primarily, so he writes primarily what will and must be spoken, reckoning the others, though primaries also, yet, in respect to him, secondaries and servants; as sitters or models in the studio of a painter, or as assistants who bring building materials to an architect.

For poetry was all written before time was, and whenever we are so finely organized that we can penetrate into that region where the air is music, we hear those primal warblings, and attempt to write them down, but we lose ever and anon a word, or a verse, and substitute something of our own, and thus miswrite the poem. The men of more delicate ear write down these cadences more faithfully, and these transcripts, though imperfect, become the songs of the nations. For nature is as truly beautiful as it is good, or as it is reasonable, and must as much appear, as it must be done, or be known. Words and deeds are quite indifferent modes of the divine energy. Words are also actions, and actions are a kind of words.

The sign and credentials of the poet are, that he announces that which no man foretold. He is the true and only doctor,[8] he knows and tells; he is the only teller of news, for he was present and privy to the appearance which he describes. He is a beholder of ideas, and utterer of the necessary and casual. For we do not speak now of men of poetical talents, or of industry and skill in metre, but of the true poet. I took part in a conversation the other day, concerning a recent writer of lyrics, a man of subtle mind, whose head appeared to be a music-box of delicate tunes and rhythms, and whose skill, and command of language, we could not sufficiently praise. But when the question arose, whether he was not only a lyrist, but a poet, we were obliged to confess that he is plainly a contemporary, not an eternal man. He does not stand out of our low limitations, like a Chimborazo[9] under the line, running up from the torrid base through all the climates of the globe, with belts of the herbage of every latitude on its high and mottled sides; but this genius is the landscape-garden of a modern house, adorned with fountains and statues, with well-bred men and women standing and sitting in the walks and terraces. We hear, through all the varied music, the ground-tone of conventional life. Our poets are men of talents who sing, and not the children of music. The argument is secondary, the finish of the verses is primary.

For it is not metres, but a metre-making argument, that makes a poem,—a thought so passionate and alive, that, like the spirit of a plant or an animal, it has an architecture of its own, and adorns nature with a new thing.[10] The thought and the form are equal in the order of time, but in the order of genesis the thought is prior to the form. The poet has a new thought: he has a whole new experience to unfold; he will tell us how it was with him, and all men will be the richer in his fortune. For, the experience of each new age requires a new confession, and the world seems always waiting for its poet. I remember, when I was young, how

---

[7] According to Greek myth, the king of Mycenae and commander of the Greek army in the Trojan war, as told in Homer's *Iliad*.
[8] Teacher.   [9] A mountain in Ecuador, south of the "line" of the equator.
[10] This sentence expresses the idea of organic form that is basic to the romantic conception of poetry.

much I was moved one morning by tidings that genius had appeared in a youth who sat near me at table. He had left his work, and gone rambling none knew whither, and had written hundreds of lines, but could not tell whether that which was in him was therein told: he could tell nothing but that all was changed,—man, beast, heaven, earth, and sea. How gladly we listened! how credulous! Society seemed to be compromised. We sat in the aurora of a sunrise which was to put out all the stars. Boston seemed to be at twice the distance it had the night before, or was much farther than that. Rome,—what was Rome? Plutarch and Shakspeare were in the yellow leaf,[11] and Homer no more should be heard of. It is much to know that poetry has been written this very day, under this very roof, by your side. What! that wonderful spirit has not expired! these stony moments are still sparkling and animated! I had fancied that the oracles were all silent, and nature had spent her fires, and behold! all night, from every pore, these fine auroras have been streaming. Every one has some interest in the advent of the poet, and no one knows how much it may concern him. We know that the secret of the world is profound, but who or what shall be our interpreter, we know not. A mountain ramble, a new style of face, a new person, may put the key into our hands. Of course, the value of genius to us is in the veracity of its report. Talent may frolic and juggle; genius realizes and adds. Mankind, in good earnest, have arrived so far in understanding themselves and their work, that the foremost watchman on the peak announces his news. It is the truest word ever spoken, and the phrase will be the fittest, most musical, and the unerring voice of the world for that time.

All that we call sacred history attests that the birth of a poet is the principal even in chronology. Man, never so often deceived, still watches for the arrival of a brother who can hold him steady to a truth, until he has made it his own. With what joy I begin to read a poem, which I confide in as an inspiration! And now my chains are to be broken; I shall mount about these clouds and opaque airs in which I live,—opaque, though they seem transparent,—and from the heaven of truth I shall see and comprehend my relations. That will reconcile me to life, and reno-vate nature, to see trifles animated by a tendency, and to know what I am doing. Life will no more be a noise; now I shall see men and women, and know the signs by which they may be discerned from fools and satans. This day shall be better than my birthday; then I became an animal: now I am invited into the science of the real. Such is the hope, but the fruition is postponed. Oftener it falls, that this winged man, who will carry me into the heaven, whirls me into mists, then leaps and frisks about with me as it were from cloud to cloud, still affirming that he is bound heavenward; and I being myself a novice, am slow in perceiving that he does not know the way into the heavens, and is merely bent that I should admire his skill to rise, like a fowl or a flying fish, a little way from the ground or the water; but the all-piercing, all-feeding, and ocular[12] air of heaven, that man shall never inhabit. I tumble down again soon into my old nooks, and lead the life of exaggerations as before, and have lost some faith in the possiblity of any guide who can lead me thither where I would be.

But leaving these victims of vanity, let us, with new hope, observe how nature, by worthier impulses, has ensured the poet's fidelity to his office of announce-ment and affirming, namely, by the beauty of things, which becomes a new, and

---

[11] Seemed old: "I have lived long enough. My way of life is fallen into the sere, the yellow leaf," from Shakespeare's *Macbeth* (V. iii. 22–23).
[12] Visible.

higher beauty, when expressed. Nature offers all her creatures to him as a picture-language. Being used as a type, a second wonderful value appears in the object, far better than its old value, as the carpenter's stretched cord, if you hold your ear close enough, is musical in the breeze. "Things more excellent than every image," says Jamblichus,[13] "are expressed through images." Things admit of being used as symbols, because nature is a symbol, in the whole, and in every part. Every line we can draw in the sand, has expression; and there is no body without its spirit or genius. All form is an effect of character; all condition, of the quality of the life; all harmony, of health; (and, for this reason, a perception of beauty should be sympathetic, or proper only to the good.) The beautiful rests on the foundations of the necessary. The soul makes the body, as the wise Spenser teaches:—

"So every spirit, as it is most pure,
And hath in it the more of heavenly light,
So it the fairer body doth procure
To habit in, and it more fairly dight,
With cheerful grace and amiable sight
For, of the soul, the body form doth take.
For soul is form, and doth the body make."[14]

Here we find ourselves, suddenly, not in a critical speculation, but in a holy place, and should go very warily and reverently. We stand before the secret of the world, there where Being passes into Appearance, and Unity into Variety.

The Universe is the externization of the soul. Wherever the life is, that bursts into appearance around it. Our science is sensual, and therefore superficial. The earth, and the heavenly bodies, physics, and chemistry, we sensually treat, as if they were self-existent; but these are the retinue of that Being we have. "The mighty heaven," said Proclus,[15] "exhibits, in its transfigurations, clear images of the splendor of intellectual perceptions; being moved in conjunction with the un-apparent periods of intellectual natures." Therefore, science always goes abreast with the just elevation of the man, keeping step with religion and metaphysics; or, the state of science is an index of our self-knowledge. Since everything in nature answers to a moral power, if any phenomenon remains brute and dark, it is because the corresponding faculty in the observer is not yet active.

No wonder, then, if these waters be so deep, that we hover over them with a religious regard. The beauty of the fable proves the importance of the sense; to the poet, and to all others; or, if you please, every man is so far a poet as to be susceptible of these enchantments of nature; for all men have the thoughts whereof the universe is the celebration. I find that the fascination resides in the symbol. Who loves nature? Who does not? Is it only poets, and men of leisure and cultivation, who live with her? No; but also hunters, farmers, grooms, and butchers, though they express their affection in their choice of life, and not in their choice of words. The writer wonders what the coachman or the hunter values in riding, in horses, and dogs. It is not superficial qualities. When you talk with him, he holds

[13] A fourth-century A.D. Neoplatonic philosopher.
[14] From "An Hymn in Honour of Beauty" (1596), by the English poet Edmund Spenser (1552?–1599).
[15] Proclus (410?–485) was a Neoplatonic philosopher who stressed the mystical possibilities of idealist philosophy.

these at as slight a rate as you. His worship is sympathetic; he has no definitions, but he is commanded in nature, by the living power which he feels to be there present. No imitation, or playing of these things, would content him; he loves the earnest of the north wind, of rain, of stone, and wood, and iron. A beauty not explicable, is dearer than a beauty which we can see to the end of. It is nature the symbol, nature certifying the supernatural, body overflowed by life, which he worships, with coarse, but sincere rites.

The inwardness, and mystery, of this attachment, drive men of every class to the use of emblems. The schools of poets, and philosophers, are not more intoxicated with their symbols, than the populace with theirs. In our political parties, compute the power of badges and emblems. See the huge wooden ball rolled by successive ardent crowds from Baltimore to Bunker hill![16] In the political processions, Lowell goes in a loom, and Lynn in a shoe, and Salem in a ship.[17] Witness the cider-barrel, the log-cabin, the hickory-stick, the palmetto,[18] and all the cognizances of party. See the power of national emblems. Some stars, lilies, leopards, a crescent, a lion, an eagle, or other figure, which came into credit God knows how, on an old rag of bunting, blowing in the wind, on a fort, at the ends of the earth, shall make the blood tingle under the rudest, or the most conventional exterior. The people fancy they hate poetry, and they are all poets and mystics!

Beyond this universality of the symbolic language, we are apprised of the divineness of this superior use of things, whereby the world is a temple, whose walls are covered with emblems, pictures, and commandments of the Deity, in this, that there is no fact in nature which does not carry the whole sense of nature; and the distinctions which we make in events, and in affairs, of low and high, honest and base, disappear when nature is used as a symbol. Thought makes everything fit for use. The vocabulary of an omniscient man would embrace words and images excluded from polite conversation. What would be base, or even obscene, to the obscene, becomes illustrious, spoken in a new connexion of thought. The piety of the Hebrew prophets purges their grossness. The circumcision is an example of the power of poetry to raise the low and offensive. Small and mean things serve as well as great symbols. The meaner the type by which a law is expressed, the more pungent it is, and the more lasting in the memories of men: just as we choose the smallest box, or case, in which any needful utensil can be carried. Bare lists of words are found suggestive, to an imaginative and excited mind; as it is related of Lord Chatham, that he was accustomed to read in Bailey's Dictionary,[19] when he was preparing to speak in Parliament. The poorest experience is rich enough for all the purposes of expressing thought. Why covet a knowledge of new facts? Day and night, house and garden, a few books, a few actions, serve us as well as would all trades and all spectacles. We are far from having exhausted the significance of the few symbols we use. We can come to use them yet with a terrible simplicity. It does not need that a poem should be long.

[16] An allusion to the political slogan "Keep the ball a-rolling," used by the supporters of William Henry Harrison in his 1840 presidential campaign.

[17] Massachusetts towns, each represented in campaign parades by a major industry: Lowell by textiles, Lynn by shoemaking, Salem by shipping.

[18] The cider-barrel and log cabin were part of Harrison's successful "Log Cabin and Hard Cider" campaign against Martin Van Buren in 1840; the palmetto State is South Carolina, which claimed to be the birthplace of Andrew Jackson (known as "Old Hickory").

[19] The English statesman William Pitt (1708–1778), earl of Chatham, celebrated for his oratory; *An Universal Etymological English Dictionary* (1721), compiled by Nathan Bailey (?–1742).

Every word was once a poem. Every new relation is a new word. Also, we use defects and deformities to a sacred purpose, so expressing our sense that the evils of the world are such only to the evil eye. In the old mythology, mythologists observe, defects are ascribed to divine natures, as lameness to Vulcan, blindness to Cupid, and the like, to signify exuberances.

For, as it is dislocation and detachment from the life of God, that makes things ugly, the poet, who re-attaches things to nature and the Whole,—and re-attaching even artificial things, and violations of nature, to nature, by a deeper insight,—disposes very easily of the most disagreeable facts. Readers of poetry see the factory-village, and the railway, and fancy that the poetry of the landscape is broken up by these: for these works of art are not yet consecrated in their reading; but the poet sees them fall within the great Order not less than the bee-hive, or the spider's geometrical web. Nature adopts them very fast into her vital circles, and the gliding train of cars she loves like her own. Besides, in a centred mind, it signifies nothing how many mechanical inventions you exhibit. Though you add millions, and never so surprising, the fact of mechanics has not gained a grain's weight. The spiritual fact remains unalterable, by many or by few particulars; as no mountain is of any appreciable height to break the curve of the sphere. A shrewd country-boy goes to the city for the first time, and the complacent citizen is not satisfied with his little wonder. It is not that he does not see all the fine houses, and know that he never saw such before, but he disposes of them as easily as the poet finds place for the railway. The chief value of the new fact, is to enhance the great and constant fact of Life, which can dwarf any and every circumstance, and to which the belt of wampum, and the commerce of America, are alike.

The world being thus put under the mind for verb and noun, the poet is he who can articulate it. For, though life is great, and fascinates, and absorbs,—and though all men are intelligent of the symbols through which it is named,—yet they cannot originally use them. We are symbols, and inhabit symbols; workmen, work, and tools, words and things, birth and death, all are emblems; but we sympathize with the symbols, and, being infatuated with the economical uses of things, we do not know that they are thoughts. The poet, by an ulterior intellectual perception, gives them power which makes their old use forgotten, and puts eyes, and a tongue, into every dumb and inanimate object. He perceives the thought's independence of the symbol, the stability of the thought, the accidency and fugacity[20] of the symbol. As the eyes of Lyncæus[21] were said to see through the earth, so the poet turns the world to glass, and shows us all things in their right series and procession. For, through that better perception, he stands one step nearer to things, and sees the flowing or metamorphosis; perceives that thought is multiform; that within the form of every creature is a force impelling it to ascend into a higher form; and, following with his eyes the life, uses the forms which express that life, and so his speech flows with the flowing of nature. All the facts of the animal economy,—sex, nutriment, gestation, birth, growth—are symbols of the passage of the world into the soul of man, to suffer there a change, and reappear a new and higher fact. He uses forms according to the life, and not according to the form. This is true science. The poet alone knows astronomy, chemistry, vegetation, and animation, for he does not stop at these facts, but employs

[20] The accidental character and fleetingness or brevity.
[21] According to Greek myth, an Argonaut who sailed with Jason to recover the Golden Fleece; supposedly, he could see through the earth.

them as signs. He knows why the plain, or meadow of space, was strown with these flowers we call suns, and moons, and stars; why the great deep is adorned with animals, with men, and gods; for, in every word he speaks he rides on them as the horses of thought.

By virtue of this science the poet is the Namer, or Language-maker, naming things sometimes after their appearance, sometimes after their essence, and giving to every one its own name and not another's, thereby rejoicing the intellect, which delights in detachment or boundary. The poets made all the words, and therefore language is the archives of history, and, if we must say it, a sort of tomb of the muses. For, though the origin of most of our words is forgotten, each word was at first a stroke of genius, and obtained currency, because for the moment it symbolized the world to the first speaker and to the hearer. The etymologist finds the deadest word to have been once a brilliant picture. Language is fossil poetry. As the limestone of the continent consists of infinite masses of the shells of animalcules, so language is made up of images, or tropes, which now, in their secondary use, have long ceased to remind us of their poetic origin. But the poet names the thing because he sees it, or comes one step nearer to it than any other. This expression, or naming, is not art, but a second nature, grown out of the first, as a leaf out of a tree. What we call nature, is a certain self-regulated motion, or change; and nature does all things by her own hands, and does not leave another to baptize her, but baptizes herself; and this through the metamorphosis again. I remember that a certain poet[22] described it to me thus:

> Genius is the activity which repairs the decays of things, whether wholly or partly of a material and finite kind. Nature, through all her kingdoms, insures herself. Nobody cares for planting the poor fungus: so she shakes down from the gills of one agaric[23] countless spores, any one of which, being preserved, transmits new billions of spores to-morrow or next day. The new agaric of this hour has a chance which the old one had not. This atom of seed is thrown into a new place, not subject to the accidents which destroyed its parent two rods off. She makes a man; and having brought him to ripe age, she will no longer run the risk of losing this wonder at a blow, but she detaches from him a new self, that the kind may be safe from accidents to which the individual is exposed. So when the soul of the poet has come to ripeness of thought, she detaches and sends away from it its poems or songs,—a fearless, sleepless, deathless progeny, which is not exposed to the accidents of the weary kingdom of time: a fearless, vivacious offspring, clad with wings (such was the virtue of the soul out of which they came), which carry them fast and far, and infix them irrecoverably into the hearts of men. These wings are the beauty of the poet's soul. The songs, thus flying immortal from their mortal parent, are pursued by clamorous flights of censures, which swarm in far greater numbers, and threaten to devour them; but these last are not winged. At the end of a very short leap they fall plump down, and rot, having received from the souls out of which they came no beautiful wings. But the melodies of the poet ascend, and leap, and pierce into the deeps of infinite time.

So far the bard taught me, using his freer speech. But nature has a higher end, in the production of new individuals, than security, namely, *ascension,* or, the passage of the soul into higher forms. I knew, in my younger days, the sculptor

---

[22] Emerson himself; the passage is from his journal.   [23] A fungus such as a mushroom.

who made the statue of the youth which stands in the public garden. He was, as I remember, unable to tell, directly, what made him happy, or unhappy, but by wonderful indirections he could tell. He rose one day, according to his habit, before the dawn, and saw the morning break, grand as the eternity out of which it came, and, for many days after, he strove to express this tranquillity, and, lo! his chisel had fashioned out of marble the form of a beautiful youth, Phosphor,[24] whose aspect is such, that, it is said, all persons who look on it become silent. The poet also resigns himself to his mood, and that thought which agitated him is expressed, but *alter idem*,[25] in a manner totally new. The expression is organic, or, the new type which things themselves take when liberated. As, in the sun, objects paint their images on the retina of the eye, so they, sharing the aspiration of the whole universe, tend to paint a far more delicate copy of their essence in his mind. Like the metamorphosis of things into higher organic forms, is their change into melodies. Over everything stands its dæmon, or soul, and, as the form of the thing is reflected by the eye, so the soul of the thing is reflected by a melody. The sea, the mountain-ridge, Niagara, and every flower-bed, pre-exist, or super-exist, in pre-cantations,[26] which sail like odors in the air, and when any man goes by with an ear sufficiently fine, he overhears them, and endeavors to write down the notes, without diluting or depraving them. And herein is the legitimation of criticism, in the mind's faith, that the poems are a corrupt version of some text in nature, with which they ought to be made to tally. A rhyme in one of our sonnets should not be less pleasing than the iterated nodes of a sea-shell, or the resembling difference of a group of flowers. The pairing of the birds is an idyl, not tedious as our idyls are; a tempest is a rough ode without falsehood or rant; a summer, with its harvest sown, reaped, and stored, is an epic song, subordinating how many admirably executed parts. Why should not the symmetry and truth that modulate these, glide into our spirits, and we participate the invention of nature?

This insight, which expresses itself by what is called Imagination, is a very high sort of seeing, which does not come by study, but by the intellect being where and what it sees, by sharing the path, or circuit of things through forms, and so making them translucid to others. The path of things is silent. Will they suffer a speaker to go with them? A spy they will not suffer; a lover, a poet, is the transcendency of their own nature,—him they will suffer. The condition of true naming, on the poet's part, is his resigning himself to the divine *aura* which breathes through forms, and accompanying that.

It is a secret which every intellectual man quickly learns, that beyond the energy of his possessed and conscious intellect, he is capable of a new energy (as of an intellect doubled on itself), by abandonment to the nature of things; that, beside his privacy of power as an individual man, there is a great public power, on which he can draw, by unlocking, at all risks, his human doors, and suffering the ethereal tides to roll and circulate through him: then he is caught up into the life of the Universe, his speech is thunder, his thought is law, and his words are universally intelligible as the plants and animals. The poet knows that he speaks adequately, then only when he speaks somewhat wildly, or, "with the flower of the mind," not with the intellect, used as an organ, but with the intellect released from all service, and suffered to take its direction from its celestial life; or, as the ancients were wont to express themselves, not with intellect alone, but with the intellect inebri-

---

[24] According to Greek myth, a god associated with the morning star.
[25] "The same, yet different" (Latin).   [26] Pre-incantations, prophetic incantations.

ated by nectar. As the traveller who has lost his way, throws his reins on his horse's neck, and trusts to the instinct of the animal to find his road, so must we do with the divine animal who carries us through this world. For if in any manner we can stimulate this instinct, new passages are opened for us into nature, the mind flows into and through things hardest and highest, and the metamorphosis is possible.

This is the reason why bards love wine, mead,[27] narcotics, coffee, tea, opium, the fumes of sandal-wood and tobacco, or whatever other procurers of animal exhilaration. All men avail themselves of such means as they can, to add this extraordinary power to their normal powers; and to this end they prize conversation, music, pictures, sculpture, dancing, theatres, travelling, war, mobs, fires, gaming, politics, or love, or science, or animal intoxication, which are several coarser or finer *quasi*-mechanical substitutes for the true nectar, which is the ravishment of the intellect by coming nearer to the fact. These are auxiliaries to the centrifugal tendency of a man, to his passage out into free space, and they help him to escape the custody of that body in which he is pent up, and of that jail-yard of individual relations in which he is enclosed. Hence a great number of such as were professionally expressors of Beauty, as painters, poets, musicians, and actors, have been more than others wont to lead a life of pleasure and indulgence; all but the few who received the true nectar; and, as it was a spurious mode of attaining freedom, as it was an emancipation not into the heavens, but into the freedom of baser places, they were punished for that advantage they won, by a dissipation and deterioration. But never can any advantage be taken of nature by a trick. The spirit of the world, the great calm presence of the creator, comes not forth to the sorceries of opium or of wine. The sublime vision comes to the pure and simple soul in a clean and chaste body. That is not an inspiration which we owe to narcotics, but some counterfeit excitement and fury. Milton says, that the lyric poet may drink wine and live generously, but the epic poet, he who shall sing of the gods, and their descent unto men, must drink water out of a wooden bowl.[28] For poetry is not 'Devil's wine,' but God's wine. It is with this as it is with toys. We fill the hands and nurseries of our children with all manner of dolls, drums and horses, withdrawing their eyes from the plain face and sufficing objects of nature, the sun, and moon, the animals, the water, and stones, which should be their toys. So the poet's habit of living should be set on a key so low, that the common influences should delight him. His cheerfulness should be the gift of the sunlight; the air should suffice for his inspiration, and he should be tipsy with water. That spirit which suffices quiet hearts, which seems to come forth to such from every dry knoll of sere grass, from every pine-stump, and half-imbedded stone, on which the dull March sun shines, comes forth to the poor and hungry, and such as are of simple taste. If thou fill thy brain with Boston and New York, with fashion and covetousness, and wilt stimulate thy jaded senses with wine and French coffee, thou shalt find no radiance of wisdom in the lonely waste of the pinewoods.

If the imagination intoxicates the poet, it is not inactive in other men. The metamorphosis excites in the beholder an emotion of joy. The use of symbols has a certain power of emancipation and exhilaration for all men. We seem to be touched by a wand, which makes us dance and run about happily, like children. We are like persons who come out of a cave or cellar into the open air. This is the effect on us of tropes,[29] fables, oracles, and all poetic forms. Poets are thus liber-

---

[27] A liquor made of fermented honey and water.
[28] Adapted from John Milton's "Sixth Latin Elegy" (1629).
[29] Figures of speech.

ating gods. Men have really got a new sense, and found within their world, another world, or nest of worlds; for, the metamorphosis once seen, we divine that it does not stop. I will not now consider how much this makes the charm of algebra and the mathematics, which also have their tropes, but it is felt in every definition; as, when Aristotle defines *space* to be an immovable vessel, in which things are contained;—or, when Plato defines a *line* to be a flowing point; or, *figure* to be a bound of solid; and many the like. What a joyful sense of freedom we have, when Vitruvius[30] announces the old opinion of artists, that no architect can build any house well, who does not know something of anatomy. When Socrates, in Charmides,[31] tells us that the soul is cured of its maladies by certain incantations, and that these incantations are beautiful reasons, from which temperance is generated into souls; when Plato calls the world an animal; and Timæus[32] affirms that the plants also are animals; or affirms a man to be a heavenly tree, growing with his root, which is his head, upward; and, as George Chapman, following him, writes,—

> "So in our tree of man, whose nervie root
> Springs in his top;"[33]

when Orpheus speaks of hoariness as "that white flower which marks extreme old age;" when Proclus calls the universe the statue of the intellect; when Chaucer, in his praise of 'Gentilesse,'[34] compares good blood in mean condition to fire, which, though carried to the darkest house betwixt this and the mount of Caucasus, will yet hold its natural office, and burn as bright as if twenty thousand men did it behold; when John saw, in the apocalypse, the ruin of the world through evil, and the stars fall from heaven, as the figtree casteth her untimely fruit,[35] when Æsop reports the whole catalogue of common daily relations through the masquerade of birds, and beasts;[36]—we take the cheerful hint of the immortality of our essence, and its versatile habit and escapes, as when the gypsies say of themselves, "it is in vain to hang them, they cannot die."[37]

The poets are thus liberating gods. The ancient British bards had for the title of their order, "Those who are free throughout the world." They are free, and they make free. An imaginative book renders us much more service at first, by stimulating us through its tropes, than afterward, when we arrive at the precise sense of the author. I think nothing is of any value in books, excepting the transcendental and extraordinary. If a man is inflamed and carried away by his thought, to that degree that he forgets the authors and the public, and heeds only this one dream, which holds him like an insanity, let me read his paper, and you may have all the arguments and histories and criticism. All the value which attaches to Pythagoras, Paracelsus, Cornelius Agrippa, Cardan, Kepler, Swedenborg, Schelling, Oken,[38]

---

[30] Vitruvius Pollio (50?–26 B.C.), a Roman writer on architecture.
[31] One of Plato's dialogues.   [32] The principal speaker in Plato's dialogue "Timaeus."
[33] From the dedication to the translation (1614–1615) of Homer by Chapman (1559?–1634).
[34] Geoffrey Chaucer (1340?–1400), in "The Wife of Bath's Tale."
[35] The Apostle John, author of the Apocalypse, or Book of Revelation; from Revelation 6:13.
[36] In the fables of Aesop, supposedly a Greek of the sixth century B.C.
[37] From *The Zincali* (1841), by the English travel writer and novelist George Borrow (1803–1881).
[38] The sixth-century B.C. Greek mathematician Pythagoras; the Swiss alchemist Philippus Paracelsus (1493–1541); the German physician Cornelius Agrippa (1486?–1535); the Italian mathematician Jerome Cardan (1501–1576); the German astronomer Johannes Kepler (1571–1630); Emanuel Swedenborg; the German philosopher Friedrich von Schelling (1775–1854); the German naturalist Lorenz Oken (1779–1851).

or any other who introduces questionable facts into his cosmogony, as angels, devils, magic, astrology, palmistry, mesmerism, and so on, is the certificate we have of departure from routine, and that here is a new witness. That also is the best success in conversation, the magic of liberty, which puts the world, like a ball, in our hands. How cheap even the liberty then seems; how mean to study, when an emotion communicates to the intellect the power to sap and upheave nature: how great the perspective! nations, times, systems, enter and disappear, like threads in tapestry of large figure and many colors; dream delivers us to dream, and, while the drunkenness lasts, we will sell our bed, our philosophy, our religion, in our opulence.

There is good reason why we should prize this liberation. The fate of the poor shepherd, who, blinded and lost in the snowstorm, perishes in a drift within a few feet of his cottage door, is an emblem of the state of man. On the brink of the waters of life and truth, we are miserably dying. The inaccessibleness of every thought but that we are in, is wonderful. What if you come near to it,—you are as remote, when you are nearest, as when you are farthest. Every thought is also a prison: every heaven is also a prison. Therefore we love the poet, the inventor, who in any form, whether in an ode, or in an action, or in looks and behavior, has yielded us a new thought. He unlocks our chains, and admits us to a new scene.

This emancipation is dear to all men, and the power to impart it, as it must come from greater depth and scope of thought, is a measure of intellect. Therefore all books of the imagination endure, all which ascend to that truth, that the writer sees nature beneath him, and uses it as his exponent.[39] Every verse or sentence, possessing this virtue, will take care of its own immortality. The religions of the world are the ejaculations of a few imaginative men.

But the quality of the imagination is to flow, and not to freeze. The poet did not stop at the color, or the form, but read their meaning; neither may he rest in this meaning, but he makes the same objects exponents of his new thought. Here is the difference betwixt the poet and the mystic, that the last nails a symbol to one sense, which was a true sense for a moment, but soon becomes old and false. For all symbols are fluxional; all language is vehicular and transitive, and is good, as ferries and horses are, for conveyance, not as farms and houses are, for homestead. Mysticism consists in the mistake of an accidental and individual symbol for an universal one. The morning-redness happens to be the favorite meteor to the eyes of Jacob Behmen,[40] and comes to stand to him for truth and faith; and he believes should stand for the same realities to every reader. But the first reader prefers as naturally the symbol of a mother and child, or a gardener and his bulb, or a jeweller polishing a gem. Either of these, or of a myriad more, are equally good to the person to whom they are significant. Only they must be held lightly, and be very willingly translated into the equivalent terms which others use. And the mystic must be steadily told,—All that you say is just as true without the tedious use of that symbol as with it. Let us have a little algebra, instead of this trite rhetoric,—universal signs, instead of these village symbols,—and we shall both be gainers. The history of hierarchies seems to show, that all religious error consisted in making the symbol too stark and solid, and, at last, nothing but an excess of the organ of language.

Swedenborg, of all men in the recent ages, stands eminently for the translator of nature into thought. I do not know the man in history to whom things stood so

---

[39] Means of setting forth his principles.   [40] Jakob Böhme (1575–1624), a German mystic.

uniformly for words. Before him the metamorphosis continually plays. Everything on which his eye rests, obeys the impulses of moral nature. The figs become grapes whilst he eats them. When some of his angels affirmed a truth, the laurel twig which they held blossomed in their hands. The noise which, at a distance, appeared like gnashing and thumping, on coming nearer was found to be the voice of disputants. The men, in one of his visions, seen in heavenly light, appeared like dragons, and seemed in darkness; but, to each other, they appeared as men, and, when the light from heaven shone into their cabin, they complained of the darkness, and were compelled to shut the window that they might see.

There was this perception in him, which makes the poet or seer an object of awe and terror, namely, that the same man, or society of men, may wear one aspect to themselves and their companions, and a different aspect to higher intelligences. Certain priests, whom he describes as conversing very learnedly together, appeared to the children, who were at some distance, like dead horses; and many the like misappearances. And instantly the mind inquires, whether these fishes under the bridge, yonder oxen in the pasture, those dogs in the yard, are immutably fishes, oxen, and dogs, or only so appear to me, and perchance to themselves appear upright men; and whether I appear as a man to all eyes. The Bramins[41] and Pythagoras propounded the same question, and if any poet has witnessed the transformation, he doubtless found it in harmony with various experiences. We have all seen changes as considerable in wheat and caterpillars. He is the poet, and shall draw us with love and terror, who sees, through the flowing vest, the firm nature, and can declare it.

I look in vain for the poet whom I describe. We do not, with sufficient plainness, or sufficient profoundness, address ourselves to life, nor dare we chaunt our own times and social circumstance. If we filled the day with bravery, we should not shrink from celebrating it. Time and nature yield us many gifts, but not yet the timely man, the new religion, the reconciler, whom all things await. Dante's praise is, that he dared to write his autobiography in colossal cipher, or into universality. We have yet had no genius in America, with tyrannous eye, which knew the value of our incomparable materials, and saw, in the barbarism and materialism of the times, another carnival of the same gods whose picture he so much admires in Homer; then in the middle age; then in Calvinism. Banks and tariffs, the newspaper and caucus,[42] methodism and unitarianism, are flat and dull to dull people, but rest on the same foundations of wonder as the town of Troy, and the temple of Delphi, and are as swiftly passing away. Our logrolling, our stumps[43] and their politics, our fisheries, our Negroes, and Indians, our boasts, and our repudiations,[44] the wrath of rogues, and the pusillanimity of honest men, the northern trade, the southern planting, the western clearing, Oregon, and Texas, are yet unsung. Yet America is a poem in our eyes; its ample geography dazzles the imagination, and it will not wait long for metres. If I have not found that excellent combination of gifts in my countrymen which I seek, neither could I aid myself to fix the idea of the poet by reading now and then in Chalmers's[45] collection of five centuries of English poets. These are wits, more than poets, though

[41] Brahmans, members of a priestly Hindu caste.   [42] A political meeting.
[43] Our trading political favors, our stump speeches, or impromptu political oratory.
[44] State government refusals to pay off bond issues.
[45] Alexander Chalmers (1759–1834) compiled *Works of the English Poets* (1810) in twenty-one volumes.

there have been poets among them. But when we adhere to the ideal of the poet, we have our difficulties even with Milton and Homer. Milton is too literary, and Homer too literal and historical.

But I am not wise enough for a national criticism, and must use the old largeness a little longer, to discharge my errand from the muse to the poet concerning his art.

Art is the path of the creator to his work. The paths, or methods, are ideal and eternal, though few men ever see them, not the artist himself for years, or for a lifetime, unless he come into the conditions. The painter, the sculptor, the composer, the epic rhapsodist, the orator, all partake one desire, namely, to express themselves symmetrically and abundantly, not dwarfishly and fragmentarily. They found or put themselves in certain conditions, as, the painter and sculptor before some impressive human figures; the orator, into the assembly of the people; and the others, in such scenes as each has found exciting to his intellect; and each presently feels the new desire. He hears a voice, he sees a beckoning. Then he is apprised, with wonder, what herds of dæmons hem him in. He can no more rest; he says, with the old painter, "By God, it is in me, and must go forth of me." He pursues a beauty, half seen, which flies before him. The poet pours out verses in every solitude. Most of the things he says are conventional, no doubt; but by and by he says something which is original and beautiful. That charms him. He would say nothing else but such things. In our way of talking we say, 'That is yours, this is mine;' but the poet knows well that it is not his; that it is as strange and beautiful to him as to you; he would fain hear the like eloquence at length. Once having tasted this immortal ichor,[46] he cannot have enough of it, and, as an admirable creative power exists in these intellections, it is of the last importance that these things get spoken. What a little of all we know is said! What drops of all the sea of our science are baled up! and by what accident it is that these are exposed, when so many secrets sleep in nature! Hence the neccessity of speech and song; hence these throbs and heart-beatings in the orator, at the door of the assembly, to the end, namely, that thought may be ejaculated as Logos, or Word.

Doubt not, O poet, but persist. Say, 'It is in me, and shall out,' Stand there, baulked and dumb, stuttering and stammering, hissed and hooted, stand and strive, until, at last, rage draw out of thee that *dream*-power which every night shows thee is thine own; a power transcending all limit and privacy, and by virtue of which a man is the conductor of the whole river of electricity. Nothing walks, or creeps, or grows, or exists, which must not in turn arise and walk before him as exponent of his meaning. Comes he to that power, his genius is no longer exhaustible. All the creatures, by pairs and by tribes, pour into his mind as into a Noah's ark, to come forth again to people a new world. This is like the stock of air for our respiration, or for the combustion of our fireplace, not a measure of gallons, but the entire atmosphere if wanted. And therefore the rich poets, as Homer, Chaucer, Shakspeare, and Raphael,[47] have obviously no limits to their works, except the limits of their lifetime, and resemble a mirror carried through the street, ready to render an image of every created thing.

O poet! a new nobility is conferred in groves and pastures, and not in castles, or by the sword-blade, any longer. The conditions are hard, but equal. Thou shalt leave the world, and know the muse only. Thou shalt not know any longer the

---

[46] According to Greek myth, an ethereal fluid that replaced blood in the gods' veins.
[47] Raphael Santi (1483–1520), a majestic painter of the Italian Renaissance.

times, customs, graces, politics, or opinions of men, but shalt take all from the muse. For the time of towns is tolled from the world by funereal chimes, but in nature the universal hours are counted by succeeding tribes of animals and plants, and by growth of joy on joy. God wills also that thou abdicate a duplex and manifold life, and that thou be content that others speak for thee. Others shall be thy gentlemen, and shall represent all courtesy and worldly life for thee; others shall do the great and resounding actions also. Thou shalt lie close hid with nature, and canst not be afforded to the Capitol or the Exchange.[48] The world is full of renunciations and apprenticeships, and this is thine; thou must pass for a fool and a churl for a long season. This is the screen and sheath in which Pan[49] has protected his well-beloved flower, and thou shalt be known only to thine own, and they shall console thee with tenderest love. And thou shalt not be able to rehearse the names of thy friends in thy verse, for an old shame before the holy ideal. And this is the reward: that the ideal shall be real to thee, and the impressions of the actual world shall fall like summer rain, copious, but not troublesome, to thy invulnerable essence. Thou shalt have the whole land for thy park and manor, the sea for thy bath and navigation, without tax and without envy; the woods and the rivers thou shalt own; and thou shalt possess that wherein others are only tenants and boarders. Thou true land-lord! sea-lord! air-lord! Wherever snow falls, or water flows, or birds fly, wherever day and night meet in twilight, wherever the blue heaven is hung by clouds, or sown with stars, wherever are forms with transparent boundaries, wherever are outlets into celestial space, wherever is danger, and awe, and love, there is Beauty, plenteous as rain, shed for thee, and though thou shouldst walk the world over, thou shalt not be able to find a condition inopportune or ignoble.

1844

FATE*

Delicate omens traced in air
To the lone bard true witness bare;
Birds with auguries on their wings
Chanted undeceiving things
Him to beckon, him to warn;
Well might then the poet scorn
To learn of scribe or courier
Hints writ in vaster character;
And on his mind, at dawn of day,
Soft shadows of the evening lay.
For the prevision is allied
Unto the thing so signified;
Or say, the foresight that awaits
Is the same Genius that creates.[1]

[48] The world of politics or the world of finance.
[49] According to Greek myth, the half-man, half-goat god of fields and woods.
* Presented in December 1851 as part of a lecture series entitled "The Conduct of Life" and first published in *The Conduct of Life* (1860).
[1] The epigraphic poem is Emerson's.

It chanced during one winter a few years ago, that our cities were bent on discussing the theory of the Age. By an odd coincidence, four or five noted men were each reading a discourse to the citizens of Boston or New York, on the Spirit of the Times.[2] It so happened that the subject had the same prominence in some remarkable pamphlets and journals issued in London in the same season. To me however the question of the times resolved itself into a practical question of the conduct of life. How shall I live? We are incompetent to solve the times. Our geometry cannot span the huge orbits of the prevailing ideas, behold their return and reconcile their opposition. We can only obey our own polarity. 'T is fine for us to speculate and elect our course, if we must accept an irresistable dictation.

In our first steps to gain our wishes we come upon immovable limitations. We are fired with the hope to reform men. After many experiments we find that we must begin earlier,—at school. But the boys and girls are not docile; we can make nothing of them. We decide that they are not of good stock. We must begin our reform earlier still,—at generation: that is to say there is Fate, or laws of the world.

But if there be irresistible dictation, this dictation understands itself. If we must accept Fate, we are not less compelled to affirm liberty, the significance of the individual, the grandeur of duty, the power of character. This is true, and that other is true. But our geometry cannot span these extreme points and reconcile them. What to do? By obeying each thought frankly, by harping, or, if you will, pounding on each string, we learn at last its power. By the same obedience to other thoughts we learn theirs, and then comes some reasonable hope of harmonizing them. We are sure that, though we know not how, necessity does comport with liberty, the individual with the world, my polarity with the spirit of the times. The riddle of the age has for each a private solution. If one would study his own time, it must be by this method of taking up in turn each of the leading topics which belong to our scheme of human life, and by firmly stating all that is agreeable to experience on one, and doing the same justice to the opposing facts in the others, the true limitations will appear. Any excess of emphasis on one part would be corrected, and a just balance would be made.

But let us honestly state the facts. Our America has a bad name for superficialness. Great men, great nations, have not been boasters and buffoons, but perceivers of the terror of life, and have manned themselves to face it. The Spartan, embodying his religion in his country, dies before its majesty without a question. The Turk, who believes his doom is written on the iron leaf in the moment when he entered the world, rushes on the enemy's sabre with undivided will. The Turk, the Arab, the Persian, accepts the foreordained fate:

> "On two days, it steads not to run from thy grave,
>   The appointed, and the unappointed day;
> On the first, neither balm nor physician can save,
>   Nor thee, on the second, the Universe slay."[3]

The Hindoo under the wheel, is as firm. Our Calvinists in the last generation[4] had

---

[2] Emerson lectured on this subject in New York in January 1851; English writers such as William Hazlitt (1778–1830) and John Stuart Mill (1806–1873) had addressed the theme earlier.

[3] Emerson translated these lines from a German translation of a Persian poet; in his journal he attributes them to Pindar of Rei in Kuhistan.

[4] Eighteenth-century Calvinists believed that a person's fate is predetermined by God.

something of the same dignity. They felt that the weight of the Universe held them down to their place. What could *they* do? Wise men feel that there is something which cannot be talked or voted away,—a strap or belt which girds the world:—

> "The Destiny, minister general,
> That executeth in the world o'er all,
> The purveyance which God hath seen beforne,
> So strong it is, that though the world had sworn
> The contrary of a thing by yea or nay,
> Yet sometime it shall fallen on a day
> That falleth not oft in a thousand year;
> For, certainly, our appetités here,
> Be it of war, or peace, or hate, or love,
> All this is ruled by the sight above."

CHAUCER: The Knighte's Tale.[5]

The Greek Tragedy expressed the same sense. "Whatever is fated, that will take place. The great immense mind of Jove is not to be transgressed."[6]

Savages cling to a local god of one tribe or town. The broad ethics of Jesus were quickly narrowed to village theologies, which preach an election or favoritism. And now and then an amiable parson, like Jung Stilling or Robert Huntington,[7] believes in a pistareen-Providence,[8] which, whenever the good man wants a dinner, makes that somebody shall knock at his door and leave a half-dollar. But Nature is no sentimentalist,—does not cosset[9] or pamper us. We must see that the world is rough and surly, and will not mind drowning a man or a woman, but swallows your ship like a grain of dust. The cold, inconsiderate of persons, tingles your blood, benumbs your feet, freezes a man like an apple. The diseases, the elements, fortune, gravity, lightning, respect no persons. The way of Providence is a little rude. The habit of snake and spider, the snap of the tiger and other leapers and bloody jumpers, the crackle of the bones of his prey in the coil of the anaconda,—these are in the system, and our habits are like theirs. You have just dined, and however scrupulously the slaughter-house is concealed in the graceful distance of miles, there is complicity, expensive races,—race living at the expense of race. The planet is liable to shocks from comets, perturbations from planets, rendings from earthquake and volcano, alterations of climate, precessions of equinoxes. Rivers dry up by opening of the forest. The sea changes its bed. Towns and counties fall into it. At Lisbon an earthquake killed men like flies.[10] At Naples three years ago ten thousand persons were crushed in a few minutes. The scurvy at sea, the sword of the climate in the west of Africa, at Cayenne, at Panama, at New Orleans, cut off men like a massacre. Our western prairie shakes with fever and ague. The cholera, the small-pox, have proved as mortal to some

---

[5] A modified version of lines 805–814.

[6] From *The Suppliants* (1047–1049), by the Greek tragic poet Aeschylus (525–456 B.C.); Jove (Jupiter) is the supreme god in Roman myth.

[7] Johann Heinrich Jung-Stilling (1740–1817), a German physician and mystic; actually *William* Huntington (1745–1813), an eccentric English minister.

[8] A Providence consisting of handing out small change to the needy; a pistareen is a Spanish coin of small value.

[9] Pamper.

[10] The catastrophic Lisbon earthquake of 1775; the Naples disaster occured in 1857.

tribes as a frost to the crickets, which, having filled the summer with noise, are silenced by a fall of the temperature of one night. Without uncovering what does not concern us, or counting how many species of parasites hang on a bombyx,[11] or groping after intestinal parasites or infusory biters,[12] or the obscurities of alternate generation,—the forms of the shark, the *labrus*,[13] the jaw of the seawolf paved with crushing teeth, the weapons of the grampus,[14] and other warriors hidden in the sea, are hints of ferocity in the interiors of nature. Let us not deny it up and down. Providence has a wild, rough, incalculable road to its end, and it is of no use to try to whitewash its huge, mixed instrumentalities, or to dress up that terrific benefactor in a clean shirt and white neckcloth of a student in divinity.

Will you say, the disasters which threaten mankind are exceptional, and one need not lay his account for cataclysms every day? Aye, but what happens once may happen again, and so long as these strokes are not to be parried by us they must be feared.

But these shocks and ruins are less destructive to us than the stealthy power of other laws, which act on us daily. An expense of ends to means is fate;—organization tyrannizing over character. The menagerie, or forms and powers of the spine, is a book of fate; the bill of the bird, the skull of the snake, determines tyrannically its limits. So is the scale of races, of temperaments;[15] so is sex; so is climate; so is the reaction of talents imprisoning the vital power in certain directions. Every spirit makes its house; but afterwards the house confines the spirit.

The gross lines are legible to the dull; the cabman is phrenologist[16] so far, he looks in your face to see if his shilling is sure. A dome of brow denotes one thing, a pot-belly another; a squint, a pugnose, mats of hair, the pigment of the epidermis, betray character. People seem sheathed in their tough organization. Ask Spurzheim, ask the doctors, ask Quetelet[17] if temperaments decide nothing?—or if there be anything they do not decide? Read the description in medical books of the four temperaments and you will think you are reading your own thoughts which you had not yet told. Find the part which black eyes and which blue eyes play severally in the company. How shall a man escape from his ancestors, or draw off from his veins the black drop which he drew from his father's or his mother's life? It often appears in a family as if all the qualities of the progenitors were potted in several jars,—some ruling quality in each son or daughter of the house; and sometimes the unmixed temperament, the rank unmitigated elixir, the family vice, is drawn off in a separate individual and the others are proportionally relieved. We sometimes see a change of expression in our companion and say his father or his mother comes to the windows of his eyes, and sometimes a remote relative. In different hours a man represents each of several of his ancestors, as if there were seven or eight of us rolled up in each man's skin,—seven or eight ancestors at least; and they constitute the variety of notes for that new piece of music which his life is. At the corner of the street you read the possibility of each

---

[11] A silkworm moth.   [12] Microscopic marine organisms.
[13] A heavy-lipped predatory fish.   [14] The killer whale.
[15] In ancient and medieval physiology, the mixture of four "humors" (blood, phlegm, choler, and melancholy) was believed to determine a person's temperament.
[16] According to the pseudo-science of phrenology, the conformation of the skull indicates mental abilities. Here, Emerson's cab driver seems more of a physiognomist, who predicts character from facial features.
[17] Johann Spurzheim (1776–1832), a German physician who popularized phrenology; Lambert Quételet (1796–1874), a Belgian mathematician who perfected the science of statistics.

passenger in the facial angle, in the complexion, in the depth of his eye. His parentage determines it. Men are what their mothers made them. You may as well ask a loom which weaves huckaback[18] why it does not make cashmere, as expect poetry from this engineer, or a chemical discovery from that jobber. Ask the digger in the ditch to explain Newton's laws; the fine organs of his brain have been pinched by overwork and squalid poverty from father to son for a hundred years. When each comes forth from his mother's womb, the gate of gifts closes behind him. Let him value his hands and feet, he has but one pair. So he has but one future, and that is already predetermined in his lobes and described in that little fatty face, pig-eye, and squat form. All the privilege and all the legislation of the world cannot meddle or help to make a poet or a prince of him.

Jesus said, "When he looketh on her, he hath commited adultery."[19] But he is an adulterer before he has yet looked on the woman, by the superfluity of animal and the defect of thought in his constitution. Who meets him, or who meets her, in the street, sees that they are ripe to be each other's victim.

In certain men digestion and sex absorb the vital force, and the stronger these are, the individual is so much weaker. The more of these drones perish, the better for the hive. If, later, they give birth to some superior individual, with force enough to add to this animal a new aim and a complete apparatus to work it out, all the ancestors are gladly forgotten. Most men and most women are merely one couple more. Now and then one has a new cell or camarilla[20] opened in his brain,—an architectural, a musical, or a philological[21] knack; some stray taste or talent for flowers, or chemistry, or pigments, or story-telling; a good hand for drawing, a good foot for dancing, an athletic frame for wide journeying, etc.— which skill nowise alters rank in the scale of nature, but serves to pass the time; the life of sensation going on as before. At last these hints and tendencies are fixed in one or in a succession. Each absorbs so much food and force as to become itself a new centre. The new talent draws off so rapidly the vital force that not enough remains for the animal functions, hardly enough for health; so that in the second generation, if the like genius appear, the health is visibly deteriorated and the generative force impaired.

People are born with the moral or with the material bias;—uterine brothers with this diverging destination; and I suppose, with high magnifiers, Mr. Frauenhofer or Dr. Carpenter[22] might come to distinguish in the embryo, at the fourth day,— this is a Whig, and that a Free-soiler.[23]

It was a poetic attempt to lift this mountain of Fate, to reconcile this despotism of race with liberty, which led the Hindoos to say, "Fate is nothing but the deeds committed in a prior state of existence."[24] I find the coincidence of the extremes of Eastern and Western speculation in the daring statement of Schelling,[25] "There is

---

[18] A strong linen fabric used for towels.

[19] " . . . whosoever looketh on a woman to lust after her hath committed adultery with her already in his heart," from Matthew 5:28.

[20] A small room, chamber.   [21] Literary.

[22] The German optician Joseph von Frauenhofer (1787–1826), who improved the telescope; the English physiologist William B. Carpenter (1813–1885), who wrote a treatise about the microscope.

[23] In 1851 "Whig" signified the Anti-Democratic party, and "Free-Soiler," the antislavery wing of the Democratic party.

[24] Probably not taken from one source, the quotation expresses the idea of karma.

[25] Friedrich Wilhelm Joseph von Schelling (1775–1854), a German philosopher whose work bridged German philosophical idealism and romanticism.

in every man a certain feeling that he has been what he is from all eternity, and by no means became such in time." To say it less sublimely,—in the history of the individual is always an account of his condition, and he knows himself to be a party to his present estate.

A good deal of our politics is physiological. Now and then a man of wealth in the heyday of youth adopts the tenet of broadest freedom. In England there is always some man of wealth and large connection, planting himself, during all his years of health, on the side of progress, who, as soon as he begins to die, checks his forward play, calls in his troops and becomes conservative. All conservatives are such from personal defects. They have been effeminated by position or nature, born halt and blind, through luxury of their parents, and can only, like invalids, act on the defensive. But strong natures, backwoodsmen, New Hampshire giants, Napoleons, Burkes, Broughams, Websters, Kossuths,[26] are inevitable patriots, until their life ebbs and their defects and gout, palsy and money, warp them.

The strongest idea incarnates itself in majorities and nations, in the healthiest and strongest. Probably the election goes by avoirdupois weight, and if you could weigh bodily the tonnage of any hundred of the Whig and the Democratic party in a town on the Dearborn balance,[27] as they passed the hay-scales, you could predict with certainty which party would carry it. On the whole it would be rather the speediest way of deciding the vote, to put the selectmen or the mayor and aldermen at the hay-scales.

In science we have to consider two things; power and circumstance. All we know of the egg, from each successive discovery, is, *another vesicle;*[28] and if, after five hundred years you get a better observer or a better glass, he finds, within the last observed, another. In vegetable and animal tissue it is just alike, and all that the primary power or spasm operates is still vesicles, vesicles. Yes,—but the tyrannical Circumstance! A vesicle in new circumstances, a vesicle lodged in the darkness, Oken[29] thought, became animal; in light, a plant. Lodged in the parent animal, it suffers changes which end in unsheathing miraculous capability in the unaltered vesicle, and it unlocks itself to fish, bird, or quadruped, head and foot, eye and claw. The Circumstance is Nature. Nature is what you may do. There is much you may not. We have two things,—the circumstance, and the life. Once we thought positive power was all. Now we learn that negative power, or circumstance, is half. Nature is the tyrannous circumstance, the thick skull, the sheathed snake, the ponderous, rock-like jaw; necessitated activity; violent direction; the conditions of a tool, like the locomotive, strong enough on its track, but which can do nothing but mischief off of it; or skates, which are wings on the ice but fetters on the ground.

The book of Nature is the book of Fate. She turns the gigantic pages,—leaf after leaf,—never re-turning one. One leaf she lays down, a floor of granite; then a thousand ages, and a bed of slate; a thousand ages, and a measure of coal; a thousand ages, and a layer of marl and mud: vegetable forms appear; her first misshapen animals, zoöphyte, trilobium, fish; then, saurians,[30]—rude forms, in

---

[26] Edmund Burke (1729–1797), an English statesman; Henry Peter Brougham (1778–1868), an English parliamentary leader; Daniel Webster (1782–1852), a statesman and leader of the Whig party; Lajos Kossuth (1802–1894), leader of the Hungarian fight for freedom in 1848. During Kossuth's 1851 to 1852 visit to the United States, Emerson welcomed him to Concord.

[27] A spring balance, or scale.   [28] A bladderlike vessel or sac.

[29] Lorenz Oken (1779–1851), a German naturalist who taught that all organisms are produced from cells.

[30] An animal that appears to be a plant, trilobites, fish; then lizards.

which she has only blocked her future statue, concealing under these unwieldly monsters the fine type of her coming king. The face of the planet cools and dries, the races meliorate, and man is born. But when a race has lived its term, it comes no more again.

The population of the world is a conditional population; not the best, but the best that could live now; and the scale of tribes, and the steadiness with which victory adheres to one tribe and defeat to another, is as uniform as the superposition of strata. We know in history what weight belongs to race. We see the English, French, and Germans planting themselves on every shore and market of America and Australia, and monopolizing the commerce of these countries. We like the nervous and victorious habit of our own branch of the family. We follow the step of the Jew, of the Indian, of the Negro. We see how much will has been expended to extinguish the Jew, in vain. Look at the unpalatable conclusions of Knox,[31] in his "Fragment of Races;"—a rash and unsatisfactory writer, but charged with pungent and unforgetable truths. "Nature respects race, and not hybrids." "Every race has its own *habitat*." "Detach a colony from the race, and it deteriorates to the crab."[32] See the shades of the picture. The German and Irish millions, like the Negro, have a great deal of guano[33] in their destiny. They are ferried over the Atlantic and carted over America, to ditch and to drudge, to make corn cheap and then to lie down prematurely to make a spot of green grass on the prairie.

One more fagot of these adamantine bandages[34] is the new science of Statistics. It is a rule that the most casual and extraordinary events, if the basis of population is broad enough, become matter of fixed calculation. It would not be safe to say when a captain like Bonaparte, a singer like Jenny Lind, or a navigator like Bowditch[35] would be born in Boston; but, on a population of twenty or two hundred millions, something like accuracy may be had.[36]

'T is frivolous to fix pedantically the date of particular inventions. They have all been invented over and over fifty times. Man is the arch machine of which all these shifts drawn from himself are toy models. He helps himself on each emergency by copying or duplicating his own structure, just so far as the need is. 'T is hard to find the right Homer, Zoroaster, or Menu; harder still to find the Tubal Cain, or Vulcan, or Cadmus, or Copernicus, or Fust, or Fulton;[37] the indisputable

[31] Robert Knox (1791–1862), a Scottish anatomist and ethnologist, who sought to justify racial prejudice scientifically in *The Races of Men: A Fragment* (1850).

[32] The supposed degeneration of apple trees to crabapples when not cultivated; Knox applied this analogy to colonies of people detached from the mother country.

[33] The manure of sea birds, used as fertilizer.

[34] One more bundle of these impenetrable explanations.

[35] Jenny Lind (1820–1887), a popular British coloratura soprano; Nathaniel Bowditch (1773–1838), an American mathematician and astronomer, whose *New American Practical Navigator* (1802) was widely used.

[36] Emerson's note: " 'Everything which pertains to the human species, considered as a whole, belongs to the order of physical facts. The greater the number of individuals, the more does the influence of the individual will disappear, leaving predominance to a series of general facts dependent on causes by which society exists, and is preserved.'—Quetelet."

[37] Zoroaster (6th or 7th century B.C.) was a Persian religious seer; Manu, said to be the author of the Hindu *Laws of Manu;* Tubal-Cain, "an instructor of every artificer in brass and iron," from Genesis 4:22; Vulcan, the Roman god of fire and metalworking; Cadmus, a legendary Phoenician prince who slew a dragon and saw an army spring up from its teeth, which he had scattered on the ground; Nicolaus Copernicus (1473–1543), the Polish astronomer who determined the movements of the solar system; Johann Fust (1400?–1466?), a German printer associated with the invention of movable type; Robert Fulton (1765–1815), the American inventor who designed steamboats.

inventor. There are scores and centuries of them. "The air is full of men." This kind of talent so abounds, this constructive tool-making efficiency, as if it adhered to the chemic atoms; as if the air he breathes were made of Vaucansons, Franklins, and Watts.[38]

Doubtless in every million there will be an astronomer, a mathematician, a comic poet, a mystic. No one can read the history of astronomy without perceiving that Copernicus, Newton, Laplace, are not new men, or a new kind of men, but that Thales, Anaximenes, Hipparchus, Empedocles, Aristarchus, Pythagoras, Œnipodes,[39] had anticipated them; each had the same tense geometrical brain, apt for the same vigorous computation and logic; a mind parallel to the movement of the world. The Roman mile probably rested on a measure of a degree of the meridian. Mahometan[40] and Chinese know what we know of leap-year, of the Gregorian calendar,[41] and of the precession of the equinoxes. As in every barrel of cowries brought to New Bedford there shall be one *orangia*,[42] so there will, in a dozen millions of Malays and Mahometans, be one or two astronomical skulls.[43] In a large city, the most casual things, and things whose beauty lies in their casualty, are produced as punctually and to order as the baker's muffin for breakfast. Punch[44] makes exactly one capital joke a week; and the journals contrive to furnish one good piece of news every day.

And not less work the laws of repression, the penalties of violated functions. Famine, typhus, frost, war, suicide and effete races must be reckoned calculable parts of the system of the world.

These are pebbles from the mountain, hints of the terms by which our life is walled up, and which show a kind of mechanical exactness, as of a loom or mill, in what we call casual or fortuitous events.

The force with which we resist these torrents of tendency looks so ridiculously inadequate that it amounts to little more than a criticism or a protest made by a minority of one, under compulsion of millions. I seemed in the height of a tempest to see men overboard struggling in the waves, and driven about here and there. They glanced intelligently at each other, but 't was little they could do for one another; 't was much if each could keep afloat alone. Well, they had a right to their eyebeams, and all the rest was Fate.

---

[38] Jacques de Vaucanson (1709–1782), a French mathematician and inventor of self-moving machines (automatons); the American inventor, statesman, and writer Benjamin Franklin (1706–1790); James Watt (1736–1819), the Scottish engineer who invented the modern steam engine.

[39] Sir Isaac Newton (1642–1727), the English mathematician and physicist who formulated the theory of gravity; Pierre Simon (1749–1827), marquis de Laplace, a French mathematician and astronomer; the Greek philosophers Thales (640?–546 B.C.), who taught that the earth is round and that the moon reflects light from the sun and predicted a solar eclipse, and Anaximenes of Miletus (6th century B.C.), who claimed that all substances are derived from air; Hipparchus (2d century B.C.), a Greek astronomer who discovered the precession of the equinoxes; Empedocles (5th century B.C.), a Greek philosopher and statesman who claimed to have prophetic powers; Aristarchus of Samos (3d century B.C.), a Greek astronomer who explained that the earth revolves around the sun and on its own axis; Pythagoras (6th century B.C.), a renowned Greek mathematician and philosopher; Oenopides of Chios (5th century B.C.), a Greek astronomer and mathematician who "anticipated" Pythagoras with his knowledge of the obliquity of the ecliptic.

[40] Mohammedan.

[41] The modern calendar, in use since 1582 (adopted in America in 1752), was named for Pope Gregory XIII (1502–1585).

[42] A particularly bright type of cowrie shell.

[43] Skulls with brains equipped for astronomical study.

[44] A British satirical weekly magazine; Emerson is droll about its humor.

We cannot trifle with this reality, this cropping-out in our planted gardens of the core of the world. No picture of life can have any veracity that does not admit the odious facts. A man's power is hooped in by a necessity which, by many experiments, he touches on every side until he learns its arc.

The element running through entire nature, which we popularly call Fate, is known to us as limitation. Whatever limits us we call Fate. If we are brute and barbarous, the fate takes a brute and dreadful shape. As we refine, our cheeks become finer. If we rise to spiritual culture, the antagonism takes a spiritual form. In the Hindoo fables, Vishnu follows Maya[45] through all her ascending changes, from insect and crawfish up to elephant; whatever form she took, he took the male form of that kind, until she became at last woman and goddess, and he a man and a god. The limitations refine as the soul purifies, but the ring of necessity is always perched at the top.

When the gods in the Norse heaven were unable to bind the Fenris Wolf[46] with steel or with weight of mountains,—the one he snapped and the other he spurned with his heel,—they put round his foot a limp band softer than silk or cobweb, and this held him; the more he spurned it the stiffer it drew. So soft and so stanch is the ring of Fate. Neither brandy, nor nectar, nor sulphuric ether, nor hell-fire, nor ichor,[47] nor poetry, nor genius, can get rid of this limp band. For if we give it the high sense in which the poets use it, even thought itself is not above Fate; that too must act according to eternal laws, and all that is wilful and fantastic in it is in opposition to its fundamental essence.

And last of all, high over thought, in the world of morals, Fate appears as vindicator, levelling the high, lifting the low, requiring justice in man, and always striking soon or late when justice is not done. What is useful will last; what is hurtful will sink. "The doer must suffer," said the Greeks; "you would soothe a Deity not to be soothed." "God himself cannot procure good for the wicked," said the Welsh triad. "God may consent, but only for a time," said the bard of Spain.[48] The limitation is impassable by any insight of man. In its last and loftiest ascensions, insight itself and the freedom of the will is one of its obedient members. But we must not run into generalizations too large, but show the natural bounds or essential distinctions, and seek to do justice to the other elements as well.

Thus we trace Fate in matter, mind, and morals; in race, in retardations of strata, and in thought and character as well. It is everywhere bound or limitation. But Fate has its lord; limitation its limits,—is different seen from above and from below, from within and from without. For though Fate is immense, so is Power, which is the other fact in the dual world, immense. If Fate follows and limits Power, Power attends and antagonizes Fate. We must respect Fate as natural history, but there is more than natural history. For who and what is this criticism that pries into the matter? Man is not order of nature, sack and sack, belly and members,[49] link in a chain, nor any ignominious baggage; but a stupendous antagonism, a dragging together of the poles of the Universe. He betrays his relation to

---

[45] In the Hindu trinity, Vishnu is the preserver of human beings; Maya is the goddess of illusion.

[46] According to Norse myth, a monster who was restrained by fragile bonds but whose wrath was ever threatening.

[47] According to Greek myth, an ethereal fluid that replaced blood in the gods' veins.

[48] The source of these maxims has not been identified.

[49] The dialogue between the belly and other parts of the body is given by Menenius Agrippa in Shakespeare's *Coriolanus* (I. i. 99–150).

what is below him,—thick-skulled, small-brained, fishy, quadrumanous,[50] quad-ruped ill-disguised, hardly escaped into biped,—and has paid for the new powers by loss of some of the old ones. But the lightning which explodes and fashions planets, maker of planets, and suns, is in him. On one side elemental order, sand-stone and granite, rock-ledges, peat-bog, forest, sea and shore; and on the other part thought, the spirit which composes and decomposes nature,—here they are, side by side, god and devil, mind and matter, king and conspirator, belt and spasm, riding peacefully together in the eye and brain of every man.

Nor can he blink the freewill. To hazard the contradiction,—freedom is neces-sary. If you please to plant yourself on the side of Fate, and say, Fate is all; then we say, a part of Fate is the freedom of man. Forever wells up the impulse of choosing and acting in the soul. Intellect annuls Fate. So far as a man thinks, he is free. And though nothing is more disgusting than the crowing about liberty by slaves, as most men are, and the flippant mistaking for freedom of some paper preamble like a "Declaration of Independence" or the statute right to vote, by those who have never dared to think or to act,—yet it is wholesome to man to look not at Fate, but the other way: the practical view is the other. His sound relation to these facts is to use and command, not to cringe to them. "Look not on Nature, for her name is fatal," said the oracle. The too much contemplation of these limits induces meanness. They who talk much of destiny, their birth-star, &c., are in a lower dangerous plane, and invite the evils they fear.

I cited the instinctive and heroic races as proud believers in Destiny. They conspire with it; a loving resignation is with the event. But the dogma makes a different impression when it is held by the weak and lazy. 'Tis weak and vicious people who cast the blame on Fate. The right use of Fate is to bring up our con-duct to the loftiness of nature. Rude and invincible except by themselves are the elements. So let man be. Let him empty his breast of his windy conceits, and show his lordship by manners and deeds on the scale of nature. Let him hold his purpose as with the tug of gravitation. No power, no persuasion, no bribe shall make him give up his point. A man ought to compare advantageously with a river, an oak, or a mountain. He shall have not less the flow, the expansion, and the resistance of these.

'T is the best use of Fate to teach a fatal courage. Go face the fire at sea, or the cholera in your friend's house, or the burglar in your own, or what danger lies in the way of duty,—knowing you are guarded by the cherubim of Destiny. If you believe in Fate to your harm, believe it at least for your good.

For if Fate is so prevailing, man also is part of it, and can confront fate with fate. If the Universe have these savage accidents, our atoms are as savage in resis-tance. We should be crushed by the atmosphere, but for the reaction of the air within the body. A tube made of a film of glass can resist the shock of the ocean if filled with the same water. If there be omnipotence in the stroke, there is omnipo-tence of recoil.

1. But Fate against Fate is only parrying and defence: there are also the noble creative forces. The revelation of Thought takes man out of servitude into free-dom. We rightly say of ourselves, we were born and afterward we were born again, and many times. We have successive experiences so important that the new forgets the old, and hence the mythology of the seven or the nine heavens. The day of days, the great day of the feast of life, is that in which the inward eye opens

[50] Having all four feet with opposable first digits.

to the Unity in things, to the omnipresence of law:—sees that what is must be and ought to be, or is the best. This beatitude dips from on high down on us and we see. It is not in us so much as we are in it. If the air come to our lungs, we breathe and live; if not, we die. If the light come to our eyes, we see; else not. And if truth come to our mind we suddenly expand to its dimensions, as if we grew to worlds. We are as lawgivers; we speak for Nature; we prophesy and divine.

This insight throws us on the party and interest of the Universe, against all and sundry; against ourselves as much as others. A man speaking from insight affirms of himself what is true of the mind: seeing its immortality, he says, I am immortal; seeing its invincibility, he says, I am strong. It is not in us, but we are in it. It is of the maker, not of what is made. All things are touched and changed by it. This uses and is not used. It distances those who share it from those who share it not. Those who share it not are flocks and herds. It dates from itself; not from former men or better men, gospel, or constitution, or college, or custom. Where it shines, Nature is no longer intrusive, but all things make a musical or pictorial impression. The world of men show like a comedy without laughter: populations, interests, government history; 't is all toy figures in a toy house. It does not overvalue particular truths. We hear eagerly every thought and word quoted from an intellectual man. But in his presence our own mind is roused to activity, and we forget very fast what he says, much more interested in the new play of our own thought than in any thought of his. 'T is the majesty into which we have suddenly mounted, the impersonality, the scorn of egotisms, the sphere of laws, that engage us. Once we were stepping a little this way and a little that way; now we are as men in a balloon, and do not think so much of the point we have left, or the point we would make, as of the liberty and glory of the way.

Just as much intellect as you add, so much organic power. He who sees through the design, presides over it, and must will that which must be. We sit and rule, and, though we sleep, our dream will come to pass. Our thought, though it were only an hour old, affirms an oldest necessity, not to be separated from thought, and not to be separated from will. They must always have coexisted. It apprises us of its sovereignty and godhead, which refuse to be severed from it. It is not mine or thine, but the will of all mind. It is poured into the souls of all men, as the soul itself which constitutes them men. I know not whether there be, as is alleged, in the upper region of our atmosphere, a permanent westerly current which carries with it all atoms which rise to that height, but I see that when souls reach a certain clearness of perception they accept a knowledge and motive above selfishness. A breath of will blows eternally through the universe of souls in the direction of the Right and Necessary. It is the air which all intellects inhale and exhale, and it is the wind which blows the worlds into order and orbit.

Thought dissolves the material universe by carrying the mind up into a sphere where all is plastic. Of two men, each obeying his own thought, he whose thought is deepest will be the strongest character. Always one man more than another represents the will of Divine Providence to the period.

2. If thought makes free, so does the moral sentiment. The mixtures of spiritual chemistry refuse to be analyzed. Yet we can see that with the perception of truth is joined the desire that it shall prevail; that affection is essential to will. Moreover, when a strong will appears, it usually results from a certain unity of organization, as if the whole energy of body and mind flowed in one direction. All great force is real and elemental. There is no manufacturing a strong will. There must be a pound to balance a pound. Where power is shown in will, it must rest on the

universal force. Alaric[51] and Bonaparte must believe they rest on a truth, or their will can be bought or bent. There is a bribe possible for any finite will. But the pure sympathy with universal ends is an infinite force, and cannot be bribed or bent. Whoever has had experience of the moral sentiment cannot choose but believe in unlimited power. Each pulse from that heart is an oath from the Most High. I know not what the word *sublime* means, if it be not the intimations, in this infant, of a terrific force. A text of heroism, a name and anecdote of courage, are not arguments but sallies of freedom. One of these is the verse of the Persian Hafiz,[52] "'T is written on the gate of Heaven, 'Woe unto him who suffers himself to be betrayed by Fate!'" Does the reading of history make us fatalists? What courage does not the opposite opinion show! A little whim of will to be free gallantly contending against the universe of chemistry.

But insight is not will, nor is affection will. Perception is cold, and goodness dies in wishes. As Voltaire[53] said, 't is the misfortune of worthy people that they are cowards; "*un des plus grands malheurs des honnêtes gens c'est qu'ils sont des lâches.*" There must be a fusion of these two to generate the energy of will. There can be no driving force except through the conversion of the man into his will, making him the will, and the will him. And one may say boldly that no man has a right perception of any truth who has not been reacted on by it so as to be ready to be its martyr.

The one serious and formidable thing in nature is a will. Society is servile from want of will, and therefore the world wants saviours and religions. One way is right to go; the hero sees it, and moves on that aim, and has the world under him for root and support. He is to others as the world. His approbation is honor; his dissent, infamy. The glance of his eye has the force of sunbeams. A personal influence towers up in memory only worthy, and we gladly forget numbers, money, climate, gravitation, and the rest of Fate.

We can afford to allow the limitation, if we know it is the meter of the growing man. We stand against Fate, as children stand up against the wall in their father's house and notch their height from year to year. But when the boy grows to man, and is master of the house, he pulls down that wall and builds a new and bigger. 'T is only a question of time. Every brave youth is in training to ride and rule this dragon. His science is to make weapons and wings of these passions and retarding forces. Now whether, seeing these two things, fate and power, we are permitted to believe in unity? The bulk of mankind believe in two gods. They are under one dominion here in the house, as friend and parent, in social circles, in letters, in art, in love, in religion; but in mechanics, in dealing with steam and climate, in trade, in politics, they think they come under another; and that it would be a practical blunder to transfer the method and way of working of one sphere into the other. What good, honest, generous men at home, will be wolves and foxes on 'Change![54] What pious men in the parlor will vote for what reprobates at the polls! To a certain point, they believe themselves the care of a Providence. But in a steamboat, in an epidemic, in war, they believe a malignant energy rules.

But relation and connection are not somewhere and sometimes, but everywhere and always. The divine order does not stop where their sight stops. The friendly

---

[51] Alaric (370?–410) was a Visigoth king who sacked Rome in 410.

[52] Shams ud-din Mohammed (14th century), a Persian lyric poet.

[53] Pen name of the French writer François Marie Arouet (1694–1778); Emerson translates Voltaire's statement, then quotes it in French.

[54] The stock exchange.

power works on the same rules in the next farm and the next planet. But where they have not experience they run against it and hurt themselves. Fate then is a name for facts not yet passed under the fire of thought; for causes which are unpenetrated.

But every jet of chaos which threatens to exterminate us is convertible by intellect into wholesome force. Fate is unpenetrated causes. The water drowns ship and sailor like a grain of dust. But learn to swim, trim your bark,[55] and the wave which drowned it will be cloven by it and carry it like its own foam, a plume and a power. The cold is inconsiderate of persons, tingles your blood, freezes a man like a dew-drop. But learn to skate, and the ice will give you a graceful, sweet, and poetic motion. The cold will brace your limbs and brain to genius, and make you foremost men of time. Cold and sea will train an imperial Saxon race, which nature cannot bear to lose, and after cooping it up for a thousand years in yonder England, gives a hundred Englands, a hundred Mexicos. All the bloods it shall absorb and domineer: and more than Mexicos, the secrets of water and steam, the spasms of electricity, the ductility of metals, the chariot of the air, the ruddered balloon are awaiting you.

The annual slaughter from typhus far exceeds that of war; but right drainage destroys typhus. The plague in the sea-service from scurvy is healed by lemon juice and other diets portable or procurable; the depopulation by cholera and small-pox is ended by drainage and vaccination; and every other pest is not less in the chain of cause and effect, and may be fought off. And whilst art draws out the venom, it commonly extorts some benefit from the vanquished enemy. The mischievous torrent is taught to drudge for man; the wild beasts he makes useful for food, or dress, or labor; the chemic explosions are controlled like his watch. These are now the steeds on which he rides. Man moves in all modes, by legs of horses, by wings of wind, by steam, by gas of balloon, by electricity, and stands on tiptoe threatening to hunt the eagle in his own element. There's nothing he will not make his carrier.

Steam was till the other day the devil which we dreaded. Every pot made by any human potter or brazier[56] had a hole in its cover, to let off the enemy, lest he should lift pot and roof and carry the house away. But the Marquis of Worcester,[57] Watt, and Fulton bethought themselves that where was power was not devil, but was God; that it must be availed of, and not by any means let off and wasted. Could he lift pots and roofs and houses so handily? He was the workman they were in search of. He could be used to lift away, chain and compel other devils far more reluctant and dangerous, namely cubic miles of earth, mountains, weight or resistance of water, machinery, and the labors of all men in the world; and time he shall lengthen, and shorten space.

It has not fared much otherwise with higher kinds of steam. The opinion of the million was the terror of the world, and it was attempted either to dissipate it, by amusing nations, or to pile it over with strata of society,—a layer of soldiers, over that a layer of lords, and a king on the top; with clamps and hoops of castles, garrisons, and police. But sometimes the religious principle would get in and burst the hoops and rive every mountain laid on top of it. The Fultons and Watts of

---

[55] Trim the sails of your small sailing ship.   [56] A brassworker.

[57] Edward Somerset (1601–1667), marquis of Worcester and earl of Glamorgan, a precursor of James Watt and Robert Fulton who studied mechanics and wrote *Century of Inventions* (1663), which describes a machine similar to a steam engine.

politics, believing in unity, saw that it was a power, and by satisfying it (as justice satisfies everybody), through a different disposition of society,—grouping it on a level instead of piling it into a mountain,—they have contrived to make of this terror the most harmless and energetic form of a State.

Very odious, I confess, are the lessons of Fate. Who likes to have a dapper phrenologist pronouncing on his fortunes? Who likes to believe that he has, hidden in his skull, spine, and pelvis, all the vices of a Saxon or Celtic race, which will be sure to pull him down,—with what grandeur of hope and resolve he is fired,—into a selfish, huckstering, servile, dodging animal? A learned physician tells us the fact is invariable with the Neapolitan, that when mature he assumes the forms of the unmistakable scoundrel. That is little overstated,—but may pass.

But these are magazines[58] and arsenals. A man must thank his defects, and stand in some terror of his talents. A transcendent talent draws so largely on his forces as to lame him; a defect pays him revenues on the other side. The sufferance which is the badge of the Jew, has made him, in these days, the ruler of the rulers of the earth.[59] If Fate is ore and quarry, if evil is good in the making, if limitation is power that shall be, if calamities, oppositions, and weights are wings and means,—we are reconciled.

Fate involves the melioration. No statement of the Universe can have any soundness which does not admit its ascending effort. The direction of the whole and of the parts is toward benefit, and in proportion to the health. Behind every individual closes organization; before him opens liberty,—the Better, the Best. The first and worse races are dead. The second and imperfect races are dying out, or remain for the maturing of higher. In the latest race, in man, every generosity, every new perception, the love and praise he extorts from his fellows, are certificates of advance out of fate into freedom. Liberation of the will from the sheaths and clogs of organization which he has outgrown, is the end and aim of this world. Every calamity is a spur and valuable hint: and where his endeavors do not yet fully avail, they tell as tendency. The whole circle of animal life,—tooth against tooth, devouring war, war for food, a yelp of pain and a grunt of triumph, until at last the whole menagerie, the whole chemical mass is mellowed and refined for higher use,—pleases at a sufficient perspective.

But to see how fate slides into freedom and freedom into fate, observe how far the roots of every creature run, or find if you can a point where there is no thread of connection. Our life is consentaneous[60] and far-related. This knot of nature is so well tied that nobody was ever cunning enough to find the two ends. Nature is intricate, over-lapped, interweaved and endless. Christopher Wren[61] said of the beautiful King's College chapel, that "if anybody would tell him where to lay the first stone, he would build such another." But where shall we find the first atom in this house of man, which is all consent, inosculation,[62] and balance of parts?

The web of relation is shown in *habitat,* shown in hibernation. When hibernation was observed, it was found that whilst some animals became torpid in winter, others were torpid in summer: hibernation then was a false name. The *long sleep* is not an effect of cold, but is regulated by the supply of food proper to the animal. It becomes torpid when the fruit or prey it lives on is not in season, and regains its activity when its food is ready.

[58] Storehouses.   [59] Through financial power and control of dominant banks.
[60] Suitable, lived with a single consent.
[61] The English architect (1632–1723) who designed St. Paul's Cathedral.
[62] Joining or blending to make a whole.

Eyes are found in light; ears in auricular[63] air; feet on land; fins in water; wings in the air; and each creature where it was meant to be, with a mutual fitness. Every zone has its own *Fauna*. There is adjustment between the animal and its food, its parasite, its enemy. Balances are kept. It is not allowed to diminish in numbers, nor to exceed. The like adjustments exist for man. His food is cooked when he arrives; his coal in the pit; the house ventilated; the mud of the deluge dried; his companions arrived at the same hour, and awaiting him with love, concert, laughter and tears. These are coarse adjustments, but the invisible are not less. There are more belongings to every creature than his air and his food. His instincts must be met, and he has predisposing power that bends and fits what is near him to his use. He is not possible until the invisible things are right for him, as well as the visible. Of what changes then in sky and earth, and in finer skies and earths, does the appearance of some Dante or Columbus apprise us!

How is this effected? Nature is no spendthrift, but takes the shortest way to her ends. As the general says to his soldiers, "If you want a fort, build a fort," so nature makes every creature do its own work and get its living,—is it planet, animal or tree. The planet makes itself. The animal cell makes itself;—then, what it wants. Every creature, wren or dragon, shall make its own lair. As soon as there is life, there is self-direction and absorbing and using of material. Life is freedom,—life in the direct ratio of its amount. You may be sure the new-born man is not inert. Life works both voluntarily and supernaturally in its neighborhood. Do you suppose he can be estimated by his weight in pounds, or that he is contained in his skin,—this reaching, radiating, jaculating[64] fellow? The smallest candle fills a mile with its rays, and the papillæ[65] of a man run out to every star.

When there is something to be done, the world knows how to get it done. The vegetable eye makes leaf, pericarp,[66] root, bark, or thorn, as the need is; the first cell converts itself into stomach, mouth, nose, or nail, according to the want; the world throws its life into a hero or a shepherd, and puts him where he is wanted. Dante and Columbus were Italians, in their time; they would be Russians or Americans to-day. Things ripen, new men come. The adaptation is not capricious. The ulterior aim, the purpose beyond itself, the correlation by which planets subside and crystallize, then animate beasts and men,—will not stop but will work into finer particulars, and from finer to finest.

The secret of the world is the tie between person and event. Person makes event, and event person. The "times," "the age," what is that but a few profound persons and a few active persons who epitomize the times?—Goethe, Hegel, Metternich, Adams, Calhoun, Guizot, Peel, Cobden, Kossuth, Rothschild, Astor, Brunel,[67] and the rest. The same fitness must be presumed between a man and the time and event, as between the sexes, or between a race of animals and the food it

---

[63] Audible.   [64] Throwing, hurling.   [65] Small nipplelike projections.

[66] The walls of a ripened plant ovary.

[67] Johann Wolfgang von Goethe (1749–1832), a German writer; George Wilhelm Friedrich Hegel (1770–1831), a German philosopher; Prince Klemens von Metternich (1773–1859), an Austrian statesman; John Adams (1735–1826), second U.S. president; John C. Calhoun (1782–1850), a southern politician and U.S. vice president from 1825 to 1832; François Guizot (1787–1874), a French statesman; Robert Peel (1788–1850), a British prime minister (1834–1835, 1841–1846); Richard Cobden (1804–1865), a British economist and politician; Lajos Kossuth; Meyer Rothschild (1743–1812), a German-Jewish banker; John Jacob Astor (1763–1848), an American fur trader and financier; Isambard Brunel (1806–1859), designer of the first transatlantic steamship, the *Great Western*.

eats, or the inferior races it uses. He thinks his fate alien, because the copula is hidden. But the soul contains the event that shall befall it; for the event is only the actualization of its thoughts, and what we pray to ourselves for is always granted. The event is the print of your form. It fits you like your skin. What each does is proper to him. Events are the children of his body and mind. We learn that the soul of Fate is the soul of us, as Hafiz sings,—

> "Alas! till now I had not known,
> My guide and fortune's guide are one."

All the toys that infatuate men and which they play for,—houses, land, money, luxury, power, fame, are the selfsame thing, with a new gauze or two of illusion overlaid. And of all the drums and rattles by which men are made willing to have their heads broke, and are led out solemnly every morning to parade,—the most admirable is this by which we are brought to believe that events are arbitrary and independent of actions. At the conjuror's, we detect the hair by which he moves his puppet, but we have not eyes sharp enough to descry the thread that ties cause and effect.

Nature magically suits the man to his fortunes, by making these the fruit of his character. Ducks take to the water, eagles to the sky, waders to the sea margin, hunters to the forest, clerks to counting-rooms, soldiers to the frontier. Thus events grow on the same stem with persons; are sub-persons. The pleasure of life is according to the man that lives it, and not according to the work or the place. Life is an ecstasy. We know what madness belongs to love,—what power to paint a vile object in hues of heaven. As insane persons are indifferent to their dress, diet, and other accommodations, and as we do in dreams, with equanimity, the most absurd acts, so a drop more of wine in our cup of life will reconcile us to strange company and work. Each creature puts forth from itself its own condition and sphere, as the slug sweats out its slimy house on the pear-leaf, and the wooly aphides on the apple perspire their own bed, and the fish its shell. In youth we clothe ourselves with rainbows and go as brave as the zodiac. In age we put out another sort of perspiration,—gout, fever, rheumatism, caprice, doubt, fretting and avarice.

A man's fortunes are the fruit of his character. A man's friends are his magnet-isms. We go to Herodotus and Plutarch[68] for examples of Fate; but we are examples. "*Quisque suos patimur manes.*"[69] The tendency of every man to enact all that is in his constitution is expressed in the old belief that the efforts which we make to escape from our destiny only serve to lead us into it: and I have noticed a man likes better to be complimented on his position, as the proof of the last or total excellence, than on his merits.

A man will see his character emitted in the events that seem to meet, but which exude from and accompany him. Events expand with the character. As once he found himself among toys, so now he plays a part in colossal systems, and his growth is declared in his ambition, his companions and his performance. He looks like a piece of luck, but is a piece of causation; the mosaic, angulated and ground

---

[68] Herodotus (5th century B.C.), a Greek historian known as the Father of History; Plutarch (A.D. 46?–120?), biographer who featured the "parallel lives" of eminent Greeks and Romans.

[69] "Each person undergoes his special penalty," from Book VI of Virgil's *Aeniad* (spoken to Aeneas by his father).

to fit into the gap he fills. Hence in each town there is some man who is, in his brain and performance, an explanation of the tillage, production, factories, banks, churches, ways of living and society of that town. If you do not chance to meet him, all that you see will leave you a little puzzled; if you see him it will become plain. We know in Massachusetts who built New Bedford, who built Lynn, Lowell, Lawrence, Clinton, Fitchburg, Holyoke, Portland, and many another noisy mart. Each of these men, if they were transparent, would seem to you so much men as walking cities, and wherever you put them they would build one.

History is the action and reaction of these two,—Nature and Thought; two boys pushing each other on the curbstone of the pavement. Everything is pusher or pushed; and matter and mind are in perpetual tilt and balance, so. Whilst the man is weak, the earth takes up him. He plants his brain and affections. By and by he will take up the earth, and have his gardens and vineyards in the beautiful order and productiveness of his thought. Every solid in the universe is ready to become fluid on the approach of the mind, and the power to flux it is the measure of the mind. If the wall remain adamant, it accuses the want of thought. To a subtler force it will stream into new forms, expressive of the character of the mind. What is the city in which we sit here, but an aggregate of incongruous materials which have obeyed the will of some man? The granite was reluctant, but his hands were stronger, and it came. Iron was deep in the ground and well combined with stone, but could not hide from his fires. Wood, lime, stuffs, fruits, gums, were dispersed over the earth and sea, in vain. Here they are, within reach of every man's day-labor,—what he wants of them. The whole world is the flux of matter over the wires of thought to the poles or points where it would build. The races of men rise out of the ground preoccupied with a thought which rules them, and divided into parties ready armed and angry to fight for this metaphysical abstraction. The quality of the thought differences the Egyptian and the Roman, the Austrian and the American. The men who come on the stage at one period are all found to be related to each other. Certain ideas are in the air. We are all impressionable, for we are made of them; all impressionable, but some more than others, and these first express them. This explains the curious contemporaneousness of inventions and discoveries. The truth is in the air, and the most impressionable brain will announce it first, but all will announce it a few minutes later. So women, as most susceptible, are the best index of the coming hour. So the great man, that is, the man most imbued with the spirit of the time, is the impressionable man;—of a fibre irritable and delicate, like iodine to light. He feels the infinitesimal attractions. His mind is righter than others because he yields to a current so feeble as can be felt only by a needle delicately poised.

The correlation is shown in defects. Möller,[70] in his Essay on Architecture, taught that the building which was fitted accurately to answer its end would turn out to be beautiful though beauty had not been intended. I find the like unity in human structures rather virulent and pervasive; that a crudity in the blood will appear in the argument; a hump in the shoulder will appear in the speech and handiwork. If his mind could be seen, the hump would be seen. If a man has a seesaw in his voice, it will run into his sentences, into his poem, into the structure of his fable, into his speculation, into his charity. And as every man is hunted by his own dæmon, vexed by his own disease, this checks all his activity.

---

[70] Georg Möller (1784–1852), a German architect and author of *Essay on the Origin and Progress of Gothic Architecture* (1825).

So each man, like each plant, has his parasites. A strong, astringent, bilious nature has more truculent enemies than the slugs and moths that fret my leaves. Such an one has curculios,[71] borers, knife-worms; a swindler ate him first, then a client, then a quack, then smooth, plausible gentlemen, bitter and selfish as Moloch.[72]

This correlation really existing can be divined. If the threads are there, thought can follow and show them. Especially when a soul is quick and docile, as Chaucer sings;—

> "Or if the soul of proper kind
> Be so perfect as men find,
> That it wot what is to come,
> And that he warneth all and some
> Of every of their aventures,
> By previsions or figures;
> But that our flesh hath not might
> It to understand aright
> For it is warned too darkly."[73]

Some people are made up of rhyme, coincidence, omen, periodicity, and presage; they meet the person they seek; what their companion prepares to say to them, they first say to him; and a hundred signs apprise them of what is about to befall.

Wonderful intricacy in the web, wonderful constancy in the design this vagabond life admits. We wonder how the fly finds its mate, and yet year after year, we find two men, two women, without legal or carnal tie, spend a great part of their best time within a few feet of each other. And the moral is that what we seek we shall find;[74] what we flee from flees from us; as Goethe said, "what we wish for in youth, comes in heaps on us in old age,"[75] too often cursed with the granting of our prayer: and hence the high caution, that since we are sure of having what we wish, we beware to ask only for high things.

One key, one solution to the mysteries of human condition, one solution to the old knots of fate, freedom, and foreknowledge, exists; the propounding, namely, of the double consciousness. A man must ride alternately on the horses of his private and his public nature, as the equestrians in the circus throw themselves nimbly from horse to horse, or plant one foot on the back of one and the other foot on the back of the other. So when a man is the victim of his fate, has sciatica in his loins and cramp in his mind; a club-foot and a club in his wit; a sour face, and a selfish temper; a strut in his gait and a conceit in his affection; or is ground to powder by the vice of his race;—he is to rally on his relation to the Universe, which his ruin benefits. Leaving the dæmon who suffers, he is to take sides with the Deity who secures universal benefit by his pain.

To offset the drag of temperament and race, which pulls down, learn this lesson, namely that by the cunning co-presence of two elements, which is throughout nature, whatever, lames or paralyzes you draws in with it the divinity, in some

[71] Snout beetles that harm fruit.

[72] A Canaanite fire god to whom children were offered in sacrifice; worship of Moloch was contrary to Hebrew law and condemned by the prophets.

[73] From Geoffrey Chaucer's *The House of Fame* (43–51).   [74] From Matthew 7:7.

[75] From the epigraph to the second part of Goethe's autobiography, *Poetry and Truth* (1811–1813).

form, to repay. A good intention clothes itself with sudden power. When a god wishes to ride, any chip or pebble will bud and shoot out winged feet and serve him for a horse.

Let us build altars to the Blessed Unity which holds nature and souls in perfect solution, and compels every atom to serve an universal end. I do not wonder at a snow-flake, a shell, a summer landscape, or the glory of the stars; but at the necessity of beauty under which the universe lies; that all is and must be pictorial; that the rainbow and the curve of the horizon and the arch of the blue vault are only results from the organism of the eye. There is no need for foolish amateurs to fetch me to admire a garden of flowers, or a sun-gilt cloud, or a waterfall, when I cannot look without seeing splendor and grace. How idle to choose a random sparkle here or there, when the indwelling necessity plants the rose of beauty on the brow of chaos, and discloses the central intention of Nature to be harmony and joy.

Let us build altars to the Beautiful Necessity. If we thought men were free in the sense that in a single exception one fantastical will could prevail over the law of things, it were all one as if a child's hand could pull down the sun. If in the least particular one could derange the order of nature,—who would accept the gift of life?

Let us build altars to the Beautiful Necessity, which secures that all is made of one piece; that plaintiff and defendant, friend and enemy, animal and planet, food and eater are of one kind. In astronomy is vast space but no foreign system; in geology, vast time but the same laws as to-day. Why should we be afraid of Nature, which is no other than "philosophy and theology embodied"? Why should we fear to be crushed by savage elements, we who are made up of the same elements? Let us build to the Beautiful Necessity, which makes man brave in believing that he cannot shun a danger that is appointed, nor incur one that is not; to the Necessity which rudely or softly educates him to the perception that there are no contingencies; that Law rules throughout existence; a Law which is not intelligent but intelligence;—not personal nor impersonal—it disdains words and passes understanding; it dissolves persons; it vivifies nature; yet solicits the pure in heart to draw on all its omnipotence.

1851, 1860

CONCORD HYMN*

SUNG AT THE COMPLETION OF THE BATTLE MONUMENT,
JULY 4, 1837

By the rude bridge that arched the flood,
  Their flag to April's breeze unfurled,
Here once the embattled farmers stood
  And fired the shot heard round the world.

---

* First printed as a leaflet and distributed at the dedication of the monument commemorating the Revolutionary War battles of Lexington and Concord (April 19, 1775).

The foe long since in silence slept;
  Alike the conqueror silent sleeps;
And Time the ruined bridge has swept
  Down the dark stream which seaward creeps.

On this green bank, by this soft stream,
  We set to-day a votive stone;[1]
That memory may their deed redeem,
  When, like our sires, our sons are gone.

Spirit, that made those heroes dare
  To die, and leave their children free,
Bid Time and Nature gently spare
  The shaft we raise to them and thee.

1837

EACH AND ALL*

Little thinks, in the field, yon red-cloaked clown[1]
Of thee from the hill-top looking down;
The heifer that lows in the upland farm,
Far-heard, lows not thine ear to charm;
The sexton,[2] tolling his bell at noon,
Deems not that great Napoleon
Stops his horse, and lists with delight,
Whilst his files sweep round yon Alpine height;
Nor knowest thou what argument
Thy life to thy neighbor's creed has lent.
All are needed by each one;
Nothing is fair or good alone.
I thought the sparrow's note from heaven,
Singing at dawn on the alder bough;
I brought him home, in his nest, at even;
He sings the song, but it cheers not now,
For I did not bring home the river and sky;—
He sang to my ear,—they sang to my eye.
The delicate shells lay on the shore;
The bubbles of the latest wave
Fresh pearls to their enamel gave,
And the bellowing of the savage sea
Greeted their safe escape to me.
I wiped away the weeds and foam,
I fetched my sea-born treasures home;
But the poor, unsightly, noisome things

---

[1] A stone offering made to fulfill a vow or promise.
* First published in the *Western Messenger* in 1839.
[1] A rustic person, peasant.   [2] Church caretaker, belltoller, and gravedigger.

Had left their beauty on the shore
With the sun and the sand and the wild uproar.
The lover watched his graceful maid,
As 'mid the virgin train she strayed,   30
Nor knew her beauty's best attire
Was woven still by the snow-white choir.
At last she came to his hermitage,
Like the bird from the woodlands to the cage;—
The gay enchantment was undone,
A gentle wife, but fairy none.
Then I said, 'I covet truth;
Beauty is unripe childhood's cheat;
I leave it behind with the games of youth:'—
As I spoke, beneath my feet   40
The ground-pine curled its pretty wreath,
Running over the club-moss burrs;
I inhaled the violet's breath;
Around me stood the oaks and firs;
Pine-cones and acorns lay on the ground;
Over me soared the eternal sky,
Full of light and of deity;
Again I saw, again I heard,
The rolling river, the morning bird;—
Beauty through my senses stole;   50
I yielded myself to the perfect whole.

1839

MERLIN*

I

Thy trivial harp will never please
Or fill my craving ear;
Its chords should ring as blows the breeze,
Free, peremptory, clear.
No jingling serenader's art,
Nor tinkle of piano strings,
Can make the wild blood start
In its mystic springs.
The kingly bard
Must smite the chords rudely and hard,   10
As with hammer or with mace;
That they may render back
Artful thunder, which conveys
Secrets of the solar track,
Sparks of the supersolar blaze.

* First published in *Poems* (1847); the title refers to a legendary Welsh bard and not to the magician of Arthurian romance.

Merlin's blows are strokes of fate,
Chiming with the forest tone,
When boughs buffet boughs in the wood;
Chiming with the gasp and moan
Of the ice-imprisoned flood;   20
With the pulse of manly hearts;
With the voice of orators;
With the din of city arts;
With the cannonade of wars;
With the marches of the brave;
And prayers of might from martyrs' cave.

Great is the art,
Great be the manners, of the bard.
He shall not his brain encumber
With the coil of rhythm and number;   30
But, leaving rule and pale forethought,
He shall aye[1] climb
For his rhyme.
"Pass in, pass in," the angels say,
"In to the upper doors,
Nor count compartments of the floors,
But mount to paradise
By the stairway of surprise."

Blameless master of the games,
King of sport that never shames,   40
He shall daily joy dispense
Hid in song's sweet influence.
Forms more cheerly live and go,
What time the subtle mind
Sings aloud the tune whereto
Their pulses beat,
And march their feet,
And their members are combined.
By Sybarites[2] beguiled,
He shall no task decline;   50
Merlin's mighty line
Extremes of nature reconciled,—
Bereaved a tyrant of his will,
And made the lion mild.
Songs can the tempest still,
Scattered on the stormy air,
Mould the year to fair increase,
And bring in poetic peace.

---

[1] Always.
[2] People known for a hedonistic life style; from the inhabitants of Sybaris, a Greek city in Italy known for wealth and self-indulgence (destroyed in 510 B.C.).

He shall not seek to weave,
In weak, unhappy times,   60
Efficacious rhymes;
Wait his returning strength.
Bird that from the nadir's floor
To the zenith's top can soar,—
The soaring orbit of the muse exceeds that
  journey's length.
Nor profane affect to hit
Or compass that, by meddling wit,
Which only the propitious mind
Publishes when 't is inclined.
There are open hours   70
When the God's will sallies free,
And the dull idiot might see
The flowing fortunes of a thousand years;—
Sudden, at unawares,
Self-moved, fly-to the doors,
Nor sword of angels could reveal
What they conceal.

     II
The rhyme of the poet
Modulates the king's affairs;
Balance-loving Nature   80
Made all things in pairs.
To every foot its antipode;[3]
Each color with its counter glowed;
To every tone beat answering tones,
Higher or graver;
Flavor gladly blends with flavor;
Leaf answers leaf upon the bough;
And match the paired cotyledons.[4]
Hands to hands, and feet to feet,
In one body grooms and brides;   90
Eldest rite, two married sides
In every mortal meet.
Light's far furnace shines,
Smelting balls and bars,
Forging double stars,
Glittering twins and trines.[5]
The animals are sick with love,
Lovesick with rhyme;
Each with all propitious Time
Into chorus wove.   100

---

[3] Exact opposite.   [4] A plant's first leaves.   [5] Groups of three.

Like the dancers' ordered band,
Thoughts come also hand in hand;
In equal couples mated,
Or else alternated;
Adding by their mutual gage,
One to other, health and age.
Solitary fancies go
Short-lived wandering to and fro,
Most like to bachelors,
Or an ungiven maid,   110
Not ancestors,
With no posterity to make the lie afraid,
Or keep truth undecayed.
Perfect-paired as eagle's wings,
Justice is the rhyme of things;
Trade and counting use
The self-same tuneful muse;
And Nemesis,[6]
Who with even matches odd,
Who athwart space redresses   120
The partial wrong,
Fills the just period,
And finishes the song.
Subtle rhymes, with ruin rife,
Murmur in the house of life,
Sung by the Sisters[7] as they spin;
In perfect time and measure they
Build and unbuild our echoing clay,
As the two twilights of the day
Fold us music-drunken in.   130

                                                    1846, 1847

ODE, INSCRIBED TO W. H. CHANNING*

Though loath to grieve
The evil time's sole patriot,
I cannot leave
My honied thought
For the priest's cant,
Or statesman's rant.

---

[6] According to Greek myth, the goddess of fate.
[7] According to classical myth, the Fates, three sisters who determine human destiny.
* First published in *Poems* (1847), dedicated to the prominent abolitionist and clergyman William Henry Channing (1810–1884), nephew of the Unitarian leader William Ellery Channing (1780–1842).

If I refuse
My study for their politique,
Which at the best is trick,
The angry Muse   10
Puts confusion in my brain.

But who is he that prates
Of the culture of mankind,
Of better arts and life?
Go, blindworm, go,
Behold the famous States
Harrying Mexico[1]
With rifle and with knife!

Or who, with accent bolder,
Dare praise the freedom-loving mountaineer?   20
I found by thee, O rushing Contoocook![2]
And in thy valleys, Agiochook![3]
The jackals of the negro-holder.[4]

The God who made New Hampshire
Taunted the lofty land
With little men;—
Small bat and wren
House in the oak:—
If earth-fire cleave
The upheaved land, and bury the folk,   30
The southern crocodile would grieve.[5]
Virtue palters; Right is hence;
Freedom praised, but hid;
Funeral eloquence
Rattles the coffin-lid.

What boots[6] thy zeal,
O glowing friend,
That would indignant rend
The northland from the south?
Wherefore? to what good end?   40
Boston Bay and Bunker Hill

---

[1] In the Mexican War (1846–1848), which Emerson opposed as an effort to enlarge slaveholding territories.
[2] A Native-American name for a river in New Hampshire.
[3] A Native-American name for the White Mountains of New Hampshire.
[4] Those who hunt runaway slaves for bounty. Because New Hampshire had voted Democratic, thus aligning itself with proslavery advocates, Emerson contrasts the state's natural grandeur with its citizens of his day.
[5] The slaveholding South would grieve to lose their allies in New Hampshire.
[6] Remedies, profits.

Would serve things still;[7]—
Things are of the snake.

The horseman serves the horse,
The neatherd serves the neat,[8]
The merchant serves the purse,
The eater serves his meat;
'T is the day of the chattel,[9]
Web to weave, and corn to grind;
Things are in the saddle,   50
And ride mankind.

There are two laws discrete,
Not reconciled,—
Law for man, and law for thing;
The last builds town and fleet,
But it runs wild,
And doth the man unking.

'T is fit the forest fall,
The steep be graded,
The mountain tunnelled,   60
The sand shaded,
The orchard planted,
The glebe[10] tilled,
The prairie granted,
The steamer built.

Let man serve law for man;
Live for friendship, live for love,
For truth's and harmony's behoof;
The state may follow how it can,
As Olympus follows Jove.[11]   70

  Yet do not I implore
The wrinkled shopman to my sounding woods,
Nor bid the unwilling senator
Ask votes of thrushes in the solitudes.
Every one to his chosen work;—
Foolish hands may mix and mar;
Wise and sure the issues are.
Round they roll till dark is light,
Sex to sex, and even to odd;—
The over-god   80
Who marries Right to Might,

---

[7] The heroic actions of Revolutionary War days do not save Massachusetts from compromising principle for commercial gain, from serving "things."
[8] The cowherd serves the cow.   [9] Slave.   [10] Field.
[11] As the minor deities on Mount Olympus follow Jove (Zeus), the supreme god in Greek myth.

Who peoples, unpeoples,—
He who exterminates
Races by stronger races,
Black by white faces,—
Knows to bring honey
Out of the lion;[12]
Grafts gentlest scion
On pirate and Turk.

The Cossack eats Poland,[13]   90
Like stolen fruit;
Her last noble is ruined,
Her last poet mute:
Straight, into double band
The victors divide;
Half for freedom strike and stand;—
The astonished Muse finds thousands at her side.

1847

HAMATREYA*

Bulkeley, Hunt, Willard, Hosmer, Meriam, Flint,[1]
Possessed the land which rendered to their toil
Hay, corn, roots, hemp, flax, apples, wool and wood.
Each of these landlords walked amidst his farm,
Saying, "'T is mine, my children's and my name's.
How sweet the west wind sounds in my own trees!
How graceful climb those shadows on my hill!
I fancy these pure waters and the flags[2]
Know me, as does my dog: we sympathize;
And, I affirm, my actions smack of the soil."   10

Where are these men? Asleep beneath their grounds:
And strangers, fond[3] as they, their furrows plough.
Earth laughs in flowers, to see her boastful boys
Earth-proud, proud of the earth which is not theirs;
Who steer the plough, but cannot steer their feet
Clear of the grave.

---

[12] In Judges 14:8 Samson, the Israelite judge known for his strength, discovered honey "in the carcass of a lion."

[13] Poland had been partitioned three times in the late eighteenth century, with Russia ("the Cossack") taking the largest portion.

* First published in *Poems* (1847); this poem is a version of "Maitreya," which Emerson recorded in his journal in 1845, and is an adaptation of a passage in the Hindu scripture *Vishnu Purana* (Bk. IV), which includes the character Maitreya (a variant of Hamatreya).

[1] The first settlers of Concord, Massachusetts, including Rev. Peter Bulkeley, Emerson's ancestor seven generations back.

[2] Wild irises.   [3] Naïve.

They added ridge to valley, brook to pond,
And sighed for all that bounded their domain;
"This suits me for a pasture; that's my park;
We must have clay, lime, gravel, granite-ledge,   20
And misty lowland, where to go for peat.
The land is well,—lies fairly to the south.
'T is good, when you have crossed the sea and back,
To find the sitfast acres where you left them."
Ah! the hot owner sees not Death, who adds
Him to his land, a lump of mould the more.
Hear what the Earth says:—

EARTH-SONG

"Mine and yours;
Mine, not yours.
Earth endures;   30
Stars abide—
Shine down in the old sea;
Old are the shores;
But where are old men?
I who have seen much,
Such have I never seen.

"The lawyer's deed
Ran sure,
In tail,[4]
To them, and to their heirs   40
Who shall succeed,
Without fail,
Forevermore.

"Here is the land,
Shaggy with wood,
With its old valley,
Mound and flood.
But the heritors?—
Fled like the flood's foam.
The lawyer, and the laws,
And the kingdom,
Clean swept herefrom.

"They called me theirs,
Who so controlled me;
Yet every one
Wished to stay, and is gone,
How am I theirs,
If they cannot hold me,
But I hold them?"

[4] "Entail," the legal method of designating inheritance to specific descendants.

When I heard the Earth-song   60
I was no longer brave;
My avarice cooled
Like lust in the chill of the grave.

1847

DAYS*

Daughters of Time, the hypocritic Days,
Muffled and dumb like barefoot dervishes,[1]
And marching single in an endless file,
Bring diadems and fagots[2] in their hands.
To each they offer gifts after his will,
Bread, kingdoms, stars, and sky that holds them
    all.
I, in my pleached[3] garden, watched the pomp,
Forgot my morning wishes, hastily
Took a few herbs and apples, and the Day
Turned and departed silent. I, too late,   10
Under her solemn fillet[4] saw the scorn.

1857

from JOURNALS

[On Hawthorne: May 24, 1864]

Yesterday, 23 May, we buried Hawthorne in Sleepy Hollow,[1] in a pomp of sunshine & verdure, & gentle winds. James F. Clarke[2] read the service in the Church & at the grave. Longfellow, Lowell, Holmes, Agassiz, Hoar, Dwight, Whipple, Norton, Alcott, Hillard, Fields, Judge Thomas,[3] & I, attended the hearse as pall

---

* First published in the inaugural issue of the *Atlantic Monthly* in 1857; collected in *May-Day and Other Pieces* (1867).
[1] Members of Moslem religious orders who take vows of poverty and austerity and wander as friars.
[2] Crowns and bundles of sticks.   [3] Shaded with plaited or interlaced branches.   [4] Headband.

[1] Sleepy Hollow Cemetery outside Concord, where Thoreau was buried and where Emerson would be buried.
[2] James Freeman Clarke (1810–1888), the Unitarian minister who had officiated at the wedding of Nathaniel Hawthorne and Sophia Peabody in 1842.
[3] The poets Henry Wadsworth Longfellow, James Russell Lowell, and Oliver Wendell Holmes; Louis Agassiz (1807–1873), a Swiss immigrant and renowned geologist at Harvard; Judge Ebenezer Hoar (1816–1895), brother of Charles Emerson's fiancée, Elizabeth Hoar; John S. Dwight (1813–1893), a music critic who was active at Brook Farm; Edwin Percy Whipple (1819–1886), a lecturer and literary critic; Charles Eliot Norton (1827–1908), a Harvard professor and writer; Bronson Alcott; George Hillard (1808–1879), a lawyer and writer; James T. Fields (1817–1881), Hawthorne's publisher; Benjamin Franklin Thomas (1813–1878), a Massachusetts Supreme Court judge. All (including Emerson) but Alcott, Hillard, and Thomas were members of the Saturday Club, which met at Boston's Parker House hotel for informal socializing the last Saturday of every month.

bearers. Franklin Pierce[4] was with the family. The church was copiously decorated with white flowers delicately arranged. The corpse was unwillingly
shown,—only a few moments to this company of his friends. But i[t] was noble &
serene in its aspect,—nothing amiss,—a calm & powerful head. A large company
filled the church, & the grounds of the cemetery. All was so bright & quiet, that
pain or mourning was hardly suggested, & Holmes said to me, that it looked like a
happy meeting.

Clarke in the church said, that, Hawthorne had done more justice than any
other to the shades of life, shown a sympathy with the crime in our nature, &, like
Jesus, was the friend of sinners.

I thought there was a tragic element in the event, that might be more fully
rendered—in the painful solitude of the man,—which, I suppose, could not
longer be endured, & he died of it.

I have found in his death a surprise & disappointment. I thought him a greater
man than any of his works betray, & that there was still a great deal of work in
him, & that he might one day show a purer power.

Moreover I have felt sure . . . that I could well wait his time,—his unwilling-
ness & caprice,—and might one day conquer a friendship. It would have been a
happiness, doubtless to both of us, to have come into habits of unreserved intercourse. It was easy to talk with him,—there were no barriers;—only, he said so
little, that I talked to[o] much, & stopped only because,—as he gave no indications,—I feared to exceed. He showed no egotism or self-assertion, rather a humility, &, at one time, a fear that he had written himself out.— One day, when I
found him on the top of his hill, in the woods, he paced back the path to his house,
& said, *"this path is the only remembrance of me that will remain."* Now it appears that I waited too long.

Lately, he had removed himself the more by the indignation his perverse politics & unfortunate friendship for that paltry Franklin Pierce awaked,—though it
rather moved pity for Hawthorne, & the assured belief that he would outlive it, &
come right at last.[5]

1824–1866?, 1909–1914

LETTER TO WALT WHITMAN*

Concord, Massachusetts, 21 July, 1855.

Dear Sir—I am not blind to the worth of the wonderful gift of "Leaves of Grass."
I find it the most extraordinary piece of wit and wisdom that America has yet
contributed. I am very happy in reading it, as great power makes us happy. It
meets the demand I am always making of what seemed the sterile and stingy nature, as if too much handiwork, or too much lymph[1] in the temperament, were
making our western wits fat and mean.[2]

---

[4] Pierce (1804–1869), Hawthorne's friend since college days at Bowdoin and former U.S. president
(1853–1857).
[5] Emerson heartily disapproved of Pierce's politically expedient and irresolute position on slavery.
* A response to a copy of *Leaves of Grass* (1855) that Walt Whitman sent to Emerson.
[1] Sluggishness.   [2] Small, petty.

I give you joy of your free and brave thought. I have great joy in it. I find incomparable things said incomparably well, as they must be. I find the courage of treatment which so delights us, and which large perception only can inspire.

I greet you at the beginning of a great career, which yet must have had a long foreground somewhere, for such a start. I rubbed my eyes a little, to see if this sunbeam were no illusion; but the solid sense of the book is a sober certainty. It has the best merits, namely, of fortifying and encouraging.

I did not know until I last night saw the book advertised in a newspaper that I could trust the name as real and available for a post-office.[3] I wish to see my benefactor, and have felt much like striking my tasks, and visiting New York to pay you my respects.

R.W. EMERSON
1855

Henry David Thoreau
(1817–1862)

Early in his essay "Thoreau" (1862), Ralph Waldo Emerson emphasizes on the "renunciations" that characterized the life of his Concord friend and neighbor. "He was bred to no profession," Emerson writes; "he never married; he lived alone; he never went to church; he never voted, he refused to pay a tax to the State; he ate no flesh, he drank no wine, he never knew the use of tobacco; and, though a naturalist, he used neither trap nor gun." The man Emerson eulogizes is thus defined by negation ("No college" offered him honors, "no academy" made him a member), stripped down to what he was not. Several paragraphs later, Emerson informs us bluntly that "No truer American existed than Thoreau."

Emerson's barrage of negatives corresponds in provocative ways with the chorus of negative descriptions of the United States in its early years of national existence. In *Letters From an American Farmer* (1782), for example, Michel-Guillaume Jean de Crèvecoeur depicts a new nation with "no aristocratical families, no courts, no kings, no bishops, no ecclesiastical dominion, no invisible power giving to the few a very visible one." Looking back to the years of colonial emigration, a character in Sylvester Judd's *Margaret* (1845) rejoices that much of "the Old World on its passage to the New was lost overboard," leaving our ancestors "considerably cleansed by the dashing waters of the Atlantic." The analogy is apparent: as the first Americans cast off the trappings of Europe, Thoreau casts off the paraphernalia of modern life. Emerson's arresting statement that "no truer American existed" is a tacit recognition of Thoreau's alignment with the pristine and revolutionary image of the early nation. Thoreau's admirable and abrasive power lay in the fact that he was a true indicator of what his nation originally hoped to be, the self-discovered man who prized what he was not and frequently blamed his neighbors for what they were.

Born in July 1817 in Concord, Massachusetts, Henry David Thoreau was the third child of Cynthia Dunbar and John Thoreau—his outgoing mother a descendant of a sturdy line

---

[3] Emerson is referring to getting Whitman's name and address: the first (1855) edition of *Leaves of Grass* was published anonymously.

of Scotch ancestors, his unassuming father a descendant of French Protestants. Henry's sister Helen, five years his senior, became a teacher; his brother, John, older by two years, became Henry's co-worker and closest friend; Sophia, two years younger than Henry, cared for him during his final illness and edited some of his work posthumously. Thoreau was sent to the Concord Academy, then to Harvard College (with financial assistance from Helen), graduating in 1837 without having distinguished himself academically. But he had developed an appetite for languages that began with his introduction to Greek literature by the visionary poet Jones Very (a tutor of Greek at Harvard) and continued during his temporary residence in 1835 with the maverick thinker Orestes Brownson, from whom Thoreau learned German. His wide reading in world literature is evident in the allusive style of his work.

Following his graduation from Harvard, Thoreau returned to Concord and taught briefly at a local academy. Then, in 1838, Thoreau and his brother John founded a progressive and successful school. While running this educational venture, Henry and John fell in love with the same girl, Ellen Sewall, the daughter of a Unitarian minister in Scituate, Massachusetts, whose younger brother, Edmund, was a favorite in the Thoreaus' school and whose aunt had long boarded in the Thoreau home. Each of the brothers proposed to her in 1840, first John (whom she refused) and then Henry. But Ellen's conservative father thought of Henry as a radical and ordered her to decline the proposal. Once Henry was rejected, conventional romance was no longer a part of his life. Although the school continued to prosper, John's ill health made the brothers decide to close it in 1841.

That same year Thoreau went to live and work as a handyman in the home of Ralph Waldo Emerson, whom he had come to know after his return to Concord in 1837. Through Emerson he became acquainted with such leading transcendentalist figures as Margaret Fuller, Bronson Alcott, Theodore Parker, and William Ellery Channing. Early in 1842 the death of John Thoreau from tetanus and, two weeks later, of Emerson's young son from scarlet fever doubtless brought the two men together in mutual grief. And a decision for Thoreau to range beyond Concord led him to take a position as tutor for the sons of Emerson's brother William on Staten Island in 1843.

The move was not a happy one for Thoreau, although he did meet the influential editor Horace Greeley, who would help him place his work in the years to come. Homesickness brought him back to Concord in 1844; several months later he decided to begin an experiment at Walden Pond, two miles from Concord. Emerson had purchased several acres bordering the pond, and he gave permission for Thoreau to clear the land and build a cabin. On July 4, 1845, Independence Day now made personal, Thoreau completed his cabin and began what would be twenty-six months of residence at Walden. He was now living out his experiment: seeing what was essential to life in this freedom, stripping away things extraneous to living. Biographers have shown that he did not live as a hermit; he visited with neighbors and walked into Concord frequently. But at Walden Thoreau did cultivate solitude as the condition of self-exploration. And he also wrote the first of his two books, *A Week on the Concord and Merrimack Rivers*, the conglomerate record of a two-week trip with his brother John in 1839, replete with poems, observations on nature, translations from Greek epics, and essays on such topics as fishing, Scripture, canal boats, the Concord Cattle Show, and friendship, all arranged according to the days of a single week. It is a meandering book, a journey through a writer's bountiful consciousness. Thoreau completed the manuscript in 1846, then revised and expanded it each time it was rejected by publishers—until he published an edition of one thousand copies at his own expense in 1849. Praised by friends such as George Ripley, the founder of Brook Farm, *A Week* was a commercial flop, selling approximately two hundred copies (with seventy-five other copies given away.) When the publisher returned the unsold books, Thoreau wrote in his journal,

WALDEN;

OR,

LIFE IN THE WOODS.

By HENRY D. THOREAU,
AUTHOR OF "A WEEK ON THE CONCORD AND MERRIMACK RIVERS."

I do not propose to write an ode to dejection, but to brag as lustily as chanticleer in the
morning, standing on his roost, if only to wake my neighbors up. — Page 92.

BOSTON:
TICKNOR AND FIELDS.
M DCCC LIV.

*The title page of the
first edition of*
Walden, *by Henry
David Thoreau.*

"I have now a library of nearly nine hundred volumes, over seven hundred of which I wrote myself."

By this time Thoreau had not only "travelled a good deal in Concord," as he says in the opening chapter of *Walden,* but had published more than thirty items in the transcendental periodical, *The Dial,* founded in 1840 and edited at different times during its four year existence by Margaret Fuller and by Emerson. At Emerson's request, Thoreau edited the April 1843 issue. The friendship of Emerson and Thoreau went through periods of coolness in these years and later, perhaps because Thoreau never liked being considered an Emerson clone, perhaps because Emerson did not like Thoreau's stubborn independence, perhaps because Thoreau did not live up to Emerson's expectations (or anyone else's). Even near the end of his essay on Thoreau, in a eulogizing context of admiration and respect, Emerson files a complaint by negation when he says that his friend had "no ambition."

The Mexican War broke out during Thoreau's second summer at Walden. Refusing to pay his poll tax to support what he saw as a bullying war to extend slavery, Thoreau was arrested and jailed for one night; although the evidence is inconclusive, his aunt Maria may have been the person who paid the tax to free him. He had lectured first at the Concord Lyceum in 1838 and in various small towns near Concord during the following years, at times drawing with subtle humor on his knowledge of the woods, at times developing with caustic wit the idea that most people's lives lack purpose. Now he began to speak with the sense of urgency and principle that informs an essay such as "Resistance to Civil Government" (delivered as a lecture in 1848 and published in 1849) and escalates to moral outrage in "Slavery in Massachusetts" (1854), occasioned by the return of two escaped slaves to their southern owners under the terms of the Fugitive Slave Act of 1850.

What Thoreau confronts in these essays is the question of which should take precedence: individual conscience or duly enacted law, the moral sphere or the legal. He argues that human beings owe allegiance to a higher law and thus must oppose any government whose laws violate the conscience. With unrelenting logic he advocates the radical strategy of passive resistance, something not for the faint of heart or for those afraid of losing their property, as he admits, but the ultimate weapon against tyranny. Adapted by Mahatma Gandhi in his opposition to British imperialism in India and by Martin Luther King, Jr., in his struggle for civil rights in the United States, Thoreau's doctrine of passive resistance has transcended time and place to rewrite history in the twentieth century. A growing passion for justice also led Thoreau to speak in defense of the abolitionist John Brown after Brown had been captured for his October 1859 raid on Harper's Ferry, Virginia. Thoreau had met Brown in Concord in 1857 and again in 1859. In Thoreau's lecture "A Plea for Captain John Brown" (1859), he portrays the militant Brown as a martyr to freedom.

Thoreau left Walden in September 1847 and began to write his second book while he worked in his father's pencil factory to get money to publish his first. Completed in 1849, the initial draft of *Walden* found no favor with publishers who had witnessed the dismal failure of *A Week* earlier that year. Thoreau found ready employment as a carpenter, a day-laborer, and a surveyor during the next few years, all the while perfecting the manuscript of *Walden,* which was finally published in 1854.

Walden personifies Thoreau, informing us that material possessions are burdens, bidding us to simplify life as the condition of knowing what it is, exhorting us to dramatic self-discovery: "Be a Columbus to whole new continents and worlds within you." Shaping the experience of his twenty-six months at Walden Pond into the cycle of a year, Thoreau enlists the seasons as the structuring principle of his book. And, as always, he prizes origins, the pristine quality of beginnings: "The poem of creation is uninterrupted; but few are the ears that hear it." In *Walden* Thoreau may lecture and admonish; but with reverence and nostalgic detachment he asks that we listen to the "poem of creation."

In the late 1840s and throughout the 1850s, Thoreau's excursions (as he called them) to the Maine woods and to Cape Cod took him to various New England settings that provided material for his journal and for later essays. His journal, begun in 1837 at Emerson's suggestion, developed over the years into a remarkable testimony of observation and of inner growth that scholars have begun to see as crucial to an understanding of Thoreau's life and work. His later essays, published in various periodicals and collected posthumously in *Excursions* (1863), *The Maine Woods* (1864), and *Cape Cod* (1865), show a writer probing for truth and simplicity with sporadic grace and vision. In 1850 Thoreau toured Quebec for twelve unhappy days with Ellery Channing; on this trip (remembered in *A Yankee in Canada* [1866]) he was a tourist with a bad cold—impatient, provincial, unwilling to appreciate the Canadian past or present. On a brief visit to New York City in 1856, he met Walt Whitman and once again saw his friend Horace Greeley. Plagued by bronchitis and chronic respiratory illness in the final years of life, Thoreau traveled to Minnesota in 1861, hoping to improve his health. But his physical decline was not to be arrested. Tended in his final months by his sister Sophia, who arranged his papers and correspondence according to his wishes, Thoreau died of tuberculosis in May 1862 (That disease had taken his sister Helen's life in 1848.) Buried in the lot belonging to his mother's family in the New Burying Ground outside Concord, his body was later interred in Concord's Sleepy Hollow Cemetery near the graves of Emerson, Nathaniel Hawthorne, and Bronson Alcott.

Suggested Readings: *The Writings of Henry David Thoreau*, 20 vols., 1906. *Consciousness in Concord: Thoreau's Lost Journal (1840-1841)*, ed. P. Miller, 1958. *The Writings of Henry David Thoreau*, (Princeton Edition), 25 vols. projected, 1971– . S. Paul, *The Shores of America: Thoreau's Inward Exploration*, 1958. W. Harding, *The Days of Henry David Thoreau: A Biography*, 1965. J. Porte, *Emerson and Thoreau: Transcendentalists in Conflict*, 1966. W. Glick, ed., *The Recognition of Henry Thoreau*, 1969. F. Garber, *Thoreau's Redemptive Imagination*, 1977. R. F. Sayre, *Thoreau and the American Indians*, 1977. W. Harding and M. Meyer, eds., *The New Thoreau Handbook*, 1980. S. Cavell, *The Senses of Walden*, 1981. W. Howarth, *The Book of Concord*, 1982. R. D. Richardson, *Henry Thoreau: A Life of the Mind*, 1986. R. Sattelmeyer, *Thoreau's Reading: A Study in Intellectual History*, 1988.

Texts Used: "Resistance to Civil Government": *The Writings of Henry D. Thoreau: Reform Papers*, ed. W. Glick, 1973. *Walden: The Writings: Walden*, ed. J. Lyndon Shanley, 1971. Journal entries from 1845 and 1846: *The Writings: Journal*, Vol. II: *1842–1848*, ed. R. Sattelmeyer, 1984. Entry from 1851: *The Journal of Henry D. Thoreau*, Vol. II: *1850–Sept. 15, 1851*, ed. B. Torrey and F. H. Allen, 1949.

RESISTANCE TO CIVIL GOVERNMENT*

I heartily accept the motto,—"That government is best which governs least;"[1] and I should like to see it acted up to more rapidly and systematically. Carried out, it finally amounts to this, which also I believe,—"That government is best which governs not at all;" and when men are prepared for it, that will be the kind of government which they will have. Government is at best but an expedient; but most governments are usually, and all governments are sometimes, inexpedient. The objections which have been brought against a standing army, and they are many and weighty, and deserve to prevail, may also at last be brought against a standing government. The standing army is only an arm of the standing government. The government itself, which is only the mode which the people have chosen to execute their will, is equally liable to be abused and perverted before the people can act through it. Witness the present Mexican war,[2] the work of compar-

---

* First published in *Aesthetic Papers*, edited by Elizabeth Peabody (Nathaniel Hawthorne's sister-in-law), in 1849. After Thoreau's death the essay was reprinted in *A Yankee in Canada, With Anti-Slavery and Reform Papers* (1866) with the widely known title "Civil Disobedience." Thoreau's ideas of passive resistance have found expression in Mahatma Gandhi's struggle for India's independence and Martin Luther King's advocacy of civil rights in America.

[1] Words once ascribed to Thomas Jefferson (because they capture the spirit of Jeffersonianism) but adapted from a motto that appeared on the cover of the *United States Magazine and Democratic Review* (1837–1849): "The best government is that which governs least."

[2] Thoreau presented this essay as a lecture at the Concord Lyceum (a community forum that sponsored an annual lecture series), apparently both in January and February 1848, during and just after the controversy over the Mexican War (1846–1848), which many New Englanders saw as a plan to extend slave territory to the West. His profound opposition to the war arises from his belief that human law must be subject to conscience.

atively a few individuals using the standing government as their tool; for, in the outset, the people would not have consented to this measure.

This American government,—what is it but a tradition, though a recent one, endeavoring to transmit itself unimpaired to posterity, but each instant losing some of its integrity? It has not the vitality and force of a single living man; for a single man can bend it to his will. It is a sort of wooden gun to the people themselves; and, if ever they should use it in earnest as a real one against each other, it will surely split. But it is not the less necessary for this; for the people must have some complicated machinery or other, and hear its din, to satisfy that idea of government which they have. Governments show thus how successfully men can be imposed on, even impose on themselves, for their own advantage. It is excellent, we must all allow; yet this government never of itself furthered any enterprise, but by the alacrity with which it got out of its way. *It* does not keep the country free. *It* does not settle the West. *It* does not educate. The character inherent in the American people has done all that has been accomplished; and it would have done somewhat more, if the government had not sometimes got in its way. For government is an expedient by which men would fain succeed in letting one another alone; and, as has been said, when it is most expedient, the governed are most let alone by it. Trade and commerce, if they were not made of India rubber, would never manage to bounce over the obstacles which legislators are continually putting in their way; and, if one were to judge these men wholly by the effects of their actions, and not partly by their intentions, they would deserve to be classed and punished with those mischievous persons who put obstructions on the railroads.

But, to speak practically and as a citizen, unlike those who call themselves no-government men, I ask for, not at once no government, but *at once* a better government. Let every man make known what kind of government would command his respect, and that will be one step toward obtaining it.

After all, the practical reason why, when the power is once in the hands of the people, a majority are permitted, and for a long period continue, to rule, is not because they are most likely to be in the right, nor because this seems fairest to the minority, but because they are physically the strongest. But a government in which the majority rule in all cases cannot be based on justice, even as far as men understand it. Can there not be a government in which majorities do not virtually decide right and wrong, but conscience?—in which majorities decide only those questions to which the rule of expediency is applicable? Must the citizen ever for a moment, or in the least degree, resign his conscience to the legislator? Why has every man a conscience, then? I think that we should be men first, and subjects afterward. It is not desirable to cultivate a respect for the law, so much as for the right. The only obligation which I have a right to assume, is to do at any time what I think right. It is truly enough said, that a corporation has no conscience;[3] but a corporation of conscientious men is a corporation *with* a conscience. Law never made men a whit more just; and, by means of their respect for it, even the well-disposed are daily made the agents of injustice. A common and natural result of an undue respect for law is, that you may see a file of soldiers, colonel, captain, corporal, privates, powder-monkeys[4] and all, marching in admirable order over

---

[3] The formulation of the English jurist Sir Edward Coke (1552–1634) in a landmark legal decision.
[4] Draftees who carry gunpowder to cannons. The sentence is arranged in descending order of military rank.

hill and dale to the wars, against their wills, aye, against their common sense and consciences, which makes it very steep marching indeed, and produces a palpitation of the heart. They have no doubt that it is a damnable business in which they are concerned; they are all peaceably inclined. Now, what are they? Men at all? or small moveable forts and magazines, at the service of some unscrupulous man in power? Visit the Navy Yard, and behold a marine, such a man as an American government can make, or such as it can make a man with its black arts, a mere shadow and reminiscence of humanity, a man laid out alive and standing, and already, as one may say, buried under arms with funeral accompaniments, though it may be

> "Not a drum was heard, not a funeral note,
> As his corpse to the rampart we hurried;
> Not a soldier discharged his farewell shot
> O'er the grave where our hero we buried."[5]

The mass of men serve the State thus, not as men mainly, but as machines, with their bodies. They are the standing army, and the militia, jailers, constable, *posse comitatus,*[6] etc. In most cases there is no free exercise whatever of the judgment or of the moral sense; but they put themselves on a level with wood and earth and stones, and wooden men can perhaps be manufactured that will serve the purpose as well. Such command no more respect than men of straw, or a lump of dirt. They have the same sort of worth only as horses and dogs. Yet such as these even are commonly esteemed good citizens. Others, as most legislators, politicians, lawyers, ministers, and office-holders, serve the State chiefly with their heads; and, as they rarely make any moral distinctions, they are as likely to serve the devil, without intending it, as God. A very few, as heroes, patriots, martyrs, reformers in the great sense, and *men,* serve the State with their consciences also, and so necessarily resist it for the most part; and they are commonly treated by it as enemies. A wise man will only be useful as a man, and will not submit to be "clay," and "stop a hole to keep the wind away,"[7] but leave that office to his dust at least:—

> "I am too high-born to be propertied,
> To be a secondary at control,
> Or useful serving-man and instrument
> To any sovereign state throughout the world."[8]

He who gives himself entirely to his fellow-men appears to them useless and selfish; but he who gives himself partially to them is pronounced a benefactor and philanthropist.

How does it become a man to behave toward this American government today? I answer that he cannot without disgrace be associated with it. I cannot for an instant recognize that political organization as *my* government which is the *slave's* government also.

---

[5] From "The Burial of Sir John Moore at Corunna" (1817), by the Irish poet Charles Wolfe (1791–1823).

[6] "Sheriff's posse" (Latin).   [7] From Shakespeare's *Hamlet* (V.i.236–237).

[8] From Shakespeare's *King John* (V.ii. 79–82).

All men recognize the right of revolution; that is, the right to refuse allegiance to and to resist the government, when its tyranny or its inefficiency are great and unendurable. But almost all say that such is not the case now. But such was the case, they think, in the Revolution of '75.[9] If one were to tell me that this was a bad government because it taxed certain foreign commodities brought to its ports, it is most probable that I should not make an ado about it, for I can do without them: all machines have their friction; and possibly this does enough good to counter-balance the evil. At any rate, it is a great evil to make a stir about it. But when the friction comes to have its machine, and oppression and robbery are organized, I say, let us not have such a machine any longer. In other words, when a sixth of the population of a nation which has undertaken to be the refuge of liberty are slaves, and a whole country [10] is unjustly overrun and conquered by a foreign army, and subjected to military law, I think that it is not too soon for honest men to rebel and revolutionize. What makes this duty the more urgent is the fact, that the country so overrun is not our own, but ours is the invading army.

Paley, a common authority with many on moral questions, in his chapter on the "Duty of Submission to Civil Government,"[11] resolves all civil obligation into expediency; and he proceeds to say, "that so long as the interest of the whole society requires it, that is, so long as the established government cannot be resisted or changed without public inconveniency, it is the will of God that the established government be obeyed, and no longer." . . . "This principle being admitted, the justice of every particular case of resistance is reduced to a computation of the quantity of the danger and grievance on the one side, and of the probability and expense of redressing it on the other." Of this, he says, every man shall judge for himself. But Paley appears never to have contemplated those cases to which the rule of expediency does not apply, in which a people, as well as an individual, must do justice, cost what it may. If I have unjustly wrested a plank from a drowning man, I must restore it to him though I drown myself. This, according to Paley, would be inconvenient. But he that would save his life, in such a case, shall lose it.[12] This people must cease to hold slaves, and to make war on Mexico, though it cost them their existence as a people.

In their practice, nations agree with Paley; but does any one think that Massachusetts does exactly what is right at the present crisis?

> "A drab of state, a cloth-o'-silver slut,
> To have her train borne up, and her soul trail in the dirt."[13]

Practically speaking, the opponents to a reform in Massachusetts are not a hundred thousand politicians at the South, but a hundred thousand merchants and farmers here, who are more interested in commerce and agriculture than they are in humanity, and are not prepared to do justice to the slave and to Mexico, *cost*

---

[9] The American Revolution (1775–1783).   [10] Mexico, "overrun" in the Mexican War.
[11] The full title of this chapter in *Principles of Moral and Political Philosophy* (1785), by William Paley (1743–1805), is "The Duty of Submission to Civil Government Explained." The theological utilitarianism taught by the English moralist Paley is diametrically opposed to what Thoreau advocates here.
[12] "Whosoever will save his life shall lose it: but whosoever will lose his life for my sake, the same shall save it," from Luke 9:24.
[13] From *The Revenger's Tragedy* (1607)(IV.iv. 70–72), attributed to the English dramatist Cyril Tourneur (1575?–1626).

what it may. I quarrel not with far-off foes, but with those who, near at home, co-operate with, and do the bidding of those far away, and without whom the latter would be harmless. We are accustomed to say, that the mass of men are unprepared; but improvement is slow, because the few are not materially wiser or better than the many. It is not so important that many should be as good as you, as that there be some absolute goodness somewhere; for that will leaven the whole lump.[14] There are thousands who are *in opinion* opposed to slavery and to the war, who yet in effect do nothing to put an end to them; who, esteeming themselves children of Washington and Franklin, sit down with their hands in their pockets,[15] and say that they know not what to do, and do nothing; who even postpone the question of freedom to the question of free-trade, and quietly read the prices-current along with the latest advices[16] from Mexico, after dinner, and, it may be, fall asleep over them both. What is the price-current of an honest man and patriot to-day? They hesitate, and they regret, and sometimes they petition; but they do nothing in earnest and with effect. They will wait, well-disposed, for others to remedy the evil, that they may no longer have it to regret. At most, they give only a cheap vote, and a feeble countenance and God-speed, to the right, as it goes by them. There are nine hundred and ninety-nine patrons of virtue to one virtuous man; but it is easier to deal with the real possessor of a thing than with the temporary guardian of it.

All voting is a sort of gaming, like chequers or backgammon, with a slight moral tinge to it, a playing with right and wrong, with moral questions; and betting naturally accompanies it. The character of the voters is not staked. I cast my vote, perchance, as I think right; but I am not vitally concerned that that right should prevail. I am willing to leave it to the majority. Its obligation, therefore, never exceeds that of expediency. Even voting *for the right* is *doing* nothing for it. It is only expressing to men feebly your desire that it should prevail. A wise man will not leave the right to the mercy of chance, nor wish it to prevail through the power of the majority. There is but little virtue in the action of masses of men. When the majority shall at length vote for the abolition of slavery, it will because they are indifferent to slavery, or because there is but little slavery left to be abolished by their vote. *They* will then be the only slaves. Only *his* vote can hasten the abolition of slavery who asserts his own freedom by his vote.

I hear of a convention to be held at Baltimore,[17] or elsewhere, for the selection of a candidate for the Presidency, made up chiefly of editors, and men who are politicians by profession; but I think, what is it to any independent, intelligent, and respectable man what decision they may come to, shall we not have the advantage of his wisdom and honesty, nevertheless? Can we not count upon some independent votes? Are there not many individuals in the country who do not attend conventions? But no: I find that the respectable man, so called, has immediately drifted from his position, and despairs of his country, when his country has more reason to despair of him. He forthwith adopts one of the candidates thus selected as the only *available* one, thus proving that he is himself *available* for any purposes of the demagogue. His vote is of no more worth than that of any unprincipled foreigner or hireling native, who may have been bought. Oh for a

---

[14] "Know ye not that a little leaven leaveneth the whole lump?" from I Corinthians 5:6.
[15] Who think they are the heirs of such heroes as George Washington and Benjamin Franklin and need do nothing on their own.
[16] News dispatches.   [17] The Democratic Convention, held in Baltimore in May 1848.

man who is a *man,* and, as my neighbor says, has a bone in his back which you cannot pass your hand through! Our statistics are at fault: the population has been returned too large. How many *men* are there to a square thousand miles in this country? Hardly one. Does not America offer any inducement for men to settle here? The American has dwindled into an Odd Fellow,[18]—one who may be known by the development of his organ of gregariousness,[19] and a manifest lack of intellect and cheerful self-reliance; whose first and chief concern, on coming into the world, is to see that the alms-houses are in good repair; and, before yet he has lawfully donned the virile garb,[20] to collect a fund for the support of the widows and orphans that may be; who, in short, ventures to live only by the aid of the mutual insurance company, which has promised to bury him decently.

It is not a man's duty, as a matter of course, to devote himself to the eradication of any, even the enormous wrong; he may still properly have other concerns to engage him; but it is his duty, at least, to wash his hands of it, and, if he gives it no thought longer, not to give it practically his support. If I devote myself to other pursuits and contemplations, I must first see, at least, that I do not pursue them sitting upon another man's shoulders. I must get off him first, that he may pursue his contemplations too. See what gross inconsistency is tolerated. I have heard some of my townsmen say, "I should like to have them order me out to help put down an insurrection of the slaves, or to march to Mexico,—see if I would go;" and yet these very men have each, directly by their allegiance, and so indirectly, at least, by their money, furnished a substitute. The soldier is applauded who refuses to serve in an unjust war by those who do not refuse to sustain the unjust government which makes the war; is applauded by those whose own act and authority he disregards and sets at nought; as if the State were penitent to that degree that it hired one to scourge it while it sinned, but not to that degree that it left off sinning for a moment. Thus, under the name of order and civil government, we are all made at last to pay homage to and support our own meanness. After the first blush of sin, comes its indifference and from immoral it becomes, as it were, *un*moral, and not quite unnecessary to that life which we have made.

The broadest and most prevalent error requires the most disinterested virtue to sustain it. The slight reproach to which the virtue of patriotism is commonly liable, the noble are most likely to incur. Those who, while they disapprove of the character and measures of a government, yield to it their allegiance and support, are undoubtedly its most conscientious supporters, and so frequently the most serious obstacles to reform. Some are petitioning the State to dissolve the Union, to disregard the requisitions of the President.[21] Why do they not dissolve it themselves,—the union between themselves and the State,—and refuse to pay their quota into its treasury?[22] Do not they stand in the same relation to the State, that the State does to the Union? And have not the same reasons prevented the State from resisting the Union, which have prevented them from resisting the State?

[18] The Independent Order of Odd Fellows, a benevolent fraternal organization established in 1819, adapted to Thoreau's satiric purposes as a way of saying that too many Americans are conformists.

[19] A term from the pseudoscience of phrenology (judging character from contours of the head), indicating one who loves company.

[20] Clothing that signified a Roman boy of fourteen had reached manhood.

[21] While James K. Polk, U.S. president from 1845 to 1849, sought troops and money for the war with Mexico, radical abolitionists in Massachusetts proposed leaving the Union, as they believed the conflict would expand slaveholding territory.

[22] Thoreau suggests that an individual can on principle secede from a state and refuse to pay taxes to the state treasury (and he later did just that).

How can a man be satisfied to entertain an opinion merely, and enjoy *it?* Is there any enjoyment in it, if his opinion is that he is aggrieved? If you are cheated out of a single dollar by your neighbor, you do not rest satisfied with knowing that you are cheated, or with saying that you are cheated, or even with petitioning him to pay you your due; but you take effectual steps at once to obtain the full amount, and see that you are never cheated again. Action from principle,—the perception and the performance of right,—changes things and relations; it is essentially revolutionary, and does not consist wholly with any thing which was. It not only divides states and churches, it divides families; aye, it divides the *individual,* separating the diabolical in him from the divine.

Unjust laws exist: shall we be content to obey them, or shall we endeavor to amend them, and obey them until we have succeeded, or shall we transgress them at once? Men generally, under such a government as this, think that they ought to wait until they have persuaded the majority to alter them. They think that, if they should resist, the remedy would be worse than the evil. But it is the fault of the government itself that the remedy *is* worse than the evil. *It* makes it worse. Why is it not more apt to anticipate and provide for reform? Why does it not cherish its wise minority? Why does it cry and resist before it is hurt? Why does it not encourage its citizens to be on the alert to point out its faults, and *do* better than it would have them? Why does it always crucify Christ, and excommunicate Copernicus and Luther, and pronounce Washington and Franklin rebels?[23]

One would think, that a deliberate and practical denial of its authority was the only offence never contemplated by government; else, why has it not assigned its definite, its suitable and proportionate penalty? If a man who has no property refuses but once to earn nine shillings[24] for the State, he is put in prison for a period unlimited by any law that I know, and determined only by the discretion of those who placed him there; but if he should steal ninety times nine shillings from the State, he is soon permitted to go at large again.

If the injustice is part of the necessary friction of the machine of government, let it go, let it go: perchance it will wear smooth,—certainly the machine will wear out. If the injustice has a spring, or a pulley, or a rope, or a crank, exclusively for itself, then perhaps you may consider whether the remedy will not be worse than the evil; but if it is of such a nature that it requires you to be the agent of injustice to another, then, I say, break the law. Let your life be a counter friction[25] to stop the machine. What I have to do is to see, at any rate, that I do not lend myself to the wrong which I condemn.

As for adopting the ways which the State has provided for remedying the evil, I know not of such ways. They take too much time, and a man's life will be gone. I have other affairs to attend to. I came into this world, not chiefly to make this a good place to live in, but to live in it, be it good or bad. A man has not every thing to do, but something; and because he cannot do *every thing,* it is not necessary

---

[23] Thoreau expands the notion of government to all governing bodies: the Polish astronomer Nicolaus Copernicus (1473–1543) died before he could be excommunicated by the church for maintaining that the earth is not the center of the universe; Martin Luther (1483–1546), the German leader of the Protestant Reformation, was excommunicated for his religious principles; George Washington and Benjamin Franklin were considered rebels by the British government.

[24] The $1.50 that Thoreau had refused to pay as a poll tax (a tax levied on all male citizens between ages twenty and seventy); "shilling" was then a common monetary term in New England, although there was no American coin or bill of that name.

[25] A device that slows moving parts by friction.

that he should do *something* wrong. It is not my business to be petitioning the governor or the legislature any more than it is theirs to petition me; and, if they should not hear my petition, what should I do then? But in this case the State has provided no way: its very Constitution is the evil. This may seem to be harsh and stubborn and unconciliatory; but it is to treat with the utmost kindness and consideration the only spirit that can appreciate or deserves it. So is all change for the better, like birth and death which convulse the body.

I do not hesitate to say, that those who call themselves abolitionists should at once effectually withdraw their support, both in person and property, from the government of Massachusetts, and not wait till they constitute a majority of one, before they suffer the right to prevail through them. I think that it is enough if they have God on their side, without waiting for that other one. Moreover, any man more right than his neighbors, constitutes a majority of one already.

I meet this American government, or its representative the State government, directly, and face to face, once a year, no more, in the person of its tax-gatherer; this is the only mode in which a man situated as I am necessarily meets it; and it then says distinctly, Recognize me; and the simplest, the most effectual, and, in the present posture of affairs, the indispensablest mode of treating with it on this head, of expressing your little satisfaction with and love for it, is to deny it then. My civil neighbor, the tax-gather,[26] is the very man I have to deal with,—for it is, after all, with men and not with parchment that I quarrel,—and he has voluntarily chosen to be an agent of the government. How shall he ever know well what he is and does as an officer of the government, or as a man, until he is obliged to consider whether he shall treat me, his neighbor, for whom he has respect, as a neighbor and well-disposed man, or as a maniac and disturber of the peace, and see if he can get over this obstruction to his neighborliness without a ruder and more impetuous thought or speech corresponding with his action? I know this well, that if one thousand, if one hundred, if ten men whom I could name,—if ten *honest* men only,—aye, if *one* HONEST man, in this State of Massachusetts, *ceasing to hold slaves,* were actually to withdraw from this copartnership, and be locked up in the county jail therefor, it would be the abolition of slavery in America. For it matters not how small the beginning may seem to be: what is once well done is done for ever. But we love better to talk about it: that we say is our mission. Reform keeps many scores of newspapers in its service, but not one man. If my esteemed neighbor, the State's ambassador, who will devote his days to the settlement of the question of human rights in the Council Chamber, instead of being threatened with the prisons of Carolina,[27] were to sit down the prisoner of Massachusetts, that State which is so anxious to foist the sin of slavery upon her sister,—though at present she can discover only an act of inhospitality to be the ground of a quarrel with her,—the Legislature would not wholly waive the subject the following winter.

Under a government which imprisons any unjustly, the true place for a just man is also a prison. The proper place to-day, the only place which Massachusetts has provided for her freer and less desponding spirits, is in her prisons, to be put out and locked out of the State by her own act, as they have already put themselves

---

[26] Sam Staples, Thoreau's friend and neighbor in Concord.

[27] Samuel Hoar (1778–1856), a Massachusetts senator from Concord, was sent to South Carolina in 1844 to aid African-American seamen from Massachusetts who had been imprisoned in the port of Charleston; he was expelled from Charleston by legal action.

out by their principles. It is there that the fugitive slave, and the Mexican prisoner on parole, and the Indian come to plead the wrongs of his race, should find them; on that separate, but more free and honorable ground, where the State places those who are not *with* her but *against* her,—the only house in a slave-state in which a free man can abide with honor. If any think that their influence would be lost there, and their voices no longer afflict the ear of the State, that they would not be as an enemy within its walls, they do not know by how much truth is stronger than error, nor how much more eloquently and effectively he can combat injustice who has experienced a little in his own person. Cast your whole vote, not a strip of paper merely, but your whole influence. A minority is powerless while it conforms to the majority; it is not even a minority then; but it is irresistible when it clogs by its whole weight. If the alternative is to keep all just men in prison, or give up war and slavery, the State will not hesitate which to choose. If a thousand men were not to pay their tax-bills this year, that would not be a violent and bloody measure, as it would be to pay them, and enable the State to commit violence and shed innocent blood. This is, in fact, the definition of a peaceable revolution, if any such is possible. If the tax-gatherer, or any other public officer, asks me, as one has done, "But what shall I do?" my answer is, "If you really wish to do any thing, resign your office." When the subject has refused allegiance, and the officer has resigned his office, then the revolution is accomplished. But even suppose blood should flow. Is there not a sort of blood shed when the conscience is wounded? Through this wound a man's real manhood and immortality flow out, and he bleeds to an everlasting death. I see this blood flowing now.

I have contemplated the imprisonment of the offender, rather than the seizure of his goods,—though both will serve the same purpose,—because they who assert the purest right, and consequently are most dangerous to a corrupt State, commonly have not spent much time in accumulating property. To such the State renders comparatively small service, and a slight tax is wont to appear exorbitant, particularly if they are obliged to earn it by special labor with their hands. If there were one who lived wholly without the use of money, the State itself would hesitate to demand it of him. But the rich man—not to make any invidious comparison—is always sold to the institution which makes him rich. Absolutely speaking, the more money, the less virtue; for money comes between a man and his objects, and obtains them for him; and it was certainly no great virtue to obtain it. It puts to rest many questions which he would otherwise be taxed to answer; while the only new question which it puts is the hard but superfluous one, how to spend it. Thus his moral ground is taken from under his feet. The opportunities of living are diminished in proportion as what are called the "means" are increased. The best thing a man can do for his culture when he is rich is to endeavour to carry out those schemes which he entertained when he was poor. Christ answered the Herodians[28] according to their condition. "Show me the tribute-money," said he;—and one took a penny out of his pocket;—if you use money which has the image of Cæsar on it, and which he has made current and valuable, that is, *if you are men of the State,* and gladly enjoy the advantages of Cæsar's government, then pay him back some of his own when he demands it; "Render therefore to Cæsar that which is Cæsar's, and to God those things which are God's,"[29]—

[28] Officials of Herod, a king of Judea, who were used in an attempt to trick Jesus into defying the law.
[29] From Matthew 22:16–21.

leaving them no wiser than before as to which was which; for they did not wish to know.

When I converse with the freest of my neighbors, I perceive that, whatever they may say about the magnitude and seriousness of the question, and their regard for the public tranquility, the long and the short of the matter is, that they cannot spare the protection of the existing government, and they dread the consequences of disobedience to it to their property and families. For my own part, I should not like to think that I ever rely on the protection of the State. But, if I deny the authority of the State when it presents its tax-bill, it will soon take and waste all my property, and so harass me and my children without end. This is hard. This makes it impossible for a man to live honestly and at the same time comfortably in outward respects. It will not be worth the while to accumulate property; that would be sure to go again. You must hire[30] or squat somewhere, and raise but a small crop, and eat that soon. You must live within yourself, and depend upon yourself, always tucked up and ready for a start, and not have many affairs. A man may grow rich in Turkey even, if he will be in all respects a good subject of the Turkish government. Confucius said,—"If a State is governed by the principles of reason, poverty and misery are subjects of shame; if a State is not governed by the principles of reason, riches and honors are the subjects of shame."[31] No: until I want the protection of Massachusetts to be extended to me in some distant southern port, where my liberty is endangered, or until I am bent solely on building up an estate at home by peaceful enterprise, I can afford to refuse allegiance to Massachusetts, and her right to my property and life. It costs me less in every sense to incur the penalty of disobedience to the State, than it would to obey. I should feel as if I were worth less in that case.

Some years ago, the State met me in behalf of the church, and commanded me to pay a certain sum toward the support of a clergyman whose preaching my father attended, but never I myself.[32] "Pay it," it said, "or be locked up in the jail." I declined to pay. But, unfortunately, another man saw fit to pay it. I did not see why the schoolmaster should be taxed to support the priest, and not the priest the schoolmaster; for I was not the State's schoolmaster, but I supported myself by voluntary subscription. I did not see why the lyceum[33] should not present its tax-bill, and have the State to back its demand, as well as the church. However, at the request of the selectmen, I condescended to make some such statement as this in writing:—"Know all men by these presents, that I, Henry Thoreau, do not wish to be regarded as a member of any incorporated society which I have not joined." This I gave to the town-clerk; and he has it. The State, having thus learned that I did not wish to be regarded as a member of that church, has never made a like demand on me since; though it said that it must adhere to its original presumption that time. If I had know how to name them, I should then have signed off in detail from all the societies which I never signed on to; but I did not know where to find a complete list.

I have paid no poll-tax for six years. I was put into a jail once on this account, for one night;[34] and, as I stood considering the walls of solid stone, two or three

---

[30] Rent.

[31] From the *Analects* (Bk. 13, Ch. 8) of the Chinese philosopher Confucius (551–479? B.C.).

[32] At the time in Massachusetts, local governments collected taxes for churches.

[33] The Concord Lyceum.

[34] On July 23 or 24, 1846, Thoreau spent a night in the Middlesex County jail in Concord.

feet thick, the door of wood and iron, a foot thick, and the iron grating which strained the light, I could not help being struck with the foolishness of that institution which treated me as if I were mere flesh and blood and bones, to be locked up. I wondered that it should have concluded at length that this was the best use it could put me to, and had never thought to avail itself of my services in some way. I saw that, if there was a wall of stone between me and my townsmen, there was a still more difficult one to climb or break through, before they could get to be as free as I was. I did not for a moment feel confined, and the walls seemed a great waste of stone and mortar. I felt as if I alone of all my townsmen had paid my tax. They plainly did not know how to treat me, but behaved like persons who are underbred. In every threat and in every compliment there was a blunder; for they thought that my chief desire was to stand the other side of that stone wall. I could not but smile to see how industriously they locked the door on my meditations, which followed them out again without let or hinderance, and *they* were really all that was dangerous. As they could not reach me, they had resolved to punish my body; just as boys, if they cannot come at some person against whom they have a spite, will abuse his dog. I saw that the State was half-witted, that it was timid as a lone woman with her silver spoons, and that it did not know its friends from its foes, and I lost all my remaining respect for it, and pitied it.

Thus the State never intentionally confronts a man's sense, intellectual or moral, but only his body, his senses. It is not armed with superior wit or honesty, but with superior physical strength. I was not born to be forced. I will breathe after my own fashion. Let us see who is the strongest. What force has a multitude? They only can force me who obey a higher law than I. They force me to become like themselves. I do not hear of *men* being *forced* to live this way or that by masses of men. What sort of life were that to live? When I meet a government which says to me, "Your money or your life," why should I be in haste to give it my money? It may be in a great strait, and not know what to do: I cannot help that. It must help itself; do as I do. It is not worth the while to snivel about it. I am not responsible for the successful working of the machinery of society. I am not the son of the engineer. I perceive that, when an acorn and a chestnut fall side by side, the one does not remain inert to make way for the other, but both obey their own laws, and spring and grow and flourish as best they can, till one, perchance, overshadows and destroys the other. If a plant cannot live according to its nature, it dies; and so a man.

The night in prison was novel and interesting enough. The prisoners in their shirtsleeves were enjoying a chat and the evening air in the door-way, when I entered. But the jailer[35] said, "Come, boys, it is time to lock up;" and so they dispersed, and I heard the sound of their steps returning into the hollow apartments. My room-mate was introduced to me by the jailer, as "as first-rate fellow and a clever[36] man." When the door was locked, he showed me where to hang my hat, and how he managed matters there. The rooms were whitewashed once a month; and this one, at least, was the whitest, most simply furnished, and probably the neatest apartment in the town. He naturally wanted to know where I came from, and what brought me there; and, when I had told him, I asked him in my turn how he came there, presuming him to be an honest man, of course; and, as the world goes, I believe he was. "Why," said he, "they accused me of burning a barn; but I never did it." As near as

[35] Sam Staples.   [36] Honest.

I could discover, he had probably gone to bed in a barn when drunk, and smoked his pipe there; and so a barn was burnt. He had the reputation of being a clever man, had been there some three months waiting for his trial to come on, and would have to wait as much longer; but he was quite domesticated and contented, since he got his board for nothing, and thought that he was well treated.

He occupied one window, and I the other; and I saw, that, if one stayed there long, his principal business would be to look out the window. I had soon read all the tracts that were left there, and examined where former prisoners had broken out, and where a grate had been sawed off, and heard the history of the various occupants of that room; for I found that even here there was a history and a gossip which never circulated beyond the walls of the jail. Probably this is the only house in the town where verses are composed, which are afterward printed in a circular form, but not published. I was shown quite a long list of verses which were composed by some young men who had been detected in an attempt to escape, who avenged themselves by singing them.

I pumped my fellow-prisoner as dry as I could, for fear I should never see him again; but at length he showed me which was my bed, and left me to blow out the lamp.

It was like travelling into a far country, such as I had never expected to behold, to lie there for one night. It seemed to me that I never had heard the town-clock strike before, nor the evening sounds of the village; for we slept with the windows open, which were inside the grating. It was to see my native village in the light of the middle ages, and our Concord was turned into a Rhine stream, and visions of knights and castles passed before me. They were the voices of old burghers that I heard in the streets. I was an involuntary spectator and auditor of whatever was done and said in the kitchen of the adjacent village-inn,—a wholly new and rare experience to me. It was a closer view of my native town. I was fairly inside of it. I never had seen its institutions before. This is one of its peculiar institutions; for it is a shire town.[37] I began to comprehend what its inhabitants were about.

In the morning, our breakfasts were put through the hole in the door, in small oblong-square tin pans, made to fit, and holding a pint of chocolate, with brown bread, and an iron spoon. When they called for the vessels again, I was green enough to return what bread I had left; but my comrade seized it, and said that I should lay that up for lunch or dinner. Soon after, he was let out to work at haying in a neighboring field, whither he went every day, and would not be back till noon; so he bade me good-day, saying that he doubted if he should see me again.

When I came out of prison,—for some one interfered, and paid the tax,[38]—I did not perceive that great changes had taken place on the common, such as he observed who went in a youth, and emerged a tottering and gray-headed man; and yet a change had to my eyes come over the scene,—the town, and State, and country,—greater than any that mere time could effect. I saw yet more distinctly the State in which I lived. I saw to what extent the people among whom I lived could be trusted as good neighbors and friends; that their friendship was for summer weather only; that they did not greatly purpose to do right; that they were a distinct race from me by their prejudices and superstitions, as the Chinamen and Malays are; that, in their sacrifices to humanity, they ran no risks, not even to their property; that, after all, they were not so noble but they treated the thief as he had treated them, and hoped,

[37] A county seat.
[38] It is not known for certain who paid Thoreau's tax, but his aunt Maria has been suggested.

by a certain outward observance and a few prayers, and by walking in a particular straight though useless path from time to time, to save their souls. This may be to judge my neighbors harshly; for I believe that most of them are not aware that they have such an institution as the jail in their village.

It was formerly the custom in our village, when a poor debtor came out of jail, for his acquaintances to salute him, looking through their fingers, which were crossed to represent the grating of a jail window, "How do ye do?" My neighbors did not thus salute me, but first looked at me, and then at one another, as if I had returned from a long journey. I was put into jail as I was going to the shoemaker's to get a shoe which was mended. When I was let out the next morning, I proceeded to finish my errand, and, having put on my mended shoe, joined a huckleberry party, who were impatient to put themselves under my conduct; and in half an hour,—for the horse was soon tackled,[39]—was in the midst of a huckleberry field, on one of our highest hills, two miles off; and then the State was nowhere to be seen.

This is the whole history of "My Prisons."[40]

I have never declined paying the highway tax, because I am as desirous of being a good neighbor as I am of being a bad subject; and, as for supporting schools, I am doing my part to educate my fellow-countrymen now. It is for no particular item in the tax-bill that I refuse to pay it. I simply wish to refuse allegiance to the State, to withdraw and stand aloof from it effectually. I do not care to trace the course of my dollar, if I could, till it buys a man, or a musket to shoot one with,—the dollar is innocent,—but I am concerned to trace the effects of my allegiance. In fact, I quietly declare war with the State, after my fashion, though I will still make what use and get what advantage of her I can, as is usual in such cases.

If others pay the tax which is demanded of me, from a sympathy with the State, they do but what they have already done in their own case, or rather they abet injustice to a greater extent than the State requires. If they pay the tax from a mistaken interest in the individual taxed, to save his property or prevent his going to jail, it is because they have not considered wisely how far they let their private feelings interfere with the public good.

This, then, is my position at present. But one cannot be too much on his guard in such a case, lest his action be biassed by obstinacy, or an undue regard for the opinions of men. Let him see that he does only what belongs to himself and to the hour.

I think sometimes, Why, this people mean well; they are only ignorant; they would do better if they knew how: why give your neighbors this pain to treat you as they are not inclined to? But I think, again, this is no reason why I should do as they do, or permit others to suffer much greater pain of a different kind. Again, I sometimes say to myself, When many millions of men, without heat, without ill-will, without personal feeling of any kind, demand of you a few shillings only, without the possibility, such is their constitution, of retracting or altering their present demand, and without the possibility, on your side, of appeal to any other millions, why expose yourself to this overwhelming brute force? You do not resist cold and hunger, the winds and the waves, thus obstinately; you quietly submit to

---

[39] Harnessed.

[40] A droll reference to the autobiography (1832) of the Italian poet Silvio Pellico (1789–1854), who spent years in Austrian prisons for fighting against the Austrian occupation of Italy.

a thousand similar necessities. You do not put your head into the fire. But just in proportion as I regard this as not wholly a brute force, but partly a human force, and consider that I have relations to those millions as to so many millions of men, and not of mere brute or inanimate things, I see that appeal is possible, first and instantaneously, from them to the Maker of them, and, secondly, from them to themselves. But, if I put my head deliberately into the fire, there is no appeal to fire or to the Maker of fire, and I have only myself to blame. If I could convince myself that I have any right to be satisfied with men as they are, and to treat them accordingly, and not according, in some respects, to my requisitions and expectations of what they and I ought to be, then, like a good Mussulman[41] and fatalist, I should endeavor to be satisfied with things as they are, and say it is the will of God. And, above all, there is this difference between resisting this and a purely brute or natural force, that I can resist this with some effect; but I cannot expect, like Orpheus,[42] to change the nature of the rocks and trees and beasts.

I do not wish to quarrel with any man or nation. I do not wish to split hairs, to make fine distinctions, or set myself up as better than my neighbors. I seek rather, I may say, even an excuse for conforming to the laws of the land. I am but too ready to conform to them. Indeed I have reason to suspect myself on this head;[43] and each year, as the tax-gatherer comes round, I find myself disposed to review the acts and position of the general and state governments, and the spirit of the people, to discover a pretext for conformity. I believe that the State will soon be able to take all my work of this sort out of my hands, and then I shall be no better a patriot than my fellow-countrymen. Seen from a lower point of view, the Constitution, with all its faults, is very good; the law and the courts are very respectable; even this State and this American government are, in many respects, very admirable and rare things, to be thankful for, such as a great many have described them; but seen from a point of view a little higher, they are what I have described them; seen from a higher still, and the highest, who shall say what they are, or that they are worth looking at or thinking of at all?

However, the government does not concern me much, and I shall bestow the fewest possible thoughts on it. It is not many moments that I live under a government, even in this world. If a man is thought-free, fancy-free, imagination-free, that which *is not* never for a long time appearing *to be* to him, unwise rulers or reformers cannot fatally interrupt him.

I know that most men think differently from myself; but those whose lives are by profession devoted to the study of these or kindred subjects, content me as little as any. Statesmen and legislators, standing so completely within the institution, never distinctly and nakedly behold it. They speak of moving society, but have no resting-place without it. They may be men of a certain experience and discrimination, and have no doubt invented ingenious and even useful systems, for which we sincerely thank them; but all their wit and usefulness lie within certain not very wide limits. They are wont to forget that the world is not governed by policy and expediency. Webster[44] never goes behind government, and so cannot speak with

---

[41] Moslem.

[42] According to Greek myth, a musician who played the lyre so wondrously that animate things and inanimate objects were charmed and changed.

[43] Point.

[44] Daniel Webster (1782–1852), a U.S. senator from Massachusetts who angered abolitionists with his support of the Fugitive Slave Act, which required the return of escaped slaves. Here Thoreau bemoans the fact that Webster considers the American Constitution to be the ultimate authority even on moral issues.

authority about it. His words are wisdom to those legislators who contemplate no essential reform in the existing government; but for thinkers, and those who legislate for all time, he never once glances at the subject. I know of those whose serene and wise speculations on this theme would soon reveal the limits of his mind's range and hospitality. Yet, compared with the cheap professions of most reformers, and the still cheaper wisdom and eloquence of politicians in general, his are almost the only sensible and valuable words, and we thank Heaven for him. Comparatively, he is always strong, original, and, above all, practical. Still his quality is not wisdom, but prudence. The lawyer's truth is not Truth, but consistency, or a consistent expediency. Truth is always in harmony with herself, and is not concerned chiefly to reveal the justice that may consist with wrong-doing. He well deserves to be called, as he has been called, the Defender of the Constitution. There are really no blows to be given by him but defensive ones. He is not a leader, but a follower. His leaders are the men of '87.[45] "I have never made an effort," he says, "and never propose to make an effort; I have never countenanced an effort, and never mean to countenance an effort, to disturb the arrangement as originally made, by which the various States came into the Union."[46] Still thinking of the sanction which the Constitution gives to slavery, he says, "Because it was a part of the original compact,—let it stand." Notwithstanding his special acuteness and ability, he is unable to take a fact out of its merely political relations, and behold it as it lies absolutely to be disposed of by the intellect,—what, for instance, it beho[o]ves a man to do here in America to-day with regard to slavery,—but ventures, or is driven, to make some such desperate answer as the following, while professing to speak absolutely, and as a private man,—from which what new and singular code of social duties might be inferred?—"The manner," says he, "in which the governments of those States where slavery exists are to regulate it, is for their own consideration, under their responsibility to their constituents, to the general laws of propriety, humanity, and justice, and to God. Associations formed elsewhere, springing from a feeling of humanity, or any other cause, have nothing whatever to do with it. They have never received any encouragement from me, and they never will."[47]

They who know of no purer sources of truth, who have traced up its stream no higher, stand, and wisely stand, by the Bible and the Constitution, and drink at it there with reverence and humility; but they who behold where it comes trickling into this lake or that pool, gird up their loins once more, and continue their pilgrimage toward its fountain-head.

No man with a genius for legislation has appeared in America. They are rare in the history of the world. There are orators, politicians, and eloquent men, by the thousand; but the speaker has not yet opened his mouth to speak, who is capable of settling the much-vexed questions of the day. We love eloquence for its own sake, and not for any truth which it may utter, or any heroism it may inspire. Our legislators have not yet learned the comparative value of free-trade and of freedom, of union, and of rectitude, to a nation. They have no genius or talent for comparatively humble questions of taxation and finance, commerce and manufactures and agriculture. If we were left solely to the wordy wit of legislators in

---

[45] The drafters of the Constitution in 1787.

[46] From Webster's speech on "The Admission of Texas" (December 22, 1845).

[47] Thoreau's note: "These extracts have been inserted since the Lecture was read." Thoreau quotes from speeches given by Webster in 1845 and 1848.

Congress for our guidance, uncorrected by the seasonable experience and the effectual complaints of the people, America would not long retain her rank among the nations. For eighteen hundred years, though perchance I have no right to say it, the New Testament has been written; yet where is the legislator who has wisdom and practical talent enough to avail himself of the light which it sheds on the science of legislation?

The authority of government, even such as I am willing to submit to,—for I will cheerfully obey those who know and can do better than I, and in many things even those who neither know nor can do so well,—is still an impure one: to be strictly just, it must have the sanction and consent of the governed. It can have no pure right over my person and property but what I concede to it. The progress from an absolute to a limited monarchy, from a limited monarchy to a democracy, is a progress toward a true respect for the individual. Is a democracy, such as we know it, the last improvement possible in government? Is it not possible to take a step further towards recognizing and organizing the rights of man? There will never be a really free and enlightened State, until the State comes to recognize the individual as a higher and independent power, from which all its own power and authority are derived, and treats him accordingly. I please myself with imagining a State at last which can afford to be just to all men, and to treat the individual with respect as a neighbor; which even would not think it inconsistent with its own repose, if a few were to live aloof from it, not meddling with it, nor embraced by it, who fulfilled all the duties of neighbors and fellow-men. A State which bore this kind of fruit, and suffered it to drop off as fast as it ripened, would prepare the way for a still more perfect and glorious State, which also I have imagined, but not yet anywhere seen.

1849

from WALDEN*

I: Economy

When I wrote the following pages, or rather the bulk of them, I lived alone, in the woods, a mile from any neighbor, in a house which I had built myself, on the shore of Walden Pond, in Concord, Massachusetts, and earned my living by the labor of my hands only. I lived there two years and two months. At present I am a sojourner in civilized life again.

I should not obtrude my affairs so much on the notice of my readers if very particular inquiries had not been made by my townsmen concerning my mode of life, which some would call impertinent, though they do not appear to me at all impertinent, but, considering the circumstances, very natural and pertinent. Some have asked what I got to eat; if I did not feel lonesome; if I was not afraid; and the

* First published in 1854 as *Walden, or Life in the Woods,* with Thoreau's epigraph: "I do not propose to write an ode to dejection, but to brag as lustily as chanticleer [the rooster in the medieval epic *Reynard the Fox*] in the morning, standing on his roost, if only to wake my neighbors up." While living at Walden Pond, near Concord, Massachusetts, from July 4, 1845, to September 6, 1847, Thoreau wrote *A Week on the Concord and Merrimack Rivers* (1849) and a substantial part of *Walden,* which he revised and completed between 1849 and 1854.

like. Others have been curious to learn what portion of my income I devoted to charitable purposes; and some, who have large families, how many poor children I maintained. I will therefore ask those of my readers who feel no particular interest in me to pardon me if I undertake to answer some of these questions in this book. In most books, the *I*, or first person, is omitted; in this it will be retained; that, in respect to egotism, is the main difference. We commonly do not remember that it is, after all, always the first person that is speaking. I should not talk so much about myself if there were any body else whom I knew as well. Unfortunately, I am confined to this theme by the narrowness of my experience. Moreover, I, on my side, require of every writer, first or last, a simple and sincere account of his own life, and not merely what he has heard of other men's lives; some such account as he would send to his kindred from a distant land; for if he has lived sincerely, it must have been in a distant land to me. Perhaps these pages are more particularly addressed to poor students. As for the rest of my readers, they will accept such portions as apply to them. I trust that none will stretch the seams in putting on the coat, for it may do good service to him whom it fits.

I would fain say something, not so much concerning the Chinese and Sandwich Islanders[1] as you who read these pages, who are said to live in New England; something about your condition, especially your outward condition or circumstances in this world, in this town, what it is, whether it is necessary that it be as bad as it is, whether it cannot be improved as well as not. I have travelled a good deal in Concord; and every where, in shops, and offices, and fields, the inhabitants have appeared to me to be doing penance in a thousand remarkable ways. What I have heard of Brahmins[2] sitting exposed to four fires and looking in the face of the sun; or hanging suspended, with their heads downward, over flames; or looking at the heavens over their shoulders "until it becomes impossible for them to resume their natural position, while from the twist of the neck nothing but liquids can pass into the stomach;" or dwelling, chained for life, at the foot of a tree; or measuring with their bodies, like caterpillars, the breadth of vast empires; or standing on one leg on the tops of pillars,—even these forms of conscious penance are hardly more incredible and astonishing than the scenes which I daily witness. The twelve labors of Hercules[3] were trifling in comparison with those which my neighbors have undertaken; for they were only twelve, and had an end; but I could never see that these men slew or captured any monster or finished any labor. They have no friend Iolas to burn with a hot iron the root of the hydra's head, but as soon as one head is crushed, two spring up.

I see young men, my townsmen, whose misfortune it is to have inherited farms, houses, barns, cattle, and farming tools; for these are more easily acquired than got rid of. Better if they had been born in the open pasture and suckled by a wolf,[4] that they might have seen with clearer eyes what field they were called to labor in. Who made them serfs of the soil? Why should they eat their sixty acres, when man is condemned to eat only his peck of dirt? Why should they begin digging their graves as soon as they are born? They have got to live a man's life,

---

[1] Hawaiians.

[2] Members of the highest Hindu caste; the source of Thoreau's information has not been identified.

[3] According to Greek myth, Hercules was assigned welve purifying labors; one was to slay the nine-headed monster Hydra, which he did with his friend Iolas: as Hercules cut off each head, Iolas seared the stump so a new head could not grow back.

[4] According to Roman myth, Romulus and Remus, the founders of Rome, were suckled by a she-wolf.

pushing all these things before them, and get on as well as they can. How many a poor immortal soul have I met well nigh crushed and smothered under its load, creeping down the road of life, pushing before it a barn seventy-five feet by forty, its Augean stables[5] never cleansed, and one hundred acres of land, tillage, mowing, pasture and wood-lot! The portionless, who struggle with no such unnecessary inherited encumbrances, find it labor enough to subdue and cultivate a few cubic feet of flesh.

But men labor under a mistake. The better part of the man is soon ploughed into the soil for compost. By a seeming fate, commonly called necessity, they are employed, as it says in an old book,[6] laying up treasures which moth and rust will corrupt and thieves break through and steal. It is a fool's life, as they will find when they get to the end of it, if not before. It is said that Deucalion and Pyrrha[7] created men by throwing stones over their heads behind them:—

> Inde genus durum sumus, experiensque laborum,
> Et documenta damus quâ simus origine nati.

Or, as Raleigh rhymes it in his sonorous way,—

> "From thence our kind hard-hearted is, enduring
>   pain and care,
> Approving that our bodies of a stony nature are."[8]

So much for a blind obedience to a blundering oracle, throwing the stones over their heads behind them, and not seeing where they fell.

Most men, even in this comparatively free country, through mere ignorance and mistake, are so occupied with the factitious cares and superfluously coarse labors of life that its finer fruits cannot be plucked by them. Their fingers, from excessive toil, are too clumsy and tremble too much for that. Actually, the laboring man has not leisure for a true integrity day by day; he cannot afford to sustain the manliest relations to men; his labor would be depreciated in the market. He has no time to be any thing but a machine. How can he remember well his ignorance—which his growth requires—who has so often to use his knowledge? We should feed and clothe him gratuitously sometimes, and recruit him with our cordials,[9] before we judge of him. The finest qualities of our nature, like the bloom on fruits, can be preserved only by the most delicate handling. Yet we do not treat ourselves nor one another thus tenderly.

Some of you, we all know, are poor, find it hard to live, are sometimes, as it were, gasping for breath. I have no doubt that some of you who read this book are unable to pay for all the dinners which you have actually eaten, or for the coats

---

[5] One of Hercules' labors was to clean in one day the stables in which three thousand oxen had been kept for thirty years by King Augeas (Hercules diverted two rivers through the stables).

[6] The Bible; Thoreau then paraphrases Matthew 6:19.

[7] According to Greek myth, Deucalion and his wife, Pyrrha, survived a great flood sent by Zeus, the supreme god; to repeople the earth, they threw stones over their shoulders: the stones thrown by Deucalion became men, and those thrown by Pyrrha became women.

[8] From the *Metamorphoses* of the Roman poet Ovid (43 B.C.-A.D. 18); translated from Latin in *The History of the World* (1614), by Sir Walter Raleigh (1554?–1618), an English soldier, courtier, and man of letters.

[9] Invigorate him with our medicines and liqueurs.

and shoes which are fast wearing or are already worn out, and have come to this page to spend borrowed or stolen time, robbing your creditors of an hour. It is very evident what mean and sneaking lives many of you live, for my sight has been whetted by experience; always on the limits, trying to get into business and trying to get out of debt, a very ancient slough, called by the Latins, *æs alienum,* another's brass,[10] for some of their coins were made of brass; still living, and dying, and buried by this other's brass; always promising to pay, promising to pay, to-morrow, and dying to-day, insolvent; seeking to curry favor, to get custom,[11] by how many modes, only not state-prison offences; lying, flattering, voting, contracting yourselves into a nutshell of civility, or dilating into an atmosphere of thin and vaporous generosity, that you may persuade your neighbor to let you make his shoes, or his hat, or his coat, or his carriage, or import his groceries for him; making yourselves sick, that you may lay up something against a sick day, something to be tucked away in an old chest, or in a stocking behind the plastering, or, more safely, in the brick bank; no matter where, no matter how much or how little.

I sometimes wonder that we can be so frivolous, I may almost say, as to attend to the gross but somewhat foreign form of servitude called Negro Slavery, there are so many keen and subtle masters that enslave both north and south. It is hard to have a southern overseer; it is worse to have a northern one; but worst of all when you are the slave-driver of yourself. Talk of a divinity in man! Look at the teamster on the highway, wending to market by day or night; does any divinity stir within him? His highest duty to fodder and water his horses! What is his destiny to him compared with the shipping interests? Does not he drive for Squire Make-a-stir?[12] How godlike, how immortal, is he? See how he cowers and sneaks, how vaguely all the day he fears, not being immortal nor divine, but the slave and prisoner of his own opinion of himself, a fame won by his own deeds. Public opinion is a weak tyrant compared with our own private opinion. What a man thinks of himself, that it is which determines, or rather indicates, his fate. Self-emancipation even in the West Indian provinces of the fancy and imagaination,— what Wilberforce,[13] is there to bring that about? Think, also, of the ladies of the land weaving toilet cushions,[14] against the last day, not to betray too green an interest in their fates! As if you could kill time without injuring eternity.

The mass of men lead lives of quiet desperation. What is called resignation is confirmed desperation. From the desperate city you go into the desperate country, and have to console yourself with the bravery of minks and muskrats. A stereotyped but unconscious despair is concealed even under what are called the games and amusements of mankind. There is no play in them, for this comes after work. But it is a characteristic of wisdom not to do desperate things.

When we consider what, to use the words of the catechism,[15] is the chief end of man, and what are the true necessaries and means of life, it appears as if men had deliberately chosen the common mode of living because they preferred it to any other. Yet they honestly think there is no choice left. But alert and healthy natures

---

[10] Somebody else's money (Latin).   [11] Business.   [12] An allegorical name.

[13] William Wilberforce (1759–1833), a British statesman and humanitarian instrumental in outlawing the slave trade (1807) and in abolishing slavery in the British Empire (1833). Thoreau's habit of internalizing geography is apparent here.

[14] Embroidered cushions used in ladies' dressing rooms.

[15] The Westminster Catechism in the *New England Primer* taught colonial children that the "chief end of man . . . is to glorify God and to enjoy him forever."

remember that the sun rose clear. It is never too late to give up our prejudices. No way of thinking or doing, however ancient, can be trusted without proof. What every body echoes or in silence passes by as true to-day may turn out to be falsehood to-morrow, mere smoke of opinion, which some had trusted for a cloud that would sprinkle fertilizing rain on their fields. What old people say you cannot do you try and find that you can. Old deeds for old people, and new deeds for new. Old people did not know enough once, perchance, to fetch fresh fuel to keep the fire a-going; new people put a little dry wood under a pot,[16] and are whirled round the globe with the speed of birds, in a way to kill old people, as the phrase is. Age is no better, hardly so well, qualified for an instructor as youth, for it has not profited so much as it has lost. One may almost doubt if the wisest man has learned any thing of absolute value by living. Practically, the old have no very important advice to give the young, their own experience has been so partial, and their lives have been such miserable failures, for private reasons, as they must believe; and it may be that they have some faith left which belies that experience, and they are only less young than they were. I have lived some thirty years on this planet, and I have yet to hear the first syllable of valuable or even earnest advice from my seniors. They have told me nothing, and probably cannot tell me any thing, to the purpose. Here is life, an experiment to a great extent untried by me; but it does not avail me that they have tried it. If I have any experience which I think valuable, I am sure to reflect that this my Mentors[17] said nothing about.

One farmer says to me, "You cannot live on vegetable food solely, for it furnishes nothing to make bones with;" and so he religiously devotes a part of his day to supplying his system with the raw material of bones; walking all the while he talks behind his oxen, which, with vegetable-made bones, jerk him and his lumbering plough along in spite of every obstacle. Some things are really necessaries of life in some circles, the most helpless and diseased, which in others are luxuries merely, and in others still are entirely unknown.

The whole ground of human life seems to some to have been gone over by their predecessors, both the heights and the valleys, and all things to have been cared for. According to Evelyn,[18] "the wise Solomon prescribed ordinances for the very distances of trees; and the Roman prætors have decided how often you may go into your neighbor's land to gather the acorns which fall on it without trespass, and what share belongs to that neighbor." Hippocrates[19] has even left directions how we should cut our nails; that is, even with the ends of the fingers, neither shorter nor longer. Undoubtedly the very tedium and ennui which presume to have exhausted the variety and the joys of life are as old as Adam. But man's capacities have never been measured; nor are we to judge of what he can do by any precedents, so little has been tried. Whatever have been thy failures hitherto, "be not afflicted, my child, for who shall. . .assign to thee what thou hast left undone?"[20]

We might try our lives by a thousand simple tests; as, for instance, that the same sun which ripens my beans illumines at once a system of earths like ours. If I had remembered this it would have prevented some mistakes. This was not the

---

[16] Under the boiler of a steam engine.

[17] Derived from Mentor, the teacher of Odysseus's son, Telemachus, in Homer's *Odyssey*.

[18] John Evelyn (1620–1706), a noted English diarist and author of *Sylva* (1644), a book on growing trees. Praetors were Roman officials with judicial duties.

[19] Hippocrates (460?–377? B.C.) was a renowned Greek physician whose treatises include "Air, Earth, and Locality," which deals with the effect of environment on health.

[20] From the *Vishnu Purana*, a Hindu religious text.

light in which I hoed them. The stars are the apexes of what wonderful triangles! What distant and different beings in the various mansions of the universe are contemplating the same one at the same moment! Nature and human life are as various as our several constitutions. Who shall say what prospect life offers to another? Could a greater miracle take place than for us to look through each other's eyes for an instant? We should live in all the ages of the world in an hour; ay, in all the worlds of the ages. History, Poetry, Mythology!—I know of no reading of another's experience so startling and informing as this would be.

The greater part of what my neighbors call good I believe in my soul to be bad, and if I repent of any thing, it is very likely to be my good behavior. What demon possessed me that I behaved so well? You may say the wisest thing you can old man,—you who have lived seventy years, not without honor of a kind,—I hear an irresistible voice which invites me away from all that. One generation abandons the enterprises of another like stranded vessels.

I think that we may safely trust a good deal more than we do. We may waive just so much care of ourselves as we honestly bestow elsewhere. Nature is as well adapted to our weakness as to our strength. The incessant anxiety and strain of some is a well nigh incurable form of disease. We are made to exaggerate the importance of what work we do; and yet how much is not done by us! or, what if we had been taken sick? How vigilant we are! determined not to live by faith if we can avoid it; all the day long on the alert, at night we unwillingly say our prayers and commit ourselves to uncertainties. So thoroughly and sincerely are we compelled to live, reverencing our life, and denying the possibility of change. This is the only way, we say; but there are as many ways as there can be drawn radii from one centre. All change is a miracle to contemplate; but it is a miracle which is taking place every instant. Confucius said, "To know that we know what we know, and that we do not know what we do not know, that is true knowledge."[21] When one man has reduced a fact of the imagination to be a fact to his understanding, I foresee that all men will at length establish their lives on that basis.

Let us consider for a moment what most of the trouble and anxiety which I have referred to is about, and how much it is necessary that we be troubled, or, at least, careful. It would be some advantage to live a primitive and frontier life, though in the midst of an outward civilization, if only to learn what are the gross necessaries of life and what methods have been taken to obtain them; or even to look over the old day-books of the merchants, to see what it was that men most commonly bought at the stores, what they stored, that is, what are the grossest groceries. For the improvements of ages have had but little influence on the essential laws of man's existence; as our skeletons, probably, are not to be distinguished from those of our ancestors.

By the words, *necessary of life,* I mean whatever, of all that man obtains by his own exertions, has been from the first, or from long use has become, so important to human life that few, if any, whether from savageness, or poverty, or philosophy, ever attempt to do without it. To many creatures there is in this sense but one necessary of life, Food. To the bison of the prairie it is a few inches of palatable grass, with water to drink; unless he seeks the Shelter of the forest or the mountain's shadow. None of the brute creation requires more than Food and Shelter. The necessaries of life for man in this climate may, accurately enough, be distrib-

---

[21] From the *Analects* (Bk. II, Ch. 17) of the Chinese philosopher Confucius (551?–479 B.C.).

uted under the several heads of Food, Shelter, Clothing, and Fuel; for not till we have secured these are we prepared to entertain the true problems of life with freedom and a prospect of success. Man has invented, not only houses, but clothes and cooked food; and possibly from the accidental discovery of the warmth of fire, and the consequent use of it, at first a luxury, arose the present necessity to sit by it. We observe cats and dogs acquiring the same second nature. By proper Shelter and Clothing we legitimately retain our own internal heat; but with an excess of these, or of Fuel, that is, with an external heat greater than our own internal, may not cookery properly be said to begin? Darwin, the naturalist, says of the inhabitants of Tierra del Fuego,[22] that while his own party, who were well clothed and sitting close to a fire, were far from too warm, these naked savages, who were farther off, were observed, to his great surprise, "to be streaming with perspiration at undergoing such a roasting." So, we are told, the New Hollander[23] goes naked with impunity, while the European shivers in his clothes. Is it impossible to combine the hardiness of these savages with the intellectualness of the civilized man? According to Liebig,[24] man's body is a stove, and food the fuel which keeps up the internal combustion in the lungs. In cold weather we eat more, in warm less. The animal heat is the result of a slow combustion, and disease and death take place when this is too rapid; or for want of fuel, or from some defect in the draught, the fire goes out. Of course the vital heat is not to be confounded with fire; but so much for analogy. It appears, therefore, from the above list, that the expression, *animal life,* is nearly synonymous with the expression, *animal heat;* for while Food may be regarded as the Fuel which keeps up the fire within us,—and Fuel serves only to prepare that Food or to increase the warmth of our bodies by addition from without,—Shelter and Clothing also serve only to retain the *heat* thus generated and absorbed.

The grand necessity, then, for our bodies, is to keep warm, to keep the vital heat in us. What pains we accordingly take, not only with our Food, and Clothing, and Shelter, but with our beds, which are our night-clothes, robbing the nests and breasts of birds to prepare this shelter within a shelter, as the mole has its bed of grass and leaves at the end of its burrow! The poor man is wont to complain that this is a cold world; and to cold, no less physical than social, we refer directly a great part of our ails. The summer, in some climates, makes possible to man a sort of Elysian[25] life. Fuel, except to cook his Food, is then unnecessary; the sun is his fire, and many of the fruits are sufficiently cooked by its rays; while Food generally is more various, and more easily obtained, and Clothing and Shelter are wholly or half unnecessary. At the present day, and in this country, as I find by my own experience, a few implements, a knife, an axe, a spade, a wheelbarrow, &c., and for the studious, lamplight, stationery, and access to a few books, rank next to necessaries, and can all be obtained at a trifling cost. Yet some, not wise, go to the other side of the globe, to barbarous and unhealthy regions, and devote themselves to trade for ten or twenty years, in order that they may live,—that is, keep comfortably warm,—and die in New England at last. The luxuriously rich are not simply kept comfortably warm, but unnaturally hot; as I implied before, they are cooked, of course *à la mode.*[26]

[22] Charles Darwin (1809–1882) describes the inhabitants of Tierra del Fuego, at the southern tip of South America, in his *Journal of Researches* (1839).
[23] An Aboriginal Australian.   [24] Justus von Liebig (1803–1873), a German chemist.
[25] According to Greek myth, the Elysian fields were home to the virtuous dead.
[26] In style, according to the fashion (French): by central heating.

Most of the luxuries, and many of the so called comforts of life, are not only not indispensable, but positive hinderances to the elevation of mankind. With respect to luxuries and comforts, the wisest have ever lived a more simple and meager life than the poor. The ancient philosophers, Chinese, Hindoo, Persian, and Greek, were a class than which none has been poorer in outward riches, none so rich in inward. We know not much about them. It is remarkable that *we* know so much of them as we do. The same is true of the more modern reformers and benefactors of their race. None can be an impartial or wise observer of human life but from the vantage ground of what *we* should call voluntary poverty. Of a life of luxury the fruit is luxury, whether in agriculture, or commerce, or literature, or art. There are nowadays professors of philosophy, but not philosophers. Yet it is admirable to profess because it was once admirable to live. To be a philosopher is not merely to have subtle thoughts, nor even to found a school, but so to love wisdom as to live according to its dictates, a life of simplicity, independence, magnanimity, and trust. It is to solve some of the problems of life, not only theoretically, but practically. The success of great scholars and thinkers is commonly a courtier-like success, not kingly, not manly. They make shift to live merely by conformity, practically as their fathers did, and are in no sense the progenitors of a nobler race of men. But why do men degenerate ever? What makes families run out? What is the nature of the luxury which enervates and destroys nations? Are we sure that there is none of it in our own lives? The philosopher is in advance of his age even in the outward form of his life. He is not fed, sheltered, clothed, warmed, like his contemporaries. How can a man be a philosopher and not maintain his vital heat by better methods than other men?

When a man is warmed by the several modes which I have described, what does he want next? Surely not more warmth of the same kind, as more and richer food, larger and more splendid houses, finer and more abundant clothing, more numerous incessant and hotter fires, and the like. When he has obtained those things which are necessary to life, there is another alternative than to obtain the superfluities; and that is, to adventure on life now, his vacation from humbler toil having commenced. The soil, it appears, is suited to the seed, for it has sent its radicle[27] downward, and it may now send its shoot upward also with confidence. Why has man rooted himself thus firmly in the earth, but that he may rise in the same proportion into the heavens above?—for the nobler plants are valued for the fruit they bear at last in the air and light, far from the ground, and are not treated like the humbler esculents,[28] which, though they may be biennials, are cultivated only till they have perfected their root, and often cut down at top for this purpose, so that most would not know them in their flowering season.

I do not mean to prescribe rules to strong and valiant natures, who will mind their own affairs whether in heaven or hell, and perchance build more magnificently and spend more lavishly than the richest, without ever impoverishing themselves, not knowing how they live,—if, indeed, there are any such, as has been dreamed; nor to those who find their encouragement and inspiration in precisely the present condition of things, and cherish it with the fondness and enthusiasm of lovers,—and, to some extent, I reckon myself in this number; I do not speak to those who are well employed, in whatever circumstances, and they know whether they are well employed or not;—but mainly to the mass of men who are discontented, and idly complaining of the hardness of their lot or of the times, when they

[27] Root.   [28] Edibles.

might improve them. There are some who complain most energetically and inconsolably of any, because they are, as they say, doing their duty. I also have in my
mind that seemingly wealthy, but most terribly impoverished class of all, who
have accumulated dross,[29] but know not how to use it, or get rid of it, and thus
have forged their own golden or silver fetters.

If I should attempt to tell how I have desired to spend my life in years past, it
would probably surprise those of my readers who are somewhat acquainted with
its actual history; it would certainly astonish those who know nothing about it. I
will only hint at some of the enterprises which I have cherished.

In any weather, at any hour of the day or night, I have been anxious to improve
the nick of time, and notch it on my stick[30] too; to stand on the meeting of two
eternities, the past and future, which is precisely the present moment; to toe that
line. You will pardon some obscurities, for there are more secrets in my trade than
in most men's, and yet not voluntarily kept, but inseparable from its very nature. I
would gladly tell all that I know about it, and never paint "No Admittance" on my
gate.

I long ago lost a hound, a bay horse, and a turtle-dove, and am still on their
trail.[31] Many are the travellers I have spoken concerning them, describing their
tracks and what calls they answered to. I have met one or two who had heard the
hound, and the tramp of the horse, and even seen the dove disappear behind a
cloud, and they seemed as anxious to recover them as if they had lost them themselves.

To anticipate, not the sunrise and the dawn merely, but, if possible, Nature
herself! How many mornings, summer and winter, before yet any neighbor was
stirring about his business, have I been about mine! No doubt, many of my townsmen have met me returning from this enterprise, farmers starting for Boston in the
twilight, or woodchoppers going to their work. It is true, I never assisted the sun
materially in his rising, but, doubt not, it was of the last importance only to be
present at it.

So many autumn, ay, and winter days, spent outside the town, trying to hear
what was in the wind, to hear and carry it express! I well-nigh sunk all my capital
in it, and lost my own breath into the bargain, running in the face of it. If it had
concerned either of the political parties, depend upon it, it would have appeared in
the Gazette with the earliest intelligence.[32] At other times watching from the observatory of some cliff or tree, to telegraph any new arrival; or waiting at evening
on the hill-tops for the sky to fall, that I might catch something, though I never
caught much, and that, manna-wise[33] would dissolve again in the sun.

For a long time I was reporter to a journal,[34] of no very wide circulation, whose
editor has never yet seen fit to print the bulk of my contributions, and, as is too
common with writers, I got only my labor for my pains. However, in this case my
pains were their own reward.

---

[29] The scum forming on molten metals.   [30] Make a record of it.

[31] A passage baffling even to Thoreau, who replied to a letter from his admiring friend B. B. Wiley in
1857 that the items mentioned symbolize profound losses in life, "according as I now understand my
own words." The paragraph takes on the allegorical quality of a quest for a lost condition in life.

[32] In Concord's weekly newspaper with the earliest news.

[33] In Exodus 16 manna, the food miraculously given to the Israelites on their journey out of Egypt,
melted in the sun.

[34] Probably Thoreau's own journal, on which he levied for contributions to various magazines.

For many years I was self-appointed inspector of snow storms and rain storms, and did my duty faithfully; surveyor, if not of highways, then of forest paths and all across-lot routes, keeping them open, and ravines bridged and passable at all seasons, where the public heel had testified to their utility.

I have looked after the wild stock of the town, which give a faithful herdsman a good deal of trouble by leaping fences; and I have had an eye to the unfrequented nooks and corners of the farm; though I did not always know whether Jonas or Solomon worked in a particular field to-day; that was none of my business. I have watered the red huckleberry, the sand cherry and the nettle tree, the red pine and the black ash, the white grape and the yellow violet, which might have withered else in dry seasons.

In short, I went on thus for a long time, I may say it without boasting, faithfully minding my business, till it became more and more evident that my townsmen would not after all admit me into the list of town officers, nor make my place a sinecure with a moderate allowance. My accounts, which I can swear to have kept faithfully, I have, indeed, never got audited, still less accepted, still less paid and settled. However, I have not set my heart on that.

Not long since, a strolling Indian went to sell baskets at the house of a well-known lawyer in my neighborhood. "Do you wish to buy any baskets?" he asked. "No, we do not want any," was the reply. "What!" exclaimed the Indian as he went out the gate, "do you mean to starve us?" Having seen his industrious white neighbors so well off,—that the lawyer had only to weave arguments, and by some magic wealth and standing followed, he had said to himself; I will go into business; I will weave baskets; it is a thing which I can do. Thinking that when he had made the baskets he would have done his part, and then it would be the white man's to buy them. He had not discovered that it was necessary for him to make it worth the other's while to buy them, or at least make him think that it was so, or to make something else which it would be worth his while to buy. I too had woven a kind of basket of a delicate texture, but I had not made it worth any one's while to buy them.[35] Yet not the less, in my case, did I think it worth my while to weave them, and instead of studying how to make it worth men's while to buy my baskets, I studied rather how to avoid the necessity of selling them. The life which men praise and regard as successful is but one kind. Why should we exaggerate any one kind at the expense of the others?

Finding that my fellow-citizens were not likely to offer me any room in the court house, or any curacy or living[36] any where else, but I must shift for myself, I turned my face more exclusively than ever to the woods, where I was better known. I determined to go into business at once, and not wait to acquire the usual capital, using such slender means as I had already got. My purpose in going to Walden Pond was not to live cheaply nor to live dearly there, but to transact some private business with the fewest obstacles; to be hindered from accomplishing which for want of a little common sense, a little enterprise and business talent, appeared not so sad as foolish.

I have always endeavored to acquire strict business habits; they are indispensable to every man. If your trade is with the Celestial Empire,[37] then some small

---

[35] A reference to Thoreau's first book, *A Week on the Concord and Merrimack Rivers,* which sold few copies.

[36] Any appointment as a county official, or any appointment as a clergyman, or income from a church office.

[37] China, so named because its emperors were thought to be sons of Heaven.

counting house on the coast, in some Salem harbor, will be fixture enough. You will export such articles as the country affords, purely native products, much ice and pine timber and a little granite, always in native bottoms.[38] These will be good ventures. To oversee all the details yourself in person; to be at once pilot and captain, and owner and underwriter; to buy and sell and keep the accounts; to read every letter received, and write or read every letter sent; to superintend the discharge of imports night and day; to be upon many parts of the coast almost at the same time;—often the richest freight will be discharged upon a Jersey shore;[39]— to be your own telegraph, unweariedly sweeping the horizon, speaking all passing vessels bound coastwise; to keep up a steady despatch of commodities, for the supply of such a distant and exorbitant market; to keep yourself informed of the state of the markets, prospects of war and peace every where, and anticipate the tendencies of trade and civilization,—taking advantage of the results of all exploring expeditions, using new passages and all improvements in navigation;— charts to be studied, the position of reefs and new lights and buoys to be ascertained, and ever, and ever, the logarithmic tables to be corrected, for by the error of some calculator the vessel often splits upon a rock that should have reached a friendly pier,—there is the untold fate of La Perouse;[40]—universal science to be kept pace with, studying the lives of all great discoverers and navigators, great adventurers and merchants, from Hanno and the Phœnicians[41] down to our day; in fine, account of stock to be taken from time to time, to know how you stand. It is a labor to task the faculties of a man,—such problems of profit and loss, of interest, of tare and tret,[42] and gauging of all kinds in it, as demand a universal knowledge.

I have thought that Walden Pond would be a good place for business, not solely on account of the railroad and the ice trade; it offers advantages which it may not be good policy to divulge; it is a good port and a good foundation. No Neva[43] marshes to be filled; though you must every where build on piles of your own driving. It is said that a flood-tide, with a westerly wind, and ice in the Neva, would sweep St. Petersburg from the face of the earth.

As this business was to be entered into without the usual capital, it may not be easy to conjecture where those means, that will still be indispensable to every such undertaking, were to be obtained. As for Clothing, to come at once to the practical part of the question, perhaps we are led oftener by the love of novelty, and a regard for the opinions of men, in procuring it, than by a true utility. Let him who has work to do recollect that the object of clothing is, first, to retain the vital heat, and secondly, in this state of society, to cover nakedness, and he may judge how much of any necessary or important work may be accomplished without adding to his wardrobe. Kings and queens who wear a suit but once, though made by some tailor or dress-maker to their majesties, cannot know the comfort of wearing a suit that fits. They are no better than wooden horses to hang the clean clothes on. Every day our garments become more assimilated to ourselves, receiving the im-

---

[38] Ships.   [39] Shipwrecked on the New Jersey coast.

[40] Jean François de Galaup (1741–1788?), count de la Perouse, a French explorer who disappeared after being shipwrecked in the New Hebrides, in the South Pacific.

[41] The Phoenicians and the Carthaginian navigator Hanno (6th–5th centuries B.C.) were noted for exploration and navigational skill.

[42] Commercial calculations of weight and of allowance for waste or spoilage.

[43] A river in Russia, near St. Petersburg (now Leningrad).

press of the wearer's character, until we hesitate to lay them aside, without such delay and medical appliances and some such solemnity even as our bodies. No man ever stood the lower in my estimation for having a patch in his clothes; yet I am sure that there is greater anxiety, commonly, to have fashionable, or at least clean and unpatched clothes, than to have a sound conscience. But even if the rent[44] is not mended, perhaps the worst vice betrayed is improvidence. I sometimes try my acquaintances by such tests as this;—who could wear a patch, or two extra seams only, over the knee? Most behave as if they believed that their prospects for life would be ruined if they should do it. It would be easier for them to hobble to town with a broken leg than with a broken pantaloon. Often if an accident happens to a gentleman's legs, they can be mended; but if a similar accident happens to the legs of his pantaloons, there is no help for it; for he considers, not what is truly respectable, but what is respected. We know but few men, a great many coats and breeches. Dress a scarecrow in your last shift, you standing shiftless by, who would not soonest salute the scarecrow? Passing a cornfield the other day, close by a hat and coat on a stake, I recognized the owner of the farm. He was only a little more weather-beaten than when I saw him last. I have heard of a dog that barked at every stranger who approached his master's premises with clothes on, but was easily quieted by a naked thief. It is an interesting question how far men would retain their relative rank if they were divested of their clothes. Could you, in such a case, tell surely of any company of civilized men, which belonged to the most respected class? When Madam Pfeiffer,[45] in her adventurous travels round the world, from east to west, had got so near home as Asiatic Russia, she says that she felt the necessity of wearing other than a travelling dress, when she went to meet the authorities, for she "was now in a civilized country, where—"people are judged of by their clothes." Even in our democratic New England towns the accidental possession of wealth, and its manifestation in dress and equipage alone, obtain for the possessor almost universal respect. But they who yield such respect, numerous as they are, are so far heathen, and need to have a missionary sent to them. Beside, clothes introduced sewing, a kind of work which you may call endless; a woman's dress, at least is never done.[46]

A man who has at length found something to do will not need to get a new suit to do it in; for him the old will do, that has lain dusty in the garret for an indeterminate period. Old shoes will serve a hero longer than they have served his valet,—if a hero ever has a valet,—bare feet are older than shoes, and he can make them do. Only they who go to soirées and legislative halls must have new coats, coats to change as often as the man changes in them. But if my jacket and trousers, my hat and shoes, are fit to worship God in, they will do; will they not? Who ever saw his old clothes,—his old coat, actually worn out, resolved into its primitive elements, so that it was not a deed of charity to bestow it on some poor boy, by him perchance to be bestowed on some poorer still, or shall we say richer, who could do with less? I say, beware of all enterprises that require new clothes, and not rather a new wearer of clothes. If there is not a new man, how can the new clothes be made to fit? If you have any enterprise before you, try it in your old clothes. All men want, not something to *do with*, but something to *do*, or rather

---

[44] The rip or tear.

[45] Ida Reyer Pfeiffer (1797–1858), an Austrian traveler and writer, author of *A Lady's Journey Round the World* (1852).

[46] A variant of the saying "A man works from sun to sun, but a woman's work is never done."

something to *be*. Perhaps we should never procure a new suit, however ragged or dirty the old, until we have so conducted, so enterprised or sailed in some way, that we feel like new men in the old, and that to retain it would be like keeping new wine in old bottles.[47] Our moulting season, like that of the fowls, must be a crisis in our lives. The loon retires to solitary ponds to spend it. Thus also the snake casts its slough, and the caterpillar its wormy coat, by an internal industry and expansion; for clothes are but our outmost cuticle and mortal coil. Otherwise we shall be found sailing under false colors, and be inevitably cashiered[48] at last by our own opinion, as well as that of mankind.

We don garment after garment, as if we grew like exogenous plants[49] by addition without. Our outside and often thin and fanciful clothes are our epidermis or false skin, which partakes not of our life, and may be stripped off here and there without fatal injury; our thicker garments, constantly worn, are our cellular integument, or cortex;[50] but our shirts are our liber or true bark, which cannot be removed without girdling and so destroying the man. I believe that all races at some seasons wear something equivalent to the shirt. It is desirable that a man be clad so simply that he can lay his hands on himself in the dark, and that he live in all respects so compactly and preparedly, that, if an enemy take the town, he can, like the old philosopher, walk out the gate empty-handed without anxiety. While one thick garment is, for most purposes, as good as three thin ones, and cheap clothing can be obtained at prices really to suit customers; while a thick coat can be bought for five dollars, which will last as many years, thick pantaloons for two dollars, cowhide boots for a dollar and a half a pair, a summer hat for a quarter of a dollar, and a winter cap for sixty-two and a half cents, or a better be made at home at a nominal cost, where is he so poor that, clad in such a suit, *of his own earning*, there will not be found wise men to do him reverence?

When I ask for a garment of a particular form, my tailoress tells me gravely, "They do not make them so now," not emphasizing the "They" at all, as if she quoted an authority as impersonal as the Fates,[51] and I find it difficult to get made what I want, simply because she cannot believe that I mean what I say, that I am so rash. When I hear this oracular sentence, I am for a moment absorbed in thought, emphasizing to myself each word separately that I may come at the meaning of it, that I may find out by what degree of consanguinity *They* are related to *me*, and what authority they may have in an affair which affects me so nearly; and, finally, I am inclined to answer her with equal mystery, and without any more emphasis of the "they,"—"It is true, they did not make them so recently, but they do now." Of what use this measuring of me if she does not measure my character, but only the breadth of my shoulders, as it were a peg to hang the coat on? We worship not the Graces, nor the Parcæ,[52] but Fashion. She spins and weaves and cuts with full authority. The head monkey at Paris puts on a traveller's cap, and all the monkeys in America do the same. I sometimes despair of getting any thing quite simple and honest done in this world by the help of men. They would have to be passed through a powerful press first, to squeeze their old

---

[47] "Neither do men put new wine into old bottles: else the bottles break . . . but they put new wine into new bottles, and both are preserved," from Matthew 9:17.

[48] Dismissed, fired.   [49] Plants that grow by adding exterior layers.

[50] The skin of a cell, or the outer layer; here, inner bark.

[51] According to classical myth, three goddesses who determine human destiny.

[52] According to Greek myth, the Graces were three goddesses who control pleasure, charm, and beauty; Parcae, or "birth-spirits," is a Roman name for the Fates.

notions out of them, so that they would not soon get upon their legs again, and then there would be some one in the company with a maggot in his head, hatched from an egg deposited there nobody knows when, for not even fire kills these things, and you would have lost your labor. Nevertheless, we will not forget that some Egyptian wheat is said to have been handed down to us by a mummy.[53]

On the whole, I think that it cannot be maintained that dressing has in this or any country risen to the dignity of an art. At present men make shift to wear what they can get. Like shipwrecked sailors, they put on what they can find on the beach, and at a little distance, whether of space or time, laugh at each other's masquerade. Every generation laughs at the old fashions, but follows religiously the new. We are amused at beholding the costume of Henry VIII, or Queen Elizabeth,[54] as much as if it was that of the King and Queen of the Cannibal Islands. All costume off a man is pitiful or grotesque. It is only the serious eye peering from and the sincere life passed within it, which restrain laughter and consecrate the costume of any people. Let Harlequin,[55] be taken with a fit of the colic and his trappings will have to serve that mood too. When the soldier is hit by a cannon ball rags are as becoming as purple.[56]

The childish and savage taste of men and women for new patterns keeps how many shaking and squinting through kaleidoscopes that they may discover the particular figure which this generation requires to-day. The manufacturers have learned that this taste is merely whimsical. Of two patterns which differ only by a few threads more or less of a particular color, the one will be sold readily, the other lie on the shelf, though it frequently happens that after the lapse of a season the latter becomes the most fashionable. Comparatively, tattooing is not the hideous custom which it is called. It is not barbarous merely because the printing is skin-deep and unalterable.

I cannot believe that our factory system is the best mode by which men may get clothing. The condition of the operatives[57] is becoming every day more like that of the English; and it cannot be wondered at, since, as far as I have heard or observed, the principal object is, not that mankind may be well and honestly clad, but, unquestionably, that the corporations may be enriched. In the long run men hit only what they aim at. Therefore, though they should fail immediately, they had better aim at something high.

As for a Shelter, I will not deny that this is now a necessary of life, though there are instances of men having done without it for long periods in colder countries than this. Samuel Laing[58] says that "The Laplander in his skin dress, and in a skin bag which he puts over his head and shoulders, will sleep night after night on the snow—in a degree of cold which would extinguish the life of one exposed to it in any woollen clothing." He had seen them alseep thus. Yet he adds, "They are not hardier than other people." But, probably, man did not live long on the earth without discovering the convenience which there is in a house, the domestic comforts, which phrase may have originally signified the satisfactions of the house

---

[53] The notion that wheat would grow from seeds sealed in ancient Egyptian tombs was popular in the nineteenth century.

[54] The king (1509–1547) and queen (1558–1603) of England.

[55] A character in comedy and pantomime, with masked face, multicolored tights, and frequently a shaved head.

[56] The traditional color of royalty.   [57] Factory workers.

[58] Laing (1780–1868), an English writer, wrote *Journal of a Residence in Norway* (1837).

more than of the family; though these must be extremely partial and occasional in those climates where the house is associated in our thoughts with winter or the rainy season chiefly, and two thirds of the year, except for a parasol, is unnecessary. In our climate, in the summer, it was formerly almost solely a covering at night. In the Indian gazettes[59] a wigwam was the symbol of a day's march, and a row of them cut or painted on the bark of a tree signified that so many times they had camped. Man was not made so large limbed and robust but that he must seek to narrow his world, and wall in a space such as fitted him. He was at first bare and out of doors; but though this was pleasant enough in serene and warm weather, by daylight, the rainy season and the winter, to say nothing of the torrid sun, would perhaps have nipped his race in the bud if he had not made haste to clothe himself with the shelter of a house. Adam and Eve, according to the fable,[60] wore the bower before other clothes. Man wanted a home, a place of warmth, or comfort, first of physical warmth, then the warmth of the affections.

We may imagine a time when, in the infancy of the human race, some enterprising mortal crept into a hollow in a rock for shelter. Every child begins the world again, to some extent, and loves to stay out doors, even in wet and cold. It plays house, as well as horse, having an instinct for it. Who does not remember the interest with which when young he looked at shelving rocks, or any approach to a cave? It was the natural yearning of that portion of our most primitive ancestor which still survived in us. From the cave we have advanced to roofs of palm leaves, of bark and boughs, of linen woven and stretched, of grass and straw, of boards and shingles, of stones and tiles. At last, we know not what it is to live in the open air, and our lives are domestic in more senses than we think. From the hearth to the field is a great distance. It would be well perhaps if we were to spend more of our days and nights without any obstruction between us and the celestial bodies, if the poet did not speak so much from under a roof, or the saint dwell there so long. Birds do not sing in caves, nor do doves cherish their innocence in dovecots.[61]

However, if one designs to construct a dwelling house, it behooves him to exercise a little Yankee shrewdness, lest after all he find himself in a workhouse, a labyrinth without a clew, a museum, an almshouse, a prison, or a splendid mausoleum instead. Consider first how slight a shelter is absolutely necessary. I have seen Penobscot Indians,[62] in this town, living in tents of thin cotton cloth, while the snow was nearly a foot deep around them, and I thought that they would be glad to have it deeper to keep out the wind. Formerly, when how to get my living honestly, with freedom left for my proper pursuits, was a question which vexed me even more than it does now, for unfortunately I am become somewhat callous, I used to see a large box by the railroad, six feet long by three wide, in which the laborers locked up their tools at night, and it suggested to me that every man who was hard pushed might get such a one for a dollar, and, having bored a few auger holes in it, to admit the air at least, get into it when it rained and at night, and hook down the lid, and so have freedom in his love, and in his soul be free. This did not appear the worst, nor by any means a despicable alternative. You could sit up as late as you pleased, and, whenever you got up, got abroad without any landlord or house-lord dogging you for rent. Many a man is harassed to death to

---

[59] According to Indian sign languages.
[60] Calling the biblical story of Adam and Eve a "fable" did not endear Thoreau to orthodox readers.
[61] Dovecotes, boxes for nesting birds.   [62] A tribe from northern Maine.

pay the rent of a larger and more luxurious box who would not have frozen to death in such a box as this. I am far from jesting. Economy is a subject which admits of being treated with levity, but it cannot so be disposed of. A comfortable house for a rude and hardy race, that lived mostly out of doors, was once made here almost entirely of such materials as Nature furnished ready to their hands. Gookin,[63] who was superintendent of the Indians subject to the Massachusetts Colony, writing in 1674, says, "The best of their houses are covered very neatly, tight and warm, with barks of trees, slipped from their bodies at those seasons when the sap is up, and made into great flakes, with pressure of weighty timber, when they are green. . . . The meaner sort are covered with mats which they make of a kind of bulrush, and are also indifferently tight and warm, but not so good as the former. . . . Some I have seen, sixty or a hundred feet long and thirty feet broad. . . . I have often lodged in their wigwams, and found them as warm as the best English houses." He adds, that they were commonly carpeted and lined within with well-wrought embroidered mats, and were furnished with various utensils. The Indians had advanced so far as to regulate the effect of the wind by a mat suspended over the hole in the roof and moved by a string. Such a lodge was in the first instance constructed in a day or two at most, and taken down and put up in a few hours; and every family owned one, or its apartment in one.

In the savage state every family owns a shelter as good as the best, and sufficient for its coarser and simpler wants; but I think that I speak within bounds when I say that, though the birds of the air have their nests, and the foxes their holes,[64] and the savages their wigwams, in modern civilized society not more than one half the families own a shelter. In the large towns and cities, where civilization especially prevails, the number of those who own a shelter is a very small fraction of the whole. The rest pay an annual tax for this outside garment of all, become indispensable summer and winter, which would buy a village of Indian wigwams, but now helps to keep them poor as long as they live. I do not mean to insist here on the disadvantage of hiring compared with owning, but it is evident that the savage owns his shelter because it costs so little, while the civilized man hires his commonly because he cannot afford to own it; nor can he, in the long run, any better afford to hire. But, answers one, by merely paying this tax the poor civilized man secures an abode which is a palace compared with the savage's. An annual rent of from twenty-five to a hundred dollars, these are the country rates, entitles him to the benefit of the improvements of centuries, spacious apartments, clean paint and paper, Rumford fireplace, back plastering,[65] Venetian blinds, copper pump, spring lock, a commodious cellar, and many other things. But how happens it that he who is said to enjoy these things is so commonly a *poor* civilized man, while the savage, who has them not, is rich as a savage? If it is asserted that civilization is a real advance in the condition of man,—and I think that it is, though only the wise improve their advantages,—it must be shown that it has produced better dwellings without making them more costly; and the cost of a thing is the amount of what I will call life which is required to be exchanged for it, immediately or in the long run. An average house in this neighborhood costs perhaps eight hundred dollars, and to lay up this sum will take from ten to fifteen

[63] Daniel Gookin (1612–1687), from his *Historical Collections of the Indians in New England* (1792) (Ch. III).

[64] "The foxes have holes, and the birds of the air have nests; but the Son of man hath not where to lay his head," from Matthew 8:20.

[65] A smokeless stove invented by Benjamin Thompson (1753–1814), Count Rumford; insulation.

years of the laborer's life, even if he is not encumbered with a family;—estimating the pecuniary value of every man's labor at one dollar a day, for if some receive more, others receive less;—so that he must have spent more than half his life commonly before *his* wigwam will be earned. If we suppose him to pay a rent instead, this is but a doubtful choice of evils. Would the savage have been wise to exchange his wigwam for a palace on these terms?

It may be guessed that I reduce almost the whole advantage of holding this superfluous property as a fund in store against the future, so far as the individual is concerned, mainly to the defraying of funeral expenses. But perhaps a man is not required to bury himself. Nevertheless this points to an important distinction between the civilized man and the savage; and, no doubt, they have designs on us for our benefit, in making the life of a civilized people an *institution,* in which the life of the individual is to a great extent absorbed, in order to preserve and perfect that of the race. But I wish to show at what a sacrifice this advantage is at present obtained, and to suggest that we may possibly so live as to secure all the advantage without suffering any of the disadvantage. What mean ye by saying that the poor ye have always with you, or that the fathers have eaten sour grapes, and the children's teeth are set on edge?[66]

"As I live, saith the Lord God, ye shall not have occasion any more to use this proverb in Israel."

"Behold all souls are mine; as the soul of the father, so also the soul of the son is mine: the soul that sinneth it shall die."

When I consider my neighbors, the farmers of Concord, who are at least as well off as the other classes, I find that for the most part they have been toiling twenty, thirty, or forty years, that they may become the real owners of their farms, which commonly they have inherited with encumbrances, or else bought with hired money,—and we may regard one third of that toil as the cost of their houses,—but commonly they have not paid for them yet. It is true, the encumbrances sometimes outweigh the value of the farm, so that the farm itself becomes one great encumbrance, and still a man is found to inherit it, being well acquainted with it, as he says. On applying to the assessors, I am surprised to learn that they cannot at once name a dozen in the town who own their farms free and clear. If you would know the history of these homesteads, inquire at the bank where they are mortgaged. The man who has actually paid for his farm with labor on it is so rare that every neighbor can point to him. I doubt if there are three such men in Concord. What has been said of the merchants, that a very large majority, even ninety-seven in a hundred, are sure to fail, is equally true of the farmers. With regard to the merchants, however, one of them says pertinently that a great part of their failures are not genuine pecuniary failures, but merely failures to fulfil their engagements, because it is inconvenient; that is, it is the moral character that breaks down. But this puts an infinitely worse face on the matter, and suggests, beside, that probably not even the other three succeed in saving their souls, but are perchance bankrupt in a worse sense than they who fail honestly. Bankruptcy and repudiation are the spring-boards from which much of our civilization vaults and turns its somersets, but the savage stands on the unelastic plank

---

[66] Thoreau takes exception to the words "For ye have the poor always with you," from Matthew 26:11, and to the proverb "The fathers have eaten . . .," from Ezekiel 18:2. As cryptic as they are here, the following two quotations, from Ezekiel 18:3–4, advance the idea that each person is born fresh in the Lord.

of famine. Yet the Middlesex Cattle Show goes off here with *éclat*[67] annually, as if all the joints of the agricultural machine were suent.[68]

The farmer is endeavoring to solve the problem of a livelihood by a formula more complicated than the problem itself. To get his shoestrings he speculates in herds of cattle. With consummate skill he has set his trap with a hair spring[69] to catch comfort and independence, and then, as he turned away, got his own leg into it. This is the reason he is poor; and for a similar reason we are all poor in respect to a thousand savage comforts, though surrounded by luxuries. As Chapman[70] sings,—

> "The false society of men—
> —for earthly greatness
> All heavenly comforts rarefies to air."

And when the farmer has got his house, he may not be the richer but the poorer for it, and it be the house that has got him. As I understand it, that was a valid objection urged by Momus against the house which Minerva[71] made, that she "had not made it movable, by which means a bad neighborhood might be avoided;" and it may still be urged, for our houses are such unwieldly property that we are often imprisoned rather than housed in them; and the bad neighborhood to be avoided is our own scurvy selves. I know one or two families, at least, in this town, who, for nearly a generation, have been wishing to sell their houses in the outskirts and move into the village, but have not been able to accomplish it, and only death will set them free.

Granted that the *majority* are able at last either to own or hire the modern house with all its improvements. While civilization has been improving our houses, it has not equally improved the men who are to inhabit them. It has created palaces, but it was not so easy to create noblemen and kings. And *if the civilized man's pursuits are no worthier than the savage's, if he is employed the greater part of his life in obtaining gross necessaries and comforts merely, why should he have a better dwelling than the former?*

But how do the poor *minority* fare? Perhaps it will be found, that just in proportion as some have been placed in outward circumstances above the savage, others have been degraded below him. The luxury of one class is counterbalanced by the indigence of another. On the one side is the palace, on the other are the almshouse and "silent poor".[72] The myriads who built the pyramids to be the tombs of the Pharaohs were fed on garlic,[73] and it may be were not decently buried themselves. The mason who finishes the cornice of the palace returns at night perchance to a hut not so good as a wigwam. It is a mistake to suppose that, in a country where the usual evidences of civilization exist, the condition of a very large body of the inhabitants may not be as degraded as that of savages. I refer to the degraded

---

[67] An agricultural country fair held in Concord, each September, with *éclat*, or "brilliantly" (French).
[68] Working well.   [69] A trap adjusted so carefully that a hair would spring it.
[70] George Chapman (1559?–1634), an English poet and dramatist, from *Caesar and Pompey* (1631) (V. ii).
[71] According to Greek myth, Momus was the god of mockery, criticism, and faultfinding; Minerva was the goddess of handicrafts (and of wisdom).
[72] Those who conceal their poverty to stay out of the poorhouse.
[73] The Greek historian Herodotus (480?–425? B.C.) mentions that onions and garlic were supplied to those who worked on the Egyptian pyramids.

poor, not now to the degraded rich. To know this I should not need to look farther than to the shanties which every where border our railroads, that last improvement in civilization; where I see in my daily walks human beings living in sties, and all winter with an open door, for the sake of light, without any visible, often imaginable, wood pile, and the forms of both old and young are permanently contracted by the long habit of shrinking from cold and misery, and the development of all their limbs and faculties is checked. It certainly is fair to look at that class by whose labor the works which distinguish this generation are accomplished. Such too, to a greater or less extent, is the condition of the operatives of every denomination in England, which is the great workhouse of the world. Or I could refer you to Ireland,[74] which is marked as one of the white or enlightened spots on the map. Contrast the physical condition of the Irish with that of the North American Indian, or the South Sea Islander, or any other savage race before it was degraded by contact with the civilized man. Yet I have no doubt that that people's rulers are as wise as the average of civilized rulers. Their condition only proves what squalidness may consist with civilization. I hardly need refer now to the laborers in our Southern States who produce the staple exports of this country, and are themselves a staple production of the South.[75] But to confine myself to those who are said to be in *moderate* circumstances.

Most men appear never to have considered what a house is, and are actually though needlessly poor all their lives because they think that they must have such a one as their neighbors have. As if one were to wear any sort of coat which the tailor might cut out for him, or, gradually leaving off palmleaf hat or cap of woodchuck skin, complain of hard times because he could not afford to buy him a crown! It is possible to invent a house still more convenient and luxurious than we have, which yet all would admit that man could not afford to pay for. Shall we always study to obtain more of these things, and not sometimes to be content with less? Shall the respectable citizen thus gravely teach, by precept and example, the necessity of the young man's providing a certain number of superfluous glow-shoes,[76] and umbrellas, and empty guest chambers for empty guests, before he dies? Why should not our furniture be as simple as the Arab's or the Indian's? When I think of the benefactors of the race, whom we have apotheosized as messengers from heaven, bearers of divine gifts to man, I do not see in my mind any retinue at their heels, any car-load of fashionable furniture. Or what if I were to allow—would it not be a singular allowance?—that our furniture should be more complex than the Arab's, in proportion as we are morally and intellectually his superiors! At present our houses are cluttered and defiled with it, and a good housewife would sweep out the greater part into the dust hole, and not leave her morning's work undone. Morning work! By the blushes of Aurora and the music of Memnon,[77] what should be man's *morning work* in this world? I had three pieces of limestone on my desk, but I was terrified to find that they required to be dusted daily, when the furniture of my mind was all undusted still, and I threw them out the window in disgust. How, then, could I have a furnished house? I

---

[74] The potato famine in the 1840s brought widespread hardship to Ireland, which appears as a "white" spot on the map because some early mapmakers used white to indicate settled lands and dark colors to signify unexplored terrain.

[75] Of slave breeders in the South.　　[76] Galoshes.

[77] The Roman goddess of the dawn, and the music of the king of ancient Egypt, whose statue supposedly sounded musical vibrations when struck by the first rays of the sun.

would rather sit in the open air, for no dust gathers on the grass, unless where man has broken ground.

It is the luxurious and dissipated who set the fashions which the herd so diligently follow. The traveller who stops at the best houses, so called, soon discovers this, for the publicans,[78] presume him to be a Sardanapalus,[79] and if he resigned himself to their tender mercies he would soon be completely emasculated. I think that in the railroad car we are inclined to spend more on luxury than on safety and convenience, and it threatens without attaining these to become no better than a modern drawing room, with its divans, and ottomans, and sunshades, and a hundred other oriental things, which we are taking west with us, invented for the ladies of the harem and the effeminate natives of the Celestial Empire, which Jonathan[80] should be ashamed to know the names of. I would rather sit on a pumpkin and have it all to myself, than be crowded on a velvet cushion. I would rather ride on earth in an ox cart with a free circulation, than go to heaven in the fancy car of an excursion train and breathe a *malaria* all the way.[81]

The very simplicity and nakedness of man's life in the primitive ages imply this advantage at least, that they left him still but a sojourner in nature. When he was refreshed with food and sleep he contemplated his journey again. He dwelt, as it were, in a tent in this world, and was either threading the valleys, or crossing the plains, or climbing the mountain tops. But lo! men have become the tools of their tools. The man who independently plucked the fruits when he was hungry is become a farmer; and he who stood under a tree for shelter, a housekeeper. We now no longer camp as for a night, but have settled down on earth and forgotten heaven. We have adopted Christianity merely as an improved method of *agri-culture*. We have built for this world a family mansion, and for the next a family tomb. The best works of art are the expression of man's struggle to free himself from this condition, but the effect of our art is merely to make this low state comfortable and that higher state to be forgotten. There is actually no place in this village for a work of *fine* art, if any had come down to us, to stand, for our lives, our houses and streets, furnish no proper pedestal for it. There is not a nail to hang a picture on, nor a shelf to receive the bust of a hero or a saint. When I consider how our houses are built and paid for, or not paid for, and their internal economy managed and sustained, I wonder that the floor does not give way under the visitor while he is admiring the gewgaws upon the mantel-piece, and let him through into the cellar, to some solid and honest though earthy foundation. I cannot but perceive that this so called rich and refined life is a thing jumped at, and I do not get on in the enjoyment of the *fine* arts which adorn it, my attention being wholly occupied with the jump; for I remember that the greatest genuine leap, due to human muscles alone, on record, is that of certain wandering Arabs, who are said to have cleared twenty-five feet on level ground. Without factitious[82] support, man is sure to come to earth again beyond that distance. The first question which I am tempted to put to the proprietor of such great impropriety is, Who bolsters you? Are you one of the ninety-seven who fail? or of the three who succeed? Answer me these questions, and then perhaps I may look at your bawbles and find

[78] Innkeepers.   [79] A decadent and self-indulgent ninth-century B.C. ruler of Assyria.

[80] A nickname for a Yankee or an American.

[81] An illusion to Nathaniel Hawthorne's satire on transcendentalism and liberal religion, "The Celestial Railroad" (1846); "malaria" literally means "bad air."

[82] Artificial.

them ornamental. The cart before the horse is neither beautiful nor useful. Before we can adorn our houses with beautiful objects the walls must be stripped, and our lives must be stripped, and beautiful housekeeping and beautiful living be laid for a foundation: now, a taste for the beautiful is most cultivated out of doors, where there is no house and no housekeeper.

Old Johnson,[83] in his "Wonder-Working Providence," speaking of the first settlers of this town, with whom he was contemporary, tells us that "they burrow themselves in the earth for their first shelter under some hillside, and, casting the soil aloft upon timber, they make a smoky fire against the earth, at the highest side." They did not "provide them houses," says he, "till the earth, by the Lord's blessing, brought forth bread to feed them," and the first year's crop was so light that "they were forced to cut their bread very thin for a long season." The secretary of the Province of New Netherland,[84] writing in Dutch, in 1650, for the information of those who wished to take up land there, states more particularly, that "those in New Netherland, and especially in New England, who have no means to build farm houses at first according to their wishes, dig a square pit in the ground, cellar fashion, six or seven feet deep, as long and as broad as they think proper, case the earth inside with wood all round the wall, and line the wood with the bark of trees or something else to prevent the caving in of the earth; floor this cellar with plank, and wainscot it overhead for a ceiling, raise a roof of spars clear up, and cover the spars with bark or green sods, so that they can live dry and warm in these houses with their entire families for two, three, and four years, it being understood that partitions are run through those cellars which are adapted to the size of the family. The wealthy and principal men in New England, in the beginning of the colonies, commenced their first dwelling houses in this fashion for two reasons; firstly, in order not to waste time in building, and not to want food the next season; secondly, in order not to discourage poor laboring people whom they brought over in numbers from Fatherland. In the course of three or four years, when the country became adapted to agriculture, they built themselves handsome houses, spending on them several thousands."

In this course which our ancestors took there was a show of prudence at least, as if their principle were to satisfy the more pressing wants first. But are the more pressing wants satisfied now? When I think of acquiring for myself one of our luxurious dwellings, I am deterred, for, so to speak, the country is not yet adapted to *human* culture, and we are still forced to cut our *spiritual* bread far thinner than our forefathers did their wheaten. Not that all architectural ornament is to be neglected even in the rudest periods; but let our houses first be lined with beauty, where they come in contact with our lives, like the tenement of the shellfish, and not overlaid with it. But, alas! I have been inside one or two of them, and know what they are lined with.

Though we are not so degenerate but that we might possibly live in a cave or a wigwam or wear skins to-day, it certainly is better to accept the advantages, though so dearly bought, which the invention and industry of mankind offer. In such a neighborhood as this, boards and shingles, lime and bricks, are cheaper and more easily obtained than suitable caves, or whole logs, or bark in sufficient quan-

---

[83] Edward Johnson (1598–1672), author of *Wonder-Working Providence of Sion's Saviour In New England* (1654), a history of New England settlement from 1628 to 1652.

[84] Later, the colony and then the state of New York. The Dutch provincial secretary, Cornelis van Tienhoven, is quoted from *Documentary History of the State of New-York* (1851), edited by Edmund Bailey O'Callaghan.

tities, or even well-tempered clay of flat stones. I speak understandingly on this subject, for I have made myself acquainted with it both theoretically and practically. With a little more wit we might use these materials so as to become richer than the richest now are, and make our civilization a blessing. The civilized man is a more experienced and wiser savage. But to make haste to my own experiment.

Near the end of March, 1845, I borrowed an axe and went down to the woods by Walden Pond, nearest to where I intended to build my house, and began to cut down some tall arrowy white pines, still in their youth, for timber. It is difficult to begin without borrowing, but perhaps it is the most generous course thus to permit your fellow-men to have an interest in your enterprise. The owner of the axe, as he released his hold on it, said that it was the apple of his eye; but I returned it sharper than I received it. It was a pleasant hillside where I worked, covered with pine woods, through which I looked out on the pond, and a small open field in the woods where pines and hickories were springing up. The ice in the pond was not yet dissolved, though there were some open spaces, and it was all dark colored and saturated with water. There were some slight flurries of snow during the days that I worked there; but for the most part when I came out on to the railroad, on my way home, its yellow sand heap stretched away gleaming in the hazy atmosphere, and the rails shone in the spring sun, and I heard the lark and pewee and other birds already come to commence another year with us. They were pleasant spring days, in which the winter of man's discontent[85] was thawing as well as the earth, and the life that had lain torpid began to stretch itself. One day, when my axe had come off,[86] and I had cut a green hickory for a wedge, driving it with a stone, and had placed the whole to soak in a pond hole in order to swell the wood, I saw a striped snake run into the water, and he lay on the bottom, apparently without inconvenience, as long as I staid there, or more than a quarter of an hour; perhaps because he had not yet fairly come out of the torpid state. It appeared to me that for a like reason men remain in their present low and primitive condition; but if they should feel the influence of the spring of springs arousing them, they would of necessity rise to a higher and more ethereal life. I had previously seen the snakes in frosty mornings in my path with portions of their bodies still numb and inflexible, waiting for the sun to thaw them. On the 1st of April it rained and melted the ice, and in the early part of the day, which was very foggy, I heard a stray goose groping about over the pond and cackling as if lost, or like the spirit of the fog.

So I went on for some days cutting and hewing thimber, and also studs and rafters, all with my narrow axe, not having many communicable or scholar-like thoughts, singing to myself,—

> Men say they know many things;
> Bu lo! they have taken wings,—
> The arts and sciences,
> And a thousand appliances;
> The wind that blows
> Is all that any body knows.[87]

[85] Adapted from the opening line of Shakespeare's *Richard III*.
[86] When the axe-head had come off the handle.
[87] Throughout *Walden*, the poetry not appearing in quotation marks is Thoreau's.

I hewed the main timbers six inches square, most of the studs on two sides only, and the rafters and floor timbers on one side, leaving the rest of the bark on, so that they were just as straight and much stronger than sawed ones. Each stick was carefully mortised or tenoned by its stump, for I had borrowed other tools by this time. My days in the woods were not very long ones; yet I usually carried my dinner of bread and butter, and read the newspaper in which it was wrapped, at noon, sitting amid the green pine boughs which I had cut off, and to my bread was imparted some of their fragrance, for my hands were covered with a thick coat of pitch. Before I had done I was more the friend than the foe of the pine tree, though I had cut down some of them, having become better acquainted with it. Sometimes a rambler in the wood was attracted by the sound of my axe, and we chatted pleasantly over the chips which I had made.

By the middle of April, for I made no haste in my work, but rather made the most of it, my house was framed and ready for the raising. I had already bought the shanty of James Collins, an Irishman who worked on the Fitchburg Railroad, for boards. James Collins' shanty was considered an uncommonly fine one. When I called to see it he was not at home. I walked about the outside, at first unobserved from within, the window was so deep and high. It was of small dimensions, with a peaked cottage roof, and not much else to be seen, the dirt being raised five feet all around as if it were a compost heap. The roof was the soundest part, though a good deal warped and made brittle by the sun. Door-sill there was none, but a perennial passage for the hens under the board. Mrs. C. came to the door and asked me to view it from the inside. The hens were driven in by my approach. It was dark, and had a dirt floor for the most part, dank, clammy, and aguish, only here a board and there a board which would not bear removal. She lighted a lamp to show me the inside of the roof and the walls, and also that the board floor extended under the bed, warning me not to step into the cellar, a sort of dust hole two feet deep. In her own words, they were "good boards overhead, good boards all around, and a good window,"—of two whole squares originally, only the cat had passed out that way lately. There was a stove, a bed, and a place to sit, an infant in the house where it was born, a silk parasol, gilt-framed looking-glass, and a patent new coffee mill nailed to an oak sapling, all told. The bargain was soon concluded, for James had in the mean while returned. I to pay four dollars and twenty-five cents to-night, he to vacate at five to-morrow morning, selling to nobody else meanwhile: I to take possession at six. It were well, he said, to be there early, and anticipate certain indistinct but wholly unjust claims on the score of ground rent and fuel. This he assured me was the only encumbrance. At six I passed him and his family on the road. One large bundle held their all,—bed, coffee-mill, looking-glass, hens —all but the cat, she took to the woods and became a wild cat, and, as I learned afterward, trod in a trap set for woodchucks, and so became a dead cat at last.

I took down this dwelling the same morning, drawing the nails, and removed it to the pond side by small cartloads, spreading the boards on the grass there to bleach and warp back again in the sun. One early thrush gave me a note or two as I drove along the woodland path. I was informed treacherously by a young Patrick[88] that neighbor Seeley, an Irishman, in the intervals of the carting, transferred the still tolerable, straight, and drivable nails, staples, and spikes to his pocket,

---

[88] Irishman; Thoreau uses "treacherously" (in mock-seriousness) because one Irishman is informing on another.

and then stood when I came back to pass the time of day, and look freshly up, unconcerned, with spring thoughts, at the devastation; there being a dearth of work, as he said. He was there to represent spectatordom, and help make this seemingly insignificant event one with the removal of the gods of Troy.[89]

I dug my cellar in the side of a hill sloping to the south, where a woodchuck had formerly dug his burrow, down through sumach and blackberry roots, and the lowest stain of vegetation, six feet square by seven deep, to a fine sand where potatoes would not freeze in any winter. The sides were left shelving, and not stoned; but the sun having never shone on them, the sand still keeps its place. It was but two hours' work. I took particular pleasure in this breaking of ground, for in almost all latitudes men dig into the earth for an equable temperature. Under the most splendid house in the city is still to be found the cellar where they store their roots as of old, and long after the superstructure has disappeared posterity remark its dent in the earth. The house is still but a sort of porch at the entrance of a burrow.

At length, in the beginning of May, with the help of some of my acquaintances, rather to improve so good an occasion for neighborliness than for any necessity, I set up the frame of my house. No man was ever more honored in the character of his raisers[90] than I. They are destined, I trust, to assist at the raising of loftier structures one day. I began to occupy my house on the 4th of July, as soon as it was boarded and roofed, for the boards were carefully feather-edged and lapped,[91] so that it was perfectly impervious to rain; but before boarding I laid the foundation of a chimney at one end, bringing two cartloads of stones up the hill from the pond in my arms. I built the chimney after my hoeing in the fall, before a fire became necessary for warmth, doing my cooking in the mean while out of doors on the ground, early in the morning: which mode I still think is in some respects more convenient and agreeable than the usual one. When it stormed before my bread was baked, I fixed a few boards over the fire, and sat under them to watch my loaf, and passed some pleasant hours in that way. In those days, when my hands were much employed, I read but little, but the least scraps of paper which lay on the ground, my holder, or tablecloth, afforded me as much entertainment, in fact answered the same purpose as the Iliad.[92]

It would be worth the while to build still more deliberately than I did, considering, for instance, what foundation a door, a window, a cellar, a garret, have in the nature of man, and perchance never raising any superstructure until we found a better reason for it than our temporal necessities even. There is some of the same fitness in a man's building his own house that there is in a bird's building its own nest. Who knows but if men constructed their dwellings with their own hands, and provided food the themselves and families simply and honestly enough, the poetic faculty would be universally developed, as birds universally sing when they are so engaged? But alas! we do like cowbirds and cuckoos, which lay their eggs in nests

---

[89] According to Greek myth, the city of Troy could not be conquered so long as the statue of the goddess Pallas Athena remained in the temple; the theft of the statue by the Greeks during the Trojan War thus made their conquest possible.

[90] Among the acquaintances who helped Thoreau "raise" the frame of his small house were Ralph Waldo Emerson, the educator and reformer Bronson Alcott (1799–1888), the poet William Ellery Channing (1818–1901), and the Concord farmer Edward Hosmer and his three sons.

[91] Cut, nailed, and overlapped to shed rain.

[92] Homer's epic poem about the Trojan War and the Greek victory at Troy.

which other birds have built, and cheer no traveller with their chattering and un-musical notes. Shall we forever resign the pleasure of construction to the carpenter? What does architecture amount to in the experience of the mass of men? I never in all my walks came across a man engaged in so simple and natural an occupation as building his house. We belong to the community. It is not the tailor alone who is the ninth part of a man;[93] it is as much the preacher, and the merchant, and the farmer. Where is this division of labor to end? and what object does it finally serve? No doubt another *may* also think for me; but it is not therefore desirable that he should do so to the exclusion of my thinking for myself.

True, there are architects so called in this country, and I have heard of one[94] at least possessed with the idea of making architectural ornaments have a core of truth, a necessity, and hence a beauty, as if it were a revelation to him. All very well perhaps from his point of view, but only a little better than the common dilettantism. A sentimental reformer in architecture, he began at the cornice, not at the foundation. It was only how to put a core of truth within the ornaments, that every sugar plum in fact might have an almond or caraway seed in it,—though I hold that almonds are most wholesome without the sugar,—and not how the inhabitant, the indweller, might build truly within and without, and let the ornaments take care of themselves. What reasonable man ever supposed that ornaments were something outward and in the skin merely,—that the tortoise got his spotted shell, or the shellfish its mother-o'-pearl tints, by such a contract as the inhabitants of Broadway their Trinity Church?[95] But a man has no more to do with the style of architecture of his house than a tortoise with that of its shell: nor need the soldier be so idle as to try to paint the precise *color* of his virtue on his standard. The enemy will find it out. He may turn pale when the trial comes. This man seemed to me to lean over the cornice and timidly whisper his half truth to the rude occupants who really knew it better than he. What of architectural beauty I now see, I know has gradually grown from within outward, out of the necessities and character of the indweller, who is the only builder,—out of some unconscious truthfulness, and nobleness, without ever a thought for the appearance; and whatever additional beauty of this kind is destined to be produced will be preceded by a like unconscious beauty of life. The most interesting dwellings in this country, as the painter knows, are the most unpretending, humble log huts and cottages of the poor commonly; it is the life of the inhabitants whose shells they are, and not any peculiarity in their surfaces merely, which makes them *picturesque;* and equally interesting will be the citizen's suburban box, when his life shall be as simple and as agreeable to the imagination, and there is as little straining after effect in the style of his dwelling. A great proportion of architectural ornaments are literally hollow, and a September gale would strip them off, like borrowed plumes, without injury to the substantials. They can do without *architecture* who have no olives nor wines in the cellar.[96] What if an equal ado were made about the ornaments of style in literature, and the architects of our bibles spent as much time about their cornices as the architects of our churches do? So are made the *belles-lettres* and the *beaux-arts* and their professors.[97] Much it concerns a man, for-

---

[93] A play on the proverb "Nine tailors make a man."

[94] According to Thoreau's *Journal* (January 11, 1852), this "architect" was the sculptor Horatio Greenough (1805–1852); Thoreau knew Greenough's ideas imperfectly and indirectly.

[95] A New York City church, constructed in an ornamented, Gothic style (1839–1846).

[96] Who own nothing valuable: olives and wine were expensive imports then.

[97] "Fine literature," "fine arts" (French), and those who make a living talking about them.

sooth, how a few sticks are slanted over him or under him, and what colors are daubed upon his box. It would signify somewhat, if, in any earnest sense, *he* slanted them and daubed it; but the spirit having departed out of the tenant, it is of a piece with constructing his own coffin,—the architecture of the grave, and "carpenter" is but another name for "coffin-maker." One man says, in his despair or indifference to life, take up a handful of the earth at your feet, and paint your house that color. Is he thinking of his last and narrow house?[98] Toss up a copper[99] for it as well. What an abundance of leisure he must have! Why do you take up a handful of dirt? Better paint your house your own complexion; let it turn pale or blush for you. An enterprise to improve the style of cottage architecture! When you have got my ornaments ready I will wear them.

Before winter I built a chimney, and shingled the sides of my house, which were already impervious to rain, with imperfect and sappy shingles made of the first slice of the log, whose edges I was obliged to straighten with a plane.

I have thus a tight shingled and plastered house, ten feet wide by fifteen long, and eight-feet posts, with a garret and a closet, a large window on each side, two trap doors, one door at the end, and a brick fireplace opposite. The exact cost of my house, paying the usual price for such materials as I used, but not counting the work, all of which was done by myself, was as follows; and I give the details because very few are able to tell exactly what their houses cost, and fewer still, if any, the separate cost of the various materials which compose them:—

Boards,	$8 03½,	mostly shanty boards.
Refuse shingles for roof and sides,	4 00	
Laths,	1 25	
Two second-hand windows with glass,	2 43	
One thousand old brick,	4 00	
Two casks of lime,	2 40	That was high.
Hair,	0 31	More than I needed
Mantle-tree iron,	0 15	
Nails,	3 90	
Hinges and screws,	0 14	
Latch,	0 10	
Chalk,	0 01	
Transportation,	1 40	{ I carried a good part on my back.
In all,	$28 12½	

These are all the materials excepting the timber stones and sand, which I claimed by squatter's right. I have also a small wood-shed adjoining, made chiefly of the stuff which was left after building the house.

I intend to build me a house which will surpass any on the main street in Concord in grandeur and luxury, as soon as it pleases me as much and will cost me no more than my present one.

[98] The grave or coffin.
[99] A coin with which to pay Charon, the ferryman of the dead crossing the river Styx of Greek myth.

I thus found that the student who wishes for a shelter can obtain one for a lifetime at an expense not greater than the rent which he now pays annually. If I seem to boast more than is becoming, my excuse is that I brag for humanity rather than for myself; and my shortcomings and inconsistencies do not affect the truth of my statement. Notwithstanding much cant and hypocrisy,—chaff which I find it difficult to separate from my wheat, but for which I am as sorry as any man,—I will breathe freely and stretch myself in this respect, it is such a relief to both the moral and physical system; and I am resolved that I will not through humility become the devil's attorney. I will endeavor to speak a good word for the truth. At Cambridge College[100] the mere rent of a student's room, which is only a little larger than my own, is thirty dollars each year, though the corporation had the advantage of building thirty-two side by side and under one roof, and the occupant suffers the inconvenience of many and noisy neighbors, and perhaps a residence in the fourth story. I cannot but think that if we had more true wisdom in these respects, not only less education would be needed, because, forsooth, more would already have been acquired, but the pecuniary expense of getting an education would in a great measure vanish. Those conveniences which the student requires at Cambridge or elsewhere cost him or somebody else ten times as great a sacrifice of life as they would with proper management on both sides. Those things for which the most money is demanded are never the things which the student most wants. Tuition, for instance, is an important item in the term bill, while for the far more valuable education which he gets by associating with the most cultivated of his contemporaries no charge is made. The mode of founding a college is, commonly, to get up a subscription of dollars and cents, and then following blindly the principles of a division of labor to its extreme, a principle which should never be followed but with circumspection,—to call in a contractor who makes this a subject of speculation, and he employs Irishmen or other operatives actually to lay the foundations, while the students that are to be are said to be fitting themselves for it; and for these oversights successive generations have to pay. I think that it would be *better than this,* for the students, or those who desire to be benefited by it, even to lay the foundation themselves. The student who secures his coveted leisure and retirement by systematically shirking any labor necessary to man obtains but an ignoble and unprofitable leisure, defrauding himself of the experience which alone can make leisure fruitful. "But," says one, "you do not mean that the students should go to work with their hands instead of their heads?" I do not mean that exactly, but I mean something which he might think a good deal like that; I mean that they should not *play* life, or *study* it merely, while the community supports them at this expensive game, but earnestly *live* it from beginning to end. How could youths better learn to live than by at once trying the experiment of living? Methinks that would exercise their minds as much as mathematics. If I wished a boy to know something about the arts and sciences, for instance, I would not pursue the common course, which is merely to send him into the neighborhood of some professor, where any thing is professed and practised but the art of life;—to survey the world through a telescope or a microscope, and never with his natural eye; to study chemistry, and not learn how his bread is made, or mechanics, and not learn how it is earned; to discover new satellites to Neptune, and not detect the motes in his eyes, or to what vagabond he is a satellite himself; or to be devoured by the monsters that swarm all around him, while contemplating the

---

[100] Harvard College in Cambridge, Massachusetts; Thoreau graduated there in 1837.

monsters in a drop of vinegar. Which would have advanced the most at the end of a month,—the boy who made his own jack-knife from the ore which he had dug and smelted, reading as much as would be necessary for this,—or the boy who had attended the lectures on metallurgy at the Institute in the mean while, and had received a Rodgers' penknife[101] from his father? Which would be most likely to cut his fingers?—To my astonishment I was informed on leaving college that I had studied navigation!—why, if I had taken one turn down the harbor I should have known more about it. Even the *poor* student studies and is taught only *political* economy, while that economy of living which is synonymous with philosophy is not even sincerely professed in our colleges. The consequence is, that while he is reading Adam Smith, Ricardo, and Say,[102] he runs his father in debt irretrievably.

As with our colleges, so with a hundred "modern improvements"; there is an illusion about them; there is not always a positive advance. The devil goes on exacting compound interest to the last for his early share and numerous succeeding investments in them. Our inventions are wont to be pretty toys, which distract our attention from serious things. They are but improved means to an unimproved end, an end which it was already but too easy to arrive at; as railroads lead to Boston or New York. We are in great haste to construct a magnetic telegraph from Maine to Texas; but Maine and Texas, it may be, have nothing important to communicate. Either is in such a predicament as the man who was earnest to be introduced to a distinguished deaf woman, but when he was presented, and one end of her ear trumpet was put into his hand, had nothing to say. As if the main object were to talk fast and not to talk sensibly. We are eager to tunnel under the Atlantic and bring the old world some weeks nearer to the new; but perchance the first news that will leak through into the broad, flapping American ear will be that the Princess Adelaide[103] has the whooping cough. After all, the man whose horse trots a mile in a minute does not carry the most important message; he is not an evangelist, nor does he come round eating locusts and wild honey.[104] I doubt if Flying Childers[105] ever carried a peck of corn to mill.

One says to me, "I wonder that you do not lay up money; you love to travel; you might take the cars and go to Fitchburg[106] to-day and see the country." But I am wiser than that. I have learned that the swiftest traveller is he that goes afoot. I say to my friend, Suppose we try who will get there first. The distance is thirty miles; the fare ninety cents. That is almost a day's wages. I remember when wages were sixty cents a day for laborers on this very road. Well, I start now on foot, and get there before night; I have travelled at that rate by the week together. You will in the mean while have earned your fare, and arrive there some time to-morrow, or possibly this evening, if you are lucky enough to get a job in season. Instead of going to Fitchburg, you will be working here the greater part of the

---

[101] A knife produced by the English cutlery firm of Joseph Rodgers and Sons.

[102] Classical economists: the Scottish Adam Smith (1723–1790), the English David Ricardo (1772–1823), and the French Jean Baptiste Say (1767–1832).

[103] Princess Adelaide of Orleans (1771–1847), sister of Louis-Philippe, king of France from 1830 to 1848.

[104] In Matthew 3:4 John the Baptist subsisted on locusts and wild honey while he lived in the wilderness.

[105] A famous English racehorse.

[106] Fitchburg (near Concord), Massachusetts, a small town at the end of the railroad line that ran by Walden Pond.

day. And so, if the railroad reached round the world, I think that I should keep ahead of you; and as for seeing the country and getting experience of that kind, I should have to cut your acquaintance altogether.

Such is the universal law, which no man can ever outwit, and with regard to the railroad even we may say it is as broad as it is long. To make a railroad round the world available to all mankind is equivalent to grading the whole surface of the planet. Men have an indistinct notion that if they keep up this activity of joint stocks and spades[107] long enough all will at length ride somewhere, in next to no time, and for nothing; but though a crowd rushes to the depot, and the conductor shouts "All aboard!" when the smoke is blown away and the vapor condensed, it will be perceived that a few are riding, but the rest are run over,—and it will be called, and will be "A melancholy accident." No doubt they can ride at last who shall have earned their fare, that is, if they survive so long, but they will probably have lost their elasticity and desire to travel by that time. This spending of the best part of one's life earning money in order to enjoy a questionable liberty, during the least valuable part of it, reminds me of the Englishman who went to India to make a fortune first, in order that he might return to England and live the life of a poet. He should have gone up garret at once. "What!" exclaim a million Irishmen starting up from all the shanties in the land, "is not this railroad which we have built a good thing?" Yes, I answer, *comparatively* good, that is, you might have done worse; but I wish, as you are brothers of mine, that you could have spent your time better than digging in this dirt.

Before I finished my house, wishing to earn ten or twelve dollars by some honest and agreeable method, in order to meet my unusual expenses, I planted about two acres and a half of light and sandy soil near it chiefly with beans, but also a small part with potatoes, corn, peas, and turnips. The whole lot contains eleven acres, mostly growing up to pines and hickories, and was sold the preceding season for eight dollars and eight cents an acre. One farmer said that it was "good for nothing but to raise cheeping squirrels on." I put no manure on this land, not being the owner, but merely a squatter, and not expecting to cultivate so much again, and I did not quite hoe it all once. I got out several cords of stumps in ploughing, which supplied me with fuel for a long time, and left small circles of virgin mould, easily distinguishable through the summer by the greater luxuriance of the beans there. The dead and for the most part unmerchantable wood behind my house, and the driftwood from the pond, have supplied the remainder of my fuel. I was obliged to hire a team and a man for the ploughing, though I held the plough myself. My farm outgoes for the first season were, for implements, seeds, work, etc., $14 72 1/2. The seed corn was given me. This never costs any thing to speak of, unless you plant more than enough. I got twelve bushels of beans, and eighteen bushels of potatoes, beside some peas and sweet corn. The yellow corn and turnips were too late to come to any thing. My whole income from the farm was

	$23 44.
Deducting the outgoes, ...	14 72½
there are left, ...	.$ 8 71½.

---

[107] Organizing corporations and building railroads.

beside produce consumed and on hand at the time this estimate was made of the value of $4 50,—the amount on hand much more than balancing a little grass which I did not raise. All things considered, that is, considering the importance of a man's soul and of to-day, notwithstanding the short time occupied by my experiment, nay, partly even because of its transient character, I believe that that was doing better than any farmer in Concord did that year.

The next year I did better still, for I spaded up all the land which I required, about a third of an acre, and I learned from the experience of both years, not being in the least awed by many celebrated works on husbandry, Arthur Young,[108] among the rest, that if one would live simply and eat only the crop which he raised, and raise no more than he ate, and not exchange it for an insufficient quantity of more luxurious and expensive things, he would need to cultivate only a few rods of ground, and that it would be cheaper to spade up that than to use oxen to plough it, and to select a fresh spot from time to time than to manure the old, and he could do all his necessary farm work as it were with his left hand at odd hours in the summer; and thus he would not be tied to an ox, or horse, or cow, or pig, as at present. I desire to speak impartially on this point, and as one not interested in the success or failure of the present economical and social arrangements. I was more independent than any farmer in Concord, for I was not anchored to a house or farm, but could follow the bent of my genius, which is a very crooked one, every moment. Beside being better off than they already, if my house had been burned or my crops had failed, I should have been nearly as well off as before.

I am wont to think that men are not so much the keepers of herds as herds are the keepers of men, the former are so much the freer. Men and oxen exchange work; but if we consider necessary work only, the oxen will be seen to have greatly the advantage, their farm is so much the larger. Man does some of his part of the exchange work in his six weeks of haying, and it is no boy's play. Certainly no nation that lived simply in all respects, that is, no nation of philosophers, would commit so great a blunder as to use the labor of animals. True, there never was and is not likely soon to be a nation of philosophers, nor am I certain it is desirable that there should be. However, *I* should never have broken a horse or bull and taken him to board for any work he might do for me, for fear I should become a horse-man or a herds-man merely; and if society seems to be the gainer by so doing, are we certain that what is one man's gain is not another's loss, and that the stable-boy has equal cause with his master to be satisfied? Granted that some public works would not have been constructed without this aid, and let man share the glory of such with the ox and horse; does it follow that he could not have accomplished works yet more worthy of himself in that case? When men begin to do, not merely unnecessary or artistic, but luxurious and idle work, with their assistance, it is inevitable that a few do all the exchange work with the oxen, or, in other words, become the slaves of the strongest. Man thus not only works for the animal within him, but, for a symbol of this, he works for the animal without him. Though we have many substantial houses of brick or stone, the prosperity of the farmer is still measured by the degree to which the barn overshadows the house. This town is said to have the largest houses for oxen cows and horses hereabouts, and it is not behindhand in its public buildings; but there are very few halls for free worship or free speech in this county. It should not be by their architecture, but

---

[108] Young (1741–1820) was an English writer of practical books on farming.

why not even by their power of abstract thought, that nations should seek to commemorate themselves? How much more admirable the Bhagvat-Geeta[109] than all the ruins of the East! Towers and temples are the luxury of princes. A simple and independent mind does not toil at the bidding of any prince. Genius is not a retainer to any emperor, nor is its material silver, or gold, or marble, except to a trifling extent. To what end, pray, is so much stone hammered? In Arcadia,[110] when I was there, I did not see any hammering stone. Nations are possessed with an insane ambition to perpetuate the memory of themselves by the amount of hammered stone they leave. What if equal pains were taken to smooth and polish their manners? One piece of good sense would be more memorable than a monument as high as the moon. I love better to see stones in place. The grandeur of Thebes[111] was a vulgar grandeur. More sensible is a rod[112] of stone wall that bounds an honest man's field than a hundred-gated Thebes that has wandered farther from the true end of life. The religion and civilization which are barbaric and heathenish build splendid temples; but what you might call Christianity does not. Most of the stone a nation hammers goes toward its tomb only. It buries itself alive. As for the Pyramids, there is nothing to wonder at in them so much as the fact that so many men could be found degraded enough to spend their lives constructing a tomb for some ambitious booby, whom it would have been wiser and manlier to have drowned in the Nile, and then given his body to the dogs. I might possibly invent some excuse for them and him, but I have no time for it. As for the religion and love of art of the builders, it is much the same all the world over, whether the building be an Egyptian temple or the United States Bank. It costs more than it comes to. The mainspring is vanity, assisted by a love of garlic and bread and butter. Mr. Balcom, a promising young architect, designs it on the back of his Vitruvius,[113] with hard pencil and ruler, and the job is let out to Dobson & Sons, stonecutters. When the thirty centuries begin to look down on it, mankind begin to look up at it. As for your high towers and monuments, there was a crazy fellow once in this town who undertook to dig through to China, and he got so far that, as he said, he heard the Chinese pots and kettles rattle; but I think that I shall not go out of my way to admire the hole which he made. Many are concerned about the monuments of the West and the East,—to know who built them. For my part, I should like to know who in those days did not build them,—who were above such trifling. But to proceed with my statistics.

By surveying, carpentry, and day-labor of various other kinds in the village in the mean while, for I have as many trades as fingers, I had earned $13 34. The expense of food for eight months, namely, from July 4th to March 1st, the time when these estimates were made, though I lived there more than two years,—not counting potatoes, a little green corn, and some peas, which I had raised, nor considering the value of what was on hand at the last date, was

Rice, ... $1 73½	
Molasses, ... 1 73	Cheapest form of the saccharine.

---

[109] The *Bhagavad-Gītā*, a sacred Hindu text.

[110] According to Greek myth, a place of pastoral simplicity and happiness; Thoreau imagined going there.

[111] A major city in ancient Egypt; Homer describes it in the *Iliad* as "hundred-gated."

[112] A measurement equivalent to sixteen and a half feet.

[113] Marcus Vitruvius Pollio (1st century B.C.), a Roman architect; Thoreau makes up the other names in this sentence to illustrate his point about vanity.

Rye meal, ...	1	04¾
Indian meal, . . .	0	99¾
Pork, ...	0	22
Flour, ...	0	88
Sugar, ...	0	80
Lard, ...	0	65
Apples, ...	0	25
Dried apple, . . .	0	22
Sweet potatoes, . .	0	10
One pumpkin, . .	0	6
One watermelon, .	0	2
Salt, ...	0	3

Cheaper than rye.

Costs more than Indian meal, both money and trouble.

All experiments which failed.

Yes, I did eat $8 74, all told; but I should not thus unblushingly publish my guilt, if I did not know that most of my readers were equally guilty with myself, and that their deeds would look no better in print. The next year I sometimes caught a mess of fish for my dinner, and once I went so far as to slaughter a woodchuck which ravaged my bean-field,—effect his transmigration, as a Tarter[114] would say,—and devour him, partly for experiment's sake; but though it afforded me a momentary enjoyment, notwithstanding a musky flavor, I saw that the longest use would not make that a good practice, however it might seem to have your woodchucks ready dressed by the village butcher.

Clothing and some incidental expenses within the same dates, though little can be inferred from this item, amounted to

$8 40¾

Oil and some household utensils, ... 2 00

So that all the pecuniary outgoes, excepting for washing and mending, which for the most part were done out of the house, and their bills have not yet been received,—and these are all and more than all the ways by which money necessarily goes out in this part of the world,—were

House, ...	$28 12½
Farm one year, ...	14 72½
Food eight months, ...	8 74
Clothing, etc., eight months, ...	8 40¾
Oil, etc., eight months, ...	2 00
In all, ...	$61 99¾

I address myself now to those of my readers who have a living to get. And to meet this I have for farm produce sold

	$23 44
Earned by day-labor, ...	13 34
In all, ...	$36 78,

---

[114] A tribesman of Russian Asia who believed souls pass into other bodies (transmigrate) after death.

which subtracted from the sum of the outgoes leaves a balance of $25 21³⁄4 on the
one side,—this being very nearly the means with which I started, and the measure
of expenses to be incurred,—and on the other, beside the leisure and independence and health thus secured, a comfortable house for me as long as I choose to
occupy it.

These statistics, however accidental and therefore uninstructive they may appear, as they have a certain completeness, have a certain value also. Nothing was
given me of which I have not rendered some account. It appears from the above
estimate, that my food alone cost me in money about twenty-seven cents a week.
It was, for nearly two years after this, rye and Indian meal without yeast, potatoes,
rice, a very little salt pork, molasses, and salt, and my drink water. It was fit that I
should live on rice, mainly, who loved so well the philosophy of India. To meet
the objections of some inveterate cavillers, I may as well state, that if I dined out
occasionally, as I always had done, and I trust shall have opportunities to do
again, it was frequently to the detriment of my domestic arrangements. But the
dining out, being, as I have stated, a constant element, does not in the least affect
a comparative statement like this.

I learned from my two years' experience that it would cost incredibly little
trouble to obtain one's necessary food, even in this latitude; that a man may use as
simple a diet as the animals, and yet retain health and strength. I have made a
satisfactory dinner, satisfactory on several accounts, simply off a dish of purslane
(*Portulaca oleracea*)[115] which I gathered in my cornfield, boiled and salted. I give
the Latin on account of the savoriness of the trivial name. And pray what more
can a reasonable man desire, in peaceful times, in ordinary noons, than a sufficient number of ears of green sweet-corn boiled, with the addition of salt? Even
the little variety which I used was a yielding to the demands of appetite, and not of
health. Yet men have come to such a pass that they frequently starve, not for want
of necessaries, but for want of luxuries; and I know a good woman who thinks that
her son lost his life because he took to drinking water only.

The reader will perceive that I am treating the subject rather from an economic
than a dietetic point of view, and he will not venture to put my abstemiousness to
the test unless he has a well-stocked larder.

Bread I at first made of pure Indian meal and salt, genuine hoe-cakes,[116] which
I baked before my fire out of doors on a shingle or the end of a stick of timber
sawed off in building my house; but it was wont to get smoked and to have a piny
flavor. I tried flour also; but have at last found a mixture of rye and Indian meal
most convenient and agreeable. In cold weather it was no little amusement to bake
several small loaves of this in succession, tending and turning them as carefully as
an Egyptian his hatching eggs.[117] They were a real cereal fruit which I ripened,
and they had to my senses a fragrance like that of other noble fruits, which I kept
in as long as possible by wrapping them in cloths. I made a study of the ancient
and indispensable art of bread-making, consulting such authorities as offered,
going back to the primitive days and first invention of the unleavened kind, when
from the wildness of nuts and meats men first reached the mildness and refinement
of this diet, and travelling gradually down in my studies through that accidental
souring of the dough which, it is supposed, taught the leavening process, and

[115] A flowering weed used in salads.
[116] Thin breads made of cornmeal, originally baked on a hoe.
[117] Ancient Egyptians were the first to hatch eggs in incubators.

through the various fermentations thereafter, till I came to "good, sweet, wholesome bread," the staff of life. Leaven, which some deem the soul of bread, the *spiritus*[118] which fills its cellular tissue, which is religiously preserved like the vestal fire,[119]—some precious bottle-full, I suppose, first brought over in the Mayflower, did the business for America, and its influence is still rising, swelling, spreading, in cerealian[120] billows over the land,—this seed I regularly and faithfully procured from the village, till at length one morning I forgot the rules, and scalded my yeast; by which accident I discovered that even this was not indispensable,—for my discoveries were not by the synthetic but analytic process,—and I have gladly omitted it since, though most housewives earnestly assured me that safe and wholesome bread without yeast might not be, and elderly people prophesied a speedy decay of the vital forces. Yet I find it not to be an essential ingredient, and after going without it for a year am still in the land of the living; and I am glad to escape the trivialness of carrying a bottle-full in my pocket, which would sometimes pop and discharge its contents to my discomfiture. It is simpler and more respectable to omit it. Man is an animal who more than any other can adapt himself to all climates and circumstances. Neither did I put any sal soda, or other acid or alkali, into my bread. It would seem that I made it according to the recipe which Marcus Porcius Cato[121] gave about two centuries before Christ. "Panem depsticium sic facito. Manus mortariumque bene lavato. Farinam in mortarium indito, aquæ paulatim addito, subigitoque pulchre. Ubi bene subegeris, defingito, coquitoque sub testu." Which I take to mean—"Make kneaded bread thus. Wash your hands and trough well. Put the meal into the trough, add water gradually, and knead it thoroughly. When you have kneaded it well, mould it, and bake it under a cover," that is, in a baking-kettle. Not a word about leaven. But I did not always use this staff of life. At one time, owing to the emptiness of my purse, I saw none of it for more than a month.

Every New Englander might easily raise all his own breadstuffs in this land of rye and Indian corn, and not depend on distant and fluctuating markets for them. Yet so far are we from simplicity and independence that, in Concord, fresh and sweet meal is rarely sold in the shops, and hominy and corn in a still coarser form are hardly used by any. For the most part the farmer gives to his cattle and hogs the grain of his own producing, and buys flour, which is at least no more wholesome, at a greater cost, at the store. I saw that I could easily raise my bushel or two of rye and Indian corn, for the former will grow on the poorest land, and the latter does not require the best, and grind them in a hand-mill, and so do without rice and pork; and if I must have some concentrated sweet, I found by experiment that I could make a very good molasses either of pumpkins or beets, and I knew that I needed only to set out a few maples to obtain it more easily still, and while these were growing I could use various substitutes beside those which I have named, "For," as the Forefathers sang,—

> "we can make liquor to sweeten our lips
> Of pumpkins and parsnips and walnut-tree chips."[122]

---

[118] "Breath of life" (Latin).   [119] The sacred fire of the ancient Romans.

[120] A pun on the word "cerulean" (blue).

[121] Cato (234–149 B.C.) was a Roman statesman who advocated a return to the simplicity of an agricultural state; the recipe is from his *De Agricultura*, which also contains recipes for curing hams and making cheesecake.

[122] From an untitled poem in *Historical Collections* (1839), by John Warner Barber (1798–1885).

Finally, as for salt, that grossest of groceries, to obtain this might be a fit occasion for a visit to the seashore, or, if I did without it altogether, I should probably drink the less water. I do not learn that the Indians ever troubled themselves to go after it.

Thus I could avoid all trade and barter, so far as my food was concerned, and having a shelter already, it would only remain to get clothing and fuel. The pantaloons which I now wear were woven in a farmer's family,—thank Heaven there is so much virtue still in man; for I think the fall from the farmer to the operative as great and memorable as that from the man to the farmer;—and in a new country fuel is an encumbrance. As for a habitat, if I were not permitted still to squat, I might purchase one acre at the same price for which the land I cultivated was sold—namely, eight dollars and eight cents. But as it was, I considered that I enhanced the value of the land by squatting on it.

There is a certain class of unbelievers who sometimes ask me such questions as, if I think that I can live on vegetable food alone; and to strike at the root of the matter at once,—for the root is faith,—I am accustomed to answer such, that I can live on board nails. If they cannot understand that, they cannot understand much that I have to say. For my part, I am glad to hear of experiments of this kind being tried; as that a young man tried for a fortnight to live on hard, raw corn on the ear, using his teeth for all mortar. The squirrel tribe tried the same and succeeded. The human race is interested in these experiments, though a few old women who are incapacitated for them, or who own their thirds in mills,[123] may be alarmed.

My furniture, part of which I made myself, and the rest cost me nothing of which I have not rendered an account, consisted of a bed, a table, a desk, three chairs, a looking-glass three inches in diameter, a pair of tongs and andirons, a kettle, a skillet, and a frying-pan, a dipper, a wash-bowl, two knives and forks, three plates, one cup, one spoon, a jug for oil, a jug for molasses, and a japanned[124] lamp. None is so poor that he need sit on a pumpkin. That is shiftlessness. There is a plenty of such chairs as I like best in the village garrets to be had for taking them away. Furniture! Thank God, I can sit and I can stand without the aid of a furniture warehouse. What man but a philosopher would not be ashamed to see his furniture packed in a cart and going up country exposed to the light of heaven and the eyes of men, a beggarly account of empty boxes? That is Spaulding's[125] furniture. I could never tell from inspecting such a load whether it belonged to a so called rich man or a poor one; the owner always seemed poverty-stricken. Indeed, the more you have of such things the poorer you are. Each load looks as if it contained the contents of a dozen shanties; and if one shanty is poor, this is a dozen times as poor. Pray, for what do we *move* ever but to get rid of our furniture, our *exuviæ;*[126] at last to go from this world to another newly furnished, and leave this to be burned? It is the same as if all these traps were buckled to a man's belt, and he could not move over the rough country where our lines are cast without dragging them,—dragging his trap. He was a lucky fox that left his tail in the trap. The muskrat will gnaw his third leg off to be free. No wonder man has lost his elasticity. How often he is at a dead set![127] "Sir, if I may be so bold, what

---

[123] The women who are "incapacitated" here are toothless; the others inherited the traditional third of a husband's estate and invested in mills that grind the corn for them.
[124] Decorated and lacquered in a Japanese style.   [125] Reference unidentified.
[126] "Things that can be discarded" (Latin).   [127] At a dead end.

do you mean by a dead set?" If you are a seer, whenever you meet a man you will see all that he owns, ay, and much that he pretends to disown, behind him, even to his kitchen furniture and all the trumpery which he saves and will not burn, and he will appear to be harnessed to it and making what headway he can. I think that the man is at a dead set who has got through a knot hole or gateway where his sledge load of furniture cannot follow him. I cannot but feel compassion when I hear some trig,[128] compact-looking man, seemingly free, all girded and ready, speak of his "furniture," as whether it is insured or not. "But what shall I do with my furniture?" My gay butterfly is entangled in a spider's web then. Even those who seem for a long while not to have any, if you inquire more narrowly you will find have some stored in somebody's barn. I look upon England to-day as an old gentleman who is travelling with a great deal of baggage, trumpery which has accumulated from long housekeeping, which he has not the courage to burn; great trunk, little trunk, bandbox and bundle. Throw away the first three at least. It would surpass the powers of a well man nowadays to take up his bed and walk,[129] and I should certainly advise a sick one to lay down his bed and run. When I have met an immigrant tottering under a bundle which contained his all,—looking like an enormous wen[130] which had grown out of the nape of his neck,—I have pitied him, not because that was his all, but because he had all *that* to carry. If I have got to drag my trap, I will take care that it be a light one and do not nip me in a vital part. But perchance it would be wisest never to put one's paw into it.

I would observe, by the way, that it costs me nothing for curtains, for I have no gazers to shut out but the sun and moon, and I am willing that they should look in. The moon will not sour milk nor taint meat of mine, nor will the sun injure my furniture or fade my carpet, and if he is sometimes too warm a friend, I find it still better economy to retreat behind some curtain which nature has provided, than to add a single item to the details of housekeeping. A lady once offered me a mat, but as I had no room to spare within the house, nor time to spare within or without to shake it, I declined it, preferring to wipe my feet on the sod before my door. It is best to avoid the beginnings of evil.

Not long since I was present at the auction of a deacon's effects, for his life had not been ineffectual:—

"The evil that men do lives after them."[131]

As usual, a great proportion was trumpery which had begun to accumulate in his father's day. Among the rest was a dried tapeworm. And now, after lying half a century in his garret and other dust holes, these things were not burned; instead of a *bonfire,* or purifying destruction of them, there was an *auction,* or increasing of them.[132] The neighbors eagerly collected to view them, bought them all, and carefully transported them to their garrets and dust holes, to lie there till their estates are settled, when they will start again. When a man dies he kicks the dust.

The customs of some savage nations might, perchance, be profitably imitated by us, for they at least go through the semblance of casting their slough annually;

---

[128] Trim.

[129] In Matthew 9:6 Jesus said to a man afflicted of palsy, "Arise, take up thy bed, and go unto thine house."

[130] A cyst.   [131] From Shakespeare's *Julius Caesar* (III.ii. 81).

[132] The Latin *auctio* means "to increase"; auctioneers seek to increase the price.

they have the idea of the thing, whether they have the reality or not. Would it not be well if we were to celebrate such a "busk," or "feast of first fruits," as Bartram[133] describes to have been the custom of the Mucclasse Indians? "When a town celebrates the busk," says he, "having previously provided themselves with new clothes, new pots, pans, and other household utensils and furniture, they collect all their worn out clothes and other despicable things, sweep and cleanse their houses, squares, and the whole town, of their filth, which with all the remaining grain and other old provisions they cast together into one common heap, and consume it with fire. After having taken medicine, and fasted for three days, all the fire in the town is extinguished. During this fast they abstain from the gratification of every appetite and passion whatever. A general amnesty is proclaimed; all malefactors may return to their town.—"

"On the fourth morning, the high priest, by rubbing dry wood together, produces new fire in the public square, from whence very habitation in the town is supplied with the new and pure flame."

They then feast on the new corn and fruits and dance and sing for three days, "and the four following days they receive visits and rejoice with their friends from neighboring towns who have in like manner purified and prepared themselves."

The Mexicans also practised a similar purification at the end of every fifty-two years, in the belief that it was time for the world to come to an end.

I have scarcely heard of a truer sacrament, that is, as the dictionary defines it, "outward and visible sign of an inward and spiritual grace," than this, and I have no doubt that they were originally inspired directly from Heaven to do thus, though they have no biblical record of the revelation.

For more than five years I maintained myself thus solely by the labor of my hands, and I found, that by working about six weeks in a year, I could meet all the expenses of living. The whole of my winters, as well as most of my summers, I had free and clear for study. I have thoroughly tried school-keeping, and found that my expenses were in proportion, or rather out of proportion, to my income, for I was obliged to dress and train, not to say think and believe, accordingly, and I lost my time into the bargain. As I did not teach for the good of my fellow-men, but simply for a livelihood, this was a failure. I have tried trade; but I found that it would take ten years to get under way in that, and that then I should probably be on my way to the devil. I was actually afraid that I might by that time be doing what is called a good business. When formerly I was looking about to see what I could do for a living, some sad experience in conforming to the wishes of friends being fresh in my mind to tax my ingenuity, I thought often and seriously of picking huckleberries; that surely I could do, and its small profits might suffice,— for my greatest skill has been to want but little,—so little capital it required, so little distraction from my wonted moods, I foolishly thought. While my acquaintances went unhesitatingly into trade or the professions, I contemplated this occupation as most like theirs; ranging the hills all summer to pick the berries which came in my way, and thereafter carelessly dispose of them; so, to keep the flocks of Admetus.[134] I also dreamed that I might gather the wild herbs, or carry ever-

---

[133] William Bartram (1739–1823), an American naturalist, in *Travels Through North and South Carolina* (1791).

[134] According to Greek myth, during a period of banishment from Mt. Olympus, the sun god Apollo tended the flocks of King Admetus.

greens to such villagers as loved to be reminded of the woods, even to the city, by hay-cart loads. But I have since learned that trade curses every thing it handles; and though you trade in messages from heaven, the whole curse of trade attaches to the business.

As I preferred some things to others, and especially valued my freedom, as I could fare hard and yet succeed well, I did not wish to spend my time in earning rich carpets or other fine furniture, or delicate cookery, or a house in the Grecian or the Gothic style just yet. If there are any to whom it is no interruption to acquire these things, and who know how to use them when acquired, I relinquish to them the pursuit. Some are "industrious," and appear to love labor for its own sake, or perhaps because it keeps them out of worse mischief; to such I have at present nothing to say. Those who would not know what to do with more leisure than they now enjoy, I might advise to work twice as hard as they do,—work till they pay for themselves, and get their free papers.[135] For myself I found that the occupation of a day-laborer was the most independent of any, especially as it required only thirty or forty days in a year to support one. The laborer's day ends with the going down of the sun, and he is then free to devote himself to his chosen pursuit, independent of his labor; but his employer, who speculates from month to month, has no respite from one end of the year to the other.

In short, I am convinced, both by faith and experience, that to maintain one's self on this earth is not a hardship but a pastime, if we will live simply and wisely;[136] as the pursuits of the simpler nations are still the sports of the more artificial. It is not necessary that a man should earn his living by the sweat of his brow, unless he sweats easier than I do.

One young man of my acquaintance, who has inherited some acres, told me that he thought he should live as I did, *if he had the means.* I would not have any one adopt *my* mode of living on any account; for, beside that before he has fairly learned it I may have found out another for myself, I desire that there may be as many different persons in the world as possible; but I would have each one be very careful to find out and pursue *his own* way, and not his father's or his mother's or his neighbor's instead. The youth may build or plant or sail, only let him not be hindered from doing that which he tells me he would like to do. It is by a mathematical point only that we are wise, as the sailor or the fugitive slave keeps the polestar[137] in his eye; but that is sufficient guidance for all our life. We may not arrive at our port within a calculable period, but we would preserve the true course.

Undoubtedly, in this case, what is true for one is truer still for a thousand, as a large house is not more expensive than a small one in proportion to its size, since one roof may cover, one cellar underlie, and one wall separate several apartments. But for my part, I preferred the solitary dwelling. Moreover, it will commonly be cheaper to build the whole yourself than to convince another of the advantage of the common wall; and when you have done this, the common partition, to be much cheaper, must be a thin one, and that other may prove a bad neighbor, and also not keep his side in repair. The only coöperation which is commonly possible is exceedingly partial and superficial; and what little true coöperation there is, is as

---

[135] To work off their debts as did indentured servants.

[136] A theory of Charles Fourier (1772–1837), a French social reformer and founder of agrarian cooperatives; the Brook Farm transcendentalist community used his ideas.

[137] The North Star, which gives the sailor direction and guides the escaped slave toward freedom.

if it were not, being a harmony inaudible to men. If a man has faith he will coöperate with equal faith every where; if he has not faith, he will continue to live like
the rest of the world, whatever company he is joined to. To coöperate, in the
highest as well as the lowest sense, means *to get our living together*. I heard it
proposed lately that two young men should travel together over the world, the one
without money, earning his means as he went, before the mast and behind the
plough, the other carrying a bill of exchange in his pocket. It was easy to see that
they could not long be companions or coöperate, since one would not *operate* at
all. They would part at the first interesting crisis in their adventures. Above all,
as I have implied, the man who goes alone can start today; but he who travels with
another must wait till that other is ready, and it may be a long time before they
get off.

But all this is very selfish, I have heard some of my townsmen say. I confess
that I have hitherto indulged very little in philanthropic enterprises. I have made
some sacrifices to a sense of duty, and among others have sacrificed this pleasure
also. There are those who have used all their arts to persuade me to undertake the
support of some poor family in the town; and if I had nothing to do,—for the devil
finds employment for the idle,[138]—I might try my hand at some such pastime as
that. However, when I have thought to indulge myself in this respect, and lay their
Heaven under an obligation by maintaining certain poor persons in all respects as
comfortably as I maintain myself, and have even ventured so far as to make them
the offer, they have one and all unhesitatingly preferred to remain poor. While my
townsmen and women are devoted in so many ways to the good of their fellows, I
trust that one at least may be spared to other and less humane pursuits. You must
have a genius for charity as well as for any thing else. As for Doing-good, that is
one of the professions which are full. Moreover, I have tried it fairly, and, strange
as it may seem, am satisfied that it does not agree with my constitution. Probably
I should not consciously and deliberately forsake my particular calling to do the
good which society demands of me, to save the universe from annihilation; and I
believe that a like but infinitely greater steadfastness elsewhere is all that now
preserves it. But I would not stand between any man and his genius; and to him
who does this work, which I decline, with his whole heart and soul and life, I
would say, Persevere, even if the world call it doing evil, as it is most likely they
will.

I am far from supposing that my case is a peculiar one; no doubt many of my
readers would make a similar defence. At doing something,—I will not engage
that my neighbors shall pronounce it good,—I do not hesitate to say that I should
be a capital fellow to hire; but what that is, it is for my employer to find out. What
good I do, in the common sense of that word, must be aside from my main path,
and for the most part wholly unintended. Men say, practically, Begin where you
are and such as you are, without aiming mainly to become of more worth, and
with kindness aforethought go about doing good. If I were to preach at all in this
strain, I should say rather, Set about being good. As if the sun should stop when
he had kindled his fires up to the splendor of a moon or a star of the sixth magnitude, and go about like a Robin Goodfellow,[139] peeping in at every cottage win-

---

[138] A popular proverb in Thoreau's time.

[139] A mischievous elf in folklore; personified as Puck in Shakespeare's *A Midsummer Night's
Dream*.

dow, inspiring lunatics, and tainting meats, and making darkness visible, instead of steadily increasing his genial heat and beneficence till he is of such brightness that no mortal can look him in the face, and then, and in the mean while too, going about the world in his own orbit, doing it good, or rather, as a truer philosophy has discovered, the world going about him getting good. When Phaeton,[140] wishing to prove his heavenly birth by his beneficence, had the sun's chariot but one day, and drove out of the beaten track, he burned several blocks of houses in the lower streets of heaven, and scorched the surface of the earth, and dried up every spring, and made the great desert of Sahara, till at length Jupiter hurled him headlong to the earth with a thunderbolt, and the sun, through grief at his death, did not shine for a year.

There is no odor so bad as that which arises from goodness tainted. It is human, it is divine, carrion. If I knew for a certainty that a man was coming to my house with the conscious design of doing me good, I should run for my life, as from that dry and parching wind of the African deserts called the simoom, which fills the mouth and nose and ears and eyes with dust till you are suffocated, for fear that I should get some of his good done to me,—some of its virus mingled with my blood. No,—in this case I would rather suffer evil the natural way. A man is not a good *man* to me because he will feed me if I should be starving, or warm me if I should be freezing, or pull me out of a ditch if I should ever fall into one. I can find you a Newfoundland dog that will do as much. Philanthropy is not love for one's fellow-man in the broadest sense. Howard[141] was no doubt an exceedingly kind and worthy man in his way, and has his reward; but, comparatively speaking, what are a hundred Howards to *us*, if their philanthropy do not help *us* in our best estate, when we are most worthy to be helped? I never heard of a philanthropic meeting in which it was sincerely proposed to do any good to me, or the like of me.

The Jesuits[142] were quite balked by those Indians who, being burned at the stake, suggested new modes of torture to their tormentors. Being superior to physical suffering, it sometimes chanced that they were superior to any consolation which the missionaries could offer; and the law to do as you would be done by fell with less persuasiveness on the ears of those, who, for their part, did not care how they were done by, who loved their enemies after a new fashion, and came very near freely forgiving them all they did.

Be sure that you give the poor the aid they most need, though it be your example which leaves them far behind. If you give money, spend yourself with it, and do not merely abandon it to them. We make curious mistakes sometimes. Often the poor man is not so cold and hungry as he is dirty and ragged and gross. It is partly his taste, and not merely his misfortune. If you give him money, he will perhaps buy more rags with it. I was wont to pity the clumsy Irish laborers who cut ice on the pond, in such mean and ragged clothes, while I shivered in my more tidy and somewhat more fashionable garments, till, one bitter cold day, one who had slipped into the water came to my house to warm him, and I saw him strip off three pairs of pants and two pairs of stockings ere he got down to the skin, though they were dirty and ragged enough, it is true, and that he could afford to refuse the

[140] According to Greek myth, the son of Apollo who attempted to drive his father's sun chariot.
[141] John Howard (1726?–1790), an English philanthropist and prison reformer.
[142] Missionaries of the Society of Jesus, a Roman Catholic religious order, who sought converts to Christianity among American Indians.

extra garments which I offered him, he had so many *intra*[143] ones. This ducking was the very thing he needed. Then I began to pity myself, and I saw that it would be a greater charity to bestow on me a flannel shirt than a whole slop-shop[144] on him. There are a thousand hacking at the branches of evil to one who is striking at the root, and it may be that he who bestows the largest amount of time and money on the needy is doing the most by his mode of life to produce that misery which he strives in vain to relieve. It is the pious slave-breeder devoting the proceeds of every tenth slave[145] to buy a Sunday's liberty for the rest. Some show their kindness to the poor by employing them in their kitchens. Would they not be kinder if they employed themselves there? You boast of spending a tenth part of your income in charity; may be you should spend the nine tenths so, and done with it. Society recovers only a tenth part of the property then. Is this owing to the generosity of him in whose possession it is found, or to the remissness of the officers of justice?

Philanthropy is almost the only virtue which is sufficiently appreciated by mankind. Nay, it is greatly overrated; and it is our selfishness which overrates it. A robust poor man, one sunny day here in Concord, praised a fellow-townsman to me, because, as he said, he was kind to the poor; meaning himself. The kind uncles and aunts of the race are more esteemed than its true spiritual fathers and mothers. I once heard a reverend lecturer on England, a man of learning and intelligence, after enumerating her scientific, literary, and political worthies, Shakspeare, Bacon, Cromwell, Milton, Newton,[146] and others, speak next of her Christian heroes, whom, as if his profession required it of him, he elevated to a place far above all the rest, as the greatest of the great. They were Penn, Howard, and Mrs. Fry.[147] Every one must feel the falsehood and cant of this. The last were not England's best men and women; only, perhaps, her best philanthropists.

I would not subtract any thing from the praise that is due to philanthropy, but merely demand justice for all who by their lives and works are a blessing to mankind. I do not value chiefly a man's uprightness and benevolence, which are, as it were, his stem and leaves. Those plants of whose greenness withered we make herb tea for the sick, serve but a humble use, and are most employed by quacks. I want the flower and fruit of a man; that some fragrance be wafted over from him to me, and some ripeness flavor our intercourse. His goodness must not be a partial and transitory act, but a constant superfluity, which costs him nothing and of which he is unconscious. This is a charity that hides a multitude of sins.[148] The philanthropist too often surrounds mankind with the remembrance of his own cast-off griefs as an atmosphere, and calls it sympathy. We should impart our courage, and not our despair, our health and ease, and not our disease, and take care that this does not spread by contagion. From what southern plains comes up the voice of wailing?[149] Under what latitudes reside the heathen to whom we would send light? Who is that intemperate and brutal man whom we would redeem? If any

---

[143] *Extra* means "outer," and *intra*, "inner" (Latin).   [144] A shop for cheap clothing.

[145] In the custom of tithing, one-tenth of a parishioner's income is given to support the church.

[146] The philosopher, essayist, and statesman Sir Francis Bacon (1561–1626); the revolutionary leader and Lord Protector of the Commonwealth Oliver Cromwell (1599–1658); the poet John Milton (1608–1674); the mathematician and natural philosopher Sir Isaac Newton (1642–1727).

[147] The American Quaker William Penn (1644–1718), John Howard, and the English Quaker Elizabeth Fry (1780–1845) were active in social reform.

[148] "... charity shall cover the multitude of sins," from I Peter 4:8.

[149] "*Our* southern plains," or slave states.

thing ail a man, so that he does not perform his functions, if he have a pain in his bowels even,—for that is the seat of sympathy,[150]—he forthwith sets about reforming—the world. Being a microcosm himself, he discovers, and it is a true discovery, and he is the man to make it,—that the world has been eating green apples; to his eyes, in fact, the globe itself is a great green apple, which there is danger awful to think of that the children of men will nibble before it is ripe; and straightway his drastic philanthropy seeks out the Esquimaux and the Patagonian,[151] and embraces the populous Indian and Chinese villages; and thus, by a few years of philanthropic activity, the powers in the mean while using him for their own ends, no doubt, he cures himself of his dyspepsia, the globe acquires a faint blush on one or both of its cheeks, as if it were beginning to be ripe, and life loses its crudity and is once more sweet and wholesome to live. I never dreamed of any enormity greater than I have committed. I never knew, and never shall know, a worse man than myself.

I believe that what so saddens the reformer is not his sympathy with his fellows in distress, but, though he be the holiest son of God, is his private ail. Let this be righted, let the spring come to him, the morning rise over his couch, and he will forsake his generous companions without apology. My excuse for not lecturing against the use of tobacco is, that I never chewed it; that is a penalty which reformed tobacco-chewers have to pay; though there are things enough I have chewed, which I could lecture against. If you should ever be betrayed into any of these philanthropies, do not let your left hand know what your right hand does,[152] for it is not worth knowing. Rescue the drowning and tie your shoe-strings. Take your time, and set about some free labor.

Our manners have been corrupted by communication with the saints. Our hymn-books resound with a melodious cursing of God and enduring him forever. One would say that even the prophets and redeemers had rather consoled the fears than confirmed the hopes of man. There is nowhere recorded a simple and irrepressible satisfaction with the gift of life, any memorable praise of God. All health and success does me good, however far off and withdrawn it may appear; all disease and failure helps to make me sad and does me evil, however much sympathy it may have with me or I with it. If, then, we would indeed restore mankind by truly Indian, botanic, magnetic, or natural means, let us first be as simple and well as Nature ourselves, dispel the clouds which hang over our own brows, and take up a little life into our pores. Do not stay to be an overseer of the poor, but endeavor to become one of the worthies of the world.

I read in the Gulistan, or Flower Garden, of Sheik Sadi of Shiraz,[153] that "They asked a wise man, saying; Of the many celebrated trees which the Most High God has created lofty and umbrageous, they call none azad, or free, excepting the cypress, which bears no fruit; what mystery is there in this? He replied; Each has its appropriate produce, and appointed season, during the continuance of which it is fresh and blooming, and during their absence dry and withered; to neither of which states is the cypress exposed, being always flourishing; and of this nature are the azads, or religious independents.—Fix not thy heart on that which is tran-

---

[150] An old idea held that the bowels are the source of sympathy.

[151] The Eskimo and the inhabitant of Patagonia, in southern South America.

[152] "But when thou doest alms, let not thy left hand know what thy right hand doeth," from Matthew 6:3.

[153] Muslih-ud-Din (1184?–1291), or Saadi, a Persian poet, in *Gulistān*, (1258), or *"Rose Garden."*

sitory; for the Dijlah, or Tigris, will continue to flow through Bagdad after the race of caliphs[154] is extinct: if thy hand has plenty, be liberal as the date tree; but if it affords nothing to give away, be an azad, or free man, like the cypress."

COMPLEMENTAL VERSES[155]

THE PRETENSIONS OF POVERTY

"Thou dost presume too much, poor needy wretch,
To claim a station in the firmament,
Because thy humble cottage, or thy tub,
Nurses some lazy or pedantic virtue
In the cheap sunshine or by shady springs,
With roots and pot-herbs; where thy right hand,
Tearing those humane passions from the mind,
Upon whose stocks fair blooming virtues flourish,
Degradeth nature, and benumbeth sense,
And, Gorgon-like,[156] turns active men to stone.
We not require the dull society
Of your necessitated temperance,
Or that unnatural stupidity
That knows nor joy nor sorrow; nor your forc'd
Falsely exalted passive fortitude
Above the active. This low abject brood,
That fix their seats in mediocrity,
Become your servile minds; but we advance
Such virtues only as admit excess,
Brave, bounteous acts, regal magnificence,
All-seeing prudence, magnanimity
That knows no bound, and that heroic virtue
For which antiquity hath left no name,
But patterns only, such as Hercules,
Achilles, Theseus.[157] Back to thy loath'd cell;
And when thou seest the new enlightened sphere,
Study to know but what those worthies were."

T. CAREW

II: Where I Lived, and What I Lived For

At a certain season of our life we are accustomed to consider every spot as the possible site of a house. I have thus surveyed the country on every side within a dozen miles of where I live. In imagination I have bought all the farms in succes-

---

[154] Heads of Islam.

[155] From *Coelum Britannicum* (1661), by the English poet Thomas Carew (1595?–1645?); Thoreau offered the lines, complete with his own title, as a tongue-in-cheek rebuttal to the idea set forth in "Economy."

[156] According to Greek myth, three sisters with hideous faces and glaring eyes, who turned to stone all who met their gaze.

[157] According to Greek myth, heroes: Achilles, known for leading the Trojan War and for his one vulnerable spot, his heel; Theseus, known for killing the Minotaur, a monster with the head of a bull.

sion, for all were to be bought, and I knew their price. I walked over each farmer's premises, tasted his wild apples, discoursed on husbandry with him, took his farm at his price, at any price, mortgaging it to him in my mind; even put a higher price on it,—took every thing but a deed of it,—took his word for his deed, for I dearly love to talk,—cultivated it, and him too to some extent, I trust, and withdrew when I had enjoyed it long enough, leaving him to carry it on. This experience entitled me to be regarded as a sort of real-estate broker by my friends. Wherever I sat, there I might live, and the landscape radiated from me accordingly. What is a house but a *sedes*, a seat?—better if a country seat. I discovered many a site for a house not likely to be soon improved, which some might have thought too far from the village, but to my eyes the village was too far from it. Well, there I might live, I said; and there I did live, for an hour, a summer and a winter life; saw how I could let the years run off, buffet the winter through, and see the spring come in. The future inhabitants of this region, wherever they may place their houses, may be sure that they have been anticipated. An afternoon sufficed to lay out the land into orchard woodlot and pasture, and to decide what fine oaks or pines should be left to stand before the door, and whence each blasted tree could be seen to the best advantage; and then I let it lie, fallow perchance, for a man is rich in proportion to the number of things which he can afford to let alone.

My imagination carried me so far that I even had the refusal of several farms,—the refusal was all I wanted,—but I never got my fingers burned by actual possession. The nearest that I came to actual possession was when I bought the Hollowell Place,[1] and had begun to sort my seeds, and collected materials with which to make a wheelbarrow to carry it on or off with; but before the owner gave me a deed of it, his wife—every man has such a wife—changed her mind and wished to keep it, and he offered me ten dollars to release him. Now, to speak the truth, I had but ten cents in the world, and it surpassed my arithmetic to tell, if I was that man who had ten cents, or who had a farm, or ten dollars, or all together. However, I let him keep the ten dollars and the farm too, for I had carried it far enough; or rather, to be generous, I sold him the farm for just what I gave for it, and, as he was not a rich man, made him a present of ten dollars, and still had my ten cents, and seeds, and materials for a wheelbarrow left. I found thus that I had been a rich man without any damage to my poverty. But I retained the landscape, and I have since annually carried off what it yielded without a wheelbarrow. With respect to landscapes,—

> "I am monarch of all I *survey*,
> My right there is none to dispute."[2]

I have frequently seen a poet withdraw, having enjoyed the most valuable part of a farm, while the crusty farmer supposed that he had got a few wild apples only. Why, the owner does not know it for many years when a poet has put his farm in rhyme, the most admirable kind of invisible fence, has fairly impounded it, milked it, skimmed it, and got all the cream, and left the farmer only the skimmed milk.

---

[1] A farm on the Sudbury River near Concord.

[2] From "Verses Supposed to be Written by Alexander Selkirk," by the English poet William Cowper (1731–1800). Selkirk (1676–1721) was a Scottish sailor after whom Daniel Defoe's Robinson Crusoe was modeled. Thoreau, who worked occasionally as a surveyor, plays on the word "survey."

The real attractions of the Hollowell farm, to me, were; its complete retirement, being about two miles from the village, half a mile from the nearest neighbor, and separated from the highway by a broad field; its bounding on the river, which the owner said protected it by its fogs from frosts in the spring, though that was nothing to me; the gray color and ruinous state of the house and barn, and the dilapidated fences, which put such an interval between me and the last occupant; the hollow and lichen-covered appled trees, gnawed by rabbits, showing what kind of neighbors I should have; but above all; the recollection I had of it from my earliest voyages up the river, when the house was concealed behind a dense grove of red maples, through which I heard the house-dog bark. I was in haste to buy it, before the proprietor finished getting out some rocks, cutting down the hollow apple trees, and grubbing up some young birches which had sprung up in the pasture, or, in short, had made any more of his improvements. To enjoy these advantages I was ready to carry it on; like Atlas[3] to take the world on my shoulders,—I never heard what compensation he received for that,—and do all those things which had no other motive or excuse but that I might pay for it and be unmolested in my possession of it; for I knew all the while that it would yield the most abundant crop of the kind I wanted if I could only afford to let it alone. But it turned out as I have said.

All that I could say, then, with respect to farming on a large scale, (I have always cultivated a garden,) was, that I had had my seeds ready. Many think that seeds improve with age. I have no doubt that time discriminates between the good and the bad; and when at last I shall plant, I shall be less likely to be disappointed. But I would say to my fellows, once for all, As long as possible live free and uncommitted. It makes but little difference whether you are committed to a farm or the county jail.

Old Cato,[4] whose "De Re Rusticâ" is my "Cultivator," says, and the only translation I have seen makes sheer nonsense of the passage, "When you think of getting a farm, turn it thus in your mind, not to buy greedily; nor spare your pains to look at it, and do not think it enough to go round it once. The oftener you go there the more it will please you if it is good." I think I shall not buy greedily, but go round and round it as long as I live, and be buried in it first, that it may please me the more at last.

The present was my next experiment of this kind, which I purpose to describe more at length; for convenience, putting the experience of two years into one. As I have said, I do not propose to write an ode to dejection, but to brag as lustily as chanticleer in the morning, standing on his roost, if only to wake my neighbors up.

When first I took up my abode in the woods, that is, began to spend my nights as well as days there, which, by accident, was on Independence Day, or the fourth of July, 1845, my house was not finished for winter, but was merely a defence against the rain, without plastering or chimney, the walls being of rough weather-stained boards, with wide chinks, which made it cool at night. The upright white hewn studs and freshly planed door and window casings gave it a clean and airy

---

[3] According to Greek myth, a Titan, or giant god, who was forced to support the heavens on his shoulders.

[4] Cato's *De Agricultura* was also known as *De Re Rustica;* two farming magazines named "Cultivator" were published in Thoreau's time.

look, especially in the morning, when its timbers were saturated with dew, so that I fancied by noon some sweet gum would exude from them. To my imagination it retained throughout the day more or less of this auroral[5] character, reminding me of a certain house on a mountain which I had visited the year before. This was an airy and unplastered cabin, fit to entertain a travelling god, and where a goddess might trail her garments. The winds which passed over my dwelling were such as sweep over the ridges of mountains, bearing the broken strains, or celestial parts only, of terrestrial music. The morning wind forever blows, the poem of creation is uninterrupted; but few are the ears that hear it. Olympus[6] is but the outside of the earth every where.

The only house I had been the owner of before, if I except a boat, was a tent, which I used occasionally when making excursions in the summer, and this is still rolled up in my garret; but the boat,[7] after passing from hand to hand, has gone down the stream of time. With this more substantial shelter about me, I had made some progress toward settling in the world. This frame, so slightly clad, was a sort of crystallization around me, and reacted on the builder. It was suggestive somewhat as a picture in outlines. I did not need to go out doors to take the air, for the atmosphere within had lost none of its freshness. It was not so much within doors as behind a door where I sat, even in the rainiest weather. The Harivansa[8] says, "An abode without birds is like a meat without seasoning." Such was not my abode, for I found my self suddenly neighbor to the birds; not by having imprisoned one, but having caged myself near them. I was not only nearer to some of those which commonly frequent the garden and the orchard, but to those wilder and more thrilling songsters of the forest which never, or rarely, serenade a villager,—the wood-thrush, the veery, the scarlet tanager, the field-sparrow, the whippoorwill, and many others.

I was seated by the shore of a small pond, about a mile and a half south of the village of Concord and somewhat higher than it, in the midst of an extensive wood between that town and Lincoln, and about two miles south of that our only field known to fame, Concord Battle Ground;[9] but I was so low in the woods that the opposite shore, half a mile off, like the rest, covered with wood, was my most distant horizon. For the first week, whenever I looked out on the pond it impressed me like a tarn[10] high up on the side of a mountain, its bottom far above the surface of other lakes, and, as the sun arose, I saw it throwing off its nightly clothing of mist, and here and there, by degrees, its soft ripples or its smooth reflecting surface was revealed, while the mists, like ghosts, were stealthily withdrawing in every direction into the woods, as at the breaking up of some nocturnal conventicle. The very dew seemed to hang upon the trees later into the day than usual, as on the sides of mountains.

This small lake was of most value as a neighbor in the intervals of a gentle rain storm in August, when, both air and water being perfectly still, but the sky overcast, mid-afternoon had all the serenity of evening, and the wood-thrush sang around, and was heard from shore to shore. A lake like this is never smoother than at such a time; and the clear portion of the air above it being shallow and darkened

---

[5] Morning.   [6] Mt. Olympus, home of the gods in Greek myth.
[7] Built by Thoreau, used for excursions on the Concord and Merrimack rivers, and sold to Nathaniel Hawthorne for seven dollars. Hawthorne later gave it to the poet William Ellery Channing.
[8] A Hindu religious epic of the fifth century.
[9] The site of a battle at the outset of the American Revolution, April 19, 1775.
[10] A small mountain lake.

by clouds, the water, full of light and reflections, becomes a lower heaven itself so much the more important. From a hill top near by, where the wood had been recently cut off, there was a pleasing vista southward across the pond, through a wide indentation in the hills which form the shore there, where their opposite sides sloping toward each other suggested a stream flowing out in that direction through a wooded valley, but stream there was none. That way I looked between and over the near green hills to some distant and higher ones in the horizon, tinged with blue. Indeed, by standing on tiptoe I could catch a glimpse of some of the peaks of the still bluer and more distant mountain ranges in the north-west, those true-blue coins from heaven's own mint, and also of some portion of the village. But in other directions, even from this point, I could not see over or beyond the woods which surrounded me. It is well to have some water in your neighborhood, to give buoyancy to and float the earth. One value even of the smallest well is, that when you look into it you see that the earth is not continent but insular. This is as important as that it keeps butter cool. When I looked across the pond from this peak toward the Sudbury meadows, which in time of flood I distinguished elevated perhaps by a mirage in their seething valley, like a coin in a basin, all the earth beyond the pond appeared like a thin crust insulated and floated even by this small sheet of intervening water, and I was reminded that this on which I dwelt was but *dry land*.

Though the view from my door was still more contracted, I did not feel crowded or confined in the least. There was pasture enough for my imagination. The low shrub-oak plateau to which the opposite shore arose, stretched away toward the prairies of the West and the steppes of Tartary,[11] affording ample room for all the roving families of men. "There are none happy in the world but beings who enjoy freely a vast horizon,"—said Damodara,[12] when his herds required new and larger pastures.

Both place and time were changed, and I dwelt nearer to those parts of the universe and to those eras in history which had most attracted me. Where I lived was as far off as many a region viewed nightly by astronomers. We are wont to imagine rare and delectable places in some remote and more celestial corner of the system, behind the constellation of Cassiopeia's Chair, far from noise and disturbance. I discovered that my house actually had its site in such a withdrawn, but forever new and unprofaned, part of the universe. If it were worth the while to settle in those parts near to the Pleiades of the Hyades, to Aldebaran or Altair,[13] then I was really there, or at an equal remoteness from the life which I had left behind, dwindled and twinkling with as fine a ray to my nearest neighbor, and to be seen only in moonless nights by him. Such was that part of creation where I had squatted;-

> "There was a shepherd that did live,
>   And held his thoughts as high
> As were the mounts whereon his flocks
>   Did hourly feed him by."[14]

[11] The ascending plains of Russian Asia, home of the Tartars.
[12] The Hindu god Krishna in the *Harivansa*.   [13] Constellations and stars.
[14] Anonymous lines set to music by Robert Jones in 1611 and printed in Thomas Evans's *Old Ballads* (1810).

What should we think of the shepherd's life if his flocks always wandered to higher pastures than his thoughts?

Every morning was a cheerful invitation to make my life of equal simplicity, and I may say innocence, with Nature herself. I have been as sincere a worshipper of Aurora as the Greeks.[15] I got up early and bathed in the pond; that was a religious exercise, and one of the best things which I did. They say that characters were engraven on the bathing tub of king Tching-thang[16] to this effect: "Renew thyself completely each day; do it again, and again, and forever again." I can understand that. Morning brings back the heroic ages. I was as much affected by the faint hum of a mosquito making its invisible and unimaginable tour through my apartment at earliest dawn, when I was sitting with door and windows open, as I could be by any trumpet that ever sang of fame. It was Homer's requiem; itself an Iliad and Odyssey in the air, singing its own wrath and wanderings. There was something cosmical about it; a standing advertisement, till forbidden,[17] of the everlasting vigor and fertility of the world. The morning, which is the most memorable season of the day, is the awakening hour. Then there is least somnolence in us; and for an hour, at least, some part of us awakes which slumbers all the rest of the day and night. Little is to be expected of that day, if it can be called a day, to which we are not awakened by our Genius,[18] but by the mechanical nudgings of some servitor, are not awakened by our own newly-acquired force and aspirations from within, accompanied by the undulations of celestial music, instead of factory bells, and a fragrance filling the air—to a higher life than we fell asleep from; and thus the darkness bear its fruit, and prove itself to be good, no less than the light. That man who does not believe that each day contains an earlier, more sacred, and auroral hour than he has yet profaned, has despaired of life, and is pursuing a descending and darkening way. After a partial cessation of his sensuous life, the soul of man, or its organs rather, are reinvigorated each day, and his Genius tries again what noble life it can make. All memorable events, I should say, transpire in morning time and in morning atmosphere. The Vedas[19] say, "All intelligences awake with the morning." Poetry and art, and the fairest and most memorable of the actions of men, date from such an hour. All poets and heroes, like Memnon, are the children of Aurora, and emit their music at sunrise. To him whose elastic and vigorous thought keeps pace with the sun, the day is a perpetual morning. It matters not what the clocks say or the attitudes and labors of men. Morning is when I am awake and there is a dawn in me. Moral reform is the effort to throw off sleep. Why is it that men give so poor an account of their day if they have not been slumbering? They are not such poor calculators. If they had not been overcome with drowsiness they would have performed something. The millions are awake enough for physical labor; but only one in a million is awake enough for effective intellectual exertion, only one in a hundred millions to a poetic or divine life. To be awake is to be alive. I have never yet met a man who was quite awake. How could I have looked him in the face?

We must learn to reawaken and keep ourselves awake, not by mechanical aids, but by an infinite expectation of the dawn, which does not forsake us in our

---

[15] Actually, the Roman goddess of the dawn was named Eos by the Greeks.

[16] Founder of China's Shang dynasty (1766–1122 B.C.); the injunction to renew the self is from Confucius, *The Great Learning* (Ch. 1).

[17] The letters "TF" directed a newspaper to run an advertisement until canceled.   [18] Guardian spirit.

[19] Ancient sacred Hindu scriptures.

soundest sleep. I know of no more encouraging fact than the unquestionable ability of man to elevate his life by a conscious endeavor. It is something to be able to paint a particular picture, or to carve a statue, and so to make a few objects beautiful; but it is far more glorious to carve and paint the very atmosphere and medium through which we look, which morally we can do. To affect the quality of the day, that is the highest of arts. Every man is tasked to make his life, even in its details, worthy of the contemplation of his most elevated and critical hour. If we refused, or rather used up, such paltry information as we get, the oracles would distinctly inform us how this might be done.

I went to the woods because I wished to live deliberately, to front only the essential facts of life, and see if I could not learn what it had to teach, and not, when I came to die, discover that I had not lived. I did not wish to live what was not life, living is so dear; nor did I wish to practise resignation, unless it was quite necessary. I wanted to live deep and suck out all the marrow of life, to live so sturdily and Spartan-like[20] as to put to rout all that was not life, to cut a broad swath and shave close, to drive life into a corner, and reduce it to its lowest terms, and, if it proved to be mean, why then to get the whole and genuine meanness of it, and publish its meanness to the world; or if it were sublime, to know it by experience, and be able to give a true account of it in my next excursion. For most men, it appears to me, are in a strange uncertainty about it, whether it is of the devil or of God, and have *somewhat hastily* concluded that it is the chief end of man here to "glorify God and enjoy him forever."[21]

Still we live meanly, like ants; though the fable tells us that we were long ago changed into men; like pygmies we fight with cranes;[22] it is error upon error, and clout upon clout, and our best virtue has for its occasion a superfluous and evitable wretchedness. Our life is frittered away by detail. An honest man has hardly need to count more than his ten fingers, or in extreme cases he may add his ten toes, and lump the rest. Simplicity, simplicity, simplicity! I say, let your affairs be as two or three, and not a hundred or a thousand; instead of a million count half a dozen, and keep your accounts on your thumb nail. In the midst of this chopping sea of civilized life, such are the clouds and storms and quicksands and thousand-and-one items to be allowed for, that a man has to live, if he would not founder and go to the bottom and not make his port at all, by dead reckoning, and he must be a great calculator indeed who succeeds. Simplify, simplify. Instead of three meals a day, if it be necessary eat but one; instead of a hundred dishes, five; and reduce other things in proportion. Our life is like a German Confederacy,[23] made up of petty states, with its boundary forever fluctuating, so that even a German cannot tell you how it is bounded at any moment. The nation itself, with all its so called internal improvements, which, by the way, are all external and superficial, is just such an unwieldy and overgrown establishment, cluttered with furniture and tripped up by its own traps, ruined by luxury and heedless expense, by want of calculation and a worthy aim, as the million households in the land; and the only

---

[20] With discipline and courage.

[21] Adapted from the opening lines of the "Shorter Catechism" in the *New England Primer:* "Man's chief End is to Glorify God, and to Enjoy Him for ever." *"Somewhat hastily"* puts an ironic bite to the message.

[22] According to Greek myth, the supreme god Zeus turned ants into humans to repopulate a plague-ravaged kingdom; Homer's *Iliad* (Bk. III) compares the Trojans to cranes fighting with pygmies.

[23] Until Germany was unified in 1871 by Prince Otto von Bismarck (1815–1898), it was an assemblage of minor states.

cure for it as for them is in a rigid economy, a stern and more than Spartan simplicity of life and elevation of purpose. It lives too fast. Men think that it is essential that the *Nation* have commerce, and export ice, and talk through a telegraph, and ride thirty miles an hour, without a doubt, whether *they* do or not; but whether we should live like baboons or like men, is a little uncertain. If we do not get out sleepers,[24] and forge rails, and devote days and nights to the work, but go to tinkering upon our *lives* to improve *them,* who will build railroads? And if railroads are not built, how shall we get to heaven in season? But if we stay at home and mind our business, who will want railroads? We do not ride on the railroad; it rides upon us. Did you ever think what those sleepers are that underlie the railroad? Each one is a man, an Irish-man, or a Yankee man. The rails are laid on them, and they are covered with sand, and the cars run smoothly over them. They are sound sleepers, I assure you. And every few years a new lot is laid down and run over; so that, if some have the pleasure of riding on a rail, others have the misfortune to be ridden upon. And when they run over a man that is walking in his sleep, a supernumerary sleeper in the wrong position, and wake him up, they suddenly stop the cars, and make a hue and cry about it, as if this were an exception. I am glad to know that it takes a gang of men for every five miles to keep the sleepers down and level in their beds as it is, for this is a sign that they may sometime get up again.

Why should we live with such hurry and waste of life? We are determined to be starved before we are hungry. Men say that a stitch in time saves nine, and so they take a thousand stitches to-day to save nine to-morrow. As for *work,* we haven't any of any consequence. We have the Saint Vitus' dance,[25] and cannot possibly keep our heads still. If I should only give a few pulls at the parish bell-rope, as for a fire, that is, without setting the bell,[26] there is hardly a man on his farm in the outskirts of Concord, notwithstanding that press of engagements which was his excuse so many times this morning, nor a boy, nor a woman, I might almost say, but would forsake all and follow that sound, not mainly to save property from the flames, but, if we will confess the truth, much more to see it burn, since burn it must, and we, be it known, did not set it on fire,—or to see it put out, and have a hand in it, if that is done as handsomely; yes, even if it were the parish church itself. Hardly a man takes a half hour's nap after dinner, but when he wakes he holds up his head and asks, "What's the news?" as if the rest of mankind had stood his sentinels. Some give directions to be waked every half hour, doubtless for no other purpose; and then, to pay for it, they tell what they have dreamed. After a night's sleep the news is as indispensable as the breakfast. "Pray tell me any thing new that has happened to a man any where on this globe",—and he reads it over his coffee and rolls, that a man has had his eyes gouged out this morning on the Wachito River;[27] never dreaming the while that he lives in the dark unfathomed mammoth cave[28] of this world, and has but the rudiment of an eye himself.

For my part, I could easily do without the post-office. I think that there are very few important communications made through it. To speak critically, I never received more than one or two letters in my life—I wrote this some years ago—that

---

[24] Wooden railroad ties (also, we must wake people from their lives of sleep).
[25] Chorea, a nervous disorder characterized by spasmodic twitchings.
[26] Pulling the bell rope so hard that the bell inverts.   [27] Arkansas's Ouachita River.
[28] Mammoth Cave in Kentucky, a deep cave in which blind fish had been seen.

were worth the postage. The penny-post is, commonly, an institution through which you seriously offer a man that penny for his thoughts which is so often safely offered in jest. And I am sure that I never read any memorable news in a newspaper. If we read of one man robbed, or murdered, or killed by accident, or one house burned, or one vessel wrecked, or one steamboat blown up, or one cow run over on the Western Railroad,[29] or one mad dog killed, or one lot of grasshoppers in the winter,—we never need read of another. One is enough. If you are acquainted with the principle, what do you care for a myriad instances and applications? To a philosopher all *news,* as it is called, is gossip, and they who edit and read it are old women over their tea. Yet not a few are greedy after this gossip. There was such a rush, as I hear, the other day at one of the offices to learn the foreign news by the last arrival, that several large squares of plate glass belonging to the establishment were broken by the pressure,—news which I seriously think a ready wit might write a twelvemonth or twelve years beforehand with sufficient accuracy. As for Spain, for instance, if you know how to throw in Don Carlos and the Infanta, and Don Pedro[30] and Seville and Granada, from time to time in the right proportions,—they may have changed the names a little since I saw the papers,—and serve up a bull-fight when other entertainments fail, it will be true to the letter, and give us as good an idea of the exact state or ruin of things in Spain as the most succinct and lucid reports under this head in the newspapers: and as for England, almost the last significant scrap of news from that quarter was the revolution of 1649;[31] and if you have learned the history of her crops for an average year, you never need attend to that thing again, unless your speculations are of a merely pecuniary character. If one may judge who rarely looks into the newspapers, nothing new does ever happen in foreign parts, a French revolution not excepted.

What news! how much more important to know what that is which was never old! "Kieou-pe-yu (great dignitary of the state of Wei) sent a man to Khoung-tseu[32] to know his news. Khoung-tseu caused the messenger to be seated near him, and questioned him in these terms: What is your master doing? The messenger answered with respect: My master desires to diminish the number of his faults, but he cannot accomplish it. The messenger being gone, the philosopher remarked: What a worthy messenger! What a worthy messenger!" The preacher, instead of vexing the ears of drowsy farmers on their day of rest at the end of the week,—for Sunday is the fit conclusion of an ill-spent week, and not the fresh and brave beginning of a new one,—with this one other draggle-tail of a sermon, should shout with thundering voice,—"Pause! Avast! Why so seeming fast, but deadly slow?"

Shams and delusions are esteemed for soundest truths, while reality is fabulous. If men would steadily observe realities only, and not allow themselves to be deluded, life, to compare it with such things as we know, would be like a fairy tale and the Arabian Nights' Entertainments.[33] If we respected only what is inevitable and has a right to be, music and poetry would resound along the streets.

---

[29] From Worcester, Massachusetts, to Albany, New York.

[30] Don Carlos de Borbón (1788–1855) revolted when his niece Isabella II (1830–1904), the Infanta, was named to the throne of Spain; Dom Pedro de Alcántara Bourbón (1798–1834) of Portugal overthrew his usurping brother, Dom Miguel, and established a constitutional monarchy.

[31] When the Puritan Commonwealth supplanted the English monarchy.

[32] Confucius; the episode is related in the *Analects* (Bk. XIV, Ch. 26).

[33] *The Thousand and One Nights,* a collection of ancient Oriental and Middle Eastern tales.

When we are unhurried and wise, we perceive that only great and worthy things have any permanent and absolute existence,—that petty fears and petty pleasures are but the shadow of the reality. This is always exhilarating and sublime. By closing the eyes and slumbering, and consenting to be deceived by shows, men establish and confirm their daily life of routine and habit every where, which still is built on purely illusory foundations. Children, who play life, discern its true law and relations more clearly than men, who fail to live it worthily, but who think that they are wiser by experience, that is, by failure. I have read in a Hindoo book, that "there was a king's son, who, being expelled in infancy from his native city, was brought up by a forester, and, growing up to maturity in that state, imagined himself to belong to the barbarous race with which he lived. One of his father's ministers having discovered him, revealed to him what he was, and the misconception of his character was removed, and he knew himself to be a prince. So soul," continues the Hindoo philosopher, "from the circumstances in which it is placed, mistakes its own character, until the truth is revealed to it by some holy teacher, and then it knows itself to be *Brahme*."[34] I perceive that we inhabitants of New England live this mean life that we do because our vision does not penetrate the surface of things. We think that that *is* which *appears* to be. If a man should walk through this town and see only the reality, where, think you, would the "Mill-dam"[35] go to? If he should give us an account of the realities he beheld there, we should not recognize the place in his description. Look at a meeting-house, or a court-house, or a jail, or a shop, or a dwelling-house, and say what that thing really is before a true gaze, and they would all go to pieces in your account of them. Men esteem truth remote, in the outskirts of the system, behind the farthest star, before Adam and after the last man. In eternity there is indeed something true and sublime. But all these times and places and occasions are now and here. God himself culminates in the present moment, and will never be more divine in the lapse of all the ages. And we are enabled to apprehend at all what is sublime and noble only by the perpetual instilling and drenching of the reality which surrounds us. The universe constantly and obediently answers to our conceptions; whether we travel fast or slow, the track is laid for us. Let us spend our lives in conceiving then. The poet or the artist never yet had so fair and noble a design but some of his posterity at least could accomplish it.

Let us spend one day as deliberately as Nature, and not be thrown off the track by every nutshell and mosquito's wing that falls on the rails. Let us rise early and fast, or break fast, gently and without perturbation; let company come and let company go, let the bells ring and the children cry,—determined to make a day of it. Why should we knock under and go with the stream? Let us not be upset and overwhelmed in that terrible rapid and whirlpool called a dinner, situated in the meridian shallows. Weather this danger and you are safe, for the rest of the way is down hill. With unrelaxed nerves, with morning vigor, sail by it, looking another way, tied to the mast like Ulysses.[36] If the engine whistles, let it whistle till it is hoarse for its pains. If the bell rings, why should we run? We will consider what kind of music they are like. Let us settle ourselves, and work and wedge our feet downward through the mud and slush of opinion, and prejudice, and tradition,

---

[34] In Hindu theology, Brahma, the chief member of the trinity and creator of the universe.

[35] The commercial center of Concord.

[36] In Homer's *Odyssey*, Ulysses (Odysseus) has himself tied to his ship's mast so he can hear the seductive song of the Sirens and not be lured to destruction.

and delusion, and appearance, that alluvion[37] which covers the globe, through Paris and London, through New York and Boston and Concord, through church and state, through poetry and philosophy and religion, till we come to a hard bottom and rocks in place, which we can call *reality*, and say, This is, and no mistake; and then begin, having a *point d'appui*,[38] below freshet and frost and fire, a place where you might found a wall or a state, or set a lamp-post safely, or perhaps a gauge, not a Nilometer,[39] but a Realometer, that future ages might know how deep a freshet of shams and appearances had gathered from time to time. If you stand right fronting and face to face to a fact, you will see the sun glimmer on both its surfaces, as if it were a cimeter,[40] and feel its sweet edge dividing you through the heart and marrow, and so you will happily conclude your mortal career. Be it life or death, we crave only reality. If we are really dying, let us hear the rattle in our throats and feel cold in the extremities; if we are alive, let us go about our business.

Time is but the stream I go a-fishing in. I drink at it; but while I drink I see the sandy bottom and detect how shallow it is. Its thin current slides away but eternity remains. I would drink deeper; fish in the sky, whose bottom is pebbly with stars. I cannot count one. I know not the first letter of the alphabet. I have always been regretting that I was not as wise as the day I was born. The intellect is a cleaver; it discerns and rifts its way into the secret of things. I do not wish to be any more busy with my hands than is necessary. My head is hands and feet. I feel all my best faculties concentrated in it. My instinct tells me that my head is an organ for burrowing, as some creatures use their snout and fore-paws, and with it I would mine and burrow my way through these hills. I think that the richest vein is somewhere hereabouts; so by the divining rod and thin rising vapors[41] I judge; and here I will begin to mine.

XII: Brute Neighbors

Sometimes I had a companion[1] in my fishing, who came through the village to my house from the other side of the town, and the catching of the dinner was as much a social exercise as the eating of it.

Hermit. I wonder what the world is doing now. I have not heard so much as a locust over the sweet-fern these three hours. The pigeons are all asleep upon their roosts,—no flutter from them. Was that a farmer's noon horn which sounded from beyond the woods just now? The hands are coming in to boiled salt beef and cider and Indian bread. Why will men worry themselves so? He that does not eat need not work. I wonder how much they have reaped. Who would live there where a body can never think for the barking of Bose?[2] And O, the housekeeping! to keep bright the devil's door-knobs, and scour his tubs this bright day! Better not keep a house. Say, some hollow tree; and then for morning calls and dinner-

---

[37] Alluvium, sediment deposited by flowing water.
[38] "Point of support" (French), or base of operations.
[39] A gauge used by Egyptians to measure the depth of the Nile River.
[40] A scimitar, a sword with a curved blade.
[41] In superstition, aids in locating water or precious metals underground.
[1] The younger William Ellery Channing, the "Poet" in the following dialogue with the "Hermit" (Thoreau).
[2] Then a common name for a dog.

parties! Only a woodpecker tapping. O, they swarm; the sun is too warm there; they are born too far into life for me. I have water from the spring, and a loaf of brown bread on the shelf.—Hark! I hear a rustling of the leaves. Is it some ill-fed village hound yielding to the instinct of the chase? or the lost pig which is said to be in these woods, whose tracks I saw after the rain? It comes on apace; my sumachs and sweet-briars tremble.—Eh, Mr. Poet, is it you? How do you like the world to-day?

Poet. See those clouds; how they hang! That's the greatest thing I have seen to-day. There's nothing like it in old paintings, nothing like it in foreign lands,— unless when we were off the coast of Spain. That's a true Mediterranean sky. I thought, as I have my living to get, and have not eaten to-day, that I might go a-fishing. That's the true industry for poets. It is the only trade I have learned. Come, let's along.

Hermit. I cannot resist. My brown bread will soon be gone. I will go with you gladly soon, but I am just concluding a serious meditation. I think that I am near the end of it. Leave me alone, then, for a while. But that we may not be delayed, you shall be digging the bait meanwhile. Angle-worms are rarely to be met with in these parts, where the soil was never fattened with manure; the race is nearly extinct. The sport of digging the bait is nearly equal to that of catching the fish, when one's appetite is not too keen; and this you may have all to yourself to-day. I would advise you to set in the spade down yonder among the ground-nuts, where you see the johnswort waving. I think that I may warrant you one worm to every three sods you turn up, if you look well in among the roots of the grass, as if you were weeding. Or, if you choose to go farther, it will not be unwise, for I have found the increase of fair bait to be very nearly as the squares of the distances.

Hermit alone. Let me see; where was I? Methinks I was nearly in this frame of mind; the world lay about at this angle. Shall I go to heaven or a-fishing? If I should soon bring this meditation to an end, would another so sweet occasion be likely to offer? I was as near being resolved into the essence of things as ever I was in my life. I fear my thoughts will not come back to me. If it would do any good, I would whistle for them. When they make us an offer, is it wise to say, We will think of it? My thoughts have left no track, and I cannot find the path again. What was it that I was thinking of? It was a very hazy day. I will just try these three sentences of Con-fut-see;[3] they may fetch that state about again. I know not whether it was the dumps or a budding ecstasy. Mem.[4] There never is but one opportunity of a kind.

Poet. How now, Hermit, is it too soon? I have got just thirteen whole ones, beside several which are imperfect or undersized; but they will do for the smaller fry; they do not cover up the hook so much. Those village worms are quite too large; a shiner may make a meal off one without finding the skewer.

Hermit. Well, then, let's be off. Shall we to the Concord? There's good sport there if the water be not too high.

Why do precisely these objects which we behold make a world? Why has man just these species of animals for his neighbors; as if nothing but a mouse could have filled this crevice? I suspect that Pilpay & Co.[5] have put animals to their best

[3] Confucius.   [4] Memorandum.
[5] Pilpay was the supposed author of a collection of Sanskrit animal fables; "& Co." refers to others who relate such fables.

use, for they are all beasts of burden, in a sense, made to carry some portion of our thoughts.

The mice which haunted my house were not the common ones, which are said to have been introduced into the country, but a wild native kind (*Mus leucopus*) not found in the village. I sent one to a distinguished naturalist,[6] and it interested him much. When I was building, one of these had its nest underneath the house, and before I had laid the second floor, and swept out the shavings, would come out regularly at lunch time and pick up the crumbs at my feet. It probably had never seen a man before; and it soon became quite familiar, and would run over my shoes and up my clothes. It could readily ascend the sides of the room by short impulses, like a squirrel, which it resembled in its motions. At length, as I leaned with my elbow on the bench one day, it ran up my clothes, and along my sleeve, and round and round the paper which held my dinner, while I kept the latter close, and dodged and played at bo-peep with it; and when at last I held still a piece of cheese between my thumb and finger, it came and nibbled it, sitting in my hand, and afterward cleaned its face and paws, like a fly, and walked away.

A phœbe soon built in my shed, and a robin for protection in a pine which grew against the house. In June the partridge, (*Tetrao umbellus*,) which is so shy a bird, led her brood past my windows, from the woods in the rear to the front of my house, clucking and calling to them like a hen, and in all her behavior proving herself the hen of the woods. The young suddenly disperse on your approach, at a signal from the mother, as if a whirlwind had swept them away, and they so exactly resemble the dried leaves and twigs that many a traveller has placed his foot in the midst of a brood, and heard the whir of the old bird as she flew off, and her anxious calls and mewing, or seen her trail her wings to attract his attention, without suspecting their neighborhood. The parent will sometimes roll and spin round before you in such a dishabille, that you cannot, for a few moments, detect what kind of creature it is. The young squat still and flat, often running their heads under a leaf, and mind only their mother's directions given from a distance, nor will your approach make them run again and betray themselves. You may even tread on them, or have your eyes on them for a minute, without discovering them. I have held them in my open hand at such a time, and still their only care, obedient to their mother and their instinct, was to squat there without fear or trembling. So perfect is this instinct, that once, when I had laid them on the leaves again, and one accidentally fell on its side, it was found with the rest in exactly the same position ten minutes afterward. They are not callow like the young of most birds, but more perfectly developed and precocious even than chickens. The remarkably adult yet innocent expression of their open and serene eyes is very memorable. All intelligence seems reflected in them. They suggest not merely the purity of infancy, but a wisdom clarified by experience. Such an eye was not born when the bird was, but is coeval with the sky it reflects. The woods do not yield another such a gem. The traveller does not often look into such a limpid well. The ignorant or reckless sportsman often shoots the parent at such a time, and leaves these innocents to fall a prey to some prowling beast or bird, or gradually mingle with the decaying leaves which they so much resemble. It is said that when hatched by a hen they will directly disperse on some alarm, and so are lost, for they never hear the mother's call which gathers them again. These were my hens and chickens.

[6] Louis Agassiz (1807–1873), a Swiss zoologist and geologist who came to America in 1846 and began teaching at Harvard in 1848.

It is remarkable how many creatures live wild and free though secret in the woods, and still sustain themselves in the neighborhood of towns, suspected by hunters only. How retired the otter manages to live here! He grows to be four feet long, as big as a small boy, perhaps without any human being getting a glimpse of him. I formerly saw the raccoon in the woods behind where my house is built, and probably still heard their whinnering at night. Commonly I rested an hour or two in the shade at noon, after planting, and ate my lunch, and read a little by a spring which was the source of a swamp and of a brook, oozing from under Brister's Hill, half a mile from my field. The approach to this was through a succession of descending grassy hollows, full of young pitch-pines, into a larger wood about the swamp. There, in a very secluded and shaded spot, under a spreading white-pine, there was yet a clean firm sward to sit on. I had dug out the spring and made a well of clear gray water, where I could dip up a pailful without roiling it, and thither I went for this purpose almost every day in midsummer, when the pond was warmest. Thither too the wood-cock led her brood, to probe the mud for worms, flying but a foot above them down the bank, while they ran in a troop beneath; but at last, spying me, she would leave her young and circle round and round me, nearer and nearer, till within four or five feet, pretending broken wings and legs, to attract my attention and get off her young, who would already have taken up their march, with faint wiry peep, single file through the swamp, as she directed. Or I heard the peep of the young when I could not see the parent bird. There too the turtle-doves sat over the spring, or fluttered from bough to bough of the soft white-pines over my head; or the red squirrel, coursing down the nearest bough, was particularly familiar and inquisitive. You only need sit still long enough in some attractive spot in the woods that all its inhabitants may exhibit themselves to you by turns.

I was witness to events of a less peaceful character. One day when I went out to my wood-pile, or rather my pile of stumps, I observed two large ants, the one red, the other much larger, nearly half an inch long, and black, fiercely contending with one another. Having once got hold they never let go, but struggled and wrestled and rolled on the chips incessantly. Looking farther, I was surprised to find that the chips were covered with such combatants, that it was not a *duellum,* but a *bellum,*[7] a war between two races of ants, the red always pitted against the black, and frequently two red ones to one black. The legions of these Myrmidons[8] covered all the hills and vales in my wood-yard, and the ground was already strewn with the dead and dying, both red and black. It was the only battle which I have ever witnessed, the only battle-field I ever trod while the battle was raging; internecine war; the red republicans on the one hand, and the black imperialists on the other. On every side they were engaged in deadly combat, yet without any noise that I could hear, and human soldiers never fought so resolutely. I watched a couple that were fast locked in each other's embraces, in a little sunny valley amid the chips, now at noon-day prepared to fight till the sun went down, or life went out. The smaller red champion had fastened himself like a vice to his adversary's front, and through all the tumblings on that field never for an instant ceased to gnaw at one of his feelers near the root, having already caused the other to go by the board; while the stronger black one dashed him from side to side, and, as I saw

---

[7] Not a duel but a war.

[8] As related in Homer's *Iliad,* the Myrmidons were the troops who fought under the Greek hero Achilles in the Trojan War; because *myrmex* is the Greek word for "ant," Thoreau mock-heroically connects the battle of the ants with the epic struggle of Greeks and Trojans.

on looking nearer, had already divested him of several of his members. They fought with more pertinacity than bull-dogs. Neither manifested the least disposition to retreat. It was evident that their battle-cry was Conquer or die. In the mean while there came along a single red ant on the hillside of this valley, evidently full of excitement, who either had despatched his foe, or had not yet taken part in the battle; probably the latter, for he had lost none of his limbs; whose mother had charged him to return with his shield or upon it.[9] Or perchance he was some Achilles, who had nourished his wrath apart, and had now come to avenge or rescue his Patroclus.[10] He saw this unequal combat from afar,—for the blacks were nearly twice the size of the red,—he drew near with rapid pace till he stood on his guard within half an inch of the combatants; then, watching his opportunity, he sprang upon the black warrior, and commenced his operations near the root of his right fore-leg, leaving the foe to select among his own members; and so there were three united for life, as if a new kind of attraction had been invented which put all other locks and cements to shame. I should not have wondered by this time to find that they had their respective musical bands stationed on some eminent chip, and playing their national airs the while, to excite the slow and cheer the dying combatants. I was myself excited somewhat even as if they had been men. The more you think of it, the less the difference. And certainly there is not the fight recorded in Concord history, at least, if in the history of America, that will bear a moment's comparison with this, whether for the numbers engaged in it, or for the patriotism and heroism displayed. For numbers and for carnage it was an Austerlitz or Dresden.[11] Concord Fight! Two killed on the patriots' side, and Luther Blanchard wounded! Why here every ant was a Buttrick,—"Fire! for God's sake fire!"—and thousands shared the fate of Davis and Hosmer.[12] There was not one hireling[13] there. I have no doubt that it was a principle they fought for, as much as our ancestors, and not to avoid a three-penny tax on their tea; and the results of this battle will be as important and memorable to those whom it concerns as those of the battle of Bunker Hill, at least.

I took up the chip on which the three I have particularly described were struggling, carried it into my house, and placed it under a tumbler on my window-sill, in order to see the issue. Holding a microscope[14] to the first-mentioned red ant, I saw that, though he was assiduously gnawing at the near fore-leg of his enemy, having severed his remaining feeler, his own breast was all torn away, exposing what vitals he had there to the jaws of the black warrior, whose breast-plate was apparently too thick for him to pierce; and the dark carbuncles of the sufferer's eyes shone with ferocity such as war only could excite. They struggled half an hour longer under the tumbler, and when I looked again the black soldier had severed the heads of his foes from their bodies, and the still living heads were hanging on either side of him like ghastly trophies at his saddle-bow, still apparently as firmly fastened as ever, and he was endeavoring with feeble struggles,

---

[9] Supposedly, the exhortation of a Spartan mother to her son, as reported in *Sayings of Spartan Women,* by the Greek biographer Plutarch (A.D.46?–120?).

[10] After a quarrel with the Greek leader Agamemnon during the Trojan War, the temperamental Achilles sulked in his tent until the death of his friend Patroclus brought him fiercely into battle.

[11] Battles fought during the Napoleonic Wars in the first decade of the nineteenth century.

[12] Davis and Hosmer were the only colonists killed at the American Revolutionary War battle of Concord on April 19, 1775; Blanchard and Buttrick were active in the battle. The cry "Fire! for God's sake fire!" was reportedly sounded at the outset of the battle.

[13] A mercenary soldier.   [14] A magnifying glass.

being without feelers and with only the remnant of a leg, and I know not how many other wounds, to divest himself of them; which at length, after half an hour more, he accomplished. I raised the glass, and he went off over the window-sill in that crippled state. Whether he finally survived that combat, and spent the remainder of his days in some Hotel des Invalides,[15] I do not know; but I thought that his industry would not be worth much thereafter. I never learned which party was victorious, nor the cause of the war; but I felt for the rest of that day as if I had had my feelings excited and harrowed by witnessing the struggle, the ferocity and carnage, of a human battle before my door.

Kirby and Spence tell us that the battles of ants have long been celebrated and the date of them recorded, though they say that Huber[16] is the only modern author who appears to have witnessed them. "Æneas Sylvius,"[17] say they, "after giving a very circumstantial account of one contested with great obstinacy by a great and small species on the trunk of a pear tree," adds that "'This action was fought in the pontificate of Eugenius the Fourth,[18] in the presence of Nicholas Pistoriensis, an eminent lawyer, who related the whole history of the battle with the greatest fidelity.' A similar engagement between great and small ants is recorded by Olaus Magnus,[19] in which the small ones, being victorious, are said to have buried the bodies of their own soldiers, but left those of their giant enemies a prey to the birds. This event happened previous to the expulsion of the tyrant Christiern the Second[20] from Sweden." The battle which I witnessed took place in the Presidency of Polk, five years before the passage of Webster's Fugitive-Slave Bill.[21]

Many a village Bose, fit only to course[22] a mud-turtle in a victualling cellar, sported his heavy quarters in the woods, without the knowledge of his master, and ineffectually smelled at old fox burrows and woodchucks' holes; led perchance by some slight cur which nimbly threaded the wood, and might still inspire a natural terror in its denizens;—now far behind his guide, barking like a canine bull toward some small squirrel which had treed itself for scrutiny, then, cantering off, bending the bushes with his weight, imagining that he is on the track of some stray member of the gerbille family. Once I was surprised to see a cat walking along the stony shore of the pond, for they rarely wander so far from home. The surprise was mutual. Nevertheless the most domestic cat, which has lain on a rug all her days, appears quite at home in the woods, and, by her sly and stealthy behavior, proves herself more native there than the regular inhabitants. Once, when berrying, I met with a cat with young kittens in the woods, quite wild, and they all, like their mother, had their backs up and were fiercely spitting at me. A few years before I lived in the woods there was what was called a "winged cat" in one of the

[15] At one time the soldiers' hospital in Paris; now the site of Napoleon's tomb.

[16] Pierre Huber (1777–1840), an entomologist whose *The Natural History of Ants* (1810) includes a description of ants fighting that was incorporated in Kirby and Spence's *Introduction to Entomology*.

[17] The pen name of Enea Silvio Piccolomini (1405–1464), a noted humanist scholar who became Pope Pius II (1458–1464).

[18] Gabriele Condulmer (1383–1447), a Venetian who served as Pope Eugene IV from 1431 to 1447.

[19] Magnus (1490–1557) was a Swedish bishop and historian.

[20] Christian II (1481–1559), king of Denmark and Norway (1513–1523), who conducted a massacre of Swedish nobles during his reign as king of Sweden (1520–1523). Deposed in 1523, he was imprisoned for life in 1532.

[21] In 1845: here Thoreau again criticizes Daniel Webster, senator from Massachusetts, who supported the Compromise of 1850, which strengthened the Fugitive Slave Act. James K. Polk, eleventh U.S. president (1845–1849) did not formally leave office until March, as was the custom then.

[22] Chase.

farm-houses in Lincoln nearest the pond, Mr. Gilian Baker's. When I called to see her in June, 1842, she was gone a-hunting in the woods, as was her wont, (I am not sure whether it was a male or female, and so use the more common pronoun,) but her mistress told me that she came into the neighborhood a little more than a year before, in April, and was finally taken into their house; that she was of dark brownish-gray color, with a white spot on her throat, and white feet, and had a large bushy tail like a fox; that in the winter the fur grew thick and flatted out along her sides, forming strips ten or twelve inches long by two and a half wide, and under her chin like a muff, the upper side loose, the under matted like felt, and in the spring these appendages cropped off. They gave me a pair of her "wings," which I keep still. There is no appearance of a membrane about them. Some thought it was part flying-squirrel or some other wild animal, which is not impossible, for, according to naturalists, prolific hybrids have been produced by the union of the marten and domestic cat. This would have been the right kind of cat for me to keep, if I had kept any; for why should not a poet's cat be winged as well as his horse?[23]

In the fall the loon (*Colymbus glacialis*) came, as usual, to moult and bathe in the pond, making the woods ring with his wild laughter before I had risen. At rumor of his arrival all the Mill-dam sportsmen are on the alert, in gigs and on foot, two by two and three by three, with patent rifles and conical balls[24] and spy-glasses. They come rustling through the woods like autumn leaves, at least ten men to one loon. Some station themselves on this side of the pond, some on that, for the poor bird cannot be omnipresent; if he dive here he must come up there. But now the kind October wind rises, rustling the leaves and rippling the surface of the water, so that no loon can be heard or seen, though his foes sweep the pond with spy-glasses, and make the woods resound with their discharges. The waves generously rise and dash angrily, taking sides with all waterfowl, and our sports-men must beat a retreat to town and shop and unfinished jobs. But they were too often successful. When I went to get a pail of water early in the morning I fre-quently saw this stately bird sailing out of my cove within a few rods. If I endeav-ored to overtake him in a boat, in order to see how he would manœuvre, he would dive and be completely lost, so that I did not discover him again, sometimes, till the latter part of the day. But I was more than a match for him on the surface. He commonly went off in a rain.

As I was paddling along the north shore one very calm October afternoon, for such days especially they settle on to the lakes, like the milkweed down, having looked in vain over the pond for a loon, suddenly one, sailing out from the shore toward the middle a few rods in front of me, set up his wild laugh and betrayed himself. I pursued with a paddle and he dived, but when he came up I was nearer than before. He dived again, but I miscalculated the direction he would take, and we were fifty rods apart when he came to the surface this time, for I had helped to widen the interval; and again he laughed long and loud, and with more reason than before. He manœuvred so cunningly that I could not get within half a dozen rods of him. Each time, when he came to the surface, turning his head this way and that, he coolly surveyed the water and the land, and apparently chose his course so that he might come up where there was the widest expanse of water and at the greatest distance from the boat. It was surprising how quickly he made up his

---

[23] According to Greek myth, the winged horse Pegasus represented the poet's inspiration.

[24] Special rifles and bullets.

mind and put his resolve into execution. He led me at once to the widest part of the pond, and could not be driven from it. While he was thinking one thing in his brain, I was endeavoring to divine his thought in mine. It was a pretty game, played on the smooth surface of the pond, a man against a loon. Suddenly your adversary's checker disappears beneath the board, and the problem is to place yours nearest to where his will appear again. Sometimes he would come up unexpectedly on the opposite side of me, having apparently passed directly under the boat. So long-winded was he and so unweariable, that when he had swum farthest he would immediately plunge again, nevertheless; and then no wit could divine where in the deep pond, beneath the smooth surface, he might be speeding his way like a fish, for he had time and ability to visit the bottom of the pond in its deepest part. It is said that loons have been caught in the New York lakes eighty feet beneath the surface, with hooks set for trout,—though Walden is deeper than that. How surprised must the fishes be to see this ungainly visitor from another sphere speeding his way amid their schools! Yet he appeared to know his course as surely under water as on the surface, and swam much faster there. Once or twice I saw a ripple where he approached the surface, just put his head out to reconnoitre, and instantly dived again. I found that it was as well for me to rest on my oars and wait his reappearing as to endeavor to calculate where he would rise; for again and again, when I was straining my eyes over the surface one way, I would suddenly be startled by his unearthly laugh behind me. But why, after displaying so much cunning, did he invariably betray himself the moment he came up by that loud laugh? Did not his white breast enough betray him? He was indeed a silly loon, I thought. I could commonly hear the plash of the water when he came up, and so also detected him. But after an hour he seemed as fresh as ever, dived as willingly and swam yet farther than at first. It was surprising to see how serenely he sailed off with unruffled breast when he came to the surface, doing all the work with his webbed feet beneath. His usual note was this demoniac laughter, yet somewhat like that of a water-fowl; but occasionally, when he had balked me most successfully and come up a long way off, he uttered a long-drawn unearthly howl, probably more like that of a wolf than any bird; as when a beast puts his muzzle to the ground and deliberately howls. This was his looning,—perhaps the wildest sound that is ever heard here, making the woods ring far and wide. I concluded that he laughed in derision of my efforts, confident of his own resources. Though the sky was by this time overcast, the pond was so smooth that I could see where he broke the surface when I did not hear him. His white breast, the stillness of the air, and the smoothness of the water were all against him. At length, having come up fifty rods off, he uttered one of those prolonged howls, as if calling on the god of loons to aid him, and immediately there came a wind from the east and rippled the surface, and filled the whole air with misty rain, and I was impressed as if it were the prayer of the loon answered, and his god was angry with me; and so I left him disappearing far away on the tumultuous surface.

For hours, in fall days, I watched the ducks cunningly tack and veer and hold the middle of the pond, far from the sportsman; tricks which they will have less need to practise in Louisiana bayous. When compelled to rise they would sometimes circle round and round and over the pond at a considerable height, from which they could easily see to other ponds and the river, like black motes in the sky; and, when I thought they had gone off thither long since, they would settle down by a slanting flight of a quarter of a mile on to a distant part which was left free; but what beside safety they got by sailing in the middle of Walden I do not know, unless they love its water for the same reason that I do.

XVII: Spring

The opening of large tracts by the ice-cutters commonly causes a pond to break up earlier; for the water, agitated by the wind, even in cold weather, wears away the surrounding ice. But such was not the effect on Walden that year, for she had soon got a thick new garment to take the place of the old.[1] This pond never breaks up so soon as the others in this neighborhood, on account both of its greater depth and its having no stream passing through it to melt or wear away the ice. I never knew it to open in the course of a winter, not excepting that of '52–3, which gave the ponds so severe a trial. It commonly opens about the first of April, a week or ten days later than Flint's Pond and Fair-Haven, beginning to melt on the north side and in the shallower parts where it began to freeze. It indicates better than any water hereabouts the absolute progress of the season, being least affected by transient changes of temperature. A severe cold of a few days' duration in March may very much retard the opening of the former ponds, while the temperature of Walden increases almost uninterruptedly. A thermometer thrust into the middle of Walden on the 6th of March, 1847, stood at 32°, or freezing point; near the shore at 33°; in the middle of Flint's Pond, the same day, at 32 1/2°; at a dozen rods from the shore, in shallow water, under ice a foot thick, at 36°. This difference of three and a half degrees between the temperature of the deep water and the shallow in the latter pond, and the fact that a great proportion of it is comparatively shallow, show why it should break up so much sooner than Walden. The ice in the shallowest part was at this time several inches thinner than in the middle. In midwinter the middle had been the warmest and the ice thinnest there. So, also, every one who has waded about the shores of a pond in summer must have perceived how much warmer the water is close to the shore, where only three or four inches deep, than a little distance out, and on the surface where it is deep, than near the bottom. In spring the sun not only exerts an influence through the increased temperature of the air and earth, but its heat passes through ice a foot or more thick, and is reflected from the bottom in shallow water, and so also warms the water and melts the under side of the ice, at the same time that it is melting it more directly above, making it uneven, and causing the air bubbles which it contains to extend themselves upward and downward until it is completely honey-combed, and at last disappears suddenly in a single spring rain. Ice has its grain as well as wood, and when a cake begins to rot or "comb," that is, assume the appearance of honey-comb, whatever may be its position, the air cells are at right angles with what was the water surface. Where there is a rock or a log rising near to the surface the ice over it is much thinner, and is frequently quite dissolved by this reflected heat; and I have been told that in the experiment at Cambridge to freeze water in a shallow wooden pond, though the cold air circulated underneath, and so had access to both sides, the reflection of the sun from the bottom more than counterbalanced this advantage. When a warm rain in the middle of the winter melts off the snow-ice from Walden, and leaves a hard dark or transparent ice on the middle, there will be a strip of rotten though thicker white ice, a rod or more wide, about the shores, created by this reflected heat. Also, as I have said, the

---

[1] Literally and metaphorically, the coming of spring marks the final movement of *Walden;* the renewal of life celebrated here leads into the powerful injunctions to self-discovery pervading Thoreau's "Conclusion."

bubbles themselves within the ice operate as burning glasses to melt the ice beneath.

The phenomena of the year take place every day in a pond on a small scale. Every morning, generally speaking, the shallow water is being warmed more rapidly than the deep, though it may not be made so warm after all, and every evening it is being cooled more rapidly until the morning. The day is an epitome of the year. The night is the winter, the morning and evening are the spring and fall, and the noon is the summer. The cracking and booming of the ice indicate a change of temperature. One pleasant morning after a cold night, February 24th, 1850, having gone to Flint's Pond to spend the day, I noticed with surprise, that when I struck the ice with the head of my axe, it resounded like a gong for many rods around, or as if I had struck on a tight drum-head. The pond began to boom about an hour after sunrise, when it felt the influence of the sun's rays slanted upon it from over the hills; it stretched itself and yawned like a waking man with a gradually increasing tumult, which was kept up three or four hours. It took a short siesta at noon, and boomed once more toward night, as the sun was withdrawing his influence. In the right stage of the weather a pond fires its evening gun with great regularity. But in the middle of the day, being full of cracks, and the air also being less elastic, it had completely lost its resonance, and probably fishes and muskrats could not then have been stunned by a blow on it.[2] The fishermen say that the "thundering of the pond" scares the fishes and prevents their biting. The pond does not thunder every evening, and I cannot tell surely when to expect its thundering; but though I may perceive no difference in the weather, it does. Who would have suspected so large and cold and thick-skinned a thing to be so sensitive? Yet it has its law to which it thunders obedience when it should as surely as the buds expand in the spring. The earth is all alive and covered with papillæ. The largest pond is as sensitive to atmospheric changes as the globule of mercury in its tube.

One attraction in coming to the woods to live was that I should have leisure and opportunity to see the spring come in. The ice in the pond at length begins to be honey-combed, and I can set my heel in it as I walk. Fogs and rains and warmer suns are gradually melting the snow; the days have grown sensibly longer; and I see how I shall get through the winter without adding to my wood-pile, for large fires are no longer necessary. I am on the alert for the first signs of spring, to hear the chance note of some arriving bird, or the striped squirrel's chirp, for his stores must be now nearly exhausted, or see the woodchuck venture out of his winter quarters. On the 13th of March, after I had heard the bluebird, song-sparrow, and red-wing, the ice was still nearly a foot thick. As the weather grew warmer, it was not sensibly worn away by the water, nor broken up and floated off as in rivers, but, though it was completely melted for half a rod in width about the shore, the middle was merely honey-combed and saturated with water, so that you could put your foot through it when six inches thick; but by the next day evening, perhaps, after a warm rain followed by fog, it would have wholly disappeared, all gone off with the fog, spirited away. One year I went across the middle only five days before it disappeared entirely. In 1845 Walden was first completely open on the 1st of April; in '46, the 25th of March; in '47, the 8th of April; in '51, the 28th of

---

[2] Fishermen sometimes smack the ice hard hoping to stun the fish below and make them easier to catch.

March; in '52, the 18th of April; in '53, the 23d of March; in '54, about the 7th of April.

Every incident connected with the breaking up of the rivers and ponds and the settling of the weather is particularly interesting to us who live in a climate of so great extremes. When the warmer days come, they who dwell near the river hear the ice crack at night with a startling whoop as loud as artillery, as if its icy fetters were rent from end to end, and within a few days see it rapidly going out. So the alligator comes out of the mud with quakings of the earth. One old man, who has been a close observer of Nature, and seems as thoroughly wise in regard to all her operations as if she had been put upon the stocks when he was a boy, and he had helped to lay her keel,—who has come to his growth, and can hardly acquire more of natural lore if he should live to the age of Methuselah,[3]—told me, and I was surprised to hear him express wonder at any of Nature's operations, for I thought that there were no secrets between them, that one spring day he took his gun and boat, and thought that he would have a little sport with the ducks. There was ice still on the meadows, but it was all gone out of the river, and he dropped down without obstruction from Sudbury, where he lived, to Fair-Haven Pond, which he found, unexpectedly, covered for the most part with a firm field of ice. It was a warm day, and he was surprised to see so great a body of ice remaining. Not seeing any ducks, he hid his boat on the north or back side of an island in the pond, and then concealed himself in the bushes on the south side, to await them. The ice was melted for three or four rods from the shore, and there was a smooth and warm sheet of water, with a muddy bottom, such as the ducks love, within, and he thought it likely that some would be along pretty soon. After he had lain still there about an hour he heard a low and seemingly very distant sound, but singularly grand and impressive, unlike any thing he had ever heard, gradually swelling and increasing as if it would have a universal and memorable ending, a sullen rush and roar, which seemed to him all at once like the sound of a vast body of fowl coming in to settle there, and, seizing his gun, he started up in haste and excited; but he found, to his surprise, that the whole body of the ice had started while he lay there, and drifted in to the shore, and the sound he had heard was made by its edge grating on the shore,—at first gently nibbled and crumbled off, but at length heaving up and scattering its wrecks along the island to a considerable height before it came to a stand still.

At length the sun's rays have attained the right angle, and warm winds blow up mist and rain and melt the snow banks, and the sun dispersing the mist smiles on a checkered landscape of russet and white smoking with incense, through which the traveller picks his way from islet to islet, cheered by the music of a thousand tinkling rills and rivulets whose veins are filled with the blood of winter which they are bearing off.

Few phenomena gave me more delight than to observe the forms which thawing sand and clay assume in flowing down the sides of a deep cut on the railroad through which I passed on my way to the village, a phenomenon not very common on so large a scale, though the number of freshly exposed banks of the right material must have been greatly multiplied since railroads were invented. The material was sand of every degree of fineness and of various rich colors, commonly mixed with a little clay. When the frost comes out in the spring, and even in a thawing day in the winter, the sand begins to flow down the slopes like lava,

---

[3] In Genesis 5:27, 969 years.

sometimes bursting out through the snow and overflowing it where no sand was to be seen before. Innumerable little streams overlap and interlace one with another, exhibiting a sort of hybrid product, which obeys half way the law of currents, and half way that of vegetation. As it flows it takes the forms of sappy leaves or vines, making heaps of pulpy sprays a foot or more in depth, and resembling, as you look down on them, the laciniated lobed and imbricated thalluses[4] of some lichens; or you are reminded of coral, of leopards' paws or birds' feet, of brains or lungs or bowels, and excrements of all kinds. It is a truly *grotesque* vegetation, whose forms and color we see imitated in bronze, a sort of architectural foliage more ancient and typical than acanthus, chiccory, ivy, vine, or any vegetable leaves; destined perhaps, under some circumstances, to become a puzzle to future geologists. The whole cut impressed me as if it were a cave with its stalactites laid open to the light. The various shades of the sand are singularly rich and agreeable, embracing the different iron colors, brown, gray, yellowish, and reddish. When the flowing mass reaches the drain at the foot of the bank it spreads out flatter into *strands,* the separate streams losing their semi-cylindrical form and gradually becoming more flat and broad, running together as they are more moist, till they form an almost flat *sand,* still variously and beautifully shaded, but in which you can trace the original forms of vegetation; till at length, in the water itself, they are converted into *banks,* like those formed off the mouths of rivers, and the forms of vegetation are lost in the ripple marks on the bottom.

The whole bank, which is from twenty to forty feet high, is sometimes overlaid with a mass of this kind of foliage, or sandy rupture, for a quarter of a mile on one or both sides, the produce of one spring day. What makes this sand foliage remarkable is its springing into existence thus suddenly. When I see on the one side the inert bank,—for the sun acts on one side first,—and on the other this luxuriant foliage, the creation of an hour, I am affected as if in a peculiar sense I stood in the laboratory of the Artist who made the world and me,—had come to where he was still at work, sporting on this bank, and with excess of energy strewing his fresh designs about. I feel as if I were nearer to the vitals of the globe, for this sandy overflow is something such a foliaceous[5] mass as the vitals of the animal body. You find thus in the very sands an anticipation of the vegetable leaf. No wonder that the earth expresses itself outwardly in leaves, it so labors with the idea inwardly. The atoms have already learned this law, and are pregnant by it. The overhanging leaf sees here its prototype. *Internally,* whether in the globe or animal body, it is a moist thick *lobe,* a word especially applicable to the liver and lungs and the *leaves* of fat, ($\lambda\epsilon\iota\beta\omega$, *labor, lapsus,* to flow or slip downward, a lapsing; $\lambda o\beta o\delta$, *globus,* lobe, globe; also lap, flap, and many other words,) *externally* a dry thin *leaf,* even as the *f* and *v* are a pressed and dried *b.* The radicals of lobe are *lb,* the soft mass of the *b* (single lobed, or B, double lobed,) with a liquid *l* behind it pressing it forward. In globe, *glb,* the guttural *g* adds to the meaning the capacity of the throat. The feathers and wings of birds are still drier and thinner leaves. Thus, also, you pass from the lumpish grub in the earth to the airy and fluttering butterfly. The very globe continually transcends and translates itself, and becomes winged in its orbit. Even ice begins with delicate crystal leaves, as if it had flowed into moulds which the fronds of water plants have impressed on the

---

[4] Young shoots that grow with both "laciniated" (deep, irregular) and "imbricated" (lapped over, patterned) lobes.

[5] Like a mass of foliage.

watery mirror. The whole tree itself is but one leaf, and rivers are still vaster leaves whose pulp is intervening earth, and towns and cities are the ova of insects in their axils.[6]

When the sun withdraws the sand ceases to flow, but in the morning the streams will start once more and branch and branch again into a myriad of others. You here see perchance how blood vessels are formed. If you look closely you observe that first there pushes forward from the thawing mass a stream of softened sand with a drop-like point, like the ball of the finger, feeling its way slowly and blindly downward, until at last with more heat and moisture, as the sun gets higher, the most fluid portion, in its effort to obey the law to which the most inert also yields, separates from the latter and forms for itself a meandering channel or artery within that, in which is seen a little silvery stream glancing like lightning from one stage of pulpy leaves or branches to another, and ever and anon swallowed up in the sand. It is wonderful how rapidly yet perfectly the sand organizes itself as it flows, using the best material its mass affords to form the sharp edges of its channel. Such are the sources of rivers. In the silicious matter which the water deposits is perhaps the bony system, and in the still finer soil and organic matter the fleshy fibre or cellular tissue. What is man but a mass of thawing clay? The ball of the human finger is but a drop congealed. The fingers and toes flow to their extent from the thawing mass of the body. Who knows what the human body would expand and flow out to under a more genial heaven? Is not the hand a spreading *palm* leaf with its lobes and veins? The ear may be regarded, fancifully, as a lichen, *umbilicaria*, on the side of the head, with its lobe or drop. The lip (*labium* from *labor* (?)) laps or lapses from the sides of the cavernous mouth. The nose is a manifest congealed drop or stalactite. The chin is a still larger drop, the confluent dripping of the face. The cheeks are a slide from the brows into the valley of the face, opposed and diffused by the cheek bones. Each rounded lobe of the vegetable leaf, too, is a thick and now loitering drop, larger or smaller; the lobes are the fingers of the leaf; and as many lobes as it has, in so many directions it tends to flow, and more heat or other genial influences would have caused it to flow yet farther.

Thus it seemed that this one hillside illustrated the principle of all the operations of Nature. The Maker of this earth but patented a leaf. What Champollion[7] will decipher this hieroglyphic for us, that we may turn over a new leaf at last? This phenomenon is more exhilarating to me than the luxuriance and fertility of vineyards. True, it is somewhat excrementitious in its character, and there is no end to the heaps of liver lights[8] and bowels, as if the globe were turned wrong side outward; but this suggests at least that Nature has some bowels, and there again is mother of humanity. This is the frost coming out of the ground; this is Spring. It precedes the green and flowery spring, as mythology precedes regular poetry. I know of nothing more purgative of winter fumes and indigestions. It convinces me that Earth is still in her swaddling clothes, and stretches forth baby fingers on every side. Fresh curls spring from the baldest brow. There is nothing inorganic.

---

[6] The angle between a branch or leaf and the stem out of which it grows, from the Latin *axilla*, or "armpit."

[7] Jean François Champollion (1790–1832), the French archeologist who deciphered the hieroglyphics on the Rosetta Stone (found in 1799 by Napoleon's troops near the Egyptian city of Rosetta) and thereby made it possible for scholars to learn about ancient Egyptian culture.

[8] Lungs. Many editors put a comma after "liver" to indicate the liver, the lungs, and the bowels. Immediately below, Thoreau makes use of the old belief that the bowels were the seat of compassion.

These foliaceous heaps lie along the bank like the slag of a furnace, showing that Nature is "in full blast" within. The earth is not a mere fragment of dead history, stratum upon stratum like the leaves of a book, to be studied by geologists and antiquaries chiefly, but living poetry like the leaves of a tree, which precede flowers and fruit,—not a fossil earth, but a living earth; compared with whose great central life all animal and vegetable life is merely parasitic. Its throes will heave our exuviæ from their graves. You may melt your metals and cast them into the most beautiful moulds you can; they will never excite me like the forms which this molten earth flows out into. And not only it, but the institutions upon it, are plastic like clay in the hands of the potter.

Ere long, not only on these banks, but on every hill and plain and in every hollow, the frost comes out of the ground like a dormant quadruped from its burrow, and seeks the sea with music, or migrates to other climes in clouds. Thaw with his gentle persuasion is more powerful than Thor[9] with his hammer. The one melts, the other but breaks in pieces.

When the ground was partially bare of snow, and a few warm days had dried its surface somewhat, it was pleasant to compare the first tender signs of the infant year just peeping forth with stately beauty of the withered vegetation which had withstood the winter,—life-everlasting, golden-rods, pinweeds, and graceful wild grasses, more obvious and interesting frequently than in summer even, as if their beauty was not ripe till then; even cotton-grass, cat-tails, mulleins, johnswort, hard-hack, meadow-sweet, and other strong stemmed plants, those unexhausted granaries which entertain the earliest birds,—decent weeds,[10] at least, which widowed Nature wears. I am particularly attracted by the arching and sheaf-like top of the wool-grass; it brings back the summer to our winter memories, and is among the forms which art loves to copy, and which, in the vegetable kingdom, have the same relation to types already in the mind of man that astronomy has. It is an antique style older than Greek or Egyptian. Many of the phenomena of Winter are suggestive of an inexpressible tenderness and fragile delicacy. We are accustomed to hear this king described as a rude and boisterous tyrant; but with the gentleness of a lover he adorns the tresses of Summer.

At the approach of spring the red-squirrels got under my house, two at a time, directly under my feet as I sat reading or writing, and kept up the queerest chuckling and chirruping and vocal pirouetting and gurgling sounds that ever were heard; and when I stamped they only chirruped the louder, as if past all fear and respect in their mad pranks, defying humanity to stop them. No you don't—chickaree—chickaree. They were wholly deaf to my arguments, or failed to perceive their force, and fell into a strain of invective that was irresistible.

The first sparrow of spring! The year beginning with younger hope than ever! The faint silvery warblings heard over the partially bare and moist fields from the blue-bird, the song-sparrow, and the red-wing, as if the last flakes of winter tinkled as they fell! What at such a time are histories, chronologies, traditions, and all written revelations? The brooks sing carols and glees to the spring. The marsh-hawk sailing low over the meadow is already seeking the first slimy life that awakes. The sinking sound of melting snow is heard in all dells, and the ice dis-

---

[9] According to Norse myth, the god of thunder. As pronounced with a New England accent, "thaw" and "Thor" would sound much the same.

[10] Proper attire for mourning.

solves apace in the ponds. The grass flames up on the hillsides like a spring fire,—"et primitus oritur herba imbribus primoribus evocata,"[11]—as if the earth sent forth an inward heat to greet the returning sun; not yellow but green is the color of its flame;—the symbol of perpetual youth, the grass-blade, like a long green ribbon, streams from the sod into the summer, checked indeed by the frost, but anon pushing on again, lifting its spear of last year's hay with the fresh life below. It grows as steadily as the rill oozes out of the ground. It is almost identical with that, for in the growing days of June, when the rills are dry, the grass blades are their channels, and from year to year the herds drink at this perennial green stream, and the mower draws from it betimes their winter supply. So our human life but dies down to its root, and still puts forth its green blade to eternity.

Walden is melting apace. There is a canal two rods wide along the northerly and westerly sides, and wider still at the east end. A great field of ice has cracked off from the main body. I hear a song-sparrow singing from the bushes on the shore,—*olit, olit, olit,—chip, chip, chip, che char,—che wiss, wiss, wiss.* He too is helping to crack it. How handsome the great sweeping curves in the edge of the ice, answering somewhat to those of the shore, but more regular! It is unusually hard, owing to the recent severe but transient cold, and all watered or waved like a palace floor. But the wind slides eastward over its opaque surface in vain, till it reaches the living surface beyond. It is glorious to behold this ribbon of water sparkling in the sun, the bare face of the pond full of glee and youth, as if it spoke the joy of the fishes within it, and of the sands on its shore,—a silvery sheen as from the scales of a *leuciscus*,[12] as it were all one active fish. Such is the contrast between winter and spring. Walden was dead and is alive again.[13] But this spring it broke up more steadily, as I have said.

The change from storm and winter to serene and mild weather, from dark and sluggish hours to bright and elastic ones, is a memorable crisis which all things proclaim. It is seemingly instantaneous at last. Suddenly an influx of light filled my house, though the evening was at hand, and the clouds of winter still overhung it, and the eaves were dripping with sleety rain. I looked out the window, and lo! where yesterday was cold gray ice there lay the transparent pond already calm and full of hope as on a summer evening, reflecting a summer evening sky in its bosom, though none was visible overhead, as if it had intelligence with some remote horizon. I heard a robin in the distance, the first I had heard for many a thousand years, methought, whose note I shall not forget for many a thousand more,—the same sweet and powerful song of yore. O the evening robin, at the end of a New England summer day! If I could ever find the twig he sits upon! I mean *he;* I mean *the twig.* This at least is not the *Turdus migratorius.*[14] The pitch-pines and shrub-oaks about my house, which had so long drooped, suddenly resumed their several characters, looked brighter, greener, and more erect and alive, as if effectually cleansed and restored by the rain. I knew that it would not rain any more. You may tell by looking at any twig of the forest, ay, at your very wood-pile, whether its winter is past or not. As it grew darker, I was startled by the *honking* of geese flying low over the woods, like weary travellers getting in late from southern lakes, and indulging at last in unrestrained complaint and mu-

---

[11] "And the first grass begins to grow, evoked by the first rains" (Latin), from Varro's *Rerum Rusticarum* (II.2).

[12] Freshwater fish.   [13] "For this my son was dead, and is alive again," from Luke 15:24.

[14] American robin.

tual consolation. Standing at my door, I could hear the rush of their wings; when, driving toward my house, they suddenly spied my light, and with hushed clamor wheeled and settled in the pond. So I came in, and shut the door, and passed my first spring night in the woods.

In the morning I watched the geese from the door through the mist, sailing in the middle of the pond, fifty rods off, so large and tumultuous that Walden appeared like an artificial pond for their amusement. But when I stood on the shore they at once rose up with a great flapping of wings at the signal of their commander, and when they had got into rank circled about over my head, twenty-nine of them, and then steered straight to Canada, with a regular *honk* from the leader at intervals, trusting to break their fast in muddier pools. A "plump" of ducks rose at the same time and took the route to the north in the wake of their noisier cousins.

For a week, I heard the circling groping clangor of some solitary goose in the foggy mornings, seeking its companion, and still peopling the woods with the sound of a larger life than they could sustain. In April the pigeons were seen again flying express in small flocks, and in due time I heard the martins twittering over my clearing, though it had not seemed that the township contained so many that it could afford me any, and I fancied that they were peculiarly of the ancient race that dwelt in hollow trees ere white men came. In almost all climes the tortoise and the frog are among the precursors and heralds of this season, and birds fly with song and glancing plumage, and plants spring and bloom, and winds blow, to correct this slight oscillation of the poles and preserve the equilibrium of Nature.

As every season seems best to us in its turn, so the coming in of spring is like the creation of Cosmos out of Chaos and the realization of the Golden Age.—

"Eurus ad Auroram, Nabathæaque regna recessit,
Persidaque, et radiis juga subdita matutinis."

"The East-Wind withdrew to Aurora and the Nabathæan kingdom,
And the Persian, and the ridges placed under the morning rays.

*   *   *

Man was born. Whether that Artificer of things,
The origin of a better world, made him from the divine seed;
Or the earth being recent and lately sundered from the high
Ether, retained some seeds of cognate heaven."[15]

A single gentle rain makes the grass many shades greener. So our prospects brighten on the influx of better thoughts. We should be blessed if we lived in the present always, and took advantage of every accident that befell us, like the grass which confesses the influence of the slightest dew that falls on it; and did not spend our time in atoning for the neglect of past opportunities, which we call doing our duty. We loiter in winter while it is already spring. In a pleasant spring morning all men's sins are forgiven. Such a day is a truce to vice. While such a sun holds out to burn, the vilest sinner may return. Through our own recovered innocence we discern the innocence of our neighbors. You may have known your

---

[15] From the *Metamorphoses* (Bk. I), of the Latin poet Ovid (43 B.C.–A.D. 18).

neighbor yesterday for a thief, a drunkard, or a sensualist, and merely pitied or despised him, and despaired of the world; but the sun shines bright and warm this first spring morning, re-creating the world, and you meet him at some serene work, and see how his exhausted and debauched veins expand with still joy and bless the new day, feel the spring influence with the innocence of infancy, and all his faults are forgotten. There is not only an atmosphere of good will about him, but even a savor of holiness groping for expression, blindly and ineffectually perhaps, like a new-born instinct, and for a short hour the south hill-side echoes to no vulgar jest. You see some innocent fair shoots preparing to burst from his gnarled rind and try another year's life, tender and fresh as the youngest plant. Even he has entered into the joy of his Lord. Why the jailer does not leave open his prison doors,—why the judge does not dismiss his case,—why the preacher does not dismiss his congregation! It is because they do not obey the hint which God gives them, nor accept the pardon which he freely offers to all.

"A return to goodness produced each day in the tranquil and beneficent breath of the morning, causes that in respect to the love of virtue and the hatred of vice, one approaches a little the primitive nature of man, as the sprouts of the forest which has been felled. In like manner the evil which one does in the interval of a day prevents the germs of virtues which began to spring up again from developing themselves and destroys them.

"After the germs of virtue have thus been prevented many times from developing themselves, then the beneficent breath of evening does not suffice to preserve them. As soon as the breath of evening does not suffice longer to preserve them, then the nature of man does not differ much from that of the brute. Men seeing the nature of this man like that of the brute, think that he has never possessed the innate faculty of reason. Are those the true and natural sentiments of man?"[16]

> "The Golden Age was first created, which without any avenger
> Spontaneously without law cherished fidelity and rectitude.
> Punishment and fear were not; nor were threatening words read
> On suspended brass; nor did the suppliant crowd fear
> The words of their judge; but were safe without an avenger.
> Not yet the pine felled on its mountains had descended
> To the liquid waves that it might see a foreign world,
> And mortals knew no shores but their own.

> *   *   *

> There was eternal spring, and placid zephyrs with warm
> Blasts soothed the flowers born without seed."[17]

On the 29th of April, as I was fishing from the bank of the river near the Nine-Acre-Corner bridge, standing on the quaking grass and willow roots, where the muskrats lurk, I heard a singular rattling sound, somewhat like that of the sticks which boys play with their fingers, when, looking up, I observed a very slight and graceful hawk, like a night-hawk, alternately soaring like a ripple and tumbling a rod or two over and over, showing the underside of its wings, which gleamed like a satin ribbon in the sun, or like the pearly inside of a shell. This

---

[16] From the *Book of Mencius* (VI.1).   [17] From Ovid's *Metamorphoses*, Bk. I.

sight reminded me of falconry and what nobleness and poetry are associated with that sport. The Merlin it seemed to me it might be called: but I care not for its name. It was the most ethereal flight I had ever witnessed. It did not simply flutter like a butterfly, nor soar like the larger hawks, but it sported with proud reliance in the fields of air; mounting again and again with its strange chuckle, it repeated its free and beautiful fall, turning over and over like a kite, and then recovering from its lofty tumbling, as if it had never set its foot on *terra firma*. It appeared to have no companion in the universe,—sporting there alone,—and to need none but the morning and the ether with which it played. It was not lonely, but made all the earth lonely beneath it. Where was the parent which hatched it, its kindred, and its father in the heavens? The tenant of the air, it seemed related to the earth but by an egg hatched some time in the crevice of a crag;—or was its native nest made in the angle of a cloud, woven of the rainbow's trimmings and the sunset sky, and lined with some soft midsummer haze caught up from earth? Its eyry[18] now some cliffy cloud.

Beside this I got a rare mess of golden and silver and bright cupreous[19] fishes, which looked like a string of jewels. Ah! I have penetrated to those meadows on the morning of many a first spring day, jumping from hummock to hummock, from willow root to willow root, when the wild river valley and the woods were bathed in so pure and bright a light as would have waked the dead, if they had been slumbering in their graves, as some suppose. There needs no stronger proof of immortality. All things must live in such a light. O Death, where was thy sting? O Grave, where was thy victory, then?[20]

Our village life would stagnate if it were not for the unexplored forests and meadows which surround it. We need the tonic of wilderness,—to wade sometimes in marshes where the bittern and the meadow-hen lurk, and hear the booming of the snipe; to smell the whispering sedge where only some wilder and more solitary fowl builds her nest, and the mink crawls with its belly close to the ground. At the same time that we are earnest to explore and learn all things, we require that all things be mysterious and unexplorable, that land and sea be infinitely wild, unsurveyed and unfathomed by us because unfathomable. We can never have enough of Nature. We must be refreshed by the sight of inexhaustible vigor, vast and Titanic features, the sea-coast with its wrecks, the wilderness with its living and its decaying trees, the thunder cloud, and the rain which lasts three weeks and produces freshets. We need to witness our own limits transgressed, and some life pasturing freely where we never wander. We are cheered when we observe the vulture feeding on the carrion which disgusts and disheartens us and deriving health and strength from the repast. There was a dead horse in the hollow by the path to my house, which compelled me sometimes to go out of my way, especially in the night when the air was heavy, but the assurance it gave me of the strong appetite and inviolable health of Nature was my compensation for this. I love to see that Nature is so rife with life that myriads can be afforded to be sacrificed and suffered to prey on one another; that tender organizations can be so serenely squashed out of existence like pulp,—tadpoles which herons gobble up, and tortoises and toads run over in the road; and that sometimes it has rained flesh and blood! With the liability to accident, we must see how little account is to be made of it. The impression made on a wise man is that of universal innocence.

---

[18] Aerie, or bird's nest.   [19] Copper-colored.
[20] "O death, where is thy sting? O grave, where is thy victory?" from I Corinthians 15:55.

Poison is not poisonous after all, nor are any wounds fatal. Compassion is a very untenable ground. It must be expeditious. Its pleadings will not bear to be stereo-typed.

Early in May, the oaks, hickories, maples, and other trees, just putting out amidst the pine woods around the pond, imparted a brightness like sunshine to the landscape, especially in cloudy days, as if the sun were breaking through mists and shining faintly on the hill-sides here and there. On the third or fourth of May I saw a loon in the pond, and during the first week of the month I heard the whippoorwill, the brown-thrasher, the veery, the wood-pewee, the chewink, and other birds. I had heard the wood-thrush long before. The phœbe had already come once more and looked in at my door and window, to see if my house was cavern-like enough for her, sustaining herself on humming wings with clinched talons, as if she held by the air, while she surveyed the premises. The sulphur-like pollen of the pitch-pine soon covered the pond and the stones and rotten wood along the shore, so that you could have collected a barrel-ful. This is the "sulphur showers" we hear of. Even in Calidas' drama of Sacontala,[21] we read of "rills dyed yellow with the golden dust of the lotus." And so the seasons went rolling on into summer, as one rambles into higher and higher grass.

Thus was my first year's life in the woods completed; and the second year was similar to it.[22] I finally left Walden September 6th, 1847.

XVIII: CONCLUSION

To the sick the doctors wisely recommend a change of air and scenery. Thank Heaven, here is not all the world. The buck-eye does not grow in New England, and the mocking-bird is rarely heard here. The wild-goose is more of a cosmopo-lite than we; he breaks his fast in Canada, takes a luncheon in the Ohio, and plumes himself for the night in a southern bayou. Even the bison, to some extent, keeps pace with the seasons, cropping the pastures of the Colorado only till a greener and sweeter grass awaits him by the Yellowstone. Yet we think that if rail-fences are pulled down, and stone-walls piled up on our farms, bounds are henceforth set to our lives and our fates decided. If you are chosen town-clerk, forsooth, you cannot go to Tierra del Fuego[1] this summer: but you may go to the land of infernal fire nevertheless. The universe is wider than our views of it.

Yet we should oftener look over the tafferel[2] of our craft, like curious passen-gers, and not make the voyage like stupid sailors picking oakum.[3] The other side of the globe is but the home of our correspondent. Our voyaging is only great-circle sailing,[4] and the doctors prescribe for diseases of the skin merely. One has-tens to Southern Africa to chase the giraffe; but surely that is not the game he

---

[21] The Sanskrit drama *Sacontalá,* by the fifth-century Hindu writer Cálidás. Thoreau knew this work in a translation by Sir William Jones (1746–1794), a British expert on Sanskrit.

[22] A reminder that Thoreau has shaped the experience of twenty-six months into one year.

[1] At the southernmost tip of South America; its translation from Spanish, "Land of Fire," can be juxtaposed with "the land of infernal fire," below.

[2] Rail at the ship's stern ("taffrail").

[3] Picking old rope apart so that it can be tarred and used for caulking.

[4] Sailing by the most direct route.

would be after. How long, pray, would a man hunt giraffes if he could? Snipes and woodcocks also may afford rare sport; but I trust it would be nobler game to shoot one's self.—

> "Direct your eye sight inward, and you'll find
> A thousand regions in your mind
> Yet undiscovered. Travel them, and be
> Expert in home-cosmography."[5]

What does Africa,—what does the West stand for? Is not our own interior white on the chart?[6] black though it may prove, like the coast, when discovered. Is it the source of the Nile, or the Niger, or the Mississippi, or a North-West Passage around this continent, that we would find? Are these the problems which most concern mankind? Is Franklin[7] the only man who is lost, that his wife should be so earnest to find him? Does Mr. Grinnell[8] know where he himself is? Be rather the Mungo Park, the Lewis and Clarke and Frobisher,[9] of your own streams and oceans; explore your own higher latitudes,—with shiploads of preserved meats to support you, if they be necessary; and pile the empty cans sky-high for a sign.[10] Were preserved meats invented to preserve meat merely? Nay, be a Columbus to whole new continents and worlds within you, opening new channels, not of trade, but of thought. Every man is the lord of a realm beside which the earthly empire of the Czar[11] is but a petty state, a hummock left by the ice. Yet some can be patriotic who have no *self*-respect, and sacrifice the greater to the less. They love the soil which makes their graves, but have no sympathy with the spirit which may still animate their clay. Patriotism is a maggot in their heads. What was the meaning of that South-Sea Exploring Expedition,[12] with all its parade and expense, but an indirect recognition of the fact, that there are continents and seas in the moral world, to which every man is an isthmus or an inlet, yet unexplored by him, but that it is easier to sail many thousand miles through cold and storm and cannibals, in a government ship, with five hundred men and boys to assist one, than it is to explore the private sea, the Atlantic and Pacific Ocean of one's being alone.—

> "Erret, et extremos alter scrutetur Iberos.
> Plus habet hic vitæ, plus habet ille viæ."

---

[5] From "To My Honoured Friend, Sir Ed. P. Knight," by the English poet William Habington (1605–1664).

[6] Unexplored.

[7] Sir John Franklin (1786–1847), a British explorer lost while searching for an Arctic passage from the Atlantic to the Pacific.

[8] Henry Grinnell (1799–1874), a whale-oil merchant from New York, who sponsored two attempts to find Franklin.

[9] Mungo Park (1771–1806), a Scottish explorer of Africa and author of *Travels in the Interior Districts of Africa* (1799); Meriwether Lewis (1774–1809) and William Clark (1770–1838), explorers of the American Northwest (1804–1806); Sir Martin Frobisher (1535?–1594), an English explorer of Canada.

[10] One trace of the lost Franklin expedition was a pile of empty cans that had held tinned meat.

[11] During Thoreau's lifetime, czarist Russia was the largest nation in the world.

[12] The American expedition to the Antarctic (1838–1842) led by the naval officer Charles Wilkes (1798–1877).

> Let them wander and scrutinize the outlandish Australians.
> I have more of God, they more of the road.[13]

It is not worth the while to go round the world to count the cats in Zanzibar.[14] Yet do this even till you can do better, and you may perhaps find some "Symmes' Hole"[15] by which to get at the inside at last. England and France, Spain and Portugal, Gold Coast and Slave Coast, all front on this private sea; but no bark from them has ventured out of sight of land, though it is without doubt the direct way to India. If you would learn to speak all tongues and conform to the customs of all nations, if you would travel farther than all travellers, be naturalized in all climes, and cause the Sphinx to dash her head against a stone,[16] even obey the precept of the old philosopher, and Explore thyself. Herein are demanded the eye and the nerve. Only the defeated and deserters go to the wars, cowards that run away and enlist. Start now on that farthest western way, which does not pause at the Mississippi or the Pacific, nor conduct toward a worn-out China or Japan, but leads on direct a tangent to this sphere, summer and winter, day and night, sun down, moon down, and at last earth down too.

It is said that Mirabeau[17] took to highway robbery "to ascertain what degree of resolution was necessary in order to place one's self in formal opposition to the most sacred laws of society." He declared that "a soldier who fights in the ranks does not require half so much courage as a foot-pad,"[18]—"that honor and religion have never stood in the way of a well-considered and a firm resolve." This was manly, as the world goes; and yet it was idle, if not desperate. A saner man would have found himself often enough "in formal opposition" to what are deemed "the most sacred laws of society," through obedience to yet more sacred laws, and so have tested his resolution without going out of his way. It is not for a man to put himself in such an attitude to society, but to maintain himself in whatever attitude he find himself through obedience to the laws of his being, which will never be one of opposition to a just government, if he should chance to meet with such.

I left the woods for as good a reason as I went there. Perhaps it seemed to me that I had several more lives to live, and could not spare any more time for that one. It is remarkable how easily and insensibly we fall into a particular route, and make a beaten track for ourselves. I had not lived there a week before my feet wore a path from my door to the pond-side; and though it is five or six years since I trod it, it is still quite distinct. It is true, I fear that others may have fallen into it, and so helped to keep it open. The surface of the earth is soft and impressible by the feet of men; and so with the paths which the mind travels. How worn and dusty, then, must be the highways of the world, how deep the ruts of tradition and conformity! I did not wish to take a cabin passage, but rather to go before the mast

---

[13] From the idyll "Old Man of Verona," by the Roman poet Claudian (4th-5th centuries B.C.); Thoreau substitutes "Australians" for "Spaniards," adds the word "outlandish" (perhaps in honor of the Australian outback), and inserts "of God" for "of life."

[14] In his variorum *Walden*, Harding reports that Thoreau had read Charles Pickering's *The Races of Man* (1851), which includes an account of domestic cats in Zanzibar.

[15] In 1818 Captain John Symmes (1780–1829) advanced the theory that the earth is hollow, with openings at the North and South Poles.

[16] The Sphinx killed herself in this way when Oedipus solved her riddle.

[17] Count de Mirabeau (1749–1791), a French statesman; from a passage in *Harper's New Monthly Magazine* in 1850.

[18] A robber.

on the deck of the world, for there I could best see the moonlight amid the mountains. I do not wish to go below now.

I learned this, at least, by my experiment; that if one advances confidently in the direction of his dreams, and endeavors to live the life which he has imagined, he will meet with a success unexpected in common hours. He will put some things behind, will pass an invisible boundary; new, universal, and more liberal laws will begin to establish themselves around and within him; or the old laws be expanded, and interpreted in his favor in a more liberal sense, and he will live with the license of a higher order of beings. In proportion as he simplifies his life, the laws of the universe will appear less complex, and solitude will not be solitude, nor poverty poverty, nor weakness weakness. If you have built castles in the air, your work need not be lost; that is where they should be. Now put the foundations under them.

It is a ridiculous demand which England and America make, that you shall speak so that they can understand you. Neither men nor toad-stools grow so. As if that were important, and there were not enough to understand you without them. As if Nature could support but one order of understandings, could not sustain birds as well as quadrupeds, flying as well as creeping things, and *hush* and *who,* which Bright[19] can understand, were the best English. As if there were safety in stupidity alone. I fear chiefly lest my expression may not be *extra- vagant* enough, may not wander far enough beyond the narrow limits of my daily experience, so as to be adequate to the truth of which I have been convinced. *Extra vagance!* it depends on how you are yarded. The migrating buffalo, which seeks new pastures in another latitude, is not extravagant like the cow which kicks over the pail, leaps the cow-yard fence, and runs after her calf, in milking time. I desire to speak somewhere *without* bounds; like a man in a waking moment, to men in their waking moments; for I am convinced that I cannot exaggerate enough even to lay the foundation of a true expression. Who that has heard a strain of music feared then lest he should speak extravagantly any more forever? In view of the future or possible, we should live quite laxly and undefined in front, our outlines dim and misty on that side; as our shadows reveal an insensible perspiration toward the sun. The volatile truth of our words should continually betray the inadequacy of the residual statement. Their truth is instantly *translated;* its literal monument alone remains. The words which express our faith and piety are not definite; yet they are significant and fragrant like frankincense to superior natures.

Why level downward to our dullest perception always, and praise that as common sense? The commonest sense is the sense of men asleep, which they express by snoring. Sometimes we are inclined to class those who are once-and-a-half witted with the half-witted, because we appreciate only a third part of their wit. Some would find fault with the morning-red, if they ever got up early enough. "They pretend," as I hear, "that the verses of Kabir[20] have four different senses; illusion, spirit, intellect, and the exoteric doctrine of the Vedas;" but in this part of the world it is considered a ground for complaint if a man's writings admit of more than one interpretation. While England endeavors to cure the potato-rot, will not any endeavor to cure the brain-rot, which prevails so much more widely and fatally?

[19] An ox; *hush* and *who* are commands to "go" and "stop."
[20] A Hindu mystic; the quotation, apparently translated by Thoreau, is from *Histoire de la Littérature Hindoue* (1839), by Garcin de Tassy.

I do not suppose that I have attained to obscurity, but I should be proud if no more fatal fault were found with my pages on this score than was found with the Walden ice. Southern customers objected to its blue color, which is the evidence of its purity, as if it were muddy, and preferred the Cambridge ice, which is white, but tastes of weeds. The purity men love is like the mists which envelop the earth, and not like the azure ether beyond.

Some are dinning in our ears that we Americans, and moderns generally, are intellectual dwarfs compared with the ancients, or even the Elizabethan men. But what is that to the purpose? A living dog is better than a dead lion.[21] Shall a man go and hang himself because he belongs to the race of pygmies, and not be the biggest pygmy that he can? Let every one mind his own business, and endeavor to be what he was made.

Why should we be in such desperate haste to succeed, and in such desperate enterprises? If a man does not keep pace with his companions, perhaps it is because he hears a different drummer. Let him step to the music which he hears, however measured or far away. It is not important that he should mature as soon as an apple-tree or an oak. Shall he turn his spring into summer? If the condition of things which we were made for is not yet, what were any reality which we can substitute? We will not be shipwrecked on a vain reality. Shall we with pains erect a heaven of blue glass over ourselves, though when it is done we shall be sure to gaze still at the true ethereal heaven far above, as if the former were not?

There was an artist in the city of Kouroo[22] who was disposed to strive after perfection. One day it came into his mind to make a staff. Having considered that in an imperfect work time is an ingredient, but into a perfect work time does not enter, he said to himself, It shall be perfect in all respects, though I should do nothing else in my life. He proceeded instantly to the forest for wood, being resolved that it should not be made of unsuitable material; and as he searched for and rejected stick after stick, his friends gradually deserted him, for they grew old in their works and died, but he grew not older by a moment. His singleness of purpose and resolution, and his elevated piety, endowed him, without his knowledge, with perennial youth. As he made no compromise with Time, Time kept out of his way, and only sighed at a distance because he could not overcome him. Before he had found a stock in all respects suitable the city of Kouroo was a hoary ruin, and he sat on one of its mounds to peel the stick. Before he had given it the proper shape the dynasty of the Candahars was at an end, and with the point of the stick he wrote the name of the last of that race in the sand, and then resumed his work. By the time he had smoothed and polished the staff Kalpa was no longer the pole-star; and ere he had put on the ferrule and the head adorned with precious stones, Brahma had awoke and slumbered many times. But why do I stay to mention these things? When the finishing stroke was put to his work, it suddenly expanded before the eyes of the astonished artist into the fairest of all the creations of Brahma. He had made a new system in making a staff, a world with full and fair proportions; in which, though the old cities and dynasties had passed away, fairer and more glorious ones had taken their places. And now he saw by the heap of shavings still fresh at his feet, that, for him and his work, the former lapse of time had been an illusion, and that no more time had elapsed than is required for a

---

[21] From Ecclesiastes 9:4.

[22] Thoreau's own fable, with a message that the true quest for perfection sets time aside and results in a pure creation.

single scintillation from the brain of Brahma to fall on and inflame the tinder of a mortal brain. The material was pure, and his art was pure; how could the result be other than wonderful?

No face which we can give to a matter will stead us so well at last as the truth. This alone wears well. For the most part, we are not where we are, but in a false position. Through an infirmity of our natures, we suppose a case, and put ourselves into it, and hence are in two cases at the same time, and it is doubly difficult to get out. In sane moments we regard only the facts, the case that is. Say what you have to say, not what you ought. Any truth is better than make-believe. Tom Hyde, the tinker,[23] standing on the gallows, was asked if he had any thing to say. "Tell the tailors," said he, "to remember to make a knot in their thread before they take the first stitch." His companion's prayer is forgotten.

However mean your life is, meet it and live it; do not shun it and call it hard names. It is not so bad as you are. It looks poorest when you are richest. The fault-finder will find faults even in paradise. Love your life, poor as it is. You may perhaps have some pleasant, thrilling, glorious hours, even in a poor-house. The setting sun is reflected from the windows of the alms-house as brightly as from the rich man's abode; the snow melts before its door as early in the spring. I do not see but a quiet mind may live as contentedly there, and have as cheering thoughts, as in a palace. The town's poor seem to me often to live the most independent lives of any. May be they are simply great enough to receive without misgiving. Most think that they are above being supported by the town; but it oftener happens that they are not above supporting themselves by dishonest means, which should be more disreputable. Cultivate property like a garden herb, like sage. Do not trouble yourself much to get new things, whether clothes or friends. Turn the old; return to them. Things do not change; we change. Sell your clothes and keep your thoughts. God will see that you do not want society. If I were confined to a corner of a garret all my days, like a spider, the world would be just as large to me while I had my thoughts about me. The philosopher said: "From an army of three divisions one can take away its general, and put it in disorder; from the man the most abject and vulgar one cannot take away his thought."[24] Do not seek so anxiously to be developed, to subject yourself to many influences to be played on; it is all dissipation. Humility like darkness reveals the heavenly lights. The shadows of poverty and meanness gather around us, "and lo! creation widens to our view."[25] We are often reminded that if there were bestowed on us the wealth of Crœsus,[26] our aims must still be the same, and our means essentially the same. Moreover, if you are restricted in your range by poverty, if you cannot buy books and newspapers, for instance, you are but confined to the most significant and vital experiences; you are compelled to deal with the material which yields the most sugar and the most starch. It is life near the bone where it is sweetest. You are defended from being a trifler. No man loses ever on a lower level by magnanimity on a higher. Superfluous wealth can buy superfluities only. Money is not required to buy one necessary of the soul.

---

[23] A mender of pots and pans, who is implicitly praised for his matter-of-fact words to the tailors who will sew his shroud.

[24] From the *Analects* (IX.25) of Confucius.

[25] From "Sonnet to Night" (1828), by the British theological writer Joseph Blanco White (1775–1841).

[26] The last king of Lydia, from 560 to 546 B.C., supposedly the richest man on earth.

I live in the angle of a leaden wall, into whose composition was poured a little alloy of bell metal. Often, in the repose of my mid-day, there reaches my ears a confused *tintinnabulum*[27] from without. It is the noise of my contemporaries. My neighbors tell me of their adventures with famous gentlemen and ladies, what notabilities they met at the dinner-table; but I am no more interested in such things than in the contents of the Daily Times. The interest and the conversation are about costume and manners chiefly; but a goose is a goose still, dress it as you will. They tell me of California and Texas, of England and the Indies, of the Hon. Mr. ————— of Georgia or of Massachusetts, all transient and fleeting phenomena, till I am ready to leap from their court-yard like the Mameluke bey.[28] I delight to come to my bearings,—not walk in procession with pomp and parade, in a conspicuous place, but to walk even with the Builder of the universe, if I may,—not to live in this restless, nervous, bustling, trivial Nineteenth Century, but stand or sit thoughtfully while it goes by. What are men celebrating? They are all on a committee of arrangements, and hourly expect a speech from somebody. God is only the president of the day, and Webster[29] is his orator. I love to weigh, to settle, to gravitate toward that which most strongly and rightfully attracts me;—not hang by the beam of the scale and try to weigh less,—not suppose a case, but take the case that is; to travel the only path I can, and that on which no power can resist me. It affords me no satisfaction to commence to spring an arch before I have got a solid foundation. Let us not play at kittly-benders.[30] There is a solid bottom every where. We read that the traveller asked the boy if the swamp before him had a hard bottom. The boy replied that it had. But presently the traveller's horse sank in up to the girths, and he observed to the boy, "I thought you said that this bog had a hard bottom." "So it has," answered the latter, "but you have not got half way to it yet." So it is with the bogs and quicksands of society; but he is an old boy that knows it. Only what is thought said or done at a certain rare coincidence is good. I would not be one of those who will foolishly drive a nail into mere lath and plastering; such a deed would keep me awake nights. Give me a hammer, and let me feel for the furring.[31] Do not depend on the putty. Drive a nail home and clinch it so faithfully that you can wake up in the night and think of your work with satisfaction,—a work at which you would not be ashamed to invoke the Muse. So will help you God, and so only. Every nail driven should be as another rivet in the machine of the universe, you carrying on the work.

Rather than love, than money, than fame, give me truth. I sat at a table where were rich food and wine in abundance, and obsequious attendance, but sincerity and truth were not; and I went away hungry from the inhospitable board. The hospitality was as cold as the ices. I thought that there was no need of ice to freeze them. They talked to me of the age of the wine and the fame of the vintage; but I thought of an older, a newer, and purer wine, of a more glorious vintage, which they had not got, and could not buy. The style, the house and grounds and "entertainment" pass for nothing with me. I called on the king, but he made me wait in his hall, and conducted like a man incapacitated for hospitality. There was a man in my neighborhood who lived in a hollow tree. His manners were truly regal. I should have done better had I called on him.

---

[27] Tinkling of bells.

[28] One of the Mamelukes, an Egyptian military caste, who escaped a massacre of the entire caste in 1811 by leaping from a wall onto his horse.

[29] Daniel Webster; the statement is ironic because of Thoreau's dislike for him.

[30] Skating or sliding over thin ice.   [31] Wall studs.

How long shall we sit in our porticoes practising idle and musty virtues, which any work would make impertinent? As if one were to begin the day with long-suffering, and hire a man to hoe his potatoes; and in the afternoon go forth to practise Christian meekness and charity with goodness aforethought! Consider the China pride[32] and stagnant self-complacency of mankind. This generation reclines a little to congratulate itself on being the last of an illustrious line; and in Boston and London and Paris and Rome, thinking of its long descent, it speaks of its progress in art and science and literature with satisfaction. There are the Records of the Philosophical Societies, and the public Eulogies of *Great Men!* It is the good Adam contemplating his own virtue. "Yes, we have done great deeds, and sung divine songs, which shall never die,"—that is, as long as *we* can remember them. The learned societies and great men of Assyria,—where are they? What youthful philosophers and experimentalists we are! There is not one of my readers who has yet lived a whole human life. These may be but the spring months in the life of the race. If we have had the seven-years' itch, we have not seen the seventeen-year locust yet in Concord. We are acquainted with a mere pellicle[33] of the globe on which we live. Most have not delved six feet beneath the surface, nor leaped as many above it. We know not where we are. Beside, we are sound asleep nearly half our time. Yet we esteem ourselves wise, and have an established order on the surface. Truly, we are deep thinkers, we are ambitious spirits! As I stand over the insect crawling amid the pine needles on the forest floor, and endeavoring to conceal itself from my sight, and ask myself why it will cherish those humble thoughts, and hide its head from me who might perhaps be its benefactor, and impart to its race some cheering information, I am reminded of the greater Benefactor and Intelligence that stands over me the human insect.

There is an incessant influx of novelty into the world, and yet we tolerate incredible dulness. I need only suggest what kind of sermons are still listened to in the most enlightened countries. There are such words as joy and sorrow, but they are only the burden of a psalm, sung with a nasal twang, while we believe in the ordinary and mean. We think that we can change our clothes only. It is said that the British Empire is very large and respectable, and that the United States are a first-rate power. We do not believe that a tide rises and falls behind every man which can float the British Empire like a chip, if he should ever harbor it in his mind. Who knows what sort of seventeen-year locust will next come out of the ground? The government of the world I live in was not framed, like that of Britain, in after-dinner conversations over the wire.

The life in us is like the water in the river. It may rise this year higher than man has ever known it, and flood the parched uplands; even this may be the eventful year, which will drown out all our muskrats. It was not always dry land where we dwell. I see far inland the banks which the stream anciently washed, before science began to record its freshets. Every one has heard the story which has gone the rounds of New England, of a strong and beautiful bug which came out of the dry leaf of an old table of apple-tree wood, which had stood in a farmer's kitchen for sixty years, first in Connecticut, and afterward in Massachusetts,—from an egg deposited in the living tree many years earlier still, as appeared by counting the annual layers beyond it; which was heard gnawing out for several weeks,

[32] An idea gleaned from China's isolationist position in the nineteenth century.
[33] A thin skin or film.

hatched perchance by the heat of an urn.[34] Who does not feel his faith in a resurrection and immortality strengthened by hearing of this? Who knows what beautiful and winged life, whose egg has been buried for ages under many concentric layers of woodenness in the dead dry life of society, deposited at first in the alburnum[35] of the green and living tree, which has been gradually converted into the semblance of its well-seasoned tomb,—heard perchance gnawing out now for years by the astonished family of man, as they sat round the festive board,—may unexpectedly come forth from amidst society's most trivial and handselled furniture,[36] to enjoy its perfect summer life at last!

I do not say that John or Jonathan[37] will realize all this; but such is the character of that morrow which mere lapse of time can never make to dawn. The light which puts out our eyes is darkness to us. Only that day dawns to which we are awake. There is more day to dawn. The sun is but a morning star.

THE END

1846–1854, 1854

from JOURNAL*

[*The Beginning at Walden: July 5, 1845*]

Walden Sat. July 5th–45

Yesterday I came here to live.[1] My house makes me think of some mountain houses I have seen, which seemed to have a fresher auroral atmosphere about them as I fancy of the halls of Olympus.[2] I lodged at the house of a saw-miller last summer, on the Caatskills mountains,[3] high up as Pine orchard in the blue-berry & raspberry region, where the quiet and cleanliness & coolness seemed to be all one, which had this ambrosial character. He was the miller of the Kaaterskill Falls,[4] They were a clean & wholesome family inside and out—like their house. The latter was not plastered—only lathed and the inner doors were not hung. The house seemed high placed, airy, and perfumed, fit to entertain a travelling God. It was so high indeed that all the music, the broken strains, the waifs & accompaniments of tunes, that swept over the ridge of the Caatskills, passed through its aisles. Could not man be man in such an abode? And would he ever find out this grovelling life?

---

[34] The story is related in several places, among them Timothy Dwight's *Travels in New England and New York* (1821).

[35] The young, soft wood of a stem.   [36] "Trivial" furniture that has been given away.

[37] John Bull, a common term for a Britisher, or Brother Jonathan, a common term for an American.

* Thoreau's massive journal has only begun to be studied in ways that will yield a sense of its contours and evolutionary relevance to his life. Begun in 1837 and kept until his death in 1862, the journal (amounting to more than 2 million words) is the record of Thoreau's imaginative, spiritual, and day-to-day observations about the world in which he lived and the world which he strove to create. Many of his lectures and essays came from passages in the journal, as did numerous passages in *A Week on the Concord and Merrimack Rivers* (1849) and *Walden* (1854).

[1] Thoreau moved into his cabin at Walden Pond on July 4, 1845.

[2] According to Greek myth, the summit of Mt. Olympus was the abode of the gods.

[3] The Catskill Mountains, part of the Appalachian system in New York state.   [4] In the Catskills.

It was the very light & atmosphere in which the works of Grecian art were composed, and in which they rest. They have appropriated to themselves a loftier hall than mortals ever occupy, at least on a level with the mountain brows of the world.

There was wanting a little of the glare of the lower vales and in its place a pure twilight as became the precincts of heaven Yet so equable and calm was the season there that you could not tell whether it was morning or noon or evening. Always there was the sound of the morning cricket

[On Emerson: Winter 1845–1846]

Emerson again is a critic poet philosopher—with talent not so conspicuous—not so adequate to his task——Lives a far more intense life—seeks to realize a divine life—his affections and intellect equally developed.—has advanced farther and a new heaven opens to him—Love & Friendship—Religion—Poetry—The Holy are familiar to him The life of an Artist—move variegated—more observing—finer perception—not so robust—elastic—practical enough in his own field—faithful—a judge of men

There is no such general critic of men & things—no such trustworthy & faithful man.—More of the divine realized in him than in any.

A poetic-critic—reserving the unqualified nouns for the gods

* * *

Emerson has special talents unequalled—The divine in man has had no more easy methodically distinct expression.

His personal influence upon young persons greater than any man's

In his world every man would be a poet—Love would reign—Beauty would take place—Man & nature would harmonize—

[The Fugitive Slave Law: April 1851]

In '75 two or three hundred of the inhabitants of Concord[5] assembled at one of the bridges with arms in their hands to assert the right of three millions to tax themselves, to have a voice in governing themselves. About a week ago the authorities of Boston, having the sympathy of many of the inhabitants of Concord, assembled in the gray of the dawn, assisted by a still larger armed force, to send back a perfectly innocent man, and one whom they knew to be innocent, into a slavery as complete as the world ever knew.[6] Of course it makes not the least difference—I wish you to consider this—who the man was,—whether he was Jesus Christ or another,—for inasmuch as ye did it unto the least of these his brethren ye did it unto him.[7] Do you think *he* would have stayed here in liberty and let the black man go into slavery in his stead? They sent him back, I say, to live in slavery with

[5] In the Battle of Concord at the outset of the American Revolution in 1775.

[6] On the morning of April 19, 1851, approximately three hundred armed men put the slave Thomas Simms on a ship in Boston harbor to be returned to his "owner" in Georgia under the conditions of the Fugitive Slave Law.

[7] "Inasmuch as ye have done it unto one of the least of these my brethren, ye have done it unto me," from Matthew 25:40.

other three millions—mark that—whom the same slave power, or slavish power, North and South, holds in that condition,—three millions who do not, like the first mentioned, assert the right to govern themselves but simply to run away and stay away from their prison.

Just a week afterward, those inhabitants of this town who especially sympathize with the authorities of Boston in this their deed caused the bells to be rung and the cannon to be fired to celebrate the courage and the love of liberty of those men who assembled at the bridge. As if *those* three millions had fought for the right to be free themselves, but to hold in slavery three million others. Why, gentlemen,[8] even consistency, though it is much abused, is iometimes a virtue. Every humane and intelligent inhabitant of Concord, when he or she heard those bells and those cannon, thought not so much of the events of the 19th of April, 1775, as of the event of the 12th of April, 1851.

I wish my townsmen to consider that, whatever the human law may be, neither an individual nor a nation can ever deliberately commit the least act of injustice without having to pay the penalty for it. A government which deliberately enacts injustice, and persists in it!—it will become the laughing-stock of the world.

Much as has been said about American slavery, I think that commonly we do not yet realize what slavery is. If I were seriously to propose to Congress to make mankind into sausages, I have no doubt that most would smile at my proposition and, if any believed me to be in earnest, they would think that I proposed something much worse than Congress had ever done. But, gentlemen, if any of you will tell me that to make a man into a sausage would be much worse—would be any worse—than to make him into a slave,—than it was then to enact the fugitive slave law,—I shall here accuse him of foolishness, of intellectual incapacity, of making a distinction without a difference. The one is just as sensible a proposition as the other.

When I read the account of the carrying back of the fugitive into slavery, which was read last Sunday evening, and read also what was not read here, that the man who made the prayer on the wharf was Daniel Foster[9] of *Concord,* I could not help feeling a slight degree of pride because, of all the towns in the Commonwealth, Concord was the only one distinctly named as being represented in that new tea-party, and, as she had a place in the first, so would have a place in this, the last and perhaps next most important chapter of the History of Massachusetts. But my second feeling, when I reflected how short a time that gentleman has resided in this town, was one of doubt and shame, because the *men* of Concord in recent times have done nothing to entitle them to the honor of having their town named in such a connection.

I hear a good deal said about trampling this law under foot. Why, one need not go out of his way to do that. This law lies not at the level of the head or the reason. Its natural habitat is in the dirt. It was bred and has its life only in the dust and mire, on a level with the feet; and he who walks with freedom, unless, with a

[8] As the style of this entry suggests, Thoreau was readying remarks that would publicly express his moral outrage. Much of what he says here (including the sausages example below) appears in "Slavery in Massachusetts," given as a lecture in Framington, Massachusetts, on July 4, 1854, and published in William Lloyd Garrison's *The Liberator* three weeks later.

[9] A fellow townsman of Thoreau's. The irony is heavy here.

sort of quibbling and Hindoo mercy,[10] he avoids treading on every venomous reptile, will inevitably tread on it, and so trample it under foot.

1837–1859, 1906

Margaret Fuller
(1810–1850)

Almost a century and a half after the tragedy of Margaret Fuller's death, we are beginning to acknowledge the extraordinary nature of her achievement. Fuller enjoyed international celebrity in her own day, both as a writer and as a personality; following her death in 1850, however, her reputation was obscured by a neglect condoned by most of her contemporaries. Long considered a rather bizarre figure on the periphery of American transcendentalism, Fuller has come to assume a position of significance in the history of American literature.

Sarah Margaret Fuller, the oldest of eight children, was born in Cambridgeport, Massachusetts, in 1810. Fuller's childhood was marked by imposing family responsibility (her mother, Margaret Crane, was sickly) and a precocious devotion to study. Her father, the lawyer Timothy Fuller, was a Jeffersonian democrat whose energy and discipline shaped his daughter's life as it had his own. He undertook her home education with all of the nineteenth-century vigor usually directed toward an oldest son; at age five she received a thorough grounding in Latin, for example. Although she was a remarkably intelligent child, her exhaustive education apparently provoked the nightmares and headaches from which she constantly suffered, and she later came to perceive her childhood as "unnatural." As the physical health of her mother flagged under the burdens of housekeeping and childbearing, Fuller was increasingly called upon to help with the monotonous chores that constituted nineteenth-century women's work. She tutored her younger brothers and sisters while maintaining a daunting personal schedule of study, and so passed an adolescence that formed habits of single-minded concentration and fervent dedication to intellectual pursuits.

The Fuller family moved to Cambridge proper in 1826, and Margaret entered the intellectual arena she would occupy for the rest of her life. The cultivated community of Cambridge figured nationally as the birthplace of Unitarianism and as the setting for debate over such new ideas as socialism, abolitionism, and feminism. Fuller thrived in this bracing atmosphere and soon acquired a local reputation for her intelligence and her broad range of knowledge. She and her friend Lydia Maria Child took Madame de Baronne de Staël, a revolutionary French writer, for their model, and there are interesting parallels between Fuller's life and that of de Staël, including their precocious intellectual development and informed conversation. Always tall for her age, Fuller was apparently what Victorian novelists would call "rather plain." She learned to carry herself well, however, and paid great attention to her dress; like de Staël, as Fuller grew into womanhood she became

---

[10] Mercy dictated by equivocation or by religious belief.

a striking, if not conventionally beautiful, figure. In addition to her imposing carriage, her odd habit of closing her eyes while she spoke at any length was often noted. Her appearance as well as her intellectual pursuits contributed to her reputation as something of an eccentric.

During this period in Cambridge Fuller's cousin James Freeman Clarke introduced her to Johann Wolfgang von Goethe's writing. German romanticism offered an appealing alternative to the rational pall with which Unitarianism cloaked New England's intellectual life. To Fuller, Goethe posed an ideal of the artist and thinker as public figure, a concept akin to Roman public virtue, with which she was familiar through her reading of Latin literature. She was planning to write a biography of Goethe when Timothy Fuller moved his family to a gentlemanly farm in Groton, Massachusetts, in 1833. She sorely missed the stimulating community of Cambridge; her experience of bucolic Groton may have accounted for her tepid response to the Brook Farm transcendentalist community outside Boston. In 1835 she toured New York state with friends and met the English author Harriet Martineau. When Fuller's father died suddenly of cholera in October 1835, she assumed financial responsibility for the family.

Fuller met Ralph Waldo Emerson in 1836 and shortly thereafter joined the Transcendental Club. She was always to enjoy a profound friendship with Emerson; she had great respect for him as the dominant intellect of his age. Their acquaintance was founded on such a degree of mutual admiration that it has been analyzed as a subconscious love of which Emerson's wife, Lydia, was jealous. But it is a mistake to relegate Margaret Fuller to the adulatory role of Emerson's student: she was a complex and dynamic person, able to assess Emerson's strengths and weaknesses. Not content to follow Emerson as a teacher, Fuller prevailed upon him to read Goethe and other German romantic writers and steadfastly defended the value of Italian painting in the face of Emerson's inability to appreciate art.

Always under the pressure of providing financial support for her family, Fuller taught at Bronson Alcott's radical Temple School for a brief time in 1836 and then taught for two years (1837–1839) at the progressive Green Street School. Both positions were congenial, and she earned a handsome salary at the Green Street School. But she found teaching emotionally exhausting and was discouraged that it left her little time for writing. She managed to publish an English translation of Johann Peter Eckermann's *Conversations with Goethe* in 1839, but the biography of Goethe remained unfinished. From 1839 to 1844 she conducted "conversations " for women in Boston. The conversation format, used by other speakers of the time (notably Bronson Alcott), was related to the Socratic method of teaching, in which the responsibility for learning was shared by the student, who engaged in direct discussion of the topic at hand. Fuller believed that conventional education provided only exercises in rote, especially for women, and it was her ambition to encourage women to allow their minds to range freely over a variety of subjects that had no apparent relevance to their domestic lives. Fuller's intellectual superiority and even arrogance were on display during these sessions, but she made several deep and lasting friendships among the women who paid to attend.

Emerson persuaded Fuller to assume the editorship of the newly founded transcendental journal, *The Dial,* for which she also wrote a substantial portion of the contents from 1840 to 1842. From this period comes "The Great Lawsuit," later reprinted as "Woman in the Nineteenth Century" (1845). In 1844 Fuller moved to New York City to write a regular column of literary criticism for Horace Greeley's *Tribune*. She achieved considerable influence as a critic, insisting upon the need for an original American literature and discerning the talent of Edgar Allan Poe, Nathaniel Hawthorne, and Herman Melville while they were relatively unknown. She also acquainted her audience with European literature in an effort to dispel the parochialism that she felt characterized American intellectual life. In 1846 Fuller published *Papers on Literature and Art,* a collection of her essays and reviews, and in August of that year embarked on a tour of Europe as a correspondent for the *Tribune.*

Fuller first visited England, where she met with William Wordsworth and Thomas Carlyle and Giuseppe Mazzini, an Italian patriot and revolutionary. In Paris she met the French novelist George Sand and became friendly with the Polish patriot Adam Mickiewicz. Excited by the political involvement of Mazzini and Mickiewicz, she went to Italy in spring 1847, continuing to produce copy for the *Tribune.* While there, she fell in love with the young aristocrat Marchese d'Ossoli (Giovanni Angelo Ossoli), who seemed to her to personify the romantic virtues of natural spontaneity and sympathetic feeling. She refused his early proposal of marriage, but they became lovers, and in September 1848 she gave birth to a son. This stay in Italy during the Risorgimento (the movement for Italian unification, led by Giuseppi Garibaldi) confirmed her republican sympathies, and she determined to write a history of the Italian revolution. After directing a military hospital during Garibaldi's struggle against the French in 1849, she and Ossoli left Rome for Florence, where they lived with their son while Margaret finished her manuscript. Financial difficulties made them determine to settle temporarily in the United States, where Margaret hoped to earn an income from her writing.

At this time, apparently, Ossoli and Fuller were married, possibly in anticipation of the stern reception they, as unmarried parents, would otherwise have gotten in New England. All three perished when their ship sank off Fire Island, New York, during the last hours of their voyage to America in July 1850. Fuller's body and her last manuscript were never found.

Margaret Fuller's reputation has undergone a critical change. She was probably known better in her own day as a conversationalist than as a writer, and many of her contemporaries were disappointed that the brilliance of her conversation was not adequately reflected in her prose. Her eccentricities, too, were sufficiently disconcerting to make such friends as Emerson and Hawthorne agree (rather smugly) that an early death might have been a blessing for such an unconventional figure. Her journals and correspondence were heavily edited for publication by Emerson, in compliance with his bland expectations of American womanhood. It has thus taken some time to recognize that Fuller was not merely Emerson's handmaiden, a paragon among New England blue-stockings—that she was in every way the intellectual equal of the gifted people with whom she associated in Cambridge, Concord, New York, and Europe. In her writing and in her life, she transcends her own time as a model of activism and intellectualism.

Suggested Readings: *Summer on the Lakes,* 1843. *Woman in the Nineteenth Century,* 1845. *Papers on Literature and Art,* Pt. II, 1846. *At Home and Abroad,* ed. A. B. Fuller, 1856. *The Letters of Margaret Fuller,* 4 vols., ed. R. N. Hudspeth, 1983– . W. H. Channing, J. F. Clarke, and R. W. Emerson, eds., *Memoirs of Margaret Fuller Ossoli,* 1852. B. G. Chevigny, *The Woman and the Myth: Margaret Fuller's Life and Writings,* 1976. P. Blanchard, *Margaret Fuller: From Transcendentalism to Revolution,* 1987. J. Myerson, ed., *Margaret Fuller: Essays on American Life and Letters,* 1978. M. V. Allen, *The Achievement of Margaret Fuller,* 1979.

Text Used: *The Dial,* July 1843, IV (1): 1–47.

from THE GREAT LAWSUIT*

It is worthy of remark, that, as the principle of liberty is better understood and more nobly interpreted, a broader protest is made in behalf of woman. As men become aware that all men have not had their fair chance, they are inclined to say that no women have had a fair chance. The French revolution, that strangely disguised angel, bore witness in favor of woman, but interpreted her claims no less ignorantly than those of man. Its idea of happiness did not rise beyond outward enjoyment, unobstructed by the tyranny of others. The title it gave was Citoyen, Citoyenne,[1] and it is not unimportant to woman that even this species of equality was awarded her. Before, she could be condemned to perish on the scaffold for treason, but not as a citizen, but a subject. The right, with which this title then invested a human being, was that of bloodshed and license. The Goddess of Liberty was impure. Yet truth was prophesied in the ravings of that hideous fever induced by long ignorance and abuse. Europe is conning a valued lesson from the blood-stained page. The same tendencies, farther unfolded, will bear good fruit in this country.

Yet, in this country, as by the Jews, when Moses was leading them to the promised land,[2] everything has been done that inherited depravity could, to hinder the promise of heaven from its fulfilment. The cross, here as elsewhere, has been planted only to be blasphemed by cruelty and fraud. The name of the Prince of Peace has been profaned by all kinds of injustice towards the Gentile whom he said he came to save. But I need not speak of what has been done towards the red man, the black man. These deeds are the scoff of the world; and they have been accompanied by such pious words, that the gentlest would not dare to intercede with, "Father forgive them, for they know not what they do."[3]

Here, as elsewhere, the gain of creation consists always in the growth of individual minds, which live and aspire, as flowers bloom and birds sing, in the midst of morasses; and in the continual development of that thought, the thought of human destiny, which is given to eternity to fulfil, and which ages of failure only seemingly impede. Only seemingly, and whatever seems to the contrary, this country is as surely destined to elucidate a great moral law, as Europe was to promote the mental culture of man.

---

* First published in *The Dial* in July 1843. With additions that expanded the size but not the message of the essay, it was reprinted in 1844 as *Woman in the Nineteenth Century* due, according to Fuller's preliminary footnote, to objections to the ambiguity of the first title. With considerable eloquence she says that she prefers the original title "partly for the reason others do not like it,—that is, that it requires some thought to see what it means, and might thus prepare the reader to meet me on my own ground. Besides, it offers a larger scope, and is, in that way, more just to my desire. I meant by that title to intimate the fact that, while it is the destiny of Man, in the course of the ages, to ascertain and fulfill the law of his being, so that his wife shall be seen, as a whole, to be that of an angel or messenger, the actions of prejudices and passions which attend, in the day, the growth of the individual, is continually obstructing the holy work that is to make earth a part of heaven. By Man I mean both man and woman; these are the two halves of one thought. I lay no especial stress on the welfare of either. I believe that the welfare of the one cannot be effected without that of the other. My highest wish is that this truth should be distinctly and rationally apprehended, and the conditions of life and freedom recognized as the same for the daughter and sons of time; twin exponents of a divine thought."

[1] Both words mean "citizen," the first male, the second female, equal under the law.

[2] Fuller suggests the paradox of Moses leading the Israelites out of bondage to the Promised Land while establishing a demeaning role for Israelite women.

[3] From Luke 23:34, Jesus' reference to the Roman soldiers who nailed him to the cross.

Though the national independence be blurred by the servility of individuals; though freedom and equality have been proclaimed only to leave room for a monstrous display of slave dealing, and slave keeping; though the free American so often feels himself free, like the Roman, only to pamper his appetites and his indolence through the misery of his fellow beings, still it is not in vain, that the verbal statement has been made, "All men are born free and equal."[4] There it stands, a golden certainty, wherewith to encourage the good, to shame the bad. The new world may be called clearly to perceive that it incurs the utmost penalty, if it reject the sorrowful brother. And if men are deaf, the angels hear. But men cannot be deaf. It is inevitable that an external freedom, such as has been achieved for the nation, should be so also for every member of it. That, which has once been clearly conceived in the intelligence, must be acted out. It has become a law, as irrevocable as that of the Medes in their ancient dominion.[5] Men will privately sin against it, but the law so clearly expressed by a leading mind of the age,

> "Tutti fatti a sembianza d' un Solo;
> Figli tutti d' un solo riscatto,
> In qual ora, in qual parte del suolo
> Trascorriamo quest' aura vital,
> Siam fratelli, siam stretti ad un patto:
> Maladetto colui che lo infrange,
> Che s' innalza sul fiacco che piange,
> Che contrista uno spirto immortal."[6]

> "All made in the likeness of the One,
> All children of one ransom,
> In whatever hour, in whatever part of the soil
> We draw this vital air,
> We are brothers, we must be bound by one compact,
> Accursed he who infringes it,
> Who raises himself upon the weak who weep,
> Who saddens an immortal spirit."

cannot fail of universal recognition.

We sicken no less at the pomp than the strife of words. We feel that never were lungs so puffed with the wind of declamation, on moral and religious subjects, as now. We are tempted to implore these "word-heroes," these word-Catos, word-Christs,[7] to beware of cant above all things; to remember that hypocrisy is the most hopeless as well as the meanest of crimes, and that those must surely be polluted by it, who do not keep a little of all this morality and religion for private use.[8] We feel that the mind may "grow black and rancid in the smoke" even of

---

[4] Adaptation of "all men are created equal," from the Declaration of Independence.

[5] Ancient Media was forcibly annexed to Persia around 550 B.C.; its former territory is now in West Iran and South Azerbaijan.

[6] Fuller's note: "Manzoni." Alessandro Manzoni (1785–1873), an Italian novelist, poet, and dramatist.

[7] People who talk like the heroic Roman Marcus Porcius Cato (95–46 B.C.), called "the conscience of Rome," or like Jesus—but who do nothing but talk.

[8] Fuller's note: "Dr. Johnson's one piece of advice should be written on every door; 'Clear your mind of cant.' But Byron, to whom it was so acceptable, in clearing away the noxious vine, shook down the building too. Stirling's emendation is note-worthy, 'Realize your cant, not cast it off.' "

altars. We start up from the harangue to go into our closet and shut the door. But, when it has been shut long enough, we remember that where there is so much smoke, there must be some fire; with so much talk about virtue and freedom must be mingled some desire for them; that it cannot be in vain that such have become the common topics of conversation among men; that the very newspapers should proclaim themselves Pilgrims, Puritans, Heralds of Holiness.[9] The king that maintains so costly a retinue cannot be a mere Count of Carabbas[10] fiction. We have waited here long in the dust; we are tired and hungry, but the triumphal procession must appear at last.

Of all its banners, none has been more steadily upheld, and under none has more valor and willingness for real sacrifices been shown, than that of the champions of the enslaved African.[11] And this band it is, which, partly in consequence of a natural following out of principles, partly because many women have been prominent in that cause, makes, just now, the warmest appeal in behalf of woman.

Though there has been a growing liberality on this point, yet society at large is not so prepared for the demands of this party, but that they are, and will be for some time, coldly regarded as the Jacobins[12] of their day.

"Is it not enough," cries the sorrowful trader, "that you have done all you could to break up the national Union, and thus destroy the prosperity of our country, but now you must be trying to break up family union, to take my wife away from the cradle, and the kitchen hearth, to vote at polls, and preach from a pulpit? Of course, if she does such things, she cannot attend to those of her own sphere. She is happy enough as she is. She has more leisure than I have, every means of improvement, every indulgence."

"Have you asked her whether she was satisfied with these indulgences?"

"No, but I know she is. She is too amiable to wish what would make me unhappy, and too judicious to wish to step beyond the sphere of her sex. I will never consent to have our peace disturbed by any such discussions."

"'Consent'—you? it is not consent from you that is in question, it is assent from your wife."

"Am not I the head of my house?"

"You are not the head of your wife. God has given her a mind of her own."

"I am the head and she the heart."

"God grant you play true to one another then. If the head represses no natural pulse of the heart, there can be no question as to your giving your consent. Both will be of one accord, and there needs but to present any question to get a full and true answer. There is no need of precaution, of indulgence, or consent. But our doubt is whether the heart consents with the head, or only acquiesces in its decree; and it is to ascertain the truth on this point, that we propose some liberating measures."

Thus vaguely are these questions proposed and discussed at present. But their being proposed at all implies much thought, and suggests more. Many women are considering within themselves what they need that they have not, and what they can have, if they find they need it. Many men are considering whether women are

---

[9] Common names for newspapers then.

[10] A character in *Le Chat Botté* (*Puss in Boots*), the embodiment of pride and pretension, by Charles Perrault (1628–1703).

[11] Abolitionists.

[12] A political group founded in Paris in 1789 at the outset of the French Revolution; by 1793 under Maximillian Robespierre (1758–1794) it had become a radical faction.

capable of being and having more than they are and have, and whether, if they are, it will be best to consent to improvement in their condition.

The numerous party, whose opinions are already labelled and adjusted too much to their mind to admit of any new light, strive, by lectures on some model-woman of bridal-like beauty and gentleness, by writing or lending little treatises, to mark out with due precision the limits of woman's sphere, and woman's mission, and to prevent other than the rightful shepherd from climbing the wall, or the flock from using any chance gap to run astray.

Without enrolling ourselves at once on either side, let us look upon the subject from that point of view which to-day offers. No better, it is to be feared, than a high house-top. A high hill-top, or at least a cathedral spire, would be desirable.

It is not surprising that it should be the Anti-Slavery party that pleads for woman, when we consider merely that she does not hold property on equal terms with men; so that, if a husband dies without a will, the wife, instead of stepping at once into his place as head of the family, inherits only a part of his fortune, as if she were a child, or ward only, not an equal partner.

We will not speak of the innumerable instances, in which profligate or idle men live upon the earnings of industrious wives; or if the wives leave them and take with them the children, to perform the double duty of mother and father, follow from place to place, and threaten to rob them of the children, if deprived of the rights of a husband, as they call them, planting themselves in their poor lodgings, frightening them into paying tribute by taking from them the children, running into debt at the expense of these otherwise so overtasked helots.[13] Though such instances abound, the public opinion of his own sex is against the man, and when cases of extreme tyranny are made known, there is private action in the wife's favor. But if woman be, indeed, the weaker party, she ought to have legal protection, which would make such oppression impossible.

And, knowing that there exists, in the world of men, a tone of feeling towards women as towards slaves, such as is expressed in the common phrase, "Tell that to women and children;" that the infinite soul can only work through them in already ascertained limits; that the prerogative of reason, man's highest portion, is allotted to them in a much lower degree; that it is better for them to be engaged in active labor, which is to be furnished and directed by those better able to think, etc., etc., we need not go further, for who can review the experience of last week, without recalling words which imply, whether in jest or earnest, these views, and views like these? Knowing this, can we wonder that many reformers think that measures are not likely to be taken in behalf of women, unless their wishes could be publicly represented by women?

That can never be necessary, cry the other side. All men are privately influenced by women; each has his wife, sister, or female friends, and is too much biassed by these relations to fail of representing their interests. And if this is not enough, let them propose and enforce their wishes with the pen. The beauty of home would be destroyed, the delicacy of the sex be violated, the dignity of halls of legislation destroyed, by an attempt to introduce them there. Such duties are inconsistent with those of a mother; and then we have ludicrous pictures of ladies in hysterics at the polls, and senate chambers filled with cradles.

But if, in reply, we admit as truth that woman seems destined by nature rather to the inner circle, we must add that the arrangements of civilized life had not been as yet such as to secure it to her. Her circle, if the duller, is not the quieter. If kept

---

[13] Serfs, the lowest class of serfs in ancient Sparta.

from excitement, she is not from drudgery. Not only the Indian carries the burdens of the camp, but the favorites of Louis the Fourteenth[14] accompany him in his journeys, and the washerwoman stands at her tub and carries home her work at all seasons, and in all states of health.

As to the use of the pen, there was quite as much opposition to woman's possessing herself of that help to free-agency as there is now to her seizing on the rostrum or the desk; and she is likely to draw, from a permission to plead her cause that way, opposite inferences to what might be wished by those who now grant it.

As to the possibility of her filling, with grace and dignity, any such position, we should think those who had seen the great actresses, and heard the Quaker preachers of modern times, would not doubt, that woman can express publicly the fulness of thought and emotion, without losing any of the peculiar beauty of her sex.

As to her home, she is not likely to leave it more than she now does for balls, theatres, meetings for promoting missions, revival meetings, and others to which she flies, in hope of an animation for her existence, commensurate with what she sees enjoyed by men. Governors of Ladies' Fairs are no less engrossed by such a charge, than the Governor of the State by his; presidents of Washingtonian societies,[15] no less away from home than presidents of conventions. If men look straitly to it, they will find that, unless their own lives are domestic, those of the women will not be. The female Greek, of our day, is as much in the street as the male, to cry, What news? We doubt not it was the same in Athens of old. The women, shut out from the market-place, made up for it at the religious festivals. For human beings are not so constituted, that they can live without expansion; and if they do not get it one way, must another, or perish.

And, as to men's representing women fairly, at present, while we hear from men who owe to their wives not only all that is comfortable and graceful, but all that is wise in the arrangement of their lives, the frequent remark, "You cannot reason with a woman," when from those of delicacy, nobleness, and poetic culture, the contemptuous phrase, "Women and children," and that in no light sally of the hour, but in works intended to give a permanent statement of the best experiences, when not one man in the million, shall I say, no, not in the hundred million, can rise above the view that woman was made *for man*, when such traits as these are daily forced upon the attention, can we feel that man will always do justice to the interests of woman? Can we think that he takes a sufficiently discerning and religious view of her office and destiny, ever to do her justice, except when prompted by sentiment; accidentally or transiently, that is, for his sentiment will vary according to the relations in which he is placed. The lover, the poet, the artist, are likely to view her nobly. The father and the philosopher have some chance of liberality; the man of the world, the legislator for expediency, none.

Under these circumstances, without attaching importance in themselves to the changes demanded by the champions of woman, we hail them as signs of the times. We would have every arbitrary barrier thrown down. We would have every path laid open to woman as freely as to man. Were this done, and a slight temporary fermentation allowed to subside, we believe that the Divine would ascend into nature to a height unknown in the history of past ages, and nature, thus instructed, would regulate the spheres not only so as to avoid collision, but to bring forth ravishing harmony.

[14] Courtesans, who are enslaved as much as are squaws or washerwomen.
[15] Organizations similar to the busy Daughters of the American Revolution.

Yet then, and only then, will human beings be ripe for this, when inward and outward freedom for woman, as much as for man, shall be acknowledged as a right, not yielded as a concession. As the friend of the negro assumes that one man cannot, by right, hold another in bondage, so should the friend of woman assume that man cannot, by right, lay even well-meant restrictions on woman. If the negro be a soul, if the woman be a soul, apparelled in flesh, to one master only are they accountable. There is but one law for all souls, and, if there is to be an interpreter of it, he comes not as man, or son of man, but as Son of God.

Were thought and feeling once so far elevated that man should esteem himself the brother and friend, but nowise the lord and tutor of woman, were he really bound with her in equal worship, arrangements as to function and employment would be of no consequence. What woman needs is not as a woman to act or rule, but as a nature to grow, as an intellect to discern, as a soul to live freely, and unimpeded to unfold such powers as were given her when we left our common home. If fewer talents were given her, yet, if allowed the free and full employment of these, so that she may render back to the giver his own with usury, she will not complain, nay, I dare to say she will bless and rejoice in her earthly birth-place, her earthly lot.

Let us consider what obstructions impede this good era, and what signs give reason to hope that it draws near.

I was talking on this subject with Miranda,[16] a woman, who, if any in the world, might speak without heat or bitterness of the position of her sex. Her father was a man who cherished no sentimental reverence for woman, but a firm belief in the equality of the sexes. She was his eldest child, and came to him at an age when he needed a companion. From the time she could speak and go alone, he addressed her not as a plaything, but as a living mind. Among the few verses he ever wrote were a copy addressed to this child, when the first locks were cut from her head, and the reverence expressed on this occasion for that cherished head he never belied. It was to him the temple of immortal intellect. He respected his child, however, too much to be an indulgent parent. He called on her for clear judgment, for courage, for honor and fidelity, in short for such virtues as he knew. In so far as he possessed the keys to the wonders of this universe, he allowed free use of them to her, and by the incentive of a high expectation he forbade, as far as possible, that she should let the privilege lie idle.

Thus this child was early led to feel herself a child of the spirit. She took her place easily, not only in the world of organized being, but in the world of mind. A dignified sense of self-dependence was given as all her portion, and she found it a sure anchor. Herself securely anchored, her relations with others were established with equal security. She was fortunate, in a total absence of those charms which might have drawn to her bewildering flatteries, and of a strong electric nature, which repelled those who did not belong to her, and attracted those who did. With men and women her relations were noble; affectionate without passion, intellectual without coldness. The world was free to her, and she lived freely in it. Outward adversity came, and inward conflict, but that faith and self-respect had early been awakened, which must always lead at last to an outward serenity, and an inward peace.

Of Miranda I had always thought as an example, that the restraints upon the sex were insuperable only to those who think them so, or who noisily strive to break them. She had taken a course of her own, and no man stood in her way. Many of

---

[16] The character "Miranda" reflects Fuller's experiences.

her acts had been unusual, but excited no uproar. Few helped, but none checked her; and the many men, who knew her mind and her life, showed to her confidence as to a brother, gentleness as to a sister. And not only refined, but very coarse men approved one in whom they saw resolution and clearness of design. Her mind was often the leading one, always effective.

When I talked with her upon these matters, and had said very much what I have written, she smilingly replied, And yet we must admit that I have been fortunate, and this should not be. My good father's early trust gave the first bias, and the rest followed of course. It is true that I have had less outward aid, in after years, than most women, but that is of little consequence. Religion was early awakened in my soul, a sense that what the soul is capable to ask it must attain, and that, though I might be aided by others, I must depend on myself as the only constant friend. This self-dependence, which was honored in me, is deprecated as a fault in most women. They are taught to learn their rule from without, not to unfold it from within.

This is the fault of man, who is still vain, and wishes to be more important to woman than by right he should be.

Men have not shown this disposition towards you, I said.

No, because the position I early was enabled to take, was one of self-reliance. And were all women as sure of their wants as I was, the result would be the same. The difficulty is to get them to the point where they shall naturally develop self-respect, the question how it is to be done.

Once I thought that men would help on this state of things more than I do now. I saw so many of them wretched in the connections they had formed in weakness and vanity. They seemed so glad to esteem women whenever they could!

But early I perceived that men never, in any extreme of despair, wished to be women. Where they admired any woman they were inclined to speak of her as above her sex. Silently I observed this, and feared it argued a rooted skepticism, which for ages had been fastening on the heart, and which only an age of miracles could eradicate.

Ever I have been treated with great sincerity; and I look upon it as a most signal instance of this, that an intimate friend of the other sex said in a fervent moment, that I deserved in some star to be a man. Another used as highest praise, in speaking of a character in literature, the words "a manly woman."

It is well known that of every strong woman they say she has a masculine mind.[17]

This by no means argues a willing want of generosity towards woman. Man is as generous towards her, as he knows how to be.

Wherever she has herself arisen in national or private history, and nobly shone forth in any ideal of excellence, men have received her, not only willingly, but with triumph. Their encomiums indeed are always in some sense mortifying, they show too much surprise.

In every-day life the feelings of the many are stained with vanity. Each wishes to be lord in a little world, to be superior at least over one; and he does not feel strong enough to retain a life-long ascendant over a strong nature. Only a Brutus would rejoice in a Portia.[18] Only Theseus could conquer before he wed the Ama-

---

[17] In *The Dial* Fuller gives no indication where Miranda's voice stops, but in the 1844 version this is clearly her last statement.

[18] The unfortunate wife of Brutus in Shakespeare's *Julius Caesar*.

zonian Queen.[19] Hercules wished rather to rest from his labors with Dejanira,[20] and received the poisoned robe, as a fit guerdon. The tale should be interpreted to all those who seek repose with the weak.

But not only is man vain and fond of power, but the same want[21] of development, which thus affects him morally in the intellect, prevents his discerning the destiny of woman. The boy wants no woman, but only a girl to play ball with him, and mark his pocket handkerchief.

Thus in Schiller's Dignity of Woman,[22] beautiful as the poem is, there is no "grave and perfect man," but only a great boy to be softened and restrained by the influence of girls. Poets, the elder brothers of their race, have usually seen further; but what can you expect of every-day men, if Schiller was not more prophetic as to what women must be? Even with Richter[23] one foremost thought about a wife was that she would "cook him something good."

The sexes should not only correspond to and appreciate one another, but prophesy to one another. In individual instances this happens. Two persons love in one another the future good which they aid one another to unfold. This is very imperfectly done as yet in the general life. Man has gone but little way, now he is waiting to see whether woman can keep step with him, but instead of calling out like a good brother; You can do it if you only think so, or impersonally; Any one can do what he tries to do, he often discourages with school-boy brag; Girls cant do that, girls cant play ball. But let any one defy their taunts, break through, and be brave and secure, they rend the air with shouts.

No! man is not willingly ungenerous. He wants faith and love, because he is not yet himself an elevated being. He cries with sneering skepticism; Give us a sign. But if the sign appears, his eyes glisten, and he offers not merely approval, but homage.

* * *

The reigns of Elizabeth of England and Isabella of Castile[24] foreboded this era. They expressed the beginning of the new state, while they forwarded its progress. These were strong characters, and in harmony with the wants of their time. One showed that this strength did not unfit a woman for the duties of a wife and mother; the other, that it could enable her to live and die alone. Elizabeth is certainly no pleasing example. In rising above the weakness, she did not lay aside the weaknesses ascribed to her sex; but her strength must be respected now, as it was in her own time.

We may accept it as an omen for ourselves, that it was Isabella who furnished Columbus with the means of coming hither. This land must pay back its debt to woman, without whose aid it would not have been brought into alliance with the civilized world.

1843

[19] According to Greek myth, Theseus was a hero who (among other things) defeated an invasion of the Amazons and married the Amazonian queen, Hippolyte. Fuller seems to offer this mythic episode as an example of male domination.

[20] To win back the love of the wandering Hercules, Dejanira followed the advice given years before by Nessus and sent her husband a robe permeated with a supposed love potion that turned out to be deadly poison. Fuller telescopes the details of this complex story to make it a warning against choosing an apparently docile wife. "Guerdon" means reward.

[21] Lack.

[22] A poem by Friedrich von Schiller (1759–1805), a German dramatist, poet, and historian.

[23] Jean Paul Richter (1763–1825), a German novelist whose *Levana: Or, The Doctrine of Education* (1807) exemplifies Fuller's point.

[24] Isabella I (1451–1504), queen of Castile, Spain (1474–1504).

═CONTEXTS═

Women's Rights in the 1830s

The involvement of women in the reform movements of the 1830s made women more aware of their own lack of rights. Although the editor and abolitionist leader William Lloyd Garrison encouraged equal participation of women in the fight for emancipation, social convention frowned on women speaking in public, and many reform organizations would not accept women as members. In 1839 numerous members of the American Anti-Slavery Society issued a public statement opposing the complete integration of women in the society's work. The reasoning of the petitioners, as published in the May 31, 1839, issue of the *Liberator,* closely resembles a common argument of slaveholders for depriving African Americans of their constitutional rights:

Protest

We the undersigned, members and delegates of the American Anti-Slavery Society, as a duty, and therefore a right, hereby protest against the principle, assumed by a majority of persons representing said Society at its present meeting, that women have the right of originating, debating, and voting on questions which come before said Society, and are eligible to its various offices:—and we protest against the assumption of said principle for the following, among other reasons, viz:

1. Because it is contrary to the expectation, design, and spirit of the Constitution of said Society, as clearly indicated by the proceedings of the framers of that instrument, at the commencement, in the progress, and at the completion of the work.

2. Because it is at variance with the construction of said instrument, as made known by the constant usage of the Society from its first to its present meeting.

3. Because it is repugnant to the wishes, the wisdom, or the moral sense of many of the early and present members of said Society, and devoted friends to the cause for which that Society was organized.

4. Because, though assumed by a majority of persons representing said Society in its present meeting, we believe it to be wide from the expression of the general sense of the abolitionists of this country of either sex, and, if not objected to in this formal manner, might seem to be the unqualified and unlimited sanction of the friends of the slave and the asserter of his rights.

Abolitionists against women's participation in the American Anti-Slavery Society, 1839

Declaration of Sentiments
(1848)

The Declaration of Sentiments of the Woman's Rights Convention at Seneca Falls, New York, on July 19 and 20, 1848, is the first extensive expression of the principles and grievances underlying feminists' dispute with male-dominated society. The document is at once the product of a historical moment and a voice in an evolving political dialogue. Because women's history was virtually unrecorded, the authors of the declaration knew little of the tradition they had joined. When Mary Ann McClintock, Lucretia Mott, Elizabeth Cady Stanton, and Martha C. Wright drafted the declaration, however, they commanded other valuable resources, some the common property of an age that sought a "true" social system. Karl Marx and Friedrich Engels had recently envisioned all history as class struggle; American utopianism had flourished in the 1840s, fostering such experiments as the transcendentalist cooperative community Brook Farm (1841–1847), near Bos-

This 1870 lithograph by Louis Prang & Co. shows the leading women suffragists of the mid-nineteenth century (clockwise from top): Lucretia Mott, Elizabeth Cady Stanton, Mary A. Livermore, Lydia Maria Child, Susan B. Anthony, and Grace Greenwood; Anna E. Dickinson is in the center.

ton, and the religious Oneida Community (1848–1880), in Oneida, New York. The authors understood, too, that changes in the social order were affecting women's lives in the workplace and in education. Moreover, the state of New York had recently supplanted common law with the first statute guaranteeing the property rights of married women— probably because wealthy farmers feared the spendthrift habits of sons-in-laws.

But the Declaration of Sentiments derives most immediately from its authors' experience in organized reform. Before adopting the Declaration of Independence as the model most commensurate with their ideas, they considered statements of the temperance and antislavery movements, which they knew well. Abolitionism offered particularly rich soil for the early women's movement. Along with such abolitionist women as Sarah and Angelina Grimké, Sojourner Truth, and Frances Wright, the authors had sharpened their political skills on the issue of slavery. Indeed, the Seneca Falls convention may be said to have had its inception in London in 1840, when the World Anti-Slavery Convention refused to seat American women delegates, including Stanton and Mott, who had to sit behind a curtain throughout the ten-day convention and resolved then to work for women's rights. Many men who supported the early women's movement also came from the antislavery movement, among them William Lloyd Garrison (who refused his seat at the London convention when the women were rejected) and Frederick Douglass (who signed the Declaration of Sentiments and defended women's rights in the *North Star*).

The Seneca Falls convention adopted the declaration with amendments and approved eleven of twelve resolutions unanimously. Many delegates feared that the resolution concerning the right to vote would bring ridicule on the whole endeavor, but it was narrowly sustained by the efforts of Stanton and Douglass, who argued that the vote was the only guarantee for other rights. One hundred people signed the document. Although the convention and the declaration were immediately belittled, particularly by the pulpit and the press, two weeks later a larger convention met at Rochester, New York, to reaffirm and extend the claims of the original document. The Seneca Falls declaration now stands as a landmark of the "old" feminism, the pursuit of women's political rights that extended from the American Revolution through the ratification of the Nineteenth Amendment in 1920. It serves likewise as an expression of issues central to the "new" feminism, including women's economic, social, and marital status.

Suggested Readings: *Proceedings of the Woman's Rights Conventions Held at Seneca Falls & Rochester, N. Y., July & August, 1848,* 1870, rpt. as *Woman's Rights Conventions, Seneca Falls & Rochester, 1848,* 1969. E. C. Stanton, *Eighty Years & More, 1815–1897,* 1898, rpt. 1971. E. Flexner, *Century of Struggle: The Woman's Rights Movement in the United States,* 1975. M. Gurko, *The Ladies of Seneca Falls: The Birth of the Woman's Rights Movement,* 1976. M. H. Bacon, *Valiant Friend: The Life of Lucretia Mott,* 1980. L. W. Banner, *Elizabeth Cady Stanton: A Radical for Woman's Rights,* 1980. E. Griffith, *In Her Own Right: The Life of Elizabeth Cady Stanton,* 1984.

Text Used: *Report of the Woman's Rights Convention, Held At Seneca Falls, N. Y., July 19th & 20th, 1848,* 1848.

DECLARATION OF SENTIMENTS

When, in the course of human events, it becomes necessary for one portion of the family of man to assume among the people of the earth a position different from that which they have hitherto occupied, but one to which the laws of nature and of nature's God entitle them, a decent respect to the opinions of mankind requires that they should declare the causes that impel them to such a course.

We hold these truths to be self-evident: that all men and women are created equal; that they are endowed by their Creator with certain inalienable rights, that among these are life, liberty, and the pursuit of happiness; that to secure these rights governments are instituted, deriving their just powers from the consent of the governed[.] Whenever any form of government becomes destructive of these ends, it is the right of those who suffer from it to refuse allegiance to it, and to insist upon the institution of a new government, laying its foundation on such principles, and organizing its powers in such form as to them shall seem most likely to effect their safety and happiness. Prudence, indeed, will dictate that governments long established should not be changed for light and transient causes; and accordingly, all experience hath shown that mankind are more disposed to suffer, while evils are sufferable, than to right themselves by abolishing the forms to which they were accustomed. But when a long train of abuses and usurpations, pursuing invariably the same object evinces a design to reduce them under absolute despotism, it is their duty to throw off such government, and to provide new guards for their future security. Such has been the patient sufferance of the women under this government, and such is now the necessity which constrains them to demand the equal station to which they are entitled.

The history of mankind is a history of repeated injuries and usurpations on the part of man toward woman, having in direct object the establishment of an absolute tyranny over her. To prove this, let facts be submitted to a candid world.

He has never permitted her to exercise her inalienable right to the elective franchise.

He has compelled her to submit to laws, in the formation of which she had no voice.

He has withheld from her rights which are given to the most ignorant and degraded men—both natives and foreigners.

Having deprived her of this first right of a citizen, the elective franchise, thereby leaving her without representation in the halls of legislation, he has oppressed her on all sides.

He has made her, if married, in the eye of the law, civilly dead.

He has taken from her all right in property, even to the wages she earns.

He has made her, morally, an irresponsible being, as she can commit many crimes with impunity, provided they be done in the presence of her husband. In the covenant of marriage, she is compelled to promise obedience to her husband, he becoming, to all intents and purposes, her master—the law giving him power to deprive her of her liberty, and to administer chastisement.

He has so framed the laws of divorce, as to what shall be the proper causes of divorce; in case of separation, to whom the guardianship of the children shall be given; as to be wholly regardless of the happiness of women—the law, in all cases, going upon a false supposition of the supremacy of man, and giving all power into his hands.

After depriving her of all rights as a married woman, if single and the owner of property, he has taxed her to support a government which recognizes her only when her property can be made profitable to it.

He has monopolized nearly all the profitable employments, and from those she is permitted to follow, she receives but a scanty remuneration.

He closes against her all the avenues to wealth and distinction, which he considers most honorable to himself. As a teacher of theology, medicine, or law, she is not known.

He has denied her the facilities for obtaining a thorough education—all colleges being closed against her.

He allows her in Church, as well as State, but a subordinate position, claiming Apostolic authority for her exclusion from the ministry, and, with some exceptions, from any public participation in the affairs of the Church.

He has created a false public sentiment, by giving to the world a different code of morals for men and women, by which moral delinquencies which exclude women from society, are not only tolerated but deemed of little account in man.

He has usurped the prerogative of Jehovah himself, claiming it as his right to assign for her a sphere of action, when that belongs to her conscience and to her God.

He has endeavored, in every way that he could, to destroy her confidence in her own powers, to lessen her self-respect, and to make her willing to lead a dependent and abject life.

Now, in view of this entire disfranchisement of one-half of the people of this country, their social and religious degradation,—in view of the unjust laws above mentioned, and because women do feel themselves aggrieved, oppressed, and fraudulently deprived of their most sacred rights, we insist that they have immediate admission to all the rights and privileges which belong to them as citizens of the United States.

In entering upon the great work before us, we anticipate no small amount of misconception, misrepresentation, and ridicule; but we shall use every instrumentality within our power to effect our object. We shall employ agents, circulate tracts, petition the state and national legislatures, and endeavor to enlist the pulpit and the press in our behalf. We hope this Convention will be followed by a series of Conventions, embracing every part of the country.

Firmly relying upon the final triumph of the Right and the True, we do this day affix our signatures to this declaration.

[Signatures]

RESOLUTIONS

Whereas the great precept of nature is conceded to be, "that man shall pursue his own true and substantial happiness." Blackstone, in his Commentaries, remarks, that this law of Nature being coeval with mankind, and dictated by God himself, is of course superior in obligation to any other. It is binding over all the globe, in all countries, and at all times; no human laws are of any validity if contrary to this, and such of them as are valid, derive all their force, and all their validity, and all their authority, mediately and immediately, from this original; therefore,

Resolved, That such laws as conflict, in any way, with the true and substantial happiness of woman, are contrary to the great precept of nature, and of no validity; for this is "superior in obligation to any other."

Resolved, That all laws which prevent woman from occupying such a station in society as her conscience shall dictate, or which place her in a position inferior to that of man, are contrary to the great precept of nature, and therefore of no force or authority.

Resolved, That woman is man's equal—was intended to be so by the Creator, and the highest good of the race demands that she should be recognized as such.

Resolved, That the women of this country ought to be enlightened in regard to the laws under which they live, that they may no longer publish their degradation, by declaring themselves satisfied with their present position, nor their ignorance, by asserting that they have all the rights they want.

Resolved, That inasmuch as man, while claiming for himself intellectual superiority, does [] accord to woman moral superiority, it is pre-eminently his duty to encourage her to speak, and teach, as she has an opportunity, in all religious assemblies.

Resolved, That the same amount of virtue, delicacy, and refinement of behavior, that is required of woman in the social state, should also be required of man, and the same transgressions should be visited with equal severity on both man and woman.

Resolved, That the objection of indelicacy and impropriety, which is so often brought against woman when she addresses a public audience, comes with a very ill-grace from those who encourage, by their attendance, her appearance on the stage, in the concert, or in feats of the circus.

Resolved, That woman has too long rested satisfied in the circumscribed limits which corrupt customs and a perverted application of the Scriptures have marked out for her, and that it is time she should move in the enlarged sphere which her great Creator has assigned her.

Resolved, That it is the duty of the women of this country to secure to themselves their sacred right to the elective franchise.

Resolved, That the equality of human rights results necessarily from the fact of the identity of the race in capabilities and responsibilities.

Resolved, therefore, That, being invested by the Creator with the same capabilities, and the same consciousness of responsibility for their exercise, it is demonstrably the right and duty of woman, equally with man, to promote every righteous cause, by every righteous means; and especially in regard to the great subjects of morals and religion, it is self-evidently her right to participate with her brother in teaching them, both in private and in public, by writing and by speaking, by any instrumentalities proper to be used, and in any assemblies proper to be held; and this being a self-evident truth, growing out of the divinely implanted principles of human nature, any custom or authority adverse to it, whether modern or wearing the hoary sanction of antiquity, is to be regarded as a self-evident falsehood, and at war with mankind.

Resolved, That the speedy success of our cause depends upon the zealous and untiring efforts of both men and women, for the overthrow of the monopoly of the pulpit, and for the securing to woman an equal participation with men in the various trades, professions and commerce.

1848

Fanny Fern (Sara Payson Willis)
(1811–1872)

Fanny Fern was one of the first and most popular female columnists, an innovative prose stylist admired for her social commentary and biting satire. Born Sara Payson Willis in Portland, Maine, in 1811, she briefly attended Catharine Beecher's Female Seminary, where her school compositions were sought after by the local newspaper editor. Willis began writing professionally, however, only when a series of personal disasters left her virtually destitute. Her happy first marriage, to the bank cashier Charles Eldredge in 1837, ended with Eldredge's death in 1846, just a short while after the death of her mother, sister, and firstborn daughter. Left with two children and no means of support, Willis, under pressure from her father, contracted a frustrating marriage of convenience to the merchant Samuel Farrington in 1849. Because she soon left Farrington, she was eventually divorced for desertion. Unable to support herself in the traditional women's vocations of teaching and sewing, she began to write as Fanny Fern, selling her first column for fifty cents in 1851; four years later she was paid one hundred dollars a column by the New York *Ledger*. In 1856 she married the editor and biographer James Parton, eleven years her junior, who had once resigned an editorial position rather than assent to canceling her sometimes controversial columns.

The pseudonym Fanny Fern both mimics and subtly parodies the names of popular contemporary writers such as Grace Greenwood, Fanny Foxglove, and Harriet Honeysuckle. Although she published numerous sentimental pieces, Fern also satirized sentimentality, and her essays on topics such as prostitution and prison reform are biting and acute. Her most common subject, however, was the condition of women; indeed, a persistent concern with women, minorities, and social issues places her firmly in the tradition of the reform-minded writers Lydia Maria Child and Margaret Fuller. Not surprisingly, the outspoken quality of Fern's writing caused her (like Fuller) to be deemed "unnatural" and "unfeminine." Despite such criticism, she continued to speak her mind on the foibles of society.

Fern also wrote several novels, the best of which is the autobiographical *Ruth Hall* (1854), dubbed "Ruthless Hall" by some readers. Modeled on her own career, the narrative tells the story of a woman's rise from widowhood and poverty to wealth and power as a popular columnist. The novel shocked readers accustomed to less assertive heroines but drew praise from Nathaniel Hawthorne (no lover of women's fiction), who remarked to his publisher, William Ticknor, in 1855 that Fern "writes as if the devil was in her; and that is the only condition under which a woman ever writes anything worth reading." Published before the secret of the Fern pseudonym was known, *Ruth Hall* contained scathing and easily recognized portraits of acquaintances—including one of her brother, the critic and publisher N. P. Willis, who had actively tried to thwart her writing career. The novel intensified accusations that Fern was an "unnatural" woman, but the criticism seemed not to bother the author: over the span of a long career, lasting until her death in 1872, Sara Payson Willis never doubted that women could write as well as—and typically more trenchantly than—men could.

Suggested Readings: *Hidden Hands: An Anthology of American Women Writers, 1790–1870*, ed. L. M. Freibert and B. A. White, 1985. J. Fetterley, *Provisions: A Reader From 19th-Century American Women*, 1985. J. W. Warren, "Introduction" to *Ruth Hall and Other Writings*, 1986.

Text Used: *Ruth Hall and Other Writings*, ed. J. W. Warren, 1986.

THE "COMING" WOMAN*

Men often say, "When *I* marry, my wife must be this, that and the other," enumerating all physical, mental, and moral perfections. One cannot but smile to look at the men who say these things; smile to think of the equivalent they will bring

* First published in the *New York Ledger*, February 12, 1859.

for all the amiability, beauty, health, intellectuality, domesticity, and faithfulness they so modestly require; smile to think of the perforated hearts, damaged morals, broken-down constitutions, and irritable tempers, which the bright, pure, innocent girl is to receive with her wedding ring. If one half the girls knew the previous life of the men they marry, the list of old maids would be wonderfully increased.

Doubted? Well, if there is room for a doubt now, thank God the "coming" woman's Alpha and Omega[1] will not be matrimony. *She* will not of necessity sour into a pink-nosed old maid, or throw herself at any rickety old shell of humanity, whose clothes are as much out of repair as his morals. No, the future man will have to "step lively;" *this* wife is not to be had for the whistling. He will have a long canter round the pasture for her, and then she will leap the fence and leave him limping on the ground. Thick-soled boots and skating are coming in, and "nerves," novels and sentiment (by consequence) are going out. The coming woman, as I see her, is not to throw aside her needle; neither is she to sit embroidering worsted dogs and cats, or singing doubtful love ditties, and rolling up her eyes to "the chaste moon."

Heaven forbid she should stamp round with a cigar in her mouth, elbowing her fellows, and puffing smoke in their faces; or stand on the free-love platform, *public or private—call it by what specious name you will*—wooing men who, low as they may have sunk in their own self-respect, would die before they would introduce her to the unsullied sister who shared their cradle.

Heaven forbid the coming woman should not have warm blood in her veins, quick to rush to her cheek, or tingle at her fingers' ends when her heart is astir. No, the coming woman shall be no cold, angular, flat-chested, narrow-shouldered, skimpy sharp-visaged Betsey,[2] but she shall be a bright-eyed, full-chested, broad-shouldered, large-souled, intellectual being; able to walk, able to eat, able to fulfill her maternal destiny, and able—if it so please God—to go to her grave happy, self-poised and serene, though unwedded.

1859

FASHIONABLE INVALIDISM*

I hope to live to see the time when it will be considered a *disgrace* to be sick. When people with flat chests and stooping shoulders, will creep round the back way, like other violators of known laws. Those who *inherit* sickly constitutions have my sincerest pity. I only request one favor of them, that they cease perpetuating themselves till they are physically on a sound basis. But a woman who laces so tightly that she breathes only by a rare accident; who vibrates constantly between the confectioner's shop and the dentist's office; who has ball-robes and jewels in plenty, but who owns neither an umbrella, nor a water-proof cloak, nor a pair of thick boots; who lies in bed till noon, never exercises, and complains of "total want of appetite," save for pastry and pickles, is simply a disgusting nuisance. Sentiment is all very nice; but, were I a man, I would beware of a woman who "couldn't eat." Why don't she take care of herself? Why don't she take a nice little bit of beefsteak with her breakfast, and a nice *walk*—not *ride*—after it? Why

---

[1] The first and last letters of the Greek alphabet; hence, "beginning and end."
[2] A made-up name to represent a type.
* First published in the *New York Ledger*, July 27, 1867.

don't she stop munching sweet stuff between meals? Why don't she go to bed at a decent time, and lead a clean, healthy life? The doctors and confectioners have ridden in their carriages long enough; let the butchers and shoemakers take a turn at it. A man or woman who "can't eat" is never sound on any question. It is waste breath to converse with them. They take hold of everything by the wrong handle. Of course it makes them very angry to whisper pityingly, "dyspepsia,"[1] when they advance some distorted opinion; but I always do it. They are not going to muddle my brain with their theories, because their internal works are in a state of physical disorganization. Let them go into a Lunatic Asylum and be properly treated till they can learn how they are put together, and how to manage themselves sensibly.

How I *rejoice* in a man or woman with a chest; who can look the sun in the eye, and step off as if they had not wooden legs. It is a rare sight. If a woman now has an errand round the corner, she must have a carriage to go there; and the men, more dead than alive, so lethargic are they with constant smoking, creep into cars and omnibuses, and curl up in a corner, dreading nothing so much as a little wholesome exertion. The more "tired" they are, the more diligently they smoke, like the women who drink perpetual *tea* "to keep them up."

Keep them up! Heavens! I am fifty-five, and I feel half the time as if I were just made. To be sure I was born in Maine, where the timber and the human race last; but I do not eat pastry, nor candy, nor ice-cream. I do not drink tea! I walk, not ride. I own stout boots—pretty ones, too! I have a water-proof cloak, and no diamonds. I like a nice bit of beefsteak and a glass of ale, and anybody else who wants it may eat pap.[2] I go to bed at ten, and get up a six. I dash out in the rain, because it feels good on my face. I don't care for my clothes, but I *will* be well; and after I am buried, I warn you, don't let any fresh air or sunlight down on my coffin, if you don't want me to get up.

1867

THE WORKING-GIRLS OF NEW YORK*

Nowhere more than in New York does the contest between squalor and splendor so sharply present itself. This is the first reflection of the observing stranger who walks its streets. Particularly is this noticeable with regard to its women. Jostling on the same pavement with the dainty fashionist is the care-worn working-girl. Looking at both these women, the question arises, which lives the more miserable life—she whom the world styles "fortunate," whose husband belongs to three clubs, and whose only meal with his family is an occasional breakfast, from year's end to year's end; who is as much a stranger to his own children as to the reader; whose young son of seventeen has already a detective on his track employed by his father to ascertain where and how he spends his nights and his father's money; swift retribution for that father who finds food, raiment, shelter, equipages for his

---

[1] Indigestion; the fashionable invalid would rather have a more complicated problem than indigestion.

[2] Soft food for infants or invalids.

* Published in *Folly As It Flies* (1868); the critic and editor Joyce W. Warren has found that some of Fern's columns have been cut out of the only remaining copy of the *New York Ledger;* this may have been one of them.

household; but love, sympathy, companionship—never? Or she—this other woman—with a heart quite as hungry and unappeased, who also faces day by day the same appalling question: *Is this all life has for me?*

A great book is yet unwritten about women. Michelet[1] has aired his wax-doll theories regarding them. The defender of "woman's rights" has given us her views. Authors and authoresses of little, and big repute, have expressed themselves on this subject, and none of them as yet have begun to grasp it: men—because they lack spirituality, rightly and justly to interpret women; women—because they dare not, or will not tell us that which most interests us to know. Who shall write this bold, frank, truthful book remains to be seen. Meanwhile woman's millennium is yet a great way off; and while it slowly progresses, conservatism and indifference gaze through their spectacles at the seething elements of to-day, and wonder "what ails all our women?"

Let me tell you what ails the working-girls. While yet your breakfast is progressing, and your toilet unmade, comes forth through Chatham Street and the Bowery, a long procession of them by twos and threes to their daily labor. Their breakfast, so called, has been hastily swallowed in a tenement house, where two of them share, in a small room, the same miserable bed. Of its quality you may better judge, when you know that each of these girls pays but three dollars a week for board, to the working man and his wife where they lodge.

The room they occupy is close and unventilated, with no accommodations for personal cleanliness, and so near to the little Flinegans that their Celtic night-cries[2] are distinctly heard. They have risen unrefreshed, as a matter of course, and their ill-cooked breakfast does not mend the matter. They emerge from the doorway where their passage is obstructed by "nanny goats" and ragged children rooting together in the dirt, and pass out into the street. They shiver as the sharp wind of early morning strikes their temples. There is no look of youth on their faces; hard lines appear there. Their brows are knit; their eyes are sunken; their dress is flimsy, and foolish, and tawdry; always a hat, and feather or soiled artificial flower upon it; the hair dressed with an abortive attempt at style; a soiled petticoat; a greasy dress, a well-worn sacque or shawl, and a gilt breast-pin and earrings.

Now follow them to the large, black-looking building, where several hundred of them are manufacturing hoop-skirts. If you are a woman you have worn plenty; but you little thought what passed in the heads of these girls as their busy fingers glazed the wire, or prepared the spools for covering them, or secured the tapes which held them in their places. *You* could not stay five minutes in that room, where the noise of the machinery used is so deafening, that only by the motion of the lips could you comprehend a person speaking.

Five minutes! Why, these young creatures bear it, from seven in the morning till six in the evening; week after week, month after month, with only half an hour at midday to eat their dinner of a slice of bread and butter or an apple, which they usually eat in the building, some of them having come a long distance. As I said, the roar of machinery in that room is like the roar of Niagara. Observe them as you enter. Not one lifts her head. They might as well be machines, for any interest or curiosity they show, save always to know *what o'clock it is*. Pitiful! pitiful, you

---

[1] Jules Michelet (1798–1894), a French historian, whose study *La Femme* (1859) portrays the ideal woman as pliant, submissive, and naïve. In the following sentence Fern may be speaking generically of "the defender" of woman's rights; no specific person has been identified.

[2] The crying of babies in a stereotyped Irish family, which lives close to the working-girls in this scenario.

almost sob to yourself, as you look at these young girls. *Young?* Alas! it is only in years that they are young.

1868

THE HISTORY OF OUR LATE WAR*

Many able works have already appeared on this subject, and many more will doubtless follow. But *my* History of the War is yet to be written; not indeed *by* me, but *for* me. A history which shall record, not the deeds of our Commanders and Generals, noble and great as they were, because these will scarcely fail of historical record and prominence; but *my* history shall preserve for the descendants of those who fought for our flag, the noble deeds of our *privates,* who shared the danger but missed the glory. Scattered far and wide in our remote villages—hidden away amid our mountains—struggling for daily bread in our swarming cities, are these unrecognized heroes. Travelling through our land, one meets them everywhere; but only as accident, or chance, leads to conversation with them, does the plain man by your side become transfigured in your eyes, till you feel like uncovering your head in his presence, as when one stands upon holy ground. Not only because they were brave upon the battle-field, but for their sublime self-abnegation under circumstances when the best of us might be forgiven our selfishness; in the tortures of the ambulance and hospital—quivering through the laggard hours, that might or might not bring peace and rest and health. Oh! what a book might be written upon the noble unselfishness *there* displayed; not only towards those who fought *for* our flag; but *against* it. The coveted drop of water, handed by one dying man to another, whose sufferings seemed the greater. The simple request to the physician to pass *his* wounds by, till those of another, whose existence was unknown to him a moment before, should have been alleviated. Who shall embalm us these?

Last summer, when I was away in the country, I was accustomed to row every evening at sunset on a lovely lake near by. The boatman who went with me was a sunburnt, pleasant-faced young man, whose stroke at the oar it was poetry to see. He made no conversation unless addressed, save occasionally to little Bright-Eyes, who sometimes accompanied me. One evening, as the sun set gloriously and the moon rose, and the aurora borealis was sending up flashes of rose and silver, I said, "Oh, this is too beautiful to leave. I *must* cross the lake again." I made some remark about the brilliance of the North Star, when he remaked simply, "That star was a good friend to me in the war." "Were you in the war?" asked I; "and all these evenings you have rowed a loyal woman like me about this lake, and I knew nothing of it!" Then, at my request, came the story of Andersonville,[1] and its horrors, told simply, and without a revengeful word; then the thrilling attempt at escape, through a country absolutely unknown, and swarming with danger, during which the North Star, of which I had just spoken, was his only guide. Then came a dark night, when the friendly star, alas! disappeared. But a watch,

---

* First published in the *New York Ledger,* February 15, 1868.
[1] A notorious Confederate prisoner of war camp in Georgia where more than eight thousand men died of malnutrition and other illnesses in 1864; Major Henry Wirtz, commander at Andersonville, was the only Confederate soldier executed for criminal conduct after the Civil War.

which he had saved his money to obtain, had a compass on the back of it. Still of what use was that without a light? Our boatman was a Yankee. He caught a glow-worm and pinched it. It flashed light sufficient for him to see that he was heading for one of our camps, where, after many hours of travel, he at last found safety, sinking down insensible from fatigue and hunger, as soon as he reached it. So ravenously did he eat, when food was brought, that a raging fever followed; and when he was carried, a mere skeleton, to his home on the borders of the lovely lake where we were rowing, whose peaceful flow had mocked him in dreams in that seething, noisome prison pen, he did not even recognize it. For months his mother watched his sick-bed, till reason and partial health returned—till by degrees he became what he then was.

When he had finished, I said, "Give me your hand—*both of 'em*—and God bless you!"—and—then I *mentioned* his jailers! Not a word of bitterness passed his lips—only this: "I used to gasp in the foul air at Andersonville, and think of this quiet, smooth lake, and our little house with the trees near it, and long so to see them again, and row my little boat here. But," he added, quietly, "*they* thought they were as right as we, and they *did* fight well!"

I swallowed a big lump in my throat—as our boat neared the shore, and he handed me out—and said, penitently, "Well, if *you* can forgive them, I am sure I ought to; but it will be the hardest work I ever did."—"Well, it is strange," said he: "I have often noticed it, since my return, that you who stayed at home feel more bitter about it, than we who came so near dying there of foul air and starvation."

1868

THE MODERN OLD MAID*

She don't shuffle round in "skimpt" raiment,[1] and awkward shoes, and cotton gloves, with horn side-combs fastening six hairs to her temples; nor has she a sharp nose, and angular jaw, and hollow cheeks, and only two front teeth. She don't read "Law's Serious Call,"[2] or keep a cat, or a snuff-box, or go to bed at dark, save on vestry-meeting nights, nor scowl at little children, or gather catnip, or apply a broomstick to astonished dogs.

Not a bit of it. The modern "old maid" is round and jolly, and has her full complement of hair and teeth, and two dimples in her cheek, and has a laugh as musical as a bobolink's song. She wears pretty, nicely fitting dresses too, and cunning little ornaments around her plump throat, and becoming bits of color in her hair, and at her breast, in the shape of little knots and bows; and her waist is shapely, and her hands have sparkling rings, and no knuckles;[3] and her foot is cunning, and is prisoned in a bewildering boot; and she goes to concerts and parties and suppers and lectures and matinees, and she don't go alone either; and she

---

* First published in the *New York Ledger*, June 5, 1869.
[1] Old-fashioned attire, lacking in style.
[2] *A Serious Call to a Devout and Holy Life* (1728), by the English religious writer William Law (1686–1761). Reading this book, having a cat and a snuffbox, and going to bed early are offered here as typical occupations of the traditional old maid.
[3] No red and swollen knuckles from years of household drudgery.

lives in a nice house, earned by herself, and gives jolly little teas in it. She don't care whether she is married or not, nor need she. She can afford to wait, as men often do, till they have "seen life," and when their bones are full of aches, and their blood tamed down to water, and they have done going out, and want somebody to swear at and to nurse them—then marry!

Ah! the modern old maid has her eye-teeth cut.[4] She takes care of herself, instead of her sister's nine children, through mumps, and measles, and croup, and chicken-pox, and lung fever and leprosy, and what not.

She don't work that way for no wages and bare toleration, day and night. No, sir! If she has no money, she teaches, or she lectures, or she writes books or poems, or she is a book-keeper, or she sets types, or she does anything but hang on to the skirts of somebody else's husband, and she feels well and independent in consequence, and holds up her head with the best, and asks no favors, and "*Woman's Rights*" has done it!

That awful bugbear, "Woman's Rights"! which small souled men, and, I am sorry to say, narrow *women* too, burlesque and ridicule, and won't believe in, till the Juggernaut of Progress[5] knocks them down and rides over them, because they will neither climb up on it, nor get out of the way.

The fact is, the *Modern* Old Maid is as good as the Modern Young Maid, and a great deal better, to those who have outgrown bread and butter. She has sense as well as freshness, and conversation and repartee as well as dimples and curves.

She carries a dainty parasol, and a natty little umbrella, and wears killing bonnets, and has live poets and sages and philosophers in her train, and knows how to use her eyes, and don't care if she never sees a cat, and couldn't tell a snuff-box from a patent reaper,[6] and has a bank-book and dividends; yes, sir! and her name is Phœbe or Alice; and Woman's Rights has done it.

1869

Frederick Douglass
(1818?–1895)

Among the many American books that concern themselves with the struggle for identity and liberty, one of the most powerful is Frederick Douglass's *Narrative of the Life of Frederick Douglass, an American Slave, Written by Himself* (1845). The fundamental structure of the *Narrative* is instructive: the fact that Douglass was a black man telling of his escape from slavery informs the fact that Douglass is an American who, like Benjamin Franklin, was compelled to tell his life story as a model of American individuality and initiative. Douglass focuses on those qualities of persistence, honesty, and social responsiblity that have been present in American writing since John Winthrop's speech "Model of Christian Charity" (1630). But the *Narrative* is specifically and crucially the story of a

---

[4] She is no longer naïve.

[5] In Hindu theology Juggernaut, a form of the god Vishnu, signifies a call for blind devotion or sacrifice; here, unstoppable progress.

[6] Any patented machine for reaping grain. "Phoebe" and "Alice" signify the modern old maid.

slave and his struggle for freedom. And among other important slave narratives of the antebellum period, including those of Harriet Jacobs, Solomon Northup, and Moses Roper, it has endured as the most influential and important. Douglass's astute use of irony, his avoidance of indulgent literary and polemic techniques, and his powerful effect on later African-American writers have made an enduring place for the *Narrative* in the history of American letters.

Douglass was born a slave on the eastern coast of Maryland in 1817 or 1818 with the given name Frederick Bailey. His mother, Harriet Bailey, was a slave; his white father, as he came to believe, was superintendent of the plantation on which young Frederick grew up. When he was eight Bailey was sent to work for the family of Thomas Auld in Baltimore. Despite Auld's steadfast opposition, Bailey laid the groundwork for his future success by teaching himself to read and to write. When he was sixteen, he was hired out as a field hand for Edward Covey, an overseer known for brutality and for "breaking" slaves under his authority. For the first time in Bailey's life he was whipped, made to crawl, made to doubt his strength of spirit. As related in the 1845 *Narrative*, his decision to defy Covey physically, to challenge him as one man to another, was a turning point in Bailey's life as a slave and as a human being.

With the help of Anna Murray, a free African-American woman from Baltimore, Bailey escaped from slavery in 1838. In New York City he and Anna were married; shortly afterwards they moved to New Bedford, Massachusetts, where over the next three years Bailey established himself as a leader in the abolitionist movement. By 1841 he was publicly acclaimed for his commitment to the cause of freedom and for his ability as a speaker. Shortly after he arrived in the North, he had renamed himself, replacing "Frederick Bailey" with the name of the protagonist of Sir Walter Scott's *The Lady of the Lake* (1810). It was thus as Frederick Douglass, a self-named man, that he established his authority as lecturer and writer.

Much of the detail concerning Douglass's early life and career comes from the 1845 *Narrative*. The man and the book make each other possible and reinforce a single identity, that of a writer capable of irony and nuance, aware of what his audience considers important. Douglass demonstrates a particular awareness of prominent and value-laden ideas by applying moral precepts to the crisis of slavery. His profound adherence to the laws of conscience as opposed to the laws of the land places his voice among those of Roger Williams, Thomas Jefferson, and Henry David Thoreau. Douglass's moral self-reliance is particularly evident in the crucial tenth chapter of the *Narrative*: "My long crushed spirit rose, cowardice departed, bold defiance took its place; and I now resolved that, however long I remained a slave in form, the day had passed when I would be a slave in fact." Like Thoreau in "Resistance to Civil Government" (1849), Douglass demonstrates a dominant commitment to what is *right* as opposed to what is legal in an effort to maintain the liberty of the soul in the face of the body's imprisonment.

Douglass maintains the integrity of the *Narrative* by eschewing the use of sentimental and personal stratagems to manipulate his audience. He refuses, for example, to divulge the particulars of his escape from a Baltimore shipyard in 1838 for fear of exposing the individuals who helped him and the methods he used—which he hopes may be duplicated. As a result the *Narrative* does not exploit melodramatic sequences and facile emotionalism (although it contains enough compelling detail to have made Douglass fear recapture as a slave).

Douglass's developing prominence can be measured by his ability to inspire later writers who have addressed the issue of race in American society. Charles W. Chesnutt and Booker T. Washington contributed biographies, and homage to Douglass has come from African-American writers from W. E. B. DuBois to Martin Luther King, Jr. A more profound literary influence can be found on the textual level: both the act of naming oneself as an assertion of identity and the ritual of self-actualization through violence (as we see in Douglass's fight with Edward Covey) are decisive to such novels as Richard Wright's *Black Boy* (1945), Ralph Ellison's *Invisible Man* (1952), and Toni Morrison's *Song of Solomon* (1977).

The *Narrative* of 1845 was only the beginning of Douglass's career as a writer and nationally recognized spokesman for African Americans. As Walt Whitman did with his *Leaves of Grass* (1855), Douglass spent much of his career rewriting, revising, and updating his autobiographical work. The second version of his story, *My Bondage and My Freedom*, appeared in 1855, and the third, *Life and Times of Frederick Douglass*, was published in 1881 and revised again in 1892; it reached a final length of almost eight hundred pages. However, the three later versions of Douglass's life story never achieved the authority and forthrightness of the original *Narrative*. The results of the critic Michael Meyer's comparison of specific parallel passages leave little doubt that the later versions lack the punch and immediacy of the original.

In the *Narrative* Douglass reconstructs the story of his life and the impact of his experience as a slave on a consciousness still in the making, coming in the final chapters to his self-conscious debut as a public speaker. The power of his style as a writer is apparent by contrast with the prefatory letters from the abolitionists William Lloyd Garrison and Wendell Phillips in this first edition. Whereas these letters are self-consciously didactic, almost heavy-handed in their assumption of authority, Douglass relieves the reader from the weight of instruction with the idiom of a man rather than that of a cause: "I was born in Tuckahoe, near Hillsborough, and about twelve miles from Easton, in Talbot County, Maryland." His straightforward style reveals a writer at one with his text and effectively recreates the significant details of his life.

Douglass was also a noted journalist, activist, diplomat, and novelist. His one novel, *The Heroic Slave* (1853), was loosely autobiographical and expanded his antislavery agenda. The hero, who has killed to free himself, prophetically describes the public discourse justifying the Civil War: "We struck for freedom, and if a true heart be in you, you will honor us for that deed." Douglass's recognition of the unfortunate necessity of violence and political activity within the Constitution eventually distanced him from the militant separatism of Garrison. As a journalist Douglass continued his polemic efforts on behalf of abolition; additionally, he endorsed the cause of temperance and women's rights in conjunction with Margaret Fuller, who had initially championed the *Narrative* when other abolitionists feared its intensity. Douglass's career as an editor began with the *North Star* (1847–1851); continued with the *Liberty Party Paper*, which was renamed *Frederick Douglass' Paper* (1851–1860); and concluded with *Douglass' Monthly* (1861–1863). Although he had counseled against the abolitionist John Brown's raid on the Harper's Ferry arsenal in 1859, Douglass's acquaintance with, and positive comments following, the attack placed him under suspicion of conspiracy and forced his escape to Canada. When his accusers publicly recanted, Douglass was vindicated.

Following the Civil War Douglass expanded his activities to include international diplomacy and other issues of broad political importance. From 1877 until 1886 he served as marshal and recorder of deeds for the District of Columbia. Additionally, he focused on the plight of the black race in the Caribbean as a member of the Santo Domingo commission (1871) and as U.S. consul general to Haiti (1889–1891). Upon his return to the United States, he completed the final revision of his autobiography, which now included the full story of his sojourn in England and Ireland following his initial escape from slavery nearly a half century earlier.

After Douglass's death in 1895, his authority among African Americans was recognized to a degree that perhaps no other individual has achieved. When African-American leaders became divided between the parties of assimilation and resistance, the first championed by Booker T. Washington, the second by W. E. B. Du Bois, both claimed the ideological paternity of Douglass. Douglass's importance to writers has been equally vital. His spirit informs the work of Harlem Renaissance writers as well as the current explosion of African-American literature. Perhaps no other figure in American letters is so responsible for both the public and private discourse of his people and his nation.

Suggested Readings: P. F. Foner, ed., *The Life and Writing of Frederick Douglass*, 5 vols., 1971. J. W. Blassinggame, ed., *The Frederick Douglass Papers*, 2 vols., 1979–1982. C. W. Chesnutt, *Frederick Douglass*, 1899. P. F. Foner, *Frederick Douglass: A Biography*, 1964. N. I. Huggins, *Slave and Citizen: The Life of Frederick Douglass*, 1980. W. E. Martin, Jr., *The Mind of Frederick Douglass*, 1984. H. Bloom, ed., *Narrative of the Life of Frederick Douglas: Modern Critical Interpretations*, 1988. D. W. Blight, *Frederick Douglass' Civil War: Keeping Faith in Jubilee*, 1989.

Text Used: *Narrative of the Life of Frederick Douglass, an American Slave*, 1845.

NARRATIVE OF THE LIFE OF FREDERICK DOUGLASS*

PREFACE[1]

In the month of August, 1841, I attended an anti-slavery convention in Nantucket, at which it was my happiness to become acquainted with Frederick Douglass, the writer of the following Narrative. He was a stranger to nearly every member of that body; but, having recently made his escape from the southern prison-house of bondage,[2] and feeling his curiosity excited to ascertain the principles and measures of the abolitionists,—of whom he had heard a somewhat vague description while he was a slave,—he was induced to give his attendance, on the occasion alluded to, though at that time a resident in New Bedford.

Fortunate, most fortunate occurrence!—fortunate for the millions of his manacled brethren, yet panting for deliverance from their awful thraldom!—fortunate for the cause of negro emancipation, and of universal liberty!—fortunate for the land of his birth, which he has already done so much to save and bless!—fortunate for a large circle of friends and acquaintances, whose sympathy and affection he has strongly secured by the many sufferings he has endured, by his virtuous traits of character, by his ever-abiding remembrance of those who are in bonds, as being bound with them!—fortunate for the multitudes, in various parts of our republic, whose minds he has enlightened on the subject of slavery, and who have been melted to tears by his pathos, or roused to virtuous indignation by his stirring eloquence against the enslavers of men!—fortunate for himself, as it at once brought him into the field of public usefulness, "gave the world assurance of a

---

* First printed in May 1845 by the Anti-Slavery Office in Boston, the source of the present text.

[1] Written by William Lloyd Garrison (1805–1879), a journalist, reformer, and militant spokesman for the abolitionist movement in America.

[2] Douglass escaped from the home of Hugh Auld in 1838; after settling in New Bedford, Massachusetts, he gradually became active among local abolitionists.

MAN," quickened the slumbering energies of his soul, and consecrated him to the great work of breaking the rod of the oppressor, and letting the oppressed go free!

I shall never forget his first speech at the convention—the extraordinary emotion it excited in my own mind—the powerful impression it created upon a crowded auditory, completely taken by surprise—the applause which followed from the beginning to the end of his felicitous remarks. I think I never hated slavery so intensely as at that moment; certainly, my perception of the enormous outrage which is inflicted by it, on the godlike nature of its victims, was rendered far more clear than ever. There stood one, in physical proportion and stature commanding and exact—in intellect richly endowed—in natural eloquence a prodigy—in soul manifestly "created but a little lower than the angels"[3]—yet a slave, ay, a fugitive slave,—trembling for his safety, hardly daring to believe that on the American soil, a single white person could be found who would befriend him at all hazards, for the love of God and humanity! Capable of high attainments as an intellectual and moral being—needing nothing but a comparatively small amount of cultivation to make him an ornament to society and a blessing to his race—by the law of the land, by the voice of the people, by the terms of the slave code, he was only a piece of property, a beast of burden, a chattel personal, nevertheless!

A beloved friend[4] from New Bedford prevailed on Mr. Douglass to address the convention. He came forward to the platform with a hesitancy and embarrassment, necessarily the attendants of a sensitive mind in such a novel position. After apologizing for his ignorance, and reminding the audience that slavery was a poor school for the human intellect and heart, he proceeded to narrate some of the facts in his own history as a slave, and in the course of his speech gave utterance to many noble thoughts and thrilling reflections. As soon as he had taken his seat, filled with hope and admiration, I rose, and declared that Patrick Henry,[5] of revolutionary fame, never made a speech more eloquent in the cause of liberty, than the one we had just listened to from the lips of that hunted fugitive. So I believed at that time—such is my belief now. I reminded the audience of the peril which surrounded this self-emancipated young man at the North,—even in Massachusetts, on the soil of the Pilgrim Fathers, among the descendants of revolutionary sires; and I appealed to them, whether they would ever allow him to be carried back into slavery,—law or no law, constitution or no constitution. The response was unanimous and in thunder-tones—"NO!" "Will you succor and protect him as a brother-man—a resident of the old Bay State?"[6] "YES!" shouted the whole mass, with an energy so startling, that the ruthless tyrants south of Mason and Dixon's line[7] might almost have heard the mighty burst of feeling, and recognized it as the pledge of an invincible determination, on the part of those who gave it, never to betray him that wanders, but to hide the outcast, and firmly to abide the consequences.

---

[3] "Thou hast made him [man] "a little lower than the angels," from Psalm 8:5.

[4] William C. Coffin, a prominent abolitionist in New Bedford.

[5] Henry (1736–1799), the statesman famous for his words to the Virginia House of Delegates in 1775: "I know not what course others may take, but as for me, give me liberty or give me death."

[6] Massachusetts.

[7] The Mason-Dixon line was surveyed by the English astronomers Charles Mason and Jeremiah Dixon between 1763 and 1767 to establish the boundary between Pennsylvania and Maryland; in 1779 it was extended to present-day West Virginia. Prior to the Civil War it was the boundary between slave states and free states.

It was at once deeply impressed upon my mind, that, if Mr. Douglass could be persuaded to consecrate his time and talents to the promotion of the anti-slavery enterprise, a powerful impetus would be given to it, and a stunning blow at the same time inflicted on northern prejudice against a colored complexion. I therefore endeavored to instil hope and courage into his mind, in order that he might dare to engage in a vocation so anomalous and responsible for a person in his situation; and I was seconded in this effort by warm-hearted friends, especially by the late General Agent of the Massachusetts Anti-Slavery Society, Mr. John A. Collins, whose judgment in this instance entirely coincided with my own. At first, he could give no encouragement; with unfeigned diffidence, he expressed his conviction that he was not adequate to the performance of so great a task; the path marked out was wholly an untrodden one; he was sincerely apprehensive that he should do more harm than good. After much deliberation, however, he consented to make a trial; and ever since that period, he has acted as a lecturing agent, under the auspices either of the American or the Massachusetts Anti-Slavery Society. In labors he has been most abundant; and his success in combating prejudice, in gaining proselytes, in agitating the public mind, has far surpassed the most sanguine expectations that were raised at the commencement of his brilliant career. He has borne himself with gentleness and meekness, yet with true manliness of character. As a public speaker, he excels in pathos, wit, comparison, imitation, strength of reasoning, and fluency of language. There is in him that union of head and heart, which is indispensable to an enlightenment of the heads and a winning of the hearts of others. May his strength continue to be equal to his day! May he continue to "grow in grace, and in the knowledge of God," that he may be increasingly serviceable in the cause of bleeding humanity, whether at home or abroad!

It is certainly a very remarkable fact, that one of the most efficient advocates of the slave population, now before the public, is a fugitive slave, in the person of Frederick Douglass; and that the free colored population of the United States are as ably represented by one of their own number, in the person of Charles Lenox Remond,[8] whose eloquent appeals have extorted the highest applause of multitudes on both sides of the Atlantic. Let the calumniators of the colored race despise themselves for their baseness and illiberality of spirit, and henceforth cease to talk of the natural inferiority of those who require nothing but time and opportunity to attain to the highest point of human excellence.

It may, perhaps, be fairly questioned, whether any other portion of the population of the earth could have endured the privations, sufferings and horrors of slavery, without having become more degraded in the scale of humanity than the slaves of African descent. Nothing has been left undone to cripple their intellects, darken their minds, debase their moral nature, obliterate all traces of their relationship to mankind; and yet how wonderfully they have sustained the mighty load of a most frightful bondage, under which they have been groaning for centuries! To illustrate the effect of slavery on the white man,—to show that he has no powers of endurance, in such a condition, superior to those of his black brother,—Daniel O'Connell,[9] the distinguished advocate of universal emancipation, and the mighti-

[8] Remond (1810–1873), a free-born African American and one of the first abolitionist lecturers of his race, returned from Great Britain and Ireland in 1842; under the auspices of the Massachusetts Anti-Slavery Society, he and Douglass spoke throughout the state in 1842.

[9] O'Connell (1775–1847), a leader in the struggle for Catholic emancipation and Irish independence and frequently hailed as the "Liberator."

est champion of prostrate but not conquered Ireland, relates the following anecdote in a speech delivered by him in the Conciliation Hall, Dublin, before the
Loyal National Repeal Association, March 31, 1845. "No matter," said Mr.
O'Connell, "under what specious term it may disguise itself, slavery is still hideous. *It has a natural, an inevitable tendency to brutalize every noble faculty of
man.* An American sailor, who was cast away on the shore of Africa, where he
was kept in slavery for three years, was, at the expiration of that period, found to
be imbruted and stultified—he had lost all reasoning power; and having forgotten
his native language, could only utter some savage gibberish between Arabic and
English, which nobody could understand, and which even he himself found difficulty in pronouncing. So much for the humanizing influence of THE DOMESTIC INSTI-
TUTION!" Admitting this to have been an extraordinary case of mental deterioration, it proves at least that the white slave can sink as low in the scale of humanity
as the black one.

Mr. Douglass has very properly chosen to write his own Narrative, in his own
style, and according to the best of his ability, rather than to employ some one else.
It is, therefore, entirely his own production; and, considering how long and dark
was the career he had to run as a slave,—how few have been his opportunities to
improve his mind since he broke his iron fetters,—it is, in my judgment, highly
creditable to his head and heart. He who can peruse it without a tearful eye, a
heaving breast, an afflicted spirit,—without being filled with an unutterable abhorrence of slavery and all its abettors, and animated with a determination to seek
the immediate overthrow of that execrable system,—without trembling for the
fate of this country in the hands of a righteous God, who is ever on the side of the
oppressed, and whose arm is not shortened that it cannot save,—must have a
flinty heart, and be qualified to act the part of a trafficker "in slaves and the souls
of men." I am confident that it is essentially true in all its statements; that nothing
has been set down in malice, nothing exaggerated, nothing drawn from the imagination; that it comes short of the reality, rather than overstates a single fact in
regard to SLAVERY AS IT IS.[10] The experience of Frederick Douglass, as a slave, was
not a peculiar one; his lot was not especially a hard one; his case may be regarded
as a very fair specimen of the treatment of slaves in Maryland, in which State it is
conceded that they are better fed and less cruelly treated than in Georgia, Alabama, or Louisiana. Many have suffered incomparably more, while very few on
the plantations have suffered less, than himself. Yet how deplorable was his situation! what terrible chastisements were inflicted upon his person! what still more
shocking outrages were perpetrated upon his mind! with all his noble powers and
sublime aspirations, how like a brute was he treated, even by those professing to
have the same mind in them that was in Christ Jesus! to what dreadful liabilities
was he continually subjected! how destitute of friendly counsel and aid, even in
his greatest extremities! how heavy was the midnight of woe which shrouded in
blackness the last ray of hope; and filled the future with terror and gloom! what
longings after freedom took possession of his breast, and how his misery augmented, in proportion as he grew reflective and intelligent,—thus demonstrating
that a happy slave is an extinct man! how he thought, reasoned, felt, under the
lash of the driver, with the chains upon his limbs! what perils he encountered in

[10] From the title of a well-known book on slavery, *American Slavery as It Is* (1839), by Theodore
Dwight Weld (1803–1895), a founder of the American Anti-Slavery Society in 1834.

his endeavors to escape from his horrible doom! and how signal have been his deliverance and preservation in the midst of a nation of pitiless enemies!

This Narrative contains many affecting incidents, many passages of great eloquence and power; but I think the most thrilling one of them all is the description Douglass gives of his feelings, as he stood soliloquizing respecting his fate, and the chances of his one day being a freeman, on the banks of the Chesapeake Bay—viewing the receding vessels as they flew with their white wings before the breeze, and apostrophizing them as animated by the living spirit of freedom. Who can read that passage, and be insensible to its pathos and sublimity? Compressed into it is a whole Alexandrian library[11] of thought, feeling, and sentiment—all that can, all that need be urged, in the form of expostulation, entreaty, rebuke, against that crime of crimes,—making man the property of his fellow-man! O, how accursed is that system, which entombs the godlike mind of man, defaces the divine image, reduces those who by creation were crowned with glory and honor to a level with four-footed beasts, and exalts the dealer in human flesh above all that is called God! Why should its existence be prolonged one hour? Is it not evil, only evil, and that continually? What does its presence imply but the absence of all fear of God, all regard for man, on the part of the people of the United States? Heaven speed its eternal overthrow!

So profoundly ignorant of the nature of slavery are many persons, that they are stubbornly incredulous whenever they read or listen to any recital of the cruelties which are daily inflicted on its victims. They do not deny that the slaves are held as property; but that terrible fact seems to convey to their minds no idea of injustice, exposure to outrage, or savage barbarity. Tell them of cruel scourgings, of mutilations and brandings, of scenes of pollution and blood, of the banishment of all light and knowledge, and they affect to be greatly indignant at such enormous exaggerations, such wholesale misstatements, such abominable libels on the character of the southern planters! As if all these direful outrages were not the natural results of slavery! As if it were less cruel to reduce a human being to the condition of a thing, than to give him a severe flagellation, or to deprive him of necessary food and clothing! As if whips, chains, thumb-screws, paddles, bloodhounds, overseers, drivers, patrols, were not all indispensable to keep the slaves down, and to give protection to their ruthless oppressors! As if, when the marriage institution is abolished, concubinage, adultery, and incest, must not necessarily abound; when all the rights of humanity are annihilated, any barrier remains to protect the victim from the fury of the spoiler; when absolute power is assumed over life and liberty, it will not be wielded with destructive sway! Skeptics of this character abound in society. In some few instances, their incredulity arises from a want of reflection; but, generally, it indicates a hatred of the light, a desire to shield slavery from the assaults of its foes, a contempt of the colored race, whether bond or free. Such will try to discredit the shocking tales of slaveholding cruelty which are recorded in this truthful Narrative; but they will labor in vain. Mr. Douglass has frankly disclosed the place of his birth, the names of those who claimed ownership in his body and soul, and the names also of those who committed the crimes which he has alleged against them. His statements, therefore, may easily be disproved, if they are untrue.

In the course of his Narrative, he relates two instances of murderous cruelty,— in one of which a planter deliberately shot a slave belonging to a neighboring

---

[11] The library at Alexandria in Egypt contained a treasured collection of ancient works.

plantation, who had unintentionally gotten within his lordly domain in quest of fish; and in the other, an overseer blew out the brains of a slave who had fled to a stream of water to escape a bloody scourging. Mr. Douglass states that in neither of these instances was any thing done by way of legal arrest or judicial investigation. The Baltimore American, of March 17, 1845, relates a similar case of atrocity, perpetrated with similar impunity—as follows:—"*Shooting a Slave.*—We learn, upon the authority of a letter from Charles county, Maryland, received by a gentleman of this city, that a young man, named Matthews, a nephew of General Matthews, and whose father, it is believed, holds an office at Washington, killed one of the slaves upon his father's farm by shooting him. The letter states that young Matthews had been left in charge of the farm; that he gave an order to the servant, which was disobeyed, when he proceeded to the house, *obtained a gun, and, returning, shot the servant.* He immediately, the letter continues, fled to his father's residence, where he still remains unmolested."—Let it never be forgotten, that no slaveholder or overseer can be convicted of any outrage perpetrated on the person of a slave, however diabolical it may be, on the testimony of colored witnesses, whether bond or free. By the slave code, they are adjudged to be as incompetent to testify against a white man, as though they were indeed a part of the brute creation. Hence, there is no legal protection in fact, whatever there may be in form, for the slave population; and any amount of cruelty may be inflicted on them with impunity. Is it possible for the human mind to conceive of a more horrible state of society?

The effect of a religious profession on the conduct of southern masters is vividly described in the following Narrative, and shown to be any thing but salutary. In the nature of the case, it must be in the highest degree pernicious. The testimony of Mr. Douglass, on this point, is sustained by a cloud of witnesses, whose veracity is unimpeachable. "A slaveholder's profession of Christianity is a palpable imposture. He is a felon of the highest grade. He is a man-stealer. It is of no importance what you put in the other scale."

Reader! are you with the man-stealers in sympathy and purpose, or on the side of their down-trodden victims? If with the former, then are you the foe of God and man. If with the latter, what are you prepared to do and dare in their behalf? Be faithful, be vigilant, be untiring in your efforts to break every yoke, and let the oppressed go free. Come what may—cost what it may—inscribe on the banner which you unfurl to the breeze, as your religious and political motto—"No Compromise with Slavery! No Union with Slaveholders!"

Wm. Lloyd Garrison.

Boston, May 1, 1845.

Letter from Wendell Phillips, Esq.[12]

Boston, April 22, 1845.

My Dear Friend:

You remember the old fable of "The Man and the Lion," where the lion complained that he should not be so misrepresented "when the lions wrote history."

I am glad the time has come when the "lions write history." We have been left long enough to gather the character of slavery from the involuntary evidence of

---

[12] Phillips (1811–1884) was a Boston-born lawyer who joined the Anti-Slavery Society in 1835 (after seeing Garrison mobbed by proslavery sympathizers) and became a powerful abolitionist speaker.

the masters. One might, indeed, rest sufficiently satisfied with what, it is evident, must be, in general, the results of such a relation, without seeking farther to find whether they have followed in every instance. Indeed, those who stare at the half-peck of corn a week, and love to count the lashes on the slave's back, are seldom the "stuff" out of which reformers and abolitionists are to be made. I remember that, in 1838 many were waiting for the results of the West India experiment,[13] before they could come into our ranks. Those "results" have come long ago; but, alas! few of that number have come with them, as converts. A man must be disposed to judge of emancipation by other tests than whether it has increased the produce of sugar,—and to hate slavery for other reasons than because it starves men and whips women,—before he is ready to lay the first stone of his anti-slavery life.

I was glad to learn, in your story, how early the most neglected of God's children waken to a sense of their rights, and of the injustice done them. Experience is a keen teacher; and long before you had mastered your A B C, or knew where the "white sails" of the Chesapeake were bound, you began, I see, to gauge the wretchedness of the slave, not by his hunger and want, not by his lashes and toil, but by the cruel and blighting death which gathers over his soul.

In connection with this, there is one circumstance which makes your recollectioins peculiarly valuable, and renders your early insight the more remarkable. You come from that part of the country where we are told slavery appears with its fairest features. Let us hear, then, what it is at its best estate—gaze on its bright side, if it has one; and then imagination may task her powers to add dark lines to the picture, as she travels southward to that (for the colored man) Valley of the Shadow of Death, where the Mississippi sweeps along.

Again, we have known you long, and can put the most entire confidence in your truth, candor, and sincerity. Every one who has heard you speak has felt, and, I am confident, every one who reads your book will feel, persuaded that you give them a fair specimen of the whole truth. No one-sided portrait,—no wholesale complaints,—but strict justice done, whenever individual kindliness has neutralized, for a moment, the deadly system with which it was strangely allied. You have been with us, too, some years, and can fairly compare the twilight of rights, which your race enjoy at the North, with that "noon of night" under which they labor south of Mason and Dixon's line. Tell us whether, after all, the half-free colored man of Massachusetts is worse off than the pampered slave of the rice swamps!

In reading your life, no one can say that we have unfairly picked out some rare specimens of cruelty. We know that the bitter drops, which even you have drained from the cup, are no incidental aggravations, no individual ills, but such as must mingle always and necessarily in the lot of every slave. They are the essential ingredients, not the occasional results, of the system.

After all, I shall read your book with trembling for you. Some years ago, when you were beginning to tell me your real name and birthplace, you may remember I stopped you, and preferred to remain ignorant of all. With the exception of a vague description, so I continued, till the other day, when you read me your memoirs. I hardly knew, at the time, whether to thank you or not for the sight of them, when I reflected that it was still dangerous, in Massachusetts, for honest men to tell their names! They say the fathers, in 1776, signed the Declaration of Indepen-

---

[13] Slavery in the British West Indies was ended in 1834; four years later, abolitionists were watching the consequences of that "experiment."

dence with the halter about their necks. You, too, publish your declaration of freedom with danger compassing you around. In all the broad lands which the Constitution of the United States overshadows, there is no single spot,—however narrow or desolate,—where a fugitive slave can plant himself and say, "I am safe." The whole armory of Northern Law has no shield for you. I am free to say that, in your place, I should throw the MS. into the fire.

You, perhaps, may tell your story in safety, endeared as you are to so many warm hearts by rare gifts, and a still rarer devotion of them to the service of others. But it will be owing only to your labors, and the fearless efforts of those who, trampling the laws and Constitution of the country under their feet, are determined that they will "hide the outcast," and that their hearts shall be, spite of the law, an asylum for the oppressed, if, some time or other, the humblest may stand in our streets, and bear witness in safety against the cruelties of which he has been the victim.

Yet it is sad to think, that these very throbbing hearts which welcome your story, and form your best safeguard in telling it, are all beating contrary to the "statute in such case made and provided." Go on, my dear friend, till you, and those who, like you, have been saved, so as by fire, from the dark prison-house, shall stereotype these free, illegal pulses into statutes; and New England, cutting loose from a blood-stained Union, shall glory in being the house of refuge for the oppressed;—till we no longer merely "*hide* the outcast," or make a merit of standing idly by while he is hunted in our midst; but, consecrating anew the soil of the Pilgrims as an asylum for the oppressed, proclaim our *welcome* to the slave so loudly, that the tones shall reach every hut in the Carolinas, and make the broken-hearted bondman leap up at the thought of old Massachusetts.

God speed the day!

Till then, and ever,

Yours truly,

WENDELL PHILLIPS.

CHAPTER I

I was born in Tuckahoe, near Hillsborough, and about twelve miles from Easton, in Talbot county, Maryland. I have no accurate knowledge of my age, never having seen any authentic record containing it. By far the larger part of the slaves know as little of their ages as horses know of theirs, and it is the wish of most masters within my knowledge to keep their slaves thus ignorant. I do not remember to have ever met a slave who could tell of his birthday. They seldom come nearer to it than planting-time, harvest-time, cherry-time, spring-time, or fall-time. A want of information concerning my own was a source of unhappiness to me even during childhood. The white children could tell their ages. I could not tell why I ought to be deprived of the same privilege. I was not allowed to make any inquiries of my master concerning it. He deemed all such inquiries on the part of a slave improper and impertinent, and evidence of a restless spirit. The nearest estimate I can give makes me now between twenty-seven and twenty-eight years of age. I come to this, from hearing my master say, some time during 1835, I was about seventeen years old.

My mother was named Harriet Bailey. She was the daughter of Isaac and Betsey Bailey, both colored, and quite dark. My mother was of a darker complexion than either my grandmother or grandfather.

My father was a white man. He was admitted to be such by all I ever heard speak of my parentage. The opinion was also whispered that my master was my father; but of the correctness of this opinion, I know nothing; the means of knowing was withheld from me. My mother and I were separated when I was but an infant—before I knew her as my mother. It is a common custom, in the part of Maryland from which I ran away, to part children from their mothers at a very early age. Frequently, before the child has reached its twelfth month, its mother is taken from it, and hired out on some farm a considerable distance off, and the child is placed under the care of an old woman, too old for field labor. For what this separation is done, I do not know, unless it be to hinder the development of the child's affection toward its mother, and to blunt and destroy the natural affection of the mother for the child. This is the inevitable result.

I never saw my mother, to know her as such, more than four or five times in my life; and each of these times was very short in duration, and at night. She was hired by a Mr. Stewart, who lived about twelve miles from my home. She made her journeys to see me in the night, travelling the whole distance on foot, after the performance of her day's work. She was a field hand, and a whipping is the penalty of not being in the field at sunrise, unless a slave has special permission from his or her master to the contrary—a permission which they seldom get, and one that gives to him that gives it the proud name of being a kind master. I do not recollect of ever seeing my mother by the light of day. She was with me in the night. She would lie down with me, and get me to sleep, but long before I waked she was gone. Very little communication ever took place between us. Death soon ended what little we could have while she lived, and with it her hardships and suffering. She died when I was about seven years old, on one of my master's farms, near Lee's Mill. I was not allowed to be present during her illness, at her death, or burial. She was gone long before I knew any thing about it. Never having enjoyed, to any considerable extent, her soothing presence, her tender and watchful care, I received the tidings of her death with much the same emotions I should have probably felt at the death of a stranger.

Called thus suddenly away, she left me without the slightest intimation of who my father was. The whisper that my master was my father, may or may not be true; and, true or false, it is of but little consequence to my purpose whilst the fact remains, in all its glaring odiousness, that slaveholders have ordained, and by law established, that the children of slave women shall in all cases follow the condition of their mothers; and this is done too obviously to administer to their own lusts, and made a gratification of their wicked desires profitable as well as pleasurable; for by this cunning arrangement, the slaveholder, in cases not a few, sustains to his slaves the double relation of master and father.

I know of such cases; and it is worthy of remark that such slaves invariably suffer greater hardships, and have more to contend with, than others. They are, in the first place, a constant offence to their mistress. She is ever disposed to find fault with them; they can seldom do any thing to please her; she is never better pleased than when she sees them under the lash, especially when she suspects her husband of showing to his mulatto children favors which he withholds from his black slaves. The master is frequently compelled to sell this class of his slaves, out of deference to the feelings of his white wife; and, cruel as the deed may strike any one to be, for a man to sell his own children to human flesh-mongers, it is often the dictate of humanity for him to do so; for, unless he does this, he must not only whip them himself, but must stand by and see one white son tie up his brother, of but few shades darker complexion than himself, and ply the gory lash to his naked back; and if he lisp one word of disapproval, it is set down to his parental partiality, and only makes a bad matter worse, both for himself and the slave whom he would protect and defend.

Every year brings with it multitudes of this class of slaves. It was doubtless in consequence of a knowledge of this fact, that one great statesman of the south predicted the downfall of slavery by the inevitable laws of population. Whether this prophecy is ever fulfilled or not, it is nevertheless plain that a very different-looking class of people are springing up at the south, and are now held in slavery, from those originally brought to this country from Africa; and if their increase will do no other good, it will do away the force of the argument, that God cursed Ham, and therefore American slavery is right.[14] If the lineal descendants of Ham are alone to be scripturally enslaved, it is certain that slavery at the south must soon become unscriptural; for thousands are ushered into the world, annually, who, like myself, owe their existence to white fathers, and those fathers most frequently their own masters.

I have had two masters. My first master's name was Anthony. I do not remember his first name. He was generally called Captain Anthony—a title which, I presume, he acquired by sailing a craft on the Chesapeake Bay. He was not considered a rich slaveholder. He owned two or three farms, and about thirty slaves. His farms and slaves were under the care of an overseer. The overseer's name was Plummer. Mr. Plummer was a miserable drunkard, a profane swearer, and a savage monster. He always went armed with a cowskin[15] and a heavy cudgel. I have known him to cut and slash the women's heads so horribly, that even master would be enraged at his cruelty, and would threaten to whip him if he did not mind himself. Master, however, was not a humane slaveholder. It required extraordinary barbarity on the part of an overseer to affect him. He was a cruel man, hardened by a long life of slaveholding. He would at times seem to take great pleasure in whipping a slave. I have often been awakened at the dawn of day by the most heart-rending shrieks of an own aunt of mine, whom he used to tie up to a joist, and whip upon her naked back till she was literally covered with blood. No words, no tears, no prayers, from his gory victim, seemed to move his iron heart from its bloody purpose. The louder she screamed, the harder he whipped; and where the blood ran fastest, there he whipped longest. He would whip her to make her scream, and whip her to make her hush; and not until overcome by fatigue, would he cease to swing the blood-clotted cowskin. I remember the first time I ever witnessed this horrible exhibition. I was quite a child, but I well remember it. I never shall forget it whilst I remember any thing. It was the first of a long series of such outrages, of which I was doomed to be a witness and a participant. It struck me with awful force. It was the blood-stained gate, the entrance to the hell of slavery, through which I was about to pass. It was a most terrible spectacle. I wish I could commit to paper the feelings with which I beheld it.

This occurrence took place very soon after I went to live with my old master, and under the following circumstances. Aunt Hester went out one night,—where or for what I do not know,—and happened to be absent when my master desired her presence. He had ordered her not to go out evenings, and warned her that she must never let him catch her in company with a young man, who was paying

---

[14] In Genesis 9:20–27 the biblical patriarch Noah curses his son Ham and commits him to bondage to his brothers; the passage was interpreted as scriptural authority for slavery.

[15] A whip made of cowhide.

attention to her belonging to Colonel Lloyd. The young man's name was Ned Roberts, generally called Lloyd's Ned. Why master was so careful of her, may be safely left to conjecture. She was a woman of noble form, and of graceful proportions, having very few equals, and fewer superiors, in personal appearance, among the colored or white women of our neighborhood.

Aunt Hester had not only disobeyed his orders in going out, but had been found in company with Lloyd's Ned; which circumstance, I found, from what he said while whipping her, was the chief offence. Had he been a man of pure morals himself, he might have been thought interested in protecting the innocence of my aunt; but those who knew him will not suspect him of any such virtue. Before he commenced whipping Aunt Hester, he took her into the kitchen, and stripped her from neck to waist, leaving her neck, shoulders, and back, entirely naked. He then told her to cross her hands, calling her at the same time a d— —d b— —h. After crossing her hands, he tied them with a strong rope, and led her to a stool under a large hook in the joist, put in for the purpose. He made her get upon the stool, and tied her hands to the hook. She now stood fair for his infernal purpose. Her arms were stretched up at their full length, so that she stood upon the ends of her toes. He then said to her, "Now, you d— —d b— —h, I'll learn you how to disobey my orders!" and after rolling up his sleeves, he commenced to lay on the heavy cowskin, and soon the warm, red blood (amid heart-rending shrieks from her, and horrid oaths from him) came dripping to the floor. I was so terrified and horror-stricken at the sight, that I hid myself in a closet, and dared not venture out till long after the bloody transaction was over. I expected it would be my turn next. It was all new to me. I had never seen any thing like it before. I had always lived with my grandmother on the outskirts of the plantation, where she was put to raise the children of the younger women. I had therefore been, until now, out of the way of the bloody scenes that often occurred on the plantation.

CHAPTER II

My master's family consisted of two sons, Andrew and Richard; one daughter, Lucretia, and her husband, Captain Thomas Auld. They lived in one house, upon the home plantation of Colonel Edward Lloyd. My master was Colonel Lloyd's clerk and superintendent. He was what might be called the overseer of the overseers. I spent two years of childhood on this plantation in my old master's family. It was there that I witnessed the bloody transaction recorded in the first chapter; and as I received my first impressions of slavery on this plantation, I will give some description of it, and of slavery as it there existed. The plantation is about twelve miles north of Easton, in Talbot county, and is situated on the border of Miles River. The principal products raised upon it were tobacco, corn, and wheat. These were raised in great abundance; so that, with the products of this and the other farms belonging to him, he was able to keep in almost constant employment a large sloop, in carrying them to market at Baltimore. This sloop was named Sally Lloyd, in honor of one of the colonel's daughters. My master's son-in-law, Captain Auld, was master of the vessel; she was otherwise manned by the colonel's own slaves. Their names were Peter, Isaac, Rich, and Jake. These were esteemed very highly by the other slaves, and looked upon as the privileged ones of the plantation; for it was no small affair, in the eyes of the slaves, to be allowed to see Baltimore.

Colonel Lloyd kept from three to four hundred slaves on his home plantation, and owned a large number more on the neighboring farms belonging to him. The names of the farms nearest to the home plantation were Wye Town and New Design. "Wye Town" was under the overseership of a man named Noah Willis. New Design was under the overseership of a Mr. Townsend. The overseers of these, and all the rest of the farms, numbering over twenty, received advice and direction from the managers of the home plantation. This was the great business place. It was the seat of government for the whole twenty farms. All disputes among the overseers were settled here. If a slave was convicted of any high misdemeanor, became unmanagable, or evinced a determination to run away, he was brought immediately here, severely whipped, put on board the sloop, carried to Baltimore, and sold to Austin Woolfolk, or some other slave-trader, as a warning to the slaves remaining.

Here, too, the slaves of all the other farms received their monthly allowance of food, and their yearly clothing. The men and women slaves received, as their monthly allowance of food, eight pounds of pork, or its equivalent in fish, and one bushel of corn meal. Their yearly clothing consisted of two coarse linen shirts, one pair of linen trousers, like the shirts, one jacket, one pair of trousers for winter, made of coarse negro cloth, one pair of stockings, and one pair of shoes; the whole of which could not have cost more than seven dollars. The allowance of the slave children was given to their mothers, or the old women having the care of them. The children unable to work in the field had neither shoes, stockings, jackets, nor trousers, given to them; their clothing consisted of two coarse linen shirts per year. When these failed them, they went naked until the next allowance-day. Children from seven to ten years old, of both sexes, almost naked, might be seen at all seasons of the year.

There were no beds given the slaves, unless one coarse blanket be considered such, and none but the men and women had these. This, however, is not considered a very great privation. They find less difficulty from the want of beds, than from the want of time to sleep; for when their day's work in the field is done, the most of them having their washing, mending, and cooking to do, and having few or none of the ordinary facilities for doing either of these, very many of their sleeping hours are consumed in preparing for the field the coming day; and when this is done, old and young, male and female, married and single, drop down side by side, on one common bed,—the cold, damp floor,—each covering himself or herself with their miserable blankets; and here they sleep till they are summoned to the field by the driver's horn. At the sound of this, all must rise, and be off to the field. There must be no halting; every one must be at his or her post; and woe betides them who hear not this morning summons to the field; for if they are not awakened by the sense of hearing, they are by the sense of feeling: no age nor sex finds any favor. Mr. Severe, the overseer, used to stand by the door of the quarter, armed with a large hickory stick and heavy cowskin, ready to whip any one who was so unfortunate as not to hear, or, from any other cause, was prevented from being ready to start for the field at the sound of the horn.

Mr. Severe was rightly named: he was a cruel man. I have seen him whip a woman, causing the blood to run half an hour at the time; and this, too, in the midst of her crying children, pleading for their mother's release. He seemed to take pleasure in manifesting his fiendish barbarity. Added to his cruelty, he was a profane swearer. It was enough to chill the blood and stiffen the hair of an ordinary man to hear him talk. Scarce a sentence escaped him but that was commenced or concluded by some horrid oath. The field was the place to witness his cruelty and profanity. His presence made it both the field of blood and of blasphemy. From the rising till the going down of the sun, he was cursing, raving, cutting, and slashing among the slaves of the field, in the most frightful manner. His career was short. He died very soon after I went to Colonel Lloyd's; and he died as he lived, uttering, with his dying groans, bitter curses and horrid oaths. His death was regarded by the slaves as the result of a merciful providence.

Mr. Severe's place was filled by a Mr. Hopkins. He was a very different man. He was less cruel, less profane, and made less noise, than Mr. Severe. His course was characterized by no extraordinary demonstrations of cruelty. He whipped, but seemed to take no pleasure in it. He was called by the slaves a good overseer.

The home plantation of Colonel Lloyd wore the appearance of a country village. All the mechanical operations for all the farms were performed here. The shoemaking and mending, the blacksmithing, cartwrighting, coopering, weaving, and grain-grinding, were all performed by the slaves on the home plantation. The whole place wore a business-like aspect very unlike the neighboring farms. The number of houses, too, conspired to give it advantage over the neighboring farms. It was called by the slaves the *Great House Farm*. Few privileges were esteemed higher, by the slaves of the out-farms, than that of being selected to do errands at the Great House Farm. It was associated in their minds with greatness. A representative could not be prouder of his election to a seat in the American Congress, than a slave on one of the out-farms would be of his election to do errands at the Great House Farm. They regarded it as evidence of great confidence reposed in them by their overseers; and it was on this account, as well as a constant desire to be out of the field from under the driver's lash, that they esteemed it a high privilege, one worth careful living for. He was called the smartest and most trusty fellow, who had this honor conferred upon him the most frequently. The competitors for this office sought as diligently to please their overseers, as the office-seekers in the political parties seek to please and deceive the people. The same traits of character might be seen in Colonel Lloyd's slaves, as are seen in the slaves of the political parties.

The slaves selected to go to the Great House Farm, for the monthly allowance for themselves and their fellow-slaves, were peculiarly enthusiastic. While on their way, they would make the dense old woods, for miles around, reverberate with their wild songs, revealing at once the highest joy and the deepest sadness. They would compose and sing as they went along, consulting neither time or tune. The thought that came up, came out—if not in the word, in the sound;—and as frequently in the one as in the other. They would sometimes sing the most pathetic sentiment in the most rapturous tone, and the most rapturous sentiment in the most pathetic tone. Into all of their songs they would manage to weave something of the Great House Farm. Especially would they do this, when leaving home. They would then sing most exultingly the following words:—

"I am going away to the Great House Farm!
O, yea! O, yea! O!"

This they would sing, as a chorus, to words which to many would seem unmeaning jargon, but which, nevertheless, were full of meaning to themselves. I have sometimes thought that the mere hearing of those songs would do more to impress some minds with the horrible character of slavery, than the reading of whole volumes of philosophy on the subject could do.

I did not, when a slave, understand the deep meaning of those rude and apparently incoherent songs. I was myself within the circle; so that I neither saw nor heard as those without might see and hear. They told a tale of woe which was then altogether beyond my feeble comprehension; they were tones loud, long, and deep; they breathed the prayer and complaint of souls boiling over with the bitterest anguish. Every tone was a testimony against slavery, and a prayer to God for deliverance from chains. The hearing of those wild notes always depressed my spirit, and filled me with ineffable sadness. I have frequently found myself in tears while hearing them. The mere recurrence to those songs, even now, afflicts me; and while I am writing these lines, an expression of feeling has already found its way down my cheek. To those songs I trace my first glimmering conception of the dehumanizing character of slavery. I can never get rid of that conception. Those songs still follow me, to deepen my hatred of slavery, and quicken my sympathies for my brethren in bonds. If any one wishes to be impressed with the soul-killing effects of slavery, let him go to Colonel Lloyd's plantation, and, on allowance-day, place himself in the deep pine woods, and there let him, in silence, analyze the sounds that shall pass through the chambers of his soul,—and if he is not thus impressed, it will only be because "there is no flesh in his obdurate heart."

I have often been utterly astonished, since I came to the north, to find persons who could speak of the singing, among slaves, as evidence of their contentment and happiness. It is impossible to conceive of a greater mistake. Slaves sing most when they are most unhappy. The songs of the slave represent the sorrows of his heart; and he is relieved by them, only as an aching heart is relieved by its tears. At least, such is my experience. I have often sung to drown my sorrow, but seldom to express my happiness. Crying for joy, and singing for joy, were alike uncommon to me while in the jaws of slavery. The singing of a man cast away upon a desolate island might be as appropriately considered as evidence of contentment and happiness, as the singing of a slave; the songs of the one and of the other are prompted by the same emotion.

Chapter III

Colonel Lloyd kept a large and finely cultivated garden, which afforded almost constant employment for four men, besides the chief gardener, (Mr. M'Durmond.) This garden was probably the greatest attraction of the place. During the summer months, people came from far and near—from Baltimore, Easton, and Annapolis—to see it. It abounded in fruits of almost every description, from the hardy apple of the north to the delicate orange of the south. This garden was not the least source of trouble on the plantation. Its excellent fruit was quite a temptation to the hungry swarms of boys, as well as the older slaves, belonging to the colonel, few of whom had the virtue or the vice to resist it. Scarcely a day passed, during the summer, but that some slave had to take the lash for stealing fruit. The colonel had to resort to all kinds of stratagems to keep his slaves out of the garden. The last and most successful one was that of tarring his fence all around; after which, if a slave was caught with any tar upon his person, it was deemed sufficient proof that he had either been into the garden, or had tried to get in. In either case, he was severely whipped by the chief gardener. This plan worked well; the slaves became as fearful of tar as of the lash. They seemed to realize the impossibility of touching *tar* without being defiled.

The colonel also kept a splendid riding equipage. His stable and carriage-house presented the appearance of some of our large city livery establishments. His horses were of the finest form and noblest blood. His carriage-house contained three splendid coaches, three or four gigs, besides dearborns and barouches[16] of the most fashionable style.

This establishment was under the care of two slaves—old Barney and young Barney—father and son. To attend to this establishment was their sole work. But it was by no means an easy employment; for in nothing was Colonel Lloyd more particular than in the management of his horses. The slightest inattention to these was unpardonable, and was visited upon those, under whose care they were placed, with the severest punishment; no excuse could shield them, if the colonel only suspected any want of attention to his horses—a supposition which he frequently indulged, and one which, of course, made the office of old and young Barney a very trying one. They never knew when they were safe from punishment. They were frequently whipped when least deserving, and escaped whipping when most deserving it. Every thing depended upon the looks of the horses, and the state of Colonel Lloyd's own mind when his horses were brought to him for use. If a horse did not move fast enough, or hold his head high enough, it was owing to some fault of his keepers. It was painful to stand near the stable-door, and hear the various complaints against the keepers when a horse was taken out for use. "This horse has not had proper attention. He has not been sufficiently rubbed and curried, or he has not been properly fed; his food was too wet or too dry; he got it too soon or too late; he was too hot or too cold; he had too much hay, and not enough of grain; or he had too much grain, and not enough of hay; instead of old Barney's attending to the horse, he had very improperly left it to his son." To all these complaints, no matter how unjust, the slave must answer never a word. Colonel Lloyd could not brook any contradiction from a slave. When he spoke, a slave must stand, listen, and tremble; and such was literally the case. I have seen Colonel Lloyd make old Barney, a man between fifty and sixty years of age, uncover his bald head, kneel down upon the cold, damp ground, and receive upon his naked and toil-worn shoulders more than thirty lashes at the time. Colonel Lloyd had three sons—Edward, Murray, and Daniel,—and three sons-in-law, Mr. Winder, Mr. Nicholson, and Mr. Lowndes. All of these lived at the Great House Farm, and enjoyed the luxury of whipping the servants when they pleased, from old Barney down to William Wilkes, the coach-driver. I have seen Winder make one of the house-servants stand off from him a suitable distance to be touched with the end of his whip, and at every stroke raise great ridges upon his back.

To describe the wealth of Colonel Lloyd would be almost equal to describing the riches of Job.[17] He kept from ten to fifteen house-servants. He was said to own a thousand slaves, and I think this estimate quite within the truth. Colonel Lloyd owned so many that he did not know them when he saw them; nor did all the slaves of the out-farms know him. It is reported of him, that, while riding along the road one day, he met a colored man, and addressed him in the usual manner of speaking to colored people on the public highways of the south: "Well, boy,

---

[16] Horse-drawn carriages with two or four wheels.

[17] The biblical figure who was extremely wealthy before being tested with misfortune, despite which he retained his faith.

whom do you belong to?" "To Colonel Lloyd," replied the slave. "Well, does the colonel treat you well?" "No, sir," was the ready reply. "What, does he work you too hard?" "Yes, sir." "Well, don't he give you enough to eat?" "Yes, sir, he gives me enough, such as it is."

The colonel, after ascertaining where the slave belonged, rode on; the man also went on about his business, not dreaming that he had been conversing with his master. He thought, said, and heard nothing more of the matter, until two or three weeks afterwards. The poor man was then informed by his overseer that, for having found fault with his master, he was now to be sold to a Georgia trader. He was immediately chained and handcuffed; and thus, without a moment's warning, he was snatched away, and forever sundered, from his family and friends, by a hand more unrelenting than death. This is the penalty of telling the truth, of telling the simple truth, in answer to a series of plain questions.

It is partly in consequence of such facts, that slaves, when inquired of as to their condition and the character of their masters, almost universally say they are contented, and that their masters are kind. The slaveholders have been known to send in spies among their slaves, to ascertain their views and feelings in regard to their condition. The frequency of this has had the effect to establish among the slaves the maxim, that a still tongue makes a wise head. They suppress the truth rather than take the consequences of telling it, and in so doing prove themselves a part of the human family. If they have any thing to say of their masters, it is generally in their masters' favor, especially when speaking to an untried man. I have been frequently asked, when a slave, if I had a kind master, and do not remember ever to have given a negative answer; nor did I, in pursuing this course, consider myself as uttering what was absolutely false; for I always measured the kindness of my master by the standard of kindness set up among slaveholders around us. Moreover, slaves are like other people, and imbibe prejudices quite common to others. They think their own better than that of others. Many, under the influence of this prejudice, think their own masters are better than the masters of other slaves; and this, too, in some cases, when the very reverse is true. Indeed, it is not uncommon for slaves even to fall out and quarrel among themselves about the relative goodness of their masters, each contending for the superior goodness of his own over that of the others. At the very same time, they mutually execrate their masters when viewed separately. It was so on our plantation. When Colonel Lloyd's slaves met the slaves of Jacob Jepson, they seldom parted without a quarrel about their masters; Colonel Lloyd's slaves contending that he was the richest, and Mr. Jepson's slaves that he was the smartest, and most of a man. Colonel Lloyd's slaves would boast his ability to buy and sell Jacob Jepson. Mr. Jepson's slaves would boast his ability to whip Colonel Lloyd. These quarrels would almost always end in a fight between the parties, and those that whipped were supposed to have gained the point at issue. They seemed to think that the greatness of their masters was transferable to themselves. It was considered as being bad enough to be a slave; but to be a poor man's slave was deemed a disgrace indeed!

Chapter IV

Mr. Hopkins remained but a short time in the office of overseer. Why his career was so short, I do not know, but suppose he lacked the necessary severity to suit Colonel Lloyd. Mr. Hopkins was succeeded by Mr. Austin Gore, a man possessing, in an eminent degree, all those traits of character indispensable to what is called a first-rate overseer. Mr. Gore had served Colonel Lloyd, in the capacity of overseer, upon one of the out-farms, and had shown himself worthy of the high station of overseer upon the home or Great House Farm.

Mr. Gore was proud, ambitious, and persevering. He was artful, cruel, and obdurate. He was just the man for such a place, and it was just the place for such a man. It afforded scope for the full exercise of all his powers, and he seemed to be perfectly at home in it. He was one of those who could torture the slightest look, word, or gesture, on the part of the slave, into impudence, and would treat it accordingly. There must be no answering back to him; no explanation was allowed a slave, showing himself to have been wrongfully accused. Mr. Gore acted fully up to the maxim laid down by slaveholders,—"It is better that a dozen slaves suffer under the lash, than that the overseer should be convicted, in the presence of the slaves, of having been at fault." No matter how innocent a slave might be—it availed him nothing, when accused by Mr. Gore of any misdemeanor. To be accused was to be convicted, and to be convicted was to be punished; the one always following the other with immutable certainty. To escape punishment was to escape accusation; and few slaves had the fortune to do either, under the overseership of Mr. Gore. He was just proud enough to demand the most debasing homage of the slave, and quite servile enough to crouch, himself, at the feet of the master. He was ambitious enough to be contented with nothing short of the highest rank of overseers, and persevering enough to reach the height of his ambition. He was cruel enough to inflict the severest punishment, artful enough to descend to the lowest trickery, and obdurate enough to be insensible to the voice of a reproving conscience. He was, of all the overseers, the most dreaded by the slaves. His presence was painful; his eye flashed confusion; and seldom was his sharp, shrill voice heard, without producing horror and trembling in their ranks.

Mr. Gore was a grave man, and, though a young man, he indulged in no jokes, said no funny words, seldom smiled. His words were in perfect keeping with his looks, and his looks were in perfect keeping with his words. Overseers will sometimes indulge in a witty word, even with the slaves; not so with Mr. Gore. He spoke but to command, and commanded but to be obeyed; he dealt sparingly with his words, and bountifully with his whip, never using the former where the latter would answer as well. When he whipped, he seemed to do so from a sense of duty, and feared no consequences. He did nothing reluctantly, no matter how disagreeable; always at his post, never inconsistent. He never promised but to fulfil. He was, in a word, a man of the most inflexible firmness and stone-like coolness.

His savage barbarity was equalled only by the consummate coolness with which he committed the grossest and most savage deeds upon the slaves under his charge. Mr. Gore once undertook to whip one of Colonel Lloyd's slaves, by the name of Demby. He had given Demby but few stripes, when, to get rid of the scourging, he ran and plunged himself into a creek, and stood there at the depth of his shoulders, refusing to come out. Mr. Gore told him that he would give him three calls, and that, if he did not come out at the third call, he would shoot him. The first call was given. Demby made no response, but stood his ground. The second and third calls were given with the same result. Mr. Gore then, without consultation or deliberation with any one, not even giving Demby an additional call, raised his musket to his face, taking deadly aim at his standing victim, and in an instant poor Demby was no more. His mangled body sank out of sight, and blood and brains marked the water where he had stood.

A thrill of horror flashed through every soul upon the plantation, excepting Mr. Gore. He alone seemed cool and collected. He was asked by Colonel Lloyd and my old master, why he resorted to this extraordinary expedient. His reply was, (as well as I can remember,) that Demby had become unmanageable. He was setting a dangerous example to the other slaves,—one which, if suffered to pass without some such demonstration on his part, would finally lead to the total subversion of all rule and order upon the plantation. He argued that if one slave refused to be corrected, and escaped with his life, the other slaves would soon copy the example; the result of which would be, the freedom of the slaves, and the enslavement of the whites. Mr. Gore's defence was satisfactory. He was continued in his station as overseer upon the home plantation. His fame as an overseer went abroad. His horrid crime was not even submitted to judicial investigation. It was committed in the presence of slaves, and they of course could neither institute a suit, nor testify against him; and thus the guilty perpetrator of one of the bloodiest and most foul murders goes unwhipped of justice, and uncensured by the community in which he lives. Mr. Gore lived in St. Michael's, Talbot county, Maryland, when I left there; and if he is still alive, he very probably lives there now; and if so, he is now, as he was then, as highly esteemed and as much respected as though his guilty soul had not been stained with his brother's blood.

I speak advisedly when I say this,—that killing a slave, or any colored person, in Talbot county, Maryland, is not treated as a crime, either by the courts or the community. Mr. Thomas Lanman, of St. Michael's, killed two slaves, one of whom he killed with a hatchet, by knocking his brains out. He used to boast of the commission of the awful and bloody deed. I have heard him do so laughingly, saying, among other things, that he was the only benefactor of his country in the company, and that when others would do as much as he had done, we should be relieved of "the d——d niggers."

The wife of Mr. Giles Hick, living but a short distance from where I used to live, murdered my wife's cousin, a young girl between fifteen and sixteen years of age, mangling her person in the most horrible manner, breaking her nose and breastbone with a stick, so that the poor girl expired in a few hours afterward. She was immediately buried, but had not been in her untimely grave but a few hours before she was taken up and examined by the coroner, who decided that she had come to her death by severe beating. The offence for which this girl was thus murdered was this:—She had been set that night to mind Mrs. Hick's baby, and during the night she fell asleep, and the baby cried. She, having lost her rest for several nights previous, did not hear the crying. They were both in the room with Mrs. Hicks. Mrs. Hicks, finding the girl slow to move, jumped from her bed, seized an oak stick of wood by the fireplace, and with it broke the girl's nose and breastbone, and thus ended her life. I will not say that this most horrid murder produced no sensation in the community. It did produce sensation, but not enough to bring the murderess to punishment. There was a warrant issued for her arrest, but it was never served. Thus she escaped not only punishment, but even the pain of being arraigned before a court for her horrid crime.

Whilst I am detailing bloody deeds which took place during my stay on Colonel Lloyd's plantation, I will briefly narrate another, which occurred about the same time as the murder of Demby by Mr. Gore.

Colonel Lloyd's slaves were in the habit of spending a part of their nights and Sundays in fishing for oysters, and in this way made up the deficiency of their scanty allowance. An old man belonging to Colonel Lloyd, while thus engaged, happened to get beyond the limits of Colonel Lloyd's, and on the premises of Mr. Beal Bondly. At this trespass, Mr. Bondly took offence, and with his musket came down to the shore, and blew its deadly contents into the poor old man.

Mr. Bondly came over to see Colonel Lloyd the next day, whether to pay him for his property, or to justify himself in what he had done, I know not. At any rate, this whole fiendish transaction was soon hushed up. There was very little said about it at all, and nothing done. It was a common saying, even among little white boys, that it was worth a half-cent to kill a "nigger," and a half-cent to bury one.

Chapter V

As to my own treatment while I lived on Colonel Lloyd's plantation, it was very similar to that of the other slave children. I was not old enough to work in the field, and there being little else than field work to do, I had a great deal of leisure time. The most I had to do was to drive up the cows at evening, keep the fowls out of the garden, keep the front yard clean, and run of errands for my old master's daughter, Mrs. Lucretia Auld. The most of my leisure time I spent in helping Master Daniel Lloyd in finding his birds, after he had shot them. My connection with Master Daniel was of some advantage to me. He became quite attached to me, and was a sort of protector of me. He would not allow the older boys to impose upon me, and would divide his cakes with me.

I was seldom whipped by my old master, and suffered little from any thing else than hunger and cold. I suffered much from hunger, but much more from cold. In hottest summer and coldest winter, I was kept almost naked—no shoes, no stockings, no jacket, no trousers, nothing on but a coarse tow linen shirt, reaching only to my knees. I had no bed. I must have perished with cold, but that, the coldest nights, I used to steal a bag which was used for carrying corn to the mill. I would crawl into this bag, and there sleep on the cold, damp, clay floor, with my head in and feet out. My feet have been so cracked with the frost, that the pen with which I am writing might be laid in the gashes.

We were not regularly allowanced. Our food was coarse corn meal boiled. This was called *mush*. It was put into a large wooden tray or trough, and set down upon the ground. The children were then called, like so many pigs, and like so many pigs they would come and devour the mush; some with oyster-shells, others with pieces of shingle, some with naked hands, and none with spoons. He that ate fastest got most; he that was strongest secured the best place; and few left the trough satisfied.

I was probably between seven and eight years old when I left Colonel Lloyd's plantation. I left it with joy. I shall never forget the ecstasy with which I received the intelligence that my old master (Anthony) had determined to let me go to Baltimore, to live with Mr. Hugh Auld, brother to my old master's son-in-law, Captain Thomas Auld. I received this information about three days before my departure. They were three of the happiest days I ever enjoyed. I spent the most part of all these three days in the creek, washing off the plantation scurf, and preparing myself for my departure.

The pride of appearance which this would indicate was not my own. I spent the time in washing, not so much because I wished to, but becaue Mrs. Lucretia had told me I must get all the dead skin off my feet and knees before I could go to

Baltimore; for the people in Baltimore were very cleanly, and would laugh at me if I looked dirty. Besides, she was going to give me a pair of trousers, which I should not put on unless I got all the dirt off me. The thought of owning a pair of trousers was great indeed! It was almost a sufficient motive, not only to make me take off what would be called by pig-drovers the mange, but the skin itself. I went at it in good earnest, working for the first time with the hope of reward.

The ties that ordinarily bind children to their homes were all suspended in my case. I found no severe trial in my departure. My home was charmless; it was not home to me; on parting from it, I could not feel that I was leaving any thing which I could have enjoyed by staying. My mother was dead, my grandmother lived far off, so that I seldom saw her. I had two sisters and one brother, that lived in the same house with me; but the early separation of us from our mother had well nigh blotted the fact of our relationship from our memories. I looked for home elsewhere, and was confident of finding none which I should relish less than the one which I was leaving. If, however, I found in my new home hardship, hunger, whipping, and nakedness, I had the consolation that I should not have escaped any one of them by staying. Having already had more than a taste of them in the house of my old master, and having endured them there, I very naturally inferred my ability to endure them elsewhere, and especially at Baltimore; for I had something of the feeling about Baltimore that is expressed in the proverb, that "being hanged in England is preferable to dying a natural death in Ireland." I had the strongest desire to see Baltimore. Cousin Tom, though not fluent in speech, had inspired me with that desire by his eloquent description of the place. I could never point out any thing at the Great House, no matter how beautiful or powerful, but that he had seen something at Baltimore far exceeding, both in beauty and strength, the object which I pointed out to him. Even the Great House itself, with all its pictures, was far inferior to many buildings in Baltimore. So strong was my desire, that I thought a gratification of it would fully compensate for whatever loss of comforts I should sustain by the exchange. I left without a regret, and with the highest hopes of future happiness.

We sailed out of Miles River for Baltimore on a Saturday morning. I remember only the day of the week, for at that time I had no knowledge of the days of the month, nor the months of the year. On setting sail, I walked aft, and gave to Colonel Lloyd's plantation what I hoped would be the last look. I then placed myself in the bows of the sloop, and there spent the remainder of the day in looking ahead, interesting myself in what was in the distance rather than in things near by or behind.

In the afternoon of that day, we reached Annapolis, the capital of the State. We stopped but a few moments, so that I had no time to go on shore. It was the first large town that I had ever seen, and though it would look small compared with some of our New England factory villages, I thought it a wonderful place for its size—more imposing even than the Great House Farm!

We arrived at Baltimore early on Sunday morning, landing at Smith's Wharf, not far from Bowley's Wharf. We had on board the sloop a large flock of sheep; and after aiding in driving them to the slaughter-house of Mr. Curtis on Louden Slater's Hill, I was conducted by Rich, one of the hands belonging on board of the sloop, to my new home in Alliciana Street, near Mr. Gardner's ship-yard, on Fells Point.

Mr. and Mrs. Auld were both at home, and met me at the door with their little son Thomas, to take care of whom I had been given. And here I saw what I had never seen before; it was a white face beaming with the most kindly emotions; it was the face of my new mistress, Sophia Auld. I wish I could describe the rapture that flashed through my soul as I beheld it. It was a new and strange sight to me, brightening up my pathway with the light of happiness. Little Thomas was told, there was his Freddy,—and I was told to take care of little Thomas; and thus I entered upon the duties of my new home with the most cheering prospect ahead.

I look upon my departure from Colonel Lloyd's plantation as one of the most interesting events of my life. It is possible, and even quite probable, that but for the mere circumstances of being removed from that plantation to Baltimore, I should have to-day, instead of being here seated by my own table, in the enjoyment of freedom and the happiness of home, writing this Narrative, been confined in the galling chains of slavery. Going to live at Baltimore laid the foundation, and opened the gateway, to all my subsequent prosperity. I have ever regarded it as the first plain manifestation of that kind providence which has ever since attended me, and marked my life with so many favors. I regarded the selection of myself as being somewhat remarkable. There were a number of slave children that might have been sent from the plantation to Baltimore. There were those younger, those older, and those of the same age. I was chosen from among them all, and was the first, last, and only choice.

I may be deemed superstitious, and even egotistical, in regarding this event as a special interposition of divine Providence in my favor. But I should be false to the earliest sentiments of my soul, if I suppressed the opinion. I prefer to be true to myself, even at the hazard of incurring the ridicule of others, rather than to be false, and incur my own abhorrence. From my earliest recollection, I date the entertainment of a deep conviction that slavery would not always be able to hold me within its foul embrace; and in the darkest hours of my career in slavery, this living word of faith and spirit of hope departed not from me, but remained like ministering angels to cheer me through the gloom. This good spirit was from God, and to him I offer thanksgiving and praise.

CHAPTER VI

My new mistress proved to be all she appeared when I first met her at the door,— a woman of the kindest heart and finest feelings. She had never had a slave under her control previously to myself, and prior to her marriage she had been dependent upon her own industry for a living. She was by trade a weaver; and by constant application to her business, she had been in a good degree preserved from the blighting and dehumanizing effects of slavery. I was utterly astonished at her goodness. I scarcely knew how to behave towards her. She was entirely unlike any other white woman I had ever seen. I could not approach her as I was accustomed to approach other white ladies. My early instruction was all out of place. The crouching servility, usually so acceptable a quality in a slave, did not answer when manifested toward her. Her favor was not gained by it; she seemed to be disturbed by it. She did not deem it impudent or unmannerly for a slave to look her in the face. The meanest slave was put fully at ease in her presence, and none left without feeling better for having seen her. Her face was made of heavenly smiles, and her voice of tranquil music.

But, alas! this kind heart had but a short time to remain such. The fatal poison of irresponsible power was already in her hands, and soon commenced its infernal work. That cheerful eye, under the influence of slavery, soon became red with rage; that voice, made all of sweet accord, changed to one of harsh and horrid discord; and that angelic face gave place to that of a demon.

Very soon after I went to live with Mr. and Mrs. Auld, she very kindly commenced to teach me the A, B, C. After I had learned this, she assisted me in learning to spell words of three or four letters. Just at this point of my progress, Mr. Auld found out what was going on, and at once forbade Mrs. Auld to instruct me further, telling her, among other things, that it was unlawful, as well as unsafe, to teach a slave to read.[18] To use his own words, further, he said, "If you give a nigger an inch, he will take an ell. A nigger should know nothing but to obey his master—to do as he is told to do. Learning would *spoil* the best nigger in the world. Now," said he, "if you teach that nigger (speaking of myself) how to read, there would be no keeping him. It would forever unfit him to be a slave. He would at once become unmanageable, and of no value to his master. As to himself, it could do him no good, but a great deal of harm. It would make him discontented and unhappy." These words sank deep into my heart, stirred up sentiments within that lay slumbering, and called into existence an entirely new train of thought. It was a new and special revelation, explaining dark and mysterious things, with which my youthful understanding had struggled, but struggled in vain. I now understood what had been to me a most perplexing difficulty—to wit, the white man's power to enslave the black man. It was a grand achievement, and I prized it highly. From that moment, I understood the pathway from slavery to freedom. It was just what I wanted, and I got it at a time when I the least expected it. Whilst I was saddened by the thought of losing the aid of my kind mistress, I was gladdened by the invaluable instruction which, by the merest accident, I had gained from my master. Though conscious of the difficulty of learning without a teacher, I set out with high hope, and a fixed purpose, at whatever cost of trouble, to learn how to read. The very decided manner with which he spoke, and strove to impress his wife with the evil consequences of giving me instruction, served to convince me that he was deeply sensible of the truths he was uttering. It gave me the best assurance that I might rely with the utmost confidence on the results which, he said, would flow from teaching me to read. What he most dreaded, that I most desired. What he most loved, that I most hated. That which to him was a great evil, to be carefully shunned, was to me a great good, to be diligently sought; and the argument which he so warmly urged, against my learning to read, only served to inspire me with a desire and determination to learn. In learning to read, I owe almost as much to the bitter opposition of my master, as to the kindly aid of my mistress. I acknowledge the benefit of both.

I had resided but a short time in Baltimore before I observed a marked difference, in the treatment of slaves, from that which I had witnessed in the country. A city slave is almost a freeman, compared with a slave on the plantation. He is much better fed and clothed, and enjoys privileges altogether unknown to the slave on the plantation. There is a vestige of decency, a sense of shame, that does much to curb and check those outbreaks of atrocious cruelty so commonly enacted upon the plantation. He is a desperate slaveholder, who will shock the humanity of his nonslaveholding neighbors with the cries of his lacerated slave. Few are willing to incur the odium attaching to the reputation of being a cruel master; and above all things, they would not be known as not giving a slave enough to eat.

---

[18] In some southern states it was illegal to teach a slave to read or write.

Every city slaveholder is anxious to have it known of him, that he feeds his slaves well; and it is due to them to say, that most of them do give their slaves enough to eat. There are, however, some painful exceptions to this rule. Directly opposite to us, on Philpot Street, lived Mr. Thomas Hamilton. He owned two slaves. Their names were Henrietta and Mary. Henrietta was about twenty-two years of age, Mary was about fourteen; and of all the mangled and emaciated creatures I ever looked upon, these two were the most so. His heart must be harder than stone, that could look upon these unmoved. The head, neck, and shoulders of Mary were literally cut to pieces. I have frequently felt her head, and found it nearly covered with festering sores, caused by the lash of her cruel mistress. I do not know that her master ever whipped her, but I have been an eye-witness to the cruelty of Mrs. Hamilton. I used to be in Mr. Hamilton's house nearly every day. Mrs. Hamilton used to sit in a large chair in the middle of the room, with a heavy cowskin always by her side, and scarce an hour passed during the day but was marked by the blood of one of these slaves. The girls seldom passed her without her saying, "Move faster, you *black gip!*" at the same time giving them a blow with the cowskin over the head or shoulders, often drawing the blood. She would then say, "Take that, you *black gip!*"—continuing, "If you don't move faster, I'll move you!" Added to the cruel lashings to which these slaves were subjected, they were kept nearly half-starved. They seldom knew what it was to eat a full meal. I have seen Mary contending with the pigs for the offal thrown into the street. So much was Mary kicked and cut to pieces, that she was oftener called *"pecked"* [19] than by her name.

CHAPTER VII

I lived in Master Hugh's family about seven years. During this time, I succeeded in learning to read and write. In accomplishing this, I was compelled to resort to various stratagems. I had no regular teacher. My mistress, who had kindly commenced to instruct me, had, in compliance with the advice and direction of her husband, not only ceased to instruct, but had set her face against my being instructed by any one else. It is due, however, to my mistress to say of her, that she did not adopt this course of treatment immediately. She at first lacked the depravity indispensable to shutting me up in mental darkness. It was at least necessary for her to have some training in the exercise of irresponsible power, to make her equal to the task of treating me as though I were a brute.

My mistress was, as I have said, a kind and tender-hearted woman; and in the simplicity of her soul she commenced, when I first went to live with her, to treat me as she supposed one human being ought to treat another. In entering upon the duties of a slaveholder, she did not seem to perceive that I sustained to her the relation of a mere chattel, and that for her to treat me as a human being was not only wrong, but dangerously so. Slavery proved as injurious to her as it did to me. When I went there, she was a pious, warm, and tender-hearted woman. There was no sorrow or suffering for which she had not a tear. She had bread for the hungry, clothes for the naked, and comfort for every mourner that came within her reach. Slavery soon proved its ability to divest her of these heavenly qualities. Under its influence, the tender heart became stone, and the lamblike disposition gave way to

---

[19] As if she had been brutally pecked by a chicken.

one of tiger-like fierceness. The first step in her downward course was in her ceasing to instruct me. She now commenced to practise her husband's precepts. She finally became even more violent in her opposition than her husband himself. She was not satisfied with simply doing as well as he had commanded; she seemed anxious to do better. Nothing seemed to make her more angry than to see me with a newspaper. She seemed to think that here lay the danger. I have had her rush at me with a face made all up of fury, and snatch from me a newspaper, in a manner that fully revealed her apprehension. She was an apt woman; and a little experience soon demonstrated, to her satisfaction, that education and slavery were incompatible with each other.

From this time I was most narrowly watched. If I was in a separate room any considerable length of time, I was sure to be suspected of having a book, and was at once called to give an account of myself. All this, however, was too late. The first step had been taken. Mistress, in teaching me the alphabet, had given me the *inch,* and no precaution could prevent me from taking the *ell.*

The plan which I adopted, and the one by which I was most successful, was that of making friends of all the little white boys whom I met in the street. As many of these as I could, I converted into teachers. With their kindly aid, obtained at different times and in different places, I finally succeeded in learning to read. When I was sent of errands, I always took my book with me, and by going one part of my errand quickly, I found time to get a lesson before my return. I used also to carry bread with me, enough of which was always in the house, and to which I was always welcome; for I was much better off in this regard than many of the poor white children in our neighborhood. This bread I used to bestow upon the hungry little urchins, who, in return, would give me that more valuable bread of knowledge. I am strongly tempted to give the names of two or three of those little boys, as a testimonial of the gratitude and affection I bear them; but prudence forbids;—not that it would injure me, but it might embarrass them; for it is almost an unpardonable offence to teach slaves to read in this Christian country. It is enough to say of the dear little fellows, that they lived on Philpot Street, very near Durgin and Bailey's ship-yard. I used to talk this matter of slavery over with them. I would sometimes say to them, I wished I could be as free as they would be when they got to be men. "You will be free as soon as you are twenty-one, *but I am a slave for life!* Have not I as good a right to be free as you have?" These words used to trouble them; they would express for me the liveliest sympathy, and console me with the hope that something would occur by which I might be free.

I was now about twelve years old, and the thought of being *a slave for life* began to bear heavily upon my heart. Just about this time, I got hold of a book entitled "The Columbian Orator."[20] Every opportunity I got, I used to read this book. Among much of other interesting matter, I found in it a dialogue between a master and his slave. The slave was represented as having run away from his master three times. The dialogue represented the conversation which took place between them, when the slave was retaken the third time. In this dialogue, the whole argument in behalf of slavery was brought forward by the master, all of which was disposed of by the slave. The slave was made to say some very smart as well as impressive things in reply to his master—things which had the desired though unexpected effect; for the conversation resulted in the voluntary emancipation of the slave on the part of the master.

---

[20] A popular collection of poems, speeches, dialogues, and plays.

In the same book, I met with one of Sheridan's[21] mighty speeches on and in behalf of Catholic emancipation. These were choice documents to me. I read them over and over again with unabated interest. They gave tongue to interesting thoughts of my own soul, which had frequently flashed through my mind, and died away for want of utterance. The moral which I gained from the dialogue was the power of truth over the conscience of even a slaveholder. What I got from Sheridan was a bold denunciation of slavery, and a powerful vindication of human rights. The reading of these documents enabled me to utter my thoughts, and to meet the arguments brought forward to sustain slavery; but while they relieved me of one difficulty, they brought on another even more painful than the one of which I was relieved. The more I read, the more I was led to abhor and detest my enslavers. I could regard them in no other light than a band of successful robbers, who had left their homes, and gone to Africa, and stolen us from our homes, and in a strange land reduced us to slavery. I loathed them as being the meanest as well as the most wicked of men. As I read and contemplated the subject, behold! that very discontentment which Master Hugh had predicted would follow my learning to read had already come, to torment and sting my sould to unutterable anguish. As I writhed under it, I would at times feel that learning to read had been a curse rather than a blessing. It had given me a view of my wretched condition, without the remedy. It opened my eyes to the horrible pit, but to no ladder upon which to get out. In moments of agony, I envied my fellow-slaves for their stupidity. I have often wished myself a beast. I preferred the condition of the meanest reptile to my own. Any thing, no matter what, to get rid of thinking! It was this everlasting thinking of my condition that tormented me. There was no getting rid of it. It was pressed upon me by every object within sight or hearing, animate or inanimate. The silver trump of freedom had roused my soul to eternal wakefulness. Freedom now appeared, to disappear no more forever. It was heard in every sound, and seen in every thing. It was ever present to torment me with a sense of my wretched condition. I saw nothing without seeing it, I heard nothing without hearing it, and felt nothing without feeling it. It looked from every star, it smiled in every calm, breathed in every wind, and moved in every storm.

I often found myself regretting my own existence, and wishing myself dead; and but for the hope of being free, I have no doubt but that I should have killed myself, or done something for which I should have been killed. While in this state of mind, I was eager to hear any one speak of slavery. I was a ready listener. Every little while, I could hear something about the abolitionists. It was some time before I found what the word meant. It was always used in such connections as to make it an interesting word to me. If a slave ran away and succeeded in getting clear, or if a slave killed his master, set fire to a barn, or did any thing very wrong in the mind of a slaveholder, it was spoken of as the fruit of *abolition*. Hearing the word in this connection very often, I set about learning what it meant. The dictionary afforded me little or no help. I found it was "the act of abolishing;" but then I did not know what was to be abolished. Here I was perplexed. I did not dare to ask any one about its meaning, for I was satisfied that it was something they wanted me to know very little about. After a patient waiting, I got one of our city papers, containing an account of the number of petitions from the north, praying for the abolition of slavery in the District of Columbia, and of the slave trade

---

[21] Richard Brinsley Sheridan (1751–1816), an Irish-born dramatist and political figure who spoke in favor of Catholic emancipation as a member of the British Parliament.

between the States. From this time I understood the words *abolition* and *abolition-ist,* and always drew near when that word was spoken, expecting to hear some-thing of importance to myself and fellow-slaves. The light broke in upon me by degrees. I went one day down on the wharf of Mr. Waters; and seeing two Irish-men unloading a scow of stone, I went, unasked, and helped them. When we had finished, one of them came to me and asked me if I were a slave. I told him I was. He asked, "Are ye a slave for life?" I told him that I was. The good Irishman seemed to be deeply affected by the statement. He said to the other that it was a pity so fine a little fellow as myself should be a slave for life. He said it was a shame to hold me. They both advised me to run away to the north; that I should find friends there, and that I should be free. I pretended not to be interested in what they said, and treated them as if I did not understand them; for I feared they might be treacherous. White men have been known to encourage slaves to escape, and then, to get the reward, catch them and return them to their masters. I was afraid that these seemingly good men might use me so; but I nevertheless remem-bered their advice, and from that time I resolved to run away. I looked forward to a time at which it would be safe for me to escape. I was too young to think of doing so immediately; besides, I wished to learn how to write, as I might have occasion to write my own pass. I consoled myself with the hope that I should one day find a good chance. Meanwhile, I would learn to write.

The idea as to how I might learn to write was suggested to me by being in Durgin and Bailey's ship-yard, and frequently seeing the ship carpenters, after hewing, and getting a piece of timber ready for use, write on the timber the name of that part of the ship for which it was intended. When a piece of timber was intended for the larboard side, it would be marked thus—"L." When a piece was for the starboard side, it would be marked thus—"S." A piece for the larboard side forward, would be marked thus—"L. F." When a piece was for starboard side forward, it would be marked thus—"S. F." For larboard aft, it would be marked thus—"L. A." For starboard aft, it would be marked thus—"S. A." I soon learned the names of these letters, and for what they were intended when placed upon a piece of timber in the ship-yard. I immediately commenced copying them, and in a short time was able to make the four letters named. After that, when I met with any boy who I knew could write, I would tell him I could write as well as he. The next word would be, "I don't believe you. Let me see you try it." I would then make the letters which I had been so fortunate as to learn, and ask him to beat that. In this way I got a good many lessons in writing, which it is quite possible I should never have gotten in any other way. During this time, my copy-book was the board fence, brick wall, and pavement; my pen and ink was a lump of chalk. With these, I learned mainly how to write. I then commenced and continued copy-ing the Italics in Webster's Spelling Book,[22] until I could make them all without looking on the book. By this time, my little Master Thomas had gone to school, and learned how to write, and had written over a number of copy-books. These had been brought home, and shown to some of our near neighbors, and then laid aside. My mistress used to go to class meeting at the Wilk Street meeting-house every Monday afternoon, and leave me to take care of the house. When left thus, I used to spend the time in writing in the spaces left in Master Thomas's copy-

[22] The famous *Spelling Book* (1783) devised by Noah Webster (1758–1843) from the first part of his *Grammatical Institute of the English Language* (1783–1785); used in American schools throughout the nineteenth century.

book, copying what he had written. I continued to do this until I could write a hand very similar to that of Master Thomas. Thus, after a long, tedious effort for years, I finally succeeded in learning how to write.

CHAPTER VIII

In a very short time after I went to live at Baltimore, my old master's youngest son Richard died; and in about three years and six months after his death, my old master, Captain Anthony, died, leaving only his son, Andrew, and daughter, Lucretia, to share his estate. He died while on a visit to see his daughter at Hillsborough. Cut off thus unexpectedly, he left no will as to the disposal of his property. It was therefore necessary to have a valuation of the property, that it might be equally divided between Mrs. Lucretia and Master Andrew. I was immediately sent for, to be valued with the other property. Here again my feelings rose up in detestation of slavery. I had now a new conception of my degraded condition. Prior to this, I had become, if not insensible to my lot, at least partly so. I left Baltimore with a young heart overborne with sadness, and a soul full of apprehension. I took passage with Captain Rowe, in the schooner Wild Cat, and, after a sail of about twenty-four hours, I found myself near the place of my birth. I had now been absent from it almost, if not quite, five years. I, however, remembered the place very well. I was only about five years old when I left it, to go and live with my old master on Colonel Lloyd's plantation; so that I was now between ten and eleven years old.

We were all ranked together at the valuation. Men and women, old and young, married and single, were ranked with horses, sheep, and swine. There were horses and men, cattle and women, pigs and children, all holding the same rank in the scale of being, and were all subjected to the same narrow examination. Silvery-headed age and sprightly youth, maids and matrons, had to undergo the same indelicate inspection. At this moment, I saw more clearly than ever the brutalizing effects of slavery upon both slave and slaveholder.

After the valuation, then came the division. I have no language to express the high excitement and deep anxiety which were felt among us poor slaves during this time. Our fate for life was now to be decided. We had no more voice in that decision than the brutes among whom we were ranked. A single word from the white men was enough—against all our wishes, prayers, and entreaties—to sunder forever the dearest friends, dearest kindred, and strongest ties known to human beings. In addition to the pain of separation, there was the horrid dread of falling into the hands of Master Andrew. He was known to us all as being a most cruel wretch,—a common drunkard, who had, by his reckless mismanagement and profligate dissipation, already wasted a large portion of his father's property. We all felt that we might as well be sold at once to the Georgia traders, as to pass into his hands; for we knew that that would be our inevitable condition,—a condition held by us all in the utmost horror and dread.

I suffered more anxiety than most of my fellowslaves. I had known what it was to be kindly treated; they had known nothing of the kind. They had seen little or nothing of the world. They were in very deed men and women of sorrow, and acquainted with grief. Their backs had been made familiar with the bloody lash, so that they had become callous; mine was yet tender; for while at Baltimore I got few whippings, and few slaves could boast of a kinder master and mistress than

myself; and the thought of passing out of their hands into those of Master Andrew—a man who, but a few days before, to give me a sample of his bloody
disposition, took my little brother by the throat, threw him on the ground, and
with the heel of his boot stamped upon his head till the blood gushed from his nose
and ears—was well calculated to make me anxious as to my fate. After he had
committed this savage outrage upon my brother, he turned to me, and said that
was the way he meant to serve me one of these days,—meaning, I suppose, when
I came into his possession.

Thanks to a kind Providence, I fell to the portion of Mrs. Lucretia, and was
sent immediately back to Baltimore, to live again in the family of Master Hugh.
Their joy at my return equalled their sorrow at my departure. It was a glad day to
me. I had escaped a worse than lion's jaws. I was absent from Baltimore, for the
purpose of valuation and division, just about one month, and it seemed to have
been six.

Very soon after my return to Baltimore, my mistress, Lucretia, died, leaving
her husband and one child, Amanda; and in a very short time after her death,
Master Andrew died. Now all the property of my old master, slaves included, was
in the hands of strangers,—strangers who had had nothing to do with accumulating it. Not a slave was left free. All remained slaves, from the youngest to the
oldest. If any one thing in my experience, more than another, served to deepen my
conviction of the infernal character of slavery, and to fill me with unutterable
loathing of slaveholders, it was their base ingratitude to my poor old grandmother.
She had served my old master faithfully from youth to old age. She had been the
source of all his wealth; she had peopled his plantation with slaves; she had become a great grandmother in his service. She had rocked him in infancy, attended
him in childhood, served him through life, and at his death wiped from his icy
brow the cold death-sweat, and closed his eyes forever. She was nevertheless left
a slave—a slave for life—a slave in the hands of strangers; and in their hands she
saw her children, her grandchildren, and her great-grandchildren, divided, like so
many sheep, without being gratified with the small privilege of a single word, as
to their or her own destiny. And, to cap the climax of their base ingratitude and
fiendish barbarity, my grandmother, who was now very old, having outlived my
old master and all his children, having seen the beginning and end of all of them,
and her present owners finding she was of but little value, her frame already
racked with the pains of old age, and complete helplessness fast stealing over her
once active limbs, they took her to the woods, built her a little hut, put up a little
mud-chimney, and then made her welcome to the privilege of supporting herself
there in perfect loneliness; thus virtually turning her out to die! If my poor old
grandmother now lives, she lives to suffer in utter loneliness; she lives to remember and mourn over the loss of children, the loss of grandchildren, and the loss of
great-grandchildren. They are, in the language of the slave's poet, Whittier,[23]—

> "Gone, gone, sold and gone
> To the rice swamp dank and lone,
> Where the slave-whip ceaseless swings,
> Where the noisome insect stings,
> Where the fever-demon strews

[23] John Greenleaf Whittier (1807–1892), the Massachusetts poet and abolitionist, in "The Farewell:
Of a Virginia Slave Mother to Her Daughter Sold Into Southern Bondage" (1838).

Poison with the falling dews,
Where the sickly sunbeams glare
Through the hot and misty air:—
  Gone, gone, sold and gone
  To the rice swamp dank and lone,
  From Virginia hills and waters—
  Woe is me, my stolen daughters!"

The hearth is desolate. The children, the unconscious children, who once sang and danced in her presence, are gone. She gropes her way, in the darkness of age, for a drink of water. Instead of the voices of her children, she hears by day the moans of the dove, and by night the screams of the hideous owl. All is gloom. The grave is at the door. And now, when weighed down by the pains and aches of old age, when the head inclines to the feet, when the beginning and ending of human existence meet, and helpless infancy and painful old age combine together—at this time, this most needful time, the time for the exercise of that tenderness and affection which children only can exercise towards a declining parent—my poor old grandmother, the devoted mother of twelve children, is left all alone, in yonder little hut, before a few dim embers. She stands—she sits—she staggers—she falls—she groans—she dies—and there are none of her children or grandchildren present, to wipe from her wrinkled brow the cold sweat of death, or to place beneath the sod her fallen remains. Will not a righteous God visit for these things?

In about two years after the death of Mrs. Lucretia, Master Thomas married his second wife. Her name was Rowena Hamilton. She was the eldest daughter of Mr. William Hamilton. Master now lived in St. Michael's. Not long after his marriage, a misunderstanding took place between himself and Master Hugh; and as a means of punishing his brother, he took me from him to live with himself at St. Michael's. Here I underwent another most painful separation. It, however, was not so severe as the one I dreaded at the division of property; for, during this interval, a great change had taken place in Master Hugh and his once kind and affectionate wife. The influence of brandy upon him, and of slavery upon her, had effected a disastrous change in the characters of both; so that, as far as they were concerned, I thought I had little to lose by the change. But it was not to them that I was attached. It was to those little Baltimore boys that I felt the strongest attachment. I had received many good lessons from them, and was still receiving them, and the thought of leaving them was painful indeed. I was leaving, too, without the hope of ever being allowed to return. Master Thomas had said he would never let me return again. The barrier betwixt himself and brother he considered impassable.

I then had to regret that I did not at least make the attempt to carry out my resolution to run away; for the chances of success are tenfold greater from the city than from the country.

I sailed from Baltimore for St. Michael's in the sloop Amanda, Captain Edward Dodson. On my passage, I paid particular attention to the direction which the steamboats took to go to Philadelphia. I found, instead of going down, on reaching North Point they went up the bay, in a north-easterly direction. I deemed this knowledge of the utmost importance. My determination to run away was again revived. I resolved to wait only so long as the offering of a favorable opportunity. When that came, I was determined to be off.

Chapter IX

I have now reached a period of my life when I can give dates. I left Baltimore, and went to live with Master Thomas Auld, at St. Michael's, in March, 1832. It was now more than seven years since I lived with him in the family of my old master, on Colonel Lloyd's plantation. We of course were now almost entire strangers to each other. He was to me a new master, and I to him a new slave. I was ignorant of his temper and disposition; he was equally so of mine. A very short time, however, brought us into full acquaintance with each other. I was made acquainted with his wife not less than with himself. They were well matched, being equally mean and cruel. I was now, for the first time during a space of more than seven years, made to feel the painful gnawings of hunger—a something which I had not experienced before since I left Colonel Lloyd's plantation. It went hard enough with me then, when I could look back to no period at which I had enjoyed a sufficiency. It was tenfold harder after living in Master Hugh's family, where I had always had enough to eat, and of that which was good. I have said Master Thomas was a mean man. He was so. Not to give a slave enough to eat, is regarded as the most aggravated development of meanness even among slaveholders. The rule is, no matter how coarse the food, only let there be enough of it. This is the theory; and in the part of Maryland from which I came, it is the general practice,—though there are many exceptions. Master Thomas gave us enough of neither coarse nor fine food. There were four slaves of us in the kitchen—my sister Eliza, my aunt Priscilla, Henny, and myself; and we were allowed less than a half of a bushel of corn-meal per week, and very little else, either in the shape of meat or vegetables. It was not enough for us to subsist upon. We were therefore reduced to the wretched necessity of living at the expense of our neighbors. This we did by begging and stealing, whichever came handy in the time of need, the one being considered as legitimate as the other. A great many times have we poor creatures been nearly perishing with hunger, when food in abundance lay mouldering in the safe and smoke-house,[24] and our pious mistress was aware of the fact; and yet that mistress and her husband would kneel every morning, and pray that God would bless them in basket and store!

Bad as all slaveholders are, we seldom meet one destitute of every element of character commanding respect. My master was one of this rare sort. I do not know of one single noble act ever performed by him. The leading trait in his character was meanness; and if there were any other element in his nature, it was made subject to this. He was mean; and, like most other mean men, he lacked the ability to conceal his meanness. Captain Auld was not born a slaveholder. He had been a poor man, master only of a Bay craft. He came into possession of all his slaves by marriage; and of all men, adopted slaveholders are the worst. He was cruel, but cowardly. He commanded without firmness. In the enforcement of his rules, he was at times rigid, and at times lax. At times, he spoke to his slaves with the firmness of Napoleon and the fury of a demon; at other times, he might well be mistaken for an inquirer who had lost his way. He did nothing of himself. He might have passed for a lion, but for his ears.[25] In all things noble which he

---

[24] A place to cure meat and fish by smoking, after which it could be stored and preserved in a meat safe.

[25] Probably, that his ears made him look like a jackass; he was not as powerful as he professed to be.

attempted, his own meanness shone most conspicuous. His airs, words, and actions, were the airs, words, and actions of born slaveholders, and, being assumed, were awkward enough. He was not even a good imitator. He possessed all the disposition to deceive, but wanted the power. Having no resources within himself, he was compelled to be the copyist of many, and being such, he was forever the victim of inconsistency; and of consequence he was an object of contempt, and was held as such even by his slaves. The luxury of having slaves of his own to wait upon him was something new and unprepared for. He was a slaveholder without the ability to hold slaves. He found himself incapable of managing his slaves either by force, fear, or fraud. We seldom called him "master;" we generally called him "Captain Auld," and were hardly disposed to title him at all. I doubt not that our conduct had much to do with making him appear awkward, and of consequence fretful. Our want of reverence for him must have perplexed him greatly. He wished to have us call him master, but lacked the firmness necessary to command us to do so. His wife used to insist upon our calling him so, but to no purpose. In August, 1832, my master attended a Methodist camp-meeting held in the Bay-side, Talbot county, and there experienced religion. I indulged a faint hope that his conversion would lead him to emancipate his slaves, and that, if he did not do this, it would, at any rate, make him more kind and humane. I was disappointed in both these respects. It neither made him to be humane to his slaves, nor to emancipate them. If it had any effect on his character, it made him more cruel and hateful in all his ways; for I believe him to have been a much worse man after his conversion than before. Prior to his conversion, he relied upon his own depravity to shield and sustain him in his savage barbarity; but after his conversion, he found religious sanction and support for his slaveholding cruelty. He made the greatest pretensions to piety. His house was the house of prayer. He prayed morning, noon, and night. He very soon distinguished himself among his brethren, and was soon made a class-leader and exhorter. His activity in revivals was great, and he proved himself an instrument in the hands of the church in converting many souls. His house was the preachers' home. They used to take great pleasure in coming there to put up; for while he starved us, he stuffed them. We have had three or four preachers there at a time. The names of those who used to come most frequently while I lived there, were Mr. Storks, Mr. Ewery, Mr. Humphry, and Mr. Hickey. I have also seen Mr. George Cookman at our house. We slaves loved Mr. Cookman. We believed him to be a good man. We thought him instrumental in getting Mr. Samuel Harrison, a very rich slaveholder, to emancipate his slaves; and by some means got the impression that he was laboring to effect the emancipation of all the slaves. When he was at our house, we were sure to be called in to prayers. When the others were there, we were sometimes called in and sometimes not. Mr. Cookman took more notice of us than either of the other ministers. He could not come among us without betraying his sympathy for us, and, stupid as we were, we had the sagacity to see it.

While I lived with my master in St. Michael's, there was a white young man, a Mr. Wilson, who proposed to keep a Sabbath school for the instruction of such slaves as might be disposed to learn to read the New Testament. We met but three times, when Mr. West and Mr. Fairbanks, both class-leaders, with many others, came upon us with sticks and other missiles, drove us off, and forbade us to meet again. Thus ended our little Sabbath school in the pious town of St. Michael's.

I have said my master found religious sanction for his cruelty. As an example,

I will state one of many facts going to prove the charge. I have seen him tie up a lame young woman, and whip her with a heavy cowskin upon her naked shoulders, causing the warm red blood to drip; and, in justification of the bloody deed, he would quote this passage of Scripture—"He that knoweth his master's will, and doeth it not, shall be beaten with many stripes."[26]

Master would keep this lacerated young woman tied up in this horrid situation four or five hours at a time. I have known him to tie her up early in the morning, and whip her before breakfast; leave her, go to his store, return at dinner, and whip her again, cutting her in the places already made raw with his cruel lash. The secret of master's cruelty toward "Henny" is found in the fact of her being almost helpless. When quite a child, she fell into the fire, and burned herself horribly. Her hands were so burnt that she never got the use of them. She could do very little but bear heavy burdens. She was to master a bill of expense; and as he was a mean man, she was a constant offence to him. He seemed desirous of getting the poor girl out of existence. He gave her away once to his sister; but, being a poor gift, she was not disposed to keep her. Finally, my benevolent master, to use his own words, "set her adrift to take care of herself." Here was a recently-converted man, holding on upon the mother, and at the same time turning out her helpless child, to starve and die! Master Thomas was one of the many pious slaveholders who hold slaves for the very charitable purpose of taking care of them.

My master and myself had quite a number of differences. He found me unsuitable to his purpose. My city life, he said, had had a very pernicious effect upon me. It had almost ruined me for every good purpose, and fitted me for every thing which was bad. One of my greatest faults was that of letting his horse run away, and go down to his father-in-law's farm, which was about five miles from St. Michael's. I would then have to go after it. My reason for this kind of carelessness, or carefulness, was, that I could always get something to eat when I went there. Master William Hamilton, my master's father-in-law, always gave his slaves enought to eat. I never left there hungry, no matter how great the need of my speedy return. Master Thomas at length said he would stand it no longer. I had lived with him nine months, during which time he had given me a number of severe whippings, all to no good purpose. He resolved to put me out, as he said, to be broken; and, for this purpose, he let me for one year to a man named Edward Covey. Mr. Covey was a poor man, a farm-renter. He rented the place upon which he lived, as also the hands with which he tilled it. Mr. Covey had acquired a very high reputation for breaking young slaves, and this reputation was of immense value to him. It enabled him to get his farm tilled with much less expense to himself than he could have had it done without such a reputation. Some slaveholders thought it not much loss to allow Mr. Covey to have their slaves one year, for the sake of the training to which they were subjected, without any other compensation. He could hire young help with great ease, in consequence of this reputation. Added to the natural good qualities of Mr. Covey, he was a professor of religion—a pious soul—a member and a class-leader in the Methodist church. All of this added weight to his reputation as a "nigger-breaker." I was aware of all the facts, having been made acquainted with them by a young man who had lived there. I nevertheless made the change gladly; for I was sure of getting enough to eat, which is not the smallest consideration to a hungry man.

[26] From Luke 12:47, wrenched out of context and woefully misapplied.

CHAPTER X

I left Master Thomas's house, and went to live with Mr. Covey, on the 1st of January, 1833. I was now, for the first time in my life, a field hand. In my new employment, I found myself even more awkward than a country boy appeared to be in a large city. I had been at my new home but one week before Mr. Covey gave me a very severe whipping, cutting my back, causing the blood to run, and raising ridges on my flesh as large as my little finger. The details of this affair are as follows: Mr. Covey sent me, very early in the morning of one of our coldest days in the month of January, to the woods, to get a load of wood. He gave me a team of unbroken oxen. He told me which was the in-hand ox, and which the off-hand one.[27] He then tied the end of a large rope around the horns of the in-hand ox, and gave me the other end of it, and told me, if the oxen started to run, that I must hold on upon the rope. I had never driven oxen before, and of course I was very awkward. I, however, succeeded in getting to the edge of the woods with little difficulty; but I had got a very few rods into the woods, when the oxen took fright, and started full tilt, carrying the cart against trees, and over stumps, in the most frightful manner. I expected every moment that my brains would be dashed out against the trees. After running thus for a considerable distance, they finally upset the cart, dashing it with great force against a tree, and threw themselves into a dense thicket. How I escaped death, I do not know. There I was, entirely alone, in a thick wood, in a place new to me. My cart was upset and shattered, my oxen were entangled among the young trees, and there was none to help me. After a long spell of effort, I succeeded in getting my cart righted, my oxen disentangled, and again yoked to the cart. I now proceeded with my team to the place where I had, the day before, been chopping wood, and loaded my cart pretty heavily, thinking in this way to tame my oxen. I then proceeded on my way home. I had now consumed one half of the day. I got out of the woods safely, and now felt out of danger. I stopped my oxen to open the woods gate; and just as I did so, before I could get hold of my ox-rope, the oxen again started, rushed through the gate, catching it between the wheel and the body of the cart, tearing it to pieces, and coming within a few inches of crushing me against the gate-post. Thus twice, in one short day, I escaped death by the merest chance. On my return, I told Mr. Covey what had happened, and how it happened. He ordered me to return to the woods again immediately. I did so, and he followed on after me. Just as I got into the woods, he came up and told me to stop my cart, and that he would teach me how to trifle away my time, and break gates. He then went to a large gum-tree, and with his axe cut three large switches, and, after trimming them up neatly with his pocket-knife, he ordered me to take off my clothes. I made him no answer, but stood with my clothes on. He repeated his order. I still made him no answer, nor did I move to strip myself. Upon this he rushed at me with the fierceness of a tiger, tore off my clothes, and lashed me till he had worn out his switches, cutting me so savagely as to leave the marks visible for a long time after. This whipping was the first of a number just like it, and for similar offences.

I lived with Mr. Covey one year. During the first six months, of that year, scarce a week passed without his whipping me. I was seldom free from a sore back. My awkwardness was almost always his excuse for whipping me. We were

[27] The "in-hand" ox is the one to the driver's right, the "off-hand" ox to the left.

worked fully up to the point of endurance. Long before day we were up, our horses fed, and by the first approach of day we were off to the field with our hoes and ploughing teams. Mr. Covey gave us enough to eat, but scarce time to eat it. We were often less than five minutes taking our meals. We were often in the field from the first approach of day till its last lingering ray had left us; and at saving-fodder time,[28] midnight often caught us in the field binding blades.

Covey would be out with us. The way he used to stand it, was this. He would spend the most of his afternoons in bed. He would then come out fresh in the evening, ready to urge us on with his words, example, and frequently with the whip. Mr. Covey was one of the few slaveholders who could and did work with his hands. He was a hard-working man. He knew by himself just what a man or a boy could do. There was no deceiving him. His work went on in his absence almost as well as in his presence; and he had the faculty of making us feel that he was ever present with us. This he did by surprising us. He seldom approached the spot where we were at work openly, if he could do it secretly. He always aimed at taking us by surprise. Such was his cunning, that we used to call him, among ourselves, "the snake." When we were at work in the cornfield, he would some-times crawl on his hands and knees to avoid detection, and all at once he would rise nearly in our midst, and scream out, "Ha, ha! Come, come! Dash on, dash on!" This being his mode of attack, it was never safe to stop a single minute. His comings were like a thief in the night. He appeared to us as being ever at hand. He was under every tree, behind every stump, in every bush, and at every window, on the plantation. He would sometimes mount his horse, as if bound to St. Mi-chael's, a distance of seven miles, and in half an hour afterwards you would see him coiled up in the corner of the wood-fence, watching every motion of the slaves. He would, for this purpose, leave his horse tied up in the woods. Again, he would sometimes walk up to us, and give us orders as though he was upon the point of starting on a long journey, turn his back upon us, and make as though he was going to the house to get ready; and, before he would get half way thither, he would turn short and crawl into a fence-corner, or behind some tree, and there watch us till the going down of the sun.

Mr. Covey's *forte*[29] consisted in his power to deceive. His life was devoted to planning and perpetrating the grossest deceptions. Every thing he possessed in the shape of learning or religion, he made conform to his disposition to deceive. He seemed to think himself equal to deceiving the Almighty. He would make a short prayer in the morning, and a long prayer at night; and, strange as it may seem, few men would at times appear more devotional than he. The exercises of his family devotions were always commenced with singing; and, as he was a very poor singer himself, the duty of raising the hymn generally came upon me. He would read his hymn, and nod at me to commence. I would at times do so; at others, I would not. My non-compliance would almost always produce much confusion. To show himself independent of me, he would start and stagger through with his hymn in the most discordant manner. In this state of mind, he prayed with more than ordinary spirit. Poor man! such was his disposition, and success at deceiving, I do verily believe that he sometimes deceived himself into the solemn belief, that he was a sincere worshipper of the most high God; and this, too, at a time when he may be said to have been guilty of compelling his woman slave to commit the sin of adultery. The facts in the case are these: Mr. Covey was a poor man; he was

---

[28] Harvesting time; blades are the leaves of plants.   [29] Specialty.

just commencing in life; he was only able to buy one slave; and, shocking as is the fact, he bought her, as he said, for *a breeder*. This woman was named Caroline. Mr. Covey bought her from Mr. Thomas Lowe, about six miles from St. Michael's. She was a large, able-bodied woman, about twenty years old. She had already given birth to one child, which proved her to be just what he wanted. After buying her, he hired a married man of Mr. Samuel Harrison, to live with him one year; and him he used to fasten up with her every night! The result was, that, at the end of the year, the miserable woman gave birth to twins. At this result Mr. Covey seemed to be highly pleased, both with the man and the wretched woman. Such was his joy, and that of his wife, that nothing they could do for Caroline during her confinement was too good, or too hard, to be done. The children were regarded as being quite an addition to his wealth.

If at any one time of my life more than another, I was made to drink the bitterest dregs of slavery, that time was during the first six months of my stay with Mr. Covey. We were worked in all weathers. It was never too hot or too cold; it could never rain, blow, hail, or snow, too hard for us to work in the field. Work, work, work, was scarcely more the order of the day than of the night. The longest days were too short for him, and the shortest nights too long for him. I was somewhat unmanageable when I first went there, but a few months of this discipline tamed me. Mr. Covey succeeded in breaking me. I was broken in body, soul, and spirit. My natural elasticity was crushed, my intellect languished, the disposition to read departed, the cheerful spark that lingered about my eye died; the dark night of slavery closed in upon me; and behold a man transformed into a brute!

Sunday was my only leisure time. I spent this in a sort of beast-like stupor, between sleep and wake, under some large tree. At times I would rise up, a flash of energetic freedom would dart through my soul, accompanied with a faint beam of hope, that flickered for a moment, and then vanished. I sank down again, mourning over my wretched condition. I was sometimes prompted to take my life, and that of Covey, but was prevented by a combination of hope and fear. My sufferings on this plantation seem now like a dream rather than a stern reality.

Our house stood within a few rods of the Chesapeake Bay, whose broad bosom was ever white with sails from every quarter of the habitable globe. Those beautiful vessels, robed in purest white, so delightful to the eye of freemen, were to me so many shrouded ghosts, to terrify and torment me with thoughts of my wretched condition. I have often, in the deep stillness of a summer's Sabbath, stood all alone upon the lofty banks of that noble bay, and traced, with saddened heart and tearful eye, the countless number of sails moving off to the mighty ocean. The sight of these always affected me powerfully. My thoughts would compel utterance; and there, with no audience but the Almighty, I would pour out my soul's complaint, in my rude way, with an apostrophe to the moving multitude of ships:—

"You are loosed from your moorings, and are free; I am fast in my chains, and am a slave! You move merrily before the gentle gale, and I sadly before the bloody whip! You are freedom's swift-winged angels, that fly round the world; I am confined in bands of iron! O that I were free! O, that I were on one of your gallant decks, and under your protecting wing– Alas! betwixt me and you, the turbid waters roll. Go on, go on. O that I could also go! Could I but swim! If I could fly! O, why was I born a man, of whom to make a brute! The glad ship is gone; she hides in the dim distance. I am left in the hottest hell of unending slavery. O God, save me! God, deliver me! Let me be free! Is there any God? Why am I a slave? I will run away. I will not stand it. Get caught, or get clear, I'll try it. I had as well die with ague as the fever. I have only one life to lose. I had as well be killed running as die standing. Only think of it; one hundred miles straight north, and I am free! Try it? Yes! God helping me, I will. It cannot be that I shall live and die a slave. I will take to the water. This very bay shall yet bear me into freedom. The steamboats steered in a north-east course from North Point. I will do the same; and when I get to the head of the bay, I will turn my canoe adrift, and walk straight through Delaware into Pennyslvania. When I get there, I shall not be required to have a pass; I can travel without being disturbed. Let but the first opportunity offer, and, come what will, I am off. Meanwhile, I will try to bear up under the yoke. I am not the only slave in the world. Why should I fret? I can bear as much as any of them. Besides, I am but a boy, and all boys are bound to some one. It may be that my misery in slavery will only increase my happiness when I get free. There is a better day coming."

Thus I used to think, and thus I used to speak to myself; goaded almost to madness at one moment, and at the next reconciling myself to my wretched lot.

I have already intimated that my condition was much worse, during the first six months of my stay at Mr. Covey's, than in the last six. The circumstances leading to the change in Mr. Covey's course toward me form an epoch in my humble history. You have seen how a man was made a slave; you shall see how a slave was made a man. On one of the hottest days of the month of August, 1833, Bill Smith, William Hughes, a slave named Eli, and myself, were engaged in fanning wheat.[30] Hughes was clearing the fanned wheat from before the fan, Eli was turning, Smith was feeding, and I was carrying wheat to the fan. The work was simple, requiring strength rather than intellect; yet, to one entirely unused to such work, it came very hard. About three o'clock of that day, I broke down; my strength failed me; I was seized with a violent aching of the head, attended with extreme dizziness; I trembled in every limb. Finding what was coming, I nerved myself up, feeling it would never do to stop work. I stood as long as I could stagger to the hopper with grain. When I could stand no longer, I fell, and felt as if held down by an immense weight. The fan of course stopped; every one had his own work to do; and no one could do the work of the other, and have his own go on at the same time.

Mr. Covey was at the house, about one hundred yards from the treading-yard where we were fanning. On hearing the fan stop, he left immediately, and came to the spot where we were. He hastily inquired what the matter was. Bill answered that I was sick, and there was no one to bring wheat to the fan. I had by this time crawled away under the side of the post and rail-fence by which the yard was enclosed, hoping to find relief by getting out of the sun. He then asked where I was. He was told by one of the hands. He came to the spot, and, after looking at me awhile, asked me what was the matter. I told him as well as I could, for I scarce had strength to speak. He then gave me a savage kick in the side, and told me to get up. I tried to do so, but fell back in the attempt. He gave me another kick, and again told me to rise. I again tried, and succeeded in gaining my feet; but, stooping to get the tub with which I was feeding the fan, I again staggered and fell. While down in this situation, Mr. Covey took up the hickory slat with which Hughes had been striking off the half-bushel measure, and with it gave me a heavy blow upon the head, making a large wound, and the blood ran freely; and

---

[30] Separating the wheat from the chaff.

with this again told me to get up. I made no effort to comply, having now made up my mind to let him do his worst. In a short time after receiving this blow, my head grew better. Mr. Covey had now left me to my fate. At this moment I resolved, for the first time, to go to my master, enter a complaint, and ask his protection. In order to this, I must that afternoon walk seven miles; and this, under the circumstances, was truly a severe undertaking. I was exceedingly feeble; made so as much by the kicks and blows which I received, as by the severe fit of sickness to which I had been subjected. I, however, watched my chance, while Covey was looking in an opposite direction, and started for St. Michael's. I succeeded in getting a considerable distance on my way to the woods, when Covey discovered me, and called after me to come back, threatening what he would do if I did not come. I disregarded both his calls and his threats, and made my way to the woods as fast as my feeble state would allow; and thinking I might be overhauled by him if I kept the road, I walked through the woods, keeping far enough from the road to avoid detection, and near enough to prevent losing my way I had not gone far before my little strength again failed me. I could go no farther. I fell down, and lay for a considerable time. The blood was yet oozing from the wound on my head. For a time I thought I should bleed to death; and think now that I should have done so, but that the blood so matted my hair as to stop the wound. After lying there about three quarters of an hour, I nerved myself up again, and started on my way, through bogs and briers, barefooted and bare-headed, tearing my feet sometimes at nearly every step; and after a journey of about seven miles, occupying some five hours to perform it, I arrived at master's store. I then presented an appearance enough to affect any but a heart of iron. From the crown of my head to my feet, I was covered with blood. My hair was all clotted with dust and blood; my shirt was stiff with blood. My legs and feet were torn in sundry places with briers and thorns, and were also covered with blood. I suppose I looked like a man who had escaped a den of wild beasts, and barely escaped them. In this state, I appeared before my master, humbly entreating him to interpose his authority for my protection. I told him all the circumstances as well as I could, and it seemed, as I spoke, at times to affect him. He would then walk the floor, and seek to justify Covey by saying he expected I deserved it. He asked me what I wanted. I told him, to let me get a new home; that as sure as I lived with Mr. Covey again, I should live with but to die with him; that Covey would surely kill me; he was in a fair way for it. Master Thomas ridiculed the idea that there was any danger of Mr. Covey's killing me, and said that he knew Mr. Covey; that he was a good man, and that he could not think of taking me from him; that, should he do so, he would lose the whole year's wages; that I belonged to Mr. Covey for one year, and that I must go back to him, come what might; and that I must not trouble him with any more stories, or that he would himself *get hold of me.* After threatening me thus, he gave me a very large dose of salts, telling me that I might remain in St. Michael's that night, (it being quite late,) but that I must be off back to Mr. Covey's early in the morning; and that if I did not, he would *get hold of me,* which meant that he would whip me. I remained all night, and, according to his orders, I started off to Covey's in the morning, (Saturday morning,) wearied in body and broken in spirit. I got no supper that night, or breakfast that morning. I reached Covey's about nine o'clock; and just as I was getting over the fence that divided Mrs. Kemp's fields from ours, out ran Covey with his cowskin, to give me another whipping. Before he could reach me, I succeeded in getting to the cornfield; and as the corn was very high, it afforded me the means of hiding. He seemed very angry, and searched for me a long time. My behavior was altogether unaccountable. He finally gave up the chase, thinking, I suppose, that I must come home for something to eat; he would give himself no further trouble in looking for me. I spent that day mostly in the woods, having the alternative before me,—to go home and be whipped to death, or stay in the woods and be starved to death. That night, I fell in with Sandy Jenkins, a slave with whom I was somewhat acquainted. Sandy had a free wife[31] who lived about four miles from Mr. Covey's; and it being Saturday, he was on his way to see her. I told him my circumstances, and he very kindly invited me to go home with him. I went home with him, and talked this whole matter over, and got his advice as to what course it was best for me to pursue. I found Sandy an old adviser. He told me, with great solemnity, I must go back to Covey; but that before I went, I must go with him into another part of the woods, where there was a certain *root*, which, if I would take some of it with me, carrying it *always on my right side,* would render it impossible for Mr. Covey, or any other white man, to whip me. He said he had carried it for years; and since he had done so, he had never received a blow, and never expected to while he carried it. I at first rejected the idea, that the simple carrying of a root in my pocket would have any such effect as he had said, and was not disposed to take it; but Sandy impressed the necessity with much earnestness, telling me it could do no harm, if it did no good. To please him, I at length took the root, and, according to his direction, carried it upon my right side. This was Sunday morning. I immediately started for home; and upon entering the yard gate, out came Mr. Covey on his way to meeting. He spoke to me very kindly, bade me drive the pigs from a lot near by, and passed on towards the church. Now, this singular conduct of Mr. Covey really made me begin to think that there was something in the *root* which Sandy had given me; and had it been on any other day than Sunday, I could have attributed the conduct to no other cause than the influence of that root; and as it was, I was half inclined to think the *root* to be something more than I at first had taken it to be. All went well till Monday morning. On this morning, the virtue of the *root* was fully tested. Long before daylight, I was called to go and rub, curry, and feed, the horses. I obeyed, and was glad to obey. But whilst thus engaged, whilst in the act of throwing down some blades from the loft, Mr. Covey entered the stable with a long rope; and just as I was half out of the loft, he caught hold of my legs, and was about tying me. As soon as I found what he was up to, I gave a sudden spring, and as I did so, he holding to my legs, I was brought sprawling on the stable floor. Mr. Covey seemed now to think he had me, and could do what he pleased; but at this moment—from whence came the spirit I don't know—I resolved to fight; and, suiting my action to the resolution, I seized Covey hard by the throat; and as I did so, I rose. He held on to me, and I to him. My resistance was so entirely unexpected, that Covey seemed taken all aback. He trembled like a leaf. This gave me assurance, and I held him uneasy, causing the blood to run where I touched him with the ends of my fingers. Mr. Covey soon called out to Hughes for help. Hughes came, and, while Covey held me, attempted to tie my right hand. While he was in the act of doing so, I watched my chance, and gave him a heavy kick close under the ribs. This kick fairly sickened Hughes, so that he left me in the hands of Mr. Covey. This kick had the effect of not only weakening Hughes, but Covey also. When he saw Hughes bending over with pain, his courage quailed. He asked me if I meant to persist in my resistance.

---

[31] A wife who had been freed legally and was not a slave.

I told him I did, come what might; that he had used me like a brute for six months, and that I was determined to be used so no longer. With that, he strove to drag me to a stick that was lying just out of the stable door. He meant to knock me down. But just as he was leaning over to get the stick, I seized him with both hands by his collar, and brought him by a sudden snatch to the ground. By this time, Bill came. Covey called upon him for assistance. Bill wanted to know what he could do. Covey said, "Take hold of him, take hold of him!" Bill said his master hired him out to work, and not to help to whip me; so he left Covey and myself to fight our own battle out. We were at it for nearly two hours. Covey at length let me go, puffing and blowing at a great rate, saying that if I had not resisted, he would not have whipped me half so much. The truth was, that he had not whipped me at all. I considered him as getting entirely the worst end of the bargain; for he had drawn no blood from me, but I had from him. The whole six months afterwards, that I spent with Mr. Covey, he never laid the weight of his finger upon me in anger. He would occasionally say, he didn't want to get hold of me again. "No," thought I, "you need not; for you will come off worse than you did before."

The battle with Mr. Covey was the turning-point in my career as a slave. It rekindled the few expiring embers of freedom, and revived within me a sense of my own manhood. It recalled the departed self-confidence, and inspired me again with a determination to be free. The gratification afforded by the triumph was a full compensation for whatever else might follow, even death itself. He only can understand the deep satisfaction which I experienced, who has himself repelled by force the bloody arm of slavery. I felt as I never felt before. It was a glorious resurrection, from the tomb of slavery, to the heaven of freedom. My long-crushed spirit rose, cowardice departed, bold defiance took its place; and I now resolved that, however long I might remain a slave in form, the day had passed forever when I could be a slave in fact. I did not hesitate to let it be known of me, that the white man who expected to succeed in whipping, must also succeed in killing me.

From this time I was never again what might be called fairly whipped, though I remained a slave four years afterwards. I had several fights, but was never whipped.

It was for a long time a matter of surprise to me why Mr. Covey did not immediately have me taken by the constable to the whipping-post, and there regularly whipped for the crime of raising my hand against a white man in defence of myself. And the only explanation I can now think of does not entirely satisfy me; but such as it is, I will give it. Mr. Covey enjoyed the most unbounded reputation for being a first-rate overseer and negro-breaker. It was of considerable importance to him. That reputation was at stake; and had he sent me—a boy about sixteen years old—to the public whipping-post, his reputation would have been lost; so, to save his reputation, he suffered me to go unpunished.

My term of actual service to Mr. Edward Covey ended on Christmas day, 1833. The days between Christmas and New Year's day are allowed as holidays; and, accordingly, we were not required to perform any labor, more than to feed and take care of the stock. This time we regarded as our own, by the grace of our masters; and we therefore used or abused it nearly as we pleased. Those of us who had families at a distance, were generally allowed to spend the whole six days in their society. This time, however, was spent in various ways. The staid, sober, thinking and industrious ones of our number would employ themselves in making corn-brooms, mats, horse-collars, and baskets; and another class of us would spend the time in hunting opossums, hares, and coons. But by far the larger part engaged in such sports and merriments as playing ball, wrestling, running foot-races, fiddling, dancing, and drinking whisky; and this latter mode of spending the time was by far the most agreeable to the feelings of our masters. A slave who would work during the holidays was considered by our masters as scarcely deserv-ing them. He was regarded as one who rejected the favor of his master. It was deemed a disgrace not to get drunk at Christmas; and he was regarded as lazy indeed, who had not provided himself with the necessary means, during the year, to get whisky enough to last him through Christmas.

From what I know of the effect of these holidays upon the slave, I believe them to be among the most effective means in the hands of the slaveholder in keeping down the spirit of insurrection. Were the slaveholders at once to abandon this practice, I have not the slightest doubt it would lead to an immediate insurrection among the slaves. These holidays serve as conductors, or safety-valves, to carry off the rebellious spirit of enslaved humanity. But for these, the slave would be forced up to the wildest desperation; and woe betide the slaveholder, the day he ventures to remove or hinder the operation of those conductors! I warn him that, in such an event, a spirit will go forth in their midst, more to be dreaded than the most appalling earthquake.

The holidays are part and parcel of the gross fraud, wrong, and inhumanity of slavery. They are professedly a custom established by the benevolence of the slaveholders; but I undertake to say, it is the result of selfishness, and one of the grossest frauds committed upon the down-trodden slave. They do not give the slaves this time because they would not like to have their work during its continu-ance, but because they know it would be unsafe to deprive them of it. This will be seen by the fact, that the slaveholders like to have their slaves spend those days just in such a manner as to make them as glad of their ending as of their begin-ning. Their object seems to be, to disgust their slaves with freedom, by plunging them into the lowest depths of dissipation. For instance, the slaveholders not only like to see the slave drink of his own accord, but will adopt various plans to make him drunk. One plan is, to make bets on their slaves, as to who can drink the whisky without getting drunk; and in this way they succeed in getting whole mul-titudes to drink to excess. Thus, when the slave asks for virtuous freedom, the cunning slaveholder, knowing his ignorance, cheats him with a dose of vicious dissipation, artfully labelled with the name of liberty. The most of us used to drink it down, and the result was just what might be supposed: many of us were led to think that there was little to choose between liberty and slavery. We felt, and very properly too, that we had almost as well be slaves to man as to rum. So, when the holidays ended, we staggered up from the filth of our wallowing, took a long breath, and marched to the field,—feeling, upon the whole, rather glad to go, from what our master had deceived us into a belief was freedom, back to the arms of slavery.

I have said that this mode of treatment is a part of the whole system of fraud and inhumanity of slavery. It is so. The mode here adopted to disgust the slave with freedom, by allowing him to see only the abuse of it, is carried out in other things. For instance, a slave loves molasses; he steals some. His master, in many cases, goes off to town, and buys a large quantity; he returns, takes his whip, and commands the slave to eat the molasses, until the poor fellow is made sick at the very mention of it. The same mode is sometimes adopted to make the slaves re-frain from asking for more food than their regular allowance. A slave runs through his allowance, and applies for more. His master is enraged at him; but, not willing to send him off without food, gives him more than is necessary, and compels him to eat it within a given time. Then, if he complains that he cannot eat it, he is said to be satisfied neither full nor fasting, and is whipped for being hard to please! I have an abundance of such illustrations of the same principle, drawn from my own observation, but think the cases I have cited sufficient. The practice is a very common one.

On the first of January, 1834, I left Mr. Covey, and went to live with Mr. William Freeland, who lived about three miles from St. Michael's. I soon found Mr. Freeland a very different man from Mr. Covey. Though not rich, he was what would be called an educated southern gentleman. Mr. Covey, as I have shown, was a well-trained negro-breaker and slave-driver. The former (slaveholder though he was) seemed to possess some regard for honor, some reverence for justice, and some respect for humanity. The latter seemed totally insensible to all such sentiments. Mr. Freeland had many of the faults peculiar to slave-holders, such as being very passionate and fretful; but I must do him the justice to say, that he was exceedingly free from those degrading vices to which Mr. Covey was constantly addicted. The one was open and frank, and we always knew where to find him. The other was a most artful deceiver, and could be understood only by such as were skilful enough to detect his cunningly-devised frauds. Another advantage I gained in my new master was, he made no pretensions to, or profession of, religion; and this, in my opinion, was truly a great advantage. I assert most unhesitatingly, that the religion of the south is a mere covering for the most horrid crimes,—a justifier of the most appalling barbarity,—a sanctifier of the most hateful frauds,—and a dark shelter under, which the darkest, foulest, grossest, and most infernal deeds of slaveholders find the strongest protection. Were I to be again reduced to the chains of slavery, next to that enslavement, I should regard being the slave of a religious master the greatest calamity that could befall me. (For of all slaveholders with whom I have ever met, religious slaveholders are the worst. I have ever found them the meanest and basest, the most cruel and cowardly, of all others.) It was my unhappy lot not only to belong to a religious slaveholder, but to live in a community of such religionists. Very near Mr. Freeland lived the Rev. Daniel Weeden, and in the same neighborhood lived the Rev. Rigby Hopkins. These were members and ministers in the Reformed Methodist Church. Mr. Weeden owned, among others, a woman slave, whose name I have forgotten. This woman's back, for weeks, was kept literally raw, made so by the lash of this merciless, *religious* wretch. He used to hire hands. His maxim was, Behave well or behave ill, it is the duty of a master occasionally to whip a slave, to remind him of his master's authority. Such was his theory, and such his practice.

Mr. Hopkins was even worse than Mr. Weeden. His chief boast was his ability to manage slaves. The peculiar feature of his government was that of whipping slaves in advance of deserving it. He always managed to have one or more of his slaves to whip every Monday morning. He did this to alarm their fears, and strike terror into those who escaped. His plan was to whip for the smallest offences, to prevent the commission of large ones. Mr. Hopkins could always find some excuse for whipping a slave. It would astonish one, unaccustomed to a slaveholding life, to see with what wonderful ease a slaveholder can find things, of which to make occasion to whip a slave. A mere look, word, or motion,—a mistake, accident, or want of power,—are all matters for which a slave may be whipped at any time. Does a slave look dissatisfied? It is said, he has the devil in him, and it must be whipped out. Does he speak loudly when spoken to by his master? Then he is getting high-minded, and should be taken down a button-hole lower. Does he forget to pull off his hat at the approach of a white person? Then he is wanting in reverence, and should be whipped for it. Does he ever venture to vindicate his conduct, when censured for it? Then he is guilty of impudence,—one of the greatest crimes of which a slave can be guilty. Does he ever venture to suggest a different mode of doing things from that pointed out by his master? He is indeed presumptuous, and getting above himself; and nothing less than a flogging will do for him. Does he, while ploughing, break a plough,—or, while hoeing, break a hoe? It is owing to his carelessness, and for it a slave must always be whipped. Mr. Hopkins could always find something of this sort to justify the use of the lash, and he seldom failed to embrace such opportunities. There was not a man in the whole county, with whom the slaves who had the getting their own home, would not prefer to live, rather than with this Rev. Mr. Hopkins. And yet there was not a man any where round, who made higher professions of religion, or was more active in revivals,—more attentive to the class, love-feast, prayer and preaching meetings, or more devotional in his family,—that prayed earlier, later, louder, and longer,—than this same reverend slave-driver, Rigby Hopkins.

But to return to Mr. Freeland, and to my experience while in his employment. He, like Mr. Covey, gave us enough to eat; but, unlike Mr. Covey, he also gave us sufficient time to take our meals. He worked us hard, but always between sunrise and sunset. He required a good deal of work to be done, but gave us good tools with which to work. His farm was large, but he employed hands enough to work it, and with ease, compared with many of his neighbors. My treatment, while in his employment, was heavenly, compared with what I experienced at the hands of Mr. Edward Covey.

Mr. Freeland was himself the owner of but two slaves. Their names were Henry Harris and John Harris. The rest of his hands he hired. These consisted of myself, Sandy Jenkins,[32] and Handy Caldwell. Henry and John were quite intelligent, and in a very little while after I went there, I succeeded in creating in them a strong desire to learn how to read. This desire soon sprang up in the others also. They very soon mustered up some old spelling-books, and nothing would do but that I must keep a Sabbath school. I agreed to do so, and accordingly devoted my Sundays to teaching these my loved fellow-slaves how to read. Neither of them knew his letters when I went there. Some of the slaves of the neighboring farms found what was going on, and also availed themselves of this little opportunity to learn to read. It was understood, among all who came, that there must be as little display about it as possible. It was necessary to keep our religious masters at St. Michael's unacquainted with the fact, that, instead of spending the Sabbath in wrestling, boxing, and drinking whisky, we were trying to learn how to read the will of God; for they had much rather see us engaged in those degrading sports, than to see us behaving like intellectual, moral, and accountable beings. My blood boils as I think of the bloody manner in which Messrs. Wright Fairbanks and

---

[32] Douglass's note: "This is the same man who gave me the roots to prevent my being whipped by Mr. Covey. He was 'a clever soul.' We used frequently to talk about the fight with Covey, and as often as we did so, he would claim my success as the result of the roots which he gave me. This superstition is very common among the more ignorant slaves. A slave seldom dies but that his death is attributed to trickery."

Garrison West, both class-leaders, in connection with many others, rushed in upon us with sticks and stones, and broke up our virtuous little Sabbath school, at St. Michael's—all calling themselves Christians! humble followers of the Lord Jesus Christ! But I am again disgressing.

I held my Sabbath school at the house of a free colored man, whose name I deem it imprudent to mention; for should it be known, it might embarrass him greatly, though the crime of holding the school was committed ten years ago. I had at one time over forty scholars, and those of the right sort, ardently desiring to learn. They were of all ages, though mostly men and women. I look back to those Sundays with an amount of pleasure not to be expressed. They were great days to my soul. The work of instructing my dear fellow-slaves was the sweetest engagement with which I was ever blessed. We loved each other, and to leave them at the close of the Sabbath was a severe cross indeed. When I think that these precious souls are to-day shut up in the prison-house of slavery, my feelings overcome me, and I am almost ready to ask, "Does a righteous God govern the universe? and for what does he hold the thunders in his right hand, if not to smite the oppressor, and deliver the spoiled out of the hand of the spoiler?" These dear souls came not to Sabbath school because it was popular to do so, nor did I teach them because it was reputable to be thus engaged. Every moment they spent in that school, they were liable to be taken up, and given thirty-nine lashes. They came because they wished to learn. Their minds had been starved by their cruel masters. They had been shut up in mental darkness. I taught them, because it was the delight of my soul to be doing something that looked like bettering the condition of my race. I kept up my school nearly the whole year I lived with Mr. Freeland; and, beside my Sabbath school, I devoted three evenings in the week, during the winter, to teaching the slaves at home. And I have the happiness to know, that several of those who came to Sabbath school learned how to read; and that one, at least, is now free through my agency.

The year passed off smoothly. It seemed only about half as long as the year which preceded it. I went through it without receiving a single blow. I will give Mr. Freeland the credit of being the best master I ever had, *till I became my own master*. For the ease with which I passed the year, I was, however, somewhat indebted to the society of my fellow-slaves. They were noble souls; they not only possessed loving hearts, but brave ones. We were linked and interlinked with each other. I loved them with a love stronger than any thing I have experienced since. It is sometimes said that we slaves do not love and confide in each other. In answer to this assertion, I can say, I never loved any or confided in any people more than my fellow-slaves, and especially those with whom I lived at Mr. Freeland's. I believe we would have died for each other. We never undertook to do any thing, of any importance, without a mutual consultation. We never moved separately. We were one; and as much so by our tempers and dispositions, as by the mutual hardships to which we were necessarily subjected by our condition as slaves.

At the close of the year 1834, Mr. Freeland again hired me of my master, for the year 1835. But, by this time, I began to want to live *upon free land* as well as *with Freeland;* and I was no longer content, therefore, to live with him or any other slaveholder. I began, with the commencement of the year, to prepare myself for a final struggle, which should decide my fate one way or the other. My tendency was upward. I was fast approaching manhood, and year after year had passed, and I was still a slave. These thoughts roused me—I must do something. I therefore resolved that 1835 should not pass without witnessing an attempt, on my part, to secure my liberty. But I was not willing to cherish this determination alone. My fellow-slaves were dear to me. I was anxious to have them participate with me in this, my life-giving determination. I therefore, though with great prudence, commenced early to ascertain their views and feelings in regard to their condition, and to imbue their minds with thoughts of freedom. I bent myself to devising ways and means for our escape, and meanwhile strove, on all fitting occasions, to impress them with the gross fraud and inhumanity of slavery. I went first to Henry, next to John, then to the others. I found, in them all, warm hearts and noble spirits. They were ready to hear, and ready to act when a feasible plan should be proposed. This was what I wanted. I talked to them of our want of manhood, if we submitted to our enslavement without at least one noble effort to be free. We met often, and consulted frequently, and told our hopes and fears, recounted the difficulties, real and imagined, which we should be called on to meet. At times we were almost disposed to give up, and try to content ourselves with our wretched lot; at others, we were firm and unbending in our determination to go. Whenever we suggested any plan, there was shrinking—the odds were fearful. Our path was beset with the greatest obstacles; and if we succeeded in gaining the end of it, our right to be free was yet questionable—we were yet liable to be returned to bondage. We could see no spot, this side of the ocean, where we could be free. We knew nothing about Canada. Our knowledge of the north did not extend farther than New York; and to go there, and be forever harassed with the frightful liability of being returned to slavery—with the certainty of being treated tenfold worse than before—the thought was truly a horrible one, and one which it was not easy to overcome. The case sometimes stood thus: At every gate through which we were to pass, we saw a watchman—at every ferry a guard—on every bridge a sentinel—and in every wood a patrol. We were hemmed in upon every side. Here were the difficulties, real or imagined—the good to be sought, and the evil to be shunned. On the one hand, there stood slavery, a stern reality, glaring frightfully upon us,—its robes already crimsoned with the blood of millions, and even now feasting itself greedily upon our own flesh. On the other hand, away back in the dim distance, under the flickering light of the north star, behind some craggy hill or snow-covered mountain, stood a doubtful freedom—half frozen—beckoning us to come and share its hospitality. This in itself was sometimes enough to stagger us; but when we permitted ourselves to survey the road, we were frequently appalled. Upon either side we saw grim death, assuming the most horrid shapes. Now it was starvation, causing us to eat our own flesh;—now we were contending with the waves, and were drowned;—now we were overtaken, and torn to pieces by the fangs of the terrible bloodhound. We were stung by scorpions, chased by wild beasts, bitten by snakes, and finally, after having nearly reached the desired spot,—after swimming rivers, encountering wild beasts, sleeping in the woods, suffering hunger and nakedness,—we were overtaken by our pursuers, and, in our resistance, we were shot dead upon the spot! I say, this picture sometimes appalled us, and made us

> "rather bear those ills we had,
> Than fly to others, that we knew not of."[33]

---

[33] Shakespeare's *Hamlet* (III.i.81–82).

In coming to a fixed determination to run away, we did more than Patrick Henry, when he resolved upon liberty or death. With us it was a doubtful liberty at most, and almost certain death if we failed. For my part, I should prefer death to hopeless bondage.

Sandy, one of our number, gave up the notion, but still encouraged us. Our company then consisted of Henry Harris, John Harris, Henry Bailey, Charles Roberts, and myself. Henry Bailey was my uncle, and belonged to my master. Charles married my aunt: he belonged to my master's father-in-law, Mr. William Hamilton.

The plan we finally concluded upon was, to get a large canoe belonging to Mr. Hamilton, and upon the Saturday night previous to Easter holidays, paddle directly up the Chesapeake Bay. On our arrival at the head of the bay, a distance of seventy or eighty miles from where we lived, it was our purpose to turn our canoe adrift, and follow the guidance of the north star till we got beyond the limits of Maryland. Our reason for taking the water route was, that we were less liable to be suspected as runaways; we hoped to be regarded as fishermen; whereas, if we should take the land route, we should be subjected to interruptions of almost every kind. Any one having a white face, and being so disposed, could stop us, and subject us to examination.

The week before our intended start, I wrote several protections, one for each of us. As well as I can remember, they were in the following words, to wit:—

"This is to certify that I, the undersigned, have given the bearer, my servant, full liberty to go to Baltimore, and spend the Easter holidays. Written with mine own hand, etc., 1835.
"WILLIAM HAMILTON,
"Near St. Michael's, in Talbot county, Maryland."

We were not going to Baltimore; but, in going up the bay, we went toward Baltimore, and these protections were only intended to protect us while on the bay.

As the time drew near for our departure, our anxiety became more and more intense. It was truly a matter of life and death with us. The strength of our determination was about to be fully tested. At this time, I was very active in explaining every difficulty, removing every doubt, dispelling every fear, and inspiring all with the firmness indispensable to success in our undertaking; assuring them that half was gained the instant we made the move; we had talked long enough; we were now ready to move; if not now, we never should be; and if we did not intend to move now, we had as well fold our arms, sit down, and acknowledge ourselves fit only to be slaves. This, none of us were prepared to acknowledge. Every man stood firm; and at our last meeting, we pledged ourselves afresh, in the most solemn manner, that, at the time appointed, we would certainly start in pursuit of freedom. This was in the middle of the week, at the end of which we were to be off. We went, as usual, to our several fields of labor, but with bosoms highly agitated with thoughts of our truly hazardous undertaking. We tried to conceal our feelings as much as possible; and I think we succeeded very well.

After a painful waiting, the Saturday morning, whose night was to witness our departure, came. I hailed it with joy, bring what of sadness it might. Friday night was a sleepless one for me. I probably felt more anxious than the rest, because I was, by common consent, at the head of the whole affair. The responsibility of success or failure lay heavily upon me. The glory of the one, and the confusion of the other, were alike mine. The first two hours of that morning were such as I never experienced before, and hope never to again. Early in the morning, we went, as usual, to the field. We were spreading manure; and all at once, while thus engaged, I was overwhelmed with an indescribable feeling, in the fulness of which I turned to Sandy, who was near by, and said, "We are betrayed!" "Well," said he, "that thought has this moment struck me." We said no more. I was never more certain of any thing.

The horn was blown as usual, and we went up from the field to the house for breakfast. I went for the form, more than for want of any thing to eat that morning. Just as I got to the house, in looking out at the lane gate, I saw four white men, with two colored men. The white men were on horseback, and the colored ones were walking behind, as if tied. I watched them a few moments till they got up to our lane gate. Here they halted, and tied the colored men to the gate-post. I was not yet certain as to what the matter was. In a few moments, in rode Mr. Hamilton, with a speed betokening great excitement. He came to the door, and inquired if Master William was in. He was told he was at the barn. Mr. Hamilton, without dismounting, rode up to the barn with extraordinary speed. In a few moments, he and Mr. Freeland returned to the house. By this time, the three constables rode up, and in great haste dismounted, tied their horses, and met Master William and Mr. Hamilton returning from the barn; and after talking awhile, they all walked up to the kitchen door. There was no one in the kitchen but myself and John. Henry and Sandy were up at the barn. Mr. Freeland put his head in at the door, and called me by name, saying there were some gentlemen at the door who wished to see me. I stepped to the door, and inquired what they wanted. They at once seized me, and, without giving me any satisfaction, tied me—lashing my hands closely together. I insisted upon knowing what the matter was. They at length said, that they had learned I had been in a "scrape," and that I was to be examined before my master; and if their information proved false, I should not be hurt.

In a few moments, they succeeded in tying John. They then turned to Henry, who had by this time returned, and commanded him to cross his hands. "I won't!" said Henry, in a firm tone, indicating his readiness to meet the consequences of his refusal. "Won't you?" said Tom Graham, the constable. "No, I won't!" said Henry, in a still stronger tone. With this, two of the constables pulled out their shining pistols, and swore, by their Creator, that they would make him cross his hands or kill him. Each cocked his pistol, and, with fingers on the trigger, walked up to Henry, saying, at the same time, if he did not cross his hands, they would blow his damned heart out. "Shoot me, shoot me!" said Henry; "you can't kill me but once. Shoot, shoot,—and be damned! *I won't be tied!*" This he said in a tone of loud defiance; and at the same time, with a motion as quick as lightning, he with one single stroke dashed the pistols from the hand of each constable. As he did this, all hands fell upon him, and, after beating him some time, they finally overpowered him, and got him tied.

During the scuffle, I managed, I know not how, to get my pass out, and, without being discovered, put it into the fire. We were all now tied; and just as we were to leave for Easton jail, Betsy Freeland, mother of William Freeland, came to the door with her hands full of biscuits, and divided them between Henry and John. She then delivered herself of a speech, to the following effect:—addressing herself to me, she said, "*You devil! You yellow devil!* it was you that put it into the heads of Henry and John to run away. But for you, you long-legged mulatto devil! Henry nor John would never have thought of such a thing." I made no reply, and was immediately hurried off towards St. Michael's. Just a moment previous to the scuffle with Henry, Mr. Hamilton suggested the propriety of making a search for the protections which he had understood Frederick had written for himself and the rest. But, just at the moment he was about carrying his proposal into effect, his aid was needed in helping to tie Henry; and the excitement attending the scuffle caused them either to forget, or to deem it unsafe, under the circumstances, to search. So we were not yet convicted of the intention to run away.

When we got about half way to St. Michael's, while the constables having us in charge were looking ahead, Henry inquired of me what he should do with his pass. I told him to eat it with his biscuit, and own nothing; and we passed the word around, "*Own nothing;*" and "*Own nothing!*" said we all. Our confidence in each other was unshaken. We were resolved to succeed or fail together, after the calamity had befallen us as much as before. We were now prepared for any thing. We were to be dragged that morning fifteen miles behind horses, and then to be placed in the Easton jail. When we reached St. Michael's, we underwent a sort of examination. We all denied that we ever intended to run away. We did this more to bring out the evidence against us, than from any hope of getting clear of being sold; for, as I have said, we were ready for that. The fact was, we cared but little where we went, so we went together. Our greatest concern was about separation. We dreaded that more than any thing this side of death. We found the evidence against us to be the testimony of one person; our master would not tell who it was; but we came to a unanimous decision among ourselves as to who their informant was. We were sent off to the jail at Easton. When we got there, we were delivered up to the sheriff, Mr. Joseph Graham, and by him placed in jail. Henry, John, and myself, were placed in one room together—Charles, and Henry Bailey, in another. Their object in separating us was to hinder concert.

We had been in jail scarcely twenty minutes, when a swarm of slave traders, and agents for slave traders, flocked into jail to look at us, and to ascertain if we were for sale. Such a set of beings I never saw before! I felt myself surrounded by so many fiends from perdition. A band of pirates never looked more like their father, the devil. They laughed and grinned over us, saying, "Ah, my boys! we have got you, haven't we?" And after taunting us in various ways, they one by one went into an examination of us, with intent to ascertain our value. They would impudently ask us if we would not like to have them for our masters. We would make them no answer, and leave them to find out as best they could. Then they would curse and swear at us, telling us that they could take the devil out of us in a very little while, if we were only in their hands.

While in jail, we found ourselves in much more comfortable quarters than we expected when we went there. We did not get much to eat, nor that which was very good; but we had a good clean room, from the windows of which we could see what was going on in the street, which was very much better than though we had been placed in one of the dark, damp cells. Upon the whole, we got along very well, so far as the jail and its keeper were concerned. Immediately after the holidays were over, contrary to all our expectations, Mr. Hamilton and Mr. Freeland came up to Easton, and took Charles, the two Henrys, and John, out of jail, and carried them home, leaving me alone. I regarded this separation as a final one. It caused me more pain than any thing else in the whole transaction. I was ready for any thing rather than separation. I supposed that they had consulted together, and had decided that, as I was the whole cause of the intention of the others to run away, it was hard to make the innocent suffer with the guilty; and that they had, therefore, concluded to take the others home, and sell me, as a warning to the others that remained. It is due to the noble Henry to say, he seemed almost as reluctant at leaving the prison as at leaving home to come to the prison. But we knew we should, in all probability, be separated, if we were sold; and since he was in their hands, he concluded to go peaceably home.

I was now left to my fate. I was all alone, and within the walls of a stone prison. But a few days before, and I was full of hope. I expected to have been safe in a land of freedom; but now I was covered with gloom, sunk down to the utmost despair. I thought the possibility of freedom was gone. I was kept in this way about one week, at the end of which, Captain Auld, my master, to my surprise and utter astonishment, came up, and took me out, with the intention of sending me, with a gentleman of his acquaintance, into Alabama. But, from some cause or other, he did not send me to Alabama, but concluded to send me back to Baltimore, to live again with his brother Hugh, and to learn a trade.

Thus, after an absence of three years and one month, I was once more permitted to return to my old home at Baltimore. My master sent me away, because there existed against me a very great prejudice in the community, and he feared I might be killed.

In a few weeks after I went to Baltimore, Master Hugh hired me to Mr. William Gardner, an extensive ship-builder, on Fell's Point. I was put there to learn how to calk. It, however, proved a very unfavorable place for the accomplishment of this object. Mr. Gardner was engaged that spring in building two large man-of-war brigs, professedly for the Mexican government. The vessels were to be launched in the July of that year, and in failure thereof, Mr. Gardner was to lose a considerable sum; so that when I entered, all was hurry. There was no time to learn any thing. Every man had to do that which he knew how to do. In entering the ship-yard, my orders from Mr. Gardner were, to do whatever the carpenters commanded me to do. This was placing me at the beck and call of about seventy-five men. I was to regard all these as masters. Their word was to be my law. My situation was a most trying one. At times I needed a dozen pair of hands. I was called a dozen ways in the space of a single minute. Three or four voices would strike my ear at the same moment. It was—"Fred., come help me to cant this timber here."—"Fred., come carry this timber yonder."—"Fred., bring that roller here."—"Fred., go get a fresh can of water."—"Fred., come help saw off the end of this timber."—"Fred., go quick, and get the crowbar."—"Fred., hold on the end of this fall."[34]—"Fred., go to the blacksmith's shop, and get a new punch."—"Hurra, Fred.! run and bring me a cold chisel."—"I say, Fred., bear a hand, and get up a fire as quick as lightning under that steam-box."—"Halloo, nigger! come, turn this grindstone."—"Come, come! move, move! and *bowse*[35] this timber forward."—"I say, darky, blast your eyes, why don't you heat up some pitch?"—"Halloo! halloo! halloo!" (Three voices at the same time.) "Come here!—Go there!——Hold on where you are! Damn you, if you move, I'll knock your brains out!"

This was my school for eight months; and I might have remained there longer, but for a most horrid fight I had with four of the white apprentices, in which my left eye was nearly knocked out, and I was horribly mangled in other respects.

---

[34] The end of a rope or tackle.   [35] Haul.

The facts in the case were these: Until a very little while after I went there, white and black ship-carpenters worked side by side, and no one seemed to see any impropriety in it. All hands seemed to be very well satisfied. Many of the black carpenters were freemen. Things seemed to be going on very well. All at once, the white carpenters knocked off, and said they would not work with free-colored workmen. Their reason for this, as alleged, was, that if free colored carpenters were encouraged, they would soon take the trade into their own hands, and poor white men would be thrown out of employment. They therefore felt called upon at once to put a stop to it. And, taking advantage of Mr. Gardner's necessities, they broke off, swearing they would work no longer, unless he would discharge his black carpenters. Now, though this did not extend to me in form, it did reach me in fact. My fellow-apprentices very soon began to feel it degrading to them to work with me. They began to put on airs, and talk about the "niggers" taking the country, saying we all ought to be killed; and, being encouraged by the journeymen, they commenced making my condition as hard as they could, by hectoring me around, and sometimes striking me. I, of course, kept the vow I made after the fight with Mr. Covey, and struck back again, regardless of consequences; and while I kept them from combining, I succeeded very well; for I could whip the whole of them, taking them separately. They, however, at length combined, and came upon me, armed with sticks, stones, and heavy handspikes. One came in front with a half brick. There was one at each side of me, and one behind me. While I was attending to those in front, and on either side, the one behind ran up with the handspike, and struck me a heavy blow upon the head. It stunned me. I fell, and with this they all ran upon me, and fell to beating me with their fists. I let them lay on for a while, gathering strength. In an instant, I gave a sudden surge, and rose to my hands and knees. Just as I did that, one of the number gave me, with his heavy boot, a powerful kick in the left eye. My eyeball seemed to have burst. When they saw my eye closed, and badly swollen, they left me. With this I seized the handspike, and for a time pursued them. But here the carpenters interfered, and I thought I might as well give it up. It was impossible to stand my hand against so many. All this took place in sight of not less than fifty white ship-carpenters, and not one interposed a friendly word; but some cried, "Kill the damned nigger! Kill him! kill him! He struck a white person." I found my only chance for life was in flight. I succeeded in getting away without an additional blow, and barely so; for to strike a white man is death by Lynch law,[36]—and that was the law in Mr. Gardner's ship-yard; nor is there much of any other out of Mr. Gardner's ship-yard.

I went directly home, and told the story of my wrongs to Master Hugh; and I am happy to say of him, irreligious as he was, his conduct was heavenly, compared with that of his brother Thomas under similar circumstances. He listened attentively to my narration of the circumstances leading to the savage outrage, and gave many proofs of his strong indignation at it. The heart of my once overkind mistress was again melted into pity. My puffed-out eye and blood-covered face moved her to tears. She took a chair by me, washed the blood from my face, and, with a mother's tenderness, bound up my head, covering the wounded eye with a lean piece of fresh beef. It was almost compensation for my suffering to witness,

---

[36] To be lynched without benefit of legal procedures. Originally, the term was "Lynch's law," probably after justice of the peace Charles Lynch (1736–1796), who used unconventional methods of trial and punishment.

once more, a manifestation of kindness from this, my once affectionate old mistress. Master Hugh was very much enraged. He gave expression to his feelings by pouring out curses upon the heads of those who did the deed. As soon as I got a little the better of my bruises, he took me with him to Esquire Watson's, on Bond Street, to see what could be done about the matter. Mr. Watson inquired who saw the assault committed. Master Hugh told him it was done in Mr. Gardner's ship-yard, at mid-day, where there were a large company of men at work. "As to that," he said, "the deed was done, and there was no question as to who did it." His answer was, he could do nothing in the case, unless some white man would come forward and testify. He could issue no warrant on my word. If I had been killed in the presence of a thousand colored people, their testimony combined would have been insufficient to have arrested one of the murderers. Master Hugh, for once, was compelled to say this state of things was too bad. Of course, it was impossible to get any white man to volunteer his testimony in my behalf, and against the white young men. Even those who may have sympathized with me were not prepared to do this. It required a degree of courage unknown to them to do so; for just at that time, the slightest manifestation of humanity toward a colored person was denounced as abolitionism, and that name subjected its bearer to frightful liabilities. The watchwords of the bloody-minded in that region, and in those days, were, "Damn the abolitionists!" and "Damn the niggers!" There was nothing done, and probably nothing would have been done if I had been killed. Such was, and such remains, the state of things in the Christian city of Baltimore.

Master Hugh, finding he could get no redress, refused to let me go back again to Mr. Gardner. He kept me himself, and his wife dressed my wound till I was again restored to health. He then took me into the ship-yard of which he was foreman, in the employment of Mr. Walter Price. There I was immediately set to calking, and very soon learned the art of using my mallet and irons. In the course of one year from the time I left Mr. Gardner's, I was able to command the highest wages given to the most experienced calkers. I was now of some importance to my master. I was bringing him from six to seven dollars per week. I sometimes brought him nine dollars per week: my wages were a dollar and a half a day. After learning how to calk, I sought my own employment, made my own contracts, and collected the money which I earned. My pathway became much more smooth than before; my condition was now much more comfortable. When I could get no calking to do, I did nothing. During these leisure times, those old notions about freedom would steal over me again. When in Mr. Gardner's employment, I was kept in such a perpetual whirl of excitement, I could think of nothing, scarcely, but my life; and in thinking of my life, I almost forgot my liberty. I have observed this in my experience of slavery,—that whenever my condition was improved, instead of its increasing my contentment, it only increased my desire to be free, and set me to thinking of plans to gain my freedom. I have found that, to make a contented slave, it is necessary to make a thoughtless one. It is necessary to darken his moral and mental vision, and, as far as possible, to annihilate the power of reason. He must be able to detect no inconsistencies in slavery; he must be made to feel that slavery is right; and he can be brought to that only when he ceases to be a man.

I was now getting, as I have said, one dollar and fifty cents per day. I contracted for it; I earned it; it was paid to me; it was rightfully my own; yet, upon each returning Saturday night, I was compelled to deliver every cent of that money to Master Hugh. And why? Not because he earned it,—not because he had any hand in earning it,—not because I owed it to him,—nor because he possessed the slightest shadow of a right to it; but solely because he had the power to compel me to give it up. The right of the grim-visaged pirate upon the high seas is exactly the same.

CHAPTER XI

I now come to that part of my life during which I planned, and finally succeeded in making, my escape from slavery. But before narrating any of the peculiar circumstances, I deem it proper to make known my intention not to state all the facts connected with the transaction. My reasons for pursuing this course may be understood from the following: First, were I to give a minute statement of all the facts, it is not only possible, but quite probable, that others would thereby be involved in the most embarrassing difficulties. Secondly, such a statement would most undoubtedly induce greater vigilance on the part of slaveholders than has existed heretofore among them; which would, of course, be the means of guarding a door whereby some dear brother bondman might escape his galling chains. I deeply regret the necessity that impels me to suppress any thing of importance connected with my experience in slavery. It would afford me great pleasure indeed, as well as materially add to the interest of my narrative, were I at liberty to gratify a curiosity, which I know exists in the minds of many, by an accurate statement of all the facts pertaining to my most fortunate escape. But I must deprive myself of this pleasure, and the curious of the gratification which such a statement would afford. I would allow myself to suffer under the greatest imputations which evil-minded men might suggest, rather than exculpate myself, and thereby run the hazard of closing the slightest avenue by which a brother slave might clear himself of the chains and fetters of slavery.

I have never approved of the very public manner in which some of our western friends have conducted what they call the *underground railroad*,[37] but which, I think, by their open declarations, has been made most emphatically the *upperground railroad*. I honor those good men and women for their noble daring, and applaud them for willingly subjecting themselves to bloody persecution, by openly avowing their participation in the escape of slaves. I, however, can see very little good resulting from such a course, either to themselves or the slaves escaping; while, upon the other hand, I see and feel assured that those open declarations are a positive evil to the slaves remaining, who are seeking to escape. They do nothing towards enlightening the slave, whilst they do much towards enlightening the master. They stimulate him to greater watchfulness, and enhance his power to capture his slave. We owe something to the slaves south of the line as well as to those north of it; and in aiding the latter on their way to freedom, we should be careful to do nothing which would be likely to hinder the former from escaping from slavery. I would keep the merciless slaveholder profoundly ignorant of the means of flight adopted by the slave. I would leave him to imagine himself surrounded by myriads of invisible tormentors, ever ready to snatch from his infernal grasp his trembling prey. Let him be left to feel his way in the dark; let darkness commensurate with his crime hover over him; and let him feel that at

---

[37] The method by which many slaves traveled to freedom: moving northward from designated house to designated house and from friend to friend, supposedly in great secrecy. Douglass has some understandable reservations about advertising the procedure.

every step he takes, in pursuit of the flying bondman, he is running the frightful risk of having his hot brains dashed out by an invisible agency. Let us render the tyrant no aid; let us not hold the light by which he can trace the footprints of our flying brother. But enough of this. I will now proceed to the statement of those facts, connected with my escape, for which I am alone responsible, and for which no one can be made to suffer but myself.

In the early part of the year 1838, I became quite restless. I could see no reason why I should, at the end of each week, pour the reward of my toil into the purse of my master. When I carried to him my weekly wages, he would, after counting the money, look me in the face with a robber-like fierceness, and ask, "Is this all?" He was satisfied with nothing less than the last cent. He would, however, when I made him six dollars, sometimes give me six cents, to encourage me. It had the opposite effect. I regarded it as a sort of admission of my right to the whole. The fact that he gave me any part of my wages was proof, to my mind, that he believed me entitled to the whole of them. I always felt worse for having received any thing; for I feared that the giving me a few cents would ease his conscience, and make him feel himself to be a pretty honorable sort of robber. My discontent grew upon me. I was ever on the look-out for means of escape; and, finding no direct means, I determined to try to hire my time, with a view of getting money with which to make my escape. In the spring of 1838, when Master Thomas came to Baltimore to purchase his spring goods, I got an opportunity, and applied to him to allow me to hire my time. He unhesitatingly refused my request, and told me this was another stratagem by which to escape. He told me I could go nowhere but that he could get me; and that, in the event of my running away, he should spare no pains in his efforts to catch me. He exhorted me to content myself, and be obedient. He told me, if I would be happy, I must lay out no plans for the future. He said, if I behaved myself properly, he would take care of me. Indeed, he advised me to complete thoughtlessness of the future, and taught me to depend solely upon him for happiness. He seemed to see fully the pressing necessity of setting aside my intellectual nature, in order to contentment in slavery. But in spite of him, and even in spite of myself, I continued to think, and to think about the injustice of my enslavement, and the means of escape.

About two months after this, I applied to Master Hugh for the privilege of hiring my time. He was not acquainted with the fact that I had applied to Master Thomas, and had been refused. He too, at first, seemed disposed to refuse; but, after some reflection, he granted me the privilege, and proposed the following terms: I was to be allowed all my time, make all contracts with those for whom I worked, and find my own employment; and, in return for this liberty, I was to pay him three dollars at the end of each week; find myself in calking tools, and in board and clothing. My board was two dollars and a half per week. This, with the wear and tear of clothing and calking tools, made my regular expenses about six dollars per week. This amount I was compelled to make up, or relinquish the privilege of hiring my time. Rain or shine, work or no work, at the end of each week the money must be forthcoming, or I must give up my privilege. This arrangement, it will be perceived, was decidedly in my master's favor. It relieved him of all need of looking after me. His money was sure. He received all the benefits of slaveholding without its evils; while I endured all the evils of a slave, and suffered all the care and anxiety of a freeman. I found it a hard bargain. But, hard as it was, I thought it better than the old mode of getting along. It was a step towards freedom to be allowed to bear the responsibilities of a freeman, and I was determined to hold on upon it. I bent myself to the work of making money. I was ready to work at night as well as day, and by the most untiring perseverance and industry, I made enough to meet my expenses, and lay up a little money every week. I went on thus from May till August. Master Hugh then refused to allow me to hire my time longer. The ground for his refusal was a failure on my part, one Saturday night, to pay him for my week's time. This failure was occasioned by my attending a camp meeting about ten miles from Baltimore. During the week, I had entered into an engagement with a number of young friends to start from Baltimore to the camp ground early Saturday evening; and being detained by my employer, I was unable to get down to Master Hugh's without disappointing the company. I knew that Master Hugh was in no special need of the money that night. I therefore decided to go to camp meeting, and upon my return pay him the three dollars. I staid at the camp meeting one day longer than I intended when I left. But as soon as I returned, I called upon him to pay what he considered his due. I found him very angry; he could scarce restrain his wrath. He said he had a great mind to give me a severe whipping. He wished to know how I dared go out of the city without asking his permission. I told him I hired my time, and while I paid him the price which he asked for it, I did not know that I was bound to ask him when and where I should go. This reply troubled him; and, after reflecting a few moments, he turned to me, and said I should hire my time no longer; that the next thing he should know of, I would be running away. Upon the same plea, he told me to bring my tools and clothing home forthwith. I did so; but instead of seeking work, as I had been accustomed to do previously to hiring my time, I spent the whole week without the performance of a single stroke of work. I did this in retaliation. Saturday night, he called upon me as usual for my week's wages. I told him I had no wages; I had done no work that week. Here we were upon the point of coming to blows. He raved, and swore his determination to get hold of me. I did not allow myself a single word; but was resolved, if he laid the weight of his hand upon me, it should be blow for blow. He did not strike me, but told me that he would find me in constant employment in future. I thought the matter over during the next day, Sunday, and finally resolved upon the third day of September, as the day upon which I would make a second attempt to secure my freedom. I now had three weeks during which to prepare for my journey. Early on Monday morning, before Master Hugh had time to make any engagement for me, I went out and got employment of Mr. Butler, at his ship-yard near the draw-bridge, upon what is called the City Block, thus making it unnecessary for him to seek employment for me. At the end of the week, I brought him between eight and nine dollars. He seemed very well pleased, and asked me why I did not do the same the week before. He little knew what my plans were. My object in working steadily was to remove any suspicion he might entertain of my intent to run away; and in this I succeeded admirably. I suppose he thought I was never better satisfied with my condition than at the very time during which I was planning my escape. The second week passed, and again I carried him my full wages; and so well pleased was he, that he gave me twenty-five cents, (quite a large sum for a slaveholder to give a slave,) and bade me to make a good use of it. I told him I would.

Things went on without very smoothly indeed, but within there was trouble. It is impossible for me to describe my feelings as the time of my contemplated start drew near. I had a number of warm-hearted friends in Baltimore,—friends that I loved almost as I did my life,—and the thought of being separated from them forever was painful beyond expression. It is my opinion that thousands would escape from slavery, who now remain, but for the strong cords of affection that bind them to their friends. The thought of leaving my friends was decidedly the most painful thought with which I had to contend. The love of them was my tender point, and shook my decision more than all things else. Besides the pain of separation, the dream and apprehension of a failure exceeded what I had experienced at my first attempt. The appalling defeat I then sustained returned to torment me. I felt assured that, if I failed in this attempt, my case would be a hopeless one—it would seal my fate as a slave forever. I could not hope to get off with any thing less than the severest punishment, and being placed beyond the means of escape. It required no very vivid imagination to depict the most frightful scenes through which I should have to pass, in case I failed. The wretchedness of slavery, and the blessedness of freedom, were perpetually before me. It was life and death with me. But I remained firm, and, according to my resolution, on the third day of September, 1838, I left my chains, and succeeded in reaching New York without the slightest interruption of any kind. How I did so,—what means I adopted,—what direction I travelled, and by what mode of conveyance,—I must leave unexplained, for the reasons before mentioned.

I have been frequently asked how I felt when I found myself in a free State. I have never been able to answer the question with any satisfaction to myself. It was a moment of the highest excitement I ever experienced. I suppose I felt as one may imagine the unarmed mariner to feel when he is rescued by a friendly man-of-war from the pursuit of a pirate. In writing to a dear friend, immediately after my arrival at New York, I said I felt like one who had escaped a den of hungry lions. This state of mind, however, very soon subsided; and I was again seized with a feeling of great insecurity and loneliness. I was yet liable to be taken back, and subjected to all the tortures of slavery. This in itself was enough to damp the ardor of my enthusiasm. But the loneliness overcame me. There I was in the midst of thousands, and yet a perfect stranger; without home and without friends, in the midst of thousands of my own brethren—children of a common Father, and yet I dared not to unfold to any one of them my sad condition. I was afraid to speak to any one for fear of speaking to the wrong one, and thereby falling into the hands of money-loving kidnappers, whose business it was to lie in wait for the panting fugitive, as the ferocious beasts of the forest lie in wait for their prey. The motto which I adopted when I started from slavery was this—"Trust no man!" I saw in every white man an enemy, and in almost every colored man cause for distrust. It was a most painful situation; and, to understand it, one must needs experience it, or imagine himself in similar circumstances. Let him be a fugitive slave in a strange land—a land given up to be the hunting-ground for slaveholders—whose inhabitants are legalized kidnappers—where he is every moment subjected to the terrible liability of being seized upon by his fellow-men, as the hideous crocodile seizes upon his prey!—I say, let him place himself in my situation—without home or friends—without money or credit—wanting shelter, and no one to give it—wanting bread, and no money to buy it,—and at the same time let him feel that he is pursued by merciless men-hunters, and in total darkness as to what to do, where to go, or where to stay,—perfectly helpless both as to the means of defence and means of escape,—in the midst of plenty, yet suffering the terrible gnawings of hunger,—in the midst of houses, yet having no home,—among fellow-men, yet feeling as if in the midst of wild beasts, whose greediness to swallow up the trembling and half-famished fugitive is only equalled by that with which the monsters of the deep swallow up the helpless fish upon which they subsist,—I say, let him be placed in this most trying situation,—the situation in which I was placed,—then, and not till then, will he fully appreciate the hardships of, and know how to sympathize with, the toil-worn and whip-scarred fugitive slave.

Thank Heaven, I remained but a short time in this distressed situation. I was relieved from it by the humane hand of Mr. David Ruggles,[38] whose vigilance, kindness, and perseverance, I shall never forget. I am glad of an opportunity to express, as far as words can, the love and gratitude I bear him. Mr. Ruggles is now afflicted with blindness, and is himself in need of the same kind offices which he was once so forward in the performance of toward others. I had been in New York but a few days, when Mr. Ruggles sought me out, and very kindly took me to his boarding-house at the corner of Church and Lespenard Streets. Mr. Ruggles was then very deeply engaged in the memorable *Darg* case, as well as attending to a number of other fugitive slaves, devising ways and means for their successful escape; and, though watched and hemmed in on almost every side, he seemed to be more than a match for his enemies.

Very soon after I went to Mr. Ruggles, he wished to know of me where I wanted to go; as he deemed it unsafe for me to remain in New York. I told him I was a calker, and should like to go where I could get work. I thought of going to Canada; but he decided against it, and in favor of my going to New Bedford, thinking I should be able to get work there at my trade. At this time, Anna,[39] my intended wife, came on; for I wrote to her immediately after my arrival at New York, (notwithstanding my homeless, houseless, and helpless condition,) informing her of my successful flight, and wishing her to come on forthwith. In a few days after her arrival, Mr. Ruggles called in the Rev. J. W. C. Pennington, who, in the presence of Mr. Ruggles, Mrs. Michaels, and two or three others, performed the marriage ceremony, and gave us a certificate, of which the following is an exact copy:—

"THIS may certify, that I joined together in holy matrimony Frederick Johnson[40] and Anna Murray, as man and wife, in the presence of Mr. David Ruggles and Mrs. Michaels.

"JAMES W. C. PENNINGTON.

"New York, Sept. 15, 1838."

Upon receiving this certificate, and a five-dollar bill from Mr. Ruggles, I shouldered one part of our baggage, and Anna took up the other, and we set out forthwith to take passage on board of the steamboat John W. Richmond for Newport, on our way to New Bedford. Mr. Ruggles gave me a letter to a Mr. Shaw in Newport, and told me, in case my money did not serve me to New Bedford, to stop in Newport and obtain further assistance; but upon our arrival at Newport, we were so anxious to get to a place of safety, that, notwithstanding we lacked the

---

[38] Ruggles (1810–1849), an African-American journalist and abolitionist, aided Douglass in his escape from Maryland in 1838, took him into his home, and made arrangements for his wedding before Douglass and his wife went on to New Bedford. Ruggles was also involved in a legal proceeding involving John P. Darg (1771–1852), a slaveowner who was trying to reclaim escaped slaves.

[39] Douglass's note: "She was free."

[40] Douglass's note: "I had changed my name from Frederick *Bailey* to that of *Johnson*."

necessary money to pay our fare, we decided to take seats in the stage, and promise to pay when we got to New Bedford. We were encouraged to do this by two excellent gentlemen, residents of New Bedford, whose names I afterward ascertained to be Joseph Ricketson and William C. Taber. They seemed at once to understand our circumstances, and gave us such assurance of their friendliness as put us fully at ease in their presence. It was good indeed to meet with such friends, at such a time. Upon reaching New Bedford, we were directed to the house of Mr. Nathan Johnson, by whom we were kindly received, and hospitably provided for. Both Mr. and Mrs. Johnson took a deep and lively interest in our welfare. They proved themselves quite worthy of the name of abolitionists. When the stagedriver found us unable to pay our fare, he held on upon our baggage as security for the debt. I had but to mention the fact to Mr. Johnson, and he forthwith advanced the money.

We now began to feel a degree of safety, and to prepare ourselves for the duties and responsibilities of a life of freedom. On the morning after our arrival at New Bedford, while at the breakfast-table, the question arose as to what name I should be called by. The name given me by my mother, was "Frederick Augustus Washington Bailey." I, however, had dispensed with the two middle names long before I left Maryland so that I was generally known by the name of "Frederick Bailey." I started from Baltimore bearing the name of "Stanley." When I got to New York, I again changed my name to "Frederick Johnson," and thought that would be the last change. But when I got to New Bedford, I found it necessary again to change my name. The reason of this necessity was, that there were so many Johnsons in New Bedford, it was already quite difficult to distinguish between them. I gave Mr. Johnson the privilege of choosing me a name, but told him he must not take from me the name of "Frederick." I must hold on to that, to preserve a sense of my identity. Mr. Johnson had just been reading the "Lady of the Lake," and at once suggested that my name be "Douglass."[41] From that time until now I have been called "Frederick Douglass;" and as I am more widely known by that name than by either of the others, I shall continue to use it as my own.

I was quite disappointed at the general appearance of things in New Bedford. The impression which I had received respecting the character and condition of the people of the north, I found to be singularly erroneous. I had very strangely supposed, while in slavery, that few of the comforts, and scarcely any of the luxuries, of life were enjoyed at the north, compared with what were enjoyed by the slaveholders of the south. I probably came to this conclusion from the fact that northern people owned no slaves. I supposed that they were about upon a level with the non-slaveholding population of the south. I knew *they* were exceedingly poor, and I had been accustomed to regard their poverty as the necessary consequence of their being non-slaveholders. I had somehow imbibed the opinion that, in the absence of slaves, there could be no wealth, and very little refinement. And upon coming to the north, I expected to meet with a rough, hard-handed, and uncultivated population, living in the most Spartan-like simplicity, knowing nothing of the ease, luxury, pomp, and grandeur of southern slaveholders. Such being my conjectures, any one acquainted with the appearance of New Bedford may very readily infer how palpably I must have seen my mistake.

---

[41] A central character in the narrative poem *The Lady of the Lake* (1810), by the British poet and novelist Sir Walter Scott (1771–1832).

In the afternoon of the day when I reached New Bedford, I visited the wharves, to take a view of the shipping. Here I found myself surrounded with the strongest proofs of wealth. Lying at the wharves, and riding in the stream, I saw many ships of the finest model, in the best order, and of the largest size. Upon the right and left, I was walled in by granite warehouses of the widest dimensions, stowed to their utmost capacity with the necessaries and comforts of life. Added to this, almost every body seemed to be at work, but noiselessly so, compared with what I had been accustomed to in Baltimore. There were no loud songs heard from those engaged in loading and unloading ships. I heard no deep oaths or horrid curses on the laborer. I saw no whipping of men; but all seemed to go smoothly on. Every man appeared to understand his work, and went at it with a sober, yet cheerful earnestness, which betokened the deep interest which he felt in what he was doing, as well as a sense of his own dignity as a man. To me this looked exceedingly strange. From the wharves I strolled around and over the town, gazing with wonder and admiration at the splendid churches, beautiful dwellings, and finely-cultivated gardens; evincing an amount of wealth, comfort, taste, and refinement, such as I had never seen in any part of slaveholding Maryland.

Every thing looked clean, new, and beautiful. I saw few or no dilapidated houses, with poverty-stricken inmates; no half-naked children and barefooted women, such as I had been accustomed to see in Hillsborough, Easton, St. Michael's, and Baltimore. The people looked more able, stronger, healthier, and happier, than those of Maryland. I was for once made glad by a view of extreme wealth, without being saddened by seeing extreme poverty. But the most astonishing as well as the most interesting thing to me was the condition of the colored people, a great many of whom, like myself, had escaped thither as a refuge from the hunters of men. I found many, who had not been seven years out of their chains, living in finer houses, and evidently enjoying more of the comforts of life, than the average of slaveholders in Maryland. I will venture to assert that my friend Mr. Nathan Johnson (of whom I can say with a grateful heart, "I was hungry, and he gave me meat; I was thirsty, and he gave me drink; I was a stranger, and he took me in"[42]) lived in a neater house; dined at a better table; took, paid for, and read, more newspapers; better understood the moral, religious, and political character of the nation,—than nine tenths of the slaveholders in Talbot county Maryland. Yet Mr. Johnson was a working man. His hands were hardened by toil, and not his alone, but those also of Mrs. Johnson. I found the colored people much more spirited than I had supposed they would be. I found among them a determination to protect each other from the blood-thirsty kidnapper, at all hazards. Soon after my arrival, I was told of a circumstance which illustrated their spirit. A colored man and a fugitive slave were on unfriendly terms. The former was heard to threaten the latter with informing his master of his whereabouts. Straightway a meeting was called among the colored people, under the stereotyped notice, "Business of importance!" The betrayer was invited to attend. The people came at the appointed hour, and organized the meeting by appointing a very religious old gentleman as president, who, I believe, made a prayer, after which he addressed the meeting as follows: *"Friends, we have got him here, and I would recommend that you young men just take him outside the door, and kill him!"* With this, a number of them bolted at him; but they were intercepted by

---

[42] From Matthew 25:35.

some more timid than themselves, and the betrayer escaped their vengeance, and has not been seen in New Bedford since. I believe there have been no more such threats, and should there be hereafter, I doubt not that death would be the consequence.

I found employment, the third day after my arrival, in stowing a sloop with a load of oil. It was new, dirty, and hard work for me; but I went at it with a glad heart and a willing hand. I was now my own master. It was a happy moment, the rapture of which can be understood only by those who have been slaves. It was the first work, the reward of which was to be entirely my own. There was no Master Hugh standing ready, the moment I earned the money, to rob me of it. I worked that day with a pleasure I had never before experienced. I was at work for myself and newly-married wife. It was to me the starting-point of a new existence. When I got through with that job, I went in pursuit of a job of calking; but such was the strength of prejudice against color, among the white calkers, that they refused to work with me, and of course I could get no employment.[43] Finding my trade of no immediate benefit, I threw off my calking habiliments, and prepared myself to do any kind of work I could get to do. Mr. Johnson kindly let me have his wood-horse and saw, and I very soon found myself a plenty of work. There was no work too hard—none too dirty. I was ready to saw wood, shovel coal, carry the hod, sweep the chimney, or roll oil casks,—all of which I did for nearly three years in New Bedford, before I became known to the anti-slavery world.

In about four months after I went to New Bedford, there came a young man to me, and inquired if I did not wish to take the "Liberator."[44] I told him I did; but, just having made my escape from slavery, I remarked that I was unable to pay for it then. I, however, finally became a subscriber to it. The paper came, and I read it from week to week with such feelings as it would be quite idle for me to attempt to describe. The paper became my meat and my drink. My soul was set all on fire. Its sympathy for my brethren in bonds—its scathing denunciations of slaveholders—its faithful exposures of slavery—and its powerful attacks upon the upholders of the institution—sent a thrill of joy through my soul, such as I had never felt before!

I had not long been a reader of the "Liberator," before I got a pretty correct idea of the principles, measures and spirit of the anti-slavery reform. I took right hold of the cause. I could do but little; but what I could, I did with a joyful heart, and never felt happier than when in an anti-slavery meeting. I seldom had much to say at the meetings, because what I wanted to say was said so much better by others. But, while attending an anti-slavery convention at Nantucket, on the 11th of August, 1841, I felt strongly moved to speak, and was at the same time much urged to do so by Mr. William C. Coffin, a gentleman who had heard me speak in the colored people's meeting at New Bedford. It was a severe cross, and I took it up reluctantly. The truth was, I felt myself a slave, and the idea of speaking to white people weighed me down. I spoke but a few moments, when I felt a degree of freedom, and said what I desired with considerable ease. From that time until

---

[43] Douglass's note: "I am told that colored persons can now get employment at calking in New Bedford—a result of anti-slavery effort."

[44] The best-known publication of the abolitionist movement, *The Liberator* first appeared in January 1831; in 1838 it had a circulation of about 1500 (including many African Americans) that grew to approximately 3000 in the 1850s. The last issue was published upon the ratification of the Thirteenth Amendment in 1865.

now, I have been engaged in pleading the cause of my brethren—with what success, and with what devotion, I leave those acquainted with my labors to decide.

APPENDIX

I find, since reading over the foregoing Narrative that I have, in several instances, spoken in such a tone and manner, respecting religion, as may possibly lead those unacquainted with my religious views to suppose me an opponent of all religion. To remove the liability of such misapprehension, I deem it proper to append the following brief explanation. What I have said respecting and against religion, I mean strictly to apply to the *slaveholding religion* of this land, and with no possible reference to Christianity proper; for, between the Christianity of this land, and the Christianity of Christ, I recognize the widest possible difference—so wide, that to receive the one as good, pure, and holy, is of necessity to reject the other as bad, corrupt, and wicked. To be the friend of the one, is of necessity to be the enemy of the other. I love the pure, peaceable, and impartial Christianity of Christ: I therefore hate the corrupt, slaveholding, women-whipping, cradle-plundering, partial and hypocritical Christianity of this land. Indeed, I can see no reason, but the most deceitful one, for calling the religion of this land Christianity. I look upon it as the climax of all misnomers, the boldest of all frauds, and the grossest of all libels. Never was there a clearer case of "stealing the livery of the court of heaven to serve the devil in." I am filled with unutterable loathing when I contemplate the religious pomp and show, together with the horrible inconsistencies, which every where surround me. We have men-stealers for ministers, women-whippers for missionaries, and cradle-plunderers for church members. The man who wields the blood-clotted cowskin during the week fills the pulpit on Sunday, and claims to be a minister of the meek and lowly Jesus. The man who robs me of my earnings at the end of each week meets me as a class-leader on Sunday morning, to show me the way of life, and the path of salvation. He who sells my sister, for purposes of prostitution, stands forth as the pious advocate of purity. He who proclaims it a religious duty to read the Bible denies me the right of learning to read the name of the God who made me. He who is the religious advocate of marriage robs whole millions of its sacred influence, and leaves them to the ravages of wholesale pollution. The warm defender of the sacredness of the family relation is the same that scatters whole families,—sundering husbands and wives, parents and children, sisters and brothers,—leaving the hut vacant, and the hearth desolate. We see the thief preaching against theft, and the adulterer against adultery. We have men sold to build churches, women sold to support the gospel, and babes sold to purchase Bibles for the *poor heathen! all for the glory of God and the good of souls!* The slave auctioneer's bell and the church-going bell chime in with each other, and the bitter cries of the heart-broken slave are drowned in the religious shouts of his pious master. Revivals of religion and revivals in the slave-trade go hand in hand together. The slave prison and the church stand near each other. The clanking of fetters and the rattling of chains in the prison, and the pious psalm and solemn prayer in the church, may be heard at the same time. The dealers in the bodies and souls of men erect their stand in the presence of the pulpit, and they mutually help each other. The dealer gives his blood-stained gold to support the pulpit, and the pulpit, in return, covers his infernal business with the garb of Christianity. Here we have religion and robbery the allies of each other—devils dressed in angels' robes, and hell presenting the semblance of paradise.

> "Just God! and these are they,
>   Who minister at thine altar, God of right!
> Men who their hands, with prayer and blessing, lay
>   On Israel's ark of light.[45]
>
> "What! preach, and kidnap men?
>   Give thanks, and rob thy own afflicted poor?
> Talk of thy glorious liberty, and then
>   Bolt hard the captive's door?
>
> "What! servants of thy own
>   Merciful Son, who came to seek and save
> The homeless and the outcast, fettering down
>   The tasked and plundered slave!
>
> "Pilate and Herod[46] friends!
>   Chief priests and rulers, as of old, combine!
> Just God and holy! is that church which lends
>   Strength to the spoiler thine?"[47]

The Christianity of America is a Christianity, of whose votaries it may be as truly said, as it was of the ancient scribes and Pharisees,[48] "They bind heavy burdens, and grievous to be borne, and lay them on men's shoulders, but they themselves will not move them with one of their fingers. All their works they do for to be seen of men.——They love the uppermost rooms at feasts, and the chief seats in the synagogues, ... and to be called of men, Rabbi, Rabbi.—— But woe unto you, scribes and Pharisees, hypocrites! for ye shut up the kingdom of heaven against men; for ye neither go in yourselves, neither suffer ye them that are entering to go in. Ye devour widows' houses, and for a pretence make long prayers; therefore ye shall receive the greater damnation. Ye compass sea and land to make one proselyte, and when he is made, ye make him twofold more the child of hell than yourselves.——Woe unto you, scribes and Pharisees, hypocrites! for ye pay tithe of mint, and anise, and cumin, and have omitted the weightier matters of the law, judgment, mercy, and faith; these ought ye to have done, and not to leave the other undone. Ye blind guides! which strain at a gnat, and swallow a camel. Woe unto you, scribes and Pharisees, hypocrites! for ye make clean the outside of the cup and of the platter; but within, they are full of extortion and excess.——Woe unto you, scribes and Pharisees, hypocrites! for ye are like unto whited sepulchres, which indeed appear beautiful outward, but are within full of

---

[45] The ark of the covenant, which is said to contain the word of God, the Torah.

[46] Pontius Pilate, the Roman procurator of Judea who gave Jesus up to be crucified; Herod Antipater, the local ruler of Galilee who had the head of John the Baptist brought on a platter to his stepdaughter, Salome.

[47] From John Greenleaf Whittier's poem "Clerical Oppressors" (1835?).

[48] Biblical scholars who taught Jewish law and edited and interpreted the Bible, and members of an influential Jewish sect who prided themselves on strict observance of traditional religious laws.

dead men's bones and of all uncleanness. Even so ye also outwardly appear righteous unto men, but within ye are full of hypocrisy and iniquity."[49]

Dark and terrible as is this picture, I hold it to be strictly true of the overwhelming mass of professed Christians in America. They strain at a gnat, and swallow a camel. Could any thing be more true of our churches? They would be shocked at the proposition of fellowshipping a *sheep*-stealer; and at the same time they hug to their communion a *man*-stealer, and brand me with being an infidel, if I find fault with them for it. They attend with Pharisaical strictness to the outward forms of religion, and at the same time neglect the weightier matters of the law, judgment, mercy, and faith. They are always ready to sacrifice, but seldom to show mercy. They are they who are represented as professing to love God whom they have not seen, whilst they hate their brother whom they have seen. They love the heathen on the other side of the globe. They can pray for him, pay money to have the Bible put into his hand, and missionaries to instruct him; while they despise and totally neglect the heathen at their own doors.

Such is, very briefly, my view of the religion of this land; and to avoid any misunderstanding, growing out of the use of general terms, I mean, by the religion of this land, that which is revealed in the words, deeds, and actions, of those bodies, north and south, calling themselves Christian churches, and yet in union with slaveholders. It is against religion, as presented by these bodies, that I have felt it my duty to testify.

I conclude these remarks by copying the following portrait of the religion of the south, (which is, by communion and fellowship, the religion of the north,) which I soberly affirm is "true to the life," and without caricature or the slightest exaggeration. It is said to have been drawn, several years before the present anti-slavery agitation began, by a northern Methodist preacher, who, while residing at the south, had an opportunity to see slaveholding morals, manners, and piety, with his own eyes. "Shall I not visit for these things? said the Lord. Shall not my soul be avenged on such a nation as this?"[50]

"A PARODY"[51]

"Come, saints and sinners, hear me tell
How pious priests whip Jack and Nell,
And women buy and children sell,
And preach all sinners down to hell,
    And sing of heavenly union.

"They'll bleat and baa, dona like goats,
Gorge down black sheep, and strain at motes,
Array their backs in fine black coats,
Then seize their negroes by their throats
    And choke, for heavenly union.

"They'll church you if you sip a dram,
And damn you if you steal a lamb;

---

[49] From Matthew 23, Jesus' denunciation of the hypocrisy of the scribes and Pharisees.
[50] From Jeremiah 5:9.
[51] Douglass's parody of "Heavenly Union," a hymn popular in many southern churches at the time.

Yet rob old Tony, Doll, and Sam,
Of human rights, and bread and ham;
  Kidnapper's heavenly union.

"They'll loudly talk of Christ's reward,
And bind his image with a cord,
And scold, and swing the lash abhorred,
And sell their brother in the Lord
  To handcuffed heavenly union.

"They'll read and sing a sacred song,
And make a prayer both loud and long,
And teach the right and do the wrong,
Hailing the brother, sister throng,
  With words of heavenly union.

"We wonder how such saints can sing,
Or praise the Lord upon the wing,
Who roar, and scold, and whip, and sting,
And to their slaves and mammon cling,
  In guilty conscience union.

"They'll raise tobacco, corn, and rye,
And drive, and thieve, and cheat, and lie,
And lay up treasures in the sky,
By making switch and cowskin fly,
  In hope of heavenly union.

"They'll crack old Tony on the skull,
And preach and roar like Bashan bull,[52]
Or braying ass, of mischief full,
Then seize old Jacob by the wool,
  And pull for heavenly union.

"A roaring, ranting, sleek man-thief,
Who lived on mutton, veal, and beef,
Yet never would afford relief
To needy, sable sons of grief,
  Was big with heavenly union.

"'Love not the world,' the preacher said,
And winked his eye, and shook his head;
He seized on Tom, and Dick, and Ned,
Cut short their meat, and clothes, and bread,
  Yet still loved heavenly union.

"Another preacher whining spoke
Of One whose heart for sinners broke:

---

[52] Powerful bulls mentioned in the Old Testament.

He tied old Nanny to an oak,
And drew the blood at every stroke,
  And prayed for heavenly union.

"Two others oped their iron jaws,
And waved their children-stealing paws;
There sat their children in gewgaws;
By stinting negroes' backs and maws,
  They kept up heavenly union.

"All good from Jack another takes,
And entertains their flirts and rakes,
Who dress as sleek as glossy snakes,
And cram their mouths with sweetened cakes;
  And this goes down for union."

Sincerely and earnestly hoping that this little book may do something toward throwing light on the American slave system, and hastening the glad day of deliverance to the millions of my brethren in bonds—faithfully relying upon the power of truth, love, and justice, for success in my humble efforts—and solemnly pledging my self anew to the sacred cause,—I subscribe myself,

FREDERICK DOUGLASS.

1845

—Lynn, Mass., April 28, 1845.

An 1862 photograph by Henry P. Moore showing slaves planting sweet potatoes in South Carolina. Southern plantations were dependent on the forced labor of African Americans.

Harriet Jacobs
(1813–1897)

Harriet Ann Jacobs's *Incidents in the Life of a Slave Girl: Written by Herself* (1861) is a rare narrative that explores what it was to be a black female slave in an American society dominated by white males. The first edition—with an author's preface signed by Linda Brent, Jacobs's persona, and an editor's introduction by Lydia Maria Child, the well-known abolitionist—was published without attribution to Jacobs. Earlier, Jacobs had tried to publish the work herself, without success; it appeared only with the help of Child.

Jacobs was born a slave in Edenton, North Carolina, in 1813. Orphaned as a child, she later became the property of three-year-old Matilda Norcom, whose father, James Norcom, was a physician with licentious propensities. To protect herself from his advances, Jacobs became sexually involved with a young white lawyer, Samuel Tredwell Sawyer, when she was sixteen and gave birth to two children. Her attempts to avoid victimization, however, only stoked the sexual desires of Dr. Norcom, whose wife became increasingly jealous of the attention he paid to the young slave. In desperation Jacobs was driven to hide in a boxlike crawlspace in the attic of her grandmother's house, where she stayed for seven years. She emerged only occasionally, spending most of her time reading and sewing, and finding solace in watching her children, who had been sold to their father, grow. When she fled to the North in 1842 and laid claim to her children, Dr. Norcom still posed a threat until Jacobs's freedom was purchased by the woman for whom she worked as a babysitter, Cornelia Grinnell Willis (the second Mrs. Nathaniel Willis), in 1852. Several years earlier Jacobs had met the Quaker reformer Amy Post, whose encouragement gradually led Jacobs to overcome a feeling of shame and to make her experience as a slave woman public. The resulting book, *Incidents,* brought Jacobs recognition and security. She then worked for the poor as a representative of Quakers from Philadelphia and New York and organized nursing homes and orphanages for African Americans in Savannah, Georgia. She returned North in 1868, living with her daughter until Jacobs's death in 1897.

Jacobs's persona in *Incidents,* Linda Brent, is an African-American woman struggling for freedom. Like Jacobs she proves her spirit and integrity by refusing to be seduced by a powerful and persistent master, Dr. Flint. Not only does she defy her tormentor from her coffinlike cell—she defeats him. The cell, which suggests woman's immobility, contrasts sharply with the image of running prevalent in male slave narratives. Linked with the book's main concern of freedom are issues of motherhood, domesticity, and female community. In other words, whereas *Incidents* is a slave narrative, it is also a sentimental novel clearly intended for a female audience. Its appeal lies in its depiction of male tyranny corrupting domestic values—an evil that threatens all women, not just slaves. As the editor Jean Fagan Yellin has observed, *Incidents* not only condemns American racism but challenges the patriarchy that generates it. And it does so in the voice of a woman who, by publicizing her painful experience, brought a hitherto forbidden topic—the sexual abuse of slave women—into public discussions of slavery.

Suggested Readings: *Incidents in the Life of a Slave Girl,* ed. L. M. Child, 1861. J. F. Yellin, ed., *Incidents in the Life of a Slave Girl,* 1987. J. Fetterley, "Harriet Jacobs," in *Provisions: A Reader From 19th-Century American Women,* 1985. W. L. Andrews, *To Tell a Free Story: The First Century of Afro-American Autobiography, 1760–1865,* 1986. H. Carby, *Reconstructing Womanhood,* 1987. V. Smith, *Self-Discovery and Authority in Afro-American Narrative,* 1988.

Text Used: *Incidents in the Life of a Slave Girl,* intro. by V. Smith, 1988.

from INCIDENTS IN THE LIFE OF A SLAVE GIRL*

I: CHILDHOOD

I was born a slave; but I never knew it till six years of happy childhood had passed away. My father[1] was a carpenter, and considered so intelligent and skilful in his trade, that, when buildings out of the common line were to be erected, he was sent for from long distances, to be head workman. On condition of paying his mistress two hundred dollars a year, and supporting himself, he was allowed to work at his trade, and manage his own affairs. His strongest wish was to purchase his children; but, though he several times offered his hard earnings for that purpose, he never succeeded. In complexion my parents were a light shade of brownish yellow, and were termed mulattoes. They lived together in a comfortable home; and, though we were all slaves, I was so fondly shielded that I never dreamed I was a piece of merchandise, trusted to them for safe keeping, and liable to be demanded of them at any moment. I had one brother, William, who was two years younger than myself—a bright, affectionate child. I had also a great treasure in my maternal grandmother,[2] who was a remarkable woman in many respects. She was the daughter of a planter in South Carolina, who, at his death, left her mother and his three children free, with money to go to St. Augustine, where they had relatives. It was during the Revolutionary War; and they were captured on their passage, carried back, and sold to different purchasers. Such was the story my grandmother used to tell me; but I do not remember all the particulars. She was a little girl when she was captured and sold to the keeper of a large hotel. I have often heard her tell how hard she fared during childhood. But as she grew older she evinced so much intelligence, and was so faithful, that her master and mistress could not help seeing it was for their interest to take care of such a valuable piece of property. She became an indispensable personage in the household, officiating in all capacities, from cook and wet nurse to seamstress. She was much praised for her cooking; and her nice crackers became so famous in the neighborhood that many people were desirous of obtaining them. In consequence of numerous requests of this kind, she asked permission of her mistress to bake crackers at night, after all the household work was done; and she obtained leave to do it, provided she would clothe herself and her children from the profits. Upon these terms, after working hard all day for her mistress, she began her midnight bakings, assisted by her two oldest children. The business proved profitable; and each year she laid by a little, which was saved for a fund to purchase her children. Her master died, and the property was divided among his heirs. The widow had her dower in the hotel, which she continued to keep open. My grandmother remained in her service as a slave; but her children were divided among her master's children. As she had five, Benjamin, the youngest one, was sold, in order that each heir might have an equal portion dollars and cents. There was so little difference in our ages that he seemed more like my brother than my uncle. He was a bright, handsome lad, nearly white; for he inherited the complexion my grandmother had derived from Anglo-Saxon ancestors. Though only ten years old, seven hundred

---

* An autobiographical narrative, first published privately in 1861.
[1] Daniel Jacobs (?–1826?); in writing her life story as if it were fiction, Jacobs gives Linda Brent the same (unnamed) relatives she herself had.
[2] Molly Horniblow (1771?–1853).

and twenty dollars were paid for him. His sale was a terrible blow to my grandmother; but she was naturally hopeful, and she went to work with renewed energy, trusting in time to be able to purchase some of her children. She had laid up three hundred dollars, which her mistress one day begged as a loan, promising to pay her soon. The reader probably knows that no promise or writing given to a slave is legally binding; for, according to Southern laws, a slave, *being* property, can *hold* no property. When my grandmother lent her hard earnings to her mistress, she trusted solely to her honor. The honor of a slaveholder to a slave!

To this good grandmother I was indebted for many comforts. My brother Willie and I often received portions of the crackers, cakes, and preserves, she made to sell; and after we ceased to be children we were indebted to her for many more important services.

Such were the unusually fortunate circumstances of my early childhood. When I was six years old, my mother[3] died; and then, for the first time, I learned, by the talk around me, that I was a slave. My mother's mistress was the daughter of my grandmother's mistress. She was the foster sister of my mother; they were both nourished at my grandmother's breast. In fact, my mother had been weaned at three months old, that the babe of the mistress might obtain sufficient food. They played together as children; and, when they became women, my mother was a most faithful servant to her whiter foster sister. On her death-bed her mistress promised that her children should never suffer for any thing; and during her lifetime she kept her word. They all spoke kindly of my dead mother, who had been a slave merely in name, but in nature was noble and womanly. I grieved for her, and my young mind was troubled with the thought who would now take care of me and my little brother. I was told that my home was now to be with her mistress; and I found it a happy one. No toilsome or disagreeable duties were imposed upon me. My mistress was so kind to me that I was always glad to do her bidding, and proud to labor for her as much as my young years would permit. I would sit by her side for hours, sewing diligently, with a heart as free from care as that of any free-born white child. When she thought I was tired, she would send me out to run and jump; and away I bounded, to gather berries or flowers to decorate her room. Those were happy days—too happy to last. The slave child had no thought for the morrow; but there came that blight, which too surely waits on every human being born to be a chattel.

When I was nearly twelve years old, my kind mistress[4] sickened and died. As I saw the cheek grow paler, and the eye more glassy, how earnestly I prayed in my heart that she might live! I loved her; for she had been almost like a mother to me. My prayers were not answered. She died, and they buried her in the little churchyard, where, day after day, my tears fell upon her grave.

I was sent to spend a week with my grandmother. I was now old enough to begin to think of the future; and again and again I asked myself what they would do with me. I felt sure I should never find another mistress so kind as the one who was gone. She had promised my dying mother that her children should never suffer for any thing; and when I remembered that, and recalled her many proofs of attachment to me, I could not help having some hopes that she had left me free. My friends were almost certain it would be so. They thought she would be sure to do it, on account of my mother's love and faithful service. But, alas! we all know

---

[3] Delilah Jacobs (?–1820), Molly Horniblow's daughter.
[4] Margaret Horniblow (1797–1825); the slave Molly was given the family name.

that the memory of a faithful slave does not avail much to save her children from the auction block.

After a brief period of suspense, the will of my mistress was read, and we learned that she had bequeathed me to her sister's daughter,[5] a child of five years old. So vanished our hopes. My mistress had taught me the precepts of God's Word: "Thou shalt love thy neighbor as thyself." "Whatsoever ye would that men should do unto you, do ye even so unto them."[6] But I was her slave, and I suppose she did not recognize me as her neighbor. I would give much to blot out from my memory that one great wrong. As a child, I loved my mistress; and, looking back on the happy days I spent with her, I try to think with less bitterness of this act of injustice. While I was with her, she taught me to read and spell; and for this privilege, which so rarely falls to the lot of a slave, I bless her memory.

She possessed but few slaves; and at her death those were all distributed among her relatives. Five of them were my grandmother's children, and had shared the same milk that nourished her mother's children. Notwithstanding my grandmother's long and faithful service to her owners, not one of her children escaped the auction block. These God-breathing machines are no more, in the sight of their masters, than the cotton they plant, or the horses they tend.

VI: The Jealous Mistress

I would ten thousand times rather that my children should be the half-starved paupers of Ireland than to be the most pampered among the slaves of America.[1] I would rather drudge out my life on a cotton plantation, till the grave opened to give me rest, than to live with an unprincipled master and a jealous mistress. The felon's home in a penitentiary is preferable. He may repent, and turn from the error of his ways, and so find peace; but it is not so with a favorite slave. She is not allowed to have any pride of character. It is deemed a crime in her to wish to be virtuous.

Mrs. Flint[2] possessed the key to her husband's character before I was born. She might have used this knowledge to counsel and to screen the young and the innocent among her slaves; but for them she had no sympathy. They were the objects of her constant suspicion and malevolence. She watched her husband with unceasing vigilance; but he was well practised in means to evade it. What he could not find opportunity to say in words he manifested in signs. He invented more than were ever thought of in a deaf and dumb asylum. I let them pass, as if I did not understand what he meant; and many were the curses and threats bestowed on me for my stupidity. One day he caught me teaching myself to write.[3] He frowned, as if he was not well pleased; but I suppose he came to the conclusion that such an accomplishment might help to advance his favorite scheme. Before long, notes were often slipped into my hand. I would return them, say, "I can't read them, sir." "Can't you?" he replied; "then I must read them to you." He always finished

[5] Mary Matilda Norcom (1822–?), who is named Emily Flint here.

[6] From Mark 12:31 and from Matthew 7:12, respectively.

[1] The numerous references to the potato famine in Ireland, and in some cases to Irish enslavement by the British, show an awareness of mutual hardship on the part of abolitionist writers.

[2] Linda Brent is now living in the Flint household (just as Harriet Jacobs lived in the home of Dr. and Mrs. Norcom).

[3] Ordinarily, slaves were not allowed to learn how to read and write.

the reading by asking, "Do you understand?" Sometimes he would complain of the heat of the tea room, and order his supper to be placed on a small table in the piazza. He would seat himself there with a well-satisfied smile, and tell me to stand by and brush away the flies. He would eat very slowly, pausing between the mouthfuls. These intervals were employed in describing the happiness I was so foolishly throwing away, and in threatening me with the penalty that finally awaited my stubborn disobedience. He boasted much of the forbearance he had exercised towards me, and reminded me that there was a limit to his patience. When I succeeded in avoiding opportunities for him to talk to me at home, I was ordered to come to his office, to do some errand. When there, I was obliged to stand and listen to such language as he saw fit to address to me. Sometimes I so openly expressed my contempt for him that he would become violently enraged, and I wondered why he did not strike me. Circumstanced as he was, he probably thought it was better policy to be forbearing. But the state of things grew worse and worse daily. In desperation I told him that I must and would apply to my grandmother for protection. He threatened me with death, and worse than death, if I made any complaint to her. Strange to say, I did not despair. I was naturally of a buoyant disposition, and always I had a hope of somehow getting out of his clutches. Like many a poor, simple slave before me, I trusted that some threads of joy would yet be woven into my dark destiny.

I had entered my sixteenth year, and every day it became more apparent that my presence was intolerable to Mrs. Flint. Angry words frequently passed between her and her husband. He had never punished me himself, and he would not allow any body else to punish me. In that respect, she was never satisfied; but, in her angry moods, no terms were too vile for her to bestow upon me. Yet I, whom she detested so bitterly, had far more pity for her than he had, whose duty it was to make her life happy. I never wronged her, or wished to wrong her; and one word of kindness from her would have brought me to her feet.

After repeated quarrels between the doctor and his wife, he announced his intention to take his youngest daughter, then four years old, to sleep in his apartment. It was necessary that a servant should sleep in the same room, to be on hand if the child stirred. I was selected for that office, and informed for what purpose that arrangement had been made. By managing to keep within sight of people, as much as possible, during the day time, I had hitherto succeeded in eluding my master, though a razor was often held to my throat to force me to change this line of policy. At night I slept by the side of my great aunt, where I felt safe. He was too prudent to come into her room. She was an old woman and had been in the family many years. Moreover, as a married man, and a professional man, he deemed it necessary to save appearances in some degree. But he resolved to remove the obstacle in the way of his scheme; and he thought he had planned it so that he should evade suspicion. He was well aware how much I prized my refuge by the side of my old aunt, and he determined to dispossess me of it. The first night the doctor had the little child in his room alone. The next morning, I was ordered to take my station as nurse the following night. A kind Providence interposed in my favor. During the day Mrs. Flint heard of this new arrangement, and a storm followed. I rejoiced to hear it rage.

After a while my mistress sent for me to come to her room. Her first question was, "Did you know you were to sleep in the doctor's room?"

"Yes, ma'am."

"Who told you?"

"My master."

"Will you answer truly all the questions I ask?"

"Yes, ma'am."

"Tell me, then, as you hope to be forgiven, are you innocent of what I have accused you?"

"I am."

She handed me a Bible, and said, "Lay your hand on your heart, kiss this holy book, and swear before God that you tell me the truth."

I took the oath she required, and I did it with a clear conscience.

"You have taken God's holy word to testify your innocence," said she. "If you have deceived me, beware! Now take this stool, sit down, look me directly in the face, and tell me all that has passed between your master and you."

I did as she ordered. As I went on with my account her color changed frequently, she wept, and sometimes groaned. She spoke in tones so sad, that I was touched by her grief. The tears came to my eyes; but I was soon convinced that her emotions arose from anger and wounded pride. She felt that her marriage vows were desecrated, her dignity insulted; but she had no compassion for the poor victim of her husband's perfidy. She pitied herself as a martyr; but she was incapable of feeling for the condition of shame and misery in which her unfortunate, helpless slave was placed.

Yet perhaps she had some touch of feeling for me; for when the conference was ended, she spoke kindly, and promised to protect me. I should have been much comforted by this assurance if I could have had confidence in it; but my experiences in slavery had filled me with distrust. She was not a very refined woman, and had not much control over her passions. I was an object of her jealousy, and, consequently, of her hatred; and I knew I could not expect kindness or confidence from her under the circumstances in which I was placed. I could not blame her. Slave-holders' wives feel as other women would under similar circumstances. The fire of her temper kindled from small sparks, and now the flame became so intense that the doctor was obliged to give up his intended arrangement.

I knew I had ignited the torch, and I expected to suffer for it afterwards; but I felt too thankful to my mistress for the timely aid she rendered me to care much about that. She now took me to sleep in a room adjoining her own. There I was an object of her especial care, though not of her especial comfort, for she spent many a sleepless night to watch over me. Sometimes I woke up, and found her bending over me. At other times she whispered in my ear, as though it was her husband who was speaking to me, and listened to hear what I would answer. If she startled me, on such occasions, she would glide stealthily away; and the next morning she would tell me I had been talking in my sleep, and ask who I was talking to. At last, I began to be fearful for my life. It had been often threatened; and you can imagine, better than I can describe, what an unpleasant sensation it must produce to wake up in the dead of night and find a jealous woman bending over you. Terrible as this experience was, I had fears that it would give place to one more terrible.

My mistress grew weary of her vigils; they did not prove satisfactory. She changed her tactics. She now tried the trick of accusing my master of crime, in my presence, and gave my name as the author of the accusation. To my utter astonishment, he replied, "I don't believe it; but if she did acknowledge it, you tortured her into exposing me." Tortured into exposing him! Truly, Satan had no difficulty in distinguishing the color of his soul! I understood his object in making this false representation. It was to show me that I gained nothing by seeking the protection of my mistress; that the power was still all in his own hands. I pitied Mrs. Flint. She was a second wife, many years the junior of her husband; and the hoary-headed[4] miscreant was enough to try the patience of a wiser and better woman. She was completely foiled, and knew not how to proceed. She would gladly have had me flogged for my supposed false oath; but, as I have already stated, the doctor never allowed any one to whip me. The old sinner was politic. The application of the lash might have led to remarks that would have exposed him in the eyes of his children and grandchildren. How often did I rejoice that I lived in a town where all the inhabitants knew each other! If I had been on a remote plantation, or lost among the multitude of a crowded city, I should not be a living woman at this day.

The secrets of slavery are concealed like those of the Inquisition. My master was, to my knowledge, the father of eleven slaves. But did the mothers dare to tell who was the father of their children? Did the other slaves dare to allude to it, except in whispers among themselves? No, indeed! They knew too well the terrible consequences.

My grandmother could not avoid seeing things which excited her suspicions. She was uneasy about me, and tried various ways to buy me; but the never-changing answer was always repeated: "Linda does not belong to *me*. She is my daughter's property, and I have no legal right to sell her." The conscientious man! He was too scrupulous to *sell* me; but he had no scruples whatever about committing a much greater wrong against the helpless young girl placed under his guardianship, as his daughter's property. Sometimes my persecutor would ask me whether I would like to be sold. I told him I would rather be sold to any body than to lead such a life as I did. On such occasions he would assume the air of a very injured individual, and reproach me for my ingratitude. "Did I not take you into the house, and make you the companion of my own children?" he would say. "Have I ever treated you like a negro? I have never allowed you to be punished, not even to please your mistress. And this is the recompense I get, you ungrateful girl!" I answered that he had reasons of his own for screening me from punishment, and that the course he pursued made my mistress hate me and persecute me. If I wept, he would say, "Poor child! Don't cry! don't cry! I will make peace for you with your mistress. Only let me arrange matters in my own way. Poor, foolish girl! you don't know what is for your own good. I would cherish you. I would make a lady of you. Now go, and think of all I have promised you."

I did think of it.

Reader, I draw no imaginary pictures of southern homes. I am telling you the plain truth. Yet when victims make their escape from this wild beast of Slavery, northerners consent to act the part of blood-hounds, and hunt the poor fugitive back into his den, "full of dead men's bones, and all uncleanness."[5] Nay, more, they are not only willing, but proud, to give their daughters in marriage to slaveholders. The poor girls have romantic notions of a sunny clime, and of the flowering vines that all the year round shade a happy home. To what disappointments are they destined! The young wife soon learns that the husband in whose

---

[4] Ancient.

[5] "Woe unto you, scribes and Pharisees, hypocrites! for ye are like unto whited sepulchres, which indeed appear beautiful outward, but are within full of dead men's bones, and of all uncleanness," from Matthew 23:27.

hands she has placed her happiness pays no regard to his marriage vows. Children of every shade of complexion play with her own fair babies, and too well she knows that they are born unto him of his own household. Jealousy and hatred enter the flowery home, and it is ravaged of its loveliness.

Southern women often marry a man knowing that he is the father of many little slaves. They do not trouble themselves about it. They regard such children as property, as marketable as the pigs on the plantation; and it is seldom that they do not make them aware of this by passing them into the slave-trader's hands as soon as possible, and thus getting them out of their sight. I am glad to say there are some honorable exceptions.

I have myself known two southern wives who exhorted their husbands to free those slaves towards whom they stood in a "parental relation;" and their request was granted. These husbands blushed before the superior nobleness of their wives' natures. Though they had only counselled them to do that which it was their duty to do, it commanded their respect, and rendered their conduct more exemplary. Concealment was at an end, and confidence took the place of distrust.

Though this bad institution deadens the moral sense, even in white women, to a fearful extent, it is not altogether extinct. I have heard southern ladies say of Mr. Such a one, "He not only thinks it no disgrace to be the father of those little niggers, but he is not ashamed to call himself their master. I declare, such things ought not to be tolerated in any decent society!"

XXI: The Loophole of Retreat*

A small shed had been added to my grandmother's house years ago. Some boards were laid across the joists at the top, and between these boards and the roof was a very small garret, never occupied by any thing but rats and mice. It was a pent roof, covered with nothing but shingles, according to the southern custom for such buildings. The garret was only nine feet long and seven wide. The highest part was three feet high, and sloped down abruptly to the loose board floor. There was no admission for either light or air. My uncle Philip, who was a carpenter, had very skilfully made a concealed trap-door, which communicated with the store-room. He had been doing this while I was waiting in the swamp. The storeroom opened upon a piazza. To this hole I was conveyed as soon as I entered the house. The air was stifling; the darkness total. A bed had been spread on the floor. I could sleep quite comfortably on one side; but the slope was so sudden that I could not turn on the other without hitting the roof. The rats and mice ran over my bed; but I was weary, and I slept such sleep as the wretched may, when a tempest has passed over them. Morning came. I knew it only by the noises I heard; for in my small den day and night were all the same. I suffered for air even more than for light. But I was not comfortless. I heard the voices of my children. There was joy and there was sadness in the sound. It made my tears flow. How I longed to speak to them! I was eager to look on their faces; but there was no hole, no crack,

---

* This title comes from the mock-heroic and didactic poem "The Task" (1785), by the British writer William Cowper (1731–1800). Having again refused Dr. Flint's sexual overtures, Linda Brent was sent to work on the plantation for the first time in her life. Worry over her fate and that of her children led her to run away (with the hope of rescuing the children later) and finally to hide in a small room in her grandmother's house, the "garret" she describes here.

through which I could peep. This continued darkness was oppressive. It seemed horrible to sit or lie in a cramped position day after day, without one gleam of light. Yet I would have chosen this, rather than my lot as a slave, though white people considered it an easy one; and it was so compared with the fate of others. I was never cruelly over-worked; I was never lacerated with the whip from head to foot; I was never so beaten and bruised that I could not turn from one side to the other; I never had my heel-strings cut to prevent my running away; I was never chained to a log and forced to drag it about, while I toiled in the fields from morning till night; I was never branded with hot iron, or torn by bloodhounds. On the contrary, I had always been kindly treated, and tenderly cared for, until I came into the hands of Dr. Flint. I had never wished for freedom till then. But though my life in slavery was comparatively devoid of hardships, God pity the woman who is compelled to lead such a life!

My food was passed up to me through the trap-door my uncle had contrived; and my grandmother, my uncle Phillip, and aunt Nancy would seize such opportunities as they could, to mount up there and chat with me at the opening. But of course this was not safe in the daytime. It must all be done in darkness. It was impossible for me to move in an erect position, but I crawled about my den for exercise. One day I hit my head against something, and found it was a gimlet. My uncle had left it sticking there when he made the trap-door. I was as rejoiced as Robinson Crusoe[1] could have been at finding such a treasure. It put a lucky thought into my head. I said to myself, "Now I will have some light. Now I will see my children." I did not dare to begin my work during the daytime, for fear of attracting attention. But I groped round; and having found the side next the street, where I could frequently see my children, I stuck the gimlet in and waited for evening. I bored three rows of holes, one above another; then I bored out the interstices between. I thus succeeded in making one hole about an inch long and an inch broad. I sat by it till late into the night, to enjoy the little whiff of air that floated in. In the morning I watched for my children. The first person I saw in the street was Dr. Flint. I had a shuddering, superstitious feeling that it was a bad omen. Several familiar faces passed by. At last I heard the merry laugh of children, and presently two sweet little faces were looking up at me, as though they knew I was there, and were conscious of the joy they imparted. How I longed to *tell* them I was there!

My condition was now a little improved. But for weeks I was tormented by hundreds of little red insects, fine as a needle's point, that pierced through my skin, and produced an intolerable burning. The good grandmother gave me herb teas and cooling medicines, and finally I got rid of them. The heat of my den was intense, for nothing but thin shingles protected me from the scorching summer's sun. But I had my consolations. Through my peeping-hole I could watch the children, and when they were near enough, I could hear their talk. Aunt Nancy brought me all the news she would hear at Dr. Flint's. From her I learned that the doctor had written to New York to a colored woman, who had been born and raised in our neighborhood, and had breathed his contaminating atmosphere. He offered her a reward if she could find out any thing about me. I know not what

---

[1] The well-known title character in *The Life and Strange Surprising Adventures of Robinson Crusoe* (1719), by the English novelist Daniel Defoe (1660–1731).

was the nature of her reply; but he soon after started for New York in haste, saying to his family that he had business of importance to transact. I peeped at him as he passed on his way to the steamboat. It was a satisfaction to have miles of land and water between us, even for a little while; and it was a still greater satisfaction to know that he believed me to be in the Free States. My little den seemed less dreary than it had done. He returned, as he did from his former journey to New York, without obtaining any satisfactory information. When he passed our house next morning, Benny was standing at the gate. He had heard them say that he had gone to find me, and he called out, "Dr. Flint, did you bring my mother home? I want to see her." The doctor stamped his foot at him in a rage, and exclaimed, "Get out of the way, you little damned rascal! If you don't, I'll cut off your head."

Benny ran terrified into the house, saying, "You can't put me in jail again. I don't belong to you now." It was well that the wind carried the words away from the doctor's ear. I told my grandmother of it, when we had our next conference at the trap-door; and begged of her not to allow the children to be impertinent to the irascible old man.

Autumn came, with a pleasant abatement of heat. My eyes had become accustomed to the dim light, and by holding my book or work in a certain position near the aperture I contrived to read and sew. That was a great relief to the tedious monotony of my life. But when winter came, the cold penetrated through the thin shingle roof, and I was dreadfully chilled. The winters there are not so long, or so severe, as in northern latitudes; but the houses are not built to shelter from cold, and my little den was peculiarly comfortless. The kind grandmother brought me bed-clothes and warm drinks. Often I was obliged to lie in bed all day to keep comfortable; but with all my precautions, my shoulders and feet were frostbitten. O, those long, gloomy days, with no object for my eye to rest upon, and no thoughts to occupy my mind, except the dreary past and the uncertain future! I was thankful when there came a day sufficiently mild for me to wrap myself up and sit at the loophole to watch the passers by. Southerners have the habit of stopping and talking in the streets, and I heard many conversations not intended to meet my ears. I heard slave-hunters planning how to catch some poor fugitive. Several times I heard allusions to Dr. Flint, myself, and the history of my children, who, perhaps, were playing near the gate. One would say, "I wouldn't move my little finger to catch her, as old Flint's property." Another would say, "I'll catch *any* nigger for the reward. A man ought to have what belongs to him, if he *is* a damned brute." The opinion was often expressed that I was in the Free States. Very rarely did any one suggest that I might be in the vicinity. Had the least suspicion rested on my grandmother's house, it would have been burned to the ground. But it was the last place they thought of. Yet there was no place, where slavery existed, that could have afforded me so good a place of concealment.

Dr. Flint and his family repeatedly tried to coax and bribe my children to tell something they had heard said about me. One day the doctor took them into a shop, and offered them some bright little silver pieces and gay handkerchiefs if they would tell where their mother was. Ellen shrank away from him, and would not speak; but Benny spoke up, and said, "Dr. Flint, I don't know where my mother is. I guess she's in New York; and when you go there again, I wish you'd ask her to come home, for I want to see her; but if you put her in jail, or tell her you'll cut her head off, I'll tell her to go right back."

XLI: Free at Last*

Mrs. Bruce, and every member of her family, were exceedingly kind to me. I was thankful for the blessings of my lot, yet I could not always wear a cheerful countenance. I was doing harm to no one; on the contrary, I was doing all the good I could in my small way; yet I could never go out to breathe God's free air without trepidation at my heart. This seemed hard; and I could not think it was a right state of things in any civilized country.

From time to time I received news from my good old grandmother. She could not write; but she employed others to write for her. The following is an extract from one of her last letters:—

"Dear Daughter: I cannot hope to see you again on earth; but I pray to God to unite us above, where pain will no more rack this feeble body of mine; where sorrow and parting from my children will be no more.[1] God has promised these things if we are faithful unto the end. My age and feeble health deprive me of going to church now; but God is with me here at home. Thank your brother for his kindness. Give much love to him, and tell him to remember the Creator in the days of his youth,[2] and strive to meet me in the Father's kingdom. Love to Ellen and Benjamin. Don't neglect him. Tell him for me, to be a good boy. Strive, my child; to train them for God's children. May he protect and provide for you, is the prayer of your loving old mother."

These letters both cheered and saddened me. I was always glad to have tidings from the kind, faithful old friend of my unhappy youth; but her messages of love made my heart yearn to see her before she died, and I mourned over the fact that it was impossible. Some months after I returned from my flight to New England, I received a letter from her, in which she wrote, "Dr. Flint is dead. He has left a distressed family. Poor old man! I hope he made his peace with God."

I remembered how he had defrauded my grandmother of the hard earnings she had loaned; how he had tried to cheat her out of the freedom her mistress had promised her, and how he had persecuted her children; and I thought to myself that she was a better Christian than I was, if she could entirely forgive him. I cannot say, with truth, that the news of my old master's death softened my feelings towards him. There are wrongs which even the grave does not bury. The man was odious to me while he lived, and his memory is odious now.

His departure from this world did not diminish my danger. He had threatened my grandmother that his heirs should hold me in slavery after he was gone; that I never should be free so long as a child of his survived. As for Mrs. Flint, I had seen her in deeper afflictions than I supposed the loss of her husband would be, for she had buried several children; yet I never saw any signs of softening in her heart. The doctor had died in embarrassed circumstances, and had little to will to his heirs, except such property as he was unable to grasp. I was well aware what I had to expect from the family of Flints; and my fears were confirmed by a letter

---

* After years of hiding in her grandmother's "garret," Linda Brent escaped to the North and was soon after reunited with her son and daughter. Although she found work with the Bruce family, her safety and that of her children was in doubt because of the passage of the Fugitive Slave Act of 1850, which sanctioned the return of escaped slaves to their owners in the South.

[1] " . . . and there shall be no more . . . sorrow, nor crying, neither shall there be any more pain . . . ," from Revelation 21:4.

[2] "Remember now thy Creator in the days of thy youth, while the evil days come not, nor the years draw nigh, when thou shalt say, I have no pleasure in them," from Ecclesiastes 12:1.

from the south, warning me to be on my guard, because Mrs. Flint openly declared that her daughter could not afford to lose so valuable a slave as I was.

I kept close watch of the newspapers for arrivals; but one Saturday night, being much occupied, I forgot to examine the Evening Express as usual. I went down into the parlor for it, early in the morning, and found the boy about to kindle a fire with it. I took it from him and examined the list of arrivals. Reader, if you have never been a slave, you cannot imagine the acute sensation of suffering at my heart, when I read the names of Mr. and Mrs. Dodge, at a hotel in Courtland Street. It was a third-rate hotel, and that circumstance convinced me of the truth of what I had heard, that they were short of funds and had need of my value, as *they* valued me; and that was by dollars and cents. I hastened with the paper to Mrs. Bruce. Her heart and hand were always open to every one in distress, and she always warmly sympathized with mine. It was impossible to tell how near the enemy was. He might have passed and repassed the house while we were sleeping. He might at that moment be waiting to pounce upon me if I ventured out of doors. I had never seen the husband of my young mistress, and therefore I could not distinguish him from any other stranger. A carriage was hastily ordered; and, closely veiled, I followed Mrs. Bruce, taking the baby again with me into exile. After various turnings and crossings, and returnings, the carriage stopped at the house of one of Mrs. Bruce's friends, where I was kindly received. Mrs. Bruce returned immediately, to instruct the domestics what to say if any one came to inquire for me.

It was lucky for me that the evening paper was not burned up before I had a chance to examine the list of arrivals. It was not long after Mrs. Bruce's return to her house, before several people came to inquire for me. One inquired for me, another asked for my daughter Ellen, and another said he had a letter from my grandmother, which he was requested to deliver in person.

They were told, "She *has* lived here, but she has left."

"How long ago?"

"I don't know, sir."

"Do you know where she went?"

"I do not, sir." And the door was closed.

This Mr. Dodge, who claimed me as his property, was originally a Yankee pedler in the south; then he became a merchant, and finally a slaveholder. He managed to get introduced into what was called the first society, and married Miss Emily Flint. A quarrel arose between him and her brother, and the brother cowhided him. This led to a family feud, and he proposed to remove to Virginia. Dr. Flint left him no property, and his own means had become circumscribed, while a wife and children depended upon him for support. Under these circumstances, it was very natural that he should make an effort to put me into his pocket.

I had a colored friend, a man from my native place, in whom I had the most implicit confidence. I sent for him, and told him that Mr. and Mrs. Dodge had arrived in New York. I proposed that he should call upon them to make inquiries about his friends at the south, with whom Dr. Flint's family were well acquainted. He thought there was no impropriety in his doing so, and he consented. He went to the hotel, and knocked at the door of Mr. Dodge's room, which was opened by the gentleman himself, who gruffly inquired, "What brought you here? How came you to know I was in the city?"

"Your arrival was published in the evening papers, sir; and I called to ask Mrs. Dodge about my friends at home. I didn't suppose it would give any offence."

"Where's that negro girl, that belongs to my wife?"

"What girl, sir?"

"You know well enough. I mean Linda, that ran away from Dr. Flint's plantation, some years ago. I dare say you've seen her, and know where she is."

"Yes, sir, I've seen her, and know where she is. She is out of your reach, sir."

"Tell me where she is, or bring her to me, and I will give her a chance to buy
her freedom."

"I don't think it would be of any use, sir. I have heard her say she would go to
the ends of the earth, rather than pay any man or woman for her freedom, because
she thinks she has a right to it. Besides, she couldn't do it, if she would, for she
has spent her earnings to educate her children."

This made Mr. Dodge very angry, and some high words passed between them.
My friend was afraid to come where I was; but in the course of the day I received
a note from him. I supposed they had not come from the south, in the winter, for a
pleasure excursion; and now the nature of their business was very plain.

Mrs. Bruce came to me and entreated me to leave the city the next morning.
She said her house was watched, and it was possible that some clew to me might
be obtained. I refused to take her advice. She pleaded with an earnest tenderness,
that ought to have moved me; but I was in a bitter, disheartened mood. I was
weary of flying from pillar to post. I had been chased during half my life, and it
seemed as if the chase was never to end. There I sat, in that great city, guiltless of
crime, yet not daring to worship God in any of the churches. I heard the bells
ringing for afternoon service, and, with contemptuous sarcasm, I said, "Will the
preachers take for their text, 'Proclaim liberty to the captive, and the opening of
prison doors to them that are bound'? or will they preach from the text, 'Do unto
others as ye would they should do unto you'?"[3] Oppressed Poles and Hungarians
could find a safe refuge in that city; John Mitchell[4] was free to proclaim in the
City Hall his desire for "a plantation well stocked with slaves;" but there I sat, an
oppressed American, not daring to show my face. God forgive the black and bitter
thoughts I indulged on that Sabbath day! The Scripture says, "Oppression makes
even a wise man mad;"[5] and I was not wise.

I had been told that Mr. Dodge said his wife had never signed away her right to
my children, and if he could not get me, he would take them. This it was, more
than any thing else, that roused such a tempest in my soul. Benjamin was with his
uncle William in California, but my innocent young daughter had come to spend a
vacation with me. I thought of what I had suffered in slavery at her age, and my
heart was like a tiger's when a hunter tries to seize her young.

Dear Mrs. Bruce! I seem to see the expression of her face, as she turned away
discouraged by my obstinate mood. Finding her expostulations unavailing, she
sent Ellen to entreat me. When ten o'clock in the evening arrived and Ellen had
not returned, this watchful and unwearied friend became anxious. She came to us
in a carriage, bringing a well-filled trunk for my journey—trusting that by this
time I would listen to reason. I yielded to her, as I ought to have done before.

The next day, baby and I set out in a heavy snow storm, bound for New England again. I received letters from the City of Iniquity,[6] addressed to me under an

---

[3] From Isaiah 61:1 and from Matthew 7:12, respectively.

[4] Mitchell (1815–1875) founded *The Citizen,* a New York proslavery newspaper.

[5] "Surely oppression maketh a wise man mad; and a gift destroyeth the heart," from Ecclesiastes 7:7.

[6] New York, a city of fear and danger for Linda Brent at this time.

assumed name. In a few days one came from Mrs. Bruce, informing me that my new master was still searching for me, and that she intended to put an end to this persecution by buying my freedom. I felt grateful for the kindness that prompted this offer, but the idea was not so pleasant to me as might have been expected. The more my mind had become enlightened, the more difficult it was for me to consider myself an article of property; and to pay money to those who had so grievously oppressed me seemed like taking from my sufferings the glory of triumph. I wrote to Mrs. Bruce, thanking her, but saying that being sold from one owner to another seemed too much like slavery; that such a great obligation could not be easily cancelled; and that I preferred to go to my brother in California.

Without my knowledge, Mrs. Bruce employed a gentleman in New York to enter into negotiations with Mr. Dodge. He proposed to pay three hundred dollars down, if Mr. Dodge would sell me, and enter into obligations to relinquish all claim to me or my children forever after. He who called himself my master said he scorned so small an offer for such a valuable servant. The gentleman replied, "You can do as you choose, sir. If you reject this offer you will never get any thing; for the woman has friends who will convey her and her children out of the country."

Mr. Dodge concluded that "half a loaf was better than no bread," and he agreed to the proffered terms. By the next mail I received this brief letter from Mrs. Bruce: "I am rejoiced to tell you that the money for your freedom has been paid to Mr. Dodge. Come home to-morrow. I long to see you and my sweet babe."

My brain reeled as I read these lines. A gentleman near me said, "It's true; I have seen the bill of sale." "The bill of sale!" Those words struck me like a blow. So I was *sold* at last! A human being *sold* in the free city of New York! The bill of sale is on record, and future generations will learn from it that women were articles of traffic in New York, late in the nineteenth century of the Christian religion. It may hereafter prove a useful document to antiquaries, who are seeking to measure the progress of civilization in the United States. I well know the value of that bit of paper; but much as I love freedom, I do not like to look upon it. I am deeply grateful to the generous friend who procured it, but I despise the miscreant who demanded payment for what never rightfully belonged to him or his.

I had objected to having my freedom bought, yet I must confess that when it was done I felt as if a heavy load had been lifted from my weary shoulders. When I rode home in the cars I was no longer afraid to unveil my face and look at people as they passed. I should have been glad to have met Daniel Dodge himself; to have had him seen me and known me, that he might have mourned over the untoward circumstances which compelled him to sell me for three hundred dollars.

When I reached home, the arms of my benefactress were thrown round me, and our tears mingled. As soon as she could speak, she said, "O Linda, I'm *so* glad it's all over! You wrote to me as if you thought you were going to be transferred from one owner to another. But I did not buy you for your services. I should have done just the same, if you had been going to sail for California to-morrow. I should, at least, have the satisfaction of knowing that you left me a free woman."

My heart was exceedingly full. I remembered how my poor father had tried to buy me, when I was a small child, and how he had been disappointed. I hoped his spirit was rejoicing over me now. I remembered how my good old grandmother had laid up her earnings to purchase me in later years, and how often her plans had been frustrated. How that faithful, loving old heart would leap for joy, if she could look on me and my children now that we were free! My relatives had been foiled in all their efforts, but God had raised me up a friend among strangers, who had bestowed on me the precious, long-desired boon. Friend! It is a common word, often lightly used. Like other good and beautiful things, it may be tarnished by careless handling; but when I speak of Mrs. Bruce as my friend, the word is sacred.

My grandmother lived to rejoice in my freedom; but not long after, a letter came with a black seal. She had gone "where the wicked cease from troubling, and the weary are at rest."[7]

Time passed on, and a paper came to me from the south, containing an obituary notice of my uncle Phillip. It was the only case I ever knew of such an honor conferred upon a colored person. It was written by one of his friends, and contained these words: "Now that death has laid him low, they call him a good man and a useful citizen; but what are eulogies to the black man, when the world has faded from his vision? It does not require man's praise to obtain rest in God's kingdom." So they called a colored man a *citizen!* Strange words to be uttered in that region!

Reader, my story ends with freedom; not in the usual way, with marriage.[8] I and my children are now free! We are as free from the power of slaveholders as are the white people of the north; and though that, according to my ideas, is not saying a great deal, it is a vast improvement in *my* condition. The dream of my life is not yet realized. I do not sit with my children in a home of my own. I still long for a hearthstone of my own, however humble. I wish it for my children's sake far more than for my own. But God so orders circumstances as to keep me with my friend Mrs. Bruce. Love, duty, gratitude, also bind me to her side. It is a privilege to serve her who pities my oppressed people, and who has bestowed the inestimable boon of freedom on me and my children.

It has been painful to me, in many ways, to recall the dreary years I passed in bondage. I would gladly forget them if I could. Yet the retrospection is not altogether without solace; for with those gloomy recollections come tender memories of my good old grandmother, like light fleecy clouds floating over a dark and troubled sea.

1861

Abraham Lincoln
(1809–1865)

As all American schoolchildren learn, Abraham Lincoln was born in a Hardin County, Kentucky, log cabin in 1809, spent his boyhood in Indiana, and later moved to Illinois, where he split fence rails before taking up politics and law. But Lincoln was not a child of

---

[7] From Job 3:17.   [8] As many nineteenth-century novels did.

the frontier. With the exception of a brief stay in Indiana in 1816 (months before it became a state), he never lived in a territory that had not reached statehood; moreover, he spent virtually all of his adult life in towns and cities and faced resolutely toward the centers of state and national political power. Students of Lincoln thus face a double task: to discover the man as he was and to trace the myth-making that has transmuted a canny politician into the exemplar of democracy. To seek beyond the aura of heroism and martyrdom, however, is not to diminish Lincoln or his admirers; his achievements are remarkable in their own right, and many elements of the Lincoln myth spring from qualities of the man himself. His literary achievements tend to be overlooked; his authority comes from his grace as a writer.

Lincoln was largely self-educated, both in his youth, when he had little formal schooling, and as an adult, when he taught himself the law. In 1834, four years after moving to Illinois, he was elected as a Whig to the state legislature. Two years later he passed the bar exam and began to establish himself as a shrewd advocate and skilled speaker; in 1842 he married the well-to-do Mary Todd. Elected to Congress in 1846, he served one term, during which he opposed the Mexican War as a proslavery venture, a position that alienated most of his constituents. In 1855 he ran unsuccessfully for the Senate.

Shortly afterward Lincoln joined the new Republican party and opposed Stephen Douglas for the Senate. Again he was defeated, but the campaign debates drew national attention to Lincoln and his cautious antislavery position. Rebutting Douglas at Ottawa, Illinois, Lincoln invoked the Declaration of Independence in support of the right of African Americans to "life, liberty, and the pursuit of happiness" but carefully distinguished between these "enumerated" rights and full racial equality. Judiciously and pragmatically, he shaped a politically tenable position on slavery and emerged as a leading presidential candidate. In 1860 he won a clear electoral victory as the Republican nominee, although he did not win a majority of the popular vote.

The Civil War severely tested both Lincoln and the presidency. Much of the burden of directing the war effort fell on the president. In this emergency, Lincoln assumed extraordinary executive powers, governing in part by proclamation, suspending habeas corpus, and extending military authority into civil domains. Such actions brought allegations that he had exceeded his constitutional authority.

Lincoln was assassinated by John Wilkes Booth on Good Friday, 1865, five days after the surrender of General Robert E. Lee's Confederate troops. Almost immediately, Lincoln's image was transformed from politician to redeemer and healer. Crowds of citizens mourned at his funeral train, and within weeks Walt Whitman had elegized "the sweetest, wisest soul of all my days and lands" in the poignant poem "When Lilacs Last in the Dooryard Bloom'd" (1865). As Lincoln's reputation flourished in the century and a half since his death, he has become a frequent subject of American poetry, drama, and historical fiction. His biographers include William Dean Howells, Edgar Lee Masters, and Carl Sandburg.

Suggested Readings: *The Collected Works of Abraham Lincoln*, 10 vols., ed. R. P. Basler et al., 1974. *Abraham Lincoln: A Documentary Portrait Through His Speeches and Writings*, ed. D. E. Fehrenbacher, 1977. J. G. Nicolay and J. Hay, *Abraham Lincoln*, 10 vols., 1886. W. H. Herndon and J. W. Weik, *Abraham Lincoln*, 1892. C. Sandburg, *Abraham Lincoln*, 6 vols., 1939. V. Searcher, *Lincoln Today*, 1969. C. B. Strozier, *Lincoln's Quest for Union: Public and Private Meanings*, 1987.

Text Used: *Documents of American History*, ed. H. S. Commager, 1948.

THE GETTYSBURG ADDRESS

Address Delivered at the Dedication of the Cemetery at Gettysburg November 19, 1863

Four score and seven years[1] ago our fathers brought forth on this continent, a new nation, conceived in Liberty, and dedicated to the proposition that all men are created equal.

Now we are engaged in a great civil war, testing whether that nation or any nation so conceived and so dedicated, can long endure. We are met on a great battle-field of that war. We have come to dedicate a portion of that field, as a final resting place for those who here gave their lives that that nation might live. It is altogether fitting and proper that we should do this.

But, in a larger sense, we can not dedicate—we can not consecrate—we can not hallow—this ground. The brave men, living and dead, who struggled here, have consecrated it, far above our poor power to add or detract. The world will little note, nor long remember what we say here, but it can never forget what they did here. It is for us the living, rather, to be dedicated here to the unfinished work which they who fought here have thus far so nobly advanced. It is rather for us to be here dedicated to the great task remaining before us—that from these honored dead we take increased devotion to that cause for which they gave the last full measure of devotion—that we here highly resolve that these dead shall not have died in vain—that this nation, under God, shall have a new birth of freedom—and that government of the people, by the people, for the people, shall not perish from the earth.

1863

SECOND INAUGURAL ADDRESS

March 4, 1865

Fellow-Countrymen:—At this second appearing to take the oath of the presidential office there is less occasion for an extended address than there was at the first. Then a statement somewhat in detail of a course to be pursued seemed fitting and proper. Now, at the expiration of four years, during which public declarations have been constantly called forth on every point and phase of the great contest which still absorbs the attention and engrosses the energies of the nation, little that is new could be presented. The progress of our arms, upon which all else chiefly depends, is as well known to the public as to myself, and it is, I trust, reasonably

---

[1] In 1776, the year in which the Declaration of Independence was signed.

satisfactory and encouraging to all. With high hope for the future, no prediction in regard to it is ventured.

On the occasion corresponding to this four years ago all thoughts were anxiously directed to an impending civil war. All dreaded it, all sought to avert it. While the inaugural address was being delivered from this place, devoted altogether to *saving* the Union without war, insurgent agents were in the city seeking to *destroy* it without war—seeking to dissolve the Union and divide effects by negotiation. Both parties deprecated war, but one of them would *make* war rather than let the nation survive, and the other would *accept* war rather than let it perish, and the war came.

One eighth of the whole population was colored slaves, not distributed generally over the Union, but localized in the southern part of it. These slaves constituted a peculiar and powerful interest. All knew that this interest was somehow the cause of the war. To strengthen, perpetuate, and extend this interest was the object for which the insurgents would rend the Union even by war, while the Government claimed no right to do more than to restrict the territorial enlargement of it. Neither party expected for the war the magnitude or the duration which it has already attained. Neither anticipated that the *cause* of the conflict might cease with or even before the conflict itself should cease. Each looked for an easier triumph, and a result less fundamental and astounding. Both read the same Bible and pray to the same God, and each invokes His aid against the other. It may seem strange that any men should dare to ask a just God's assistance in wringing their bread from the sweat of other men's faces, but let us judge not, that we be not judged.[1] The prayers of both could not be answered. That of neither has been answered fully. The Almighty has His own purposes. "Woe unto the world because of offenses: for it must needs be that offenses come, but woe to that man by whom the offense cometh."[2] If we shall suppose that American slavery is one of those offenses which, in the providence of God, must needs come, but which, having continued through His appointed time, He now wills to remove, and that He gives to both North and South this terrible war, as the woe due to those by whom the offense came, shall we discern therein any departure from those divine attributes which the believers in a living God always ascribe to Him? Fondly do we hope, fervently do we pray, that this mighty scourge of war may speedily pass away. Yet, if God wills that it continue until all the wealth piled by the bondsman's two hundred and fifty years of unrequited toil shall be sunk, and until every drop of blood drawn with the lash shall be paid by another drawn with the sword, as was said three thousand years ago, so still it must be said, "The judgments of the Lord are true and righteous altogether."[3]

With malice toward none, with charity for all, with firmness in the right as God gives us to see the right, let us strive on to finish the work we are in, to bind up the nation's wounds, to care for him who shall have borne the battle and for his widow and his orphan, to do all which may achieve and cherish a just and lasting peace among ourselves and with all nations.

1865

---

[1] "Judge ye not, that ye be not judged," from Matthew 7:1; the biblical cadences here enhance the solemnity and compassion of Lincoln's words.
[2] From Matthew 18:7.   [3] From Psalm 19:9.

EARLY TO MIDDLE 19TH-CENTURY POETRY

In 1820 the English critic Sydney Smith provoked indignation in the United States with a barrage of questions in the *Edinburgh Review* that began "who reads an American book?" He swirled on to ask who ("in the four quarters of the globe") admires American art, learns from American medicine, looks through American telescopes, or "drinks out of American glasses? or eats from American plates?" The most elaborate response to Smith's scornful attack came not from artists, physicians, or dishmakers but from the editor Samuel Kettell. Out of a conviction that American poetry had begun to demonstrate "a national spirit," Kettell issued his three-volume *Specimens of American Poetry* (1829), which includes the work of 189 writers, most of them contemporary. It was a decidedly uneven collection of verse. Many of Kettell's poets wrote dismal romantic stuff: a mawkish hymn to the ocean, a tearful tribute to parting, an indulgent consideration of beauty refined by consumption. Some of them addressed American topics—the monument at Bunker Hill, the Indian maiden Pocahontas—and thus pointed, however feebly, toward materials that might go into the making of a national poetry. But three of the younger writers—William Cullen Bryant, Henry Wadsworth Longfellow, and John Greenleaf Whittier—would become admired American poets in the nineteenth century. It is to Kettell's credit that he recognized their youthful promise.

Despite the limitations of quality in Kettell's anthology, the collection does suggest the role of poetry in a nation still testing the dimensions of its independence. Kettell's parade of patriotic poems, for example, is both understandable and amusing. His assessment of Bryant brings us to see something of deeper import: the appeal of conservative and didactic verse in the first half of the nineteenth century. After noting Bryant's "propriety" and love of nature, Kettell praises this model poet for upholding "a pure and classical standard in an age" that tends "toward lawless fanaticism and wildness." These last words may seem surprising to anyone who thinks the late twentieth century has a monopoly on "wildness"— and they may be exaggerated to make a point. But Kettell's description of the "age" was echoed in many newspapers and magazines throughout the 1820s and 1830s, and it provides a social backdrop against which we can measure the attraction of poetry that was comforting in its values and manner.

As a lawyer, newspaper editor, and literary critic, William Cullen Bryant understood the adjunct role of the poet in a utilitarian America and thus anticipated the practice and stance of the (younger) "Fireside Poets," so-named because families commonly read their works around the fireside: Longfellow, Whittier, Oliver Wendell Holmes, and James Russell Lowell, all of whom made important contributions to other professions. Much of Bryant's poetry offered readers a romantic sensibility familiar from the work of William Wordsworth and Samuel Taylor Coleridge. Pervading this romanticism, however, and giving it an American bias is Bryant's appreciation of native landscapes and his comforting belief that nature is a gentle and wise teacher. "To a Waterfowl" (1818) and "The Prairies" (1833) illustrate the two main articles of Bryant's poetic faith—the first with its didactic

The Erie Canal, as seen in this 1838 engraving, opened a major route to the West when it was completed in 1825, and helped further the nation's romantic expansionism.

reassurance that a benign power guides us through life, the second with its celebration of a setting "for which the speech of England has no name."

In the hands of Bryant and the Fireside Poets, American poetry came to affirm and validate social norms. The poetry they wrote could criticize social practice from a moral perspective. If Bryant's decorous work asserted a reformist faith in the benevolence of progress, that of the Fireside Poets frequently confronted social and political issues even as it proclaimed the importance of domestic values. Whittier, for example, expressed his deep abolitionist feelings in poems such as "Massachusetts to Virginia" (1843) and "Ichabod" (1850) but produced the classic memory-poem of the nineteenth century in *Snowbound* (1866), a paean to the richness of domestic harmony—nostalgic, triumphant in its recollections. Lowell used dialect and a facade of naïveté in *The Biglow Papers* (1848, 1867) to protest the Mexican War and the expansion of slavery, but he also wrote light verse and the witty *Fable for Critics* (1848) which pictures the composed Bryant in "supreme iceolation" and describes Poe as "three-fifths . . . genius and two-fifths sheer fudge." And Longfellow, the most popular poet of the century, made epic poems from the fabric of American history in such narratives as *Evangeline* (1847) and *The Song of Hiawatha* (1855), although he remained the champion of domestic piety in his best-known verse.

Bryant and the Fireside Poets produced work that incorporated American topics through the lens of a temperate romanticism. In a variety of ways they taught and affirmed traditional values, took up political causes with idealistic passion, and ranged in form from the sonnet to the epic. They personified the image of the poet as public figure, someone available for political discourse or for ceremonial occasions. In a deep and real sense, they were part of the society for which they wrote.

Although the Fireside Poets made American poetry seem chiefly a New England enterprise, a number of southern poets reminded the nation of the distinctiveness of their region in the mid-nineteenth century. *Russell's Magazine,* founded in 1857 by Paul Hamilton Hayne, provided a ready outlet for a number of poets—including Hayne, Henry Timrod, and William John Grayson—who made up the informal "Russell's Bookstore Group" in Charleston, South Carolina. The early work of both Hayne and Timrod celebrates the beauty of nature in the American South. Some of this southern poetry defends the institution of slavery: Grayson's *The Hireling and the Slave* (1854), for example, presents an idyllic portrait of slavery in contrast to the harsh life of European laborers.

Juxtaposed with such a view is the poetic vision of Frances E. W. Harper, the most notable African-American poet in the years between Phillis Wheatley (in the eighteenth century) and Paul Laurence Dunbar (at the end of the nineteenth). Many of Harper's poems portray oppression and the abuses of slavery, with dramatic eloquence. "The Slave Mother: A Tale of the Ohio" (1874) anticipates the fateful plot of Toni Morrison's *Beloved* (1987) in relating starkly the story of a mother who sacrifices her baby's life so as not to condemn the child to a life of slavery. Harper's poetry shows us the experience of oppression from the inside. Her voice authenticates pain and degradation, just as the voices of the abolitionists articulate principle.

Two major formulations of poetic theory in this period came from Edgar Allan Poe and Ralph Waldo Emerson, both poets of considerable talent. Romantic that he was in defining *beauty* as the province of the poem, Poe nonetheless stressed the importance of *form* in poetry; to him the poet was a craftsman who introduced such considerations as rhyme and meter, of tone and even length, into the making of a poem. Militantly opposed to what he called "the heresy of *The Didactic*" (and thus to the practice of the honored writers of New England), Poe defines poetry in his essay "The Poetic Principle" (1850) as *"The Rhythmical Creation of Beauty."* To Emerson, conversely, the poet is a seer or prophet who releases us from the prison of our own little worlds. In his essay "The Poet" (1844) Emerson asserts the priority of "thought" in the genesis of a poem; "it is not metres but a metre-making argument, that makes a poem, a thought so passionate and alive, that, like the spirit of a thought or an animal, it has an architecture of its own, and adorns nature with a new thing." The form of a poem is thus organic, expressive, profoundly liberating.

Poe and Emerson visualized the possibilities of poetry in diametrically opposed ways, Poe in a way that intrigued the French symbolists and some modernist poets, Emerson in a way that appealed to any number of romantic poets but principally and dramatically to his contemporary, Walt Whitman. In "The Poet," Emerson laments the fact that the United States had not yet produced a writer who realized "the value of our incomparable materials." He called for a poet who could exalt the details of American life: such things as political caucuses, logrolling, and

---

==CONTEXTS==

The Abolition Movement

In the 1830s America experienced a resurgence of antislavery sentiment, largely due to three factors: the debates over slavery in conventions called for the purpose of rewriting state constitutions; Nat Turner's Rebellion in Virginia in 1831; and the publication of the *Liberator,* a radical abolitionist newspaper by William Lloyd Garrison (1805–1879) calling for the immediate, unconditional emancipation of all slaves in America. Garrison's weekly was launched on January 1, 1831, and continued publication for thirty-four years, folding its doors only after slavery had been abolished by the Thirteenth Amendment to the Constitution. (Garrison was the first editor to print the poems of John Greenleaf Whittier, a fellow abolitionist and a founder of the American Anti-Slavery Society.) Garrison's statement of his aims and purposes, reprinted below from the first issue, alarmed northern moderates, outraged southerners, and caused a split between those who called for the gradual end of slavery and those who wanted its immediate end.

Commencement of the *Liberator*

Assenting to the "self-evident truth" maintained in the American Declaration of Independence, "that all men are created equal, and endowed by their Creator with certain inalienable rights—among which are life, liberty, and the pursuit of happiness," I shall strenuously contend for the immediate enfranchisement of our slave population. In Park Street Church, on the Fourth of July, 1829, in an address on slavery, I unreflectingly assented to the popular but pernicious doctrine of gradual abolition. I seize this opportunity to make a full and unequivocal recantation, and thus publicly to ask pardon of my God, of my country, and of my brethren, the poor slaves, for having uttered a sentiment so full of timidity, injustice and absurdity. A similar recantation, from my pen, was published in the *Genius of Universal Emancipation,* at Baltimore, in September, 1829. My conscience is now satisfied.

I am aware, that many object to the severity of my language; but is there not cause for severity? I will be as harsh as truth, and as uncompromising as justice. On this subject, I do not wish to think, or speak, or write, with moderation. No! no! Tell a man, whose house is on fire, to give a moderate alarm; tell him to moderately rescue his wife from the hands of the ravisher; tell the mother to gradually extricate her babe from the fire into which it has fallen; but urge me not to use moderation in a cause like the present! I am in earnest. I will not equivocate—I will not excuse—I will not retreat a single inch—AND I WILL BE HEARD. The apathy of the people is enough to make every statue leap from its pedestal, and to hasten the resurrection of the dead.

William Lloyd Garrison, 1831

---

western clearing "are flat and dull to dull people," he argues, but they "rest on the same foundations of wonder as the town of Troy, and the temple of Delphos." Emerson admits that he is not the poet to celebrate these "unsung" aspects of American life, but he asserts that "America is a poem in our eyes," that "its ample geography dazzles the imagination." A decade later Walt Whitman began to write this vast poem. With egocentric grace he remarked to the journalist J. T. Trowbridge, "I had been simmering, simmering, simmering; Emerson brought me to a boil."

What Whitman extracted from Emerson and from the democratic nation that had grown awkwardly through the first half of the nineteenth century was the crucial idea of "self." The first edition of *Leaves of Grass* appeared in 1855 and evoked strong reactions from other writers: Whittier threw his gift copy into the fireplace, Lowell reportedly refused to read it, and Emerson praised it warmly. Notwithstanding the small sales of the book, Whitman published a second edition in 1856 and a third in 1860 (there were nine in all). Each edition grew, adjusting and rearranging its vision, absorbing the experience of the nation into the democratic and collective self at the center. Radically different in form and substance from any previous poetry, Whitman's *Leaves* celebrates the self as encompassing, expansive, boastfully inclusive in its vision. No longer is it necessary to have history and legend to forge an epic: as Whitman makes clear in the remarkable preface to the 1855 edition of *Leaves* and in that volume's "Song of Myself," the human being, body and soul (which are one), becomes epic in importance, deserving of epic treatment in a land of epic proportions.

Devastating and crippling, the Civil War gave American poets a tragic subject of their own, a gathering event for the expression of grief. From different perspectives Whitman, Herman Melville, and Henry Timrod wrote poems about individual battles and individual soldiers dead or broken in body. Tempered in assertion, solemn in tone, the poems in Whitman's *Drum-Taps* (1865) display a haunting sorrow, the consequence of a shattered optimism that found deepest expression in his tribute to Abraham Lincoln, "When Lilacs Last in the Dooryard Bloom'd." By comparison with these meditations on death, the poems in Melville's *Battle-Pieces* (1866) seem distanced, almost frozen with commemorative pride in the heroism and suffering of the war. Even the delicate portrait of "The College Colonel" is restrained, mannered, austere in its reckoning of pain.

Whereas Whitman and Melville write about the consequences of battle from fixed perspectives after-the-fact, three poems by Timrod frame the Civil War from developing points of view in Charleston, South Carolina. *Ethnogenesis,* written in 1861 during sessions of the Confederate Congress (but not published until 1873), is not so much a war poem as a founding statement that hails the Confederacy, congratulates the South for its character and climate, and predicts victory over the North. "Charleston" (1862) portrays that southern city in portentous calm, awaiting the clash of arms that will bring "triumph or the tomb." And the "Ode" (1867) to the Confederate dead buried at Magnolia Cemetery honors the "martyrs of a fallen cause" whose "defeated valor" hallows the earth forever.

Among American poets only Whitman emerged from the trauma of the Civil War with hope for the future. His optimism was qualified, his flagrant boasting about America a thing of the past. Yet, so great was his faith in democracy, so firm was his commitment to the future, that Whitman in *Democratic Vistas* (1871) came to see the war years as "the years of parturition," the years of the birth of the country. In April 1865 Bryant published "Abraham Lincoln," honoring the president who had seen the nation through four years of strife. It is a polished and accomplished poem, deserving of the praise Samuel Kettell gave Bryant's work in 1829. But to read that poem alongside Whitman's "When Lilacs Last in the Dooryard Bloom'd," written in the same year, is to see that a revolution had occurred in American poetry, radical beyond Bryant's powers, encompassing beyond what Kettell could have foreseen. With Walt Whitman's "barbaric yawp" (as he termed it in *Song of Myself*), poetry in America became American poetry.

William Cullen Bryant
(1794–1878)

William Cullen Bryant, lawyer, journalist, literary critic, and romantic nature poet, was one of the most dominant literary figures of his age. A member of the Knickerbocker group and other literary societies, he spent his life close to the arts. He was among the first to call for a truly American literature and the first American poet to achieve international acclaim. The son of a physician father and a mother who was a descendant of the Puritan John Alden, Bryant was born in 1794 in Cummington, Massachusetts, and educated early at the hands of country Calvinist ministers. When he was thirteen, he published *The Embargo* (1808), a satire in verse on the political policies of Thomas Jefferson. He entered Williams College in 1810 but left after less than a year and embarked on the study of law. Admitted to the bar in 1814, he established a law practice in Great Barrington, Massachusetts, and married Fanny Fairchild in 1821.

Bryant gave up his legal work to pursue a career in journalism. In 1825 he moved to New York City and began editing the *New York Review*. A year later he became an assistant editor of the New York *Evening Post*, and in 1829 he assumed the editorship of this prestigious journal, a position he held until his death in 1878. Bryant occupies a central place in the history of American journalism.

Bryant's poetry is important as a transition between the neoclassical tendencies of the early republic and the American romanticism that would follow. Bryant published his first collection of poetry, *Poems*, in 1821; it includes "Thanatopsis," perhaps his most famous poem, originally drafted around 1811. As a forerunner of the romantic movement in America, he led the literary revolt against neoclassicism in part by stressing the use of American materials, including the American landscape. Bryant claimed from his earliest childhood to be "a delighted observer of external nature," and his poetry is filled with images drawn from his youth in the Berkshires of Massachusetts. The major themes in his work include nature, mutability, death, the past, and poetry itself. Insistently didactic, his poetry repeatedly suggests the moral and spiritual perfection to be found in the contemplation of nature. Many of his best poems are meditative and describe the goodness of nature in detail.

In keeping with Bryant's romantic inclinations, his poetry also shows remarkable range in terms of metrical freedom and experimentation. A meticulous craftsman, Bryant became a master of poetic forms; during the final decade of his life he translated Homer's *Iliad* (1870) and *Odyssey* (1871–1872) into simple and effective blank verse. As his work

Pictured in Kindred Spirits *(1849), by Asher Durand, are William Cullen Bryant, poet, and Thomas Cole, landscape painter, in a setting that exemplifies the romantic ideal of harmony between nature and people.*

demonstrates, Bryant was interested in scientific progress and perhaps even more so in politics—advocating the rights of labor unions, free trade, and a free press. His concern for human rights is evident in his stand against slavery and in his interest in the traditions of Native Americans. An exceptionally prominent figure in his own time, Bryant continued writing and publishing until his death. His limited reputation today seems scant appreciation for a lifetime of measured but definite achievement.

Suggested Readings: *The Letters of William Cullen Bryant*, ed. W. C. Bryant II and T. G. Voss, 4 vols., 1975–1984. C. S. Johnson, *Politics and a Bellyful: The Journalistic Career of William Cullen Bryant*, 1962. H. H. Peckham, *Gotham Yankee: A Biography of William Cullen Bryant*, 1971. C. H. Brown, *William Cullen Bryant*, 1972. J. T. Phair, *A Bibliography of William Cullen Bryant and His Critics, 1808-1972*, 1975.

Text Used: "The Poet" and "Abraham Lincoln": *The Poetical Works of William Cullen Bryant*, ed. P. Godwin, Vol. II, 1883, rpt. 1967. All else: *The Poetical Works*, Vol. I.

THANATOPSIS*

To him who in the love of Nature holds
Communion with her visible forms, she speaks
A various language; for his gayer hours
She has a voice of gladness, and a smile
And eloquence of beauty, and she glides
Into his darker musings, with a mild
And healing sympathy, that steals away
Their sharpness, ere he is aware. When thoughts
Of the last bitter hour come like a blight
Over thy spirit, and sad images   10
Of the stern agony, and shroud, and pall,
And breathless darkness, and the narrow house,
Make thee to shudder, and grow sick at heart;—
Go forth, under the open sky, and list
To Nature's teachings, while from all around—
Earth and her waters, and the depths of air—
Comes a still voice.—[1]

                Yet a few days, and thee
The all-beholding sun shall see no more
In all his course; nor yet in the cold ground,
Where thy pale form was laid, with many tears,   20
Nor in the embrace of ocean, shall exist
Thy image. Earth, that nourished thee, shall claim
Thy growth, to be resolved to earth again,
And, lost each human trace, surrendering up
Thine individual being, shalt thou go
To mix for ever with the elements,
To be a brother to the insensible rock
And to the sluggish clod, which the rude swain[2]
Turns with his share,[3] and treads upon. The oak
Shall send his roots abroad, and pierce thy mould.   30

   Yet not to thine eternal resting-place
Shalt thou retire alone, nor couldst thou wish
Couch more magnificent. Thou shalt lie down
With patriarchs of the infant world—with kings,
The powerful of the earth—the wise, the good,
Fair forms, and hoary seers of ages past,
All in one mighty sepulchre. The hills
Rock-ribbed and ancient as the sun,—the vales
Stretching in pensive quietness between;

---

* First published in part in the *North American Review* (1817) and revised into the present form for publication in Bryant's *Poems* (1821). The Greek word "thanatopsis" means "meditation on death."
[1] From this point to the end of the poem, nature in its entirety speaks in "a still voice" of stoic authority.
[2] Farmer.   [3] Plowshare.

The venerable woods—rivers that move   40
In majesty, and the complaining brooks
That make the meadows green; and, poured round
     all,
Old Ocean's gray and melancholy waste,—
Are but the solemn decorations all
Of the great tomb of man. The golden sun,
The planets, all the infinite host of heaven,
Are shining on the sad abodes of death,
Through the still lapse of ages. All that tread
The globe are but a handful to the tribes
That slumber in its bosom.—Take the wings   50
Of morning, pierce the Barcan wilderness,[4]
Or lose thyself in the continuous woods
Where rolls the Oregon,[5] and hears no sound,
Save his own dashings—yet the dead are there:
And millions in those solitudes, since first
The flight of years began, have laid them down
In their last sleep—the dead reign there alone.
So shalt thou rest, and what if thou withdraw
In silence from the living, and no friend
Take note of thy departure? All that breathe   60
Will share thy destiny. The gay will laugh
When thou art gone, the solemn brood of care
Plod on, and each one as before will chase
His favorite phantom; yet all these shall leave
Their mirth and their employments, and shall come
And make their bed with thee. As the long train
Of ages glides away, the sons of men,
The youth in life's fresh spring, and he who goes
In the full strength of years, matron and maid,
The speechless babe, and the gray-headed man—
Shall one by one be gathered to thy side,   70
By those, who in their turn shall follow them.
     So live, that when thy summons comes to join
The innumerable caravan, which moves
To that mysterious realm, where each shall take
His chamber in the silent halls of death,
Thou go not, like the quarry-slave at night,
Scourged to his dungeon, but, sustained and soothed
By an unfaltering trust, approach thy grave,
Like one who wraps the drapery of his couch   80
About him, and lies down to pleasant dreams.

                                  1811?, 1817

---

[4] The Libyan desert of Barca.
[5] The Native-American name for Oregon's Columbia River.

TO A WATERFOWL*

Whither, midst falling dew,
While glow the heavens with the last steps of day,
Far, through their rosy depths, dost thou pursue
Thy solitary way?

Vainly the fowler's eye
Might mark thy distant flight to do thee wrong,
As, darkly painted on the crimson sky,
Thy figure floats along.

Seek'st thou the plashy[1] brink
Of weedy lake, or marge of river wide,   10
Or where the rocking billows rise and sink
On the chafed ocean-side?

There is a Power whose care
Teaches thy way along that pathless coast—
The desert and illimitable air—
Lone wandering, but not lost.

All day thy wings have fanned,
At that far height, the cold, thin atmosphere,
Yet stoop not, weary, to the welcome land,
Though the dark night is near.   20

And soon that toil shall end;
Soon shalt thou find a summer home, and rest,
And scream among thy fellows; reeds shall bend,
Soon, o'er thy sheltered nest.

Thou'rt gone, the abyss of heaven
Hath swallowed up thy form; yet, on my heart
Deeply has sunk the lesson thou hast given,
And shall not soon depart.

He who, from zone to zone,
Guides through the boundless sky thy certain flight,   30
In the long way that I must tread alone,
Will lead my steps aright.

                                                  1815, 1818

---

* First published in the *North American Review* (1818).   [1] Marshy.

THE AFRICAN CHIEF*

Chained in the market-place he stood,
A man of giant frame,
Amid the gathering multitude
That shrunk to hear his name[1]—
All stern of look and strong of limb,
His dark eye on the ground:—
And silently they gazed on him,
As on a lion bound.

Vainly, but well that chief had fought,
He was a captive now,   10
Yet pride, that fortune humbles not,
Was written on his brow.
The scars his dark broad bosom wore
Showed warrior true and brave;
A prince among his tribe before,
He could not be a slave.[2]

Then to his conqueror he spake:
"My brother is a king;
Undo this necklace from my neck,
And take this bracelet ring,   20
And send me where my brother reigns,
And I will fill thy hands
With store of ivory from the plains,
And gold-dust from the sands."

"Not for thy ivory nor thy gold
Will I unbind thy chain;
That bloody hand shall never hold
The battle-spear again.
A price that nation never gave[3]
Shall yet be paid for thee;   30
For thou shalt be the Christian's slave,
In lands beyond the sea."

Then wept the warrior chief, and bade[4]
To shred his locks away;
And one by one, each heavy braid
Before the victor lay.
Thick were the platted locks, and long,
And closely hidden there
Shone many a wedge of gold among
The dark and crisped hair.   40

* First published in the *United States Review* (1826).
[1] The scene is a marketplace in Africa where this mighty chief stands to be sold to slave traders; apparently his name is well known, for the multitude shrinks back when they hear it.
[2] Meant literally and forcefully, this line anticipates the poem's tragic ending.
[3] A price beyond what anyone ever paid will be "paid for thee."   [4] Told them to.

"Look, feast thy greedy eye with gold
Long kept for sorest need;
Take it—thou askest sums untold—
And say that I am freed.

Take it—my wife, the long, long day,
Weeps by the cocoa-tree,
And my young children leave their play,
And ask in vain for me."

"I take thy gold, but, I have made
Thy fetters fast and strong,
And ween[5] that by the cocoa-shade   50
Thy wife will wait thee long."
Strong was the agony that shook
The captive's frame to hear,
And the proud meaning of his look
Was changed to mortal fear.

His heart was broken—crazed his brain:
At once his eye grew wild;
He struggled fiercely with his chain,
Whispered, and wept, and smiled;   60
Yet wore not long those fatal bands,
And once, at shut of day,
They drew him forth upon the sands,
The foul hyena's prey.[6]

1825, 1826

THE POET*

Thou, who wouldst wear the name
Of poet mid thy brethren of mankind,
And clothe in words of flame
Thoughts that shall live within the general mind!
Deem not the framing of a deathless lay
The pastime of a drowsy summer day.

But gather all thy powers,
And wreak them[1] on the verse that thou dost weave,
And in thy lonely hours,

---

[5] Know.

[6] The ending is suggested not only by line 16 but by the fact that the chief smiles after experiencing fear and wildness: he is so attuned to his surroundings that nature, in the form of a savage hyena, takes away his life before he can be sold into bondage. Bryant's stance against slavery was strong, although his best-known poems would hardly attest to the fact.

* First published in *Thirty Poems* (1864).   [1] Release them, apply them fully.

At silent morning or at wakeful eve,   10
While the warm current tingles through thy veins,
Set forth the burning words in fluent strains.

No smooth array of phrase,
Artfully sought and ordered though it be,
Which the cold rhymer lays
Upon his page with languid industry,
Can wake the listless pulse to livelier speed,
Or fill with sudden tears the eyes that read.

The secret wouldst thou know
To touch the heart or fire the blood at will?   20
Let thine own eyes o'erflow;
Let thy lips quiver with the passionate thrill;
Seize the great thought, ere yet its power be past,
And bind, in words, the fleet emotion fast.

Then, should thy verse appear
Halting and harsh, and all unaptly wrought,
Touch the crude line with fear,
Save in the moment of impassioned thought;
Then summon back the original glow, and mend
The strain with rapture that with fire was penned.   30

Yet let no empty gust
Of passion find a utterance in thy lay,
A blast that whirls the dust
Along the howling street and dies away;
But feelings of calm power and mighty sweep,
Like currents journeying through the windless deep.

Seek'st thou, in living lays,
To limn[2] the beauty of the earth and sky?
Before thine inner gaze
Let all that beauty in clear vision lie;   40
Look on it with exceeding love, and write
The words inspired by wonder and delight.

Of tempests wouldst thou sing,
Or tell of battles—make thyself a part
Of the great tumult; cling
To the tossed wreck with terror in thy heart;
Scale, with the assaulting host, the rampart's height,
And strike and struggle in the thickest fight.

So shalt thou frame a lay[3]
That haply may endure from age to age,   50
And they who read shall say:

---

[2] Paint, portray.   [3] A song or poem.

"What witchery hangs upon this poet's page!
What art is his the written spells to find
That sway from mood to mood the willing mind!"

1863, 1864

ABRAHAM LINCOLN*

Oh, slow to smite and swift to spare,
Gentle and merciful and just!
Who, in the fear of God, didst bear
The sword of power, a nation's trust!

In sorrow by thy bier we stand,
Amid the awe that hushes all,
And speak the anguish of a land
That shook with horror at thy fall.

Thy task is done; the bond[1] are free:
We bear thee to an honored grave.   10
Whose proudest monument shall be
The broken fetters[2] of the slave.

Pure was thy life; its bloody close
Hath placed thee with the sons of light,
Among the noble host of those
Who perished in the cause of Right.

1865

Henry Wadsworth Longfellow
(1807–1882)

Henry Wadsworth Longfellow was the most widely read American poet in the nineteenth century. The sales of his poems suggest his immense popularity: his first collection, *Voices of the Night* (1839), sold 43,000 copies; *The Song of Hiawatha* (1855) sold 30,000 copies within six months; and *The Courtship of Miles Standish* (1858) sold an astonishing 15,000

---

* First published in the New York *Evening Post,* April 26, 1865. The poem was written at the request of the Committee on Arrangements and read to a gathering of mourners on April 24, 1865, when Lincoln's funeral procession passed through New York City. Lincoln had been assassinated on April 24, 1865.
[1] Slaves.   [2] Shackles.

A portrait of Longfellow's three daughters.

copies on its first day of publication. So great was his fame in England that he was the first American to have his bust preserved in Poet's Corner of Westminster Abbey after his death in 1882. With James Russell Lowell, John Greenleaf Whittier, and Oliver Wendell Holmes, Longfellow was one of the culturally approved "Fireside Poets," whose works became standard educational fare throughout the nation. Master of a wide range of verse forms, Longfellow was particularly adept as a writer of ballads, sonnets, and narrative poems.

Longfellow was born in 1807 in Portland, Maine, then a part of Massachusetts, into a long-established family that could trace its ancestry back to the *Mayflower*. He attended Portland Academy and later Bowdoin College, where he was a classmate of Nathaniel Hawthorne. Upon graduation in 1825, Longfellow accepted a professorship in modern languages at Bowdoin, and the college sent him to Europe for three years of preparatory study in Europe. In 1829 he assumed his post at Bowdoin. Longfellow held positions in the field of modern foreign language at Harvard University as well. In 1835 he returned to Europe for intense language study, particularly German, in preparation for his Harvard appointment. On the journey, however, his wife since 1831, Mary Potter, died after a miscarriage. From 1836 to 1854 he was chairman of modern languages at Harvard; during that time he met and married the heiress Frances Appleton. After eighteen years of marriage, during which she bore three daughters and two sons, she was killed in a house fire in 1861.

Given his training in foreign languages, and his immersion in foreign culture, it is not surprising that Longfellow remained interested in foreign literature and the classics throughout his long career, from his collection of European poetry in *Poets and Poetry of Europe* (1845) to his *Tales of a Wayside Inn* (1863) and his translation of Dante's *Divine Comedy* (1867). Although his knowledge of other literary traditions, particularly Germanic and Scandinavian, allowed him to borrow from a virtual storehouse of poetry, Longfellow demonstrated great versatility in his use of prosody and poetic forms. And like William Cullen Bryant and other writers concerned to create an American literature, Longfellow used his talents to explore American history, legends, and folklore. Works such as *Evangeline* (1847), *Hiawatha*, and *The Courtship of Miles Standish* attest to this considerable effort.

Longfellow was a deeply traditional writer, a poet of assurance whose commitment to the values of domesticity endeared him to a wide audience. By considering that *Hiawatha* and the first edition of Walt Whitman's *Leaves of Grass* were published in the same year, 1855, we get a sense of American poetry at a crossroads—Longfellow offering the public what it wanted, Whitman offering the same public what it had to have. Because the twentieth century has come to prefer Whitman, we have tended to neglect the work of our public poet par excellence—along with that of the other Fireside Poets. Yet, even from our perspective, many of Longfellow's shorter lyrics, and especially the more personal of his sonnets, command respect and admiration.

Suggested Readings: *Kavanagh, A Tale*, ed. J. Downey, 1965. *The Poetical Works of Longfellow*, 1893, rpt. 1975. *The Letters of Henry Wadsworth Longfellow*, 6 vols., ed. A. Hilen, 1966–1982. S. Longfellow, *The Life of Henry Wadsworth Longfellow*, 3 vols., 1886, rpt. 1969. N. Arvin, *Longfellow: His Life and Work*, 1963. C. B. Williams, *Henry Wadsworth Longfellow*, 1964. L. R. Thompson, *Young Longfellow (1807–1843)*, 1969. E. Wagenknecht, *Henry Wadsworth Longfellow, His Poetry and Prose*, 1986.

Text Used: *The Complete Poetical Works of Henry Wadsworth Longfellow*, 1922.

MEZZO CAMMIN*

Written at Boppard on the Rhine, August 25, 1842, just before leaving for home.

Half of my life is gone, and I have let
    The years slip from me and have not fulfilled
    The aspiration of my youth, to build
Some tower of song with lofty parapet.

---

* First published posthumously in the *Life of Henry Wadsworth Longfellow* (1886), edited by Samuel Longfellow (1819–1892), Henry's brother. The title is taken from the opening line of Dante's *Divine Comedy*, "*Nel mezzo del cammin di nostra vita*" ("Midway along the path of life"); Longfellow wrote the poem when he was thirty-five, half of the biblical allotment of threescore and ten years (Psalm 89:10).

Not indolence, nor pleasure, nor the fret
   Of restless passions that would not be stilled,
   But sorrow, and a care that almost killed,[1]
   Kept me from what I may accomplish yet;
Though, half-way up the hill, I see the Past
   Lying beneath me with its sounds and sights,—   10
   A city in the twilight dim and vast,
With smoking roofs, soft bells, and gleaming lights,—
   And hear above me on the autumnal blast
   The cataract of Death far thundering from the heights.

                                              1842, 1886

THE JEWISH CEMETERY AT NEWPORT*

How strange it seems! These Hebrews in their graves,
   Close by the street of this fair seaport town,
Silent beside the never-silent waves,
   At rest in all this moving up and down!

The trees are white with dust, that o'er their sleep
   Wave their broad curtains in the south-wind's breath,
While underneath these leafy tents they keep
   The long, mysterious Exodus[1] of Death.

And these sepulchral stones, so old and brown,
   That pave with level flags[2] their burial-place,   10
Seem like the tablets of the Law, thrown down
   And broken by Moses at the mountain's base.[3]

The very names recorded here are strange,
   Of foreign accent, and of different climes;
Alvares and Rivera[4] interchange
   With Abraham and Jacob[5] of old times.

"Blessed be God, for he created Death!"
   The mourners said, "and Death is rest and peace;"
Then added, in the certainty of faith,
   "And giveth Life that nevermore shall cease."   20

---

[1] The death of Longfellow's first wife, Mary Potter, in 1835.
* First published in *Putnam's Monthly Magazine* in 1854. Newport is a seaport town in Rhode Island.
[1] A journey; the biblical book of Exodus tells of the journey of the Israelites from Egypt.
[2] Flagstones; the stones in this extant cemetery are flat with the ground.
[3] In Exodus 32:1–19, when Moses came down from the mountain and saw the Israelites worshipping an idol, he broke the stone tablets inscribed with the Ten Commandments.
[4] Names (on the gravestones) of Jews who had come from Portugal and Spain.
[5] Old Testament patriarchs.

Closed are the portals of their Synagogue.
  No Psalms of David now the silence break,
No Rabbi reads the ancient Decalogue[6]
  In the grand dialect the Prophets spake.

Gone are the living, but the dead remain,
  And not neglected; for a hand unseen,
Scattering its bounty, like a summer rain,
  Still keeps their graves and their remembrance green.

How came they here? What burst of Christian hate,
  What persecution, merciless and blind,   30
Drove o'er the sea—that desert desolate—
  These Ishmaels and Hagars[7] of mankind?

They lived in narrow streets and lanes obscure,
  Ghetto and Judenstrass,[8] in mirk and mire;
Taught in the school of patience to endure
  The life of anguish and the death of fire.

All their lives long, with the unleavened bread
  And bitter herbs of exile and its fears,
The wasting famine of the heart they fed,
  And slaked its thirst with marah[9] of their tears.   40

Anathema maranatha![10] was the cry
  That rang from town to town, from street to street:
At every gate the accursed Mordecai[11]
  Was mocked and jeered, and spurned by Christian feet.

Pride and humiliation hand in hand
  Walked with them through the world where'er they went;
Trampled and beaten were they as the sand,
  And yet unshaken as the continent.

For in the background figures vague and vast
  Of patriarchs and of prophets rose sublime,   50
And all the great traditions of the Past
  They saw reflected in the coming time.

And thus forever with reverted look
  The mystic volume of the world they read,
Spelling it backward, like a Hebrew book,[12]
  Till life became a Legend of the Dead.

---

[6] The Ten Commandments.   [7] Outcasts and pariahs (see Genesis 16 and 21).
[8] "Street of Jews" (German).   [9] "Bitterness" (Hebrew).
[10] "If any man does not love the Lord Jesus Christ, let him be anathema. Maranatha," from I Corinthians 16:22–23: this cry rang after the Jews.
[11] In Esther 5–7, a Jewish leader reviled by the Persians.
[12] Hebrew is read from right to left.

But ah! what once has been shall be no more!
  The groaning earth in travail and in pain
Brings forth its races, but does not restore,
  And the dead nations never rise again.   60

1852, 1854

MILTON*

I pace the sounding sea-beach and behold
  How the voluminous billows roll and run,
  Upheaving and subsiding, while the sun
  Shines through their sheeted emerald far unrolled,
And the ninth wave,[1] slow gathering fold by fold
  All its loose-flowing garments into one,
  Plunges upon the shore, and floods the dun
Pale reach of sands, and changes them to gold.
So in majestic cadence rise and fall
  The mighty undulations of thy song,   10
  O sightless bard, England's Mæonides![2]
And ever and anon, high over all
  Uplifted, a ninth wave superb and strong,
  Floods all the soul with its melodious seas.

1873?, 1875

NATURE†

As a fond mother, when the day is o'er,
  Leads by the hand her little child to bed,
  Half willing, half reluctant to be led,
  And leave his broken playthings on the floor,
Still gazing at them through the open door,
  Nor wholly reassured and comforted
  By promises of others in their stead,
Which, though more splendid, may not please him more:
So Nature deals with us, and takes away
  Our playthings one by one, and by the hand   10
  Leads us to rest so gently, that we go
Scarce knowing if we wish to go or stay,
  Being too full of sleep to understand
  How far the unknown transcends the what we know.

1874, 1875

---

* First published in the *Atlantic Monthly* in 1875, this sonnet is a tribute to the English poet John Milton (1608–1674), author of the epic poem *Paradise Lost* (1667).
[1] Supposedly the strongest in a series of waves.
[2] The Greek epic poet Homer, said to have been blind, like Milton.
† First published in the *Atlantic Monthly* in 1875.

THE CROSS OF SNOW*

In the long, sleepless watches of the night,
   A gentle face—the face of one long dead—
   Looks at me from the wall, where round its head
   The night-lamp casts a halo of pale light.
Here in this room she died; and soul more white
   Never through martyrdom of fire was led
   To its repose; nor can in books be read
   The legend of a life more benedight.[1]
There is a mountain in the distant West
   That, sun-defying, in its deep ravines   10
   Displays a cross of snow upon its side.
Such is the cross I wear upon my breast
   These eighteen years, through all the changing scenes
   And seasons, changeless since the day she died.

                          1879, 1886

John Greenleaf Whittier
(1807–1892)

Born on a farm north of Boston near Haverhill, Massachusetts, in 1807, John Greenleaf Whittier received a relatively scant education at the area's District School, followed by a brief two-term stint at Haverhill Academy. In contrast to his contemporary Henry Wadsworth Longfellow, for whom poetry seemed to come naturally, Whittier conscientiously learned his craft, modeling his early work on that of the Scottish poet Robert Burns. Before he turned twenty-five Whittier had produced many amateurish poems that can be seen as workshop experiences, preludes to his later successes. His first published piece was printed in 1826 in the Newburyport, Massachusetts, *Free Press,* a newspaper run by William Lloyd Garrison, who encouraged Whittier to pursue writing as a career and became his lifelong friend and associate in abolitionist and other reform causes.

    Whittier was raised as a Quaker, and the tenets of that religion influenced his life and his work. His great cause was abolitionism, which he began to champion as early as the 1830s. Valuing the virtue of direct communication, he used his talent as a writer of poetry and of newspaper editorials to raise public awareness of the slavery issue. In 1833 he published *Justice and Expediency,* an abolitionist pamphlet that brought him into the public eye and coincided with his election as a delegate to the National Anti-Slavery Conven-

---

* First published posthumously in the *Life of Henry Wadsworth Longfellow* (1886), edited by Samuel Longfellow (1819–1892), Henry's brother. Like "Mezzo Cammin," this poem is deeply personal, a meditation on the enduring grief Longfellow carried with him after the tragic death of his second wife by fire. It is interesting that these two poems, among Longfellow's most accomplished, were considered too private to share with his public. His almost stereotyped image as a public poet does not reflect all of his abilities.
[1] Blessed.

*John Brown leaving jail, on his way to be executed; etching
by Thomas Hoovenden (1885). Courtesy of the New York
Historical Society.*

tion in Philadelphia. In 1835 he was elected to a term in the Massachusetts legislature and
was active in the Whig party. Later, in 1839, he helped to found the Liberty party, which
had its basis in abolitionism. For much of his life Whittier edited various reform journals,
including *The Pennsylvania Freeman* in Philadelphia and the *National Era* in Washington,
D.C. He paid for his principles in these years by being mobbed and stoned and made the
target of gunfire.

Whittier wrote one lengthy work of fiction, *Leaves From Margaret Smith's Journal in
the Province of Massachusetts Bay* (1849), which explores the temper of the Puritan mind
prior to the Salem witchcraft trials of 1692. During this middle period of his career, however, much of his creative energy went into the writing of antislavery poems ("Massachusetts to Virginia" among them), which were collected in *Voices of Freedom* (1846); together with the later "Ichabod" (1850) and "Laus Deo!" (1865), these poems stand as
examples of the writer's deep commitment to human justice. Yet, Whittier's reputation
does not rest exclusively on political verse: he was considered one of the "Fireside Poets"
and much of his poetry is rooted in the traditions of New England country life. After the
Civil War he celebrated the values of that life in his "winter idyl," *Snow-Bound* (1866). In
that poem Whittier portrays rural New England with compelling authority, carefully de-

picting the virtues of domesticity in a time gone by. *Snow-Bound* is a masterful triumph of nostalgia, with its implicit contrast between the safety and simple pleasures of the past, and the turmoil and complexity of the present.

In ill health, Whittier spent his later years in the family home he had inherited in Amesbury, Massachusetts, and in nearby Danvers. He died of a stroke in Hampton Falls, New Hampshire, in 1892. Poet of the conscience and poet of the hearth, Whittier's work continues to speak to the issues of a later day as it spoke to those of his own.

Suggested Readings: *Whittier on Writers and Writing: The Uncollected Critical Writings of John Greenleaf Whittier*, ed. E. H. Cady and H. H. Clark, 1950. *Letters of John Greenleaf Whittier*, 3 vols., ed. J. B. Pickard, 1975. E. Wagenknecht, *John Greenleaf Whittier: A Portrait in Paradox*, 1967. J. A. Pollard, *John Greenleaf Whittier, Friend of Man*, 1969. R. P. Warren, *John Greenleaf Whittier's Poetry: An Appraisal and a Selection*, 1971. J. K. Kribbs, ed., *Critical Essays on John Greenleaf Whittier*, 1980. R. H. Woodwell, *John Greenleaf Whittier: A Biography*, 1985.

Texts Used: "Massachusetts to Virginia" and "Ichabod!": *The Poetical Works of John Greenleaf Whittier*, Vol. I, 1884. "Snow-Bound": *The Poetical Works*, Vol. III.

MASSACHUSETTS TO VIRGINIA*

The blast from Freedom's Northern hills, upon its Southern way,
Bears greetings to Virginia from Massachusetts Bay:—
No word of haughty challenging, nor battle bugle's peal,
Nor steady tread of marching files, nor clang of horsemen's steel.

No trains of deep-mouthed cannon along our highways go,—
Around our silent arsenals untrodden lies the snow;
And to the land-breeze of our ports, upon their errands far,
A thousand sails of commerce swell, but none are spread for war.

We hear thy threats, Virginia! thy stormy words and high,
Swell harshly on the Southern winds which melt along our sky;   10
Yet, not one brown, hard hand foregoes its honest labor here,—
No hewer of our mountain oaks suspends his axe in fear.

Wild are the waves which lash the reefs along St. George's bank,—[1]
Cold on the shore of Labrador the fog lies white and dank;
Through storm and wave and blinding mist stout are the hearts which man
The fishing-smacks of Marblehead, the sea-boats of Cape Ann.[2]

---

* Read at the Essex County Anti-Slavery Convention on January 2, 1843, and published that month in *The Liberator*. Whittier's note: "Written on reading an account of the proceedings of the citizens of Norfolk, Va., in reference to George Latimer, the alleged fugitive slave, who was seized in Boston without warrant at the request of James B. Grey, of Norfolk, claiming to be his master. The case caused great excitement North and South, and led to the presentation of a petition to Congress, signed by more than fifty thousand citizens of Massachusetts, calling for such laws and proposed amendments to the Constitution as should relieve the Commonwealth from all further participation in the crime of oppression. George Latimer himself was finally given his free papers for the sum of four hundred dollars."

[1] Off the coast of Newfoundland.   [2] On the Massachusetts coast.

The cold north light and wintry sun glare on their icy forms,
Bent grimly o'er their straining lines or wrestling with the storms;
Free as the winds they drive before, rough as the waves they roam,
They laugh to scorn the slaver's threat against their rocky home.   20

What means the Old Dominion?[3] Hath she forgot the day
When o'er her conquered valleys swept the Briton's steel array?
How side by side, with sons of hers, the Massachusetts men
Encountered Tarleton's charge of fire, and stout Cornwallis,[4] then?

Forgets she how the Bay State,[5] in answer to the call
Of her old House of Burgesses, spoke out from Faneuil Hall?[6]
When, echoing back her Henry's[7] cry, came pulsing on each breath
Of Northern winds, the thrilling sounds of "LIBERTY OR DEATH!"

What asks the Old Dominion? If now her sons have proved
False to their fathers' memory,—false to the faith they loved,   30
If she can scoff at Freedom, and its great charter[8] spurn,
Must we of Massachusetts from truth and duty turn?

We hunt your bondmen,[9] flying from Slavery's hateful hell,—
Our voices, at your bidding, take up the bloodhound's yell,—
We gather, at your summons, above our fathers' graves,
From Freedom's holy altar-horns[10] to tear your wretched slaves!

Thank God! not yet so vilely can Massachusetts bow;
The spirit of her early time is with her even now;
Dream not because her Pilgrim blood moves slow and calm and cool,
She thus can stoop her chainless neck, a sister's slave and tool!   40

All that a *sister* State should do, all that a *free* State may,
Heart, hand, and purse we proffer, as in our early day;
But that one dark loathsome burden ye must stagger with alone,
And reap the bitter harvest which ye yourselves have sown!

Hold, while ye may, your struggling slaves, and burden God's free air
With woman's shriek beneath the lash, and manhood's wild despair;
Cling closer to the "cleaving curse"[11] that writes upon your plains
The blasting of Almighty wrath against a land of chains.

[3] Virginia.
[4] British generals who commanded troops in Virginia during the American Revolution.
[5] Massachusetts.
[6] The lower house in Virginia's colonial legislature; the famous meeting hall in Boston.
[7] The Virginia statesman Patrick Henry (1736–1799).   [8] The Declaration of Independence.
[9] Slaves. Fugitive Slave Laws required northern states to return runaway slaves to the South; later, with the Compromise of 1850, the situation grew worse.
[10] In I Kings 1:50–53 and 2:28, outcasts seeking asylum could grasp horns protruding from the altars of Israelites.
[11] See Deuteronomy 13:12–17.

Still shame your gallant ancestry, the cavaliers of old,
By watching round the shambles[12] where human flesh is sold,—   50
Gloat o'er the new-born child, and count his market value, when
The maddened mother's cry of woe shall pierce the slaver's den!
Lower than plummet[13] soundeth, sink the Virginia name;
Plant, if ye will, your fathers' graves with rankest weeds of shame;
Be, if ye will, the scandal of God's fair universe,—
We wash our hands forever of your sin and shame and curse.

A voice from lips whereon the coal from Freedom's shrine hath been,[14]
Thrilled, as but yesterday, the hearts of Berkshire's mountain men:[15]
The echoes of that solemn voice are sadly lingering still
In all our sunny valleys, on every wind-swept hill.   60

And when the prowling man-thief[16] came hunting for his prey
Beneath the very shadow of Bunker's shaft[17] of gray,
How, through the free lips of the son, the father's warning spoke;
How, from its bonds of trade and sect, the Pilgrim city[18] broke!

A hundred thousand right arms were lifted up on high,—
A hundred thousand voices sent back their loud reply;
Through the thronged towns of Essex[19] the startling summons rang,
And up from bench and loom and wheel her young mechanics sprang!

The voice of free, broad Middlesex,—of thousands as of one,—
The shaft of Bunker calling to that of Lexington,—   70
From Norfolk's ancient villages, from Plymouth's rocky bound
To where Nantucket[20] feels the arms of ocean close her round;—
From rich and rural Worcester, where through the calm repose
Of cultured vales and fringing woods the gentle Nashua[21] flows,
To where Wachuset's[22] wintry blasts the mountain larches stir,
Swelled up to Heaven the thrilling cry of "God save Latimer!"

And sandy Barnstable rose up, wet with the salt sea spray,—
And Bristol sent her answering shout down Narragansett Bay![23]
Along the broad Connecticut[24] old Hampden felt the thrill,
And the cheer of Hampshire's woodmen swept down from Holyoke Hill.   80

---

[12] Slaughterhouse for animals, where slave markets were set up.
[13] A lead weight for "sounding" or measuring water depth.
[14] "Then flew one of the seraphims unto me, having a live coal . . . from off the altar: And he laid it upon my mouth, and said, Lo, . . . thine iniquity is taken away, and thy sin purged," from Isaiah 6:6–7.
[15] Men from the Berkshire Mountains of western Massachusetts.   [16] Slave hunter.
[17] The Bunker Hill monument on the site of the early Revolutionary War battle.   [18] Boston.
[19] Whittier's home county; the following stanzas name other counties in Massachusetts (Middlesex, Norfolk, Plymouth, Worcester, Barnstable, Bristol, Hampden, and Hampshire) to suggest the wide opposition to George Latimer's arrest.
[20] An island off the Massachusetts coast.   [21] A river in Massachusetts.
[22] A mountain in Massachusetts.   [23] The bay off Rhode Island and Massachusetts.
[24] The Connecticut River.

The voice of Massachusetts! Of her free sons and daughters,—
Deep calling unto deep aloud,[25]—the sound of many waters!
Against the burden of that voice what tyrant power shall stand?
No fetters in the Bay State! No slave upon her land!

Look to it well, Virginians! In calmness we have borne,
In answer to our faith and trust, your insult and your scorn;
You've spurned our kindest counsels,—you've hunted for our lives,—
And shaken round our hearths and homes your manacles and gyves![26]
We wage no war,—we lift no arm,—we fling no torch within
The fire-damps[27] of the quaking mine beneath your soil of sin;   90
We leave ye with your bondmen, to wrestle, while ye can,
With the strong upward tendencies and godlike soul of man!

But for us and for our children, the vow which we have given
For freedom and humanity is registered in heaven;
No slave-hunt in our borders,—no pirate on our strand!
No fetters in the Bay State,—no slave upon our land!

                                                                    1843

ICHABOD!*

So fallen! so lost! the light withdrawn
    Which once he wore!
The glory from his gray hairs gone
    Forevermore!

Revile him not,—the Tempter hath
    A snare for all;
And pitying tears, not scorn and wrath,
    Befit his fall!

O, dumb be passion's stormy rage,
    When he who might   10
Have lighted up and led his age,
    Falls back in night.

Scorn! would the angels laugh, to mark
    A bright soul driven,
Fiend-goaded, down the endless dark,
    From hope and heaven!

---

[25] "Deep calleth unto deep at the noise of thy waterspouts: all thy waves and thy billows are gone over me," from Psalm 42:7.
[26] Leg chains.   [27] The methane-gas mixture found in underground mines.
* First published in *Songs of Labor, and Other Poems* (1850). The title is from I Samuel 4:21: "And she named the child Ichabod, saying, The glory is departed from Israel." The poem is a castigation of Daniel Webster (1782–1852), U.S. senator from Massachusetts who championed the Compromise of 1850 and thus helped to strengthen the provisions of the Fugitive Slave Act.

Let not the land once proud of him
    Insult him now,
Nor brand with deeper shame his dim,
    Dishonored brow.   20

But let its humbled sons, instead,
    From sea to lake,
A long lament, as for the dead,
    In sadness make.

Of all we loved and honored, naught
    Save power remains,—
A fallen angel's pride of thought,
    Still strong in chains.

All else is gone; from those great eyes
    The soul has fled: 30
When faith is lost, when honor dies,
    The man is dead!

Then, pay the reverence of old days
    To his dead fame;
Walk backward, with averted gaze,[1]
    And hide the shame!

1850

SNOW-BOUND*

A Winter Idyl

"As the Spirits of Darkness be stronger in the dark, so Good Spirits which be Angels of Light are augmented not only by the Divine light of the Sun, but also by our common Wood Fire: and as the celestial Fire drives away dark spirits, so also this our Fire of Wood doth the same."
            COR. AGRIPPA, *Occult Philosophy*, Book I. chap. v.[1]

[1] As did Noah's children, to avoid the sight of their father lying drunk and naked in his tent, in Genesis 9:20–23.

* Written in 1865 and 1866 and first published as a small volume in 1866. In a prefatory note inserted in the 1891 edition, Whittier mentions that storytelling was a major "resource" during long winter evenings in the family farmhouse when he was a boy, and dedicates his poem to the memory of that household. Members of the "Whittier homestead" (all mentioned in the poem) were his mother and father, his brother and two sisters, an aunt and uncle ("both unmarried"), and the district schoolmaster, who was then boarding with them. And a volatile young woman, Whittier goes on to say, was included in the snow-bound circle: Harriet Livermore, then boarding about two miles away, who spent much of her life traveling in Europe and Asia preaching the Second Coming of Christ. As an old woman she was found "wandering in Syria with a tribe of Arabs, who with the Oriental notion that madness is inspiration, accepted her as their prophetess and leader." It is small wonder that Whittier describes Livermore in the poem as a "not unfeared, half-welcome guest."

[1] Heinrich Cornelius Agrippa (1486–1525), a German physician and student of occult science.

"Announced by all the trumpets of the sky,
Arrives the snow; and, driving o' er the fields,
Seems nowhere to alight; the whited air
Hides hills and woods, the river and the heaven,
And veils the farm-house at the garden's end.
The sled and traveller stopped, the courier's feet
Delayed, all friends shut out, the housemates sit
Around the radiant fireplace, enclosed
In a tumultuous privacy of storm."[2]

EMERSON

The sun that brief December day
Rose cheerless over hills of gray,
And, darkly circled, gave at noon
A sadder light than waning moon.
Slow tracing down the thickening sky
Its mute and ominous prophecy,
A portent seeming less than threat,
It sank from sight before it set.
A chill no coat, however stout,
Of homespun stuff could quite shut out,   10
A hard, dull bitterness of cold,
    That checked, mid-vein, the circling race
    Of life-blood in the sharpened face,
The coming of the snow-storm told.
The wind blew east:[3] we heard the roar
Of Ocean on his wintry shore,
And felt the strong pulse throbbing there
Beat with low rhythm our inland air.

Meanwhile we did our nightly chores,—
Brought in the wood from out of doors,   20
Littered[4] the stalls, and from the mows[5]
Raked down the herd's-grass for the cows:
Heard the horse whinnying for his corn;
And, sharply clashing horn on horn,
Impatient down the stanchion[6] rows
The cattle shake their walnut bows;
While, peering from his early perch
Upon the scaffold's pole of birch,
The cock his crested helmet bent
And down his querulous challenge sent.   30

Unwarmed by any sunset light
The gray day darkened into night,
A night made hoary with the swarm

---

[2] From Ralph Waldo Emerson's "The Snow-Storm" (1841).
[3] From the East, so they could hear the "roar" of the Atlantic Ocean.
[4] Put down straw for bedding.   [5] Haymows.
[6] Adjustable braces fixed to posts that hold an animal's neck in place during feeding or milking; they are shaped like bows and made of walnut.

And whirl-dance of the blinding storm,
As zigzag wavering to and fro
Crossed and recrossed the wingéd snow:
And ere the early bedtime came
The white drift piled the window-frame,
And through the glass the clothes-line posts
Looked in like tall and sheeted ghosts.   40

So all night long the storm roared on:
The morning broke without a sun;
In tiny spherule[7] traced with lines
Of Nature's geometric signs,
In starry flake, and pellicle,[8]
All day the hoary[9] meteor fell;
And, when the second morning shone,
We looked upon a world unknown,
On nothing we could call our own.
Around the glistening wonder bent   50
The blue walls of the firmament,
No cloud above, no earth below,—
A universe of sky and snow!
The old familiar sights of ours
Took marvellous shapes; strange domes and towers
Rose up where sty or corn-crib stood,
Or garden wall, or belt of wood;
A smooth white mound the brush-pile showed,
A fenceless drift what once was road;
The bridle-post an old man sat   60
With loose-flung coat and high cocked hat;
The well-curb had a Chinese roof;
And even the long sweep,[10] high aloof,
In its slant splendor, seemed to tell
Of Pisa's leaning miracle.[11]

A prompt, decisive man, no breath
Our father wasted: "Boys, a path!"
Well pleased, (for when did farmer boy
Count such a summons less than joy?)
Our buskins[12] on our feet we drew;   70
    With mittened hands, and caps drawn low,
    To guard our necks and ears from snow
We cut the solid whiteness through.
And, where the drift was deepest, made
A tunnel walled and overlaid
With dazzling crystal: we had read
Of rare Aladdin's wondrous cave,

---

[7] A small spherical body.   [8] A thin crust of crystals.   [9] Ancient.
[10] Well-sweep, a pole used to raise the well bucket.
[11] The leaning tower of Pisa in Italy.   [12] Boots.

And to our own his name we gave,
With many a wish the luck were ours
To test his lamp's supernal powers.   80
We reached the barn with merry din,
And roused the prisoned brutes within.
The old horse thrust his long head out,
And grave with wonder gazed about;
The cock his lusty greeting said,
And forth his speckled harem led;
The oxen lashed their tails, and hooked,[13]
And mild reproach of hunger looked;
The hornéd patriarch of the sheep,
Like Egypt's Amun[14] roused from sleep,   90
Shook his sage head with gesture mute,
And emphasized with stamp of foot.

All day the gusty north-wind bore
The loosening drift its breath before;
Low circling round its southern zone,
The sun through dazzling snow-mist shone.
No church-bell lent its Christian tone
To the savage air, no social smoke
Curled over woods of snow-hung oak.
A solitude made more intense   100
By dreary-voicéd elements,
The shrieking of the mindless wind,
The moaning tree-boughs swaying blind,
And on the glass the unmeaning beat
Of ghostly finger-tips of sleet.
Beyond the circle of our hearth
No welcome sound of toil or mirth
Unbound the spell, and testified
Of human life and thought outside.
We minded that the sharpest ear   110
The buried brooklet could not hear,
The music of whose liquid lip
Had been to us companionship,
And, in our lonely life, had grown
To have an almost human tone.

As night drew on, and, from the crest
Of wooded knolls that ridged the west,
The sun, a snow-blown traveller, sank
From sight beneath the smothering bank,
We piled, with care, our nightly stack   120
Of wood against the chimney-back,—
The oaken log, green, huge, and thick,

---

[13] Hooked their horns: bent their heads sideways.
[14] According to Egyptian myth, a god with a ram's head.

And on its top the stout back-stick;
The knotty forestick laid apart,
And filled between with curious art
The ragged brush; then, hovering near,
We watched the first red blaze appear,
Heard the sharp crackle, caught the gleam
On whitewashed wall and sagging beam,
Until the old, rude-furnished room   130
Burst, flower-like, into rosy bloom;
While radiant with a mimic flame
Outside the sparkling drift became,
And through the bare-boughed lilac-tree
Our own warm hearth seemed blazing free.
The crane and pendent trammels[15] showed,
The Turks' heads[16] on the andirons glowed;
While childish fancy, prompt to tell
The meaning of the miracle,
Whispered the old rhyme: "*Under the tree,*   140
When fire outdoors burns merrily,
There the witches are making tea."

The moon above the eastern wood
Shone at its full; the hill-range stood
Transfigured in the silver flood,
Its blown snows flashing cold and keen,
Dead white, save where some sharp ravine
Took shadow, or the sombre green
Of hemlocks turned to pitchy black
Against the whiteness at their back.   150
For such a world and such a night
Most fitting that unwarming light,
Which only seemed where'er it fell
To make the coldness visible.

Shut in from all the world without,
We sat the clean-winged hearth about,
Content to let the north-wind roar
In baffled rage at pane and door,
While the red logs before us beat
The frost-line back with tropic heat;   160
And ever, when a louder blast
Shook beam and rafter as it passed,
The merrier up its roaring draught
The great throat of the chimney laughed,
The house-dog on his paws outspread
Laid to the fire his drowsy head,
The cat's dark silhouette on the wall

---

[15] Pothooks.   [16] Turbanlike designs.

A couchant[17] tiger's seemed to fall;
And, for the winter fireside meet,
Between the andirons' straddling feet,   170
The mug of cider simmered slow,
The apples sputtered in a row,
And, close at hand, the basket stood
With nuts from brown October's wood.

What matter how the night behaved?
What matter how the north-wind raved?
Blow high, blow low, not all its snow
Could quench our hearth-fire's ruddy glow.
O Time and Change!—with hair as gray
As was my sire's that winter day,   180
How strange it seems, with so much gone
Of life and love, to still live on!
Ah, brother![18] only I and thou
Are left of all that circle now,—
The dear home faces whereupon
That fitful firelight paled and shone.
Henceforward, listen as we will,
The voices of that hearth are still;
Look where we may, the wide earth o'er,
Those lighted faces smile no more.   190
We tread the paths their feet have worn,
    We sit beneath their orchard-trees,
    We hear, like them, the hum of bees
And rustle of the bladed corn;
We turn the pages that they read,
    Their written words we linger o'er,
But in the sun they cast no shade,
No voice is heard, no sign is made,
    No step is on the conscious floor!
Yet Love will dream, and Faith will trust,   200
(Since He who knows our need is just,)
That somehow, somewhere, meet we must.
Alas for him who never sees
The stars shine through his cypress-trees!
Who, hopeless, lays his dead away,
Nor looks to see the breaking day
Across the mournful marbles[19] play!
Who hath not learned, in hours of faith,
    The truth to flesh and sense unknown,
That Life is ever lord of Death,   210
    And Love can never lose its own!

---

[17] Lying down with head raised.   [18] Matthew Whittier (1812–1883).   [19] Tombstones of marble.

We sped the time with stories old,
Wrought puzzles out, and riddles told,
Or stammered from our school-book lore
"The Chief of Gambia's golden shore."[20]
How often since, when all the land
Was clay in Slavery's shaping hand,
As if a trumpet called, I've heard
Dame Mercy Warren's[21] rousing word:
"Does not the voice of reason cry,   220
    Claim the first right which Nature gave,
From the red scourge of bondage fly,
    Nor deign to live a burdened slave!"
Our father rode again his ride
On Memphremagog's[22] wooded side;
Sat down again to moose and samp[23]
In trapper's hut and Indian camp;
Lived o'er the old idyllic ease
Beneath St. François'[24] hemlock-trees;
Again for him the moonlight shone   230
On Norman cap and bodiced zone;[25]
Again he heard the violin play
Which led the village dance away,
And mingled in its merry whirl
The grandam and the laughing girl.
Or, nearer home, our steps he led
Where Salisbury's[26] level marshes spread
    Mile-wide as flies the laden bee;
Where merry mowers, hale and strong,
Swept, scythe on scythe, their swaths along   240
    The low green prairies of the sea.
We shared the fishing off Boar's Head,[27]
    And round the rocky Isles of Shoals[28]
    The hake-broil[29] on the drift-wood coals;
The chowder on the sand-beach made,
Dipped by the hungry, steaming hot,
With spoons of clam-shell from the pot.
We heard the tales of witchcraft old,

---

[20] From "The African Chief," an antislavery poem by Sarah Wentworth Morton (1759–1846).

[21] Mercy Otis Warren (1728–1814), whose *History of the Rise, Progress, and Termination of the American Revolution* (1805) is valuable as a contemporary record of events; however, the poem quoted is by Sarah Wentworth Morton.

[22] A lake between Vermont and Quebec. As Whittier says in his 1891 preface, his father told stories of travels in Canada.

[23] Sat down to eat moose and cornmeal mush.

[24] A village north of Lake Memphremagog.

[25] Whittier's father remembers the dress of French-Canadian women, the cap like those worn in Normandy, France, and the bodices around their waists.

[26] A town in northeast Massachusetts.   [27] A headland on the New England coast.

[28] Off the New Hampshire coast.

[29] A variety of cod, commonly broiled over an open fire.

And dream and sign and marvel told
To sleepy listeners as they lay   250
Stretched idly on the salted hay,
    Adrift along the winding shores,
When favoring breezes deigned to blow
The square sail of the gundelow[30]
    And idle lay the useless oars.

Our mother, while she turned her wheel
Or run the new-knit stocking-heel,
Told how the Indian hordes came down
At midnight on Cocheco town,[31]
And how her own great-uncle bore   260
His cruel scalp-mark to fourscore.
Recalling, in her fitting phrase,
    So rich and picturesque and free,
    (The common unrhymed poetry
Of simple life and country ways,)
The story of her early days,—
She made us welcome to her home;
Old hearths grew wide to give us room;
We stole with her a frightened look
At the gray wizard's conjuring-book,[32]   270
The fame whereof went far and wide
Through all the simple country side;
We heard the hawks at twilight play,
The boat-horn on Piscataqua,
The loon's weird laughter far away;
We fished her little trout-brook, knew
What flowers in wood and meadow grew,
What sunny hillsides autumn-brown
She climbed to shake the ripe nuts down,
Saw where in sheltered cove and bay   280
The ducks' black squadron anchored lay,
And heard the wild-geese calling loud
Beneath the gray November cloud.

Then, haply, with a look more grave,
And soberer tone, some tale she gave
From painful Sewell's ancient tome,[33]
Beloved in every Quaker home,
Of faith fire-winged by martyrdom,

[30] Flat-bottomed boat.

[31] A village near Dover, New Hampshire, on the Cocheco River; in his 1891 preface Whittier says his mother knew of "strange people" who lived on the Piscataqua and Cocheco rivers.

[32] Agrippa's *Occult Philosophy*.

[33] William Sewell or Sewal (1650–1725), whose *History of the Quakers* (1725) detailed the persecutions the Quakers suffered at the hands of the Puritans in the seventeenth century. Whittier, a Quaker, owned a copy of the book.

Or Chalkley's Journal,[34] old and quaint,—
Gentlest of skippers, rare sea-saint!—   290
Who, when the dreary calms prevailed,
And water-butt and bread-cask failed,
And cruel, hungry eyes pursued
His portly presence mad for food,
With dark hints muttered under breath
Of casting lots for life or death,
Offered, if Heaven withheld supplies,
To be himself the sacrifice.
Then, suddenly, as if to save
The good man from his living grave,   300
A ripple on the water grew,
A school of porpoise flashed in view.
"Take, eat,"[35] he said, "and be content;
These fishes in my stead are sent
By Him who gave the tangled ram
To spare the child of Abraham."[36]

Our uncle, innocent of books,
Was rich in lore of fields and brooks,
The ancient teachers never dumb
Of Nature's unhoused lyceum.[37]   310
In moons and tides and weather wise,
He read the clouds as prophecies,
And foul or fair could well divine,
By many an occult hint and sign,
Holding the cunning-warded keys[38]
To all the woodcraft mysteries;
Himself to Nature's heart so near
That all her voices in his ear
Of beast or bird had meanings clear,
Like Apollonius[39] of old,   320
Who knew the tales the sparrows told,
Or Hermes,[40] who interpreted
What the sage cranes of Nilus said;
A simple, guileless, childlike man,
Content to live where life began;

---

[34] The sea-going Quaker Thomas Chalkley (1675–1741) published his *Journal* in 1747.

[35] Christ's words to the Apostles: "Take, eat; this is my body," from Matthew 26:26.

[36] In Genesis 22:8–13, Abraham was willing to obey God by sacrificing his son Isaac; a ram was given in Isaac's place.

[37] Public lecture hall. "My uncle," Whittier writes in his 1891 preface, "had many stories of hunting and fishing and some of witchcraft and superstition."

[38] Keys with intricate notches; hence, keys to "woodcraft mysteries."

[39] Appollonius of Tyana (1st century B.C.), a Greek philosopher and mystic who supposedly had miraculous powers.

[40] Hermes Trismegistus, legendary Egyptian author of books on magic; here he is said to have interpreted motions of cranes along the Nile ("Nilus") River.

Strong only on his native grounds,
The little world of sights and sounds
Whose girdle was the parish bounds,
Whereof his fondly partial pride
The common features magnified,   330
As Surrey hills to mountains grew
In White of Selborne's[41] loving view,—
He told how teal and loon he shot,
And how the eagle's eggs he got,
The feats on pond and river done,
The prodigies of rod and gun;
Till, warming with the tales he told,
Forgotten was the outside cold,
The bitter wind unheeded blew,
From ripening corn the pigeons flew,   340
The partridge drummed i' the wood, the mink
Went fishing down the river-brink.
In fields with bean or clover gay,
The woodchuck, like a hermit gray,
    Peered from the doorway of his cell;
The muskrat plied the mason's trade,
And tier by tier his mud-walls laid;
And from the shagbark overhead
    The grizzled squirrel dropped his shell.

Next, the dear aunt, whose smile of cheer   350
And voice in dreams I see and hear,—
The sweetest woman ever Fate
Perverse denied a household mate,
Who, lonely, homeless, not the less
Found peace in love's unselfishness,
And welcome wheresoe'er she went,
A calm and gracious element,
Whose presence seemed the sweet income
And womanly atmosphere of home,—
Called up her girlhood memories,   360
The huskings and the apple-bees,
The sleigh-rides and the summer sails,
Weaving through all the poor details
And homespun warp of circumstance
A golden woof-thread of romance.
For well she kept her genial mood
And simple faith of maidenhood;
Before her still a cloud-land lay,
The mirage loomed across her way;
The morning dew, that dries so soon   370
With others, glistened at her noon;

[41] *The Natural History and Antiquities of Selborne* (1789), by Gilbert White (1720–1793) of Surrey, England.

Through years of toil and soil and care,
From glossy tress to thin gray hair,
All unprofaned she held apart
The virgin fancies of the heart.
Be shame to him of woman born
Who hath for such but thought of scorn.

There, too, our elder sister plied
Her evening task the stand beside;
A full, rich nature, free to trust,   380
Truthful and almost sternly just,
Impulsive, earnest, prompt to act,
And make her generous thought a fact,
Keeping with many a light disguise
The secret of self-sacrifice.
O heart sore-tried! thou hast the best
That Heaven itself could give thee,—rest,
Rest from all bitter thoughts and things!
    How many a poor one's blessing went
    With thee beneath the low green tent   390
Whose curtain never outward swings!

As one who held herself a part
Of all she saw, and let her heart
    Against the household bosom lean,
Upon the motley-braided mat
Our youngest and our dearest sat,
Lifting her large, sweet, asking eyes,
    Now bathed within the eternal green
And holy peace of Paradise.
O, looking from some heavenly hill,   400
    Or from the shade of saintly palms,
    Or silver reach of river calms,
Do those large eyes behold me still?
With me one little year ago:—
The chill weight of the winter snow
    For months upon her grave has lain;
And now, when summer south-winds blow
    And brier and harebell bloom again,
I tread the pleasant paths we trod,
I see the violet-sprinkled sod   410
Whereon she leaned, too frail and weak
The hillside flowers she loved to seek,
Yet following me where'er I went
With dark eyes full of love's content.
The birds are glad; the brier-rose fills
The air with sweetness; all the hills
Stretch green to June's unclouded sky;
But still I wait with ear and eye
For something gone which should be nigh,

A loss in all familiar things,   420
In flower that blooms and bird that sings.
And yet, dear heart! remembering thee,
   Am I not richer than of old?
Safe in thy immortality,
   What change can reach the wealth I hold?
   What chance can mar the pearl and gold
Thy love hath left in trust with me?
And while in life's late afternoon,
   Where cool and long the shadows grow,
I walk to meet the night that soon   430
   Shall shape and shadow overflow,
I cannot feel that thou art far,
Since near at need the angels are;
And when the sunset gates unbar,
   Shall I not see thee waiting stand,
And, white against the evening star,
   The welcome of thy beckoning hand?

Brisk wielder of the birch and rule,
The master of the district school
Held at the fire his favored place,   440
Its warm glow lit a laughing face
Fresh-hued and fair, where scarce appeared
The uncertain prophecy of beard.
He teased the mitten-blinded cat,
Played cross-pins on my uncle's hat,
Sang songs, and told us what befalls
In classic Dartmouth's college halls.
Born the wild Northern hills among,
From whence his yeoman father wrung
By patient toil subsistence scant,   450
Not competence and yet not want,
He early gained the power to pay
His cheerful, self-reliant way;
Could doff at ease his scholar's gown
To peddle wares from town to town;
Or through the long vacation's reach
In lonely lowland districts teach,
Where all the droll experience found
At stranger hearths in boarding round,
The moonlit skater's keen delight,   460
The sleigh-drive through the frosty night,
The rustic party, with its rough
Accompaniment of blind-man's-buff,
And whirling plate,[42] and forfeits paid,
His winter task a pastime made.

[42] A children's game of spinning a pewter plate on its edge longer than others can, with the losers paying a penalty.

Happy the snow-locked homes wherein
He tuned his merry violin,
Or played the athlete in the barn,
Or held the good dame's winding-yarn,
Or mirth-provoking versions told   470
Of classic legends rare and old,
Wherein the scenes of Greece and Rome
Had all the commonplace of home,
And little seemed at best the odds
'Twixt Yankee pedlers and old gods;
Where Pindus-born Aracthus[43] took
The guise of any grist-mill brook,
And dread Olympus[44] at his will
Became a huckleberry hill.

A careless boy that night he seemed;   480
    But at his desk he had the look
And air of one who wisely schemed,
    And hostage from the future took
    In trainéd thought and lore of book.
Large-brained, clear-eyed,—of such as he
Shall Freedom's young apostles be,
Who, following in War's bloody trail,[45]
Shall every lingering wrong assail;
All chains from limb and spirit strike,
Uplift the black and white alike;   490
Scatter before their swift advance
The darkness and the ignorance,
The pride, the lust, the squalid sloth,
Which nurtured Treason's monstrous growth,
Made murder pastime, and the hell
Of prison-torture possible;
The cruel lie of caste refute,
Old forms remould, and substitute
For Slavery's lash the freeman's will,
For blind routine, wise-handed skill;   500
A school-house plant on every hill,
Stretching in radiate nerve-lines thence
The quick wires of intelligence;[46]
Till North and South together brought
Shall own the same electric thought,
In peace a common flag salute,
And, side by side in labor's free
And unresentful rivalry,
Harvest the fields wherein they fought.

[43] A river in Greece originating in the Pindus Mountains.
[44] According to Greek myth, Mt. Olympus was the abode of the gods.
[45] In the classroom, the schoolmaster follows the progress of the Civil War in the context of its moral issues.
[46] Communication by telegraph.

Another guest[47] that winter night   510
Flashed back from lustrous eyes the light.
Unmarked by time, and yet not young,
The honeyed music of her tongue
And words of meekness scarcely told
A nature passionate and bold,
Strong, self-concentred, spurning guide,
Its milder features dwarfed beside
Her unbent will's majestic pride.
She sat among us, at the best,
A not unfeared, half-welcome guest,   520
Rebuking with her cultured phrase
Our homeliness of words and ways.
A certain pard-like,[48] treacherous grace
     Swayed the lithe limbs and drooped the lash,
     Lent the white teeth their dazzling flash;
     And under low brows, black with night,
     Rayed out at times a dangerous light;
The sharp heat-lightnings of her face
Presaging ill to him whom Fate
Condemned to share her love or hate.   530
A woman tropical, intense
In thought and act, in soul and sense,
She blended in a like degree
The vixen and the devotee,
Revealing with each freak or feint
     The temper of Petruchio's Kate,[49]
The raptures of Siena's saint.[50]
Her tapering hand and rounded wrist
Had facile power to form a fist;
The warm, dark languish of her eyes   540
Was never safe from wrath's surprise.
Brows saintly calm and lips devout
Knew every change of scowl and pout;
And the sweet voice had notes more high
And shrill for social battle-cry.

Since then what old cathedral town
Has missed her pilgrim staff and gown,
What convent-gate has held its lock
Against the challenge of her knock!
Through Smyrna's[51] plague-hushed thoroughfares,   550
Up sea-set Malta's[52] rocky stairs,
Gray olive slopes of hills that hem
Thy tombs and shrines, Jerusalem,
Or startling on her desert throne

---

[47] Harriet Livermore.   [48] Leopardlike.
[49] The explosive heroine tamed by Petruchio in Shakespeare's *Taming of the Shrew.*
[50] St. Catherine (1347–1380) of Siena, Italy.   [51] Now Izmir in Turkey.
[52] A mountainous island in the Mediterranean Sea, south of Sicily.

The crazy Queen of Lebanon[53]
With claims fantastic as her own,
Her tireless feet have held their way;
And still, unrestful, bowed, and gray,
She watches under Eastern skies,
    With hope each day renewed and fresh,   560
    The Lord's quick coming in the flesh,
Whereof she dreams and prophesies!

Where'er her troubled path may be,
    The Lord's sweet pity with her go!
The outward wayward life we see,
    The hidden springs we may not know.
Nor is it given us to discern
    What threads the fatal sisters spun,[54]
    Through what ancestral years has run
The sorrow with the woman born,   570
What forged her cruel chain of moods,
What set her feet in solitudes,
    And held the love within her mute,
What mingled madness in the blood,
    A life-long discord and annoy,
    Water of tears with oil of joy,
And hid within the folded bud
    Perversities of flower and fruit.
It is not ours to separate
The tangled skein of will and fate,   580
To show what metes and bounds should stand
Upon the soul's debatable land,
And between choice and Providence
Divide the circle of events;
    But He who knows our frame is just,
Merciful and compassionate,
And full of sweet assurances
And hope for all the language is.
    That He remembereth we are dust![55]

At last the great logs, crumbling low,   590
Sent out a dull and duller glow,
The bull's-eye watch[56] that hung in view,
Ticking its weary circuit through,
Pointed with mutely-warning sign
Its black hand to the hour of nine.
That sign the pleasant circle broke:

---

[53] Lady Hester Stanhope (1776–1839), an eccentric Englishwoman who settled in Lebanon in 1810 and ruled despotically over a small area of the land. Harriet Livermore lived with her for a while before the two quarreled about accompanying Christ into Jerusalem at the time of the Second Coming.
[54] The three Fates of Greek myth, who spin the thread of life, measure it, and cut it off.
[55] "For he knoweth our frame; he remembereth that we are dust," from Psalm 103:14.
[56] A globe-shaped watch, with thick glass facing; not for the wrist.

My uncle ceased his pipe to smoke,
Knocked from its bowl the refuse gray
And laid it tenderly away,
Then roused himself to safely cover   600
The dull red brands with ashes over.
And while, with care, our mother laid
The work aside, her steps she stayed
One moment, seeking to express
Her grateful sense of happiness
For food and shelter, warmth and health,
And love's contentment more than wealth,
With simple wishes (not the weak,
Vain prayers which no fulfilment seek,
But such as warm the generous heart,   610
O'er-prompt to do with Heaven its part)
That none might lack, that bitter night,
For bread and clothing, warmth and light.

Within our beds awhile we heard
The wind that round the gables roared,
With now and then a ruder shock,
Which made our very bedsteads rock.
We heard the loosened clapboards tost,
The board-nails snapping in the frost;
And on us, through the unplastered wall,   620
Felt the light sifted snow-flakes fall.
But sleep stole on, as sleep will do
When hearts are light and life is new;
Faint and more faint the murmurs grew,
Till in the summer-land of dreams
They softened to the sound of streams,
Low stir of leaves, and dip of oars,
And lapsing waves on quiet shores.

Next morn we wakened with the shout
  Of merry voices high and clear;
  And saw the teamsters[57] drawing near   630
To break the drifted highways out.
Down the long hillside treading slow
We saw the half-buried oxen go,
Shaking the snow from heads uptost,
Their straining nostrils white with frost.
Before our door the straggling train
Drew up, an added team to gain.
The elders threshed their hands a-cold,
  Passed, with the cider-mug, their jokes   640
  From lip to lip; the younger folks
Down the loose snow-banks, wrestling, rolled,
Then toiled again the cavalcade

---

[57] Those in the business of hauling with a team of horses; here, plowing drifted snow.

O'er windy hill, through clogged ravine,
And woodland paths that wound between
Low drooping pine-boughs winter-weighed.
From every barn a team afoot,
At every house a new recruit,
Where, drawn by Nature's subtlest law,
Haply the watchful young men saw   650
Sweet doorway pictures of the curls
And curious eyes of merry girls,
Lifting their hands in mock defence
Against the snow-ball's compliments,
And reading in each missive tost
The charm with Eden never lost.

We heard once more the sleigh-bells' sound;
    And, following where the teamsters led,
The wise old Doctor went his round,
Just pausing at our door to say,   660
In the brief autocratic way
Of one who, prompt at Duty's call,
Was free to urge her claim on all,
    That some poor neighbor sick abed
At night our mother's aid would need.
For, one in generous thought and deed,
    What mattered in the sufferer's sight
    The Quaker matron's inward light,
The Doctor's mail[58] of Calvin's creed?
All hearts confess the saints elect   670
    Who, twain in faith, in love agree,
And melt not in an acid sect
    The Christian pearl of charity!

So days went on: a week had passed
Since the great world was heard from last.
The Almanac was studied o'er,
Read and reread our little store,
Of books and pamphlets, scarce a score;
One harmless novel, mostly hid
From younger eyes, a book forbid,   680
And poetry, (or good or bad,
A single book was all we had,)
Where Ellwood's[59] meek, drab-skirted Muse,
    A stranger to the heathen Nine,
    Sang, with a somewhat nasal whine,
The wars of David and the Jews.

---

[58] Whittier questions the importance of the difference between his mother's "inward light" (the Quaker center of belief) and the doctor's armorlike Calvinist creed of predestination when the two people are together "in generous thought and deed."

[59] The English Quaker Thomas Ellwood (1639–1714), who wrote the poem *Davideis* (1712), epic in length but not, according to Whittier, in inspiration; Ellwood's "drab-skirted Muse" knows nothing of the Muses of Greek mythology and brings him to write boringly of biblical themes.

At last the floundering carrier bore
The village paper to our door.
Lo! broadening outward as we read,
To warmer zones the horizon spread;   690
In panoramic length unrolled
We saw the marvels that it told.
Before us passed the painted Creeks,[60]
    And daft McGregor on his raids
      In Costa Rica's everglades.
And up Taygetos winding slow
Rode Ypsilanti's Mainote Greeks,
A Turk's head at each saddle-bow![61]
Welcome to us its week-old news,
Its corner for the rustic Muse,   700
    Its monthly gauge of snow and rain,
Its record, mingling in a breath
The wedding knell and dirge of death;
Jest, anecdote, and love-lorn tale,
The latest culprit sent to jail;
Its hue and cry of stolen and lost,
Its vendue[62] sales and goods at cost,
    And traffic calling loud for gain.
We felt the stir of hall and street,
The pulse of life that round us beat;   710
The chill embargo of the snow
Was melted in the genial glow;
Wide swung again our ice-locked door,
And all the world was ours once more!

Clasp, Angel of the backward look
    And folded wings of ashen gray
    And voice of echoes far away,
The brazen covers of thy book;
The weird palimpsest[63] old and vast,
Wherein thou hid'st the spectral past;   720
Where, closely mingling, pale and glow
The characters of joy and woe;
The monographs of outlived years,
Or smile-illumed or dim with tears,
    Green hills of life that slope to death,
And haunts of home, whose vistaed trees
Shade off to mournful cypresses
    With the white amaranths[64] underneath.

[60] The newspaper broadens their horizons with news of the Creek Indians, defeated in the Creek War of 1813 to 1814 (and then moved from their homes in Georgia and Alabama to what is now Oklahoma) and news of the Scottish adventurer Gregor MacGregor (who failed in an attempt to colonize Costa Rica in 1819) and of the Greek revolutionary patriot Alexander Ypsilanti (who defeated the Turks at Mt. Taygetos in 1820). All this news was probably not in one issue.

[61] The defeated Turks were decapitated, and their heads mounted on saddles as trophies of victory.

[62] Auction.   [63] Parchment with original writing faintly visible beneath later writing.

[64] Legendary unfading flowers.

Even while I look, I can but heed
   The restless sands' incessant fall,   730
Importunate hours that hours succeed,
Each clamorous with its own sharp need,
   And duty keeping pace with all.
Shut down and clasp the heavy lids;
I hear again the voice that bids
The dreamer leave his dream midway
For larger hopes and graver fears:
Life greatens in these later years,
The century's aloe[65] flowers to-day!

Yet, haply, in some lull of life,   740
Some Truce of God which breaks its strife,
The worldling's eyes shall gather dew,
   Dreaming in throngful city ways
Of winter joys his boyhood knew;
And dear and early friends—the few
Who yet remain—shall pause to view
   These Flemish pictures of old days;[66]
Sit with me by the homestead hearth,
And stretch the hands of memory forth
   To warm them at the wood-fire's blaze!   750
And thanks untraced to lips unknown
Shall greet me like the odors blown
From unseen meadows newly mown,
Or lilies floating in some pond,
Wood-fringed, the wayside gaze beyond;
The traveller owns the grateful sense
Of sweetness near, he knows not whence,
And, pausing, takes with forehead bare
The benediction of the air.

1865–1866, 1866

Frances E. W. Harper
(1825–1911)

A brilliant speaker, a writer of essays, short fiction, and a novel, Frances E. W. Harper is best known today for her stirring oratorical poetry. During her lifetime she was probably the most popular African-American poet. Born in 1825 to free parents in Baltimore—in the slave state of Maryland—Frances Ellen Watkins was orphaned at age three and raised

---

[65] A fabled plant said to bloom only once each century.
[66] Seventeenth-century Flemish painters were known for the realistic detail with which they depicted domestic scenes.

by an aunt and uncle. She attended a school for free African Americans, conducted by her uncle in Baltimore. In 1850 she moved to the North and obtained a teaching position at Union Seminary (later Wilberforce University), near Columbus, Ohio. Morally drawn to the antislavery cause, she worked actively for the Underground Railroad and began to lecture widely on abolition. She delivered her first abolitionist speech in 1854 in New Bedford, Massachusetts, and was later employed as a lecturer by the Anti-Slavery Society of Maine. In 1860 she married Fenton Harper, a widowed father, and ceased her public work for a time, settling on a farm in Ohio and giving birth to a daughter. After her husband died in 1863, Harper moved to Philadelphia and resumed her career as a lecturer. Nearly fifty years passed until her death of heart disease in 1911.

The four volumes of poetry for which Harper is known reflect her commitment to the causes of abolition and women's rights. Her most famous collection, *Poems on Miscellaneous Subjects,* was published in 1854 and went through numerous editions. The ambitious *Moses: A Story of the Nile* (1869) has deep historical resonance, though its allegorical flourishes make it unfashionably abstract for many readers. A volume entitled *Poems* (1871), however, draws poignantly on Harper's experience in the South during the years of Reconstruction. Her last significant book of poetry, *Sketches of Southern Life* (1872), provides an emotional picture of the conditions Harper had found in her travels. By means of a central character named Aunt Chloe, Harper explores the divergence between the dream of equality and the stark reality of discrimination.

Dedicated to Harper's daughter, *Iola Leroy: Or, Shadows Uplifted* (1892) is an ambitious novel split curiously in two parts, the first focused on historical settings and issues (the Civil War and Reconstruction), the second on Iola's search for her mother and for happiness in marriage. Along with a number of nineteenth-century writers, including Samuel Woodworth in *The Mysterious Chief* (1816), James Fenimore Cooper in *The Spy* (1821), and John William DeForest in *Miss Ravenel's Conversion From Secession to Loyalty* (1867), Harper found it difficult to merge historical and personal narrative into unified form. Yet, the themes of *Iola Leroy* and Harper's skill at characterization mark the novel as a provocative achievement.

Confident of her talents as a speaker, Harper made major contributions to the traditions of oral poetry. As Maryemma Graham, an editor of Harper's work, has observed, informing that work was a deep sense of piety fostered by the Bible and by the specific example of John Greenleaf Whittier and of Henry Wadsworth Longfellow. Not only do Harper's best poems bring piety and passion to an engagement with social issues, but they dramatize the importance of a convincing poetic voice—thereby remaining vital.

Suggested Readings: *Poems on Miscellaneous Subjects,* 1854, rpt. 1969. *Iola Leroy: Or, Shadows Uplifted,* 1892, rpt. 1988. *Idylls of the Bible,* 1901, rpt. 1975. M. H. Washington, *Invented Lives,* 1985. H. V. Carby, *Reconstructing Womanhood,* 1987. M. Graham, "Introduction," in *Complete Poems of Frances E. W. Harper,* 1988.

Text Used: *Complete Poems of Frances E. W. Harper,* ed. M. Graham, 1988.

THE SLAVE AUCTION*

The sale began—young girls were there,
Defenceless in their wretchedness,
Whose stifled sobs of deep despair
Revealed their anguish and distress.

* First published in *Poems on Miscellaneous Subjects* (1854).

And mothers stood with streaming eyes,
  And saw their dearest children sold;
Unheeded rose their bitter cries,
  While tyrants bartered them for gold.

And woman, with her love and truth—
  For these in sable forms may dwell—   10
Gaz'd on the husband of her youth,
  With anguish none may paint or tell.

And men, whose sole crime was their hue,
  The impress of their Maker's hand,
And frail and shrinking children, too,
  Were gathered in that mournful band.

Ye who have laid your love to rest,
  And wept above their lifeless clay,
Know not the anguish of that breast,
  Whose lov'd are rudely torn away.   20

Ye may not know how desolate
  Are bosoms rudely forced to part,
And how a dull and heavy weight
  Will press the life-drops from the heart.

                                        1854

BURY ME IN A FREE LAND*

Make me a grave where'er you will,
In a lowly plain, or a lofty hill,
Make it among earth's humblest graves,
But not in a land where men are slaves.

I could not rest if around my grave
I heard the steps of a trembling slave:
His shadow above my silent tomb
Would make it a place of fearful gloom.

I could not rest if I heard the tread
Of a coffie gang to the shambles led,[1]   10

---

* First published in *The Liberator*, William Lloyd Garrison's abolitionist weekly, in 1864; included in *Poems* (1871).

[1] A train of men or women bound together like beasts (a slave caravan) led to a place for slaughtering animals for meat.

And the mother's shriek of wild despair
Rise like a curse on the trembling air.

I could not sleep if I saw the lash
Drinking her blood at each fearful gash,
And I saw her babes torn from her breast,
Like trembling doves from their parent nest.

I'd shudder and start if I heard the bay
Of blood-hounds seizing their human prey,
And I heard the captive plead in vain
As they bound afresh his galling chain.   20

If I saw young girls from their mother's arms
Bartered and sold for their youthful charms,
My eye would flash with a mournful flame,
My death-paled cheek grow red with shame.

I would sleep, dear friends, where bloated might
Can rob no man of his dearest right;
My rest shall be calm in any grave
Where none can call his brother a slave.

I ask no monument, proud and high
To arrest the gaze of the passers-by;   30
All that my yearning spirit craves,
Is bury me not in a land of slaves.

1864

THE SLAVE MOTHER*

A Tale of the Ohio[1]

I have but four, the treasures of my soul,
    They lay like doves around my heart;
I tremble lest some cruel hand
    Should tear my household wreaths apart.

My baby girl, with childish glance,
    Looks curious in my anxious eye,
She little knows that for her sake
    Deep shadows round my spirit lie.

---

* First published in the twentieth edition of *Poems on Miscellaneous Subjects* (1874).
[1] The Ohio River.

My playful boys could I forget,
  My home might seem a joyous spot,   10
But with their sunshine mirth I blend
  The darkness of their future lot.

And thou my babe, my darling one,
  My last, my loved, my precious child,
Oh! when I think upon thy doom
  My heart grows faint and then throbs wild.

The Ohio's bridged and spanned with ice,
  The northern star is shining bright,
I'll take the nestlings of my heart
  And search for freedom by its light.   20

Winter and night were on the earth,
  And feebly moaned the shivering trees,
A sigh of winter seemed to run
  Through every murmur of the breeze.

She fled,[2] and with her children all,
  She reached the stream and crossed it o'er,
Bright visions of deliverance came
  Like dreams of plenty to the poor.

Dreams! vain dreams, heroic mother,
  Give all thy hopes and struggles o'er,   30
The pursuer is on thy track,
  And the hunter at thy door.

Judea's[3] refuge cities had power
  To shelter, shield and save,
E'en Rome had altars, 'neath whose shade
  Might crouch the wan and weary slave.[4]

But Ohio had no sacred fane,[5]
  To human rights so consecrated,
Where thou may'st shield thy hapless ones
  From their darkly gathering fate.   40

Then, said the mournful mother,
  If Ohio cannot save,
I will do a deed for freedom,
  Shalt find each child a grave.

---

[2] Here the point of view changes from first person to that of an omniscient spectator, giving an added perspective to the plight of the slave mother. The two points of view alternate throughout the remainder of the poem.
   [3] A division of Palestine under the Romans; the cities of Judea could offer protection to outcasts.
[4] The altar would afford asylum to the slave.   [5] Temple or church.

I will save my precious children
  From their darkly threatened doom,
I will hew their path to freedom
  Through the portals of the tomb.

A moment in the sunlight,
  She held a glimmering knife,   50
The next moment she had bathed it
  In the crimson fount of life.

They snatched away the fatal knife,
  Her boys shrieked wild with dread;
The baby girl was pale and cold,
  They raised it up, the child was dead.

Sends this deed of fearful daring
  Through my country's heart no thrill,
Do the icy hands of slavery
  Every pure emotion chill?   60

Oh! if there is any honor,
  Truth or justice in the land,
Will ye not, us men and Christians,
  On the side of freedom stand?

1874

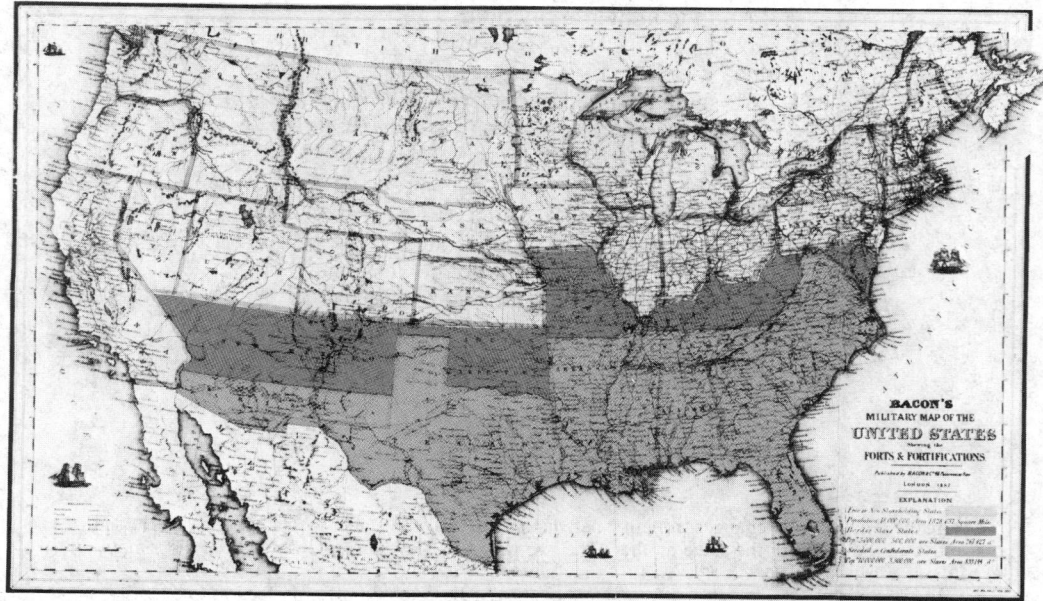

An 1862 map of the United States showing: light area, the free or nonslaveholding states; dark area, the border slave states; medium area, the seceded or Confederate states.

Henry Timrod
(1828–1867)

Henry Timrod was born in Charleston, South Carolina, in 1828. During his youth he studied at several schools in Charleston and went on to enroll at Franklin College (now the University of Georgia) in Athens in 1845. A year later, short of money and plagued by ill health, he returned to Charleston to study law. There he developed friendships with several men in Charleston's active literary community, among them Paul Hamilton Hayne (with whom Timrod founded *Russell's Magazine* in 1857), the scholar Basil Gildersleeve, and the novelist William Gilmore Simms. Timrod soon gave up the study of law and turned to the classics, hoping for a college professorship. But he was forced to settle for various positions as a tutor on plantations. Meanwhile, he spent holidays with his literary friends in Charleston and wrote poetry (as he had since his days in college), which was published in newspapers and, under the pseudonym Aglaus, in the *Southern Literary Messenger*. In 1860 his small volume *Poems* was published by the Boston firm of Ticknor and Fields and brought him national, albeit fleeting, praise.

Like many southern writers of the time, Timrod found his life and his poetry changed by the Civil War. For several months he served as clerk in the Confederate Army, but his perilous health foreclosed any career as a soldier. Instead, he wrote poems in support of the southern cause, transforming his interest in nature poetry to poems of war—its glory and ultimate tragedy. Timrod's early war poems, such as "Ethnogenesis" (1861), reveal his enthusiasm for, and confidence in, the Confederacy. As the war dragged on and his health failed, however, the problematic outcome of the military struggle generated the kind of ambivalent vision he explored stoically in "Charleston" (1862). Later poems, including "Ode Sung at the Occasion of Decorating the Graves of the Confederate Dead" (1867), mourn the fate of "martyrs of a fallen cause." During the final years of the war, Timrod moved to Columbia, South Carolina, as an editor of the *South Carolinian* daily newspaper. He married Kate S. Goodwin (to whom his poem *Katie* [1884] is dedicated) in 1864 and had a son the following year. But events proved devastating for him: not only did he witness the burning of Columbia in February 1865, but his son died later that year. Following the war, Timrod's health continued to deteriorate while he worked at a series of low-paying jobs. He died of tuberculosis aggravated by poor nutrition in 1867.

Known as the "Laureate of the Confederacy," Timrod expressed the range of emotions associated with the South during the Civil War. With its elevated diction and conventional anthems of praise, his poetry has seemed cloying to some modern readers. Nevertheless, as Edd Winfield Parks, a biographer, has observed, the spiritual history of the Confederacy can be traced in Timrod's work. What Timrod gives us is the emotional genesis of a lost-cause mentality that would later haunt (and serve) southern writers as diverse as Margaret Mitchell, William Faulkner, and Walker Percy.

Suggested Readings: P. H. Hayne, ed., *The Poems of Henry Timrod*, 1872, rpt. 1972. G. A. Cardwell, Jr., *The Uncollected Poems of Henry Timrod*, 1942. E. W. Parks and A. W. Parks, eds., *Collected Poems: A Variorum Edition*, 1965. J. B. Hubbell, *The Last Years of Henry Timrod*, 1941. E. W. Parks, *Henry Timrod*, 1964.

Text Used: *Poems of Henry Timrod*, 1901.

CHARLESTON*

Calm as that second summer which precedes
    The first fall of the snow,
In the broad sunlight of heroic deeds,
    The City bides the foe.

As yet, behind their ramparts stern and proud,
    Her bolted thunders sleep—
Dark Sumter,[1] like a battlemented cloud,
    Looms o'er the solemn deep.

No Calpe[2] frowns from lofty cliff or scar
    To guard the holy strand;   10
But Moultrie[3] holds in leash her dogs of war
    Above the level sand.

And down the dunes a thousand guns lie couched,
    Unseen, beside the flood—
Like tigers in some Orient jungle crouched
    That wait and watch for blood.

Meanwhile, through streets still echoing with trade,
    Walk grave and thoughtful men,
Whose hands may one day wield the patriot's blade
    As lightly as the pen.   20

And maidens, with such eyes as would grow dim
    Over a bleeding hound,
Seem each one to have caught the strength of him
    Whose sword she sadly bound.

Thus girt without and garrisoned at home,
    Day patient following day,
Old Charleston looks from roof, and spire, and dome,
    Across her tranquil bay.

Ships, through a hundred foes, from Saxon lands
    And spicy Indian ports.[4]   30
Bring Saxon steel and iron to her hands,
    And Summer to her courts.[5]

But still, along yon dim Atlantic line,
    The only hostile smoke

---

* First published in the December 13,1862, issue of the Charleston *Mercury*.
[1] Fort Sumter, at the entrance to Charleston harbor, was the scene of the first incident of the Civil War: advocates of secession fired on the fort.
[2] Rock of Gibraltar.
[3] The fort on Sullivan's Island off Charleston, named for the Revolutionary War general William Moultrie (1730–1805).
[4] From England and northern Europe and from ports in the West Indies.
[5] Courtyards, where happiness is still possible.

Creeps like a harmless mist above the brine,
　From some frail, floating oak.

Shall the Spring dawn, and she still clad in smiles,
　And with an unscathed brow,
Rest in the strong arms of her palm-crowned isles,[6]
　As fair and free as now?　　　　　　　　　　　40

We know not; in the temple of the Fates
　God has inscribed her doom;
And, all untroubled in her faith, she waits
　The triumph or the tomb.

　　　　　　　　　　　　　　　　　　1862

ODE*

SUNG ON THE OCCASION OF DECORATING THE GRAVES OF THE CONFEDERATE
DEAD, AT MAGNOLIA CEMETERY, CHARLESTON, S. C., 1867

I

Sleep sweetly in your humble graves,
　Sleep, martyrs of a fallen cause;
Though yet no marble column craves
　The pilgrim here to pause.

II

In seeds of laurel in the earth
　The blossom of your fame is blown,
And somewhere, waiting for its birth,
　The shaft is in the stone!

III

Meanwhile, behalf the tardy years
　Which keep in trust your storied tombs,　　　　10
Behold! your sisters bring their tears,
　And these memorial blooms.

IV

Small tributes! but your shades[1] will smile
　More proudly on these wreaths today,
Than when some cannon-moulded pile
　Shall overlook this bay.

V

Stoop, angels, hither from the skies!
　There is no holier spot of ground
Than where defeated valor lies,
　By mourning beauty crowned!　　　　　　　20

　　　　　　　　　　　　　　　　　　1866

---

[6] The islands off the South Carolina coast, which have palm trees.
　* Sung on Decoration Day (Memorial Day) at the Magnolia Cemetery in Charleston on June 16,
1866, and first printed in the *Charleston Courier* on June 18, 1866.
[1] Spirits.

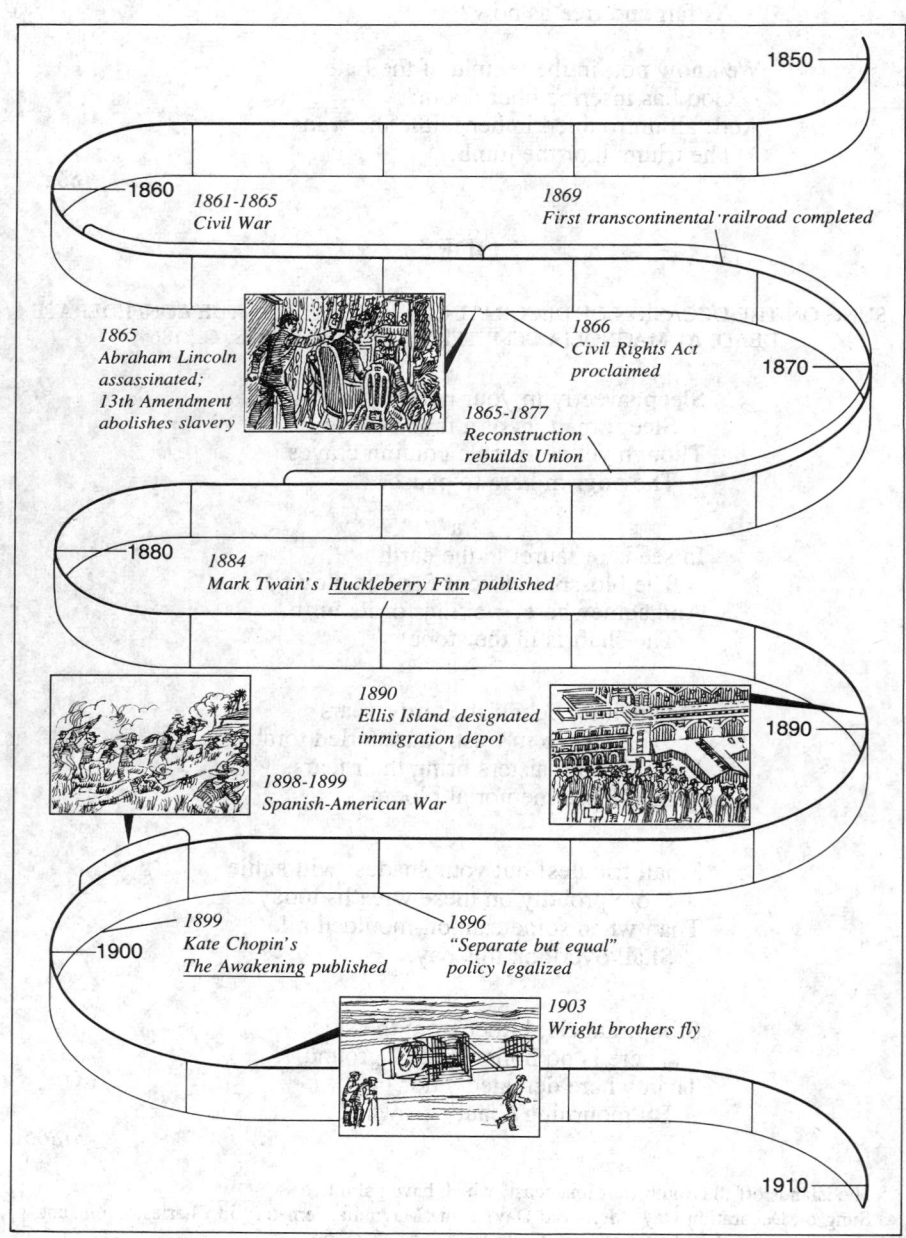

1850

1860

1861-1865
Civil War

1869
First transcontinental railroad completed

1865
Abraham Lincoln
assassinated;
13th Amendment
abolishes slavery

1866
Civil Rights Act
proclaimed

1870

1865-1877
Reconstruction
rebuilds Union

1880

1884
Mark Twain's Huckleberry Finn *published*

1890
Ellis Island designated
immigration depot

1890

1898-1899
Spanish-American War

1899
Kate Chopin's
The Awakening *published*

1896
"Separate but equal"
policy legalized

1900

1903
Wright brothers fly

1910

PART FOUR

Expansion and National Redefinition

The Late 19th Century

The assassination of Abraham Lincoln only five days after General Robert E. Lee's surrender in Appomattox Court House, Virginia, in 1865 was an eerie precursor of the violence and profound disruption that continued to characterize American life even after the Civil War had officially ended. The meaning of the Civil War remained contested. To many northerners the war had increasingly come to have a moral component. Victory seemed to validate the increased power of the central government, which had directed the war, and also to commit the nation to a revolution in race relations. For many white southerners, defeat in war signified simply an end to claims of southern independence and to the system of slavery. Many thought they could return to life as it had been before the guns fired on Fort Sumter in Charleston: that is, to a system of race relations in which whites were dominant and blacks were submissive, and to a political system in which the white men who had controlled politics would resume their seats in Congress and in state legislatures as though nothing had happened.

Reconstruction

National politics were poisoned by a struggle among former Unionists about what ought to be done to "reconstruct" the defeated South. This was especially true after the former Confederate states passed "Black Codes," laws ostensibly intended to grant freedpeople civil rights—to marry, to testify in court, to hold property, to sue and be sued—but that in fact created second-class citizenships. The Black Codes generally forbade African Americans to marry whites, to bear arms, to possess alcoholic beverages, to be on the streets after dark, and to claim seats on public conveyances. As the level of violence in the South rose, the distance between President Andrew Johnson and Congress also grew. Congress had to override presidential vetoes in order to establish its most important Reconstruction legislation, notably the Freedmen's Bureau, the Civil Rights Act of 1866, and the Reconstruction Act of 1867. The Freedmen's Bureau was empowered to establish courts to protect the lives of freedpeople, to feed and clothe refugees, and to supervise the renting of land confiscated from Confederates to loyal refugees and freedpeople. The Civil Rights Act of 1866 guaranteed ex-slaves the right to own property, to make contracts, and to enforce their claims in court. The Reconstruction Act of 1867 divided the South into five military districts in which military officers would maintain order, register voters, and supervise the creation of new state constitutions that guaranteed suffrage to African-American men. The struggle between Congress and the President ended with the impeachment and trial of Andrew Johnson in 1868; one vote short of the required two-thirds majority, he was not convicted, but the stigma of being the first president to be impeached made him politically helpless for the rest of his term.

To make change permanent, Congress amended the Constitution in 1868. The Fourteenth Amendment was the most significant single act of the postwar years. It defines as citizens "all persons born or naturalized in the United States" and guarantees all Americans "equal protection of the laws." The Fourteenth Amendment in effect requires the states as well as the federal government to enforce the provisions of the Bill of Rights and has remained central to American civil liberties since its passage.

The second section of the Fourteenth Amendment canceled the "three-fifths" clause of the Constitution, set up by the Three-Fifths Compromise, and guaranteed suffrage to African-American men by penalizing states that did not permit all adult men to vote by cutting their representation in Congress. In framing the guarantee clause this way, however, Congress for the first time introduced the word "male" into the Constitution and explicitly made gender a limiting factor in interpreting constitutional rights. This was done despite the bitter protest of women's suffrage organizations; ironically, it was never enforced to protect the rights of African-American male voters. The Fifteenth Amendment, passed in 1870, straightforwardly prohibits states from denying the right to vote on the basis of race, color, or previous condition of servitude. It does not guarantee suffrage to women, who began to urge a separate constitutional amendment on their own behalf. Northerners were much more willing to insist on suffrage for African-American men in the South than in the North: in referendums held in nine northern states between 1865 and 1869, suffrage for African-American men was voted down in all except Iowa and Minnesota.

In areas where the Union had been in control during the war, such as the Sea Islands off Georgia, some freedpeople had worked forty-acre plots of confiscated land. Many African Americans expected that this policy would be extended and that, with the defeat of slavery, each former slave would receive "forty acres and a mule." But although Congress was reluctantly willing to offer citizenship rights to African Americans, it was not prepared to offer them either the education or the economic security that would transform the dependent relations of slavery into authentic independence. Education was left to the states and to voluntary organizations. Federal troops were used to enforce traditional property relations, and in the years after the war former slaves became tenant farmers bound to their former masters by a series of contractual arrangements. Through sharecropping, freedpeople used landlords' land and supplies and in return gave up one-half to two-thirds of what was produced. By making the ex-slaves indebted to country stores and dependent on landowners for seed for the following year's crop, share-cropping maintained the hierarchy of race relations within the structure of political freedom.

A decade after Appomattox, a special electoral commission, voting along party lines, awarded contested electoral votes to Rutherford B. Hayes, the Republican presidential candidate. Democratic resentment at the "stolen" election was soothed by a "compromise" in which Hayes and the Republicans promised to support federal economic aid to railroad development in the South and to let white southerners handle local race relations. The few troops still in the South were withdrawn.

In the absence of northern control, a "New South" developed, characterized by the exclusion of African Americans from both voting and officeholding and by the erasure of the reforms Reconstruction legislatures had undertaken, notably in support for public education. Mass media throughout the South stereotyped African Americans as childlike fools or degenerates, and state legislation disfranchised African Americans by imposing poll taxes and manipulative literacy tests. In the 1890s a new wave of legislation excluded African Americans from public places, inventing a new system of segregation in which railroads, libraries, restaurants, schools, hospitals, cemetaries, and prisons were different for blacks and whites. According to the Supreme Court ruling *Plessy* v. *Ferguson* of 1896, segregation with roughly equal though separate facilities was not a denial of equal protection under the law. Subsequent courts made no effort to ensure actual "equality" of public accomodations. Systematically excluded from the skilled trades, southern African Americans were pushed into marginal jobs even more extensively than they had been under slavery; it has been estimated that at the end of the Civil War, at least fifty percent of all skilled craftsmen in the South were African Americans, but by the 1890s that figure had dropped below ten percent. The new system was maintained by intimidation and violence: 1400 African-American men were hanged, shot, or burned alive in lynchings during the 1890s alone.

Expansion

The Civil War was succeeded by an undeclared civil war against the Native Americans of the Great Plains. The violence intensified with the completion of the transcontinental railway and the coming of more white settlers. Native Americans watched with dismay the near-extermination of the buffalo; some 13 million were killed by 1883. When the federal government allowed gold prospectors to enter the Black Hills of South Dakota and of Wyoming, the Sioux fought back to protect their land and their holy places. Although they were victorious over General George Custer at the Battle of the Little Bighorn in 1876, they were defeated elsewhere, and their hero, Chief Crazy Horse, was killed. Congress ceased to treat the tribes as independent nations. The Dawes Severalty Act of 1887 entitled each head of household to only 160 acres of land, thus forcing the Native Americans into agriculture rather than hunting and transforming relationships within the tribes as well as the relationship of the tribes to the federal government.

Some works of literature and art, such as The Spirit of the Frontier *(1872), by John Dost, helped transform the harsh realities of frontier life into a myth of limitless opportunity.*

The expansionist vision that haunted relationships with Native Americans also affected foreign policy. On overseas expansion, however, there was considerably more ambivalence: "We want no unwilling citizens to enter our Union," Theodore Roosevelt wrote in 1886. But as American economic interests overseas increased, as exports grew (more than three hundred percent between 1870 and 1900), and as European imperialism closed major markets off to American trade, overseas expansion seemed increasingly attractive to more people. American planters and the American ambassador to Hawaii supported a successful coup against Queen Liliuokalani, who had challenged American domination of the sugar market in 1893; five years later the Hawaiian islands were annexed. The United States intervened to assist the Cuban resistance to Spain in 1898 but quickly transformed an act of assistance to a claim for empire. After the battleship *Maine* blew up in Havana harbor, President William McKinley declared war on Spain, although no one knows if Spain was responsible for the explosion. The fighting, which lasted only ten weeks, was distinctly one-sided. The result of the Spanish-American War was not only the establishment of Cuban independence but also the achievement of a stable environment for American sugar producers and exporters and the annexation of other Spanish possessions: the Philippines, Puerto Rico, and Guam. In the Philippines American expansion faced intense resistance from the native people, who maintained a bloody and bitter guerilla war for three years.

═CONTEXTS═

The Westward Expansion After 1865

By the late 1860s, exploitation of the last frontier in North America, the Great Plains/Rocky Mountain region, was well under way. The scarcity of cheap, fertile land in the East and Far West spurred westward migration, as did the passage of the Homestead Act of 1862, by which Congress gave 160 acres of land to each permanent settler in exchange for a small fee. The British historian James Bryce (1838–1922) twice visited the American West in the 1880s. In his book on American custom and culture, *The American Commonwealth* (1893), he attempted to define the western character and in so doing perpetuates old myths that seem to honor white mercantile expansionism.

The American Commonwealth

It is the most enterprising and unsettled Americans that come West; and when they have left their old haunts, broken their old ties, resigned the comforts and pleasures of their former homes, they are resolved to obtain the wealth and success for which they have come. They throw themselves into work with a feverish yet sustained intensity. They rise early, they work all day, they have few pleasures, few opportunities for relaxation. I remember in the young city of Seattle on Puget Sound to have found business in full swing at seven o'clock A.M.: the shops open, the streets full of people. Everything is speculative, land (or, as it is usually called, "real estate") most so, the value of lots of ground rising or falling perhaps two or three hundred per cent in the year. No one has any fixed occupation; he is a storekeeper to-day, a ranchman to-morrow, a miner next week. . . . Few men stay in one of the newer cities more than a few weeks or months; to have been there a whole year is to be an old inhabitant, an oracle if you have succeeded, a by-word if you have not, for to prosper in the West you must be able to turn your hand to anything, and seize the chance to-day which everyone else will have seen to-morrow.

*   *   *

These people are intoxicated by the majestic scale of the nature in which their lot is cast, enormous mineral deposits, boundless prairies, forests which, even squandered—wickedly squandered—as they now are, will supply timber to the United States for centuries; a soil which, with the rudest cultivation, yields the most abundant crops, a populous continent for their market. They see all round them railways being built, telegraph wires laid, steamboat lines across the Pacific projected, cities springing up in the solitudes, and settlers making the wilderness to blossom like the rose. Their imagination revels in these sights and signs of progress, and they gild their own struggles for fortune with the belief that they are the missionaries of civilization and the instruments of Providence in the greatest work the world has seen. . . .

James Bryce, 1893

Industrialization and Immigration

One of the most striking exhibits of the Great Centennial Exposition in Philadelphia in 1876 was the Corliss engine. Like the rest of its companions in Machinery Hall, the Corliss engine would have been inconceivable in 1776. It was an emblem of "smokestack America" and the extraordinary productivity of an economy dependent on heavy industry. In addition to the consumer goods—textiles, clothing, processed grains—turned out by pre-Civil War factories, the new industry emphasized mining, metal processing, and the manufacture of machinery. Vast sums of capital sustained a phenomenal output of the basic metals: iron, steel, and copper. A new technology of steel—iron refined in a Bessemer converter—cut the cost in half and revolutionized the production of rails, engines, and bridges. A new technology of brake and gear design transformed railcars. The result was a change in the scale of economic activity: with a national transportation system, the entire nation could be treated as a single market. And even that market was to broaden after Orville and Wilbur Wright made the first sustained airplane flight in Kitty Hawk, North Carolina, in 1903.

The industrial economy had what seemed like an insatiable demand for workers, as the number of jobs increased some four hundred percent during the second half of the nineteenth century. But factory owners rarely hired African Americans, for whom factory work would have represented a major improvement in situation. Instead employers recruited what seemed like a limitless supply of Europeans. Fourteen million immigrants entered between 1860 and 1900, nearly three times as many as in the forty years before the Civil War. Some of the Europeans—notably Jews—were forced from their native lands by religious and political persecution; most others left because of overpopulation, by the consolidation of land, and by desperate poverty. They were attracted to the United States by economic opportunity, commonly in the form of advertisements for labor.

In 1890 Ellis Island, New York, was opened as a receiving depot for immigration. American law welcomed immigrants: through the process of naturalization, virtually unknown elsewhere, foreigners could become citizens with exactly the same legal status as the native-born. In this sense America really was a "Promised Land." Other new countries—Canada, Australia, Argentina—also were populated by European immigrants, but from only a few nationalities: eighty percent of Argentina's immigrants came from Italy and Spain, and seventy-five percent of Canadian immigrants were from English-speaking countries. But immigration to the United States was characterized by many language groups and nationalities: British, German, Irish, Italian, Polish, Hungarian, Russian, and Scandinavian. The Chinese, however, met great hostility: race riots in San Francisco in 1877 marked the beginning of a campaign that culminated in the Chinese Exclusion Act of 1882, which prohibited the immigration of both skilled and unskilled Chinese workers.

The work immigrants found was hard and often precarious. Working-class families relied upon the work of adult women as well as adult men. By 1900 twenty percent of adult women were in the paid labor force, and many more earned money by taking in boarders or laundry at home. Working-class families also relied on the labor of their children, who were generally in their early teens when they left school. The immigrants entered an erratic economy, highly vulnerable to boom and bust business cycles. Particularly severe depressions occurred between 1873 and 1878 and again between 1893 and 1897. It is estimated that between one-quarter and one-third of the work force was unemployed at some time every year during the late nineteenth century, when there was no unemployment insurance in the United States. Still, perhaps one-fifth of the immigrants managed to climb into the middle class, and many children of immigrants improved on the situation of their parents.

The last quarter of the nineteenth century was a time of major working-class protest, in which railroad workers played a leading part. In 1888 1 out of 357 railroad workers in the United States was killed on the job, and 1 out of 35 injured. (In England, by comparison, railroad work killed 1 out of 875 and injured 1 out of 158 [Nell Painter, *Standing at Armageddon*, 1987].) In 1877 railroad workers staged the first national industrial strike, and for the first time on a national scale, the military was called out to break it. Fourteen hundred strikes, involving nearly half a million workers, were called in 1886 alone, and all the major ones failed. With virtually no evidence, eight anarchists were convicted of planting a bomb at the Haymarket Square protest against the McCormick Reaper Company in Chicago. The defeat of strikes gradually demoralized the Knights of Labor, which had sought to represent the interests of labor as a whole. In the 1890s the American Federation of Labor, which stressed the interests of skilled workers, replaced it as the leading voice of organized workers.

Social Change

Changes in industry were accompanied by changes in bureaucracy, in the family, and in education. Like industrial changes, bureaucratic changes had begun almost unnoticed during the Civil War. The invention of the typewriter in 1876 provided a technical tool by which to record business transactions—as well as to write literary works more efficiently—and was part of a great explosion of paperwork that accompanied the transformed economy. During the Civil War government agencies facing a shortage of men became the first workplaces in America in which men and women worked side by side doing similar jobs. By the end of the century many middle-class men and women worked in large hierarchical bureaucracies, their reward security rather than Horatio Alger's dream of fortune.

At the urging of Anthony Comstock, the head of the New York Society for the Suppression of Vice, Congress provided severe penalties for the transportation by mail not only of pornographic materials but of all materials "for the prevention of conception." However, birth rates continued to decline in the late nineteenth century. In 1860 each American woman bore on average 5.2 children, but in 1900 the figure had dropped to 3.6. The decline was even sharper among the business and professional classes, in which families with only 2 children were increasingly common. Middle-class families believed that they could provide their children with more advantages, such as higher education, if the children were fewer in

=CONTEXTS=

The Chicago Riots

One of the most intense labor struggles in American history was the nationwide crusade for the eight-hour workday. At its 1884 national convention in Chicago, the Federation of Organized Trades and Labor Unions of the United States and Canada (the forerunner of the American Federation of Labor) delivered an ultimatum: on May 1, 1886, an eight-hour system would go into effect nationally, or strikes and demonstrations would be held to convince rebellious employers to comply.

At the McCormick Reaper Company on May 3, 1886, Chicago police opened fire on a crowd of strikers, killing and wounding several men. When workers held a protest meeting near Chicago's Haymarket Square the following evening, a bomb was thrown into the ranks of the police, trying to stop the meeting. The officers in turn opened fire on the crowd. Seventy people were wounded, and seven police officers died. Eight anarchists were blamed for the bombing and convicted of murder—although the bombthrower was never apprehended. The trial became the *cause célèbre* for liberals, including the novelist William Dean Howells. Four of the defendants were hanged, a fifth killed himself in his cell, and the others received lengthy prison terms. In 1893 the latter were pardoned by the reform governor of Illinois, John Peter Altgeld, who decided that the evidence failed to link them to the bombing.

The night before the Haymarket Riot, anarchists distributed to striking workers a circular, introduced as evidence in the trial:

REVENGE!

—

Workingmen, to Arms!!!

Your masters sent out their bloodhounds — the police --; they killed six of your brothers at McCormicks this afternoon. They killed the poor wretches, because they, like you, had the courage to disobey the supreme will of your bosses. They killed them, because they dared ask for the shortenin of the hours of toil. They killed them to show you, 'Free American Citizens", that you must be satisfied and contended with whatever your bosses condescend to allow you, or you will get killed!

You have for years endured the most abject humiliations; you have for years suffered unmeasurable iniquities; you have worked yourself to death; you have endured the pangs of want and hunger; your Children you have sacrificed to the factory-lords — in short: You have been miserable and obedient slave all these years: Why? To satisfy the insatiable greed, to fill the coffers of your lazy thieving master? When you ask them now to lessen your burden, he sends his bloodhounds out to shoot you, kill you!

If you are men, if you are the sons of your grand sires, who have shed their blood to free you, then you will rise in your might, Hercules, and destroy the hideous monster that seeks to destroy you. To arms we call you, to arms!

Your Brothers.

Anonymous circular, 1886

Author, educator, reformer, and 1931 Nobel Peace Prize winner, Jane Addams experimented with new teaching methods at her famous community center, Hull House, which she founded in Chicago in 1889.

number. Between 1870 and 1900 the number of public high schools increased from 160 to 6,000, and in 1900 nearly two-thirds of the states had laws for compulsory schooling. The number of students in colleges and universities rose sharply as new institutions were founded, and the impact was particularly great for women. Between 1890 and 1900 the proportion of female college graduates rose from thirteen to twenty percent. Many members of this first sizable generation of women graduates emerged with a strong sense of civic obligation, and many—notably Jane Addams of Chicago's Hull House—were stimulated to found settlement houses and social-service agencies and to address the major social problems of the new industrial society.

LATE 19TH-CENTURY POETRY

The publication of Walt Whitman's *Leaves of Grass* in 1855 signaled the coming of age of poetry in the United States. In his essay "The Poet" (1844), Ralph Waldo Emerson had announced that "America is a poem in our eyes" and called for a writer, as yet unknown, who could exalt the dazzling geography of national life. A decade later Whitman embraced the task of writing this vibrant poem. With egocentric generosity he remarked to the journalist J. T. Trowbridge, "I had been simmering, simmering, simmering; Emerson brought me to a boil."

At the time of Whitman's dramatic accomplishment American poetry was characterized to a large extent by the work of such writers as Henry Wadsworth Longfellow, John Greenleaf Whittier, Oliver Wendell Holmes, and James Russell Lowell. To be sure, other poets had developed and were developing noteworthy perspectives on art and on society, as evidenced by the gnostic reflections of Emerson, the craftmanship of Edgar Allan Poe, the southern voices of Henry Timrod and Paul Hamilton Hayne, and the eloquence of Frances E. W. Harper in her portrayals of human oppression. But the most popular and ubiquitous poetry at the time Whitman began to write was that of the so-called Fireside Poets: Longfellow, Whittier, Holmes, and Lowell, whose work provided instruction for the classroom and piety for the home. These writers incorporated American topics into their poetry through the lens of a temperate romanticism. In a variety of ways they affirmed traditional values and championed moral causes with idealistic passion. Whitter's devotion to the abolitionist movement, for example, brought Frederick Douglass to call him the "slave's poet" in Douglass's autobiographical *Narrative* (1845). Yet in *Snowbound* (1866), Whittier produced the classic memory poem of the nineteenth century, a nostalgic tribute to the values of home and hearth. Content with established forms, the Fireside Poets were public figures, writers available for political discourse or for ceremonial occasions. In a fundamental way they were part of the grateful society for which they wrote.

Radically different in form and content from previous or contemporary poetry, Whitman's *Leaves of Grass* celebrates the grandeur of the democratic "self," body and soul, male and female: no longer is it necessary to forge an epic from history and legend, as Whitman makes clear in the remarkable preface to the 1855 edition of *Leaves* and in "Song of Myself"; the human being is epic in potential, deserving of epic treatment in a land of epic proportions. Undaunted by the poor sales of his book, Whitman published a second edition in 1856 and a much enlarged edition in 1860; there were nine editions in all, the final one completed in the year of his death, 1892. As different as Whitman's poetic credo was from that of Ezra Pound in the early decades of the twentieth century, the imperious Pound (with his passion for a poetry fresh and uncompromised by habit) found it necessary to treat Whitman's achievement with grudging respect. In a poem first entitled "A Truce" and then "A Pact" (1916), Pound addresses Whitman as a reluctant "grown child" coming to a "pig-headed father." Then comes a significant admission: "It was you that broke the new wood, / Now is a time for carving." Among nineteenth-century American poets only Whitman elicits this kind of concession from Pound; only Whitman brings Pound to say "We have one sap and one root— / Let there be commerce between us."

From Pound's perspective, the persistent influence of the Fireside Poets throughout the final decades of the nineteenth century put a damper on poetic initiative and innovation. With his interest in history, he had no concern for the way Whittier and Longfellow came to be revered as guardians of virtue who made society's way of wanting poetry their way of writing it. For a different reason it was not possible for him (or for nineteenth-century readers) to appreciate the distinctive achievement of Emily Dickinson, who saw only a dozen of her 1,776 poems published during her lifetime—and those with misgivings.

Like Whitman, Dickinson was a poet of striking originality. Whereas his poetic impulse led to stylistic expansiveness and discursiveness, however, hers yielded spareness and a determined lack of excess. Whereas he reached out to include the world in his utterance, she looked within to define a world bright with surprise, startling in its scope. Definition is an integral part of Dickinson's poetic mode: in defining such virtues as faith and hope and such emotions as elysium (happiness) and remorse, she translates them into a personal idiom in which we meet and know them afresh. "Renunciation is a piercing virtue," she asserts in a poem that enacts a central paradox of her work, the idea that one knows best by not having: thus "Success is counted sweetest," as she writes, "By those who ne'er succeed."

In her personal life Dickinson rejected the standard nineteenth-century roles for women, preferring an unfettered existence that left her the necessary time for thinking and writing; similarly, throughout her career as a poet in the 1860s and 1870s, she often moved beyond conventional usage in matters of syntax, capitalization, and punctuation. Perhaps her most-remarked stylistic idiosyncrasy is her use of the dash as a principal mark of punctuation. Her preference for the dash (sometimes tilting up, sometimes slightly down) over the period may be a private way of directing the reading of her poems; it may also suggest a rejection of finality in experience, a belief that conventional signs in human discourse oversimplify reality.

The work of other poets in the second half of the nineteenth century suggests that the period was not given over to revolutionary breakthroughs of form and idiom but was also a time of applying traditional modes of expression to a postbellum world and of perfecting established poetic techniques. The reclusive Henry Goddard Tuckerman and the politically active Emma Lazarus, for example, extended the resources of the sonnet in markedly different ways: the former in three inner-directed sonnet sequences written around 1870 but not published until 1931, the latter in protests against mistreatment of Jews in Europe and in the very public "The New Colossus" (1883), the sonnet carved on the pedestal of the Statue of Liberty. That poem includes words that are better known than the poet herself: "Give me your tired, your poor, / Your huddled masses yearning to breathe free." It was an ideal to which Lazarus dedicated herself wholeheartedly.

The rhythms of African-American folk speech and those of nature transposed to metrical patterns are registered, respectively and with mixed success, in the poetry of Paul Laurence Dunbar and of Sidney Lanier. Dunbar cultivated a poetic voice rooted in present realities yet aware of the past and of rich folk traditions. Praised by the novelist and editor William Dean Howells in a preface to *Lyrics of Lowly Life* (1896), Dunbar's dialect poems give a popular version of speech patterns from plantation life infused with a romantic combination of pathos and humor. In other poems of the 1890s ("We Wear the Mask" [1896], for example), Dunbar demonstrates an ironic understanding of what it is to be an African American in a race-conscious United States.

Much of Sidney Lanier's poetry portrays nature in the American South. But

---

═CONTEXTS═

The Completion of the Transcontinental Railway

The building of the transcontinental railway in the 1860s linked the West with eastern markets, encouraged settlement of the Great Plains, and brought about the extermination of the buffalo and the massacre of the Plains Indians. The government-created Union Pacific and the California-chartered Central Pacific railroads competed for government land grants and loans based on the miles of track laid. Their race across deserts and through mountains ended 1,776 miles of rails later on May 10, 1869, when the westbound tracks of the Union Pacific met the eastbound tracks of the Central Pacific in Promontory, Utah. Amidst cheers, a golden spike was driven into one of the ties, signaling completion of the line.

Chinese, African-American, Irish, and Mormon laborers had successfully hauled engines, rails, and other supplies across mountains, negotiated swamps, spanned gorges, blasted through granite walls in the Sierras (marking the first use of nitroglycerine in America), and built towns along the railroad's path virtually overnight. With a rapidity never before dreamed of, the tracks were laid by an assembly-line method, described in the *Cincinnati Gazette* in June 1867:

The trucks, each drawn by two horses, ply between the track-layers and their supplies. One of these trucks takes on a load of rails, about forty, with the proper proportion of spikes and chairs, making a load, when the horses are started off on a full gallop for the track-layers. On each side of these trucks are rollers to facilitate running off the iron.

The rails within reach, parties of five men stand on either side. One in the rear throws a rail upon the rollers, three in advance seize it, and run out with it to the proper distance. The chairs have, meantime, been set under the last rails placed.

The two men in the rear, with a single swing, force the end of the rail into the chair, and the chief of the squad calls out "Down," in a tone that equals the "Forward" to an army. Every thirty seconds there came that brave "Down," "Down," on either side of the track. They were the pendulum beats of a mighty era; they marked the time of the march and its regulation beat.

Cincinnati Gazette, 1867

---

there is a difference between the work of Lanier and that of his southern colleagues Henry Timrod and Paul Hamilton Hayne: for Lanier was not only a musician (at one time a flutist in the Peabody Orchestra in Baltimore); he was a theorist deeply concerned with the relationship of music and the cadences of poetry. In "The Symphony" (1875) he adapts words to the various instruments of an orchestra to construct a symphonic dialogue about economic and aesthetic matters. And in such poems as "The Marshes of Glynn" (1878) and "March Song—at Sunset" (1882), he captures in fascinating if somewhat ponderous detail the diurnal rhythms of marsh and seacoast in Glynn County, Georgia.

Julia A. Moore, the Sweet Singer of Michigan, by common consent the worst poet the nation has ever produced, should not be overlooked in this discussion. There has always been bad poetry, verse that makes us wince, in every nation and time. Moore's *The Sweet Singer of Michigan Salutes the Public* (1876) takes its place with the most fatuous and maudlin. Unconscious of her parodic talent and

Crowded and unsanitary conditions created hardships for the thousands of urban poor, as shown here on Hester Street in New York City in 1890. Such a setting was used by Stephen Crane in Maggie.

startling grammatical lapses, Moore specialized in obituary poems, saccharine verses on death: "Little Henry" died as an infant; "Little Andrew" drowned at the age of two; "Little Minnie" passed away suddenly when she was four; little "Hattie House" (age six) died "at play" after falling into "a fit"; in the most tragic case of all, "Little Libbie," a "dear little child of ten," choked to death "on a piece of beef." Poems such as these may have inspired the hilarious "Ode to Stephen Dowling Bots, Dec'd" in Mark Twain's *Adventures of Huckleberry Finn* (1884). In *Following the Equator* (1897), Mark Twain notes that the Sweet Singer of Michigan had brought joy to his heart for twenty years.

Caustic and filled with self-awareness, the poetry of Stephen Crane thrives on cosmic irony. At first glance some of his poems (all written in the 1890s) might seem to resemble those of Emily Dickinson. But Crane's poems lack Dickinson's specificity and verbal texture; for the most part they are bitter parables of human destiny played out in an uncaring universe. Properly disciplined and expressed, however, the ironic vision that pervades Crane's fiction can generate a poem such as "Do not weep, maiden, for war is kind" (1899), in which the experience of loss is magnified by the muted and sardonic tone.

Set in a context of interesting poetry of uneven quality, the work of Whitman and of Dickinson constitutes the major poetic achievement of the late nineteenth century. More than that, it exercised a lasting influence on the accomplishments of such early twentiety-century modernists as Ezra Pound, T. S. Eliot, Hilda Doolittle, William Carlos Williams, and Hart Crane. In many ways it continues to affect the writing of poetry in a postmodern era searching for fresh ways of visualizing our common humanity.

Walt Whitman
(1819–1892)

Walt Whitman owes his considerable prominence in American literary history to a single volume of poetry, *Leaves of Grass,* which he first published in 1855 and continued to rework through eight subsequent editions until his death in 1892. Whitman's poetry is marked by startling innovations in style and content that not only reflect the contemporary transition from romanticism to realism, but that signal the liberation of American literature from its European parentage and from the domination of the New England intellectual establishment. A politicized and self-conscious writer, Whitman adapted the romantic concept of the poet as national bard, developing and enacting the role of the American poet as a personification of the democratic ideal: the preeminently common man. In his poetry he celebrates his own vigor as a poet and a man and the dynamic diversity that characterized mid-nineteenth-century America.

Walter Whitman, Jr., the second of eight surviving children, was born on May 31, 1819, in rural West Hills, Long Island. His mother, Louisa Van Velsor, was an energetic woman of Dutch extraction to whom he was devoted. His father had farmed a share of the large tract of land on eastern Long Island that had been owned by the Whitmans since the seventeenth century, but he moved his family to Brooklyn to work as a carpenter when Walt was just four. A noticeable strain of instability ran through the family: Whitman's father was probably an alcoholic; a feeble-minded brother required lifelong care; another died, syphilitic, in a mental institution; and a sister suffered from neurologic problems and depression. A penchant for solitude earned young Walt a reputation for eccentricity.

Whitman's father was a friend of Thomas Paine and an avid reader of political literature. Discourse in the Whitman household was thus imbued with eighteenth-century liberalism, and the individualistic and egalitarian premise of the senior Whitman's politics remained a permanent influence. The family also supported the views of the Scottish feminist Fanny Wright and subscribed to her radical newspaper, *The Free Enquirer.* As a youth Walt looked to the leaders of the American Revolution, especially George Washington, as heroes, and one of Whitman's most important childhood memories centered on seeing the Marquis de Lafayette at an Independence Day ceremony.

Whitman's liberal political beliefs were matched by a nonsectarian religious outlook, an outlook associated with the tolerance that had historically characterized the Dutch of his maternal ancestry. His family was familiar with eighteenth-century deism and was much influenced by the Quaker preacher Elias Hicks, whose earthbound religious philosophy bore some resemblance to Ralph Waldo Emerson's. Throughout his life Whitman valued the quiet introspection and the humanitarianism that are fundamental to Quaker belief.

Despite the senior Whitman's political and philosophical interests, the family did not represent the learned tradition of, say, a Henry Adams; nevertheless, Whitman was well read, and many of the classics of western literature were available to him. In addition to his father's political pamphlets, he read at an early age the novels of Sir Walter Scott, Charles Dickens, and George Sand. Whitman knew the Bible well and had read Greek drama and the writings of Homer, Epicurus, and Lucretius, as well as the work of Shakespeare, Dante, John Milton, and the English romantic poets. The thread of mysticism running through Whitman's poetry may owe something to his reading of Indian literature, especially the Hindu *Bhagavad-Gita* and the Vedic Upanishads.

One of the most important elements of Whitman's thought is his glorification of the experiences of the common man. His own life was composed of such experiences. He left school when he was twelve to become a printer's apprentice, and by nineteen he was editing the weekly *Long Islander*. He taught school in rural Long Island from 1836 to 1841 and then took up his journalistic career once again, editing and writing for newspapers in Brooklyn, New York City, and New Orleans. In 1842 he published *Franklin Evans: Or, the Inebriate,* a formula-ridden and forgettable temperance novel. During these years Whitman developed a camaraderie with stagecoach drivers and with other working-class men, thus demonstrating an egalitarian politics even in his social life. He also became an avid theatergoer and enthusiast of Italian opera. He continued doing newspaper work into the 1850s, writing political editorials and sentimental poems and stories.

In 1855 Whitman published (at his own expense) *Leaves of Grass,* a curious, slim volume of twelve untitled poems prefaced by nine pages of rambling prose and an engraved daguerreotype of the anonymous author. This portrait of the artist as a relaxed young man, casually clothed, one hand resting on his hip, conveys the essence of Whitman's concept of himself as poet: "one of the roughs," he called himself, a man of the quotidian world, curious, confident, and aware. Whitman sent a gift copy of *Leaves of Grass* to Ralph Waldo Emerson, who responded in a now-famous letter greeting the author "at the beginning of a great career" and congratulating him on having produced "the most extraordinary bit of wit and wisdom that America has yet contributed." Despite Emerson's acclaim, this first edition of Whitman's poetry knew little critical success, except for some anonymous and positive reviews written by Whitman himself.

The 1855 preface, which did not appear in subsequent editions of *Leaves of Grass,* is now regarded as an American literary manifesto on the order of Emerson's *American Scholar* (1837) and "The Poet" (1844), to which it is indebted. In it Whitman foreshadows a countercultural poetics that neglects ordinary conventions of versification to exploit the "brawny" richness of Americanized English, "the dialect of common sense." He defines "the greatest poet" as one who "says to the past, Rise and walk before me that I may realize you," as someone connected realistically with his own time and place yet transcending it to "glow for a moment on the extremist verge." The style of the preface is eccentric, punctuated by numerous ellipses and characterized by the declamatory tone of a voice crying in the wilderness; it is the sound of a new voice calling attention to itself. Whitman sings of the beauty of America that coexists with the spiritual beauty of the American people. He hails his country as the ultimate democracy in which citizens can enjoy "the President's taking off his hat to them not they to him."

"Song of Myself" (untitled until 1881) is probably the best known and most significant of the twelve poems in this first edition. In this poem of 1346 lines, the poet celebrates his individuality, the authenticity of his own experiences in nature and in American society, and the diversity of the American population with whom he identifies. Whitman's style here reflects his rejection of nineteenth-century poetic convention and draws its strength from structural and rhythmic patterns similar to the language of biblical texts. Much critical notice has been given to the "chanting" voice of "Song of Myself"; the primitive power of the poem originates partly in the cumulative effect of Whitman's descriptive catalogues, which build in force to a mythic authority.

During the year following the first edition of *Leaves of Grass,* Whitman continued to do

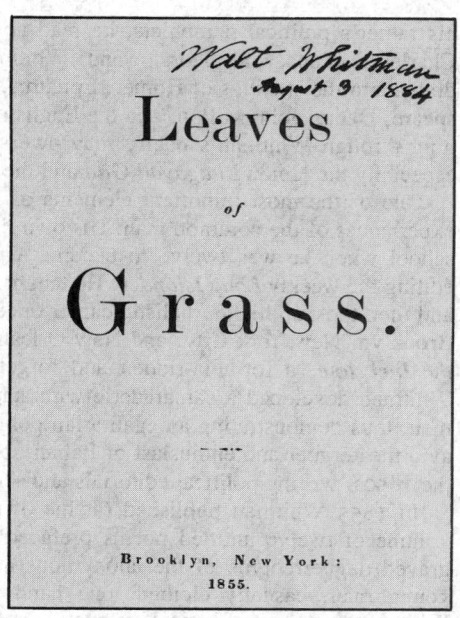

Walt Whitman
August 9 1884

Leaves

of

Grass.

- -.-

Brooklyn, New York:
1855.

The frontispiece and title page of the first edition of Walt Whitman's Leaves of Grass.

newspaper work and promoted the sale of his book. He flaunted Emerson's personal letter of congratulation in newspaper advertisements and on the spine of the second edition, a bit of self-promotion that many (but apparently not Emerson) found offensive. Whitman's preoccupation with personal image (evident even in the studied insouciance of the first edition daguerreotype), is part of his chosen subject, the dignity of the individual human being; yet, there remains a quality of self-interest in his search for identity that allows some to dismiss him as insincere and affected. Certainly, it can be said that one literary tradition in which Whitman participated fully was the age-old quest for fame. He seemed to have achieved some measure of it in 1855 and 1856, when he was visited by Emerson, Henry David Thoreau, and Bronson Alcott. In 1856 Whitman published a second edition of *Leaves of Grass,* which contains the important addition of the "Sun-Down Poem" (later called "Crossing Brooklyn Ferry"). At this time he worked as an editor at the Brooklyn *Times* and began working on the group of homoerotic poems known as the "Calamus" poems. In 1860 he published a third edition of *Leaves of Grass,* which includes the sexually frank "Enfans d'Adam" (later titled "Children of Adam") and "Calamus" poems as well as the important metaphorical account of the poet's assumption of his vocation, "A Word Out of the Sea" (later titled "Out of the Cradle Endlessly Rocking"). Whitman was always concerned about the sexually explicit nature of some of his work, and Emerson had tried, to no avail, to persuade him not to publish "Enfans d'Adam." Upon the publication of this third edition, the doors of Boston's literary elite were slammed in Whitman's face, in smarting contrast to the effusive reception that had earlier greeted him. The 1860 edition is considered critically important, however, because it marks the conclusion of Whitman's interest in the creative and procreative aspect of his poetic role; henceforth, Whitman's poetry would convey an emphasis on the poet as cultural prophet.

In 1862 Whitman traveled to Washington, D.C., to care for his brother George, who had been wounded in the Civil War. Whitman had always visited the sick among his Brooklyn acquaintances, and he now found himself performing that same humanitarian service among his brother's many wounded comrades. He was greatly appreciated as a cheering presence and worked arduously as a hospital attendant, sometimes assisting during medical procedures. These experiences and his general political interest in Abraham Lincoln's presidential election and in the Civil War provide the subject for *Drum-Taps*, a group of poems published in 1865. The volume was subsequently issued as a "sequel" with the addition of the magnificent elegy of Lincoln, "When Lilacs Last in the Dooryard Bloom'd," and was incorporated, with the *Passage to India* (1871) poems, in the 1872 edition of *Leaves of Grass*.

In Washington in 1865 Whitman worked for six months in the Army Paymaster's Office but lost his job when the supervisor discovered the erotic nature of his poetry. Whitman was given a new job in the Attorney General's office, however, by William O'Connor, a friend who wrote the appreciative biography *The Good Gray Poet* (1866). In 1871 Whitman published *Democratic Vistas*, a prose pamphlet that explores the cultural possibilities of democracy. In 1873 he suffered a paralytic stroke, after which he was moved to the Camden, New Jersey, home of his brother George to recuperate.

Whitman's poetic power, many feel, diminished after the 1860 edition of *Leaves of Grass*. When he had recovered physically from the events of 1873, he did not produce anything of substance, with the exception of *Specimen Days*, a volume of prose published in 1882. But his popular reputation grew in these later years, and he came to be lionized in Camden in much the same way Emerson had been in Concord. Whitman issued subsequent editions of *Leaves of Grass* in 1876, 1881, and 1891 to 1892 despite continuing threats of suppression because of the candid quality of his poetry. He died in Camden on March 26, 1892. A century later Whitman's celebration of democracy, diversity, and his own vitality remains for us the quintessential expression of the American artist.

Suggested Readings: *The Complete Prose Works of Walt Whitman*, Vol. II, 1902. *Leaves of Grass*, 1860 edition, ed. R. H. Pearce, 1961. *Walt Whitman: The Correspondence*, 6 vols., ed. E. H. Miller, 1961–1977. *The Collected Writings of Walt Whitman*, ed. G. W. Allen and S. Bradley, 1961– . H. Traubel, *With Walt Whitman in Camden*, 6 vols., 1906. G. W. Allen, *The Solitary Singer: A Critical Biography of Walt Whitman*, 1955, rpt. 1985. R. Asselineau, *The Evolution of Walt Whitman*, 1962. J. C. Smuts, *Walt Whitman: A Study in the Evolution of a Personality*, 1973. J. Woodress, ed., *Critical Essays on Walt Whitman*, 1983. G. W. Allen, *The New Walt Whitman Handbook*, 1986. G. Hutchinson, *The Ecstatic Whitman: Literary Shamanism and the Crisis of the Union*, 1986. M. W. Thomas, *The Lunar Light of Whitman's Poetry*, 1987. K. C. Larson, *Whitman's Drama of Consensus*, 1988. B. Erkkila, *Whitman the Political Poet*, 1989. E. H. Miller, *Walt Whitman's "Song of Myself": A Mosaic of Interpretations*, 1989. K. M. Price, *Whitman and Tradition*, 1990.

Texts Used: "Preface" and poems: *Leaves of Grass*, ed. H. W. Blodgett and S. Bradley, 1965. All else: *The Complete Prose Works*, Vol. I.

from   **LEAVES OF GRASS**

PREFACE TO THE 1855 EDITION*

America does not repel the past or what it has produced under its forms or amid other politics or the idea of castes or the old religions. . . . accepts the lesson with calmness . . . is not so impatient as has been supposed that the slough[1] still sticks

---

* Omitted from later editions, although much of the preface material is retained in the poems added to those editions. The ellipses and idiosyncratic spellings are Whitman's.
[1] The outer, discarded skin of a snake.

to opinions and manners and literature while the life which served its requirements has passed into the new life of the new forms . . . perceives that the corpse is slowly borne from the eating and sleeping rooms of the house . . . perceives that it waits a little while in the door . . . that it was fittest for its days . . . that its action has descended to the stalwart and wellshaped heir who approaches . . . and that he shall be fittest for his days.

The Americans of all nations at any time upon the earth have probably the fullest poetical nature. The United States themselves are essentially the greatest poem. In the history of the earth hitherto the largest and most stirring appear tame and orderly to their ampler largeness and stir. Here at last is something in the doings of man that corresponds with the broadcast doings of the day and night. Here is not merely a nation but a teeming nation of nations. Here is action untied from strings necessarily blind to particulars and details magnificently moving in vast masses. Here is the hospitality which forever indicates heroes. . . . Here are the roughs and beards and space and ruggedness and nonchalance that the soul loves. Here the performance disdaining the trivial unapproached in the tremendous audacity of its crowds and groupings and the push of its perspective spreads with crampless and flowing breadth and showers its prolific and splendid extravagance. One sees it must indeed own the riches of the summer and winter, and need never be bankrupt while corn grows from the ground or the orchards drop apples or the bays contain fish or men beget children upon women.

Other states indicate themselves in their deputies. . . . but the genius of the United States is not best or most in its executives or legislatures, nor in its ambassadors or authors or colleges or churches or parlors, nor even in its newspapers or inventors . . . but always most in the common people. Their manners speech dress friendships—the freshness and candor of their physiognomy—the picturesque looseness of their carriage . . . their deathless attachment to freedom—their aversion to anything indecorous or soft or mean—the practical acknowledgment of the citizens of one state by the citizens of all other states—the fierceness of their roused resentment—their curiosity and welcome of novelty—their self-esteem and wonderful sympathy—their susceptibility to a slight—the air they have of persons who never knew how it felt to stand in the presence of superiors—the fluency of their speech—their delight in music, the sure symptom of manly tenderness and native elegance of soul . . . their good temper and open-handedness—the terrible significance of their elections—the President's taking off his hat to them not they to him—these too are unrhymed poetry. It awaits the gigantic and generous treatment worthy of it.

The largeness of nature or the nation were monstrous without a corresponding largeness and generosity of the spirit of the citizen. Not nature nor swarming states nor streets and steamships nor prosperous business nor farms nor capital nor learning may suffice for the ideal of man . . . nor suffice the poet. No reminiscences may suffice either. A live nation can always cut a deep mark and can have the best authority the cheapest . . . namely from its own soul. This is the sum of the profitable uses of individuals or states and of present action and grandeur and of the subjects of poets.—As if it were necessary to trot back generation after generation to the eastern records! As if the beauty and sacredness of the demonstrable must fall behind that of the mythical! As if men do not make their mark out of any times! As if the opening of the western continent by discovery and what has transpired since in North and South America were less than the small theatre of the antique or the aimless sleep-walking of the middle ages! The pride of the United

States leaves the wealth and finesse of the cities and all returns of commerce and agriculture and all the magnitude of geography or shows of exterior victory to enjoy the breed of fullsized men or one fullsized man unconquerable and simple.

The American poets are to enclose old and new for America is the race of races. Of them a bard[2] is to be commensurate with a people. To him the other continents arrive as contributions . . . he gives them reception for their sake and his own sake. His spirit responds to his country's spirit. . . . he incarnates its geography and natural life and rivers and lakes. Mississippi with annual freshets and changing chutes, Missouri and Columbia and Ohio and Saint Lawrence with the falls and beautiful masculine Hudson, do not embouchure[3] where they spend themselves more than they embouchure into him. The blue breadth over the inland sea of Virginia and Maryland and the sea off Massachusetts and Maine and over Manhattan bay and over Champlain and Erie and over Ontario and Huron and Michigan and Superior, and over the Texan and Mexican and Floridian and Cuban seas and over the seas off California and Oregon, is not tallied by the blue breadth of the waters below more than the breadth of above and below is tallied by him. When the long Atlantic coast stretches longer and the Pacific coast stretches longer he easily stretches with them north or south. He spans between them also from east to west and reflects what is between them. On him rise solid growths that offset the growths of pine and cedar and hemlock and liveoak and locust and chestnut and cypress and hickory and limetree and cottonwood and tuliptree and cactus and wildvine and tamarind and persimmon. . . . and tangles as tangled as any canebrake or swamp. . . . and forests coated with transparent ice and icicles hanging from the boughs and crackling in the wind. . . . and sides and peaks of mountains. . . . and pasturage sweet and free as savannah or upland or prairie. . . . with flights and songs and screams that answer those of the wildpigeon and highhold[4] and orchard oriole and coot and surf-duck and redshouldered-hawk and fish-hawk and white-ibis and indian-hen and cat-owl and water-pheasant and qua-bird and pied-sheldrake and blackbird and mockingbird and buzzard and condor and night-heron and eagle. To him the hereditary countenance descends both mother's and father's. To him enter the essences of the real things and past and present events—of the enormous diversity of temperature and agriculture and mines—the tribes of red aborigines—the weatherbeaten vessels entering new ports or making landings on rocky coasts—the first settlements north or south— the rapid stature and muscle—the haughty defiance of '76,[5] and the war and peace and formation of the constitution. . . . the union always surrounded by blatherers and always calm and impregnable—the perpetual coming of immigrants—the wharf hem'd cities and superior marine[6]—the unsurveyed interior—the loghouses and clearings and wild animals and hunters and trappers. . . . the free commerce—the fisheries and whaling and golddigging—the endless gestation of new states—the convening of Congress every December,[7] the members duly coming up from all climates and the uttermost parts. . . . the noble character of the young mechanics[8] and of all free American workmen and workwomen. . . . the general ardor and friendliness and enterprise—the perfect equality of the female with the male. . . . the large amativeness[9]—the fluid movement of the population—the

---

[2] A national or tribal poet, traditionally in the epic or heroic vein; one who sustained and continued the oral tradition of the people.
[3] Pour out.   [4] Woodpecker.   [5] The Declaration of Independence.
[6] Maritime industry.   [7] Before 1933 Congress convened on the first Monday in December.
[8] Manual laborers.   [9] Amorousness.

factories and mercantile life and laborsaving machinery—the Yankee swap[10]—the New-York firemen and the target excursion[11]—the southern plantation life—the character of the northeast and of the northwest and southwest—slavery and the tremulous spreading of hands to protect it, and the stern opposition to it which shall never cease till it ceases or the speaking of tongues and the moving of lips cease. For such the expression of the American poet is to be transcendant and new. It is to be indirect and not direct or descriptive or epic. Its quality goes through these to much more. Let the age and wars of other nations be chanted and their eras and characters be illustrated and that finish the verse. Not so the great psalm of the republic. Here the theme is creative and has vista. Here comes one among the wellbeloved stonecutters and plans with decision and science and sees the solid and beautiful forms of the future where there are now no solid forms.

Of all nations the United States with veins full of poetical stuff most need poets and will doubtless have the greatest and use them the greatest. Their Presidents shall not be their common referee so much as their poets shall. Of all mankind the great poet is the equable man. Not in him but off from him things are grotesque or eccentric or fail of their sanity. Nothing out of its place is good and nothing in its place is bad. He bestows on every object or quality its fit proportions neither more nor less. He is the arbiter of the diverse and he is the key. He is the equalizer of his age and land. . . . he supplies what wants supplying and checks what wants checking. If peace is the routine out of him speaks the spirit of peace, large, rich, thrifty, building vast and populous cities, encouraging agriculture and the arts and commerce—lighting the study of man, the soul, immortality—federal, state or municipal government, marriage, health, freetrade, intertravel by land and sea. . . . nothing too close, nothing too far off . . . the stars not too far off. In war he is the most deadly force of the war. Who recruits him recruits horse and foot[12] . . . he fetches parks of artillery[13] the best that engineer ever knew. If the time becomes slothful and heavy he knows how to arouse it . . . he can make every word he speaks draw blood. Whatever stagnates in the flat[14] of custom or obedience or legislation he never stagnates. Obedience does not master him, he masters it. High up out of reach he stands turning a concentrated light . . . he turns the pivot with his finger . . . he baffles the swiftest runners as he stands and easily overtakes and envelops them. The time straying toward infidelity and confections and persiflage he withholds by his steady faith . . . he spreads out his dishes . . . he offers the sweet firmfibred meat that grows men and women. His brain is the ultimate brain. He is no arguer . . . he is judgment. He judges not as the judge judges but as the sun falling around a helpless thing. As he sees the farthest he has the most faith. His thoughts are the hymns of the praise of things. In the talk on the soul and eternity and God off of his equal plane he is silent. He sees eternity less like a play with a prologue and denouement. . . . he sees eternity in men and women . . . he does not see men and women as dreams or dots. Faith is the antiseptic of the soul . . . it pervades the common people and preserves them . . . they never give up believing and expecting and trusting. There is that indescribable freshness and unconsciousness about an illiterate person that humbles and mocks the power of the noblest expressive genius. The poet sees for a certainty how one not a great artist may be just as sacred and perfect as the

---

[10] A shrewd deal, from the reputation of New Englanders (Yankees) for hard bargaining.
[11] The outing to a shooting match.   [12] Cavalry and infantry.
[13] Local militias commonly drilled in city parks, which in times of need became supply depots.
[14] Low, marshy land.

greatest artist. . . . The power to destroy or remould is freely used by him but never the power of attack. What is past is past. If he does not expose superior models and prove himself by every step he takes he is not what is wanted. The presence of the greatest poet conquers . . . not parleying or struggling or any prepared attempts. Now he has passed that way see after him! there is not left any vestige of despair or misanthropy or cunning or exclusiveness or the ignominy of a nativity or color or delusion of hell or the necessity of hell. . . . and no man thenceforward shall be degraded for ignorance or weakness or sin.

The greatest poet hardly knows pettiness or triviality. If he breathes into any thing that was before thought small it dilates with the grandeur and life of the universe. He is a seer. . . . he is individual . . . he is complete in himself. . . . the others are as good as he, only he sees it and they do not. He is not one of the chorus. . . . he does not stop for any regulation . . . he is the president of regulation. What the eyesight does to the rest he does to the rest. Who knows the curious mystery of the eyesight? The other senses corroborate themselves, but this is removed from any proof but its own and foreruns the identities of the spiritual world. A single glance of it mocks all the investigations of man and all the instruments and books of the earth and all reasoning. What is marvellous? what is unlikely? what is impossible or baseless or vague? after you have once just opened the space of a peachpit and given audience to far and near and to the sunset and had all things enter with electric swiftness softly and duly without confusion or jostling or jam.

The land and sea, the animals fishes and birds, the sky of heaven and the orbs, the forests mountains and rivers, are not small themes . . . but folks expect of the poet to indicate more than the beauty and dignity which always attach to dumb real objects . . . . they expect him to indicate the path between reality and their souls. Men and women perceive the beauty well enough. .probably as well as he. The passionate tenacity of hunters, woodmen, early risers, cultivators of gardens and orchards and fields, the love of healthy women for the manly form, seafaring persons, drivers of horses, the passion for light and the open air, all is an old varied sign of the unfailing perception of beauty and of a residence of the poetic in outdoor people. They can never be assisted by poets to perceive . . . some may but they never can. The poetic quality is not marshalled in rhyme or uniformity or abstract addresses to things nor in melancholy complaints or good precepts, but is the life of these and much else and is in the soul. The profit of rhyme is that it drops seeds of a sweeter and more luxuriant rhyme, and of uniformity that it conveys itself into its own roots in the ground out of sight. The rhyme and uniformity of perfect poems show the free growth of metrical laws and bud from them as unerringly and loosely as lilacs or roses on a bush, and take shapes as compact as the shapes of chestnuts and oranges and melons and pears, and shed the perfume impalpable to form. The fluency and ornaments of the finest poems or music or orations or recitations are not independent but dependent. All beauty comes from beautiful blood and a beautiful brain. If the greatnesses are in conjunction in a man or woman it is enough . . . . the fact will prevail through the universe . . . . but the gaggery[15] and gilt of a million years will not prevail. Who troubles himself about his ornaments or fluency is lost. This is what you shall do: Love the earth and sun and the animals, despise riches, give alms to every one that asks, stand up for the stupid and crazy, devote your income and labor to others,

---

[15] Falseness.

hate tyrants, argue not concerning God, have patience and indulgence toward the people, take off your hat to nothing known or unknown or to any man or number of men, go freely with powerful uneducated persons and with the young and with the mothers of families, read these leaves in the open air every season of every year of your life, re-examine all you have been told at school or church or in any book, dismiss whatever insults your own soul, and your very flesh shall be a great poem and have the richest fluency not only in its words but in the silent lines of its lips and face and between the lashes of your eyes and in every motion and joint of your body. . . . . The poet shall not spend his time in unneeded work. He shall know that the ground is always ready ploughed and manured . . . . others may not know it but he shall. He shall go directly to the creation. His trust shall master the trust of everything he touches . . . . and shall master all attachment.

The known universe has one complete lover and that is the greatest poet. He consumes an eternal passion and is indifferent which chance happens and which possible contingency of fortune or misfortune and persuades daily and hourly his delicious pay. What balks or breaks others is fuel for his burning progress to contact and amorous joy. Other proportions of the reception of pleasure dwindle to nothing to his proportions. All expected from heaven or from the highest he is rapport with in the sight of the daybreak or a scene of the winter woods or the presence of children playing or with his arm round the neck of a man or woman. His love above all love has leisure and expanse . . . . he leaves room ahead of himself. He is no irresolute or suspicious lover . . . he is sure . . . he scorns intervals. His experience and the showers and thrills are not for nothing. Nothing can jar him . . . . suffering and darkness cannot—death and fear cannot. To him complaint and jealousy and envy are corpses buried and rotten in the earth . . . . he saw them buried. The sea is not surer of the shore or the shore of the sea than he is of the fruition of his love and of all perfection and beauty.

The fruition of beauty is no chance of hit or miss . . . it is inevitable as life . . . . it is exact and plumb as gravitation. From the eyesight proceeds another eyesight and from the hearing proceeds another hearing and from the voice proceeds another voice eternally curious of the harmony of things with man. To these respond perfections not only in the committees that were supposed to stand for the rest but in the rest themselves just the same. These understand the law of perfection in masses and floods . . . that its finish is to each for itself and onward from itself . . . that it is profuse and impartial . . . that there is not a minute of the light or dark nor an acre of the earth or sea without it—nor any direction of the sky nor any trade or employment nor any turn of events. This is the reason that about the proper expression of beauty there is precision and balance . . . one part does not need to be thrust above another. The best singer is not the one who has the most lithe and powerful organ . . . the pleasure of poems is not in them that take the handsomest measure and similes and sound.

Without effort and without exposing in the least how it is done the greatest poet brings the spirit of any or all events and passions and scenes and persons some more and some less to bear on your individual character as you hear or read. To do this well is to compete with the laws that pursue and follow time. What is the purpose must surely be there and the clue of it must be there . . . . and the faintest indication is the indication of the best and then becomes the clearest indication. Past and present and future are not disjoined but joined. The greatest poet forms the consistence of what is to be from what has been and is. He drags the dead out of their coffins and stands them again on their feet . . . . he says to the past, Rise and walk before me that I may realize you. He learns the lesson. . . . he places himself where the future becomes present. The greatest poet does not only dazzle his rays over character and scenes and passions . . . he finally ascends and finishes all . . . he exhibits the pinnacles that no man can tell what they are for or what is beyond. . . . he glows a moment on the extremest verge. He is most wonderful in his last half-hidden smile or frown . . . by that flash of the moment of parting the one that sees it shall be encouraged or terrified afterward for many years. The greatest poet does not moralize or make applications of morals . . . he knows the soul. The soul has that measureless pride which consists in never acknowledging any lessons but its own. But it has sympathy as measureless as its pride and the one balances the other and neither can stretch too far while it stretches in company with the other. The inmost secrets of art sleep with the twain. The greatest poet has lain close betwixt both and they are vital in his style and thoughts.

The art of art, the glory of expression and the sunshine of the light of letters is simplicity. Nothing is better than simplicity . . . . nothing can make up for excess or for the lack of definiteness. To carry on the heave of impulse and pierce intellectual depths and give all subjects their articulations are powers neither common nor very uncommon. But to speak in literature with the perfect rectitude and insousiance[16] of the movements of animals and the unimpeachableness of the sentiment of trees in the woods and grass by the roadside is the flawless triumph of art. If you have looked on him who has achieved it you have looked on one of the masters of the artists of all nations and times. You shall not contemplate the flight of the graygull over the bay or the mettlesome action of the blood horse or the tall leaning of sunflowers on their stalk or the appearance of the sun journeying through heaven or the appearance of the moon afterward with any more satisfaction than you shall contemplate him. The greatest poet has less a marked style and is more the channel of thoughts and things without increase or diminution, and is the free channel of himself. He swears to his art, I will not be meddlesome, I will not have in my writing any elegance or effect or originality to hang in the way between me and the rest like curtains. I will have nothing hang in the way, not the richest curtains. What I tell I tell for precisely what it is. Let who may exalt or startle or fascinate or sooth I will have purposes as health or heat or snow has and be as regardless of observation. What I experience or portray shall go from my composition without a shred of my composition. You shall stand by my side and look in the mirror with me.

The old red blood and stainless gentility of great poets will be proved by their unconstraint. A heroic person walks at his ease through and out of that custom or precedent or authority that suits him not. Of the traits of the brotherhood of writers savans[17] musicians inventors and artists nothing is finer than silent defiance advancing from new free forms. In the need of poems philosophy politics mechanism science behaviour, the craft of art, an appropriate native grand-opera, shipcraft, or any craft, he is greatest forever and forever who contributes the greatest original practical example. The cleanest expression is that which finds no sphere worthy of itself and makes one.

The messages of great poets to each man and woman are, Come to us on equal terms, Only then can you understand us, We are no better than you, What we enclose you enclose, What we enjoy you may enjoy. Did you suppose there could

---

[16] Indifference.   [17] Savants, or learned men.

be only one Supreme? We affirm there can be unnumbered Supremes, and that one does not countervail another any more than one eyesight countervails another . . and that men can be good or grand only of the consciousness of their supremacy within them. What do you think is the grandeur of storms and dismemberments and the deadliest battles and wrecks and the wildest fury of the elements and the power of the sea and the motion of nature and of the throes of human desires and dignity and hate and love? It is that something in the soul which says, Rage on, Whirl on, I tread master here and everywhere, Master of the spasms of the sky and of the shatter of the sea, Master of nature and passion and death, And of all terror and all pain.

The American bards shall be marked for generosity and affection and for encouraging competitors . . They shall be kosmos . . without monopoly or secresy . . glad to pass any thing to any one . . hungry for equals night and day. They shall not be careful of riches and privilege . . . . they shall be riches and privilege . . . . they shall perceive who the most affluent man is. The most affluent man is he that confronts all the shows he sees by equivalents out of the stronger wealth of himself. The American bard shall delineate no class of persons nor one or two out of the strata of interests nor love most nor truth most nor the soul most nor the body most . . . . and not be for the eastern states more than the western or the northern states more than the southern.

Exact science and its practical movements are no checks on the greatest poet but always his encouragement and support. The outset and remembrance are there . . there the arms that lifted him first and brace him best. . . . there he returns after all his goings and comings. The sailor and traveler . . the anatomist, chemist, astronomer, geologist, phrenologist, spiritualist, mathematician, historian and lexicographer are not poets, but they are the lawgivers of poets and their construction underlies the structure of every perfect poem. No matter what rises or is uttered they sent the seed of the conception of it . . . of them and by them stand the visible proofs of souls . . . . . always of their fatherstuff must be begotten the sinewy races of bards. If there shall be love and content between the father and the son and if the greatness of the son is the exuding of the greatness of the father there shall be love between the poet and the man of demonstrable science. In the beauty of poems are the tuft and final applause of science.

Great is the faith of the flush of knowledge and of the investigation of the depths of qualities and things. Cleaving and circling here swells the soul of the poet yet is president of itself always. The depths are fathomless and therefore calm. The innocence and nakedness are resumed . . . they are neither modest nor immodest. The whole theory of the special and supernatural and all that was twined with it or educed[18] out of it departs as a dream. What has ever happened . . . . what happens and whatever may or shall happen, the vital laws enclose all . . . . they are sufficent for any case and for all cases . . . none to be hurried or retarded . . . . any miracle of affairs or persons inadmissible in the vast clear scheme where every motion and every spear of grass and the frames and spirits of men and women and all that concerns them are unspeakably perfect miracles all referring to all and each distinct and in its place. It is also not consistent with the reality of the soul to admit that there is anything in the known universe more divine than men and women.

[18] Drawn forth.

Men and women and the earth and all upon it are simply to be taken as they are, and the investigation of their past and present and future shall be unintermitted and shall be done with perfect candor. Upon this basis philosophy speculates ever looking toward the poet, ever regarding the eternal tendencies of all toward happiness never inconsistent with what is clear to the senses and to the soul. For the eternal tendencies of all toward happiness make the only point of sane philosophy. Whatever comprehends less than that . . . whatever is less than the laws of light and of astronomical motion . . . or less than the laws that follow the thief the liar the glutton and the drunkard through this life and doubtless afterward . . . . . . or less than vast stretches of time or the slow formation of density or the patient upheaving of strata—is of no account. Whatever would put God in a poem or system of philosophy as contending against some being or influence is also of no account. Sanity and ensemble characterise the great master . . . spoilt in one principle all is spoilt. The great master has nothing to do with miracles. He sees health for himself in being one of the mass . . . . he sees the hiatus in singular eminence. To the perfect shape comes common ground. To be under the general law is great for that is to correspond with it. The master knows that he is unspeakably great and that all are unspeakably great. . . . that nothing for instance is greater than to conceive children and bring them up well . . . that to be is just as great as to perceive or tell.

In the make of the great masters the idea of political liberty is indispensible. Liberty takes the adherence of heroes wherever men and women exist . . . . but never takes any adherence or welcome from the rest more than from poets. They are the voice and exposition of liberty. They out of ages are worthy the grand idea . . . . to them it is confided and they must sustain it. Nothing has precedence of it and nothing can warp or degrade it. The attitude of great poets is to cheer up slaves and horrify despots. The turn of their necks, the sound of their feet, the motions of their wrists, are full of hazard to the one and hope to the other. Come nigh them awhile and though they neither speak or advise you shall learn the faithful American lesson. Liberty is poorly served by men whose good intent is quelled from one failure or two failures or any number of failures, or from the casual indifference or ingratitude of the people, or from the sharp show of the tushes[19] of power, or the bringing to bear soldiers and cannon or any penal statutes. Liberty relies upon itself, invites no one, promises nothing, sits in calmness and light, is positive and composed, and knows no discouragement. The battle rages with many a loud alarm and frequent advance and retreat . . . . the enemy triumphs . . . . the prison, the handcuffs, the iron necklace and anklet, the scaffold, garrote and leadballs do their work . . . . the cause is asleep . . . . the strong throats are choked with their own blood . . . . the young men drop their eyelashes toward the ground when they pass each other . . . . and is liberty gone out of that place? No never. When liberty goes it is not the first to go nor the second or third to go . . it waits for all the rest to go . . it is the last. . . When the memories of the old martyrs are faded utterly away . . . . when the large names of patriots are laughed at in the public halls from the lips of the orators . . . . when the boys are no more christened after the same but christened after tyrants and traitors instead . . . . when the laws of the free are grudgingly permitted and laws for informers and bloodmoney are sweet to the taste of the people . . . .

---

[19] Tusks.

when I and you walk abroad upon the earth stung with compassion at the sight of numberless brothers answering our equal friendship and calling no man master— and when we are elated with noble joy at the sight of slaves . . . . when the soul retires in the cool communion of the night and surveys its experience and has much extasy over the word and deed that put back a helpless innocent person into the gripe of the gripers or into any cruel inferiority . . . . when those in all parts of these states who could easier realize the true American character but do not yet—when the swarms of cringers, suckers, doughfaces,[20] lice of politics, planners of sly involutions for their own preferment to city offices or state legislatures or the judiciary or congress or the presidency, obtain a response of love and natural deference from the people whether they get the offices or no . . . . when it is better to be a bound booby[21] and rogue in office at a high salary than the poorest free mechanic or farmer with his hat unmoved from his head and firm eyes and a candid and generous heart . . . . and when servility by town or state or the federal government or any oppression on a large scale or small scale can be tried on without its own punishment following duly after in exact proportion against the smallest chance of escape . . . . or rather when all life and all the souls of men and women are discharged from any part of the earth—then only shall the instinct of liberty be discharged from that part of the earth.

As the attributes of the poets of the kosmos concentre in the real body and soul and in the pleasure of things they possess the superiority of genuineness over all fiction and romance. As they emit themselves facts are showered over with light . . . . the daylight is lit with more volatile light . . . . also the deep between the setting and rising sun goes deeper many fold. Each precise object or condition or combination or process exhibits a beauty . . . . the multiplication table its—old age its—the carpenter's trade its—the grand-opera its . . . . the hugehulled clean-shaped New-York clipper at sea under steam or full sail gleams with unmatched beauty . . . . the American circles and large harmonies of government gleam with theirs . . . . and the commonest definite intentions and actions with theirs. The poets of the kosmos advance through all interpositions and coverings and turmoils and stratagems to first principles. They are of use . . . . they dissolve poverty from its need and riches from its conceit. You large proprietor they say shall not realize or perceive more than any one else. The owner of the library is not he who holds a legal title to it having bought and paid for it. Any one and every one is owner of the library who can read the same through all the varieties of tongues and subjects and styles, and in whom they enter with ease and take residence and force toward paternity and maternity, and make supple and powerful and rich and large. . . . . These American states strong and healthy and accomplished shall receive no pleasure from violations of natural models and must not permit them. In paintings or mouldings or carvings in mineral or wood, or in the illustrations of books or newspapers, or in any comic or tragic prints, or in the patterns of woven stuffs or any thing to beautify rooms or furniture or costumes, or to put upon cornices or monuments or on the prows of sterns of ships, or to put anywhere before the human eye indoors or out, that which distorts honest shapes or which creates unearthly beings or places or contingencies is a nuisance and revolt. Of the human form especially it is so great it must never be made ridiculous. Of ornaments to a work nothing outre[22] can be allowed . . but those ornaments can

---

[20] Swindlers; changeable, unscrupulous people.   [21] A political fool who owes favors.
[22] Extravagant, improper.

be allowed that conform to the perfect facts of the open air and that flow out of the nature of the work and come irrepressibly from it and are necessary to the completion of the work. Most works are most beautiful without ornament. . . Exaggerations will be revenged in human physiology. Clean and vigorous children are jetted[23] and conceived only in those communities where the models of natural forms are public every day. . . . . Great genius and the people of these states must never be demeaned to romances. As soon as histories are properly told there is no more need of romances.

The great poets are also to be known by the absence in them of tricks and by the justification of perfect personal candor. Then folks echo a new cheap joy and a divine voice leaping from their brains: How beautiful is candor! All faults may be forgiven of him who has perfect candor. Henceforth let no man of us lie, for we have seen that openness wins the inner and outer world and that there is no single exception, and that never since our earth gathered itself in a mass have deceit or subterfuge or prevarication attracted its smallest particle or the faintest tinge of a shade—and that through the enveloping wealth and rank of a state or the whole republic of states a sneak or sly person shall be discovered and despised . . . . and that the soul has never been once fooled and never can be fooled . . . . and thrift without the loving nod of the soul is only a fœtid puff . . . . and there never grew up in any of the continents of the globe nor upon any planet or satellite or star, nor upon the asteroids, nor in any part of ethereal space, nor in the midst of density, nor under the fluid wet of the sea, nor in that condition which precedes the birth of babes, nor at any time during the changes of life, nor in that condition that follows what we term death, nor in any stretch of abeyance or action afterward of vitality, nor in any process of formation or reformation anywhere, a being whose instinct hated the truth.

Extreme caution or prudence, the soundest organic health, large hope and comparison and fondness for women and children, large alimentiveness[24] and destructiveness and causality, with a perfect sense of the oneness of nature and the propriety of the same spirit applied to human affairs . . these are called up of the float[25] of the brain of the world to be parts of the greatest poet from his birth out of his mother's womb and from her birth out of her mother's. Caution seldom goes far enough. It has been thought that the prudent citizen was the citizen who applied himself to solid gains and did well for himself and his family and completed a lawful life without debt or crime. The greatest poet sees and admits these economies as he sees the economies of food and sleep, but has higher notions of prudence than to think he gives much when he gives a few slight attentions at the latch of the gate. The premises of the prudence of life are not the hospitality of it or the ripeness and harvest of it. Beyond the independence of a little sum laid aside for burial-money, and of a few clapboards around and shingles overhead on a lot of American soil owned, and the easy dollars that supply the year's plain clothing and meals, the melancholy prudence of the abandonment of such a great being as a man is to the toss and pallor of years of moneymaking with all their scorching days and icy nights and all their stifling deceits and underhanded dodgings, or infinitesimals of parlors, or shameless stuffing while others starve . . and all the loss of the bloom and odor of the earth and of the flowers and atmosphere and of the sea and of the true taste of the women and men you pass or have to do with in youth or middle age, and the issuing sickness and desperate revolt at the

---

[23] Ejaculated.   [24] Love of food.   [25] Buoyancy.

close of a life without elevation or naivete, and the ghastly chatter of a death without serenity or majesty, is the great fraud upon modern civilization and fore-thought, blotching the surface and system which civilization undeniably drafts, and moistening with tears the immense features it spreads and spreads with such velocity before the reached kisses of the soul. . . Still the right explanation re-mains to be made about prudence. The prudence of the mere wealth and respecta-bility of the most esteemed life appears too faint for the eye to observe at all when little and large alike drop quietly aside at the thought of the prudence suitable for immortality. What is wisdom that fills the thinness of a year or seventy or eighty years to wisdom spaced out by ages and coming back at a certain time with strong reinforcements and rich presents and the clear faces of wedding-guests as far as you can look in every direction running gaily toward you? Only the soul is of itself . . . . all else has reference to what ensues. All that a person does or thinks is of consequence. Not a move can a man or woman make that affects him or her in a day or a month or any part of the direct lifetime or the hour of death but the same affects him or her onward afterward through the indirect lifetime. The indi-rect is always as great and real as the direct. The spirit receives from the body just as much as it gives to the body. Not one name of word or deed . . not of venereal sores or discolorations . . not the privacy of the onanist[26] . . not of the putrid veins of gluttons or rumdrinkers . . . not peculation[27] or cunning or betrayal or murder . . no serpentine poison of those that seduce women . . not the foolish yielding of women . . not prostitution . . not of any depravity of young men . . not of the attainment of gain by discreditable means . . not any nastiness of appe-tite . . not any harshness of officers to men or judges to prisoners or fathers to sons or sons to fathers or of husbands to wives or bosses to their boys . . not of greedy looks or malignant wishes . . . nor any of the wiles practised by people upon themselves . . . ever is or ever can be stamped on the programme but it is duly realized and returned, and that returned in further performances . . . and they returned again. Nor can the push of charity or personal force ever be any thing else than the profoundest reason, whether it bring arguments to hand or no. No specification is necessary . . to add or subtract or divide is in vain. Little or big, learned or unlearned, white or black, legal or illegal, sick or well, from the first inspiration down the windpipe to the last expiration out of it, all that a male or female does that is vigorous and benevolent and clean is so much sure profit to him or her in the unshakable order of the universe and through the whole scope of it forever. If the savage or felon is wise it is well. . . . if the greatest poet or savan is wise it is simply the same . . if the President or chief justice is wise it is the same . . if the young mechanic or farmer is wise it is no more or less . . if the prostitute is wise it is no more nor less. The interest will come round . . all will come round. All the best actions of war and peace . . . all help given to relatives and strangers and the poor and old and sorrowful and young children and widows and the sick, and to all shunned persons . . all furtherance of fugitives and of the escape of slaves . . all the self-denial that stood steady and aloof on wrecks and saw others take the seats of the boats . . . all offering of substance or life for the good old cause, or for a friend's sake or opinion's sake . . . all pains of en-thusiasts scoffed at by their neighbors . . all the vast sweet love and precious suffering of mothers . . . all honest men baffled in strifes recorded or unre-corded . . . . all the grandeur and good of the few ancient nations whose frag-ments of annals we inherit . . and all the good of the hundreds of far mightier and

---

[26] Masturbator, after Onan, the son of Judah, in Genesis 38:9.   [27] Embezzlement.

more ancient nations unknown to us by name or date or location. . . . all that was ever manfully begun, whether it succeeded or no. . . . all that has at any time been well suggested out of the divine heart of man or by the divinity of his mouth or by the shaping of his great hands . . and all that is well thought or done this day on any part of the surface of the globe . . or on any of the wandering stars or fixed stars by those there as we are here . . or that is henceforth to be well thought or done by you whoever you are, or by any one—these singly and wholly inured at their time and inure now and will inure always to the identities from which they sprung or shall spring . . . Did you guess any of them lived only its moment? The world does not so exist . . no parts palpable or impalpable so exist . . . no result exists now without being from its long antecedent result, and that from its antecedent, and so backward without the farthest mentionable spot coming a bit nearer the beginning than any other spot. . . . . Whatever satisfies the soul is truth. The prudence of the greatest poet answers at last the craving and glut of the soul, is not contemptuous of less ways of prudence if they conform to its ways, puts off nothing, permits no let-up for its own case or any case, has no particular sabbath or judgment-day, divides not the living from the dead or the righteous from the unrighteous, is satisfied with the present, matches every thought or act by its correlative, knows no possible forgiveness or deputed atonement . . knows that the young man who composedly periled his life and lost it has done exceeding well for himself, while the man who has not periled his life and retains it to old age in riches and ease has perhaps achieved nothing for himself worth mentioning . . and that only that person has no great prudence to learn who has learnt to prefer real longlived things, and favors body and soul the same, and perceives the indirect assuredly following the direct, and what evil or good he does leaping onward and waiting to meet him again—and who in his spirit in any emergency whatever neither hurries or avoids death.

The direct trial of him who would be the greatest poet is today. If he does not flood himself with the immediate age as with vast oceanic tides . . . . . and if he does not attract his own land body and soul to himself and hang on its neck with incomparable love and plunge his semitic muscle[28] into its merits and demerits . . . and if he be not himself the age transfigured . . . . and if to him is not opened the eternity which gives similitude to all periods and locations and processes and animate and inanimate forms, and which is the bond of time, and rises up from its inconceivable vagueness and infiniteness in the swimming shape of today, and is held by the ductile anchors of life, and makes the present spot the passage from what was to what shall be, and commits itself to the representation of this wave of an hour and this one of the sixty beautiful children of the wave— let him merge in the general run and wait his development. . . . . . . Still the final test of poems or any character or work remains. The prescient poet projects himself centuries ahead and judges performer or performance after the changes of time. Does it live through them? Does it still hold on untired? Will the same style and the direction of genius to similar points be satisfactory now? Has no new discovery in science or arrival at superior planes of thought and judgment and behaviour fixed him or his so that either can be looked down upon? Have the marches of tens and hundreds and thousands of years made willing detours to the right hand and the left hand for his sake? Is he beloved long and long after he is buried? Does the young man think often of him? and the young woman think often of him? and do the middleaged and the old think of him?

---

[28] Whitman's euphemism for penis.

A great poem is for ages and ages in common and for all degrees and complexions and all departments and sects and for a woman as much as a man and a man as much as a woman. A great poem is no finish to a man or woman but rather a beginning. Has any one fancied he could sit at last under some due authority and rest satisfied with explanations and realize and be content and full? To no such terminus does the greatest poet bring . . . he brings neither cessation or sheltered fatness and ease. The touch of him tells in action. Whom he takes he takes with firm sure grasp into live regions previously unattained . . . . thenceforward is no rest . . . . they see the space and ineffable sheen that turn the old spots and lights into dead vacuums. The companion of him beholds the birth and progress of stars and learns one of the meanings. Now there shall be a man cohered out of tumult and chaos . . . . the elder encourages the younger and shows him how . . . they two shall launch off fearlessly together till the new world fits an orbit for itself and looks unabashed on the lesser orbits of the stars and sweeps through the ceaseless rings and shall never be quiet again.

There will soon be no more priests. Their work is done. They may wait awhile . . perhaps a generation or two . . dropping off by degrees. A superior breed shall take their place. . . . the gangs of kosmos and prophets en masse shall take their place. A new order shall arise and they shall be the priests of man, and every man shall be his own priest. The churches built under their umbrage[29] shall be the churches of men and women. Through the divinity of themselves shall the kosmos and the new breed of poets be interpreters of men and women and of all events and things. They shall find their inspiration in real objects today, symptoms of the past and future . . . . They shall not deign to defend immortality or God or the perfection of things or liberty or the exquisite beauty and reality of the soul. They shall arise in America and be responded to from the remainder of the earth.

The English language befriends the grand American expression. . . . it is brawny enough and limber and full enough. On the tough stock of a race who through all change of circumstance was never without the idea of political liberty, which is the animus of all liberty, it has attracted the terms of daintier and gayer and subtler and more elegant tongues. It is the powerful language of resistance . . . it is the dialect of common sense. It is the speech of the proud and melancholy races and of all who aspire. It is the chosen tongue to express growth faith self-esteem freedom justice equality friendliness amplitude prudence decision and courage. It is the medium that shall well nigh express the inexpressible.

No great literature nor any like style of behaviour or oratory or social intercourse or household arrangements or public institutions or the treatment by bosses of employed people, nor executive detail of the army or navy, nor spirit of legislation or courts or police or tuition or architecture or songs or amusements or the costumes of young men, can long elude the jealous and passionate instinct of American standards. Whether or no the sign appears from the mouths of the people, it throbs a live interrogation in every freeman's and freewoman's heart after that which passes by, or this built to remain. Is it uniform with my country? Are its disposals without ignominious distinctions? Is it for the evergrowing communes of brothers and lovers, large, well-united, proud beyond the old models, generous beyond all models? Is it something grown fresh out of the fields or drawn from the sea for use to me today here? I know that what answers for me an American must answer for any individual or nation that serves for a part of my materials. Does this answer? or is it without reference to universal needs? or

[29] Shade, shelter.

sprung of the needs of the less developed society of special ranks? or old needs of pleasure overlaid by modern science and form? Does this acknowledge liberty with audible and absolute acknowledgment, and set slavery at nought for life and death? Will it help breed one goodshaped and wellhung man, and a woman to be his perfect and independent mate? Does it improve manners? Is it for the nursing of the young of the republic? Does it solve[30] readily with the sweet milk of the nipples of the breasts of the mother of many children? Has it too the old ever-fresh forbearance and impartiality? Does it look with the same love on the last born and on those hardening toward stature, and on the errant, and on those who disdain all strength of assault outside of their own?

The poems distilled from other poems will probably pass away. The coward will surely pass away. The expectation of the vital and great can only be satisfied by the demeanor of the vital and great. The swarms of the polished deprecating and reflectors and the polite float off and leave no remembrance. America prepares with composure and goodwill for the visitors that have sent word. It is not intellect that is to be their warrant and welcome. The talented, the artist, the ingenious, the editor, the statesman, the erudite . . they are not unappreciated . . they fall in their place and do their work. The soul of the nation also does its work. No disguise can pass on it . . no disguise can conceal from it. It rejects none, it permits all. Only toward as good as itself and toward the like of itself will it advance half-way. An individual is as superb as a nation when he has the qualities which make a superb nation. The soul of the largest and wealthiest and proudest nation may well go half-way to meet that of its poets. The signs are effectual. There is no fear of mistake. If the one is true the other is true. The proof of a poet is that his country absorbs him as affectionately as he has absorbed it.

1855

from INSCRIPTIONS*

ONE'S-SELF I SING

One's-Self I sing, a simple separate person,
Yet utter the word Democratic, the word En-Masse.

Of physiology from top to toe I sing,
Not physiognomy[1] alone nor brain alone is worthy for the Muse, I say the
    Form complete is worthier far,
The Female equally with the Male I sing.

Of Life immense in passion, pulse, and power,
Cheerful, for freest action form'd under the laws divine,
The Modern Man I sing.

1867

---

[30] Dissolve.
    * Group title for the opening nine poems of the 1871 edition of *Leaves of Grass*, increased to include twenty-four poems in 1881.
    [1] The art of judging human character from physical characteristics, especially facial features.

SHUT NOT YOUR DOORS*

Shut not your doors to me proud libraries,
For that which was lacking on all your well-fill'd shelves, yet needed most,
  I bring,
Forth from the war emerging, a book I have made,
The words of my book nothing, the drift of it every thing,
A book separate, not link'd with the rest nor felt by the intellect,
But you ye untold latencies will thrill to every page.

1865

SONG OF MYSELF†

1

I celebrate myself, and sing myself,
And what I assume you shall assume,
For every atom belonging to me as good belongs to you.

I loafe and invite my soul,
I lean and loafe at my ease observing a spear of summer grass.
My tongue, every atom of my blood, form'd from this soil, this air,
Born here of parents born here from parents the same, and their parents
  the same,
I, now thirty-seven years old in perfect health begin,
Hoping to cease not till death.

Creeds and schools in abeyance,   10
Retiring back a while sufficed at what they are, but never forgotten,
I harbor for good or bad, I permit to speak at every hazard,
Nature without check with original energy.

2

Houses and rooms are full of perfumes, the shelves are crowded with
  perfumes,
I breathe the fragrance myself and know it and like it,
The distillation would intoxicate me also, but I shall not let it.

The atmosphere is not a perfume, it has no taste of the distillation, it is
  odorless,
It is for my mouth forever, I am in love with it,
I will go to the bank by the wood and become undisguised and naked,
I am mad for it to be in contact with me.   20
The smoke of my own breath,

---

* First appeared in *Drum-Taps* (1865), revised, and added to "Inscriptions" in 1881.
  † Appeared in the 1855 edition of *Leaves of Grass* untitled and without subdivisions. In the 1856 edition it was titled "Poem of Walt Whitman, an American," and in 1860 and later editions, "Walt Whitman." Not until 1881 did it appear as "Song of Myself."

Echoes, ripples, buzz'd whispers, love-root, silk-thread, crotch and vine,
My respiration and inspiration, the beating of my heart, the passing of
     blood and air through my lungs,
The sniff of green leaves and dry leaves, and of the shore and dark-color'd
     sea-rocks, and of hay in the barn,
The sound of the belch'd words of my voice loos'd to the eddies of the wind,
A few light kisses, a few embraces, a reaching around of arms,
The play of shine and shade on the trees as the supple boughs wag,
The delight alone or in the rush of the streets, or along the fields and
     hill-sides,
The feeling of health, the full-noon trill, the song of me rising from bed
     and meeting the sun.

Have you reckon'd a thousand acres much? have you reckon'd the
     earth much?   30
Have you practis'd so long to learn to read?
Have you felt so proud to get at the meaning of poems?

Stop this day and night with me and you shall possess the origin of
     all poems,
You shall possess the good of the earth and sun, (there are millions of suns
     left,)
You shall no longer take things at second or third hand, nor look through
     the eyes of the dead, nor feed on the spectres in books,
You shall not look through my eyes either, nor take things from me,
You shall listen to all sides and filter them from yourself.

                                      3
I have heard what the talkers were talking, the talk of the beginning
     and the end,
But I do not talk of the beginning or the end.

There was never any more inception than there is now,   40
Nor any more youth or age than there is now,
And will never be any more perfection than there is now,
Nor any more heaven or hell than there is now.

Urge and urge and urge,
Always the procreant urge of the world.

Out of the dimness opposite equals advance, always substance and
     increase, always sex,
Always a knit of identity, always distinction, always a breed of life.

To elaborate is no avail, learn'd and unlearn'd feel that it is so.

Sure as the most certain sure, plumb in the uprights, well entretied,[1]
     braced in the beams,
Stout as a horse, affectionate, haughty, electrical,   50

---

[1] Cross-braced or supported.

I and this mystery here we stand.
Clear and sweet is my soul, and clear and sweet is all that is not my soul.

Lack one lacks both, and the unseen is proved by the seen,
Till that becomes unseen and receives proof in its turn.

Showing the best and dividing it from the worst, age vexes age,
Knowing the perfect fitness and equanimity of things, while they discuss
    I am silent, and go bathe and admire myself.

Welcome is every organ and attribute of me, and of any man hearty
    and clean,
Not an inch nor a particle of an inch is vile, and none shall be less familiar
    than the rest.

I am satisfied—I see, dance, laugh, sing;
As the hugging and loving bed-fellow[2] sleeps at my side through the
    night, and withdraws at the peep of the day with stealthy tread,   60
Leaving me baskets cover'd with white towels swelling the house with
    their plenty,
Shall I postpone my acceptation and realization and scream at my eyes,
That they turn from gazing after and down the road,
And forthwith cipher[3] and show me to a cent,
Exactly the value of one and exactly the value of two, and which
    is ahead?

                                   4
Trippers and askers[4] surround me,
People I meet, the effect upon me of my early life or the ward and city I
    live in, or the nation,
The latest dates, discoveries, inventions, societies, authors old and new,
My dinner, dress, associates, looks, compliments, dues,
The real or fancied indifference of some man or woman I love,   70
The sickness of one of my folks or of myself, or ill-doing or loss or lack
    of money, or depressions or exaltations,
Battles, the horrors of fratricidal war, the fever of doubtful news, the
    fitful events;
These come to me days and nights and go from me again,
But they are not the Me myself.

Apart from the pulling and hauling stands what I am,
Stands amused, complacent, compassionating, idle, unitary,
Looks down, is erect, or bends an arm on an impalpable certain rest,
Looking with side-curved head curious what will come next,
Both in and out of the game and watching and wondering at it.

Backward I see in my own days where I sweated through fog with
    linguists and contenders,   80
I have no mockings or arguments, I witness and wait.

---

[2] In the 1855 version, God is the "loving bed-fellow."   [3] Calculate.
[4] Travelers and solicitors.

5

I believe in you my soul, the other I am must not abase itself to you,
And you must not be abased to the other.

Loafe with me on the grass, loose the stop from your throat,
Not words, not music or rhyme I want, not custom or lecture, not even
    the best,
Only the lull I like, the hum of your valvèd voice.

I mind how once we lay such a transparent summer morning,
How you settled your head athwart my hips and gently turn'd over
    upon me.
And parted the shirt from my bosom-bone, and plunged your tongue to
    my bare-stript heart,
And reach'd till you felt my beard, and reach'd till you held my feet.   90

Swiftly arose and spread around me the peace and knowledge that pass
    all the argument of the earth,
And I know that the hand of God is the promise of my own,
And I know that the spirit of God is the brother of my own,
And that all the men ever born are also my brothers, and the women my
    sisters and lovers,
And that a kelson[5] of the creation is love,
And limitless are leaves stiff or drooping in the fields,
And brown ants in the little wells beneath them,
And mossy scabs of the worm fence,[6] heap'd stones, elder, mullein and
    poke-weed.

6

A child said *What is the grass?* fetching it to me with full hands;
How could I answer the child? I do not know what it is any more
    than he.   100

I guess it must be the flag of my disposition, out of hopeful green
    stuff woven.

Or I guess it is the handkerchief of the Lord,
A scented gift and remembrancer designedly dropt,
Bearing the owner's name someway in the corners, that we may see and
    remark, and say *Whose?*

Or I guess the grass is itself a child, the produced babe of the vegetation.

Or I guess it is a uniform hieroglyphic,
And it means, Sprouting alike in broad zones and narrow zones,
Growing among black folks as among white,
Kanuck, Tuckahoe,[7] Congressman, Cuff,[8] I give them the same, I
    receive them the same.

---

[5] Keelson, or timbers that brace a ship's keel.   [6] An undulating or zigzag fence of split rails.
[7] A French-Canadian; a native of Tidewater Virginia.   [8] An African American.

And now it seems to me the beautiful uncut hair of graves.   110

Tenderly will I use you curling grass,
It may be you transpire from the breasts of young men,
It may be if I had known them I would have loved them,
It may be you are from old people, or from offspring taken soon out of
    their mothers' laps,
And here you are the mothers' laps.

This grass is very dark to be from the white heads of old mothers,
Darker than the colorless beards of old men,
Dark to come from under the faint red roofs of mouths.

O I perceive after all so many uttering tongues,
And I perceive they do not come from the roofs of mouths for nothing.   120

I wish I could translate the hints about the dead young men and women,
And the hints about old men and mothers, and the offspring taken soon
    out of their laps.

What do you think has become of the young and old men?
And what do you think has become of the women and children?

They are alive and well somewhere,
The smallest sprout shows there is really no death,
And if ever there was it led forward life, and does not wait at the end to
    arrest it,
And ceas'd the moment life appear'd.

All goes onward and outward, nothing collapses,
And to die is different from what any one supposed, and luckier.   130

7

Has any one supposed it lucky to be born?
I hasten to inform him or her it is just as lucky to die, and I know it.

I pass death with the dying and birth with the new-wash'd babe, and am
    not contain'd between my hat and boots,
And peruse manifold objects, no two alike and every one good,
The earth good and the stars good, and their adjuncts all good.

I am not an earth nor an adjunct of an earth,
I am the mate and companion of people, all just as immortal and
    fathomless as myself,
(They do not know how immortal, but I know.)

Every kind for itself and its own, for me mine male and female,
For me those that have been boys and that love women,   140
For me the man that is proud and feels how it stings to be slighted,
For me the sweet-heart and the old maid, for me mothers and the mothers
    of mothers,

For me lips that have smiled, eyes that have shed tears,
For me children and the begetters of children.

Undrape! you are not guilty to me, nor stale nor discarded,
I see through the broadcloth and gingham whether or no,
And am around, tenacious, acquisitive, tireless, and cannot be
    shaken away.

8

The little one sleeps in its cradle,
I lift the gauze and look a long time, and silently brush away flies with
    my hand.

The youngster and the red-faced girl turn aside up the busy hill,   150
I peeringly view them from the top.

The suicide sprawls on the bloody floor of the bedroom,
I witness the corpse with its dabbled hair, I note where the pistol
    has fallen.

The blab of the pave,[9] tires of carts, sluff of boot-soles, talk of
    the promenaders,
The heavy omnibus, the driver with his interrogating thumb, the clank of
    the shod horses on the granite floor,
The snow-sleighs, clinking, shouted jokes, pelts of snow-balls,
The hurrahs for popular favorites, the fury of rous'd mobs,
The flap of the curtain'd litter, a sick man inside borne to the hospital,
The meeting of enemies, the sudden oath, the blows and fall,
The excited crowd, the policeman with his star quickly working his
    passage to the centre of the crowd,   160
The impassive stones that receive and return so many echoes,
What groans of over-fed or half-starv'd who fall sunstruck or in fits,
What exclamations of women taken suddenly who hurry home and give
    birth to babes,
What living and buried speech is always vibrating here, what howls
    restrain'd by decorum,
Arrests of criminals, slights, adulterous offers made, acceptances,
    rejections with convex lips,
I mind them or the show or resonance of them—I come and I depart.

9

The big doors of the country barn stand open and ready,
The dried grass of the harvest-time loads the slow-drawn wagon,
The clear light plays on the brown gray and green intertinged,
The armfuls are pack'd to the sagging mow.   170

I am there, I help, I came stretch'd atop of the load,
I felt its soft jolts, one leg reclined on the other,
I jump from the cross-beams and seize the clover and timothy,
And roll head over heels and tangle my hair full of wisps.

[9] Street talk.

10

Alone far in the wilds and mountains I hunt,
Wandering amazed at my own lightness and glee,
In the late afternoon choosing a safe spot to pass the night,
Kindling a fire and broiling the fresh-kill'd game,
Falling asleep on the gather'd leaves with my dog and gun by my side.

The Yankee clipper is under her sky-sails,[10] she cuts the sparkle
    and scud,   180
My eyes settle the land, I bend at her prow or shout joyously from
    the deck.

The boatmen and clam-diggers arose early and stopt for me,
I tuck'd my trowser-ends in my boots and went and had a good time;
You should have been with us that day round the chowder-kettle.

I saw the marriage of the trapper in the open air in the far west, the bride
    was a red girl,
Her father and his friends sat near cross-legged and dumbly smoking,
    they had moccasins to their feet and large thick blankets hanging from
    their shoulders,
On a bank lounged the trapper, he was drest mostly in skins, his
    luxuriant beard and curls protected his neck, he held his bride by
    the hand,
She had long eyelashes, her head was bare, her coarse straight locks
    descended upon her voluptuous limbs and reach'd to her feet.[11]

The runaway slave came to my house and stopt outside,
I heard his motions crackling the twigs of the woodpile,   190
Through the swung half-door of the kitchen I saw him limpsy and weak,
And went where he sat on a log and led him in and assured him,
And brought water and fill'd a tub for his sweated body and bruis'd feet,
And gave him a room that enter'd from my own, and gave him some
    coarse clean clothes,
And remember perfectly well his revolving eyes and his awkwardness,
And remember putting plasters on the galls of his neck and ankles;
He staid with me a week before he was recuperated and pass'd north,
I had him sit next me at table, my fire-lock[12] lean'd in the corner.

11

Twenty-eight young men bathe by the shore,
Twenty-eight young men and all so friendly;   200
Twenty-eight years of womanly life and all so lonesome.

She owns the fine house by the rise of the bank,
She hides handsome and richly drest aft the blinds of the window.

[10] Top sails; scud is sea foam.
[11] This stanza is based on the painting *The Trapper's Bride,* by Alfred Jacob Miller (1810–1874).
[12] Gun.

Which of the young men does she like the best?
Ah the homeliest of them is beautiful to her.

Where are you off to, lady? for I see you,
You splash in the water there, yet stay stock still in your room.

Dancing and laughing along the beach came the twenty-ninth bather,
The rest did not see her, but she saw them and loved them.

The beards of the young men glisten'd with wet, it ran from their
    long hair,   210
Little streams pass'd all over their bodies.

An unseen hand also pass'd over their bodies,
It descended tremblingly from their temples and ribs.

The young men float on their backs, their white bellies bulge to the sun,
    they do not ask who seizes fast to them,
They do not know who puffs and declines with pendant and
    bending arch,
They do not think whom they souse with spray.

12

The butcher-boy puts off his killing-clothes, or sharpens his knife at the
    stall in the market,
I loiter enjoying his repartee and his shuffle and break-down.[13]

Blacksmiths with grimed and hairy chests environ the anvil,
Each has his main-sledge, they are all out, there is a great heat in
    the fire.   220

From the cinder-strew'd threshold I follow their movements,
The lithe sheer[14] of their waists plays even with their massive arms,
Overhand the hammers swing, overhand so slow, overhand so sure,
They do no hasten, each man hits in his place.

13

The negro holds firmly the reins of his four horses, the block swags
    underneath on its tied-over chain,
The negro that drives the long dray[15] of the stone-yard, steady and tall he
    stands pois'd on one leg on the string piece,[16]
His blue shirt exposes his ample neck and breast and loosens over his
    hip-band,
His glance is calm and commanding, he tosses the slouch of his hat away
    from his forehead,

---

[13] Two popular minstrel-show steps: the shuffle, a sliding, slow step; the break-down, faster and un-
inhibited.
    [14] Upward curve.   [15] A low, heavy cart for haulage.
    [16] A heavy timber used to shore up construction or to brace a load.

The sun falls on his crispy hair and mustache, falls on the black of his
   polish'd and perfect limbs.

I behold the picturesque giant and love him, and I do not stop there,   230
I go with the team also.

In me the caresser of life wherever moving, backward as well as
   forward sluing,[17]
To niches aside and junior[18] bending, not a person or object missing,
Absorbing all to myself and for this song.

Oxen that rattle the yoke and chain or halt in the leafy shade, what is that
   you express in your eyes?
It seems to me more than all the print I have read in my life.

My tread scares the wood-drake and wood-duck on my distant and day-
   long ramble,
They rise together, they slowly circle around.

I believe in those wing'd purposes,
And acknowledge red, yellow, white, playing within me,   240
And consider green and violet and the tufted crown intentional,
And do not call the tortoise unworthy because she is not something else,
And the jay in the woods never studied the gamut,[19] yet trills pretty
   well to me,
And the look of the bay mare shames silliness out of me.

14

The wild gander leads his flock through the cool night,
Ya-honk he says, and sounds it down to me like an invitation,
The pert[20] may suppose it meaningless, but I listening close,
Find its purpose and place up there toward the wintry sky.

The sharp-hoof'd moose of the north, the cat on the house-sill, the
   chickadee, the prairie dog,
The litter of the grunting sow as they tug at her teats,   250
The brood of the turkey-hen and she with her half-spread wings,
I see in them and myself the same old law.

The press of my foot to the earth springs a hundred affections,
They scorn the best I can do to relate them.
I am enamour'd of growing out-doors,
Of men that live among cattle or taste of the ocean or woods,
Of the builders and steerers of ships and the wielders of axes and mauls,
   and the drivers of horses,
I can eat and sleep with them week in and week out.

---

[17] Twisting.   [18] Lesser.
[19] Never practiced musical scales.   [20] The bold.

What is commonest, cheapest, nearest, easiest, is Me,
Me going in for my chances, spending for vast returns,   260
Adorning myself to bestow myself on the first that will take me,
Not asking the sky to come down to my good will,
Scattering it freely forever.

15

The pure contralto sings in the organ loft,
The carpenter dresses his plank, the tongue of his foreplane whistles its
    wild ascending lisp,
The married and unmarried children ride home to their Thanksgiving
    dinner,
The pilot seizes the king-pin,[21] he heaves down with a strong arm,
The mate stands braced in the whale-boat, lance and harpoon are ready,
The duck-shooter walks by silent and cautious stretches,
The deacons are ordain'd with cross'd hands at the altar,   270
The spinning-girl retreats and advances to the hum of the big wheel,
The farmer stops by the bars[22] as he walks on a First-day loafe[23] and
    looks at the oats and rye,
The lunatic is carried at last to the asylum a confirm'd case,
(He will never sleep any more as he did in the cot in his mother's
    bed-room;)
The jour printer[24] with gray head and gaunt jaws works at his case,
He turns his quid of tobacco while his eyes blurr with the manuscript;
The malform'd limbs are tied to the surgeon's table,
What is removed drops horribly in a pail;
The quadroon[25] girl is sold at the auction-stand, the drunkard nods by the
    bar-room stove,
The machinist rolls up his sleeves, the policeman travels his beat, the
    gate-keeper marks who pass,   280
The young fellow drives the express-wagon, (I love him, though I do not
    know him;)
The half-breed straps on his light boots to compete in the race,
The western turkey-shooting draws old and young, some lean on their
    rifles, some sit on logs,
Out from the crowd steps the marksman, takes his position, levels
    his piece;
The groups of newly-come immigrants cover the wharf or levee,
As the woolly-pates[26] hoe in the sugar-field, the overseer views them
    from his saddle,
The bugle calls in the ball-room, the gentlemen run for their partners, the
    dancers bow to each other,
The youth lies awake in the cedar-roof'd garret and harks to the
    musical rain,

[21] The extended spoke of the pilot wheel.   [22] Fence rails.
[23] The Quaker designation for the first day of the week: Sunday, a day of leisure.
[24] Journeyman printer, working out his case of typefaces.
[25] One-quarter black (with one black grandparent).   [26] African-American slaves.

The Wolverine[27] sets traps on the creek that helps fill the Huron,
The squaw wrapt in her yellow-hemm'd cloth is offering moccasins and
    bead-bags for sale,   290
The connoisseur peers along the exhibition-gallery with half-shut eyes
    bent sideways,
As the deck-hands make fast the steamboat the plank is thrown for the
    shore-going passengers,
The young sister holds out the skein while the elder sister winds it off in
    a ball, and stops now and then for the knots,
The one-year wife is recovering and happy having a week ago borne her
    first child,
The clean-hair'd Yankee girl works with her sewing-machine or in the
    factory or mill,
The paving-man leans on his two-handed rammer, the reporter's lead
    flies swiftly over the note-book, the sign-painter is lettering with blue
    and gold,
The canal boy trots on the tow-path,[28] the book-keeper counts at his
    desk, the shoemaker waxes his thread,
The conductor beats time for the band and all the performers follow him,
The child is baptized, the convert is making his first professions,
The regatta is spread on the bay, the race is begun, (how the white
    sails sparkle!)   300
The drover watching his drove sings out to them that would stray,
The pedler sweats with his pack on his back, (the purchaser higgling
    about the odd cent;)
The bride unrumples her white dress, the minute-hand of the clock
    moves slowly,
The opium-eater reclines with rigid head and just-open'd lips,
The prostitute draggles her shawl, her bonnet bobs on her tipsy and
    pimpled neck,
The crowd laugh at her blackguard oaths, the men jeer and wink to
    each other,
(Miserable! I do not laugh at your oaths nor jeer you;)
The President holding a cabinet council is surrounded by the
    great Secretaries,
On the piazza walk three matrons stately and friendly with
    twined arms,
The crew of the fish-smack pack repeated layers of halibut in the hold,   310
The Missourian crosses the plains toting his wares and his cattle,
As the fare-collector goes through the train he gives notice by the
    jingling of loose change,
The floor-men are laying the floor, the tinners are tinning[29] the roof, the
    masons are calling for mortar,
In single file each shouldering his nod pass onward the laborers;
Seasons pursuing each other the indescribable crowd is gather'd, it is the
    fourth of Seventh-month,[30] (what salutes of cannon and small arms!)

---

[27] Michigan resident.   [28] A path along which draft animals tow canal barges.
[29] Repairing a sheet-metal roof.
[30] The Quaker designation for the Fourth of July.

Seasons pursuing each other the plougher ploughs, the mower mows,
    and the winter-grain falls in the ground;
Off on the lakes the pike-fisher watches and waits by the hole in the
    frozen surface,
The stumps stand thick round the clearing, the squatter strikes deep with
    his axe,
Flatboatmen make fast towards dusk near the cotton-wood or
    pecan-trees,
Coon-seekers[31] go through the regions of the Red river or through those
    drain'd by the Tennessee, or through those of the Arkansas,   320
Torches shine in the dark that hangs on the Chattahooche
    or Altamahaw,[32]
Patriarchs sit at supper with sons and grandsons and great-grandsons
    around them,
In walls of adobie, in canvas tents, rest hunters and trappers after their
    day's sport,
The city sleeps and the country sleeps,
The living sleep for their time, the dead sleep for their time,
The old husband sleeps by his wife and the young husband sleeps by
    his wife;
And these tend inward to me, and I tend outward to them,
And such as it is to be of these more or less I am,
And of these one and all I weave the song of myself.

16

I am of old and young, of the foolish as much as the wise,   330
Regardless of others, ever regardful of others,
Maternal as well as paternal, a child as well as a man,
Stuff'd with the stuff that is coarse and stuff'd with the stuff that is fine,
One of the Nation of many nations, the smallest the same and the largest
    the same,
A Southerner soon as a Northerner, a planter nonchalant and hospitable
    down by the Oconee[33] I live,
A Yankee bound my own way ready for trade, my joints the limberest
    joints on earth and the sternest joints on earth,
A Kentuckian walking the vale of the Elkhorn[34] in my deer-skin leggings,
    a Louisianian or Georgian,
A boatman over lakes or bays or along coasts, a Hoosier, Badger,
    Buckeye;[35]
At home on Kanadian snow-shoes or up in the bush, or with fishermen
    off Newfoundland,
At home in the fleet of ice-boats, sailing with the rest and tacking,   340
At home on the hills of Vermont or in the woods of Maine, or the
    Texan ranch,

---

[31] Racoon hunters; the Red River borders Texas and Oklahoma.
[32] Rivers in Alabama and Louisiana.
[33] A river in Georgia.
[34] A river in Nebraska.
[35] An inhabitant of Indiana, Wisconsin, and Ohio, respectively.

Comrade of Californians, comrade of free North-Westerners, (loving
   their big proportions,)
Comrade of raftsmen and coalmen, comrade of all who shake hands and
   welcome to drink and meat,
A learner with the simplest, a teacher of the thoughtfullest,
A novice beginning yet experient of myriads of seasons,
Of every hue and caste am I, of every rank and religion,
A farmer, mechanic, artist, gentleman, sailor, quaker,
Prisoner, fancy-man,[36] rowdy, lawyer, physician, priest.

I resist any thing better than my own diversity,
Breathe the air but leave plenty after me,   350
And am not stuck up, and am in my place.

(The moth and the fish-eggs are in their place,
The bright suns I see and the dark suns I cannot see are in their place,
The palpable is in its place and the impalpable is in its place.)

17

These are really the thoughts of all men in all ages and lands, they are
   not original with me,
If they are not yours as much as mine they are nothing, or next to nothing,
If they are not the riddle and the untying of the riddle they are nothing,
If they are not just as close as they are distant they are nothing.

This is the grass that grows wherever the land is and the water is,
This the common air that bathes the globe.   360

18

With music strong I come, with my cornets and my drums,
I play not marches for accepted victors only, I play marches for
   conquer'd and slain persons.

Have you heard that it was good to gain the day?
I also say it is good to fall, battles are lost in the same spirit in which
   they are won.

I beat and pound for the dead,
I blow through my embouchures[37] my loudest and gayest for them.

Vivas to those who have fail'd!
And to those whose war-vessels sank in the sea!
And to those themselves who sank in the sea!
And to all generals that lost engagements, and all overcome heroes!   370
And the numberless unknown heroes equal to the greatest heroes known!

---

[36] A pimp.   [37] Mouthpieces of wind and brass instruments.

19

This is the meal equally set, this the meat for natural hunger,
It is for the wicked just the same as the righteous, I make appointments
    with all,
I will not have a single person slighted or left away,
The kept-woman, sponger, thief, are hereby invited,
The heavy-lipp'd slave is invited, the venerealee[38] is invited;
There shall be no difference between them and the rest.

This is the press of a bashful hand, this the float and odor of hair,
This the touch of my lips to yours, this the murmur of yearning,
This the far-off depth and height reflecting my own face,   380
This the thoughtful merge of myself, and the outlet again.

Do you guess I have some intricate purpose?
Well I have, for the Fourth-month[39] showers have, and the mica on the
    side of a rock has.

Do you take it I would astonish?
Does the daylight astonish? does the early redstart twittering through
    the woods?
Do I astonish more than they?

This hour I tell things in confidence,
I might not tell everybody, but I will tell you.

20

Who goes there? hankering, gross, mystical, nude;
How is it I extract strength from the beef I eat?   390

What is a man anyhow? what am I? what are you?

All I mark as my own you shall offset it with your own,
Else it were time lost listening to me.

I do not snivel that snivel the world over,
That months are vacuums and the ground but wallow and filth.

Whimpering and truckling fold with powders for invalids,[40] conformity,
    goes to the fourth-remov'd,[41]
I wear my hat as I please indoors or out.

Why should I pray? why should I venerate and be ceremonious?

---

[38] One infected with a venereal disease or obsessed with sexual desire.   [39] April.
  [40] Whimpering and yielding are appropriate medicines to be combined with the other powders administered to invalids.
  [41] Those removed from society.

Having pried through the strata, analyzed to a hair, counsel'd with
    doctors and calculated close,
I find no sweeter fat than sticks to my own bones.   400

In all people I see myself, none more and not one a barley-corn less,
And the good or bad I say of myself I say of them.

I know I am solid and sound,
To me the converging objects of the universe perpetually flow,
All are written to me, and I must get what the writing means.

I know I am deathless,
I know this orbit of mine cannot be swept by a carpenter's compass,
I know I shall not pass like a child's carlacue[42] cut with a burnt stick
    at night.

I know I am august,
I do not trouble my spirit to vindicate itself or be understood,   410
I see that the elementary laws never apologize,
(I reckon I behave no prouder than the level I plant my house by,
    after all.)

I exist as I am, that is enough,
If no other in the world be aware I sit content,
And if each and all be aware I sit content.

One world is aware and by far the largest to me, and that is myself,
And whether I come to my own to-day or in ten thousand or ten
    million years,
I can cheerfully take it now, or with equal cheerfulness I can wait.
My foothold is tenon'd and mortis'd[43] in granite,
I laugh at what you call dissolution,   420
And I know the amplitude of time.

21

I am the poet of the Body and I am the poet of the Soul,
The pleasures of heaven are with me and the pains of hell are with me,
The first I graft and increase upon myself, the latter I translate into a
    new tongue.

I am the poet of the woman the same as the man,
And I say it is as great to be a woman as to be a man,
And I say there is nothing greater than the mother of men.

I chant the chant of dilation or pride,
We have had ducking and deprecating about enough,
I show that size is only development.   430

---

[42] A curlicue, here a brief pattern of light "cut" in the darkness by the glowing end of a burning stick.
[43] Joined with interlocking pieces.

Have you outstript the rest? are you the President?
It is a trifle, they will more than arrive there every one, and still pass on.

I am he that walks with the tender and growing night,
I call to the earth and sea half-held by the night.

Press close bare-bosom'd night—press close magnetic nourishing night!
Night of south winds—night of the large few stars!
Still nodding night—mad naked summer night.

Smile O voluptuous cool-breath'd earth!
Earth of the slumbering and liquid trees!
Earth of departed sunset—earth of the mountains misty-topt!   440
Earth of the vitreous[44] pour of the full moon just tinged with blue!
Earth of shine and dark mottling the tide of the river!
Earth of the limpid gray of clouds brighter and clearer for my sake!
Far-swooping elbow'd earth—rich apple blossom'd earth!
Smile, for your lover comes.

Prodigal, you have given me love—therefore I to you give love!
O unspeakable passionate love.

22

You sea! I resign myself to you also—I guess what you mean,
I behold from the beach your crooked inviting fingers,
I believe you refuse to go back without feeling of me,   450
We must have a turn together, I undress, hurry me out of sight of
    the land,
Cushion me soft, rock me in billowy drowse,
Dash me with amorous wet, I can repay you.

Sea of stretch'd ground-swells,
Sea breathing broad and convulsive breaths,
Sea of the brine of life and of unshovell'd yet always-ready graves,
Howler and scooper of storms, capricious and dainty sea,
I am integral with you, I too am of one phase and of all phases.

Partaker of influx and efflux, I, extoller of hate and conciliation,
Extoller of amies[45] and those that sleep in each others' arms.   460

I am he attesting sympathy,
(Shall I make my list of things in the house and skip the house that
    supports them?)

I am not the poet of goodness only, I do not decline to be the poet of
    wickedness also.

What blurt is this about virtue and about vice?
Evil propels me and reform of evil propels me, I stand indifferent,

---

[44] Glasslike.   [45] "Friends" or "lovers" (French).

My gait is no fault-finder's or rejecter's gait,
I moisten the roots of all that has grown.

Did you fear some scrofula[46] out of the unflagging pregnancy?
Did you guess the celestial laws are yet to be work'd over and rectified?

I find one side a balance and the antipodal side a balance,   470
Soft doctrine as steady help as stable doctrine,
Thoughts and deeds of the present our rouse and early start.

This minute that comes to me over the past decillions,[47]
There is no better than it and now.

What behaved well in the past or behaves well to-day is not such
    a wonder,
The wonder is always and always how there can be a mean man or
    an infidel.

                                      23
Endless unfolding of words of ages!
And mine a word of the modern, the word En-Masse.

A word of the faith that never balks,
Here or henceforward it is all the same to me, I accept Time
    absolutely.   480

It alone is without flaw, it alone rounds and completes all,
That mystic baffling wonder alone completes all.

I accept Reality and dare not question it,
Materialism first and last imbuing.

Hurrah for positive science! long live exact demonstration!
Fetch stonecrop[48] mixt with cedar and branches of lilac,
This is the lexicographer, this the chemist, this made a grammar of the
    old cartouches,[49]
These mariners put the ship through dangerous unknown seas,
This is the geologist, this works with the scalpel, and this is a
    mathematician.

Gentlemen, to you the first honors always!   490
Your facts are useful, and yet they are not my dwelling,
I but enter by them to an area of my dwelling.

---

[46] A form of tuberculosis involving swelling of the lymph glands and inflammation of the joints;
"scrofulous" carries a connotation of moral degeneracy.
[47] Many years: one followed by thirty-three zeros.
[48] A plant used as a medicinal herb.
[49] Deciphered the Egyptian hieroglyphs carved in oblong or oval figures.

Less the reminders of properties told my words,
And more the reminders they of life untold, and of freedom and
    extrication,
And make short account of neuters and geldings, and favor men and
    women fully equipt,
And beat the gong of revolt, and stop with fugitives and them that plot
    and conspire.

24

Walt Whitman, a kosmos, of Manhattan the son,
Turbulent, fleshy, sensual, eating, drinking and breeding,
No sentimentalist, no stander above men and women or apart
    from them,
No more modest than immodest.   500

Unscrew the locks from the doors!
Unscrew the doors themselves from their jambs!

Whoever degrades another degrades me,
And whatever is done or said returns at last to me.

Through me the afflatus[50] surging and surging, through me the current
    and index.

I speak the pass-word primeval, I give the sign of democracy,
By God! I will accept nothing which all cannot have their counterpart
    of on the same terms.

Through me many long dumb voices,
Voices of the interminable generations of prisoners and slaves,
Voices of the diseas'd and despairing and of thieves and dwarfs,   510
Voices of cycles of preparation and accretion,
And of the threads that connect the stars, and of wombs and of the
    father-stuff,
And of the rights of them the others are down upon,
Of the deform'd, trivial, flat, foolish, despised,
Fog in the air, beetles rolling balls of dung.

Through me forbidden voices,
Voices of sexes and lusts, voices veil'd and I remove the veil,
Voices indecent by me clarified and transfigur'd.

I do not press my fingers across my mouth,
I keep as delicate around the bowels as around the head and heart,   520
Copulation is no more rank to me than death is.

---

[50] A divine wind, communicating knowledge or inspiration.

I believe in the flesh and the appetites,
Seeing, hearing, feeling, are miracles, and each part and tag of me is a
  miracle.

Divine am I inside and out, and I make holy whatever I touch or am
  touch'd from,
The scent of these arm-pits aroma finer than prayer,
This head more than churches, bibles, and all the creeds.

If I worship one thing more than another it shall be the spread of my
  own body, or any part of it,
Translucent mould of me it shall be you!
Shaded ledges and rests it shall be you!
Firm masculine colter[51] it shall be you!   530
Whatever goes to the tilth[52] of me it shall be you!
You my rich blood! your milky stream pale strippings of my life!
Breast that presses against other breasts it shall be you!
My brain it shall be your occult convolutions!
Root of wash'd sweet-flag![53] timorous pond-snipe! nest of guarded
  duplicate eggs! it shall be you!
Mix'd tussled hay of head, beard, brawn, it shall be you!
Trickling sap of maple, fibre of manly wheat, it shall be you!
Sun so generous it shall be you!
Vapors lighting and shading my face it shall be you!
You sweaty brooks and dews it shall be you!   540
Winds whose soft-tickling genitals rub against me it shall be you!
Broad muscular fields, branches of live oak, loving lounger in my
  winding paths, it shall be you!
Hands I have taken, face I have kiss'd, mortal I have ever touch'd, it
  shall be you.

I dote on myself, there is that lot of me and all so luscious,
Each moment and whatever happens thrills me with joy,
I cannot tell how my ankles bend, nor whence the cause of my
  faintest wish,
Nor the cause of the friendship I emit, nor the cause of the friendship I
  take again.

That I walk up my stoop, I pause to consider if it really be,
A morning-glory at my window satisfies me more than the
  metaphysics of books.

To behold the day-break!   550
The little light fades the immense and diaphanous shadows,
The air tastes good to my palate.

---

[51] A sharp blade that cuts the ground in front of a plowshare.   [52] Cultivation.
[53] The aromatic root of the calamus plant.

Hefts[54] of the moving world at innocent gambols silently rising freshly
    exuding,
Scooting obliquely high and low.

Something I cannot see puts upward libidinous prongs,
Seas of bright juice suffuse heaven.

The earth by the sky staid with, the daily close of their junction,
The heav'd challenge from the east that moment over my head,
The mocking taunt, See then whether you shall be master!

25

Dazzling and tremendous how quick the sun-rise would kill me,   560
If I could not now and always send sun-rise out of me.

We also ascend dazzling and tremendous as the sun,
We found our own O my soul in the calm and cool of the daybreak.

My voice goes after what my eyes cannot reach,
With the twirl of my tongue I encompass worlds and volumes of worlds.

Speech is the twin of my vision, it is unequal to measure itself,
It provokes me forever, it says sarcastically,
Walt you contain enough, why don't you let it out then?

Come now I will not be tantalized, you conceive too much of
    articulation,
Do you not know O speech how the buds beneath you are folded?   570
Waiting in gloom, protected by frost,
The dirt receding before my prophetical screams,
I underlying causes to balance them at last,
My knowledge my live parts, it keeping tally with the meaning of all
    things,
Happiness, (which whoever hears me let him or her set out in search of
    this day.)

My final merit I refuse you, I refuse putting from me what I really am,
Encompass worlds, but never try to encompass me,
I crowd your sleekest and best by simply looking toward you.

Writing and talk do not prove me,
I carry the plenum[55] of proof and every thing else in my face,   580
With the hush of my lips I wholly confound the skeptic.

26

Now I will do nothing but listen,
To accrue what I hear into this song, to let sounds contribute toward it.

---

[54] The most massive parts.   [55] Fullness.

I hear bravuras of birds, bustle of growing wheat, gossip of flames, clack
    of sticks cooking my meals,
I hear the sound I love, the sound of the human voice,
I hear all sounds running together, combined, fused or following,
Sounds of the city and sounds out of the city, sounds of the day and night,
Talkative young ones to those that like them, the loud laugh of work-
    people at their meals,
The angry base[56] of disjointed friendship, the faint tones of the sick,
The judge with hands tight to the desk, his pallid lips pronouncing a
    death-sentence,   590
The heave'e'yo of stevedores unlading ships by the wharves, the refrain
    of the anchor-lifters,
The ring of alarm-bells, the cry of fire, the whirr of swift-streaking
    engines and hose-carts with premonitory tinkles and color'd lights,
The steam-whistle, the solid roll of the train of approaching cars,
The slow march play'd at the head of the association marching two
    and two,
(They go to guard some corpse, the flag-tops are draped with black
    muslin.)

I hear the violoncello, ('tis the young man's heart's complaint,)
I hear the key'd cornet, it glides quickly in through my ears,
It shakes mad-sweet pangs through my belly and breast.

I hear the chorus, it is a grand opera,
Ah this indeed is music—this suits me.   600

A tenor large and fresh as the creation fills me,
The orbic flex of his mouth is pouring and filling me full.

I hear the train'd soprano (what work with hers is this?)
The orchestra whirls me wider than Uranus[57] flies,
It wrenches such ardors from me I did not know I possess'd them,
It sails me, I dab with bare feet, they are lick'd by the indolent waves,
I am cut by bitter and angry hail, I lose my breath,
Steep'd amid honey'd morphine, my windpipe throttled in fakes[58]
    of death,
At length let up again to feel the puzzle of puzzles,
And that we call Being.   610

27

To be in any form, what is that?
(Round and round we go, all of us, and ever come back thither,)
If nothing lay more develop'd the quahaug[59] in its callous shell were
    enough.

---

[56] Bass.
[57] Then thought to be the most remote planet; it orbits the sun at a mean distance of nearly 2 million miles.
[58] Coils of rope.   [59] Quahog, an edible Atlantic clam.

Mine is no callous shell,
I have instant conductors all over me whether I pass or stop,
They seize every object and lead it harmlessly through me.

I merely stir, press, feel with my fingers, and am happy,
To touch my person to some one else's is about as much as I can stand.

28

Is this then a touch? quivering me to a new identity,
Flames and ether making a rush for my veins,   620
Treacherous tip of me reaching and crowing to help them,
My flesh and blood playing out lightning to strike what is hardly
    different from myself,
On all sides prurient provokers stiffening my limbs,
Straining the udder of my heart for its withheld drip,
Behaving licentious toward me, taking no denial,
Depriving me of my best as for a purpose,
Unbuttoning my clothes, holding me by the bare waist,
Deluding my confusion with the calm of the sunlight and pasture-fields,
Immodestly sliding the fellow-senses away,
They bribed to swap off with touch and go and graze at the edges of me,   630
No consideration, no regard for my draining strength or my anger,
Fetching the rest of the herd around to enjoy them a while,
Then all uniting to stand on a headland and worry me.

The sentries desert every other part of me,
They have left me helpless to a red marauder,
They all come to the headland to witness and assist against me.

I am given up by traitors,
I talk wildly, I have lost my wits, I and nobody else am the greatest
    traitor,
I went myself first to the headland, my own hands carried me there.

You villain touch! what are you doing? my breath is tight in its throat,   640
Unclench your floodgates, you are too much for me.

29

Blind loving wrestling touch, sheath'd hooded sharp-tooth'd touch!
Did it make you ache so, leaving me?

Parting track'd by arriving, perpetual payment of perpetual loan,
Rich showering rain, and recompense richer afterward.

Sprouts take and accumulate, stand by the curb prolific and vital,
Landscapes projected masculine, full-sized and golden.

30

All truths wait in all things,
They neither hasten their own delivery nor resist it,

They do not need the obstetric forceps of the surgeon,   650
The insignificant is as big to me as any,
(What is less or more than a touch?)

Logic and sermons never convince,
The damp of the night drives deeper into my soul.

(Only what proves itself to every man and woman is so,
Only what nobody denies is so.)

A minute and a drop of me settle my brain,
I believe the soggy clods shall become lovers and lamps,
And a compend[60] of compends is the meat of a man or woman,
And a summit and flower there is the feeling they have for each other,   660
And they are to branch boundlessly out of that lesson until it becomes
    omnific,
And until one and all shall delight us, and we them.

31

I believe a leaf of grass is no less than the journey-work of the stars,
And the pismire[61] is equally perfect, and a grain of sand, and the egg of
    the wren,
And the tree-toad is a chef-d'œuvre[62] for the highest,
And the running blackberry would adorn the parlors of heaven,
And the narrowest hinge in my hand puts to scorn all machinery,
And the cow crunching with depress'd head surpasses any statue,
And a mouse is miracle enough to stagger sextillions[63] of infidels.

I find I incorporate gneiss,[64] coal, long-threaded moss, fruits, grains,
    esculent roots,   670
And am stucco'd with quadrupeds and birds all over,
And have distanced what is behind me for good reasons,
But call any thing back again when I desire it.

In vain the speeding or shyness,
In vain the plutonic rocks[65] send their old heat against my approach,
In vain the mastodon retreats beneath its own powder'd bones,
In vain objects stand leagues off and assume manifold shapes,
In vain the ocean settling in hollows and the great monsters lying low,
In vain the buzzard houses herself with the sky,
In vain the snake slides through the creepers and logs,   680
In vain the elk takes to the inner passes of the woods,
In vain the razor-bill'd auk sails far north to Labrador,
I follow quickly, I ascend to the nest in the fissure of the cliff.

---

[60] A compendium or short summary, especially of a very broad subject.   [61] Ant.
[62] A masterpiece (French).   [63] A large number: one followed by twenty-one zeros.
[64] Layered, coarse-grained metamorphic rock.
[65] Rock formed from molten material beneath the earth's crust; from the Roman god Pluto, the ruler of the Underworld.

32

I think I could turn and live with animals, they are so placid and self-
    contain'd,
I stand and look at them long and long.

They do not sweat and whine about their condition,
They do not lie awake in the dark and weep for their sins,
They do not make me sick discussing their duty to God,
Not one is dissatisfied, not one is demented with the mania of owning
    things,
Not one kneels to another, nor to his kind that lived thousands of
    years ago,   690
Not one is respectable or unhappy over the whole earth.

So they show their relations to me and I accept them,
They bring me tokens of myself, they evince them plainly in their
    possession.

I wonder where they get those tokens,
Did I pass that way huge times ago and negligently drop them?

Myself moving forward then and now and forever,
Gathering and showing more always and with velocity,
Infinite and omnigenous,[66] and the like of these among them,
Not too exclusive toward the reachers of my remembrancers,
Picking out here one that I love, and now go with him on brotherly
    terms.   700

A gigantic beauty of a stallion, fresh and responsive to my caresses,
Head high in the forehead, wide between the ears,
Limbs glossy and supple, tail dusting the ground,
Eyes full of sparkling wickedness, ears finely cut, flexibly moving.

His nostrils dilate as my heels embrace him,
His well-built limbs tremble with pleasure as we race around and return.

I but use you a minute, then I resign you, stallion,
Why do I need your paces when I myself out-gallop them?
Even as I stand or sit passing faster than you.

33

Space and Time! now I see it is true, what I guess'd at,   710
What I guess'd when I loaf'd on the grass,
What I guess'd while I lay alone in my bed,
And again as I walk'd the beach under the paling stars of the morning.

[66] Of all forms.

My ties and ballasts leave me, my elbows rest in sea-gaps,[67]
I skirt sierras, my palms cover continents,
I am afoot with my vision.

By the city's quadrangular houses—in log huts, camping with
    lumbermen,
Along the ruts of the turnpike, along the dry gulch and rivulet bed,
Weeding my onion-patch or hoeing rows of carrots and parsnips,
    crossing savannas, trailing in forests,
Prospecting, gold-digging, girdling the trees of a new purchase,   720
Scorch'd ankle-deep by the hot sand, hauling by boat down the shallow
    river,
Where the panther walks to and fro on a limb overhead, where the buck
    turns furiously at the hunter,
Where the rattlesnake suns his flabby length on a rock, where the otter is
    feeding on fish,
Where the alligator in his tough pimples sleeps by the bayou,
Where the black bear is searching for roots or honey, where the beaver
    pats the mud with his paddle-shaped tail;
Over the growing sugar, over the yellow-flower'd cotton plant, over the
    rice in its low moist field,
Over the sharp-peak'd farm house, with its scallop'd scum and slender
    shoots from the gutters,[68]
Over the western persimmon, over the long-leav'd corn, over the
    delicate blue-flower flax,
Over the white and brown buckwheat, a hummer and buzzer[69] there with
    the rest,
Over the dusky green of the rye as it ripples and shades in the breeze;   730
Scaling mountains, pulling myself cautiously up, holding on by low
    scragged[70] limbs,
Walking the path worn in the grass and beat through the leaves of the
    brush,
Where the quail is whistling betwixt the woods and the wheat-lot,
Where the bat flies in the Seventh-month eve, where the great goldbug[71]
    drops through the dark,
Where the brook puts out of the roots of the old tree and flows to the
    meadow,
Where cattle stand and shake away flies with the tremulous shuddering
    of their hides,
Where the cheese-cloth hangs in the kitchen, where andirons straddle the
    hearth-slab, where cobwebs fall in festoons from the rafters;
Where trip-hammers crash, where the press is whirling its cylinders,
Wherever the human heart beats with terrible throes under its ribs,
Where the pear-shaped balloon is floating aloft, (floating in it myself
    and looking composedly down,)   740

---

[67] Estuaries, inlets.
[68] Patterns of sediment washed down from the roof peaks, and shoots of plants that have colonized
the sediment deposited in the rain-gutters.
[69] A hummingbird and a bee.   [70] Low-growing.   [71] A beetle.

Where the life-car[72] is drawn on the slip-noose, where the heat hatches
    pale-green eggs in the dented sand,
Where the she-whale swims with her calf and never forsakes it,
Where the steam-ship trails hind-ways its long pennant of smoke,
Where the fin of the shark cuts like a black chip out of the water,
Where the half-burn'd brig[73] is riding on unknown currents,
Where shells grow to her slimy deck, where the dead are corrupting
    below;
Where the dense-starr'd flag is borne at the head of the regiments,
Approaching Manhattan up by the long-stretching island,
Under Niagara, the cataract[74] falling like a veil over my countenance,
Upon a door-step, upon the horse-block[75] of hard wood outside,   750
Upon the race-course, or enjoying picnics or jibs or a good game of
    baseball,
At he-festivals, with blackguard gibes, ironical license, bull-dances,[76]
    drinking, laughter,
At the cider-mill tasting the sweets of the brown mash, sucking the
    juice through a straw,
At apple-peelings wanting kisses for all the red fruit I find,
At musters,[77] beach-parties, friendly bees, huskings,[78] house-raisings;
Where the mocking-bird sounds his delicious gurgles, cackles, screams,
    weeps,
Where the hay-rick[79] stands in the barn-yard, where the dry-stalks are
    scatter'd, where the brood-cow waits in the hovel,
Where the bull advances to do his masculine work, where the stud to the
    mare, where the cock is treading the hen,
Where the heifers browse, where geese nip their food with short jerks,
Where sun-down shadows lengthen over the limitless and lonesome
    prairie,   760
Where herds of buffalo make a crawling spread of the square miles far
    and near,
Where the humming-bird shimmers, where the neck of the long-lived
    swan is curving and winding,
Where the laughing-gull scoots by the shore, where she laughs her near-
    human laugh,
Where bee-hives range on a gray bench in the garden half hid by the high
    weeds,
Where band-neck'd partridges roost in a ring on the ground with their
    heads out,
Where burial coaches enter the arch'd gates of a cemetery,
Where winter wolves bark amid wastes of snow and icicled trees,
Where the yellow-crown'd heron comes to the edge of the marsh at night
    and feeds upon small crabs,

[72] A watertight "car" that moves on ropes, used to evacuate ships.
[73] A brigantine, or two-masted ship.   [74] Large waterfall.   [75] A step to aid in mounting horses.
[76] Country dances in which men danced with men, due to a shortage of women.
[77] Military assemblies or community gatherings.
[78] Social events for the completion of a labor-intensive task such as quilting or preserving; corn-husking.
[79] Hayracks, from which livestock eat hay.

Where the splash of swimmers and divers cools the warm noon,
Where the katy-did works her chromatic reed[80] on the walnut-tree over
    the well,   770
Through patches of citrons[81] and cucumbers with silver-wired leaves,
Through the salt-lick or orange glade, or under conical firs,
Through the gymnasium, through the curtain'd saloon, through the
    office or public hall;
Pleas'd with the native and pleas'd with the foreign, pleas'd with the
    new and old,
Pleas'd with the homely woman as well as the handsome,
Pleas'd with the quakeress as she puts off her bonnet and talks
    melodiously,
Pleas'd with the tune of the choir of the whitewash'd church,
Pleas'd with the earnest words of the sweating Methodist preacher,
    impress'd seriously at the camp-meeting;
Looking in at the shop windows of Broadway the whole forenoon,
    flatting the flesh of my nose on the thick plate glass,
Wandering the same afternoon with my face turn'd up to the clouds, or
    down a lane or along the beach,   780
My right and left arms round the sides of two friends, and I in the
    middle;
Coming home with the silent and dark-cheek'd bush-boy, (behind me he
    rides at the drape[82] of the day,)
Far from the settlements studying the print of animals' feet, or the
    moccasin print,
By the cot in the hospital reaching lemonade to a feverish patient,
Nigh the coffin'd corpse when all is still, examining with a candle;
Voyaging to every port to dicker and adventure,
Hurrying with the modern crowd as eager and fickle as any,
Hot toward one I hate, ready in my madness to knife him,
Solitary at midnight in my back yard, my thoughts gone from me a
    long while,
Walking the old hills of Judæa with the beautiful gentle God by
    my side,   790
Speeding through space, speeding through heaven and the stars,
Speeding amid the seven satellites and the broad ring,[83] and the
    diameter of eighty thousand miles,
Speeding with tail'd meteors, throwing fire-balls like the rest,
Carrying the crescent child that carries its own full mother in its belly,[84]
Storming, enjoying, planning, loving, cautioning,
Backing and filling, appearing and disappearing,
I tread day and night such roads.

I visit the orchards of spheres and look at the product,
And look at quintillions[85] ripen'd and look at quintillions green.

---

[80] Colorful harmony.   [81] An edible type of watermelon.   [82] Close.
[83] The seven planets then known and the rings of Saturn.
[84] A crescent moon, with the full moon palely visible.   [85] Many: one followed by eighteen zeros.

I fly those flights of a fluid and swallowing soul,   800
My course runs below the soundings of plummets.

I help myself to material and immaterial,
No guard can shut me off, no law prevent me.

I anchor my ship for a little while only,
My messengers continually cruise away or bring their returns to me.

I go hunting polar furs and the seal, leaping chasms with a pike-pointed
   staff, clinging to topples[86] of brittle and blue.

I ascend to the foretruck,[87]
I take my place late at night in the crow's-nest,
We sail the arctic sea, it is plenty light enough,
Through the clear atmosphere I stretch around on the wonderful beauty,   810
The enormous masses of ice pass me and I pass them, the scenery is
   plain in all directions,
The white-topt mountains show in the distance, I fling out my fancies
   toward them,
We are approaching some great battle-field in which we are soon to be
   engaged,
We pass the colossal outposts of the encampment, we pass with still feet
   and caution,
Or we are entering by the suburbs some vast and ruin'd city,
The blocks and fallen architecture more than all the living cities of
   the globe.

I am a free companion, I bivouac by invading watchfires,
I turn the bridegroom out of bed and stay with the bride myself,
I tighten her all night to my thighs and lips.

My voice is the wife's voice, the screech by the rail of the stairs,   820
They fetch my man's body up dripping and drown'd.

I understand the large hearts of heroes,
The courage of present times and all times,
How the skipper saw the crowded and rudderless wreck of the steam-
   ship, and Death chasing it up and down the storm,
How he knuckled tight and gave not back an inch, and was faithful of
   days and faithful of nights,
And chalk'd in large letters on a board, *Be of good cheer, we will not
   desert you;*
How he follow'd with them and tack'd with them three days and would
   not give it up,
How he saved the drifting company at last,

---

[86] Fallen, or "toppled" chunks of ice.   [87] The platform of a foremast.

How the lank loose-gown'd women look'd when boated from the side of
   their prepared graves,
How the silent old-faced infants and the lifted sick, and the sharp-lipp'd
   unshaved men;   830
All this I swallow, it tastes good, I like it well, it becomes mine,
I am the man, I suffer'd, I was there.[88]
The disdain and calmness of martyrs,
The mother of old, condemn'd for a witch, burnt with dry wood, her
   children gazing on,
The hounded slave that flags in the race, leans by the fence, blowing,
   cover'd with sweat,
The twinges that sting like needles his legs and neck, the murderous
   buckshot and the bullets,
All these I feel or am.

I am the hounded slave, I wince at the bite of the dogs,
Hell and despair are upon me, crack and again crack the marksmen,
I clutch the rails of the fence, my gore dribs,[89] thinn'd with the ooze of
   my skin,   840
I fall on the weeds and stones,
The riders spur their unwilling horses, haul close,
Taunt my dizzy ears and beat me violently over the head with whip-
   stocks.

Agonies are one of my changes of garments,
I do not ask the wounded person how he feels, I myself become the
   wounded person,
My hurts turn livid upon me as I lean on a cane and observe.

I am the mash'd fireman with breast-bone broken,
Tumbling walls buried me in their debris,
Heat and smoke I inspired,[90] I heard the yelling shouts of my comrades,
I heard the distant click of their picks and shovels,   850
They have clear'd the beams away, they tenderly lift me forth.

I lie in the night air in my red shirt, the pervading hush is for my sake,
Painless after all I lie exhausted but not so unhappy,
White and beautiful are the faces around me, the heads are bared of
   their fire-caps,
The kneeling crowd fades with the light of the torches.

Distant and dead resuscitate,
They show as the dial or move as the hands of me, I am the
   clock myself.

I am an old artillerist, I tell of my fort's bombardment,
I am there again.

---

[88] At the wreck of the *San Francisco,* caught in a storm only one day out from New York. The ship
drifted in high seas from December 23, 1853 to January 5, 1854.
[89] Drips.   [90] Inhaled.

Again the long roll of the drummers, 860
Again the attacking cannon, mortars,
Again to my listening ears the cannon responsive.

I take part, I see and hear the whole,
The cries, curses, roar, the plaudits for well-aim'd shots,
The ambulanza slowly passing trailing its red drip,
Workmen searching after damages, making indispensable repairs,
The fall of grenades through the rent roof, the fan-shaped explosion,
The whizz of limbs, heads, stone, wood, iron, high in the air.

Again gurgles the mouth of my dying general, he furiously waves with
    his hand,
He gasps through the clot *Mind not me—mind—the entrenchments.* 870

34

Now I tell what I knew in Texas in my early youth,
(I tell not the fall of Alamo,
Not one escaped to tell the fall of Alamo,
The hundred and fifty are dumb yet at Alamo,)
'Tis the tale of the murder in cold blood of four hundred and twelve
    young men.[91]

Retreating they had form'd in a hollow square with their baggage for
    breastworks,
Nine hundred lives out of the surrounding enemy's, nine times their
    number, was the price they took in advance,
Their colonel was wounded and their ammunition gone,
They treated for an honorable capitulation, receiv'd writing and seal,
    gave up their arms and march'd back prisoners of war.

They were the glory of the race of rangers, 880
Matchless with horse, rifle, song, supper, courtship,
Large, turbulent generous, handsome, proud, and affectionate,
Bearded, sunburnt, drest in the free costume of hunters,
Not a single one over thirty years of age.

The second First-day morning they were brought out in squads and
    massacred, it was beautiful early summer,
The work commenced about five o'clock and was over by eight.

None obey'd the command to kneel,
Some made a mad and helpless rush, some stood stark and straight,
A few fell at once, shot in the temple or heart, the living and dead lay
    together,
The maim'd and mangled dug in the dirt, the new-comers saw
    them there, 890
Some half-kill'd attempted to crawl away,

[91] A massacre near what is now Goliad, Texas, in March 1836; Whitman had never been in Texas.

These were despatch'd with bayonets or batter'd with the blunts of
    muskets,
A youth not seventeen years old seiz'd his assassin till two more came to
    release him,
The three were all torn and cover'd with the boy's blood.

At eleven o'clock began the burning of the bodies;
That is the tale of the murder of the four hundred and twelve young men.

35
Would you hear of an old-time-sea-fight?[92]
Would you learn who won by the light of the moon and stars?
List to the yarn, as my grandmother's father the sailor told it to me.

Our foe was no skulk in his ship I tell you, (said he,)   900
His was the surly English pluck, and there is no tougher or truer, and
    never was, and never will be;
Along the lower'd eve he came horribly raking[93] us.

We closed with him, the yards entangled, the cannon touch'd,
My captain lash'd fast[94] with his own hands.

We had receiv'd some eighteen pound shots under the water,
On our lower-gun-deck two large pieces had burst at the first fire, killing
    all around and blowing up overhead.

Fighting at sun-down, fighting at dark,
Ten o'clock at night, the full moon well up, our leaks on the gain, and
    five feet of water reported,[95]
The master-at-arms loosing the prisoners confined in the after-hold to
    give them a chance for themselves.

The transit to and from the magazine[96] is now stopt by the sentinels,   910
They see so many strange faces they do not know whom to trust.

Our frigate takes fire,
The other asks if we demand quarter[97]?
If our colors are struck and the fighting done?[98]

Now I laugh content, for I hear the voice of my little captain,
We have not struck, he composedly cries, *we have just begun our
    part of the fighting.*

---

[92] The sea battle between the American ship *Bonhomme Richard*, commanded by John Paul Jones,
and the British ship *Serapis* on September 23, 1779; in this battle Jones uttered the famous words, "I
have not yet begun to fight."
[93] Aiming heavy gunfire along the length of.   [94] Lashed the two ships fast to one another.
[95] Jones reported that the *Bonhomme Richard* took on five feet of water during the battle.
[96] Ammunition storeroom.   [97] Mercy.
[98] The British thought the Americans, whose flag had been shot away, were surrendering.

Only three guns are in use,
One is directed by the captain himself against the enemy's mainmast,
Two well serv'd with grape and canister[99] silence his musketry and
    clear his decks.

The tops[100] alone second the fire of this little battery, especially the
    main-top,   920
The hold out bravely during the whole of the action.

Not a moment's cease,
The leaks gain fast on the pumps, the fire eats toward the powder-
    magazine.

One of the pumps has been shot away, it is generally thought we are
    sinking.

Serene stands the little captain,
He is not hurried, his voice is neither high nor low,
His eyes give more light to us than our battle-lanterns.

Toward twelve there in the beams of the moon they surrender to us.

36

Stretch'd and still lies the midnight,
Two great hulls motionless on the breast of the darkness,   930
Our vessel riddled and slowly sinking, preparations to pass to the one
    we have conquer'd,
The captain on the quarter-deck coldly giving his orders through a
    countenance white as a sheet,
Near by the corpse of the child that serv'd in the cabin,
The dead face of an old salt with long white hair and carefully curl'd
    whiskers,
The flames spite of all that can be done flickering aloft and below,
The husky voices of the two or three officers yet fit for duty,
Formless stacks of bodies and bodies by themselves, dabs of flesh upon
    the masts and spars,
Cut of cordage, dangle of rigging, slight shock of the soothe of waves,
Black and impassive guns, litter of powder-parcels, strong scent,
A few large stars overhead, silent and mournful shining,   940
Delicate sniffs of sea-breeze, smells of sedgy grass and fields by the
    shore, death-messages given in charge to survivors,
The hiss of the surgeon's knife, the gnawing teeth of this saw,
Wheeze, cluck, swash of falling blood, short wild scream, and long,
    dull, tapering groan,
These so, these irretrievable.

---

[99] Grape-size and smaller iron balls fired from the cannon.
[100] Marksmen firing from platforms on the ship's masts.

37

You laggards there on guard! look to your arms!
In at the conquer'd doors they crowd! I am possess'd!
Embody all presences outlaw'd or suffering,
See myself in prison shaped like another man,
And feel the dull unintermitted pain.

For me the keepers of convicts shoulder their carbines and keep watch,   950
It is I let out in the morning and barr'd at night.

Not a mutineer walks handcuff'd to jail but I am handcuff'd to him and
    walk by his side,
(I am less the jolly one there, and more the silent one with sweat on my
    twitching lips.)

Not a youngster is taken for larceny but I go up too, and am tried and
    sentenced.

Not a cholera patient lies at the last gasp but I also lie at the last gasp,
My face is ash-color'd, my sinews gnarl, away from me people retreat.

Askers embody themselves in me and I am embodied in them,
I project my hat,[101] sit shame-faced, and beg.

38

Enough! enough! enough!
Somehow I have been stunn'd. Stand back!   960
Give me a little time beyond my cuff'd head, slumbers, dreams, gaping,
I discover myself on the verge of a usual mistake.

That I could forget the mockers and insults!
That I could forget the trickling tears and the blows of the bludgeons
    and hammers!
That I could look with a separate look on my own crucifixion and bloody
    crowning.

I remember now,
I resume the overstaid fraction,
The grave of rock multiplies what has been confided to it, or to any
    graves,
Corpses rise, gashes heal, fastenings roll from me.

I troop forth replenish'd with supreme power, one of an average
    unending procession,   970
Inland and sea-coast we go, and pass all boundary lines,
Our swift ordinances on their way over the whole earth,
The blossoms we wear in our hats the growth of thousands of years.

---

[101] Extend my hat (as though to beg for money).

Eleves,[102] I salute you! come forward!
Continue your annotations, continue your questionings.

39

The friendly and flowing savage, who is he?
Is he waiting for civilization, or past it and mastering it?

Is he some Southwesterner rais'd out-doors? is he Kanadian?
Is he from the Mississippi country? Iowa, Oregon, California?
The mountains? prairie-life, bush-life? or sailor from the sea?   980

Wherever he goes men and women accept and desire him,
They desire he should like them, touch them, speak to them, stay
   with them.

Behavior lawless as snow-flakes, words simple as grass, uncomb'd head,
   laughter, and naiveté,
Slow-stepping feet, common features, common modes and emanations,
They descend in new forms from the tips of his fingers,
They are wafted with the odor of his body or breath, they fly out of the
   glance of his eyes.

40

Flaunt of the sunshine I need not your bask—lie over!
You light surfaces only, I force surfaces and depths also.

Earth! you seem to look for something at my hands,
Say, old top-knot,[103] what do you want?   990

Man or woman, I might tell how I like you, but cannot,
And might tell what it is in me and what it is in you, but cannot,
And might tell that pining I have, that pulse of my nights and days.

Behold, I do not give lectures or a little charity,
When I give I give myself.

You there, impotent, loose in the knees,
Open your scarf'd chops[104] till I blow grit[105] within you,
Spread your palms and lift the flaps of your pockets,
I am not to be denied, I compel, I have stores plenty and to spare,
And any thing I have I bestow.   1000

I do not ask who you are, that is not important to me,
You can do nothing and be nothing but what I will infold you.

---

[102] "Students" or "disciples" (French).
[103] "Indian": Certain tribes of Native Americans wore an ornament or tuft of hair on the top of the
head.
[104] Lined and weathered jaws.   [105] Breathe courage.

To cotton-field drudge or cleaner of privies I lean,
On his right cheek I put the family kiss,
And in my soul I swear I never will deny him.

On women fit for conception I start bigger and nimbler babes,
(This day I am jetting the stuff of far more arrogant republics.)

To any one dying, thither I speed and twist the knob of the door,
Turn the bed-clothes toward the foot of the bed,
Let the physician and the priest go home.   1010

I seize the descending man and raise him with resistless will,
O despairer, here is my neck,
By God, you shall not go down! hang your whole weight upon me.

I dilate you with tremendous breath, I buoy you up,
Every room of the house do I fill with an arm'd force,
Lovers of me, bafflers of graves.

Sleep—I and they keep guard all night,
Not doubt, not decease shall dare to lay finger upon you,
I have embraced you, and henceforth possess you to myself,
And when you rise in the morning you will find what I tell you is so.   1020

41
I am he bringing help for the sick as they pant on their backs,
And for strong upright men I bring yet more needed help.

I heard what was said of the universe,
Heard it and heard it of several thousand years;
It is middling well as far as it goes—but is that all?

Magnifying and applying come I,
Outbidding at the start the old cautious hucksters,
Taking myself the exact dimensions of Jehovah,[106]
Lithographing Kronos, Zeus his son, and Hercules his grandson,
Buying drafts of Osiris, Isis, Belus, Brahma, Buddha,   1030
In my portfolio placing Manito loose, Allah on a leaf, the crucifix
    engraved,
With Odin and the hideous-faced Mexitli[107] and every idol and image,
Taking them all for what they are worth and not a cent more,
Admitting they were alive and did the work of their days,

---

[106] The Judeo-Christian God.
[107] The Titan, or giant god, Kronos (or Cronus) was the supreme god in Greek myth until he was overthrown by his son Zeus; Hercules, the son of Zeus and Alcmene, was known for his strength; Osiris and Isis, the Egyptian god and goddess of fertility; Belus, an Assyrian god-king; Brahma, the supreme Hindu god; Buddha, Siddhartha Gautama (6th century B.C.), founder of Buddhism; Manito, the Algonquian Indian god of nature; Allah, the Muslim God; Odin, the supreme Norse god; Mexitli, an Aztec war god.

(They bore mites as for unfledg'd birds who have now to rise and fly and
    sing for themselves,)
Accepting the rough deific sketches to fill out better in myself,
    bestowing them freely on each man and woman I see,
Discovering as much or more in a framer framing a house,
Putting higher claims for him there with his roll'd-up sleeves driving the
    mallet and chisel,
Not objecting to special revelations, considering a curl of smoke or a
    hair on the back of my hand just as curious as any revelation,
Lads ahold of fire-engines and hook-and-ladder ropes no less to me than
    the gods of the antique wars,   1040
Minding their voices peal through the crash of destruction,
Their brawny limbs passing safe over charr'd laths, their white foreheads
    whole and unhurt out of the flames;
By the mechanic's wife with her babe at her nipple interceding for every
    person born,
Three scythes at harvest whizzing in a row from three lusty angels with
    shirts bagg'd out at their waists,
The snag-tooth'd hostler[108] with red hair redeeming sins past and to
    come,
Selling all he possesses, traveling on foot to fee lawyers for his brother
    and sit by him while he is tried for forgery;
What was strewn in the amplest strewing the square rod about me, and
    not filling the square rod then,
The bull and the bug[109] never worshipp'd half enough,
Dung and dirt more admirable than was dream'd,
The supernatural of no account, myself waiting my time to be one of
    the supremes,   1050
The day getting ready for me when I shall do as much good as the best,
    and be as prodigious;
By my life-lumps![110] becoming already a creator,
Putting myself here and now to the ambush'd womb of the shadows.

42

A call in the midst of the crowd,
My own voice, orotund sweeping and final.

Come my children,
Come my boys and girls, my women, household and intimates,
Now the performer launches his nerve, he has pass'd his prelude on the
    reeds within.

Easily written loose-finger'd chords—I feel the thrum of your climax
    and close.

---

[108] Stableman.   [109] The bull was worshipped by Greeks, Egyptians, and Moslems; the beetle, by
Egyptians.
[110] Testicles.

My head slues round on my neck,   1060
Music rolls, but not from the organ,
Folks are around me, but they are no household of mind.

Ever the hard unsunk ground,
Ever the eaters and drinkers, ever the upward and downward sun, ever
    the air and the ceaseless tides,
Ever myself and my neighbors, refreshing, wicked, real,
Ever the old inexplicable query, ever that thorn'd thumb, that breath of
    itches and thirsts,
Ever the vexer's *hoot! hoot!* till we find where the sly one hides and
    bring him forth,
Ever love, ever the sobbing liquid of life,
Ever the bandage under the chin, ever the trestles[111] of death.

Here and there with dimes on the eyes walking,[112]   1070
To feed the greed of the belly the brains liberally spooning,
Tickets buying, taking, selling, but in to the feast never once going,
Many sweating, ploughing, thrashing, and then the chaff for payment
    receiving,
A few idly owning, and they the wheat continually claiming.

This is the city and I am one of the citizens,
Whatever interests the rest interests me, politics, wars, markets,
    newspapers, schools,
The mayor and councils, banks, tariffs, steamships, factories, stocks,
    stores, real estate and personal estate.

The little plentiful manikins skipping around in collars and tail'd coats,
I am aware who they are, (they are positively not worms or fleas,)
I acknowledge the duplicates of myself, the weakest and shallowest is
    deathless with me,   1080
What I do and say the same waits for them,
Every thought that flounders in me the same flounders in them.

I know perfectly well my own egotism,
Know my omnivorous lines and must not write any less,
And would fetch you whoever you are flush with myself.

Not words of routine this song of mine,
But abruptly to question, to leap beyond yet nearer bring;
This printed and bound book—but the printer and the printing-office
    boy?
The well-taken photographs—but your wife or friend close and solid in
    your arms?
The black ship mail'd with iron, her mighty guns in her turrets—but the
    pluck of the captain and engineers?   1090

---

[111] Sawhorses or other supports for a coffin.
[112] Coins placed on the eyes of the dead; also, the greedy.

In the houses the dishes and fare and furniture—but the host and hostess,
    and the look out of their eyes?
The sky up there—yet here or next door, or across the way?
The saints and sages in history—but you yourself?
Sermons, creeds, theology—but the fathomless human brain,
And what is reason? and what is love? and what is life?

43

I do not despise you priests, all time, the world over,
My faith is the greatest of faiths and the least of faiths,
Enclosing worship ancient and modern and all between ancient and
    modern,
Believing I shall come again upon the earth after five thousand years,
Waiting responses from oracles, honoring the gods, saluting the sun,   1100
Making a fetich[113] of the first rock or stump, powowing with sticks in the
    circle of obis,[114]
Helping the llama or brahmin[115] as he trims the lamps of the idols,
Dancing yet through the streets in a phallic procession, rapt and austere
    in the woods a gymnosophist,[116]
Drinking mead[117] from the skull-cup, to Shastas and Vedas[118] admirant,
    minding the Koran,
Walking the teokallis,[119] spotted with gore from the stone and knife,
    beating the serpent-skin drum,
Accepting the Gospels, accepting him that was crucified, knowing
    assuredly that he is divine,
To the mass kneeling or the puritan's prayer rising, or sitting patiently in
    a pew,
Ranting and frothing in my insane crisis, or waiting dead-like till my
    spirit arouses me,
Looking forth on pavement and land, or outside of pavement and land,
Belonging to the winders of the circuit of circuits.   1110

One of that centripetal and centrifugal gang I turn and talk like a man
    leaving charges before a journey.

Down-hearted doubters dull and excluded,
Frivolous, sullen, moping, angry, affected, dishearten'd, atheistical,
I know every one of you, I know the sea of torment, doubt, despair and
    unbelief.

How the flukes splash!
How they contort rapid as lightning, with spasms and spouts of blood!

Be at peace bloody flukes[120] of doubters and sullen mopers,
I take my place among you as much as among any,

---

[113] A fetish, or primitive object of worship.   [114] Charms used in sorcery, of African origin.
[115] Lama (or Tibetan high priest) or member of the highest Hindu caste.
[116] Member of an ascetic Hindu sect.
[117] An alcoholic beverage made from fermented honey and water.
[118] Books of Hindu law (Shastras) and Hindu sacred writings, respectively.
[119] An Aztec temple where human sacrifice was conducted.   [120] The tail fins of stricken whales.

The past is the push of you, me, all, precisely the same,
And what is yet untried and afterward is for you, me, all, precisely
   the same.   1120

I do not know what is untried and afterward,
But I know it will in its turn prove sufficient, and cannot fail.

Each who passes is consider'd, each who stops is consider'd, not a single
   one can it fail.

It cannot fail the young man who died and was buried,
Nor the young woman who died and was put by his side,
Nor the little child that peep'd in at the door, and then drew back and
   was never seen again,
Nor the old man who has lived without purpose, and feels it with
   bitterness worse than gall,
Nor him in the poor house tubercled by rum and the bad disorder,[121]
Nor the numberless slaughter'd and wreck'd, nor the brutish koboo
   call'd the ordure[122] of humanity,
Nor the sacs merely floating with open mouths for food to slip in,   1130
Nor any thing in the earth, or down in the oldest graves of the earth,
Nor any thing in the myriads of spheres, nor the myriads of myriads that
   inhabit them,
Nor the present, nor the least wisp that is known.

44

It is time to explain myself—let us stand up.

What is known I strip away,
I launch all men and women forward with me into the Unknown.

The clock indicates the moment—but what does eternity indicate?

We have thus far exhausted trillions of winters and summers,
There are trillions ahead, and trillions ahead of them.

Births have brought us richness and variety,   1140
And other births will bring us richness and variety.

I do not call one greater and one smaller,
That which fills its period and place is equal to any.

Were mankind murderous or jealous upon you, my brother, my sister?
I am sorry for you, they are not murderous or jealous upon me,
All has been gentle with me, I keep no account with lamentation,
(What have I to do with lamentation?)

I am an acme of things accomplish'd, and I am encloser of things to be.

---

[121] Syphilis.   [122] Native of Sumatra; excrement.

My feet strike an apex of the apices of the stairs,
On every step bunches of ages, and larger bunches between the steps,   1150
All below duly travel'd, and still I mount and mount.

Rise after rise bow the phantoms behind me,
Afar down I see the huge first Nothing, I know I was even there,
I waited unseen and always, and slept through the lethargic mist,
And took my time, and took no hurt from the fetid carbon.

Long I was hugg'd close—long and long.

Immense have been the preparations for me,
Faithful and friendly the arms that have help'd me.

Cycles ferried my cradle, rowing and rowing like cheerful boatmen,
For room to me stars kept aside in their own rings,   1160
They sent influences to look after what was to hold me.

Before I was born out of my mother generations guided me,
My embryo has never been torpid, nothing could overlay it.

For it the nebula cohered to an orb,
The long slow strata piled to rest it on,
Vast vegetables gave it sustenance,
Monstrous sauroids[123] transported it in their mouths and deposited it
    with care.

All forces have been steadily employ'd to complete and delight me,
Now on this spot I stand with my robust soul.

45

O span of youth! ever-push'd elasticity!   1170
O manhood, balanced, florid and full.

My lovers suffocate me,
Crowding my lips, thick in the pores of my skin,
Jostling me through streets and public halls, coming naked to me at
    night,
Crying by day *Ahoy!* from the rocks of the river, swinging and chirping
    over my head,
Calling my name from flower-beds, vines, tangled underbrush,
Lighting on every moment of my life,
Bussing[124] my body with soft balsamic busses,
Noiselessly passing handfuls out of their hearts and giving them to
    be mine.

Old age superbly rising! O welcome, ineffable grace of dying days!   1180

---

[123] Lizardlike reptiles; here, dinosaurs.   [124] Kissing.

Every condition promulges[125] not only itself, it promulges what grows
    after and out of itself,
And the dark hush promulges as much as any.

I open my scuttle[126] at night and see the far-sprinkled systems,
And all I see multiplied as high as I can cipher edge but the rim of the
    farther systems.

Wider and wider they spread, expanding, always expanding,
Outward and outward and forever outward.

My sun has his sun and round him obediently wheels,
He joins with his partners a group of superior circuit,
And greater sets follow, making specks of the greatest inside them.

There is no stoppage and never can be stoppage,   1190
If I, you, and the worlds, and all beneath or upon their surfaces, were
    this moment reduced back to a pallid float,[127] it would not avail in
    the long run,
We should surely bring up again where we now stand,
And surely go as much farther, and then farther and farther.

A few quadrillions of eras, a few octillions[128] of cubic leagues, do not
    hazard the span or make it impatient,
They are but parts, any thing is but a part.

See ever so far, there is limitless space outside of that,
Count ever so much, there is limitless time around that.

My rendezvous is appointed, it is certain,
The Lord will be there and wait till I come on perfect terms,
The great Camerado,[129] the lover true for whom I pine will be there.   1200

46

I know I have the best of time and space, and was never measured and
    never will be measured.

I tramp a perpetual journey, (come listen all!)
My signs are a rain-proof coat, good shoes, and a staff cut from the
    woods,
No friend of mine takes his ease in my chair,
I have no chair, no church, no philosophy,
I lead no man to a dinner-table, library, exchange,[130]
But each man and each woman of you I lead upon a knoll,
My left hand hooking you round the waist,
My right hand pointing to landscapes of continents and the public road.

---

[125] Promulgates or publicly advocates.   [126] Roof hatch.   [127] Returned to a primordial soup.
[128] One followed by twenty-seven zeros.   [129] Comrade.   [130] Stock exchange.

Not I, not any one else can travel that road for you,   1210
You must travel it for yourself.
It is not far, it is within reach,
Perhaps you have been on it since you were born and did not know,
Perhaps it is everywhere on water and on land.

Shoulder your duds dear son, and I will mine, and let us hasten forth,
Wonderful cities and free nations we shall fetch[131] as we go.

If you tire, give me both burdens, and rest the chuff[132] of your hand on
    my hip,
And in due time you shall repay the same service to me,
For after we start we never lie by again.

This day before dawn I ascended a hill and look'd at the crowded
    heaven,   1220
And I said to my spirit *When we become the enfolders of those orbs,*
    and the pleasure and knowledge of every thing in them, shall we be
    fill'd and satisfied then?
And my spirit said *No, we but level that lift[133] to pass and continue*
    beyond.

You are also asking me questions and I hear you,
I answer that I cannot answer, you must find out for yourself.

Sit a while dear son,
Here are biscuits to eat and here is milk to drink,
But as soon as you sleep and renew yourself in sweet clothes, I kiss you
    with a good-by kiss and open the gate for your egress hence.

Long enough have you dream'd contemptible dreams,
Now I wash the gum from your eyes,
You must habit yourself to the dazzle of the light and of every moment
    of your life.   1230

Long have you timidly waded holding a plank by the shore,
Now I will you to be a bold swimmer,
To jump off in the midst of the sea, rise again, nod to me, shout, and
    laughingly dash with your hair.

47

I am the teacher of athletes,
He that by me spreads a wider breast than my own proves the width of
    my own,
He most honors my style who learns under it to destroy the teacher.

The boy I love, the same becomes a man not through derived power, but
    in his own right,

---

[131] Reach.   [132] The fleshy part of the palm.   [133] Elevation.

Wicked rather than virtuous out of conformity or fear,
Fond of his sweetheart, relishing well his steak,
Unrequited love or a slight cutting him worse than sharp steel cuts,   1240
First-rate to ride, to fight, to hit the bull's eye, to sail a skiff, to sing a
    song or play on the banjo,
Preferring scars and the beard and faces pitted with small-pox over all
    latherers,
And those well-tann'd to those that keep out of the sun.

I teach straying from me, yet who can stray from me?
I follow you whoever you are from the present hour,
My words itch at your ears till you understand them.

I do not say these things for a dollar or to fill up the time while I wait
    for a boat,
(It is you talking just as much as myself, I act as the tongue of you,
Tied in your mouth, in mine it begins to be loosen'd.)

I swear I will never again mention love or death inside a house,   1250
And I swear I will never translate myself at all, only to him or her who
    privately stays with me in the open air.

If you would understand me go to the heights or water-shore,
The nearest gnat is an explanation, and a drop or motion of waves a key,
The maul, the oar, the hand-saw, second my words.

No shutter'd room or school can commune with me,
But roughs and little children better than they.

The young mechanic is closest to me, he knows me well,
The woodman that takes his axe and jug with him shall take me with him
    all day,
The farm-boy ploughing in the field feels good at the sound of my voice,
In vessels that sail my words sail, I go with fishermen and seamen and
    love them.   1260

The soldier camp'd or upon the march is mine,
On the night ere the pending battle many seek me, and I do not fail them,
On that solemn night (it may be their last) those that know me seek me.

My face rubs to the hunter's face when he lies down alone in his blanket,
The driver thinking of me does not mind the jolt of his wagon,
The young mother and old mother comprehend me,
The girl and the wife rest the needle a moment and forget where they are,
They and all would resume what I have told them.

48

I have said that the soul is not more than the body,
And I have said that the body is not more than the soul,   1270
And nothing, not God, is greater to one than one's self is,

And whoever walks a furlong without sympathy walks to his own funeral
    drest in his shroud,
And I or you pocketless of a dime may purchase the pick of the earth,
And to glance with an eye or show a bean in its pod confounds the
    learning of all times,
And there is no trade or employment but the young man following it
    may become a hero,
And there is no object so soft but it makes a hub for the wheel'd
    universe,
And I say to any man or woman, Let your soul stand cool and composed
    before a million universes.

And I say to mankind, Be not curious about God,
For I who am curious about each am not curious about God,
(No array of terms can say how much I am at peace about God
    and about death.)   1280

I hear and behold God in every object, yet understand God not in the
    least,
Nor do I understand who there can be more wonderful than myself.

Why should I wish to see God better than this day?
I see something of God each hour of the twenty-four, and each moment
    then,
In the faces of men and women I see God, and in my own face in the
    glass,
I find letters from God dropt in the street, and every one is sign'd by
    God's name,
And I leave them where they are, for I know that wheresoe'er I go,
Others will punctually come for ever and ever.

49
And as to you Death, and you bitter hug of mortality, it is idle to try to
    alarm me.

To his work without flinching the accoucheur[134] comes,   1290
I see the elder-hand pressing receiving supporting,
I recline by the sills of the exquisite flexible doors,
And mark the outlet, and mark the relief and escape.

And as to you Corpse I think you are good manure, but that does not
    offend me,
I smell the white roses sweet-scented and growing,
I reach to the leafy lips, I reach to the polish'd breasts of melons.

And as to you Life I reckon you are the leavings of many deaths,
(No doubt I have died myself ten thousand times before.)

---

[134] Midwife or obstetrician.

I hear you whispering there O stars of heaven,
O suns—O grass of graves—O perpetual transfers and promotions,   1300
If you do not say any thing how can I say any thing?

Of the turbid pool that lies in the autumn forest,
Of the moon that descends the steeps of the soughing[135] twilight,
Toss, sparkles of day and dusk—toss on the black stems that decay in
   the muck,
Toss to the moaning gibberish of the dry limbs.

I ascend from the moon, I ascend from the night,
I perceive that the ghastly glimmer is noonday sunbeams reflected,
And debouch[136] to the steady and central from the offspring great
   or small.

50

There is that in me—I do not know what it is—but I know it is in me.

Wrench'd and sweaty—calm and cool then my body becomes,   1310
I sleep—I sleep long.

I do not know it—it is without name—it is a word unsaid,
It is not in any dictionary, utterance, symbol.

Something it swings on more than the earth I swing on,
To it the creation is the friend whose embracing awakes me.

Perhaps I might tell more. Outlines! I plead for my brothers and sisters.

Do you see O my brothers and sisters?
It is not chaos or death—it is form, union, plan—it is eternal life—it
   is Happiness.

51

The past and present wilt—I have fill'd them, emptied them,
And proceed to fill my next fold of the future.   1320

Listener up there! what have you to confide to me?
Look in my face while I snuff the sidle of evening,[137]
(Talk honestly, no one else hears you, and I stay only a minute longer.)

Do I contradict myself?
Very well then I contradict myself,
(I am large, I contain multitudes.)

I concentrate toward them that are nigh, I wait on the door-slab.

Who has done his day's work? who will soonest be through with his
   supper?
Who wishes to walk with me?

---

[135] Murmuring.   [136] Emerge, or flow outward from a narrow place into open country.
[137] The fading twilight.

Will you speak before I am gone? will you prove already too late?   1330

52

The spotten hawk swoops by and accuses me, he complains of my gab
    and my loitering.

I too am not a bit tamed, I too am untranslatable,
I sound my barbaric yawp over the roofs of the world.

The last scud[138] of day holds back for me,
It flings my likeness after the rest and true as any on the
    shadow'd wilds,
It coaxes me to the vapor and the dusk.

I depart as air, I shake my white locks at the runaway sun,
I effuse[139] my flesh in eddies, and drift it in lacy jags.

I bequeath myself to the dirt to grow from the grass I love,
If you want me again look for me under your boot-soles.   1340

You will hardly know who I am or what I mean,
But I shall be good health to you nevertheless,
And filter and fibre your blood.

Failing to fetch me at first keep encouraged,
Missing me one place search another,
I stop somewhere waiting for you.

1855

from   CHILDREN OF ADAM*

ONCE I PASS'D THROUGH A POPULOUS CITY

Once I pass'd through a populous city imprinting my brain for future
    use with its shows, architecture, customs, traditions,
Yet now of all that city I remember only a woman I casually met
    there who detain'd me for love of me,
Day by day and night by night we were together—all else has
    long been forgotten by me,
I remember I say only that woman who passionately clung to me,
Again we wander, we love, we separate again,
Again she holds me by the hand, I must not go.
I see her close beside me with silent lips sad and tremulous.

1860

---

138 Mist.   139 Pour forth.
* Fifteen poems were included in the group "Enfans d' Adam" in the 1860 edition of *Leaves of Grass;*
by 1871 sixteen poems comprised "Children of Adam."

FACING WEST FROM CALIFORNIA'S SHORES*

Facing west from California's shores,
Inquiring, tireless, seeking what is yet unfound.
I, a child, very old, over waves, towards the house of maternity,[1]
   the land of migrations, look afar,
Look off the shores of my Western sea, the circle almost circled;
For starting westward from Hindustan,[2] from the vales of Kashmere,[3]
From Asia, from the north, from the God, the sage, and the hero,
From the south, from the flowery peninsulas and the spice islands,[4]
Long having wander'd since, round the earth having wander'd
Now I face home again, very pleas'd and joyous,
(But where is what I started for so long ago?
And why is it yet unfound?)

1860

AS ADAM EARLY IN THE MORNING

As Adam early in the morning,
Walking forth from the bower refresh'd with sleep,
Behold me where I pass, hear my voice, approach,
Touch me, touch the palm of your hand to my body as I pass,
Be not afraid of my body.

1861

from CALAMUS†

IN PATHS UNTRODDEN[1]

In paths untrodden,
In the growth by margins of pond-waters,
Escaped from the life that exhibits itself,
From all the standards hitherto publish'd, from the pleasure,
   profits, conformities,
Which too long I was offering to feed my soul,
Clear to me now standards not yet publish'd, clear to me that my soul,
That the soul of the man I speak for rejoices in comrades,

---

* Originally untitled; first appeared with this title in the 1867 edition of *Leaves of Grass*.
[1] Asia, believed to be the birthplace of civilization.   [2] India.
[3] Kashmir, a mountainous region adjacent to India, Pakistan, and Tibet.
[4] Indonesia.
† Forty-five poems were included in this group in the 1860 edition of *Leaves of Grass;* by the 1881 edition, there were thirty-nine. Whitman defined calamus as "the very large & aromatic grass, or rush, growing about water-ponds in the valleys—spears about three feet high—often called 'sweet flag'—grows all over the Northern and Middle States. . . . "
[1] First appeared with this title in the 1867 edition of *Leaves of Grass*.

Here by myself away from the clank of the world,
Tallying and talk'd to here by tongues aromatic,
No longer abash'd, (for in this secluded spot I can respond as I
    would not dare elsewhere,)   10
Strong upon me the life that does not exhibit itself, yet contains
    all the rest,
Resolv'd to sing no songs to-day but those of manly attachment,
Projecting them along that substantial life,
Bequeathing hence types of athletic love,
Afternoon this delicious Ninth-month in my forty-first year,[2]
I proceed for all who are or have been young men,
To tell the secret of my nights and days,
To celebrate the need of comrades.

1860

RECORDERS AGES HENCE*

Recorders ages hence,
Come, I will take you down underneath this impassive[1] exterior, I
    will tell you what to say to me,
Publish my name and hang up my picture as that of the tenderest lover,
The friend the lover's portrait, of whom his friend his lover was fondest,
Who was not proud of his songs, but of the measureless ocean of
    love within him, and freely pour'd it forth,
Who often walk'd lonesome walks thinking of his dear friends,
    his lovers,
Who pensive away from one he lov'd often lay sleepless and
    dissatisfied at night,
Who knew too well the sick, sick dread lest the one he lov'd
    might secretly be indifferent to him,
Whose happiest days were far away through fields, in woods, on
    hills, he and another wandering hand in hand, they twain
    apart from other men,
Who oft as he saunter'd the streets curv'd with his arm the shoulder
    of his friend, while the arm of his friend rested upon him also.   10

1860

I SAW IN LOUISIANA A LIVE-OAK GROWING†

I saw in Louisiana a live-oak growing,
All alone stood it and the moss hung down from the branches,
Without any companion it grew there uttering joyous leaves of
    dark greed,

---

[2] September 1859, from the Quaker numerical designations for months.
* First appeared with this title in 1867.   [1] Unemotional.
† First appeared with this title in the 1867 edition of *Leaves of Grass*.

And its look, rude, unbending, lusty, made me think of myself,
But I wonder'd how it could utter joyous leaves standing alone
   there without its friend near, for I knew I could not,
And I broke off a twig with a certain number of leaves upon it,
   and twined around it a little moss,
And brought it away, and I have placed it in sight in my room,
It is not needed to remind me as of my own dear friends,
(For I believe lately I think of little else than of them,)
Yet it remains to me a curious token, it makes me think of manly love;   10
For all that, and though the live-oak glistens there in Louisiana
   solitary in a wide flat space,
Uttering joyous leaves all its life without a friend a lover near,
I know very well I could not.

                                           1860

CROSSING BROOKLYN FERRY*

I

Flood-tide below me! I see you face to face!
Clouds of the west—sun there half an hour high—I see you
   also face to face.

Crowds of men and women attired in the usual costumes, how
   curious you are to me!
On the ferry-boats the hundreds and hundreds that cross, returning
   home, are more curious to me than you suppose,
And you that shall cross from shore to shore years hence are more
   to me, and more in my meditations, than you might suppose.

2

The impalpable sustenance of me from all things at all hours of
   the day,
The simple, compact, well-join'd scheme, myself disintegrated,
   every one disintegrated yet part of the scheme,
The similitudes of the past and those of the future,
The glories strung like beads on my smallest sights and hearings,
   on the walk in the street and the passage over the river,
The current rushing so swiftly and swimming with me far away,   10
The others that are to follow me, the ties between me and them,
The certainty of others, the life, love, sight, hearing of others.

Others will enter the gates of the ferry and cross from shore to shore,
Others will watch the run of the flood-tide,
Others will see the shipping of Manhattan north and west, and the
   heights of Brooklyn to the south and east,

---

* Titled "Sun-Down Poem" in the 1856 edition of *Leaves of Grass;* first appeared with this title in the
1860 edition.

Others will see the islands large and small;
Fifty years hence, others will see them as they cross, the sun half
   an hour high,
A hundred years hence, or ever so many hundred years hence,
   others will see them,
Will enjoy the sunset, the pouring-in of the flood-tide, the falling-
   back to the sea of the ebb-tide.

3

It avails not, time nor place—distance avails not,   20
I am with you, you men and women of a generation, or ever so
   many generations hence,
Just as you feel when you look on the river and sky, so I felt,
Just as any of you is one of a living crowd, I was one of a crowd,
Just as you are refresh'd by the gladness of the river and the bright
   flow, I was refresh'd,
Just as you stand and lean on the rail, yet hurry with the swift
   current, I stood yet was hurried,
Just as you look on the numberless masts of ships and the thick-
   stemm'd pipes of steamboats, I look'd.

I too many and many a time cross'd the river of old,
Watched the Twelfth-month[1] sea-gulls, saw them high in the air
   floating with motionless wings, oscillating their bodies,
Saw how the glistening yellow lit up parts of their bodies and left the
   rest in strong shadow,
Saw the slow-wheeling circles and the gradual edging toward the south,   30
Saw the reflection of the summer sky in the water,
Had my eyes dazzled by the shimmering track of beams,
Look'd at the fine centrifugal spokes of light round the shape of my
   head in the sunlit water,
Look'd on the haze on the hills southward and south-westward,
Look'd on the vapor as it flew in fleeces tinged with violet,
Look'd toward the lower bay to notice the vessels arriving,
Saw their approach, saw aboard those that were near me,
Saw the white sails of schooners and sloops, saw the ships at anchor,
The sailors at work in the rigging or out astride the spars,
The round masts, the swinging motion of the hulls, the slender
   serpentine pennants,   40
The large and small steamers in motion, the pilots in their pilot-
   houses,
The white wake left by the passage, the quick tremulous whirl of
   the wheels,
The flags of all nations, the falling of them at sunset,
The scallop-edged waves in the twilight, the ladled cups, the
   frolicsome crests and glistening,
The stretch afar growing dimmer and dimmer, the gray walls of
   the granite storehouses by the docks,

---

[1] December, from the Quaker numerical designations for months.

On the river the shadowy group, the big steam-tug closely flank'd
    on each side by the barges, the hay-boat, the belated lighter,[2]
On the neighboring shore the fires from the foundry chimneys
    burning high and glaringly into the night,
Casting their flicker of black contrasted with wild red and yellow light
    over the tops of houses, and down into the clefts of streets.

4

These and all else were to me the same as they are to you,
I loved well those cities, loved well the stately and rapid river,   50
The men and women I saw were all near to me,
Others the same—others who look back on me because I look'd
    forward to them,
(The time will come, though I stop here to-day and to-night.)

5

What is it then between us?
What is the count of the scores or hundreds of years between us?

Whatever it is, it avails not—distance avails not, and place avails not,
I too lived, Brooklyn of ample hills was mine,
I too walk'd the streets of Manhattan island, and bathed in the waters
    around it,
I too felt the curious abrupt questionings stir within me,
In the day among crowds of people sometimes they came upon me,   60
In my walks home late at night or as I lay in my bed they came upon me,
I too had been struck from the float forever held in solution,
I too had receiv'd identity by my body,
That I was I knew was of my body, and what I should be I knew I
    should be of my body.

6

It is not upon you alone the dark patches fall,
The dark threw its patches down upon me also,
The best I had done seem'd to me blank and suspicious,
My great thoughts as I supposed them, were they not in reality meagre?
Nor is it you alone who know what it is to be evil,
I am he who knew what it was to be evil,   70
I too knitted the old knot of contrariety,
Blabb'd, blush'd, resented, lied, stole, grudg'd,
Had guile, anger, lust, hot wishes I dared not speak,
Was wayward, vain, greedy, shallow, sly, cowardly, malignant,
The wolf, the snake, the hog, not wanting[3] in me,
The cheating look, the frivolous word, the adulterous wish, not
    wanting,
Refusals, hates, postponements, meanness, laziness, none of these
    wanting,

Was one with the rest, the days, and haps[4] of the rest,
Was call'd by my nighest[5] name by clear loud voices of young men
    as they saw me approaching or passing,

---

[2] A barge used to load or to lighten (unload) cargo ships.
[3] Lacking.   [4] Chance happenings.   [5] Nearest, most familiar.

Felt their arms on my neck as I stood, or the negligent leaning of
    their flesh against me as I sat,   80
Saw many I loved in the street or ferry-boat or public assembly, yet
    never told them a word,
Lived the same life with the rest, the same old laughing, gnawing,
    sleeping,
Play'd the part that still looks back on the actor or actress,
The same old role, the role that is what we make it, as great as we like,
Or as small as we like, or both great and small.

7

Closer yet I approach you,
What thought you have of me now, I had as much of you—I laid in
    my stores in advance,
I consider'd long and seriously of you before you were born.

Who was to know what should come home to me?
Who knows but I am enjoying this?   90
Who knows, for all the distance, but I am as good as looking at
    you now, for all you cannot see me?

8

Ah, what can ever be more stately and admirable to me than mast-
    hemm'd Manhattan?
River and sunset and scallop-edg'd waves of flood-tide?
The sea-gulls oscillating their bodies, the hay-boat in the twilight,
    and the belated lighter?
What gods can exceed these that clasp me by the hand, and with
    voices I love call me promptly and loudly by my nighest
    name as I approach?
What is more subtle than this which ties me to the woman or man that
    looks in my face?
Which fuses me into you now, and pours my meaning into you?

We understand then do we not?
What I promis'd without mentioning it, have you not accepted?
What the study could not teach—what the preaching could not
    accomplish is accomplish'd, is it not?   100

9

Flow on, river! flow with the flood-tide, and ebb with the ebb-tide!
Frolic on, crested and scallop-edg'd waves!
Gorgeous clouds of the sunset! drench with your splendor me, or the
    men and women generations after me!
Cross from shore to shore, countless crowds of passengers!
Stand up, tall masts of Mannahatta! stand up, beautiful hills of Brooklyn!
Throb, baffled and curious brain! throw out questions and answers!
Suspend here and everywhere, eternal float of solution!
Gaze, loving and thirsting eyes, in the house or street or public
    assembly!

Sound out, voices of young men! loudly and musically call me by
    my nighest name!
Live, old life! play the part that looks back on the actor or actress!   110
Play the old role, the role that is great or small according as one
    makes it!
Consider, you who peruse me, whether I may not in unknown ways
    be looking upon you;
Be firm, rail over the river, to support those who lean idly, yet
    haste with the hasting current;
Fly on, sea-birds! fly sideways, or wheel in large circles high in
    the air;
Receive the summer sky, you water, and faithfully hold it till all
    downcast eyes have time to take it from you!
Diverge, fine spokes of light, from the shape of my head, or any
    one's head, in the sunlit water!
Come on, ships from the lower bay! pass up or down, white-sail'd
    schooners, sloops, lighters!
Flaunt away, flags of all nations! be duly lower'd at sunset!
Burn high your fires, foundry chimneys! cast black shadows at
    nightfall! cast red and yellow light over the tops of the
    houses!
Appearances, now or henceforth, indicate what you are,   120
You necessary film, continue to envelop the soul,
About my body for me, and your body for you, be hung our
    divinest aromas,
Thrive, cities—bring your freight, bring your shows, ample and
    sufficient rivers,
Expand, being than which none else is perhaps more spiritual,
Keep your places, objects than which none else is more lasting.

You have waited, you always wait, you dumb, beautiful ministers,
We receive you with free sense at last, and are insatiate henceforward,
Not you any more shall be able to foil us, or withhold yourselves from us,
We use you, and do not cast you aside—we plant you permanently
    within us,
We fathom you not—we love you—there is perfection in you also,   130
You furnish your parts toward eternity,
Great or small, you furnish your parts toward the soul.

1856

from   Sᴇᴀ-Dʀɪꜰᴛ*

OUT OF THE CRADLE ENDLESSLY ROCKING[1]

Out of the cradle endlessly rocking,
Out of the mocking-bird's throat, the musical shuttle,

---

* Eleven poems compiled in the 1881 edition of *Leaves of Grass*.
[1] First appeared as "A Child's Reminiscence" in the December 24, 1859, issue of the New York
Saturday Press and with this title in the 1871 edition of *Leaves of Grass*.

Out of the Ninth-month[2] midnight,
Over the sterile sands and the fields beyond, where the child leaving
   his bed wander'd alone, bareheaded, barefoot,
Down from the shower'd halo,
Up from the mystic play of shadows twining and twisting as if they
   were alive,
Out from the patches of briers and blackberries,
From the memories of the bird that chanted to me,
From your memories sad brother, from the fitful risings and fallings
   I heard,
From under that yellow half-moon late-risen and swollen as if with tears,   10
From those beginning notes of yearning and love there in the mist,
From the thousand responses of my heart never to cease,
From the myriad thence-arous'd words,
From the word stronger and more delicious than any,
From such as now they start the scene revisiting,
As a flock, twittering, rising, or overhead passing,
Borne hither, ere all eludes me, hurriedly,
A man, yet by these tears a little boy again,
Throwing myself on the sand, confronting the waves,
I, chanter of pains and joys, uniter of here and hereafter,   20
Taking all hints to use them, but swiftly leaping beyond them,
A reminiscence sing.

Once Paumanok,[3]
When the lilac-scent was in the air and Fifth-month[4] grass was
   growing,
Up this seashore in some briers,
Two feather'd guests from Alabama, two together,
And their nest, and four light-green eggs spotted with brown,
And every day the he-bird to and fro near at hand,
And every day the she-bird crouch'd on her nest, silent, with
   bright eyes,
And every day I, a curious boy, never too close, never disturbing
   them,   30
Cautiously peering, absorbing, translating.

Shine! shine! shine!
Pour down your warmth, great sun!
While we bask, we two together.

Two together!
Winds blow south, or winds blow north,
Day come white, or night come black,
Home, or rivers and mountains from home,
Singing all time, minding no time,
While we two keep together.   40

---

[2] September, from the Quaker numerical designations for months; perhaps reflective of the nine-month-long human gestational cycle.
[3] A Native-American name for Long Island.   [4] May.

Till of a sudden,
May-be kill'd, unknown to her mate,
One forenoon the she-bird crouch'd not on the nest,
Nor return'd that afternoon, nor the next,
Nor ever appear'd again.

And thenceforward all summer in the sound of the sea,
And at night under the full of the moon in calmer weather,
Over the hoarse surging of the sea,
Or flitting from brier to brier by day,
I saw, I heard at intervals the remaining one, the he-bird,   50
The solitary guest from Alabama.

Blow! blow! blow!
Blow up sea-winds along Paumanok's shore;
I wait and I wait till you blow my mate to me.

Yes, when the stars glisten'd,
All night long on the prong of a moss-scallop'd stake,
Down almost amid the slapping waves,
Sat the lone singer wonderful causing tears.

He call'd on his mate,
He pour'd forth the meanings which I of all men know.   60

Yes my brother I know,
The rest might not, but I have treasur'd every note,
For more than once dimly down to the beach gliding,
Silent, avoiding the moonbeams, blending myself with the shadow,
Recalling now the obscure shapes, the echoes, the sounds and
    sights after their sorts,
The white arms out in the breakers tirelessly tossing,
I, with bare feet, a child, the wind wafting my hair,
Listen'd long and long.

Listen'd to keep, to sing, now translating the notes,
Following you my brother,   70

Soothe! soothe! soothe!
Close on its wave soothes the wave behind,
And again another behind embracing and lapping, every one close,
But my love soothes not me, not me.

Low hangs the moon, it rose late,
It is lagging—O I think it is heavy with love, with love.

O madly the sea pushes upon the land,
With love, with love.

O night! do I not see my love fluttering out among the breakers?
What is that little black thing I see there in the white?   80

Loud! loud! loud!
Loud I call to you, my love!

High and clear I shoot my voice over the waves,
Surely you must know who is here, is here,
You must know who I am, my love.

Low-hanging moon!
What is that dusky spot in your brown yellow?
O it is the shape, the shape of my mate!
O moon do not keep her from me any longer.

Land! land! O land!   90
Whichever way I turn, O I think you could give me my mate back
    again if you only would,
For I am almost sure I see her dimly whichever way I look.

O rising stars!
Perhaps the one I want so much will rise, will rise with some of you.

O throat! O trembling throat!
Sound clearer through the atmosphere!
Pierce the woods, the earth,
Somewhere listening to catch you must be the one I want.

Shake out carols!
Solitary here, the night's carols!   100
Carols of lonesome love! death's carols!
Carols under that lagging, yellow, waning moon!
O under that moon where she droops almost down into the sea!
O reckless despairing carols.

But soft! sink low!
Soft! let me just murmur,
And do you wait a moment you husky-nois'd sea,
For somewhere I believe I heard my mate responding to me,
So faint, I must be still, be still to listen,
But not altogether still, for then she might not come immediately
    to me.   110

Hither my love!
Here I am! here!
With this just-sustain'd note I announce myself to you,
This gentle call is for you my love, for you.

Do not be decoy'd elsewhere,
That is the whistle of the wind, it is not my voice,
That is the fluttering, the fluttering of the spray,
Those are the shadows of leaves.

O darkness! O in vain!
O I am very sick and sorrowful.   120

O brown halo in the sky near the moon, drooping upon the sea!
O troubled reflection in the sea!
O throat! O throbbing heart!
And I singing uselessly, uselessly all the night.

O past! O happy life! O songs of joy!
In the air, in the woods, over fields,
Loved! loved! loved! loved! loved!
But my mate no more, no more with me!
We two together no more.

The aria sinking,   130
All else continuing, the stars shining,
The winds blowing, the notes of the bird continuous echoing,
With angry moans the fierce old mother incessantly moaning,
On the sands of Paumanok's shore gray and rustling,
The yellow half-moon enlarged, sagging down, drooping, the face
    of the sea almost touching,
The boy ecstatic, with his bare feet the waves, with his hair the
    atmosphere dallying,
The love in the heart long pent, now loose, now at last tumultuously
    bursting,
The aria's meaning, the ears, the soul, swiftly depositing,
The strange tears down the cheeks coursing,
The colloquy there, the trio, each uttering,   140
The undertone, the savage old mother incessantly crying,
To the boy's soul's questions sullenly timing, some drown'd secret
    hissing,
To the outsetting bard.

Demon or bird! (said the boy's soul,)
Is it indeed toward your mate you sing? or is it really to me?
For I, that was a child, my tongue's use sleeping, now I have
    heard you,
Now in a moment I know what I am for, I awake,
And already a thousand singers, a thousand songs, clearer, louder
    and more sorrowful than yours,
A thousand warbling echoes have started to life within me, never
    to die.

O you singer solitary, singing by yourself, projecting me,   150
O solitary me listening, never more shall I cease perpetuating you,
Never more shall I escape, never more the reverberations,
Never more the cries of unsatisfied love be absent from me,
Never again leave me to be the peaceful child I was before what there
    in the night,
By the sea under the yellow and sagging moon,

The messenger there arous'd, the fire, the sweet hell within,
The unknown want, the destiny of me.

O give me the clew! (it lurks in the night here somewhere,)
O if I am to have so much, let me have more!

A word then, (for I will conquer it,)   160
The word final, superior to all,
Subtle, sent up—what is it?—I listen;
Are you whispering it, and have been all the time, you sea-waves?
Is that it from your liquid rims, and wet sands?

Whereto answering, the sea,
Delaying not, hurrying not,
Whisper'd me through the night, and very plainly before day-break,
Lisp'd to me the low and delicious word death,
And again death, death, death, death,
Hissing melodious, neither like the bird nor like my arous'd child's
    heart,   170
But edging near as privately for me rustling at my feet,
Creeping thence steadily up to my ears and laving me softly all over,
Death, death, death, death, death.

Which I do not forget,
But fuse the song of my dusky demon and brother,
That he sang to me in the moonlight on Paumanok's gray beach,
With the thousand responsive songs at random,
My own songs awaked from that hour,
And with them the key, the word up from the waves,
The word of the sweetest song and all songs,   180
That strong and delicious word which, creeping to my feet,
(Or like some old crone rocking the cradle, swathed in sweet
    garments, bending aside,)
The sea whisper'd me.

1859

from   BY THE ROADSIDE*

WHEN I HEARD THE LEARN'D ASTRONOMER[1]

When I heard the learn'd astronomer,
When the proofs, the figures, were ranged in columns before me,
When I was shown the charts and diagrams, to add, divide, and
    measure them,

* Twenty-nine poems that appeared in various sections of *Leaves of Grass* and *Drum-Taps* (1865)
until grouped with this title in the 1881 edition of *Leaves*.
[1] First published in *Drum-Taps* (1865) and eventually added to "By the Roadside" in the 1881 edition
of *Leaves of Grass*.

When I sitting heard the astronomer where he lectured with much
    applause in the lecture-room,
How soon unaccountable I became tired and sick,
Till rising and gliding out I wander'd off by myself,
In the mystical moist night-air, and from time to time,
Look'd up in perfect silence at the stars.

1865

from   Drum-Taps*

BEAT! BEAT! DRUMS![1]

Beat! beat! drums!—blow! bugles! blow!
Through the windows—through doors—burst like a ruthless force,
Into the solemn church, and scatter the congregation,
Into the school where the scholar is studying;
Leave not the bridegroom quiet—no happiness must he have now
    with his bride,
Nor the peaceful farmer any peace, ploughing his field or gathering
    his grain,
So fierce you whirr and pound you drums—so shrill you bugles blow.

Beat! beat! drums!—blow! bugles! blow!
Over the traffic of cities—over the rumble of wheels in the streets;
Are beds prepared for sleepers at night in the houses? no sleepers
    must sleep in those beds,   10
No bargainers' bargains by day—no brokers or speculators—would
    they continue?
Would the talkers be talking? would the singer attempt to sing?
Would the lawyer rise in the court to state his case before the judge?
Beat! beat! drums!—blow! bugles! blow!
Then rattle quicker, heavier drums—you bugles wilder blow.
Make no parley—stop for no expostulation,
Mind not the timid—mind not the weeper or prayer,
Mind not the old man beseeching the young man,
Let not the child's voice be heard, nor the mother's entreaties,
Make even the trestles to shake the dead where they lie awaiting
    the hearses,   20
So strong you thump O terrible drums—so loud you bugles blow.

1861

---

* First published separately with fifty-three poems in 1865; revised with eighteen new poems as
"Sequel to Drum-Taps" (1865–1866)—a volume that received unenthusiastic reviews—and added to
the 1867 edition of *Leaves of Grass,* ultimately as a group of forty-three poems in the 1881 edition.
  [1] First published simultaneously in *Harper's Weekly* and the New York *Ledger* on September 28,
1861.

VIGIL STRANGE I KEPT ON THE FIELD ONE NIGHT

Vigil strange I kept on the field one night;
When you my son and my comrade dropt at my side that day,
One look I but gave which your dear eyes return'd with a look I
    shall never forget,
One touch of your hand to mine O boy, reach'd up as you lay
    on the ground,
Then onward I sped in the battle, the even-contested battle,
Till late in the night reliev'd to the place at last again I made my way,
Found you in death so cold dear comrade, found your body son
    of responding kisses, (never again on earth responding,)
Bared your face in the starlight, curious the scene, cool blew the
    moderate night-wind,
Long there and then in vigil I stood, dimly around me the battle-
    field spreading,
Vigil wondrous and vigil sweet there in the fragrant silent night,   10
But not a tear fell, not even a long-drawn sigh, long, long I gazed,
Then on the earth partially reclining sat by your side leaning my chin
    in my hands,
Passing sweet hours, immortal and mystic hours with you dearest
    comrade—not a tear, not a word,
Vigil of silence, love and death, vigil for you my son and my soldier,
As onward silently stars aloft, eastward new ones upward stole,
Vigil final for you brave boy, (I could not save you, swift was your
    death,
I faithfully loved you and cared for you living, I think we shall surely
    meet again,)
Till at latest lingering of the night, indeed just as the dawn appear'd,
My comrade I wrapt in his blanket, envelop'd well his form,
Folded the blanket well, tucking it carefully over head and carefully
    under feet,   20
And there and then and bathed by the rising sun, my son in his
    grave, in his rude-dug grave I deposited,
Ending my vigil strange with that, vigil of night and battle-field dim,
Vigil for boy of responding kisses, (never again on earth responding,)
Vigil for comrade swiftly slain, vigil I never forget, how as day
    brighten'd,
I rose from the chill ground and folded my soldier well in his blanket,
And buried him where he fell.

1865

A MARCH IN THE RANKS HARD-PREST, AND THE ROAD UNKNOWN

A march in the ranks hard-prest, and the road unknown,
A route through a heavy wood with muffled steps in the darkness,
Our army foil'd with loss severe, and the sullen remnant retreating,

Till after midnight glimmer upon us the lights of a dim-lighted building,
We come to an open space in the woods, and halt by the dim-lighted
    building,
'Tis a large old church at the crossing roads, now an impromptu hospital,
Entering but for a minute I see a sight beyond all the pictures and
    poems ever made,
Shadows of deepest, deepest black, just lit by moving candles and lamps,
And by one great pitchy torch stationary with wild red flame and clouds
    of smoke,
By these, crowds, groups of forms vaguely I see on the floor, some
    in the pews laid down,   10
At my feet more distinctly a soldier, a mere lad, in danger of bleeding
    to death, (he is shot in the abdomen,)
I stanch the blood temporarily, (the youngster's face is white as a lily,)
Then before I depart I sweep my eyes o'er the scene fain to absorb it all,
Faces, varieties, postures beyond description, most in obscurity,
    some of them dead,
Surgeons operating, attendants holding lights, the smell of ether,
    the odor of blood,
The crowd, O the crowd of the bloody forms, the yard outside also fill'd,
Some on the bare ground, some on planks or stretchers, some in the
    death-spasm sweating,
An occasional scream or cry, the doctor's shouted orders or calls,
The glisten of the little steel instruments catching the glint of the
    torches,
These I resume as I chant, I see again the forms, I smell the odor,   20
Then hear outside the orders given, *Fall in, my men, fall in;*
But first I bend to the dying lad, his eyes open, a half-smile gives
    he me,
Then the eyes close, calmly close, and I speed forth to the darkness,
Resuming, marching, ever in darkness marching, on in the ranks,
The unknown road still marching.

                                 1865

A SIGHT IN CAMP IN THE DAYBREAK
GRAY AND DIM

A sight in camp in the daybreak gray and dim,
As from my tent I emerge so early sleepless,
As slow I walk in the cool fresh air the path near by the hospital tent,
Three forms I see on stretchers lying, brought out there untended lying,
Over each the blanket spread, ample brownish woolen blanket,
Gray and heavy blanket, folding, covering all.

Curious I halt and silent stand,
Then with light fingers I from the face of the nearest the first just lift
    the blanket;

Who are you elderly man so gaunt and grim, with well-gray'd hair,
    and flesh all sunken about the eyes?
Who are you my dear comrade?   10
Then to the second I step—and who are you my child and darling?
Who are you sweet boy with cheeks yet blooming?

Then to the third—a face nor child nor old, very calm, as of beautiful
    yellow-white ivory;
Young man I think I know you—I think this face is the face of the
    Christ himself,
Dead and divine and brother of all, and here again he lies.

1865

DIRGE FOR TWO VETERANS*

    The last sunbeam
Lightly falls from the finish'd Sabbath,
On the pavement here, and there beyond it is looking,
    Down a new-made double grave.

    Lo, the moon ascending,
Up from the east the silvery round moon,
Beautiful over the house-tops, ghastly, phantom moon,
    Immense and silent moon.

    I see a sad procession,
And I hear the sound of coming full-key'd bugles,   10
All the channels of the city streets they're flooding,
    As with voices and with tears.

    I hear the great drums pounding,
And the small drums steady whirring,
And every blow of the great convulsive drums,
    Strikes me through and through.

    For the son is brought with the father,
(In the foremost ranks of the fierce assault they fell,
Two veterans son and father dropt together,
    And the double grave awaits them.)   20

    Now nearer blow the bugles,
And the drums strike more convulsive,
And the daylight o'er the pavement quite has faded,
    And the strong dead-march enwraps me.

---

* First appeared in the "Sequel to Drum-Taps" (1865–1866).

In the eastern sky up-buoying,
The sorrowful vast phantom moves illumin'd,
('Tis some mother's large transparent face,
    In heaven brighter growing.)

O strong dead-march you please me!
O moon immense with your silvery face you soothe me!   30
O my soldiers twain! O my veterans passing to burial!
    What I have I also give you.

The moon gives you light,
And the bugles and the drums give you music,
And my heart, O my soldiers, my veterans,
    My heart gives you love.

                                                                1865–1866

            from   MEMORIES OF PRESIDENT LINCOLN*

WHEN LILACS LAST IN THE DOORYARD BLOOM'D[1]

1

When lilacs last in the dooryard bloom'd,
And the great star[2] early droop'd in the western sky in the night,
I mourn'd, and yet shall mourn with ever-returning spring.

Ever-returning spring, trinity sure to me you bring,
Lilac blooming perennial and drooping star in the west,
And thought of him I love.

2

O powerful western fallen star!
O shades of night—O moody, tearful night!
O great star disappear'd—O the black murk that hides the star!
O cruel hands that hold me powerless—O helpless soul of me!   10
O harsh surrounding cloud that will not free my soul.

3

In the dooryard fronting an old farm-house near the white-wash'd palings,
Stands the lilac-bush tall-growing with heart-shaped leaves of rich green,
With many a pointed blossom rising delicate, with the perfume strong
    I love,
With every leaf a miracle—and from this bush in the dooryard,

---

* Four poems first grouped as "President Lincoln's Burial Hymn" in the 1871 edition of *Leaves of Grass* and with this title in the 1881 edition.
[1] First appeared in the "Sequel to Drum-Taps"(1865–1866).   [2] Venus.

With delicate-color'd blossoms and heart-shaped leaves of rich green,
A sprig with its flower I break.

4

In the swamp in secluded recesses,
A shy and hidden bird is warbling a song.

Solitary the thrush,   20
The hermit withdrawn to himself, avoiding the settlements,
Sings by himself a song.

Song of the bleeding throat,
Death's outlet song of life, (for well dear brother I know,
If thou wast not granted to sing thou would'st surely die.)

5

Over the breast of the spring, the land, amid cities,
Amid lanes and through old woods, where lately the violets peep'd
    from the ground, spotting the gray debris,
Amid the grass in the fields each side of the lanes, passing the endless
    grass,
Passing the yellow-spear'd wheat, every grain from its shroud in the
    dark-brown fields uprisen,
Passing the apple-tree blows³ of white and pink in the orchards,   30
Carrying a corpse to where it shall rest in the grave,
Night and day journeys a coffin.⁴

6

Coffin that passes through lanes and streets,
Through day and night with the great cloud darkening the land,
With the pomp of the inloop'd flags with the cities draped in black,
With the show of the States themselves as of crape-veil'd women standing,
With processions long and winding and the flambeaus⁵ of the night,
With the countless torches lit, with the silent sea of faces and the
    unbared heads,
With the waiting depot, the arriving coffin, and the sombre faces,
With dirges through the night, with the thousand voices rising strong
    and solemn,   40
With all the mournful voices of the dirges pour'd around the coffin,
The dim-lit churches and the shuddering organs—where amid these
    you journey,
With the tolling tolling bells' perpetual clang,
Here, coffin that slowly passes,
I give you my sprig of lilac.

³ Blossoms.
⁴ Lincoln's body was transported by train from Washington, D.C., to Springfield, Illinois, for burial
after he was assassinated in April 1865.
⁵ Torches or candles.

7

(Nor for you, for one alone,
Blossoms and branches green to coffins all I bring,
For fresh as the morning, thus would I chant a song for you O sane
    and sacred death.

All over bouquets of roses,
O death, I cover you over with roses and early lilies,   50
But mostly and now the lilac that blooms the first,
Copious I break, I break the sprigs from the bushes,
With loaded arms I come, pouring for you,
For you and the coffins all of you O death.)

8

O western orb sailing the heaven,
Now I know what you must have meant as a month since I walk'd,
As I walk'd in silence the transparent shadowy night,
As I saw you had something to tell as you bent to me night after night,
As you droop'd from the sky low down as if to my side, (while the
    other stars all look'd on,)
As we wander'd together the solemn night, (for something I know not
    what kept me from sleep,)   60
As the night advanced, and I saw on the rim of the west how full you
    were of woe,
As I stood on the rising ground in the breeze in the cool transparent night,
As I watch'd where you pass'd and was lost in the netherward black of
    the night,
As my soul in its trouble dissatisfied sank, as where you sad orb,
Concluded, dropt in the night, and was gone.

9

Sing on there in the swamp,
O singer bashful and tender, I hear your notes, I hear your call,
I hear, I come presently, I understand you,
But a moment I linger, for the lustrous star has detain'd me,
The star my departing comrade holds and detains me.   70

10

O how shall I warble myself for the dead one there I loved?
And how shall I deck my song for the large sweet soul that has gone?
And what shall my perfume be for the grave of him I love?

Sea-winds blown from east and west,
Blown from the Eastern sea and blown from the Western sea, till
    there on the prairies meeting,
These and with these and the breath of my chant,
I'll perfume the grave of him I love.

11

O what shall I hang on the chamber walls?
And what shall the pictures be that I hang on the walls,
To adorn the burial-house of him I love?   80

Pictures of growing spring and farms and homes,
With the Fourth-month[6] eve at sundown, and the gray smoke lucid
    and bright,
With floods of the yellow gold of the gorgeous, indolent, sinking
    sun, burning, expanding the air,
With the fresh sweet herbage under foot, and the pale green leaves of
    the trees prolific,
In the distance the flowing glaze, the breast of the river, with a
    wind-dapple here and there,
With ranging hills on the banks, with many a line against the sky, and
    shadows,
And the city at hand with dwellings so dense, and stacks of chimneys,
And all the scenes of life and the workshops, and the workmen homeward
    returning.

12

Lo, body and soul—this land,
My own Manhattan with spires, and the sparkling and hurrying tides,
    and the ships,   90
The varied and ample land, the South and the North in the light, Ohio's
    shores and flashing Missouri,
And ever the far-spreading prairies cover'd with grass and corn.

Lo, the most excellent sun so calm and haughty,
The violet and purple morn with just-felt breezes,
The gentle soft-born measureless light
The miracle spreading bathing all, the fulfill'd noon,
The coming eve delicious, the welcome night and the stars,
Over my cities shining all, enveloping man and land.

13

Sing on, sing on you gray-brown bird,
Sing from the swamps, the recesses, pour your chant from the bushes,   100
Limitless out of the dusk, out of the cedars and pines.

Sing on dearest brother, warble your reedy song,
Loud human song, with voice of uttermost woe.

O liquid and free and tender!
O wild and loose to my soul—O wondrous singer!
You only I hear—yet the star holds me, (but will soon depart,)
Yet the lilac with mastering odor holds me.

14

Now while I sat in the day and look'd forth,
In the close of the day with its light and the fields of spring, and
    the farmers preparing their crops,
In the large unconscious scenery of my land with its lakes and forests,   110

---

[6] April, from the Quaker numerical designations for months.

In the heavenly aerial beauty, (after the perturb'd winds and the storms,)
Under the arching heavens of the afternoon swift passing, and the voices
   of children and women,
The many-moving sea-tides, and I saw the ships how they sail'd,
And the summer approaching with richness, and the fields all busy
   with labor,
And the infinite separate houses, how they all went on, each with
   its meals and minutia of daily usages,
And the streets how their throbbings throbb'd, and the cities pent—lo,
   then and there,
Falling upon them all and among them all, enveloping me with the rest,
Appear'd the cloud, appear'd the long black trail,
And I knew death, its thought, and the sacred knowledge of death.

Then with the knowledge of death as walking one side of me,   120
And the thought of death close-walking the other side of me,
And I in the middle as with companions, and as holding the hands
   of companions,
I fled forth to the hiding receiving night that talks not,
Down to the shores of the water, the path by the swamp in the dimness,
To the solemn shadowy cedars and ghostly pines so still.

And the singer so shy to the rest receiv'd me,
The gray-brown bird I know receiv'd us comrades three,
And he sang the carol of death, and a verse for him I love.

From deep secluded recesses,
From the fragrant cedars and the ghostly pines so still,   130
Came the carol of the bird.

And the charm of the carol rapt me,
As I held as if by their hands my comrades in the night,
And the voice of my spirit tallied the song of the bird.

Come lovely and soothing death,
Undulate round the world, serenely arriving, arriving,
In the day, in the night, to all, to each,
Sooner or later delicate death.

Prais'd be the fathomless universe,
For life and joy, and for objects and knowledge curious,   140
And for love, sweet love—but praise! praise! praise!
For the sure-enwinding arms of cool-enfolding death.

Dark mother always gliding near with soft feet,
Have none chanted for thee a chant of fullest welcome?
Then I chant it for thee, I glorify thee above all,
I bring thee a song that when thou must indeed come, come unfalteringly.

Approach strong deliveress,
When it is so, when thou hast taken them I joyously sing the dead,

Lost in the loving floating ocean of thee,
Laved in the flood of thy bliss O death.   150

From me to thee glad serenades,
Dances for thee I propose saluting thee, adornments and feastings
    for thee,
And the sights of the open landscape and the high-spread sky are fitting,
And life and the fields, and the huge and thoughtful night.

The night in silence under many a star,
The ocean shore and the husky whispering wave whose voice I know,
And the soul turning to thee O vast and well-veil'd death,
And the body gratefully nestling close to thee.

Over the tree-tops I float thee a song,
Over the rising and sinking waves, over the myriad fields and the
    prairies wide,   160
Over the dense-pack'd cities all and the teeming wharves and ways,
I float this carol with joy, with joy to thee O death.

                    15

To the tally of my soul,
Loud and strong kept up the gray-brown bird,
With pure deliberate notes spreading filling the night.

Loud in the pines and cedars dim,
Clear in the freshness moist and the swamp-perfume,
And I with my comrades there in the night.

While my sight that was bound in my eyes unclosed,
As to long panoramas of visions.   170

And I saw askant[7] the armies,
I saw as in noiseless dreams hundreds of battle-flags,
Borne through the smoke of the battles and pierc'd with missiles I
    saw them,
And carried hither and yon through the smoke, and torn and bloody,
And at last but a few shreds left on the staffs, (and all in silence,)
And the staffs all splinter'd and broken.

I saw battle-corpses, myriads of them,
And the white skeletons of young men, I saw them,
I saw the debris and debris of all the slain soldiers of the war,
But I saw they were not as was thought,   180
They themselves were fully at rest, they suffer'd not,
The living remain'd and suffer'd, the mother suffer'd,
And the wife and the child and the musing comrade suffer'd,
And the armies that remain'd suffer'd.

---

[7] From the corner of the eye, obliquely.

16

Passing the visions, passing the night,
Passing, unloosing the hold of my comrades' hands,
Passing the song of the hermit bird and the tallying song of my soul,
Victorious song, death's outlet song, yet varying ever-altering song,
As low and wailing, yet clear the notes, rising and falling, flooding
    the night,
Sadly sinking and fainting, as warning and warning, and yet again
    bursting with joy,   190
Covering the earth and filling the spread of the heaven,
As that powerful psalm in the night I heard from recesses,
Passing, I leave thee lilac with heart-shaped leaves,
I leave thee there in the door-yard, blooming, returning with spring.

I cease from my song for thee,
From my gaze on thee in the west, fronting the west, communing with thee,
O comrade lustrous with silver face in the night.

Yet each to keep and all, retrievements out of the night,
The song, the wondrous chant of the gray-brown bird,
And the tallying chant, the echo arous'd in my soul,   200
With the lustrous and drooping star with the countenance full of woe,
With the holders holding my hand nearing the call of the bird,
Comrades mine and I in the midst, and their memory ever to keep,
    for the dead I loved so well,
For the sweetest, wisest soul of all my days and lands—and this for his
    dear sake,
Lilac and star and bird twined with the chant of my soul,
There in the fragrant pines and the cedars dusk and dim.

1865–1866

PASSAGE TO INDIA*

I

Singing my days,
Singing the great achievements of the present,
Singing the strong light works of engineers,
Our modern wonders, (the antique ponderous Seven[1] outvied,)
In the Old World the east the Suez canal,[2]
The New by its mighty railroad spann'd,[3]

---

* First published as the title poem of a volume of seventy-five poems in 1871 and in the 1871 edition
of *Leaves of Grass*.
[1] The Seven Wonders of the Ancient World: the pyramids of Egypt; the Temple of Artemis at Ephesus, in Asia Minor; the hanging gardens of Babylon; the Mausoleum at Halicarnassus, in Asia
Minor; the Pharos, or lighthouse, at Alexandria, Egypt; the statue of Zeus at Olympia, Greece; and
the Colossus of Rhodes.
[2] Begun in April 1859 and completed in November 1869.
[3] The Union Pacific and Central Pacific railroads, joined at Promontory, Utah, in May 1869.

The seas inlaid with eloquent gentle wires;[4]
Yet first to sound, and ever sound, the cry with thee O soul,
The Past! the Past! the Past!

The Past—the dark unfathom'd retrospect!   10
The teeming gulf—the sleepers and the shadows!
The past—the infinite greatness of the past!
For what is the present after all but a growth out of the past?
(As a projectile form'd, impell'd, passing a certain line, still keeps on,
So the present, utterly form'd, impell'd by the past.)

2

Passage O soul to India!
Eclaircise[5] the myths Asiatic, the primitive fables.

Not you alone proud truths of the world,
Nor you alone ye facts of modern science,
But myths and fables of eld,[6] Asia's, Africa's fables,   20
The far-darting beams of the spirit, the unloos'd dreams,
The deep diving bibles and legends,
The daring plots of the poets, the elder religions;
O you temples fairer than lilies pour'd over by the rising sun!
O you fables spurning the known, eluding the hold of the known,
    mounting to heaven!
You lofty and dazzling towers, pinnacled, red as roses, burnish'd with
    gold!
Towers of fables immortal fashion'd from mortal dreams!
You too I welcome and fully the same as the rest!
You too with joy I sing.

Passage to India!   30
Lo, soul, seest thou not God's purpose from the first?
The earth to be spann'd, connected by network,
The races, neighbors, to marry and be given in marriage,
The oceans to be cross'd, the distant brought near,
The lands to be welded together.

A worship new I sing,
You captains, voyagers, explorers, yours,
You engineers, you architects, machinists, yours,
You, not for trade or transportation only,
But in God's name, and for thy sake O soul.   40

3

Passage to India!
Lo soul for thee of tableaus twain,
I see in one the Suez canal initiated, open'd,

[4] The Trans-Atlantic cable, completed in 1866.
[5] Make clear, explain; from *éclair*, "a flash of illumination" (French).   [6] Old, or antiquity.

I see the procession of steamships, the Empress Eugenie's[7] leading
   the van,
I mark from on deck the strange landscape, the pure sky, the level
   sand in the distance,
I pass swiftly the picturesque groups, the workmen gather'd,
The gigantic dredging machines.

In one again, different, (yet thine, all thine, O soul, the same,)
I see over my own continent the Pacific railroad surmounting every
   barrier,[8]
I see continual trains of cars winding along the Platte carrying freight
   and passengers,   50
I hear the locomotives rushing and roaring, and the shrill steam-whistle,
I hear the echoes reverberate through the grandest scenery in the world,
I cross the Laramie plains, I note the rocks in grotesque shapes, the buttes,
I see the plentiful larkspur and wild onions, the barren, colorless,
   sage-deserts,
I see in glimpses afar or towering immediately above me the great
   mountains, I see the Wind river and the Wahsatch mountains,
I see the Monument mountain and the Eagle's Nest, I pass the
   Promontory, I ascend the Nevadas,
I scan the noble Elk mountain and wind around its base,
I see the Humboldt range, I thread the valley and cross the river,
I see the clear waters of Lake Tahoe, I see forests of majestic pines,
Or crossing the great desert, the alkaline plains, I behold enchanting
   mirages of waters and meadows,   60
Marking through these and after all, in duplicate slender lines,
Bridging the three or four thousand miles of land travel,
Tying the Eastern to the Western sea,
The road between Europe and Asia.

(Ah Genoese[9] thy dream! thy dream!
Centuries after thou art laid in thy grave,
The shore thou foundest verifies thy dream.)

              4
Passage to India!
Struggles of many a captain, tales of many a sailor dead,
Over my mood stealing and spreading they come,   70
Like clouds and cloudlets in the unreach'd sky.

Along all history, down the slopes,
As a rivulet running, sinking now, and now again to the surface rising,
A ceaseless thought, a varied train—lo, soul, to thee, thy sight, they rise,
The plans, the voyages again, the expeditions;
Again Vasco de Gama[10] sails forth,

---

[7] Eugénie de Guzmán (1853–1920), wife of Napoleon III and empress of France (1853–1871).
[8] Along the route from Omaha to San Francisco.
[9] Christopher Columbus, a native of Genoa, Italy.
[10] Da Gama (1469?–1524), a Portuguese navigator, was the first European to sail around southern Africa to India.

Again the knowledge gain'd, the mariner's compass,
Lands found and nations born, thou born America,
For purpose vast, man's long probation fill'd,
Thou rondure[11] of the world at last accomplish'd.   80

                              5

O vast Rondure, swimming in space,
Cover'd all over with visible power and beauty,
Alternate light and day and the teeming spiritual darkness,
Unspeakable high processions of sun and moon and countless stars above,
Below, the manifold grass and waters, animals, mountains, trees,
With inscrutable purpose, some hidden prophetic intention,
Now first it seems my thought begins to span thee.

Down from the gardens of Asia descending radiating,
Adam and Eve appear, then their myriad progeny after them,
Wandering, yearning, curious, with restless explorations,   90
With questionings, baffled, formless, feverish, with never-happy hearts,
With that sad incessant refrain, *Wherefore unsatisfied soul?* and *Whither
    O mocking life?*

Ah who shall soothe these feverish children?
Who justify these restless explorations?
Who speak the secret of impassive earth?
Who bind it to us? what is this separate Nature so unnatural?
What is this earth to our affections? (unloving earth, without a throb
    to answer ours,
Cold earth, the place of graves.)

Yet soul be sure the first intent remains, and shall be carried out,
Perhaps even how the time has arrived.   100

After the seas are all cross'd, (as they seem already cross'd,)
After the great captains and engineers have accomplish'd their work,
After the noble inventors, after the scientists, the chemist, the
    geologist, ethnologist,
Finally shall come the poet worthy that name,
The true son of God shall come singing his songs.

Then not your deeds only O voyagers, O scientists and inventors, shall
    be justified,
All these hearts as of fretted children shall be sooth'd,
All affection shall be fully responded to, the secret shall be told,
All these separations and gaps shall be taken up and hook'd and link'd
    together,
The whole earth, this cold, impassive, voiceless earth, shall be
    completely justified,   110
Trinitas[12] divine shall be gloriously accomplish'd and compacted by
    the true son of God, the poet,

---

[11] Encirclement.   [12] The Holy Trinity (an attempt at Spanish).

(He shall indeed pass the straits and conquer the mountains,
He shall double the cape of Good Hope to some purpose,)
Nature and Man shall be disjoin'd and diffused no more,
The true son of God shall absolutely fuse them.

6

Year at whose wide-flung door I sing!
Year of the purpose accomplish'd!
Year of the marriage of continents, climates and oceans!
(No mere doge of Venice[13] now wedding the Adriatic,)
I see O year in you the vast terraqueous globe given and giving all,   120
Europe to Asia, Africa join'd, and they to the New World,
The lands, geographies, dancing before you, holding a festival garland,
As brides and bridegrooms hand in hand.

Passage to India!
Cooling airs from Caucasus[14] far, soothing cradle of man,
The river Euphrates[15] flowing, the past lit up again.
Lo soul, the retrospect brought forward,
The old, most populous, wealthiest of earth's lands,
The streams of the Indus and the Ganges[16] and their many affluents,
(I my shores of America walking to-day behold, resuming all,)   130
The tale of Alexander[17] on his warlike marches suddenly dying,
On one side China and on the other side Persia and Arabia,
To the south the great seas and the bay of Bengal,
The flowing literatures, tremendous epics, religions, castes,
Old occult Brahma interminably far back, the tender and junior Buddha,[18]
Central and southern empires and all their belongings, possessors,
The wars of Tamerlane, the reign of Aurungzebe,[19]
The traders, rulers, explorers, Moslems, Venetians, Byzantium, the
      Arabs, Portuguese,
The first travelers famous yet, Marco Polo, Batouta the Moor,[20]
Doubts to be solv'd, the map incognita,[21] blanks to be fill'd,   140
The foot of man unstay'd, the hands never at rest,
Thyself O soul that will not brook a challenge.

---

[13] The doge, or chief magistrate, each year cast a ring into the sea to symbolize the marriage of the Adriatic Sea and the city-state of Venice.

[14] The mountainous region in Russia between the Black and Caspian Sea.

[15] A river originating in Turkey and flowing into the Persian Gulf, one of four rivers said to flow from the Garden of Eden; the Euphrates Valley was considered the cradle of Western civilization.

[16] Great rivers of India.

[17] Alexander III (356–323 B.C.), or Alexander the Great, king of Macedon (336–323 B.C.), who extended his empire as far as the Indus River and died on his return from an invasion of India.

[18] Brahma was the supreme Hindu god; Buddha, or Siddhartha Gautama (6th century B.C.), founder of Buddhism.

[19] Tamerlane (1336?–1405) was the Mongol conqueror of southern and western Asia; Aurungzebe (1618–1707) was the self-proclaimed "Conquerer of the World."

[20] Polo (1254–1324), the famed Venetian traveler, was in China from 1271 to 1295; Batouta (1303–1377) was an explorer of Asia and Africa.

[21] Unknown.

The mediæval navigators rise before me,
The world of 1492, with its awaken'd enterprise,
Something swelling in humanity now like the sap of the earth in spring,
The sunset splendor of chivalry declining.

And who art thou sad shade?
Gigantic, visionary, thyself a visionary,
With majestic limbs and pious beaming eyes,
Spreading around with every look of thine a golden world,   150
Enhuing it with gorgeous hues.

As the chief histrion,[22]
Down to the footlights walks in some great scena,
Dominating the rest I see the Admiral[23] himself,
(History's type of courage, action, faith,)
Behold him sail from Palos[24] leading his little fleet,
His voyage behold, his return, his great fame,
His misfortunes, calumniators, behold him a prisoner, chain'd,
Behold his dejection, poverty, death.

(Curious in time I stand, noting the efforts of heroes,   160
Is the deferment long? bitter the slander, poverty, death?
Lies the seed unreck'd[25] for centuries in the ground? lo, to God's
    due occasion,
Uprising in the night, its sprouts, blooms,
And fills the earth with use and beauty.)

7

Passage indeed O soul to primal thought,
Not lands and seas alone, thy own clear freshness,
The young maturity of brood and bloom,
To realms of budding bibles.

O soul, repressless, I with thee and thou with me,
Thy circumnavigation of the world begin,   170
Of man, the voyage of his mind's return,
To reason's early paradise,
Back, back to wisdom's birth, to innocent intuitions,
Again with fair creation.

8

O we can wait no longer,
We too take ship O soul,
Joyous we too launch out on trackless seas,
Fearless for unknown shores on waves of ecstasy to sail,
Amid the wafting winds, (thou pressing me to thee, I thee to me, O soul,)

[22] Actor.   [23] Columbus.
[24] The Spanish port from which Columbus sailed in August 1492.   [25] Unnoticed or disregarded.

Caroling free, singing our song of God,   180
Chanting our chant of pleasant exploration.

With laugh and many a kiss,
(Let others deprecate, let others weep for sin, remorse, humiliation,)
O soul thou pleasest me, I thee.

Ah more than any priest O soul we too believe in God,
But with the mystery of God we dare not dally.

O soul thou pleasest me, I thee,
Sailing these seas or on the hills, or waking in the night,
Thoughts, silent thoughts, of Time and Space and Death, like waters
    flowing,
Bear me indeed as through the regions infinite,   190
Whose air I breathe, whose ripples hear, lave me all over,
Bathe me O God in thee, mounting to thee,
I and my soul to range in range of thee.

O Thou transcendent,
Nameless, the fibre and the breath,
Light of the the light, shedding forth universes, thou centre of them,
Thou mightier centre of the true, the good, the loving,
Thou moral, spiritual fountain—affection's source—thou reservoir,
(O pensive soul of me—O thirst unsatisfied—waitest not there?
Waitest not haply for us somewhere there the Comrade perfect?)   200
Thou pulse—thou motive of the stars, suns, systems,
That, circling, move in order, safe, harmonious,
Athwart the shapeless vastnesses of space,
How should I think, how breathe a single breath, how speak, if, out
    of myself,
I could not launch, to those, superior universes?

Swiftly I shrivel at the thought of God,
At Nature and its wonders, Time and Space and Death,
But that I, turning, call to thee O soul, thou actual Me,
And lo, thou gently masterest the orbs,
Thou matest Time, smilest content at Death,   210
And fillest, swellest full the vastnesses of Space.

Greater than stars or suns,
Bounding O soul thou journeyest forth;
What love than thine and ours could wider amplify?
What aspirations, wishes, outvie thine and ours O soul?
What dreams of the ideal? what plans of purity, perfection, strength?
What cheerful willingness for others' sake to give up all?
For others' sake to suffer all?

Reckoning ahead O soul, when thou, the time achiev'd,
The seas all cross'd, weather'd the capes, the voyage done,   220
Surrounded, copest, frontest God, yieldest, the aim attain'd,
As fill'd with friendship, love complete, the Elder Brother found,
The Younger melts in fondness in his arms.

9

Passage to more than India!
Are thy wings plumed indeed for such far flights?
O soul, voyagest thou indeed on voyages like those?
Disportest thou on waters such as those?
Soundest below the Sanscrit and the Vedas?[26]
Then have thy bent[27] unleash'd.

Passage to you, your shores, ye aged fierce enigmas!   230
Passage to you, to mastership of you, ye strangling problems!
You, strew'd with the wrecks of skeletons, that, living, never
    reach'd you.

Passage to more than India!
O secret of the earth and sky!
Of you O waters of the sea! O winding creeks and rivers!
Of you O woods and fields! of you strong mountains of my land!
Of you O prairies! of you gray rocks!
O morning red! O clouds! O rain and snows!
O day and night, passage to you!

O sun and moon and all your stars! Sirius and Jupiter!   240
Passage to you!

Passage, immediate passage! the blood burns in my veins!
Away O soul! hoist instantly the anchor!
Cut the hawsers—haul out—shake out every sail!
Have we not stood here like trees in the ground long enough?
Have we not grovel'd here long enough, eating and drinking like
    mere brutes?
Have we not darken'd and dazed ourselves with books long enough?

Sail forth—steer for the deep waters only,
Reckless O soul, exploring, I with thee, and thou with me,
For we are bound where mariner has not yet dared to go,   250
And we will risk the ship, ourselves and all.

O my brave soul!
O farther farther sail!

---

[26] Ancient Hindu scriptures written in Sanskrit.   [27] Energy.

O daring joy, but safe! are they not all the seas of God?
O farther, farther, farther sail!

1871

from   FROM NOON TO STARRY NIGHT*

TO A LOCOMOTIVE IN WINTER[1]

Thee for my recitative,[2]
Thee in the driving storm even as now, the snow, the winter-day declining,
Thee in thy panoply,[3] thy measur'd dual throbbing and thy beat convulsive,
Thy black cylindric body, golden brass and silvery steel,
Thy ponderous side-bars, parallel and connecting rods, gyrating, shuttling
    at thy sides,
Thy metrical, now swelling pant and roar, now tapering in the distance,
Thy great protruding head-light fix'd in front,
Thy long, pale, floating vapor-pennants, tinged with delicate purple,
The dense and murky clouds out-belching from thy smoke-stack,
Thy knitted frame, thy springs and valves, the tremulous twinkle of
    thy wheels,   10
Thy train of cars behind, obedient, merrily following,
Through gale or calm, now swift, now slack, yet steadily careering;
Type of the modern—emblem of motion and power—pulse of the
    continent,
For once come serve the Muse and merge in verse, even as here I see thee,
With storm and buffeting gusts of wind and falling snow,
By day thy warning ringing bell to sound its notes,
By night thy silent signal lamps to swing.

Fierce-throated beauty!
Roll through my chant with all thy lawless music, thy swinging lamps
    at night,
Thy madly-whistled laughter, echoing, rumbling like an earthquake,
    rousing all,   20
Law of thyself complete, thine own track firmly holding,
(No sweetness debonair of tearful harp or glib piano thine,)
Thy trills of shrieks by rocks and hills return'd,
Launch'd o'er the prairies wide, across the lakes,
To the free skies unpent and glad and strong.

1876

---

* Twenty-two poems that first appeared in the 1881 edition of *Leaves of Grass*.
[1] First published in the New York *Daily Tribune* on February 19, 1876.
[2] In musical terminology, an intermediate form between speaking and singing: a particularly apt
mode of address for Whitman, who is both conversational and celebratory.
[3] Armor.

from   FIRST ANNEX: SANDS AT SEVENTY*

DEATH OF GENERAL GRANT[1]

As one by one withdraw the lofty actors,
From that great play on history's stage eterne,
That lurid, partial act of war and peace—of old and new contending,
Fought out through wrath, fears, dark dismays, and many a long suspense;
All past—and since, in countless graves receding, mellowing,
Victor's and vanquish'd—Lincoln's and Lee's[2]—now thou with them,
Man of the mighty days—and equal to the days!
Thou from the prairies!—tangled and many-vein'd and hard has been
   thy part,
To admiration has it been enacted!

1885

from   SECOND ANNEX: GOOD-BYE MY FANCY†

OSCEOLA[1]

[When I was nearly grown to manhood in Brooklyn, New York, (middle of 1838,) I met one of the return'd U. S. Marines from Fort Moultrie, S. C., and had long talks with him—learn'd the occurrence below described—death of Osceola. The latter was a young, brave, leading Seminole in the Florida war of that time—was surrender'd to our troops, imprison'd and literally died of "a broken heart," at Fort Moultrie. He sicken'd of his confinement—the doctor and officers made every allowance and kindness possible for him; then the close:]

When his hour for death had come,
He slowly rais'd himself from the bed on the floor,
Drew on his war-dress, shirt, leggings, and girdled the belt around his waist,
Call'd for vermilion paint (his looking-glass was held before him,)
Painted half his face and neck, his wrists, and back-hands.
Put the scalp-knife carefully in his belt—then lying down, resting a moment,
Rose again, half sitting, smiled, gave in silence his extended hand to each
   and all,

---

* First published with prose pieces in *November Boughs* (1888); added to the 1884 reprint of *Leaves of Grass*.

[1] First appeared in *Harper's Weekly* on May 16, 1885, although Ulysses S. Grant (1822–1885), eighteenth U.S. president (1869–1877), did not die until July 23, 1885.

[2] Abraham Lincoln and Robert E. Lee.

† Thirty-one poems and prose pieces added to the 1891–1892 edition of *Leaves of Grass*.

[1] First published in *Monson's Illustrated World* in April 1890. Osceola (?–1838) was a brave leader in the second Seminole War (1835–1837) who was seized and imprisoned while working toward a truce; he died after four months in captivity. The bracketed note is Whitman's.

Sank faintly low to the floor (tightly grasping the tomahawk handle,)
Fix'd his look on wife and little children—the last:

(And here a line in memory of his name and death.)

1890

L. OF G.'S PURPORT*

Not to exclude or demarcate, or pick out evils from their formidable
    masses (even to expose them,)
But add, fuse, complete, extend—and celebrate the immortal and
    the good.

Haughty this song, its words and scope,
To span vast realms of space and time,
Evolution—the cumulative—growths and generations.
Begun in ripen'd youth and steadily pursued,
Wandering, peering, dallying with all—war, peace, day, and night
    absorbing,
Never even for one brief hour abandoning my task,
I end it here in sickness, poverty, and old age.

I sing of life, yet mind me well of death: 10
To-day shadowy Death dogs my steps, my seated shape, and has for years—
Draws sometimes close to me, as face to face.

1891

from   *SPECIMEN DAYS†*

ABRAHAM LINCOLN

August 12th.[1863]—I see the President almost every day, as I happen to live
where he passes to or from his lodgings out of town. He never sleeps at the White
House during the hot season, but has quarters at a healthy location some three
miles north of the city, the Soldiers' Home, a United States military establishment. I saw him this morning about 8 1/2 coming in to business, riding on Vermont Avenue, near L Street. He always has a company of twenty-five or thirty

---

* A statement of Whitman's intent in writing *Leaves of Grass*.
    † *Specimen Days and Collect* (1882) is Whitman's autobiographical narrative consisting of prefaces
and essays.

cavalry, with sabres drawn and held upright over their shoulders. They say this guard was against his personal wish, but he let his counselors have their way. The party makes no great show in uniform or horses. Mr. Lincoln on the saddle generally rides a good-sized, easy-going gray horse, is dress'd in plain black, somewhat rusty and dusty, wears a black stiff hat, and looks about as ordinary in attire, etc., as the commonest man. A lieutenant, with yellow straps, rides at his left, and following behind, two by two, come the cavalry men, in their yellow-striped jackets. They are generally going at a slow trot, as that is the pace set them by the one they wait upon. The sabres and accoutrements[1] clank, and the entirely unornamental *cortège*[2] as it trots towards Lafayette Square arouses no sensation, only some curious stranger stops and gazes. I see very plainly Abraham Lincoln's dark brown face, with the deep-cut lines, the eyes, always to me with a deep latent sadness in the expression. We have got so that we exchange bows, and very cordial ones. Sometimes the President goes and comes in an open barouche.[3] The cavalry always accompany him, with drawn sabres. Often I notice as he goes out evenings—and sometimes in the morning, when he returns early—he turns off and halts at the large and handsome residence of the Secretary of War, on K Street, and holds conference there. If in his barouche, I can see from my window he does not alight, but sits in his vehicle, and Mr. Stanton[4] comes out to attend him. Sometimes one of his sons, a boy of ten or twelve, accompanies him, riding at his right on a pony. Earlier in the summer I occasionally saw the President and his wife, toward the latter part of the afternoon, out in a barouche, on a pleasure ride through the city. Mrs. Lincoln was dress'd in complete black, with a long crape veil. The equipage is of the plainest kind, only two horses, and they nothing extra. They pass'd me once very close, and I saw the President in the face fully, as they were moving slowly, and his look, though abstracted, happen'd to be directed steadily in my eye. He bow'd and smiled, but far beneath his smile I noticed well the expression I have alluded to. None of the artists or pictures has caught the deep, though subtle and indirect expression of this man's face. There is something else there. One of the great portrait painters of two or three centuries ago is needed.

Two Brothers, One South, One North

May 28–9. [1865]—I staid to-night a long time by the bedside of a new patient, a young Baltimorean, aged about 19 years, W. S. P., (2d Maryland, southern,) very feeble, right leg amputated, can't sleep hardly at all—has taken a great deal of morphine, which, as usual, is costing more than it comes to. Evidently very intelligent and well bred—very affectionate—held on to my hand, and put it by his face, not willing to let me leave. As I was lingering, soothing him in his pain, he says to me suddenly, "I hardly think you know who I am—I don't wish to

---

[1] Miscellaneous equipment of a soldier.

[2] "Retinue" (French) ceremonial procession.

[3] A four-wheeled carriage with an outside seat for the driver and a top that could be raised to cover the back seat.

[4] Edwin Masters Stanton (1814–1869), U.S. secretary of war from 1862 to 1868.

impose upon you—I am a rebel soldier." I said I did not know that, but it made no difference. Visiting him daily for about two weeks after that, while he lived, (death had mark'd him, and he was quite alone,) I loved him much, always kiss'd him, and he did me. In an adjoining ward I found his brother, an officer of rank, a Union soldier, a brave and religious man, (Col. Clifton K. Prentiss, sixth Maryland infantry, Sixth corps, wounded in one of the engagements at Petersburg, April 2—linger'd, suffer'd much, died in Brooklyn, Aug. 20, '65).[1] It was in the same battle both were hit. One was a strong Unionist, the other Secesh;[2] both fought on their respective sides, both badly wounded, and both brought together here after a separation of four years. Each died for his cause.

═CONTEXTS═

The Move to the Cities

Post-Civil War America was characterized by the national drive to develop the material resources of the West. Towns and cities grew at a spectacular rate as miners, cattlemen, cowboys, farmers, and indigent immigrants traveled the railways, looking for land and work. William Fraser Rae (1835–1905), a correspondent for the London *Daily News,* was one of the first to take the trip by rail from New York to San Francisco. In his book *Westward by Rail: The New Route to the East* (1871), he describes Omaha, whose rapid growth was typical of American cities in the post-Civil War era:

Over the Rocky Mountains

Omaha is one of those American cities which seem to spring up, flourish, and wax great in the twinkling of an eye. Its history dates from 1854. In that year a few squatters fixed their residence in this section of what was then the Territory of Nebraska, which was regarded as in the heart of the Far West. Situated on the bank of the Missouri River, at a point almost equidistant between the Atlantic and Pacific Oceans, Omaha had many natural advantages, and these have been turned to profitable account since the Pacific Railway has furnished the opportunity. Certain it is that the city's prospects are bright. In 1860 the population did not exceed 1,883; now the number of inhabitants is estimated at 20,000. There are many manufactories within its bounds, one distillery, and several breweries. In the year 1868–9 the sales of the merchants were upwards of a million and a quarter sterling. Like most American cities it possesses two daily newspapers, the one the Republican the other the Democratic organ. Four other journals are published at longer intervals. Of schools, both public and private, there is abundance. The churches are fifteen in number. There are eleven hotels, of which one or two are first-class establishments. That this progress should have been made within the space of a few short years is not only marvellous, but inspires hope that the city's future will be a great and an enviable one. . . .

William Fraser Rae, 1871

---

[1] This information was added after the essay was first written.   [2] A secessionist.

Emily Dickinson
(1830–1886)

"The Banquet of Abstemiousness / Defaces that of wine": that line from a poem by Emily Dickinson sets forth a perspective that permeates both her life and her poetic vision. Dickinson cared little for quantity, for multitude, for aggregating things or experiences. Outwardly her life was quiet, uncluttered by the public activities that customarily measure development or success. She died in the village of Amherst, Massachusetts, in 1886 in the same house in which she had been born in 1830. She traveled outside Massachusetts only once, in 1855, when she accompanied her father to Philadelphia and to Washington, D.C. During the last fifteen years of her life in Amherst she restricted her movements severely, rarely leaving her house and garden. In no way, however, was this election of privacy an abandonment of life; as the documents in the biographer Jay Leyda's *The Years and Hours of Emily Dickinson* (1960) testify, Dickinson's steady focus on an inner world was deliberate, purposeful, the condition of creativity. To prefer the "banquet of abstemiousness" means to find more in less, to nourish oneself on the quality of experience rather than on the plentiful menu of social convention. Making such a perspective possible for Dickinson was her extreme sensitivity to the outside world, her inclination not to let the obligations and institutions of society regulate her life; in later years simply receiving a letter or conversing with a visitor was an overpowering experience for her, at once intense, animating, and threatening.

The second child of Edward and Emily Norcross Dickinson, the poet-to-be had a devoted brother, Austin, one year her senior, and a protective younger sister, Lavinia. The family lived quietly, secure financially: Dickinson's imposing father was a lawyer and at one time a member of Congress, her mother, a woman of retiring habit, apparently remote from her children. In this family, genuinely supportive yet with no insistent habits of sociality, Dickinson could be herself, could play the games of childhood as a young girl, could withdraw to think and write as her imagination cultivated privacy. When she was seventeen she attended Amherst Academy and the nearby Mount Holyoke Female Seminary for one year. But she returned home the following year, willingly and with the ready assent of her parents.

Dickinson's attachment not only to members of her family but to those she knew well constituted a meaningful dimension of her life. Among her friends was Helen Hunt Jackson, also from Amherst, who began publishing poetry in the 1860s (when Dickinson was writing a poem almost every day) and repeatedly urged her friend to bring her work before the public. Jackson's novel *Mercy Philbrick's Choice* (1876) is thought to be a portrait of Dickinson; the forceful and romantic figure of Rev. Charles Wadsworth, doubtless the subject of eloquent poems of separation, made a deep imprint on her emotions and her imagination. The family friend Judge Otis P. Lord was a treasured part of Dickinson's life; apparently Judge Lord suggested marriage when Dickinson was fifty years old and accepted her refusal with an understanding that matched his longtime admiration. And the sympathetic critic Thomas Wentworth Higginson was for years her confidante about mat-

An 1858 lithograph of the Dickinson homestead on Main Street, Amherst, Massachusetts, where Emily Dickinson spent most of her life.

ters of poetry. Above all, Dickinson's sister-in-law, Susan Gilbert Dickinson, who lived next door ("a hedge away," as an early poem says), was a person whom Dickinson regarded with a unique love and openness throughout her adult life.

Domestic tension was far from unknown in the Dickinson household: the thirteen-year love affair between Austin Dickinson and Mabel Loomis Todd, the wife of David Peck Todd, a professor of astronomy at Amherst, brought increasing stress into the environment. We can only surmise what Dickinson thought of this affair (which became common knowledge in the family) and the swirling emotions it must have caused her. For a while at least it seems to have bonded her all the more closely to her sister-in-law, Susan, not out of a knowing pity but out of a glorification of their role as sisters.

In a letter to her vacationing sister-in-law in 1871, Dickinson adopted the same perspective that informs her statement about the "Banquet of Abstemiousness": "To miss you, Sue, is power. The stimulus of Loss makes most Possession mean." A virtual signature of her way of expressing emotion, this idea of feeding on emptiness has profound implications for Dickinson's poetry. "Success is counted sweetest," she writes, "By those who ne'er succeed." Similarly, "Water, is taught by thirst." In "I had been hungry, all the Years," the poet finds that hunger is a way "Of Persons outside Windows / The Entering—takes away." What such poems confidently assert amounts to a paradoxical theory of knowledge, the idea that a person knows something best, most keenly, by not having it. In fashioning this perspective Dickinson's poems formulate a poetics of deprivation that has its roots in the stern moral dictates of the Puritans of an earlier Massachusetts. Dickinson secularizes Puritan "thou shalt nots" and makes the injunctions part of her mode of expression. Additionally, with the announcement that "My business is circumference," she encircles her world, makes it her own with a startling range of definitions (of hope, exultation, remorse), describes its citizens (crickets, robins, hummingbirds), and presides over its parade of death and celebration with a "self," an "I," that is whimsical, ironic, insistent, and terribly aware of loss, both individual and universal.

What Dickinson says and how she says it are finally inseparable; they come together in a remarkable idiom that consists of the elliptical quality of her lines, her use of syntax, slant (imperfect) rhyme, punctuation, and capitalization, and even the unconventional use of articles: when she writes in "A Bird came down the Walk" that the bird drank "A Dew / from a convenient Grass," the reader sees that her way of using language extends originality to minute detail. Few writers succeed in creating a genuine idiom in which the world is transformed by language into something original, fresh with discovery. Along with Walt Whitman and Mark Twain in nineteenth-century American literature, Dickinson is one of the few, and the only one whose idiom was fully arrayed from the beginning of her career. Although she liked to read a number of nineteenth-century British writers, among them John Keats, Charlotte and Emily Brönte, Robert and Elizabeth Barrett Browning, and George Eliot, Dickinson's reading had no discernable effect on the style of her poetry. She knew the Bible well, as evidenced by her numerous allusions to biblical events. But even these episodes are made part of the idiom that serves as Dickinson's way of apprehending the world: thus, in the early poem "A little East of Jordan," the story of Jacob wrestling with an angel becomes "A Gymnast and an Angel / Did wrestle long and hard."

Dickinson's concern with herself as the center of her world is reminiscent of Henry David Thoreau, who advocates self-exploration as the only worthy kind of travel. In her assumptions about the individual's access to the infinite, she enacts even more distinctively the precepts of Ralph Waldo Emerson's brand of self-reliance. And, to borrow a term from Emerson's essay "The Poet" (1844), we may say that she rules over the world of her poetry with the "tyrannous eye" Emerson thought so necessary. In so doing, she comes to a triumphant sense of her importance as a woman: "I'm 'wife'—I've finished that . . . / I'm Czar—I'm 'Woman' now," she writes in one poem; "Title divine—is mine!" she begins another; and although "Sages" might think her life small, it "Swelled—like Horizons—in my breast." Without the benefit of committees and organizations, Dickinson celebrated her autonomy as an individual and as a woman.

Like any aspiring poet, even one desirous of maintaining privacy, Dickinson wanted to have some outside estimate of her work. Accordingly, in April 1862 she wrote to Higginson, enclosing four poems, to ask if her work was "alive." By this time Dickinson had a developing sense of herself as a poet, which Higginson encouraged without understanding the full range of its passion and depth or the poems it generated. Nonetheless, Higginson's liberal attention over the years was a boon to Dickinson, something deeply appreciated, as her letters show.

As we have learned from the invaluable *Manuscript Books of Emily Dickinson* (1981), edited by the critic Ralph Franklin, Dickinson assembled her poems privately and systematically over a period of years. Her method of composition was to write out a draft of a poem on a sheet of paper or whatever was at hand—the back of a used envelope, at some times, a scrap of paper at others. She would assemble a number of such drafts, then, at a later time, copy them onto folded sheets of unlined paper, frequently adding alternative choices for words of which she was unsure. Arranging these folded sheets in a pile, she would punch two holes on the left-hand side and tie them together with string, thus making packets of sixteen or more pages, called "fascicles," with about twenty poems in each packet. Franklin prints these fascicles in *The Manuscript Books,* supplies lists of the poems in each fascicle, and adds photostats so that it is possible to see Dickinson's handwriting, her alternate words, idiosyncratic punctuation, and capitalization, as well as the unconventional line breaks she sometimes made.

Only a dozen of Dickinson's poems were published during her lifetime, and she seems neither to have sought nor welcomed their publication. As she said in an 1862 letter to Higginson, publication was "foreign" to her thought. After her death recognition of her achievement came slowly because of the circumstances of publication. When Lavinia found over a thousand poems loose or bound in fascicles, she gave them to Susan with an apparent intention of seeing them in print. After two years she retrieved the poems and asked Higginson and Mabel Loomis Todd (herself a writer and poet) to edit them for publication. Accordingly, Higginson and Todd selected poems for a volume published in 1890 (*Poems*) and another in 1891 (*Poems: Second Series*), and in 1896 Todd edited a third selection of Dickinson's poems (*Poems: Third Series*). Although these editions attracted considerable interest, they performed a disservice to the poems Dickinson actually wrote: for they made Dickinson's poetry as conventional as possible by assigning titles, adjusting syntax, inserting regular punctuation, altering the text in some cases to make lines more "readable," and arranging the poems in such categories as Nature, Death, Love, and Friendship. Not until Thomas Johnson's three-volume edition of the poems appeared in 1955 were adequate texts of Dickinson's poems made public. Johnson not only edited the poems with scrupulous care but studied Dickinson's handwriting and the evidence in letters so that he could number them according to their approximate dates of composition. Thus, the numbers given to Dickinson's poems in all recent collections are those assigned by Johnson. Together with fellow editor Theodora Ward, Johnson also brought out three volumes of Dickinson's letters in 1958. Frequently, Dickinson included poems as part of these striking documents; at other times the cadences of her poetry emerge from her prose so that poems seem to evolve in the context of a letter. And in many of her letters the singular idiom of the poetry takes impressionistic form: "Friday I tasted life," she wrote to her close friend Mrs. J. G. Holland in 1866: "A circus passed the house—still I feel the red in my mind though the drums are out."

Dickinson's poetry has attracted the attention of musicians and composers in the twentieth century. Aaron Copland's "Twelve Poems by Emily Dickinson" (1950), written for solo voice and piano, includes "I felt a Funeral, in my Brain" and "There came a Wind like a Bugle." John Adams's "Harmonium" (1981) features a chorus singing the words of "Wild Nights—Wild Nights!" and "Because I Could Not Stop for Death." These notable compositions evidence more than a fashionable interest in the work of a major poet. For, as a number of scholars have pointed out, Dickinson's metrical patterns derive primarily from the prosody of hymns to which she was exposed in her early life. The poetry specialist Mary Favret has observed that many of Dickinson's poems can be sung to the melody of "Amazing Grace" and to the far different beat of "Battle Hymn of the Republic." The critic Susan Gubar adds "The Yellow Rose of Texas" to this list and makes a point of having students who might yawn at an introduction to "prosody" sing Dickinson poems to all three melodies in order to discover how music and words do and do not fit.

Dickinson has also been honored by the practice and testimony of poets in the twentieth century. A number of American poets, among them William Carlos Williams, Hart Crane, Richard Wilbur, and Adrienne Rich, have looked to her work for a renewed sense of the possibilities of more recent poetry. In selecting the "Banquet of Abstemiousness" as the surest way of knowing the intensity of life and the dimensions of modern consciousness, Dickinson has left a legacy of abundance to poets and readers alike.

Suggested Readings: *The Letters of Emily Dickinson*, 3 vols., ed. T. H. Johnson and T. Ward, 1958. *The Years and Hours of Emily Dickinson*, 2 vols., ed. J. Leyda, 1960. *A Concordance to the*

Poems of Emily Dickinson, ed. S. P. Rosenbaum, 1964. *The Manuscript Books of Emily Dickinson,*
2 vols., ed. R. W. Franklin, 1981. T. H. Johnson, *Emily Dickinson: An Interpretive Biography,*
1955. C. R. Anderson, *Emily Dickinson's Poetry,* 1960. A. J. Gelpi, *Emily Dickinson: The Mind of
the Poet,* 1965. J. Cody, *After Great Pain: The Inner Life of Emily Dickinson,* 1971. I. N. Kher, *The
Landscape of Absence: Emily Dickinson's Poetry,* 1974. R. B. Sewall, *The Life of Emily Dickinson,*
2 vols., 1974. S. Cameron, *Lyric Time: Dickinson and the Limits of Genre,* 1979. A. Rich,
"Vesuvius at Home: The Power of Emily Dickinson," 1976, rpt. in *On Lies, Secrets and Silence:
Selected Prose 1966–1978,* 1979. M. Homan, *Women Writers and Poetic Identity,* 1980. B. A.
Clarke Mossberg, *Emily Dickinson: When a Writer Is a Daughter,* 1982. S. Juhasz, ed., *Feminist
Critics Read Emily Dickinson,* 1983. P. Longsworth, *Austin and Mabel: The Amherst Affair,* 1983.
V. R. Pollak, *Dickinson: The Anxiety of Gender,* 1984. J. Loving, *Emily Dickinson: The Poet on the
Second Story,* 1986. C. G. Wolff, *Emily Dickinson,* 1986. J. Dobson, *Dickinson and the Strategies
of Reticence: The Woman Writer in Nineteenth-Century America,* 1989.

Texts Used: *The Poems of Emily Dickinson,* 3 vols., ed. T. H. Johnson, 1951, 1955.

59*

A little East of Jordan,
Evangelists record,
A Gymnast and an Angel[1]
Did wrestle long and hard –

Till morning touching mountain –
And Jacob, waxing strong,
The Angel begged permission
To Breakfast – to return –

Not so, said cunning Jacob!
"I will not let thee go   10
Except thou bless me" – Stranger![2]
The which acceded to –

Light swung the silver fleeces
"Peniel" Hills[3] beyond,
And the bewildered Gymnast
Found he had worsted God!

                                        1858?, 1890

67

Success is counted sweetest
By those who ne'er succeed.
To comprehend a nectar[1]
Requires sorest need.

* Dickinson titled few of her poems; they were numbered by Thomas Johnson in his *Poems of Emily
Dickinson* (1955).
[1] In Genesis 32, the biblical patriarch Jacob (here a "Gymnast") wrestles with an angel.
[2] According to Thomas Johnson, Dickinson later penciled in the alternative word "Signor."
[3] "And Jacob called the name of the place Peniel: for I have seen God face to face, and my life is
preserved," from Genesis 32:30.
[1] According to classical myth, the drink of the gods; here, any celebratory beverage.

Not one of all the purple Host
Who took the Flag[2] today
Can tell the definition
So clear of Victory

As he defeated – dying –
On whose forbidden ear   10
The distant strains of triumph
Burst agonized and clear!

1859?, 1878

76

Exultation is the going
Of an inland soul to sea
Past the houses – past the headlands –
Into deep Eternity –

Bred as we, among the mountains,
Can the sailor understand
The divine intoxication
Of the first league out from land?

1859?, 1890

125

For each extatic[1] instant
We must an anguish pay
In keen and quivering ratio
To the extasy.

For each beloved hour
Sharp pittances of years –
Bitter contested farthings[2] –
And Coffers[3] heaped with Tears!

1859?, 1891

130

These are the days when Birds come back –
A very few – a Bird or two –
To take a backward look.

---

[2] Who captured the enemy flag in battle.
[1] Ecstatic.   [2] British coins of little value.   [3] Trunks or chests for holding valuables.

These are the days when skies resume
The old – old sophistries[1] of June –
A blue and gold mistake.

Oh fraud that cannot cheat the Bee –
Almost thy plausibility
Induces my belief.

Till ranks of seeds their witness bear –   10
And softly thro' the altered air
Hurries a timid leaf.

Oh Sacrament of summer days,
Oh Last Communion[2] in the Haze –
Permit a child to join.

Thy sacred emblems to partake –
Thy consecrated bread to take
And thine immortal wine!

1859?, 1890

135

Water, is taught by thirst.[1]
Land – by the Oceans passed.
Transport – by throe[2] –
Peace – by it's battles told –
Love, by Memorial Mold[3] –
Birds, by the Snow.

1859?, 1896

185

"Faith" is a fine invention
When Gentlemen can *see* –
But *Microscopes* are prudent
In an Emergency.

1860?, 1891

---

[1] Deceptive reasonings in subtle form.
[2] Dickinson compares the death of nature in autumn to the death of Christ commemorated in the sacrament of communion. The metaphors of the final stanza extend the comparison.
[1] We learn the value of water by being thirsty. Each line of the poem offers another instance of what we know or learn by not having it.
[2] We learn rapture by experiencing anguish.
[3] A memorial photograph or pictorial representation.

199

I'm "wife" – I've finished that[1] –
That other state –
I'm Czar – I'm "Woman" now –
It's safer so –

How odd the Girl's life looks
Behind this soft Eclipse –
I think that Earth feels so
To folks in Heaven – now –

This being comfort – then
That other kind – was pain –   10
But why compare?
I'm "Wife"! Stop there!

1860?, 1890

214*

I taste a liquor never brewed –
From Tankards scooped in Pearl –
Not all the Frankfort Berries[1]
Yield such an Alcohol!

Inebriate of Air – am I –
And Debauchee of Dew –
Reeling – thro endless summer days –
From inns of Molten Blue –

When "Landlords" turn the drunken Bee
Out of the Foxglove's door –   10
When Butterflies – renounce their "drams" –
I shall but drink the more!

Till Seraphs swing their snowy Hats[2] –
And Saints – to windows run –
To see the little Tippler
From Manzanilla come![3]

1860?, 1861

---

[1] Although Dickinson never married, this poem announces a triumphant sense of having graduated from the life of a girl to that of a woman; her feeling of being a "wife" was possibly brought about by her love for Rev. Charles Wadsworth.

* Published anonymously as "The May-Wine" in the *Springfield Daily Republican* on May 4, 1861.

[1] Dickinson's manuscript offers "Vats upon the Rhine" as an alternative for "Frankfort Berries."

[2] Till angels swing their halos.

[3] Dickinson apparently associated Manzanilla, Cuba, with rum; she supplied the alternative final line, "Leaning against the – Sun."

241

I like a look of Agony,
Because I know it's true –
Men do not sham Convulsion,
Nor simulate, a Throe[1] –

The Eyes glaze once – and that is Death –
Impossible to feign
The Beads upon the Forehead
By homely Anguish strung.

1861?, 1890

258

There's a certain Slant of light,
Winter Afternoons –
That oppresses, like the Heft[1]
Of Cathedral Tunes –

Heavenly Hurt, it gives us –
We can find no scar,
But internal difference,
Where the Meanings, are –

None may teach it – Any[2] –
'Tis the Seal Despair –   10
An imperial affliction
Sent us of the Air –

When it comes, the Landscape listens –
Shadows – hold their breath –
When it goes, 'tis like the Distance
On the look of Death –

1861?, 1890

280

I felt a Funeral, in my Brain,
And Mourners to and fro
Kept treading – treading – till it seemed
That Sense was breaking through[1] –

[1] Pain or anguish.
[1] Weight, bulk.   [2] Anything: Dickinson's personal idiom here compresses "anything" to "any."
[1] Breaking down, giving way; the poem continues to develop the idea of the faculties disintegrating and concludes with the climactic breaking of "Reason."

And when they all were seated,
A Service, like a Drum –
Kept beating – beating – till I thought
My Mind was going numb –

And then I heard them lift a Box
And creak across my Soul   10
With those same Boots of Lead, again,
Then Space – began to toll,

As[2] all the Heavens were a Bell,
And Being, but an Ear,
And I, and Silence, some strange Race
Wrecked, solitary, here –

And then a Plank in Reason, broke,
And I dropped down, and down –
And hit a World, at every plunge,
And Finished knowing – then –   20

1861?, 1896

285

The Robin's my Criterion for Tune –
Because I grow – where Robins do –
But, were I Cuckoo born[1] –
I'd swear by him –
The ode familiar – rules the Noon –
The Buttercup's, my Whim for Bloom –
Because, we're Orchard sprung –
But, were I Britain born,
I'd Daisies spurn –
None but the Nut – October fit –   10
Because, through dropping it,
The seasons flit – I'm taught –
Without the Snow's Tableau
Winter, were lie – to me –
Because I see – New Englandly –
The Queen, discerns like me –
Provincially –

1861?, 1929

---

[2] As if: Dickinson's personal idiom uses the elliptical substitution of "As" for "As if."
[1] If I had been born where the cuckoo is a common bird, I'd take his song as "normal."

293

I got so I could hear his name –
Without – Tremendous gain –
That Stop-sensation – on my Soul –
And Thunder – in the Room –

I got so I could walk across
That Angle in the floor,
Where he turned so, and I turned – how –
And all our Sinew tore –

I got so I could stir the Box –
In which his letters grew[1]   10
Without that forcing, in my breath –
As Staples – driven through –

Could dimly recollect a Grace –
I think, they call it "God" –
Renowned to ease Extremity –
When Formula, had failed –

And shape my Hands –
Petition's way,
Tho' ignorant of a word
That Ordination[2] – utters –   20

My Business, with the Cloud,
If any Power behind it, be,
Not subject to Despair –
It care, in some remoter way,
For so minute affair
As Misery –
Itself, too great, for interrupting – more –

                                        1861?, 1929

328

A bird came down the Walk –
He did not know I saw –
He bit an Angleworm in halves
And ate the fellow, raw,

---

[1] I could look through the box in which the number of his letters grew. Dickinson's elliptical style is evident.
[2] To the ministry.

And then he drank a Dew
From a convenient Grass –
And then hopped sidewise to the Wall
To let a Beetle pass –

He glanced with rapid eyes
That hurried all around –   10
They looked like frightened Beads, I thought –
He stirred his Velvet Head

Like one in danger, Cautious,
I offered him a Crumb
And he unrolled his feathers
And rowed him softer home –

Than Oars divide the Ocean,
Too silver for a seam –
Or Butterflies, off Banks of Noon
Leap, plashless[1] as they swim.   20

                                   1862?, 1891

336

The face I carry with me – last –
When I go out of Time –
To take my Rank – by – in the West –
That face – will just be thine –

I'll hand it to the Angel –
That – Sir – was my Degree –
In Kingdoms – you have heard the Raised[1] –
Refer to – possibly.

He'll take it – scan it – step aside –
Return – with such a crown   10
As Gabriel – never capered at –
And beg me put it on –

And then – he'll turn me round and round –
To an admiring sky –
As one that bore her Master's name –
Sufficient Royalty!

                                   1862?, 1945

[1] Splashless.
[1] Those who have died and been resurrected to glory in Heaven.

341

After great pain, a formal feeling comes –
The Nerves sit ceremonious, like Tombs –
The stiff Heart questions was it He, that bore,
And Yesterday, or Centuries before?

The Feet, mechanical, go round –
Of ground, or Air, or Ought[1] –
A Wooden way
Regardless grown,
A Quartz contentment, like a stone –

This is the Hour of Lead –   10
Remembered, if outlived,
As Freezing persons, recollect the Snow –
First – Chill – then Stupor – then the letting go –

                                                    1862?, 1929

348

I dreaded that first Robin, so,
But He is mastered, now,
I'm some accustomed to Him grown,
He hurts a little, though –

I thought if I could only live
Till that first Shout got by –
Not all Pianos in the Woods
Had power to mangle me –

I dared not meet the Daffodils –
For fear their Yellow Gown   10
Would pierce me with a fashion
So foreign to my own –

I wished the Grass would hurry –
So – when 'twas time to see –
He'd be too tall, the tallest one
Could stretch – to look at me –

I could not bear the Bees should come,
I wished they'd stay away
In those dim countries where they go,
What word had they, for me?   20

---

[1] A double meaning: anything (from Dickinson's spelling of "aught"), and obligation (the feet simply do what they are obliged to do, mechanically, without thought).

They're here, though; not a creature failed –
No Blossom stayed away
In gentle deference to me –
The Queen of Calvary[1] –

Each one salutes me, as he goes,
And I, my childish Plumes,
Lift, in bereaved acknowledgement
Of their unthinking Drums –

1862?, 1891

401

What Soft – Cherubic Creatures –
These Gentlewomen are –
One would as soon assault a Plush[1] –
Or violate a Star –

Such Dimity[2] Convictions –
A Horror so refined
Of freckled Human Nature[3] –
Of Deity – ashamed[4] –

It's such a common – Glory –
A Fisherman's – Degree[5] –   10
Redemption – Brittle Lady –
Be so – ashamed of Thee –

1862?, 1896

435

Much Madness is divinest Sense –
To a discerning Eye –
Much Sense – the starkest Madness –
'Tis the Majority
In this, as All, prevail –
Assent – and you are sane –
Demur – you're straightway dangerous –
And handled with a Chain –

1862?, 1890

---

[1] The hill near Jerusalem on which Christ was crucified. The idea of the poem is that spring arrives with all its new life despite the suffering of the speaker.
   [1] A cloth with long, soft pile.   [2] A thin, sheer cotton fabric.   [3] With spots or imperfections.
   [4] "For whosoever shall be ashamed of me and of my words, of him shall the Son of man be ashamed, when he shall come in his own glory," from Luke 9:26.
   [5] To be like the Apostles (who were fishermen) is common and ordinary, according to the "Gentle-women."

441*

This is my letter to the World
That never wrote to Me –
The simple News that Nature told –
With tender Majesty

Her Message is committed
To Hands I cannot see –
For love of Her – Sweet – countrymen –
Judge tenderly – of Me

1862?, 1890

449

I died for Beauty – but was scarce
Adjusted in the Tomb
When One who died for Truth, was lain
In an adjoining Room –

He questioned softly "Why I failed"?[1]
"For Beauty", I replied –
"And I – for Truth – Themself are One –
We Bretheren, are", He said –

And so, as Kinsmen, met a Night –
We talked between the Rooms –   10
Until the Moss had reached our lips –
And covered up – our names –

1862?, 1890

465

I heard a Fly buzz – when I died –
The Stillness in the Room
Was like the Stillness in the Air –
Between the Heaves of Storm –

The Eyes around – had wrung them dry –
And Breaths were gathering firm
For that last Onset – when the King
Be witnessed – in the Room –

---

* Although Thomas Wentworth Higginson (1823–1911) and Mabel Loomis Todd (1856–1932) inserted this poem just after the table of contents and before the selections in *Poems* (1890), there is no evidence that Dickinson thought of it as an introduction to her poetry. Higginson also published it as one of fourteen poems in an article he wrote for the *Christian Union* in September 1890.
[1] Died.

I willed my Keepsakes – Signed away
What portion of me be   10
Assignable – and then it was
There interposed a Fly –

With Blue – uncertain stumbling Buzz –
Between the light – and me –
And then the Windows failed – and then
I could not see to see –

                                                        1862?, 1896

511

If you were coming in the Fall,
I'd brush the Summer by
With half a smile, and half a spurn,
As Housewives do, a Fly.

If I could see you in a year,
I'd wind the months in balls –
And put them each in separate Drawers,
For fear the numbers fuse[1] –

If only Centuries, delayed,
I'd count them on my Hand,   10
Subtracting, till my fingers dropped
Into Van Dieman's Land.[2]

If certain, when this life was out –
That your's and mine, should be
I'd toss it yonder, like a Rind,
And take Eternity –

But, now, uncertain of the length
Of this, that is between,
It goads me, like the Goblin Bee –
That will not state – it's sting.   20

                                                        1862?, 1890

512

The Soul has Bandaged moments –
When too appalled to stir –
She feels some ghastly Fright come up
And stop to look at her –

---

[1] Would melt together.   [2] An early name for Tasmania.

Salute her – with long fingers –
Caress her freezing hair –
Sip, Goblin, from the very lips
The Lover – hovered – o'er –
Unworthy, that a thought so mean
Accost a Theme – so – fair –   10

The soul has moments of Escape –
When bursting all the doors –
She dances like a Bomb, abroad,
And swings upon the Hours,

As do the Bee – delirious borne –
Long Dungeoned from his Rose –
Touch Liberty – then know no more,
But Noon, and Paradise –

The Soul's retaken moments –
When, Felon led along,   20
With shackles on the plumed feet,
And staples, in the Song,

The Horror welcomes her, again,
These, are not brayed of Tongue –

                                          1862?, 1945

526

To hear an Oriole sing
May be a common thing –
Or only a divine.

It is not of the Bird
Who sings the same, unheard,
As unto Crowd –

The Fashion of the Ear
Attireth that it hear
In Dun,[1] or fair –

So whether it be Rune,[2]   10
Or whether it be none
Is of within.

The "Tune is in the Tree – "
The Skeptic – showeth me –
"No Sir! In Thee!"

                                          1862?, 1891

---

[1] A color of low brilliance and saturation.
[2] A character of the alphabet used by Teutonic peoples from approximately the third century A.D.

579

I had been hungry, all the Years –
My Noon had Come – to dine –
I trembling drew the Table near –
And touched the Curious Wine –

'Twas this on Tables I had seen –
When turning, hungry, Home
I looked in Windows, for the Wealth
I could not hope – for Mine –

I did not know the ample Bread –
'Twas so unlike the Crumb   10
The Birds and I, had often shared
In Nature's – Dining Room –

The Plenty hurt me – 'twas so new –
Myself felt ill – and odd –
As Berry – of a Mountain Bush –
Transplanted – to the Road –

Nor was I hungry – so I found
That Hunger – was a way
Of Persons outside Windows –
The Entering – takes away –   20

1862?, 1891

585

I like to see it lap the Miles –
And lick the Valleys up –
And stop to feed itself at Tanks –
And then – prodigious step

Around a Pile of Mountains –
And supercilious peer
In Shanties – by the sides of Roads –
And then a Quarry pare

To fit it's sides
And crawl between   10
Complaining all the while
In horrid – hooting stanza –
Then chase itself down Hill –

And neigh like Boanerges[1] –
Then – prompter than a Star

---

[1] "Sons of Thunder" (Greek): originally a term describing the active evangelizing of the Apostles John and James; here, any loud preacher or orator.

Stop – docile and omnipotent
At it's[2] own stable door –

1862?, 1891

636

The Way I read a Letter's – this –
'Tis first – I lock the Door –
And push it with my fingers – next –
For transport it be sure[1] –

And then I go the furthest off
To counteract a knock –
Then draw my little Letter forth
And slowly pick the lock[2] –

Then – glancing narrow, at the Wall –
And narrow at the floor   10
For firm Conviction of a Mouse
Not exorcised before –

Peruse how infinite I am
To no one that You – know –
And sigh for lack of Heaven – but not
The Heaven God bestow –

1862?, 1891

640

I cannot live with You –
It would be Life –
And Life is over there –
Behind the Shelf

The Sexton[1] keeps the Key to –
Putting up
Our Life – His Porcelain –
Like a Cup –

Discarded of the Housewife –
Quaint – or Broke –   10

---

[2] Dickinson consistently makes the error of using this contraction for a possessive.
[1] A line rich in ambiguity: on the most literal level, "to make sure the letter has been transported to her"; on an emotional level, "to be sure of the happiness contained inside."
[2] Open the letter very carefully.
[1] A church caretaker, bellringer, and gravedigger.

A newer Sevres[2] pleases –
Old Ones crack –

I could not die – with You –
For One must wait
To shut the Other's Gaze down –
You – could not –

And I – Could I stand by –
And see You – freeze –
Without my Right of Frost –
Death's privilege?   20

Nor could I rise – with You –
Because Your Face
Would put out Jesus' –
That New Grace

Glow plain – and foreign
On my homesick Eye –
Except that You than He
Shone closer by –

They'd judge Us – How –
For You – served Heaven[3] – You know,   30
Or sought to –
I could not –

Because You saturated Sight –
And I had no more Eyes
For sordid excellence
As Paradise

And were You lost, I would be –
Though My Name
Rang loudest
On the Heavenly fame –   40

And were You – saved –
And I – condemned to be
Where You were not –
That self – were Hell to Me –

So We must meet apart –
You there – I – here –
With just the Door ajar

---

[2] Fine porcelain china made in Sèvres, France.
[3] The poem supposedly registers Dickinson's feelings about Rev. Charles Wadsworth, who had moved to California.

That Oceans are – and Prayer –
And that White Sustenance –
Despair –   50

1862?, 1890

650

Pain – has an Element of Blank –
It cannot recollect
When it begun – or if there were
A time when it was not –

It has no Future – but itself –
It's Infinite contain[1]
It's Past – enlightened to perceive
New Periods – of Pain.

1862?, 1890

657

I dwell in Possibility –
A fairer House than Prose –
More numerous of Windows –
Superior – for Doors –

Of Chambers as the Cedars –
Impregnable of Eye[1] –
And for an Everlasting Roof
The Gambrels[2] of the Sky –

Of Visiters – the fairest –
For Occupation – This –   10
The spreading wide my narrow Hands
To gather Paradise –

1862?, 1929

712

Because I could not stop for Death –
He kindly stopped for me –

---

[1] To make this line more conventional, Thomas Wentworth Higginson (1823–1911) and Mabel Loomis Todd (1856–1932) altered it in *Poems* (1890) to "Its infinite realms contain."
[1] Impenetrable to the eye.   [2] Angled roofs.

The Carriage held but just Ourselves –
And Immortality.

We slowly drove – He knew no haste
And I had put away
My labor and my leisure too,
For His Civility –

We passed the School, where Children strove
At Recess – in the Ring –   10
We passed the Fields of Gazing Grain –
We passed the Setting Sun –

Or rather – He passed Us –
The Dews drew quivering and chill –
For only Gossamer, my Gown –
My Tippet – only Tulle[1] –

We paused before a House that seemed
A Swelling of the Ground –
The Roof was scarce'y visible –
The Cornice[2] – in the Ground –   20

Since then – 'tis Centuries – and yet
Feels shorter than the Day
I first surmised the Horses Heads
Were toward Eternity –

1863?, 1890

725

Where Thou art – that – is Home –
Cashmere – or Calvary[1] – the same –
Degree – or Shame –
I scarce esteem Location's Name –
So I may Come –

What Thou dost – is Delight –
Bondage as Play – be sweet –
Imprisonment – Content –
And Sentence – Sacrament –
Just We two – meet –   10

Where Thou art not – is Wo –
Tho' Bands of Spices – row –

---

[1] My cape or scarf, made only of a thin netlike fabric.   [2] Decorative molding just below a roof.
[1] Kashmir is a mountainous region adjacent to India, Pakistan, and Tibet; Calvary is the hill near Jerusalem where Christ was crucified. Being with her lover is so paramount that these places and everything else become the same to the speaker.

What Thou dost not – Despair –
Tho' Gabriel – praise me – Sir –

1863?, 1929

732

She rose to His Requirement – dropt
The Playthings of Her Life
To take the honorable Work
Of Woman, and of Wife –

If ought[1] She missed in Her new Day,
Of Amplitude, or Awe –
Or first Prospective – Or the Gold
In using, wear away,

It lay unmentioned – as the Sea
Develope Pearl, and Weed,   10
But only to Himself – be known
The Fathoms they abide[2] –

1863?, 1890

754

My Life had stood – a Loaded Gun –
In Corners – till a Day
The Owner passed – identified –
And carried Me away –

And now We roam in Sovreign Woods –
And now We hunt the Doe –
And every time I speak for Him –
The Mountains straight reply –

And do I smile, such cordial light
Upon the Valley glow –   10
It is as a Vesuvian face[1]
Had let it's pleasure through –

And when at Night – Our good Day done –
I guard My Master's Head –
'Tis better than the Eider-Duck's
Deep[2] Pillow – to have shared –

---

[1] Aught, anything.   [2] Only the sea knows how deep its creatures live.
[1] Capable of erupting like Italy's Mt. Vesuvius.   [2] Downy.

To foe of His – I'm deadly foe –
None stir the second time –
On whom I lay a Yellow Eye[3] –
Or an emphatic Thumb –   20

Though I than He – may longer live
He longer must – than I –
For I have but the power to kill,
Without – the power to die –

1863?, 1929

765

You constituted Time –
I deemed Eternity
A Revelation of Yourself –
'Twas therefore Deity

The Absolute – removed
The Relative away –
That I unto Himself adjust
My slow idolatry –

1863?, 1945

771

None can experience stint
Who Bounty – have not known –
The fact of Famine – could not be
Except for Fact of Corn –

Want – is a meagre Art
Acquired by Reverse –
The Poverty that was not Wealth –
Cannot be Indigence

1863?, 1945

997

Crumbling is not an instant's Act
A fundamental pause
Delapidation's processes
Are organized Decays.

---

[3] A metaphor for a hunter's deadly eye; similarly, an "emphatic Thumb" rubs things out.

'Tis first a Cobweb on the Soul
A Cuticle[1] of Dust
A Borer in the Axis[2]
An Elemental Rust –

Ruin is formal – Devils work
Consecutive and slow –   10
Fail in an instant, no man did
Slipping – is Crashe's law.[3]

1865?, 1945

1068

Further in Summer than the Birds
Pathetic from the Grass
A minor Nation celebrates
It's unobtrusive Mass.

No Ordinance[1] be seen
So gradual the Grace
A pensive Custom it becomes
Enlarging Loneliness.

Antiquest[2] felt at Noon
When August burning low   10
Arise this spectral Canticle[3]
Repose to typify

Remit as yet no Grace
No Furrow on the Glow
Yet a Druidic[4] Difference
Enhances Nature now

1866?, 1891

1072

Title divine – is mine!
The Wife – without the Sign!
Acute Degree – conferred on me –

---

[1] A thin, dead covering.   [2] Something that makes a small hole at the center.
[3] According to the critic Charles Anderson, Dickinson may have made up a person named Crashe, and thus "Crashe's law" (like Newton's law), to give mock authority to her point about "Crumbling" being a slow process. If so, "Crashe" is ironic for a process so prolonged and "formal."
[1] A prescribed practice that, in the context of "Mass" and "Grace," takes on the connotation of religious ritual.
[2] Most antique; in one version of the poem Dickinson had "antiquer."
[3] A song or hymn; a biblical song of praise.
[4] The Druids were pre-Christian, Celtic nature worshipers.

Empress of Calvary![1]
Royal – all but the Crown!
Betrothed – without the swoon
God sends us Women –
When you – hold – Garnet to Garnet –
Gold – to Gold –
Born – Bridalled – Shrouded –   10
In a Day –
"My Husband" – women say –
Stroking the Melody –
Is *this* – the way?

1862?, 1924

1078

The Bustle in a House
The Morning after Death
Is solemnest of industries
Enacted upon Earth –

The Sweeping up the Heart
And putting Love away
We shall not want to use again
Until Eternity.

1866?, 1890

1100*

The last Night that She lived
It was a Common Night
Except the Dying – this to Us
Made Nature different

We noticed smallest things –
Things overlooked before
By this great light upon our Minds
Italicized – as 'twere.

As We went out and in
Between Her final Room   10

---

[1] The hill near Jerusalem on which Christ was crucified. Dickinson evokes the idea of suffering in a situation that yields the closeness but not the fact of marriage.

* Written about the daughter of Mr. and Mrs. L. M. Hills, Laura Dickey, who died at her parents' home in Amherst on May 3, 1866. The Hills were the Dickinsons' neighbors.

And Rooms where Those to be alive
Tomorrow were, a Blame

That Others could exist
While She must finish quite
A Jealousy for Her arose
So nearly infinite –

We waited while She passed –
It was a narrow time –
Too jostled were Our Souls to speak
At length the notice came.   20

She mentioned, and forgot –
Then lightly as a Reed
Bent to the Water, struggled scarce –
Consented, and was dead –

And We – We placed the Hair –
And drew the Head erect –
And then as awful leisure was
Belief to regulate –

                                        1866?, 1890

1129

Tell all the Truth but tell it slant –
Success in Circuit lies
Too bright for our infirm Delight
The Truth's superb surprise
As Lightning to the Children eased
With explanation kind
The Truth must dazzle gradually
Or every man be blind –

                                        1868?, 1945

1331

Wonder – is not precisely Knowing
And not precisely Knowing not –
A beautiful but bleak condition
He has not lived who has not felt –

Suspense – is his maturer Sister –
Whether Adult Delight is Pain

Or of itself a new misgiving –
This is the Gnat that mangles men[1] –

1874?, 1945

1333

A little Madness in the Spring
Is wholesome even for the King,
But God be with the Clown –
Who ponders this tremendous scene –
This whole Experiment of Green –
As if it were his own!

1875?, 1914

1463

A Route of Evanescence[1]
With a revolving Wheel –
A Resonance of Emerald –
A Rush of Cochineal[2] –
And every Blossom on the Bush
Adjusts it's tumbled Head –
The mail from Tunis,[3] probably,
An easy Morning's Ride –

1879?, 1891

1540

As imperceptibly as Grief
The Summer lapsed away –
Too imperceptible at last
To seem like Perfidy[1] –
A Quietness distilled
As Twilight long begun,
Or Nature spending with herself
Sequestered Afternoon –
The Dusk drew earlier in –

[1] The tiny question or consideration that confuses human beings.
[1] Vanishing from sight. This poem describes a hummingbird.   [2] A red dye.   [3] A city in Tunisia.
[1] A violation of faith.

The Morning foreign shone –   10
A courteous, yet harrowing Grace,
As Guest, that would be gone –
And thus, without a Wing
Or service of a Keel[2]
Our Summer made her light escape
Into the Beautiful.

                                           1865 – 1882, 1891

1670

In Winter in my Room
I came upon a Worm
Pink lank and warm
But as he was a worm
And worms presume
Not quite with him at home
Secured him by a string
To something neighboring
And went along.
A Trifle afterward   10
A thing occurred
I'd not believe it if I heard
But state with creeping blood
A snake with mottles rare
Surveyed my chamber floor
In feature as the worm before
But ringed with power
The very string with which
I tied him – too
When he was mean and new   20
That string was there –

I shrank – "How fair you are"!
Propitiation's claw[1] –
"Afraid he hissed
Of me"?
"No cordiality" –
He fathomed me –
Then to a Rhythm *Slim*[2]
Secreted in his Form
As Patterns swim   30
Projected him.[3]

---

[2] Without the use of a ship.
[1] The above statement was meant to propitiate, or appease, the snake.   [2] Cunning, sly.
[3] He projected himself, glided toward me.

That time I flew
Both eyes his way
Lest he pursue
Nor ever ceased to run
Till in a distant Town
Towns on from mine
I set me down
This was a dream –

1914

1732

My life closed twice before its close;
It yet remains to see
If Immortality unveil
A third event to me,

So huge, so hopeless to conceive
As these that twice befel.
Parting is all we know of heaven,
And all we need of hell.

1896

1755

To make a prairie it takes a clover and one bee,
One clover, and a bee,
And revery.
The revery alone will do,
If bees are few.

1896

1760

Elysium[1] is as far as to
The very nearest Room
If in that Room a Friend await
Felicity or Doom –

What fortitude the Soul contains,
That it can so endure
The accent of a coming Foot –
The opening of a Door –

1882?, 1890

---

[1] According to Greek myth, the home of the virtuous after death; here, Paradise or happiness.

Emma Lazarus
(1849–1887)

Many readers who have never heard of Emma Lazarus are familiar with two lines of her most famous poem, "The New Colossus" (1883): "Give me your tired, your poor, / Your huddled masses yearning to breathe free." Inscribed on the base of the Statue of Liberty, this sonnet epitomizes the spirit of Lazarus's writing. Her most important work consistently supports the dignity of the poor and downtrodden. Specifically, her strongest and most passionate poetry protests the mistreatment of her people, the Jews.

Born to a cultured and cosmopolitan New York family in 1849, Lazarus showed in her teens a talent for languages, learning German, French, and Italian with enviable skill. She read voraciously the work of such English writers as Shakespeare, Keats, Shelley, and Tennyson and that of the Americans Ralph Waldo Emerson and Henry Wadsworth Longfellow. She soon began writing poetry and published her first book of verse, *Poems and Translations* (1860), when she was seventeen. Most of these early poems cultivate a popular romantic spirit, using conventional poetic forms and diction. Lazarus sent a copy of her first book to Emerson, and despite the flowery quality of some of the poems, he became a friend and occasional mentor. In 1871 she published a second volume, *Admetus and Other Poems,* which she dedicated to Emerson. She turned to fiction in 1874 with the novel *Alide,* based on the life of the German writer Johann Wolfgang von Goethe. Lazarus's interest in German romantic literature is also attested by her excellent translation of the *Poems and Ballads* of Heinrich Heine in 1881.

Lazarus's discovery of her need to write about Jewish themes came about when she became indignantly aware of the Russian pogroms of the early 1880s and the persecution of Jews in Europe. The critic E. C. Stedman helped Lazarus discover her voice at this time by urging her to write about her Jewish heritage. Once she realized the extent of anti-Semitic purges in Germany and Russia, she became a poet with a sacred cause and wrote both poetry and prose about the injustices meted out to her people. An advocate of the establishment of a Jewish state in Palestine, she organized relief work for the persecuted Jews. *Songs of a Semite,* published in 1882, reflects Lazarus's Jewish themes in poems such as "The Banner of the Jew" and in the verse drama "The Dance to Death," which is based on the hysterical accusation that Jews had poisoned wells and brought on the Black Death in Thuringia, in central Germany, during the twelfth century.

Although she wrote eloquently about the mistreatment of Jews, Lazarus worked with other subjects and forms as well. Not only did she translate the work of Heine but also that of the German dramatist and poet Friedrich von Schiller, the French writers Victor Hugo and Alexandre Dumas père, and several medieval Hebrew poets. She also wrote essays on American writers and on socialism. A few months before her death in 1887, she published "By the Waters of Babylon," a series of prose poems, in the *Century Illustrated Monthly Magazine.* In short, Lazarus's work reflects the broad interests of an intelligent student of languages and of history who found her most powerful voice in championing her own rich heritage.

Suggested Readings: *Songs of a Semite,* 1882, rpt. 1966. *Poems,* 1889. H. E. Jacobs, *The World of Emma Lazarus,* 1949. E. Merriam, *Emma Lazarus: Woman With a Torch,* 1956. C. Angoff, *Emma Lazarus: Poet, Jewish Activist, Pioneer Zionist,* 1979. D. Vogel, *Emma Lazarus,* 1980.

Text Used: "In the Jewish Synagogue at Newport": *Emma Lazarus: Selections From Her Poetry and Prose,* ed. M. U. Schappes, 1967. "The New Colossus": *The Poems of Emma Lazarus,* Vol. I, 1888. "1492": *The Poems of Emma Lazarus,* Vol. II, 1888.

IN THE JEWISH SYNAGOGUE AT NEWPORT*

Here, where the noises of the busy town,
   The ocean's plunge and roar can enter not,
We stand and gaze around with tearful awe,
   And muse upon the consecrated spot.

No signs of life are here: the very prayers
   Inscribed around are in a language dead;[1]
The light of the "perpetual lamp" is spent
   That an undying radiance was to shed.

What prayers were in this temple offered up,
   Wrung from sad hearts that knew no joy on earth,   10
By these lone exiles of a thousand years,
   From the fair sunrise land that gave them birth!

Now as we gaze, in this new world of light,
   Upon this relic of the days of old,
The present vanishes, and tropic bloom
   And Eastern towns and temples we behold.

Again we see the patriarch with his flocks,
   The purple seas, the hot blue sky o'erhead,
The slaves of Egypt,—omens, mysteries,—
   Dark fleeing hosts by flaming angels led.   20

A wondrous light upon a sky-kissed mount,
   A man[2] who reads Jehovah's written law,
'Midst blinding glory and effulgence rare,
   Unto a people prone with reverent awe.

The pride of luxury's barbaric pomp,
   In the rich court of royal Solomon[3]—
Alas! we wake: one scene alone remains,—
   The exiles by the streams of Babylon.[4]

Our softened voices send us back again
   But mournful echoes through the empty hall;   30
Our footsteps have a strange, unnatural sound,
   And with unwonted gentleness they fall.

The weary ones, the sad, the suffering,
   All found their comfort in the holy place,
And children's gladness and men's gratitude
   Took voice and mingled in the chant of praise.

---

* First published in *Poems and Translations* (1867). The poem has interesting similarities to "The Jewish Cemetery at Newport" (1854), by Henry Wadsworth Longfellow, a poet Lazarus admired.
[1] Hebrew.   [2] Moses.
[3] The proverbial wise king of ancient Israel, son and successor of King David.
[4] An ancient city of Mesopotamia, on the Euphrates River, where the Hebrews were exiled.

The funeral and the marriage, now, alas!
   We know not which is sadder to recall;
For youth and happiness have followed age,
   And green grass lieth gently over all.   40

And still the sacred shrine is holy yet,
   With its lone floors where reverent feet once trod.
Take off your shoes as by the burning bush,
   Before the mystery of death and God.

            1867

THE NEW COLOSSUS*

Not like the brazen giant of Greek fame,[1]
With conquering limbs astride from land to land;
Here at our sea-washed, sunset gates shall stand
A mighty woman with a torch, whose flame
Is the imprisoned lightning, and her name
Mother of Exiles. From her beacon-hand
Glows world-wide welcome; her mild eyes command
The air-bridged harbor that twin cities[2] frame.
"Keep, ancient lands, your storied pomp!" cries she
With silent lips. "Give me your tired, your poor,   10
Your huddled masses yearning to breathe free,
The wretched refuse of your teeming shore.
Send these, the homeless, tempest-tost to me,
I lift my lamp beside the golden door!"

            1883

1492

Thou two-faced year,[1] Mother of Change and Fate,
Didst weep when Spain cast forth with flaming sword,
The children of the prophets of the Lord,
Prince, priest, and people, spurned by zealot hate.
Hounded from sea to sea, from state to state,

---

* This sonnet is inscribed on the base of the Statue of Liberty in New York harbor. The "old" Colossus, the Colossus of Rhodes, was a gigantic statue of the Greek god Apollo erected at the entrance to the harbor at Rhodes about 280 B.C. to celebrate a military victory.

[1] In these opening lines Lazarus establishes the difference between the Colossus at Rhodes and the Statue of Liberty, the "new" Colossus, designed by the French sculptor Frederic Auguste Bartholdi (1834–1904) and originally named "Liberty Enlightening the World." It was presented to the United States by the Franco-American Union to commemorate the American Revolution; formally dedicated in 1886, it became a national monument in 1924.

[2] The closest cities to Liberty Island, where the statue is located, are New York City (specifically Brooklyn), on the New York side, and Jersey City, on the New Jersey side.

[1] The "two-faced" year 1492 wept at the persecution of Jews in Spain, then smiled at the unveiling of a "virgin world," America, in which ancient prejudice had no reality.

> The West refused them, and the East abhorred.
> No anchorage the known world could afford,
> Close-locked was every port, barred every gate.
> Then smiling, thou unveil'dst, O two-faced year,
> A virgin world where doors of sunset part,   10
> Saying, "Ho, all who weary, enter here!
> There falls each ancient barrier that the art
> Of race or creed or rank devised, to rear
> Grim bulwarked hatred between heart and heart!"

1883

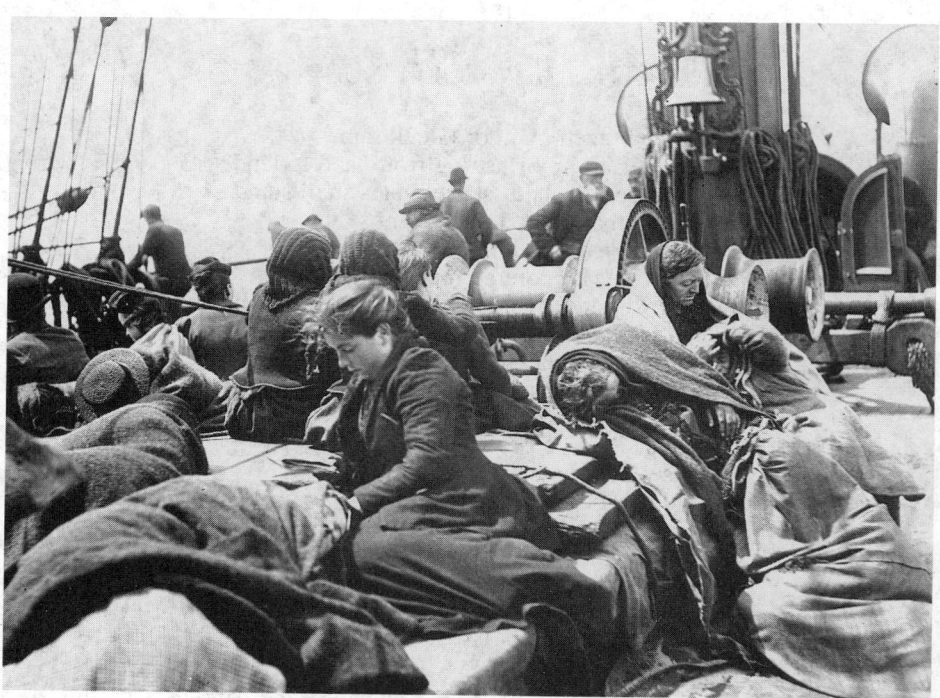

Typically fleeing near-starvation in Europe, immigrants spent their last funds to book passage on the decks of ships like the S.S. Pennland, *photographed in 1893.*

Paul Laurence Dunbar

(1872–1906)

Paul Laurence Dunbar was born in Dayton, Ohio, in 1872 to parents who had been slaves in Kentucky. The only African American in his class, he excelled as a student in the Dayton public schools and went on to become the editor of his high school student magazine and to write the school song for his graduation. After finishing high school, however, Dunbar found his opportunities severely limited. Financially unable to attend college, he worked at a number of menial positions. He became an elevator operator for several months, then took a temporary job, arranged for him by Frederick Douglass, in the Haiti building at the 1894 Chicago World's Fair. During this period of instability Dunbar began to write poetry.

Oak and Ivy (1893) and *Majors and Minors* (1895)—both published at his own expense—were Dunbar's first collections of verse. William Dean Howells's favorable full-page review of *Majors and Minors* in *Harper's Weekly* gave Dunbar sudden recognition and launched his career as a writer. He became very popular, in demand for readings of his work as well as for lectures. In 1896 he published *Lyrics of Lowly Life,* a compilation of the best pieces from his first two books along with some newer poems. This collection helped to secure his growing reputation, and he traveled as far as England in 1897 to read his poetry. Upon Dunbar's return from England in 1898, he married Alice Ruth Moore and accepted a position as an assistant in the Library of Congress.

Unfortunately, the hectic lifestyle that accompanied Dunbar's success took its toll on the young writer. By 1899 he had contracted tuberculosis; he spent one winter in Colorado in the hope that his health would improve, but it began to fail rapidly. No longer able to make public appearances, he returned to Dayton and made a stubborn effort to go on writing. His marriage also deteriorated at this time; after only four years Dunbar and his wife separated. He died at the age of thirty-three in 1906.

Although Dunbar has achieved some recognition for his work in standard, or "literary," English (a recognition he definitely wanted), he has been more highly acclaimed for his dialect verse. He was popular during a time when literary regionalism and the use of dialect were much in fashion, and his acquaintance with African-American speech patterns and customs helped him to depict aspects of African-American life with a grace that appealed to many readers. Because such writers as Thomas Nelson Page, Robert Burns, and James Whitcomb Riley influenced Dunbar's work, some of his poetry has a sentimental flavor. Dunbar also wrote some conventional short fiction and four novels, the most interesting of which, *The Sport of the Gods* (1902), concerns a southern African-American family in Harlem. His primary gift, however, was lyric, not narrative: in the rhythms of his dialect poems and in the more intense rhetoric of his sonnets is heard a voice both playful and serious, both popular and filled with the anguish of our history.

Suggested Readings: *Oak and Ivy,* 1893. *Lyrics of Lowly Life,* 1896. *The Uncalled: A Novel,* 1898, rpt. 1972. *Lyrics of the Hearthside,* 1899, rpt. 1988. *Complete Poems,* 1980. L. K. Wiggins, *The Life and Works of Paul Laurence Dunbar,* 1907, rpt. 1971. A. D. Nelson, *Paul Laurence Dunbar: Poet Laureate of the Negro Race,* 1914. V. Lawson, *Dunbar Critically Examined,* 1941. V. Cunningham, *Paul Laurence Dunbar and His Song,* 1947. A. Gayle, Jr., *Oak and Ivy: A Biography of Paul Laurence Dunbar,* 1971. J. Martin, ed., *A Singer in the Rain: Reinterpretations of Paul Laurence Dunbar,* 1975. P. Revell, *Paul Laurence Dunbar,* 1979.

Text Used: *The Complete Poems of Paul Laurence Dunbar,* 1913.

WE WEAR THE MASK*

We wear the mask that grins and lies,
It hides our cheeks and shades our eyes,—
This debt we pay to human guile;

* Included in *Lyrics of Lowly Life* (1896).

With torn and bleeding hearts we smile,
And mouth with myriad subtleties.

Why should the world be overwise,
In counting all our tears and sighs?
Nay, let them only see us, while
   We wear the mask.

We smile, but, O great Christ, our cries   10
To thee from tortured souls arise.
We sing, but oh the clay is vile
Beneath our feet, and long the mile;
But let the world dream otherwise,
   We wear the mask!

1896

HARRIET BEECHER STOWE*

She told the story,[1] and the whole world wept
   At wrongs and cruelties it had not known
   But for this fearless woman's voice alone.
She spoke to consciences that long had slept:
Her message, Freedom's clear reveille, swept
   From heedless hovel to complacent throne.
   Command and prophecy were in the tone
And from its sheath the sword of justice leapt.
Around two peoples swelled a fiery wave,
   But both came forth transfigured from the flame.   10
Blest be the hand that dared be strong to save,
   And blest be she who in our weakness came—
Prophet and priestess! At one stroke she gave
   A race to freedom and herself to fame.

1899

DOUGLASS†

Ah, Douglass, we have fall'n on evil days,
   Such days as thou, not even thou didst know,
   When thee, the eyes of that harsh long ago

---

* Included in *Lyrics of the Hearthside* (1899); Stowe (1811–1896) was influenced by abolitionists at the theological seminary run by her father, Lyman Beecher (1775–1863).

[1] *Uncle Tom's Cabin: Or, Life Among the Lowly* (1852), Stowe's famous novel that sold more than 300,000 copies in its first year of publication and kindled widespread opposition to slavery in the United States.

† Included in *Lyrics of Love and Laughter* (1903); Frederick Douglass (1818–1895), who escaped from slavery in 1838 and thereafter lectured to antislavery societies. His autobiographical *Narrative of the Life of Frederick Douglass* (1845) is an eloquent account of his experiences as a slave and of his escape to the North.

Saw, salient, at the cross of devious ways,
And all the country heard thee with amaze.
    Not ended then, the passionate ebb and flow,
    The awful tide that battled to and fro;
We ride amid a tempest of dispraise.

Now, when the waves of swift dissension swarm,
    And Honor, the strong pilot, lieth stark,   10
Oh, for thy voice high-sounding o'er the storm,
    For thy strong arm to guide the shivering bark,
The blast-defying power of thy form,
    To give us comfort through the lonely dark.

1903

BOOKER T. WASHINGTON*

The word is writ that he who runs may read.
What is the passing breath of earthly fame?
But to snatch glory from the hands of blame—
That is to be, to live, to strive indeed.
A poor Virginia cabin gave the seed,
And from its dark and lowly door there came
A peer of princes in the world's acclaim,
A master spirit for the nation's need.
Strong, silent, purposeful beyond his kind,
    The mark of rugged force on brow and lip,   10
Straight on he goes, nor turns to look behind
    Where hot the hounds come baying at his hip;
With one idea foremost in his mind,
    Like the keen prow of some on-forging ship.

1903

LATE 19TH-CENTURY NONFICTION PROSE

At the time of the American Revolution nonfiction prose served primarily a political purpose. In the first half of the nineteenth century it functioned in the climate of an American romanticism to assert the significance of the democratic self. And in the late nineteenth century it evolved again in style and substance to express the situation of different groups within the nation—African Americans striving to define their freedom, immigrants confronting the issue of identity in a new land, and others exploring the resources of journalism, literary theory, travel writing, and

---

* Included in *Lyrics of Love and Laugher* (1903); Washington (1856–1915), an African-American educational leader who was hailed by many, black and white, in the United States. He continued his work despite criticism by those who disapproved of his position on the separation of the races. His books include an autobiography, *Up From Slavery* (1901).

historical inquiry. The genre of nonfiction prose remained vibrant precisely because it was so changeable in form, so responsive to personal and social issues.

During the final decades of the nineteenth century, substantial contributions to the genre were made in the area of autobiography. Earlier writers such as Mary Rowlandson, Benjamin Franklin, Harriet Jacobs, and Frederick Douglass had used forms of autobiography to illustrate their travails or to offer to the public their personal visions of Americanness. The autobiographical impulse continued unabated as the nineteenth century drew to a close. In different ways William Dean Howells, Henry James, and Mark Twain described their lives in volumes that remain of great importance to students of their work; yet, despite their manifest narrative skills, none of these writers fashioned autobiographies with the social and historical significance of Booker T. Washington's *Up From Slavery* (1901), W. E. B. Du Bois's *The Souls of Black Folk* (1903), or Henry Adams's *The Education of Henry Adams* (1907).

In *Up From Slavery* the acclaimed educator Washington encouraged members of his own race and soothed nervous white readers with the story of his Horatio Alger-like rise to success. By telling so optimistic a story, however, excusing white cruelty that he knew first-hand, encouraging blacks to take up practical and vocational training, and celebrating the virtues of hard work and selflessness, Washington (as he was aware) drew criticism for what seemed a conciliatory vision. Du Bois, for one, advocated an alternative, more assertive role for African Americans with his contributions to the founding of the National Association for the Advancement of Colored People, his work as editor of *The Crisis* magazine, and his collection of essays and meditations, *The Souls of Black Folk*. With a quiet audacity that enlarges our sense of what autobiography can be, that prophetic book reaches beyond the story of an individual life to offer the collective story of a race articulated by a writer who (as he says) is "bone of the bone and flesh of the flesh" of those for whom he speaks.

The use of an unconventional narrative technique likewise distinguishes *The Education of Henry Adams*. Adams, a historian and direct descendant of two of America's early presidents, intended his autobiography for selected friends only. Privately printed in 1907, it was published for the public at large in 1918, after Adams's death. By choosing to write of himself in the third person (a technique Norman Mailer would later adopt in such works as *The Armies of the Night* [1968]), Adams managed to distance himself from his own experience. The perspective he adopted allowed him at least implicitly to criticize the romantic insistence on the self that had informed the nonfiction work of his predecessors. It also allowed him to pass over portions of his life that he wished not to discuss—his wife's suicide in 1885, for example, an event with lasting repercussions that resulted in his "posthumous existence" and introduced a despondent tone to *The Education*. Adams's preoccupation with the impersonal forces of the modern world and with the superior virtues of centuries past are vividly documented in his autobiography. In a nation that was reeling from rapid change and in part recoiling from the sheer numbers of new immigrants, his passion for order along with his undeniable anti-Semitism must have appealed to some readers. The lasting reputation of *The Education*, however, is a consequence of a narrative voice that is at

The grandeur of the buildings and monuments of The World's Columbian Exposition, Chicago, 1893 (shown in this 1894 painting by Theodore Robinson), demonstrated America's technological and industrial innovations and its new wealth and power.

once nostalgic and intelligent, scrupulous in its search for values in history, and prescient in its ability to identify forces that have dominated life in the twentieth century.

As a tidal wave of immigration brought millions to America's shores in the 1880s and 1890s, Michel-Guillaume Jean de Crèvecoeur's old question, "What is an American?" took on a new and sometimes heated relevance. The subject of immigration was debated in magazines; it was even considered by the U.S. Congress. No one handled the subject with greater enthusiasm and passion than did immigrants themselves, men and women who used autobiographical forms to point to their distinctive place in the American mainstream. Such figures as the Danish-born journalist Jacob Riis and the Polish-born writer Mary Antin, both nineteenth-century arrivals who lived well into the twentieth century, described in memorable self-portraits immigrant life and the achievement of becoming "American": Riis in *The Making of an American* (1901) and Antin in *The Promised Land* (1912). The latter is an extended version of *From Plotzk to Boston*, which Antin wrote in Yiddish as a young girl and translated into English for publication in 1899.

=CONTEXTS=

The Birth of Labor Unions

Between 1870 and 1890 America experienced a wave of industrial growth. Older industries such as beef packing and garment making were expanding; giant industries such as steel making and oil refining were developing due to technological inventions and new techniques. The resulting rapid rise of urban industrial centers across America occurred without systematic planning or control. During this chaotic period, as the populations of America's cities doubled (or tripled), Americans were faced with the new urban problems of fire protection, garbage collection, waste elimination, street paving, clean water supplies, and even organized crime. The American city, celebrated by America's great writers before the Civil War, was now descried by them in its commercial greed and industrial heartlessness as a force of anticivilization.

New ways of running factories and managing offices (corporations, trusts, holding companies, and monopolies among them) were started, and the trend toward "bigness" in business was born. As factories grew, communication between owners and workers stopped: employment conditions worsened, and the need for organized labor arose. By 1884, worsening factory conditions had caused over seven hundred thousand frustrated workers to join the Knights of Labor, then the most important labor union. Before the Civil War three out of five Americans worked on a farm; by 1880 more worked in factories than in farms; after 1880 immigrants from eastern and southern Europe (who so needed work that they accepted low wages and long hours) displaced many Americans from their factory jobs. For the first time, workers in America faced long bouts of unemployment. In an April 1885 editorial published in the *North American Review,* Terence V. Powderly (1849–1924), a leading spokesman for the Knights of Labor and champion of the eight-hour workday, shows why labor unions were needed:

The Army of the Discontented

. . . When the President of the United States issued his Thanksgiving proclamation in 1884, there were millions of men and women in want of bread, notwithstanding "the abundant harvests and continued prosperity which God hath vouchsafed to this nation," and the cry, not of thanksgiving, went up from millions of farmers of "Too much wheat!" Doubting as to the exact meaning of the Creator in growing so much wheat, they invoked the aid of such institutions as the Chicago Board of Trade, in the hope of thwarting the will of God by cornering wheat. These men invoked blessings on their Thanksgiving dinners, and thanked God for the turkey, while they hoarded the wheat away from those who asked for bread.

Give men shorter hours in which to labor, and you give them more time to study and learn why bread is so scarce while wheat is so plenty. . . .

Terence V. Powderly, 1885

While immigrants explored the difficult experience of coming to a new home, a number of prominent American writers described the fashionable experience of visiting Europe in the decades following the Civil War. Among Mark Twain's numerous books of travels, *The Innocents Abroad* (1869) stands out for its irreverent (and self-deprecating) account of a journey to Europe and the Middle East. His *A Tramp Abroad* (1880) and *Following the Equator* (1897) are erratic in form and lumpy with detail; their episodes of genuine humor tend to give way to observations that seem strained and grim. Nonetheless, these books do suggest that the market for travel à la Twain remained steady. William Dean Howells had the opportunity to gather material for *Venetian Life* (1866) and *Italian Journeys* (1867), volumes richly appreciative of art and culture, during his four years at the U.S. consulate in Venice in the early 1860s. Henry James's travel writing includes the accomplished sketches of Italy, France, and England that he collected in *Portraits of Places* (1883), the cosmopolitan perspectives of *Essays in London and Elsewhere* (1893), and the revealing (and self-revelatory) assessments of American society that make up *The American Scene* (1907), written after his many years of residence in England.

To note that Howells and James also wrote impressive volumes of literary criticism and biography—*Criticism and Fiction* (1891) and *My Mark Twain* (1910) by Howells, for example; *Hawthorne* (1879) and *Partial Portraits* (1888) by James—is to understand that these novelists contributed significantly to the achievement of nonfiction prose. A series of essays written at the turn of the century made another novelist, Frank Norris, a leading exponent of naturalism. In "A Plea for Romantic Fiction" (1901), Norris admits that realism can be "respectable as a church and proper as a deacon," such as "the novels of Mr. Howells"; but his preference was for fiction that plumbs the extraordinary secrets of the heart and soul. That kind of fiction Norris labels "Romance" or, in its contemporary form, "naturalism." Despite his reservations about realism, Norris echoed the appreciation of Howells sounded by many writers and critics. During his years of writing the "Editor's Study" column in *Harper's Monthly,* Howells promoted the cause of various types of fiction: he praised the work of established European realists and championed that of new American writers, among them Stephen Crane, Hamlin Garland, Sarah Orne Jewett, Paul Laurence Dunbar, and Abraham Cahan.

Both Howells and Twain came to their literary endeavors by way of newspaper work. The anecdotal quality of a volume such as Howells's *Literary Friends and Acquaintances* (1900) suggests the manner in which reporting and editorial-writing affected the pace and style of his writing. With Twain the case is even more obvious. In *Roughing It* (1872), for example, Twain interspersed the realistic account of his trip westward with set pieces similar to the humorous feature articles that often appeared in the newspapers of the time (a straightforward tribute to pony express riders, the account of a buffalo that climbed a tree, the story of Jim Blaine's grandfather's ram). What results is a book that is realistic yet hyperbolic, fact spiced with the oral traditions of the tall tale.

In his own distinctive way, Stephen Crane extended the range of journalism in the 1890s to achieve a remarkable blending of forms. Crane wrote *The Red Badge of Courage* (1895), his classic account of a youth maturing in the context of the Civil War, at a time when he had not seen war; yet, as a consequence of that novel and his previous experience in journalism, he became a correspondent in the Greco-Turkish war and the Spanish-American War in Cuba in the late 1890s. His war dispatches, like his other newspaper stories, bring an impressionistic prose to bear on the material he reports. Whether Crane is writing of a night spent with the homeless men of the Bowery in New York City ("An Experiment in Misery" [1894]), giving his personal account of survival in a lifeboat between Cuba and Florida ("Stephen Crane's Own Story" [1897]), or supplying an explanation of how a child may have been brainwashed after witnessing a murder ("An Illusion in Red and White" [1900]), his laconic prose, ironic posture, and introduction of dialogue into newspaper articles (as these were) leads to a point at which fact and fiction become indistinguishable parts of a new form, immersed in the event. Crane's journalistic prose courts a world in which language must take on new burdens because reality, increasingly bizarre, threatens to outstrip the imagination; his work anticipates such varied twentieth-century experiments in form as Truman Capote's *In Cold Blood* (1966), subtitled "A Non-Fiction Novel," and Carl Bernstein and Bob Woodward's *All the President's Men* (1974). Crane's achievement, along with that of Du Bois, Adams, Antin, and others, demonstrates that the essential thrust of nonfiction prose in the late nineteenth century was to forge an awareness of what America had become, and out of that awareness to point unblinkingly to the problems and opportunities that would be part of a new century.

Henry Adams
(1838–1918)

The achievement of Henry Adams is inseparable from his personal and family history, making it appropriate that his reputation should rest largely on his searching and ironic autobiography, *The Education of Henry Adams* (1907). Henry Brooks Adams was born in 1838 in Boston and raised there and in nearby Quincy. Two strains of American culture were available to young Henry: one, the heritage of public service embodied by his great-grandfather John Adams (second president of the United States), his grandfather John Quincy Adams (sixth president of the United States), and his father, the diplomat Charles Francis Adams; another, the path of State Street commerce set forth by his wealthy maternal grandfather. The latter path Adams rejected when he was a boy of age ten. The issue at stake in that choice—the divorce of practical power and social ideals—would lead Adams through a lifetime of study.

After graduating from Harvard University in 1858, Adams traveled to Berlin to study law but left his studies to make a grand tour of Europe, with the help of the Adams name. Back in the United States he became his father's private secretary, first in Washington and then in England during the Civil War. With some misgivings, he returned to Harvard in 1870 to teach medieval history. Although Adams was not a trained medievalist and later deprecated his teaching, his courses were well received, and he remained at Harvard for seven years. During this period he accepted the editorship of the *North American Review* and, in perceptive essays that had little tangible effect, criticized political corruption and individual abuses of wealth.

In 1877 Adams moved to Washington, D.C., to him the center of power, and directed his interest in national politics into his work in American history. Not only does his *Docu-*

ments Relating to New England Federalism, 1800–1815 (1877) vindicate the principled politics of John Quincy Adams; his biography *The Life of Albert Gallatin* (1879) shows Gallatin, a contemporary of John Adams and Thomas Jefferson, to be, like them, an embodiment of eighteenth-century integrity. Adams next began work on the nine-volume *History of the United States of America During the Administrations of Thomas Jefferson and James Madison* (1889–1891). As he had done before, he relied on historical documents to tell the story, attempting to write "scientific" history by stating the facts severely and with minimal comment, "in such order as seemed rigorously consequent," as he put it in *The Education.* The result, a major study of the period, remains valuable today.

In 1872 Adams had married Marian Hooper, the daughter of a wealthy Boston surgeon. She and Adams became prominent members of Washington society, forming close ties with the diplomat John Hay and the geologist Clarence King and friendships with such well-known persons as Henry James, who sketched them as the Bonnycastles in "Pandora" (1884). The protagonists of Adams's two novels may have been modeled on his wife, although many readers detect as much of Henry Adams as of Marian Adams in the characters. In *Democracy* (1880), an anonymously written satire of political corruption, Madeline Lee goes to Washington to find the springs of power in government but discovers only low conniving in high places. In *Esther* (1884), published under the pseudonym Frances Snow Compton, young Esther Dudley is sent on a search for a principle of order that will give meaning and purpose to life. Esther owes her name to the protagonist of Nathaniel Hawthorne's tale "Old Esther Dudley" (1839), about a forlorn American Loyalist who believes that "Heaven's cause and the King's are one." Adams's Esther, searching for an analogous connection in a scientific age, finds nothing that can fulfill both her mind and her heart.

Marian Adams committed suicide in December 1885—undoubtedly depressed over the death of her father and perhaps driven by her position as a thoughtful woman fettered by masculine society. Adams commissioned a memorial from a friend, the sculptor Augustus Saint-Gaudens, and referred to the enigmatic figure as "The Peace of God." (From another perspective, Mark Twain called it "Grief.") Marian's suicide shattered Adams's life. He finished the projects that he had begun in her lifetime and withdrew with the feeling that life was over, that, according to *The Education,* "the rest mattered so little."

Yet, it is the "rest" of Adams's work that has come to matter so much. In 1894 he was elected president of the American Historical Association; his inaugural address, "The Tendency of History," articulated the "dynamic theory of history" that would inform his best work, most notably *Mont-Saint-Michel and Chartres* (1904) and *The Education.* In these studies Adams undertakes to determine the place of human beings as a force in a world of forces. Force, for Adams, is both philosophical and physical, mental and material: "anything that does, or helps to do work," be it man, the sun, or a mathematical point, he asserts in *The Education.* Adams now pursued knowledge from different premises than fact and sequence. Starting from "the point of history when man held the highest idea of himself as a unit in a unified universe" (the thirteenth century, as manifested in "Amiens Cathedral and the works of Thomas Aquinas"), Adams proposed to "measure motion down to his own time, without assuming anything as true or untrue, except relation."

Mont-Saint-Michel and Chartres is Adams's compelling "Study of Thirteenth-Century Unity" in the great cathedrals of northwestern France. Here disparate forces—wealth and knowledge, skill and faith—had been marshalled by the power of the Virgin to attract the mind: with arches and buttresses human beings had elevated stone, dissipated strain, and opened room for art and instruction. In *The Education,* subtitled "A Study of Twentieth-Century Multiplicity," Adams traces the proliferation of forces in the modern world; such things as democracy, capitalism, electricity, and radium attract the mind, he feels, but to no discernible purpose. Alleging that his own education had failed to prepare him to be a

Extraordinary in size and power, late nineteenth-century industrial machines were objects of awe and secular worship. "The Dynamo and the Virgin" is based on the machines Henry Adams saw at the 1900 Universal Exposition in Paris.

force among twentieth-century forces, Adams nevertheless tenuously hoped that education is still possible, that the mind can respond with a necessary "jump." *The Education* was first published in a 1907 private edition of one hundred copies, which a few privileged readers were to correct and return. Not until October 1918, six months after Adams's death, did the book reach the public. It was awarded a Pulitzer Prize in 1919.

Suggested Readings: *The Education of Henry Adams,* ed. E. Samuels, 1973. *The Letters of Henry Adams,* 6 vols., ed. J. C. Levenson et al., 1982–1988. *Novels, Mont-Saint-Michel, The Education,* 1983. E. Samuels, *The Young Henry Adams,* 1948. W. H. Jordy, *Henry Adams: Scientific Historian,* 1952. J. C. Levenson, *The Mind and Art of Henry Adams,* 1957. E. Samuels, *Henry Adams: The Middle Years,* 1958. G. Hochfield, *Henry Adams: An Introduction and Interpretation,* 1962. E. Samuels, *Henry Adams: The Major Phase,* 1964. J. C. Rowe, *Henry Adams and Henry James: The Emergence of a Modern Consciousness,* 1976. E. N. Harbert, *The Force So Much Closer Home: Henry Adams and the Adams Family,* 1977. R. P. Blackmur, *Henry Adams,* 1980. W. Dusinberre, *Henry Adams: The Myth of Failure,* 1980. J. F. Byrnes, *The Virgin of Chartres: An Intellectual and Psychological History of Henry Adams,* 1981. W. Wasserstrom, *The Ironies of Progress,* 1984. C. Tichi, "Dynamo, Virgin, Engineer," in *Shifting Gears: Technology, Literature, Culture in Modernist America,* 1987.

Text Used: *The Education of Henry Adams: An Autobiography,* 1927.

from THE EDUCATION OF HENRY ADAMS*

Chapter XXV: The Dynamo and the Virgin (1900)[1]

Until the Great Exposition of 1900 closed its doors in November,[2] Adams haunted it, aching to absorb knowledge, and helpless to find it. He would have liked to know how much of it could have been grasped by the best-informed man in the world. While he was thus meditating chaos, Langley[3] came by, and showed it to him. At Langley's behest, the Exhibition dropped its superfluous rags and stripped itself to the skin, for Langley knew what to study, and why, and how; while Adams might as well have stood outside in the night, staring at the Milky Way. Yet Langley said nothing new, and taught nothing that one might not have learned from Lord Bacon, three hundred years before; but though one should have known the "Advancement of Science" as well as one knew the "Comedy of Errors,"[4] the literary knowledge counted for nothing until some teacher should show how to apply it. Bacon took a vast deal of trouble in teaching King James I[5] and his subjects, American or other, towards the year 1620, that true science was the development or economy of forces; yet an elderly American in 1900 knew neither the formula nor the forces; or even so much as to say to himself that his historical business in the Exposition concerned only the economies or developments of force since 1893, when he began the study at Chicago.[6]

Nothing in education is so astonishing as the amount of ignorance it accumulates in the form of inert facts. Adams had looked at most of the accumulations of art in the storehouses called Art Museums; yet he did not know how to look at the art exhibits of 1900. He had studied Karl Marx[7] and his doctrines of history with profound attention, yet he could not apply them at Paris. Langley, with the ease of a great master of experiment, threw out of the field every exhibit that did not reveal a new application of force, and naturally threw out, to begin with, almost the whole art exhibit. Equally, he ignored almost the whole industrial exhibit. He led his pupil directly to the forces. His chief interest was in new motors to make his airship feasible, and he taught Adams the astonishing complexities of the new

---

* Adams assesses the contemporary world through selected facts from his own life and study, although he insistently distances personal experience by writing of himself in the third person.

[1] Adams's attempt to find order and value in the present as well as in the past leads him to contemplate the development of impersonal "forces" in the modern world; these he juxtaposes with the harmony of previous centuries and other cultures, once experienced as "force," now regarded as symbol. Here, the "Dynamo" represents the forces of the modern world, the "Virgin" that of a world gone by.

[2] The Universal Exposition, or World's Fair, held in Paris from April to November 1900.

[3] Samuel Pierpont Langley (1834–1906), an American scientist, inventor of the bolometer for recording variations in solar radiation, founder of the Smithsonian Astrophysical Observatory (1890), and designer of the first airplane to fly successfully (1896).

[4] Actually, *The Advancement of Learning* (1605), by the English natural philosopher Sir Francis Bacon (1561–1626); an early Shakespearean comedy.

[5] James I (1566–1625) was king of England from 1603 to 1625.

[6] The Columbian Exposition held at Chicago in 1893; in Ch. XXII of *The Education*, Adams tells how the exhibits kindled his interest in the "economy of forces."

[7] Marx (1818–1883), a German social philosopher, founder (with Friedrich Engels) of modern socialism and communism, and author of *Das Kapital* (3 vols., 1867–1894), in which he uses the concept of dialectical materialism to analyze economic and social history.

Daimler[8] motor, and of the automobile, which, since 1893, had become a nightmare at a hundred kilometres an hour, almost as destructive as the electric tram which was only ten years older; and threatening to become as terrible as the locomotive steam-engine itself, which was almost exactly Adams's own age.

Then he showed his scholar the great hall of dynamos, and explained how little he knew about electricity or force of any kind, even of his own special sun, which spouted heat in inconceivable volume, but which, as far as he knew, might spout less or more, at any time, for all the certainty he felt in it. To him, the dynamo itself was but an ingenious channel for conveying somewhere the heat latent in a few tons of poor coal hidden in a dirty engine-house carefully kept out of sight; but to Adams the dynamo became a symbol of infinity. As he grew accustomed to the great gallery of machines, he began to feel the forty-foot dynamos as a moral force much as the early Christians felt the Cross. The planet itself seemed less impressive, in its old-fashioned, deliberate, annual or daily revolution, than this huge wheel, revolving within arm's length at some vertiginous speed, and barely murmuring—scarcely humming an audible warning to stand a hair's-breadth further for respect of power—while it would not wake the baby lying close against its frame. Before the end, one began to pray to it; inherited instinct taught the natural expression of man before silent and infinite force. Among the thousand symbols of ultimate energy, the dynamo was not so human as some, but it was the most expressive.

Yet the dynamo, next to the steam-engine, was the most familiar of exhibits. For Adams's objects its value lay chiefly in its occult mechanism. Between the dynamo in the gallery of machines and the engine-house outside, the break of continuity amounted to abysmal fracture for a historian's objects. No more relation could he discover between the steam and the electric current than between the Cross and the cathedral. The forces were interchangeable if not reversible, but he could see only an absolute *fiat* in electricity as in faith. Langley could not help him. Indeed, Langley seemed to be worried by the same trouble, for he constantly repeated that the new forces were anarchical, and specially that he was not responsible for the new rays, that were little short of parricidal in their wicked spirit towards science. His own rays, with which he had doubled the solar spectrum, were altogether harmless and beneficent; but Radium denied its God—or, what was to Langley the same thing, denied the truths of his Science.[9] The force was wholly new.

A historian who asked only to learn enough to be as futile as Langley or Kelvin,[10] made rapid progress under this teaching, and mixed himself up in the tangle of ideas until he achieved a sort of Paradise of ignorance vastly consoling to his fatigued senses. He wrapped himself in vibrations and rays which were new, and he would have hugged Marconi and Branly[11] had he met them, as he hugged the dynamo; while he lost his arithmetic in trying to figure out the equation between

[8] Gottlieb Daimler (1834–1900), a German engineer, inventor, and pioneer automobile manufacturer who constructed the first high-speed internal combustion engine in 1885.

[9] The spontaneous transformation of radium through radioactive emission could not be explained by the existing paradigm that distinguished between matter and energy; hence, radium seemed to deny the "truths" of science.

[10] William Thomson (1824–1907), Baron Kelvin, a British mathematician and physicist, whose work in thermodynamics established the law of the conservation of energy.

[11] Guglielmo Marconi (1874–1937), an Italian physicist and inventor of wireless telegraphy in 1905, who (with Karl Braun) received the Nobel Prize for physics in 1909; Édouard Branly (1844–1940), a French physicist and inventor of the Branly "coherer" for distinguishing radio waves.

the discoveries and the economies of force. The economies, like the discoveries, were absolute, supersensual, occult; incapable of expression in horse-power. What mathematical equivalent could he suggest as the value of a Branly coherer? Frozen air, or the electric furnace, had some scale of measurement, no doubt, if somebody could invent a thermometer adequate to the purpose; but X-rays[12] had played no part whatever in man's consciousness, and the atom itself had figured only as a fiction of thought. In these seven years man had translated himself into a new universe which had no common scale of measurement with the old. He had entered a supersensual world, in which he could measure nothing except by chance collisions of movements imperceptible to his senses, perhaps even imperceptible to his instruments, but perceptible to each other, and so to some known ray at the end of the scale. Langley seemed prepared for anything, even for an indeterminable number of universes interfused—physics stark mad in metaphysics.

Historians undertake to arrange sequences,—called stories, or histories—assuming in silence a relation of cause and effect. These assumptions, hidden in the depths of dusty libraries, have been astounding, but commonly unconscious and childlike; so much so, that if any captious critic were to drag them to light, historians would probably reply, with one voice, that they had never supposed themselves required to know what they were talking about. Adams, for one, had toiled in vain to find out what he meant. He had even published a dozen volumes of American history for no other purpose than to satisfy himself whether, by the severest process of stating, with the least possible comment, such facts as seemed sure, in such order as seemed rigorously consequent, he could fix for a familiar moment a necessary sequence of human movement. The result had satisfied him as little as at Harvard College. Where he saw sequence, other men saw something quite different, and no one saw the same unit of measure. He cared little about his experiments and less about his statesmen, who seemed to him quite as ignorant as himself and, as a rule, no more honest; but he insisted on a relation of sequence, and if he could not reach it by one method, he would try as many methods as science knew. Satisfied that the sequence of men led to nothing and that the sequence of their society could lead no further, while the mere sequence of time was artificial, and the sequence of thought was chaos, he turned at last to the sequence of force; and thus it happened that, after ten years' pursuit, he found himself lying in the Gallery of Machines at the Great Exposition of 1900, his historical neck broken by the sudden irruption of forces totally new.

Since no one else showed much concern, an elderly person without other cares had no need to betray alarm. The year 1900 was not the first to upset schoolmasters. Copernicus and Galileo[13] had broken many professorial necks about 1600; Columbus had stood the world on its head towards 1500; but the nearest approach to the revolution of 1900 was that of 310, when Constantine set up the Cross.[14] The rays that Langley disowned, as well as those which he fathered, were occult,

---

[12] Discovered by the German physicist Wilhelm Conrad Roentgen (1845–1923), who received the first Nobel Prize in physics (1901).

[13] Nicholaus Copernicus (1473–1543), a Polish astronomer who determined the movements of the solar system; Galileo Galilei (1564–1642), an Italian astronomer and physicist who supported Copernican ideas rather than the classical Ptolemaic theory that the earth is the center of the universe.

[14] The Roman Emperor Constantine the Great (A.D. 288?–337) introduced Christianity to the Roman Empire after the battle at Mulvian Bridge in A.D. 312. Adams dates the introduction at A.D. 310, when Constantine began his reign.

supersensual, irrational; they were a revelation of mysterious energy like that of the Cross; they were what, in terms of mediæval science, were called immediate modes of the divine substance.

The historian was thus reduced to his last resources. Clearly if he was bound to reduce all these forces to a common value, this common value could have no measure but that of their attraction on his own mind. He must treat them as they had been felt; as convertible, reversible, interchangeable attractions on thought. He made up his mind to venture it; he would risk translating rays into faith. Such a reversible process would vastly amuse a chemist, but the chemist could not deny that he, or some of his fellow physicists, could feel the force of both. When Adams was a boy in Boston, the best chemist in the place had probably never heard of Venus except by way of scandal, or of the Virgin except as idolatry;[15] neither had he heard of dynamos or automobiles or radium; yet his mind was ready to feel the force of all, though the rays were unborn and the women were dead.

Here opened another totally new education, which promised to be by far the most hazardous of all. The knife-edge along which he must crawl, like Sir Lancelot[16] in the twelfth century, divided two kingdoms of force which had nothing in common but attraction. They were as different as a magnet is from gravitation, supposing one knew what a magnet was, or gravitation, or love. The force of the Virgin was still felt at Lourdes,[17] and seemed to be as potent as X-rays; but in America neither Venus nor Virgin ever had value as force—at most as sentiment. No American had ever been truly afraid of either.

This problem in dynamics gravely perplexed an American historian. The Woman had once been supreme; in France she still seemed potent, not merely as a sentiment, but as a force. Why was she unknown in America? For evidently America was ashamed of her, and she was ashamed of herself, otherwise they would not have strewn fig-leaves so profusely all over her. When she was a true force, she was ignorant of fig-leaves, but the monthly-magazine-made American female had not a feature that would have been recognized by Adam.[18] The trait was notorious, and often humorous, but any one brought up among Puritans knew that sex was sin. In any previous age, sex was strength. Neither art nor beauty was needed. Every one, even among Puritans, knew that neither Diana of the Ephesians[19] nor any of the Oriental goddesses was worshipped for her beauty. She was goddess because of her force; she was the animated dynamo; she was reproduction—the greatest and most mysterious of all energies; all she needed was to be fecund. Singularly enough, not one of Adams's many schools of education had ever drawn his attention to the opening lines of Lucretius, though they were perhaps the finest in all Latin literature, where the poet invoked Venus exactly as Dante invoked the Virgin:—

---

[15] The "chemist," or druggist, would know of Venus (the Roman goddess of love) only from dispensing medicine for venereal disease, and as a Bostonian descended from the Puritans would think of the Virgin Mary as an object of idolatry.

[16] The heroic knight in *Lancelot,* by the French poet Chrétien de Troyes (12th century); Lancelot was once obliged to crawl across a bridge consisting of a long knife in order to rescue Queen Guinevere.

[17] The famous shrine in southwestern France where the Virgin Mary is reported to have appeared to St. Bernadette in 1858; since then the shrine has been known for miraculous cures.

[18] The Woman, originally a "true force" in her nakedness and sensuality, has been turned into the stylishly-clad "American female" that the biblical Adam would not recognize by the popular monthly magazines.

[19] According to Greek myth, the ancient city of Ephesus in Asia Minor was sacred to Artemis (Diana to the Romans), a virgin huntress but also a goddess of maternity.

"Quae quoniam rerum naturam *sola* gubernas."[20]

The Venus of Epicurean philosophy survived in the Virgin of the Schools:[21]—

"Donna, sei tanto grande, e tanto vali,
Che qual vuol grazia, e a te non ricorre,
Sua disianza vuol volar senz' ali."[22]

All this was to American thought as though it had never existed. The true American knew something of the facts, but nothing of the feelings; he read the letter, but he never felt the law. Before this historical chasm, a mind like that of Adams felt itself helpless; he turned from the Virgin to the Dynamo as though he were a Branly coherer. On one side, at the Louvre and at Chartres,[23] as he knew by the record of work actually done and still before his eyes, was the highest energy ever known to man, the creator of four-fifths of his noblest art, exercising vastly more attraction over the human mind than all the steam-engines and dynamos ever dreamed of; and yet this energy was unknown to the American mind. An American Virgin would never dare command; an American Venus would never dare exist.

The question, which to any plain American of the nineteenth century seemed as remote as it did to Adams, drew him almost violently to study, once it was posed; and on this point Langleys were as useless as though they were Herbert Spencers[24] or dynamos. The idea survived only as art. There one turned as naturally as though the artist were himself a woman. Adams began to ponder, asking himself whether he knew of any American artist who had ever insisted on the power of sex, as every classic had always done; but he could think only of Walt Whitman; Bret Harte,[25] as far as the magazines would let him venture; and one or two painters, for the flesh-tones. All the rest had used sex for sentiment, never for force; to them, Eve was a tender flower, and Herodias[26] an unfeminine horror. American art, like the American language and American education, was as far as possible sexless. Society regarded this victory over sex as its greatest triumph, and the historian readily admitted it, since the moral issue, for the moment, did not con-

---

[20] "Since you alone govern the nature of things" (Latin), from *On the Nature of Things*, by the Roman philosophical poet Lucretius (99?–55? B.C.), addressed to Venus.

[21] In the following lines from Dante Alighieri (1265–1321), the magnetism of the pagan Venus survived the adjustments made by medieval scholastic philosophers in presenting the figure of the Virgin Mary.

[22] "Lady, thou art so great and so triumphant, / that if there be one who would have grace and does not turn to thee, / his longing seeks to fly without wings" (Italian), from Dante's *Paradiso* (XXXIII 13–15).

[23] Formerly a palace, the Louvre is a renowned museum of art in Paris; the medieval cathedral of Chartres, France, is praised for its Gothic spires. Adams treated the importance of this cathedral in *Mont-Saint-Michel and Chartres: A Study of Thirteenth-Century Unity* (1904, 1913). *The Education*, in contrast, is designed to be "A Study of Twentieth-Century Multiplicity."

[24] Spencer (1820–1893) was an English popularizer of Charles Darwin's evolutionary theories; Adams suggests that Spencer's interpretations were flimsy.

[25] Whitman's *Leaves of Grass* (1855) treats sex prominently as a major force in human life; Bret Harte (1836–1902) portrayed prostitutes sentimentally in such stories as "The Outcasts of Poker Flat" (1869). Adams may be the only writer who ever saw similarities in the work of Whitman and of Harte.

[26] King Herod's wife, who instructed her daughter to ask for the head of John the Baptist as a reward for her dancing (see Matthew 14:8).

cern one who was studying the relations of unmoral force. He cared nothing for the sex of the dynamo until he could measure its energy.

Vaguely seeking a clue, he wandered through the art exhibit, and, in his stroll, stopped almost every day before St. Gaudens's General Sherman,[27] which had been given the central post of honor. St. Gaudens himself was in Paris, putting on the work his usual interminable last touches, and listening to the usual contradictory suggestions of brother sculptors. Of all the American artists who gave to American art whatever life it breathed in the seventies, St. Gaudens was perhaps the most sympathetic, but certainly the most inarticulate. General Grant or Don Cameron[28] had scarcely less instinct of rhetoric than he. All the others—the Hunts, Richardson, John La Farge, Stanford White[29]—were exuberant; only St. Gaudens could never discuss or dilate on an emotion, or suggest artistic arguments for giving to his work the forms that he felt. He never laid down the law, or affected the despot, or became brutalized like Whistler[30] by the brutalities of his world. He required no incense; he was no egoist; his simplicity of thought was excessive; he could not imitate, or give any form but his own to the creations of his hand. No one felt more strongly than he the strength of other men, but the idea that they could affect him never stirred an image in his mind.

This summer his health was poor and his spirits were low. For such a temper, Adams was not the best companion, since his own gaiety was not *folle*;[31] but he risked going now and then to the studio on Mont Parnasse[32] to draw him out for a stroll in the Bois de Boulogne, or dinner as pleased his moods, and in return St. Gaudens sometimes let Adams go about in his company.

Once St. Gaudens took him down to Amiens, with a party of Frenchmen, to see the cathedral. Not until they found themselves actually studying the sculpture of the western portal, did it dawn on Adams's mind that, for his purposes, St. Gaudens on that spot had more interest to him than the cathedral itself. Great men before great monuments express great truths, provided they are not taken too solemnly. Adams never tired of quoting the supreme phrase of his idol Gibbon,[33] before the Gothic cathedrals: "I darted a contemptuous look on the stately monuments of superstition." Even in the footnotes of his history, Gibbon had never inserted a bit of humor more human than this, and one would have paid largely for a photograph of the fat little historian, on the background of Notre Dame of

---

[27] A statue of William Tecumseh Sherman (1820–1891), a Union general in the Civil War, by the American sculptor Augustus St. Gaudens (1848–1907); then situated in Paris, the statue is now in Central Park, New York City.

[28] James Donald Cameron (1833–1918), U.S. Senator and secretary of war under the eighteenth president, Ulysses S. Grant (1822–1885).

[29] The brothers William Morris Hunt (1824–1879), an eminent painter, and Richard Morris Hunt (1828–1895), an architect and founder of an architectural studio in New York City; Henry Hobson Richardson (1838–1886), an architect noted for his "Richardson Romanesque" style, as seen in Trinity Church, Boston (1872–1877); La Farge (1835–1910), a mural painter and designer of stained glass; White (1853–1906), an architect famous for the Washington Arch and the Century Club in New York City.

[30] James Abbott McNeill Whistler (1834–1903), a painter and lithographer who acquired a reputation as a dandy and publicity seeker when he lived in London in the 1860s.

[31] "Wild" (French).

[32] A Left Bank section of Paris frequented by writers and artists; the Bois de Boulogne is a wooded park on the outskirts of Paris.

[33] Edward Gibbon (1737–1794), an English historian and author of *The Decline and Fall of the Roman Empire* (6 vols., 1776–1788) and the autobiographical *Memoirs of His Life and Writings* (1796); Adams apparently paraphrases from a February 1763 entry in Gibbon's journal.

Amiens, trying to persuade his readers—perhaps himself—that he was darting a contemptuous look on the stately monument, for which he felt in fact the respect which every man of his vast study and active mind always feels before objects worthy of it; but besides the humor, one felt also the relation. Gibbon ignored the Virgin, because in 1789 religious monuments were out of fashion. In 1900 his remark sounded fresh and simple as the green fields to ears that had heard a hundred years of other remarks, mostly no more fresh and certainly less simple. Without malice, one might find it more instructive than a whole lecture of Ruskin.[34] One sees what one brings, and at that moment Gibbon brought the French Revolution. Ruskin brought reaction against the Revolution. St. Gaudens had passed beyond all. He liked the stately monuments much more than he liked Gibbon or Ruskin; he loved their dignity; their unity; their scale; their lines; their lights and shadows; their decorative sculpture; but he was even less conscious than they of the force that created it all—the Virgin, the Woman—by whose genius "the stately monuments of superstition" were built, through which she was expressed. He would have seen more meaning in Isis[35] with the cow's horns, at Edfoo, who expressed the same thought. The art remained, but the energy was lost even upon the artist.

Yet in mind and person St. Gaudens was a survival of the 1500s; he bore the stamp of the Renaissance, and should have carried an image of the Virgin round his neck, or stuck in his hat, like Louis XI.[36] In mere time he was a lost soul that had strayed by chance into the twentieth century, and forgotten where it came from. He writhed and cursed at his ignorance, much as Adams did at his own, but in the opposite sense. St. Gaudens was a child of Benvenuto Cellini,[37] smothered in an American cradle. Adams was a quintessence of Boston, devoured by curiosity to think like Benvenuto. St. Gaudens's art was starved from birth, and Adams's instinct was blighted from babyhood. Each had but half of a nature, and when they came together before the Virgin of Amiens they ought both to have felt in her the force that made them one; but it was not so. To Adams she became more than ever a channel of force; to St. Gaudens she remained as before a channel of taste.

For a symbol of power, St. Gaudens instinctively preferred the horse, as was plain in his horse and Victory of the Sherman monument. Doubtless Sherman also felt it so. The attitude was so American that, for at least forty years, Adams had never realized that any other could be in sound taste. How many years had he taken to admit a notion of what Michael Angelo and Rubens[38] were driving at? He could not say; but he knew that only since 1895 had he begun to feel the Virgin or Venus as force, and not everywhere even so. At Chartres—perhaps at Lourdes—possibly at Cnidos if one could still find there the divinely naked Aphrodite of

---

[34] John Ruskin (1819–1900), an English critic of art and architecture, especially that of the Italian Renaissance.
[35] Adams saw a statue of the Egyptian goddess Isis at Edfu ("Edfoo") on the Nile River in 1873 and again in 1893.
[36] Louis XI (1423–1483) was a politically and militarily active king of France (1461–1483); fearing assassination in his later days, he frequently disguised himself as a holy pilgrim.
[37] Cellini (1500–1571), an Italian sculptor and metalsmith and author of a picaresque autobiography, a major document of the sixteenth century.
[38] Michelangelo (1475–1564), an Italian artist and sculptor and chief architect of St. Peter's Cathedral in Rome. Peter Paul Rubens (1577–1640), an eminent Flemish painter; "Venus and Adonis" is among his principal works.

Praxiteles[39]—but otherwise one must look for force to the goddesses of Indian mythology. The idea died out long ago in the German and English stock. St. Gaudens at Amiens was hardly less sensitive to the force of the female energy than Matthew Arnold at the Grande Chartreuse.[40] Neither of them felt goddesses as power—only as reflected emotion, human expression, beauty, purity, taste, scarcely even as sympathy. They felt a railway train as power; yet they, and all other artists, constantly complained that the power embodied in a railway train could never be embodied in art. All the steam in the world could not, like the Virgin, build Chartres.

Yet in mechanics, whatever the mechanicians might think, both energies acted as interchangeable forces on man, and by action on man all known force may be measured. Indeed, few men of science measured force in any other way. After once admitting that a straight line was the shortest distance between two points, no serious mathematician cared to deny anything that suited his convenience, and rejected no symbol, unproved or unproveable, that helped him to accomplish work. The symbol was force, as a compass-needle or a triangle was force, as the mechanist might prove by losing it, and nothing could be gained by ignoring their value. Symbol or energy, the Virgin had acted as the greatest force the Western world ever felt, and had drawn man's activities to herself more strongly than any other power, natural or supernatural, had ever done; the historian's business was to follow the track of the energy; to find where it came from and where it went to; its complex source and shifting channels; its values, equivalents, conversions. It could scarcely be more complex than radium; it could hardly be deflected, diverted, polarized, absorbed more perplexingly than other radiant matter. Adams knew nothing about any of them, but as a mathematical problem of influence on human progress, though all were occult, all reacted on his mind, and he rather inclined to think the Virgin easiest to handle.

The pursuit turned out to be long and tortuous, leading at last into the vast forests of scholastic science. From Zeno to Descartes, hand in hand with Thomas Aquinas, Montaigne, and Pascal,[41] one stumbled as stupidly as though one were still a German student of 1860. Only with the instinct of despair could one force one's self into this old thicket of ignorance after having been repulsed at a score of entrances more promising and more popular. Thus far, no path had led anywhere, unless perhaps to an exceedingly modest living. Forty-five years of study had proved to be quite futile for the pursuit of power; one controlled no more force in 1900 than in 1850, although the amount of force controlled by society had enormously increased. The secret of education still hid itself somewhere behind ignorance, and one fumbled over it as feebly as ever. In such labyrinths, the staff is a force almost more necessary than the legs; the pen becomes a sort of blind-man's dog, to keep him from falling into the gutters. The pen works for itself, and acts like a hand, modelling the plastic material over and over again to the form that suits it best. The form is never arbitrary, but is a sort of growth like crystalli-

---

[39] A famous fourth-century B.C. Greek sculptor whose renowned "Aphrodite of Cnidus" (a city in Asia Minor) exists only in a copy at the Vatican in Rome.

[40] Arnold (1822–1888) was a British poet whose "Stanzas From the Grande Chartreuse" (a monastery of the Carthusian monks, an order founded in 1086) laments the loss of medieval religious faith.

[41] Adams refers to studies that took him from one philosopher to another: from the Greek Zeno (366?–264 B.C.) to the French René Descartes (1596–1650) and the unlikely trio of the theologically oriented Thomas Aquinas (1225?–1274), the French skeptic Michel de Montaigne (1533–1592), and the French scientist and religious thinker Blaise Pascal (1623–1662).

zation, as any artist knows too well; for often the pencil or pen runs into side-paths and shapelessness, loses its relations, stops or is bogged. Then it has to return on its trail, and recover, if it can, its line of force. The result of a year's work depends more on what is struck out than on what is left in; on the sequence of the main lines of thought, than on their play or variety. Compelled once more to lean heavily on this support, Adams covered more thousands of pages with figures as formal as though they were algebra, laboriously striking out, altering, burning, experimenting, until the year had expired, the Exposition had long been closed, and winter drawing to its end, before he sailed from Cherbourg,[42] on January 19, 1901, for home.

1907

═CONTEXTS═

The World's Columbian Exposition of 1893

The World's Columbian Exposition, held in Chicago in 1893 to commemorate the four hundredth anniversary of Christopher Columbus's discovery of America, marked the first time that machines were used for fun at a fair. (The fact that Chicago won the right to house the fair illustrates the rising status of the West in national affairs.) On the Midway, spectators sampled a range of amusements, including George Ferris's wheel, hot-air balloon rides, artificial ice for warm-weather skating, an electrified house demonstrating the practical applications of electricity, Buffalo Bill's Wild West Show, Scott Joplin's ragtime piano-playing, and the hootchy-kootchy dancing of Little Egypt. In the numerous exhibition halls, spectators heard the pianist Ignace Paderewski play Chopin, attended intellectual congresses on such hotly debated topics as the Victorian stereotyping of women, and saw demonstrations of the latest inventions—the phonograph and Linotype. The Pullman car, a railroad car with folding upper berths, was displayed in the Transportation Building, the uncluttered lines of which clashed with the ornate, gilded facades of the exhibition halls. The waters of nearby Lake Michigan fed a network of manmade lagoons within the fair itself and served as an exotic backdrop to the 65,000 exhibits from 47 different countries, displayed on the 686-acre fairground.

An observer of the fair, Charles Eliot Norton (1827–1908), co-editor of the *North American Review* with James Russell Lowell, offered this view:

The Great American Fair

The great Fair was indeed a superb and appropriate symbol of our great nation, in its noble general design and in the inequalities of its execution; in its unexampled display of industrial energy and practical capacity; in the absence of the higher works of the creative imagination; in its incongruities, its mingling of noble realities and ignoble pretences, in its refinements cheek-by-jowl with vulgarities, in its order and its confusion—in its heterogeneousness and in its unity.

Charles Eliot Norton, 1894?

---

[42] A port in France.

Booker T. Washington
(1856–1915)

The son of a black woman named Jane and an anonymous white plantation owner, Booker T. Washington was born into slavery in 1856. After the Civil War ended, he and his mother moved to Malden, West Virginia. There he worked as a salt packer, a coal miner, and a house servant and, when he could, attended the local school out of a desire to read and write. In 1872 he made his famous five-hundred-mile journey, partly on foot, to enroll in the Hampton Institute in Virginia, a school established by the American Missionary Association to train African-American teachers and to promote the study of agriculture and trade.

After graduating from Hampton in 1875, Washington moved back to Malden to become an itinerant teacher; he established, among other things, a library and a night school. Several years later he accepted an invitation from the founder of the Hampton Institute, Samuel Chapman Armstrong, to return there to teach and to conduct an experimental program for the instruction of Native-American students. In 1881 Washington, helped by Armstrong's recommendation, was invited to become the principal of an industrial school for ex-slaves in Tuskegee, Alabama. Through hard work and perseverance he built it up from a $2,000 legislative appropriation to a college with 2500 students, 111 buildings, and 3500 acres of land by the time of his death in 1915. He used the system at Hampton Institute as his primary model in creating the Tuskegee Institute, with one major difference: instead of using a predominately white faculty, Washington employed black teachers.

Both his "Atlanta Exposition Address" (an 1895 speech given at the Cotton States and International Exposition) and his autobiography, *Up From Slavery* (1901), demonstrate the manner in which Washington's skills as orator and writer brought him to national attention. Popularly known as the "Atlanta Compromise," Washington's influential speech set a practical and conciliatory agenda for African Americans in society: let African Americans, he counseled, be given the opportunity to improve their economic condition; let them (as a trade-off) overlook matters of human and political rights. Given the racial tumult in the South in the late nineteenth century, the tenor of this speech brought many blacks and whites alike to see Washington as a welcome and uniquely qualified peacemaker, the leading African-American spokesman. His position was enhanced by the publication of *Up From Slavery*, a compelling autobiography that both appropriated and validated Franklinesque virtues of diligence and hard work. Further honors came from an appreciative white world when Washington received an honorary degree from Harvard University and dined at the White House with President Theodore Roosevelt.

For his many accomplishments Washington was hailed as the "Moses of his race." Even W. E. B. Du Bois admitted Washington's predominance as a spokesman for African Americans. But to Du Bois and to an increasing number of blacks, especially those who came of age after World War I, Washington's ideas seemed to accept racial inequality, to bargain for the doctrine of "separate but unequal," to play the white man's game. Washington remains a significant figure—significant to some for the limitations of his vision.

Suggested Readings: *The Future of the American Negro*, 1899. *Working With the Hands*, 1904. *The Booker T. Washington Papers*, ed. L. R. Harlan, 1972– . B. Matthews, *Booker T. Washington: Educator and Interracial Interpreter*, 1948. A. Meier, *Negro Thought in America, 1880–1915*, 1963. E. L. Thornborough, *Booker T. Washington*, 1969. Louis R. Harlan, *Booker T. Washington: The*

Making of a Black Leader, 1865–1901, 1972. R. B. Stepto, *From Behind the Veil: A Study of Afro-American Narrative*, 1979. L. R. Harlan, *Booker T. Washington: The Wizard of Tuskegee, 1901–1915*, 1983. R. Smock, ed., *Booker T. Washington in Perspective: Essays of Louis R. Harlan*, 1988.

Text Used: *Up From Slavery*, 1901.

from UP FROM SLAVERY*

Chapter XIV: The Atlanta Exposition Address[1]

The Atlanta Exposition, at which I had been asked to make an address as a representative of the Negro race, as stated in the last chapter, was opened with a short address from Governor Bullock. After other interesting exercises, including an invocation from Bishop Nelson,[2] of Georgia, a dedicatory ode by Albert Howell, Jr., and addresses by the President of the Exposition and Mrs. Joseph Thompson, the President of the Woman's Board, Governor Bullock introduced me with the words, "We have with us to-day a representative of Negro enterprise and Negro civilization."

When I arose to speak, there was considerable cheering, especially from the coloured people. As I remember it now, the thing that was uppermost in my mind was the desire to say something that would cement the friendship of the races and bring about hearty cooperation between them. So far as my outward surroundings were concerned, the only thing that I recall distinctly now is that when I got up, I saw thousands of eyes looking intently into my face. The following is the address which I delivered:—

Mr. President and Gentlemen of the Board of Directors and Citizens.

One-third of the population of the South is of the Negro race. No enterprise seeking the material, civil, or moral welfare of this section can disregard this element of our population and reach the highest success. I but convey to you, Mr. President and Directors, the sentiment of the masses of my race when I say that in no way have the value and manhood of the American Negro been more fittingly and generously recognized than by the managers of this magnificent Exposition at every stage of its progress. It is a recognition that will do more to cement the friendship of the two races than any occurrence since the dawn of our freedom.

Not only this, but the opportunity here afforded will awaken among us a new era of industrial progress. Ignorant and inexperienced, it is not strange that in the first years of our new life we began at the top instead of at the bottom; that a seat in Congress or the state legislature was more sought than real estate or industrial skill; that the political convention of stump speaking had more attractions than starting a dairy farm or truck garden.

---

* First published serially in *The Outlook* from November 3, 1900, to February 23, 1901, and in book form in 1901.
[1] Washington delivered this address at the opening ceremonies of the Cotton States and International Exposition in Atlanta, September 18, 1895.
[2] Cleland Kinlock Nelson (1852–1917), Episcopal bishop of Atlanta (1907–1917).

A ship lost at sea for many days suddenly sighted a friendly vessel. From the mast of the unfortunate vessel was seen a signal, "Water, water; we die of thirst!" The answer from the friendly vessel at once came back, "Cast down your bucket where you are." A second time the signal, "Water, water; send us water!" ran up from the distressed vessel, and was answered, "Cast down your bucket where you are." And a third and fourth signal for water was answered, "Cast down your bucket where you are." The captain of the distressed vessel, at last heeding the injunction, cast down his bucket, and it came up full of fresh, sparkling water from the mouth of the Amazon River. To those of my race who depend on bettering their condition in a foreign land or who underestimate the importance of cultivating friendly relations with the Southern white man, who is their next-door neighbour, I would say: "Cast down your bucket where you are"—cast it down in making friends in every manly way of the people of all races by whom we are surrounded.

Cast it down in agriculture, mechanics, in commerce, in domestic service, and in the professions. And in this connection it is well to bear in mind that whatever other sins the South may be called to bear, when it comes to business, pure and simple, it is in the South that the Negro is given a man's chance in the commercial world, and in nothing is this Exposition more eloquent than in emphasizing this chance. Our greatest danger is that in the great leap from slavery to freedom we may overlook the fact that the masses of us are to live by the productions of our hands, and fail to keep in mind that we shall prosper in proportion as we learn to dignify and glorify common labour and put brains and skill into the common occupations of life; shall prosper in proportion as we learn to draw the line between the superficial and the substantial, the ornamental gewgaws of life and the useful. No race can prosper till it learns that there is as much dignity in tilling a field as in writing a poem. It is at the bottom of life we must begin, and not at the top. Nor should we permit our grievances to overshadow our opportunities.

To those of the white race who look to the incoming of those of foreign birth and strange tongue and habits for the prosperity of the South, were I permitted I would repeat what I say to my own race, "Cast down your bucket where you are." Cast it down among the eight millions of Negroes whose habits you know, whose fidelity and love you have tested in days when to have proved treacherous meant the ruin of your firesides. Cast down your bucket among these people who have, without strikes and labour wars, tilled your fields, cleared your forests, builded your railroads and cities, and brought forth treasures from the bowels of the earth, and helped make possible this magnificent representation of the progress of the South. Casting down your bucket among my people, helping and encouraging them as you are doing on these grounds, and to education of head, hand, and heart, you will find that they will buy your surplus land, make blossom the waste places in your fields, and run your factories. While doing this, you can be sure in the future, as in the past, that you and your families will be surrounded by the most patient, faithful, law-abiding, and unresentful people that the world has seen. As we have proved our loyalty to you in the past, in nursing your children, watching by the sick-bed of your mothers and fathers, and often following them with tear-dimmed eyes to their graves, so in the future, in our humble way, we shall stand by you with a devotion that no foreigner can approach, ready to lay down our lives, if need be, in defence of yours, interlacing our industrial, commercial, civil, and religious life with yours in a way that shall make the interests of both races one. In all things that are purely social we can be as separate as the fingers, yet one as the hand in all things essential to mutual progress.

There is no defence or security for any of us except in the highest intelligence and development of all. If anywhere there are efforts tending to curtail the fullest growth of the Negro, let these efforts be turned into stimulating, encouraging, and making him the most useful and intelligent citizen. Effort or means so invested will pay a thousand per cent interest. These efforts will be twice blessed—"blessing him that gives and him that takes."[3]

There is no escape through law of man or God from the inevitable:—

> The laws of changeless justice bind
> Oppressor with oppressed;
> And close as sin and suffering joined
> We march to fate abreast.[4]

Nearly sixteen millions of hands will aid you in pulling the load upward, or they will pull against you the load downward. We shall constitute one-third and more of the ignorance and crime of the South, or one-third its intelligence and progress; we shall contribute one-third to the business and industrial prosperity of the South, or we shall prove a veritable body of death, stagnating, depressing, retarding every effort to advance the body politic.

Gentlemen of the Exposition, as we present to you our humble effort at an exhibition of our progress, you must not expect overmuch. Starting thirty years ago with ownership here and there in a few quilts and pumpkins and chickens (gathered from miscellaneous sources), remember the path that has led from these to the inventions and production of agricultural implements, buggies, steam-engines, newspapers, books, statuary, carving, paintings, the management of drug-stores and banks, has not been trodden without contact with thorns and thistles. While we take pride in what we exhibit as a result of our independent efforts, we do not for a moment forget that our part in this exhibition would fall far short of your expectations but for the constant help that has come to our educational life, not only from the Southern states, but especially from Northern philanthropists, who have made their gifts a constant stream of blessing and encouragement.

The wisest among my race understand that the agitation of questions of social equality is the extremest folly, and that progress in the enjoyment of all the privileges that will come to us must be the result of severe and constant struggle rather than of artificial forcing. No race that has anything to contribute to the markets of the world is long in any degree ostracized. It is important and right that all privileges of the law be ours, but it is vastly more important that we be prepared for the exercises of these privileges. The opportunity to earn a dollar in a factory just now is worth infinitely more than the opportunity to spend a dollar in an opera-house.

In conclusion, may I repeat that nothing in thirty years has given us more hope and encouragement, and drawn us so near to you of the white race, as this opportunity offered by the Exposition; and here bending, as it were, over the altar that represents the results of the struggles of your race and mine, both starting practically empty-handed three decades ago, I pledge that in your effort to work out the great and intricate problem which God has laid at the doors of the South, you shall have at all times the patient, sympathetic help of my race; only let this be constantly in mind, that, while from representations in these buildings of the product

---

[3] From Shakespeare's *Merchant of Venice* (IV.i.1670): "It blesseth him that gives and him that takes."

[4] From "Song of the Negro Boatman," by the poet John Greenleaf Whittier (1807–1892).

of field, of forest, of mine, of factory, letters, and art, much good will come, yet far above and beyond material benefits will be that higher good, that, let us pray God, will come, in a blotting out of sectional differences and racial animosities and suspicions, in a determination to administer absolute justice, in a willing obedience among all classes to the mandates of law. This, this, coupled with our material prosperity, will bring into our beloved South a new heaven and a new earth.

The first thing that I remember, after I had finished speaking, was that Governor Bullock rushed across the platform and took me by the hand, and that others did the same. I received so many and such hearty congratulations that I found it difficult to get out of the building. I did not appreciate to any degree, however, the impression which my address seemed to have made, until the next morning, when I went into the business part of the city. As soon as I was recognized, I was surprised to find myself pointed out and surrounded by a crowd of men who wished to shake hands with me. This was kept up on every street on to which I went, to an extent which embarrassed me so much that I went back to my boarding-place. The next morning I returned to Tuskegee.[5] At the station in Atlanta, and at almost all of the stations at which the train stopped between that city and Tuskegee, I found a crowd of people anxious to shake hands with me.

The papers in all parts of the United States published the address in full, and for months afterward there were complimentary editorial references to it. Mr. Clark Howell, the editor of the Atlanta *Constitution*, telegraphed to a New York paper, among other words, the following, "I do not exaggerate when I say that Professor Booker T. Washington's address yesterday was one of the most notable speeches, both as to character and as to the warmth of its reception, ever delivered to a Southern audience. The address was a revelation. The whole speech is a platform upon which blacks and whites can stand with full justice to each other."

The Boston *Transcript* said editorially: "The speech of Booker T. Washington at the Atlanta Exposition, this week, seems to have dwarfed all the other proceedings and the Exposition itself. The sensation that it has caused in the press has never been equalled."

I very soon began receiving all kinds of propositions from lecture bureaus, and editors of magazines and papers, to take the lecture platform, and to write articles. One lecture bureau offered me fifty thousand dollars, or two hundred dollars a night and expenses, if I would place my services at its disposal for a given period. To all these communications I replied that my life-work was at Tuskegee; and that whenever I spoke it must be in the interests of the Tuskegee school and my race, and that I would enter into no arrangements that seemed to place a mere commercial value upon my services.

Some days after its delivery I sent a copy of my address to the President of the United States, the Hon. Grover Cleveland.[6] I received from him the following autograph reply:—

> Gray Gables, Buzzard's Bay, Mass.,
> October 6, 1895.

[5] Tuskegee, Alabama, where Washington had founded the Tuskegee Institute, a school for training African-American teachers, in 1881.

[6] Cleveland (1837–1908) was the twenty-second (1885–1889) and twenty-fourth (1893–1897) U.S. president.

BOOKER T. WASHINGTON, ESQ.:

My Dear Sir: I thank you for sending me a copy of your address delivered at the Atlanta Exposition.

I thank you with much enthusiasm for making the address. I have read it with intense interest, and I think the Exposition would be fully justified if it did not do more than furnish the opportunity for its delivery. Your words cannot fail to delight and encourage all who wish well for your race; and if our coloured fellow-citizens do not from your utterances gather new hope and form new determinations to gain every valuable advantage offered them by their citizenship, it will be strange indeed.

Yours very truly,

GROVER CLEVELAND.

Later I met Mr. Cleveland, for the first time, when, as President, he visited the Atlanta Exposition. At the request of myself and others he consented to spend an hour in the Negro Building, for the purpose of inspecting the Negro exhibit and of giving the coloured people in attendance an opportunity to shake hands with him. As soon as I met Mr. Cleveland I became impressed with his simplicity, greatness, and rugged honesty. I have met him many times since then, both at public functions and at his private residence in Princeton, and the more I see of him the more I admire him. When he visited the Negro Building in Atlanta he seemed to give himself up wholly, for that hour, to the coloured people. He seemed to be as careful to shake hands with some old coloured "auntie" clad partially in rags, and to take as much pleasure in doing so, as if he were greeting some millionnaire. Many of the coloured people took advantage of the occasion to get him to write his name in a book or on a slip of paper. He was as careful and patient in doing this as if he were putting his signature to some great state document.

Mr. Cleveland has not only shown his friendship for me in many personal ways, but has always consented to do anything I have asked of him for our school. This he has done, whether it was to make a personal donation or to use his influence in securing the donations of others. Judging from my personal acquaintance with Mr. Cleveland, I do not believe that he is conscious of possessing any colour prejudice. He is too great for that. In my contact with people I find that, as a rule, it is only the little, narrow people who live for themselves, who never read good books, who do not travel, who never open up their souls in a way to permit them to come into contact with other souls—with the great outside world. No man whose vision is bounded by colour can come into contact with what is highest and best in the world. In meeting men, in many places, I have found that the happiest people are those who do the most for others; the most miserable are those who do the least. I have also found that few things, if any, are capable of making one so blind and narrow as race prejudice. I often say to our students, in the course of my talks to them on Sunday evenings in the chapel, that the longer I live and the more experience I have of the world, the more I am convinced that, after all, the one thing that is most worth living for—and dying for, if need be—is the opportunity of making some one else more happy and more useful.

The coloured people and the coloured newspapers at first seemed to be greatly pleased with the character of my Atlanta address, as well as with its reception. But after the first burst of enthusiasm began to die away, and the coloured people began reading the speech in cold type, some of them seemed to feel that they had been hypnotized. They seemed to feel that I had been too liberal in my remarks toward the Southern whites, and that I had not spoken out strongly enough for what they termed the "rights" of the race. For a while there was a reaction, so far as a certain element of my own race was concerned, but later these reactionary ones seemed to have been won over to my way of believing and acting.

While speaking of changes in public sentiment, I recall that about ten years after the school at Tuskegee was established, I had an experience that I shall never forget. Dr. Lyman Abbott,[7] then the pastor of Plymouth Church, and also editor of the *Outlook* (then the *Christian Union*), asked me to write a letter for his paper giving my opinion of the exact condition, mental and moral, of the coloured ministers in the South, as based upon my observations. I wrote the letter, giving the exact facts as I conceived them to be. The picture painted was a rather black one—or, since I am black, shall I say "white"? It could not be otherwise with a race but a few years out of slavery, a race which had not had time or opportunity to produce a competent ministry.

What I said soon reached every Negro minister in the country, I think, and the letters of condemnation which I received from them were not few. I think that for a year after the publication of this article every association and every conference or religious body of any kind, of my race, that met, did not fail before adjourning to pass a resolution condemning me, or calling upon me to retract or modify what I had said. Many of these organizations went so far in their resolutions as to advise parents to cease sending their children to Tuskegee. One association even appointed a "missionary" whose duty it was to warn the people against sending their children to Tuskegee. This missionary had a son in the school, and I noticed that, whatever the "missionary" might have said or done with regard to others, he was careful not to take his son away from the institution. Many of the coloured papers, especially those that were the organs of religious bodies, joined in the general chorus of condemnation or demands for retraction.

During the whole time of the excitement, and through all the criticism, I did not utter a word of explanation or retraction. I knew that I was right, and that time and the sober second thought of the people would vindicate me. It was not long before the bishops and other church leaders began to make a careful investigation of the conditions of the ministry, and they found out that I was right. In fact, the oldest and most influential bishop in one branch of the Methodist Church said that my words were far too mild. Very soon public sentiment began making itself felt, in demanding a purifying of the ministry. While this is not yet complete by any means, I think I may say, without egotism, and I have been told by many of our most influential ministers, that my words had much to do with starting a demand for the placing of a higher type of men in the pulpit. I have had the satisfaction of having many who once condemned me thank me heartily for my frank words.

The change of the attitude of the Negro ministry, so far as regards myself, is so complete that at the present time I have no warmer friends among any class than I have among the clergymen. The improvement in the character and life of the Negro ministers is one of the most gratifying evidences of the progress of the race.

---

[7] Abbott (1835–1922) was a Congregationalist minister, pastor of Plymouth Church in Brooklyn, New York, and editor of *The Christian Examiner* (1870–1893) and of its successor, *The Outlook* (1893–1935).

My experience with them, as well as other events in my life, convince me that the thing to do, when one feels sure that he has said or done the right thing, and is condemned, is to stand still and keep quiet. If he is right, time will show it.

In the midst of the discussion which was going on concerning my Atlanta speech, I received the letter which I give below, from Dr. Gilman,[8] the President of Johns Hopkins University, who had been made chairman of the judges of award in connection with the Atlanta Exposition:—

> Johns Hopkins University, Baltimore,
> President's Office, September 30, 1895.

> Dear Mr. Washington: Would it be agreeable to you to be one of the Judges of Award in the Department of Education at Atlanta? If so, I shall be glad to place your name upon the list. A line by telegraph will be welcomed.
>> Yours very truly,
>> D. C. Gilman.

I think I was even more surprised to receive this invitation than I had been to receive the invitation to speak at the opening of the Exposition. It was to be a part of my duty, as one of the jurors, to pass not only upon the exhibits of the coloured schools, but also upon those of the white schools. I accepted the position, and spent a month in Atlanta in performance of the duties which it entailed. The board of jurors was a large one, consisting in all of sixty members. It was about equally divided between Southern white people and Northern white people. Among them were college presidents, leading scientists and men of letters, and specialists in many subjects. When the group of jurors to which I was assigned met for organization, Mr. Thomas Nelson Page,[9] who was one of the number, moved that I be made secretary of that division, and the motion was unanimously adopted. Nearly half of our division were Southern people. In performing my duties in the inspection of the exhibits of white schools I was in every case treated with respect, and at the close of our labours I parted from my associates with regret.

I am often asked to express myself more freely than I do upon the political condition and the political future of my race. These recollections of my experience in Atlanta give me the opportunity to do so briefly. My own belief is, although I have never before said so in so many words, that the time will come when the Negro in the South will be accorded all the political rights which his ability, character, and material possessions entitle him to. I think, though, that the opportunity to freely exercise such political rights will not come in any large degree through outside or artificial forcing, but will be accorded to the Negro by the Southern white people themselves, and that they will protect him in the exercise of those rights. Just as soon as the South gets over the old feeling that it is being forced by "foreigners," or "aliens," to do something which it does not want to do, I believe

---

[8] Daniel Coit Gilman (1831–1908), president of the University of California (1872–1875), and first president of Johns Hopkins University (1876–1901) and of the Carnegie Institution (1901–1904).

[9] Page (1853–1922) was a Virginia-born author of novels set in the old South and during Reconstruction and served as U.S. ambassador to Italy (1913–1919).

that the change in the direction that I have indicated is going to begin. In fact, there are indications that it is already beginning in a slight degree.

Let me illustrate my meaning. Suppose that some months before the opening of the Atlanta Exposition there had been a general demand from the press and public platform outside the South that a Negro be given a place on the opening programme, and that a Negro be placed upon the board of jurors of award. Would any such recognition of the race have taken place? I do not think so. The Atlanta officials went so far as they did because they felt it to be a pleasure, as well as a duty, to reward what they considered merit in the Negro race. Say what we will, there is something in human nature which we cannot blot out, which makes one man, in the end, recognize and reward merit in another, regardless of colour or race.

I believe it is the duty of the Negro—as the greater part of the race is already doing—to deport himself modestly in regard to political claims, depending upon the slow but sure influences that proceed from the possession of property, intelligence, and high character for the full recognition of his political rights. I think that the according of the full exercise of political rights is going to be a matter of natural, slow growth, not an over-night, gourd-vine affair. I do not believe that the Negro should cease voting, for a man cannot learn the exercise of self-government by ceasing to vote, any more than a boy can learn to swim by keeping out of the water, but I do believe that in his voting he should more and more be influenced by those of intelligence and character who are his next-door neighbours.

I know coloured men who, through the encouragement, help, and advice of Southern white people, have accumulated thousands of dollars' worth of property, but who, at the same time, would never think of going to those same persons for advice concerning the casting of their ballots. This, it seems to me, is unwise and unreasonable, and should cease. In saying this I do not mean that the Negro should truckle, or not vote from principle, for the instant he ceases to vote from principle he loses the confidence and respect of the Southern white man even.

I do not believe that any state should make a law that permits an ignorant and poverty-stricken white man to vote, and prevents a black man in the same condition from voting. Such a law is not only unjust, but it will react, as all unjust laws do, in time; for the effect of such a law is to encourage the Negro to secure education and property, and at the same time it encourages the white man to remain in ignorance and poverty. I believe that in time, through the operation of intelligence and friendly race relations, all cheating at the ballot-box in the South will cease. It will become apparent that the white man who begins by cheating a Negro out of his ballot soon learns to cheat a white man out of his, and that the man who does this ends his career of dishonesty by the theft of property or by some equally serious crime. In my opinion, the time will come when the South will encourage all of its citizens to vote. It will see that it pays better, from every standpoint, to have healthy, vigorous life than to have that political stagnation which always results when one-half of the population has no share and no interest in the Government.

As a rule, I believe in universal, free suffrage, but I believe that in the South we are confronted with peculiar conditions that justify the protection of the ballot in many of the states, for a while at least, either by an educational test, a property test, or by both combined; but whatever tests are required, they should be made to apply with equal and exact justice to both races.

1900–1901

W. E. B. Du Bois
(1868–1963)

In the "Forethought" to *The Souls of Black Folk* (1903), William Edward Burghardt Du Bois made the following provocative statement: "Herein lie buried many things which if read with patience may show the strange meaning of being black here in the dawning of the twentieth century." Near the end of the twentieth century, the import of these words and of the experiences out of which they came has become clearer than ever before. We have begun to see that anyone who hopes to understand the meaning of black experience in American society must pay attention to Du Bois and to his ideas about racial diversity and conflict in the United States.

Born in 1868 in Great Barrington, Massachusetts, Du Bois was educated at Fisk University in Nashville, Harvard University, and the University of Berlin. He dedicated his intellectual energies to the then new discipline of sociology. If his education differed from that of other African Americans, his life experiences were distinct from those of most sociologists. During his summers as an undergraduate at Fisk, for example, he taught at African-American schools in rural Tennessee and thus came to know chronic racial oppression in a deeply personal way. As a young sociologist living in the North, however, Du Bois began his professional career as the product of his scholarly training. His study *The Philadelphia Negro* (1899) manifests an objective approach to its subject, a detached marshaling of evidence.

When Du Bois settled in Atlanta in 1897, an environment of racist violence brought him to realize that his race and his professional training could no longer be separated. On his way to visit the folk writer Joel Chandler Harris (creator of the Uncle Remus stories), he saw a lynched African-American man hanging in a storefront window. The brutality of such spectacles led Du Bois to write *The Souls of Black Folk,* a compelling mélange of exhortation, sociological survey, folk study, autobiography, and realist narrative. In this volume he sets himself in vehement opposition to the doctrine of acceptance and compromise articulated by Booker T. Washington at the Atlanta Exposition in 1895. Du Bois argues that blacks will never be a part of white America, that they should educate themselves not as members of a white industrial society but rather as members of a black and ancient race. In *The Souls of Black Folk* Du Bois also found the idiom that would characterize his expanding career as champion of black dignity. He extended his ideas to include black experience globally, until his death in Ghana in 1963.

Du Bois fashioned a voice of resistance and a mode of perception that have become beacons for black writers in the twentieth century. As different as they are, such writers as James Weldon Johnson and Jean Toomer, Langston Hughes and Malcolm X, Ralph Ellison and Toni Morrison have described "the strange meaning of being black" in America as unique in its complexity and in the resonance of its pain. In doing so, they—like Du Bois before them—have converted suppression to achievement, "invisibility" to a determined quest for self-affirming identity.

Suggested Readings: *The Philadelphia Negro: A Social Study,* 1899. *W. E. B. Du Bois Speaks: Speeches and Addresses,* ed. P. S. Foner, 1970. *The Emerging Thought of W. E. B. Du Bois: Essays* *and Editorials From the "Crisis"*, ed. H. L. Moon, 1972. *The Correspondence of W. E. B. Du Bois*, 3 vols., ed. H. Aptheker, 1973–1978. F. L. Broderick, *W. E. B. DuBois: Negro Leader in a Time of Crisis*, 1959. E. M. Rudwick, *W. E. B. Du Bois: A Study in Minority Group Leadership*, 1961. J. H. Franklin, *From Slavery to Freedom: A History of American Negroes*, 1967. A. Rampersad, *The Art and Imagination of W. E. B. Du Bois*, 1976. J. B. Moore, *W. E. B. Du Bois*, 1981. J. P. De Marco, *The Social Thought of W. E. B. Du Bois*, 1983. W. L. Andrews, *Critical Essays on W. E. B. Du Bois*, 1985.

Text Used: *The Souls of Black Folk: Essays and Sketches*, 1903.

from THE SOULS OF BLACK FOLK*

III: OF MR. BOOKER T. WASHINGTON AND OTHERS†

From birth till death enslaved; in word, in deed, unmanned!

Hereditary bondsmen! Know ye not
Who would be free themselves must strike the blow?

BYRON.[1]

Easily the most striking thing in the history of the American Negro since 1876[2] is the ascendancy of Mr. Booker T. Washington.[3] It began at the time when war memories and ideals were rapidly passing; a day of astonishing commercial development was dawning; a sense of doubt and hesitation overtook the freedmen's sons,—then it was that his leading began. Mr. Washington came, with a simple definite programme, at the psychological moment when the nation was a little ashamed of having bestowed so much sentiment on Negroes, and was concentrating its energies on Dollars. His programme of industrial education, conciliation of the South, and submission and silence as to civil and political rights, was not wholly original; the Free Negroes from 1830 up to war-time had striven to build

---

* This collection of fourteen essays on the social and spiritual world in which African Americans lived at the beginning of the twentieth century was first published in 1903.

† An essay first published in the *Guardian*, July 27, 1902.

[1] From *Childe Harold's Pilgrimage* (11. 74.710, 11.76.720–721), by the English romantic poet George Gordon (1788–1824), Lord Byron. The music that follows is from the refrain of a spiritual, what Du Bois calls a "Sorrow Song," entitled "A Great Camp-Meeting in de Promised Land." The words are "Going to mourn and never tire, / Mourn and never tire, mourn and never tire."

[2] The year marking the end of Reconstruction in the South.

[3] Washington (1856?–1915), the renowned African-American educator who founded Tuskegee Institute in Alabama and was an influential spokesman for African Americans; his address at the Atlanta Exposition in 1895 brought him to national prominence.

industrial schools, and the American Missionary Association had from the first taught various trades; and Price[4] and others had sought a way of honorable alliance with the best of the Southerners. But Mr. Washington first indissolubly linked these things; he put enthusiasm, unlimited energy, and perfect faith into this programme, and changed it from a by-path into a veritable Way of Life. And the tale of the methods by which he did this is a fascinating study of human life.

It startled the nation to hear a Negro advocating such a programme after many decades of bitter complaint; it startled and won the applause of the South, it interested and won the admiration of the North; and after a confused murmur of protest, it silenced if it did not convert the Negroes themselves.

To gain the sympathy and cooperation of the various elements comprising the white South was Mr. Washington's first task; and this, at the time Tuskegee was founded, seemed, for a black man, well-nigh impossible. And yet ten years later it was done in the word spoken at Atlanta: "In all things purely social we can be as separate as the five fingers, and yet one as the hand in all things essential to mutual progress." This "Atlanta Compromise"[5] is by all odds the most notable thing in Mr. Washington's career. The South interpreted it in different ways: the radicals received it as a complete surrender of the demand for civil and political equality; the conservatives, as a generously conceived working basis for mutual understanding. So both approved it, and to-day its author is certainly the most distinguished Southerner since Jefferson Davis,[6] and the one with the largest personal following.

Next to this achievement comes Mr. Washington's work in gaining place and consideration in the North. Others less shrewd and tactful had formerly essayed to sit on these two stools and had fallen between them; but as Mr. Washington knew the heart of the South from birth and training, so by singular insight he intuitively grasped the spirit of the age which was dominating the North. And so thoroughly did he learn the speech and thought of triumphant commercialism, and the ideals of material prosperity, that the picture of a lone black boy poring over a French grammar amid the weeds and dirt of a neglected home soon seemed to him the acme of absurdities.[7] One wonders what Socrates and St. Francis of Assisi would say to this.

And yet this very singleness of vision and thorough oneness with his age is a mark of the successful man. It is as though Nature must needs make men narrow in order to give them force. So Mr. Washington's cult has gained unquestioning followers, his work has wonderfully prospered, his friends are legion, and his enemies are confounded. To-day he stands as the one recognized spokesman of his ten million fellows, and one of the most notable figures in a nation of seventy millions. One hesitates, therefore, to criticize a life which, beginning with so little, has done so much. And yet the time is come when one may speak in all

[4] Thomas Frederick Price (1860–1919), a Roman Catholic priest who was a founder of the American Missionary Association.

[5] "Compromise" is Du Bois's term for what Washington proposed in his Atlanta address: an emphasis on vocational training for African Americans rather than an insistence on civil and social rights. Washington intended to promote racial harmony and to prepare young men and women for employment.

[6] Davis (1809–1889) was a U.S. senator from Mississippi (1847–1851, 1857–1861) and secretary of war (1853–1857) under the fourteenth President, Franklin Pierce (1804–1869); Davis became president of the Confederacy during the Civil War.

[7] Washington encountered this situation during his travels in the South and lamented the futility of such study when practical skills seemed so necessary (in *Up From Slavery* [1901], Ch. VIII).

sincerity and utter courtesy of the mistakes and shortcomings of Mr. Washington's career, as well as of his triumphs, without being thought captious or envious, and without forgetting that it is easier to do ill than well in the world.

The criticism that has hitherto met Mr. Washington has not always been of this broad character. In the South especially has he had to walk warily to avoid the harshest judgments,—and naturally so, for he is dealing with the one subject of deepest sensitiveness to that section. Twice—once when at the Chicago celebration of the Spanish-American War he alluded to the color-prejudice that is "eating away the vitals of the South," and once when he dined with President Roosevelt[8]—has the resulting Southern criticism been violent enough to threaten seriously his popularity. In the North the feeling has several times forced itself into words, that Mr. Washington's counsels of submission overlooked certain elements of true manhood, and that his educational programme was unnecessarily narrow. Usually, however, such criticism has not found open expression, although, too, the spiritual sons of the Abolitionists have not been prepared to acknowledge that the schools founded before Tuskegee, by men of broad ideals and self-sacrificing spirit, were wholly failures or worthy of ridicule. While, then, criticism has not failed to follow Mr. Washington, yet the prevailing public opinion of the land has been but too willing to deliver the solution of a wearisome problem into his hands, and say, "If that is all you and your race ask, take it."

Among his own people, however, Mr. Washington has encountered the strongest and most lasting opposition, amounting at times to bitterness, and even to-day continuing strong and insistent even though largely silenced in outward expression by the public opinion of the nation. Some of this opposition is, of course, mere envy; the disappointment of displaced demagogues and the spite of narrow minds. But aside from this, there is among educated and thoughtful colored men in all parts of the land a feeling of deep regret, sorrow, and apprehension at the wide currency and ascendancy which some of Mr. Washington's theories have gained. These same men admire his sincerity of purpose, and are willing to forgive much to honest endeavor which is doing something worth the doing. They cooperate with Mr. Washington as far as they conscientiously can; and, indeed, it is no ordinary tribute to this man's tact and power that, steering as he must between so many diverse interests and opinions, he so largely retains the respect of all.

But the hushing of the criticism of honest opponents is a dangerous thing. It leads some of the best of the critics to unfortunate silence and paralysis of effort, and others to burst into speech so passionately and intemperately as to lose listeners. Honest and earnest criticism from those whose interests are most nearly touched,—criticism of writers by readers, of government by those governed, of leaders by those led,—this is the soul of democracy and the safeguard of modern society. If the best of the American Negroes receive by outer pressure a leader whom they had not recognized before, manifestly there is here a certain palpable gain. Yet there is also irreparable loss,—a loss of that peculiarly valuable education which a group receives when by search and criticism it finds and commissions its own leaders. The way in which this is done is at once the most elementary and the nicest problem of social growth. History is but the record of such group-leadership; and yet how infinitely changeful is its type and character! And of all types and kinds, what can be more instructive than the leadership of a group within a

---

[8] Theodore Roosevelt (1858–1919), twenty-sixth U.S. president (1901–1909). Different groups in different parts of the country criticized Washington for attending this dinner in 1901.

group?—that curious double movement where real progress may be negative and actual advance be relative retrogression. All this is the social student's inspiration and despair.

Now in the past the American Negro has had instructive experience in the choosing of group leaders, founding thus a peculiar dynasty which in the light of present conditions is worth while studying. When sticks and stones and beasts form the sole environment of a people, their attitude is largely one of determined opposition to and conquest of natural forces. But when to earth and brute is added an environment of men and ideas, then the attitude of the imprisoned group may take three main forms,—a feeling of revolt and revenge; an attempt to adjust all thought and action to the will of the greater group; or, finally, a determined effort at self-realization and self-development despite environing opinion. The influence of all of these attitudes at various times can be traced in the history of the American Negro, and in the evolution of his successive leaders.

Before 1750, while the fire of African freedom still burned in the veins of the slaves, there was in all leadership or attempted leadership but the one motive of revolt and revenge,—typified in the terrible Maroons, the Danish blacks, and Cato of Stono,[9] and veiling all the Americas in fear of insurrection. The liberalizing tendencies of the latter half of the eighteenth century brought, along with kindlier relations between black and white, thoughts of ultimate adjustment and assimilation. Such aspiration was especially voiced in the earnest songs of Phyllis, in the martyrdom of Attucks, the fighting of Salem and Poor, the intellectual accomplishments of Banneker and Derham, and the political demands of the Cuffes.[10]

Stern financial and social stress after the war cooled much of the previous humanitarian ardor. The disappointment and impatience of the Negroes at the persistence of slavery and serfdom voiced itself in two movements. The slaves in the South, aroused undoubtedly by vague rumors of the Haytian revolt, made three fierce attempts at insurrection,—in 1800 under Gabriel in Virginia, in 1822 under Vesey in Carolina, and in 1831 again in Virginia under the terrible Nat Turner.[11] In the Free States, on the other hand, a new and curious attempt at self-development was made. In Philadelphia and New York color-prescription led to a withdrawal of Negro communicants from white churches and the formation of a peculiar socio-religious institution among the Negroes known as the African Church,—an organization still living and controlling in its various branches over a million of men.

---

[9] Fugitive slaves from the West Indies and Guiana in the seventeenth and eighteenth centuries, or their descendants; slaves in the Danish West Indies, who revolted in 1733 because of food shortages; Cato of Stono, North Carolina, who led a slave insurrection in 1739 during which twenty-five whites were killed.

[10] Notable eighteenth-century African Americans: the poet Phillis Wheatley (1753?–1784); Crispus Attucks (1723?–1770), the leader of colonists killed by British troops in the "Boston Massacre"; Peter Salem (?–1816), the patriot who shot Major Pitcairn in the Battle of Bunker Hill during the Revolutionary War; Salem Poor (1747–?), a soldier who fought at Bunker Hill and Valley Forge; Benjamin Banneker (1731–1806), a Maryland mathematician who published his astronomical calculations from 1791 to 1797 in his *Almanack and Ephemeris;* James Derham (1762–?), an eminent New Orleans physician who bought his freedom in 1783; Paul Cuffe (1759–1817), a Massachusetts organizer of a movement to settle free blacks in African colonies.

[11] Gabriel (1775?–1800) was hanged after his aborted attempt to attack Richmond, Virginia, with a thousand slaves; Denmark Vesey (1767?–1822), after purchasing his freedom in 1800, was hanged for leading a slave uprising in North Carolina; Turner (1800–1831) was hanged for commanding approximately sixty slaves in an insurrection in Southampton County, Virginia.

Walker's[12] wild appeal against the trend of the times showed how the world was changing after the coming of the cotton-gin. By 1830 slavery seemed hopelessly fastened on the South, and the slaves thoroughly cowed into submission. The free Negroes of the North, inspired by the mulatto immigrants from the West Indies, began to change the basis of their demands; they recognized the slavery of slaves, but insisted that they themselves were freemen, and sought assimilation and amalgamation with the nation on the same terms with other men. Thus, Forten and Purvis of Philadelphia, Shad of Wilmington, Du Bois of New Haven, Barbadoes of Boston,[13] and others, strove singly and together as men, they said, not as slaves; as "people of color," not as "Negroes." The trend of the times, however, refused them recognition save in individual and exceptional cases, considered them as one with all the despised blacks, and they soon found themselves striving to keep even the rights they formerly had of voting and working and moving as freemen. Schemes of migration and colonization arose among them; but these they refused to entertain, and they eventually turned to the Abolition movement as a final refuge.

Here, led by Remond, Nell, Wells-Brown, and Douglass,[14] a new period of self-assertion and self-development dawned. To be sure, ultimate freedom and assimilation was the ideal before the leaders, but the assertion of the manhood rights of the Negro by himself was the main reliance, and John Brown's raid[15] was the extreme of its logic. After the war and emancipation, the great form of Frederick Douglass, the greatest of American Negro leaders, still led the host. Self-assertion, especially in political lines, was the main programme, and behind Douglass came Elliot, Bruce, and Langston, and the Reconstruction politicians, and, less conspicuous but of greater social significance Alexander Crummell and Bishop Daniel Payne.[16]

---

[12] David Walker (1785?–1830), a free-born African American, who urged blacks to unite against slavery in his pamphlet, *Walker's Appeal,* in Boston in 1831.

[13] James Forten (1766–1842), a drummer-boy during the American Revolution, later a prosperous manufacturer of sailboat equipment in Philadelphia; Robert Purvis (1810–1898), president of the Underground Railroad and co-founder of the American Anti-Slavery Society in 1833; Abraham Shadd (?–1860?), a Delaware delegate to the first National Negro Convention in 1830 and president of the third Convention in 1833; Alexander Du Bois (1803–1887), active in the Negro Episcopal church in Massachusetts and grandfather of W. E. B. Du Bois; James G. Barbadoes, a Massachusetts delegate to the first National Negro Convention.

[14] African-American leaders whose careers spanned the Civil War: Charles Lenox Remond (1810–1873), an abolitionist and powerful orator from Salem, Massachusetts, who served as recruiting officer for the Massachusetts militia during the Civil War; William Cooper Nell (1816–1874), an abolitionist and the first African American to secure a U.S. government appointment (as postal clerk), instrumental in extending equal opportunities to all schoolchildren in Boston; William Wells Brown (1816?–1884), a writer whose works included an autobiographical *Narrative* (1847) and *Clotel: Or, The President's Daughter* (1853), the first published novel by an African American; Frederick Douglass (1817–1895), author of the *Narrative of the Life of Frederick Douglass* (1845), later U.S. minister to Haiti and U.S. marshal of the District of Columbia.

[15] Brown (1800–1859) was a white abolitionist who led a raid on the U.S. armory in Harper's Ferry, Virginia, in October 1859. He was captured, tried, and hanged in December 1859.

[16] African Americans whose careers flourished in the latter half of the nineteenth century: Robert Brown Elliot (1842–1884), a graduate of Eton in England and U.S. congressman from South Carolina; Blanche K. Bruce (1841–1898), a Virginia-born slave educated at Oberlin College in Ohio, U.S. Senator from Mississippi (1875–1881); John Mercer Langston (1829–1897), an educator, lawyer, president of the Virginia Normal and Collegiate Institute (1885–1888), and U.S. congressman from Virginia (1888–1890); Crummell (1819–1898) was an Episcopal missionary in Liberia for twenty years after being educated at Cambridge University in England; Payne (1811–1893) was bishop of the African Methodist Episcopal church and president of Wilberforce University (1863–1870).

Then came the Revolution of 1876, the suppression of the Negro votes, the changing and shifting of ideals, and the seeking of new lights in the great night. Douglass, in his old age, still bravely stood for the ideals of his early manhood,— ultimate assimilation *through* self-assertion, and on no other terms. For a time Price arose as a new leader, destined, it seemed, not to give up, but to re-state the old ideals in a form less repugnant to the white South. But he passed away in his prime. Then came the new leader. Nearly all the former ones had become leaders by the silent suffrage of their fellows, had sought to lead their own people alone, and were usually, save Douglass, little known outside their race. But Booker T. Washington arose as essentially the leader not of one race but of two,—a compromiser between the South, the North, and the Negro. Naturally the Negroes resented, at first bitterly, signs of compromise which surrendered their civil and political rights, even though this was to be exchanged for larger chances of economic development. The rich and dominating North, however, was not only weary of the race problem, but was investing largely in Southern enterprises, and welcomed any method of peaceful cooperation. Thus, by national opinion, the Negroes began to recognize Mr. Washington's leadership; and the voice of criticism was hushed.

Mr. Washington represents in Negro thought the old attitude of adjustment and submission; but adjustment at such a peculiar time as to make his programme unique. This is an age of unusual economic development, and Mr. Washington's programme naturally takes an economic cast, becoming a gospel of Work and Money to such an extent as apparently almost completely to overshadow the higher aims of life. Moreover, this is an age when the more advanced races are coming in closer contact with the less developed races, and the race-feeling is therefore intensified; and Mr. Washington's programme practically accepts the alleged inferiority of the Negro races. Again, in our own land, the reaction from the sentiment of war time has given impetus to race-prejudice against Negroes, and Mr. Washington withdraws many of the high demands of Negroes as men and American citizens. In other periods of intensified prejudice all the Negro's tendency to self-assertion has been called forth; at this period a policy of submission is advocated. In the history of nearly all other races and peoples the doctrine preached at such crises has been that manly self-respect is worth more than lands and houses, and that a people who voluntarily surrender such respect, or cease striving for it, are not worth civilizing.

In answer to this, it has been claimed that the Negro can survive only through submission. Mr. Washington distinctly asks that black people give up, at least for the present, three things,—

First, political power,

Second, insistence on civil rights,

Third, higher education of Negro youth,—

and concentrate all their energies on industrial education, the accumulation of wealth, and the conciliation of the South. This policy has been courageously and insistently advocated for over fifteen years, and has been triumphant for perhaps ten years. As a result of this tender of the palm-branch, what has been the return? In these years there have occurred:

1. The disfranchisement of the Negro.

2. The legal creation of a distinct status of civil inferiority for the Negro.

3. The steady withdrawal of aid from institutions for the higher training of the Negro.

These movements are not, to be sure, direct results of Mr. Washington's teachings; but his propaganda has, without a shadow of doubt, helped their speedier accomplishment. The question then comes: Is it possible, and probable, that nine millions of men can make effective progress in economic lines if they are deprived of political rights, made a servile caste, and allowed only the most meagre chance for developing their exceptional men? If history and reason give any distinct answer to these questions, it is an emphatic *No*. And Mr. Washington thus faces the triple paradox of his career:

1. He is striving nobly to make Negro artisans business men and property-owners; but it is utterly impossible, under modern competitive methods, for workingmen and property-owners to defend their rights and exist without the right of suffrage.

2. He insists on thrift and self-respect, but at the same time counsels a silent submission to civic inferiority such as is bound to sap the manhood of any race in the long run.

3. He advocates common-school[17] and industrial training, and depreciates institutions of higher learning; but neither the Negro common-schools, nor Tuskegee itself, could remain open a day were it not for teachers trained in Negro colleges, or trained by their graduates.

This triple paradox in Mr. Washington's position is the object of criticism by two classes of colored Americans. One class is spiritually descended from Toussaint the Savior,[18] through Gabriel, Vesey, and Turner, and they represent the attitude of revolt and revenge; they hate the white South blindly and distrust the white race generally, and so far as they agree on definite action, think that the Negro's only hope lies in emigration beyond the borders of the United States. And yet, by the irony of fate, nothing has more effectually made this programme seem hopeless than the recent course of the United States toward weaker and darker peoples in the West Indies, Hawaii, and the Philippines,—for where in the world may we go and be safe from lying and brute force?

The other class of Negroes who cannot agree with Mr. Washington has hitherto said little aloud. They deprecate the sight of scattered counsels, of internal disagreement; and especially they dislike making their just criticism of a useful and earnest man an excuse for a general discharge of venom from small-minded opponents. Nevertheless, the questions involved are so fundamental and serious that it is difficult to see how men like the Grimkes, Kelly Miller, J. W. E. Bowen,[19] and other representatives of this group, can much longer be silent. Such men feel in conscience bound to ask of this nation three things:

1. The right to vote.

2. Civic equality.

3. The education of youth according to ability.

They acknowledge Mr. Washington's invaluable service in counselling patience and courtesy in such demands; they do not ask that ignorant black men vote when ignorant whites are debarred, or that any reasonable restrictions in the suffrage

---

[17] Free public schools.

[18] François Dominique Toussaint L'Ouverture (1774?–1803), a self-educated freed slave, leader of the 1791 slave rebellion in Haiti that led to Haitian independence; treacherously seized by the French in 1802, he died in a dungeon in France, a symbol of the fight for individual freedom and national independence.

[19] The brothers Archibald (1849–1930) and Francis (1850–1937) Grimké, who demonstrated a concern for African-American affairs after the Civil War; Miller (1863–1939) was dean of Howard University in the 1890s; John Wesley Edward Bowen (1855–?), a Methodist clergyman and then president of Gammon Theological Seminary in Atlanta.

should not be applied; they know that the low social level of the mass of the race is responsible for much discrimination against it, but they also know, and the nation knows, that relentless color-prejudice is more often a cause than a result of the Negro's degradation; they seek the abatement of this relic of barbarism, and not its systematic encouragement and pampering by all agencies of social power from the Associated Press to the Church of Christ. They advocate, with Mr. Washington, a broad system of Negro common schools supplemented by thorough industrial training; but they are surprised that a man of Mr. Washington's insight cannot see that no such educational system ever has rested or can rest on any other basis than that of the well-equipped college and university, and they insist that there is a demand for a few such institutions throughout the South to train the best of the Negro youth as teachers, professional men, and leaders.

This group of men honor Mr. Washington for his attitude of conciliation toward the white South; they accept the "Atlanta Compromise" in its broadest interpretation; they recognize, with him, many signs of promise, many men of high purpose and fair judgment, in this section; they know that no easy task has been laid upon a region already tottering under heavy burdens. But, nevertheless, they insist that the way to truth and right lies in straightforward honesty, not in indiscriminate flattery; in praising those of the South who do well and criticising uncompromisingly those who do ill; in taking advantage of the opportunities at hand and urging their fellows to do the same, but at the same time in remembering that only a firm adherence to their higher ideals and aspirations will ever keep those ideals within the realm of possibility. They do not expect that the free right to vote, to enjoy civic rights, and to be educated, will come in a moment; they do not expect to see the bias and prejudices of years disappear at the blast of a trumpet; but they are absolutely certain that the way for a people to gain their reasonable rights is not by voluntarily throwing them away and insisting that they do not want them; that the way for a people to gain respect is not by continually belittling and ridiculing themselves; that, on the contrary, Negroes must insist continually, in season and out of season, that voting is necessary to modern manhood, that color discrimination is barbarism, and that black boys need education as well as white boys.

In failing thus to state plainly and unequivocally the legitimate demands of their people, even at the cost of opposing an honored leader, the thinking classes of American Negroes would shirk a heavy responsibility,—a responsibility to themselves, a responsibility to the struggling masses, a responsibility to the darker races of men whose future depends so largely on this American experiment, but especially a responsibility to this nation,—this common Fatherland. It is wrong to encourage a man or a people in evil-doing; it is wrong to aid and abet a national crime simply because it is unpopular not to do so. The growing spirit of kindliness and reconciliation between the North and South after the frightful differences of a generation ago ought to be a source of deep congratulation to all, and especially to those whose mistreatment caused the war; but if that reconciliation is to be marked by the industrial slavery and civic death of those same black men, with permanent legislation into a position of inferiority, then those black men, if they are really men, are called upon by every consideration of patriotism and loyalty to oppose such a course by all civilized methods, even though such opposition involves disagreement with Mr. Booker T. Washington. We have no right to sit silently by while the inevitable seeds are sown for a harvest of disaster to our children, black and white.

First, it is the duty of black men to judge the South discriminatingly. The present generation of Southerners are not responsible for the past, and they should not be blindly hated or blamed for it. Furthermore, to no class is the indiscriminate endorsement of the recent course of the South toward Negroes more nauseating than to the best thought of the South. The South is not "solid"; it is a land in the ferment of social change, wherein forces of all kinds are fighting for supremacy; and to praise the ill the South is to-day perpetrating is just as wrong as to condemn the good. Discriminating and broad-minded criticism is what the South needs,— needs it for the sake of her own white sons and daughters, and for the insurance of robust, healthy mental and moral development.

To-day even the attitude of the Southern whites toward the blacks is not, as so many assume, in all cases the same; the ignorant Southerner hates the Negro, the workingmen fear his competition, the money-makers wish to use him as a laborer, some of the educated see a menace in his upward development, while others— usually the sons of the masters—wish to help him to rise. National opinion has enabled this last class to maintain the Negro common schools, and to protect the Negro partially in property, life, and limb. Through the pressure of the money-makers, the Negro is in danger of being reduced to semi-slavery, especially in the country districts; the workingmen, and those of the educated who fear the Negro, have united to disfranchise him, and some have urged his deportation; while the passions of the ignorant are easily aroused to lynch and abuse any black man. To praise this intricate whirl of thought and prejudice is nonsense; to inveigh indis-criminately against "the South" is unjust; but to use the same breath in praising Governor Aycock, exposing Senator Morgan, arguing with Mr. Thomas Nelson Page, and denouncing Senator Ben Tillman,[20] is not only sane, but the imperative duty of thinking black men.

It would be unjust to Mr. Washington not to acknowledge that in several in-stances he has opposed movements in the South which were unjust to the Negro; he sent memorials to the Louisiana and Alabama constitutional conventions, he has spoken against lynching, and in other ways has openly or silently set his influ-ence against sinister schemes and unfortunate happenings. Notwithstanding this, it is equally true to assert that on the whole the distinct impression left by Mr. Wash-ington's propaganda is, first, that the South is justified in its present attitude to-ward the Negro because of the Negro's degradation; secondly, that the prime cause of the Negro's failure to rise more quickly is his wrong education in the past; and, thirdly, that his future rise depends primarily on his own efforts. Each of these propositions is a dangerous half-truth. The supplementary truths must never be lost sight of: first, slavery and race-prejudice are potent if not sufficient causes of the Negro's position; second, industrial and common-school training were necessarily slow in planting because they had to await the black teachers trained by higher institutions,—it being extremely doubtful if any essentially dif-ferent development was possible, and certainly a Tuskegee was unthinkable be-

---

[20] Charles Brantley Aycock (1859–1912), governor of North Carolina (1901–1905); Edward Denison Morgan (1811–1883), governor of New York (1859–1863) and U.S. senator (1863–1869), who voted with the minority in President Andrew Johnson's veto of the Freedman's Bureau bill and later to try Johnson for impeachment; Page (1853–1922) was a Virginia-born writer and diplomat whose novels contributed to romantic legends of life in the South before the Civil War; Benjamin Ryan Tillman (1847–1918), governor of South Carolina (1890–1894) and U.S. senator (1895–1918), who designed the article requiring literacy and property qualifications for voting during the South Carolina constitutional conventional, making it virtually impossible for freed slaves to vote, and advocated the repeal of the Fifteenth Amendment (ratified in 1870), which gave all (male) U.S. citizens the right to vote regardless of race, color, or "previous condition of servitude."

fore 1880; and, third, while it is a great truth to say that the Negro must strive and strive mightily to help himself, it is equally true that unless his striving be not simply seconded, but rather aroused and encouraged, by the initiative of the richer and wiser environing group, he cannot hope for great success.

In his failure to realize and impress this last point, Mr. Washington is especially to be criticised. His doctrine has tended to make the whites, North and South, shift the burden of the Negro problem to the Negro's shoulders and stand aside as critical and rather pessimistic spectators; when in fact the burden belongs to the nation, and the hands of none of us are clean if we bend not our energies to righting these great wrongs.

The South ought to be led, by candid and honest criticism, to assert her better self and do her full duty to the race she has cruelly wronged and is still wronging. The North—her co-partner in guilt—cannot salve her conscience by plastering it with gold. We cannot settle this problem by diplomacy and suaveness, by "policy" alone. If worse come to worst, can the moral fibre of this country survive the slow throttling and murder of nine millions of men?

The black men of America have a duty to perform, a duty stern and delicate,—a forward movement to oppose a part of the work of their greatest leader. So far as Mr. Washington preaches Thrift, Patience, and Industrial Training for the masses, we must hold up his hands and strive with him, rejoicing in his honors and glorying in the strength of this Joshua[21] called of God and of man to lead the headless host. But so far as Mr. Washington apologizes for injustice, North or South, does not rightly value the privilege and duty of voting, belittles the emasculating effects of caste distinctions, and opposes the higher training and ambition of our brighter minds,—so far as he, the South, or the Nation, does this,—we must unceasingly and firmly oppose them. By every civilized and peaceful method we must strive for the rights which the world accords to men, clinging unwaveringly to those great words which the sons of the Fathers would fain forget: "We hold these truths to be self-evident: That all men are created equal; that they are endowed by their Creator with certain unalienable rights; that among these are life, liberty, and the pursuit of happiness."

1903

LATE 19TH-CENTURY FICTION

The central movement in American fiction in the last half of the nineteenth century was the development of realism. The realistic novel had been a salient feature of the literary landscape in Europe for several decades before realism took hold in America. Through his reviews and columns in the *Atlantic Monthly* and *Harper's,* William Dean Howells introduced French and Russian novelists to the reading public. He also recognized the promise of America's new and innovative writers, among them Charles W. Chesnutt, Sarah Orne Jewett, and Stephen Crane. As a practicing novelist Howells avoided the bizarre and the heroic out of a conviction that the proper task of the serious American writer is to delineate the details of everyday existence. To portray life realistically, he felt, is to portray it as most readers know it. In his more than two dozen novels, Howells examined a broad

---

[21] The Old Testament successor of Moses who led the Israelites into Canaan.

range of middle-class life in late nineteenth-century American settings, affirming its values and criticizing with a sometimes withering touch its moral shortcomings. He wrote of weakness, self-indulgence, and divorce in *A Modern Instance* (1882); the amorality of the business world in *The Rise of Silas Lapham* (1885); and the complex issues of workers' rights and socialist goals in *A Hazard of New Fortunes* (1890).

As a novelist Howells displayed considerable insight into the motives and convictions of his characters. Yet, his sensitivity to character serves large social concerns: for Howells's great subject is life in society, the analysis of ethical conduct in a world devoid of absolutes. Conversely, his friend Henry James was absorbed with what we might call the inner life. Throughout a lengthy career, in such early works as *The American* (1877) and *Daisy Miller* (1879) and in such accomplished late novels as *The Wings of the Dove* (1902), *The Ambassadors* (1903), and *The Golden Bowl* (1904), James explored with increasing sophistication and acuity the contrast between American "innocence" and European "experience." His Gothic dramas of the mind, chief among them "The Turn of the Screw" (1898) and "The Jolly Corner" (1908), manipulate ghostly conventions with a similar concern for character and for psychological validity. James's evocative stories of artists and writers, often wry and always compassionate, as shown by "The Real Thing" (1892) and "The Death of the Lion" (1894), reveal still another aspect of his achievement in fiction. So do *The Bostonians* (1886), a provocative portrait of human relationships in the context of the feminist movement, and *What Maisie Knew* (1897), a novel of adult misunderstandings told through the medium of a little girl's mind. Whatever his subject, James's concern for psychological realism remained constant.

Unlike Howells or James, Mark Twain had roots in the fiction of the pre-Civil War Southwest Humorists, whose use of the oral tale and vernacular speech left a rich legacy for later writers. Twain did write a number of novels that make little or no use of such a tradition: *The Prince and the Pauper* (1882), *A Connecticut Yankee in King Arthur's Court* (1889), and *The Tragedy of Pudd'nhead Wilson* (1894) suggest his interest in a variety of locales and themes. First and foremost, however, Twain's achievement was one of language and place. In *The Adventures of Tom Sawyer* (1876) he deals with the setting he knew best to tell a boy's story from a perspective at once good-natured, satirical, and nostalgic; in the anecdotal *Life on the Mississippi* (1883) he joyfully recalls his boyhood years on the river and bemoans the manner in which commerce had converted adventure to matters of dollars and cents; and in *Adventures of Huckleberry Finn* (1884) he brings language and place together to create an idiom as vital to American prose fiction as the achievement of Walt Whitman and Emily Dickinson is to American poetry. In *Huckleberry Finn* Twain's use of the vernacular is vibrant, metaphorically fresh. It allows him to describe customs and attitudes with precision, to give a rambunctious scrutiny of small-town river life in its generosity and cruelty, and yet to preserve the innocence of the narrator, Huckleberry Finn, throughout what the critic James M. Cox (in *Mark Twain: The Fate of Humor* [1978]) has called a sad and inevitable initiation into the moral dimensions of life. With its unique blending of naïveté and knowledge, the language of Huckleberry Finn is a notable contribution to the development of realism in American fiction.

The image of the locomotive on the western plains—"the machine in the garden"—depicted in this 1871 engraving of a Kansas-Pacific Railroad train, symbolized human intrusion into the wilderness.

A native-born impulse toward realism, nourished by authors who sought to portray the manner in which lives are conditioned by regional environments, was also evident in the late nineteenth century. The term "local-color writing" conventionally applied to the fiction of those authors has long had the unintentional effect of measuring the quality of such work according to quantitative standards. The cameolike achievement of the best regional fiction evokes condescending praise if we assume that excellence comes only on a grand scale, that the scope of Harriet Beecher Stowe's *Uncle Tom's Cabin* (1851–1852) or Henry James's *Portrait of a Lady* (1881) takes precedence over the focus of stories such as Constance Fenimore Woolson's "King David" (1878) and Mary E. Wilkins Freeman's "A Village Singer" (1891). Just as music criticism assesses the quality of a sonata without measuring it against the dimensions of a symphony, so literary criticism stands in need of perspectives to describe achievement in regional writing.

With their expert use of dialect and their dispassionate observation of characters needing to feel important or at least useful in their restrictive environments, the stories of Woolson and of Freeman put us inside the worlds of which they write, that of the South during Reconstruction in Woolson's *Rodman the Keeper* (1880), that of New England village life in Freeman's *A New England Nun* (1891). The work of Sarah Orne Jewett enlarges this tradition of unpretentious distinction with

=CONTEXTS=

Regionalism

Regionalistic literature deals with the conditions and environment of a specific geographic area. Authors in this tradition make use of a region's folklore and history and show how they affect the lives of the inhabitants. Bret Harte (1836–1902), a noted regional author, gained fame as an adept observer of character and conditions in middle nineteenth-century northern California. Though best known for his colorful portraits of California frontier life, Harte subordinates local-color interests to the more universal issues of personal courage and moral ambiguity. His most widely acclaimed work, "The Luck of Roaring Camp" (1868), has served as a model for many tales of the Old West. The opening paragraph typifies life in the gold fields and mining camps of California's gold-rush days:

The Luck of Roaring Camp

There was a commotion in Roaring Camp. It could not have been a fight, for in 1850 that was not novel enough to have called together the entire settlement. The ditches and claims were not only deserted, but "Tuttle's grocery" had contributed its gamblers, who, it will be remembered, calmly continued their game the day that French Pete and Kanaka Joe shot each other to death over the bar in the front room. The whole camp was collected before a rude cabin on the outer edge of the clearing. Conversation was carried on in a low tone, but the name of a woman was frequently repeated. It was a name familiar enough in the camp,—"Cherokee Sal."

Perhaps the less said of her the better. She was a coarse, and it is to be feared, a very sinful woman. But at that time she was the only woman in Roaring Camp. . . .

Regional authors typically use peculiar dialects to convey regional color. Harte uses this technique in the miner Stumpy's speech to the Roaring Camp crowd at the christening of the child of the dead Cherokee Sal:

"It ain't my style to spoil fun, boys," said the little man, stoutly eying the faces around him, "but it strikes me that this thing ain't exactly on the squar. It's playing it pretty low down on this yer baby to ring in fun on him that he ain't goin' to understand. And ef there's goin' to be any godfathers 'round, I'd like to see who's got any better rights than me."

Bret Harte, 1868

stories set in her native state of Maine; from the promise of *Deephaven* (1877) to the achievement of *Country of the Pointed Firs* (1896), Jewett's work demonstrates how character and locale interact. To appreciate her stories is to understand why Jewett exercised so important an influence on the fiction of Willa Cather (as Cather gracefully acknowledges in *Not Under Forty* [1936]).

The most popular books in the second half of the nineteenth century were those published in the Dime Novel series, originated by Erastus F. Beadle, and those that made up the various series written by Horatio Alger, Jr. Paperback dime novels (which actually sold for a nickel) were immensely popular with soldiers during the Civil War and with the general public until the 1890s. Melodramatic and ridden with formula, they were written (generally for $75) by various authors under a baffling array of pseudonyms and deal chiefly with the American Revolution and with episodes of frontier fighting. By 1865 the publishing firm of Beadle & Adams had sold more than four million dime novels, among them Ann Sophia Stephens's *Malaeska: The Indian Wife of the White Hunter* (1860), which sold 300,000 copies.

Moralistic critics objected to the extravagance of dime novels the way some people objected to comic books a century later. But no moralist could find fault with the 119 books written by Horatio Alger, Jr., an estimated twenty million copies of which were sold in the late nineteenth century. Among the most popular were those in the Ragged Dick Series (begun in 1867), the Luck and Pluck Series (begun in 1869), and the Tattered Tom Series (begun in 1871). Invariably, Alger's young (and poor) heroes shine shoes or sell newspapers; just as invariably, they discover that working hard and being good lead to fame and fortune. Life is that simple in Alger novels, which deplore liquor and idleness and show that virtue leads to financial rewards.

Understandably, readers were also drawn to fiction that portrays, in different ways, the complexities of human life. In her stories of Cajun society in Louisiana, Kate Chopin employed both realistic techniques and the emphasis on rootedness that is an essential part of regional writing. Similarly, she brought a strong sense of the French-Catholic ambience of New Orleans to *The Awakening* (1899), her memorable account of Edna Pontellier's futile attempt to balance her role as a wife and her existence as a woman. Told in the first person (and based on her own experience), Charlotte Perkins Gilman's landmark story "The Yellow Wallpaper" (1892) moves disjointedly from realistic awareness to visions of fantasy and terror as it portrays the mind of a woman virtually suffocating from her physician-husband's efforts to restore her to health. The different and distinctive worlds of Charles W. Chesnutt can be seen in the stories that make up *The Conjure Woman* (1899) and those collected in *The Wife of His Youth* (1899), the first a series of dialect tales, the second a set of realistic fictions centering on conflicts of loyalties. The surface joviality of *The Conjure Woman* and the role of coincidence in parts of *The Wife of His Youth* do not obscure the books' underlying tone. What Howells said in reviewing Chesnutt's novel *The Marrow of Tradition* (1901) for the *North American Review* applies to both collections of stories: "bitter, bitter," but "powerful."

Realism prizes accuracy, as Frank Norris correctly observes in his 1896 essay on the French novelist Émile Zola. But naturalism, according to Norris, distorts, probes, and caricatures in its efforts to get at the truths of human life that lie beneath the drama of the commonplace. As a literary movement arriving with force at the end of the nineteenth century, naturalism was a way of seeing human beings "twisted from the ordinary" (in Norris's words), "wrenched" from the uneventful. In novels such as *Vandover and the Brute* (published posthumously in 1914) and *McTeague* (1899), Norris enacts his ideas with characteristic energy: beneath the socialized exterior of life lie elemental forces that erupt into the lives of Vandover and McTeague and plunge them into worlds deformed with pain and tragedy.

Whereas Norris's fiction stresses elemental forces at odds with social constraints, the work of other naturalists tends to portray human beings overwhelmed by environmental forces. In many of Jack London's stories and novels, the struggle to stay alive in settings desolate and threatening is the focus of the narrative; setting becomes the adversary in these tales, mighty in its power to erase life. More complex is the work of Stephen Crane. Crane emphasized the grinding and overwhelming power of environment, social and economic, in *Maggie: A Girl of the Streets* (1893) and in *George's Mother* (1896) but developed a prose both supple and impressionistic to tell the ironic story of Henry Fleming's maturation in *The Red Badge of Courage* (1895), in which the sun mirrors emotional states, and the struggle for survival in "The Open Boat" (1898), in which nature is flatly indifferent to human hopes and prayers. Likewise ironic is "The Bride Comes to Yellow Sky" (1898), a western comedy of manners that punctures the glamor of a gunfighter era Crane would deny ever existed. Naturalism was significant in shaping Crane's fiction. But anyone who writes of women working "in various shades of yellow discontent" or a character living through the "red years" of his youth (as Crane does in *Maggie*) is cultivating an impressionistic style that resists a rigid adherence to naturalism. The work of Theodore Dreiser in the twentieth century would give naturalism its fullest place in American fiction. That work would take its place beside the fiction of Edith Wharton, Willa Cather, and other writers who invoked new strategies of expression to explore the human condition.

Mark Twain (Samuel Clemens)
(1835–1910)

Born in the hamlet of Florida, Missouri, in 1835, Samuel Langhorne Clemens grew up in the Mississippi River town of Hannibal that he later fictionalized as St. Petersburg in *The Adventures of Tom Sawyer* (1876) and *Adventures of Huckleberry Finn* (1884). His father, John Marshall Clemens, was a hopeful but struggling lawyer, postmaster, justice of the peace, and storekeeper. John Clemens had failed in a move westward after he married the vivacious Jane Lampton in Adair Country, Kentucky, in 1823; the couple wound up in Missouri, where John, ever dignified, strove toward success until his death in 1847. From Jane Lampton Clemens, blessed with a good sense of humor to go with her hard life, Samuel Clemens may have learned at least the rudiments of the deadpan humor he later perfected. As his friend and biographer Albert Bigelow Paine notes, Clemens remembered his mother's way of saying something humorous with the air of not seeing its humor at all. He admired that type of delivery.

After the death of his father, twelve-year-old Samuel was apprenticed to a local printer; four years later, having learned the trade, he went to work for his older brother Orion, who had become a publisher in Hannibal. But in 1853 young Clemens decided to roam: he traveled to St. Louis, Cincinnati, Philadelphia, New York, and other cities, working in printing establishments often on a daily basis to earn his way. During this time he also visited and worked in Keokuk, Iowa, and it was in the Keokuk *Saturday Post* in the late 1850s that he published three humorous accounts of his experiences on the Mississippi River under the unlikely pseudonym of Thomas Jefferson Snodgrass. He likewise reached back to his days on the river when he adopted his enduring pseudonym from the riverboat cry of "Mark Twain" (signifying "two fathoms deep," and therefore a safe channel) for the sketches of mining life and western adventure he wrote for newspapers in Nevada and California in 1863 and 1864.

At age twenty-one Clemens signed on with the experienced Horace Bixby to serve an apprenticeship of eighteen months as a cub riverboat pilot, after which he fulfilled a childhood ambition and became a licensed pilot on the Mississippi River. Not only did the job give him status among those connected with riverboat commerce; it also gave him deep inner satisfaction, the product of a way of life that he saw as authentic, without sham. Writing as Mark Twain almost two decades later, he looked back on those pre-Civil War days with reverent pleasure in *Old Times on the Mississippi* (1875), a series of seven articles written for the *Atlantic Monthly,* then edited by his friend William Dean Howells.

When the Civil War brought an end to commercial traffic on the Mississippi River, Clemens spent several weeks in an irregular unit of the Confederate Army, an experience he recalled in "The Private History of a Campaign That Failed," published in the *Century Magazine* in 1885. Typically, he exaggerated his military misadventures with an ever-developing sense of language and pace and the effects to be gained by reprise and audacious changes in tone. "The Private History" is comic with sudden interludes of seriousness, humorous at the expense of fellow-soldiers with boomerang thrusts reserved for the soldier-writer, who concludes his account of an inglorious career by saying, "I knew more about retreating than the man that invented retreating." One of Mark Twain's most endearing traits as a humorist was his willingness to make a target of himself: "I am a great and sublime fool," he once wrote to his friend Howells; "but then I am God's fool, & all His works must be contemplated with respect."

Late in 1861, Clemens, no longer part of the amateur militia, accompanied his brother Orion to the Nevada Territory: an official trip for Orion, who had been appointed secretary of the territory by President Abraham Lincoln; an adventure for Samuel, who hoped to get rich mining silver but wound up mining his experiences for sketches in the Virginia City *Territorial Enterprise*. Clemens was officially known as Mark Twain by 1865, when he published his version of a well-known tall tale, "Jim Smiley and His Jumping Frog" (later called "The Notorious Jumping Frog of Calaveras County") in the New York *Saturday Press*. The story brought an appreciative national audience to Mark Twain at his unbuckled best.

After traveling east in 1866, Twain sailed the following year on the excursion ship *Quaker City,* touring Mediterranean countries and the Holy Land as a correspondent for the New York *Tribune* and the San Francisco *Alta California*. His letters to these newspapers were shaped into his first book, *The Innocents Abroad* (1869); both the letters and the book were immensely popular for their satire of "Old World" institutions and manners and for their good-natured account of provincial attitudes among the American "pilgrims." Although it thrives on stereotypes, Twain's narrative voice in *The Innocents Abroad* sets the conditions for humor, from his observations on the gradual demise of the diaries-of-the-trip begun by many passengers to his wide-eyed report that the legendary Sea of Galilee was really no bigger than Lake Tahoe.

The success of his first book gave Twain some remunerative years as a writer and lecturer. During this period he met, courted, and married (in 1870) Olivia Langdon, the daughter of a wealthy coal merchant in Elmira, New York. If part of Mark Twain remained irreverent and wild, another part now yearned for social solidity; the couple built a mansion in Hartford, Connecticut, and became established members of the community. And almost because they were opposites in temperament and background—with her refinement and his roughneck ways—their relationship was mutually rewarding, despite the tendency of some recent critics to see Olivia as one who stifled her husband's lusty imagination. Twain could contrive an elaborate letter to Howells claiming that Howells had called someone "a quadrilateral, astronomical, incandescent sonuvabitch"; at the same time he could play "Youth" to Olivia's "Angel" and depend on a gentility as authentic as the riverboat experiences that had made him Mark Twain.

The pace of Twain's career accelerated in the 1870s. In 1872 he published *Roughing It*, an unbridled account of his adventures in Nevada and California, complete with outlandish tall tales and satirical broadsides. The following year, in collaboration with the journalist Charles Dudley Warner, he brought out *The Gilded Age*, a flimsy attempt at a novel, which nonetheless gave a name to an era of rampant capitalism in nineteenth-century American history. And in 1876 he returned to the surer ground of childhood memories in Hannibal with *Tom Sawyer*, a book filled with nostalgia for a simple world of good and bad and dominated by a narrative voice that mocks both patent medicines and the romantic pretensions of its young protagonist. In *Tom Sawyer* we first see Tom and Huckleberry Finn operating as a pair: Tom as society's hero, the entrepreneur who gets other boys to whitewash the family fence; Huck as the asocial sidekick who enjoys an unschooled and unwashed life and sleeps in discarded barrels. Whereas it is evident from the very beginning of *Tom Sawyer* that Tom has complete (and sometimes tiresome) authority over Huck in all matters referring to society and to books, it is also evident that he knows the power of Huck's reputation: asked why he arrived late for school, Tom replies, "I stopped to talk with Huckleberry Finn." Characteristically, Tom knows how to unload a bombshell in the schoolroom; he is a master at gauging "effects."

Perhaps because the figure of Huckleberry Finn had a latent energy that could not be realized in the tidy world of *Tom Sawyer*, in which fate metes out punishment and society dispenses rewards, Twain began writing *Adventures of Huckleberry Finn* in 1876. Working on it intermittently, struggling with elements of plot, and taking time to write *The Prince and the Pauper* in 1882, he did not finish the new novel until 1883, and even then

An illustration by E. W. Kemble from the first edition of Mark Twain's Adventures of Huckleberry Finn.

took seven additional months for revision. The master step in the book that became his classic was to make Huckleberry Finn the narrator. Twain thereby relied not only on his knowledge of the river and of small-town life in the antebellum South but on all he had assimilated about the vibrancy and freshness of vernacular speech—extending its resources far beyond what other writers had done, sacrificing nothing by way of description and character portrayal, converting the world Huckleberry Finn sees and hears and smells into an idiom that has remained vital for more than a century. First and foremost, *Huckleberry Finn* is a triumph of language. "All modern American literature comes from one book by Mark Twain called *Huckleberry Finn,*" writes Ernest Hemingway in *The Green Hills of Africa* (1935), a resounding tribute even when adjusted for exaggeration. Such was not the opinion of genteel readers who greeted the book in the 1880s, however; many thought the book vulgar and trashy, and the public library in Concord, Massachusetts, banned the novel from its shelves. One hundred years later *Huckleberry Finn* still offends some readers, who view its racial epithets out of context and overlook the education that rubs off on the unsuspecting Huck from his association with the runaway slave Jim. It is not surprising that Twain's novel continues to trouble readers; for it makes us confront in unrelenting terms the pain, and shame, of our history.

By 1885 fame and fortune had come to Mark Twain, and the future appeared even brighter. His large investment in the Charles R. Webster and Company publishing firm looked like a stroke of genius when the company brought out the remarkably successful *Personal Memoirs of U. S. Grant* (1885). And the automatic typesetting machine of James W. Paige, heavily underwritten by Twain for more than a dozen years, seemed like an invention that would secure the future for those wise enough to read it. But Webster's firm, unable to repeat its commercial success, foundered and eventually failed after the financial panic of 1893. And Paige's typesetter became a total loss because of unforeseen competition from the superior Linotype machine. Before the final collapse of these two ventures, which sent Twain into bankruptcy, *A Connecticut Yankee in King Arthur's Court* (1889) suggested his frustration: ostensibly a comic satire on medieval superstition and cant, the novel becomes a scathing indictment of nineteenth-century "progress," astonishing in its violence, disturbing in its vision. *The Tragedy of Pudd'nhead Wilson* (1894) extends that vision, spinning out its contrived plot on issues of slavery and nurture with little to offset a tone of disdain. To protect some property from creditors, the bankrupt Twain went so far as to copyright *Pudd'nhead* in Olivia's name.

With some hope and little inspiration Twain turned back to his best-known characters in *Tom Sawyer Abroad* (1894) and *Tom Sawyer, Detective* (1896), both narrated by Huckleberry Finn, and embarked on a round-the-world lecture trip—out of which came *Following the Equator* (1897), a travel book that understandably lacks the buoyancy of his earlier work. Although he finished paying off his debts in 1898, personal tragedy followed him at this time: his oldest daughter, Susy, died of meningitis while he and Olivia were abroad, and Olivia's health began a gradual decline that made her an invalid until her death in 1904. Emotionally and psychologically battered, unable to recover the perspective on himself that had made his humor possible, Twain's work began to evince a general pessimism. His love affair with language had never faltered: *Connecticut Yankee* and *Puddn'head Wilson* contain admirable cadences of style, remarkable juxtapositions of word and event, and Huckleberry Finn's voice has moments of genuine vigor in the later novels he narrates. But *what* Twain said in works such as *The Man That Corrupted Hadleyburg* (1900), *What Is Man?* (1906), the "The Mysterious Stranger" manuscripts (arranged into one narrative by Paine in 1916, published in their entirety in 1969), and the posthumously published *The War Prayer* (1923) and *Letters From the Earth* (1963) reveals an increasing despair about the "awful human race."

In the years before his death in 1910, Twain was a renowned and highly respected public figure despite his disillusionment with the human race. The acclaim was richly deserved. For this writer, "the Lincoln of our literature," according to Howells in *My Mark Twain* (1910), raised the act of storytelling to high art. Twain's special talent was to introduce the flavor of oral speech, its vernacular rhythms and turns of phrase, into prose of lasting appeal. At his best, in *Huckleberry Finn,* he turns that prose into an instrument that measures the moral dimensions of our humanity.

Suggested Readings: *The Writings of Mark Twain,* 37 vols., ed. A. B. Paine, 1922–1925. *The Correspondence of Samuel L. Clemens and William Dean Howells, 1872–1910,* ed. H. N. Smith and W. Gibson, 1960. *The Mark Twain Papers,* ed. F. Anderson et al., 1967– . *The Works of Mark Twain,* ed. J. Gerber et al., 1972– . W. D. Howells, *My Mark Twain,* 1910. A. B. Paine, *Mark Twain: A Biography,* 3 vols., 1912. B. DeVoto, *The Ordeal of Mark Twain,* 1932. W. Blair, *Mark Twain and Huck Finn,* 1960. P. Fatout, *Mark Twain on the Lecture Circuit,* 1960. R. Salomon, *Twain and the Image of History,* 1961. H. N. Smith, *Mark Twain: The Development of a Writer,* 1962. J. M. Cox, *Mark Twain: The Fate of Humor,* 1966. J. Kaplan, *Mr. Clemens and Mark Twain,* 1966. H. Hill, *Mark Twain, God's Fool,* 1973. W. Gibson, *The Art of Mark Twain,* 1976. D. Sloane, *Mark Twain as a Literary Comedian,* 1979. L. J. Budd, *Our Mark Twain: The Making of His Public Personality,* 1983. E. Emerson, *The Authentic Mark Twain: A Literary Biography of Samuel Clemens,* 1984. E. Long, *The New Mark Twain Handbook,* 1985. F. G. Robinson, *In Bad Faith: The Dynamics of Deception in Mark Twain's America,* 1986. S. Gillman, *Dark Twins: Imposture and Identity in Mark Twain's America,* 1989. J. Lauber, *The Inventions of Mark Twain,* 1990.

Texts Used: "The Notorious Jumping Frog of Calaveras County": *Sketches: New and Old,* 1917. "The Private History of a Campaign That Failed": *The American Claimant and Other Stories and Sketches,* 1924. "Fenimore Cooper's Literary Offenses": *In Defense of Harriet Shelley and Other Essays,* 1925. *Adventures of Huckleberry Finn,* 1885 (some spelling from first edition corrected).

THE NOTORIOUS JUMPING FROG
OF CALAVERAS COUNTY*

In compliance with the request of a friend of mine, who wrote me from the East, I called on good-natured, garrulous old Simon Wheeler, and inquired after my friend's friend, Leonidas W. Smiley, as requested to do, and I hereunto append the result. I have a lurking suspicion that *Leonidas W.* Smiley is a myth; that my friend never knew such a personage; and that he only conjectured that if I asked old Wheeler about him, it would remind him of his infamous *Jim* Smiley, and he would go to work and bore me to death with some exasperating reminiscence of him as long and as tedious as it should be useless to me. If that was the design, it succeeded.

I found Simon Wheeler dozing comfortably by the bar-room stove of the dilapidated tavern in the decayed mining camp of Angel's,[1] and I noticed that he was fat and bald-headed, and had an expression of winning gentleness and simplicity upon his tranquil countenance. He roused up, and gave me good day. I told him that a friend of mine had commissioned me to make some inquiries about a cherished companion of his boyhood named *Leonidas W.* Smiley—*Rev. Leonidas W.* Smiley, a young minister of the Gospel, who he had heard was at one time a

---

* First published in the New York *Saturday Press* on November 18, 1865, as "Jim Smiley and His Jumping Frog," revised as "The Celebrated Jumping Frog of Calaveras County," and revised again with the title here. Mark Twain's note: "pronounced Cal-e-*va*-ras."
[1] In Calaveras County, California.

resident of Angel's Camp. I added that if Mr. Wheeler could tell me anything about this Rev. Leonidas W. Smiley, I would feel under many obligations to him.

Simon Wheeler backed me into a corner and blockaded me there with his chair, and then sat down and reeled off the monotonous narrative which follows this paragraph. He never smiled, he never frowned, he never changed his voice from the gentle-flowing key to which he tuned his initial sentence, he never betrayed the slightest suspicion of enthusiasm; but all through the interminable narrative there ran a vein of impressive earnestness and sincerity, which showed me plainly that, so far from his imagining that there was anything ridiculous or funny about his story, he regarded it as a really important matter, and admired its two heroes as men of transcendent genius in *finesse*. I let him go on in his own way, and never interrupted him once.

"Rev. Leonidas W. H'm, Reverend Le—well, there was a feller here once by the name of *Jim* Smiley, in the winter of '49—or maybe it was the spring of '50—I don't recollect exactly, somehow, though what makes me think it was one or the other is because I remember the big flume[2] warn't finished when he first come to the camp; but anyway, he was the curiousest man about always betting on anything that turned up you ever see, if he could get anybody to bet on the other side; and if he couldn't he'd change sides. Any way that suited the other man would suit *him*—any way just so's he got a bet, *he* was satisfied. But still he was lucky, uncommon lucky; he most always come out winner. He was always ready and laying for a chance; there couldn't be no solit'ry thing mentioned but that feller'd offer to bet on it, and take ary side you please, as I was just telling you. If there was a horse-race, you'd find him flush or you'd find him busted at the end of it; if there was a dog-fight, he'd bet on it; if there was a cat-fight, he'd bet on it; if there was a chicken-fight, he'd bet on it; why, if there was two birds setting on a fence, he would bet you which one would fly first; or if there was a camp-meeting, he would be there reg'lar to bet on Parson Walker, which he judged to be the best exhorter about here, and so he was too, and a good man. If he even see a straddle-bug[3] start to go anywheres, he would bet you how long it would take him to get to—to wherever he was going to, and if you took him up, he would foller that straddle-bug to Mexico but what he would find out where he was bound for and how long he was on the road. Lots of the boys here has seen that Smiley, and can tell you about him. Why, it never made no difference to *him*—he'd bet on *any* thing—the dangdest feller. Parson Walker's wife laid very sick once, for a good while, and it seemed as if they warn't going to save her; but one morning he come in, and Smiley up and asked him how she was, and he said she was considerable better—thank the Lord for his inf'nite mercy—and coming on so smart that with the blessing of Prov'dence she'd get well yet; and Smiley, before he thought, says, 'Well, I'll resk two-and-a-half she don't anyway.'

"Thish-yer Smiley had a mare—the boys called her the fifteen-minute nag, but that was only in fun, you know, because of course she was faster than that—and he used to win money on that horse, for all she was so slow and always had the asthma, or the distemper, or the consumption, or something of that kind. They used to give her two or three hundred yards' start, and then pass her under way; but always at the fag end of the race she'd get excited and desperate like, and

---

[2] A ravine with a stream running through it; in mining, an inclined channel made of wood, through which water is brought to the site.

[3] A type of beetle, also called tumble-bug or tumble-dung.

come cavorting and straddling up, and scattering her legs around limber, sometimes in the air, and sometimes out to one side among the fences, and kicking up m-o-r-e dust and raising m-o-r-e racket with her coughing and sneezing and blowing her nose—and *always* fetch up at the stand just about a neck ahead, as near as you could cipher it down.

"And he had a little small bull-pup, that to look at him you'd think he warn't worth a cent but to set around and look ornery and lay for a chance to steal something. But as soon as money was up on him he was a different dog; his under-jaw'd begin to stick out like the fo'castle of a steamboat, and his teeth would uncover and shine like the furnaces. And a dog might tackle him and bully-rag him, and bite him, and throw him over his shoulder two or three times, and Andrew Jackson—which was the name of the pup—Andrew Jackson would never let on but what *he* was satisfied, and hadn't expected nothing else—and the bets being doubled and doubled on the other side all the time, till the money was all up; and then all of a sudden he would grab that other dog jest by the j'int of his hind leg and freeze to it—not chaw, you understand, but only just grip and hang on till they throwed up the sponge, if it was a year. Smiley always come out winner on that pup, till he harnessed a dog once that didn't have no hind legs, because they'd been sawed off in a circular saw, and when the thing had gone along far enough, and the money was all up, and he come to make a snatch for his pet holt, he see in a minute how he'd been imposed on, and how the other dog had him in the door, so to speak, and he 'peared surprised, and then he looked sorter discouraged-like, and didn't try no more to win the fight, and so he got shucked out bad. He give Smiley a look, as much as to say his heart was broke, and it was *his* fault, for putting up a dog that hadn't no hind legs for him to take holt of, which was his main dependence in a fight, and then he limped off a piece and laid down and died. It was a good pup, was that Andrew Jackson, and would have made a name for hisself if he'd lived, for the stuff was in him and he had genius—I know it, because he hadn't no opportunities to speak of, and it don't stand to reason that a dog could make such a fight as he could under them circumstances if he hadn't no talent. It always makes me feel sorry when I think of that last fight of his'n, and the way it turned out.

"Well, thish-yer Smiley had rat-tarriers, and chicken cocks, and tomcats and all them kind of things, till you couldn't rest, and you couldn't fetch nothing for him to bet on but he'd match you. He ketched a frog one day, and took him home, and said he cal'lated to educate him; and so he never done nothing for three months but set in his back yard and learn that frog to jump. And you bet you he *did* learn him too. He'd give him a little punch behind, and the next minute you'd see that frog whirling in the air like a doughnut—see him turn one summerset,[4] or maybe a couple, if he got a good start, and come down flat-footed and all right, like a cat. He got him up so in the matter of ketching flies, and kep' him in practice so constant, that he'd nail a fly every time as fur as he could see him. Smiley said all a frog wanted was education, and he could do 'most anything—and I believe him. Why, I've seen him set Dan'l Webster down here on this floor—Dan'l Webster was the name of the frog—and sing out, 'Flies, Dan'l, flies!' and quicker'n you could wink he'd spring straight up and snake a fly off'n the counter there, and flop down on the floor ag'in as solid as a gob of mud, and fall to scratching the side of his head with his hind foot as indifferent as if he hadn't no idea he'd been doin'

---

[4] Somersault.

any more'n any frog might do. You never see a frog so modest and straight-for'ard as he was, for all he was so gifted. And when it come to fair and square jumping on a dead level, he could get over more ground at one straddle than any animal of his breed you ever see. Jumping on a dead level was his strong suit, you understand; and when it come to that, Smiley would ante up money on him as long as he had a red.[5] Smiley was monstrous proud of his frog, and well he might be, for fellers that had traveled and been everywheres all said he laid over any frog that ever *they* see.

"Well, Smiley kep' the beast in a little lattice box, and he used to fetch him down-town sometimes and lay for a bet. One day a feller—a stranger in the camp, he was—come acrost him with his box, and says:

"'What might it be that you've got in the box?'

"And Smiley says, sorter indifferent-like, 'It might be a parrot, or it might be a canary, maybe, but it ain't—it's only just a frog.'

"And the feller took it, and looked at it careful, and turned it round this way and that, and says, 'H'm—so 'tis. Well, what's *he* good for?'

"'Well,' Smiley says, easy and careless, 'he's good enough for *one* thing, I should judge—he can outjump any frog in Calaveras County.'

"The feller took the box again, and took another long, particular look, and give it back to Smiley, and says, very deliberate, 'Well,' he says, 'I don't see no p'ints about that frog that's any better'n any other frog.'

"'Maybe you don't,' Smiley says. 'Maybe you understand frogs and maybe you don't understand 'em; maybe you've had experience, and maybe you ain't only a amature, as it were. Anyways, I've got *my* opinion and I'll resk forty dollars that he can outjump any frog in Calaveras County.'

"And the feller studied a minute, and then says, kinder sadlike, 'Well, I'm only a stranger here, and I ain't got no frog; but if I had a frog, I'd bet you.'

"And then Smiley says, 'That's all right—that's all right—if you'll hold my box a minute, I'll go and get you a frog.' And so the feller took the box, and put up his forty dollars along with Smiley's, and set down to wait.

"So he set there a good while thinking and thinking to himself, and then he got the frog out and prized his mouth open and took a teaspoon and filled him full of quail-shot—filled him pretty near up to his chin—and set him on the floor. Smiley he went to the swamp and slopped around in the mud for a long time, and finally he ketched a frog, and fetched him in, and give him to this feller, and says:

"'Now, if you're ready, set him alongside of Dan'l, with his fore paws just even with Dan'l's, and I'll give the word.' Then he says, 'One—two—three—*git!*' and him and the feller touched up the frogs from behind, and the new frog hopped off lively, but Dan'l give a heave, and hysted up his shoulders—so—like a Frenchman, but it warn't no use—he couldn't budge; he was planted as solid as a church, and he couldn't no more stir than if he was anchored out. Smiley was a good deal surprised, and he was disgusted too, but he didn't have no idea what the matter was, of course.

"The feller took the money and started away; and when he was going out at the door, he sorter jerked his thumb over his shoulder—so—at Dan'l, and says again, very deliberate, 'Well,' he says, '*I* don't see no p'ints about that frog that's any better'n any other frog.'

"Smiley he stood scratching his head and looking down at Dan'l a long time,

---

[5] A red cent, a penny.

and at last he says, 'I do wonder what in the nation that frog throw'd off for—I wonder if there ain't something the matter with him—he 'pears to look mighty baggy, somehow.' And he ketched Dan'l by the nap of the neck, and hefted him, and says, 'Why blame my cats if he don't weigh five pound!' and turned him upside down and he belched out a double handful of shot. And then he see how it was, and he was the maddest man—he set the frog down and took out after that feller, but he never ketched him. And—"

[Here Simon Wheeler heard his name called from the front yard, and got up to see what was wanted.] And turning to me as he moved away, he said: "Just set where you are stranger, and rest easy—I ain't going to be gone a second."

But, by your leave, I did not think that a continuation of the history of the enterprising vagabond *Jim* Smiley would be likely to afford me much information concerning the Rev. *Leonidas W.* Smiley, and so I started away.

At the door I met the sociable Wheeler returning, and he buttonholed me and recommenced:

"Well, thish-yer Smiley had a yailer one-eyed cow that didn't have no tail, only just a short stump like a bannanner, and—"

However, lacking both time and inclination, I did not wait to hear about the afflicted cow, but took my leave.

1865

THE PRIVATE HISTORY OF A CAMPAIGN
THAT FAILED*

You have heard from a great many people who did something in the war;[1] is it not fair and right that you listen a little moment to one who started out to do something in it, but didn't? Thousands entered the war, got just a taste of it, and then stepped out again permanently. These, by their very numbers, are respectable, and are therefore entitled to a sort of voice—not a loud one, but a modest one; not a boastful one, but an apologetic one. They ought not to be allowed much space among better people—people who did something. I grant that; but they ought at least to be allowed to state why they didn't do anything, and also to explain the process by which they didn't do anything. Surely this kind of light must have a sort of value.

Out West[2] there was a good deal of confusion in men's minds during the first months of the great trouble—a good deal of unsettledness, of leaning first this way, then that, then the other way. It was hard for us to get our bearings. I call to mind an instance of this. I was piloting on the Mississippi when the news came that South Carolina had gone out of the Union on the 20th of December, 1860. My pilot mate was a New-Yorker. He was strong for the Union; so was I. But he would not listen to me with any patience; my loyalty was smirched, to his eye, because my father had owned slaves. I said, in palliation of this dark fact, that I had heard my father say, some years before he died, that slavery was a great wrong, and that he would free the solitary negro he then owned if he could think it

---

* First published in the *Century Magazine*, December 1885.   [1] The Civil War (1861–1865).
[2] In Missouri, where Twain lived.

right to give away the property of the family when he was so straitened in means. My mate retorted that a mere impulse was nothing—anybody could pretend to a good impulse; and went on decrying my Unionism and libeling my ancestry. A month later the secession atmosphere had considerably thickened on the Lower Mississippi, and I became a rebel; so did he. We were together in New Orleans the 26th of January, when Louisiana went out of the Union. He did his full share of the rebel shouting, but was bitterly opposed to letting me do mine. He said that I came of bad stock—of a father who had been willing to set slaves free. In the following summer he was piloting a Federal gunboat and shouting for the Union again, and I was in the Confederate army. I held his note for some borrowed money. He was one of the most upright men I ever knew, but he repudiated that note without hesitation because I was a rebel and the son of a man who owned slaves.

In that summer—of 1861—the first wash of the wave of war broke upon the shores of Missouri. Our state was invaded by the Union forces. They took possession of St. Louis, Jefferson Barracks,[3] and some other points. The Governor, Calib Jackson, issued his proclamation calling out fifty thousand militia to repel the invader.

I was visiting in the small town where my boyhood had been spent—Hannibal, Marion County. Several of us got together in a secret place by night and formed ourselves into a military company. One Tom Lyman, a young fellow of a good deal of spirit but of no military experience, was made captain; I was made second lieutenant. We had no first lieutenant; I do not know why; it was long ago. There were fifteen of us. By the advice of an innocent connected with the organization we called ourselves the Marion Rangers. I do not remember that any one found fault with the name. I did not; I thought it sounded quite well. The young fellow who proposed this title was perhaps a fair sample of the kind of stuff we were made of. He was young, ignorant, good-natured, well-meaning, trivial, full of romance, and given to reading chivalric novels and singing forlorn love-ditties. He had some pathetic little nickel-plated aristocratic instincts, and detested his name, which was Dunlap; detested it, partly because it was nearly as common in that region as Smith, but mainly because it had a plebeian sound to his ear. So he tried to ennoble it by writing it in this way: *d'Unlap*. That contented his eye, but left his ear unsatisfied, for people gave the new name the same old pronunciation—emphasis on the front end of it. He then did the bravest thing that can be imagined—a thing to make one shiver when one remembers how the world is given to resenting shams and affectations; he began to write his name so: *d'Un Lap*. And he waited patiently through the long storm of mud that was flung at this work of art, and he had his reward at last; for he lived to see that name accepted, and the emphasis put where he wanted it by people who had known him all his life, and to whom the tribe of Dunlaps had been as familiar as the rain and the sunshine for forty years. So sure of victory at last is the courage that can wait. He said he had found, by consulting some ancient French chronicles, that the name was rightly and originally written d'Un Lap; and said that if it were translated into English it would mean Peterson: *Lap*, Latin or Greek, he said, for stone or rock, same as the French *pierre*, that is to say, Peter: *d'*, of or from; *un*, a or one; hence, d'Un Lap, of or from a stone or a Peter; that is to say, one who is the son of a stone, the son of a Peter—Peterson. Our militia company were not learned, and

[3] An army camp near St. Louis.

the explanation confused them; so they called him Peterson Dunlap. He proved useful to us in his way; he named our camps for us, and he generally struck a name that was "no slouch," as the boys said.

That is one sample of us. Another was Ed Stevens, son of the town jeweler—trim-built, handsome, graceful, neat as a cat; bright, educated, but given over entirely to fun. There was nothing serious in life to him. As far as he was concerned, this military expedition of ours was simply a holiday. I should say that about half of us looked upon it in the same way; not consciously, perhaps, but unconsciously. We did not think; we were not capable of it. As for myself, I was full of unreasoning joy to be done with turning out of bed at midnight and four in the morning for a while;[4] grateful to have a change, new scenes, new occupations, a new interest. In my thoughts that was as far as I went; I did not go into the details; as a rule, one doesn't at twenty-four.

Another sample was Smith, the blacksmith's apprentice. This vast donkey had some pluck, of a slow and sluggish nature, but a soft heart; at one time he would knock a horse down for some impropriety and at another he would get homesick and cry. However, he had one ultimate credit to his account which some of us hadn't; he stuck to the war, and was killed in battle at last.

Jo Bowers, another sample, was a huge, good-natured, flax-headed lubber; lazy, sentimental, full of harmless brag, a grumbler by nature; an experienced, industrious, ambitious, and often quite picturesque liar, and yet not a successful one, for he had had no intelligent training, but was allowed to come up just any way. This life was serious enough to him, and seldom satisfactory. But he was a good fellow, anyway, and the boys all liked him. He was made orderly sergeant; Stevens was made corporal.

These samples will answer—and they are quite fair ones. Well, this herd of cattle started for the war. What could you expect of them? They did as well as they knew how; but, really, what was justly to be expected of them? Nothing, I should say. That is what they did.

We waited for a dark night, for caution and secrecy were necessary; then, toward midnight, we stole in couples and from various directions to the Griffith place, beyond the town; from that point we set out together on foot. Hannibal lies at the extreme southeastern corner of Marion County, on the Mississippi River; our objective point was the hamlet of New London, ten miles away, in Ralls County.

The first hour was all fun, all idle nonsense and laughter. But that could not be kept up. The steady trudging came to be like work; the play had somehow oozed out of it; the stillness of the woods and the somberness of the night began to throw a depressing influence over the spirits of the boys, and presently the talking died out and each person shut himself up in his own thoughts. During the last half of the second hour nobody said a word.

Now we approached a log farm-house where, according to report, there was a guard of five Union soldiers. Lyman called a halt; and there, in the deep gloom of the overhanging branches, he began to whisper a plan of assault upon that house, which made the gloom more depressing than it was before. It was a crucial moment; we realized, with a cold suddenness, that here was no jest—we were standing face to face with actual war. We were equal to the occasion. In our response there was no hesitation, no indecision: we said that if Lyman wanted to meddle

---

[4] As a riverboat pilot on the Mississippi, Twain would have watches at these and other hours.

with those soldiers, he could go ahead and do it; but if he waited for us to follow him, he would wait a long time.

Lyman urged, pleaded, tried to shame us, but it had no effect. Our course was plain, our minds were made up: we would flank the farm-house—go out around. And that was what we did.

We struck into the woods and entered upon a rough time, stumbling over roots, getting tangled in vines, and torn by briers. At last we reached an open place in a safe region, and sat down, blown and hot, to cool off and nurse our scratches and bruises. Lyman was annoyed, but the rest of us were cheerful; we had flanked the farm-house, we had made our first military movement, and it was a success; we had nothing to fret about, we were feeling just the other way. Horse-play and laughing began again; the expedition was become a holiday frolic once more.

Then we had two more hours of dull trudging and ultimate silence and depression; then, about dawn, we straggled into New London, soiled, heel-blistered, fagged with our little march, and all of us except Stevens in a sour and raspy humor and privately down on the war. We stacked our shabby old shotguns in Colonel Ralls's barn, and then went in a body and breakfasted with that veteran of the Mexican War.[5] Afterward he took us to a distant meadow, and there in the shade of a tree we listened to an old-fashioned speech from him, full of gunpowder and glory, full of that adjective-piling, mixed metaphor and windy declamation which were regarded as eloquence in that ancient time and that remote region; and then he swore us on the Bible to be faithful to the State of Missouri and drive all invaders from her soil, no matter whence they might come or under what flag they might march. This mixed us considerably, and we could not make out just what service we were embarked in; but Colonel Ralls, the practised politician and phrase-juggler, was not similarly in doubt; he knew quite clearly that he had invested us in the cause of the Southern Confederacy. He closed the solemnities by belting around me the sword which his neighbor, Colonel Brown, had worn at Buena Vista and Molino del Rey;[6] and he accompanied this act with another impressive blast.

Then we formed in line of battle and marched four miles to a shady and pleasant piece of woods on the border of the far-reaching expanses of a flowery prairie. It was an enchanting region for war—our kind of war.

We pierced the forest about half a mile, and took up a strong position, with some low, rocky, and wooded hills behind us, and a purling, limpid creek in front. Straightway half the command were in swimming and the other half fishing. The ass with the French name gave this position a romantic title, but it was too long, so the boys shortened and simplified it to Camp Ralls.

We occupied an old maple-sugar camp, whose half-rotted troughs were still propped against the trees. A long corn-crib served for sleeping-quarters for the battalion. On our left, half a mile away, were Mason's farm and house; and he was a friend to the cause. Shortly after noon the farmers began to arrive from several directions, with mules and horses for our use, and these they lent us for as long as the war might last, which they judged would be about three months. The animals were of all sizes, all colors, and all breeds. They were mainly young and frisky, and nobody in the command could stay on them long at a time; for we were town boys, and ignorant of horsemanship. The creature that fell to my share was a very small mule, and yet so quick and active that it could throw me without diffi-

[5] The war between Mexico and the United States (1846–1848).   [6] Mexican War battles.

culty; and it did this whenever I got on it. Then it would bray—stretching its neck out, laying its ear back, and spreading its jaws till you could see down to its works. It was a disagreeable animal in every way. If I took it by the bridle and tried to lead it off the grounds, it would sit down and brace back, and no one could budge it. However, I was not entirely destitute of military resources, and I did presently manage to spoil this game; for I had seen many a steamboat aground in my time, and knew a trick or two which even a grounded mule would be obliged to respect. There was a well by the corn-crib; so I substituted thirty fathom of rope for the bridle, and fetched him home with the windlass.[7]

I will anticipate here sufficiently to say that we did learn to ride, after some days' practice, but never well. We could not learn to like our animals; they were not choice ones, and most of them had annoying peculiarities of one kind or another. Stevens's horse would carry him, when he was not noticing, under the huge excrescences which form on the trunks of oak-trees, and wipe him out of the saddle; in this way Stevens got several bad hurts. Sergeant Bowers's horse was very large and tall, with slim, long legs, and looked like a railroad bridge. His size enabled him to reach all about, and as far as he wanted to, with his head; so he was always biting Bowers's legs. On the march, in the sun, Bowers slept a good deal; and as soon as the horse recognized that he was asleep he would reach around and bite him on the leg. His legs were black and blue with bites. This was the only thing that could ever make him swear, but this always did; whenever his horse bit him he always swore, and of course Stevens, who laughed at everything, laughed at this, and would even get into such convulsions over it as to lose his balance and fall off his horse; and then Bowers, already irritated by the pain of the horse-bite, would resent the laughter with hard language, and there would be a quarrel; so that horse made no end of trouble and bad blood in the command.

However, I will get back to where I was—our first afternoon in the sugar-camp. The sugar-troughs came very handy as horse-troughs, and we had plenty of corn to fill them with. I ordered Sergeant Bowers to feed my mule; but he said that if I reckoned he went to war to be a dry-nurse to a mule it wouldn't take me very long to find out my mistake. I believed that this was insubordination, but I was full of uncertainties about everything military, and so I let the thing pass, and went and ordered Smith, the blacksmith's apprentice, to feed the mule; but he merely gave me a large, cold, sarcastic grin, such as an ostensibly seven-year-old horse gives you when you lift his lip and find he is fourteen, and turned his back on me. I then went to the captain, and asked if it were not right and proper and military for me to have an orderly. He said it was, but as there was only one orderly in the corps, it was but right that he himself should have Bowers on his staff. Bowers said he wouldn't serve on anybody's staff; and if anybody thought he could make him, let him try it. So, of course, the thing had to be dropped; there was no other way.

Next, nobody would cook; it was considered a degradation; so we had no dinner. We lazied the rest of the pleasant afternoon away, some dozing under the trees, some smoking cob-pipes and talking sweethearts and war, some playing games. By late supper-time all hands were famished; and to meet the difficulty all hands turned to, on an equal footing, and gathered wood, built fires, and cooked the meal. Afterward everything was smooth for a while; then trouble broke out between the corporal and the sergeant, each claiming to rank the other. Nobody

---

[7] Any machine for hoisting or hauling; here a homemade means of winding the mule in with the rope.

knew which was the higher office; so Lyman had to settle the matter by making the rank of both officers equal. The commander of an ignorant crew like that has many troubles and vexations which probably do not occur in the regular army at all. However, with the song-singing and yarn-spinning around the camp-fire, everything presently became serene again; and by and by we raked the corn down level in one end of the crib, and all went to bed on it, tying a horse to the door, so that he would neigh if any one tried to get in.[8]

We had some horsemanship drill every forenoon; then, afternoons, we rode off here and there in squads a few miles, and visited the farmers' girls, and had a youthful good time, and got an honest good dinner or supper, and then home again to camp, happy and content.

For a time life was idly delicious, it was perfect; there was nothing to mar it. Then came some farmers with an alarm one day. They said it was rumored that the enemy were advancing in our direction from over Hyde's prairie. The result was a sharp stir among us, and general consternation. It was a rude awakening from our pleasant trance. The rumor was but a rumor—nothing definite about it; so, in the confusion, we did not know which way to retreat. Lyman was for not retreating at all in these uncertain circumstances; but he found that if he tried to maintain that attitude he would fare badly, for the command were in no humor to put up with insubordination. So he yielded the point and called a council of war—to consist of himself and the three other officers; but the privates made such a fuss about being left out that we had to allow them to remain, for they were already present, and doing the most of the talking too. The question was, which way to retreat; but all were so flurried that nobody seemed to have even a guess to offer. Except Lyman. He explained in a few calm words that, inasmuch as the enemy were approaching from over Hyde's prairie, our course was simple: all we had to do was not to retreat *toward* him; any other direction would answer our needs perfectly. Everybody saw in a moment how true this was, and how wise; so Lyman got a great many compliments. It was now decided that we should fall back on Mason's farm.

It was after dark by this time, and as we could not know how soon the enemy might arrive, it did not seem best to try to take the horses and things with us; so we only took the guns and ammunition, and started at once. The route was very rough and hilly and rocky, and presently the night grew very black and rain began to fall; so we had a troublesome time of it, struggling and stumbling along in the dark; and soon some person slipped and fell, and then the next person behind stumbled over him and fell, and so did the rest, one after the other; and then Bowers came, with a keg of powder in his arms, while the command were all mixed together, arms and legs, on the muddy slope; and so he fell, of course, with the keg, and this started the whole detachment down the hill in a body, and they landed in the brook at the bottom in a pile, and each that was undermost pulling the hair and scratching and biting those that were on top of him; and those that were being scratched and bitten scratching and biting the rest in their turn, and all saying they would die before they would ever go to war again if they ever got out

---

[8] Twain's note: "It was always my impression that that was what the horse was there for, and I know that it was also the impression of at least one other of the command, for we talked about it at the time, and admired the military ingenuity of the device; but when I was out West, three years ago, I was told by Mr. A. G. Fuqua, a member of our company, that the horse was his; that the leaving him tied at the door was a matter of mere forgetfulness, and that to attribute it to intelligent invention was to give him quite too much credit. In support of his position he called my attention to the suggestive fact that the artifice was not employed again. I had not thought of that before."

of this brook this time, and the invader might rot for all they cared, and the country along with him—and all such talk as that, which was dismal to hear and take part in, in such smothered, low voices, and such a grisly dark place and so wet, and the enemy, maybe, coming any moment.

The keg of powder was lost, and the guns, too; so the growling and complaining continued straight along while the brigade pawed around the pasty hillside and slopped around in the brook hunting for these things; consequently we lost considerable time at this; and then we heard a sound, and held our breath and listened, and it seemed to be the enemy coming, though it could have been a cow, for it had a cough like a cow; but we did not wait, but left a couple of guns behind and struck out for Mason's again as briskly as we could scramble along in the dark. But we got lost presently among the rugged little ravines, and wasted a deal of time finding the way again, so it was after nine when we reached Mason's stile at last; and then before we could open our mouths to give the countersign several dogs came bounding over the fence, with great riot and noise, and each of them took a soldier by the slack of his trousers and began to back away with him. We could not shoot the dogs without endangering the persons they were attached to; so we had to look on helpless at what was perhaps the most mortifying spectacle of the Civil War. There was light enough, and to spare, for the Masons had now run out on the porch with candles in their hands. The old man and his son came and undid the dogs without difficulty, all but Bowers's; but they couldn't undo his dog, they didn't know his combination; he was of the bull kind, and seemed to be set with a Yale time-lock; but they got him loose at last with some scalding water, of which Bowers got his share and returned thanks. Peterson Dunlap afterward made up a fine name for this engagement, and also for the night march which preceded it, but both have long ago faded out of my memory.

We now went into the house, and they began to ask us a world of questions, whereby it presently came out that we did not know anything concerning who or what we were running from; so the old gentleman made himself very frank, and said we were a curious breed of soldiers, and guessed we could be depended on to end up the war in time, because no government could stand the expense of the shoe-leather we should cost it trying to follow us around. "Marion *Rangers!* good name, b'gosh!" said he. And wanted to know why we hadn't had a picket-guard at the place where the road entered the prairie, and why we hadn't sent out a scouting party to spy out the enemy and bring us an account of his strength, and so on, before jumping up and stampeding out of a strong position upon a mere vague rumor—and so on, and so forth, till he made us all feel shabbier than the dogs had done, not half so enthusiastically welcome. So we went to bed shamed and low-spirited; except Stevens. Soon Stevens began to devise a garment for Bowers which could be made to automatically display his battle-scars to the grateful, or conceal them from the envious, according to his occasions; but Bowers was in no humor for this, so there was a fight, and when it was over Stevens had some battle-scars of his own to think about.

Then we got a little sleep. But after all we had gone through, our activities were not over for the night; for about two o'clock in the morning we heard a shout of warning from down the lane, accompanied by a chorus from all the dogs, and in a moment everybody was up and flying around to find out what the alarm was about. The alarmist was a horseman who gave notice that a detachment of Union soldiers was on its way from Hannibal with orders to capture and hang any bands like ours which it could find, and said we had no time to lose. Farmer Mason was in a flurry this time himself. He hurried us out of the house with all haste, and sent one of his negroes with us to show us where to hide ourselves and our telltale guns among the ravines half a mile away. It was raining heavily.

We struck down the lane, then across some rocky pasture-land which offered good advantages for stumbling; consequently we were down in the mud most of the time, and every time a man went down he blackguarded the war, and the people that started it, and everybody connected with it, and gave himself the master dose of all for being so foolish as to go into it. At last we reached the wooded mouth of a ravine, and there we huddled ourselves under the streaming trees, and sent the negro back home. It was a dismal and heart-breaking time. We were like to be drowned with the rain, deafened with the howling wind and the booming thunder, and blinded by the lighting. It was, indeed, a wild night. The drenching we were getting was misery enough, but a deeper misery still was the reflection that the halter might end us before we were a day older. A death of this shameful sort had not occurred to us as being among the possibilities of war. It took the romance all out of the campaign, and turned our dreams of glory into a repulsive nightmare. As for doubting that so barbarous an order had been given, not one of us did that.

The long night wore itself out at last, and then the negro came to us with the news that the alarm had manifestly been a false one, and that breakfast would soon be ready. Straightway we were light-hearted again, and the world was bright, and life as full of hope and promise as ever—for we were young then. How long ago that was! Twenty-four years.

The mongrel child of philology[9] named the night's refuge Camp Devastation, and no soul objected. The Masons gave us a Missouri country breakfast, in Missourian abundance, and we needed it: hot biscuits; hot "wheat bread," prettily criss-crossed in a lattice pattern on top; hot corn-pone; fried chicken; bacon, coffee, eggs, milk, buttermilk, etc.; and the world may be confidently challenged to furnish the equal of such a breakfast, as it is cooked in the South.

We stayed several days at Mason's; and after all these years the memory of the dullness, and stillness, and lifelessness of that slumberous farm-house still oppresses my spirit as with a sense of the presence of death and mourning. There was nothing to do, nothing to think about; there was no interest in life. The male part of the household were away in the fields all day, the women were busy and out of our sight; there was no sound but the plaintive wailing of a spinning-wheel, forever moaning out from some distant room—the most lonesome sound in nature, a sound steeped and sodden with homesickness and the emptiness of life. The family went to bed about dark every night, and as we were not invited to intrude any new customs we naturally followed theirs. Those nights were a hundred years long to youths accustomed to being up till twelve. We lay awake and miserable till that hour every time, and grew old, and decrepit waiting through the still eternities for the clock-strikes. This was no place for town boys. So at last it was with something very like joy that we received news that the enemy were on our track again. With a new birth of the old warrior spirit we sprang to our places in line of battle and fell back on Camp Ralls.

Captain Lyman had taken a hint from Mason's talk, and he now gave orders that our camp should be guarded against surprise by the posting of pickets. I was ordered to place a picket at the forks of the road in Hyde's prairie. Night shut

---

[9] Peterson Dunlap; philology means scholarship, the love of learning and literature.

down black and threatening. I told Sergeant Bowers to go out to that place and stay till midnight; and, just as I was expecting, he said he wouldn't do it. I tried to get others to go, but all refused. Some excused themselves on account of the weather; but the rest were frank enough to say they wouldn't go in any kind of weather. This kind of thing sounds odd now, and impossible, but there was no surprise in it at the time. On the contrary, it seemed a perfectly natural thing to do. There were scores of little camps scattered over Missouri where the same thing was happening. These camps were composed of young men who had been born and reared to a sturdy independence, and who did not know what it meant to be ordered around by Tom, Dick, and Harry, whom they had known familiarly all their lives, in the village or on the farm. It is quite within the probabilities that this same thing was happening all over the South. James Redpath[10] recognized the justice of this assumption, and furnished the following instance in support of it. During a short stay in East Tennessee he was in a citizen colonel's tent one day talking, when a big private appeared at the door, and, without salute or other circumlocution, said to the colonel:

"Say, Jim, I'm a-goin' home for a few days."

"What for?"

"Well, I hain't b'en there for a right smart while, and I'd like to see how things is comin' on."

"How long are you going to be gone?"

"'Bout two weeks."

"Well, don't be gone longer than that; and get back sooner if you can."

That was all, and the citizen officer resumed his conversation where the private had broken it off. This was in the first months of the war, of course. The camps in our part of Missouri were under Brigadier-General Thomas H. Harris. He was a townsman of ours, a first-rate fellow, and well liked; but we had all familiarly known him as the sole and modest-salaried operator in our telegraph-office, where he had to send about one despatch a week in ordinary times, and two when there was a rush of business; consequently, when he appeared in our midst one day, on the wing, and delivered a military command of some sort, in a large military fashion, nobody was surprised at the response which he got from the assembled soldiery:

"Oh, now, what'll you take to *don't,* Tom Harris?"

It was quite the natural thing. One might justly imagine that we were hopeless material for war. And so we seemed, in our ignorant state; but there were those among us who afterward learned the grim trade; learned to obey like machines; became valuable soldiers; fought all through the war, and came out at the end with excellent records. One of the very boys who refused to go out on picket duty that night, and called me an ass for thinking he would expose himself to danger in such a foolhardy way, had become distinguished for intrepidity before he was a year older.

I did secure my picket that night—not by authority, but by diplomacy. I got Bowers to go by agreeing to exchange ranks with him for the time being, and go along and stand the watch with him as his subordinate. We stayed out there a couple of dreary hours in the pitchy darkness and the rain, with nothing to modify the dreariness but Bowers's monotonous growlings at the war and the weather; then we began to nod, and presently found it next to impossible to stay in the

[10] Redpath (1833–1891), a Scottish-born journalist, was a correspondent for the New York *Tribune.*

saddle; so we gave up the tedious job, and went back to the camp without waiting for the relief guard. We rode into camp without interruption or objection from anybody, and the enemy could have done the same, for there were no sentries. Everybody was asleep; at midnight there was nobody to send out another picket, so none was sent. We never tried to establish a watch at night again, as far as I remember, but we generally kept a picket out in the daytime.

In that camp the whole command slept on the corn in the big corn-crib; and there was usually a general row before morning, for the place was full of rats, and they would scramble over the boys' bodies and faces, annoying and irritating everybody; and now and then they would bite some one's toe, and the person who owned the toe would start up and magnify his English and begin to throw corn in the dark. The ears were half as heavy as bricks, and when they struck they hurt. The persons struck would respond, and inside of five minutes every man would be locked in a death-grip with his neighbor. There was a grievous deal of blood shed in the corn-crib, but this was all that was spilt while I was in the war. No, that is not quite true. But for one circumstance it would have been all. I will come to that now.

Our scares were frequent. Every few days rumors would come that the enemy were approaching. In these cases we always fell back on some other camp of ours; we never stayed where we were. But the rumors always turned out to be false; so at last even we began to grow indifferent to them. One night a negro was sent to our corn-crib with the same old warning: the enemy was hovering in our neighborhood. We all said let him hover. We resolved to stay still and be comfortable. It was a fine warlike resolution, and no doubt we all felt the stir of it in our veins—for a moment. We had been having a very jolly time, that was full of horse-play and school-boy hilarity; but that cooled down now, and presently the fast-waning fire of forced jokes and forced laughs died out altogether, and the company became silent. Silent and nervous. And soon uneasy—worried—apprehensive. We had said we would stay, and we were committed. We could have been persuaded to go, but there was nobody brave enough to suggest it. An almost noiseless movement presently began in the dark by a general but unvoiced impulse. When the movement was completed each man knew that he was not the only person who had crept to the front wall and had his eye at a crack between the logs. No, we were all there; all there with our hearts in our throats, and staring out toward the sugar-troughs where the forest footpath came through. It was late, and there was a deep woodsy stillness everywhere. There was a veiled moonlight, which was only just strong enough to enable us to mark the general shape of objects. Presently a muffled sound caught our ears, and we recognized it as the hoof-beats of a horse or horses. And right away a figure appeared in the forest path; it could have been made of smoke, its mass had so little sharpness of outline. It was a man on horseback, and it seemed to me that there were others behind him. I got hold of a gun in the dark, and pushed it through a crack between the logs, hardly knowing what I was doing, I was so dazed with fright. Somebody said "Fire!" I pulled the trigger. I seemed to see a hundred flashes and hear a hundred reports; then I saw the man fall down out of the saddle. My first feeling was of surprised gratification; my first impulse was an apprentice-sportsman's impulse to run and pick up his game. Somebody said, hardly audibly, "Good—we've got him!—wait for the rest." But the rest did not come. We waited—listened—still no more came. There was not a sound, not the whisper of a leaf; just perfect stillness; an uncanny kind of stillness, which was all the more uncanny on account of the damp, earthy, late-night smells now rising and pervading it. Then, wondering, we crept stealthily out, and approached the man. When we got to him the moon revealed him distinctly. He was lying on his back, with his arms abroad; his mouth was open and his chest heaving with long gasps, and his white shirt-front was all splashed with blood. The thought shot through me that I was a murderer; that I had killed a man—a man who had never done me any harm. That was the coldest sensation that ever went through my marrow. I was down by him in a moment, helplessly stroking his forehead; and I would have given anything then—my own life freely—to make him again what he had been five minutes before. And all the boys seemed to be feeling in the same way; they hung over him, full of pitying interest, and tried all they could to help him, and said all sorts of regretful things. They had forgotten all about the enemy; they thought only of this one forlorn unit of the foe. Once my imagination persuaded me that the dying man gave me a reproachful look out of his shadowy eyes, and it seemed to me that I could rather he had stabbed me than done that. He muttered and mumbled like a dreamer in his sleep about his wife and his child; and I thought with a new despair, "This thing that I have done does not end with him; it falls upon *them* too, and they never did me any harm, any more than he."

In a little while the man was dead. He was killed in war; killed in fair and legitimate war; killed in battle, as you may say; and yet he was as sincerely mourned by the opposing force as if he had been their brother. The boys stood there a half-hour sorrowing over him, and recalling the details of the tragedy, and wondering who he might be, and if he were a spy, and saying that if it were to do over again they would not hurt him unless he attacked them first. It soon came out that mine was not the only shot fired; there were five others—a division of the guilt which was a great relief to me, since it in some degree lightened and diminished the burden I was carrying. There were six shots fired at once; but I was not in my right mind at the time, and my heated imagination had magnified my one shot into a volley.

The man was not in uniform, and was not armed. He was a stranger in the country; that was all we ever found out about him. The thought of him got to preying upon me every night; I could not get rid of it. I could not drive it away, the taking of that unoffending life seemed such a wanton thing. And it seemed an epitome of war; that all war must be just that—the killing of strangers against whom you feel no personal animosity; strangers whom, in other circumstances, you would help if you found them in trouble, and who would help you if you needed it.[11] My campaign was spoiled. It seemed to me that I was not rightly equipped for this awful business; that war was intended for men, and I for a child's nurse. I resolved to retire from this avocation of sham soldiership while I could save some remnant of my self-respect. These morbid thoughts clung to me against reason; for at bottom I did not believe I had touched that man. The law of probabilities decreed me guiltless of his blood; for in all my small experience with guns I had never hit anything I had tried to hit, and I knew I had done my best to hit him. Yet there was no solace in the thought. Against a diseased imagination demonstration goes for nothing.

The rest of my war experience was of a piece with what I have already told of it. We kept monotonously falling back upon one camp or another, and eating up the farmers and their families. They ought to have shot us; on the contrary, they

---

[11] A memorable definition of war from a very serious Twain.

were as hospitably kind and courteous to us as if we had deserved it. In one of these camps we found Ab Grimes, an Upper Mississippi pilot,[12] who afterward became famous as a dare-devil rebel spy, whose career bristled with desperate adventures. The look and style of his comrades suggested that they had not come into the war to play, and their deeds made good the conjecture later. They were fine horsemen and good revolver shots; but their favorite arm was the lasso. Each had one at his pommel, and could snatch a man out of the saddle with it every time, on a full gallop, at any reasonable distance.

In another camp the chief was a fierce and profane old blacksmith of sixty, and he had furnished his twenty recruits with gigantic home-made bowie-knives, to be swung with two hands, like the *machetes* of the Isthmus. It was a grisly spectacle to see that earnest band practising their murderous cuts and slashes under the eye of that remorseless old fanatic.

The last camp which we fell back upon was in a hollow near the village of Florida, where I was born—in Monroe County. Here we were warned one day that a Union colonel was sweeping down on us with a whole regiment at his heel. This looked decidedly serious. Our boys went apart and consulted; then we went back and told the other companies present that the war was a disappointment to us, and we were going to disband. They were getting ready themselves to fall back on some place or other, and we were only waiting for General Tom Harris, who was expected to arrive at any moment; so they tried to persuade us to wait a little while, but the majority of us said no, we were accustomed to falling back, and didn't need any of Tom Harris's help; we could get along perfectly well without him—and save time, too. So about half of our fifteen, including myself, mounted and left on the instant; the others yielded to persuasion and stayed—stayed through the war.

An hour later we met General Harris on the road, with two or three people in his company—his staff, probably, but we could not tell; none of them were in uniform; uniforms had not come into vogue among us yet. Harris ordered us back; but we told him there was a Union colonel coming with a whole regiment in his wake, and it looked as if there was going to be a disturbance; so we had concluded to go home. He raged a little, but it was of no use; our minds were made up. We had done our share; had killed one man, exterminated one army, such as it was; let him go and kill the rest, and that would end the war. I did not see that brisk young general again until last year; then he was wearing white hair and whiskers.

In time I came to know that Union colonel whose coming frightened me out of the war and crippled the Southern cause to that extent—General Grant. I came within a few hours of seeing him when he was as unknown as I was myself; at a time when anybody could have said, "Grant?—Ulysses S. Grant?[13] I do not remember hearing the name before." It seems difficult to realize that there was once a time when such a remark could be rationally made; but there *was,* and I was within a few miles of the place and the occasion, too, though proceeding in the other direction.

The thoughtful will not throw this war paper of mine lightly aside as being valueless. It has this value: it is a not unfair picture of what went on in many and many a militia camp in the first months of the rebellion, when the green recruits

---

[12] A riverboat pilot.
[13] Grant (1822–1885) became commander in chief of the Union Armies and later the eighteenth U.S. president (1869–1877).

were without discipline, without the steadying and heartening influence of trained leaders; when all their circumstances were new and strange, and charged with exaggerated terrors, and before the invaluable experience of actual collision in the field had turned them from rabbits into soldiers. If this side of the picture of that early day has not before been put into history, then history has been to that degree incomplete, for it had and has its rightful place there. There was more Bull Run[14] material scattered through the early camps of this country than exhibited itself at Bull Run. And yet it learned its trade presently, and helped to fight the great battles later. I could have become a soldier myself if I had waited. I had got part of it learned; I knew more about retreating than the man that invented retreating.

1885

FENIMORE COOPER'S LITERARY OFFENSES*

The Pathfinder and *The Deerslayer*[1] stand at the head of Cooper's novels as artistic creations. There are others of his works which contain parts as perfect as are to be found in these, and scenes even more thrilling. Not one can be compared with either of them as a finished whole.

The defects in both of these tales are comparatively slight. They were pure works of art.—PROF. LOUNSBURY[2]

The five tales reveal an extraordinary fullness of invention.

. . . One of the very greatest characters in fiction, Natty Bumppo. . . .

The craft of the woodsman, the tricks of the trapper, all the delicate art of the forest, were familiar to Cooper from his youth up.—PROF. BRANDER MATTHEWS[3]

Cooper is the greatest artist in the domain of romantic fiction yet produced by America.—WILKIE COLLINS[4]

It seems to me that it was far from right for the Professor of English Literature in Yale, the Professor of English Literature in Columbia, and Wilkie Collins to deliver opinions on Cooper's literature without having read some of it. It would have been much more decorous to keep silent and let persons talk who have read Cooper.

Cooper's art has some defects. In one place in *Deerslayer,* and in the restricted space of two-thirds of a page, Cooper has scored 114 offenses against literary art out of a possible 115. It breaks the record.

---

[14] A small stream in northeast Virginia, the site of two Union defeats during the Civil War: in the first Battle of Bull Run (or Manassas), July 21, 1861, General Stonewall Jackson and other Confederate forces routed the inexperienced Union troops; in the second Battle of Bull Run, August 29–30, 1862, Confederate forces under Jackson and General James Longstreet twice repulsed Union troops under General John Pope.

* First published in the *North American Review,* July 1895. The American novelist James Fenimore Cooper (1789–1851) wrote the five Leather-Stocking Tales that Twain discusses. Twain indulges his talent for humorous exaggeration in detailing Cooper's "literary offenses," but other evidence makes it clear that he liked neither the type of adventure story Cooper wrote nor Cooper's wordy style.

[1] Published in 1840 and 1841, respectively. *The Deerslayer,* the final novel in the Leather-Stocking series, presents Cooper's protagonist, Natty Bumppo, at his youngest and most innocent.

[2] Thomas R. Lounsbury (1838–1915), a noted scholar and author of *James Fenimore Cooper* (1882).

[3] Matthews (1852–1929) had written an appreciative essay on Cooper in 1889, the centennial of Cooper's birth.

[4] William Wilkie Collins (1824–1889), an English novelist, author of *The Woman in White* (1860) and *The Moonstone* (1868).

There are nineteen rules governing literary art in the domain of romantic fiction—some say twenty-two. In *Deerslayer* Cooper violated eighteen of them. These eighteen require:

1. That a tale shall accomplish something and arrive somewhere. But the *Deerslayer* tale accomplishes nothing and arrives in the air.

2. They require that the episodes of a tale shall be necessary parts of the tale, and shall help to develop it. But as the *Deerslayer* tale is not a tale, and accomplishes nothing and arrives nowhere, the episodes have no rightful place in the work, since there was nothing for them to develop.

3. They require that the personages in a tale shall be alive, except in the case of corpses, and that always the reader shall be able to tell the corpses from the others. But this detail has often been overlooked in the *Deerslayer* tale.

4. They require that the personages in a tale, both dead and alive, shall exhibit a sufficient excuse for being there. But this detail also has been overlooked in the *Deerslayer* tale.

5. They require that when the personages of a tale deal in conversation, the talk shall sound like human talk, and be talk such as human beings would be likely to talk in the given circumstances, and have a discoverable meaning, also a discoverable purpose, and a show of relevancy, and remain in the neighborhood of the subject in hand, and be interesting to the reader, and help out the tale, and stop when the people cannot think of anything more to say. But this requirement has been ignored from the beginning of the *Deerslayer* tale to the end of it.

6. They require that when the author describes the character of a personage in his tale, the conduct and conversation of that personage shall justify said description. But this law gets little or no attention in the *Deerslayer* tale, as Natty Bumppo's case will amply prove.

7. They require that when a personage talks like an illustrated, gilt-edged, tree-calf, hand-tooled, seven-dollar Friendship's Offering[5] in the beginning of a paragraph, he shall not talk like a negro minstrel in the end of it. But this rule is flung down and danced upon in the *Deerslayer* tale.

8. They require that crass stupidities shall not be played upon the reader as "the craft of the woodsman, the delicate art of the forest," by either the author or the people in the tale. But this rule is persistently violated in the *Deerslayer* tale.

9. They require that the personages of a tale shall confine themselves to possibilities and let miracles alone; or, if they venture a miracle, the author must so plausibly set it forth as to make it look possible and reasonable. But these rules are not respected in the *Deerslayer* tale.

10. They require that the author shall make the reader feel a deep interest in the personages of his tale and in their fate; and that he shall make the reader love the good people in the tale and hate the bad ones. But the reader of the *Deerslayer* tale dislikes the good people in it, is indifferent to the others, and wishes they would all get drowned together.

11. They require that the characters in a tale shall be so clearly defined that the reader can tell beforehand what each will do in a given emergency. But in the *Deerslayer* tale this rule is vacated.

In addition to these large rules there are some little ones. These require that the author shall

12. *Say* what he is proposing to say, not merely come near it.

---

[5] An invented name for the type of gift book typically filled with sentimental verse and flowery language; "gilt-edged, tree-calf, hand-tooled," are terms for an expensive, elegantly bound book.

13. Use the right word, not its second cousin.
14. Eschew surplusage.
15. Not omit necessary details.
16. Avoid slovenliness of form.
17. Use good grammar.
18. Employ a simple and straightforward style.

Even these seven are coldly and persistently violated in the *Deerslayer* tale.

Cooper's gift in the way of invention was not a rich endowment; but such as it was he liked to work it, he was pleased with the effects, and indeed he did some quite sweet things with it. In his little box of stage-properties he kept six or eight cunning devices, tricks, artifices for his savages and woodsmen to deceive and circumvent each other with, and he was never so happy as when he was working these innocent things and seeing them go. A favorite one was to make a moccasined person tread in the tracks of the moccasined enemy, and thus hide his own trail. Cooper wore out barrels and barrels of moccasins in working that trick. Another stage-property that he pulled out of his box pretty frequently was his broken twig. He prized his broken twig above all the rest of his effects, and worked it the hardest. It is a restful chapter in any book of his when somebody doesn't step on a dry twig and alarm all the reds and whites for two hundred yards around. Every time a Cooper person is in peril, and absolute silence is worth four dollars a minute, he is sure to step on a dry twig. There may be a hundred handier things to step on, but that wouldn't satisfy Cooper. Cooper requires him to turn out and find a dry twig; and if he can't do it, go and borrow one. In fact, the Leatherstocking Series ought to have been called the Broken Twig Series.

I am sorry there is not room to put in a few dozen instances of the delicate art of the forest, as practised by Natty Bumppo and some of the other Cooperian experts. Perhaps we may venture two or three samples. Cooper was a sailor—a naval officer; yet he gravely tells us how a vessel, driving toward a lee shore[6] in a gale, is steered for a particular spot by her skipper because he knows of an *undertow* there which will hold her back against the gale and save her. For just pure woodcraft, or sailorcraft, or whatever it is, isn't that neat? For several years Cooper was daily in the society of artillery, and he ought to have noticed that when a cannon-ball strikes the ground it either buries itself or skips a hundred feet or so; skips again a hundred feet or so—and so on, till finally it gets tired and rolls. Now in one place he loses some "females"—as he always calls women—in the edge of a wood near a plain at night in a fog, on purpose to give Bumppo a chance to show off the delicate art of the forest before the reader. These mislaid people are hunting for a fort. They hear a cannon-blast, and a cannon-ball presently comes rolling into the wood and stops at their feet. To the females this suggests nothing. The case is very different with the admirable Bumppo. I wish I may never know peace again if he doesn't strike out promptly and *follow the track* of that cannon-ball across the plain through the dense fog and find the fort. Isn't it a daisy? If Cooper had any real knowledge of Nature's ways of doing things, he had a most delicate art in concealing the fact. For instance: one of his acute Indian experts, Chingachgook[7] (pronounced Chicago, I think), has lost the trail of a per-

---

[6] The shore protected from the wind. Cooper wrote a number of sea novels, among them *The Pilot* (1823) and *The Two Admirals* (1842); one of the Leather-Stocking Tales, *The Pathfinder* (1840), has a lengthy section that takes place on Lake Huron.

[7] A Mohican chief, Natty Bumppo's friend and companion in four of the Leather-Stocking Tales (Chingachgook dies in *The Pioneers* [1823], well before the time covered in *The Prairie* [1827]).

son he is tracking through the forest. Apparently that trail is hopelessly lost. Neither you nor I could ever have guessed out the way to find it. It was very different with Chicago. Chicago was not stumped for long. He turned a running stream out of its course, and there, in the slush in its old bed, were that person's moccasin tracks.[8] The current did not wash them away, as it would have done in all other like cases—no, even the eternal laws of Nature have to vacate when Cooper wants to put up a delicate job of woodcraft on the reader.

We must be a little wary when Brander Matthews tell us that Cooper's books "reveal an extraordinary fullness of invention." As a rule, I am quite willing to accept Brander Matthews's literary judgments and applaud his lucid and graceful phrasing of them; but that particular statement needs to be taken with a few tons of salt. Bless your heart, Cooper hadn't any more invention than a horse; and I don't mean a high-class horse, either; I mean a clothes-horse. It would be very difficult to find a really clever "situation" in Cooper's books, and still more difficult to find one of any kind which he has failed to render absurd by his handling of it. Look at the episodes of "the caves"; and at the celebrated scuffle between Maqua[9] and those others on the table-land a few days later; and at Hurry Harry's[10] queer water-transit from the castle to the ark; and at Deerslayer's half-hour with his first corpse;[11] and at the quarrel between Hurry Harry and Deerslayer later; and at—but choose for yourself; you can't go amiss.

If Cooper had been an observer his inventive faculty would have worked better; not more interestingly, but more rationally, more plausibly. Cooper's proudest creations in the way of "situations" suffer noticeably from the absence of the observer's protecting gift. Cooper's eye was splendidly inaccurate. Cooper seldom saw anything correctly. He saw nearly all things as through a glass eye, darkly. Of course a man who cannot see the commonest little every-day matters accurately is working at a disadvantage when he is constructing a "situation." In the *Deerslayer* tale Cooper has a stream which is fifty feet wide where it flows out of a lake; it presently narrows to twenty as it meanders along for no given reason, and yet when a stream acts like that it ought to be required to explain itself. Fourteen pages later the width of the brook's outlet from the lake has suddenly shrunk thirty feet, and become "the narrowest part of the stream." This shrinkage is not accounted for. The stream has bends in it, a sure indication that it has alluvial banks and cuts them; yet these bends are only thirty and fifty feet long. If Cooper had been a nice and punctilious observer he would have noticed that the bends were oftener nine hundred feet long than short of it.

Cooper made the exit of that stream fifty feet wide, in the first place, for no particular reason; in the second place, he narrowed it to less than twenty to accommodate some Indians. He bends a "sapling" to the form of an arch over this narrow passage, and conceals six Indians in its foliage. They are "laying" for a settler's scow or ark which is coming up the stream on its way to the lake; it is being hauled against the stiff current by a rope whose stationary end is anchored in the lake; its rate of progress cannot be more than a mile an hour. Cooper describes the

---

[8] An incident in *The Last of the Mohicans* (1826); actually, Uncas, Chingachgook's son, performs this wondrous feat of tracking.

[9] An evil Huron chief in *The Last of the Mohicans*.

[10] Hurry Harry March, an amoral white hunter in *The Deerslayer*.

[11] In a memorable scene in *The Deerslayer,* young Natty Bumppo ("Deerslayer") kills his first human being in single combat and remains with his dying foe until the end. This Huron Indian names Natty "Hawkeye" in tribute to his marksmanship.

ark, but pretty obscurely. In the matter of dimensions "it was little more than a modern canal-boat." Let us guess, then, that it was about one hundred and forty feet long. It was of "greater breadth than common." Let us guess, then, that it was about sixteen feet wide. This leviathan had been prowling down bends which were but a third as long as itself, and scraping between banks where it had only two feet of space to spare on each side. We cannot too much admire this miracle. A low-roofed log dwelling occupies "two-thirds of the ark's length"—a dwelling ninety feet long and sixteen feet wide, let us say—a kind of vestibule train. The dwelling has two rooms—each forty-five feet long and sixteen feet wide, let us guess. One of them is the bedroom of the Hutter girls, Judith and Hetty; the other is the parlor in the daytime, at night it is papa's bedchamber. The ark is arriving at the stream's exit now, whose width has been reduced to less than twenty feet to accommodate the Indians—say to eighteen. There is a foot to spare on each side of the boat. Did the Indians notice that there was going to be a tight squeeze there? Did they notice that they could make money by climbing down out of that arched sapling and just stepping aboard when the ark scraped by? No, other Indians would have noticed these things, but Cooper's Indians never notice anything. Cooper thinks they are marvelous creatures for noticing, but he was almost always in error about his Indians. There was seldom a sane one among them.

The ark is one hundred and forty-feet long; the dwelling is ninety feet long. The idea of the Indians is to drop softly and secretly from the arched sapling to the dwelling as the ark creeps along under it at the rate of a mile an hour, and butcher the family. It will take the ark a minute and a half to pass under. It will take the ninety-foot dwelling a minute to pass under. Now, then, what did the six Indians do? It would take you thirty years to guess, and even then you would have to give it up, I believe. Therefore, I will tell you what the Indians did. Their chief, a person of quite extraordinary intellect for a Cooper Indian, warily watched the canal-boat as it squeezed along under him, and when he had got his calculations fined down to exactly the right shade, as he judged, he let go and dropped. And *missed the house!* That is actually what he did. He missed the house, and landed in the stern of the scow. It was not much of a fall, yet it knocked him silly. He lay there unconscious. If the house had been ninety-seven feet long he would have made the trip. The fault was Cooper's, not his. The error lay in the construction of the house. Cooper was no architect.

There still remained in the roost five Indians. The boat has passed under and is now out of their reach. Let me explain what the five did—you would not be able to reason it out for yourself. No. 1 jumped for the boat, but fell in the water astern of it. Then No. 2 jumped for the boat, but fell in the water still farther astern of it. Then No. 3 jumped for the boat, and fell a good way astern of it. Then No. 4 jumped for the boat, and fell in the water *away* astern. Then even No. 5 made a jump for the boat—for he was a Cooper Indian. In the matter of intellect, the difference between a Cooper Indian and the Indian that stands in front of the cigar-shop is not spacious. The scow episode is really a sublime burst of invention; but it does not thrill, because the inaccuracy of the details throws a sort of air of fictitiousness and general improbability over it. This comes of Cooper's inadequacy as an observer.

The reader will find some examples of Cooper's high talent for inaccurate observation in the account of the shooting-match in *The Pathfinder*.

A common wrought nail was driven lightly into the target, its head having been first touched with paint.

The color of the paint is not stated—an important omission, but Cooper deals freely in important omissions. No, after all, it was not an important omission; for this nail-head is a *hundred yards from* the marksmen, and could not be seen by them at that distance, no matter what its color might be. How far can the best eyes see a common house-fly? A hundred yards? It is quite impossible. Very well; eyes that cannot see a house-fly that is a hundred yards away cannot see an ordinary nail-head at that distance, for the size of the two objects is the same. It takes a keen eye to see a fly or a nail-head at fifty yards—one hundred and fifty feet. Can the reader do it?

The nail was lightly driven, its head painted, and game called. Then the Cooper miracles began. The bullet of the first marksman chipped an edge of the nail-head; the next man's bullet drove the nail a little way into the target—and removed all the paint. Haven't the miracles gone far enough now? Not to suit Cooper; for the purpose of this whole scheme is to show off his prodigy, Deerslayer-Hawkeye-Long-Rifle-Leatherstocking-Pathfinder-Bumppo[12] before the ladies.

"Be all ready to clench it, boys!" cried out Pathfinder, stepping into his friend's tracks the instant they were vacant. "Never mind a new nail; I can see that, though the paint is gone, and what I can see I can hit at a hundred yards, though it were only a mosquito's eye. Be ready to clench!"

The rifle cracked, the bullet sped its way, and the head of the nail was buried in the wood, covered by the piece of flattened lead.

There, you see, is a man who could hunt flies with a rifle, and command a ducal salary in a Wild West show to-day if we had him back with us.

The recorded feat is certainly surprising just as it stands; but it is not surprising enough for Cooper. Cooper adds a touch. He has made Pathfinder do this miracle with another man's rifle; and not only that, but Pathfinder did not have even the advantage of loading it himself. He had everything against him, and yet he made that impossible shot; and not only made it, but did it with absolute confidence, saying, "Be ready to clench." Now a person like that would have undertaken that same feat with a brickbat, and with Cooper to help he would have achieved it, too.

Pathfinder showed off handsomely that day before the ladies. His very first feat was a thing which no Wild West show can touch. He was standing with the group of marksmen, observing—a hundred yards from the target, mind; one Jasper raised his rifle and drove the center of the bull's-eye. Then the Quartermaster fired. The target exhibited no result this time. There was a laugh. "It's a dead miss," said Major Lundie. Pathfinder waited an impressive moment or two; then said, in that calm, indifferent, know-it-all way of his, "No, Major, he has covered Jasper's bullet, as will be seen if any one will take the trouble to examine the target."

Wasn't it remarkable! How *could* he see that little pellet fly through the air and enter that distant bullet-hole? Yet that is what he did; for nothing is impossible to a

---

[12] Various names Natty Bumppo earns in the Leather-Stocking Tales.

Cooper person. Did any of those people have any deep-seated doubts about this thing? No; for that would imply sanity, and these were all Cooper people.

> The respect for Pathfinder's skill and for his *quickness and accuracy of sight* [the italics are mine] was so profound and general, that the instant he made this declaration the spectators began to distrust their own opinions, and a dozen rushed to the target in order to ascertain the fact. There, sure enough, it was found that the Quartermaster's bullet had gone through the hole made by Jasper's, and that, too, so accurately as to require a minute examination to be certain of the circumstance, which, however, was soon clearly established by discovering one bullet over the other in the stump against which the target was placed.

They made a "minute" examination; but never mind, how could they know that there were two bullets in that hole without digging the latest one out? for neither probe nor eyesight could prove the presence of any more than one bullet. Did they dig? No; as we shall see. It is the Pathfinder's turn now; he steps out before the ladies, takes aim, and fires.

But, alas! here is a disappointment; an incredible, an unimaginable disappointment—for the target's aspect is unchanged; there is nothing there but that same old bullet-hole!

> "If one dared to hint at such a thing," cried Major Duncan, "I should say that the Pathfinder has also missed the target!"

As nobody had missed it yet, the "also" was not necessary; but never mind about that, for the Pathfinder is going to speak.

> "No, no, Major," said he, confidently, "that *would* be a risky declaration. I didn't load the piece, and can't say what was in it, but if it was lead, you will find the bullet driving down those of the Quartermaster and Jasper, else is not my name Pathfinder."
>
> A shout from the target announced the truth of this assertion.

Is the miracle sufficient as it stands? Not for Cooper. The Pathfinder speaks again, as he "now slowly advances toward the stage occupied by the females":

> "That's not all, boys, that's not all; if you find the target touched at all, I'll own to a miss. The Quartermaster cut the wood, but you'll find no wood cut by that last messenger."

The miracle is at last complete. He knew—doubtless *saw*—at the distance of a hundred yards—that his bullet had passed into the hole *without fraying the edges*. There were now three bullets in that one hole—three bullets embedded processionally in the body of the stump back of the target. Everybody knew this—somehow or other—and yet nobody had dug any of them out to make sure.[13] Cooper is not a close observer, but he is interesting. He is certainly always that, no matter

---

[13] This episode takes place pretty much as Twain recounts it.

what happens. And he is more interesting when he is not noticing what he is about than when he is. This is a considerable merit.

The conversations in the Cooper books have a curious sound in our modern ears. To believe that such talk really ever came out of people's mouths would be to believe that there was a time when time was of no value to a person who thought he had something to say; when it was the custom to spread a two-minute remark out to ten; when a man's mouth was a rolling-mill, and busied itself all day long in turning four-foot pigs[14] of thought into thirty-foot bars of conversational railroad iron by attenuation; when subjects were seldom faithfully stuck to, but the talk wandered all around and arrived nowhere; when conversations consisted mainly of irrelevancies, with here and there a relevancy, a relevancy with an embarrassed look, as not being able to explain how it got there.

Cooper was certainly not a master in the construction of dialogue. Inaccurate observation defeated him here as it defeated him in so many other enterprises of his. He even failed to notice that the man who talks corrupt English six days in the week must and will talk it on the seventh, and can't help himself. In the *Deerslayer* story he lets Deerslayer talk the showiest kind of book-talk sometimes, and at other times the basest of base dialects. For instance, when some one asks him if he has a sweetheart, and if so, where she abides, this is his majestic answer:

> "She's in the forest—hanging from the boughs of the trees, in a soft rain—in the dew on the open grass—the clouds that float about in the blue heavens—the birds that sing in the woods—the sweet springs where I slake my thirst—and in all the other glorious gifts that come from God's Providence!"

And he preceded that, a little before, with this:

> "It consarns me as all things that touches a fri'nd consarns a fri'nd."

And this is another of his remarks:

> "If I was Injin born, now, I might tell of this, or carry in the scalp and boast of the expl'ite afore the whole tribe; or if my inimy had only been a bear"—[and so on].

We cannot imagine such a thing as a veteran Scotch Commander-in-Chief comporting himself in the field like a windy melodramatic actor, but Cooper could. On one occasion Alice and Cora were being chased by the French through a fog in the neighborhood of their father's fort:[15]

> "*Point de quartier aux coquins!*"[16] cried an eager pursuer, who seemed to direct the operations of the enemy.
> "Stand firm and be ready, my gallant 60ths!" suddenly exclaimed a voice above them; "wait to see the enemy; fire low, and sweep the glacis."[17]

---

[14] Ingots of metal rolled into railroad tracks.
[15] The British Fort William Henry in *The Last of the Mohicans*.
[16] "Show no mercy to the rascals!" (French).
[17] Clear the field in front of the wall of the fort.

"Father! father" exclaimed a piercing cry from out the mist; "it is I! Alice! thy own Elsie! O! save your daughters!"

"Hold!" shouted the former speaker, in the awful tones of parental agony, the sound reaching even to the woods, and rolling back in solemn echo. "'Tis she! God has restored me my children! Throw open the sally-port;[18] to the field, 60ths, to the field! pull not a trigger, lest ye kill my lambs! Drive off these dogs of France with your steel!"

Cooper's word-sense was singularly dull. When a person has a poor ear for music he will flat and sharp right along without knowing it. He keeps near the tune, but it is *not* the tune. When a person has a poor ear for words, the result is a literary flatting and sharping; you perceive what he is intending to say, but you also perceive that he doesn't *say* it. This is Cooper. He was not a word-musician. His ear was satisfied with the *approximate* word. I will furnish some circumstantial evidence in support of this charge. My instances are gathered from half a dozen pages of the tale called *Deerslayer*. He uses "verbal" for "oral"; "precision" for "facility"; "phenomena" for "marvels"; "necessary" for "predetermined"; "unsophisticated" for "primitive"; "preparation" for "expectancy"; "rebuked" for "subdued"; "dependent on" for "resulting from"; "fact" for "condition"; "fact" for "conjecture"; "precaution" for "caution"; "explain" for "determine"; "mortified" for "disappointed"; "meretricious" for "factitious"; "materially" for "considerably"; "decreasing" for "deepening"; "increasing" for "disappearing"; "embedded" for "inclosed"; "treacherous" for "hostile"; "stood" for "stooped"; "softened" for "replaced"; "rejoined" for "remarked"; "situation" for "condition"; "different" for "differing"; "insensible" for "unsentient"; "brevity" for "celerity"; "distrusted" for "suspicious"; "mental imbecility" for "imbecility"; "eyes" for "sight"; "counteracting" for "opposing"; "funeral obsequies" for "obsequies."

There have been daring people in the world who claimed that Cooper could write English, but they are all dead now—all dead but Lounsbury. I don't remember that Lounsbury makes the claim in so many words, still he makes it, for he says that *Deerslayer* is a "pure work of art." Pure, in that connection, means faultless—faultless in all details—and language is a detail. If Mr. Lounsbury had only compared Cooper's English with the English which he writes himself—but it is plain that he didn't; and so it is likely that he imagines until this day that Cooper's is as clean and compact as his own. Now I feel sure, deep down in my heart, that Cooper wrote about the poorest English that exists in our language, and that the English of *Deerslayer* is the very worst that even Cooper ever wrote.

I may be mistaken, but it does seem to me that *Deerslayer* is not a work of art in any sense; it does seem to me that it is destitute of every detail that goes to the making of a work of art; in truth, it seems to me that *Deerslayer* is just simply a literary *delirium tremens*.[19]

A work of art? It has no invention; it has no order, system, sequence, or result; it has no lifelikeness, no thrill, no stir, no seeming of reality; its characters are confusedly drawn, and by their acts and words they prove that they are not the sort of people the author claims that they are; its humor is pathetic; its pathos is funny;

---

[18] A door in the wall of a fort through which troops can rush out.
[19] "Trembling delirium" (Latin): a violent delirium, induced by excessive and prolonged use of alcohol.

its conversations are—oh! indescribable; its love-scenes odious; its English a crime against the language.

Counting these out, what is left is Art. I think we must all admit that.

1893, 1895

from ADVENTURES OF HUCKLEBERRY FINN*

(*Tom Sawyer's Comrade*[1]).

SCENE: THE MISSISSIPPI VALLEY.
TIME: FORTY TO FIFTY YEARS AGO.[2]

NOTICE.

Persons attempting to find a motive in this narrative will be prosecuted; persons attempting to find a moral in it will be banished; persons attempting to find a plot in it will be shot.

BY ORDER OF THE AUTHOR
PER G. G., CHIEF OF ORDNANCE.

EXPLANATORY.

In this book a number of dialects are used, to wit: the Missouri negro dialect; the extremest form of the backwoods South-Western dialect; the ordinary "Pike-County"[3] dialect; and four modified varieties of this last. The shadings have not been done in a hap-hazard fashion or by guess-work; but pains-takingly, and with the trustworthy guidance and support of personal familiarity with these several forms of speech.

I make this explanation for the reason that without it many readers would suppose that all these characters were trying to talk alike and not succeeding.

THE AUTHOR.

CHAPTER I

You don't know about me, without you have read a book by the name of "The Adventures of Tom Sawyer," but that ain't no matter. That book was made by Mr. Mark Twain, and he told the truth, mainly. There was things which he

---

* First published in England in 1884; the first American edition was in 1885.
[1] Twain had already published *The Adventures of Tom Sawyer* in 1876.
[2] That would put the setting between 1835 and 1845.   [3] In Missouri.

stretched, but mainly he told the truth. That is nothing. I never seen anybody but lied, one time or another, without it was Aunt Polly, or the widow, or maybe Mary.[4] Aunt Polly—Tom's Aunt Polly, she is—and Mary, and the Widow Douglas, is all told about in that book—which is mostly a true book; with some stretchers, as I said before.

Now the way that the book winds up, is this: Tom and me found the money that the robbers hid in the cave and it made us rich. We got six thousand dollars apiece—all gold. It was an awful sight of money when it was piled up. Well, Judge Thatcher, he took it and put it out at interest, and it fetched us a dollar a day apiece, all the year round—more than a body could tell what to do with. The Widow Douglas, she took me for her son, and allowed she would sivilize me; but it was rough living in the house all the time, considering how dismal regular and decent the widow was in all her ways; and so when I couldn't stand it no longer, I lit out. I got into my old rags, and my sugar-hogshead[5] again, and was free and satisfied. But Tom Sawyer, he hunted me up and said he was going to start a band of robbers, and I might join if I would go back to the widow and be respectable. So I went back.

The widow she cried over me, and called me a poor lost lamb, and she called me a lot of other names, too, but she never meant no harm by it. She put me in them new clothes again, and I couldn't do nothing but sweat and sweat, and feel all cramped up. Well, then, the old thing commenced again. The widow rung a bell for supper, and you had to come on time. When you got to the table you couldn't go right to eating, but you had to wait for the widow to tuck down her head and grumble a little over the victuals, though there warn't really anything the matter with them. That is, nothing only everything was cooked by itself. In a barrel of odds and ends it is different; things get mixed up, and the juice kind of swaps around, and the things go better.

After supper she got out her book and learned me about Moses and the Bulrushers;[6] and I was in a sweat to find out all about him; but by-and-by she let it out that Moses had been dead a considerable long time; so then I didn't care no more about him; because I don't take no stock in dead people.

Pretty soon I wanted to smoke, and asked the widow to let me. But she wouldn't. She said it was a mean practice and wasn't clean, and I must try to not do it any more. That is just the way with some people. They get down on a thing when they don't know nothing about it. Here she was a bothering about Moses, which was no kin to her, and no use to anybody, being gone, you see, yet finding a power of fault with me for doing a thing that had some good in it. And she took snuff too; of course that was all right, because she done it herself.

Her sister, Miss Watson, a tolerable slim old maid, with goggles on, had just come to live with her, and took a set at me now, with a spelling-book. She worked me middling hard for about an hour, and then the widow made her ease up. I couldn't stood it much longer. Then for an hour it was deadly dull, and I was fidgety. Miss Watson would say, "Don't put your feet up there, Huckleberry;" and "don't scrunch up like that, Huckleberry—set up straight;" and pretty soon she would say, "Don't gap[7] and stretch like that, Huckleberry—why don't you try to behave?" Then she told me all about the bad place, and I said I wished I was

---

[4] Tom Sawyer's cousin.   [5] A large barrel.
[6] In Exodus 2:1–10 the pharaoh's daughter finds the infant Moses in a basket made of bulrushes.
[7] Yawn.

there. She got mad, then, but I didn't mean no harm. All I wanted was to go somewheres; all I wanted was a change, I warn't particular. She said it was wicked to say what I said; said she wouldn't say it for the whole world; *she* was going to live so as to go to the good place. Well, I couldn't see no advantage in going where she was going, so I made up my mind I wouldn't try for it. But I never said so, because it would only make trouble, and wouldn't do no good.

Now she had got a start, and she went on and told me all about the good place. She said all a body would have to do there was to go around all day long with a harp and sing, forever and ever. So I didn't think much of it. But I never said so. I asked her if she reckoned Tom Sawyer would go there, and, she said, not by a considerable sight. I was glad about that, because I wanted him and me to be together.

Miss Watson she kept pecking at me, and it got tiresome and lonesome. By-and-by they fetched the niggers[8] in and had prayers, and then everybody was off to bed. I went up to my room with a piece of candle and put it on the table. Then I set down in a chair by the window and tried to think of something cheerful, but it warn't no use. I felt so lonesome I most wished I was dead. The stars was shining, and the leaves rustled in the woods ever so mournful; and I heard an owl, away off, who-whooing about somebody that was dead, and a whippowill and a dog crying about somebody that was going to die; and the wind was trying to whisper something to me and I couldn't make out what it was, and so it made the cold shivers run over me. Then away out in the woods I heard that kind of a sound that a ghost makes when it wants to tell about something that's on its mind and can't make itself understood, and so can't rest easy in its grave and has to go about that way every night grieving. I got so down-hearted and scared, I did wish I had some company. Pretty soon a spider went crawling up my shoulder, and I flipped it off and it lit in the candle; and before I could budge it was all shriveled up. I didn't need anybody to tell me that that was an awful bad sign and would fetch me some bad luck, so I was scared and most shook the clothes off of me. I got up and turned around in my tracks three times and crossed my breast every time; and then I tied up a little lock of my hair with a thread to keep witches away. But I hadn't no confidence. You do that when you've lost a horse-shoe that you've found, instead of nailing it up over the door, but I hadn't ever heard anybody say it was any way to keep off bad luck when you'd killed a spider.

I set down again, a shaking all over, and got out my pipe for a smoke; for the house was all as still as death, now, and so the widow wouldn't know. Well, after a long time I heard the clock away off in the town go boom—boom—boom—twelve licks—and all still again—stiller than ever. Pretty soon I heard a twig snap, down in the dark amongst the trees—something was a stirring. I set still and listened. Directly I could just barely hear a "*me-you! me-yow!*" down there. That was good! Says I, "*me-yow! me-yow!*" as soft as I could, and then I put out the light and scrambled out of the window onto the shed. Then I slipped down to the ground and crawled in amongst the trees, and sure enough there was Tom Sawyer waiting for me.

[8] This term, a corruption of "Negro," has long been the most highly charged and offensive word in American English. Prior to the Civil War it was frequently used as a synonym for "slave," and Huckleberry Finn uses it descriptively, without personal derision, even when he decides to go to Hell rather than let his friend Jim remain in captivity. The use of the term here is part of Twain's effort to reproduce with social realism the speech of this particular time and place. Twain makes us wince by touching the raw nerve of our history.

from   CHAPTER II

We went tip-toeing along a path amongst the trees back towards the end of the widow's garden, stooping down so as the branches wouldn't scrape our heads. When we was passing by the kitchen I fell over a root and made a noise. We scrouched down and laid still. Miss Watson's big nigger, named Jim, was setting in the kitchen door; we could see him pretty clear, because there was a light behind him. He got up and stretched his neck out about a minute, listening. Then he says,

"Who dah?"

He listened some more; then he come tip-toeing down and stood right between us; we could a touched him, nearly. Well, likely it was minutes and minutes that there warn't a sound, and we all there so close together. There was a place on my ankle that got to itching; but I dasn't scratch it; and then my ear begun to itch; and next my back, right between my shoulders. Seemed like I'd die if I couldn't scratch. Well, I've noticed that thing plenty of times since. If you are with the quality, or at a funeral, or trying to go to sleep when you ain't sleepy—if you are anywheres where it won't do for you to scratch, why you will itch all over in upwards of a thousand places. Pretty soon Jim says:

"Say—who is you? Whar is you? Dog my cats ef I didn' hear sumf'n. Well, I knows what I's gwyne to do. I's gwyne to set down here and listen tell I hears it agin."

So he set down on the ground betwixt me and Tom. He leaned his back up against a tree, and stretched his legs out till one of them most touched one of mine. My nose begun to itch. It itched till the tears come into my eyes. But I dasn't scratch. Then it begun to itch on the inside. Next I got to itching underneath. I didn't know how I was going to set still. This miserableness went on as much as six or seven minutes; but it seemed a sight longer than that. I was itching in eleven different places now. I reckoned I couldn't stand it more'n a minute longer, but I set my teeth hard and got ready to try. Just then Jim begun to breathe heavy; next he begun to snore—and then I was pretty soon comfortable again.

Tom he made a sign to me—kind of a little noise with his mouth—and we went creeping away on our hands and knees. When we was ten foot off, Tom whispered to me and wanted to tie Jim to the tree for fun; but I said no; he might wake and make a disturbance, and then they'd find out I warn't in. Then Tom said he hadn't got candles enough, and he would slip in the kitchen and get some more. I didn't want him to try. I said Jim might wake up and come. But Tom wanted to resk it; so we slid in there and got three candles, and Tom laid five cents on the table for pay. Then we got out, and I was in a sweat to get away; but nothing would do Tom but he must crawl to where Jim was, on his hands and knees, and play something on him. I waited, and it seemed a good while, everything was so still and lonesome.

As soon as Tom was back, we cut along the path, around the garden fence, and by-and-by fetched up on the steep top of the hill the other side of the house. Tom said he slipped Jim's hat off of his head and hung it on a limb right over him, and Jim stirred a little, but he didn't wake. Afterwards Jim said the witches bewitched him and put him in a trance, and rode him all over the State, and then set him under the trees again and hung his hat on a limb to show who done it. And next time Jim told it he said they rode him down to New Orleans; and after that, every time he told it he spread it more and more, till by-and-by he said they rode him all over the world, and tired him most to death, and his back was all over saddle-boils. Jim was monstrous proud about it, and he got so he wouldn't hardly notice the other niggers. Niggers would come miles to hear Jim tell about it, and he was more looked up to than any nigger in that country. Strange niggers[1] would stand with their mouths open and look him all over, same as if he was a wonder. Niggers is always talking about witches in the dark by the kitchen fire; but whenever one was talking and letting on to know all about such things, Jim would happen in and say, "Hm! What you know 'bout witches?" and that nigger was corked up and had to take a back seat. Jim always kept that five-center piece around his neck with a string and said it was a charm the devil give to him with his own hands and told him he could cure anybody with it and fetch witches whenever he wanted to, just by saying something to it; but he never told what it was he said to it. Niggers would come from all around there and give Jim anything they had, just for a sight of that five-center piece; but they wouldn't touch it, because the devil had had his hands on it. Jim was most ruined, for a servant, because he got so stuck up on account of having seen the devil and been rode by witches.

* * *

from CHAPTER VI

Well, pretty soon the old man was up and around again, and then he went for Judge Thatcher in the courts to make him give up that money, and he went for me, too, for not stopping school. He catched me a couple of times and thrashed me, but I went to school just the same, and dodged him or out-run him most of the time. I didn't want to go to school much, before, but I reckoned I'd go now to spite pap. That law trial was a slow business; appeared like they warn't ever going to get started on it; so every now and then I'd borrow two or three dollars off of the judge for him, to keep from getting a cowhiding. Every time he got money he got drunk; and every time he got drunk he raised Cain[1] around town; and every time he raised Cain he got jailed. He was just suited—this kind of thing was right in his line.

He got to hanging around the widow's too much, and so she told him at last, that if he didn't quit using[2] around there she would make trouble for him. Well, *wasn't* he mad? He said he would show who was Huck Finn's boss. So he watched out for me one day in the spring, and catched me, and took me up the river about three mile, in a skiff, and crossed over to the Illinois shore where it was woody and there warn't no houses but an old log hut in a place where the timber was so thick you couldn't find it if you didn't know where it was.

He kept me with him all the time, and I never got a chance to run off. We lived in that old cabin, and he always locked the door and put the key under his head, nights. He had a gun which he had stole, I reckon, and we fished and hunted, and that was what we lived on. Every little while he locked me in and went down to the store, three miles, to the ferry, and traded fish and game for whisky and fetched it home and got drunk and had a good time, and licked me. The widow

---

[1] Who do not live in the area.
[1] Created a great commotion; after the oldest son of Adam and Eve in Genesis 4: Cain killed his brother, Abel.
[2] Making a habit of loitering.

she found out where I was, by-and-by, and she sent a man over to try to get hold of me, but pap drove him off with the gun, and it warn't long after that till I was used to being where I was, and liked it, all but the cowhide part.

It was kind of lazy and jolly, laying off comfortable all day, smoking and fishing, and no books nor study. Two months or more run along, and my clothes got to be all rags and dirt, and I didn't see how I'd ever got to like it so well at the widow's, where you had to wash, and eat on a plate, and comb up, and go to bed and get up regular, and be forever bothering over a book and have old Miss Watson pecking at you all the time. I didn't want to go back no more. I had stopped cussing, because the widow didn't like it; but now I took to it again because pap hadn't no objections. It was pretty good times up in the woods there, take it all around.

But by-and-by pap got too handy with his hick'ry, and I couldn't stand it. I was all over welts. He got to going away so much, too, and locking me in. Once he locked me in and was gone three days. It was dreadful lonesome. I judged he had got drowned and I wasn't ever going to get out any more. I was scared. I made up my mind I would fix up some way to leave there. I had tried to get out of that cabin many a time, but I couldn't find no way. There warn't a window to it big enough for a dog to get through. I couldn't get up the chimbly, it was too narrow. The door was thick solid oak slabs. Pap was pretty careful not to leave a knife or anything in the cabin when he was away; I reckon I had hunted the place over as much as a hundred times; well, I was 'most all the time at it, because it was about the only way to put in the time. But this time I found something at last; I found an old rusty wood-saw without any handle; it was laid in between a rafter and the clapboards of the roof. I greased it up and went to work. There was an old horse-blanket nailed against the logs at the far end of the cabin behind the table, to keep the wind from blowing through the chinks and putting the candle out. I got under the table and raised the blanket and went to work to saw a section of the big bottom log out, big enough to let me through. Well, it was a good long job, but I was getting towards the end of it when I heard pap's gun in the woods. I got rid of the signs of my work, and dropped the blanket and hid my saw, and pretty soon pap come in.

* * *

from   Chapter VII

"Git up! what you 'bout!"

I opened my eyes and looked around, trying to make out where I was. It was after sun-up, and I had been sound asleep. Pap was standing over me, looking sour—and sick, too. He says—

"What you doin' with this gun?"

I judged he didn't know nothing about what he had been doing, so I says:

"Somebody tried to get in, so I was laying for him."

"Why didn't you roust me out?"

"Well I tried to, but I couldn't; I couldn't budge you."

"Well, all right. Don't stand there palavering[1] all day, but out with you and see if there's a fish on the lines for breakfast. I'll be along in a minute.

---

[1] Jabbering.

He unlocked the door and I cleared out, up the river bank. I noticed some pieces of limbs and such things floating down, and a sprinkling of bark; so I knowed the river had begun to rise. I reckoned I would have great times, now, if I was over at the town. The June rise used to be always luck for me; because as soon as that rise begins, here comes cord-wood[2] floating down, and pieces of log rafts—sometimes a dozen logs together; so all you have to do is to catch them and sell them to the wood yards and the sawmill.

I went along up the bank with one eye out for pap and 'tother one out for what the rise might fetch along. Well, all at once, here comes a canoe; just a beauty, too, about thirteen or fourteen foot long, riding high like a duck. I shot head first off of the bank, like a frog, clothes and all on, and struck out for the canoe. I just expected there'd be somebody laying down in it, because people often done that to fool folks, and when a chap had pulled a skiff out most to it they'd raise up and laugh at him. But it warn't so this time. It was a drift-canoe, sure enough, and I clumb in and paddled her ashore. Thinks I, the old man will be glad when he sees this—she's worth ten dollars. But when I got to shore pap wasn't in sight yet, and as I was running her into a little creek like a gully, all hung over with vines and willows, I struck another idea; I judged I'd hide her good, and then, stead of taking to the woods when I run off, I'd go down the river about fifty mile and camp in one place for good, and not have such a rough time tramping on foot.

It was pretty close to the shanty, and I thought I heard the old man coming, all the time; but I got her hid; and then I out and looked around a bunch of willows, and there was the old man down the path apiece just drawing a bead on a bird with his gun. So he hadn't seen anything.

When he got along, I was hard at it taking up a "trot" line.[3] He abused me a little for being so slow, but I told him I fell in the river and that was what made me so long. I knowed he would see I was wet, and then he would be asking questions. We got five cat-fish off of the lines and went home.

While we laid off, after breakfast, to sleep up, both of us being about wore out, I got to thinking that if I could fix up some way to keep pap and the widow from trying to follow me, it would be a certainer thing than trusting to luck to get far enough off before they missed me; you see, all kinds of things might happen. Well, I didn't see no way for a while, but by-and-by pap raised up a minute, to drink another barrel of water, and he says:

"Another time a man comes a-prowling round here, you roust me out, you hear? That man warn't here for no good. I'd a shot him. Next time, you roust me out, you hear?"

Then he dropped down and went to sleep again—but what he had been saying give me the very idea I wanted. I says to myself, I can fix it now so nobody won't think of following me.

About twelve o'clock we turned out and went along up the bank. The river was coming up pretty fast, and lots of drift-wood going by on the rise. By-and-by, along comes part of a log raft—nine logs fast together. We went out with the skiff and towed it ashore. Then we had dinner. Anybody but pap would a waited and seen the day through, so as to catch more stuff; but that warn't pap's style. Nine logs was enough for one time; he must shove right over to town and sell. So he locked me in and took the skiff and started off towing the raft about half-past

---

[2] Wood cut into four-foot lengths.
[3] A fishing line strung across a stream from which hooks are attached at intervals.

three. I judged he wouldn't come back that night. I waited till I reckoned he had got a good start, then I out with my saw and went to work on that log again. Before he was 'tother side of the river I was out of the hole; him and his raft was just a speck on the water away off yonder.

I took the sack of corn meal and took it to where the canoe was hid, and shoved the vines and branches apart and put it in; then I done the same with the side of bacon; then the whisky jug; I took all the coffee and sugar there was, and all the ammunition; I took the wadding; I took the bucket and gourd, I took a dipper and a tin cup, and my old saw and two blankets, and the skillet and the coffee-pot. I took fish-lines and matches and other things—everything that was worth a cent. I cleaned out the place. I wanted an axe, but there wasn't any, only the one out at the wood pile, and I knowed why I was going to leave that. I fetched out the gun, and now I was done.

I had wore the ground a good deal, crawling out of the hole and dragging out so many things. So I fixed that as good as I could from the outside by scattering dust on the place, which covered up the smoothness and the sawdust. Then I fixed the piece of log back into its place, and put two rocks under it and one against it to hold it there,—for it was bent up at that place, and didn't quite touch ground. If you stood four or five foot away and didn't know it was sawed, you wouldn't ever notice it; and besides, this was the back of the cabin and it warn't likely anybody would go fooling around there.

It was all grass clear to the canoe; so I hadn't left a track. I followed around to see. I stood on the bank and looked out over the river. All safe. So I took the gun and went up a piece into the woods and was hunting around for some birds, when I see a wild pig; hogs soon went wild in them bottoms after they had got away from the prairie farms. I shot this fellow and took him into camp.

I took the axe and smashed in the door—I beat it and hacked it considerable, a-doing it. I fetched the pig in and took him back nearly to the table and hacked into his throat with the ax, and laid him down on the ground to bleed—I say ground, because it *was* ground—hard packed, and no boards. Well, next I took an old sack and put a lot of big rocks in it,—all I could drag—and I started it from the pig and dragged it to the door and through the woods down to the river and dumped it in, and down it sunk, out of sight. You could easy see that something had been dragged over the ground. I did wish Tom Sawyer was there, I knowed he would take an interest in this kind of business, and throw in the fancy touches. Nobody could spread himself like Tom Sawyer in such a thing as that.

Well, last I pulled out some of my hair, and bloodied the ax good, and stuck it on the back side, and slung the ax in the corner. Then I took up the pig and held him to my breast with my jacket (so he couldn't drip) till I got a good piece below the house and then dumped him into the river. Now I thought of something else. So I went and got the bag of meal and my old saw out of the canoe and fetched them to the house. I took the bag to where it used to stand, and ripped a hole in the bottom of it with the saw, for there warn't no knives and forks on the place—pap done everything with his clasp-knife, about the cooking. Then I carried the sack about a hundred yards across the grass and through the willows east of the house, to a shallow lake that was five mile wide and full of rushes—and ducks too, you might say, in the season. There was a slough or a creek leading out of it on the other side, that went miles away, I don't know where, but it didn't go to the river. The meal sifted out and made a little track all the way to the lake. I dropped pap's whetstone there too, so as to look like it had been done by accident. Then I tied up the rip in the meal sack with a string, so it wouldn't leak no more, and took it and my saw to the canoe again.

It was about dark, now; so I dropped the canoe down the river under some willows that hung over the bank, and waited for the moon to rise. I made fast to a willow; then I took a bite to eat, and by-and-by laid down in the canoe to smoke a pipe and lay out a plan. I says to myself, they'll follow the track of that sackful of rocks to the shore and then drag the river for me. And they'll follow that meal track to the lake and go browsing down the creek that leads out of it to find the robbers that killed me and took the things. They won't ever hunt the river for anything but my dead carcass. They'll soon get tired of that, and won't bother no more about me. All right; I can stop anywhere I want to. Jackson's Island[4] is good enough for me; I know that island pretty well, and nobody ever comes there. And then I can paddle over to town, nights, and slink around and pick up things I want. Jackson's Island's the place.

* * *

from   Chapter VIII

* * *

. . . . So I took my gun and slipped off towards where I had run across that camp fire, stopping every minute or two to listen. But I hadn't no luck, somehow; I couldn't seem to find the place. But by-and-by sure enough, I catched a glimpse of fire, away through the trees. I went for it, cautious and slow. By-and-by I was close enough to have a look, and there laid a man on the ground. It most give me the fan-tods.[1] He had a blanket around his head, and his head was nearly in the fire. I set there behind a clump of bushes, in about six foot of him, and kept my eyes on him steady. It was getting gray daylight, now. Pretty soon he gapped, and stretched himself, and hove off the blanket, and it was Miss Watson's Jim! I bet I was glad to see him. I says:

"Hello, Jim!" and skipped out.

He bounced up and stared at me wild. Then he drops down on his knees, and puts his hands together and says:

"Doan' hurt me—don't! I hain't ever done no harm to a ghos'. I awluz liked dead people, en done all I could for 'em. You go en git in de river agin, whah you b'longs, en doan' do nuffn to Ole Jim, 'at 'uz awluz yo' fren'."

Well, I warn't long making him understand I warn't dead. I was ever so glad to see Jim. I warn't lonesome, now. I told him I warn't afraid of *him* telling the people where I was. I talked along, but he only set there and looked at me; never said nothing. Then I says:

"It's good daylight. Le's get breakfast. Make up your camp fire good."

"What's de use er makin' up de camp fire to cook strawbries en sich truck? But you got a gun, hain't you? Den we kin git sumfn better den strawbries."

"Strawberries and such truck," I says. "Is that what you live on?"

"I couldn' git nuffn else," he says.

"Why, how long you been on the island, Jim?"

"I come heah de night arter you's killed."

---

[4] An island to which Tom Sawyer, Joe Harper, and Huck sneak away in *Tom Sawyer*.
[1] The willies, the nervous fidgets.

"What, all that time?"

"Yes-indeedy."

"And ain't you had nothing but that kind of rubbage to eat?"

"No, sah—nuffn else."

"Well, you must be most starved, ain't you?"

"I reck'n I could eat a hoss. I think I could. How long you ben on de islan'?"

"Since the night I got killed."

"No! W'y, what has you lived on? But you got a gun. Oh, yes, you got a gun. Dat's good. Now you kill sumfn en I'll make up de fire."

So we went over to where the canoe was, and while he built a fire in a grassy open place amongst the trees, I fetched meal and bacon and coffee, and coffee-pot and frying-pan, and sugar and tin cups, and the nigger was set back considerable, because he reckoned it was all done with witchcraft. I catched a good big cat-fish, too, and Jim cleaned him with his knife, and fried him.

When breakfast was ready, we lolled on the grass and eat it smoking hot. Jim laid it in with all his might, for he was most about starved. Then when we had got pretty well stuffed, we laid off and lazied.

By-and-by Jim says:

"But looky here, Huck, who wuz it dat 'uz killed in dat shanty, ef it warn't you?"

Then I told him the whole thing, and he said it was smart. He said Tom Sawyer couldn't get up no better plan than what I had. Then I says:

"How do you come to be here, Jim, and how'd you get here?"

He looked pretty uneasy, and didn't say nothing for a minute. Then he says:

"Maybe I better not tell."

"Why, Jim?"

"Well, dey's reasons. But you wouldn' tell on me ef I 'uz to tell you, would you, Huck?"

"Blamed if I would, Jim."

"Well, I b'lieve you, Huck. I—I *run off*."

"Jim!"

"But mind, you said you wouldn't tell—you know you said you wouldn't tell, Huck."

"Well, I did. I said I wouldn't, and I'll stick to it. Honest *injun* I will. People would call me a low down Ablitionist[2] and despise me for keeping mum—but that don't make no difference. I ain't agoing to tell, and I ain't agoing back there anyways. So now, le's know all about it."

"Well, you see, it 'uz dis way. Ole Missus—dat's Miss Watson—she pecks on me all de time, en treats me pooty rough, but she awluz said she wouldn' sell me down to Orleans. But I noticed dey wuz a nigger trader roun' de place considable, lately, en I begin to git oneasy. Well, one night I creeps to de do', pooty late, en de do' warn't quite shet, en I hear ole missus tell de widder she gwyne to sell me down to Orleans,[3] but she didn' want to, but she could git eight hund'd dollars for me, en it 'uz sich a big stack o' money she couldn' resis'. De widder she try to git her to say she wouldn' do it, but I never waited to hear de res'. I lit out mighty quick, I tell you.

---

[2] Abolitionist.

[3] New Orleans; to be "sold down the river," separated from family, and sent to work as a field hand on a large plantation was a fate understandably feared by slaves.

"I tuck out en shin down de hill en 'spec to steal a skift 'long de sho' som'ers 'bove de town, but dey wuz people a-stirrin' yit, so I hid in de ole tumble-down cooper shop[4] on de bank to wait for everybody to go 'way. Well, I wuz dah all night. Dey wuz somebody roun' all de time. 'Long 'bout six in de mawnin', skifts begin to go by, en 'bout eight er nine every skift dat went 'long wuz talkin' 'bout how yo' pap come over to de town en say you's killed. Dese las' skifts wuz full o' ladies en genlmen agoin' over for to see de place. Sometimes dey'd pull up at de sho' en take a res' b'fo' dey started acrost, so by de talk I got to know all 'bout de killin'. I 'uz powerful sorry you's killed, Huck, but I ain't no mo', now.

"I laid dah under de shavins all day. I 'uz hungry, but I warn't afeard; bekase I knowed ole missus en de widder wuz goin' to start to de camp-meetn' right arter breakfas' en be gone all day, en dey knows I goes off wid de cattle 'bout daylight, so dey wouldn' 'spec to see me roun' de place, en so dey wouldn' miss me tell arter dark in de evenin'. De yuther servants wouldn' miss me, kase dey'd shin out en take holiday, soon as de ole folks 'uz out'n de way.

"Well, when it come dark I tuck out up de river road, en went 'bout two mile er more to whah dey warn't no houses. I'd made up my mine 'bout what I's agwyne to do. You see ef I kep' on tryin' to git away afoot, de dogs 'ud track me; ef I stole a skift to cross over, dey'd miss dat skift, you see, en dey'd know 'bout whah I'd lan' on de yuther side en whah to pick up my track. So I says, a raff is what I's arter; it doan' *make* no track.

"I see a light a-comin' roun' de p'int, bymeby, so I wade' in en shove' a log ahead o' me, en swum more'n half-way acrost de river, en got in 'mongst de drift-wood, en kep' my head down low, en kinder swum agin de current tell de raff come along. Den I swum to de stern uv it, en tuck aholt. It clouded up en 'uz pooty dark for a little while. So I clumb up en laid down on de planks. De men 'uz all 'way yonder in de middle, whah de lantern wuz. De river wuz arisin' en dey wuz a good current; so I reck'n'd 'at by fo' in de mawnin' I'd be twenty-five mile down de river, en den I'd slip in, jis' b'fo' daylight, en swim asho' en take to de woods on de Illinoi side.

"But I didn' have no luck. When we 'uz mos' down to de head er de islan', a man begin to come aft wid de lantern. I see it warn't no use fer to wait, so I slid overboard, en struck out fer de islan'. Well, I had a notion I could lan' mos' anywhers, but I couldn't—bank too bluff. I'uz mos' to de foot er de islan' b'fo' I foun' a good place. I went into de woods en jedged I wouldn' fool wid raffs no mo', long as dey move de lantern roun' so. I had my pipe en a plug er dog-leg,[5] en some matches in my cap, en dey warn't wet, so I 'uz all right."

"And so you ain't had no meat nor bread to eat all this time? Why didn't you get mud-turkles?"

"How you gwyne to git'm? You can't slip up on um en grab um; en how's a body gwyne to hit um wid a rock? How could a body do it in de night? en I warn't gwyne to show mysef on de bank in de daytime."

"Well, that's so. You've had to keep in the woods all the time, of course. Did you hear 'em shooting the cannon?"

"Oh, yes. I knowed dey was arter you. I see um go by heah; watched um thoo de bushes."

Some young birds come along, flying a yard or two at a time and lighting. Jim

---

[4] Barrel-maker's shop.
[5] Cheap leaf chewing tobacco, twisted into the shape of a dog's hind leg.

said it was a sign it was going to rain. He said it was a sign when young chickens flew that way, and so he reckoned it was the same way when young birds done it. I was going to catch some of them, but Jim wouldn't let me. He said it was death. He said his father laid mighty sick once, and some of them catched a bird, and his old granny said his father would die, and he did.

And Jim said you musn't count the things you are going to cook for dinner, because that would bring bad luck. The same if you shook the table-cloth after sundown. And he said if a man owned a bee-hive, and that man died, the bees must be told about it before sun-up next morning, or else the bees would all weaken down and quit work and die. Jim said bees wouldn't sting idiots; but I didn't believe that, because I had tried them lots of times myself, and they wouldn't sting me.

I had heard about some of these things before, but not all of them. Jim knowed all kinds of signs. He said he knowed most everything. I said it looked to me like all the signs was about bad luck, and so I asked him if there warn't any good-luck signs. He says:

"Mighty few—an' *dey* ain' no use to a body. What you want to know when good luck's a-comin for? want to keep it off?" And he said: "Ef you's got hairy arms en a hairy breas', it's a sign dat you's agwyne to be rich. Well, dey's some use in a sign like dat, 'kase it's so fur ahead. You see, maybe you's got to be po' a long time fust, en so you might git discourage' en kill yo'sef 'f you didn' know by de sign dat you gwyne to be rich bymeby."

"Have you got hairy arms and a hairy breast, Jim?"

"What's de use to ax dat question? don' you see I has?"

"Well, are you rich?"

"No, but I ben rich wunst, and gwyne to be rich agin. Wunst I had foteen dollars, but I tuck to specalat'n', en got busted out."

"What did you speculate in, Jim?"

"Well, fust I tackled stock."

"What kind of stock?"

"Why, live stock. Cattle, you know. I put ten dollars in a cow. But I ain' gwyne to resk no mo' money in stock. De cow up 'n' died on my han's."

"So you lost the ten dollars."

"No, I didn' lose it all. I on'y los' 'bout nine of it. I sole de hide en taller[6] for a dollar en ten cents."

"You had five dollars and ten cents left. Did you speculate any more?"

"Yes. You know dat one-laigged nigger dat b'longs to old Misto Bradish? well, he sot up a bank, en say anybody dat put in a dollar would git fo' dollars mo' at de en' er de year. Well, all de niggers went in, but dey didn' have much. I wuz de on'y one dat had much. So I stuck out for mo' dan fo' dollars, en I said 'f I didn't git it I'd start a bank mysef. Well o' course dat nigger want' to keep me out er de business, bekase he say dey warn't business 'nough for two banks, so he say I could put in my five dollars en he pay me thirty-five at de en' er de year.

"So I done it. Den I reck'n'd I'd inves' de thirty-five dollars right off en keep things a-movin'. Dey wuz a nigger name' Bob, dat had ketched a wood-flat,[7] en his marster didn' know it; en I bought it off'n him en told him to take de thirty-five dollars when de en' er de year come; but somebody stole de wood-flat dat

---

[6] Tallow.

[7] A flat-bottomed boat used for carrying wood. Jim makes a point that Bob's "marster didn' know it" because slaves were forbidden to own property; the "marster" would have taken the boat.

night, en nex' day de one-laigged nigger say de bank's busted. So dey didn' none uv us git no money."

"What did you do with the ten cents, Jim?"

"Well, I'uz gwyne to spen' it, but I had a dream, en de dream tole me to give it to a nigger name' Balum—Balum's Ass[8] dey call him for short, he's one er dem chuckle-heads, you know. But he's lucky, dey say, en I see I warn't lucky. De dream say let Balum inves' de ten cents en he'd make a raise for me. Well, Balum he tuck de money, en when he wuz in church he hear de preacher say dat whoever give to de po' len' to de Lord, en boun' to git his money back a hund'd times. So Balum he tuck en give de ten cents to de po,' en laid low to see what wuz gwyne to come of it."

"Well, what did come of it, Jim?"

"Nuffn' never come of it. I couldn' manage to k'leck dat money no way; en Balum he couldn'. I ain' gwyne to len' no mo' money 'dout I see de security. Boun' to git yo' money back a hund'd times, de preacher says! Ef I could git de ten *cents* back, I'd call it squah, en be glad er de chanst."

"Well, it's all right, anyway, Jim, long as you're going to be rich again some time or other."

"Yes—en I's rich now, come to look at it. I owns mysef, en I's wuth eight hund'd dollars. I wisht I had de money, I wouldn' want no mo'."

CHAPTER XV

We judged that three nights more would fetch us to Cairo,[1] at the bottom of Illinois, where the Ohio River comes in, and that was what we was after. We would sell the raft and get on a steamboat and go way up the Ohio amongst the free States, and then be out of trouble.

Well, the second night a fog begun to come on, and we made for a tow-head to tie to, for it wouldn't do to try to run in fog; but when I paddled ahead in the canoe, with the line, to make fast, there warn't anything but little saplings to tie to. I passed the line around one of them right on the edge of the cut bank,[2] but there was a stiff current, and the raft come booming down so lively she tore it out by the roots and away she went. I see the fog closing down, and it made me so sick and scared I couldn't budge for most a half a minute it seemed to me—and then there warn't no raft in sight; you couldn't see twenty yards. I jumped into the canoe and run back to the stern and grabbed the paddle and set her back a stroke. But she didn't come. I was in such a hurry I hadn't untied her. I got up and tried to untie her, but I was so excited my hands shook so I couldn't hardly do anything with them.

As soon as I got started I took out after the raft, hot and heavy, right down the tow-head. That was all right as far as it went, but the tow-head warn't sixty yards long, and the minute I flew by the foot of it I shot out into the solid white fog, and hadn't no more idea which way I was going than a dead man.

---

[8] In Numbers 22:21–34 the biblical Balaam, blind to an angel's presence, was saved from destruction by the ass upon which he rode; here, Balaam is blind to anything but literal meaning.

[1] Pronounced KAY-ro. Because southern Illinois was heavily proslavery in sentiment in the 1840s, Jim would stand a better chance of reaching freedom if he could get farther north, up the Ohio River. Huck does not consider the possible difficulties of a boy selling a raft and then buying steamboat tickets for himself and for Jim; what he proposes is more a hope than a realistic plan.

[2] A steep river bank shaped ("cut") by the force of the current.

Thinks I, it won't do to paddle; first I know I'll run into the bank or a tow-head or something; I got to set still and float, and yet it's mighty fidgety business to have to hold your hands still at such a time. I whooped and listened. Away down there, somewheres, I hears a small whoop, and up comes my spirits. I went tearing after it, listening sharp to hear it again. The next time it come, I see I warn't heading for it but heading away to the right of it. And the next time, I was heading away to the left of it—and not gaining on it much, either, for I was flying around, this way and that and 'tother, but it was going straight ahead all the time.

I did wish the fool would think to beat a tin pan, and beat it all the time, but he never did, and it was the still places between the whoops that was making the trouble for me. Well, I fought along, and directly I hears the whoop *behind* me. I was tangled good, now. That was somebody else's whoop, or else I was turned around.

I throwed the paddle down. I heard the whoop again; it was behind me yet, but in a different place; it kept coming, and kept changing its place, and I kept answering, till by-and-by it was in front of me again and I knowed the current had swung the canoe's head down stream and I was all right, if that was Jim and not some other raftsman hollering. I couldn't tell nothing about voices in a fog, for nothing don't look natural nor sound natural in a fog.

The whooping went on, and in about a minute I come a booming down on a cut bank with smoky ghosts of big trees on it, and the current throwed me off to the left and shot by, amongst a lot of snags that fairly roared, the current was tearing by them so swift.

In another second or two it was solid white and still again. I set perfectly still, then, listening to my heart thump, and I reckon I didn't draw a breath while it thumped a hundred.

I just give up, then. I knowed what the matter was. That cut bank was an island, and Jim had gone down 'tother side of it. It warn't no tow-head, that you could float by in ten minutes. It had the big timber of a regular island; it might be five or six mile long and more than a half a mile wide.

I kept quiet, with my ears cocked, about fifteen minutes, I reckon. I was floating along, of course, four or five mile an hour; but you don't ever think of that. No, you *feel* like you are laying dead still on the water; and if a little glimpse of a snag slips by, you don't think to yourself how fast *you're* going, but you catch your breath and think, my! how that snag's tearing along. If you think it ain't dismal and lonesome out in a fog that way, by yourself, in the night, you try it once—you'll see.

Next, for about a half an hour, I whoops now and then; at last I hears the answer a long ways off, and tries to follow it, but I couldn't do it, and directly I judged I'd got into a nest of tow-heads, for I had little dim glimpses of them on both sides of me, sometimes just a narrow channel between; and some that I couldn't see, I knowed was there, because I'd hear the wash of the current against the old dead brush and trash that hung over the banks. Well, I warn't long losing the whoops, down amongst the tow-heads; and I only tried to chase them a little while, anyway, because it was worse than chasing a Jack-o-lantern.[3] You never knowed a sound dodge around so, and swap places so quick and so much.

I had to claw away from the bank pretty lively, four or five times, to keep from knocking the islands out of the river; and so I judged the raft must be butting into

---

[3] An elusive light that appears over marshy grounds at night, supposedly caused by the combustion of marsh gas; popularly called will-o'-the-wisp.

the bank every now and then, or else it would get further ahead and clear out of hearing—it was floating a little faster than what I was.

Well, I seemed to be in the open river again, by-and-by, but I couldn't hear no sign of a whoop nowheres. I reckoned Jim had fetched up on a snag, maybe, and it was all up with him. I was good and tired, so I laid down in the canoe and said I wouldn't bother no more. I didn't want to go to sleep, of course; but I was so sleepy I couldn't help it; so I thought I would take just one little cat-nap.

But I reckon it was more than a cat-nap, for when I waked up the stars was shining bright, the fog was all gone, and I was spinning down a big bend stern first. First I didn't know where I was; I thought I was dreaming; and when things begun to come back to me, they seemed to come up dim out of last week.

It was a monstrous big river here, with the tallest and the thickest kind of timber on both banks; just a solid wall, as well as I could see, by the stars. I looked away down stream, and seen a black speck on the water. I took out after it; but when I got to it it warn't nothing but a couple of saw-logs made fast together. Then I see another speck, and chased that; then another, and this time I was right. It was the raft.

When I got to it Jim was setting there with his head down between his knees, asleep, with his right arm hanging over the steering oar. The other oar was smashed off, and the raft was littered up with leaves and branches and dirt. So she'd had a rough time.

I made fast and laid down under Jim's nose on the raft, and begun to gap, and stretch my fists out against Jim, and says:

"Hello, Jim, have I been asleep? Why didn't you stir me up?"

"Goodness gracious, is dat you, Huck? En you ain' dead—you ain' drownded—you's back agin? It's too good for true, honey, it's too good for true. Lemme look at you, chile, lemme feel o' you. No, you ain' dead! you's back agin, 'live en soun', jis de same ole Huck—de same ole Huck, thanks to goodness!"

"What's the matter with you, Jim? You been a drinking?"

"Drinkin'? Has I ben a drinkin'? Has I had a chance to be a drinkin'?"

"Well, then, what makes you talk so wild?"

"How does I talk wild?"

"*How?* why, hain't you been talking about my coming back, and all that stuff, as if I'd been gone away?"

"Huck—Huck Finn, you look me in de eye; look me in de eye. *Hain't* you ben gone away?"

"Gone away? Why, what in the nation do you mean? *I* hain't been gone anywheres. Where would I go to?"

"Well, looky here, boss, dey's sumf'n wrong, dey is. Is I *me*, or who *is* I? Is I heah, or whah *is* I? Now dat's what I wants to know?"

"Well, I think you're here, plain enough, but I think you're a tangle-headed old fool, Jim."

"I is, is I? Well you answer me dis. Didn't you tote out de line in de canoe, fer to make fas' to de tow-head?"

"No, I didn't. What tow-head? I hain't seen no tow-head."

"You hain't seen no tow-head? Looky here—didn't de line pull loose en de raf' go a hummin' down de river, en leave you en de canoe behine in de fog?"

"What fog?"

"Why *de* fog. De fog dat's ben aroun' all night. En didn't you whoop, en didn't I whoop, tell we got mix' up in de islands en one un us got los' en 'tother one was jis' as good as los', 'kase he didn't know whah he wuz? En didn't I bust up agin a lot er dem islands en have a turrible time en mos' git drownded? Now ain' dat so, boss—ain't it so? You answer me dat."

"Well, this is too many for me, Jim. I hain't seen no fog, nor no islands, nor no troubles, nor nothing. I been setting here talking with you all night till you went to sleep about ten minutes ago, and I reckon I done the same. You couldn't a got drunk in that time, so of course you've been dreaming."

"Dad fetch it, how is I gwyne to dream all dat in ten minutes?"

"Well, hang it all, you did dream it, because there didn't any of it happen."

"But Huck, it's all jis' as plain to me as—"

"It don't make no difference how plain it is, there ain't nothing in it. I know, because I've been here all the time."

Jim didn't say nothing for about five minutes, but set there studying over it. Then he says:

"Well, den, I reck'n I did dream it, Huck; but dog my cats ef it ain't de power-fullest dream I ever see. En I hain't ever had no dream b'fo' dat's tired me like dis one."

"Oh, well, that's all right, because a dream does tire a body like everything, sometimes. But this one was a staving[4] dream—tell me all about it, Jim."

So Jim went to work and told me the whole thing right through, just as it happened, only he painted it up considerable. Then he said he must start in and "'terpret" it, because it was sent for a warning. He said the first tow-head stood for a man that would try to do us some good, but the current was another man that would get us away from him. The whoops was warnings that would come to us every now and then, and if we didn't try hard to make out to understand them they'd just take us into bad luck, 'stead of keeping us out of it. The lot of tow-heads was troubles we was going to get into with quarrelsome people and all kinds of mean folks, but if we minded our business and didn't talk back and aggravate[5] them, we would pull through and get out of the fog and into the big clear river,[5] which was the free States, and wouldn't have no more trouble.

It had clouded up pretty dark just after I got onto the raft, but it was clearing up again, now.

"Oh, well, that's all interpreted well enough, as far as it goes, Jim," I says; "but what does *these* things stand for?"

It was the leaves and rubbish on the raft, and the smashed oar. You could see them first rate, now.

Jim looked at the trash, and then looked at me, and back at the trash again. He had got the dream fixed so strong in his head that he couldn't seem to shake it loose and get the facts back into its place again, right away. But when he did get the thing straightened around, he looked at me steady, without ever smiling, and says:

"What do dey stan' for? I's gwyne to tell you. When I got all wore out wid work, en wid de callin' for you, en went to sleep, my heart wuz mos' broke bekase you wuz los', en I didn' k'yer no mo' what become er me en de raf'. En when I wake up en fine you back agin', all safe en soun', de tears come en I could a got down on my knees en kiss' yo' foot I's so thankful. En all you wuz thinkin 'bout wuz how you could make a fool uv ole Jim wid a lie. Dat truck dah is *trash;* en trash is what people is dat puts dirt on de head er dey fren's en makes 'em ashamed."

---

[4] Graphic and involved.   [5] The Ohio River.

Then he got up slow, and walked to the wigwam, and went in there, without saying anything but that. But that was enough. It made me feel so mean I could almost kissed *his* foot to get him to take it back.

It was fifteen minutes before I could work myself up to go and humble myself to a nigger—but I done it, and I warn't ever sorry for it afterwards, neither. I didn't do him no more mean tricks, and I wouldn't done that one if I'd a knowed it would make him feel that way.

CHAPTER XVI

We slept most all day, and started out at night, a little ways behind a monstrous long raft that was as long going by as a procession. She had four long sweeps[1] at each end, so we judged she carried as many as thirty men, likely. She had five big wigwams aboard, wide apart, and an open camp fire in the middle, and a tall flag-pole at each end. There was a power of style about her. It *amounted* to something being a raftsman on such a craft as that.

We went drifting down into a big bend, and the night clouded up and got hot. The river was very wide, and was walled with solid timber on both sides; you couldn't see a break in it hardly ever, or a light. We talked about Cairo, and wondered whether we would know it when we got to it. I said likely we wouldn't, because I had heard say there warn't but about a dozen houses there, and if they didn't happen to have them lit up, how was we going to know we was passing a town? Jim said if the two big rivers joined together there, that would show. But I said maybe we might think we was passing the foot of an island and coming into the same old river again. That disturbed Jim—and me too. So the question was, what to do? I said, paddle ashore the first time a light showed, and tell them pap was behind, coming along with a trading-scow, and was a green hand at the business, and wanted to know how far it was to Cairo. Jim thought it was a good idea, so we took a smoke on it and waited.

There warn't nothing to do, now, but to look out sharp for the town, and not pass it without seeing it. He said he'd be mighty sure to see it, because he'd be a free man the minute he seen it, but if he missed it he'd be in the slave country again and no more show[2] for freedom. Every little while he jumps up and says:

"Dah she is!"

But it warn't. It was Jack-o-lanterns, or lightning-bugs; so he set down again, and went to watching, same as before. Jim said it made him all over trembly and feverish to be so close to freedom. Well, I can tell you it made me all over trembly and feverish, too, to hear him, because I begun to get it through my head that he *was* most free—and who was to blame for it? Why, *me*. I couldn't get that out of my conscience, no how nor no way. It got to troubling me so I couldn't rest; I couldn't stay still in one place. It hadn't ever come home to me before, what this thing was that I was doing. But now it did; and it staid with me, and scorched me more and more. I tried to make out to myself that *I* warn't to blame, because *I* didn't run Jim off from his rightful owner; but it warn't no use, conscience up and says, every time, "But you knowed he was running for his freedom, and you could a paddled ashore and told somebody." That was so—I couldn't get around that, noway. That was where it pinched. Conscience says to me, "What had poor Miss Watson done to you, that you could see her nigger go off right under your

---

[1] Long oars used for steering rafts of this sort.   [2] Chance.

eyes and never say one single word? What did that poor old woman do to you, that you could treat her so mean? Why, she tried to learn you your book, she tried to learn you your manners, she tried to be good to you every way she knowed how. *That's* what she done."

I got to feeling so mean and so miserable I most wished I was dead. I fidgeted up and down the raft, abusing myself to myself, and Jim was fidgeting up and down past me. We neither of us could keep still. Every time he danced around and says, "Dah's Cairo!" it went through me like a shot, and I thought if it *was* Cairo I reckoned I would die of miserableness.

Jim talked out loud all the time while I was talking to myself. He was saying how the first thing he would do when he got to a free State he would go to saving up money and never spend a single cent, and when he got enough he would buy his wife, which was owned on a farm close to where Miss Watson lived; and then they would both work to buy the two children, and if their master wouldn't sell them, they'd get an Ab'litionist to go and steal them.

It most froze me to hear such talk. He wouldn't ever dared to talk such talk in his life before. Just see what a difference it made in him the minute he judged he was about free. It was according to the old saying, "give a nigger an inch and he'll take an ell." Thinks I, this is what comes of my not thinking. Here was this nigger which I had as good as helped to run away, coming right out flat-footed and saying he would steal his children—children that belonged to a man I didn't even know; a man that hadn't ever done me no harm.

I was sorry to hear Jim say that, it was such a lowering of him. My conscience got to stirring me up hotter than ever, until at last I says to it, "Let up on me—it ain't too late, yet—I'll paddle ashore at the first light, and tell." I felt easy, and happy, and light as a feather, right off. All my troubles was gone. I went to looking out sharp for a light, and sort of singing to myself. By-and-by one showed. Jim sings out:

"We's safe, Huck, we's safe! Jump up and crack yo' heels, dat's de good ole Cairo at las', I jis knows it!"

I says:

"I'll take the canoe and go see, Jim. It mightn't be, you know."

He jumped and got the canoe ready, and put his old coat in the bottom for me to set on, and give me the paddle; and as I shoved off, he says:

"Pooty soon I'll be a-shout'n for joy, en I'll say, it's all on accounts o' Huck; I's a free man, en I couldn't ever ben free ef it hadn' ben for Huck; Huck done it. Jim won't ever forget you, Huck; you's de bes' fren' Jim's ever had; en you's de *only* fren' ole Jim's got now."

I was paddling off, all in a sweat to tell on him; but when he says this, it seemed to kind of take the tuck all out of me. I went along slow then, and I warn't right down certain whether I was glad I started or whether I warn't. When I was fifty yards off, Jim says:

"Dah you goes, de ole true Huck; de on'y white genlman dat ever kep' his promise to ole Jim."

Well, I just felt sick. But I says, I *got* to do it—I can't get *out* of it. Right then, along comes a skiff with two men in it, with guns, and they stopped and I stopped. One of them says:

"What's that, yonder?"

"A piece of a raft," I says.

"Do you belong on it?"

"Yes, sir."

"Any men on it?"

"Only one, sir."

"Well, there's five niggers run off to-night, up yonder above the head of the bend. Is your man white or black?"

I didn't answer up prompt. I tried to, but the words wouldn't come. I tried, for a second or two, to brace up and out with it, but I warn't man enough—hadn't the spunk of a rabbit. I see I was weakening; so I just give up trying, and up and says—

"He's white."

"I reckon we'll go and see for ourselves."

"I wish you would," says I, "because it's pap that's there, and maybe you'd help me tow the raft ashore where the light is. He's sick—and so is mam and Mary Ann."

"Oh, the devil! we're in a hurry, boy. But I s'pose we've got to. Come—buckle to your paddle, and let's get along."

I buckled to my paddle and they laid to their oars. When we had made a stroke or two, I says:

"Pap'll be mighty much obleeged to you, I can tell you. Everybody goes away when I want them to help me tow the raft ashore, and I can't do it by myself."

"Well, that's infernal mean. Odd, too. Say, boy, what's the matter with your father?"

"It's the—a—the—well, it ain't anything, much."

They stopped pulling. It warn't but a mighty little ways to the raft, now. One says:

"Boy, that's a lie. What *is* the matter with your pap? Answer up square, now, and it'll be the better for you."

"I will sir, I will, honest—but don't leave us, please. It's the—the—gentlemen, if you'll only pull ahead, and let me heave you the head-line, you won't have to come a-near the raft—please do."

"Set her back, John, set her back!" says one. They backed water. "Keep away, boy—keep to looard.[3] Confound it, I just expect the wind has blowed it to us. Your pap's got the small-pox,[4] and you know it precious well. Why didn't you come out and say so? Do you want to spread it all over?"

"Well," says I, a-blubbering, "I've told everybody before, and then they just went away and left us."

"Poor devil, there's something in that. We are right down sorry for you, but we—well, hang it, we don't want the small-pox, you see. Look here, I'll tell you what to do. Don't you try to land by yourself, or you'll smash everything to pieces. You float along down about twenty miles and you'll come to a town on the left-hand side of the river. It will be long after sun-up, then, and when you ask for help, you tell them your folks are all down with chills and fever. Don't be a fool again, and let people guess what is the matter. Now we're trying to do you a kindness; so you just put twenty miles between us, that's a good boy. It wouldn't do any good to land yonder where the light is—it's only a wood-yard. Say—I reckon your father's poor, and I'm bound to say he's in pretty hard luck. Here—

---

[3] Leeward, away from the wind.

[4] Huck allows the men to name a disease they fear; smallpox was highly infectious and often fatal at the time.

I'll put a twenty dollar gold piece on this board, and you get it when it floats by. I feel mighty mean to leave you, but my kingdom! it won't do to fool with small-pox, don't you see?"

"Hold on, Parker," says the other man, "here's a twenty to put on the board for me. Good-bye, boy, you do as Mr. Parker told you, and you'll be all right."

"That's so, my boy—good-bye, good-bye. If you see any runaway niggers, you get help and nab them, and you can make some money by it."

"Good-bye, sir," says I, "I won't let no runaway niggers get by me if I can help it."

They went off, and I got aboard the raft, feeling bad and low, because I knowed very well I had done wrong, and I see it warn't no use for me to try to learn to do right; a body that don't get *started* right when he's little, ain't got no show—when the pinch comes there ain't nothing to back him up and keep him to his work, and so he gets beat. Then I thought a minute, and says to myself, hold on—s'pose you'd a done right and give Jim up; would you felt better than what you do now? No, says I, I'd feel bad—I'd feel just the same way I do now. Well, then, says I, what's the use you learning to do right, when it's troublesome to do right and ain't no trouble to do wrong, and the wages is just the same? I was stuck. I couldn't answer that. So I reckoned I wouldn't bother no more about it, but after this always do whichever come handiest at the time.

I went into the wigwam; Jim warn't there. I looked all around; he warn't anywhere. I says:

"Jim!"

"Here I is, Huck. Is dey out o' sight yit? Don't talk loud."

He was in the river, under the stern oar, with just his nose out. I told him they was out of sight, so he come aboard. He says:

"I was a-listening' to all de talk, en I slips into de river en was gwyne to shove for sho' if dey come aboard. Den I was gwyne to swim to de raf' agin when dey was gone. But lawsy, how you did fool 'em, Huck! Dat *wuz* de smartes' dodge! I tell you, chile, I 'speck it save' old Jim—ole Jim ain't gwyne to forgit you for dat, honey."

Then we talked about the money. It was a pretty good raise, twenty dollars apiece. Jim said we could take deck passage[5] on a steamboat now, and the money would last us as far as we wanted to go in the free States. He said twenty mile more warn't far for the raft to go, but he wished we was already there.

Towards daybreak we tied up, and Jim was mighty particular about hiding the raft good. Then he worked all day fixing things in bundles, and getting all ready to quit rafting.

That night about ten we hove in sight of the lights of a town away down in a left-hand bend.

I went off in the canoe, to ask about it. Pretty soon I found a man out in the river with a skiff, setting a trot-line. I ranged up and says:

"Mister, is that town Cairo?"

"Cairo? no. You must be a blame' fool."

"What town is it mister?"

"If you want to know, go and find out. If you stay here botherin' around me for about a half a minute longer, you'll get something you don't want."

---

[5] Without a cabin, the cheapest way to travel; the forty dollars makes the hope of steamboating to freedom seem more feasible.

I paddled to the raft. Jim was awful disappointed, but I said never mind, Cairo would be the next place, I reckoned.

We passed another town before daylight, and I was going out again; but it was high ground, so I didn't go. No high ground about Cairo, Jim said. I had forgot it. We laid up for the day, on a tow-head tolerable close to the left-hand bank. I begun to suspicion something. So did Jim. I says:

"Maybe we went by Cairo in the fog that night."

He says:

"Doan' less' talk about it, Huck. Po' niggers can't have no luck. I awluz 'spected dat rattle-snake skin warn't done wid it's work."

"I wish I'd never seen that snake-skin, Jim—I do wish I'd never laid eyes on it."

"It ain't yo' fault, Huck; you didn' know. Don't you blame yo'self 'bout it."

When it was daylight, here was the clear Ohio water in shore, sure enough, and outside was the old regular Muddy! So it was all up with Cairo.[6]

We talked it all over. It wouldn't do to take to the shore; we couldn't take the raft up the stream, of course. There warn't no way but to wait for dark, and start back in the canoe and take the chances. So we slept all day amongst the cottonwood thicket, so as to be fresh for the work, and when we went back to the raft about dark the canoe was gone!

We didn't say a word for a good while. There warn't anything to say. We both knowed well enough it was some more work of the rattle-snake skin; so what was the use to talk about it? It would only look like we was finding fault, and that would be bound to fetch more bad luck—and keep on fetching it, too, till we knowed enough to keep still.

By-and-by we talked about what we better do, and found there warn't no way but just to go along down with the raft till we got a chance to buy a canoe to go back in. We warn't going to borrow it when there warn't anybody around, the way pap would do, for that might set people after us.

So we shoved out, after dark, on the raft.

Anybody that don't believe yet, that it's foolishness to handle a snake-skin, after all that that snake-skin done for us, will believe it now, if they read on and see what more it done for us.

The place to buy canoes is off of rafts laying up at shore. But we didn't see no rafts laying up; so we went along during three hours and more. Well, the night got gray, and ruther thick, which is the next meanest thing to fog. You can't tell the shape of the river, and you can't see no distance. It got to be very late and still, and then along comes a steamboat up the river. We lit the lantern, and judged she would see it. Up-stream boats didn't generly come close to us; they go out and follow the bars and hunt for easy water under the reefs; but nights like this they bull right up the channel against the whole river.

We could hear her pounding along, but we didn't see her good till she was close. She aimed right for us. Often they do that and try to see how close they can come without touching; sometimes the wheel bites off a sweep, and then the pilot sticks his head out and laughs, and thinks he's mighty smart. Well, here she comes, and we said she was going to try to shave us; but she didn't seem to be sheering off a bit. She was a big one, and she was coming in a hurry, too, looking

---

[6] The relatively clear water of the Ohio River flowing near the eastern shore of the Mississippi tells Jim and Huck that they have passed the confluence of the two rivers at Cairo.

like a black cloud with rows of glow-worms around it; but all of a sudden she bulged out, big and scary, with a long row of wide-open furnace doors shining like red-hot teeth, and her monstrous bows and guards hanging right over us. There was a yell at us, and a jingling of bells to stop the engines, a pow-wow of cussing, and whistling of steam—and as Jim went overboard on one side and I on the other, she come smashing straight through the raft.

I dived—and I aimed to find the bottom, too, for a thirty-foot wheel had got to go over me, and I wanted it to have plenty of room. I could always stay under water a minute; this time I reckon I staid under water a minute and a half. Then I bounced for the top in a hurry, for I was nearly busting. I popped out to my arm-pits and blowed the water out of my nose, and puffed a bit. Of course there was a booming current; and of course that boat started her engines again ten seconds after she stopped them, for they never cared much for raftsmen; so now she was churning along up the river, out of sight in the thick weather, though I could hear her.

I sung out for Jim about a dozen times, but I didn't get any answer; so I grabbed a plank that touched me while I was "treading water," and struck out for shore, shoving it ahead of me. But I made out to see that the drift of the current was towards the left-hand shore,[7] which meant that I was in a crossing; so I changed off and went that way.

It was one of these long, slanting, two-mile crossings; so I was a good long time in getting over. I made a safe landing, and clum up the bank. I couldn't see but a little ways, but I went poking along over rough ground for a quarter of a mile or more, and then I run across a big old-fashioned double log house before I noticed it. I was going to rush by and get away, but a lot of dogs jumped out and went to howling and barking at me, and I knowed better than to move another peg.

Chapter XVII

In about half a minute somebody spoke out of a window, without putting his head out, and says:

"Be done, boys! Who's there?"

I says:

"It's me."

"Who's me?"

"George Jackson, sir."

"What do you want?"

"I don't want nothing, sir. I only want to go along by, but the dogs won't let me."

"What are you prowling around here this time of night, for—hey?"

"I warn't prowling around, sir; I fell overboard off of the steam-boat."

"Oh you did, did you? Strike a light there, somebody. What did you say your name was?"

"George Jackson, sir, I'm only a boy."

"Look here; if you're telling the truth, you needn't be afraid—nobody 'll hurt you. But don't try to budge; stand right where you are. Rouse out Bob and Tom, some of you, and fetch the guns. George Jackson, is there anybody with you?"

---

[7] Kentucky, where the following two chapters are set.

"No sir, nobody."

I heard the people stirring around in the house, now, and see a light. The man sung out:

"Snatch that light away, Betsy, you old fool—aint's you got any sense? Put it on the floor behind the front door. Bob, if you and Tom are ready, take your places."

"All ready."

"Now, George Jackson, do you know the Shepherdsons?"

"No, sir—I never heard of them."

"Well, that may be so, and it mayn't. Now, all ready. Step forward, George Jackson. And mind, don't you hurry—come mighty slow. If there's anybody with you, let him keep back—if he shows himself he'll be shot. Come along, now. Come slow; push the door open, yourself—just enough to squeeze in, d' you hear?"

I didn't hurry, I couldn't if I'd a wanted to. I took one slow step at a time, and there warn't a sound, only I thought I could hear my heart. The dogs were as still as the humans, but they followed a little behind me. When I got to the three log door-steps, I heard them unlocking and unbarring and unbolting. I put my hand on the door and pushed it a little and a little more, till somebody said, "There, that's enough—put your head in." I done it, but I judged they would take it off.

The candle was on the floor, and there they all was, looking at me, and me at them, for about a quarter of a minute. Three big men with guns pointed at me, which made me wince, I tell you; the oldest, gray and about sixty, the other two thirty or more—all of them fine and handsome—and the sweetest old gray-headed lady, and back of her two young women which I couldn't see right well. The old gentleman says:

"There—I reckon it's all right. Come in."

As soon as I was in, the old gentleman he locked the door and barred it and bolted it, and told the young men to come in with their guns, and they all went in a big parlor that had a new rag carpet on the floor, and got together in a corner that was out of range of the front windows—there warn't none on the side. They held the candle, and took a good look at me, and all said "Why *he* ain't a Shepherdson—no, there ain't any Shepherdson about him." Then the old man said he hoped I wouldn't mind being searched for arms, because he didn't mean no harm by it—it was only to make sure. So he didn't pry into my pockets, but only felt outside with his hands, and said it was all right. He told me to make myself easy and at home, and tell all about myself; but the old lady says:

"Why bless you, Saul, the poor thing's as wet as he can be; and don't you reckon it may be he's hungry?"

"True for you, Rachel—I forgot."

So the old lady says:

"Betsy" (this was a nigger woman), "you fly around and get him something to eat, as quick as you can, poor thing; and one of you girls go and wake up Buck and tell him—Oh, here he is himself. Buck, take this little stranger and get the wet clothes off from him and dress him up in some of yours that's dry."

Buck looked about as old as me—thirteen or fourteen[1] or along there, though he was a little bigger than me. He hadn't on anything but a shirt, and he was very frowsy-headed. He come in gaping and digging one fist into his eyes, and he was dragging a gun along with the other one. He says:

---

[1] In a notebook entry Twain characterizes Huck as "a boy of 14."

"Ain't they no Shepherdsons around?"

They said, no, 'twas a false alarm.

"Well," he says, "if they'd a ben some, I reckon I'd a got one."

They all laughed, and Bob says:

"Why, Buck, they might have scalped us all, you've been so slow in coming."

"Well, nobody come after me, and it ain't right. I'm always kep' down; I don't get no show."

"Never mind, Buck, my boy," says the old man, "you'll have show enough, all in good time, don't you fret about that. Go 'long with you now, and do as your mother told you."

When we got up stairs to his room, he got me a coarse shirt and a roundabout[2] and pants of his, and I put them on. While I was at it he asked me what my name was, but before I could tell him, he started to telling me about a blue jay and a young rabbit he had catched in the woods day before yesterday, and he asked me where Moses was when the candle went out. I said I didn't know; I hadn't heard about it before, no way.

"Well, guess," he says.

"How'm I going to guess," says I, "when I never heard tell about it before?"

"But you can guess, can't you? It's just as easy."

"*Which* candle?" I says.

"Why, any candle," he says.

"I don't know where he was," says I; "where was he?"

"Why he was in the *dark!* That's where he was!"

"Well, if you knowed where he was, what did you ask me for?"

"Why, blame it, it's a riddle, don't you see? Say, how long are you going to stay here? You got to stay always. We can just have booming times—they don't have no school now. Do you own a dog? I've got a dog—and he'll go in the river and bring out chips that you throw in. Do you like to comb up, Sundays, and all that kind of foolishness? You bet I don't, but ma she makes me. Confound these ole britches, I reckon I'd better put 'em on, but I'd ruther not, it's so warm. Are you all ready? All right—come along, old hoss."

Cold corn-pone, cold corn-beef, butter and butter-milk—that is what they had for me down there, and there ain't nothing better that ever I've come across yet. Buck and his ma and all of them smoked cob pipes, except the nigger woman, which was gone, and the two young women. They all smoked and talked, and I eat and talked. The young women had quilts around them, and their hair down their backs. They all asked me questions, and I told them how pap and me and all the family was living on a little farm down at the bottom of Arkansaw, and my sister Mary Ann run off and got married and never was heard of no more, and Bill went to hunt them and he warn't heard of no more, and Tom and Mort died, and then there warn't nobody but just me and pap left, and he was just trimmed down to nothing, on account of his troubles; so when he died I took what there was left, because the farm didn't belong to us, and started up the river, deck passage, and fell overboard; and that was how I come to be here. So they said I could have a home there as long as I wanted it. Then it was most daylight, and everybody went to bed, and I went to bed with Buck, and when I waked up in the morning, drat it all, I had forgot what my name was. So I laid there about an hour trying to think, and when Buck waked up, I says:

"Can you spell, Buck?"

---

[2] A short jacket.

"Yes," he says.

"I bet you can't spell my name," says I.

"I bet you what you dare I can," says he.

"All right," says I, "go ahead."

"G-o-r-g-e J-a-x-o-n—there now," he says.

"Well," says I, "you done it, but I didn't think you could. It ain't no slouch of a name to spell—right off without studying."

I set it down, private, because somebody might want *me* to spell it, next, and so I wanted to be handy with it and rattle it off like I was used to it.

It was a mighty nice family, and a mighty nice house, too. I hadn't seen no house out in the country before that was so nice and had so much style. It didn't have an iron latch on the front door, nor a wooden one with a buckskin string, but a brass knob to turn, the same as houses in a town. There warn't no bed in the parlor, not a sign of a bed; but heaps of parlors in towns has beds in them. There was a big fireplace that was bricked on the bottom, and the bricks were kept clean and red by pouring water on them and scrubbing them with another brick; sometimes they washed them over with red water-paint that they call Spanish-brown, same as they do in town. They had big brass dog-irons that could hold up a saw-log.[3] There was a clock on the middle of the mantel-piece, with a picture of a town painted on the bottom half of the glass front, and a round place in the middle of it for the sun, and you could see the pendulum swing behind it. It was beautiful to hear that clock tick; and sometimes when one of these peddlers had been along and scoured her up and got her in good shape, she would start in and strike a hundred and fifty before she got tuckered out. They wouldn't took any money for her.

Well, there was a big outlandish parrot on each side of the clock, made out of something like chalk, and painted up gaudy. By one of the parrots was a cat made of crockery, and a crockery dog by the other; and when you pressed down on them they squeaked, but didn't open their mouths nor look different nor interested. They squeaked through underneath. There was a couple of big wild-turkey-wing fans spread out behind those things. On a table in the middle of the room was a kind of a lovely crockery basket that had apples and oranges and peaches and grapes piled up in it which was much redder and yellower amd prettier than real ones is, but they warn't real because you could see where pieces had got chipped off and showed the white chalk or whatever it was, underneath.

This table had a cover made out of beautiful oil-cloth, with a red and blue spread-eagle painted on it, and a painted border all around. It come all the way from Philadelphia, they said. There was some books too, piled up perfectly exact, on each corner of the table. One was a big family Bible, full of pictures. One was "Pilgrim's Progress," about a man that left his family it didn't say why. I read considerable in it now and then. The statements was interesting, but tough. Another was "Friendship's Offering," full of beautiful stuff and poetry; but I didn't read the poetry. Another was Henry Clay's Speeches, and another was Dr. Gunn's Family Medicine,[4] which told you all about what to do if a body was sick or dead.

---

[3] Andirons that could hold a log large enough to be sawed into planks.

[4] The Grangerford library consists of a Bible; *The Pilgrim's Progress* (1678), a dream allegory by the English preacher and writer John Bunyan (1628–1688); *Friendship's Offering,* a popular gift book containing sentimental verse and pious prose; the "Speeches" of Henry Clay (1777–1852), a noted politician and orator from Kentucky; and Dr. Gunn's *Domestic Medicine* (1830). The furnishings of this household clearly give the impressionable Huck a sense of class and dignity; the irony is that this "cultured" family is involved in a blood feud.

There was a Hymn Book, and a lot of other books. And there was nice split-bottom chairs, and perfectly sound, too—not bagged down in the middle and busted, like an old basket.

They had pictures hung on the walls—mainly Washingtons and Lafayettes, and battles, and Highland Marys,[5] and one called "Signing the Declaration." There was some that they called crayons, which one of the daughters which was dead made her own self when she was only fifteen years old. They was different from any pictures I ever see before; blacker, mostly, than is common. One was a woman in a slim black dress, belted small under the arm-pits, with bulges like a cabbage in the middle of the sleeves, and a large black scoop-shovel bonnet with a black veil, and white slim ankles crossed about with black tape, and very wee black slippers, like a chisel, and she was leaning pensive on a tombstone on her right elbow, under a weeping willow, and her other hand hanging down her side holding a white handkerchief and a reticule, and underneath the picture it said "Shall I Never See Thee More Alas." Another one was a young lady with her hair all combed up straight to the top of her head, and knotted there in front of a comb like a chair-back, and she was crying into a handkerchief and had a dead bird laying on its back in her other hand with its heels up, and underneath the picture it said "I Shall Never Hear Thy Sweet Chirrup More Alas." There was one where a young lady was at a window looking up at the moon, and tears running down her cheeks; and she had an open letter in one hand with black sealing-wax showing on one edge of it, and she was mashing a locket with a chain to it against her mouth, and underneath the picture it said "And Art Thou Gone Yes Thou Art Gone Alas." These was all nice pictures, I reckon, but I didn't somehow seem to take to them, because if ever I was down a little, they always give me the fan-tods. Everybody was sorry she died, because she had laid out a lot more of these pictures to do, and a body could see by what she had done what they had lost. But I reckoned, that with her disposition, she was having a better time in the graveyard. She was at work on what they said was her greatest picture when she took sick, and every day and every night it was her prayer to be allowed to live till she got it done, but she never got the chance. It was a picture of a young woman in a long white gown, standing on the rail of a bridge all ready to jump off, with her hair all down her back, and looking up to the moon, with the tears running down her face, and she had two arms folded across her breast, and two arms stretched out in front, and two more reaching up towards the moon—and the idea was, to see which pair would look best and then scratch out all the other arms; but, as I was saying, she died before she got her mind made up, and now they kept this picture over the head of the bed in her room, and every time her birthday come they hung flowers on it. Other times it was hid with a little curtain. The young woman in the picture had a kind of a nice sweet face, but there was so many arms it made her look too spidery, seemed to me.

This young girl kept a scrap-book when she was alive, and used to paste obituaries and accidents and cases of patient suffering in it out of the *Presbyterian Observer,* and write poetry after them out of her own head. It was very good

---

[5] Marquis de Lafayette (1757–1834) was a French general and statesman who served in the Continental army during the American Revolution. The pictures are selected to suggest the taste of the region at this time: "Highland Mary" is Mary Campbell, an early love of the Scottish poet Robert Burns (1759–1796), who wrote several elegies in her honor, among them "To Mary in Heaven."

poetry. This is what she wrote about a boy by the name of Stephen Dowling Bots that fell down a well and was drownded:

ODE TO STEPHEN DOWLING BOTS, DEC'D.[6]

And did young Stephen sicken,
   And did young Stephen die?
And did the sad hearts thicken,
   And did the mourners cry?

No; such was not the fate of
   Young Stephen Dowling Bots;
Though sad hearts round him thickened,
   'Twas not from sickness' shots.

No whooping-cough did rack his frame,
   Nor measles drear, with spots;
Not these impaired the sacred name
   Of Stephen Dowling Bots.

Despised love struck not with woe
   That head of curly knots,
Nor stomach troubles laid him low,
   Young Stephen Dowling Bots.

O no. Then list with tearful eye,
   Whilst I his fate do tell.
His soul did from this cold world fly,
   By falling down a well.

They got him out and emptied him;
   Alas it was too late;
His spirit was gone for to sport aloft
   In the realms of the good and great.

If Emmeline Grangerford could make poetry like that before she was fourteen, there ain't no telling what she could a done by-and-by. Buck said she could rattle off poetry like nothing. She didn't ever have to stop to think. He said she would slap down a line, and if she couldn't find anything to rhyme with it she would just scratch it out and slap down another one, and go ahead. She warn't particular, she could write about anything you choose to give her to write about, just so it was sadful. Every time a man died, or a woman died, or a child died, she would be on hand with her "tribute" before he was cold. She called them tributes. The neigh-

---

[6] Deceased. This parodic poem was probably occasioned by the work of Julia A. Moore (1847–1920), whose book of sentimental verse *The Sweet Singer of Michigan Salutes the Public* appeared in 1876. Moore specialized in "obituary" poems evoked by the death of children. In *Following the Equator* (1897), Twain said that *The Sweet Singer of Michigan* had brought joy to his heart for twenty years.

bors said it was the doctor first, then Emmeline, then the undertaker—the undertaker never got in ahead of Emmeline but once, and then she hung fire on a rhyme for the dead person's name, which was Whistler. She warn't ever the same, after that; she never complained, but she kind of pined away and did not live long. Poor thing, many's the time I made myself go up to the little room that used to be hers and get out her poor old scrapbook and read in it when her pictures had been aggravating me and I had soured on her a little. I liked all that family, dead ones and all, and warn't going to let anything come between us. Poor Emmeline made poetry about all the dead people when she was alive, and it didn't seem right that there warn't nobody to make some about her, now she was gone; so I tried to sweat out a verse or two myself, but I couldn't seem to make it go, somehow. They kept Emmeline's room trim and nice and all the things fixed in it just the way she liked to have them when she was alive, and nobody ever slept there. The old lady took care of the room herself, though there was plenty of niggers, and she sewed there a good deal and read her Bible there, mostly.

Well, as I was saying about the parlor, there was beautiful curtains on the windows: white, with pictures painted on them, of castles with vines all down the walls, and cattle coming down to drink. There was a little old piano, too, that had tin pans in it,[7] I reckon, and nothing was ever so lovely as to hear the young ladies sing, "The Last Link is Broken" and play "The Battle of Prague"[8] on it. The walls of all the rooms was plastered, and most had carpets on the floors, and the whole house was whitewashed on the outside.

It was a double house, and the big open place betwixt them was roofed and floored, and sometimes the table was set there in the middle of the day, and it was a cool, comfortable place. Nothing couldn't be better. And warn't the cooking good, and just bushels of it too!

Chapter XVIII

Col. Grangerford was a gentleman, you see. He was a gentleman all over; and so was his family. He was well born, as the saying is, and that's worth as much in a man as it is in a horse, so the Widow Douglas said, and nobody ever denied that she was of the first aristocracy in our town; and pap he always said it, too, though he warn't no more quality than a mud-cat,[1] himself. Col. Grangerford was very tall and very slim, and had a darkish-paly complexion, not a sign of red in it anywheres; he was clean-shaved every morning, all over his thin face, and he had the thinnest kind of lips, and the thinnest kind of nostrils, and a high nose, and heavy eyebrows, and the blackest kind of eyes, sunk so deep back that they seemed like they was looking out of caverns at you, as you may say. His forehead was high, and his hair was black and straight, and hung to his shoulders. His hands was long and thin, and every day of his life he put on a clean shirt and a full suit from head to foot made out of linen so white it hurt your eyes to look at it; and on Sundays he wore a blue tail-coat with brass buttons on it. He carried a mahogany cane with a silver head to it. There warn't no frivolishness about him, not a

---

[7] Some pianos in the nineteenth century were equipped with cymbals and other percussion devices that responded to foot pedals.

[8] "The Last Link Is Broken" (1840?) is a sentimental song by William Clifton; "The Battle of Prague" (1788) is a flamboyant piano piece by the Czech composer Franz Kotzwara that attempts to recreate the sounds of a military battle.

[1] A catfish.

bit, and he warn't ever loud. He was as kind as he could be—you could feel that, you know, and so you had confidence. Sometimes he smiled, and it was good to see; but when he straightened himself up like a liberty-pole,[2] and the lightning begun to flicker out from under his eyebrows you wanted to climb a tree first, and find out what the matter was afterwards. He didn't ever have to tell anybody to mind their manners—everybody was always good mannered where he was. Everybody loved to have him around, too; he was sunshine most always—I mean he made it seem like good weather. When he turned into a cloud-bank it was awful dark for a half a minute and that was enough; there wouldn't nothing go wrong again for a week.

When him and the old lady come down in the morning, all the family got up out of their chairs and give them good-day, and didn't set down again till they had set down. Then Tom and Bob went to the sideboard where the decanters was, and mixed a glass of bitters and handed it to him, and he held it in his hand and waited till Tom's and Bob's was mixed, and then they bowed and said "Our duty to you, sir and madam;" and *they* bowed the least bit in the world and said thank you, and so they drank, all three, and Bob and Tom poured a spoonful of water on the sugar and the mite of whisky or apple brandy in the bottom of their tumblers, and give it to me and Buck, and we drank to the old people too.

Bob was the oldest, and Tom was next. Tall, beautiful men with very broad shoulders and brown faces, and long black hair and black eyes. They dressed in white linen from head to foot, like the old gentleman, and wore broad Panama hats.

Then there was Miss Charlotte, she was twenty-five, and tall and proud and grand, but as good as she could be, when she warn't stirred up; but when she was, she had a look that would make you wilt in your tracks, like her father. She was beautiful.

So was her sister, Miss Sophia, but it was a different kind. She was gentle and sweet, like a dove, and she was only twenty.

Each person had their own nigger to wait on them—Buck, too. My nigger had a monstrous easy time, because I warn't used to having anybody do anything for me, but Buck's was on the jump most of the time.

This was all there was of the family, now; but there used to be more—three sons; they got killed; and Emmeline that died.

The old gentleman owned a lot of farms, and over a hundred niggers. Sometimes a stack of people would come there, horseback, from ten or fifteen mile around, and stay five or six days, and have such junketings round about and on the river, and dances and picnics in the woods, day-times, and balls at the house, nights. These people was mostly kin-folks of the family. The men brought their guns with them. It was a handsome lot of quality, I tell you.

There was another clan of aristocracy around there—five or six families— mostly of the name of Shepherdson. They was as high-toned, and well born, and rich and grand, as the tribe of Grangerfords. The Shepherdsons and the Grangerfords used the same steamboat landing, which was about two mile above our house; so sometimes when I went up there with a lot of our folks I used to see a lot of the Shepherdsons there, on their fine horses.

One day Buck and me was away out in the woods, hunting, and heard a horse coming. We was crossing the road. Buck says:

---

[2] A flagpole.

"Quick! Jump for the woods!"

We done it, and then peeped down the woods through the leaves. Pretty soon a splendid young man come galloping down the road, setting his horse easy and looking like a soldier. He had his gun across his pommel. I had seen him before. It was young Harney Shepherdson. I heard Buck's gun go off at my ear, and Harney's hat tumbled off from his head. He grabbed his gun and rode straight to the place where we was hid. But we didn't wait. We started through the woods on a run. The woods warn't thick, so I looked over my shoulder, to dodge the bullet, and twice I seen Harney cover Buck with his gun; and then he rode away the way he come—to get his hat, I reckon, but I couldn't see. We never stopped running till we got home. The old gentleman's eyes blazed a minute—'twas pleasure, mainly, I judged—then his face sort of smoothed down, and he says, kind of gentle:

"I don't like that shooting from behind a bush. Why didn't you step into the road, my boy?"

"The Shepherdsons don't, father. They always take advantage."

Miss Charlotte she held her head up like a queen while Buck was telling his tale, and her nostrils spread and her eyes snapped. The two young men looked dark, but never said nothing. Miss Sophia she turned pale, but the color come back when she found the man warn't hurt.

Soon as I could get Buck down by the corn-cribs under the trees by ourselves, I says:

"Did you want to kill him, Buck?"

"Well, I bet I did."

"What did he do to you?"

"Him? He never done nothing to me."

"Well, then, what did you want to kill him for?"

"Why nothing—only it's on account of the feud."

"What's a feud?"

"Why, where was you raised? Don't you know what a feud is?"

"Never heard of it before—tell me about it."

"Well," says Buck, "a feud is this way. A man has a quarrel with another man, and kills him; then that other man's brother kills *him;* then the other brothers, on both sides, goes for one another; then the *cousins* chip in—and by-and-by everybody's killed off, and there ain't no more feud. But it's kind of slow, and takes a long time."

"Has this one been going on long, Buck?"

"Well, I should *reckon!* it started thirty year ago, or som'ers along there. There was trouble 'bout something and then a lawsuit to settle it; and the suit went agin one of the men, and so he up and shot the man that won the suit—which he would naturally do, of course. Anybody would."

"What was the trouble about, Buck?—land?"

"I reckon maybe—I don't know."

"Well, who done the shooting?—was it a Grangerford or a Shepherdson?"

"Laws, how do *I* know? it was so long ago."

"Don't anybody know?"

"Oh, yes, pa knows, I reckon, and some of the other old folks; but they don't know, now, what the row was about in the first place."

"Has there been many killed, Buck?"

"Yes—right smart chance of funerals. But they don't always kill. Pa's got a few buck-shot in him; but he don't mind it 'cuz he don't weigh much anyway. Bob's been carved up some with a bowie, and Tom's been hurt once or twice."

"Has anybody been killed this year, Buck?"

"Yes, we got one and they got one. 'Bout three months ago my cousin Bud, fourteen year old, was riding through the woods on t'other side of the river, and didn't have no weapon with him, which was blame' foolishness, and in a lonesome place he hears a horse a-coming behind him, and sees old Baldy Shepherdson a-linkin' after him with his gun in his hand and his white hair a-flying in the wind; and 'stead of jumping off and taking to the brush, Bud 'lowed he could outrun him; so they had it, nip and tuck, for five mile or more, the old man a-gaining all the time; so at last Bud seen it warn't any use, so he stopped and faced around so as to have the bullet holes in front, you know, and the old man he rode up and shot him down. But he didn't git much chance to enjoy his luck, for inside of a week our folks laid *him* out."

"I reckon that old man was a coward, Buck."

"I reckon he *warn't* a coward. Not by a blame' sight. There ain't a coward amongst them Shepherdsons—not a one. And there ain't no cowards amongst the Grangerfords, either. Why, that old man kep' up his end in a fight one day, for a half an hour, against three Grangerfords, and come out winner. They was all a-horseback; he lit off of his horse and got behind a little wood-pile, and kep' his horse before him to stop the bullets; but the Grangerfords staid on their horses and capered around the old man, and peppered away at him, and he peppered away at them. Him and his horse both went home pretty leaky and crippled, but the Grangerfords had to be *fetched* home—and one of 'em was dead, and another died the next day. No, sir, if a body's out hunting for cowards, he don't want to fool away any time amongst them Shepherdsons, becuz they don't breed any of that *kind*."

Next Sunday we all went to church, about three mile, everybody a-horseback. The men took their guns along, so did Buck, and kept them betweeen their knees or stood them handy against the wall. The Shepherdsons done the same. It was pretty ornery preaching—all about brotherly love, and such-like tiresomeness; but everybody said it was a good sermon, and they all talked it over going home, and had such a powerful lot to say about faith, and good works, and free grace, and preforeordestination,[3] and I don't know what all, that it did seem to me to be one of the roughest Sundays I had run across yet.

About an hour after dinner everybody was dozing around, some in their chairs and some in their rooms, and it got to be pretty dull. Buck and a dog was stretched out on the grass in the sun, sound asleep. I went up to our room, and judged I would take a nap myself. I found that sweet Miss Sophia standing in her door, which was next to ours, and she took me in her room and shut the door very soft, and asked me if I liked her, and I said I did; and she asked me if I would do something for her and not tell anybody, and I said I would. Then she said she'd forgot her Testament, and left it in the seat at church, between two other books and would I slip out quiet and go there and fetch it to her, and not say nothing to nobody. I said I would. So I slid out and slipped off up the road, and there warn't anybody at the church, except maybe a hog or two, for there warn't any lock on

---

[3] Huck combines the terms "predestination" and "foreordination" to make this jawbreaking word.

the door, and hogs likes a puncheon floor[4] in summer-time because it's cool. If you notice, most folks don't go to church only when they've got to; but a hog is different.

Says I to myself something's up—it ain't natural for a girl to be in such a sweat about a Testament; so I give it a shake, and out drops a little piece of paper with "*Half-past two*" wrote on it with a pencil. I ransacked it, but couldn't find anything else. I couldn't make anything out of that, so I put the paper in the book again, and when I got home and up stairs, there was Miss Sophia in her door waiting for me. She pulled me in and shut the door; then she looked in the Testament till she found the paper, and as soon as she read it she looked glad; and before a body could think, she grabbed me and give me a squeeze, and said I was the best boy in the world, and not to tell anybody. She was mighty red in the face, for a minute, and her eyes lighted up and it made her powerful pretty. I was a good deal astonished, but when I got my breath I asked her what the paper was about, and she asked me if I had read it, and I said no, and she asked me if I could read writing, and I told her "no, only coarse-hand,"[5] and then she said the paper warn't anything but a book-mark to keep her place, and I might go and play now.

I went off down to the river, studying over this thing, and pretty soon I noticed that my nigger was following along behind. When we was out of sight of the house, he looked back and around a second, and then comes a-running, and says:

"Mars Jawge, if you'll come down into de swamp, I'll show you a whole stack o' water-moccasins."

Thinks I, that's mighty curious; he said that yesterday. He oughter know a body don't love water-moccasins enough to go around hunting for them. What is he up to anyway? So I says—

"All right, trot ahead."

I followed a half a mile, then he struck out over the swamp and waded ankle deep as much as another half mile. We come to a little flat piece of land which was dry and very thick with trees and bushes and vines, and he says—

"You shove right in dah, jist a few steps, Mars Jawge, dah's whah dey is. I's seed 'm befo', I don't k'yer to see 'em no mo'. "

Then he slopped right along and went away, and pretty soon the trees hid him. I poked into the place a-ways, and come to a little open patch as big as a bedroom, all hung around with vines, and found a man laying there asleep—and by jings it was my old Jim!

I waked him up, and I reckoned it was going to be a grand surprise to him to see me again, but it warn't. He nearly cried, he was so glad, but he warn't surprised. He said he swum along behind me, that night, and heard me yell every time, but dasn't answer, because he didn't want nobody to pick *him* up, and take him into slavery again. Says he—

"I got hurt a little, en couldn't swim fas', so I wuz a considable ways behine you, towards de las'; when you landed I reck'ned I could ketch up wid you on de lan' 'dout havin' to shout at you, but when I see dat house I begin to go slow. I 'uz off too fur to hear what dey say to you—I wuz 'fraid o' de dogs—but when it 'uz all quiet agin, I knowed you's in de house, so I struck out for de woods to wait for day. Early in de mawnin' some er de niggers come along, gwyne to de fields, en dey tuck me en showed me dis place, whah de dogs can't track me on accounts

---

[4] A floor of log slabs set into the ground.   [5] Block printing by hand.

o' de water, en dey brings me truck to eat every night, en tells me how you's a gitt'n along."

"Why didn't you tell my Jack to fetch me here sooner, Jim?"

"Well, 'twarn't no use to 'sturb you, Huck, tell we could do sumfn—but we's all right now. I ben a-buyin' pots en pans en vittles, as I got a chanst, en a patching' up de raf' nights, when—"

"*What* raft, Jim?"

"Our ole raf'."

"You mean to say our old raft warn't smashed all to flinders?"

"No, she warn't. She was tore up a good deal—one en' of her was—but dey warn't no great harm done, on'y our traps was mos' all los'. Ef we hadn' dive' so deep en swum so fur under water, en de night hadn' ben so dark, en we warn't so sk'yerd, en ben sich punkin-heads, as de sayin' is, we'd a seed de raf'. But it's jis' as well we didn't, 'kase now she's all fixed up agin mos' as good as new, en we's got a new lot o'stuff, too, in de place o' what 'uz los'. "

"Why, how did you get hold of the raft again, Jim—did you catch her?"

"How I gwyne to ketch her, en I out in de woods? No, some er de niggers foun' her ketched on a snag, along heah in de ben', en dey hid her in a crick, 'mongst de willows, en dey wuz so much jawin' 'bout which un 'um she b'long to de mos', dat I come to heah 'bout it pooty soon, so I ups en settles de trouble by tellin' 'um she don't b'long to none uv um, but to you en me; en I ast 'm if dey gwyne to grab a young white genlman's propaty, en git a hid'n for it? Den I gin 'm ten cents apiece, en dey 'uz mighty well satisfied, en wisht some mo' raf's 'ud come along en make 'm rich agin. Dey's mighty good to me, dese niggers is, en whatever I wants 'm to do fur me, I doan't have to ast 'm twice, honey. Dat Jack's a good nigger, en pooty smart."

"Yes, he is. He ain't ever told me you was here; told me to come, and he'd show me a lot of water-moccasins. If anything happens, *he* ain't mixed up in it. He can say he never seen us together, and it'll be the truth."

I don't want to talk much about the next day. I reckon I'll cut it pretty short. I waked up about dawn, and was agoing to turn over and go to sleep again, when I noticed how still it was—didn't seem to be anybody stirring. That warn't usual. Next I noticed that Buck was up and gone. Well, I gets up, a-wondering, and goes down stairs—nobody around; everything as still as a mouse. Just the same outside; thinks I, what does it mean? Down by the wood-pile I comes across my Jack, and says:

"What's it all about?"

Says he:

"Don't you know, Mars Jawge?"

"No," says I, "I don't."

"Well, den, Miss Sophia's run off! 'deed she has. She run off in de night, sometime—nobody don't know jis' when—run off to git married to dat young Harney Shepherdson, you know—leastways, so dey 'spec. De fambly foun' it out, 'bout half an hour ago—maybe a little mo'—en' I *tell* you dey warn't no time los'. Sich another hurryin' up guns en hosses *you* never see! De women folks has gone for to stir up de relations, en ole Mars Saul en de boys tuck dey guns en rode up de river road for to try to ketch dat young man en kill him 'fo' he kin git across de river wid Mis Sophia. I reck'n dey's gwyne to be mighty rough times."

"Buck went off 'thout waking me up."

"Well I reck'n he *did!* Dey warn't gwyne to mix you up in it. Mars Buck he loaded up his gun en 'lowed he's gwyne to fetch home a Shepherdson or bust. Well, dey'll be plenty un 'm dah, I reck'n, en you bet you he'll fetch one ef he gits a chanst."

I took up the river road as hard as I could put. By-and-by I begin to hear guns a good ways off. When I come in sight of the log store and the wood-pile where the steamboats lands, I worked along under the trees and brush till I got to a good place, and then I clumb up into the forks of a cotton-wood that was out of reach, and watched. There was a wood-rank[6] four foot high, a little ways in front of the tree, and first I was going to hide behind that; but maybe it was luckier I didn't.

There was four or five men cavorting around on their horses in the open place before the log store, cussing and yelling, and trying to get at a couple of young chaps that was behind the wood-rank alongside of the steamboat landing—but they couldn't come it. Every time one of them showed himself on the river side of the wood-pile he got shot at. The two boys was squatting back to back behind the pile, so they could watch both ways.

By-and-by the men stopped cavorting around and yelling. They started riding towards the store; then up gets one of the boys, draws a steady bead over the wood-rank, and drops one of them out of his saddle. All the men jumped off of their horses and grabbed the hurt one and started to carry him to the store; and that minute the two boys started on the run. They got half-way to the tree I was in before the men noticed. Then the men see them, and jumped on their horses and took out after them. They gained on the boys, but it didn't do no good, the boys had too good a start; they got to the wood-pile that was in front of my tree, and slipped in behind it, and so they had the bulge[7] on the men again. One of the boys was Buck, and the other was a slim young chap about nineteen years old.

The men ripped around awhile, and then rode away. As soon as they was out of sight, I sung out to Buck and told him. He didn't know what to make of my voice coming out of the tree, at first. He was awful surprised. He told me to watch out sharp and let him know when the men come in sight again; said they was up to some devilment or other—wouldn't be gone long. I wished I was out of that tree, but I dasn't come down. Buck begun to cry and rip, and 'lowed that him and his cousin Joe (that was the other young chap) would make up for this day, yet. He said his father and his two brothers was killed, and two or three of the enemy. Said the Shepherdsons laid for them, in ambush. Buck said his father and brothers ought to waited for their relations—the Shepherdsons was too strong for them. I asked him what was become of young Harney and Miss Sophia. He said they'd got across the river and was safe. I was glad of that; but the way Buck did take on because he didn't manage to kill Harney that day he shot at him—I hain't ever heard anything like it.

All of a sudden, bang! bang! bang! goes three or four guns— the men had slipped around through the woods and come in from behind without their horses! The boys jumped for the river—both of them hurt—and as they swum down the current the men run along the bank shooting at them and singing out, "Kill them, kill them!" It made me so sick I most fell out of the tree. I ain't agoing to tell *all* that happened—it would make me sick again if I was to do that. I wished I hadn't ever come ashore that night, to see such things. I ain't ever going to get shut of them—lots of times I dream about them.

---

[6] A stack of firewood.   [7] The edge, the advantage.

I staid in the tree till it begun to get dark, afraid to come down. Sometimes I heard guns away off in the woods; and twice I seen little gangs of men gallop past the log store with guns; so I reckoned the trouble was still agoing on. I was mighty down-hearted; so I made up my mind I wouldn't ever go anear that house again, because I reckoned I was to blame, somehow. I judged that that piece of paper meant that Miss Sophia was to meet Harney somewheres at half-past two and run off; and I judged I ought to told her father about that paper and the curious way she acted, and then maybe he would a locked her up and this awful mess wouldn't ever happened.

When I got down out of the tree, I crept along down the river bank a piece, and found the two bodies laying in the edge of the water, and tugged at them till I got them ashore; then I covered up their faces, and got away as quick as I could. I cried a little when I was covering up Buck's face, for he was mighty good to me.

It was just dark, now. I never went near the house, but struck through the woods and made for the swamp. Jim warn't on his island, so I tramped off in a hurry for the crick, and crowded through the willows, red-hot to jump aboard and get out of that awful country—the raft was gone! My souls, but I was scared! I couldn't get my breath for most a minute. Then I raised a yell. A voice not twenty-five foot from me, says—

"Good lan'! is dat you, honey? Doan' make no noise."

It was Jim's voice—nothing ever sounded so good before. I run along the bank a piece and got aboard, and Jim he grabbed me and hugged me, he was so glad to see me. He says—

"Laws bless you, chile, I 'uz right down sho' you's dead agin. Jack's been heah, he say he reck'n you's ben shot, kase you didn' come home no mo'; so I's jes' dis minute a startin' de raf' down towards de mouf er de crick, so's to be all ready for to shove out en leave soon as Jack comes agin en tells me for certain you *is* dead. Lawsy, I's mighty glad to git you back agin, honey."

I says—

"All right—that's mighty good; they won't find me, and they'll think I've been killed, and floated down the river—there's something up there that'll help them to think so—so don't you lose no time, Jim, but just shove off for the big water as fast as ever you can."

I never felt easy till the raft was two mile below there and out in the middle of the Mississippi. Then we hung up our signal lantern, and judged that we was free and safe once more. I hadn't had a bite to eat since yesterday; so Jim he got out some corn-dodgers[8] and buttermilk, and pork and cabbage, and greens—there ain't nothing in the world so good, when it's cooked right—and whilst I eat my supper we talked, and had a good time. I was powerful glad to get away from the feuds, and so was Jim to get away from the swamp. We said there warn't no home like a raft, after all. Other places do seem so cramped up and smothery, but a raft don't. You feel mighty free and easy and comfortable on a raft.

from CHAPTER XXXI

We dasn't stop again at any town, for days and days; kept right along down the river. We was down south in the warm weather, now, and a mighty long ways from home. We begun to come to trees with Spanish moss on them, hanging

---

[8] Hard-baked cornmeal cakes.

down from the limbs like long gray beards. It was the first I ever see it growing, and it made the woods look solemn and dismal. So now the frauds reckoned they was out of danger, and they begun to work the villages again.

First they done a lecture on temperance; but they didn't make enough for them both to get drunk on. Then in another village they started a dancing school; but they didn't know no more how to dance than a kangaroo does; so the first prance they made, the general public jumped in and pranced them out of town. Another time they tried a go at yellocution; but they didn't yellocute long till the audience got up and give them a solid good cussing and made them skip out. They tackled missionarying, and mesmerizering, and doctoring, and telling fortunes, and a little of everything; but they couldn't seem to have no luck. So at last they got just about dead broke, and laid around the raft, as she floated along, thinking, and thinking, and never saying nothing, by the half a day at a time, and dreadful blue and desperate.

And at last they took a change, and begun to lay their heads together in the wigwam and talk low and confidential two or three hours at a time. Jim and me got uneasy. We didn't like the look of it. We judged they was studying up some kind of worse deviltry than ever. We turned it over and over, and at last we made up our minds they was going to break into somebody's house or store, or was going into the counterfeit-money business, or something. So then we was pretty scared, and made up an agreement that we wouldn't have nothing in the world to do with such actions, and if we ever got the least show we would give them the cold shake, and clear out and leave them behind. Well, early one morning we hid the raft in a good safe place about two mile below a little bit of a shabby village, named Pikesville, and the king he went ashore, and told us all to stay hid whilst he went up to town and smelt around to see if anybody had got any wind of the Royal Nonesuch there yet. ("House to rob, you *mean*," says I to myself; "and when you get through robbing it you'll come back here and wonder what's become of me and Jim and the raft—and you'll have to take it out in wondering.") And he said if he warn't back by midday, the duke and me would know it was all right, and we was to come along.

So we staid where was was. The duke he fretted and sweated around, and was in a mighty sour way. He scolded us for everything, and we couldn't seem to do nothing right; he found fault with every little thing. Something was a-brewing, sure. I was good and glad when midday come and no king; we could have a change, anyway—and maybe a chance for *the* change, on top of it. So me and the duke went up to the village, and hunted around there for the king, and by-and-by we found him in the back room of a little low doggery,[1] very tight, and a lot of loafers bullyragging him for sport, and he a cussing and threatening with all his might, and so tight he couldn't walk, and couldn't do nothing to them. The duke he began to abuse him for an old fool, and the king begun to sass back; and the minute they was fairly at it, I lit out, and shook the reefs out of[2] my hind legs, and spun down the river road like a deer—for I see our chance; and I made up my mind that it would be a long day before they ever see me and Jim again. I got down there all out of breath but loaded up with joy, and sung out—

"Set her loose, Jim, we're all right, now!"

But there warn't no answer, and nobody come out of the wigwam. Jim was gone! I set up a shout—and then another—and then another one; and run this way

---

[1] Cheap saloon.   [2] Stretched out.

and that in the woods, whooping and screeching; but it warn't no use—old Jim was gone. Then I set down and cried; I couldn't help it. But I couldn't set still long. Pretty soon I went out on the road, trying to think what I better do, and I run across a boy walking, and asked him if he'd seen a strange nigger, dressed so and so, and he says:

"Yes."

"Whereabouts?" says I.

"Down to Silas Phelps's place, two mile below here. He's a runaway nigger, and they've got him. Was you looking for him?"

"You bet I ain't! I run across him in the woods about an hour or two ago, and he said if I hollered he'd cut my livers out—and told me to lay down and stay where I was; and I done it. Been there ever since; afeard to come out."

"Well," he says, "you needn't be afeard no more, becuz they've got him. He run off f'm down South, som'ers."

"It's a good job they got him."

"Well, I *reckon!* There's two hunderd dollars reward on him. It's like picking up money out'n the road."

"Yes, it is—and *I* could a had it if I'd been big enough; I see him *first*. Who nailed him?"

"It was an old fellow—a stranger—and he sold out his chance in him for forty dollars, becuz he's got to go up the river and can't wait. Think o' that, now! You bet *I'd* wait, if it was seven year."

"That's me, every time," says I. "But maybe his chance ain't worth no more than that, if he'll sell it so cheap. Maybe there's something ain't straight about it."

"But it *is*, though—straight as a string. I see the handbill myself. It tells all about him, to a dot—paints him like a picture, and tells the plantation he's frum, below New*rleans*. No-sirree-*bob*, they ain't no trouble 'bout *that* speculation, you bet you. Say, gimme a chaw tobacker, won't ye?"

I didn't have none, so he left. I went to the raft, and set down in the wigwam to think. But I couldn't come to nothing. I thought till I wore my head sore, but I couldn't see no way out of the trouble. After all this long journey, and after all we'd done for them scoundrels, here was it all come to nothing, everything all busted up and ruined, because they could have the heart to serve Jim such a trick as that, and make him a slave again all his life, and amongst strangers, too, for forty dirty dollars.

Once I said to myself it would be a thousand times better for Jim to be a slave at home where his family was, as long as he'd *got* to be a slave, and so I'd better write a letter to Tom Sawyer and tell him to tell Miss Watson where he was. But I soon give up that notion, for two things: she'd be mad and disgusted at his rascality and ungratefulness for leaving her, and so she'd sell him straight down the river again; and if she didn't, everybody naturally despises an ungrateful nigger, and they'd make Jim feel it all the time, and so he'd feel ornery and disgraced. And then think of *me!* It would get all around, that Huck Finn helped a nigger to get his freedom; and if I was to ever see anybody from that town again, I'd be ready to get down and lick his boots for shame. That's just the way: a person does a low-down thing, and then he don't want to take no consequences of it. Thinks as long as he can hide it, it ain't no disgrace. That was my fix exactly. The more I studied about this, the more my conscience went to grinding me, and the more wicked and low-down and ornery I got to feeling. And at last, when it hit me all of a sudden that here was the plain hand of Providence slapping me in the face and letting me know my wickedness was being watched all the time from up there in heaven, whilst I was stealing a poor old woman's nigger that hadn't ever done me no harm, and now was showing me there's One that's always on the lookout, and ain't agoing to allow no such miserable doings to go only just so fur and no further, I most dropped in my tracks I was so scared. Well, I tried the best I could to kinder soften it up somehow for myself, by saying I was brung up wicked, and so I warn't so much to blame; but something inside of me kept saying, "There was the Sunday school, you could a gone to it; and if you'd a done it they'd a learnt you, there, that people that acts as I'd been acting about that nigger goes to everlasting fire."

It made me shiver. And I about made up my mind to pray; and see if I couldn't try to quit being the kind of a boy I was, and be better. So I kneeled down. But the words wouldn't come. Why wouldn't they? It warn't no use to try and hide it from Him. Nor from *me,* neither. I knowed very well why they wouldn't come. It was because my heart warn't right; it was because I warn't square; it was because I was playing double. I was letting *on* to give up sin, but away inside of me I was holding on to the biggest one of all. I was trying to make my mouth *say* I would do the right thing and the clean thing, and go and write to that nigger's owner and tell where he was; but deep down in me I knowed it was a lie—and He knowed it. You can't pray a lie—I found that out.

So I was full of trouble, full as I could be; and didn't know what to do. At last I had an idea; and I says, I'll go and write the letter—and *then* see if I can pray. Why, it was astonishing, the way I felt as light as a feather, right straight off, and my troubles all gone. So I got a piece of paper and a pencil, all glad and excited, and set down and wrote:

> Miss Watson your runaway nigger Jim is down here two mile below Pikesville and Mr. Phelps has got him and he will give him up for the reward if you send.
>
> HUCK FINN.

I felt good and all washed clean of sin for the first time I had ever felt so in my life, and I knowed I could pray now. But I didn't do it straight off, but laid the paper down and set there thinking—thinking how good it was all this happened so, and how near I come to being lost and going to hell. And went on thinking. And got thinking over our trip down the river; and I see Jim before me, all the time, in the day, and in the night-time, sometimes moonlight, sometimes storms, and we a floating along, talking, and singing, and laughing. But somehow I couldn't seem to strike no places to harden me against him, but only the other kind. I'd see him standing my watch on top of his'n, stead of calling me, so I could go on sleeping; and see him how glad he was when I come back out of the fog; and when I come to him again in the swamp, up there where the feud was; and such-like times; and would always call me honey, and pet me, and do everything he could think of for me, and how good he always was; and at last I struck the time I saved him by telling the men we had small-pox aboard, and he was so grateful, and said I was the best friend old Jim ever had in the world, and the *only* one he's got now; and then I happened to look around, and see that paper.

It was a close place. I took it up, and held it in my hand. I was a trembling, because I'd got to decide, forever, betwixt two things, and I knowed it. I studied a minute, sort of holding my breath, and then says to myself:

"All right, then, I'll *go* to hell"—and tore it up.[3]

It was awful thoughts, and awful words, but they was said. And I let them stay said; and never thought no more about reforming. I shoved the whole thing out of my head; and said I would take up wickedness again, which was in my line, being brung up to it, and the other warn't. And for a starter I would go to work and steal Jim out of slavery again; and if I could think up anything worse, I would do that, too; because as long as I was in, and in for good, I might as well go the whole hog.

* * *

from   CHAPTER **XXXII**

* * *

I went right along, not fixing up any particular plan, but just trusting to Providence to put the right words in my mouth when the time come; for I'd noticed that Providence always did put the right words in my mouth, if I left it alone.

When I got half-way, first one hound and then another got up and went for me, and of course I stopped and faced them, and kept still. And such another pow-wow as they made! In a quarter of a minute I was a kind of a hub of a wheel, as you may say—spokes made out of dogs—circle of fifteen of them packed together around me, with their necks and noses stretched up towards me, a barking and howling; and more a coming; you could see them sailing over fences and around corners from everywheres.

A nigger woman come tearing out of the kitchen with a rolling-pin in her hand, singing out, "Begone! *you* Tige! you Spot! begone, sah!" and she fetched first one and then another of them a clip and sent him howling, and then the rest followed; and the next second, half of them come back, wagging their tails around me and making friends with me. There ain't no harm in a hound, nohow.

And behind the woman comes a little nigger girl and two little nigger boys, without anything on but tow-linen shirts, and they hung onto their mother's gown, and peeped out from behind her at me, bashful, the way they always do. And here comes the white woman running from the house, about forty-five or fifty year old, bareheaded, and her spinning-stick in her hand; and behind her comes her little white children, acting the same way the little niggers was doing. She was smiling all over so she could hardly stand—and says:

"It's *you*, at last!—*ain't* it?"

I out with a "Yes'm," before I thought.

She grabbed me and hugged me tight; and then gripped me by both hands and shook and shook; and the tears come in her eyes, and run down over; and she couldn't seem to hug and shake enough, and kept saying, "You don't look as much like your mother as I reckoned you would, but law sakes, I don't care for that, I'm *so* glad to see you! Dear, dear, it does seem like I could eat you up! Childern, it's your cousin Tom!—tell him howdy."

---

[3] Twain once said that Huckleberry Finn was a boy "with a stout heart and a deformed conscience," Huck's heart being human and his conscience social. Here Huck's heart wins out; he becomes morally heroic at the moment he thinks he will go to Hell.

But they ducked their heads, and put their fingers in theirs mouths, and hid behind her. So she run on:

"Lize, hurry up and get him a hot breakfast, right away—or did you get your breakfast on the boat?"

I said I had got it on the boat. So then she started for the house, leading me by the hand, and the children tagging after. When we got there, she set me down in a split-bottomed chair, and set herself down on a little low stool in front of me, holding both of my hands, and says:

"Now I can have a *good* look at you; and laws-a-me, I've been hungry for it a many and a many a time, all these long years, and it's come at last! We been expecting you a couple of days and more. What's kep' you?—boat get aground?"

"Yes'm—she—"

"Don't say yes'm—say Aunt Sally. Where'd she get aground?"

I didn't rightly know what to say, because I didn't know whether the boat would be coming up the river or down. But I go a good deal on instinct; and my instinct said she would be coming up—from down towards Orleans. That didn't help me much, though; for I didn't know the names of bars down that way. I see I'd got to invent a bar, or forget the name of the one we got aground on—or— Now I struck an idea, and fetched it out:

"It warn't the grounding—that didn't keep us back but a little. We blowed out a cylinder-head."

"Good gracious! Anybody hurt?"

"No'm. Killed a nigger."

"Well, it's lucky; because sometimes people do get hurt. Two years ago last Christmas, your uncle Silas was coming up from Newrleans on the old *Lally Rook*,[1] and she blowed out a cylinder-head and crippled a man. And I think he died afterwards. He was a Babtist. Your uncle Silas knowed a family in Baton Rouge that knowed his people very well. Yes, I remember, now he *did* die. Mortification[2] set in, and they had to amputate him. But it didn't save him. Yes, it was mortification—that was it. He turned blue all over, and died in the hope of a glorious resurrection. They say he was a sight to look at. Your uncle's been up to the town every day to fetch you. And he's gone again, not more'n an hour ago; he'll be back any minute, now. You must a met him on the road, didn't you?—oldish man, with a—"

"No, I didn't see nobody, Aunt Sally. The boat landed just at daylight, and I left my baggage on the wharf-boat[3] and went looking around the town and out a piece in the country, to put in the time and not get here too soon; and so I come down the back way."

"Who'd you give the baggage to?"

"Nobody."

"Why, child, it'll be stole!"

"Not where *I* hid it I reckon it won't," I says.

"How'd you get your breakfast so early on the boat?"

It was kinder thin ice, but I says:

---

[1] Named for the princess in *Lalla Rookh* (1817), a series of oriental tales in verse that are connected by a story in prose, by the English writer Thomas Moore (1779-1852).
[2] Gangrene.   [3] Landing dock.

"The captain see me standing around, and told me I better have something to eat before I went ashore; so he took me in the texas to the officers' lunch,[4] and give me all I wanted."

I was getting so uneasy I couldn't listen good. I had my mind on the children all the time; I wanted to get them out to one side, and pump them a little, and find out who I was. But I couldn't get no show, Mrs. Phelps kept it up and run on so. Pretty soon she made the cold chills streak all down my back, because she says:

"But here we're a running on this way, and you hain't told me a word about Sis, nor any of them. Now I'll rest my works a little, and you start up yourn; just tell me *everything*—tell me all about 'm all—every one of 'm; and how they are, and what they're doing, and what they told you to tell me; and every last thing you can think of."

Well, I see I was up a stump—and up it good. Providence had stood by me this fur, all right, but I was hard and tight aground, now. I see it warn't a bit of use to try to go ahead—I'd *got* to throw up my hand. So I says to myself, here's another place where I got to resk the truth. I opened my mouth to begin; but she grabbed me and hustled me in behind the bed, and says:

"Here he comes! stick your head down lower—there, that'll do; you can't be seen, now. Don't you let on you're here. I'll play a joke on him. Childern, don't you say a word."

I see I was in a fix, now. But it warn't no use to worry; there warn't nothing to do but just hold still, and try and be ready to stand from under when the lightning struck.

I had just one little glimpse of the old gentleman when he come in, then the bed hid him. Mrs. Phelps she jumps for him and says:

"Has he come?"

"No," says her husband.

"Good-*ness* gracious!" she says, "what in the world *can* have become of him?"

"I can't imagine," says the old gentleman; "and I must say, it makes me dreadful uneasy."

"Uneasy!" she says, "I'm ready to go distracted! He *must* a come; and you've missed him along the road. I *know* it's so—something *tells* me so."

"Why Sally, I *couldn't* miss him along the road—*you* know that."

"But oh, dear, dear, what *will* Sis say? He must a come! You must a missed him. He—"

"Oh, don't distress me any more'n I'm already distressed. I don't know what in the world to make of it. I'm at my wit's end, and I don't mind acknowledging 't I'm right down scared. But there's no hope that he's come; for he *couldn't* come and me miss him. Sally, it's terrible—just terrible—something's happened to the boat, sure!"

"Why, Silas! Look yonder!—up the road!—ain't that somebody coming?"

He sprung to the window at the head of the bed, and that give Mrs. Phelps the chance she wanted. She stooped down quick, at the foot of the bed, and give me a pull, and out I come; and when he turned back from the window, there she stood, a-beaming and a-smiling like a house afire, and I standing pretty meek and sweaty alongside. The old gentleman stared, and says:

---

[4] Officer's mess, or dining room.

"Why, who's that?"

"Who do you reckon 't is?"

"I hain't no idea. Who *is* it?"

"It's *Tom Sawyer!*"

By jings, I most slumped through the floor. But there warn't no time to swap knives;[5] the old man grabbed me by the hand and shook, and kept on shaking; and all the time, how the woman did dance around and laugh and cry; and then how they both did fire off questions about Sid, and Mary, and the rest of the tribe.

But if they was joyful, it warn't nothing to what I was; for it was like being born again, I was so glad to find out who I was. Well, they froze to me for two hours; and at last when my chin was so tired it couldn't hardly go, any more, I had told them more about my family—I mean the Sawyer family—than ever happened to any six Sawyer families. And I explained all about how we blowed out a cylinder-head at the mouth of White River and it took us three days to fix it. Which was all right, and worked first rate; because *they* didn't know but what it would take three days to fix it. If I'd a called it a bolt-head it would a done just as well.

Now I was feeling pretty comfortable all down one side, and pretty uncomfortable all up the other. Being Tom Sawyer was easy and comfortable; and it stayed easy and comfortable till by-and-by I hear a steamboat coughing along down the river—then I says to myself, spose Tom Sawyer come down on that boat?—and spose he steps in here, any minute, and sings out my name before I can throw him a wink to keep quiet? Well, I couldn't *have* it that way—it wouldn't do at all. I must go up the road and waylay him. So I told the folks I reckoned I would go up to the town and fetch down my baggage. The old gentleman was for going along with me, but I said no, I could drive the horse myself, and I druther he wouldn't take no trouble about me.

from   CHAPTER XXXIII

So I started for town, in the wagon, and when I was half-way I see a wagon coming, and sure enough it was Tom Sawyer, and I stopped and waited till he come along. I says "Hold on!" and it stopped alongside, and his mouth opened up like a trunk, and staid so; and he swallowed two or three times like a person that's got a dry throat, and then says:

"I hain't ever done you no harm. You know that. So then, what you want to come back and ha'nt *me* for?"

I says:

"I hain't come back—I hain't been *gone*."

When he heard my voice, it righted him up some, but he warn't quite satisfied yet. He says:

"Don't you play nothing on me, because I wouldn't on you. Honest injun, now, you ain't a ghost?"

"Honest injun, I ain't," I says.

"Well—I—I—well, that ought to settle it, of course; but I can't somehow seem to understand it, no way. Looky here, warn't you ever murdered *at all?*"

---

[5] Change plans.

"No. I warn't ever murdered at all—I played it on them. You come in here and feel of me if you don't believe me."

So he done it; and it satisfied him; and he was that glad to see me again, he didn't know what to do. And he wanted to know all about it right off; because it was a grand adventure, and mysterious, and so it hit him where he lived. But I said, leave it alone till by-and-by; and told his driver to wait, and we drove off a little piece, and I told him the kind of fix I was in, and what did he reckon we better do? He said, let him alone a minute, and don't disturb him. So he thought and thought, and pretty soon he says:

"It's all right, I've got it. Take my trunk in your wagon, and let on it's your'n; and you turn back and fool along slow, so as to get to the house about the time you ought to; and I'll go towards town a piece, and take a fresh start, and get there a quarter or a half an hour after you; and you needn't let on to know me, at first."

I says:

"All right; but wait a minute. There's one more thing—a thing that *nobody* don't know but me. And that is, there's a nigger here that I'm a trying to steal out of slavery—and his name is *Jim*—old Miss Watson's Jim."

He says:

"What! Why Jim is—"

He stopped and went to studying. I says:

"*I* know what you'll say. You'll say it's dirty low-down business; but what if it is?—*I*'m low down; and I'm agoing to steal him, and I want you to keep mum and not let on. Will you?"

His eye lit up, and he says:

"I'll *help* you steal him!"

Well, I let go all holts then, like I was shot. It was the most astonishing speech I ever heard—and I'm bound to say Tom Sawyer fell, considerable, in my estimation. Only I couldn't believe it. Tom Sawyer a *nigger stealer!*

"Oh, shucks," I says, "you're joking."

"I ain't joking, either."

"Well, then," I says, "joking or no joking, if you hear anything said about a runaway nigger, don't forget to remember that *you* don't know nothing about him, and *I* don't know nothing about him."

Then we took the trunk and put it in my wagon, and he drove off his way, and I drove mine. But of course I forgot all about driving slow, on accounts of being glad and full of thinking; so I got home a heap too quick for that length of a trip. The old gentleman was at the door, and he says:

"Why, this is wonderful. Who ever would a thought it was in that mare to do it. I wish we'd a timed her. And she hain't sweated a hair—not a hair. It's wonderful. Why, I wouldn't take a hunderd dollars for that horse now; I wouldn't, honest; and yet I'd a sold her for fifteen before, and thought 'twas all she was worth."

That's all he said. He was the innocentest, best old soul I ever see. But it warn't surprising; because he warn't only just a farmer, he was a preacher, too, and had a little one-horse log church down back of the plantation, which he built it himself at his own expense, for a church and school-house, and never charged nothing for his preaching, and it was worth it, too. There was plenty other farmer-preachers like that, and done the same way, down South.

* * *

from   Chapter XXXIV

We stopped talking, and got to thinking.

By-and-by Tom says:

"Looky here, Huck, what fools we are, to not think of it before! I bet I know where Jim is."

"No! Where?"

"In that hut down by the ash-hopper. Why, looky here. When we was at dinner, didn't you see a nigger man go in there with some vittles?"

"Yes."

"What did you think the vittles was for?"

"For a dog."

"So'd I. Well, it wasn't for a dog."

"Why?"

"Because part of it was watermelon."

"So it was—I noticed it. Well, it does beat all, that I never thought about a dog not eating watermelon. It shows how a body can see and don't see at the same time."

"Well, the nigger unlocked the padlock when he went in, and he locked it again when he come out. He fetched uncle a key, about the time we got up from table— same key, I bet. Watermelon shows man, lock shows prisoner; and it ain't likely there's two prisoners on such a little plantation, and where the people's all so kind and good. Jim's the prisoner. All right—I'm glad we found it out detective fashion; I wouldn't give shucks for any other way. Now you work your mind and study out a plan to steal Jim, and I will study out one, too; and we'll take the one we like the best."

What a head for just a boy to have! If I had Tom Sawyer's head, I wouldn't trade it off to be a duke, nor mate of a steamboat, nor clown in a circus, nor nothing I can think of. I went to thinking out a plan, but only just to be doing something. I knowed very well where the right plan was going to come from. Pretty soon, Tom says:

"Ready?"

"Yes," I says.

"All right—bring it out."

"My plan is this," I says, "We can easy find out if it's Jim in there. Then get up my canoe to-morrow night, and fetch my raft over from the island. Then the first dark night that comes, steal the key out of the old man's britches, after he goes to bed, and shove off down the river on the raft, with Jim, hiding daytimes and running nights, the way me and Jim used to do before. Wouldn't that plan work?"

"*Work?* Why cert'nly, it would work, like rats a fighting. But it's too blame' simple; there ain't nothing *to* it. What's the good of a plan that ain't no more trouble than that? It's as mild as goose-milk. Why, Huck, it wouldn't make no more talk than breaking into a soap factory."

I never said nothing, because I warn't expecting nothing different; but I knowed mighty well that whenever he got *his* plan ready it wouldn't have none of them objections to it.

And it didn't. He told me what it was, and I see in a minute it was worth fifteen of mine, for style, and would make Jim just as free a man as mine would, and maybe get us all killed besides. So I was satisfied, and said we would waltz in on it. I needn't tell what it was, here, because I knowed it wouldn't stay the way it was. I knowed he would be changing it around, every which way, as we went along, and heaving in new bullinesses wherever he got a chance. And that is what he done.

Well, one thing was dead sure; and that was, that Tom Sawyer was in earnest and was actly going to help steal that nigger out of slavery. That was the thing that was too many for me. Here was a boy that was respectable, and well brung up; and had a character to lose; and folks at home that had characters; and he was bright and not leather-headed; and knowing and not ignorant; and not mean, but kind; and yet here he was, without any more pride, or rightness, or feeling, than to stoop to this business, and make himself a shame, and his family a shame, before everybody. I *couldn't* understand it, no way at all. It was outrageous, and I knowed I ought to just up and tell him so; and so be his true friend, and let him quit the thing right where he was, and save himself. And I *did* start to tell him; but he shut me up, and says:

"Don't you reckon I know what I'm about? Don't I generly know what I'm about?"

"Yes."

"Didn't I *say* I was going to help steal the nigger?"

"Yes."

"*Well* then."

That's all he said, and that's all I said. It warn't no use to say any more; because when he said he'd do a thing, he always done it. But *I* couldn't make out how he was willing to go into this thing; so I just let it go, and never bothered no more about it. If he was bound to have it so, *I* couldn't help it.

* * *

Chapter XXXV

It would be most an hour, yet, till breakfast, so we left, and struck down into the woods; because Tom said we got to have *some* light to see how to dig by, and a lantern makes too much, and might get us into trouble; what we must have was a lot of them rotten chunks that's called fox-fire[1] and just makes a soft kind of a glow when you lay them in a dark place. We fetched an armful and hid it in the weeds, and set down to rest, and Tom says, kind of dissatisfied:

"Blame it, this whole thing is just as easy and awkard as it can be. And so it makes it so rotten difficult to get up a difficult plan. There ain't no watchman to be drugged—now there *ought* to be a watchman. There ain't even a dog to give a sleeping-mixture to. And there's Jim chained by one leg, with a ten-foot chain, to the leg of his bed: why, all you got to do is to lift up the bedstead and slip off the chain. And Uncle Silas he trusts everybody; sends the key to the punkin-headed nigger, and don't send nobody to watch the nigger. Jim could a got out of that window hole before this, only there wouldn't be no use trying to travel with a ten-foot chain on his leg. Why, drat it, Huck, it's the stupidest arrangement I ever see. You got to invent *all* the difficulties. Well, we can't help it, we got to do the best we can with the materials we've got. Anyhow, there's one thing—there's more honor in getting him out through a lot of difficulties and dangers, where

---

[1] The phosphorescent glow of fungus on rotting wood.

there warn't one of them furnished to you by the people who it was their duty to furnish them, and you had to contrive them all out of your own head. Now look at just that one thing of the lantern. When you come down to the cold facts, we simply got to *let on* that a lantern's resky. Why, we could work with a torchlight procession if we wanted to, *I* believe. Now, whilst I think of it, we got to hunt up something to make a saw out of, the first chance we get."

"What do we want of a saw?"

"What do we *want* of it? Hain't we got to saw the leg of Jim's bed off, so as to get the chain loose?"

"Why, you just said a body could lift up the bedstead and slip the chain off."

"Well, if that ain't just like you, Huck Finn. You *can* get up the infant-schooliest ways of going at a thing. Why, hain't you ever read any books at all?—Baron Trenck, nor Casanova, nor Benvenuto Chelleeny, nor Henri IV.,[2] nor none of them heroes? Whoever heard of getting a prisoner loose in such an old-maidy way as that? No; the way all the best authorities does, is to saw the bed-leg in two, and leave it just so, and swallow the sawdust, so it can't be found, and put some dirt and grease around the sawed place so the very keenest seneskal[3] can't see no sign of it's being sawed, and thinks the bed-leg is perfectly sound. Then, the night you're ready, fetch the leg a kick, down she goes; slip off your chain, and there you are. Nothing to do but hitch your rope-ladder to the battlements, shin down it, break your leg in the moat—because a rope-ladder is nineteen foot too short, you know—and there's your horses and your trusty vassles, and they scoop you up and fling you across a saddle and away you go, to your native Langudoc, or Navarre,[4] or wherever it is. It's gaudy, Huck. I wish there was a moat to this cabin. If we get time, the night of the escape, we'll dig one."

I says:

"What do we want of a moat, when we're going to snake him out from under the cabin?"

But he never heard me. He had forgot me and everything else. He had his chin in his hand, thinking. Pretty soon, he sighs, and shakes his head; then sighs again, and says:

"No, it wouldn't do—there ain't necessity enough for it."

"For what?" I says.

"Why, to saw Jim's leg off," he says.

"Good land!" I says, "why, there ain't *no* necessity for it. And what would you want to saw his leg off for, anyway?"

"Well, some of the best authorities has done it. They couldn't get the chain off, so they just cut their hand off, and shoved. And a leg would be better still. But we got to let that go. There ain't necessity enough in this case; and besides, Jim's a nigger and wouldn't understand the reasons for it, and how it's the custom in Europe; so we'll let it go. But there's one thing—he can have a rope-ladder; we can tear up our sheets and make him a rope-ladder easy enough. And we can send it to him in a pie; it's mostly done that way. And I've et worse pies."

"Why, Tom Sawyer, how you talk," I says; "Jim ain't got no use for a rope-ladder."

---

[2] Baron Friedrich von Trenck (1726–1794), an Austrian soldier; the Italian lover Giovanni Giacomo Casanova (1725–1798); Benvenuto Cellini (1500–1571), an Italian artist; and Henry IV (1553–1610), king of France (1589–1610): all attempted daring escapes.

[3] Seneschal, a high-ranking official in important medieval households.

[4] Provinces in southern France and in the Pyrenees (between France and Spain), respectively.

"He *has* got use for it. How *you* talk, you better say; you don't know nothing about it. He's *got* to have a rope ladder; they all do."

"What in the nation can he *do* with it?"

"*Do* with it? He can hide it in his bed, can't he? That's what they all do; and *he's* got to, too. Huck, you don't ever seem to want to do anything that's regular; you want to be starting something fresh all the time. Spose he *don't* do nothing with it? ain't it there in his bed, for a clew, after he's gone? and don't you reckon they'll want clews? Of course they will. And you wouldn't leave them any? That would be a *pretty* howdy-do, *wouldn't* it! I never heard of such a thing."

"Well," I says, "if it's in the regulations, and he's got to have it, all right, let him have it; because I don't wish to go back on no regulations; but there's one thing, Tom Sawyer—if we go to tearing up our sheets to make Jim a rope-ladder, we're going to get into trouble with Aunt Sally, just as sure as you're born. Now, the way I look at it, a hickry-bark ladder don't cost nothing, and don't waste nothing, and is just as good to load up a pie with, and hide in a straw tick, as any rag ladder you can start; and as for Jim, he ain't had no experience, and so *he* don't care what kind of a——"

"Oh, shucks, Huck Finn, if I was as ignorant as you, I'd keep still—that's what *I'd* do. Who ever heard of a state prisoner escaping by a hickry-bark ladder? Why, it's perfectly ridiculous."

"Well, all right, Tom, fix it your own way; but if you'll take my advice, you'll let me borrow a sheet off of the clothes-line."

He said that would do. And that give him another idea, and he says:

"Borrow a shirt, too."

"What do we want of a shirt, Tom?"

"Want it for Jim to keep a journal on."

"Journal your granny—*Jim* can't write."

"Spose he *can't* write—he can make marks on the shirt, can't he, if we make him a pen out of an old pewter spoon or a piece of an old iron barrel-hoop?"

"Why, Tom, we can pull a feather out of a goose and make him a better one; and quicker, too."

"*Prisoners* don't have geese running around the donjon-keep to pull pens out of, you muggins. They *always* make their pens out of the hardest, toughest, troublesomest piece of old brass candlestick or something like that they can get their hands on; and it takes them weeks and weeks, and months and months to file it out, too, because they've got to do it by rubbing it on the wall. *They* wouldn't use a goose-quill if they had it. It ain't regular."

"Well, then, what'll we make him the ink out of?"

"Many makes it out of iron-rust and tears; but that's the common sort and women; the best authorities uses their own blood. Jim can do that; and when he wants to send any little common ordinary mysterious message to let the world know where he's captivated, he can write it on the bottom of a tin plate with a fork and throw it out of the window. The Iron Mask[5] always done that, and it's a blame' good way, too."

"Jim ain't got no tin plates. They feed him in a pan."

"That ain't anything; we can get him some."

---

[5] The protagonist in the romantic novel *Le Vicomte de Bragelonne* (1848–1850), or "*The Viscount of Bragelonne*" (French), by Alexandre Dumas (1802–1870); part of it was translated in the 1850s as *The Man in the Iron Mask*.

"Can't nobody *read* his plates."

"That ain't got nothing to *do* with it, Huck Finn. All *he's* got to do is to write on the plate and throw it out. You don't *have* to be able to read it. Why, half the time you can't read anything a prisoner writes on a tin plate, or anywhere else."

"Well, then, what's the sense in wasting the plates?"

"Why, blame it all, it ain't the *prisoner's* plates."

"But it's *somebody's* plates, ain't it?"

"Well, spos'n it is? What does the *prisoner* care whose——"

He broke off there, because we heard the breakfast-horn blowing. So we cleared out for the house.

Along during that morning I borrowed a sheet and a white shirt off of the clothes-line; and I found an old sack and put them in it, and we went down and got the fox-fire, and put that in too. I called it borrowing, because that was what pap always called it; but Tom said it warn't borrowing, it was stealing. He said we was representing prisoners; and prisoners don't care how they get a thing so they get it, and nobody don't blame them for it, either. It ain't no crime in a prisoner to steal the thing he needs to get away with, Tom said; it's his right; and so, as long as we was representing a prisoner, we had a perfect right to steal anything on this place we had the least use for, to get ourselves out of prison with. He said if we warn't prisoners it would be a very different thing, and nobody but a mean ornery person would steal when he warn't a prisoner. So we allowed we would steal everything there was that come handy. And yet he made a mighty fuss, one day, after that, when I stole a watermelon out of the nigger patch[6] and eat it; and he made me go and give the niggers a dime, without telling them what it was for. Tom said that what he meant was, we could steal anything we *needed*. Well, I says, I needed the watermelon. But he said I didn't need it to get out of prison with, there's where the difference was. He said if I'd a wanted it to hide a knife in, and smuggle it to Jim to kill the seneskal with, it would a been all right. So I let it go at that, though I couldn't see no advantage in my representing a prisoner, if I got to set down and chaw over a lot of gold-leaf[7] distinctions like that, every time I see a chance to hog a watermelon.

Well, as I was saying, we waited that morning till everybody was settled down to business, and nobody in sight around the yard; then Tom he carried the sack into the lean-to whilst I stood off a piece to keep watch. By-and-by he come out, and we went and set down on the wood-pile, to talk. He says:

"Everything's all right, now, except tools; and that's easy fixed."

"Tools?" I says.

"Yes."

"Tools for what?"

"Why, to dig with. We ain't agoing to *gnaw* him out, are we?"

"Ain't them old crippled picks and things in there good enough to dig a nigger out with?" I says.

He turns on me looking pitying enough to make a body cry, and says:

"Huck Finn, did you *ever* hear of a prisoner having picks and shovels, and all the modern conveniences in his wardrobe to dig himself out with? Now I want to ask you—if you got any reasonableness in you at all—what kind of a show would *that* give him to be a hero? Why, they might as well lend him the key, and done with it. Picks and shovels—why they wouldn't furnish 'em to a king."

---

[6] A slave's garden for growing fruits and vegetables.   [7] Flimsy, thin as gold leaf.

"Well, then," I says, "if we don't want the picks and shovels, what do we want?"

"A couple of case-knives."[8]

"To dig the foundations out from under that cabin with?"

"Yes."

"Confound it, it's foolish, Tom."

"It don't make no difference how foolish it is, it's the *right* way—and it's the regular way. And there ain't no *other* way, that ever *I* heard of, and I've read all the books that gives any information about these things. They always dig out with a case-knife—and not through dirt, mind you; generly it's through solid rock. And it takes them weeks and weeks and weeks, and for ever and ever. Why, look at one of them prisoners in the bottom dungeon of the Castle Deef,[9] in the harbor of Marseilles, that dug himself out that way; how long was *he* at it, you reckon?"

"I don't know."

"Well, guess."

"I don't know. A month and a half?"

"*Thirty-seven year*—and he come out in China. *That's* the kind. I wish the bottom of *this* fortress was solid rock."

"*Jim* don't know nobody in China."

"What's *that* got to do with it? Neither did that other fellow. But you're always a-wandering off on a side issue. Why can't you stick to the main point?"

"All right—*I* don't care where he comes out, so he *comes* out; and Jim don't, either, I reckon. But there's one thing, anyway—Jim's too old to be dug out with a case-knife. He won't last."

"Yes he will *last*, too. You don't reckon it's going to take thirty-seven years to dig out through a *dirt* foundation, do you?"

"How long will it take, Tom?"

"Well, we can't resk being as long as we ought to, because it mayn't take very long for Uncle Silas to hear from down there by New Orleans. He'll hear Jim ain't from there. Then his next move will be to advertise Jim, or something like that. So we can't resk being as long digging him out as we ought to. By rights I reckon we ought to be a couple of years; but we can't. Things being so uncertain, what I recommend is this: that we really dig right in, as quick as we can; and after that, we can *let on*, to ourselves, that we was at it thirty-seven years. Then we can snatch him out and rush him away the first time there's an alarm. Yes, I reckon that'll be the best way."

"Now, there's *sense* in that," I says. "Letting on don't cost nothing; letting on ain't no trouble; and if it's any object, I don't mind letting on we was at it a hundred and fifty year. It wouldn't strain me none, after I got my hand in. So I'll mosey along now, and smouch a couple of case-knives."

"Smouch three," he says; "we want one to make a saw out of."

"Tom, if it ain't unregular and irreligious to sejest it," I says, "there's an old rusty saw-blade around yonder sticking under the weatherboarding behind the smoke-house."

He looked kind of weary and discouraged-like, and says:

"It ain't no use to try to learn you nothing, Huck. Run along and smouch the knives—three of them." So I done it.

---

[8] Kitchen knives.   [9] The Chateau d'If, the prison in Dumas's *Count of Monte Cristo* (1845).

CHAPTER THE LAST

The first time I catched Tom, private, I asked him what was his idea, time of the evasion?—what it was he'd planned to do if the evasion worked all right and he managed to set a nigger free that was already free before? And he said, what he had planned in his head, from the start, if we got Jim out all safe, was for us to run him down the river, on the raft, and have adventures plumb to the mouth of the river, and then tell him about his being free, and take him back up home on a steamboat, in style, and pay him for his lost time, and write word ahead and get out all the niggers around, and have them waltz him into town with a torchlight procession and a brass band, and then he would be a hero, and so would we. But I reckened it was about as well the way it was.

We had Jim out of the chains in no time, and when Aunt Polly and Uncle Silas and Aunt Sally found out how good he helped the doctor nurse Tom, they made a heap of fuss over him, and fixed him up prime, and give him all he wanted to eat, and a good time, and nothing to do. And we had him up to the sick-room; and had a high talk; and Tom give Jim forty dollars for being prisoner for us so patient, and doing it up so good, and Jim was pleased most to death, and busted out, and says:

"*Dah*, now, Huck, what I tell you?—what I tell you up dah on Jackson islan'? I *tole* you I got a hairy breas', en what's de sign un it; en I *tole* you I ben rich wunst, en gwineter to be rich *agin;* en it's come true; en heah she *is! Dah*, now! doan' talk to *me*—signs is *signs*, mine I tell you; en I knowed jis' 's well 'at I 'uz gwineter be rich agin as I's a stannin' heah dis minute!"

And then Tom he talked along, and talked along, and says, le's all three slide out of here, one of these nights, and get an outfit, and go for howling adventures amongst the Injuns, over in the Territory, for a couple of weeks or two; and I says, all right, that suits me, but I ain't got no money for to buy the outfit, and I reckon I couldn't get none from home, because it's likely pap's been back before now, and got it all away from Judge Thatcher and drunk it up.

"No he hain't," Tom says; "it's all there, yet—six thousand dollars and more; and your pap hain't ever been back since. Hadn't when I come away, anyhow."

Jim says, kind of solemn:

"He ain't a comin' back no mo', Huck."

I says:

"Why, Jim?"

"Nemmine why, Huck—but he ain't comin' back no mo'."

But I kept at him; so at last he says:

"Doan' you 'member de house dat was float'n down de river, en dey wuz a man in dah, kivered up, en I went in en unkivered him and didn' let you come in? Well, den, you k'n git yo' money when you wants it; kase dat wuz him."

Tom's most well, now, and got his bullet around his neck on a watch-guard for a watch, and is always seeing what time it is, and so there ain't nothing more to write about, and I am rotten glad of it, because if I'd a knowed what a trouble it was to make a book I wouldn't a tackled it and ain't agoing to no more. But I reckon I got to light out for the Territory ahead of the rest, because Aunt Sally she's going to adopt me and sivilize me and I can't stand it. I been there before.

THE END. YOURS TRULY, HUCK FINN.

1876–1883, 1884

Sarah Orne Jewett
(1849–1909)

In the short story "A White Heron" (1886), Sylvia wavers between directing a handsome ornithologist to the elusive heron's nest and saving the bird, eventually choosing silence and the green world of nature over the money and approval the young man from "the great world" offers. Her silence admits Sylvia into Sarah Orne Jewett's coterie of strong, independent females who choose the best lives they can with the meager resources that small, late nineteenth-century New England towns provided. Born the second daughter of Theodore Herman Jewett, a physician, and the former Caroline Frances Perry in 1849, Theodora Sarah Orne Jewett—who quickly dropped her first name—grew up in South Berwick, Maine, an inland port past its heyday, a place of remembered grandeur and romance. Because she suffered from arthritis as a child, and because her father doted on her, she often accompanied him on his rounds rather than going to school. During these visits, Jewett grew to appreciate both the people and the landscape of her region.

Jewett's father also encouraged her interest in literature; later, he urged her to "tell things *just as they are*," as stated in *Sarah Orne Jewett's Letters* (1967). Jewett followed this admonition in depicting the idiom, ideals, and environments of the elderly women whose strength and courage she admired. Influenced by the example of Harriet Beecher Stowe's narrative of the Maine coast, *The Pearl of Orr's Island* (1862), Jewett began her literary career while still in her teens, publishing short fiction in magazines including the *Atlantic Monthly,* then edited by William Dean Howells. With his encouragement, she collected her sketches into the volume *Deephaven* (1877), named for one of her fictional Maine towns. Over the next twenty-five years Jewett published thirteen volumes of fiction, including *A Country Doctor* (1884)—in which a New England girl refuses an offer of marriage so that she might become a doctor—and *A Marsh Island* (1885).

Jewett is ranked highly among New England local-color writers, particularly for *The Country of the Pointed Firs* (1896), a work Willa Cather considered one of the three greatest American masterpieces (along with Nathaniel Hawthorne's *Scarlet Letter* [1850] and Mark Twain's *Adventures of Huckleberry Finn* [1884]). Despite this high praise, Jewett's novel-in-sketches is not well known; in *Short Fiction* (1979) the critic Barbara Solomon ascribes its neglect to its being "so thoroughly a woman's book about the world of women," a world of visiting and reminiscing, of quiet contemplation. With unerring pictorial detail, Jewett presents the limited world of Dunnet Landing as a place of few men and many strong women who live in close relationships to the land and sea, an economically declining and yet restorative, psychologically vivifying place.

Like many of her characters, Jewett did not marry; her closest relationships were with women, particularly her publisher's wife, Annie Adams Fields. After James Fields died in 1881 Jewett and Fields began living together platonically in a "Boston marriage." Although Jewett's career ended prematurely (after an injury in a carriage accident), she had already preserved the flavor of a New England soon to vanish under the pressures of industrialization. Several months after suffering a crippling stroke in 1909, she died in South Berwick in the house in which she was born.

Suggested Readings: *The Country of the Pointed Firs,* 1896. *The Best Short Stories of Sarah Orne Jewett,* intro. W. Cather, 1927, rpt. 1965. *Deephaven and Other Stories,* ed. R. Cary, 1966. *The*

Uncollected Short Stories of Sarah Orne Jewett, ed. R. Cary, 1971. R. Cary, *Sarah Orne Jewett,* 1962. F. O. Matthiessen, *Sarah Orne Jewett,* 1965. R. Cary, ed., *Appreciation of Sarah Orne Jewett: 29 Interpretive Essays,* 1973. G. L. Nagel, *Critical Essays on Sarah Orne Jewett,* 1984. S. W. Sherman, *Sarah Orne Jewett, An American Persephone,* 1989.

Text Used: *Tales of New England,* 1890.

A WHITE HERON*

I

The woods were already filled with shadows one June evening, just before eight o'clock, though a bright sunset still glimmered faintly among the trunks of the trees. A little girl was driving home her cow, a plodding, dilatory, provoking creature in her behavior, but a valued companion for all that. They were going away from the western light, and striking deep into the dark woods, but their feet were familiar with the path, and it was no matter whether their eyes could see it or not.

There was hardly a night the summer through when the old cow could be found waiting at the pasture bars; on the contrary, it was her greatest pleasure to hide herself away among the high huckleberry bushes, and though she wore a loud bell she had made the discovery that if one stood perfectly still it would not ring. So Sylvia had to hunt for her until she found her, and call Co'! Co'! with never an answering Moo, until her childish patience was quite spent. If the creature had not given good milk and plenty of it, the case would have seemed very different to her owners. Besides, Sylvia had all the time there was, and very little use to make of it. Sometimes in pleasant weather it was a consolation to look upon the cow's pranks as an intelligent attempt to play hide and seek, and as the child had no playmates she lent herself to this amusement with a good deal of zest. Though this chase had been so long that the wary animal herself had given an unusual signal of her whereabouts, Sylvia had only laughed when she came upon Mistress Moolly at the swamp-side, and urged her affectionately homeward with a twig of birch leaves. The old cow was not inclined to wander farther, she even turned in the right direction for once as they left the pasture, and stepped along the road at a good pace. She was quite ready to be milked now, and seldom stopped to browse. Sylvia wondered what her grandmother would say because they were so late. It was a great while since she had left home at half past five o'clock, but everybody knew the difficulty of making this errand a short one. Mrs. Tilley had chased the hornéd torment too many summer evenings herself to blame any one else for lingering, and was only thankful as she waited that she had Sylvia, nowadays, to give such valuable assistance. The good woman suspected that Sylvia loitered occasionally on her own account; there never was such a child for straying about out-of-doors since the world was made! Everybody said that it was a good change for a little maid who had tried to grow for eight years in a crowded manufacturing town, but, as for Sylvia herself, it seemed as if she never had been alive at all

---

* First published in Jewett's collection *A White Heron and Other Stories* (1886).

before she came to live at the farm. She thought often with wistful compassion of a wretched dry geranium that belonged to a town neighbor.

"'Afraid of folks,'" old Mrs. Tilley said to herself, with a smile, after she had made the unlikely choice of Sylvia from her daughter's houseful of children, and was returning to the farm. "'Afraid of folks,' they said! I guess she won't be troubled no great with 'em up to the old place!" When they reached the door of the lonely house and stopped to unlock it, the cat came to purr loudly, and rub against them, a deserted pussy, indeed, but fat with young robins, Sylvia whispered that this was a beautiful place to live in, and she never should wish to go home.

The companions followed the shady wood-road, the cow taking slow steps, and the child very fast ones. The cow stopped long at the brook to drink, as if the pasture were not half a swamp, and Sylvia stood still and waited, letting her bare feet cool themselves in the shoal water, while the great twilight moths struck softly against her. She waded on through the brook as the cow moved away, and listened to the thrushes with a heart that beat fast with pleasure. There was a stirring in the great boughs overhead. They were full of little birds and beasts that seemed to be wide-awake, and going about their world, or else saying good-night to each other in sleepy twitters. Sylvia herself felt sleepy as she walked along. However, it was not much farther to the house, and the air was soft and sweet. She was not often in the woods so late as this, and it made her feel as if she were a part of the gray shadows and the moving leaves. She was just thinking how long it seemed since she first came to the farm a year ago, and wondering if everything went on in the noisy town just the same as when she was there; the thought of the great red-faced boy who used to chase and frighten her made her hurry along the path to escape from the shadow of the trees.

Suddenly this little woods-girl is horror-stricken to hear a clear whistle not very far away. Not a bird's whistle, which would have a sort of friendliness, but a boy's whistle, determined, and somewhat aggressive. Sylvia left the cow to whatever sad fate might await her, and stepped discreetly aside into the bushes, but she was just too late. The enemy had discovered her, and called out in a very cheerful and persuasive tone, "Halloa, little girl, how far is it to the road?" and trembling Sylvia answered almost inaudibly, "A good ways."

She did not dare to look boldly at the tall young man, who carried a gun over his shoulder, but she came out of her bush and again followed the cow, while he walked alongside.

"I have been hunting for some birds," the stranger said kindly, "and I have lost my way, and need a friend very much. Don't be afraid," he added gallantly. "Speak up and tell me what your name is, and whether you think I can spend the night at your house, and go out gunning early in the morning."

Sylvia was more alarmed than before. Would not her grandmother consider her much to blame? But who could have foreseen such an accident as this? It did not appear to be her fault, and she hung her head as if the stem of it were broken, but managed to answer "Sylvy," with much effort when her companion again asked her name.

Mrs. Tilley was standing in the doorway when the trio came into view. The cow gave a loud moo by way of explanation.

"Yes, you'd better speak up for yourself, you old trial! Where'd she tucked herself away this time, Sylvy?" Sylvia kept an awed silence; she knew by instinct that her grandmother did not comprehend the gravity of the situation. She must be mistaking the stranger for one of the farmer-lads of the region.

The young man stood his gun beside the door, and dropped a heavy game-bag beside it; then he bade Mrs. Tilley good-evening, and repeated his wayfarer's story, and asked if he could have a night's lodging.

"Put me anywhere you like," he said. "I must be off early in the morning, before day; but I am very hungry, indeed. You can give me some milk at any rate, that's plain."

"Dear sakes, yes," responded the hostess, whose long slumbering hospitality seemed to be easily awakened. "You might fare better if you went out on the main road a mile or so, but you're welcome to what we've got. I'll milk right off, and you make yourself at home. You can sleep on husks or feathers," she proffered graciously. "I raised them all myself. There's good pasturing for geese just below here towards the ma'sh. Now step round and set a plate for the gentleman, Sylvy!" And Sylvia promptly stepped. She was glad to have something to do, and she was hungry herself.

It was a surprise to find so clean and comfortable a little dwelling in this New England wilderness. The young man had known the horrors of its most primitive housekeeping, and the dreary squalor of that level of society which does not rebel at the companionship of hens. This was the best thrift of an old-fashioned farm-stead, though on such a small scale that it seemed like a hermitage. He listened eagerly to the old woman's quaint talk, he watched Sylvia's pale face and shining gray eyes with ever growing enthusiasm, and insisted that this was the best supper he had eaten for a month; then, afterward, the new-made friends sat down in the doorway together while the moon came up.

Soon it would be berry-time, and Sylvia was a great help at picking. The cow was a good milker, though a plaguy[1] thing to keep track of, the hostess gossiped frankly, adding presently that she had buried four children, so that Sylvia's mother, and a son (who might be dead) in California were all the children she had left. "Dan, my boy, was a great hand to go gunning," she explained sadly. "I never wanted for pa'tridges or gray squer'ls while he was to home. He's been a great wand'rer, I expect, and he's no hand to write letters. There, I don't blame him, I'd ha' seen the world myself if it had been so I could."

"Sylvia takes after him," the grandmother continued affectionately, after a minute's pause. "There ain't a foot o' ground she don't know her way over, and the wild creatur's counts her one o' themselves. Squer'ls she'll tame to come an' feed right out o' her hands, and all sorts o' birds. Last winter she got the jay-birds to bangeing[2] here, and I believe she'd 'a' scanted herself of her own meals to have plenty to throw out amongst 'em, if I had n't kep' watch. Anything but crows, I tell her, I'm willin' to help support,—though Dan he went an' tamed one o' them that did seem to have reason same as folks. It was round here a good spell after he went away. Dan an' his father they did n't hitch,—but he never held up his head ag'in after Dan had dared him an' gone off."

The guest did not notice this hint of family sorrows in his eager interest in something else.

"So Sylvy knows all about birds, does she?" he exclaimed, as he looked round at the little girl who sat, very demure but increasingly sleepy, in the moonlight. "I am making a collection of birds myself. I have been at it ever since I was a boy."

---

[1] Annoying.   [2] Gathering or hanging around leisurely, a New England term.

(Mrs. Tilley smiled.) "There are two or three very rare ones I have been hunting for these five years. I mean to get them on my own ground if they can be found."

"Do you cage 'em up?" asked Mrs. Tilley doubtfully, in response to this enthusiastic announcement.

"Oh, no, they're stuffed and preserved, dozens and dozens of them," said the ornithologist, "and I have shot or snared every one myself. I caught a glimpse of a white heron three miles from here on Saturday, and I have followed it in this direction. They have never been found in this district at all. The little white heron, it is," and he turned again to look at Sylvia with the hope of discovering that the rare bird was one of her acquaintances.

But Sylvia was watching a hop-toad in the narrow footpath.

"You would know the heron if you saw it," the stranger continued eagerly. "A queer tall white bird with soft feathers and long thin legs. And it would have a nest perhaps in the top of a high tree, made of sticks, something like a hawk's nest."

Sylvia's heart gave a wild beat; she knew that strange white bird, and had once stolen softly near where it stood in some bright green swamp grass, away over at the other side of the woods. There was an open place where the sunshine always seemed strangely yellow and hot, where tall, nodding rushes grew, and her grandmother had warned her that she might sink in the soft black mud underneath and never be heard of more. Not far beyond were the salt marshes and beyond those was the sea, the sea which Sylvia wondered and dreamed about, but never had looked upon, though its great voice could often be heard above the noise of the woods on stormy nights.

"I can't think of anything I should like so much as to find that heron's nest," the handsome stranger was saying. "I would give ten dollars to anybody who could show it to me," he added desperately, "and I mean to spend my whole vacation hunting for it if need be. Perhaps it was only migrating, or had been chased out of its own region by some bird of prey."

Mrs. Tilley gave amazed attention to all this, but Sylvia still watched the toad, not divining, as she might have done at some calmer time, that the creature wished to get to its hole under the doorstep, and was much hindered by the unusual spectators at that hour of the evening. No amount of thought, that night, could decide how many wished-for treasures the ten dollars, so lightly spoken of, would buy.

The next day the young sportsman hovered about the woods, and Sylvia kept him company, having lost her first fear of the friendly lad, who proved to be most kind and sympathetic. He told her many things about the birds and what they knew and where they lived and what they did with themselves. And he gave her a jack-knife, which she thought as great a treasure as if she were a desert-islander. All day long he did not once make her troubled or afraid except when he brought down some unsuspecting singing creature from its bough. Sylvia would have liked him vastly better without his gun; she could not understand why he killed the very birds he seemed to like so much. But as the day waned, Sylvia still watched the young man with loving admiration. She had never seen anybody so charming and delightful; the woman's heart, asleep in the child, was vaguely thrilled by a dream of love. Some premonition of that great power stirred and swayed these young foresters who traversed the woodlands with soft-footed silent care. They stopped to listen to a bird's song; they pressed forward again eagerly, parting the branches,—speaking to each other rarely and in whispers; the young man going first and Sylvia following, fascinated, a few steps behind, with her gray eyes dark with excitement.

She grieved because the longed-for white heron was elusive, but she did not lead the guest, she only followed, and there was no such thing as speaking first. The sound of her own unquestioned voice would have terrified her,—it was hard enough to answer yes or no when there was need of that. At last evening began to fall, and they drove the cow home together, and Sylvia smiled with pleasure when they came to the place where she heard the whistle and was afraid only the night before.

II

Half a mile from home, at the farther edge of the woods, where the land was highest, a great pine-tree stood, the last of its generation. Whether it was left for a boundary mark, or for what reason, no one could say; the woodchoppers who had felled its mates were dead and gone long ago, and a whole forest of sturdy trees, pines and oaks and maples, had grown again. But the stately head of this old pine towered above them all and made a landmark for sea and shore miles and miles away. Sylvia knew it well. She had always believed that whoever climbed to the top of it could see the ocean; and the little girl had often laid her hand on the great rough trunk and looked up wistfully at those dark boughs that the wind always stirred, no matter how hot and still the air might be below. Now she thought of the tree with a new excitement, for why, if one climbed it at break of day, could not one see all the world, and easily discover whence the white heron flew, and mark the place, and find the hidden nest?

What a spirit of adventure, what wild ambition! What fancied triumph and delight and glory for the later morning when she could make known the secret! It was almost too real and too great for the childish heart to bear.

All night the door of the little house stood open, and the whippoorwills came and sang upon the very step. The young sportsman and his old hostess were sound asleep, but Sylvia's great design kept her broad awake and watching. She forgot to think of sleep. The short summer night seemed as long as the winter darkness, and at last when the whippoorwills ceased, and she was afraid the morning would after all come too soon, she stole out of the house and followed the pasture path through the woods, hastening toward the open ground beyond, listening with a sense of comfort and companionship to the drowsy twitter of a half-awakened bird, whose perch she had jarred in passing. Alas, if the great wave of human interest which flooded for the first time this dull little life should sweep away the satisfactions of an existence heart to heart with nature and the dumb life of the forest!

There was the huge tree asleep yet in the paling moonlight, and small and hopeful Sylvia began with utmost bravery to mount to the top of it, with tingling, eager blood coursing the channels of her whole frame, with her bare feet and fingers, that pinched and held like bird's claws to the monstrous ladder reaching up, up, almost to the sky itself. First she must mount the white oak tree that grew alongside, where she was almost lost among the dark branches and the green leaves heavy and wet with dew; a bird fluttered off its nest, and a red squirrel ran to and fro and scolded pettishly at the harmless housebreaker. Sylvia felt her way easily. She had often climbed there, and knew that higher still one of the oak's upper branches chafed against the pine trunk, just where its lower boughs were set close together. There, when she made the dangerous pass from one tree to the other, the great enterprise would really begin.

She crept out along the swaying oak limb at last, and took the daring step across into the old pine-tree. The way was harder than she thought; she must reach far and hold fast, the sharp dry twigs caught and held her and scratched her like angry talons, the pitch made her thin little fingers clumsy and stiff as she went round and round the tree's great stem, higher and higher upward. The sparrows and robins in the woods below were beginning to wake and twitter to the dawn, yet it seemed much lighter there aloft in the pine-tree, and the child knew that she must hurry if her project were to be of any use.

The tree seemed to lengthen itself out as she went up, and to reach farther and farther upward. It was like a great main-mast to the voyaging earth; it must truly have been amazed that morning through all its ponderous frame as it felt this determined spark of human spirit creeping and climbing from higher branch to branch. Who knows how steadily the least twigs held themselves to advantage this light, weak creature on her way! The old pine must have loved his new dependent. More than all the hawks, and bats, and moths, and even the sweet-voiced thrushes, was the brave, beating heart of the solitary gray-eyed child. And the tree stood still and held away the winds that June morning while the dawn grew bright in the east.

Sylvia's face was like a pale star, if one had seen it from the ground, when the last thorny bough was past, and she stood trembling and tired but wholly triumphant, high in the tree-top. Yes, there was the sea with the dawning sun making a golden dazzle over it, and toward that glorious east flew two hawks with slow-moving pinions.[3] How low they looked in the air from that height when before one had only seen them far up, and dark against the blue sky. Their gray feathers were as soft as moths; they seemed only a little way from the tree, and Sylvia felt as if she too could go flying away among the clouds. Westward, the woodlands and farms reached miles and miles into the distance; here and there were church steeples, and white villages; truly it was a vast and awesome world.

The birds sang louder and louder. At last the sun came up bewilderingly bright. Sylvia could see the white sails of ships out at sea, and the clouds that were purple and rose-colored and yellow at first began to fade away. Where was the white heron's nest in the sea of green branches, and was this wonderful sight and pageant of the world the only reward for having climbed to such a giddy height? Now look down again, Sylvia, where the green marsh is set among the shining birches and dark hemlocks; there where you saw the white heron once you will see him again; look, look! a white spot of him like a single floating feather comes up from the dead hemlock and grows larger, and rises, and comes close at last, and goes by the landmark pine with steady sweep of wing and outstretched slender neck and crested head. And wait! wait! do not move a foot or a finger, little girl, do not send an arrow of light and consciousness from your two eager eyes, for the heron has perched on a pine bough not far beyond yours, and cries back to his mate on the nest, and plumes his feathers for the new day!

The child gives a long sigh a minute later when a company of shouting catbirds comes also to the tree, and vexed by their fluttering and lawlessness the solemn heron goes away. She knows his secret now, the wild, light, slender bird that floats and wavers, and goes back like an arrow presently to his home in the green world beneath. Then Sylvia, well satisfied, makes her perilous way down again, not daring to look far below the branch she stands on, ready to cry sometimes because her fingers ache and her lamed feet slip. Wondering over and over

---

[3] Wings or wing feathers.

again what the stranger would say to her, and what he would think when she told him how to find his way straight to the heron's nest.

"Sylvy, Sylvy!" called the busy old grandmother again and again, but nobody answered, and the small husk bed was empty, and Sylvia had disappeared.

The guest waked from a dream, and remembering his day's pleasure hurried to dress himself that it might sooner begin. He was sure from the way the shy little girl looked once or twice yesterday that she had at least seen the white heron, and now she must really be persuaded to tell. Here she comes now, paler than ever, and her worn old frock is torn and tattered, and smeared with pine pitch. The grandmother and the sportsman stand in the door together and question her, and the splendid moment has come to speak of the dead hemlock-tree by the green marsh.

But Sylvia does not speak after all, though the old grandmother fretfully rebukes her, and the young man's kind appealing eyes are looking straight in her own. He can make them rich with money; he has promised it, and they are poor now. He is so well worth making happy, and he waits to hear the story she can tell.

No, she must keep silence! What is it that suddenly forbids her and makes her dumb? Has she been nine years growing, and now, when the great world for the first time puts out a hand to her, must she thrust it aside for a bird's sake? The murmur of the pine's green branches is in her ears, she remembers how the white heron came flying through the golden air and how they watched the sea and the morning together, and Sylvia cannot speak; she cannot tell the heron's secret and give its life away.

Dear loyalty, that suffered a sharp pang as the guest went away disappointed later in the day, that could have served and followed him and loved him as a dog loves! Many a night Sylvia heard the echo of his whistle haunting the pasture path as she came home with the loitering cow. She forgot even her sorrow at the sharp report of his gun and the piteous sight of thrushes and sparrows dropping silent to the ground, their songs hushed and their pretty feathers stained and wet with blood. Were the birds better friends than their hunter might have been,—who can tell? Whatever treasures were lost to her, woodlands and summer-time, remember! Bring your gifts and graces and tell your secrets to this lonely country child!

1886

Kate Chopin
(1851–1904)

The publication of *The Awakening* in 1899 shocked readers who were accustomed to thinking of Kate Chopin's stories as "agreeable" sketches of Creole and Cajun life. Along with the theme of infidelity, the manifest sensuality of the novel evoked condemnation from many quarters. Recalling that "Miss Chopin" had created "sweet and lovable characters," an unidentified admonitory reviewer said it was wrong for this writer of "great refinement and poetic grace to enter the overworked field of sex fiction." To examine *The Awakening* in the context of Chopin's earlier fiction, however, is to see that it entered no field, over-worked or not; rather, it extended the borders of an area in which Chopin had long been working. Nor were the gender issues that the work raises new to her writings. As Chopin biographer Per Seyersted has noted, the heroines of Chopin's three earliest stories could be labeled as "feminine," "emancipated," and "modern," respectively, in the existentialist writer Simone de Beauvoir's sense of these terms—suggesting that Chopin was long pre-occupied with female characters who sought to establish and maintain their identities in a partriarchal society.

Katherine O'Flaherty was born in St. Louis in 1851 to Thomas O'Flaherty, a wealthy merchant, and Eliza Faris, a French Creole aristocrat. After losing her father in a train wreck in 1855, young Kate spent much of her time listening to her great-grandmother, Mme. Charleville, describe Natchitoches (pronounced Nack-uh-tush) Parish in Louisiana and embellish the already racy histories of the settlers of St. Louis. Later, Kate received a Catholic convent-school education before entering St. Louis society as one of the promi-nent belles of 1868. Although she complained to her diary that St. Louis party life was "a nuisance," she participated fully before marrying Oscar Chopin, a Louisiana native, in 1870 and moving to New Orleans. The two had six children, for whom Kate Chopin cared dutifully; the Chopins ran a cotton plantation and a general store. In 1879 the young family moved to Cloutierville in Natchitoches Parish, where they remained until Oscar's death from swamp fever in 1883. The grief-stricken widow continued her husband's business for a year before returning to St. Louis, where she again faced the death of a loved one when her mother died suddenly in 1885.

Hoping to dispel some of her despair, Chopin's physician and close friend, Frederick Kolbenheyer, encouraged her to read more widely and to begin writing fiction. Chopin attempted poetry as well as short stories; in fact, her first printed work is a short poem, "If It Might Be," which appeared in the magazine *America* in January 1889. Quickly recog-nizing that her work was "crude and unformed," Chopin studied "to better her style," emulating the New England local-color writers Sarah Orne Jewett and Mary E. Wilkins Freeman as well as the French naturalists Gustave Flaubert, Émile Zola, and Guy de Maupassant. At the same time, Kolbenheyer encouraged her to read the work of the biolo-gists Charles Darwin and Thomas H. Huxley and of the philosopher Herbert Spencer; their work contributed to her own version of naturalism.

Chopin's novel from this period, *At Fault* (1890), received far less acclaim than did the short stories she wrote for *Vogue, Century, Harper's Young People,* and similar maga-zines. In 1894 she published twenty-three of these stories under the title *Bayou Folk,* a collection one critic termed "the best literary work that has come out of the Southland in a long time" (although another praised it more faintly as a group of "clever and charming" vignettes of Creole life). Both this collection and the subsequent *A Night in Acadie* (1897) were generally well received; yet, laudatory as most of Chopin's contemporaries were, they seem to have regarded her fiction as limited in scope and regional in achievement. Perhaps they overlooked what we see as fundamental human issues because of precon-ceived ideas about the work of local-color writers and because Chopin rarely loaded her fiction with moral judgments. However, even in her early stories she addresses problems of race and class tensions, of racially mixed marriage, of women choosing between mar-riage and career, of people considering divorce, and of couples seeking to have "modern" marriages in which the woman is not a subjugated figure. This range of concerns (sug-gested in such stories as "Désirée's Baby" [1893] and "The Storm" [1898]) demonstrates Chopin's continued interest in confronting the problems that exist both for women who accept conventional roles and women who seek to reject them. Her emphasis on women's

THE
AWAKENING
BY
KATE CHOPIN

MDCCCXCIX

The cover of the first edition of Kate Chopin's Awakening.

struggles becomes still more obvious: within weeks of receiving the preliminary reviews of *Bayou Folk,* Chopin wrote "The Story of an Hour" (1894), the startling sketch of Louise Mallard's reaction to her husband's supposed death, and an eloquent example of how Chopin conflated issues of freedom, personal identity, and marital status.

Issues of female identity and autonomy are most apparent in Chopin's masterpiece, *The Awakening.* Set on Grand Isle (a resort island off the Louisiana coast) and in New Orleans, the novel contrasts Edna Pontellier with the perfect "mother-woman" and the eccentric artist, one readily accepted by society, the other tolerated—and implies that this same society cannot imagine the kind of autonomy Edna seeks. Although she is similar to Flaubert's Emma Bovary in enjoying her sexual liberation, Edna is less concerned with the erotic than with the close connections she perceives between sexual and social independence. The story of Edna's growth toward personal, emotional, and sexual liberation concludes, however, not only with the heroine's suicide, but in effect with the author's artistic death. Within months after its publication, *The Awakening* was banned by St. Louis libraries, Chopin's third collection of stories was refused by her publisher, and former friends lost interest in her company. That combination of events prompted her to cease writing almost entirely; she died soon afterward in 1904. Virtually dismissed from the literary scene, Chopin was not rediscovered and reassessed as a writer until the 1950s. In the decades since, scholars have come to value her work as a link between local-color writing and naturalism and to praise her insight into the profound relation between the quest for female autonomy and social attitudes toward sexuality and motherhood.

Suggested Readings: *Bayou Folk,* ed. W. Berthoff, 1970. *Portraits: Short Stories by Kate Chopin,* ed. H. Taylor, 1979. *The Awakening and Selected Stories,* ed. S. M. Gilbert, 1984. D. Rankin, *Kate Chopin and Her Creole Stories,* 1932. M. Springer, *Edith Wharton and Kate Chopin: A Reference Guide,* 1976. P. Seyersted, *Kate Chopin: A Critical Biography,* 1980. H. Bloom, ed., *Kate Chopin,* 1987. T. Bonner, *The Kate Chopin Companion: With Chopin's Translations From French Fiction,* 1988. W. Martin, ed., *New Essays on The Awakening,* 1988. A. S. Elfenbien, *Women on the Color Line: Evolving Stereotypes and the Writings of George Washington Cable, Grace King, and Kate Chopin,* 1989. H. Taylor, *Gender, Race, and Region in the Writings of Grace King, Ruth McEnery Stuart, and Kate Chopin,* 1989.

Text Used: *The Complete Works of Kate Chopin,* Vol. I, ed. P. Seyersted, 1969.

DÉSIRÉE'S BABY*

As the day was pleasant, Madame Valmondé drove over to L'Abri[1] to see Désirée and the baby.

It made her laugh to think of Désirée with a baby. Why, it seemed but yesterday that Désirée was little more than a baby herself; when Monsieur in riding through the gateway of Valmondé had found her lying asleep in the shadow of the big stone pillar.

The little one awoke in his arms and began to cry for "Dada." That was as much as she could do or say. Some people thought she might have strayed there of her own accord, for she was of the toddling age. The prevailing belief was that she had been purposely left by a party of Texans, whose canvas-covered wagon, late in the day, had crossed the ferry that Coton Maïs kept, just below the plantation. In time Madame Valmondé abandoned every speculation but the one that Désirée had been sent to her by a beneficent Providence to be the child of her affection, seeing that she was without child of the flesh. For the girl grew to be beautiful and gentle, affectionate and sincere,—the idol of Valmondé.

It was no wonder, when she stood one day against the stone pillar in whose shadow she had lain asleep, eighteen years before, that Armand Aubigny riding by and seeing her there, had fallen in love with her. That was the way all the Aubignys fell in love, as if struck by a pistol shot. The wonder was that he had not loved her before; for he had known her since his father brought him home from Paris, a boy of eight, after his mother died there. The passion that awoke in him that day, when he saw her at the gate, swept along like an avalanche, or like a prairie fire, or like anything that drives headlong over all obstacles.

Monsieur Valmondé grew practical and wanted things well considered: that is, the girl's obscure origin. Armand looked into her eyes and did not care. He was reminded that she was nameless. What did it matter about a name when he could give her one of the oldest and proudest in Louisiana? He ordered the *corbeille*[2]

---

* First published in *Vogue* in 1893.   [1] "Refuge" (French), an ironic name for a plantation.
[2] Wedding presents given by a bridegroom (French).

from Paris, and contained himself with what patience he could until it arrived; then they were married.

Madame Valmondé had not seen Désirée and the baby for four weeks. When she reached L'Abri she shuddered at the first sight of it, as she always did. It was a sad looking place, which for many years had not known the gentle presence of a mistress, old Monsieur Aubigny having married and buried his wife in France, and she having loved her own land too well ever to leave it. The roof came down steep and black like a cowl, reaching out beyond the wide galleries that encircled the yellow stuccoed house. Big, solemn oaks grew close to it, and their thick-leaved, far-reaching branches shadowed it like a pall. Young Aubigny's rule was a strict one, too, and under it his negroes had forgotten how to be gay, as they had been during the old master's easy-going and indulgent lifetime.

The young mother was recovering slowly, and lay full length, in her soft white muslins and laces, upon a couch. The baby was beside her, upon her arm, where he had fallen asleep, at her breast. The yellow nurse woman sat beside a window fanning herself.

Madame Valmondé bent her portly figure over Désirée and kissed her, holding her an instant tenderly in her arms. Then she turned to the child.

"This is not the baby!" she exclaimed, in startled tones. French was the language spoken at Valmondé in those days.

"I knew you would be astonished," laughed Désirée, "at the way he has grown. The little *cochon de lait!*[3] Look at his legs, mamma, and his hands and finger-nails,—real finger-nails. Zandrine had to cut them this morning. Isn't it true, Zandrine?"

The woman bowed her turbaned head majestically, "Mais si,[4] Madame."

"And the way he cries," went on Désirée, "is deafening. Armand heard him the other day as far away as La Blanche's cabin."

Madame Valmondé had never removed her eyes from the child. She lifted it and walked with it over to the window that was lightest. She scanned the baby narrowly, then looked as searchingly at Zandrine, whose face was turned to gaze across the fields.

"Yes, the child has grown, has changed," said Madame Valmondé, slowly, as she replaced it beside its mother. "What does Armand say?"

Désirée's face became suffused with a glow that was happiness itself.

"Oh, Armand is the proudest father in the parish, I believe, chiefly because it is a boy, to bear his name; though he says not,—that he would have loved a girl as well. But I know it isn't true. I know he says that to please me. And mamma," she added, drawing Madame Valmondé's head down to her, and speaking in a whisper, "he hasn't punished one of them—not one of them—since baby is born. Even Négrillon, who pretended to have burnt his leg that he might rest from work—he only laughed, and said Négrillon was a great scamp. Oh, mamma, I'm so happy; it frightens me."

What Désirée said was true. Marriage, and later the birth of his son had softened Armand Aubigny's imperious and exacting nature greatly. This was what made the gentle Désirée so happy, for she loved him desperately. When he frowned she trembled, but loved him. When he smiled, she asked no greater

---

[3] "Suckling-pig" (French), used as an endearment.   [4] "But yes" (French).

blessing of God. But Armand's dark, handsome face had not often been disfigured by frowns since the day he fell in love with her.

When the baby was about three months old, Désirée awoke one day to the conviction that there was something in the air menacing her peace. It was at first too subtle to grasp. It had only been a disquieting suggestion; an air of mystery among the blacks; unexpected visits from far-off neighbors who could hardly account for their coming. Then a strange, an awful change in her husband's manner, which she dared not ask him to explain. When he spoke to her, it was with averted eyes, from which the old love-light seemed to have gone out. He absented himself from home; and when there, avoided her presence and that of her child, without excuse. And the very spirit of Satan seemed suddenly to take hold of him in his dealings with the slaves. Désirée was miserable enough to die.

She sat in her room, one hot afternoon, in her *peignoir,*[5] listlessly drawing through her fingers the strands of her long, silky brown hair that hung about her shoulders. The baby, half naked, lay asleep upon her own great mahogany bed, that was like a sumptuous throne, with its satin-lined half-canopy. One of La Blanche's little quadroon[6] boys—half naked too—stood fanning the child slowly with a fan of peacock feathers. Désirée's eyes had been fixed absently and sadly upon the baby, while she was striving to penetrate the threatening mist that she felt closing about her. She looked from her child to the boy who stood beside him, and back again; over and over. "Ah!" It was a cry that she could not help; which she was not conscious of having uttered. The blood turned like ice in her veins, and a clammy moisture gathered upon her face.

She tried to speak to the little quadroon boy; but no sound would come, at first. When he heard his name uttered, he looked up, and his mistress was pointing to the door. He laid aside the great, soft fan, and obediently stole away, over the polished floor, on his bare tiptoes.

She stayed motionless, with gaze riveted upon her child, and her face the picture of fright.

Presently her husband entered the room, and without noticing her, went to a table and began to search among some papers which covered it.

"Armand," she called to him, in a voice which must have stabbed him, if he was human. But he did not notice. "Armand," she said again. Then she rose and tottered towards him. "Armand," she panted once more, clutching his arm, "look at our child. What does it mean? tell me."

He coldly but gently loosened her fingers from about his arm and thrust the hand away from him. "Tell me what it means!" she cried despairingly.

"It means," he answered lightly, "that the child is not white; it means that you are not white."

A quick conception of all that this accusation meant for her nerved her with unwonted courage to deny it. "It is a lie; it is not true, I am white! Look at my hair, it is brown; and my eyes are gray, Armand, you know they are gray. And my skin is fair," seizing his wrist. "Look at my hand; whiter than yours, Armand," she laughed hysterically.

"As white as La Blanche's," he returned cruelly; and went away leaving her alone with their child.

---

[5] A loose dressing gown (French).   [6] Of one-quarter African ancestry.

When she could hold a pen in her hand, she sent a despairing letter to Madame Valmondé.

"My mother, they tell me I am not white. Armand has told me I am not white. For God's sake tell them it is not true. You must know it is not true. I shall die. I must die. I cannot be so unhappy, and live."

The answer that came was as brief:

"My own Désirée: Come home to Valmondé; back to your mother who loves you. Come with your child."

When the letter reached Désirée she went with it to her husband's study, and laid it open upon the desk before which he sat. She was like a stone image: silent, white, motionless after she placed it there.

In silence he ran his cold eyes over the written words. He said nothing. "Shall I go, Armand?" she asked in tones sharp with agonized suspense.

"Yes, go."

"Do you want me to go?"

"Yes, I want you to go."

He thought Almighty God had dealt cruelly and unjustly with him; and felt, somehow, that he was paying Him back in kind when he stabbed thus into his wife's soul. Moreover he no longer loved her, because of the unconscious injury she had brought upon his home and his name.

She turned away like one stunned by a blow, and walked slowly towards the door, hoping he would call her back.

"Good-by, Armand," she moaned.

He did not answer her. That was his last blow at fate.

Désirée went in search of her child. Zandrine was pacing the sombre gallery with it. She took the little one from the nurse's arms with no word of explanation, and descending the steps, walked away, under the live-oak branches.

It was an October afternoon; the sun was just sinking. Out in the still fields the negroes were picking cotton.

Désirée had not changed the thin white garment nor the slippers which she wore. Her hair was uncovered and the sun's rays brought a golden gleam from its brown meshes. She did not take the broad, beaten road which led to the far-off plantation of Valmondé. She walked across a deserted field, where the stubble bruised her tender feet, so delicately shod, and tore her thin gown to shreds.

She disappeared among the reeds and willows that grew thick along the banks of the deep, sluggish bayou; and she did not come back again.

Some weeks later there was a curious scene enacted at L'Abri. In the centre of the smoothly swept back yard was a great bonfire. Armand Aubigny sat in the wide hallway that commanded a view of the spectacle; and it was he who dealt out to a half dozen negroes the material which kept this fire ablaze.

A graceful cradle of willow, with all its dainty furbishings, was laid upon the pyre, which had already been fed with the richness of a priceless *layette*.[7] Then there were silk gowns, and velvet and satin ones added to these; laces, too, and embroideries; bonnets and gloves; for the *corbeille* had been of rare quality.

The last thing to go was a tiny bundle of letters; innocent little scriblings that

---

[7] Clothes and linens for a baby (French).

Désirée had sent to him during the days of their espousal. There was the remnant of one back in the drawer from which he took them. But it was not Désirée's; it was part of an old letter from his mother to his father. He read it. She was thanking God for the blessing of her husband's love:—

"But, above all," she wrote, "night and day, I thank the good God for having so arranged our lives that our dear Armand will never know that his mother, who adores him, belongs to the race that is cursed with the brand of slavery."

1892, 1893

THE STORY OF AN HOUR*

Knowing that Mrs. Mallard was afflicted with a heart trouble, great care was taken to break to her as gently as possible the news of her husband's death.

It was her sister Josephine who told her, in broken sentences; veiled hints that revealed in half concealing. Her husband's friend Richards was there, too, near her. It was he who had been in the newspaper office when intelligence of the railroad disaster was received, with Brently Mallard's name leading the list of "killed." He had only taken the time to assure himself of its truth by a second telegram, and had hastened to forestall any less careful, less tender friend in bearing the sad message.

She did not hear the story as many women have heard the same, with a paralyzed inability to accept its significance. She wept at once, with sudden, wild abandonment, in her sister's arms. When the storm of grief had spent itself she went away to her room alone. She would have no one follow her.

There stood, facing the open window, a comfortable, roomy armchair. Into this she sank, pressed down by a physical exhaustion that haunted her body and seemed to reach into her soul.

She could see in the open square before her house the tops of trees that were all aquiver with the new spring life. The delicious breath of rain was in the air. In the street below a peddler was crying his wares. The notes of a distant song which some one was singing reached her faintly, and countless sparrows were twittering in the eaves.

There were patches of blue sky showing here and there through the clouds that had met and piled one above the other in the west facing her window.

She sat with her head thrown back upon the cushion of the chair, quite motionless, except when a sob came up into her throat and shook her, as a child who has cried itself to sleep continues to sob in its dreams.

She was young, with a fair, calm face, whose lines bespoke repression and even a certain strength. But now there was a dull stare in her eyes, whose gaze was fixed away off yonder on one of those patches of blue sky. It was not a glance of reflection, but rather indicated a suspension of intelligent thought.

There was something coming to her and she was waiting for it, fearfully. What was it? She did not know; it was too subtle and elusive to name. But she felt it,

---

* First published in *Vogue* in 1894 as "The Dream of an Hour."

creeping out of the sky, reaching toward her through the sounds, the scents, the color that filled the air.

Now her bosom rose and fell tumultuously. She was beginning to recognize this thing that was approaching to possess her, and she was striving to beat it back with her will—as powerless as her two white slender hands would have been.

When she abandoned herself a little whispered word escaped her slightly parted lips. She said it over and over under her breath: "free, free, free!" The vacant stare and the look of terror that had followed it went from her eyes. They stayed keen and bright. Her pulses beat fast, and the coursing blood warmed and relaxed every inch of her body.

She did not stop to ask if it were or were not a monstrous joy that held her. A clear and exalted perception enabled her to dismiss the suggestion as trivial.

She knew that she would weep again when she saw the kind, tender hands folded in death; the face that had never looked save with love upon her, fixed and gray and dead. But she saw beyond that bitter moment a long procession of years to come that would belong to her absolutely. And she opened and spread her arms out to them in welcome.

There would be no one to live for her during those coming years: she would live for herself. There would be no powerful will bending hers in that blind persistence with which men and women believe they have a right to impose a private will upon a fellow-creature. A kind intention or a cruel intention made the act seem no less a crime as she looked upon it in that brief moment of illumination.

And yet she had loved him—sometimes. Often she had not. What did it matter! What could love, the unsolved mystery, count for in face of this possession of self-assertion which she suddenly recognized as the strongest impulse of her being!

"Free! Body and soul free!" she kept whispering.

Josephine was kneeling before the closed door with her lips to the keyhole, imploring for admission, "Louise, open the door! I beg; open the door—you will make yourself ill. What are you doing, Louise? For heaven's sake open the door."

"Go away. I am not making myself ill." No; she was drinking in a very elixir of life through that open window.

Her fancy was running riot along those days ahead of her. Spring days, and summer days, and all sorts of days that would be her own. She breathed a quick prayer that life might be long. It was only yesterday she had thought with a shudder that life might be long.

She arose at length and opened the door to her sister's importunities. There was a feverish triumph in her eyes, and she carried herself unwittingly like a goddess of Victory. She clasped her sister's waist, and together they descended the stairs. Richards stood waiting for them at the bottom.

Some one was opening the front door with a latchkey. It was Brently Mallard who entered, a little travel-stained, composedly carrying his grip-sack and umbrella. He had been far from the scene of accident, and did not even know there had been one. He stood amazed at Josephine's piercing cry; at Richards' quick motion to screen him from the view of his wife.

But Richards was too late.

When the doctors came they said she had died of heart disease—of joy that kills.

1894

Charles W. Chesnutt
(1858–1932)

Although he was born in 1858 in Cleveland, Ohio, and spent much of his childhood and adult life in that area, Charles Waddell Chesnutt set most of his fiction in the South. When he was eight his parents moved the family back to Fayetteville, North Carolina (which they had fled during the Civil War), and Chesnutt remained there until he was twenty-five. During these formative years he married Susan Perry from Fayetteville (in 1878) and developed an interest in the regional folkways that later became an integral part of his fiction.

Chesnutt was a light-skinned African American who could probably have "passed" for white had he desired to do so. However, he chose to live and work as a black, a choice that limited his career opportunities but did not stop him from achieving success. Largely self-educated, he became a teacher and by age twenty-two was the principal of the State Colored Normal School in Fayetteville. Hoping for greater opportunity, he went to New York City in 1883 and became a legal stenographer. Six months later he and his wife moved to Cleveland, where he passed the Ohio bar exam with high marks and established a successful legal-stenography firm. Chesnutt remained a court reporter until his death in 1932.

Chesnutt's first nationally recognized publication, "The Goophered Grapevine," appeared in the August 1887 issue of the *Atlantic Monthly*. This piece combined dialect with Chesnutt's awareness of southern folk customs. In 1899 his first collection of short stories, *The Conjure Woman,* was published. The narrator of these tales, an ex-slave named Uncle Julius McAdoo, was influenced in part by Joel Chandler Harris's figure Uncle Remus, although the powerful irony of such stories as "Sis' Becky's Pickaninny" comes directly from Chesnutt's personal vision. Later in 1899 Chesnutt published a biography of Frederick Douglass, *Life of Frederick Douglass,* and a second volume of short stories, *The Wife of His Youth and Other Stories of the Color Line.* Following these works came three novels more explicit in their criticism of American society: *The House Behind the Cedars* (1900), *The Marrow of Tradition* (1901), and *The Colonel's Dream* (1905).

Throughout his work Chesnutt was concerned with the racial situation in the post-Civil War South. Many of his stories deal with light-skinned blacks passing for white, with racial intermarriage, and with racial tensions arising from economic and social conditions. His belief that African Americans should be assimilated into the American mainstream was tempered by his perception of racial injustice. As a conservative Chesnutt believed that assimilation can best occur when African Americans are educated for careers that match their abilities. As a realist he deplored the manner in which the evils of prejudice choked off such possibilities.

Chesnutt wrote six novels after 1905, none of them published. But he remained active in civic and professional affairs in Cleveland. In 1928 the National Association for the Advancement of Colored People awarded him the Spingarn Medal for his "pioneer work as a literary artist depicting the life and struggles of Americans of Negro descent, and for his long and useful career as scholar, worker, and freeman of one of America's greatest cities."

Suggested Readings: *The Conjure Woman*, 1899. *The Marrow of Tradition*, 1901. *The Colonel's Dream*, 1905. *The Short Fiction of Charles W. Chesnutt*, ed. S. L. Render, 1980. H. M. Chesnutt, *Charles Waddell Chesnutt, Pioneer of the Color Line*, 1952. J. N. Heermance, *Charles W. Chesnutt: America's First Great Black Novelist*, 1974. C. W. Ellison and E. W. Metcalf, Jr., *Charles W. Chesnutt: A Reference Guide*, 1977. F. R. Keller, *An American Crusade: The Life of Charles Waddell Chesnutt*, 1978. W. L. Andrews, *The Literary Career of Charles W. Chesnutt*, 1980. S. L. Render, *Charles W. Chesnutt*, 1980.

Text Used: *The Wife of His Youth and Other Stories of the Color Line*, 1899.

THE PASSING OF GRANDISON*

I

When it is said that it was done to please a woman, there ought perhaps to be enough said to explain anything; for what a man will not do to please a woman is yet to be discovered. Nevertheless, it might be well to state a few preliminary facts to make it clear why young Dick Owens tried to run one of his father's negro men off to Canada.

In the early fifties,[1] when the growth of anti-slavery sentiment and the constant drain of fugitive slaves into the North had so alarmed the slaveholders of the border States as to lead to the passage of the Fugitive Slave Law,[2] a young white man from Ohio, moved by compassion for the sufferings of a certain bondman who happened to have a "hard master," essayed to help the slave to freedom. The attempt was discovered and frustrated; the abductor was tried and convicted for slave-stealing, and sentenced to a term of imprisonment in the penitentiary. His death, after the expiration of only a small part of the sentence, from cholera contracted while nursing stricken fellow prisoners, lent to the case a melancholy interest that made it famous in anti-slavery annals.

Dick Owens had attended the trial. He was a youth of about twenty-two, intelligent, handsome, and amiable, but extremely indolent, in a graceful and gentlemanly way; or, as old Judge Fenderson put it more than once, he was lazy as the Devil,—a mere figure of speech, of course, and not one that did justice to the Enemy of Mankind. When asked why he never did anything serious, Dick would good-naturedly reply, with a well-modulated drawl, that he didn't have to. His father was rich; there was but one other child, an unmarried daughter, who because of poor health would probably never marry, and Dick was therefore heir presumptive to a large estate. Wealth or social position he did not need to seek, for he was born to both. Charity Lomax had shamed him into studying law, but notwithstanding an hour or so a day spent at old Judge Fenderson's office, he did not make remarkable headway in his legal studies.

"What Dick needs," said the judge, who was fond of tropes,[3] as became a scholar, and of horses, as was befitting a Kentuckian, "is the whip of necessity, or

---

* First published in the *Atlantic Monthly* in July 1898.   [1] The 1850s.
[2] Enacted in 1850, it allowed slaves who had escaped to free states to be recaptured and returned to their owners and made aiding an escaping slave illegal.
[3] Figures of speech; a rhetorical device, as in the metaphor "whip of necessity."

the spur of ambition. If he had either, he would soon need the snaffle to hold him back."

But all Dick required, in fact, to prompt him to the most remarkable thing he accomplished before he was twenty-five, was a mere suggestion from Charity Lomax. The story was never really known to but two persons until after the war, when it came out because it was a good story and there was no particular reason for its concealment.

Young Owens had attended the trial of this slave-stealer, or martyr,—either or both,—and, when it was over, had gone to call on Charity Lomax, and, while they sat on the veranda after sundown, had told her all about the trial. He was a good talker, as his career in later years disclosed, and described the proceedings very graphically.

"I confess," he admitted, "that while my principles were against the prisoner, my sympathies were on his side. It appeared that he was of good family, and that he had an old father and mother, respectable people, dependent upon him for support and comfort in their declining years. He had been led into the matter by pity for a negro whose master ought to have been run out of the county long ago for abusing his slaves. If it had been merely a question of old Sam Briggs's negro, nobody would have cared anything about it. But father and the rest of them stood on the principle of the thing, and told the judge so, and the fellow was sentenced to three years in the penitentiary."

Miss Lomax had listened with lively interest.

"I've always hated old Sam Briggs," she said emphatically, "ever since the time he broke a negro's leg with a piece of cordwood.[4] When I hear of a cruel deed it makes the Quaker blood that came from my grandmother assert itself. Personally I wish that all Sam Briggs's negroes would run away. As for the young man, I regard him as a hero. He dared something for humanity. I could love a man who would take such chances for the sake of others."

"Could you love me, Charity, if I did something heroic?"

"You never will, Dick. You're too lazy for any use. You'll never do anything harder than playing cards or fox-hunting."

"Oh, come now, sweetheart! I've been courting you for a year, and it's the hardest work imaginable. Are you never going to love me?" he pleaded.

His hand sought hers, but she drew it back beyond his reach.

"I'll never love you, Dick Owens, until you have done something. When that time comes, I'll think about it."

"But it takes so long to do anything worth mentioning, and I don't want to wait. One must read two years to become a lawyer, and work five more to make a reputation. We shall both be gray by then."

"Oh, I don't know," she rejoined. "It doesn't require a lifetime for a man to prove that he is a man. This one did something, or at least tried to."

"Well, I'm willing to attempt as much as any other man. What do you want me to do, sweetheart? Give me a test."

"Oh, dear me!" said Charity, "I don't care what you *do*, so you do *something*. Really, come to think of it, why should I care whether you do anything or not?"

"I'm sure I don't know why you should, Charity," rejoined Dick humbly, "for I'm aware that I'm not worthy of it."

---

[4] Wood stacked in a cord, a pile of a specific size.

"Except that I do hate," she added, relenting slightly, "to see a really clever man so utterly lazy and good for nothing."

"Thank you, my dear; a word of praise from you has sharpened my wits already. I have an idea! Will you love me if *I* run a negro off to Canada?"

"What nonsense!" said Charity scornfully. "You must be losing your wits. Steal another man's slave, indeed, while your father owns a hundred!"

"Oh, there'll be no trouble about that," responded Dick lightly; "I'll run off one of the old man's; we've got too many anyway. It may not be quite as difficult as the other man found it, but it will be just as unlawful, and will demonstrate what I am capable of."

"Seeing's believing," replied Charity. "Of course, what you are talking about now is merely absurd. I'm going away for three weeks, to visit my aunt in Tennessee. If you're able to tell me, when I return, that you've done something to prove your quality, I'll—well, you may come and tell me about it."

II

Young Owens got up about nine o'clock next morning, and while making his toilet put some questions to his personal attendant, a rather bright looking young mulatto[5] of about his own age.

"Tom," said Dick.

"Yas, Mars Dick," responded the servant.

"I'm going on a trip North. Would you like to go with me?"

Now, if there was anything that Tom would have liked to make, it was a trip North. It was something he had long contemplated in the abstract, but had never been able to muster up sufficient courage to attempt in the concrete. He was prudent enough, however, to dissemble his feelings.

"I wouldn't min' it, Mars Dick, ez long ez you'd take keer er me an' fetch me home all right."

Tom's eyes belied his words, however, and his young master felt well assured that Tom needed only a good opportunity to make him run away. Having a comfortable home, and a dismal prospect in case of failure, Tom was not likely to take any desperate chances; but young Owens was satisfied that in a free State but little persuasion would be required to lead Tom astray. With a very logical and characteristic desire to gain his end with the least necessary expenditure of effort, he decided to take Tom with him, if his father did not object.

Colonel Owens had left the house when Dick went to breakfast, so Dick did not see his father till luncheon.

"Father," he remarked casually to the colonel, over the fried chicken, "I'm feeling a trifle run down. I imagine my health would be improved somewhat by a little travel and change of scene."

"Why don't you take a trip North?" suggested his father. The colonel added to paternal affection a considerable respect for his son as the heir of a large estate. He himself had been "raised" in comparative poverty, and had laid the foundations of his fortune by hard work; and while he despised the ladder by which he had climbed, he could not entirely forget it, and unconsciously manifested, in his in-

---

[5] A person with one black and one white parent.

tercourse with his son, some of the poor man's deference toward the wealthy and well-born.

"I think I'll adopt your suggestion, sir," replied the son, "and run up to New York; and after I've been there awhile I may go on to Boston for a week or so. I've never been there, you know."

"There are some matters you can talk over with my factor[6] in New York," rejoined the colonel, "and while you are up there among the Yankees, I hope you'll keep your eyes and ears open to find out what the rascally abolitionists are saying and doing. They're becoming altogether too active for our comfort, and entirely too many ungrateful niggers are running away. I hope the conviction of that fellow yesterday may discourage the rest of the breed. I'd just like to catch any one trying to run off one of my darkeys. He'd get short shrift; I don't think any Court would have a chance to try him."

"They are a pestiferous lot," assented Dick, "and dangerous to our institutions. But say, father, if I go North I shall want to take Tom with me."

Now, the colonel, while a very indulgent father, had pronounced views on the subject of negroes, having studied them, as he often said, for a great many years, and, as he asserted oftener still, understanding them perfectly. It is scarcely worth while to say, either, that he valued more highly than if he had inherited them the slaves he had toiled and schemed for.

"I don't think it safe to take Tom up North," he declared, with promptness and decision. "He's a good enough boy, but too smart to trust among those low-down abolitionists. I strongly suspect him of having learned to read, though I can't imagine how. I saw him with a newspaper the other day, and while he pretended to be looking at a woodcut, I'm almost sure he was reading the paper. I think it by no means safe to take him."

Dick did not insist, because he knew it was useless. The colonel would have obliged his son in any other matter, but his negroes were the outward and visible sign of his wealth and station, and therefore sacred to him.

"Whom do you think it safe to take?" asked Dick. "I suppose I'll have to have a body-servant."

"What's the matter with Grandison?" suggested the colonel. "He's handy enough, and I reckon we can trust him. He's too fond of good eating, to risk losing his regular meals; besides, he's sweet on your mother's maid, Betty, and I've promised to let 'em get married before long. I'll have Grandison up, and we'll talk to him. Here, you boy Jack," called the colonel to a yellow youth in the next room who was catching flies and pulling their wings off to pass the time, "go down to the barn and tell Grandison to come here."

"Grandison," said the colonel, when the negro stood before him, hat in hand.

"Yas, marster."

"Haven't I always treated you right?"

"Yas, marster."

"Haven't you always got all you wanted to eat?"

"Yas, marster."

"And as much whiskey and tobacco as was good for you, Grandison?"

"Y-a-s, marster."

"I should just like to know, Grandison, whether you don't think yourself a

[6] Business agent.

great deal better off than those poor free negroes down by the plank road, with no kind master to look after them and no mistress to give them medicine when they're sick and—and"—

"Well, I sh'd jes' reckon I is better off, suh, dan dem low-down free niggers, suh! Ef anybody ax 'em who dey b'long ter, dey has ter say nobody, er e'se lie erbout it. Anybody ax me who I b'longs ter, I ain' got no 'casion ter be shame' ter tell 'em, no, suh, 'deed I ain', suh!"

The colonel was beaming. This was true gratitude, and his feudal heart thrilled at such appreciative homage. What cold-blooded, heartless monsters they were who would break up this blissful relationship of kindly protection on the one hand, of wise subordination and loyal dependence on the other! The colonel always became indignant at the mere thought of such wickedness.

"Grandison," the colonel continued, "your young master Dick is going North for a few weeks, and I am thinking of letting him take you along. I shall send you on this trip, Grandison, in order that you may take care of your young master. He will need some one to wait on him, and no one can ever do it so well as one of the boys brought up with him on the old plantation. I am going to trust him in your hands, and I'm sure you'll do your duty faithfully, and bring him back home safe and sound—to old Kentucky."

Grandison grinned. "Oh yas, marster, I'll take keer er young Mars Dick."

"I want to warn you, though, Grandison," continued the colonel impressively, "against these cussed abolitionists, who try to entice servants from their comfortable homes and their indulgent masters, from the blue skies, the green fields, and the warm sunlight of their southern home, and send them away off yonder to Canada, a dreary country, where the woods are full of wildcats and wolves and bears, where the snow lies up to the eaves of the houses for six months of the year, and the cold is so severe that it freezes your breath and curdles your blood; and where, when runaway niggers get sick and can't work, they are turned out to starve and die, unloved and uncared for. I reckon, Grandison, that you have too much sense to permit yourself to be led astray by any such foolish and wicked people."

"'Deed, suh, I would n' low none er dem cussed, low-down abolitioners ter come nigh me, suh. I'd—I'd—would I be 'lowed ter hit 'em, suh?"

"Certainly, Grandison," replied the colonel, chuckling, "hit 'em as hard as you can. I reckon they'd rather like it. Begad, I believe they would! It would serve 'em right to be hit by a nigger!"

"Er ef I didn't hit 'em, suh," continued Grandison reflectively, "I'd tell Mars Dick, en *he'd* fix 'em. He'd smash de face off'n 'em, suh, I jes' knows he would."

"Oh yes, Grandison, your young master will protect you. You need fear no harm while he is near."

"Dey won't try ter steal me, will dey, marster?" asked the negro, with sudden alarm.

"I don't know, Grandison," replied the colonel, lighting a fresh cigar. "They're a desperate set of lunatics, and there's no telling what they may resort to. But if you stick close to your young master, and remember always that he is your best friend, and understands your real needs, and has your true interests at heart, and if you will be careful to avoid strangers who try to talk to you, you'll stand a fair chance of getting back to your home and your friends. And if you please your master Dick, he'll buy you a present, and a string of beads for Betty to wear when you and she get married in the fall."

"Thanky, marster, thanky, suh," replied Grandison, oozing gratitude at every pore; "you is a good marster, to be sho', suh; yas, 'deed you is. You kin jes' bet me and Mars Dick gwine git 'long jes' lack I wuz own boy ter Mars Dick. En it won't be my fault ef he don' want me fer his boy all de time, w'en we come back home ag'in."

"All right, Grandison, you may go now. You needn't work any more to-day, and here's a piece of tobacco for you off my own plug."

"Thanky, marster, thanky, marster! You is de bes' marster any nigger ever had in dis worl'." And Grandison bowed and scraped and disappeared round the corner, his jaws closing around a large section of the colonel's best tobacco.

"You may take Grandison," said the colonel to his son. "I allow he's abolitionist-proof."

III

Richard Owens, Esq., and servant, from Kentucky, registered at the fashionable New York hostelry for Southerners in those days, a hotel where an atmosphere congenial to Southern institutions was sedulously maintained. But there were negro waiters in the dining-room, and mulatto bell-boys, and Dick had no doubt that Grandison, with the native gregariousness and garrulousness of his race, would foregather and palaver with them sooner or later, and Dick hoped that they would speedily inoculate him with the virus of freedom. For it was not Dick's intention to say anything to his servant about his plan to free him, for obvious reasons. To mention one of them, if Grandison should go away, and by legal process be recaptured, his young master's part in the matter would doubtless become known, which would be embarrassing to Dick, to say the least. If, on the other hand, he should merely give Grandison sufficient latitude, he had no doubt he would eventually lose him. For while not exactly skeptical about Grandison's perfervid loyalty, Dick had been a somewhat keen observer of human nature, in his own indolent way, and based his expectations upon the force of the example and argument that his servant could scarcely fail to encounter. Grandison should have a fair chance to become free by his own initiative; if it should become necessary to adopt other measures to get rid of him, it would be time enough to act when the necessity arose; and Dick Owens was not the youth to take needless trouble.

The young master renewed some acquaintances and made others, and spent a week or two very pleasantly in the best society of the metropolis, easily accessible to a wealthy, well-bred young Southerner, with proper introductions. Young women smiled on him, and young men of convivial habits pressed their hospitalities; but the memory of Charity's sweet, strong face and clear blue eyes made him proof against the blandishments of the one sex and the persuasions of the other. Meanwhile he kept Grandison supplied with pocket-money, and left him mainly to his own devices. Every night when Dick came in he hoped he might have to wait upon himself, and every morning he looked forward with pleasure to the prospect of making his toilet[7] unaided. His hopes, however, were doomed to disappoint-

---

[7] Dressing himself.

ment, for every night when he came in Grandison was on hand with a bootjack, and a nightcap mixed for his young master as the colonel had taught him to mix it, and every morning Grandison appeared with his master's boots blacked and his clothes brushed, and laid his linen out for the day.

"Grandison," said Dick one morning, after finishing his toilet, "this is a chance of your life to go around among your own people and see how they live. Have you met any of them?"

"Yas, suh, I's seen some of 'em. But I don' keer nuffin fer 'em, suh. Dey're diffe'nt f'm de niggers down ou' way. Dey 'lows dey're free, but dey ain' got sense 'nuff ter know dey ain' half as well off as dey would be down Souf, whar dey'd be 'preciated."

When two weeks had passed without any apparent effect of evil example upon Grandison, Dick resolved to go on to Boston, where he thought the atmosphere might prove more favorable to his ends. After he had been at the Revere House for a day or two without losing Grandison, he decided upon slightly different tactics.

Having ascertained from a city directory the addresses of several well-known abolitionists, he wrote them each a letter something like this:—

DEAR FRIEND AND BROTHER:—

A wicked slaveholder from Kentucky, stopping at the Revere House, has dared to insult the liberty-loving people of Boston by bringing his slave into their midst. Shall this be tolerated? Or shall steps be taken in the name of liberty to rescue a fellow-man from bondage? For obvious reasons I can only sign myself,

A FRIEND OF HUMANITY.

That his letter might have an opportunity to prove effective, Dick made it a point to send Grandison away from the hotel on various errands. On one of these occasions Dick watched him for quite a distance down the street. Grandison had scarcely left the hotel when a long-haired, sharp-featured man came out behind him, followed him, soon overtook him, and kept along beside him until they turned the next corner. Dick's hopes were roused by this spectacle, but sank correspondingly when Grandison returned to the hotel. As Grandison said nothing about the encounter, Dick hoped there might be some self-consciousness behind this unexpected reticence, the results of which might develop later on.

But Grandison was on hand again when his master came back to the hotel at night, and was in attendance again in the morning, with hot water, to assist at his master's toilet. Dick sent him on further errands from day to day, and upon one occasion came squarely up to him—inadvertently of course—while Grandison was engaged in conversation with a young white man in clerical garb. When Grandison saw Dick approaching, he edged away from the preacher and hastened toward his master, with a very evident expression of relief upon his countenance.

"Mars Dick," he said, "dese yer abolitioners is jes' pesterin' de life out er me tryin' ter git me ter run away. I don' pay no 'tention ter 'em, but dey riles me so sometimes dat I'm feared I'll hit some of 'em some er dese days, an' dat mought git me inter trouble. I ain' said nuffin' ter you 'bout it, Mars Dick, fer I did n' wanter 'sturb yo' min'; but I don' like it, suh; no, suh, I don'! Is we gwine back home 'fo' long, Mars Dick?"

"We'll be going back soon enough," replied Dick somewhat shortly, while he inwardly cursed the stupidity of a slave who could be free and would not, and registered a secret vow that if he were unable to get rid of Grandison without assassinating him, and were therefore compelled to take him back to Kentucky, he would see that Grandison got a taste of an article of slavery that would make him regret his wasted opportunities. Meanwhile he determined to tempt his servant yet more strongly.

"Grandison," he said next morning, "I'm going away for a day or two, but I shall leave you here. I shall lock up a hundred dollars in this drawer and give you the key. If you need any of it, use it and enjoy yourself,—spend it all if you like,—for this is probably the last chance you'll have for some time to be in a free State, and you'd better enjoy your liberty while you may."

When he came back a couple of days later and found the faithful Grandison at his post, and the hundred dollars intact, Dick felt seriously annoyed. His vexation was increased by the fact that he could not express his feelings adequately. He did not even scold Grandison; how could he, indeed, find fault with one who so sensibly recognized his true place in the economy of civilization, and kept it with such touching fidelity?

"I can't say a thing to him," groaned Dick. "He deserves a leather medal, made out of his own hide tanned. I reckon I'll write to father and let him know what a model servant he has given me."

He wrote his father a letter which made the colonel swell with pride and pleasure. "I really think," the colonel observed to one of his friends, "that Dick ought to have the nigger interviewed by the Boston papers, so that they may see how contented and happy our darkeys really are."

Dick also wrote a long letter to Charity Lomax, in which he said, among other things, that if she knew how hard he was working, and under what difficulties, to accomplish something serious for her sake, she would no longer keep him in suspense, but overwhelm him with love and admiration.

Having thus exhausted without result the more obvious methods of getting rid of Grandison, and diplomacy having also proved a failure, Dick was forced to consider more radical measures. Of course he might run away himself, and abandon Grandison, but this would be merely to leave him in the United States, where he was still a slave, and where, with his notions of loyalty, he would speedily be reclaimed. It was necessary, in order to accomplish the purpose of his trip to the North, to leave Grandison permanently in Canada, where he would be legally free.

"I might extend my trip to Canada," he reflected, "but that would be too palpable. I have it! I'll visit Niagara Falls on the way home, and lose him on the Canada side. When he once realizes that he is actually free, I'll warrant that he'll stay."

So the next day saw them westward bound, and in due course of time, by the somewhat slow conveyances of the period, they found themselves at Niagara. Dick walked and drove about the Falls for several days, taking Grandison along with him on most occasions. One morning they stood on the Canadian side, watching the wild whirl of the waters below them.

"Grandison," said Dick, raising his voice above the roar of the cataract,[8] "do you know where you are now?"

"I's wid you, Mars Dick; dat's all I keers."

"You're now in Canada, Grandison, where your people go when they run away from their masters. If you wished Grandison, you might walk away from me this very minute, and I could not lay my hand upon you to take you back."

---

[8] Large waterfall.

Grandison looked around uneasily.

"Let's go back ober de ribber, Mars Dick. I's feared I'll lose you ovuh heah, an' den I won' hab no marster, an' won't nebber be able to git back home no mo'."

Discouraged, but not yet hopeless, Dick said, a few minutes later,—

"Grandison, I'm going up the road a bit, to the inn over yonder. You stay here until I return. I'll not be gone a great while."

Grandison's eyes opened wide and he looked somewhat fearful.

"Is dey any er dem dadblasted abolitioners roun' heah, Mars Dick?"

"I don't imagine that there are," replied his master, hoping there might be. "But I'm not afraid of *your* running away, Grandison. I only wish I were," he added to himself.

Dick walked leisurely down the road to where the whitewashed inn, built of stone, with true British solidity, loomed up through the trees by the roadside. Arrived there he ordered a glass of ale and a sandwich, and took a seat at a table by a window, from which he could see Grandison in the distance. For a while he hoped that the seed he had sown might have fallen on fertile ground, and that Grandison, relieved from the restraining power of a master's eye, and finding himself in a free country, might get up and walk away; but the hope was vain, for Grandison remained faithfully at his post, awaiting his master's return. He had seated himself on a broad flat stone, and turning his eyes away from the grand and awe-inspiring spectacle that lay close at hand, was looking anxiously toward the inn where his master sat cursing his ill-timed fidelity.

By and by a girl came into the room to serve his order, and Dick very naturally glanced at her; and as she was young and pretty and remained in attendance, it was some minutes before he looked for Grandison. When he did so his faithful servant had disappeared.

To pay his reckoning and go away without the change was a matter quickly accomplished. Retracing his footsteps toward the Falls, he saw, to his great disgust, as he approached the spot where he had left Grandison, the familiar form of his servant stretched out on the ground, his face to the sun, his mouth open, sleeping the time away, oblivious alike to the grandeur of the scenery, the thunderous roar of the cataract, or the insidious voice of sentiment.

"Grandison," soliloquized his master, as he stood gazing down at his ebony encumbrance, "I do not deserve to be an American citizen; I ought not to have the advantages I possess over you; and I certainly am not worthy of Charity Lomax, if I am not smart enough to get rid of you. I have an idea! You shall yet be free, and I will be the instrument of your deliverance. Sleep on, faithful and affectionate servitor, and dream of the blue grass and the bright skies of old Kentucky, for it is only in your dreams that you will ever see them again!"

Dick retraced his footsteps towards the inn. The young woman chanced to look out of the window and saw the handsome young gentleman she had waited on a few minutes before, standing in the road a short distance away, apparently engaged in earnest conversation with a colored man employed as a hostler[9] for the inn. She thought she saw something pass from the white man to the other, but at that moment her duties called her away from the window, and when she looked out again the young gentleman had disappeared, and the hostler, with two other young men of the neighborhood, one white and one colored, were walking rapidly towards the Falls.

---

[9] Innkeeper.

IV

Dick made the journey homeward alone, and as rapidly as the conveyances of the day would permit. As he drew near home his conduct in going back without Grandison took on a more serious aspect than it had borne at any previous time, and although he had prepared the colonel by a letter sent several days ahead, there was still the prospect of a bad quarter of an hour with him; not, indeed, that his father would upbraid him, but he was likely to make searching inquiries. And notwithstanding the vein of quiet recklessness that had carried Dick through his preposterous scheme, he was a very poor liar, having rarely had occasion or inclination to tell anything but the truth. Any reluctance to meet his father was more than offset, however, by a stronger force drawing him homeward, for Charity Lomax must long since have returned from her visit to her aunt in Tennessee.

Dick got off easier than he had expected. He told a straight story, and a truthful one, so far as it went.

The colonel raged at first, but rage soon subsided into anger, and anger moderated into annoyance, and annoyance into a sort of garrulous sense of injury. The colonel thought he had been hardly used; he had trusted this negro, and he had broken faith. Yet, after all, he did not blame Grandison so much as he did the abolitionists, who were undoubtedly at the bottom of it.

As for Charity Lomax, Dick told her, privately of course, that he had run his father's man, Grandison, off to Canada, and left him there.

"Oh, Dick," she had said with shuddering alarm, "what have you done? If they knew it they'd send you to the penitentiary, like they did that Yankee."

"But they don't know it," he had replied seriously; adding, with an injured tone, "you don't seem to appreciate my heroism like you did that of the Yankee; perhaps it's because I wasn't caught and sent to the penitentiary. I thought you wanted me to do it."

"Why, Dick Owens!" she exclaimed. "You know I never dreamed of any such outrageous proceeding.

"But I presume I'll have to marry you," she concluded, after some insistence on Dick's part, "if only to take care of you. You are too reckless for anything; and a man who goes chasing all over the North, being entertained by New York and Boston society and having negroes to throw away, needs some one to look after him."

"It's a most remarkable thing," replied Dick fervently, "that your views correspond exactly with my profoundest convictions. It proves beyond question that we were made for one another."

They were married three weeks later. As each of them had just returned from a journey, they spent their honeymoon at home.

A week after the wedding they were seated one afternoon, on the piazza of the colonel's house, where Dick had taken his bride, when a negro from the yard ran down the land and threw open the big gate for the colonel's buggy to enter. The colonel was not alone. Beside him, ragged and travel-stained, bowed with weariness, and upon his face a haggard look that told of hardship and privation, sat the lost Grandison.

The colonel alighted at the steps.

"Take the lines, Tom," he said to the man who had opened the gate, "and drive round to the barn. Help Grandison down,—poor devil, he's so stiff he can hardly move!—and get a tub of water and wash him and rub him down, and feed him, and give him a big drink of whiskey, and then let him come round and see his young master and his new mistress."

The colonel's face wore an expression compounded of joy and indignation,—joy at the restoration of a valuable piece of property; indignation for reasons he proceeded to state.

"It's astounding, the depths of depravity the human heart is capable of! I was coming along the road three miles away, when I heard some one call me from the roadside. I pulled up the mare, and who should come out of the woods but Grandison. The poor nigger could hardly crawl along, with the help of a broken limb. I was never more astonished in my life. You could have knocked me down with a feather. He seemed pretty far gone,—he could hardly talk above a whisper,—and I had to give him a mouthful of whiskey to brace him up so he could tell his story. It's just as I thought from the beginning, Dick; Grandison had no notion of running away; he knew when he was well off, and where his friends were. All the persuasions of abolition liars and runaway niggers did not move him. But the desperation of those fanatics knew no bounds; their guilty consciences gave them no rest. They got the notion somehow that Grandison belongs to a nigger-catcher, and had been brought North as a spy to help capture ungrateful runaway servants. They actually kidnaped him—just think of it!—and gagged him and bound him and threw him rudely into a wagon, and carried him into the gloomy depths of a Canadian forest, and locked him in a lonely hut, and fed him on bread and water for three weeks. One of the scoundrels wanted to kill him, and persuaded the others that it ought to be done; but they got to quarreling about how they should do it, and before they had their minds made up Grandison escaped, and, keeping his back steadily to the North Star, made his way, after suffering incredible hardships, back to the old plantation, back to his master, his friends, and his home. Why, it's as good as one of Scott's novels! Mr. Simms[10] or some other one of our Southern authors ought to write it up."

"Don't you think, sir," suggested Dick, who had calmly smoked his cigar throughout the colonel's animated recital, "that that kidnaping yarn sounds a little improbable? Isn't there some more likely explanation?"

"Nonsense, Dick; it's the gospel truth! Those infernal abolitionists are capable of anything—everything! Just think of their locking the poor, faithful nigger up, beating him, kicking him, depriving him of his liberty, keeping him on bread and water for three long, lonesome weeks, and he all the time pining for the old plantation!"

There were almost tears in the colonel's eyes at the picture of Grandison's sufferings that he conjured up. Dick still professed to be slightly skeptical, and met Charity's severely questioning eye with bland unconsciousness.

The colonel killed the fatted calf for Grandison, and for two or three weeks the returned wanderer's life was a slave's dream of pleasure. His fame spread throughout the county, and the colonel gave him a permanent place among the house servants, where he could always have him conveniently at hand to relate his adventures to admiring visitors.

About three weeks after Grandison's return the colonel's faith in sable humanity was rudely shaken, and its foundations almost broken up. He came near losing

---

[10] The Scottish poet and novelist Sir Walter Scott (1771–1832), author of such famous historical romances as *Lady of the Lake* (1810) and *Ivanhoe* (1819); William Gilmore Simms (1806–1870), of Charleston, South Carolina, author of historical romances set in the American South, among them *Guy Rivers* (1834) and *The Partisan* (1835).

his belief in the fidelity of the negro to his master,—the servile virtue most highly prized and most sedulously cultivated by the colonel and his kind. One Monday morning Grandison was missing. And not only Grandison, but his wife, Betty the maid; his mother, aunt Eunice; his father, uncle Ike; his brothers, Tom and John, and his little sister Elsie, were likewise absent from the plantation; and a hurried search and inquiry in the neighborhood resulted in no information as to their whereabouts. So much valuable property could not be lost without an effort to recover it, and the wholesale nature of the transaction carried consternation to the hearts of those whose ledgers were chiefly bound in black. Extremely energetic measures were taken by the colonel and his friends. The fugitives were traced, and followed from point to point, on their northward run through Ohio. Several times the hunters were close upon their heels, but the magnitude of the escaping party begot unusual vigilance on the part of those who sympathized with the fugitives, and strangely enough, the underground railroad[11] seemed to have had its tracks cleared and signals set for this particular train. Once, twice, the colonel thought he had them, but they slipped through his fingers.

One last glimpse he caught of his vanishing property, as he stood, accompanied by a United States marshal, on a wharf at a port on the south shore of Lake Erie. On the stern of a small steamboat which was receding rapidly from the wharf, with her nose pointing toward Canada, there stood a group of familiar dark faces, and the look they cast backward was not one of longing for the fleshpots of Egypt. The colonel saw Grandison point him out to one of the crew of the vessel, who waved his hand derisively toward the colonel. The latter shook his fist impotently—and the incident was closed.

1898

Charlotte Perkins Gilman
(1860–1935)

At age twenty Charlotte Perkins composed a brief note "to gather strength from" and put it on her dresser mirror. "If I live, (as I do,) for others," the note began, "if all my high desires for self-improvement are solely with a view to the elevation of the race—if my mission is to lead a self-sacrificing life . . . to teach and guide, to love, protect and care for—then it behooves me to crush all personal sorrow and drop the whole ground of self-interest forever. Neither is this Quixotic or impossible." Perkins's rigorous self-discipline and unyielding commitment to social improvement enabled her to become one of the strongest turn-of-the-century feminist voices despite a debilitating "nerve-ruin" that grievously impaired her ability to read and frequent periods of despair, during which nearly all activity was impossible.

The second child of Fredric Beecher Perkins and Mary Fitch, Charlotte Anna Perkins was born in Hartford, Connecticut, in 1860. Her father abandoned the family shortly after her birth, and although she later beseeched him to write more frequently, he remained

---

[11] A pre-Civil War system of helping fugitive slaves move North to freedom.

remote. She did, however, know his family and proudly claimed her relation to her great-aunt Harriet Beecher Stowe. Family background notwithstanding, Mary Perkins and her son and daughter suffered poverty so severe that they were forced to move nineteen times in eighteen years. More distressing to Charlotte was her mother's response to hardship and disappointment: determined never to have her children suffer because of unfulfilled hopes and expectations, Mary Perkins withheld outward shows of affection, motherly hugs and kisses, and forbade Charlotte to enjoy such pleasures as reading novels or cultivating an "inner world" of imagination.

After briefly attending the Rhode Island School of Design, Charlotte enjoyed some success painting flowers and teaching art. In 1882 she met Charles Walter Stetson, a painter from Providence, who soon proposed marriage. Declining immediately, she subsequently reconsidered; after two years of wavering, uncertain whether marriage would fit into her plans for a life of service to society, she married Stetson in May 1884. Although the two were happy together, she noted in her autobiography, first published in 1935, that "something was going wrong from the start," like a "gray fog [that] drifted across my mind, a cloud that grew and darkened." This cloud of depression did not abate after the birth of their daughter in 1885, nor was it alleviated by the "rest-cure" prescribed by the noted physician S. Weir Mitchell. On the contrary, following his advice she "came perilously near to losing [her] mind."

In 1887, realizing the inherent dangers of remaining married, the Stetsons agreed to divorce, and Charlotte Perkins and her daughter moved to Pasadena the next autumn, aided by the writer Grace Channing. Although Perkins's four years in California were the hardest of her life, her feeling of being "finally free" (though a "wreck") in 1890 resulted in the production of some of her best work. Her acclaimed story "The Yellow Wallpaper," written at that time, chronicles the breakdown and progressive decline of a patient who follows the "rest-cure" (she sent a copy of this story to Dr. Mitchell and later heard that he changed his treatment of nervous prostration after reading it). At about this time she began lecturing professionally, most often to women's and labor groups. However, her efforts netted barely enough money for survival. Given her poor health and scanty income, Perkins reluctantly decided that her daughter should live with Charles Stetson and his new wife, Grace Channing, a decision for which Perkins was publicly condemned.

On her own in California, Perkins supported herself through writing, lecturing, teaching, and editing. "The Yellow Wallpaper" appeared in *The New England Magazine* in 1892 (later William Dean Howells included it in a collection of great American stories). Written in only fifty-eight days, her most influential book, *Women and Economics* (1898), argues that women's economic dependence on men is detrimental to both genders because it limits the ability of women to exercise their creativity in nondomestic fields. In this and later works (*Concerning Children* [1900], *The Home* [1904], and *Human Work* [1904]), she advanced her ideas for child-care centers, kitchenless homes, and professional housekeeping as ways to give women more usable time and children more effective supervision.

In 1900 Perkins married her cousin George Houghton Gilman, with whom she had had a long epistolary courtship. They remained together, happily, until his sudden death in 1934. He provided much support while she wrote, edited, published, and distributed *Forerunner*, a one-woman journal that appeared from 1909 to 1916, as well as *Man-Made World* (1911), *Herland* (serialized in *Forerunner* in 1915), *With Her in Ourland* (1916), and *His Religion and Hers* (1923). These late works maintain that women's nurturing, life-sustaining efforts are preferable to the bellicose tendencies of men, that a feminine influence is needed in national and international affairs as well as in religion, and that the female is "the primary type of the human species" (a claim she discussed with Lester Ward, a noted sociologist).

Gilman was influential as a public speaker, lecturing to a variety of audiences, including women's clubs, church groups, and college students. She traveled both nationally and internationally as a delegate to suffrage conventions and spoke at the International Suffrage Convention in Budapest in 1913. In the 1920s, however, her constituency waned. And in 1935, suffering from breast cancer, she ended her life with chloroform because of her conviction that "when all usefulness is over, when one is assured of unavoidable and imminent death, it is the simplest of human rights to choose a quick and easy death in place of a slow and horrible one." Gilman's works were largely forgotten for almost fifty years after her death, but now, as the era Gilman referred to as the "woman's century" comes to a close, they are being reclaimed as significant early contributions to the feminist tradition in America.

Suggested Readings: *His Religion and Hers: A Study of the Faith of Our Fathers and the Work of Our Mothers,* 1923, rpt. 1976. *The Living of Charlotte Perkins Gilman: An Autobiography,* 1935, rpt. 1972. *Herland,* 1979. *The Charlotte Perkins Gilman Reader: The Yellow Wallpaper and Other Fiction,* ed. A. J. Lane, 1980. M. A. Hill, *Charlotte Perkins Gilman: The Making of a Radical Feminist, 1860–1896,* 1980. G. Scharnhorst, *Charlotte Perkins Gilman,* 1985. P. W. Allen, *Building Domestic Liberty: Charlotte Perkins Gilman's Architectural Feminism,* 1988. S. L. Meyering, ed., *Charlotte Perkins Gilman: The Woman and Her Work,* 1989. A. J. Lane, *To "Herland" and Beyond: The Life and Work of Charlotte Perkins Gilman,* 1990.

Text Used: *The New England Magazine,* V (5):647–656, January 1892.

THE YELLOW WALL-PAPER*

It is very seldom that mere ordinary people like John and myself secure ancestral halls for the summer.

A colonial mansion, a hereditary estate, I would say a haunted house, and reach the height of romantic felicity—but that would be asking too much of fate!

Still I will proudly declare that there is something queer about it.

Else, why should it be let so cheaply? And why have stood so long untenanted?

John laughs at me, of course, but one expects that in marriage.

John is practical in the extreme. He has no patience with faith, an intense horror of superstition, and he scoffs openly at any talk of things not to be felt and seen and put down in figures.

John is a physician, and *perhaps*—(I would not say it to a living soul, of course, but this is dead paper and a great relief to my mind—) *perhaps* that is one reason I do not get well faster.

You see he does not believe I am sick!

And what can one do?

If a physician of high standing, and one's own husband, assures friends and relatives that there is really nothing the matter with one but temporary nervous depression—a slight hysterical tendency[1]—what is one to do?

My brother is also a physician, and also of high standing, and he says the same thing.

---

* First published in *The New England Magazine* in January 1892.

[1] In the late nineteenth century the term "hysteria" was used to describe a number of emotional problems to which women were supposedly liable, among them anxiety, depression, and stress.

So I take phosphates or phosphites[2]—whichever it is, and tonics, and journeys, and air, and exercise, and am absolutely forbidden to "work" until I am well again.

Personally, I disagree with their ideas.

Personally, I believe that congenial work, with excitement and change, would do me good.

But what is one to do?

I did write for a while in spite of them; but it *does* exhaust me a good deal—having to be so sly about it, or else meet with heavy opposition.

I sometimes fancy that in my condition if I had less opposition and more society and stimulus—but John says the very worst thing I can do is to think about my condition, and I confess it always makes me feel bad.

So I will let it alone and talk about the house.

The most beautiful place! It is quite alone, standing well back from the road, quite three miles from the village. It makes me think of English places that you read about, for there are hedges and walls and gates that lock, and lots of separate little houses for the gardeners and people.

There is a *delicious* garden! I never saw such a garden—large and shady, full of box-bordered paths, and lined with long grape-covered arbors with seats under them.

There were greenhouses, too, but they are all broken now.

There was some legal trouble, I believe, something about the heirs and co-heirs; anyhow, the place has been empty for years.

That spoils my ghostliness, I am afraid, but I don't care—there is something strange about the house—I can feel it.

I even said so to John one moonlight evening, but he said what I felt was a *draught,* and shut the window.

I get unreasonably angry with John sometimes. I'm sure I never used to be so sensitive. I think it is due to this nervous condition.

But John says if I feel so, I shall neglect proper self-control; so I take pains to control myself—before him, at least, and that makes me very tired.

I don't like our room a bit. I wanted one downstairs that opened on the piazza and had roses all over the window, and such pretty old-fashioned chintz hangings! but John would not hear of it.

He said there was only one window and not room for two beds, and no near room for him if he took another.

He is very careful and loving, and hardly lets me stir without special direction.

I have a schedule prescription for each hour in the day; he takes all care from me, and so I feel basely ungrateful not to value it more.

He said we came here solely on my account, that I was to have perfect rest and all the air I could get. "Your exercise depends on your strength, my dear," said he, "and your food somewhat on your appetite; but air you can absorb all the time." So we took the nursery at the top of the house.

It is a big, airy room, the whole floor nearly, with windows that look all ways, and air and sunshine galore. It was nursery first and then playroom and gymnasium, I should judge; for the windows are barred for little children, and there are rings and things in the walls.

The paint and paper look as if a boys' school had used it. It is stripped off—the paper—in great patches all around the head of my bed, about as far as I can reach,

---

[2] Carbonated water with a small amount of acid phosphate, flavored with a fruit syrup.

and in a great place on the other side of the room low down. I never saw a worse paper in my life.

One of those sprawling flamboyant patterns committing every artistic sin.

It is dull enough to confuse the eye in following, pronounced enough to constantly irritate and provoke study, and when you follow the lame uncertain curves for a little distance they suddenly commit suicide—plunge off at outrageous angles, destroy themselves in unheard of contradictions.

The color is repellant, almost revolting; a smouldering unclean yellow, strangely faded by the slow-turning sunlight.

It is a dull yet lurid orange in some places, a sickly sulphur tint in others.

No wonder the children hated it! I should hate it myself if I had to live in this room long.

There comes John, and I must put this away,—he hates to have me write a word.

We have been here two weeks, and I haven't felt like writing before, since that first day.

I am sitting by the window now, up in this atrocious nursery, and there is nothing to hinder my writing as much as I please, save lack of strength.

John is away all day, and even some nights when his cases are serious.

I am glad my case is not serious!

But these nervous troubles are dreadfully depressing.

John does not know how much I really suffer. He knows there is no *reason* to suffer, and that satisfies him.

Of course it is only nervousness. It does weigh on me so not to do my duty in any way!

I meant to be such a help to John, such a real rest and comfort, and here I am a comparative burden already!

Nobody would believe what an effort it is to do what little I am able,—to dress and entertain, and order things.

It is fortunate Mary is so good with the baby. Such a dear baby!

And yet I *cannot* be with him, it makes me so nervous.

I suppose John never was nervous in his life. He laughs at me so about this wall-paper!

At first he meant to repaper the room, but afterwards he said that I was letting it get the better of me, and that nothing was worse for a nervous patient than to give way to such fancies.

He said that after the wall-paper was changed it would be the heavy bedstead, and then the barred windows, and then that gate at the head of the stairs, and so on.

"You know the place is doing you good," he said, "and really, dear, I don't care to renovate the house just for a three months' rental."

"Then do let us go downstairs," I said, "there are such pretty rooms there."

Then he took me in his arms and called me a blessed little goose, and said he would go down cellar, if I wished, and have it whitewashed into the bargain.

But he is right enough about the beds and windows and things.

It is an airy and comfortable room as any one need wish, and, of course, I would not be so silly as to make him uncomfortable just for a whim.

I'm really getting quite fond of the big room, all but that horrid paper.

Out of one window I can see the garden, those mysterious deep-shaded arbors, the riotous old-fashioned flowers, and bushes and gnarly trees.

Out of another I get a lovely view of the bay and a little private wharf belonging to the estate. There is a beautiful shaded lane that runs down there from the house. I always fancy I see people walking in these numerous paths and arbors, but John has cautioned me not to give way to fancy in the least. He says that with my imaginative power and habit of story-making, a nervous weakness like mine is sure to lead to all manner of excited fancies, and that I ought to use my will and good sense to check the tendency. So I try.

I think sometimes that if I were only well enough to write a little it would relieve the press of ideas and rest me.

But I find I get pretty tired when I try.

It is so discouraging not to have any advice and companionship about my work. When I get really well, John says we will ask Cousin Henry and Julia down for a long visit; but he says he would as soon put fireworks in my pillow-case as to let me have those stimulating people about now.

I wish I could get well faster.

But I must not think about that. This paper looks to me as if it *knew* what a vicious influence it had!

There is a recurrent spot where the pattern lolls like a broken neck and two bulbous eyes stare at you upside down.

I get positively angry with the impertinence of it and the everlastingness. Up and down and sideways they crawl, and those absurd, unblinking eyes are everywhere. There is one place where two breaths didn't match, and the eyes go all up and down the line, one a little higher than the other.

I never saw so much expression in an inanimate thing before, and we all know how much expression they have! I used to lie awake as a child and get more entertainment and terror out of blank walls and plain furniture than most children could find in a toy-store.

I remember what a kindly wink the knobs of our big, old bureau used to have, and there was one chair that always seemed like a strong friend.

I used to feel that if any of the other things looked too fierce I could always hop into that chair and be safe.

The furniture in this room is no worse than inharmonious, however, for we had to bring it all from downstairs. I suppose when this was used as a playroom they had to take the nursery things out, and no wonder! I never saw such ravages as the children have made here.

The wall-paper, as I said before, is torn off in spots, and it sticketh closer than a brother[3]—they must have had perserverance as well as hatred.

Then the floor is scratched and gouged and splintered, the plaster itself is dug out here and there, and this great heavy bed which is all we found in the room, looks as if it had been through the wars.

"But I don't mind it a bit—only the paper.

There comes John's sister. Such a dear girl as she is, and so careful of me! I must not let her find me writing.

She is a perfect and enthusiastic housekeeper, and hopes for no better profession. I verily believe she thinks it is the writing which made me sick!

But I can write when she is out, and see her a long way off from these windows.

---

[3] A biblical maxim suddenly springs to the narrator's mind: "There is a friend that sticketh closer than a brother," from Proverbs 18:24.

There is one that commands the road, a lovely shaded winding road, and one that just looks off over the country. A lovely country, too, full of great elms and velvet meadows.

This wallpaper has a kind of sub-pattern in a different shade, a particularly irritating one, for you can only see it in certain lights, and not clearly then.

But in the places where it isn't faded and where the sun is just so—I can see a strange, provoking, formless sort of figure, that seems to skulk about behind that silly and conspicuous front design.

There's sister on the stair!

Well, the Fourth of July is over! The people are all gone and I am tired out. John thought it might do me good to see a little company, so we just had mother and Nellie and the children down for a week.

Of course I didn't do a thing. Jennie sees to everything now.

But it tired me all the same.

John says if I don't pick up faster he shall send me to Weir Mitchell[4] in the fall.

But I don't want to go there at all. I had a friend who was in his hands once, and she says he is just like John and my brother, only more so!

Besides, it is such an undertaking to go so far.

I don't feel as if it was worth while to turn my hand over for anything, and I'm getting dreadfully fretful and querulous.

I cry at nothing, and cry most of the time.

Of course I don't when John is here, or anybody else, but when I am alone.

And I am alone a good deal just now. John is kept in town very often by serious cases, and Jennie is good and lets me alone when I want her to.

So I walk a little in the garden or down that lovely lane, sit on the porch under the roses, and lie down up here a good deal.

I'm getting really fond of the room in spite of the wallpaper. Perhaps *because* of the wallpaper.

It dwells in my mind so!

I lie here on this great immovable bed—it is nailed down, I believe—and follow that pattern about by the hour. It it as good as gymnastics, I assure you. I start, we'll say, at the bottom, down in the corner over there where it has not been touched, and I determine for the thousandth time that I *will* follow that pattern to some sort of a conclusion.

I know a little of the principle of design, and I know this thing was not arranged on any laws of radiation, or alternation, or repetition, or symmetry, or anything else that I ever heard of.

It is repeated, of course, by the breadths, but not otherwise.

Looked at in one way each breadth stands alone, the bloated curves and flourishes—a kind of "debased Romanesque" with *delirium tremens*[5]—go waddling up and down in isolated columns of fatuity.

But, on the other hand, they connect diagonally, and the sprawling outlines run off in great slanting waves of optic horror, like a lot of wallowing seaweeds in full chase.

---

[4] S. Weir Mitchell (1829–1914), an American physician, a specialist in nervous disorders, whose "rest-cure" for "hysteria" Gilman had undergone. Mitchell was supposedly the model for the nerve specialist in William Dean Howells's *The Shadow of a Dream* (1890); he later became a novelist.

[5] Romanesque architecture is elaborately ornamented; the narrator now sees the wallpaper designs not only as elaborate but as "debased" and afflicted with a violent and trembling delirium.

The whole thing goes horizontally, too, at least it seems so, and I exhaust myself in trying to distinguish the order of its going in that direction.

They have used a horizontal breadth for a frieze,[6] and that adds wonderfully to the confusion.

There is one end of the room where it is almost intact, and there, when the crosslights fade and the low sun shines directly upon it, I can almost fancy radiation after all,—the interminable grotesque seem to form around a common centre and rush off in headlong plunges of equal distraction.

It makes me tired to follow it. I will take a nap I guess.

I don't know why I should write this.

I don't want to.

I don't feel able.

And I know John would think it absurd. But I *must* say what I feel and think in some way—it is such a relief!

But the effort is getting to be greater than the relief.

Half the time now I am awfully lazy, and lie down ever so much.

John says I mustn't lose my strength, and has me take cod liver oil and lots of tonics and things, to say nothing of ale and wine and rare meat.

Dear John! He loves me very dearly, and hates to have me sick. I tried to have a real earnest reasonable talk with him the other day, and tell him how I wish he would let me go and make a visit to Cousin Henry and Julia.

But he said I wasn't able to go, nor able to stand it after I got there; and I did not make out a very good case for myself, for I was crying before I had finished.

It is getting to be a great effort for me to think straight. Just this nervous weakness I suppose.

And dear John gathered me up in his arms, and just carried me upstairs and laid me on the bed, and sat by me and read to me till it tired my head.

He said I was his darling and his comfort and all he had, and that I must take care of myself for his sake, and keep well.

He says no one but myself can help me out of it, that I must use my will and self-control and not let any silly fancies run away with me.

There's one comfort, the baby is well and happy, and does not have to occupy this nursery with the horrid wallpaper.

If we had not used it, that blessed child would have! What a fortunate escape! Why, I wouldn't have a child of mine, an impressionable little thing, live in such a room for worlds.

I never thought of it before, but it is lucky that John kept me here after all, I can stand it so much easier than a baby, you see.

Of course I never mention it to them any more—I am too wise,—but I keep watch of it all the same.

There are things in that paper that nobody knows but me, or ever will.

Behind that outside pattern the dim shapes get clearer every day.

It is always the same shape, only very numerous.

And it is like a woman stooping down and creeping about behind that pattern. I don't like it a bit. I wonder—I begin to think—I wish John would take me away from here!

It is so hard to talk with John about my case, because he is so wise, and because he loves me so.

---

[6] An ornamental band that serves as a border where a wall meets the ceiling.

But I tried last night.

It was moonlight. The moon shines in all around just as the sun does.

I hate to see it sometimes, it creeps so slowly, and always comes in by one window or another.

John was asleep and I hated to waken him, so I kept still and watched the moonlight on that undulating wallpaper till I felt creepy.

The faint figure behind seemed to shake the pattern, just as if she wanted to get out.

I got up softly and went to feel and see if the paper *did* move, and when I came back John was awake.

"What is it, little girl?" he said. "Don't go walking about like that—you'll get cold."

I thought it was a good time to talk, so I told him that I really was not gaining here, and that I wished he would take me away.

"Why, darling!" said he, "our lease will be up in three weeks, and I can't see how to leave before.

"The repairs are not done at home, and I cannot possibly leave town just now. Of course if you were in any danger, I could and would, but you really are better, dear, whether you can see it or not. I am a doctor, dear, and I know. You are gaining flesh and color, your appetite is better, I feel really much easier about you."

"I don't weigh a bit more," said I, "nor as much; and my appetite may be better in the evening when you are here, but it is worse in the morning when you are away!"

"Bless her little heart!" said he with a big hug, "she shall be as sick as she pleases! But now let's improve the shining hours[7] by going to sleep, and talk about it in the morning!"

"And you won't go away?" I asked gloomily.

"Why, how can I, dear? It is only three weeks more and then we will take a nice little trip of a few days while Jennie is getting the house ready. Really dear you are better!"

"Better in body perhaps—" I began, and stopped short, for he sat up straight and looked at me with such a stern, reproachful look that I could not say another word.

"My darling," said he, "I beg of you, for my sake and for our child's sake, as well as for your own, that you will never for one instant let that idea enter your mind! There is nothing so dangerous, so fascinating, to a temperament like yours. It is a false and foolish fancy. Can you not trust me as a physician when I tell you so?"

So of course I said no more on that score, and we went to sleep before long. He thought I was asleep first, but I wasn't, and lay there for hours trying to decide whether that front pattern and the back pattern really did more together or separately.

On a pattern like this, by daylight, there is a lack of sequence, a defiance of law, that is a constant irritant to a normal mind.

The color is hideous enough, and unreliable enough, and infuriating enough, but the pattern is torturing.

---

[7] "How doth the little busy bee / Improve each shining hour," from the poem "Against Idleness and Mischief" in *Divine Songs for Children*, by Isaac Watts (1674–1748). The smug superiority of Watts's lines matches that of John's demeanor toward his wife.

You think you have mastered it, but just as you get well underway in following, it turns a back-somersault and there you are. It slaps you in the face, knocks you down, and tramples upon you. It is like a bad dream.

The outside pattern is a florid arabesque, reminding one of a fungus. If you can imagine a toadstool in joints, an interminable string of toadstools, budding and sprouting in endless convolutions—why, that is something like it.

That is, sometimes!

There is one marked peculiarity about this paper, a thing nobody seems to notice but myself, and that is that it changes as the light changes.

When the sun shoots in through the east window—I always watch for that first long, straight ray—it changes so quickly that I never can quite believe it.

That is why I watch it always.

By moonlight—the moon shines in all night when there is a moon—I wouldn't know it was the same paper.

At night in any kind of light, in twilight, candlelight, lamplight, and worst of all by moonlight, it becomes bars! The outside pattern I mean, and the woman behind it is as plain as can be.

I didn't realize for a long time what the thing was that showed behind, that dim sub-pattern, but now I am quite sure it is a woman.

By daylight she is subdued, quiet. I fancy it is the pattern that keeps her so still. It is so puzzling. It keeps me quiet by the hour.

I lie down ever so much now. John says it is good for me, and to sleep all I can.

Indeed he started the habit by making me lie down for an hour after each meal.

It is a very bad habit I am convinced, for you see I don't sleep.

And that cultivates deceit, for I don't tell them I'm awake—O no!

The fact is I am getting a little afraid of John.

He seems very queer sometimes, and even Jennie has an inexplicable look.

It strikes me occasionally, just as a scientific hypothesis,—that perhaps it is the paper!

I have watched John when he did not know I was looking, and come into the room suddenly on the most innocent excuses, and I've caught him several times *looking at the paper!* And Jennie too. I caught Jennie with her hand on it once.

She didn't know I was in the room, and when I asked her in a quiet, a very quiet voice, with the most restrained manner possible, what she was doing with the paper—she turned around as if she had been caught stealing, and looked quite angry—asked me why I should frighten her so!

Then she said that the paper stained everything it touched, that she had found yellow smooches on all my clothes and John's, and she wished we would be more careful!

Did not that sound innocent? But I know she was studying that pattern, and I am determined that nobody shall find it out but myself!

Life is very much more exciting now than it used to be. You see I have something more to expect, to look forward to, to watch. I really do eat better, and am more quiet than I was.

John is so pleased to see me improve! He laughed a little the other day, and said I seemed to be flourishing in spite of my wall-paper.

I turned it off with a laugh. I had no intention of telling him it was *because* of the wall-paper—he would make fun of me. He might even want to take me away.

I don't want to leave now until I have found it out. There is a week more, and I think that will be enough.

I'm feeling ever so much better! I don't sleep much at night, for it is so interesting to watch developments; but I sleep a good deal in the daytime.

In the daytime it is tiresome and perplexing.

There are always new shoots on the fungus, and new shades of yellow all over it. I cannot keep count of them, though I have tried conscientiously.

It is the strangest yellow, that wall-paper! It makes me think of all the yellow things I ever saw—not beautiful ones like buttercups, but old foul, bad yellow things.

But there is something else about that paper—the smell! I noticed it the moment we came into the room, but with so much air and sun it was not bad. Now we have had a week of fog and rain, and whether the windows are open or not, the smell is here.

It creeps all over the house.

I find it hovering in the dining-room, skulking in the parlor, hiding in the hall, lying in wait for me on the stairs.

It gets into my hair.

Even when I go to ride, if I turn my head suddenly and surprise it—there is that smell!

Such a peculiar odor, too! I have spent hours in trying to analyze it, to find what it smelled like.

It is not bad—at first, and very gentle, but quite the subtlest, most enduring odor I ever met.

In this damp weather it is awful, I wake up in the night and find it hanging over me.

It used to disturb me at first. I thought seriously of burning the house—to reach the smell.

But now I am used to it. The only thing I can think of that it is like is the *color* of the paper! A yellow smell.

There is a very funny mark on this wall, low down, near the mopboard. A streak that runs round the room. It goes behind every piece of furniture, except the bed, a long, straight, even *smooch,* as if it had been rubbed over and over.

I wonder how it was done and who did it, and what they did it for. Round and round and round—round and round and round—it makes me dizzy!

I really have discovered something at last.

Through watching so much at night, when it changes so, I have finally found out.

The front pattern *does* move—and no wonder! The woman behind shakes it!

Sometimes I think there are a great many women behind, and sometimes only one, and she crawls around fast, and her crawling shakes it all over.

Then in the very bright spots she keeps still, and in the very shady spots she just takes hold of the bars and shakes them hard.

And she is all the time trying to climb through. But nobody could climb through that pattern—it strangles so; I think that is why it has so many heads.

They get through, and then the pattern strangles them off and turns them upside down, and makes their eyes white!

If those heads were covered or taken off it would not be half so bad.

I think that woman gets out in the daytime!

And I'll tell you why—privately—I've seen her!

I can see her out of every one of my windows!

It is the same woman, I know, for she is always creeping, and most women do not creep by daylight.

I see her in that long shaded lane, creeping up and down. I see her in those dark grape arbors, creeping all around the garden.

I see her on that long road under the trees, creeping along, and when a carriage comes she hides under the blackberry vines.

I don't blame her a bit. It must be very humiliating to be caught creeping by daylight!

I always lock the door when I creep by daylight. I can't do it at night, for I know John would suspect something at once.

And John is so queer now, that I don't want to irritate him. I wish he would take another room! Besides, I don't want anybody to get that woman out at night but myself.

I often wonder if I could see her out of all the windows at once.

But, turn as fast as I can, I can only see out of one at one time.

And though I always see her, she *may* be able to creep faster than I can turn!

I have watched her sometimes away off in the open country, creeping as fast as a cloud shadow in a high wind.

If only that top pattern could be gotten off from the under one! I mean to try it, little by little.

I have found out another funny thing, but I shan't tell it this time! It does not do to trust people too much.

There are only two more days to get this paper off, and I believe John is beginning to notice. I don't like the look in his eyes.

And I heard him ask Jennie a lot of professional questions about me. She had a very good report to give.

She said I slept a good deal in the daytime.

John knows I don't sleep very well at night, for all I'm so quiet!

He asked me all sorts of questions, too, and pretended to be very loving and kind.

As if I couldn't see through him!

Still, I don't wonder he acts so, sleeping under this paper for three months.

It only interests me, but I feel sure John and Jennie are secretly affected by it.

Hurrah! This is the last day, but it is enough. John to stay in town over night, and won't be out until this evening.

Jennie wanted to sleep with me—the sly thing! but I told her I should undoubtedly rest better for a night all alone.

That was clever, for really I wasn't alone a bit! As soon as it was moonlight and that poor thing began to crawl and shake the pattern, I got up and ran to help her.

I pulled and she shook, I shook and she pulled, and before morning we had peeled off yards of that paper.

A strip about as high as my head and half around the room.

And then when the sun came and that awful pattern began to laugh at me, I declared I would finish it to-day!

We go away to-morrow, and they are moving all my furniture down again to leave things as they were before.

Jennie looked at the wall in amazement, but I told her merrily that I did it out of pure spite at the vicious thing.

She laughed and said she wouldn't mind doing it herself, but I must not get tired.

How she betrayed herself that time!

But I am here, and no person touches this paper but me,—not *alive!*

She tried to get me out of the room—it was too patent! But I said it was so quiet and empty and clean now that I believed I would lie down again and sleep all I could; and not to wake me even for dinner—I would call when I woke.

So now she is gone, and the servants are gone, and the things are gone, and there is nothing left but that great bedstead nailed down, with the canvas mattress we found on it.

We shall sleep downstairs to-night, and take the boat home to-morrow.

I quite enjoy the room, now it is bare again.

How those children did tear about here!

This bedstead is fairly gnawed!

But I must get to work.

I have locked the door and thrown the key down into the front path.

I don't want to go out, and I don't want to have anybody come in, till John comes.

I want to astonish him.

I've got a rope up here than even Jennie did not find. If that woman does get out, and tries to get away, I can tie her!

But I forgot I could not reach far without anything to stand on!

This bed will *not* move!

I tried to lift and push it until I was lame, and then I got so angry I bit off a little piece at one corner—but it hurt my teeth.

Then I peeled off all the paper I could reach standing on the floor. It sticks horribly and the pattern just enjoys it! All those strangled heads and bulbous eyes and waddling fungus growths just shriek with derision!

I am getting angry enough to do something desperate. To jump out of the window would be admirable exercise, but the bars are too strong even to try.

Besides I wouldn't do it. Of course not. I know well enough that a step like that is improper and might be misconstrued.

I don't like to *look* out of the windows even—there are so many of these creeping women, and they creep so fast.

I wonder if they all come out of that wall-paper as I did?

But I am securely fastened now by my well-hidden rope—you don't get *me* out in the road there!

I suppose I shall have to get back behind the pattern when it comes night, and that is hard!

It is so pleasant to be out in this great room and creep around as I please!

I don't want to go outside. I won't, even if Jennie asks me to.

For outside you have to creep on the ground, and everything is green instead of yellow.

But here I can creep smoothly on the floor, and my shoulder just fits in that long smooch around the wall, so I cannot lose my way.

Why there's John at the door!

It is no use, young man, you can't open it!

How he does call and pound!

Now he's crying for an axe.

It would be a shame to break down that beautiful door!

"John dear!" said I in the gentlest voice, "the key is down by the front steps, under a plaintain leaf!"

That silenced him for a few moments.

Then he said—very quietly indeed, "Open the door, my darling!"

"I can't," said I. "The key is down by the front door under a plantain leaf!"

And then I said it again, several times, very gently and slowly, and said it so often that he had to go and see, and he got it of course, and came in. He stopped short by the door.

"What is the matter?" he cried. "For God's sake, what are you doing!"

I kept on creeping just the same, but I looked at him over my shoulder.

"I've got out at last," said I, "in spite of you and Jane? And I've pulled off most of the paper, so you can't put me back!"

Now why should that man have fainted? But he did, and right across my path by the wall, so that I had to creep over him every time!

1892

Henry James
(1843–1916)

According to Edith Wharton, Henry James "was greater than his works, much greater—and that is saying a good deal." The statement is generous, the tribute to the man heightened by an acknowledgment of the quality of his work. But the generosity of Wharton's appraisal has not found easy consensus in the twentieth century. Indeed, few writers have aroused admiration and antagonism in such measure as has Henry James. At times his monolithic presence has diverted attention from his work and converted his importance into the appearance of stuffy self-importance. Some readers attending to the work have been critical of James's frequent portrayal of naïve, even coarse, Americans among cultivated Europeans, especially in the light of his own expatriation; others claim to have stumbled through his dense fiction as they would through a cluttered Victorian parlor; still others have detected a studied and dogmatic quality in the nonfictional prose that makes a condescending fussbudget of the *doyen* of American fiction. Despite the difficulties James poses, however, he remains a formidable novelist and theoretician with a substantial claim to having revolutionized the novel in English.

Henry James, Jr., was born in New York City in 1843 into a family that enjoyed upper middle-class prosperity as the result of shrewd land purchases by Henry's paternal grandfather, an Irish immigrant. James's father, Henry, Sr., was an energetic thinker and writer with a cork leg, whose eccentricity was to some extent balanced by the quiet stability of Mary Walsh James, the novelist's mother. The restlessness of Henry, Sr., led him to promote the theology of the Swedish mystic Emanuel Swedenborg without ever bringing the recognition Henry, Sr., sought through his writing. And his roving spirit and independent pedagogical interests led him to move his family frequently between Europe and various homes in the United states in search of educational opportunities for his children. Young James thus developed an early familiarity with European society and the American community in Europe. His older brother, William, was to attain prominence as a psychologist and become the leading exponent of pragmatism as an ethical and philosophical position. James also had two younger brothers, Wilkinson and Robertson, whose adult lives were adventurous but undistinguished; and a sister, Alice, a highly intelligent woman best known for her lifelong neurasthenia, a type of neurosis Henry and, to an even greater degree, William seem to have shared.

James's reminiscences, published as *A Small Boy and Others* (1913) and *Notes of a Son and Brother* (1914), describe a socially secure childhood, rich in privileged associations. He remembers, for example, the guest bedroom referred to as "Mr. Emerson's room," an avuncular William Thackeray admiring the buttons on his jacket, and an occasion when Washington Irving delivered the news that Margaret Fuller had just drowned. As a young boy, James demonstrated a consuming interest in the family library, especially in the works of Charles Dickens and in books of engravings.

James was always interested in art, and he and William took painting lessons together, but Henry soon recognized that his own gifts lay elsewhere. It is likely, however, that his concern for the visual affected his characteristically detailed depiction of fictional scenes, commonly transmitted by highly observant narrators. One of his most important early friendships was that of the American painter, John LaFarge, who encouraged James to write. The James family spent time in Newport, Rhode Island, and eventually settled in Cambridge, Massachusetts. Henry spent a year at a Swiss engineering school and a year at Harvard Law School, half-heartedly conceding to parental attempts to direct him toward a career, while he grew in the conviction that writing was his intended profession. His first published pieces, an anonymous tale in the *Continental Monthly* and a book review for *The North American Review* (edited by Charles Eliot Norton and James Russell Lowell), both appeared in 1864. He began to write travel articles as well as reviews and short fiction, publishing frequently in the *Atlantic Monthly*. He enjoyed a lifelong friendship with the editor of the *Atlantic*, William Dean Howells. Although he would come to see Howells as a novelist of limited power and scope, James continued to respect Howells for his generous encouragement of new writers. Together, James and Howells are now viewed as leading figures of American realism.

James spent a year alone in Europe from 1869 to 1870. He toured England and stayed for a time in London, where family connections permitted him access to pleasant society. He traveled to the continent, where he found France and Italy, especially Florence, particularly congenial. Indeed, his enthusiasm for Italy marked the beginning of a permanent affection for that country. While abroad he was devastated to hear of the death of his cousin, Minny Temple, to whom he may have been romantically attracted and for whom he felt tremendous admiration. Even in his immediate grief, he recognized that Minny would survive in his imagination. The later characterizations of Isabel Archer in *The Portrait of a Lady* (1881) and especially Millie Theale in *The Wings of the Dove* (1902) owe much to James's perception of Minny as a prototypical American girl—bright, sensitive, and refined yet irrepressibly spirited and gay.

James's awareness of himself as an author developed during this early stay in Europe: he quite consciously realized that he was gathering material for future writing, and he expressed a commitment to earning an income from his pen. When he came back to his family in Cambridge, he spent two years writing articles and short fiction for magazines—a period he afterward referred to as "brooding exile," marking time until he could return to Europe. That opportunity came when he was asked to accompany his sister and their aunt on a European tour in 1872. He traveled as a working writer, submitting travel sketches to the *Nation* during his stay. James remained in Europe after the tour ended, and he continued to write for the *Atlantic* and *Galaxy*. In 1875 he published *Transatlantic Sketches* and the short novel *A Passionate Pilgrim* before returning to Cambridge, Massachusetts, in July of that year. In October he set sail once again for Europe and stayed for a time in Paris, where he frequently visited with his fellow novelists Ivan Turgenev, Gustave Flaubert, Alphonse Daudet, and Émile Zola. James moved on to London and, with rare interruptions, made England his home for the rest of his life.

James's fiction is usually divided into three periods, the first inaugurated with the publication of *Roderick Hudson* in 1876. During this early period James wrote *The American* (1877), *The Europeans* (1878), *Daisy Miller* (1879), *Washington Square* (1881), and *The Portrait of a Lady*. The promising note struck by *Roderick Hudson*, the story of an American sculptor in Italy, would sound throughout James's career: the situation of the American in Europe and the contrast between American and European temperaments and moral codes recur in his fiction. On the basis of this contrast, some readers have imputed to James a snobbish rejection of a native land he regarded as provincial and a wish to acquire the sophistication and culture he identified with Europeans; others note that the strength and innocence exhibited by his American characters emerge as the ultimate values of his fiction.

Like Honoré de Balzac—whom he regarded as his most important model—James was an astute social chronicler. Although E. M. Forster, an English novelist, has argued that the refined detail of James's social observations becomes trivial in the absence of more profound concerns, it is these very details that yield characters such as Madame Merle in *The Portrait of a Lady* and Lambert Strether in *The Ambassadors* and ultimately such themes as the unlived life and the negating power of self-absorbtion. Except for *Daisy Miller,* which attracted international attention to its author, James was never a bestselling writer, but he developed a devoted audience among critics and readers and was able to earn a living from his writing. He also enjoyed the society of the artistic and intellectual circles of his day.

James is as important a theoretician of fiction as he is a novelist. In addition to an appreciative critical biography of Nathaniel Hawthorne (1879) and *French Poets and Novelists* (1878), his essay "The Art of Fiction" (1888) is a highly significant statement of fictional principles. He wrote unique prefaces to the New York edition of his works, in each providing information about the "germ" of a novel and compelling insight into its composition. Selections from his voluminous notebooks have been edited and published since his death, and many of his sketches, reviews, and other essays have been published in various collections. James is considered a master of psychological realism and is always concerned with nuance of character and the subtleties of motivation and perception. For their mastery of these aspects of fiction writing, he admired George Eliot and, above all, the French and Russian realists Balzac, Flaubert, Zola, and Turgenev. It was his aim to refine and order the form of fiction to accommodate the exact and plenteous detail of these writers.

James's middle period is marked by *The Bostonians* (1886), *The Princess Casamassima* (1886), and *The Tragic Muse* (1889). At this time he put off novel-writing to write for the theater but found virtually no success. In 1895 he returned to fiction, writing tales and novellas, such as *What Maisie Knew* (1897), *The Spoils of Poynton* (1897), and the psychological thriller "The Turn of the Screw" (1898). Critics generally point out that the scenic techniques of the fiction he wrote at this time are informed by the dramatic method he had studied in the previous five years. The poet Stephen Spender claims that James revolutionized the modern novel with his manner of relating "scene" to the emotional development of the characters. In 1898 James purchased Lamb House in Rye, Sussex, and

The frontispiece of the first edition of Henry James's Daisy Miller.

continued to enjoy an active social life as the intimate of such prominent figures as the American painter John Singer Sargent and Edith Wharton.

Out of the final period of James's writing came such accomplished tales as "The Beast in the Jungle" (1903) and "The Jolly Corner" (1906) as well as the novels *The Wings of the Dove, The Ambassadors* (1903), and *The Golden Bowl* (1904). (He left unfinished at his death in 1916 *The Ivory Tower* and *The Sense of the Past,* both published a year later.) His most significant technical innovations in these later novels have to do with narrative point of view; the editor Percy Lubbock has noted the consummate craftsmanship of *The Ambassadors,* for example, which enables James to convey the details of the story through the perspective of a single character while depicting the expanding perceptions of that character. James's technical progress in this direction served as a model for James Joyce, Virginia Woolf, and other writers who would go on to employ the stream-of-consciousness method of narration. The waggish observation that "Henry James chewed more than he could bite off" is a recurrent criticism of this late fiction, which is known for its fulsome prose, its difficult, sometimes obscure, grammatical constructions, and its meticulous detail. But James's attention to language derives from a profound concern that the reader know his characters in all their complexity and experience his fictional world in the fullest possible way.

When Great Britain was drawn into World War I, James became a British citizen as a gesture of loyalty to his adopted country and in despair over what he perceived as America's failure to support Britain's defense. He was granted the Royal Order of Merit on New Year's Day, 1916—the only novelist beside George Meredith and Thomas Hardy to have been so honored. Henry James remains one of the most productive and influential writers in the history of the novel. Like Balzac and Dickens, he has left a valuable record of an age that has since disappeared. Just as importantly, he has directed writers of fiction to a closer scrutiny of their craft and has clarified the critical reader's assessment of how social and psychological reality can be presented in fiction. To judge by the quality of his achievement as theoretician and writer of fiction, his claims as an artist rest secure.

Suggested Readings: *The Novels and Tales of Henry James* (New York edition), 26 vols., 1907–1917, rpt. 1962–1965. *The Art of the Novel: Critical Prefaces*, ed. R. Blackmur, 1943. *The Notebooks of Henry James*, ed. F. O. Matthiessen and K. Murdock, 1947. *Stories of the Supernatural*, ed. L. Edel, 1949. *Autobiography*, 3 vols., ed. F. W. Dupee, 1956. *The Complete Tales of Henry James*, 12 vols., ed. L. Edel, 1962–1965. *The Letters of Henry James*, 4 vols., ed L. Edel, 1975–1984. L. Edel, *Henry James*, 5 vols., 1953–1972. Q. Anderson, *The American Henry James*, 1957. C. Wegelin, *The Image of Europe in Henry James*, 1958. R. Poirier, *The Comic Sense of Henry James: A Study of the Early Novels*, 1960. J. Ward, *The Imagination of Disaster: Evil in the Fiction of Henry James*, 1961. D. Krook, *The Ordeal of Consciousness in Henry James*, 1962. L. Holland, *The Expense of Vision: Essays on the Craft of Henry James*, 1964. M. Banta, *Henry James and the Occult*, 1972. O. Cargill, *The Novels of Henry James*, 1975. W. R. Veeder, *The Lesson of the Master*, 1975. J. Rowe, *Henry Adams and Henry James*, 1976. R. Yeazell, *Language and Knowledge in the Late Novels of Henry James*, 1976. D. Fogel, *Henry James and the Structure of the Romantic Imagination*, 1981. M. E. Jacobson, *Henry James and the Mass Market*, 1983. M. Seltzer, *Henry James and the Art of Power*, 1984. L. Edel, *Henry James: A Life*, 1985. D. McWhirter, *Desire and Love in Henry James: A Study of the Late Novels*, 1989.

Texts Used: "The Real Thing": *The Novels and Tales of Henry James* (New York edition), Vol. XVIII, 1909. "The Jolly Corner": *The Novels and Tales*, Vol. XVII, 1909. "The Art of Fiction": *Partial Portraits*, 1911.

THE REAL THING*

I

When the porter's wife, who used to answer the house-bell, announced "A gentleman and a lady, sir," I had, as I often had in those days—the wish being father to the thought—an immediate vision of sitters. Sitters my visitors in this case proved to be; but not in the sense I should have preferred. There was nothing at first however to indicate that they mightn't have come for a portrait. The gentleman, a man of fifty, very high and very straight, with a moustache slightly grizzled and a dark grey walking-coat admirably fitted, both of which I noted professionally—I don't mean as a barber or yet as a tailor—would have struck me as a celebrity if celebrities often were striking. It was a truth of which I had for some time been conscious that a figure with a good deal of frontage[1] was, as one might say, almost never a public institution. A glance at the lady helped to remind me of this paradoxical law: she also looked too distinguished to be a "personality." Moreover one would scarcely come across two variations together.

Neither of the pair immediately spoke—they only prolonged the preliminary gaze suggesting that each wished to give the other a chance. They were visibly

---

* First published in *Black and White* (1892).   [1] An imposing figure.

shy; they stood there letting me take them in—which, as I afterwards perceived, was the most practical thing they could have done. In this way their embarrassment served their cause. I had seen people painfully reluctant to mention that they desired anything so gross as to be represented on canvas; but the scruples of my new friends appeared almost insurmountable. Yet the gentleman might have said "I should like a portrait of my wife," and the lady might have said "I should like a portrait of my husband." Perhaps they weren't husband and wife—this naturally would make the matter more delicate. Perhaps they wished to be done together—in which case they ought to have brought a third person to break the news.

"We come from Mr. Rivet," the lady finally said with a dim smile that had the effect of a moist sponge passed over a "sunk"[2] piece of painting, as well as a vague allusion to vanished beauty. She was as tall and straight, in her degree, as her companion, and with ten years less to carry. She looked as sad as a woman could look whose face was not charged with expression; that is her tinted oval mask showed waste as an exposed surface shows friction. The hand of time had played over her freely, but to an effect of elimination. She was slim and stiff, and so well-dressed, in dark blue cloth, with lappets[3] and pockets and buttons, that it was clear she employed the same tailor as her husband. The couple had an indefinable air of prosperous thrift—they evidently got a good deal of luxury for their money. If I was to be one of their luxuries it would behove me to consider my terms.

"Ah Claude Rivet recommended me?" I echoed; and I added that it was very kind of him, though I could reflect that, as he only painted landscape, this wasn't a sacrifice.

The lady looked very hard at the gentleman, and the gentleman looked round the room. Then staring at the floor a moment and stroking his moustache, he rested his pleasant eyes on me with the remark: "He said you were the right one."

"I try to be, when people want to sit."

"Yes, we should like to," said the lady anxiously.

"Do you mean together?"

My visitors exchanged a glance. "If you could do anything with *me* I suppose it would be double," the gentleman stammered.

"Oh yes, there's naturally a higher charge for two figures than for one."

"We should like to make it pay," the husband confessed.

"That's very good of you," I returned, appreciating so unwonted a sympathy—for I supposed he meant pay the artist.

A sense of strangeness seemed to dawn on the lady.

"We mean for the illustrations—Mr. Rivet said you might put one in."

"Put in—an illustration?" I was equally confused.

"Sketch her off, you know," said the gentleman, colouring.

It was only then that I understood the service Claude Rivet had rendered me; he had told them how I worked in black-and-white, for magazines, for story-books, for sketches of contemporary life, and consequently had copious employment for models. These things were true, but it was not less true—I may confess it now; whether because the aspiration was to lead to everything or to nothing I leave the reader to guess—that I couldn't get the honours, to say nothing of the emoluments,[4] of a great painter of portraits out of my head. My "illustrations" were my pot-boilers; I looked to a different branch of art—far and away the most interest-

---

[2] Faded or dull.   [3] Folds or flaps.   [4] Profits.

ing it had always seemed to me—to perpetuate my fame. There was no shame in looking to it also to make my fortune; but that fortune was by so much further from being made from the moment my visitors wished to be "done" for nothing. I was disappointed; for in the pictorial sense I had immediately *seen* them. I had seized their type—I had already settled what I would do with it. Something that wouldn't absolutely have pleased them, I afterwards reflected.

"Ah you're—you're—a—?" I began as soon as I had mastered my surprise. I couldn't bring out the dingy word "models": it seemed so little to fit the case.

"We haven't had much practice," said the lady.

"We've got to *do* something, and we've thought that an artist in your line might perhaps make something of us," her husband threw off. He further mentioned that they didn't know many artists and that they had gone first, on the off-chance—he painted views of course, but sometimes put in figures; perhaps I remembered—to Mr. Rivet, whom they had met a few years before at a place in Norfolk where he was sketching.

"We used to sketch a little ourselves," the lady hinted.

"It's very awkward, but we absolutely *must* do something," her husband went on.

"Of course we're not so *very* young," she admitted with a wan smile.

With the remark that I might as well know something more about them the husband had handed me a card extracted from a neat new pocket-book—their appurtenances[5] were all of the freshest—and inscribed with the words "Major Monarch." Impressive as these words were they didn't carry my knowledge much further; but my visitor presently added: "I've left the army and we've had the misfortune to lose our money. In fact our means are dreadfully small."

"It's awfully trying—a regular strain," said Mrs. Monarch.

They evidently wished to be discreet—to take care not to swagger because they were gentlefolk. I felt them willing to recognise this as something of a drawback, at the same time that I guessed at an underlying sense—their consolation in adversity—that they *had* their points. They certainly had; but these advantages struck me as preponderantly social; such for instance as would help to make a drawing-room look well. However, a drawing-room was always, or ought to be, a picture.

In consequence of his wife's allusion to their age Major Monarch observed: "Naturally it's more for the figure that we thought of going in. We can still hold ourselves up." On the instant I saw that the figure was indeed their strong point. His "naturally" didn't sound vain, but it lighted up the question. "*She* has the best one," he continued, nodding at his wife with a pleasant after-dinner absence of circumlocution. I could only reply, as if we were in fact sitting over our wine, that this didn't prevent his own from being very good; which led him in turn to make answer: "We thought that if you ever had to do people like us we might be something like it. *She* particularly—for a lady in a book, you know."

I was so amused by them that, to get more of it, I did my best to take their point of view; and though it was an embarrassment to find myself appraising physically, as if they were animals on hire or useful blacks, a pair whom I should have expected to meet only in one of the relations in which criticism is tacit, I looked at Mrs. Monarch judicially enough to be able to exclaim after a moment with conviction: "Oh yes, a lady in a book!" She was singularly like a bad illustration.

---

[5] Belongings, accessories.

"We'll stand up, if you like," said the Major; and he raised himself before me with a really grand air.

I could take his measure at a glance—he was six feet two and a perfect gentleman. It would have paid any club in process of formation and in want of a stamp to engage him at a salary to stand in the principal window. What struck me at once was that in coming to me they had rather missed their vocation; they could surely have been turned to better account for advertising purposes. I couldn't of course see the thing in detail, but I could see them make somebody's fortune—I don't mean their own. There was something in them for a waistcoat-maker, an hotel-keeper or a soap-vendor. I could imagine "We always use it" pinned on their bosoms with the greatest effect; I had a vision of the brilliancy with which they would launch a table d'hôte.[6]

Mrs. Monarch sat still, not from pride but from shyness, and presently her husband said to her: "Get up, my dear, and show how smart you are." She obeyed, but she had no need to get up to show it. She walked to the end of the studio and then came back blushing, her fluttered eyes on the partner of her appeal. I was reminded of an incident I had accidentally had a glimpse of in Paris—being with a friend there, a dramatist about to produce a play, when an actress came to him to ask to be entrusted with a part. She went through her paces before him, walked up and down as Mrs. Monarch was doing. Mrs. Monarch did it quite well, but I abstained from applauding. It was very odd to see such people apply for such poor pay. She looked as if she had ten thousand a year. Her husband had used the word that described her: she was in the London current jargon essentially and typically "smart." Her figure was, in the same order of ideas, conspicuously and irreproachably "good." For a woman of her age her waist was surprisingly small; her elbow moreover had the orthodox crook. She held her head at the conventional angle, but why did she come to *me?* She ought to have tried on jackets at a big shop. I feared my visitors were not only destitute but "artistic"—which would be a great complication. When she sat down again I thanked her, observing that what a draughtsman most valued in his model was the faculty of keeping quiet.

"Oh, *she* can keep quiet," said Major Monarch. Then he added jocosely: "I've always kept her quiet."

"I'm not a nasty fidget, am I?" It was going to wring tears from me, I felt, the way she hid her head, ostrich-like, in the other broad bosom.

The owner of this expanse addressed his answer to me. "Perhaps it isn't out of place to mention—because we ought to be quite business-like, oughtn't we?—that when I married her she was known as the Beautiful Statue."

"Oh dear!" said Mrs. Monarch ruefully.

"Of course I should want a certain amount of expression," I rejoined.

"Of *course!*"—and I had never heard such unanimity.

"And then I suppose you know that you'll get awfully tired."

"Oh we *never* get tired!" they eagerly cried.

"Have you had any kind of practice?"

They hesitated—they looked at each other. "We've been photographed—*immensely*," said Mrs. Monarch.

"She means the fellows have asked us themselves," added the Major.

---

[6] A common table for guests at a hotel or restaurant.

"I see—because you're so good-looking."

"I don't know what they thought, but they were always after us."

"We always got our photographs for nothing," smiled Mrs. Monarch.

"We might have brought some, my dear," her husband remarked.

"I'm not sure we have any left. We've given quantities away," she explained to me.

"With our autographs and that sort of thing," said the Major.

"Are they to be got in the shops?" I enquired as a harmless pleasantry.

"Oh yes, *hers*—they used to be."

"Not now," said Mrs. Monarch with her eyes on the floor.

II

I could fancy the "sort of thing" they put on the presentation copies of their photographs, and I was sure they wrote a beautiful hand. It was odd how quickly I was sure of everything that concerned them. If they were now so poor as to have to earn shillings and pence they could never have had much of a margin. Their good looks had been their capital, and they had good-humouredly made the most of the career that this resource marked out for them. It was in their faces, the blankness, the deep intellectual repose of the twenty years of country-house[7] visiting that had given them pleasant intonations. I could see the sunny drawing-rooms, sprinkled with periodicals she didn't read, in which Mrs. Monarch had continuously sat; I could see the wet shrubberies in which she had walked, equipped to admiration for either exercise. I could see the rich covers[8] the Major had helped to shoot and the wonderful garments in which, late at night, he repaired to the smoking-room to talk about them. I could imagine their leggings and waterproofs, their knowing tweeds and rugs, their rolls of sticks and cases of tackle and neat umbrellas; and I could evoke the exact appearance of their servants and the compact variety of their luggage on the platforms of country stations.

They gave small tips, but they were liked; they didn't do anything themselves, but they were welcome. They looked so well everywhere; they gratified the general relish for stature, complexion and "form." They knew it without fatuity or vulgarity, and they respected themselves in consequence. They weren't superficial; they were thorough and kept themselves up—it had been their line. People with such a taste for activity had to have some line. I could feel how even in a dull house they could have been counted on for the joy of life. At present something had happened—it didn't matter what, their little income had grown less, it had grown least—and they had to do something for pocket-money. Their friends could like them, I made out, without liking to support them. There was something about them that represented credit—their clothes, their manners, their type; but if credit is a large empty pocket in which an occasional chink reverberates, the chink at least must be audible. What they wanted of me was to help to make it so. Fortunately they had no children—I soon divined that. They would also perhaps wish our relations to be kept secret: this was why it was "for the figure"—the reproduction of the face would betray them.

---

[7] A country estate of the well-to-do.   [8] Game birds taken out of hiding places.

I liked them—I felt, quite as their friends must have done—they were so simple; and I had no objection to them if they would suit. But somehow with all their perfections I didn't easily believe in them. After all they were amateurs, and the ruling passion of my life was the detestation of the amateur. Combined with this was another perversity—an innate preference for the represented subject over the real one: the defect of the real one was so apt to be a lack of representation. I liked things that appeared; then one was sure. Whether they *were* or not was a subordinate and almost always a profitless question. There were other considerations, the first of which was that I already had two or three recruits in use, notably a young person with big feet, in alpaca,[9] from Kilburn, who for a couple of years had come to me regularly for my illustrations and with whom I was still—perhaps ignobly—satisfied. I frankly explained to my visitors how the case stood, but they had taken more precautions than I supposed. They had reasoned out their opportunity, for Claude Rivet had told them of the projected *édition de luxe* of one of the writers of our day—the rarest of the novelists—who, long neglected by the multitudinous vulgar and dearly prized by the attentive (need I mention Philip Vincent?) had had the happy fortune of seeing, late in life, the dawn and then the full light of a higher criticism; an estimate in which on the part of the public there was something really of expiation. The edition preparing, planned by a publisher of taste, was practically an act of high reparation; the wood-cuts with which it was to be enriched were the homage of English art to one of the most independent representatives of English letters. Major and Mrs. Monarch confessed to me they had hoped I might be able to work *them* into my branch of the enterprise. They knew I was to do the first of the books, "Rutland Ramsay," but I had to make clear to them that my participation in the rest of the affair—this first book was to be a test—must depend on the satisfaction I should give. If this should be limited my employers would drop me with scarce common forms. It was therefore a crisis for me, and naturally I was making special preparations, looking about for new people, should they be necessary, and securing the best types. I admitted however that I should like to settle down to two or three good models who would do for everything.

"Should we have often to—a—put on special clothes?" Mrs. Monarch timidly demanded.

"Dear yes—that's half the business."

"And should we be expected to supply our own costumes?"

"Oh no; I've got a lot of things. A painter's models put on—or put off—anything he likes."

"And you mean—a—the same?"

"The same?"

Mrs. Monarch looked at her husband again.

"Oh she was just wondering," he explained, "if the costumes are in *general* use." I had to confess that they were, and I mentioned further that some of them—I had a lot of genuine greasy last-century things—had served their time, a hundred years ago, on living world-stained men and women; on figures not perhaps so far removed, in that vanished world, from *their* type, the Monarchs', *quoi!*[10] of a breeched and bewigged age. "We'll put on anything that *fits*," said the Major.

---

[9] Dressed in alpaca wool.   [10] "What!" (French).

"Oh I arrange that—they fit in the pictures."

"I'm afraid I should do better for the modern books. I'd come as you like," said Mrs. Monarch.

"She has got a lot of clothes at home: they might do for contemporary life," her husband continued.

"Oh I can fancy scenes in which you'd be quite natural." And indeed I could see the slipshod rearrangements of stale properties—the stories I tried to produce pictures for without the exasperation of reading them—whose sandy tracts the good lady might help to people. But I had to return to the fact that for this sort of work—the daily mechanical grind—I was already equipped: the people I was working with were fully adequate.

"We only thought we might be more like *some* characters," said Mrs. Monarch mildly, getting up.

Her husband also rose; he stood looking at me with a dim wistfulness that was touching in so fine a man. "Wouldn't it be rather a pull sometimes to have—a—to have—?" He hung fire;[11] he wanted me to help him by phrasing what he meant. But I couldn't—I didn't know. So he brought it out awkwardly: "The *real* thing; a gentleman, you know, or a lady." I was quite ready to give a general assent—I admitted that there was a great deal in that. This encouraged Major Monarch to say, following up his appeal with an unacted gulp: "It's awfully hard—we've tried everything." The gulp was communicative; it proved too much for his wife. Before I knew it Mrs. Monarch had dropped again upon a divan[12] and burst into tears. Her husband sat down beside her, holding one of her hands; whereupon she quickly dried her eyes with the other, while I felt embarrassed as she looked up at me. "There isn't a confounded job I haven't applied for—waited for—prayed for. You can fancy we'd be pretty bad first. Secretaryships and that sort of thing? You might as well ask for a peerage. I'd be *anything*—I'm strong; a messenger or a coalheaver. I'd put on a gold-laced cap and open carriage-doors in front of the haberdasher's; I'd hang about a station to carry portmanteaux;[13] I'd be a postman. But they won't *look* at you; there are thousands as good as yourself already on the ground. *Gentlemen*, poor beggars, who've drunk their wine, who've kept their hunters!"

I was as reassuring as I knew how to be, and my visitors were presently on their feet again while, for the experiment, we agreed on an hour. We were discussing it when the door opened and Miss Churm came in with a wet umbrella. Miss Churm had to take the omnibus to Maida Vale and then walk half a mile. She looked a trifle blowsy and slightly splashed. I scarcely ever saw her come in without thinking afresh how odd it was that, being so little in herself, she should yet be so much in others. She was a meagre little Miss Churm, but was such an ample heroine of romance. She was only a freckled cockney, but she could represent everything, from a fine lady to a shepherdess; she had the faculty as she might have had a fine voice or long hair. She couldn't spell and she loved beer, but she had two or three "points," and practice, and a knack, and mother-wit, and a whimsical sensibility, and a love of the theatre, and seven sisters, and not an ounce of respect, especially for the *h*.[14] The first thing my visitors saw was that her umbrella was wet, and in

[11] Delayed expressing himself.   [12] A long, backless couch.
[13] Large leather suitcases with two hinged compartments.
[14] In the cockney dialect of London's East End, the *h*'s are dropped from words.

their spotless perfection they visibly winced at it. The rain had come on since their arrival.

"I'm all in a soak; there *was* a mess of people in the 'bus. I wish you lived near a stytion," said Miss Churm. I requested her to get ready as quickly as possible, and she passed into the room in which she always changed her dress. But before going out she asked me what she was to get into this time.

"It's the Russian princess, don't you know?" I answered; "the one with the 'golden eyes,' in black velvet, for the long thing in the *Cheapside*."[15]

"Golden eyes? I *say!*" cried Miss Churm, while my companions watched her with intensity as she withdrew. She always arranged herself, when she was late, before I could turn round; and I kept my visitors a little on purpose, so that they might get an idea, from seeing her, what would be expected of themselves. I mentioned that she was quite my notion of an excellent model—she was really very clever.

"Do you think she looks like a Russian princess?" Major Monarch asked with lurking alarm.

"When I make her, yes."

"Oh if you have to *make* her—!" he reasoned, not without point.

"That's the most you can ask. There are so many who are not makeable."

"Well now, *here's* a lady"—and with a persuasive smile he passed his arm into his wife's—"who's already made!"

"Oh I'm not a Russian princess," Mrs. Monarch protested a little coldly. I could see she had known some and didn't like them. There at once was a complication of a kind I never had to fear with Miss Churm.

This young lady came back in black velvet—the gown was rather rusty and very low on her lean shoulders—and with a Japanese fan in her red hands. I reminded her that in the scene I was doing she had to look over some one's head. "I forget whose it is; but it doesn't matter. Just look over a head."

"I'd rather look over a stove," said Miss Churm; and she took her station near the fire. She fell into position, settled herself into a tall attitude, gave a certain backward inclination to her head and a certain forward droop to her fan, and looked, at least to my prejudiced sense, distinguished and charming, foreign and dangerous. We left her looking so while I went downstairs with Major and Mrs. Monarch.

"I believe I could come about as near it as that," said Mrs. Monarch.

"Oh you think she's shabby, but you must allow for the alchemy of art."

However, they went off with an evident increase of comfort founded on their demonstrable advantage in being the real thing. I could fancy them shuddering over Miss Churm. She was very droll about them when I went back, for I told her what they wanted.

"Well, if *she* can sit I'll tyke to bookkeeping," said my model.

"She's very ladylike," I replied as an innocent form of aggravation.

"So much the worse for *you*. That means she can't turn round."

"She'll do for the fashionable novels."

"Oh yes, she'll *do* for them!" my model humorously declared. "Ain't they bad enough without her?" I had often sociably denounced them to Miss Churm.

---

[15] An imaginary magazine named after a London business street.

III

It was for the elucidation of a mystery in one of these works that I first tried Mrs. Monarch. Her husband came with her, to be useful if necessary—it was sufficiently clear that as a general thing he would prefer to come with her. At first I wondered if this were for "propriety's" sake—if he were going to be jealous and meddling. The idea was too tiresome, and if it had been confirmed it would speedily have brought our acquaintance to a close. But I soon saw there was nothing in it and that if he accompanied Mrs. Monarch it was—in addition to the chance of being wanted—simply because he had nothing else to do. When they were separate his occupation was gone and they never *had* been separate. I judged rightly that in their awkward situation their close union was their main comfort and that this union had no weak spot. It was a real marriage, an encouragement to the hesitating, a nut for pessimists to crack. Their address was humble—I remember afterwards thinking it had been the only thing about them that was really professional—and I could fancy the lamentable lodgings in which the Major would have been left alone. He could sit there more or less grimly with his wife—he couldn't sit there anyhow without her.

He had too much tact to try and make himself agreeable when he couldn't be useful; so when I was too absorbed in my work to talk he simply sat and waited. But I liked to hear him talk—it made my work, when not interrupting it, less mechanical, less special. To listen to him was to combine the excitement of going out with the economy of staying at home. There was only one hindrance—that I seemed not to know any of the people this brilliant couple had known. I think he wondered extremely, during the term of our intercourse, whom the deuce I *did* know. He hadn't a stray sixpence of an idea to fumble for, so we didn't spin it very fine; we confined ourselves to questions of leather and even of liquor—saddlers and breeches-makers and how to get excellent claret cheap—and matters like "good trains" and the habits of small game. His lore on these last subjects was astonishing—he managed to interweave the station-master with the ornithologist. When he couldn't talk about greater things he could talk cheerfully about smaller, and since I couldn't accompany him into reminiscences of the fashionable world he could lower the conversation without a visible effort to my level.

So earnest a desire to please was touching in a man who could so easily have knocked one down. He looked after the fire and had an opinion on the draught of the stove without my asking him, and I could see that he thought many of my arrangements not half knowing. I remember telling him that if I were only rich I'd offer him a salary to come and teach me how to live. Sometimes he gave a random sigh of which the essence might have been: "Give me even such a bare old barrack as *this,* and I'd do something with it!" When I wanted to use him he came alone; which was an illustration of the superior courage of women. His wife could bear her solitary second floor, and she was in general more discreet; showing by various small reserves that she was alive to the propriety of keeping our relations markedly professional—not letting them slide into sociability. She wished it to remain clear that she and the Major were employed, not cultivated, and if she approved of me as a superior, who could be kept in his place, she never thought me quite good enough for an equal.

She sat with great intensity, giving the whole of her mind to it, and was capable of remaining for an hour almost as motionless as before a photographer's lens. I could see she had been photographed often, but somehow the very habit that made her good for that purpose unfitted her for mine. At first I was extremely pleased with her ladylike air, and it was a satisfaction, on coming to follow her lines, to see how good they were and how far they could lead the pencil. But after a little skirmishing I began to find her too insurmountably stiff; do what I would with it my drawing looked like a photograph or a copy of a photograph. Her figure had no variety of expression—she herself had no sense of variety. You may say that this was my business and was only a question of placing her. Yet I placed her in every conceivable position and she managed to obliterate their differences. She was always a lady certainly and into the bargain was always the same lady. She was the real thing, but always the same thing. There were moments when I rather writhed under the serenity of her confidence that she *was* the real thing. All her dealings with me and all her husband's were an implication that this was lucky for *me*. Meanwhile I found myself trying to invent types that approached her own, instead of making her own transform itself—in the clever way that was not impossible for instance to poor Miss Churm. Arrange as I would and take the precautions as I would, she always came out, in my pictures, too tall—landing me in the dilemma of having represented a fascinating woman as seven feet high, which (out of respect perhaps to my own very much scantier inches) was far from my idea of such a personage.

The case was worse with the Major—nothing I could do would keep *him* down, so that he became useful only for the representation of brawny giants. I adored variety and range, I cherished human accidents, the illustrative note; I wanted to characterise closely, and the thing in the world I most hated was the danger of being ridden by a type. I had quarrelled with some of my friends about it; I had parted company with them for maintaining that one *had* to be, and that if the type was beautiful—witness Raphael and Leonardo[16]—the servitude was only a gain. I was neither Leonardo nor Raphael—I might only be a presumptuous young modern searcher; but I held that everything was to be sacrificed sooner than character. When they claimed that the obsessional form could easily *be* character I retorted, perhaps superficially, "Whose?" It couldn't be everybody's—it might end in being nobody's.

After I had drawn Mrs. Monarch a dozen times I felt surer even than before that the value of such a model as Miss Churm resided precisely in the fact that she had no positive stamp, combined of course with the other fact that what she did have was a curious and inexplicable talent for imitation. Her usual appearance was like a curtain which she could draw up at request for a capital performance. This performance was simply suggestive; but it was a word to the wise—it was vivid and pretty. Sometimes even I thought it, though she was plain herself, too insipidly pretty; I made it a reproach to her that the figures drawn from her were monotonously (*bêtement*,[17] as we used to say) graceful. Nothing made her more angry: it was so much her pride to feel she could sit for characters that had nothing in common with each other. She would accuse me at such moments of taking away her "reputytion."

It suffered a certain shrinkage, this queer quantity, from the repeated visits of my new friends. Miss Churm was greatly in demand, never in want of employment, so I had no scruple in putting her off occasionally, to try them more at my ease. It was certainly amusing at first to do the real thing—it was amusing to do

---

[16] The famous Italian painters Raffaelo Sanzio (1483–1520) and Leonardo da Vinci (1452–1519).
[17] "Stupidly" (French).

Major Monarch's trousers. They *were* the real thing, even if he did come out colossal. It was amusing to do his wife's back hair—it was so mathematically neat—and the particular "smart" tension of her tight stays.[18] She lent herself especially to positions in which the face was somewhat averted or blurred; she abounded in ladylike back views and *profils perdus*.[19] When she stood erect she took naturally one of the attitudes in which court-painters represent queens and princesses; so that I found myself wondering whether, to draw out this accomplishment, I couldn't get the editor of the *Cheapside* to publish a really royal romance, "A Tale of Buckingham Palace." Sometimes however the real thing and the make-believe came into contact; by which I mean that Miss Churm, keeping an appointment or coming to make one on days when I had much work in hand, encountered her invidious rivals. The encounter was not on their part, for they noticed her no more than if she had been the housemaid; not from intentional loftiness, but simply because as yet, professionally, they didn't know how to fraternise, as I could imagine they would have liked—or at least that the Major would. They couldn't talk about the omnibus—they always walked; and they didn't know what else to try—she wasn't interested in good trains or cheap claret. Besides, they must have felt—in the air—that she was amused at them, secretly derisive of their ever knowing how. She wasn't a person to conceal the limits of her faith if she had had a chance to show them. On the other hand Mrs. Monarch didn't think her tidy; for why else did she take pains to say to me—it was going out of the way, for Mrs. Monarch—that she didn't like dirty women?

One day when my young lady happened to be present with my other sitters—and she even dropped in, when it was convenient, for a chat—I asked her to be so good as to lend a hand in getting tea, a service with which she was familiar and which was one of a class that, living as I did in a small way, with slender domestic resources, I often appealed to my models to render. They liked to lay hands on my property, to break the sitting, and sometimes the china—it made them feel Bohemian.[20] The next time I saw Miss Churm after this incident she surprised me greatly by making a scene about it—she accused me of having wished to humiliate her. She hadn't resented the outrage at the time, but had seemed obliging and amused, enjoying the comedy of asking Mrs. Monarch, who sat vague and silent, whether she would have cream and sugar, and putting an exaggerated simper into the question. She had tried intonations—as if she too wished to pass for the real thing—till I was afraid my other visitors would take offence.

Oh they were determined not to do this, and their touching patience was the measure of their great need. They would sit by the hour, uncomplaining, till I was ready to use them; they would come back on the chance of being wanted and would walk away cheerfully if it failed. I used to go to the door with them to see in what magnificent order they retreated. I tried to find other employment for them—I introduced them to several artists. But they didn't "take," for reasons I could appreciate, and I became rather anxiously aware that after such disappointments they fell back upon me with a heavier weight. They did me the honour to think me most *their* form. They weren't romantic enough for the painters, and in those days there were few serious workers in black-and-white. Besides, they had

---

[18] Stiffenings in a corset.
[19] "Lost profiles" (French), or poses that show a face looking back over the shoulder.
[20] Artistic or unconventional.

on supplying the right essence for my pictorial vindication of our fine novelist. They knew that for this undertaking I should want no costume-effects, none of the frippery[21] of past ages—that it was a case in which everything would be contemporary and satirical and presumably genteel. If I could work them into it their future would be assured, for the labour would of course be long and the occupation steady.

One day Mrs. Monarch came without her husband—she explained his absence by his having had to go to the City.[22] While she sat there in her usual relaxed majesty there came at the door a knock which I immediately recognised as the subdued appeal of a model out of work. It was followed by the entrance of a young man whom I at once saw to be a foreigner and who proved in fact an Italian acquainted with no English word but my name, which he uttered in a way that made it seem to include all others. I hadn't then visited his country, nor was I proficient in his tongue; but as he was not so meanly constituted—what Italian is?—as to depend only on that member for expression he conveyed to me, in familiar but graceful mimicry, that he was in search of exactly the employment in which the lady before me was engaged. I was not struck with him at first, and while I continued to draw I dropped few signs of interest or encouragement. He stood his ground however—not importunately, but with a dumb dog-like fidelity in his eyes that amounted to innocent impudence, the manner of a devoted servant—he might have been in the house for years—unjustly suspected. Suddenly it struck me that this very attitude and expression made a picture; whereupon I told him to sit down and wait till I should be free. There was another picture in the way he obeyed me, and I observed as I worked that there were others still in the way he looked wonderingly, with his head thrown back, about the high studio. He might have been crossing himself in Saint Peter's.[23] Before I finished I said to myself "The fellow's a bankrupt orange-monger, but a treasure."

When Mrs. Monarch withdrew he passed across the room like a flash to open the door for her, standing there with the rapt pure gaze of the young Dante spellbound by the young Beatrice.[24] As I never insisted, in such situations, on the blankness of the British domestic, I reflected that he had the making of a servant—and I needed one, but couldn't pay him to be only that—as well as of a model; in short I resolved to adopt my bright adventurer if he would agree to officiate in the double capacity. He jumped at my offer, and in the event my rashness—for I had really known nothing about him—wasn't brought home to me. He proved a sympathetic though a desultory ministrant, and had in a wonderful degree the *sentiment de la pose*.[25] It was uncultivated, instinctive, a part of the happy instinct that had guided him to my door and helped him to spell out my name on the card nailed to it. He had had no other introduction to me than a guess, from the shape of my high north window, seen outside, that my place was a studio and that as a studio it would contain an artist. He had wandered to England in search of fortune, like other itinerants, and had embarked, with a partner and a small green hand-cart, on the sale of penny ices. The ices had melted away and the

[21] Cheap, gaudy clothes.
[22] London's financial and commercial district.   [23] Cathedral in the Vatican, Rome.
[24] Beatrice Portinari (1266–1290), the inspiration for the Italian poet Dante Alighieri (1265–1321), and a character in his *Divine Comedy*.
[25] Instinct for posing (French).

reddish stripes and his name was Oronte. He was sallow but fair, and when I put him into some old clothes of my own he looked like an Englishman. He was as good as Miss Churm, who could look, when requested, like an Italian.

IV

I thought Mrs. Monarch's face slightly convulsed when, on her coming back with her husband, she found Oronte installed. It was strange to have to recognise in a scrap of a lazzarone[26] a competitor to her magnificent Major. It was she who scented danger first, for the Major was anecdotically unconscious. But Oronte gave us tea, with a hundred eager confusions—he had never been concerned in so queer a process—and I think she thought better of me for having at last an "establishment." They saw a couple of drawings that I had made of the establishment, and Mrs. Monarch hinted that it never would have struck her he had sat for them. "Now the drawings you make from *us,* they look exactly like us," she reminded me, smiling in triumph; and I recognised that this was indeed just their defect. When I drew the Monarchs I couldn't anyhow get away from them—get into the character I wanted to represent; and I hadn't the least desire my model should be discoverable in my picture. Miss Churm never was, and Mrs. Monarch thought I hid her, very properly, because she was vulgar; whereas if she was lost it was only as the dead who go to heaven are lost—in the gain of an angel the more.

By this time I had got a certain start with "Rutland Ramsay," the first novel in the great projected series; that is I had produced a dozen drawings, several with the help of the Major and his wife, and I had sent them in for approval. My understanding with the publishers, as I have already hinted, had been that I was to be left to do my work, in this particular case, as I liked, with the whole book committed to me; but my connexion with the rest of the series was only contingent. There were moments when, frankly, it *was* a comfort to have the real thing under one's hand; for there were characters in "Rutland Ramsay" that were very much like it. There were people presumably as erect as the Major and women of as good a fashion as Mrs. Monarch. There was a great deal of country-house life—treated, it is true, in a fine fanciful ironical generalised way—and there was a considerable implication of knickerbockers and kilts. There were certain things I had to settle at the outset; such things for instance as the exact appearance of the hero and the particular bloom and figure of the heroine. The author of course gave me a lead, but there was margin for interpretation. I took the Monarchs into my confidence, I told them frankly what I was about, I mentioned my embarrassments and alternatives. "Oh take *him!* Mrs. Monarch murmured sweetly, looking at her husband; and "What could you want better than my wife?" the Major enquired with the comfortable candour that now prevailed between us.

I wasn't obliged to answer these remarks—I was only obliged to place my sitters. I wasn't easy in mind, and I postponed a little timidly perhaps the solving of my question. The book was a large canvas, the other figures were numerous, and I worked off at first some of the episodes in which the hero and the heroine were not concerned. When once I had set *them* up I should have to stick to them— I couldn't make my young man seven feet high in one place and five feet nine in another. I inclined on the whole to the latter measurement, though the Major more

---

[26] A beggar or cad (Italian).

than once reminded me that *he* looked about as young as any one. It was indeed quite possible to arrange him, for the figure, so that it would have been difficult to detect his age. After the spontaneous Oronte had been with me a month, and after I had given him to understand several times over that his native exuberance would presently constitute an insurmountable barrier to our further intercourse, I waked to a sense of his heroic capacity. He was only five feet seven, but the remaining inches were latent. I tried him almost secretly at first, for I was really rather afraid of the judgement my other models would pass on such a choice. If they regarded Miss Churm as little better than a snare what would they think of the representation by a person so little the real thing as an Italian street-vendor of a protagonist formed by a public school?

If I went a little in fear of them it wasn't because they bullied me, because they had got an oppressive foothold, but because in their really pathetic decorum and mysteriously permanent newness they counted on me so intensely. I was therefore very glad when Jack Hawley came home: he was always of such good counsel. He painted badly himself, but there was no one like him for putting his finger on the place. He had been absent from England for a year; he had been somewhere—I don't remember where—to get a fresh eye. I was in a good deal of dread of any such organ, but we were old friends; he had been away for months and a sense of emptiness was creeping into my life. I hadn't dodged a missile for a year.

He came back with a fresh eye, but with the same old black velvet blouse, and the first evening he spent in my studio we smoked cigarettes till the small hours. He had done no work himself, he had only got the eye; so the field was clear for the production of my little things. He wanted to see what I had produced for the *Cheapside,* but he was disappointed in the exhibition. That at least seemed the meaning of two or three comprehensive groans which, as he lounged on my big divan, his leg folded under him, looking at my latest drawings, issued from his lips with the smoke of the cigarette.

"What's the matter with you?" I asked.

"What's the matter with *you?*"

"Nothing save that I'm mystified."

"You are indeed. You're quite off the hinge. What's the meaning of this new fad?" And he tossed me, with visible irreverence, a drawing in which I happened to have depicted both my elegant models. I asked if he didn't think it good, and he replied that it struck him as execrable, given the sort of thing I had always represented myself to him as wishing to arrive at; but I let that pass—I was so anxious to see exactly what he meant. The two figures in the picture looked colossal, but I supposed this was *not* what he meant, inasmuch as, for aught he knew to the contrary, I might have been trying for some such effect. I maintained that I was working exactly in the same way as when he last had done me the honour to tell me I might do something some day. "Well, there's a screw loose somewhere," he answered; "wait a bit and I'll discover it." I depended upon him to do so: where else was the fresh eye? But he produced at last nothing more luminous than "I don't know—I don't like your types." This was lame for a critic who had never consented to discuss with me anything but the question of execution, the direction of strokes and the mystery of values.

"In the drawings you've been looking at I think my types are very handsome."

"Oh they won't do!"

"I've been working with new models."

"I see you have. *They* won't do."

"Are you very sure of that?"

"Absolutely—they're stupid."

"You mean *I* am—for I ought to get round that."

"You *can't*—with such people. Who are they?"

I told him, so far as was necessary, and he concluded heartlessly: "Ce sont des gens qu'il faut mettre à la porte."[27]

"You've never seen them; they're awfully good"—I flew to their defence.

"Not seen them? Why all this recent work of yours drops to pieces with them. It's all I want to see of them."

"No one else has said anything against it—the *Cheapside* people are pleased."

"Every one else is an ass, and the *Cheapside* people the biggest asses of all. Come, don't pretend at this time of day to have pretty illusions about the public, especially about publishers and editors. It's not for *such* animals you work—it's for those who know, *coloro che sanno*,[28] so keep straight for *me* if you can't keep straight for yourself. There was a certain sort of thing you used to try for—and a very good thing it was. But this twaddle isn't *in* it." When I talked with Hawley later about "Rutland Ramsay" and its possible successors he declared that I must get back into my boat again or I should go to the bottom. His voice in short was the voice of warning.

I noted the warning, but I didn't turn my friends out of doors. They bored me a good deal; but the very fact that they bored me admonished me not to sacrifice them—if there was anything to be done with them—simply to irritation. As I look back at this phase they seem to me to have pervaded my life not a little. I have a vision of them as most of the time in my studio, seated against the wall on an old velvet bench to be out of the way, and resembling the while a pair of patient courtiers in a royal ante-chamber. I'm convinced that during the coldest weeks of the winter they held their ground because it saved them fire. Their newness was losing its gloss, and it was impossible not to feel them objects of charity. Whenever Miss Churm arrived they went away, and after I was fairly launched in "Rutland Ramsay" Miss Churm arrived pretty often. They managed to express to me tacitly that they supposed I wanted her for the low life of the book, and I let them suppose it, since they had attempted to study the work—it was lying about the studio—without discovering that it dealt only with the highest circles. They had dipped into the most brilliant of our novelists without deciphering many passages. I still took an hour from them, now and again, in spite of Jack Hawley's warning: it would be time enough to dismiss them, if dismissal should be necessary, when the rigour of the season was over. Hawley had made their acquaintance—he had met them at my fireside—and thought them a ridiculous pair. Learning that he was a painter they tried to approach him, to show him too that they were the real thing; but he looked at them, across the big room, as if they were miles away; they were a compendium of everything he most objected to in the social system of his country. Such people as that, all convention and patent-leather, with ejaculations that stopped conversation, had no business in a studio. A studio was a place to learn to see, and how could you see through a pair of feather-beds?

The main inconvenience I suffered at their hands was that at first I was shy of letting it break upon them that my artful little servant had begun to sit to me for

---

[27] "They are people who should be shown the door" (French).

[28] "Those who know" (Italian): from Dante's *Inferno* (IV. 131).

"Rutland Ramsay." They knew I had been odd enough—they were prepared by this time to allow oddity to artists—to pick a foreign vagabond out of the streets when I might have had a person with whiskers and credentials; but it was some time before they learned how high I rated his accomplishments. They found him in an attitude more than once, but they never doubted I was doing him as an organ-grinder. There were several things they never guessed, and one of them was that for a striking scene in the novel, in which a footman briefly figured, it occurred to me to make use of Major Monarch as the menial. I kept putting this off, I didn't like to ask him to don the livery—besides the difficulty of finding a livery to fit him. At last, one day late in the winter, when I was at work on the despised Oronte, who caught one's idea on the wing, and was in the glow of feeling myself go very straight, they came in, the Major and his wife, with their society laugh about nothing (there was less and less to laugh at); came in like country-callers—they always reminded me of that—who have walked across the park after church and are presently persuaded to stay to luncheon. Luncheon was over, but they could stay to tea—I knew they wanted it. The fit was on me, however, and I couldn't let my ardour cool and my work wait, with the fading daylight, while my model prepared it. So I asked Mrs. Monarch if she would mind laying it out—a request which for an instant brought all the blood to her face. Her eyes were on her husband's for a second, and some mute telegraphy passed between them. Their folly was over the next instant; his cheerful shrewdness put an end to it. So far from pitying their wounded pride, I must add, I was moved to give it as complete a lesson as I could. They bustled about together and got out the cups and saucers and made the kettle boil. I know they felt as if they were waiting on my servant, and when the tea was prepared I said: "He'll have a cup, please—he's tired." Mrs. Monarch brought him one where he stood, and he took it from her as if he had been a gentleman at a party squeezing a crush-hat with an elbow.

Then it came over me that she had made a great effort for me—made it with a kind of nobleness—and that I owed her a compensation. Each time I saw her after this I wondered what the compensation could be. I couldn't go on doing the wrong thing to oblige them. Oh it *was* the wrong thing, the stamp of the work for which they sat—Hawley was not the only person to say it now. I sent in a large number of the drawings I had made for "Rutland Ramsay," and I received a warning that was more to the point than Hawley's. The artistic adviser of the house for which I was working was of opinion that many of my illustrations were not what had been looked for. Most of these illustrations were the subjects in which the Monarchs had figured. Without going into the question of what *had* been looked for, I had to face the fact that at this rate I shouldn't get the other books to do. I hurled myself in despair on Miss Churm—I put her through all her paces. I not only adopted Oronte publicly as my hero, but one morning when the Major looked in to see if I didn't require him to finish a *Cheapside* figure for which he had begun to sit the week before, I told him I had changed my mind—I'd do the drawing from my man. At this my visitor turned pale and stood looking at me. "Is *he* your idea of an English gentleman?" he asked.

I was disappointed, I was nervous, I wanted to get on with my work; so I replied with irritation: "Oh my dear Major—I can't be ruined for *you!*"

It was a horrid speech, but he stood another moment—after which, without a word, he quitted the studio. I drew a long breath, for I said to myself that I shouldn't see him again. I hadn't told him definitely that I was in danger of having my work rejected, but I was vexed at his not having felt the catastrophe in the air, read with me the moral of our fruitless collaboration, the lesson that in the deceptive atmosphere of art even the highest respectability may fail of being plastic.[29]

I didn't owe my friends money, but I did see them again. They reappeared together three days later, and, given all the other facts, there was something tragic in that one. It was a clear proof they could find nothing else in life to do. They had threshed the matter out in a dismal conference—they had digested the bad news that they were not in for the series. If they weren't useful to me even for the *Cheapside* their function seemed difficult to determine, and I could only judge at first that they had come, forgivingly, decorously, to take a last leave. This made me rejoice in secret that I had little leisure for a scene; for I had placed both my other models in position together and I was pegging away at a drawing from which I hoped to derive glory. It had been suggested by the passage in which Rutland Ramsay, drawing up a chair to Artemisia's piano-stool, says extraordinary things to her while she ostensibly fingers out a difficult piece of music. I had done Miss Churm at the piano before—it was an attitude in which she knew how to take on an absolutely poetic grace. I wished the two figures to "compose" together with intensity, and my little Italian had entered perfectly into my conception. The pair were vividly before me, the piano had been pulled out; it was a charming show of blended youth and murmured love, which I had only to catch and keep. My visitors stood and looked at it, and I was friendly to them over my shoulder.

They made no response, but I was used to silent company and went on with my work, only a little disconcerted—even though exhilarated by the sense that *this* was at least the ideal thing—at not having got rid of them after all. Presently I heard Mrs. Monarch's sweet voice beside or rather above me: "I wish her hair were a little better done." I looked up and she was staring with a strange fixedness at Miss Churm, whose back was turned to her. "Do you mind my just touching it?" she went on—a question which made me spring up for an instant as with the instinctive fear that she might do the young lady a harm. But she quieted me with a glance I shall never forget—I confess I should like to have been able to paint *that*—and went for a moment to my model. She spoke to her softly, laying a hand on her shoulder and bending over her; and as the girl, understanding, gratefully assented, she disposed her rough curls, with a few quick passes, in such a way as to make Miss Churm's head twice as charming. It was one of the most heroic personal services I've ever seen rendered. Then Mrs. Monarch turned away with a low sigh and, looking about her as if for something to do, stooped to the floor with a noble humility and picked up a dirty rag that had dropped out of my paint-box.

The Major meanwhile had also been looking for something to do, and, wandering to the other end of the studio, saw before him my breakfast-things neglected, unremoved. "I say, can't I be useful *here?*" he called out to me with an irrepressible quaver. I assented with a laugh that I fear was awkward, and for the next ten minutes, while I worked, I heard the light clatter of china and the tinkle of spoons and glass. Mrs. Monarch assisted her husband—they washed up my crockery, they put it away. They wandered off into my little scullery, and I afterwards found that they had cleaned my knives and that my slender stock of plate had an unprec-

---

[29] May be too stiff for artistic expression.

edented surface. When it came over me, the latent eloquence of what they were doing, I confess that my drawing was blurred for a moment—the picture swam. They had accepted their failure, but they couldn't accept their fate. They had bowed their heads in bewilderment to the perverse and cruel law in virtue of which the real thing could be so much less precious than the unreal; but they didn't want to starve. If my servants were my models, then my models might be my servants. They would reverse the parts—the others would sit for the ladies and gentlemen and *they* would do the work. They would still be in the studio—it was an intense dumb appeal to me not to turn them out. "Take us on," they wanted to say— "we'll do *anything*."

My pencil dropped from my hand; my sitting was spoiled and I got rid of my sitters, who were also evidently rather mystified and awestruck. Then, alone with the Major and his wife I had a most uncomfortable moment. He put their prayer into a single sentence: "I say, you know—just let *us* do for you, can't you?" I couldn't—it was dreadful to see them emptying my slops; but I pretended I could, to oblige them, for about a week. Then I gave them a sum of money to go away, and I never saw them again. I obtained the remaining books, but my friend Hawley repeats that Major and Mrs. Monarch did me a permanent harm, got me into false ways. If it be true I'm content to have paid the price—for the memory.

1892

THE JOLLY CORNER*

I

"Every one asks me what I 'think' of everything," said Spencer Brydon; "and I make answer as I can—begging or dodging the question, putting them off with any nonsense. It wouldn't matter to any of them really," he went on, "for, even were it possible to meet in that stand-and-deliver way so silly a demand on so big a subject, my 'thoughts' would still be almost altogether about something that concerns only myself." He was talking to Miss Staverton, with whom for a couple of months now he had availed himself of every possible occasion to talk; this disposition and this resource, this comfort and support, as the situation in fact presented itself, having promptly enough taken the first place in the considerable array of rather unattenuated surprises attending his so strangely belated return to America. Everything was somehow a surprise; and that might be natural when one had so long and so consistently neglected everything, taken pains to give surprises so much margin for play. He had given them more than thirty years—thirty-three, to be exact; and they now seemed to him to have organised their performance quite on the scale of that licence. He had been twenty-three on leaving New York—he was fifty-six to-day: unless indeed he were to reckon as he had sometimes, since his repatriation, found himself feeling; in which case he would have lived longer than is often allotted to man. It would have taken a century, he repeatedly said to himself, and said also to Alice Staverton, it would have taken a longer

* First published in the *English Review* in December 1908.

absence and a more averted mind than those even of which he had been guilty, to pile up the differences, the newnesses, the queernesses, above all the bignesses, for the better or the worse, that at present assaulted his vision wherever he looked.

The great fact all the while however had been the incalculability; since he *had* supposed himself, from decade to decade, to be allowing, and in the most liberal and intelligent manner, for brilliancy of change. He actually saw that he had allowed for nothing; he missed what he would have been sure of finding, he found what he would never have imagined. Proportions and values were upside-down; the ugly things he had expected, the ugly things of his far-away youth, when he had too promptly waked up to a sense of the ugly—these uncanny phenomena placed him rather, as it happened, under the charm; whereas the "swagger" things, the modern, the monstrous, the famous things, those he had more particularly, like thousands of ingenuous enquirers every year, come over to see, were exactly his sources of dismay. They were as so many set traps for displeasure, above all for reaction, of which his restless tread was constantly pressing the spring. It was interesting, doubtless, the whole show, but it would have been too disconcerting hadn't a certain finer truth saved the situation. He had distinctly not, in this steadier light, come over *all* for the monstrosities; he had come, not only in the last analysis but quite on the face of the act, under an impulse with which they had nothing to do. He had come—putting the thing pompously—to look at his "property," which he had thus for a third of a century not been within four thousand miles of; or, expressing it less sordidly, he had yielded to the humour of seeing again his house on the jolly corner, as he usually, and quite fondly, described it—the one in which he had first seen the light, in which various members of his family had lived and had died, in which the holidays of his overschooled boyhood had been passed and the few social flowers of his chilled adolescence gathered, and which, alienated then for so long a period, had, through the successive deaths of his two brothers and the termination of old arrangements, come wholly into his hands. He was the owner of another, not quite so "good"—the jolly corner having been, from far back, superlatively extended and consecrated; and the value of the pair represented his main capital, with an income consisting, in these later years, of their respective rents which (thanks precisely to their original excellent type) had never been depressingly low. He could live in "Europe," as he had been in the habit of living, on the product of these flourishing New York leases, and all the better since, that of the second structure, the mere number in its long row, having within a twelvemonth fallen in, renovation at a high advance had proved beautifully possible.

These were items of property indeed, but he had found himself since his arrival distinguishing more than ever between them. The house within the street, two bristling blocks westward, was already in course of reconstruction as a tall mass of flats; he had acceded, some time before, to overtures for this conversion—in which, now that it was going forward, it had been not the least of his astonishments to find himself able, on the spot, and though without a previous ounce of such experience, to participate with a certain intelligence, almost with a certain authority. He had lived his life with his back so turned to such concerns and his face addressed to those of so different an order that he scarce knew what to make of this lively stir, in a compartment of his mind never yet penetrated, of a capacity for business and a sense for construction. These virtues, so common all round him now, had been dormant in his own organism—where it might be said of them perhaps that they had slept the sleep of the just. At present, in the splendid autumn weather—the autumn at least was a pure boon in the terrible place—he loafed about his "work" undeterred, secretly agitated; not in the least "minding" that the whole proposition, as they said, was vulgar and sordid, and ready to climb ladders, to walk the plank, to handle materials and look wise about them, to ask questions, in fine, and challenge explanations and really "go into" figures.

It amused, it verily quite charmed him; and, by the same stroke, it amused, and even more, Alice Staverton, though perhaps charming her perceptibly less. She wasn't however going to be better-off for it, as *he* was—and so astonishingly much: nothing was now likely, he knew, ever to make her better-off than she found herself, in the afternoon of life, as the delicately frugal possessor and tenant of the small house in Irving Place to which she had subtly managed to cling through her almost unbroken New York career. If he knew the way to it now better than to any other address among the dreadful multiplied numberings which seemed to him to reduce the whole place to some vast ledger-page, overgrown, fantastic, of ruled and criss-crossed lines and figures—if he had formed, for his consolation, that habit, it was really not a little because of the charm of his having encountered and recognised, in the vast wilderness of the wholesale, breaking through the mere gross generalisation of wealth and force and success, a small still scene where items and shades, all delicate things, kept the sharpness of the notes of a high voice perfectly trained, and where economy hung about like the scent of a garden. His old friend lived with one maid and herself dusted her relics and trimmed her lamps and polished her silver; she stood off, in the awful modern crush, when she could, but she sallied forth and did battle when the challenge was really to "spirit," the spirit she after all confessed to, proudly and a little shyly, as to that of the better time, that of *their* common, their quite far-away and antediluvian social period and order. She made use of the street-cars when need be, the terrible things that people scrambled for as the panic-stricken at sea scramble for the boats; she affronted, inscrutably, under stress, all the public concussions and ordeals; and yet, with that slim mystifying grace of her appearance, which defied you to say if she were a fair young woman who looked older through trouble, or a fine smooth older one who looked young through successful indifference; with her precious reference, above all, to memories and histories into which he could enter, she was as exquisite for him as some pale pressed flower (a rarity to begin with), and, failing other sweetnesses, she was a sufficient reward of his effort. They had communities of knowledge, "their" knowledge (this discriminating possessive was always on her lips) of presences of the other age, presences all overlaid, in his case, by the experience of a man and the freedom of a wanderer, overlaid by pleasure, by infidelity, by passages of life that were strange and dim to her, just by "Europe" in short, but still unobscured, still exposed and cherished, under that pious visitation of the spirit from which she had never been diverted.

She had come with him one day to see how his "apartment-house" was rising; he had helped her over gaps and explained to her plans, and while they were there had happened to have, before her, a brief but lively discussion with the man in charge, the representative of the building-firm that had undertaken his work. He had found himself quite "standing-up" to this personage over a failure on the latter's part to observe some detail of one of their noted conditions, and had so lucidly argued his case that, besides ever so prettily flushing, at the time, for sympathy in his triumph, she had afterwards said to him (though to a slightly greater effect of irony) that he had clearly for too many years neglected a real gift. If he had but stayed at home he would have anticipated the inventor of the skyscraper. If he had but stayed at home he would have discovered his genius in time really to start some new variety of awful architectural hare and run it till it burrowed in a gold-mine. He was to remember these words, while the weeks elapsed, for the small silver ring they had sounded over the queerest and deepest of his own lately most disguised and most muffled vibrations.

It had begun to be present to him after the first fortnight, it had broken out with the oddest abruptness, this particular wanton wonderment: it met him there—and this was the image under which he himself judged the matter, or at least, not a little, thrilled and flushed with it—very much as he might have been met by some strange figure, some unexpected occupant, at a turn of one of the dim passages of an empty house. The quaint analogy quite hauntingly remained with him, when he didn't indeed rather improve it by a still intenser form: that of his opening a door behind which he would have made sure of finding nothing, a door into a room shuttered and void, and yet so coming, with a great suppressed start, on some quite erect confronting presence, something planted in the middle of the place and facing him through the dusk. After that visit to the house in construction he walked with his companion to see the other and always so much the better one, which in the eastward direction formed one of the corners, the "jolly" one precisely, of the street now so generally dishonoured and disfigured in its westward reaches, and of the comparatively conservative Avenue.[1] The Avenue still had pretensions, as Miss Staverton said, to decency; the old people had mostly gone, the old names were unknown, and here and there an old association seemed to stray, all vaguely, like some very aged person, out too late, whom you might meet and feel the impulse to watch or follow, in kindness, for safe restoration to shelter.

They went in together, our friends; he admitted himself with his key, as he kept no one there, he explained, preferring, for his reasons, to leave the place empty, under a simple arrangement with a good woman living in the neighbourhood and who came for a daily hour to open windows and dust and sweep. Spencer Brydon had his reasons and was growingly aware of them; they seemed to him better each time he was there, though he didn't name them all to his companion, any more than he told her as yet how often, how quite absurdly often, he himself came. He only let her see for the present, while they walked through the great blank rooms, that absolute vacancy reigned and that, from top to bottom, there was nothing but Mrs. Muldoon's broomstick, in a corner, to tempt the burglar. Mrs. Muldoon was then on the premises, and she loquaciously attended the visitors, preceding them from room to room and pushing back shutters and throwing up sashes—all to show them, as she remarked, how little there was to see. There was little indeed to see in the great gaunt shell where the main dispositions and the general apportionment of space, the style of an age of ampler allowances, had nevertheless for its master their honest pleading message, affecting him as some good old servant's, some lifelong retainer's appeal for a character, or even for a retiring-pension; yet it was also a remark of Mrs. Muldoon's that, glad as she was to oblige him by her noonday round, there was a request she greatly hoped he would never make of her. If he should wish her for any reason to come in after dark she would just tell him, if he "plased," that he must ask it of somebody else.

The fact that there was nothing to see didn't militate for the worthy woman against what one *might* see, and she put it frankly to Miss Staverton that no lady could be expected to like, could she? "craping up to thim top storeys in the ayvil

[1] Fifth Avenue, a fashionable street in New York City.

hours." The gas and the electric light were off the house, and she fairly evoked a gruesome vision of her march through the great grey rooms—so many of them as there were too!—with her glimmering taper. Miss Staverton met her honest glare with a smile and the profession that she herself certainly would recoil from such an adventure. Spencer Brydon meanwhile held his peace—for the moment; the question of the "evil" hours in his old home had already become too grave for him. He had begun some time since to "crape," and he knew just why a packet of candles addressed to that pursuit had been stowed by his own hand, three weeks before, at the back of a drawer of the fine old sideboard that occupied, as a "fixture," the deep recess in the dining-room. Just now he laughed at his companions—quickly however changing the subject; for the reason that, in the first place, his laugh struck him even at that moment as starting the odd echo, the conscious human resonance (he scarce knew how to qualify it) that sounds made while he was there alone sent back to his ear or his fancy; and that, in the second, he imagined Alice Staverton for the instant on the point of asking him, with a divination, if he ever so prowled. There were divinations he was unprepared for, and he had at all events averted enquiry by the time Mrs. Muldoon had left them, passing on to other parts.

There was happily enough to say, on so consecrated a spot, that could be said freely and fairly; so that a whole train of declarations was precipitated by his friend's having herself broken out, after a yearning look round: "But I hope you don't mean they want you to pull *this* to pieces!" His answer came, promptly, with his re-awakened wrath: it was of course exactly what they wanted, and what they were "at" him for, daily, with the iteration of people who couldn't for their life understand a man's liability to decent feelings. He had found the place, just as it stood and beyond what he could express, an interest and a joy. There were values other than the beastly rent-values, and in short, in short—! But it was thus Miss Staverton took him up. "In short you're to make so good a thing of your skyscraper that, living in luxury on *those* ill-gotten gains, you can afford for a while to be sentimental here!" Her smile had for him, with the words, the particular mild irony with which he found half her talk suffused; an irony without bitterness and that came, exactly, from her having so much imagination—not, like the cheap sarcasms with which one heard most people, about the world of "society," bid for the reputation of cleverness, from nobody's really having any. It was agreeable to him at this very moment to be sure that when he had answered, after a brief demur, "Well yes: so, precisely, you may put it!" her imagination would still do him justice. He explained that even if never a dollar were to come to him from the other house he would nevertheless cherish this one; and he dwelt, further, while they lingered and wandered, on the fact of the stupefaction he was already exciting, the positive mystification he felt himself create.

He spoke of the value of all he read into it, into the mere sight of the walls, mere shapes of the rooms, mere sound of the floors, mere feel, in his hand, of the old silver-plated knobs of the several mahogany doors, which suggested the pressure of the palms of the dead; the seventy years of the past in fine that these things represented, the annals of nearly three generations, counting his grandfather's, the one that had ended there, and the impalpable ashes of his long-extinct youth, afloat in the very air like microscopic motes. She listened to everything; she was a woman who answered intimately but who utterly didn't chatter. She scattered abroad therefore no cloud of words; she could assent, she could agree, above all she could encourage, without doing that. Only at the last she went a little further than he had done himself. "And then how do you know! You may still, after all, want to live here." It rather indeed pulled him up, for it wasn't what he had been thinking, at least in her sense of the words. "You mean I may decide to stay on for the sake of it?"

"Well, *with* such a home—!" But, quite beautifully, she had too much tact to dot so monstrous an *i*, and it was precisely an illustration of the way she didn't rattle. How could any one—of any wit—insist on any one else's "wanting" to live in New York?

"Oh," he said, "I *might* have lived here (since I had my opportunity early in life); I might have put in here all these years. Then everything would have been different enough—and, I dare say, 'funny' enough. But that's another matter. And then the beauty of it—I mean of my perversity, of my refusal to agree to a 'deal'—is just in the total absence of a reason. Don't you see that if I had a reason about the matter at all it would *have* to be the other way, and would then be inevitably a reason of dollars? There are no reasons here *but* of dollars. Let us therefore have none whatever—not the ghost of one."

They were back in the hall then for departure, but from where they stood the vista was large, through an open door, into the great square main saloon, with its almost antique felicity of brave spaces between windows. Her eyes came back from that reach and met his own a moment. "Are you very sure the 'ghost' of one doesn't, much rather, serve—?"

He had a positive sense of turning pale. But it was as near as they were then to come. For he made answer, he believed, between a glare and a grin: "Oh ghosts— of course the place must swarm with them! I should be ashamed of it if it didn't. Poor Mrs. Muldoon's right, and it's why I haven't asked her to do more than look in."

Miss Staverton's gaze again lost itself, and things she didn't utter, it was clear, came and went in her mind. She might even for the minute, off there in the fine room, have imagined some element dimly gathering. Simplified like the death-mask of a handsome face, it perhaps produced for her just then an effect akin to the stir of an expression in the "set" commemorative plaster. Yet whatever her impression may have been she produced instead a vague platitude. "Well, if it were only furnished and lived in—!"

She appeared to imply that in case of its being still furnished he might have been a little less opposed to the idea of a return. But she passed straight into the vestibule, as if to leave her words behind her, and the next moment he had opened the house-door and was standing with her on the steps. He closed the door and, while he re-pocketed his key, looking up and down, they took in the compara-tively harsh actuality of the Avenue, which reminded him of the assault of the outer light of the Desert on the traveller emerging from an Egyptian tomb. But he risked before they stepped into the street his gathered answer to her speech. "For me it *is* lived in. For me it *is* furnished." At which it was easy for her to sigh "Ah yes—!" all vaguely and discreetly; since his parents and his favourite sister, to say nothing of other kin, in numbers, had run their course and met their end there. That represented, within the walls, ineffaceable life.

It was a few days after this that, during an hour passed with her again, he had expressed his impatience of the too flattering curiosity—among the people he met—about his appreciation of New York. He had arrived at none at all that was socially producible, and as for that matter of his "thinking" (thinking the better or the worse of anything there) he was wholly taken up with one subject of thought.

It was mere vain egoism, and it was moreover, if she liked, a morbid obsession. He found all things come back to the question of what he personally might have been, how he might have led his life and "turned out," if he had not so, at the outset, given it up. And confessing for the first time to the intensity within him of this absurd speculation—which but proved also, no doubt, the habit of too self-ishly thinking—he affirmed the impotence there of any other source of interest, any other native appeal. "What would it have made of me, what would it have made of me? I keep for ever wondering, all idiotically; as if I could possibly know! I see what it has made of dozens of others, those I meet, and it positively aches within me, to the point of exasperation, that it would have made something of me as well. Only I can't make out *what,* and the worry of it, the small rage of curiosity never to be satisfied, brings back what I remember to have felt, once or twice, after judging best, for reasons, to burn some important letter unopened. I've been sorry, I've hated it—I've never known what was in the letter. You may of course say it's a trifle—!"

"I don't say it's a trifle," Miss Staverton gravely interrupted.

She was seated by her fire, and before her, on his feet and restless, he turned to and fro between this intensity of his idea and a fitful and unseeing inspection, through his single eye-glass, of the dear little old objects on her chimney-piece. Her interruption made him for an instant look at her harder. "I shouldn't care if you did!" he laughed, however; "and it's only a figure, at any rate, for the way I now feel. *Not* to have followed my perverse young course—and almost in the teeth of my father's curse, as I may say; not to have kept it up, so, 'over there,' from that day to this, without a doubt or a pang; not, above all, to have liked it, to have loved it, so much, loved it, no doubt, with such an abysmal conceit of my own preference: some variation from *that,* I say, must have produced some differ-ent effect for my life and for my 'form.' I should have stuck here—if it had been possible; and I was too young, at twenty-three, to judge, *pour deux sous,*[2] whether it *were* possible. If I had waited I might have seen it was, and then I might have been, by staying here, something nearer to one of these types who have been hammered so hard and made so keen by their conditions. It isn't that I admire them so much—the question of any charm in them, or of any charm, beyond that of the rank money-passion, exerted by their conditions *for* them, has nothing to do with the matter: it's only a question of what fantastic, yet perfectly possible, de-velopment of my own nature I mayn't have missed. It comes over me that I had then a strange *alter ego* deep down somewhere within me, as the full-blown flower is in the small tight bud, and that I just took the course, I just transferred him to the climate, that blighted him for once and for ever."

"And you wonder about the flower," Miss Staverton said. "So do I, if you want to know; and so I've been wondering these several weeks. I believe in the flower," she continued, "I feel it would have been quite splendid, quite huge and monstrous."

"Monstrous above all!" her visitor echoed; "and I imagine, by the same stroke, quite hideous and offensive."

"You don't believe that," she returned; "if you did you wouldn't wonder. You'd know, and that would be enough for you. What you feel—and what I feel *for* you—is that you'd have had power."

"You'd have liked me that way?" he asked.

---

[2] "For two cents" (French).

She barely hung fire.[3] "How should I not have liked you?"

"I see. You'd have liked me, have preferred me, a billionaire!"

"How should I not have liked you?" she simply again asked.

He stood before her still—her question kept him motionless. He took it in, so much there was of it; and indeed his not otherwise meeting it testified to that. "I know at least what I am," he simply went on; "the other side of the medal's clear enough. I've not been edifying—I believe I'm thought in a hundred quarters to have been barely decent. I've followed strange paths and worshipped strange gods; it must have come to you again and again—in fact you've admitted to me as much—that I was leading, at any time these thirty years, a selfish frivolous scandalous life. And you see what it has made of me."

She just waited, smiling at him. "You see what it has made of *me*."

"Oh you're a person whom nothing can have altered. You were born to be what you are, anywhere, anyway: you've the perfection nothing else could have blighted. And don't you see how, without my exile, I shouldn't have been waiting till now—!" But he pulled up for the strange pang.

"The great thing to see," she presently said, "seems to me to be that it has spoiled nothing. It hasn't spoiled your being here at last. It hasn't spoiled this. It hasn't spoiled your speaking—" She also however faltered.

He wondered at everything her controlled emotion might mean. "Do you believe then—too dreadfully!—that I *am* as good as I might ever have been?"

"Oh no! Far from it!" With which she got up from her chair and was nearer to him. "But I don't care," she smiled.

"You mean I'm good enough?"

She considered a little. "Will you believe it if I say so? I mean will you let that settle your question for you?" And then as if making out in his face that he drew back from this, that he had some idea which, however absurd, he couldn't yet bargain away: "Oh you don't care either—but very differently: you don't care for anything but yourself."

Spencer Brydon recognised it—it was in fact what he had absolutely professed. Yet he importantly qualified. "*He* isn't myself. He's the just so totally other person. But I do want to see him," he added. "And I can. And I shall."

Their eyes met for a minute while he guessed from something in hers that she divined his strange sense. But neither of them otherwise expressed it, and her apparent understanding, with no protesting shock, no easy derision, touched him more deeply than anything yet, constituting for his stifled perversity, on the spot, an element that was like breatheable air. What she said however was unexpected. "Well, *I've* seen him."

"You—?"

"I've seen him in a dream."

"Oh a 'dream'—!" It let him down.

"But twice over," she continued. "I saw him as I see you now."

"You've dreamed the same dream—?"

"Twice over," she repeated. "The very same."

This did somehow a little speak to him, as it also gratified him. "You dream about me at that rate?"

"Ah about *him!*" she smiled.

His eyes again sounded her. "Then you know all about him." And as she said nothing more: "What's the wretch like?"

---

[3] Kept from saying.

She hesitated, and it was as if he were pressing her so hard that, resisting for reasons of her own, she had to turn away. "I'll tell you some other time!"

II

It was after this that there was most of a virtue for him, most of a cultivated charm, most of a preposterous secret thrill, in the particular form of surrender to his obsession and of address to what he more and more believed to be his privilege. It was what in these weeks he was living for—since he really felt life to begin but after Mrs. Muldoon had retired from the scene and, visiting the ample house from attic to cellar, making sure he was alone, he knew himself in safe possession and, as he tacitly expressed it, let himself go. He sometimes came twice in the twenty-four hours; the moments he liked best were those of gathering dusk, of the short autumn twilight; this was the time of which, again and again, he found himself hoping most. Then he could, as seemed to him, most intimately wander and wait, linger and listen, feel his fine attention, never in his life before so fine, on the pulse of the great vague place: he preferred the lampless hour and only wished he might have prolonged each day the deep crepuscular spell. Later—rarely much before midnight, but then for a considerable vigil—he watched with his glimmering light; moving slowly, holding it high, playing it far, rejoicing above all, as much as he might, in open vistas, reaches of communication between rooms and by passages; the long straight chance or show, as he would have called it, for the revelation he pretended to invite. It was a practice he found he could perfectly "work" without exciting remark; no one was in the least the wiser for it; even Alice Staverton, who was moreover a well of discretion, didn't quite fully imagine.

He let himself in and let himself out with the assurance of calm proprietorship; and accident so far favoured him that, if a fat Avenue "officer" had happened on occasion to see him entering at eleven-thirty, he had never yet, to the best of his belief, been noticed as emerging at two. He walked there on the crisp November nights, arrived regularly at the evening's end; it was as easy to do this after dining out as to take his way to a club or to his hotel. When he left his club, if he hadn't been dining out, it was ostensibly to go to his hotel; and when he left his hotel, if he had spent a part of the evening there, it was ostensibly to go to his club. Everything was easy in fine; everything conspired and promoted: there was truly even in the strain of his experience something that glossed over, something that salved and simplified, all the rest of consciousness. He circulated, talked, renewed, loosely and pleasantly, old relations—met indeed, so far as he could, new expectations and seemed to make out on the whole that in spite of the career, of such different contacts, which he had spoken of to Miss Staverton as ministering so little, for those who might have watched it, to edification, he was positively rather liked than not. He was a dim secondary social success—and all with people who had truly not an idea of him. It was all mere surface sound, this murmur of their welcome, this popping of their corks—just as his gestures of response were the extravagant shadows, emphatic in proportion as they meant little, of some game of *ombres chinoises*.[4] He projected himself all day, in thought, straight over the bristling line of hard unconscious heads and into the other, the real, the waiting life; the life that, as soon as he had heard behind him the click of his great house-door,

---

[4] "Chinese shadows" (French): a show in which actors' shadows are projected onto a screen.

began for him, on the jolly corner, as beguilingly as the slow opening bars of some rich music follows the tap of the conductor's wand.

He always caught the first effect of the steel point of his stick on the old marble of the hall pavement, large black-and-white squares that he remembered as the admiration of his childhood and that had then made in him, as he now saw, for the growth of an early conception of style. This effect was the dim reverberating tinkle as of some far-off bell hung who should say where?—in the depths of the house, of the past, of that mystical other world that might have flourished for him had he not, for weal or woe, abandoned it. On this impression he did ever the same thing; he put his stick noiselessly away in a corner—feeling the place once more in the likeness of some great glass bowl, all precious concave crystal, set delicately humming by the play of a moist finger round its edge. The concave crystal held, as it were, this mystical other world, and the indescribably fine murmur of its rim was the sigh there, the scarce audible pathetic wail to his strained ear, of all the old baffled forsworn possibilities. What he did therefore by this appeal of his hushed presence was to wake them into such measure of ghostly life as they might still enjoy. They were shy, all but unappeasably shy, but they weren't really sinister; at least they weren't as he had hitherto felt them—before they had taken the Form he so yearned to make them take, the Form he at moments saw himself in the light of fairly hunting on tiptoe, the points of his evening-shoes, from room to room and from storey to storey.

That was the essence of his vision—which was all rank folly, if one would, while he was out of the house and otherwise occupied, but which took on the last verisimilitude as soon as he was placed and posted. He knew what he meant and what he wanted; it was as clear as the figure on a cheque presented in demand for cash. His *alter ego* "walked"—that was the note of his image of him, while his image of his motive for his own odd pastime was the desire to waylay him and meet him. He roamed, slowly, warily, but all restlessly, he himself did—Mrs. Muldoon had been right, absolutely, with her figure of their "craping"; and the presence he watched for would roam restlessly too. But it would be as cautious and as shifty; the conviction of its probable, in fact its already quite sensible, quite audible evasion of pursuit grew for him from night to night, laying on him finally a rigour to which nothing in his life had been comparable. It had been the theory of many superficially-judging persons, he knew, that he was wasting that life in a surrender to sensations, but he had tasted of no pleasure so fine as his actual tension, had been introduced to no sport that demanded at once the patience and the nerve of this stalking of a creature more subtle, yet at bay perhaps more formidable, than any beast of the forest. The terms, the comparisons, the very practices of the chase positively came again into play; there were even moments when passages of his occasional experience as a sportsman, stirred memories, from his younger time, of moor and mountain and desert, revived for him—and to the increase of his keenness—by the tremendous force of analogy. He found himself at moments—once he had placed his single light on some mantel-shelf or in some recess—stepping back into shelter or shade, effacing himself behind a door or in an embrasure, as he had sought of old the vantage of rock and tree; he found himself holding his breath and living in the joy of the instant, the supreme suspense created by big game alone.

He wasn't afraid (though putting himself the question as he believed gentlemen on Bengal tiger-shoots or in close quarters with the great bear of the Rockies had been known to confess to having put it); and this indeed—since here at least he might be frank!—because of the impression, so intimate and so strange, that he himself produced as yet a dread, produced certainly a strain, beyond the liveliest he was likely to feel. They fell for him into categories, they fairly became familiar, the signs, for his own perception, of the alarm his presence and his vigilance created; though leaving him always to remark, portentously, on his probably having formed a relation, his probably enjoying a consciousness, unique in the experience of man. People enough, first and last, had been in terror of apparitions, but who had ever before so turned the tables and become himself, in the apparitional world, an incalculable terror? He might have found this sublime had he quite dared to think of it; but he didn't too much insist, truly, on that side of his privilege. With habit and repetition he gained to an extraordinary degree the power to penetrate the dusk of distances and the darkness of corners, to resolve back into their innocence the treacheries of uncertain light, the evil-looking forms taken in the gloom by mere shadows, by accidents of the air, by shifting effects of perspective; putting down his dim luminary he could still wander on without it, pass into other rooms and, only knowing it was there behind him in case of need, see his way about, visually project for his purpose a comparative clearness. It made him feel, this acquired faculty, like some monstrous stealthy cat; he wondered if he would have glared at these moments with large shining yellow eyes, and what it mightn't verily be, for the poor hard-pressed *alter ego,* to be confronted with such a type.

He liked however the open shutters; he opened everywhere those Mrs. Muldoon had closed, closing them as carefully afterwards, so that she shouldn't notice: he liked—oh this he did like, and above all in the upper rooms!—the sense of the hard silver of the autumn stars through the window-panes, and scarcely less the flare of the street-lamps below, the white electric lustre which it would have taken curtains to keep out. This was human actual social; this was of the world he had lived in, and he was more at his ease certainly for the countenance, coldly general and impersonal, that all the while and in spite of his detachment it seemed to give him. He had support of course mostly in the rooms at the wide front and the prolonged side; it failed him considerably in the central shades and the parts at the back. But if he sometimes, on his rounds, was glad of his optical reach, so none the less often the rear of the house affected him as the very jungle of his prey. The place was there more subdivided; a large "extension" in particular, where small rooms for servants had been multiplied, abounded in nooks and corners, in closets and passages, in the ramifications especially of an ample back staircase over which he leaned, many a time, to look far down—not deterred from his gravity even while aware that he might, for a spectator, have figured some solemn simpleton playing at hide-and-seek. Outside in fact he might himself make that ironic *rapprochement;*[5] but within the walls, and in spite of the clear windows, his consistency was proof against the cynical light of New York.

It had belonged to that idea of the exasperated consciousness of his victim to become a real test for him; since he had quite put it to himself from the first that, oh distinctly! he could "cultivate" his whole perception. He had felt it as above all open to cultivation—which indeed was but another name for his manner of spending his time. He was bringing it on, bringing it to perfection, by practice; in consequence of which it had grown so fine that he was now aware of impressions, attestations of his general postulate, that couldn't have broken upon him at once.

[5] Bringing together, comparison (French).

This was the case more specifically with a phenomenon at last quite frequent for him in the upper rooms, the recognition—absolutely unmistakeable, and by a turn dating from a particular hour, his resumption of his campaign after a diplomatic drop, a calculated absence of three nights—of his being definitely followed, tracked at a distance carefully taken and to the express end that he should the less confidently, less arrogantly, appear to himself merely to pursue. It worried, it finally quite broke him up, for it proved, of all the conceivable impressions, the one least suited to his book. He was kept in sight while remaining himself—as regards the essence of his position—sightless, and his only recourse then was in abrupt turns, rapid recoveries of ground. He wheeled about, retracing his steps, as if he might so catch in his face at least the stirred air of some other quick revolution. It was indeed true that his fully dislocalised thought of these manœuvres recalled to him Pantaloon, at the Christmas farce, buffeted and tricked from behind by ubiquitous Harlequin;[6] but it left intact the influence of the conditions themselves each time he was re-exposed to them, so that in fact this association, had he suffered it to become constant, would on a certain side have but ministered to his intenser gravity. He had made, as I have said, to create on the premises the baseless sense of a reprieve, his three absences; and the result of the third was to confirm the after-effect of the second.

On his return, that night—the night succeeding his last intermission—he stood in the hall and looked up the staircase with a certainty more intimate than any he had yet known. "He's *there,* at the top, and waiting—not, as in general, falling back for disappearance. He's holding his ground, and it's the first time—which is a proof, isn't it? that something has happened for him." So Brydon argued with his hand on the banister and his foot on the lowest stair; in which position he felt as never before the air chilled by his logic. He himself turned cold in it, for he seemed of a sudden to know what now was involved. "Harder pressed?—yes, he takes it in, with its thus making clear to him that I've come, as they say, 'to stay.' He finally doesn't like and can't bear it, in the sense, I mean, that his wrath, his menaced interest, now balances with his dread. I've hunted him till he has 'turned': that, up there, is what has happened—he's the fanged or the antlered animal brought at last to bay." There came to him, as I say—but determined by an influence beyond my notation!—the acuteness of this certainty; under which however the next moment he had broken into a sweat that he would as little have consented to attribute to fear as he would have dared immediately to act upon it for enterprise. It marked none the less a prodigious thrill, a thrill that represented sudden dismay, no doubt, but also represented, and with the selfsame throb, the strangest, the most joyous, possibly the next minute almost the proudest, duplication of consciousness.

"He has been dodging, retreating, hiding, but now, worked up to anger, he'll fight!"—this intense impression made a single mouthful, as it were, of terror and applause. But what was wondrous was that the applause, for the felt fact, was so eager, since, if it was his other self he was running to earth, this ineffable identity was thus in the last resort not unworthy of him. It bristled there—somewhere near at hand, however unseen still—as the hunted thing, even as the trodden worm of the adage *must* at last bristle; and Brydon at this instant tasted probably of a sensation more complex than had ever before found itself consistent with sanity. It was

---

[6] Pantaloon and Harlequin, traditional characters in pantomime, are known for playing tricks on others.

as if it would have shamed him that a character so associated with his own should triumphantly succeed in just skulking, should to the end not risk the open; so that the drop of this danger was, on the spot, a great lift of the whole situation. Yet with another rare shift of the same subtlety he was already trying to measure by how much more he himself might now be in peril of fear; so rejoicing that he could, in another form, actively inspire that fear, and simultaneously quaking for the form in which he might passively know it.

The apprehension of knowing it must after a little have grown in him, and the strangest moment of his adventure perhaps, the most memorable or really most interesting, afterwards, of his crisis, was the lapse of certain instants of concentrated conscious *combat,* the sense of a need to hold on to something, even after the manner of a man slipping and slipping on some awful incline; the vivid impulse, above all, to move, to act, to charge, somehow and upon something—to show himself, in a word, that he wasn't afraid. The state of "holding-on" was thus the state to which he was momentarily reduced; if there had been anything, in the great vacancy, to seize, he would presently have been aware of having clutched it as he might under a shock at home have clutched the nearest chair-back. He had been surprised at any rate—of this he *was* aware—into something unprecedented since his original appropriation of the place; he had closed his eyes, held them tight, for a long minute, as with that instinct of dismay and that terror of vision. When he opened them the room, the other contiguous rooms, extraordinarily, seemed lighter—so light, almost, that at first he took the change for day. He stood firm, however that might be, just where he had paused; his resistance had helped him—it was as if there were something he had tided over. He knew after a little what this was—it had been in the imminent danger of flight. He had stiffened his will against going; without this he would have made for the stairs, and it seemed to him that, still with his eyes closed, he would have descended them, would have known how, straight and swiftly, to the bottom.

Well, as he had held out, here he was—still at the top, among the more intricate upper rooms and with the gauntlet[7] of the others, of all the rest of the house, still to run when it should be his time to go. He would go at his time—only at his time: didn't he go every night very much at the same hour? He took out his watch—there was light for that: it was scarcely a quarter past one, and he had never withdrawn so soon. He reached his lodgings for the most part at two—with his walk of a quarter of an hour. He would wait for the last quarter—he wouldn't stir till then; and he kept his watch there with his eyes on it, reflecting while he held it that this deliberate wait, a wait with an effort, which he recognised, would serve perfectly for the attestation he desired to make. It would prove his courage—unless indeed the latter might most be proved by his budging at last from his place. What he mainly felt now was that, since he hadn't originally scuttled, he had his dignities—which had never in his life seemed so many—all to preserve and to carry aloft. This was before him in truth as a physical image, an image almost worthy of an age of greater romance. That remark indeed glimmered for him only to glow the next instant with a finer light; since what age of romance, after all, could have matched either the state of his mind or, "objectively," as they said, the wonder of his situation? The only difference would have been that, brandishing his dignities over his head as in a parchment scroll, he might then—that is

---

[7] From "run the gauntlet," a former punishment in which a man ran between two rows of men who struck him with switches (whipping sticks) as he passed.

in the heroic time—have proceeded downstairs with a drawn sword in his other grasp.

At present, really, the light he had set down on the mantel of the next room would have to figure his sword; which utensil, in the course of a minute, he had taken the requisite number of steps to possess himself of. The door between the rooms was open, and from the second another door opened to a third. These rooms, as he remembered, gave all three upon a common corridor as well, but there was a fourth, beyond them, without issue save through the preceding. To have moved, to have heard his step again, was appreciably a help; though even in recognising this he lingered once more a little by the chimney-piece on which his light had rested. When he next moved, just hesitating where to turn, he found himself considering a circumstance that, after his first and comparatively vague apprehension of it, produced in him the start that often attends some pang of recollection, the violent shock of having ceased happily to forget. He had come into sight of the door in which the brief chain of communication ended and which he now surveyed from the nearer threshold, the one not directly facing it. Placed at some distance to the left of this point, it would have admitted him to the last room of the four, the room without other approach or egress, had it not, to his intimate conviction, been closed *since* his former visitation, the matter probably of a quarter of an hour before. He stared with all his eyes at the wonder of the fact, arrested again where he stood and again holding his breath while he sounded its sense. Surely it had been *subsequently* closed—that is it had been on his previous passage indubitably open!

He took it full in the face that something had happened between—that he couldn't not have noticed before (by which he meant on his original tour of all the rooms that evening) that such a barrier had exceptionally presented itself. He had indeed since that moment undergone an agitation so extraordinary that it might have muddled for him any earlier view; and he tried to convince himself that he might perhaps then have gone into the room and, inadvertently, automatically, on coming out, have drawn the door after him. The difficulty was that this exactly was what he never did; it was against his whole policy, as he might have said, the essence of which was to keep vistas clear. He had them from the first, as he was well aware, quite on the brain: the strange apparition, at the far end of one of them, of his baffled "prey" (which had become by so sharp an irony so little the term now to apply!) was the form of success his imagination had most cherished, projecting into it always a refinement of beauty. He had known fifty times the start of perception that had afterwards dropped; had fifty times gasped to himself "There!" under some fond brief hallucination. The house, as the case stood, admirably lent itself; he might wonder at the taste, the native architecture of the particular time, which could rejoice so in the multiplication of doors—the opposite extreme to the modern, the actual almost complete proscription of them; but it had fairly contributed to provoke this obsession of the presence encountered telescopically, as he might say, focussed and studied in diminishing perspective and as by a rest for the elbow.

It was with these considerations that his present attention was charged—they perfectly availed to make what he saw portentous. He *couldn't,* by any lapse, have blocked that aperture; and if he hadn't, if it was unthinkable, why what else was clear but that there had been another agent? Another agent?—he had been catching, as he felt, a moment back, the very breath of him; but when had he been so close as in this simple, this logical, this completely personal act? It was so logical, that is, that one might have *taken* it for personal; yet for what did Brydon take it, he asked himself, while, softly panting, he felt his eyes almost leave their sockets. Ah this time at last they *were,* the two, the opposed projections of him, in presence; and this time, as much as one would, the question of danger loomed. With it rose, as not before, the question of courage—for what he knew the blank face of the door to say to him was "Show us how much you have!" It stared, it glared back at him with that challenge; it put to him the two alternatives: should he just push it open or not? Oh to have this consciousness was to *think*—and to think, Brydon knew, as he stood there, was, with the lapsing moments, not to have acted! Not to have acted—that was the misery and the pang—was even still not to act; was in fact *all* to feel the thing in another, in a new and terrible way. How long did he pause and how long did he debate? There was presently nothing to measure it; for his vibration had already changed—as just by the effect of its intensity. Shut up there, at bay, defiant, and with the prodigy of the thing palpably proveably *done,* thus giving notice like some stark signboard—under that accession of accent the situation itself had turned; and Brydon at last remarkably made up his mind on what it had turned to.

It had turned altogether to a different admonition; to a supreme hint, for him, of the value of Discretion! This slowly dawned, no doubt—for it could take its time; so perfectly, on his threshold, had he been stayed, so little as yet had he either advanced or retreated. It was the strangest of all things that now when, by his taking ten steps and applying his hand to a latch, or even his shoulder and his knee, if necessary, to a panel, all the hunger of his prime need might have been met, his high curiosity crowned, his unrest assuaged—it was amazing, but it was also exquisite and rare, that insistence should have, at a touch, quite dropped from him. Discretion—he jumped at that; and yet not, verily, at such a pitch, because it saved his nerves or his skin, but because, much more valuably, it saved the situation. When I say he "jumped" at it I feel the consonance of this term with the fact that—at the end indeed of I know not how long—he did move again, he crossed straight to the door. He wouldn't touch it—it seemed now that he might *if* he would: he would only just wait there a little, to show, to prove, that he wouldn't. He had thus another station, close to the thin partition by which revelation was denied him; but with his eyes bent and his hands held off in a mere intensity of stillness. He listened as if there had been something to hear, but this attitude, while it lasted, was his own communication. "If you won't then—good: I spare you and I give up. You affect me as by the appeal positively for pity: you convince me that for reasons rigid and sublime—what do I know?—we both of us should have suffered. I respect them then, and, though moved and privileged as, I believe, it has never been given to man, I retire, I renounce—never, on my honour, to try again. So rest for ever—and let *me!*"

That, for Brydon was the deep sense of this last demonstration—solemn, measured, directed, as he felt it to be. He brought it to a close, he turned away; and now verily he knew how deeply he had been stirred. He retraced his steps, taking up his candle, burnt, he observed, well-nigh to the socket, and marking again, lighten it as he would, the distinctness of his footfall; after which, in a moment, he knew himself at the other side of the house. He did here what he had not yet done at these hours—he opened half a casement, one of those in the front, and let in the air of the night; a thing he would have taken at any time previous for a sharp rupture of his spell. His spell was broken now, and it didn't matter—broken by his concession and his surrender, which made it idle henceforth that he should ever come back. The empty street—its other life so marked even by the great lamplit vacancy—was within call, within touch; he stayed there as to be in it again, high above it though he was still perched; he watched as for some comforting common fact, some vulgar human note, the passage of a scavenger or a thief, some night-bird however base. He would have blessed that sign of life; he would have welcomed positively the slow approach of his friend the policeman, whom he had hitherto only sought to avoid, and was not sure that if the patrol had come into sight he mightn't have felt the impulse to get into relation with it, to hail it, on some pretext, from his fourth floor.

The pretext that wouldn't have been too silly or too compromising, the explanation that would have saved his dignity and kept his name, in such a case, out of the papers, was not definite to him: he was so occupied with the thought of recording his Discretion—as an effect of the vow he had just uttered to his intimate adversary—that the importance of this loomed large and something had overtaken all ironically his sense of proportion. If there had been a ladder applied to the front of the house, even one of the vertiginous perpendiculars employed by painters and roofers and sometimes left standing overnight, he would have managed somehow, astride of the window-sill, to compass by outstretched leg and arm that mode of descent. If there had been some such uncanny thing as he had found in his room at hotels, a workable fire-escape in the form of notched cable or a canvas shoot, he would have availed himself of it as a proof—well, of his present delicacy. He nursed that sentiment, as the question stood, a little in vain, and even—at the end of he scarce knew, once more, how long—found it, as by the action on his mind of the failure of response of the outer world, sinking back to vague anguish. It seemed to him he had waited an age for some stir of the great grim hush; the life of the town was itself under a spell—so unnaturally, up and down the whole prospect of known and rather ugly objects, the blankness and the silence lasted. Had they ever, he asked himself, the hard-faced houses, which had begun to look livid in the dim dawn, had they ever spoken so little to any need of his spirit? Great builded voids, great crowded stillnesses put on, often, in the heart of cities, for the small hours, a sort of sinister mask, and it was of this large collective negation that Brydon presently became conscious—all the more that the break of day was, almost incredibly, now at hand, proving to him what a night he had made of it.

He looked again at his watch, saw what had become of his time-values (he had taken hours for minutes—not, as in other tense situations, minutes for hours) and the strange air of the streets was but the weak, the sullen flush of a dawn in which everything was still locked up. His choked appeal from his own open window had been the sole note of life, and he could but break off at last as for a worse despair. Yet while so deeply demoralised he was capable again of an impulse denoting—at least by his present measure—extraordinary resolution; of retracing his steps to the spot where he had turned cold with the extinction of his last pulse of doubt as to there being in the place another presence than his own. This required an effort strong enough to sicken him; but he had his reason, which overmastered for the moment everything else. There was the whole of the rest of the house to traverse, and how should he screw himself to that if the door he had seen closed were at present open? He could hold to the idea that the closing had practically been for him an act of mercy, a chance offered him to descend, depart, get off the ground and never again profane it. This conception held together, it worked; but what it meant for him depended now clearly on the amount of forbearance his recent action, or rather his recent inaction, had engendered. The image of the "presence," whatever it was, waiting there for him to go—this image had not yet been so concrete for his nerves as when he stopped short of the point at which certainty would have come to him. For, with all his resolution, or more exactly with all his dread, he did stop short—he hung back from really seeing. The risk was too great and his fear too definite: it took at this moment an awful specific form.

He knew—yes, as he had never known anything—that, *should* he see the door open, it would all too abjectly be the end of him. It would mean that the agent of his shame—for his shame was the deep abjection—was once more at large and in general possession; and what glared him thus in the face was the act that this would determine for him. It would send him straight about to the window he had left open, and by that window, be long ladder and dangling rope as absent as they would, he saw himself uncontrollably insanely fatally take his way to the street. The hideous chance of this he at least could avert; but he could only avert it by recoiling in time from assurance. He had the whole house to deal with, this fact was still there; only he now knew that uncertainty alone could start him. He stole back from where he had checked himself—merely to do so was suddenly like safety—and, making blindly for the greater staircase, left gaping rooms and sounding passages behind. Here was the top of the stairs, with a fine large dim descent and three spacious landings to mark off. His instinct was all for mildness, but his feet were harsh on the floors, and, strangely, when he had in a couple of minutes become aware of this, it counted somehow for help. He couldn't have spoken, the tone of his voice would have scared him, and the common conceit or resource of "whistling in the dark" (whether literally or figuratively) have appeared basely vulgar; yet he liked none the less to hear himself go, and when he had reached his first landing—taking it all with no rush, but quite steadily—that stage of success drew from him a gasp of relief.

The house, withal, seemed immense, the scale of space again inordinate; the open rooms, to no one of which his eyes deflected, gloomed in their shuttered state like mouths of caverns; only the high skylight that formed the crown of the deep well created for him a medium in which he could advance, but which might have been, for queerness of colour, some watery under-world. He tried to think of something noble, as that his property was really grand, a splendid possession; but this nobleness took the form too of the clear delight with which he was finally to sacrifice it. They might come in now, the builders, the destroyers—they might come as soon as they would. At the end of two flights he had dropped to another zone, and from the middle of the third, with only one more left, he recognised the influence of the lower windows, of half-drawn blinds, of the occasional gleam of street-lamps, of the glazed spaces of the vestibule, This was the bottom of the sea, which showed an illumination of its own and which he even saw paved—when at a given moment he drew up to sink a long look over the banisters—with the marble squares of his childhood. By that time indubitably he felt, as he might have said in a commoner cause, better; it had allowed him to stop and draw breath, and the ease increased with the sight of the old black-and-white slabs. But what he most felt was that now surely, with the element of impunity pulling him as by hard firm hands, the case was settled for what he might have seen above had he dared that last look. The closed door, blessedly remote now, was still closed—and he had only in short to reach that of the house.

He came down further, he crossed the passage forming the access to the last flight; and if here again he stopped an instant it was almost for the sharpness of the thrill of assured escape. It made him shut his eyes—which opened again to the straight slope of the remainder of the stairs. Here was impunity still, but impunity almost excessive; inasmuch as the sidelights and the high fan-tracery of the entrance were glimmering straight into the hall; an appearance produced, he the next instant saw, by the fact that the vestibule gaped wide, that the hinged halves of the inner door had been thrown far back. Out of that again the *question* sprang at him, making his eyes, as he felt, half-start from his head, as they had done, at the top of the house, before the sign of the other door. If he had left that one open, hadn't he left this one closed, and wasn't he now in *most* immediate presence of some inconceivable occult activity? It was as sharp, the question, as a knife in his side, but the answer hung fire still and seemed to lose itself in the vague darkness to which the thin admitted dawn, glimmering archwise over the whole outer door, made a semicircular margin, a cold silvery nimbus that seemed to play a little as he looked—to shift and expand and contract.

It was as if there had been something within it, protected by indistinctness and corresponding in extent with the opaque surface behind, the painted panels of the last barrier to his escape, of which the key was in his pocket. The indistinctness mocked him even while he stared, affected him as somehow shrouding or challenging certitude, so that after faltering an instant on his step he let himself go with the sense that here *was* at last something to meet, to touch, to take, to know—something all unnatural and dreadful, but to advance upon which was the condition for him either of liberation or of supreme defeat. The penumbra,[8] dense and dark, was the virtual screen of a figure which stood in it as still as some image erect in a niche or as some black-vizored sentinel guarding a treasure. Brydon was to know afterwards, was to recall and make out, the particular thing he had believed during the rest of his descent. He saw, in its great grey glimmering margin, the central vagueness diminish, and he felt it to be taking the very form toward which, for so many days, the passion of his curiosity had yearned. It gloomed, it loomed, it was something, it was somebody, the prodigy of a personal presence.

Rigid and conscious, spectral yet human, a man of his own substance and stature waited there to measure himself with his power to dismay. This only could it be—this only till he recognised, with his advance, that what made the face dim was the pair of raised hands that covered it and in which, so far from being offered in defiance, it was buried as for dark deprecation. So Brydon, before him, took him in; with every fact of him now, in the higher light, hard and acute—his planted stillness, his vivid truth, his grizzled bent head and white masking hands, his queer actuality of evening-dress, of dangling double eye-glass, of gleaming silk lappet[9] and white linen, of pearl button and gold watch-guard and polished shoe. No portrait by a great modern master could have presented him with more intensity, thrust him out of his frame with more art, as if there had been "treatment," of the consummate sort, in his every shade and salience. The revulsion, for our friend, had become, before he knew it, immense—this drop, in the act of apprehension, to the sense of his adversary's inscrutable manœuvre. That meaning at least, while he gaped, it offered him; for he could but gape at his other self in this other anguish, gape as a proof that *he,* standing there for the achieved, the enjoyed, the triumphant life, couldn't be faced in his triumph. Wasn't the proof in the splendid covering hands, strong and completely spread?—so spread and so

---

[8] A partial shadow surrounding the complete shadow of an opaque body.   [9] A fold of a garment.

intentional that, in spite of a special verity that surpassed every other, the fact that one of these hands had lost two fingers, which were reduced to stumps, as if accidentally shot away, the face was effectually guarded and saved.

"Saved," though, *would* it be?—Brydon breathed his wonder till the very impunity of his attitude and the very insistence of his eyes produced, as he felt, a sudden stir which showed the next instant as a deeper portent, while the head raised itself, the betrayal of a braver purpose. The hands, as he looked, began to move, to open; then, as if deciding in a flash, dropped from the face and left it uncovered and presented. Horror, with the sight, had leaped into Brydon's throat, gasping there in a sound he couldn't utter; for the bared identity was too hideous as *his*, and his glare was the passion of his protest. The face, *that* face, Spencer Brydon's?—he searched it still, but looking away from it in dismay and denial, falling straight from his height of sublimity. It was unknown, inconceivable, awful, disconnected from any possibility—! He had been "sold," he inwardly moaned, stalking such game as this: the presence before him was a presence, the horror within him a horror, but the waste of his nights had been only grotesque and the success of his adventure an irony. Such an identity fitted his at *no* point, made its alternative monstrous. A thousand times yes, as it came upon him nearer now—the face was the face of a stranger. It came upon him nearer now, quite as one of those expanding fantastic images projected by the magic lantern of childhood; for the stranger, whoever he might be, evil, odious, blatant, vulgar, had advanced as for aggression, and he knew himself give ground. Then harder pressed still, sick with the force of his shock, and falling back as under the hot breath and the roused passion of a life larger than his own, a rage of personality before which his own collapsed, he felt the whole vision turn to darkness and his very feet give way. His head went round; he was going; he had gone.

III

What had next brought him back, clearly—though after how long?—was Mrs. Muldoon's voice, coming to him from quite near, from so near that he seemed presently to see her as kneeling on the ground before him while he lay looking up at her; himself not wholly on the ground, but half-raised and upheld—conscious, yes, of tenderness of support and, more particularly, of a head pillowed in extraordinary softness and fainly refreshing fragrance. He considered, he wondered, his wit but half at his service; then another face intervened, bending more directly over him, and he finally knew that Alice Staverton had made her lap an ample and perfect cushion to him, and that she had to this end seated herself on the lowest degree of the staircase, the rest of his long person remaining stretched on his old black-and-white slabs. They were cold, these marble squares of his youth; but *he* somehow was not, in this rich return of consciousness—the most wonderful hour, little by little, that he had ever known, leaving him, as it did, so gratefully, so abysmally passive, and yet as with a treasure of intelligence waiting all round him for quiet appropriation; dissolved, he might call it, in the air of the place and producing the golden glow of a late autumn afternoon. He had come back, yes— come back from further away than any man but himself had ever travelled; but it was strange how with this sense what he had come back *to* seemed really the great thing, and as if his prodigious journey had been all for the sake of it. Slowly but surely his consciousness grew, his vision of his state thus completing itself: he had been miraculously *carried* back—lifted and carefully borne as from where he had been picked up, the uttermost end of an interminable grey passage. Even with this he was suffered to rest, and what had now brought him to knowledge was the break in the long mild motion.

It had brought him to knowledge, to knowledge—yes, this was the beauty of his state; which came to resemble more and more that of a man who has gone to sleep on some news of a great inheritance, and then, after dreaming it away, after profaning it with matters strange to it, has waked up again to serenity of certitude and has only to lie and watch it grow. This was the drift of his patience—that he had only to let it shine on him. He must moreover, with intermissions, still have been lifted and borne; since why and how else should he have known himself, later on, with the afternoon glow intenser, no longer at the foot of his stairs— situated as these now seemed at that dark other end of his tunnel—but on a deep window-bench of his high saloon, over which had been spread, couch-fashion, a mantle of soft stuff lined with grey fur that was familiar to his eyes and that one of his hands kept fondly feeling as for its pledge of truth. Mrs. Muldoon's face had gone, but the other, the second he had recognised, hung over him in a way that showed how he was still propped and pillowed. He took it all in, and the more he took it the more it seemed to suffice: he was as much at peace as if he had had food and drink. It was the two women who had found him, on Mrs. Muldoon's having plied, at her usual hour, her latch-key—and on her having above all arrived while Miss Staverton still lingered near the house. She had been turning away, all anxiety, from worrying the vain bell-handle—her calculation having been of the hour of the good woman's visit; but the latter, blessedly, had come up while she was still there, and they had entered together. He had then lain, beyond the vestibule, very much as he was lying now—quite, that is, as he appeared to have fallen, but all so wondrously without bruise or gash; only in a depth of stupor. What he most took in, however, at present, with the steadier clearance, was that Alice Staverton had for a long unspeakable moment not doubted he was dead.

"It must have been that I *was*." He made it out as she held him. "Yes—I can only have died. You brought me literally to life. Only," he wondered, his eyes rising to her, "only, in the name of all the benedictions, how?"

It took her but an instant to bend her face and kiss him, and something in the manner of it, and in the way her hands clasped and locked his head while he felt the cool charity and virtue of her lips, something in all this beatitude somehow answered everything. "And now I keep you," she said.

"Oh keep me, keep me!" he pleaded while her face still hung over him: in response to which it dropped again and stayed close, clingingly close. It was the seal of their situation—of which he tasted the impress for a long blissful moment in silence. But he came back. "Yet how did you know—?"

"I was uneasy. You were to have come, you remember—and you had sent no word."

"Yes, I remember—I was to have gone to you at one to-day." It caught on to their "old" life and relation—which were so near and so far. "I was still out there in my strange darkness—where was it, what was it? I must have stayed there so long." He could but wonder at the depth and the duration of his swoon.

"Since last night?" she asked with a shade of fear for her possible indiscretion.

"Since this morning—it must have been: the cold dim dawn of to-day. Where have I been," he vaguely wailed, "where have I been?" He felt her hold him close, and it was as if this helped him now to make in all security his mild moan. "What a long dark day!"

All in her tenderness she had waited a moment. "In the cold dim dawn?" she quavered.

But he had already gone on piecing together the parts of the whole prodigy. "As I didn't turn up you came straight—?"

She barely cast about. "I went first to your hotel—where they told me of your absence. You had dined out last evening and hadn't been back since. But they appeared to know you had been at your club."

"So you had the idea of *this*—?"

"Of what?" she asked in a moment.

"Well—of what has happened."

"I believed at least you'd have been here. I've known, all along," she said, "that you've been coming."

"'Known' it—?"

"Well, I've believed it. I said nothing to you after that talk we had a month ago—but I felt sure. I knew you *would*," she declared.

"That I'd persist, you mean?"

"That you'd see him."

"Ah, but I didn't!" cried Brydon with his long wail. "There's somebody—an awful beast; whom I brought, too horribly, to bay. But it's not me."

At this she bent over him again, and her eyes were in his eyes. "No—it's not you." And it was as if, while her face hovered, he might have made out in it, hadn't it been so near, some particular meaning blurred by a smile. "No, thank heaven," she repeated—"it's not you! Of course it wasn't to have been."

"Ah but it *was*," he gently insisted. And he stared before him now as he had been staring for so many weeks. "I was to have known myself."

"You couldn't!" she returned consolingly. And then reverting, and as if to account further for what she had herself done, "But it wasn't only *that*, that you hadn't been at home," she went on. "I waited till the hour at which we had found Mrs. Muldoon that day of my going with you; and she arrived, as I've told you, while, failing to bring any one to the door, I lingered in my despair on the steps. After a little, if she hadn't come, by such a mercy, I should have found means to hunt her up. But it wasn't," said Alice Staverton, as if once more with her fine intention—"it wasn't only that."

His eyes, as he lay, turned back to her. "What more then?"

She met it, the wonder she had stirred. "In the cold dim dawn, you say? Well, in the cold dim dawn of this morning I too saw you."

"Saw *me*—?"

"Saw *him*," said Alice Staverton. "It must have been at the same moment."

He lay an instant taking it in—as if he wished to be quite reasonable. "At the same moment?"

"Yes—in my dream again, the same one I've named to you. He came back to me. Then I knew it for a sign. He had come to you."

At this Brydon raised himself; he had to see her better. She helped him when she understood his movement, and he sat up, steadying himself beside her there on the window-bench and with his right hand grasping her left. "*He* didn't come to me."

"You came to yourself," she beautifully smiled.

"Ah I've come to myself now—thanks to you, dearest. But this brute, with his awful face—this brute's a black stranger. He's none of *me,* even as I *might* have been," Brydon sturdily declared.

But she kept the clearness that was like the breath of infallibility. "Isn't the whole point that you'd have been different?"

He almost scowled for it. "As different as *that*—?"

Her look again was more beautiful to him than the things of this world. "Haven't you exactly wanted to know *how* different? So this morning," she said, "you appeared to me."

"Like *him?*"

"A black stranger!"

"Then how did you know it was I?"

"Because, as I told you weeks ago, my mind, my imagination, had worked so over what you might, what you mightn't have been—to show you, you see, how I've thought of you. In the midst of that you came to me—that my wonder might be answered. So I knew," she went on; "and believed that, since the question held you too so fast, as you told me that day, you too would see for yourself. And when this morning I again saw I knew it would be because you had—and also then, from the first moment, because you somehow wanted me. *He* seemed to tell me of that. So why," she strangely smiled, "shouldn't I like him?"

It brought Spencer Brydon to his feet. "You 'like' that horror—?"

"I *could* have liked him. And to me," she said, "he was no horror. I had accepted him."

"'Accepted'—?" Brydon oddly sounded.

"Before, for the interest of his difference—yes. And as *I* didn't disown him, as *I* knew him—which you at last, confronted with him in his difference, so cruelly didn't, my dear—well, he must have been, you see, less dreadful to me. And it may have pleased him that I pitied him."

She was beside him on her feet, but still holding his hand—still with her arm supporting him. But though it all brought for him thus a dim light, "You 'pitied' him?" he grudgingly, resentfully asked.

"He has been unhappy, he has been ravaged," she said.

"And haven't I been unhappy? Am not I—you've only to look at me!—ravaged?"

"Ah I don't say I like him *better,*" she granted after a thought. "But he's grim, he's worn—and things have happened to him. He doesn't make shift, for sight, with your charming monocle."

"No"—it struck Brydon: "I couldn't have sported mine 'downtown.' They'd have guyed[10] me there."

"His great convex pince-nez[11]—I saw it, I recognised the kind—is for his poor ruined sight. And his poor right hand—!"

"Ah!" Brydon winced—whether for his proved identity or for his lost fingers. Then, "He has a million a year," he lucidly added. "But he hasn't you."

"And he isn't—no, he isn't—*you!*" she murmured as he drew her to his breast.

1908

---

[10] Teased.   [11] Eyeglasses held on the face by a spring that pinches the nose.

THE ART OF FICTION*

I should not have affixed so comprehensive a title to these few remarks, necessarily wanting in any completeness upon a subject the full consideration of which would carry us far, did I not seem to discover a pretext for my temerity in the interesting pamphlet lately published under this name by Mr. Walter Besant. Mr. Besant's lecture at the Royal Institution—the original form of his pamphlet—appears to indicate that many persons are interested in the art of fiction, and are not indifferent to such remarks, as those who practise it may attempt to make about it. I am therefore anxious not to lose the benefit of this favourable association, and to edge in a few words under cover of the attention which Mr. Besant is sure to have excited. There is something very encouraging in his having put into form certain of his ideas on the mystery of story-telling.

It is a proof of life and curiosity—curiosity on the part of the brotherhood of novelists as well as on the part of their readers. Only a short time ago it might have been supposed that the English novel was not what the French call *discutable*.[1] It had no air of having a theory, a conviction, a consciousness of itself behind it—of being the expression of an artistic faith, the result of choice and comparison. I do not say it was necessarily the worse for that: it would take much more courage than I possess to intimate that the form of the novel as Dickens and Thackeray (for instance) saw it had any taint of incompleteness. It was, however, *naïf*[2] (if I may help myself out with another French word); and evidently if it be destined to suffer in any way for having lost its *naïveté* it has now an idea of making sure of the corresponding advantages. During the period I have alluded to there was a comfortable, good-humoured feeling abroad that a novel is a novel, as a pudding is a pudding, and that our only business with it could be to swallow it. But within a year or two, for some reason or other, there have been signs of returning animation—the era of discussion would appear to have been to a certain extent opened. Art lives upon discussion, upon experiment, upon curiosity, upon variety of attempt, upon the exchange of views and the comparison of standpoints; and there is a presumption that those times when no one has anything particular to say about it, and has no reason to give for practice or preference, though they may be times of honour, are not times of development—are times, possibly even, a little of dulness. The successful application of any art is a delightful spectacle, but the theory too is interesting; and though there is a great deal of the latter without the former I suspect there has never been genuine success that has not had a latent core of conviction. Discussion, suggestion, formulation, these things are fertilising when they are frank and sincere. Mr. Besant has set an excellent example in saying what he thinks, for his part, about the way in which fiction should be written, as well as about the way in which it should be published; for his view of the "art," carried on into an appendix, covers that too. Other labourers in the same field will doubtless take up the argument, they will give it the light of their experience, and the effect will surely be to make our interest in the novel a little more

---

* First published in *Longman's Magazine* in 1884, written in response to a lecture on fiction given by the English novelist and critic Sir Walter Besant (1836–1901) at the Royal Institution in London on April 25, 1884.
[1] "Disputable," "debatable" (French).   [2] "Naïve" (French).

what it had for some time threatened to fail to be—a serious, active, inquiring interest, under protection of which this delightful study may, in moments of confidence, venture to say a little more what it thinks of itself.

It must take itself seriously for the public to take it so. The old superstition about fiction being "wicked" has doubtless died out in England; but the spirit of it lingers in a certain oblique regard directed toward any story which does not more or less admit that it is only a joke. Even the most jocular novel feels in some degree the weight of the proscription that was formerly directed against literary levity: the jocularity does not always succeed in passing for orthodoxy. It is still expected, though perhaps people are ashamed to say it, that a production which is after all only a "make-believe" (for what else is a "story"?) shall be in some degree apologetic—shall renounce the pretension of attempting really to represent life. This, of course, any sensible, wide-awake story declines to do, for it quickly perceives that the tolerance granted to it on such a condition is only an attempt to stifle it disguised in the form of generosity. The old evangelical hostility to the novel, which was as explicit as it was narrow, and which regarded it as little less favourable to our immortal part than a stage-play, was in reality far less insulting. The only reason for the existence of a novel is that it does attempt to represent life. When it relinquishes this attempt, the same attempt that we see on the canvas of the painter, it will have arrived at a very strange pass. It is not expected of the picture that it will make itself humble in order to be forgiven; and the analogy between the art of the painter and the art of the novelist is, so far as I am able to see, complete. Their inspiration is the same, their process (allowing for the different quality of the vehicle), is the same, their success is the same. They may learn from each other, they may explain and sustain each other. Their cause is the same, and the honour of one is the honour of another. The Mahometans[3] think a picture an unholy thing, but it is a long time since any Christian did, and it is therefore the more odd that in the Christian mind the traces (dissimulated though they may be) of a suspicion of the sister art should linger to this day. The only effectual way to lay it to rest is to emphasise the analogy to which I just alluded—to insist on the fact that as the picture is reality, so the novel is history. That is the only general description (which does it justice) that we may give of the novel. But history also is allowed to represent life; it is not, any more than painting, expected to apologise. The subject-matter of fiction is stored up likewise in documents and records, and if it will not give itself away, as they say in California, it must speak with assurance, with the tone of the historian. Certain accomplished novelists have a habit of giving themselves away which must often bring tears to the eyes of people who take their fiction seriously. I was lately struck, in reading over many pages of Anthony Trollope,[4] with his want of discretion in this particular. In a digression, a parenthesis or an aside, he concedes to the reader that he and this trusting friend are only "making believe." He admits that the events he narrates have not really happened, and that he can give his narrative any turn the reader may like best. Such a betrayal of a sacred office seems to me, I confess, a terrible crime; it is what I mean by the attitude of apology, and it shocks me every whit as much in Trollope as it would have shocked me in Gibbon or Macaulay.[5] It implies that the

---

[3] Mohammedans; the Muslim religion at one time forbade figural representations.
[4] Trollope (1815–1882) was an English novelist.
[5] Edward Gibbon (1737–1794) and Thomas Babington Macaulay (1800–1859): English historians.

novelist is less occupied in looking for the truth (the truth, of course I mean, that he assumes, the premises that we must grant him, whatever they may be), than the historian, and in doing so it deprives him at a stroke of all his standing-room. To represent and illustrate the past, the actions of men, is the task of either writer, and the only difference that I can see is, in proportion as he succeeds, to the honour of the novelist, consisting as it does in his having more difficulty in collecting his evidence, which is so far from being purely literary. It seems to me to give him a great character, the fact that he has at once so much in common with the philosopher and the painter; this double analogy is a magnificent heritage.

It is of all this evidently that Mr. Besant is full when he insists upon the fact that fiction is one of the *fine* arts, deserving in its turn of all the honours and emoluments that have hitherto been reserved for the successful profession of music, poetry, painting, architecture. It is impossible to insist too much on so important a truth, and the place that Mr. Besant demands for the work of the novelist may be represented, a trifle less abstractly, by saying that he demands not only that it shall be reputed artistic, but that it shall be reputed very artistic indeed. It is excellent that he should have struck this note, for his doing so indicates that there was need of it, that his proposition may be to many people a novelty. One rubs one's eyes at the thought; but the rest of Mr. Besant's essay confirms the revelation. I suspect in truth that it would be possible to confirm it still further, and that one would not be far wrong in saying that in addition to the people to whom it has never occurred that a novel ought to be artistic, there are a great many others who, if this principle were urged upon them, would be filled with an indefinable mistrust. They would find it difficult to explain their repugnance, but it would operate strongly to put them on their guard. "Art," in our Protestant communities, where so many things have got so strangely twisted about, is supposed in certain circles to have some vaguely injurious effect upon those who make it an important consideration, who let it weigh in the balance. It is assumed to be opposed in some mysterious manner to morality, to amusement, to instruction. When it is embodied in the work of the painter (the sculptor is another affair!) you know what it is: it stands there before you, in the honesty of pink and green and a gilt frame; you can see the worst of it at a glance, and you can be on your guard. But when it is introduced into literature it becomes more insidious—there is danger of its hurting you before you know it. Literature should be either instructive or amusing, and there is in many minds an impression that these artistic preoccupations, the search for form, contribute to neither end, interfere indeed with both. They are too frivolous to be edifying, and too serious to be diverting; and they are moreover priggish and paradoxical and superfluous. That, I think, represents the manner in which the latent thought of many people who read novels as an exercise in skipping would explain itself if it were to become articulate. They would argue, of course, that a novel ought to be "good," but they would interpret this term in a fashion of their own, which indeed would vary considerably from one critic to another. One would say that being good means representing virtuous and aspiring characters, placed in prominent positions; another would say that it depends on a "happy ending," on a distribution at the last of prizes, pensions, husbands, wives, babies, millions, appended paragraphs, and cheerful remarks. Another still would say that it means being full of incident and movement, so that we shall wish to jump ahead, to see who was the mysterious stranger, and if the stolen will was ever found, and shall not be distracted from this pleasure by any tiresome analysis or "description." But they would all agree that the "artistic" idea would spoil some of their fun. One would hold it accountable for all the description, another would see it revealed in the absence of sympathy. Its hostility to a happy ending would be evident, and it might even in some cases render any ending at all impossible. The "ending" of a novel is, for many persons, like that of a good dinner, a course of dessert and ices, and the artist in fiction is regarded as a sort of meddlesome doctor who forbids agreeable aftertastes. It is therefore true that this conception of Mr. Besant's of the novel as a superior form encounters not only a negative but a positive indifference. It matters little that as a work of art it should really be as little or as much of its essence to supply happy endings, sympathetic characters, and an objective tone, as if it were a work of mechanics: the association of ideas, however incongruous, might easily be too much for it if an eloquent voice were not sometimes raised to call attention to the fact that it is at once as free and as serious a branch of literature as any other.

Certainly this might sometimes be doubted in presence of the enormous number of works of fiction that appeal to the credulity of our generation, for it might easily seem that there could be no great character in a commodity so quickly and easily produced. It must be admitted that good novels are much compromised by bad ones, and that the field at large suffers discredit from overcrowding. I think, however, that this injury is only superficial, and that the super-abundance of written fiction proves nothing against the principle itself. It has been vulgarised, like all other kinds of literature, like everything else to-day, and it has proved more than some kinds accessible to vulgarisation. But there is as much difference as there ever was between a good novel and a bad one: the bad is swept with all the daubed canvases and spoiled marble into some unvisited limbo, or infinite rubbish-yard beneath the back-windows of the world, and the good subsists and emits its light and stimulates our desire for perfection. As I shall take the liberty of making but a single criticism of Mr. Besant, whose tone is so full of the love of his art, I may as well have done with it at once. He seems to me to mistake in attempting to say so definitely beforehand what sort of an affair the good novel will be. To indicate the danger of such an error as that has been the purpose of these few pages; to suggest that certain traditions on the subject, applied *a priori,* have already had much to answer for, and that the good health of an art which undertakes so immediately to reproduce life must demand that it be perfectly free. It lives upon exercise, and the very meaning of exercise is freedom. The only obligation to which in advance we may hold a novel, without incurring the accusation of being arbitrary, is that it be interesting. That general responsibility rests upon it, but it is the only one I can think of. The ways in which it is at liberty to accomplish this result (of interesting us) strike me as innumerable, and such as can only suffer from being marked out or fenced in by prescription. They are as various as the temperament of man, and they are successful in proportion as they reveal a particular mind, different from others. A novel is in its broadest definition a personal, a direct impression of life: that, to begin with, constitutes its value, which is greater or less according to the intensity of the impression. But there will be no intensity at all, and therefore no value, unless there is freedom to feel and say. The tracing of a line to be followed, of a tone to be taken, of a form to be filled out, is a limitation of that freedom and a suppression of the very thing that we are most curious about. The form, it seems to me, is to be appreciated after the fact: then the author's choice has been made, his standard has been indicated; then we can follow lines and directions and compare tones and resemblances. Then in a word we can enjoy one of the most charming of pleasures, we can estimate quality, we can apply the test of execution. The execution belongs to the author alone; it is what is most personal to him, and we measure him by that. The advantage, the luxury, as well as the torment and responsibility of the novelist, is that there is no limit to what he may attempt as an executant—no limit to his possible experiments, efforts, discoveries, successes. Here it is especially that he works, step by step, like his brother of the brush, of whom we may always say that he has painted his picture in a manner best known to himself. His manner is his secret, not necessarily a jealous one. He cannot disclose it as a general thing if he would; he would be at a loss to teach it to others. I say this with a due recollection of having insisted on the community of method of the artist who paints a picture and the artist who writes a novel. The painter *is* able to teach the rudiments of his practice, and it is possible, from the study of good work (granted the aptitude), both to learn how to paint and to learn how to write. Yet it remains true, without injury to the *rapprochement*,[6] that the literary artist would be obliged to say to his pupil much more than the other, "Ah, well, you must do it as you can!" It is a question of degree, a matter of delicacy. If there are exact sciences, there are also exact arts, and the grammar of painting is so much more definite that it makes the difference.

I ought to add, however, that if Mr. Besant says at the beginning of his essay that the "laws of fiction may be laid down and taught with as much precision and exactness as the laws of harmony, perspective, and proportion," he mitigates what might appear to be an extravagance by applying his remark to "general" laws, and by expressing most of these rules in a manner with which it would certainly be unaccommodating to disagree. That the novelist must write from his experience, that his "characters must be real and such as might be met with in actual life;" that "a young lady brought up in a quiet country village should avoid descriptions of garrison life," and "a writer whose friends and personal experiences belong to the lower middle-class should carefully avoid introducing his characters into society;" that one should enter one's notes in a common-place book; that one's figures should be clear in outline; that making them clear by some trick of speech or of carriage is a bad method, and "describing them at length" is a worse one; that English Fiction should have a "conscious moral purpose;" that "it is almost impossible to estimate too highly the value of careful workmanship—that is, of style;" that "the most important point of all is the story," that "the story is everything": these are principles with most of which it is surely impossible not to sympathise. That remark about the lower middle-class writer and his knowing his place is perhaps rather chilling; but for the rest I should find it difficult to dissent from any one of these recommendations. At the same time, I should find it difficult positively to assent to them, with the exception, perhaps, of the injunction as to entering one's notes in a common-place book. They scarcely seem to me to have the quality that Mr. Besant attributes to the rules of the novelist—the "precision and exactness" of "the laws of harmony, perspective, and proportion." They are suggestive, they are even inspiring, but they are not exact, though they are doubtless as much so as the case admits of: which is a proof of that liberty of interpretation for which I just contended. For the value of these different injunctions—so beautiful and so vague—is wholly in the meaning one attaches to them. The characters,

---

[6] Bringing together, comparison (French).

the situation, which strike one as real will be those that touch and interest one most, but the measure of reality is very difficult to fix. The reality of Don Quixote or of Mr. Micawber[7] is a very delicate shade; it is a reality so coloured by the author's vision that, vivid as it may be, one would hesitate to propose it as a model: one would expose one's self to some very embarrassing questions on the part of a pupil. It goes without saying that you will not write a good novel unless you possess the sense of reality; but it will be difficult to give you a recipe for calling that sense into being. Humanity is immense, and reality has a myriad forms; the most one can affirm is that some of the flowers of fiction have the odour of it, and others have not; as for telling you in advance how your nosegay should be composed, that is another affair. It is equally excellent and inconclusive to say that one must write from experience; to our supposititious aspirant such a declaration might savour of mockery. What kind of experience is intended, and where does it begin and end? Experience is never limited, and it is never complete; it is an immense sensibility, a kind of huge spiderweb of the finest silken threads suspended in the chamber of consciousness, and catching every airborne particle in its tissue. It is the very atmosphere of the mind; and when the mind is imaginative—much more when it happens to be that of a man of genius—it takes to itself the faintest hints of life, it converts the very pulses of the air into revelations. The young lady living in a village has only to be a damsel upon whom nothing is lost to make it quite unfair (as it seems to me) to declare to her that she shall have nothing to say about the military. Greater miracles have been seen than that, imagination assisting, she should speak the truth about some of these gentlemen. I remember an English novelist, a woman of genius, telling me that she was much commended for the impression she had managed to give in one of her tales of the nature and way of life of the French Protestant youth. She had been asked where she learned so much about this recondite being, she had been congratulated on her peculiar opportunities. These opportunities consisted in her having once, in Paris, as she ascended a staircase, passed an open door where, in the household of a *pasteur*,[8] some of the young Protestants were seated at table round a finished meal. The glimpse made a picture; it lasted only a moment, but that moment was experience. She had got her direct personal impression, and she turned out her type. She knew what youth was, and what Protestantism; she also had the advantage of having seen what it was to be French, so that she converted these ideas into a concrete image and produced a reality. Above all, however, she was blessed with the faculty which when you give it an inch takes an ell, and which for the artist is a much greater source of strength than any accident of residence or of place in the social scale. The power to guess the unseen from the seen, to trace the implication of things, to judge the whole piece by the pattern, the condition of feeling life in general so completely that you are well on your way to knowing any particular corner of it—this cluster of gifts may almost be said to constitute experience, and they occur in country and in town, and in the most differing stages of education. If experience consists of impressions, it may be said that impressions *are* experience, just as (have we not seen it?) they are the very air we breathe.

---

[7] The hero of *Don Quixote* (1605, 1616), by Miguel de Cervantes (1547–1616), and a character in *David Copperfield* (1849–1850), by Charles Dickens (1812–1870).

[8] "Pastor" (French).

Therefore, if I should certainly say to a novice, "Write from experience and experience only," I should feel that this was rather a tantalising monition if I were not careful immediately to add, "Try to be one of the people on whom nothing is lost!"

I am far from intending by this to minimise the importance of exactness—of truth of detail. One can speak best from one's own taste, and I may therefore venture to say that the air of reality (solidity of specification) seems to me to be the supreme virtue of a novel—the merit on which all its other merits (including that conscious moral purpose of which Mr. Besant speaks) helplessly and submissively depend. If it be not there they are all as nothing, and if these be there, they owe their effect to the success with which the author has produced the illusion of life. The cultivation of this success, the study of this exquisite process, form, to my taste, the beginning and the end of the art of the novelist. They are his inspiration, his despair, his reward, his torment, his delight. It is here in very truth that he competes with life; it is here that he competes with his brother the painter in *his* attempt to render the look of things, the look that conveys their meaning, to catch the colour, the relief, the expression, the surface, the substance of the human spectacle. It is in regard to this that Mr. Besant is well inspired when he bids him take notes. He cannot possibly take too many, he cannot possibly take enough. All life solicits him, and to "render" the simplest surface, to produce the most momentary illusion, is a very complicated business. His case would be easier, and the rule would be more exact, if Mr. Besant had been able to tell him what notes to take. But this, I fear, he can never learn in any manual; it is the business of his life. He has to take a great many in order to select a few, he has to work them up as he can, and even the guides and philosophers who might have most to say to him must leave him alone when it comes to the application of precepts, as we leave the painter in communion with his palette. That his characters "must be clear in outline," as Mr. Besant says—he feels that down to his boots; but how he shall make them so is a secret between his good angel and himself. It would be absurdly simple if he could be taught that a great deal of "description" would make them so, or that on the contrary the absence of description and the cultivation of dialogue, or the absence of dialogue and the multiplication of "incident," would rescue him from his difficulties. Nothing, for instance, is more possible than that he be of a turn of mind for which this odd, literal opposition of description and dialogue, incident and description, has little meaning and light. People often talk of these things as if they had a kind of internecine distinctness, instead of melting into each other at every breath, and being intimately associated parts of one general effort of expression. I cannot imagine composition existing in a series of blocks, nor conceive, in any novel worth discussing at all, of a passage of description that is not in its intention narrative, a passage of dialogue that is not in its intention descriptive, a touch of truth of any sort that does not partake of the nature of incident, or an incident that derives its interest from any other source than the general and only source of the success of a work of art—that of being illustrative. A novel is a living thing, all one and continuous, like any other organism, and in proportion as it lives will it be found, I think, that in each of the parts there is something of each of the other parts. The critic who over the close texture of a finished work shall pretend to trace a geography of items will mark some frontiers as artificial, I fear, as any that have been known to history. There is an old-fashioned distinction between the novel of character and the novel of incident which must have cost many a smile to the intending fabulist who was keen about his work. It appears to me as little to the point as the equally celebrated distinction between the novel and the romance—to answer as little to any reality. There are bad novels and good novels, as there are bad pictures and good pictures; but that is the only distinction in which I see any meaning, and I can as little imagine speaking of a novel of character as I can imagine speaking of a picture of character. When one says picture one says of character, when one says novel one says of incident, and the terms may be transposed at will. What is character but the determination of incident? What is incident but the illustration of character? What is either a picture or a novel that is *not* of character? What else do we seek in it and find in it? It is an incident for a woman to stand up with her hand resting on a table and look out at you in a certain way; or if it be not an incident I think it will be hard to say what it is. At the same time it is an expression of character. If you say you don't see it (character in *that—allons donc!*[9]), this is exactly what the artist who has reasons of his own for thinking he *does* see it undertakes to show you. When a young man makes up his mind that he has not faith enough after all to enter the church as he intended, that is an incident, though you may not hurry to the end of the chapter to see whether perhaps he doesn't change once more. I do not say that these are extraordinary or startling incidents. I do not pretend to estimate the degree of interest proceeding from them, for this will depend upon the skill of the painter. It sounds almost puerile to say that some incidents are intrinsically much more important than others, and I need not take this precaution after having professed my sympathy for the major ones in remarking that the only classification of the novel that I can understand is into that which has life and that which has it not.

The novel and the romance, the novel of incident and that of character—these clumsy separations appear to me to have been made by critics and readers for their own convenience, and to help them out of some of their occasional queer predicaments, but to have little reality or interest for the producer, from whose point of view it is of course that we are attempting to consider the art of fiction. The case is the same with another shadowy category which Mr. Besant apparently is disposed to set up—that of the "modern English novel"; unless indeed it be that in this matter he has fallen into an accidental confusion of stand-points. It is not quite clear whether he intends the remarks in which he alludes to it to be didactic or historical. It is as difficult to suppose a person intending to write a modern English as to suppose him writing an ancient English novel: that is a label which begs the question. One writes the novel, one paints the picture, of one's language and of one's time, and calling it modern English will not, alas! make the difficult task any easier. No more, unfortunately, will calling this or that work of one's fellow-artist a romance—unless it be, of course, simply for the pleasantness of the thing, as for instance when Hawthorne gave this heading to his story of *Blithedale*.[10] The French, who have brought the theory of fiction to remarkable completeness, have but one name for the novel, and have not attempted smaller things in it, that I can see, for that. I can think of no obligation to which the "romancer" would not be

---

[9] "Come now!" or "Nonsense!" (French).
[10] Nathaniel Hawthorne's novel *The Blithedale Romance* (1852).

held equally with the novelist; the standard of execution is equally high for each. Of course it is of execution that we are talking—that being the only point of a novel that is open to contention. This is perhaps too often lost sight of, only to produce interminable confusions and cross-purposes. We must grant the artist his subject, his idea, his *donnée*:[11] our criticism is applied only to what he makes of it. Naturally I do not mean that we are bound to like it or find it interesting: in case we do not our course is perfectly simple—to let it alone. We may believe that of a certain idea even the most sincere novelist can make nothing at all, and the event may perfectly justify our belief; but the failure will have been a failure to execute, and it is in the execution that the fatal weakness is recorded. If we pretend to respect the artist at all, we must allow him his freedom of choice, in the face, in particular cases, of innumerable presumptions that the choice will not fructify. Art derives a considerable part of its beneficial exercise from flying in the face of presumptions, and some of the most interesting experiments of which it is capable are hidden in the bosom of common things. Gustave Flaubert has written a story[12] about the devotion of a servant-girl to a parrot, and the production, highly finished as it is, cannot on the whole be called a success. We are perfectly free to find it flat, but I think it might have been interesting; and I, for my part, am extremely glad he should have written it; it is a contribution to our knowledge of what can be done—or what cannot. Ivan Turgénieff has written a tale[13] about a deaf and dumb serf and a lap-dog, and the thing is touching, loving, a little masterpiece. He struck the note of life where Gustave Flaubert missed it—he flew in the face of a presumption and achieved a victory.

Nothing, of course, will ever take the place of the good old fashion of "liking" a work of art or not liking it: the most improved criticism will not abolish that primitive, that ultimate test. I mention this to guard myself from the accusation of intimating that the idea, the subject, of a novel or a picture, does not matter. It matters, to my sense, in the highest degree, and if I might put up a prayer it would be that artists should select none but the richest. Some, as I have already hastened to admit, are much more remunerative than others, and it would be a world happily arranged in which persons intending to treat them should be exempt from confusions and mistakes. This fortunate condition will arrive only, I fear, on the same day that critics become purged from error. Meanwhile, I repeat, we do not judge the artist with fairness unless we say to him, "Oh, I grant you your starting-point, because if I did not I should seem to prescribe to you, and heaven forbid I should take that responsibility. If I pretend to tell you what you must not take, you will call upon me to tell you then what you must take; in which case I shall be prettily caught. Moreover, it isn't till I have accepted your data that I can begin to measure you. I have the standard, the pitch; I have no right to tamper with your flute and then criticise your music. Of course I may not care for your idea at all; I may think it silly, or stale, or unclean; in which case I wash my hands of you altogether. I may content myself with believing that you will not have succeeded in being interesting, but I shall, of course, not attempt to demonstrate it, and you will be as indifferent to me as I am to you. I needn't remind you that there are all

---

[11] "A given" (French): a premise.
[12] "Un Coeur Simple" (1877), by the French novelist Flaubert (1821–1880).
[13] "Mumu" (1856), by the Russian novelist Turgenev (1818–1883).

sorts of tastes: who can know it better? Some people, for excellent reasons, don't like to read about carpenters; others, for reasons even better, don't like to read about courtesans. Many object to Americans. Others (I believe they are mainly editors and publishers) won't look at Italians. Some readers don't like quiet subjects; others don't like bustling ones. Some enjoy a complete illusion, others the consciousness of large concessions. They choose their novels accordingly, and if they don't care about your idea they won't, *a fortiori*,[14] care about your treatment."

So that it comes back very quickly, as I have said, to the liking: in spite of M. Zola,[15] who reasons less powerfully than he represents, and who will not reconcile himself to this absoluteness of taste, thinking that there are certain things that people ought to like, and that they can be made to like. I am quite at a loss to imagine anything (at any rate in this matter of fiction) that people *ought* to like or to dislike. Selection will be sure to take care of itself, for it has a constant motive behind it. That motive is simply experience. As people feel life, so they will feel the art that is most closely related to it. This closeness of relation is what we should never forget in talking of the effort of the novel. Many people speak of it as a factitious, artificial form, a product of ingenuity, the business of which is to alter and arrange the things that surround us, to translate them into conventional, traditional moulds. This, however, is a view of the matter which carries us but a very short way, condemns the art to an eternal repetition of a few familiar *clichés*, cuts short its development, and leads us straight up to a dead wall. Catching the very note and trick, the strange irregular rhythm of life, that is the attempt whose strenuous force keeps Fiction upon her feet. In proportion as in what she offers us we see life *without* rearrangement do we feel that we are touching the truth; in proportion as we see it *with* rearrangement do we feel that we are being put off with a substitute, a compromise and convention. It is not uncommon to hear an extraordinary assurance of remark in regard to this matter of rearranging, which is often spoken of as if it were the last word of art. Mr. Besant seems to me in danger of falling into the great error with his rather unguarded talk about "selection." Art is essentially selection, but it is a selection whose main care is to be typical, to be inclusive. For many people art means rose-coloured window-panes, and selection means picking a bouquet for Mrs. Grundy.[16] They will tell you glibly that artistic considerations have nothing to do with the disagreeable, with the ugly; they will rattle off shallow commonplaces about the province of art and the limits of art till you are moved to some wonder in return as to the province and the limits of ignorance. It appears to me that no one can ever have made a seriously artistic attempt without becoming conscious of an immense increase—a kind of revelation—of freedom. One perceives in that case—by the light of a heavenly ray—that the province of art is all life, all feeling, all observation, all vision. As Mr. Besant so justly intimates, it is all experience. That is a sufficient answer to those who maintain that it must not touch the sad things of life, who stick into its divine unconscious bosom little prohibitory inscriptions on the end of sticks, such as we see in public gardens—"It is forbidden to walk on the grass; it

---

[14] "With greater reason" (Latin).

[15] Émile Zola (1840–1902), a French naturalistic novelist and critic; James says that Zola's criticism is less powerful than his fiction.

[16] A character in the play *Speed the Plow* (1798), by Thomas Morton (1764–1838); she has become a symbol of prudishness.

is forbidden to touch the flowers; it is not allowed to introduce dogs or to remain after dark; it is requested to keep to the right." The young aspirant in the line of fiction whom we continue to imagine will do nothing without taste, for in that case his freedom would be of little use to him; but the first advantage of his taste will be to reveal to him the absurdity of the little sticks and tickets. If he have taste, I must add, of course he will have ingenuity, and my disrespectful reference to that quality just now was not meant to imply that it is useless in fiction. But it is only a secondary aid; the first is a capacity for receiving straight impressions.

Mr. Besant has some remarks on the question of "the story" which I shall not attempt to criticise, though they seem to me to contain a singular ambiguity, because I do not think I understand them. I cannot see what is meant by talking as if there were a part of a novel which is the story and part of it which for mystical reasons is not—unless indeed the distinction be made in a sense in which it is difficult to suppose that any one should attempt to convey anything. "The story," if it represents anything, represents the subject, the idea, the *donnée* of the novel; and there is surely no "school"—Mr. Besant speaks of a school—which urges that a novel should be all treatment and no subject. There must assuredly be something to treat; every school is intimately conscious of that. This sense of the story being the idea, the starting-point, of the novel, is the only one that I see in which it can be spoken of as something different from its organic whole; and since in proportion as the work is successful the idea permeates and penetrates it, informs and animates it, so that every word and every punctuation point contribute directly to the expression, in that proportion do we lose our sense of the story being a blade which may be drawn more or less out of its sheath. The story and the novel, the idea and the form, are the needle and thread, and I never heard of a guild of tailors who recommended the use of the thread without the needle, or the needle without the thread. Mr. Besant is not the only critic who may be observed to have spoken as if there were certain things in life which constitute stories, and certain others which do not. I find the same odd implication in an entertaining article in the *Pall Mall Gazette,* devoted, as it happens, to Mr. Besant's lecture. "The story is the thing!" says this graceful writer, as if with a tone of opposition to some other idea. I should think it was, as every painter who, as the time for "sending in" his picture[17] looms in the distance, finds himself still in quest of a subject—as every belated artist not fixed about his theme will heartily agree. There are some subjects which speak to us and others which do not, but he would be a clever man who should undertake to give a rule—an index expurgatorius[18]—by which the story and the no-story should be known apart. It is impossible (to me at least) to imagine any such rule which shall not be altogether arbitrary. The writer in the *Pall Mall* opposes the delightful (as I suppose) novel of *Margot la Balafrée*[19] to certain tales in which "Bostonian nymphs" appear to have "rejected English dukes for psychological reasons." I am not acquainted with the romance just designated, and can scarcely forgive the *Pall Mall* critic for not mentioning the name of the author, but the title appears to refer to a lady who may have received a scar in some heroic adventure. I am inconsolable at not being acquainted with this epi-

[17] Submitting his painting for exhibition.
[18] Index of forbidden readings (Latin): a standard by which to judge.
[19] *Margot the Scarfaced Woman,* an 1884 novel by the French novelist Fortuné du Boisgobey (1821–1891).

sode, but am utterly at a loss to see why it is a story when the rejection (or acceptance) of a duke is not, and why a reason, psychological or other, is not a
subject when a cicatrix[20] is. They are all particles of the multitudinous life with
which the novel deals, and surely no dogma which pretends to make it lawful to
touch the one and unlawful to touch the other will stand for a moment on its feet.
It is the special picture that must stand or fall, according as it seem to possess truth
or to lack it. Mr. Besant does not, to my sense, light up the subject by intimating
that a story must, under penalty of not being a story, consist of "adventures." Why
of adventures more than of green spectacles? He mentions a category of impossible things, and among them he places "fiction without adventure." Why without
adventure, more than without matrimony, or celibacy, or parturition,[21] or cholera,
or hydropathy, or Jansenism?[22] This seems to me to bring the novel back to the
hapless little *rôle* of being an artificial, ingenious thing—bring it down from its
large, free character of an immense and exquisite correspondence with life. And
what *is* adventure, when it comes to that, and by what sign is the listening pupil to
recognise it? It is an adventure—an immense one—for me to write this little article; and for a Bostonian nymph to reject an English duke is an adventure only less
stirring, I should say, than for an English duke to be rejected by a Bostonian
nymph. I see dramas within dramas in that, and innumerable points of view. A
psychological reason is, to my imagination, an object adorably pictorial; to catch
the tint of its complexion—I feel as if that idea might inspire one to Titianesque[23]
efforts. There are few things more exciting to me, in short, than a psychological
reason, and yet, I protest, the novel seems to me the most magnificent form of art.
I have just been reading, at the same time, the delightful story of *Treasure Island,*[24] by Mr. Robert Louis Stevenson and, in a manner less consecutive, the last
tale from M. Edmond de Goncourt, which is entitled *Chérie.*[25] One of these works
treats of murders, mysteries, islands of dreadful renown, hairbreadth escapes, miraculous coincidences and buried doubloons. The other treats of a little French girl
who lived in a fine house in Paris, and died of wounded sensibility because no one
would marry her. I call *Treasure Island* delightful, because it appears to me to
have succeeded wonderfully in what it attempts; and I venture to bestow no epithet
upon *Chérie,* which strikes me as having failed deplorably in what it attempts—
that is in tracing the development of the moral consciousness of a child. But one
of these productions strikes me as exactly as much of a novel as the other, and as
having a "story" quite as much. The moral consciousness of a child is as much a
part of life as the islands of the Spanish Main, and the one sort of geography
seems to me to have those "surprises" of which Mr. Besant speaks quite as much
as the other. For myself (since it comes back in the last resort, as I say, to the
preference of the individual), the picture of the child's experience has the advantage that I can at successive steps (an immense luxury, near to the "sensual pleasure" of which Mr. Besant's critic in the *Pall Mall* speaks) say Yes or No, as it
may be, to what the artist puts before me. I have been a child in fact, but I have
been on a quest for a buried treasure only in supposition, and it is a simple acci-

---

[20] A scar.   [21] Childbirth.
[22] The doctrine of the Dutch theologian Bishop Cornelis Jansen (1585–1638), emphasizing predestination and the necessity of belonging to the Catholic Church.
[23] Like the work of Titian (1477–1576), an Italian painter known for his use of color.
[24] An 1883 novel by the English writer Stevenson (1850–1894).
[25] An 1884 novel by Edmond Louis Antoine de Goncourt (1822–1896), a French novelist who collaborated with his brother, Jules Alfred Huot de Goncourt (1830–1870).

dent that with M. de Goncourt I should have for the most part to say No. With George Eliot,[26] when she painted that country with a far other intelligence, I always said Yes.

The most interesting part of Mr. Besant's lecture is unfortunately the briefest passage—his very cursory allusion to the "conscious moral purpose" of the novel. Here again it is not very clear whether he be recording a fact or laying down a principle; it is a great pity that in the latter case he should not have developed his idea. This branch of the subject is of immense importance, and Mr. Besant's few words point to considerations of the widest reach, not to be lightly disposed of. He will have treated the art of fiction but superficially who is not prepared to go every inch of the way that these considerations will carry him. It is for this reason that at the beginning of these remarks I was careful to notify the reader that my reflections on so large a theme have no pretension to be exhaustive. Like Mr. Besant, I have left the question of the morality of the novel till the last, and at the last I find I have used up my space. It is a question surrounded with difficulties, as witness the very first that meets us, in the form of a definite question, on the threshold. Vagueness, in such a discussion, is fatal, and what is the meaning of your morality and your conscious moral purpose? Will you not define your terms and explain how (a novel being a picture) a picture can be either moral or immoral? You wish to paint a moral picture or carve a moral statue: will you not tell us how you would set about it? We are discussing the Art of Fiction; questions of art are questions (in the widest sense) of execution; questions of morality are quite another affair, and will you not let us see how it is that you find it so easy to mix them up? These things are so clear to Mr. Besant that he has deduced from them a law which he sees embodied in English Fiction, and which is "a truly admirable thing and a great cause for congratulation." It is a great cause for congratulation indeed when such thorny problems become as smooth as silk. I may add that in so far as Mr. Besant perceives that in point of fact English Fiction has addressed itself preponderantly to these delicate questions he will appear to many people to have made a vain discovery. They will have been positively struck, on the contrary, with the moral timidity of the usual English novelist; with his (or with her) aversion to face the difficulties with which on every side the treatment of reality bristles. He is apt to be extremely shy (whereas the picture that Mr. Besant draws is a picture of boldness), and the sign of his work, for the most part, is a cautious silence on certain subjects. In the English novel (by which of course I mean the American as well), more than in any other, there is a traditional difference between that which people know and that which they agree to admit that they know, that which they see and that which they speak of, that which they feel to be a part of life and that which they allow to enter into literature. There is the great difference, in short, between what they talk of in conversation and what they talk of in print. The essence of moral energy is to survey the whole field, and I should directly reverse Mr. Besant's remark and say not that the English novel has a purpose, but that it has a diffidence. To what degree a purpose in a work of art is a source of corruption I shall not attempt to inquire; the one that seems to me least dangerous is the purpose of making a perfect work. As for our novel, I may say lastly on this score that as we find it in England to-day it strikes me as addressed in a large degree to "young people," and that this in itself constitutes a presumption that it will be rather shy. There are certain things which it is generally agreed not to discuss, not

---

[26] Pseudonym for Mary Ann Evans (1819–1880), the English author of *Silas Marner* (1861).

even to mention, before young people. That is very well, but the absence of discussion is not a symptom of the moral passion. The purpose of the English novel—"a truly admirable thing, and a great cause for congratulation"—strikes me therefore as rather negative.

There is one point at which the moral sense and the artistic sense lie very near together; that is in the light of the very obvious truth that the deepest quality of a work of art will always be the quality of the mind of the producer. In proportion as that intelligence is fine will the novel, the picture, the statue partake of the substance of beauty and truth. To be constituted of such elements is, to my vision, to have purpose enough. No good novel will ever proceed from a superficial mind; that seems to me an axiom which, for the artist in fiction, will cover all needful moral ground: if the youthful aspirant take it to heart it will illuminate for him many of the mysteries of "purpose." There are many other useful things that might be said to him, but I have come to the end of my article, and can only touch them as I pass. The critic in the *Pall Mall Gazette,* whom I have already quoted, draws attention to the danger, in speaking of the art of fiction, of generalising. The danger that he has in mind is rather, I imagine, that of particularising, for there are some comprehensive remarks which, in addition to those embodied in Mr Besant's suggestive lecture, might without fear of misleading him be addressed to the ingenuous student. I should remind him first of the magnificence of the form that is open to him, which offers to sight so few restrictions and such innumerable opportunities. The other arts, in comparison, appear confined and hampered; the various conditions under which they are exercised are so rigid and definite. But the only condition that I can think of attaching to the composition of the novel is, as I have already said, that it be sincere. This freedom is a splendid privilege, and the first lesson of the young novelist is to learn to be worthy of it. "Enjoy it as it deserves," I should say to him; "take possession of it, explore it to its utmost extent, publish it, rejoice in it. All life belongs to you, and do not listen either to those who would shut you up into corners of it and tell you that it is only here and there that art inhabits, or to those who would persuade you that this heavenly messenger wings her way outside of life altogether, breathing a superfine air, and turning away her head from the truth of things. There is no impression of life, no manner of seeing it and feeling it, to which the plan of the novelist may not offer a place; you have only to remember that talents so dissimilar as those of Alexandre Dumas and Jane Austen,[27] Charles Dickens and Gustave Flaubert have worked in this field with equal glory. Do not think too much about optimism and pessimism; try and catch the colour of life itself. In France to-day we see a prodigious effort (that of Emile Zola, to whose solid and serious work no explorer of the capacity of the novel can allude without respect), we see an extraordinary effort vitiated by a spirit of pessimism on a narrow basis. M. Zola is magnificent, but he strikes an English reader as ignorant; he has an air of working in the dark; if he had as much light as energy, his results would be of the highest value. As for the aberrations of a shallow optimism, the ground (of English fiction especially) is strewn with their brittle particles as with broken glass. If you must indulge in conclusions, let them have the taste of a wide knowledge. Remember that your first duty is to be as complete as possible—to make as perfect a work. Be generous and delicate and pursue the prize."

1884

---

[27] The French novelist and playwright Dumas (1802–1870) wrote *The Count of Monte Cristo* (1844); the English novelist Austen (1775–1817) wrote *Pride and Prejudice* (1813).

=CONTEXTS=

The Birth of the Movies

In 1877 Governor Leland Stanford of California, wishing to win his bet that, at some point in their stride, horses suspend all four hooves at the same time, hired the photographer Eadweard Muybridge (1830–1904) to provide visual proof. With the aid of the chief engineer of the Southern Pacific Railroad, Muybridge set up a system of magnetic releases to trigger a series of cameras. The resulting photographs of horses in motion marked the first time in history that live action was continuously recorded on film.

The significance of Muybridge's work, which led to the invention of the first practical motion picture camera in 1889 (the kinetograph, developed at the Edison laboratories in New Jersey), eluded some of his contemporaries. In a letter to Muybridge, Thomas Edison (1847–1931) expressed doubt about the future of "moving pictures":

> . . . [I have] built a little instrument which I call a kinetograph with a nickel & slot but I am very doubtful if there is any commercial feature in it & fear they will not earn their cost. These Zootropic devices are of too sentimental a character to get the public to invest in.
>
> Thomas Edison, 1894

However, when Edison opened the first Kinetoscope Parlor later that year, it met with huge success. Soon delighted patrons in penny arcades across the nation eagerly peered into the coin-operated machines to view quarter-minute films of Buffalo Bill waving to them from horseback. Motion pictures had been born.

William Dean Howells
(1837–1920)

In the final decade of the nineteenth century William Dean Howells was commonly considered the "dean" of American letters. As the editor of *Harper's* magazine, he spoke with authority on contemporary writers and on the nature of realism in American fiction; as an experienced novelist he commanded the respect of public and critics alike. In the late twentieth century Howells's reputation has declined: along with Mark Twain and Henry James, he is known as a nineteenth-century American realist; yet, unlike Twain and James (with whom Howells shared life-long friendships), he has failed to find a wide audience among readers of American literature. Because he wrote in an age when readers were accustomed to apocalyptic events and highly embroidered fiction, it has been easy to overlook Howells's insistence on portraying ordinary people involved with the problems of everyday life. Deliberately, in accordance with his theories of realism in American fiction, Howells's novels are not flashy, and yet their truthfulness and skillful style provide insights into human character that many writers never develop.

Born in Martin's Ferry, Ohio, in 1837, Howells worked with words from an early age when he began setting type for his father's newspaper. He read widely and taught himself a reading knowledge of several languages. In the process, he developed his own literary ambitions, as he reveals in such works as *My Literary Passions* (1895) and *Literary Friends and Acquaintance* (1900). As a young man he moved from jobs as typesetter and reporter to news editor and editorial writer on the Cincinnati *Gazette* and the *Ohio State Journal* in Columbus. His break into wider social circles occurred after his campaign biography of Abraham Lincoln in 1860, when Howells was appointed consul to Venice. When he returned from Italy in 1865, he became assistant editor of the *Atlantic Monthly,* then editor in chief in 1871. During his ten years as editor of this prestigious magazine and his later years at *Harper's,* Howells acquired great authority in the world of letters. Able to aid or thwart careers, he took his responsibility seriously, championing writers who showed promise, tactfully criticizing without meanness, and maintaining a standard of professionalism previously unknown in periodicals.

Howells's integrity pervades his many novels as well as his critical writings. Characteristically, his fiction portrays the daily lives of contemporary people in ways that reveal universal human emotions. Out of a belief that melodramatic excess distorts the representation of life, he wrote such arresting studies of moral behavior as *A Modern Instance* (1882), *The Rise of Silas Lapham* (1885), and *The Landlord at Lion's Head* (1897), all of which show the vulnerability that underlies human postures of strength and ambition. Howells believed that a novelist should focus on character, then attend to the incidents that grow out of character.

Critical response to Howells has varied from adulation during his life to dismissal by such writers as H. L. Mencken and Sinclair Lewis, both of whom saw Howells as prudish and old-fashioned. Mencken deplored Howells's literary descent from Jane Austen and Washington Irving and preferred the raucous vigor of François Rabelais and Geoffrey Chaucer. Howells is worth reading, however, precisely because he is not raucous, because his work exhibits a profound awareness of pretension and human frailty. In his biography of Howells, Edwin H. Cady refers to the "quiet heartbreak" implicit in many of Howells's novels. It is the signature of a writer who found the truths of human character in the lives we ordinarily lead.

Suggested Readings: *A Modern Instance,* 1882. *The Rise of Silas Lapham,* 1885. *A Hazard of New Fortunes,* 1890. *Literature and Life: Studies,* 1902. *My Mark Twain,* 1910. *Literary Friends and Acquaintance,* ed. D. F. Hiatt and E. H. Cady, 1968. *A Selected Edition of W. D. Howells,* 1968– . J. L. Woodress, *Howells and Italy,* 1952. E. H. Cady, *The Road to Realism: The Early Years, 1837–1885,* 1956. E. H. Cady, *The Realist at War: The Mature Years, 1885–1920,* 1958. E. H. Cady and D. L. Frazier. eds., *The War of the Critics Over William Dean Howells,* 1962. K. Vanderbilt, *The Achievement of William Dean Howells,* 1968. K. S. Lynn, *William Dean Howells,* 1971. G. N. Bennett, *The Realism of William Dean Howells,* 1973. K. Eble, *William Dean Howells,* 1982. J. W. Crowley, *The Black Heart's Truth: The Early Career of W. D. Howells,* 1985. E. Nettels, *Language, Race, and Social Class in Howells's America,* 1988. J. W. Crowley, ed., *The Mask of Fiction: Essays on W. D. Howells,* 1989.

Text Used: *Between the Dark and the Daylight: Romances,* 1907.

EDITHA*

The air was thick with the war[1] feeling, like the electricity of a storm which has not yet burst. Editha sat looking out into the hot spring afternoon, with her lips

---

* First published in *Harper's Monthly* in 1905; appeared in book form in *Between the Dark and the Daylight: Romances* (1907).

[1] Just before the Spanish-American War in 1898.

parted, and panting with the intensity of the question whether she could let him go. She had decided that she could not let him stay, when she saw him at the end of the still leafless avenue, making slowly up towards the house, with his head down and his figure relaxed. She ran impatiently out on the veranda, to the edge of the steps, and imperatively demanded greater haste of him with her will before she called aloud to him: "George!"

He had quickened his pace in mystical response to her mystical urgence, before he could have heard her; now he looked up and answered. "Well?"

"Oh, how united we are!" she exulted, and then she swooped down the steps to him. "What is it?" she cried.

"It's war," he said, and he pulled her up to him and kissed her.

She kissed him back intensely, but irrelevantly, as to their passion, and uttered from deep in her throat, "How glorious!"

"It's war," he repeated, without consenting to her sense of it; and she did not know just what to think at first. She never knew what to think of him; that made his mystery, his charm. All through their courtship, which was contemporaneous with the growth of the war feeling, she had been puzzled by his want of seriousness about it. He seemed to despise it even more than he abhorred it. She could have understood his abhorring any sort of bloodshed; that would have been a survival of his old life when he thought he would be a minister, and before he changed and took up the law. But making light of a cause so high and noble seemed to show a want of earnestness at the core of his being. Not but that she felt herself able to cope with a congenital defect of that sort, and make his love for her save him from himself. Now perhaps the miracle was already wrought in him. In the presence of the tremendous fact that he announced, all triviality seemed to have gone out of him; she began to feel that. He sank down on the top step, and wiped his forehead with his handkerchief, while she poured out upon him her question of the origin and authenticity of his news.

All the while, in her duplex emotioning, she was aware that now at the very beginning she must put a guard upon herself against urging him, by any word or act, to take the part that her whole soul willed him to take, for the completion of her ideal of him. He was very nearly perfect as he was, and he must be allowed to perfect himself. But he was peculiar, and he might very well be reasoned out of his peculiarity. Before her reasoning went her emotioning: her nature pulling upon his nature, her womanhood upon his manhood, without her knowing the means she was using to the end she was willing. She had always supposed that the man who won her would have done something to win her; she did not know what, but something. George Gearson had simply asked her for her love, on the way home from a concert, and she gave her love to him, without, as it were, thinking. But now, it flashed upon her, if he could do something worthy to *have* won her—be a hero, *her* hero—it would be even better than if he had done it before asking her; it would be grander. Besides, she had believed in the war from the beginning.

"But don't you see, dearest," she said, "that it wouldn't have come to this if it hadn't been in the order of Providence? And I call any war glorious that is for the liberation of people who have been struggling for years against the cruelest oppression. Don't you think so, too?"

"I suppose so," he returned, languidly. "But war! Is it glorious to break the peace of the world?"

"That ignoble peace! It was no peace at all, with that crime and shame at our very gates." She was conscious of parroting the current phrases of the newspapers, but it was no time to pick and choose her words. She must sacrifice anything to the high ideal she had for him, and after a good deal of rapid argument she ended with the climax: "But now it doesn't matter about the how or why. Since the war has come, all that is gone. There are no two sides any more. There is nothing now but our country."

He sat with his eyes closed and his head leant back against the veranda, and he remarked, with a vague smile, as if musing aloud, "Our country—right or wrong."[2]

"Yes, right or wrong!" she returned, fervidly. "I'll go and get you some lemonade." She rose rustling, and whisked away; when she came back with two tall glasses of clouded liquid on a tray, and the ice clunking in them, he still sat as she had left him, and she said, as if there had been no interruption: "But there is no question of wrong in this case. I call it a sacred war. A war for liberty and humanity, if ever there was one. And I know you will see it just as I do, yet."

He took half the lemonade at a gulp, and he answered as he set the glass down: "I know you always have the highest ideal. When I differ from you I ought to doubt myself."

A generous sob rose in Editha's throat for the humility of a man, so very nearly perfect, who was willing to put himself below her.

Besides, she felt, more subliminally, that he was never so near slipping through her fingers as when he took that meek way.

"You shall not say that! Only, for once I happen to be right." She seized his hand in her two hands, and poured her soul from her eyes into his. "Don't you think so?" she entreated him.

He released his hand and drank the rest of his lemonade, and she added, "Have mine, too," but he shook his head in answering, "I've no business to think so, unless I act so, too."

Her heart stopped a beat before it pulsed on with leaps that she felt in her neck. She had noticed that strange thing in men: they seemed to feel bound to do what they believed, and not think a thing was finished when they said it, as girls did. She knew what was in his mind, but she pretended not, and she said, "Oh, I am not sure," and then faltered.

He went on as if to himself, without apparently heeding her: "There's only one way of proving one's faith in a thing like this."

She could not say that she understood, but she did understand.

He went on again. "If I believed—if I felt as you do about this war—Do you wish me to feel as you do?"

Now she was really not sure; so she said: "George, I don't know what you mean?"

He seemed to muse away from her as before. "There is a sort of fascination in it. I suppose that at the bottom of his heart every man would like at times to have his courage tested, to see how he would act."

"How can you talk in that ghastly way?"

"It *is* rather morbid. Still, that's what it comes to, unless you're swept away by ambition or driven by conviction. I haven't the conviction or the ambition, and the other thing is what it comes to with me. I ought to have been a preacher, after all; then I couldn't have asked it of myself, as I must now I'm a lawyer. And you believe it's a holy war, Editha?" he suddenly addressed her. "Oh, I know you do! But you wish me to believe so, too?"

---

[2] A phrase coined in 1816 by the American naval hero Stephen Decatur (1779–1820); the modern equivalent is "America: love it or leave it."

She hardly knew whether he was mocking or not, in the ironical way he always had with her plainer mind. But the only thing was to be outspoken with him.

"George, I wish you to believe whatever you think is true, at any and every cost. If I've tried to talk you into anything, I take it all back."

"Oh, I know that, Editha. I know how sincere you are, and how—I wish I had your undoubting spirit! I'll think it over; I'd like to believe as you do. But I don't, now; I don't, indeed. It isn't this war alone; though this seems peculiarly wanton and needless; but it's every war—so stupid; it makes me sick. Why shouldn't this thing have been settled reasonably?"

"Because," she said, very throatily again, "God meant it to be war."

"You think it was God? Yes, I suppose that is what people will say."

"Do you suppose it would have been war if God hadn't meant it?"

"I don't know. Sometimes it seems as if God had put this world into men's keeping to work it as they pleased."

"Now, George, that is blasphemy."

"Well, I won't blaspheme. I'll try to believe in your pocket Providence," he said, and then he rose to go.

"Why don't you stay to dinner?" Dinner at Balcom's Works was at one o'clock.

"I'll come back to supper, if you'll let me. Perhaps I shall bring you a convert."

"Well, you may come back, on that condition."

"All right. If I don't come, you'll understand."

He went away without kissing her, and she felt it a suspension of their engagement. It all interested her intensely; she was undergoing a tremendous experience, and she was being equal to it. While she stood looking after him, her mother came out through one of the long windows onto the veranda, with a catlike softness and vagueness.

"Why didn't he stay to dinner?"

"Because—because—war has been declared," Editha pronounced, without turning.

Her mother said, "Oh, my!" and then said nothing more until she had sat down in one of the large Shaker chairs[3] and rocked herself for some time. Then she closed whatever tacit passage of thought there had been in her mind with the spoken words: "Well, I hope *he* won't go."

"And *I* hope he *will*," the girl said, and confronted her mother with a stormy exaltation that would have frightened any creature less unimpressionable than a cat.

Her mother rocked herself again for an interval of cogitation. What she arrived at in speech was: "Well, I guess you've done a wicked thing, Editha Balcom."

The girl said, as she passed indoors through the same window her mother had come out by: "I haven't done anything—yet."

In her room, she put together all her letters and gifts from Gearson, down to the withered petals of the first flower he had offered, with that timidity of his veiled in that irony of his. In the heart of the packet she enshrined her engagement ring which she had restored to the pretty box he had brought it her in. Then she sat down, if not calmly yet strongly, and wrote:

---

[3] Furniture made by the Shaker religious community, noted for its simplicity and lack of ornamentation.

"GEORGE:—I understood when you left me. But I think we had better emphasize your meaning that if we cannot be one in everything we had better be one in nothing. So I am sending these things for your keeping till you have made up your mind.

"I shall always love you, and therefore I shall never marry any one else. But the man I marry must love his country first of all, and be able to say to me,

" 'I could not love thee, dear, so much,
Loved I not honor more.'[4]

"There is no honor above America with me. In this great hour there is no other honor.

"Your heart will make my words clear to you. I had never expected to say so much, but it has come upon me that I must say the utmost.

EDITHA."

She thought she had worded her letter well, worded it in a way that could not be bettered; all had been implied and nothing expressed.

She had it ready to send with the packet she had tied with red, white, and blue ribbon, when it occurred to her that she was not just to him, that she was not giving him a fair chance. He had said he would go and think it over, and she was not waiting. She was pushing, threatening, compelling. That was not a woman's part. She must leave him free, free, free. She could not accept for her country or herself a forced sacrifice.

In writing her letter she had satisfied the impulse from which it sprang; she could well afford to wait till he had thought it over. She put the packet and the letter by, and rested serene in the consciousness of having done what was laid upon her by her love itself to do, and yet used patience, mercy, justice.

She had her reward. Gearson did not come to tea, but she had given him till morning, when, late at night there came up from the village the sound of a fife and drum, with a tumult of voices, in shouting, singing, and laughing. The noise drew nearer and nearer; it reached the street end of the avenue; there it silenced itself, and one voice, the voice she knew best, rose over the silence. It fell; the air was filled with cheers; the fife and drum struck up, with the shouting, singing, and laughing again, but now retreating; and a single figure came hurrying up the avenue.

She ran down to meet her lover and clung to him. He was very gay, and he put his arm round her with a boisterous laugh. "Well, you must call me Captain now; or Cap, if you prefer; that's what the boys call me. Yes, we've had a meeting at the town-hall, and everybody has volunteered; and they selected me for captain, and I'm going to the war, the big war, the glorious war, the holy war ordained by the pocket Providence that blesses butchery. Come along; let's tell the whole family about it. Call them from their downy beds, father, mother, Aunt Hitty, and all the folks!"

But when they mounted the veranda steps he did not wait for a larger audience; he poured the story out upon Editha alone.

"There was a lot of speaking, and then some of the fools set up a shout for me. It was all going one way, and I thought it would be a good joke to sprinkle a little cold water on them. But you can't do that with a crowd that adores you. The first

[4] From "To Lucasta, Going to the Wars," by the English poet Richard Lovelace (1618–1658).

thing I knew I was sprinkling hell-fire on them. 'Cry havoc, and let slip the dogs of war.'[5] That was the style. Now that it had come to the fight, there were no two parties; there was one country, and the thing was to fight to a finish as quick as possible. I suggested volunteering then and there, and I wrote my name first of all on the roster. Then they elected me—that's all. I wish I had some ice-water."

She left him walking up and down the veranda, while she ran for the ice-pitcher and a goblet, and when she came back he was still walking up and down, shouting the story he had told her to her father and mother, who had come out more sketchily dressed than they commonly were by day. He drank goblet after goblet of the ice-water without noticing who was giving it, and kept on talking, and laughing through his talk wildly. "It's astonishing," he said, "how well the worse reason looks when you try to make it appear the better. Why, I believe I was the first convert to the war in that crowd to-night! I never thought I should like to kill a man; but now I shouldn't care; and the smokeless powder lets you see the man drop that you kill. It's all for the country! What a thing it is to have a country that *can't* be wrong, but if it is, is right, anyway!"

Editha had a great, vital thought, an inspiration. She set down the ice-pitcher on the veranda floor, and ran up-stairs and got the letter she had written him. When at last he noisily bade her father and mother, "Well, good-night. I forgot I woke you up; I sha'n't want any sleep myself," she followed him down the avenue to the gate. There, after the whirling words that seemed to fly away from her thoughts and refuse to serve them, she made a last effort to solemnize the moment that seemed so crazy, and pressed the letter she had written upon him.

"What's this?" he said. "Want me to mail it?"

"No, no. It's for you. I wrote it after you went this morning. Keep it—keep it—and read it sometime—" She thought, and then her inspiration came: "Read it if ever you doubt what you've done, or fear that I regret your having done it. Read it after you've started."

They strained each other in embraces that seemed as ineffective as their words, and he kissed her face with quick, hot breaths that were so unlike him, that made her feel as if she had lost her old lover and found a stranger in his place. The stranger said: "What a gorgeous flower you are, with your red hair, and your blue eyes that look black now, and your face with the color painted out by the white moonshine! Let me hold you under the chin, to see whether I love blood, you tiger-lily!" Then he laughed Gearson's laugh, and released her, scared and giddy. Within her wilfulness she had been frightened by a sense of subtler force in him, and mystically mastered as she had never been before.

She ran all the way back to the house, and mounted the steps panting. Her mother and father were talking of the great affair. Her mother said: "Wa'n't Mr. Gearson in rather of an excited state of mind? Didn't you think he acted curious?"

"Well, not for a man who'd just been elected captain and had set 'em up for the whole of Company A," her father chuckled back.

"What in the world do you mean, Mr. Balcom? Oh! There's Editha!" She offered to follow the girl indoors.

"Don't come, mother!" Editha called, vanishing.

Mrs. Balcom remained to reproach her husband. "I don't see much of anything to laugh at."

"Well, it's catching. Caught it from Gearson. I guess it won't be much of a

---

[5] From Shakespeare's *Julius Caesar* (III.i.273).

war, and I guess Gearson don't think so, either. The other fellows will back down as soon as they see we mean it. I wouldn't lose any sleep over it. I'm going back to bed, myself."

Gearson came again next afternoon, looking pale and rather sick, but quite himself, even to his languid irony. "I guess I'd better tell you, Editha, that I consecrated myself to your god of battles last night by pouring too many libations to him down my own throat. But I'm all right now. One has to carry off the excitement, somehow."

"Promise me," she commanded, "that you'll never touch it again!"

"What! Not let the cannikin[6] clink? Not let the soldier drink? Well, I promise."

"You don't belong to yourself now; you don't even belong to *me*. You belong to your country, and you have a sacred charge to keep yourself strong and well for your country's sake. I have been thinking, thinking all night and all day long."

"You look as if you had been crying a little, too," he said, with his queer smile.

"That's all past. I've been thinking, and worshipping *you*. Don't you suppose I know all that you've been through, to come to this? I've followed you every step from your old theories and opinions."

"Well, you've had a long row to hoe."

"And I know you've done this from the highest motives—"

"Oh, there won't be much pettifogging[7] to do till this cruel war is—"

"And you haven't simply done it for my sake. I couldn't respect you if you had."

"Well, then we'll say I haven't. A man that hasn't got his own respect intact wants the respect of all the other people he can corner. But we won't go into that. I'm in for the thing now, and we've got to face our future. My idea is that this isn't going to be a very protracted struggle; we shall just scare the enemy to death before it comes to a fight at all. But we must provide for contingencies, Editha. If anything happens to me—"

"Oh, George!" She clung to him, sobbing.

"I don't want you to feel foolishly bound to my memory. I should hate that, wherever I happened to be."

"I am yours, for time and eternity—time and eternity." She liked the words; they satisfied her famine for phrases.

"Well, say eternity; that's all right; but time's another thing; and I'm talking about time. But there is something! My mother! If anything happens—"

She winced, and he laughed. "You're not the bold soldier-girl of yesterday!" Then he sobered. "If anything happens, I want you to help my mother out. She won't like my doing this thing. She brought me up to think war a fool thing as well as a bad thing. My father was in the Civil War; all through it; lost his arm in it." She thrilled with the sense of the arm round her; what if that should be lost? He laughed as if divining her: "Oh, it doesn't run in the family, as far as I know!" Then he added, gravely: "He came home with misgivings about war, and they grew on him. I guess he and mother agreed between them that I was to be brought up in his final mind about it; but that was before my time. I only knew him from

[6] Cup; an allusion to Shakespeare's *Othello* (II.iii.71–75).
[7] Being unduly concerned with trivial matters.

my mother's report of him and his opinions; I don't know whether they were hers first; but they were hers last. This will be a blow to her. I shall have to write and tell her—"

He stopped, and she asked: "Would you like me to write, too, George?"

"I don't believe that would do. No, I'll do the writing. She'll understand a little if I say that I thought the way to minimize it was to make war on the largest possible scale at once—that I felt I must have been helping on the war somehow if I hadn't helped keep it from coming, and I knew I hadn't; when it came, I had no right to stay out of it."

Whether his sophistries[8] satisfied him or not, they satisfied her. She clung to his breast, and whispered, with closed eyes and quivering lips: "Yes, yes, yes!"

"But if anything should happen, you might go to her and see what you could do for her. You know? It's rather far off; she can't leave her chair—"

"Oh, I'll go, if it's the ends of the earth! But nothing will happen! Nothing *can!* I—"

She felt herself lifted with his rising, and Gearson was saying, with his arm still round her, to her father: "Well, we're off at once, Mr. Balcom. We're to be formally accepted at the capital, and then bunched up with the rest somehow, and sent into camp somewhere, and got to the front as soon as possible. We all want to be in the van,[9] of course; we're the first company to report to the Governor. I came to tell Editha, but I hadn't got round to it."

She saw him again for a moment at the capital, in the station, just before the train started southward with his regiment. He looked well, in his uniform, and very soldierly, but somehow girlish, too, with his clean-shaven face and slim figure. The manly eyes and the strong voice satisfied her, and his preoccupation with some unexpected details of duty flattered her. Other girls were weeping and bemoaning themselves, but she felt a sort of noble distinction in the abstraction, the almost unconsciousness, with which they parted. Only at the last moment he said: "Don't forget my mother. It mayn't be such a walk-over as I supposed," and he laughed at the notion.

He waved his hand to her as the train moved off—she knew it among a score of hands that were waved to other girls from the platform of the car, for it held a letter which she knew was hers. Then he went inside the car to read it, doubtless, and she did not see him again. But she felt safe for him through the strength of what she called her love. What she called her God, always speaking the name in a deep voice and with the implication of a mutual understanding, would watch over him and keep him and bring him back to her. If with an empty sleeve, then he should have three arms instead of two, for both of hers should be his for life. She did not see, though, why she should always be thinking of the arm his father had lost.

There were not many letters from him, but they were such as she could have wished, and she put her whole strength into making hers such as she imagined he could have wished, glorifying and supporting him. She wrote to his mother glorifying him as their hero, but the brief answer she got was merely to the effect that

---

[8] Reasonings that are subtly false, used here by George to cover up his misgivings about volunteering.

[9] Vanguard, the first division to go into battle.

Mrs. Gearson was not well enough to write herself, and thanking her for her letter by the hand of some one who called herself "Yrs truly, Mrs. W. J. Andrews."

Editha determined not to be hurt, but to write again quite as if the answer had been all she expected. Before it seemed as if she could have written, there came news of the first skirmish, and in the list of the killed, which was telegraphed as a trifling loss on our side, was Gearson's name. There was a frantic time of trying to make out that it might be, must be, some other Gearson; but the name and the company and the regiment and the State were too definitely given.

Then there was a lapse into depths out of which it seemed as if she never could rise again; then a lift into clouds far above all grief, black clouds, that blotted out the sun, but where she soared with him, with George—George! She had the fever that she expected of herself, but she did not die in it; she was not even delirious, and it did not last long. When she was well enough to leave her bed, her one thought was of George's mother, of his strangely worded wish that she should go to her and see what she could do for her. In the exaltation of the duty laid upon her—it buoyed her up instead of burdening her—she rapidly recovered.

Her father went with her on the long railroad journey from northern New York to western Iowa; he had business out at Davenport, and he said he could just as well go then as any other time; and he went with her to the little country town where George's mother lived in a little house on the edge of the illimitable corn-fields, under trees pushed to a top of the rolling prairie. George's father had settled there after the Civil War, as so many other old soldiers had done; but they were Eastern people, and Editha fancied touches of the East in the June rose over-hanging the front door, and the garden with early summer flowers stretching from the gate of the paling fence.

It was very low inside the house, and so dim, with the closed blinds, that they could scarcely see one another: Editha tall and black in her crapes[10] which filled the air with the smell of their dyes; her father standing decorously apart with his hat on his forearm, as at funerals; a woman rested in a deep arm-chair, and the woman who had let the strangers in stood behind the chair.

The seated woman turned her head round and up, and asked the woman behind the chair: "*Who* did you say?"

Editha, if she had done what she expected of herself, would have gone down on her knees at the feet of the seated figure and said, "I am George's Editha," for answer.

But instead of her own voice she heard that other woman's voice, saying: "Well, I don't know as I *did* get the name just right. I guess I'll have to make a little more light in here," and she went and pushed two of the shutters ajar.

Then Editha's father said, in his public will-now-address-a-few-remarks tone: "My name is Balcom, ma'am—Junius H. Balcom, of Balcom's Works, New York; my daughter—"

"Oh!" the seated woman broke in, with a powerful voice, the voice that always surprised Editha from Gearson's slender frame. "Let me see you. Stand round where the light can strike on your face," and Editha dumbly obeyed. "So, you're Editha Balcom," she sighed.

---

[10] Thin, crinkled fabrics; Victorian women wore black clothing to signify their mourning over a death. Because they could not buy ready-to-wear clothes, they had to dye the clothes they already had.

"Yes," Editha said, more like a culprit than a comforter.

"What did you come for?" Mrs. Gearson asked.

Editha's face quivered and her knees shook. "I came—because—because George—" She could go no further.

"Yes," the mother said, "he told me he had asked you to come if he got killed. You didn't expect that, I suppose, when you sent him."

"I would rather have died myself than done it!" Editha said, with more truth in her deep voice than she ordinarily found in it. "I tried to leave him free—"

"Yes, that letter of yours, that came back with his other things, left him free."

Editha saw now where George's irony came from.

"It was not to be read before—unless—until— I told him so," she faltered.

"Of course, he wouldn't read a letter of yours, under the circumstances, till he thought you wanted him to. Been sick?" the woman abruptly demanded.

"Very sick," Editha said, with self-pity.

"Daughter's life," her father interposed, "was almost despaired of, at one time."

Mrs. Gearson gave him no heed. "I suppose you would have been glad to die, such a brave person as you! I don't believe *he* was glad to die. He was always a timid boy, that way; he was afraid of a good many things; but if he was afraid he did what he made up his mind to. I suppose he made up his mind to go, but I knew what it cost him by what it cost me when I heard of it. I had been through *one* war before. When you sent him you didn't expect he would get killed."

The voice seemed to compassionate Editha, and it was time. "No," she huskily murmured.

"No, girls don't; women don't, when they give their men up to their country. They think they'll come marching back, somehow, just as gay as they went, or if it's an empty sleeve, or even an empty pantaloon, it's all the more glory, and they're so much the prouder of them, poor things!"

The tears began to run down Editha's face; she had not wept till then; but it was now such a relief to be understood that the tears came.

"No, you didn't expect him to get killed," Mrs. Gearson repeated, in a voice which was startlingly like George's again. "You just expected him to kill some one else, some of those foreigners, that weren't there because they had any say about it, but because they had to be there, poor wretches—conscripts, or whatever they call 'em. You thought it would be all right for my George, *your* George, to kill the sons of those miserable mothers and the husbands of those girls that you would never see the faces of." The woman lifted her powerful voice in a psalmlike note. "I thank my God he didn't live to do it! I thank my God they killed him first, and that he ain't livin' with their blood on his hands!" She dropped her eyes, which she had raised with her voice, and glared at Editha. "What you got that black on for?" She lifted herself by her powerful arms so high that her helpless body seemed to hang limp its full length. "Take it off, take it off, before I tear it from your back!"

The lady who was passing the summer near Balcom's Works was sketching Editha's beauty, which lent itself wonderfully to the effects of a colorist. It had come to that confidence which is rather apt to grow between artist and sitter, and Editha had told her everything.

"To think of your having such a tragedy in your life!" the lady said. She added: "I suppose there are people who feel that way about war. But when you consider

the good this war has done—how much it has done for the country! I can't understand such people, for my part. And when you had come all the way out there to
console her—got up out of a sick-bed! Well!"

"I think," Editha said, magnanimously, "she wasn't quite in her right mind; and
so did papa."

"Yes," the lady said, looking at Editha's lips in nature and then at her lips in
art, and giving an empirical touch to them in the picture. "But how dreadful of
her! How perfectly—excuse me—how *vulgar!*"

A light broke upon Editha in the darkness which she felt had been without a
gleam of brightness for weeks and months. The mystery that had bewildered her
was solved by the word; and from that moment she rose from grovelling in shame
and self-pity, and began to live again in the ideal.

1905

Stephen Crane
(1871–1900)

When he published *Maggie: A Girl of the Streets* under the pseudonym Johnston Smith in
1893, Stephen Crane was twenty-one years old. Contemporaries could not have known
that this young writer had less than a decade to live, nor would they have guessed that
during his brief career he would complete several novels and novellas, numerous short
stories and sketches, and two volumes of poetry. In the 1890s, however, Crane's importance as a writer came to be recognized by such colleagues as Joseph Conrad, Hamlin
Garland, William Dean Howells, and Henry James.

Crane, the fourteenth child of Methodist minister Jonathan Townley Crane and social
activist Mary Helen Peck, was born in 1871 in Newark, New Jersey. The family moved
several times and settled in Port Jervis, New York, when Crane was seven. While his
father was pastor of Drew Methodist Church at Port Jervis, young Stephen led a vigorous,
out-of-doors life, spending hours on foot and on horseback in nearby Sullivan County. He
eventually turned his experiences among the forests and hills of this area into his discerning sketches of Sullivan County and its inhabitants. In 1888 Crane attended a military
academy, Claverack College in New York, and became a cadet captain before leaving
school in 1890. That same year he enrolled as an engineering student in Lafayette College
in Pennsylvania for one term, then—restless and ever more intent on becoming a writer—
transferred to Syracuse University, where he worked as a correspondent for the New York
Tribune, wrote some of his early stories, and earned a varsity letter playing baseball.

In 1891 Crane moved to New York City and began to work as a freelance writer for the
Tribune. Living in New York gave him the opportunity to observe life in the slums, and
Crane was quick to turn these observations into frank depictions, fictional and nonfictional, of the brutal and typically short lives of slum dwellers. With its stark, ironic portrayal of life and death among residents of New York City's Bowery, *Maggie* stands as
one of the earliest works of American naturalism. Crane later published other works dealing with New York tenement life, among them the novel *George's Mother* (1896) and

stories that deal unflinchingly with sex, violence, and the bleak cycle of poverty. But Crane did not believe that vice was confined to the back lots and dirty apartments of Rum Alley and Devil's Row. In *The Monster* (1899) he explores an even more insidious form of human cruelty as the people of a small town ostracize a disfigured African-American servant and his protector, whose child the servant had rescued from a fire.

If Crane's career as a novelist began with *Maggie*, it reached its apex with *The Red Badge of Courage* (1895), the ironic and measured account of a young man's responses to battle in the Civil War. His career now firmly established with this narrative of a war he had never seen, Crane worked as a war correspondent first in Greece and then in Cuba during the Spanish-American War. During this time he lived a life as dangerous as those lived by many of his characters. Running guns to Cuba in winter 1896–1897, Crane and three other men underwent the ordeal related in "The Open Boat" (1897) and "Stephen Crane's Own Story" (1897). In writing about war experiences Crane was unsparing in his depiction of the mechanized horror of death by shelling and rifle volley.

Crane occasionally tempered his stark vision of life in the slums or on the battlefield with lighter, humorous pieces such as some of the Sullivan County sketches or "The Bride Comes to Yellow Sky" (1898). He had an eye for unusual settings or characters, from the embarrassed marshall in "Yellow Sky" to the edgy, snowbound guests of "The Blue Hotel" (1898), who elicit the tragic fate they fear. During the last years of his life he traveled extensively to Mexico, the West, Ireland, and England, always alert for material with the potential for his distinctive treatment. In England he met the novelist Joseph Conrad, who became Crane's close friend. Crane's physical constitution could not ultimately

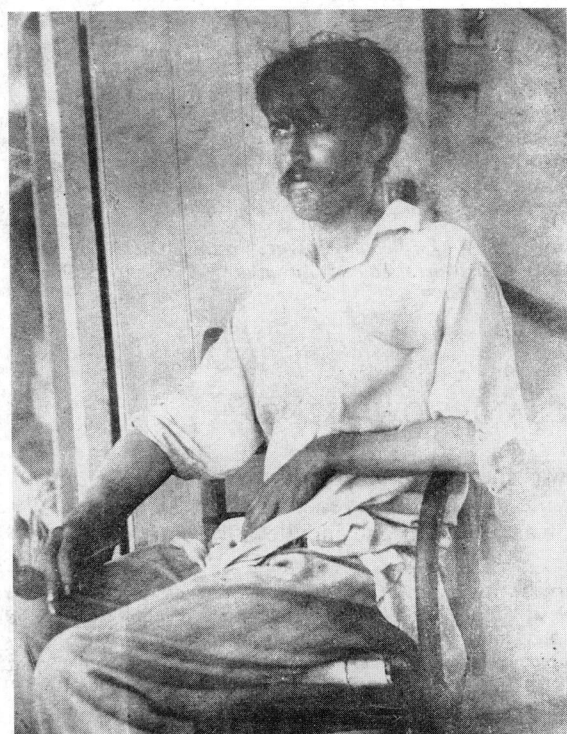

Stephen Crane after the sinking of the Commodore, *the basis for "The Open Boat" : the frontispiece in Crane's* Tales of Adventure.

match the energy he spent in maintaining his prodigious literary output. In 1898, while covering the Puerto Rico campaign of the Spanish-American War for the New York *Journal,* Crane fell ill with fever and returned to recuperate in America. He was suffering, however, from a more serious illness, tuberculosis. Stricken with the disease, he continued to write, completing several books during the last year and a half of his life. Knowing that he might not live to finish his novel *The O'Ruddy* (1903), Crane arranged for Robert Barr, an editor and novelist, to complete it according to Crane's notes. Crane died of tuberculosis in a sanitarium at Badenweiler, Germany, in 1900, half a year into the new century whose dark events seemed prophesied by the tone of his fiction.

Although both of his parents were active in church affairs and social reforms, Crane did not share their unbending faith in a universe ordered by God's Providence, as the recurrent themes of his work demonstrate. His characters suffer and die generally without a sense of purpose or even the knowledge of the correspondent in "The Open Boat," who comes to recognize that nature is "indifferent, flatly indifferent," to the struggles of human beings. Much of Crane's poetry addresses similar concerns in caustic parables that appeal for ultimate meaning but end in mockery and existential confusion. Some poems, too (chief among them "Do not weep maiden, for war is kind" [1896]), enact the pervasive irony of Crane's work with a distilled bitterness. Whether writing of the chance events that determine the fate of men in an open boat or that lead to cowardice and heroism on the battlefield, Crane left a unique naturalist legacy of style and substance to twentieth-century readers. If Frank Norris directs our attention to threatening primitive instincts within "civilized" human beings, if Theodore Dreiser focuses on individuals with (as he says) their "tremendous urges" and "pathetic equipment," Crane treats us to the spectacle of the universe as cosmic joke—grim, freighted with irony, unintelligible to its victims.

Suggested Readings: *Stephen Crane: Letters,* ed. R. W. Stallman and L. Gilkes, 1960. *The Poems of Stephen Crane: A Critical Edition,* ed. J. Katz, 1966. *The Works of Stephen Crane,* 10 vols., ed. F. Bowers, 1969–1975. J. Berryman, *Stephen Crane,* 1950, rpt. 1980. D. Hoffman, *The Poetry of Stephen Crane,* 1956. E. Solomon, *Stephen Crane: From Parody to Realism,* 1966. D. Gibson, *The Fiction of Stephen Crane,* 1968. R. W. Stallman, *Stephen Crane: A Biography,* 1968. M. Holton, *Cylinder of Vision: The Fiction and Journalistic Writing of Stephen Crane,* 1972. F. Bergon, *Stephen Crane's Artistry,* 1975. E. H. Cady, *Stephen Crane,* 1980. J. Nagel, *Stephen Crane and Literary Impressionism,* 1980. D. Halliburton, *The Color of the Sky: A Study of Stephen Crane,* 1989.

Texts Used: "Stephen Crane's Own Story": *The Works: Reports of War,* Vol. IX, 1971. "The Open Boat" and "The Bride Comes to Yellow Sky": *The Works: Tales of Adventure,* Vol. V, 1970. Poems: *The Works: Poems and Literary Remains,* Vol. X, 1975.

STEPHEN CRANE'S OWN STORY*

JACKSONVILLE, FLA., Jan. 6.—It was the afternoon of New Year's. The *Commodore* lay at her dock in Jacksonville and negro stevedores[1] processioned steadily toward her with box after box of ammunition and bundle after bundle of rifles.

---

* Crane sailed from Jacksonville, Florida, on the steamer *Commodore* on New Year's Day of 1897 to cover the Cuban Revolution for the New York *Press;* the ship, which carried munitions for the revolutionaries, sank the next morning, and Crane and three other men survived in a ten-foot dinghy that reached Daytona Beach the following day. On January 6 Crane published this newspaper story of the perilous adventure; six months later he published a fictional companion-piece, "The Open Boat."
[1] Workers who load and unload ships in port.

Her hatch, like the mouth of a monster, engulfed them. It might have been the feeding time of some legendary creature of the sea. It was in broad daylight and the crowd of gleeful Cubans on the pier did not forbear to sing the strange patriotic ballads of their island.

Everything was perfectly open. The *Commodore* was cleared with a cargo of arms and munitions for Cuba. There was none of that extreme modesty about the proceeding which had marked previous departures of the famous tug. She loaded up as placidly as if she were going to carry oranges to New York, instead of Remingtons[2] to Cuba. Down the river, furthermore, the revenue cutter *Boutwell,* the old isosceles triangle that protects United States interests in the St. Johns,[3] lay at anchor, with no sign of excitement aboard her.

On the decks of the *Commodore* there were exchanges of farewells in two languages. Many of the men who were to sail upon her had many intimates in the old Southern town, and we who had left our friends in the remote North received our first touch of melancholy on witnessing these strenuous and earnest good-bys.

It seems, however, that there was more difficulty at the custom house. The officers of the ship and the Cuban leaders were detained there until a mournful twilight settled upon the St. Johns, and through a heavy fog the lights of Jacksonville blinked dimly.

Then at last the *Commodore* swung clear of the dock, amid a tumult of good-bys. As she turned her bow toward the distant sea the Cubans ashore cheered and cheered. In response the *Commodore* gave three long blasts of her whistle, which even to this time impressed me with their sadness. Somehow they sounded as wails.

Then at last we began to feel like filibusters.[4] I don't suppose that the most stolid brain could contrive to believe that there is not a mere trifle of danger in filibustering, and so as we watched the lights of Jacksonville swing past us and heard the regular thump, thump, thump of the engines we did considerable reflecting.

But I am sure that there was no hifalutin emotions visible upon any of the faces which fronted the speeding shore. In fact, from cook's boy to captain, we were all enveloped in a gentle satisfaction and cheerfulness.

But less than two miles from Jacksonville this atrocious fog caused the pilot to ram the bow of the *Commodore* hard upon the mud, and in this ignominious position we were compelled to stay until daybreak.

It was to all of us more than a physical calamity. We were now no longer filibusters. We were men on a ship stuck in the mud. A certain mental somersault was made once more necessary. But word had been sent to Jacksonville to the captain of the revenue cutter *Boutwell,* and Captain Kilgore turned out promptly and generously fired up his old triangle and came at full speed to our assistance. She dragged us out of the mud and again we headed for the mouth of the river. The revenue cutter pounded along a half mile astern of us, to make sure that we did not take on board at some place along the river men for the Cuban army.

This was the early morning of New Year's Day, and the fine golden Southern sunlight fell full upon the river. It flashed over the ancient *Boutwell* until her white sides gleamed like pearl and her rigging was spun into little threads of gold. Cheers greeted the old *Commodore* from passing ships and from the shore. It was a cheerful, almost merry, beginning to our voyage.

---

[2] Rifles.   [3] A river in northeast Florida.   [4] Military adventurers; here, gun runners.

At Mayport, however, we changed our river pilot for a man who could take her to open sea, and again the *Commodore* was beached. The *Boutwell* was fussing around us in her venerable way, and, upon seeing our predicament, she came again to assist us, but this time with engines reversed the *Commodore* dragged herself away from the grip of the sand and again the *Commodore* headed for the open sea.

The captain of the revenue cutter grew curious. He hailed the *Commodore:* "Are you fellows going to sea to-day?"

Captain Murphy of the *Commodore* called back: "Yes, sir." And then as the whistle of the *Commodore* saluted him Captain Kilgore doffed his cap and said: "Well, gentlemen, I hope you have a pleasant cruise," and this was our last words from shore.

When the *Commodore* came to the enormous rollers that flee over the bar, a certain light-heartedness departed from the throats of the ship's company. The *Commodore* began to turn handsprings, and by the time she had gotten fairly to sea and turned into the eye of the roaring breeze that was blowing from the southeast there was an almost general opinion on board the vessel that a life on the rolling wave was not the finest thing in the world. On deck amidships lay five or six Cubans, limp, forlorn and infinitely depressed. In the bunks below lay more Cubans, also limp, forlorn and infinitely depressed. In the captain's quarters, back of the pilot house, the Cuban leaders were stretched out in postures of complete contentment to this terrestrial realm of their stomachs.

The *Commodore* was heavily laden and in this strong sea she rolled like a rubber ball. She appeared to be a gallant sea boat and bravely flung off the waves that swarmed over her bow. At this time the first mate was at the wheel, and I remember how proud he was of the ship as she dashed the white foaming waters aside and arose to the swells like a duck.

"Ain't she a daisy?" said he. But she certainly did do a remarkable lot of pitching, and presently even some American seamen were made ill by the long wallowing motion of the ship. A squall confronted us dead ahead and in the impressive twilight of this New Year's Day the *Commodore* steamed sturdily toward a darkened part of the horizon. The State of Florida is very large when you look at it from an airship, but it is as narrow as a sheet of paper when you look at it sideways. The coast was merely a faint streak.

As darkness came upon the waters the *Commodore's* wake was a broad, flaming path of blue and silver phosphorescence, and as her stout bow lunged at the great black waves she threw flashing, roaring cascades to either side. And all that was to be heard was the rhythmical and mighty pounding of the engines.

Being an inexperienced filibuster, the writer had undergone considerable mental excitement since the starting of the ship, and consequently he had not yet been to sleep, and so I went to the first mate's bunk to indulge myself in all the physical delights of holding one's self in bed. Every time the ship lurched I expected to be fired through a bulkhead, and it was neither amusing nor instructive to see in the dim light a certain accursed valise aiming itself at the top of my stomach with every lurch of the ship.

The cook was asleep on a bench in the galley. He was of a portly and noble exterior, and by means of a checker board he had himself wedged on this bench in such a manner that the motion of the ship would be unable to dislodge him. He awoke as I entered the galley, and, feeling moved, he delivered himself of some dolorous sentiments. "God," he said, in the course of his observations, "I don't feel right about this ship somehow. It strikes me that something is going to happen to us. I don't know what it is, but the old ship is going to get it in the neck, I think."

"Well, how about the men on board of her?" said I. "Are any of us going to get out, prophet?"

"Yes," said the cook, "sometimes I have these damned feelings come over me, and they are always right, and it seems to me somehow that you and I will both get out and meet again somewhere, down at Coney Island, perhaps, or some place like that."

Finding it impossible to sleep, I went back to the pilot house. An old seaman named Tom Smith, from Charleston, was then at the wheel. In the darkness I could not see Tom's face, except at those times when he leaned forward to scan the compass and the dim light from the box came upon his weather-beaten features.

"Well, Tom," said I, "how do you like filibustering?"

He said: "I think I am about through with it. I've been in a number of these expeditions, and the pay is good, but I think if I ever get back safe this time I will cut it."

I sat down in the corner of the pilot house and went almost to sleep. In the meantime the captain came on duty and he was standing near me when the chief engineer rushed up the stairs and cried hurriedly to the captain that there was something wrong in the engine room. He and the captain departed swiftly. I was drowsing there in my corner when the captain returned, and, going to the door of the little room directly back of the pilot house, cried to the Cuban leader:

"Say, can't you get those fellows to work? I can't talk their language and I can't get them started. Come on and get them going."

The Cuban leader turned to me then and said: "Go help in the fire-room. They are going to bail with buckets."

The engine room, by the way, represented a scene at this time taken from the middle kitchen of hades. In the first place, it was insufferably warm, and the lights burned faintly in a way to cause mystic and grewsome shadows. There was a quantity of soapish sea water swirling and sweeping and swishing among machinery that roared and banged and clattered and steamed, and in the second place, it was a devil of a ways down below.

Here I first came to know a certain young oiler named Billy Higgins. He was sloshing around this inferno filling buckets with water and passing them to a chain of men that extended up to the ship's side. Afterward we got orders to change our point of attack on the water and to operate through a little door on the windward side of the ship that led into the engine room.

During this time there was much talk of pumps out of order and many other statements of a mechanical kind, which I did not altogether comprehend, but understood to mean that there was a general and sudden ruin in the engine room.

There was no particular agitation at this time, and even later there was never a panic on board the *Commodore*. The party of men who worked with Higgins and me at this time were all Cubans, and we were under the direction of the Cuban leaders. Presently we were ordered again to the afterhold, and there was some hesitation about going into the abominable fire-room again, but Higgins dashed down the companionway with a bucket.

The heat and hard work in the fire-room affected me and I was obliged to come on deck again. Going forward I heard as I went talk of lowering the boats. Near the corner of the galley the mate was talking with a man.

"Why don't you send up a rocket?" said this unknown person. And the mate replied: "What the hell do we want to send up a rocket for? The ship is all right."

Returning with a little rubber and cloth overcoat, I saw the first boat about to be lowered. A certain man was the first person in this first boat, and they were handing him in a valise about as large as a hotel. I had not entirely recovered from my astonishment and pleasure in witnessing this noble deed, when I saw another valise go to him. This valise was not perhaps so large as a hotel, but it was a big valise anyhow. Afterward there went to him something which looked to me like an overcoat.

Seeing the chief engineer leaning out of his little window, I remarked to him: "What do you think of that blank, blank, blank?"

"Oh, he's a bird," said the old chief.

It was now that was heard the order to get away the lifeboat, which was stowed on top of the deckhouse. The deckhouse was a mighty slippery place, and with each roll of the ship the men there thought themselves likely to take headers into the deadly black sea. Higgins was on top of the deckhouse, and, with the first mate and two colored stokers, we wrestled with that boat, which I am willing to swear weighed as much as a Broadway cable car. She might have been spiked to the deck. We could have pushed a little brick schoolhouse along a corduroy road as easily as we could have moved this boat. But the first mate got a tackle to her from a leeward davit, and on the deck below the captain corralled enough men to make an impression upon the boat. We were ordered to cease hauling then, and in this lull the cook of the ship came to me and said: "What are you going to do?"

I told him of my plans, and he said: "Well, my God, that's what I am going to do."

Now the whistle of the *Commodore* had been turned loose, and if there ever was a voice of despair and death it was in the voice of this whistle. It had gained a new tone. It was as if its throat was already choked by the water, and this cry on the sea at night, with a wind blowing the spray over the ship, and the waves roaring over the bow, and swirling white along the decks, was to each of us probably a song of man's end.

It was now that the first mate showed a sign of losing his grip. To us who were trying in all stages of competence and experience to launch the lifeboat he raged in all terms of fiery satire and hammer-like abuse. But the boat moved at last and swung down toward the water.

Afterward when I went aft I saw the captain standing with his arm in a sling, holding on to a stay with his one good hand and directing the launching of the boat. He gave me a five-gallon jug of water to hold, and asked me what I was going to do. I told him what I thought was about the proper thing, and he told me that the cook had the same idea, and ordered me to go forward and be ready to launch the ten-foot dingy. I remember very well that he turned then to swear at a colored stoker who was prowling around, done up in life preservers until he looked like a feather bed.

I went forward with my five-gallon jug of water, and when the captain came we launched the dingy, and they put me over the side to fend her off from the ship with an oar.

They handed me down the water jug, and then the cook came into the boat, and we sat there in the darkness, wondering why, by all our hopes of future happiness, the captain was so long in coming over the side and ordering us away from the doomed ship.

The captain was waiting for the other boat to go. Finally he hailed in the darkness: "Are you all right, Mr. Graines?"

The first mate answered: "All right, sir."

"Shove off then," cried the captain. The captain was just about to swing over the rail when a dark form came forward and a voice said: "Captain, I go with you."

The captain answered: "Yes, Billy; get in."

It was Billy Higgins, the oiler. Billy dropped into the boat and a moment later the captain followed, bringing with him an end of about forty yards of lead line. The other end was attached to the rail of the ship. As we swung back to leaward the captain said: "Boys, we will stay right near the ship till she goes down."

This cheerful information, of course, filled us all with glee. The line kept us headed properly into the wind and as we rode over the monstrous roarers we saw upon each rise the swaying lights of the dying *Commodore*.

When came the gray shade of dawn, the form of the *Commodore* grew slowly clear to us as our little ten-foot boat rose over each swell. She was floating with such an air of buoyancy that we laughed when we had time, and said: "What a guy[5] it would be on those other fellows if she didn't sink at all."

But later we saw men aboard of her, and later still they began to hail us. I had forgotten to mention that previously we had loosened the end of the lead line and dropped much further to leeward. The men on board were a mystery to us, of course, as we had seen all the boats leave the ship. We rowed back to the ship, but did not approach too near, because we were four men in a ten-foot boat, and we knew that the touch of a hand on our gunwale would assuredly swamp us.

The first mate cried out from the ship that the third boat had foundered alongside. He cried that they had made rafts and wished us to tow them. The captain said: "All right."

Their rafts were floating astern.

"Jump in," cried the captain, but here was a singular and most harrowing hesitation. There were five white men and two negroes. This scene in the gray light of morning impressed one as would a view into some place where ghosts move slowly. These seven men on the stern of the sinking *Commodore* were silent. Save the words of the mate to the captain there was no talk. Here was death, but here also was a most singular and indefinable kind of fortitude.

Four men, I remember, clambered over the railing and stood there watching the cold, steely sheen of the sweeping waves.

"Jump," cried the captain again. The old chief engineer first obeyed the order. He landed on the outside raft and the captain told him how to grip the raft, and he obeyed as promptly and as docilely as a scholar in riding school.

[5] A joke, a tease.

A stoker followed him, and then the first mate threw his hands over his head and plunged into the sea. He had no life belt, and for my part, even when he did this horrible thing, I somehow felt that I could see in the expression of his hands, and in the very toss of his head, as he leaped thus to death, that it was rage, rage, rage unspeakable that was in his heart at the time.

And then I saw Tom Smith, the man who was going to quit filibustering after this expedition, jump to a raft and turn his face toward us. On board the *Commodore* three men strode, still in silence and with their faces turned toward us. One man had his arms folded and was leaning against the deckhouse. His feet were crossed, so that the toe of his left foot pointed downward. There they stood gazing at us, and neither from the deck nor from the rafts was a voice raised. Still was there this silence.

The colored stoker on the first raft threw us a line and we began to tow. Of course, we perfectly understood the absolute impossiblity of any such thing; our dingy was within the six inches of the water's edge, there was an enormous sea running, and I knew that under the circumstances a tugboat would have no light task in moving these rafts. But we tried it, and would have continued to try it indefinitely, but that something critical came to pass. I was at an oar and so faced the rafts. The cook controlled the line. Suddenly the boat began to go backward, and then we saw this negro on the first raft pulling on the line hand over hand and drawing us to him.

He had turned into a demon. He was wild, wild as a tiger. He was crouched on this raft and ready to spring. Every muscle of him seemed to be turned into an elastic spring. His eyes were almost white. His face was the face of a lost man reaching upward, and we knew that the weight of his hand on our gunwale doomed us. The cook let go of the line.

We rowed around to see if we could not get a line from the chief engineer, and all this time, mind you, there were no shrieks, no groans, but silence, silence and silence, and then the *Commodore* sank. She lurched to windward, then swung afar back, righted and dove into the sea, and the rafts were suddenly swallowed by this frightful maw of the ocean. And then by the men on the ten-foot dingy were words said that were still not words, something far beyond words.

The lighthouse of Mosquito Inlet stuck up above the horizon like the point of a pin. We turned our dingy toward the shore. The history of life in an open boat for thirty hours would no doubt be very instructive for the young, but none is to be told here now. For my part I would prefer to tell the story at once, because from it would shine the splendid manhood of Captain Edward Murphy and of William Higgins, the oiler, but let it suffice at this time to say that when we were swamped in the surf and making the best of our way toward the shore the captain gave orders amid the wildness of the breakers as clearly as if he had been on the quarterdeck of a battleship.

John Kitchell of Daytona came running down the beach, and as he ran the air was filled with clothes. If he had pulled a single lever and undressed, even as the fire horses harness, he could not to me seem to have stripped with more speed. He dashed into the water and grabbed the cook. Then he went after the captain, but the captain sent him to me, and then it was that we saw Billy Higgins lying with his forehead on sand that was clear of the water, and he was dead.

1897

THE OPEN BOAT*

A TALE INTENDED TO BE AFTER THE FACT. BEING THE EXPERIENCE OF FOUR
MEN FROM THE SUNK STEAMER COMMODORE

I

None of them knew the color of the sky. Their eyes glanced level, and were fastened upon the waves that swept toward them. These waves were of the hue of slate, save for the tops, which were of foaming white, and all of the men knew the colors of the sea. The horizon narrowed and widened, and dipped and rose, and at all times its edge was jagged with waves that seemed thrust up in points like rocks.

Many a man ought to have a bath-tub larger than the boat which here rode upon the sea. These waves were most wrongfully and barbarously abrupt and tall, and each froth-top was a problem in small boat navigation.

The cook squatted in the bottom and looked with both eyes at the six inches of gunwale which separated him from the ocean. His sleeves were rolled over his fat forearms, and the two flaps of his unbuttoned vest dangled as he bent to bail out the boat. Often he said: "Gawd! That was a narrow clip." As he remarked it he invariably gazed eastward over the broken sea.

The oiler,[1] steering with one of the two oars in the boat, sometimes raised himself suddenly to keep clear of water that swirled in over the stern. It was a thin little oar and it seemed often ready to snap.

The correspondent, pulling at the other oar, watched the waves and wondered why he was there.

The injured captain, lying in the bow, was at this time buried in that profound dejection and indifference which comes, temporarily at least, to even the bravest and most enduring when, willy nilly, the firm fails, the army loses, the ship goes down. The mind of the master of a vessel is rooted deep in the timbers of her, though he command for a day or a decade, and this captain had on him the stern impression of a scene in the grays of dawn of seven turned faces, and later a stump of a top-mast with a white ball on it that slashed to and fro at the waves, went low and lower, and down. Thereafter there was something strange in his voice. Although steady, it was deep with mourning, and of a quality beyond oration or tears.

"Keep 'er a little more south, Billie," said he.

" 'A little more south,' sir," said the oiler in the stern.

A seat in this boat was not unlike a seat upon a bucking broncho, and, by the same token, a broncho is not much smaller. The craft pranced and reared, and plunged like an animal. As each wave came, and she rose for it, she seemed like a

---

* First published in *Scribner's Magazine* in June 1897. Crane sailed from Jacksonville, Florida, on the steamer *Commodore* on New Year's Day of 1897 to cover the Cuban Revolution for the New York *Press;* the ship, which carried munitions for the revolutionaries, sank the next morning, and Crane and three other men survived in a ten-foot dinghy that reached Daytona Beach the following day. On January 6 Crane wrote his newspaper story of the perilous adventure, "Stephen Crane's Own Story"; six months later he published this fictional account.

[1] A crewman who oils machinery in the ship's engine room.

horse making at a fence outrageously high. The manner of her scramble over these walls of water is a mystic thing, and, moreover, at the top of them were ordinarily these problems in white water, the foam racing down from the summit of each wave, requiring a new leap, and a leap from the air. Then, after scornfully bumping a crest, she would slide, and race, and splash down a long incline and arrive bobbing and nodding in front of the next menace.

A singular disadvantage of the sea lies in the fact that after successfully surmounting one wave you discover that there is another behind it just as important and just as nervously anxious to do something effective in the way of swamping boats. In a ten-foot dingey one can get an idea of the resources of the sea in the line of waves that is not probable to the average experience, which is never at sea in a dingey. As each slaty wall of water approached, it shut all else from the view of the men in the boat, and it was not difficult to imagine that this particular wave was the final outburst of the ocean, the last effort of the grim water. There was a terrible grace in the move of the waves, and they came in silence, save for the snarling of the crests.

In the wan light, the faces of the men must have been gray. Their eyes must have glinted in strange ways as they gazed steadily astern. Viewed from a balcony, the whole thing would doubtlessly have been weirdly picturesque. But the men in the boat had no time to see it, and if they had had leisure there were other things to occupy their minds. The sun swung steadily up the sky, and they knew it was broad day because the color of the sea changed from slate to emerald-green, streaked with amber lights, and the foam was like tumbling snow. The process of the breaking day was unknown to them. They were aware only of this effect upon the color of the waves that rolled toward them.

In disjointed sentences the cook and the correspondent argued as to the difference between a life-saving station and a house of refuge. The cook had said: "There's a house of refuge just north of the Mosquito Inlet Light, and as soon as they see us, they'll come off in their boat and pick us up."

"As soon as who see us?" said the correspondent.

"The crew," said the cook.

"Houses of refuge don't have crews," said the correspondent. "As I understand them, they are only places where clothes and grub are stored for the benefit of shipwrecked people. They don't carry crews."

"Oh, yes, they do," said the cook.

"No, they don't," said the correspondent.

"Well, we're not there yet, anyhow," said the oiler, in the stern.

"Well," said the cook, "perhaps it's not a house of refuge that I'm thinking of as being near Mosquito Inlet Light. Perhaps it's a life-saving station."

"We're not there yet," said the oiler, in the stern.

II

As the boat bounced from the top of each wave, the wind tore through the hair of the hatless men, and as the craft plopped her stern down again the spray slashed past them. The crest of each of these waves was a hill, from the top of which the men surveyed, for a moment, a broad tumultuous expanse, shining and wind-riven. It was probably splendid. It was probably glorious, this play of the free sea, wild with lights of emerald and white and amber.

"Bully good thing it's an on-shore wind," said the cook. "If not, where would we be? Wouldn't have a show."

"That's right," said the correspondent.

The busy oiler nodded his assent.

Then the captain, in the bow, chuckled in a way that expressed humor, contempt, tragedy, all in one. "Do you think we've got much of a show, now, boys?" said he.

Whereupon the three were silent, save for a trifle of hemming and hawing. To express any particular optimism at this time they felt to be childish and stupid, but they all doubtless possessed this sense of the situation in their mind. A young man thinks doggedly at such times. On the other hand, the ethics of their condition was decidedly against any open suggestion of hopelessness. So they were silent.

"Oh, well," said the captain, soothing his children, "we'll get ashore all right."

But there was that in his tone which made them think, so the oiler quoth: "Yes! If this wind holds!"

The cook was bailing. "Yes! If we don't catch hell in the surf."

Canton flannel gulls[2] flew near and far. Sometimes they sat down on the sea, near patches of brown sea-weed that rolled over the waves with a movement like carpets on a line in a gale. The birds sat comfortably in groups, and they were envied by some in the dingey, for the wrath of the sea was no more to them than it was to a covey of prairie chickens a thousand miles inland. Often they came very close and stared at the men with black bead-like eyes. At these times they were uncanny and sinister in their unblinking scrutiny, and the men hooted angrily at them, telling them to be gone. One came, and evidently decided to alight on the top of the captain's head. The bird flew parallel to the boat and did not circle, but made short sidelong jumps in the air in chicken-fashion. His black eyes were wistfully fixed upon the captain's head. "Ugly brute," said the oiler to the bird. "You look as if you were made with a jack-knife." The cook and the correspondent swore darkly at the creature. The captain naturally wished to knock it away with the end of the heavy painter,[3] but he did not dare do it, because anything resembling an emphatic gesture would have capsized this freighted boat, and so with his open hand, the captain gently and carefully waved the gull away. After it had been discouraged from the pursuit the captain breathed easier on account of his hair, and others breathed easier because the bird struck their minds at this time as being somehow grewsome and ominous.

In the meantime the oiler and the correspondent rowed. And also they rowed.

They sat together in the same seat, and each rowed an oar. Then the oiler took both oars; then the correspondent took both oars; then the oiler; then the correspondent. They rowed and they rowed. The very ticklish part of the business was when the time came for the reclining one in the stern to take his turn at the oars. By the very last star of truth, it is easier to steal eggs from under a hen than it was to change seats in the dingey. First the man in the stern slid his hand along the thwart and moved with care, as if he were of Sèvres.[4] Then the man in the rowing

---

[2] The gulls look like cotton flannel from Canton, China.
[3] The coiled end of a rope used to fasten the boat to a wharf.
[4] Delicate porcelain made in Sèvres, France.

seat slid his hand along the other thwart. It was all done with the most extraordinary care. As the two sidled past each other, the whole party kept watchful eyes on the coming wave, and the captain cried: "Look out now! Steady there!"

The brown mats of sea-weed that appeared from time to time were like islands, bits of earth. They were travelling, apparently, neither one way nor the other. They were, to all intents, stationary. They informed the men in the boat that it was making progress slowly toward the land.

The captain, rearing cautiously in the bow, after the dingey soared on a great swell, said that he had seen the light-house at Mosquito Inlet. Presently the cook remarked that he had seen it. The correspondent was at the oars, then, and for some reason he too wished to look at the light-house, but his back was toward the far shore and the waves were important, and for some time he could not seize an opportunity to turn his head. But at last there came a wave more gentle than the others, and when at the crest of it he swiftly scoured the western horizon.

"See it?" said the captain.

"No," said the correspondent, slowly, "I didn't see anything."

"Look again," said the captain. He pointed. "It's exactly in that direction."

At the top of another wave, the correspondent did as he was bid, and this time his eyes chanced on a small still thing on the edge of the swaying horizon. It was precisely like the point of a pin. It took an anxious eye to find a light-house so tiny.

"Think we'll make it, Captain?"

"If this wind holds and the boat don't swamp, we can't do much else," said the captain.

The little boat, lifted by each towering sea, and splashed viciously by the crests, made progress that in the absence of sea-weed was not apparent to those in her. She seemed just a wee thing wallowing, miraculously, top-up, at the mercy of five oceans. Occasionally, a great spread of water, like white flames, swarmed into her.

"Bail her, cook," said the captain, serenely.

"All right, Captain," said the cheerful cook.

III

It would be difficult to describe the subtle brotherhood of men that was here established on the seas. No one said that it was so. No one mentioned it. But it dwelt in the boat, and each man felt it warm him. They were a captain, an oiler, a cook, and a correspondent, and they were friends, friends in a more curiously iron-bound degree than may be common. The hurt captain, lying against the water-jar in the bow, spoke always in a low voice and calmly, but he could never command a more ready and swiftly obedient crew than the motley three of the dingey. It was more than a mere recognition of what was best for the common safety. There was surely in it a quality that was personal and heartfelt. And after this devotion to the commander of the boat there was this comradeship that the correspondent, for instance, who had been taught to be cynical of men, knew even at the time was the best experience of his life. But no one said that it was so. No one mentioned it.

"I wish we had a sail," remarked the captain. "We might try my overcoat on the end of an oar and give you two boys a chance to rest." So the cook and the correspondent held the mast and spread wide the overcoat. The oiler steered, and the little boat made good way with her new rig. Sometimes the oiler had to scull sharply to keep a sea from breaking into the boat, but otherwise sailing was a success.

Meanwhile the light-house had been growing slowly larger. It had now almost assumed color, and appeared like a little gray shadow on the sky. The man at the oars could not be prevented from turning his head rather often to try for a glimpse of this little gray shadow.

At last, from the top of each wave the men in the tossing boat could see land. Even as the light-house was an upright shadow on the sky, this land seemed but a long black shadow on the sea. It certainly was thinner than paper. "We must be about opposite New Smyrna," said the cook, who had coasted this shore often in schooners. "Captain, by the way, I believe they abandoned that life-saving station there about a year ago."

"Did they?" said the captain.

The wind slowly died away. The cook and the correspondent were not now obliged to slave in order to hold high the oar. But the waves continued their old impetuous swooping at the dingey, and the little craft, no longer under way, struggled woundily over them. The oiler or the correspondent took the oars again.

Shipwrecks are *apropos* of nothing. If men could only train for them and have them occur when the men had reached pink condition, there would be less drowning at sea. Of the four in the dingey none had slept any time worth mentioning for two days and two nights previous to embarking in the dingey, and in the excitement of clambering about the deck of a foundering ship they had also forgotten to eat heartily.

For these reasons, and for others, neither the oiler nor the correspondent was fond of rowing at this time. The correspondent wondered ingenuously how in the name of all that was sane could there be people who thought it amusing to row a boat. It was not an amusement; it was a diabolical punishment, and even a genius of mental aberrations could never conclude that it was anything but a horror to the muscles and a crime against the back. He mentioned to the boat in general how the amusement of rowing struck him, and the weary-faced oiler smiled in full sympathy. Previously to the foundering, by the way, the oiler had worked double-watch in the engine-room of the ship.

"Take her easy, now, boys," said the captain. "Don't spend yourselves. If we have to run a surf you'll need all your strength, because we'll sure have to swim for it. Take your time."

Slowly the land arose from the sea. From a black line it became a line of black and a line of white—trees and sand. Finally, the captain said that he could make out a house on the shore. "That's the house of refuge, sure," said the cook. "They'll see us before long, and come out after us."

The distant light-house reared high. "The keeper ought to be able to make us out now, if he's looking through a glass," said the captain. "He'll notify the life-saving people."

"None of those other boats could have got ashore to give word of the wreck," said the oiler, in a low voice. "Else the life-boat would be out hunting us."

Slowly and beautifully the land loomed out of the sea. The wind came again. It had veered from the northeast to the southeast. Finally, a new sound struck the ears of the men in the boat. It was the low thunder of the surf on the shore. "We'll never be able to make the light-house now," said the captain. "Swing her head a little more north, Billie."

" 'A little more north,' sir," said the oiler.

Whereupon the little boat turned her nose once more down the wind, and all but the oarsman watched the shore grow. Under the influence of this expansion doubt and direful apprehension was leaving the minds of the men. The management of the boat was still most absorbing, but it could not prevent a quiet cheerfulness. In an hour, perhaps, they would be ashore.

Their back-bones had become thoroughly used to balancing in the boat and they now rode this wild colt of a dingey like circus men. The correspondent thought that he had been drenched to the skin, but happening to feel in the top pocket of his coat, he found therein eight cigars. Four of them were soaked with sea-water; four were perfectly scatheless. After a search, somebody produced three dry matches, and thereupon the four waifs rode impudently in their little boat, and with an assurance of an impending rescue shining in their eyes, puffed at the big cigars and judged well and ill of all men. Everybody took a drink of water.

IV

"Cook," remarked the captain, "there don't seem to be any signs of life about your house of refuge."

"No," replied the cook. "Funny they don't see us!"

A broad stretch of lowly coast lay before the eyes of the men. It was of dunes topped with dark vegetation. The roar of the surf was plain, and sometimes they could see the white lip of a wave as it spun up the beach. a tiny house was blocked out black upon the sky. Southward, the slim light-house lifted its little gray length.

Tide, wind, and waves were swinging the dingey northward. "Funny they don't see us," said the men.

The surf's roar was here dulled, but its tone was, nevertheless, thunderous and mighty. As the boat swam over the great rollers, the men sat listening to this roar. "We'll swamp sure," said everybody.

It is fair to say here that there was not a life-saving station within twenty miles in either direction, but the men did not know this fact and in consequence they made dark and opprobrious remarks concerning the eyesight of the nation's life-savers. Four scowling men sat in the dingey and surpassed records in the invention of epithets.

"Funny they don't see us."

The light-heartedness of a former time had completely faded. To their sharp-ened minds it was easy to conjure pictures of all kinds of incompetency and blind-ness and, indeed, cowardice. There was the shore of the populous land, and it was bitter and bitter to them that from it came no sign.

"Well," said the captain, ultimately, "I suppose we'll have to make a try for ourselves. If we stay out here too long, we'll none of us have strength left to swim after the boat swamps."

And so the oiler, who was at the oars, turned the boat straight for the shore. There was a sudden tightening of muscles. There was some thinking.

"If we don't all get ashore—" said the captain. "If we don't all get ashore, I suppose you fellows know where to send news of my finish?"

They then briefly exchanged some addresses and admonitions. As for the reflections of the men, there was a great deal of rage in them. Perchance they might be formulated thus: "If I am going to be drowned—if I am going to be drowned— if I am going to be drowned, why, in the name of the seven mad gods who rule the sea, was I allowed to come thus far and contemplate sand and trees? Was I brought here merely to have my nose dragged away as I was about to nibble the sacred cheese of life? It is preposterous. If this old ninny-woman, Fate, cannot do better than this, she should be deprived of the management of men's fortunes. She is an old hen who knows not her intention. If she has decided to drown me, why did she not do it in the beginning and save me all this trouble. The whole affair is absurd. . . . But, no, she cannot mean to drown me. She dare not drown me. She cannot drown me. Not after all this work." Afterward the man might have had an impulse to shake his fist at the clouds. "Just you drown me, now, and then hear what I call you!"

The billows that came at this time were more formidable. They seemed always just about to break and roll over the little boat in a turmoil of foam. There was a preparatory and long growl in the speech of them. No mind unused to the sea would have concluded that the dingey could ascend these sheer heights in time. The shore was still afar. The oiler was a wily surfman. "Boys," he said, swiftly, "she won't live three minutes more and we're too far out to swim. Shall I take her to sea again, Captain?"

"Yes! Go ahead!" said the captain.

This oiler, by a series of quick miracles, and fast and steady oarsmanship, turned the boat in the middle of the surf and took her safely to sea again.

There was a considerable silence as the boat bumped over the furrowed sea to deeper water. Then somebody in gloom spoke. "Well, anyhow, they must have seen us from the shore by now."

The gulls went in slanting flight up the wind toward the gray desolate east. A squall, marked by dingy clouds, and clouds brick-red, like smoke from a burning building, appeared from the southeast.

"What do you think of those life-saving people? Ain't they peaches?"

"Funny they haven't seen us."

"Maybe they think we're out here for sport! Maybe they think we're fishin'. Maybe they think we're damned fools."

It was a long afternoon. A changed tide tried to force them southward, but wind and wave said northward. Far ahead, where coast-line, sea, and sky formed their mighty angle, there were little dots which seemed to indicate a city on the shore.

"St. Augustine?"

The captain shook his head. "Too near Mosquito Inlet."

And the oiler rowed, and then the correspondent rowed. Then the oiler rowed. It was a weary business. The human back can become the seat of more aches and pains than are registered in books for the composite anatomy of a regiment. It is a limited area, but it can become the theatre of innumerable muscular conflicts, tangles, wrenches, knots, and other comforts.

"Did you ever like to row, Billie?" asked the correspondent.

"No," said the oiler. "Hang it."

When one exchanged the rowing-seat for a place in the bottom of the boat, he suffered a bodily depression that caused him to be careless of everything save an obligation to wiggle one finger. There was cold sea-water swashing to and fro in the boat, and he lay in it. His head, pillowed on a thwart, was within an inch of the swirl of a wave crest, and sometimes a particularly obstreperous sea came in-board and drenched him once more. But these matters did not annoy him. It is almost certain that if the boat had capsized he would have tumbled comfortably out upon the ocean as if he felt sure that it was a great soft mattress.

"Look! There's a man on the shore!"

"Where?"

"There! See 'im? See 'im?"

"Yes, sure! He's walking along."

"Now he's stopped. Look! He's facing us!"

"He's waving at us!"

"So he is! By thunder!"

"Ah, now, we're all right! Now we're all right! There'll be a boat out here for us in half an hour."

"He's going on. He's running. He's going up to that house there."

The remote beach seemed lower than the sea, and it required a searching glance to discern the little black figure. The captain saw a floating stick and they rowed to it. A bath-towel was by some weird chance in the boat, and, tying this on the stick, the captain waved it. The oarsman did not dare turn his head, so he was obliged to ask questions.

"What's he doing now?"

"He's standing still again. He's looking, I think. . . . There he goes again. Toward the house. . . . Now he's stopped again."

"Is he waving at us?"

"No, not now! he was, though."

"Look! There comes another man!"

"He's running."

"Look at him go, would you."

"Why, he's on a bicycle. Now he's met the other man. They're both waving at us. Look!"

"There comes something up the beach."

"What the devil is that thing?"

"Why, it looks like a boat."

"Why, certainly it's a boat."

"No, it's on wheels."

"Yes, so it is. Well, that must be the life-boat. They drag them along shore on a wagon."

"That's the life-boat, sure."

"No, by————, it's—it's an omnibus."

"I tell you it's a life-boat."

"It is not! It's an omnibus. I can see it plain. See? One of those big hotel omnibuses."

"By thunder, you're right. It's an omnibus, sure as fate. What do you suppose they are doing with an omnibus? Maybe they are going around collecting the life-crew, hey?"

"That's it, likely. Look! There's a fellow waving a little black flag. He's standing on the steps of the omnibus. There come those other two fellows. Now they're all talking together. Look at the fellow with the flag. Maybe he ain't waving it!"

"That ain't a flag, is it? That's his coat. Why, certainly, that's his coat."

"So it is. It's his coat. He's taken it off and is waving it around his head. But would you look at him swing it!"

"Oh, say, there isn't any life-saving station there. That's just a winter resort hotel omnibus that has brought over some of the boarders to see us drown."

"What's that idiot with the coat mean? What's he signaling, anyhow?"

"It looks as if he were trying to tell us to go north. There must be a life-saving station up there."

"No! He thinks we're fishing. Just giving us a merry hand. See? Ah, there, Willie."

"Well, I wish I could make something out of those signals. What do you suppose he means?"

"He don't mean anything. He's just playing."

"Well, if he'd just signal us to try the surf again, or to go to sea and wait, or go north, or go south, or go to hell—there would be some reason in it. But look at him. He just stands there and keeps his coat revolving like a wheel. The ass!"

"There come more people."

"Now there's quite a mob. Look! Isn't that a boat?"

"Where? Oh, I see where you mean. No, that's no boat."

"That fellow is still waving his coat."

"He must think we like to see him do that. Why don't he quit it. It don't mean anything."

"I don't know. I think he is trying to make us go north. It must be that there's a life-saving station there somewhere."

"Say, he ain't tired yet. Look at 'im wave."

"Wonder how long he can keep that up. He's been revolving his coat ever since he caught sight of us. He's an idiot. Why aren't they getting men to bring a boat out. A fishing boat—one of those big yawls—could come out here all right. Why don't he do something?"

"Oh, it's all right, now."

"They'll have a boat out here for us in less than no time, now that they've seen us."

A faint yellow tone came into the sky over the low land. The shadows on the sea slowly deepened. The wind bore coldness with it, and the men began to shiver.

"Holy smoke!" said one, allowing his voice to express his impious mood, "if we keep on monkeying out here! If we've got to flounder out here all night!"

"Oh, we'll never have to stay here all night! Don't you worry. They've seen us now, and it won't be long before they'll come chasing out after us."

The shore grew dusky. The man waving a coat blended gradually into this gloom, and it swallowed in the same manner the omnibus and the group of people. The spray, when it dashed uproariously over the side, made the voyagers shrink and swear like men who were being branded.

"I'd like to catch the chump who waved the coat. I feel like soaking him one, just for luck."

"Why? What did he do?"

"Oh, nothing, but then he seemed so damned cheerful."

In the meantime the oiler rowed, and the correspondent rowed, and then the oiler rowed. Gray-faced and bowed forward, they mechanically, turn by turn, plied the leaden oars. The form of the light-house had vanished from the southern horizon, but finally a pale star appeared, just lifting from the sea. The streaked saffron in the west passed before the all-merging darkness, and the sea to the east was black. The land had vanished, and was expressed only by the low and drear thunder of the surf.

"If I am going to be drowned—if I am going to be drowned—if I am going to be drowned, why, in the name of the seven mad gods who rule the sea, was I allowed to come thus far and contemplate sand and trees? Was I brought here merely to have my nose dragged away as I was about to nibble the sacred cheese of life?"

The patient captain, drooped over the water-jar, was sometimes obliged to speak to the oarsman.

"Keep her head up! Keep her head up!"

" 'Keep her head up,' sir." The voices were weary and low.

This was surely a quiet evening. All save the oarsman lay heavily and listlessly in the boat's bottom. As for him, his eyes were just capable of noting the tall black waves that swept forward in a most sinister silence, save for an occasional subdued growl of a crest.

The cook's head was on a thwart, and he looked without interest at the water under his nose. He was deep in other scenes. Finally he spoke. "Billie," he murmured, dreamfully, "what kind of pie do you like best?"

V

"Pie," said the oiler and the correspondent, agitatedly. "Don't talk about those things, blast you!"

"Well," said the cook, "I was just thinking about ham sandwiches, and———"

A night on the sea in an open boat is a long night. As darkness settled finally, the shine of the light, lifting from the sea in the south, changed to full gold. On the northern horizon a new light appeared, a small bluish gleam on the edge of the waters. These two lights were the furniture of the world. Otherwise there was nothing but waves.

Two men huddled in the stern, and distances were so magnificent in the dingey that the rower was enabled to keep his feet partly warmed by thrusting them under his companions. Their legs indeed extended far under the rowing-seat until they touched the feet of the captain forward. Sometimes, despite the efforts of the tired oarsman, a wave came piling into the boat, an icy wave of the night, and the chilling water soaked them anew. They would twist their bodies for a moment and groan, and sleep the dead sleep once more, while the water in the boat gurgled about them as the craft rocked.

The plan of the oiler and the correspondent was for one to row until he lost the ability, and then arouse the other from his sea-water couch in the bottom of the boat.

The oiler plied the oars until his head drooped forward, and the overpowering sleep blinded him. And he rowed yet afterward. Then he touched a man in the bottom of the boat, and called his name. "Will you spell me for a little while?" he said, meekly.

"Sure, Billie," said the correspondent, awakening and dragging himself to a sitting position. They exchanged places carefully, and the oiler, cuddling down in the sea-water at the cook's side, seemed to go to sleep instantly.

The particular violence of the sea had ceased. The waves came without snarling. The obligation of the man at the oars was to keep the boat headed so that the tilt of the rollers would not capsize her, and to preserve her from filling when the crests rushed past. The black waves were silent and hard to be seen in the darkness. Often one was almost upon the boat before the oarsman was aware.

In a low voice the correspondent addressed the captain. He was not sure that the captain was awake, although this iron man seemed to be always awake. "Captain, shall I keep her making for that light north, sir?"

The same steady voice answered him. "Yes. Keep it about two points off the port bow."

The cook had tied a life-belt around himself in order to get even the warmth which this clumsy cork contrivance could donate, and he seemed almost stove-like when a rower, whose teeth invariably chattered wildly as soon as he ceased his labor, dropped down to sleep.

The correspondent, as he rowed, looked down at the two men sleeping under foot. The cook's arm was around the oiler's shoulders, and, with their fragmentary clothing and haggard faces, they were the babes of the sea, a grotesque rendering of the old babes in the wood.

Later he must have grown stupid at his work, for suddenly there was a growling of water, and a crest came with a roar and a swash into the boat, and it was a wonder that it did not set the cook afloat in his life-belt. The cook continued to sleep, but the oiler sat up, blinking his eyes and shaking with the new cold.

"Oh, I'm awful sorry, Billie," said the correspondent, contritely.

"That's all right, old boy," said the oiler, and lay down again and was asleep.

Presently it seemed that even the captain dozed, and the correspondent thought that he was the one man afloat on all the oceans. The wind had a voice as it came over the waves, and it was sadder than the end.

There was a long, loud swishing astern of the boat, and a gleaming trail of phosphorescence, like blue flame, was furrowed on the black waters. It might have been made by a monstrous knife.

Then there came a stillness, while the correspondent breathed with the open mouth and looked at the sea.

Suddenly there was another swish and another long flash of bluish light, and this time it was alongside the boat, and might almost have been reached with an oar. The correspondent saw an enormous fin speed like a shadow through the water, hurling the crystalline spray and leaving the long glowing trail.

The correspondent looked over his shoulder at the captain. His face was hidden, and he seemed to be asleep. He looked at the babes of the sea. They certainly were asleep. So, being bereft of sympathy, he leaned a little way to one side and swore softly into the sea.

But the thing did not then leave the vicinity of the boat. Ahead or astern, on one side or the other, at intervals long or short, fled the long sparkling streak, and there was to be heard the whiroo of the dark fin. The speed and power of the thing was greatly to be admired. It cut the water like a gigantic and keen projectile.

The presence of this biding thing did not affect the man with the same horror that it would if he had been a picnicker. He simply looked at the sea dully and swore in an undertone.

Nevertheless, it is true that he did not wish to be alone with the thing. He wished one of his companions to awaken by chance and keep him company with it. But the captain hung motionless over the water-jar and the oiler and the cook in the bottom of the boat were plunged in slumber.

VI

"If I am going to be drowned—if I am going to be drowned—if I am going to be drowned, why, in the name of the seven mad gods who rule the sea, was I allowed to come thus far and contemplate sand and trees?"

During this dismal night, it may be remarked that a man would conclude that it was really the intention of the seven mad gods to drown him, despite the abominable injustice of it. For it was certainly an abominable injustice to drown a man who had worked so hard, so hard. The man felt it would be a crime most unnatural. Other people had drowned at sea since galleys swarmed with painted sails, but still——

When it occurs to a man that nature does not regard him as important, and that she feels she would not maim the universe by disposing of him, he at first wishes to throw bricks at the temple, and he hates deeply the fact that there are no bricks and no temples. Any visible expression of nature would surely be pelleted with his jeers.

Then, if there be no tangible thing to hoot he feels, perhaps, the desire to confront a personification and indulge in pleas, bowed to one knee, and with hands supplicant, saying: "Yes, but I love myself."

A high cold star on a winter's night is the word he feels that she says to him. Thereafter he knows the pathos of his situation.

The men in the dingey had not discussed these matters, but each had, no doubt, reflected upon them in silence and according to his mind. There was seldom any expression upon their faces save the general one of complete weariness. Speech was devoted to the business of the boat.

To chime the notes of his emotion, a verse mysteriously entered the correspondent's head. He had even forgotten that he had forgotten this verse, but it suddenly was in his mind.

> A soldier of the Legion lay dying in Algiers,
> There was lack of woman's nursing, there was dearth of woman's tears;
> But a comrade stood beside him, and he took that comrade's hand,
> And he said: "I never more shall see my own, my native land."[5]

In his childhood, the correspondent had been made acquainted with the fact that a soldier of the Legion lay dying in Algiers, but he had never regarded it as important. Myriads of his school-fellows had informed him of the soldier's plight, but the dinning had naturally ended by making him perfectly indifferent. He had never considered it his affair that a soldier of the Legion lay dying in Algiers, nor had it appeared to him as a matter for sorrow. It was less to him than the breaking of a pencil's point.

Now, however, it quaintly came to him as a human, living thing. It was no longer merely a picture of a few throes in the breast of a poet, meanwhile drinking tea and warming his feet at the grate; it was an actuality—stern, mournful, and fine.

The correspondent plainly saw the soldier. He lay on the sand with his feet out straight and still. While his pale left hand was upon his chest in an attempt to thwart the going of his life, the blood came between his fingers. In the far Alge-

---

[5] Adapted from the poem "Bingen on the Rhine" (1883), by Caroline E. S. Norton (1808–1877).

rian distance, a city of low square forms was set against a sky that was faint with the last sunset hues. The correspondent, plying the oars and dreaming of the slow and slower movements of the lips of the soldier, was moved by a profound and perfectly impersonal comprehension. He was sorry for the soldier of the Legion who lay dying in Algiers.

The thing which had followed the boat and waited had evidently grown bored at the delay. There was no longer to be heard the slash of the cut-water, and there was no longer the flame of the long trail. The light in the north still glimmered, but it was apparently no nearer to the boat. Sometimes the boom of the surf rang in the correspondent's ears, and he turned the craft seaward then and rowed harder. Southward, some one had evidently built a watch-fire on the beach. It was too low and too far to be seen, but it made a shimmering, roseate reflection upon the bluff back of it, and this could be discerned from the boat. The wind came stronger, and sometimes a wave suddenly raged out like a mountain-cat and there was to be seen the sheen and sparkle of a broken crest.

The captain, in the bow, moved on his water-jar and sat erect. "Pretty long night," he observed to the correspondent. He looked at the shore. "Those life-saving people take their time."

"Did you see that shark playing around?"

"Yes, I saw him. He was a big fellow, all right."

"Wish I had known you were awake."

Later the correspondent spoke into the bottom of the boat.

"Billie!" There was a slow and gradual disentanglement. "Billie, will you spell me?"

"Sure," said the oiler.

As soon as the correspondent touched the cold comfortable sea-water in the bottom of the boat, and had huddled close to the cook's life-belt he was deep in sleep, despite the fact that his teeth played all the popular airs. This sleep was so good to him that it was but a moment before he heard a voice call his name in a tone that demonstrated the last stages of exhaustion. "Will you spell me?"

"Sure, Billie."

The light in the north had mysteriously vanished, but the correspondent took his course from the wide-awake captain.

Later in the night they took the boat farther out to sea, and the captain directed the cook to take one oar at the stern and keep the boat facing the seas. He was to call out if he should hear the thunder of the surf. This plan enabled the oiler and the correspondent to get respite together. "We'll give those boys a chance to get into shape again," said the captain. They curled down and, after a few preliminary chatterings and trembles, slept once more the dead sleep. Neither knew they had bequeathed to the cook the company of another shark, or perhaps the same shark.

As the boat caroused on the waves, spray occasionally bumped over the side and gave them a fresh soaking, but this had no power to break their repose. The ominous slash of the wind and the water affected them as it would have affected mummies.

"Boys," said the cook, with the notes of every reluctance in his voice, "she's drifted in pretty close. I guess one of you had better take her to sea again." The correspondent, aroused, heard the crash of the toppled crests.

As he was rowing, the captain gave him some whiskey and water, and this steadied the chills out of him. "If I can ever get ashore and anybody shows me even a photograph of an oar————"

At last there was a short conversation.

"Billie. . . . Billie, will you spell me?"

"Sure," said the oiler.

VII

When the correspondent again opened his eyes, the sea and the sky were each of the gray hue of the dawning. Later, carmine and gold was painted upon the waters. The morning appeared finally, in its splendor, with a sky of pure blue, and the sunlight flamed on the tips of the waves.

On the distant dunes were set many little black cottages, and a tall white windmill reared above them. No man, nor dog, nor bicycle appeared on the beach. The cottages might have formed a deserted village.

The voyagers scanned the shore. A conference was held in the boat. "Well," said the captain, "if no help is coming, we might better try a run through the surf right away. If we stay out here much longer we will be too weak to do anything for ourselves at all." The others silently acquiesced in this reasoning. The boat was headed for the beach. The correspondent wondered if none ever ascended the tall wind-tower, and if then they never looked seaward. This tower was a giant, standing with its back to the plight of the ants. It represented in a degree, to the correspondent, the serenity of nature amid the struggles of the individual—nature in the wind, and nature in the vision of men. She did not seem cruel to him then, nor beneficent, nor treacherous, nor wise. But she was indifferent, flatly indifferent. It is, perhaps, plausible that a man in this situation, impressed with the unconcern of the universe, should see the innumerable flaws of his life and have them taste wickedly in his mind and wish for another chance. A distinction between right and wrong seems absurdly clear to him, then, in this new ignorance of the grave-edge, and he understands that if he were given another opportunity he would mend his conduct and his words, and be better and brighter during an introduction, or at a tea.

"Now, boys," said the captain, "she is going to swamp sure. All we can do is to work her in as far as possible, and then when she swamps, pile out and scramble for the beach. Keep cool now, and don't jump until she swamps sure."

The oiler took the oars. Over his shoulders he scanned the surf. "Captain," he said, "I think I'd better bring her about, and keep her head-on to the seas and back her in."

"All right, Billie," said the captain. "Back her in." The oiler swung the boat then and, seated in the stern, the cook and the correspondent were obliged to look over their shoulders to contemplate the lonely and indifferent shore.

The monstrous inshore rollers heaved the boat high until the men were again enabled to see the white sheets of water scudding up the slanted beach. "We won't get in very close," said the captain. Each time a man could wrest his attention from the rollers, he turned his glance toward the shore, and in the expression of the eyes during this contemplation there was a singular quality. The correspondent, observing the others, knew that they were not afraid, but the full meaning of their glances was shrouded.

As for himself, he was too tired to grapple fundamentally with the fact. He tried to coerce his mind into thinking of it, but the mind was dominated at this time by the muscles, and the muscles said they did not care. It merely occurred to him that if he should drown it would be a shame.

There were no hurried words, no pallor, no plain agitation. The men simply looked at the shore. "Now, remember to get well clear of the boat when you jump," said the captain.

Seaward the crest of a roller suddenly fell with a thunderous crash, and the long white comber came roaring down upon the boat.

"Steady now," said the captain. The men were silent. They turned their eyes from the shore to the comber and waited. The boat slid up the incline, leaped at the furious top, bounced over it, and swung down the long back of the wave. Some water had been shipped and the cook bailed it out.

But the next crest crashed also. The tumbling boiling flood of white water caught the boat and whirled it almost perpendicular. Water swarmed in from all sides. The correspondent had his hands on the gunwale at this time, and when the water entered at that place he swiftly withdrew his fingers, as if he objected to wetting them.

The little boat, drunken with this weight of water, reeled and snuggled deeper into the sea.

"Bail her out, cook! Bail her out," said the captain.

"All right, Captain," said the cook.

"Now, boys, the next one will do for us, sure," said the oiler. "Mind to jump clear of the boat."

The third wave moved forward, huge, furious, implacable. It fairly swallowed the dingey, and almost simultaneously the men tumbled into the sea. A piece of life-belt had lain in the bottom of the boat, and as the correspondent went overboard he held this to his chest with his left hand.

The January water was icy, and he reflected immediately that it was colder than he had expected to find it off the coast of Florida. This appeared to his dazed mind as a fact important enough to be noted at the time. The coldness of the water was sad; it was tragic. This fact was somehow so mixed and confused with his opinion of his own situation that it seemed almost a proper reason for tears. The water was cold.

When he came to the surface he was conscious of little but the noisy water. Afterward he saw his companions in the sea. The oiler was ahead in the race. He was swimming strongly and rapidly. Off to the correspondent's left, the cook's great white and corked back bulged out of the water, and in the rear the captain was hanging with his one good hand to the keel of the overturned dingey.

There is a certain immovable quality to a shore, and the correspondent wondered at it amid the confusion of the sea.

It seemed also very attractive, but the correspondent knew that it was a long journey, and he paddled leisurely. The piece of life-preserver lay under him, and sometimes he whirled down the incline of a wave as if he were on a hand-sled.

But finally he arrived at a place in the sea where travel was beset with difficulty. He did not pause swimming to inquire what manner of current had caught him, but there his progress ceased. The shore was set before him like a bit of scenery on a stage, and he looked at it and understood with his eyes each detail of it.

As the cook passed, much farther to the left, the captain was calling to him, "Turn over on your back, cook! Turn over on your back and use the oar."

"All right, sir." The cook turned on his back, and, paddling with an oar, went ahead as if he were a canoe.

Presently the boat also passed to the left of the correspondent with the captain clinging with one hand to the keel. He would have appeared like a man raising himself to look over a board fence, if it were not for the extraordinary gymnastics of the boat. The correspondent marvelled that the captain could still hold to it.

They passed on, nearer to shore—the oiler, the cook, the captain—and following them went the water-jar, bouncing gayly over the seas.

The correspondent remained in the grip of this strange new enemy—a current. The shore, with its white slope of sand and its green bluff, topped with little silent cottages, was spread like a picture before him. It was very near to him then, but he was impressed as one who in a gallery looks at a scene from Brittany or Holland.

He thought: "I am going to drown? Can it be possible? Can it be possible? Can it be possible?" Perhaps an individual must consider his own death to be the final phenomenon of nature.

But later a wave perhaps whirled him out of this small deadly current, for he found suddenly that he could again make progress toward the shore. Later still, he was aware that the captain, clinging with one hand to the keel of the dingey, had his face turned away from the shore and toward him, and was calling his name. "Come to the boat! Come to the boat!"

In his struggle to reach the captain and the boat, he reflected that when one gets properly wearied, drowning must really be a comfortable arrangement, a cessation of hostilities accompanied by a large degree of relief, and he was glad of it, for the main thing in his mind for some moments had been horror of the temporary agony. He did not wish to be hurt.

Presently he saw a man running along the shore. He was undressing with most remarkable speed. Coat, trousers, shirt, everything flew magically off him.

"Come to the boat," called the captain.

"All right, Captain." As the correspondent paddled, he saw the captain let himself down to bottom and leave the boat. Then the correspondent performed his one little marvel of the voyage. A large wave caught him and flung him with ease and supreme speed completely over the boat and far beyond it. It struck him even then as an event in gymnastics, and a true miracle of the sea. An overturned boat in the surf is not a plaything to a swimming man.

The correspondent arrived in water that reached only to his waist, but his condition did not enable him to stand for more than a moment. Each wave knocked him into a heap, and the under-tow pulled at him.

Then he saw the man who had been running and undressing, and undressing and running, come bounding into the water. He dragged ashore the cook, and then waded toward the captain, but the captain waved him away, and sent him to the correspondent. He was naked, naked as a tree in winter, but a halo was about his head, and he shone like a saint. He gave a strong pull, and a long drag, and a bully heave at the correspondent's hand. The correspondent, schooled in the minor formulæ, said: "Thanks, old man." But suddenly the man cried: "What's that?" He pointed a swift finger. The correspondent said: "Go."

In the shallows, face downward, lay the oiler. His forehead touched sand that was periodically, between each wave, clear of the sea.

The correspondent did not know all that transpired afterward. When he achieved safe ground he fell, striking the sand with each particular part of his body. It was as if he had dropped from a roof, but the thud was grateful to him.

It seems that instantly the beach was populated with men with blankets, clothes, and flasks, and women with coffee-pots and all the remedies sacred to their minds. The welcome of the land to the men from the sea was warm and generous, but a still and dripping shape was carried slowly up the beach, and the land's welcome for it could only be the different and sinister hospitality of the grave.

When it came night, the white waves paced to and fro in the moonlight, and the wind brought the sound of the great sea's voice to the men on shore, and they felt that they could then be interpreters.

1897

THE BRIDE COMES TO YELLOW SKY*

I

The great Pullman[1] was whirling onward with such dignity of motion that a glance from the window seemed simply to prove that the plains of Texas were pouring eastward. Vast flats of green grass, dull-hued spaces of mesquite and cactus, little groups of frame houses, woods of light and tender trees, all were sweeping into the east, sweeping over the horizon, a precipice.

A newly married pair had boarded this coach at San Antonio. The man's face was reddened from many days in the wind and sun, and a direct result of his new black clothes was that his brick-colored hands were constantly performing in a most conscious fashion. From time to time he looked down respectfully at his attire. He sat with a hand on each knee, like a man waiting in a barber's shop. The glances he devoted to other passengers were furtive and shy.

The bride was not pretty, nor was she very young. She wore a dress of blue cashmere, with small reservations of velvet here and there and with steel buttons abounding. She continually twisted her head to regard her puff sleeves, very stiff, straight, and high. They embarrassed her. It was quite apparent that she had cooked, and that she expected to cook, dutifully. The blushes caused by the careless scrutiny of some passengers as she had entered the car were strange to see upon this plain, under-class countenance, which was drawn in placid, almost emotionless lines.

They were evidently very happy. "Ever been in a parlor-car before?" he asked, smiling with delight.

"No," she answered. "I never was. It's fine, ain't it?"

---

* First published in *McClure's Magazine* in America and in *Chapman's Magazine* in England in February 1898.
[1] A railroad passenger car with convertible sleeping berths, named for its inventor, G. M. Pullman (1831–1897).

"Great! And then after a while we'll go forward to the diner and get a big lay-out. Finest meal in the world. Charge a dollar."

"Oh, do they?" cried the bride. "Charge a dollar? Why, that's too much—for us—ain't it, Jack?"

"Not this trip, anyhow," he answered bravely. "We're going to go the whole thing."

Later, he explained to her about the trains. "You see, it's a thousand miles from one end of Texas to the other, and this train runs right across it and never stops but four times." He had the pride of an owner. He pointed out to her the dazzling fittings of the coach, and in truth her eyes opened wider as she contemplated the sea-green figured velvet, the shining brass, silver, and glass, the wood that gleamed as darkly brilliant as the surface of a pool of oil. At one end a bronze figure sturdily held a support for a separated chamber, and at convenient places on the ceiling were frescoes in olive and silver.

To the minds of the pair, their surroundings reflected the glory of their marriage that morning in San Antonio. This was the environment of their new estate, and the man's face in particular beamed with an elation that made him appear ridiculous to the negro porter. This individual at times surveyed them from afar with an amused and superior grin. On other occasions he bullied them with skill in ways that did not make it exactly plain to them that they were being bullied. He subtly used all the manners of the most unconquerable kind of snobbery. He oppressed them, but of this oppression they had small knowledge, and they speedily forgot that infrequently a number of travelers covered them with stares of derisive enjoyment. Historically there was supposed to be something infinitely humorous in their situation.

"We are due in Yellow Sky at 3.42," he said, looking tenderly into her eyes.

"Oh, are we?" she said, as if she had not been aware of it. To evince surprise at her husband's statement was part of her wifely amiability. She took from a pocket a little silver watch, and as she held it before her and stared at it with a frown of attention, the new husband's face shone.

"I bought it in San Anton' from a friend of mine," he told her gleefully.

"It's seventeen minutes past twelve," she said, looking up at him with a kind of shy and clumsy coquetry. A passenger, noting this play, grew excessively sardonic, and winked at himself in one of the numerous mirrors.

At last they went to the dining-car. Two rows of negro waiters in glowing white suits surveyed their entrance with the interest and also the equanimity of men who had been forewarned. The pair fell to the lot of a waiter who happened to feel pleasure in steering them through their meal. He viewed them with the manner of a fatherly pilot, his countenance radiant with benevolence. The patronage entwined with the ordinary deference was not plain to them. And yet as they returned to their coach they showed in their faces a sense of escape.

To the left, miles down a long purple slope, was a little ribbon of mist where moved the keening Rio Grande. The train was approaching it at an angle, and the apex was Yellow Sky. Presently it was apparent that as the distance from Yellow Sky grew shorter, the husband became commensurately restless. His brick-red hands were more insistent in their prominence. Occasionally he was even rather absent-minded and far-away when the bride leaned forward and addressed him.

As a matter of truth, Jack Potter was beginning to find the shadow of a deed weigh upon him like a leaden slab. He, the town marshal of Yellow Sky, a man known, liked, and feared in his corner, a prominent person, had gone to San Antonio to meet a girl he believed he loved, and there, after the usual prayers, had actually induced her to marry him, without consulting Yellow Sky for any part of the transaction. He was now bringing his bride before an innocent and unsuspecting community.

Of course, people in Yellow Sky married as it pleased them in accordance with a general custom; but such was Potter's thought of his duty to his friends, or of their idea of his duty, or of an unspoken form which does not control men in these matters, that he felt he was heinous. He had committed an extraordinary crime. Face to face with this girl in San Antonio, and spurred by his sharp impulse, he had gone headlong over all the social hedges. At San Antonio he was like a man hidden in the dark. A knife to sever any friendly duty, any form, was easy to his hand in that remote city. But the hour of Yellow Sky, the hour of daylight, was approaching.

He knew full well that his marriage was an important thing to his town. It could only be exceeded by the burning of the new hotel. His friends would not forgive him. Frequently he had reflected on the advisability of telling them by telegraph, but a new cowardice had been upon him. He feared to do it. And now the train was hurrying him toward a scene of amazement, glee, reproach. He glanced out of the window at the line of haze swinging slowly in toward the train.

Yellow Sky had a kind of brass band which played painfully to the delight of the populace. He laughed without heart as he thought of it. If the citizens could dream of his prospective arrival with his bride, they would parade the band at the station and escort them, amid cheers and laughing congratulations, to his adobe home.

He resolved that he would use all the devices of speed and plains-craft in making the journey from the station to his house. Once within that safe citadel, he could issue some sort of a vocal bulletin, and then not go among the citizens until they had time to wear off a little of their enthusiasm.

The bride looked anxiously at him. "What's worrying you, Jack?"

He laughed again. "I'm not worrying, girl. I'm only thinking of Yellow Sky."

She flushed in comprehension.

A sense of mutual guilt invaded their minds and developed a finer tenderness. They looked at each other with eyes softly aglow. But Potter often laughed the same nervous laugh. The flush upon the bride's face seemed quite permanent.

The traitor to the feelings of Yellow Sky narrowly watched the speeding landscape. "We're nearly there," he said.

Presently the porter came and announced the proximity of Potter's home. He held a brush in his hand and, with all his airy superiority gone, he brushed Potter's new clothes as the latter slowly turned this way and that way. Potter fumbled out a coin and gave it to the porter as he had seen others do. It was a heavy and muscle-bound business, as that of a man shoeing his first horse.

The porter took their bag, and as the train began to slow they moved forward to the hooded platform of the car. Presently the two engines and their long string of coaches rushed into the station of Yellow Sky.

"They have to take water here," said Potter, from a constricted throat and in mournful cadence as one announcing death. Before the train stopped his eye had swept the length of the platform, and he was glad and astonished to see there was none upon it but the station-agent, who, with a slightly hurried and anxious air, was walking toward the water-tanks. When the train had halted, the porter alighted first and placed in position a little temporary step.

"Come on, girl," said Potter hoarsely. As he helped her down they each laughed on a false note. He took the bag from the negro, and bade his wife cling to his arm. As they slunk rapidly away, his hang-dog glance perceived that they were unloading the two trunks, and also that the station-agent far ahead near the baggage-car had turned and was running toward him, making gestures. He laughed, and groaned as he laughed, when he noted the first effect of his marital bliss upon Yellow Sky. He gripped his wife's arm firmly to his side, and they fled. Behind them the porter stood chuckling fatuously.

II

The California Express on the Southern Railway was due at Yellow Sky in twenty-one minutes. There were six men at the bar of the Weary Gentleman saloon. One was a drummer[2] who talked a great deal and rapidly; three were Texans who did not care to talk at that time; and two were Mexican sheep-herders who did not talk as a general practice in the Weary Gentleman saloon. The bar-keeper's dog lay on the board-walk that crossed in front of the door. His head was on his paws, and he glanced drowsily here and there with the constant vigilance of a dog that is kicked on occasion. Across the sandy street were some vivid green grass plots, so wonderful in appearance amid the sands that burned near them in a blazing sun that they caused a doubt in the mind. They exactly resembled the grass mats used to represent lawns on the stage. At the cooler end of the railway station a man without a coat sat in a tilted chair and smoked his pipe. The fresh-cut bank of the Rio Grande circled near the town, and there could be seen beyond it a great plum-colored plain of mesquite.

Save for the busy drummer and his companions in the saloon, Yellow Sky was dozing. The new-comer leaned gracefully upon the bar, and recited many tales with the confidence of a bard who has come upon a new field.

"———and at the moment that the old man fell down stairs with the bureau in his arms, the old woman was coming up with two scuttles[3] of coal, and, of course———"

The drummer's tale was interrupted by a young man who suddenly appeared in the open door. He cried: "Scratchy Wilson's drunk, and has turned loose with both hands." The two Mexicans at once set down their glasses and faded out of the rear entrance of the saloon.

The drummer, innocent and jocular, answered: "All right, old man. S'pose he has. Come in and have a drink, anyhow."

But the information had made such an obvious cleft in every skull in the room that the drummer was obliged to see its importance. All had become instantly morose. "Say," said he, mystified, "what is this?" His three companions made the

---

[2] A traveling salesman.   [3] Buckets with a wide lip.

introductory gesture of eloquent speech, but the young man at the door forestalled them.

"It means, my friend," he answered, as he came into the saloon, "that for the next two hours this town won't be a health resort."

The bar-keeper went to the door and locked and barred it. Reaching out of the window, he pulled in heavy wooden shutters and barred them. Immediately a solemn, chapel-like gloom was upon the place. The drummer was looking from one to another.

"But say," he cried, "what is this, anyhow? You don't mean there is going to be a gun-fight?"

"Don't know whether there'll be a fight or not," answered one man grimly. "But there'll be some shootin'—some good shootin'."

The young man who had warned them waved his hand. "Oh, there'll be a fight fast enough, if anyone wants it. Anybody can get a fight out there in the street. There's a fight just waiting."

The drummer seemed to be swayed between the interest of a foreigner and a perception of personal danger.

"What did you say his name was?" he asked.

"Scratchy Wilson,"[4] they answered in chorus.

"And will he kill anybody? What are you going to do? Does this happen often? Does he rampage around like this once a week or so? Can he break in that door?"

"No, he can't break down that door," replied the bar-keeper. "He's tried it three times. But when he comes you'd better lay down on the floor, stranger. He's dead sure to shoot at it, and a bullet may come through."

Thereafter the drummer kept a strict eye upon the door. The time had not yet been called for him to hug the floor, but as a minor precaution he sidled near to the wall. "Will he kill anybody?" he said again.

The men laughed low and scornfully at the question.

"He's out to shoot, and he's out for trouble. Don't see any good in experimentin' with him."

"But what do you do in a case like this? What do you do?"

A man responded: "Why, he and Jack Potter———"

But, in chorus, the other men interrupted: "Jack Potter's in San Anton'."

"Well, who is he? What's he got to do with it?"

"Oh, he's the town marshal. He goes out and fights Scratchy when he gets on one of these tears."

"Wow," said the drummer, mopping his brow. "Nice job he's got."

The voices had toned away to mere whisperings. The drummer wished to ask further questions which were born of an increasing anxiety and bewilderment; but when he attempted them, the men merely looked at him in irritation and motioned him to remain silent. A tense waiting hush was upon them. In the deep shadows of the room their eyes shone as they listened for sounds from the street. One man made three gestures at the bar-keeper, and the latter, moving like a ghost, handed him a glass and a bottle. The man poured a full glass of whisky, and set down the

---

[4] Scratchy Wilson appears as Jack Potter's deputy in Crane's story "Moonlight on the Snow," published posthumously in 1901.

bottle noiselessly. He gulped the whisky in a swallow, and turned again toward the door in immovable silence. The drummer saw that the bar-keeper, without a sound, had taken a Winchester from beneath the bar. Later he saw this individual beckoning to him, so he tiptoed across the room.

"You better come with me back of the bar."

"No, thanks," said the drummer, perspiring. "I'd rather be where I can make a break for the back door."

Whereupon the man of bottles made a kindly but peremptory gesture. The drummer obeyed it, and finding himself seated on a box with his head below the level of the bar, balm was laid upon his soul at sight of various zinc and copper fittings that bore a resemblance to armor-plate. The bar-keeper took a seat comfortably upon an adjacent box.

"You see," he whispered, "this here Scratchy Wilson is a wonder with a gun— a perfect wonder—and when he goes on the war trail, we hunt our holes—naturally. He's about the last one of the old gang that used to hang out along the river here. He's a terror when he's drunk. When he's sober he's all right—kind of simple—wouldn't hurt a fly—nicest fellow in town. But when he's drunk— whoo!"

There were periods of stillness. "I wish Jack Potter was back from San Anton'," said the bar-keeper. "He shot Wilson up once—in the leg—and he would sail in and pull out the kinks in this thing."

Presently they heard from a distance the sound of a shot, followed by three wild yowls. It instantly removed a bond from the men in the darkened saloon. There was a shuffling of feet. They looked at each other. "Here he comes," they said.

III

A man in a maroon-colored flannel shirt, which had been purchased for purposes of decoration and made, principally, by some Jewish women on the east side of New York, rounded a corner and walked into the middle of the main street of Yellow Sky. In either hand the man held a long, heavy blue-black revolver. Often he yelled, and these cries rang through a semblance of a deserted village, shrilly flying over the roofs in a volume that seemed to have no relation to the ordinary vocal strength of a man. It was as if the surrounding stillness formed the arch of a tomb over him. These cries of ferocious challenge rang against walls of silence. And his boots had red tops with gilded imprints, of the kind beloved in winter by little sledding boys on the hillsides of New England.

The man's face flamed in a rage begot of whisky. His eyes, rolling and yet keen for ambush, hunted the still door-ways and windows. He walked with the creeping movement of the midnight cat. As it occurred to him, he roared menacing information. The long revolvers in his hands were as easy as straws; they were moved with an electric swiftness. The little fingers of each hand played sometimes in a musician's way. Plain from the low collar of the shirt, the cords of his neck straightened and sank, straightened and sank, as passion moved him. The only sounds were his terrible invitations. The calm adobes preserved their demeanor at the passing of this small thing in the middle of the street.

There was no offer of fight; no offer of fight. The man called to the sky. There were no attractions. He bellowed and fumed and swayed his revolvers here and everywhere.

The dog of the bar-keeper of the Weary Gentleman saloon had not appreciated the advance of events. He yet lay dozing in front of his master's door. At sight of the dog, the man paused and raised his revolver humorously. At sight of the man, the dog sprang up and walked diagonally away, with a sullen head and growling. The man yelled, and the dog broke into a gallop. As it was about to enter an alley, there was a loud noise, a whistling, and something spat the ground directly before it. The dog screamed, and, wheeling in terror, galloped headlong in a new direction. Again there was a noise, a whistling, and sand was kicked viciously before it. Fear-stricken, the dog turned and flurried like an animal in a pen. The man stood laughing, his weapons at his hips.

Ultimately the man was attracted by the closed door of the Weary Gentleman saloon. He went to it, and hammering with a revolver, demanded drink.

The door remaining imperturbable, he picked a bit of paper from the walk and nailed it to the framework with a knife. He then turned his back contemptuously upon this popular resort, and walking to the opposite side of the street, and spinning there on his heel quickly and lithely, fired at the bit of paper. He missed it by a half inch. He swore at himself, and went away. Later, he comfortably fusilladed[5] the windows of his most intimate friend. The man was playing with this town. It was a toy for him.

But still there was no offer of fight. The name of Jack Potter, his ancient antagonist, entered his mind, and he concluded that it would be a glad thing if he should go to Potter's house and by bombardment induce him to come out and fight. He moved in the direction of his desire, chanting Apache scalp-music.

When he arrived at it, Potter's house presented the same still, calm front as had the other adobes. Taking up a strategic position, the man howled a challenge. But this house regarded him as might a great stone god. It gave no sign. After a decent wait, the man howled further challenges, mingling with them wonderful epithets.

Presently there came the spectacle of a man churning himself into deepest rage over the immobility of a house. He fumed at it as the winter wind attacks a prairie cabin in the North. To the distance there should have gone the sound of a tumult like the fighting of two hundred Mexicans. As necessity bade him, he paused for breath or to reload his revolvers.

IV

Potter and his bride walked sheepishly and with speed. Sometimes they laughed together shamefacedly and low.

"Next corner, dear," he said finally.

They put forth the efforts of a pair walking bowed against a strong wind. Potter was about to raise a finger to point the first appearance of the new home when, as they circled the corner, they came face to face with a man in a maroon-colored

---

[5] Rapidly shot at.

shirt who was feverishly pushing cartridges into a large revolver. Upon the instant the man dropped this revolver to the ground, and, like lightning, whipped another from its holster. The second weapon was aimed at the bridegroom's chest.

There was a silence. Potter's mouth seemed to be merely a grave for his tongue. He exhibited an instinct to at once loosen his arm from the woman's grip, and he dropped the bag to the sand. As for the bride, her face had gone as yellow as old cloth. She was a slave to hideous rites gazing at the apparitional snake.

The two men faced each other at a distance of three paces. He of the revolver smiled with a new and quiet ferocity. "Tried to sneak up on me," he said. "Tried to sneak up on me!" His eyes grew more baleful. As Potter made a slight movement, the man thrust his revolver venomously forward. "No, don't you do it, Jack Potter. Don't you move a finger toward a gun just yet. Don't move an eyelash. The time has come for me to settle with you, and I'm goin' to do it my own way and loaf along with no interferin'. So if you don't want a gun bent on you, just mind what I tell you."

Potter looked at his enemy. "I ain't got a gun on me, Scratchy," he said. "Honest, I ain't." He was stiffening and steadying, but yet somewhere at the back of his mind a vision of the Pullman floated, the sea-green figured velvet, the shining brass, silver, and glass, the wood that gleamed as darkly brilliant as the surface of a pool of oil—all the glory of the marriage, the environment of the new estate. "You know I fight when it comes to fighting, Scratchy Wilson, but I ain't got a gun on me. You'll have to do all the shootin' yourself."

His enemy's face went livid. He stepped forward and lashed his weapon to and fro before Potter's chest. "Don't you tell me you ain't got no gun on you, you whelp. Don't tell me no lie like that. There ain't a man in Texas ever seen you without no gun. Don't take me for no kid." His eyes blazed with light, and his throat worked like a pump.

"I ain't takin' you for no kid," answered Potter. His heels had not moved an inch backward. "I'm takin' you for a———fool. I tell you I ain't got a gun, and I ain't. If you're goin' to shoot me up, you better begin now. You'll never get a chance like this again."

So much enforced reasoning had told on Wilson's rage. He was calmer. "If you ain't got a gun, why ain't you got a gun?" he sneered. "Been to Sunday-school?"

"I ain't got a gun because I've just come from San Anton' with my wife. I'm married," said Potter. "And if I'd thought there was going to be any galoots like you prowling around when I brought my wife home, I'd had a gun, and don't you forget it."

"Married!" said Scratchy, not at all comprehending.

"Yes, married. I'm married," said Potter distinctly.

"Married?" said Scratchy. Seemingly for the first time he saw the drooping drowning woman at the other man's side. "No!" he said. He was like a creature allowed a glimpse of another world. He moved a pace backward, and his arm with the revolver dropped to his side. "Is this—is this the lady?" he asked.

"Yes, this is the lady," answered Potter.

There was another period of silence.

"Well," said Wilson at last, slowly, "I s'pose it's all off now."

"It's all off if you say so, Scratchy. You know I didn't make the trouble." Potter lifted his valise.

"Well, I 'low it's off, Jack," said Wilson. He was looking at the ground. "Married!" He was not a student of chivalry; it was merely that in the presence of this foreign condition he was a simple child of the earlier plains. He picked up his starboard[6] revolver, and placing both weapons in their holsters, he went away. His feet made funnel-shaped tracks in the heavy sand.

1898

from   THE BLACK RIDERS AND OTHER LINES*

I

Black riders came from the sea.
There was clang and clang of spear and shield,
And clash and clash of hoof and heel,
Wild shouts and the wave of hair
In the rush upon the wind:
Thus the ride of sin.

XIX

A god in wrath
Was beating a man;
He cuffed him loudly
With thunderous blows
That rang and rolled over the earth.
All people came running.
The man screamed and struggled.
And bit madly at the feet of the god.
The people cried,
"Ah, what a wicked man!"   10
And—
"Ah, what a redoubtable god!"

XXIV

I saw a man pursuing the horizon;
Round and round they sped.

---

[6] Right-hand side.
* These poems were published without titles in Crane's collection *The Black Riders and Other Lines* in 1895.

I was disturbed at this;
I accosted the man.
"It is futile," I said.
"You can never———"

"You lie," he cried,
And ran on.

from   WAR IS KIND*

69

Do not weep, maiden, for war is kind.
Because your lover threw wild hands toward the sky
And the affrighted steed ran on alone,
Do not weep.
War is kind.

   Hoarse, booming drums of the regiment
   Little souls who thirst for fight,
   These men were born to drill and die
   The unexplained glory flies above them
   Great is the battle-god, great, and his kingdom———   10
   A field where a thousand corpses lie.

Do not weep, babe, for war is kind.
Because your father tumbled in the yellow trenches,
Raged at his breast, gulped and died,
Do not weep.
War is kind.

   Swift, blazing flag of the regiment
   Eagle with crest of red and gold,
   These men were born to drill and die
   Point for them the virtue of slaughter   20
   Make plain to them the excellence of killing
   And a field where a thousand corpses lie.

Mother whose heart hung humble as a button
On the bright splendid shroud of your son,
Do not weep.
War is kind.

                                                    1895, 1896

* These poems were published without titles in Crane's collection *War Is Kind* in 1899.

89

A man said to the universe:
"Sir, I exist!"
"However," replied the universe,
"The fact has not created in me
"A sense of obligation."

1894, 1899

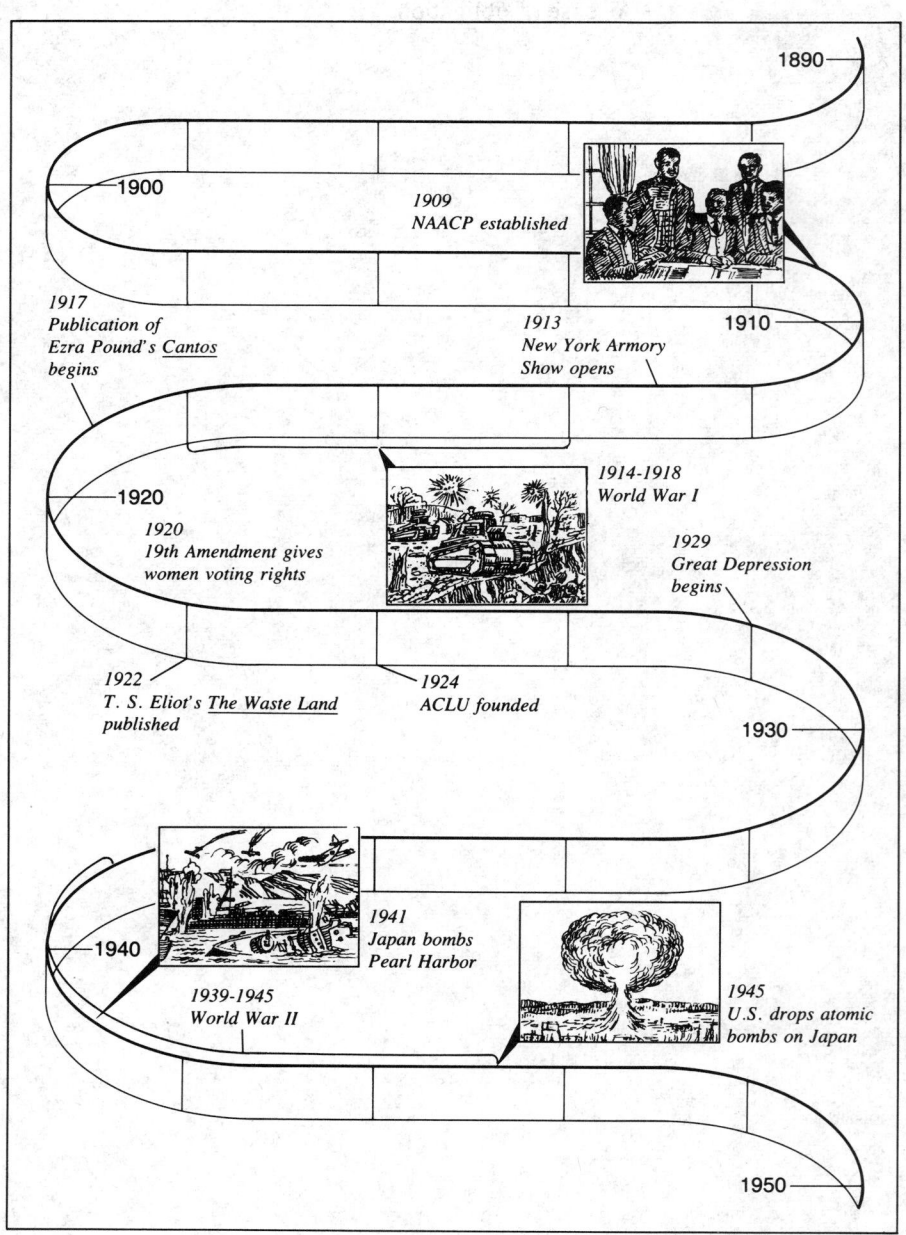

1890

1900

1909
NAACP established

1917
Publication of
Ezra Pound's *Cantos*
begins

1913
New York Armory
Show opens

1910

1914-1918
World War I

1920

1920
19th Amendment gives
women voting rights

1929
Great Depression
begins

1922
T. S. Eliot's *The Waste Land*
published

1924
ACLU founded

1930

1941
Japan bombs
Pearl Harbor

1940

1939-1945
World War II

1945
U.S. drops atomic
bombs on Japan

1950

PART FIVE

America in the World Community

The Early 20th Century

Children born in the final years of the nineteenth century were young adults during World War I and were likely to send their sons to fight in World War II. In the interwar years their life chances would be curtailed by a severe economic depression; they would experience the anguish of watching what seemed like an inexorable rise of fascism and tyranny around the world. But the century opened bravely. A generation of progressive reformers, supported in many of their concerns by President Theodore Roosevelt, believed that human intelligence could solve the problems of urbanization, immigration, education, and public health. In state after state, new laws limited work hours of women and children, set the standards for decent working conditions, and made basic education compulsory. The membership of trade unions doubled between 1915 and 1920. Progressive mayors promoted public libraries and museums, sought to eliminate graft and corruption from civic building projects, and lowered fees for public services. Federal legislation provided for the regulation and inspection of food and drugs, including eliminating the cocaine that had originally been an ingredient in Coca-Cola. It was possible to anticipate that future generations could be protected from exploitation and that decent living standards were within the reach of all Americans.

But for many the reforms came too slowly and too late. On March 25, 1911, nearly 150 young female garment workers died when a fire broke out in the factory of the Triangle Shirtwaist Company in Manhattan; the owners had kept the doors to the fire escapes locked so that workers could not take breaks from their work and union organizers could not enter. Passers-by watched in horror as forty-six young women jumped out windows; some jumped in groups, holding hands. Among the watchers was a young social worker, Frances Perkins, who would dedicate her life to improving factory conditions and whom Franklin D. Roosevelt would appoint to his cabinet as secretary of labor in 1933. She was the first female member of a presidential cabinet.

Progressive reformers could be ambivalent on racial issues; Theodore Roosevelt invited Booker T. Washington to dinner at the White House but also ordered the dishonorable discharge of 167 African-American soldiers after a race riot in

Brownsville, Texas, although charges could not be proved against any of them. In 1909 a coalition of white and black reformers, led by W. E. B. Du Bois, Mary White Ovington, and Oswald Garrison Villard (grandson of the abolitionist William Lloyd Garrison), organized the National Association for the Advancement of Colored People to resist lynching, promote better race relations, and support the interests of African Americans.

World War I

World War I broke out in Europe in 1914 between the Allies (Great Britain, Belgium, France, and Russia) and the Central Powers (Germany, Austria-Hungary, and Bulgaria). Tensions from colonial rivalries and nationalist sentiment exploded after the assassination of Austria's Archduke Francis Ferdinand in June 1914. President Woodrow Wilson called upon Americans to remain neutral in thought and in action. What was neutral behavior, however, was not always obvious. For example, British passenger liners commonly carried war supplies. When German submarines sunk these ships, such as the *Lusitania* in 1915, they did so on the grounds that the ships contributed to the war effort. Wilson's secretary of state, William Jennings Bryan, thought the Germans had drawn an obvious conclusion and urged Wilson to forbid Americans to travel on belligerent ships. But Wilson took the position that a German attack on any U.S. ship would constitute an act of aggression. When in 1917 Germany announced that it would sink on sight any ship heading for England or France and then sunk five American merchant ships in a two-week period in March, Wilson called for a declaration of war. Framing it in terms of a war to stabilize democracy, he promised that the fight would be for freedom of the seas, the self-determination of small nations and colonial peoples, and "a concert of free peoples as shall bring peace and safety to all nations and make the world itself at last free."

American intervention came at a crucial time: the "Great War" had bled both sides of nearly a generation of young men. The British lost 900,000 men, the French 1.4 million, the Russians 1.7 million; in contrast, Americans lost 50,000 men. At least an equal number were wounded. But the addition of American troops in the late stages of fighting provided a crucial margin for allied victory. African-American leaders, W. E. B. Du Bois among them, urged their followers to support the war, but upon enlisting African Americans found themselves assigned to segregated units and required to do menial labor. Female suffragists had believed that women had a special responsibility to oppose war, but when the United States entered, most suffrage groups stifled their opposition and joined the patriotic campaign. Seizing upon the contradiction between a war to make the world safe for democracy and the denial of democratic participation to women, they persuaded Wilson to drop his opposition to women's suffrage. The result of a major lobbying effort was the passage of the Nineteenth Amendment to the Constitution in 1919, which gives women the right to vote.

Other groups, notably socialists, bitterly opposed intervention; they found that once war was declared neither the government nor much of the American public

New weapons, such as machine guns and poison gas, along with disease and the tactics of trench warfare, led to at least ten million deaths in World War I.

tolerated criticism. The Espionage Act of 1917 permitted the government to ban "treasonous" materials from the mails without specifying what constitutes treason; the Sedition Act of 1918 made punishable any "disloyal, profane, scurrilous, or abusive language about the form of government." More than one thousand people were convicted under these statutes, including many who had printed or distributed pamphlets opposing American intervention in Europe or in Russia, and these convictions were upheld by the Supreme Court. Freedom of speech and of the press were thus bitterly contested during the war years. The American Civil Liberties Union would be founded in 1924 to articulate the broad principles of the right to speak, write, and publish.

The peace that was negotiated at Versailles, France, in 1919 was a complex one. The negotiators were grimly distressed by the success of the Russian Revolution and by the fear that a proletarian revolution might spread outside the Soviet Union. The United States briefly sent troops that supported resistance to Nikolai Lenin, leader of the Russian Revolution. The European negotiators were determined to punish Germany and to pay for the restoration of their own economies through German reparations. But the Treaty of Versailles did create independent states from the defunct Austro-Hungarian empire—not only Austria and Hungary but also Poland, Yugoslavia, and Czechoslovakia. It established some guidelines for the treatment of colonies, and it established the League of Nations, which, it was hoped, would fulfill Wilson's promise of a "concert of free peoples."

In the aftermath of World War I, frightened by the Russian Revolution, Americans refused to join the League of Nations. Superpatriotism built on fear; in 1920 the Ku Klux Klan—racist, anti-Semitic, anti-Catholic, and generally xenophobic—claimed over 100,000 members; it grew fastest in the Midwest. Although American radical organizations were in fact losing members, a "Red scare," fear of communism, spread and contributed to the passage of laws severely restricting European immigration and virtually eliminating Asian immigration. In the 1930s these laws would even effectively bar the entry of refugees from Adolf Hitler's terror. (They did not, however, restrict immigration from Western Hemisphere countries: by the end of the 1920s one out of five people in Los Angeles was of Mexican origin.) In 1920 two Italian immigrants, the anarchists Nicola Sacco and Bartolomeo Vanzetti, were convicted for murdering a guard and a paymaster during a payroll robbery in South Braintree, Massachusetts. Many liberals believed the evidence was flimsy and that Sacco and Vanzetti were sentenced because they were foreign. Intellectuals, writers, and artists rallied to their defense. Carl Sandburg, Katherine Anne Porter, and Edna St. Vincent Millay were among the many writers who protested the conviction; Ben Shahn created twenty-three paintings in protest. Nevertheless, Sacco and Vanzetti were executed in 1927.

Consumerism and Technology

The 1920s was the high-water mark of a revolution in consumer goods and communications technology that had been underway since the 1890s. By the end of the 1920s nearly half the nation's households had telephones, and an equal number had radios. The first commercial radio station opened in 1920: car radios came into use in 1927. Radio shaped a national audience for music, news, stories—weekly comedy series and daytime soap operas—and sports; the World Series was first broadcast in 1921. Other developments also created national audiences and national standards of taste in the 1920s, helping to break down regional variations in culture. Magazines such as *The Saturday Evening Post* and *The Ladies' Home Journal* had national circulations of over 2.5 million. An estimated 100 million people a week went to movies, and the first "talkies" appeared in movie theatres in 1927. The Book-of-the-Month Club, founded in 1926, invigorated the national circulation of a limited range of titles. New automobile technology widened horizons; by the end of the 1920s there was one car for every five people. Explaining why her family had chosen to buy a car before installing running water, one rural woman explained to an inquiring sociologist, "You can't go to town in a bathtub."

Mass circulation of magazines and of broadcasts also helped to shape national patterns of consumption, and national advertising became a big business. Advertisers leaned heavily on the latest findings of psychologists in their efforts to influence purchasing behavior; advertisements stressed that the purchase of particular objects would solve consumers' insecurities and contribute to their personal happiness. Metaphors of consumption as the route to psychological security would persist throughout the twentieth century.

The Great Depression

The stock-market crash of October 1929 brought a startling halt to the prosperity that had characterized the 1920s. President Herbert Hoover moved more aggressively than had any president before him to use federal power to address the economic crisis. But it was not enough for national boards and committees to call upon businesses for voluntary actions. By 1932 85,000 businesses had failed, and many others had cut back their operations; hundreds of thousands of people (one out of four by 1933) had lost their jobs. President Franklin D. Roosevelt's New Deal reform policy, initiated in 1933, was an amalgam of support for economic planning and for welfare programs. Claiming that "the only thing we have to fear is fear itself," Roosevelt enthusiastically and aggressively used the power of government action to address economic problems, particularly in the legislation proposed to Congress during the first hundred days of his presidency. His Works Progress Administration funded jobs for the unemployed and was a boon to writers and artists. The WPA's Federal Writers' Project employed some five thousand writers to produce state guidebooks, historians to interview hundreds of former slaves, and librarians and historians to catalogue the holdings of major manuscript libraries and state archives. The WPA's Federal Theater Project commissioned plays, hired directors and actors, and made tickets available at low prices to working people.

The Great Depression was not fully resolved until the demands of production for World War II redefined the economy. But the New Deal transformed the relationship between government and the economy in ways that still endure, giving the federal government extensive regulatory power over the stock market, banks, agriculture, unions, corporations, electrical and subsequently atomic energy, transportation, and welfare (notably social security and related legislation). Much of the welfare legislation had first been sketched out by progressive reformers working in the cities and the states; now the reformers clustered around Eleanor Roosevelt, forming an effective lobbying group for the interests of women, children, and the poor within the Roosevelt administration. Notable reformers included Florence Kelley, head of the National Consumers' League, who had begun her career at Jane Addams's Hull House; Grace Abbott, head of the Children's Bureau of the Department of Labor; Harry Hopkins, a New York social worker; and Molly Dewson, head of the Women's Division of the Democratic National Committee.

Social Change

Economics, psychology, and sex roles intertwined in the 1930s. Divorce rates declined; so did marriage and birth rates, as people postponed setting up or enlarging households. In 1936 Margaret Sanger, a nurse, successfully tested federal bans on birth-control devices by importing a clearly marked package of diaphragms from Japan and challenging customs officials to confiscate it. Afterward, doctors were generally free to dispense birth-control information. A few states continued to make it illegal to sell birth control devices, however, (the ban lasted into the 1960s in Connecticut), and abortion generally remained illegal. An estimated nine thousand women died each year from abortions performed in unsanitary and unprofessional conditions during the 1930s.

Although the proportion of women who worked for wages steadily rose, as did the proportions of married working women and of working mothers, public-opinion polls regularly reported that both men and women felt wives should not work. Many states and the federal government adopted laws forbidding more than one member of a household from holding civil service jobs; invariably the person who lost the job in such cases was the wife. Many school districts forbade the employment of married women as school teachers. New Deal relief programs typically ignored women's needs; the Civilian Conservation Corps, for example, hired only young men. Domestic servants, generally African American and female, were totally excluded from Social Security coverage and from the Fair Labor Standards Act.

World War II

The 1930s was also a time of great international tension as fascism rose in Europe and the democracies seemed powerless—or unwilling—to resist. Americans had generally concluded from the disaster of World War I that wars did not solve international problems and that compromises should be made with Adolph Hitler and Benito Mussolini in the hope of maintaining American neutrality. In the Far East, Japan aggressively sought to establish its own rule in China, Malaya (now part of Malaysia), and Burma. Many on the political Left, including writers such a Ernest Hemingway and John Dos Passos, supported the Loyalists (those opposing Gen. Francisco Franco's revolt) during the Spanish Civil War (1936–1939). Over three thousand Americans formed the Abraham Lincoln Brigade and went to Spain to fight as volunteers, but they were a tiny minority. Germany, seeking new territory, annexed its close neighbors from 1936 to 1939, with little resistance from the rest of Europe. When in 1938 German armies occupied Czechoslovakia, Americans were sympathetic to the Czechs but silent; Americans were also shocked, but not into action, when news came in summer 1939 of a Nazi-Soviet Non-Aggression Pact. When Germany invaded Poland in September 1939, England and France declared war on Germany, but the United States remained neutral.

Germany and its allies, Fascist Italy and Japan, known as the Axis powers, expanded their territorial holdings worldwide. By the end of 1940 German armies had established control of Norway, Denmark, Belgium, Luxembourg, the Netherlands, and most of France. Not until 1941 did a vigorous lend-lease program make ships and goods available to Great Britain and, after Germany broke the Nazi-Soviet pact, to the Soviet Union as well. During 1941 the United States gradually became a major supporter of the Allied powers (which included Great Britain, the Soviet Union, and France); still, the Japanese attack on Pearl Harbor on December

═CONTEXTS═

Proletarian Fiction

Between the two world wars many writers became increasingly critical of American capitalism and materialism. These writers saw American life as a response to political, social, and economic conditions and related these conditions to the theories of Karl Marx (1818–1883). A leader in this movement was John Dos Passos (1896–1970). He examined the problems of materialism inherent in the lives of all Americans—rich and poor, new immigrant and established businessman. American materialism, Dos Passos felt, creates class distinctions and encourages personal greed.

In his later novels Dos Passos depicts the fragmentation of American society, caused by class divisions and by the Great Depression. He structures his narratives around such varied sources as personal reflection, historical fact, and fictional elements, all woven into an eclectic blend. The disjointedness of this blend suggests that the American "rags to riches" myth leads only to alienation and moral decay. In *The Big Money* (1936), the final volume of his *USA* trilogy (collected in 1938), he uses verbal montages of newsreel headlines to simulate the confusing and contradictory information to which we are subjected:

The Big Money

Newsreel LXVIII

WALL STREET STUNNED

This is not Thirtyeight but it's old Ninetyseven
You must put her in Center on time

MARKET SURE TO RECOVER FROM SLUMP

DECLINE IN CONTRACTS

POLICE TURN MACHINE GUNS ON COLORADO MINE STRIKERS
KILL 5 WOUND 40

sympathizers appeared on the scene just as thousands of office workers were pouring out of the buildings at the lunch hour. As they raised their placard high and started an indefinite march from one side to the other, they were jeered and hooted not only by the office workers but also by workmen on a building under construction

NEW METHODS OF SELLING SEEN

RESCUE CREWS TRY TO UPEND ILL-FATED CRAFT
WHILE WAITING FOR PONTOONS

He looked 'round an' said to his black greasy fireman
Jus' shovel in a little more coal
And when we cross that White Oak Mountain
You can watch your Ninety-seven roll

I find your column interesting and need advice. I have saved four thousand dollars which I want to invest for a better income. Do you think I might buy stocks?

John Dos Passos, 1936

7, 1941, came as a shock and a surprise to a largely unprepared nation. A few days later Hitler declared war on the United States.

At the time of the attack, more than half the Japanese Americans in the United States were American citizens. In an atmosphere of post-Pearl Harbor hysteria, fueled by long-standing racism, those of Japanese descent on the West Coast, whether citizens or not, were forced to abandon their property and moved to primitive relocation camps. Not until 1983 did Congress formally acknowledge that they had constituted no threat to American security and promise to pay modest reparations. As the United States entered the 1990s, however, money for the reparation had not been allocated.

Thirteen million men and 350,000 women served in a global war. When the United States entered the war in 1942, it was unprepared to launch an invasion of Europe, so the Soviet Union continued to lead the fight against Germany. The Soviets lost at least twenty million people, some eight percent of their population; in the 1990s these estimates have been raised to forty million. The German advance was stopped at the bitter and costly Battle of Stalingrad in winter 1942–1943. Joseph Stalin would never forgive the United States and England, unprepared as they were, for refusing to launch a large-scale invasion of Europe at that time, which would have forced Germany to fight on two fronts at once. (England and the United States did initiate a successful offensive in North Africa.) By mid-1943 the Allies had conquered Italy and were planning a major invasion of the European continent. However, D-day, the Allied invasion of Normandy, did not take place until June 6, 1944. The scale of fighting in the last months of the war was unprecedented: over a million Allied troops landed in Europe in June alone. News had come from many reliable sources of the systematic murder of millions of Jews by the Nazis, but Allied forces refused to target concentration camps or even railroad lines to the camps. When Allied troops entered the camps, such as Auschwitz and Buchenwald, after Germany's surrender in May 1945, they were shocked and surprised by the evidence of genocide—the Holocaust—they encountered.

Meanwhile, Japan had moved quickly after Pearl Harbor, capturing the Philippines, Burma, and Malaya within three months. Although the fight against Germany was carried on with the Allies, the United States alone fought Japan in the Pacific. The death toll in the Pacific was very high as American forces had to move from island to island, expelling the Japanese. By August 1944 American planes were bombing Tokyo, but Japanese resistance continued, even past the final defeat of Germany in spring 1945.

Whereas much of Europe was devastated or radically realigned by World War II, the United States (and the Soviet Union) emerged as global superpowers. The U.S. government's role in the economy, strengthened during the New Deal years, grew even stronger during the war. The United States became the "arsenal of democracy," building some 300,000 airplanes, 88,000 tanks, and 3,000 ships. Industrial production and corporate profits doubled in the five years after the war ended. Scarce products were rationed; some items that would have competed with war production, such as cars, were not made at all. Tax rates were raised, and a payroll deduction was established for income taxes. Many Americans were drawn

During World War II over six million women worked in traditionally male jobs in factories supporting the war effort, and earned the nickname "Rosie the Riveter." When the war ended, most found themselves replaced by returning servicemen.

into the war industry: a national recruitment campaign explicitly attacked old stereotypes against working women, substituting "Rosie the Riveter" as the model woman in her country's service. Most working women had actually been in the paid labor force before the war; now they moved into skilled jobs at better pay. Both the civilian and military communities remained strictly segregated by race. African Americans held only menial jobs in the navy and the lowest ranking jobs in the army.

Even before the United States had entered the war, it had secretly entered the race to build an atomic bomb. Many of the scientists who worked on the bomb were refugees from Germany and Italy. When Harry S. Truman succeeded to the presidency after Roosevelt's death in spring 1945, the war in Europe was virtually over, but the war in Japan continued. Truman received conflicting advice about whether or not to use the bomb. On the one hand, Japanese resistance in the Pacific had been intense, and there was every reason to expect it would continue were there to be an invasion of Japan. Most Americans thought the United States had sacrificed enough and wanted a quick end to the war, an end without the

Soviet Union's help, so there would be no need for compromise with the Soviets after the war. Some Americans thought the bomb was proper repayment for Pearl Harbor and were less inhibited about dropping it against Asians than they would have been against Europeans. On the other hand, many scientists who appreciated the damage the bomb could do urged that Truman simply demonstrate its capabilities, hoping to frighten the Japanese into surrender.

The bomb dropped on Hiroshima on August 6, 1945, killed 100,000 people. When Japan did not surrender immediately, another was dropped on Nagasaki, killing 60,000. Many thousands more died of radiation poisoning not long after. When J. Robert Oppenheimer, leader of the Manhattan Project, which developed the bomb, saw its first test he thought of a line from the Sanskrit book of verse Bhagavad-Gītā (first or second century A.D.): "I am become death, the destroyer of worlds."

EARLY 20TH-CENTURY POETRY

Unlike American fiction, which had taken on a fresh strength and national identity, American poetry in the early twentieth century was weak and imitative, offering few models for a young poet who wished, in Ezra Pound's words, to "make it new." Walt Whitman's death in 1892 had marked the end of an era, and young poets such as Pound and T. S. Eliot felt compelled to look abroad for inspiration. In a lecture given in Dublin in 1936, Eliot, at the height of his international fame, recollected that in his formative years even the contemporary English poets had little to offer him, while "there were no American poets at all."

The years between Eliot's birth in 1888 and Hart Crane's in 1899 were probably the most important in the history of American poetry. Modernism, a movement marked by a need to impose internal order within a chaotic world, began at this time. Crane in his youth had access to a native American tradition that had not existed for Pound, Eliot, Wallace Stevens, or William Carlos Williams. Emily Dickinson's poetry had been discovered, and a revival of Herman Melville's work was under way: the canon of twentieth-century American literature was taking shape. More importantly, Crane found himself heir to a new poetic, formed in large part by those American poets born in the 1880s. Writing to his friend and fellow poet Allen Tate, Crane spoke of his immediate predecessors—especially Pound and Eliot—as if they were already modern masters. Assuming the mantle of Whitman, Crane made a visionary pilgrimage through America's geographical and emotional space. His epic poem *The Bridge* (1930) celebrates the Brooklyn Bridge as both an architectural achievement and a symbol of American modernity.

By convention the major American poets of this time are divided into those who, like Pound and Eliot, chose expatriation and played a crucial role in creating an "international modernism," and those who stayed in America and sought a "native American modernism." This distinction holds a rough truth but needs many qualifications. Pound and Eliot, and Henry James before them, always considered themselves American writers who had chosen expatriation in order to gain

Marcel Duchamp's cubist painting
Nude Descending a Staircase *(1912)*
shocked visitors at the New York
Armory Show in 1913. Modernist
writers of the period were also
breaking conventions.

perspective on their native land. The first section of Pound's essay *Patria Mia* (1950, written in 1912) opens with "America, my country." From his early essays on American literature and society through the autobiographical writing of *Indiscretions* (1920) to the American history cantos of the 1930s, Pound remained a man of only one country.

Eliot's "Americanness" is less obvious but no less profound, as Pound argues in a 1920 exchange with William Carlos Williams. Williams felt that the "academic" nature of Eliot's early poetry threatened to stifle a more spontaneous regional American form and typically compensated for his sense of isolation and belatedness by casting Eliot in the role of cultural traitor. Pound shrewdly turned the tables by calling Williams a newly arrived outsider objective enough to survive the American experience; Pound and Eliot, by contrast, were deeply infected with the American virus by way of their Puritan inheritances. In this exchange Williams becomes the foreign bystander, Pound and Eliot the ingrained natives.

Whereas Pound remained to the end a rambunctious American abroad, Eliot assimilated British culture until he became an Englishman superficially, even choosing British citizenship in 1927. But Eliot viewed himself as a foreigner abroad. He believed that no one could properly appreciate him without understanding those deep attachments to the American landscape and to the American past that are the imaginative sources of much of his best work, especially the poems of *Four Quartets* (1935–1942). Eliot is buried in the village of East Coker, in western England, the home of his ancestors before they pioneered in the New World in the seventeenth century. Inscribed around the memorial tablet in the village church are the mottoes that frame Eliot's poem *East Coker* (1940), part of *Four Quartets:* "In my beginning is my end" and "In my end is my beginning."

Conversely, the modernist poets who remained in the States were much more international in their outlooks and styles than has been claimed. The poetry of Robert Frost, who has been called the quintessential poet "in the American grain," was first recognized (by Ezra Pound) during his 1913 to 1915 stay in England; his friendship with the British poet Edward Thomas, formed then, was probably the most decisive event in Frost's poetic life. The apparent simplicity of Frost's poems is deceptive: the poems reveal an enigmatic art in which the seemingly benign pastoral surface conceals dark and ironic possibilities. His landscapes are landscapes of the inner self, and he belongs not to a region but to the larger world of the great tragic realists.

Wallace Stevens never traveled abroad but in college learned of the modern French poets and later kept in touch with international developments in the art world. A businessman and a poet, Stevens knew poetry, like life, to be a necessary and unending oscillation between the worlds of fact and of the imagination. His is a philosophical poetry that uses concrete images from American life in fleshing out difficult abstractions. The depiction of Stevens as a mannered creator of poems about poetry ignores the range of his subjects and of his styles. Stevens was not an aesthete unattached to society but a poet of everyday American reality, a reality always transformed by a cosmopolitan imagination.

Even William Carlos Williams, the most relentlessly "local" of all the early modernists, felt that he needed the stimulus of European experimental writing to keep his style fresh and responsive. Williams sat in his third-floor study in Rutherford, New Jersey, contemplating the local scene but seeing it through the eyes of Paris; Ezra Pound looked out at the Italian landscape from his apartment in Rapallo but wrote his cantos on American history. These are the complementary images of modern American poetry. The common aim of the modern poets was to be American without being provincial, to celebrate the local without falling into the narrowness of local color.

The contrasts and similarities between Pound/Eliot and Stevens/Williams/Frost form a useful paradigm under which other poets can be considered. Marianne Moore witnessed the modernism movement from its beginnings to its close, and her reviews provide the most balanced assessment available of her great contemporaries. Her neat poetic world is governed by an aesthetic that combines Pound's emphasis on the concrete image with Williams's stress on the details of ordinary life. A poet's poet because of her attention to technique, Moore resembles other modernist poets while remaining uniquely herself.

Allen Tate was the most prominent member of the Fugitives, a group of southern poets and critics that included Robert Penn Warren and John Crowe Ransom. During the 1920s and 1930s they celebrated the values of a vanishing agricultural South. Their emphasis on authority and tradition, derived from T. S. Eliot, was grounded in the tragic course of southern history. Tate's "Ode to the Confederate Dead" (1928) shows that the techniques of international modernism were easily adaptable to regional values and voices.

In some ways the Harlem Renaissance of the 1920s fits the broad pattern of regionalism. The writers who gathered in New York City's Harlem district celebrated African-American culture, including its myths, language, and sense of community. Along with such fiction writers as Zora Neale Hurston, the poets—Countee Cullen, James Weldon Johnson, and Langston Hughes among them—frankly addressed racial issues and incorporated characters from contemporary life into their poetry. Hughes's poems transcribe blues songs, jazz rhythms, and vernacular speech, creating a mythology of twentieth-century African-American life that transcends the merely local. Like other American poets of his time whose work has endured, Hughes reminds us that the more rooted and particular an artist is, the better his or her chance of achieving an enduring and universal audience.

A common aim of early twentieth-century poets was the creation of a long poem under the stylistic conditions of modernist poetry, conditions best defined by a brief rehearsal of the imagist movement. "Imagism" is a term invented by Ezra Pound to publicize his own poetry and that of some friends, including Hilda Doolittle. When she submitted a group of her finely chiseled poems to *Poetry* magazine, Pound insisted that she sign them "H. D., *Imagiste*." In a series of his own in *Poetry* (1912–1913), Pound sought to give the movement a theoretical underpinning. Imagism aimed to treat subjects directly, to use only words that contribute to a poem's presentation, and to compose with the rhythm of a musical phrase, not with that of a metronome. The rules laid out in these essays had a profound impact on the course of modern American literature. For example, the crisp, clean style of Ernest Hemingway reflects that author's deep debt to Pound.

As a movement imagism was short-lived, part of the politics of literature. The term is still used to represent the tendencies in early modern American poetry toward a conversational style and sharp, concrete, visual presentation. The goal was to scrub the palette clean of poetic diction and begin again with the primary colors of observed reality and overheard speech. That aim was well suited to the short poem, such as Pound's exemplary imagist poem "In a Station of the Metro" (1913).

How could such an aesthetic, with its emphasis on the concise and on simultaneity of effect, be accommodated in the long poem? As early as 1914 Pound was asking this question because the writing of a long poem traditionally is the validation of a poet's art. The history of modern American poetry is in a way a history of the search for a long form that would preserve the effects the modernist poets had achieved in their early, short poems. Pound's *Hugh Selwyn Mauberley* (1920), Eliot's *The Waste Land* (1922), Stevens's *The Comedian as the Letter C* (1923), and Williams's *Spring and All* (1923) were early attempts to solve this problem; Hart Crane's *The Bridge,* Eliot's *Four Quartets,* Stevens's long poems of the 1930s and 1940s, and Williams's *Paterson* (1946–1963) were later attempts. The most heroic example is Pound's *The Cantos* (1917–1959), for over fifty years the focus of his creative life and unfinished at his death.

The American modernist poet had to discover sources of order other than those

=CONTEXTS=

The Harlem Renaissance

An increased sociopolitical consciousness among African Americans in urban centers after World War I gave rise to a flowering of African-American literature and art. This movement, centered primarily in the Harlem area of New York City, has been called the Harlem Renaissance. Countee Cullen (1903–1946) was a central poet of the Harlem Renaissance. His poetry typically deals with the problems of African-American experience in the United States, the struggle to fuse latent African roots with the practical problems of racism in America. Cullen sought to validate the dignity and secure the basic human rights of African Americans. In "Heritage," Cullen attempts to regain his sense of his ancestral roots.

Heritage

What is Africa to me:
Copper sun or scarlet sea,
Jungle star or jungle track,
Strong bronzed men, or regal black
Women from whose loins I sprang
When the birds of Eden sang?
One three centuries removed
From the scenes his fathers loved,
Spicy grove, cinnamon tree,
What is Africa to me?

* * *

So I lie, who find no peace
Night or day, no slight release
From the unremmittant beat
Made by cruel padded feet
Walking through my body's street.
Up and down they go, and back,
Treading out a jungle track.

* * *

All day long and all night through,
One thing only must I do:
Quench my pride and cool my blood,
Lest I perish in the flood. . . .
Not yet has my heart or head
In the least way realized
They and I are civilized.

Countee Cullen, 1925

available to his or her predecessors. The traditional frames of plot and drama could not contain the conflicting energies of contemporary experience. The poet felt compelled to express through form and language the discontinuities and fragmentation of the world outside the poem. The result was a variety of poetic strategies, ranging from Eliot's orchestration of literary allusions and historical references in *The Waste Land* to Williams's interweaving of poetry and historical prose in *Paterson*. In some ways *Paterson* is the culmination of the modernist ambition to combine in a single work high and low culture, history and current events, ordinary speech and the "distinguished" language of poetry.

Robert Frost
(1874–1963)

Robert Frost's first book was not published until he was nearly forty, yet by the time of his death in 1963, he was America's best-known poet. Millions of people had watched the windswept New England sage recite a poem at John F. Kennedy's televised presidential inauguration in 1961. The public image Frost created for himself was insistently rural, regional, and American. But he was born in San Francisco, grew up in a California factory town, and first gained literary recognition in England. The kindly philosopher image was somewhat a mask. Letters, biographies, and critical studies published after Frost's death reveal cruelty, tragedy, and despair. Fear and uncertainty are major themes of his work. In the essay "The Figure a Poem Makes" (1939), he defines poetry as "a momentary stay against confusion." Writing in forms based on iambic lines and colloquial speech patterns, he positioned himself against both nothingness and the free verse experiments of modernists such as Ezra Pound and T. S. Eliot.

Robert Lee Frost was born in 1874 to William Prescott Frost, Jr., of New Hampshire and Isabelle Moodie of Scotland. William, a journalist, was a heavy drinker, sometimes brutal and impetuous. Although a northerner, he had tried to enlist in the Confederate army while he was an adolescent, and named his son after General Robert E. Lee. When William died at age thirty-four, Isabelle followed his instructions to bury him in Lowell, Massachusetts. She stayed east and eventually opened a private school. Her son at first resisted school, and Isabelle indulged his lack of discipline. In high school he pursued classics and romantic poetry, interests his mother had sparked by reading him heroic tales. He studied hard and graduated as co-valedictorian and class poet. The other valedictorian was his future wife, Elinor White. Frost entered Dartmouth College but quickly dropped out. Despite his hounding White to quit college and marry him, she insisted on finishing her degree. Frost went so far as to expose himself to the dangers of Virginia's Dismal Swamp to win her over. They were finally married in 1895.

Frost attended Harvard University from 1897 to 1899, a period he later considered a turning point. There he was stimulated by the philosophy lectures of George Santayana and by the work of psychologist/philosopher William James and could measure himself against current cultural authorities. Ill health forced him to drop out after eighteen months; by this time the Frosts had two children. The oldest died in 1900, and Frost's mother, too, died that year. To help the couple, Frost's grandfather bought a farm for them to live on in Derry, New Hampshire. When his grandfather died in 1901, Frost received the farm and an annuity but had never acknowledged his grandfather's generosity. By 1907 the Frosts had five children. The annuity allowed Frost to write, though he had little other income. Guilty for placing his art above his family and still lacking an audience, Frost made the years in Derry among his most productive in both farming and writing.

As did other poets of the American literary renaissance in the 1910s, Frost left the unreceptive United States for England; he arrived in London with his family in September 1912. A month later he found a publisher for his first poetry collection, *A Boy's Will* (1913). In May Ezra Pound published a review of it in *Poetry,* the first important American notice of Frost's work. Frost selected and arranged the poems—generally love lyrics for Elinor—to trace a boy's development from self-centered idealism to maturity. Some of the early poems are awkwardly poetic, but others, such as "Mowing," show that even before reaching London's responsive literary scene Frost had mastered the crafting of colloquial language. His second book, *North of Boston,* was published in 1914. Pound enthusiastically reviewed it for *Poetry,* but some readers had trouble understanding Frost's technique and mistook his lines for free verse. A poem commonly considered his finest, "After Apple-Picking," is part of this collection, as are "The Wood-Pile" and "Home Burial." Frost insisted that the latter poem, written around 1912, was not autobiographical, but Elinor's reaction to their son's death had been similar to the mother's reaction in the poem.

The Frosts returned to the United States in 1915 after the outbreak of World War I. Henry Holt had already published an American edition of *North of Boston* and, within months, also issued *A Boy's Will.* Over the next four years Frost was named Phi Beta Kappa poet at Tufts and Harvard Universities, was elected to the National Institute of Arts and Letters and hired to teach at Amherst College, and received his first of forty-four honorary degrees. He began to create the farmer-moralist disguise for his increasingly attentive public. Holt rushed his third collection, *Mountain Interval,* into print in 1916. A dozen of the poems dated from the Derry years; Frost considered "An Old Man's Winter Night" the best of these.

Even at the height of his career Frost did not make a living from the sale of his books. In 1920 he began what he called "barding around"—serving as poet in residence at colleges and universities. He provided the first modern example of this role, which became common by the 1960s. For six years Frost moved back and forth between Amherst and the University of Michigan, then spent twelve years at Amherst, four at Harvard, and six at Dartmouth. In the 1920s he began a summer tradition of lecturing at the Bread Loaf School of English and Writers' Conference in Vermont. He returned to Amherst in 1949 with a life appointment.

New Hampshire (1923) won Frost the first of four Pulitzer Prizes. The collection includes "Dust of Snow," "Nothing Gold Can Stay," and "Stopping by Woods on a Snowy Evening" (which he rightly saw as his best chance to be remembered). That "Stopping by Woods" is repeatedly discussed stems from the ambiguity of the speaker's choice between safety and the unknown—a theme that has preoccupied many American writers—and from the hypnotic sounds that undermine the speaker's apparently choosing his human duties over the lure of death. *New Hampshire* also includes conservative social comments in verse. Somewhere between these comments and the lyrics is Frost's philosophical self-defense in "For Once, Then, Something."

Frost continued to publish poems of social and political comment, to the dismay of critics who looked to him for lyric perfection and universal themes. One such poem is

Robert Frost, age 86, reciting his poem "The Gift Outright" at the inauguration of President John F. Kennedy in January 1961.

"The Bear," from his 1928 collection *West-Running Brook*. The book poses disturbing uncertainties about man's prowess and importance. In "Spring Pools," the poet cannot identify the power that must destroy to create fleeting beauty, a power at the heart of nature's cycles. "Acquainted With the Night," for Frost uncharacteristically surreal, shows comfortless isolation in the city.

Frost won a second Pulitzer Prize for his 1930 edition of *Collected Poems,* but the decade that would most grimly dramatize his vision had begun. One daughter died of complications after childbirth in 1934; another suffered an emotional breakdown. Elinor died four years later; during her last days she refused to let her husband enter her room. In 1940 their second son committed suicide. Meanwhile, Frost lost the near-unanimous praise his poetry had received since his return from England. The Great Depression was underway, and war was brewing in Europe as Adolph Hitler and Benito Mussolini amassed power. Although *A Further Range* (1935) garnered Frost's third Pulitzer Prize, influential critics regarded some of its poems as insensitive to victims of the Depression and lacking in commitment against fascism.

A Further Range includes some of Frost's most enduring poems, "Desert Places," "Design," and "Provide, Provide." The generalized background to these poems, what Frost (in a 1935 letter to the *Amherst Student*) called "hugeness and confusion shading away . . . into black and utter chaos," may have been his way of translating modern upheaval into poetic material he could skillfully control. An early version of the sonnet "Design" was written in 1912 to defend the philosopher Henri Bergson against charges of atheism. The finished poem, first published in 1922, explores the ambiguities of whiteness—a theme Melville had made centrally American in *Moby-Dick* (1851). "Design" offers two equally terrifying possibilities: that events are ruled by divine plan, in which case man is powerless, or that they occur by mindless chance.

Frost's fourth Pulitzer Prize was awarded for *A Witness Tree,* published in 1942. He dedicated the volume to Kathleen Morrison, the wife of a Harvard professor. Following Frost's tragedies of the 1930s, his grown children accusing him of having sacrificed them for art, he sank into a depression deep enough to hamper his tending to daily tasks. Morrison helped him reorganize his life. *A Witness Tree* includes "The Gift Outright," the poem he later recited at President Kennedy's inauguration, as well as "The Silken Tent," "Come In," and "Never Again Would Birds' Song Be the Same." "The Silken Tent" is a love sonnet that portrays a woman, drawing attention to the intricacies of metaphor rather than to the woman herself. In contrast, "The Subverted Flower," another poem in the collection, has seemed to some readers to be unexpectedly revealing of Frost's relationship with his wife. First drafted, Frost claimed, before 1913, the poem is a nightmarish sexual encounter between a boy and a girl. The boy coerces, as Frost did when Elinor was in college; the girl recoils. Biographers have speculated that Frost withheld the poem from publication until after Elinor's death to save her from embarrassment.

At age seventy Frost took up, in different forms, a religious question he had explored before, most notably in "After Apple Picking": can a man's best efforts ever satisfy God? *A Masque of Reason* (1945) and *A Masque of Mercy* (1947) are comic-serious dramatic narratives; the former concerns Job's suffering, and the latter, Jonah's rebellion. The question became a plea for acceptability in *A Sermon* (1947), which Frost delivered at a synagogue in Cincinnati. The way to salvation is a theme of his last great poem, "Directive," published in *Steeple Bush* (1947). Frost had been delighted to learn that Christ spoke in parables to conceal salvation from those who do not deserve it. The key word in "Directive," Frost explained, is source. For him the source was art (as reported in 1967 by Theodore Morrison in *Atlantic Monthly*): "You can't be saved unless you understand poetry—or you can't be saved unless you have some poetry in you."

Frost's last years were filled with public honors. For his *Complete Poems* (1949) he received a gold medal from the Limited Editions Club. The U.S. Senate sent him greetings on his seventy-seventh birthday. The state government of Vermont named a mountain after him. The State Department sent him to Brazil and London. He was named Consultant in Poetry to the Library of Congress, took part in Kennedy's presidential inauguration, and received a Congressional Medal of Honor. Just before Frost's death he received the Bollingen Prize. To his distress, he was never awarded a Nobel Prize.

At age eighty-eight, after recovering from a critical bout of pneumonia, his sight and hearing impaired, Frost made an official visit to the Soviet Union. He spent ninety minutes talking with Premier Nikita Khrushchev, but Frost's press report of this conversation confused and angered many Americans. He quoted Khrushchev as saying modern liberals were "too liberal to fight." Frost, obsessed with satirizing liberals, thought the remark was a "good crack." But in the cold-war atmosphere of the early 1960s, it was interpreted to mean that the premier believed Kennedy's Democratic administration would not resist Soviet expansion. Frost did not hear from the president again and died in 1963, four months after his trip.

A public that had worshipped the white-haired country sage was unprepared for the unpleasant biographical details that were published by Lawrance Thompson between 1966 and 1976. Yet, some of his poems reveal the compulsions, cynicism, and anguish that his public image perhaps masked. Frost's later work signals that he may have convinced even himself that his job was to make homespun pronouncements. He could not have been fully convinced: in his last poetry collection, *In the Clearing* (1962), Frost returned to the uncertainties of the dark woods.

Suggested Readings: *Dedication/The Gift Outright/The Inaugural Address*, 1961. *Selected Prose of Robert Frost*, 1966. *Robert Frost on Writing*, ed. E. Barry, 1972. *Robert Frost: Poetry and Prose*, ed. E. C. Lathem and L. Thompson, 1972. F. Lentricchia, *Robert Frost: Modern Poetics and the Landscapes of Self*, 1975. R. Poirier, *Robert Frost: The Work of Knowing*, 1977. L. W. Wagner, ed., *Robert Frost: The Critical Reception*, 1977. P. L. Gerber, *Robert Frost*, 1982. L. Thompson, *Robert Frost: A Biography*, abridged by E. C. Lathem, 1982. D. J. Hall, *Robert Frost: Contours of Belief*, 1984.

Text Used: *The Poetry of Robert Frost*, ed. E. C. Lathem, 1969.

THE PASTURE

I'm going out to clean the pasture spring;
I'll only stop to rake the leaves away
(And wait to watch the water clear, I may):
I shan't be gone long.—You come too.

I'm going out to fetch the little calf
That's standing by the mother. It's so young
It totters when she licks it with her tongue.
I shan't be gone long.—You come too.

1913

MOWING

There was never a sound beside the wood but one,
And that was my long scythe whispering to the ground.
What was it it whispered? I knew not well myself;
Perhaps it was something about the heat of the sun,
Something, perhaps, about the lack of sound—
And that was why it whispered and did not speak.
It was no dream of the gift of idle hours,
Or easy gold at the hand of fay[1] or elf:
Anything more than the truth would have seemed too weak
To the earnest love that laid the swale[2] in rows,   10
Not without feeble-pointed spikes of flowers
(Pale orchises), and scared a bright green snake.
The fact is the sweetest dream that labor knows.
My long scythe whispered and left the hay to make.

1913

---

[1] A fairy.   [2] A low-lying marshland.

HOME BURIAL

He saw her from the bottom of the stairs
Before she saw him. She was starting down,
Looking back over her shoulder at some fear.
She took a doubtful step and then undid it
To raise herself and look again. He spoke
Advancing toward her: "What is it you see
From up there always?—for I want to know."
She turned and sank upon her skirts at that,
And her face changed from terrified to dull.
He said to gain time: "What is it you see?"   10
Mounting until she cowered under him.
"I will find out now—you must tell me, dear."
She, in her place, refused him any help,
With the least stiffening of her neck and silence.
She let him look, sure that he wouldn't see,
Blind creature; and awhile he didn't see.
But at last he murmured, "Oh," and again, "Oh."

"What is it—what?" she said.

                        "Just that I see."

"You don't," she challenged. "Tell me what it is."

"The wonder is I didn't see at once.   20
I never noticed it from here before.
I must be wonted[1] to it—that's the reason.
The little graveyard where my people are!
So small the window frames the whole of it.
Not so much larger than a bedroom, is it?
There are three stones of slate and one of marble,
Broad-shouldered little slabs there in the sunlight
On the sidehill. We haven't to mind *those*.
But I understand: it is not the stones,
But the child's mound—"

                        "Don't, don't, don't,
    don't," she cried.   30

She withdrew, shrinking from beneath his arm
That rested on the banister, and slid downstairs;
And turned on him with such a daunting look,
He said twice over before he knew himself:
"Can't a man speak of his own child he's lost?"

"Not you!—Oh, where's my hat? Oh, I don't need it!
I must get out of here. I must get air.—
I don't know rightly whether any man can."

---

[1] Accustomed.

"Amy! Don't go to someone else this time.
Listen to me. I won't come down the stairs."   40
He sat and fixed his chin between his fists.
"There's something I should like to ask you, dear."

"You don't know how to ask it."

                              "Help me, then."

Her fingers moved the latch for all reply.

"My words are nearly always an offense.
I don't know how to speak of anything
So as to please you. But I might be taught,
I should suppose. I can't say I see how.
A man must partly give up being a man
With womenfolk. We could have some arrangement   50
By which I'd bind myself to keep hands off
Anything special you're a-mind to name.
Though I don't like such things 'twixt those that love.
Two that don't love can't live together without them
But two that do can't live together with them."
She moved the latch a little. "Don't—don't go.
Don't carry it to someone else this time.
Tell me about it if it's something human.
Let me into your grief. I'm not so much
Unlike other folks as your standing there   60
Apart would make me out. Give me my chance.
I do think, though, you overdo it a little.
What was it brought you up to think it the thing
To take your mother-loss of a first child
So inconsolably—in the face of love.
You'd think his memory might be satisfied—"

"There you go sneering now!"
                              "I'm not, I'm not!
You make me angry. I'll come down to you.
God, what a woman! And it's come to this,
A man can't speak of his own child that's dead."   70

"You can't because you don't know how to speak.
If you had any feelings, you that dug
With your own hand—how could you?—his little grave;
I saw you from that very window there,
Making the gravel leap and leap in air,
Leap up, like that, like that, and land so lightly
And roll back down the mound beside the hole.
I thought, Who is that man? I didn't know you.
And I crept down the stairs and up the stairs
To look again, and still your spade kept lifting.   80
Then you came in. I heard your rumbling voice

Out in the kitchen, and I don't know why,
But I went near to see with my own eyes.
You could sit there with the stains on your shoes
Of the fresh earth from your own baby's grave
And talk about your everyday concerns.
You had stood the spade up against the wall
Outside there in the entry, for I saw it."

"I shall laugh the worst laugh I ever laughed.
I'm cursed. God, if I don't believe I'm cursed."   90

"I can repeat the very words you were saying:
'Three foggy mornings and one rainy day
Will rot the best birch fence a man can build.'
Think of it, talk like that at such a time!
What had how long it takes a birch to rot
To do with what was in the darkened parlor?
You *couldn't* care! The nearest friends can go
With anyone to death, comes so far short
They might as well not try to go at all.
No, from the time when one is sick to death,   100
One is alone, and he dies more alone.
Friends make pretense of following to the grave,
But before one is in it, their minds are turned
And making the best of their way back to life
And living people, and things they understand.
But the world's evil. I won't have grief so
If I can change it. Oh, I won't, I won't!"

"There, you have said it all and you feel better.
You won't go now. You're crying. Close the door.
The heart's gone out of it: why keep it up?   110
Amy! There's someone coming down the road!"

"*You*—oh, you think the talk is all. I must go—
Somewhere out of this house. How can I make you—"

"If—you—do!" She was opening the door wider.
"Where do you mean to go? First tell me that.
I'll follow and bring you back by force. I *will!*—"

                                                1912?, 1914

AFTER APPLE-PICKING

My long two-pointed ladder's sticking through a tree
Toward heaven still,
And there's a barrel that I didn't fill
Beside it, and there may be two or three

Apples I didn't pick upon some bough.
But I am done with apple-picking now.
Essence of winter sleep is on the night,
The scent of apples: I am drowsing off.
I cannot rub the strangeness from my sight
I got from looking through a pane of glass   10
I skimmed this morning from the drinking trough
And held against the world of hoary grass.
It melted, and I let it fall and break.
But I was well
Upon my way to sleep before it fell,
And I could tell
What form my dreaming was about to take.
Magnified apples appear and disappear,
Stem end and blossom end,
And every fleck of russet showing clear.   20
My instep arch not only keeps the ache,
It keeps the pressure of a ladder-round.
I feel the ladder sway as the boughs bend.
And I keep hearing from the cellar bin
The rumbling sound
Of load on load of apples coming in.
For I have had too much
Of apple-picking: I am overtired
Of the great harvest I myself desired.
There were ten thousand thousand fruit to touch,   30
Cherish in hand, lift down, and not let fall.
For all
That struck the earth,
No matter if not bruised or spiked with stubble,
Went surely to the cider-apple heap
As of no worth.
One can see what will trouble
This sleep of mine, whatever sleep it is.
Were he not gone,
The woodchuck could say whether it's like his   40
Long sleep, as I describe its coming on,
Or just some human sleep.

1914

THE WOOD-PILE

Out walking in the frozen swamp one gray day,
I paused and said, "I will turn back from here.
No, I will go on farther—and we shall see."
The hard snow held me, save where now and then
One foot went through. The view was all in lines
Straight up and down of tall slim trees

Too much alike to mark or name a place by
So as to say for certain I was here
Or somewhere else: I was just far from home.
A small bird flew before me. He was careful   10
To put a tree between us when he lighted,
And say no word to tell me who he was
Who was so foolish as to think what *he* thought.
He thought that I was after him for a feather—
The white one in his tail; like one who takes
Everything said as personal to himself.
One flight out sideways would have undeceived him.
And then there was a pile of wood for which
I forgot him and let his little fear
Carry him off the way I might have gone,   20
Without so much as wishing him good-night.
He went behind it to make his last stand.
It was a cord of maple, cut and split
And piled—and measured, four by four by eight.
And not another like it could I see.
No runner tracks in this year's snow looped near it.
And it was older sure than this year's cutting,
Or even last year's or the year's before.
The wood was gray and the bark warping off it
And the pile somewhat sunken. Clematis[1]   30
Had wound strings round and round it like a bundle.
What held it, though, on one side was a tree
Still growing, and on one a stake and prop,
These latter about to fall. I thought that only
Someone who lived in turning to fresh tasks
Could so forget his handiwork on which
He spent himself, the labor of his ax,
And leave it there far from a useful fireplace
To warm the frozen swamp as best it could
With the slow smokeless burning of decay.   40

1914

THE OVEN BIRD*

There is a singer everyone has heard,
Loud, a mid-summer and a mid-wood bird,
Who makes the solid tree trunks sound again.
He says that leaves are old and that for flowers
Mid-summer is to spring as one to ten.
He says the early petal-fall is past,
When pear and cherry bloom went down in showers

---

[1] A flowering vine of the buttercup family.
* The American warbler, which builds a dome-shaped nest on the ground.

On sunny days a moment overcast;
And comes that other fall we name the fall.
He says the highway dust is over all.   10
The bird would cease and be as other birds
But that he knows in singing not to sing.
The question that he frames in all but words
Is what to make of a diminished thing.

1916

BIRCHES

When I see birches bend to left and right
Across the lines of straighter darker trees,
I like to think some boy's been swinging them.
But swinging doesn't bend them down to stay
As ice storms do. Often you must have seen them
Loaded with ice a sunny winter morning
After a rain. They click upon themselves
As the breeze rises, and turn many-colored
As the stir cracks and crazes their enamel.
Soon the sun's warmth makes them shed crystal shells   10
Shattering and avalanching on the snow crust—
Such heaps of broken glass to sweep away
You'd think the inner dome of heaven had fallen.
They are dragged to the withered bracken by the load,
And they seem not to break; though once they are bowed
So low for long, they never right themselves:
You may see their trunks arching in the woods
Years afterwards, trailing their leaves on the ground
Like girls on hands and knees that throw their hair
Before them over their heads to dry in the sun.   20
But I was going to say when Truth broke in
With all her matter of fact about the ice storm,
I should prefer to have some boy bend them
As he went out and in to fetch the cows—
Some boy too far from town to learn baseball,
Whose only play was what he found himself,
Summer or winter, and could play alone.
One by one he subdued his father's trees
By riding them down over and over again
Until he took the stiffness out of them,   30
And not one but hung limp, not one was left
For him to conquer. He learned all there was
To learn about not launching out too soon
And so not carrying the tree away
Clear to the ground. He always kept his poise
To the top branches, climbing carefully

With the same pains you use to fill a cup
Up to the brim, and even above the brim.
Then he flung outward, feet first, with a swish,
Kicking his way down through the air to the ground.   40
So was I once myself a swinger of birches.
And so I dream of going back to be.
It's when I'm weary of considerations,
And life is too much like a pathless wood
Where your face burns and tickles with the cobwebs
Broken across it, and one eye is weeping
From a twig's having lashed across it open.
I'd like to get away from earth awhile
And then come back to it and begin over.
May no fate willfully misunderstand me   50
And half grant what I wish and snatch me away
Not to return. Earth's the right place for love:
I don't know where it's likely to go better.
I'd like to go by climbing a birch tree,
And climb black branches up a snow-white trunk
Toward heaven, till the tree could bear no more,
But dipped its top and set me down again.
That would be good both going and coming back.
One could do worse than be a swinger of birches.

1914?, 1916

"OUT, OUT—"*

The buzz saw snarled and rattled in the yard
And made dust and dropped stove-length sticks of wood,
Sweet-scented stuff when the breeze drew across it.
And from there those that lifted eyes could count
Five mountain ranges one behind the other
Under the sunset far into Vermont.
And the saw snarled and rattled, snarled and rattled,
As it ran light, or had to bear a load.
And nothing happened: day was all but done.
Call it a day, I wish they might have said   10
To please the boy by giving him the half hour
That a boy counts so much when saved from work.
His sister stood beside them in her apron
To tell them "Supper." At the word, the saw,
As if to prove saws knew what supper meant,
Leaped out at the boy's hand, or seemed to leap—
He must have given the hand. However it was,
Neither refused the meeting. But the hand!
The boy's first outcry was a rueful laugh,

* "Out, out brief candle! / Life's but a walking shadow," from Shakespeare's *Macbeth* (V.v.23–24).

As he swung toward them holding up the hand,   20
Half in appeal, but half as if to keep
The life from spilling. Then the boy saw all—
Since he was old enough to know, big boy
Doing a man's work, though a child at heart—
He saw all spoiled. "Don't let him cut my hand off—
The doctor, when he comes. Don't let him, sister!"
So. But the hand was gone already.
The doctor put him in the dark of ether.
He lay and puffed his lips out with his breath.
And then—the watcher at his pulse took fright.   30
No one believed. They listened at his heart.
Little—less—nothing!—and that ended it.
No more to build on there. And they, since they
Were not the one dead, turned to their affairs.

1916

STOPPING BY WOODS ON A SNOWY EVENING

Whose woods these are I think I know.
His house is in the village, though;
He will not see me stopping here
To watch his woods fill up with snow.

My little horse must think it queer
To stop without a farmhouse near
Between the woods and frozen lake
The darkest evening of the year.

He gives his harness bells a shake
To ask if there is some mistake.   10
The only other sound's the sweep
Of easy wind and downy flake.

The woods are lovely, dark, and deep,
But I have promises to keep,
And miles to go before I sleep,
And miles to go before I sleep.

1923

ONCE BY THE PACIFIC

The shattered water made a misty din.
Great waves looked over others coming in,
And thought of doing something to the shore
That water never did to land before.

The clouds were low and hairy in the skies,
Like locks blown forward in the gleam of eyes.
You could not tell, and yet it looked as if
The shore was lucky in being backed by cliff,
The cliff in being backed by continent;
It looked as if a night of dark intent   10
Was coming, and not only a night, an age.
Someone had better be prepared for rage.
There would be more than ocean-water broken
Before God's last *Put out the Light* was spoken.[1]

1928

ACQUAINTED WITH THE NIGHT

I have been one acquainted with the night.
I have walked out in rain—and back in rain.
I have outwalked the furthest city light.

I have looked down the saddest city lane.
I have passed by the watchman on his beat
And dropped my eyes, unwilling to explain.

I have stood still and stopped the sound of feet
When far away an interrupted cry
Came over houses from another street,

But not to call me back or say good-by;   10
And further still at an unearthly height
One luminary clock against the sky

Proclaimed the time was neither wrong nor right.
I have been one acquainted with the night.

1928

DESIGN

I found a dimpled spider, fat and white,
On a white heal-all,[1] holding up a moth
Like a white piece of rigid satin cloth—
Assorted characters of death and blight
Mixed ready to begin the morning right,
Like the ingredients of a witches' broth—
A snow-drop spider, a flower like a froth,
And dead wings carried like a paper kite.

[1] In Genesis 1:3 God created the world, saying " . . . Let there be light."
[1] A medicinal plant whose flowers are generally blue.

What had that flower to do with being white,
The wayside blue and innocent heal-all?   10
What brought the kindred spider to that height,
Then steered the white moth thither in the night?
What but design of darkness to appall?—
If design govern in a thing so small.[2]

1922, 1936

THE SILKEN TENT

She is as in a field a silken tent
At midday when a sunny summer breeze
Has dried the dew and all its ropes relent,
So that in guys[1] it gently sways at ease,
And its supporting central cedar pole,
That is its pinnacle to heavenward
And signifies the sureness of the soul,
Seems to owe naught to any single cord,
But strictly held by none, is loosely bound
By countless silken ties of love and thought   10
To everything on earth the compass round,
And only by one's going slightly taut
In the capriciousness of summer air
Is of the slightest bondage made aware.

1939, 1942

COME IN

As I came to the edge of the woods,
Thrush music—hark!
Now if it was dusk outside,
Inside it was dark.

Too dark in the woods for a bird
By sleight of wing
To better its perch for the night,
Though it still could sing.

The last of the light of the sun
That had died in the west   10
Still lived for one song more
In a thrush's breast.

---

[2] Design, or order, in nature has been cited as proof of God's existence.
[1] Ropes or chains for support.

Far in the pillared dark
Thrush music went—
Almost like a call to come in
To the dark and lament.

But no, I was out for stars:
I would not come in.
I meant not even if asked,
And I hadn't been.   20

1941, 1942

NEVER AGAIN WOULD BIRDS' SONG BE THE SAME

He would declare and could himself believe
That the birds there in all the garden round
From having heard the daylong voice of Eve
Had added to their own an oversound,
Her tone of meaning but without the words.
Admittedly an eloquence so soft
Could only have had an influence on birds
When call or laughter carried it aloft.
Be that as may be, she was in their song.
Moreover her voice upon their voices crossed   10
Had now persisted in the woods so long
That probably it never would be lost.
Never again would birds' song be the same.
And to do that to birds was why she came.

1942

DIRECTIVE

Back out of all this now too much for us,
Back in a time made simple by the loss
Of detail, burned, dissolved, and broken off
Like graveyard marble sculpture in the weather,
There is a house that is no more a house
Upon a farm that is no more a farm
And in a town that is no more a town.
The road there, if you'll let a guide direct you
Who only has at heart your getting lost,
May seem as if it should have been a quarry—   10
Great monolithic knees the former town
Long since gave up pretense of keeping covered.
And there's a story in a book about it:
Besides the wear of iron wagon wheels

The ledges show lines ruled southeast-northwest,
The chisel work of an enormous Glacier
That braced his feet against the Arctic Pole.
You must not mind a certain coolness from him
Still said to haunt this side of Panther Mountain.
Nor need you mind the serial ordeal   20
Of being watched from forty cellar holes
As if by eye pairs out of forty firkins.[1]
As for the woods' excitement over you
That sends light rustle rushes to their leaves,
Charge that to upstart inexperience.
Where were they all not twenty years ago?
They think too much of having shaded out
A few old pecker-fretted[2] apple trees.
Make yourself up a cheering song of how
Someone's road home from work this once was,   30
Who may be just ahead of you on foot
Or creaking with a buggy load of grain.
The height of the adventure is the height
Of country where two village cultures faded
Into each other. Both of them are lost.
And if you're lost enough to find yourself
By now, pull in your ladder road behind you
And put a sign up CLOSED to all but me.
Then make yourself at home. The only field
Now left's no bigger than a harness gall.[3]   40
First there's the children's house of make-believe,
Some shattered dishes underneath a pine,
The playthings in the playhouse of the children.
Weep for what little things could make them glad.
Then for the house that is no more a house,
But only a belilaced cellar hole,
Now slowly closing like a dent in dough.
This was no playhouse but a house in earnest.
Your destination and your destiny's
A brook that was the water of the house,   50
Cold as a spring as yet so near its source,
Too lofty and original to rage.
(We know the valley streams that when aroused
Will leave their tatters hung on barb and thorn.)
I have kept hidden in the instep arch
Of an old cedar at the waterside
A broken drinking goblet like the Grail[4]
Under a spell so the wrong ones can't find it,
So can't get saved, as Saint Mark says they mustn't.[5]

[1] Small wooden barrels.   [2] Marked by woodpecker holes.
[3] A sore on a horse's skin, from the rubbing of the harness.
[4] The cup Jesus used at the Last Supper and the object of medieval quests.
[5] "He that believeth and is baptized shall be saved; but he that believeth not shall be damned," from Mark 16:16.

(I stole the goblet from the children's playhouse.)   60
Here are your waters and your watering place.
Drink and be whole again beyond confusion.

1946, 1947

Wallace Stevens
(1879–1955)

Wallace Stevens, born in 1879 in Reading, Pennsylvania, was the son of a prominent lawyer and a former schoolteacher. Looking back at this typical, prosperous American family, Stevens felt he had inherited his practical side from his father and his imaginative side from his mother. The well-to-do Stevens family was prominent in the Dutch Reform Church, and young Wallace attended Evangelical Lutheran elementary schools and the Reading Boys' High School before entering Harvard University in 1897.

At Harvard, where his more influential professors included Charles Townsend Copeland, Barrett Wendell, and George Santayana, Stevens became an agnostic, a position he firmly maintained until his final deathbed conversion to Roman Catholicism. In fact, much of his later poetry deals with the process of finding through poetry some recompense for the loss of faith. During his Harvard years he also wrote for the *Harvard Advocate*, served on its editorial board, and in 1900 became its president. The March 10, 1900, issue of the *Harvard Advocate*, the first with Stevens in control, included a poem, a short story, and three editorials by Stevens, who apparently had to supplement the magazine by adding his own material.

He left Harvard without a degree in June 1900 and moved to New York City to try his hand at journalism. But the life of a journalist left him lonely and depressed—even then he apparently sensed a need for something more than the reality in which journalists are caught up. At the urging and with the support of his father, he entered New York Law School in 1901. He graduated less than two years later and was admitted to the New York Bar Association in 1904. In the succeeding years, Stevens worked for a number of New York law firms, until finally in 1909 he obtained a job with American Bonding Company of Baltimore. The job gave him the financial security he needed to marry Elsie Viola Kachel, whom he had met about four years earlier on one of his trips to his parents' home in Reading. The wedding took place in September 1909, and the Stevenses lived in New York City for the next seven years.

Perhaps coincidentally, Stevens's poetic aspirations did not surface again until after his father died in 1911. At about this time Stevens became more actively involved with the writers and painters of New York City's Greenwich Village and befriended Marianne Moore and William Carlos Williams. Gradually, as a result of this involvement his interest in oriental literature, the French symbolists, and modern painting intensified. The New York Armory Show of 1913, which introduced the early modern masters to the American public, was for Stevens and many of his contemporaries a watershed experience. It stimulated a lifelong interest in painting and an enthusiasm for the avant-garde in all the arts.

In 1914 Stevens began publishing in earnest, and his career in writing poetry was underway. His early poems reveal the oriental and French influences, a love of color, and, perhaps most important, a celebration of sensual experience as a replacement for an absent God. In those early poems he created stylized symbolic landscapes, responded to the imagists by crystallizing human experience in sharp haiku-like stanzas, and explored the limits of human perception. The intense excitement generated by Stevens's engagement with modernism resulted in some of his best and most anthologized work, including "Sunday Morning," "Peter Quince at the Clavier" (both published in 1915), and "Thirteen Ways of Looking at a Blackbird" (1917). Nevertheless, for financial security Stevens took a job with the Hartford Accident and Indemnity Company in 1916; he eventually was named a vice-president there and until his death remained an insurance lawyer in Hartford.

By the time Stevens's first poetry collection, *Harmonium*, appeared in 1923, Stevens had published nearly one hundred poems in various "little magazines" and anthologies. His interest in language, in word play, and in the imagination's transformation of sensual experience was beginning to take precedence over his interest in images and in sensual experience for its own sake. "Nuances of a Theme by Williams" (about William Carlos Williams, notorious as a spokesman for the senses), "Anecdote of the Jar," and the companion poems "The Snow Man" and "Tea at the Palaz of Hoon," are Stevens's meditations on the barrenness of the natural world, the insufficiency of mere things, and the necessity of both the order-producing intelligence and the transforming imagination. "The Emperor of Ice-Cream" and "The Snow Man" look clearly at the finality of death and at the reality of life in a universe without God, especially when this reality is not transformed by the human imagination.

In 1924 Stevens's daughter, Holly, was born, and he took a self-imposed sabbatical from poetry—perhaps because he felt he had said everything he had to say in *Harmonium*, perhaps to concentrate on his career and his family. After publishing "Sea Surface Full of Clouds" (1924) he all but retired from writing poetry until 1930. In the years before returning to serious poetry, however, Stevens immersed himself in poetic theory; he read the modern French critics on "pure poetry," and reread the canon of literary criticism. This was essential preparation for his later work, with its never-ending quest for the possible, impossible poem, for what in *The Necessary Angel* (1951) he calls the "supreme fiction."

Stevens's next book, *Ideas of Order* (1935), reveals a new sensibility, a new orientation of thought and feeling. This is perhaps most apparent in "The Idea of Order at Key West," in which a woman's voice makes "the sky acutest at its vanishing." When the singing ends the poet can step back and comment on the song, the town, the lights, the sea, the night, and the "blessed rage for order," which may, in the mind of the poet/maker, pull it all together. The conflict between reality and the imagination presented in "The Idea of Order at Key West" is a theme that permeates Stevens's later work. Both "Mozart, 1935" and "Anglais Mort à Florence" are concerned with the poet's struggle to wring some compensation from an unfeeling world, and they are grounded in the conflict between the "hoo-hoo-hoo" of the dreary present "where music fails" and the imaginatively charged, imaginatively colored past.

The Man With the Blue Guitar and Other Poems (1937) marked the beginning of a highly productive period for Stevens, culminating in *Parts of a World* (1942) and *Notes Toward a Supreme Fiction* (1942). His poems from this period deal with "the incessant conjunctions between things as they are and things imagined," as Stevens explains on the dust jacket of *Blue Guitar*. Two poems representative of this period, "A Postcard From the Volcano" (1936) and "Study of Two Pears" (1942), emphasize the meagerness of a world without imagination. Despite the similarities between them, both poems give additional insight, add something to our understanding of the conjunction of imagination and reality. The poems, like each of the stanzas in Stevens's early "Thirteen Ways of Looking at a Blackbird," view reality from a significantly different, uniquely illuminating perspective.

Stevens's aesthetic philosophy is embodied in the poems of the early 1940s, especially

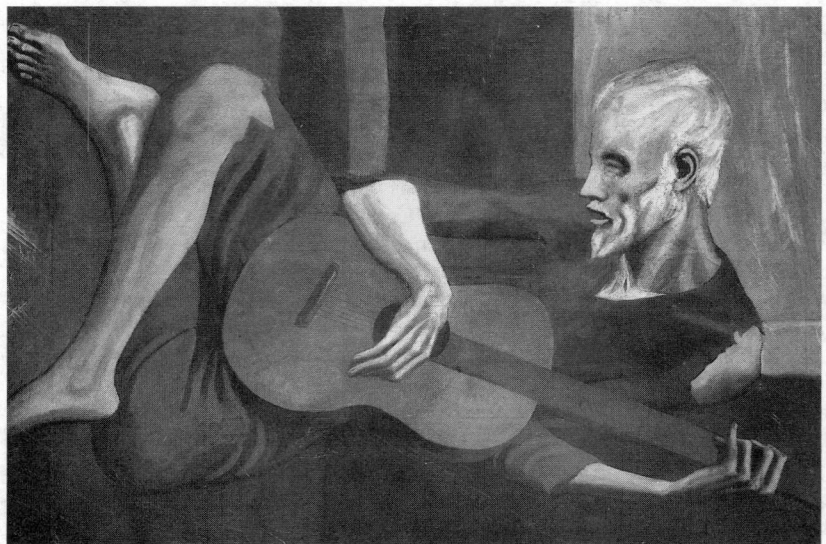

Picasso's early modernist painting The Old Guitarist *(1903) is believed to have inspired Wallace Stevens's poem "The Man With the Blue Guitar."*

"Of Modern Poetry," "Mrs. Alfred Uruguay," and "Asides on an Oboe," and is the reason *Notes Toward a Supreme Fiction* was written (all four published in 1942). The latter long poem, of central importance in the Stevens canon, is actually thirty-one short poems, each composed of seven three-line stanzas. The thirty-one poems are divided into three sets that focus on what Stevens felt to be a necessary if not sufficient condition of the ultimate poem—it must be abstract; it must change; and it must give pleasure. The three sets of poems are parallel in structure so that each poem (canto) is connected to the corresponding poems in the other two sets. Stevens's exploration of aesthetic philosophy, his groping toward the supreme fiction, is present not only in his poetry but also in his critical essays. *The Necessary Angel*, subtitled *Essays in Reality and the Imagination*, contains many passages that help shed light on some of his more difficult later poems. The essay "The Noble Rider and the Sound of Words" (delivered as a lecture in 1941) is especially helpful as preparation for reading his meditative, philosophical poems of the early 1940s, in particular "Mrs. Alfred Uruguay" and *Notes Toward a Supreme Fiction*.

After writing *Notes Toward a Supreme Fiction* when he was sixty-two, an age when so many other poets would be in decline, Stevens continued to write poems, including those in *Transport to Summer* (1947) and in *The Auroras of Autumn* (1950). He also wrote a significant part of a third book, *The Rock*, which he appended to *Collected Poems* (1954). That volume's last ten poems, all written after Stevens's sixty-eighth year, illustrate his continuing poetic strength. In many of these poems (such as "Large Red Man Reading," "This Solitude of Cataracts," and "The River of Rivers in Connecticut") Stevens, like the pre-Socratic philosopher Heraclitus, is concerned with the impossibility of stepping into the same river twice and with the incessant flux of the natural world, treating this flux with characteristic depth, sophistication, and verve. Among these later poems are "To an Old Philosopher in Rome," his moving tribute to the dying Santayana (perhaps the finest poem of Stevens's later period and certainly one of the strongest poems in the Stevens canon), and "The Course of a Particular," a poem in which the "cry of leaves that do not transcend themselves" in the final analysis "concerns no one at all."

Stevens was awarded the Pulitzer Prize for poetry for the 1955 edition of *Collected Poems* and was preparing his acceptance speech when he succumbed to cancer in August 1955. His poetry lives on, and his position as one of the most important poets of the twentieth century has become more firmly established with each succeeding generation. Readers continue to discover "something there" and to respond both to the imaginative force of the early poems that celebrate the beauty inherent in the physical, natural world and to the imaginative force of the later poems that celebrate the mind in the act of creating the supreme fiction, of finding what will suffice.

Suggested Readings: *Harmonium*, 1923, 1937. *Notes Toward a Supreme Fiction*, 1942. *The Collected Poems of Wallace Stevens*, 1954. *Letters of Wallace Stevens*, ed. H. Stevens, 1966. J. N. Riddel, *The Clairvoyant Eye: The Poetry and Poetics of Wallace Stevens*, 1965. R. Sukenick, *Wallace Stevens: Musing the Obscure*, 1967. H. H. Vendler, *On Extended Wings: Wallace Stevens' Longer Poems*, 1969. A. W. Litz, *Introspective Voyager: The Poetic Development of Wallace Stevens*, 1972. H. Bloom, *Wallace Stevens: The Poems of Our Climate*, 1977. F. Doggett, *Stevens' Poetry of Thought*, 1980. M. J. Bates, *Wallace Stevens: A Mythology of Self*, 1985. B. J. Leggett, *Wallace Stevens and Poetic Theory*, 1987.

Text Used: *The Palm at the End of the Mind*, ed. H. Stevens, 1971.

SUNDAY MORNING*

I

Complacencies of the peignoir, and late
Coffee and oranges in a sunny chair,
And the green freedom of a cockatoo
Upon a rug mingle to dissipate
The holy hush of ancient sacrifice.
She dreams a little, and she feels the dark
Encroachment of that old catastrophe,
As a calm darkens among water-lights.
The pungent oranges and bright, green wings
Seem things in some procession of the dead,   10
Winding across wide water, without sound.
The day is like wide water, without sound,
Stilled for the passing of her dreaming feet
Over the seas, to silent Palestine,
Dominion of the blood and sepulchre.[1]

II

Why should she give her bounty to the dead?
What is divinity if it can come
Only in silent shadows and in dreams?
Shall she not find in comforts of the sun,
In pungent fruit and bright, green wings, or else   20
In any balm or beauty of the earth,

---

* First published in a shortened version in *Poetry* in 1915 with the stanzas ordered I, VIII, IV, V, VII. According to Stevens it is "simply an expression of paganism, although, of course, I did not think I was expressing paganism when I wrote it" (*Letters of Wallace Stevens*, 1977).
[1] The site of blood sacrifices, such as that of Jesus, and sacred tombs.

Things to be cherished like the thought of heaven?
Divinity must live within herself:
Passions of rain, or moods in falling snow;
Grievings in loneliness, or unsubdued
Elations when the forest blooms; gusty
Emotions on wet roads on autumn nights;
All pleasures and all pains, remembering
The bough of summer and the winter branch.
These are the measures destined for her soul.   30

III

Jove[2] in the clouds had his inhuman birth.
No mother suckled him, no sweet land gave
Large-mannered motions to his mythy mind.
He moved among us, as a muttering king,
Magnificent, would move among his hinds,[3]
Until our blood, commingling, virginal,
With heaven, brought such requital to desire
The very hinds discerned it, in a star.
Shall our blood fail? Or shall it come to be
The blood of paradise? And shall the earth   40
Seem all of paradise that we shall know?
The sky will be much friendlier then than now,
A part of labor and a part of pain,
And next in glory to enduring love,
Not this dividing and indifferent blue.

IV

She says, "I am content when wakened birds,
Before they fly, test the reality
Of misty fields, by their sweet questionings;
But when the birds are gone, and their warm fields
Return no more, where, then, is paradise?"   50
There is not any haunt of prophecy,
Nor any old chimera[4] of the grave,
Neither the golden underground,[5] nor isle
Melodious, where spirits gat them home,
Nor visionary south, nor cloudy palm
Remote on heaven's hill, that has endured
As April's green endures; or will endure
Like her remembrance of awakened birds,
Or her desire for June and evening, tipped
By the consummation of the swallow's wings.   60

V

She says "But in contentment I still feel
The need of some imperishable bliss."

[2] According to Roman myth, Jupiter, the supreme god.
[3] Shepherds, those who saw the star of Bethlehem, which marked the birth of Jesus.
[4] According to Greek myth, a fire-breathing monster.
[5] According to Greek myth, Elysium, the resting place of the virtuous.

Death is the mother of beauty; hence from her,
Alone, shall come fulfilment to our dreams
And our desires. Although she strews the leaves
Of sure obliteration on our paths,
The path sick sorrow took, the many paths
Where triumph rang its brassy phrase, or love
Whispered a little out of tenderness,
She makes the willow shiver in the sun   70
For maidens who were wont to sit and gaze
Upon the grass, relinquished to their feet.
She causes boys to pile new plums and pears
On disregarded plate.[6] The maidens taste
And stray impassioned in the littering leaves.

VI

Is there no change of death in paradise?
Does ripe fruit never fall? Or do the boughs
Hang always heavy in that perfect sky,
Unchanging, yet so like our perishing earth,
With rivers like our own that seek for seas   80
They never find, the same receding shores
That never touch with inarticulate pang?
Why set the pear upon those river-banks
Or spice the shores with odors of the plum?
Alas, that they should wear our colors there,
The silken weavings of our afternoons,
And pick the strings of our insipid lutes!
Death is the mother of beauty, mystical,
Within whose burning bosom we devise
Our earthly mothers waiting, sleeplessly.   90

VII

Supple and turbulent, a ring of men
Shall chant in orgy on a summer morn
Their boisterous devotion to the sun,
Not as a god, but as a god might be,
Naked among them, like a savage source.
Their chant shall be a chant of paradise,
Out of their blood, returning to the sky;
And in their chant shall enter, voice by voice,
The windy lake wherein their lord delights,
The trees, like serafin,[7] and echoing hills,   100
That choir among themselves long afterward.
They shall know well the heavenly fellowship
Of men that perish and of summer morn.

---

[6] Stevens's note: "Plate is used in the sense of so-called family plate. Disregarded refers to the disuse into which things fall that have been possessed for a long time. I mean, therefore, that death releases and renews. What the old have come to disregard, the young inherit and make use of" (*Letters*).

[7] Seraphim, or angels.

And whence they came and whither they shall go
The dew upon their feet shall manifest.[8]

VIII

She hears, upon that water without sound,
A voice that cries, "The tomb in Palestine
Is not the porch of spirits lingering.
It is the grave of Jesus, where he lay."
We live in an old chaos of the sun,   110
Or old dependency of day and night,
Or island solitude, unsponsored, free,
Of that wide water, inescapable.
Deer walk upon our mountains, and the quail
Whistle about us their spontaneous cries;
Sweet berries ripen in the wilderness;
And, in the isolation of the sky,
At evening, casual flocks of pigeons make
Ambiguous undulations as they sink,
Downward to darkness, on extended wings.   120

1915, 1923

THIRTEEN WAYS OF LOOKING AT A BLACKBIRD*

I
Among twenty snowy mountains,
The only moving thing
Was the eye of the blackbird.

II
I was of three minds,
Like a tree
In which there are three blackbirds.

III
The blackbird whirled in the autumn winds.
It was a small part of the pantomime.

IV
A man and a woman
Are one.
A man and a woman and a blackbird
Are one.   10

---

[8] Stevens's note: "Life is as fugitive as dew upon the feet of men dancing in dew. Men do not either come from any direction or disappear in any direction. Life is as meaningless as dew. Now these ideas are not bad in a poem. But they are a frightful bore when converted as above" (*Letters*).

* Stevens's note: "This group of poems is not meant to be a collection of epigrams or ideas, but of sensations" (*Letters of Wallace Stevens*, 1977).

V

I do not know which to prefer,
The beauty of inflections
Or the beauty of innuendoes,
The blackbird whistling
Or just after.

VI

Icicles filled the long window
With barbaric glass.
The shadow of the blackbird   20
Crossed it, to and fro.

The mood
Traced in the shadow
An indecipherable cause.

VII

O thin men of Haddam,[1]
Why do you imagine golden birds?
Do you not see how the blackbird
Walks around the feet
Of the women about you?

VIII

I know noble accents   30
And lucid, inescapable rhythms;
But I know, too,
That the blackbird is involved
In what I know.

IX

When the blackbird flew out of sight,
It marked the edge
Of one of many circles.

X

At the sight of blackbirds
Flying in a green light,
Even the bawds of euphony[2]   40
Would cry out sharply.

XI

He rode over Connecticut
In a glass coach.
Once, a fear pierced him,

---

[1] Haddam, Connecticut.
[2] Stevens's note: "[I] intended [that] the bawds of euphony would suddenly cease to be academic and express themselves sharply: naturally, with pleasure, etc." (*Letters*).

In that he mistook
The shadow of his equipage
For blackbirds.

XII

The river is moving.
The blackbird must be flying.[3]

XIII

It was evening all afternoon.   50
It was snowing
And it was going to snow.
The blackbird sat
In the cedar-limbs.[4]

1923

NUANCES OF A THEME BY WILLIAMS*

It's a strange courage
you give me, ancient star:

Shine alone in the sunrise
toward which you lend no part![1]

I

Shine alone, shine nakedly, shine like bronze,
that reflects neither my face nor any inner part
of my being, shine like fire, that mirrors nothing.

II

Lend no part to any humanity that suffuses
you in its own light.
Be not chimera[2] of morning,
Half-man, half-star.
Be not an intelligence,
Like a widow's bird
Or an old horse.   10

1919, 1923

---

[3] Stevens's note: "[The point] is the compulsion frequently back of the things that we do" (*Letters*).
[4] Stevens's note: "[I wanted this stanza to] convey despair" (*Letters*).
* William Carlos Williams (1883–1963).
[1] "El Hombre," published in Williams's *¡Al Que Quiere!* (1917).
[2] According to Greek myth, a fire-breathing monster.

ANECDOTE OF THE JAR

I placed a jar in Tennessee,
And round it was, upon a hill.
It made the slovenly wilderness
Surround that hill.

The wilderness rose up to it,
And sprawled around, no longer wild.
The jar was round upon the ground
And tall and of a port in air.

It took dominion everywhere.
The jar was gray and bare.   10
It did not give of bird or bush,
Like nothing else in Tennessee.

1919, 1923

THE SNOW MAN*

One must have a mind of winter
To regard the frost and the boughs
Of the pine-trees crusted with snow;

And have been cold a long time
To behold the junipers shagged with ice,
The spruces rough in the distant glitter

Of the January sun; and not to think
Of any misery in the sound of the wind,
In the sound of a few leaves,

Which is the sound of the land   10
Full of the same wind
That is blowing in the same bare place

For the listener, who listens in the snow,
And, nothing himself, beholds
Nothing that is not there and the nothing that is.

1921, 1923

---

* Stevens's note: "[This poem is] an example of the necessity of identifying oneself with reality in order to understand and enjoy it" (*Letters of Wallace Stevens*, 1977).

TEA AT THE PALAZ OF HOON*

Not less because in purple I descended
The western day through what you called
The loneliest air, not less was I myself.

What was the ointment sprinkled on my beard?
What were the hymns that buzzed beside my ears?
What was the sea whose tide swept through me there?

Out of my mind the golden ointment rained,
And my ears made the blowing hymns they heard.
I was myself the compass of that sea:

I was the world in which I walked, and what I saw   10
Or heard or felt came not but from myself;
And there I found myself more truly and more strange.

1923

THE EMPEROR OF ICE-CREAM†

Call the roller of big cigars,
The muscular one, and bid him whip
In kitchen cups concupiscent curds.[1]
Let the wenches dawdle in such dress
As they are used to wear, and let the boys
Bring flowers in last month's newspapers.
Let be be finale of seem.[2]
The only emperor is the emperor of ice-cream.

Take from the dresser of deal,[3]
Lacking the three glass knobs, that sheet   10
On which she embroidered fantails[4] once
And spread it so as to cover her face.

---

* Stevens's note: ". . . Hoon could be . . . the son of old man Hoon. He sounds like a Dutchman. I think the word is probably an automatic cipher for 'the loneliest air,' that is to say, the expanse of sky and space" (*Letters of Wallace Stevens*, 1977).

† Stevens's note: "This poem is an instance of letting myself go. Poems of this sort are the pleasantest on which to look back, because they seem to remain fresher than others" (*Letters of Wallace Stevens*, 1977).

[1] Stevens's note: [These words] have no genealogy; they are merely expressive. . . . They express the concupiscence of life, but, by contrast with the things in relation to them in the poem, they express or accentuate life's destitution, and it is this that gives them something more than a cheap lustre" (*Letters*).

[2] Stevens's note: "The true sense is let being become the conclusion or denouement of appearing to be: in short, icecream is an absolute good. The poem is obviously not about icecream, but about being as distinguished from seeming to be" (*Letters*).

[3] A dresser of cheap wood.   [4] Fantail pigeons.

If her horny feet protrude, they come
To show how cold she is, and dumb.
Let the lamp affix its beam.
The only emperor is the emperor of ice-cream.

1922, 1923

THE IDEA OF ORDER AT KEY WEST*

She sang beyond the genius of the sea.
The water never formed to mind or voice,
Like a body wholly body, fluttering
Its empty sleeves; and yet its mimic motion
Made constant cry, caused constantly a cry,
That was not ours although we understood,
Inhuman, of the veritable ocean.

The sea was not a mask. No more was she.
The song and water were not medleyed sound
Even if what she sang was what she heard,   10
Since what she sang was uttered word by word.
It may be that in all her phrases stirred
The grinding water and the gasping wind;
But it was she and not the sea we heard.

For she was the maker of the song she sang.
The ever-hooded, tragic-gestured sea
Was merely a place by which she walked to sing.
Whose spirit is this? we said, because we knew
It was the spirit that we sought and knew
That we should ask this often as she sang.   20

If it was only the dark voice of the sea
That rose, or even colored by many waves;
If it was only the outer voice of sky
And cloud, of the sunken coral water-walled,
However clear, it would have been deep air,
The heaving speech of air, a summer sound
Repeated in a summer without end
And sound alone. But it was more than that,
More even than her voice, and ours, among
The meaningless plungings of water and the wind,   30
Theatrical distances, bronze shadows heaped
On high horizons, mountainous atmospheres
Of sky and sea.

---

* Stevens's note: "In 'The Idea of Order at Key West,' life has ceased to be a matter of chance. It may be that every man introduces his own order into the life about him . . ." (*Letters of Wallace Stevens*, 1977).

It was her voice that made
The sky acutest at its vanishing.
She measured to the hour its solitude.
She was the single artificer of the world
In which she sang. And when she sang, the sea,
Whatever self it had, became the self
That was her song, for she was the maker. Then we,   40
As we beheld her striding there alone,
Knew that there never was a world for her
Except the one she sang and, singing, made.

Ramon Fernandez,[1] tell me, if you know,
Why, when the singing ended and we turned
Toward the town, tell why the glassy lights,
The lights in the fishing boats at anchor there,
As the night descended, tilting in the air,
Mastered the night and portioned out the sea,
Fixing emblazoned zones and fiery poles,   50
Arranging, deepening, enchanting night.

Oh! Blessed rage for order, pale Ramon,
The maker's rage to order words of the sea,
Words of the fragrant portals, dimly-starred,
And of ourselves and of our origins,
In ghostlier demarcations, keener sounds.

                                                    1934, 1935

ANGLAIS MORT À FLORENCE*

A little less returned for him each spring.
Music began to fail him. Brahms, although
His dark familiar, often walked apart.

His spirit grew uncertain of delight,
Certain of its uncertainty, in which
That dark companion left him unconsoled

For a self returning mostly memory.
Only last year he said that the naked moon
Was not the moon he used to see, to feel

(In the pale coherences of moon and mood   10
When he was young), naked and alien,
More leanly shining from a lankier sky.

---

[1] Fernandez (1894–1944) was a French literary critic, but Stevens repeatedly denied that he was consciously thinking of any real person when he wrote this poem.

* "An Englishman Who Died in Florence" (French). Stevens's note: "[This poem reveals a] strong spirit [that] stands by its own strength [without] the aid of philosophy, religion and one thing or another" (*Letters of Wallace Stevens*, 1977).

Its ruddy pallor had grown cadaverous.
He used his reason, exercised his will,
Turning in time to Brahms as alternate

In speech. He was that music and himself.
They were particles of order, a single majesty:
But he remembered the time when he stood alone.   20

He stood at last by God's help and the police;
But he remembered the time when he stood alone.
He yielded himself to that single majesty;

But he remembered the time when he stood alone,
When to be and delight to be seemed to be one,
Before the colors deepened and grew small.

1936

OF HARTFORD IN A PURPLE LIGHT

A long time you have been making the trip
From Havre[1] to Hartford, Master Soleil,[2]
Bringing the lights of Norway[3] and all that.

A long time the ocean has come with you,
Shaking the water off, like a poodle,
That splatters incessant thousands of drops,

Each drop a petty tricolor. For this,
The aunts in Pasadena, remembering,
Abhor the plaster of the western horses,

Souvenirs of museums. But, Master, there are   10
Lights masculine and lights feminine.
What is this purple, this parasol,

This stage-light of the Opera?
It is like a region full of intonings.
It is Hartford seen in a purple light.

A moment ago, light masculine,
Working, with big hands, on the town,
Arranged its heroic attitudes.

But now as in an amour of women
Purple sets purple round. Look, Master,   20
See the river, the railroad, the cathedral . . .

---

[1] Le Havre, France.   [2] "Sun" (French).   [3] The aurora borealis, or northern lights.

When male light fell on the naked back
Of the town, the river, the railroad were clear.
Now, every muscle slops away.

Hi! Whisk it, poodle, flick the spray
Of the ocean, ever-freshening,
On the irised hunks; the stone bouquet.

1942

ASIDES ON THE OBOE

The prologues are over. It is a question, now,
Of final belief. So, say that final belief
Must be in a fiction. It is time to choose.

I

That obsolete fiction of the wide river in
An empty land;[1] the gods that Boucher[2] killed;
And the metal heroes that time granulates—
The philosophers' man alone still walks in dew,
Still by the sea-side mutters milky lines
Concerning an immaculate imagery.
If you say on the hautboy man[3] is not enough,   10
Can never stand as god, is ever wrong
In the end, however naked, tall, there is still
The impossible possible philosophers' man,
The man who has had the time to think enough,
The central man, the human globe, responsive
As a mirror with a voice, the man of glass,
Who in a million diamonds sums us up.

II

He is the transparence of the place in which
He is and in his poems we find peace.
He sets this peddler's pie and cries in summer,   20
The glass man, cold and numbered, dewily cries,
"Thou art not August unless I make thee so."
Clandestine steps upon imagined stairs
Climb through the night, because his cuckoos call.

III

One year, death and war prevented the jasmine scent
And the jasmine islands were bloody martyrdoms.
How was it then with the central man? Did we

---

[1] According to Greek myth, the souls of the newly dead had to cross the river Styx to reach the "empty" land of the dead.
[2] Jacques Boucher de Crèvecoeur de Perthes (1788–1868), a French archeologist and writer who proved that humans existed in prehistoric times, thereby refuting popular creation theories.
[3] A hero (from "haut" for "tall" [French]); a hautboy is an oboe.

Find peace? We found the sum of men. We found,
If we found the central evil, the central good.
We buried the fallen without jasmine crowns.   30
There was nothing he did not suffer, no; nor we.

It was not as if the jasmine ever returned.
But we and the diamond globe at last were one.
We had always been partly one. It was as we came
To see him, that we were wholly one, as we heard
Him chanting for those buried in their blood,
In the jasmine haunted forests, that we knew
The glass man, without external reference.

1942

SO-AND-SO RECLINING ON HER COUCH

On her side, reclining on her elbow.
This mechanism, this apparition,
Suppose we call it Projection A.

She floats in air at the level of
The eye, completely anonymous,
Born, as she was, at twenty-one,

Without lineage or language, only
The curving of her hip, as motionless gesture,
Eyes dripping blue, so much to learn.

If just above her head there hung,   10
Suspended in air, the slightest crown
Of Gothic prong and practick[1] bright,

The suspension, as in solid space,
The suspending hand withdrawn, would be
An invisible gesture. Let this be called

Projection B. To get at the thing
Without gestures is to get at it as
Idea. She floats in the contention, the flux

Between the thing as idea and
The idea as thing. She is half who made her.   20
This is the final Projection, C.

The arrangement contains the desire of
The artist. But one confides in what has no
Concealed creator. One walks easily

---

[1] Practice, customary practice and law.

The unpainted shore, accepts the world
As anything but sculpture. Good-bye,
Mrs. Pappadopoulos, and thanks.

1947

ANGEL SURROUNDED BY PAYSANS*

One of the countrymen:
                                    There is
A welcome at the door to which no one comes?
The angel:
I am the angel of reality,[1]
Seen for a moment standing in the door.

I have neither ashen wing nor wear of ore
And live without a tepid aureole,[2]

Or stars that follow me, not to attend,
But, of my being and its knowing, part.   10

I am one of you and being one of you
Is being and knowing what I am and know.

Yet I am the necessary angel of earth,
Since, in my sight, you see the earth again,

Cleared of its stiff and stubborn, man-locked set,
And, in my hearing, you hear its tragic drone

Rise liquidly in liquid lingerings,
Like watery words awash; like meanings said

By repetitions of half-meanings. Am I not,
Myself, only half of a figure of a sort,   20

A figure half seen, or seen for a moment, a man
Of the mind, an apparition apparelled in

---

* "Peasants" (French). This poem is Stevens's response to Pierre Tal Coat's painting *Still Life*. Stevens's notes: "The angel is the Venetian glass bowl on the left with the little spray of leaves in it. The peasants are the terrines [earthenware dishes], bottles, and the glasses that surround it"; "[The point of this poem] is that there must be in the world about us things that solace us quite as fully as any heavenly visitation could" (*Letters of Wallace Stevens,* 1977).
[1] In this poem, in contrast to much of Stevens's work, "reality and contact with it are the great blessings"; apparently, Stevens is rebelling against "recently [having] been fitted into too many philosophic frames" (*Letters*).
[2] A halo.

Apparels of such lightest look that a turn
Of my shoulder and quickly, too quickly, I am gone?

1950

THE COURSE OF A PARTICULAR

Today the leaves cry, hanging on branches swept by wind,
Yet the nothingness of winter becomes a little less.
It is still full of icy shades and shapen snow.

The leaves cry . . . One holds off and merely hears the cry.
It is a busy cry, concerning someone else.
And though one says that one is part of everything,

There is a conflict, there is a resistance involved;
And being part is an exertion that declines:
One feels the life of that which gives life as it is.

The leaves cry. It is not a cry of divine attention,   10
Nor the smoke-drift of puffed-out heroes, nor human cry.
It is the cry of leaves that do not transcend themselves,

In the absence of fantasia, without meaning more
Than they are in the final finding of the ear, in the thing
Itself, until, at last, the cry concerns no one at all.

1951, 1957

TO AN OLD PHILOSOPHER IN ROME*

On the threshold of heaven, the figures in the street
Become the figures of heaven, the majestic movement
Of men growing small in the distances of space,
Singing, with smaller and still smaller sound,
Unintelligible absolution and an end—

---

* This poem was written one year before the death of George Santayana (1863–1952), an American poet and philosopher who in 1912 retired from teaching at Harvard University and spent the rest of his life in Italy. Stevens writes of his early encounters with Santayana at Harvard: "While I did not take any of his courses and never heard him lecture, he invited me to come to see him a number of times and, in that way, I came to know him a little. I read several poems to him and he expressed his own view of the subject of them in a sonnet ['Cathedrals by the Sea . . .'{1901}] which he sent me, and which is in one of his books. . . . I always came away from my visits with him feeling that he made up in the most genuine way for many things that I needed. He was then still definitely a poet" (*Letters of Wallace Stevens,* 1977).

The threshold, Rome, and that more merciful Rome
Beyond, the two alike in the make of the mind.
It is as if in a human dignity
Two parallels become one, a perspective, of which
Men are part both in the inch and in the mile.   10

How easily the blown banners change to wings
Things dark on the horizons of perception
Become accompaniments of fortune, but
Of the fortune of the spirit, beyond the eye,
Not of its sphere, and yet not far beyond,

The human end in the spirit's greatest reach,
The extreme of the known in the presence of the extreme
Of the unknown. The newsboys' muttering
Becomes another murmuring; the smell
Of medicine, a fragrantness not to be spoiled   20

The bed, the books, the chair, the moving nuns,
The candle as it evades the sight, these are
The sources of happiness in the shape of Rome,
A shape within the ancient circles of shapes,
And these beneath the shadow of a shape

In a confusion on bed and books, a portent
On the chair, a moving transparence on the nuns,
A light on the candle tearing against the wick
To join a hovering excellence, to escape
From fire and be part only of that of which   30

Fire is the symbol: the celestial possible.
Speak to your pillow as if it was yourself.
Be orator but with an accurate tongue
And without eloquence, O, half-asleep,
Of the pity that is the memorial of this room,

So that we feel, in this illumined large,
The veritable small, so that each of us
Beholds himself in you, and hears his voice
In yours, master and commiserable man,
Intent on your particles of nether-do,   40

Your dozing in the depths of wakefulness,
In the warmth of your bed, at the edge of your chair, alive
Yet living in two worlds, impenitent
As to one, and, as to one, most penitent,
Impatient for the grandeur that you need

In so much misery; and yet finding it
Only in misery, the afflatus of ruin,

Profound poetry of the poor and of the dead,
As in the last drop of the deepest blood,
As it falls from the heart and lies there to be seen,   50

Even as the blood of an empire, it might be,
For a citizen of heaven though still of Rome.
It is poverty's speech that seeks us out the most.
It is older than the oldest speech of Rome.
This is the tragic accent of the scene.

And you—it is you that speak it, without speech,
The loftiest syllables among loftiest things,
The one invulnerable man among
Crude captains, the naked majesty, if you like,
Of bird-nest arches and of rain-stained vaults.   60

The sounds drift in. The buildings are remembered.
The life of the city never lets go, nor do you
Ever want it to. It is part of the life in your room.
Its domes are the architecture of your bed.
The bells keep on repeating solemn names

In choruses and choirs of choruses,
Unwilling that mercy should be a mystery
Of silence, that any solitude of sense
Should give you more than their peculiar chords
And reverberations clinging to whisper still.   70

It is a kind of total grandeur at the end,
With every visible thing enlarged and yet
No more than a bed, a chair and moving nuns,
The immensest theatre, the pillared porch,
The book and candle in your ambered room,

Total grandeur of a total edifice,
Chosen by an inquisitor of structures
For himself. He stops upon this threshold,
As if the design of all his words takes form
And frame from thinking and is realized.   80

1951, 1954

OF MERE BEING

The palm at the end of the mind,
Beyond the last thought, rises
In the bronze decor,

A gold-feathered bird
Sings in the palm, without human meaning,
Without human feeling, a foreign song.

You know then that it is not the reason
That makes us happy or unhappy.
The bird sings. Its feathers shine.

The palm stands on the edge of space.   10
The wind moves slowly in the branches.
The bird's fire-fangled feathers dangle down.

1955, 1957

William Carlos Williams
(1883–1963)

William Carlos Williams's career culminated with *Paterson,* his epic poem with prose passages, published between 1946 and 1963. As Williams said in his autobiography (1951), *Paterson* was written about the "whole knowable world" surrounding him in his own region of New Jersey, a region transformed through his poetic vision. His career as a poet merged with his perceptions and experiences as a physician. His verse forms are apparently simple, in keeping with the simplicity of his poetic subjects: events from everyday life, which range from a commonplace, natural setting noted by the poet/physician on his way to the "contagious hospital" in "Spring and All," the title poem of his 1923 collection, to the painterly lyricism captured in perhaps his most famous short poem, "The Red Wheelbarrow," from the same volume.

Williams was born in 1883 in Rutherford, New Jersey, near the city of Paterson. He attended medical school at the University of Pennsylvania, where he specialized in pediatrics and befriended the poets Ezra Pound, Marianne Moore, and Hilda Doolittle. Although Williams viewed his career in medicine as a means of support for his poetic career, for more than forty years he was a dedicated physician, and that dedication is evident in the tone and subjects of his poetry. He married Florence Herman in 1912, and the marriage lasted until his death, giving rise to two sons and such love poems as "Asphodel, That Greeny Flower" (1955). In 1924 and 1927 he journeyed to Europe, where he furthered his friendship with Ezra Pound and met James Joyce. Later in life Williams made trips for lectures and poetry readings, but he spent most of his time practicing medicine in Rutherford. Williams wrote poetry after caring for patients during the day and kept abreast of developments in modernist poetry through extensive reading and visits to New York City to meet painters and poets, including Marianne Moore and Wallace Stevens.

A late bloomer as a poet, Williams struggled for years to overcome the Keatsian style of his early verse. He finally found his own voice in *Kora in Hell* (1920), *Sour Grapes* (1921), and especially *Spring and All*. Like Pound, Williams wanted to "make it new," but

Charles Demuth's watercolor Tuberoses *(1922) was owned by William Carlos Williams, whose poems reflect his love of natural beauty, as is apparent in his poems "The Pot of Flowers" (based on this painting) and "The Wildflower."*

unlike Pound he believed that the scene of his poetry should be America and that he should be an American poet speaking from within that scene, as exemplified by *Paterson* and *In the American Grain* (1925), now recognized as a major essay on American culture. He felt that his poetry should not aspire to the international intellectualism of T. S. Eliot but that it should be more than the regionalism of Robert Frost.

Williams's poetry transmutes the commonplace and everyday through his poetic process. His meticulous selection of visual detail and careful diction show his talent for the poetic picture; in fact, Williams had at one time studied painting. Williams's early work tended to consist of concise poems with vivid, sensuous images. Some of these poems, such as "The Red Wheelbarrow" and "The Pot of Flowers," from *Spring and All,* show his rendering of "painterly" detail. In "The Red Wheelbarrow" the poet presents an apparently simple picture of a red wheelbarrow "glazed with rain / water" standing "beside the white / chickens." Williams demands that the reader sense the picture of a wheelbarrow and the interaction of the picture's details, but he makes no comments about this picture except that "so much depends" upon it. We as readers are expected to supply our own interpretation. Williams aimed to render the linguistic image with little or no authorial intrusion or comment. Williams's precept "no ideas but in things" represents a tendency in twentieth-century poetry. He believed that the poet need make no comment "about" the content of the poetry. Although some critics have argued that Williams's poems lack emotional depth or intellectual profundity, the poems should be read within the context of his intention to create poetry that produces its own effect directly, much in the manner of painting, and that shows the promptings of the traditional American belief in the value of practicality.

In the 1930s Williams began writing fiction. The short-story collections *The Knife of the Times* (1932) and *Life Along the Passaic River* (1938) and the novels *White Mule* (1937), *In the Money* (1940), and *The Build-Up* (1952) accompanied his essays and poems. He attempted to counter the powerful influences of Eliot and of the New Critics by establishing "little" magazines with an alternative view, and actively participated in community and political events. After World War II Williams was denied the post of Consultant in Poetry at the Library of Congress because his leftist or liberal views clashed with the conservatism of that time.

From 1946 to 1958 the five books comprising *Paterson* were published, even though Williams suffered a heart attack in 1948 and a series of disabling strokes, beginning in 1951, that forced him to retire from the medical profession. (An incomplete sixth book came out in 1963.) *The Desert Music* was published in 1954 and *Pictures From Brueghel* in 1962, but Williams had to stop writing in 1961. His poetic influence can be seen in a generation of younger poets, including the beat poets, the Black Mountain group, the San Francisco poets, and the New York school. Common among these poets was the use of the American idiom in poetry; an openness of form with a corresponding openness of experience rather than a shaping of experience toward preordained conclusions; a predilection for concrete imagery; and an awareness that poems are made of words, not ideas, and that language is the poet's primary raw material. The traditional well-made poem, with beginning, middle, and end, was replaced by the absence of closure, by a play of language that invited the reader to participate in the poem and to determine its meaning. Poetry, like life, was to be open-ended.

Late in his career Williams gained wide recognition. He received a National Book Award in 1950 for part of *Paterson,* the Bollingen Prize in 1953, and a Pulitzer Prize in 1963 for *Pictures From Brueghel.* Although he felt himself to be underrated, his poetic influence has been persistent and widespread. Whereas a Europeanized mentality dominated the poetry of the American expatriate poets such as Pound and Eliot, Williams centered his interest on a local American scene, in the manner of Walt Whitman and Emily Dickinson.

Williams's most obvious poetic ancestor is Whitman: both poets borrowed from and celebrated the common life of America. However, Williams differed from Whitman by making details significant in themselves, by tightening the poetic line, by emphasizing language's material aspects, and by carefully composing painterly poems. Whitman is typically described as the father of open-form poetry in America, and the freedom allowed by that open form found many descendants. Perhaps his most innovative and distinguished descendant was Williams. His poetic form depends on the line, which he wanted to contain rhythm within itself and which carried rhythm from line to line. Williams's lines vary in length, and in his later verse he experimented with a long line broken into three segments. A tension exists between Williams's need to vary the line, breaking or interrupting traditional linear form, and his need to retain the traces of formal poetic composition in the line, which can be deceptively simple.

Paterson has been received both positively and negatively by critics. The nature of modernism makes the construction of the long poem difficult by rejecting the forms that traditionally create coherence, such as transition, narrative sequentiality, and linearity. Modernist strategies in poetry, in keeping with trends in philosophy, art, sculpture, and music, interrupt or rupture formalist assumptions. The long modernist poem, typified by Eliot's *The Waste Land* (1922), consists of fragments juxtaposed against a unifying background of myth. In *Paterson* Dr. Paterson is Dr. Williams himself, who observes the city and comments on it. The poet celebrates the presence of masses of ordinary men and women but without sentimentality. Dr. Paterson helps organize the poem's fragments, which consist of persons from local legend and history, newspaper fragments and sections from history books, sections of verse, and unabridged letters from friends, all set against the background of industry, marriage, and language—subjects that were important to Williams throughout his life as a poet.

Suggested Readings: *The Tempers*, 1913. *Al Que Quiere!*, 1917. *Sour Grapes*, 1921. *Spring and All*, 1923. *In the American Grain*, 1925. *The Descent of Winter*, 1928. *The Knife of the Times*, 1932. *An Early Martyr*, 1935. *Adam and Eve and the City*, 1936. *White Mule*, 1937. *Life Along the Passaic River*, 1938. *In the Money*, 1940. *The Wedge*, 1944. *Paterson*, Bks. I–V, 1946–1963. *The Autobiography of William Carlos Williams*, 1951. *The Desert Music*, 1954. *Pictures From Brueghel and Other Poems*, 1962. B. Dijkstra, *The Hieroglyphics of a New Speech: Cubism, Stieglitz, and the Early Poetry of William Carlos Williams*, 1969. J. E. Breslin, *William Carlos Williams, An American Artist*, 1970. M. Weaver, *William Carlos Williams: The American Background*, 1971. P. L. Mariani, *William Carlos Williams: The Poet and His Critics*, 1976. R. Coles, *William Carlos Williams: The Knack of Survival*, 1980. P. L. Mariani, *William Carlos Williams: A New World Naked*, 1981.

Texts Used: "Landscape With the Fall of Icarus": *The Collected Poems of William Carlos Williams*, Vol. II: 1939–1962, ed. C. MacGowan, 1988. All else: *The Collected Poems*, Vol. I: 1909–1939, ed. A. W. Litz and C. MacGowan.

TRACT*

I will teach you my townspeople
how to perform a funeral—
for you have it over a troop
of artists—
unless one should scour the world—
you have the ground sense necessary.

See! the hearse leads.
I begin with a design for a hearse.
For Christ's sake not black—
nor white either—and not polished!   10
Let it be weathered—like a farm wagon—
with gilt wheels (this could be
applied fresh at small expense)
or no wheels at all:
a rough dray to drag over the ground.

Knock the glass out!
My God—glass, my townspeople!
For what purpose? Is it for the dead
to look out or for us to see
how well he is housed or to see   20
the flowers or the lack of them—
or what?
To keep the rain and snow from him?
He will have a heavier rain soon:
pebbles and dirt and what not.
Let there be no glass—

* Williams's note: "I was always searching for a regular format of the line, just as I wanted to be regular in my life—to conform. But I thought my friends were damn fools, because they didn't know any better way of conducting their lives. Still they conformed better than I to a code. I wanted to conform but I couldn't so I wrote my poetry."

and no upholstery, phew!
and no little brass rollers
and small easy wheels on the bottom—
my townspeople what are you thinking of?   30

A rough plain hearse then
with gilt wheels and no top at all.
On this the coffin lies
by its own weight.

                No wreaths please—
especially no hot house flowers.
Some common memento is better,
something he prized and is known by:
his old clothes—a few books perhaps—
God knows what! You realize   40
how we are about these things
my townspeople—
something will be found—anything
even flowers if he had come to that.
So much for the hearse.

For heaven's sake though see to the driver!
Take off the silk hat! In fact
that's no place at all for him—
up there unceremoniously
dragging our friend out to his own dignity!   50
Bring him down—bring him down!
Low and inconspicuous! I'd not have him ride
on the wagon at all—damn him—
the undertaker's understrapper!
Let him hold the reins
and walk at the side
and inconspicuously too!

Then briefly as to yourselves:
Walk behind—as they do in France,
seventh class, or if you ride   60
Hell take curtains! Go with some show
of inconvenience; sit openly—
to the weather as to grief.
Or do you think you can shut grief in?
What—from us? We who have perhaps
nothing to lose? Share with us
share with us—it will be money
in your pockets.

                Go now
I think you are ready.   70

1917

EL HOMBRE*

It's a strange courage
you give me ancient star:

Shine alone in the sunrise
toward which you lend no part!

1917

PORTRAIT OF A LADY†

Your thighs are appletrees
whose blossoms touch the sky.
Which sky? The sky
where Watteau¹ hung a lady's
slipper. Your knees
are a southern breeze—or
a gust of snow. Agh! what
sort of man was Fragonard?²
—as if that answered
anything. Ah, yes—below   10
the knees, since the tune
drops that way, it is
one of those white summer days,
the tall grass of your ankles
flickers upon the shore—
Which shore?—
the sand clings to my lips—
Which shore?
Agh, petals maybe. How
should I know?   20
Which shore? Which shore?
I said petals from an appletree.

1920, 1934

---

* "The Man" (Spanish); Wallace Stevens's interpretation of this poem is his "Nuances of a Theme by Williams" (1919).

† Compare this poem with T. S. Eliot's "Portrait of a Lady" (1915) and Ezra Pound's "Portrait d'une Femme" (1912).

¹ Jean Antoine Watteau (1684–1721), a French Rococo artist who painted conventional shepherds and shepherdesses, rustic dances, and fashionably dressed lovers.

² Jean-Honoré Fragonard (1732–1806), a French painter and engraver; much in demand for his light-hearted and exquisite paintings of fashionable youths in amorous play with their mistresses and other subjects glorifying love and beauty. In Fragonard's *The Swing* (1766?) a girl has kicked her slipper into the air.

THE LATE SINGER

Here it is spring again
and I still a young man!
I am late at my singing.
The sparrow with the black rain on his breast
has been at his cadenzas[1] for two weeks past:
What is it that is dragging at my heart?
The grass by the back door
is stiff with sap.
The old maples are opening
their branches of brown and yellow moth-flowers.   10
A moon hangs in the blue
in the early afternoons over the marshes.
I am late at my singing.

1921

OVERTURE TO A DANCE OF LOCOMOTIVES*

Men with picked voices chant the names
of cities in a huge gallery: promises
that pull through descending stairways
to a deep rumbling.

                        The rubbing feet
of those coming to be carried quicken a
grey pavement into soft light that rocks
to and fro, under the domed ceiling,
across and across from pale
earthcolored walls of bare limestone.   10

Covertly the hands of a great clock
go round and round! Were they to
move quickly and at once the whole
secret would be out and the shuffling
of all ants be done forever.

A leaning pyramid of sunlight, narrowing
out at a high window, moves by the clock:
disaccordant hands straining out from
a center: inevitable postures infinitely
repeated—   20
two—twofour—twoeight!
Porters in red hats run on narrow platforms.
This way ma'am!
                        —important not to take

[1] Elaborate solo musical passages.
* Williams's note: "Pennsylvania Station."

the wrong train!
                Lights from the concrete
ceiling hang crooked but—
                    Poised horizontal
on glittering parallels the dingy cylinders
packed with a warm glow—inviting entry—   30
pull against the hour. But brakes can
hold a fixed posture till—
                  The whistle!

Not twoeight. Not twofour. Two!
Gliding windows. Colored cooks sweating
in a small kitchen. Taillights—

In time: twofour!
In time: twoeight!

—rivers are tunneled: trestles
cross oozy swampland: wheels repeating   40
the same gesture remain relatively
stationary: rails forever parallel
return on themselves infinitely.
                The dance is sure.

                     1920, 1921

SPRING AND ALL*

By the road to the contagious hospital
under the surge of the blue
mottled clouds driven from the
northeast—a cold wind. Beyond, the
waste of broad, muddy fields
brown with dried weeds, standing and fallen

patches of standing water
the scattering of tall trees

All along the road the reddish
purplish, forked, upstanding, twiggy   10
stuff of bushes and small trees
with dead, brown leaves under them
leafless vines—

Lifeless in appearance, sluggish
dazed spring approaches—

---

* In *Spring and All* (1923) Williams identified poems by roman numerals; he later added titles and used the volume's title for the poem numbered I.

They enter the new world naked,
cold, uncertain of all
save that they enter. All about them
the cold, familiar wind—

Now the grass, tomorrow   20
the stiff curl of wildcarrot leaf

One by one objects are defined—
It quickens: clarity, outline of leaf

But now the stark dignity of
entrance—Still, the profound change
has come upon them: rooted, they
grip down and begin to awaken

1923

THE RED WHEELBARROW*

so much depends
upon

a red wheel
barrow

glazed with rain
water

beside the white
chickens

1923

THE WILDFLOWER†

Black eyed susan
rich orange
round the purple core

the white daisy
is not
enough

Crowds are white
as farmers
who live poorly

* Numbered XXII in the 1923 edition of *Spring and All*.
† The final poem, numbered XXVII, in the 1923 edition of *Spring and All*.

But you   10
are rich
in savagery—

Arab
Indian
dark woman

                                              1923

THE ATTIC WHICH IS DESIRE*

the unused tent
of

bare beams
beyond which

directly wait
the night

and day—
Here

from the street
by   10

```
*   *   *
*   S   *
*   O   *
*   D   *
*   A   *
*   *   *
```

ringed with
running lights

the darkened
pane

exactly
down the center

is
transfixed

                                              1930

* The poem describes the view from the window of Williams's attic study in Rutherford, New Jersey, including a visual imitation of a street sign.

THIS IS JUST TO SAY

I have eaten
the plums
that were in
the icebox

and which
you were probably
saving
for breakfast

Forgive me
they were delicious   10
so sweet
and so cold

1934

THE LOCUST TREE IN FLOWER

[*First Version*]

Among
the leaves
bright

green
of wrist-thick
tree

and old
stiff broken
branch

ferncool   10
swaying
loosely strung—

come May
again
white blossom

clusters
hide
to spill

their sweets
almost   20
unnoticed

down
and quickly
fall

1933

THE LOCUST TREE IN FLOWER

[*Second Version*]

Among
of
green

stiff
old
bright

broken
branch
come

white   10
sweet
May

again

1935

THE YACHTS*

contend in a sea which the land partly encloses
shielding them from the too-heavy blows
of an ungoverned ocean which when it chooses

tortures the biggest hulls, the best man knows
to pit against its beatings, and sinks them pitilessly.
Mothlike in mists, scintillant[1] in the minute

brilliance of cloudless days, with broad bellying sails
they glide to the wind tossing green water
from their sharp prows while over them the crew crawls

---

* Williams's notes: "A *very* vague imitation of Dante. I was quickly carried away by my own feel-ings." "The yachts do not sink but go on with the race while only *in the imagination* are they seen to flounder. It is a false situation which the yachts typify with the beauty of their movements while the real situation (of the poor) is desperate while 'the skillful yachts pass over.' "

[1] Sparkling, brilliant.

ant-like, solicitously grooming them, releasing,   10
making fast as they turn, lean far over and having
caught the wind again, side by side, head for the mark.

In a well guarded arena of open water surrounded by
lesser and greater craft which, sycophant, lumbering
and flittering follow them, they appear youthful, rare

as the light of a happy eye, live with the grace
of all that in the mind is fleckless, free and
naturally to be desired. Now the sea which holds them

is moody, lapping their glossy sides, as if feeling
for some slightest flaw but fails completely.   20
Today no race. Then the wind comes again. The yachts

move, jockeying for a start, the signal is set and they
are off. Now the waves strike at them but they are too
well made, they slip through, though they take in canvas.

Arms with hands grasping seek to clutch at the prows.
Bodies thrown recklessly in the way are cut aside.
It is a sea of faces about them in agony, in despair

until the horror of the race dawns staggering the mind,
the whole sea become an entanglement of watery bodies
lost to the world bearing what they cannot hold. Broken,   30

beaten, desolate, reaching from the dead to be taken up
they cry out, failing, failing! their cries rising
in waves still as the skillful yachts pass over.

1935

FINE WORK WITH PITCH AND COPPER

Now they are resting
in the fleckless light
separately in unison

like the sacks
of sifted stone stacked
regularly by twos

about the flat roof
ready after lunch
to be opened and strewn

The copper in eight   10
foot strips has been
beaten lengthwise

down the center at right
angles and lies ready
to edge the coping[1]

One still chewing
picks up a copper strip
and runs his eye along it

1936

from   *PICTURES FROM BRUEGHEL**

II: LANDSCAPE WITH THE FALL OF ICARUS[1]

According to Brueghel[2]
when Icarus fell
it was spring

a farmer was ploughing
his field
the whole pageantry

of the year was
awake tingling
near

the edge of the sea   10
concerned
with itself

sweating in the sun
that melted
the wings' wax

unsignificantly
off the coast
there was

---

[1] The top layer of a masonry wall; generally sloped to carry off water.
* Pieter Brueghel the Elder (1525?–1569), a Flemish painter.
[1] According to Greek myth, Icarus was a young man whose father, Daedalus, made wings for him, attached by wax. Icarus flew too near the sun; the wax melted, and he fell into the sea and drowned. His story symbolizes arrogance or over-reaching.
[2] Brueghel painted *Landscape With the Fall of Icarus* (1555?), in a corner of which Icarus's leg protrudes from the sea; a farmer ploughing and a delicate sailing ship nearby are unconcerned by his fall.

a splash quite unnoticed
this was   20
Icarus drowning

1962

=CONTEXTS=

Women Writers After World War I

During the years after World War I, feminist voices challenging the traditional roles
of women began to meet increasing hostility in a society dominated by patriarchal
values. Women's demands for greater personal freedom were met with the renewed
insistence that women retain their traditional positions as wives, mothers, and upholders of religious and domestic values, with few vocational opportunities or legal
rights. In literary and academic circles, women's writing was devalued as sentimental and lacking in intellectual sophistication. At this time the reputations of such
established female authors as Willa Cather and Edith Wharton began to decline, and
many other women were excluded from the central canon of "serious" literature.
The works of new modernist (predominantly male) poets, including T. S. Eliot and
Ezra Pound, were admired by scholars for their difficulty and allusiveness. Many of
the critics who acclaimed these male poets dismissed women's poetry as overly
emotional and too personal. Even when women used modernist forms, as did Hilda
Doolittle (H. D.), their work was generally seen as derivative and simplistic.

The poetry of Edna St. Vincent Millay (1892–1950) refigures conventional images of women as poets of love and emotion. In her use of the sonnet form, traditionally a vehicle for conventional expressions of love, Millay at once invokes and
debunks the expected perspective of women authors. By pointing out that love may
not be the only important thing for women, the poem challenges the era's typical
attitudes about women. Millay foregoes the accepted stance of the sentimental female poet, twisting the traditional love poem into an ironic examination of love's
transience.

Love Is Not All

Love is not all; it is not meat nor drink
Nor slumber nor a roof against the rain
Nor yet a floating spar to men that sink
And rise and sink and rise and sink again;
Love can not fill the thickened lung with breath,
Nor clean the blood, nor set the fractured bone;
Yet many a man is making friends with death
Even as I speak, for lack of love alone.
It well may be that in a difficult hour,
Pinned down by pain and moaning for release,
Or nagged by want past resolution's power,
I might be driven to sell your love for peace,
Or trade the memory of this night for food.
It well may be. I do not think I would.

Edna St. Vincent Millay, 1931

Hilda Doolittle (H. D.)
(1886–1961)

Although Hilda Doolittle is best known as an imagist poet, this label inadequately describes the range of her literary voice. Following the more purely imagistic work in her first book of verse, *Sea Garden* (1916), she wrote epics, novels, plays, translations, essays, and memoirs, many of which remain unpublished or out of print. She left America in 1911, living in Europe through two wars and returning only on brief visits. She lived at the center of modernist literature in Paris and London among the major writers of her time, leaving her own indelible mark on the literature of the day.

Doolittle was born into a strict Moravian community in Bethlehem, Pennsylvania, in 1886 and lived there until she was nine. (The Moravians were a Protestant sect founded in the eighteenth century.) Her mother was an artist who taught painting and music; her father was a professor of astronomy. At age fifteen Doolittle met and fell in love with the poet Ezra Pound. Their relationship, portrayed in various poems, is also described in her prose memoir *End to Torment* (1958). After a brief engagement opposed by her parents and doomed by Pound's other romantic entanglements, the couple continued a difficult friendship for many years. Doolittle was indebted to Pound for encouraging her to read the classics, for introducing her to writers abroad, and for grabbing three poems out of her hand one afternoon in 1912 at the tea room in the British Museum. Recognizing that the poems exemplified and embodied poetic theories he and the poet T. E. Hulme were developing, Pound immediately revised the poems, scrawled "H. D., Imagiste" at the bottom, and sent them off to the founder of *Poetry* magazine, Harriet Monroe. In his letter to Monroe he called the poems "modern," "laconic," "objective," and "direct." The poems were published in January 1913, and imagism was born.

H. D.'s poems happened to correspond with Pound's theories about poetry, and a few months after the poems appeared he published his definition of imagism in an issue of *Poetry*. An image, Pound asserted, is "that which presents an intellectual and emotional complex in an instant of time." For all the audacity with which Pound remade Hilda Doolittle into H. D.—creating the imagist movement as a vehicle for promoting her work—he did launch her literary career and teach the public how to read her work. (The imagist movement, from which Pound fairly early disassociated himself, lasted until 1917, when the last imagist anthology was published.)

During the imagism years, H. D. was romantically involved with both men and women; she married the poet Richard Aldington in 1913. Two years later she delivered a still-born baby, and the marriage, troubled already, became intolerable to her. When Aldington entered the British army in 1916, H. D. became an editor of the *Egoist* and published *Sea Garden*. Aldington's affairs further damaged the marriage, and the couple separated in 1918 (and eventually divorced in 1937). From 1915 to 1918 she maintained an intense relationship with the novelist D. H. Lawrence, who abruptly broke with her. In 1918 H. D.'s brother died in combat in World War I; her father died soon after; she was separated from Aldington; Lawrence had recently abandoned her; and she was pregnant and suffering from severe influenza. After H. D. gave birth to a daughter, the financial and emotional assistance of a wealthy young admirer, Winifred Ellerman, gave the poet a new life. Ellerman, who wrote under the pen name Bryher, became H. D.'s lover and longtime friend. In her prose fiction *Palimpsest* (1926), H. D. dedicated Part VI of "Let Zeus Record" ("Stars wheel in purple") to Bryher. During the next few years H. D., her daughter, and Bryher traveled—notably to New York City, where they met the poet Marianne Moore, and to Greece and Crete, where H. D. had visionary experiences that were to inform her work thereafter. She continued to write, funded by money from her parents and from Bryher. H. D.'s *Collected Poems* was published in 1925. Between travels, she lived in London and in Switzerland (joined there by her ailing mother), remaining with Bryher through the 1920s and early 1930s.

In 1933 H. D. began to undergo psychoanalysis with Sigmund Freud and returned for a few months as a student as well as a patient in 1934. Through analysis she overcame the writer's block she had been experiencing and achieved a new understanding and a belief in herself as a writer. She recounts this profound experience in *Tribute to Freud* (1956), a prose work examining her search for the underlying patterns that guided her behavior and formed her identity. At Freud's insistence she also wrote about her time with Pound and with Aldington, recorded in *Bid Me to Live* (1960). Throughout the rest of the 1930s H. D. published poetry and prose as well as translations of the tragedies of Euripides.

Years of productivity followed, but in 1945 H. D. suffered a nervous breakdown. After six months of recovery in Switzerland her creativity was renewed. She finished her remarkable trilogy of *The Walls Do No Fall* (1944), *Tribute to Angels* (1945), and *Flowering of the Rod* (1946), works inspired by her years in London during World War II, in which she explores in long meditative poems the role of matriarchal goddesses and poets. Aside from various volumes of prose and poetry, she wrote her last important work, *Helen in Egypt* (1961), then. An epic based on variants of the Greek myth about Helen of Troy, *Helen in Egypt* interweaves poetry and prose as the poet explores Helen's search for identity.

The last years of H. D.'s life were spent alone, mainly in Swiss and Italian hotels. Toward the end of her life, when Pound was still at St. Elizabeth's Hospital in Washington, D.C., she renewed their correspondence, as she did later with Aldington. In fact, the renewal characterizing her later years extended to an awakened appreciation of her work. In 1960, a year before her death, H. D. became the first woman to win the poetry award of the American Academy of Arts and Letters. Although her poetry of the 1910s and 1920s had been highly praised, later critics typically complained of her move away from imagism. With the 1970s and 1980s revival of female writers, H. D. regained critical attention, although her Greek masks and myths remain a barrier to many readers. Her work in reinterpreting myths and telling the untold stories of mythic characters from the woman's perspective parallels the work of Louise Bogan and anticipates the poetry of Adrienne Rich, Muriel Rukeyser, and May Sarton.

Suggested Readings: *Palimpsest*, 1926. *Tribute to Freud*, 1956, 1974. *Bid Me to Live*, 1960, 1983. *Helen in Egypt*, 1961. *HERmione*, 1981. L. Freibert, "Conflict and Creativity in the World of H. D.," *Journal of Women's Studies in Literature*, 1 (Summer):258–271, 1979. S. S. Friedman, *Psyche Reborn: The Emergence of H. D.*, 1981. A. Ostriker, "The Thieves of Language: Women Poets and Revisionist Mythmaking," *Signs*, 9 (Autumn):68–90, 1982. J. S. Robinson, *H. D.: The Life and Work of an American Poet*, 1982. B. Guest, *Herself Defined: The Poet H. D. and Her World*, 1984.

Text Used: *Collected Poems: 1912–1944*, ed. L. L. Martz, 1983.

PEAR TREE

Silver dust
lifted from the earth,
higher than my arms reach,
you have mounted,
O silver,
higher than my arms reach
you front us with great mass;

no flower ever opened
so staunch a white leaf,
no flower ever parted silver   10
from such rare silver;

O white pear,
your flower-tufts
thick on the branch
bring summer and ripe fruits
in their purple hearts.

1916

HELEN*

All Greece hates
the still eyes in the white face,
the lustre as of olives
where she stands,
and the white hands.

All Greece reviles
the wan face when she smiles,
hating it deeper still
when it grows wan and white,
remembering past enchantments   10
and past ills.

Greece sees unmoved,
God's daughter,[1] born of love,
the beauty of cool feet
and slenderest knees,

---

* Helen of Troy, beautiful wife of King Menelaus of Greece; according to Greek myth, her abduction by the Trojan prince Paris led to the Trojan War, which Greece won.
[1] Helen was the daughter of the supreme god, Zeus, and Leda, a mortal woman.

could love indeed the maid,
only if she were laid,
white ash amid funereal cypresses.

1924

from   SIGIL

XI

If you take the moon in your hands
and turn it round
(heavy, slightly tarnished platter)
you're there;

if you pull dry sea-weed from the sand
and turn it round
and wonder at the underside's bright amber,
your eyes

look out as they did here,
(you don't remember)   10
when my soul turned round,

perceiving the other-side of everything,
mullein-leaf,[1] dog-wood leaf, moth-wing
and dandelion-seed under the ground.

1931

from   THE MYSTERIES*

Renaissance Choros[1]

VI

"The mysteries remain,
I keep the same
cycle of seed-time

---

[1] A tall plant of the figwort family.

* The Eleusinian mysteries of Greek myth: associated with the earth goddess Demeter and the god of wine, Dionysus (or Iacchus). At the celebration of the mysteries, Iacchus was represented carrying a torch, and the word "Iacchus" was repeated.

[1] A band of dancers or singers in ancient Greece.

and of sun and rain;
Demeter in the grass
I multiply,
renew and bless
Iacchus in the vine;
I hold the law,
I keep the mysteries true,   10
the first of these
to name the living, dead;
I am red wine and bread.

I keep the law,
I hold the mysteries true,
I am the vine,
the branches, you
and you."

1931

Ezra Pound
(1885–1972)

Ezra Pound decisively affected the course of twentieth-century literature. Born in Hailey, Idaho, in 1885, Ezra Weston Loomis Pound and his family moved to Wyncote, Pennsylvania, a Philadelphia suburb, when he was less than two years old. "The Pound Era" began around the turn of the twentieth century, when Pound determined that by age thirty he would know more about poetry than anyone else living. He attended Hamilton College (in Clinton, New York) and the University of Pennsylvania, from which he earned an M.A. in 1906. Encouraged by his college friend William Carlos Williams and by his sweetheart, Hilda Doolittle (H. D.), Pound began a comprehensive study of poetry in English, Spanish, French, Italian, Provençal, Latin, and Greek (and later, Chinese). Pound's early friendship with two of the other major American poets of his generation helped put him at the center of artistic and intellectual activity, a position he occupied wherever he lived.

After four months of teaching at Wabash College in Indiana, Pound left for Venice in 1908, in part because of his disenchantment with academia and in part because of a scandal over a female overnight visitor. From there, with his first, self-published book of poetry in hand, he went to London. That book, *A Lume Spento* ("With Tapers Quenched" [1908]), was well received, and by the following year he had published three more. Making the acquaintance of the man whom he considered the finest living English-language poet, William Butler Yeats, Pound both learned from Yeats and taught him. In 1914 Pound married Dorothy Shakespear, the daughter of a friend of Yeats, and he served as Yeats's secretary for two winters between 1914 and 1916 at Stone Cottage, Sussex, England. Pound and Yeats exchanged views on writing, each altering his style as a result of the interaction.

From left to right, the Irish writer James Joyce, Ezra Pound, the English writer Ford Madox Ford, and the American lawyer and book collector John Quinn (who bought the manuscript of T. S. Eliot's The Waste Land*), in Pound's Paris studio in 1923.*

The London years were frenetic: Pound lectured on romance literature, published several volumes of verse and criticism, translated medieval Italian poetry, and became foreign editor of the important new Chicago magazine *Poetry*. He championed the poetry of Hilda Doolittle through his association with the imagist movement, editing the anthology *Des Imagistes* (1914). Working with the notebooks of the Orientalist Ernest Fenollosa, Pound began an exploration of Chinese poetry and thought that would continue for fifty years. In 1914 and 1915 he was closely associated with the vorticist movement in the arts and with Wyndham Lewis's shocking new journal, *Blast*.

In 1915 Pound began writing his great work, *The Cantos,* which spanned from 1917 to 1959 and were collected in *The Cantos of Ezra Pound* (1986). From that time through the early 1920s Pound was an indefatigable advocate of the poems and prose of James Joyce and of the poetry and criticism of T. S. Eliot, and was instrumental in gaining attention for their work. He also became associated with the Socialist journal *The New Age* and began a slow conversion from aestheticism to social engagement, a change in his view of the role of the poet in society, hastened by the onset of World War I and its enormous waste of life and talent. Some of Pound's more extreme positions offended members of the British literary establishment, and he found many magazines closed to his work. After trying to make a living writing music criticism (under the pseudonym William Atheling), art criticism (under the pseudonym B. H. Dias), and literary criticism (in his own name) for *The New Age,* Pound left London for Paris at the end of 1920.

Paris after the war was the scene of intense American expatriate literary and artistic activity. Due to a favorable exchange rate, the cost of living was inexpensive, and Pound fitted in well. His own work, though, was not progressing, a result of his characteristic generosity toward other artists and of the excitement of a major metropolis. In 1924 he moved to Rapallo, a small resort town east of Genoa on the Italian Riviera, where he remained for the next twenty-one years. Rapallo was a conducive location for work, and Pound had finished his first thirty cantos by 1930, when the onset of the worldwide Great Depression revived his interests in politics and economics. Throughout the 1930s Pound increasingly became an active advocate of needed economic and monetary reform, advancing positions that, slightly ahead of their time, were thought eccentric by academic economists of the period.

More ominous was Pound's growing enthusiasm for anti-Semitism and for Italian fascism—sparked by the 1932 celebration of the tenth anniversary of the institution of fascism in Italy and by a private meeting with the charismatic Italian dictator Benito Mussolini in January 1933. Particularly after Italian banking-reform legislation was passed in 1936, Pound believed that Mussolini was putting into effect economic changes similar to those that the poet advocated, and his support for the Fascist regime grew. When World War II broke out in 1939 Pound found himself in a difficult position. With his wife, his companion (Olga Rudge), one of his children, and his parents all living in Italy, Pound found leaving Italy impossible. Out of personal conviction and the necessity of earning a living, he began working as a propagandist for Italian radio. When the United States entered the war late in 1941, Pound stopped broadcasting but resumed after a hiatus of several months. Indicted for radio treason by an American grand jury in July 1943, he was arrested in May 1945 and imprisoned for six months in a disciplinary training camp in Pisa, where he was held in a steel cage until he suffered a temporary physical and mental collapse.

Brought to Washington, D.C., Pound was found unfit to stand trial for reason of insanity and was confined to St. Elizabeth's Hospital, a sanitarium, until 1958. The publication of *The Pisan Cantos* (1948) earned him the first Bollingen Prize in 1949 and occasioned a storm of controversy over his wartime role. Through a constant stream of literary correspondence and visiting poets, the St. Elizabeth's years were productive ones for Pound, but he was also in contact with a group of racist and right-wing fanatics who did little to help his reputation as a political reactionary. Upon his release Pound returned to Italy where, after suffering ill health, he lapsed into depression and rarely spoke during the final years of his life. He died in Venice in 1972 and was buried there.

Apart from the Bollingen Prize and a $2000 award given by *The Dial* magazine in 1928, major honors eluded Pound during his lifetime. His importance as a poet could not be denied, but his support for the Italian Fascist regime and the anti-Semitism that surfaced in some of his work disturbed critics and readers, who responded by carefully partitioning his work from his life. Pound and his generation continue to have a major impact on both American and world poetry, and *The Cantos* in particular has survived the transition from the modern to the postmodern period remarkably well.

The Cantos, Pound's epic of fifty years' making, is a formidable piece of high modernist poetry, comparable in difficulty to James Joyce's *Ulysses* (1922). The verse is densely allusive with occasional fragments of Greek, Latin, Chinese, French, Italian, Spanish, and Provençal. *The Cantos* ranges through human history in Pound's search for high points of cultural achievement as well as for explanations of why civilizations decay. "Canto I" typifies his historical quest. Like Odysseus he offers blood for ghosts and will allow only those past figures who can offer important insights to speak. Pound had perhaps the most vivid historical imagination of any poet. When he presents a historical figure, such as Sigismundo Malatesta, the hero of Cantos VIII through XI, the reader enters the world of a fifteenth-century Italian condottiere (a mercenary soldier) whose violence in battle is accompanied by an aesthetic ideal that helps to initiate the Renaissance in Italy. The difficulties of reading *The Cantos* are formidable but only at first. Once a source is found, a quotation translated, or an allusion understood, the problems disappear. Pound is ultimately very precise and very clear.

Although Pound wrote some of the most beautiful lyric poetry in English, he was not primarily a lyric poet. A didactic poet, he took seriously the nineteenth century's claim that poets authoritatively address the largest concerns of their culture. He believed, with Percy Bysshe Shelley, that the poet is the unacknowledged legislator of the world. Pound's frequent allusions serve a serious point: he wishes the reader to go beyond *The Cantos* and consider and read the works of those poets to whom he alludes—Dante and Ovid, the philosophers Confucius and Karl Marx, and the politicians Thomas Jefferson and John Adams. Although *The Cantos,* with its open-ended nature and lengthy genesis, cannot be said to possess the organic form, a fusing of form and content, of many other works of literature, it does cohere. The reader who progresses through the poems and reads the books Pound recommends acquires a true liberal education. The references, repeated and varied, become clearer, the meaning more precise. *The Cantos* are also what T. S. Eliot called "a reticent autobiography," presenting the record of the life of one man, a man who was in contact with the most vital currents of twentieth-century art, literature, and thought.

Pound's poetry is collected in three volumes: *Collected Early Poems of Ezra Pound* (1982), *Personae* (1990), Pound's own choice of the short poems he wished to remain in print, and his life's work, *The Cantos*. His poetic practice was attentive to the role of translation in a nation's literature. He produced several volumes of translation, most notably *The Translations of Ezra Pound* (1953) and the works of Confucius (*Confucius* [1969] and *Shih-Ching* [1954]).

There is no denying Pound's central position in twentieth-century literature. We need only consider Pound's role as a critic. For Pound, who went back to the Greek root of the word, a critic is someone who chooses, someone who determines what work is good and worthy of attention, and what is spurious and outmoded. Pound discovered, fostered, and taught the following writers: Basil Bunting, Hilda Doolittle (whom he renamed H. D.), T. S. Eliot, Ernest Hemingway, James Joyce, Marianne Moore, Robert Frost, William Carlos Williams, and Louis Zukofsky. In some measure they all owe their success to Pound. Without question he was the preeminent critic of his century, perhaps of any century.

Beyond that, he served his art. When he first began his study he found poetry lagging behind the prose art of novelists such as Gustave Flaubert and Stendhal (Marie-Henri Beyle); by the 1920s Pound had restored it to renewed status and seriousness. For Pound was a serious artist, and his understanding of the techniques of verse has never been matched. Through his translations he brought into English poetry the attained maxima in the three effects he considered most essential to poetry: melopoiea, the art of musically charging language (in which he was unsurpassed); phanopoiea, the art of visually charging language; and logopoeia, the art of charging language through the interplay of word connotations. Pound's criticism was addressed to the young, and if there exists a single place where young poets can turn to learn all the possibilities of their craft, that place is in the work of Ezra Pound, who by his criticism and practice so greatly enhanced the resources of the poet's art and so energetically revitalized the English language.

Suggested Readings: *Personae,* 1909. *Hugh Selwyn Mauberley,* 1920. *Selected Poems,* ed. T. S. Eliot, 1928. *ABC of Reading,* 1934. *Make It New,* 1934. *Pisan Cantos,* 1948. *Patria Mia,* 1950. *The Cantos of Ezra Pound,* 1964, rpt. 1986. *Literary Essays,* ed. T. S. Eliot, 1968. *Confucius: The Great Digest, The Unwobbling Pivot, The Analects,* 1969. *Late Cantos and Fragments,* 1969. *Pound-*

Joyce: Letters and Essays, 1970. *Selected Letters, 1907–1941*, ed. D. D. Paige, 1951. *Collected Early Poems*, 1982. H. Kenner, *The Poetry of Ezra Pound*, 1951. C. Emery, *Ideas Into Action: A Study of Pound's Cantos*, 1958. E. Davis, *Vision Fugitive: Ezra Pound's Economics*, 1968. K. K. Ruthven, *A Guide to Ezra Pound's Personae*, 1969. H. Witemeyer, *The Poetry of Ezra Pound: Forms and Renewal, 1908–1920*, 1969. N. Stock, *The Life of Ezra Pound*, 1970. M. Alexander, *The Poetic Achievement of Ezra Pound*, 1979. C. F. Terrell, *A Companion to the Cantos of Ezra Pound*, 2 vols., 1980, 1984. I. F. A. Bell, *Critic as Scientist: The Modernist Poetics of Ezra Pound*, 1981. D. Gallup, *Ezra Pound: A Bibliography*, 1983. H. Carpenter, *A Serious Character*, 1988.

Text Used: *Personae: The Shorter Poems of Ezra Pound*, ed. L. Baechler and A. W. Litz, 1990.

THE TREE

I stood still and was a tree amid the wood,
Knowing the truth of things unseen before;
Of Daphne[1] and the laurel bow
And that god-feasting couple old
That grew elm-oak amid the wold.
'Twas not until the gods had been
Kindly entreated, and been brought within
Unto the hearth of their heart's home
That they might do this wonder thing;
Nathless[2] I have been a tree amid the wood   10
Any many a new thing understood
That was rank folly to my head before.

1908

SESTINA: ALTAFORTE*

LOQUITUR: *En* Bertrans de Born.[1]
Dante Alighieri[2] put this man in hell for that he was a stirrer
up of strife.
Eccovi![3]
Judge ye!
Have I dug him up again?
The scene is at his castle, Altaforte. "Papiols" is his jongleur.[4]
"The Leopard," the *device* of Richard Cœur de Lion.[5]

---

[1] According to Greek myth, the nymph Daphne is changed into a laurel tree to escape the sun god Apollo, who is pursuing her.
[2] Nonetheless.
* "Very loud" (Italian); the sestina is one of the most difficult poetic forms because it is based on a fixed pattern of line endings. Pound departs from the form slightly in Stanza IV (l. 21 should end with "music," and l. 22, with "rejoicing") and more noticeably in Stanza VII (which should have six lines, with all six end words used).
[1] "Speaker" (Latin): Lord Bertrans de Born.
[2] The Italian poet Dante (1265–1321), best known for his *Divine Comedy*, which describes a journey through Hell, Purgatory, and Paradise.
[3] "Here you are" (Italian).   [4] "Juggler" (French).
[5] "Richard the Lion-Hearted" (French): Richard I (1157–1199), king of England from 1189 to 1199.

I

Damn it all! all this our South stinks peace.
You whoreson dog, Papiols, come! Let's to music!
I have no life save when the swords clash.
But ah! when I see the standards gold, vair, purple, opposing
And the broad fields beneath them turn crimson,
Then howl I my heart nigh mad with rejoicing.

II

In hot summer have I great rejoicing
When the tempests kill the earth's foul peace,
And the lightnings from black heav'n flash crimson,
And the fierce thunders roar me their music   10
And the winds shriek through the clouds mad, opposing,
And through all the riven skies God's swords clash.

III

Hell grant soon we hear again the swords clash!
And the shrill neighs of destriers in battle rejoicing,
Spiked breast to spiked breast opposing!
Better one hour's stour[6] than a year's peace
With fat boards, bawds, wine and frail music!
Bah! there's no wine like the blood's crimson!

IV

And I love to see the sun rise blood-crimson.
And I watch his spears through the dark clash   20
And it fills all my heart with rejoicing
And pries wide my mouth with fast music
When I see him so scorn and defy peace,
His lone might 'gainst all darkness opposing.

V

The man who fears war and squats opposing
My words for stour, hath no blood of crimson
But is fit only to rot in womanish peace
Far from where worth's won and the swords clash
For the death of such sluts I go rejoicing;
Yea, I fill all the air with my music.   30

---

[6] Combat, conflict.

VI

Papiols, Papiols, to the music!
There's no sound like to swords swords opposing,
No cry like the battle's rejoicing
When our elbows and swords drip the crimson
And our charges 'gainst "The Leopard's" rush clash.
May God damn for ever all who cry "Peace!"

VII

And let the music of the swords make them crimson!
Hell grant soon we hear again the swords clash!
Hell blot black for alway the thought "Peace"!

1909

PORTRAIT D'UNE FEMME*

Your mind and you are our Sargasso Sea,[1]
London has swept about you this score years
And bright ships left you this or that in fee:
Ideas, old gossip, oddments of all things,
Strange spars of knowledge and dimmed wares of price.
Great minds have sought you—lacking someone else.
You have been second always. Tragical?
No. You preferred it to the usual thing:
One dull man, dulling and uxorious,
One average mind—with one thought less, each year.   10
Oh, you are patient, I have seen you sit
Hours, where something might have floated up.
And now you pay one. Yes, you richly pay.
You are a person of some interest, one comes to you
And takes strange gain away:
Trophies fished up; some curious suggestion;
Fact that leads nowhere; and a tale or two,
Pregnant with mandrakes,[2] or with something else
That might prove useful and yet never proves,
That never fits a corner or shows use,   20
Or finds its hour upon the loom of days:
The tarnished, gaudy, wonderful old work;
Idols and ambergris[3] and rare inlays,

---

* "Portrait of a Lady" (French).
[1] A North Atlantic sea noted for its abundant seaweed, thought to entrap ships.
[2] The forked root of the mandrake, a plant in the nightshade family, was thought to promote conception.
[3] A waxy substance, from the intestines of sperm whales, that is used in perfumes.

These are your riches, your great store; and yet
For all this sea-hoard of deciduous things,
Strange woods half sodden, and new brighter stuff:
In the slow float of differing light and deep,
No! there is nothing! In the whole and all,
Nothing that's quite your own.
           Yet this is you.   30

1912

THE RETURN*

See, they return; ah, see the tentative
Movements, and the slow feet,
The trouble in the pace and the uncertain
Wavering!

See, they return, one, and by one,
With fear, as half-awakened;
As if the snow should hesitate
And murmur in the wind,
          and half turn back;
These were the "Wing'd-with-Awe,"   10
          Inviolable.

Gods of the winged shoe![1]
With them the silver hounds,
          sniffing the trace of air!

Haie! Haie![2]
        These were the swift to harry;
These the keen-scented;
These were the souls of blood.

Slow on the leash,
          pallid the leash-men!   20

1912

THE GARDEN

En robe de parade. —SAMAIN[1]

Like a skein[2] of loose silk blown against a wall
She walks by the railing of a path in Kensington Gardens,[3]

---

* Considered by the Irish writer William Butler Yeats (1865–1939) the most beautiful free verse poem in English.
[1] The Greek god Hermes and the Roman god Mercury, who served as messengers to the other gods.
[2] A French exclamation for calling the hounds to get in line.
[1] "Dressed for an outing" (French), from *Au Jardin de l'Infante* (1893), by Albert Samain (1858–1900).
[2] A coil.   [3] A large public park in London.

And she is dying piece-meal[4]
　　of a sort of emotional anæmia.

And round about there is a rabble
Of the filthy, sturdy, unkillable infants of the very poor.
They shall inherit the earth.

In her is the end[5] of breeding.
Her boredom is exquisite and excessive.
She would like some one to speak to her,　　　　　　　　　　10
And is almost afraid that I
　　will commit that indiscretion.

1913

LIU CH'E*

The rustling of the silk is discontinued,
Dust drifts over the court-yard,
There is no sound of foot-fall, and the leaves
Scurry into heaps and lie still,
And she the rejoicer of the heart is beneath them:

A wet leaf that clings to the threshold.

1914

IN A STATION OF THE METRO**

The apparition of these faces in the crowd;
Petals on a wet, black bough.

1913, 1916

THE RIVER-MERCHANT'S WIFE: A LETTER†

While my hair was still cut straight across my forehead[1]
I played about the front gate, pulling flowers.
You came by on bamboo stilts, playing horse,

---

[4] Gradually.　　[5] Here, both result and finish.
 * According to T. S. Eliot, Pound was the inventor of Chinese poetry in our time. Here, the sparse style presents a situation but leaves to the reader the task of drawing conclusions. The Chinese emperor Liu Ch'e (156–87 B.C.), Pound believed, was a fellow imagist.
 ** The Paris subway.
 † Translated and adapted from a Chinese poem by Li Po (701–762).　　[1] As a child.

You walked about my seat, playing with blue plums.
And we went on living in the village of Chokan:[2]
Two small people, without dislike or suspicion.

At fourteen I married My Lord you.
I never laughed, being bashful.
Lowering my head, I looked at the wall.
Called to, a thousand times, I never looked back.   10

At fifteen I stopped scowling,
I desired my dust to be mingled with yours
Forever and forever and forever.
Why should I climb the look out?

At sixteen you departed,
You went into far Ku-to-en,[3] by the river of swirling eddies,
And you have been gone five months.
The monkeys make sorrowful noise overhead.

You dragged your feet when you went out.
By the gate now, the moss is grown, the different mosses,   20
Too deep to clear them away!
The leaves fall early this autumn, in wind.
The paired butterflies are already yellow with August
Over the grass in the West garden;
They hurt me. I grow older.
If you are coming down through the narrows of the river Kiang,[4]
Please let me know beforehand,
And I will come out to meet you
                    As far as Cho-fū-Sa.[5]

By Rihaku[6]
1915

Marianne Moore
(1887–1972)

In the introduction to *A Marianne Moore Reader* (1961), the poet responds to a remark about her poetry—"Why the many quotation marks?"—by posing another question: "When a thing has been said so well that it could not be said better, why paraphrase it? Hence, my writing is, if not a cabinet of fossils, a kind of collection of flies in amber."

---

[2] Ch'ang-kan, a suburb of Nanking.   [3] Yen-yu-tui, an island in the dangerous river Ch'u-t'ang.
[4] The river Ch'u-t'ang.   [5] Ch'ang-feng-sha, several hundred miles up river from Nanking.
[6] The Japanese name of Li Po.

The publication of the *Reader* coincided with Marianne Moore's emergence as a public figure: the grand dame of American letters, an avid baseball fan who once threw out the 1968 season's first ball in Yankee Stadium, a consultant to Ford Motors in naming a new car model, and the frequently photographed poet with black tricorn hat and white gloves. Less and less she is viewed as the "flies in amber" poet who borrowed from newspapers and nature magazines; more and more she is prized as one of the twentieth century's most startling literary intelligences.

Until age seven, Moore, born in 1887 in Kirkwood, Missouri, lived with her brother, mother, and grandfather, a Presbyterian minister; Moore's father had deserted them. After her grandfather's death the family moved to Pennsylvania, where Moore entered Bryn Mawr College in 1905. Upon graduation she taught stenography at the United States Indian School in Carlisle, Pennsylvania, and in 1918 moved with her mother to Brooklyn, New York, to be near Moore's brother, a New Jersey chaplain. Moore acknowledged her mother as her most perceptive and harshest critic as well as her housemate; their relationship informed Moore's poetry for many years.

Moore's poems were first published in Bryn Mawr's student magazine. Her first book, *Poems,* appeared in 1921; her second, *Observations,* in 1924; and her third, *Selected Poems,* not until 1935. From 1925 until 1929 Moore edited the *Dial,* a literary journal begun by Margaret Fuller and Ralph Waldo Emerson in the 1840s. Moore wrote no poetry then but published essays and reviews, establishing herself as a prose stylist. She later wrote essays on Ezra Pound and T. S. Eliot, among others. Her most famous essay, "Humility, Concentration, and Gusto" (1948), argues that those qualities are essential to good verse.

Moore's coming of age as a writer parallels the flowering of modernism. Fellow modernists Eliot and Pound were ardent admirers of Moore, and there was reciprocal influence among them; her correspondence with Pound stretched over decades. Criticized for her use of direct and paraphrased quotations, "phrasings," Moore by no means originated the technique: both Eliot and Pound borrowed freely from other sources. Indeed, Moore's comment in the foreword to *A Marianne Moore Reader* about *Marriage* (1923), a lengthy poem in which Adam and Eve come to life, could be made about Eliot's poem *The Waste Land* (1922): "The thing (I would hardly call it a poem) is . . . a little anthology of statements that took my fancy—phrasings that I liked."

An avid baseball fan, Marianne Moore threw out the first ball at Yankee Stadium to open the 1968 season.

In 1941 Moore published *What are Years?* The title poem, written on the eve of World War II, considers such conflict-prompted ruminations as the natures of guilt and of innocence and the absence of safety. A more dramatic situation than Moore usually chose, the subject of war allowed her stringent moral concerns to take center stage. "We don't want war," she wrote in "Humility, Concentration, and Gusto," "but it does conduce to humility." That quality of humility is evoked and celebrated in "What are Years?" Moore's war poems, like most of her work, are poems of conscience, of elevated perception.

For many years Moore's achievements were either neglected or viewed as some sort of literary curiosity, primarily because of her gender. The poetry of the early twentieth-century's best-known female poets, Elinor Wylie and Edna St. Vincent Millay, reflects highly traditional conceptions of prosody, although Millay countered conventional ideas about women's roles. Poetry by women was limited to, and by, romantic and overly pastoral views of nature. Although Moore ironically led a quieter, more traditional life than did her more outspoken female contemporaries, she was clearly an odd duck.

Moore's poetry set her apart not only from Wylie and Millay but from Eliot and Pound as well. Commonly criticized for writing only syllabic, merely descriptive verse that is not poetry at all, Moore used complex and highly original techniques of language and syntax in treating "unpoetic" subjects such as unusual animals, baseball, and objets d'art. Because Moore tried for natural and conversational language and syntax, her poetry is characterized by an elevated style true to turn-of-the-century speech, which may not seem to possess the rhythms of modern speech. Moore masterfully manipulated language and syntax to create poems in which both poet and reader see through the examined objects to something larger. The true subject of many of her poems is the nature of perception. These poems, such as "Bowls" (1935) and "In the Days of Prismatic Color" (1924), typically begin on one tangent and end seemingly far afield on another.

"Nine Nectarines" (1935), "The Steeple-Jack" (1935, 1961) and to some extent "A Grave" (1924) more directly explore the nature of perception. Several of Moore's poems begin with an art-related image: "Nine Nectarines" is much like a still-life, whereas "When I Buy Pictures" (1921) examines an art that is anything but still. As finely detailed as any Albrecht Dürer etching, "The Steeple-Jack," originally one-third of the longer poem "Part of a Novel, Part of a Poem, Part of a Play" (1932), begins serenely but abruptly changes from an "etched" stillness to a "whirlwind" of confusion. Moore thereby introduces the element of danger, which clearly presents itself and demands to be taken into account. Danger is a very real element in other poems as well, such as "A Grave," in which the sea is a metaphor for death.

Moore's critical regard rose with the publication of *Collected Poems* (1951), which received a Pulitzer Prize, a National Book Award, and the Bollingen Prize. In 1954 she published the translation *The Fables of La Fontaine* (Jean de La Fontaine), a project begun after Moore's mother's death in 1947. Growing older Moore wrote fewer and less expansive poems, the intellectual rigor of her early poems replaced by a comparatively relaxed tone of voice, as in "Baseball and Writing" (1966).

Despite its title Moore's 1967 *Complete Poems* is by no means complete. Numerous poems are missing, and Moore notes in the preface that "omissions are not accidents." She radically revised others, turning many early syllabic poems into freer forms. Like other modernist poets Moore felt that revision is essential to the poetic process. Moore, who died in 1972, presented in *Complete Poems* the body of work she meant to preserve. Yet, the omitted poems, like all her poems, are treasures of language and intellect, of feeling and precision.

Suggested Readings: *Poems*, 1921. *Observations*, 1924. *The Pangolin and Other Verse*, 1936. *What Are Years?* 1941. *Nevertheless*, 1944. *The Fables of La Fontaine*, 1954. *Like a Bulwark*, 1956. *O to Be a Dragon*, 1959. *Tell Me, Tell Me*, 1967. *The Complete Prose of Marianne Moore*, 1986. R.

Jarrell, "Two Essays on Marianne Moore," in *Poetry and the Age*, 1973. E. Bishop, "Efforts of Affection," in *The Collected Prose*, 1984. R. P. Blackmur, "The Method of Marianne Moore," in *Selected Essays of R. P. Blackmur*, 1986. G. Schulman, *Marianne Moore: The Poetry of Engagement*, 1986.

Texts Used: "Poetry": *Collected Poems*, 1955. All else: *Complete Poems*, 1981.

WHEN I BUY PICTURES

or what is closer to the truth,
when I look at that of which I may regard myself as the
        imaginary possessor,
I fix upon what would give me pleasure in my average moments:
the satire upon curiosity in which no more is discernible
than the intensity of the mood,
or quite the opposite—the old thing, the medieval decorated
           hat-box,
in which there are hounds with waists diminishing like the
        waist of the hour-glass,
and deer and birds and seated people;
it may be no more than a square of parquetry;[1] the literal
        biography perhaps,
in letters standing well apart upon a parchment-like expanse;   10
an artichoke in six varieties of blue; the snipe-legged
       hieroglyphic in three parts;
the silver fence protecting Adam's grave,[2] or Michael taking
       Adam by the wrist.[3]
Too stern an intellectual emphasis upon this quality or that
      detracts from one's enjoyment.
It must not wish to disarm anything; nor may the approved
      triumph easily be honored—
that which is great because something else is small.
It comes to this: of whatever sort it is,
it must be "lit with piercing glances into the life of things";[4]
it must acknowledge the spiritual forces which have made it.

                   1921

POETRY*

I, too, dislike it: there are things that are important beyond
  all this fiddle.

---

[1] Inlaid woodwork in geometric forms, used especially in flooring.
[2] Moore's note: " 'A silver fence was erected by Constantine to enclose the grave of Adam.' *Literary Digest*, January 5, 1918, descriptive paragraph with photograph."
[3] Saint Michael, the archangel expelling Adam from Eden.
[4] Moore's note: "A. R. Gordon, *The Poets of the Old Testament* (Hodder and Stoughton, 1919)."
* A revised version of this poem, consisting largely of the first three lines only, was published in *The Complete Poems* (1967).

Reading it, however, with a perfect contempt for it, one
    discovers in
it after all, a place for the genuine.
    Hands that can grasp, eyes
    that can dilate, hair that can rise
        if it must, these things are important not because a

high-sounding interpretation can be put upon them but be-
    cause they are
useful. When they become so derivative as to become
    unintelligible,
the same thing may be said for all of us, that we
    do not admire what
    we cannot understand: the bat
        holding on upside down or in quest of something to

eat, elephants pushing, a wild horse taking a roll, a tireless
    wolf under
a tree, the immovable critic twitching his skin like a horse
    that feels a flea, the base-
ball fan, the statistician—
    nor is it valid
        to discriminate against 'business documents and

school-books';[1] all these phenomena are important. One
    must make a distinction
however: when dragged into prominence by half poets,
    the result is not poetry,
nor till the poets among us can be
    'literalists of
    the imagination'[2]—above
        insolence and triviality and can present

for inspection, 'imaginary gardens with real toads in them',
    shall we have
it. In the meantime, if you demand on the one hand,
the raw material of poetry in
    all its rawness and
    that which is on the other hand
        genuine, you are interested in poetry.

1921

10

20

---

[1] Moore's note: "*Diary of Tolstoy* (Dutton), p. 84. 'Where the boundary between prose and poetry lies, I shall never be able to understand. The question is raised in manuals of style, yet the answer to it lies beyond me. Poetry is verse; prose is not verse. Or else poetry is everything with the exception of business documents and school books.' "

[2] Moore's note: "*Yeats: Ideas of Good and Evil* (A. H. Bullen), p. 182. 'The limitation of his view was from the very intensity of his vision; he was a too literal realist of imagination, as others are of nature; and because he believed that the figures seen by the mind's eye, when exalted by inspiration, were "eternal existences," symbols of divine essences, he hated every grace of style that might obscure their lineaments.' "

THE STEEPLE-JACK*

Dürer[1] would have seen a reason for living
    in a town like this, with eight stranded whales
to look at; with the sweet sea air coming into your house
on a fine day, from water etched
    with waves as formal as the scales
on a fish.

One by one in two's and three's, the seagulls keep
    flying back and forth over the town clock,
or sailing around the lighthouse without moving their wings—
rising steadily with a slight   10
    quiver of the body—or flock
mewing where

a sea the purple of the peacock's neck is
    paled to greenish azure as Dürer changed
the pine green of the Tyrol[2] to peacock blue and guinea
gray.[3] You can see a twenty-five-
    pound lobster; and fish nets arranged
to dry. The

whirlwind fife-and-drum of the storm bends the salt
    marsh grass, disturbs stars in the sky and the   20
star on the steeple; it is a privilege to see so
much confusion. Disguised by what
    might seem the opposite, the sea-
side flowers and

trees are favored by the fog so that you have
    the tropics at first hand: the trumpet-vine,
fox-glove, giant snap-dragon, a salpiglossis[4] that has
spots and stripes; morning-glories, gourds,
    or moon-vines trained on fishing-twine
at the back door;   30

cat-tails, flags, blueberries and spiderwort,
    striped grass, lichens, sunflowers, asters, daisies—
yellow and crab-claw ragged sailors[5] with green bracts[6]—toad-plant,
petunias, ferns; pink lilies, blue
    ones, tigers; poppies; black sweet-peas.
The climate

---

* A person who builds or repairs steeples.
[1] Albrecht Dürer (1471–1528), a German painter and engraver.
[2] An Alpine region in western Austria and northern Italy.   [3] Gray speckled with white.
[4] A Chilean annual plant of the nightshade family, cultivated for long-stalked, trumpet-shaped flowers.
[5] Bluebottles, or cornflowers.   [6] Leaves.

is not right for the banyan, frangipani, or
          jack-fruit trees; or for exotic serpent
life. Ring lizard and snake-skin for the foot, if you see fit;
but here they've cats, not cobras, to   40
          keep down the rats. The diffident
little newt

with white pin-dots on black horizontal spaced-
          out bands lives here; yet there is nothing that
ambition can buy or take away. The college student
named Ambrose sits on the hillside
          with his not-native books and hat
and sees boats

at sea progress white and rigid as if in
          a groove. Liking an elegance of which   50
the source is not bravado, he knows by heart the antique
sugar-bowl shaped summer-house of
          interlacing slats, and the pitch
of the church

spire, not true, from which a man in scarlet lets
          down a rope as a spider spins a thread;
he might be part of a novel, but on the sidewalk a
sign says C. J. Poole, Steeple-Jack,
          in black and white; and one in red
and white says   60

Danger. The church portico has four fluted
          columns, each a single piece of stone, made
modester by white-wash. This would be a fit haven for
waifs, children, animals, prisoners,
          and presidents who have repaid
sin-driven

senators by not thinking about them. The
          place has a school-house, a post-office in a
store, fish-houses, hen-houses, a three-masted
          schooner on   70
the stocks. The hero, the student,
          the steeple-jack, each in his way,
is at home.

It could not be dangerous to be living
          in a town like this, of simple people,
who have a steeple-jack placing danger-signs by the church
while he is gilding the solid-
          pointed star, which on a steeple
stands for hope.

                                                                    1932

NINE NECTARINES*

Arranged by two's as peaches are,
at intervals that all may live—
   eight and a single one, on twigs that
   grew the year before—they look like
a derivative;
   although not uncommonly
the opposite is seen—
nine peaches on a nectarine.
   Fuzzless through slender crescent leaves
      of green or blue or
      both, in the Chinese style, the four   10

   pairs' half-moon leaf-mosaic turns
out to the sun the sprinkled blush
   of puce[1]-American-Beauty pink
   applied to bees-wax gray by the
uninquiring brush
   of mercantile bookbinding.
Like the peach *Yu,* the red-
cheeked peach which cannot aid the dead,
      but eaten in time prevents death,   20
      the Italian
      peach-nut, Persian plum, Ispahan[2]

   secluded wall-grown nectarine,
as wild spontaneous fruit was
   found in China first. But was it wild?
   Prudent de Candolle would not say.
One perceives no flaws
   in this emblematic group
of nine, with leaf window
unquilted by *curculio*[3]   30
      which someone once depicted on
      this much-mended plate
      or in the also accurate

   unantlered moose or Iceland horse
or ass asleep against the old
      thick, low-leaning nectarine that is the

---

* Moore's note: " 'The Chinese believed the oval peaches, which are very red on one side, to be a symbol of long life. . . . According to the word of Chin-noug-king, the peach *Yu* prevents death. If it is not eaten in time, it at least preserves the body from decay until the end of the world.' Alphonse de Candolle, *Origin of Cultivated Plants* (Appleton, 1886)." De Candolle (1806–1893) was a Swiss botanist. The ellipsis is Moore's.
[1] Brownish purple.   [2] A Persian city.   [3] A beetle with a long snout.

color of the shrub-tree's brownish
flower.

.   .   .   .   .   .

A Chinese "understands
the spirit of the wilderness"
and the nectarine-loving kylin[4]
of pony appearance—the long-
tailed or the tailless
small cinnamon-brown, common
camel-haired unicorn
with antelope feet and no horn,
here enameled on porcelain.
It was a Chinese
who imagined this masterpiece.

1935

WHAT ARE YEARS?

What is our innocence,
what is our guilt? All are
naked, none is safe. And whence
is courage: the unanswered question,
the resolute doubt,—
dumbly calling, deafly listening—that
in misfortune, even death,
encourages others
and in its defeat, stirs

the soul to be strong? He
sees deep and is glad, who
accedes to mortality
and in his imprisonment rises
upon himself as
the sea in a chasm, struggling to be
free and unable to be,
in its surrendering
finds its continuing.

So he who strongly feels,
behaves. The very bird,
grown taller as he sings, steels
his form straight up. Though he is captive,
his mighty singing

40

10

20

---

[4] Moore's note: "[A] Chinese unicorn. . . . It has the body of a stag, with a single horn, the tail of a cow, horse's hoofs, a yellow belly, and hair of five colours."

says, satisfaction is a lowly
thing, how pure a thing is joy.
    This is mortality,
    this is eternity.

1941

A JELLY-FISH

Visible, invisible,
    a fluctuating charm
an amber-tinctured amethyst
    inhabits it, your arm
approaches and it opens
    and it closes; you had meant
to catch it and it quivers;
    you abandon your intent.

1959

BASEBALL AND WRITING*

Suggested by post-game broadcasts.

Fanaticism? No. Writing is exciting
and baseball is like writing.
    You can never tell with either
      how it will go
      or what you will do;
    generating excitement—
    a fever in the victim—
    pitcher, catcher, fielder, batter.
      Victim in what category?
*Owl*man watching from the press box?   10
      To whom does it apply?
      Who is excited? Might it be I?

It's a pitcher's battle all the way—a duel—
a catcher's, as, with cruel
    puma paw, Elston Howard lumbers lightly
      back to plate. (His spring
      de-winged a bat swing.)
    They have that killer instinct;
yet Elston—whose catching

---

* An avid baseball fan, Moore refers throughout to various members of the New York Yankees during the early 1960s.

arm has hurt them all with the bat—   20
    when questioned, says, unenviously,
"I'm very satisfied. We won."
    Shorn of the batting crown,[1] says, "We";
robbed by a technicality.

When three players on a side play three positions
and modify conditions,
    the massive run need not be everything.
      "Going, going . . . " Is
    it? Roger Maris
has it, running fast. You will   30
never see a finer catch. Well . . .
    "Mickey,[2] leaping like the devil"—why
      gild it, although deer sounds better—
snares what was speeding towards its treetop nest,
    one-handing the souvenir-to-be
    meant to be caught by you or me.

Assign Yogi Berra to Cape Canaveral;
he could handle any missile.
    He is no feather. "Strike! . . . Strike *two!*"
      Fouled back. A blur.   40
    It's gone. You would infer
that the bat had eyes.
He put the wood to that one.
Praised, Skowron says, "Thanks, Mel.[3]
I think I helped a *little* bit."
      All business, each, and modesty.
    Blanchard, Richardson, Kubek, Boyer.[4]
    In that galaxy of nine, say which
    won the pennant? *Each*. It was he.

Those two magnificent saves from the knee—throws   50
by Boyer, finesses in twos—
    like Whitey's[5] three kinds of pitch and pre-
      diagnosis
    with pick-off psychosis.
    Pitching is a large subject.
Your arm, too true at first, can learn to
catch the corners—even trouble
    Mickey Mantle. ("Grazed a Yankee!
My baby pitcher, Montejo!"[6]
    With some pedagogy,[7]   60
    you'll be touch, premature prodigy.)

---

[1] An accolade for the player with the highest batting average in a given year.   [2] Mickey Mantle.
[3] Bill ("Moose") Skowron; Mel Stottlemeyer.
[4] Johnny Blanchard, Bobby Richardson, Tony Kubek, Clete Boyer.   [5] Whitey Ford.
[6] Manny Montejo, of the Detroit Tigers.   [7] Instruction.

They crowd him and curve him and aim for the knees. Trying
indeed! The secret implying:
  "I can stand here, bat held steady."
    One may suit him;
    none has hit him.
  Imponderables smite him.
  Muscle kinks, infections, spike wounds
  require food, rest, respite from ruffians. (Drat it!
    Celebrity costs privacy!)
Cow's milk, "tiger's milk," soy milk, carrot juice,
    brewer's yeast (high-potency)—
    concentrates presage victory

sped by Luis Arroyo, Hector Lopez—
deadly in a pinch. And "Yes,
  it's work; I want you to bear down,
    but enjoy it
    while you're doing it."
  Mr. Houk and Mr. Sain,[8]
  If you have a rummage sale,
  don't sell Roland Sheldon or Tom Tresh.
    Studded with stars in belt and crown,
the Stadium is an adastrium.[9]
    O flashing Orion,[10]
    your stars are muscled like the lion.

1966

T. S. Eliot
(1888–1965)

In April 1956 Thomas Stearns Eliot gave the lecture "The Frontiers of Criticism" in a
stadium at the University of Minnesota. Fourteen thousand people heard him speak. Today
such vast crowds seem to gather only for rock bands, sporting events, and presidential
candidates. That so many people were interested in hearing T. S. Eliot points to his position late in life as the leading poet and man of letters of his day.

Eliot was born in St. Louis to a transplanted New England family: his grandfather
founded Washington University in St. Louis; his father ran a brick-manufacturing firm;
and his mother fostered Eliot's interest in literature. A 1910 Harvard University graduate,
he earned an M.A. in Sanskrit and philosophy from Harvard in 1914. Eliot then settled in

[8] Ralph Houk and Johnny Sain, then in management positions.
[9] Probably coined from *ad astrum*, "to the star" (Latin).
[10] An equatorial constellation, the hunter.

England and did not visit the United States until eighteen years had passed. He married Vivienne Haigh-Wood in 1915 and worked as a bank clerk in London from 1918 to 1924. His wife's continuous illnesses and his father's disapproval and subsequent death led Eliot to an emotional breakdown. (Vivienne, ultimately institutionalized, died in 1947.)

Recovered, Eliot went on to edit the journals *The Egoist* and *The Criterion* (which he founded in 1922 and continued to edit until 1939). In 1927 he took British citizenship and joined the Anglican church, actions that had profound effects on the content and scope of his poetry. Despite his adopted citizenship, Eliot retained an American sensibility. In a 1959 interview for *Writers at Work,* Eliot said of his poetry that "in its sources, in its emotional springs, it comes from America."

Shortly after moving to England, Eliot met Ezra Pound. In September 1914 Pound wrote to Harriet Monroe, the editor of *Poetry* magazine, that Eliot "has actually trained himself *and* modernized himself *on his own*." Pound's comment focuses on Eliot's education and poetic craftsmanship. Eliot was well read (or "trained") in a number of languages and traditions, including Latin and Greek classics, French and German, and Eastern philosophy. Eliot started "modernizing himself," using techniques that Pound thought essential for the revitalization of poetry, by reading French symbolist poetry, which he first encountered in Arthur Symons's *The Symbolist Movement in Literature* (1899). That book led Eliot to read the poetry of Jules Laforgue, from which he learned the technique of introverted irony and of splitting the personality into two, techniques that Eliot used in his first volume of poems, *Prufrock and Other Observations* (1917).

In "The Love Song of J. Alfred Prufrock," the first poem in that volume, Prufrock, a mild, ineffectual man approaching middle age, discusses with himself visiting a woman to make some sort of declaration. He is the victim of an overactive imagination that paralyzes him with scenarios of the fool he might appear to be. The first image in the poem, "the evening spread out against the sky / Like a patient etherized upon a table," is notable not only for its antiromantic shock value, but also as a description of Prufrock himself. Prufrock finally decides that it is too late to visit the woman and takes no action at all. The doubling of his personality into "you and I" is Laforgian, as is the irony in the poem, which Prufrock directs at himself. He compares his indecision with that of Hamlet, a heroic figure, and thinks that he is more like Polonius, an officious busybody who might start a scene but would never be the central character.

"Sweeney Among the Nightingales" appeared in Eliot's second volume, *Poems* (1920). Many of the poems of that volume were written in quatrains, because Eliot and Pound decided that free verse had been overused and that they should try to work in a tighter form. "Sweeney" exemplifies the way Eliot conflates past and present. The poem seems to be leading to some dreadful action against Sweeney although nothing dreadful actually occurs in the poem. Eliot parallels Sweeney's plight with that of Agamemnon, the Greek commander in the Trojan War, killed by his wife on his return from Troy, and with the fate of Philomela, a princess of Athens, turned into a nightingale after her brother-in-law raped her and cut out her tongue. Eliot is not saying that the past is better than the present or vice-versa. Rather, he makes Sweeney (the present) seem more heroic by drawing him together with Agamemnon (the past) and at the same time deflates Agamemnon's heroism by comparing him with Sweeney. Further, Eliot suggests the unheroic aspect of Agamemnon's career, the aspect that caused his wife's deadly hatred.

This complicated use of the past is further developed in Eliot's next major poem, *The Waste Land,* published in 1922, as was James Joyce's *Ulysses.* In his essay "*Ulysses,* Order and Myth" (appearing in *The Dial,* November 1923) Eliot describes Joyce's "mythic method" as "manipulating a continuous parallel between contemporaneity and antiquity," providing a means "of controlling, of ordering, of giving a shape and a significance to the immense panorama of futility and anarchy which is contemporary history." This description applies as well to Eliot's method in *The Waste Land,* which has been thought to be emblematic of the despair felt after World War I. The poem combines fragments of the literature of the past, "shoring" them against the ruins of contemporary society.

The Waste Land became more disjunct, or fragmented, as a result of Ezra Pound's input. His editing removed abstraction, description, and narration and focused on concrete images, in the process making the poem less conventional in rhyme and meter. The disjunctive quality of the poem makes it difficult for the reader to organize into a whole. Eliot's first note to the poem indicates one way, pointing the reader to Jessie Weston's anthropological study of the Grail legend, *From Ritual to Romance* (1920), as an important source for the poem. Weston's book ties the Arthurian Grail legends to pre-Christian fertility myths found in many cultures. In the Arthurian versions a knight must go to the Chapel Perilous and ask questions about the objects he sees there, which usually include a lance and a cup. Asking the appropriate questions results in the healing of the wounded Fisher King and his land, both of which have been rendered sterile. Eliot also recognizes the influence of James G. Frazer's *The Golden Bough* (1907–1915), a compendium of worldwide myths and ritual practices that finds similarities in myths of different cultures. This comparative approach to culture lies behind Eliot's conflation of Eastern and Western religion, myth, and literature in *The Waste Land.*

Whereas many of Eliot's shorter poems are dramatic monologues, *The Waste Land* contains a series of voices, generally unidentified, speaking in sequence. The voices are filtered through the consciousness of Tiresias, the blind seer who has been both male and female. In the poem's landscape of urban and rural desert, the speakers are involved in fruitless sexual relationships and prefer death to the rebirth possible only if rain comes to the Waste Land, if the questions are asked and the Fisher King healed. Voices ask questions throughout the poem, but none of the questions seems to be the right one: while a damp wind blows and the thunder rolls at the end of the poem, no rain falls.

After *The Waste Land* Eliot published *The Hollow Men* (1925), which seems a distillation of the material of *The Waste Land.* At this point Eliot had to find some new poetic avenue; he could go no further with that material. Out of his conversion to Anglicanism came *Ash-Wednesday* (1930) and his Ariel poems (from the Old Testament name for Jerusalem). Each published separately as a sort of Christmas card, the Ariel poems deal with a yearning for revelation, a seeking of fulfillment within a world lacking faith and certainty. *Journey of the Magi* (1927), the first of the Ariel poems, is a dramatic monologue spoken by one of the Magi after returning from the visit to the Christ child. He has seen the beginning of the New Dispensation but has no knowledge of the sacrifice yet to be made. He is caught between the old and the new, waiting for some revelation that he has no assurance will ever come. The despair in the Magus's words reflects the despair Eliot saw in so much of the early twentieth century: an old faith fading with no new faith to take its place. Eliot chose to revive the old faith in his own life, deciding that no other could do as well.

In *Marina* (1930), the last of the Ariel poems, Shakespeare's Pericles awakens to discover his lost daughter. In this dramatic monologue Pericles speaks of his wonder and joy. The fullness of revelation seems to be his, as the event for which he has long wished has finally happened. Eliot juxtaposes a quotation from the Roman philosopher/dramatist Seneca, however, to show the opposite possibility: Hercules awakens from madness to find his children dead by his own hand. Pericles' joy must be understood in contrast to the other extreme.

In the 1930s Eliot wrote the verse dramas *Murder in the Cathedral* (1935) and *The Family Reunion* (1939). However, with the intervention of World War II and the closing

Antonello da Messina's striking painting The Crucifixion *(1455?), which T. S. Eliot saw in Antwerp, heightened Eliot's interest in religious themes and images.*

of London theaters, Eliot returned to writing nondramatic poetry. In 1935 he had written *Burnt Norton* (1936), which begins with passages taken from *Murder in the Cathedral*. Then he wrote three more poems using the same structure and themes—time and eternity, memory and history—and named the group *Four Quartets* (1943). *East Coker* (1940), the second of the four, is concerned with Eliot's family history and the history of England. Whereas *Burnt Norton* speculates on what might have happened, *East Coker* focuses on what has happened. The other two poems in the cycle are *The Dry Salvages* (1941) and *Little Gidding* (1942).

East Coker is the English village from which Eliot's family migrated to America in the seventeenth century. Eliot roots the poem and his family in the English Renaissance, a time of growth and change in literature, science, and exploration. The motto of Mary, Queen of Scots, whose end came from a beheading ax, reminds the reader of the cyclical nature of life: the earth, composed of "flesh, fur and faeces," is part of growth and change. As the other quartets are tied to air, fire, and water, *East Coker* is the quartet of earth—the earth of burial, the earth of rebirth in the cyclical pattern of the seasons. Part four of *East Coker* uses the metaphor of the wounded surgeon (Christ) to discuss the paradoxical nature of mankind's salvation. The dying that is inevitable can be redeemed by the wounded surgeon; "dying of the absolute paternal care" gives life. The paradoxes of Christianity take human beings beyond the cyclical living and dying of earth. The poet seeks to find the "still point," the eternal, but the cycles of change, death, and rebirth make such stillness difficult to obtain. Eliot has moved beyond the despair of *The Waste Land* to a vision of life that includes death and rebirth, not fearing or denying the possibility of renewal.

After *Four Quartets* Eliot wrote almost no nondramatic poetry. He returned to the stage with three more verse plays, of which the most successful was *The Cocktail Party* (1950). In 1948 he won the Nobel Prize for literature and the British Order of Merit. Eliot received numerous other awards and was met by huge crowds wherever he went. At age sixty-eight he married his longtime secretary, Valerie Fletcher. He died in 1965, and his ashes are buried in the church at East Coker.

Suggested Readings: *The Sacred Wood*, 1920. *The Use of Poetry and the Use of Criticism*, 1933. *Selected Essays*, 1950. *On Poetry and Poets*, 1957. *Collected Plays*, 1962. *Collected Poems 1909–1962*, 1963. *To Criticise the Critic*, 1965. *The Waste Land, a Facsimile and Transcripts of the Original Drafts*, ed. V. Eliot, 1971. *Selected Prose of T. S. Eliot*, ed. F. Kermode, 1975. *The Letters of T. S. Eliot*, Vol. 1, ed. V. Eliot, 1988. H. Gardner, *The Art of T. S. Eliot*, 1949. N. Frye, *T. S. Eliot*, 1963. D. C. Gallup, *T. S. Eliot: A Bibliography*, 1969. A. W. Litz, ed., *Eliot in His Time: Essays on the Occasion of the Fiftieth Anniversary of The Waste Land*, 1973. L. Gordon, *Eliot's Early Years*, 1977. H. Gardner, *The Composition of Four Quartets*, 1978. J. Reibetanz, *A Reading of Four Quartets*, 1983. P. Ackroyd, *T. S. Eliot: A Life*, 1984. R. Bush, *T. S. Eliot: A Study in Character and Style*, 1984. L. Gordon, *Eliot's New Life*, 1988.

Text Used: *The Complete Poems and Plays*, 1969.

THE LOVE SONG OF J. ALFRED PRUFROCK*

> *S'io credessi che mia risposta fosse*
> *a persona che mai tornasse al mondo,*
> *questa fiamma staria senza più scosse.*
> *Ma per ciò che giammai di questo fondo*
> *non torno vivo alcun, s'i'odo il vero,*
> *senza tema d'infamia ti rispondo.*[1]

    Let us go then, you and I,
When the evening is spread out against the sky
Like a patient etherised upon a table;
Let us go, through certain half-deserted streets,
The muttering retreats
Of restless nights in one-night cheap hotels
And sawdust restaurants with oyster-shells:
Streets that follow like a tedious argument
Of insidious intent
To lead you to an overwhelming question . . .   10
Oh, do not ask, 'What is it?'
Let us go and make our visit.

    In the room the women come and go
Talking of Michelangelo.

---

* First published in *Poetry* in 1915 and collected in Eliot's first volume of poems, *Prufrock and Other Observations* (1917); the ellipses are Eliot's.

[1] "If I thought my reply were to one who could return to the world, this flame would stop flickering. But since no one returns alive from this pit, if what I hear is true, I answer you without fear of dishonor" (Italian), from *Inferno* (XXVII. 61–66), by Dante Alighieri (1265–1321). Spoken to the character Dante by Guido da Montefeltro, who, while wrapped in flame, confesses to the sin of fraudulent counseling.

The yellow fog that rubs its back upon the window-panes,
The yellow smoke that rubs its muzzle on the window-panes,
Licked its tongue into the corners of the evening,
Lingered upon the pools that stand in drains,
Let fall upon its back the soot that falls from chimneys,
Slipped by the terrace, made a sudden leap,   20
And seeing that it was a soft October night,
Curled once about the house, and fell asleep.

And indeed there will be time
For the yellow smoke that slides along the street
Rubbing its back upon the window-panes;
There will be time, there will be time
To prepare a face to meet the faces that you meet;
There will be time to murder and create,
And time for all the works and days[2] of hands
That lift and drop a question on your plate;   30
Time for you and time for me,
And time yet for a hundred indecisions,
And for a hundred visions and revisions,
Before the taking of a toast and tea.

In the room the women come and go
Talking of Michelangelo.

And indeed there will be time
To wonder, 'Do I dare?' and, 'Do I dare?'
Time to turn back and descend the stair,
With a bald spot in the middle of my hair—   40
(They will say: 'How his hair is growing thin!')
My morning coat, my collar mounting firmly to the chin,
My necktie rich and modest, but asserted by a simple pin—
(They will say: 'But how his arms and legs are thin!')
Do I dare
Disturb the universe?
In a minute there is time
For decisions and revisions which a minute will reverse.

For I have known them all already, known them all—
Have known the evenings, mornings, afternoons,   50
I have measured out my life with coffee spoons;
I know the voices dying with a dying fall
Beneath the music from a farther room.
    So how should I presume?

And I have known the eyes already, known them all—
The eyes that fix you in a formulated phrase,
And when I am formulated, sprawling on a pin,

[2] *Works and Days,* an agricultural poem by the Greek poet Hesiod (8th century B.C.).

When I am pinned and wriggling on the wall,
Then how should I begin
To spit out all the butt-ends of my days and ways?   60
    And how should I presume?

And I have known the arms already, known them all—
Arms that are braceleted and white and bare
(But in the lamplight, downed with light brown hair!)
Is it perfume from a dress
That makes me so digress?
Arms that lie along a table, or wrap about a shawl.
    And should I then presume?
    And how should I begin?

                    .   .   .   .

Shall I say, I have gone at dusk through narrow streets   70
And watched the smoke that rises from the pipes
Of lonely men in shirt-sleeves, leaning out of windows? . . .

I should have been a pair of ragged claws
Scuttling across the floors of silent seas.

                    .   .   .   .

And the afternoon, the evening, sleeps so peacefully!
Smoothed by long fingers,
Asleep . . . tired . . . or it malingers,
Stretched on the floor, here beside you and me.
Should I, after tea and cakes and ices,
Have the strength to force the moment to its crisis?   80
But though I have wept and fasted, wept and prayed,
Though I have seen my head (grown slightly bald)
        brought in upon a platter,[3]
I am no prophet—and here's no great matter;
I have seen the moment of my greatness flicker,
And I have seen the eternal Footman hold my coat, and snicker,
And in short, I was afraid.

And would it have been worth it, after all,
After the cups, the marmalade, the tea,
Among the porcelain, among some talk of you and me,
Would it have been worth while,   90
To have bitten off the matter with a smile,
To have squeezed the universe into a ball[4]
To roll it towards some overwhelming question,

---

[3] In Matthew 14:3–11, when Salome, Herodias's daughter, pleased Herod with her dancing, he promised her anything she requested. She asked for and received the head of the prophet John the Baptist on a platter.
[4] "Let us roll all our strength and all / Our sweetness up into one ball / And tear our pleasures with rough strife / Through the iron gates of life," from "To His Coy Mistress," by the English poet Andrew Marvell (1621–1628).

To say: 'I am Lazarus, come from the dead,[5]
Come back to tell you all, I shall tell you all'—
If one, settling a pillow by her head,
 Should say: 'That is not what I meant at all.
 That is not it, at all.'

 And would it have been worth it, after all,
Would it have been worth while,   100
After the sunsets and the dooryards and the sprinkled streets,
After the novels, after the teacups, after the skirts that trail along
  the floor—
And this, and so much more?—
It is impossible to say just what I mean!
But as if a magic lantern threw the nerves in patterns on a screen:
Would it have been worth while
If one, settling a pillow or throwing off a shawl,
And turning toward the window, should say:
 'That is not it at all,
 That is not what I meant, at all.'   110

   . . . . .

 No! I am not Prince Hamlet, nor was meant to be;
Am an attendant lord, one that will do
To swell a progress,[6] start a scene or two,
Advise the prince; no doubt, an easy tool,
Deferential, glad to be of use,
Politic, cautious, and meticulous;
Full of high sentence,[7] but a bit obtuse;
At times, indeed, almost ridiculous—
Almost, at times, the Fool.

 I grow old . . . I grow old . . .   120
I shall wear the bottoms of my trousers rolled.

 Shall I part my hair behind? Do I dare to eat a peach?
I shall wear white flannel trousers, and walk upon the beach.
I have heard the mermaids singing, each to each.

I do not think that they will sing to me.
I have seen them riding seaward on the waves
Combing the white hair of the waves blown back
When the wind blows the water white and black.

We have lingered in the chambers of the sea
By sea-girls wreathed with seaweed red and brown   130
Till human voices wake us, and we drown.

            1910–1911, 1915

---

[5] In John 11:1–44 Jesus raised Lazarus from the dead. [6] A royal procession.
[7] Judgment or opinion.

COUSIN NANCY

Miss Nancy Ellicott
Strode across the hills and broke them,
Rode across the hills and broke them—
The barren New England hills—
Riding to hounds
Over the cow-pasture.

Miss Nancy Ellicott smoked
And danced all the modern dances;
And her aunts were not quite sure how they felt about it,
But they knew that it was modern.   10

Upon the glazen shelves kept watch
Matthew and Waldo,[1] guardians of the faith,
The army of unalterable law.[2]

1917

SWEENEY AMONG THE NIGHTINGALES*

ὤμοι, πέπληγμαι καιρίαν πληγὴν ἔσω.[1]

Apeneck Sweeney spreads his knees
Letting his arms hang down to laugh,
The zebra stripes along his jaw
Swelling to maculate[2] giraffe.

The circles of the stormy moon
Slide westward toward the River Plate,[3]
Death and the Raven[4] drift above
And Sweeney guards the hornèd gate.[5]

---

[1] Matthew Arnold (1822–1888) and Ralph Waldo Emerson (1803–1882), guardians of Victorian moral and literary standards.

[2] In the sonnet "Lucifer in Starlight," by the English novelist and poet George Meredith (1829–1909), Lucifer (the Devil) soars over the earth until he looks up: "He reached a middle height, and at the stars, / Which are the brain of heaven, he looked, and sank. / Around the ancient track marched, rank on rank, / The army of unalterable law."

* Eliot's symbolic character Sweeney, a vulgar person, is introduced in "Mr. Eliot's Sunday Morning Service" (1918) and appears again in such poems as "Sweeney Erect" (1919), *The Waste Land* (1922), and *Sweeney Agonistes* (1926–1927).

[1] "Alas, I have been struck by a mortal blow," from *Agamemnon* (l.1343), by the Greek tragedian Aeschylus (525?–456 B.C.): the last words of Agamemnon, the leader of the Greeks in the Trojan War, who was killed in his bath by his wife, Clytemnestra.

[2] Spotted, blotched.   [3] The Río de la Plata, an estuary between Uruguay and Argentina.

[4] The southern constellation Corvus, the Crow.

[5] According to Greek myth, one of the two gates of the dead. False dreams come to humans through the ivory gate, true dreams through the horn gate.

Gloomy Orion and the Dog[6]
Are veiled; and hushed the shrunken seas;   10
The person in the Spanish cape
Tries to sit on Sweeney's knees

Slips and pulls the table cloth
Overturns a coffee-cup,
Reorganised upon the floor
She yawns and draws a stocking up;

The silent man in mocha brown
Sprawls at the window-sill and gapes;
The waiter brings in oranges
Bananas figs and hothouse grapes;   20

The silent vertebrate in brown
Contracts and concentrates, withdraws;
Rachel *née* Rabinovitch
Tears at the grapes with murderous paws;

She and the lady in the cape
Are suspect, thought to be in league;
Therefore the man with heavy eyes
Declines the gambit, shows fatigue,

Leaves the room and reappears
Outside the window, leaning in,   30
Branches of wistaria
Circumscribe a golden grin;

The host with someone indistinct
Converses at the door apart,
The nightingales[7] are singing near
The Convent of the Sacred Heart,

And sang within the bloody wood
When Agamemnon cried aloud
And let their liquid siftings fall
To stain the stiff dishonoured shroud.   40

1918

---

[6] The equatorial constellation of the hunter, and the nearby "Dog Star," Sirius, the hunter's dog.

[7] According to Greek myth, Philomela was raped by her brother-in-law, Tereus, who cut out her tongue to prevent her from identifying him as her attacker. She wove a tapestry showing what had happened and sent it to her sister, Procne. Philomela was turned into a nightingale, Procne into a swallow.

THE WASTE LAND*

*'Nam Sibyllam quidem Cumis ego ipse oculis meis vidi in ampulla pendere, et cum illi
pueri dicerent: Σίβυλλα τί θέλεις; respondebat illa: ἀποθανεῖν θέλω.'*[1]

For Ezra Pound
il miglior fabbro.[2]

I. The Burial of the Dead[3]

April is the cruellest month, breeding
Lilacs out of the dead land, mixing
Memory and desire, stirring
Dull roots with spring rain.
Winter kept us warm, covering
Earth in forgetful snow, feeding
A little life with dried tubers.
Summer surprised us, coming over the Starnbergersee[4]
With a shower of rain; we stopped in the colonnade,
And went on in sunlight, into the Hofgarten,[5]   10
And drank coffee, and talked for an hour.
Bin gar keine Russin, stamm' aus Litauen, echt deutsch.[6]
And when we were children, staying at the arch-duke's,
My cousin's, he took me out on a sled,
And I was frightened. He said, Marie,
Marie, hold on tight. And down we went.

---

* Eliot states in *The Frontiers of Criticism* (1956), "When it came to print *The Waste Land* as a little book [1922]—for the poem on its first appearance in *The Dial* [1922] and in *The Criterion* [1922] had no notes whatever—it was discovered that the poem was inconveniently short, so I set to work to expand the notes, in order to provide a few more pages of printed matter. . . . " Eliot's note: "Not only the title, but the plan and a good deal of the incidental symbolism of the poem were suggested by Miss Jessie L. Weston's book on the Grail legend: *From Ritual to Romance* (Cambridge [1920]). Indeed, so deeply am I indebted, Miss Weston's book will elucidate the difficulties of the poem much better than my notes can do; and I recommend it (apart from the great interest of the book itself) to any who think such elucidation of the poem worth the trouble. To another work of anthropology I am indebted in general, one which has influenced our generation profoundly; I mean *The Golden Bough* [(1890), by the Scottish anthropologist Sir James Frazer]; I have used especially the two volumes *Adonis, Attis, Osiris.* Anyone who is acquainted with these works will immediately recognise in the poem certain references to vegetation ceremonies."

[1] "For I myself with my own eyes saw the Sibyl of Cumae hanging in a bottle, and when the boys asked her: 'Sibyl, what do you want?' she responded, 'I want to die,'" from *Satyricon* (Ch. 48), by the Roman satirist Petronius (?–A.D. 66). According to Roman myth, the sun god Apollo granted the sibyl (a prophetess) immortality, but, having forgotten to ask for eternal youth, she was doomed to perpetual old age.

[2] "The best maker" (Italian), from *Purgatorio* (XXVI.117), by Dante Alighieri (1265–1321). Dante praises the Italian poet Guido Guinizelli (1240?–1274), who responds that the Provençal poet Arnaut Daniel (12th century B.C.) is the best maker of poetry. Pound (1885–1972) edited *The Waste Land*.

[3] The burial service in the Anglican *Book of Common Prayer*.

[4] A lake south of Munich.   [5] A public garden in Munich.

[6] "I am not at all Russian, I come from Lithuania, a real German" (German).

In the mountains, there you feel free.
I read, much of the night, and go south in the winter.

What are the roots that clutch, what branches grow
Out of this stony rubbish? Son of man,[7]   20
You cannot say, or guess, for you know only
A heap of broken images, where the sun beats,
And the dead tree gives no shelter, the cricket no relief,[8]
And the dry stone no sound of water. Only
There is shadow under this red rock,
(Come in under the shadow of this red rock),
And I will show you something different from either
Your shadow at morning striding behind you
Or your shadow at evening rising to meet you;
I will show you fear in a handful of dust.   30
                      Frisch weht der Wind[9]
                      Der Heimat zu
                      Mein Irisch Kind
                      Wo weilest du?
'You gave me hyacinths first a year ago;
'They called me the hyacinth girl.'[10]
—Yet when we came back, late, from the hyacinth garden,
Your arms full, and your hair wet, I could not
Speak, and my eyes failed, I was neither
Living nor dead, and I knew nothing,   40
Looking into the heart of light, the silence.
Oed' und leer das Meer.[11]

Madame Sosostris, famous clairvoyante,
Had a bad cold, nevertheless
Is known to be the wisest woman in Europe,
With a wicked pack of cards.[12] Here, said she,
Is your card, the drowned Phoenician Sailor,

---

[7] Eliot's note: "Cf. Ezekiel II, i," in which God tells the "Son of man," the prophet Ezekiel, "Stand upon thy feet, and I will speak unto thee."

[8] Eliot's note: "Cf. Ecclesiastes XII, v," in which old age is said to be a time when "the grasshopper shall be a burden, and desire shall fail."

[9] "Fresh blows the wind / to the homeland / my Irish child / where are you waiting?" (German). Eliot's note: "V. *Tristan und Isolde*, I. verses 5–8," an opera by Richard Wagner (1813–1883).

[10] According to Greek myth, Hyacinthus was a youth accidentally killed by Apollo, who resurrected the boy as a flower, the hyacinth, which came to symbolize rebirth.

[11] "Empty and barren is the sea" (German). Eliot's note: "Id. III, verse 24." Near the end of Wagner's opera, the dying Tristan is told that his love Isolde's ship cannot be seen.

[12] Eliot's note: "I am not familiar with the exact constitution of the Tarot pack of cards, from which I have obviously departed to suit my own convenience. The Hanged Man, a member of the traditional pack, fits my purpose in two ways: because he is associated in my mind with the Hanged God of Frazer, and because I associate him with the hooded figure in the passage of the disciples of Emmaus in Part V. The Phoenician Sailor and the Merchant appear later; also the 'crowds of people,' and Death by Water is executed in Part IV. The Man with Three Staves (an authentic member of the Tarot pack) I associate, quite arbitrarily, with the Fisher King himself."

(Those are pearls that were his eyes.[13] Look!)
Here is Belladonna, the Lady of the Rocks,[14]
The lady of situations.   50
Here is the man with three staves, and here the Wheel,
And here is the one-eyed merchant, and this card,
Which is blank, is something he carries on his back,
Which I am forbidden to see. I do not find
The Hanged Man. Fear death by water.
I see crowds of people, walking round in a ring.
Thank you. If you see dear Mrs. Equitone,
Tell her I bring the horoscope myself:
One must be so careful these days.

        Unreal City,[15]   60
Under the brown fog of a winter dawn,
A crowd flowed over London Bridge, so many,
I had not thought death had undone so many.[16]
Sighs, short and infrequent, were exhaled,[17]
And each man fixed his eyes before his feet.
Flowed up the hill and down King William Street,
To where Saint Mary Woolnoth[18] kept the hours
With a dead sound on the final stroke of nine.[19]
There I saw one I knew, and stopped him, crying: 'Stetson!
'You who were with me in the ships at Mylae![20]   70
'That corpse you planted last year in your garden,
'Has it begun to sprout? Will it bloom this year?
'Or has the sudden frost disturbed its bed?
'O keep the Dog far hence, that's friend to men,[21]

---

[13] In Shakespeare's *The Tempest* (I.ii.397–402) Ariel sings to Ferdinand, who fears that his father has drowned: "Full fathom five thy father lies, / Of his bones are coral made: / Those are pearls that were his eyes: / Nothing of him that doth fade, / But doth suffer a sea-change / Into something rich and strange."

[14] "Beautiful lady" (Italian), the poisonous plant nightshade and a cosmetic; also the Virgin Mary of the painting *Madonna of the Rocks*, by Leonardo da Vinci.

[15] Eliot's note: "Cf. Baudelaire: 'Fourmillante cité, cité pleine de rêves, / Où le spectre en plein jour raccroche le passant' " (French): "Swarming city, city full of dreams, / Where the specter in broad daylight accosts the passerby," from *Les Fleurs du Mal* (*The Flowers of Evil*, 1857), by the French symbolist Charles Baudelaire (1821–1867).

[16] Eliot's note: "Cf. *Inferno*, III, 55–57: 'si lunga tratta / di gente, ch'io non avrei mai creduto / che morte tanta n'avesse disfatta' " (Italian): "such a long train / of people, I should not have believed / that death had undone so many." Entering the Inferno, Dante sees the hordes of people who made no choices in life and therefore have been rejected by both Heaven and Hell.

[17] Eliot's note: "Cf. *Inferno*, IV, 25–27: 'Quivi, secondo che per ascoltare, / non avea piante ma' che di sospiri, / che l'aura eterna facevan tremare' " (Italian): "Here, to judge by hearing, there was no weeping but sighs / that made the eternal air tremble." Dante is in the first circle of the Inferno, Limbo, where the virtuous non-Christians suffer only from the fact that they can never see God.

[18] A London church.

[19] Eliot's note: "A phenomenon which I have often noticed."

[20] The site of a Roman naval victory against Carthage (260 B.C.).

[21] Eliot's note: "Cf. the Dirge in Webster's *White Devil*." The play *The White Devil or Vittoria Corombona* (1610?), by John Webster (1580?–1625?), ends, "But keep the wolf far thence, that's foe to men; / For with his nails he'll dig them up again."

'Or with his nails he'll dig it up again!
'You! hypocrite lecteur!—mon semblable,—mon frère!'[22]

II. A Game of Chess[23]

The Chair she sat in, like a burnished throne,[24]
Glowed on the marble, where the glass
Held up by standards wrought with fruited vines
From which a golden Cupidon[25] peeped out   80
(Another hid his eyes behind his wing)
Doubled the flames of sevenbranched candelabra
Reflecting light upon the table as
The glitter of her jewels rose to meet it,
From satin cases poured in rich profusion.
In vials of ivory and coloured glass
Unstoppered, lurked her strange synthetic perfumes,
Unguent, powdered, or liquid—troubled, confused
And drowned the sense in odours; stirred by the air
That freshened from the window, these ascended   90
In fattening the prolonged candle-flames,
Flung their smoke into the laquearia,[26]
Stirring the pattern on the coffered ceiling.
Huge sea-wood fed with copper
Burned green and orange, framed by the coloured stone,
In which sad light a carvèd dolphin swam.
Above the antique mantel was displayed
As though a window gave upon the sylvan scene[27]
The change of Philomel, by the barbarous king[28]
So rudely forced; yet there the nightingale[29]   100
Filled all the desert with inviolable voice

[22] Eliot's note: "V. Baudelaire, Preface to *Fleurs du Mal*." The prefatory poem to this volume, titled "Au Lecteur" ("To the Reader") ends with the line, "You! Hypocritical reader!—my counterpart,—my brother!"

[23] Probably refers to one of two plays by Thomas Middleton (1570?–1627): *A Game at Chesse* (1624), a political satire, or *Women Beware Women* (1657), in which a woman is seduced while her mother-in-law plays chess nearby.

[24] Eliot's note: "Cf. *Antony and Cleopatra*, II, ii, 1. 190." In this Shakespeare play, Enobarbus, attempting to describe Cleopatra to Roman friends, begins his famous speech, "The barge she sat in, like a burnish'd throne."

[25] A statue of the Roman god of love, Cupid.

[26] Eliot's note: "Laquearia. V. *Aeneid*, I, 726: dependent lychni laquearibus aureis incensi, et noctem flammis funalia vincunt" (Latin): "from the golden paneled ceiling hang lamps, and the torches conquer the night with their flames," a description of the banquet hall where Aeneas is welcomed to Carthage by Queen Dido, who later kills herself after Aeneas abandons her to found Rome.

[27] Eliot's note: "Sylvan scene. V. Milton, *Paradise Lost*, IV, 140." In this epic by John Milton (1608–1674), Satan comes to Eden and sees "A Silvan Scene, and as the ranks ascend / Shade above shade, a woody Theatre / Of stateliest view" (140–142).

[28] Eliot's note: "V. Ovid, *Metamorphoses*, VI, Philomela." In this narrative poem by the Roman Ovid (43 B.C.–A.D. 17?), Philomela is raped by King Tereus of Thrace, her brother-in-law, who cuts out her tongue to silence her; the gods transform her into a nightingale. Note the contrast from the Edenic sylvan scene of the previous line.

[29] Eliot's note: "Cf. Part III, l. 204" (of *The Waste Land*).

And still she cried, and still the world pursues,
'Jug Jug'[30] to dirty ears.
And other withered stumps of time
Were told upon the walls; staring forms
Leaned out, leaning, hushing the room enclosed.
Footsteps shuffled on the stair.
Under the firelight, under the brush, her hair
Spread out in fiery points
Glowed into words, then would be savagely still.   110

   'My nerves are bad to-night. Yes, bad. Stay with me.
Speak to me. Why do you never speak. Speak.
      What are you thinking of? What thinking? What?
I never know what you are thinking. Think.'

   I think we are in rats' alley[31]
Where the dead men lost their bones.

   'What is that noise?'
                    The wind under the door.[32]
'What is that noise now? What is the wind doing?'
                    Nothing again nothing.   120
                                        'Do
'You know nothing? Do you see nothing? Do you remember
Nothing?'

   I remember
Those are pearls that were his eyes.
'Are you alive, or not? Is there nothing in your head?'[33]
                                        But
O O O O that Shakespeherian Rag[34]—
It's so elegant
So intelligent   130
'What shall I do now? What shall I do?
I shall rush out as I am, and walk the street
With my hair down, so. What shall we do tomorrow?
What shall we ever do?'
                    The hot water at ten.
And if it rains, a closed car at four.
And we shall play a game of chess,
Pressing lidless eyes and waiting for a knock upon the door.[35]

---

[30] A standard Elizabethan transcription of the nightingale's song.
[31] Eliot's note: "Cf. Part III, l. 195" (of *The Waste Land*).
[32] Eliot's note: "Cf. Webster: 'Is the wind in that door still?' " In Webster's *The Devil's Law Case* (1619?) (III.ii), a doctor makes this comment when an attack fails to kill the victim, who is still breathing.
[33] Eliot's note: "Cf. Part I, l. 37, 48" (of *The Waste Land*).
[34] "The Shakespearian Rag" (1912), lyrics by Gene Buck and Herman Ruby, music by Dave Stamper, contains the chorus: "That Shakespearian rag, / Most intelligent, very elegant. . . . "
[35] Eliot's note: "Cf. the game of chess in Middleton's *Women Beware Women*."

When Lil's husband got demobbed,[36] I said—
I didn't mince my words, I said to her myself,   140
HURRY UP PLEASE ITS TIME[37]
Now Albert's coming back, make yourself a bit smart.
He'll want to know what you done with that money he gave you
To get yourself some teeth. He did, I was there.
You have them all out, Lil, and get a nice set,
He said, I swear, I can't bear to look at you.
And no more can't I, I said, and think of poor Albert,
He's been in the army four years, he wants a good time,
And if you don't give it him, there's others will, I said.
Oh is there, she said. Something o' that, I said.   150
Then I'll know who to thank, she said, and give me a straight look.
HURRY UP PLEASE ITS TIME
If you don't like it you can get on with it, I said.
Others can pick and choose if you can't.
But if Albert makes off, it won't be for lack of telling.
You ought to be ashamed, I said, to look so antique.
(And her only thirty-one.)
I can't help it, she said, pulling a long face,
It's them pills I took, to bring it off, she said.
(She's had five already, and nearly died of young George.)   160
The chemist[38] said it would be all right, but I've never been the same.
You *are* a proper fool, I said.
Well, if Albert won't leave you alone, there it is, I said,
What you get married for if you don't want children?
HURRY UP PLEASE ITS TIME
Well, that Sunday Albert was home, they had a hot gammon,[39]
And they asked me in to dinner, to get the beauty of it hot—
HURRY UP PLEASE ITS TIME
HURRY UP PLEASE ITS TIME
Goonight Bill. Goonight Lou. Goonight May. Goonight.   170
Ta ta. Goonight. Goonight.
Good night, ladies, good night, sweet ladies, good night, good night.[40]

III. THE FIRE SERMON[41]

The river's tent is broken; the last fingers of leaf
Clutch and sink into the wet bank. The wind
Crosses the brown land, unheard. The nymphs are departed.
Sweet Thames, run softly, till I end my song.[42]
The river bears no empty bottles, sandwich papers,

[36] Slang for "demobilized from the army," a change made by Pound.
[37] A typical announcement of closing-time in a London pub.
[38] Pharmacist.   [39] Ham or bacon.
[40] From Shakespeare's *Hamlet* (IV.v. 74–75), spoken by Ophelia.   [41] Buddha's Fire Sermon.
[42] Eliot's note: "V. Spenser, *Prothalamion*": the refrain to the 1596 marriage song by Edmund Spenser (1552?–1599).

Silk handkerchiefs, cardboard boxes, cigarette ends
Or other testimony of summer nights. The nymphs are departed.
And their friends, the loitering heirs of City directors;[43]   180
Departed, have left no addresses.
By the waters of Leman I sat down and wept . . . [44]
Sweet Thames, run softly till I end my song,
Sweet Thames, run softly, for I speak not loud or long.
But at my back in a cold blast I hear[45]
The rattle of the bones, and chuckle spread from ear to ear.
A rat crept softly through the vegetation
Dragging its slimy belly on the bank
While I was fishing in the dull canal
On a winter evening round behind the gashouse   190
Musing upon the king my brother's wreck
And on the king my father's death before him.[46]
White bodies naked on the low damp ground
And bones cast in a little low dry garret,
Rattled by the rat's foot only, year to year.
But at my back from time to time I hear[47]
The sound of horns and motors, which shall bring[48]
Sweeney to Mrs. Porter in the spring.
O the moon shone bright on Mrs. Porter[49]
And on her daughter   200
They wash their feet in soda water
Et O ces voix d'enfants, chantant dans la coupole![50]

Twit twit twit
Jug jug jug jug jug jug
So rudely forc'd.
Tereu[51]

---

[43] Business directors in London's financial sector, the City.

[44] After "By the rivers of Babylon, there we sat down, yea, we wept, when we remembered Zion," from Psalm 137:1. Léman is the French name for Lake Geneva, Switzerland.

[45] After "But at my back I always hear / Time's wingéd chariot hurrying near . . . ," from the poem "To His Coy Mistress" (21–22), by Andrew Marvell (1621–1678). The speaker, in his attempt to seduce his lady, reminds her of the inevitable passing of time.

[46] Eliot's note: "Cf. *The Tempest,* I, ii." Ferdinand, son of the king of Naples, says, "Sitting on a bank, / Weeping again the King my father's wreck, / This music crept by me on the waters."

[47] Eliot's note: "Cf. Marvell, *To His Coy Mistress.*"

[48] Eliot's note: "Cf. Day, *Parliament of Bees:* 'When of the sudden, listening, you shall hear, / A noise of horns and hunting, which shall bring / Actaeon to Diana in the spring, / Where all shall see her naked skin. . . . '" According to classical myth, Actaeon, as punishment for seeing naked Diana (the Roman goddess of the hunt) bathing, was turned into a stag and killed by his own hounds. *Parliament of Bees* (1607?) is a satirical play by John Day (1574–1640?).

[49] Eliot's note: "I do not know the origin of the ballad from which these lines are taken: it was reported to me from Sydney, Australia." In the song, a favorite of British troops during World War I, Mrs. Porter and her daughter are prostitutes. Eliot uses the character Sweeney throughout his poetry as a vulgar person.

[50] "And oh those voices of children, singing in the cupola!" (French): Eliot's note: "V. Verlaine, *Parsifal,*" the concluding line of a sonnet by the French symbolist poet Paul Verlaine (1844–1896). In Wagner's opera *Parsifal* (1882), before the knight Parsifal can approach the Holy Grail, his feet must be washed.

[51] Short for Tereus, representing the nightingale's song.

Unreal City
Under the brown fog of a winter noon
Mr. Eugenides, the Smyrna[52] merchant
Unshaven, with a pocket full of currants[53]   210
C.i.f. London: documents at sight,
Asked me in demotic[54] French
To luncheon at the Cannon Street Hotel[55]
Followed by a weekend at the Metropole.

At the violet hour, when the eyes and back
Turn upward from the desk, when the human engines waits
Like a taxi throbbing waiting,
I Tiresias, though blind, throbbing between two lives,[56]
Old man with wrinkled female breasts, can see
At the violet hour, the evening hour that strives   220
Homeward, and brings the sailor home from sea,[57]
The typist home at teatime, clears her breakfast, lights
Her stove, and lays out food in tins.
Out of the window perilously spread
Her drying combinations touched by the sun's last rays,
On the divan are piled (at night her bed)
Stockings, slippers, camisoles, and stays.
I Tiresias, old man with wrinkled dugs
Perceived the scene, and foretold the rest—
I too awaited the expected guest.   230
He, the young man carbuncular, arrives,
A small house agent's clerk, with one bold stare,
One of the low on whom assurance sits
As a silk hat on a Bradford[58] millionaire.
The time is now propitious, as he guesses,

[52] A port in Turkey.

[53] Eliot's note: "The currants were quoted at a price 'cost insurance and freight to London'; and the Bill of Lading, etc., were to be handed to the buyer upon payment of the sight draft."

[54] Popular, vernacular.

[55] A London hotel next to a station, typically full of travelers from Europe; the Metropole is a luxury hotel in Brighton, England.

[56] Eliot's note: "Tiresias, although a mere spectator and not indeed a 'character,' is yet the most important personage in the poem, uniting all the rest. Just as the one-eyed merchant, seller of currants, melts into the Phoenician Sailor, and the latter is not wholly distinct from Ferdinand Prince of Naples, so all the women are one woman, and the two sexes meet in Tiresias. What Tiresias *sees*, in fact, is the substance of the poem. The whole passage from Ovid is of great anthropological interest. . . . " Eliot then quotes from Ovid's *Metamorphoses* (III.320–338): the story of Tiresias, who upon seeing two snakes mating, strikes them and is turned into a woman. Seven years later he comes upon them again, strikes them, and is turned back into a man. Because he has been both man and woman, Tiresias is called upon to settle a quarrel between Jove and Juno (the supreme Roman god and goddess) concerning whether men or women have more pleasure in love. Tiresias's answer that women have more pleasure angered Juno, who struck him blind. To compensate for the loss of sight, Jove granted Tiresias the gift of prophesy.

[57] Eliot's note: "This may not appear as exact as Sappho's lines, but I had in mind the 'longshore' or 'dory' fisherman, who returns at nightfall." Sappho (early 6th century B.C.) was a Greek lyric poet; another source is "Requiem" by Robert Louis Stevenson (1850–1894): "Home is the sailor, home from the sea. . . . "

[58] An English Midlands industrial town where fortunes were made during World War I.

The meal is ended, she is bored and tired,
Endeavours to engage her in caresses
Which still are unreproved, if undesired.
Flushed and decided, he assaults at once;
Exploring hands encounter no defence;   240
His vanity requires no response,
And makes a welcome of indifference.
(And I Tiresias have foresuffered all
Enacted on this same divan or bed;
I who have sat by Thebes below the wall[59]
And walked among the lowest of the dead.)
Bestows one final patronising kiss,
And gropes his way, finding the stairs unlit . . .

    She turns and looks a moment in the glass,
Hardly aware of her departed lover;   250
Her brain allows one half-formed thought to pass:
'Well now that's done: and I'm glad it's over.'
When lovely woman stoops to folly and[60]
Paces about her room again, alone,
She smoothes her hair with automatic hand,
And puts a record on the gramophone.

    'This music crept by me upon the waters'[61]
And along the Strand, up Queen Victoria Street.
O City city, I can sometimes hear
Beside a public bar in Lower Thames Street,   260
The pleasant whining of a mandoline
And a clatter and a chatter from within
Where fishermen lounge at noon: where the walls
Of Magnus Martyr hold[62]
Inexplicable splendour of Ionian white and gold.

            The river sweats[63]
            Oil and tar
            The barges drift

[59] Below the wall of Thebes stretched the marketplace where Tiresias prophesized.

[60] Eliot's note: "V. Goldsmith, the song in *The Vicar of Wakefield*": a 1766 novel by Oliver Goldsmith (1728–1774), in which Olivia, having been seduced, sings, "When lovely woman stoops to folly / And finds too late that men betray, / What charm can soothe her melancholy, / What art can wash her guilt away? / The only art her guilt to cover, / To hide her shame from every eye, / To give repentance to her lover / And wring his bosom—is to die."

[61] Eliot's note: "V. *The Tempest*, as above."

[62] Eliot's note: "The interior of St. Magnus Martyr is to my mind one of the finest among Wren's interiors. See *The Proposed Demolition of Nineteen City Churches:* (P. S. King & Son, Ltd.)." St. Magnus Martyr, a church designed by the English architect Sir Christopher Wren (1632–1723), is in London, as are the other sites mentioned.

[63] Eliot's note: "The Song of the (three) Thames-daughters begins here. From line 292 to 306 inclusive they speak in turn. V. *Götterdämmerung*, III, i: the Rhine-daughters." Lines 277–278 and 290–291 are the refrain of the Rhine maidens, who sing of the deterioration of the Rhine River, in Wagner's 1874 opera ("*Twilight of the Gods*" [German]): Eliot adapts the song to the Thames River.

With the turning tide
Red sails   270
Wide
To leeward, swing on the heavy spar.
The barges wash
Drifting logs
Down Greenwich reach
Past the Isle of Dogs.[64]
   Weialala leia
   Wallala leialala

Elizabeth and Leicester[65]
Beating oars   280
The stern was formed
A gilded shell
Red and gold
The brisk swell
Rippled both shores
Southwest wind
Carried down stream
The peal of bells
White towers
   Weialala leia   290
   Wallala leialala

'Trams and dusty trees.
Highbury bore me. Richmond and Kew[66]
Undid me. By Richmond I raised my knees
Supine on the floor of a narrow canoe.'

'My feet are at Moorgate,[67] and my heart
Under my feet. After the event
He wept. He promised "a new start."
I made no comment. What should I resent?'

'On Margate Sands.[68]   300
I can connect

---

[64] A peninsula in the Thames River, across from the borough of Greenwich, where Elizabeth I (1533–1603), queen of England from 1558 to 1603, was born.

[65] Eliot's note: "V. Froude, *Elizabeth,* Vol. I, ch. iv, letter of De Quadra to Philip of Spain: 'In the afternoon we were in a barge, watching the games on the river. (The queen) was alone with Lord Robert and myself on the poop, when they began to talk nonsense, and went so far that Lord Robert at last said, as I was on the spot there was no reason why they should not be married if the queen pleased.'" The English historian James Anthony Froude (1818–1894) wrote of the love affair between Elizabeth I and the earl of Leicester, Robert Dudley (1532?–1588). Bishop De Quadra was the Spanish ambassador to England; the poop is a raised deck at a ship's stern.

[66] Eliot's note: "Cf. *Purgatorio,* V. 133: 'Ricorditi di me, che son la Pia; / 'Siena mi fe', disfecemi Maremma'": "Remember me, who am Pia; Siena made me, Maremma unmade me" (Italian). In the Antepurgatory Dante meets Pia, one of those who died without last rites, probably because her jealous husband had her killed because of suspicion of adultery. She was born in Siena and died in Maremma. Highbury is a London suburb; Richmond, a borough of London; Kew, a London district noted for its botanical garden.

[67] A London slum. [68] A resort on the Thames.

Nothing with nothing.
The broken fingernails of dirty hands.
My people humble people who expect
Nothing.'
    la la

To Carthage then I came[69]

Burning burning burning burning[70]
O Lord Thou pluckest me out[71]
O Lord Thou pluckest   310

burning

IV. Death By Water[72]

Phlebas the Phoenician, a fortnight dead,
Forgot the cry of gulls, and the deep sea swell
And the profit and loss.
              A current under sea
Picked his bones in whispers. As he rose and fell
He passed the stages of his age and youth
Entering the whirlpool.
              Gentile or Jew
O you who turn the wheel and look to windward,   320
Consider Phlebas, who was once handsome and tall as you.

V. What the Thunder Said[73]

  After the torchlight red on sweaty faces
After the frosty silence in the gardens
After the agony in stony places
The shouting and the crying
Prison and palace and reverberation

---

[69] Eliot's note: "V. St. Augustine's *Confessions:* 'to Carthage then I came, where a cauldron of unholy loves sang all about mine ears': from the autobiography (III. i) of St. Augustine (354–430).

[70] Eliot's note: "The complete text of the Buddha's Fire Sermon (which corresponds in importance to the Sermon on the Mount) from which these words are taken, will be found translated in the late Henry Clarke Warren's *Buddhism in Translation* (Harvard Oriental Series). Mr. Warren was one of the great pioneers of Buddhist studies in the Occident." Buddha's sermon calls for a life free of passion, which he symbolized by fire; for the Sermon on the Mount, see Matthew 5.

[71] Eliot's note: "From St. Augustine's *Confessions* again. The collocation of these two representatives of eastern and western asceticism, as the culmination of this part of the poem, is not an accident."

[72] This section, which Pound shortened considerably, was originally written in French as the conclusion to Eliot's poem "Dans le Restaurant" (1920), or "In the Restaurant."

[73] Eliot's note: "In the first part of Part V three themes are employed: the journey to Emmaus, the approach to the Chapel Perilous (see Miss Weston's book) and the present decay of eastern Europe." In Luke 24:13–35 two disciples meet Christ on the road to Emmaus after his resurrection; the first nine lines deal with the events from Jesus' betrayal to his crucifixion. In the *Upanishads*, Vedic holy books, thunder is the language of god.

Of thunder of spring over distant mountains
He who was living is now dead
We who were living are now dying
With a little patience   330

    Here is no water but only rock
Rock and no water and the sandy road
The road winding above among the mountains
Which are mountains of rock without water
If there were water we should stop and drink
Amongst the rock one cannot stop or think
Sweat is dry and feet are in the sand
If there were only water amongst the rock
Dead mountain mouth of carious[74] teeth that cannot spit
Here one can neither stand nor lie nor sit   340
There is not even silence in the mountains
But dry sterile thunder without rain
There is not even solitude in the mountains
But red sullen faces sneer and snarl
From doors of mudcracked houses
                                   If there were water
   And no rock
   If there were rock
   And also water
   And water
   A spring   350
   A pool among the rock
   If there were the sound of water only
   Not the cicada
   And dry grass singing
   But sound of water over a rock
   Where the hermit-thrush sings in the pine trees
   Drip drop drip drop drop drop drop[75]
   But there is no water

Who is the third who walks always beside you?[76]
When I count, there are only you and I together   360
But when I look ahead up the white road

---

[74] Decaying.

[75] Eliot's note: "This is *Turdus aonalaschkae pallasii*, the hermit-thrush which I have heard in Quebec Province. Chapman says (*Handbook of Birds of Eastern North America*) 'it is most at home in secluded woodland and thickety retreats. . . . Its notes are not remarkable for variety or volume, but in purity and sweetness of tone and exquisite modulation they are unequalled.' Its 'water-dripping song' is justly celebrated." Frank Michler Chapman (1864–1945), an ornithologist, published this *Handbook* in 1895.

[76] Eliot's note: "The following lines were stimulated by the account of one of the Antarctic expeditions (I forget which, but I think one of Shackleton's): it was related that the party of explorers, at the extremity of their strength, had the constant delusion that there was *one more member* than could actually be counted." In Luke 24:13–34 a stranger appears to the two disciples journeying to Emmaus affter Jesus' death; the stranger is Jesus himself. Sir Ernest Henry Shackleton (1874–1922) was a British explorer who made three expeditions to Antarctica.

There is always another one walking beside you
Gliding wrapt in a brown mantle, hooded
I do not know whether a man or a woman
—But who is that on the other side of you?

What is that sound high in the air[77]
Murmur of maternal lamentation
Who are those hooded hordes swarming
Over endless plains, stumbling in cracked earth
Ringed by the flat horizon only   370
What is the city over the mountains
Cracks and reforms and bursts in the violet air
Falling towers
Jerusalem Athens Alexandria
Vienna London
Unreal

A woman drew her long black hair out tight
And fiddled whisper music on those strings
And bats with baby faces in the violet light
Whistled, and beat their wings   380
And crawled head downward down a blackened wall
And upside down in air were towers
Tolling reminiscent bells, that kept the hours
And voices singing out of empty cisterns and exhausted wells.

In this decayed hole among the mountains
In the faint moonlight, the grass is singing
Over the tumbled graves, about the chapel[78]
There is the empty chapel, only the wind's home.
It has no windows, and the door swings,
Dry bones can harm no one.   390
Only a cock stood on the rooftree
Co co rico co co rico[79]
In a flash of lightning. Then a damp gust
Bringing rain

Ganga[80] was sunken, and the limp leaves
Waited for rain, while the black clouds
Gathered far distant, over Himavant.[81]

---

[77] Eliot's note: "Cf. Hermann Hesse, *Blick ins Chaos* . . . ": "*A Glimpse Into Chaos*" (German), a 1920 book by Hesse (1877–1962). Eliot then quotes a passage from the book, translated as, "Already half of Europe, already at least half of Eastern Europe, is on the way to chaos, going drunk in holy madness along the edge of the abyss and sings, sings drunkenly and hymnlike as Dmitri Karamazov sang. The bourgeois laughs, shocked, at these songs; the saint and the prophet hear them with tears." The passage refers to the Russian Revolution in 1917; Karamazov is a character in *The Brothers Karamazov* (1880), by Feodor Dostoevski (1821–1881).

[78] The Chapel Perilous of the Arthurian Grail legend, where a knight must go in search of the Holy Grail.

[79] According to folklore, a cock's crowing indicates that a ghost has departed.

[80] The Ganges River in India, sacred to Hindus.   [81] The Himalayas.

The jungle crouched, humped in silence.
The spoke the thunder
D<small>A</small>   400
Datta:[82] what have we given?
My friend, blood shaking my heart
The awful daring of a moment's surrender
Which an age of prudence can never retract
By this, and this only, we have existed
Which is not to be found in our obituaries
Or in memories draped by the beneficent spider[83]
Or under seals broken by the lean solicitor
In our empty rooms
D<small>A</small>   410
Dayadhvam: I have heard the key[84]
Turn in the door once and turn once only
We think of the key, each in his prison
Thinking of the key, each confirms a prison
Only at nightfall, aethereal rumours
Revive for a moment a broken Coriolanus[85]
D<small>A</small>
Damyata: The boat responded
Gaily, to the hand expert with sail and oar
The sea was calm, your heart would have responded   420
Gaily, when invited, beating obedient
To controlling hands

                              I sat upon the shore
Fishing,[86] with the arid plain behind me
Shall I at least set my lands in order?[87]
London Bridge is falling down falling down falling down

---

[82] Eliot's note: "Datta, dayadvam, damyata" ("Give, sympathise, control" [Sanskrit]). The fable of the meaning of the Thunder is found in the *Brihadaranyaka-Upanishad,* 5, 1. A translation is found in Deussen's *Sechzig Upanishads des Veda,* p. 489." According to Hindu Theology, "Da" is the command of the god Prajapati; thunder, god's voice, commands that humans practice alms-giving, sympathy, and self-control. Paul Deussen (1845–1919) was a German philosopher and Sanskrit scholar who wrote *Sixty Vedic Upanishads.*

[83] Eliot's note: "Cf. Webster, *The White Devil,* V, vi: ' . . . they'll remarry / Ere the worm pierce your winding-sheet, ere the spider / Make a thin curtain for your epitaphs.' "

[84] Eliot's note: "Cf. *Inferno,* XXXIII, 46: 'ed io senti chiavar l'uscio di sotto / all'orribile torre.' Also F. H. Bradley, *Appearance and Reality,* p. 346. 'My external sensations are no less private to myself than are my thoughts or my feelings. In either case my experience falls within my own circle, a circle closed on the outside; and, with all its elements alike, every sphere is opaque to the others which surround it. . . . In brief, regarded as an existence which appears in a soul, the whole world for each is peculiar and private to that soul.' " "And I heard them below locking the door / of the horrible tower" (Italian), spoken by Count Ugolino, whom Dante meets in Circle 9 of the Inferno, among those who were traitors to their countries. Ugolino was locked in a tower with his sons and grandsons and left to starve.

[85] Gaius Marcius Coriolanus (5th century B.C.), a Roman hero who became *Coriolanus* (1608), the excessively proud protagonist of Shakespeare's play ruined by his inability to sympathize with Rome's common people.

[86] Eliot's note: "V. Weston: *From Ritual to Romance;* chapter on the Fisher King." The Fisher King symbolizes resurrection.

[87] "Thus saith the Lord, Set thine house in order: for thou shalt die, and not live," from Isaiah 38:1.

Poi s'ascose nel foco che gli affina[88]
Quando fiam uti chelidon—O swallow swallow[89]
Le Prince d'Aquitaine à la tour abolie[90]
These fragments I have shored against my ruins   430
Why then Ile fit you. Hieronymo's mad againe.[91]
Datta. Dayadhvam. Damyata.
    Shantih shantih shantih[92]

1921, 1922

from *FOUR QUARTETS**

EAST COKER[1]

I

In my beginning is my end.[2] In succession
Houses rise and fall, crumble, are extended,
Are removed, destroyed, restored, or in their place
Is an open field, or a factory, or a by-pass.
Old stone to new building, old timber to new fires,
Old fires to ashes, and ashes to the earth
Which is already flesh, fur and faeces,
Bone of man and beast, cornstalk and leaf.
Houses live and die: there is a time for building
And a time for living and for generation   10

[88] Eliot's note: V. *Purgatorio,* XXVI, 48. "'Ara vos prec er aquella valor / "que vos condus al som de l'escalina, / "sovegna vos a temps de ma dolor." / Poi s'ascose nel foco che li affina.'" "'I pray you now in the name of that virtue / that guides you to the top of this stair [paradise], / remember in good time my suffering.' / Then he hid himself in the purifying fire." On Ledge 7 of Purgatory, among the Lustful, Dante meets the poet Arnaut Daniel: Daniel speaks in Provençal; Dante, in Italian.

[89] "When shall I be like the swallow?" (Latin). Eliot's note: "V. *Pervigilium Veneris.* Cf. Philomela in Parts II and III." In the version of the myth in the anonymous poem "The Vigil of Venus," Philomela is turned into a swallow.

[90] "The Prince of Aquitaine at the ruined tower" (French). Eliot's note: "V. Gerard de Nerval, Sonnet *El Desdichado.*" The prince has been disinherited in this sonnet from *Les Chimères* (1854), or "*The Chimeras*" (French), by the French writer de Nerval (1808–1855).

[91] Eliot's note: "V. Kyd's *Spanish Tragedy.*" "Why then Ile fit [supply] you" refers to Hieronymo's plan to gain revenge while performing a play that has been requested by those he seeks to kill, from a 1594 drama by the English playwright Thomas Kyd (1557?–1595?). "Hieronymo's mad againe" refers to the play's subtitle. Hieronymo bites out his tongue at the end of the play.

[92] Eliot's note: "Shantih. Repeated as here, a formal ending to an Upanishad. 'The Peace which passeth understanding' is our equivalent to this word."

* A group of poems with the same structure and themes—time and eternity, memory and history—published separately as *Burnt Norton* (1936), *East Coker* (1940), *The Dry Salvages* (1941), and *Little Gidding* (1942); they were collected as *Four Quartets* in 1943.

[1] The English village from which Eliot's seventeenth-century ancestors set forth on their journey to the New World.

[2] The motto of Mary Stuart (1542–1587), queen of Scots, was "*En ma fin est mon commencement*": "In my end is my beginning" (French).

And a time for the wind to break the loosened pane
And to shake the wainscot[3] where the field-mouse trots
And to shake the tattered arras[4] woven with a silent motto.

In my beginning is my end. Now the light falls
Across the open field, leaving the deep lane
Shuttered with branches, dark in the afternoon,
Where you lean against a bank while a van passes,
And the deep lane insists on the direction
Into the village, in the electric heat
Hypnotised. In a warm haze the sultry light   20
Is absorbed, not refracted, by grey stone.
The dahlias sleep in the empty silence.
Wait for the early owl.

                              In that open field
If you do not come too close, if you do not come too close,
On a summer midnight, you can hear the music
Of the weak pipe and the little drum
And see them dancing around the bonfire
The association of man and woman
In daunsinge, signifying matrimonie—   30
A dignified and commodious sacrament.
Two and two, necessarye coniunction,
Holding eche other by the hand or the arm[5]
Whiche betokeneth concorde. Round and round the fire
Leaping through the flames, or joined in circles,
Rustically solemn or in rustic laughter
Lifting heavy feet in clumsy shoes,
Earth feet, loam[6] feet, lifted in country mirth
Mirth of those long since under earth
Nourishing the corn. Keeping time,   40
Keeping the rhythm in their dancing
As in their living in the living seasons
The time of the seasons and the constellations
The time of milking and the time of harvest
The time of the coupling of man and woman
And that of beasts. Feet rising and falling.
Eating and drinking. Dung and death.

Dawn points, and another day
Prepares for heat and silence. Out at sea the dawn wind
Wrinkles and slides. I am here   50
Or there, or elsewhere. In my beginning.

---

[3] A wood lining or paneling on walls.   [4] An elaborate type of tapestry.
[5] From Bk. I, Ch. 12 of *The Boke Named the Governour* (1531), by Thomas Elyot (1490?–1546), an ancestor of Eliot.
[6] A rich soil.

II

What is the late November doing
With the disturbance of the spring
And creatures of the summer heat,
And snowdrops writhing under feet
And hollyhocks that aim too high
Red into grey and tumble down
Late roses filled with early snow?
Thunder rolled by the rolling stars
Simulates triumphal cars   60
Deployed in constellated wars
Scorpion[7] fights against the Sun
Until the Sun and Moon go down
Comets weep and Leonids[8] fly
Hunt the heavens and the plains
Whirled in a vortex that shall bring
The world to that destructive fire
Which burns before the ice-cap reigns.

    That was a way of putting it—not very satisfactory:
A periphrastic[9] study in a worn-out poetical fashion,   70
Leaving one still with the intolerable wrestle
With words and meanings. The poetry does not matter.
It was not (to start again) what one had expected.
What was to be the value of the long looked forward to,
Long hoped for calm, the autumnal serenity
And the wisdom of age? Had they deceived us,
Or deceived themselves, the quiet-voiced elders,
Bequeathing us merely a receipt for deceit?
The serenity only a deliberate hebetude,[10]
The wisdom only the knowledge of dead secrets   80
Useless in the darkness into which they peered
Or from which they turned their eyes. There is, it seems to us,
At best, only a limited value
In the knowledge derived from experience.
The knowledge imposes a pattern, and falsifies,
For the pattern is new in every moment
And every moment is a new and shocking
Valuation of all we have been. We are only undeceived
Of that which, deceiving, could no longer harm.
In the middle, not only in the middle of the way   90
But all the way, in a dark wood,[11] in a bramble,

---

[7] The constellation Scorpio and the sign of the zodiac for October–November.
[8] Meteor showers that appear to originate from the constellation Leo, the lion.
[9] Roundabout, using many words when one or a few will do.
[10] Dullness, lethargy.
[11] In the *Inferno,* by Dante Alighieri (1265–1321), Dante has lost his way in a dark wood "in the middle of the journey of our life" (I.1).

On the edge of a grimpen,[12] where is no secure foothold,
And menaced by monsters, fancy lights,
Risking enchantment. Do not let me hear
Of the wisdom of old men, but rather of their folly,
Their fear of fear and frenzy, their fear of possession,
Of belonging to another, or to others, or to God.
The only wisdom we can hope to acquire
Is the wisdom of humility: humility is endless.

The houses are all gone under the sea. 100

The dancers are all gone under the hill.

III

O dark dark dark.[13] They all go into the dark,
The vacant interstellar spaces, the vacant into the vacant,
The captains, merchant bankers, eminent men of letters,
The generous patrons of art, the statesmen and the rulers,
Distinguished civil servants, chairman of many committees,
Industrial lords and petty contractors, all go into the dark,
And dark the Sun and Moon, and the Almanach de Gotha[14]
And the Stock Exchange Gazette, the Directory of Directors,
And cold the sense and lost the motive of action. 110
And we all go with them, into the silent funeral,
Nobody's funeral, for there is no one to bury.
I said to my soul, be still, and let the dark come upon you
Which shall be the darkness of God. As, in a theatre,
The lights are extinguished, for the scene to be changed
With a hollow rumble of wings, with a movement of darkness on
        darkness,
And we know that the hills and the trees, the distant panorama
And the bold imposing façade are all being rolled away—
Or as, when an underground train, in the tube, stops too long between
        stations
And the conversation rises and slowly fades into silence 120
And you see behind every face the mental emptiness deepen
Leaving only the growing terror of nothing to think about;
Or when, under ether, the mind is conscious but conscious of
        nothing—
I said to my soul, be still, and wait without hope

---

[12] In *The Hound of the Baskervilles* (1902), by Sir Arthur Conan Doyle (1859–1930), the great Grimpen Mire swallows anything that gets caught in its mud. The huge hound that scares people literally to death is hidden on solid ground in the center of the mire.

[13] "O dark, dark, dark, amid the blaze of noon, / Irrecoverably dark, total Eclipse / Without all hope of day!" from *Samson Agonistes* (1671) (XI. 80–82), by John Milton (1608–1674).

[14] An international gazette that includes genealogical, diplomatic, and statistical information; first published in 1763 by Johann George Justus Perthes (1749–1816) of Gotha, Germany, it appears annually.

For hope would be hope for the wrong thing; wait without love
For love would be love of the wrong thing; there is yet faith
But the faith and the love and the hope are all in the waiting.
Wait without thought, for you are not ready for thought:
So the darkness shall be the light, and the stillness the dancing.
Whisper of running streams, and winter lightning.   130
The wild thyme unseen and the wild strawberry,
The laughter in the garden, echoed ecstasy
Not lost, but requiring, pointing to the agony
Of death and birth.
                You say I am repeating
Something I have said before. I shall say it again.
Shall I say it again? In order to arrive there,
To arrive where you are, to get from where you are not,
    You must go by a way wherein there is no ecstasy.
In order to arrive at what you do not know   140
    You must go by a way which is the way of ignorance.
In order to possess what you do not possess
    You must go by the way of dispossession.
In order to arrive at what you are not
    You must go through the way in which you are not.
And what you do not know is the only thing you know
And what you own is what you do not own
And where you are is where you are not.

IV

The wounded surgeon plies the steel
That questions the distempered part;   150
Beneath the bleeding hands we feel
The sharp compassion of the healer's art
Resolving the enigma of the fever chart.

Our only health is the disease
If we obey the dying nurse
Whose constant care is not to please
But to remind of our, and Adam's curse,[15]
And that, to be restored, our sickness must grow worse.

The whole earth is our hospital
Endowed by the ruined millionaire,   160
Wherein, if we do well, we shall
Die of the absolute paternal care
That will not leave us, but prevents us everywhere.

---

[15] "Because thou . . . hast eaten of the tree [of knowledge of good and evil] of which I [the Lord] commanded thee, saying, thou shalt not eat of it: cursed is the ground for thy sake; in sorrow shalt thou eat of it all the days of thy life," from Genesis 3:17.

The chill ascends from feet to knees,
The fever sings in mental wires.
If to be warmed, then I must freeze
And quake in frigid purgatorial fires
Of which the flame is roses, and the smoke is briars.

The dripping blood our only drink,
The bloody flesh our only food:[16]   170
In spite of which we like to think
That we are sound, substantial flesh and blood—
Again, in spite of that, we call this Friday good.[17]

V

So here I am, in the middle way, having had twenty years—
Twenty years largely wasted, the years of *l'entre deux guerres*[18]—
Trying to learn to use words, and every attempt
Is a wholly new start, and a different kind of failure
Because one has only learnt to get the better of words
For the thing one no longer has to say, or the way in which
One is no longer disposed to say it. And so each venture   180
Is a new beginning, a raid on the inarticulate
With shabby equipment always deteriorating
In the general mess of imprecision of feeling,
Undisciplined squads of emotion. And what there is to conquer
By strength and submission, has already been discovered
Once or twice, or several times, by men whom one cannot hope
To emulate—but there is no competition—
There is only the fight to recover what has been lost
And found and lost again and again: and now, under conditions
That seem unpropitious. But perhaps neither gain nor loss.   190
For us, there is only the trying. The rest is not our business.

Home is where one starts from. As we grow older
The world becomes stranger, the pattern more complicated
Of dead and living. Not the intense moment
Isolated, with no before and after,
But a lifetime burning in every moment
And not the lifetime of one man only
But of old stones that cannot be deciphered.
There is a time for the evening under starlight,
A time for the evening under lamplight   200

---

[16] The blood and flesh of the crucified Jesus: in Matthew 26:26–28, " . . . Jesus took bread . . . and gave it to the disciples, and said, Take, eat; this is my body. And he took the cup . . . and gave it to them, saying, Drink ye all of it; For this is my blood. . . . "
[17] Good Friday, the Friday before Easter, commemorates Jesus' crucifixion.
[18] "Between two wars" (French).

(The evening with the photograph album).
Love is most nearly itself
When here and now cease to matter.
Old men ought to be explorers
Here and there does not matter
We must be still and still moving
Into another intensity
For a further union, a deeper communion
Through the dark cold and the empty desolation,
The wave cry, the wind cry, the vast waters   210
Of the petrel[19] and the porpoise. In my end is my beginning.

1940

=CONTEXTS=

New Criticism

In the late 1930s the state of English studies in American universities led the poet/
editor John Crowe Ransom (1888–1974) to pose certain fundamental questions
about the business of literary scholarship:

What Is Criticism?

"Easier to ask, What is criticism not? It is an act now notoriously arbitrary and
undefined. We feel certain that the critical act is not one of those which the
professors of literature habitually perform, and cause their students to perform. And it is our melancholy impression that it is not often cleanly performed in those loose compositions, by writers of perfectly indeterminate
qualifications, that appear in print as reviews of books."

John Crowe Ransom, 1938

Determined that literary studies should occupy a place of respect in universities,
Ransom and other scholars such as Cleanth Brooks (1906–) and Robert Penn Warren (1905–1990) sought to mold literary criticism into more of a "hard science"
while still maintaining a somewhat mystical reverence for literary texts themselves.
"Criticism," Ransom continues, "must become more scientific, or precise and systematic. . . . " Ransom and other New Critics, as they called themselves, were after
a more "objective" treatment of literature, specifically poetry. They wanted to deal
specifically with the literary object itself and avoid entanglement in external matters,
including historical comment, airy impressionism, psychological evaluations of the
author, and other techniques that deal with abstract and isolated elements of a work.
Rather, the New Criticism focused on elements of a poem—such as meter, texture,
tone, syntax, and patterns of imagery—as they relate to the work as a whole, an
organic unity.

---

[19] A small marine bird.

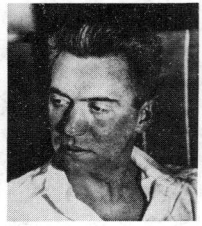

Hart Crane
(1899–1932)

Hart Crane's poetry makes enormous demands upon its readers. Its dense web of figurative language, violations of customary syntax, and exotic diction all aspire to the verbal music with which Crane casts his poetic spell. For Crane these intricacies were necessities rather than obstacles to the kind of poetry he was after. Adherence to such exacting standards of literary achievement places the artist in a precarious position. Crane's poems at times waver between magnificence and murkiness, a characteristic that had led some critics (perhaps unfairly) to call Crane a "splendid failure." But Crane insisted that a poet must risk criticism "in the conquest of consciousness." The fruits of this risk turned out to be some of the most original and beautiful passages of poetry available in American literature.

Born into a well-to-do family in Garrettsville, Ohio, in 1899, Harold Hart Crane began writing poetry while he was in high school. He published his first poem, a tribute to the Irish writer Oscar Wilde, at age seventeen. During parts of 1917, 1918, and 1919, Crane lived in New York City, immersing himself in Greenwich Village's thriving bohemian art world and publishing poems in several "little" magazines, including the *Little Review,* an important vehicle for the experimental work of major modernist writers, such as James Joyce, T. S. Eliot, and Ezra Pound. Crane spent much of the next four years in Cleveland, working in his father's candy company (which developed Life Savers), in advertising, and at other jobs. During these years he carried on energetic correspondences with a number of writers, including Sherwood Anderson and Allen Tate. Despite enduring emotionally draining conflicts with his divorced parents—conflicts that would plague Crane all his life—he was writing the poems that mark the beginning of his mature work: "My Grandmother's Love Letters" (1920), "Chaplinesque" (1921), and "For the Marriage of Faustus and Helen" (1922). Among others, his most ambitious project, *The Bridge* (1930), an epic poem he described as a "mystical synthesis of America," was conceived at this time, though not completed until 1929.

The next few years were Crane's most productive ones. After returning to New York City in 1923, he composed many of the poems collected in his first book, *White Buildings* (1926), including "Voyages," a sequence of six love poems inspired by an intense homosexual relationship. For much of 1926 he stayed at his grandmother's plantation on the Isle of Pines, near Cuba; that summer, in a burst of creativity during which he felt as if he were "dancing on dynamite," he wrote much of *The Bridge.* Following this active period Crane began to lose confidence in his abilities, giving himself over more completely than ever before to heavy drinking and sometimes-dangerous homosexual encounters with sailors. Chronically short of money, he moved restlessly from New York to Hollywood, Paris, and Ohio, until a Guggenheim Fellowship took him to Mexico in 1931. While he had planned to work on an epic about the Aztec emperor Montezuma, he was disheartened by the negative critical reception of *The Bridge* and wrote very little except for "The Broken Tower" (1932), a poem that communicates Crane's anguished uncertainty about his poetic achievement yet reaffirms his faith in the imagination. In 1932, while returning by boat to New York City from Mexico, he jumped to his death.

Although Crane was very much attracted to the formal experimentalism of modernism and at times wrote in free verse, he commonly employed traditional metrical and stanzaic patterns, relying instead on unorthodox uses of figurative language. Underlying all his work is an essentially romantic notion of creativity, a predisposition that Crane felt necessary to defend at a time when many intellectuals and artists were denigrating romanticist poets. Defending his poetry against the charge that its opaque conceits were inadmissible, Crane embraced Samuel Coleridge's conviction that poetic genius "cannot be lawless," because "the power of acting creatively under laws of its own origination" is exactly what constitutes that genius. In a letter to the photographer Alfred Stieglitz, Crane complained that he had "to combat everyday those really sincere people, but limited, who deny the superior logic of metaphor in favor of their more perfect sums, divisions, subtractions." Crane sought to create what he called an "interior form," in which he could "dye" the words to take on a slightly different meaning than they would normally have.

Crane shared the belief in this distinction between poetic language and ordinary discourse with T. S. Eliot and with the French symbolist poets they both admired, but Crane resisted the cultural pessimism that marked the work of Eliot and many other writers in the wake of World War I. Calling Eliot's *The Waste Land* (1922) "good, of course, but so damned dead," Crane declared his intention to "take Eliot as a point of departure toward an almost complete reverse of direction" and "apply as much of his erudition and technique as I can absorb and assemble toward a more positive, or (if [I] must put it so in a sceptical age) ecstatic goal."

Crane's most ambitious statement of this "ecstatic goal" is *The Bridge,* a long work composed of fifteen individual poems in which the personal quest for transcendent experience is coupled with a Whitmanesque vision of national destiny. The Brooklyn Bridge, with which the poem begins and ends, is the book's controlling symbol, an object of beauty that to Crane embodied the promise of a marriage between the forces of modern technology and older notions of spiritual aspirations. Like Walt Whitman, with whom he strongly identified in temperament if not in style, Crane believed a poet ought to (in Whitman's words) "flood himself with the immediate age," not reject it, as Crane felt Eliot had done. Crane's belief that it was thus incumbent upon poetry to "absorb the machine, i.e., *acclimatize* it as naturally and casually as trees," takes shape in the presence of numerous images of modern technology in *The Bridge.* But Crane feared that his personal associations of the bridge with spiritual and idealistic national aspirations were not shared by the culture as a whole, that instead "the bridge as a symbol today has no significance beyond an economical approach to shorter hours, quicker lunches, behaviorism and toothpicks." In the face of overwhelming obstacles and imminent disillusionment, *The Bridge* affirms the individual's commitment to a visionary goal.

Suggested Readings: *White Buildings,* 1926. *The Bridge,* 1930. *The Letters of Hart Crane: 1916–1932,* ed. B. Weber, 1965. *The Complete Poems and Selected Letters and Prose of Hart Crane,* ed. B. Weber, 1966. *Letters of Hart Crane and His Family,* ed. T. S. W. Lewis, 1974. *Hart Crane and Yvor Winters: Their Literary Correspondence,* ed. T. Parkinson, 1978. P. Horton, *Hart Crane: The Life of an American Poet,* 1937. H. Leibowitz, *Hart Crane: An Introduction to the Poetry,* 1968. J. Unterecker, *Voyager: A Life of Hart Crane,* 1969. S. Paul, *Hart's Bridge,* 1972. A. Trachtenberg, ed. *Hart Crane: A Collection of Critical Essays,* 1982. E. Brunner, *Splendid Failure: Hart Crane and the Making of "The Bridge",* 1985. H. Bloom, ed., *Hart Crane,* 1986. M. F. Bennett, *Unfractioned Idiom: Hart Crane and Modernism,* 1987. L. Edelman, *Transmemberment of Song: Hart Crane's Anatomies of Rhetoric and Desire,* 1987.

Text Used: *The Poems of Hart Crane,* ed. M. Simon, 1986.

MY GRANDMOTHER'S LOVE LETTERS

There are no stars tonight
But those of memory.
Yet how much room for memory there is
In the loose girdle of soft rain.

There is even room enough
For the letters of my mother's mother,
Elizabeth,
That have been pressed so long
Into a corner of the roof
That they are brown and soft,   10
And liable to melt as snow.

Over the greatness of such space
Steps must be gentle.
It is all hung by an invisible white hair.
It trembles as birch limbs webbing the air.

And I ask myself:

"Are your fingers long enough to play
Old keys that are but echoes:
Is the silence strong enough
To carry back the music to its source   20
And back to you again
As though to her?"

Yet I would lead my grandmother by the hand
Through much of what she would not understand;
And so I stumble. And the rain continues on the roof
With such a sound of gently pitying laughter.

                                                      1926

CHAPLINESQUE*

We make our meek adjustments,
Contented with such random consolations

---

* Crane admired the ability of the comedian Charlie Chaplin (1889–1977) to make sentimentality "transcend itself into a new kind of tragedy, eccentric, homely and yet brilliant." Inspired by Chaplin's film *The Kid* (1921), Crane explained to a friend that "Poetry . . . is so crowded out of the humdrum, rushing, mechanical scramble of today that the man who would preserve them must duck and camouflage for dear life to keep them or keep himself from annihilation. . . . I have tried to express these 'social sympathies' in words corresponding somewhat to the antics of the actor."

As the wind deposits
In slithered and too ample pockets.

For we can still love the world, who find
A famished kitten[1] on the step, and know
Recesses for it from the fury of the street,
Or warm torn elbow coverts.

We will sidestep, and to the final smirk
Dally the doom of that inevitable thumb   10
That slowly chafes its puckered index toward us,
Facing the dull squint with what innocence
And what surprise!

And yet these fine collapses are not lies
More than the pirouettes of any pliant cane;
Our obsequies[2] are, in a way, no enterprise.
We can evade you, and all else but the heart:
What blame to us if the heart live on.

The game enforces smirks; but we have seen
The moon in lonely alleys make   20
A grail of laughter of an empty ash can,
And through all sound of gaiety and quest
Have heard a kitten in the wilderness.

1926

AT MELVILLE'S TOMB*

Often beneath the wave, wide from this ledge
The dice of drowned men's bones he saw bequeath
An embassy.[1] Their numbers as he watched,
Beat on the dusty shore and were obscured.

---

[1] Here, symbolizing poetry.   [2] Burial rights; here, suggesting obsequious behavior.

* A tribute to Herman Melville (1819–1891) that first appeared in *Poetry* magazine in October 1926, but only after an exchange of letters between its editor, Harriet Monroe (1860–1936), and Crane about the propriety of the poem's unorthodox imagery. In the course of this exchange, which was published with the poem, Crane not only explicated several of his images, but also defended the authority of a poet to base a poem on the "so-called illogical impingements of the connotations of words on the consciousness" rather than on "logically rigid significations." Crane argued that the articulation of "fresh concepts, more inclusive evaluations" is the proper "province of poetry," and that in quest of these a poet must rely on "something like short-hand as compared to usual description."

[1] Crane's note: "Dice bequeath an embassy, in the first place, by being ground (in this connection only, of course) in little cubes from the bones of drowned men by the action of the sea, and are finally thrown up on the sand, having 'numbers' but no identification. These being the bones of dead men who never completed their voyage, it seems legitimate to refer to them as the only surviving evidence of certain messages undelivered, mute evidence of certain things, experiences that the dead mariners might have had to deliver. Dice as a symbol of chance and circumstance is also implied."

And wrecks passed without sound of bells,
The calyx[2] of death's bounty giving back
A scattered chapter, livid hieroglyph,
The portent wound in corridors of shells.

Then in the circuit calm of one vast coil,
Its lashings charmed and malice reconciled,   10
Frosted eyes there were that lifted altars;[3]
And silent answers crept across the stars.

Compass, quadrant and sextant contrive
No farther tides . . . [4] High in the azure steeps
Monody[5] shall not wake the mariner.
This fabulous shadow only the sea keeps.

1926

VOYAGES*

I

Above the fresh ruffles of the surf
Bright striped urchins flay each other with sand.
They have contrived a conquest for shell shucks,
And their fingers crumble fragments of baked weed
Gaily digging and scattering.

And in answer to their treble interjections
The sun beats lightning on the waves,
The waves fold thunder on the sand;
And could they hear me I would tell them:

---

[2] Crane's note: "This calyx refers in a double ironic sense both to a cornucopia and the vortex made by a sinking vessel. As soon as the water has closed over a ship, this whirlpool sends up broken spars, wreckage, etc., which can be alluded to as livid *hieroglyphs,* making a *scattered chapter* so far as any complete record of the recent ship and her crew is concerned. In fact, about as much definite knowledge might come from all this as anyone might gain from the roar of his own veins, which is easily heard (haven't you ever done it?) by holding a shell close to one's ear."

[3] Crane's note: "Refers simply to a conviction that a man, not knowing perhaps a definite god yet being endowed with a reverence for deity—such a man naturally postulates a deity somehow, and the altar of that deity by the very *action* of the eyes *lifted* in searching."

[4] Crane's note: "Hasn't it often occurred that instruments originally invented for record and computation have inadvertently so extended the concepts of the entity they were invented to measure (concepts of space, etc.) in the mind and imagination that employed them, that they may metaphorically be said to have extended the original boundaries of the entity measured? This little bit of 'relativity' ought not to be discredited in poetry now that scientists are proceeding to measure the universe on principles of pure *ratio,* quite as metaphorical, so far as previous standards of scientific methods extended, as some of the axioms in Job."

[5] The title of an 1891 Melville poem: a monotonous sound or tone, as of waves.

* Comprised of a series of six poems published separately.

O brilliant kids, frisk with your dog,   10
Fondle your shells and sticks, bleached
By time and the elements; but there is a line
You must not cross nor ever trust beyond it
Spry cordage of your bodies to caresses
Too lichen-faithful[1] from too wide a breast.
The bottom of the sea is cruel.

II

—And yet this great wink of eternity,
Of rimless floods, unfettered leewardings,[2]
Samite[3] sheeted and processioned where
Her undinal[4] vast belly moonward bends,   20
Laughing the wrapt inflections of our love;

Take this Sea, whose diapason[5] knells
On scrolls of silver snowy sentences,
The sceptred terror of whose sessions rends
As her demeanors motion well or ill,
All but the pieties of lovers' hands.

And onward, as bells off San Salvador
Salute the crocus lustres of the stars,
In these poinsettia meadows of her tides,—
Adagios of islands,[6] O my Prodigal,   30
Complete the dark confessions her veins spell.

Mark how her turning shoulders wind the hours,
And hasten while her penniless rich palms
Pass superscription of bent foam and wave,—
Hasten, while they are true,—sleep, death, desire,
Close round one instant in one floating flower.

Bind us in time, O Seasons clear, and awe.
O minstrel galleons of Carib fire,
Bequeath us to no earthly shore until
Is answered in the vortex of our grave   40
The seal's wide spindrift[7] gaze toward paradise.

---

[1] A lichen is a symbiotic relationship between a fungus and an alga: a close relationship.
[2] Leeward is the direction toward which the wind blows.
[3] Heavy silk fabric threaded with gold, worn in the Middle Ages.
[4] According to folklore, Undine is a female water spirit who acquired a soul after marrying a human.
[5] The range of a musical instrument or voice.
[6] Crane's note: "the reference is to the motion of a boat through islands clustered thickly, the rhythm of the motion, etc. And it seems a much more direct and creative statement than any more logical employment of words such as 'coasting slowly through the islands,' besides ushering in a whole world of music."
[7] Spray blown from a rough surf.

III

Infinite consanguinity it bears—
This tendered theme of you that light
Retrieves from sea plains where the sky
Resigns a breast that every wave enthrones;
While ribboned water lanes I wind
Are laved and scattered with no stroke
Wide from your side, whereto this hour
The sea lifts, also, reliquary[8] hands.

And so, admitted through black swollen gates   50
That must arrest all distance otherwise,—
Past whirling pillars and lithe pediments,[9]
Light wrestling there incessantly with light,
Star kissing star through wave on wave unto
Your body rocking!
               and where death, if shed,
Presumes no carnage, but this single change,—
Upon the steep floor flung from dawn to dawn
The silken skilled transmemberment[10] of song;

Permit me voyage, love, into your hands . . .   60

IV

Whose counted smile of hours and days, suppose
I know as spectrum of the sea and pledge
Vastly now parting gulf on gulf of wings
Whose circles bridge, I know, (from palms to the severe
Chilled albatross's white immutability)
No stream of greater love advancing now
Than, singing, this mortality alone
Through clay aflow immortally to you.

All fragrance irrefragably,[11] and claim
Madly meeting logically in this hour   70
And region that is ours to wreathe again,
Portending eyes and lips and making told
The chancel[12] port and portion of our June—

[8] A container in which relics are kept and displayed.
[9] Triangular ornamental features in Grecian-style architecture.
[10] A term Crane coined, indicating both metamorphosis, as in transfiguration or transformation, and disintegration.
[11] Indisputably.   [12] The part of a church near the altar.

Shall they not stem and close in our own steps
Bright staves of flowers and quills today as I
Must first be lost in fatal tides to tell?

In signature of the incarnate word
The harbor shoulders to resign in mingling
Mutual blood, transpiring as foreknown
And widening noon within your breast for gathering   80
All bright insinuations that my years have caught
For islands where must lead inviolably
Blue latitudes and levels of your eyes,—

In this expectant, still exclaim receive
The secret oar and petals of all love.

                                 V

Meticulous, past midnight in clear rime,[13]
Infrangible[14] and lonely, smooth as though cast
Together in one merciless white blade—
The bay estuaries fleck the hard sky limits.

—As if too brittle or too clear to touch!   90
The cables of our sleep so swiftly filed,
Already hang, shred ends from remembered stars.
One frozen trackless smile . . . What words
Can strangle this deaf moonlight? For we

Are overtaken. Now no cry, no sword
Can fasten or deflect this tidal wedge,
Slow tyranny of moonlight, moonlight loved
And changed . . . "There's

Nothing like this in the world," you say,
Knowing I cannot touch your hand and look   100
Too, into that godless cleft of sky
Where nothing turns but dead sands flashing.

"—And never to quite understand!" No,
In all the argosy[15] of your bright hair I dreamed
Nothing so flagless as this piracy.

                         But now
Draw in your head, alone and too tall here.
Your eyes already in the slant of drifting foam;
Your breath sealed by the ghosts I do not know:
Draw in your head and sleep the long way home.   110

---

[13] Frost.   [14] Unbreakable.   [15] A large merchant ship or fleet of ships.

VI

Where icy and bright dungeons lift
Of swimmers their lost morning eyes,
And ocean rivers, churning, shift
Green borders under stranger skies,

Steadily as a shell secretes
Its beating leagues of monotone,
Or as many waters trough the sun's
Red kelson[16] past the cape's wet stone;

O rivers mingling toward the sky
And harbor of the phoenix'[17] breast—   120
My eyes pressed black against the prow,
—Thy derelict and blinded guest

Waiting, afire, what name, unspoke,
I cannot claim: let thy waves rear
More savage than the death of kings,
Some splintered garland for the seer.

Beyond siroccos[18] harvesting
The solstice thunders, crept away,
Like a cliff swinging or a sail
Flung into April's inmost day—   130

Creation's blithe and petalled word
To the lounged goddess when she rose
Conceding dialogue with eyes
That smile unsearchable repose—

Still fervid covenant, Belle Isle,
—Unfolded floating dais before
Which rainbows twine continual hair—
Belle Isle, white echo of the oar!

The imaged Word, it is, that holds
Hushed willows anchored in its glow.   140
It is the unbetrayable reply
Whose accent no farewell can know.

1921–1924, 1926

---

[16] Keelson, structural support inside a ship's hull along the keel.
[17] According to Egyptian myth, a bird that lives for hundreds of years, sets itself on fire, and arises from the ashes: a symbol of immortality.
[18] Hot, oppressive winds.

from *THE BRIDGE**

TO BROOKLYN BRIDGE[1]

How many dawns, chill from his rippling rest
The seagull's wings shall dip and pivot him,
Shedding white rings of tumult, building high
Over the chained bay waters Liberty—

Then, with inviolate curve, forsake our eyes
As apparitional as sails that cross
Some page of figures to be filed away;
—Till elevators drop us from our day . . .

I think of cinemas, panoramic sleights
With multitudes bent toward some flashing scene   10
Never disclosed, but hastened to again,
Foretold to other eyes on the same screen;

And Thee,[2] across the harbor, silver-paced
As though the sun took step of thee, yet left
Some motion ever unspent in thy stride,—
Implicitly thy freedom staying thee!

Out of some subway scuttle, cell or loft
A bedlamite[3] speeds to thy parapets,
Tilting there momently, shrill shirt ballooning,
A jest falls from the speechless caravan.   20

Down Wall,[4] from girder into street noon leaks,
A rip-tooth of the sky's acetylene;
All afternoon the cloud-flown derricks turn . . .
Thy cables breathe the North Atlantic still.

And obscure as that heaven of the Jews,
Thy guerdon[5] . . . Accolade thou dost bestow
Of anonymity time cannot raise:
Vibrant reprieve and pardon thou dost show.

---

* A long poem, published in 1930, consisting of an opening proem (introduction)—"To Brooklyn Bridge"—and eight succeeding sections: "Ave Maria," "Powhatan's Daughter," "Cutty Sark," "Cape Hatteras," "Three Songs," "Quaker Hill," "The Tunnel," and "Atlantis." The ellipses are Crane's.
   [1] A suspension bridge designed by John A. Roebling (1806–1869) and built from 1869 to 1883; it spans the East River from Brooklyn to Manhattan.
   [2] Brooklyn Bridge.   [3] An insane person: after Bedlam, an insane asylum in London.
   [4] New York City's Wall Street.   [5] A reward.

O harp and altar, of the fury fused,
(How could mere toil align thy choiring strings!)   30
Terrific threshold of the prophet's pledge,
Prayer of pariah, and the lover's cry,—

Again the traffic lights that skim thy swift
Unfractioned idiom, immaculate sigh of stars,
Beading thy path—condense eternity:
And we have seen night lifted in thine arms.

Under thy shadow by the piers I waited;
Only in darkness is thy shadow clear.
The City's fiery parcels all undone,
Already snow submerges an iron year . . .   40

O Sleepless as the river under thee,
Vaulting the sea, the prairies' dreaming sod,
Unto us lowliest sometime sweep, descend
And of the curveship[6] *lend a myth to God.*

1926–1927, 1930

THE BROKEN TOWER

The bell-rope that gathers God at dawn
Dispatches me as though I dropped down the knell
Of a spent day—to wander the cathedral lawn
From pit to crucifix, feet chill on steps from hell.

Have you not heard, have you not seen that corps
Of shadows in the tower, whose shoulders sway
Antiphonal carillons[1] launched before
The stars are caught and hived in the sun's ray?

The bells, I say, the bells break down their tower;
And swing I know not where. Their tongues engrave   10
Membrane through marrow, my long-scattered score
Of broken intervals . . . And I, their sexton[2] slave!

Oval encyclicals[3] in canyons heaping
The impasse high with choir. Banked voices slain!
Pagodas, campaniles[4] with reveilles outleaping—
O terraced echoes prostrate on the plain! . . .

---

[6] A term Crane coined.
[1] Bells that produce harmonies through opposing sounds.
[2] A church caretaker, bellringer and gravedigger.
[3] Papal letters circulated to the bishops of a whole church or in one country.
[4] Free-standing church towers.

And so it was I entered the broken world
To trace the visionary company of love, its voice
An instant in the wind (I know not whither hurled)
But not for long to hold each desperate choice.   20

My word I poured. But was it cognate, scored
Of that tribunal monarch of the air
Whose thigh embronzes earth, strikes crystal Word
In wounds pledged once to hope,—cleft to despair?

The steep encroachments of my blood left me
No answer (could blood hold such a lofty tower
As flings the question true?)—or is it she
Whose sweet mortality stirs latent power?—

And through whose pulse I hear, counting the strokes
My veins recall and add, revived and sure   30
The angelus[5] of wars my chest evokes:
What I hold healed, original now, and pure . . .

And builds, within, a tower that is not stone
(Not stone can jacket heaven)—but slip
Of pebbles,—visible wings of silence sown
In azure circles, widening as they dip

The matrix of the heart, lift down the eye
That shrines the quiet lake and swells a tower . . .
The commodious, tall decorum of that sky
Unseals her earth, and lifts love in its shower.   40

1932

Louise Bogan
(1897–1970)

Not until nearly fifteen years after Louise Bogan's death, with the publication of Elizabeth Frank's biography *Louise Bogan, A Portrait* (1985), did the "rough and vulgar facts" of Bogan's life come to light. In her poems we read of passion and grief, but we do not know what prompted the poetry. A formal, tightly controlled, discrete verse, Bogan's poetry fell out of fashion when free verse and explicitly autobiographical poetry were the dominant

---

[5] The Roman Catholic prayer that commemorates the Incarnation of Christ; or the bell rung to announce this thrice-daily prayer.

trends. Interest in her life and in her work is growing, however, with particular attention to her slim volume of collected verse, *The Blue Estuaries* (1968). Most of the poems in this volume were originally published in the 1920s and 1930s. Thereafter she wrote a few poems and some (uncollected) fiction and continued to write remarkable reviews as poetry critic for the *New Yorker,* a job she held for thirty-eight years.

Bogan was born in 1897 in Livermore Falls, a small mill town in Maine. She spent her early years with her family in Maine, New Hampshire, and Massachusetts among various boarding houses. Her parents' marriage was extremely troubled, and her mother engaged in a series of affairs, all of which the child was aware of. Bogan's formal education took place, except for one year at Boston College, in Boston's Girls' Latin School, where she was rigorously trained in the classics and was already writing poetry. She has said that by age eighteen she had learned every essential of her trade. Bogan married Curt Alexander, an army man, in 1916 but found both him and army life to her dislike and left with their only child, a daughter. He died in 1920, when Bogan was living in New York City's Greenwich Village. There Bogan, at age twenty-two, was already gaining a reputation as a gifted lyric poet and met friends she was to have for life, notably the writers Edmund Wilson, Malcolm Cowley, and Rolfe Humphries. Yet, though her work was going well, she suffered the first of several emotional breakdowns.

In 1923 Bogan's first book of verse, *Body of this Death,* was published, and she married the writer Raymond Holden in 1925. Her second book, *Dark Summer* (1929), received quiet, if favorable, reviews. However, Bogan suffered from depression in the early 1930s and twice checked herself into New York's Neurological Institute. In her letters she writes of having gone "to the ninth circle of hell" and back. Her second marriage fell apart, and she divorced at age thirty-seven. During the 1930s Bogan traveled on fellowships and continued writing, her last collection of new work, *The Sleeping Fury,* coming out in 1937.

Thereafter, Bogan struggled mainly to write criticism and stave off depression. In 1954 she was elected to the Academy of American Poets and published *Collected Poems,* for which she shared a Bollingen Prize with Léonie Adams. Bogan spent much of her last years alone, although she kept up her lively and witty correspondence with friends. She died in 1970, alone in her apartment opposite the Neurological Institute. The importance of Bogan's work in the canon of modern poetry is now established, her poetry recognized once again, and with considerable enthusiasm, for its technical grace, lyric perfection, and hard-earned wisdom.

Suggested Readings: *Achievement in American Poetry, 1900–1950,* 1951. *A Poet's Alphabet: Reflections on the Literary Art and Vocation,* ed. R. Phelps and R. Limmer, 1970. *What the Woman Lived: Selected Letters of Louise Bogan 1920–1970,* ed. R. Limmer, 1973. *Journey Around My Room: The Autobiography of Louise Bogan, A Mosaic,* ed. R. Limmer, 1980. M. Collins, ed., *Critical Essays on Louise Bogan,* 1984. E. Frank, *Louise Bogan, A Portrait,* 1985. G. Bowles, *Louise Bogan's Aesthetic of Limitation,* 1987.

Text Used: *The Blue Estuaries: Poems 1923–1968,* 1968.

SONNET

Dark, underground, is furnished with the bone;
The tool's lost, and the counter in the game.

Eaten as though by water or by flame
The elaborate craft built up from wood and stone.

Words made of breath, these also are undone,
And greedy sight abolished in its claim.
Light fails from ruin and from wall the same;
The loud sound and pure silence fall as one.

Worn flesh at last is history and treasure
Unto itself; its scars it still can keep,   10
Received from love, from memory's false measure,
From pain, from the long dream drawn back in sleep.

Attest, poor body, with what scars you have,
That you left life, to come down to the grave.

1929

SINGLE SONNET

Now, you great stanza, you heroic mould,
Bend to my will, for I must give you love:
The weight in the heart that breathes, but cannot move,
Which to endure flesh only makes so bold.

Take up, take up, as it were lead or gold
The burden; test the dreadful mass thereof.
No stone, slate, metal under or above
Earth, is so ponderous, so dull, so cold.

Too long as ocean bed bears up the ocean,
As earth's core bears the earth, have I borne this;   10
Too long have lovers, bending for their kiss,
Felt bitter force cohering without motion.

Staunch meter, great song, it is yours, at length,
To prove how stronger you are than my strength.

1930

ITALIAN MORNING

Half circle's come before we know.
Full in the falling arc, we hear
Our heel give earth a lonely blow.
We place the hour and name the year.

High in a room long since designed
For our late visit under night,
We sleep: we wake to watch the lined
Wave take strange walls with counterfeit light.

The big magnolia, like a hand,
Repeats our flesh. (O bred to love,   10
Gathered to silence!) In a land
Thus garnished, there is time enough

To pace the rooms where painted swags[1]
Of fruit and flower in pride depend,
Stayed as we are not. The hour wags
Deliberate, and great arches bend

In long perspective past our eye.

Mutable body, and brief name,
Confront, against an early sky,
This marble herb, and this stone flame.   20

1930

EVENING IN THE SANITARIUM*

The free evening fades, outside the windows fastened with decorative
    iron grilles.
The lamps are lighted; the shades drawn; the nurses are watching a
    little.
It is the hour of the complicated knitting on the safe bone needles; of
    the games of anagrams and bridge;
The deadly game of chess; the book held up like a mask.

The period of the wildest weeping, the fiercest delusion, is over.
The women rest their tired half-healed hearts; they are almost well.
Some of them will stay almost well always: the blunt-faced woman
    whose thinking dissolved
Under academic discipline; the manic-depressive girl
Now leveling off; one paranoiac afflicted with jealousy.
Another with persecution. Some alleviation has been possible.   10

O fortunate bride, who never again will become elated after childbirth!
O lucky older wife, who has been cured of feeling unwanted!
To the suburban railway station you will return, return,

[1] Decorations hanging in a curve between two points.
* First published in 1941 with the subtitle "Imitated From Auden." Bogan much admired the work of
the English poet W. H. Auden (1907–1973), who became an American citizen in 1946.

To meet forever Jim home on the 5:35.
You will be again as normal and selfish and heartless as anybody else.

There is life left: the piano says it with its octave smile.
The soft carpets pad the thump and splinter of the suicide to be.
Everything will be splendid: the grandmother will not drink habitually.
The fruit salad will bloom on the plate like a bouquet
And the garden produce the blue-ribbon aquilegia.[1]   20

The cats will be glad; the fathers feel justified; the mothers relieved.
The sons and husbands will no longer need to pay the bills.
Childhoods will be put away, the obscene nightmare abated.

At the ends of the corridors the baths are running.
Mrs. C. again feels the shadow of the obsessive idea.
Miss R. looks at the mantel-piece, which must mean something.

1941

NIGHT

The cold remote islands
And the blue estuaries
Where what breathes, breathes
The restless wind of the inlets,
And what drinks, drinks
The incoming tide;

Where shell and weed
Wait upon the salt wash of the sea,
And the clear nights of stars
Swing their lights westward   10
To set behind the land;

Where the pulse clinging to the rocks
Renews itself forever;
Where, again on cloudless nights,
The water reflects
The firmament's partial setting;

—O remember
In your narrowing dark hours
That more things move
Than blood in the heart.   20

1968

---

[1] Columbine, a blue-flowered plant of the Rocky Mountains.

=CONTEXTS=

The Southern Agrarians

In the American South of the early 1920s a literary revival, known as the Southern Renaissance, took shape. Though the authors of the Southern Renaissance moved beyond the strictures of "regional" literature and approached more universal concerns, they continued the traditions of the local-color writers and retained a distinctive southern flavor. In his poem "Vision by Sweetwater" (1927), John Crowe Ransom (1888–1974), a prominent Southern Renaissance writer, contrasts the peacefulness of antebellum southern life with the debased state of the post-Reconstruction South:

Vision by Sweetwater

Go and ask Robin to bring the girls over
To Sweetwater, said my Aunt; and that was why
It was like a dream of ladies sweeping by
The willows, clouds, deep meadowgrass, and river.

Robin's sisters and my Aunt's lily daughter
Laughed and talked, and tinkled light as wrens
If there were a little colony all hens
To go walking by the steep turn of Sweetwater.

Let them alone, dear Aunt, just for one minute
Till I go fishing in the dark of my mind:
Where have I seen before, against the wind,
These bright virgins, robed and bare of bonnet,

Flowing with music of their strange quick tongue
And adventuring with delicate paces by the stream,—
Myself a child, old suddenly at the scream
From one of the white throats which it hid among?

John Crowe Ransom, 1927

The proponents of the movement of regional pride known as agrarianism, including Ransom, Allen Tate, and Robert Penn Warren (1905–1990), were concerned that industrialization would overwhelm the Old South's pastoral way of life. This way of life involved an organic relationship between humans and nature, a relationship that would be destroyed, agrarians feared, by the introduction of smoke-belching factories, the diminished importance of the individual, and other trappings of industrialism. Some southerners also feared that an industrial economy, with its need for cheap sources of labor, would allow African Americans a more stable economic footing in the South. The agrarians' inability to reconcile the values of the rural South with the needs and rights of its African-American population contributed to the ultimate failure of agrarianism to hold the line against industrialism.

Langston Hughes
(1902–1967)

Langston Hughes's contributions to African-American literature span the period from the Harlem Renaissance of the 1920s to the Black Arts movement of the late 1960s. Known as the "bard of Harlem," he wrote poems, plays, fiction, and nonfiction; edited anthologies; and encouraged such younger writers as Gwendolyn Brooks and Alice Walker. Hughes was born in Joplin, Missouri, in 1902. In 1903 his father, Jessie Nathaniel Hughes, left for Mexico in search of economic opportunities. His mother, Carrie Mercer Langston, moved frequently, working as a newspaperwoman and stenographer. Hughes occasionally traveled with her but resided in Lawrence, Kansas, with his maternal grandmother, a woman honored as the last surviving widow of a slave killed in John Brown's 1859 raid. After her death in 1915 Hughes briefly stayed with devoutly religious friends of hers. From 1916 to 1920 he lived with his mother, new stepfather, and stepbrother in Cleveland, Ohio, where he attended high school. The more liberal of his white schoolmates, children of European immigrants, introduced him to continental philosophy and Marxism.

At age eighteen Hughes wrote his most anthologized poem, "The Negro Speaks of Rivers," while crossing the Mississippi by train on his way to Mexico to spend a year with his father. The poem was accepted by W. E. B. DuBois's magazine *Crisis*. Hughes enrolled at Columbia University in 1920 but dropped out after a year to immerse himself in the people, night life, and folk forms that shaped the Harlem Renaissance. Working to free writing from European traditions, he innovated forms based on African-American culture.

Throughout his life Hughes traveled extensively. His travels enabled him to form friendships with writers of different backgrounds, stretching both his thinking about the responsibilities of artists and his own literary practice. His translations introduced Caribbean, Latin American, and African poets to American readers. Hughes first went to Africa as a cabin boy on a freighter in 1923 and to Paris the following year. There, the writer/educator Alain Locke made Hughes a part of the Harlem Renaissance by including the poet's work in the anthology *The New Negro* (1925).

Back in the States, Hughes met the novelist Arna Bontemps, with whom he collaborated for several decades on children's books and anthologies. *The Weary Blues,* Hughes's first poetry book, was published in 1926; his second book of poems, *Fine Clothes to the Jew,* appeared in 1927. Some black reviewers objected to both books' stance against middle-class assimilation of African Americans. That summer Charlotte Mason, one of Hughes's several white patrons, provided support for him to begin his first novel. However, their differences surfaced by the time that novel, *Not Without Laughter,* was published in 1930. Mason saw black culture as white Americans' connection to the primitive, whereas Hughes increasingly wrote to protest the social conditions of a racist society.

By this time Hughes had finished college at Lincoln University (he was later awarded two honorary doctorates). The Great Depression had so deprived the Harlem Renaissance of its wealthy audience that the movement had dispersed. Hughes was determined to make a living as a writer. In Chapel Hill, North Carolina, in 1931, an unofficial student paper published Hughes's "Christ in Alabama," a poem about nine young black men who were unjustly jailed for the rapes of two white prostitutes. The audience at Hughes's subsequent poetry reading in Chapel Hill nearly rioted. Elsewhere audiences packed his readings. In 1932 he visited Russia, where he met the communist writer Arthur Koestler. Hughes and Koestler explored Soviet Asia and debated the roles of social goals and individual desires in art. Hughes defended the artist's autonomy, but the discussions revived his interest in leftist thought. His poetry of this period rings with the language of proletarian revolution.

Hughes's drama *Mulatto* played on Broadway from 1935 to 1936. As a correspondent for the *Baltimore Afro-American* in 1937, he covered the Spanish Civil War and met the influential literary figures Ernest Hemingway, André Malraux, and Pablo Neruda in Madrid. In Los Angeles in 1939 Hughes founded the New Negro Theater, wrote a screenplay, and completed the first part of his autobiography, *The Big Sea* (1940). Over the next three years he received a fellowship to write historical plays and, in Chicago, founded the Skyloft Players, who performed his musical *The Sun Do More* (1941).

Hughes returned to New York City when his book *Shakespeare in Harlem* was published in 1942. He wrote slogans to sell U.S. Defense Bonds and a weekly column for the *Chicago Defender*, an African-American newspaper, where his first of five short stories of Harlem folk philosopher Jesse B. Semple (nicknamed "Simple") were published. Semple's female counterpart, Madam Alberta K. Johnson, appeared in the poems of *One-Way Ticket* (1949). His long poem *Montage of a Dream Deferred* was published in 1951. Reviews of his work remain mixed: critics have recognized the modernism of Hughes's restraint, but some have had reservations about the folk elements.

In 1953 Hughes was called before Senator Joseph McCarthy's subcommittee on subversive activities and testified about his involvement with communism in the 1930s. As had other black intellectuals, Hughes saw communism's interest in the poor as potentially helpful to African Americans. Until 1959 he was listed by the FBI as a security risk. After 1960, however, he visited Africa and Europe many times on cultural grants from the State Department. In varied forms of satire, the poems in *Ask Your Mama* (1961), considered by some his greatest work, discuss the rising anger against bigotry of the 1960s. The status of African Americans was changing, but Hughes saw the change as slow and regressive. The prolific writer died in 1967, shortly after the publication of *The Panther and the Lash: Poems of Our Times* and shortly before major upheavals in the civil rights movement.

Suggested Readings: *The Weary Blues*, 1926. *Not Without Laughter*, 1930. *The Dream Keeper and Other Poems*, 1932. *Scottsboro Limited: Four Poems and a Play in Verse*, 1932. *The Ways of White Folks*, 1934. *The Big Sea: An Autobiography*, 1940. *One-Way Ticket*, 1949. *Montage of a Dream Deferred*, 1951. *I Wonder As I Wander: An Autobiographical Journey*, 1956. *The Langston Hughes Reader*, 1958. *The Best of Simple*, 1961. *Fight for Freedom: The Story of the NAACP*, 1962. D. C. Dickinson, *A Bio-Bibliography of Langston Hughes, 1902–1967*, 1967. N. Huggins, *Harlem Renaissance*, 1971. R. K. Barksdale, *Langston Hughes: The Poet and His Critics*, 1977. F. Berry, *Langston Hughes: Before and Beyond Harlem*, 1983. A. Rampersad, *The Life of Langston Hughes*, 2 vols., 1986–1988. R. B. Miller, *The Art and Imagination of Langston Hughes*, 1989.

Text Used: *Selected Poems of Langston Hughes*, 1970.

THE NEGRO SPEAKS OF RIVERS

I've known rivers:
I've known rivers ancient as the world and older than the
    flow of human blood in human veins.

My soul has grown deep like the rivers.

I bathed in the Euphrates[1] when dawns were young.
I built my hut near the Congo[2] and it lulled me to sleep.
I looked upon the Nile and raised the pyramids above it.
I heard the singing of the Mississippi when Abe Lincoln
    went down to New Orleans, and I've seen its muddy
    bosom turn all golden in the sunset.   10

I've known rivers:
Ancient, dusky rivers.

My soul has grown deep like the rivers.

1920, 1921

THE WEARY BLUES

Droning a drowsy syncopated tune,
Rocking back and forth to a mellow croon,
    I heard a Negro play.
Down on Lenox Avenue[1] the other night
By the pale dull pallor of an old gas light
    He did a lazy sway. . . .
    He did a lazy sway. . . .
To the tune o' those Weary Blues.
With his ebony hands on each ivory key
He made that poor piano moan with melody.   10
    O Blues!
Swaying to and fro on his rickety stool
He played that sad raggy tune like a musical fool.
    Sweet Blues!
Coming from a black man's soul.
    O Blues!
In a deep song voice with a melancholy tone
I heard that Negro sing, that old piano moan—
    "Ain't got nobody in all this world,
    Ain't got nobody but ma self.   20
    I's gwine to quit ma frownin'
    And put ma troubles on the shelf."
Thump, thump, thump, went his foot on the floor.
He played a few chords then he sang some more—
    "I got the Weary Blues

---

[1] The Euphrates River, the cradle of ancient Babylonian civilization, flows from eastern Turkey
through Syria and Iraq into the Persian Gulf.
[2] The Congo River, which flows through West Central Africa into the Atlantic.
[1] In New York City's Harlem.

And I can't be satisfied.
Got the Weary Blues
And can't be satisfied—
I ain't happy no mo'
And I wish that I had died." 30
And far into the night he crooned that tune.
The stars went out and so did the moon.
The singer stopped playing and went to bed
While the Weary Blues echoed through his head.
He slept like a rock or a man that's dead.

1923, 1926

DREAM BOOGIE

Good morning, daddy!
Ain't you heard
The boogie-woogie[1] rumble
Of a dream deferred?

Listen closely:
You'll hear their feet
Beating out and beating out a—

You think
It's a happy beat?

Listen to it closely: 10
Ain't you heard
something underneath
like a—

What did I say?

Sure,
I'm happy!
Take it away!

Hey, pop!
Re-bop!
Mop! 20

Y-e-a-h!

1951

---

[1] A percussive style of playing blues on the piano, characterized by a steady rhythmic bass and a series of improvised melodic variations.

THEME FOR ENGLISH B

The instructor said,

> *Go home and write*
> *a page tonight.*
> *And let that page come out of you—*
> *Then, it will be true.*

I wonder if it's that simple?
I am twenty-two, colored, born in Winston-Salem.
I went to school there, then Durham,[1] then here
to this college[2] on the hill above Harlem.
I am the only colored student in my class.   10
The steps from the hill lead down into Harlem,
through a park, then I cross St. Nicholas,[3]
Eighth Avenue, Seventh, and I come to the Y,[4]
the Harlem Branch Y, where I take the elevator
up to my room, sit down, and write this page:

It's not easy to know what is true for you or me
at twenty-two, my age. But I guess I'm what
I feel and see and hear, Harlem, I hear you:
hear you, hear me—we two—you, me, talk on this page.
(I hear New York, too.) Me—who?   20
Well, I like to eat, sleep, drink, and be in love.
I like to work, read, learn, and understand life.
I like a pipe for a Christmas present,
or records—Bessie, bop, or Bach.[5]
I guess being colored doesn't make me *not* like
the same things other folks like who are other races.
So will my page be colored that I write?
Being me, it will not be white.
But it will be
a part of you, instructor.   30
You are white—
yet a part of me, as I am a part of you.
That's American.
Sometimes perhaps you don't want to be a part of me.
Nor do I often want to be a part of you.
But we are, that's true!
As I learn from you,

---

[1] Cities in North Carolina.   [2] Columbia University.
[3] An avenue east of the Columbia University campus.
[4] The Young Men's Christian Association (YMCA).
[5] The famous African-American blues singer Bessie Smith (1898?–1937); jazz, often played very fast, characterized by harmonic complexity, convoluted melodic lines, and constant shifting of accent; the German composer and organist Johann Sebastian Bach (1685–1750).

I guess you learn from me—
although you're older—and white—
and somewhat more free.   40

This is my page for English B.

1951

HARLEM

What happens to a dream deferred?

Does it dry up
like a raisin in the sun?
Or fester like a sore—
And then run?
Does it stink like rotten meat?
Or crust and sugar over—
like a syrupy sweet?

Maybe it just sags
like a heavy load.

Or does it explode?

1951

EARLY 20TH-CENTURY FICTION

The early years of the twentieth century were marked by a series of political and cultural disruptions, both international and domestic. During that time, traditional political structures were globally destabilized. Europe's empires were either diminishing greatly or were being replaced by new regimes, and the United States was replacing them in arbitrating international affairs. As the political maps were being redrawn and the lessons of history reassessed, developments in physics, philosophy, and psychiatry combined to discredit the most fundamental assumptions about the stability and the validity of our perceptions of reality. Increasingly dehumanizing industrialization, World War I, the 1917 Russian Revolution, the revolt of disenfranchised women everywhere, and the disillusioning rise and fall of western economies in the 1920s and 1930s all contributed to a growing dissatisfaction with traditional values. This distrust produced radical changes in literary tastes and techniques in Europe and the United States.

The naturalism movement that had begun in the late 1800s continued into the early 1900s. Naturalism, in which environmental forces overwhelm individual will, was dominated by the work of Theodore Dreiser. In his novel *Sister Carrie* (1900) it is chance that causes a safe to shut accidentally at a pivotal moment, leaving George Hurstwood a thief and leading to his horrible downfall, which might easily have been averted. And in *The Financier* (1912) Dreiser evidences his belief in environmental determinism as the young Frank Cowperwood observes an octopus and a squid in the same fishtank; over the period of a few days, the octopus thrives while the squid perishes, simply, Dreiser shows, because of the "random" ability of one to consume the other.

Edith Wharton, a friend and admirer of Henry James, treated in her own novels many of the ethical issues she found in his novels. Like James, she was most comfortable examining American mores from a distance: leaving her husband and her country, she moved to France. There she wrote incisively ironic and lucid fiction, much of it concerning married American women. James's influence is apparent in Wharton's finely crafted studies of the leisured and horrifyingly empty lives of upper-class women in the years prior to World War I.

Gertrude Stein was notable for following James and Wharton in their expatriation and for promptly rejecting the social standards and rituals they dissected in their exquisitely polished prose. Stein also rejected that prose style itself. She went beyond Wharton's lucid criticisms of women's place in the American family to pioneer the alternative lifestyle of the uncloseted lesbian, unapologetically appropriating a degree of sexual license that was denied less presumptuous women throughout the century. Stein and her lifelong companion, Alice B. Toklas, were frequently visited at their home in Paris by an international collection of writers, artists, sculptors, and painters. Mingling the aesthetics of guests Pablo Picasso, Ezra Pound, Henri Matisse, and James Joyce, Stein wrote experimental narratives applying avant-garde theories of sculpture to prose. In her novel *Tender Buttons* (1914) her incantatory, primitive pattern of repeating phrases with slight variations imitates the simplification and fragmentation of cubist painting. Although her commonly unintelligible writing was more often discussed than read, she stimulated writers such as Ernest Hemingway and William Faulkner, members of what she labeled "the lost generation," as they searched for new modes of expressing their postwar grief and confusion.

One influential proponent of Stein's simplified, fragmented, prose was her friend Sherwood Anderson. Anderson, too, experimented with consciously primitive prose styles and multiple points of view. In Anderson's story "The Book of the Grotesque," included in his best-known collection, *Winesburg, Ohio* (1919), an elderly author tries to write a book envisioning truth and beauty, but his vision devolves into nightmare. By the 1920s many nineteenth-century moral certainties were suspect, replaced by the queasily uncertain principles of pluralism and subjectivity. Anderson's work—tame enough today but in its time shocking for its sexual candor as well as its stylistic innovations—dramatized the despair and liberation of artists caught unprepared for the political, aesthetic, and sexual emancipations of the flapper era.

Hemingway, influenced by Anderson and Stein, responded to the moral void following World War I with tales of physically and philosophically courageous

St. Louis singer-dancer sensation Josephine Baker moved to Paris in 1925 and helped introduce American jazz there. Receiving the Legion of Honor for her resistance work during World War II, she founded an orphanage for all races—her "experiment in brotherhood"—in the 1950s.

Anne Porter's stories, collected in *Flowering Judas* (1930) and *Pale Horse, Pale Rider* (1939). But the southern states produced by far the greatest number of regionalist authors. The Southern Renaissance, beginning in the 1920s, generated a chorus of lyrical celebrations and lamentations. Thomas Wolfe nostalgically retold his North Carolina childhood and youth in a series of long novels, beginning with *Look Homeward, Angel* (1929).

Many authors of the early twentieth century wrote with horrified vividness of the economic devastations during the Great Depression of the 1930s. The depression was especially ruinous in rural communities, and John Steinbeck recorded with sympathy and humor its catastrophic effects in those communities. His novel *The Grapes of Wrath* (1939) follows the westward migration of Oklahoma sharecroppers fleeing the desperately impoverished midwestern Dust Bowl. Steinbeck was less concerned with technically innovative prose styles than with political and social documentation of the period. In this undertaking he continued a tradition of social criticism in American fiction, traceable through Theodore Dreiser's *Sister Carrie;* Sinclair Lewis's *Main Street* (1920), *Babbitt* (1922), and *Arrowsmith* (1925); and the novels of John Dos Passos, particularly his anti-World War I novel, *Three Soldiers* (1921), and his *U.S.A.* trilogy (1938). Each of these authors championed the poor, the unemployed, and the dehumanized worker; each criticized the growth of mechanized industry and the concomitant deification of material goods and profits. Distrusting capitalist society and its promises, these authors found an increasing readership as the depression lingered. Although many authors—at best employed only marginally—had themselves been severely affected by the depression, the government funded Federal Writers' Project, part of Franklin D. Roosevelt's New Deal, provided support for unemployed writers. The FWP allowed such writers as Zora Neale Hurston, Saul Bellow, Tillie Olsen, John Cheever, and Richard Wright to get back on their feet. Thereafter, politically engaged writers, like many American readers in the 1930s and 1940s, gained interest in the growing Socialist and Communist reform movements. After World War II disrupted the 1940s, a new generation of politically conscious writers with new voices and new literary tools continued this tradition.

═CONTEXTS═

Reform Writers

During the 1920s and 1930s many American writers became disillusioned with the brutality of twentieth-century industrial life. They were critical of the destructive effects of runaway capitalism on humanity and in their works sought to expose these ills.

Notable among these reform writers is Upton Sinclair (1878–1968), whose works typically depict the horror of working-class life in the industrial age. His 1906 novel *The Jungle,* with its graphic depictions of the dehumanizing effects of industry, resulted in the passage of legislation toward improvements in the sanitation of meat packing and processing.

The Jungle depicts a Lithuanian immigrant family's struggles to make a living and fulfill the "American Dream." Shortly after arriving in the New World, the realities of industrial life become clear to the immigrants. They are beset from the beginning by political corruption, brutal working conditions, and bitter poverty (as in the excerpt below). In the end the family dissolves, but a glimmer of hope is cast by the protagonist's drift toward the Communist party.

The Jungle

A very few days of practical experience in this land of high wages had been sufficient to make clear to them the cruel fact that it was also a land of high prices, and that in it the poor man was almost as poor as in any other corner of the earth; and so there vanished in a night all the wonderful dreams of wealth that had been haunting Jurgis. What had made the discovery all the more painful was that they were spending, at American prices, money which they had earned at home rates of wages—and so were really being cheated by the world!

Upton Sinclair, 1906

Edith Wharton
(1862–1937)

Born in 1862, Edith Newbold Jones was the youngest child of George Frederic Jones and Lucretia Stevens Rhinelander, members of the wealthy "Old New York" society. In 1866, with their financial state impaired by the post-Civil War inflation, the Joneses went to Europe in order to economize. Edith spent much of her early childhood traveling in France, Italy, and Germany. After their return to America she enjoyed summers in Newport, Rhode Island, and winters in New York City. She eagerly read the classics in her father's library, where she discovered "the Old Testament, the Apocalypse and the Eliza-

Edith Wharton in 1905.

bethan dramatists," as noted by R. W. B. Lewis in his 1975 Pulitzer Prize-winning biography of Wharton.

Although her family disapproved of literary activities and expected Edith to become a conventional society matron, a different destiny seemed ordained by her ability to read easily in several languages and by the private printing of her first volume of poetry when she was sixteen—a year before she made her debutante appearance. Like Kate Chopin, Edith Jones had to curb her desire for reading and "making up" bits of writing in order to participate in the social world of the debutante. Through that world she met the Bostonian Edward ("Teddy") Robbins Wharton, whom she married in 1885. The two had a childless and leisure-filled marriage, dividing their time between New York, Newport, Boston, and

Europe and even taking a cruise on the Aegean Sea in 1888 that Wharton described in a letter as "the greatest step forward in [her] making." Although Teddy appears to have been a decent and considerate husband, the marriage was clearly not a happy one. Indeed, the literary critic Edmund Wilson suggests that Wharton began writing in earnest at the recommendation of the "nerve specialist" Dr. S. Weir Mitchell, who treated her for a "paralyzing melancholy" that recurred from the early 1890s until 1902, the year her husband's mental illness became quite evident. Whether invigorated by her journey or seeking a happier world through her imagination, Wharton did begin to write seriously, publishing poetry and stories in major magazines, including *Scribner's, Harper's,* and the *Century.* Produced with the Boston architect Ogden Codman, Jr., her first lengthy work—*The Decoration of Houses* (1897)—combined an interest in interior design with developing writing abilities.

Although Wharton complained in her autobiography, *A Backward Glance* (1934), that she had little encouragement during this period, her short-story collections *The Greater Inclination* (1899) and *Crucial Instances* (1901) brought her enough assurance as a writer to feel that she needed to build a haven where she could work without interruption. "The Mount," in Lenox, Massachusetts, not only offered her solitude but provided her with a vantage for observing the land and the people who would figure prominently in her rural fiction. The novellas and the novel (*The Valley of Decision* [1902]) of this period reflect Wharton's "apprenticeship," an experimentation with both the forms and the themes that would recur in her more mature works—including tales of the supernatural; the relationships between artistry, artists, and life; variations on the international theme; and reflections on the problems of the marriage market.

Wharton did not meet Henry James until 1902, but the similarity between her early themes and those that James addressed is striking, although the stylistic strategies deployed by the two differ greatly. In contrast to James's indirection, for example, Wharton's *The House of Mirth* (1905) demonstrates her preference for straightforward examination and presentation. Frankly and somewhat sardonically *The House of Mirth* combines the tenets of the genteel novel of manners with the harsh determinism of Charles Darwin or Herbert Spencer in order to examine both the intricacies of old New York City's elite inner circle and the specific problems of Lily Bart, a slightly unconventional woman in that world. Although she would like to belong to a "republic of the spirit," Bart cannot break free of the social constraints within which she has been born; she is stifled in a world in which women should simply be lovely wives and good hostesses.

Despite dissimilarities in their subjects, many of Wharton's best stories of this period share a preoccupation with exploring a protagonist's responses to socially imposed restrictions. *The Reef* (1912), *The Custom of the Country* (1913), and the Pulitzer Prize-winning *The Age of Innocence* (1920) all consider the social forces that tightly regulate personal and sexual relationships, dictating which alliances are acceptable and which are not. *Ethan Frome* (1911) and *Summer* (1917) explore the limitations imposed not by the inner circle of New York but by the communal standards of rural New England. The protagonists' struggles to live happily despite communal standards typically force them to consider divorce or to give up a lover. These tensions are so pervasive in Wharton's fiction perhaps because she was herself in a dilemma akin to the ones she described. Around 1910 she was involved in a passionate affair with her longtime friend Morton Fullerton, a relationship that she understood to be temporary but nevertheless forced both her and Teddy to recognize the deficiencies of their marriage. Selling "The Mount," they moved to France for Teddy's health; however, he had another nervous breakdown and was subsequently confined to a sanitorium. The couple divorced in 1913, and Wharton poured her energy into the civilian war efforts in France. She incorporated some of her experiences into nonfictional work and into her two war novels, *The Marne* (1918) and *A Son at the Front* (1923).

Although her late writings are generally regarded as less successful than *The House of Mirth* or *The Age of Innocence*, Wharton remained highly acclaimed. In 1923 she became the first woman to receive a Doctor of Letters from Yale University; in 1930 she and Mary E. Wilkins Freeman were the first two women to receive gold medals from the National Institute of Arts and Letters; and in 1934 she was selected for membership in the American Academy of Arts and Letters. As such wide acknowledgment suggests, her best work—typically ironic and carefully modulated in tone—addresses fundamental questions of the survival of weak or disenfranchised individuals in self-promoting societies that can be vicious simply through unquestioning allegiance to their own standards.

Suggested Readings: *The House of Mirth,* 1905. *The Age of Innocence,* 1920. *A Backward Glance,* 1934. *The World Over,* 1936. *The Edith Wharton Reader,* ed. L. Auchincloss, 1965. *The Collected Short Stories of Edith Wharton,* ed. R. W. B. Lewis, 1968. *The Letters of Edith Wharton,* ed. R. W. B. Lewis and N. Lewis, 1988. B. Nevius, *Edith Wharton: A Study of Her Fiction,* 1961. R. W. B. Lewis, *Edith Wharton: A Biography,* 1975. G. Lindberg, *Edith Wharton and the Novel of Manners,* 1975. M. B. McDowell, *Edith Wharton,* 1976. C. G. Wolff, *A Feast of Words: The Triumph of Edith Wharton,* 1977. E. Ammons, *Edith Wharton's Argument With America,* 1980. W. Gimbel, *Edith Wharton: Orphancy and Survival,* 1984. J. Fryer, *Felicitous Space: The Imaginative Structures of Edith Wharton and Willa Cather,* 1986. J. Goodwyn, *Edith Wharton: Traveller in the Land of Letters,* 1990. P. Vita-Finzi, *Edith Wharton and the Art of Fiction,* 1990.

Text Used: *The Descent of Man and Other Stories,* 1904.

THE OTHER TWO*

I

Waythorn, on the drawing-room hearth, waited for his wife to come down to dinner.

It was their first night under his own roof, and he was surprised at his thrill of boyish agitation. He was not so old, to be sure—his glass[1] gave him little more than the five-and-thirty years to which his wife confessed—but he had fancied himself already in the temperate zone; yet here he was listening for her step with a tender sense of all it symbolized, with some old trail of verse about the garlanded nuptial door-posts floating through his enjoyment of the pleasant room and the good dinner just beyond it.

They had been hastily recalled from their honeymoon by the illness of Lily Haskett, the child of Mrs. Waythorn's first marriage. The little girl, at Waythorn's desire, had been transferred to his house on the day of her mother's wedding, and the doctor, on their arrival, broke the news that she was ill with typhoid, but declared that all the symptoms were favourable. Lily could show twelve years of unblemished health, and the case promised to be a light one. The nurse spoke as reassuringly, and after a moment of alarm Mrs. Waythorn had adjusted herself to the situation. She was very fond of Lily—her affection for the child had perhaps been her decisive charm in Waythorn's eyes—but she had the perfectly balanced nerves which her little girl had inherited, and no woman ever wasted less tissue in unproductive worry. Waythorn was therefore quite prepared to see her come in

---

* First published in *The Descent of Man and Other Stories* (1904). The ellipses are Wharton's.
[1] Mirror.

presently, a little late because of a last look at Lily, but as serene and well-appointed as if her good-night kiss had been laid on the brow of health. Her composure was restful to him; it acted as ballast to his somewhat unstable sensibilities. As he pictured her bending over the child's bed he thought how soothing her presence must be in illness: her very step would prognosticate recovery.

His own life had been a gray one, from temperament rather than circumstance, and he had been drawn to her by the unperturbed gaiety which kept her fresh and elastic at an age when most women's activities are growing either slack or febrile. He knew what was said about her; for, popular as she was, there had always been a faint undercurrent of detraction. When she had appeared in New York, nine or ten years earlier, as the pretty Mrs. Haskett whom Gus Varick had unearthed somewhere—was it in Pittsburg or Utica?—society, while promptly accepting her, had reserved the right to cast a doubt on its own discrimination. Enquiry, however, established her undoubted connection with a socially reigning family, and explained her recent divorce as the natural result of a runaway match at seventeen; and as nothing was known of Mr. Haskett it was easy to believe the worst of him.

Alice Haskett's remarriage with Gus Varick was a passport to the set whose recognition she coveted, and for a few years the Varicks were the most popular couple in town. Unfortunately the alliance was brief and stormy, and this time the husband had his champions. Still, even Varick's staunchest supporters admitted that he was not meant for matrimony, and Mrs. Varick's grievances were of a nature to bear the inspection of the New York courts. A New York divorce is in itself a diploma of virtue,[2] and in the semi-widowhood of this second separation Mrs. Varick took on an air of sanctity, and was allowed to confide her wrongs to some of the most scrupulous ears in town. But when it was known that she was to marry Waythorn there was a momentary reaction. Her best friends would have preferred to see her remain in the rôle of the injured wife, which was as becoming to her as crape to a rosy complexion. True, a decent time had elapsed, and it was not even suggested that Waythorn had supplanted his predecessor. People shook their heads over him, however, and one grudging friend, to whom he affirmed that he took the step with his eyes open, replied oracularly: "Yes—and with your ears shut."

Waythorn could afford to smile at these innuendoes. In the Wall Street phrase, he had 'discounted' them. He knew that society has not yet adapted itself to the consequences of divorce, and that till the adaptation takes place every woman who uses the freedom the law accords her must be her own social justification. Waythorn had an amused confidence in his wife's ability to justify herself. His expectations were fulfilled, and before the wedding took place Alice Varick's group had rallied openly to her support. She took it all imperturbably: she had a way of surmounting obstacles without seeming to be aware of them, and Waythorn looked back with wonder at the trivialities over which he had worn his nerves thin. He had the sense of having found refuge in a richer, warmer nature than his own, and his satisfaction, at the moment, was humorously summed up in the thought that his wife, when she had done all she could for Lily, would not be ashamed to come down and enjoy a good dinner.

The anticipation of such enjoyment was not, however, the sentiment expressed

---

[2] Because adultery was the only ground for divorce in New York state in the early 1900s, the party that sued for divorce seemed virtuous.

by Mrs. Waythorn's charming face when she presently joined him. Though she had put on her most engaging tea-gown she had neglected to assume the smile that went with it, and Waythorn thought he had never seen her look so nearly worried.

"What is it?" he asked. "Is anything wrong with Lily?"

"No; I've just been in and she's still sleeping." Mrs. Waythorn hesitated. "But something tiresome has happened."

He had taken her two hands, and now perceived that he was crushing a paper between them.

"This letter?"

"Yes—Mr. Haskett has written—I mean his lawyer has written."

Waythorn felt himself flush uncomfortably. He dropped his wife's hands. "What about?"

"About seeing Lily. You know the courts——"

"Yes, yes," he interrupted nervously.

Nothing was known about Haskett in New York. He was vaguely supposed to have remained in the outer darkness from which his wife had been rescued, and Waythorn was one of the few who were aware that he had given up his business in Utica and followed her to New York in order to be near his little girl. In the days of his wooing, Waythorn had often met Lily on the doorstep, rosy and smiling, on her way "to see papa."

"I am so sorry," Mrs. Waythorn murmured.

He roused himself. "What does he want?"

"He wants to see her. You know she goes to him once a week."

"Well—he doesn't expect her to go to him now, does he?"

"No—he has heard of her illness; but he expects to come here."

"Here?"

Mrs. Waythorn reddened under his gaze. They looked away from each other.

"I'm afraid he has the right. . . . You'll see. . . ." She made a proffer of the letter.

Waythorn moved away with a gesture of refusal. He stood staring about the softly lighted room, which a moment before had seemed so full of bridal intimacy.

"I'm so sorry," she repeated. "If Lily could have been moved——"

"That's out of the question," he returned impatiently.

"I suppose so."

Her lip was beginning to tremble, and he felt himself a brute.

"He must come, of course," he said. "When is—his day?"

"I'm afraid—to-morrow."

"Very well. Send a note in the morning."

The butler entered to announce dinner.

Waythorn turned to his wife. "Come—you must be tired. It's beastly, but try to forget about it," he said, drawing her hand through his arm.

"You're so good, dear. I'll try," she whispered back.

Her face cleared at once, and as she looked at him across the flowers, between the rosy candle-shades, he saw her lips waver back into a smile.

"How pretty everything is!" she sighed luxuriously.

He turned to the butler. "The champagne at once, please. Mrs. Waythorn is tired."

In a moment or two their eyes met above the sparkling glasses. Her own were quite clear and untroubled: he saw that she had obeyed his injunction and forgotten.

II

Waythorn, the next morning, went down town earlier than usual. Haskett was not likely to come till the afternoon, but the instinct of flight drove him forth. He meant to stay away all day—he had thoughts of dining at his club. As his door closed behind him he reflected that before he opened it again it would have admitted another man who had as much right to enter it as himself, and the thought filled him with a physical repugnance.

He caught the "elevated"[3] at the employés' hour, and found himself crushed between two layers of pendulous humanity. At Eighth Street the man facing him wriggled out, and another took his place. Waythorn glanced up and saw that it was Gus Varick. The men were so close together that it was impossible to ignore the smile of recognition on Varick's handsome overblown face. And after all—why not? They had always been on good terms, and Varick had been divorced before Waythorn's attentions to his wife began. The two exchanged a word on the perennial grievance of the congested trains, and when a seat at their side was miraculously left empty the instinct of self-preservation made Waythorn slip into it after Varick.

The latter drew the stout man's breath of relief. "Lord—I was beginning to feel like a pressed flower." He leaned back, looking unconcernedly at Waythorn. "Sorry to hear that Sellers is knocked out again."

"Sellers?" echoed Waythorn, starting at his partner's name.

Varick looked surprised. "You didn't know he was laid up with the gout?"

"No, I've been away—I only got back last night." Waythorn felt himself reddening in anticipation of the other's smile.

"Ah—yes; to be sure. And Seller's attack came on two days ago. I'm afraid he's pretty bad. Very awkward for me, as it happens, because he was just putting through a rather important thing for me."

"Ah?" Waythorn wondered vaguely since when Varick had been dealing in "important things." Hitherto he had dabbled only in the shallow pools of speculation, with which Waythorn's office did not usually concern itself.

It occurred to him that Varick might be talking at random, to relieve the strain of their propinquity. That strain was becoming momentarily more apparent to Waythorn, and when, at Cortlandt Street, he caught sight of an acquaintance, and had a sudden vision of the picture he and Varick must present to an initiated eye, he jumped up with a muttered excuse.

"I hope you'll find Sellers better," said Varick civilly, and he stammered back: "If I can be of any use to you———" and let the departing crowd sweep him to the platform.

At his office he heard that Sellers was in fact ill with the gout, and would probably not be able to leave the house for some weeks.

"I'm sorry it should have happened so, Mr. Waythorn," the senior clerk said with affable significance. "Mr. Sellers was very much upset at the idea of giving you such a lot of extra work just now."

"Oh, that's no matter," said Waythorn hastily. He secretly welcomed the pressure of additional business, and was glad to think that, when the day's work was over, he would have to call at his partner's on the way home.

He was late for luncheon, and turned in at the nearest restaurant instead of

---

[3] A train on rails set above street level, hence "elevated."

going to his club. The place was full, and the waiter hurried him to the back of the room to capture the only vacant table. In the cloud of cigar-smoke Waythorn did not at once distinguish his neighbours; but presently, looking about him, he saw Varick seated a few feet off. This time, luckily, they were too far apart for conversation, and Varick, who faced another way, had probably not even seen him; but there was an irony in their renewed nearness.

Varick was said to be fond of good living, and as Waythorn sat despatching his hurried luncheon he looked across half enviously at the other's leisurely degustation of his meal. When Waythorn first saw him he had been helping himself with critical deliberation to a bit of Camembert at the ideal point of liquefaction, and now, the cheese removed, he was just pouring his *café double*[4] from its little two-storied earthen pot. He poured slowly, his ruddy profile bent above the task, and one be-ringed white hand steadying the lid of the coffee-pot; then he stretched his other hand to the decanter of cognac at his elbow, filled a liqueur-glass, took a tentative sip, and poured the brandy into his coffee-cup.

Waythorn watched him in a kind of fascination. What was he thinking of— only of the flavour of the coffee and the liqueur? Had the morning's meeting left no more trace in his thoughts than on his face? Had his wife so completely passed out of his life that even this odd encounter with her present husband, within a week after her remarriage, was no more than an incident in his day? And as Waythorn mused, another idea struck him: had Haskett ever met Varick as Varick and he had just met? The recollection of Haskett perturbed him, and he rose and left the restaurant, taking a circuitous way out to escape the placid irony of Varick's nod.

It was after seven when Waythorn reached home. He thought the footman who opened the door looked at him oddly.

"How is Miss Lily?" he asked in haste.

"Doing very well, sir. A gentleman————"

"Tell Barlow to put off dinner for half an hour," Waythorn cut him off, hurrying upstairs.

He went straight to his room and dressed without seeing his wife. When he reached the drawing-room she was there, fresh and radiant. Lily's day had been good; the doctor was not coming back that evening.

At dinner Waythorn told her of Seller's illness and of the resulting complications. She listened sympathetically, adjuring him not to let himself be overworked, and asking vague feminine questions about the routing of the office. Then she gave him the chronicle of Lily's day; quoted the nurse and doctor, and told him who had called to enquire. He had never seen her more serene and unruffled. It struck him, with a curious pang, that she was very happy in being with him, so happy that she found a childish pleasure in rehearsing the trivial incidents of her day.

After dinner they went to the library, and the servant put the coffee and liqueurs on a low table before her and left the room. She looked singularly soft and girlish, in her rosy pale dress, against the dark leather of one of his bachelor armchairs. A day earlier the contrast would have charmed him.

He turned away now, choosing a cigar with affected deliberation.

---

[4] "Double coffee" (French): strong coffee in which water drips through the grounds in individual servings. Varick's manner with the Camembert cheese, the coffee, and the cognac functions as part of Wharton's characterization.

"Did Haskett come?" he asked, with his back to her.

"Oh, yes—he came."

"You didn't see him, of course?"

She hesitated a moment. "I let the nurse see him."

That was all. There was nothing more to ask. He swung round toward her, applying a match to his cigar. Well, the thing was over for a week, at any rate. He would try not to think of it. She looked up at him, a trifle rosier than usual, with a smile in her eyes.

"Ready for your coffee, dear?"

He leaned against the mantelpiece, watching her as she lifted the coffee-pot. The lamplight struck a gleam from her bracelets and tipped her soft hair with brightness. How light and slender she was, and how each gesture flowed into the next! She seemed a creature all compact of harmonies. As the thought of Haskett receded, Waythorn felt himself yielding again to the joy of possessorship. They were his, those white hands with their flitting motions, his the light haze of hair, the lips and eyes. . . .

She set down the coffee-pot, and reaching for the decanter of cognac, measured off a liqueur-glass and poured it into his cup.

Waythorn uttered a sudden exclamation.

"What is the matter?" she said, startled.

"Nothing; only—I don't take cognac in my coffee."

"Oh, how stupid of me," she cried.

Their eyes met, and she blushed a sudden agonized red.

III

Ten days later, Mr. Sellers, still house-bound, asked Waythorn to call on his way down town.

The senior partner, with his swaddled foot propped up by the fire, greeted his associate with an air of embarrassment.

"I'm sorry, my dear fellow; I've got to ask you to do an awkward thing for me."

Waythorn waited, and the other went on, after a pause apparently given to the arrangement of his phrases: "The fact is, when I was knocked out I had just gone into a rather complicated piece of business for—Gus Varick."

"Well?" said Waythorn, with an attempt to put him at his ease.

"Well—it's this way: Varick came to me the day before my attack. He had evidently had an inside tip from somebody, and had made about a hundred thousand. He came to me for advice, and I suggested his going in with Vanderlyn."

"Oh, the deuce!" Waythorn exclaimed. He saw in a flash what had happened. The investment was an alluring one, but required negotiation. He listened quietly while Sellers put the case before him, and, the statement ended, he said: "You think I ought to see Varick?"

"I'm afraid I can't as yet. The doctor is obdurate. And this thing can't wait. I hate to ask you, but no one else in the office knows the ins and outs of it."

Waythorn stood silent. He did not care a farthing for the success of Varick's venture, but the honour of the office was to be considered, and he could hardly refuse to oblige his partner.

"Very well," he said, "I'll do it."

That afternoon, apprised by telephone, Varick called at the office. Waythorn, waiting in his private room, wondered what the others thought of it. The newspapers, at the time of Mrs. Waythorn's marriage, had acquainted their readers with every detail of her previous matrimonial ventures, and Waythorn could fancy the clerks smiling behind Varick's back as he was ushered in.

Varick bore himself admirably. He was easy without being undignified, and Waythorn was conscious of cutting a much less impressive figure. Varick had no experience of business, and the talk prolonged itself for nearly an hour while Waythorn set forth with scrupulous precision the details of the proposed transaction.

"I'm awfully obliged to you," Varick said as he rose. "The fact is I'm not used to having much money to look after, and I don't want to make an ass of myself——" He smiled, and Waythorn could not help noticing that there was something pleasant about his smile. "It feels uncommonly queer to have enough cash to pay one's bills. I'd have sold my soul for it a few years ago!"

Waythorn winced at the allusion. He had heard it rumoured that a lack of funds had been one of the determining causes of the Varick separation, but it did not occur to him that Varick's words were intentional. It seemed more likely that the desire to keep clear of embarrassing topics had fatally drawn him into one. Waythorn did not wish to be outdone in civility.

"We'll do the best we can for you," he said. "I think this is a good thing you're in."

"Oh, I'm sure it's immense. It's awfully good of you——" Varick broke off, embarrassed. "I suppose the thing's settled now—but if——"

"If anything happens before Sellers is about, I'll see you again," said Waythorn quietly. He was glad, in the end, to appear the more self-possessed of the two.

.　　　.　　　.　　　.　　　.　　　.

The course of Lily's illness ran smooth, and as the days passed Waythorn grew used to the idea of Haskett's weekly visit. The first time the day came round, he stayed out late, and questioned his wife as to the visit on his return. She replied at once that Haskett had merely seen the nurse downstairs, as the doctor did not wish any one in the child's sick-room till after the crisis.

The following week Waythorn was again conscious of the recurrence of the day, but had forgotten it by the time he came home to dinner. The crisis of the disease came a few days later, with a rapid decline of fever, and the little girl was pronounced out of danger. In the rejoicing which ensued, the thought of Haskett passed out of Waythorn's mind, and one afternoon, letting himself into the house with a latch-key, he went straight to his library without noticing a shabby hat and umbrella in the hall.

In the library he found a small effaced-looking man with a thinnish gray beard sitting on the edge of the chair. The stranger might have been a piano-tuner, or one of those mysteriously efficient persons who are summoned in emergencies to adjust some detail of the domestic machinery. He blinked at Waythorn through a pair of gold-rimmed spectacles and said mildly: "Mr. Waythorn, I presume? I am Lily's father."

Waythorn flushed. "Oh——" he stammered uncomfortably. He broke off, disliking to appear rude. Inwardly he was trying to adjust the actual Haskett to the image of him projected by his wife's reminiscences. Waythorn had been allowed to infer that Alice's first husband was a brute.

"I am sorry to intrude," said Haskett, with his over-the-counter politeness.

"Don't mention it," returned Waythorn, collecting himself. "I suppose the nurse has been told?"

"I presume so. I can wait," said Haskett. He had a resigned way of speaking, as though life had worn down his natural powers of resistance.

Waythorn stood on the threshold, nervously pulling off his gloves.

"I'm sorry you've been detained. I will send for the nurse," he said; and as he opened the door he added with an effort: "I'm glad we can give you a good report of Lily." He winced as the *we* slipped out, but Haskett seemed not to notice it.

"Thank you, Mr. Waythorn. It's been an anxious time for me."

"Ah, well, that's past. Soon she'll be able to go to you." Waythorn nodded and passed out.

In his own room he flung himself down with a groan. He hated the womanish sensibility which made him suffer so acutely from the grotesque chances of life. He had known when he married that his wife's former husbands were both living, and that amid the multiplied contacts of modern existence there were a thousand chances to one that he would run against one or the other, yet he found himself as much disturbed by his brief encounter with Haskett as though the law had not obligingly removed all difficulties in the way of their meeting.

Waythorn sprang up and began to pace the room nervously. He had not suffered half as much from his two meetings with Varick. It was Haskett's presence in his own house that made the situation so intolerable. He stood still, hearing steps in the passage.

"This way, please," he heard the nurse say. Haskett was being taken upstairs, then: not a corner of the house but was open to him. Waythorn dropped into another chair, staring vaguely ahead of him. On his dressing-table stood a photograph of Alice, taken when he had first known her. She was Alice Varick then— how fine and exquisite he had thought her! Those were Varick's pearls about her neck. At Waythorn's instance they had been returned before her marriage. Had Haskett ever given her any trinkets—and what had become of them, Waythorn wondered? He realized suddenly that he knew very little of Haskett's past or present situation; but from the man's appearance and manner of speech he could reconstruct with curious precision the surroundings of Alice's first marriage. And it startled him to think that she had, in the background of her life, a phase of existence so different from anything with which he had connected her. Varick, whatever his faults, was a gentleman, in the conventional, traditional sense of the term: the sense which at that moment seemed, oddly enough, to have most meaning to Waythorn. He and Varick had the same social habits, spoke the same language, understood the same allusions. But this other man . . . it was grotesquely uppermost in Waythorn's mind that Haskett had worn a made-up tie attached with an elastic. Why should that ridiculous detail symbolize the whole man? Waythorn was exasperated by his own paltriness, but the fact of the tie expanded, forced itself on him, became as it were the key to Alice's past. He could see her, as Mrs. Haskett, sitting in a "front parlour" furnished in plush, with a pianola, and a copy of "Ben Hur" on the centre-table.[5] He could see her going to the theatre with Hasket—or perhaps even to a "Church Sociable"—she in a "picture hat" and Haskett in a black frock-coat, a little creased, with the made-up tie on an elastic. On the way home they would stop and look at the illuminated shop-windows, linger-

---

[5] Waythorn sees her as hopelessly middle class, with an overfurnished ("plush") parlour; a pianola, or mechanical piano player; and a copy of *Ben Hur* (1880), by the American soldier and writer General Lew Wallace (1827–1905); *Ben Hur* sold approximately two million copies.

ing over the photographs of New York actresses. On Sunday afternoons Haskett would take her for a walk, pushing Lily ahead of them in a white enamelled perambulator, and Waythorn had a vision of the people they would stop and talk to. He could fancy how pretty Alice must have looked, in a dress adroitly constructed from the hints of a New York fashion-paper, and how she must have looked down on the other women, chafing at her life, and secretly feeling that she belonged in a bigger place.

For the moment his foremost thought was one of wonder at the way in which she had shed the phase of existence which her marriage with Haskett implied. It was as if her whole aspect, every gesture, every inflection, every allusion, were a studied negation of that period of her life. If she had denied being married to Haskett she could hardly have stood more convicted of duplicity than in this obliteration of the self which had been his wife.

Waythorn started up, checking himself in the analysis of her motives. What right had he to create a fantastic effigy of her and then pass judgment on it? She had spoken vaguely of her first marriage as unhappy, had hinted, with becoming reticence, that Haskett had wrought havoc among her young illusions. . . . It was a pity for Waythorn's peace of mind that Haskett's very inoffensiveness shed a new light on the nature of those illusions. A man would rather think that his wife has been brutalized by her first husband than that the process has been reversed.

IV

"Mr. Waythorn, I don't like that French governess of Lily's."

Haskett, subdued and apologetic, stood before Waythorn in the library, revolving his shabby hat in his hand.

Waythorn, surprised in his armchair over the evening paper, stared back perplexedly at his visitor.

"You'll excuse my asking to see you," Haskett continued. "But this is my last visit, and I thought if I could have a word with you it would be a better way than writing to Mrs. Waythorn's lawyer."

Waythorn rose uneasily. He did not like the French governess either; but that was irrelevant.

"I am not so sure of that," he returned stiffly; "but since you wish it I will give your message to—my wife." He always hesitated over the possessive pronoun in addressing Haskett.

The latter sighed. "I don't know as that will help much. She didn't like it when I spoke to her."

Waythorn turned red. "When did you see her?" he asked.

"Not since the first day I came to see Lily—right after she was taken sick. I remarked to her then that I didn't like the governess."

Waythorn made no answer. He remembered distinctly that, after that first visit, he had asked his wife if she had seen Haskett. She had lied to him then, but she had respected his wishes since; and the incident cast a curious light on her character. He was sure she would not have seen Haskett that first day if she had divined that Waythorn would object, and the fact that she did not divine it was almost as disagreeable to the latter as the discovery that she had lied to him.

"I don't like the woman," Haskett was repeating with mild persistency. "She ain't straight, Mr. Waythorn—she'll teach the child to be underhand. I've noticed a change in Lily—she's too anxious to please—and she don't always tell the truth.

She used to be the straightest child, Mr. Waythorn————" He broke off, his voice a little thick. "Not but what I want her to have a stylish education," he ended.

Waythorn was touched. "I'm sorry, Mr. Haskett; but frankly, I don't quite see what I can do."

Haskett hesitated. Then he laid his hat on the table, and advanced to the hearth-rug, on which Waythorn was standing. There was nothing aggressive in his manner, but he had the solemnity of a timid man resolved on a decisive measure.

"There's just one thing you can do, Mr. Waythorn," he said. "You can remind Mrs. Waythorn that, by the decree of the courts, I am entitled to have a voice in Lily's bringing up." He paused, and went on more deprecatingly: "I'm not the kind to talk about enforcing my rights, Mr. Waythorn. I don't know as I think a man is entitled to rights he hasn't known how to hold on to; but this business of the child is different. I've never let go there—and I never mean to."

The scene left Waythorn deeply shaken. Shamefacedly, in indirect ways, he had been finding out about Haskett; and all that he had learned was favourable. The little man, in order to be near his daughter, had sold out his share in a profitable business in Utica, and accepted a modest clerkship in a New York manufacturing house. He boarded in a shabby street and had few acquaintances. His passion for Lily filled his life. Waythorn felt that this exploration of Haskett was like groping about with a dark-lantern in his wife's past; but he saw now that there were recesses his lantern had not explored. He had never enquired into the exact circumstances of his wife's first matrimonial rupture. On the surface all had been fair. It was she who had obtained the divorce, and the court had given her the child. But Waythorn knew how many ambiguities such a verdict might cover. The mere fact that Haskett retained a right over his daughter implied an unsuspected compromise. Waythorn was an idealist. He always refused to recognize unpleasant contingencies till he found himself confronted with them, and then he saw them followed by a spectral train of consequences. His next days were thus haunted, and he determined to try to lay the ghosts by conjuring them up in his wife's presence.

When he repeated Haskett's request a flame of anger passed over her face; but she subdued it instantly and spoke with a slight quiver of outraged motherhood.

"It is very ungentlemanly of him," she said.

The word grated on Waythorn. "That is neither here nor there. It's a bare question of rights."

She murmured: "It's not as if he could ever be a help to Lily————"

Waythorn flushed. This was even less to his taste. "The question is," he repeated, "what authority has he over her?"

She looked downward, twisting herself a little in her seat. "I am willing to see him—I thought you objected," she faltered.

In a flash he understood that she knew the extent of Haskett's claims. Perhaps it was not the first time she had resisted them.

"My objecting has nothing to do with it," he said coldly; "if Haskett has a right to be consulted you must consult him."

She burst into tears, and he saw that she expected him to regard her as a victim.

Haskett did not abuse his rights. Waythorn had felt miserably sure that he would not. But the governess was dismissed, and from time to time the little man demanded an interview with Alice. After the first outburst she accepted the situation with her usual adaptability. Haskett had once reminded Waythorn of the piano-tuner, and Mrs. Waythorn, after a month or two, appeared to class him with that domestic familiar. Waythorn could not but respect the father's tenacity. At first he had tried to cultivate the suspicion that Haskett might be "up to" something, that he had an object in securing a foothold in the house. But in his heart Waythorn was sure of Haskett's single-mindedness; he even guessed in the latter a mild contempt for such advantages as his relation with the Waythorns might offer. Haskett's sincerity of purpose made him invulnerable, and his successor had to accept him as a lien on the property.

Mr. Sellers was sent to Europe to recover from his gout, and Varick's affairs hung on Waythorn's hands. The negotiations were prolonged and complicated; they necessitated frequent conferences between the two men, and the interests of the firm forbade Waythorn's suggesting that his client should transfer his business to another office.

Varick appeared well in the transaction. In moments of relaxation his coarse streak appeared, and Waythorn dreaded his geniality; but in the office he was concise and clear-headed, with a flattering deference to Waythorn's judgment. Their business relations being so affably established, it would have been absurd for the two men to ignore each other in society. The first time they met in a drawing-room, Varick took up their intercourse in the same easy key, and his hostess's grateful glance obliged Waythorn to respond to it. After that they ran across each other frequently, and one evening at a ball Waythorn, wandering through the remoter rooms, came upon Varick seated beside his wife. She coloured a little, and faltered in what she was saying; but Varick nodded to Waythorn without rising, and the latter strolled on.

In the carriage, on the way home, he broke out nervously: "I didn't know you spoke to Varick."

Her voice trembled a little. "It's the first time—he happened to be standing near me; I didn't know what to do. It's so awkward, meeting everywhere—and he said you had been very kind about some business."

"That's different," said Waythorn.

She paused a moment. "I'll do just as you wish," she returned pliantly. "I thought it would be less awkward to speak to him when we meet."

Her pliancy was beginning to sicken him. Had she really no will of her own—no theory about her relation to these men? She had accepted Haskett—did she mean to accept Varick? It was "less awkward," as she had said, and her instinct was to evade difficulties or to circumvent them. With sudden vividness Waythorn saw how the instinct had developed. She was "as easy as an old shoe"—a shoe that too many feet had worn. Her elasticity was the result of tension in too many different directions. Alice Haskett—Alice Varick—Alice Waythorn—she had been each in turn, and had left hanging to each name a little of her privacy, a little of her personality, a little of the inmost self where the unknown god abides.

"Yes—it's better to speak to Varick," said Waythorn wearily.

V

The winter wore on, and society took advantage of the Waythorns' acceptance of Varick. Harassed hostesses were grateful to them for bridging over a social difficulty, and Mrs. Waythorn was held up as a miracle of good taste. Some experimental spirits could not resist the diversion of throwing Varick and his for-

Kinship

mer wife together, and there were those who thought he found a zest in the propinquity. But Mrs. Waythorn's conduct remained irreproachable. She neither avoided Varick nor sought him out. Even Waythorn could not but admit that she had discovered the solution of the newest social problem.

He had married her without giving much thought to that problem. He had fancied that a woman can shed her past like a man. But now he saw that Alice was bound to hers both by the circumstances which forced her into continued relation with it, and by the traces it had left on her nature. With grim irony Waythorn compared himself to a member of a syndicate. He held so many shares in his wife's personality and his predecessors were his partners in the business. If there had been any element of passion in the transaction he would have felt less deteriorated by it. The fact that Alice took her change of husbands like a change of weather reduced the situation to mediocrity. He could have forgiven her for blunders, for excesses; for resisting Haskett, for yielding to Varick; for anything but her acquiescence and her tact. She reminded him of a juggler tossing knives; but the knives were blunt and she knew they would never cut her.

And then, gradually, habit formed a protecting surface for his sensibilities. If he paid for each day's comfort with the small change of his illusions, he grew daily to value the comfort more and set less store upon the coin. He had drifted into a dulling propinquity with Haskett and Varick and he took refuge in the cheap revenge of satirizing the situation. He even began to reckon up the advantages which accrued from it, to ask himself if it were not better to own a third of a wife who knew how to make a man happy than a whole one who had lacked opportunity to acquire the art. For it *was* an art, and made up, like all others, of concessions, eliminations and embellishments; of lights judiciously thrown and shadows skilfully softened. His wife knew exactly how to manage the lights, and he knew exactly to what training she owed her skill. He even tried to trace the source of his obligations, to discriminate between the influences which had combined to produce his domestic happiness: he perceived that Haskett's commonness had made Alice worship good breeding, while Varick's liberal construction of the marriage bond had taught her to value the conjugal virtues; so that he was directly indebted to his predecessors for the devotion which made his life easy if not inspiring.

From this phase he passed into that of complete acceptance. He ceased to satirize himself because time dulled the irony of the situation and the joke lost its humour with its sting. Even the sight of Haskett's hat on the hall table had ceased to touch the springs of epigram. The hat was often seen there now, for it had been decided that it was better for Lily's father to visit her than for the little girl to go to his boarding-house. Waythorn, having acquiesced in this arrangement, had been surprised to find how little difference it made. Haskett was never obtrusive, and the few visitors who met him on the stairs were unaware of his identity. Waythorn did not know how often he saw Alice, but with himself Haskett was seldom in contact.

One afternoon, however, he learned on entering that Lily's father was waiting to see him. In the library he found Haskett occupying a chair in his usual provisional way. Waythorn always felt grateful to him for not leaning back.

"I hope you'll excuse me, Mr. Waythorn," he said, rising. "I wanted to see Mrs. Waythorn about Lily, and your man asked me to wait here till she came in."

"Of course," said Waythorn, remembering that a sudden leak had that morning given over the drawing-room to the plumbers.

He opened his cigar-case and held it out to his visitor, and Haskett's acceptance seemed to mark a fresh stage in their intercourse. The spring evening was chilly, and Waythorn invited his guest to draw up his chair to the fire. He meant to find an excuse to leave Haskett in a moment; but he was tired and cold, and after all the little man no longer jarred on him.

The two were enclosed in the intimacy of their blended cigar-smoke when the door opened and Varick walked into the room. Waythorn rose abruptly. It was the first time that Varick had come to the house, and the surprise of seeing him, combined with the singular inopportuneness of his arrival, gave a new edge to Waythorn's blunted sensibilities. He stared at his visitor without speaking.

Varick seemed too preoccupied to notice his host's embarrassment.

"My dear fellow," he exclaimed in his most expansive tone, "I must apologize for tumbling in on you in this way, but I was too late to catch you down town, and so I thought————"

He stopped short, catching sight of Haskett, and his sanguine colour deepened to a flush which spread vividly under his scant blond hair. But in a moment he recovered himself and nodded slightly. Haskett returned the bow in silence, and Waythorn was still groping for speech when the footman came in carrying a tea-table.

The intrusion offered a welcome vent to Waythorn's nerves. "What the deuce are you bringing this here for?" he said sharply.

"I beg your pardon, sir, but the plumbers are still in the drawing-room, and Mrs. Waythorn said she would have tea in the library." The footman's perfectly respectful tone implied a reflection on Waythorn's reasonableness.

"Oh, very well," said the latter resignedly, and the footman proceeded to open the folding tea-table and set out its complicated appointments. While this interminable process continued the three men stood motionless, watching it with a fascinated stare, till Waythorn, to break the silence, said to Varick: "Won't you have a cigar?"

He held out the case he had just tendered to Haskett, and Varick helped himself with a smile. Waythorn looked about for a match, and finding none, proffered a light from his own cigar. Haskett, in the background, held his ground mildly, examining his cigar-tip now and then, and stepping forward at the right moment to knock its ashes into the fire.

The footman at last withdrew, and Varick immediately began: "If I could just say half a word to you about this business————"

"Certainly," stammered Waythorn; "in the dining-room————"

But as he placed his hand on the door it opened from without, and his wife appeared on the threshold.

She came in fresh and smiling, in her street dress and hat, shedding a fragrance from the boa[6] which she loosened in advancing.

"Shall we have tea in here, dear?" she began; and then she caught sight of Varick. Her smile deepened, veiling a slight tremor of surprise.

"Why, how do you do?" she said with a distinct note of pleasure.

As she shook hands with Varick she saw Haskett standing behind him. Her smile faded for a moment, but she recalled it quickly, with a scarcely perceptible side-glance at Waythorn.

"How do you do, Mr. Haskett?" she said, and shook hands with him a shade less cordially.

---

[6] A fluffy wrap-around scarf, named humorously for the boa constrictor.

The three men stood awkwardly before her, till Varick, always the most self-possessed, dashed into an explanatory phrase.

"We—I had to see Waythorn a moment on business," he stammered, brick-red from chin to nape.

Haskett stepped forward with his air of mild obstinacy. "I am sorry to intrude; but you appointed five o'clock————" he directed his resigned glance to the timepiece on the mantel.

She swept aside their embarrassment with a charming gesture of hospitality.

"I'm so sorry—I'm always late; but the afternoon was so lovely." She stood drawing off her gloves, propitiatory and graceful, diffusing about her a sense of ease and familiarity in which the situation lost its grotesqueness. "But before talking business," she added brightly, "I'm sure every one wants a cup of tea."

She dropped into her low chair by the tea-table, and the two visitors, as if drawn by her smile, advanced to receive the cups she held out.

She glanced about for Waythorn, and he took the third cup with a laugh.

1904

Theodore Dreiser
(1871–1945)

The twelfth of thirteen children of a German Catholic immigrant father and a Mennonite mother, Theodore Dreiser was born in 1871 in Terre Haute, Indiana. His childhood was a harsh one, clouded by poverty and the severe religious code of his parents. Dreiser's father lost his job when a woolen mill he managed burned down, and for some years afterward the family was frequently separated while both parents and the older children sought employment. One of Dreiser's sisters was involved in an affair with a married man that provided the basis for Dreiser's first novel, *Sister Carrie* (1900). Dreiser's older brother Paul made a living in New York City as the composer of Tin Pan Alley tunes, among them "On the Banks of the Wabash" (1899), on which Dreiser may have collaborated, and "My Gal Sal" (1905). During his infrequent but dramatic visits home, Paul provided his brother with a tantalizing model of the success that seemed so accessible in large cities. After Dreiser graduated from high school in 1889 in Warsaw, Indiana, a sympathetic high school teacher, Mildred Fielding, paid his expenses to attend Indiana University. But Dreiser left after one year, unconvinced that academic studies had relevance for his life.

Like many American writers, Dreiser turned to journalism for an income; for the next few years he did freelance magazine writing and newspaper reporting in Chicago, St. Louis (where he met Sara White, whom he married in 1898), Pittsburgh, and New York. He was dazzled by the burgeoning consumer society of urban America, and his experiences in these cities sharpened his taste for a material standard of living beyond anything he had ever known. His sense of himself as an outsider accounts for much that is characteristic in his fiction: the hunger for wealth of such young protagonists as Frank Cowperwood in *The Financier* and Clyde Griffiths in *An American Tragedy*, the accumulation of detail upon which Dreiser's power as a naturalist is based.

Sister Carrie was all but suppressed by Dreiser's publisher when it became apparent that the frank narrative of a girl's sexual compromise and success as an actress would not find favor among genteel readers. But Dreiser persisted with his writing and his vision of the force of environment in shaping human lives: he published *Jennie Gerhardt* in 1911; two volumes of a trilogy, *The Financier* in 1912 and *The Titan* in 1914; and *The "Genius"* in 1915. No longer dependent upon journalism for an income, he also produced essays and plays during these years and wrote several short stories centered in the consciousness of young women, notably "The Second choice" (1918). The publication of *An American Tragedy* in 1925, however, brought him his greatest measure of fame.

Dreiser's novels are informed by a fatalistic belief in the power of circumstance, resulting largely from his conviction that American society values material success above all else. They depict candidly, almost amorally, and with cumulative force the appeal of the world and of the flesh; typically, his characters live in places where avarice and ruthlessness bring rewards, where innocence and trust are exploited. Despite an ungainly prose style that remains part of his signature as a writer, Dreiser is deservedly regarded as a leading exponent of naturalism in American fiction.

Throughout his life Dreiser continued to look for answers, for systems that would place him on the inside. After a visit to Russia in 1927, he became an advocate of socialism; he later became a student of Eastern philosophy. Despite his failing health, Dreiser married his mistress of twenty-five years, Helen Richardson, in mid-1944; he died in Hollywood in late 1945. Two labored but interesting novels were published posthumously: *The Bulwark* (1946) and *The Stoic* (1947), the final volume of the Frank Cowperwood trilogy begun years before with *The Financier* and *The Titan*.

Suggested Readings: *An American Tragedy*, 1925. *The Letters of Theodore Dreiser*, 3 vols., ed. R. Elias, 1959. *Theodore Dreiser: A Selection of Uncollected Poems*, ed. D. Pizer, 1977. *Sister Carrie*, ed. J. Berkey and A. Winters, 1981. *American Diaries, 1902–1926*, ed. T. Riggio, 1982. R. Elias, *Theodore Dreiser, Apostle of Nature*, 1949, rpt. 1970. H. P. Dreiser, *My Life With Dreiser*, 1951. C. Shapiro, *Theodore Dreiser: Our Bitter Patriot*, 1962. W. A. Swanberg, *Dreiser*, 1965. R. Lehan, *Theodore Dreiser: His World and His Novels*, 1969. E. Moers, *Two Dreisers: The Man and the Novelist*, 1969. D. Pizer, *The Novels of Theodore Dreiser*, 1976. L. Hussman, *Dreiser and His Fiction*, 1983. J. Griffin, *The Small Canvas: An Introduction to Dreiser's Short Stories*, 1985. R. Lingeman, *Theodore Dreiser: At the Gates of the City*, 1986.

Text Used: *Free and Other Stories*, 1918.

THE SECOND CHOICE*

SHIRLEY DEAR:
    You don't want the letters. There are only six of them, anyhow, and think, they're all I have of you to cheer me on my travels. What good would they be to you—little bits of notes telling me you're sure to meet me—but me—think of me! If I send them to you, you'll tear them up, whereas if you leave them with me I can dab them with musk and ambergris and keep them in a little silver box, always beside me.
    Ah, Shirley dear, you really don't know how sweet I think you are, how dear! There isn't a thing we have ever done together that isn't as clear in my mind as this

---

* First published in *Cosmopolitan* in February 1918 and collected in *Free and Other Stories* the same year. The asterisks are Dreiser's.

great big skyscraper over the way here in Pittsburgh, and far more pleasing. In fact, my thoughts of you are the most precious and delicious things I have, Shirley.

But I'm too young to marry now. You know that, Shirley, don't you? I haven't placed myself in any way yet, and I'm so restless that I don't know whether I ever will, really. Only yesterday, old Roxbaum—that's my new employer here—came to me and wanted to know if I would like an assistant overseership on one of his coffee plantations in Java,[1] said there would not be much money in it for a year or two, a bare living, but later there would be more—and I jumped at it. Just the thought of Java and going there did that, although I knew I could make more staying right here. Can't you see how it is with me, Shirl? I'm too restless and too young. I couldn't take care of you right, and you wouldn't like me after a while if I didn't.

But ah, Shirley sweet, I think the dearest things of you! There isn't an hour, it seems, but some little bit of you comes back—a dear, sweet bit—the night we sat on the grass in Tregore Park and counted the stars through the trees; that first evening at Sparrows Point when we missed the last train and had to walk to Langley. Remember the tree-toads, Shirl? And then that warm April Sunday in Atholby woods! Ah, Shirl, you don't want the six notes! Let me keep them. But think of me, will you, sweet, wherever you go and whatever you do? I'll always think of you, and wish that you had met a better, saner man than me, and that I really could have married you and been all you wanted me to be. By-by, sweet. I may start for Java within the month. If so, and you would want them, I'll sent you some cards from there—if they have any.

Your worthless,

ARTHUR.

She sat and turned the letter in her hand, dumb with despair. It was the very last letter she would ever get from him. Of that she was certain. He was gone now, once and for all. She had written him only once, not making an open plea but asking him to return her letters, and then there had come this tender but evasive reply, saying nothing of a possible return but desiring to keep her letters for old times' sake—the happy hours they had spent together.

The happy hours! Oh, yes, yes, yes—the happy hours!

In her memory now, as she sat here in her home after the day's work, meditating on all that had been in the few short months since he had come and gone, was a world of color and light—a color and a light so transfiguring as to seem celestial, but now, alas, wholly dissipated. It had contained so much of all she had desired—love, romance, amusement, laughter. He had been so gay and thoughtless, or headstrong, so youthfully romantic, and with such a love of play and change and to be saying and doing anything and everything. Arthur could dance in a gay way, whistle, sing after a fashion, play. He could play cards and do tricks, and he had such a superior air, so genial and brisk, with a kind of innate courtesy in it and yet an intolerance for slowness and stodginess or anything dull or dingy, such as characterized—— But here her thoughts fled from him. She refused to think of any one but Arthur.

Sitting in her little bedroom now, off the parlor on the ground floor in her home in Bethune Street, and looking out over the Kessels' yard, and beyond that—there being no fences in Bethune Street—over the "yards" or lawns of the Pollards, Bakers, Cryders, and others, she thought of how dull it must all have seemed to

---

[1] On the Malay Archipelago.

him, with his fine imaginative mind and experiences, his love of change and gay-ety, his atmosphere of something better than she had ever known. How little she had been fitted, perhaps, by beauty or temperament to overcome this—the some-thing—dullness in her work or her home, which possibly had driven him away. For, although many had admired her to date, and she was young and pretty in her simple way and constantly receiving suggestions that her beauty was disturbing to some, still, he had not cared for her—he had gone.

And now, as she meditated, it seemed that this scene, and all that it stood for—her parents, her work, her daily shuttling to and fro between the drug com-pany for which she worked and this street and house—was typical of her life and what she was destined to endure always. Some girls were so much more fortunate. They had fine clothes, fine homes, a world of pleasure and opportunity in which to move. They did not have to scrimp and save and work to pay their own way. And yet she had always been compelled to do it, but had never complained until now—or until he came, and after. Bethune Street, with its commonplace front yards and houses nearly all alike, and this house, so like the others, room for room and porch for porch, and her parents, too, really like all the others, had seemed good enough, quite satisfactory, indeed, until then. But now, now!

Here, in their kitchen, was her mother, a thin, pale, but kindly woman, peeling potatoes and washing lettuce, and putting a bit of steak or a chop or a piece of liver in a frying-pan day after day, morning and evening, month after month, year after year. And next door was Mrs. Kessel doing the same thing. And next door Mrs. Cryder. And next door Mrs. Pollard. But, until now, she had not thought it so bad. But now—now—oh! And on all the porches or lawns all along this street were the husbands and fathers, mostly middle-aged or old men like her father, reading their papers or cutting the grass before dinner, or smoking and meditating afterward. Her father was out in front now, a stooped, forbearing, meditative soul, who had rarely anything to say—leaving it all to his wife, her mother, but who was fond of her in his dull, quiet way. He was a pattern-maker by trade, and had come into possession of this small, ordinary home via years of toil and sav-ing, her mother helping him. They had no particular religion, as he often said, thinking reasonably human conduct a sufficient passport to heaven, but they had gone occasionally to the Methodist Church over in Nicholas Street, and she had once joined it. But of late she had not gone, weaned away by the other common-place pleasures of her world.

And then in the midst of it, the dull drift of things, as she now saw them to be, he had come—Arthur Bristow—young, energetic, good-looking, ambitious, dreamful, and instanter, and with her never knowing quite how, the whole thing had been changed. He had appeared so swiftly—out of nothing, as it were.

Previous to him had been Barton Williams, stout, phlegmatic, good-natured, well-meaning, who was, or had been before Arthur came, asking her to marry him, and whom she allowed to half assume that she would. She had liked him in a feeble, albeit, as she thought, tender way, thinking him the kind, according to the logic of her neighborhood, who would make her a good husband, and, until Arthur appeared on the scene, had really intended to marry him. It was not really a love-match, as she saw now, but she thought it was, which was much the same thing, perhaps. But, as she now recalled, when Arthur came, how the scales fell from her eyes! In a trice, as it were, nearly, there was a new heaven and a new earth. Arthur had arrived, and with him a sense of something different.

Mabel Gove had asked her to come over to her house in Westleigh, the adjoining suburb, for Thanksgiving eve and day, and without a thought of any thing, and because Barton was busy handling a part of the work in the despatcher's office of the Great Eastern and could not see her, she had gone. And then, to her surprise and strange, almost ineffable delight, the moment she had seen him, he was there—Arthur, with his slim, straight figure and dark hair and eyes and clean-cut features, as clean and attractive as those of a coin. And as he had looked at her and smiled and narrated humorous bits of things that had happened to him, something had come over her—a spell—and after dinner they had all gone round to Edith Barringer's to dance, and there as she had danced with him, somehow, without any seeming boldness on his part, he had taken possesion of her, as it were, drawn her close, and told her she had beautiful eyes and hair and such a delicately rounded chin, and that he thought she danced gracefully and was sweet. She had nearly fainted with delight.

"Do you like me?" he had asked in one place in the dance, and, in spite of herself, she had looked up into his eyes, and from that moment she was almost mad over him, could think of nothing else but his hair and eyes and his smile and his graceful figure.

Mabel Gove had seen it all, in spite of her determination that no one should, and on their going to bed later, back at Mabel's home, she had whispered:

"Ah, Shirley, I saw. You like Arthur, don't you?"

"I think he's very nice," Shirley recalled replying, for Mabel knew of her affair with Barton and liked him, "But I'm not crazy over him." And for this bit of treason she had sighed in her dreams nearly all night.

And the next day, true to a request and a promise made by him, Arthur had called again at Mabel's to take her and Mabel to a "movie" which was not so far away, and from there they had gone to an ice-cream parlor, and during it all, when Mabel was not looking, he had squeezed her arm and hand and kissed her neck, and she had held her breath, and her heart had seemed to stop.

"And now you're going to let me come out to your place to see you, aren't you?" he had whispered.

And she had replied, "Wednesday evening," and then written the address on a little piece of paper and given it to him.

But now it was all gone, gone!

This house, which now looked so dreary—how romantic it had seemed that first night *he* called—the front room with its commonplace furniture, and later in the spring, the veranda, with its vines just sprouting, and the moon in May. Oh, the moon in May, and June and July, when he was here! How she had lied to Barton to make evenings for Arthur, and occasionally to Arthur to keep him from contact with Barton. She had not even mentioned Barton to Arthur because—because—well, because Arthur was so much better, and somehow (she admitted it to herself now) she had not been sure that Arthur would care for her long, if at all, and then—well, and then, to be quite frank, Barton might be good enough. She did not exactly hate him because she had found Arthur—not at all. She still liked him in a way—he was so kind and faithful, so very dull and straightforward and thoughtful of her, which Arthur was certainly not. Before Arthur had appeared, as she well remembered, Barton had seemed to be plenty good enough—in fact, all that she desired in a pleasant, companionable way, calling for her, taking her places, bringing her flowers and candy, which Arthur rarely did, and for that, if nothing more, she could not help continuing to like him and to feel sorry for him, and, besides, as she had admitted to herself before, if Arthur left her—* * * * *

Weren't his parents better off than hers—and hadn't he a good position for such a man as he—one hundred and fifty dollars a month and the certainty of more later on? A little while before meeting Arthur, she had thought this very good, enough for two to live on at least, and she had thought some of trying it at some time or other—but now—now——

And that first night he had called—how well she remembered it—how it had transfigured the parlor next this in which she was now, filling it with something it had never had before, and the porch outside, too, for that matter, with its gaunt, leafless vine, and this street, too, even—dull, commonplace Bethune Street. There had been a flurry of snow during the afternoon while she was working at the store, and the ground was white with it. All the neighboring homes seemed to look sweeter and happier and more inviting than ever they had as she came past them, with their lights peeping from under curtains and drawn shades. She had hurried into hers and lighted the big red-shaded parlor lamp, her one artistic treasure, as she thought, and put it near the piano, between it and the window, and arranged the chairs, and then bustled to the task of making herself as pleasing as she might. For him she had gotten out her one best filmy house dress and done up her hair in the fashion she thought most becoming—and that he had not seen before—and powdered her cheeks and nose and darkened her eyelashes, as some of the girls at the store did, and put on her new gray satin slippers, and then, being so arrayed, waited nervously, unable to eat anything or to think of anything but him.

And at last, just when she had begun to think he might not be coming, he had appeared with that arch smile and a "Hello! It's here you live, is it? I was wondering. George, but you're twice as sweet as I thought you were, aren't you?" And then, in the little entryway, behind the closed door, he had held her and kissed her on the mouth a dozen times while she pretended to push against his coat and struggle and say that her parents might hear.

And, oh, the room afterward, with him in it in the red glow of the lamp, and with his pale handsome face made handsomer thereby, as she thought! He had made her sit near him and had held her hands and told her about his work and his dreams—all that he expected to do in the future—and then she had found herself wishing intensely to share just such a life—his life—anything that he might wish to do; only, she kept wondering, with a slight pain, whether he would want her to—he was so young, dreamful, ambitious, much younger and more dreamful than herself, although, in reality, he was several years older.

And then followed that glorious period from December to this late September, in which everything which was worth happening in love had happened. Oh, those wondrous days the following spring, when, with the first burst of buds and leaves, he had taken her one Sunday to Atholby, where all the great woods were, and they had hunted spring beauties in the grass, and sat on a slope and looked at the river below and watched some boys fixing up a sailboat and setting forth in it quite as she wished she and Arthur might be doing—going somewhere together—far, far away from all commonplace things and life! And then he had slipped his arm about her and kissed her cheek and neck, and tweaked her ear and smoothed her hair—and oh, there on the grass, with the spring flowers about her and a canopy of small green leaves above, the perfection of love had come—love so wonderful that the mere thought of it made her eyes brim now! And then had been days, Saturday afternoons and Sundays, at Atholby and Sparrows Point, where the great beach was, and in lovely Tregore Park, a mile or two from her home, where they could go of an evening and sit in or near the pavilion and have ice-cream and dance or watch the dancers. Oh, the stars, the winds, the summer breath of those days! Ah, me! Ah, me!

Naturally, her parents had wondered from the first about her and Arthur, and her and Barton, since Barton had already assumed a proprietary interest in her and she had seemed to like him. But then she was an only child and a pet, and used to presuming on that, and they could not think of saying anything to her. After all, she was young and pretty and was entitled to change her mind; only, only—she had had to indulge in a career of lying and subterfuge in connection with Barton, since Arthur was headstrong and wanted every evening that he chose—to call for her at the store and keep her down-town to dinner and a show.

Arthur had never been like Barton, shy, phlegmatic, obedient, waiting long and patiently for each little favor, but, instead, masterful and eager, rifling her of kisses and caresses and every delight of love, and teasing and playing with her as a cat would a mouse. She could never resist him. He demanded of her her time and her affection without let or hindrance. He was not exactly selfish or cruel, as some might have been, but gay and unthinking at times, unconsciously so, and yet loving and tender at others—nearly always so. But always he would talk of things in the future as if they really did not include her—and this troubled her greatly—of places he might go, things he might do, which, somehow, he seemed to think or assume that she could not or would not do with him. He was always going to Australia sometime, he thought, in a business way, or to South Africa, or possibly to India. He never seemed to have any fixed clear future for himself in mind.

A dreadful sense of helplessness and of impending disaster came over her at these times, of being involved in some predicament over which she had no control, and which would lead her on to some sad end. Arthur, although plainly in love, as she thought, and apparently delighted with her, might not always love her. She began, timidly at first (and always, for that matter), to ask him pretty, seeking questions about himself and her, whether their future was certain to be together, whether he really wanted her—loved her—whether he might not want to marry some one else or just her, and whether she wouldn't look nice in a pearl satin wedding-dress with a long creamy veil and satin slippers and a bouquet of bridal-wreath. She had been so slowly but surely saving to that end, even before he came, in connection with Barton; only, after *he* came, all thought of the import of it had been transferred to him. But now, also, she was beginning to ask herself sadly, "Would it ever be?" He was so airy, so inconsequential, so ready to say: "Yes, yes," and "Sure, sure! That's right! Yes, indeedy; you bet! Say, kiddie, but you'll look sweet!" but, somehow, it had always seemed as if this whole thing were a glorious interlude and that it could not last. Arthur was too gay and ethereal and too little settled in his own mind. His ideas of travel and living in different cities, finally winding up in New York or San Francisco, but never with her exactly until she asked him, was too ominous, although he always reassured her gaily: "Of course! Of course!" But somehow she could never believe it really, and it made her intensely sad at times, horribly gloomy. So often she wanted to cry, and she could scarcely tell why.

And then, because of her intense affection for him, she had finally quarreled with Barton, or nearly that, if one could say that one ever really quarreled with him. It had been because of a certain Thursday evening a few weeks before about which she had disappointed him. In a fit of generosity, knowing that Arthur was coming Wednesday, and because Barton had stopped in at the store to see her, she had told him that he might come, having regretted it afterward, so enamored was she of Arthur. And then when Wednesday came, Arthur had changed his mind, telling her he would come Friday instead, but on Thursday evening he had stopped in at the store and asked her to go to Sparrows Point, with the result that she had no time to notify Barton. He had gone to the house and sat with her parents until ten-thirty, and then, a few days later, although she had written him offering an excuse, had called at the store to complain slightly.

"Do you think you did just right, Shirley? You might have sent word, mightn't you? Who was it—the new fellow you won't tell me about?"

Shirley flared on the instant.

"Supposing it was? What's it to you? I don't belong to you yet, do I? I told you there wasn't any one, and I wish you'd let me alone about that. I couldn't help it last Thursday—that's all—and I don't want you to be fussing with me—that's all. If you don't want to, you needn't come any more, anyhow."

"Don't say that, Shirley," pleaded Barton. "You don't mean that. I won't bother you, though, if you don't want me any more."

And because Shirley sulked, not knowing what else to do, he had gone and she had not seen him since.

And then sometime later when she had thus broken with Barton, avoiding the railway station where he worked, Arthur had failed to come at his appointed time, sending no word until the next day, when a note came to the store saying that he had been out of town for his firm over Sunday and had not been able to notify her, but that he would call Tuesday. It was an awful blow. At the time, Shirley had a vision of what was to follow. It seemed for the moment as if the whole world had suddenly been reduced to ashes, that there was nothing but black charred cinders anywhere—she felt that about all life. Yet it all came to her clearly then that this was but the beginning of just such days and just such excuses, and that soon, soon, he would come no more. He was beginning to be tired of her and soon he would not even make excuses. She felt it, and it froze and terrified her.

And then, soon after, the indifference which she feared did follow—almost created by her own thoughts, as it were. First, it was a meeting he had to attend somewhere one Wednesday night when he was to have come for her. Then he was going out of town again, over Sunday. Then he was going away for a whole week—it was absolutely unavoidable, he said, his commercial duties were increasing—and once he had casually remarked that nothing could stand in the way where she was concerned—never! She did not think of reproaching him with this; she was too proud. If he was going, he must go. She would not be willing to say to herself that she had ever attempted to hold any man. But, just the same, she was agonized by the thought. When he was with her, he seemed tender enough; only, at times, his eyes wandered and he seemed slightly bored. Other girls, particularly pretty ones, seemed to interest him as much as she did.

And the agony of the long days when he did not come any more for a week or two at a time! The waiting, the brooding, the wondering, at the store and here in her home—in the former place making mistakes at times because she could not get her mind off him and being reminded of them, and here at her own home at nights, being so absent-minded that her parents remarked on it. She felt sure that her parents must be noticing that Arthur was not coming any more, or as much as he had—for she pretended to be going out with him, going to Mabel Gove's instead—and that Barton had deserted her too, he having been driven off by her indifference, never to come any more, perhaps, unless she sought him out.

And then it was that the thought of saving her own face by taking up with Barton once more occurred to her, of using him and his affections and faithfulness and dulness, if you will, to cover up her own dilemma. Only, this ruse was not to be tried until she had written Arthur this one letter—a pretext merely to see if there was a single ray of hope, a letter to be written in a gentle-enough way and asking for the return of the few notes she had written him. She had not seen him now in nearly a month, and the last time she had, he had said he might soon be compelled to leave her awhile—to go to Pittsburgh to work. And it was his reply to this that she now held in her hand—from Pittsburgh! It was frightful! The future without him!

But Barton would never know really what had transpired, if she went back to him. In spite of all her delicious hours with Arthur, she could call him back, she felt sure. She had never really entirely dropped him, and he knew it. He had bored her dreadfully on occasion, arriving on off days when Arthur was not about, with flowers or candy, or both, and sitting on the porch steps and talking of the railroad business and of the whereabouts and doings of some of their old friends. It was shameful, she had thought at times, to see a man so patient, so hopeful, so good-natured as Barton, deceived in this way, and by her, who was so miserable over another. Her parents must see and know, she had thought at these times, but still, what else was she to do?

"I'm a bad girl," she kept telling herself. "I'm all wrong. What right have I to offer Barton what is left?" But still, somehow, she realized that Barton, if she chose to favor him, would only to be too grateful for even the leavings of others where she was concerned, and that even yet, if she but deigned to crook a finger, she could have him. He was so simple, so good-natured, so stolid and matter of fact, so different to Arthur whom (she could not help smiling at the thought of it) she was loving now about as Barton loved her—slavishly, hopelessly.

And then, as the days passed and Arthur did not write any more—just this one brief note—she at first grieved horribly, and then in a fit of numb despair attempted, bravely enough from one point of view, to adjust herself to the new situation. Why should she despair? Why die of agony where there were plenty who would still sigh for her—Barton among others? She was young, pretty, very—many told her so. She could, if she chose, achieve a vivacity which she did not feel. Why should she brook this unkindness without a thought of retaliation? Why shouldn't she enter upon a gay and heartless career, indulging in a dozen flirtations at once—dancing and killing all thoughts of Arthur in a round of frivolities? There were many who beckoned to her. She stood at her counter in the drug store on many a day and brooded over this, but at the thought of which one to begin with, she faltered. After her late love, all were so tame, for the present anyhow.

And then—and then—always there was Barton, the humble or faithful, to whom she had been so unkind and whom she had used and whom she still really liked. So often self-reproaching thoughts in connection with him crept over her. He must have known, must have seen how badly she was using him all this while, and yet he had not failed to come and come, until she had actually quarreled with him, and any one would have seen that it was literally hopeless. She could not help remembering, especially now in her pain, that he adored her. He was not calling on her now at all—by her indifference she had finally driven him away— but a word, a word— She waited for days, weeks, hoping against hope, and then————

The office of Barton's superior in the Great Eastern terminal had always made him an easy object for her blandishments, coming and going, as she frequently did, via this very station. He was in the office of the assistant train-despatcher on the ground floor, where passing to and from the local, which, at times, was quicker than a street-car, she could easily see him by peering in; only, she had carefully avoided him for nearly a year. If she chose now, and would call for a message-blank at the adjacent telegraph-window which was a part of his room, and raised her voice as she often had in the past, he could scarcely fail to hear, if he did not see her. And if he did, he would rise and come over—of that she was sure, for he never could resist her. It had been a wile of hers in the old days to do this or to make her presence felt by idling outside. After a month of brooding, she felt that she must act—her position as a deserted girl was too much. She could not stand it any longer really—the eyes of her mother, for one.

It was six-fifteen one evening when, coming out ot the store in which she worked, she turned her step disconsolately homeward. Her heart was heavy, her face rather pale and drawn. She had stopped in the store's retiring-room before coming out to add to her charms as much as possible by a little powder and rouge and to smooth her hair. It would not take much to reallure her former sweetheart, she felt sure—and yet it might not be so easy after all. Suppose he had found another? But she could not believe that. It had scarcely been long enough since he had last attempted to see her, and he was really so very, very fond of her and so faithful. He was too slow and certain in his choosing—he had been so with her. Still, who knows? With this thought, she went forward in the evening, feeling for the first time the shame and pain that comes of deception, the agony of having to relinquish an ideal and the feeling of despair that comes to those who find themselves in the position of suppliants, stooping to something which in better days and better fortune they would not know. Arthur was the cause of this.

When she reached the station, the crowd that usually filled it at this hour was swarming. There were so many pairs like Arthur and herself laughing and hurrying away or so she felt. First glancing in the small mirror of a weighing scale to see if she were still of her former charm, she stopped thoughtfully at a little flower stand which stood outside, and for a few pennies purchased a tiny bunch of violets. She then went inside and stood near the window, peering first furtively to see if he were present. He was. Bent over his work, a green shade over his eyes, she could see his stolid, genial figure at a table. Stepping back a moment to ponder, she finally went forward and, in a clear voice, asked,

"May I have a blank,[2] please?"

The infatuation of the discarded Barton was such that it brought him instantly to his feet. In his stodgy, stocky way he rose, his eyes glowing with a friendly hope, his mouth wreathed in smiles, and came over. At the sight of her, pale, but pretty—paler and prettier, really, than he had ever seen her—he thrilled dumbly.

"How are you, Shirley?" he asked sweetly, as he drew near, his eyes searching her face hopefully. He had not seen her for so long that he was intensely hungry, and her paler beauty appealed to him more than ever. Why wouldn't she have him? he was asking himself. Why wouldn't his persistent love yet win her? Perhaps it might. "I haven't seen you in a month of Sundays, it seems. How are the folks?"

"They're all right, Bart," she smiled archly, "and so am I. How have you been?

---

[2] A blank form on which to write the message for a telegram.

It has been a long time since I've seen you. I've been wondering how you were. Have you been all right? I was just going to send a message."

As he had approached, Shirley had pretended at first not to see him, a moment later to affect surprise, although she was really suppressing a heavy sigh. The sight of him, after Arthur, was not reassuring. Could she really interest herself in him any more? Could she?

"Sure, sure," he replied genially; "I'm always all right. You couldn't kill me, you know. Not going away, are you, Shirl?" he queried interestedly.

"No; I'm just telegraphing to Mabel. She promised to meet me to-morrow, and I want to be sure she will."

"You don't come past here as often as you did, Shirley," he complained tenderly. "At least, I don't seem to see you so often," he added with a smile. "It isn't anything I have done, is it?" he queried, and then, when she protested quickly, added: "What's the trouble, Shirl? Haven't been sick, have you?"

She affected all her old gaiety and ease, feeling as though she would like to cry.

"Oh, no," she returned; "I've been all right. I've been going through the other door, I suppose, or coming in and going out on the Langdon Avenue car." (This was true, because she had been wanting to avoid him.) "I've been in such a hurry, most nights, that I haven't had time to stop, Bart. You know how late the store keeps us at times."

He remembered, too, that in the old days she had made time to stop or meet him occasionally.

"Yes, I know," he said tactfully. "But you haven't been to any of our old card-parties either of late, have you? At least, I haven't seen you. I've gone to two or three, thinking you might be there."

That was another thing Arthur had done—broken up her interest in these old store and neighborhood parties and a banjo-and-mandolin club to which she had once belonged. They had all seemed so pleasing and amusing in the old days—but now—* * * * In those days Bart had been her usual companion when his work permitted.

"No," she replied evasively, but with a forced air of pleasant remembrance; "I have often thought of how much fun we had at those, though. It was a shame to drop them. You haven't seen Harry Stull or Trina Task recently, have you?" she inquired, more to be saying something than for any interest she felt.

He shook his head negatively, then added:

"Yes, I did, too; here in the waiting-room a few nights ago. They were coming down-town to a theater, I suppose."

His face fell slightly as he recalled how it had been their custom to do this, and what their one quarrel had been about. Shirley noticed it. She felt the least bit sorry for him, but much more for herself, coming back so disconsolately to all this.

"Well, you're looking as pretty as ever, Shirley," he continued, noting that she had not written the telegram and that there was something wistful in her glance. "Prettier, I think," and she smiled sadly. Every word that she tolerated from him was as so much gold to him, so much of dead ashes to her. "You wouldn't like to come down some evening this week and see 'The Mouse-Trap,' would you? We haven't been to a theater together in I don't know when." His eyes sought hers in a hopeful, doglike way.

So—she could have him again—that was the pity of it! To have what she really did not want, did not care for! At the least nod now he would come, and this very devotion made it all but worthless, and so sad. She ought to marry him now for certain, if she began in this way, and could in a month's time if she chose, but oh, oh—could she? For the moment she decided that she could not, would not. If he had only repulsed her—told her to go—ignored her—but no; it was her fate to be loved by him in this moving, pleading way, and hers not to love him as she wished to love—to be loved. Plainly, he needed some one like her, whereas she, she——. She turned a little sick, a sense of the sacrilege of gaiety at this time creeping into her voice, and exclaimed:

"No, no!" Then seeing his face change, a heavy sadness come over it, "Not this week, anyhow, I mean" ("Not so soon," she had almost said). "I have several engagements this week and I'm not feeling well. But"—seeing his face change, and the thought of her own state returning—"you might come out to the house some evening instead, and then we can go some other time."

His face brightened intensely. It was wonderful how he longed to be with her, how the least favor from her comforted and lifted him up. She could see also now, however, how little it meant to her, how little it could ever mean, even if to him it was heaven. The old relationship would have to be resumed in toto, once and for all, but did she want it that way now that she was feeling so miserable about this other affair? As she meditated, these various moods racing to and fro in her mind, Barton seemed to notice, and now it occurred to him that perhaps he had not pursued her enough—was too easily put off. She probably did like him yet. This evening, her present visit, seemed to prove it.

"Sure, sure!" he agreed. "I'd like that. I'll come out Sunday, if you say. We can go any time to the play. I'm sorry, Shirley, if you're not feeling well. I've thought of you a lot these days. I'll come out Wednesday, if you don't mind."

She smiled a wan smile. It was all so much easier than she had expected—her triumph—and so ashenlike in consequence, a flavor of dead-sea fruit and defeat about it all, that it was pathetic. How could she, after Arthur? How could he, really?

"Make it Sunday," she pleaded, naming the farthest day off, and then hurried out.

Her faithful lover gazed after her, while she suffered an intense nausea. To think—to think—it should all be coming to this! She had not used her telegraph-blank, and now had forgotten all about it. It was not the simple trickery that discouraged her, but her own future which could find no better outlet than this, could not rise above it apparently, or that she had no heart to make it rise above it. Why couldn't she interest herself in some one different to Barton? Why did she have to return to him? Why not wait and meet some other—ignore him as before? But no, no; nothing mattered now—no one—it might as well be Barton really as any one, and she would at least make him happy and at the same time solve her own problem. She went out into the train-shed and climbed into her train. Slowly, after the usual pushing and jostling of a crowd, it drew out toward Latonia, that suburban region in which her home lay. As she rode, she thought.

"What have I just done? What am I doing?" she kept asking herself as the clacking wheels on the rails fell into a rhythmic dance and the houses of the brown, dry endless city fled past in a maze. "Severing myself decisively from the past—the happy past—for supposing, once I am married, Arthur should return and want me again—suppose! Suppose!"

Below at one place, under a shed, were some market-gardeners disposing of the last remnants of their day's wares–a sickly, dull life, she thought. Here was

Rutgers Avenue, with its line of red street-cars, many wagons and tracks and counter-streams of automobiles—how often had she passed it morning and evening in a shuttle-like way, and how often would, unless she got married! And here, now, was the river flowing smoothly between its banks lined with coal-pockets and wharves—away, away to the huge deep sea which she and Arthur had enjoyed so much. Oh, to be in a small boat and drift out, out into the endless, restless, pathless deep! Somehow the sight of this water, to-night and every night, brought back those evenings in the open with Arthur at Sparrows Point, the long line of dancers in Eckert's Pavilion, the woods at Atholby, the park with the dancers in the pavilion—she choked back a sob. Once Arthur had come this way with her on just such an evening as this, pressing her hand and saying how wonderful she was. Oh, Arthur! Arthur! And now Barton was to take his old place again—forever, no doubt. She could not trifle with her life longer in this foolish way, or his. What was the use? But think of it!

Yes, it must be—forever now, she told herself. She must marry. Time would be slipping by and she would become too old. It was her only future—marriage. It was the only future she had ever contemplated really, a home, children, the love of some man whom she could love as she loved Arthur. Ah, what a happy home that would have been for her! But now, now——

But there must be no turning back now, either. There was no other way. If Arthur ever came back—but fear not, he wouldn't! She had risked so much and lost—lost him. Her little venture into true love had been such a failure. Before Arthur had come all had been well enough. Barton, stout and simple and frank and direct, had in some way—how, she could scarcely realize now—offered sufficient of a future. But now, now! He had enough money, she knew, to build a cottage for the two of them. He had told her so. He would do his best always to make her happy, she was sure of that. They could live in about the state her parents were living in—or a little better, not much—and would never want. No doubt there would be children, because he craved them—several of them—and that would take up her time, long years of it—the sad, gray years! But then Arthur, whose children she would have thrilled to bear, would be no more, a mere memory—think of that!—and Barton, the dull, the commonplace, would have achieved his finest dream—and why?

Because love was a failure for her—that was why—and in her life there could be no more true love. She would never love any one again as she had Arthur. It could not be, she was sure of it. He was too fascinating, too wonderful. Always, always, wherever she might be, whoever she might marry, he would be coming back, intruding between her and any possible love, receiving any possible kiss. It would be Arthur she would be loving or kissing. She dabbed at her eyes with a tiny handkerchief, turned her face close to the window and stared out, and then as the environs of Latonia came into view, wondered (so deep is romance): What if Arthur should come back at some time—or now! Supposing he should be here at the station now, accidentally or on purpose, to welcome her, to soothe her weary heart. He had met her here before. How she would fly to him, lay her head on his shoulder, forget forever that Barton ever was, that they had ever separated for an hour. Oh, Arthur! Arthur!

But no, no; here was Latonia—here the viaduct over her train, the long business street and the cars marked "Center" and "Langdon Avenue" running back into the great city. A few blocks away in treeshaded Bethune Street, duller and plainer than ever, was her parents' cottage and the routine of that old life which

was now, she felt, more fully fastened upon her than ever before—the lawnmowers, the lawns, the front porches all alike. Now would come the going to and fro
of Barton to business as her father and she now went to business, her keeping
house, cooking, washing ironing, sewing for Barton as her mother now did these
things for her father and herself. And she would not be in love really, as she
wanted to be. Oh, dreadful! She could never escape it really, now that she could
endure it less, scarcely for another hour. And yet she must, must, for the sake
of—for the sake of—she closed her eyes and dreamed.

She walked up the street under the trees, past the houses and lawns all alike to
her own, and found her father on their veranda reading the evening paper. She
sighed at the sight.

"Back, daughter?" he called pleasantly.

"Yes."

"Your mother is wondering if you would like steak or liver for dinner. Better
tell her."

"Oh, it doesn't matter."

She hurried into her bedroom, threw down her hat and gloves, and herself on
the bed to rest silently, and groaned in her soul. To think that it had all come to
this!—Never to see him any more!—To see only Barton, and marry him and live
in such a street, have four or five children, forget all her youthful companion-
ships—and all to save her face before her parents, and her future. Why must it be?
Should it be, really? She choked and stifled. After a little time her mother, hearing
her come in, came to the door—thin, practical, affectionate, conventional.

"What's wrong, honey? Aren't you feeling well tonight? Have you a headache?
Let me feel."

Her thin cool fingers crept over her temples and hair. She suggested something
to eat or a headache powder right away.

"I'm all right, mother. I'm just not feeling well now. Don't bother. I'll get up
soon. Please don't."

"Would you rather have liver or steak to-night, dear?"

"Oh, anything—nothing—please don't bother—steak will do—anything"—if
only she could get rid of her and be at rest!

Her mother looked at her and shook her head sympathetically, then retreated
quietly, saying no more. Lying so, she thought and thought—grinding, destroying
thoughts about the beauty of the past, the darkness of the future—until able to
endure them no longer she got up and, looking distractedly out of the window into
the yard and the house next door, stared at her future fixedly. What should she do?
What should she really do? There was Mrs. Kessel in her kitchen getting her
dinner as usual, just as her own mother was now, and Mr. Kessel out on the front
porch in his shirt-sleeves reading the evening paper. Beyond was Mr. Pollard in
his yard, cutting the grass. All along Bethune Street were such houses and such
people—simple, commonplace souls all—clerks, managers, fairly successful
craftsmen, like her father and Barton, excellent in their way but not like Arthur the
beloved, the lost—and here was she, perforce, or by decision of necessity, soon
to be one of them, in some such street as this no doubt, forever and —. For the
moment it choked and stifled her.

She decided that she would not. No, no, no! There must be some other way—
many ways. She did not have to do this unless she really wished to—would not—
only—. Then going to the mirror she looked at her face and smoothed her hair.

"But what's the use?" she asked of herself wearily and resignedly after a time.

"Why should I cry? Why shouldn't I marry Barton? I don't amount to anything, anyhow. Arthur wouldn't have me. I wanted him, and I am compelled to take some one else—or no one—what difference does it really make who? My dreams are too high, that's all. I wanted Arthur, and he wouldn't have me. I don't want Barton, and he crawls at my feet. I'm a failure, that's what's the matter with me."

And then, turning up her sleeves and removing a fichu[3] which stood out too prominently from her breast, she went into the kitchen and, looking about for an apron, observed:

"Can't I help? Where's the tablecloth?" and finding it among napkins and silverware in a drawer in the adjoining room, proceeded to set the table.

1918

Willa Cather
(1873–1947)

The narrator of *O Pioneers!* (1913) observes that "there are only two or three human stories, and they go on repeating themselves as fiercely as if they had never happened before." Throughout her career, Willa Cather recorded these primary tales of struggle and aspiration, situating them upon various frontiers that evoke a sense of promise and of promise lost. Some of the frontiers required pioneers who were strong in body and spirit (Alexandra Bergson of *O Pioneers!* and Ántonia Shimerda of *My Ántonia* [1918], for example). Others called for trailblazers who channeled their vitality and courage into artistry or worlds of the spirit.

Willela ("Willie") Cather was born near Winchester, Virginia, in 1873. At age nine she moved with her family to Webster County, Nebraska, and later to Red Cloud, Nebraska—much the same trip Jim Burden makes in *My Ántonia*. Like Jim, she befriended many of the immigrants whose trials and perseverance would become an enduring part of her fiction. At the University of Nebraska in the 1890s she studied the classics and published lively reviews of cultural events in the Lincoln newspaper. She moved to Pittsburgh in 1896 to edit *Home Monthly* magazine. In 1905 Cather's first short-story collection, *The Troll Garden,* appeared, with its moving contrasts between the starkness of the prairies and the evocative world of art. Although this period of her life remains mysterious (because she burned most of her letters), her roommate Isabelle McClung seems to have been her closest companion in Pittsburgh. In 1906 Cather moved to New York to work at *McClure's Magazine;* there she met Edith Lewis, who became her lifelong companion until Cather's death in 1947. In Boston soon thereafter, Cather had the good fortune to meet Sarah Orne Jewett, whose advice on writing affected both the content and the style of Cather's work.

Her atypical first novel, *Alexander's Bridge,* was serialized in *McClure's* in 1912. After that false start (as she saw it), Cather took Jewett's advice to write about what she

[3] A three-cornered cape.

knew and produced *O Pioneers!* and *The Song of the Lark* (1915). In *My Ántonia* Cather portrays the heroic Ántonia through the eyes of Jim Burden, whose unfulfilling life in the East leads him to recapture the memories of his youth—and to bring them into the present. In this novel, too, Cather dramatizes gender roles more directly than in her previous works. Despite her growing reputation, she became disillusioned with the materialism and lack of value in modern life—as evidenced in her Pulitzer Prize-winning war novel, *One of Ours* (1922), and in a book of essays, *Not Under Forty* (1936), in which she asserts that "the world broke in two in 1922 or thereabouts." After finishing the novel *A Lost Lady* (1923), she began to turn her imagination toward historically remote locales in a search for meaning and order, first, tentatively, in *The Professor's House* (1925), then in the quiet harmony of *Death Comes for the Archbishop* (1927) and the resolute domesticity of *Shadows on the Rock* (1931). The Nebraska prairie had served Cather's early fiction well: in these later narratives her lifelong reverence for the Southwest and an interest in seventeenth-century Quebec took her again to primary human stories of struggle and achievement.

Suggested Readings: *My Ántonia*, 1918. *The Novels and Stories of Willa Cather*, 13 vols., 1937–1941. *On Writing: Critical Studies on Writing as Art*, 1949. *The Kingdom of Art: Willa Cather's First Principles and Critical Statements, 1893–1896*, ed. B. Slote, 1966. *Willa Cather's Collected Short Fiction*, ed. V. Faulkner, 1970. *April Twilights: Poems by Willa Cather*, 1976. E. K. Brown and L. Edel, *Willa Cather: A Critical Biography*, 1953. E. S. Sergeant, *Willa Cather, A Memoir*, 1963. P. C. Robinson, *Willa, The Life of Willa Cather*, 1983. S. O'Brien, *Willa Cather: The Emerging Voice*, 1987. J. Woodress, *Willa Cather: A Literary Life*, 1987. H. Lee, *Willa Cather: Double Lives*, 1990.

Text Used: *Youth and the Bright Medusa*, 1937.

An early 1900s photograph of Red Cloud, Nebraska, the pioneer town in which Willa Cather was raised—and the source of some of her best fiction.

A WAGNER MATINÉE*

I received one morning a letter, written in pale ink on glassy, blue-lined note-paper, and bearing the postmark of a little Nebraska town. This communication, worn and rubbed, looking as if it had been carried for some days in a coat pocket that was none too clean, was from my Uncle Howard, and informed me that his wife had been left a small legacy by a bachelor relative, and that it would be necessary for her to go to Boston to attend to the settling of the estate. He requested me to meet her at the station and render her whatever services might be necessary. On examining the date indicated as that of her arrival, I found it to be no later than to-morrow. He had characteristically delayed writing until, had I been away from home for a day, I must have missed my aunt altogether.

The name of my Aunt Georgiana opened before me a gulf of recollection so wide and deep that, as the letter dropped from my hand, I felt suddenly a stranger to all the present conditions of my existence, wholly ill at ease and out of place amid the familiar surroundings of my study. I became, in short, the gangling farmer-boy my aunt had known, scourged with chilblains[1] and bashfulness, my hands cracked and sore from the corn-husking. I sat again before her parlour organ, fumbling the scales with my stiff, red fingers, while she, beside me, made canvas mittens for the huskers.

The next morning, after preparing my landlady for a visitor, I set out for the station. When the train arrived, I had some difficulty in finding my aunt. She was the last of the passengers to alight, and it was not until I got her into the carriage that she seemed really to recognize me. She had come all the way in a day coach; her linen duster had become black with soot and her black bonnet grey with dust during the journey. When we arrived at my boarding-house, the landlady put her to bed at once and I did not see her again until the next morning.

Whatever shock Mrs. Springer experienced at my aunt's appearance, she considerately concealed. As for myself, I saw my aunt's battered figure with that feeling of awe and respect with which we behold explorers who have left their ears and fingers north of Franz-Josef Land,[2] or their health somewhere along the Upper Congo.

My Aunt Georgiana had been a music-teacher at the Boston Conservatory, somewhere back in the late sixties. One summer, while visiting in the little village among the Green Mountains where her ancestors had dwelt for generations, she had kindled the callow fancy of my uncle, Howard Carpenter, then an idle, shiftless boy of twenty-one. When she returned to her duties in Boston, Howard followed her, and the upshot of this infatuation was that she eloped with him, eluding the reproaches of her family and the criticism of her friends by going with him to the Nebraska frontier. Carpenter, who, of course, had no money, took up a homestead in Red Willow County, fifty miles from the railroad. There they had measured off their land themselves, driving across the prairie in a wagon, to the wheel of which they had tied a red cotton handkerchief, and counting its revolutions. They built a dugout in the red hillside, one of those cave dwellings whose immates

---

* First published in *Everybody's Magazine* in 1904, revised, and collected in *The Troll Garden* in 1905. This version, from *Youth and the Bright Medusa* (1937), incorporates additional revisions made by Cather. The title refers to Richard Wagner (1813–1883), a renowned German composer of operas.

[1] Sores or swellings caused by exposure to cold.

[2] An archipelago in the Arctic Ocean that was annexed by Soviet Russia in 1928.

so often reverted to primitive conditions. Their water they got from the lagoons where the buffalo drank, and their slender stock of provisions was always at the mercy of bands of roving Indians. For thirty years my aunt had not been farther than fifty miles from the homestead.

I owed to this woman most of the good that ever came my way in my boyhood, and had a reverential affection for her. During the years when I was riding herd for my uncle, my aunt, after cooking the three meals—the first of which was ready at six o'clock in the morning—and putting the six children to bed, would often stand until midnight at her ironing-board, with me at the kitchen table beside her, hearing me recite Latin declensions and conjugations, gently shaking me when my drowsy head sank down over a page of irregular verbs. It was to her, at her ironing or mending, that I read my first Shakespeare, and her old textbook on mythology was the first that ever came into my empty hands. She taught me my scales and exercises on the little parlour organ which her husband had bought her after fifteen years during which she had not so much as seen a musical instrument. She would sit beside me by the hour, darning and counting, while I struggled with the "Joyous Farmer." She seldom talked to me about music, and I understood why. Once when I had been doggedly beating out some easy passages from an old score of "Euryanthe"[3] I had found among her music-books, she came up to me and, putting her hands over my eyes, gently drew my head back upon her shoulder, saying tremulously, "Don't love it so well, Clark, or it may be taken from you."

When my aunt appeared on the morning after her arrival in Boston, she was still in a semi-somnambulant state. She seemed not to realize that she was in the city where she had spent her youth, the place longed for hungrily half a lifetime. She had been so wretchedly train-sick throughout the journey that she had no recollection of anything but her discomfort, and, to all intents and purposes, there were but a few hours of nightmare between the farm in Red Willow County and my study on Newbury Street. I had planned a little pleasure for her that afternoon, to repay her for some of the glorious moments she had given me when we used to milk together in the straw-thatched cow-shed and she, because I was more than usually tired, or because her husband had spoken sharply to me, would tell me of the splendid performance of the "Huguenots"[4] she had seen in Paris, in her youth.

At two o'clock the Symphony Orchestra was to give a Wagner program, and I intended to take my aunt; though, as I conversed with her, I grew doubtful about her enjoyment of it. I suggested our visiting the Conservatory and the Common before lunch, but she seemed altogether too timid to wish to venture out. She questioned me absently about various changes in the city, but she was chiefly concerned that she had forgotten to leave instructions about feeding half-skimmed milk to a certain weakling calf, "old Maggie's calf, you know, Clark," she explained, evidently having forgotten how long I had been away. She was further troubled because she had neglected to tell her daughter about the freshly opened kit of mackerel in the cellar, which would spoil if it were not used directly.

I asked her whether she had ever heard any of the Wagnerian operas, and found that she had not, though she was perfectly familiar with their respective situations, and had once possessed the piano score of "The Flying Dutchman."[5] I began to

---

[3] An opera by Carl Maria von Weber (1786–1826) first performed in Vienna in 1823.
[4] An opera by Giacomo Meyerbeer (1791–1864) first performed in Paris in 1836.
[5] A Wagner opera completed in 1841 and first performed in Dresden in 1843.

think it would be best to get her back to Red Willow County without waking her, and regretted having suggested the concert.

From the time we entered the concert hall, however, she was a trifle less passive and inert, and for the first time seemed to perceive her surroundings. I had felt some trepidation lest she might become aware of her queer, country clothes, or might experience some painful embarrassment at stepping suddenly into the world to which she had been dead for more than a quarter of a century. But, again, I found how superficially I had judged her. She sat looking about her with eyes as impersonal, almost as stony, as those with which the granite Rameses[6] in a museum watches the froth and fret that ebbs and flows about his pedestal. I have seen this same aloofness in old miners who drift into the Brown Palace Hotel at Denver, their pockets full of bullion, their linen soiled, their haggard faces unshaven; standing in the thronged corridors as solitary as though they were still in a frozen camp on the Yukon.

The matinée audience was made up chiefly of women. One lost the contour of faces and figures, indeed any effect of line whatever, and there was only the colour of bodices past counting, the shimmer of fabrics soft and firm, silky and sheer; red, mauve, pink, blue, lilac, purple, écru, rose, yellow, cream, and white, all the colours that an impressionist finds in a sunlit landscape, with here and there the dead shadow of a frock coat. My Aunt Georgiana regarded them as though they had been so many daubs of tube-paint on a palette.

When the musicians came out and took their places, she gave a little stir of anticipation, and looked with quickening interest down over the rail at that invariable grouping, perhaps the first wholly familiar thing that had greeted her eye since she had left old Maggie and her weakling calf. I could feel how all those details sank into her soul, for I had not forgotten how they had sunk into mine when I came fresh from ploughing forever and forever between green aisles of corn, where, as in a treadmill, one might walk from daybreak to dusk without perceiving a shadow of change. The clean profiles of the musicians, the gloss of their linen, the dull black of their coats, the beloved shapes of the instruments, the patches of yellow light on the smooth, varnished bellies of the 'cellos and the bass viols in the rear, the restless, wind-tossed forest of fiddle necks and bows—I recalled how, in the first orchestra I ever heard, those long bow-strokes seemed to draw the heart out of me, as a conjurer's stick reels out yards of paper ribbon from a hat.

The first number was the "Tannhäuser"[7] overture. When the horns drew out the first strain of the Pilgrims' Chorus, Aunt Georgiana clutched my coat-sleeve. Then it was I first realized that for her this broke a silence of thirty years. I saw again the tall, naked house on the prairie, black and grim as a wooden fortress; the black pond where I had learned to swim, its margin pitted with sun-dried cattle tracks; the rain-gullied clay banks about the naked house, the four dwarf ash seedlings where the dish-cloths were always hung to dry before the kitchen door. The world there was the flat world of the ancients; to the east, a cornfield that stretched to daybreak; to the west, a corral that reached to sunset; between, the conquests of peace, dearer-bought than those of war.

The overture closed, my aunt released my coat-sleeve, but she said nothing. She sat quietly looking at the orchestra. What, I wondered, did she get from it?

---

[6] A statue of one of several Egyptian kings, or pharaohs.

[7] A Wagner opera (first performed in Dresden in 1845) in which the minstrel knight Tannhauser joins a group of pilgrims journeying to Rome.

She had been a good pianist in her day, I knew, and her musical education had been broader than that of most music-teachers of a quarter of a century ago. She had often told me of Mozart's operas and Meyerbeer's, and I could remember hearing her sing, years ago, certain melodies of Verdi.[8] When I had fallen ill with a fever in her house, she used to sit by my cot in the evening—when the cool night wind blew in through the faded mosquito netting tacked over the window and I lay watching a certain bright star that burned red above the cornfield—and sing "Home to our mountains, O, let us return!" in a way fit to break the heart of a Vermont boy near dead of homesickness already.

I watched her closely through the prelude to "Tristan and Isolde,"[9] trying vainly to conjecture what that seething turmoil of strings and winds might mean to her, but she sat mutely staring at the violin bows that drove obliquely downward, like the streaks of rain in a summer shower. Had this music any message for her? Had she enough left to at all comprehend this power which had kindled the world since she had left it? I was in a fever of curiosity, but Aunt Georgiana preserved her utter immobility throughout the number from "The Flying Dutchman," though her fingers worked mechanically upon her black dress, as if, of themselves, they were recalling the piano score they had once played. Poor hands! They had been stretched and twisted into mere tentacles to hold and lift and knead with; on one of them a thin, worn band that had once been a wedding ring. As I pressed and gently quieted one of those groping hands, I remembered their services for me in other days.

Soon after the tenor began the "Prize Song,"[10] I heard a quick-drawn breath and turned to my aunt. Her eyes were closed, but the tears were glistening on her cheeks, and I think, in a moment more, they were in my eyes as well. It never really died, then—the soul which can suffer so excruciatingly and so interminably; it withers to the outward eye only; like that strange moss which can lie on a dusty shelf half a century and yet, if placed in water, grows green again.

During the intermission before the second half, I questioned my aunt and found that the "Prize Song" was not new to her. Some years before there had drifted to the farm in Red Willow County a young German, a tramp cow-puncher, who had sung in the chorus at Bayreuth[11] when he was a boy, along with the other peasant boys and girls. Of a Sunday morning he used to sit on his gingham-sheeted bed in the hands' bedroom which opened off the kitchen, cleaning the leather of his boots and saddle, singing the 'Prize Song,' while my aunt went about her work in the kitchen. She had hovered over him until she had prevailed upon him to join the country church, though his sole fitness for this step, in so far as I could gather, lay in his boyish face and his possession of this divine melody. Shortly afterward, he had gone to town on the Fourth of July, been drunk for several days, lost his money at a faro table, ridden a saddled Texas steer on a bet, and disappeared with a fractured collar-bone. All this my aunt told me huskily, wanderingly, during the intermission.

"Well, we have come to better things than the old "Trovatore"[12] at any rate, Aunt Georgie?" I asked, with a well-meant effort at jocularity.

[8] Wolfgang Amadeus Mozart (1756–1791); Giuseppe Verdi (1813–1901): composers of grand opera.
[9] A Wagner opera first performed in Munich in 1865.
[10] A famous song from Act III of Wagner's *Die Meistersinger* (1867), or *"The Mastersingers"* (German).
[11] A city in Bavaria. The "tramp cow-puncher" from Bayreuth (a wandering Dutchman himself) sings the famous aria from *The Flying Dutchman*.
[12] A Verdi opera first performed in Rome in 1853.

Her lip quivered and she hastily put her handkerchief up to her mouth. From behind it she murmured, "And you have been hearing this ever since you left me, Clark?" Her question was the gentlest and saddest of reproaches.

The second half of the programme consisted of four numbers from the "Ring"[13] and closed with Siegfried's funeral march. Throughout these I felt that my aunt had drifted quite away from me. From time to time her eyes looked up at the lights, burning softly under their dull glass globes.

The deluge of sound poured on and on; I never knew what she found in the shining current of it; I never knew how far it bore her, or past what happy islands. From the trembling of her face I could well believe that before the last number she had been carried out where the myriad graves are, into the grey, nameless burying grounds of the sea; or into some world of death vaster yet, where, from the beginning of the world, hope has lain down with hope and dream with dream and, renouncing, slept.

The concert was over; the people filed out of the hall chattering and laughing, glad to relax and find the living level again, but my kinswoman made no effort to rise. The harpist slipped the green felt cover over his instrument; the flute-players shook the water from their mouthpieces; the men of the orchestra went out one by one, leaving the stage to the chairs and music-stands, empty as a winter cornfield.

I spoke to my aunt. She turned to me with a sad little smile. "I don't want to go, Clark. I suppose we must."

I understood. For her, just outside the concert hall, lay the black pond with the cattle-tracked bluffs; the tall, unpainted house, with weather-curled boards, naked as a tower; the crook-backed ash seedlings where the dish-cloths hung to dry; the gaunt, moulting turkeys picking up refuse about the kitchen door.

1904

Gertrude Stein
(1874–1946)

Gertrude Stein, one of the twentieth century's most original literary minds, was born in Allegheny, Pennsylvania, in 1874 to prosperous, assimilated German-Jewish immigrants. Her father had followed his father in operating a successful textile and clothing business, enlarging the family fortune through real-estate speculation and other investments. The youngest of seven children, she was a pampered child. From 1875 to 1879 the Steins lived in Vienna and Paris, moving to Oakland, California, in 1880. After both parents had died by 1891, the five remaining children received comfortable inheritances. Gertrude later relied on the freedom this income gave her: able to ignore the pressures of finding a market for her writing, she could pursue her uncompromising experimentations in literary form.

---

[13] *Der Ring des Nibelungen* ("The Ring of the Nibelungs" [German]), a cycle of four Wagner operas performed individually from 1869 to 1876 and as a complete cycle in Bayreuth in 1876. Siegfried's funeral march is from the third of these operas, *Siegfried*.

In 1892 Stein accompanied her brother Leo to Harvard University and enrolled in the "Harvard Annex" for women (now Radcliffe). She soon entered the orbit of Harvard's famous psychologist and philosopher William James, whose theories of consciousness as the subjective streams of "concrete particular I's and you's" underlie Stein's early writings. Under James's tutelage she participated in laboratory experiments in automatic writing, publishing the results of her own experiment, "Cultivated Motor Automatism: A Study of Character in Its Relation to Attention," in Harvard's *Psychological Review* in 1898. When Leo began graduate study in biology at Johns Hopkins University in 1897, Gertrude enrolled in the Johns Hopkins School of Medicine, which had only recently begun to admit women students. From then until about 1914 the independent, eccentric sister and brother made a home together.

Stein seemed headed toward an auspicious career as a pioneering female scientist. However, entangled in an unhappy lesbian triangle (which provided the then-unpublishable subject of her first novel, *Q.E.D.* [1950]) and aware of Leo's flagging interest in his studies, Stein neglected her own courses. When her impulsive brother resolved to go to Europe to study painting, she soon followed him to 27 *rue de Fleurus,* the home that she would occupy for many years and make famous as a premier gathering-place for artists and intellectuals of the Parisian and expatriate avant-garde.

Together, Gertrude and Leo set about building a remarkable private collection of modern art. They first bought works by established recent artists, such as Paul Gaugin, Auguste Renoir, and Paul Cézanne. In the process the Steins supported several struggling painters, including Henri Matisse and Pablo Picasso, who in 1906 painted a now-famous portrait of Gertrude Stein and who became a lifelong friend. At this time she was writing the three-part *Three Lives* (1909), which blends subject matter familiar to late nineteenth-century naturalistic fiction—the experiences and sexuality of immigrant and black

Pablo Picasso's 1906 painting of Gertrude Stein. (The Metropolitan Museum of Art, bequest of Gertrude Stein, 1946)

women—with a literary style formed from her absorption of the psychological and aesthetic principles of William James, Gustave Flaubert, and Cézanne. Despite poor sales, the work (which contains "The Gentle Lena") earned critical success; some readers, including the critics Mabel Dodge and Carl Van Vechten, became dedicated promoters of Stein's work. Soon the *rue de Fleurus* household changed permanently, when Alice B. Toklas moved in as Stein's self-effacing companion, secretary, and lover; their mutual devotion lasted until Stein's death.

Between 1906 and 1908 Stein wrote an enormous, ponderous novel, *The Making of Americans* (not published until 1925), based largely on memories of her family. She pushed her experiments in exposition and narration further in a series of short "word portraits" of friends and relatives. The 1913 New York Armory show introduced the challenging new European art forms to a mainly querulous American public. In an art magazine accompanying the exhibition, an essay by Mabel Dodge on Stein's writings linked Stein's name, in the minds of eager journalists, to the European innovations: her American reputation was made by their parodies and ridicule. Her most radical prose experiment, *Tender Buttons* (1914), a series of asyntactical entries "about" the immediate environment of the household, appeared in the wake of and furthered this publicity. The popular view of Stein was tempered by the enthusiastic reception her work received from established American cultural figures such as Sherwood Anderson and the photographer Alfred Stieglitz.

Meanwhile, Stein had steadily consolidated her position at the center of the Parisian avant-garde: she met and hosted an amazing array of European and American talents. She and Toklas did volunteer relief work during World War I. After Stein's return to Paris in 1918, more visiting writers and artists sought her acquaintance and typically received her advice. She published works in "little" magazines and with small, ephemeral presses but kept a large pile of manuscripts in a cabinet; many of these were published posthumously. Extending her formal experiments to drama, she wrote numerous short plays. In 1926 Stein accepted an invitation to speak at Oxford University; her lecture, "Composition as Explanation," was the first of many public lectures she gave during the 1920s and 1930s.

In 1930 Stein and Toklas decided to publish Stein's works themselves, creating their press, Plain Editions. However, the memoir *The Autobiography of Alice B. Toklas* (1933), written by Stein from Toklas's viewpoint, brought the resolute inventor of intransigent literary experiments into the world of commercial publishing: the book became a bestseller and was serialized in the *Atlantic Monthly*. For the first time Stein earned substantial royalties for her work and was courted by publishers, such as Bennett Cerf, who printed one Stein book per year as long as she provided them. The American popularity of *Toklas,* casual and anecdotal, aroused interest in the modernist opera by Stein and composer Virgil Thomson, *Four Saints in Three Acts,* which premiered in 1934 and caused considerable high-society excitement. Later that year Stein and Toklas began a highly-publicized American tour, discovering firsthand the potential impact of the American publicity machine: lights in New York's Times Square flashed "GERTRUDE STEIN HAS ARRIVED IN NEW YORK." Stein lectured to large audiences across the country; she and Toklas took tea with Eleanor Roosevelt at the White House.

After returning to France in 1935, Stein produced several more books, some in a difficult-to-read style, some in a more accessible style. The tour yielded volumes of her lectures, *The Geographical History of America* (1935), and *Everybody's Autobiography* (1937), but none repeated the success of *Toklas.* When France fell to the Germans during World War II, Stein and Toklas moved to the South of France, despite the risk they faced as Jews and, later, as enemy nationals. Stein's account of the occupation of France, *Wars I Have Seen,* was published in 1945. In 1946 she died of cancer. Her obituaries tended to emphasize her celebrity status, forceful personality, and illustrious acquaintances, giving only a decorous, qualified praise to her works. Stein the author has begun to be fully appreciated only since the 1960s. The renewed interest in Stein by writers and critics alike is reflected in the dozens of books about her and her work that have been published in the decades after her death.

Suggested Readings: *Tender Buttons*, 1914. *The Making of Americans*, 1925. *The Autobiography of Alice B. Toklas*, 1933. *Four Saints in Three Acts*, with V. Thomson, 1934. *Lectures in America*, 1935. *Everybody's Autobiography*, 1937. *Selected Writings of Gertrude Stein*, ed. C. Van Vechten, 1946. *Yes Is for a Very Young Man*, 1946. *The Yale Edition of the Unpublished Writings of Gertrude Stein*, 8 vols., ed. C. Van Vechten, 1951–1958. *Gertrude Stein: Writings and Lectures, 1909–1945*, ed. P. Meyerowitz, 1967. *Gertrude Stein on Picasso*, ed. E. Burns, 1970. *Dear Sammy: Letters From Gertrude Stein and Alice B. Toklas*. ed. S. M. Steward, 1977. A. B. Toklas, *What Is Remembered*, 1963. R. Bridgman, *Gertrude Stein in Pieces*, 1970. J. R. Mellow, *Charmed Circle: Gertrude Stein and Company*, 1974. W. Steiner, *Exact Resemblance to Exact Resemblance: The Literary Portraiture of Gertrude Stein*, 1978. M. J. Hoffman, ed., *Critical Essays on Gertrude Stein*, 1986. S. Neuman, and I. B. Nadel, eds., *Gertrude Stein and the Making of Literature*, 1988. H. S. Chessman, *The Public Is Invited to the Dance: Representation, the Body, and Dialogue in Gertrude Stein*, 1989.

Text Used: *Three Lives*, 1933.

THE GENTLE LENA*

Lena was patient, gentle, sweet and german. She had been a servant for four years and had liked it very well.

Lena had been brought from Germany to Brigepoint by a cousin and had been in the same place there for four years.

This place Lena had found very good. There was a pleasant, unexacting mistress and her children, and they all liked Lena very well.

There was a cook there who scolded Lena a great deal but Lena's german patience held no suffering and the good incessant woman really only scolded so for Lena's good.

Lena's german voice when she knocked and called the family in the morning was as awakening, as soothing, and as appealing, as a delicate soft breeze in midday, summer. She stood in the hallway every morning a long time in her unexpectant and unsuffering german patience calling to the young ones to get up. She would call and wait a long time and then call again, always even, gentle, patient, while the young ones fell back often into that precious, tense, last bit of sleeping that gives a strength of joyous vigor in the young, over them that have come to the readiness of middle age, in their awakening.

Lena had good hard work all morning, and on the pleasant, sunny afternoons she was sent out into the park to sit and watch the little two year old girl baby of the family.

---

* The third story of Stein's *Three Lives* (1909), like the first, "The Good Anna," describes the life of a German-born immigrant woman in the fictional American town of Bridgepoint. The long middle story is "Melanctha." Lena was drawn in part from Lena Lebender, the German immigrant housekeeper at the Baltimore home Stein shared with her brother, Leo. Another influence was *Trois Contes* (1877), or "*Three Tales*," by the French novelist Gustave Flaubert (1821–1880), which Stein was then translating into English. When *Three Lives* was first printed, its copy editors, thinking that an author named Stein might not have herself mastered English, offered to correct the "errors" in her prose.

The other girls, all them that make the pleasant, lazy crowd, that watch the children in the sunny afternoons out in the park, all liked the simple, gentle, german Lena very well. They all, too, liked very well to tease her, for it was so easy to make her mixed and troubled, and all helpless, for she could never learn to know just what the other quicker girls meant by the queer things they said.

The two or three of these girls, the ones that Lena always sat with, always worked together to confuse her. Still it was pleasant, all this life for Lena.

The little girl fell down sometimes and cried, and then Lena had to soothe her. When the little girl would drop her hat, Lena had to pick it up and hold it. When the little girl was bad and threw away her playthings, Lena told her she could not have them and took them from her to hold until the little girl should need them.

It was all a peaceful life for Lena, almost as peaceful as a pleasant leisure. The other girls, of course, did tease her, but then that only made a gentle stir within her.

Lena was a brown and pleasant creature, brown as blonde races often have them brown, brown, not with the yellow or the red or the chocolate brown of sun burned countries, but brown with the clear color laid flat on the light toned skin beneath, the plain, spare brown that makes it right to have been made with hazel eyes, and not too abundant straight, brown hair, hair that only later deepens itself into brown from the straw yellow of a german childhood.

Lena had the flat chest, straight back and forward falling shoulders of the patient and enduring working woman, though her body was now still in its milder girlhood and work had not yet made these lines too clear.

The rarer feeling that there was with Lena, showed in all the even quiet of her body movements, but in all it was the strongest in the patient, old-world ignorance, and earth made pureness of her brown, flat, soft featured face. Lena had eyebrows that were a wondrous thickness. They were black, and spread, and very cool, with their dark color and their beauty, and beneath them were her hazel eyes, simple and human, with the earth patience of the working, gentle, german woman.

Yes it was all a peaceful life for Lena. The other girls, of course, did tease her, but then that only made a gentle stir within her.

"What you got on your finger Lena," Mary, one of the girls she always sat with, one day asked her. Mary was good natured, quick, intelligent and Irish.

Lena had just picked up the fancy paper made accordion that the little girl had dropped beside her, and was making it squeak sadly as she pulled it with her brown strong, awkward finger.

"Why, what is it, Mary, paint?" said Lena, putting her finger to her mouth to taste the dirt spot.

"That's awful poison Lena, don't you know?" said Mary, "that green paint that you just tasted."

Lena has sucked a good deal of the green paint from her finger. She stopped and looked hard at the finger. She did not know just how much Mary meant by what she said.

"Ain't it poison, Nellie, that green paint, that Lena sucked just now," said Mary. "Sure it is Lena, its real poison, I ain't foolin' this time anyhow."

Lena was a little troubled. She looked hard at her finger where the paint was, and she wondered if she had really sucked it.

It was still a little wet on the edges and she rubbed it off a long time on the inside of her dress, and in between she wondered and looked at the finger and thought, was it really poison that she had just tasted.

"Ain't it too bad, Nellie, Lena should have sucked that," Mary said.

Nellie smiled and did not answer. Nellie was dark and thin, and looked Italian. She had a big mass of black hair that she wore high up on her head, and that made her face look very fine.

Nellie always smiled and did not say much, and then she would look at Lena to perplex her.

And so they all three sat with their little charges in the pleasant sunshine a long time. And Lena would often look at her finger and wonder if it was really poison that she had just tasted and then she would rub her finger on her dress a little harder.

Mary laughed at her and teased her and Nellie smiled a little and looked queerly at her.

Then it came time, for it was growing cooler, for them to drag together the little ones, who had begun to wander, and to take each one back to its own mother. And Lena never knew for certain whether it was really poison, that green stuff that she had tasted.

During these four years of service, Lena always spent her Sundays out at the house of her aunt, who had brought her four years before to Bridgepoint.

This aunt, who had brought Lena, four years before, to Bridgepoint, was a hard, ambitious, well meaning, german woman. Her husband was a grocer in the town, and they were very well to do. Mrs. Haydon, Lena's aunt, had two daughters who were just beginning as young ladies, and she had a little boy who was not honest and who was very hard to manage.

Mrs. Haydon was a short, stout, hard built, german woman. She always hit the ground very firmly and compactly as she walked. Mrs. Haydon was all a compact and well hardened mass, even to her face, reddish and darkened from its early blonde, with its hearty, shiny, cheeks, and doubled chin well covered over with the uproll from her short, square neck.

The two daughters, who were fourteen and fifteen, looked like unkneaded, unformed mounds of flesh beside her.

The elder girl, Mathilda, was blonde, and slow, and simple, and quite fat. The younger, Bertha, who was almost as tall as her sister, was dark, and quicker, and she was heavy, too, but not really fat.

These two girls the mother had brought up very firmly. They were well taught for their position. They were always both well dressed, in the same kinds of hats and dresses, as is becoming in two german sisters. The mother liked to have them dressed in red. Their best clothes were red dresses, made of good heavy cloth, and strongly trimmed with braid of a glistening black. They had stiff, red felt hats, trimmed with black velvet ribbon, and a bird. The mother dressed matronly, in a bonnet and in black, always sat between her two big daughters, firm, directing, and repressed.

The only weak spot in this good woman's conduct was the way she spoiled her boy who was not honest and who was very hard to manage.

The father of this family was a decent, quiet, heavy, and uninterfering german man. He tried to cure the boy of his bad ways, and make him honest, but the mother could not make herself let the father manage, and so the boy was brought up very badly.

Mrs. Haydon's girls were now only just beginning as young ladies, and so to get her niece, Lena, married, was just then the most important thing that Mrs. Haydon had to do.

Mrs. Haydon had four years before gone to Germany to see her parents, and had taken the girls with her. This visit had been for Mrs. Haydon most successful, though her children had not liked it very well.

Mrs. Haydon was a good and generous woman, and she patronized her parents grandly, and all the cousins who came from all about to see her. Mrs. Haydon's people were of the middling class of farmers. They were not peasants, and they lived in a town of some pretension, but it all seemed very poor and smelly to Mrs. Haydon's american born daughters.

Mrs. Haydon liked it all. It was familiar, and then here she was so wealthy and important. She listened and decided, and advised all of her relations how to do things better. She arranged their present and their future for them, and showed them how in the past they had been wrong in all their methods.

Mrs. Haydon's only trouble was with her two daughters, whom she could not make behave well to her parents. The two girls were very nasty to all their numerous relations. Their mother could hardly make them kiss their grandparents, and every day the girls would get a scolding. But then Mrs. Haydon was so very busy that she did not have time to really manage her stubborn daughters.

These hard working, earth-rough german cousins were to these american born children, ugly and dirty and as far below them as were italian or negro workmen, and they could not see how their mother could ever bear to touch them, and then all the women dressed so funny, and were worked all rough and different.

The two girls stuck up their noses at them all, and always talked in English to each other about how they hated all these people and how they wished their mother would not do so. The girls could talk some German, but they never chose to use it.

It was her eldest brother's family that most interested Mrs. Haydon. Here there were eight children, and out of the eight, five of them were girls.

Mrs. Haydon thought it would be a fine thing to take one of these girls back with her to Bridgepoint and get her well started. Everybody liked that she should do so, and they were all willing that it should be Lena.

Lena was the second girl in her large family. She was at this time just seventeen years old. Lena was not an important daughter in the family. She was always sort of dreamy and not there. She worked hard and went very regularly at it, but even good work never seemed to bring her near.

Lena's age just suited Mrs. Haydon's purpose. Lena could first go out to service, and learn how to do things, and then, when she was a little older, Mrs. Haydon could get her a good husband. And then Lena was so still and docile, she would never want to do things her own way. And then, too, Mrs. Haydon, with all her hardness had wisdom, and she could feel the rarer strain there was in Lena.

Lena was willing to go with Mrs. Haydon. Lena did not like her german life very well. It was not the hard work but the roughness that disturbed her. The people were not gentle, and the men when they were glad were very boisterous, and would lay hold of her and roughly tease her. They were good people enough around her, but it was all harsh and dreary for her.

Lena did not really know that she did not like it. She did not know that she was always dreamy and not there. She did not think whether it would be different for her away off there in Bridgepoint. Mrs. Haydon took her and got her different kinds of dresses, and then took her with them to the steamer. Lena did not really know what it was that had happened to her.

Mrs. Haydon, and her daughters, and Lena traveled second class on the steamer. Mrs. Haydon's daughters hated that their mother should take Lena. They hated to have a cousin, who was to them, little better than a nigger, and then everybody on the steamer there would see her. Mrs. Haydon's daughters said things like this to their mother, but she never stopped to hear them, and the girls did not dare to make their meaning very clear. And so they could only go on hating Lena hard, together. They could not stop her from going back with them to Bridgepoint.

Lena was very sick on the voyage. She thought, surely before it was over that she would die. She was so sick she could not even wish that she had not started. She could not eat, she could not moan, she was just blank and scared, and sure that every minute she would die. She could not hold herself in, nor help herself in her trouble. She just staid where she had been put, pale, and scared, and weak, and sick, and sure that she was going to die.

Mathilda and Bertha Haydon had no trouble from having Lena for a cousin on the voyage, until the last day that they were on the ship, and by that time they had made their friends and could explain.

Mrs. Haydon went down every day to Lena, gave her things to make her better, held her head when it was needful, and generally was good and did her duty by her.

Poor Lena had no power to be strong in such trouble. She did not know how to yield to her sickness nor endure. She lost all her little sense of being in her suffering. She was so scared, and then at her best, Lena, who was patient, sweet and quiet, had not self-control, nor any active courage.

Poor Lena was so scared and weak, and every minute she was sure that she would die.

After Lena was on land again a little while, she forgot all her bad suffering. Mrs. Haydon got her the good place, with the pleasant unexacting mistress, and her children, and Lena began to learn some English and soon was very happy and content.

All her Sundays out Lena spent at Mrs. Haydon's house. Lena would have liked much better to spend her Sundays with the girls she always sat with, and who often asked her, and who teased her and made a gentle stir within her, but it never came to Lena's unexpectant and unsuffering german nature to do something different from what was expected of her, just because she would like it that way better. Mrs. Haydon had said that Lena was to come to her house every other Sunday, and so Lena always went there.

Mrs. Haydon was the only one of her family who took any interest in Lena. Mr. Haydon did not think much of her. She was his wife's cousin and he was good to her, but she was for him stupid, and a little simple, and very dull, and sure some day to need help and to be in trouble. All young poor relations, who were brought from Germany to Bridgepoint were sure, before long, to need help and to be in trouble.

The little Haydon boy was always very nasty to her. He was a hard child for any one to manage, and his mother spoiled him very badly. Mrs. Haydon's daughters as they grew older did not learn to like Lena any better. Lena never knew that she did not like them either. She did not know that she was only happy with the other quicker girls, she always sat with in the park, and who laughed at her and always teased her.

Mathilda Haydon, the simple, fat, blonde, older daughter felt very badly that she had to say that this was her cousin Lena, this Lena who was little better for her than a nigger. Mathilda was an overgrown, slow, flabby, blonde, stupid, fat girl, just beginning as a woman; thick in her speech and dull and simple in her mind, and very jealous of all her family and of other girls, and proud that she could have good dresses and new hats and learn music, and hating very badly to have a cousin who was a common servant. And then Mathilda remembered very strongly that dirty nasty place that Lena came from and that Mathilda had so turned up her nose at, and where she had been made so angry because her mother scolded her and liked all those rough cow-smelly people.

Then, too, Mathilda would get very mad when her mother had Lena at their parties, and when she talked about how good Lena was, to certain german mothers in whose sons, perhaps, Mrs. Haydon might find Lena a good husband. All this would make the dull, blonde, fat Mathilda very angry. Sometimes she would get so angry that she would, in her thick, slow way, and with jealous anger blazing in her light blue eyes, tell her mother that she did not see how she could like that nasty Lena; and then her mother would scold Mathilda, and tell her that she knew her cousin Lena was poor and Mathilda must be good to poor people.

Mathilda Haydon did not like relations to be poor. She told all her girl friends what she thought of Lena, and so the girls would never talk to Lena at Mrs. Haydon's parties. But Lena in her unsuffering and unexpectant patience never really knew that she was slighted. When Mathilda was with her girls in the street or in the park and would see Lena, she always turned up her nose and barely nodded to her, and then she would tell her friends how funny her mother was to take care of people like that Lena, and how, back in Germany, all Lena's people lived just like pigs.

The younger daughter, the dark, large, but not fat, Bertha Haydon, who was very quick in her mind, and in her ways, and who was the favorite with her father, did not like Lena, either. She did not like her because for her Lena was a fool and so stupid, and she would let those Irish and Italian girls laugh at her and tease her, and everybody always made fun of Lena, and Lena never got mad, or even had sense enough to know that they were all making an awful fool of her.

Bertha Haydon hated people to be fools. Her father, too, thought Lena was a fool, and so neither the father nor the daughter ever paid any attention to Lena, although she came to their house every other Sunday.

Lena did not know how all the Haydons felt. She came to her aunt's house all her Sunday afternoons that she had out, because Mrs. Haydon had told her she must do so. In the same way Lena always saved all of her wages. She never thought of any way to spend it. The german cook, the good woman who always scolded Lena, helped her to put it in the bank each month, as soon as she got it. Sometimes before it got into the bank to be taken care of, somebody would ask Lena for it. The little Haydon boy sometimes asked and would get it, and sometimes some of the girls, the ones Lena always sat with, needed some more money; but the german cook, who always scolded Lena, saw to it that this did not happen very often. When it did happen she would scold Lena very sharply, and for the next few months she would not let Lena touch her wages, but put it in the bank for her on the same day that Lena got it.

So Lena always saved her wages, for she never thought to spend them, and she always went to her aunt's house for her Sundays because she did not know that she could do anything different.

Mrs. Haydon felt more and more every year that she had done right to bring Lena back with her, for it was all coming out just as she had expected. Lena was good and never wanted her own way, she was learning English, and saving all her wages, and soon Mrs. Haydon would get her a good husband.

All these four years Mrs. Haydon was busy looking around among all the german people that she knew for the right man to be Lena's husband, and now at last she was quite decided.

The man Mrs. Haydon wanted for Lena was a young german-american tailor, who worked with his father. He was good and all the family were very saving, and Mrs. Haydon was sure that this would be just right for Lena, and then too, this young tailor always did whatever his father and his mother wanted.

This old german tailor and his wife, the father and the mother of Herman Kreder, who was to marry Lena Mainz, were very thrifty, careful people. Herman was the only child they had left with them, and he always did everything they wanted. Herman was now twenty-eight years old, but he had never stopped being scolded and directed by his father and his mother. And now they wanted to see him married.

Herman Kreder did not care much to get married. He was a gentle soul and a little fearful. He had a sullen temper, too. He was obedient to his father and his mother. He always did his work well. He often went out on Saturday nights and on Sundays, with other men. He liked it with them but he never became really joyous. He liked to be with men and he hated to have women with them. He was obedient to his mother, but he did not care much to get married.

Mrs. Haydon and the elder Kreders had often talked the marriage over. They all three liked it very well. Lena would do anything that Mrs. Haydon wanted, and Herman was always obedient in everything to his father and his mother. Both Lena and Herman were saving and good workers and neither of them ever wanted their own way.

The elder Kreders, everybody knew, had saved up all their money, and they were hard, good german people, and Mrs. Haydon was sure that with these people Lena would never be in any trouble. Mr. Haydon would not say anything about it. He knew old Kreder had a lot of money and owned some good houses, and he did not care what his wife did with that simple, stupid Lena, so long as she would be sure never to need help or to be in trouble.

Lena did not care much to get married. She liked her life very well where she was working. She did not think much about Herman Kreder. She thought he was a good man and she always found him very quiet. Neither of them ever spoke much to the other. Lena did not care much just then about getting married.

Mrs. Haydon spoke to Lena about it very often. Lena never answered anything at all. Mrs. Haydon thought, perhaps Lena did not like Herman Kreder. Mrs. Haydon could not believe that any girl not even Lena, really had no feeling about getting married.

Mrs. Haydon spoke to Lena very often about Herman. Mrs. Haydon sometimes got very angry with Lena. She was afraid that Lena, for once, was going to be stubborn, now when it was all fixed right for her to be married.

"Why you stand there so stupid, why don't you answer, Lena," said Mrs. Haydon one Sunday, at the end of a long talking that she was giving Lena about Herman Kreder, and about Lena's getting married to him.

"Yes ma'am," said Lena, and then Mrs. Haydon was furious with this stupid Lena. "Why don't you answer with some sense, Lena, when I ask you if you don't like Herman Kreder. You stand there so stupid and don't answer just like you ain't heard a word what I been saying to you. I never see anybody like you, Lena. If you going to burst out at all, why don't you burst out sudden instead of standing there so silly and don't answer. And here I am so good to you, and find you a good husband so you can have a place to live in all your own. Answer me,

Lena, don't you like Herman Kreder? He is a fine young fellow, almost too good for you, Lena, when you stand there so stupid and don't make no answer. There ain't many poor girls that get the chance you got now to get married."

"Why, I do anything you say, Aunt Mathilda. Yes, I like him. He don't say much to me, but I guess he is a good man, and I do anything you say for me to do."

"Well then Lena, why you stand there so silly all the time and not answer when I asked you."

"I didn't hear you say you wanted I should say anything to you. I didn't know you wanted me to say nothing. I do whatever you tell me it's right for me to do. I marry Herman Kreder, if you want me."

And so for Lena Mainz the match was made.

Old Mrs. Kreder did not discuss the matter with her Herman. She never thought that she needed to talk such things over with him. She just told him about getting married to Lena Mainz who was a good worker and very saving and never wanted her own way, and Herman made his usual little grunt in answer to her.

Mrs. Kreder and Mrs. Haydon fixed the day and made all the arrangements for the wedding and invited everybody who ought to be there to see them married.

In three months Lena Mainz and Herman Kreder were to be married.

Mrs. Haydon attended to Lena's getting all the things that she needed. Lena had to help a good deal with the sewing. Lena did not sew very well. Mrs. Haydon scolded because Lena did not do it better, but then she was very good to Lena, and she hired a girl to come and help her. Lena still stayed on with her pleasant mistress, but she spent all her evenings and her Sundays with her aunt and all the sewing.

Mrs. Haydon got Lena some nice dresses. Lena liked that very well. Lena liked having new hats even better, and Mrs. Haydon had some made for her by a real milliner who made them very pretty.

Lena was nervous these days, but she did not think much about getting married. She did not know really what it was, that, which was always coming nearer.

Lena liked the place where she was with the pleasant mistress and the good cook, who always scolded, and she liked the girls she always sat with. She did not ask if she would like being married any better. She always did whatever her aunt said and expected, but she was always nervous when she saw the Kreders with their Herman. She was excited and she liked her new hats, and everybody teased her and every day her marrying was coming nearer, and yet she did not really know what it was, this that was about to happen to her.

Herman Kreder knew more what it meant to be married and he did not like it very well. He did not like to see girls and he did not want to have to have one alway near him. Herman always did everything that his father and his mother wanted and now they wanted that he should be married.

Herman had a sullen temper; he was gentle and he never said much. He liked to go out with other men, but he never wanted that there should be any women with them. The men all teased him about getting married. Herman did not mind the teasing but he did not like very well the getting married and having a girl always with him.

Three days before the wedding day, Herman went away to the country to be gone over Sunday. He and Lena were to be married Tuesday afternoon. When the day came Herman had not been seen or heard from.

The old Kreder couple had not worried much about it. Herman always did everything they wanted and he would surely come back in time to get married. But when Monday night came, and there was no Herman, they went to Mrs. Haydon to tell her what had happened.

Mrs. Haydon got very much excited. It was hard enough to work so as to get everything all ready, and then to have that silly Herman go off that way, so no one could tell what was going to happen. Here was Lena and everything all ready, and now they would have to make the wedding later so that they would know that Herman would be sure to be there.

Mrs. Haydon was very much excited, and then she could not say much to the old Kreder couple. She did not want to make them angry, for she wanted very badly now that Lena should be married to their Herman.

At last it was decided that the wedding should be put off a week longer. Old Mr. Kreder would go to New York to find Herman, for it was very likely that Herman had gone there to his married sister.

Mrs. Haydon sent word around, about waiting until a week from that Tuesday, to everybody that had been invited, and then Tuesday morning she sent for Lena to come down to see her.

Mrs. Haydon was very angry with poor Lena when she saw her. She scolded her hard because she was so foolish, and now Herman had gone off and nobody could tell where he had gone to, and all because Lena always was so dumb and silly. And Mrs. Haydon was just like a mother to her, and Lena always stood there so stupid and did not answer what anybody asked her, and Herman was so silly too, and now his father had to go and find him. Mrs. Haydon did not think that any old people should be good to their children. Their children always were so thankless, and never paid any attention, and older people were always doing things for their good. Did Lena think it gave Mrs. Haydon any pleasure, to work so hard to make Lena happy, and get her a good husband, and then Lena was so thankless and never did anything that anybody wanted. It was a lesson to poor Mrs. Haydon not to do things any more for anybody. Let everybody take care of themselves and never come to her with any troubles; she knew better now than to meddle to make other people happy. It just made trouble for her and her husband did not like it. He always said she was too good, and nobody ever thanked her for it, and there Lena was always standing stupid and not answering anything anybody wanted. Lena could always talk enough to those silly girls she liked so much, and always sat with, but who never did anything for her except to take away her money, and here was her aunt who tried so hard and was so good to her and treated her just like one of her own children and Lena stood there, and never made any answer and never tried to please her aunt, or to do anything that her aunt wanted. "No, it ain't no use your standin' there and cryin', now, Lena. Its too late now to care about that Herman. You should have cared some before, and then you wouldn't have to stand and cry now, and be a disappointment to me, and then I get scolded by my husband for taking care of everybody, and nobody ever thankful. I am glad you got the sense to feel sorry now, Lena, anyway, and I try to do what I can to help you out in your trouble, only you don't deserve to have anybody take any trouble for you. But perhaps you know better next time. You go home now and take care you don't spoil your clothes and that new hat, you had no business to be wearin' that this morning, but you ain't got no sense at all, Lena. I never in my life see anybody be so stupid."

Mrs. Haydon stopped and poor Lena stood there in her hat, all trimmed with pretty flowers, and the tears coming out of her eyes, and Lena did not know what it was that she had done, only she was not going to be married and it was a disgrace for a girl to be left by a man on the very day she was to be married.

Lena went home all alone, and cried in the street car.

Poor Lena cried very hard all alone in the street car. She almost spoiled her new hat with her hitting it against the window in her crying. Then she remembered that she must not do so.

The conductor was a kind man and he was very sorry when he saw her crying. "Don't feel so bad, you get another feller, you are such a nice girl," he said to make her cheerful. "But Aunt Mathilda said now, I never get married," poor Lena sobbed out for her answer. "Why you really got trouble like that," said the conductor, "I just said that now to josh you. I didn't ever think you really was left by a feller. He must be a stupid feller. But don't you worry, he wasn't much good if he could go away and leave you, lookin' to be such a nice girl. You just tell all your trouble to me, and I help you." The car was empty and the conductor sat down beside her to put his arm around her, and to be a comfort to her. Lena suddenly remembered where she was, and if she did things like that her aunt would scold her. She moved away from the man into the corner. He laughed, "Don't be scared," he said, "I wasn't going to hurt you. But you just keep up your spirit. You are a real nice girl, and you'll be sure to get a real good husband. Don't you let nobody fool you. You're all right and I don't want to scare you."

The conductor went back to his platform to help a passenger get on the car. All the time Lena stayed in the street car, he would come in every little while and reassure her, about her not to feel so bad about a man who hadn't no more sense than to go away and leave her. She'd be sure yet to get a good man, she needn't be so worried, he frequently assured her.

He chatted with the other passenger who had just come in, a very well dressed old man, and then with another who came in later, a good sort of a working man, and then another who came in, a nice lady, and he told them all about Lena's having trouble, and it was too bad there were men who treated a poor girl so badly. And everybody in the car was sorry for poor Lena and the workman tried to cheer her, and the old man looked sharply at her, and said she looked like a good girl, but she ought to be more careful and not be so careless, and things like that would not happen to her, and the nice lady went and sat beside her and Lena liked it, though she shrank away from being near her.

So Lena was feeling a little better when she got off the car, and the conductor helped her, and he called out to her, "You be sure you keep up a good heart now. He wasn't no good that feller and you were lucky for to lose him. You'll get a real man yet, one that will be better for you. Don't you be worried, you're a real nice girl as I ever see in such trouble," and the conductor shook his head and went back into his car to talk it over with the other passengers he had there.

The german cook, who always scolded Lena, was very angry when she heard the story. She never did think Mrs. Haydon would do so much for Lena, though she was always talking so grand about what she could do for everybody. The good german cook always had been a little distrustful of her. People who always thought they were so much never did really do things right for anybody. Not that Mrs. Haydon wasn't a good woman. Mrs. Haydon was a real, good, german woman, and she did really mean to do well by her niece Lena. The cook knew that very well, and she had always said so, and she always had liked and respected Mrs. Haydon, who always acted very proper to her, and Lena was so backward, when there was a man to talk to, Mrs. Haydon did have hard work when she tried to marry Lena. Mrs. Haydon was a good woman, only she did talk sometimes too grand. Perhaps this trouble would make her see it wasn't always so easy to do, to make everybody do everything just like she wanted. The cook was very sorry now for Mrs. Haydon. All this must be such a disappointment, and such a worry to her, and she really had always been very good to Lena. But Lena had better go and put on her other clothes and stop with all that crying. That wouldn't do nothing now to help her, and if Lena would be a good girl, and just be real patient, her aunt would make it all come out right yet for her. "I just tell Mrs. Aldrich, Lena, you stay here yet a little longer. You know she is always so good to you, Lena, and I know she let you, and I tell her all about that stupid Herman Kreder. I got no patience, Lena, with anybody who can be so stupid. You just stop now with your crying, Lena, and take off them good clothes and put them away so you don't spoil them when you need them, and you can help me with the dishes and everything will come off better for you. You see if I ain't right by what I tell you. You just stop crying now Lena quick, or else I scold you."

Lena still choked a little and was very miserable inside her but she did everything just as the cook told her.

The girls Lena always sat with were very sorry to see her look so sad with her trouble. Mary the Irish girl sometimes got very angry with her. Mary was always very hot when she talked of Lena's aunt Mathilda, who thought she was so grand, and had such stupid, stuck up daughters. Mary wouldn't be a fat fool like that ugly tempered Mathilda Haydon, not for anything anybody could ever give her. How Lena could keep on going there so much when they all always acted as if she was just dirt to them, Mary never could see. But Lena never had any sense of how she should make people stand round for her, and that was always all the trouble with her. And poor Lena, she was so stupid to be sorry for losing that gawky fool who didn't ever know what he wanted and just said "ja" to his mamma and his papa, like a baby, and was scared to look at a girl straight, and then sneaked away the last day like as if somebody was going to do something to him. Disgrace, Lena talking about disgrace! It was a disgrace for a girl to be seen with the likes of him, let alone to be married to him. But that poor Lena, she never did know how to show herself off for what she was really. Disgrace to have him go away and leave her. Mary would just like to get a chance to show him. If Lena wasn't worth fifteen like Herman Kreder, Mary would just eat her own head all up. It was a good riddance Lena had of that Herman Kreder and his stingy, dirty parents, and if Lena didn't stop crying about it,—Mary would just naturally despise her.

Poor Lena, she knew very well how Mary meant it all, this she was always saying to her. But Lena was very miserable inside her. She felt the disgrace it was for a decent german girl that a man should go away and leave her. Lena knew very well that her aunt was right when she said the way Herman had acted to her was a disgrace to everyone that knew her. Mary and Nellie and the other girls she always sat with were always very good to Lena but that did not make her trouble any better. It was a disgrace the way Lena had been left, to any decent family, and that could never be made any different to her.

And so the slow days wore on, and Lena never saw her Aunt Mathilda. At last on Sunday she got word by a boy to go and see her aunt Mathilda. Lena's heart beat quick for she was very nervous now with all this that had happened to her. She went just as quickly as she could to see her Aunt Mathilda.

Mrs. Haydon quick, as soon as she saw Lena, began to scold her for keeping her aunt waiting so long for her, and for not coming in all the week to see her, to see if her aunt should need her, and so her aunt had to send a boy to tell her. But it was easy, even for Lena, to see that her aunt was not really angry with her. It wasn't Lena's fault, went on Mrs. Haydon, that everything was going to happen all right for her. Mrs. Haydon was very tired taking all this trouble for her, and when Lena couldn't even take trouble to come and see her aunt, to see if she needed anything to tell her. But Mrs. Haydon really never minded things like that when she could do things for anybody. She was tired now, all the trouble she had been taking to make things right for Lena, but perhaps now Lena heard it she would learn a little to be thankful to her. "You get all ready to be married Tuesday. Lena, you hear me," said Mrs. Haydon to her. "You come here Tuesday morning and I have everything all ready for you. You wear your new dress I got you, and your hat with all them flowers on it, and you be very careful coming you don't get your things all dirty, you so careless all the time, Lena, and not thinking, and you act sometimes you never got no head at all on you. You go home, now, and you tell your Mrs. Aldrich that you leave her Tuesday. Don't you go forgetting now, Lena, anything I ever told you what you should do to be careful. You be a good girl, now Lena. You get married Tuesday to Herman Kreder." And that was all Lena ever knew of what had happened all this week to Herman Kreder. Lena forgot there was anything to know about it. She was really to be married Tuesday, and her Aunt Mathilda said she was a good girl, and now there was no disgrace left upon her.

Lena now fell back into the way she always had of being always dreamy and not there, the way she always had been, except for the few days she was so excited, because she had been left by a man the very day she was to have been married. Lena was a little nervous all these last days, but she did not think much about what it meant for her to be married.

Herman Kreder was not so content about it. He was quiet and was sullen and he knew he could not help it. He knew now he just had to let himself get married. It was not that Herman did not like Lena Mainz. She was as good as any other girl could be for him. She was a little better perhaps than other girls he saw, she was so very quiet, but Herman did not like to always have to have a girl around him. Herman had always done everything that his mother and his father wanted. His father had found him in New York, where Herman had gone to be with his married sister.

Herman's father when he had found him coaxed Herman a long time and went on whole days with his complaining to him, always troubled but gentle and quite patient with him; and always he was worrying to Herman about what was the right way his boy Herman should always do, always whatever it was his mother ever wanted from him, and always Herman never made him any answer.

Old Mr. Kreder kept on saying to him, he did not see how Herman could think now, it could be any different. When you make a bargain you just got to stick right to it, that was the only way old Mr. Kreder could ever see it, and saying you would get married to a girl and she got everything all ready, that was a bargain just like one you make in business and Herman he had made it, and now Herman he would just have to do it, old Mr. Kreder didn't see there was any other way a good boy like his Herman had, to do it. And then too that Lena Mainz was such a nice girl and Herman hadn't ought to really give his father so much trouble and make him pay out all that money, to come all the way to New York just to find him, and they both lose all that time from their working, when all Herman had to do was just to stand up, for an hour, and then he would be all right married, and it would be all over for him, and then everything at home would never be any different to him.

And his father went on; there was his poor mother saying always how her Herman always did everything before she ever wanted, and now just because he got notions in him, and wanted to show people how he could be stubborn, he was making all this trouble for her, and making them pay all that money just to run around and find him. "You got no idea Herman, how bad mama is feeling about the way you been acting Herman," said old Mr. Kreder to him. "She says she never can understand how you can be so thankless Herman. It hurts her very much you been so stubborn, and she find you such a nice girl for you, like Lena Mainz who is always just so quiet and always saves up all her wages, and she never wanting her own way at all like some girls are always all the time to have it, and your mama trying so hard, just so you could be comfortable Herman to be married, and then you act so stubborn Herman. You like all young people Herman, you think only about yourself, and what you are just wanting, and your mama she is thinking only what is good for you to have, for you in the future. Do you think your mama wants to have a girl around to be a bother, for herself, Herman. Its just for you Herman she is always thinking, and she talks always about how happy she will be, when she sees her Herman married to a nice girl, and then when she fixed it all up so good for you, so it never would be any bother to you, just the way she wanted you should like it, and you say yes all right, I do it, and then you go away like this and act stubborn, and make all this trouble everybody to take for you, and we spend money, and I got to travel all round to find you. You come home now with me Herman and get married, and I tell your mama she better not say anything to you about how much it cost me to come all the way to look for you—Hey Herman," said his father coaxing, "Hey, you come home now and get married. All you got to do Herman is just to stand up for an hour Herman, and then you don't never to have any more bother to it—Hey Herman!—you come home with me to-morrow and get married. Hey Herman."

Herman's married sister liked her brother Herman, and she had always tried to help him, when there was anything she knew he wanted. She liked it that he was so good and always did everything that their father and their mother wanted, but still she wished it could be that he could have more his own way, if there was anything he ever wanted.

But now she thought Herman with his girl was very funny. She wanted that Herman should be married. She thought it would do him lots of good to get married. She laughed at Herman when she heard the story. Until his father came to find him, she did not know why it was Herman had come just then to New York to see her. When she heard the story she laughed a good deal at her brother Herman and teased him a good deal about his running away, because he didn't want to have a girl to be all the time around him.

Herman's married sister liked her brother Herman, and she did not want him not to like to be with women. He was good, her brother Herman, and it would surely do him good to get married. It would make him stand up for himself stronger. Herman's sister always laughed at him and always she would try to reassure him. "Such a nice man as my brother Herman acting like as if he was afraid of women. Why the girls all like a man like you Herman, if you didn't always run away when you saw them. It do you good really Herman to get married, and then you got somebody you can boss around when you want to. It do you good Herman to get married, you see if you don't like it, when you really done it. You go along home now with papa, Herman and get married to that Lena. You don't know how nice you like it Herman when you try once how you can do it. You just don't be afraid of nothing, Herman. You good enough for any girl to marry, Herman. Any girl be glad to have a man like you to be always with them Herman. You just go along home with papa and try it what I say, Herman. Oh you so funny Herman, when you sit there, and then run away and leave your girl behind you. I know she is crying like anything Herman for to lose you. Don't be bad to her Herman. You go along home with papa now and get married Herman. I'd be awful ashamed Herman, to really have a brother didn't have spirit enough to get married, when a girl is just dying for to have him. You always like me to be with you Herman. I don't see why you say you don't want a girl to be all the time around you. You always been good to me Herman, and I know you always be good to that Lena, and you soon feel just like as if she had always been there with you. Don't act like as if you wasn't a nice strong man, Herman. Really I laugh at you Herman, but you know I like awful well to see you real happy. You go home and get married to that Lena, Herman. She is a real pretty girl and real nice and good and quiet and she make my brother Herman very happy. You just stop your fussing now with Herman, papa. He go with you to-morrow papa, and you see he like it so much to be married, he make everybody laugh just to see him be so happy. Really truly, that's the way it will be with you Herman. You just listen to me what I tell you Herman." And so his sister laughed at him and reassured him, and his father kept on telling what the mother always said about her Herman, and he coaxed him and Herman never said anything in answer, and his sister packed his things up and was very cheerful with him, and she kissed him, and then she laughed and then she kissed him, and his father went and bought the tickets for the train, and at last late on Sunday he brought Herman back to Bridgepoint with him.

It was always very hard to keep Mrs. Kreder from saying what she thought, to her Herman, but her daughter had written her a letter, so as to warn her not to say anything about what he had been doing, to him, and her husband came in with Herman and said, "Here we are come home mama, Herman and me, and we are very tired it was so crowded coming," and then he whispered to her. "You be good to Herman, mama, he didn't mean to make us so much trouble," and so old Mrs. Kreder, held in what she felt was so strong in her to say to her Herman. She just said very stiffly to him, "I'm glad to see you come home to-day, Herman." Then she went to arrange it all with Mrs. Haydon.

Herman was now again just like he always had been, sullen and very good, and very quiet, and always ready to do whatever his mother and his father wanted. Tuesday morning came, Herman got his new clothes on and went with his father and his mother to stand up for an hour and get married. Lena was there in her new dress, and her hat with all the pretty flowers, and she was very nervous for now she knew she was really very soon to be married. Mrs. Haydon had everything all ready. Everybody was there just as they should be and very soon Herman Kreder and Lena Mainz were married.

When everything was really over, they went back to the Kreder house together. They were all now to live together, Lena and Herman and the old father and the old mother, in the house where Mr. Kreder had worked so many years as a tailor, with his son Herman always there to help him.

Irish Mary had often said to Lena she never did see how Lena could ever want to have anything to do with Herman Kreder and his dirty stingy parents. The old Kreders were to an Irish nature, a stingy, dirty couple. They had not the free-hearted, thoughtless, fighting, mud bespattered, ragged, peat-smoked cabin dirt that irish Mary knew and could forgive and love. Theirs was the german dirt of saving, of being dowdy and loose and foul in your clothes so as to save them and yourself in washing, having your hair greasy to save it in the soap and drying, having your clothes dirty, not in freedom, but because so it was cheaper, keeping the house close and smelly because so it cost less to get it heated, living so poorly not only so as to save money but so they should never even know themselves that they had it, working all the time not only because from their nature they just had to and because it made them money but also that they never could be put in any way to make them spend their money.

This was the place Lena now had for her home and to her it was very different than it could be for an irish Mary. She too was german and was thrifty, though she was always so dreamy and not there. Lena was always careful with things and she always saved her money, for that was the only way she knew how to do it. She never had taken care of her own money and she never had thought how to use it.

Lena Mainz had been, before she was Mrs. Herman Kreder, always clean and decent in her clothes and in her person, but it was not because she ever thought about it or really needed so to have it, it was the way her people did in the german country where she came from, and her Aunt Mathilda and the good german cook who always scolded, had kept her on and made her, with their scoldings, always more careful to keep clean and to wash real often. But there was no deep need in all this for Lena and so, though Lena did not like the old Kreders, though she really did not know that, she did not think about their being stingy dirty people.

Herman Kreder was cleaner than the old people, just because it was his nature to keep cleaner, but he was used to his mother and his father, and he never thought that they should keep things cleaner. And Herman too always saved all his money, except for that little beer he drank when he went out with other men of an evening the way he always liked to do it, and he never thought of any other way to spend it. His father had always kept all the money for them and he always was doing business with it. And then too Herman really had no money, for he always had worked for his father, and his father had never thought to pay him.

And so they began all four to live in the Kreder house together, and Lena began soon with it to look careless and a little dirty, and to be more lifeless with it, and nobody ever noticed much what Lena wanted, and she never really knew herself what she needed.

The only real trouble that came to Lena with their living all four there together, was the way old Mrs. Kreder scolded. Lena had always been used to being scolded, but this scolding of old Mrs. Kreder was very different from the way she ever before had had to endure it.

Herman, now he was married to her, really liked Lena very well. He did not care very much about her but she never was a bother to him being there around him, only when his mother worried and was nasty to them because Lena was so careless, and did not know how to save things right for them with their eating, and all the other ways with money, that the old woman had to save it.

Herman Kreder had always done everything his mother and his father wanted but he did not really love his parents very deeply. With Herman it was always only that he hated to have any struggle. It was all always all right with him when he could just go along and do the same thing over every day with his working, and not to hear things, and not to have people make him listen to their anger. And now his marriage, and he just knew it would, was making trouble for him. It made him hear more what his mother was always saying, with her scolding. He had to really hear it now because Lena was there, and she was so scared and dull always when she heard it. Herman knew very well with his mother, it was all right if one ate very little and worked hard all day and did not hear her when she scolded, the way Herman always had done before they were so foolish about his getting married and having a girl there to be all the time around him, and now he had to help her so the girl could learn too, not to hear it when his mother scolded, and not to look so scared, and not to eat much, and always to be sure to save it.

Herman really did not know very well what he could do to help Lena to understand it. He could never answer his mother back to help Lena, that never would make things any better for her, and he never could feel in himself any way to comfort Lena, to make her strong not to hear his mother, in all the awful ways she always scolded. It just worried Herman to have it like that all the time around him. Herman did not know much about how a man could make a struggle with a mother, to do much to keep her quiet, and indeed Herman never knew much how to make a struggle against anyone who really wanted to have anything very badly. Herman all his life never wanted anything so badly, that he would really make a struggle against any one to get it. Herman all his life only wanted to live regular and quiet, and not talk much and to do the same way every day like every other with his working. And now his mother had made him get married to this Lena and now with his mother making all that scolding, he had all this trouble and this worry always on him.

Mrs. Haydon did not see Lena now very often. She had not lost her interest in her niece Lena, but Lena could not come much to her house to see her, it would not be right, now Lena was a married woman. And then too Mrs. Haydon had her hands full just then with her two daughters, for she was getting them ready to find them good husbands, and then too her own husband now worried her very often about her always spoiling that boy of hers, so he would be sure to turn out no good and be a disgrace to a german family, and all because his mother always spoiled him. All these things were very worrying now to Mrs. Haydon, but still she wanted to be good to Lena, though she could not see her very often. She only saw her when Mrs. Haydon went to call on Mrs. Kreder or when Mrs. Kreder came to see Mrs. Haydon, and that never could be very often. Then too these days Mrs. Haydon could not scold Lena, Mrs. Kreder was always there with her, and it would not be right to scold Lena when Mrs. Kreder was there, who had now the real right to do it. And so her aunt always said nice things now to Lena, and though Mrs. Haydon sometimes was a little worried when she saw Lena looking sad and not careful, she did not have time just then to really worry much about it.

Lena now never any more saw the girls she always used to sit with. She had no way now to see them and it was not in Lena's nature to search out ways to see them, nor did she now ever think much of the days when she had been used to see them. They never any of them had come to the Kreder house to see her. Not even Irish Mary had ever thought to come to see her. Lena had been soon forgotten by them. They had soon passed away from Lena and now Lena never thought any more that she had ever known them.

The only one of her old friends who tried to know what Lena liked and what she needed, and who always made Lena come to see her, was the good german cook who had always scolded. She now scolded Lena hard for letting herself go so, and going out when she was looking so untidy. "I know you going to have a baby Lena, but that's no way for you to be looking. I am ashamed most to see you

come and sit here in my kitchen, looking so sloppy and like you never used to
Lena. I never see anybody like you Lena. Herman is very good to you, you always say so, and he don't treat you bad ever though you don't deserve to have
anybody good to you, you so careless all the time, Lena, letting yourself go like
you never had anybody tell you what was the right way you should know how to
be looking. No, Lena, I don't see no reason you should let yourself go so and look
so untidy Lena, so I am ashamed to see you sit there looking so ugly, Lena. No
Lena that ain't no way ever I see a woman make things come out better, letting
herself go so every way and crying all the time like as if you had real trouble. I
never wanted to see you marry Herman Kreder, Lena, I knew what you got to
stand with that old woman always, and that old man, he is so stingy too and he
don't say things out but he ain't any better in his heart than his wife with her bad
ways, I know that Lena, I know they don't hardly give you enough to eat, Lena, I
am real sorry for you Lena, you know that Lena, but that ain't any way to be
going round so untidy Lena, even if you have got all that trouble. You never see
me do like that Lena, though sometimes I got a headache so I can't see to stand to
be working hardly, and nothing comes right with all my cooking, but I always see
Lena, I look decent. That's the only way a german girl can make things come out
right Lena. You hear me what I am saying to you Lena. Now you eat something
nice Lena, I got it all ready for you, and you wash up and be careful Lena and the
baby will come all right to you, and then I make your Aunt Mathilda see that you
live in a house soon all alone with Herman and your baby, and then everything go
better for you. You hear me what I say to you Lena. Now don't let me ever see
you come looking like this any more Lena, and you just stop with that always
crying. You ain't got no reason to be sitting there now with all that crying, I never
see anybody have trouble it did them any good to do the way you are doing, Lena.
You hear me Lena. You go home now and you be good the way I tell you Lena,
and I see what I can do. I make your Aunt Mathilda make old Mrs. Kreder let you
be till you get your baby all right. Now don't you be scared and so silly Lena. I
don't like to see you act so Lena when really you got a nice man and so many
things really any girl should be grateful to be having. Now you go home Lena
to-day and you do the way I say, to you, and I see what I can do to help you."

   "Yes Mrs. Aldrich" said the good german woman to her mistress later, "Yes
Mrs. Aldrich that's the way it is with them girls when they want so to get married.
They dont know when they got it good Mrs. Aldrich. They never know what it is
they're really wanting when they got it, Mrs. Aldrich. There's that poor Lena, she
just been here crying and looking so careless so I scold her, but that was no good
that marrying for that poor Lena, Mrs. Aldrich. She do look so pale and sad now
Mrs. Aldrich, it just break my heart to see her. She was a good girl was Lena,
Mrs. Aldrich, and I never had no trouble with her like I got with so many young
girls nowadays, Mrs. Aldrich, and I never see any girl any better to work right
than our Lena, and now she got to stand it all the time with that old woman Mrs.
Kreder. My! Mrs. Aldrich, she is a bad old woman to her. I never see Mrs.
Aldrich how old people can be so bad to young girls and not have no kind of
patience with them. If Lena could only live with her Herman, he ain't so bad the
way men are, Mrs. Aldrich, but he is just the way always his mother wants him,
he ain't got no spirit in him, and so I don't really see no help for that poor Lena. I
know her aunt, Mrs. Haydon, meant it all right for her Mrs. Aldrich, but poor
Lena, it would be better for her if her Herman had stayed there in New York that
time he went away to leave her. I don't like it the way Lena is looking now, Mrs.

Aldrich. She looks like as if she don't have no life left in her hardly, Mrs. Aldrich, she just drags around and looks so dirty and after all the pains I always took to teach her and to keep her nice in her ways and looking. It don't do no good to them, for them girls to get married Mrs. Aldrich, they are much better when they only know it, to stay in a good place when they got it, and keep on regular with their working. I don't like it the way Lena looks now Mrs. Aldrich. I wish I knew some way to help that poor Lena, Mrs. Aldrich, but she is a bad old woman, that old Mrs. Kreder, Herman's mother. I speak to Mrs. Haydon real soon, Mrs. Aldrich, I see what we can do now to help that poor Lena."

These were really bad days for poor Lena. Herman always was real good to her and now he even sometimes tried to stop his mother from scolding Lena. "She ain't well now mama, you let her be now you hear me. You tell me what it is you want she should be doing, I tell her. I see she does it right just the way you want it mama. You let be, I say now mama, with that always scolding Lena. You let be, I say now, you wait till she is feeling better." Herman was getting really strong to struggle, for he could see that Lena with that baby working hard inside her, really could not stand it any longer with his mother and the awful ways she always scolded.

It was a new feeling Herman now had inside him that made him feel he was strong to make a struggle. It was new for Herman Kreder really to be wanting something, but Herman wanted strongly now to be a father, and he wanted badly that his baby should be a boy and healthy. Herman never had cared really very much about his father and his mother, though always, all his life, he had done everything just as they wanted, and he had never really cared much about his wife, Lena, though he always had been very good to her, and had always tried to keep his mother off her, with the awful way she always scolded, but to be really a father of a little baby, that feeling took hold of Herman very deeply. He was almost ready, so as to save his baby from all trouble, to really make a strong struggle with his mother and with his father, too, if he would not help him to control his mother.

Sometimes Herman even went to Mrs. Haydon to talk all this trouble over. They decided then together, it was better to wait there all four together for the baby, and Herman could make Mrs. Kreder stop a little with her scolding, and then when Lena was a little stronger, Herman should have his own house for her, next door to his father, so he could always be there to help him in his working, but so they could eat and sleep in a house where the old woman could not control them and they could not hear her awful scolding.

And so things went on, the same way, a little longer. Poor Lena was not feeling any joy to have a baby. She was scared the way she had been when she was so sick on the water. She was scared now every time when anything would hurt her. She was scared and still and lifeless, and sure that every minute she would die. Lena had no power to be strong in this kind of trouble, she could only sit still and be scared, and dull, and lifeless, and sure that every minute she would die.

Before very long, Lena had her baby. He was a good, healthy little boy, the baby. Herman cared very much to have the baby. When Lena was a little stronger he took a house next door to the old couple, so he and his own family could eat and sleep and do the way they wanted. This did not seem to make much change now for Lena. She was just the same as when she was waiting with her baby. She just dragged around and was careless with her clothes and all lifeless, and she acted always and lived on just as if she had no feeling. She always did everything regular with the work, the way she always had had to do it, but she never got back any spirit in her. Herman was always good and kind, and always helped her with her working. He did everything he knew to help her. He always did all the active new things in the house and for the baby. Lena did what she had to do the way she always had been taught it. She always just kept going now with her working, and she was always careless, and dirty, and a little dazed, and lifeless. Lena never got any better in herself of this way of being that she had had ever since she had been married.

Mrs. Haydon never saw any more of her niece, Lena. Mrs. Haydon had now so much trouble with her own house, and her daughters getting married, and her boy, who was growing up, and who always was getting so much worse to manage. She knew she had done right by Lena. Herman Kreder was a good man, she would be glad to get one so good, sometimes, for her own daughters, and now they had a home to live in together, separate from the old people, who had made their trouble for them. Mrs. Haydon felt she had done very well by her niece, Lena, and she never thought now she needed any more to go and see her. Lena would do very well now without her aunt to trouble herself any more about her.

The good german cook who had always scolded, still tried to do her duty like a mother to poor Lena. It was very hard now to do right by Lena. Lena never seemed to hear now what anyone was saying to her. Herman was always doing everything he could to help her. Herman always, when he was home, took good care of the baby. Herman loved to take care of his baby. Lena never thought to take him out or to do anything she didn't have to.

The good cook sometimes made Lena come to see her. Lena would come with her baby and sit there in the kitchen, and watch the good woman cooking, and listen to her sometimes a little, the way she used to, while the good german woman scolded her for going around looking so careless when now she had no trouble, and sitting there so dull, and always being just so thankless. Sometimes Lena would wake up a little and get back into her face her old, gentle, patient, and unsuffering sweetness, but mostly Lena did not seem to hear much when the good german woman scolded. Lena always like it when Mrs. Aldrich her good mistress spoke to her kindly, and then Lena would seem to go back and feel herself to be like she was when she had been in service. But mostly Lena just lived along and was careless in her clothes, and dull, and lifeless.

By and by Lena had two more little babies. Lena was not so much scared now when she had the babies. She did not seem to notice very much when they hurt her, and she never seemed to feel very much now about anything that happened to her.

They were very nice babies, all these three that Lena had, and Herman took good care of them always. Herman never really cared much about his wife, Lena. The only things Herman ever really cared for were his babies. Herman always was very good to his children. He always had a gentle, tender way when he held them. He learned to be very handy with them. He spent all the time he was not working, with them. By and by he began to work all day in his own home so that he could have his children always in the same room with him.

Lena always was more and more lifeless and Herman now mostly never thought about her. He more and more took all the care of their three children. He saw to their eating right and their washing, and he dressed them every morning, and he taught them the right way to do things, and he put them to their sleeping, and he was now always every minute with them. Then there was to come to them, a fourth baby. Lena went to the hospital near by to have the baby. Lena seemed to be going to have much trouble with it. When the baby was come out at last, it was like its mother lifeless. While it was coming, Lena had grown very pale and sicker. When it was all over Lena had died, too, and nobody knew just how it had happened to her.

The good german cook who had always scolded Lena, and had always to the last day tried to help her, was the only one who ever missed her. She remembered how nice Lena had looked all the time she was in service with her, and how her voice had been so gentle and sweet-sounding, and how she always was a good girl, and how she never had to have any trouble with her, the way she always had with all the other girls who had been taken into the house to help her. The good cook sometimes spoke so of Lena when she had time to have a talk with Mrs. Aldrich, and this was all the remembering there now ever was of Lena.

Herman Kreder now always lived very happy, very gentle, very quiet, very well content alone with his three children. He never had a woman any more to be all the time around him. He always did all his own work in his house, when he was through every day with the work he was always doing for his father. Herman always was alone, and he always worked alone, until his little ones were big enough to help him. Herman Kreder was very well content now and he always lived very regular and peaceful, and with every day just like the next one, always alone now with his three good, gentle children.

FINIS

1909

An organized women's suffrage movement that began in the 1890s led to the passage of the Nineteenth Amendment in 1920. Here, women in 1913 are demonstrating for the right to vote.

Katherine Anne Porter
(1890–1980)

Details about Katherine Anne Porter did not become available until Joan Givner's biography *Katherine Anne Porter: A Life* was published in 1982. In interview after interview Porter retold and revised the story of her life, changing the details of her ancestors, birthdate, religion, schooling, number of husbands, and working habits to suit the picture of herself she wanted to present. Porter—who was baptized Callie Russell and changed her name on her twenty-fifth birthday—was born in 1890 in Indian Creek, Texas, to rather poor parents. Her mother died when Porter was two, and the family spent many years with her grandmother in worse poverty than before. Porter's father slid into depression after his wife died and seems to have never fully recovered.

After leaving school in 1906, Porter married for the first of four times and converted from Methodism to Catholicism, her husband's religion. Divorced nine years later, she worked briefly at her childhood aspiration of becoming an actress. Beginning in 1916 Porter earned money as a journalist in Dallas and then Denver; a year later she nearly died of influenza, during a period she describes in the novella *Pale Horse, Pale Rider* (1939). Her entire life Porter struggled with financial difficulties, poor physical and mental health, and failed relationships.

In 1918 a job with *Magazine of Mexico* brought Porter to Mexico for the first time. To Porter Mexico was her "familiar country," and it indeed provided some of the richest material for her fiction.

During the 1920s and 1930s she immersed herself in the revolutionary and artistic communities of Mexico: she taught dance, studied folk art, witnessed revolutions, and, above all, wrote. Although the bulk of her writing during this period was journalistic, she took copious notes on people she met, stories she heard, and experiences she had. It was in Mexico City that she met the young woman courted by the fat revolutionary depicted in the strong "Flowering Judas" (1930). The two women visited prisoners, one of whom died of a drug overdose. In 1929, while visiting friends in New York City, Porter wrote the story at one sitting, taking her title from T. S. Eliot's "Gerontion" (1920), in which Christ comes "in depraved May, dogwood and chestnut, flowering judas". She said repeatedly in interviews that she never deliberately put symbols in her stories—they were just naturally there. She said of "Flowering Judas" that in fact a judas tree, which symbolizes betrayal, was part of the original experience. Although she had published her first story, "María Concepción," in 1922 (when she was thirty-two), not until the publication of "Flowering Judas" did friends and editors suggest she publish a collection of short stories.

On a Guggenheim Fellowship Porter traveled to Europe in 1931. This ocean crossing became the subject of her only novel, *Ship of Fools* (1962), which she wrote intermittently over a period of thirty years. Its publication was announced several times before the book was actually finished, and Porter was seventy-two when the novel was finally published. In it she depicts the variously ridiculous, nasty, insincere, and illusioned lives of travelers set against the backdrop of the looming Nazi threat. Not a critical success, *Ship of Fools* earned tremendous popular success—it remained a best seller almost a year and was made into a movie. Although critics thought she should keep to writing short stories, the novel's financial success allowed her to stop teaching and going on lecture tours, which had supported her. Porter then settled in Washington, D.C., where in her last years she gathered her nonfiction for publication and worked on a biography of the clergyman Cotton Mather, which she never completed.

Though she was sometimes called a southern writer, Porter did not think of herself that way. She resisted the label, preferring to think of herself as a Southerner who happened to write wonderful fiction with characters not confined to regional habits of speech, thought, and manner. She always pointed out that although her youth was spent in parts of Texas, the rest of her life was spent in New York, Chicago, California, Mexico, Paris, Berlin, Bermuda, and elsewhere. Porter was in a nursing home in Maryland when she died in 1980.

Porter is typically viewed as a "stylist" and a "writer's writer," terms that annoyed her considerably. She is compared with Henry James and Gustave Flaubert for her finely wrought fiction pieces. Joan Givner calls Porter's style "restrained" and "lyrical," carried by an undercurrent of complicated irony and morality. As noted in Givner's biography, in a 1965 interview she said, "I was brought up in the generations that Miss [Gertrude] Stein described as 'lost,' but I'll be damned if I ever was lost. I always knew where I was. I sometimes wondered how I was going to get out of it, but I knew where I was and how I got there." Porter painstakingly crafted her stories word by word and rarely let editors change her work.

Porter's reputation is based primarily on the short fiction she produced during the first half of her life and her many self-dramatizing interviews. She also published a volume of essays and occasional writings, *The Days Before,* in 1952. She procrastinated regularly, always opting for distractions while complaining about the interruptions of work or company or travel. Nevertheless, she managed to produce a considerable body of work that earned her much acclaim, which took the form of a National Book Award and Pulitzer Prize for her *Collected Stories* (1965) and the Gold Medal for Fiction in 1967.

Suggested Readings: *Hacienda,* 1934. *Pale Horse, Pale Rider: Three Short Novels,* 1935. *Ship of Fools,* 1962. *Collected Stories,* 1967. *The Collected Essays and Occasional Writings of Katherine Anne Porter,* 1970. G. Hendrick, *Katherine Anne Porter,* 1965. G. Core and L. Hartley, eds., *Katherine Anne Porter: A Critical Symposium,* 1969. J. Givner, *Katherine Anne Porter: A Life,* 1982. J. Givner, ed., *Katherine Anne Porter: Conversations,* 1987.

Text Used: *Flowering Judas and Other Stories,* 1935.

FLOWERING JUDAS*

Braggioni sits heaped upon the edge of a straight-backed chair much too small for him, and sings to Laura in a furry, mournful voice. Laura has begun to find reasons for avoiding her own house until the latest possible moment, for Braggioni is there almost every night. No matter how late she is, he will be sitting there with a surly, waiting expression, pulling at his kinky yellow hair, thumbing the strings of his guitar, snarling a tune under his breath. Lupe the Indian maid meets Laura at the door, and says with a flicker of a glance towards the upper room, "He waits."

---

* The title story of Porter's first published volume, *Flowering Judas and Other Stories,* which was expanded in 1935. The Judas tree, or cercis, was named for Judas Iscariot, Jesus' betrayer, who supposedly hanged himself on one such tree.

Laura wishes to lie down, she is tired of her hairpins and the feel of her long tight sleeves, but she says to him, "Have you a new song for me this evening?" If he says yes, she asks him to sing it. If he says no, she remembers his favorite one, and asks him to sing it again. Lupe brings her a cup of chocolate and a plate of rice, and Laura eats at the small table under the lamp, first inviting Braggioni, whose answer is always the same: "I have eaten, and besides, chocolate thickens the voice."

Laura says, "Sing, then," and Braggioni heaves himself into song. He scratches the guitar familiarly as though it were a pet animal, and sings passionately off key, taking the high notes in a prolonged painful squeal. Laura, who haunts the markets listening to the ballad singers, and stops every day to hear the blind boy playing his reed-flute in Sixteenth of September Street,[1] listens to Braggioni with pitiless courtesy, because she dares not smile at his miserable performance. Nobody dares to smile at him. Braggioni is cruel to everyone, with a kind of specialized insolence, but he is so vain of his talents, and so sensitive to slights, it would require a cruelty and vanity greater than his own to lay a finger on the vast cureless wound of his self-esteem. It would require courage, too, for it is dangerous to offend him, and nobody has this courage.

Braggioni loves himself with such tenderness and amplitude and eternal charity that his followers—for he is a leader of men, a skilled revolutionist, and his skin has been punctured in honorable warfare—warm themselves in the reflected glow and say to each other: "He has a real nobility, a love of humanity raised above mere personal affections." The excess of this self-love has flowed out, inconveniently for her, over Laura, who, with so many others, owes her comfortable situation and her salary to him. When he is in a very good humor, he tells her, "I am tempted to forgive you for being a *gringa. Gringita!*"[2] and Laura, burning, imagines herself leaning forward suddenly, and with a sound back-handed slap wiping the suety smile from his face. If he notices her eyes at these moments he gives no sign.

She knows what Braggioni would offer her, and she must resist tenaciously without appearing to resist, and if she could avoid it she would not admit even to herself the slow drift of his intention. During these long evenings which have spoiled a long month for her, she sits in her deep chair with an open book on her knees, resting her eyes on the consoling rigidity of the printed page when the sight and sound of Braggioni singing threaten to identify themselves with all her remembered afflictions and to add their weight to her uneasy premonitions of the future. The gluttonous bulk of Braggioni has become a symbol of her many disillusions, for a revolutionist should be lean, animated by heroic faith, a vessel of abstract virtues. This is nonsense, she knows it now and is ashamed of it. Revolution must have leaders, and leadership is a career for energetic men. She is, her comrades tell her, full of romantic error, for what she defines as cynicism in them is merely "a developed sense of reality." She is almost too willing to say, "I am wrong, I suppose I don't really understand the principles," and afterward she makes a secret truce with herself, determined not to surrender her will to such expedient logic. But she cannot help feeling that she has been betrayed irreparably by the disunion between her way of living and her feeling of what life should be, and at times she is almost contented to rest in this sense of grievance as a private

---

[1] A street in Mexico City named for the first day of the Mexican Revolution in 1910.

[2] "American girl. Little American girl!" (Spanish), said mockingly.

store of consolation. Sometimes she wishes to run away, but she stays. Now she longs to fly out of this room, down the narrow stairs, and into the street where the houses lean together like conspirators under a single mottled lamp, and leave Braggioni singing to himself.

Instead she looks at Braggioni, frankly and clearly, like a good child who understands the rules of behavior. Her knees cling together under sound blue serge, and her round white collar is not purposely nun-like. She wears the uniform of an idea, and has renounced vanities. She was born Roman Catholic, and in spite of her fear of being seen by someone who might make a scandal of it, she slips now and again into some crumbling little church, kneels on the chilly stone, and says a Hail Mary on the gold rosary she bought in Tehuantepec.[3] It is no good and she ends by examining the altar with its tinsel flowers and ragged brocades, and feels tender about the battered doll-shape of some male saint whose white, lace-trimmed drawers hang limply around his ankles below the hieratic dignity of his velvet robe. She has encased herself in a set of principles derived from her early training, leaving no detail of gesture or of personal taste untouched, and for this reason she will not wear lace made on machines. This is her private heresy, for in her special group the machine is sacred, and will be the salvation of the workers. She loves fine lace, and there is a tiny edge of fluted cobweb on this collar, which is one of twenty precisely alike, folded in blue tissue paper in the upper drawer of her clothes chest.

Braggioni catches her glance solidly as if he had been waiting for it, leans forward, balancing his paunch between his spread knees, and sings with tremendous emphasis, weighing his words. He has, the song relates, no father and no mother, nor even a friend to console him; lonely as a wave of the sea he comes and goes, lonely as a wave. His mouth opens round and yearns sideways, his balloon cheeks grow oily with the labor of song. He bulges marvelously in his expensive garments. Over his lavender collar, crushed upon a purple necktie, held by a diamond hoop: over his ammunition belt of tooled leather worked in silver, buckled cruelly around his grasping middle: over the tops of his glossy yellow shoes Braggioni swells with ominous ripeness, his mauve silk hose stretched taut, his ankles bound with the stout leather thongs of his shoes.

When he stretches his eyelids at Laura she notes again that his eyes are the true tawny yellow cat's eye. He is rich, not in money, he tells her, but in power and this power brings with it the blameless ownership of things, and the right to indulge his love of small luxuries. "I have a taste for the elegant refinements," he said once, flourishing a yellow silk handkerchief before her nose. "Smell that? It is Jockey Club, imported from New York." Nonetheless he is wounded by life. He will say so presently. "It is true everything turns to dust in the hand, to gall on the tongue." He sighs and his leather belt creaks like a saddle girth. "I am disappointed in everything as it comes. Everything." He shakes his head. "You, poor thing, you will be disappointed too. You are born for it. We are more alike than you realize in some things. Wait and see. Some day you will remember what I have told you, you will know that Braggioni was your friend."

Laura feels a slow chill, a purely physical sense of danger, a warning in her blood that violence, mutilation, a shocking death, wait for her with lessening patience. She has translated this fear into something homely, immediate, and some-

---

[3] A town in southern Mexico.

times hesitates before crossing the street. "My personal fate is nothing, except as the testimony of a mental attitude," she reminds herself, quoting from some forgotten philosophic primer, and is sensible enough to add, "Anyhow, I shall not be killed by an automobile if I can help it."

"It may be true I am as corrupt, in another way, as Braggioni," she thinks in spite of herself, "as callous, as incomplete," and if this is so, any kind of death seems preferable. Still she sits quietly, she does not run. Where could she go? Uninvited she has promised herself to this place; she can no longer imagine herself as living in another country, and there is no pleasure in remembering her life before she came here.

Precisely what is the nature of this devotion, its true motives, and what are its obligations? Laura cannot say. She spends part of her days in Xochimilco,[4] near by, teaching Indian children to say in English, "The cat is on the mat." When she appears in the classroom they crowd about her with smiles on their wise, innocent, clay-colored faces, crying, "Good morning, my titcher!" in immaculate voices, and they make of her desk a fresh garden of flowers every day.

During her leisure she goes to union meetings and listens to busy important voices quarreling over tactics, methods, internal politics. She visits the prisoners of her own political faith in their cells, where they entertain themselves with counting cockroaches, repenting of their indiscretions, composing their memoirs, writing out manifestoes and plans for their comrades who are still walking about free, hands in pockets, sniffing fresh air. Laura brings them food and cigarettes and a little money, and she brings messages disguised in equivocal phrases from the men outside who dare not set foot in the prison for fear of disappearing into the cells kept empty for them. If the prisoners confuse night and day, and complain, "Dear little Laura, time doesn't pass in this infernal hole, and I won't know when it is time to sleep unless I have a reminder," she brings them their favorite narcotics, and says in a tone that does not wound them with pity, "Tonight will really be night for you," and though her Spanish amuses them, they find her comforting, useful. If they lose patience and all faith, and curse the slowness of their friends in coming to their rescue with money and influence, they trust her not to repeat everything, and if she inquires, "Where do you think we can find money, or influence?" they are certain to answer, "Well, there is Braggioni, why doesn't he do something?"

She smuggles letters from headquarters to men hiding from firing squads in back streets in mildewed houses, where they sit in tumbled beds and talk bitterly as if all Mexico were at their heels, when Laura knows positively they might appear at the band concert in the Alameda[5] on Sunday morning, and no one would notice them. But Braggioni says, "Let them sweat a little. The next time they may be careful. It is very restful to have them out of the way for a while." She is not afraid to knock on any door in any street after midnight, and enter in the darkness, and say to one of these men who is really in danger: "They will be looking for you—seriously—tomorrow morning after six. Here is some money from Vicente. Go to Vera Cruz[6] and wait."

She borrows money from the Roumanian agitator to give to his bitter enemy the

---

[4] A town near Mexico City known for its floating gardens.
[5] A large park in Mexico City.
[6] A city on the Gulf of Mexico.

Polish agitator. The favor of Braggioni is their disputed territory, and Braggioni holds the balance nicely, for he can use them both. The Polish agitator talks love to her over café tables, hoping to exploit what he believes is her secret sentimental preference for him, and he gives her misinformation which he begs her to repeat as the solemn truth to certain persons. The Roumanian is more adroit. He is generous with his money in all good causes, and lies to her with an air of ingenuous candor, as if he were her good friend and confidant. She never repeats anything they may say. Braggioni never asks questions. He has other ways to discover all that he wishes to know about them.

Nobody touches her, but all praise her gray eyes, and the soft, round under lip which promises gayety, yet is always grave, nearly always firmly closed: and they cannot understand why she is in Mexico. She walks back and forth on her errands, with puzzled eyebrows, carrying her little folder of drawings and music and school papers. No dancer dances more beautifully than Laura walks, and she inspires some amusing, unexpected ardors, which cause little gossip, because nothing comes of them. A young captain who had been a soldier in Zapata's[7] army attempted, during a horseback ride near Cuernavaca, to express his desire for her with the noble simplicity befitting a rude folk-hero: but gently, because he was gentle. This gentleness was his defeat, for when he alighted, and removed her foot from the stirrup, and essayed to draw her down into his arms, her horse, ordinarily a tame one, shied fiercely, reared and plunged away. The young hero's horse careered blindly after his stable-mate, and the hero did not return to the hotel until rather late that evening. At breakfast he came to her table in full charro dress, gray buckskin jacket and trousers with strings of silver buttons down the leg, and he was in a humorous, careless mood. "May I sit with you?" and "You are a wonderful rider. I was terrified that you might be thrown and dragged. I should never have forgiven myself. But I cannot admire you enough for your riding!"

"I learned to ride in Arizona," said Laura.

"If you will ride with me again this morning, I promise you a horse that will not shy with you," he said. But Laura remembered that she must return to Mexico City at noon.

Next morning the children made a celebration and spent their playtime writing on the blackboard, "We lov ar ticher," and with tinted chalks they drew wreaths of flowers around the words. The young hero wrote her a letter: "I am a very foolish, wasteful, impulsive man. I should have first said I love you, and then you would not have run away. But you shall see me again." Laura thought, "I must send him a box of colored crayons," but she was trying to forgive herself for having spurred her horse at the wrong moment.

A brown, shock-haired youth came and stood in her patio one night and sang like a lost soul for two hours, but Laura could think of nothing to do about it. The moonlight spread a wash of gauzy silver over the clear spaces of the garden, and the shadows were cobalt blue. The scarlet blossoms of the Judas tree were dull purple, and the names of the colors repeated themselves automatically in her mind, while she watched not the boy, but his shadow, fallen like a dark garment across the fountain rim, trailing in the water. Lupe came silently and whispered expert counsel in her ear: "If you will throw him one little flower, he will sing

---

[7] Emiliano Zapata (1877?–1919), one of the leaders of the Mexican Revolution; the city of Cuernavaca is south of Mexico City.

another song or two and go away." Laura threw the flower, and he sang a last song and went away with the flower tucked in the band of his hat. Lupe said, "He is one of the organizers of the Typographers Union, and before that he sold corridos in the Merced market,[8] and before that, he came from Guanajuato,[9] where I was born. I would not trust any man, but I trust least those from Guanajuato."

She did not tell Laura that he would be back again the next night, and the next, nor that he would follow her at a certain fixed distance around the Merced market, though the Zócolo,[10] up Francisco I. Madero Avenue, and so along the Paseo de la Reforma to Chapultepec Park, and into the Philosopher's Footpath, still with that flower withering in his hat, and an indivisible attention in his eyes.

Now Laura is accustomed to him, it means nothing except that he is nineteen years old and is observing a convention with all propriety, as though it were founded on a law of nature, which in the end it might well prove to be. He is beginning to write poems which he prints on a wooden press, and he leaves them stuck like handbills in her door. She is pleasantly disturbed by the abstract, unhurried watchfulness of his black eyes which will in time turn easily towards another object. She tells herself that throwing the flower was a mistake, for she is twenty-two years old and knows better; but she refuses to regret it, and persuades herself that her negation of all external events as they occur is a sign that she is gradually perfecting herself in the stoicism she strives to cultivate against that disaster she fears, though she cannot name it.

She is not at home in the world. Every day she teaches children who remain strangers to her, though she loves their tender round hands and their charming opportunist savagery. She knocks at unfamiliar doors not knowing whether a friend or a stranger shall answer, and even if a known face emerges from the sour gloom of that unknown interior, still it is the face of a stranger. No matter what this stranger says to her, nor what her message to him, the very cells of her flesh reject knowledge and kinship in one monotonous word. No. No. No. She draws her strength from this one holy talismanic word which does not suffer her to be led into evil. Denying everything, she may walk anywhere in safety, she looks at everything without amazement.

No, repeats this firm unchanging voice of her blood; and she looks at Braggioni without amazement. He is a great man, he wishes to impress this simple girl who covers her great round breasts with thick dark cloth, and who hides long, invaluably beautiful legs under a heavy skirt. She is almost thin except for the incomprehensible fullness of her breasts, like a nursing mother's, and Braggioni, who considers himself a judge of women, speculates again on the puzzle of her notorious virginity, and takes the liberty of speech which she permits without a sign of modesty, indeed, without any sort of sign, which is disconcerting.

"You think you are so cold, *gringita!* Wait and see. You will surprise yourself some day! May I be there to advise you!" He stretches his eyelids at her, and his ill-humored cat's eyes waver in a separate glance for the two points of light marking the opposite ends of a smoothly drawn path between the swollen curve of her

---

[8] "Ballads" (Spanish) in the open-air market in Mexico City.

[9] A city northwest of Mexico City.

[10] The common name of Mexico City's Constitution Square; Madero (1873–1913) was a revolutionary leader and president of Mexico (1911–1913). "Boulevard of the Reformation" (Spanish); Chapultepec is a fortress on a hill near Mexico City.

breasts. He is not put off by that blue serge, nor by her resolutely fixed gaze. There is all the time in the world. His cheeks are bellying with the wind of the song. "O girl with the dark eyes," he sings, and reconsiders. "But yours are not dark. I can change all that. O girl with the green eyes, you have stolen my heart away!" then his mind wanders to the song, and Laura feels the weight of his attention being shifted elsewhere. Singing thus, he seems harmless, he is quite harmless, there is nothing to do but sit patiently and say "No," when the moment comes. She draws a full breath, and her mind wanders also, but not far. She dares not wander too far.

Not for nothing has Braggioni taken pains to be a good revolutionist and a professional lover of humanity. He will never die of it. He has the malice, the cleverness, the wickedness, the sharpness of wit, the hardness of heart, stipulated for loving the world profitably. *He will never die of it.* He will live to see himself kicked out from his feeding trough by other hungry world-saviors. Traditionally he must sing in spite of his life which drives him to bloodshed, he tells Laura, for his father was a Tuscany[11] peasant who drifted to Yucatan and married a Maya woman: a woman of race, an aristocrat. They gave him the love and knowledge of music, thus: and under the rip of his thumbnail, the strings of the instrument complain like exposed nerves.

Once he was called Delgadito[12] by all the girls and married women who ran after him; he was so scrawny all his bones showed under his thin cotton clothing, and he could squeeze his emptiness to the very backbone with his two hands. He was a poet and the revolution was only a dream then; too many women loved him and sapped away his youth, and he could never find enough to eat anywhere, anywhere! Now he is a leader of men, crafty men who whisper in his ear, hungry men who wait for hours outside his office for a word with him, emaciated men with wild faces who waylay him at the street gate with a timid, "Comrade, let me tell you . . ." and they blow the foul breath from their empty stomachs in his face.

He is always sympathetic. He gives them handfuls of small coins from his own pocket, he promises them work, there will be demonstrations, they must join the unions and attend the meetings, above all they must be on the watch for spies. They are closer to him than his own brothers, without them he can do nothing—until tomorrow, comrade!

Until tomorrow. "They are stupid, they are lazy, they are treacherous, they would cut my throat for nothing," he says to Laura. He has good food and abundant drink, he hires an automobile and drives in the Paseo on Sunday morning, and enjoys plenty of sleep in a soft bed beside a wife who dares not disturb him; and he sits pampering his bones in easy billows of fat, singing to Laura, who knows and thinks these things about him. When he was fifteen, he tried to drown himself because he loved a girl, his first love, and she laughed at him. "A thousand women have paid for that," and his tight little mouth turns down at the corners. Now he perfumes his hair with Jockey Club, and confides to Laura: "One woman is really as good as another for me, in the dark. I prefer them all."

His wife organizes unions among the girls in the cigarette factories, and walks in picket lines, and even speaks at meetings in the evening. But she cannot be

---

[11] A region of central Italy; Mexico's Yucatan Peninsula has been home to the Maya Indians since long before the arrival of Europeans in the sixteenth century.
[12] "Skinny" (Spanish).

brought to acknowledge the benefits of true liberty. "I tell her I must have my freedom, net. She does not understand my point of view." Laura has heard this many times. Braggioni scratches the guitar and meditates. "She is an instinctively virtuous woman, pure gold, no doubt of that. If she were not, I should lock her up, and she knows it."

His wife, who works so hard for the good of the factory girls, employs part of her leisure lying on the floor weeping because there are so many women in the world, and only one husband for her, and she never knows where nor when to look for him. He told her: "Unless you can learn to cry when I am not here, I must go away for good." That day he went away and took a room at the Hotel Madrid.

It is this month of separation for the sake of higher principles that has been spoiled not only for Mrs. Braggioni, whose sense of reality is beyond criticism, but for Laura, who feels herself bogged in a nightmare. Tonight Laura envies Mrs. Braggioni, who is alone, and free to weep as much as she pleases about a concrete wrong. Laura has just come from a visit to the prison, and she is waiting for tomorrow with a bitter anxiety as if tomorrow may not come, but time may be caught immovable in this hour, with herself transfixed, Braggioni singing on forever, and Eugenio's body not yet discovered by the guard.

Braggioni says: "Are you going to sleep?" Almost before she can shake her head, he begins telling her about the May-day disturbances coming on in Morelia,[13] for the Catholics hold a festival in honor of the Blessed Virgin, and the Socialists celebrate their martyrs on that day. "There will be two independent processions, starting from either end of town, and they will march until they meet, and the rest depends . . ." He asks her to oil and load his pistols. Standing up, he unbuckles his ammunition belt, and spreads it laden across her knees. Laura sits with the shells slipping through the cleaning cloth dipped in oil, and he says again he cannot understand why she works so hard for the revolutionary idea unless she loves some man who is in it. "Are you not in love with someone?" "No," says Laura. "And no one is in love with you?" "No." "Then it is your own fault. No woman need go begging. Why, what is the matter with you? The legless beggar woman in the Alameda has a perfectly faithful lover. Did you know that?"

Laura peers down the pistol barrel and says nothing, but a long, slow faintness rises and subsides in her; Braggioni curves his swollen fingers around the throat of the guitar and softly smothers the music out of it, and when she hears him again he seems to have forgotten her, and is speaking in the hypnotic voice he uses when talking in small rooms to a listening, close-gathered crowd. Some day this world, now seemingly so composed and eternal, to the edges of every sea shall be merely a tangle of gaping trenches, of crashing walls and broken bodies. Everything must be torn from its accustomed place where it has rotted for centuries, hurled skyward and distributed, cast down again clean as rain, without separate identity. Nothing shall survive that the stiffened hands of poverty have created for the rich and no one shall be left alive except the elect spirits destined to procreate a new world cleansed of cruelty and injustice, ruled by benevolent anarchy: "Pistols are good, I love them, cannon are even better, but in the end I pin my faith to good dynamite," he concludes, and strokes the pistol lying in her hands. "Once I dreamed of destroying this city, in case it offered resistance to General Ortíz,[14] but it fell into his hands like an overripe pear."

---

[13] A city west of Mexico City.
[14] Pascual Ortíz Rubio (1877–1963), a revolutionary leader and president of Mexico (1930–1932).

He is made restless by his own words, rises and stands waiting. Laura holds up the belt to him: "Put that on, and go kill somebody in Morelia, and you will be happier," she says softly. The presence of death in the room makes her bold. "Today, I found Eugenio going into a stupor. He refused to allow me to call the prison doctor. He had taken all the tablets I brought him yesterday. He said he took them because he was bored."

"He is a fool, and his death is his own business," says Braggioni, fastening his belt carefully.

"I told him if he had waited only a little while longer, you would have got him set free," says Laura. "He said he did not want to wait."

"He is a fool and we are well rid of him," says Braggioni, reaching for his hat.

He goes away. Laura knows his mood has changed, she will not see him any more for a while. He will send word when he needs her to go on errands into strange streets, to speak to the strange faces that will appear, like clay masks with the power of human speech, to mutter their thanks to Braggioni for his help. Now she is free, and she thinks, I must run while there is time. But she does not go.

Braggioni enters his own house where for a month his wife has spent many hours every night weeping and tangling her hair upon her pillow. She is weeping now, and she weeps more at the sight of him, the cause of all her sorrows. He looks about the room. Nothing is changed, the smells are good and familiar, he is well acquainted with the woman who comes toward him with no reproach except grief on her face. He says to her tenderly: "You are so good, please don't cry any more, you dear good creature." She says, "Are you tired, my angel? Sit here and I will wash your feet." She brings a bowl of water, and kneeling, unlaces his shoes, and when from her knees she raises her sad eyes under her blackened lids, he is sorry for everything, and bursts into tears. "Ah, yes, I am hungry, I am tired, let us eat something together," he says, between sobs. His wife leans her head on his arm and says, "Forgive me!" and this time he is refreshed by the solemn, endless rain of her tears.

Laura takes off her serge dress and puts on a white linen nightgown and goes to bed. She turns her head a little to one side, and lying still, reminds herself that it is time to sleep. Numbers tick in her brain like little clocks, soundless doors close of themselves around her. If you would sleep, you must not remember anything, the children will say tomorrow, good morning, my teacher, the poor prisoners who come every day bringing flowers to their jailor. 1-2-3-4-5—it is monstrous to confuse love with revolution, night with day, life with death—ah, Eugenio!

The tolling of the midnight bell is a signal, but what does it mean? Get up, Laura, and follow me: come out of your sleep, out of your bed, out of this strange house. What are you doing in this house? Without a word, without fear she rose and reached for Eugenio's hand, but he eluded her with a sharp, sly smile and drifted away. This is not all, you shall see—Murderer, he said, follow me, I will show you a new country, but it is far away and we must hurry. No, said Laura, not unless you take my hand, no; and she clung first to the stair rail, and then to the topmost branch of the Judas tree that bent down slowly and set her upon the earth, and then to the rocky ledge of a cliff, and then to the jagged wave of a sea that was not water but a desert of crumbling stone. Where are you taking me, she asked in wonder but without fear. To death, and it is a long way off, and we must hurry, said Eugenio. No, said Laura, not unless you take my hand. Then eat these flowers, poor prisoner, said Eugenio in a voice of pity, take and eat: and from the

Judas tree he stripped the warm bleeding flowers, and held them to her lips. She saw that his hand was fleshless, a cluster of small white petrified branches, and his eye sockets were without light, but she ate the flowers greedily for they satisfied both hunger and thirst. Murderer! said Eugenio, and Cannibal! This is my body and my blood. Laura cried No! and at the sound of her own voice, she awoke trembling, and was afraid to sleep again.

1930

F. Scott Fitzgerald
(1896–1940)

Near the end of F. Scott Fitzgerald's novel *The Great Gatsby* (1925), Jay Gatsby's father shows the narrator, Nick Carraway, a book Jay had owned as a boy. On the flyleaf Gatsby (then known by his true, prosaic name, Jimmy Gatz) had written a detailed daily schedule of activities for self-improvement. The passage clearly alludes to the *Autobiography* (1867) of Benjamin Franklin, who had designed charts and calendars to outline an optimistic "campaign for moral perfection," according to which a person could theoretically eliminate all personality flaws—effectively making oneself anew—simply by sticking to the schedule. In *Gatsby* Fitzgerald conveys the young Gatz's Franklinesque determination to remake himself by means of such scheduling: "dumbbell exercise and wall-scaling" (6:15–6:30 A.M.), the study of "elocution, poise, and how to attain it" (5:00–6:00 P.M.), the "study [of] needed inventions" (7:00–9:00 P.M.), and so on. That this document is produced by Mr. Gatz after his son, the rich, awe-inspiring party-giver Gatsby, is dead is a central irony of the novel. Readers learn along with Nick that young Jimmy Gatz's self-perfection schemes had led him to "success" as a bootlegger and a fraud.

The late eighteenth century had Benjamin Franklin; the late nineteenth century, Horatio Alger, whose inspirational rags-to-riches stories for boys preached the gospel of the Protestant ethic—success through humble diligence. F. Scott Fitzgerald gave the early twentieth century Jay Gatsby both to continue and subvert the tradition. Gatz/Gatsby had exploited the myth of the self-made man, acquiring a new identity and an enormous illegal fortune by playing upon gullible Americans who, like Nick Carraway, believed in the myth. The irony of Jimmy Gatz's fabrication of "Jay Gatsby" sheds light on the career of Fitzgerald, who lived that traditional American myth as well as investigated its condition in an era that seemed to have superseded Franklin's pragmatic moral earnestness in favor of a remorseless opportunism, a worship of prosperity and pleasure.

Jimmy Gatz started out in North Dakota and ended up murdered in "West Egg," a wealthy Long Island suburb; Fitzgerald came from St. Paul, Minnesota, and unhappily wound up in that factory of American self-fabrication, Hollywood. He was born the only child of Irish Catholic parents in 1896 and named Frances Scott Key Fitzgerald, after the author of "The Star-Spangled Banner," a distant maternal ancestor. Fitzgerald's mother, a descendant of well-to-do Southerners, was the daughter of one of St. Paul's most prominent businessmen. Married relatively late to Edward Fitzgerald, Mollie McQuillan inherited money that kept the family near the upper middle-class life style to which they were accustomed. Edward's business failures made this legacy all the more important, for Mollie had great plans for her son in the business world. His own youthful dreams of literary fame were just as great.

Fitzgerald was sent to a Catholic boarding school in New Jersey in 1911 and, barely passing his entrance exams, entered Princeton University in 1914. He compiled a very poor record during his college years, but academia was hardly his main concern. He later called the Princeton of his era "the pleasantest country club in America," and from the start he strove assiduously to exploit its opportunities for social success. No natural athlete, he tried in vain to make the football team; that failure never ceased festering. He compensated by making his way into undergraduate literary circles. Two fellow Princetonians, John Peale Bishop and Edmund Wilson, were to be valued supporters and friends—and sometimes harsh critics—throughout Fitzgerald's literary career.

In spring 1917 America entered World War I in Europe. Dropping out of Princeton in his senior year, Fitzgerald obtained an infantry commission. Convinced he would die on the battlefield, he furiously began writing a novel aptly called "The Romantic Egoist," intending to leave the world evidence of his genius. In fact, he never shipped out. While in training camp near Montgomery, Alabama, Fitzgerald met Zelda Sayre, a vivacious eighteen-year-old socialite, at a country club ball and soon fell in love with her. Zelda and her parents balked at the idea of her marrying an unpublished aspiring writer, so, with his discharge in hand, Fitzgerald headed to New York alone to make his fame and fortune.

What ensued looks in retrospect like a sad parody of the Franklin or Alger myth, specially adapted to the literary world. A young editor at Scribners, Max Perkins, thought "The Romantic Egoist" showed great promise, but the house declined to publish it without revision. Fitzgerald landed a job in an advertising agency and spent nights writing stories, verse, and revising his novel, which garnered 122 rejection slips in spring 1919. But when he sent his novel back to Scribners, Perkins backed it wholeheartedly and persuaded his senior colleagues to accept it. They could hardly have regretted the decision: *This Side of Paradise* (1920), as the book was renamed, sold out its first printing in three days, went through twelve printings in two years, and made Fitzgerald an instant celebrity. Partly autobiographical, it portrayed "the contemporary American in adolescence and young manhood," and both book and author rose upon a groundswell of enthusiasm for the values and concerns of youth. Poetic and irreverent in message and style, it seemed to speak for a whole generation and to affront and ignore the older representatives of established American society. Princeton president John Grier Hibben wrote Fitzgerald to say he was "grieved" by the novel's depiction of the "calculation and snobbishness" of university men, but other readers celebrated the work for its "self-criticism."

Soon Fitzgerald was quoted widely in the popular press as an authority on the new social and sexual mores of 1920. Interviews and articles with titles such as "Fitzgerald, Flappers, and Fame" treated him as the "Flapper Philosopher." One week after publication of *This Side of Paradise,* Fitzgerald married Zelda, seemingly inaugurating the new American decade that in a later book he named "the Jazz Age." It was the beginning of the illusory identity "F. Scott Fitzgerald"—the embodiment of 1920s hedonism—that the real Fitzgerald was never be able to shed. New York gloriously feted him, twenty-three, and Zelda, nineteen. They danced in the fountain outside the Plaza Hotel; they rode atop taxis; the bootleg alcohol flowed. Fitzgerald somehow managed to keep writing, producing the short-story collections *Flappers and Philosophers* (1920) and *Tales of the Jazz Age* (1922) and the novel *The Beautiful and Damned* (1922).

The Fitzgeralds bought a house in Great Neck, the Long Island town on which West Egg of *The Great Gatsby* was modeled. Financially imprudent, to say the least—their monthly budget shows generous sums earmarked for such uses as "wild parties"—they soon found themselves heavily in debt. Fitzgerald attempted to ease their debt by writing numerous magazine pieces, including a self-mocking essay entitled "How to Live on $36,000 a Year" for the *Saturday Evening Post* (April 5, 1924)—while most Americans earned about $1,500 a year.

In 1921 a daughter, their only child, was born. In summer 1924 the Fitzgeralds went abroad, ostensibly for a less costly life style. They settled on the French Riviera, and Fitzgerald worked on *The Great Gatsby*. The novel is now considered his finest, perhaps one of the best novels written by an American. Yet, when it appeared in 1925 it was greeted with only modest praise (although T. S. Eliot considered it "the first step that American fiction has taken since Henry James"), and its sales were half those of *This Side of Paradise*. By the time the novel was published, the Fitzgeralds were in Paris, where they met Ernest Hemingway, Gertrude Stein, Ezra Pound, and others; but Fitzgerald kept his distance from Paris's expatriate literary life, writing only for American magazines and seeking no entry into French intellectual circles. He and Zelda continued their inebriated high jinks with desperate gaiety. In the 1931 story "Babylon Revisited," Fitzgerald's memories of this time of dissipation in Paris were expressed by his protagonist, Charlie Wales—memories of "champagne dinners and long luncheons that began at two and ended in a blurred and vague twilight," of relentless "catering to vice and waste." Plans were underway for a fourth novel, but it was 1934 before *Tender Is the Night* appeared.

In the late 1920s and the 1930s the money continued to come in: in 1928 the *Saturday Evening Post* paid Fitzgerald $4,000 per short story. However, in his personal ledger of that year he made the entry "Thirty-two years old . . . OMINOUS No Real Progress in ANY way + *wrecked myself with dozens of people*." He had most conspicuously wrecked himself with Zelda, as she had with him: their marriage, already strained by infidelities on both sides, threatened to collapse. The couple's deterioration had vaguely been predicted in *The Beautiful and the Damned*.

A writer of promise and an aspiring dancer, Zelda Fitzgerald was frustrated by her husband's greater success and resented his rather condescending encouragement of her efforts. In 1930 she suffered a breakdown and was diagnosed as schizophrenic; from then until her death in 1947 she spent much time in asylums and clinics. It was in December 1930 while Zelda was undergoing treatment in Switzerland that Fitzgerald wrote "Babylon Revisited." They returned to America in 1931, and Zelda entered a hospital near Baltimore and worked determinedly on an autobiographical novel, *Save Me the Waltz*. At first furious, Fitzgerald eventually helped warm Max Perkins to the book, which was published in 1932 to poor sales and reviews.

In summer 1932 he worked hard at his long-deferred novel *Tender Is the Night,* a subtle examination of the process by which the protagonist, a gifted doctor, "betrays his genius" by becoming involved with a group of dissolute American expatriates in Europe. Fitzgerald felt that he had committed such a self-betrayal, and his portrait of Dick and Nicole Diver conveys much of the contempt, remorse, and pity with which he regarded himself and Zelda. Written in the midst of the Great Depression, when American literary concerns were predominantly social and political, the novel did not sell well. To many readers its story of pleasure-seeking expatriates seemed a vestige of the roaring twenties. The poet Horace Gregory summed up many critics' views of *Tender Is the Night* by writing that, though superficially appealing, the novel never criticizes "the entire system which has made such creatures as [Fitzgerald's characters] possible."

Responding to his doctor's advice, Fitzgerald made several unsuccessful attempts to give up drinking; he was hospitalized for alcoholism several times from 1933 on. He continued to produce magazine stories and essays—publishing one last story collection, *Taps at Reveille,* in 1935—but he was increasingly regarded as a rather pathetic has-been. He turned his own "betrayal of his genius" into marketable subject matter for a series of alternately self-critical and self-pitying articles for *Esquire,* beginning with "The Crack-Up" in late 1935. Fitzgerald was censured by a cutting comment in Hemingway's story "The Snows of Kilimanjaro" (1936) and publicly humiliated on his fortieth birthday by a *New York Post* article entitled "The Other Side of Paradise / Scott Fitzgerald, 40, / Engulfed in Despair / Broken in Health He Spends Birthday Re- / gretting That He Has Lost Faith in His Star." The drinking and debts worsened.

In 1937 Fitzgerald went to Hollywood, hired as a screenwriter by Metro-Goldwyn-Mayer. Much of his initial salary of $1,000 a week was spent on Zelda's hospitalization and their daughter's college tuition as well as on his many debts. He began an affair with Sheilah Graham, a Hollywood gossip columnist, that lasted until his death. Although Fitzgerald earned more money in Hollywood than he had ever made from his fiction and worked on many film scripts (including a stint on *Gone With the Wind* [1939]), he never became the top movie writer he hoped to be. In late 1940, at the nadir of his career but with a new novel well underway, Fitzgerald died suddenly of a heart attack. Ironically, his literary reputation was soon steadily revived, partly through the efforts of the critic Edmund Wilson, Fitzgerald's college friend. Wilson oversaw publication of that unfinished novel, *The Last Tycoon* (1941), and *The Crack-Up* (1945), a selection of Fitzgerald's writings from the 1930s. *The Stories of F. Scott Fitzgerald* (1951), edited by Malcolm Cowley, continued the resurgence of interest in Fitzgerald's work.

Suggested Readings: *This Side of Paradise,* 1920. *The Beautiful and Damned,* 1922. *Tales of the Jazz Age,* 1922. *The Great Gatsby,* 1925. *Tender Is the Night,* 1934. *The Last Tycoon,* 1941. *The Crack-Up,* ed. E. Wilson, 1945. *Correspondence of F. Scott Fitzgerald,* eds. M. J. Bruccoli and M. M. Duggan, 1980. A. Kazin, ed. *F. Scott Fitzgerald: The Man and His Work,* 1951. S. Graham and R. Grant, *Beloved Infidel,* 1958. A. Mizener, *The Far Side of Paradise,* 1965. S. Perosa, *The Art of F. Scott Fitzgerald,* trans. C. Matz and S. Perosa, 1965. M. Cowley, and R. Cowley, eds. *Fitzgerald and the Jazz Age,* 1966. M. R. Stern, *The Golden Moment: The Novels of F. Scott Fitzgerald,* 1970. M. J. Bruccoli, *F. Scott Fitzgerald: A Descriptive Bibliography,* 1972. R. A. Gallo, *F. Scott Fitzgerald,* 1978. M. J. Bruccoli, ed., *Some Kind of Epic Grandeur: The Life of F. Scott Fitzgerald,* 1981. S. Donaldson, *Fool for Love: F. Scott Fitzgerald,* 1983.

Text Used: *The Stories of F. Scott Fitzgerald,* 1951.

BABYLON REVISITED*

"And where's Mr. Campbell?" Charlie asked.

"Gone to Switzerland. Mr. Campbell's a pretty sick man, Mr. Wales."

"I'm sorry to hear that. And George Hardt?" Charlie inquired.

"Back in America, gone to work."

"And where is the Snow Bird?"[1]

"He was in here last week. Anyway, his friend, Mr. Schaeffer, is in Paris."

---

* Babylon is an ancient city-kingdom in Southwest Asia where the Israelites fled into exile after the destruction of the first Temple (587 B.C.); the name is synonymous with civic corruption and perverse luxury. The story was first published in the *Saturday Evening Post* on February 21, 1931, and collected in *Taps at Reveille* (1935).

[1] Slang for a cocaine ("snow") addict who also sometimes sells the drug.

Two familiar names from the long list of a year and a half ago. Charlie scribbled an address in his notebook and tore out the page.

"If you see Mr. Schaeffer, give him this," he said. "It's my brother-in-law's address. I haven't settled on a hotel yet."

He was not really disappointed to find Paris was so empty. But the stillness in the Ritz bar[2] was strange and portentous. It was not an American bar any more—he felt polite in it, and not as if he owned it. It had gone back into France. He felt the stillness from the moment he got out of the taxi and saw the doorman, usually in a frenzy of activity at this hour, gossiping with a *chasseur*[3] by the servants' entrance.

Passing through the corridor, he heard only a single, bored voice in the once-clamorous women's room. When he turned into the bar he traveled the twenty feet of green carpet with his eyes fixed straight ahead by old habit; and then, with his foot firmly on the rail, he turned and surveyed the room, encountering only a single pair of eyes that fluttered up from a newspaper in the corner. Charlie asked for the head barman, Paul, who in the latter days of the bull market had come to work in his own custom-built car—disembarking, however, with due nicety at the nearest corner. But Paul was at his country house today and Alix giving him information.

"No, no more," Charlie said, "I'm going slow these days."

Alix congratulated him: "You were going pretty strong a couple of years ago."

"I'll stick to it all right," Charlie assured him. "I've stuck to it for over a year and a half now."

"How do you find conditions in America?"

"I haven't been to America for months. I'm in business in Prague, representing a couple of concerns there. They don't know about me down there."

Alix smiled.

"Remember the night of George Hardt's bachelor dinner here?" said Charlie. "By the way, what's become of Claude Fessenden?"

Alix lowered his voice confidentially: "He's in Paris, but he doesn't come here any more. Paul doesn't allow it. He ran up a bill of thirty thousand francs, charging all his drinks and his lunches, and usually his dinner, for more than a year. And when Paul finally told him he had to pay, he gave him a bad check."

Alix shook his head sadly.

"I don't understand it, such a dandy fellow. Now he's all bloated up—"He made a plump apple of his hands.

Charlie watched a group of strident queens[4] installing themselves in a corner.

"Nothing affects them," he thought. "Stocks rise and fall, people loaf or work, but they go on forever." The place oppressed him. He called for the dice and shook with Alix for the drink.

"Here for long, Mr. Wales?"

"I'm here for four or five days to see my little girl."

"Oh-h! You have a little girl?"

Outside, the fire-red, gas-blue, ghost-green signs shone smokily through the tranquil rain. It was late afternoon and the streets were in movement; the *bistros*

---

[2] The bar at the Ritz Hotel in Paris, a prime gathering spot for rich Americans; Fitzgerald mentions many well-known Parisian locales.
[3] A hotel porter (French).   [4] Male homosexuals.

gleamed. At the corner of the Boulevard des Capucines he took a taxi. The Place de la Concorde[5] moved by in pink majesty; they crossed the logical Seine, and Charlie felt the sudden provincial quality of the left bank.[6]

Charlie directed his taxi to the Avenue de l'Opera, which was out of his way. But he wanted to see the blue hour spread over the magnificent façade, and imagine that the cab horns, playing endlessly the first few bars of *Le Plus que Lent*,[7] were the trumpets of the Second Empire. They were closing the iron grill in front of Brentano's Book-store, and people were already at dinner behind the trim little bourgeois hedge of Duval's. He had never eaten at a really cheap restaurant in Paris. Five-course dinner, four francs fifty, eighteen cents, wine included. For some odd reason he wished that he had.

As they rolled on to the Left Bank and he felt its sudden provincialism, he thought, "I spoiled this city for myself. I didn't realize it, but the days came along one after another, and then two years were gone, and everything was gone, and I was gone."

He was thirty-five, and good to look at. The Irish mobility of his face was sobered by a deep wrinkle between his eyes. As he rang his brother-in-law's bell in the Rue Palatine, the wrinkle deepened till it pulled down his brows; he felt a cramping sensation in his belly. From behind the maid who opened the door darted a lovely little girl of nine who shrieked "Daddy!" and flew up, struggling like a fish, into his arms. She pulled his head around by one ear and set her cheek against his.

"My old pie," he said.

"Oh, daddy, daddy, daddy, daddy, dads, dads, dads!"

She drew him into the salon, where the family waited, a boy and a girl his daughter's age, his sister-in-law and her husband. He greeted Marion with his voice pitched carefully to avoid either feigned enthusiasm or dislike, but her response was more frankly tepid, though she minimized her expression of unalterable distrust by directing her regard toward his child. The two men clasped hands in a friendly way and Lincoln Peters rested his for a moment on Charlie's shoulder.

The room was warm and comfortably American. The three children moved intimately about, playing through the yellow oblongs that led to other rooms; the cheer of six o'clock spoke in the eager smacks of the fire and the sounds of French activity in the kitchen. But Charlie did not relax; his heart sat up rigidly in his body and he drew confidence from his daughter, who from time to time came close to him, holding in her arms the doll he had brought.

"Really extremely well," he declared in answer to Lincoln's question. "There's a lot of business there that isn't moving at all, but we're doing even better than ever. In fact, damn well. I'm bringing my sister over from America next month to keep house for me. My income last year was bigger than it was when I had money. You see, the Czechs————"

---

[5] A famous square in Paris; symbolic in that Charlie Wales is in Paris to reach a "concord" with his past and with his sister-in-law, the legal guardian of his daughter.

[6] He crosses from the cosmopolitan Right Bank of the Seine River to the less pretentious Left Bank, where the Peterses live.

[7] "The slowest of the slow" (French), the title of a waltz by Claude Debussy (1862–1918), to express the mood of Parisian cafés and cabarets. The Second Empire (1852–1871) in France was the period of modernization and expansion under Louis Napoleon (1808–1873), Emperor Napoleon III; the broad boulevards of Paris were laid out then.

His boasting was for a specific purpose; but after a moment, seeing a faint restiveness in Lincoln's eye, he changed the subject:

"Those are fine children of yours, well brought up, good manners."

"We think Honoria's a great little girl too."

Marion Peters came back from the kitchen. She was a tall woman with worried eyes, who had once possessed a fresh American loveliness. Charlie had never been sensitive to it and was always surprised when people spoke of how pretty she had been. From the first there had been an instinctive antipathy between them.

"Well, how do you find Honoria?" she asked.

"Wonderful. I was astonished how much she's grown in ten months. All the children are looking well."

"We haven't had a doctor for a year. How do you like being back in Paris?"

"It seems very funny to see so few Americans around."

"I'm delighted," Marion said vehemently. "Now at least you can go into a store without their assuming you're a millionaire. We've suffered like everybody,[8] but on the whole it's a good deal pleasanter."

"But it was nice while it lasted," Charlie said. "We were sort of royalty, almost infallible, with a sort of magic around us. In the bar this afternoon"—he stumbled, seeing his mistake—"there wasn't a man I knew."

She looked at him keenly. "I should think you'd have had enough of bars."

"I only stayed a minute. I take one drink every afternoon, and no more."

"Don't you want a cocktail before dinner?" Lincoln asked.

"I take only one drink every afternoon, and I've had that."

"I hope you keep to it," said Marion.

Her dislike was evident in the coldness with which she spoke, but Charlie only smiled; he had larger plans. Her very aggressiveness gave him an advantage, and he knew enough to wait. He wanted them to initiate the discussion of what they knew had brought him to Paris.

At dinner he couldn't decide whether Honoria was most like him or her mother. Fortunate if she didn't combine the traits of both that had brought them to disaster. A great wave of protectiveness went over him. He thought he knew what to do for her. He believed in character; he wanted to jump back a whole generation and trust in character again as the eternally valuable element. Everything else wore out.

He left soon after dinner, but not to go home. He was curious to see Paris by night with clearer and more judicious eyes than those of other days. He bought a *strapontin*[9] for the Casino and watched Josephine Baker go through her chocolate arabesques.

After an hour he left and strolled toward Montmartre, up the Rue Pigalle[10] into the Place Blanche. The rain had stopped and there were a few people in evening clothes disembarking from taxis in front of cabarets, and *cocottes*[11] prowling singly or in pairs, and many Negroes. He passed a lighted door from which issued

---

[8] Two years after the 1929 crash of the American stock market, the depression hit Paris, decimating its large American colony.

[9] A low-priced flip-up seat in a theater or cabaret (French); here, a ticket for such a seat. Josephine Baker (1906–1975) was an African-American singer and dancer whose erotic performances made her the rage of Paris nightclubs in the 1920s and 1930s.

[10] A district of risqué night life; Fitzgerald names several popular clubs, such as Bricktop's.

[11] "Prostitutes" (French).

music, and stopped with the sense of familiarity; it was Bricktop's, where he had parted with so many hours and so much money. A few doors farther on he found another ancient rendezvous and incautiously put his head inside. Immediately an eager orchestra burst into sound, a pair of professional dancers leaped to their feet and a maître d'hôtel swooped toward him, crying, "Crowd just arriving, sir!" But he withdrew quickly.

"You have to be damn drunk," he thought.

Zelli's was closed, the bleak and sinister cheap hotels surrounding it were dark; up in the Rue Blanche there was more light and a local, colloquial French crowd. The Poet's Cave had disappeared, but the two great mouths of the Café of Heaven and the Café of Hell still yawned—even devoured, as he watched, the meager contents of a tourist bus—a German, a Japanese, and an American couple who glanced at him with much frightened eyes.

So much for the effort and ingenuity of Montmartre. All the catering to vice and waste was on an utterly childish scale, and he suddenly realized the meaning of the word "dissipate"—to dissipate into thin air; to make nothing out of something. In the little hours of the night every move from place to place was an enormous human jump, an increase of paying for the privilege of slower and slower motion.

He remembered thousand-franc notes given to an orchestra for playing a single number, hundred-franc notes tossed to a doorman for calling a cab.

But it hadn't been given for nothing.

It had been given, even the most wildly squandered sum, as an offering to destiny that he might not remember the things most worth remembering, the things that now he would always remember—his child taken from his control, his wife escaped to a grave in Vermont.

In the glare of a *brasserie*[12] a woman spoke to him. He bought her some eggs and coffee, and then, eluding her encouraging stare, gave her a twenty-franc note and took a taxi to his hotel.

II

He woke upon a fine fall day—football weather. The depression of yesterday was gone and he liked the people on the streets. At noon he sat opposite Honoria at Le Grand Vatel, the only restaurant he could think of not reminiscent of champagne dinners and long luncheons that began at two and ended in a blurred and vague twilight.

"Now, how about vegetables? Oughtn't you to have some vegetables?"

"Well, yes."

"Here's *épinards* and *chou-fleur* and carrots and *haricots*."[13]

"I'd like *chou-fleur*."

"Wouldn't you like to have two vegetables?"

"I usually only have one at lunch."

The waiter was pretending to be inordinately fond of children. *"Qu'elle est mignonne la petite! Elle parle exactement comme une Française."*[14]

---

[12] A restaurant and bar (French).   [13] "Spinach," "cauliflower," "beans" (French).
[14] "What a little darling she is! She speaks just like a French girl" (French).

"How about dessert? Shall we wait and see?"

The waiter disappeared. Honoria looked at her father expectantly.

"What are we going to do?"

"First, we're going to that toy store in the Rue Saint-Honoré and buy you anything you like. And then we're going to the vaudeville at the Empire."

She hesitated. "I like it about the vaudeville, but not the toy store."

"Why not?"

"Well, you brought me this doll." She had it with her. "And I've got lots of things. And we're not rich any more, are we?"

"We never were. But today you are to have anything you want."

"All right," she agreed resignedly.

When there had been her mother and a French nurse he had been inclined to be strict; now he extended himself, reached out for a new tolerance; he must be both parents to her and not shut any of her out of communication.

"I want to get to know you," he said gravely. "First let me introduce myself. My name is Charles J. Wales, of Prague."

"Oh, daddy!" her voice cracked with laughter.

"And who are you, please?" he persisted, and she accepted a rôle immediately: "Honoria Wales, Rue Palatine, Paris."

"Married or single?"

"No, not married. Single."

He indicated the doll. "But I see you have a child, madame."

Unwilling to disinherit it, she took it to her heart and thought quickly: "Yes, I've been married, but I'm not married now. My husband is dead."

He went on quickly, "And the child's name?"

"Simone. That's after my best friend at school."

"I'm very pleased that you're doing so well at school."

"I'm third this month," she boasted. "Elsie"—that was her cousin—"is only about eighteenth, and Richard is about at the bottom."

"You like Richard and Elsie, don't you?"

"Oh, yes. I like Richard quite well and I like her all right."

Cautiously and casually he asked: "And Aunt Marion and Uncle Lincoln—which do you like best?"

"Oh, Uncle Lincoln, I guess."

He was increasingly aware of her presence. As they came in, a murmur of " . . . adorable" followed them, and now the people at the next table bent all their silences upon her, staring as if she were something no more conscious than a flower.

"Why don't I live with you?" she asked suddenly. "Because mamma's dead?"

"You must stay here and learn more French. It would have been hard for daddy to take care of you so well."

"I don't really need much taking care of any more. I do everything for myself."

Going out of the restaurant, a man and a woman unexpectedly hailed him.

"Well, the old Wales!"

"Hello there, Lorraine. . . . Dunc."

Sudden ghosts out of the past: Duncan Schaeffer, a friend from college. Lorraine Quarrles, a lovely, pale blonde of thirty; one of a crowd who had helped them make months into days in the lavish times of three years ago.

"My husband couldn't come this year," she said, in answer to his question.

"We're poor as hell. So he gave me two hundred a month and told me I could do my worst on that. . . . This is your little girl?"

"What about coming back and sitting down?" Duncan asked.

"Can't do it." He was glad for an excuse. As always, he felt Lorraine's passionate, provocative attraction, but his own rhythm was different now.

"Well, how about dinner?" she asked.

"I'm not free. Give me your address and let me call you."

"Charlie, I believe you're sober," she said judicially. "I honestly believe he's sober, Dunc. Pinch him and see if he's sober."

Charlie indicated Honoria with his head. They both laughed.

"What's your address?" said Duncan skeptically.

He hesitated, unwilling to give the name of his hotel.

"I'm not settled yet. I'd better call you. We're going to see the vaudeville at the Empire."

"There! That's what I want to do," Lorraine said. "I want to see some clowns and acrobats and jugglers. That's just what we'll do, Dunc."

"We've got to do an errand first," said Charlie. "Perhaps we'll see you there."

"All right, you snob. . . . Good-by, beautiful little girl."

"Good-by."

Honoria bobbed politely.

Somehow, an unwelcome encounter. They liked him because he was functioning, because he was serious; they wanted to see him, because he was stronger than they were now, because they wanted to draw a certain sustenance from his strength.

At the Empire, Honoria proudly refused to sit upon her father's folded coat. She was already an individual with a code of her own, and Charlie was more and more absorbed by the desire of putting a little of himself into her before she crystallized utterly. It was hopeless to try to know her in so short a time.

Between the acts they came upon Duncan and Lorraine in the lobby where the band was playing.

"Have a drink?"

"All right, but not up at the bar. We'll take a table."

"The perfect father."

Listening abstractedly to Lorraine, Charlie watched Honoria's eyes leave their table and he followed them wistfully about the room, wondering what they saw. He met her glance and she smiled.

"I liked that lemonade," she said.

What had she said? What had he expected? Gong home in a taxi afterward, he pulled her over until her head rested against his chest.

"Darling, do you ever think about your mother?"

"Yes, sometimes," she answered vaguely.

"I don't want you to forget her. Have you got a picture of her?"

"Yes, I think so. Anyhow, Aunt Marion has. Why don't you want me to forget her?"

"She loved you very much."

"I loved her too."

They were silent for a moment.

"Daddy, I want to come and live with you," she said suddenly.

His heart leaped; he had wanted it to come like this.

"Aren't you perfectly happy?"

"Yes, but I love you better than anybody. And you love me better than anybody, don't you, now that mummy's dead?"

"Of course I do. But you won't always like me best, honey. You'll grow up and meet somebody your own age and go marry him and forget you ever had a daddy."

"Yes, that's true," she agreed tranquilly.

He didn't go in. He was coming back at nine o'clock and he wanted to keep himself fresh and new for the thing he must say then.

"When you're safe inside, just show yourself in that window."

"All right. Good-by, dads, dads, dads, dads."

He waited in the dark street until she appeared, all warm and glowing, in the window above and kissed her fingers out into the night.

III

They were waiting. Marion sat behind the coffee service in a dignified black dinner dress that just faintly suggested mourning. Lincoln was walking up and down with the animation of one who had already been talking. They were as anxious as he was to get into the question. He opened it almost immediately:

"I supposed you know what I want to see you about—why I really came to Paris."

Marion played with the black stars on her necklace and frowned.

"I'm awfully anxious to have a home," he continued. "And I'm awfully anxious to have Honoria in it. I appreciate your taking in Honoria for her mother's sake, but things have changed now"—he hesitated and then continued more forcibly—"changed radically with me, and I want to ask you to reconsider the matter. It would be silly for me to deny that about three years ago I was acting badly————"

Marion looked up at him with hard eyes.

"—but all that's over. As I told you, I haven't had more than a drink a day for over a year, and I take that drink deliberately, so that the idea of alcohol won't get too big in my imagination. You see the idea?"

"No," said Marion succinctly.

"It's a sort of stunt I set myself. It keeps the matter in proportion."

"I get you," said Lincoln. "You don't want to admit it's got any attraction for you."

"Something like that. Sometimes I forget and don't take it. But I try to take it. Anyhow, I couldn't afford to drink in my position. The people I represent are more than satisfied with what I've done, and I'm bringing my sister over from Burlington to keep house for me, and I want awfully to have Honoria too. You know that even when her mother and I weren't getting along well we never let anything that happened touch Honoria. I know she's fond of me and I know I'm able to take care of her and—well, there you are. How do you feel about it?"

He knew that now he would have to take a beating. It would last an hour or two hours, and it would be difficult, but if he modulated his inevitable resentment to the chastened attitude of the reformed sinner, he might win his point in the end.

Keep your temper, he told himself. You don't want to be justified. You want Honoria.

Lincoln spoke first: "We've been talking it over ever since we got your letter last month. We're happy to have Honoria here. She's a dear little thing, and we're glad to be able to help her, but of course that isn't the question————"

Marion interrupted suddenly. "How long are you going to stay sober, Charlie?" she asked.

"Permanently, I hope."

"How can anybody count on that?"

"You know I never did drink heavily until I gave up business and came over here with nothing to do. Then Helen and I began to run around with————"

"Please leave Helen out of it. I can't bear to hear you talk about her like that."

He stared at her grimly; he had never been certain how fond of each other the sisters were in life.

"My drinking only lasted about a year and a half—from the time we came over until I—collapsed."

"It was time enough."

"It was time enough," he agreed.

"My duty is entirely to Helen," she said. "I try to think what she would have wanted me to do. Frankly, from the night you did that terrible thing you haven't really existed for me. I can't help that. She was my sister."

"Yes."

"When she was dying she asked me to look out for Honoria. If you hadn't been in a sanitarium then, it might have helped matters."

He had no answer.

"I'll never in my life be able to forget the morning when Helen knocked at my door, soaked to the skin and shivering, and said you'd locked her out."

Charlie gripped the sides of the chair. This was more difficult than he expected; he wanted to launch out into a long expostulation and explanation, but he only said: "The night I locked her out—" and she interrupted, "I don't feel up to going over that again."

After a moment's silence Lincoln said: "We're getting off the subject. You want Marion to set aside her legal guardianship and give you Honoria. I think the main point for her is whether she has confidence in you or not."

"I don't blame Marion," Charlie said slowly, "but I think she can have entire confidence in me. I had a good record up to three years ago. Of course, it's within human possibilities I might go wrong any time. But if we wait much longer I'll lose Honoria's childhood and my chance for a home." He shook his head, "I'll simply lose her, don't you see?"

"Yes, I see," said Lincoln.

"Why didn't you think of all this before?" Marion asked.

"I suppose I did, from time to time, but Helen and I were getting along badly. When I consented to the guardianship, I was flat on my back in a sanitarium and the market had cleaned me out. I knew I'd acted badly, and I thought if it would bring any peace to Helen, I'd agree to anything. But now it's different. I'm functioning, I'm behaving damn well, so far as————"

"Please don't swear at me," Marion said.

He looked at her, startled. With each remark the force of her dislike became more and more apparent. She had built up all her fear of life into one wall and faced it toward him. This trivial reproof was possibly the result of some trouble with the cook several hours before. Charlie became increasingly alarmed at leaving Honoria in this atmosphere of hostility against himself; sooner or later it would come out, in a word here, a shake of the head there, and some of that distrust would be irrevocably implanted in Honoria. But he pulled his temper down out of his face and shut it up inside him; he had won a point, for Lincoln realized the absurdity of Marion's remark and asked her lightly since when she had objected to the word "damn."

"Another thing," Charlie said: "I'm able to give her certain advantages now. I'm going to take a French governess to Prague with me. I've got a lease on a new apartment————"

He stopped, realizing he was blundering. They couldn't be expected to accept with equanimity the fact that his income was again twice as large as their own.

"I suppose you can give her more luxuries than we can," said Marion. "When you were throwing away money we were living along watching every ten francs. . . . I suppose you'll start doing it again."

"Oh, no," he said. "I've learned. I've worked hard for ten years, you know— until I got lucky in the market, like so many people. Terribly lucky. It didn't seem any use working any more, so I quit."

There was a long silence. All of them felt their nerves straining, and for the first time in a year Charlie wanted a drink. He was sure now that Lincoln Peters wanted him to have his child.

Marion shuddered suddenly; part of her saw that Charlie's feet were planted on the earth now, and her own maternal feeling recognized the naturalness of his desire; but she had lived for a long time with a prejudice—a prejudice founded on a curious disbelief in her sister's happiness, and which, in the shock of one terrible night, had turned to hatred for him. It had all happened at a point in her life where the discouragement of ill health and adverse circumstances made it necessary for her to believe in tangible villainy and a tangible villain.

"I can't help what I think!" she cried out suddenly. "How much you were responsible for Helen's death, I don't know. It's something you'll have to square with your own conscience."

An electric current of agony surged through him; for a moment he was almost on his feet, an unuttered sound echoing in his throat. He hung on to himself for a moment, another moment.

"Hold on there," said Lincoln uncomfortably. "I never thought you were responsible for that."

"Helen died of heart trouble," Charlie said dully.

"Yes, heart trouble." Marion spoke as if the phrase had another meaning for her.

Then, in the flatness that followed her outburst, she saw him plainly and she knew he had somehow arrived at control over the situation. Glancing at her husband, she found no help from him, and as abruptly as if it were a matter of no importance, she threw up the sponge.

"Do what you like!" she cried, springing up from her chair. "She's your child. I'm not the person to stand in your way. I think if it were my child I'd rather see her—" She managed to check herself. "You two decide it. I can't stand this. I'm sick. I'm going to bed."

She hurried from the room; after a moment Lincoln said:

"This has been a hard day for her. You know how strongly she feels—" His voice was almost apologetic: "When a woman gets an idea in her head."

"Of course."

"It's going to be all right. I think she sees now that you—can provide for the child, and so we can't very well stand in your way or Honoria's way."

"Thank you, Lincoln."

"I'd better go along and see how she is."

"I'm going."

He was still trembling when he reached the street, but a walk down the Rue Bonaparte to the *quais*[15] set him up, and as he crossed the Seine, fresh and new by the *quai* lamps, he felt exultant. But back in his room he couldn't sleep. The image of Helen haunted him. Helen whom he had loved so until they had sense-lessly begun to abuse each other's love, tear it into shreds. On that terrible February night that Marion remembered so vividly, a slow quarrel had gone on for hours. There was a scene at the Florida, and then he attempted to take her home, and then she kissed young Webb at a table; after that there was what she had hysterically said. When he arrived home alone he turned the key in the lock in wild anger. How could he know she would arrive an hour later alone, that there would be a snowstorm in which she wandered about in slippers, too confused to find a taxi? Then the aftermath, her escaping pneumonia by a miracle, and all the attendant horror. They were "reconciled," but that was the beginning of the end, and Marion, who had seen with her own eyes and who imagined it to be one of many scenes from her sister's martyrdom, never forgot.

Going over it again brought Helen nearer, and in the white, soft light that steals upon half sleep near morning he found himself talking to her again. She said that he was perfectly right about Honoria and that she wanted Honoria to be with him. She said she was glad he was being good and doing better. She said a lot of other things—very friendly things—but she was in a swing in a white dress, and swinging faster and faster all the time, so that at the end he could not hear clearly all that she said.

IV

He woke up feeling happy. The door of the world was open again. He made plans, vistas, futures for Honoria and himself, but suddenly he grew sad, remembering all the plans he and Helen had made. She had not planned to die. The present was the thing—work to do and someone to love. But not to love too much, for he knew the injury that a father can do to a daughter or a mother to a son by attaching them too closely: afterward, out in the world, the child would seek in the marriage partner the same blind tenderness and, failing probably to find it, turn against love and life.

It was another bright, crisp day. He called Lincoln Peters at the bank where he worked and asked if he could count on taking Honoria when he left for Prague. Lincoln agreed that there was no reason for delay. One thing—the legal guardian-ship. Marion wanted to retain that a while longer. She was upset by the whole

---

[15] "Embankments" (French); here, along the Seine.

matter, and it would oil things if she felt that the situation was still in her control for another year. Charlie agreed, wanting only the tangible, visible child.

Then the question of a governess. Charles sat in a gloomy agency and talked to a cross Béarnaise and to a buxom Breton peasant,[16] neither of whom he could have endured. There were others whom he would see tomorrow.

He lunched with Lincoln Peters at Griffons, trying to keep down his exultation.

"There's nothing quite like your own child," Lincoln said. "But you understand how Marion feels too."

"She's forgotten how hard I worked for seven years there," Charlie said. "She just remembers one night."

"There's another thing." Lincoln hesitated. "While you and Helen were tearing around Europe throwing money away, we were just getting along. I didn't touch any of the prosperity because I never got ahead enough to carry anything but my insurance. I think Marion felt there was some kind of injustice in it—you not even working toward the end, and getting richer and richer."

"It went just as quick as it came," said Charlie.

"Yes, a lot of it stayed in the hands of *chasseurs* and saxophone players and maîtres d'hôtel—well, the big party's over now. I just said that to explain Marion's feeling about those crazy years. If you drop in about six o'clock tonight before Marion's too tired, we'll settle the details on the spot."

Back at his hotel, Charlie found a *pneumatique*[17] that had been redirected from the Ritz bar where Charlie had left his address for the purpose of finding a certain man.

> "DEAR CHARLIE: You were so strange when we saw you the other day that I wondered if I did something to offend you. If so, I'm not conscious of it. In fact, I have thought about you too much for the last year, and it's always been in the back of my mind that I might see you if I came over here. We *did* have such good times that crazy spring, like the night you and I stole the butcher's tricycle, and the time we tried to call on the president and you had the old derby rim and the wire cane. Everybody seems so old lately, but I don't feel old a bit. Couldn't we get together some time today for old time's sake? I've got a vile hang-over for the moment, but will be feeling better this afternoon and will look for you about five in the sweatshop at the Ritz.
>
>   "Always devotedly,
>   "LORRAINE."

His first feeling was one of awe that he had actually, in his mature years, stolen a tricycle and pedaled Lorraine all over the Étoile[18] between the small hours and dawn. In retrospect it was a nightmare. Locking out Helen didn't fit in with any other act of his life, but the tricycle incident did—it was one of many. How many weeks or months of dissipation to arrive at that condition of utter irresponsibility?

He tried to picture how Lorraine had appeared to him then—very attractive;

---

[16] Wales interviews two women: one from Béarn, in southwestern France, the other from Brittany, in northwestern France.

[17] An express message sent through a pneumatic tube (French).

[18] The Place de l'Étoile, the Parisian square in which the Arc de Triomphe stands.

Helen was unhappy about it, though she said nothing. Yesterday, in the restaurant, Lorraine had seemed trite, blurred, worn away. He emphatically did not want to see her, and he was glad Alix had not given away his hotel address. It was a relief to think, instead, of Honoria, to think of Sundays spent with her and of saying good morning to her and of knowing she was there in his house at night, drawing her breath in the darkness.

At five he took a taxi and bought presents for all the Peters—a piquant cloth doll, a box of Roman soldiers, flowers for Marion, big linen handkerchiefs for Lincoln.

He saw, when he arrived in the apartment, that Marion had accepted the inevitable. She greeted him now as though he were a recalcitrant member of the family, rather than a menacing outsider. Honoria had been told she was going; Charlie was glad to see that her tack made her conceal her excessive happiness. Only on his lap did she whisper her delight and the question "When?" before she slipped away with the other children.

He and Marion were alone for a minute in the room, and on an impulse he spoke out boldly:

"Family quarrels are bitter things. They don't go according to any rules. They're not like aches or wounds; they're more like splits in the skin that won't heal because there's not enough material. I wish you and I could be on better terms."

"Some things are hard to forget," she answered. "It's a question of confidence." There was no answer to this and presently she asked, "When do you propose to take her?"

"As soon as I can get a governess. I hoped the day after tomorrow."

"That's impossible. I've got to get her things in shape. Not before Saturday."

He yielded. Coming back into the room, Lincoln offered him a drink.

"I'll take my daily whisky," he said.

It was warm here, it was a home, people together by a fire. The children felt very safe and important; the mother and father were serious, watchful. They had things to do for the children more important than his visit here. A spoonful of medicine was, after all, more important than the strained relations between Marion and himself. They were not dull people, but they were very much in the grip of life and circumstances. He wondered if he couldn't do something to get Lincoln out of his rut at the bank.

A long peal at the door-bell; the *bonne à tout faire*[19] passed through and went down the corridor. The door opened upon another long ring, and then voices, and the three in the salon looked up expectantly; Richard moved to bring the corridor within his range of vision, and Marion rose. Then the maid came back along the corridor, closely followed by the voices, which developed under the light into Duncan Schaeffer and Lorraine Quarrles.

They were gay, they were hilarious, they were roaring with laughter. For a moment Charlie was astounded; unable to understand how they ferreted out the Peters' address.

"Ah-h-h!" Duncan wagged his finger roguishly at Charlie. "Ah-h-h!"

They both slid down another cascade of laughter. Anxious and at a loss, Char-

---

[19] "Maid of all work" (French), a housemaid. The Peters's modest circumstances permit them to have one servant for all household chores.

lie shook hands with them quickly and presented them to Lincoln and Marion. Marion nodded, scarcely speaking. She had drawn back a step toward the fire; her little girl stood beside her, and Marion put an arm about her shoulder.

With growing annoyance at the intrusion, Charlie waited for them to explain themselves. After some concentration Duncan said:

"We came to invite you out to dinner. Lorraine and I insist that all this chi-chi, cagy business 'bout your address got to stop."

Charlie came closer to them, as if to force them backward down the corridor.

"Sorry, but I can't. Tell me where you'll be and I'll phone you in half an hour."

This made no impression. Lorraine sat down suddenly on the side of a chair, and focusing her eyes on Richard, cried, "Oh, what a nice little boy! Come here, little boy." Richard glanced at his mother, but did not move. With a perceptible shrug of her shoulders, Lorraine turned back to Charlie:

"Come and dine. Sure your cousins won' mine. See you so sel'om. Or sol-emn."

"I can't," said Charlie sharply. "You two have dinner and I'll phone you."

Her voice became suddenly unpleasant. "All right, we'll go. But I remember once when you hammered on my door at four A. M. I was enough of a good sport to give you a drink. Come on, Dunc."

Still in slow motion, with blurred, angry faces, with uncertain feet, they retired along the corridor.

"Good night," Charlie said.

"Good night!" responded Lorraine emphatically.

When he went back into the salon Marion had not moved, only now her son was standing in the circle of her other arm. Lincoln was still swinging Honoria back and forth like a pendulum from side to side.

"What an outrage!" Charlie broke out. "What an absolute outrage!"

Neither of them answered. Charlie dropped into an armchair, picked up his drink, set it down again and said:

"People I haven't seen for two years having the colossal nerve———"

He broke off. Marion had made the sound "Oh!" in one swift, furious breath, turned her body from him with a jerk and left the room.

Lincoln set down Honoria carefully.

"You children go in and start your soup," he said, and when they obeyed, he said to Charlie:

"Marion's not well and she can't stand shocks. That kind of people make her really physically sick."

"I didn't tell them to come here. They wormed your name out of somebody. They deliberately———"

"Well, it's too bad. It doesn't help matters. Excuse me a minute."

Left alone, Charlie sat tense in his chair. In the next room he could hear the children eating, talking in monosyllables, already oblivious to the scene between their elders. He heard a murmur of conversation from a farther room and then the ticking bell of a telephone receiver picked up, and in a panic he moved to the other side of the room and out of earshot.

In a minute Lincoln came back. "Look here, Charlie. I think we'd better call off dinner for tonight. Marion's in bad shape."

"Is she angry with me?"

"Sort of," he said, almost roughly. "She's not strong and———"

"You mean she's changed her mind about Honoria?"

"She's pretty bitter right now. I don't know. You phone me at the bank tomorrow."

"I wish you'd explain to her I never dreamed these people would come here. I'm just as sore as you are."

"I couldn't explain anything to her now."

Charlie got up. He took his coat and hat and started down the corridor. Then he opened the door of the dining room and said in a strange voice, "Good night, children."

Honoria rose and ran around the table to hug him.

"Good night, sweetheart," he said vaguely, and then trying to make his voice more tender, trying to conciliate something, "Good night, dear children."

V

Charlie went directly to the Ritz bar with the furious idea of finding Lorraine and Duncan, but they were not there, and he realized that in any case there was nothing he could do. He had not touched his drink at the Peters', and now he ordered a whisky-and-soda. Paul came over to say hello.

"It's a great change," he said sadly. "We do about half the business we did. So many fellows I hear about back in the States lost everything, maybe not in the first crash, but then in the second. Your friend George Hardt lost every cent, I hear. Are you back in the States?"

"No, I'm in business in Prague."

"I heard that you lost a lot in the crash."

"I did," and he added grimly, "but I lost everything I wanted in the boom."

"Selling short."

"Something like that."

Again the memory of those days swept over him like a nightmare—the people they had met travelling; then people who couldn't add a row of figures or speak a coherent sentence. The little man Helen had consented to dance with at the ship's party, who had insulted her ten feet from the table; the women and girls carried screaming with drink or drugs out of public places——

—The men who locked their wives out in the snow, because the snow of twenty-nine wasn't real snow. If you didn't want it to be snow, you just paid some money.

He went to the phone and called the Peters' apartment; Lincoln answered.

"I called up because this thing is on my mind. Has Marion said anything definite?"

"Marion's sick," Lincoln answered shortly. "I know this thing isn't altogether your fault, but I can't have her go to pieces about it. I'm afraid we'll have to let it slide for six months; I can't take the chance of working her up to this state again."

"I see."

"I'm sorry, Charlie."

He went back to his table. His whisky glass was empty, but he shook his head when Alix looked at it questioningly. There wasn't much he could do now except send Honoria some things; he would send her a lot of things tomorrow. He thought rather angrily that this was just money—he had given so many people money. . . .

"No, no more," he said to another waiter. "What do I owe you?"

He would come back some day; they couldn't make him pay forever. But he wanted his child, and nothing was much good now, beside that fact. He wasn't young any more, with a lot of nice thoughts and dreams to have by himself. He was absolutely sure Helen wouldn't have wanted him to be so alone.

1931

A February 1926 Life *magazine cover by John Held, Jr., expresses the youthful spirit of the "flappers" during the prosperous "roaring twenties," before the stock-market crash of 1929 and the subsequent Great Depression.*

Zora Neale Hurston
(1901?–1960)

Zora Neale Hurston was the most prolific African-American female writer from the 1920s through the 1950s. She published an autobiography, novels, folklore, short stories, and essays. Although she earned critical acclaim (as well as controversy), her life ended in a welfare hospital, and she was buried in 1960 in an unmarked grave.

Hurston was born about 1901 in Eatonville, Florida, the all-black town featured in her most accomplished novel, *Their Eyes Were Watching God* (1937). When her mother died, the thirteen-year-old Hurston, rejected by her father and stepmother, was passed to various relatives. She eventually set out on her own. While attending Howard University, she met Professor Alain Locke, who encouraged her to move to New York City. Already publishing stories and gaining attention in the early 1920s, Hurston burst upon the Harlem Renaissance at its height. The Harlem Renaissance emerged after World War I, when the wartime race riots had subsided. A new enthusiasm for Harlem and its so-called primitive music, literature, and art made Harlem a cultural capital for African Americans in the 1920s. Hurston fit right in, documenting the black experience as she lived it and observed it.

On a scholarship Hurston entered Barnard College, where she studied with the noted anthropologist Franz Boas. Under his influence she began defining part of her life's work: to record black life. With encouragement and private funding she collected the songs, customs, tales, anecdotes, and games she later published in the voodoo stories *Mules and Men* (1935) and incorporated into her fiction. For many years she had difficulty publishing her research, although she was able to produce musical revues of the folklore.

After Hurston finished the short story "The Gilded Six-Bits" (1933), she began to write a novel—*Jonah's Gourd Vine* (1934)—based on an idea she got from her publisher. *Their Eyes Were Watching God*, published three years later, was written in only seven weeks while Hurston continued her folklore research in the Caribbean. In this acclaimed novel, Hurston combines themes from her earlier work, especially love, community, marriage, and inner spiritual life. Her second folklore collection, *Tell My Horse* (1938), was less successful. Her novel *Moses, Man of the Mountain* (1939), a reworking of the Moses legend for African Americans, followed. After producing her autobiography, *Dust Tracks on a Road* (1942), Hurston began teaching and writing magazine pieces. Her last novel, *Seraph on the Suwanee*, was published in 1948 but failed terribly; that same year she was arrested for child molestation. Although the charge was dropped, Hurston never fully recovered from the ensuing scandal. She spent the last ten years of her life barely surviving financially.

Hurston was not uniformly admired. Although she celebrated black culture, many critics, including Richard Wright, complained that she was on the sidelines politically. She did not explicitly address racial and class issues, and when she publicly denounced desegregation, her audience became even more critical. But changes in popular and critical tastes have resulted in renewed interest and re-publication of Hurston's work. Such interest was initially fostered by advocates of neglected female writers—especially black female writers—but critics have begun to assess and appreciate the universal concerns at the heart of her work and that work's pervading poetic sensibility. Contemporary writers such as Alice Walker now claim Hurston as a literary influence.

Suggested Readings: *Jonah's Gourd Vine*, 1934. *Mules and Men*, 1935. *Their Eyes Were Watching God*, 1937. *Voodoo Gods*, 1939. *The Man of the Mountain*, 1941. *Dust Tracks on a Road*, 1942. *Seraph on the Suwanee*, 1948. *Spunk: The Selected Stories of Zora Neale Hurston*, 1985. R. Hemenway, *Zora Neale Hurston: A Literary Biography*, 1977. L. P. Howard, *Zora Neale Hurston*, 1980. B. Bell, *The Afro-American Novel and Its Tradition*, 1987.

Text Used: *I Love Myself When I Am Laughing . . . And Then Again When I Am Looking Mean and Impressive*, ed. A. Walker, 1979.

HOW IT FEELS TO BE COLORED ME

I am colored but I offer nothing in the way of extenuating circumstances except the fact that I am the only Negro in the United States whose grandfather on the mother's side was *not* an Indian chief.

I remember the very day that I became colored. Up to my thirteenth year I lived in the little Negro town of Eatonville, Florida. It is exclusively a colored town. The only white people I knew passed through the town going to or coming from Orlando. The native whites rode dusty horses, the Northern tourists chugged down the sandy village road in automobiles. The town knew the Southerners and never stopped cane chewing when they passed. But the Northerners were something else again. They were peered at cautiously from behind curtains by the timid. The more venturesome would come out on the porch to watch them go past and got just as much pleasure out of the tourists as the tourists got out of the village.

The front porch might seem a daring place for the rest of the town, but it was a gallery seat for me. My favorite place was atop the gate-post. Proscenium[1] box for a born first-nighter. Not only did I enjoy the show, but I didn't mind the actors knowing that I liked it. I usually spoke to them in passing. I'd wave at them and when they returned my salute, I would say something like this: "Howdy-do-well-I-thank-you-where-you-goin'?" Usually automobile or the horse paused at this, and after a queer exchange of compliments, I would probably "go a piece of the way" with them, as we say in farthest Florida. If one of my family happened to come to the front in time to see me, of course negotiations would be rudely broken off. But even so, it is clear that I was the first "welcome-to-our-state" Floridian, and I hope the Miami Chamber of Commerce will please take notice.

During this period, white people differed from colored to me only in that they rode through town and never lived there. They liked to hear me "speak pieces" and sing and wanted to see me dance the parse-me-la, and gave me generously of their small silver for doing these things, which seemed strange to me for I wanted to do them so much that I needed bribing to stop. Only they didn't know it. The colored people gave no dimes. They deplored any joyful tendencies in me, but I

---

[1] The theater area closest to the stage.

was their Zora nevertheless. I belonged to them, to the nearby hotels, to the county—everybody's Zora.

But changes came in the family when I was thirteen, and I was sent to school in Jacksonville. I left Eatonville, the town of the oleanders, as Zora. When I disembarked from the river-boat at Jacksonville, she was no more. It seemed that I had suffered a sea change. I was not Zora of Orange County any more. I was now a little colored girl. I found it out in certain ways. In my heart as well as in the mirror. I became a fast brown—warranted not to rub nor run.

But I am not tragically colored. There is no great sorrow dammed up in my soul, nor lurking behind my eyes. I do not mind at all. I do not belong to the sobbing school of Negrohood who hold that nature somehow has given them a lowdown dirty deal and whose feelings are all hurt about it. Even in the helter-skelter skirmish that is my life, I have seen that the world is to the strong regardless of a little pigmentation more or less. No, I do not weep at the world—I am too busy sharpening my oyster knife.

Someone is always at my elbow reminding me that I am the granddaughter of slaves. It fails to register depression with me. Slavery is sixty years in the past. The operation was successful and the patient is doing well, thank you. The terrible struggle that made me an American out of a potential slave said "On the line!" The Reconstruction said "Get set!" and the generation before said "Go!" I am off to a flying start and I must not halt in the stretch to look behind and weep. Slavery is the price I paid for civilization, and the choice was not with me. It is a bully adventure and worth all that I have paid through my ancestors for it. No one on earth ever had a greater chance for glory. The world to be won and nothing to be lost. It is thrilling to think—to know that for any act of mine, I shall get twice as much praise or twice as much blame. It is quite exciting to hold the center of the national stage, with the spectators not knowing whether to laugh or to weep.

The position of my white neighbor is much more difficult. No brown specter pulls up a chair beside me when I sit down to eat. No dark ghost thrusts its leg against mine in bed. The game of keeping what one has is never so exciting as the game of getting.

I do not always feel colored. Even now I often achieve the unconscious Zora of Eatonville before the Hegira.[2] I feel most colored when I am thrown against a sharp white background.

For instance at Barnard.[3] "Beside the waters of the Hudson" I feel my race. Among the thousand white persons, I am a dark rock surged upon, and overswept, but through it all, I remain myself. When covered by the waters, I am; and the ebb but reveals me again.

Sometimes it is the other way around. A white person is set down in our midst, but the contrast is just as sharp for me. For instance, when I sit in the drafty basement that is The New World Cabaret[4] with a white person, my color comes. We enter chatting about any little nothing that we have in common and are seated by the jazz waiters. In the abrupt way that jazz orchestras have, this one plunges into a number. It loses no time in circumlocutions, but gets right down to busi-

---

[2] The flight of Mohammed from Mecca (A.D. 622), or any journey undertaken to seek refuge from danger.
[3] Barnard College in New York City, near the Hudson River.
[4] A popular Harlem nightclub in the 1920s.

ness. It constricts the thorax and splits the heart with its tempo and narcotic harmonies. This orchestra grows rambunctious, rears on its hind legs and attacks the tonal veil with primitive fury, rending it, clawing it until it breaks through to the jungle beyond. I follow those heathen—follow them exultingly. I dance wildly inside myself; I yell within, I whoop; I shake my assegai[5] above my head, I hurl it true to the mark *yeeeeooww!* I am in the jungle and living in the jungle way. My face is painted red and yellow and my body is painted blue. My pulse is throbbing like a war drum. I want to slaughter something—give pain, give death to what, I do not know. But the piece ends. The men of the orchestra wipe their lips and rest their fingers. I creep back slowly to the veneer we call civilization with the last tone and find the white friend sitting motionless in his seat, smoking calmly.

"Good music they have here," he remarks, drumming the table with his fingertips.

Music. The great blobs of purple and red emotion have not touched him. He has only heard what I felt. He is far away and I see him but dimly across the ocean and the continent that have fallen between us. He is so pale with his whiteness then and I am *so* colored.

At certain times I have no race. I am *me*. When I set my hat at a certain angle and saunter down Seventh Avenue, Harlem City, feeling as snooty as the lions in front of the Forty-Second Street Library, for instance. So far as my feelings are concerned, Peggy Hopkins Joyce[6] on the Boule Mich[7] with her gorgeous raiment, stately carriage, knees knocking together in a most aristocratic manner, has nothing on me. The cosmic Zora emerges. I belong to no race nor time. I am the eternal feminine with its string of beads.

I have no separate feeling about being an American citizen and colored. I am merely a fragment of the Great Soul that surges within the boundaries. My country, right or wrong.

Sometimes, I feel discriminated against, but it does not make me angry. It merely astonishes me. How *can* any deny themselves the pleasure of my company? It's beyond me.

But in the main, I feel like a brown bag of miscellany propped against a wall. Against a wall in company with other bags, white, red and yellow. Pour out the contents, and there is discovered a jumble of small things priceless and worthless. A first-water[8] diamond, an empty spool, bits of broken glass, lengths of string, a key to a door long since crumbled away, a rusty knife-blade, old shoes saved for a road that never was and never will be, a nail bent under the weight of things too heavy for any nail, a dried flower or two still a little fragrant. In your hand is the brown bag. On the ground before you is the jumble it held—so much like the jumble in the bags, could they be emptied, that all might be dumped in a single heap and the bags refilled without altering the content of any greatly. A bit of colored glass more or less would not matter. Perhaps that is how the Great Stuffer of Bags filled them in the first place—who knows?

1933

---

[5] A thin spear or light javelin used by some southern African tribes.
[6] A famous American heiress and socialite.
[7] Boulevard St. Michel, a well-known street in Paris, that runs near the Sorbonne and through the "Latin Quarter."
[8] Of the best quality.

With millions unemployed during the Great Depression, apple sellers (like those here in 1930) were a common sight on city streets, as people sought to earn a living.

William Faulkner
(1897–1962)

"Tell them I was born in 1826 of a Negro slave and an alligator." So responded William Faulkner in a 1931 interview (L. H. Cox, *William Faulkner,* 1982) when asked about his childhood. An intensely private man who resented public curiosity about his personal life, he remarked in a 1949 letter to the writer Malcolm Cowley that it was his "ambition to be, as a private individual, abolished and voided from history, leaving it markless, no refuse save the printed books. . . . It is my aim, and every effort bent, that the sum and history of my life, which in the same sentence is my obit and epitaph too, shall be them both: He made the books and he died." Despite his refusal to divulge personal information, Faulkner set all his major fiction in Mississippi, which he cherished as his "little postage stamp of native ground," and drew many of his characters and plots from his early experiences and from family memories and legends.

Born in New Albany, Mississippi, in 1897 (the family soon moved to nearby Oxford), William Cuthbert Falkner was the oldest son of Murray Cuthbert Falkner and Maud Butler and the great-grandson of Colonel William Clark Falkner. (The author added the "u" later.) The colonel's dramatic life inspired such characters as Colonel Sartoris of *Sartoris* (1929) and Thomas Sutpen of *Absalom, Absalom!* (1936). A lawyer and lieutenant in the Mexican War, the colonel had stabbed a man to death in self-defense and shot another; he also was a writer, an infantry captain during the Civil War, and founder of the Ripley Railroad (later the Gulf and Chicago Railroad). He died when he was shot in the head at close range by a former stockholder in the railroad. The violence continued in the Falkner family for two generations.

Faulkner's formal education ended after the eleventh grade; by then Faulkner was already an avid reader and writer of poetry. His first published work, *The Marble Faun* (1924), was a collection of verse, and years later he described himself not as a novelist or short-story writer but as a failed poet. After his high school sweetheart, Estelle Oldham, married a more financially secure man, Faulkner left Oxford in 1918 and enlisted in the British Royal Air Force in Canada (as he did not meet U.S. requirements) to play an active role in World War I. The war ended before he reached Europe, though, and he returned home—with a limp and a story of a metal plate in his head, both of which he claimed were the result of war wounds.

Faulkner began to publish poems—both his own and translations from French symbolists—and critical pieces in local newspapers, and in 1920 he wrote the verse play *Marionettes* (not published until 1975). Seeking to support himself, he drifted from job to job, finally becoming postmaster at the University of Mississippi. Forced to resign, however, Faulkner went to New Orleans in 1924. There he met the fiction writer Sherwood Anderson, who encouraged Faulkner to develop his prose style and to draw on his home region for material. When Faulkner left for Europe in 1925, he had with him the manuscript of a completed novel about life in postwar America, *Soldier's Pay*, which Anderson had recommended to his publisher; the novel appeared in 1926. Faulkner traveled in Italy, France, and England and lived in Paris for several months, where he frequented the Louvre and the Luxembourg galleries. He continued to write, working on a novel about the place of artists in society; the novel was published in 1927 as *Mosquitoes*.

Back in Mississippi in late 1925, Faulkner turned to projects with southern settings in which he introduced fictional families, including the aristocratic Sartorises. "Flags in the Dust," the novel about the Sartorises and their community, later called Yoknapatawpha County, was rejected several times before it was finally published in heavily edited form in 1929 as *Sartoris* (the original manuscript appeared posthumously in 1973). Meanwhile, he had resumed his romance with Estelle Oldham, now a divorcée with two young children. Faulkner and Oldham married in 1929, and the family of four settled into a large, dilapidated house, Rowan Oak. A daughter born in 1931 died after just nine days; another was born in 1933.

Despite the financial pressure placed on Faulkner by the sudden acquisition of a family and house, the years around 1930 were among his most productive. *The Sound and the Fury*, his favorite novel, was published in 1929; it is the story of Caddy Compson and the disintegration of the Compson family amidst the decline of the Old South. Exhibiting Faulkner's fascination with subjective rather than chronological time, the novel is divided into four sections, each presented from a different perspective and written in a different style. Caddy's brothers narrate the first three sections; only in the third-person narration of Dilsey, the cook, is the account sequential.

The Sound and the Fury earned Faulkner more critical attention than he had yet received but not the money that he badly needed. Working as a supervisor on the night shift

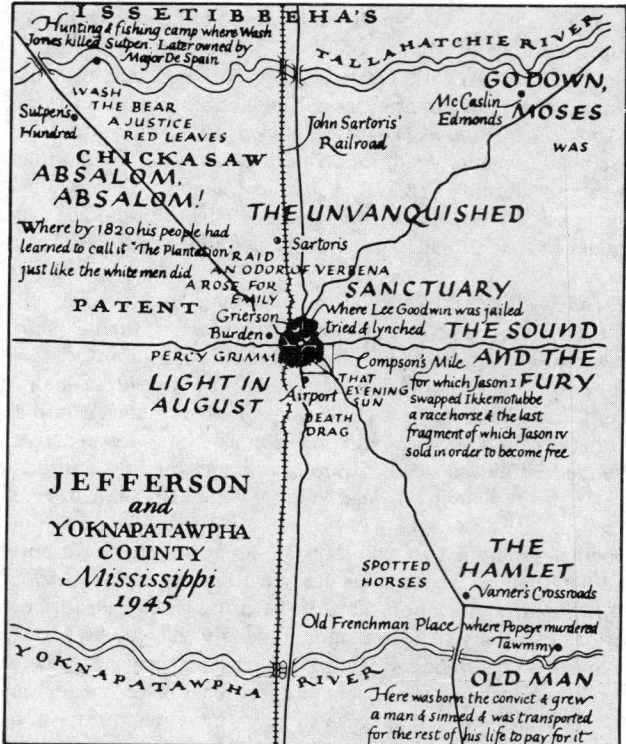

This is one of several maps that William Faulkner provided of his fictional city Jefferson in the imaginary Yoknapatawpha County, Mississippi.

at a local power plant, he wrote his next masterpiece, *As I Lay Dying* (1930), the story of a six-day journey a poor family undertakes to transport their dead mother for burial in Jefferson, the Yoknapatawpha County seat. Like *The Sound and the Fury*, *As I Lay Dying* is comprised of interior monologues; each of fifteen different characters perceives the events differently. His next novel, *Sanctuary* (1931), which deals with urban corruption, prostitution, and drugs and describes a brutal rape, increased the charges of bad taste and sensationalism that *As I Lay Dying* had brought on Faulkner.

Before he began his next novel, *Light in August* (1932), Faulkner turned his attention to the immediately marketable form of the short story, yet the stories that he wrote then—published in national magazines such as the *Saturday Evening Post, Scribner's,* and *Harper's* and collected in *These 13* (1931)—are anything but formulaic. *These 13* is divided into three sections: the first consists of World War I stories; the second relates the history of Yoknapatawpha County; and the third, which includes "That Evening Sun" and "A Rose for Emily," focuses on the contemporary community of Jefferson and its separate black and white quarters. The stories use many of the same techniques and involve many of the same characters that his novels do. "That Evening Sun," about Nancy, an African-American washerwoman and temporary cook for the Compson family, and narrated by Quentin Compson, takes place roughly eight years before the events of *The Sound and the Fury*. As is true of all Faulkner's novels, the reader must distinguish between the narrator's relating of events and the events themselves: the Compson children are unable to understand when Nancy tells Jesus, her threatening lover, that the "watermelon" under her dress "never come off your vine." The first-person narrator of "A Rose for Emily," one of

Faulkner's most masterful and popular stories, constantly misinterprets actions and events as he recalls the story of Miss Emily's tragic love affair with Homer Barron. Teasing readers who confuse "time with its mathematical progression," the narrative moves back and forth in time, memory following upon memory. Both stories display Faulkner's keen awareness of the inequities and peculiar ironies of race relations in the South. " 'I can't hang around white man's kitchen. . . . But white men can hang around mine,' " Jesus remarks in "That Evening Sun."

These 13 was very favorably received, but Faulkner still faced economic pressures, and when Metro-Goldwyn-Mayer offered him a six-week contract as a screenwriter in 1932 for $500 a week, he accepted. "Nothing can injure a man's writing if he's a first rate writer," he later told an interviewer; "the problem does not apply if he is not first rate, because he has already sold his soul for a swimming pool" (Cox, 1982). Faulkner developed a close working relationship with the director Howard Hawks but was not happy in Hollywood and returned to Mississippi in 1933, where he continued to experiment with novelistic form. *Absalom, Absalom!*, the story of the rise and fall of Thomas Sutpen, who had sought to found a dynasty in the post-Civil War South, is variously told by four different speakers (including Quentin Compson) who impose different interpretations on the events they narrate. Between 1933 and 1940 Faulkner published a novel almost every year and continued to write stories. (It was then that he began working on his novelette "The Bear," one of seven stories in the acclaimed *Go Down, Moses* [1942].) In 1937 he was corresponding with Maurice Coindreau, a French critic and translator, who introduced Faulkner's work to France via translations of *The Sound and the Fury* and *As I Lay Dying* and who is largely responsible for Faulkner's high reputation there. The philosopher/writer Jean-Paul Sartre wrote that *"Pour les jeunes en France, Faulkner c'est un dieu,"* or "For the young people of France, Faulkner is a god" (J. Blotner, *Faulkner*, 1984). Faulkner continued to work intermittently in Hollywood, contributing to the scripts for Howard Hawk's *To Have and Have Not* (1945) and *The Big Sleep* (1946), both starring Humphrey Bogart and Lauren Bacall.

With the onset of World War II Faulkner's concern with social problems, always present in his work, moved to the forefront. His writing became less experimental and more traditional; he began a series of books—*The Hamlet* (1940), *The Town* (1957), and *The Mansion* (1959), the so-called Snopes Trilogy—about the rise of the "poor white trash" Snopes family and the fall of the old southern gentry in Yoknapatawpha County. His reputation in America was strengthened with the 1946 publication of Malcolm Cowley's edition of *The Portable Faulkner*, for which Faulkner wrote an appendix on the history of the Compson family, beginning with the Native-American Ikkemotubbe and ending with the Compson's cook, Dilsey. In 1948 Faulkner wrote to his publisher that he had half of a novel written, the story of "a Negro [who is] in jail accused of murder and waiting for the white folks to drag him out and pour gasoline over him and set him on fire, [and who] is the detective, solves the crime because he goddamn has to to keep from being lynched." The novel, published in 1948 as *Intruder in the Dust*, is perhaps the strongest expression of the antiracist theme he had examined throughout his works; it led to the highest honor of his life, the 1950 Nobel Prize for literature. Typically reluctant to put himself in the public eye, Faulkner initially balked at attending the award ceremony in Stockholm. In the end he not only attended, but also delivered one of the most memorable laureate's speeches in the history of the prize. "The award was made, not to me, but to my works," he said. Of the $30,000 prize, he set apart $25,000 for the William Faulkner Foundation, to provide educational scholarships for African-American Mississippians and financial encouragement for Latin-American writers.

His post-Nobel years brought him numerous honors. In 1950 he received the Howells

In 1951

Medal from the American Academy of Arts and Letters; in 1951 he was awarded both the National Book Award for fiction and the French Legion of Honor; and in 1955 his parable *A Fable* (1954) earned him a Pulitzer Prize. Though he continued to write, he increasingly assumed the role of sage. A frequent lecturer at college campuses, he refused to accept honorary degrees, saying that to do so "would be an insult to all those who have gained degrees by means of . . . long and arduous devotion" (Cox, 1982). Faulkner spoke out on civil rights issues in his native South and even undertook various State Department assignments between 1954 and 1961, traveling to South America, Japan, Manila, Europe, and Iceland. Faulkner was awarded another Pulitzer Prize for *The Reivers* (1962), a fictional "reminiscence" told by Lucius Priest to his grandson. In summer 1962 Faulkner suffered a severe back injury; the day after he was admitted to a hospital, he died at age sixty-five of a heart attack. He left behind a considerable body of work that accomplished what he expressed in his Nobel speech as the writer's duty: to write about the human "soul, a spirit capable of compassion and sacrifice and endurance."

Suggested Readings: *The Marble Faun,* 1924. *Soldier's Pay,* 1927. *The Sound and the Fury,* 1929. *As I Lay Dying,* 1930. *These 13,* 1931. *Light in August,* 1932. *Absalom, Absalom!,* 1936. *Go Down, Moses and Other Stories,* 1942. *Requiem for a Nun,* 1951. *A Fable,* 1954. *The Reivers,* 1962. *Essays, Speeches & Public Letters,* ed. J. B. Meriwether, 1966. *Uncollected Stories of William Faulkner,* 1979. I. Howe, *William Faulkner: A Critical Study,* 1962. O. W. Vickery, *The Novels of William Faulkner: A Critical Interpretation,* 1964. M. Millgate, *The Achievement of William Faulkner,* 1966. L. Wagner-Martin, *William Faulkner: Four Decades of Criticism,* 1973. J. T. Irwin, *Doubling and Incest/Repetition and Revenge: A Speculative Reading of Faulkner,* 1975. D. L. Mintner, *William Faulkner: His Life and Work,* 1980. C. Brooks, *William Faulkner: First Encounters,* 1983. T. M. Davis, *Faulkner's "Negro": Art and the Southern Context,* 1983. E. Peters, *William Faulkner: The Yoknapatawpha World and Black Being,* 1983. J. L. Blotner, *Faulkner: A Biography,* 1984.

Text Used: *Collected Stories of William Faulkner,* 1977.

A ROSE FOR EMILY

I

When Miss Emily Grierson died, our whole town went to her funeral: the men through a sort of respectful affection for a fallen monument, the women mostly out of curiosity to see the inside of her house, which no one save an old manservant—a combined gardener and cook—had seen in at least ten years.

It was a big, squarish frame house that had once been white, decorated with cupolas and spires and scrolled balconies in the heavily lightsome style of the seventies, set on what had once been our most select street. But garages and cotton gins had encroached and obliterated even the august names of that neighborhood; only Miss Emily's house was left, lifting its stubborn and coquettish decay above the cotton wagons and the gasoline pumps—an eyesore among eyesores. And now Miss Emily had gone to join the representatives of those august names where they lay in the cedar-bemused cemetery among the ranked and anonymous graves of Union and Confederate soldiers who fell at the battle of Jefferson.[1]

---

[1] The seat of Faulkner's fictional Yoknapatawpha county, Jefferson is clearly his home town of Oxford, Mississippi.

Alive, Miss Emily had been a tradition, a duty, and a care; a sort of hereditary obligation upon the town, dating from that day in 1894 when Colonel Sartoris, the mayor—he who fathered the edict that no Negro woman should appear on the streets without an apron—remitted her taxes, the dispensation dating from the death of her father on into perpetuity. Not that Miss Emily would have accepted charity. Colonel Sartoris invented an involved tale to the effect that Miss Emily's father had loaned money to the town, which the town, as a matter of business, preferred this way of repaying. Only a man of Colonel Sartoris' generation and thought could have invented it, and only a woman could have believed it.

When the next generation, with its more modern ideas, became mayors and aldermen, this arrangement created some little dissatisfaction. On the first of the year they mailed her a tax notice. February came, and there was no reply. They wrote her a formal letter, asking her to call at the sheriff's office at her convenience. A week later the mayor wrote her himself, offering to call or to send his car for her, and received in reply a note on paper of an archaic shape, in a thin, flowing calligraphy in faded ink, to the effect that she no longer went out at all. The tax notice was also enclosed, without comment.

They called a special meeting of the Board of Aldermen. A deputation waited upon her, knocked at the door through which no visitor had passed since she ceased giving china-painting lessons eight or ten years earlier. They were admitted by the old Negro into a dim hall from which a stairway mounted into still more shadow. It smelled of dust and disuse—a close, dank smell. The Negro led them into the parlor. It was furnished in heavy, leather-covered furniture. When the Negro opened the blinds of one window, they could see that the leather was cracked; and when they sat down, a faint dust rose sluggishly about their thighs, spinning with slow motes in the single sun-ray. On a tarnished gilt easel before the fireplace stood a crayon portrait of Miss Emily's father.

They rose when she entered—a small, fat woman in black, with a thin gold chain descending to her waist and vanishing into her belt, leaning on an ebony cane with a tarnished gold head. Her skeleton was small and spare; perhaps that was why what would have been merely plumpness in another was obesity in her. She looked bloated, like a body long submerged in motionless water, and of that pallid hue. Her eyes, lost in the fatty ridges of her face, looked like two small pieces of coal pressed into a lump of dough as they moved from one face to another while the visitors stated their errand.

She did not ask them to sit. She just stood in the door and listened quietly until the spokesman came to a stumbling halt. Then they could hear the invisible watch ticking at the end of the gold chain.

Her voice was dry and cold. "I have no taxes in Jefferson. Colonel Sartoris explained it to me. Perhaps one of you can gain access to the city records and satisfy yourselves."

"But we have. We are the city authorities, Miss Emily. Didn't you get a notice from the sheriff, signed by him?"

"I received a paper, yes," Miss Emily said. "Perhaps he considers himself the sheriff . . . I have no taxes in Jefferson."

"But there is nothing on the books to show that, you see. We must go by the—"

"See Colonel Sartoris. I have no taxes in Jefferson."

"But, Miss Emily—"

"See Colonel Sartoris." (Colonel Sartoris had been dead almost ten years.) "I have no taxes in Jefferson. Tobe!" The Negro appeared. "Show these gentlemen out."

II

So she vanquished them, horse and foot,[2] just as she had vanquished their fathers thirty years before about the smell. That was two years after her father's death and a short time after her sweetheart—the one we believed would marry her—had deserted her. After her father's death she went out very little; after her sweetheart went away, people hardly saw her at all. A few of the ladies had the temerity to call, but were not received, and the only sign of life about the place was the Negro man—a young man then—going in and out with a market basket.

"Just as if a man—any man—could keep a kitchen properly," the ladies said; so they were not surprised when the smell developed. It was another link between the gross, teeming world and the high and mighty Griersons.

A neighbor, a woman, complained to the mayor, Judge Stevens, eighty years old.

"But what will you have me do about it, madam?" he said.

"Why, send her word to stop it," the woman said. "Isn't there a law?"

"I'm sure that won't be necessary," Judge Stevens said. "It's probably just a snake or a rat that nigger of hers killed in the yard. I'll speak to him about it."

The next day he received two more complaints, one from a man who came in diffident deprecation. "We really must do something about it, Judge. I'd be the last one in the world to bother Miss Emily, but we've got to do something." That night the Board of Aldermen met—three graybeards and one younger man, a member of the rising generation.

"It's simple enough," he said. "Send her word to have her place cleaned up. Give her a certain time to do it in, and if she don't . . ."

"Dammit, sir," Judge Stevens said, "will you accuse a lady to her face of smelling bad?"

So the next night, after midnight, four men crossed Miss Emily's lawn and slunk about the house like burglars, sniffing along the base of the brickwork and at the cellar openings while one of them performed a regular sowing motion with his hand out of a sack slung from his shoulder. They broke open the cellar door and sprinkled lime there, and in all the outbuildings. As they recrossed the lawn, a window that had been dark was lighted and Miss Emily sat in it, the light behind her, and her upright torso motionless as that of an idol. They crept quietly across the lawn and into the shadow of the locusts that lined the street. After a week or two the smell went away.

That was when people had begun to feel really sorry for her. People in our town, remembering how old lady Wyatt, her great-aunt, had gone completely crazy at last, believed that the Griersons held themselves a little too high for what they really were. None of the young men were quite good enough for Miss Emily and such. We had long thought of them as a tableau, Miss Emily a slender figure in white in the background, her father a spraddled silhouette in the foreground, his back to her and clutching a horsewhip, the two of them framed by the back-flung front door. So when she got to be thirty and was still single, we were not pleased exactly, but vindicated; even with insanity in the family she wouldn't have turned down all of her chances if they had really materialized.

[2] Completely, as in the defeat of an army's cavalry (horses) and infantry (foot).

When her father died, it got about that the house was all that was left to her; and in a way, people were glad. At last they could pity Miss Emily. Being left alone, and a pauper, she had become humanized. Now she too would know the old thrill and the old despair of a penny more or less.

The day after his death all the ladies prepared to call at the house and offer condolence and aid, as is our custom. Miss Emily met them at the door, dressed as usual and with no trace of grief on her face. She told them that her father was not dead. She did that for three days, with the ministers calling on her, and the doctors, trying to persuade her to let them dispose of the body. Just as they were about to resort to law and force, she broke down, and they buried her father quickly.

We did not say she was crazy then. We believed she had to do that. We remembered all the young men her father had driven away, and we knew that with nothing left, she would have to cling to that which had robbed her, as people will.

III

She was sick for a long time. When we saw her again, her hair was cut short, making her look like a girl, with a vague resemblance to those angels in colored church windows—sort of tragic and serene.

The town had just let the contracts for paving the sidewalks, and in the summer after her father's death they began the work. The construction company came with niggers and mules and machinery, and a foreman named Homer Barron, a Yankee—a big, dark, ready man, with a big voice and eyes lighter than his face. The little boys would follow in groups to hear him cuss the niggers, and the niggers singing in time to the rise and fall of picks. Pretty soon he knew everybody in town. Whenever you heard a lot of laughing anywhere about the square, Homer Barron would be in the center of the group. Presently we began to see him and Miss Emily on Sunday afternoons driving in the yellow-wheeled buggy and the matched team of bays from the livery stable.

At first we were glad that Miss Emily would have an interest, because the ladies all said, "Of course a Grierson would not think seriously of a Northerner, a day laborer." But there were still others, older people, who said that even grief could not cause a real lady to forget *noblesse oblige*[3]—without calling it *noblesse oblige*. They just said, "Poor Emily. Her kinsfolk should come to her." She had some kin in Alabama; but years ago her father had fallen out with them over the estate of old lady Wyatt, the crazy woman, and there was no communication between the two families. They had not even been represented at the funeral.

And as soon as the old people said, "Poor Emily," the whispering began. "Do you suppose it's really so?" they said to one another. "Of course it is. What else could . . . " This behind their hands; rustling of craned silk and satin behind jalousies closed upon the sun of Sunday afternoon as the thin, swift clop-clop-clop of the matched team passed: "Poor Emily."

She carried her head high enough—even when we believed that she was fallen. It was as if she demanded more than ever the recognition of her dignity as the last Grierson; as if it had wanted that touch of earthiness to reaffirm her imperviousness. Like when she bought the rat poison, the arsenic. That was over a year after

---

[3] "High birth obligates" (French): the obligation of honorable, generous, and responsible behavior associated with high rank or birth.

they had begun to say "Poor Emily," and while the two female cousins were visiting her.

"I want some poison," she said to the druggist. She was over thirty then, still a slight woman, though thinner than usual, with cold, haughty black eyes in a face the flesh of which was strained across the temples and about the eyesockets as you imagine a lighthouse-keeper's face ought to look. "I want some poison," she said.

"Yes, Miss Emily. What kind? For rats and such? I'd recom——"

"I want the best you have. I don't care what kind."

The druggist named several. "They'll kill anything up to an elephant. But what you want is——"

"Arsenic," Miss Emily said. "Is that a good one?"

"Is . . . arsenic? Yes, ma'am. But what you want——"

"I want arsenic."

The druggist looked down at her. She looked back at him, erect, her face like a strained flag. "Why, of course," the druggist said. "If that's what you want. But the law requires you to tell what you are going to use it for."

Miss Emily just stared at him, her head tilted back in order to look him eye for eye, until he looked away and went and got the arsenic and wrapped it up. The Negro delivery boy brought her the package; the druggist didn't come back. When she opened the package at home there was written on the box, under the skull and bones: "For rats."

IV

So the next day we all said, "She will kill herself"; and we said it would be the best thing. When she had first begun to be seen with Homer Barron, we had said, "She will marry him." Then we said, "She will persuade him yet," because Homer himself had remarked—he liked men, and it was known that he drank with the younger men in the Elks' Club—that he was not a marrying man. Later we said, "Poor Emily" behind the jalousies as they passed on Sunday afternoon in the glittering buggy, Miss Emily with her head high and Homer Barron with his hat cocked and a cigar in his teeth, reins and whip in a yellow glove.

Then some of the ladies began to say that it was a disgrace to the town and a bad example to the young people. The men did not want to interfere, but at last the ladies forced the Baptist minister—Miss Emily's people were Episcopal—to call upon her. He would never divulge what happened during that interview, but he refused to go back again. The next Sunday they again drove about the streets, and the following day the minister's wife wrote to Miss Emily's relations in Alabama.

So she had blood-kin under her roof again and we sat back to watch developments. At first nothing happened. Then we were sure that they were to be married. We learned that Miss Emily had been to the jeweler's and ordered a man's toilet set in silver, with the letters H. B. on each piece. Two days later we learned that she had bought a complete outfit of men's clothing, including a nightshirt, and we said, "They are married." We were really glad. We were glad because the two female cousins were even more Grierson than Miss Emily had ever been.

So we were not surprised when Homer Barron—the streets had been finished some time since—was gone. We were a little disappointed that there was not a public blowing-off, but we believed that he had gone on to prepare for Miss Emily's coming, or to give her a chance to get rid of the cousins. (By that time it was a cabal, and we were all Miss Emily's allies to help circumvent the cousins.)

Sure enough, after another week they departed. And, as we had expected all along, within three days Homer Barron was back in town. A neighbor saw the Negro man admit him at the kitchen door at dusk one evening.

And that was the last we saw of Homer Barron. And of Miss Emily for some time. The Negro man went in and out with the market basket, but the front door remained closed. Now and then we would see her at the window for a moment, as the men did that night when they sprinkled the lime, but for almost six months she did not appear on the streets. Then we knew that this was to be expected too; as if that quality of her father which had thwarted her woman's life so many times had been too virulent and too furious to die.

When we next saw Miss Emily, she had grown fat and her hair was turning gray. During the next few years it grew grayer and grayer until it attained an even pepper-and salt iron-gray, when it ceased turning. Up to the day of her death at seventy-four it was still that vigorous iron-gray, like the hair of an active man.

From that time on her front door remained closed, save for a period of six or seven years, when she was about forty, during which she gave lessons in china-painting. She fitted up a studio in one of the downstairs rooms, where the daughters and granddaughters of Colonel Sartoris' contemporaries were sent to her with the same regularity and in the same spirit that they were sent to church on Sundays with a twenty-five-cent piece for the collection plate. Meanwhile her taxes had been remitted.

Then the newer generation became the backbone and the spirit of the town, and the painting pupils grew up and fell away and did not send their children to her with boxes of color and tedious brushes and pictures cut from the ladies' magazines. The front door closed upon the last one and remained closed for good. When the town got free postal delivery, Miss Emily alone refused to let them fasten the metal numbers above her door and attach a mailbox to it. She would not listen to them.

Daily, monthly, yearly we watched the Negro grow grayer and more stooped, going in and out with the market basket. Each December we sent her a tax notice, which would be returned by the post office a week later, unclaimed. Now and then we would see her in one of the downstairs windows—she had evidently shut up the top floor of the house—like the carven torso of an idol in a niche, looking or not looking at us, we could never tell which. Thus she passed from generation to generation—dear, inescapable, impervious, tranquil, and perverse.

And so she died. Fell ill in the house filled with dust and shadows, with only a doddering Negro man to wait on her. We did not even know she was sick; we had long since given up trying to get any information from the Negro. He talked to no one, probably not even to her, for his voice had grown harsh and rusty, as if from disuse.

She died in one of the downstairs rooms, in a heavy walnut bed with a curtain, her gray head propped on a pillow yellow and moldy with age and lack of sunlight.

V

The Negro met the first of the ladies at the front door and let them in, with their hushed, sibilant voices and their quick, curious glances, and then he disappeared. He walked right through the house and out the back and was not seen again.

The two female cousins came at once. They held the funeral on the second day, with the town coming to look at Miss Emily beneath a mass of bought flowers, with the crayon face of her father musing profoundly above the bier and the ladies sibilant and macabre; and the very old men—some in their brushed Confederate uniforms—on the porch and the lawn, talking of Miss Emily as if she had been a contemporary of theirs, believing that they had danced with her and courted her perhaps, confusing time with its mathematical progression, as the old do, to whom all the past is not a diminishing road but, instead, a huge meadow which no winter ever quite touches, divided from them now by the narrow bottle-neck of the most recent decade of years.

Already we knew that there was one room in that region above stairs which no one had seen in forty years, and which would have to be forced. They waited until Miss Emily was decently in the ground before they opened it.

The violence of breaking down the door seemed to fill this room with pervading dust. A thin, acrid pall as of the tomb seemed to lie everywhere upon this room decked and furnished as for a bridal: upon the valance curtains of faded rose color, upon the rose-shaded lights, upon the dressing table, upon the delicate array of crystal and the man's toilet things backed with tarnished silver, silver so tarnished that the monogram was obscured. Among them lay a collar and tie, as if they had just been removed, which, lifted, left upon the surface a pale crescent in the dust. Upon a chair hung the suit, carefully folded; beneath it the two mute shoes and the discarded socks.

The man himself lay in the bed.

For a long while we just stood there, looking down at the profound and fleshless grin. The body had apparently once lain in the attitude of an embrace, but now the long sleep that outlasts love, that conquers even the grimace of love, had cuckolded him. What was left of him, rotted beneath what was left of the nightshirt, had become inextricable from the bed in which he lay; and upon him and upon the pillow beside him lay that even coating of the patient and biding dust.

Then we noticed that in the second pillow was the indentation of a head. One of us lifted something from it; and leaning forward, that faint and invisible dust dry and acrid in the nostrils, we saw a long strand of iron-gray hair.

1930

THAT EVENING SUN*

I

Monday is no different from any other weekday in Jefferson[1] now. The streets are paved now, and the telephone and electric companies are cutting down more and more of the shade trees—the water oaks, the maples and locusts and elms—to make room for iron poles bearing clusters of bloated and ghostly and bloodless

---

* First published in the *American Mercury* in March 1931 and collected in *These 13* (1931). The title is probably based on W. C. Handy's song "St. Louis Blues" (1914), in which a woman sings of her unfaithful lover. "Hate to see de ev'nin' sun go down. / 'Cause my baby, he done lef' dis town."

[1] The seat of Faulkner's fictional Yoknapatawpha County, Jefferson is clearly his hometown of Oxford, Mississippi.

grapes, and we have a city laundry which makes the rounds on Monday morning, gathering the bundles of clothes into bright-colored, specially-made motor cars: the soiled wearing of a whole week now flees apparitionlike behind alert and irritable electric horns, with a long diminishing noise of rubber and asphalt like tearing silk, and even the Negro women who still take in white people's washing after the old custom, fetch and deliver it in automobiles.

But fifteen years ago, on Monday morning the quiet, dusty, shady streets would be full of Negro women with, balanced on their steady, turbaned heads, bundles of clothes tied up in sheets, almost as large as cotton bales, carried so without touch of hand between the kitchen door of the white house and the blackened washpot beside a cabin door in Negro Hollow.

Nancy would set her bundle on the top of her head, then upon the bundle in turn she would set the black straw sailor hat which she wore winter and summer. She was tall, with a high, sad face sunken a little where her teeth were missing. Sometimes we would go a part of the way down the lane and across the pasture with her, to watch the balanced bundle and the hat that never bobbed nor wavered, even when she walked down into the ditch and up the other side and stooped through the fence. She would go down on her hands and knees and crawl through the gap, her head rigid, uptilted, the bundle steady as a rock or a balloon, and rise to her feet again and go on.

Sometimes the husbands of the washing women would fetch and deliver the clothes, but Jesus never did that for Nancy, even before father told him to stay away from our house, even when Dilsey was sick and Nancy would come to cook for us.

And then about half the time we'd have to go down the lane to Nancy's cabin and tell her to come on and cook breakfast. We would stop at the ditch, because father told us to not have anything to do with Jesus—he was a short black man, with a razor scar down his face—and we would throw rocks at Nancy's house until she came to the door, leaning her head around it without any clothes on.

"What yawl mean, chunking my house?" Nancy said. "What you little devils mean?"

"Father says for you to come on and get breakfast," Caddy said. "Father says it's over a half an hour now, and you've got to come this minute."

"I aint studying no breakfast," Nancy said. "I going to get my sleep out."

"I bet you're drunk," Jason said. "Father says you're drunk. Are you drunk, Nancy?"

"Who says I is?" Nancy said. "I got to get my sleep out. I aint studying no breakfast."

So after a while we quit chunking the cabin and went back home. When she finally came, it was too late for me to go to school. So we thought it was whisky until that day they arrested her again and they were taking her to jail and they passed Mr Stovall. He was the cashier in the bank and a deacon in the Baptist church, and Nancy began to say:

"When you going to pay me, white man? When you going to pay me, white man? It's been three times now since you paid me a cent—" Mr Stovall knocked her down, but she kept on saying, "When you going to pay me, white man? It's been three times now since—" until Mr Stovall kicked her in the mouth with his heel and the marshal caught Mr Stovall back, and Nancy lying in the street, laughing. She turned her head and spat out some blood and teeth and said, "It's been three times now since he paid me a cent."

That was how she lost her teeth, and all that day they told about Nancy and Mr Stovall, and all that night the ones that passed the jail could hear Nancy singing and yelling. They could see her hands holding to the window bars, and a lot of them stopped along the fence, listening to her and to the jailer trying to make her stop. She didn't shut up until almost daylight, when the jailer began to hear a bumping and scraping upstairs and he went up there and found Nancy hanging from the window bar. He said that it was cocaine and not whisky, because no nigger would try to commit suicide unless he was full of cocaine, because a nigger full of cocaine wasn't a nigger any longer.

The jailer cut her down and revived her; then he beat her, whipped her. She had hung herself with her dress. She had fixed it all right, but when they arrested her she didn't have on anything except a dress and so she didn't have anything to tie her hands with and she couldn't make her hands let go of the window ledge. So the jailer heard the noise and ran up there and found Nancy hanging from the window, stark naked, her belly already swelling out a little, like a little balloon.

When Dilsey was sick in her cabin and Nancy was cooking for us, we could see her apron swelling out; that was before father told Jesus to stay away from the house. Jesus was in the kitchen, sitting behind the stove, with his razor scar on his black face like a piece of dirty string. He said it was a watermelon that Nancy had under her dress.

"It never come off of your vine, though," Nancy said.

"Off of what vine?" Caddy said.

"I can cut down the vine it did come off of," Jesus said.

"What makes you want to talk like that before these children?" Nancy said. "Whyn't you go on to work? You done et. You want Mr Jason to catch you hanging around his kitchen, talking that way before these chillen?"

"Talking what way?" Caddy said. "What vine?"

"I cant hang around white man's kitchen," Jesus said. "But white man can hang around mine. White man can come in my house, but I cant stop him. When white man want to come in my house, I aint got no house. I cant stop him, but he cant kick me outen it. He cant do that."

Dilsey was still sick in her cabin. Father told Jesus to stay off our place. Dilsey was still sick. It was a long time. We were in the library after supper.

"Isn't Nancy through in the kitchen yet?" mother said. "It seems to me that she has had plenty of time to have finished the dishes."

"Let Quentin go and see," father said. "Go and see if Nancy is through, Quentin. Tell her she can go on home."

I went to the kitchen. Nancy was through. The dishes were put away and the fire was out. Nancy was sitting in a chair, close to the cold stove. She looked at me.

"Mother wants to know if you are through," I said.

"Yes," Nancy said. She looked at me. "I done finished." She looked at me.

"What is it?" I said. "What is it?"

"I aint nothing but a nigger," Nancy said. "It aint none of my fault."

She looked at me, sitting in the chair before the cold stove, the sailor hat on her head. I went back to the library. It was the cold stove and all, when you think of a kitchen being warm and busy and cheerful. And with a cold stove and the dishes all put away, and nobody wanting to eat at that hour.

"Is she through?" mother said.

"Yessum," I said.

"What is she doing?" mother said.

"She's not doing anything. She's through."

"I'll go and see," father said.

"Maybe she's waiting for Jesus to come and take her home," Caddy said.

"Jesus is gone," I said. Nancy told us how one morning she woke up and Jesus was gone.

"He quit me," Nancy said. "Done gone to Memphis, I reckon. Dodging them city *po*-lice for a while, I reckon."

"And a good riddance," father said. "I hope he stays there."

"Nancy's scaired of the dark," Jason said.

"So are you," Caddy said.

"I'm not," Jason said.

"Scairy cat," Caddy said.

"I'm not," Jason said.

"You, Candace!" mother said. Father came back.

"I am going to walk down the lane with Nancy," he said. "She says that Jesus is back."

"Has she seen him?" mother said.

"No. Some Negro sent her word that he was back in town. I wont be long."

"You'll leave me alone, to take Nancy home?" mother said. "Is her safety more precious to you than mine?"

"I wont be long," father said.

"You'll leave these children unprotected, with that Negro about?"

"I'm going too," Caddy said, "Let me go, Father."

"What would he do with them, if he were unfortunate enough to have them?" father said.

"I want to go, too," Jason said.

"Jason!" mother said. She was speaking to father. You could tell that by the way she said the name. Like she believed that all day father had been trying to think of doing the thing she wouldn't like the most, and that she knew all the time that after a while he would think of it. I stayed quiet, because father and I both knew that mother would want him to make me stay with her if she just thought of it in time. So father didn't look at me. I was the oldest. I was nine and Caddy was seven and Jason was five.

"Nonsense," father said. "We wont be long."

Nancy had her hat on. We came to the lane. "Jesus always been good to me," Nancy said. "Whenever he had two dollars, one of them was mine." We walked in the lane. "If I can just get through the lane." Nancy said, "I be all right then."

The lane was always dark. "This is where Jason got scared on Hallowe'en," Caddy said.

"I didn't," Jason said.

"Cant Aunt Rachel do anything with him?" father said. Aunt Rachel was old. She lived in a cabin beyond Nancy's, by herself. She had white hair and she smoked a pipe in the door, all day long; she didn't work any more. They said she was Jesus' mother. Sometimes she said she was and sometimes she said she wasn't any kin to Jesus.

"Yes, you did," Caddy said. "You were scairder than Frony. You were scairder than T.P. even. Scairder than niggers."

"Cant nobody do nothing with him," Nancy said. "He say I done woke up the devil in him and aint but one thing going to lay it down again."

"Well, he's gone now," father said. "There's nothing for you to be afraid of now. And if you'd just let white men alone."

"Let what white men alone?" Caddy said. "How let them alone?"

"He aint gone nowhere," Nancy said. "I can feel him. I can feel him now, in this lane. He hearing us talk, every word, hid somewhere, waiting. I aint seen him, and I aint going to see him again but once more, with that razor in his mouth. That razor on that string down his back, inside his shirt. And then I aint going to be even surprised."

"I wasn't scaired," Jason said.

"If you'd behave yourself, you'd have kept out of this," father said. "But it's all right now. He's probably in St. Louis now. Probably got another wife by now and forgot all about you."

"If he has, I better not find out about it," Nancy said. "I'd stand there right over them, and every time he wropped her, I'd cut that arm off. I'd cut his head off and I'd slit her belly and I'd shove—"

"Hush," father said.

"Slit whose belly, Nancy?" Caddy said.

"I wasn't scaired," Jason said. "I'd walk right down this lane by myself."

"Yah," Caddy said. "You wouldn't dare to put your foot down in it if we were not here too."

II

Dilsey was still sick, so we took Nancy home every night until mother said, "How much longer is this going on? I to be left alone in this big house while you take home a frightened Negro?

We fixed a pallet,[2] in the kitchen for Nancy. One night we waked up, hearing the sound. It was not singing and it was not crying, coming up the dark stairs. There was a light in mother's room and we heard father going down the hall, down the back stairs, and Caddy and I went into the hall. The floor was cold. Our toes curled away from it while we listened to the sound. It was like singing and it wasn't like singing, like the sounds that Negroes make.

Then it stopped and we heard father going down the back stairs, and we went to the head of the stairs. Then the sound began again, in the stairway, not loud, and we could see Nancy's eyes halfway up the stairs, against the wall. They looked like cat's eyes do, like a big cat against the wall, watching us. When we came down the steps to where she was, she quit making the sound again, and we stood there until father came back up from the kitchen, with his pistol in his hand. He went back down with Nancy and they came back with Nancy's pallet.

We spread the pallet in our room. After the light in mother's room went off, we could see Nancy's eyes again. "Nancy," Caddy whispered, "are you asleep, Nancy?"

Nancy whispered something. It was oh or no, I dont know which. Like nobody had made it, like it came from nowhere and went nowhere, until it was like Nancy was not there at all; that I had looked so hard at her eyes on the stairs that they had got printed on my eyeballs, like the sun does when you have closed your eyes and there is no sun. "Jesus," Nancy whispered. "Jesus."

---

[2] A temporary bed, typically on the floor.

"Was it Jesus?" Caddy said. "Did he try to come into the kitchen?"

"Jesus," Nancy said. Like this: Jeeeeeeeeeeeeeeeeus, until the sound went out, like a match or a candle does.

"It's the other Jesus she means," I said.

"Can you see us, Nancy?" Caddy whispered. "Can you see our eyes too?"

"I aint nothing but a nigger," Nancy said. "God knows. God knows."

"What did you see down there in the kitchen?" Caddy whispered. "What tried to get in?"

"God knows," Nancy said. We could see her eyes. "God knows."

Dilsey got well. She cooked dinner. "You'd better stay in bed a day or two longer," father said.

"What for?" Dilsey said. "If I had been a day later, this place would be to rack and ruin. Get on out of here now, and let me get my kitchen straight again."

Dilsey cooked supper too. And that night, just before dark, Nancy came into the kitchen.

"How do you know he's back?" Dilsey said. "You aint seen him."

"Jesus is a nigger," Jason said.

"I can feel him," Nancy said. "I can feel him laying yonder in the ditch."

"Tonight?" Dilsey said. "Is he there tonight?"

"Dilsey's a nigger too," Jason said.

"You try to eat something," Dilsey said.

"I dont want nothing," Nancy said.

"I aint a nigger," Jason said.

"Drink some coffee," Dilsey said. She poured a cup of coffee for Nancy. "Do you know he's out there tonight? How come you know it's tonight?"

"I know," Nancy said. "He's there, waiting. I know. I done lived with him too long. I know what he is fixing to do fore he know it himself."

"Drink some coffee," Dilsey said. Nancy held the cup to her mouth and blew into the cup. Her mouth pursed out like a spreading adder's, like a rubber mouth, like she had blown all the color out of her lips with blowing the coffee.

"I aint a nigger," Jason said. "Are you a nigger, Nancy?"

"I hellborn, child," Nancy said. "I wont be nothing soon. I going back where I come from soon."

III

She began to drink the coffee. While she was drinking, holding the cup in both hands, she began to make the sound again. She made the sound into the cup and the coffee sploshed out onto her hands and her dress. Her eyes looked at us and she sat there, her elbows on her knees, holding the cup in both hands, looking at us across the wet cup, making the sound. "Look at Nancy," Jason said. "Nancy cant cook for us now. Dilsey's got well now."

"You hush up," Dilsey said. Nancy held the cup in both hands, looking at us, making the sound, like there were two of them: one looking at us and the other making the sound. "Whyn't you let Mr Jason telefoam the marshal?" Dilsey said. Nancy stopped then, holding the cup in her long brown hands. She tried to drink some coffee again, but it sploshed out of the cup, onto her hands and her dress, and she put the cup down. Jason watched her.

"I cant swallow it," Nancy said. "I swallows but it wont go down me."

"You go down to the cabin," Dilsey said. "Frony will fix you a pallet and I'll be there soon."

"Wont no nigger stop him," Nancy said.

"I aint a nigger," Jason said. "Am I, Dilsey?"

"I reckon not," Dilsey said. She looked at Nancy. "I dont reckon so. What you going to do, then?"

Nancy looked at us. Her eyes went fast, like she was afraid there wasn't time to look, without hardly moving at all. She looked at us, at all three of us at one time. "You member that night I stayed in yawls' room?" she said. She told about how we waked up early the next morning, and played. We had to play quiet, on her pallet, until father woke up and it was time to get breakfast. "Go and ask your maw to let me stay here tonight," Nancy said. "I wont need no pallet. We can play some more."

Caddy asked mother. Jason went too. "I cant have Negroes sleeping in the bedrooms," mother said. Jason cried. He cried until mother said he couldn't have any dessert for three days if he didn't stop. Then Jason said he would stop if Dilsey would make a chocolate cake. Father was there.

"Why dont you do something about it?" mother said. "What do we have officers for?"

"Why is Nancy afraid of Jesus?" Caddy said. "Are you afraid of father, mother?"

"What could the officers do?" father said. "If Nancy hasn't seen him, how could the officers find him?"

"Then why is she afraid?" mother said.

"She says he is there. She says she knows he is there tonight."

"Yet we pay taxes," mother said. "I must wait here alone in this big house while you take a Negro woman home."

"You know that I am not lying outside with a razor," father said.

"I'll stop if Dilsey will make a chocolate cake," Jason said. Mother told us to go out and father said he didn't know if Jason would get a chocolate cake or not, but he knew what Jason was going to get in about a minute. We went back to the kitchen and told Nancy.

"Father said for you to go home and lock the door, and you'll be all right," Caddy said. "All right from what, Nancy? Is Jesus mad at you?" Nancy was holding the coffee cup in her hands again, her elbows on her knees and her hands holding the cup between her knees. She was looking into the cup. "What have you done that made Jesus mad?" Caddy said. Nancy let the cup go. It didn't break on the floor, but the coffee spilled out, and Nancy sat there with her hands still making the shape of the cup. She began to make the sound again, not loud. Not singing and not unsinging. We watched her.

"Here," Dilsey said. "You quit that, now. You get aholt of yourself. You wait here. I going to get Versh to walk home with you." Dilsey went out.

We looked at Nancy. Her shoulders kept shaking, but she quit making the sound. We watched her. "What's Jesus going to do to you?" Caddy said. "He went away."

Nancy looked at us. "We had fun that night I stayed in yawls' room, didn't we?"

"I didn't," Jason said. "I didn't have any fun."

"You were asleep in mother's room," Caddy said. "You were not there."

"Let's go down to my house and have some more fun," Nancy said.

"Mother wont let us," I said. "It's too late now."

"Dont bother her," Nancy said. "We can tell her in the morning. She wont mind."

"She wouldn't let us," I said.

"Dont ask her now," Nancy said. "Dont bother her now."

"She didn't say we couldn't go," Caddy said.

"We didn't ask," I said.

"If you go, I'll tell," Jason said.

"We'll have fun," Nancy said. "They won't mind, just to my house. I been working for yawl a long time. They won't mind."

"I'm not afraid to go," Caddy said. "Jason is the one that's afraid. He'll tell."

"I'm not," Jason said.

"Yes, you are," Caddy said, "You'll tell."

"I won't tell," Jason said. "I'm not afraid."

"Jason ain't afraid to go with me," Nancy said. "Is you, Jason?"

"Jason is going to tell," Caddy said. The lane was dark. We passed the pasture gate. "I bet if something was to jump out from behind that gate, Jason would holler."

"I wouldn't," Jason said. We walked down the lane. Nancy was talking loud.

"What are you talking so loud for, Nancy?" Caddy said.

"Who; me?" Nancy said. "Listen at Quentin and Caddy and Jason saying I'm talking loud."

"You talk like there was five of us here," Caddy said. "You talk like father was here too."

"Who; me talking loud, Mr Jason?" Nancy said.

"Nancy called Jason 'Mister,' " Caddy said.

"Listen how Caddy and Quentin and Jason talk," Nancy said.

"We're not talking loud," Caddy said. "You're the one that's talking like father—"

"Hush," Nancy said; "hush, Mr Jason."

"Nancy called Jason 'Mister' aguh—"

"Hush," Nancy said. She was talking loud when we crossed the ditch and stooped through the fence where she used to stoop through with the clothes on her head. Then we came to her house. We were going fast then. She opened the door. The smell of the house was like the lamp and the smell of Nancy was like the wick, like they were waiting for one another to begin to smell. She lit the lamp and closed the door and put the bar up. Then she quit talking loud, looking at us.

"What're we going to do?" Caddy said.

"What do yawl want to do?" Nancy said.

"You said we would have some fun," Caddy said.

There was something about Nancy's house; something you could smell besides Nancy and the house. Jason smelled it, even. "I don't want to stay here," he said. "I want to go home."

"Go home, then," Caddy said.

"I don't want to go by myself," Jason said.

"We're going to have some fun," Nancy said.

"How?" Caddy said.

Nancy stood by the door. She was looking at us, only it was like she had emptied her eyes, like she had quit using them. "What do you want to do?" she said.

"Tell us a story," Caddy said. "Can you tell a story?"

"Yes," Nancy said.

"Tell it," Caddy said. We looked at Nancy. "You don't know any stories."

"Yes," Nancy said. "Yes, I do."

She came and sat in a chair before the hearth. There was a little fire there. Nancy built it up, when it was already hot inside. She built a good blaze. She told a story. She talked like her eyes looked, like her eyes watching us and her voice talking to us did not belong to her. Like she was living somewhere else, waiting somewhere else. She was outside the cabin. Her voice was inside and the shape of her, the Nancy that could stoop under a barbed wire fence with a bundle of clothes balanced on her head as though without weight, like a balloon, was there. But that was all. "And so this here queen come walking up to the ditch, where that bad man was hiding. She was walking up to the ditch, and she say, 'If I can just get past this here ditch,' was what she say . . . "

"What ditch?" Caddy said. "A ditch like that one out there? Why did a queen want to go into a ditch?"

"To get to her house," Nancy said. She looked at us. "She had to cross the ditch to get into her house quick and bar the door."

"Why did she want to go home and bar the door?" Caddy said.

IV

Nancy looked at us. She quit talking. She looked at us. Jason's legs stuck straight out of his pants where he sat on Nancy's lap. "I don't think that's a good story," he said. "I want to go home."

"Maybe we had better," Caddy said. She got up from the floor. "I bet they are looking for us right now." She went toward the door.

"No," Nancy said. "Don't open it." She got up quick and passed Caddy. She didn't touch the door, the wooden bar.

"Why not?" Caddy said.

"Come back to the lamp," Nancy said. "We'll have fun. You don't have to go."

"We ought to go," Caddy said. "Unless we have a lot of fun." She and Nancy came back to the fire, the lamp.

"I want to go home," Jason said. "I'm going to tell."

"I know another story," Nancy said. She stood close to the lamp. She looked at Caddy, like when your eyes look up at a stick balanced on your nose. She had to look down to see Caddy, but her eyes looked like that, like when you are balancing a stick.

"I won't listen to it," Jason said. "I'll bang on the floor."

"It's a good one," Nancy said. "It's better than the other one."

"What's it about?" Caddy said. Nancy was standing by the lamp. Her hand was on the lamp, against the light, long and brown.

"Your hand is on that hot globe," Caddy said. "Don't it feel hot to your hand?"

Nancy looked at her hand on the lamp chimney. She took her hand away, slow. She stood there, looking at Caddy, wringing her long hand as though it were tied to her wrist with a string.

"Let's do something else," Caddy said.

"I want to go home," Jason said.

"I got some popcorn," Nancy said. She looked at Caddy and then at Jason and then at me and then at Caddy again. "I got some popcorn."

"I don't like popcorn," Jason said. "I'd rather have candy."

Nancy looked at Jason. "You can hold the popper." She was still wringing her hand; it was long and limp and brown.

"All right," Jason said. "I'll stay a while if I can do that. Caddy can't hold it. I'll want to go home again if Caddy holds the popper."

Nancy built up the fire. "Look at Nancy putting her hands in the fire," Caddy said. "What's the matter with you, Nancy?"

"I got popcorn," Nancy said. "I got some." She took the popper from under the bed. It was broken. Jason began to cry.

"Now we can't have any popcorn," he said.

"We ought to go home, anyway," Caddy said. "Come on, Quentin."

"Wait," Nancy said; "wait. I can fix it. Don't you want to help me fix it?"

"I don't think I want any," Caddy said. "It's too late now."

"You help me, Jason," Nancy said. "Don't you want to help me?"

"No," Jason said. "I want to go home."

"Hush," Nancy said; "hush. Watch. Watch me. I can fix it so Jason can hold it and pop the corn." She got a piece of wire and fixed the popper.

"It won't hold good," Caddy said.

"Yes, it will," Nancy said. "Yawl watch. Yawl help me shell some corn."

The popcorn was under the bed too. We shelled it into the popper and Nancy helped Jason hold the popper over the fire.

"It's not popping," Jason said. "I want to go home."

"You wait," Nancy said. "It'll begin to pop. We'll have fun then." She was sitting close to the fire. The lamp was turned up so high it was beginning to smoke.

"Why don't you turn it down some?" I said.

"It's all right," Nancy said. "I'll clean it. Yawl wait. The popcorn will start in a minute."

"I don't believe it's going to start," Caddy said. "We ought to start home, anyway. They'll be worried."

"No," Nancy said. "It's going to pop. Dilsey will tell um yawl with me. I been working for yawl long time. They won't mind if yawl at my house. You wait, now. It'll start popping any minute now."

Then Jason got some smoke in his eyes and he began to cry. He dropped the popper into the fire. Nancy got a wet rag and wiped Jason's face, but he didn't stop crying.

"Hush," she said, "Hush." But he didn't hush. Caddy took the popper out of the fire.

"It's burned up," she said. "You'll have to get some more popcorn, Nancy."

"Did you put all of it in?" Nancy said.

"Yes," Caddy said. Nancy looked at Caddy. Then she took the popper and opened it and poured the cinders into her apron and began to sort the grains, her hands long and brown, and we watching her.

"Haven't you got any more?" Caddy said.

"Yes," Nancy said; "yes. Look. This here ain't burnt. All we need to do is—"

"I want to go home," Jason said. "I'm going to tell."

"Hush," Caddy said. We all listened. Nancy's head was already turned toward the barred door, her eyes filled with red lamplight. "Somebody is coming," Caddy said.

Then Nancy began to make that sound again, not loud, sitting there above the fire, her long hands dangling between her knees; all of a sudden water began to come out on her face in big drops, running down her face, carrying in each one a little turning ball of firelight like a spark until it dropped off her chin. "She's not crying," I said.

"I ain't crying," Nancy said. Her eyes were closed. "I ain't crying. Who is it?"

"I don't know," Caddy said. She went to the door and looked out. "We've got to go now," she said. "Here comes father."

"I'm going to tell," Jason said. "Yawl made me come."

The water still ran down Nancy's face. She turned in her chair. "Listen. Tell him. Tell him we going to have fun. Tell him I take good care of yawl until in the morning. Tell him to let me come home with yawl and sleep on the floor. Tell him I won't need no pallet. We'll have fun. You member last time how we had so much fun?"

"I didn't have fun," Jason said. "You hurt me. You put smoke in my eyes. I'm going to tell."

V

Father came in. He looked at us. Nancy did not get up.

"Tell him," she said.

"Caddy made us come down here," Jason said. "I didn't want to."

Father came to the fire. Nancy looked up at him. "Can't you go to Aunt Rachel's and stay?" he said. Nancy looked up at father, her hands between her knees. "He's not here," father said. "I would have seen him. There's not a soul in sight."

"He in the ditch," Nancy said. "He waiting in the ditch yonder."

"Nonsense," father said. He looked at Nancy. "Do you know he's there?"

"I got the sign," Nancy said.

"What sign?"

"I got it. It was on the table when I come in. It was a hog-bone, with blood meat still on it, laying by the lamp. He's out there. When yawl walk out that door, I gone."

"Gone where, Nancy?" Caddy said.

"I'm not a tattletale," Jason said.

"Nonsense," father said.

"He out there," Nancy said. "He looking through that window this minute, waiting for yawl to go. Then I gone."

"Nonsense," father said. "Lock up your house and we'll take you on to Aunt Rachel's."

"'Twont do no good," Nancy said. She didn't look at father now, but he looked down at her, at her long, limp, moving hands. "Putting it off wont do no good."

"Then what do you want to do?" father said.

"I don't know," Nancy said. "I can't do nothing. Just put it off. And that don't do no good. I reckon it belong to me. I reckon what I going to get ain't no more than mine."

"Get what?" Caddy said. "What's yours?"

"Nothing," father said. "You all must get to bed."

"Caddy made me come," Jason said.

"Go on to Aunt Rachel's," father said.

"It won't do no good," Nancy said. She sat before the fire, her elbows on her knees, her long hands between her knees. "When even your own kitchen wouldn't do no good. When even if I was sleeping on the floor in the room with your chillen, and the next morning there I am, and blood—"

"Hush," father said. "Lock the door and put out the lamp and go to bed."

"I scared of the dark," Nancy said. "I scared for it to happen in the dark."

"You mean you're going to sit right here with the lamp lighted?" father said. Then Nancy began to make the sound again, sitting before the fire, her long hands between her knees. "Ah, damnation," father said. "Come along, chillen. It's past bedtime."

"When yawl go home, I gone," Nancy said. She talked quieter now, and her face looked quiet, like her hands. "Anyway, I got my coffin money saved up with Mr. Lovelady." Mr. Lovelady was a short, dirty man who collected the Negro insurance, coming around to the cabins or the kitchens every Saturday morning, to collect fifteen cents. He and his wife lived at the hotel. One morning his wife committed suicide. They had a child, a little girl. He and the child went away. After a week or two he came back alone. We would see him going along the lanes and the back streets on Saturday mornings.

"Nonsense," father said. "You'll be the first thing I'll see in the kitchen tomorrow morning."

"You'll see what you'll see, I reckon," Nancy said. "But it will take the Lord to say what that will be."

VI

We left her sitting before the fire.

"Come and put the bar up," father said. But she didn't move. She didn't look at us again, sitting quietly there between the lamp and the fire. From some distance down the lane we could look back and see her through the open door.

"What, Father?" Caddy said. "What's going to happen?"

"Nothing," father said. Jason was on father's back, so Jason was the tallest of all of us. We went down into the ditch. I looked at it, quiet. I couldn't see much where the moonlight and the shadows tangled.

"If Jesus is hid here, he can see us, cant he?" Caddy said.

"He's not there," father said. "He went away a long time ago."

"You made me come," Jason said, high; against the sky it looked like father had two heads, a little one and a big one. "I didn't want to."

We went up out of the ditch. We could still see Nancy's house and the open door, but we couldn't see Nancy now, sitting before the fire with the door open, because she was tired. "I just done got tired," she said. "I just a nigger. It ain't no fault of mine."

But we could hear her, because she began just after we came up out of the ditch, the sound that was not singing and not unsinging. "Who will do our washing now, Father?" I said.

"I'm not a nigger," Jason said, high and close above father's head.

"You're worse," Caddy said, "you are a tattletale. If something was to jump out, you'd be scairder than a nigger."

"I wouldn't," Jason said.

"You'd cry," Caddy said.

"Caddy," father said.

"I wouldn't!" Jason said.

"Scairy cat," Caddy said.

"Candace!" father said.

1931

Ernest Hemingway
(1899–1961)

Born in 1899 in Oak Park, Illinois, a prosperous suburb of Chicago, Ernest Miller Hemingway grew up as the third child, the oldest son, of six children in a comfortable, devout Protestant family. His parents were dynamic, spirited individuals: Clarence Edmond Hemingway was a general practitioner and an avid sportsman; his wife, Grace Hall, had relinquished a potential operatic career in favor of marriage and devoted her talents to teaching music and to the promotion of religion and high culture in her household. From the time Ernest Hemingway was a few months old, the family regularly spent summers at a cottage in upper Michigan, where the boy acquired his lifelong passion for hunting and fishing. The landscape was to provide the setting for some of Hemingway's greatest stories, including "Big Two-Hearted River" (1925).

By the time Hemingway was eighteen, America had entered World War I, and he faced a choice about his future. Having decided not to attend college, he spent six months working as a cub reporter for the Kansas City *Star* and discovered a boundless enthusiasm, which never left him, for the "romance of journalism." Hemingway longed to participate in the war in Europe, but an inherited eye problem precluded military service. Searching for alternatives, he and two of his closest friends made a pact to volunteer as ambulance drivers for the Red Cross, and in spring 1918 he found himself aboard a ship bound for France.

What he saw and experienced during the next months in Europe affected him deeply and lastingly. "I was an awful dope when I went to the last war," he recalled in a 1942 letter to the editor Maxwell Perkins. "I can remember just thinking that we were the home team and the Austrians were the visiting team." Not only were Hemingway's illusions shattered by constant exposure to the wounded and the dead, but while serving in northern Italy in early July he was badly injured by shrapnel. Sent to the Red Cross Hospital in Milan, he began a long convalescence, which was enlivened by a brief romance with a beautiful American nurse. Before long the other nurses took to exhibiting the handsome young Hemingway to visitors as a "prize specimen of a wounded hero." Despite his bravado and the obvious pleasure he got from this attention, Hemingway was troubled by a sense that his preferment was undeserved, his suffering much less than those of others. Such feelings were only heightened when he was decorated for valor (for carrying to safety a soldier more seriously wounded than himself) and when he was singled out, limping down the gangplank upon his return to New York in January 1919, by an interview-seeking New York *Sun* reporter as an American hero who had "defied the shrapnel of the Central Powers" (January 22, 1919).

Back in America Hemingway gradually recovered from his injuries and renewed two prewar passions, fishing trips to northern Michigan and journalism. He wrote for the Toronto *Star* and the monthly *Cooperative Commonwealth*. He found himself increasingly at odds with his parents, especially his mother, who criticized him for what she saw as his laziness and impiety. In 1921 he married Hadley Richardson and briefly lived with her in Chicago. Later that year the couple set out for Paris, armed with letters of introduction from the fiction writer Sherwood Anderson to numerous influential figures in Parisian ex-patriate society. Hadley would count on a small income from a trust fund, and Ernest would write for the Toronto *Star* while attempting to begin his literary career.

Hemingway's years in Paris have achieved the status of legend in literary history and popular consciousness: it was there that the "lost generation"—as the avant-garde author and art collector Gertrude Stein called the loosely-knit group of artists and writers centered on the Left Bank of the Seine River—took shape and fostered a revolution in aesthetic style and sensibility. With the aid of Anderson's letters, Hemingway met the bookstore proprietor Sylvia Beach, Stein, Ezra Pound, F. Scott Fitzgerald, and many others. Writing in cafés and rented rooms, Hemingway crafted the distinctive prose style—marked by clipped declarative sentences and suggestive understatement—that characterizes his work. In a series of short stories and several novels of extraordinary power, he drew on his reporter's sense of economy of expression as well as on his experience of war and injury. Nick Adams, the protagonist of "Big Two-Hearted River" and numerous other tales, became an exemplar of Hemingway's personal artistic and ethical "code," a man who had suffered debilitating wounds and emotional distresses but who tried to cope with them with quiet dignity, resignation, and grace.

"Big Two-Hearted River" dates from Hemingway's time in Paris in the early 1920s and was originally published in the expatriate magazine *This Quarter* and in the collection *In Our Time* in 1925. After returning from the war in Europe Hemingway went on several recuperative fishing expeditions in summer 1919, one to Michigan's upper peninsula, the site of Nick Adams's solitary journey. Hemingway, according to a letter he wrote to the author Malcolm Cowley in 1948, was limping so slowly in getting off the train at Seney, Michigan, that the brakeman called out to the engineer to wait because of the "cripple." Hearing himself called a cripple so shocked him that he "stopped being one in [my] mind." True or not, this story speaks of Hemingway's desire for an emotional and imaginative "cure" to purge the profound disturbances of the war and the feelings of shame and complicity it had inculcated in him.

Yet, "Big Two-Hearted River" makes no mention of war or physical injury; it is a prime example of what Hemingway called his "iceberg" principle of fiction. Like an iceberg, a story should be "seven-eighths under water for every part that shows," Hemingway noted in a 1958 interview in *Paris Review*. In "Big Two-Hearted River" Nick's intense concentration on the details of making his camp, cooking his meals, and preparing to fish draw their significance from precisely what is unspecified in the story, the obscure cause and context of his anxiety and unhappiness. The solitary expedition becomes a ritual of healing, each step of which must be taken in its turn. Nick's repeated efforts to restrain his thoughts and actions are related in a prose that pares itself down to an insistent staccato at moments of special intensity.

Hemingway's work in the early 1920s was quickly seized upon for its "new, tough, severe and satisfying beauty"; the influential critic Edmund Wilson helped promote the young writer's "strikingly original" stories. After producing *The Torrents of Spring*, (1926), a slight parody of Sherwood Anderson's *Dark Laughter* (1925), Hemingway published his first serious novel, *The Sun Also Rises* (1926). Greeted with widespread enthusiasm, it sealed "lost generationism" as a phenomenon of popular culture. The taciturn Jake Barnes, emasculated by his war injuries, narrates the cycle of tawdry amusements and betrayals of a group of jaded, hard-drinking expatriates in Paris and Spain. Jake's stoic endurance of jealousy and frustration contrasts sharply with the selfishness and narcissism of his companions and with the self-dramatizing machismo of the young Spanish bullfighter who becomes involved with them. The peaceful center of the work is an account of the fishing trip taken by Jake and his friend Bill to Spain's Basque region for a temporary escape. The quiet camaraderie of the two men and their shared appreciation for the fishing ritual seem to represent the best that the Hemingway world has to offer.

The Sun Also Rises was followed in 1927 by the short-story collection *Men Without Women* and in 1929 by the novel *A Farewell to Arms*, both of which enhanced Hemingway's reputation as a tough-minded realist, unafraid of depicting emotional and sexual issues long considered taboo. In *A Farewell to Arms* Hemingway creates a sympathetic portrait of an American army deserter, Frederic Henry. Hemingway used his own 1918 hospital stay in Milan as the springboard for his tale of Henry's escape from the war with Catherine Barkley, an English nurse; Catherine subsequently dies giving birth to their illegitimate child.

Hemingway's early fiction had been so influential that as early as 1931 critics were referring to a "Hemingway school" of fiction. But after the 1920s his fame as a public personality outstripped the critical appraisal of his writings. He began to suffer from the loss of novelty in his work. Furthermore, readers whose moral tolerance had been strained by *A Farewell to Arms* refused to countenance the even greater "licentiousness" they saw in ensuing books. Hemingway did not help his cause with *Death in the Afternoon* (1932), a nonfiction meditation on bullfighting, or *Green Hills of Africa* (1935), a thinly veiled fictional account of an East African safari. Both received mixed reviews and were faulted for the frequent, strident editorial passages, their "small-boy wickedness of vocabulary," and their "he-mannish" posturing. Although his novel *To Have and Have Not* (1937) enjoyed large sales, it received a similar critical reception. Throughout the decade, however, Hemingway produced noteworthy short stories, including some of his greatest—such as "A Way You'll Never Be" (1932), "A Clean, Well-Lighted Place" (1933), "The Snows of Kilimanjaro" (1936), and "The Short Happy Life of Francis Macomber" (1936).

Ernest Hemingway's public image as a "he-man" author was promoted by frequent news stories of his adventures and sporting activities. Here, he is on a hunting trip in 1941.

Hollywood versions of *A Farewell to Arms* and *To Have and Have Not* converted Hemingway's works into star vehicles for Gary Cooper and Humphrey Bogart, diluted Hemingway to the American cinema audience, and distorted his plots by adding happy endings, all while increasing his fame and income. Hemingway's 1940 novel about the Spanish civil war, *For Whom the Bell Tolls*, salvaged his literary reputation, but there were to be further ups and downs. His novel *Across the River and Into the Trees* (1950) was disappointing; the novella *The Old Man and the Sea* (1952), which first appeared in *Life* magazine, was greeted with "a chorus of relief" and hailed as a triumph for the aging master, earning him a Pulitzer Prize. In 1954 Hemingway was awarded the Nobel Prize for literature. Though he subsequently worked on several projected novels, he never published another during his lifetime.

The public persona "Papa" Hemingway assiduously cultivated—hirsute, no-nonsense, a "man's man" as a writer, sportsman, and daredevil—masked many deep-seated insecurities about his creativity and sexuality. Married four times, he remained a sexual adventurer and braggart, attempting to dominate each of the very independent women with whom he became involved. During World War II he yearned, as he had done in World War I, for an opportunity to prove himself in battle. He offered his services to the FBI, establishing an amateur anti-Fascist intelligence and paramilitary organization in Cuba, where he had a home. Later in the war he toured Allied installations in Europe as a correspondent for *Collier's* magazine. His avidity for "blood-sports"—bullfighting, big-game hunting, marlin fishing—was another form of demonstrating manliness. Perhaps the most telling irony of Hemingway's life is in the manner of his death: when in 1961, ill, depressed, and subject to extreme paranoia, he took his own life (as his father had), he did so violently, shooting himself in the forehead with a double-barreled shotgun.

Suggested Readings: *In Our Time*, 1925. *The Sun Also Rises*, 1926. *A Farewell to Arms*, 1929. *To Have and Have Not*, 1937. *The Fifth Column and the First Forty-Nine Stories*, 1938. *For Whom the Bell Tolls*, 1940. *The Old Man and the Sea*, 1952. *A Moveable Feast*, 1964. *The Nick Adams Stories*, ed. P. Young, 1972. R. P. Weeks, ed., *Hemingway: A Collection of Critical Essays*, 1962. C. Baker, *Ernest Hemingway: A Life Story*, 1969. C. Baker, *Hemingway: The Writer as Artist*, 1972. S. Donaldson, *By Force of Will: The Life and Art of Ernest Hemingway*, 1977. J. M. Flora, *Hemingway's Nick Adams*, 1982. J. Nagel, *Ernest Hemingway: The Writer in Context*, 1984. P. Griffin, *Along With Youth: Hemingway, The Early Years*, 1985.

Text Used: *The Short Stories of Ernest Hemingway*, 1987.

BIG TWO-HEARTED RIVER*

PART I

The train went on up the track out of sight, around one of the hills of burnt timber. Nick sat down on the bundle of canvas and bedding the baggage man had pitched out of the door of the baggage car. There was no town, nothing but the rails and the burned-over country. The thirteen saloons that had lined the one street of Seney[1] had not left a trace. The foundations of the Mansion House hotel stuck up

* First published in *In Our Time* (1925); the main character, Nick Adams, appears in numerous other Hemingway stories. Although Hemingway chose this river—to the Northeast of Seney, Michigan, the setting of this story—for the "poetry" of its name, the river at Seney is actually the Fox River.

[1] Twice destroyed by forest fires, Seney, a railroad town in Michigan's Upper Peninsula (between Lakes Superior and Michigan), was a "virtual ghost town" when Hemingway visited it in 1919.

above the ground. The stone was chipped and split by the fire. It was all that was left of the town of Seney. Even the surface had been burned off the ground.

Nick looked at the burned-over stretch of hillside, where he had expected to find the scattered houses of the town and then walked down the railroad track to the bridge over the river. The river was there. It swirled against the log spiles[2] of the bridge. Nick looked down into the clear, brown water, colored from the pebbly bottom, and watched the trout keeping themselves steady in the current with wavering fins. As he watched them they changed their positions by quick angles, only to hold steady in the fast water again. Nick watched them a long time.

He watched them holding themselves with their noses into the current, many trout in deep, fast moving water, slightly distorted as he watched far down through the glassy convex surface of the pool, its surface pushing and swelling smooth against the resistance of the log-driven piles of the bridge. At the bottom of the pool were the big trout. Nick did not see them at first. Then he saw them at the bottom of the pool, big trout looking to hold themselves on the gravel bottom in a varying mist of gravel and sand, raised in spurts by the current.

Nick looked down into the pool from the bridge. It was a hot day. A kingfisher flew up the stream. It was a long time since Nick had looked into a stream and seen trout. They were very satisfactory. As the shadow of the kingfisher moved up the stream, a big trout shot upstream in a long angle, only his shadow marking the angle, then lost his shadow as he came through the surface of the water, caught the sun, and then, as he went back into the stream under the surface, his shadow seemed to float down the stream with the current, unresisting, to his post under the bridge where he tightened facing up into the current.

Nick's heart tightened as the trout moved. He felt all the old feeling.

He turned and looked down the stream. It stretched away, pebbly-bottomed with shallows and big boulders and a deep pool as it curved away around the foot of a bluff.

Nick walked back up the ties to where his pack lay in the cinders beside the railway track. He was happy. He adjusted the pack harness around the bundle, pulling straps tight, slung the pack on the back, got his arms through the shoulder straps and took some of the pull off his shoulders by leaning his forehead against the wide band of the tump-line.[3] Still, it was too heavy. It was much too heavy. He had his leather rod-case in his hand and leaning forward to keep the weight of the pack high on his shoulders he walked along the road that paralleled the railway track, leaving the burned town behind in the heat, and then turned off around a hill with a high, fire-scarred hill on either side onto a road that went back into the country. He walked along the road feeling the ache from the pull of the heavy pack. The road climbed steadily. It was hard work walking up-hill. His muscles ached and the day was hot, but Nick felt happy. He felt he had left everything behind, the need for thinking, the need to write, other needs. It was all back of him.

From the time he had gotten down off the train and the baggage man had thrown his pack out of the open car door things had been different. Seney was burned, the country was burned over and changed, but it did not matter. It could not all be burned. He knew that. He hiked along the road, sweating in the sun, climbing to cross the range of hills that separated the railway from the pine plains.

---

[2] Stakes or timbers used for support.
[3] A strap stretched across the forehead to help support a backpack.

The road ran on, dipping occasionally, but always climbing. Nick went on up. Finally the road after going parallel to the burnt hillside reached the top. Nick leaned back against a stump and slipped out of the pack harness. Ahead of him, as far as he could see, was the pine plain. The burned country stopped off at the left with the range of hills. On ahead islands of dark pine trees rose out of the plain. Far off to the left was the line of the river. Nick followed it with his eye and caught glints of the water in the sun.

There was nothing but the pine plain ahead of him, until the far blue hills that marked the Lake Superior height of land. He could hardly see them, faint and far away in the heat-light over the plain. If he looked too steadily they were gone. But if he only half-looked they were there, the far-off hills of the height of land.

Nick sat down against the charred stump and smoked a cigarette. His pack balanced on the top of the stump, harness holding ready, a hollow molded in it from his back. Nick sat smoking, looking out over the country. He did not need to get his map out. He knew where he was from the position of the river.

As he smoked, his legs stretched out in front of him, he noticed a grasshopper walk along the ground and up onto his woolen sock. The grasshopper was black. As he had walked along the road, climbing, he had started many grasshoppers from the dust. They were all black. They were not the big grasshoppers with yellow and black or red and black wings whirring out from their black wing sheathing as they fly up. These were just ordinary hoppers, but all a sooty black in color. Nick had wondered about them as he walked, without really thinking about them. Now, as he watched the black hopper that was nibbling at the wool of his sock with its fourway lip, he realized that they had all turned black from living in the burned-over land. He realized that the fire must have come the year before, but the grasshoppers were all black now. He wondered how long they would stay that way.

Carefully he reached his hand down and took hold of the hopper by the wings. He turned him up, all his legs walking in the air, and looked at his jointed belly. Yes, it was black too, iridescent where the back and head were dusty.

"Go on, hopper," Nick said, speaking out loud for the first time. "Fly away somewhere."

He tossed the grasshopper up into the air and watched him sail away to a charcoal stump across the road.

Nick stood up. He leaned his back against the weight of his pack where it rested upright on the stump and got his arms through the shoulder straps. He stood with the pack on his back on the brow of the hill looking out across the country, toward the distant river and then struck down the hillside away from the road. Underfoot the ground was good walking. Two hundred yards down the hillside the fire line stopped. Then it was sweet fern, growing ankle high, to walk through, and clumps of jack pines; a long undulating country with frequent rises and descents, sandy underfoot and the country alive again.

Nick kept his direction by the sun. He knew where he wanted to strike the river and he kept on through the pine plain, mounting small rises to see other rises ahead of him and sometimes from the top of a rise a great solid island of pines off to his right or his left. He broke off some sprigs of the heathery sweet fern, and put them under his pack straps. The chafing crushed it and he smelled it as he walked.

He was tired and very hot, walking across the uneven, shadeless pine plain. At any time he knew he could strike the river by turning off to his left. It could not be more than a mile away. But he kept on toward the north to hit the river as far upstream as he could go in one day's walking.

For some time as he walked Nick had been in sight of one of the big islands of pine standing out above the rolling high ground he was crossing. He dipped down and then as he came slowly up to the crest of the bridge he turned and made toward the pine trees.

There was no underbrush in the island of pine trees. The trunks of the trees went straight up or slanted toward each other. The trunks were straight and brown without branches. The branches were high above. Some interlocked to make a solid shadow on the brown forest floor. Around the grove of trees was a bare space. It was brown and soft underfoot as Nick walked on it. This was the over-lapping of the pine needle floor, extending out beyond the width of the high branches. The trees had grown tall and the branches moved high, leaving in the sun this bare space they had once covered with shadow. Sharp at the edge of this extension of the forest floor commenced the sweet fern.

Nick slipped off his pack and lay down in the shade. He lay on his back and looked up into the pine trees. His neck and back and the small of his back rested as he stretched. The earth felt good against his back. He looked up at the sky, through the branches, and then shut his eyes. He opened them and looked up again. There was a wind high up in the branches. He shut his eyes again and went to sleep.

Nick woke stiff and cramped. The sun was nearly down. His pack was heavy and the straps painful as he lifted it on. He leaned over with the pack on and picked up the leather rod-case and started out from the pine trees across the sweet fern swale, toward the river. He knew it could not be more than a mile.

He came down a hillside covered with stumps into a meadow. At the edge of the meadow flowed the river. Nick was glad to get to the river. He walked up-stream through the meadow. His trousers were soaked with the dew as he walked. After the hot day, the dew had come quickly and heavily. The river made no sound. It was too fast and smooth. At the edge of the meadow, before he mounted to a piece of high ground to make camp, Nick looked down the river at the trout rising. They were rising to insects come from the swamp on the other side of the stream when the sun went down. The trout jumped out of the water to take them. While Nick walked through the little stretch of meadow alongside the stream, trout had jumped high out of water. Now as he looked down the river, the insects must be settling on the surface, for the trout were feeding steadily all down the stream. As far down the long stretch as he could see, the trout were rising, making circles all down the surface of the water, as though it were starting to rain.

The ground rose, wooded and sandy, to overlook the meadow, the stretch of river and the swamp. Nick dropped his pack and rod-case and looked for a level piece of ground. He was very hungry and he wanted to make his camp before he cooked. Between two jack pines, the ground was quite level. He took the ax out of the pack and chopped out two projecting roots. That leveled a piece of ground large enough to sleep on. He smoothed out the sandy soil with his hand and pulled all the sweet fern bushes by their roots. His hands smelled good from the sweet fern. He smoothed the uprooted earth. He did not want anything making lumps under the blankets. When he had the ground smooth, he spread his three blankets. One he folded double, next to the ground. The other two he spread on top.

With the ax he slit off a bright slab of pine from one of the stumps and split it into pegs for the tent. He wanted them long and solid to hold in the ground. With the tent unpacked and spread on the ground, the pack, leaning against a jackpine, looked much smaller. Nick tied the rope that served the tent for a ridge-pole to the trunk of one of the pine trees and pulled the tent up off the ground with the other end of the rope and tied it to the other pine. The tent hung on the rope like a canvas blanket on a clothesline. Nick poked a pole he had cut up under the back peak of the canvas and then made it a tent by pegging out the sides. He pegged the sides out taut and drove the pegs deep, hitting them down into the ground with the flat of the ax until the rope loops were buried and the canvas was drum tight.

Across the open mouth of the tent Nick fixed cheesecloth to keep out mosquitoes. He crawled inside under the mosquito bar with various things from the pack to put at the head of the bed under the slant of the canvas. Inside the tent the light came through the brown canvas. It smelled pleasantly of canvas. Already there was something mysterious and homelike. Nick was happy as he crawled inside the tent. He had not been unhappy all day. This was different though. Now things were done. There had been this to do. Now it was done. It had been a hard trip. He was very tired. That was done. He had made his camp. He was settled. Nothing could touch him. It was a good place to camp. He was there, in the good place. He was in his home where he had made it. Now he was hungry.

He came out, crawling under the cheesecloth. It was quite dark outside. It was lighter in the tent.

Nick went over to the pack and found, with his fingers, a long nail in a paper sack of nails, in the bottom of the pack. He drove it into the pine tree, holding it close and hitting it gently with the flat of the ax. He hung the pack up on the nail. All his supplies were in the pack. They were off the ground and sheltered now.

Nick was hungry. He did not believe he had ever been hungrier. He opened and emptied a can of pork and beans and a can of spaghetti into the frying pan.

"I've got a right to eat this kind of stuff, if I'm willing to carry it," Nick said. His voice sounded strange in the darkening woods. He did not speak again.

He started a fire with some chunks of pine he got with the ax from a stump. Over the fire he stuck a wire grill, pushing the four legs down into the ground with his boot. Nick put the frying pan on the grill over the flames. He was hungrier. The beans and spaghetti warmed. Nick stirred them and mixed them together. They began to bubble, making little bubbles that rose with difficulty to the surface. There was a good smell. Nick got out a bottle of tomato catchup and cut four slices of bread. The little bubbles were coming faster now. Nick sat down beside the fire and lifted the frying pan off. He poured about half the contents out into the tin plate. It spread slowly on the plate. Nick knew it was too hot. He poured on some tomato catchup. He knew the beans and spaghetti were still too hot. He looked at the fire, then at the tent, he was not going to spoil it all by burning his tongue. For years he had never enjoyed fried bananas because he had never been able to wait for them to cool. His tongue was very sensitive. He was very hungry. Across the river in the swamp, in the almost dark, he saw a mist rising. He looked at the tent once more. All right. He took a full spoonful from the plate.

"Chrise," Nick said, "Geezus Chrise," he said happily.

He ate the whole plateful before he remembered the bread. Nick finished the second plateful with the bread, mopping the plate shiny. He had not eaten since a cup of coffee and a ham sandwich in the station restaurant at St. Ignace.[4] It had been a very fine experience. He had been that hungry before, but had not been

---

[4] An Upper Peninsula town southeast of Seney on the Strait of Mackinac in Lake Michigan.

able to satisfy it. He could have made camp hours before if he had wanted to. There were plenty of good places to camp on the river. But this was good.

Nick tucked two big chips of pine under the grill. The fire flared up. He had forgotten to get water for the coffee. Out of the pack he got a folding canvas bucket and walked down the hill, across the edge of the meadow, to the stream. The other bank was in the white mist. The grass was wet and cold as he knelt on the bank and dipped the canvas bucket into the stream. It bellied and pulled hard in the current. The water was ice cold. Nick rinsed the bucket and carried it full up to the camp. Up away from the stream it was not so cold.

Nick drove another big nail and hung up the bucket full of water. He dipped the coffee pot half full, put some more chips under the grill onto the fire and put the pot on. He could not remember which way he made coffee. He could remember an argument about it with Hopkins, but not which side he had taken. He decided to bring it to a boil. He remembered now that was Hopkins's way. He had once argued about everything with Hopkins. While he waited for the coffee to boil, he opened a small can of apricots. He liked to open cans. He emptied the can of apricots out into a tin cup. While he watched the coffee on the fire, he drank the juice syrup of the apricots, carefully at first to keep from spilling, then meditatively, sucking the apricots down. They were better than fresh apricots.

The coffee boiled as he watched. The lid came up and coffee and grounds ran down the side of the pot. Nick took it off the grill. It was a triumph for Hopkins. He put sugar in the empty apricot cup and poured some of the coffee out to cool. It was too hot to pour and he used his hat to hold the handle of the coffee pot. He would not let it steep in the pot at all. Not the first cup. It should be straight Hopkins all the way. Hop deserved that. He was a very serious coffee drinker. He was the most serious man Nick had ever known. Not heavy, serious. That was a long time ago. Hopkins spoke without moving his lips. He had played polo. He made millions of dollars in Texas. He had borrowed carfare to go to Chicago, when the wire came that his first big well had come in. He could have wired for money. That would have been too slow. They called Hop's girl the Blonde Venus. Hop did not mind because she was not his real girl. Hopkins said very confidently that none of them would make fun of his real girl. He was right. Hopkins went away when the telegram came. That was on the Black River.[5] It took eight days for the telegram to reach him. Hopkins gave away his .22 caliber Colt automatic pistol to Nick. He gave his camera to Bill. It was to remember him always by. They were all going fishing again next summer. The Hop Head was rich. He would get a yacht and they would all cruise along the north shore of Lake Superior. He was excited but serious. They said good-bye and all felt bad. It broke up the trip. They never saw Hopkins again. That was a long time ago on the Black River.

Nick drank the coffee, the coffee according to Hopkins. The coffee was bitter. Nick laughed. It made a good ending to the story. His mind was starting to work. He knew he could choke it because he was tired enough. He spilled the coffee out of the pot and shook the grounds loose into the fire. He lit a cigarette and went inside the tent. He took off his shoes and trousers, sitting on the blankets, rolled the shoes up inside the trousers for a pillow and got in between the blankets.

Out through the front of the tent he watched the glow of the fire, when the night wind blew on it. It was a quiet night. The swamp was perfectly quiet. Nick

---

[5] Near the northern tip of Michigan's Lower Peninsula; Hemingway fished it in summer 1919.

stretched under the blanket comfortably. A mosquito hummed close to his ear. Nick sat up and lit a match. The mosquito was on the canvas, over his head. Nick moved the match quickly up to it. The mosquito made a satisfactory hiss in the flame. The match went out. Nick lay down again under the blanket. He turned on his side and shut his eyes. He was sleepy. He felt sleep coming. He curled up under the blanket and went to sleep.

PART II

In the morning the sun was up and the tent was starting to get hot. Nick crawled out under the mosquito netting stretched across the mouth of the tent, to look at the morning. The grass was wet on his hands as he came out. He held his trousers and his shoes in his hands. The sun was just up over the hill. There was the meadow, the river and the swamp. There were birch trees in the green of the swamp on the other side of the river.

The river was clear and smoothly fast in the early morning. Down about two hundred yards were three logs all the way across the stream. They made the water smooth and deep above them. As Nick watched, a mink crossed the river on the logs and went into the swamp. Nick was excited. He was excited by the early morning and the river. He was really too hurried to eat breakfast, but he knew he must. He built a little fire and put on the coffee pot.

While the water was heating in the pot he took an empty bottle and went down over the edge of the high ground to the meadow. The meadow was wet with dew and Nick wanted to catch grasshoppers for bait before the sun dried the grass. He found plenty of good grasshoppers. They were at the base of the grass stems. Sometimes they clung to a grass stem. They were cold and wet with the dew, and could not jump until the sun warmed them. Nick picked them up, taking only the medium-sized brown ones, and put them into the bottle. He turned over a log and just under the shelter of the edge were several hundred hoppers. It was a grasshopper lodging house. Nick put about fifty of the medium browns into the bottle. While he was picking up the hoppers the others warmed in the sun and commenced to hop away. They flew when they hopped. At first they made one flight and stayed stiff when they landed, as though they were dead.

Nick knew that by the time he was through with breakfast they would be as lively as ever. Without dew in the grass it would take him all day to catch a bottle full of good grasshoppers and he would have to crush many of them, slamming at them with his hat. He washed his hands at the stream. He was excited to be near it. Then he walked up to the tent. The hoppers were already jumping stiffly in the grass. In the bottle, warmed by the sun, they were jumping in a mass. Nick put in a pine stick as a cork. It plugged the mouth of the bottle enough, so the hoppers could not get out and left plenty of air passage.

He had rolled the log back and knew he could get grasshoppers there every morning.

Nick laid the bottle full of jumping grasshoppers against a pine trunk. Rapidly he mixed some buckwheat flour with water and stirred it smooth, one cup of flour, one cup of water. He put a handful of coffee in the pot and dipped a lump of grease out of a can and slid it sputtering across the hot skillet. On the smoking skillet he poured smoothly the buckwheat batter. It spread like lava, the grease spitting sharply. Around the edges the buckwheat cake began to firm, then brown, then crisp. The surface was bubbling slowly to porousness. Nick pushed under the browned under surface with a fresh pine chip. He shook the skillet sideways and the cake was loose on the surface. I won't try and flop it, he thought. He slid the chip of clean wood all the way under the cake, and flopped it over onto its face. It sputtered in the pan.

When it was cooked Nick regreased the skillet. He used all the batter. It made another big flapjack and one smaller one.

Nick ate a big flapjack and a smaller one, covered with apple butter. He put apple butter on the third cake, folded it over twice, wrapped it in oiled paper and put it in his shirt pocket. He put the apple butter jar back in the pack and cut bread for two sandwiches.

In the pack he found a big onion. He sliced it in two and peeled the silky outer skin. Then he cut one half into slices and made onion sandwiches. He wrapped them in oiled paper and buttoned them in the other pocket of his khaki shirt. He turned the skillet upside down on the grill, drank the coffee, sweetened and yellow brown with the condensed milk in it, and tidied up the camp. It was a good camp.

Nick took his fly rod out of the leather rod-case, jointed it, and shoved the rod-case back into the tent. He put on the reel and threaded the line through the guides. He had to hold it from hand to hand, as he threaded it, or it would slip back through its own weight. It was a heavy, double tapered fly line. Nick had paid eight dollars for it a long time ago. It was made heavy to lift back in the air and come forward flat and heavy and straight to make it possible to cast a fly which has no weight. Nick opened the aluminum leader[6] box. The leaders were coiled between the damp flannel pads. Nick had wet the pads at the water cooler on the train up to St. Ignace. In the damp pads the gut leaders had softened and Nick unrolled one and tied it by a loop at the end to the heavy fly line. He fastened a hook on the end of the leader. It was a small hook; very thin and springy.

Nick took it from his hook book, sitting with the rod across his lap. He tested the knot and the spring of the rod by pulling the line taut. It was a good feeling. He was careful not to let the hook bite into his finger.

He started down to the stream, holding his rod, the bottle of grasshoppers hung from his neck by a thong tied in half hitches around the neck of the bottle. His landing net hung by a hook from his belt. Over his shoulder was a long flour sack tied at each corner into an ear. The cord went over his shoulder. The sack flapped against his legs.

Nick felt awkward and professionally happy with all his equipment hanging from him. The grasshopper bottle swung against his chest. In his shirt the breast pockets bulged against him with the lunch and his fly book.

He stepped into the stream. It was a shock. His trousers clung tight to his legs. His shoes felt the gravel. The water was a rising cold shock.

Rushing, the current sucked against his legs. Where he stepped in, the water was over his knees. He waded with the current. The gravel slid under his shoes. He looked down at the swirl of water below each leg and tipped up the bottle to get a grasshopper.

The first grasshopper gave a jump in the neck of the bottle and went out into the water. He was sucked under in the whirl by Nick's right leg and came to the surface a little way down stream. He floated rapidly, kicking. In a quick circle, breaking the smooth surface of the water, he disappeared. A trout had taken him.

---

[6] A short length of gut or wire used to attach a hook to a fishing line.

Another hopper poked his face out of the bottle. His antennæ wavered. He was getting his front legs out of the bottle to jump. Nick took him by the head and held him while he threaded the slim hook under his chin, down through his thorax and into the last segments of his abdomen. The grasshopper took hold of the hook with his front feet, spitting tobacco juice on it. Nick dropped him into the water.

Holding the rod in his right hand he let out line against the pull of the grasshopper in the current. He stripped off line from the reel with his left hand and let it run free. He could see the hopper in the little waves of the current. It went out of sight.

There was a tug on the line. Nick pulled against the taut line. It was his first strike. Holding the now living rod across the current, he brought in the line with his left hand. The rod bent in jerks, the trout pumping against the current. Nick knew it was a small one. He lifted the rod straight up in the air. It bowed with the pull.

He saw the trout in the water jerking with his head and body against the shifting tangent of the line in the stream.

Nick took the line in his left hand and pulled the trout, thumping tiredly against the current, to the surface. His back was mottled the clear, water-over-gravel color, his side flashing in the sun. The rod under his right arm, Nick stooped, dipping his right hand into the current. He held the trout, never still, with his moist right hand, while he unhooked the barb from his mouth, then dropped him back into the stream.

He hung unsteadily in the current, then settled to the bottom beside a stone. Nick reached down his hand to touch him, his arm to the elbow under water. The trout was steady in the moving stream, resting on the gravel, beside a stone. As Nick's fingers touched him, touched his smooth, cool, underwater feeling he was gone, gone in a shadow across the bottom of the stream.

He's all right, Nick thought. He was only tired.

He had wet his hand before he touched the trout, so he would not disturb the delicate mucus that covered him. If a trout was touched with a dry hand, a white fungus attacked the unprotected spot. Years before when he had fished crowded streams, with fly fishermen ahead of him and behind him, Nick had again and again come on dead trout, furry with white fungus, drifted against a rock, or floating belly up in some pool. Nick did not like to fish with other men on the river. Unless they were of your own party, they spoiled it.

He wallowed down the stream, above his knees in the current, through the fifty yards of shallow water above the pile of logs that crossed the stream. He did not rebait his hook and held it in his hand as he waded. He was certain he could catch small trout in the shallows, but he did not want them. There would be no big trout in the shallows this time of day.

Now the water deepened up his thighs sharply and coldly. Ahead was the smooth dammed-back flood of water above the logs. The water was smooth and dark; on the left, the lower edge of the meadow; on the right the swamp.

Nick leaned back against the current and took a hopper from the bottle. He threaded the hopper on the hook and spat on him for good luck. Then he pulled several yards of line from the reel and tossed the hopper out ahead onto the fast, dark water. It floated down towards the logs, then the weight of the line pulled the bait under the surface. Nick held the rod in his right hand, letting the line run out through his fingers.

There was a long tug. Nick struck and the rod came alive and dangerous, bent double, the line tightening, coming out of water, tightening, all in a heavy, dangerous, steady pull. Nick felt the moment when the leader would break if the strain increased and let the line go.

The reel ratcheted into a mechanical shriek as the line went out in a rush. Too fast. Nick could not check it, the line rushing out, the reel note rising as the line ran out.

With the core of the reel showing, his heart feeling stopped with the excitement, leaning back against the current that mounted icily his thighs, Nick thumbed the reel hard with his left hand. It was awkward getting his thumb inside the fly reel frame.

As he put on pressure the line tightened into sudden hardness and beyond the logs a huge trout went high out of water. As he jumped, Nick lowered the tip of the rod. But he felt, as he dropped the tip to ease the strain, the moment when the strain was too great; the hardness too tight. Of course, the leader had broken. There was no mistaking the feeling when all spring left the line and it became dry and hard. Then it went slack.

His mouth dry, his heart down, Nick reeled in. He had never seen so big a trout. There was a heaviness, a power not to be held, and then the bulk of him as he jumped. He looked as broad as a salmon.

Nick's hand was shaky. He reeled in slowly. The thrill had been too much. He felt, vaguely, a little sick, as though it would be better to sit down.

The leader had broken where the hook was tied to it. Nick took it in his hand. He thought of the trout somewhere on the bottom, holding himself steady over the gravel, far down below the light, under the logs, with the hook in his jaw. Nick knew the trout's teeth would cut through the snell of the hook. The hook would imbed itself in his jaw. He'd bet the trout was angry. Anything that size would be angry. That was a trout. He had been solidly hooked. Solid as a rock. He felt like a rock, too, before he started off. By God, he was a big one. By God, he was the biggest one I ever heard of.

Nick climbed out onto the meadow and stood, water running down his trousers and out of his shoes, his shoes squlchy. He went over and sat on the logs. He did not want to rush his sensations any.

He wriggled his toes in the water, in his shoes, and got out a cigarette from his breast pocket. He lit it and tossed the match into the fast water below the logs. A tiny trout rose at the match, as it swung around in the fast current. Nick laughed. He would finish the cigarette.

He sat on the logs, smoking, drying in the sun, the sun warm on his back, the river shallow ahead entering the woods, curving into the woods, shallows, light glittering, big water-smooth rocks, cedars along the bank and white birches, the logs warm in the sun, smooth to sit on, without bark, gray to the touch; slowly the feeling of disappointment left him. It went away slowly, the feeling of disappointment that came sharply after the thrill that made his shoulders ache. It was all right now. His rod lying out on the logs, Nick tied a new hook on the leader, pulling the gut tight until it grimped into itself in a hard knot.

He baited up, then picked up the rod and walked to the far end of the logs to get into the water, where it was not too deep. Under and beyond the logs was a deep pool. Nick walked around the shallow shelf near the swamp shore until he came out on the shallow bed of the stream.

On the left, where the meadow ended and the woods began, a great elm tree was uprooted. Gone over in a storm, it lay back into the woods, its roots clotted with dirt, grass growing in them, rising a solid bank beside the stream. The river cut to the edge of the uprooted tree. From where Nick stood he could see deep channels, like ruts, cut in the shallow bed of the stream by the flow of the current. Pebbly where he stood and pebbly and full of boulders beyond; where it curved near the tree roots, the bed of the stream was marly and between the ruts of deep water green weed fronds swung in the current.

Nick swung the rod back over his shoulder and forward, and the line, curving forward, laid the grasshopper down on one of the deep channels in the weeds. A trout struck and Nick hooked him.

Holding the rod far out toward the uprooted tree and sloshing backward in the current, Nick worked the trout, plunging, the rod bending alive, out of the danger of the weeds into the open river. Holding the rod, pumping alive against the current, Nick brought the trout in. He rushed, but always came, the spring of the rod yielding to the rushes, sometimes jerking under water, but always bringing him in. Nick eased downstream with the rushes. The rod above his head he led the trout over the net, then lifted.

The trout hung heavy in the net, mottled trout back and silver sides in the meshes. Nick unhooked him; heavy sides, good to hold, big undershot jaw, and slipped him, heaving and big sliding, into the long sack that hung from his shoulders in the water.

Nick spread the mouth of the sack against the current and it filled, heavy with water. He held it up, the bottom in the stream, and the water poured out through the sides. Inside at the bottom was the big trout, alive in the water.

Nick moved downstream. The sack out ahead of him sunk heavy in the water, pulling from his shoulders.

It was getting hot, the sun hot on the back of his neck.

Nick had one good trout. He did not care about getting many trout. Now the stream was shallow and wide. There were trees along both banks. The trees of the left bank made short shadows on the current in the forenoon sun. Nick knew there were trout in each shadow. In the afternoon, after the sun had crossed toward the hills, the trout would be in the cool shadows on the other side of the stream.

The very biggest ones would lie up close to the bank. You could always pick them up there on the Black. When the sun was down they all moved out into the current. Just when the sun made the water blinding in the glare before it went down, you were liable to strike a big trout anywhere in the current. It was almost impossible to fish then, the surface of the water was blinding as a mirror in the sun. Of course, you could fish upstream, but in a stream like the Black, or this, you had to wallow against the current and in a deep place, the water piled up on you. It was no fun to fish upstream with this much current.

Nick moved along through the shallow stretch watching the banks for deep holes. A beech tree grew close beside the river, so that the branches hung down into the water. The stream went back in under the leaves. There were always trout in a place like that.

Nick did not care about fishing that hole. He was sure he would get hooked in the branches.

It looked deep though. He dropped the grasshopper so the current took it under water, back in under the overhanging branch. The line pulled hard and Nick struck. The trout threshed heavily, half out of water in the leaves and branches. The line was caught. Nick pulled hard and the trout was off. He reeled in and holding the hook in his hand, walked down the stream.

Ahead, close to the left bank, was a big log. Nick saw it was hollow; pointing up river the current entered it smoothly, only a little ripple spread each side of the log. The water was deepening. The top of the hollow log was gray and dry. It was partly in the shadow.

Nick took the cork out of the grasshopper bottle and a hopper clung to it. He picked him off, hooked him and tossed him out. He held the rod far out so that the hopper on the water moved into the current flowing into the hollow log. Nick lowered the rod and the hopper floated in. There was a heavy strike. Nick swung the rod against the pull. It felt as though he were hooked into the log itself, except for the live feeling.

He tried to force the fish out into the current. It came, heavily.

The line went slack and Nick thought the trout was gone. Then he saw him, very near, in the current, shaking his head, trying to get the hook out. His mouth was clamped shut. He was fighting the hook in the clear flowing current.

Looping in the line with his left hand, Nick swung the rod to make the line taut and tried to lead the trout toward the net, but he was gone, out of sight, the line pumping. Nick fought him against the current, letting him thump in the water against the spring of the rod. He shifted the rod to his left hand, worked the trout upstream, holding his weight, fighting on the rod, and then let him down into the net. He lifted him clear of the water, a heavy half circle in the net, the net dripping, unhooked him and slid him into the sack.

He spread the mouth of the sack and looked down in at the two big trout alive in the water.

Through the deepening water, Nick waded over to the hollow log. He took the sack off, over his head, the trout flopping as it came out of water, and hung it so the trout were deep in the water. Then he pulled himself up on the log and sat, the water from his trousers and boots running down into the stream. He laid his rod down, moved along to the shady end of the log and took the sandwiches out of his pocket. He dipped the sandwiches in the cold water. The current carried away the crumbs. He ate the sandwiches and dipped his hat full of water to drink, the water running out through his hat just ahead of his drinking.

It was cool in the shade, sitting on the log. He took a cigarette out and struck a match to light it. The match sunk into the gray wood, making a tiny furrow. Nick leaned over the side of the log, found a hard place and lit the match. He sat smoking and watching the river.

Ahead the river narrowed and went into a swamp. The river became smooth and deep and the swamp looked solid with cedar trees, their trunks close together, their branches solid. It would not be possible to walk through a swamp like that. The branches grew so low. You would have to keep almost level with the ground to move at all. You could not crash through the branches. That must be why the animals that lived in swamps were built the way they were, Nick thought.

He wished he had brought something to read. He felt like reading. He did not feel like going on into the swamp. He looked down the river. A big cedar slanted all the way across the stream. Beyond that the river went into the swamp.

Nick did not want to go in there now. He felt a reaction against deep wading with the water deepening up under his armpits, to hook big trout in places impossible to land them. In the swamp the banks were bare, the big cedars came together overhead, the sun did not come through, except in patches; in the fast deep water, in the half light, the fishing would be tragic. In the swamp fishing was a tragic adventure. Nick did not want it. He did not want to go down the stream any further today.

He took out his knife, opened it and stuck it in the log. Then he pulled up the sack, reached into it and brought out one of the trout. Holding him near the tail, hard to hold, alive, in his hand, he whacked him against the log. The trout quivered, rigid. Nick laid him on the log in the shade and broke the neck of the other fish the same way. He laid them side by side on the log. They were fine trout.

Nick cleaned them, slitting them from the vent to the tip of the jaw. All the insides and the gills and tongue came out in one piece. They were both males; long gray-white strips of milt,[7] smooth and clean. All the insides clean and compact, coming out all together. Nick tossed the offal ashore for the minks to find.

He washed the trout in the stream. When he held them back up in the water they looked like live fish. Their color was not gone yet. He washed his hands and dried them on the log. Then he laid the trout on the sack spread out on the log, rolled them up in it, tied the bundle and put it in the landing net. His knife was still standing, blade stuck in the log. He cleaned it on the wood and put it in his pocket.

Nick stood up on the log, holding his rod, the landing net hanging heavy, then stepped into the water and splashed ashore. He climbed the bank and cut up into the woods, toward the high ground. He was going back to camp. He looked back. The river just showed through the trees. There were plenty of days coming when he could fish the swamp.

1924, 1925

---

[7] Fish sperm, or the reproductive glands that produce it; symbolically, the male fish, full of sperm, may refer obliquely to young men of Nick's age.

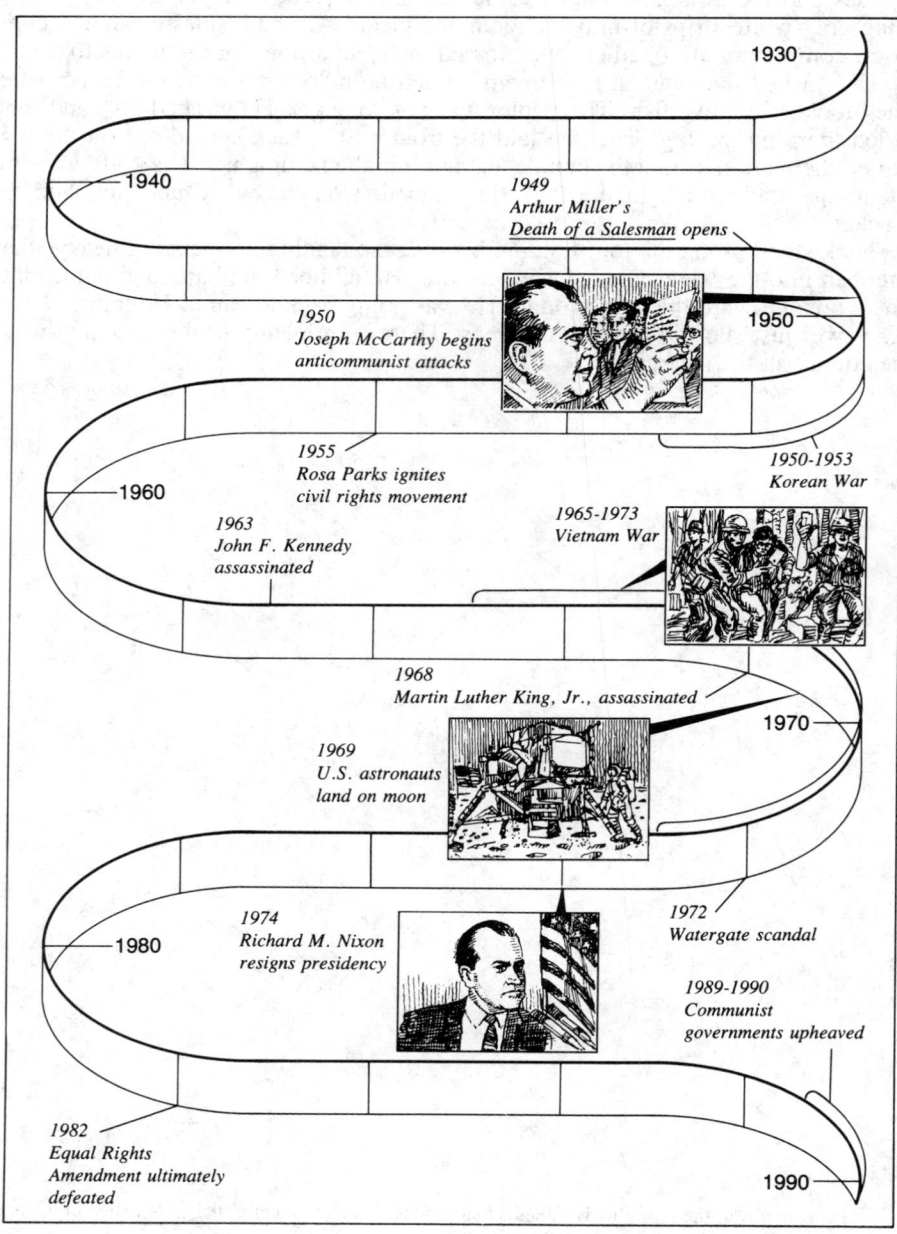

1930

1940

1949
Arthur Miller's
Death of a Salesman opens

1950
Joseph McCarthy begins
anticommunist attacks

1950

1950-1953
Korean War

1955
Rosa Parks ignites
civil rights movement

1960

1963
John F. Kennedy
assassinated

1965-1973
Vietnam War

1968
Martin Luther King, Jr., assassinated

1970

1969
U.S. astronauts
land on moon

1972
Watergate scandal

1974
Richard M. Nixon
resigns presidency

1980

1989-1990
Communist
governments upheaved

1982
Equal Rights
Amendment ultimately
defeated

1990

PART SIX

Diversity, Technology, and Social Change

The Middle to Late 20th Century

In the distant future it may be said that World War II did not really come to an end until autumn 1989, when a democratic upheaval swept Eastern Europe, when the Berlin Wall was demolished, and when the rivalries between the United States and the Soviet Union (dating from the world-war years) seemed well on the way to resolution. The power of Fascist regimes at their height in 1942 stretched from Mongolia to Burma to the Marshall Islands in the Pacific; from the outskirts of Moscow to Europe's Atlantic Coast; from Casablanca to Cairo in North Africa. Genocide for Jews and Gypsies, ruthless management of prisoners of war, and harsh occupation of conquered territories suggested what the defeated could expect. The triumph of the Allied powers over Germany and Japan in 1945 ended a nightmare. But embedded in the triumph were its own tragedies, and the postwar generations would not find it easy to maintain the peace for which they longed. An oxymoronic epithet would describe the era: it would be called the "cold war."

Savoring their triumph, and determined to make it more lasting than victory in World War I had been, the Allies moved to make the United Nations a permanent forum for international dialogue. Understanding that the seeds of war had grown in the festering wounds of a demoralized political system and a bankrupt economy in Germany, the United States moved quickly to make postwar economic reconstruction possible: the Marshall Plan provided $17 billion over four years for sixteen nations, including the western portion of a divided Germany. Western Europe was restored to economic health quickly, as was Japan, where a peace treaty and a democratic constitution were imposed. Forbidden to build armies, Japan and West Germany concentrated on economic rebuilding. In less than a generation their economies were robust and competitive, their political systems authentically democratic.

Within the United States the advent of peace also signaled great opportunities, as manufacturing responded to the demand for consumer goods that it had been unable to satisfy during the war. A generous "G.I. Bill" gave returning veterans priority for many jobs, small-business loans, low-interest mortgages, and tuition subsidies for vocational schools and for colleges. Into college streamed millions of returning veterans, many from working-class families, who before the war would have found college far out of their reach. New colleges and universities were founded, and older ones expanded. College education became vastly more accessible and would remain so. In 1940 less than ten percent of eighteen- to twenty-four-year-olds were enrolled in college; by 1980 over thirty-five percent of that group were. An unintentional result of the G.I. Bill was the expansion of the gap between middle-class men and women in the accessibility of college education. Although all veterans were eligible for its benefits, only a very small fraction of veterans—mostly army nurses and members of the Women's Army Corps—were women. Not until 1978 would the gap between male and female college students be closed.

But tragedies were also inherited from World War II. Chief among them was the abuse of atomic energy: the race with German scientists to build an atomic bomb was quickly replaced by a race with Soviet scientists to build a hydrogen bomb, powered by fusion and many times more destructive than the atomic bomb. Americans had long been suspicious of the Soviet Union as a tyranny and had entered into the wartime alliance only out of necessity; now that the war was over, American suspicions resumed their force. These suspicions were heightened by the widespread feeling that the United States had been too slow in appreciating the Fascist threat in the 1930s. Many Americans were determined not to repeat that mistake. For its part the Soviet Union felt the Allies had delayed opening a second front while the Soviets faced the German threat virtually alone. (Estimates of the number of USSR citizens who died in World War II, once thought to be 20 million, were revised in 1990 to about 40 million; that is, nearly one out of five of the Soviet population may have perished in the war.) The Soviets were determined to make a third twentieth-century invasion from the West impossible, demanding that Germany be inhibited from rebuilding its strength and that regimes in Eastern Europe be friendly ones. Russian troops were in place in Eastern Europe as Germany was defeated, and they showed no anxiety to leave; neither the United States nor Great Britain was prepared to remove them by force. Instead, the United States took the position that it would seek to "contain" Soviet expansion by a military alliance, the North Atlantic Treaty Organization (NATO) and by a massive increase in its own military spending. But it would not intervene to challenge the boundaries of the Soviet sphere of influence. When East Germans rebelled in 1953, when Hungarians revolted in 1956, and when Czechs rose in 1968, the United States kept its distance lest a major war would ensue.

In the Far East the United States took a stricter line. Although it had long worried about the corrupt regime of Chiang Kai-shek in China, the United States refused diplomatic overtures made by Chou En-lai's and Mao Tse-tung's victorious Communists in 1949. When North Korean troops invaded South Korea in 1950, President Harry S. Truman concluded that the Soviet Union was responsible. Once the United Nations Security Council agreed, Truman bypassed Congress and ordered two American army divisions into action. The Korean War, which lasted until 1953, demonstrated American's willingness to "contain" communism anywhere on the globe. Meanwhile, the South Korean dictator Syngman Rhee was defined as a "gallant ally." Historian William Chafe has observed that "through such logic the United States seriously impaired its credibility with Third World countries, neutrals, even allies" (*The Unfinished Journey,* 1986). Similar themes would emerge during the next decade's involvement in Vietnam.

Anxieties about international relations infused domestic politics in the postwar years. Fear of communism abroad spilled over into fear of Communists at home. Although membership in the American Communist party had declined sharply after World War II, many Americans were convinced that Communists were actively seeking to subvert the U.S. government. The McCarran Internal Security Act of 1950 illegalized "substantially contributing" to establishing a dictatorship in the United States. In the late 1940s Truman established a program to search for people suspected of subversive activity, and the House Un-American Activities Committee embarked on a major investigation of the motion-picture industry in 1947. Ten screenwriters, including Dalton Trumbo, were sent to federal prison for refusing to testify; many other writers and actors were informally blacklisted and forced out of their profession by rumor and innuendo. African-American writers and artists, among them the distinguished scholar and National Association for the Advancement of Colored People (NAACP) founder W. E. B. DuBois, and the great singer and actor Paul Robeson, were accused of Communist cooperation; while they were abroad, their passports were confiscated. Through most of the 1950s Joseph McCarthy, who had had an undistinguished career as a senator from Wisconsin, accused hundreds of people of being Communist agents or sympathizers—"fellow travelers." His accusations, which had virtually no evidence, were generally enough to ruin careers, until in 1954 he attacked the army itself. In one of the first sets of congressional hearings to be televised, millions of people watched as his accusations were shown to be groundless. During the 1953 production of Arthur Miller's *The Crucible,* which shows how easily suspicion and dread were spread in the Salem witchcraft trials in colonial Massachusetts, everyone in the audience knew Miller was writing about his own time.

The Civil Rights Movement

The civil rights revolution had many of its origins in World War II. Millions of black soldiers had been drafted to fight for democracy in a segregated army in which they were commanded by white officers. Millions of African-American men and women had worked in defense plants. Returning veterans were outraged by the continuation of segregation and by lynchings. Not until African-American civil rights leaders threatened a massive civil disobedience campaign in 1948 did Truman issue an executive order ending discrimination in the armed forces, but the army was not actually desegregated until after the Korean War, and the navy remained segregated long after that. The federal government did not defend African Americans against violence and intimidation when they attempted to vote. And in 1955 fourteen-year-old Emmett Till, visiting Mississippi from Chicago, was murdered because he had not been deferential to whites in a grocery store.

The NAACP brought lawsuits challenging claims that states were providing "separate but equal" educational facilities, beginning with "law schools" that were

---

=CONTEXTS=

The Civil Rights Movement

Throughout the 1950s and 1960s African Americans continued to struggle vigorously for the basic rights to which they were entitled. This struggle was centered in the activities of the Congress of Racial Equality, the Southern Christian Leadership Conference, and the Student Nonviolent Coordinating Committee. Martin Luther King, Jr. (1929–1968), head of the SCLC, was a major force in this movement. He delivered his "I Have A Dream" speech during a civil rights march on Washington, D.C., on August 28, 1963:

I Have a Dream

Five score years ago a great American in whose symbolic shadow we stand today signed the Emancipation Proclamation. This momentous decree is a great beacon light of hope to millions of Negro slaves who had been seared in the flames of withering injustice. It came as a joyous daybreak to end the long night of their captivity. But 100 years later, the Negro still is not free. One hundred years later the life of the Negro is still badly crippled by the manacles of segregation and the chains of discrimination. One hundred years later the Negro lives on a lonely island of poverty in the midst of a vast ocean of material prosperity. One hundred years later the Negro still languishe[s] in the corners of American society and finds himself in exile in his own land. . . .

We must forever conduct our struggle on the high plane of dignity and discipline. We must not allow our creative protests to degenerate into physical violence. Again and again we must rise to the majestic heights of meeting physical force with soul force. . . .

. . . I have a dream that my four little children will one day live in a nation where they will not be judged by the color of their skin but by the content of their character. . . .

When we allow freedom to ring—when we let it ring from every city and every hamlet, from every state and every city, we will be able to speed up that day when all God's children, black men and white men, Jews and Gentiles, Protestants and Catholics, will be able to join hands and sing in the words of the old Negro spiritual, "Free at last, Free at last! Great God a-mighty, We are free at last!"

Martin Luther King, Jr., 1963

---

one-room facilities with one teacher and no books. In the landmark case of *Brown* v. *Board of Education* in 1954, a legal team brilliantly led by attorney Thurgood Marshall argued that no separate facilities *could* be equal because separation itself stigmatized African Americans as different and unequal. Chief Justice Earl Warren had supported the relocation of Japanese Americans during World War II but had come to regret that decision bitterly. In 1954 he took a leading role in persuading his fellow justices not only to declare "separate but equal" a denial of equal protection of the law, but to do so unanimously. The Supreme Court, however, could only declare what the law was. Although President Dwight D. Eisenhower had moved effectively to desegregate the army, he was critical of the *Brown* decision and did not move to enforce it, even rhetorically. Although most southern states had been ready to comply with the court's decision, they gradually moved to resist or circumvent it. Children trying to register at Central High School in Little Rock, Arkansas, in 1957 were surrounded and intimidated by hostile crowds. Other children were met by hostility and violence, inside and outside schools. Tax funds were used to pay tuition at "private" schools for white children. Embittered by the law's failure to protect them, African Americans became ever more skeptical of whites' protestations of equality.

In autumn 1955 Rosa Parks, secretary of the Montgomery, Alabama, NAACP branch, felt the time had come; when a bus driver insisted she move to the segregated back of the bus, she refused. She was arrested, and her colleagues—veterans of efforts to desegregate drinking fountains and the police force—embarked on a massive boycott of the public buses of Montgomery. The boycott lasted a year and a month. It brought together Montgomery's black community (who, by walking long distances to work each day, dramatically demonstrated that they would make major practical sacrifices rather than absorb the continued humiliation of segregation), the national black community, and ultimately a national community of whites moved by the demonstrations. They catapulted to national visibility and leadership the young minister Martin Luther King, Jr. whose moving speeches articulated the high moral principles that placed the boycott on a level with other classic struggles for liberty and justice.

In 1960 four African-American college freshmen in Greensboro, North Carolina, sat down at a segregated lunch counter and refused to obey management's demand that they leave. The following day more African-American students joined them. The "sit-in" movement became a national protest, enlarged to claim not only a seat at a lunch counter or on a bus, but full economic, educational, and political freedom. It was met with violence, brutality, and murder. It also resulted in federal legislation that outlawed racial discrimination in public accommodations; prohibited hiring on the basis of race, sex, religion, or national origin; and authorized federal examiners to register African-American voters when local officials would not.

Gender Equality Movements

The women's movement of the middle to late twentieth century had its roots in World War II and in the civil rights movement. During the war women's participation in the paid work force was a welcome contribution to the economy. Many married women entered the paid work force, and women who were already working found highly improved opportunities and salaries. African-American women gained skilled jobs in manufacturing for the first time. When the war was over, however, these women lost their jobs to returning veterans; worse, they lost the seniority that would have made them candidates for subsequent openings. Few women could afford to stop working; instead they moved into part-time or underpaid, less-skilled work. They typically carried with them memories of better times, and the conviction that their daughters should have greater opportunities than they had. In 1963, when the President's Commission on the Status of Women documented widespread legal discrimination, the average working woman earned sixty-three percent of what the average working man earned; that figure actually declined to fifty-seven percent in the next decade. Meanwhile, young women working in the civil rights movement came to criticize attitudes that considered them inferior to their male colleagues and learned effective tactics for demanding social and cultural change.

In the 1970s feminists launched a wide-ranging criticism of legal and social practice. They demanded equal employment opportunities; access to safe, legal abortion; and equal access to credit, to fringe benefits, and to education. Their criticism of colleges and universities focused both on the exclusion of women from college faculties and on the curriculum itself. Feminists questioned the absence of women's experience from fields as diverse as psychology, economics, history, and literature; they also questioned decisions as to what texts deserve to be labeled "classic" and what authors should be presented to the next generation as indispensable to the well-educated person.

A series of Supreme Court decisions in the early 1970s established for the first time in American history that discrimination based solely on sex could under certain conditions be unconstitutional. In an effort to make this interpretation permanent, Congress passed a proposed Equal Rights Amendment to the Constitution in 1972. It was quickly ratified by thirty of the required thirty-eight states, but thereafter progress on passage was stopped by a strong conservative movement claiming that women already have sufficient protection by law.

During the 1970s radical feminists developed the argument that gender itself is socially constructed. "Sex" refers to biological differences that are unchanging, but "gender" involves the *meaning* that a particular society and culture attaches to sexual difference. In "consciousness-raising" groups, women shared painful memories of making their way in a society that put limits on their aspirations and constrained their choices. They reinterpreted behavior they had once thought to be "natural" as in fact learned behavior, the result of socialization. Lesbians offered the most intense critique of a society that permitted heterosexual men to set the norms; along with gay men, lesbians publicly claimed the legitimacy of their own sexual choices. These claims were embodied in part by public gestures such as parades, in part by the direct challenging of laws that barred lesbians and gay men from careers in teaching or in the military, and in part by the renegotiation of institutional regulations that denied equal treatment to partners in homosexual relationships.

The Vietnam War Years

Throughout the 1960s much American foreign policy continued to be framed in cold-war terms, and the tension between the United States and communism was assumed to be permanent. One region in which this tension exploded was southeast Asia. Ho Chi Minh had led a nationalist resistance to Japanese occupation

Visitors to the black marble Vietnam War Memorial in Washington, D.C., take pencil rubbings of the names of loved ones killed in the controversial war in Southeast Asia.

during World War II; this resistance continued when Vietnam was returned to the French. It was strong enough to force the French out, despite American military and economic aid. Vietnam was divided, with Ho presiding over the North. Understanding that he was allied with Communists, believing that the crucial errors of the 1930s had been the failure to stop Hitler's advances early enough, and fearing that if one region fell to the Communists others would follow like "falling dominos" (in Eisenhower's words), the United States began to support Ho's enemies in South Vietnam, sending first a secret CIA mission, then military advisors, and ultimately combat troops in 1965. At the time of President John F. Kennedy's assassination in 1963, there were some 16,000 military advisors; by 1966 there were 385,000 military personnel; at the end of Lyndon Johnson's term as president in 1968, there were 500,000.

The immediacy of news coverage provided by electronic media made Vietnam the "living-room war," and America was not ready for what it saw. Criticism of the Vietnam intervention grew at home, particularly on college campuses, where students who had worked for civil rights brought to college campuses the strategies they had learned in the South. In the mid-1960s they transformed the culture of American college life by demanding student participation in setting university policy, in curriculum change, and often in demanding admission of minority students. College students bitterly questioned the need to spend lives in defending an undemocratic regime in South Vietnam, questioned the domino theory, and questioned the cold war itself. They attacked their own universities for maintaining ROTC programs, which prepared students for Vietnam service, and for accepting federal grants for military research. By the late 1960s it was possible to identify a "counterculture" of young people who opposed the war and believed in the possibility of an American society driven by harmony and cooperation rather than by competition and individualism.

The year 1968 was a deeply tragic one. The incompatibility of the war in Vietnam and a liberal reform agenda at home so exhausted and depressed Lyndon Johnson that he declined to run for a second term as president. Robert F. Kennedy and Martin Luther King, Jr., two political leaders whose heroic and inclusive vision promised to heal the divisions of American society, were assassinated within two months of each other. The Democratic National Convention in Chicago took place amid a virtual police riot against antiwar demonstrators: while the police used mace and tear gas, protesters chanted to television cameras, "The whole world is watching!" Republican candidate Richard M. Nixon used consensus language in his campaign, promising to "bring the country together," but domestic politics remained polarized throughout his time in office.

Nixon adopted the policy of a gradual withdrawal of American ground troops but an escalation of air power in Vietnam. In an effort to interdict the flow of supplies from North Vietnam, Nixon approved an invasion of Cambodia in 1970. When college students throughout America demonstrated in protest, local police and National Guard units were called out to silence them. At a peaceable rally at Kent State University in Ohio, four students were killed and eleven wounded; at Jackson State College, an African-American college in Mississippi, police fired into a dormitory, killing two innocent students. During the next five years, under a policy of "Vietnamization," American troops were slowly withdrawn from Vietnam. The peace accords that were signed in January 1973 permitted the North Vietnamese to keep their troops in the South. By 1975 the South Vietnamese forces had crumbled, and the last Americans fled in an ignominious retreat. Overloaded helicopters desperately fled Saigon, unable to carry even those Vietnamese who had cooperated most closely with Americans and therefore faced the most extreme reprisals.

The Postwar Years

American public opinion was partly assuaged for the failures of Vietnam by Nixon's restoration of diplomatic relations with China in 1972 after twenty-five years. The United States agreed to withdraw troops stationed in Taiwan, while the Chinese promised to urge North Vietnam to accept a negotiated settlement, and trade relations were opened. Nixon also initiated a major breakthrough in relations with the Soviet Union, including a Strategic Arms Limitation Treaty (SALT-I), signed in 1972.

Nixon was re-elected in 1972 by the largest majority ever claimed by a Republican presidential candidate. But in late 1973 Vice-President Spiro Agnew, facing

The "space race" that began in 1957 with the Soviet Union's launching of Sputnik I, the first artificial satellite, eventually led to the landing of Americans on the moon on July 20, 1969.

charges of income-tax evasion and bribery, was forced to resign. During Nixon's presidential campaign, five burglars sponsored by his campaign committee had been caught breaking into the Democratic National Headquarters at the Watergate Hotel in Washington, D.C. As discovered by two reporters for the *Washington Post*, the break-in was part of a "dirty tricks" campaign against Democratic candidates, complete with massive illegal fundraising. A Select Senate Committee and the House Judiciary Committee heard testimony on wiretapping, perjury, and blackmail, emanating from the executive office. When tape recordings—which Nixon had himself ordered to be made—provided evidence of a criminal conspiracy to obstruct justice, Nixon, facing increasingly likely impeachment proceedings, resigned.

"American politics oscillated wildly during the seventies," writes William Chafe, "giving the Democrats their greatest majority in the postwar era in 1974, and then in 1980 doing the same for the Republicans. . . . No one seemed able to find answers capable of forging a new consensus" (*The Unfinished Journey*, 1986). The oscillation continued into the 1980s, when Congress was often controlled by Democrats, while the White House was held by Republicans. The economy was equally difficult to interpret. Massive deficits characterized the federal budget for two decades. These deficits are generally traced to Lyndon Johnson's fear of raising taxes to pay for the expenses of Vietnam (lest opposition to taxes turn into opposition to foreign policy) and to Richard Nixon's monetary policies, which permitted an inflation rate of ten percent in 1973. Ronald Reagan made an attack on the deficit a major part of his platform in 1980 and again in 1984, but the deficit continued to grow, due in large part to heightened military spending.

For many, especially the well educated, professional opportunities improved in the 1970s and 1980s. This was particularly true for college-educated women. Desegregated schools and changes in job expectations enabled more African-American families to reach middle-class status. But there was also a downward spiral: for the first time sociologists could identify a permanent "underclass." Two-thirds of all adults classified as poor in 1980 were women; the "feminization of poverty" developed first among African Americans. Poverty had many political consequences, among them demoralization; the lowest voting rates are found in the poorest neighborhoods.

In 1893 the historian Frederick Jackson Turner suggested that the frontier experience was at the core of what was distinctive about American society; "frontier" was a metaphor for limitless possibility, for resources waiting to be claimed and used, for plenty and prosperity. American political metaphor in the twentieth century has stressed both "new" and "limitless"—FDR spoke of a New Deal, JFK of a New Frontier. The landing of U.S. astronauts on the moon on July 20, 1969, opened a truly limitless frontier in space. Americans had traditionally described their society as free of the distinctions of class, race, and gender; political rhetoric insisted that all were equal and that any existing distinctions would soon erode. American society would always have room for upward mobility. In the postwar years the United States was indisputably the most economically prosperous nation in the world. Ironically, American aid to nations destroyed in World War II enabled those nations to build economies that, by the end of the 1980s, were competitive with the U.S. economy. Social critics of the postwar years denied the "melting pot" and insisted on acknowledging the depths of prejudice and discrimination that characterized American society. As the 1990s began, Americans cheered the end of the cold war and the emergence of stronger economies among their allies and burgeoning democracies among their former enemies. But they also worried about America's ability to retain its character as a multiracial, multiethnic society both prosperous and free.

MIDDLE TO LATE 20TH-CENTURY DRAMA

By the end of the nineteenth century, the American theater was thoroughly encrusted with tired conventions borrowed mostly from European traditions. Great actors overshadowed both playwrights and their plays; melodrama flourished at the expense of language and of the complexities of social relations. But by about 1912 the situation began to change, with the appearance of "little theaters" in several cities. Several of them—the Provincetown Players, the Neighborhood Playhouse, and the Washington Square Players—became the voices of change.

The Provincetown Players was founded in 1915 by a small group headed by the writer Susan Glaspell and her husband, George Gram Cook, to encourage new American dramatists. The group gave its first performances in a small theater on a wharf in Provincetown, Massachusetts; by the next summer the program included *Bound East for Cardiff*, by the young Eugene O'Neill. The season was such a success that the group took over a playhouse in New York City and remained there until 1929. The Provincetown Players created an audience for serious American drama and provided a forum for O'Neill's experimental works, such as *The Emperor Jones* (1920).

Established in 1915 in New York City, the Neighborhood Playhouse and the Washington Square Players also attempted to raise the standards of the American stage. Such problems as rising costs and competition with Broadway forced these groups to disband before long. But an outgrowth of the defunct Washington Square Players was the Theatre Guild founded in 1919. The first commercially successful theater group committed to producing quality plays, the guild initially produced works by the leading European playwrights but in 1923 mounted Elmer Rice's *Adding Machine* and in 1928 started to produce O'Neill's plays for its subscription audience. From then on the Guild aggressively sought new American playwrights. It also established a permanent acting company and began to perform works in repertory.

By 1920 O'Neill, already heralded as America's most promising playwright, had his first full-length play, *Beyond the Horizon* (1920), presented on Broadway to critical acclaim. A prolific writer, he completed about twenty-five full-length plays, among them such masterpieces as *Desire Under the Elms* (1924), *Mourning Becomes Electra* (1931), and *The Iceman Cometh* (1946). Although O'Neill experimented with symbolism, expressionism, and novel technical devices (the use of masks and extended asides), his greatest plays reveal that he was a master of realistic tragedy. He began what was later recognized as the "shrinking" of the American stage: a preoccupation with physical and psychological space, compressed and pressing in on the characters.

During the 1930s a new group of dramatists gained prominence. The fame of Maxwell Anderson rests on his efforts to revive poetic drama in such historical plays as *Mary of Scotland* (1933). Robert B. Sherwood's best works were the realistic-allegoric melodrama *The Petrified Forest* (1935) and the semifarcical *Idiot's Delight* (1936). Lillian Hellman's third and finest play, *The Little Foxes* (1939), depicts the ruthless infighting of a rapacious southern family. The first two plays of William Saroyan, *My Heart's in the Highlands* (1939) and *The Time of Your Life* (1939), celebrate the eccentric life.

The social consciousness evident in Hellman's and Sherwood's work was evident elsewhere in the theater. The country was still in the midst of the Great Depression. As part of the Works Progress Administration, the government created the Federal Theatre Project in 1935 to provide work for unemployed theater professionals and to provide inexpensive, uncensored theater. At its peak, the project employed ten thousand people and set up numerous semiautonomous companies that offered audiences a broad range of theatrical fare. Among its controversial innovations was the Living Newspaper, documentary plays dramatizing daily events. With the Federal Theatre Project's support, numerous African-American theater groups sprang up in Harlem and elsewhere. Some productions, such as Orson Welles's all-black staging of *Macbeth* (1935), became nationally celebrated. However, in 1939 Congress abolished the project in response to conservative opposition to what was seen as the left-wing propagandistic tone of many of the productions. Despite its relatively brief life, the Federal Theatre is the closest America has come to having a national theater.

Another influential and politically involved theatrical organization, the Group Theatre, was founded in 1931 by Harold Clurman, Cheryl Crawford, and Lee Strasberg, who had broken away from the Theatre Guild. Committed leftists, Clurman and Strasberg wanted a theater that reflected their political views and tried to counteract the notion that social concern is death to art. Until it disbanded in 1940, the Group Theatre was perhaps the most potent artistic force in American theater. Beside producing works of socially conscious playwrights such as Sidney Kingsley, Irwin Shaw, and Marc Blitzstein, it introduced Clifford Odets, the leading playwright of left-wing protest, with productions of *Awake and Sing* (1935), *Waiting for Lefty* (1935), and *Golden Boy* (1937).

Of the playwrights writing on the eve of World War II, the most significant beside O'Neill may have been Thornton Wilder. His universal tale of smalltown life, *Our Town* (1938), is one of the best-known and most popular American dramas. *The Skin of Our Teeth* (1942), an allegory based on humankind's fight for survival, was another critical and commercial success for Wilder. His use of theatrical devices taken from surrealism, futurism, and expressionism placed him among experimental writers such as O'Neill and influenced European playwrights such as Friedrich Durrenmatt and Eugene Ionesco. Yet, Wilder's plays are accessible to the average theatergoer, mostly because of the simplicity of their subject matter.

Between the world wars American theater won international acclaim. But with the exception of O'Neill and Wilder, there were no real innovators, or artistic movements. Part of the reason was economic. In 1928, just before the depression, there were fifteen hundred theaters across the country, but on the eve of World War II, the number had dwindled to about two hundred. The development of sound films in 1928, coupled with their low admission prices, made it nearly impossible for theaters to compete with movies. Rising production costs, partly caused by the increasing power of theatrical unions, worsened the situation. Theater managers then had to attract the popular audience, a group notoriously disinterested in risky plays or artistic experimentation.

During World War II the musical became the most popular form of theater and, as has been frequently said, reached its maturity. *Oklahoma* (1943), by Richard Rodgers and Oscar Hammerstein II, was the first musical to integrate song and story and one of the first to integrate modern American dance. Later Rodgers and Hammerstein productions, such as *Carousel* (1945), *South Pacific* (1949), and *The King and I* (1951), cemented the place of musicals in American theater.

After the war two major new dramatists—Tennessee Williams and Arthur Miller—appeared and came to master expressionistic drama. Williams's first success, *The Glass Menagerie* (1945), manipulates theme and place in exploring the

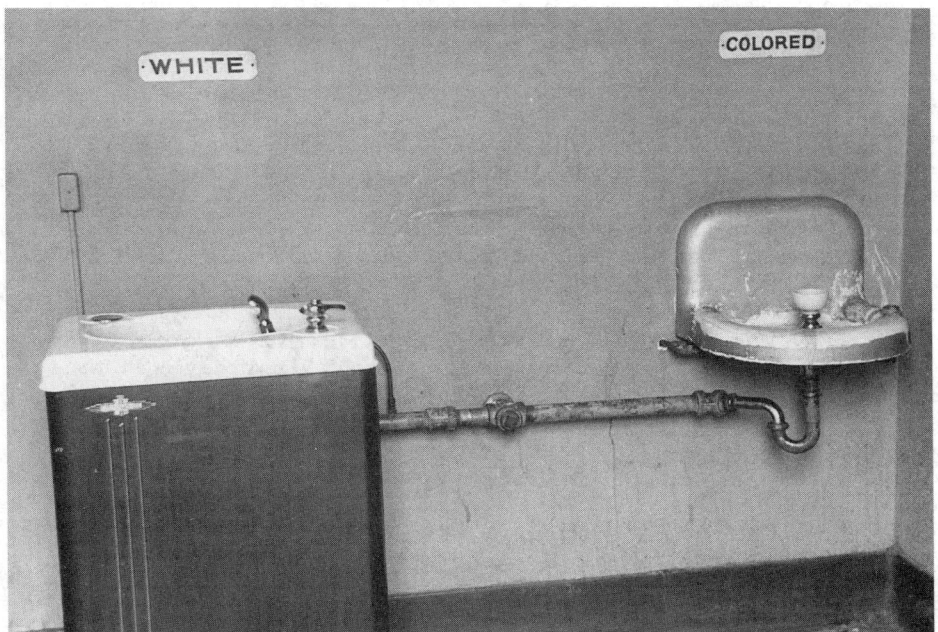

Even drinking fountains in the South were racially segregated before the Civil Rights Act of 1964.

characters' inner and often unconscious motivation. In his many later acclaimed plays, Williams's protagonists are misfits or lost souls, out of sync with normal people, who physically and morally humiliate them. Miller first achieved recognition with *All My Sons* (1947) and was further lauded for *Death of a Salesman* (1949). Miller's best works are powerful and dramatic moral statements about the individual's responsibility to preserve his or her integrity in a society that demands the opposite. Miller was himself a prominent character in a political drama that unfolded in the later 1940s and early 1950s: the anticommunism panic that led to the investigations of the House Committee on Un-American Activities. Many well-known playwrights were brought before the infamous House Committee. The plays of the time reflected the horror of members of the artistic community who watched the integrity of friends crumble and were themselves called upon to answer the question, "Are you now, or have you ever been, a member of the Communist party?" Clifford Odets and Elia Kazan were forever linked to those who named names before the committee. Miller wrote the play *The Crucible* (1953) to protest the injustice of the "witchhunts"; Lillian Hellman wrote memorable letters in which she states her refusal to implicate colleagues, and she produced *Scoundrel Time* (1976), an account of her own experiences, and those of her friends, during the McCarthy era.

One of the most powerful influences on the theater in the mid-1950s was the Actor's Studio, a workshop for professional actors. Founded in 1950 by Elia Kazan, Robert Lewis, and Cheryl Crawford, it was the leading proponent of

═CONTEXTS═

Archetypal Criticism

Archetypal criticism is a way of understanding literature in terms of certain recurring patterns, thought to originate in the subconscious mind. The Canadian literary critic Northrop Frye (1912–), author of *Anatomy of Criticism* (1957), sought for literary criticism a sense of methodological discipline more common among the "hard sciences." For Frye this involved the construction of a single, overriding hypothesis of literature that could act as a cohesive force in criticism. He found this in his theory of literary "archetypes," recurring structures in literature that are reducible to common elements of the subconscious mind. The conflict between father and son, for example, assumes archetypal dimensions in Arthur Miller's *Death of a Salesman*. Frye explains his theory in this excerpt from the essay "The Archetypes of Literature" (1951):

The Archetypes of Literature

It is clear that criticism cannot be systematic unless there is a quality in literature which enables it to be so, an order of words corresponding to the order of nature in the natural sciences. An archetype should be not only a unifying category of criticism, but itself a part of a total form, and it leads us at once to the question of what sort of total form criticism can see in literature. . . . Total literary history moves from the primitive to the sophisticated, and here we glimpse the possibility of seeing literature as a complication of a relatively restricted and simple group of formulas that can be studied in primitive culture. If so, then the search for archetypes is a kind of literary anthropology, concerned with the way that literature is informed by pre-literary categories such as ritual, myth and folk tale. We next realize that the relation between these categories and literature is by no means purely one of descent, as we find them reappearing in the greatest classics—in fact there seems to be a general tendency on the part of the great classics to revert to them.

Northrop Frye, 1951

"method" acting, which encourages performers to probe their own feelings as the way to find a character's psychological truth, sometimes, its critics claimed, at the expense of technique. The Actor's Studio established special units for directors, playwrights, and production. But by 1962, when the production unit was created, the studio's influence was already waning as American theater began to turn from the psychological realism expounded by Lee Strasberg, its leading advocate.

It was during the 1950s that Off Broadway theaters became prominent. By renting cheap, and in some cases nontheatrical, space, Off Broadway producers kept production costs and ticket costs down. The low overhead and the necessity of adapting to unusual stages encouraged experimentation. The 1952 revival of Williams's *Summer and Smoke* (1947), an artistic and commercial triumph, suggested that small theaters might be able to mount productions of higher quality than the larger, more commercial playhouses. By the mid-1950s Off Broadway productions outnumbered those on Broadway, were more diverse, and emphasized repertory. However, Off Broadway did not tend to be experimental either in writing or staging and did not seriously challenge the dominance of Broadway.

During the 1960s regional American theaters developed, and women's and minority theater gained in prominence. African-American theater flourished with the establishment of the Black Arts Theater School in New York City in 1964. By 1968 about forty African-American arts organizations existed, including the New York-based Negro Ensemble Company, which aimed to continuously present black drama "without regard to the whims of commercial theater." This increased African-American consciousness in the theater spawned such new playwrights as James Baldwin, Lorraine Hansberry, Ed Bullins, Douglas Turner Ward, Amiri Baraka (LeRoi Jones), Ntozake Shange, and August Wilson. Hansberry was probably the most critically acclaimed, although in her brief lifetime she completed only two plays—*A Raisin in the Sun* (1959) and *The Sign in Sidney Brustein's Window* (1964).

One of the important dramatists to emerge in the 1960s was Edward Albee. In works such as *The American Dream* (1961) and *Who's Afraid of Virginia Woolf?* (1962), he combined fantasy and reality. Critics proclaimed him the first American absurdist dramatist, in the tradition of the Irish playwright Samuel Beckett.

During the 1960s Off Off Broadway assumed the role Off Broadway had played in the 1950s. Off Off Broadway groups of the 1960s, generally working without pay and on tiny budgets, produced hundreds of plays by new playwrights, including Ronald Tavel, Charles Ludlam, Lanford Wilson, Maria Irene Fornès, Terrence McNally, Adrienne Kennedy, Luís Valdez, David Mamet, and Sam Shepard. Such writers moved American drama from the realism of Miller and Williams toward more experimental forms. Of the Off-Off Broadway organizations promoting this change, some of the most influential have been the Living Theater, La Mama Experimental Theater, the Ridiculous Theater Company, and the Public Theater.

Created in 1947 by the husband-and-wife team of Julian Beck and Judith Malina, the Living Theater reached its zenith during the 1960s and 1970s. The group's productions emphasized improvisation, ritual actions, nonverbal communications, and other devices from the Theater of Cruelty (based on the theories of the French actor and director Antonin Artaud). In one of the Living Theater's most celebrated productions, *Paradise Now* (1968), the actors confronted members of the audience, seeking to insult and humiliate them. Such radical efforts to involve playgoers were attacked as counterproductive, and the Living Theater has never regained its former influence. In contrast, La Mama, the Ridiculous Theater Company, and the Public Theater are all still potent forces in American theater. Under the energetic guidance of La Mama's founder, Elaine Stewart, that group has mounted avant-garde performances since 1962. The Ridiculous Theater Company was headed by Charles Ludlam until his death. At the forefront of gay drama, the group has presented fantasies based on myths derived from the popular culture, with the key roles played by female impersonators. And since Joseph Papp transformed New York City's Astor Library into the Public Theater in 1967, that group has continued to present new playwrights, such as Charles Gordone and David Rabe.

The most prolific and successful of the new writers to have originated in Off Off Broadway is Sam Shepard, whose works were first produced in 1967 and contain a wide variety of American stereotypes, from rock stars to cowboys to gangsters. His plays, such as *Buried Child* (1978) and *A Lie of the Mind* (1985), have been acclaimed for their imaginative language, a mix of slang, rock and roll, and B-movie dialogue.

Experimental theater has continued in new forms. One of them is performance art, which developed out of experimental "happenings" staged during the 1960s when performers combined elements from other media such as dance, film, and music. Today's performance artists, such as Laurie Anderson and Robert Wilson, still rely on mixed media to highlight dramatic intent. And if Wilson and Anderson represent the radical extreme of American theater, new dramatists such as Wendy Wasserstein, Angus Wilson, and David Henry Hwang fit more into the mainstream. Their work, and that of Michael Bennett and Stephen Sondheim, innovative artists in the field of musical drama, has proven successful even on Broadway. According to Hwang, "American theater is beginning to discover . . . Black theater, women's theater, gay theater, Asian American theater, Hispanic theater." But as the twentieth century draws to a close, the theater is struggling with the entertainment industry—movies and television—to maintain itself as a vital community, one engaged in artistic renewal.

Eugene O'Neill
(1888–1953)

The private life of a theatrical family typically includes the extension of drama from the stage to the household; daily occurrences become small melodramatic scenes insisting on crisis and resolution. The circumstances of Eugene O'Neill's upbringing have all the elements, as O'Neill was himself excruciatingly aware, of a play by the man from whom O'Neill took his literary models, August Strindberg. In O'Neill's life and his work, as in Strindberg's plays, to be a member of a family is to participate in extravagant lies to conceal from public view the family's inner weaknesses and moral blight. Awash in alcohol and addiction and suffering under what he perceived as the "tyrannies" of Irish Catholicism, O'Neill's family life prepared him for the manic velocity of his early manhood.

Eugene Gladstone O'Neill was born in New York City in 1888. His father, James O'Neill, was an actor famous for his portrayal of the hero in *The Count of Monte Cristo*, a potboiler by the playwright Alexander Dumas. James shunted his family from town to town on the American theater circuit. In the midst of this rootless life, the only measure of consistency was James O'Neill's nightly performance as the Count of Monte Cristo—a drudgery that went on for thirty years. The O'Neills traveled from hotel to hotel, trying to keep some semblance of a home. O'Neill's mother, Ella Quinlan, became ill while she was pregnant with her second child; the child later died. The family held James O'Neill at fault for engaging the services of the least expensive physician available. She had been treated with morphine, a drug to which she remained addicted for the rest of her life. Eugene O'Neill's memories of this childhood were agonizingly recreated in his masterpiece, *Long Day's Journey Into Night*, which was written in 1940 but first produced in 1956.

Rebellious and unhappy through years of parochial school training, O'Neill entered Princeton University in 1906, only to be expelled a year later because of a prank. Although he married Kathleen Jenkins, a New York socialite, in 1909, O'Neill succumbed to the romantic lure of life at sea. He drifted aimlessly from port to port but returned home in 1911 and soon afterward made a feeble attempt at suicide. In 1912 O'Neill divorced his wife and became severely ill with tuberculosis; he entered Gaylord Farm Sanatorium in Wallingford, Connecticut, for treatment. Because his grandfather had died from the disease, O'Neill considered his own death imminent (but that was not to occur until 1953). At the sanatorium he read extensively, from European philosophy to plays. He began to form his own belief about the grim fate determining all existence, the destructive cycles of struggle and defeat.

When O'Neill left the sanatorium in June 1913, he was surprised and grateful to be alive and devoted himself to the writing profession. While writing his early plays, O'Neill studied at Harvard University with George Pierce Baker, who instructed many of the early twentieth-century playwrights and was then considered the father of American drama. O'Neill's first plays, primarily one-act plays, evoke the melodrama that had surrounded him and that he had survived, but in his later plays great emotion coexists with a skepticism that deflates it. Even as O'Neill, in emulation of Strindberg, turned to realism, his work retained an almost tidal emotion while concentrating upon the increasingly narrow worlds of the family.

In 1915 O'Neill moved to Provincetown, Massachusetts; while there he courted Agnes Boulton, who in 1918 became his second wife. In 1916 the Provincetown Players produced his play *Bound East for Cardiff*. The focus of the Players, a group of playwrights and actors committed to American theater and American plays, was unusual in a time when theater groups tended to borrow plays from abroad. In retrospect, the arrival of Eugene O'Neill in Provincetown might be seen as the beginning of modern American theater, because his name and twentieth-century American drama would become indissolubly linked. This link has regrettably caused some equally important American playwrights to be lost in O'Neill's shadow. Susan Glaspell and George Cook, for example, members of the Provincetown Players, were significant for their own works and for their dedication to a theater struggling to get out from under the pervading influences of European drama as well as for their careful nurturing of O'Neill's early work.

Cook's commitment to the scope of O'Neill's talent took physical shape in the set Cook created for *The Emperor Jones* (1920). The dome setting cost the Players' entire budget, but the conception was arresting. O'Neill calls for drumbeats throughout the play to signal changes in emotion: fear, confusion, triumph. Most of the play is delivered in soliloquies, with other characters often privy to the speeches.

O'Neill's special abilities as a playwright were widely appreciated with the 1920 New York production of *Beyond the Horizon*. The play, a Pulitzer Prize winner, depicts the failure and disillusionment of a poor farming family, the Mayos. O'Neill's subsequent play *Anna Christie* (1921), a revision of the unsuccessful *Chris Christopherson*, earned the playwright another Pulitzer Prize. Yet another modern American tragedy, *Anna Christie* represented a "backward look" to O'Neill, who favored the experimental use of sound and character development of *The Emperor Jones*. He returned to experimenting with other forms in plays such as *The Hairy Ape* (1922) and *All God's Chillun Got Wings* (1924).

A scene from a production of O'Neill's Desire Under the Elms.

Desire Under the Elms, produced in 1924, won O'Neill even wider critical acclaim. By setting the play on the Cabot Farm in Connecticut, O'Neill gave it a degree of intimacy (he had just purchased a thirty-acre estate in Ridgefield, Connecticut); by setting it in 1850, he gave it a degree of distance. Through an intricate network of marriages and deceit, the Cabot family vies for possession of the farm. The aging patriarch Ephraim Cabot returns to his farm with a new, young wife, the scheming former housemaid Abbie Putnam. Eben, Ephraim's third son, vengefully begins an affair with Abbie as he was convinced that Ephraim had killed Eben's mother through overwork. The illegitimate birth of a child parented by Eben and Abbie sets the family further at odds. Eben announces his plan to desert Abbie, and, in a desperate attempt to prove that she loves him and does not want his family's farm, she murders the child.

Watching over these melodramatic struggles are the elms that with "crushing, jealous absorption" brood over the house with a "sinister maternity." O'Neill's fascination with Greek tragedy invites a comparison to Medea, a sorceress who kills her children. *Desire Under the Elms* was O'Neill's first attempt at writing in the tradition of Greek tragedy. Abbie is carefully patterned after Phaedra, the queen in Euripedes's play *Hippolytus* whose desire for her husband's son is uncontrollable.

O'Neill's first Broadway play, *Marco Millions,* was produced in 1928. A complex allegory of religion, commerce, and salvation, the play traces the movement of the main character, Marco Polo, from poet to salesman through a course that includes a papal visit. While at work on his other plays, O'Neill began the trilogy *Mourning Becomes Electra,* written in France between 1929 and 1931 after O'Neill had divorced his second wife and married his third wife, Carlotta Monterey. *Mourning Becomes Electra* consists of three sections—*The Homecoming, The Hunted,* and *The Haunted*—in which O'Neill sought to give a modern psychological approximation of the Greek tragedy's sense of fate. The play went through many drafts and revisions as O'Neill used Aeschylus's *Oresteia* as his model.

In the Pulitzer Prize winning *Strange Interlude* (1928) O'Neill revived the use of soliloquy in performance. More than just a halt in the dramatic action or the necessary introduction of pertinent information by the character, soliloquies in many of O'Neill's plays abruptly shift the audience's perception of a character's state of mind or motive. Allowing some dramatic tension, depending on who overhears the soliloquy, this device reminded critics of the finest Renaissance creations.

Year after year O'Neill produced plays that have endured in American theater. *The Iceman Cometh* (1946) captures the rosy, transitory glow of the drinking house. Set in Harry Hope's Saloon and Boardinghouse, the characters spin dreams and tell lies to pass the time. They await the arrival of Hickey, a traveling salesman who makes an annual visit to drink, buy drinks, celebrate Harry's birthday, and joke about his own wife's affair with the iceman. Hickey arrives sober and proceeds to dispel everyone's dreams, returning them to the image of their own devastating failures. The play ends when Hickey confesses that he murdered his wife to end the suffering he had been causing her, and Don Parritt, a character hiding from the police, admits that he has turned his mother in for money. O'Neill's women are a constant reminder of failure. *The Iceman Cometh*, written in 1939, was not produced until 1946 and was the last new play to be produced on Broadway in O'Neill's lifetime. When the play was revived on Broadway in 1958, more than four years after O'Neill's death, it renewed interest in his work, beginning new productions that offered critical reinterpretations of his most powerful plays.

Elements of O'Neill's family life appear in all his plays—domineering fathers riding their children, drunken men contemplating their failures, women at once guilt ridden and contemptuous—but in *Long Day's Journey Into Night* the family is portrayed with a painful accuracy that lays bare the soul-sickness of years of entanglements, blame, guilt, and sorrow that underlie a cultivated appearance of propriety. O'Neill's painstaking control is apparent in his elaborate, exacting stage directions and instructions about how the lines should be delivered (and thus how they should be received). Like a choreographer, O'Neill positions the family members where a loss of poise or balance leads to an unraveling or to self-exposure.

Mary Tyrone, the mother in *Long Day's Journey*, moves from blame to sudden revelation to confused detachment, all in the course of a single speech. Her recent return from a sanatorium, where she was "treated" for morphine addiction, is the object of her husband's and her sons' fragile hope that "this time" will be "different." As the precarious peace crumbles, the stress on all the characters is revealed. Over and over old stories of betrayal and wrongdoing are told to excuse present shortcomings. The elaborate dance of the two sons, Jamie and Edmund (whose continual coughing echoes in the house, grimly diagnosing his tuberculosis), moves between their own despair and their united fury at their father's miserly ways. The story O'Neill tells in *Long Day's Journey* is painful not only because of the clear, autobiographical elements, but also because as an American playwright—whose most famous colleagues in twentieth-century theater consistently represent either their own or their families' alcoholism—he is telling a peculiarly American story of what lies between the appearance and the reality of American family life.

Like *Long Day's Journey, A Moon for the Misbegotten* (1952) stretches time to create a sense of endlessness. The actual length of time, however, is an effect of O'Neill's subtle manipulation of the characters' behavior as they change in response to situations unbearably and destructively repetitive. He composed *A Moon for the Misbegotten,* which is said to deal with his brother Jamie's deterioration, in 1943 after O'Neill had supposedly retired. He wrote continuously throughout his life, and some of his "lost" plays, never produced, were published as late as 1972. His complex, vivid works and his varied role in American theater earned him a Nobel Prize for literature in 1936 and deserve renewed attention from contemporary audiences.

Suggested Readings: *Beyond the Horizon,* 1920. *The Emperor Jones,* 1920. *Anna Christie,* 1921. *The Hairy Ape,* 1922. *All God's Chillun Got Wings,* 1924. *Strange Interlude,* 1928. *Mourning Becomes Electra,* 1931. *The Iceman Cometh,* 1946. *A Moon for the Misbegotten,* 1947. *Long Day's Journey Into Night,* 1956. *A Touch of the Poet,* 1957. *Ten "Lost" Plays,* ed. B. Cerf, 1963. *Poems 1912–1944,* ed. D. C. Gallup, 1980. E. A. Engel, *The Haunted Heroes of Eugene O'Neill,* 1953. J. Gassner, *Eugene O'Neill,* 1965. J. H. Raleigh, *The Plays of Eugene O'Neill,* 1965. E. Tornqvuist, *A Drama of Souls,* 1968. A. and B. Gelb, *O'Neill,* 1973. L. Schaeffer, *Eugene O'Neill: Son and Artist,* 1973. C. W. E. Bigsby, *20th-Century American Drama,* 1984. H. Bloom, ed., *Eugene O'Neill: Modern Critical Interpretations,* 1987.

Text Used: *The Plays of Eugene O'Neill,* 1924.

DESIRE UNDER THE ELMS

CHARACTERS

EPHRAIM CABOT

SIMEON

PETER } *his sons*

EBEN

ABBIE PUTNAM

YOUNG GIRL, TWO FARMERS, *the* FIDDLER, *a* SHERIFF, *and other folk from the neighboring farms.*

The action of the entire play takes place in, and immediately outside of, the Cabot farmhouse in New England, in the year 1850. The south end of the house faces front to a stone wall with a wooden gate at center opening on a country road. The house is in good condition but in need of paint. Its walls are a sickly grayish, the green of the shutters faded. Two enormous elms are on each side of the house. They bend their trailing branches down over the roof. They appear to protect and at the same time subdue. There is a sinister maternity in their aspect, a crushing, jealous absorption. They have developed from their intimate contact with the life of man in the house an appalling humaneness. They brood oppressively over the house. They are like exhausted women resting their sagging breasts and hands and hair on its roof, and when it rains their tears trickle down monotonously and rot on the shingles.

There is a path running from the gate around the right corner of the house to the front door. A narrow porch is on this side. The end wall facing us has two windows in its upper story, two larger ones on the floor below. The two upper are those of the father's bedroom and that of the brothers. On the left, ground floor, is the kitchen — on the right, the parlor, the shades of which are always drawn down.

PART I, SCENE I

(Exterior of the farmhouse. It is sunset of a day at the beginning of summer in the year 1850. There is no wind and everything is still. The sky above the roof is suffused with deep colors, the green of the elms glows, but the house is in shadow, seeming pale and washed out by contrast.)

(A door opens and Eben Cabot comes to the end of the porch and stands look-ing down the road to the right. He has a large bell in his hand and this he swings mechanically, awakening a deafening clangor. Then he puts his hands on his hips and stares up at the sky. He sighs with a puzzled awe and blurts out with halting appreciation.)

EBEN: God! Purty! *(His eyes fall and he stares about him frowningly. He is twenty-five, tall and sinewy. His face is well formed, good-looking, but its expres-sion is resentful and defensive. His defiant, dark eyes remind one of a wild ani-mal's in captivity. Each day is a cage in which he finds himself trapped but in-wardly unsubdued. There is a fierce repressed vitality about him. He has black hair, mustache, a thin curly trace of beard. He is dressed in rough farm clothes.)*

(He spits on the ground with intense disgust, turns, and goes back into the house.)
(Simeon and Peter come in from their work in the fields. They are tall men, much older than their half-brother [Simeon is thirty-nine and Peter thirty-seven], built on a squarer, simpler model, fleshier in body, more bovine and homelier in face, shrewder and more practical. Their shoulders stoop a bit from years of farm work. They clump heavily along in their clumsy thick-soled boots caked with earth. Their clothes, their faces, hands, bare arms, and throats are earth-stained. They smell of earth. They stand together for a moment in front of the house and, as if with the one impulse, stare dumbly up at the sky, leaning on their hoes. Their faces have a compressed, unresigned expression. As they look upward, this softens.)

SIMEON *(grudgingly)*:   Purty.
PETER: Ay-eh.
SIMEON *(suddenly)*:   Eighteen years ago.
PETER: What?
SIMEON: Jenn. My woman. She died.
PETER: I'd fergot.
SIMEON: I rec'lect—now an' agin. Makes it lonesome. She'd hair long's a hoss' tail—an' yaller like gold!
PETER: Waal—she's gone. *(This with indifferent finality—then after a pause.)* They's gold in the West, Sim.
SIMEON *(still under the influence of sunset—vaguely)*:   In the sky?
PETER: Waal—in a manner o' speakin'—that's the promise. *(Growing ex-cited.)* Gold in the sky—in the West—Golden Gate—Californi-a!—Goldest West!—fields o' gold!
SIMEON *(excited in his turn)*:   Fortunes layin' just atop o' the ground waitin' t' be picked! Solomon's mines, they says! *(For a moment they continue looking up at the sky—then their eyes drop.)*
PETER *(with sardonic bitterness)*:   Here—it's stones atop o' the ground—

stones atop o' stones—makin' stone walls—year atop o' year—him 'n' yew 'n' me 'n' then Eben—makin' stone walls fur him to fence us in!

SIMEON: We've wuked. Give our strength. Give our years. Plowed 'em under in the ground—(*He stamps rebelliously.*)—rottin'—makin' soil for his crops! (*A pause.*) Waal—the farm pays good for hereabouts.

PETER: If we plowed in Californi-a, they'd be lumps o' gold in the furrow!

SIMEON: Californi-a's t'other side o' earth, a'most. We got t' calc'late—

PETER (*after a pause*):   'Twould be hard fur me, too, to give up what we've 'arned here by our sweat. (*A pause. Eben sticks his head out of the dining room window, listening.*)

SIMEON: Ay-eh. (*A pause.*) Mebbe—he'll die soon.

PETER (*doubtfully*):   Mebbe.

SIMEON: Mebbe—fur all we knows—he's dead now.

PETER: Ye'd need proof.

SIMEON: He's been gone two months—with no word.

PETER: Left us in the fields an evenin' like this. Hitched up an' druv off into the West. That's plum onnateral. He hain't never been off this farm 'ceptin' t' the village in thirty year or more, not since he married Eben's maw. (*A pause. Shrewdly.*) I calc'late we might git him declared crazy by the court.

SIMEON: He skinned 'em too slick. He got the best o' all on 'em. They'd never b'lieve him crazy. (*A pause.*) We got t' wait—till he's underground.

EBEN: (*with a sardonic chuckle*):   Honor thy father! (*They turn startled, and stare at him. He grins, then scowls.*) I pray he's died. (*They stare at him. He continues matter-of-factly.*) Supper's ready.

SIMEON AND PETER (*together*):   Ay-eh.

EBEN: (*gazing up at the sky*):   Sun's downin' purty.

SIMEON AND PETER (*together*):   Ay-eh. They's gold in the West.

EBEN: Ay-eh. (*Pointing.*) Yonder atop o' the hill pasture, ye mean?

SIMEON AND PETER (*together*):   In Californi-a!

EBEN: Hunh? (*Stares at them indifferently for a second, then drawls.*) Waal—supper's gittin' cold. (*He turns back into kitchen.*)

SIMEON (*startled—smacks his lips*):   I air hungry!

PETER (*sniffing*):   I smells bacon!

SIMEON (*with hungry appreciation*):   Bacon's good!

PETER (*in same tone*):   Bacon's bacon! (*They turn, shouldering each other, their bodies bumping and rubbing together as they hurry clumsily to their food, like two friendly oxen toward their evening meal. They disappear around the right corner of house and can be heard entering the door.*)

SCENE II

(*The color fades from the sky. Twilight begins. The interior of the kitchen is now visible. A pine table is at center, a cook-stove in the right rear corner, four rough wooden chairs, a tallow candle on the table. In the middle of the rear wall is fastened a big advertising poster with a ship in full sail and the word "California" in big letters. Kitchen utensils hang from nails. Everything is neat and in order but the atmosphere is of a men's camp kitchen rather than that of a home.*)

(*Places for three are laid. Eben takes boiled potatoes and bacon from the stove and puts them on the table, also a loaf of bread and a crock of water. Simeon and*

*Peter shoulder in, slump down in their chairs without a word. Eben joins them.
The three eat in silence for a moment, the two elder as naturally unrestrained as
beasts of the field, Eben picking at his food without appetite, glancing at them
with a tolerant dislike.)*

SIMEON (*suddenly turns to Eben*):   Looky here! Ye'd oughtn't t' said that,
Eben.

PETER: 'Twa'n't righteous.

EBEN: What?

SIMEON: Ye prayed he'd died.

EBEN: Waal—don't yew pray it? (*A pause.*)

PETER: He's our Paw.

EBEN (*violently*):   Not mine!

SIMEON (*dryly*):   Ye'd not let no one else say that about yer Maw! Ha! (*He
gives one abrupt sardonic guffaw. Peter grins.*)

EBEN (*very pale*):   I meant—I hain't his'n—I hain't like him—he hain't me!

PETER (*dryly*):   Wait till ye've growed his age!

EBEN (*intensely*):   I'm Maw—every drop o' blood! (*A pause. They stare at him
with indifferent curiosity.*)

PETER (*reminiscently*):   She was good t' Sim 'n' me. A good Stepmaw's
scurse.

SIMEON: She was good t' everyone.

EBEN (*greatly moved, gets to his feet and makes an awkward bow to each of
them—stammering*):   I be thankful t' ye. I'm her—her heir. (*He sits down in
confusion.*)

PETER (*after a pause—judicially*):   She was good even t' him.

EBEN (*fiercely*):   An' fur thanks he killed her!

SIMEON (*after a pause*):   No one never kills nobody. It's allus somethin'.
That's the murderer.

EBEN: Didn't he slave Maw t' death?

PETER: He's slaved himself t' death. He's slaved Sim 'n' me 'n' yew t'
death—on'y none o' us hain't died—yit.

SIMEON: It's somethin'—drivin' him—t' drive us!

EBEN (*vengefully*):   Waal—I hold him t' jedgment! (*Then scornfully.*) Somethin'! What's somethin'?

SIMEON: Dunno.

EBEN (*sardonically*):   What's drivin' yew to Californi-a, mebbe? (*They look at
him in surprise.*) Oh, I've heerd ye! (*Then, after a pause.*) But ye'll never go t'
the gold fields!

PETER (*Assertively*):   Mebbe!

EBEN: Whar'll ye git the money?

PETER: We kin walk. It's an a'mighty ways—Californi-a—but if yew was t'
put all the steps we've walked on this farm end t' end we'd be in the moon!

EBEN: The Injuns'll skulp ye on the plains.

SIMEON (*with grim humor*):   We'll mebbe make 'em pay a hair fur a hair!

EBEN (*decisively*):   But t'aint that. Ye won't never go because ye'll wait here
fur yer share o' the farm, thinkin' allus he'll die soon.

SIMEON (*after a pause*):   We've a right.

PETER: Two-thirds belongs t'us.

EBEN (*jumping to his feet*):   Ye've no right! She wa'n't yewr Maw! It was her
farm! Didn't he steal it from her? She's dead. It's my farm.

SIMEON (*sardonically*):   Tell that t' Paw—when he comes! I'll bet ye a dollar he'll laugh—fur once in his life. Ha! (*He laughs himself in one single mirthless bark.*)

PETER (*amused in turn, echoes his brother*):   Ha!

SIMEON (*after a pause*):   What've ye got held agin us, Eben? Year arter year it's skulked in yer eye—somethin'.

PETER: Ay-eh.

EBEN: Ay-eh. They's somethin'. (*Suddenly exploding.*) Why didn't ye never stand between him 'n' my Maw when he was slavin' her to her grave—t' pay her back fur the kindness she done t' yew? (*There is a long pause. They stare at him in surprise.*)

SIMEON: Waal—the stock'd got t' be watered.

PETER: 'R they was woodin' t' do.

SIMEON: 'R plowin'.

PETER: 'R hayin'.

SIMEON: 'R spreadin' manure.

PETER: 'R weedin'.

SIMEON: 'R prunin'.

PETER: 'R milkin'.

EBEN (*breaking in harshly*):   An' makin' walls—stone atop o' stone—makin' walls till yer heart's a stone ye heft up out o' the way o' growth onto a stone wall t' wall in yer heart!

SIMEON (*matter-of-factly*):   We never had no time t' meddle.

PETER (*to Eben*):   Yew was fifteen afore yer Maw died—an' big fur yer age. Why didn't ye never do nothin'?

EBEN (*harshly*):   They was chores t' do, wa'n't they? (*A pause—then slowly.*) It was on'y arter she died I come to think o' it. Me cookin'—doin' her work—that made me know her, suffer her sufferin'—she'd come back t'help—come back t' bile potatoes—come back t' fry bacon—come back t' bake biscuits—come back all cramped up t' shake the fire, an' carry ashes, her eyes weepin' an' bloody with smoke an' cinders same's they used t' be. She still comes back—stands by the stove thar in the evenin'—she can't find it nateral sleepin' an' restin' in peace. She can't git used t' bein' free—even in her grave.

SIMEON: She never complained none.

EBEN: She'd got too tired. She'd got too used t' bein' too tired. That was what he done. (*With vengeful passion.*) An' sooner'r later, I'll meddle. I'll say the thin's I didn't say then t' him! I'll yell 'em at the top o' my lungs. I'll see t' it my Maw gits some rest an' sleep in her grave! (*He sits down again, relapsing into a brooding silence. They look at him with a queer indifferent curiosity.*)

PETER (*after a pause*):   Whar in tarnation d'ye s'pose he went, Sim?

SIMEON: Dunno. He druv off in the buggy, all spick an' span, with the mare all breshed an' shiny, druv off clackin' his tongue an' wavin' his whip. I remember it right well. I was finishin' plowin', it was spring an' May an' sunset, an' gold in the West, an' he druv off into it. I yells "Whar ye goin', Paw?" an' he hauls up by the stone wall a jiffy. His old snake's eyes was glitterin' in the sun like he'd been drinkin' a jugful an' he says with a mule's grin: "Don't ye run away till I come back!"

PETER: Wonder if he knowed we was wantin' fur Californi-a?

SIMEON: Mebbe. I didn't say nothin' and he says, lookin' kinder queer an' sick: "I been hearin' the hens cluckin' an' the roosters crowin' all the durn day. I been listenin' t' the cows lowin' an' everythin' else kickin' up till I can't stand it no more. It's spring an' I'm feelin' damned," he says. "Damned like an old bare hickory tree fit on'y fur burnin'," he says. An' then I calc'late I must've looked a mite hopeful, fur he adds real spry and vicious: "But don't git no fool idee I'm dead. I've sworn t' live a hundred an' I'll do it, if on'y t' spite yer sinful greed! An' now I'm ridin' out t' learn God's message t' me in the spring, like the prophets done. An' yew git back t' yer plowin'," he says. An' he druv off singin' a hymn. I thought he was drunk—'r I'd stopped him goin'.

EBEN (*scornfully*): No, ye wouldn't! Ye're scared o' him. He's stronger—inside—than both o' ye put together!

PETER (*sardonically*): An' yew—be yew Samson?[1]

EBEN: I'm gittin' stronger. I kin feel it growin' in me—growin' an' growin'—till it'll bust out—! (*He gets up and puts on his coat and a hat. They watch him, gradually breaking into grins. Eben avoids their eyes sheepishly.*) I'm goin' out fur a spell—up the road.

PETER: T' the village.

SIMEON: T' see Minnie?

EBEN (*defiantly*): Ay-eh!

PETER (*jeeringly*): The Scarlet Woman!

SIMEON: Lust—that's what's growin' in ye!

EBEN: Waal—she's purty!

PETER: She's been purty fur twenty year.

SIMEON: A new coat o' paint'll make a heifer out of forty.

EBEN: She hain't forty!

PETER: If she hain't, she's teeterin' on the edge.

EBEN (*desperately*): What d'yew know—

PETER: All they is . . . Sim knew her—an' then me arter—

SIMEON: An' Paw kin tell yew somethin' too! He was fust!

EBEN: D'ye mean t' say he . . . ?

SIMEON (*with a grin*): Ay-eh! We air his heirs in everythin'!

EBEN (*intensely*): That's more to it! That grows on it! It'll bust soon! (*Then violently.*) I'll go smash my fist in her face! (*He pulls open the door in rear violently.*)

SIMEON (*with a wink at Peter—drawlingly*): Mebbe—but the night's wa'm—purty—by the time ye git thar mebbe ye'll kiss her instead!

PETER: Sart'n he will! (*They both roar with coarse laughter. Eben rushes out and slams the door—then the outside front door—comes around the corner of the house and stands still by the gate, staring up at the sky.*)

SIMEON (*looking after him*): Like his Paw.

PETER: Dead spit an' image!

SIMEON: Dog'll eat dog!

PETER: Ay-eh. (*Pause. With yearning.*) Mebbe a year from now we'll be in Californi-a.

SIMEON: Ay-eh. (*A pause. Both yawn.*) Let's git t'bed. (*He blows out the candle. They go out door in rear. Eben stretches his arms up to the sky—rebelliously.*)

EBEN: Waal—thar's a star, an' somewhar's they's him, an' here's me, an'

---

[1] In the Old Testament, a hero known for his great strength.

thar's Min up the road—in the same night. What if I does kiss her? She's like t'night, she's soft 'n' wa'm, her eyes kin wink like a star, her mouth's wa'm, her arms're wa'm, she smells like a wa'm plowed field, she's purty . . . Ay-eh! By God A'mighty she's purty, an' I don't give a damn how many sins she's sinned afore mine or who she's sinned 'em with, my sin's as purty as any one on 'em! *(He strides off down the road to the left.)*

Scene III

(It is the pitch darkness just before dawn. Eben comes in from the left and goes around to the porch, feeling his way, chuckling bitterly and cursing half-aloud to himself.)

EBEN: The cussed old miser! *(He can be heard going in the front door. There is a pause as he goes upstairs, then a loud knock on the bedroom door of the brothers.)* Wake up!

SIMEON *(startledly)*:   Who's thar?

EBEN *(Pushing open the door and coming in, a lighted candle in his hand. The bedroom of the brothers is revealed. Its ceiling is the sloping roof. They can stand upright only close to the center dividing wall of the upstairs. Simeon and Peter are in a double bed, front. Eben's cot is to the rear. Eben has a mixture of silly grin and vicious scowl on his face.)*: I be!

PETER *(angrily)*:   What in hell's-fire . . . ?

EBEN: I got news fur ye! Ha! *(He gives one abrupt sardonic guffaw.)*

SIMEON *(angrily)*:   Couldn't ye hold it 'til we'd got our sleep?

EBEN: It's nigh sunup. *(Then explosively.)* He's gone an' married agen!

SIMEON AND PETER *(explosively)*:   Paw?

EBEN: Got himself hitched to a female 'bout thirty-five—an' purty, they says . . .

SIMEON *(aghast)*:   It's a durn lie!

PETER: Who says?

SIMEON: They been stringin' ye!

EBEN: Think I'm a dunce, do ye? The hull village says. The preacher from New Dover, he brung the news—told it t'our preacher—New Dover, that's whar the old loon got himself hitched—that's whar the woman lived—

PETER *(no longer doubting—stunned)*:   Waal . . . !

SIMEON *(the same)*:   Waal . . . !

EBEN *(sitting down on a bed—with vicious hatred)*:   Ain't he a devil out o' hell? It's jest t' spite us—the damned old mule!

PETER *(after a pause)*:   Everythin'll go t'her now.

SIMEON: Ay-eh. *(A pause—dully.)* Waal—if it's done—

PETER: It's done us. *(Pause—then persuasively.)* They's gold in the fields o' Californi-a, Sim. No good a-stayin' here now.

SIMEON: Jest what I was a-thinkin'. *(Then with decision.)* S'well fust's last! Let's light out and git this mornin'.

PETER: Suits me.

EBEN: Ye must like walkin'.

SIMEON *(sardonically)*:   If ye'd grow wings on us we'd fly thar!

EBEN: Ye'd like ridin' better—on a boat, wouldn't ye? *(Fumbles in his pocket and takes out a crumpled sheet of foolscap.)* Waal, if ye sign this ye kin ride on a boat. I've had it writ out an' ready in case ye'd ever go. It says fur three hundred dollars t' each ye agree yewr shares o' the farm is sold t' me. (*They look suspiciously at the paper. A pause.*)

SIMEON (*wonderingly*):   But if he's hitched agen—

PETER: An' whar'd yew git that sum o' money, anyways?

EBEN (*cunningly*):   I know whar it's hid. I been waitin'—Maw told me. She knew whar it lay fur years, but she was waitin' . . . It's her'n—the money he hoarded from her farm an' hid from Maw. It's my money by rights now.

PETER: Whar's it hid?

EBEN (*cunningly*):   Whar yew won't never find it without me. Maw spied on him—'r she'd never knowed. (*A pause. They look at him suspiciously, and he at them.*) Waal, is it fa'r trade?

SIMEON: Dunno.

PETER: Dunno.

SIMEON (*looking at window*):   Sky's grayin'.

PETER: Ye better start the fire, Eben.

SIMEON: An' fix some vittles.

EBEN: Ay-eh. (*Then with a forced jocular heartiness.*) I'll git ye a good one. If ye're startin' t' hoof it t' Californi-a ye'll need somethin' that'll stick t' yer ribs. (*He turns to the door, adding meaningly.*) But ye kin ride on a boat if ye'll swap. (*He stops at the door and pauses. They stare at him.*)

SIMEON (*suspiciously*):   Whar was ye all night?

EBEN (*defiantly*):   Up t' Min's. (*Then slowly.*) Walkin' thar, fust I felt 's if I'd kiss her; then I got a-thinkin' o' what ye'd said o' him an' her an' I says, I'll bust her nose fur that! Then I got t' the village an' heerd the news an' I got madder'n hell an' run all the way t' Min's not knowin' what I'd do— (*He pauses—then sheepishly but more defiantly.*) Waal—when I seen her, I didn't hit her—nor I didn't kiss her nuther—I begun t'beller like a calf an' cuss at the same time, I was so durn mad—an' she got scared—an' I jest grabbed holt an' tuk her! (*Proudly.*) Yes, sirree! I tuk her. She may've been his'n—an' your'n, too—but she's mine now!

SIMEON (*dryly*):   In love, air yew?

EBEN (*with lofty scorn*):   Love! I don't take no stock in sech slop!

PETER (*winking at Simeon*):   Mebbe Eben's aimin' t' marry, too.

SIMEON: Min'd make a true faithful he'pmeet! (*They snicker.*)

EBEN: What do I care fur her—'ceptin' she's round an' wa'm? The p'int is she was his'n—an' now she b'longs t' me! (*He goes to the door—then turns—rebelliously.* An' Min hain't sech a bad un. They's worse'n Min in the world, I'll bet ye! Wait'll we see this cow the Old Man's hitched t'! She'll beat Min, I got a notion! (*He starts to go out.*)

SIMEON (*suddenly*):   Mebbe ye'll try t' make her your'n, too?

PETER: Ha! (*He gives a sardonic laugh of relish at this idea.*)

EBEN (*spitting with disgust*):   Her—here—sleepin' with him—stealin' my Maw's farm! I'd as soon pet a skunk 'r kiss a snake! (*He goes out. The two stare after him suspiciously. A pause. They listen to his steps receding.*)

PETER: He's startin' the fire.

SIMEON: I'd like t' ride t' Californi-a—but—

PETER: Min might o' put some scheme in his head.

SIMEON: Mebbe it's all a lie 'bout Paw marryin'. We'd best wait an' see the bride.

PETER: An' don't sign nothin' till we does!

SIMEON: Nor till we've tested it's good money! (*Then with a grin.*) But if Paw's hitched we'd be sellin' Eben somethin' we'd never git nohow!

PETER: We'll wait an' see. (*Then with sudden vindictive anger.*) An' till he comes, let's yew 'n' me not wuk a lick, let Eben tend to thin's if he's a mind t', let's us jest sleep an' eat an' drink likker, an' let the hull damned farm go t' blazes!

SIMEON (*excitedly*):   By God, we've 'arned a rest! We'll play rich fur a change. I hain't a-going to stir outa bed till breakfast's ready.

PETER: An' on the table!

SIMEON (*after a pause—thoughtfully*):   What d'ye calc'late she'll be like—our new Maw? Like Eben thinks?

PETER: More'n' likely.

SIMEON (*vindictively*):   Waal—I hope she's a she-devil that'll make him wish he was dead an' livin' in the pit o' hell fur comfort!

PETER (*fervently*):   Amen!

SIMEON (*imitating his father's voice*):   "I'm ridin' out t' learn God's message t' me in the spring like the prophets done," he says. I'll bet right then an' thar he knew plumb well he was goin' whorin', the stinkin' old hypocrite!

SCENE IV

(*Same as Scene II—shows the interior of the kitchen with a lighted candle on table. It is a gray dawn outside. Simeon and Peter are just finishing their breakfast. Eben sits before his plate of untouched food, brooding frowningly.*)

PETER (*glancing at him rather irritably*):   Lookin' glum don't help none.

SIMEON (*sarcastically*):   Sorrowin' over his lust o' the flesh!

PETER (*with a grin*):   Was she yer fust?

EBEN (*angrily*):   None o' yer business. (*A pause.*) I was thinkin' o' him. I got a notion he's gittin' near—I kin feel him comin' on like yew kin feel malaria chill afore it takes ye.

PETER: It's too early yet.

SIMEON: Dunno. He'd like t' catch us nappin'—jest t' have somethin' t' hoss us 'round over.

PETER (*Mechanically gets to his feet. Simeon does the same.*):   Waal—let's git t'wuk. (*They both plod mechanically toward the door before they realize. Then they stop short.*)

SIMEON (*grinning*):   Ye're a cussed fool, Pete—and I be wuss! Let him see we hain't wukin'! We don't give a durn!

PETER (*as they go back to the table*):   Not a damned durn! It'll serve t' show him we're done with him. (*They sit down again. Eben stares from one to the other with surprise.*)

SIMEON (*grins at him*):   We're aimin' t' start bein' lilies o' the field.

PETER: Nary a toil 'r spin 'r lick o' wuk do we put in!

SIMEON: Ye're sole owner—till he comes—that's what ye wanted. Waal, ye got t' be sole hand, too.

PETER: The cows air bellerin'. Ye better hustle at the milkin'.

EBEN (*with excited joy*):   Ye mean ye'll sign the paper?

SIMEON (*dryly*):   Mebbe.

PETER: Mebbe.

SIMEON: We're considerin'. (*Peremptorily.*) Ye better git t' wuk.

EBEN (*with queer excitement*):   It's Maw's farm agen! It's my farm! Them's my cows! I'll milk my durn fingers off fur cows o' mine! (*He goes out door in rear, they stare after him indifferently.*)

SIMEON: Like his Paw.

PETER: Dead spit 'n' image!

SIMEON: Waal—let dog eat dog! (*Eben comes out of front door and around the corner of the house. The sky is beginning to grow flushed with sunrise. Eben stops by the gate and stares around him with glowing, possessive eyes. He takes in the whole farm with his embracing glance of desire.*)

EBEN: It's purty! It's damned purty! It's mine! (*He suddenly throws his head back boldly and glares with hard, defiant eyes at the sky.*) Mine, d'ye hear? Mine! (*He turns and walks quickly off left, rear, toward the barn. The two brothers light their pipes.*)

SIMEON (*putting his muddy boots up on the table, tilting back his chair, and puffing defiantly*): Waal—this air solid comfort—fur once.

PETER: Ay-eh. (*He follows suit. A pause. Unconsciously they both sigh.*)

SIMEON (*suddenly*):   He never was much o' a hand at milkin', Eben wa'n't.

PETER (*with a snort*):   His hands air like hoofs! (*A pause.*)

SIMEON: Reach down the jug thar! Let's take a swaller. I'm feelin' kind o' low.

PETER: Good idee! (*He does so—gets two glasses—they pour out drinks of whisky.*) Here's t' the gold in Californi-a!

SIMEON: An' luck t' find it! (*They drink—puff resolutely—sigh—take their feet down from the table.*)

PETER: Likker don't 'pear t' sot right.

SIMEON: We hain't used t' it this early. (*A pause. They become very restless.*)

PETER: Gittin' close in this kitchen.

SIMEON (*with immense relief*):   Let's git a breath o' air. (*They arise briskly and go out rear—appear around house and stop by the gate. They stare up at the sky with a numbed appreciation.*)

PETER: Purty!

SIMEON: Ay-eh. Gold's t' the East now.

PETER: Sun's startin' with us fur the Golden West.

SIMEON (*staring around the farm, his compressed face tightened, unable to conceal his emotion*): Waal—it's our last mornin'—mebbe.

PETER (*the same*):   Ay-eh.

SIMEON (*stamps his foot on the earth and addresses it desperately*):   Waal—ye've thirty year o' me buried in ye—spread out over ye—blood an' bone an' sweat—rotted away—fertilizin' ye—richin' yer soul—prime manure, by God, that's what I been t' ye!

PETER: Ay-eh! An' me.

SIMEON: An' yew, Peter. (*He sighs—then spits.*) Waal—no use'n cryin' over spilt milk.

PETER: They's gold in the West—an' freedom, mebbe. We been slaves t' stone walls here.

SIMEON (*defiantly*):   We hain't nobody's slaves from this out—nor nothin's slaves nuther. (*A pause—restlessly.*) Speaking o' milk, wonder how Eben's managin'?

PETER: I s'pose he's managin'.

SIMEON: Mebbe we'd ought t' help—this once.

PETER: Mebbe. The cows knows us.

SIMEON: An' likes us. They don't know him much.

PETER: An' the hosses, an' pigs, an' chickens. They don't know him much.

SIMEON: They knows us like brothers—an' likes us! (*Proudly.*) Hain't we raised 'em t' be fust-rate, number one prize stock?

PETER: We hain't—not no more.

SIMEON (*dully*): I was fergittin'. (*Then resignedly.*) Waal, let's go help Eben a spell an' git waked up.

PETER: Suits me. (*They are starting off down left, rear, for the barn when Eben appears from there hurrying toward them, his face excited.*)

EBEN (*breathlessly*): Waal—har they be! The old mule an' the bride! I seen 'em from the barn down below at the turnin'.

PETER: How could ye tell that far?

EBEN: Hain't I as far-sight as he's near-sight? Don't I know the mare 'n' buggy, an' two people settin' in it? Who else . . . ? An' I tell ye I kin feel 'em a-comin', too! (*He squirms as if he had the itch.*)

PETER (*beginning to be angry*): Waal—let him do his own unhitchin'!

SIMEON (*angry in his turn*): Let's hustle in an' git our bundles an' be a-goin' as he's a-comin'. I don't want never t' step inside the door agen arter he's back. (*They both start back around the corner of the house. Eben follows them.*)

EBEN (*anxiously*): Will ye sign it afore ye go?

PETER: Let's see the color o' the old skinflint's money an' we'll sign. (*They disappear left. The two brothers clump upstairs to get their bundles. Eben appears in the kitchen, runs to window, peers out, comes back and pulls up a strip of flooring in under stove, takes out a canvas bag and puts it on table, then sets the floorboard back in place. The two brothers appear a moment after. They carry old carpetbags.*)

EBEN (*puts his hand on bag guardingly*): Have ye signed?

SIMEON (*shows paper in his hand*): Ay-eh. (*Greedily.*) Be that the money?

EBEN (*opens bag and pours out pile of twenty-dollar gold pieces*): Twenty-dollar pieces—thirty on 'em. Count 'em. (*Peter does so, arranging them in stacks of five, biting one or two to test them.*)

PETER: Six hundred. (*He puts them in bag and puts it inside his shirt carefully.*)

SIMEON (*handing paper to Eben*): Har ye be.

EBEN (*after a glance, folds it carefully and hides it under his shirt—gratefully*): Thank yew.

PETER: Thank yew fur the ride.

SIMEON: We'll send ye a lump o' gold fur Christmas. (*A pause. Eben stares at them and they at him.*)

PETER (*awkwardly*): Waal—we're a-goin'.

SIMEON: Comin' out t' the yard?

EBEN: No. I'm waitin' in here a spell. (*Another silence. The brothers edge awkwardly to door in rear—then turn and stand.*)

SIMEON: Waal—good-by.

PETER: Good-by.

EBEN: Good-by. (*They go out. He sits down at the table, faces the stove and pulls out the paper. He looks from it to the stove. His face, lighted up by the shaft of sunlight from the window, has an expression of trance. His lips move. The two brothers come out to the gate.*)

PETER (*looking off toward barn*):   Thar he be—unhitchin'.

SIMEON (*with a chuckle*):   I'll bet ye he's riled!

PETER: An' thar she be.

SIMEON: Let's wait 'n' see what our new Maw looks like.

PETER (*with a grin*):   An' give him our partin' cuss!

SIMEON (*grinning*):   I feel like raisin' fun. I feel light in my head an' feet.

PETER: Me, too. I feel like laffin' till I'd split up the middle.

SIMEON: Reckon it's the likker?

PETER: No. My feet feel itchin' t' walk an' walk—an' jump high over thin's—an' . . .

SIMEON: Dance? (*A pause.*)

PETER (*puzzled*):   It's plumb onnateral.

SIMEON (*a light coming over his face*):   I calc'late it's 'cause school's out. It's holiday. Fur once we're free!

PETER (*dazedly*):   Free?

SIMEON: The halter's broke—the harness is busted—the fence bars is down—the stone walls air crumblin' an' tumblin'! We'll be kickin' up an' tearin' away down the road!

PETER (*drawing a deep breath—oratorically*):   Anybody that wants this stinkin' old rock-pile of a farm kin hev it. T'ain't our'n, no sirree!

SIMEON (*takes the gate off its hinges and puts it under his arm*):   We harby 'bolishes shet gates, an' open gates, an' all gates, by thunder!

PETER: We'll take it with us fur luck an' let 'er sail free down some river.

SIMEON (*as a sound of voices comes from left, rear*):   Har they comes! (*The two brothers congeal into two stiff, grim-visaged statues. Ephraim Cabot and Abbie Putnam come in. Cabot is seventy-five, tall and gaunt, with great, wiry, concentrated power, but stoop-shouldered from toil. His face is as hard as if it were hewn out of a boulder, yet there is a weakness in it, a petty pride in its own narrow strength. His eyes are small, close together, and extremely near-sighted, blinking continually in the effort to focus on objects, their stare having a straining, ingrowing quality. He is dressed in his dismal black Sunday suit. Abbie is thirty-five, buxom, full of vitality. Her round face is pretty but marred by its rather gross sensuality. There is strength and obstinacy in her jaw, a hard determination in her eyes, and about her whole personality the same unsettled, untamed, desperate quality which is so apparent in Eben.*)

CABOT (*as they enter—a queer strangled emotion in his dry cracking voice*): Har we be t'hum, Abbie.

ABBIE (*with lust for the word*):   Hum! (*Her eyes gloating on the house without seeming to see the two stiff figures at the gate.*) It's purty—purty! I can't b'lieve it's r'ally mine.

CABOT (*sharply*):   Yewr'n? Mine! (*He stares at her penetratingly. She stares back. He adds relentingly.*) Our'n—mebbe! It was lonesome too long. I was growin' old in the spring. A hum's got t' hev a woman.

ABBIE (*her voice taking possession*):   A woman's got t' hev a hum!

CABOT (*nodding uncertainly*):   Ay-eh. (*Then irritably.*) Whar be they? Ain't thar nobody about—'r wukin'—'r nothin'?

ABBIE (*Sees the brothers. She returns their stare of cold appraising contempt with interest—slowly.*):   Thar's two men loafin' at the gate an' starin' at me like a couple o' strayed hogs.

CABOT (*straining his eyes*):   I kin see 'em—but I can't make out . . .

SIMEON: It's Simeon.

PETER: It's Peter.

CABOT (*exploding*):   Why hain't ye wukin'?

SIMEON (*dryly*):   We're waitin' t' welcome ye hum—yew an' the bride!

CABOT (*confusedly*):   Huh? Waal—this be yer new Maw, boys. (*She stares at them and they at her.*)

SIMEON (*turns away and spits contemptuously*):   I see her!

PETER (*spits also*):   An' I see her!

ABBIE (*with the conqueror's conscious superiority*):   I'll go in an' look at *my* house. (*She goes slowly around to porch.*)

SIMEON (*with a snort*):   *Her* house!

PETER (*calls after her*):   Ye'll find Eben inside. Ye better not tell him it's *yewr* house.

ABBIE (*mouthing the name*):   Eben. (*Then quietly.*) I'll tell Eben.

CABOT (*with a contemptuous sneer*):   Ye needn't heed Eben. Eben's a dumb fool—like his Maw—soft an' simple!

SIMEON (*with his sardonic burst of laughter*):   Ha! Eben's a chip o' yew—spit 'n' image—hard 'n' bitter's a hickory tree! Dog'll eat dog. He'll eat ye yet, old man!

CABOT (*commandingly*):   Ye git t' wuk.

SIMEON (*as Abbie disappears in house—winks at Peter and says tauntingly*):   So that thar's our new Maw, be it? Whar in hell did ye dig her up? (*He and Peter laugh.*)

PETER: Ha! Ye'd better turn her in the pen with the other sows. (*They laugh uproariously, slapping their thighs.*)

CABOT (*so amazed at their effrontery that he stutters in confusion*):   Simeon! Peter! What's come over ye? Air ye drunk?

SIMEON: We're free, old man—free o' yew an' the hull damned farm! (*They grow more and more hilarious and excited.*)

PETER: An' we're startin' out fur the gold fields o' Californi-a!

SIMEON: Ye kin take this place an' burn it!

PETER: An' bury it—fur all we cares!

SIMEON: We're free, old man! (*He cuts a caper.*)

PETER: Free! (*He gives a kick in the air.*)

SIMEON (*in a frenzy*):   Whoop!

PETER: Whoop! (*They do an absurd Indian war dance about the old man who is petrified between rage and the fear that they are insane.*)

SIMEON: We're free as Injuns! Lucky we don't skulp ye!

PETER: An' burn yer barn an' kill the stock!

SIMEON: An' rape yer new woman! Whoop! (*He and Peter stop their dance, holding their sides, rocking with wild laughter.*)

CABOT (*edging away*):   Lust fur gold—fur the sinful, easy gold o' Californi-a! It's made ye mad!

SIMEON (*tauntingly*):   Wouldn't ye like us to send ye back some sinful gold, ye old sinner?

PETER: They's gold besides what's in Californi-a! (*He retreats back beyond the vision of the old man and takes the bag of money and flaunts it in the air above his head, laughing.*)

SIMEON: And sinfuller, too!

PETER: We'll be voyagin' on the sea! Whoop! (*He leaps up and down.*)

SIMEON: Livin' free! Whoop! (*He leaps in turn.*)

CABOT (*suddenly roaring with rage*):   My cuss on ye!

SIMEON: Take our'n in trade fur it! Whoop!

CABOT: I'll hev ye both chained up in the asylum!

PETER: Ye old skinflint! Good-by!

SIMEON: Ye old blood sucker! Good-by!

CABOT: Go afore I . . . !

PETER: Whoop! (*He picks a stone from the road. Simeon does the same.*)

SIMEON: Maw'll be in the parlor.

PETER: Ay-eh! One! Two!

CABOT (*frightened*):   What air ye . . . ?

PETER: Three! (*They both throw, the stones hitting the parlor window with a crash of glass, tearing the shade.*)

SIMEON: Whoop!

PETER: Whoop!

CABOT (*in a fury now, rushing toward them*):   If I kin lay hands on ye—I'll break yer bones fur ye! (*But they beat a capering retreat before him, Simeon with the gate still under his arm. Cabot comes back, panting with impotent rage. Their voices as they go off take up the song of the gold-seekers to the old tune of "Oh, Susannah!"*)

"I jumped aboard the Liza ship,
And traveled on the sea,
And every time I thought of home
I wished it wasn't me!
Oh! Californi-a,
That's the land fur me!
I'm off to Californi-a!
With my wash bowl on my knee."

(*In the meantime, the window of the upper bedroom on right is raised and Abbie sticks her head out. She looks down at Cabot—with a sigh of relief.*)

ABBIE: Waal—that's the last o' them two, hain't it? (*He doesn't answer. Then in possessive tones.*) This here's a nice bedroom, Ephraim. It's a r'al nice bed. Is it my room, Ephraim?

CABOT (*grimly—without looking up*):   Our'n! (*She cannot control a grimace of aversion and pulls back her head slowly and shuts the window. A sudden horrible thought seems to enter Cabot's head.*) They been up to somethin'! Mebbe—mebbe they've pizened the stock—'r somethin'! (*He almost runs off down toward the barn. A moment later the kitchen door is slowly pushed open and Abbie enters. For a moment she stands looking at Eben. He does not notice her at first. Her eyes take him in penetratingly with a calculating appraisal of his strength as against hers. But under this her desire is dimly awakened by his youth and good looks. Suddenly he becomes conscious of her presence and looks up. Their eyes meet. He leaps to his feet, glowering at her speechlessly.*)

ABBIE (*in her most seductive tones which she uses all through this scene*):   Be you—Eben? I'm Abbie— (*She laughs.*) I mean, I'm yer new Maw.

EBEN (*viciously*):   No, damn ye!

ABBIE (*as if she hadn't heard—with a queer smile*):   Yer Paw's spoke a lot o' yew. . . .

EBEN: Ha!

ABBIE: Ye mustn't mind him. He's an old man. (*A long pause. They stare at each other.*) I don't want t' pretend playin' Maw t' ye, Eben. (*Admiringly.*) Ye're too big an' too strong fur that. I want t' be frens with ye. Mebbe with me fur a fren ye'd find ye'd like livin' here better. I kin make it easy fur ye with him, mebbe. (*With a scornful sense of power.*) I calc'late I kin git him t' do most anythin' fur me.

EBEN (*with bitter scorn*):   Ha! (*They stare again, Eben obscurely moved, physically attracted to her—in forced stilted tones.*) Yew kin go t' the devil!

ABBIE (*calmly*):   If cussin' me does ye good, cuss all ye've a mind t'. I'm all prepared t' have ye agin me—at fust. I don't blame ye nuther. I'd feel the same at any stranger comin' t' take my Maw's place. (*He shudders. She is watching him carefully.*) Yew must've cared a lot fur yewr Maw, didn't ye? My Maw died afore I'd growed. I don't remember her none. (*A pause.*) But yew won't hate me long, Eben. I'm not the wust in the world—an' yew an' me've got a lot in common. I kin tell that by lookin' at ye. Waal—I've had a hard life, too—oceans o' trouble an' nuthin' but wuk fur reward. I was a orphan early an' had t' wuk fur others in other folks' hums. Then I married an' he turned out a drunken spreer an' so he had to wuk fur others an' me too agen in other folks' hums, an' the baby died, an' my husband got sick an' died too, an' I was glad sayin' now I'm free fur once, on'y I diskivered right away all I was free fur was t' wuk agen in other folks' hums, doin' other folks' wuk till I'd most give up hope o' ever doin' my own wuk in my own hum, an' then your Paw come. . . . (*Cabot appears returning from the barn. He comes to the gate and looks down the road the brothers have gone. A faint strain of their retreating voices is heard: "Oh, Californi-a! That's the place for me." He stands glowering, his fist clenched, his face grim with rage.*)

EBEN (*fighting against his growing attraction and sympathy—harshly*): An' bought yew—like a harlot! (*She is stung and flushes angrily. She has been sincerely moved by the recital of her troubles. He adds furiously.*) An' the price he's payin' ye—this farm—was my Maw's, damn ye!—an' mine now!

ABBIE (*with a cool laugh of confidence*):   Yewr'n? We'll see 'bout that! (*Then strongly.*) Waal—what if I did need a hum? What else'd I marry an old man like him fur?

EBEN (*maliciously*):   I'll tell him ye said that!

ABBIE (*smiling*):   I'll say ye're lyin' a-purpose—an' he'll drive ye off the place!

EBEN: Ye devil!

ABBIE (*defying him*):   This be my farm—this be my hum—this be my kitchen—!

EBEN (*furiously, as if he were going to attack her*):   Shut up, damn ye!

ABBIE (*walks up to him—a queer coarse expression of desire in her face and body—slowly*): An' upstairs—that be my bedroom—an' my bed! (*He stares into her eyes, terribly confused and torn. She adds softly.*) I hain't bad nor mean—'ceptin' fur an enemy—but I got t' fight fur what's due me out o' life, if I ever 'spect t' git it. (*Then putting her hand on his arm—seductively.*) Let's yew 'n' me be frens, Eben.

EBEN (*stupidly—as if hypnotized*):   Ay-eh. (*Then furiously flinging off her arm.*) No, ye durned old witch! I hate ye! (*He rushes out the door.*)

ABBIE (*looks after him smiling satisfiedly—then half to herself, mouthing the word*): Eben's nice. (*She looks at the table, proudly.*) I'll wash up *my* dishes now.

(*Eben appears outside, slamming the door behind him. He comes around corner, stops on seeing his father, and stands staring at him with hate.*)

CABOT (*raising his arms to heaven in the fury he can no longer control*): Lord God o' Hosts,[2] smite the undutiful sons with Thy wust cuss!

EBEN (*breaking in violently*):   Yew 'n' yewr God! Allus cussin' folks—allus naggin' 'em!

CABOT (*oblivious to him—summoningly*):   God o' the old! God o' the lonesome!

EBEN (*mockingly*):   Naggin' His sheep t' sin! T' hell with yewr God! (*Cabot turns. He and Eben glower at each other.*)

CABOT (*harshly*):   So it's yew. I might've knowed it. (*Shaking his finger threateningly at him.*) Blasphemin' fool! (*Then quickly.*) Why hain't ye t' wuk?

EBEN: Why hain't yew? They've went. I can't wuk it all alone.

CABOT (*contemptuously*):   Nor noways! I'm wuth ten o' ye yit, old's I be! Ye'll never be more'n half a man! (*Then, matter-of-factly.*) Waal—let's git t' the barn. (*They go. A last faint note of the "Californi-a" song is heard from the distance. Abbie is washing her dishes.*)

PART II, SCENE I

(*The exterior of the farmhouse, as in Part I—a hot Sunday afternoon two months later. Abbie, dressed in her best, is discovered sitting in a rocker at the end of the porch. She rocks listlessly, enervated by the heat, staring in front of her with bored, half-closed eyes.*)

(*Eben sticks his head out of his bedroom window. He looks around furtively and tries to see—or hear—if anyone is on the porch, but although he has been careful to make no noise, Abbie has sensed his movement. She stops rocking, her face grows animated and eager, she waits attentively. Eben seems to feel her presence, he scowls back his thoughts of her and spits with exaggerated disdain—then withdraws back into the room. Abbie waits, holding her breath as she listens with passionate eagerness for every sound within the house.*)

(*Eben comes out. Their eyes meet; his falter. He is confused, he turns away and slams the door resentfully. At this gesture, Abbie laughs tantalizingly, amused but at the same time piqued and irritated. He scowls, strides off the porch to the path and starts to walk past her to the road with a grand swagger of ignoring her existence. He is dressed in his store suit, spruced up, his face shines from soap and water. Abbie leans forward on her chair, her eyes hard and angry now, and, as he passes her, gives a sneering, taunting chuckle.*)

EBEN (*stung—turns on her furiously*):   What air yew cacklin' 'bout?

ABBIE (*triumphant*):   Yew!

EBEN: What about me?

ABBIE: Ye look all slicked up like a prize bull.

EBEN (*with a sneer*):   Waal—ye hain't so durned purty yerself, be ye? (*They stare into each other's eyes, his held by hers in spite of himself, hers glowingly possessive. Their physical attraction becomes a palpable force quivering in the hot air.*)

[2]Eucharistic wafers, consecrated for the ceremony of Holy Communion.

ABBIE (*softly*): Ye don't mean that, Eben. Ye may think ye mean it, mebbe, but ye don't. Ye can't. It's agin nature, Eben. Ye been fightin' yer nature ever since the day I come—tryin' t' tell yerself I hain't purty t'ye. (*She laughs a low humid laugh without taking her eyes from his. A pause—her body squirms desirously—she murmurs languorously.*) Hain't the sun strong an' hot? Ye kin feel it burnin' into the earth—Nature—makin' thin's grow—bigger 'n' bigger—burnin' inside ye—makin' ye want t' grow—into somethin' else—till ye're jined with it—an' it's your'n—but it owns ye, too—an' makes ye grow bigger—like a tree—like them elums—(*She laughs again softly, holding his eyes. He takes a step toward her, compelled against his will.*) Nature'll beat ye, Eben. Ye might's well own up t' it fust 's last.

EBEN (*trying to break from her spell—confusedly*): If Paw'd hear ye goin' on . . . (*Resentfully.*) But ye've made such a damned idjit out o' the old devil . . . ! (*Abbie laughs.*)

ABBIE: Waal—hain't it easier fur yew with him changed softer?

EBEN (*defiantly*): No. I'm fightin' him—fightin' yew—fightin' fur Maw's rights t' her hum! (*This breaks her spell for him. He glowers at her.*) An' I'm onto ye. Ye hain't foolin' me a mite. Ye're aimin' t' swaller up everythin' an' make it your'n. Waal, you'll find I'm a heap sight bigger hunk nor yew kin chew! (*He turns from her with a sneer.*)

ABBIE (*trying to regain her ascendancy—seductively*): Eben!

EBEN: Leave me be! (*He starts to walk away.*)

ABBIE (*more commandingly*): Eben!

EBEN (*stops—resentfully*): What d'ye want?

ABBIE (*trying to conceal a growing excitement*): Whar air ye goin'?

EBEN (*with malicious nonchalance*): Oh—up the road a spell.

ABBIE: T' the village?

EBEN (*airily*): Mebbe.

ABBIE (*excitedly*): T' see Min, I s'pose?

EBEN: Mebbe.

ABBIE (*weakly*): What d'ye want t' waste time on her fur?

EBEN (*revenging himself now—grinning at her*): Ye can't beat Nature, didn't ye say? (*He laughs and again starts to walk away.*)

ABBIE (*bursting out*): An ugly old hake!

EBEN (*with a tantalizing sneer*): She's purtier'n yew be!

ABBIE: That every wuthless drunk in the country has . . .

EBEN (*tauntingly*): Mebbe—but she's better'n yew. She owns up fa'r 'n' squar' t' her doin's.

ABBIE (*furiously*): Don't ye dare compare . . .

EBEN: She don't go sneakin' an' stealin'—what's mine.

ABBIE (*savagely seizing on his weak point*): Your'n? Yew mean—my farm?

EBEN: I mean the farm yew sold yerself fur like any other old whore—my farm!

ABBIE (*stung—fiercely*): Ye'll never live t' see the day when even a stinkin' weed on it'll belong t' ye! (*Then in a scream.*) Git out o' my sight! Go on t' yer slut—disgracin' yer Paw 'n' me! I'll git yer Paw t' horsewhip ye off the place if I want t'! Ye're only livin' here 'cause I tolerate ye! Git along! I hate the sight o' ye! (*She stops, panting and glaring at him.*)

EBEN (*returning her glance in kind*): An' I hate the sight o' yew! (*He turns and strides off up the road. She follows his retreating figure with concentrated hate. Old Cabot appears coming up from the barn. The hard, grim expression of his face has changed. He seems in some queer way softened, mellowed. His eyes have taken on a strange, incongruous dreamy quality. Yet there is no hint of physical weakness about him—rather he looks more robust and younger. Abbie sees him and turns away quickly with unconcealed aversion. He comes slowly up to her.)*

CABOT (*mildly*):   War yew an' Eben quarrelin' agen?

ABBIE (*shortly*):   No.

CABOT: Ye was talkin' a'mighty loud. (*He sits down on the edge of porch.*)

ABBIE (*snappishly*):   If ye heerd us they hain't no need askin' questions.

CABOT: I didn't hear what ye said.

ABBIE (*relieved*):   Waal—it wa'n't nothin' t' speak on.

CABOT (*after a pause*):   Eben's queer.

ABBIE (*bitterly*):   He's the dead spit 'n' image o' yew!

CABOT (*queerly interested*):   D'ye think so, Abbie? (*After a pause, ruminatingly.*) Me 'n' Eben's allus fit 'n' fit. I never could b'ar him noways. He's so thunderin' soft—like his Maw.

ABBIE (*scornfully*):   Ay-eh! 'Bout as soft as yew be!

CABOT (*as if he hadn't heard*):   Mebbe I been too hard on him.

ABBIE (*jeeringly*):   Waal—ye're gittin' soft now—soft as slop! That's what Eben was sayin'.

CABOT (*his face instantly grim and ominous*):   Eben was sayin'? Waal, he'd best not do nothin' t' try me 'r he'll soon diskiver. . . . (*A pause. She keeps her face turned away. His gradually softens. He stares up at the sky.*) Purty, hain't it?

ABBIE (*crossly*):   I don't see nothin' purty.

CABOT: The sky. Feels like a wa'm field up thar.

ABBIE (*sarcastically*):   Air yew aimin' t' buy up over the farm too? (*She snickers contemptuously.*)

CABOT (*strangely*):   I'd like t' own my place up thar. (*A pause.*) I'm gittin' old, Abbie. I'm gittin' ripe on the bough. (*A pause. She stares at him mystified. He goes on.*) It's allus lonesome cold in the house —even when it's bilin' hot outside. Hain't yew noticed?

ABBIE: No.

CABOT: It's wa'm down t' the barn—nice smellin' an' warm—with the cows. (*A pause.*) Cows is queer.

ABBIE: Like yew?

CABOT: Like Eben. (*A pause.*) I' gittin' t' feel resigned t' Eben—jest as I got t' feel 'bout his Maw. I'm gittin' t' learn to b'ar his softness—jest like her'n. I calc'late I c'd a'most take t' him—if he wa'n't sech a dumb fool! (*A pause.*) I s'pose it's old age a-creepin' in my bones.

ABBIE (*indifferently*):   Waal—ye hain't dead yet.

CABOT (*roused*):   No, I hain't, yew bet—not by a hell of a sight—I'm sound 'n' tough as hickory! (*Then moodily.*) But arter three score and ten the Lord warns ye t' prepare. (*A pause.*) That's why Eben's come in my head. Now that his cussed sinful brothers is gone their path t' hell, they's no one left but Eben.

ABBIE (*resentfully*):   They's me, hain't they? (*Agitatedly.*) What's all this sudden likin' ye've tuk to Eben? Why don't ye say nothin' 'bout me? Hain't I yer lawful wife?

CABOT (*simply*):   Ay-eh. Ye be. (*A pause—he stares at her desirously—his eyes grow avid—then with a sudden movement he seizes her hands and squeezes them, declaiming in a queer camp meeting preacher's tempo.)* Yew air my Rose o' Sharon! Behold, yew air fair; yer eyes air doves; yer lips air like scarlet; yer two breasts air like two fawns; yer navel be like a round goblet; yer belly be like a heap o' wheat . . . *(He covers her hand with kisses. She does not seem to notice. She stares before her with hard angry eyes.)*

ABBIE *(jerking her hands away—harshly)*:   So ye're plannin' t' leave the farm t' Eben, air ye?

CABOT *(dazedly)*:   Leave . . . ? *(Then with resentful obstinacy.)* I hain't a-givin' it t' no one!

ABBIE *(remorselessly)*:   Ye can't take it with ye.

CABOT *(thinks a moment—then reluctantly)*:   No, I calc'late not. *(After a pause—with a strange passion.)* But if I could, I would, by the Eternal! 'R if I could, in my dyin' hour, I'd set it afire an' watch it burn—this house an' every ear o' corn an' every tree down t' the last blade o' hay! I'd sit an' know it was all a-dying with me an' no one else'd ever own what was mine, what I'd made out o' nothin' with my own sweat 'n' blood! *(A pause—then he adds with a queer affection.)* 'Ceptin' the cows. Them I'd turn free.

ABBIE *(harshly)*:   An' me?

CABOT *(with a queer smile)*:   Ye'd be turned free, too.

ABBIE *(furiously)*:   So that's the thanks I git fur marryin' ye—t' have ye change kind to Eben who hates ye, an' talk o' turnin' me out in the road.

CABOT *(hastily)*:   Abbie! Ye know I wa'n't. . . .

ABBIE *(vengefully)*:   Just let me tell ye a thing or two 'bout Eben! Whar's he gone? T' see that harlot, Min! I tried fur t' stop him. Disgracin' yew an' me—on the Sabbath, too!

CABOT *(rather guiltily)*:   He's a sinner—nateral-born. It's lust eatin' his heart.

ABBIE *(enraged beyond endurance—wildly vindictive)*:   An' his lust fur me! Kin ye find excuses fur that?

CABOT *(stares at her—after a dead pause)*:   Lust—fur yew?

ABBIE *(defiantly)*:   He was tryin' t' make love t' me—when ye heerd us quarrelin'.

CABOT *(stares at her—then a terrible expression of rage comes over his face— he springs to his feet shaking all over)*: By the A'mighty God—I'll end him!

ABBIE *(frightened now for Eben)*:   No! Don't ye!

CABOT *(violently)*:   I'll git the shotgun an' blow his soft brains t' the top o' them elums!

ABBIE *(throwing her arms around him)*:   No, Ephraim!

CABOT *(pushing her away violently)*:   I will, by God!

ABBIE *(in a quieting tone)*:   Listen, Ephraim. 'Twa'n't nothin' bad—on'y a boy's foolin'—'twa'an't meant serious—jest jokin' an' teasin' . . . .

CABOT: Then why did ye say—lust?

ABBIE: It must hev sounded wusser'n I meant. An' I was mad at thinkin'— ye'd leave him the farm.

CABOT *(quieter but still grim and cruel)*:   Waal then, I'll horsewhip him off the place if that much'll content ye.

ABBIE *(reaching out and taking his hand)*:   No. Don't think o' me! Ye mustn't drive him off. 'Tain't sensible. Who'll ye get to help ye on the farm? They's no one hereabouts.

CABOT *(considers this—then nodding his appreciation)*:   Ye got a head on ye. *(Then irritably.)* Waal, let him stay. *(He sits down on the edge of the porch. She sits beside him. He murmurs contemptuously.*) I oughtn't t' git riled so—at that 'ere fool calf. (*A pause.*) But har's the p'int. What son o' mine'll keep on here t' the farm—when the Lord does call me? Simeon an' Peter air gone t' hell—an' Eben's follerin' 'em.

ABBIE: They's me.

CABOT: Ye're on'y a woman.

ABBIE: I'm yewr wife.

CABOT: That hain't me. A son is me—my blood—mine. Mine ought t' git mine. An' then it's still mine—even though I be six foot under. D'ye see?

ABBIE (*giving him a look of hatred*):   Ay-eh. I see. (*She becomes very thoughtful, her face growing shrewd, her eyes studying Cabot craftily.*)

CABOT: I'm gittin' old—ripe on the bough. (*Then with a sudden forced reassurance.*) Not but what I hain't a hard nut t' crack even yet—an' fur many a year t' come! By the Etarnal, I kin break most o' the young fellers' backs at any kind o' work any day o' the year!

ABBIE (*suddenly*):   Mebbe the Lord'll give *us* a son.

CABOT (*turns and stares at her eagerly*):   Ye mean—a son—t' me 'n' yew?

ABBIE (*with a cajoling smile*):   Ye're a strong man yet, hain't ye? 'Tain't noways impossible, be it? We know that. Why d'ye stare so? Hain't ye never thought o' that afore? I been thinkin' o' it all along. Ay-eh—an' I been prayin' it'd happen, too.

CABOT (*his face growing full of joyous pride and a sort of religious ecstasy*): Ye been prayin', Abbie?—fur a son?—t' us?

ABBIE: Ay-eh. (*With a grim resolution.*) I want a son now.

CABOT (*excitedly clutching both of her hands in his*):   It'd be the blessin' o' God, Abbie—the blessin' o' God A'mighty on me—in my old age—in my lonesomeness! They hain't nothin' I wouldn't do fur ye then, Abbie. Ye'd hev on'y t' ask it—anythin' ye'd a mind t'!

ABBIE (*interrupting*):   Would ye will the farm t' me then—t' me an' it . . . ?

CABOT (*vehemently*):   I'd do anythin' ye axed, I tell ye! I swar it! May I be everlastin' damned t' hell if I wouldn't! (*He sinks to his knees pulling her down with him. He trembles all over with the fervor of his hopes.*) Pray t' the Lord agen, Abbie. It's the Sabbath! I'll jine ye! Two prayers air better nor one. "An' God hearkened unto Rachel"![3] An' God hearkened unto Abbie! Pray, Abbie! Pray fur him to hearken! (*He bows his head, mumbling. She pretends to do likewise but gives him a side glance of scorn and triumph.*)

SCENE II

(*About eight in the evening. The interior of the two bedrooms on the top floor is shown. Eben is sitting on the side of his bed in the room on the left. On account of the heat he has taken off everything but his undershirt and pants. His feet are bare. He faces front, brooding moodily, his chin propped on his hands, a desperate expression on his face.*)

(*In the other room Cabot and Abbie are sitting side by side on the edge of their bed, an old four-poster with feather mattress. He is in his nightshirt, she in her*

---

[3]A paraphrase of Genesis 30:22; Rachel, a wife of Jacob, had been childless, but God allowed her to conceive a son, Joseph.

nightdress. He is still in the queer, excited mood into which the notion of a son has thrown him. Both rooms are lighted dimly and flickeringly by tallow candles.)

CABOT: The farm needs a son.

ABBIE: I need a son.

CABOT: Ay-eh. Sometimes ye air the farm an' sometimes the farm be yew. That's why I clove t' ye in my lonesomeness. (*A pause. He pounds his knee with his fist.*) Me an' the farm has got t' beget a son!

ABBIE: Ye'd best go t' sleep. Ye're gittin' thin's all mixed.

CABOT *(with an impatient gesture)*:   No, I hain't. My mind's clear's a well. Ye don't know me, that's it. (*He stares hopelessly at the floor.*)

ABBIE *(indifferently)*:   Mebbe. (*In the next room Eben gets up and paces up and down distractedly. Abbie hears him. Her eyes fasten on the intervening wall with concentrated attention. Eben stops and stares. Their hot glances seem to meet through the wall. Unconsciously he stretches out his arms for her and she half rises. Then aware, he mutters a curse at himself and flings himself face downward on the bed, his clenched fists above his head, his face buried in the pillow. Abbie relaxes with a faint sigh but her eyes remain fixed on the wall; she listens with all her attention for some movement from Eben.*)

CABOT *(suddenly raises his head and looks at her—scornfully)*:   Will ye ever know me—'r will any man 'r woman? (*Shaking his head.*) No. I calc'late wa'n't t' be. (*He turns away. Abbie looks at the wall. Then, evidently unable to keep silent about his thoughts, without looking at his wife, he puts out his hand and clutches her knee. She starts violently, looks at him, sees he is not watching her, concentrates again on the wall, and pays no attention to what he says.*) Listen Abbie. When I come here fifty odd year ago—I was jest twenty an' the strongest an' hardest ye ever seen—ten times as strong an' fifty times as hard as Eben. Waal—this place was nothin' but fields o' stones. Folks laughed when I tuk it. They couldn't know what I knowed. When ye kin make corn sprout out o' stones, God's livin' in yew! They wa'n't strong enuf fur that! They reckoned God was easy. They laughed. They don't laugh no more. Some died hereabouts. Some went West an' died. They're all underground—fur follerin' arter an easy God. God hain't easy. (*He shakes his head slowly.*) An' I growed hard. Folks kept allus sayin' he's a hard man like 'twas sinful t' be hard, so's at last I said back at 'em: Waal then, by thunder, ye'll git me hard an' see how ye like it! (*Then suddenly.*) But I give in t' weakness once. 'Twas arter I'd been here two year. I got weak—despairful—they was so many stones. They was a party leavin', givin' up, goin' West. I jined 'em. We tracked on 'n on. We come t' broad medders, plains, whar the soil was black an' rich as gold. Nary a stone. Easy. Ye'd on'y to plow an' sow an' then set an' smoke yer pipe an' watch thin's grow. I could o' been a rich man—but somethin' in me fit me an' fit me—the voice o' God sayin': "This hain't wuth nothin' t' Me. Git ye back t' hum!" I got afeerd o' that voice an' I lit out back t' hum here, leavin' my claim an' crops t' whoever'd a mind t' take 'em. Ay-eh. I actoolly give up what was rightful mine! God's hard, not easy! God's in the stones! Build my church on a rock—out o' stones an' I'll be in them! That's what He meant t' Peter! (*He sighs heavily—a pause.*) Stones. I picked 'em up an' piled 'em into walls. Ye kin read the years o' my life in them walls, every day a hefted stone, climbin' over the hills up and down, fencin' in the fields that was mine, whar I'd made thin's grow out o' nothin'—like the will o' God, like the servant o' His hand. It wa'n't easy. It was hard an' He made me hard fur it. (*He *pauses.*) All the time I kept gittin' lonesomer. I tuk a wife. She bore Simeon an' Peter. She was a good woman. She wuked hard. We was married twenty year. She never knowed me. She helped but she never knowed what she was helpin'. I was allus lonesome. She died. After that it wa'n't so lonesome fur a spell. (*A pause.*) I lost count o' the years. I had no time t' fool away countin' 'em. Sim an' Peter helped. The farm growed. It was all mine! When I thought o' that I didn't feel lonesome. (*A pause.*) But ye can't hitch yer mind t' one thin' day an' night. I tuk another wife—Eben's Maw. Her folks was contestin' me at law over my deeds t' the farm—my farm! That's why Eben keeps a-talkin' his fool talk o' this bein' his Maw's farm. She bore Eben. She was purty—but soft. She tried t' be hard. She couldn't. She never knowed me nor nothin'. It was lonesomer 'n hell with her. After a matter o' sixteen odd years, she died. (*A pause.*) I lived with the boys. They hated me 'cause I was hard. I hated them 'cause they was soft. They coveted the farm without knowin' what it meant. It made me bitter 'n wormwood. It aged me—them coveting what I'd made fur mine. Then this spring the call come—the voice o' God cryin' in my wilderness, in my lonesomeness—t' go out an' seek an' find! (*Turning to her with strange passion.*) I sought ye an' I found ye! Yew air my Rose o' Sharon! Yer eyes air like. . . . (*She has turned a blank face, resentful eyes to his. He stares at her for a moment—then harshly.*) Air ye any the wiser fur all I've told ye?

ABBIE (*confusedly*):   Mebbe.

CABOT (*pushing her away from him—angrily*):   Ye don't know nothin'—nor never will. If ye don't hev a son t' redeem ye. . . . (*This in a tone of cold threat.*)

ABBIE (*resentfully*):   I've prayed, hain't I?

CABOT (*bitterly*):   Pray agen—fur understandin'!

ABBIE (*a veiled threat in her tone*):   Ye'll have a son out o' me, I promise ye.

CABOT: How kin ye promise?

ABBIE: I got second-sight mebbe. I kin foretell. (*She gives a queer smile.*)

CABOT: I believe ye have. Ye give me the chills sometimes. (*He shivers.*) It's cold in this house. It's oneasy. They's thin's pokin' about in the dark—in the corners. (*He pulls on his trousers, tucking in his nightshirt, and pulls on his boots.*)

ABBIE (*surprised*):   Whar air ye goin'?

CABOT (*queerly*):   Down whar it's restful—whar it's warm—down t' the barn. (*Bitterly.*) I kin talk t' the cows. They know. They know the farm an' me. They'll give me peace. (*He turns to go out the door.*)

ABBIE (*a bit frightenedly*):   Air ye ailin' tonight, Ephraim?

CABOT: Growin'. Growin' ripe on the bough. (*He turns and goes, his boots clumping down the stairs. Eben sits up with a start, listening. Abbie is conscious of his movement and stares at the wall. Cabot comes out of the house around the corner and stands by the gate, blinking at the sky. He stretches up his hands in a tortured gesture.*) God A'mighty, call from the dark! (*He listens as if expecting an answer. Then his arms drop, he shakes his head and plods off toward the barn. Eben and Abbie stare at each other through the wall. Eben sighs heavily and Abbie echoes it. Both become terribly nervous, uneasy. Finally Abbie gets up and listens, her ear to the wall. He acts as if he saw every move she was making, he becomes resolutely still. She seems driven into a decision—goes out the door in rear determinedly. His eyes follow her. Then as the door of his room is opened softly, he turns away, waits in an attitude of strained fixity. Abbie stands for a second staring at him, her eyes burning with desire. Then with a little cry she runs over and throws her arms about his neck, she pulls his head back and covers his mouth with kisses. At first, he submits dumbly; then he puts his arms about her neck and returns her kisses, but finally, suddenly aware of his hatred, he hurls her away from him, springing to his feet. They stand speechless and breathless, panting like two animals.)*

ABBIE (*at last—painfully*):   Ye shouldn't Eben—ye shouldn't—I'd make ye happy!

EBEN (*harshly*):   I don't want t' be happy—from yew!

ABBIE (*helplessly*):   Ye do, Eben! Ye do! Why d'ye lie?

EBEN (*viciously*):   I don't take t'ye, I tell ye! I hate the sight o' ye!

ABBIE (*with an uncertain troubled laugh*):   Waal, I kissed ye anyways—an' ye kissed back—yer lips was burnin'—ye can't lie 'bout that! (*Intensely.*) If ye don't care, why did ye kiss me back—why was yer lips burnin'?

EBEN (*wiping his mouth*):   It was like pizen on 'em. (*Then tauntingly.*) When I kissed ye back, mebbe I thought 'twas someone else.

ABBIE (*wildly*):   Min?

EBEN: Mebbe.

ABBIE (*torturedly*):   Did ye go t' see her? Did ye r'ally go? I thought ye mightn't. Is that why ye throwed me off jest now?

EBEN (*sneeringly*):   What if it be?

ABBIE (*raging*):   Then ye're a dog, Eben Cabot!

EBEN (*threateningly*):   Ye can't talk that way t' me!

ABBIE (*with a shrill laugh*):   Can't I? Did ye think I was in love with ye—a weak thin' like yew? Not much! I on'y wanted ye fur a purpose o' my own—an' I'll hev ye fur it yet 'cause I'm stronger'n yew be!

EBEN (*resentfully*):   I knowed well it was on'y part o' yer plan t' swaller everythin'!

ABBIE (*tauntingly*):   Mebbe!

EBEN (*furious*):   Git out o' my room!

ABBIE: This air my room an' ye're on'y hired help!

EBEN (*threateningly*):   Git out afore I murder ye!

ABBIE (*quite confident now*):   I hain't a mite afeerd. Ye want me, don't ye? Yes, ye do! An' yer Paw's son'll never kill what he wants! Look at yer eyes! They's lust fur me in 'em, burnin' 'em up! Look at yer lips now! They're tremblin' an' longin' t' kiss me, an' yer teeth t' bite! (*He is watching her now with a horrible fascination. She laughs a crazy triumphant laugh.*) I'm a-goin' t' make all o' this hum my hum! They's one room hain't mine yet, but it's a-goin' t' be tonight. I'm a-goin' down now an' light up! (*She makes him a mocking bow.*) Won't ye come courtin' me in the best parlor, Mister Cabot?

EBEN (*staring at her—horribly confused—dully*):   Don't ye dare! It hain't been opened since Maw died an' was laid out thar! Don't ye . . . ! (*But her eyes are fixed on his so burningly that his will seems to wither before hers. He stands swaying toward her helplessly.*)

ABBIE (*holding his eyes and putting all her will into her words as she backs out the door*): I'll expect ye afore long, Eben.

EBEN (*Stares after her for a while, walking toward the door. A light appears in the parlor window. He murmurs.*): In the parlor? (*This seems to arouse connotations, for he comes back and puts on his white shirt, collar, half ties the tie mechanically, puts on coat, takes his hat, stands barefooted looking about him in bewilderment, mutters wonderingly.*) Maw! Whar air yew? (*Then goes slowly toward the door in rear.*)

Scene III

(A few minutes later. The interior of the parlor is shown. A grim, repressed room like a tomb in which the family has been interred alive. Abbie sits on the edge of the horsehair sofa. She has lighted all the candles and the room is revealed in all its preserved ugliness. A change has come over the woman. She looks awed and frightened now, ready to run away.)

(The door is opened and Eben appears. His face wears an expression of obsessed confusion. He stands staring at her, his arms hanging disjointedly from his shoulders, his feet bare, his hat in his hand.)

ABBIE *(after a pause—with a nervous, formal politeness)*:   Won't ye set?

EBEN *(dully)*:   Ay-eh. *(Mechanically he places his hat carefully on the floor near the door and sits stiffly beside her on the edge of the sofa. A pause. They both remain rigid, looking straight ahead with eyes full of fear.)*

ABBIE: When I fust come in—in the dark—they seemed somethin' here.

EBEN *(simply)*:   Maw.

ABBIE: I kin still feel—somethin'. . . .

EBEN: It's Maw.

ABBIE: At fust I was feered o' it. I wanted t' yell an' run. Now—since yew come—seems like it's growin' soft an' kind t' me. *(Addressing the air—queerly.)* Thank yew.

EBEN: Maw allus loved me.

ABBIE: Mebbe it knows I love yew, too. Mebbe that makes it kind t' me.

EBEN *(dully)*:   I dunno. I should think she'd hate ye.

ABBIE *(with certainty)*:   No. I kin feel it don't—not no more.

EBEN: Hate ye fur stealin' her place—here in her hum—settin' in her parlor whar she was laid— *(He suddenly stops, staring stupidly before him.)*

ABBIE: What is it, Eben?

EBEN *(in a whisper)*:   Seems like Maw didn't want me t' remind ye.

ABBIE *(excitedly)*:   I knowed, Eben! It's kind t' me! It don't b'ar me no grudges fur what I never knowed an' couldn't help!

EBEN: Maw b'ars him a grudge.

ABBIE: Waal, so does all o' us.

EBEN: Ay-eh. *(With passion.)* I does, by God!

ABBIE *(taking one of his hands in hers and patting it)*:   Thar! Don't git riled thinkin' o' him. Think o' yer Maw who's kind t' us. Tell me about yer Maw, Eben.

EBEN: They hain't nothin' much. She was kind. She was good.

ABBIE *(Putting one arm over his shoulder. He does not seem to notice—passionately.)*: I'll be kind an' good t' ye!

EBEN: Sometimes she used t' sing fur me.

ABBIE: I'll sing fur ye!

EBEN: This was her hum. This was her farm.

ABBIE: This is my hum! This is my farm!

EBEN: He married her t' steal 'em. She was soft an' easy. He couldn't 'preciate her.

ABBIE: He can't 'preciate me!

EBEN: He murdered her with his hardness.

ABBIE: He's murderin' me!

EBEN: She died. (*A pause.*) Sometimes she used to sing fur me. (*He bursts into a fit of sobbing.*)

ABBIE (*both her arms around him—with wild passion*):   I'll sing fur ye! I'll die fur ye! (*In spite of her overwhelming desire for him, there is a sincere maternal love in her manner and voice—a horribly frank mixture of lust and mother love.*) Don't cry, Eben! I'll take yer Maw's place! I'll be everythin' she was t' ye! Let me kiss ye, Eben! (*She pulls his head around. He makes a bewildered pretense of resistance. She is tender.*) Don't be afeered! I'll kiss ye pure, Eben—same's if I was a Maw t' ye—an' ye kin kiss me back 's if yew was my son—my boy— sayin' good-night t' me! Kiss me, Eben. (*They kiss in restrained fashion. Then suddenly wild passion overcomes her. She kisses him lustfully again and again and he flings his arms about her and returns her kisses. Suddenly, as in the bedroom, he frees himself from her violently and springs to his feet. He is trembling all over, in a strange state of terror. Abbie strains her arms toward him with fierce pleading.*) Don't ye leave me, Eben! Can't ye see it hain't enuf—lovin' ye like a Maw—can't ye see it's got t' be that an' more—much more—a hundred times more—fur me t' be happy—fur yew t' be happy?

EBEN (*to the presence he feels in the room*):   Maw! Maw! What d'ye want? What air ye tellin' me?

ABBIE: She's tellin' ye t' love me. She knows I love ye an' I'll be good t' ye. Can't ye feel it? Don't ye know? She's tellin' ye t' love me, Eben!

EBEN: Ay-eh. I feel—mebbe she—but—I can't figger out—why—when ye've stole her place—here in her hum—in the parlor whar she was—

ABBIE (*fiercely*):   She knows I love ye!

EBEN (*his face suddenly lighting up with a fierce, triumphant grin*):   I see it! I sees why. It's her vengeance on him—so's she kin rest quiet in her grave!

ABBIE (*wildly*):   Vengeance o' God on the hull o' us! What d'we give a durn? I love ye, Eben! God knows I love ye! (*She stretches out her arms for him.*)

EBEN (*throws himself on his knees beside the sofa and grabs her in his arms— releasing all his pent-up passion*): An' I love ye, Abbie!—now I kin say it! I been dyin' fur want o' ye—every hour since ye come! I love ye! (*Their lips meet in a fierce, bruising kiss.*)

SCENE IV

(*Exterior of the farmhouse. It is just dawn. The front door at right is opened and Eben comes out and walks around to the gate. He is dressed in his working clothes. He seems changed. His face wears a bold and confident expression, he is grinning to himself with evident satisfaction. As he gets near the gate, the window of the parlor is heard opening and the shutters are flung back and Abbie sticks her head out. Her hair tumbles over her shoulders in disarray, her face is flushed, she looks at Eben with tender, languorous eyes and calls softly.*)

ABBIE: Eben. (*As he turns—playfully.*) Jest one more kiss afore ye go. I'm goin' to miss ye fearful all day.

EBEN: An' me yew, ye kin bet! (*He goes to her. They kiss several times. He draws away, laughingly.*) Thar. That's enuf, hain't it? Ye won't hev none left fur next time.

ABBIE: I got a million o' 'em left fur yew! (*Then a bit anxiously.*) D'ye r'ally love me, Eben?

EBEN (*emphatically*):   I like ye better'n any gal I ever knowed! That's gospel!

ABBIE: Likin' hain't lovin'.

EBEN: Waal then—I love ye. Now air yew satisfied?

ABBIE: Ay-eh, I be. (*She smiles at him adoringly.*)

EBEN: I better git t' the barn. The old critter's liable t' suspicion an' come sneakin' up.

ABBIE (*with a confident laugh*):   Let him! I kin allus pull the wool over his eyes. I'm goin' t' leave the shutters open and let in the sun 'n' air. This room's been dead long enuf. Now it's goin' t' be my room!

EBEN (*frowning*):   Ay-eh.

ABBIE (*hastily*):   I meant—our room.

EBEN: Ay-eh.

ABBIE: We made it our'n last night, didn't we? We give it life—our lovin' did. (*A pause.*)

EBEN (*with a strange look*):   Maw's gone back t' her grave. She kin sleep now.

ABBIE: May she rest in peace! (*Then tenderly rebuking.*) Ye oughtn't t' talk o' sad thin's—this mornin'.

EBEN: It jest come up in my mind o' itself.

ABBIE: Don't let it. (*He doesn't answer. She yawns.*) Waal, I'm a-goin' t' steal a wink o' sleep. I'll tell the Old Man I hain't feelin' pert. Let him git his own vittles.

EBEN: I see him comin' from the barn. Ye better look smart an' git upstairs.

ABBIE: Ay-eh. Good-by. Don't ferget me. (*She throws him a kiss. He grins—then squares his shoulders and awaits his father confidently. Cabot walks slowly up from the left, staring up at the sky with a vague face.*)

EBEN (*jovially*):   Mornin', Paw. Star-gazin' in daylight?

CABOT: Purty, hain't it?

EBEN (*looking around him possessively*):   It's a durned purty farm.

CABOT: I mean the sky.

EBEN (*grinning*):   How d'ye know? Them eyes o' your'n can't see that fur. (*This tickles his humor and he slaps his thigh and laughs.*) Ho-ho! That's a good un!

CABOT (*grimly sarcastic*):   Ye're feelin' right chipper, hain't ye? Whar'd ye steal the likker?

EBEN (*good-naturedly*):   'Tain't likker. Jest life. (*Suddenly holding out his hand—soberly.*) Yew 'n' me is quits. Let's shake hands.

CABOT (*suspiciously*):   What's come over ye?

EBEN: Then don't. Mebbe it's jest as well. (*A moment's pause.*) What's come over me? (*Queerly.*) Didn't ye feel her passin'—goin' back t' her grave?

CABOT (*dully*):   Who?

EBEN: Maw. She kin rest now an' sleep content. She's quit with ye.

CABOT (*confusedly*):   I rested. I slept good—down with the cows. They know how t' sleep. They're teachin' me.

EBEN (*suddenly jovial again*):   Good fur the cows! Waal—ye better git t' work.

CABOT (*grimly amused*):   Air yew bossin' me, ye calf?

EBEN (*beginning to laugh*):   Ay-eh! I'm bossin' yew! Ha-ha-ha! See how ye like it! Ha-ha-ha! I'm the prize rooster o' this roost. Ha-ha-ha! (*He goes off toward the barn laughing.*)

CABOT (*looks after him with scornful pity*):   Soft-headed. Like his Maw. Dead spit 'n' image. No hope in him! (*He spits with contemptuous disgust.*) A born fool! (*Then matter-of-factly.*) Waal—I'm gittin' peckish. (*He goes toward door.*)

PART III, SCENE I

(*A night in late spring the following year. The kitchen and the two bedrooms upstairs are shown. The two bedrooms are dimly lighted by a tallow candle in each. Eben is sitting on the side of the bed in his room, his chin propped on his fists, his face a study of the struggle he is making to understand his conflicting emotions. The noisy laughter and music from below where a kitchen dance is in progress annoy and distract him. He scowls at the floor.*)

(*In the next room a cradle stands beside the double bed.*)

(*In the kitchen all is festivity. The stove has been taken down to give more room to the dancers. The chairs, with wooden benches added, have been pushed back against the walls. On these are seated, squeezed in tight against one another, farmers and their wives and their young folks of both sexes from the neighboring farms. They are all chattering and laughing loudly. They evidently have some secret joke in common. There is no end of winking, of nudging, of meaning nods of the head toward Cabot who, in a state of extreme hilarious excitement increased by the amount he has drunk, is standing near the rear door where there is a small keg of whisky and serving drinks to all the men. In the left corner, front, dividing the attention with her husband, Abbie is sitting in a rocking chair, a shawl wrapped about her shoulders. She is very pale, her face is thin and drawn, her eyes are fixed anxiously on the open door in rear as if waiting for someone.*)

(*The musician is tuning up his fiddle, seated in the far right corner. He is a lanky young fellow with a long, weak face. His pale eyes blink incessantly and he grins about him slyly with a greedy malice.*)

ABBIE (*suddenly turning to a young girl on her right*):   Whar's Eben?

YOUNG GIRL (*eyeing her scornfully*):   I dunno, Mrs. Cabot. I hain't seen Eben in ages. (*Meaningly.*) Seems like he's spent most o' his time t' hum since yew come.

ABBIE (*vaguely*):   I tuk his Maw's place.

YOUNG GIRL: Ay-eh. So I've heerd. (*She turns away to retail this bit of gossip to her mother sitting next to her. Abbie turns to her left to a big stoutish middle-aged man whose flushed face and starting eyes show the amount of "likker" he has consumed.*)

ABBIE: Ye hain't seen Eben, hev ye?

MAN: No, I hain't. (*Then he adds with a wink.*) If yew hain't, who would?

ABBIE: He's the best dancer in the county. He'd ought t' come an' dance.

MAN (*with a wink*): Mebbe he's doin' the dutiful an' walkin' the kid t' sleep. It's a boy, hain't it?

ABBIE (*nodding vaguely*):   Ay-eh—born two weeks back—purty's a picter.

MAN: They all is—t' their Maws. (*Then in a whisper, with a nudge and a leer.*) Listen, Abbie—if ye ever git tired o' Eben, remember me! Don't fergit now! (*He looks at her uncomprehending face for a second—then grunts disgustedly.*) Waal—guess I'll likker agin. (*He goes over and joins Cabot who is arguing noisily with an old farmer over cows. They all drink.*)

ABBIE (*this time appealing to nobody in particular*):   Wonder what Eben's a-doin'? (*Her remark is repeated down the line with many a guffaw and titter until it reaches the fiddler. He fastens his blinking eyes on Abbie.*)

FIDDLER (*raising his voice*):   Bet I kin tell ye, Abbie, what Eben's doin'! He's down t' the church offerin' up prayers o' thanksgivin'. (*They all titter expectantly.*)

A MAN: What fur? (*Another titter.*)

FIDDLER: 'Cause unto him a— (*He hesitates just long enough.*) brother is born! (*A roar of laughter. They all look from Abbie to Cabot. She is oblivious, staring at the door. Cabot, although he hasn't heard the words, is irritated by the laughter and steps forward, glaring about him. There is an immediate silence.*)

CABOT: What're ye all bleatin' about—like a flock o' goats? Why don't ye dance, damn ye? I axed ye here t'dance—t' eat, drink an' be merry—an' thar ye set cacklin' like a lot o' wet hens with the pip! Ye've swilled my likker an' guzzled my vittles like hogs, hain't ye? Then dance fur me, can't ye? That's fa'r an' squar', hain't it? (*A grumble of resentment goes around but they are all evidently in too much awe of him to express it openly.*)

FIDDLER (*slyly*):   We're waitin' fur Eben. (*A suppressed laugh.*)

CABOT (*with a fierce exultation*):   T'hell with Eben! Eben's done fur now! I got a new son! (*His mood switching with drunken suddenness.*) But ye needn't t' laugh at Eben, none o' ye! He's my blood, if he be a dumb fool. He's better nor any o' yew! He kin do a day's work a'most up t' what I kin–an' that'd put any o' yew pore critters t' shame!

FIDDLER: An' he kin do a good night's work, too! (*A roar of laughter.*)

CABOT: Laugh, ye damn fools! Ye're right jist the same, Fiddler. He kin work day an' night too, like I kin, if need be!

OLD FARMER (*from behind the keg where he is weaving drunkenly back and forth—with great simplicity*): They hain't many t' touch ye, Ephraim—a son at seventy-six. That's a hard man fur ye! I be on'y sixty-eight an' I couldn't do it. (*A roar of laughter in which Cabot joins uproariously.*)

CABOT (*slapping him on the back*):   I'm sorry fur ye, Hi. I'd never suspicion sech weakness from a boy like yew!

OLD FARMER: An' I never reckoned yew had it in ye nuther, Ephraim. (*There is another laugh.*)

CABOT (*suddenly grim*):   I got a lot in me—a hell of a lot—folks don't know on. (*Turning to the fiddler.*) Fiddle 'er up, durn ye! Give 'em somethin' t' dance t'! What air ye, an ornament? Hain't this a celebration? Then grease yer elbow an' go it!

FIDDLER (*seizes a drink which the Old Farmer holds out to him and downs it*):   Here goes! (*He starts to fiddle "Lady of the Lake." Four young fellows and four girls form in two lines and dance a square dance. The Fiddler shouts directions for the different movements, keeping his words in the rhythm of the music and interspersing them with jocular personal remarks to the dancers themselves. The people seated along the walls stamp their feet and clap their hands in unison. Cabot is especially active in this respect. Only Abbie remains apathetic, staring at the door as if she were alone in a silent room.*)

FIDDLER: Swing your partner t' the right! That's it, Jim! Give her a b'ar hug. Her Maw hain't lookin'. (*Laughter.*) Change partners! That suits ye, don't it, Essie, now ye got Reub afore ye? Look at her redden up, will ye? Waal, life is short an' so's love, as the feller says. (*Laughter.*)

CABOT (*excitedly, stamping his foot*):   Go it, boys! Go it, gals!

FIDDLER (*with a wink at the others*):   Ye're the spryest seventy-six ever I sees, Ephraim! Now if ye'd on'y good eyesight . . . ! (*Suppressed laughter. He gives Cabot no chance to retort but roars.*) Promenade! Ye're walkin' like a bride down the aisle, Sarah! Waal, while they's life they's allus hope, I've heerd tell. Swing your partner to the left! Gosh A'mighty, look at Johnny Cook high-steppin'! They hain't goin' t' be much strength left fur howin' in the corn lot t'morrow. (*Laughter.*)

CABOT: Go it! Go it! (*Then suddenly, unable to restrain himself any longer, he prances into the midst of the dancers, scattering them, waving his arms about wildly.*) Ye're all hoofs! Git out o' my road! Give me room! I'll show ye dancin'. Ye're all too soft! (*He pushes them roughly away. They crowd back toward the walls, muttering, looking at him resentfully.*)

FIDDLER (*jeeringly*):   Go it, Ephraim! Go it! (*He starts "Pop, Goes the Weasel," increasing the tempo with every verse until at the end he is fiddling crazily as fast as he can go.*)

CABOT (*Starts to dance, which he does very well and with tremendous vigor. Then he begins to improvise, cuts incredibly grotesque capers, leaping up and cracking his heels together, prancing around in a circle with body bent in an Indian war dance, then suddenly straightening up and kicking as high as he can with both legs. He is like a monkey on a string. And all the while he intersperses his antics with shouts and derisive comments.*): Whoop! Here's dancin' fur ye! Whoop! See that! Seventy-six, if I'm a day! Hard as iron yet! Beatin' the young 'uns like I allus done! Look at me! I'd invite ye t' dance on my hundredth birthday on'y ye'll all be dead by then. Ye're a sickly generation! Yer hearts air pink, not red! Yer veins is full o' mud an' water! I be the on'y man in the county! Whoop! See that! I'm a Injun! I've killed Injuns in the West afore ye was born—an' skulped 'em too! They's a arrer wound on my backside I c'd show ye! The hull tribe chased me. I outrun 'em all—with the arrer stuck in me! An' I tuk vengeance on 'em. Ten eyes fur an eye, that was my motter! Whoop! Look at me! I kin kick the ceilin' off the room! Whoop!

FIDDLER (*stops playing—exhaustedly*):   God A'mighty, I got enuf. Ye got the devil's strength in ye.

CABOT (*delightedly*):   Did I beat yew, too? Waal, ye played smart. Hev a swig. (*He pours whisky for himself and Fiddler. They drink. The others watch Cabot silently with cold, hostile eyes. There is a dead pause. The Fiddler rests. Cabot leans against the keg, panting, glaring around him confusedly. In the room above, Eben gets to his feet and tiptoes out the door in rear, appearing a moment later in the other bedroom. He moves silently, even frightenedly, toward the cradle and stands there looking down at the baby. His face is as vague as his reactions are confused, but there is a trace of tenderness, of interested discovery. At the same moment that he reaches the cradle, Abbie seems to sense something. She gets up weakly and goes to Cabot.*)

ABBIE: I'm goin' up t' the baby.

CABOT (*with real solicitation*):   Air ye able fur the stairs? D'ye want me t' help ye, Abbie?

ABBIE: No, I'm able. I'll be down agen soon.

CABOT: Don't ye git wore out! He needs ye, remember—our son does! (*He grins affectionately, patting her on the back. She shrinks from his touch.*)

ABBIE (*dully*):   Don't—tech me. I'm goin'—up. (*She goes. Cabot looks after her. A whisper goes around the room. Cabot turns. It ceases. He wipes his forehead streaming with sweat. He is breathing pantingly.*)

CABOT: I'm a-goin' out t' git fresh air. I'm feelin' a mite dizzy. Fiddle up thar! Dance, all o' ye! Here's likker fur them as wants it. Enjoy yerselves. I'll be back. (*He goes, closing the door behind him.*)

FIDDLER (*sarcastically*): Don't hurry none on our account! (*A suppressed laugh. He imitates Abbie.*) Whar's Eben? (*More laughter.*)

A WOMAN (*loudly*): What's happened in this house is plain as the nose on yer face! (*Abbie appears in the doorway upstairs and stands looking in surprise and adoration at Eben who does not see her.*)

A MAN: Ssshh! He's li'ble t' be listenin' at the door. That'd be like him. (*Their voices die to an intensive whispering. Their faces are concentrated on this gossip. A noise as of dead leaves in the wind comes from the room. Cabot has come out from the porch and stands by the gate, leaning on it, staring at the sky blinkingly. Abbie comes across the room silently. Eben does not notice her until quite near.*)

EBEN (*starting*): Abbie!

ABBIE: Sshh! (*She throws her arms around him. They kiss—then bend over the cradle together.*) Ain't he purty?—dead spit 'n' image o' yew!

EBEN (*pleased*): Air he? I can't tell none.

ABBIE: E-zactly like!

EBEN (*frowningly*): I don't like this. I don't like lettin' on what's mine's his'n. I been doin' that all my life. I'm gittin' t' the end o' b'arin' it!

ABBIE (*putting her finger on his lips*): We're doin' the best we kin. We got t' wait. Somethin's bound t' happen. (*She puts her arms around him.*) I got t' go back.

EBEN: I'm goin' out. I can't b'ar it with the fiddle playin' an' the laughin'.

ABBIE: Don't git feelin' low. I love ye, Eben. Kiss me. (*He kisses her. They remain in each other's arms.*)

CABOT (*at the gate, confusedly*): Even the music can't drive it out—somethin'. Ye kin feel it droppin' off the elums, climbin' up the roof, sneakin' down the chimney, pokin' in the corners! They's no peace in houses, they's no rest livin' with folks. Somethin's always livin' with ye. (*With a deep sigh.*) I'll go t' the barn an' rest a spell. (*He goes wearily toward the barn.*)

FIDDLER (*tuning up*): Let's celebrate the old skunk gittin' fooled! We kin have some fun now he's went. (*He starts to fiddle "Turkey in the Straw." There is real merriment now. The young folks get up to dance.*)

SCENE II

(*A half hour later—exterior—Eben is standing by the gate looking up at the sky, an expression of dumb pain bewildered by itself on his face. Cabot appears, returning from the barn, walking wearily, his eyes on the ground. He sees Eben and his whole mood immediately changes. He becomes excited, a cruel, triumphant grin comes to his lips, he strides up and slaps Eben on the back. From within comes the whining of the fiddle and the noise of stamping feet and laughing voices.*)

CABOT: So har ye be!

EBEN (*startled, stares at him with hatred for a moment—then dully*): Ay-eh.

CABOT (*surveying him jeeringly*): Why hain't ye been in t' dance? They was all axin' fur ye.

EBEN: Let 'em ax!

CABOT: They's a hull passel o' purty gals.

EBEN: T' hell with 'em!

CABOT: Ye'd ought t' be marryin' one o' 'em soon.

EBEN: I hain't marryin' no one.

CABOT: Ye might 'arn a share o' a farm that way.

EBEN (*with a sneer*):   Like yew did, ye mean? I hain't that kind.

CABOT (*stung*):   Ye lie! 'Twas yer Maw's folks aimed t' steal my farm from me.

EBEN: Other folks don't say so. (*After a pause—defiantly.*) An' I got a farm, anyways!

CABOT (*derisively*):   Whar?

EBEN (*stamps a foot on the ground*):   Har!

CABOT (*throws his head back and laughs coarsely*):   Ho-ho! Ye hev, hev ye? Waal, that's a good un!

EBEN (*controlling himself—grimly*):   Ye'll see!

CABOT (*stares at him suspiciously, trying to make him out—a pause—then with scornful confidence*): Ay-eh. I'll see. So'll ye. It's ye that's blind—blind as a mole underground. (*Eben suddenly laughs, one short sardonic bark: "Ha." A pause. Cabot peers at him with renewed suspicion.*) What air ye hawin' 'bout? (*Eben turns away without answering. Cabot grows angry.*) God A'mighty, yew air a dumb dunce! They's nothin' in that thick skull o' your'n but noise—like a empty keg it be! (*Eben doesn't seem to hear. Cabot's rage grows.*) Yewr farm! God A'mighty! If ye wa'n't a born donkey ye'd know ye'll never own stick nor stone on it, specially now arter him bein' born. It's his'n, I tell ye—his'n arter I die—but I'll live a hundred jest t' fool ye all—an' he'll be growed then—yewr age a'most! (*Eben laughs again his sardonic "Ha." This drives Cabot into a fury.*) Ha? Ye think ye kin git 'round that someways, do ye? Waal, it'll be her'n, too— Abbie's—ye won't git 'round her—she knows yer tricks—she'll be too much fur ye—she wants the farm her'n—she was afeerd o' ye—she told me ye was sneakin' 'round tryin' t' make love t' her t' git her on yer side . . . ye . . . ye mad fool, ye! (*He raises his clenched fists threateningly.*)

EBEN (*is confronting him, choking with rage*):   Ye lie, ye old skunk! Abbie never said no sech thing!

CABOT (*suddenly triumphant when he sees how shaken Eben is*):   She did. An' I says, I'll blow his brains t' the top o' them elums—an' she says no, that hain't sense, who'll ye git t'help ye on the farm in his place—an' then she says yew'n me ought t' have a son—I know we kin, she says—an' I says, if we do, ye kin have anythin' I've got ye've a mind t'. An' she says, I wants Eben cut off so's this farm'll be mine when ye die! (*With terrible gloating.*) An' that's what's happened, hain't it? An' the farm's her'n! An' the dust o' the road—that's you'rn! Ha! Now who's hawin'?

EBEN (*has been listening, petrified with grief and rage—suddenly laughs wildly and brokenly*): Ha-ha-ha! So that's her sneakin' game—all along!—like I suspicioned at fust—t' swaller it all—an' me, too . . . ! (*Madly.*) I'll murder her! (*He springs toward the porch but Cabot is quicker and gets in between.*)

CABOT: No, ye don't!

EBEN: Git out o' my road! (*He tries to throw Cabot aside. They grapple in what becomes immediately a murderous struggle. The old man's concentrated strength is too much for Eben. Cabot gets one hand on his throat and presses him back across the stone wall. At the same moment, Abbie comes out on the porch. With a stifled cry she runs toward them.*)

ABBIE: Eben! Ephraim! (*She tugs at the hand on Eben's throat.*) Let go, Ephraim! Ye're chokin' him!

CABOT (*Removes his hand and flings Eben sideways full length on the grass, gasping and choking. With a cry, Abbie kneels beside him, trying to take his head on her lap, but he pushes her away. Cabot stands looking down with fierce triumph.*): Ye needn't t've fret, Abbie, I wa'n't aimin' t' kill him. He hain't wuth hangin' fur—not by a hell of a sight! (*More and more triumphantly.*) Seventy-six an' him not thirty yit—an' look whar he be fur thinkin' his Paw was easy! No, by God, I hain't easy! An' him upstairs, I'll raise him t' be like me! (*He turns to leave them.*) I'm goin' in an' dance!—sing an' celebrate! (*He walks to the porch—then turns with a great grin.*) I don't calc'late it's left in him, but if he gits pesky, Abbie, ye jest sing out. I'll come a-runnin' an' by the Etarnal, I'll put him across my knee an' birch him! Ha-ha-ha! (*He goes into the house laughing. A moment later his loud "whoop" is heard.*)

ABBIE (*tenderly*):   Eben. Air ye hurt? (*She tries to kiss him but he pushes her violently away and struggles to a sitting position.*)

EBEN (*gaspingly*):   T'hell—with ye!

ABBIE (*not believing her ears*):   It's me, Eben—Abbie—don't ye know me?

EBEN (*glowering at her with hatred*):   Ay-eh—I know ye—now! (*He suddenly breaks down, sobbing weakly.*)

ABBIE (*fearfully*):   Eben—what's happened t' ye—why did ye look at me 's if ye hated me?

EBEN (*violently, between sobs and gasps*):   I do hate ye! Ye're a whore—a damn trickin' whore!

ABBIE (*shrinking back horrified*):   Eben! Ye don't know what ye're sayin'!

EBEN (*scrambling to his feet and following her—accusingly*):   Ye're nothin' but a stinkin' passel o' lies! Ye've been lyin' t' me every word ye spoke, day an' night, since we fust—done it. Y've kept sayin' ye loved me. . . .

ABBIE (*frantically*):   I do love ye! (*She takes his hand but he flings hers away.*)

EBEN (*unheeding*):   Ye've made a fool o' me—a sick, dumb fool—a-purpose! Ye've been on'y playin' yer sneakin', stealin' game all along—gittin' me t' lie with ye so's ye'd hev a son he'd think was his'n, an' makin' him promise he'd give ye the farm and let me eat dust, if ye did git him a son! (*Staring at her with anguished, bewildered eyes.*) They must be a devil livin' in ye! T'ain't human t' be as bad as that be!

ABBIE (*stunned—dully*):   He told yew . . . ?

EBEN: Hain't it true? It hain't no good in yew lyin'.

ABBIE (*pleadingly*):   Eben, listen—ye must listen—it was long ago—afore we done nothin'—yew was scornin' me—goin' t' see Min—when I was lovin' ye— an' I said it t' him t' git vengeance on ye!

EBEN (*Unheedingly. With tortured passion.*):   I wish ye was dead! I wish I was dead along with ye afore this come! (*Ragingly.*) But I'll git my vengeance too! I'll pray Maw t' come back t' help me—t' put her cuss on yew an' him!

ABBIE (*brokenly*):   Don't ye, Eben! Don't ye! (*She throws herself on her knees before him, weeping.*) I didn't mean t' do bad t'ye! Fergive me, won't ye?

EBEN (*not seeming to hear her—fiercely*):   I'll git squar' with the old skunk— an' yew! I'll tell him the truth 'bout the son he's so proud o'! Then I'll leave ye here t' pizen each other—with Maw comin' out o' her grave at nights—an' I'll go t' the gold fields o' Californi-a whar Sim an' Peter be!

ABBIE (*terrified*):   Ye won't—leave me? Ye can't!

EBEN (*with fierce determination*):   I'm a-goin', I tell ye! I'll git rich thar an' come back an' fight him fur the farm he stole—an' I'll kick ye both out in the road—t' beg an' sleep in the woods—an' yer son along with ye—t' starve an' die! (*He is hysterical at the end.*)

ABBIE (*with a shudder—humbly*):   He's yewr son, too, Eben.

EBEN (*torturedly*):   I wish he never was born! I wish he'd die this minit! I wish I'd never sot eyes on him! It's him—yew havin' him—a-purpose t' steal—that's changed everythin'!

ABBIE (*gently*):   Did ye believe I loved ye—afore he come?

EBEN: Aye-eh—like a dumb ox!

ABBIE: An' ye don't believe no more?

EBEN: B'lieve a lyin' thief! Ha!

ABBIE (*shudders—then humbly*):   An' did ye r'ally love me afore?

EBEN (*brokenly*):   Ay-eh—an' ye was trickin' me!

ABBIE: An' ye don't love me now!

EBEN (*violently*):   I hate ye, I tell ye!

ABBIE: An' ye're truly goin' West—goin' t' leave me—all account o' him being born?

EBEN: I'm a-goin' in the mornin'—or may God strike me t' hell!

ABBIE (*after a pause—with dreadful cold intensity—slowly*):   If that's what his comin's done t' me—killin' yewr love—takin' yew away—my on'y joy—the on'y joy I ever knowed—like heaven t' me—purtier'n heaven—then I hate him, too, even if I be his Maw!

EBEN (*bitterly*):   Lies! Ye love him! He'll steal the farm fur ye! (*Brokenly.*) But t'ain't the farm so much—not no more—it's yew foolin' me—gittin' me t' love ye—lyin' yew loved me—jest t' git a son t' steal!

ABBIE (*distractedly*):   He won't steal! I'd kill him fust! I do love ye! I'll prove t' ye . . . !

EBEN (*harshly*):   T'ain't no use lyin' no more. I'm deaf t' ye! (*He turns away.*) I hain't seein' ye agen. Good-by!

ABBIE (*pale with anguish*):   Hain't ye even goin' t' kiss me—not once—arter all we loved?

EBEN (*in a hard voice*):   I hain't wantin' t' kiss ye never agen! I'm wantin' t' forgit I ever sot eyes on ye!

ABBIE: Eben!—ye mustn't—wait a spell—I want t' tell ye. . . .

EBEN: I'm a-goin' in t' git drunk. I'm a-goin' t' dance.

ABBIE (*clinging to his arm—with passionate earnestness*):   If I could make it—'s if he'd never come up between us—if I could prove t' ye I wa'n't schemin' t' steal from ye—so's everythin' could be jest the same with us, lovin' each other jest the same, kissin' an' happy the same's we've been happy afore he come—if I could do it—ye'd love me agen, wouldn't ye? Ye'd kiss me agen? Ye wouldn't never leave me, would ye?

EBEN (*moved*):   I calc'late not. (*Then shaking her hand off his arm—with a bitter smile.*) But ye hain't God, be ye?

ABBIE (*exultantly*):   Remember y've promised! (*Then with strange intensity.*) Mebbe I kin take back one thin' God does!

EBEN (*peering at her*):   Ye're gittin' cracked, hain't ye? (*Then going toward door.*) I'm a-goin' t' dance.

ABBIE (*calls after him intensely*):   I'll prove t' ye! I'll prove I love ye bettter'n. . . . (*He goes in the door, not seeming to hear. She remains standing where she is, looking after him—then she finishes desperately.*) Better'n everythin' else in the world!

Scene III

(Just before dawn in the morning—shows the kitchen and Cabot's bedroom. In the kitchen, by the light of a tallow candle on the table, Eben is sitting, his chin propped on his hands, his drawn face blank and expressionless. His carpetbag is on the floor beside him. In the bedroom, dimly lighted by a small whale-oil lamp, Cabot lies asleep. Abbie is bending over the cradle, listening, her face full of terror yet with an undercurrent of desperate triumph. Suddenly, she breaks down and sobs, appears about to throw herself on her knees beside the cradle; but the old man turns restlessly, groaning in his sleep, and she controls herself, and, shrinking away from the cradle with a gesture of horror, backs swiftly toward the door in rear and goes out. A moment later she comes into the kitchen and, running to Eben, flings her arms about his neck and kisses him wildly. He hardens himself, he remains unmoved and cold, he keeps his eyes straight ahead.)

ABBIE *(hysterically)*:   I done it, Eben! I told ye I'd do it! I've proved I love ye—better'n everythin'—so's ye can't never doubt me no more!

EBEN *(dully)*:   Whatever ye done, it hain't no good now.

ABBIE *(wildly)*:   Don't ye say that! Kiss me, Eben, won't ye? I need ye t' kiss me arter what I done! I need ye t' say ye love me!

EBEN *(kisses her without emotion—dully)*:   That's fur good-by. I'm a-goin' soon.

ABBIE: No! No! Ye won't go—not now!

EBEN *(going on with his own thoughts)*:   I been a-thinkin'—an' I hain't goin' t' tell Paw nothin'. I'll leave Maw t' take vengeance on ye. If I told him, the old skunk'd jest be stinkin' mean enuf to take it out on that baby. *(His voice showing emotion in spite of him.)* An' I don't want nothin' bad t' happen t' him. He hain't t' blame fur yew. *(He adds with a certain queer pride.)* An' he looks like me! An' by God, he's mine! An' some day I'll be a-comin' back an' . . . !

ABBIE *(too absorbed in her own thoughts to listen to him—pleadingly)*: They's no cause fur ye t' go now—they's no sense—it's all the same's it was—they's nothin' come b'tween us now—arter what I done!

EBEN *(Something in her voice arouses him. He stares at her a bit frightenedly.)*: Ye look mad, Abbie. What did ye do?

ABBIE: I—I killed him, Eben.

EBEN *(amazed)*:   Ye killed him?

ABBIE *(dully)*:   Ay-eh.

EBEN *(recovering from his astonishment—savagely)*:   An' serves him right! But we got t' do somethin' quick t' make it look s'if the old skunk'd killed himself when he was drunk. We kin prove by 'em all how drunk he got.

ABBIE *(wildly)*:   No! No! Not him! *(Laughing distractedly.)* But that's what I ought t' done, hain't it? I oughter killed him instead! Why didn't ye tell me?

EBEN *(appalled)*:   Instead? What d'ye mean?

ABBIE: Not him.

EBEN *(his face grown ghastly)*:   Not—not that baby!

ABBIE *(dully)*:   Ay-eh!

EBEN *(falls to his knees as if he'd been struck—his voice trembling with horror)*:   Oh, God A'mighty! A'mighty God! Maw, whar was ye, why didn't ye stop her?

ABBIE *(simply)*:   She went back t' her grave that night we fust done it, remember? I hain't felt her about since. *(A pause. Eben hides his head in his hands, trembling all over as if he had the ague. She goes on dully.*) I left the piller over his little face. Then he killed himself. He stopped breathin'. (*She begins to weep softly.*)

EBEN (*rage beginning to mingle with grief*):   He looked like me. He was mine, damn ye!

ABBIE (*slowly and brokenly*):   I didn't want t' do it. I hated myself fur doin' it. I loved him. He was so purty—dead spit 'n' image o' yew. But I loved yew more—an' yew was goin' away—far off whar I'd never see ye agen, never kiss ye, never feel ye pressed agin me agen—an' ye said ye hated me fur havin' him— ye said ye hated him an' wished he was dead—ye said if it hadn't been fur him comin' it'd be the same's afore between us.

EBEN (*unable to endure this, springs to his feet in a fury, threatening her, his twitching fingers seeming to reach out for her throat*): Ye lie! I never said—I never dreamed ye'd—I'd cut off my head afore I'd hurt his finger!

ABBIE (*piteously, sinking on her knees*):   Eben, don't ye look at me like that— hatin' me—not after what I done fur ye—fur us—so's we could be happy agen—

EBEN (*furiously now*):   Shut up, or I'll kill ye! I see yer game now—the same old sneakin' trick—ye're aimin' t' blame me fur the murder ye done!

ABBIE (*moaning—putting her hands over her ears*):   Don't ye, Eben! Don't ye! (*She grasps his legs.*)

EBEN (*his mood suddenly changing to horror, shrinks away from her*):   Don't ye tech me! Ye're pizen! How could ye—t' murder a pore little critter—Ye must've swapped yer soul t' hell! (*Suddenly raging.*) Ha! I kin see why ye done it! Not the lies ye jest told—but 'cause ye wanted t' steal agen—steal the last thin' ye'd left me—my part o' him—no, the hull o' him—ye saw he looked like me— ye knowed he was all mine—an' ye couldn't b'ar it—I know ye! Ye killed him fur bein' mine! (*All this has driven him almost insane. He makes a rush past her for the door—then turns—shaking both fists at her, violently.*) But I'll take vengeance now! I'll git the Sheriff! I'll tell him everythin'! Then I'll sing "I'm off to Californi-a!" an' go—gold—Golden Gate—gold sun—fields o' gold in the West! (*This last he half shouts, half croons incoherently, suddenly breaking off passionately.*) I'm a-goin' fur the Sheriff t' come an' git ye! I want ye tuk away, locked up from me! I can't stand t' luk at ye! Murderer an' thief 'r not, ye still tempt me! I'll give ye up t' the Sheriff! (*He turns and runs out, around the corner of house, panting and sobbing, and breaks into a swerving spring down the road.*)

ABBIE (*struggling to her feet, runs to the door, calling after him*):   I love ye, Eben! I love ye! (*She stops at the door weakly, swaying, about to fall.*) I don't care what ye do—if ye'll on'y love me agen—(*She falls limply to the floor in a faint.*)

SCENE IV

(*About an hour later. Same as Scene III. Shows the kitchen and Cabot's bedroom. It is after dawn. The sky is brilliant with the sunrise. In the kitchen, Abbie sits at the table, her body limp and exhausted, her head bowed down over her arms, her face hidden. Upstairs, Cabot is still asleep but awakens with a start. He looks toward the window and gives a snort of surprise and irritation—throws back the covers and begins hurriedly pulling on his clothes. Without looking behind him, he begins talking to Abbie whom he supposes beside him.*)

CABOT: Thunder 'n' lightin', Abbie! I hain't slept this late in fifty year! Looks 's if the sun was full riz a'most. Must've been the dancin' an' likker. Must be gittin' old. I hope Eben's t' wuk. Ye might've tuk the trouble t' rouse me, Abbie. (*He turns—sees no one there—surprised.*) Waal—whar air she? Gittin' vittles, I calc'late. (*He tiptoes to the cradle and peers down—proudly.*) Mornin', sonny. Purty's a picter! Sleepin' sound. He don't beller all night like most o' 'em. (*He goes quietly out the door in rear—a few moments later enters kitchen—sees Abbie—with satisfaction.*) So thar ye be. Ye got any vittles cooked?

ABBIE (*without moving*):   No.

CABOT (*coming to her, almost sympathetically*):   Ye feelin' sick?

ABBIE: No.

CABOT (*Pats her on shoulder. She shudders.*):   Ye'd best lie down a spell. (*Half jocularly.*) Yer son'll be needin' ye soon. He'd ought t' wake up with a gnashin' appetite, the sound way he's sleepin'.

ABBIE (*shudders—then in a dead voice*):   He hain't never goin' t' wake up.

CABOT (*jokingly*):   Takes after me this mornin'. I hain't slept so late in . . .

ABBIE: He's dead.

CABOT (*stares at her—bewilderedly*):   What. . . .

ABBIE: I killed him.

CABOT (*stepping back from her—aghast*):   Air ye drunk—'r crazy—'r . . . ?

ABBIE (*suddenly lifts her head and turns on him—wildly*):   I killed him, I tell ye! I smothered him. Go up an' see if ye don't b'lieve me!

(*Cabot stares at her a second, then bolts out the rear door, can be heard bounding up the stairs, and rushes into the bedroom and over to the cradle. Abbie has sunk back lifelessly into her former position. Cabot puts his hand down on the body in the crib. An expression of fear and horror comes over his face.*)

CABOT (*shrinking away—tremblingly*):   God A'mighty! God A'mighty. (*He stumbles out the door—in a short while returns to the kitchen—comes to Abbie, the stunned expression still on his face—hoarsely.*) Why did ye do it? Why? (*As she doesn't answer, he grabs her violently by the shoulder and shakes her.*) I ax ye why ye done it! Ye'd better tell me 'r . . . !

ABBIE (*gives him a furious push which sends him staggering back and springs to her feet—with wild rage and hatred*): Don't ye dare tech me! What right hev ye t' question me 'bout him? He wa'n't yewr son! Think I'd have a son by yew? I'd die fust! I hate the sight o' ye an' allus did! It's yew I should've murdered, if I'd had good sense! I hate ye! I love Eben. I did from the fust. An' he was Eben's son— mine an' Eben's—not your'n!

CABOT (*stands looking at her dazedly—a pause—finding his words with an effort—dully*): That was it—what I felt—pokin' round the corners—while ye lied—holdin' yerself from me—sayin' ye'd a'ready conceived—(*He lapses into crushed silence—then with a strange emotion.*) He's dead, sart'n. I felt his heart. Pore little critter! (*He blinks back one tear, wiping his sleeve across his nose.*)

ABBIE (*hysterically*):   Don't ye! Don't ye! (*She sobs unrestrainedly.*)

CABOT (*with a concentrated effort that stiffens his body into a rigid line and hardens his face into a stony mask—through his teeth to himself*): I got t' be—like a stone—a rock o' jedgment! (*A pause. He gets complete control over himself— harshly.*) If he was Eben's, I be glad he air gone! An' mebbe I suspicioned it all along. I felt they was somethin' onnateral—somewhars—the house got so lonesome—an' cold—drivin' me down t' the barn—t' the beasts o' the field. . . . Ay-eh. I must've suspicioned—somethin'. Ye didn't fool me—not altogether, leastways—I'm too old a bird—growin' ripe on the bough . . . .(*He becomes aware he is wandering, straightens again, looks at Abbie with a cruel grin.*) So ye'd liked t' hev murdered me 'stead o' him, would ye! Waal, I'll live to a hundred! I'll live t' see ye hung! I'll deliver ye up t' the jedgment o' God an' the law! I'll git the Sheriff now. (*Starts for the door.*)

ABBIE (*dully*): Ye needn't. Eben's gone fur him.

CABOT (*amazed*): Eben—gone fur the Sheriff?

ABBIE: Ay-eh.

CABOT: T' inform agen ye?

ABBIE: Ay-eh.

CABOT (*considers this—a pause—then in a hard voice*): Waal, I'm thankful fur him savin' me the trouble. I'll git t' wuk. (*He goes to the door—then turns—in a voice full of strange emotion.*) He'd ought t' been my son, Abbie. Ye'd ought t' loved me. I'm a man. If ye'd loved me, I'd never told no Sheriff on ye no matter what ye did, if they was t' brile me alive!

ABBIE (*defensively*): They's more to it nor yew know, makes him tell.

CABOT (*dryly*): Fur yewr sake, I hope they be. (*He goes out—comes around to the gate—stares up at the sky. His control relaxes. For a moment he is old and weary. He murmurs despairingly.*) God A'mighty, I be lonesomer'n ever! (*He hears running footsteps from the left, immediately is himself again. Eben runs in, panting exhaustedly, wild-eyed and mad looking. He lurches through the gate. Cabot grabs him by the shoulder. Eben stares at him dumbly.*) Did ye tell the Sheriff?

EBEN (*nodding stupidly*): Ay-eh.

CABOT (*gives him a push away that sends him sprawling—laughing with withering contempt*): Good fur ye! A prime chip o' yer Maw ye be! (*He goes toward the barn, laughing harshly. Eben scrambles to his feet. Suddenly Cabot turns—grimly threatening.*) Git off this farm when the Sheriff takes her—or, by God, he'll have t' come back an' git me fur murder, too! (*He stalks off. Eben does not appear to have heard him. He runs to the door and comes into the kitchen. Abbie looks up with a cry of anguished joy. Eben stumbles over and throws himself on his knees beside her sobbing brokenly.*)

EBEN: Fergive me!

ABBIE (*happily*): Eben! (*She kisses him and pulls his head over against her breast.*)

EBEN: I love ye! Fergive me!

ABBIE (*ecstatically*): I'd fergive ye all the sins in hell fur sayin' that! (*She kisses his head, pressing it to her with a fierce passion of possession.*)

EBEN (*brokenly*): But I told the Sheriff. He's comin' fur ye!

ABBIE: I kin b'ar what happens t' me—now!

EBEN: I woke him up. I told him. He says, wait 'til I git dressed. I was waiting. I got to thinkin' o' yew. I got to thinkin' how I'd loved ye. It hurt like somethin' was bustin' in my chest an' head. I got t' cryin'. I knowed sudden I loved ye yet, an' allus would love ye!

ABBIE (*caressing his hair—tenderly*): My boy, hain't ye?

EBEN: I begun t' run back. I cut across the fields an' through the woods. I thought ye might have time t' run away—with me—an' . . .

ABBIE (*shaking her head*): I got t' take my punishment—t' pay fur my sin.

EBEN: Then I want t' share it with ye.

ABBIE: Ye didn't do nothin'.

EBEN: I put it in yer head. I wisht he was dead! I as much as urged ye t' do it!

ABBIE: No. It was me alone!

EBEN: I'm as guilty as yew be! He was the child o' our sin.

ABBIE (*lifting her head as if defying God*):   I don't repent that sin! I hain't askin' God t' fergive that!

EBEN: Nor me—but it led up t' the other—an' the murder ye did, ye did 'count o' me—an' it's my murder, too, I'll tell the Sheriff—an' if ye deny it, I'll say we planned it t'gether—an' they'll all b'lieve me, fur they suspicion everythin' we've done, an' it'll seem likely an' true to 'em. An' it is true—way down. I did help ye—somehow.

ABBIE (*laying her head on his—sobbing*):   No! I don't want yew t' suffer!

EBEN: I got t' pay fur my part o' the sin! An' I'd suffer wuss leavin' ye, goin' West, thinkin' o' ye day an' night, bein' out when yew was in—(*Lowering his voice.*) 'r bein' alive when yew was dead. (*A pause.*) I want t' share with ye, Abbie—prison 'r death 'r hell 'r anythin'! (*He looks into her eyes and forces a trembling smile.*) If I'm sharin' with ye, I won't feel lonesome, leastways.

ABBIE (*weakly*):   Eben! I won't let ye! I can't let ye!

EBEN (*kissing her—tenderly*):   Ye can't he'p yerself. I got ye beat fur once!

ABBIE (*forcing a smile—adoringly*):   I hain't beat—s'long's I got ye!

EBEN (*hears the sound of feet outside*):   Sshh! Listen! They've come t' take us!

ABBIE: No, it's him. Don't give him no chance to fight ye, Eben. Don't say nothin'—no matter what he says. An' I won't neither. (*It is Cabot. He comes up from the barn in a great state of excitement and strides into the house and then into the kitchen. Eben is kneeling beside Abbie, his arm around her, hers around him. They stare straight ahead.*)

CABOT (*Stares at them, his face hard. A long pause—vindictively.*):   Ye make a slick pair o' murderin' turtle doves! Ye'd ought t' be both hung on the same limb an' left thar t' swing in the breeze an' rot—a warnin' t' old fools like me t' b'ar their lonesomeness alone—an' fur young fools like ye t' hobble their lust. (*A pause. The excitement returns to his face, his eyes snap, he looks a bit crazy.*) I couldn't work today. I couldn't take no interest. T' hell with the farm! I'm leavin' it! I've turned the cows an' other stock loose! I've druv 'em into the woods whar they kin be free! By freein' 'em, I'm freein' myself! I'm quittin' here today! I'll set fire t' house an' barn an' watch 'em burn, an' I'll leave yer Maw t' haunt the ashes, an' I'll will the fields back t' God, so that nothin' human kin never touch 'em! I'll be a-goin' to Californi-a—t' jine Simeon an' Peter—true sons o' mine if they be dumb fools—an' the Cabots'll find Solomon's Mines t'gether! (*He suddenly cuts a mad caper.*) Whoop! What was the song they sung? "Oh, Californi-a! That's the land fur me." (*He sings this—then gets on his knees by the floorboard under which the money was hid.*) An' I'll sail thar on one o' the finest clippers I kin find! I've got the money! Pity ye didn't know whar this was hidden so's ye could steal. . . . (*He has pulled up the board. He stares—feels—stares again. A pause of dead silence. He slowly turns, slumping into a sitting position on the floor, his eyes like those of a dead fish, his face the sickly green of an attack of nausea. He swallows painfully several times—forces a weak smile at last.*) So—ye did steal it!

EBEN (*emotionlessly*):   I swapped it t' Sim an' Peter fur their share o' the farm—t' pay their passage t' Californi-a.

CABOT (*with one sardonic*):   Ha! (*He begins to recover. Gets slowly to his feet—strangely.*) I calc'late God give it to 'em—not yew! God's hard, not easy! Mebbe they's easy gold in the West but it hain't God's gold. It hain't fur me. I kin hear His voice warnin' me agen t' be hard an' stay on my farm. I kin see his hand usin' Eben t' steal t' keep me from weakness. I kin feel I be in the palm o' His hand, His fingers guidin' me. (*A pause—then he mutters sadly.*) It's a-goin' t' be lonesomer now than ever it war afore—an' I'm gittin' old, Lord—ripe on the bough. . . . (*Then stiffening.*) Waal—what d'ye want? God's lonesome, hain't He? God's hard an' lonesome! (*A pause. The Sheriff with two men comes up the road from the left. They move cautiously to the door. The Sheriff knocks on it with the butt of his pistol.*)

SHERIFF: Open in the name o' the law! (*They start.*)

CABOT: They've come fur ye. (*He goes to the rear door.*) Come in, Jim! (*The three men enter. Cabot meets them in doorway.*) Jest a minit, Jim. I got 'em safe here. (*The Sheriff nods. He and his companions remain in the doorway.*)

EBEN (*suddenly calls*):   I lied this mornin', Jim. I helped her to do it. Ye kin take me, too.

ABBIE (*brokenly*):   No!

CABOT: Take 'em both. (*He comes forward—stares at Eben with a trace of grudging admiration.*) Purty good—fur yew! Waal, I got t' round up the stock. Good-by.

EBEN: Good-by.

ABBIE: Good-by. (*Cabot turns and strides past the men—comes out and around the corner of the house, his shoulders squared, his face stony, and stalks grimly toward the barn. In the meantime the Sheriff and men have come into the room.*)

SHERIFF (*embarrassedly*):   Waal—we'd best start.

ABBIE: Wait. (*Turns to Eben.*) I love ye, Eben.

EBEN: I love ye, Abbie. (*They kiss. The three men grin and shuffle embarrassedly. Eben takes Abbie's hand. They go out the door in rear, the men following, and come from the house, walking hand in hand to the gate. Eben stops there and points to the sunrise sky.*) Sun's a-rizin'. Purty, hain't it?

ABBIE: Ay-eh. (*They both stand for a moment looking up raptly in attitudes strangely aloof and devout.*)

SHERIFF (*looking around at the farm enviously—to his companions*):   It's a jim-dandy farm, no denyin'. Wished I owned it!

1924

Tennessee Williams
(1911–1983)

Born Thomas Lanier Williams in Columbus, Mississippi, in 1911, Tennessee Williams inherited a culture of disappointment, a shabby gentility. He was in part raised by his grandparents, thereby absorbing a tradition many years older than the world of his peers.

Young Thomas, his mother, and his sister Rose moved frequently. Leaving the quiet, orderly Episcopalian rectories of the churches in which his grandfather preached, the boy ultimately settled in St. Louis, in a chaos only slightly mitigated by his grandmother's presence. Williams's father was a traveling shoe salesman who visited the family periodically but, when his son was seven, was made a sales manager of a St. Louis shoe company and wanted to establish a home. That home, however, was filled with violence and drinking. Rose Williams, the model for many of her brother's later fragile female characters, suffered not only the terror of her father's rage but the fear that her mother, constantly ill, would die. Both as a brother and an artist, Williams was preoccupied with Rose. Over the years she was taken from treatment to treatment, gradually deteriorating; she was one of the first Americans to undergo a frontal lobotomy.

Many of Williams's characters whose brutal masculinity menaces the gentler characters around them may have been created in memory of the father Williams openly "hated." Williams's father, who called his son "Miss Nancy," had little time for a boy who read and stayed close to his mother's side. As an adolescent Williams, finding himself in a society that was all too ready to adopt his father's scorn, took to the solitary pursuits of reading and writing. He attended, but dropped out of, the University of Missouri and Washington University in St. Louis, and spent three years working in a shoe factory. He then returned to college and, in his mid-twenties, earned a B.A. from the University of Iowa. While in college Williams began writing plays and won prizes for fiction. He experimented with different forms, but his short stories were his first works to be published, in "little" magazines.

After college Williams spent brief periods in numerous cities, doing menial jobs and writing. It was then that he gave himself the romanticized name "Tennessee." The theatrical agent Audrey Wood found Williams' work promising and contacted him in 1939 to offer her services as an agent. (Their partnership would last for most of his career.) In 1940 the Theater Guild produced his *Battle of Angels* in Boston. The play took up many of the themes of later Williams plays, but its plot was unwieldy and its subject matter received mixed reviews. (It was revised and later released as *Orpheus Descending* [1957].) Throughout his career Williams considered topics shunned by the public: incest, adultery, homosexuality, cannibalism, and mental illness. In the aftermath of the failure of *Battle of Angels,* Williams eventually took a job in Hollywood, writing movie scripts. While writing not-so-successful screenplays, Williams turned his rejected screenplay "The Gentleman Caller" into the play *The Glass Menagerie* (1944), a New York Drama Critics' Circle Award winner.

Williams is known for his eery, evocative creation of characters whose oddities render them unfit for the "normal" world. These unusual characters are set in the South in a world that eastern audiences had not seen or understood. That world that insulates itself in stories of lost glory, languishing in the closeted, dark experiences of characters such as Laura in *The Glass Menagerie.* As Laura turns her glass unicorn, a mystical, tinkling sound begins before the background music drifts out; Williams's language is there first, delicately combining filaments of daydreaming, languor, and confinement. His refrain is in his lyrical language, the richness of rhythm created by monologue and musing.

For the Wingfields, the family of *The Glass Menagerie,* life takes on the sheen of disappointment, polished only by dreams. While Tom—the narrator, frustrated writer, and Laura's brother—dreams of getting away from the family, and Amanda—the mother—fantasizes about gentler, easier times, Laura lives precariously in a world of glass, blown into shape by imagination and longing. The story, like a musicbox figurine, revolves around the expected arrival of the visitor, the "Gentleman Caller." For the life of a young and slightly "odd" woman and her anxious mother pining away in a dingy apartment in St. Louis in the late 1930s, the gentleman caller's visit is anticipated as a rescue, the possible

A scene from a production of Tennessee Williams's The Glass Menagerie.

salvation of marriage and escape. But the arrival of Jim O'Connor, the Gentleman Caller, proves to be a cruel blow. Reality is always desperately harsh in Williams's plays as characters' worst fears are confirmed and surpassed. The pain of loss is typically so intense as to seem indulgent, as if pain for its own pleasure, delicious anguish, is the dubious reward for perpetual expectation.

If we follow Williams's directive to read his plays as autobiographical pieces (a practice to be undertaken with healthy skepticism because such interpretation can flatten rich, ambiguous characters and settings), his next big success matured from his own childhood and isolated longings as a young writer to the conflicts of class and temperament contained in adult liaisons. *A Streetcar Named Desire* opened in New York in 1947 and won a Pulitzer Prize in 1948. The play exists, however, in the American memory as a film, and even those who know little of the theater are likely to know Marlon Brando's Stanley Kowalski character. His "Stella!" echoes down from 1951 to the present, bringing with it the powerful contrast between fame in American theater and the more lucrative, widespread fame in Hollywood.

Back and forth across a dilapidated street in the New Orleans French Quarter run two streetcars, one named Desire, the other Cemeteries. Somehow, as Williams's life had thus far progressed, he seemed to have always been on his way to this street. As the characters appear, weaving in and out to the sounds of a blues piano, lovers shouting, and air moving audibly through the languor of humid speech, the story shapes itself into an atmospheric tale of heat and mistrust. What ease and passion there is between Stella and Stanley Kowalski is a tale that has been told before the play begins. Their connection is one of powerful attraction and learned acceptance: Stella's past as a genteel southern girl seems gratefully relinquished for the vitality of Stanley's physical presence. Their Eden is interrupted as the play opens with the arrival of Blanche DuBois, Stella's sister, an affected, girlish schoolteacher whose disbelief at the poverty into which Stella has married immediately begins to erode the Kowalskis' ease. Social strictures are evoked subtly, the sense that some presence of authority has arrived and the couple must now curtail their energy, must now behave in their small, cramped apartment. Williams clearly represents the struggles of class inherent in this seemingly classless society.

In some ways Blanche represents the world of the imagination as does Laura in *The Glass Menagerie*. With paper lanterns to soften the effects of harsh light, coy slips into French or German, and educated conversation, Blanche stands in contrast to Stanley's blunt sensuality and uncultured manners. She sadly mirrors the position of the artist in the everyday world. While Blanche upholds the code for a woman, particularly a southern woman, of soft lies and supposed purity, her vitality, mirrored in Stanley's passion, is suppressed. Williams accurately portrays a society uncomfortable with its own imagination, which seems to hold unbearable secrets.

In his subsequent plays Williams continued to create intricate relationships among families threatening to reveal the secret lives of their members. *Cat on a Hot Tin Roof* (1955), which earned Williams a second Pulitzer Prize, expands the vista of the cramped apartment to the large plantation house. But the scenes are generally limited to the bedroom, that of Brick and Maggie, a couple locked in a struggle over sexuality. The question of homosexuality hangs in the air quite realistically but is never asked directly. Williams's own homosexuality was the subject of much attention throughout his artistic career. Within the theater community, Williams and his longtime lover, Frank Merlo, were accepted, but the theater-going society was capable of petty judgments and bigotry.

Williams's determined investigation of sexuality included incest, rape, castration, nymphomania, and pedophilia. His screenplay *Baby Doll* (1956), created from two of his one-act plays, features a young bride who sleeps in a crib. The image of her manipulative and oppressive infantilization is a stark challenge to American sexual mores, often heinous in the prudery that hides the sexualization of little girls, the false comfort of "Papas." And in his novelette *The Roman Spring of Mrs. Stone* (1950) and play *Sweet Bird of Youth* (1959), Williams depicts the sordid relationship between an aging actress and a kept young man.

Williams peopled his plays with characters who had lived in isolation and exclusion. *The Night of the Iguana* (1962) was written and produced while Williams was suffering from complications due to drug addiction. Taking place in 1940, the play gathers together a defrocked Episcopalian minister, a Nantucket artist and spinster, her grandfather, a practicing poet, a group of American women on tour, Germans exultant over Adolph Hitler's early war victories, and the keeper of the hotel where they are all staying. A one-day journey into the cycles of life and death accompanied by guilt (religious and sexual), confusion, and fanaticism, *The Night of the Iguana* is considered Williams's last great work for the theater. The play received immediate attention and won the New York Drama Critics Circle Award.

Williams continued to compose for the theater, but his worsening physical and mental health is clear in the first-draft title page of *The Two-Character Play* (1969), written "from the state of lunacy. . . . It is the story of the last six to seven years of the 1960s. The play is about disorientation—these people are lost as I am. They are two sides of one person." A play-within-a-play, Williams portrays a brother and a sister at a play called "The Two-Character Play." As he does in the comical *The Rose Tattoo* (1950) and in the violent *Suddenly Last Summer* (1958), Williams uses that motif to reexamine, obsessively, his own fears about his sister, Rose, her breakdowns, and her operation. Williams was aware that his own breakdown was imminent, the years of drugs and alcohol having completely taxed his system.

Through the last thirteen years of his life, Tennessee Williams wrote continually. He completed such plays as *Small Craft Warnings* (1972) and numerous nondramatic works, including the novel *Noise and the World of Reason* (1975), in which a homosexual writer recalls his youth and his search for love, the poetry collection *Androgyne, Mon Amour* (1977), and *Memoirs* (1975). His recovery from seizures suffered during drug withdrawal was miraculous, though his continuing alcoholism crippled his strength. His accidental death by choking in 1983 shocked the theater community. Williams left behind a body of work, powerful and prolific, that challenged and revived the American stage.

Suggested Readings: *Summer and Smoke*, 1947. *A Streetcar Named Desire*, 1947. *The Rose Tattoo*, 1950. *Camino Real*, 1953. *Cat on a Hot Tin Roof*, 1955. *Suddenly Last Summer*, 1958. *Sweet Bird of Youth*, 1959. *The Night of the Iguana*, 1962. S. Falk, *Tennessee Williams*, 1961. N. Tischler, *Tennessee Williams, Rebellious Puritan*, 1961. E. Jackson, *The Broken World of Tennessee Williams*, 1965. G. Maxwell, *Tennessee Williams and Friends: An Informal Biography*, 1965. S. Stanton, *Tennessee Williams: A Collection of Critical Essays*, 1977. F. Hirsch, *A Portrait of the Artist: The Plays of Tennessee Williams*, 1979. C. W. E. Bigsby, *20th-Century American Drama*, Vol. II, 1984. H. Bloom, ed., *Tennessee Williams: Modern Critical Interpretations*, 1987.

Text Used: *The Glass Menagerie*, 1945.

THE GLASS MENAGERIE

Nobody, not even the rain, has such small hands. —E. E. Cummings

CHARACTERS

AMANDA WINGFIELD, *the mother. A little woman of great but confused vitality clinging frantically to another time and place. Her characterization must be carefully created, not copied from type. She is not paranoiac, but her life is paranoia. There is much to admire in Amanda, and as much to love and pity as there is to laugh at. Certainly she has endurance and a kind of heroism, and though her foolishness makes her unwittingly cruel at times, there is tenderness in her slight person.*

LAURA WINGFIELD, *her daughter. Amanda, having failed to establish contact with reality, continues to live vitally in her illusions, but Laura's situation is even graver. A childhood illness has left her crippled, one leg slightly shorter than the other, and held in a brace. This defect need not be more than suggested on the stage. Stemming from this, Laura's separation increases till she is like a piece of her own glass collection, too exquisitely fragile to move from the shelf.*

TOM WINGFIELD, *her son. And the narrator of the play. A poet with a job in a warehouse. His nature is not remorseless, but to escape from a trap he has to act without pity.*

JIM O'CONNOR, *the gentleman caller. A nice, ordinary, young man.*

SCENE: *An alley in St. Louis.*
Part I: *Preparation for a Gentleman Caller.*
Part II: *The Gentleman Calls.*
Time: *Now and the Past.*

SCENE I

(The Wingfield apartment is in the rear of the building, one of those vast hive-like conglomerations of cellular living-units that flower as warty growths in over-crowded urban centers of lower middle-class population and are symptomatic of the impulse of this largest and fundamentally enslaved section of American society to avoid fluidity and differentiation and to exist and function as one interfused mass of automatism.)

(The apartment faces an alley and is entered by a fire escape, a structure whose name is a touch of accidental poetic truth, for all of these huge buildings are always burning with the slow and implacable fires of human desperation. The fire escape is included in the set—that is, the landing of it and steps descending from it.)

(The scene is memory and is therefore nonrealistic. Memory takes a lot of poetic license. It omits some details; others are exaggerated, according to the emotional value of the articles it touches, for memory is seated predominantly in the heart. The interior is therefore rather dim and poetic.)

(At the rise of the curtain, the audience is faced with the dark, grim rear wall of the Wingfield tenement. This building, which runs parallel to the footlights, is flanked on both sides by dark, narrow alleys which run into murky canyons of tangled clotheslines, garbage cans, and the sinister latticework of neighboring fire escapes. It is up and down these side alleys that exterior entrances and exits are made, during the play. At the end of Tom's opening commentary, the dark tenement wall slowly reveals (by means of a transparency) the interior of the ground floor Wingfield apartment.)

(Downstage is the living room, which also serves as a sleeping room for Laura, the sofa unfolding to make her bed. Upstage, center, and divided by a wide arch or second proscenium[1] with transparent faded portieres[2] (or second curtain), is the dining room. In an old-fashioned what-not in the living room are seen scores of transparent glass animals. A blown-up photograph of the father hangs on the wall of the living room, facing the audience, to the left of the archway. It is the face of a very handsome young man in a doughboy's First World War cap. He is gallantly smiling, ineluctably smiling, as if to say, "I will be smiling forever.")

(The audience hears and sees the opening scene in the dining room through both the transparent fourth wall of the building and the transparent gauze portieres of the dining-room arch. It is during this revealing scene that the fourth wall slowly ascends, out of sight. This transparent exterior wall is not brought down again until the very end of the play, during Tom's final speech.)

(The narrator is an undisguised convention of the play. He takes whatever license with dramatic convention as is convenient to his purposes.)

(Tom enters dressed as a merchant sailor from alley, stage left, and strolls across the front of the stage to the fire escape. There he stops and lights a cigarette. He addresses the audience.)

TOM: Yes, I have tricks in my pocket, I have things up my sleeve. But I am the opposite of a stage magician. He gives you illusion that has the appearance of truth. I give you truth in the pleasant disguise of illusion. To begin with, I turn back time. I reverse it to that quaint period, the thirties, when the huge middle class of America was matriculating in a school for the blind. Their eyes had failed

---

[1] The separation of the stage from the audience.   [2] Drapes, generally heavy.

them, or they had failed their eyes, and so they were having their fingers pressed forcibly down on the fiery Braille alphabet of a dissolving economy. In Spain there was revolution. Here there was only shouting and confusion. In Spain there was Guernica.[3] Here there were disturbances of labor, sometimes pretty violent, in otherwise peaceful cities such as Chicago, Cleveland, Saint Louis . . . . This is the social background of the play.

(*Music.*)

The play is memory. Being a memory play, it is dimly lighted, it is sentimental, it is not realistic. In memory everything seems to happen to music. That explains the fiddle in the wings. I am the narrator of the play, and also a character in it. The other characters are my mother, Amanda, my sister, Laura, and a gentleman caller who appears in the final scenes. He is the most realistic character in the play, being an emissary from a world of reality that we were somehow set apart from. But since I have a poet's weakness for symbols, I am using this character also as a symbol; he is the long delayed but always expected something that we live for. There is a fifth character in the play who doesn't appear except in this larger-than-life photograph over the mantel. This is our father who left us a long time ago. He was a telephone man who fell in love with long distances; he gave up his job with the telephone company and skipped the light fantastic out of town . . . The last we heard of him was a picture postcard from Mazatlan, on the Pacific coast of Mexico, containing a message of two words—"Hello—Goodbye!" and no address. I think the rest of the play will explain itself. . . .

(*Amanda's voice becomes audible through the portieres.*)
    (*Legend on Screen: "Où Sont les Neiges."*[4])
    (*He divides the portieres and enters the upstage area.*)
    (*Amanda and Laura are seated at a drop-leaf table. Eating is indicated by gestures without food or utensils. Amanda faces the audience. Tom and Laura are seated in profile.*)
    (*The interior has lit up softly and through the scrim we see Amanda and Laura seated at the table in the upstage area.*)

AMANDA (*calling*):   Tom?
TOM: Yes, Mother.
AMANDA: We can't say grace until you come to the table!
TOM: Coming, Mother. (*He bows slightly and withdraws, reappearing a few moments later in his place at the table.*)
AMANDA (*to her son*): Honey, don't *push* with your *fingers*. If you have to push with something, the thing to push with is a crust of bread. And chew—chew! Animals have sections in their stomachs which enable them to digest food without mastication, but human beings are supposed to chew their food before they swallow it down. Eat food leisurely, son, and really enjoy it. A well-cooked meal has lots of delicate flavors that have to be held in the mouth for appreciation. So chew your food and give your salivary glands a chance to function!

---

[3] A town in northern Spain bombed by German Fascist sympathizers in 1937 during the Spanish civil war (1936–1939).
    [4] "Where are the snows of yesteryear?" (French) from "Ballade des Dames du Temps Jadis" ("Ballad of the Ladies of Bygone Times"), by François Villon (1431–?).

(Tom deliberately lays his imaginary fork down and pushes his chair back from the table.)

TOM: I haven't enjoyed one bite of this dinner because of your constant directions on how to eat it. It's you that makes me rush through meals with your hawk-like attention to every bite I take. Sickening—spoils my appetite—all this discussion of animals' secretion—salivary glands—mastication!

AMANDA *(lightly)*:   Temperament like a Metropolitan[5] star! *(He rises and crosses downstage.)* You're not excused from the table.

TOM: I'm getting a cigarette.

AMANDA: You smoke too much.

(Laura rises.)

LAURA: I'll bring in the blanc mange.[6]

(He remains standing with his cigarette by the portieres during the following.)

AMANDA *(rising)*:   No, sister, no, sister—you be the lady this time and I'll be the darky.

LAURA: I'm already up.

AMANDA: Resume your seat, little sister—I want you to stay fresh and pretty—for gentlemen callers!

LAURA: I'm not expecting any gentlemen callers.

AMANDA *(Crossing out to kitchenette. Airily.)*:   Sometimes they come when they are least expected! Why, I remember one Sunday afternoon in Blue Mountain—*(Enters kitchenette.)*

TOM: I know what's coming!

LAURA: Yes. But let her tell it.

TOM: Again?

LAURA: She loves to tell it.

(Amanda returns with bowl of dessert.)

AMANDA: One Sunday afternoon in Blue Mountain—your mother received—*seventeen!*—gentlemen callers! Why, sometimes there weren't chairs enough to accommodate them all. We had to send the nigger over to bring in folding chairs from the parish house.

TOM *(remaining at portieres)*:   How did you entertain those gentlemen callers?

AMANDA: I understood the art of conversation!

TOM: I bet you could talk.

AMANDA: Girls in those days *knew* how to talk, I can tell you.

TOM: Yes?

(Image.   Amanda as a girl on a porch greeting callers.)

AMANDA: They knew how to entertain their gentlemen callers. It wasn't enough for a girl to be possessed of a pretty face and a graceful figure—although I wasn't slighted in either respect. She also needed to have a nimble wit and a tongue to meet all occasions.

TOM: What did you talk about?

[5] New York City's Metropolitan Opera House.
[6] A molded, jellylike dessert.

AMANDA: Things of importance going on in the world! Never anything coarse or common or vulgar. *(She addresses Tom as though he were seated in the vacant chair at the table though he remains by portieres. He plays this scene as though he held the book.)* My callers were gentlemen—all! Among my callers were some of the most prominent young planters of the Mississippi Delta—planters and sons of planters!

(Tom motions for music and a spot of light on Amanda.)
    (Her eyes lift, her face glows, her voice becomes rich and elegiac.)
    (Screen legend: "Où Sont les Neiges.")

There was young Champ Laughlin who later became vice-president of the Delta Planters Bank. Hadley Stevenson who was drowned in Moon Lake and left his widow one hundred and fifty thousand in Government bonds. There were the Cutrere brothers, Wesley and Bates. Bates was one of my bright particular beaux! He got in a quarrel with that wild Wainright boy. They shot it out on the floor of Moon Lake Casino. Bates was shot through the stomach. Died in the ambulance on his way to Memphis. His widow was also well-provided for, came into eight or ten thousand acres, that's all. She married him on the rebound—never loved her—carried my picture on him the night he died! And there was that boy that every girl in the Delta had set her cap for! That beautiful, brilliant young Fitzhugh boy from Greene County!

TOM: What did he leave his widow?

AMANDA: He never married! Gracious, you talk as though all of my old admirers had turned up their toes to the daisies!

TOM: Isn't this the first you mentioned that still survives?

AMANDA: That Fitzhugh boy went North and made a fortune—came to be known as the Wolf of Wall Street! He had the Midas touch, whatever he touched turned to gold! And I could have been Mrs. Duncan J. Fitzhugh, mind you! But— I picked your *father!*

LAURA *(rising)*:   Mother, let me clear the table.

AMANDA: No, dear, you go in front and study your typewriter chart. Or practice your shorthand a little. Stay fresh and pretty!—It's almost time for our gentlemen callers to start arriving. *(She flounces girlishly toward the kitchenette.)* How many do you suppose we're going to entertain this afternoon?

(Tom throws down the paper and jumps up with a groan.)

LAURA *(alone in the dining room)*:   I don't believe we're going to receive any, Mother.

AMANDA *(reappearing, airily)*:   What? No one—not one? You must be joking! *(Laura nervously echoes her laugh. She slips in a fugitive manner through the half-open portieres and draws them gently behind her. A shaft of very clear light is thrown on her face against the faded tapestry of the curtains. Music: "The Glass Menagerie" under faintly. Lightly.)* Not one gentleman caller? It can't be true! There must be a flood, there must have been a tornado!

LAURA: It isn't a flood, it's not a tornado, Mother. I'm just not popular like you were in Blue Mountain. . . . *(Tom utters another groan. Laura glances at him with a faint, apologetic smile. Her voice catching a little.)* Mother's afraid I'm going to be an old maid.

(The scene dims out with "Glass Menagerie" music.)

SCENE II

("Laura, Haven't You Ever Liked Some Boy?")
   (On the dark stage the screen is lighted with the image of blue roses.)
   (Gradually Laura's figure becomes apparent and the screen goes out.)
   (The music subsides.)
   (Laura is seated in the delicate ivory chair at the small clawfoot table.)
   (She wears a dress of soft violet material for a kimono—her hair tied back from her forehead with a ribbon.)
   (She is washing and polishing her collection of glass.)
   (Amanda appears on the fire escape steps. At the sound of her ascent, Laura catches her breath, thrusts the bowl of ornaments away and seats herself stiffly before the diagram of the typewriter keyboard as though it held her spellbound. Something has happened to Amanda. It is written in her face as she climbs to the landing: a look that is grim and hopeless and a little absurd.)
   (She has on one of those cheap or imitation velvety-looking cloth coats with imitation fur collar. Her hat is five or six years old, one of those dreadful cloche hats that were worn in the late twenties, and she is clasping an enormous black patent-leather pocketbook with nickel clasp and initials. This is her full-dress outfit, the one she usually wears to the D.A.R.[7])
   (Before entering she looks through the door.)
   (She purses her lips, opens her eyes wide, rolls them upward and shakes her head.)
   (Then she slowly lets herself in the door. Seeing her mother's expression Laura touches her lips with a nervous gesture.)

LAURA: Hello, Mother, I was—*(She makes a nervous gesture toward the chart on the wall. Amanda leans against the shut door and stares at Laura with a martyred look.)*

AMANDA: Deception? Deception? *(She slowly removes her hat and gloves, continuing the swift suffering stare. She lets the hat and gloves fall on the floor—a bit of acting.)*

LAURA *(shakily)*:   How was the D.A.R. meeting? *(Amanda slowly opens her purse and removes a dainty white handkerchief which she shakes out delicately and delicately touches to her lips and nostrils.)* Didn't you go to the D.A.R. meeting, Mother?

AMANDA *(faintly, almost inaudibly)*:—No.—No. *(Then more forcibly).* I did not have the strength—to go to the D.A.R. In fact, I did not have the courage! I wanted to find a hole in the ground and hide myself in it forever! *(She crosses slowly to the wall and removes the diagram of the typewriter keyboard. She holds it in front of her for a second, staring at it sweetly and sorrowfully—then bites her lips and tears it in two pieces.)*

LAURA *(faintly)*:   Why did you do that, Mother? *(Amanda repeats the same procedure with the chart of the Gregg Alphabet.)* Why are you—

AMANDA: Why? Why? How old are you, Laura?

LAURA: Mother, you know my age.

AMANDA: I thought that you were an adult; it seems that I was mistaken. *(She crosses slowly to the sofa and sinks down and stares at Laura.)*

---

[7] To a meeting of the Daughters of the American Revolution, a conservative, patriotic society for women whose ancestors fought in the Revolutionary War.

LAURA: Please don't stare at me, Mother.

(*Amanda closes her eyes and lowers her head. Count ten.*)

AMANDA: What are we going to do, what is going to become of us, what is the future?

(*Count ten.*)

LAURA: Has something happened, Mother? (*Amanda draws a long breath and takes out the handkerchief again. Dabbing process.*) Mother, has—something happened?

AMANDA: I'll be all right in a minute. I'm just bewildered—(*Count five.*)—by life. . . .

LAURA: Mother, I wish that you would tell me what's happened.

AMANDA: As you know, I was supposed to be inducted into my office at the D.A.R. this afternoon. (*Image: a swarm of typewriters.*) But I stopped off at Rubicam's Business College to speak to your teachers about your having a cold and ask them what progress they thought you were making down there.

LAURA: Oh. . . .

AMANDA: I went to the typing instructor and introduced myself as your mother. She didn't know who you were. Wingfield, she said. We don't have any such student enrolled at the school! I assured her she did, that you had been going to classes since early in January. "I wonder," she said, "if you could be talking about that terribly shy little girl who dropped out of school after only a few days' attendance?" "No," I said, "Laura, my daughter, has been going to school every day for the past six weeks!" "Excuse me," she said. She took the attendance book out and there was your name, unmistakably printed, and all the dates you were absent until they decided that you had dropped out of school. I still said, "No, there must have been some mistake! There must have been some mix-up in the records!" And she said, "No—I remember her perfectly now. Her hands shook so that she couldn't hit the right keys! The first time we gave a speed test, she broke down completely—was sick at the stomach and almost had to be carried into the wash-room! After that morning she never showed up any more. We phoned the house but never got any answer"—while I was working at Famous and Barr,[8] I suppose, demonstrating those—Oh! I felt so weak I could barely keep on my feet. I had to sit down while they got me a glass of water! Fifty dollars' tuition, all of our plans —my hopes and ambitions for you—just gone up the spout, just gone up the spout like that. (*Laura draws a long breath and gets awkwardly to her feet. She crosses to the victrola and winds it up.*) What are you doing?

LAURA: Oh! (*She releases the handle and returns to her seat.*)

AMANDA: Laura, where have you been going when you've gone out pretending that you were going to business college?

LAURA: I've just been going out walking.

AMANDA: That's not true.

LAURA: It is. I just went walking.

AMANDA: Walking? Walking? In winter? Deliberately courting pneumonia in that light coat? Where did you walk to, Laura?

LAURA: All sorts of places—mostly in the park.

AMANDA: Even after you'd started catching that cold?

---

[8] A St. Louis department store.

LAURA: It was the lesser of two evils, Mother. (*Image: winter scene in park.*) I couldn't go back up. I—threw up—on the floor!

AMANDA: From half past seven till after five every day you mean to tell me you walked around in the park, because you wanted to make me think that you were still going to Rubicam's Business College?

LAURA: It wasn't as bad as it sounds. I went inside places to get warmed up.

AMANDA: Inside where?

LAURA: I went in the art museum and the bird houses at the Zoo. I visited the penguins every day! Sometimes I did without lunch and went to the movies. Lately I've been spending most of my afternoons in the Jewel-box, that big glass house where they raise the tropical flowers.

AMANDA: You did all this to deceive me, just for the deception? (*Laura looks down.*) Why?

LAURA: Mother, when you're disappointed, you get that awful suffering look on your face, like the picture of Jesus' mother in the museum!

AMANDA: Hush!

LAURA: I couldn't face it.

(Pause. A whisper of strings.)
(Legend: "The Crust of Humility.")

AMANDA (*hopelessly fingering the huge pocketbook*):   So what are we going to do the rest of our lives? Stay home and watch the parades go by? Amuse ourselves with the glass menagerie, darling? Eternally play those worn-out phonograph records your father left as a painful reminder of him? We won't have a business career—we've given that up because it gave us nervous indigestion! (*Laughs wearily.*) What is there left but dependency all our lives? I know so well what becomes of unmarried women who aren't prepared to occupy a position. I've seen such pitiful cases in the South—barely tolerated spinsters living upon the grudging patronage of sister's husband or brother's wife!—stuck away in some little mousetrap of a room—encouraged by one in-law to visit another—little birdlike women without any nest—eating the crust of humility all their life! Is that the future that we've mapped out for ourselves? I swear it's the only alternative I can think of! It isn't a very pleasant alternative, is it? Of course—some girls do *marry*. (*Laura twists her hands nervously.*) Haven't you ever liked some boy?

LAURA: Yes. I liked one once. (*Rises.*) I came across his picture a while ago.

AMANDA (*with some interest*):   He gave you his picture?

LAURA: No, it's in the yearbook.

AMANDA (*disappointed*):   Oh—a high-school boy.

(Screen image: Jim as high school hero bearing a silver cup.)

LAURA: Yes. His name was Jim. (*Laura lifts the heavy annual from the clawfoot table.*) Here he is in *The Pirates of Penzance*.[9]

AMANDA (*absently*):   The what?

LAURA: The operetta the senior class put on. He had a wonderful voice and we sat across the aisle from each other Mondays, Wednesdays, and Fridays in the Aud. Here he is with the silver cup for debating! See his grin?

AMANDA (*absently*):   He must have had a jolly disposition.

LAURA: He used to call me—Blue Roses.

---

[9] A Gilbert and Sullivan comic light opera (1879).

(Image: blue roses.)

AMANDA: Why did he call you such a name as that?

LAURA: When I had that attack of pleurosis[10]—he asked me what was the matter when I came back. I said pleurosis—he thought that I said Blue Roses! So that's what he always called me after that. Whenever he saw me, he'd holler, "Hello, Blue Roses!" I didn't care for the girl that he went out with. Emily Meisenbach. Emily was the best-dressed girl at Soldan. She never struck me, though, as being sincere . . . It says in the Personal Section—they're engaged. That's— six years ago! They must be married by now.

AMANDA: Girls that aren't cut out for business careers usually wind up married to some nice man. *(Gets up with a spark of revival.)* Sister, that's what you'll do!

(Laura utters a startled, doubtful laugh. She reaches quickly for a piece of glass.)

LAURA: But, Mother—

AMANDA: Yes? *(Crossing to photograph.)*

LAURA *(in a tone of frightened apology)*:   I'm—crippled!

(Image: screen.)

AMANDA: Nonsense! Laura, I've told you never, never to use that word. Why, you're not crippled, you just have a little defect—hardly noticeable, even! When people have some slight disadvantage like that, they cultivate other things to make up for it—develop charm—and vivacity—and—*charm!* That's all you have to do! *(She turns again to the photograph.)* One thing your father had *plenty of*— was *charm!*

(Tom motions to the fiddle in the wings.)
  (The scene fades out with music.)

Scene III

(Legend on screen: "After the Fiasco—")
  (Tom speaks from the fire escape landing.)

TOM: After the fiasco at Rubicam's Business College, the idea of getting a gentleman caller for Laura began to play a more important part in Mother's calculations. It became an obsession. Like some archetype of the universal unconscious, the image of the gentleman caller haunted our small apartment. . . . *(Image: young man at door with flowers.)* An evening at home rarely passed without some allusion to this image, this specter, this hope. . . . Even when he wasn't mentioned, his presence hung in Mother's preoccupied look and in my sister's frightened, apologetic manner—hung like a sentence passed upon the Wingfields! Mother was a woman of action as well as words. She began to take logical steps in the planned direction. Late that winter and in the early spring—realizing that extra money would be needed to properly feather the nest and plume the bird—she conducted a vigorous campaign on the telephone, roping in subscribers to one of those magazines for matrons called *The Home-maker's Companion,* the type of journal that features the serialized sublimations of ladies of letters who think in terms of delicate cuplike breasts, slim, tapering waists,

---

[10] A respiratory inflammation.

rich, creamy thighs, eyes like wood smoke in autumn, fingers that soothe and caress like strains of music, bodies as powerful as Etruscan sculpture.

(Screen image: glamor magazine cover.)

(Amanda enters with phone on long extension cord. She is spotted in the dim stage.)

AMANDA: Ida Scott? This is Amanda Wingfield! We *missed* you at the D.A.R. last Monday! I said to myself: She's probably suffering with that sinus condition! How is that sinus condition? Horrors! Heaven have mercy!—You're a Christian martyr, yes, that's what you are, a Christian martyr! Well, I just now happened to notice that your subscription to the *Companion*'s about to expire! Yes, it expires with the next issue, honey!—just when that wonderful new serial by Bessie Mae Hopper is getting off to such an exciting start. Oh, honey, it's something that you can't miss! You remember how *Gone With the Wind* took everybody by storm? You simply couldn't go out if you hadn't read it. All everybody *talked* was Scarlett O'Hara. Well, this is a book that critics already compare to *Gone With the Wind*. It's the *Gone With the Wind* of the post-World War generation!—What?— Burning?—Oh, honey, don't let them burn, go take a look in the oven and I'll hold the wire! Heavens—I think she's hung up!

(Dim out.)

(Legend on screen: "You Think I'm in Love with Continental Shoemakers?")

(Before the stage is lighted, the violent voices of Tom and Amanda are heard.)

(They are quarreling behind the portieres. In front of them stands Laura with clenched hands and panicky expression.)

(A clear pool of light on her figure throughout this scene.)

TOM: What in Christ's name am I—

AMANDA (*shrilly*): Don't you use that—

TOM: Supposed to do!

AMANDA: Expression! Not in my—

TOM: Ohhh!

AMANDA: Presence! Have you gone out of your senses?

TOM: I have, that's true, *driven* out!

AMANDA: What is the matter with you, you—big—big—IDIOT!

TOM: Look—I've got *no thing,* no single thing—

AMANDA: Lower your voice!

TOM: In my life here that I can call my OWN! Everything is—

AMANDA: Stop that shouting!

TOM: Yesterday you confiscated my books! You had the nerve to—

AMANDA: I took that horrible novel back to the library—yes! That hideous book by that insane Mr. Lawrence.[11] (*Tom laughs wildly.*) I cannot control the output of diseased minds or people who cater to them— (*Tom laughs still more wildly.*) BUT I WON'T ALLOW SUCH FILTH BROUGHT INTO MY HOUSE! No, no, no, no, no!

TOM: House, house! Who pays rent on it, who makes a slave of himself to—

AMANDA (*fairly screeching*) Don't you DARE to—

TOM: No, no, *I* musn't say things! *I've* got to just—

AMANDA: Let me tell you—

TOM: I don't want to hear any more! (*He tears the portieres open. The upstage area is lit with a turgid smoky red glow.*)

---

[11] D. H. Lawrence (1885–1930), an English poet and fiction writer.

(Amanda's hair is in metal curlers and she wears a very old bathrobe, much too large for her slight figure, a relic of the faithless Mr. Wingfield.)

(An upright typewriter and a wild disarray of manuscripts are on the dropleaf table. The quarrel was probably precipitated by Amanda's interruption of his creative labor. A chair lying overthrown on the floor.)

(Their gesticulating shadows are cast on the ceiling by the fiery glow.)

AMANDA: You *will* hear more, you—

TOM: No, I won't hear more, I'm going out!

AMANDA: You come right back in—

TOM: Out, out out! Because I'm—

AMANDA: Come back here, Tom Wingfield! I'm not through talking to you!

TOM: Oh, go—

LAURA *(desperately)*: Tom!

AMANDA: You're going to listen, and no more insolence from you! I'm at the end of my patience! *(He comes back toward her.)*

TOM: What do you think I'm at? Aren't I supposed to have any patience to reach the end of, Mother? I know, I know. It seems unimportant to you, what I'm *doing*—what I *want* to do—having a little *difference* between them! You don't think that—

AMANDA: I think you've been doing things that you're ashamed of. That's why you act like this. I don't believe that you go every night to the movies. Nobody goes to the movies night after night. Nobody in their right minds goes to the movies as often as you pretend to. People don't go to the movies at nearly midnight, and movies don't let out at two A.M. Come in stumbling. Muttering to yourself like a maniac! You get three hours' sleep and then go to work. Oh, I can picture the way you're doing down there. Moping, doping, because you're in no condition.

TOM *(wildly)*:   No, I'm in no condition!

AMANDA: What right have you got to jeopardize your job? Jeopardize the security of us all? How do you think we'd manage if you were—

TOM: Listen! You think I'm crazy *about* the *warehouse*? *(He bends fiercely toward her slight figure.)* You think I'm in love with the Continental Shoemakers? You think I want to spend fifty-five *years* down there in that—*celotex interior!* with—*fluorescent—tubes!* Look! I'd rather somebody picked up a crowbar and battered out my brains—than go back mornings! I *go!* Every time you come in yelling that God damn *"Rise and Shine!" "Rise and Shine!"* I say to myself, "How *lucky dead* people are!" But I get up. I *go!* For sixty-five dollars a month I give up all that I dream of doing and being *ever!* And you say self—*self*'s all I ever think of. Why, listen, if self is what I thought of, Mother, I'd be where he is—GONE! *(Pointing to father's picture.)* As far as the system of transportation reaches! *(He starts past her. She grabs his arm.)* Don't grab at me, Mother!

AMANDA: Where are you going?

TOM: I'm going to the *movies!*

AMANDA: I don't believe that lie!

TOM *(Crouching toward her, overtowering her tiny figure. She backs away, gasping.)*:   I'm going to opium dens! Yes, opium dens, dens of vice and criminals' hangouts, Mother. I've joined the Hogan gang,[12] I'm a hired assassin, I carry a tommy-gun in a violin case! I run a string of cathouses in the Valley! They

[12] A major criminal organization in St. Louis in the 1930s.

call me Killer, Killer Wingfield, I'm leading a double life, a simple, honest ware-house worker by day, by night, a dynamic *czar* of the *underworld, Mother.* I go to gambling casinos, I spin away fortunes on the roulette table! I wear a patch over one eye and a false mustache, sometimes I put on green whiskers. On those occa-sions they call me—*El Diablo!*[13] Oh, I could tell you things to make you sleep-less! My enemies plan to dynamite this place. They're going to blow us all sky-high some night! I'll be glad, very happy, and so will you! You'll go up, up on a broomstick, over Blue Mountain with seventeen gentlemen callers! You ugly—babbling old—*witch* . . . . (*He goes through a series of violent, clumsy move-ments, seizing his overcoat, lunging to the door, pulling it fiercely open. The women watch him, aghast. His arm catches in the sleeve of the coat as he strug-gles to pull it on. For a moment he is pinioned by the bulky garment. With an outraged groan he tears the coat off again, splitting the shoulders of it, and hurls it across the room. It strikes against the shelf of Laura's glass collection, there is a tinkle of shattering glass. Laura cries out as if wounded.*)

(*Music legend: "The Glass Menagerie."*)

   LAURA (*shrilly*):   My glass!—menagerie. . . . (*She covers her face and turns away.*)

(*But Amanda is still stunned and stupefied by the "ugly witch" so that she barely notices this occurrence. Now she recovers her speech.*)

   AMANDA (*in an awful voice*):   I won't speak to you—until you apologize! (*She crosses through portieres and draws them together behind her. Tom is left with Laura. Laura clings weakly to the mantel with her face averted. Tom stares at her stupidly for a moment. Then he crosses to shelf. Drops awkwardly to his knees to collect the fallen glass, glancing at Laura as if he would speak but couldn't.*)

(*"The Glass Menagerie" steals in as the scene dims out.*)

SCENE IV

(*The interior is dark. Faint light in the alley.*)
   (*A deep-voiced bell in a church is tolling the hour of five as the scene com-mences.*)
   (*Tom appears at the top of the alley. After each solemn boom of the bell in the tower, he shakes a little noisemaker or rattle as if to express the tiny spasm of man in contrast to the sustained power and dignity of the Almighty. This and the un-steadiness of his advance make it evident that he has been drinking.*)
   (*As he climbs the few steps to the fire escape landing light steals up inside. Laura appears in nightdress, observing Tom's empty bed in the front room.*)
   (*Tom fishes in his pockets for the door key, removing a motley assortment of articles in the search, including a perfect shower of movie ticket stubs and an empty bottle. At last he finds the key, but just as he is about to insert it, it slips from his fingers. He strikes a match and crouches below the door.*)

   TOM (*bitterly*):   One crack—and it falls through!

---

[13] "The Devil" (Spanish).

(*Laura opens the door.*)

LAURA: Tom! Tom, what are you doing?

TOM: Looking for a door key.

LAURA: Where have you been all this time?

TOM: I have been to the movies.

LAURA: All this time at the movies?

TOM: There was a very long program. There was a Garbo picture and a Mickey Mouse and a travelogue and a newsreel and a preview of coming attractions. And there was an organ solo and a collection for the milk fund—simultaneously—which ended up in a terrible fight between a fat lady and an usher!

LAURA (*innocently*): Did you have to stay through everything?

TOM: Of course! And, oh, I forgot! There was a big stage show! The headliner on this stage show was Malvolio the Magician. He performed wonderful tricks, many of them, such as pouring water back and forth between pitchers. First it turned to wine and then it turned to beer and then it turned to whiskey. I know it was whiskey it finally turned into because he needed somebody to come up out of the audience to help him, and I came up—both shows! It was Kentucky Straight Bourbon. A very generous fellow, he gave souvenirs. (*He pulls from his back pocket a shimmering rainbow-colored scarf.*) He gave me this. This is his magic scarf. You can have it, Laura. You wave it over a canary cage and you get a bowl of goldfish. You wave it over the goldfish bowl and they fly away canaries. . . . But the wonderfullest trick of all was the coffin trick. We nailed him into a coffin and he got out of the coffin without removing one nail. (*He has come inside.*) There is a trick that would come in handy for me—get me out of this 2 by 4 situation! (*Flops onto bed and starts removing shoes.*)

LAURA: Tom—Shhh!

TOM: What you shushing me for?

LAURA: You'll wake up Mother.

TOM: Goody, goody! Pay 'er back for all those "Rise an' Shines." (*Lies down, groaning.*) You know it don't take much intelligence to get yourself into a nailed-up coffin, Laura. But who in hell ever got himself out of one without removing one nail?

(*As if in answer, the father's grinning photograph lights up.*)

(*Scene dims out.*)

(*Immediately following: The church bell is heard striking six. At the sixth stroke the alarm clock goes off in Amanda's room, and after a few moments we hear her calling: "Rise and Shine! Rise and Shine! Laura, go tell your brother to rise and shine!"*)

TOM (*sitting up slowly*): I'll rise—but I won't shine.

(*The light increases.*)

AMANDA: Laura, tell your brother his coffee is ready.

(*Laura slips into front room.*)

LAURA: Tom! it's nearly seven. Don't make Mother nervous. (*He stares at her stupidly. Beseechingly.*) Tom, speak to Mother this morning. Make up with her, apologize, speak to her!

TOM: She won't to me. It's her that started not speaking.

LAURA: If you just say you're sorry she'll start speaking.

TOM: Her not speaking—is that such a tragedy?

LAURA: Please—please!

AMANDA *(calling from kitchenette)*:   Laura, are you going to do what I asked you to do, or do I have to get dressed and go out myself?

LAURA: Going, going—soon as I get on my coat! *(She pulls on a shapeless felt hat with nervous, jerky movement, pleadingly glancing at Tom. Rushes awkwardly for coat. The coat is one of Amanda's, inaccurately made over, the sleeves too short for Laura.)* Butter and what else?

AMANDA *(entering upstage)*:   Just butter. Tell them to charge it.

LAURA: Mother, they make such faces when I do that.

AMANDA: Sticks and stones may break my bones, but the expression on Mr. Garfinkel's face won't harm us! Tell your brother his coffee is getting cold.

LAURA *(at door)*:   Do what I asked you, will you, will you, Tom?

(He looks sullenly away.)

AMANDA: Laura, go now or just don't go at all!

LAURA *(rushing out)*:   Going—going! *(A second later she cries out. Tom springs up and crosses to the door. Amanda rushes anxiously in. Tom opens the door.)*

TOM: Laura?

LAURA: I'm all right. I slipped, but I'm all right.

AMANDA *(peering anxiously after her)*:   If anyone breaks a leg on those fire escape steps, the landlord ought to be sued for every cent he possesses! *(She shuts door. Remembers she isn't speaking and returns to other room.)*

(As Tom enters listlessly for his coffee, she turns her back to him and stands rigidly facing the window on the gloomy gray vault of the areaway. Its light on her face with its aged but childish features is cruelly sharp, satirical as a Daumier[14] print.)

(Music under: "Ave Maria.")

(Tom glances sheepishly but sullenly at her averted figure and slumps at the table. The coffee is scalding hot; he sips it and gasps and spits it back in the cup. At his gasp, Amanda catches her breath and half turns. Then catches herself and turns back to window.)

(Tom blows on his coffee, glancing sidewise at his mother. She clears her throat. Tom clears his. He starts to rise. Sinks back down again, scratches his head, clears his throat again. Amanda coughs. Tom raises his cup in both hands to blow on it, his eyes staring over the rim of it at his mother for several moments. Then he slowly sets the cup down and awkwardly and hesitantly rises from the chair.)

TOM *(hoarsely)*:   Mother. I—I apologize. Mother. *(Amanda draws a quick, shuddering breath. Her face works grotesquely. She breaks into childlike tears.)* I'm sorry for what I said, for everything that I said, I didn't mean it.

AMANDA *(sobbingly)*:   My devotion has made me a witch and so I make myself hateful to my children!

TOM: *No, you don't.*

AMANDA: I worry so much, don't sleep, it makes me nervous!

TOM *(gently)*:   I understand that.

[14] Honoré Daumier (1808–1879), a French caricaturist.

AMANDA: I've had to put up a solitary battle all these years. But you're my right-hand bower![15] Don't fall down, don't fail!

TOM (*gently*):   I try, Mother.

AMANDA (*with great enthusiasm*):   Try and you will SUCCEED! (*The notion makes her breathless.*) Why, you—you're just *full* of natural endowments! Both of my children—they're *unusual* children! Don't you think I know it? I'm so— *proud!* Happy and—feel I've—so much to be thankful for but—Promise me one thing, son!

TOM: What, Mother?

AMANDA: Promise, son, you'll—never be a drunkard!

TOM (*turns to her grinning*):   I will never be a drunkard, Mother.

AMANDA: That's what frightened me, so, that you'd be drinking! Eat a bowl of Purina!

TOM: Just coffee, Mother.

AMANDA: Shredded wheat biscuit?

TOM: No, no, Mother, just coffee.

AMANDA: You can't put in a day's work on an empty stomach. You've got ten minutes—don't gulp! Drinking too-hot liquids makes cancer of the stomach. . . . Put cream in.

TOM: No, thank you.

AMANDA: To cool it.

TOM: No! No, thank you, I want it black.

AMANDA: I know, but it's not good for you. We have to do all that we can to build ourselves up. In these trying times we live in, all that we have to cling to is—each other. . . . That's why it's so important to—Tom, I—I sent out your sister so I could discuss something with you. If you hadn't spoken I would have spoken to you. (*Sits down.*)

TOM (*gently*):   What is it, Mother, that you want to discuss?

AMANDA: *Laura!*

(*Tom puts his cup down slowly.*)
    (*Legend on screen: "Laura."*)
    (*Music: "The Glass Menagerie."*)

TOM: —Oh.—Laura . . .

AMANDA (*touching his sleeve*):   You know how Laura is. So quiet but—still water runs deep! She notices things and I think she—broods about them. (*Tom looks up.*) A few days ago I came in and she was crying.

TOM: What about?

AMANDA: You.

TOM: Me?

AMANDA: She has an idea that you're not happy here.

TOM: What gave her that idea?

AMANDA: What gives her any idea? However, you do act strangely. I—I'm not criticizing, understand *that!* I know your ambitions do not lie in the ware-house, that like everybody in the whole wide world —you've had to—make sacri-fices, but—Tom—Tom—life's not easy, it calls for—Spartan endurance! There's so many things in my heart that I cannot describe to you! I've never told you but I—*loved your father.* . . .

[15] An anchor at the front of a ship.

TOM (*gently*):   I know that, Mother.

AMANDA: And you—when I see you taking after his ways! Staying out late— and—well, you *had* been drinking the night you were in that—terrifying condition! Laura says that you hate the apartment and that you go out nights to get away from it! Is that true, Tom?

TOM: No. You say there's so much in your heart that you can't describe to me. That's true of me, too. There's so much in my heart that I can't describe to *you!* So let's respect each other's—

AMANDA: But, why—*why*, Tom—are you always so *restless?* Where do you go to, nights?

TOM: I—go to the movies.

AMANDA: Why do you go to the movies so much, Tom?

TOM: I go to the movies because—I like adventure. Adventure is something I don't have much of at work, so I go to the movies.

AMANDA: But, Tom, you go to the movies *entirely* too *much!*

TOM: I like a lot of adventure.

(*Amanda looks baffled, then hurt. As the familiar inquisition resumes he becomes hard and impatient again. Amanda slips back into her querulous attitude toward him.*)

(*Image on screen: sailing vessel with Jolly Roger.*[16])

AMANDA: Most young men find adventure in their careers.

TOM: Then most young men are not employed in a warehouse.

AMANDA: The world is full of young men employed in warehouses and offices and factories.

TOM: Do all of them find adventure in their careers?

AMANDA: They do or they do without it! Not everybody has a craze for adventure.

TOM: Man is by instinct a lover, a hunter, a fighter, and none of those instincts are given much play at the warehouse!

AMANDA: Man is by instinct! Don't quote instinct to me! Instinct is something that people have got away from! It belongs to animals! Christian adults don't want it!

TOM: What do Christian adults want, then, Mother?

AMANDA: Superior things! Things of the mind and the spirit! Only animals have to satisfy instincts! Surely your aims are somewhat higher than theirs! Than monkeys—pigs—

TOM: I reckon they're not.

AMANDA: You're joking. However, that isn't what I wanted to discuss.

TOM (*rising*): I haven't much time.

AMANDA (*pushing his shoulders*): Sit down.

TOM: You want me to punch in red[17] at the warehouse, Mother?

AMANDA: You have five minutes. I want to talk about Laura.

(*Legend: "Plans and Provisions."*)

TOM: All right! What about Laura?

AMANDA: We have to be making plans and provisions for her. She's older than

---

[16] The pirates' flag, black with white skull and crossbones.   [17] Arrive late for work.

you, two years, and nothing has happened. She just drifts along doing nothing. It frightens me terribly how she just drifts along.

TOM: I guess she's the type that people call home girls.

AMANDA: There's no such type, and if there is, it's a pity! That is unless the home is hers, with a husband!

TOM: What?

AMANDA: Oh, I can see the handwriting on the wall as plain as I see the nose in front of my face! It's terrifying! More and more you remind me of your father! He was out all hours without explanation—Then *left! Goodbye!* And me with a bag to hold. I saw that letter you got from the Merchant Marine. I know what you're dreaming of. I'm not standing here blindfolded. Very well, then. Then *do* it! But not till there's somebody to take your place.

TOM: What do you mean?

AMANDA: I mean that as soon as Laura has got somebody to take care of her, married, a home of her own, independent—why, then you'll be free to go wherever you please, on land, on sea, whichever way the wind blows you! But until that time you've got to look out for your sister. I don't say me because I'm old and don't matter! I say for your sister because she's young and dependent. I put her in business college—a dismal failure! Frightened her so it made her sick to her stomach. I took her over to the Young People's League at the church. Another fiasco. She spoke to nobody, nobody spoke to her. Now all she does is fool with those pieces of glass and play those worn-out records. What kind of a life is that for a girl to lead!

TOM: What can I do about it?

AMANDA: Overcome selfishness! Self, self, self is all that you ever think of! (*Tom springs up and crosses to get his coat. It is ugly and bulky. He pulls on a cap with earmuffs.*) Where is your muffler? Put your wool muffler on! (*He snatches it angrily from the closet and tosses it around his neck and pulls both ends tight.*) Tom! I haven't said what I had in mind to ask you.

TOM: I'm too late to—

AMANDA (*Catching his arms—very importunately. Then shyly*): Down at the warehouse, aren't there some—nice young men?

TOM: No!

AMANDA: There *must* be—*some* . . .

TOM: Mother—

(*Gesture.*)

AMANDA: Find out one that's clean-living—doesn't drink and—ask him out for sister!

TOM: What?

AMANDA: For *sister!* To *meet!* Get *acquainted!*

TOM (*stamping to door*): Oh, my go-osh!

AMANDA: Will you? (*He opens door. Imploringly.*) Will you? (*He starts down.*) Will you? *Will* you, dear?

TOM (*calling back*): YES!

(*Amanda closes the door hesitantly and with a troubled but faintly hopeful expression.*)
(*Screen image: glamor magazine cover.*)
(*Spot*[18] *Amanda at phone.*)

[18] Spotlight on.

AMANDA: Ella Cartwright? This is Amanda Wingfield! How are you, honey? How is that kidney condition? (*Count five.*) *Horrors!* (*Count five.*) You're a Christian martyr, yes, honey, that's what you are, a Christian martyr! Well, I just happened to notice in my little red book that your subscription to the *Companion* has just run out! I knew that you wouldn't want to miss out on the wonderful serial starting in this new issue. It's by Bessie Mae Hopper, the first thing she's written since *Honeymoon for Three.* Wasn't that a strange and interesting story? Well, this one is even lovelier, I believe. It has a sophisticated society background. It's all about the horsey set on Long Island!

(*Fade out.*)

SCENE V

(*Legend on screen: "Annunciation." Fade with music.*)
    (*It is early dusk of a spring evening. Supper has just been finished in the Wing-field apartment. Amanda and Laura in light colored dresses are removing dishes from the table, in the upstage area, which is shadowy, their movements formal-ized almost as a dance or ritual, their moving forms as pale and silent as moths.*)
    (*Tom, in white shirt and trousers, rises from the table and crosses toward the fire escape.*)

AMANDA (*as he passes her*): Son, will you do me a favor?
TOM: What?
AMANDA: Comb your hair! You look so pretty when your hair is combed! (*Tom slouches on sofa with evening paper. Enormous caption "Franco*[19] *Tri-umphs."*) There is only one respect in which I would like you to emulate your father.
TOM: What respect is that?
AMANDA: The care he always took of his appearance. He never allowed him-self to look untidy. (*He throws down the paper and crosses to fire escape.*) Where are you going?
TOM: I'm going out to smoke.
AMANDA: You smoke too much. A pack a day at fifteen cents a pack. How much would that amount to in a month? Thirty times fifteen is how much, Tom? Figure it out and you will be astounded at what you could save. Enough to give you a night school course in accounting at Washington U! Just think what a won-derful thing that would be for you, son!

(*Tom is unmoved by the thought.*)

TOM: I'd rather smoke. (*He steps out on landing, letting the screen door slam.*)
AMANDA (*sharply*): I know! That's the tragedy of it. . . . (*Alone, she turns to look at her husband's picture.*)

(*Dance music: "All the World is Waiting for the Sunrise!"*)

TOM (*to the audience*): Across the alley from us was the Paradise Dance Hall. On evenings in spring the windows and doors were open and the music came

---

[19] Francisco Franco (1892–1975), Fascist Spanish dictator who came to power after the Spanish civil war.

outdoors. Sometimes the lights were turned out except for a large glass sphere that hung from the ceiling. It would turn slowly about and filter the dusk with delicate rainbow colors. Then the orchestra played a waltz or a tango, something that had a slow and sensuous rhythm. Couples would come outside, to the relative privacy of the alley. You could see them kissing behind ash-pits and telephone poles. This was the compensation for lives that passed like mine, without any change or adventure. Adventure and change were imminent in this year. They were waiting around the corner for all these kids. Suspended in the mist over Berchtesgaden,[20] caught in the folds of Chamberlain's umbrella—In Spain there was Guernica! But here there was only hot swing music and liquor, dance halls, bars, and movies, and sex that hung in the gloom like a chandelier and flooded the world with brief, deceptive rainbows. . . . All the world was waiting for bombardments!

(Amanda turns from the picture and comes outside.)

AMANDA *(sighing)*: A fire escape landing's a poor excuse for a porch. *(She spreads a newspaper on a step and sits down, gracefully and demurely as if she were settling into a swing on a Mississippi veranda.)* What are you looking at?

TOM: The moon.

AMANDA: Is there a moon this evening?

TOM: It's rising over Garfinkel's Delicatessen.

AMANDA: So it is! A little silver slipper of a moon. Have you made a wish on it yet?

TOM: Um-hum.

AMANDA: What did you wish for?

TOM: That's a secret.

AMANDA: A secret, huh? Well, I won't tell mine either. I will be just as mysterious as you.

TOM: I bet I can guess what yours is.

AMANDA: Is my head so transparent?

TOM: You're not a sphinx.

AMANDA: No, I don't have secrets. I'll tell you what I wished for on the moon. Success and happiness for my precious children! I wish for that whenever there's a moon, and when there isn't a moon, I wish for it, too.

TOM: I thought perhaps you wished for a gentleman caller.

AMANDA: Why do you say that?

TOM: Don't you remember asking me to fetch one?

AMANDA: I remember suggesting that it would be nice for your sister if you brought home some nice young man from the warehouse. I think I've made that suggestion more than once.

TOM: Yes, you have made it repeatedly.

AMANDA: Well?

TOM: We are going to have one.

AMANDA: *What?*

TOM: A gentleman caller!

(The annunciation is celebrated with music.)
   (Amanda rises.)

---

[20] The German town where the British prime minister Neville Chamberlain met with Adolph Hitler and signed the Munich Pact to avoid World War II; Chamberlain and the umbrella he carried became symbolic of unsuccessful attempts to pacify evil forces.

(Image on screen: caller with bouquet.)

AMANDA: You mean you have asked some nice young man to come over?

TOM: Yep. I've asked him to dinner.

AMANDA: You really did?

TOM: I did!

AMANDA: You did, and did he—*accept?*

TOM: He did!

AMANDA: Well, well—well, well! That's—lovely!

TOM: I thought that you would be pleased.

AMANDA: It's definite, then?

TOM: Very definite.

AMANDA: Soon?

TOM: Very soon.

AMANDA: For heaven's sake, stop putting on and tell me some things, will you?

TOM: What things do you want me to tell you?

AMANDA: *Naturally* I would like to know when he's *coming!*

TOM: He's coming tomorrow.

AMANDA: *Tomorrow?*

TOM: Yep. Tomorrow.

AMANDA: But, Tom!

TOM: Yes, Mother?

AMANDA: Tomorrow gives me no time!

TOM: Time for what?

AMANDA: Preparations! Why didn't you phone me at once, as soon as you asked him, the minute that he accepted? Then, don't you see, I could have been getting ready!

TOM: You don't have to make any fuss.

AMANDA: Oh, Tom, Tom, Tom, of course I have to make a fuss! I want things nice, not sloppy! Not thrown together. I'll certainly have to do some fast thinking, won't I?

TOM: I don't see why you have to think at all.

AMANDA: You just don't know. We can't have a gentleman caller in a pigsty! All my wedding silver has to be polished, the monogrammed table linen ought to be laundered! The windows have to be washed and fresh curtains put up. And how about clothes? We have to *wear* something, don't we?

TOM: Mother, this boy is no one to make a fuss over!

AMANDA: Do you realize he's the first young man we've introduced to your sister? It's terrible, dreadful, disgraceful that poor little sister has never received a single gentleman caller! Tom, come inside! (*She opens the screen door.*)

TOM: What for?

AMANDA: I want to ask you some things.

TOM: If you're going to make such a fuss, I'll call it off, I'll tell him not to come.

AMANDA: You certainly won't do anything of the kind. Nothing offends people worse than broken engagements. It simply means I'll have to work like a Turk! We won't be brilliant, but we'll pass inspection. Come on inside. (*Tom follows, groaning.*) Sit down.

TOM: Any particular place you would like me to sit?

AMANDA: Thank heavens I've got that new sofa! I'm also making payments on a floor lamp I'll have sent out! And put the chintz covers on, they'll brighten things up! Of course I'd hoped to have these walls repapered. . . . What is the young man's name?

TOM: His name is O'Connor.

AMANDA: That, of course, means fish—tomorrow is Friday![21] I'll have that salmon loaf—with Durkee's dressing! What does he do? He works at the warehouse?

TOM: Of course! How else would I—

AMANDA: Tom, he—doesn't drink?

TOM: Why do you ask me that?

AMANDA: Your father *did!*

TOM: Don't get started on that!

AMANDA: He *does* drink, then?

TOM: Not that I know of!

AMANDA: Make sure, be certain! The last thing I want for my daughter's a boy who drinks!

TOM: Aren't you being a little premature? Mr. O'Connor has not yet appeared on the scene!

AMANDA: But will tomorrow. To meet your sister, and what do I know about his character? Nothing! Old maids are better off than wives of drunkards!

TOM: Oh, my God!

AMANDA: Be still!

TOM (*leaning forward to whisper*): Lots of fellows meet girls whom they don't marry!

AMANDA: Oh, talk sensibly, Tom—and don't be sarcastic! (*She has gotten a hairbrush.*)

TOM: What are you doing?

AMANDA: I'm brushing that cowlick down! What is this young man's position at the warehouse?

TOM (*submitting grimly to the brush and the interrogation*): This young man's position is that of a shipping clerk, Mother.

AMANDA: Sounds to me like a fairly responsible job, the sort of a job *you* would be in if you just had more *get-up*. What is his salary? Have you got any idea?

TOM: I would judge it to be approximately eighty-five dollars a month.

AMANDA: Well—not princely, but—

TOM: Twenty more than I make.

AMANDA: Yes, how well I know! But for a family man, eighty-five dollars a month is not much more than you can just get by on. . . .

TOM: Yes, but Mr. O'Connor is not a family man.

AMANDA: He might be, mightn't he? Some time in the future?

TOM: I see. Plans and provisions.

AMANDA: You are the only young man that I know of who ignores the fact that the future becomes the present, the present the past, and the past turns into everlasting regret if you don't plan for it!

TOM: I will think that over and see what I can make of it.

AMANDA: Don't be supercilious with your mother! Tell me some more about this—what do you call him?

---

[21] Catholics were then prohibited from eating meat on Fridays.

TOM: James D. O'Connor. The D. is for Delaney.

AMANDA: Irish on *both* sides! *Gracious!* And doesn't drink?

TOM: Shall I call him up and ask him right this minute?

AMANDA: The only way to find out about those things is to make discreet inquiries at the proper moment. When I was a girl in Blue Mountain and it was suspected that a young man drank, the girl whose attentions he had been receiving, if any girl *was*, would sometimes speak to the minister of his church, or rather her father would if her father was living, and sort of feel him out on the young man's character. That is the way such things are discreetly handled to keep a young woman from making a tragic mistake!

TOM: Then how did you happen to make a tragic mistake?

AMANDA: That innocent look of your father's had everyone fooled! He *smiled*—the world was *enchanted!* No girl can do worse than put herself at the mercy of a handsome appearance! I hope that Mr. O'Connor is not too good-looking.

TOM: No, he's not too good-looking. He's covered with freckles and hasn't too much of a nose.

AMANDA: He's not right-down homely, though?

TOM: Not right-down homely. Just medium homely, I'd say.

AMANDA: Character's what to look for in a man.

TOM: That's what I've always said, Mother.

AMANDA: You've never said anything of the kind and I suspect you would never give it a thought.

TOM: Don't be suspicious of me.

AMANDA: At least I hope he's the type that's up and coming.

TOM: I think he really goes in for self-improvement.

AMANDA: What reason have you to think so?

TOM: He goes to night school.

AMANDA (*beaming*): Splendid! What does he do, I mean study?

TOM: Radio engineering and public speaking!

AMANDA: Then he has visions of being advanced in the world! Any young man who studies public speaking is aiming to have an executive job some day! And radio engineering? A thing for the future! Both of these facts are very illuminating. Those are the sort of things that a mother should know concerning any young man who comes to call on her daughter. Seriously or—not.

TOM: One little warning. He doesn't know about Laura. I didn't let on that we had dark ulterior motives. I just said, why don't you come have dinner with us? He said okay and that was the whole conversation.

AMANDA: I bet it was! You're eloquent as an oyster. However, he'll know about Laura when he gets here. When he sees how lovely and sweet and pretty she is, he'll thank his lucky stars he was asked to dinner.

TOM: Mother, you mustn't expect too much of Laura.

AMANDA: What do you mean?

TOM: Laura seems all those things to you and me because she's ours and we love her. We don't even notice she's crippled anymore.

AMANDA: Don't say crippled! You know that I never allow that word to be used!

TOM: But face facts, Mother. She is and—that's not all—

AMANDA: What do you mean "not all"?

TOM: Laura is very different from other girls.

AMANDA: I think the difference is all to her advantage.

TOM: Not quite all—in the eyes of others—strangers—she's terribly shy and lives in a world of her own and those things make her seem a little peculiar to people outside the house.

AMANDA: Don't say peculiar.

TOM: Face the facts. She is.

(The dance-hall music changes to a tango that has a minor and somewhat ominous tone.)

AMANDA: In what way is she peculiar—may I ask?

TOM *(gently)*: She lives in a world of her own—a world of—little glass ornaments, Mother. . . . *(Gets up. Amanda remains holding brush, looking at him, troubled.)* She plays old phonograph records and—that's about all—*(He glances at himself in the mirror and crosses to door.)*

AMANDA *(sharply)*: Where are you going?

TOM: I'm going to the movies. *(Out screen door.)*

AMANDA: Not to the movies, every night to the movies! *(Follows quickly to screen door.)* I don't believe you always go to the movies! *(He is gone. Amanda looks worriedly after him for a moment. Then vitality and optimism return and she turns from the door. Crossing to portieres.)* Laura! Laura! *(Laura answers from kitchenette.)*

LAURA: Yes, Mother.

AMANDA: Let those dishes go and come in front! *(Laura appears with dish towel. Gaily.)* Laura, come here and make a wish on the moon!

LAURA *(entering)*: Moon—moon?

AMANDA: A little silver slipper of a moon. Look over your left shoulder, Laura, and make a wish! *(Laura looks faintly puzzled as if called out of sleep. Amanda seizes her shoulders and turns her at an angle by the door.)* Now! Now, darling, *wish!*

LAURA: What shall I wish for, Mother?

AMANDA *(her voice trembling and her eyes suddenly filling with tears)*: Happiness! Good Fortune!

(The violin rises and the stage dims out.)

SCENE VI

(Image: high school hero.)

TOM: And so the following evening I brought Jim home to dinner. I had known Jim slightly in high school. In high school Jim was a hero. He had tremendous Irish good nature and vitality with the scrubbed and polished look of white chinaware. He seemed to move in a continual spotlight. He was a star in basketball, captain of the debating club, president of the senior class and the glee club and he sang the male lead in the annual light operas. He was always running or bounding, never just walking. He seemed always at the point of defeating the law of gravity. He was shooting with such velocity through his adolescence that you would logically expect him to arrive at nothing short of the White House by the time he was thirty. But Jim apparently ran into more interference after his graduation from Soldan. His speed had definitely slowed. Six years after he left high school he was holding a job that wasn't much better than mine.

(Image: clerk.)

He was the only one at the warehouse with whom I was on friendly terms. I was valuable to him as someone who could remember his former glory, who had seen him win basketball games and the silver cup in debating. He knew of my secret practice of retiring to a cabinet of the washroom to work on poems when business was slack in the warehouse. He called me Shakespeare. And while the other boys in the warehouse regarded me with suspicious hostility, Jim took a humorous attitude toward me. Gradually his attitude affected the others, their hostility wore off and they also began to smile at me as people smile at an oddly fashioned dog who trots across their path at some distance.

I knew that Jim and Laura had known each other at Soldan, and I had heard Laura speak admiringly of his voice. I didn't know if Jim remembered her or not. In high school Laura had been as unobtrusive as Jim had been astonishing. If he did remember Laura, it was not as my sister, for when I asked him to dinner, he grinned and said, "You know, Shakespeare, I never thought of you as having folks!"

He was about to discover that I did. . . .

(Light up stage.)
    (Legend on screen: "The Accent of a Coming Foot.")
    (Friday evening. It is about five o'clock of a late spring evening which comes "scattering poems in the sky.")
    (A delicate lemony light is in the Wingfield apartment.)
    (Amanda has worked like a Turk in preparation for the gentleman caller. The results are astonishing. The new floor lamp with its rose-silk shade is in place, a colored paper lantern conceals the broken light fixture in the ceiling, new billowing white curtains are at the windows, chintz covers are on chairs and sofa, a pair of new sofa pillows make their initial appearance.)
    (Open boxes and tissue paper are scattered on the floor.)
    (Laura stands in the middle with lifted arms while Amanda crouches before her, adjusting the hem of the new dress, devout and ritualistic. The dress is colored and designed by memory. The arrangement of Laura's hair is changed; it is softer and more becoming. A fragile, unearthly prettiness has come out in Laura: she is like a piece of translucent glass touched by light, given a momentary radiance, not actual, not lasting.)

AMANDA *(impatiently)*: Why are you trembling?
LAURA: Mother, you've made me so nervous!
AMANDA: How have I made you nervous?
LAURA: By all this fuss! You make it seem so important!
AMANDA: I don't understand you, Laura. You couldn't be satisfied with just sitting home, and yet whenever I try to arrange something for you, you seem to resist it. *(She gets up.)* Now take a look at yourself. No, wait! Wait just a moment—I have an idea!
LAURA: What is it now?

(Amanda produces two powder puffs which she wraps in handkerchiefs and stuffs in Laura's bosom.)

LAURA: Mother, what are you doing?
AMANDA: They call them "Gay Deceivers"!
LAURA: I won't wear them!

AMANDA: You will!

LAURA: Why should I?

AMANDA: Because, to be painfully honest, your chest is flat.

LAURA: You make it seem like we were setting a trap.

AMANDA: All pretty girls are a trap, a pretty trap, and men expect them to be. (*Legend: "A Pretty Trap."*) Now look at yourself, young lady. This is the prettiest you will ever be! I've got to fix myself now! You're going to be surprised by your mother's appearance! (*She crosses through portieres, humming gaily.*)

(*Laura moves slowly to the long mirror and stares solemnly at herself.*)

(*A wind blows the white curtains inward in a slow, graceful motion and with a faint, sorrowful sighing.*)

AMANDA (*offstage*): It isn't dark enough yet. (*She turns slowly before the mirror with a troubled look.*)

(*Legend on screen: "This is My Sister: Celebrate Her with Strings!" Music.*)

AMANDA (*laughing, off*): I'm going to show you something. I'm going to make a spectacular appearance!

LAURA: What is it, Mother?

AMANDA: Possess your soul in patience—you will see! Something I've resurrected from that old trunk! Styles haven't changed so terribly much after all. . . . (*She parts the portieres.*) Now just look at your mother! (*She wears a girlish frock of yellowed voile with a blue silk sash. She carries a bunch of jonquils—the legend of her youth is nearly revived. Feverishly.*) This is the dress in which I led the cotillion. Won the cakewalk twice at Sunset Hill, wore one spring to the Governor's ball in Jackson![22] See how I sashayed around the ballroom, Laura? (*She raises her skirt and does a mincing step around the room.*) I wore it on Sundays for my gentlemen callers! I had it on the day I met your father—I had malaria fever all that spring. The change of climate from East Tennessee to the Delta—weakened resistance—I had a little temperature all the time—not enough to be serious—just enough to make me restless and giddy! Invitations poured in—parties all over the Delta!—"Stay in bed," said Mother, "you have fever!"—but I just wouldn't.—I took quinine but kept on going, going!—Evenings, dances!—Afternoons, long, long rides! Picnics—lovely!—So lovely, that country in May.—All lacy with dogwood, literally flooded with jonquils!—That was the spring I had the craze for jonquils. Jonquils became an absolute obsession. Mother said, "Honey, there's no more room for jonquils." And still I kept on bringing in more jonquils. Whenever, wherever I saw them, I'd say, "Stop! Stop! I see jonquils!" I made the young men help me gather the jonquils! It was a joke, Amanda and her jonquils! Finally there were no more vases to hold them, every available space was filled with jonquils. No vases to hold them? All right, I'll hold them myself! And then I— (*She stops in front of the picture. Music.*) met your father! Malaria fever and jonquils and then—this—boy. . . . (*She switches on the rose-colored lamp.*) I hope they get here before it starts to rain. (*She crosses upstage and places the jonquils in bowl on table.*) I gave your brother a little extra change so he and Mr. O'Connor could take the service car home.

LAURA (*with altered look*): What did you say his name was?

AMANDA: O'Connor.

---

[22] Jackson, Mississippi.

LAURA: What is his first name?

AMANDA: I don't remember. Oh, yes, I do. It was—Jim!

(Laura sways slightly and catches hold of a chair.)
  (Legend on screen: "Not Jim!")

LAURA *(faintly)*: Not—Jim!

AMANDA: Yes, that was it, it was Jim! I've never known a Jim that wasn't nice!

(Music: ominous.)

LAURA: Are you sure his name is Jim O'Connor?

AMANDA: Yes. Why?

LAURA: Is he the one that Tom used to know in high school?

AMANDA: He didn't say so. I think he just got to know him at the warehouse.

LAURA: There was a Jim O'Connor we both knew in high school—*(Then, with effort.)* If that is the one that Tom is bringing to dinner—you'll have to excuse me, I won't come to the table.

AMANDA: What sort of nonsense is this?

LAURA: You asked me once if I'd ever liked a boy. Don't you remember I showed you this boy's picture?

AMANDA: You mean the boy you showed me in the yearbook?

LAURA: Yes, that boy.

AMANDA: Laura, Laura, were you in love with that boy?

LAURA: I don't know, Mother. All I know is I couldn't sit at the table if it was him!

AMANDA: It won't be him! It isn't the least bit likely. But whether it is or not, you will come to the table. You will not be excused.

LAURA: I'll have to be, Mother.

AMANDA: I don't intend to humor your silliness, Laura. I've had too much from you and your brother, both! So just sit down and compose yourself till they come. Tom has forgotten his key so you'll have to let them in, when they arrive.

LAURA *(panicky)*: Oh, Mother—*you* answer the door!

AMANDA *(lightly)*: I'll be in the kitchen—busy!

LAURA: Oh, Mother, please answer the door, don't make me do it!

AMANDA *(crossing into kitchenette)*: I've got to fix the dressing for the salmon. Fuss, fuss—silliness!—over a gentleman caller!

(Door swings shut. Laura is left alone.)
  (Legend: "Terror!")
  (She utters a low moan and turns off the lamp—sits stiffly on the edge of the sofa, knotting her fingers together.)
  (Legend on screen: "The Opening of a Door!")
  (Tom and Jim appear on the fire escape steps and climb to landing. Hearing their approach, Laura rises with a panicky gesture. She retreats to the portieres.)
  (The doorbell. Laura catches her breath and touches her throat. Low drums.)

AMANDA *(calling)*: Laura, sweetheart! The door!

(Laura stares at it without moving.)

JIM: I think we just beat the rain.

TOM: Uh-huh. *(He rings again, nervously. Jim whistles and fishes for a cigarette.)*

AMANDA (*very, very gaily*): Laura, that is your brother and Mr. O'Connor! Will you let them in, darling?

(*Laura crosses toward kitchenette door.*)

LAURA (*breathlessly*): Mother—you go to the door!

(*Amanda steps out of kitchenette and stares furiously at Laura. She points imperiously at the door.*)

LAURA: Please, please!
AMANDA (*in a fierce whisper*): What is the matter with you, you silly thing?
LAURA (*desperately*): Please, you answer it, *please!*
AMANDA: I told you I wasn't going to humor you, Laura. Why have you chosen this moment to lose your mind?
LAURA: Please, please, please, you go!
AMANDA: You'll have to go to the door because I can't!
LAURA (*despairingly*): I can't either!
AMANDA: *Why?*
LAURA: I'm *sick!*
AMANDA: I'm sick, too—of your nonsense! Why can't you and your brother be normal people? Fantastic whims and behavior! (*Tom gives a long ring.*) Preposterous goings on! Can you give me one reason—(*Calls out lyrically.*) COMING! JUST ONE SECOND!—why should you be afraid to open a door? Now you answer it, Laura!
LAURA: Oh, oh, oh . . . (*She returns through the portieres. Darts to the victrola and winds it frantically and turns it on.*)
AMANDA: Laura Wingfield, you march right to that door!
LAURA: Yes—yes, Mother!

(*A faraway, scratchy rendition of "Dardanella" softens the air and gives her strength to move through it. She slips to the door and draws it cautiously open.*)
(*Tom enters with the caller, Jim O'Connor.*)

TOM: Laura, this is Jim. Jim, this is my sister, Laura.
JIM (*stepping inside*): I didn't know that Shakespeare had a sister!
LAURA (*retreating stiff and trembling from the door*): How—how do you do?
JIM (*heartily extending his hand*): Okay!

(*Laura touches it hesitantly with hers.*)

JIM: Your hand's *cold*, Laura!
LAURA: Yes, well—I've been playing the victrola. . . .
JIM: Must have been playing classical music on it! You ought to play a little hot swing music to warm you up!
LAURA: Excuse me—I haven't finished playing the victrola. . . .

(*She turns awkwardly and hurries into the front room. She pauses a second by the victrola. Then catches her breath and darts through the portieres like a frightened deer.*)

JIM (*grinning*): What was the matter?

TOM: Oh—with Laura? Laura is—terribly shy.

JIM: Shy, huh? Its unusual to meet a shy girl nowadays. I don't believe you ever mentioned you had a sister.

TOM: Well, now you know. I have one. Here is the *Post Dispatch.*[23] You want a piece of it?

JIM: Uh-huh.

TOM: What piece? The comics?

JIM: Sports! (*Glances at it.*) Ole Dizzy Dean[24] is on his bad behavior.

TOM (*disinterest*): Yeah? (*Lights cigarette and crosses back to fire escape door.*)

JIM: Where are *you* going?

TOM: I'm going out on the terrace.

JIM (*goes after him*): You know, Shakespeare—I'm going to sell you a bill of goods!

TOM: What goods?

JIM: A course I'm taking.

TOM: Huh?

JIM: In public speaking! You and me, we're not the warehouse type.

TOM: Thanks—that's good news. But what has public speaking got to do with it?

JIM: It fits you for—executive positions!

TOM: Awww.

JIM: I tell you it's done a helluva lot for me.

(Image: executive at desk.)

TOM: In what respect?

JIM: In every! Ask yourself what is the difference between you an' me and men in the office down front? Brain?—No!—Ability?—No! Then what? Just one little thing—

TOM: What is that one little thing?

JIM: Primarily it amounts to—social poise! Being able to square up to people and hold your own on any social level!

AMANDA (*offstage*): Tom?

TOM: Yes, Mother?

AMANDA: Is that you and Mr. O'Connor?

TOM: Yes, Mother.

AMANDA: Well, you just make yourselves comfortable in there.

TOM: Yes, Mother.

AMANDA: Ask Mr. O'Connor if he would like to wash his hands.

JIM: Aw,—no—no—thank you—I took care of that at the warehouse. Tom—

TOM: Yes?

JIM: Mr. Mendoza was speaking to me about you.

TOM: Favorably?

JIM: What do you think?

TOM: Well—

---

[23] The *St. Louis Post Dispatch.*
[24] Jerome Herman Dean (1911–1974), a renowned pitcher for the St. Louis Cardinals (1932–1938).

JIM: You're going to be out of a job if you don't wake up.

TOM: I am waking up—

JIM: You show no signs.

TOM: The signs are interior.

(Image on screen: the sailing vessel with Jolly Roger again.)

TOM: I'm planning to change. *(He leans over the rail speaking with quiet exhilaration. The incandescent marquees and signs of the first-run movie houses light his face from across the alley. He looks like a voyager.)* I'm right at the point of committing myself to a future that doesn't include the warehouse and Mr. Mendoza or even a night school course in public speaking.

JIM: What are you gassing about?

TOM: I'm tired of the movies.

JIM: Movies!

TOM: Yes, movies! Look at them—*(A wave toward the marvels of Grand Avenue.)* All of those glamorous people—having adventures—hogging it all, gobbling the whole thing up! You know what happens? People go to the *movies* instead of *moving!* Hollywood characters are supposed to have all the adventures for everybody in America, while everybody in America sits in a dark room and watches them have them! Yes, until there's a war. That's when adventure becomes available to the masses! *Everyone's* dish, not only Gable's! Then the people in the dark room come out of the dark room to have some adventures themselves—Goody, goody! —It's our turn now, to go to the South Sea Island—to make a safari—to be exotic, far-off! —But I'm not patient. I don't want to wait till then. I'm tired of the *movies* and I am *about* to *move!*

JIM *(incredulously)*: Move?

TOM: Yes.

JIM: When?

TOM: Soon!

JIM: Where? Where?

(Theme three music seems to answer the question, while Tom thinks it over. He searches among his pockets.)

TOM: I'm starting to boil inside. I know I seem dreamy, but inside—well, I'm boiling! Whenever I pick up a shoe, I shudder a little thinking how short life is and what I am doing! —Whatever that means. I know it doesn't mean shoes—except as something to wear on a traveler's feet! *(Finds paper.)* Look—

JIM: What?

TOM: I'm a member.

JIM *(reading)*: The Union of Merchant Seamen.

TOM: I paid my dues this month, instead of the light bill.

JIM: You will regret it when they turn the lights off.

TOM: I won't be here.

JIM: How about your mother?

TOM: I'm like my father. The bastard son of a bastard! See how he grins? And he's been absent going on sixteen years!

JIM: You're just talking, you drip. How does your mother feel about it?

TOM: Shhh! —Here comes Mother! Mother is not acquainted with my plans!

AMANDA *(enters portieres)*: Where are you all?

TOM: On the terrace, Mother.

(They start inside. She advances to them. Tom is distinctly shocked at her appearance. Even Jim blinks a little. He is making his first contact with girlish Southern vivacity and in spite of the night school course in public speaking is somewhat thrown off the beam by the unexpected outlay of social charm.)

(Certain responses are attempted by Jim but are swept aside by Amanda's gay laughter and chatter. Tom is embarrassed but after the first shock Jim reacts very warmly. Grins and chuckles, is altogether won over.)

(Image: Amanda as a girl.)

AMANDA *(coyly smiling, shaking her girlish ringlets)*: Well, well, well, so this is Mr. O'Connor. Introductions entirely unnecessary. I've heard so much about you from my boy. I finally said to him, Tom—good gracious! —why don't you bring this paragon to supper? I'd like to meet this nice young man at the warehouse! —Instead of just hearing him sing your praises so much! I don't know why my son is so standoffish—that's not Southern behavior! Let's sit down and—I think we could stand a little more air in here! Tom, leave the door open. I felt a nice fresh breeze a moment ago. Where has it gone to? Mmm, so warm already! And not quite summer, even. We're going to burn up when summer really gets started. However, we're having—we're having a very light supper. I think light things are better fo' this time of year. The same as light clothes are. Light clothes an' light food are what warm weather calls fo'. You know our blood gets so thick during th' winter—it takes a while fo' us to *adjust* ou'selves! —when the season changes . . . It's come so quick this year. I wasn't prepared. All of a sudden— heavens! Already summer! —I ran to the trunk an' pulled out this light dress— Terribly old! Historical almost! But feels so good—so good an' co-ol, y'know. . . .

TOM: Mother—

AMANDA: Yes, honey?

TOM: How about—supper?

AMANDA: Honey, you go ask Sister if supper is ready! You know that Sister is in full charge of supper! Tell her you hungry boys are waiting for it. *(To Jim.)* Have you met Laura?

JIM: She—

AMANDA: Let you in? Oh, good, you've met already! It's rare for a girl as sweet an' pretty as Laura to be domestic! But Laura is, thank heavens, not only pretty but also very domestic. I'm not at all. I never was a bit. I never could make a thing but angel food cake. Well, in the South we had so many servants. Gone, gone, gone. All vestiges of gracious living! Gone completely! I wasn't prepared for what the future brought me. All of my gentlemen callers were sons of planters and so of course I assumed that I would be married to one and raise my family on a large piece of land with plenty of servants. But man proposes—and woman accepts the proposal!—To vary that old, old saying a little bit—I married no planter! I married a man who worked for the telephone company!—That gallantly smiling gentleman over there! *(Points to the picture.)* A telephone man who—fell in love with long distance!—Now he travels and I don't even know where!—But what am I going on for about my—tribulations! Tell me yours—I hope you don't have any! Tom?

TOM *(returning)*: Yes, Mother?

AMANDA: Is supper nearly ready?

TOM: It looks to me like supper is on the table.

AMANDA: Let me look—(*She rises prettily and looks through portieres.*) Oh, lovely!—But where is Sister?

TOM: Laura is not feeling well and she says that she thinks she'd better not come to the table.

AMANDA: What?—Nonsense!—Laura? Oh, Laura!

LAURA (*off stage, faintly*): Yes, Mother.

AMANDA: You really must come to the table. We won't be seated until you come to the table! Come in, Mr. O'Connor. You sit over there, and I'll—Laura? Laura Wingfield! You're keeping us waiting, honey! We can't say grace until you come to the table!

(*The back door is pushed weakly open and Laura comes in. She is obviously quite faint, her lips trembling, her eyes wide and staring. She moves unsteadily toward the table.*)

(*Legend: "Terror!"*)

(*Outside a summer storm is coming abruptly. The white curtains billow inward at the windows and there is a sorrowful murmur and deep blue dusk.*)

(*Laura suddenly stumbles—she catches at a chair with a faint moan.*)

TOM: Laura!

AMANDA: Laura! (*There is a clap of thunder.*) (*Legend: "Ah!"*) (*Despairingly.*) Why, Laura, you *are* sick, darling! Tom, help your sister into the living room, dear! Sit in the living room, Laura—rest on the sofa. Well! (*To the gentleman caller.*) Standing over the hot stove made her ill!—I told her that it was just too warm this evening, but—(*Tom comes back in. Laura is on the sofa.*) Is Laura all right now?

TOM: Yes.

AMANDA: What *is* that? Rain? A nice cool rain has come up! (*She gives the gentleman caller a frightened look.*) I think we may—have grace—now . . . (*Tom looks at her stupidly.*) Tom, honey—you say grace!

TOM: Oh . . . "For these and all thy mercies—"(*They bow their heads, Amanda stealing a nervous glance at Jim. In the living room Laura, stretched on the sofa, clenches her hand to her lips, to hold back a shuddering sob.*) God's Holy Name be praised—

(*The scene dims out.*)

SCENE VII

(*A Souvenir*)

(*Half an hour later. Dinner is just being finished in the upstage area which is concealed by the drawn portieres.*)

(*As the curtain rises Laura is still huddled upon the sofa, her feet drawn under her, her head resting on a pale blue pillow, her eyes wide and mysteriously watchful. The new floor lamp with its shade of rose-colored silk gives a soft, becoming light to her face, bringing out the fragile, unearthly prettiness which usually escapes attention. There is a steady murmur of rain, but it is slackening and stops soon after the scene begins; the air outside becomes pale and luminous as the moon breaks out.*)

(A moment after the curtain rises, the lights in both rooms flicker and go out.)

JIM: Hey, there, Mr. Light Bulb!

(Amanda laughs nervously.)
(Legend: "Suspension of a Public Service.")

AMANDA: Where was Moses when the lights went out? Ha-ha. Do you know the answer to that one, Mr. O'Connor?

JIM: No, Ma'am, what's the answer?

AMANDA: In the dark! *(Jim laughs appreciably.)* Everybody sit still. I'll light the candles. Isn't it lucky we have them on the table? Where's a match? Which of you gentlemen can provide a match?

JIM: Here.

AMANDA: Thank you, sir.

JIM: Not at all, Ma'am!

AMANDA: I guess the fuse has burnt out. Mr. O'Connor, can you tell a burnt-out fuse? I know I can't and Tom is a total loss when it comes to mechanics. *(Sound: getting up: voices recede a little to kitchenette.)* Oh, be careful you don't bump into something. We don't want our gentleman caller to break his neck. Now wouldn't that be a fine howdy-do?

JIM: Ha-ha! Where is the fuse box?

AMANDA: Right here next to the stove. Can you see anything?

JIM: Just a minute.

AMANDA: Isn't electricity a mysterious thing? Wasn't it Benjamin Franklin who tied a key to a kite? We live in such a mysterious universe, don't we? Some people say that science clears up all the mysteries for us. In my opinion it only creates more! Have you found it yet?

JIM: No, Ma'am. All these fuses look okay to me.

AMANDA: Tom!

TOM: Yes, Mother?

AMANDA: That light bill I gave you several days ago. The one I told you we got the notices about?

TOM: Oh.—Yeah.

(Legend: "Ha!")

AMANDA: You didn't neglect to pay it by any chance?

TOM: Why, I—

AMANDA: Didn't! I might have known it!

JIM: Shakespeare probably wrote a poem on that light bill, Mrs. Wingfield.

AMANDA: I might have known better than to trust him with it! There's such a high price for negligence in this world!

JIM: Maybe the poem will win a ten-dollar prize.

AMANDA: We'll just have to spend the remainder of the evening in the nineteenth century, before Mr. Edison made the Mazda lamp![25]

JIM: Candlelight is my favorite kind of light.

AMANDA: That shows you're romantic! But that's no excuse for Tom. Well, we got through dinner. Very considerate of them to let us get through dinner before they plunged us into everlasting darkness, wasn't it, Mr. O'Connor?

---

[25] The first incandescent lamp.

JIM: Ha-ha!

AMANDA: Tom, as a penalty for your carelessness you can help me with the dishes.

JIM: Let me give you a hand.

AMANDA: Indeed you will not!

JIM: I ought to be good for something.

AMANDA: Good for something? (*Her tone is rhapsodic.*) You? Why, Mr. O'Connor, nobody, *nobody*'s given me this much entertainment in years—as you have!

JIM: Aw, now, Mrs. Wingfield!

AMANDA: I'm not exaggerating, not one bit! But Sister is all by her lonesome. You go keep her company in the parlor! I'll give you this lovely old candelabrum that used to be on the altar at the church of the Heavenly Rest. It was melted a little out of shape when the church burnt down. Lightning struck it one spring. Gypsy Jones was holding a revival at the time and he intimated that the church was destroyed because the Episcopalians gave card parties.

JIM: Ha-ha.

AMANDA: And how about coaxing Sister to drink a little wine? I think it would be good for her! Can you carry both at once?

JIM: Sure. I'm Superman!

AMANDA: Now, Thomas, get into this apron!

(*The door of kitchenette swings closed on Amanda's gay laughter; the flickering light approaches the portieres.*)

(*Laura sits up nervously as he enters. Her speech at first is low and breathless from the almost intolerable strain of being alone with a stranger.*)
(*The legend: "I Don't Suppose You Remember Me at All!"*)
(*In her first speeches in this scene, before Jim's warmth overcomes her paralyzing shyness, Laura's voice is thin and breathless as though she has just run up a steep flight of stairs.*)
(*Jim's attitude is gently humorous. In playing this scene it should be stressed that while the incident is apparently unimportant, it is to Laura the climax of her secret life.*)

JIM: Hello, there, Laura.

LAURA (*faintly*):   Hello. (*She clears her throat.*)

JIM: How are you feeling now? Better?

LAURA: Yes. Yes, thank you.

JIM: This is for you. A little dandelion wine. (*He extends it toward her with extravagant gallantry.*)

LAURA: Thank you.

JIM: Drink it—but don't get drunk! (*He laughs heartily. Laura takes the glass uncertainly; laughs shyly.*) Where shall I set the candles?

LAURA: Oh—oh, anywhere . . .

JIM: How about here on the floor? Any objections?

LAURA: No.

JIM: I'll spread a newspaper under to catch the drippings. I like to sit on the floor. Mind if I do?

LAURA: Oh, no.

JIM: Give me a pillow?

LAURA: What?

JIM: A pillow!

LAURA: Oh . . . (*Hands him one quickly.*)

JIM: How about you? Don't you like to sit on the floor?

LAURA: Oh—yes.

JIM: Why don't you, then?

LAURA: I—will.

Take a pillow! (*Laura does. Sits on the other side of the candelabrum. Jim crosses his legs and smiles engagingly at her.*) I can't hardly see you sitting way over there.

LAURA: I can—see you.

JIM: I know, but that's not fair, I'm in the limelight. (*Laura moves her pillow closer.*) Good! Now I can see you! Comfortable?

LAURA: Yes.

JIM: So am I. Comfortable as a cow. Will you have some gum?

LAURA: No, thank you.

JIM: I think that I will indulge, with your permission. (*Musingly unwraps it and holds it up.*) Think of the fortune made by the guy that invented the first piece of chewing gum. Amazing, huh? The Wrigley Building is one of the sights of Chicago.—I saw it summer before last when I went up to the Century of Progress.[26] Did you take in the Century of Progress?

LAURA: No, I didn't.

JIM: Well, it was quite a wonderful exposition. What impressed me most was the Hall of Science. Gives you an idea of what the future will be in America, even more wonderful than the present time is! (*Pause. Smiling at her.*) Your brother tells me you're shy. Is that right, Laura?

LAURA: I—don't know.

JIM: I judge you to be an old-fashioned type of girl. Well, I think that's a pretty good type to be. Hope you don't think I'm being too personal—do you?

LAURA (*hastily, out of embarrassment*): I believe I *will* take a piece of gum, if you—don't mind. (*Clearing her throat.*) Mr. O'Connor, have you—kept up with your singing?

JIM: Singing? Me?

LAURA: Yes. I remember what a beautiful voice you had.

JIM: When did you hear me sing?

(*Voice offstage in the pause.*)

VOICE (*offstage*): O blow, ye winds, heigh-ho,
 A-roving I will go!
  I'm off to my love
   With a boxing glove—
 Ten thousand miles away!

JIM: You say you've heard me sing?

LAURA: Oh, yes! Yes, very often . . . I—don't suppose you remember me—at all?

JIM (*smiling doubtfully*): You know I have an idea I've seen you before. I had that idea soon as you opened the door. It seemed almost like I was about to re-

---

[26] A world's fair (1933–1934) to celebrate Chicago's centennial.

member your name. But the name that I started to call you—wasn't a name! And so I stopped myself before I said it.

LAURA: Wasn't it—Blue Roses?

JIM (*Springs up. Grinning.*): Blue Roses! My gosh, yes—Blue Roses! That's what I had on my tongue when you opened the door! Isn't it funny what tricks your memory plays? I didn't connect you with the high school somehow or other. But that's where it was; it was high school. I didn't even know you were Shakespeare's sister! Gosh, I'm sorry.

LAURA: I didn't expect you to. You—barely knew me!

JIM: But we did have a speaking acquaintance, huh?

LAURA: Yes, we—spoke to each other.

JIM: When did you recognize me?

LAURA: Oh, right away!

JIM: Soon as I came in the door?

LAURA: When I heard your name I thought it was probably you. I knew that Tom used to know you a little in high school. So when you came in the door—Well, then I was—sure.

JIM: Why didn't you *say* something, then?

LAURA (*breathlessly*): I didn't know what to say, I was —too surprised!

JIM: For goodness' sakes! You know, this sure is funny!

LAURA: Yes! Yes, isn't it, though . . .

JIM: Didn't we have a class in something together?

LAURA: Yes, we did.

JIM: What class was that?

LAURA: It was—singing—Chorus!

JIM: Aw!

LAURA: I sat across the aisle from you in the Aud.

JIM: Aw.

LAURA: Mondays, Wednesdays, and Fridays.

JIM: Now I remember—you always came in late.

LAURA: Yes, it was so hard for me, getting upstairs. I had that brace on my leg—it clumped so loud!

JIM: I never heard any clumping.

LAURA (*wincing at the recollection*): To me it sounded like—thunder!

JIM: Well, well, well, I never even noticed.

LAURA: And everybody was seated before I came in. I had to walk in front of all those people. My seat was in the back row. I had to go clumping all the way up the aisle with everyone watching!

JIM: You shouldn't have been self-conscious.

LAURA: I know, but I was. It was always such a relief when the singing started.

JIM: Aw, yes, I've placed you now! I used to call you Blue Roses. How was it that I got started calling you that?

LAURA: I was out of school a little while with pleurosis. When I came back you asked me what was the matter. I said I had pleurosis—you thought I said Blue Roses. That's what you always called me after that!

JIM: I hope you didn't mind.

LAURA: Oh, no—I liked it. You see, I wasn't acquainted with many—people. . . .

JIM: As I remember you sort of stuck by yourself.

LAURA: I—I—never had much luck at—making friends.

JIM: I don't see why you wouldn't.

LAURA: Well, I—started out badly.

JIM: You mean being—

LAURA: Yes, it sort of—stood between me—

JIM: You shouldn't have let it!

LAURA: I know, but it did, and—

JIM: You were shy with people!

LAURA: I tried not to be but never could—

JIM: Overcome it?

LAURA: No, I—I never could!

JIM: I guess being shy is something you have to work out of kind of gradually.

LAURA (*sorrowfully*): Yes—I guess it—

JIM: Takes time!

LAURA: Yes—

JIM: People are not so dreadful when you know them. That's what you have to remember! And everybody has problems, not just you, but practically everybody has got some problems. You think of yourself as having the only problems, as being the only one who is disappointed. But just look around you and you will see lots of people as disappointed as you are. For instance, I hoped when I was going to high school that I would be further along at this time, six years later, than I am now—You remember that wonderful write-up I had in *The Torch?*

LAURA: Yes! (*She rises and crosses to table.*)

JIM: It said I was bound to succeed in anything I went into! (*Laura returns with the annual.*) Holy Jeez! *The Torch!* (*He accepts it reverently. They smile across it with mutual wonder. Laura crouches beside him and they begin to turn through it. Laura's shyness is dissolving in his warmth.*)

LAURA: Here you are in *Pirates of Penzance!*

JIM (*wistfully*): I sang the baritone lead in that operetta.

LAURA (*rapidly*): So—*beautifully!*

JIM (*protesting*): Aw—

LAURA: Yes, yes—beautifully—beautifully!

JIM: You heard me?

LAURA: All three times!

JIM: No!

LAURA: Yes!

JIM: All three performances?

LAURA (*looking down*): Yes.

JIM: Why?

LAURA: I—wanted to ask you to—autograph my program.

JIM: Why didn't you ask me to?

LAURA: You were always surrounded by your own friends so much that I never had a chance to.

JIM: You should have just—

LAURA: Well, I—thought you might think I was—

JIM: Thought I might think you was—what?

LAURA: Oh—

JIM (*with reflective relish*): I was beleaguered by females in those days.

LAURA: You were terribly popular!

JIM: Yeah—

LAURA: You had such a—friendly way—

JIM: I was spoiled in high school.

LAURA: Everybody—liked you!

JIM: Including you?

LAURA: I—yes, I—I did, too—(*She gently closes the book in her lap.*)

JIM: Well, well, well!—Give me that program, Laura. (*She hands it to him.*
He signs it with a flourish.) There you are—better late than never!

LAURA: Oh, I—what a—surprise!

JIM: My signature isn't worth very much right now. But some day—maybe—
it will increase in value! Being disappointed is one thing and being discouraged is
something else. I am disappointed but I am not discouraged. I'm twenty-three
years old. How old are you?

LAURA: I'll be twenty-four in June.

JIM: That's not old age!

LAURA: No, but—

JIM: You finished high school?

LAURA (*with difficulty*): I didn't go back.

JIM: You mean you dropped out?

LAURA: I made bad grades in my final examinations. (*She rises and replaces*
the book and the program. Her voice strained.) How is—Emily Meisenbach getting along?

JIM: Oh, that kraut-head!

LAURA: Why do you call her that?

JIM: That's what she was.

LAURA: You're not still—going with her?

JIM: I never see her.

LAURA: It said in the Personal Section that you were—engaged!

JIM: I know, but I wasn't impressed by that—propaganda!

LAURA: It wasn't—the truth?

JIM: Only in Emily's optimistic opinion!

LAURA: Oh—

(*Legend: "What Have You Done since High School?"*)
(*Jim lights a cigarette and leans indolently back on his elbows smiling at Laura*
with a warmth and charm which lights her inwardly with altar candles. She re-
mains by the table and turns in her hands a piece of glass to cover her tumult.)

JIM (*after several reflective puffs on a cigarette*): What have you done since
high school? (*She seems not to hear him.*) Huh? (*Laura looks up.*) I said what
have you done since high school, Laura?

LAURA: Nothing much.

JIM: You must have been doing something these six long years.

LAURA: Yes.

JIM: Well, then, such as what?

LAURA: I took a business course at business college—

JIM: How did that work out?

LAURA: Well, not very—well—I had to drop out, it gave me—indigestion—

(*Jim laughs gently.*)

JIM: What are you doing now?

LAURA: I don't do anything—much. Oh, please don't think I sit around doing nothing! My glass collection takes up a good deal of my time. Glass is something you have to take good care of.

JIM: What did you say—about glass?

LAURA: Collection I said—I have one— (*She clears her throat and turns away again, acutely shy.*)

JIM (*abruptly*): You know what I judge to be the trouble with you? Inferiority complex! Know what that is? That's what they call it when someone low-rates himself! I understand it because I had it, too. Although my case was not so aggravated as yours seems to be. I had it until I took up public speaking, developed my voice, and learned that I had an aptitude for science. Before that time I never thought of myself as being outstanding in any way whatsoever! Now I've never made a regular study of it, but I have a friend who says I can analyze people better than doctors that make a profession of it. I don't claim that to be necessarily true, but I can sure guess a person's psychology, Laura! (*Takes out his gum.*) Excuse me, Laura. I always take it out when the flavor is gone. I'll use this scrap of paper to wrap it in. I know how it is to get it stuck on a shoe. Yep—that's what I judge to be your principal trouble. A lack of confidence in yourself as a person. You don't have the proper amount of faith in yourself. I'm basing that fact on a number of your remarks and also on certain observations I've made. For instance that clumping you thought was so awful in high school. You say that you even dreaded to walk into class. You see what you did? You dropped out of school, you gave up an education because of a clump, which as far as I know was practically nonexistent! A little physical defect is what you have. Hardly noticeable even! Magnified thousands of times by imagination! You know what my strong advice to you is? Think of yourself as *superior* in some way!

LAURA: In what way would I think?

JIM: Why, man alive, Laura! Just look about you a little. What do you see? A world full of common people! All of 'em born and all of 'em going to die! Which of them has one-tenth of your good points! Or mine! Or anyone else's, as far as that goes—Gosh! Everybody excels in some one thing. Some in many! (*Unconsciously glances at himself in the mirror.*) All you've got to do is discover in *what!* Take me, for instance. (*He adjusts his tie at the mirror.*) My interest happens to lie in electro-dynamics. I'm taking a course in radio engineering at night school, Laura, on top of a fairly responsible job at the warehouse. I'm taking that course and studying public speaking.

LAURA: Ohhhh.

JIM: Because I believe in the future of television! (*Turning back to her.*) I wish to be ready to go up right along with it. Therefore I'm planning to get in on the ground floor. In fact, I've already made the right connections and all that remains is for the industry itself to get under way! Full steam—(*His eyes are starry.*) Knowledge—Zzzzzp! Money—Zzzzzzp!—Power! That's the cycle democracy is built on! (*His attitude is convincingly dynamic. Laura stares at him, even her shyness eclipsed in her absolute wonder. He suddenly grins.*) I guess you think I think a lot of myself!

LAURA: No—o-o-o, I—

JIM: Now how about you? Isn't there something you take more interest in than anything else?

LAURA: Well, I do—as I said—have my—glass collection—

(*A peal of girlish laughter from the kitchen.*)

JIM: I'm not right sure I know what you're talking about. What kind of glass is it?

LAURA: Little articles of it, they're ornaments mostly! Most of them are little animals made out of glass, the tiniest little animals in the world. Mother calls them a glass menagerie! Here's an example of one, if you'd like to see it! This one is one of the oldest. It's nearly thirteen. (*He stretches out his hand.*) (*Music: "The Glass Menagerie."*) Oh, be careful—if you breathe, it breaks!

JIM: I'd better not take it. I'm pretty clumsy with things.

LAURA: Go on, I trust you with him! (*Places it in his palm.*) There now— you're holding him gently! Hold him over the light, he loves the light! You see how the light shines through him?

JIM: It sure does shine!

LAURA: I shouldn't be partial, but he is my favorite one.

JIM: What kind of a thing is this one supposed to be?

LAURA: Haven't you noticed the single horn on his forehead?

JIM: A unicorn, huh?

LAURA: Mmm-hmmm!

JIM: Unicorns, aren't they extinct in the modern world?

LAURA: I know!

JIM: Poor little fellow, he must feel sort of lonesome.

LAURA (*smiling*): Well, if he does he doesn't complain about it. He stays on a shelf with some horses that don't have horns and all of them seem to get along nicely together.

JIM: How do you know?

LAURA (*lightly*): I haven't heard any arguments among them!

JIM (*grinning*): No arguments, huh? Well, that's a pretty good sign! Where shall I set him?

LAURA: Put him on the table. They all like a change of scenery once in a while!

JIM (*stretching*): Well, well, well, well—Look how big my shadow is when I stretch!

LAURA: Oh, oh, yes—it stretches across the ceiling!

JIM (*crossing to door*): I think it's stopped raining. (*Opens fire escape door.*) Where does the music come from?

LAURA: From the Paradise Dance Hall across the alley.

JIM: How about cutting the rug a little, Miss Wingfield?

LAURA: Oh, I—

JIM: Or is your program filled up? Let me have a look at it. (*Grasps imaginary card.*) Why, every dance is taken! I'll just have to scratch some out. (*Waltz music: "La Golondrina."*) Ahhh, a waltz! (*He executes some sweeping turns by himself then holds his arms toward Laura.*)

LAURA (*breathlessly*): I—can't dance!

JIM: There you go, that inferiority stuff!

LAURA: I've never danced in my life!

JIM: Come on, try!

LAURA: Oh, but I'd step on you!

JIM: I'm not made out of glass.

LAURA: How—how—how do we start?

JIM: Just leave it to me. You hold your arms out a little.

LAURA: Like this?

JIM: A little bit higher. Right. Now don't tighten up, that's the main thing about it—relax.

LAURA (*laughing breathlessly*): It's hard not to.

JIM: Okay.

LAURA: I'm afraid you can't budge me.

JIM: What do you bet I can't? (*He swings her into motion.*)

LAURA: Goodness, yes, you can!

JIM: Let yourself go, now, Laura, just let yourself go.

LAURA: I'm—

JIM: Come on!

LAURA: Trying!

JIM: Not so stiff—Easy does it!

LAURA: I know but I'm—

JIM: Loosen th' backbone! There now, that's a lot better.

LAURA: Am I?

JIM: Lots, lots better! (*He moves her about the room in a clumsy waltz.*)

LAURA: Oh, my!

JIM: Ha-ha!

LAURA: Oh, my goodness!

JIM: Ha-ha-ha! (*They suddenly bump into the table. Jim stops.*) What did we hit on?

LAURA: Table.

JIM: Did something fall off it? I think—

LAURA: Yes.

JIM: I hope that it wasn't the little glass horse with the horn!

LAURA: Yes.

JIM: Aw, aw, aw. Is it broken?

LAURA: Now it is just like all the other horses.

JIM: It's lost its—

LAURA: Horn! It doesn't matter. Maybe it's a blessing in disguise.

JIM: You'll never forgive me. I bet that that was your favorite piece of glass.

LAURA: I don't have favorites much. It's no tragedy, Freckles. Glass breaks so easily. No matter how careful you are. The traffic jars the shelves and things fall off them.

JIM: Still I'm awfully sorry that I was the cause.

LAURA (*smiling*): I'll just imagine he had an operation. The horn was removed to make him feel less—freakish! (*They both laugh.*) Now he will feel more at home with the other horses, the ones that don't have horns . . .

JIM: Ha-ha, that's very funny! (*Suddenly serious.*) I'm glad to see that you have a sense of humor. You know—you're—well—very different! Surprisingly different from anyone else I know! (*His voice becomes soft and hesitant with a genuine feeling.*) Do you mind me telling you that? (*Laura is abashed beyond speech.*) I mean it in a nice way . . . . (*Laura nods shyly, looking away.*) You make me feel sort of—I don't know how to put it! I'm usually pretty good at expressing things, but—This is something that I don't know how to say! (*Laura touches her throat and clears it—turns the broken unicorn in her hands.*) (*Even softer.*) Has anyone ever told you that you were pretty? (*Pause: Music.*) (*Laura looks up slowly, with wonder, and shakes her head.*) Well, you are! In a very different way from anyone else. And all the nicer because of the difference, too. (*His voice becomes low and husky. Laura turns away, nearly faint with the nov-*

elty of her emotions.) I wish that you were my sister. I'd teach you to have some confidence in yourself. The different people are not like other people, but being different is nothing to be ashamed of. Because other people are not such wonderful people. They're one hundred times one thousand. You're one times one! They walk all over the earth. You just stay here. They're common as—weeds, but— you—well, you're—*Blue Roses!*

(Image on screen: blue roses.)
  (Music changes.)

LAURA: But blue is wrong for—roses . . .
JIM: It's right for you—You're—pretty!
LAURA: In what respect am I pretty?
JIM: In all respects—believe me! Your eyes—your hair—are pretty! Your hands are pretty! (*He catches hold of her hand.*) You think I'm making this up because I'm invited to dinner and have to be nice. Oh, I could do that! I could put on an act for you, Laura, and say lots of things without being very sincere. But this time I am. I'm talking to you sincerely. I happened to notice you had this inferiority complex that keeps you from feeling comfortable with people. Somebody needs to build your confidence up and make you proud instead of shy and turning away and—blushing—Somebody ought to—Ought to—*kiss* you, Laura! (*His hand slips slowly up her arm to her shoulder.*) (*Music swells tumultuously.*) (*He suddenly turns her about and kisses her on the lips. When he releases her Laura sinks on the sofa with a bright, dazed look. Jim backs away and fishes in his pocket for a cigarette.*) (*Legend on screen: "Souvenir."*) Stumble-john! (*He lights the cigarette, avoiding her look. There is a peal of girlish laughter from Amanda in the kitchen. Laura slowly raises and opens her hand. It still contains the little broken glass animal. She looks at it with a tender, bewildered expression.*) Stumble-john! I shouldn't have done that—That was way off the beam. You don't smoke, do you? (*She looks up, smiling, not hearing the question. He sits beside her a little gingerly. She looks at him speechlessly—waiting. He coughs decorously and moves a little farther aside as he considers the situation and senses her feelings, dimly, with perturbation. Gently.*) Would you—care for a—mint? (*She doesn't seem to hear him but her look grows brighter even.*) Peppermint—Life Saver? My pocket's a regular drugstore—wherever I go . . . (*He pops a mint in his mouth. Then gulps and decides to make a clean breast of it. He speaks slowly and gingerly.*) Laura, you know, if I had a sister like you, I'd do the same thing as Tom. I'd bring out fellows and—introduce her to them. The right type of boys of a type to—appreciate her. Only—well—he made a mistake about me. Maybe I've got no call to be saying this. That may not have been the idea in having me over. But what if it was? There's nothing wrong about that. The only trouble is that in my case—I'm not in a situation to—do the right thing. I can't take down your number and say I'll phone. I can't call up next week and—ask for a date. I thought I had better explain the situation in case you misunderstood it and—hurt your feelings. . . . (*Pause. Slowly, very slowly, Laura's look changes, her eyes returning slowly from his to the ornament in her palm.*)

(Amanda utters another gay laugh in the kitchen.)

LAURA (*faintly*): You—won't—call again?
JIM: No Laura, I can't. (*He rises from the sofa.*) As I was just explaining, I've—got strings on me, Laura, I've—been going steady! I go out all the time

with a girl named Betty. She's a home-girl like you, and Catholic, and Irish, and in a great many ways we—get along fine. I met her last summer on a moonlight boat trip up the river to Alton,[27] on the *Majestic*. Well—right away from the start it was—love! (*Legend: Love!*) (*Laura sways slightly forward and grips the arm of the sofa. He fails to notice, now enrapt in his own comfortable being.*) Being in love has made a new man of me! (*Leaning stiffly forward, clutching the arm of the sofa, Laura struggles visibly with her storm. But Jim is oblivious, she is a long way off.*) The power of love is really pretty tremendous! Love is something that— changes the whole world, Laura! (*The storm abates a little and Laura leans back. He notices her again.*) It happened that Betty's aunt took sick, she got a wire and had to go to Centralia.[28] So Tom—when he asked me to dinner—I naturally just accepted the invitation, not knowing that you—that he—that I—(*He stops awkwardly.*) Huh—I'm a stumble-john! (*He flops back on the sofa. The holy candles on the altar of Laura's face have been snuffed out! There is a look of almost infinite desolation. Jim glances at her uneasily.*) I wish that you would—say something. (*She bites her lip which was trembling and then bravely smiles. She opens her hand again on the broken glass ornament. Then she gently takes his hand and raises it level with her own. She carefully places the unicorn in the palm of his hand, then pushes his fingers closed upon it.*) What are you—doing that for? You want me to have him?—Laura? (*She nods.*) What for?

LAURA: A—souvenir . . .

(*She rises unsteadily and crouches beside the victrola to wind it up.*)
(*Legend on screen: "Things Have a Way of Turning out so Badly."*)
(*Or Image: "Gentleman Caller Waving Good-bye!—Gaily."*)
(*At this moment Amanda rushes brightly back in the front room. She bears a pitcher of fruit punch in an old-fashioned cut-glass pitcher and a plate of macaroons. The plate has a gold border and poppies painted on it.*)

AMANDA: Well, well, well! Isn't the air delightful after the shower? I've made you children a little liquid refreshment. (*Turns gaily to the gentleman caller.*) Jim, do you know that song about lemonade?
"Lemonade, lemonade
Made in the shade and stirred with a spade—
Good enough for any old maid!"
JIM (*uneasily*): Ha-ha! No—I never heard it.
AMANDA: Why, Laura! You look so serious!
JIM: We were having a serious conversation.
AMANDA: Good! Now you're better acquainted!
JIM (*uncertainly*): Ha-ha! Yes.
AMANDA: You modern young people are much more serious-minded than my generation. I was so gay as a girl!
JIM: You haven't changed, Mrs. Wingfield.
AMANDA: Tonight I'm rejuvenated! The gaiety of the occasion, Mr. O'Connor! (*She tosses her head with a peal of laughter. Spills lemonade.*) Oooo! I'm baptizing myself!
JIM: Here—let me—
AMANDA (*setting the pitcher down*): There now. I discovered we had some maraschino cherries. I dumped them in, juice and all!

[27] Alton, Illinois.   [28] Centralia, Illinois.

JIM: You shouldn't have gone to that trouble, Mrs. Wingfield.

AMANDA: Trouble, trouble? Why it was loads of fun! Didn't you hear me cutting up in the kitchen? I bet your ears were burning! I told Tom how outdone with him I was for keeping you to himself so long a time! He should have brought you over much, much sooner! Well, now that you've found your way, I want you to be a very frequent caller! Not just occasional but all the time. Oh, we're going to have a lot of gay times together! I see them coming! Mmm, just breathe that air! So fresh, and the moon's so pretty! I'll skip back out—I know where my place is when young folks are having a—serious conversation!

JIM: Oh, don't go out, Mrs. Wingfield. The fact of the matter is I've got to be going.

AMANDA: Going, now? You're joking! Why, it's only the shank of the evening, Mr. O'Connor!

JIM: Well, you know how it is.

AMANDA: You mean you're a young workingman and have to keep workingmen's hours. We'll let you off early tonight. But only on the condition that next time you stay later. What's the best night for you? Isn't Saturday night the best night for you workingmen?

JIM: I have a couple of time clocks to punch, Mrs. Wingfield. One at morning, another one at night!

AMANDA: My, but you *are* ambitious! You work at night, too?

JIM: No, Ma'am, not work but—Betty! (*He crosses deliberately to pick up his hat. The band at the Paradise Dance Hall goes into a tender waltz.*)

AMANDA: Betty? Betty? Who's—Betty! (*There is an ominous cracking sound in the sky.*)

JIM: Oh, just a girl. The girl I go steady with! (*He smiles charmingly. The sky falls.*)

(*Legend: "The Sky Falls."*)

AMANDA (*a long-drawn exhalation*): Ohhhh . . . Is it a serious romance, Mr. O'Connor?

JIM: We're going to be married the second Sunday in June.

AMANDA: Ohhhh—how nice! Tom didn't mention that you were engaged to be married.

JIM: The cat's not out of the bag at the warehouse yet. You know how they are. They call you Romeo and stuff like that. (*He stops at the oval mirror to put on his hat. He carefully shapes the brim and the crown to give a discreetly dashing effect.*) It's been a wonderful evening, Mrs. Wingfield. I guess this is what they mean by Southern hospitality.

AMANDA: It really wasn't anything at all.

JIM: I hope it don't seem like I'm rushing off. But I promised Betty I'd pick her up at the Wabash depot, an' by the time I get my jalopy down there her train'll be in. Some women are pretty upset if you keep 'em waiting.

AMANDA: Yes, I know—The tyranny of women! (*Extends her hand.*) Goodbye, Mr. O'Connor. I wish you luck—and happiness—and success! All three of them, and so does Laura!—Don't you, Laura?

LAURA: Yes!

JIM (*taking her hand*) Good-bye, Laura. I'm certainly going to treasure that souvenir. And don't you forget the good advice I gave you. (*Raises his voice to a cheery shout.*) So long, Shakespeare! Thanks again, ladies—Good night!

(He grins and ducks jauntily out.)

(Still bravely grimacing, Amanda closes the door on the gentleman caller. Then she turns back to the room with a puzzled expression. She and Laura don't dare to face each other. Laura crouches beside the victrola to wind it.)

AMANDA *(faintly)*: Things have a way of turning out so badly. I don't believe that I would play the victrola. Well, well—well—Our gentleman caller was engaged to be married! Tom!

TOM *(from back)*: Yes, Mother?

AMANDA: Come in here a minute. I want to tell you something awfully funny.

TOM *(enters with macaroon and a glass of the lemonade)*: Has the gentleman caller gotten away already?

AMANDA: The gentleman caller has made an early departure. What a wonderful joke you played on us!

TOM: How do you mean?

AMANDA: You didn't mention that he was engaged to be married.

TOM: Jim? Engaged?

AMANDA: That's what he just informed us.

TOM: I'll be jiggered! I didn't know about that.

AMANDA: That seems very peculiar.

TOM: What's peculiar about it?

AMANDA: Didn't you call him your best friend down at the warehouse?

TOM: He is, but how did I know?

AMANDA: It seems extremely peculiar that you wouldn't know your best friend was going to be married!

TOM: The warehouse is where I work, not where I know things about people!

AMANDA: You don't know things anywhere! You live in a dream; you manufacture illusions! *(He crosses to door.)* Where are you going?

TOM: I'm going to the movies.

AMANDA: That's right, now that you've had us make such fools of ourselves. The effort, the preparations, all the expense! The new floor lamp, the rug, the clothes for Laura! All for what? To entertain some other girl's fiancé! Go to the movies, go! Don't think about us, a mother deserted, an unmarried sister who's crippled and has no job! Don't let anything interfere with your selfish pleasure! Just go, go, go—to the movies!

TOM: All right, I will! The more you shout about my selfishness to me the quicker I'll go, and I won't go to the movies!

AMANDA: Go, then! Then go to the moon—you selfish dreamer!

(Tom smashes his glass on the floor. He plunges out on the fire escape, slamming the door. Laura screams—cut by door.)

(Dance hall music up. Tom goes to the rail and grips it desperately, lifting his face in the chill white moonlight penetrating the narrow abyss of the alley.)

(Legend on screen: "And so Good-bye . . . ")

(Tom's closing speech is timed with the interior pantomime. The interior scene is played as though viewed through soundproof glass. Amanda appears to be making a comforting speech to Laura who is huddled upon the sofa. Now that we cannot hear the mother's speech, her silliness is gone and she has dignity and tragic beauty. Laura's dark hair hides her face until at the end of the speech she lifts it to smile at her mother. Amanda's gestures are slow and graceful, almost dancelike, as she comforts the daughter. At the end of her speech she glances a

moment at the father's picture—then withdraws through the portieres. At close of
Tom's speech, Laura blows out the candles, ending the play.)

TOM: I didn't go to the moon, I went much further—for time is the longest
distance between two places—Not long after that I was fired for writing a poem
on the lid of a shoebox. I left Saint Louis. I descended the steps of this fire escape
for a last time and followed, from then on, in my father's footsteps, attempting to
find in motion what was lost in space—I traveled around a great deal. The cities
swept about me like dead leaves, leaves that were brightly colored but torn away
from the branches. I would have stopped, but I was pursued by something. It
always came upon me unawares, taking me altogether by surprise. Perhaps it was
a familiar bit of music. Perhaps it was only a piece of transparent glass—Perhaps
I am walking along a street at night, in some strange city, before I have found
companions. I pass the lighted window of a shop where perfume is sold. The
window is filled with pieces of colored glass, tiny transparent bottles in delicate
colors, like bits of a shattered rainbow. Than all at once my sister touches my
shoulder. I turn around and look into her eyes . . . Oh, Laura, Laura, I tried to
leave you behind me, but I am more faithful than I intended to be! I reach for a
cigarette, I cross the street, I run into the movies or a bar, I buy a drink, I speak to
the nearest stranger—anything that can blow your candles out! (*Laura bends over
the candles.*)—for nowadays the world is lit by lightning! Blow out your candles,
Laura—and so good-bye. . . .

(*She blows the candles out.*)
   (*The scene dissolves.*)

1944, 1945

MIDDLE TO LATE 20TH-CENTURY POETRY

After World War II the influence of the modernists remained strong. The new
generation of poets had the unenviable task of fashioning their own styles in the
living shadows of Ezra Pound, William Carlos Williams, Wallace Stevens, Robert
Frost, W. H. Auden (who, having emigrated to America in 1939, became a citizen in 1946), and especially T. S. Eliot. During the 1940s and 1950s these great
modernists were not only still publishing major collections, but gaining in literary
stature. For most modernists the primary question had been how and what to write
after Eliot's *The Waste Land* (1922). Although *Four Quartets* (1943) had supplanted it as Eliot's vision of the quintessential modern long poem, neither the rest
of his generation nor the next caught up with him or discovered a way to escape
his authority easily.

World War II forced a decisive break in world history. Emerging from the
conflict, the United States assumed the role of superpower. Artistically, this dominance was reflected in America's replacing England as the center of poetry. Despite Eliot's shadow, young American postwar poets inherited a confidence for
which the previous generation had had to fight. This confidence was solidified by
the newfound importance of poetry in American colleges and universities. Many

John Crowe Ransom established the journal Kenyon Review *at Kenyon College in 1937. Since then, increasing numbers of colleges have become centers of literary activities.*

young poets learned their craft by studying literature, whereas the previous generation had been largely self-taught. By 1950 poets and poetry had become fixtures on campuses in New York City, New Haven, Cambridge, Nashville, Ann Arbor, Berkeley, and elsewhere. During the late 1940s and early 1950s, many of the new generation of poets—including W. S. Merwin, Robert Lowell, James Merrill, James Wright, Richard Wilbur, Adrienne Rich, and John Ashbery—went abroad, financed either by private funds or by fellowships and grants. Yet, no one city became a foreign literary center, as Paris had in the 1920s, and these poets did not follow in the footsteps of Pound and Eliot, who lived abroad permanently.

The accent on the individual is the signature of postmodern poetry, an appellation given to poetry that appeared after 1945 and differs stylistically from the poetry of the modernists. Individual, if not personal, experience came to be not only acceptable as subject matter and stance, but assumed. And with the shift to postmodernism came a shift in poetry criticism. The most significant critical movement of the 1940s and the 1950s was the so-called New Criticism, led by the poet/critics I. A. Richards, John Crowe Ransom, R. P. Blackmur, Robert Penn Warren, and Cleanth Brooks. Influenced by the formal, classical, and impersonal elements in Eliot's poetry and criticism, the New Critics saw the poem as an independent whole (a self-contained object) whose meaning could be interpreted by close textual analysis without reference to either the author's intention or the reader's emotional response. In their own poetry the New Critics employed tradi-

=CONTEXTS==

Psychoanalytic Criticism

Psychoanalytic criticism involves the examination of literary works and their authors in terms of the theories of psychoanalysis, especially those of Sigmund Freud (1856–1939). In the essay "Freud and Literature" (1941), the writer Lionel Trilling (1905–1975) finds "literary affinities" to certain elements of Freudian psychology. In making connections between the functions of the mind as Freud understood them and the interpretation of literature, Trilling writes:

Freud and Literature

The whole notion of rich ambiguity in literature, of the interplay between the apparent meaning and the latent—not "hidden"—meaning, has been reinforced by the Freudian concepts, perhaps even received its first impetus from them.

Specifically of poetry, he says:

Of all the mental systems, the Freudian psychology is the one which makes poetry indigenous to the very constitution of the mind. Indeed, the mind, as Freud sees it, is in the greater part of its tendency exactly a poetry-making organ. This puts the case too strongly, no doubt, for it seems to make the working of the unconscious mind equivalent to poetry itself, forgetting that between the unconscious mind and the finished poem there supervene the social intention and the formal control of the conscious mind. Yet the statement has at least the virtue of counterbalancing the belief, so commonly expressed or implied, that the very opposite is true, and that poetry is a kind of beneficent aberration of the mind's right course.

                                                          Lionel Trilling, 1941

tional forms in writing objective, "impersonal" poems. Some young poets showed the influence of the New Criticism in their first volumes: Randall Jarrell's *Blood for a Stranger* (1942), Robert Lowell's *Lord Weary's Castle* (1946), John Berryman's *The Dispossessed* (1948), and Theodore Roethke's *Lost Son and Other Poems* (1948). These poets later freed themselves in varying degrees from its restraints. Other young poets, such as Elizabeth Bishop, admired by her peers for her technical elegance, were relatively untouched by the New Critics, as her first volume, *North and South* (1946), shows. Richard Wilbur, who published his first book of poetry, *The Beautiful Changes* in 1947, also remained a formalist. But the New Criticism, which had quickly become entrenched in academia, reached its zenith in 1956 with the revised edition of Brooks and Warren's 1938 *Understanding Poetry*, a college textbook that taught students how to "read" poetry according to the editors' canons.

By 1960 other views of poetry began to be heard. In his highly influential anthology *The New American Poetry*, published that year, Donald Allen included the work of post-World War II poets who represented, he claimed in his introduction, "the avant-garde, the true continuers of the modern movement in American poetry." Their common characteristic was "a total rejection of all those qualities typical of academic verse." Allen divided these poets into such groups as the Black Mountain School, the beats, and the New York School, although he recognized that this categorization was flexible.

Many of the Black Mountain poets—most of them affiliated with Black Mountain College in North Carolina—followed the theories of the college's rector, the poet Charles Olson. He advocated "projective verse," or poems as "open fields" conducting energy from poet to reader. Open forms included irregular meter and placement of lines and phrases over the page, as dictated by the poet's "breath." Members of the Black Mountain School included Robert Creeley, Robert Duncan, and the English poet Denise Levertov, after she emigrated to America following the war.

Allen Ginsberg's long poem "Howl" (1956) ushered in the beat generation of poets. In "Howl," Ginsberg explained, he sought to write with the "freedom of personal-thought rhythms as they occur." As Walt Whitman had done the century before, Ginsberg lengthened the traditional poetic line and extended the subject matter of poetry to embrace the often raw, dirty, ugly side of life and to protest public complacency, espousing instead freer lifestyles. Indeed, the term "beat" linked poets who shared Ginsberg's views to such underground alternatives as drugs, political radicalism, and homosexuality. Yet, it also connected them to another, more inward path of revolt, that achieved through the "beatitude" offered by the Eastern religious cults popular during the 1960s and 1970s. Ginsberg wrote and read "Howl" in San Francisco, which had become a center of beat activities during the 1950s, primarily through the efforts of beat poets such as Lawrence Ferlinghetti, who ran the influential City Lights bookstore, and Kenneth Rexroth.

Another opening of poetic content and form was initiated by the New York poets. Influenced by abstract-expressionist and surrealist painters, Frank O'Hara, John Ashbery, and James Schuyler wrote verse that, like abstract expressionism, concentrates on the act of composition itself and on capturing the moment that occasioned it. O'Hara's *Lunch Poems* (1964), written like notebook jottings, exemplifies the lighthearted, casual quality found in much of these poets' work. Of the New York poets, Ashbery has gone on to develop a far more complex style, as in his long poem "Self-Portrait in a Convex Mirror" (1975), which explores the tension between a completed work of art and the poet using all his energy to write about it.

A less radical expansion of poetry originated in the confessional verse of the 1950s and 1960s. The first volume by W. D. Snodgrass, *Heart's Needle* (1959), consisting of poems on his divorce, spurred Robert Lowell to write the family history poems of *Life Studies* (1959). Confessional verse was characterized by the unflinching candor with which these poets and others, including John Berryman in *The Dream Songs* (1964, 1969), Anne Sexton in *To Bedlam and Part Way Back* (1960), and Sylvia Plath in *Ariel* (1965), examined the most painful elements of their private lives—alcoholism, mental breakdowns, suicide attempts, and adultery. Yet, although they opened poetry to new subject matter, these poets tended to employ more formal verse styles than did the Black Mountain poets, the beats, and the New York poets. The tension in confessional poetry, in fact, arises from the friction between the personal, often shocking subject matter and the form (or its vestiges) that strives to contain it.

As many Americans, especially the young, turned increasingly to social protest in the 1960s, poetry of social protest came to the forefront, as it had in the 1930s. Adrienne Rich, Robert Lowell, Denise Levertov, and Allen Ginsberg wrote poems attacking America's involvement in the Vietnam War—and in the process both continued and changed the focus of Jarrell's war poetry of World War II. Rich passionately addresses the issues of women's liberation in *Diving Into the Wreck* (1973) and of lesbianism in *Sources* (1983), whereas Amiri Baraka angrily advocates African-American separatism and (later) revolution in his poetry of *The Dead Lecturer* (1964) and *In Our Terribleness* (1971) and in his prose. Such works, which explore the moral questions underlying the social issues of the times, would have been unlikely if post-World War II poets had not expanded the permissible range of subject matter and form.

Today's poets are taking full advantage of this previous experimentation. Written in formal verse, James Merrill's trilogy of book-length poems, *The Changing Light at Sandover* (1983), boldly attempts to construct an epic poem, using the brief lyric as its essential building block. Other notable recent poets, including Galway Kinnell, James Wright, A. R. Ammons, and Robert Hass, have in varying degrees replaced strict forms by looser ones, typically dispensing with rhyme and meter to emphasize metaphor and image, juxtaposition, lineation, and rhythm. Poets such as Lawson Inada, Paula Gunn Allen, Maxine Kumin, Simon Ortíz, Alberto Ríos, Louise Erdrich, and William Stafford write poetry firmly rooted in their ethnic heritage and/or explore regional landscapes. Poetry has once again been redefined in the generations of the postmodernists.

Theodore Roethke
(1908–1963)

Theodore Roethke was born in Saginaw, Michigan, in 1908. Much of Roethke's childhood was spent in intimate contact with the world within the greenhouse operated by his father, a successful florist who died when the poet was fifteen. This early death, and his ambivalent feelings for his father, are recurrent themes in Roethke's poems, but these poems are not as frankly autobiographical as the confessional poetry of Roethke's contemporaries Robert Lowell and Sylvia Plath.

After graduating from the University of Michigan in 1929 and spending a year at Harvard University, Roethke embarked on a series of teaching jobs. At Lafayette College in Pennsylvania he established important friendships with the poets Louise Bogan, Stanley Kunitz, and Rolfe Humphries; at Bennington College in Vermont he met the intellectually stimulating critic Kenneth Burke. From 1947 until his sudden death in 1963, Roethke taught at the University of Washington in Seattle, where the poets Carolyn Kizer, Richard Hugo, David Wagoner, and James Wright were among the many students captivated by Roethke's intensity.

Roethke's "greenhouse" poems stem from a rediscovery of his childhood. The highly unconventional free-verse greenhouse poems in *The Lost Son and Other Poems* (1948) brought the literary world to attention. Some of these poems scrutinize a subterranean realm of leaf mold, mildew, and roots; other poems are interior monologues written in the meditative yet anxious voice of a child. In both cases Roethke asks us to recognize our kinship with the "subhuman" order of life. Roethke's contemporaries recognized the publication of *The Lost Son* as an important event.

Although Roethke's creative breakthrough was accomplished in free verse, he never forsook traditional poetic forms. A poem like "The Waking" (1953), a highly successful villanelle—a complex and demanding verse form of French origin—shows that Roethke was capable of working within traditional forms while addressing a theme implicit in the greenhouse poems: that the unconscious is our most reliable guide to spiritual progress. In "The Waking" he writes that we "wake to sleep," not to our rational, conscious powers. Indeed, he is at times excessively derisive of reason. Roethke seeks instead a return to a primordial category of consciousness and situates himself within American and British traditions of romanticism. In his nature poems he manifests Ralph Waldo Emerson's desire to explore the near-familiar; Roethke's focus on the child amounts to an innovative revival of William Wordsworth's reverence for the intuitive wisdom of childhood. (The title of Roethke's third book, *Praise to the End!* [1951], comes from Book I of *The Prelude* [1850], Wordsworth's long autobiographical poem.) The affirmative counterpart to the traumatized voice of Roethke's "The Lost Son" is evident in the numerous children's nonsense poems and other humorous pieces in *Words for the Wind* (1958) and *I Am! Says the Lamb* (1961). Equally playful are Roethke's late and beautiful love poems, such as "I Knew a Woman" (1958), replete with erotic puns.

Roethke's craving for recognition was answered late in life. He received a Pulitzer Prize in 1954 for *The Waking, Poems: 1933–1953;* National Book Awards in 1959 for *Words for the Wind* and in 1964 for *The Far Field;* and the Bollingen Prize in 1959 for *Words for the Wind*. Despite these achievements and his students' admiration, Roethke's life was marked by personal anguish, periods of heavy drinking, and the need for frequent reassurances from friends about the quality of his poetry. After 1935 he was plagued by a series of emotional breakdowns. Several of these breakdowns warranted hospitalization, but Roethke managed to write some of his best poems during these difficult periods.

Suggested Readings: *Open House*, 1941. *The Lost Son and Other Poems*, 1948. *Praise to the End!*, 1951. *The Waking, Poems: 1933–1953*, 1953. *Words for the Wind*, 1958. *The Far Field*, 1965. *On the Poet and His Craft: Selected Prose of Theodore Roethke*, ed. R. J. Mills, Jr., 1965. K. Malkoff, *Theodore Roethke: An Introduction to the Poetry*, 1966. A. Seager, *The Glass House: The Life of Theodore Roethke*, 1968. J. La Belle, *The Echoing Wood of Theodore Roethke*, 1976. H. Bloom, ed. *Theodore Roethke*, 1988. P. Balakian, *Theodore Roethke's Far Fields: The Evolution of His Poetry*, 1989.

Text Used: *The Collected Poems of Theodore Roethke*, 1975.

MY PAPA'S WALTZ*

The whiskey on your breath
Could make a small boy dizzy;
But I hung on like death:
Such waltzing was not easy.

We romped until the pans
Slid from the kitchen shelf;
My mother's countenance
Could not unfrown itself.

The hand that held my wrist
Was battered on one knuckle;   10
At every step you missed
My right ear scraped a buckle.

You beat time on my head
With a palm caked hard by dirt,
Then waltzed me off to bed
Still clinging to your shirt.

1942

ROOT CELLAR

Nothing would sleep in that cellar, dank as a ditch,
Bulbs broke out of boxes hunting for chinks in the dark,
Shoots dangled and drooped,
Lolling obscenely from mildewed crates,
Hung down long yellow evil necks, like tropical snakes.
And what a congress of stinks!—
Roots ripe as old bait,
Pulpy stems, rank, silo-rich,[1]
Leaf-mold, manure, lime, piled against slippery planks.
Nothing would give up life: 10
Even the dirt kept breathing a small breath.

1946, 1948

* First published in *Harper's Bazaar* in 1942.
[1] Stored for a long time.

THE LOST SON

I. THE FLIGHT

At Woodlawn[1] I heard the dead cry:
I was lulled by the slamming of iron,
A slow drip over stones,
Toads brooding wells.
All the leaves stuck out their tongues;
I shook the softening chalk of my bones,
Saying,
Snail, snail, glister[2] me forward,
Bird, soft-sigh me home,
Worm, be with me.   10
This is my hard time.

Fished in an old wound,
The soft pond of repose;
Nothing nibbled my line,
Not even the minnows came.

Sat in an empty house
Watching shadows crawl,
Scratching.
There was one fly.

Voice, come out of the silence.   20
Say something.
Appear in the form of a spider
Or a moth beating the curtain.

Tell me:
Which is the way I take;
Out of what door do I go,
Where and to whom?

      Dark hollows said, lee to the wind,
      The moon said, back of an eel,
      The salt said, look by the sea,   30
      Your tears are not enough praise,
      You will find no comfort here,
      In the kingdom of bang and blab.[3]

---

[1] A cemetery.
[2] An archaic variant of glisten; snails produce a mucus trail along which they glide.
[3] Noise and idle chatter.

Running lightly over spongy ground,
Past the pasture of flat stones,
The three elms,
The sheep strewn on a field,
Over a rickety bridge
Toward the quick-water, wrinkling and rippling.

Hunting along the river,   40
Down among the rubbish, the bug-riddled foliage,
By the muddy pond-edge, by the bog-holes,
By the shrunken lake, hunting, in the heat of summer.

The shape of a rat?
    It's bigger than that.
    It's less than a leg
    And more than a nose,
    Just under the water
    It usually goes.

Is it soft like a mouse?   50
Can it wrinkle its nose?
Could it come in the house
On the tips of its toes?

Take the skin of a cat
And the back of an eel,
Then roll them in grease,—
That's the way it would feel.

It's sleek as an otter
With wide webby toes
Just under the water   60
It usually goes.

2. THE PIT

Where do the roots go?
    Look down under the leaves.
Who put the moss there?
    These stones have been here too long.
Who stunned the dirt into noise?
    Ask the mole, he knows.
I feel the slime of a wet nest.
    Beware Mother Mildew.
Nibble again, fish nerves.   70

3. The Gibber[4]

At the wood's mouth,
By the cave's door,
I listened to something
I had heard before.

Dogs of the groin
Barked and howled,
The sun was against me,
The moon would not have me.

The weeds whined,
The snakes cried,   80
The cows and briars
Said to me: Die.

What a small song. What slow clouds. What dark water.
Hath the rain a father? All the caves are ice. Only the snow's here.
I'm cold. I'm cold all over. Rub me in father and mother.
Fear was my father, Father Fear.
His look drained the stones.

What gliding shape
Beckoning through halls,
Stood poised on the stair,   90
Fell dreamily down?

From the mouths of jugs
Perched on many shelves,
I saw substance flowing
That cold morning.

Like a slither of eels
That watery cheek
As my own tongue kissed
My lips awake.

Is this the storm's heart? The ground is unstilling itself.   100
My veins are running nowhere. Do the bones cast out their fire?
Is the seed leaving the old bed? These buds are live as birds.
Where, where are the tears of the world?
Let the kisses resound, flat like a butcher's palm;
Let the gestures freeze; our doom is already decided.
All the windows are burning! What's left of my life?

---

[4] Unintelligible chatter; also a pouch at the base of some flowers.

I want the old rage, the lash of primordial milk!
Goodbye, goodbye, old stones, the time-order is going,
I have married my hands to perpetual agitation,
I run, I run to the whistle of money.   110

    Money money money
    Water water water

    How cool the grass is.
    Has the bird left?
    The stalk still sways.
    Has the worm a shadow?
    What do the clouds say?

    These sweeps of light undo me.
    Look, look, the ditch is running white!
    I've more veins than a tree!   120
    Kiss me, ashes, I'm falling through a dark swirl.

4. The Return

    The way to the boiler was dark,
    Dark all the way,
    Over slippery cinders
    Through the long greenhouse.

    The roses kept breathing in the dark.
    They had many mouths to breathe with.
    My knees made little winds underneath
    Where the weeds slept.

    There was always a single light   130
    Swinging by the fire-pit,[5]
    Where the fireman pulled out roses,
    The big roses, the big bloody clinkers.[6]

    Once I stayed all night.
    The light in the morning came slowly over the white
    Snow.
    There were many kinds of cool
    Air.
    Then came steam.

    Pipe-knock.[7]   140

---

[5] The heat source of the boiler that keeps the greenhouse temperature high.
[6] Fused residue from burnt coals, still red-hot ("bloody").   [7] The knocking of radiator pipes.

Scurry of warm over small plants.
Ordnung! ordnung![8]
Papa is coming!

A fine haze moved off the leaves;
Frost melted on far panes;
The rose, the chrysanthemum turned toward the light.
Even the hushed forms, the bent yellowy weeds
Moved in a slow up-sway.

5. "IT WAS BEGINNING WINTER"

It was beginning winter,
An in-between time,   150
The landscape still partly brown:
The bones of weeds kept swinging in the wind,
Above the blue snow.

It was beginning winter,
The light moved slowly over the frozen field,
Over the dry seed-crowns,
The beautiful surviving bones
Swinging in the wind.

Light traveled over the wide field;
Stayed.   160
The weeds stopped swinging.
The mind moved, not alone,
Through the clear air, in the silence.

Was it light?
Was it light within?
Was it light within light?
Stillness becoming alive,
Yet still?

A lively understandable spirit
Once entertained you.   170
It will come again.
Be still.
Wait.

1946, 1948

---

[8] "Order! Order!" (German).

THE WAKING

I wake to sleep, and take my waking slow.
I feel my fate in what I cannot fear.
I learn by going where I have to go.

We think by feeling. What is there to know?
I hear my being dance from ear to ear.
I wake to sleep, and take my waking slow.

Of those so close beside me, which are you?
God bless the Ground! I shall walk softly there,
And learn by going where I have to go.

Light takes the Tree; but who can tell us how?   10
The lowly worm climbs up a winding stair;
I wake to sleep, and take my waking slow.

Great Nature has another thing to do
To you and me; so take the lively air,
And, lovely, learn by going where to go.

This shaking keeps me steady. I should know.
What falls away is always. And is near.
I wake to sleep, and take my waking slow.
I learn by going where I have to go.

1952, 1953

I KNEW A WOMAN

I knew a woman, lovely in her bones,
When small birds sighed, she would sigh back at them;
Ah, when she moved, she moved more ways than one:
The shapes a bright container can contain!
Of her choice virtues only gods should speak,
Or English poets who grew up on Greek
(I'd have them sing in chorus, cheek to cheek).

How well her wishes went! She stroked my chin,
She taught me Turn, and Counter-turn, and Stand;[1]
She taught me Touch, that undulant white skin;   10
I nibbled meekly from her proffered hand;

---

[1] Strophe, antistrophe, and epode, or the three stanzas around which the odes of the Greek poet Pindar (522–442 B.C.) are organized. Usually elevated in tone, Pindaric odes have a complex metrical structure reflecting the dance movements they were written to accompany. The pattern of the strophe is repeated in the antistrophe but not in the concluding epode.

She was the sickle; I, poor I, the rake,
Coming behind her for her pretty sake
(But what prodigious mowing we did make).

Love likes a gander, and adores a goose:
Her full lips pursed, the errant note to seize;
She played it quick, she played it light and loose;
My eyes, they dazzled at her flowing knees;
Her several parts could keep a pure repose,
Or one hip quiver with a mobile nose   20
(She moved in circles, and those circles moved).

Let seed be grass, and grass turn into hay:
I'm martyr to a motion not my own;
What's freedom for? To know eternity.
I swear she cast a shadow white as stone.
But who would count eternity in days?
These old bones live to learn her wanton ways:
(I measure time by how a body sways).

                                             1958

IN A DARK TIME*

In a dark time, the eye begins to see,
I meet my shadow in the deepening shade;
I hear my echo in the echoing wood—
A lord of nature weeping to a tree.
I live between the heron[1] and the wren,
Beasts of the hill and serpents of the den.

What's madness but nobility of soul
At odds with circumstance? The day's on fire!
I know the purity of pure despair,
My sh dow pinn d against a sweating wall.   10
That ice among the rocks—is it a cave,
Or wi ling path? The edge is what I have.

A steady storm of correspondences!
A night flowing with birds, a ragged moon,
And in broad day the midnight come again!
A man goes far to find out what he is—
Death of the self in a long, tearless night,
All natural shapes blazing unnatural light.

* Roethke's note: "[The poem is] a drive toward God; an effort to break through the barrier of rational experience."
[1] Roethke's note: "A symbol of purity, wisdom, toughness."

Dark, dark my light, and darker my desire.
My soul, like some heat-maddened summer fly,   20
Keeps buzzing at the sill. Which I is *I*?
A fallen man, I climb out of my fear.
The mind enters itself, and God the mind,
And one is One, free in the tearing[2] wind.

1964

Elizabeth Bishop
(1911–1979)

Elizabeth Bishop's titles for three of her major collections of poems—*North & South* (1946), *Questions of Travel* (1965), and *Geography III* (1976)—appropriately allude to her life and to the subject of much of her work. Bishop was a poet whose early losses and uprootedness are reflected in her adult travels and in poems tentatively addressing questions of "place," of travel and geography. Bishop relied on the intricate details of observation, translating them into descriptions of external landscapes that yield, though somewhat obliquely, the more elusive internal landscape of the self. To Bishop that internal landscape can be apprehended by knowing precisely where we are geographically and by understanding the complex relationship between that location and where we could be or could have chosen to be. Whereas the poem "Questions of Travel" asks "Should we have stayed at home and thought of here?" and "'*Should we have stayed at home, / wherever that may be?*',", the poet contends that "*the choice is never wide and never free.*"

If the poems address questions of place, the poet and her work are likewise difficult to place. Highly descriptive and typically formal, the poetry is not easily defined in relation to any specific movement. Belonging to no particular school of poetry, Bishop remained, by her work and by her character and life style, essentially outside the literary circles of her contemporaries. A poet who did not necessarily think of herself as a writer, she remarked in a 1978 interview with Elizabeth Spires (in *Poets at Work* [1989]) that "there's nothing more embarrassing than being a poet, really." A woman who, until late in her career, was too shy to give readings or to teach, Bishop established and maintained significant relationships with the poets Marianne Moore and Robert Lowell.

Born in Worcester, Massachusetts, in 1911 to parents of Canadian descent, Bishop spent her early childhood with her maternal grandparents in Nova Scotia, a landscape to which she returned in much of her poetry. Her father had died soon after her birth; in 1916 her mother, who had suffered a series of breakdowns, was committed to a mental hospital and remained there until her death in 1934. For Bishop, who never saw her mother again after the last breakdown, itinerancy became a way of life when she was soon sent to her paternal grandparents in Worcester. There she became severely ill. When she went to live with an aunt in Boston, continued ill health—bronchitis, chronic asthma, and eczema—

---

[2] Roethke's note: "I feel there is hope in the ambiguity of 'tearing'—that the ambient air itself . . . [is] capable of pity."

*A 1976 drawing of
Elizabeth Bishop by
Darcy Penteado.*

kept her out of school for long periods at a time. Bishop did not begin a steady formal education until she went away to boarding school in Natick, Massachusetts. She entered Vassar College in 1930 as a music composition major but dreaded the performances required of her. After giving up music she studied English and shortly before graduation met Marianne Moore. They began a lifelong friendship lasting until Moore's death in 1972.

After graduating with an A.B. in 1934, Bishop traveled to Europe, North Africa, and Mexico, and her poems began to appear in such periodicals as the *Partisan Review* and *Poetry*. Although Bishop's poems were published as early as 1935, she did not bring out her first collection, *North & South,* until 1946, about the time the poet Randall Jarrell introduced her to Robert Lowell. In 1938 she went to Key West, where she stayed for extended periods until the late 1940s. She traveled to South America in 1951, settling in Río de Janiero for nearly twenty years, and once took a trip down the Amazon River.

Bishop's travels and foreign residences are not surprising, as she had been a child with no permanent home nor a sense of one. "I was always sort of a guest, and I think I've always felt that way," she told Spires. As traveler and carefully inquisitive poet she was not unlike her "Sandpiper" (1965), ". . . preoccupied, / looking for something, something, something." Although Bishop claimed she had not really "been anywhere at all," her poems are deeply connected to the various landscapes she inhabited, particularly the northern ones of New England and Nova Scotia and the southern ones of Key West and South America. Characterized by repetition, rhyme and partial rhyme, they are rarely self-referential, focusing instead on the precise detail of what lies before the poet's eye, "preoccupied" with naturalizing for the self the specifics of geographic location.

Yet, such poems as "The Map" (1946), "The Imaginary Iceberg" (1946), "Questions of Travel," and "The Moose" (1976) tentatively probe the interior landscape of the self, subtly excavating the shadowy worlds of borders, the places between and beneath what is most apparently visible, what is highlighted in the deceptively simple surface descriptions of the poems. "We'd rather have the iceberg than the ship, / although it meant the end of travel," writes Bishop in "The Imaginary Iceberg," for it "cuts its facets from within" and, like the soul, is "self-made from elements least visible." Maintaining a straightforward and modest tone but authoritative control over material, Bishop's poems tend to pivot on a series of questions or qualified, provisional assertions: "the art of losing's not too hard to master / though it may look like (*Write* it!) like disaster," Bishop claims in "One Art" (1976).

Returning to the United States in the early 1970s, Bishop taught at a number of universities, including Harvard, and lived in Boston from 1974 until her sudden death in 1979. The posthumously published *Elizabeth Bishop: The Collected Prose* (1984) includes the much-noted short story "In the Village." She translated the work of several Brazilian poets and *The Diary of "Helena Morley"* (1957). The first woman and the first American to win the prestigious Books Abroad/Neustadt International Prize for literature (1976), Bishop received such honors as two Guggenheim Fellowships, the Houghton Mifflin Poetry Award (for *North & South*), a Pulitzer Prize for *Poems: North & South—A Cold Spring* (1955), a National Book Award for *The Complete Poems* (1969), and the National Book Critics' Circle Award for *Geography III*. Widely acclaimed yet always on the edge of mainstream literary life, Bishop was not unlike her "imaginary iceberg," her epithets "self-made" and "least visible" applicable to the internal landscapes lying beneath her carefully constructed descriptions and to her poetic persona.

Suggested Readings: *North & South*, 1946. *Poems: North & South—A Cold Spring*, 1955. *The Ballad of the Burglar of Babylon*, 1968. *Questions of Travel*, 1968. *Geography III*, 1976. *The Collected Prose*, 1984. J. H. Miller, *Poets of Reality: Six Twentieth-Century Writers*, 1965. A. Stevenson, *Elizabeth Bishop*, 1966. A. Brown, "Elizabeth Bishop in Brazil," in *Southern Review*, 13:688–704 (Autumn) 1977. A. S. Ostriker, *Stealing the Language: The Emergence of Women's Poetry in America*, 1986. H. Vendler, "The Poems of Elizabeth Bishop," in *Critical Inquiry*, 13(4): 825–838, (Summer) 1987. D. Kalstone, *Becoming a Poet: Elizabeth Bishop With Marianne Moore and Robert Lowell*, ed. R. Hemenway, 1989. E. Spires, "An Afternoon With Elizabeth Bishop," in *Poets at Work: The PARIS REVIEW Interviews*, ed. G. Plimpton, 1989.

Text Used: *The Complete Poems: 1927–1979*, 1983.

THE MAP

Land lies in water; it is shadowed green.
Shadows, or are they shallows, at its edges
showing the line of long sea-weeded ledges
where weeds hang to the simple blue from green.
Or does the land lean down to lift the sea from under,
drawing it unperturbed around itself?
Along the fine tan sandy shelf
is the land tugging at the sea from under?

The shadow of Newfoundland lies flat and still.
Labrador's yellow, where the moony Eskimo   10

has oiled it. We can stroke these lovely bays,
under a glass as if they were expected to blossom,
or as if to provide a clean cage for invisible fish.
The names of seashore towns run out to sea,
the names of cities cross the neighboring mountains
—the printer here experiencing the same excitement
as when emotion too far exceeds its cause.
These peninsulas take the water between thumb and finger
like women feeling for the smoothness of yard-goods.

Mapped waters are more quiet than the land is,   20
lending the land their waves' own conformation:
and Norway's hare runs south[1] in agitation,
profiles investigate the sea, where land is.
Are they assigned, or can the countries pick their colors?
—What suits the character or the native waters best.
Topography displays no favorites; North's as near as West.
More delicate than the historians' are the map-makers' colors.

1946

THE IMAGINARY ICEBERG

We'd rather have the iceberg than the ship,
although it meant the end of travel.
Although it stood stock-still like cloudy rock
and all the sea were moving marble.
We'd rather have the iceberg than the ship;
we'd rather own this breathing plain of snow
though the ship's sails were laid upon the sea
as the snow lies undissolved upon the water.
O solemn, floating field,
are you aware an iceberg takes repose   10
with you, and when it wakes may pasture on your snows?

This is a scene a sailor'd give his eyes for.
The ship's ignored. The iceberg rises
and sinks again; its glassy pinnacles
correct elliptics in the sky.
This is a scene where he who treads the boards
is artlessly rhetorical. The curtain
is light enough to rise on finest ropes
that airy twists of snow provide.
The wits of these white peaks   20
spar with the sun. Its weight the iceberg dares
upon a shifting stage and stands and stares.

---

[1] A reference to Norway's shape; its "head" is pointed southward, with the upper portion in the Atlantic and the lower portion in Skagerrak, the broad arm of the North Sea.

This iceberg cuts its facets from within.
Like jewelry from a grave
it saves itself perpetually and adorns
only itself, perhaps the snows
which so surprise us lying on the sea.
Goody-bye, we say, good-bye, the ship steers off
where waves give in to one another's waves
and clouds run in a warmer sky.   30
Icebergs behoove the soul
(both being self-made from elements least visible)
to see them so: fleshed, fair, erected indivisible.

1946

THE BIGHT*

[*On my birthday*]

At low tide like this how sheer the water is.
White, crumbling ribs of marl[1] protrude and glare
and the boats are dry, the pilings dry as matches.
Absorbing, rather than being absorbed,
the water in the bight doesn't wet anything,
the color of the gas flame turned as low as possible.
One can smell it turning to gas; if one were Baudelaire[2]
one could probably hear it turning to marimba music.[3]
The little ocher dredge at work off the end of the dock
already plays the dry perfectly off-beat claves.[4]   10
The birds are outsize. Pelicans crash
into his peculiar gas unnecessarily hard,
it seems to me, like pickaxes,
rarely coming up with anything to show for it,
and going off with humorous elbowings.
Black-and-white man-of-war birds soar
on impalpable drafts
and open their tails like scissors on the curves
or tense them like wishbones, till they tremble.
The frowsy sponge boats keep coming in   20

---

* A bay formed by a curve in a river or coastline.
[1] A soft, crumbly mixture of clay, sand, and limestone in varying proportions, typically containing shell fragments.
[2] The French poet Charles Baudelaire (1821–1867), whose aesthetic ideas were the source of the symbolist movement.
[3] Latin dance music based on a syncopated rhythm of alternating phrases of three and two beats, played by a musical instrument resembling a xylophone, consisting of a series of hard wooden bars with resonators, struck with small mallets.
[4] A pair of cylindrical hardwood sticks that make a hollow sound when struck together, used as a percussion instrument in Latin music.

with the obliging air of retrievers,
bristling with jackstraw gaffs and hooks[5]
and decorated with bobbles of sponges.
There is a fence of chicken wire along the dock
where, glinting like little plowshares,
the blue-gray shark tails are hung up to dry
for the Chinese-restaurant trade.
Some of the little white boats are still piled up
against each other, or lie on their sides, stove in,
and not yet salvaged, if they ever will be, from the last bad storm,   30
like torn-open, unanswered letters.
The bight is littered with old correspondences.
Click. Click. Goes the dredge,
and brings up a dripping jawful of marl.
All the untidy activity continues,
awful but cheerful.

1955

QUESTIONS OF TRAVEL

There are too many waterfalls here; the crowded streams
hurry too rapidly down to the sea,
and the pressure of so many clouds on the mountaintops
makes them spill over the sides in soft slow-motion,
turning to waterfalls under our very eyes.
—For if those streaks, those mile-long, shiny, tearstains,
aren't waterfalls yet,
in a quick age or so, as ages go here,
they probably will be.
But if the streams and clouds keep travelling, travelling,   10
the mountains look like the hulls of capsized ships,
slime-hung and barnacled.

Think of the long trip home.
Should we have stayed at home and thought of here?
Where should we be today?
Is it right to be watching strangers in a play
in this strangest of theatres?
What childishness is it that while there's a breath of life
in our bodies, we are determined to rush
to see the sun the other way around?   20
The tiniest green hummingbird in the world?
To stare at some inexplicable old stonework,
inexplicable and impenetrable,
at any view,

[5] Large, strong hooks on a pole used in catching large sponges; here, hooks on a sponge-catching
boat to hold the catch.

instantly seen and always, always delightful?
Oh, must we dream our dreams
and have them, too?
And have we room
for one more folded sunset, still quite warm?

But surely it would have been a pity   30
not to have seen the trees along this road,
really exaggerated in their beauty,
not to have seen them gesturing
like noble pantomimists, robed in pink.
—Not to have had to stop for gas and heard
the sad, two-noted, wooden tune
of disparate wooden clogs
carelessly clacking over
a grease-stained filling-station floor.
(In another country the clogs would all be tested.   40
Each pair there would have identical pitch.)
—A pity not to have heard
the other, less primitive music of the fat brown bird
who sings above the broken gasoline pump
in a bamboo church of Jesuit baroque:[1]
three towers, five silver crosses.
—Yes, a pity not to have pondered,
blurr'dly and inconclusively,
on what connection can exist for centuries
between the crudest wooden footwear   50
and, careful and finicky,
the whittled fantasies of wooden cages.
—Never to have studied history in
the weak calligraphy of songbirds' cages.
—And never to have had to listen to rain
so much like politicians' speeches:
two hours of unrelenting oratory
and then a sudden golden silence
in which the traveller takes a notebook, writes:

"Is it lack of imagination that makes us come   60
to imagined places, not just stay at home?
Or could Pascal[2] have been not entirely right
about just sitting quietly in one's room?

Continent, city, country, society:
the choice is never wide and never free.
And here, or there . . . No. Should we have stayed at home,
wherever that may be?"

1965

---

[1] A seventeenth-century architectural style first brought to South America by the Jesuits.
    [2] Blaise Pascal (1623–1662), a French mathematician, physicist, and philosopher who entered a convent in 1654 and argued for the necessity of mystic faith in understanding the universe.

POEM

About the size of an old-style dollar bill,
American or Canadian,
mostly the same whites, gray greens, and steel grays
—this little painting (a sketch for a larger one?)
has never earned any money in its life.
Useless and free, it has spent seventy years
as a minor family relic
handed along collaterally to owners
who looked at it sometimes, or didn't bother to.

It must be Nova Scotia; only there   10
does one see gabled wooden houses
painted that awful shade of brown.
The other houses, the bits that show, are white.
Elm trees, low hills, a thin church steeple
—that gray-blue wisp—or is it? In the foreground
a water meadow with some tiny cows,
two brushstrokes each, but confidently cows;
two minuscule white geese in the blue water,
back-to-back, feeding, and a slanting stick.
Up closer, a wild iris, white and yellow,   20
fresh-squiggled from the tube.
The air is fresh and cold; cold early spring
clear as gray glass; a half inch of blue sky
below the steel-gray storm clouds.
(They were the artist's specialty.)
A specklike bird is flying to the left.
Or is it a flyspeck looking like a bird?

Heavens, I recognize the place, I know it!
It's behind—I can almost remember the farmer's name.
His barn backed on that meadow. There it is,   30
titanium white, one dab. The hint of steeple,
filaments of brush-hairs, barely there,
must be the Presbyterian church.
Would that be Miss Gillespie's house?
Those particular geese and cows
are naturally before my time.

A sketch done in an hour, "in one breath,"
once taken from a trunk and handed over.
*Would you like this? I'll probably never
have room to hang these things again.*   40
*Your Uncle George, no, mine, my Uncle George,
he'd be your great-uncle, left them all with Mother
when he went back to England.*
You know, he was quite famous, an R.A.[1] . . .

---

[1] An artist elected to England's Royal Academy.

I never knew him. We both knew this place,
apparently, this literal small backwater,
looked at it long enough to memorize it,
our years apart. How strange. And it's still loved,
or its memory is (it must have changed a lot).
Our visions coincided—"visions" is   50
too serious a word—our looks, two looks:
art "copying from life" and life itself,
life and the memory of it so compressed
they've turned into each other. Which is which?
Life and the memory of it cramped,
dim, on a piece of Bristol board,[2]
dim, but how live, how touching in detail
—the little that we get for free,
the little of our earthly trust. Not much.
About the size of our abidance   60
along with theirs: the munching cows,
the iris, crisp and shivering, the water
still standing from spring freshets,
the yet-to-be-dismantled elms, the geese.

1976

IN THE WAITING ROOM

In Worcester, Massachusetts,
I went with Aunt Consuelo
to keep her dentist's appointment
and sat and waited for her
in the dentist's waiting room.
It was winter. It got dark
early. The waiting room
was full of grown-up people,
arctics and overcoats,
lamps and magazines.   10
My aunt was inside
what seemed like a long time
and while I waited I read
the *National Geographic*
(I could read) and carefully
studied the photographs:
the inside of a volcano,
black, and full of ashes;
then it was spilling over
in rivulets of fire.   20
Osa and Martin Johnson[1]

---

[2] A smooth pasteboard used by artists.
[1] Osa Johnson (1894–1953) and her husband, Martin Johnson (1884–1937), filmed Africa's vanishing wildlife for the American Museum of Natural History.

dressed in riding breeches,
laced boots, and pith helmets.
A dead man slung on a pole
—"Long Pig,"² the caption said.
Babies with pointed heads
wound round and round with string;
black, naked women with necks
wound round and round with wire
like the necks of light bulbs.   30
Their breasts were horrifying.
I read it right straight through.
I was too shy to stop.
And then I looked at the cover:
the yellow margins, the date.

Suddenly, from inside,
came an *oh!* of pain
—Aunt Consuelo's voice—
not very loud or long.
I wasn't at all surprised;   40
even then I knew she was
a foolish, timid woman.
I might have been embarrassed,
but wasn't. What took me
completely by surprise
was that it was *me:*
my voice, in my mouth.
Without thinking at all
I was my foolish aunt,
I—we—were falling, falling,   50
our eyes glued to the cover
of the *National Geographic,*
February, 1918.

I said to myself: three days
and you'll be seven years old.
I was saying it to stop
the sensation of falling off
the round, turning world
into cold, blue-black space.
But I felt: you are an *I,*   60
you are an *Elizabeth,*
you are one of *them.*
Why should you be one, too?
I scarcely dared to look
to see what it was I was.
I gave a sidelong glance
—I couldn't look any higher—
at shadowy gray knees,

²The name Polynesian cannibals use for a dead person.

trousers and skirts and boots
and different pairs of hands   70
lying under the lamps.
I knew that nothing stranger
had ever happened, that nothing
stranger could ever happen.

Why should I be my aunt,
or me, or anyone?
What similarities—
boots, hands, the family voice
I felt in my throat, or even
the *National Geographic*   80
and those awful hanging breasts—
held us all together
or made us all just one?
How—I didn't know any
word for it—how "unlikely" . . .
How had I come to be here,
like them, and overhear
a cry of pain that could have
got loud and worse but hadn't?

The waiting room was bright   90
and too hot. It was sliding
beneath a big black wave,
another, and another.

Then I was back in it.
the War[3] was on. Outside,
in Worcester, Massachusetts,
were night and slush and cold,
and it was still the fifth
of February, 1918.

1976

THE MOOSE

For Grace Bulmer Bowers[1]

From narrow provinces
of fish and bread and tea,
home of the long tides

[3] World War I (1914–1918).
[1] Bishop's maternal aunt.

where the bay leaves the sea
twice a day and takes
the herrings long rides,

where if the river
enters or retreats
in a wall of brown foam
depends on if it meets   10
the bay coming in,
the bay not at home;

where, silted red,
sometimes the sun sets
facing a red sea,
and others, veins the flats'
lavender, rich mud
in burning rivulets;

on red, gravelly roads,
down rows of sugar maples,   20
past clapboard farmhouses
and neat, clapboard churches,
bleached, ridged as clamshells,
past twin silver birches,

through late afternoon
a bus journeys west,
the windshield flashing pink,
pink glancing off of metal,
brushing the dented flank
of blue, beat-up enamel;   30

down hollows, up rises,
and waits, patient, while
a lone traveller gives
kisses and embraces
to seven relatives
and a collie supervises.

Goodbye to the elms,
to the farm, to the dog.
The bus starts. The light
grows richer; the fog,   40
shifting, salty, thin,
comes closing in.

Its cold, round crystals
form and slide and settle
in the white hens' feathers,
in gray glazed cabbages,

on the cabbage roses
and lupins[2] like apostles;

the sweet peas cling
to their wet white string
on the whitewashed fences;   50
bumblebees creep
inside the foxgloves,
and evening commences.

One stop at Bass River.
Then the Economies—
Lower, Middle, Upper;
Five Islands, Five Houses,[3]
where a woman shakes a tablecloth
out after supper.   60

A pale flickering. Gone.
The Tantramar marshes
and the smell of salt hay.
An iron bridge trembles
and a loose plank rattles
but doesn't give way.

On the left, a red light
swims through the dark:
a ship's port lantern.
Two rubber boots show,   70
illuminated, solemn.
A dog gives one bark.

A woman climbs in
with two market bags,
brisk, freckled, elderly.
"A grand night. Yes, sir,
all the way to Boston."
She regards us amicably.

Moonlight as we enter
the New Brunswick woods,   80
hairy, scratchy, splintery;
moonlight and mist
caught in them like lamb's wool
on bushes in a pasture.

---

[2] Lupines, plants of the pea family.   [3] Sites in Nova Scotia.

The passengers lie back.
Snores. Some long sighs.
A dreamy divagation
begins in the night,
a gentle, auditory,
slow hallucination. . . .   90

In the creakings and noises,
an old conversation
—not concerning us,
but recognizable, somewhere,
back in the bus:
Grandparents' voices

uninterruptedly
talking, in Eternity:
names being mentioned,
things cleared up finally;   100
what he said, what she said,
who got pensioned;

deaths, deaths and sicknesses;
the year he remarried;
the year (something) happened.
She died in childbirth.
That was the son lost
when the schooner foundered.

He took to drink. Yes.
She went to the bad.   110
When Amos began to pray
even in the store and
finally the family had
to put him away.

"Yes . . ." that peculiar
affirmative. "Yes . . ."
A sharp, indrawn breath,
half groan, half acceptance,
that means "Life's like that.
We know *it* (also death)."   120

Talking the way they talked
in the old featherbed,
peacefully, on and on,
dim lamplight in the hall,
down in the kitchen, the dog
tucked in her shawl.

Now, it's all right now
even to fall asleep
just as on all those nights.
—Suddenly the bus driver   130
stops with a jolt,
turns off his lights.

A moose has come out of
the impenetrable wood
and stands there, looms, rather,
in the middle of the road.
It approaches; it sniffs at
the bus's hot hood.

Towering, antlerless,
high as a church,   140
homely as a house
(or, safe as houses).
A man's voice assures us
"Perfectly harmless. . . ."

Some of the passengers
exclaim in whispers,
childishly, softly,
"Sure are big creatures."
"It's awful plain."
"Look! It's a she!"   150

Taking her time,
she looks the bus over,
grand, otherworldly.
Why, why do we feel
(we all feel) this sweet
sensation of joy?

"Curious creatures,"
says our quiet driver,
rolling his *r*'s.
"Look at that, would you."   160
Then he shifts gears.
For a moment longer,

by craning backward,
the moose can be seen
on the moonlit macadam;
then there's a dim
smell of moose, an acrid
smell of gasoline.

1976

Randall Jarrell
(1914–1965)

Randall Jarrell was at his most eloquent when he was writing of America's involvement in World War II. Born in Nashville in 1914, Jarrell lived in California until he was twelve. He then returned to Nashville and stayed with his recently divorced mother. There Jarrell later did undergraduate and graduate work at Vanderbilt University, where he studied with the poet John Crowe Ransom. Jarrell spent much of his life teaching literature at Kenyon and Sarah Lawrence Colleges and at the Universities of Texas and North Carolina. One of only a handful of poets able to write about World War II from the perspective of a serviceman, he served as an Air Force pilot from 1942 to 1946. Jarrell's poems, many of which are dramatic monologues from the viewpoint of pilots or prisoners of war, do not glorify war; they return it to a human scale. "The Death of the Ball Turret Gunner" (1945), Jarrell's best-known war poem, is successful precisely for the way it equates death with rebirth.

In addition to writing war poems, Jarrell authored four children's books and translated fairy tales, including those of the Brothers Grimm. He typically imbued the speakers of his dramatic monologues, regardless of their age, with the guilelessness and remembered innocence of childhood. His poem "90 North" (1942) explores that innocence and the sad experience of those who have reached adulthood: "Pain comes from the darkness / And we call it wisdom. It is pain." At once lyric and dramatic, introspective and declarative, "90 North" seems finally an extended metaphor for the failure of metaphor to do life justice and for the sometimes misleading nature of words.

Jarrell survived the war. America did, too, though not undamaged, and was soon launched into an era marked by the growth of suburbs. This America (and its inhabitants), revitalized after the war, was Jarrell's second great subject. His two final collections of poetry—*The Woman at the Washington Zoo* (1960), a National Book Award winner, and the posthumously published *The Lost World* (1965)—contain a number of dramatic monologues delivered by women. Most notable from these collections is "Next Day" (from *The Lost World*), set in a grocery store and delivered while the speaker moves "from Cheer to Joy, from Joy to All."

In October 1965 while out walking, Jarrell was struck and killed by a passing motorist. The month before, in a letter to the poet and novelist Robert Penn Warren, Jarrell had noted, "I haven't written any poems [lately], but I've been thinking about the passage of time, and what it's like to live a certain number of years in the world, that I think it's sure to turn into some poems in the long run." Jarrell was widely acknowledged by his contemporaries as the best poet/critic of his generation. His essays and reviews are collected in several volumes, including *Poetry and the Age* (1953), which contains the influential essay "The Obscurity of the Poet"; *A Sad Heart at the Supermarket* (1962); and *Kipling, Auden & Co.* (1980). He also authored *Pictures From an Institution* (1954), a satirical novel about college life.

Suggested Readings: *Blood for a Stranger*, 1942. *Losses*, 1948. *The Seven-League Crutches*, 1951. *Poetry and the Age*, 1953. *Pictures From an Institution*, 1954. *The Woman at the Washington Zoo*, 1960. *Selected Poems*, 1964. *The Lost World*, 1965. *The Third Book of Criticism*, 1965. M. L. Rosenthal, *The Modern Poets: A Critical Introduction*, 1960. R. Lowell et al., eds., *Randall Jarrell, 1914–1965*, 1967. E. Simpson, *Poets in Their Youth, A Memoir*, 1983. J. A. Bryant, Jr., *Under-*

standing Randall Jarrell, 1986. R. Lowell, "Randall Jarrell," in *Collected Prose,* 1987. H. Vendler, "Randall Jarrell," in *The Music of What Happens,* 1988.

Text Used: *The Complete Poems,* 1969.

90 NORTH*

At home, in my flannel gown, like a bear to its floe,
I clambered to bed; up the globe's impossible sides
I sailed all night—till at last, with my black beard,
My furs and my dogs, I stood at the northern pole.

There in the childish night my companions lay frozen,
The stiff furs knocked at my starveling throat,
And I gave my great sigh: the flakes came huddling,
Were they really my end? In the darkness I turned to my rest.

—Here, the flag snaps in the glare and silence
Of the unbroken ice. I stand here,   10
The dogs bark, my beard is black, and I stare
At the North Pole . . .
                                  And now what? Why, go back.

Turn as I please, my step is to the south.
The world—my world spins on this final point
Of cold and wretchedness: all lines, all winds
End in this whirlpool I at last discover.

And it is meaningless. In the child's bed
After the night's voyage, in that warm world
Where people work and suffer for the end
That crowns the pain—in that Cloud-Cuckoo-Land[1]   20

I reached my North and it had meaning.
Here at the actual pole of my existence,
Where all that I have done is meaningless,
Where I die or live by accident alone—

Where, living or dying, I am still alone;
Here where North, the night, the berg of death
Crowd me out of the ignorant darkness,
I see at last that all the knowledge

---

* The latitude of the North Pole.
[1] Fantasy land: an imaginary city built in the sky by cuckoos, in the comic drama *The Birds* (414 B.C.), by the Greek satirist Aristophanes (450?–388? B.C.).

I wrung from the darkness—that the darkness flung me—
Is worthless as ignorance: nothing comes from nothing,   30
The darkness from the darkness. Pain comes from the darkness
And we call it wisdom. It is pain.

                                                                    1942

THE DEATH OF THE BALL TURRET GUNNER*

From my mother's sleep I fell into the State,
And I hunched in its belly till my wet fur froze.
Six miles from earth, loosed from its dream of life,
I woke to black flak[1] and the nightmare fighters.
When I died they washed me out of the turret with a hose.

                                                                    1945

THE WOMAN AT THE WASHINGTON ZOO

The saris[1] go by me from the embassies.

Cloth from the moon. Cloth from another planet.
They look back at the leopard like the leopard.

And I. . . .
                this print of mine, that has kept its color
Alive through so many cleanings; this dull null
Navy I wear to work, and wear from work, and so
To my bed, so to my grave, with no
Complaints, no comment: neither from my chief,
The Deputy Chief Assistant, nor his chief—
Only I complain. . . . this serviceable   10
Body that no sunlight dyes, no hand suffuses
But, dome-shadowed, withering among columns,
Wavy beneath fountains—small, far-off, shining
In the eyes of animals, these beings trapped
As I am trapped but not, themselves, the trap,
Aging, but without knowledge of their age,

---

* Jarrell's note: "A ball turret was a plexiglass sphere set into the belly of a B-17 or B-24 [bomber], and inhabited by two .50 caliber machine-guns and one man, a short, small man. When this gunner tracked with his machine-guns a fighter attacking his bomber from below, he revolved with the turret; hunched upside-down in his little sphere, he looked like the foetus in the womb. The fighters which attacked him were armed with cannon firing explosive shells. The hose was a steam hose."

[1] The noise and fire of anti-aircraft guns.

[1] The wrapped outer garments of Hindu women.

Kept safe here, knowing not of death, for death—
Oh, bars of my own body, open, open!

The world goes by my cage and never sees me.   20
And there come not to me, as come to these,
The wild beasts, sparrows pecking the llamas' grain,
Pigeons settling on the bears' bread, buzzards
Tearing the meat the flies have clouded. . . .
                                    Vulture,
When you come for the white rat that the foxes left,
Take off the red helmet of your head, the black
Wings that have shadowed me, and step to me as man:
The wild brother at whose feet the white wolves fawn,
To whose hand of power the great lioness
Stalks, purring. . . .
                        You know what I was,
You see what I am: change me, change me!   30
                                                    1960

BATS

A bat is born
Naked and blind and pale.
His mother makes a pocket of her tail
And catches him. He clings to her long fur
By his thumbs and toes and teeth.
And then the mother dances through the night
Doubling and looping, soaring, somersaulting—
Her baby hangs on underneath.
All night, in happiness, she hunts and flies.
Her high sharp cries   10
Like shining needlepoints of sound
Go out into the night and, echoing back,
Tell her what they have touched.
She hears how far it is, how big it is,
Which way it's going:
She lives by hearing.
The mother eats the moths and gnats she catches
In full flight; in full flight
The mother drinks the water of the pond
She skims across. Her baby hangs on tight.   20
Her baby drinks the milk she makes him
In moonlight or starlight, in mid-air.
Their single shadow, printed on the moon
Or fluttering across the stars,
Whirls on all night; at daybreak
The tired mother flaps home to her rafter.

The others all are there.
They hang themselves up by their toes,
They wrap themselves in their brown wings.
Bunched upside-down, they sleep in air.   30
Their sharp ears, their sharp teeth, their quick sharp faces
Are dull and slow and mild.
All the bright day, as the mother sleeps,
She folds her wings about her sleeping child.

1965

John Berryman
(1914–1972)

The madness and eloquence that characterize John Berryman's poetry are very much the madness and eloquence of the twentieth century—the political and social upheavals, the obsessions with loss. Berryman was born John Smith in McAlester, Oklahoma, in 1914, the first year of World War I. When he was twelve his father shot himself to death. This event haunted Berryman for the rest of his life and reappears obsessively in his poetry. After his mother remarried he took the surname of his stepfather. Educated at Columbia University and Clare College in Cambridge, England, Berryman subsequently taught literature and the history of civilization at Princeton and Harvard Universities and the Universities of Cincinnati and Minnesota. His first published book was *Poems* (1942). He followed it by *The Dispossessed* (1948) and achieved recognition with the long lyric poem *Homage to Mistress Bradstreet* (1956). In 1965 he received a Pulitzer Prize for *77 Dream Songs* (1964), which became the first section of *The Dream Songs* (1969). By the end of Berryman's life, the number of "dream songs" totaled 385.

Berryman's poetry was a continued if troubled apprenticeship to any number of difficult masters. William Butler Yeats profoundly influenced Berryman's early poems, and echoes of W. H. Auden and Robert Lowell may also be heard. Nevertheless, some of these poems bear suggestions of the brilliance that *The Dream Songs* later captured. What makes "The Ball Poem" (1942) and a handful of other poems stand out from the mass of Berryman's early work is their psychological acuity: they demonstrate unapologetically the bounds and rebounds of a mind profoundly unsettled by loss.

Homage to Mistress Bradstreet, the poem that defines and exemplifies the middle years of Berryman's career, in many ways prefigures *The Dream Songs,* most notably in the use of inversion and forced diction. "When I finally woke up to the fact that I was involved in a long poem," he recollected in the essay "One Answer to a Question" (1976), "one of my first thoughts was: Narrative! let's have narrative, and at least one dominant personality, and no fragmentation!" The poem takes for its subject the life of the seventeenth-century Puritan poet Anne Bradstreet, who Berryman describes as "this boring high-minded Puritan woman." *Homage to Mistress Bradstreet* allowed Berryman to show in a historical character how the personal and the spiritual life of a poet can become the stuff of a poem. At times the lyric sequence takes the form of a conversation between Bradstreet and a twentieth-century poet, most likely Berryman himself, although he denied that. In the end Mistress Bradstreet is as much a fictional creation as is Henry, the protagonist of *The Dream Songs*. Henry's last name is never revealed with certainty: it changes, as Berryman's had.

In "One Answer to a Question" Berryman describes the form of *The Dream Songs* as "eighteen-line sections, three six-line stanzas, each normally (for feet) 5–5–3–5–5–3, variously rhymed and not but mostly rhymed with great strictness." This stanzaic structure commonly breaks down. For example, "A Strut for Roethke," the eighteenth Dream Song, has twenty lines; the extra two form a bridge between the first and second stanzas. And the seventy-seventh dream song has a haunting one-line bridge: "—Come away, Mr. Bones." Some critics have suggested that Henry's unnamed friend, the speaker who implores Mr. Bones to "come away," is Death. Whether or not this is true, in a number of the later dream songs Berryman certainly mourns the death of many of his closest friends, among them the poets Randall Jarrell and Delmore Schwartz. "I'm cross with god who has wrecked this generation," begins dream song number 153. This poem cites the deaths not only of Jarrell and Schwartz, but also of Theodore Roethke, R. P. Blackmur, and Sylvia Plath, each of whom was a contemporary or near-contemporary of Berryman. Yet, for all the despair and the numerous losses they record, *The Dream Songs* struggle to find laughter in the wreckage. At their best they make tragedy of the commonplace and comedy of tragedy. That Henry and his vaudevillian friend speak at times in the dialect of minstrels is unfortunate, as their patter can be—and has been—misconstrued as racist. Nonetheless, the diction Berryman chose for *The Dream Songs* seems appropriate to the dark comedy of Henry's life.

After the publication of *The Dream Songs*, Berryman seemed to flounder. The "I" of his later poems appears to lapse into the voice of the poet himself. Although many of these later poems share the diction and the stanzaic structure Berryman originated in *The Dream Songs*, they are more self-indulgent than self-revelatory and lack his characteristic eloquence. As the years passed, the suffering caused by his father's death continued unabated. Alcoholism, clinical depression, and three failed marriages further eroded his emotional and physical stamina. In 1972, at age fifty-seven, Berryman committed suicide by jumping off a Minneapolis bridge.

Suggested Readings: *Homage to Mistress Bradstreet*, 1956. *77 Dream Songs*, 1964. *Berryman's Sonnets*, 1967. *Delusions, Etc.*, 1972. *Recovery*, 1973. *The Freedom of the Poet*, 1976. *Henry's Fate*, 1977. M. L. Rosenthal, *The New Poets: American and British Poetry Since World War II*, 1967. E. Simpson, *Poets in Their Youth: A Memoir*, 1983. E. M. Halliday, *John Berryman and the Thirties: A Memoir*, 1987. R. Lowell, "John Berryman," in *Robert Lowell: Collected Prose*, 1987. J. D. McClatchy, "John Berryman: The Impediments of Salvation," in *White Paper*, 1989.

Texts Used: *The Dream Songs*, 1969. All else: *Collected Poems: 1937–1971*, ed. C. Thornburg, 1989.

THE BALL POEM

What is the boy now, who has lost his ball,
What, what is he to do? I saw it go
Merrily bouncing, down the street, and then
Merrily over—there it is in the water!

No use to say 'O there are other balls':
An ultimate shaking grief fixes the boy
As he stands rigid, trembling, staring down
All his young days into the harbour where
His ball went. I would not intrude on him,
A dime, another ball, is worthless. Now   10
He senses first responsibility
In a world of possessions. People will take balls,
Balls will be lost always, little boy,
And no one buys a ball back. Money is external.
He is learning, well behind his desperate eyes,
The epistemology of loss, how to stand up
Knowing what every man must one day know
And most know many days, how to stand up
And gradually light returns to the street,
A whistle blows, the ball is out of sight,   20
Soon part of me will explore the deep and dark
Floor of the harbour . . I am everywhere,
I suffer and move, my mind and my heart move
With all that move me, under the water
Or whistling, I am not a little boy.

                                                    1948

THE SONG OF THE TORTURED GIRL

After a little I could not have told—
But no one asked me this—why I was there.
I asked. The ceiling of that place was high
And there were sudden noises, which I made.
I must have stayed there a long time today:
My cup of soup was gone when they brought me back.

Often 'Nothing worse now can come to us'
I thought, the winter the young men stayed away,
My uncle died, and mother broke her crutch.
And then the strange room where the brightest light   ♠   10
Does not shine on the strange men: shines on me.
I feel them stretch my youth and throw a switch.

Through leafless branches the sweet wind blows
Making a mild sound, softer than a moan;
High in a pass once where we put our tent,
Minutes I lay awake to hear my joy.
—I no longer remember what they want.—
Minutes I lay awake to hear my joy.

                                                    1948

from **THE DREAM SONGS***

I

Huffy Henry hid   the day,
unappeasable Henry sulked.
I see his point,—a trying to put things over.
It was the thought that they thought
they could *do* it made Henry wicked & away.
But he should have come out and talked.

All the world like a woolen lover
once did seem on Henry's side.
Then came a departure.
Thereafter nothing fell out as it might or ought.   10
I don't see how Henry, pried
open for all the world to see, survived.

What he has now to say is a long
wonder the world can bear & be.
Once in a sycamore I was glad
all at the top, and I sang.
Hard on the land wears the strong sea
and empty grows every bed.

1958, 1959

14

Life, friends, is boring. We must not say so.
After all, the sky flashes, the great sea yearns,
we ourselves flash and yearn,
and moreover my mother told me as a boy
(repeatingly) 'Ever to confess you're bored
means you have no

Inner Resources.' I conclude now I have no
inner resources, because I am heavy bored.
Peoples bore me,

---

* Most of these poems were first published in *77 Dream Songs* (1967) or in *His Toy, His Dream, His Rest* (1968) and then collected in *The Dream Songs* (1969). Throughout the "dream songs" appear Berryman's persona, Henry, and Henry's alter ego, Mister Bones (a name given to the character who rattled bones as a sound effect in minstrel shows). Berryman's note: "The poem, then, whatever its wide cast of characters, is essentially about an imaginary character (not the poet, not me) named Henry, a white American in early middle age sometimes in blackface, who has suffered an irreversible loss and talks about himself sometimes in the first person, sometimes in the third, sometimes even in the second; he has a friend, never named, who addresses him as Mr. Bones and variants thereof. Requiescant in pace ["Rest in peace" (Latin)]."

literature bores me, especially great literature,   10
Henry bores me, with his plights & gripes
as bad as achilles,[1]

who loves people and valiant art, which bores me.
And the tranquil hills, & gin, look like a drag
and somehow a dog
has taken itself & its tail considerably away
into mountains or sea or sky, leaving
behind: me, wag.

1964

18

A STRUT FOR ROETHKE*

Westward, hit a low note, for a roarer lost
across the Sound but north from Bremerton,[1]
hit a way down note.
And never cadenza[2] again of flowers, or cost.
Him who could really do that cleared his throat
& staggered on.

The bluebells, pool-shallows, saluted his over-needs,
while the clouds growled, heh-heh, & snapped, & crashed.

No stunt he'll ever unflinch once more will fail
(O lucky fellow, eh Bones?)—drifted off upstairs,   10
downstairs, somewheres.
No more daily, trying to hit the head on the nail:
thirstless: without a think in his head:
back from wherever, with it said.

Hit a high long note, for a lover found
needing a lower into friendlier ground
to bug among worms no more
around um jungles where ah blurt 'What for?'
Weeds, too, he favoured as   most men don't favour men.
The Garden Master's gone.[3]   20

1964

---

[1] The hero of *The Iliad,* by the Greek epic poet Homer (8th century B.C.); because of injured pride, Achilles sulked in his tent, refusing to fight the Trojans.
* The poet Theodore Roethke (1908–1963).
[1] A city in Washington State on the Puget Sound; at the time of his death, Roethke was teaching at the University of Washington.
[2] An elaborate musical passage played solo.
[3] Roethke's father and grandfather were greenhouse keepers; his poems are filled with allusions to botanical growth.

29

There sat down, once, a thing on Henry's heart
so heavy, if he had a hundred years
& more, & weeping, sleepless, in all them time
Henry could not make good.
Starts again always in Henry's ears
the little cough somewhere, an odour, a chime.

And there is another thing he has in mind
like a grave Sienese face[1] a thousand years
would fail to blur the still profiled reproach of. Ghastly,
with open eyes, he attends, blind.   10
All the bells say: too late. This is not for tears;
thinking.

But never did Henry, as he thought he did,
end anyone and hacks her body up
and hide the pieces, where they may be found.
He knows: he went over everyone, & nobody's missing.
Often he reckons, in the dawn, them up.
Nobody is ever missing.

1960

40

I'm scared a lonely. Never see my son,
easy be not to see anyone,
combers[1] out to sea
know they're goin somewhere but not me.
Got a little poison, got a little gun,
I'm scared a lonely.

I'm scared a only one thing, which is me,
from othering I don't take nothin, see,
for any hound dog's sake.
But this is where I livin, where I rake   10
my leaves and cop[2] my promise, this' where we
cry oursel's awake.

Wishin was dyin but I gotta make
it all this way to that bed on these feet
where peoples said to meet.

---

[1] Like a face seen in the religious paintings by thirteenth- and fourteenth-century Italian artists in Siena.
[1] Long, breaking waves.   [2] Back down on, go back on.

Maybe but even if I see my son
forever never, get back on the take,
free, black & forty-one.[3]

1964

76

HENRY'S CONFESSION

Nothin very bad happen to me lately.
How you explain that?—I explain that, Mr Bones,
terms o' your bafflin odd sobriety.
Sober as man can get, no girls, no telephones,
what could happen bad to Mr Bones?
—*If* life is a handkerchief sandwich,

in a modesty of death I join my father
who dared so long agone leave me.
A bullet on a concrete stoop
close by a smothering southern sea   10
spreadeagled on an island, by my knee.
—You is from hunger, Mr Bones,

I offers you this handkerchief, now set
your left foot by my right foot,
shoulder to shoulder, all that jazz,
arm in arm, by the beautiful sea,
hum a little, Mr Bones.
—I saw nobody coming, so I went instead.

1964

77

Seedy Henry rose up shy in de world
& shaved & swung his barbells, duded Henry up
and p.a.'d[1] poor thousands of persons on topics of grand
moment to Henry, ah to those less & none.
Wif a book of his in either hand
he is stript down to move on.

—Come away, Mr Bones.

---

[3] A play on "free, white, and twenty-one," a colloquialism for "legally independent."
[1] Publicly addressed (from "P. A. system").

—Henry is tired of the winter,
& haircuts, & a squeamish comfy   ruin-prone proud national
   mind,   & Spring (in the city so called).
Henry likes Fall.   10
Hé would be prepared to líve in a world of Fáll
for ever, impenitent Henry.
But the snows and summers grieve & dream;

thése fierce & airy occupations, and love,
raved away so many of Henry's years
it is a wonder that, with in each hand
one of his own mad books and all,
ancient fires for eyes, his head full
& his heart full, he's making ready to move on.

1964

127

Again, his friend's death made the man sit still
and freeze inside—his daughter won first prize—
his wife scowled over at him—
It seemed to be Hallowe'en.
His friend's death had been adjudged suicide,
which dangles a trail

longer than Henry's chill, longer than his loss
and longer than the letter that he wrote
that day to the widow
to find out what the hell had happened thus.   10
All souls converge upon a hopeless mote
tonight, as though

the throngs of souls in hopeless pain rise up
to say they cannot care, to say they abide
whatever is to come.
My air is flung with souls which will not stop
and among them hangs a soul that has not died
and refuses to come home.

1968

153

I'm cross with god who has wrecked this generation.
First he seized Ted, then Richard, Randall, and now Delmore.[1]
In between he gorged on Sylvia Plath.

---

[1] The poets Theodore Roethke (1908–1963); R. P. Blackmur (1904–1965), a critic as well; Randall
Jarrell (1914–1965); Delmore Schwartz (1913–1966); also, Plath (1932–1963).

That was a first rate haul. He left alive
fools I could number like a kitchen knife
but Lowell he did not touch.[2]

Somewhere the enterprise continues, not—
yellow the sun lies on the baby's blouse—
in Henry's staggered thought.
I suppose the word would be, we must submit.   10
Later.
I hang, and I will not be part of it.

A friend of Henry's contrasted God's career
with Mozart's,[3] leaving Henry with nothing to say
but praise for a word so apt.
We suffer on, a day, a day, a day.
And never again can come, like a man slapped,
news like this

1968

157

Ten Songs, one solid block of agony,
I wrote for him,[1] and then I wrote no more.
His sad ghost must aspire
free of my love to its own post, that ghost,
among its fellows, Mozart's, Bach's,[2] Delmore's
free of its careful body

high in the shades which line that avenue
where I will gladly walk, beloved of one,
and listen to the Buddha.
His work downhill, I don't conceal from you,   10
ran and ran out. The brain shook as if stunned,
I hope he's over that,

flame may his glory in that other place,
for he was fond of fame, devoted to it,
and every first-rate soul
has sacrifices which it puts in play,
I hope he's sitting with his peers: sit, sit,
& recover & be whole.

1968

---

[2] In contrast to the other poets mentioned, Robert Lowell (1917–1977) was still alive when Berryman wrote this.

[3] The Austrian composer Wolfgang Amadeus Mozart (1756–1791).

[1] The poet Delmore Schwartz (1913–1966).

[2] The Austrian composer Wolfgang Amadeus Mozart (1756–1791); the German organist and composer Johann Sebastian Bach (1685–1750).

187

Them lady poets must not marry, pal.
Miss Dickinson[1]—fancy in Amherst bedding hér.
Fancy a lark with Sappho,[2]
a tumble in the bushes with Miss Moore,[3]
a spoon with Emily, while Charlotte glare.[4]
Miss Bishop's[5] too noble-O.

That was the lot. And two of them are here
as yet, and—and: Sylvia Plath is not.[6]
She—she her credentials
has handed in, leaving alone two tots   10
and widower to what he makes of it—
surviving guy, &

when Tolstoy's pathetic widow doing her whung[7]
(after them decades of marriage) & kids, she decided he was *queer*
& loving his agent.
Wherefore he rush off, leaving two journals, & die.
It is a true error to marry with poets
or to be by them.

1968

366

Chilled in this Irish pub I wish my loves
well, well to strangers, well to all his friends,
seven or so in number,
I forgive my enemies, especially two,
races his heart, at so much magnanimity,
can it at all be true?

—Mr Bones, you on a trip outside yourself.
Has you seen a medicine man? You sound will-like,
a testament & such.
Is you going?—Oh, I suffer from a strike   10
& a strike & three balls: I stand up for much,
Wordsworth[1] & that sort of thing.

---

[1] Emily Dickinson (1830–1886), born in Amherst, Massachusetts, where she lived all her life.
[2] A seventh-century B.C. Greek lyric poet (female).
[3] Marianne Moore (1887–1972).
[4] Here, Berryman converts the verb "to spoon," or "to make love with kisses and carresses," into a noun; the Brönte sisters: Emily (1818–1845) and Charlotte (1816–1855), English novelists and poets.
[5] Elizabeth Bishop (1911–1979).
[6] When Berryman wrote this, both Bishop and Moore were alive, but Plath (1932–1963) was not.
[7] After 48 years of marriage to Sonya Andreyevna Bers, his worsening marital situation drove the Russian novelist Leo Tolstoy (1828–1910) to flee home secretly; several days later he died of pneumonia at the remote railway junction of Astapovo. The "agent" is probably Tolstoy's disciple V. G. Chertkov.
[1] The English poet William Wordsworth (1770–1850).

The pitcher dreamed. He threw a hazy curve,
I took it in my stride & out I struck,
lonesome Henry.
These Songs are not meant to be understood, you understand.
They are only meant to terrify & comfort.
Lilac was found in his hand.

1968

William Stafford
(1914–   )

The poetry of William Stafford is, in every sense of the word, conversational. It is a dialogue between the poet and his various subjects: the past, both personal and historical; the natural world, its rewards and diminishing returns; the act of writing. For Stafford, the poet is not sacred; rather, the poetry is itself sacred. In many ways Stafford is a direct poetic descendant of William Wordsworth, emphasizing feeling first and then thought. It is easy to see Stafford's poems as manifestations of Wordsworth's view of poetry as "the spontaneous overflow of powerful feelings [taking] its origin from emotion recollected in tranquility," as Stafford's poem "After Arguing Against the Contention That Art Must Come From Discontent" (1982) ultimately contends. Stafford, the author of numerous essays on the nature and composition of poetry, possesses an eloquence that is at once uniquely American yet, unlike the eloquence of Walt Whitman, for example, is neither partisan nor nationalistic. However, Stafford's vision, like Whitman's, is expansive. Despite the brevity of Stafford's poems, their pace is unhurried: they are as declarative as they are meditative.

Born in 1914 in Hutchinson, Kansas, Stafford earned degrees from the Universities of Kansas and Iowa. During World War II he was a conscientious objector and worked in a public-service camp. His essays on the writing and teaching of poetry are collected in two volumes, *Writing the Australian Crawl* (1978) and *You Must Revise Your Life* (1986). Since 1948 Stafford has lived in Portland, Oregon, where he has been a professor at Lewis and Clark College.

Whereas Stafford's poems cannot be called nationalistic, they have typically, though wrongly, been called regional because he has spent the greater part of his life in, and has written about, the American Northwest. To label Stafford "regional" is to categorize superficially a writer who has never truly been a part of either the academic community or the East Coast literary community. In the preface to his collection *An Oregon Message* (1987), he writes: "My poems are organically grown, and it is my habit to allow language its freedom and confidence. Each poem is a miracle that has been invited to happen." There is verve in Stafford's emphasis on the "freedom and confidence" of language. Stafford was influenced not by the language of Wallace Stevens or of T. S. Eliot but by the language of William Carlos Williams and to some extent that of Robert Frost. Stafford is not a poet of unadorned speech: Stafford's poems tend to consist of a direct address from writer to reader, whether that reader is a specific individual—a number of Stafford's later poems are addressed to his mother—or any individual. Such an address occurs at the close of

"Traveling Through the Dark" (1962), from the National Book Award winner by the same name and perhaps his best-known poem. In this poem Stafford addresses a doe, dead at roadside, and her unborn fawn as well as the poet and reader. Poet and reader share complicity in the act of disposing of the body, if only, Stafford would seem to argue, because such acts have consequences for all of "us."

Suggested Readings: *Down in My Heart,* 1947. *West of Your City,* 1960. *Traveling Through the Dark,* 1962. *Allegiances,* 1970. *Writing the Australian Crawl,* 1978. *You Must Revise Your Life,* 1986. R. Howard, *Alone With America: Essays on the Art of Poetry in America Since 1950,* 1969. J. Holden, *The Mark to Turn: A Reading of William Stafford's Poetry,* 1976. G. S. Lensing and R. Moran, *Four Poets and the Emotive Imagination: Robert Bly, James Wright, Louis Simpson and William Stafford,* 1976. L. Wagner, *American Modern: Essays in Fiction and Poetry,* 1980. R. Jackson, *Acts of Mind,* 1983.

Texts Used: "After Arguing Against the Contention That Art Must Come From Discontent": *A Glass Face in the Rain,* 1982. "An Oregon Message," 1987. All else: *Stories That Could Be True: New and Collected Poems,* 1977.

AT THE BOMB TESTING SITE

At noon in the desert a panting lizard
waited for history, its elbows tense,
watching the curve of a particular road
as if something might happen.

It was looking at something farther off
than people could see, an important scene
acted in stone for little selves
at the flute end of consequences.

There was just a continent without much on it
under a sky that never cared less.   10
Ready for a change, the elbows waited.
The hands gripped hard on the desert.

1960

from **IN MEDIAS RES**

TRAVELING THROUGH THE DARK

Traveling through the dark I found a deer
dead on the edge of the Wilson River road.
It is usually best to roll them into the canyon:
that road is narrow; to swerve might make more dead.

By glow of the tail-light I stumbled back of the car
and stood by the heap, a doe, a recent killing;

she had stiffened already, almost cold.
I dragged her off; she was large in the belly.

My fingers touching her side brought me the reason—
her side was warm; her fawn lay there waiting,   10
alive, still, never to be born.
Beside that mountain road I hesitated.

The car aimed ahead its lowered parking lights;
under the hood purred the steady engine.
I stood in the glare of the warm exhaust turning red;
around our group I could hear the wilderness listen.

I thought hard for us all—my only swerving—,
then pushed her over the edge into the river.

1962

THE FARM ON THE GREAT PLAINS*

A telephone line goes cold;
birds tread it wherever it goes.
A farm back of a great plain
tugs an end of the line.

I call that farm every year,
ringing it, listening, still;
no one is home at the farm,
the line gives only a hum.

Some year I will ring the line
on a night at last the right one,   10
and with an eye tapered for braille
from the phone on the wall

I will see the tenant who waits—
the last one left at the place;
through the dark my braille eye
will lovingly touch his face.

"Hello, is Mother at home?"
No one is home today.
"But Father—he should be there."
No one—no one is here.   20

"But you—are you the one . . . ?"
Then the line will be gone

---

* In Kansas, where Stafford was born and raised.

because both ends will be home:
no space, no birds, no farm.

My self will be the plain,
wise as winter is gray,
pure as cold posts go
pacing toward what I know.

1966

THE EPITAPH ENDING IN AND

In the last storm, when hawks
blast upward and a dove is
driven into the grass, its broken wings
a delicate design, the air between
wracked thin where it stretched before,
a clear spring bent close too often
(that Earth should ever have such wings
burnt on in blind color!), this will be
good as an epitaph:

Doves did not know where to fly, and   10

1966

ACCOUNTABILITY

Cold nights outside the taverns in Wyoming
pickups and big semi's[1] lounge idling, letting their
haunches twitch now and then in gusts of powder snow,
their owners inside for hours, forgetting as well
as they can the miles, the circling plains, the still town
that connects to nothing but cold and space and a few
stray ribbons of pavement, icy guides to nothing
but bigger towns and other taverns that glitter and wait:
Denver, Cheyenne.

Hibernating in the library of the school on the hill   10
a few pieces by Thomas Aquinas or Saint Teresa[2]
and the fragmentary explorations of people like Alfred
North Whitehead[3] crouch and wait amid research folders

---

[1] Semi-trailer: a detachable trailer and the truck it pulls, generally an eighteen-wheeled truck.
[2] Saint Thomas Aquinas (1225?–1274) was an Italian theologian and philosopher who systematized
Catholic theology; Teresa (1515–1582) was a Spanish saint known for her mystical visions.
[3] Whitehead (1861–1947) was an English mathematician and philosopher.

on energy and military recruitment posters glimpsed
by the hard stars. The school bus by the door, a yellow
mound, clangs open and shut as the wind finds a loose
door and worries it all night, letting the hollow
students count off and break up and blow away
over the frozen ground.

1977

AFTER ARGUING AGAINST THE CONTENTION THAT ART MUST COME FROM DISCONTENT

Whispering to each handhold, "I'll be back,"
I go up the cliff in the dark. One place
I loosen a rock and listen a long time
till it hits, faint in the gulf, but the rush
of the torrent almost drowns it out, and the wind—
I almost forgot the wind: it tears at your side
or it waits and then buffets; you sag outward. . . .

I remember they said it would be hard. I scramble
by luck into a little pocket out of
the wind and begin to beat on the stones   10
with my scratched numb hands, rocking back and forth
in silent laughter there in the dark—
"Made it again!" Oh how I love this climb!
—the whispering to stones, the drag, the weight
as your muscles crack and ease on, working
right. They are back there, discontent,
waiting to be driven forth. I pound
on the earth, riding the earth past the stars:
"Made it again! Made it again!"

1982

AN OREGON MESSAGE

When we first moved here,[1] pulled
the trees in around us, curled
our backs to the wind, no one
had ever hit the moon—no one.
Now our trees are safer than the stars,
and only other people's neglect
is our precious and abiding shell,
pierced by meteors, radar, and the telephone.

[1] Stafford moved to Portland, Oregon, in 1948.

From our snug place we shout
religiously for attention, in order to hide: 10
only silence or evasion will bring
dangerous notice, the hovering hawk
of the state, or the sudden quiet stare
and fatal estimate of an alerted neighbor.

This message we smuggle out in
its plain cover, to be opened
quietly: Friends everywhere—
we are alive! Those moon rockets
have missed millions of secret
places! Best wishes.   20

Burn this.

1987

Robert Lowell
(1917–1977)

Born in 1917, Robert Traill Spence Lowell, Jr., was the only child of Charlotte Winslow and Robert Traill Spence Lowell, a naval officer who was talked into leaving the navy and becoming a stockbrocker (a job at which he had little success). The Lowells came from a prominent New England intellectual family that included James Russell Lowell, a nineteenth-century poet and editor, and Amy Lowell, an imagist poet. Throughout his poetic career Robert Lowell struggled to come to terms with his patrician family background. In a memoir of his childhood, "Antebellum Boston" (1957) Lowell draws a comparison between himself and the author Henry Adams, a member of another venerable Boston family. Written when Lowell was forty, his memoir displays perhaps the most characteristic feature of his poetry: the marriage, uneasy though it might be, of personal and historical points of view.

After graduating form St. Mark's preparatory school, Lowell began undergraduate studies at Harvard University but left after two years. At the urging of the poet Allen Tate, Lowell entered Kenyon College in Ohio, where his instructors and acquaintances included Tate and his wife, Caroline Gordon; John Crowe Ransom; Ford Madox Ford; Peter Taylor; and Randall Jarrell. After leaving Kenyon, Lowell studied with Robert Penn Warren and Cleanth Brooks at Louisiana State University. Many of Lowell's teachers were proponents of the New Criticism. Although Lowell adopted many of the formal tenets of his teachers, biographical—and autobiographical—material came to be so important in Lowell's work that his poems cannot be analyzed without in some fashion considering the life behind the poems. Lowell's relatives and friends all appear as characters in his poetry, even though certain truths were altered to meet the needs and requirements of the poems.

In 1940 Lowell graduated as Kenyon's valedictorian; also during that year he married Jean Stafford, a novelist, and converted to Roman Catholicism. His conversion, though temporary, was to affect his poetry throughout the 1940s. In a 1971 interview with the writer Ian Hamilton, Lowell explained: "I was born a nonbelieving Protestant New Englander; my parents and everyone I saw were nonbelieving Protestant New Englanders . . . From zealous, atheist Calvinist to a believing Catholic is no great leap." At the outset of World War II, Lowell attempted to enlist in the navy, following family tradition, but was turned down because of bad eyesight. So when he soon received orders from the army, Lowell sent a letter to President Franklin Delano Roosevelt in which he declared himself a conscientious objector. Lowell was sentenced in 1943 to a year and a day in prison. He spent five months in prison and served the rest of his term as an attendant in a Connecticut hospital. His poem "Memories of West Street and Lepke" (1959) describes the first days of his incarceration, in a New York City jail.

In 1944 Lowell's first poetry collection, *Land of Unlikeness*, was privately published. Its poems, many about religious subjects, are heavy with symbolism. A number of these poems appear in revised form in Lowell's second book, *Lord Weary's Castle* (1946), for which he received a Pulitzer Prize. *Lord Weary's Castle* includes two of Lowell's most famous poems, "Mr. Edwards and the Spider" and "The Quaker Graveyard in Nantucket." The former copiously quotes the writings of Jonathan Edwards, an eighteenth-century Puritan revivalist minister and essayist, particularly his sermon "Sinners in the Hands of an Angry God" (1741). The latter poem, dedicated to Lowell's cousin Warren Winslow, who drowned at sea during World War II, shows the influence of John Milton's "Lycidas" (1637), Herman Melville's *Moby Dick* (1851), and T. S. Eliot's *Four Quartets* (1943)—especially "The Dry Salvages," published only a few years before "Quaker Graveyard." Not long after the release of *Lord Weary's Castle*, Lowell had a mental breakdown, the first of several that would plague him over the three decades until his death.

Lowell experimented with form, most notably dramatic monologue, in *The Mills of the Kavanaughs* (1951). An even greater change is evident in *Life Studies* (1959), considered by many to be his greatest work and also one of the most influential poetry collections of his generation. The collection begins with the prose memoir "91 Revere Street," one of the few chapters of Lowell's proposed autobiography that he was able to finish, and the only chapter published during his lifetime. Its title is the street address where Lowell and his mother lived while his father, a naval commander, was under orders to reside on the naval base in Boston. Although this memoir seems to stand apart from the poems in *Life Studies*, those poems illuminate the prose recollection.

Life Studies contains poems (such as "Beyond the Alps") that flow naturally from his earlier work. The poems of the final section of *Life Studies* generated great criticism as well as praise; in these poems Lowell shows off his "new" style. These frankly autobiographical, confessional poems, like most poems in the collection, are written in free verse. Long admired for his technical mastery and compressed syntax, Lowell worked with lines and stanzas that are untraditional yet controlled. The poems range from the poet's childhood memories of the Lowell family, as in "My Last Afternoon With Uncle Devereaux Winslow," to searing and sordid accounts of the adult poet's hospitalization for chronic manic depression, as in "Waking in the Blue." The collection ends with "Skunk Hour," dedicated to Elizabeth Bishop and modeled after her poem "The Armadillo" (1965). Many of its lines and images can be traced to such sources as the poetry of Johann Hölderlin and John Milton's *Paradise Lost* (1667). In "Skunk Hour" Lowell struggles with the religion of his family, a struggle less narrative than thematic, less explicit than implicit. Set in a small town in Maine, the poem suggests sickness in both landscape ("The season's ill")

The Massachusetts 54th, under Colonel Robert Gould Shaw, was the first African-American regiment to fight in the Civil War and is remembered in Robert Lowell's poem "For the Union Dead."

and the poet himself ("My mind's not right"). The poet travels from desperation to an ambiguous affirmation of life.

Lowell followed the personal history of *Life Studies* with *For the Union Dead* (1964), which continues his personal/historical explorations—returning, for example, to Jonathan Edwards for subject matter. The fiercely moral and intensely personal title poem commemorates, among other things, Col. Robert Shaw's Civil War regiment of African-American soldiers, the bronze monument dedicated to those soldiers (located in Boston), the victims of the atomic bomb, and the civil rights movement in the South during the late 1950s and early 1960s. Yet, perhaps nowhere in his entire body of work do Lowell's moral, historical, and personal concerns manifest themselves more than in the long collection *Notebook 1967–68* (1969). Although the volume includes dozens of sonnetlike sections, Lowell thought of *Notebook* as a single poem, his life story in fourteen-line, unrhymed verse. With numerous revisions, the political and historical poems of *Notebook* were published as *History* (1973), and the more personal poems appeared in *For Lizzie and Harriet* (1973), which concerns Lowell's breakup with his second wife (the critic and novelist Elizabeth Hardwick) and their only child, Harriet. Lowell had become a public figure by this time due to his refusal to attend a White House Festival of the Arts, his support of the presidential campaign of Senator Eugene McCarthy, and his vocal opposition to America's involvement in Vietnam—an involvement he actively protested and for which he was arrested.

The Dolphin (1973) is another volume of fourteen-line sections of verse and a personal history. The collection deals with the relationship between art and experience; with his third marriage, to the English novelist Lady Caroline Blackwood; and with the birth of their son. In *The Dolphin*, the personal triumphs over the historical—some of its poems detail the pain of his divorce from Hardwick and chronicle his continued episodes of manic depression. His final collection, *Day by Day*, is a loosely constructed, almost relaxed volume that ends with the poem "Epilogue," seen by some as Lowell's poetic masterpiece. Published in 1977, the year of Lowell's sudden death from a heart attack, *Day by Day* seems heavy with a sense of resignation, of acceptance, as if Lowell knew that he would soon die.

Suggested Readings: *Lord Weary's Castle*, 1946. *The Mills of the Kavanaughs*, 1951. *Life Studies*, 1959. *For the Union Dead*, 1964. *The Old Glory*, 1968. *Notebooks, 1967–1968*, 1970. *For Lizzie and Harriet*, 1973. *The Dolphin*, 1973. *Collected Prose*, 1988. H. B. Stapler, *Robert Lowell: The First Twenty Years*, 1961. W. J. Martz, *The Achievement of Robert Lowell*, 1966. T. Parkinson, ed., *Robert Lowell: A Collection of Critical Essays*, 1968. S. G. Axelrod, *Robert Lowell: Life and Art*, 1978. H. Vendler, "Robert Lowell," in *Part of Nature, Part of Us: Modern American Poets*, 1980. I. Hamilton, *Robert Lowell, A Biography*, 1982. R. V. Hallberg, *American Poetry and Culture, 1945–80*, 1985. S. G. Axelrod and H. Deese, *Robert Lowell: Essays on the Poetry*, 1986.

Texts Used: "Epilogue": *Day by Day*, 1977. All else: *Selected Poems*, 1976.

THE QUAKER GRAVEYARD IN NANTUCKET

[FOR WARREN WINSLOW, DEAD AT SEA]*

*Let man have dominion over the fishes of the sea and the fowls of the air
and the beasts of the whole earth, and every creeping creature
that moveth upon the earth.*[1]

I

A brackish reach of shoal off Madaket[2]—
The sea was still breaking violently and night
Had steamed into our North Atlantic Fleet,
When the drowned sailor clutched the drag-net. Light
Flashed from his matted head and marble feet,
He grappled at the net
With the coiled, hurdling muscles of his thighs:
The corpse was bloodless, a botch of reds and whites,
Its open, staring eyes
Were lustreless dead-lights[3]   10
Or cabin-windows on a stranded hulk
Heavy with sand. We weight the body, close
Its eyes and heave it seaward whence it came,[4]

---

* Lowell's cousin died when his naval ship sank during World War II.
[1] From Genesis 1:26.
[2] Siasconset, a town on Nantucket Island, off Cape Cod.
[3] Strong covers placed over a ship's porthole cabin window in stormy weather. Lines 4–11 are based on "The Shipwreck," the first chapter of *Cape Cod* (1865), by Henry David Thoreau (1817–1862).
[4] All life is thought to have developed from a primordial "sea."

Where the heel-headed dogfish barks its nose
On Ahab's[5] void and forehead; and the name
Is blocked in yellow chalk.
Sailors, who pitch this portent at the sea
Where dreadnaughts shall confess
Its hell-bent deity,
When you are powerless   20
To sand-bag this Atlantic bulwark, faced
By the earth-shaker,[6] green, unwearied, chaste
In his steel scales; ask for no Orphean lute
To pluck life back.[7] The guns of the steeled fleet
Recoil and then repeat
The hoarse salute.

II

Whenever winds are moving and their breath
Heaves at the roped-in bulwarks of this pier,
The terns and sea-gulls tremble at your death
In these home waters. Sailor, can you hear   30
The Pequod's sea wings, beating landward, fall
Headlong and break on our Atlantic wall
Off 'Sconset,[8] where the yawing S-boats[9] splash
The bellbuoy, with ballooning spinnakers,
As the entangled, screeching mainsheet clears
The blocks: off Madaket, where lubbers[10] lash
The heavy surf and throw their long lead squids
For blue-fish? Sea-gulls blink their heavy lids
Seaward. The winds' wings beat upon the stones,
Cousin, and scream for you and the claws rush   40
At the sea's throat and wring it in the slush
Of this old Quaker graveyard where the bones
Cry out in the long night for the hurt beast
Bobbing by Ahab's whaleboats in the East.

III

All you recovered from Poseidon died
With you, my cousin, and the harrowed brine
Is fruitless on the blue beard of the god,
Stretching beyond us to the castles in Spain,
Nantucket's westward haven. To Cape Cod
Guns, cradled on the tide,   50
Blast the eelgrass about a waterclock[11]
Of bilge and backwash, roil the salt and sand

---

[5] The captain of the whaler *Pequod* in *Moby-Dick* (1851), by Herman Melville (1819–1891).
[6] The god of the sea and of earthquakes: Poseidon to the Greeks, Neptune to the Romans.
[7] According to Greek myth, Orpheus's music so charmed Hades, the god of the Underworld, that he allowed Orpheus to try to bring his wife, Eurydice, back to earth.
[8] A town on Nantucket Island.   [9] Wildly steering racing yachts.
[10] Landlubbers: inexperienced sailors.   [11] A device for measuring time by the flow of water.

Lashing earth's scaffold, rock
Our warships in the hand
Of the great God; where time's contrition blues
Whatever it was these Quaker sailors,[12] lost
In the mad scramble of their lives. They died
When time was open-eyed,
Wooden and childish, only bones abide
There, in the nowhere, where their boats were tossed   60
Sky-high, where mariners had fabled news
Of IS,[13] the whited monster. What it cost
Them is their secret. In the sperm-whale's slick
I see the Quakers drown and hear their cry:
"If God himself had not been on our side,
If God himself had not been on our side,
When the Atlantic rose against us, why,
Then it had swallowed us up quick."

IV

This is the end of the whaleroad[14] and the whale
Who spewed Nantucket bones on the thrashed swell   70
And stirred the troubled waters to whirlpools
To send the Pequod packing off to hell:
This is the end of them, three-quarters fools,
Snatching at straws to sail
Seaward and seaward on the turntail whale,
Spouting out blood and water as it rolls,
Sick as a dog to these Atlantic shoals:
Clamavimus,[15] O depths. Let the sea-gulls wail

For water, for the deep where the high tide
Mutters to its hurt self, mutters and ebbs.   80
Waves wallow in their wash, go out and out,
Leave only the death-rattle of the crabs,
The beach increasing, its enormous snout
Sucking the ocean's side.
This is the end of running on the waves;
We are poured out like water. Who will dance
The mast-lashed master of Leviathans[16]
Up from this field of Quakers in their unstoned graves?

V

When the whale's viscera go and the roll
Of its corruption overruns this world   90

---

[12] Many Nantucket sailors were Quakers.
[13] A being of great force: Jesus Salvator, a sacrificial victim, as the whale was thought to be a victim of the Quakers; Revelation 17:8 speaks of a " . . . beast that was and is not and yet is."
[14] The sea.
[15] "We have cried" (Latin); after Psalm 130:1, "Out of the depths I have cried unto thee, O Lord."
[16] In the Old Testament, sea monsters, typically whales.

Beyond tree-swept Nantucket and Woods Hole[17]
And Martha's Vineyard, Sailor, will your sword
Whistle and fall and sink into the fat?
In the great ash-pit of Jehoshaphat[18]
The bones cry for the blood of the white whale,
The fat flukes arch and whack about its ears,
The death-lance churns into the sanctuary, tears
The gun-blue swingle,[19] heaving like a flail,
And hacks the coiling life out: it works and drags
And rips the sperm-whale's midriff into rags,   100
Gobbets of blubber spill to wind and weather,
Sailor, and gulls go round the stoven timbers
Where the morning stars sing out together
And thunder shakes the white surf and dismembers
The red flag hammered in the mast-head.[20] Hide,
Our steel, Jonas Messias,[21] in Thy side.

VI

OUR LADY OF WALSINGHAM[22]

There once the penitents took off their shoes
And then walked barefoot the remaining mile;
And the small trees, a stream and hedgerows file
Slowly along the munching English lane,   110
Like cows to the old shrine, until you lose
Track of your dragging pain.
The stream flows down under the druid tree,[23]
Shiloah's[24] whirlpools gurgle and make glad
The castle of God. Sailor, you were glad
And whistled Sion by that stream.[25] But see:

Our Lady, too small for her canopy,
Sits near the altar. There's no comeliness
At all or charm in that expressionless
Face with its heavy eyelids. As before,   120
This face, for centuries a memory,

---

[17] A town on the Massachusetts coast, across from the island of Martha's Vineyard.

[18] The "valley of decision," site of the Last Judgment (see Joel 3:11–16). Lowell's note: "The day of judgment. The world, according to some prophets, will end in fire."

[19] A knifelike wooden instrument used to clean flax or hemp by beating or scraping.

[20] At the end of *Moby-Dick* the sail of the sinking *Pequod* is nailed to the mast like a flag.

[21] A combination of Jonah, the Old Testament prophet who was swallowed by a whale, and Jesus, the New Testament Messiah. Here, Jonah's emergence from the whale is prophetic of Jesus' resurrection.

[22] A medieval shrine dedicated to the Virgin Mary in Walsingham Priory, Norfolk, England; details from E. I. Watkin's *Catholic Art and Culture*.

[23] The oak tree, sacred to ancient pagan Celtic Druids.   [24] The town Shiloh, in ancient Palestine.

[25] The stream on Mount Sion (or Zion) that flows past God's Temple in Jerusalem (see Isaiah 8:6); in Isaiah 51:2 the redeemed come "singing into Zion."

Non est species, neque decor,[26]
Expressionless, expresses God: it goes
Past castled Sion. She knows what God knows,
Not Calvary's Cross nor crib at Bethlehem[27]
Now, and the world shall come to Walsingham.

VII

The empty winds are creaking and the oak
Splatters and splatters on the cenotaph,[28]
The boughs are trembling and a gaff[29]
Bobs on the untimely stroke   130
Of the greased wash exploding on a shoal-bell
In the old mouth of the Atlantic. It's well;
Atlantic, you are fouled with the blue sailors,
Sea-monsters, upward angel, downward fish:[30]
Unmarried and corroding, spare of flesh
Mart once of supercilious, wing'd clippers,
Atlantic, where your bell-trap guts its spoil
You could cut the brackish winds with a knife
Here in Nantucket, and cast up the time
When the Lord God formed man from the sea's slime   140
And breathed into this face the breath of life,
And blue-lung'd combers lumbered to the kill.
The Lord survives the rainbow of His will.[31]

1946

MR. EDWARDS AND THE SPIDER*

I saw the spiders marching through the air,
Swimming from tree to tree that mildewed day
    In latter August when the hay
    Came creaking to the barn. But where
        The wind is westerly,
Where gnarled November makes the spiders fly
Into the apparitions of the sky,
    They purpose nothing but their ease and die
Urgently beating east to sunrise and the sea;

---

[26] "There is neither form nor beauty" (Latin).
[27] Not the site of Jesus' crucifixion nor that of his birth.
[28] An empty tomb or monument erected in honor of someone buried elsewhere.
[29] A pole with a hook used in catching large fish.
[30] After Book I (462–463) of *Paradise Lost* (1667), by John Milton (1608–1674).
[31] In Genesis 9:11 God makes a covenant with Noah that the earth would never again be plagued by a Great Flood.

* Jonathan Edwards (1703–1758) was a Puritan minister and theologian. The first stanza is derived from the essay "Of Insects," which Edwards wrote in 1715.

What are we in the hands of the great God?[1]   10
It was in vain you set up thorn and briar
    In battle array against the fire
    And treason crackling in your blood;
        For the wild thorns grow tame
    And will do nothing to oppose the flame;
    Your lacerations tell the losing game
    You play against a sickness past your cure.
How will the hands be strong? How will the heart endure?

A very little thing, a little worm,
Or hourglass-blazoned spider,[2] it is said,   20
    Can kill a tiger. Will the dead
    Hold up his mirror and affirm
        To the four winds the smell
    And flash of his authority? It's well
    If God who holds you to the pit of hell,
    Much as one holds a spider, will destroy,
Baffle and dissipate your soul. As a small boy

On Windsor Marsh,[3] I saw the spider die
When thrown into the bowels of fierce fire:
    There's no long struggle, no desire   30
    To get up on its feet and fly—
        It stretches out its feet
    And dies. This is the sinner's last retreat;
    Yes, and no strength exerted on the heat
    Then sinews the abolished will, when sick
And full of burning, it will whistle on a brick.

But who can plumb the sinking of that soul?
Josiah Hawley,[4] picture yourself cast
    Into a brick-kiln where the blast
    Fans your quick vitals to a coal—   40
        If measured by a glass,
    How long would it seem burning! Let there pass
    A minute, ten, ten trillion; but the blaze
    Is infinite, eternal: this is death,
To die and know it. This is the Black Widow, death.

1946

---

[1] After Edwards's famous sermon *Sinners in the Hands of an Angry God* (1741), based on Ezekiel
22:14: "Can thine heart endure, or can thine hands be strong, in the days that I shall deal with thee?"
In the sermon God dangles sinners like spiders above a bottomless pit.
    [2] On the underside of the abdomen of the poisonous female black widow spider is a red, hourglass-
shaped mark.
    [3] Near East Windsor, Connecticut, where Edwards spent his boyhood.
    [4] Edwards's uncle, whose suicide Edwards blamed on the Devil.

from LIFE STUDIES*

I

MY LAST AFTERNOON
WITH UNCLE DEVEREUX WINSLOW[1]

1922: THE STONE PORCH OF MY GRANDFATHER'S[2] SUMMER HOUSE

I

"I won't go with you. I want to stay with Grandpa!"
That's how I threw cold water
on my Mother and Father's
watery martini pipe dreams at Sunday dinner.
. . . Fontainebleau, Mattapoisett,[3] Puget Sound. . . .
Nowhere was anywhere after a summer
at my Grandfather's farm.
Diamond-pointed, athirst and Norman,[4]
its alley of poplars
paraded from Grandmother's rose garden   10
to a scary stand of virgin pine,
scrub, and paths forever pioneering.

One afternoon in 1922,
I sat on the stone porch, looking through
screens as black-grained as drifting coal.
Tockytock, tockytock
clumped our Alpine, Edwardian[5] cuckoo clock,
slung with strangled, wooden game.
Our farmer was cementing a root-house[6] under the hill.
One of my hands was cool on a pile   20
of black earth, the other warm
on a pile of lime. All about me
were the works of my Grandfather's hands:
snapshots of his *Liberty Bell* silver mine;

---

* Lowell's four-part collection of highly personal poetry and prose, published in 1959.
[1] An uncle on Lowell's mother's side; the Winslow family was as patrician as was the Lowell family.
The ellipses are Lowell's.
[2] Arthur Winslow, Lowell's maternal grandfather, a financial entrepreneur from Boston.
[3] A wealthy Paris suburb and location of a royal chateau; a summer resort town in southeastern
Massachusetts.
[4] A style of architecture that flourished in Normandy, France, and, after the Norman conquest (1066),
in England; characterized by massive construction, round arches over recessed doors and windows,
and carvings.
[5] In the style prominent during the reign of Edward VII.
[6] A storage place for bulbs and root vegetables.

his high school at *Stuttgart am Neckar;*[7]
stogie-brown beams; fools'-gold nuggets;
octagonal red tiles,
sweaty with a secret dank, crummy with ant-stale;
a Rocky Mountain chaise longue,
its legs, shellacked saplings.   30
A pastel-pale Huckleberry Finn
fished with a broom straw in a basin
hollowed out of a millstone.
Like my Grandfather, the décor
was manly, comfortable,
overbearing, disproportioned.

What were those sunflowers? Pumpkins floating shoulder-high?
It was sunset, Sadie and Nellie
bearing pitchers of ice-tea,
oranges, lemons, mint, and peppermints,   40
and the jug of shandygaff,
which Grandpa made by blending half and half
yeasty, wheezing homemade sarsaparilla with beer.
The farm, entitled *Char-de-sa*
in the Social Register,
was named for my Grandfather's children:
Charlotte, Devereux, and Sarah.
No one had died there in my lifetime . . .
Only Cinder, our Scottie puppy
paralyzed from gobbling toads.   50
I sat mixing black earth and lime.

II

I was five and a half.
My formal pearl gray shorts
had been worn for three minutes.
My perfection was the Olympian[8]
poise of my models in the imperishable autumn
display windows
of Rogers Peet's boys' store below the State House
in Boston. Distorting drops of water
pinpricked my face in the basin's mirror.   60
I was a stuffed toucan
with a bibulous, multicolored beak.

III

Up in the air
by the lakeview window in the billiards-room,
lurid in the doldrums of the sunset hour,
my Great Aunt Sarah

---

[7] "Stuttgart on the Neckar [River]" (German).   [8] Like the gods of Mt. Olympus of classical myth.

was learning *Samson and Delilah*.[9]
She thundered on the keyboard of her dummy piano,
with gauze curtains like a boudoir table,
accordionlike yet soundless.   70
It had been bought to spare the nerves
of my Grandmother,
tone-deaf, quick as a cricket,
now needing a fourth for "Auction,"[10]
and casting a thirsty eye
on Aunt Sarah, risen like the phoenix[11]
from her bed of troublesome snacks and Tauchnitz classics.[12]

Forty years earlier,
twenty, auburn headed,
grasshopper notes of genius!   80
Family gossip says Aunt Sarah
tilted her archaic Athenian nose
and jilted an Astor.[13]
Each morning she practiced
on the grand piano at Symphony Hall,
deathlike in the off-season summer—
its naked Greek statues draped with purple
like the saints in Holy Week. . . .
On the recital day, she failed to appear.

                          IV

I picked with a clean finger nail at the blue anchor   90
on my sailor blouse washed white as a spinnaker.
What in the world was I wishing?
    . . . A sail-colored horse browsing in the bullrushes . . .
A fluff of the west wind puffing
my blouse, kiting me over our seven chimneys,
troubling the waters. . . .
As small as sapphires were the ponds: *Quittacus, Snippituit,*
and *Assawompset*,[14] halved by "the Island,"
where my Uncle's duck blind[15]
floated in a barrage of smoke-clouds.   100
Double-barreled shotguns
stuck out like bundles of baby crow-bars.
A single sculler[16] in a camouflaged kayak
was quacking to the decoys. . . .

---

[9] An 1877 opera by the French composer Camille Saint-Saëns (1835–1921).
[10] Auction bridge, which requires four players.
[11] According to Egyptian myth, a bird that sets itself on fire and rises anew from the ashes.
[12] German-produced, paper-covered English editions of standard British and American works.
[13] A member of a wealthy German-American family.   [14] In southeastern Massachusetts.
[15] A structure that conceals a duck hunter from the prey.
[16] The oarsman in a racing boat (or kayak).

At the cabin between the waters,
the nearest windows were already boarded.
Uncle Devereux was closing camp for the winter.
As if posed for "the engagement photograph,"
he was wearing his severe
war-uniform of a volunteer Canadian officer.   110
Daylight from the doorway riddled his student posters,
tacked helter-skelter on walls as raw as a boardwalk.
Mr. Punch,[17] a water melon in hockey tights,
was tossing off a decanter of Scotch.
La Belle France[18] in a red, white and blue toga
was accepting the arm of her "protector,"
the ingenu and porcine Edward VII.[19]
The pre-war music hall belles
had goose necks, glorious signatures, beauty-moles,
and coils of hair like rooster tails.   120
The finest poster was two or three young men in khaki kilts
being bushwhacked on the veldt[20]—
They were almost life-size. . . .
My Uncle was dying at twenty-nine.
"You are behaving like children,"
said my Grandfather,
when my Uncle and Aunt left their three baby daughters,
and sailed for Europe on a last honeymoon . . .
I cowered in terror.
I wasn't a child at all—   130
unseen and all-seeing, I was Agrippina[21]
in the Golden House of Nero. . . .
Near me was the white measuring-door
my Grandfather had penciled with my Uncle's heights.
In 1911, he had stopped growing at just six feet.
While I sat on the tiles,
and dug at the anchor on my sailor blouse,
Uncle Devereux stood behind me.
He was as brushed as Bayard, our riding horse.
His face was putty.   140
His blue coat and white trousers
grew sharper and straighter.
His coat was a blue jay's tail,

---

[17] The cartoon figure of a plump Englishman, the emblem of the English humor magazine *Punch*, established in 1841.

[18] The female emblem of France.

[19] A poster showing Edward VII (1841–1910), king of Great Britain and Ireland (1901–1910), well known as a ladies' man, with his arm around La Belle France; it commemorates the Entente Cordiale, an informal understanding between France and England (1904).

[20] Open, grassy country in South Africa; in the Boer War (1899–1902) Britain defeated the South African republics of the Orange Free State and the Transvaal.

[21] Julia Agrippina II (A.D. 15?–59), mother of the Roman emperor Nero; she was murdered on his orders. After a fire that destroyed much of Rome in A.D. 64, Nero erected his "Golden House" between two of Rome's seven hills, decorating it with gold and precious stones and then taxing the provinces to pay for it.

his trousers were solid cream from the top of the bottle.
He was animated, hierarchical,
like a ginger snap man in a clothes-press.
He was dying of the incurable Hodgkin's disease. . . .
My hands were warm, then cool, on the piles
of earth and lime,
a black pile and a white pile. . . .   150
Come winter,
Uncle Devereux would blend to the one color.

                                                          1959

THE NEO-CLASSICAL URN

I rub my head and find a turtle shell
stuck on a pole,
each hair electrical
with charges, and the juice alive
with ferment. Bubbles drive
the motor, always purposeful . . .
Poor head!
How its skinny shell once hummed,
as I sprinted down the colonnade
of bleaching pines, cylindrical   10
clipped trunks without a twig between them. Rest!
I cound not rest. At full run on the curve,
I left the cast stone statue of a nymph,
her soaring armpits and her one bare breast,
gray from the rain and graying in the shade,
as on, on, in sun, the pathway now a dyke,
I swerved between two water bogs,
two seines[1] of moss, and stooped to snatch
the painted turtles on dead logs.
In that season of joy,   20
my turtle catch
was thirty-three,
dropped splashing in our garden urn,
like money in the bank,
the plop and splash
of turtle on turtle,
fed raw gobs of hash . . .

Oh neo-classical white urn, Oh nymph,
Oh lute! The boy was pitiless who strummed
their elegy,   .   30
for as the month wore on,
the turtles rose,

[1] Large fishing nets with floats along the top and weights along the bottom.

and popped up dead on the stale scummed
surface—limp wrinkled heads and legs withdrawn
in pain. What pain? A turtle's nothing. No
grace, no cerebration, less free will
than the mosquito I must kill—
nothings! Turtles! I rub my skull,
that turtle shell,
and breathe their dying smell,   40
still watch their crippled last survivors pass,
and hobble humpbacked through the grizzled grass.

1964

FOR THE UNION DEAD*

"Relinquunt omnia servare rem publicam."[1]

The old South Boston Aquarium stands
in a Sahara of snow now. Its broken windows are boarded.
The bronze weathervane cod has lost half its scales.
The airy tanks are dry.

Once my nose crawled like a snail on the glass;
my hand tingled
to burst the bubbles
drifting from the noses of the cowed, compliant fish.

My hand draws back. I often sigh still
for the dark downward and vegetating kingdom   10
of the fish and reptile. One morning last March,
I pressed against the new barbed and galvanized

fence on the Boston Common. Behind their cage,
yellow dinosaur steamshovels were grunting
as they cropped up tons of mush and grass
to gouge their underworld garage.

Parking spaces luxuriate like civic
sandpiles in the heart of Boston.
A girdle of orange, Puritan-pumpkin colored girders
braces the tingling Statehouse,   20

* First published as "Colonel Shaw and the Massachusetts 54th" in the 1960 edition of *Life Studies* and with this title as the title poem of Lowell's 1964 collection. Colonel Robert Shaw (1837–1863) led the first African-American regiment (of enlistees) in the Civil War.
  [1] "They give up everything to serve the republic" (Latin); after the inscription on the monument to Shaw, sculpted by Augustus Saint-Gaudens (1848–1907), which stands at the edge of Boston Common, a public park across from the Boston State House.

shaking over the excavations, as it faces Colonel Shaw
and his bell-cheeked Negro infantry
on St. Gaudens' shaking Civil War relief,
propped by a plank splint against the garage's earthquake.

Two months after marching through Boston,
half the regiment was dead;
at the dedication,
William James[2] could almost hear the bronze Negroes breathe.

Their monument sticks like a fishbone
in the city's throat.   30
Its Colonel is as lean
as a compass-needle.

He has an angry wrenlike vigilance,
a greyhound's gentle tautness;
he seems to wince at pleasure,
and suffocate for privacy.

He is out of bounds now. He rejoices in man's lovely,
peculiar power to choose life and die—
when he leads his black soldiers to death,
he cannot bend his back.   40

On a thousand small town New England greens,
the old white churches hold their air
of sparse, sincere rebellion; frayed flags
quilt the graveyards of the Grand Army of the Republic.[3]

The stone statues of the abstract Union Soldier
grow slimmer and younger each year—
wasp-waisted, they doze over muskets
and muse through their sideburns . . .

Shaw's father wanted no monument
except the ditch,   50
where his son's body was thrown
and lost with his "niggers."[4]

---

[2] William James (1842–1910), a philosopher and psychologist (and brother of Henry James), who in his "Oration at the Dedication of the Monument" in May 1897 said, "There on foot go the dark outcasts, so true to nature that one can almost hear them breathing as they march."
[3] An organization for Union and Confederate Civil War veterans.
[4] The name a Confederate officer used for Shaw's troops: on July 18, 1863, Shaw and most of his men were killed during an attack against Fort Wagner in South Carolina; the Confederates buried them in a common grave.

The ditch is nearer.
There are no statues for the last war[5] here;
on Boylston Street,[6] a commercial photograph
shows Hiroshima boiling

over a Mosler Safe,[7] the "Rock of Ages"
that survived the blast. Space is nearer.
When I crouch to my television set,
the drained faces of Negro school-children rise like balloons.[8]   60

Colonel Shaw
is riding on his bubble,
he waits
for the blessèd break.

The Aquarium is gone. Everywhere,
giant finned cars nose forward like fish;
a savage servility
slides by on grease.

1960

READING MYSELF

Like thousands, I took just pride and more than just,
struck matches that brought my blood to a boil;
I memorized the tricks to set the river on fire—
somehow never wrote something to go back to.
Can I suppose I am finished with wax flowers
and have earned my grass on the minor slopes of Parnassus[1] . . . .
No honeycomb is built without a bee
adding circle to circle, cell to cell,
the wax and honey of a mausoleum—
this round dome proves its maker is alive;   10
the corpse of the insect lives embalmed in honey,
prays that its perishable work live long
enough for the sweet-tooth bear to desecrate—
this open book . . . my open coffin.

---

[5] World War II (1939–1945).   [6] A street in central Boston.
[7] A brand of safe that was photographed as intact in Hiroshima after the nuclear bomb was dropped there in 1945; "Rock of Ages" is a hymn written in 1775 by Augustus Montague Toplady (1740–1778).
[8] Probably in relation to civil rights demonstrations of the 1960s to enforce the desegregation of schools afforded by the *Brown* v. *Board of Education of Topeka* decision of 1954.
[1] A mountain in Greece; according to Greek myth, the seat of music and poetry.

EPILOGUE*

Those blessèd structures, plot and rhyme—
why are they no help to me now
I want to make
something imagined, not recalled?
I hear the noise of my own voice:
The painter's vision is not a lens,
it trembles to caress the light.
But sometimes everything I write
with the threadbare art of my eye
seems a snapshot,   10
lurid, rapid, garish, grouped,
heightened from life,
yet paralyzed by fact.
All's misalliance.
Yet why not say what happened?
Pray for the grace of accuracy
Vermeer[1] gave to the sun's illumination
stealing like the tide across a map
to his girl solid with yearning.
We are poor passing facts,   20
warned by that to give
each figure in the photograph
his living name.

1977

Gwendolyn Brooks
(1917–   )

Gwendolyn Brooks was the first female African-American poet to be recognized in America by the critics and public alike. Although too young to have been part of the Harlem Renaissance, which was waning at the beginning of the Great Depression, Brooks corresponded with and met poets who had made their reputations in Harlem—notably Langston Hughes and James Weldon Johnson, both of whom encouraged her. Each recognized her talent and similar focus on writing about black people in a spirit of dignity and honesty, as well as her technical expertise in doing so.

Brooks was born in Topeka, Kansas, in 1917 and raised in Chicago, her home for most of her life. As a child she wrote poetry; at age thirteen her first poem was published in a children's magazine. At sixteen she met Langston Hughes, whose serious attention to her

---

* Published in *Day by Day* (1977) shortly before Lowell's death.
[1] Jan Vermeer (1632–1675), a Dutch painter (mostly of interiors), celebrated for his reproduction of the tones of daylight.

work made a great impression on her. The two later became friends. Brooks graduated from Wilson Junior College in Chicago in 1936 and worked briefly as a maid and then as secretary to a spiritual advisor (she hated both jobs). Years later she drew upon this experience for the title poem of *In the Mecca* (1968). In 1938 she joined the National Association for the Advancement of Colored People Youth Council, where she met Henry Blakely, whom she married in 1939. The two moved into a crowded apartment, later depicted in her poetry, which was being published regularly in the Chicago *Defender*. The early 1940s were highly creative years for her: she took a writing workshop and wrote most of the poems in *A Street in Bronzeville* (1945), named for an African-American neighborhood in Chicago. She submitted her poems to *Harper's* where the author Richard Wright read them and recommended publication with additional poems. The volume came out to excellent reviews, many praising the poignant portraits of African-American life, rendered in formal eloquence and everyday speech.

Prizes and fellowships (including two Guggenheim Fellowships) followed, allowing Brooks to travel and write. To the surprise of many and the discomfort of a few, in 1950 she became the first black Pulitzer Prize recipient. Her prize-winning book, *Annie Allen* (1949), is a collection of poems about a young black girl coming of age while trying to reconcile her conflicting romantic dreams and dismal realities. A turning point in Brooks's life came in 1967 after she attended the Second Black Writers' Conference at Fisk University in Nashville. As she recounted in an interview (in *Black Women Writers at Work* [1983], edited by Claudia Tate), "The poets among them felt that black poets should write as blacks, about blacks, address themselves *to* blacks. I had never thought deliberately in such terms." Her work since then shows a deepened political consciousness as she confronts racial and social oppression with less irony and more urgency.

After meeting members of a Chicago street gang called the Blackstone Rangers, she began her lifelong involvement in teaching, funding, and promoting young African-American writers. In 1968 she was named Poet Laureate of Illinois, after Carl Sandburg, and in the early 1970s she traveled through East and West Africa, returning more strongly committed than ever to her work for her people. She told Tate that her poetry is meant to "be presented in a tavern atmosphere—on a street corner." Through the years her rhythms and forms have become looser, but she continues experimenting with ballad and sonnet stanzas, mixing free and blank verse, and playing with words in a serious and impatient way.

Suggested Readings: *A Street in Bronzeville*, 1945. *Annie Allen*, 1949. *Maud Martha*, 1953. *The Bean Eaters*, 1960. *In the Mecca*, 1963. *Riot*, 1969. *The World of Gwendolyn Brooks*, 1971. *Report From Part One*, 1972. J. N. Loff, "Gwendolyn Brooks: A Bibliography," in *College Language Association Journal*, 17 (September): 21–32, 1973. H. B. Shaw, *Gwendolyn Brooks*, 1980. C. Tate, ed. *Black Women Writers at Work*, 1983. D. H. Melhem, *Gwendolyn Brooks: Poetry and the Heroic Voice*, 1987. M. K. Mootry and G. Smith, eds, *A Life Distilled: Gwendolyn Brooks, Her Poetry and Fiction*, 1987.

Text Used: *Selected Poems*, 1963.

from   A STREET IN BRONZEVILLE

THE MOTHER

Abortions will not let you forget.
You remember the children you got that you did not get,
The damp small pulps with a little or with no hair,
The singers and workers that never handled the air.

You will never neglect or beat
Them, or silence or buy with a sweet.
You will never wind up the sucking-thumb
Or scuttle off ghosts that come.
You will never leave them, controlling your luscious sigh,
Return for a snack of them, with gobbling mother-eye.   10

I have heard in the voices of the wind the voices of my dim killed children.
I have contracted. I have eased
My dim dears at the breasts they could never suck.
I have said, Sweets, if I sinned, if I seized
Your luck
And your lives from your unfinished reach,
If I stole your births and your names,
Your straight baby tears and your games,
Your stilted or lovely loves, your tumults, your marriages, aches, and your
     deaths,
If I poisoned the beginnings of your breaths,   20
Believe than even in my deliberateness I was not deliberate.
Though why should I whine,
Whine that the crime was other than mine?—
Since anyhow you are dead.
Or rather, or instead,
You were never made.
But that too, I am afraid,
Is faulty: oh, what shall I say, how is the truth to be said?
You were born, you had body, you died.
It is just that you never giggled or planned or cried.   30

Believe me, I loved you all.
Believe me, I knew you, though faintly, and I loved, I loved you
All.

1945

A SONG IN THE FRONT YARD

I've stayed in the front yard all my life.
I want a peek at the back
Where it's rough and untended and hungry weed grows.
A girl gets sick of a rose.

I want to go in the back yard now
And maybe down the alley,
To where the charity children play.
I want a good time today.

They do some wonderful things.
They have some wonderful fun.   10
My mother sneers, but I say it's fine
How they don't have to go in at quarter to nine.

My mother, she tells me that Johnnie Mae
Will grow up to be a bad woman.
That George'll be taken to Jail soon or late
(On account of last winter he sold our back gate).

But I say it's fine. Honest, I do.
And I'd like to be a bad woman, too,
And wear the brave stockings of night-black lace
And strut down the streets with paint on my face.   20

1945

THE BEAN EATERS

They eat beans mostly, this old yellow pair.
Dinner is a casual affair.
Plain chipware on a plain and creaking wood,
Tin flatware.

Two who are Mostly Good.
Two who have lived their day,
But keep on putting on their clothes
And putting things away.

And remembering . . .
Remembering, with twinklings and twinges,   10
As they lean over the beans in their rented back room that is full of beads and
    receipts and dolls and cloths, tobacco crumbs, vases and fringes.

1960

WE REAL COOL

The Pool Players.
Seven at the Golden Shovel.[1]

We real cool. We
Left school. We

Lurk late. We
Strike straight. We

Sing sin. We
Thin gin. We

Jazz June. We
Die soon.

1960

---

[1] A Chicago pool hall.

Richard Wilbur
(1921–   )

"My first poems were written in answer to the inner and outer disorders of the Second World War and they helped me, as poems should, to take ahold [*sic*] of raw events and convert them, provisionally, into experience." So writes Richard Wilbur in the essay "On My Own Work," included in his collection of critical prose, *Responses* (1976). Since the publication of Wilbur's first book, *The Beautiful Changes and Other Poems* (1947), when he was twenty-six, critics have praised his superb ear, technical perfection, and talent as a formalist. With praise of his skill has come the suspicion that Wilbur is somehow too conventional, too safe, and too optimistic. For Wilbur, the conversion of raw events into experience—to order his world into meter, rhythm, and rhyme through stanzaic forms—is verification, an act of affirmation, albeit an unfashionable one.

Wilbur, who typically sets his poems in natural landscapes or incorporates specific details of nature, was born in New York City in 1921 and grew up on a farm in North Caldwell, New Jersey. Soon after graduating from Amherst College in 1942, Wilbur entered the army and served in the infantry in Italy and France until 1945. He later went to Harvard University and in 1947 received an M.A. in English and had *The Beautiful Changes* published. He had begun teaching at Harvard in 1950 when his second book, *Ceremony and Other Poems*, came out. The book includes some of his translations of French plays, which early established his reputation as a distinguished translator. On a Guggenheim Fellowship he then went to New Mexico; with a grant from the Academy of Arts and Letters he traveled to Rome. There he finished his first of several Molière translations, which earned him a Bollingen Prize in 1963.

Since 1954 Wilbur has taught at Wellesley College, Wesleyan University, and Smith College. In 1956 his third book of verse, *Things of This World* (in which "Love Calls Us to the Things of This World" appears), won a Pulitzer Prize and a National Book Award. The title of this book has particular significance for Wilbur, who is consistently concerned with "things." In a 1977 *Paris Review* interview, "The Art of Poetry," Wilbur remarked that he has "considerable respect for the actual and physical. We are all kickers of stones, you know. . . . " He has continued to present reality through imagery in such collections as *Advice to a Prophet* (1961) and *The Mind-Reader* (1976).

Unlike the confessional poetry of some of Wilbur's contemporaries, such as Robert Lowell, Wilbur has deliberately avoided the explicitly intimate, asserting in "The Art of Poetry" that impersonal poems are "more honest and usable." Through the years his work has become simpler, he claims, and critics have noted that his poetry has become more personal and direct. Wilbur's lyrics are characterized by elegance, wit, and sheer loveliness of melody. In his lyrics he tries to "lay claim to as much of the world as possible through uttering the names of things."

Suggested Readings: *The Beautiful Changes and Other Poems*, 1947. *A Bestiary*, 1955. *Things of This World*, 1956. *Advice to a Prophet*, 1961. *The Poems of Richard Wilbur*, 1963. *The Mind-Reader*, 1976. *Responses, Prose Pieces: 1953–1976*, 1976. D. L. Hill, *Richard Wilbur*, 1968. J. P. Field, *Richard Wilbur: A Bibliographical Checklist*, 1971. W. Salinger, ed., *Richard Wilbur's Creation*, 1983.

Text Used: *New and Collected Poems*, 1988.

LOVE CALLS US TO THE THINGS OF THIS WORLD

The eyes open to a cry of pulleys,
And spirited from sleep, the astounded soul
Hangs for a moment bodiless and simple
As false dawn.
                    Outside the open window
The morning air is all awash with angels.

Some are in bed-sheets, some are in blouses,
Some are in smocks: but truly there they are.
Now they are rising together in calm swells
Of halcyon feeling, filling whatever they wear   10
With the deep joy of their impersonal breathing;

Now they are flying in place, conveying
The terrible speed of their omnipresence, moving
And staying like white water; and now of a sudden
They swoon down into so rapt a quiet
That nobody seems to be there.
                              The soul shrinks

From all that it is about to remember,
From the punctual rape of every blessèd day,
And cries,   20
          "Oh, let there be nothing on earth but laundry,
Nothing but rosy hands in the rising steam
And clear dances done in the sight of heaven."

Yet, as the sun acknowledges
With a warm look the world's hunks and colors,
The soul descends once more in bitter love
To accept the waking body, saying now
In a changed voice as the man yawns and rises,

"Bring them down from their ruddy gallows;
Let there be clean linen for the backs of thieves;   30
Let lovers go fresh and sweet to be undone,
And the heaviest nuns walk in a pure floating
Of dark habits,
                keeping their difficult balance."

1956

FOR DUDLEY*

Even when death has taken
An exceptional man,
It is common things which touch us, gathered
In the house that proved a hostel.

---

* Dudley Fitts (1903–1968), an educator and translator of classical literature.

Though on his desk there lie
The half of a sentence
Not to be finished by us, who lack
His gaiety, his Greek,

It is the straight back
Of a good woman   10
Which now we notice. For her guests' hunger
She sets the polished table.

And now the quick sun,
Rounding the gable,
Picks out a chair, a vase of flowers,
Which had stood till then in shadow.

It is the light of which
Achilles[1] spoke,
Himself a shadow then, recalling
The splendor of mere being.   20

As if we were perceived
From a black ship—
A small knot of island folk,
The Light-Dwellers, pouring

A life to the dark sea—
All that we do
Is touched with ocean, yet we remain
On the shore of what we know.

We say that we are behaving
As he would have us—   30
He who was brave and loved this world,
Who did not hold with weeping,

Yet in the mind as in
The shut closet
Where his coats hang in black procession,
There is a covert muster.
One is moved to turn to him,
The exceptional man,
Telling him all these things, and waiting
For the deft, lucid answer.   40

At the sound of that voice's deep
Specific silence,
The sun winks and fails in the window.
Light perpetual keep him.

1969

---

[1] According to Greek myth, the warrior who led the Greeks in the Trojan War; the hero of the *Iliad*, by Homer (8th? century B.C.).

TO THE ETRUSCAN POETS*

Dream fluently, still brothers, who when young
Took with your mother's milk the mother tongue,

In which pure matrix, joining world and mind,
You strove to leave some line of verse behind

Like a fresh track across a field of snow,
Not reckoning that all could melt and go.

1975

THE WRITER

In her room at the prow of the house
Where light breaks, and the windows are tossed with linden,
My daughter is writing a story.

I pause in the stairwell, hearing
From her shut door a commotion of typewriter-keys
Like a chain hauled over a gunwale.

Young as she is, the stuff
Of her life is a great cargo, and some of it heavy:
I wish her a lucky passage.

But now it is she who pauses,   10
As if to reject my thought and its easy figure.
A stillness greatens, in which

The whole house seems to be thinking,
And then she is at it again with a bunched clamor
Of strokes, and again is silent.

I remember the dazed starling
Which was trapped in that very room, two years ago;
How we stole in, lifted a sash

And retreated, not to affright it;
And how for a helpless hour, through the crack of the door,   20
We watched the sleek, wild, dark

And iridescent creature
Batter against the brilliance, drop like a glove
To the hard floor, or the desk-top,

* First published in the *Ontario Review* in 1975. The Etruscans were the people of Etruria, a region in Italy (now Tuscany and part of Umbria), who flourished in the sixth century B.C.

And wait then, humped and bloody,
For the wits to try it again; and how our spirits
Rose when, suddenly sure,

It lifted off from a chair-back,
Beating a smooth course for the right window
And clearing the sill of the world.   30

It is always a matter, my darling,
Of life or death, as I had forgotten. I wish
What I wished you before, but harder.

1976

LYING*

To claim, at a dead party, to have spotted a grackle,[1]
When in fact you haven't of late, can do no harm.
Your reputation for saying things of interest
Will not be marred, if you hasten to other topics,
Nor will the delicate web of human trust
Be ruptured by that airy fabrication.
Later, however, talking with toxic zest
Of golf, or taxes, or the rest of it
Where the beaked ladle plies the chuckling ice,
You may enjoy a chill of severance, hearing   10
Above your head the shrug of unreal wings.
Not that the world is tiresome in itself:
We know what boredom is: it is a dull
Impatience or a fierce velleity,[2]
A champing wish, stalled by our lassitude,
To make or do. In the strict sense, of course,
We invent nothing, merely bearing witness
To what each morning brings again to light:
Gold crosses, cornices, astonishment
Of panes, the turbine-vent which natural law   20
Spins on the grill-end of the diner's roof,
Then grass and grackles or, at the end of town
In sheen-swept pastureland, the horse's neck
Clothed with its usual thunder, and the stones
Beginning now to tug their shadows in
And track the air with glitter. All these things
Are there before us; there before we look
Or fail to look; there to be seen or not
By us, as by the bee's twelve thousand eyes,
According to our means and purposes.   30

* First published in the *New Yorker* in 1987.   [1] A blackbird.
[2] A wish; one that generally does not lead to an action.

So too with strangeness not to be ignored,
Total eclipse or snow upon the rose,
And so with that most rare conception, nothing.
What is it, after all, but something missed?
It is the water of a dried-up well
Gone to assail the cliffs of Labrador.
There is what galled the arch-negator,[3] sprung
From Hell to probe with intellectual sight
The cells and heavens of a given world
Which he could take but as another prison: 40
Small wonder that, pretending not to be,
He drifted through the bar-like boles[4] of Eden
In a *black mist low creeping,* dragging down
And darkening with moody self-absorption
What, when he left it, lifted and, if seen
From the sun's vantage, seethed with vaulting hues.
Closer to making than the deftest fraud
Is seeing how the catbird's tail was made
To counterpoise, on the mock-orange spray,
Its light, up-tilted spine; or, lighter still,   50
How the shucked tunic of an onion, brushed
To one side on a backlit chopping-board
And rocked by trifling currents, prints and prints
Its bright, ribbed shadow like a flapping sail.
Odd that a thing is most itself when likened:
The eye mists over, basil hints of clove,
The river glazes toward the dam and spills
To the drubbed[5] rocks below its crashing cullet,[6]
And in the barnyard near the sawdust-pile
Some great thing is tormented. Either it is   60
A trap torn loose and in the groaning wind
Now puffed, now flattened, or a hip-shot beast
Which tries again, and once again, to rise.
What, though for pain there is no other word,
Finds pleasure in the cruellest simile?
It is something in us like the catbird's song
From neighbor bushes in the grey of morning
That, harsh or sweet, and of its own accord,
Proclaims its many kin. It is a chant
Of the first springs, and it is tributary   70
To the great lies told with the eyes half-shut
That have the truth in view: the tale of Chiron[7]
Who, with sage head, wild heart, and planted hoof
Instructed brute Achilles in the lyre,
Or of the garden where we first mislaid
Simplicity of wish and will, forgetting

---

[3] The Devil.   [4] Tree trunks.   [5] Beaten, weathered.   [6] "Little neck" (French).
[7] According to Greek myth, a wise and just centaur (half man, half horse) who reared the warrior Achilles from infancy, teaching him to ride and hunt and instructing him in the art of healing.

Out of what cognate splendor all things came
To take their scattering names; and nonetheless
That matter of a baggage-train surprised
By a few Gascons[8] in the Pyrenees   80
Which, having worked three centuries and more
In the dark caves of France, poured out at last
The blood of Roland,[9] who to Charles his king
And to the dove that hatched the dove-tailed world
Was faithful unto death, and shamed the Devil.

1987

Denise Levertov
(1923–   )

Denise Levertov was born in Essex, England, in 1923. Her mother was Welsh; her father, a Russian Jew of Hasidic ancestry, had converted to Christianity and became an Anglican minister. Levertov's parents were prisoners of war in Germany during World War I and assisted in the relocation of Jewish refugees during World War II. Levertov was educated at home amid literary, religious, and political discussions in many languages. She drew upon that education in her poetry: the title poems "The Jacob's Ladder" (1961) and "O Taste and See" (1964), for example, reveal the influence of her (informal) religious training.

The Double Image, Levertov's first book of poetry, was written during World War II and published in London in 1946. Its formal, melancholy style is like that of other neo-romantic British poets of the 1940s. In 1947 she married an American soldier, the writer Mitchell Goodman, and the following year the couple moved to New York. Their son Nikolai was born in 1949, the year Levertov's poetry was anthologized in *The New British Poets.* Her second book, *Here and Now,* appeared in 1957, just after Levertov became a U.S. citizen. Its style and focus show that she had transformed herself into an American poet; her work was soon published in an American anthology, *The New American Poets* (1959). Levertov acknowledged the influence of William Carlos Williams in this metamorphosis. His poetics directed her attention to the poetry of idiomatic speech and reenforced her movement away from the nostalgia of her early work and toward immediate everyday experience. Another influence in this direction was a group of avant-garde poets teaching at Black Mountain College near Asheville, North Carolina. She considered two of those poets, Robert Creeley and Robert Duncan, the finest poets of her generation.

In the 1960s and 1970s Levertov became active in the protests against the Vietnam War, and her poetry reflected these political concerns. Her war poetry, collected in *To Stay Alive* (1971), records the poet's pilgrimage through years of urban unrest, student

---

[8] Natives of Gascony, a region in southwest France along the Pyrenees Mountains.
[9] A legendary hero of the epic *Chanson de Roland* ("*Song of Roland*" [French]), one of twelve paladins, or knights of the emperor Charlemagne (742–814), or Charles the Great.

protest, and war resistance. A number of the earlier poems in the volume were written after the death of Levertov's sister Olga, an activist who encouraged Levertov's social commitment. *The Freeing of the Dust* (1975) maps another spiritual journey, one that follows Levertov's divorce and a visit to Hanoi. Throughout the 1980s she remained politically outspoken, working and writing against nuclear proliferation and American military involvement in Central America. She has been known to disrupt the complacency of a poetry reading by demanding that the audience act on a pressing social issue.

Levertov has been influential as a teacher and theorist and has translated poetry from several languages. In her own poetry she rejects both traditional forms and free verse and seeks instead an "organic form," which grows from the poet's inner voice and opposes "normal" rules of form or of content. Experiences, she believes, have their own internal form that must be discovered and expressed in the movement of a poem. Although she does not define herself as a feminist, her attention to the occurrences of daily life, expressed in sensuous detail, has produced much writing concerned with women's common experiences. Prose analyses of her own creative process are collected in *Poet in the World* (1973). And she has since published numerous volumes of poetry, including *Oblique Players* (1984) and *Breathing the Water* (1987).

Suggested Readings: *Here and Now,* 1956. *The Sorrow Dance,* 1967. *Footprints,* 1972. *The Poet in the World,* 1974. *The Freeing of the Dust,* 1975. *Collected Earlier Poems: 1940–1960,* 1979. *Poems 1960–1967,* 1983. *Oblique Players,* 1984. *Selected Poems,* 1986. *Poems 1968–1972,* 1987. C. Altieri, *Enlarging the Temple: New Directions in Poetry During the 1960's,* 1980. R. Howard, *Alone With America: Essays on the Art of Poetry in the United States Since 1950,* 1980. H. Marten, *Understanding Denise Levertov,* 1988. L. W. Wagner, *Denise Levertov,* 1967. L. W. Wagner, ed., *Denise Levertov: In Her Own Province,* 1979.

Texts Used: *The Jacob's Ladder,* 1961. "The Ache of Marriage": *New Directions in Prose and Poetry 18.* ed. J. Laughlin, 1964. *O Taste and See,* 1964.

THE JACOB'S LADDER*

    The stairway is not
    a thing of gleaming strands
    a radiant evanescence
    for angels' feet that only glance in their tread, and need not
    touch the stone.

    It is of stone.
    A rosy stone that takes
    a glowing tone of softness
    only because behind it the sky is a doubtful, a doubting
    night gray.   10

    A stairway of sharp
    angles, solidly built.
    One sees that the angels must spring

---

* In Genesis 28:12 the patriarch Jacob saw in a dream "a ladder set up on the earth, and the top of it reached to heaven: and behold the angels of God ascending and descending on it."

down from one step to the next, giving a little
lift of the wings:

and a man climbing
must scrape his knees, and bring
the grip of his hands into play. The cut stone
consoles his groping feet. Wings brush past him.
The poem ascends.   20

1958

THE ACHE OF MARRIAGE

The ache of marriage:

thigh and tongue, beloved,
are heavy with it,
it throbs in the teeth

We look for communion
and are turned away, beloved,
each and each

It is leviathan[1] and we
in its belly
looking for joy, some joy   10
not to be known outside it

two by two in the ark of
the ache of it

1964

O TASTE AND SEE

The world is
not with us enough.[1]
O taste and see[2]

the subway Bible poster said,
meaning **The Lord,** meaning
if anything all that lives
to the imagination's tongue,

---

[1] A biblical sea monster, a whale or a large reptile.
[1] After the sonnet "The World Is Too Much With Us" (1807), by the English poet William Wordsworth (1770–1850).
[2] "O taste and see that the Lord is good," from Psalm 34:8.

grief, mercy, language,
tangerine, weather, to
breathe them, bite,   10
savor, chew, swallow, transform

into our flesh our
deaths, crossing the street, plum, quince,
living in the orchard and being

hungry, and plucking
the fruit.

1964

Allen Ginsberg
(1926–   )

"My poetry is Angelical Ravings," said Allen Ginsberg in 1959 (Lewis Hyde, *On the Poetry of Allen Ginsberg,* 1984), but critical response has been divided about whether his poetry is indeed angelic, merely a stream of ravings, or not poetry at all. A mythic figure in American culture, particularly as a leader of the beat poets, Ginsberg engendered and continues to sustain the numerous legends about him. He was born in 1926 in Newark, New Jersey, to a father who taught high school English and was a published poet and to a mother who was mentally ill and institutionalized throughout much of her life. Ginsberg attended Columbia University, where he studied and struggled with Lionel Trilling and Mark Van Doren, who both became critics and educators. After a school suspension and a subsequent stay at a mental institution (where he met Carl Solomon, a fellow patient to whom the poem "Howl" [1956] is dedicated), Ginsberg earned a B.A. in 1948. His already turbulent life changed dramatically that year when, alone and depressed, he read William Blake's poems and experienced a series of visions or "beatific illuminations" in which he "saw the universe unfold in [his] brain" and heard the voice of Blake speaking to him directly (Hyde, 1984). From that moment Ginsberg attained a sense of vocation as a poet whose visions would enlighten him in the same intense way. Years of travel and experimentation with drugs followed, but the visions did not reappear.

Ginsberg lived with his father in Paterson, New Jersey, for a time in the late 1940s and there met the poet William Carlos Williams, who later wrote the introduction to "Howl." In 1954 Ginsberg found his way to San Francisco, which was then bursting with poetic life, primarily under the influence of the poet Kenneth Rexroth. It was there that Lawrence Ferlinghetti's City Lights Bookshop released "Howl," the poem that made Ginsberg's reputation. In an obscenity trial following the poem's publication, Ferlinghetti was charged with disseminating "indecent writing." Although the judge ruled in favor of Ferlinghetti on the basis of freedom of speech, reviews of the poem were generally negative. Similar objections to Ginsberg's personal references—to his mother's madness and his guiltless homosexuality—would be raised throughout his career. Nonetheless, Ginsberg was thrust into the public eye and has remained there ever since.

After "Howl" Ginsberg traveled the world—to Tangier, Spain, France, Chile—and returned to the United States to give readings of his work. His readings became "performances," and he became a popular speaker on college campuses. Leading the beat poets in their anti-intellectual and anti-establishment efforts in the 1950s, Ginsberg proclaimed individual expression as paramount, a philosophy reflected in his prosody. Based not on traditional metrics but on the single breath unit ("one physical and mental inspiration of thought contained in the elastic of a breath" [Hyde, 1984]), Ginsberg's poetic line is like that of Walt Whitman and characterized by Ginsberg's own long "breath."

During the 1960s Ginsberg was involved with Vietnam War protests and the civil rights movement; he gradually turned to Eastern philosophies and became a Buddhist. In addition to the collections *The Fall of America* (1972), and *Howl and Other Poems* (1956), his collection *Kaddish and Other Poems* (1961), of which the title poem laments the recent death of Ginsberg's mother, gained widespread recognition. Ginsberg has won such awards as a Guggenheim Fellowship, a National Book Award for *Fall*, and a medal from the National Arts Club. And in 1990 he was honored with an American Book Award for his lifetime achievement in contributing "to literary excellence in America."

Suggested Readings: *Howl and Other Poems*, 1956. *Kaddish and Other Poems*, 1961. *The Fall of America, Poems of These States*, 1972. *Mind Breaths*, 1978. T. Clark, "Allen Ginsberg: An Interview," in *Writers at Work: The Paris Review Interviews*, Third Series, 1967. J. Kramer, *Allen Ginsberg in America*, 1969. T. F. Merrill, *Allen Ginsberg*, 1969. *To Eberhart From Ginsberg: A Letter About Howl 1956*, 1976. L. Hyde, ed., *On the Poetry of Allen Ginsberg*, 1984.

Text Used: *Collected Poems: 1947–1980*, 1988.

HOWL

*For Carl Solomon**

I

I saw the best minds of my generation destroyed by madness, starving hysterical
    naked,
dragging themselves through the negro streets at dawn looking for an angry fix,
angelheaded hipsters burning for the ancient heavenly connection[1] to the starry
    dynamo in the machinery of night,
who poverty and tatters and hollow-eyed and high sat up smoking in the
    supernatural darkness of cold-water flats floating across the tops of cities
    contemplating jazz,
who bared their brains to Heaven under the El[2] and saw Mohammedan angels
    staggering on tenement roofs illuminated,
who passed through universities with radiant cool eyes hallucinating Arkansas

---

* Solomon (1928–   ) was a fellow patient of Ginsberg's at the Columbia Psychiatric Institute in New York City in 1949; part of the poem is thought to be based on Solomon's "apocryphal history" of adventures.
[1] Dope supplier.   [2] The elevated railway system in New York City.

and Blake-light[3] tragedy among the scholars of war,
who were expelled from the academies for crazy & publishing obscene odes
    on the windows of the skull,[4]
who cowered in unshaven rooms in underwear, burning their money in
    wastebaskets and listening to the Terror through the wall,
who got busted in their pubic beards returning through Laredo[5] with a belt of
    marijuana for New York,
who ate fire in paint hotels or drank turpentine in Paradise Alley,[6] death, or
    purgatoried their torsos night after night   10
with dreams, with drugs, with waking nightmares, alcohol and cock and
    endless balls,
incomparable blind streets of shuddering cloud and lightning in the mind leaping
    toward poles of Canada & Paterson,[7] illuminating all the motionless world of
    Time between,
Peyote[8] solidities of halls, backyard green tree cemetery dawns, wine
    drunkenness over the rooftops, storefront boroughs of teahead joyride neon
    blinking traffic light, sun and moon and tree vibrations in the roaring winter
    dusks of Brooklyn, ashcan rantings and kind king light of mind,
who chained themselves to subways for the endless ride from Battery[9] to holy
    Bronx on benzedrine until the noise of wheels and children brought them
    down shuddering mouth-wracked and battered bleak of brain all drained of
    brilliance in the drear light of Zoo,[10]
who sank all night in submarine light of Bickford's[11] floated out and sat through
    the stale beer afternoon in desolate Fugazzi's[12] listening to the crack of doom
    on the hydrogen jukebox,
who talked continuously seventy hours from park to pad to bar to Bellevue[13] to
    museum to the Brooklyn Bridge,
a lost battalion of platonic conversationalists jumping down the stoops off
    fire escapes off windowsills off Empire State out of the moon,
yacketayakking screaming vomiting whispering facts and memories and
    anecdotes and eyeball kicks and shocks of hospitals and jails and wars,
whole intellects disgorged in total recall for seven days and nights with
    brilliant eyes, meat for the Synagogue cast on the pavement,
who vanished into nowhere Zen New Jersey leaving a trail of ambiguous
    picture postcards of Atlantic City Hall,   20
suffering Eastern sweats and Tangerian bone-grindings and migraines of

---

[3] Ginsberg experienced a mystical vision while he read the work of the English poet William Blake (1757–1827).
[4] In 1945 Ginsberg was expelled from Columbia University for drawing and writing obscenities on his dormitory windows.
[5] Laredo, Texas, on the Mexican border.
[6] Ginsberg's note: "A slum courtyard N. Y. Lower East Side, site of Kerouac's *Subterraneans*, 1958": a beat novel by Jack Kerouac (1922–1969).
[7] Paterson, New Jersey, where Ginsberg lived for a few years and met William Carlos Williams (1883–1963), author of the long poem *Paterson* (1946–1963).
[8] Mescal, portions of a cactus that Mexican Indians chew in religious ceremonies for their hallucinogenic effects.
[9] Battery Park, at the southern end of Manhattan.
[10] The Bronx Zoo, at the northern end of the N.Y.C. subway line.
[11] The all-night cafeteria where Ginsberg worked while he was a Columbia student.
[12] A bar near Greenwich Village where beats gathered.
[13] A New York public hospital with a psychiatric clinic.

China[14] under junk-withdrawal in Newark's bleak furnished room,
who wandered around and around at midnight in the railroad yard wondering
     where to go, and went, leaving no broken hearts,
who lit cigarettes in boxcars boxcars boxcars racketing through snow toward
     lonesome farms in grandfather night,
who studied Plotinus Poe St. John of the Cross[15] telepathy and bop kabbalah[16]
     because the cosmos instinctively vibrated at their feet in Kansas,
who loned it through the streets of Idaho seeking visionary indian angels
     who were visionary indian angels,
who thought they were only mad when Baltimore gleamed in supernatural ecstasy,
who jumped in limousines with the Chinaman of Oklahoma on the impulse of
     winter midnight streetlight smalltown rain,
who lounged hungry and lonesome through Houston seeking jazz or sex or
     soup, and followed the brilliant Spaniard to converse about America and
     Eternity, a hopeless task, and so took ship to Africa,
who disappeared into the volcanoes of Mexico leaving behind nothing but
     the shadow of dungarees and the lava and ash of poetry scattered in fireplace
     Chicago,
who reappeared on the West Coast investigating the FBI in beards and shorts
     with big pacifist eyes sexy in their dark skin passing out incomprehensible
     leaflets,   30
who burned cigarette holes in their arms protesting the narcotic tobacco haze
     of Capitalism,
who distributed Supercommunist pamphlets in Union Square[17] weeping and
     undressing while the sirens of Los Alamos[18] wailed them down, and wailed
     down Wall,[19] and the Staten Island ferry also wailed,
who broke down crying in white gymnasiums naked and trembling before
     the machinery of other skeletons,
who bit detectives in the neck and shrieked with delight in policecars for
     committing no crime but their own wild cooking pederasty and intoxication,
who howled on their knees in the subway and were dragged off the roof
     waving genitals and manuscripts,
who let themselves be fucked in the ass by saintly motorcyclists, and screamed
     with joy,
who blew and were blown by those human seraphim, the sailors, caresses of
     Atlantic and Caribbean love,
who balled in the morning in the evenings in rosegardens and the grass of
     public parks and cemeteries scattering their semen freely to whomever come
     who may,
who hiccuped endlessly trying to giggle but wound up with a sob behind a
     partition in a Turkish Bath when the blond & naked angel came to pierce
     them with a sword,

[14] African and Asian drug sources.
[15] Plotinus (A.D. 205?–270) was a Roman neo-Platonic philosopher; the poet and writer Edgar Allan
Poe (1809–1849); Juan de Yepes y Álvaraz (1542–1591), a Spanish mystic poet.
[16] The bop style of jazz developed in the 1940s and 1950s; the mystical tradition of interpreting
Hebrew scripture.
[17] Once a meeting place for radical speakers and protesters in New York City.
[18] The New Mexico site for the research and development of the atomic bomb.
[19] Wall Street; also, Jerusalem's Wailing Wall (thought to be part of the wall surrounding the temple
of King Herod (73–4 B.C.) of Judea, where Jews have traditionally gathered for prayer.

who lost their loveboys to the three old shrews of fate[20] the one eyed shrew of
   the heterosexual dollar the one eyed shrew that winks out of the womb and
   the one eyed shrew that does nothing but sit on her ass and snip the
   intellectual golden threads of the craftsman's loom,   40
who copulated ecstatic and insatiate with a bottle of beer a sweetheart a
   package of cigarettes a candle and fell off the bed, and continued along the
   floor and down the hall and ended fainting on the wall with a vision of ultimate
   cunt and come eluding the last gyzym of consciousness,
who sweetened the snatches of a million girls trembling in the sunset, and
   were red eyed in the morning but prepared to sweeten the snatch of the sunrise,
   flashing buttocks under barns and naked in the lake,
who went out whoring through Colorado in myriad stolen night-cars, N.C.,[21]
   secret hero of these poems, cocksman and Adonis[22] of Denver—joy to the
   memory of his innumerable lays of girls in empty lots & diner backyards,
   moviehouses' rickety rows, on mountaintops in caves or with gaunt waitresses
   in familiar roadside lonely petticoat upliftings & especially secret gas-station
   solipsisms[23] of johns, & hometown alleys too,
who faded out in vast sordid movies, were shifted in dreams, woke on a
   sudden Manhattan, and picked themselves up out of basements hungover with
   heartless Tokay[24] and the horrors of Third Avenue iron dreams & stumbled to
   unemployment offices,
who walked all night with their shoes full of blood on the snowbank docks
   waiting for a door in the East River to open to a room full of steamheat
   and opium,
who created great suicidal dramas on the apartment cliff-banks of the Hudson[25]
   under the wartime blue floodlight of the moon & their heads shall be crowned
   with laurel in oblivion,
who ate the lamb stew of the imagination or digested the crab at the muddy
   bottom of the rivers of Bowery,[26]
who wept at the romance of the streets with their pushcarts full of onions and
   bad music,
who sat in boxes breathing in the darkness under the bridge, and rose up to
   build harpsichords in their lofts,
who coughed on the sixth floor of Harlem crowned with flame under the
   tubercular sky surrounded by orange crates of theology,   50
who scribbled all night rocking and rolling over lofty incantations which in
   the yellow morning were stanzas of gibberish,
who cooked rotten animals lung heart feet tail borsht[27] & tortillas dreaming of
   the pure vegetable kingdom,
who plunged themselves under meat trucks looking for an egg,

---

[20] The Fates: according to Roman myth, three goddesses of destiny who determine the course of
human lives.

[21] Neal Cassady (1926–1968), a beat writer and friend of Ginsberg and Kerouac on whom Kerouac
based the character Dean Moriarty in *On the Road* (1957).

[22] According to Greek myth, a handsome young man loved by Aphrodite, goddess of love.

[23] Philosophical theories by which only the self exists, so that all experience is subjective.

[24] A cheap, fortified wine favored by alcoholic derelicts.

[25] The high-rise apartment houses atop the cliffs of the Palisades along the Hudson River.

[26] The lower part of Third Avenue in New York City, frequented by alcoholic derelicts.

[27] Borscht, Russian beet soup.

who threw their watches off the roof to cast their ballot for Eternity outside
of Time, & alarm clocks fell on their heads every day for the next decade,

who cut their wrists three times successively unsuccessfully, gave up and
were forced to open antique stores where they thought they were growing old
and cried,

who were burned alive in their innocent flannel suits on Madison Avenue[28]
amid blasts of leaden verse & the tanked-up clatter of the iron regiments of
fashion & the nitroglycerine shrieks of the fairies of advertising & the mustard
gas of sinister intelligent editors, or were run down by the drunken taxicabs of
Absolute Reality,

who jumped off the Brooklyn Bridge this actually happened and walked away
unknown and forgotten into the ghostly daze of Chinatown soup alleyways &
firetrucks, not even one free beer,

who sang out of their windows in despair, fell out of the subway window,
jumped in the filthy Passaic,[29] leaped on negroes, cried all over the street,
danced on broken wineglasses barefoot smashed phonograph records of
nostalgic European 1930s German jazz finished the whiskey and threw up
groaning into the bloody toilet, moans in their ears and the blast of colossal
steamwhistles,

who barreled down the highways of the past journeying to each other's
hotrod-Golgotha[30] jail-solitude watch or Birmingham jazz incarnation,

who drove crosscountry seventytwo hours to find out if I had a vision or you
had a vision or he had a vision to find out Eternity,

who journeyed to Denver, who died in Denver, who came back to Denver
& waited in vain, who watched over Denver & brooded & loned in Denver
and finally went away to find out the Time, & now Denver is lonesome for
her heroes,

who fell on their knees in hopeless cathedrals praying for each other's
salvation and light and breasts, until the soul illuminated its hair for a second,

who crashed through their minds in jail waiting for impossible criminals
with golden heads and the charm of reality in their hearts who sang sweet
blues to Alcatraz,

who retired to Mexico to cultivate a habit, or Rocky Mount to tender Buddha
or Tangiers to boys or Southern Pacific to the black locomotive[31] or Harvard
to Narcissus to Woodlawn[32] to the daisychain or grave,

who demanded sanity trials accusing the radio of hypnotism & were left with
their insanity & their hands & a hung jury,

who threw potato salad at CCNY[33] lecturers on Dadaism and subsequently
presented themselves on the granite steps of the madhouse with shaven heads
and harlequin speech of suicide, demanding instantaneous lobotomy,

60

[28] The traditional location of New York advertising agencies whose conformist employees wore gray flannel suits as a "uniform" for success.

[29] The Passaic River, which flows past Paterson, New Jersey.

[30] "Place of a Skull" (Hebrew): Calvary, the site of Jesus' crucifixion.

[31] William Burroughs (1914–   ), a beat writer and drug addict, lived in Mexico and Tangier, Morocco; Kerouac lived in Rocky Mount, North Carolina; Cassady worked for the Southern Pacific Railroad.

[32] According to Greek myth, Narcissus was a youth who fell in love with his own reflection in a pool; Woodlawn is a cemetery in the Bronx.

[33] The City College of New York; the dada cult (1916–1922) was an artistic and literary movement emphasizing the irrational and the absurd.

and who were given instead the concrete void of insulin Metrazol[34] electricity
hydrotherapy psychotherapy occupational therapy pingpong & amnesia,
who in humorless protest overturned only one symbolic pingpong table,
resting briefly in catatonia,
returning years later truly bald except for a wig of blood, and tears and fingers,
to the visible madman doom of the wards of the madtowns of the East,
Pilgrim State's Rockland's and Greystone's[35] foetid halls, bickering with the
echoes of the soul, rocking and rolling in the midnight solitude-bench
dolmen-realms[36] of love, dream of life a nightmare, bodies turned to stone as
heavy as the moon,   70
with mother finally******, and the last fantastic book flung out of the
tenement window, and the last door closed at 4 A.M. and the last telephone
slammed at the wall in reply and the last furnished room emptied down to the
last piece of mental furniture, a yellow paper rose twisted on a wire hanger
in the closet, and even that imaginary nothing but a hopeful little bit of
hallucination—
ah, Carl, while you are not safe I am not safe, and now you're really in the
total animal soup of time—
and who therefore ran through the icy streets obsessed with a sudden flash of
the alchemy of the use of the ellipse the catalog the meter & the vibrating
plane,
who dreamt and made incarnate gaps in Time & Space through images
juxtaposed, and trapped the archangel of the soul between 2 visual images and
joined the elemental verbs and set the noun and dash of consciousness together
jumping with sensation of Pater Omnipotens Aeterna Deus[37]
to recreate the syntax and measure of poor human prose and stand before you
speechless and intelligent and shaking with shame, rejected yet confessing out
the soul to conform to the rhythm of thought in his naked and endless head,
the madman bum and angel beat in Time, unknown, yet putting down here
what might be left to say in time come after death,
and rose reincarnate in the ghostly clothes of jazz in the goldhorn shadow of
the band and blew the suffering of America's naked mind for love into an
eli eli lamma lamma sabacthani[38] saxophone cry that shivered the cities down
to the last radio
with the absolute heart of the poem of life butchered out of their own bodies
good to eat a thousand years.

II

What sphinx[39] of cement and aluminum bashed open their skulls and ate up
their brains and imagination?

---

[34] The brand name of pentylenetetrazol, a drug used in shock therapy.

[35] Hospitals for the insane, near New York City. Solomon spent time at Pilgrim State and Rockland;
Ginsberg's mother, institutionalized at Greystone since the late 1940s, died there in 1956.

[36] Dolmens are neolithic tombs consisting of a large, flat rock laid across upright rocks.

[37] "All-powerful Father, Eternal God" (Latin), from a 1904 letter by the French painter Paul Cézanne
(1839–1906).

[38] "My God, my God, why have you forsaken me?" (Aramaic), from Matthew 27:46, Jesus' last
words on the cross.

[39] A mythical beast with a lion's body and a human head.

Moloch![40] Solitude! Filth! Ugliness! Ashcans and unobtainable dollars!
  Children screaming under the stairways! Boys sobbing in armies! Old men
  weeping in the parks!   80
Moloch! Moloch! Nightmare of Moloch! Moloch the loveless! Mental
  Moloch! Moloch the heavy judger of men!
Moloch the incomprehensible prison! Moloch the crossbone soulless jailhouse
  and Congress of sorrows! Moloch whose buildings are judgment! Moloch the
  vast stone of war! Moloch the stunned governments!
Moloch whose mind is pure machinery! Moloch whose blood is running
  money! Moloch whose fingers are ten armies! Moloch whose breast is a
  cannibal dynamo! Moloch whose ear is a smoking tomb!
Moloch whose eyes are a thousand blind windows! Moloch whose skyscrapers
  stand in the long streets like endless Jehovahs![41] Moloch whose factories
  dream and croak in the fog! Moloch whose smokestacks and antennae crown
  the cities!
Moloch whose love is endless oil and stone! Moloch whose soul is electricity
  and banks! Moloch whose poverty is the specter of genius! Moloch whose fate
  is a cloud of sexless hydrogen! Moloch whose name is the Mind!
Moloch in whom I sit lonely! Moloch in whom I dream Angels! Crazy in
  Moloch! Cocksucker in Moloch! Lacklove and manless in Moloch!
Moloch who entered my soul early! Moloch in whom I am a consciousness
  without a body! Moloch who frightened me out of my natural ecstasy! Moloch
  whom I abandon! Wake up in Moloch! Light streaming out of the sky!
Moloch! Moloch! Robot apartments! invisible suburbs! skeleton treasures!
  blind capitals! demonic industries! spectral nations! invincible madhouses!
  granite cocks! monstrous bombs!
They broke their backs lifting Moloch to Heaven! Pavements, trees, radios,
  tons! lifting the city to Heaven which exists and is everywhere about us!
Visions! omens! hallucinations! miracles! ecstasies! gone down the
  American river!   90
Dreams! adorations! illuminations! religions! the whole boatload of sensitive
  bullshit!
Breakthroughs! over the river! flips and crucifixions! gone down the flood!
  Highs! Epiphanies! Despairs! Ten years' animal screams and suicides!
  Minds! New loves! Mad generation! down on the rocks of Time!
Real holy laughter in the river! They saw it all! the wild eyes! the holy yells!
  They bade farewell! They jumped off the roof! to solitude! waving! carrying
  flowers! Down to the river! into the street!

III

Carl Solomon! I'm with you in Rockland
  where you're madder than I am
I'm with you in Rockland
  where you must feel very strange

---

[40] Ginsberg's note: "Or Molech, the Canaanite fire god, whose worship was marked by parents burning their children as propitiatory sacrifice. 'And thou shalt not let any of thy seed pass through the fire to Molech' (Leviticus 18:21)."
[41] Judeo-Christian Gods.

I'm with you in Rockland
  where you imitate the shade of my mother
I'm with you in Rockland
  where you've murdered your twelve secretaries
I'm with you in Rockland
  where you laugh at this invisible humor
I'm with you in Rockland
  where we are great writers on the same dreadful typewriter
I'm with you in Rockland
  where your condition has become serious and is reported on the radio   100
I'm with you in Rockland
  where the faculties of the skull no longer admit the worms of the senses
I'm with you in Rockland
  where you drink the tea of the breasts of the spinsters of Utica
I'm with you in Rockland
  where you pun on the bodies of your nurses the harpies of the Bronx
I'm with you in Rockland
  where you scream in a straightjacket that you're losing the game of the
  actual pingpong of the abyss
I'm with you in Rockland
  where you bang on the catatonic piano the soul is innocent and immortal
  it should never die ungodly in an armed madhouse
I'm with you in Rockland
  where fifty more shocks will never return your soul to its body again from
  its pilgrimage to a cross in the void
I'm with you in Rockland
  where you accuse your doctors of insanity and plot the Hebrew socialist
  revolution against the fascist national Golgotha
I'm with you in Rockland
  where you will split the heavens of Long Island and resurrect your living
  human Jesus from the superhuman tomb
I'm with you in Rockland
  where there are twenty-five thousand mad comrades all together singing the
  final stanzas of the Internationale[42]
I'm with you in Rockland
  where we hug and kiss the United States under our bedsheets the United
  States that coughs all night and won't let us sleep   110
I'm with you in Rockland
  where we wake up electrified out of the coma by our own souls' airplanes
  roaring over the roof they've come to drop angelic bombs the hospital
  illuminates itself   imaginary walls collapse   O skinny legions run outside
  O starry-spangled shock of mercy the eternal war is here   O victory forget
  your underwear we're free
I'm with you in Rockland
  in my dreams you walk dripping from a sea-journey on the highway across
  America in tears to the door of my cottage in the Western night
                                                          1955–1956, 1956

---

[42] The national anthem of the Soviet Union from the Russian Revolution (1917) to World War II
(1944).

A SUPERMARKET IN CALIFORNIA

What thoughts I have of you tonight, Walt Whitman,[1] for I walked down the sidestreets under the trees with a headache self-conscious looking at the full moon.

In my hungry fatigue, and shopping for images, I went into the neon fruit supermarket, dreaming of your enumerations!

What peaches and what penumbras![2] Whole families shopping at night! Aisles full of husbands! Wives in the avocados, babies in the tomatoes! —and you, García Lorca,[3] what were you doing down by the watermelons?

I saw you, Walt Whitman, childless, lonely old grubber, poking among the meats in the refrigerator and eyeing the grocery boys.

I heard you asking questions of each: Who killed the pork chops? What price bananas? Are you my Angel?

I wandered in and out of the brilliant stacks of cans following you, and followed in my imagination by the store detective.

We strode down in the open corridors together in our solitary fancy tasting artichokes, possessing every frozen delicacy, and never passing the cashier.

Where are we going, Walt Whitman? The doors close in an hour. Which way does your beard point tonight?

(I touch your book and dream of our odyssey in the supermarket and feel absurd.)

Will we walk all night through solitary streets? The trees add shade to shade, lights out in the houses, we'll both be lonely.

Will we stroll dreaming to the lost America of love past blue automobiles in driveways, home to our silent cottage?

Ah, dear father, graybeard, lonely old courage-teacher, what America did you have when Charon[4] quit poling his ferry and you got out on a smoking bank and stood watching the boat disappear on the black waters of Lethe?

1955, 1956

AMERICA

America I've given you all and now I'm nothing.
America two dollars and twentyseven cents January, 17, 1956.
I can't stand my own mind.
America when will we end the human war?
Go fuck yourself with your atom bomb.

---

[1] Ginsberg deeply admired the poet Whitman (1819–1892), to whom he has frequently been compared.

[2] Partly lighted areas.

[3] Federico García Lorca (1899–1936), a Spanish poet and playwright; in his *Collected Poems* (1984) Ginsberg notes García Lorca's poem "Ode to Walt Whitman": like Whitman's and Ginsberg's poetry, García Lorca's is homoerotic.

[4] According to Greek myth, the boatman who ferried the dead across the Lethe, the river of forgetfulness in Hades, the Underworld.

I don't feel good don't bother me.
I won't write my poem till I'm in my right mind.
America when will you be angelic?
When will you take off your clothes?
When will you look at yourself through the grave?   10
When will you be worthy of your million Trotskyites?[1]
America why are your libraries full of tears?
America when will you send your eggs to India?
I'm sick of your insane demands.
When can I go into the supermarket and buy what I need with my good looks?
America after all it is you and I who are perfect not the next world.
Your machinery is too much for me.
You made me want to be a saint.
There must be some other way to settle this argument.
Burroughs[2] is in Tangiers I don't think he'll come back it's sinister.   20
Are you being sinister or is this some form of practical joke?
I'm trying to come to the point.
I refuse to give up my obsession.
America stop pushing I know what I'm doing.
America the plum blossoms are falling.
I haven't read the newspapers for months, everyday somebody goes on trial
    for murder.
America I feel sentimental about the Wobblies.[3]
America I used to be a communist when I was a kid I'm not sorry.
I smoke marijuana every chance I get.
I sit in my house for days on end and stare at the roses in the closet.   30
When I go to Chinatown I get drunk and never get laid.
My mind is made up there's going to be trouble.
You should have seen me reading Marx.[4]
My psychoanalyst thinks I'm perfectly right.
I won't say the Lord's Prayer.
I have mystical visions and cosmic vibrations.
America I still haven't told you what you did to Uncle Max after he came
    over from Russia.
I'm addressing you.
Are you going to let your emotional life be run by Time Magazine?
I'm obsessed by Time Magazine.   40
I read it every week.
Its cover stares at me every time I slink past the corner candystore.
I read it in the basement of the Berkeley Public Library.
It's always telling me about responsibility. Businessmen are serious. Movie
    producers are serious. Everybody's serious but me.
It occurs to me that I am America.
I am talking to myself again.

---

[1] Supporters of the Russian Communist leader Leon Trotsky (1877–1940).
[2] William Burroughs (1914–   ), a beat writer then living in Morocco.
[3] A nickname for members of the radical Industrial Workers of the World, an organization of unions, formed in 1905.
[4] The German political philosopher and the founder of modern socialism, Karl Marx (1818–1883).

Asia is rising against me.
I haven't got a chinaman's chance.
I'd better consider my national resources.
My national resources consist of two joints of marijuana millions of genitals
    an unpublishable private literature that jetplanes 1400 miles an hour and
    twentyfive-thousand mental institutions.   50
I say nothing about my prisons nor the millions of underprivileged who live in
    my flowerpots under the light of five hundred suns.
I have abolished the whorehouses of France, Tangiers is the next to go. My
    ambition is to be President despite the fact that I'm a Catholic.

America how can I write a holy litany in your silly mood?
I will continue like Henry Ford my strophes[5] are as individual as his
    automobiles more so they're all different sexes.
America I will sell you strophes $2500 apiece $500 down on your old strophe
America free Tom Mooney[6]
America save the Spanish Loyalists[7]
America Sacco & Vanzetti must not die[8]
America I am the Scottsboro boys.[9]   60
America when I was seven momma took me to Communist Cell meetings
    they sold us garbanzos[10] a handful per ticket a ticket costs a nickel and the
    speeches were free everybody was angelic and sentimental about the workers
    it was all so sincere you have no idea what a good thing the party was in 1935
    Scott Nearing was a grand old man a real mensch[11] Mother Bloor the
    Silk-strikers' Ewig-Weibliche[12] made me cry I once saw the Yiddish orator
    Israel Amter[13] plain. Everybody must have been a spy.
America you don't really want to go to war.
America it's them bad Russians.
Them Russians them Russians and them Chinamen. And them Russians.
The Russia wants to eat us alive. The Russia's power mad. She wants to take
    our cars from out our garages.
Her wants to grab Chicago. Her needs a Red *Reader's Digest*. Her wants our
    auto plants in Siberia. Him big bureaucracy running our fillingstations.
That no good. Ugh. Him make Indians learn read. Him need big black
    niggers. Hah. Her make us all work sixteen hours a day. Help.

---

[5] Stanzas.
[6] Mooney (1882–1942) was an American labor leader imprisoned in 1916 for bomb throwing and pardoned in 1939.
[7] In the Spanish Civil War (1936–1939), foreign supporters of the Spanish government against the Fascist general Francisco Franco (1892–1975).
[8] Nicola Sacco (1891–1927) and Bartolomeo Vanzetti (1888–1927), Italian-American anarchists convicted of robbery and murder in Massachusetts and executed despite international protests over their innocence.
[9] Nine black youths arrested in 1931 in Scottsboro, Alabama, for the rape of two white women; amid widespread protests of racism, they were eventually released.
[10] Chickpeas.
[11] A real sensible, mature person (Yiddish). Scott Nearing (1883–1983) and Ella Reeve Bloor (1862–1951) were American Communist leaders.
[12] "Eternally feminine" (German), the eternal woman.
[13] Amter (1881–1954) was an American Communist leader.

America this is quite serious.
America this is the impression I get from looking in the television set.
America is this correct?   70
I'd better get right down to the job.
It's true I don't want to join the Army or turn lathes in precision parts
   factories, I'm nearsighted and psychopathic anyway.
America I'm putting my queer shoulder to the wheel.

1956

ODE TO FAILURE

Many prophets have failed, their voices silent
ghost-shouts in basements nobody heard dusty laughter in family attics
nor glanced them on park benches weeping with relief under empty sky
Walt Whitman viva'd[1] local losers—courage to Fat Ladies in the Freak
   Show! nervous prisoners whose mustached lips dripped sweat on chow lines—
Mayakovsky cried, Then die! my verse, die like the workers' rank & file
   fusilladed in Petersburg![2]
Prospero[3] burned his Power books & plummeted his magic wand to the bottom
   of dragon seas
Alexander the Great[4] failed to find more worlds to conquer!
O Failure I chant your terrifying name, accept me your 54 year old Prophet
   epicking[5] Eternal Flop! I join your Pantheon[6] of mortal bards, & hasten this
   ode with high blood pressure
rushing to the top of my skull as if I wouldn't last another minute, like the
   Dying Gaul![7] to   10
You, Lord of blind Monet, deaf Beethoven, armless Venus de Milo,
   headless Winged Victory![8]
I failed to sleep with every bearded rosy-cheeked boy I jacked off over
My tirades destroyed no Intellectual Unions of KGB & CIA in turtlenecks &
   underpants, their woolen suits & tweeds
I never dissolved Plutonium or dismantled the nuclear Bomb before my skull
   lost hair

---

[1] Whitman (1819–1892) applauded.
[2] "Let glory / disconsolate widow frail / trudge after genius / in funeral anthems / Die, my verse / die,
like the rank and file," from "At the Top of My Voice" (1930), by the Russian poet Vladimir May-
akovski (1893–1930).
[3] The magician in Shakespeare's *Tempest* who abandons his magic.
[4] Alexander III (356–323 B.C.), king of Macedonia (336–323 B.C.) and conquerer of Asia Minor,
Egypt, Babylon, and central Asia.
[5] Ginsberg has made a verb out of "epic."
[6] A building in which a nation's famous dead are entombed.
[7] A Roman copy of an original bronze statue (230–220 B.C.) of a dying warrior; the Gauls were Celtic
peoples in Europe (1st to 5th centuries B.C.).
[8] The French painter Claude Monet (1840–1926), whose eyesight was failing in his later years; the
German romantic composer Ludwig van Beethoven (1770–1827), who went deaf around 1819; the
famous armless statue (150? B.C.) of Venus, Greek goddess of love; a headless sculpture (200–190
B.C.) of Nike of Samothrace, the winged Greek goddess of victory.

I have not yet stopped the Armies of entire Mankind in their march toward
   World War III
I never got to Heaven, Nirvana,[9] X, Whatchamacallit, I never left Earth,
I never learned to die.

1980

James Merrill
(1926–)

James Merrill's career has long been an anomaly: he is a formalist in an age of free verse,
a poet of technical elegance and virtuosity in an age of plain speech. Merrill was born in
New York City in 1926 to Hellen Ingram and Charles Merrill, a wealthy financier who
helped found the world-famous brokerage house Merrill, Lynch. James Merrill was just
sixteen when his first book, a privately published collection entitled *Jim's Book* (1942),
appeared. Since 1950, when his *First Poems* was published, Merrill has written books of
poetry, novels, plays, and a collection of prose.

    While Merrill was an undergraduate at Amherst College, he was deeply influenced by
the French novelist Marcel Proust. Merrill has borrowed the Proustian usage of memory to
analyze and liberate the true meaning of the past. Childhood typically surfaces as a subject
for Merrill, as does daily home life. A sequence of seven sonnets, "The Broken Home"
(1966), recounts the breakup of his parents' marriage against the backdrop of the country's
charged atmosphere between the two world wars, a time when women lobbied for the
vote, expatriatism became fashionable, and the battle between the sexes broke out on the
domestic front: "Father Time and Mother Earth, / a marriage on the rocks."

    Two of the volumes constituting the middle part of Merrill's career—*Nights and Days*
(1960) and *The Fire Screen* (1964)—depict experiences in Greece, where Merrill spent
part of each year, and in Stonington, Connecticut, a village on the Long Island Sound,
where the poet made his American home. Although some of his work is continental, Merrill is a singularly American poet influenced as much by Americans such as Henry James
as by the Greek poet C. P. Cavafy and by Proust. In the all-American collection *Braving
the Elements* (1969), Merrill plays out his preoccupations in the context of America's Far
West. In these books as in his earlier work, sensuous descriptions of the outside world are
used to shed light on interior psychological states or truths. One of these truths, about
which Merrill is increasingly frank, is his own homosexuality.

    In 1977 Merrill received the Pulitzer Prize for poetry for *Divine Comedies,* which in-
cludes the long narrative *The Book of Ephraim. The Book of Ephraim* became the first part
of his trilogy of book-length poems, *The Changing Light at Sandover* (1982). The other
two parts are *Mirabell: Books of Number* (1978) and *Scripts for the Pageant* (1980). *The
Changing Light* chronicles Merrill's experiments with a Ouija board (a device that supposedly conveys messages from spirits) to contact the dead, such as W. H. Auden and Marianne Moore. Felt by many to be Merrill's crowning achievement, *The Changing Light* is a
massive, highly original and integrative work of the imagination. It represents the poet's

---

[9] A place or condition of great peace or bliss.

courageous effort to locate all the sources of his creative nourishment: scientific theories, metaphysical occurrences, historical events, human beings, even life in other worlds.

Merrill's recent poems deal with concerns of age, the fits and starts of memory, and death. "Farewell Performance," from *The Inner Room* (1988), embraces each of these subjects, placing them in the context of a ballet. The poem is an elegy for Merrill's friend David Kalstone, a literary critic who died of AIDS in 1986. It expresses the restorative if transient nature of art, which "cures affliction."

Suggested Readings: *First Poems*, 1950. *The Seraglio*, 1957. *The (Diblos) Notebook*, 1965. *Nights and Days*, 1966. *Divine Comedies*, 1976. *The Changing Light at Sandover*, 1982. *Recitative*, 1986. D. Kalstone, *Five Temperaments*, 1977. J. Moffet, *James Merrill: An Introduction to the Poetry*, 1984. R. von Hallberg, "James Merrill: Revealing by Obscuring," in *American Poetry and Culture, 1945–1980*, 1985. S. Yenser, *The Consuming Myth: The Work of James Merrill*, 1987. H. Vendler, "James Merrill," in *The Music of What Happens*, 1988.

Texts Used: "Charles on Fire": *From the First Nine*, 1982. "Farewell Performance": *The Innter Room*, 1988.

CHARLES ON FIRE

Another evening we sprawled about discussing
Appearances. And it was the consensus
That while uncommon physical good looks
Continued to launch one, as before, in life
(Among its vaporous eddies and false calms),
Still, as one of us said into his beard,
"Without your intellectual and spiritual
Values, man, you are sunk." No one but squared
The shoulders of his own unloveliness.
Long-suffering Charles, having cooked and served the meal,   10
Now brought out little tumblers finely etched
He filled with amber liquor and then passed.
"Say," said the same young man, "in Paris, France,
They do it this way"—bounding to his feet
And touching a lit match to our host's full glass.
A blue flame, gentle, beautiful, came, went
Above the surface. In a hush that fell
We heard the vessel crack. The contents drained
As who should step down from a crystal coach.
Steward of spirits, Charles's glistening hand   20
All at once gloved itself in eeriness.
The moment passed. He made two quick sweeps and
Was flesh again. "It couldn't matter less,"
He said, but with a shocked, unconscious glance
Into the mirror. Finding nothing changed,
He filled a fresh glass and sank down among us.

1966

FAREWELL PERFORMANCE

*for DK**

Art. It cures affliction. As lights go down and
Maestro lifts his wand, the unfailing sea change
starts within us. Limber alembics[1] once more
make of the common

lot a pure, brief gold. At the end our bravos
call them back, sweat-soldered and leotarded,
back, again back—anything not to face the
fact that it's over.

You are gone. You'd caught like a cold their airy
lust for essence. Now, in the furnace parched to   10
ten or twelve light handfuls, a mortal gravel
sifted through fingers,

coarse yet grayly glimmering sublimate of
palace days, Strauss, Sidney,[2] the lover's plaintive
Can't we just be friends? which your breakfast phone call
clothed in amusement,

this is what we paddled a neighbor's dinghy
out to scatter—Peter who grasped the buoy,
I who held the box underwater, freeing
all it contained. Past   20

sunny, fluent soundings that gruel of selfhood
taking manlike shape for one last jeté on
ghostly—wait, ah!—point into darkness vanished.
High up, a gull's wings

clapped. The house lights (always supposing, caro,
Earth remains your house) at their brightest set the
scene for good: true colors, the sun-warm hand to
cover my wet one. . . .

Back they come. How you would have loved it. We in
turn have risen. Pity and terror done with,   30
programs furled, lips parted, we jostle forward
eager to hail them,

---

* David Kalstone (1932–1986), a literary critic and friend of Merrill's.
[1] Any devices that refine or purify.
[2] The German composer Richard Strauss (1864–1949); Sir Philip Sidney (1554–1586), an English courtier and poet who served on diplomatic missions for Elizabeth I (1533–1603), queen of England (1558–1603).

more, to join the troupe—will a friend enroll us
one fine day? Strange, though. For up close their magic
self-destructs. Pale, dripping, with downcast eyes they've
seen where it led you.

1988

Anne Sexton
(1928–1974)

Born Anne Harvey in 1928 in Newton, Massachusetts, Anne Sexton was a descendant of the Pilgrims. At an early age she wrote poetry but soon abandoned her efforts. In 1948, after briefly attending Garland Junior College, she married Alfred Sexton; they had two girls. Sexton suffered from, and was often hospitalized for, chronic acute depression; several times she attempted suicide. After the first attempt, one of her doctors suggested that she return to writing poetry, which she admitted gave her a feeling of purpose. After attending poetry workshops led by John Holmes and by Robert Lowell at Boston University, Sexton published her first book, *To Bedlam and Part Way Back* (1960). It describes her breakdown and life in a mental hospital and attempts to heal domestic wounds after her discharge. Because these poems tend to be harrowingly autobiographical, Sexton was, along with Lowell, Sylvia Plath, and W. D. Snodgrass, labeled a "confessional" poet. Like them she wrote poems chronicling her relationship to such raw subjects as mental breakdowns, guilt, madness, and suicide. In Sexton's work these subjects serve as vehicles by which to examine myth and religion, sin and redemption, love (both sexual and romantic) and its withdrawal, memory and the imagination.

In her early poems especially, Sexton was influenced by Theodore Roethke, Elizabeth Bishop, and May Swenson, in addition to Plath, Lowell, and Snodgrass. Sexton's early work met with almost immediate success. For *Live or Die* (1966) she received a Pulitzer Prize. Yet, the critical reception of her work has varied. Some contemporary critics dismissed Sexton for her incomplete formal education and her unsparing exploration of subjects previously deemed improper for poetry. Others, however, praised her work for the same reasons. Early feminists saw in Sexton a spokesperson for their cause and particularly applauded the poems in *Transformations* (1971), which they saw as feminist reenactments of Grimm's fairy tales. Like some of her early admirers, more recent critics have acknowledged the poet's startling use of metaphor and imagery, perhaps in part the result of her many years in psychoanalysis.

Toward the end of Sexton's life, her own critical standards relaxed somewhat. Her later poems are less formal and intimate, more fluid and in some cases incantatory, than her early poems are. In 1974, depressed by the dissolution of her marriage and by fears that her creative powers were diminishing, Sexton committed suicide. She left behind a body of work that is highly original and compelling though sadly reflective of her slow emotional deterioration.

Suggested Readings: *To Bedlam and Part Way Back*, 1960. *All My Pretty Ones*, 1962. *Live or Die*, 1966. *Anne Sexton: A Self-Portrait in Letters*, 1977. *The Complete Poems*, 1981. *No Evil Star: Selected Essays, Interviews and Prose*, 1985. *Love Poems of Anne Sexton*, 1989. J. D. McClatchy, ed., *Anne Sexton: The Artist and Her Critics*, 1978. D. H. George, *Oedipus Anne: The Poetry of Anne Sexton*, 1987. S. E. Colburn, ed., *Anne Sexton: Telling the Tale*, 1988. D. H. George, *Sexton: Selected Criticism*, 1988. C. H. Barnard, *Anne Sexton*, 1989.

Text Used: *Selected Poems*, 1988.

HER KIND

I have gone out, a possessed witch,
haunting the black air, braver at night;
dreaming evil, I have done my hitch
over the plain houses, light by light:
lonely thing, twelve-fingered,[1] out of mind.
A woman like that is not a woman, quite.
I have been her kind.

I have found the warm caves in the woods,
filled them with skillets, carvings, shelves,
closets, silks, innumerable goods;   10
fixed the suppers for the worms and the elves:
whining, rearranging the disaligned.
A woman like that is misunderstood.
I have been her kind.

I have ridden in your cart, driver,
waved my nude arms at villages going by,
learning the last bright routes, survivor
where your flames still bite my thigh
and my ribs crack where your wheels wind.
A woman like that is not ashamed to die.   20
I have been her kind.

1960

THE TRUTH THE DEAD KNOW

*For my mother, born March 1902, died March 1959,
and my father, born February 1900, died June 1959*

Gone, I say and walk from church,
refusing the stiff procession to the grave,
letting the dead ride alone in the hearse.
It is June. I am tired of being brave.

[1] Possession of a sixth finger per hand has been considered a sign of witchcraft.

We drive to the Cape.[1] I cultivate
myself where the sun gutters from the sky,
where the sea swings in like an iron gate
and we touch. In another country people die.

My darling, the wind falls in like stones
from the whitehearted water and when we touch   10
we enter touch entirely. No one's alone.
Men kill for this, or for as much.

And what of the dead? They lie without shoes
in their stone boats. They are more like stone
than the sea would be if it stopped. They refuse
to be blessed, throat, eye and knucklebone.

1962

ALL MY PRETTY ONES*

Father, this year's jinx rides us apart
where you followed our mother to her cold slumber;
a second shock boiling its stone to your heart,
leaving me here to shuffle and disencumber
you from the residence you could not afford:
a gold key, your half of a woolen mill,
twenty suits from Dunne's, an English Ford,
the love and legal verbiage of another will,
boxes of pictures of people I do not know.
I touch their cardboard faces. They must go.   10

But the eyes, as thick as wood in this album,
hold me. I stop here, where a small boy
waits in a ruffled dress for someone to come . . .
for this soldier who holds his bugle like a toy
or for this velvet lady who cannot smile.
Is this your father's father, this commodore
in a mailman suit? My father, time meanwhile
has made it unimportant who you are looking for.
I'll never know what these faces are all about.
I lock them into their book and throw them out.   20

This is the yellow scrapbook that you began
the year I was born; as crackling now and wrinkly

---

[1] Cape Cod.
* From Shakespeare's *Macbeth* (IV. iii. 216): Macduff's response upon learning that Macbeth has had his wife and children murdered.

as tobacco leaves: clippings where Hoover[1] outran
the Democrats, wiggling his dry finger at me
and Prohibition; news where the *Hindenburg*[2] went
down and recent years where you went flush
on war. This year, solvent but sick, you meant
to marry that pretty widow in a one-month rush.
But before you had that second chance, I cried
on your fat shoulder. Three days later you died.   30

These are the snapshots of marriage, stopped in places.
Side by side at the rail toward Nassau[3] now;
here, with the winner's cup at the speedboat races,
here, in tails at the Cotillion,[4] you take a bow,
here, by our kennel of dogs with their pink eyes,
running like show-bred pigs in their chain-link pen;
here, at the horseshow where my sister wins a prize;
and here, standing like a duke among groups of men.
Now I fold you down, my drunkard, my navigator,
my first lost keeper, to love or look at later.   40

I hold a five-year diary that my mother kept
for three years, telling all she does not say
of your alcoholic tendency. You overslept,
she writes. My God, father, each Christmas Day
with your blood, will I drink down your glass
of wine? The diary of your hurly-burly years
goes to my shelf to wait for my age to pass.
Only in this hoarded span will love persevere.
Whether you are pretty or not, I outlive you,
bend down my strange face to yours and forgive you.   50

1962

US

I was wrapped in black
fur and white fur and
you undid me and then
you placed me in gold light

---

[1] Herbert Hoover (1874–1964), the Republican candidate for president in 1928, who won a landslide victory over his Democratic rival, Alfred E. Smith (1873–1944), and served as the thirty-first U.S. president (1929–1933); Prohibition was in effect until shortly after he left office.
[2] The helium-filled passenger blimp that crashed in Lakehurst, New Jersey, in 1937, after exploding in midair.
[3] The capital of the Bahama Islands.
[4] A formal ball; generally one at which debutantes are introduced.

and then you crowned me,
while snow fell outside
the door in diagonal darts.
While a ten-inch snow
came down like stars
in small calcium fragments,   10
we were in our own bodies
(that room that will bury us)
and you were in my body
(that room that will outlive us)
and at first I rubbed your
feet dry with a towel
because I was your slave
and then you called me princess.
Princess!

Oh then   20
I stood up in my gold skin
and I beat down the psalms
and I beat down the clothes
and you undid the bridle
and you undid the reins
and I undid the buttons,
the bones, the confusions,
the New England postcards,
the January ten o'clock night,
and we rose up like wheat,   30
acre after acre of gold,
and we harvested,
we harvested.

                                                    1969

John Ashbery
(1927–   )

More than any of his contemporaries, John Ashbery explores through the tenor of his poems what might be called the vehicle of imagination: the vast possibilities of imagination as a habit of mind and a habit of language. His nontraditional poems encompass advertisement and cliché, popular song and the history of poetry, as well as original thoughts and ideas. Ashbery's work reflects all that the twentieth century offers. It has been said that his poetry suffers from an intensely private dialogue with the self, that only Ashbery can understand Ashbery; it has been argued that the poet's dialogue with the self covers all possible subjects at once. Even a cursory reading reveals the inclusiveness of Ashbery's poems, most of which require numerous readings.

Like Scheherazade (the title of a 1985 Ashbery poem), the narrator of the ancient tales of *The Arabian Nights* who told continuously open-ended stories to save herself from execution, Ashbery constructs tales that flow one into the next. Scheherazade and the cartoon character Popeye (in the sestina "Farm Implements and Rutabagas in a Landscape" [1985]) flow into and out of the novelist Gertrude Stein and the poet Andrew Marvell, who in turn flow into and out of the painters Jackson Pollack and Parmigianino. Ashbery, a noted art historian and art critic, alludes as naturally to art and artists as to the artifacts of daily life and popular culture. The artistic movements of surrealism and abstract expressionism strongly influence his writings.

This all-encompassing approach, with its borrowings and abstractions, places Ashbery firmly in line with the modernism of Ezra Pound, T. S. Eliot, and Marianne Moore. Yet, Ashbery's "respect for things as they are" (to borrow the title of his 1982 essay on the artist Fairfield Porter) suggests that the poet is ultimately less modern than postmodern. By and large, Ashbery's poetry resists explication. It is as much about the process and experience of reading as it is about the process and experience of writing, with both reader and poet engaged in a common act of perception. Ashbery's poems seem to absorb all that falls under the poet's attention.

Dazzling and difficult, Ashbery's poetry has not always met with critical regard. Although his first volume, *Some Trees* (1956), was selected by the poet W. H. Auden for the Yale Series of Younger Poets (an award given only to poets under age forty), its poems baffled some critics and most readers. During the 1950s Ashbery was a "member," along with James Schuyler and Frank O'Hara, of the so-called New York school of poetry, a response to the New York school of abstract art.

The Tennis Court Oath (1962), Ashbery's second volume of poems, shows the influence of Wallace Stevens. Ashbery's "Painter," for example, echoes Stevens's "Idea of Order at Key West" (1936). Although the comparison of Ashbery to Stevens is a common one, few American poets writing in the last half of the twentieth century have escaped that comparison. Ashbery seemed, at first, either unwilling or unable to conceal the influence, but as his work progressed he lost those echoes and the sentimentality that tends to come of such imitation. However, his poems lost none of the flash, the verbal and philosophical acrobatics, that characterize his early work; the recent poems seem less contrived and more relaxed. They are also less formal, largely abandoning rhyme and meter for forms much more fluid and even experimental. Ashbery's prose poems, though comparatively few in number, are among his best. His book *Three Poems* (1972) consists of three extended prose poems.

Ashbery's most celebrated work is the introspective "Self-Portrait in a Convex Mirror," the title poem of his 1975 book that won a Pulitzer Prize, the National Book Award, and the National Book Critics' Circle Award. As the title suggests, that poem is an extended meditation on the natures of art and the self. The poet's formal explorations continued in *Shadow Train* (1981), a volume of sixteen-line poems that in their logic and composition resemble the sonnet, though they are unrhymed and lack regular meter.

In recent years, Ashbery's attention has turned to the issues of age, death, and memory, as in "Forgotten Sex," from *April Galleons* (1987). Although some critics have seen it as Ashbery's tribute to those who have died of AIDS, the poem functions, as do all of his poems, on a much less specific level. "Forgotten Sex" suggests a special place and time out of which a world is created, a world in which "Sweetness of things late, a memory for particulars / As lively as though they happened still" looms large.

Born in Rochester, New York, in 1927, Ashbery was educated at Harvard, Columbia, and New York universities. For a number of years he lived in France, first as a Fulbright scholar and later as an art critic and a literary critic. But Ashbery moved back to New

York in 1965 and became an art critic for *Newsweek*. His literary contributions go beyond poetry and criticism: he co-authored the novel *A Nest of Ninnies* (1969) with James Schuyler and wrote the one-act plays *The Heroes* (1952) and *The Philosopher* (1962) as well as the three-act *Compromise* (1956).

Suggested Readings: *Some Trees*, 1956. *A Nest of Ninnies*, with J. Schuyler, 1969. *Three Poems*, 1972. *Self-Portrait in a Convex Mirror*, 1975. *Shadow Train*, 1981. D. Kalstone, *Five Temperaments*, 1977. D. Lehman, ed., *Beyond Amazement: New Essays on John Ashbery*, 1980. R. von Hallberg, "Robert Creeley and John Ashbery: Systems," in *American Poetry and Culture, 1945–1980*, 1985. A. Corn, "A Magma of Interiors: John Ashbery's 'Self-Portrait in a Convex Mirror,'" in *The Metamorphoses of Metaphor*, 1987. H. Vendler, "John Ashbery, Louise Glück," in *The Music of What Happens*, 1988.

Texts Used: "Frost": *April Galleons*, 1988. All else: *Selected Poems*, 1985.

SOME TREES

These are amazing: each
Joining a neighbor, as though speech
Were a still performance.
Arranging by chance

To meet as far this morning
From the world as agreeing
With it, you and I
Are suddenly what the trees try

To tell us we are:
That their merely being there   10
Means something; that soon
We may touch, love, explain.

And glad not to have invented
Such comeliness, we are surrounded:
A silence already filled with noises,
A canvas on which emerges

A chorus of smiles, a winter morning.
Placed in a puzzling light, and moving,
Our days put on such reticence
These accents seem their own defense.   20

1956

THE PAINTER

Sitting between the sea and the buildings
He enjoyed painting the sea's portrait.
But just as children imagine a prayer

Is merely silence, he expected his subject
To rush up the sand, and, seizing a brush,
Plaster its own portrait on the canvas.

So there was never any paint on his canvas
Until the people who lived in the buildings
Put him to work: "Try using the brush
As a means to an end. Select, for a portrait,   10
Something less angry and large, and more subject
To a painter's moods, or, perhaps, to a prayer."

How could he explain to them his prayer
That nature, not art, might usurp the canvas?
He chose his wife for a new subject,
Making her vast, like ruined buildings,
As if, forgetting itself, the portrait
Had expressed itself without a brush.

Slightly encouraged, he dipped his brush
In the sea, murmuring a heartfelt prayer: 20
"My soul, when I paint this next portrait
Let it be you who wrecks the canvas."
The news spread like wildfire through the buildings:
He had gone back to the sea for his subject.

Imagine a painter crucified by his subject!
Too exhausted even to lift his brush,
He provoked some artists leaning from the buildings
To malicious mirth: "We haven't a prayer
Now, of putting ourselves on canvas,
Or getting the sea to sit for a portrait!"   30

Others declared it a self-portrait.
Finally all indications of a subject
Began to fade, leaving the canvas
Perfectly white. He put down the brush.
At once a howl, that was also a prayer,
Arose from the overcrowded buildings.

They tossed him, the portrait, from the tallest of the building
And the sea devoured the canvas and the brush
As though his subject had decided to remain a prayer.

                                                    1956

RIVERS AND MOUNTAINS

On the secret map the assassins
Cloistered, the Moon River was marked
Near the eighteen peaks and the city

Of humiliation and defeat—wan ending
Of the trail among dry, papery leaves
Gray-brown quills like thoughts
In the melodious but vast mass of today's
Writing through fields and swamps
Marked, on the map, with little bunches of weeds.
Certainly squirrels lived in the woods   10
But devastation and dull sleep still
Hung over the land, quelled
The rioters turned out of sleep in the peace of prisons
Singing on marble factory walls
Deaf consolation of minor tunes that pack
The air with heavy invisible rods
Pent in some sand valley from
Which only quiet walking ever instructs.
The bird flew over and
Sat—there was nothing else to do.   20
Do not mistake its silence for pride or strength
Or the waterfall for a harbor
Full of light boats that is there
Performing for thousands of people
In clothes some with places to go
Or games. Sometimes over the pillar
Of square stones its impact
Makes a light print.

So going around cities
To get to other places you found   30
It all on paper but the land
Was made of paper processed
To look like ferns, mud or other
Whose sea unrolled its magic
Distances and then rolled them up
Its secret was only a pocket
After all but some corners are darker
Than these moonless nights spent as on a raft
In the seclusion of a melody heard
As though through trees   40
And you can never ignite their touch
Long but there were homes
Flung far out near the asperities
Of a sharp, rocky pinnacle
And other collective places
Shadows of vineyards whose wine
Tasted of the forest floor
Fisheries and oyster beds
Tides under the pole
Seminaries of instruction, public   50
Places for electric light
And the major tax assessment area

Wrinkled on the plan
Of election to public office
Sixty-two years old bath and breakfast
The formal traffic, shadows
To make it not worth joining
After the ox had pulled away the cart.

Your plan was to separate the enemy into two groups
With the razor-edged mountains between.   60
It worked well on paper
But their camp had grown
To be the mountains and the map
Carefully peeled away and not torn
Was the light, a tender but tough bark
On everything. Fortunately the war was solved
In another way by isolating the two sections
Of the enemy's navy so that the mainland
Warded away the big floating ships.
Light bounced off the ends   70
Of the small gray waves to tell
Them in the observatory
About the great drama that was being won
To turn off the machinery
And quietly move among the rustic landscape
Scooping snow off the mountains rinsing
The coarser ones that love had
Slowly risen in the night to overflow
Wetting pillow and petal
Determined to place the letter   80
On the unassassinated president's desk
So that a stamp could reproduce all this
In detail, down to the last autumn leaf
And the affliction of June ride
Slowly out into the sun-blackened landscape.

1966

FARM IMPLEMENTS AND RUTABAGAS
IN A LANDSCAPE*

The first of the undecoded messages read: "Popeye[1] sits in thunder,
Unthought of. From that shoebox of an apartment,
From livid curtain's hue, a tangram emerges: a country."
Meanwhile the Sea Hag was relaxing on a green couch: "How pleasant

---

* A spoof of titles traditionally given to landscape paintings.
[1] All names in the poem are those of characters in the Popeye comic strip, created by Segar.

To spend one's vacation *en la casa de Popeye*,"[2] she scratched
Her cleft chin's solitary hair. She remembered spinach

And was going to ask Wimpy if he had bought any spinach.
"M'love," he intercepted, "the plains are decked out in thunder
Today, and it shall be as you wish." He scratched
The part of his head under his hat. The apartment   10
Seemed to grow smaller. "But what if no pleasant
Inspiration plunge us now to the stars? *For this is my country*."

Suddenly they remembered how it was cheaper in the country.
Wimpy was thoughtfully cutting open a number 2 can of spinach
When the door opened and Swee'pea crept in. "How pleasant!"
But Swee'pea looked morose. A note was pinned to his bib. "Thunder
And tears are unavailing," it read. "Henceforth shall Popeye's apartment
Be but remembered space, toxic or salubrious, whole or scratched."

Olive came hurtling through the window; its geraniums scratched
Her long thigh. "I have news!" she gasped. "Popeye, forced as you know to
     flee the country   20
One musty gusty evening, by the schemes of his wizened, duplicate father,
     jealous of the apartment
And all that it contains, myself and spinach
In particular, heaves bolts of loving thunder
At his own astonished becoming, rupturing the pleasant

Arpeggio[3] of our years. No more shall pleasant
Rays of the sun refresh your sense of growing old, nor the scratched
Tree-trunks and mossy foliage, only immaculate darkness and thunder."
She grabbed Swee'pea. "I'm taking the brat to the country."
"But you can't do that—he hasn't even finished his spinach,"
Urged the Sea Hag, looking fearfully around at the apartment.   30

But Olive was already out of earshot. Now the apartment
Succumbed to a strange new hush. "Actually it's quite pleasant
Here," thought the Sea Hag. "If this is all we need fear from spinach
Then I don't mind so much. Perhaps we could invite Alice the Goon over"—
     she scratched
One dug pensively—"but Wimpy is such a country
Bumpkin, always burping like that." Minute at first, the thunder
Soon filled the apartment. It was domestic thunder,
The color of spinach. Popeye chuckled and scratched
His balls: it sure was pleasant to spend a day in the country.

                                                            1966

---

[2] "In Popeye's house" (Spanish). When Ashbery wrote the poem, the strip was appearing in New York City only in the Spanish-language newspaper *El Diario*.
[3] A chord whose notes are played in quick succession rather than simultaneously.

WET CASEMENTS*

When Eduard Raban, coming along the passage,
walked into the open doorway, he saw that it was
raining. It was not raining much.
    —KAFKA, *Wedding Preparations in the Country*[1]

The concept is interesting: to see, as though reflected
In streaming windowpanes, the look of others through
Their own eyes. A digest of their correct impressions of
Their self-analytical attitudes overlaid by your
Ghostly transparent face. You in falbalas[2]
Of some distant but not too distant era, the cosmetics,
The shoes perfectly pointed, drifting (how long you
Have been drifting; how long I have too for that matter)
Like a bottle-imp[3] toward a surface which can never be approached,
Never pierced through into the timeless energy of a present   10
Which would have its own opinions on these matters,
Are an epistemological snapshot of the processes
That first mentioned your name at some crowded cocktail
Party long ago, and someone (not the person addressed)
Overheard it and carried that name around in his wallet
For years as the wallet crumbled and bills slid in
And out of it. I want that information very much today,

Can't have it, and this makes me angry.
I shall use my anger to build a bridge like that
Of Avignon,[4] on which people may dance for the feeling   20
Of dancing on a bridge. I shall at last see my complete face
Reflected not in the water but in the worn stone floor of my bridge.

I shall keep to myself.
I shall not repeat others' comments about me.

                                        1975

MY EROTIC DOUBLE

He says he doesn't feel like working today.
It's just as well. Here in the shade
Behind the house, protected from street noises,
One can go over all kinds of old feeling,
Throw some away, keep others.

*Window frames that open on hinges along the side.
[1] A novel fragment (1907) by the Czech writer Franz Kafka (1883–1924).
[2] Flounces or trimmings for women's garments.   [3] A genie of the bottle.
[4] A city in southeast France.

                                      The wordplay
Between us gets very intense when there are
Fewer feelings around to confuse things.
Another go-round? No, but the last things
You always find to say are charming, and rescue me   10
Before the night does. We are afloat
On our dreams as on a barge made of ice,
Shot through with questions and fissures of starlight
That keep us awake, thinking about the dreams
As they are happening. Some occurrence. You said it.

I said it but I can hide it. But I choose not to.
Thank you. You are a very pleasant person.
Thank you. You are too.

                                               1979

FROST

Trapped in the wrong dream, you turn
Out of an alley into a wide, weak street   Mirrors
Fall from trees, and it could be time
To refinance the mess of starting
And staying put. But rumors feed this.
The distant passage is then always sublime
And well-lit for some, a curious picture
Of longing and distress for others.

Meanwhile the only tall thing
Of importance dismantles himself,   10
Transparent in places, sometimes opaque
And more beautiful for the scenes
That might be projected on him. The secret
Chamber is one, where only the king
Could come, and now two or three young people
Can sit, uneasy and comfortable, discussing
Bicycles, the bone: any of the smaller anythings.
Which is quite nice, but darkness
Seems to fall more quickly, to accrue more in this sudden
Place, made of a name cut out of a map.   20

One gets closer to nervousness then.
It needn't be so. Things are stranger elsewhere.
Here in the dark the keeping of secrets
Is dense, that's all. There are still a few common
Names for things around; even they don't have to be
Used. Only I wish
There was some way of not getting more thoughtful,

Of not bruising the obvious shadow for which
There is a reason. Am I poor?
Have I worn out God's welcome?   30
There is enough dark green to cover us,
Yet will we always be speechless to the end,
Unable to say the familiar things?

1984

W. S. Merwin
(1927–   )

After the publication of the poetry collection *The Lice* (1967), W. S. Merwin was acclaimed by many critics as the representative poet of the 1960s. Though the events to which the book refers are rarely named, its spare, highly controlled poems convey an unmistakable rage at the political and ecological crises of the time—the Vietnam War in particular—and an overwhelming sense of despair. Merwin's work during this period amounts to an indictment of what he has called "a society whose triumphs . . . emerge as new symbols of death, and that feeds itself by poisoning the earth. . . . " Upon receiving the Pulitzer Prize for poetry in 1971 for *The Carrier of Ladders* (1970), he publicly declared that he would donate most of the prize money to the draft-resistance movement.

This sense that humanity has betrayed both its natural environment and its own primal foundations informs Merwin's attitude toward language as well. Characterized by the desire to avoid the "very dangerous human arrogance" of using language "to possess the world" and by the need to transcend the "ego-bound, historical, culturally brainwashed, incredibly limited moment," Merwin's poems are often hushed, inhabited by a disembodied voice that suggests the inadequacy of language rather than its power. Thus, the humble posture he strikes in a poem such as "For the Anniversary of My Death" (1967), which ends with the speaker "bowing not knowing to what," reflects Merwin's conviction that a poet should not use rhetoric as an "emotional screen." Knowing that he is drawn to words like "silence," "darkness," and "emptiness," Merwin explains in an interview that he has tried to guard against falling into a merely habitual rhetoric because those words would then "have an emptiness which obscures their real emptiness; they can become sentimental."

The son of a Presbyterian minister, William Stanley Merwin was born in 1927 in New York City and grew up in Union City, New Jersey, and Scranton, Pennsylvania. He associates his initiation into writing with his father's religious vocation: "I started writing hymns for my father almost as soon as I could write at all, illustrating them. I recall some rather stern little pieces addressed . . . to backsliders, but I can remember too wondering whether there might not be some liberating mode" (from a 1984 interview with L. Edwin Folsom). With the help of a scholarship, he attended Princeton University, where he studied with, and was influenced by, the writers John Berryman and R. P. Blackmur, to whom the collection *The Moving Target* (1963) is dedicated. During Merwin's college years he admired Ezra Pound, a poet to whom he still feels a tremendous debt. Merwin says he was "marked . . . for life" by the visit he made in 1946 to Pound in Washington, D.C., at St. Elizabeth's Hospital for the criminally insane; Merwin, like Pound, became a student of foreign languages and a reader of medieval poetry, especially the work of Dante and of François Villon.

After graduating with a B.A. in romance languages from Princeton in 1947, Merwin went abroad. He worked as a tutor in France, Portugal, and Majorca (where he tutored the son of the British writer Robert Graves) and as a translator in London, where he got involved with the theater. Upon returning to the United States in 1956, Merwin wrote several plays for the Poets' Theater in Cambridge, Massachusetts. In 1952 his first volume of poems, *A Mask for Janus,* won the Yale Younger Poets Award, chosen by the poet W. H. Auden. Auden praised Merwin for his command of a wide range of traditional poetic forms, including such folk forms as the ballad—a reflection of Merwin's long-standing interest in oral literature.

By the end of the 1950s, after having been very well received by the literary world, Merwin experienced something of a crisis in his work and, he says in an interview, "virtually stopped writing poetry." During these years he broke away from traditional metrical and stanzaic patterns and was engaged in a process of "strengthening by compressing and intensifying, of getting down to what was really essential." In his fourth book, *The Drunk in the Furnace* (1960), Merwin turned to autobiographical themes, writing poems about his family and his childhood in Scranton. His next collection, *The Moving Target* (1963), represents a major turning point: he began to omit all punctuation from his poems, a practice that since the 1960s has become one of the distinctive characteristics of his verse. "Punctuation," writes Merwin, "seemed to staple the poem to the page, but if I took those staples out the poem lifted itself right up off the page."

In addition to his numerous collections of poetry and of prose, Merwin has established himself as an important and innovative translator of works in various languages and a wide range of styles, from Sanskrit love poetry to French symbolist poetry to Asian proverbs. Partly on the advice of Ezra Pound, Merwin started translating as an exercise that he hoped would help his own writing. Pound's suggestion that he write English versions of Spanish romances eventually led to Merwin's translations of two medieval epics, the Spanish *The Poem of the Cid* (1959) and the French *Song of Roland* (1963). He has worked on material that reflects his thematic and formal interests, even if that material is written in languages in which he has no firsthand knowledge. *Asian Figures* (1973), for example, consists of English adaptations of proverbs from a variety of Asian languages and embodies Merwin's attraction to compact forms.

Merwin recently made Hawaii his primary residence. At work on a book of prose about Hawaii, he is combing oral histories and essays in an effort to tell what he believes is the largely ignored story of how the U.S. military has desecrated Kaho'Olawe, an uninhabited island sacred to the Hawaiian people, by using the island as a bombing target. Merwin has described this project as a "gathering together of almost all of my interests . . . ," including opposing "the destruction of the earth for abstract and greedy reasons."

Suggested Readings: *A Mask for Janus,* 1952. *The Drunk in the Furnace,* 1960. *The Lice,* 1967. *The Carrier of Ladders,* 1970. *The Miner's Pale Children,* 1970. *The Compass Flower,* 1977. *Houses and Travellers,* 1977. *Unframed Originals: Recollections,* 1982. *Regions of Memory: Uncollected Prose,* ed. E. Folsom and C. Nelson, 1987. J. Vernon, in *American Poetry Review,* Jan.–Feb., 1978. C. Davis, *W. S. Merwin,* 1981. C. Nelson and E. Folsom, eds., *W. S. Merwin: Essays on the Poetry,* 1987.

Texts Used: "Thanks": *The Rain in the Trees,* 1988. All else: *Selected Poems,* 1988.

ONE-EYE

("In the country of the blind the one-eyed man is king.")*

On that vacant day
After kicking and moseying[1] here and there
For some time, he lifted that carpet-corner
   His one eye-lid, and the dyed light
Leapt at him from all sides like dogs. Also hues
That he had never heard of, in that place
   Were bleeding and playing.

Even so, it was
Only at the grazing of light fingers
Over his face, unannounced, and then his   10
   Sight of many mat eyes, paired white
Irises like dried peas looking, that it dawned
On him: his sidelong idling had found
   The country of the blind.

Whose swarming digits
Knew him at once: their king, come to them
Out of a saying. And chanting an anthem
   Unto his one eye, to the dry
Accompaniment that their leaping fingers made
Flicking round him like locusts in a cloud,   20
   They took him home with them.

Their shapely city
Shines like a suit. On a plain chair he was set
In a cloak of hands, and crowned, to intricate
   Music. They sent him their softest
Daughters, clad only in scent and their own
Vast ears, meantime making different noises
   In each ante-chamber.

They can be wakened
Sometimes by a feather falling on the next   30
Floor, and they keep time by the water-clocks'[2]
   Dropping even when they sleep. Once
He would expound to them all, from his only
Light, day breaking, the sky spiked and the
   Earth amuck with color,

And they would listen,
Amazed at his royalty, gaping like
Sockets, and would agree, agree, blank
   As pearls. At the beginning.

---

* From the short story "The Country of the Blind" (1911), by the English writer H. G. Wells (1866–1946).
[1] Strolling.   [2] Clocks that operate by the flow of water.

Alone in brightness, soon he spoke of it   40
In sleep only; "Look, look," he would call out
   In the dark only.

   Now in summer gaudy
With birds he says nothing; of their thefts, often
Beheld, and their beauties, now for a long time
   Nothing. Nothing, day after day,
To see the black thumb as big as a valley
Over their heads descending silently
   Out of a quiet sky.

1960

THE DRUNK IN THE FURNACE

   For a good decade
The furnace stood in the naked gully, fireless
And vacant as any hat. Then when it was
No more to them than a hulking black fossil
To erode unnoticed with the rest of the junk-hill
By the poisonous creek, and rapidly to be added
   To their ignorance,

   They were afterwards astonished
To confirm, one morning, a twist of smoke like a pale
Resurrection, staggering out of its chewed hole,   10
And to remark then other tokens that someone,
Cosily bolted behind the eye-holed iron
Door of the drafty burner, had there established
   His bad castle.

   Where he gets his spirits
It's a mystery. But the stuff keeps him musical:
Hammer-and-anvilling with poker and bottle
To his jugged bellowings, till the last groaning clang
As he collapses onto the rioting
Springs of a litter of car-seats ranged on the grates,   20
   To sleep like an iron pig.

   In their tar-paper church
On a text about stoke-holes that are sated never
Their Reverend lingers. They nod and hate trespassers.
When the furnace wakes, though, all afternoon
Their witless offspring flock like piped rats[1] to its siren
Crescendo, and agape on the crumbling ridge
   Stand in a row and learn.

1956, 1960

---

[1] From the German folk tale of the Pied Piper of Hamelin, who lured rats out of town with his flute playing but, angered at not being paid, also lured away the children.

THE ANIMALS

All these years behind windows
With blind crosses sweeping the tables

And myself tracking over empty ground
Animals I never saw

I with no voice

Remembering names to invent for them
Will any come back will one

Saying yes

Saying look carefully yes
We will meet again   10

1967

FOR THE ANNIVERSARY OF MY DEATH

Every year without knowing it I have passed the day
When the last fires will wave to me
And the silence will set out
Tireless traveller
Like the beam of a lightless star

Then I will no longer
Find myself in life as in a strange garment
Surprised at the earth
And the love of one woman
And the shamelessness of men   10
As today writing after three days of rain
Hearing the wren sing and the falling cease
And bowing not knowing to what

1967

THE JUDGMENT OF PARIS*

Long afterwards
the intelligent could deduce what had been offered
and not recognized
and they suggest that bitterness should be confined
to the fact that the gods chose for their arbiter
a mind and character so ordinary
albeit a prince

* According to Greek myth, a golden apple marked "To the Fairest," thrown by Eris (the goddess of discord) was claimed by three goddesses: Hera (the supreme goddess), Athena (the goddess of wisdom and warfare), and Aphrodite (the goddess of love); to settle the dispute, Zeus (the supreme god) advised them to consult Paris, the son of King Priam of Troy.

and brought up as a shepherd[1]
a calling he must have liked
for he had returned to it   10

when they stood before him
the three
naked feminine deathless
and he realized that he was clothed
in nothing but mortality
the strap of his quiver of arrows crossing
between his nipples
making it seem stranger

and he knew he must choose
and on that day   20
the one with the gray eyes[2] spoke first
and whatever she said he kept
thinking he remembered
but remembered it woven with confusion and fear
the two faces that he called father
the first sight of the palace
where the brothers were strangers
and the dogs watched him and refused to know him
she made everything clear she was dazzling she
offered it to him   30
to have for his own but what he saw
was the scorn above her eyes
and her words of which he understood few
all said to him *Take wisdom*
take power
you will forget anyway

the one with the dark eyes[3] spoke
and everything she said
he imagined he had once wished for
but in confusion and cowardice   40
the crown
of his father the crowns the crowns bowing to him
his name everywhere like grass
only he and the sea
triumphant
she made everything sound possible she was
dazzling she offered it to him
to hold high but what he saw

---

[1] Because of a prophecy that Paris would bring destruction to Troy, he was left to die as an infant in the wilderness but, unbeknown to the king, was raised by one of his own shepherds.

[2] Athena, who promised Paris victory in battles if he chose her.

[3] Hera, who promised to make Paris ruler of the world.

was the cruelty around her mouth
and her words of which he understood more   50
all said to him *Take pride*
take glory
you will suffer anyway

the third one[4] the color of whose eyes
later he could not remember
spoke last and slowly and
of desire and it was his
though up until then he had been
happy with his river nymph[5]
here was his mind   60
filled utterly with one girl gathering
yellow flowers
and no one like her
the words
made everything seem present
almost present
present
they said to him *Take*
her
you will lose her anyway   70

it was only when he reached out to the voice
as though he could take the speaker
herself
that his hand filled with
something to give
but to give to only one of the three
an apple as it is told
discord itself in a single fruit its skin ,
already carved
To the fairest   80

then a mason working above the gates of Troy
in the sunlight thought he felt the stone
shiver

in the quiver on Paris's back the head
of the arrow for Achilles' heel[6]
smiled in its sleep

---

[4] Aphrodite, who promised Paris the fairest woman in the world—Helen, the wife of the Spartan king Menelaus. Paris chose Aphrodite and incurred the hatred of Hera and Athena; the events led to the Trojan War, in which the Greeks fought to restore Helen to Menelaus.
[5] The nymph Oenone.
[6] Paris killed the hero Achilles by shooting an arrow into his one vulnerable spot, his heel.

and Helen stepped from the palace to gather
as she would do every day in that season
from the grove the yellow ray flowers tall
as herself   90

whose roots are said to dispel pain

                                                                                 1970

FLIES

On the day when the flies were made
death was a garden
already without walls
without apples
with nowhere to look back to
all that day the stars could be seen
black points
in the eyes of flies
and the only sound was the roar of the flies
until the sun went down   10

each day after that something else was made
and something else with no name
was a garden
which the flies never saw
what they saw was not there
with no end
no apples
ringed with black stars
that no one heard
and they flew in it happily all day   20
wearing mourning

                                                                                 1973

THANKS*

Listen
with the night falling we are saying thank you
we are stopping on the bridges to bow from the railings
we are running out of the glass rooms
with our mouths full of food to look at the sky
and say thank you
we are standing by the water thanking it
standing by the windows looking out
in our directions

* First published in *The Nation*.

back from a series of hospitals back from a mugging   10
after funerals we are saying thank you
after the news of the dead
whether or not we knew them we are saying thank you

over telephones we are saying thank you
in doorways and in the backs of cars and in elevators
remembering wars and the police at the door
and the beatings on stairs we are saying thank you
in the banks we are saying thank you
in the faces of the officials and the rich
and of all who will never change   20
we go on saying thank you thank you

with the animals dying around us
taking our feelings we are saying thank you
with the forests falling faster than the minutes
of our lives we are saying thank you
with the words going out like cells of a brain
with the cities growing over us
we are saying thank you faster and faster
with nobody listening we are saying thank you
thank you we are saying and waving   30
dark though it is

1988

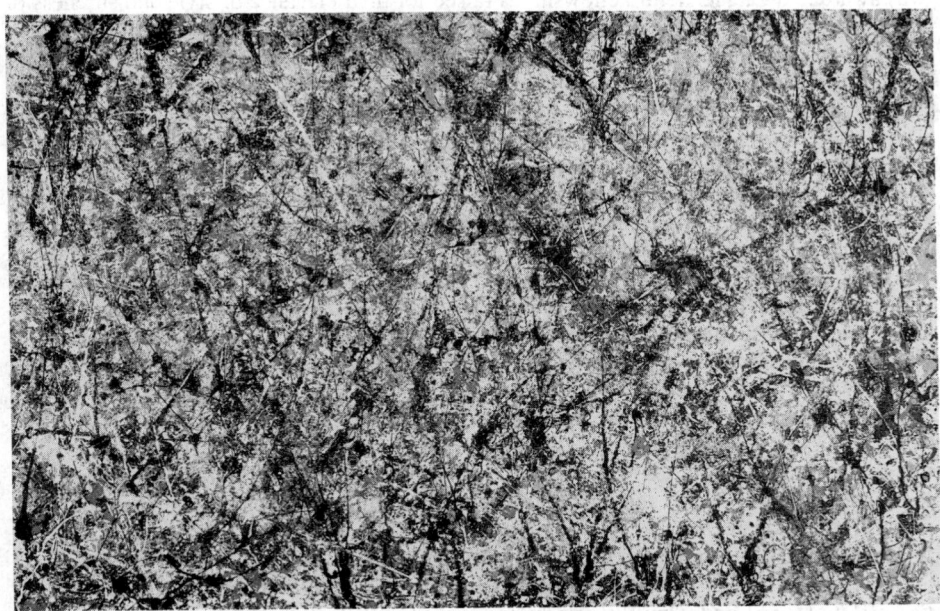

Jackson Pollock's Number 1, 1950 (Lavender Mist) *(1950) is an example of abstract expressionism. Pollock's radical techniques, such as dripping paint on a canvas, helped generate experimentation in abstract expression in literature as well.*

Adrienne Rich
(1929–   )

The title of Adrienne Rich's first book, *A Change of World* (1951), aptly describes all of Rich's subsequent work: poems and essays that celebrate and speak for women. Rich is trying to change the very consciousness of the world. By daring and even insisting on confronting the myths by which we live, myths handed from generation to generation, Rich aims to change our world by changing how we imagine ourselves in it. To say the unspoken and to banish the silences, she walks a dangerous path with few guides to follow. Achieving remarkable success in both the academic and popular communities, Rich has nonetheless managed to find her way in book after book—undoing and redoing the sense of self, the sense of what is essential, and the sense of what is possible.

Born in Baltimore in 1929, Rich grew up feeling "vaguely Episcopal" in a southern family, with a Jewish father and non-Jewish mother. Not until the late 1940s, when Rich was attending Radcliffe College, did she begin to claim Jewish identity. In her prose collection *Blood, Bread and Poetry* (1986), she describes the ambiguity of her childhood and her early sense of being "split at the root," a metaphor she probes in much of her work. Rich graduated from Radcliffe in 1951, the year *A Change of World*, chosen by the poet W. H. Auden for the Yale Younger Poets Award, was published. The following year she was awarded a Guggenheim Fellowship. Praised for their elegance of style and sureness of technique, both her first volume of poems and her second, *The Diamond Cutters* (1955), radiate her training in the traditional and early modern masters, including Auden.

In 1953 Rich married Alfred Conrad, an economist from an Orthodox Jewish family, and by the time she was thirty she had given birth to three children. The family lived in Cambridge, Massachusetts, where Conrad taught at Harvard University. Rich also began to teach and has since taught at several colleges, including Swarthmore College and Columbia, Rutgers and Cornell Universities. Concerned primarily with motherhood during the Cambridge years, Rich snatched moments to write and won a second Guggenheim Fellowship in 1961. Eight years elapsed between the publication of her second volume and her third, *Snapshots of a Daughter-in-Law* (1963). The "snapshot" format of the title poem reflects the stolen fragments of time during which she wrote and the progress of her emerging feminist consciousness. Piecing together bits of insights and incongruities that unsettled her and unsettle her readers, she wrote the title poem, she says in the essay "When We Dead Awaken" (1971), "in a longer, looser mode than I'd ever trusted myself with before. It was an extraordinary relief to write that poem. It strikes me now as too literary, too dependent on allusions; I hadn't found the courage yet to do without authority or even to use the pronoun 'I'—the woman in the poem is always 'she.'" *Snapshots* announced a tremendous leap in Rich's thinking and writing, and pointed to her abandonment of traditional forms and subjects.

Rich's poetry became more experimental in the 1960s—and more overtly political and feminist. What had earlier been ambiguous became declarative in her collections *Necessities of Life* (1966) and *The Will to Change* (1968). When Rich and her family moved to New York in 1966, she began teaching at City College, where she became involved with the school's open admissions policy and with the civil rights movement. In "When We Dead Awaken" she says that the social justice movement during those years "lifted [her] out of a sense of personal frustration and hopelessness," helping her to clarify those convictions that would shape her feminist philosophy. Although Rich's move from the personal to the social delineates her ever-emerging perspective on gender and sexual issues, hers is not a universal poetry but an emphatically feminine one. "Time is male," she writes in "Snapshots of a Daughter-in-Law," and accordingly, "universal" to her has meant nonfemale.

After her husband committed suicide in 1970, Rich wrote *Diving Into the Wreck* (1973), an angry, pained collection that plunges into the depths of her being. In it she continues to confront the sexual politics and inherited myths that had left her bitter and to voice the themes of marginality, power and powerlessness, and rage against the forced silence of generations. A book written a few years later, *The Dream of a Common Language* (1978), is even by its title more hopeful, the rage redirected to a dream and hope for communication. As exemplified in the twenty-one love poems collected in that volume, a "common language" is not a universal one, but one vital and true to those who speak it. Detailing a lesbian relationship, these poems articulate a love taboo in lyric poetry of the traditional poets.

In 1974 Rich received a National Book Award, which she accepted with the poet Audre Lourde on behalf of all women. In the mid-1970s Rich moved in with the writer Michelle Cliff and began to edit the feminist journal *Sinister Wisdom* with her. For Rich there is no distinction between the political and the personal, the political and the poetic, the political and the feminine. Whereas in the earlier prose collection *Of Woman Born* (1976) she explodes the myths of motherhood, in her essay "Compulsory Heterosexuality and the Lesbian Experience" (1981), she explodes the myths of heterosexuality. Rich contends that because sexuality has been determined by society through training and the models given in the media and in literature, heterosexuality is enforced and hence not natural. These deliberate shatterings of traditional beliefs and, as Rich says, "re-visions" of the female experience dictate a corresponding change in our vision of humanity.

Suggested Readings: *Snapshots of a Daughter-in-Law: Poems 1954–1962*, 1963. *Diving Into the Wreck*, 1973. *Of Woman Born: Motherhood as Experience and Institution*, 1976. *The Dream of a Common Language: Poems 1974–1977*, 1978. *On Lies, Secrets and Silence: Selected Prose 1966–78*, 1979. *Blood, Bread and Poetry: Selected Prose 1979–1985*, 1986. B. Gelpi and A. Gelpi, ed., *Adrienne Rich's Poetry, A Norton Critical Edition*, 1975. D. Kalstone, *Five Temperaments*, 1977. J. R. Cooper, *Reading Adrienne Rich: Reviews and Re-Visions 1951–1981*, 1984. C. Keyes, *The Aesthetics of Power: The Poetry of Adrienne Rich*, 1986.

Texts Used: "In Memoriam: D. K.": *Time's Power*, 1989. All else: *The Fact of a Doorframe: Poems Selected and New, 1950–1984*, 1984.

LIVING IN SIN

She had thought the studio would keep itself;
no dust upon the furniture of love.
Half heresy, to wish the taps[1] less vocal,
the panes relieved of grime. A plate of pears,
a piano with a Persian shawl, a cat
stalking the picturesque amusing mouse
had risen at his urging.
Not that at five each separate stair would writhe

---

[1] Water faucets.

under the milkman's tramp; that morning light
so coldly would delineate the scraps   10
of last night's cheese and three sepulchral[2] bottles;
that on the kitchen shelf among the saucers
a pair of beetle-eyes would fix her own—
envoy from some village in the moldings . . .
Meanwhile, he, with a yawn,
sounded a dozen notes upon the keyboard,
declared it out of tune, shrugged at the mirror,
rubbed at his beard, went out for cigarettes;
while she, jeered by the minor demons,
pulled back the sheets and made the bed and found   20
a towel to dust the table-top,
and let the coffee-pot boil over on the stove.
By evening she was back in love again,
though not so wholly but throughout the night
she woke sometimes to feel the daylight coming
like a relentless milkman up the stairs.

1955

SNAPSHOTS OF A DAUGHTER-IN-LAW

I.

You, once a belle in Shreveport,[1]
with henna-colored hair, skin like a peachbud,
still have your dresses copied from that time,
and play a Chopin[2] prelude
called by Cortot:[3] *"Delicious recollections
float like perfume through the memory."*

Your mind now, moldering like wedding-cake,
heavy with useless experience, rich
with suspicion, rumor, fantasy,
crumbling to pieces under the knife-edge   10
of mere fact. In the prime of your life.

Nervy, glowering, your daughter
wipes the teaspoons, grows another way.

2.

Banging the coffee-pot into the sink
she hears the angels chiding, and looks out
past the raked gardens to the sloppy sky.
Only a week since They said: *Have no patience.*

---

[2] Ghostly.
[1] Shreveport, Louisiana.   [2] The Polish composer and pianist Frederic Chopin (1810–1849).
[3] Alfred Cortot (1877–1962), a famous French pianist; from the preface to his *Chopin: 24 Preludes*
(1930), specifically Prelude No. 7.

The next time it was: *Be insatiable.*
Then: *Save yourself; others you cannot save.*
Sometimes she's let the tapstream scald her arm,   20
a match burn to her thumbnail,

or held her hand above the kettle's snout
right in the woolly steam. They are probably angels,
since nothing hurts her anymore, except
each morning's grit blowing into her eyes.

3.

A thinking woman sleeps with monsters.
The beak that grips her, she becomes. And Nature,
that sprung-lidded, still commodious
steamer-trunk of *tempora* and *mores*[4]
gets stuffed with it all: The mildewed orange-flowers,   30
the female pills,[5] the terrible breasts
of Boadicea[6] beneath flat foxes' heads and orchids.

Two handsome women, gripped in argument,
each proud, acute, subtle, I hear scream
across the cut glass and majolica[7]
like Furies[8] cornered from their prey:
The argument *ad feminam*,[9] all the old knives
that have rusted in my back, I drive in yours,
ma semblable, ma soeur![10]

4.

Knowing themselves too well in one another: 40
their gifts no pure fruition, but a thorn,
the prick filed sharp against a hint of scorn . . .
Reading while waiting
for the iron to heat,
writing, *My Life had stood—a Loaded Gun*—[11]
in that Amherst pantry while the jellies boil and scum,
or, more often,
iron-eyed and beaked and purposed as a bird,
dusting everything on the whatnot every day of life.

---

[4] "Times," "customs" (Latin).   [5] Medication for menstrual pain.
[6] Boadicea (?–A.D. 62), queen of the Iceni (Britons of Norfolk and Suffolk), led an unsuccessful revolt against Roman rulers.
[7] A modern imitation of Italian Renaissance pottery, both characterized by rich colors, glaze, and ornamentation.
[8] According to Greek myth, goddesses of vengeance.
[9] "To the woman" (Latin): the feminine version of *ad hominem*, an argument appealing to the emotions rather than to reason.
[10] "My like, my sister!" (French), after the final line of the poem "Au Lecteur," by the French poet Charles Baudelaire (1821–1867); Rich changes "brother" to "sister."
[11] Rich's note: "*Emily Dickinson, Complete Poems*, ed. T. H. Johnson, 1960, p. 369": from poem 754 by Emily Dickinson (1830–1886), who lived her entire life in Amherst, Massachusetts.

5.

Dulce ridens, dulce loquens,[12]   50
she shaves her legs until they gleam
like petrified mammoth-tusk.

6.

When to her lute Corinna sings[13]
neither words nor music are her own;
only the long hair dipping
over her cheek, only the song
of silk against her knees
and these
adjusted in reflections of an eye.

Poised, trembling and unsatisfied, before   60
an unlocked door, that cage of cages,
tell us, you bird, you tragical machine—
is this *fertilisante douleur?*[14] Pinned down
by love, for you the only natural action,
are you edged more keen
to prise the secrets of the vault? has Nature shown
her household books to you, daughter-in-law,
that her sons never saw?

7.

"To have in this uncertain world some stay
which cannot be undermined, is   70
of the utmost consequence."[15]
                              Thus wrote
a woman, partly brave and partly good,
who fought with what she partly understood.
Few men about her would or could do more,
hence she was labeled harpy, shrew and whore.

8.

"You all die at fifteen," said Diderot,[16]
and turn part legend, part convention.

[12] "Sweetly smiling, sweetly speaking" (Latin), from Ode XXII, "Integer vitae" (23–24), by the Roman poet Horace (65–8 B.C.).

[13] The first line of a song by the English poet and composer Thomas Campion (1567–1620).

[14] "Fertilizing [or life-giving] sorrow" (French).

[15] Rich's note: "From Mary Wollstonecraft, *Thoughts on the Education of Daughters,* London, 1787." An early feminist, Wollstonecraft (1759–1797), best known for her *Vindication of the Rights of Women* (1792), advocated equality and companionship between the sexes and education for women.

[16] Denis Diderot (1713–1784), a French encyclopedist, philosopher, critic, and playwright. Rich's note: "'You all die at fifteen': '*Vous mourez toutes à quinze ans,*' from the *Lettres à Sophie Volland,* quoted by Simone de Beauvoir in *Le Deuxième Sexe,* Vol. II, pp. 123–124." The French writer de Beauvoir (1908–1986) published *Le Deuxième Sexe,* or "The Second Sex" (French), in 1949.

Still, eyes inaccurately dream
behind closed windows blankening with steam.   80
Deliciously, all that we might have been,
all that we were—fire, tears,
wit, taste, martyred ambition—
stirs like the memory of refused adultery
the drained and flagging bosom of our middle years.

9.

*Not that it is done well, but
that it is done at all?*[17] Yes, think
of the odds! or shrug them off forever.
This luxury of the precocious child,
Time's precious chronic invalid,—   90
would we, darlings, resign it if we could?
Our blight has been our sinecure:
mere talent was enough for us—
glitter in fragments and rough drafts.

Sigh no more, ladies.
                    Time is male
and in his cups drinks to the fair.
Bemused by gallantry, we hear
our mediocrities over-praised,
indolence read as abnegation,   100
slattern thought styled intuition,
every lapse forgiven, our crime
only to cast too bold a shadow
or smash the mold straight off.

For that, solitary confinement,
tear gas, attrition shelling.
Few applicants for that honor.

10.
                    Well,
she's long about her coming, who must be
more merciless to herself than history.   110
Her mind full to the wind, I see her plunge
breasted and glancing through the currents,
taking the light upon her
at least as beautiful as any boy
or helicopter,[18]

---

[17] After a remark by the English man-of-letters, poet, biographer, and lexicographer Samuel Johnson (1709–1784) to his biographer James Boswell (1740–1795) in 1763: "Sir, a woman's preaching is like a dog's walking on his hinder legs. It is not done well; but you are surprised to find it done at all."

[18] Rich's note: "She comes down from the remoteness of ages, from Thebes, from Crete, from Chichén-Itzá; and she is also the totem set deep in the African jungle; she is a helicopter and she is a bird; and there is this, the greatest wonder of all: under her tinted hair the forest murmur becomes a thought and words issue from her breasts," from de Beauvoir's *Le Deuxième Sexe*.

> poised, still coming,
> her fine blades making the air wince
> but her cargo
> no promise then:
> delivered   120
> palpable
> ours.

1958–1960, 1963

FACE TO FACE

Never to be lonely like that—
the Early American figure on the beach
in black coat and knee-breeches
scanning the didactic storm in privacy,

never to hear the prairie wolves
in their lunar hilarity
circling one's little all, one's claim
to be Law and Prophets

for all that lawlessness,
never to whet the appetite   10
weeks early, for a face, a hand
longed-for and dreaded—

How people used to meet!
starved, intense, the old
Christmas gifts saved up till spring,
and the old plain words,

and each with his God-given secret,
spelled out through months of snow and silence,
burning under the bleached scalp; behind dry lips
a loaded gun.[1]   20

1965, 1966

ORION*

Far back when I went zig-zagging
through tamarack[1] pastures
you were my genius, you

---

[1] "My Life had stood—a Loaded Gun—," from poem 754 by Emily Dickinson (1830–1886).
* The equatorial constellation of the hunter Orion; according to Greek myth, Artemis (goddess of the moon and the hunt) loved Orion but accidentally killed him, so she placed him in the sky as a constellation.
[1] The American larch tree, a member of the pine family.

my cast-iron Viking, my helmed[2]
lion-heart king[3] in prison.
Years later now you're young

my fierce half-brother, staring
down from that simplified west
your breast open, your belt[4] dragged down
by an oldfashioned thing, a sword   10
the last bravado you won't give over
though it weighs you down as you stride

and the stars in it are dim[5]
and maybe have stopped burning.
But you burn, and I know it;
as I throw back my head to take you in
an old transfusion happens again:
divine astronomy is nothing to it.

Indoors I bruise and blunder,
break faith, leave ill enough   20
alone, a dead child born in the dark.
Night cracks up over the chimney,
pieces of time, frozen geodes[6]
come showering down in the grate.

A man reaches behind my eyes
and finds them empty
a woman's head turns away
from my head in the mirror
children are dying my death
and eating crumbs of my life.   30

Pity is not your forte.
Calmly you ache up there
pinned aloft in your crow's nest,[7]
my speechless pirate!
You take it all for granted
and when I look you back

it's with a starlike eye
shooting its cold and egotistical spear
where it can do least damage.

---

[2] Helmeted.
[3] Richard I (1157–1199), king of England (1189–1199) and named Richard the Lion-Hearted; he was captured in Austria in 1192 and held until he was ransomed in 1194.
[4] Orion's belt and sword are formed by stars in the constellation.
[5] Of the seven stars of Orion, only two—Rigel and Betelgeuse— are bright.
[6] Globular stones with a crystal-lined cavity.   [7] A lookout platform near the top of a ship's mast.

Breathe deep! No hurt, no pardon   40
out here in the cold with you
you with your back to the wall.[8]

1965, 1969

A VALEDICTION FORBIDDING MOURNING*

My swirling wants. Your frozen lips.
The grammar turned and attacked me.
Themes, written under duress.
Emptiness of the notations.

They gave me a drug that slowed the healing of wounds.

I want you to see this before I leave:
the experience of repetition as death
the failure of criticism to locate the pain
the poster in the bus that said:
my bleeding is under control.   10

A red plant in a cemetery of plastic wreaths.

A last attempt: the language is a dialect called metaphor.
These images go unglossed: hair, glacier, flashlight.
When I think of a landscape I am thinking of a time.
When I talk of taking a trip I mean forever.
I could say: those mountains have a meaning
but further than that I could not say.

To do something very common, in my own way.

1970, 1971

FROM A SURVIVOR

The pact that we[1] made was the ordinary pact
of men and women in those days

---

[8] Rich's note: "One of two phrases suggested by Gottfried Benn's essay, 'Artists and Old Age' in *Primal Vision*, edited by E. B. Ashton, New Directions." The German poet and essayist Benn (1886–1956) advises modern artists, "Don't lose sight of the cold and egotistical element in your mission. . . . With your back to the wall, care-worn and weary, in the gray light of the void, read Job and Jeremiah and keep going."

* Also the title of a famous poem by John Donne (1572–1631).

[1] Rich and her husband, the economist Alfred Conrad (1924–1970); they were married in 1953.

I don't know who we thought we were
that our personalities
could resist the failures of the race

Lucky or unlucky, we didn't know
the race had failures of that order
and that we were going to share them

Like everybody else, we thought of ourselves as special

Your body is as vivid to me   10
as it ever was: even more

since my feeling for it is clearer:
I know what it could and could not do

it is no longer
the body of a god
or anything with power over my life

Next year it would have been 20 years
and you are wastefully dead[2]
who might have made the leap
we talked, too late, of making   20

which I live now
not as a leap
but a succession of brief, amazing movements

each one making possible the next

1972

IN MEMORIAM: D. K.*

A man walking on the street
feels unwell   has felt unwell
all week, a little   Yet the flowers crammed
in pots on the corner: furled anemones:
he knows they open
burgundy, violet, pink, amarillo[1]
all the way to their velvet cores
The flowers hanging over the fence: fuchsias:
each tongued, staring,   all of a fire:
the flowers   He who has   10

---

[2] Conrad committed suicide.
* David Kalstone (1932–1986), a literary critic.   [1] "Yellow" (Spanish).

been happy oftener than sad
carelessly happy   well oftener than sick
one of the lucky   is thinking about death
and its music   about poetry
its translations of his life
And what good will it do you
to go home and put on the Mozart Requiem?[2]
Read Keats?[3]   How will culture cure you?

Poor, unhappy

unwell culture   what can it sing or say   20
six weeks from now, to you?

Give me your living hand   If I could take the hour
death moved into you   undeclared, unnamed
—even if sweet, if I could take that hour

between my forceps   tear at it like a monster
wrench it out of your flesh   dissolve its shape in quicklime
and make you well again

no, not again

but still. . . .

1986, 1989

In the 1960s and 1970s the proposed Equal Rights Amendment, calling for full equality for women, was ratified in many states but failed to gain the necessary majority for passage by the 1982 deadline. Here, pro-ERA demonstrators marched in Chicago in 1980.

---

[2] The unfinished requiem mass by the Austrian composer Wolfgang Amadeus Mozart (1756–1791).
[3] The English poet John Keats (1795–1821).

Sylvia Plath
(1932–1963)

"Sylvia Plath," the critic George Stade has written, "would have been a good poet even if she had not committed suicide, but not exactly the poet she has since become" (in N. H. Stelnor, *A Closer Look at Ariel*, 1973). Plath's poetic reputation is indeed a posthumous phenomenon. Her *Collected Poems* (1981) earned a Pulitzer Prize nearly twenty years after her death. Her most acclaimed collection of poetry, *Ariel* (1965)—which her husband, the English poet Ted Hughes, published two years after her death—immediately transformed the image readers had of her from a promising talent to a major lyric voice. In the *Ariel* poems, most of which she wrote in furious bursts in the last months of her life, the pared-down syntax, stark imagery, and incantatory tone create a haunting vision of tormented intensity that the student of Plath finds difficult to reconcile with the fabric of much of her life. Commonly called a confessional poet, Plath derived much of the raw material for her work from her life—yet, more important is the way in which she created a personal mythology transcending the facts and events of simple autobiography.

Born in 1932 in Boston, Plath was the eldest child of Otto Emil Plath, a German immigrant, and Aurelia Schoeber, the daughter of Austrian immigrants. Otto Plath was a professor of biology and an entomologist (one who studies insects), specializing in bees, at Boston University, where he also taught German for scientists; his wife had a graduate degree in German. The family lived in the coastal town of Winthrop, Massachusetts, and Sylvia enjoyed a seemingly happy childhood, playing by the sea. The apparent idyll ended when her father began to suffer from diabetes, which required the amputation of a gangrenous leg and claimed his life in 1940. Aurelia Plath moved her family to Wellesley, Massachusetts, and began to teach at Boston University.

Sylvia Plath began to write poetry early; her first published poem, called simply "Poem," appeared in 1940 in the *Boston Sunday Herald* when she was eight. She excelled academically in high school and dutifully submitted forty-five pieces to *Seventeen* magazine before one was finally published in 1950. That year she won a full scholarship to Smith College in Massachusetts, where she continued her academic achievements. Plath published stories and poems in magazines, won two Smith poetry prizes, and was elected to Phi Beta Kappa. She also won a fiction contest sponsored by *Mademoiselle* magazine: the prize included a paid trip to New York, where she worked as a guest editor on the magazine. During her month in Manhattan she interviewed writers and poets, including Anthony Hecht, Richard Wilbur, George Steiner, and Elizabeth Bowen. When Plath returned home to Wellesley for the rest of her summer vacation, she became increasingly anxious and depressed. One day when her family was out, she hid in the basement and swallowed a large number of sleeping pills. She was found three days later and was rushed to a hospital, where she began psychotherapy and electric shock therapy. Plath's doctors allowed her to return to college that winter, and despite her setback she graduated summa cum laude in 1955, with a Fulbright scholarship to Cambridge University in hand.

Plath studied for two years at Newnham College, Cambridge, and toured Europe during breaks. In February 1956 she met Ted Hughes, whose work she had read and admired; in April she wrote an ecstatic letter home to her brother (in *Letters Home*, 1975): "[I] am

*Sylvia Plath's own
sketch* The Docks,
Portland, Maine.

writing poetry as I never have before; and it is the best, because I am strong in myself and in love with the only man in the world who is my match." The two were married in June 1956 and, after spending the summer in Spain, settled into a flat near Cambridge, where she continued her studies and he taught at a nearby secondary school. In 1957 they moved to America, where Plath had been offered an instructorship in English at her alma mater and Hughes taught creative writing at the University of Massachusetts. Teaching left them little time for their own writing, though, and they decided to leave their jobs at the end of the academic year.

The couple returned to England in 1959; shortly thereafter Plath's first child, a daughter, was born and her first collection of poetry, *The Colossus* (1960), was accepted for publication. She began work on a novel, *The Bell Jar*, based on her former psychiatric experiences. During the summer, she and Hughes bought a house in Devon, England, and early in 1962 she gave birth to a son. The year 1962 was an agonizing one for Plath: she was sick much of the time; her marriage was suffering, too, and she and Hughes separated; and she moved her two children to London during the coldest winter in England in 150 years. In January 1963 *The Bell Jar* appeared, under the pseudonym Victoria Lucas. Plath took to rising at four in the morning to write before her children awoke. She was working on the *Ariel* poems at an astonishing pace, turning out two, sometimes three poems a day. Alone, sick, and exhausted, in February 1963 at six in the morning, Plath prepared breakfast for her children, brought it up to them before they woke, went downstairs, and took her own life by inhaling gas from the oven.

Plath says in *The Poet Speaks* (1977) that "birds, bees, spring, fall, all those subjects . . . are absolute gifts to the person who doesn't have any interior experience to write about." Much of the poetry included in *The Colossus* and in the two collections that Ted Hughes published in 1971, *Crossing the Water* and *Winter Trees,* records a keen appreciation of, and an intense reaction to, nature. It also reveals Plath's careful attention to stanzaic form, rhythm, and sound patterns. In "Blackberrying," from *Crossing the Water,* natural objects are so fraught with symbolic, larger-than-life significance as to threaten the identity of the persona; yet Plath also maintains regular stanzaic form and creates a resonant beat. In the *Ariel* poems, of which Plath wrote to her mother in 1962 (in *Letters Home*), "I am writing the best poems of my life; they will make my name," the powerful symbolism and relentless scrutiny of a persona alternately victimized and triumphant combine with hypnotic rhythms and insistent sound patterns to mark the height of Plath's poetic achievement. But as she committed suicide well before *Ariel* was published, she was never to enjoy that achievement.

Suggested Readings: *The Colossus,* 1960. *The Bell Jar* (pseud. Victoria Lucas), 1963. *Ariel,* 1965. *Crossing the Water*, 1971. *Winter Trees,* 1971. *Letters Home: Correspondence 1950–63; ed. A. S. Plath,* 1975. *Johnny Panic* and the *Bible of Dreams: Short Stories, Prose and Diary Excerpts,* 1977. *The Journals of Sylvia Plath,* ed. T. Hughes and McCullough, 1982. A. Alvarez, *The Savage God: A Study of Suicide,* 1972. E. Aird, *Sylvia Plath,* 1973. M. Dickie, *Sylvia Plath and Ted Hughes,* 1979. L. Wagner, ed., *Critical Essays on Sylvia Plath,* 1984. L. Wagner-Martin, *Sylvia Plath: A Biography,* 1987. H. Bloom, ed., *Sylvia Plath,* 1988. A. Stevenson, *Bitter Fame: A Life of Sylvia Plath,* 1989. S. G. Axelrod, *Sylvia Plath: The Wound and the Cure of Words,* 1990.

Text Used: *The Collected Poems,* ed. T. Hughes, 1981.

TULIPS*

The tulips are too excitable, it is winter here.
Look how white everything is, how quiet, how snowed-in.
I am learning peacefulness, lying by myself quietly
As the light lies on these white walls, this bed, these hands.
I am nobody; I have nothing to do with explosions.
I have given my name and my day-clothes up to the nurses
And my history to the anesthetist and my body to surgeons.

They have propped my head between the pillow and the sheet-cuff
Like an eye between two white lids that will not shut.
Stupid pupil, it has to take everything in.   10
The nurses pass and pass, they are no trouble,
They pass the way gulls pass inland in their white caps,
Doing things with their hands, one just the same as another,
So it is impossible to tell how many there are.

My body is a pebble to them, they tend it as water
Tends to the pebbles it must run over, smoothing them gently.
They bring me numbness in their bright needles, they bring me sleep.
Now I have lost myself I am sick of baggage———

---

* Written in March 1961; that winter Plath had suffered a miscarriage, and in March she was hospitalized for an appendectomy.

My patent leather overnight case like a black pillbox,
My husband and child[1] smiling out of the family photo;   20
Their smiles catch onto my skin, little smiling hooks.

I have let things slip, a thirty-year-old cargo boat
Stubbornly hanging on to my name and address.
They have swabbed me clear of my loving associations.
Scared and bare on the green plastic-pillowed trolley
I watched my teaset, my bureaus of linen, my books
Sink out of sight, and the water went over my head.
I am a nun now, I have never been so pure.

I didn't want any flowers, I only wanted
To lie with my hands turned up and be utterly empty.   30
How free it is, you have no idea how free————
The peacefulness is so big it dazes you,
And it asks nothing, a name tag, a few trinkets.
It is what the dead close on, finally; I imagine them
Shutting their mouths on it, like a Communion tablet.[2]

The tulips are too red in the first place, they hurt me.
Even through the gift paper I could hear them breathe
Lightly, through their white swaddlings, like an awful baby.
Their redness talks to my wound, it corresponds.
They are subtle: they seem to float, though they weigh me down,   40
Upsetting me with their sudden tongues and their color,
A dozen red lead sinkers round my neck.

Nobody watched me before, now I am watched.
The tulips turn to me, and the window behind me
Where once a day the light slowly widens and slowly thins,
And I see myself, flat, ridiculous, a cut-paper shadow
Between the eye of the sun and the eyes of the tulips,
And I have no face, I have wanted to efface myself.
The vivid tulips eat my oxygen.

Before they came the air was calm enough,   50
Coming and going, breath by breath, without any fuss.
Then the tulips filled it up like a loud noise.
Now the air snags and eddies round them the way a river
Snags and eddies round a sunken rust-red engine.
They concentrate my attention, that was happy
Playing and resting without committing itself.

---

[1] Plath's husband was the English poet Ted Hughes (1930–   ); their daughter, Frieda, was born in April 1960.
[2] During the Christian sacrament of Communion to commemorate Christ's death, a tablet or wafer (symbolizing the body of Christ) is eaten.

The walls, also, seem to be warming themselves.
The tulips should be behind bars like dangerous animals;
They are opening like the mouth of some great African cat,
And I am aware of my heart: it opens and closes   60
Its bowl of red blooms out of sheer love of me.
The water I taste is warm and salt, like the sea,
And comes from a country far away as health.

1961, 1965

LADY LAZARUS*

I have done it again.
One year in every ten
I manage it———

A sort of walking miracle, my skin
Bright as a Nazi lampshade,[1]
My right foot

A paperweight,
My face a featureless, fine
Jew linen.

Peel off the napkin   10
O my enemy.
Do I terrify?———

The nose, the eye pits, the full set of teeth?
The sour breath
Will vanish in a day.

Soon, soon the flesh
The grave cave ate will be
At home on me

And I a smiling woman.
I am only thirty.   20
And like the cat I have nine times to die.

This is Number Three.
What a trash
To annihilate each decade.

---

* In John 11:39–44 Jesus raised Lazarus, the brother of Mary, from the dead; Plath refers to her own suicide attempts.
[1] In Nazi concentration camps the skin of victims was sometimes made into lampshades.

What a million filaments.
The peanut-crunching crowd
Shoves in to see

Them unwrap me hand and foot————
The big strip tease.
Gentlemen, ladies   30

These are my hands
My knees.
I may be skin and bone,

Nevertheless, I am the same, identical woman.
The first time it happened I was ten.
It was an accident.

The second time I meant
To last it out and not come back at all.
I rocked shut

As a seashell.   40
They had to call and call
And pick the worms off me like sticky pearls.

Dying
Is an art, like everything else.
I do it exceptionally well.

I do it so it feels like hell.
I do it so it feels real.
I guess you could say I've a call.

It's easy enough to do it in a cell.
It's easy enough to do it and stay put.   50
It's the theatrical

Comeback in broad day
To the same place, the same face, the same brute
Amused shout:

'A miracle!'
That knocks me out.
There is a charge

For the eyeing of my scars, there is a charge
For the hearing of my heart————
It really goes.   60

And there is a charge, a very large charge
For a word or a touch
Or a bit of blood

Or a piece of my hair or my clothes.
So, so, Herr Doktor.[2]
So, Herr Enemy.

I am your opus,
I am your valuable,
The pure gold baby

That melts to a shriek.   70
I turn and burn.
Do not think I underestimate your great concern.

Ash, ash—
You poke and stir.
Flesh, bone, there is nothing there———

A cake of soap,
A wedding ring,
A gold filling.

Herr God, Herr Lucifer
Beware   80
Beware.

Out of the ash
I rise[3] with my red hair
And I eat men like air.

                                                            1962, 1965

THE BEE MEETING*

Who are these people at the bridge to meet me? They are the villagers———
The rector, the midwife, the sexton,[1] the agent for bees.
In my sleeveless summery dress I have no protection,
And they are all gloved and covered, why did nobody tell me?
They are smiling and taking out veils tacked to ancient hats.

I am nude as a chicken neck, does nobody love me?
Yes, here is the secretary of bees with her white shop smock,
Buttoning the cuffs at my wrists and the slit from my neck to my knees.
Now I am milkweed silk, the bees will not notice.
They will not smell my fear, my fear, my fear.   10

---

[2] "Mr. Doctor" (German).

[3] Like the phoenix, a mythical bird that supposedly sets itself on fire and rises anew from its own ashes.

* Plath's father, Otto Plath (1885–1940), was a biologist and author of *Bumble Bees and Their Ways* (1934). While living in Devon, England, she kept a hive of bees and attended meetings of the Bee-keepers Association.

[1] A church caretaker, bellringer, and gravedigger.

Which is the rector now, is it that man in black?
Which is the midwife, is that her blue coat?
Everybody is nodding a square black head, they are knights in visors,
Breastplates of cheesecloth knotted under the armpits.
Their smiles and their voices are changing. I am led through a beanfield.

Strips of tinfoil winking like people,
Feather dusters fanning their hands in a sea of bean flowers,
Creamy bean flowers with black eyes and leaves like bored hearts.
Is it blood clots the tendrils are dragging up that string?
No, no, it is scarlet flowers that will one day be edible.   20

Now they are giving me a fashionable white straw Italian hat
And a black veil that molds to my face, they are making me one of them.
They are leading me to the shorn grove, the circle of hives.
Is it the hawthorn[2] that smells so sick?
The barren body of hawthorn, etherizing its children.

Is it some operation that is taking place?
It is the surgeon my neighbors are waiting for,
This apparition in a green helmet,
Shining gloves and white suit.
Is it the butcher, the grocer, the postman, someone I know?   30

I cannot run, I am rooted, and the gorse[3] hurts me
With its yellow purses, its spiky armory.
I could not run without having to run forever.
The white hive is snug as a virgin,
Sealing off her brood[4] cells, her honey, and quietly humming.

Smoke rolls and scarves in the grove.
The mind of the hive thinks this is the end of everything.
Here they come, the outriders, on their hysterical elastics.[5]
If I stand very still, they will think I am cow-parsley,
A gullible head untouched by their animosity,   40

Not even nodding, a personage in a hedgerow.
The villagers open the chambers, they are hunting the queen.
Is she hiding, is she eating honey? She is very clever.
She is old, old, old, she must live another year, and she knows it.
While in their fingerjoint cells the new virgins

Dream of a duel they will win inevitably,
A curtain of wax dividing them from the bride flight,
The upflight of the murderess[6] into a heaven that loves her.
The villagers are moving the virgins, there will be no killing.
The old queen does not show herself, is she so ungrateful?   50

[2] A spring shrub of the rose family, with fragrant flowers and small red fruits.
[3] A spiny, yellow-flowered shrub.   [4] Breeding.
[5] The bees that left the hive return quickly.   [6] The queen bee.

I am exhausted, I am exhausted————
Pillar of white in a blackout of knives.
I am the magician's girl who does not flinch.
The villagers are untying their disguises, they are shaking hands.
Whose is that long white box in the grove, what have they accomplished, why am
    I cold.

1962, 1965

ARIEL*

Stasis[1] in darkness.
Then the substanceless blue
Pour of tor[2] and distances.

God's lioness,
How one we grow,
Pivot of heels and knees!—The furrow

Splits and passes, sister to
The brown arc
Of the neck I cannot catch,

Nigger-eye   10
Berries cast dark
Hooks————

Black sweet blood mouthfuls,
Shadows.
Something else

Hauls me through air————
Thighs, hair;
Flakes from my heels.

White
Godiva,[3] I unpeel————   20
Dead hands, dead stringencies.

And now I
Foam to wheat, a glitter of seas.
The child's cry

* The horse Plath rode in Devon, England, during the two years she lived there; a name for Jerusalem, meaning "lion of God" (Hebrew); also, the sprite of fire and air in Shakespeare's *Tempest*.
[1] A state of balance or equilibrium.   [2] A high, craggy hill.
[3] Lady Godiva, a noblewoman who supposedly rode naked on horseback through Coventry, England
(1040), to get feudal obligations and taxes reduced.

Melts in the wall.
And I
Am the arrow,

The dew that flies
Suicidal, at one with the drive
Into the red   30

Eye, the cauldron of morning.

1962, 1965

DADDY*

You do not do, you do not do
Any more, black shoe
In which I have lived like a foot
For thirty years, poor and white,
Barely daring to breathe or Achoo.

Daddy, I have had to kill you.
You died before I had time———
Marble-heavy, a bag full of God,
Ghastly statue with one gray toe[1]
Big as a Frisco seal   10

And a head in the freakish Atlantic
Where it pours bean green over blue
In the waters off beautiful Nauset.[2]
I used to pray to recover you.
Ach, du.[3]

In the German tongue, in the Polish town[4]
Scraped flat by the roller
Of wars, wars, wars.
But the name of the town is common.
My Polack friend   20

---

* Plath's note: "The poem is spoken by a girl with an Electra complex [a tendency for a daughter to be attached to her father and hostile to her mother]. Her father died while she thought he was God. Her case is complicated by the fact that her father was also a Nazi and her mother very possibly part Jewish. In the daughter the two strains marry and paralyze each other—she has to act out the awful little allegory before she is free of it."

[1] The result of diabetes-induced gangrene; Plath's father, Otto Plath (1885–1940) had died from the disease.

[2] The Native-American name for Eastham, Cape Cod.

[3] "Ah, you" (German); the first of several references to her father's German background.

[4] Grasbow, where Otto Plath was born.

Says there are a dozen or two.
So I never could tell where you
Put your foot, your root,
I never could talk to you.
The tongue stuck in my jaw.

It stuck in a barb wire snare.
Ich, ich, ich, ich,[5]
I could hardly speak.
I thought every German was you.
And the language obscene   30

An engine, an engine
Chuffing[6] me off like a Jew.
A Jew to Dachau, Auschwitz, Belsen.[7]
I began to talk like a Jew.
I think I may well be a Jew.

The snows of the Tyrol,[8] the clear beer of Vienna
Are not very pure or true.
With my gipsy ancestress and my weird luck
And my Taroc pack[9] and my Taroc pack
I may be a bit of a Jew.   40

I have always been scared of *you,*
With your Luftwaffe,[10] your gobbledygoo.
And your neat mustache
And your Aryan[11] eye, bright blue.
Panzer-man, panzer-man,[12] O You————

Not God but a swastika[13]
So black no sky could squeak through.
Every woman adores a Fascist,
The boot in the face, the brute
Brute heart of a brute like you.   50

You stand at the blackboard, daddy,[14]
In the picture I have of you,
A cleft in your chin instead of your foot
But no less a devil for that, no not
Any less the black man who

---

[5] "I, I, I, I" (German).   [6] Chugging.
[7] Nazi concentration camps in Poland (Auschwitz) and Germany.
[8] Tirol, an Alpine region in Austria and Italy.
[9] A variant of Tarot, ancient fortune-telling cards.   [10] The Nazi air force.
[11] In Nazi ideology, the "superior" race of Nordic people of non-Jewish descent.
[12] A soldier in the Nazi tank division.   [13] A Greek cross, a symbol used by the Nazi party.
[14] Otto Plath taught biology at Boston University.

Bit my pretty red heart in two.
I was ten when they buried you.
At twenty I tried to die
And get back, back, back to you.[15]
I thought even the bones would do.   60

But they pulled me out of the sack,
And they stuck me together with glue.
And then I knew what to do.
I made a model of you,
A man in black with a Meinkampf[16] look

And a love of the rack and the screw.
And I said I do, I do.
So daddy, I'm finally through.
The black telephone's off at the root,
The voices just can't worm through.   70

If I've killed one man, I've killed two———
The vampire who said he was you
And drank my blood for a year,
Seven years, if you want to know.
Daddy, you can lie back now.

There's a stake in your fat black heart
And the villagers never liked you.
They are dancing and stamping on you.
They always *knew* it was you.
Daddy, daddy, you bastard, I'm through.   80

1962, 1965

NICK AND THE CANDLESTICK*

I am a miner. The light burns blue.
Waxy stalactites[1]
Drip and thicken, tears

The earthen womb
Exudes from its dead boredom.
Black bat airs

---

[15] Plath first attempted suicide when she was home from college during summer break.
[16] Hitler's autobiography of his youth, *Mein Kampf* ("My Struggle" [German]), published in 1925, before his political rise.
* Plath's son, Nicholas, born in January 1962.
[1] Deposits of calcium carbonate that hang like icicles from the roof or sides of a cavern.

Wrap me, raggy shawls,
Cold homicides.
They weld to me like plums.

Old cave of calcium   10
Icicles, old echoer.
Even the newts are white,

Those holy Joes.
And the fish, the fish————
Christ! they are panes of ice,

A vice of knives,
A piranha
Religion, drinking

Its first communion[2] out of my live toes.
The candle   20
Gulps and recovers its small altitude,

Its yellows hearten.
O love, how did you get here?
O embryo

Remembering, even in sleep,
Your crossed position.
The blood blooms clean

In you, ruby.
The pain
You wake to is not yours.   30

Love, love,
I have hung our cave with roses,
With soft rugs————

The last of Victoriana.[3]
Let the stars
Plummet to their dark address,

Let the mercuric
Atoms that cripple drip
Into the terrible well,

---

[2] A Christian sacrament in which bread and wine are consumed as a commemoration of Jesus' death.
[3] Objects typical of the Victorian era, during the reign (1837–1901) of Queen Victoria (1819–1901) of Great Britain and Ireland.

You are the one   40
Solid the spaces lean on, envious.
You are the baby in the barn.

1962, 1965

EDGE*

The woman is perfected.
Her dead

Body wears the smile of accomplishment,
The illusion of a Greek necessity

Flows in the scrolls of her toga,
Her bare

Feet seem to be saying:
We have come so far, it is over.

Each dead child coiled, a white serpent,
One at each little   10

Pitcher of milk, now empty.[1]
She has folded

Them back into her body as petals
Of a rose close when the garden

Stiffens and odors bleed
From the sweet, deep throats of the night flower.

The moon has nothing to be sad about,
Staring from her hood of bone.

She is used to this sort of thing.
Her blacks crackle and drag.   20

1963, 1965

---

* Plath's husband, Ted Hughes (1930–   ), suggests in "Notes on the Chronological Order of Sylvia Plath's Poems" (1966) that this poem was written a week before she committed suicide in February 1963.
[1] At the time of Plath's death, her daughter was nearly three years old and her son just over one year.

Amiri Baraka (LeRoi Jones)
(1934–   )

Amiri Baraka was born LeRoi Jones in Newark, New Jersey, in 1934 and educated at Rutgers and Howard Universities. After he spent nearly three years in the U.S. Air Force, Jones immersed himself in the bohemian scene of New York City's Greenwich Village in 1957 while he worked toward an M.A. in German literature at Columbia University and at the New School for Social Research. Jones and his wife, Hettie Cohen, edited *Yugen,* an avant-garde journal. Consistently a social critic and literary innovator, Jones has passed through a series of transformations, adjusting his aesthetics, his politics, and his personal life in resistance to the changing imbalances in mainstream American culture. A visit to Cuba in 1960 marked a turning point, the beginning of his movement toward politically engaged art.

In 1960 Jones's poetry was included in *The New American Poetry,* an influential anthology that brought together a diverse collection of post-World War II poets—nearly all white—who rejected traditional forms. "MY POETRY is whatever I think I am," Jones wrote in his statement at the end of the volume. "I CAN BE ANYTHING I CAN. I make a poetry with what I feel is useful & can be saved out of all the garbage of our lives."

Struggling against the silence of printed poetry, Jones wrote for the theater. His plays *Dutchman* and *The Slave,* produced Off Broadway in 1964, won awards and critical acclaim. His writing of the early 1960s shows conflicts about his position in white society, doubts about beat poetics, and a search, through music criticism, for the criteria of a new African-American aesthetic.

In 1965, after the assassination of the Black Muslim leader Malcolm X, Jones entered a decade of African-American nationalist activism. He divorced his white wife and moved from Greenwich Village to Harlem. There he founded the Black Arts Theater School, which served as a model for black theaters throughout America. In 1966 he returned to Newark, where he founded the Spirit House Theater. Jones adopted the Muslim name Imamu (spiritual leader) Amiri (blessed) Baraka (prince) in 1968, and his new wife, Sylvia Robinson, took the name Amina Baraka. His co-editorship of *Black Fire: An Anthology of African-American Writing* (1968) was a major contribution to the African-American arts movement. Baraka's two mixed-media works of 1970, *In Our Terribleness* and *It's Nation Time,* drew on Kawaida, an African value system emphasizing collectivity, self-determination, creativity, and faith.

Much of the work of Baraka's black nationalist period was fiercely antiwhite. This stance changed by 1974 as he adopted Marxism. Dropping the religious title "Imamu," Baraka revised his leadership role, becoming an African studies professor and an artist/worker. He has succeeded at raising political and historical awareness through poetry of struggle and theater of ideas.

Suggested Readings: *Preface to a Twenty Volume Suicide Note,* 1961. *Blues People: Negro Music in White America,* 1963. *The System of Dante's Hell,* 1965. *Four Black Revolutionary Plays,* 1969. *The Motion of History and Other Plays,* 1978. *Selected Plays and Prose of Amiri Baraka/LeRoi Jones,* 1979. *The Autobiography of LeRoi Jones/Amiri Baraka,* 1984. *Daggers and Javelins: Essays, 1974–1979,* 1984. K. W. Benston, *Baraka: The Renegade and the Mask,* 1976. K. W. Benston, *Imamu Amiri Baraka (LeRoi Jones): A Collection of Critical Essays,* 1976. W. Sollers, *Amiri Baraka/LeRoi Jones: The Quest for a "Populist Modernism",* 1978. L. W. Brown, *Amiri Baraka,* 1980. H. C. Lacey, *To Raise, Destroy, and Create: The Poetry, Drama, and Fiction of Imamu Amiri*

Baraka (LeRoi Jones), 1981. W. J. Harris, *The Poetry and Poetics of Amiri Baraka: The Jazz Aesthetic,* 1985.

Texts Used: "I Substitute for the Dead Lecturer" and "Political Poem": *The Dead Lecturer,* 1964. "Legacy" *Black Magic,* 1969. All else: *Selected Poetry of Amiri Baraka/LeRoi Jones,* 1979.

PREFACE TO A TWENTY VOLUME SUICIDE NOTE

(For Kellie Jones,[1] born 16 May 1959)

Lately, I've become accustomed to the way
The ground opens up and envelops me
Each time I go out to walk the dog.
Or the broad edged silly music the wind
Makes when I run for a bus . . .

Things have come to that.

And now, each night I count the stars,
And each night I get the same number.
And when they will not come to be counted,
I count the holes they leave.   10

Nobody sings anymore.

And then last night, I tiptoed up
To my daughter's room and heard her
Talking to someone, and when I opened
The door, there was no one there . . .
Only she on her knees, peeking into

Her own clasped hands.

                                          1957, 1961

I SUBSTITUTE FOR THE DEAD LECTURER

What is most precious, because
it is lost. What is lost,
because it is most
precious.

They have turned, and say that I am dying. That
I have thrown
my life

---

[1] The daughter of Baraka (when he was still LeRoi Jones) and his wife Hettie Cohen.

away. They
have left me alone, where
there is no one, nothing
save who I am. Not a note
nor a word.

    Cold air batters
the poor (and their minds   10
turn open
like sores). What kindness
What wealth
can I offer? Except
what is, for me,
ugliest. What is
for me, shadows, shrieking
phantoms. Except
they have need
of life. Flesh   20
at least,
        should be theirs.

The Lord has saved me
to do this. The Lord
has made me strong. I
am as I must have
myself. Against all
thought, all music, all
my soft loves.

    For all these wan roads   30
I am pushed to follow, are
my own conceit. A simple muttering
elegance, slipped in my head
pressed on my soul, is my heart's
worth. And I am frightened
that the flame of my sickness
will burn off my face. And leave
the bones, my stewed black skull,
an empty cage of failure.

                                  1964

POLITICAL POEM

(for Basil)

Luxury, then, is a way of
being ignorant, comfortably
An approach to the open market

of least information. Where theories
can thrive, under heavy tarpaulins
without being cracked by ideas.

(I have not seen the earth for years
and think now possibly "dirt" is
negative, positive, but clearly
social. I cannot plant a seed, cannot   10
recognize the root with clearer dent
than indifference. Though I eat
and shit as a natural man. (Getting up
from the desk to secure a turkey sandwich
and answer the phone: the poem undone
undone by my station, by my station,
and the bad words of Newark.[1]) Raised up
to the breech, we seek to fill for this
crumbling century. The darkness of love,
in whose sweating memory all error is forced.   20

Undone by the logic of any specific death. (Old gentlemen
who still follow fires, tho are quieter
and less punctual. It is a polite truth
we are left with. Who are you? What are you
saying? Something to be dealt with, as easily.
The noxious game of reason, saying, "No, No,
you cannot feel," like my dead lecturer
lamenting thru gipsies his fast suicide.

1964

A POEM FOR BLACK HEARTS

For Malcolm's[1] eyes, when they broke
the face of some dumb white man, For
Malcolm's hands raised to bless us
all black and strong in his image
of ourselves, For Malcolm's words
fire darts, the victor's tireless
thrusts, words hung above the world
change as it may, he said it, and
for this he was killed, for saying,

---

[1] In the mid-1960s Baraka began to concentrate his activities in Newark, New Jersey.
[1] Malcolm X (1925–1965), a civil rights leader and Black Muslim activist who was assassinated.

and feeling, and being/change, all   10
collected hot in his heart, For Malcolm's
heart, raising us above our filthy cities,
for his stride, and his beat, and his address
to the gray monsters of the world, For Malcolm's
pleas for your dignity, black men, for your life,
black man, for the filling of your minds
with righteousness, For all of him dead and
gone and vanished from us, and all of him which
clings to our speech black god of our time.
For all of him, and all of yourself, look up,   20
black man, quit stuttering and shuffling, look up,
black man, quit whining and stooping, for all of him,
For Great Malcolm a prince of the earth, let nothing in us rest
until we avenge ourselves for his death, stupid animals
that killed him, let us never breathe a pure breath if
we fail and white men call us faggots till the end of
the earth.

1967

LEGACY

(For Blues People)

In the south, sleeping against
the drugstore, growling under
the trucks and stoves, stumbling
through and over the cluttered eyes
of early mysterious night. Frowning
drunk waving moving a hand or lash.
Dancing kneeling reaching out, letting
a hand rest in shadows. Squatting
to drink or pee. Stretching to climb
pulling themselves onto horses near   10
where there was sea (the old songs
lead you to believe). Riding out
from this town, to another, where
it is also black. Down a road
where people are asleep. Towards
the moon or the shadows of houses.
Towards the songs' pretended sea.

1967

Paula Gunn Allen
(1939–   )

Born in 1939 in Cubero, New Mexico, Paula Gunn Allen was raised in that village at the edge of the Laguna Indian Pueblo. Of Laguna, Sioux, and Lebanese ancestry, Allen grew up in a family in which, according to her, English was only one of the five languages in which the family conversed. In *Songs From This Earth on Turtle's Back* (1983, edited by Joseph Bruchac) Allen has said of her complicated heritage, "My poetry, my poetics and my aesthetics all arise out of this chaotic mix, this primordial soup. Melting pots hold no terrors for me because I am one." After receiving a master of fine arts degree from the University of Oregon and Ph.D. from the University of New Mexico, Allen taught at Fort Lewis College in Durango, Colorado. Subsequently, in California she has directed programs for, and has taught, Native-American studies.

A poet, novelist, essayist, and critic, Allen has published more than half a dozen collections of verse, including the acclaimed *Skins and Bones* (1988); a novel, *The Woman Who Owned the Shadows* (1983); two major critical studies of Native-American literature, *Studies in Native American Literature* (1983) and *The Sacred Hoop: Recovering the Feminine in American Indian Traditions* (1986); and numerous uncollected poems, stories, and essays. Of her primary interest in Native-American culture and literature, Allen states in the essay "The Autobiography of a Confluence" (1987), "I was told over and over, 'Never forget that you're Indian.' My mother said it. Nor did she say, 'Remember that you are part Indian.' "

The author's intense concern for what being Native American and being a mixed-blooded woman in contemporary America means is central to her poetry and fiction. Again and again in her poems and in her long and short fiction, Allen draws upon Native-American mythology, in particular the oral tradition of southwestern tribes, to explore and define her own life and the lives of those around her. In some of her poems, such as "Coyote Jungle" (1988), she calls upon Coyote, a trickster figure of Native-American legend. She also typically focuses the reader's attention on the dilemmas that confront women and addresses the choices available to today's women. Simultaneously, Allen identifies closely with, and writes about, the landscape. "[Native Americans] are the land," Allen declares in "IYANI: It Goes This Way" (1981). "To the best of my understanding, that is the fundamental idea embedded in Native American life and culture in the Southwest."

Suggested Readings: *The Blind Lion*, 1975. *Coyote's Daylight Trip*, 1978. *A Cannon Between My Knees*, 1981. *Starchild*, 1981. *Shadow Country*, 1982. *The Woman Who Owned the Shadows*, 1983. *The Sacred Hoop: Recovering the Feminine in American Indian Traditions*, 1986. H. A. Baker, Jr., ed., *Three American Literatures: Essays in Chicano, Native American, Asian-American Literature for Teachers of American Literature*, 1982. K. Lincoln, *Native American Renaissance*, 1983. J. Ruppert, "Paula Gunn Allen and Joy Harjo: Closing the Distance Between Personal and Mythic Space," in *American Indian Quarterly*, 7(1): 27–40, 1983. L. Owens and T. Colonnese, *American Indian Novelists: An Annotated Critical Bibliography*, 1985. G. Vizenor, *Narrative Chance: Postmodern Discourse on Native American Literatures*, 1989.

Text Used: *Skins and Bones: Poems 1979–1987*, 1988.

C'KOY'U, OLD WOMAN*

old woman there in the earth
outside you we wait
do you dream of birth, bring
what is outside   inside?

        old
            woman inside
              old
                  woman outside

              old woman there in the sky
              we are waiting inside you   10
              dreaming your dream of birthing
              get what is inside/outside

          a hey a hey a hey a ho
          a hey a hey a hey a ho
          a hi oh ho a hi oh ho
          a hey a hey a hey a ho

                                      1988

POCAHONTAS TO HER ENGLISH HUSBAND, JOHN ROLFE†

In a way, then, Pocahontas was a kind of traitor to her people. . . . Perhaps I am being a little too hard on her. The crucial point, it seems to me, is to remember that Pocahontas was a hostage. Would she have converted freely to Christianity if she had not been in captivity? There is no easy answer to this question other than to note that once she was free to do what she wanted, she avoided her own people like the plague. . . .

Pocahontas was a white dream—a dream of cultural superiority.

                —CHARLES LARSON, *American Indian Fiction*[1]

Had I not cradled you in my arms
oh beloved perfidious one,
you would have died.

---

* In the Laguna language, "c'koy'u" means "old woman."

† The princess Pocahontas (1595?–1617), daughter of Powhatan, the chief of the Wampanoag Indians, married Rolfe (1585–1622), an English colonist and a founder of Jamestown, Virginia (1607), in 1614. She is said to have saved the life of Captain John Smith (1580–1631), another Jamestown colonist, in 1608 by holding his head in her arms to prevent Powhatan's warriors from clubbing him to death.

[1] Published in 1978.

And how many times did I pluck you
from certain death in the wilderness—
my world through which you stumbled
as though blind?
Had I not set you tasks
your masters far across the sea
would have abandoned you—
did abandon you, as many times   10
they left you
to reap the harvest of their lies.
Still you survived, oh my fair husband,
and brought them gold
wrung from a harvest I taught you
to plant. Tobacco.
It is not without irony that by this crop
your descendants die, for other
powers than you know
take part in this and all things.   20
And indeed I did rescue you—
not once but a thousand thousand times
and in my arms you slept, a foolish child,
and under my protecting gaze you played,
chattering nonsense about a God
you had not wit to name. I'm sure
you wondered at my silence, saying I was
a simple wanton,[2] a savage maid,
dusky daughter of heathen sires   30
who cartwheeled naked through the muddy towns
who would learn the ways of grace only
by your firm guidance, through
your husbandly rule:
no doubt, no doubt.
I spoke little, you said.
And you listened less,
but played with your gaudy dreams
and sent ponderous missives to the throne
striving thereby to curry favor   40
with your king.[3]
I saw you well. I
understood your ploys and still
protected you, going so far as to die
in your keeping—a wasting,
putrefying Christian death[4]—and you,
deceiver, whiteman, father of my son,
survived, reaping wealth greater

---

[2] A lewd or lascivious person.
[3] James I (1566–1625), king of England (1603–1625).
[4] Pocahontas probably died from tuberculosis.

than any you had ever dreamed
from what I taught you and   50
from the wasting of my bones.

1988

COYOTE JUNGLE*

The man across from me
sits tight, holding
together all the plans
of another time,
pointed toe edging
cautious toward a future
of electronic landscape.
Even the forests
have been wired, plugged in
to terminals far away.   10
He doesn't understand
that the furrow on his
forehead was transferred
from the furrows he once turned
on the land, embedded there
by lightning flash that stunned
him, knocked him silly
as he sat on the tractor
waiting out Nebraska storm.
On that day,   20
Earth marked him as her own,
and blinded by that light
to tractor hum and rich,
new-turned clods,
he walked to town
carrying nothing but a small
squat black box[1] for doctoring
and a stranger's way of knowing.
Now he sits near me,
squinting into the velvet dark   30
of technological truth,
muttering with vanished wizards:

DO WHAT THOU WILT
SHALL BE THE WHOLE OF THE LAW

---

* According to Native-American legend, the coyote is a trickster who assumes many forms and shapes.
[1] A box containing natural remedies carried by Native-American medicine men.

and there casts the enchantment
that will frame our lives anew.
He does not comprehend
the fire-studded darkness
of the words that fall: *silver,*
camphor, mercury, copper, gold,   40
iron, brass and *lead,* ancient
ritual revitalized on smog-
heavy mountain air.
Jeremiah in the wild,
Coyote hunched on the northeast border of urban sprawl
he grows sheep and doctors
broken pets;
he builds strong fences
to cradle baby and wife in,   50
he speaks words to banish
terror in face of the dark
he knows he is facing:
goddam coyotes,
I'd like to see em raise em
in the cities, like
em to see the gutted bellies
of the lambs those varmints
leave behind.

1988

WEED

She stood, a weed tall in the sun.
She grew like that and went
over it again and again trying to be tall
trying not to die in the drying sun
the seeming turbulence of waiting
the sun so yellow
so still

There was nothing else to do. It was like that
in her day, and the sun who rose so bright
so full of fire reminded her of that.   10
It was the sun that did it; it was the rain.
She stood it all, and more:
the water pounding from the high rock face
of the mesas[1] that made her yard

[1] High plateaus or flat tablelands with steep sides; common in the southwestern United States.

she knew where she was growing. Didn't
she know what sun will do, what happens to weeds
when their growing time's done? Didn't she care?
She got the sun into her, though.
The fire. She drank the rain for fuel.
She stood there in the day, growing,   20
trying to stand tall like a right weed would.

The drying was part of it.
The dying. Come from heat, the transformation
of fire. The rain helped because it understood
why she just stood there, growing,
tall in the heat and bright.

                                                  1988

MYTH/TELLING—DREAM/SHOWING

I.

so where do we go next?
(into sunrise)

2.

there is all the clutter:
on the walls, the table top,
in the sink, all over the counters,
on the stove, the sofa, the floors.

3.

the bird, yellow, green and blue
who lives in a cage with an open door
chirps now and then. drops onto the table
for breakfast.   10

4.

the cloud in the north, she said.
she meant the united states.

5.

I don't care, he said. I love
the united states. it isn't fair.
I never killed any indians. I am not
responsible for what my ancestors did.
I love the wilderness, he said. the indians
can't keep me out of it.

6.

and then there's the indian woman
who hates in herself what is white.   20
says she sees it like vomit. like
a crippled withered leg she must drag
with her everywhere she goes.

7.

and there is all the litter. the hours
passing. the exhaustion. the cloud
that is what I have to do today. not
go to the water. not go to the mesa.[1]
go into the city. the cloud.

8.

the indian woman is cursed with lupus.[2]
a blood disease. in which your blood   30
devours you.

9.

the white man goes to yosemite
on vacation. it's his recreation.
yes, says another man, black. it's
your recreation, but it's their life.

10.

the north of here is oregon, washington.
mt. st. helen's.[3] that cloud.

11.

the bird dreams in his cage.
about lunch. he doesn't dream of trees.
he never saw one, doesn't know what they are.   40

12.

I have to put my feathers on.
go through the door that opens.
into wilderness. city traffic.
bird-empty streets.

---

[1] A high plateau or flat tableland with steep sides; common in the southwestern United States.
[2] An inflammatory disease in which the body's immunological system attacks itself.
[3] A volcano in Washington state.

13.

if dawn comes (if corn comes).
if it is sunrise. that soft and blessing.
where someone is going, next.
if spring comes. (summer-people time.)
corn-is-growing time.
where/when-someone-is-going-next time.   50

1988

Simon J. Ortiz
(1941–   )

Simon J. Ortiz was born in 1941 in the Acoma Pueblo Indian tribe's village of McCartys,
New Mexico ("Deetziyama" to its Acoma inhabitants), and raised there. "My childhood
was the oral tradition of the Acoma Pueblo people," Ortiz says in his autobiographical
essay "The Language We Know" (1987). "The language I spoke was that of a struggling
people who held ferociously to a heritage, culture, language, and land despite the odds
posed them by the forces surrounding them since 1540 A.D., the advent of Euro-American
colonization." When he began elementary school in the Bureau of Indian Affairs day
school on the Acoma reservation, Ortiz spoke only the language of the Acoma people.
Immediately, like countless Native-American children since the late 1800s, he found himself forced to learn English and punished when he spoke his native language. Despite such
coercion, Ortiz learned English rapidly because of his love for "language, the sound,
meaning, and magic of language."

From the reservation school Oritz entered the army briefly and attended the University
of New Mexico. He went on to receive a masters degree in writing from the University of
Iowa International Writing Program and has published more than a dozen books. In 1980
he was invited to Washington, D.C., to take part in the White House Salute to Poetry and
American Poets, and in 1982 he received a Pushcart Prize for his poetry collection *From
Sand Creek* (1981). In addition to serving as lieutenant governor of the Acoma Pueblo,
Ortiz has taught Native-American literature and creative writing at such schools as the
University of New Mexico and at San Diego State University and has directed the creative
writing program at Sinte Gleska College in South Dakota. He has edited such publications
as the Navajo *Rough Rock News* and *Wanbli Ho,* a Native-American literary magazine, as
well as collections of Native-American prose and poetry, such as the short-fiction collection *Earth Power Coming* (1983).

Ortiz's works, both poetry and fiction, merge a distinctly political concern for contemporary Native-American existence with the ancient knowledge and traditions of his Acoma
heritage. Much of his poetry is intended to be narrated. Coyote, his traditional Native-
American trickster figure, appears in poems such as "The Creation, According to Coyote"
(1976)—with the hint of satire that typically accompanies tricksters—to remind the

speaker of his people's origins. In the poem "A Story of How a Wall Stands" (1976) Ortiz recalls with emblematic force the skill of his father and of the Acoma people as stoneworkers for generations. Permeating Ortiz's free-form verse are the traditional storyteller's voice and the rhythms and patterns of Native-American ceremony and song. Deeply immersed in his tribe's oral tradition—the ceremony, mythology, and storytelling—Ortiz says in "The Language We Know," "I don't remember a world without language. . . . It is language that brings us into being in order to know life."

Suggested Readings: *A Good Journey,* 1977. *Fight Back: For the Sake of the People, for the Sake of Land,* 1980. *Fightin': New and Collected Short Stories,* 1983. Ed., *Earth Power Coming: Short Fiction in Native American Literature,* 1988. "Always the Stories: A Brief History and Thoughts on My Writing," in *Coyote Was Here: Essays on Contemporary Native American Literary and Political Mobilization,* ed. B. Scholer, 1984. K. Lincoln, *Native American Renaissance,* 1983. K. Lincoln, "The Poetry of Simon Ortiz," in *Coyote Was Here,* ed. B. Scholer, 1984. P. G. Allen, *The Sacred Hoop: Recovering the Feminine in American Indian Traditions,* 1986. A. Wiget, *Simon Ortiz,* 1986. A. Krupat, *The Voice in the Margin: Native American Literature and the Canon,* 1989.

Texts Used: "Grief" and "The Sky Is Brilliant": *From Sand Creek,* 1981. All else: *Going for the Rain,* 1976.

DRY ROOT IN A WASH*

the sand is a fine grit
and warm to the touch.
An old juniper root
lies by the cutbank[1] of sand;
it lingers, waiting
for the next month of rain.

I feel like saying,
It will rain, but you know
better than I these centuries
don't mean much   10
for anyone to be waiting.

Upstream, towards the mountains,
the Shiwana[2] work for rain.

They know we're waiting.

Underneath the fine sand
it is cool
with crystalline moisture,
the forming rain.

1976

---

* The dry bed of a stream.   [1] A steep stream bank.
[2] A society of men who are said to bring rain through prayers and observances in a religious ceremony that requires sacred objects.

A STORY OF HOW A WALL STANDS

At Acu,[1] there is a wall almost 400 years old which supports hundreds of tons of dirt and bones—it's a graveyard built on a steep incline—and it looks like it's about to fall down the incline but will not for a long time.

My father, who works with stone,
says, "That's just the part you see,
the stones which seem to be
just packed in on the outside,"
and with his hands puts the stone and mud
in place. "Underneath
what looks like loose stone,
there is stone woven together."
He ties one hand over the other,
fitting like the bones of his hands   10
and fingers. "That's what is holding it together."

"It is built that carefully,"
he says, "the mud mixed
to a certain texture," patiently
"with the fingers," worked
in the palm of his hand. "So that
placed between the stones, they hold
together for a long, long time."

He tells me those things,
the story of them worked   20
with his fingers, in the palm
of his hands, working the stone
and the mud until they become
the wall that stands a long, long time.

1976

WIND AND GLACIER VOICES

Laguna[1] man said,
I only heard that glacier scraping
once, thirty thousand years ago.
My daughter was born then.
                    —a storytelling, continuing
                         voice—
West of Yuma,[2] a brown man murmurs

---

[1] The Acoma Pueblo in New Mexico, where Ortiz was born and raised.
[1] A Native-American tribe of New Mexico.   [2] Yuma, Arizona.

the motion of the solar wind.[3]
                              —a harsh, searing
                              voice—   10

Please don't tell me
how to live;
I've always lived this way.
                              —a protesting
                              voice—

the last time I was in Fargo[4]
I thought I heard the echo
of a glacier scraping.
                              —a remembering,
                              beckoning   20
                              voice—

And the wind, solar,
the big wind will come.
Solar, it will come.
Solar, it will come.
It will pass by and through
and with everything.
                              —a longing, whispering,
                              prophetic
                              voice—   30

                                                        1976

THE CREATION, ACCORDING TO COYOTE*

"First of all, it's all true."
Coyote, he says this, this way,
humble yourself, motioning and meaning
what he says.

You were born when you came
from that body, the earth;
your black head burst from granite,
the ashes cooling,

until it began to rain.   10
It turned muddy then,
and then green and brown things
came without legs.

---

[3] Streams of electrically charged gas particles emitted by the sun.   [4] Fargo, North Dakota.
* According to Native-American legend, the coyote is a trickster who assumes many shapes and forms.

They looked strange.
Everything was strange.
There was nothing to know then,

until later, Coyote told me this,
and he was b.s.-ing probably,
two sons were born,
Uyuyayeh and Masaweh.

They were young then,   20
and then later on they were older.

And then the people were wondering
what was above
they had heard rumors.

But, you know, Coyote,
he was mainly bragging
when he said (I think),
"My brothers, the Twins then said,
'Let's lead these poor creatures
and save them.'"   30

And later on, they came to light
after many exciting and colorful
and tragic things of adventure;
and this is the life, all these, all these.

My uncle told me all this, that time.
Coyote told me too, but you know
how he is, always talking to the gods,
the mountains, the stone all around.

And you know, I believe him.

1976

from   *FROM SAND CREEK**

GRIEF

Grief
memorizes this grass.
Raw

---

* A series of untitled poems and interspersed prose taken from Ortiz's own experiences as a recovering U.S. Army veteran. Sand Creek, in southeastern Colorado, is the site of a slaughter of Cheyennes and Arapahos by U.S. troops in November 1864.

courage,
           believe it,
red-eyed and urgent,
stalking Denver.
Like stone,
like steel,
the hone and sheer gone,   10
just the brute
and perceptive angle left.

Like courage,
           believe it,

left still;
the words from then
talk like that.

Believe it.

                                                    1981

THE SKY IS BRILLIANT

The sky is brilliant
and expansive like the universe
on the concave of my eye.
My mind is a cove
                       of light
shining upon a vista
of a grassed great plain.
I know
there is a world
peopled with love.   10
I know
there are people
                who speak
not in undertones
but gallantly and joyously,
who are valorous
with simple courage.
But looking at the VA[1] hospital
fortressed with dike walls
in defense against the rising   20
Arkansas River,[2] I see
a train that carries dreams
and freedom away.

---

[1] Veteran's Administration.   [2] A river in southeastern Colorado.

                              Thunder rises
              in me and its waves empty me.
                                          O
              train and people and plains,
              look at me and the hospital
              where stricken men and broken boys
              are mortared and sealed   30
              into its defensive walls. O look,
              now.

                                                              1981

Louise Glück
(1943–   )

The world as portrayed in Louise Glück's poems is a world of archetypes, newly fashioned or traditional, a world in which the gods of myth—their tragedies, seductions and reprisals—are the figurative equals of "you" and "I." It is a world of children who sense "the great human subjects: time which breeds loss, desire, the world's beauty," Glück explains in the essay "Education of the Poet" (1988). Where autobiography figures in her work (as it does in such poems as "Dedication to Hunger" (1980), poems with the common subject of renunciation), such detail becomes a sort of epic, or extended simile, a device John Milton used in *Paradise Lost* (1667).

Glück's "you" and "I" are typically meant to represent men and women, respectively: "male and female, thrust and ache," as she writes in "Palais des Arts" (1980). From the striking absence of personal pronouns in her early poems to the encompassing "you" and "I" of her later ones, her subjects are treated distinctively, as though Glück was desperately trying to learn how to write "I" and mean something larger than mere autobiography. Life as a subject for poetry is denied its specificity and is thereby not demystified but mystified.

If in Glück's poetry men and women are meant to be figurative, then so are their offspring. In "The Drowned Children," from *Descending Figure* (1980), she writes "You see, they have no judgment. / So it is natural that they should drown." These children, "lost / in the waters, blue and permanent," might well lack judgment, yet they are among the poet's most prescient characters. "Gretel in Darkness" (from her widely acclaimed *The House on Marshland* [1975]) reimagines the Grimm's fairytale, escalating the violence of the original, so that even children seem to wage war with one another. "All who would have seen us dead / are dead," Gretel addresses her brother; "I killed for you." Glück also retells ancient myths conveyed by means of direct address. In "Mythic Fragment" (1985) she distills the story of Daphne and Apollo.

Such archetypal and mythical tendencies and ambitions commonly seem at odds with both the plainspoken and formalist currents of much contemporary poetry; they are also potential invitations to excess. Excess is rare, though, in Glück's poetry. Her language is mannered but careful, her technique one of almost rigid control. The poems in her collection *Ararat* (1990) are even more pared down than are her earlier poems. In that book, a series of short verses linked as a single narrative, her imagery and honesty are paramount. If her poems have ancestors, they are surely the poems of William Blake and Emily Dickinson, not only in their shared obsessions with archetype and the created world, but also in their short trimeter lines. Even so, Glück's poems at times echo those of Elizabeth Bishop, of Robert Lowell, and of Stanley Kunitz (with whom Glück studied at Columbia University during the early 1960s).

Born in 1943 in New York City, Glück was raised on Long Island and attended Sarah Lawrence College and Columbia University. At age twenty-five she published her first collection, *Firstborn* (1968). For her poetry she has received numerous grants and awards such as a National Endowment for the Arts grant, a Guggenheim Fellowship, and a National Book Critics' Circle Award for *The Triumph of Achilles* (1985). She has taught at Goddard College in Vermont, at Warren Wilson College in North Carolina, and at Williams College.

Suggested Readings: *The House on Marshland*, 1975. *Ararat*, 1990. H. Vendler, "Louise Glück," in *Part of Nature, Part of Us: Modern American Poets*, 1980. H. Vendler, "John Ashbery, Louise Glück" in *The Music of What Happens*, 1988.

Texts Used: "Cottonmouth Country": *Firstborn*, 1968. "The Drowned Children" and "Palais des Arts": *Descending Figure*, 1980. All else: *The Triumph of Achilles*, 1985.

COTTONMOUTH COUNTRY*

Fish bones walked the waves off Hatteras.[1]
And there were other signs
That Death wooed us, by water, wooed us
By land: among the pines
An uncurled cottonmouth that rolled on moss
Reared in the polluted air.
Birth, not death, is the hard loss.
I know. I also left a skin there.

1967

THE DROWNED CHILDREN†

You see, they have no judgment.
So it is natural that they should drown,
first the ice taking them in
and then, all winter, their wool scarves
floating behind them as they sink
until at last they are quiet.
And the pond lifts them in its manifold dark arms.

---

* Water moccasin country, the southeastern United States; first published in the *New American Review*, Number 1, 1967.
[1] An island off North Carolina.
† First published in the *New Yorker*.

But death must come to them differently,
so close to the beginning.
As though they had always been   10
blind and weightless. Therefore
the rest is dreamed, the lamp,
the good white cloth that covered the table,
their bodies.

And yet they hear the names they used
like lures slipping over the pond:
What are you waiting for
come home, come home, lost
in the waters, blue and permanent.

1980

PALAIS DES ARTS*

Love long dormant showing itself:
the large expected gods
caged really, the columns
sitting on the lawn, as though perfection
were not timeless but stationary—that
is the comedy, she thinks,
that they are paralyzed. Or like the matching swans,
insular, circling the pond: restraint so passionate
implies possession. They hardly speak.
On the other bank, a small boy throws bits of bread   10
into the water. The reflected monument
is stirred, briefly, stricken with light—
She can't touch his arm in innocence again.
They have to give that up and begin
as male and female, thrust and ache.

1980

MYTHIC FRAGMENT

When the stern god[1]
approached me with his gift
my fear enchanted him
so that he ran more quickly
through the wet grass, as he insisted,
to praise me. I saw captivity

---

* "Palace of the Arts" (French).
[1] Apollo (the sun god of Greek myth), who courted the nymph Daphne.

in praise; against the lyre,
I begged my father in the sea
to save me.[2] When
the god arrived, I was nowhere,   10
I was in a tree forever. Reader,
pity Apollo: at the water's edge,
I turned from him, I summoned
my invisible father—as
I stiffened in the god's arms,
of his encompassing love
my father made
no other sign from the water.

1985

ELMS

All day I tried to distinguish
need from desire. Now, in the dark,
I feel only bitter sadness for us,
the builders, the planers of wood,
because I have been looking
steadily at these elms
and seen the process that creates
the writhing, stationary tree
is torment, and have understood
it will make no forms but twisted forms.   10

1985

HORSE*

What does the horse give you
that I cannot give you?

I watch you when you are alone,
when you ride into the field behind the dairy,
your hands buried in the mare's
dark mane.

Then I know what lies behind your silence:
scorn, hatred of me, of marriage. Still,
you want me to touch you; you cry out
as brides cry, but when I look at you I see   10
there are no children in your body.
Then what is there?

---

[2] According to the myth, she begged her father, the river god Peneus, to help her avoid the god's
pursuit and was transformed into a laurel tree.
   * First published in *Antaeus*.

Nothing, I think. Only haste
to die before I die.

In a dream, I watched you ride the horse
over the dry fields and then
dismount: you two walked together;
in the dark, you had no shadows.
But I felt them coming toward me
since at night they go anywhere,   20
they are their own masters.

Look at me. You think I don't understand?
What is the animal
if not passage out of this life?

1985

MIDDLE TO LATE 20TH-CENTURY FICTION

Since World War II American fiction has been distinguished by an unprecedented heterogeneity of genre, subject, and theme and by a comparable elasticity in form and language. World War II, the Korean War, and the Vietnam War generated a large body of literature documenting the newly realized capacity for cruelty and self-destruction, glorifying individual instances of wartime courage and generosity, and, more typically, condemning American participation in foreign conflicts. The efflorescence of regionalism begun in the Southern Renaissance earlier in the twentieth century continued, with new energies. American audiences learned in the second half of the century to read not only the literatures of marginalized foreign countries but those of historically voiceless American factions, authors who would have been ignored prior to World War II for reasons of religion, race, or gender. In the 1940s and 1950s they began demanding to be heard and were gradually and slowly allowed to enrich American literature. And the paranoia engendered by the cold war and McCarthyism during the 1950s provoked a new form of popular fiction, the spy novel, and bolstered the popularity of a related genre, the mystery novel.

World War II was the favored topic of the American novel in the late 1940s and early 1950s. Some novelists used the arena of the war to portray the individual's impotence and insignificance in the universe; others transformed wartime exigencies into political allegories of peacetime society. One of the most successful World War II novels was one of the first, Norman Mailer's *The Naked and the Dead* (1948). Mailer's realistic and comprehensive portrayal of an infantry platoon fighting the Japanese in the Pacific earned him great critical acclaim and several critical accusations of romanticism. His search for a hero suitable to the nuclear age found no ideal figure in *The Naked and the Dead,* but Mailer clearly admired the characters wielding military authority.

=CONTEXTS=

Historical Interpretation

The historical interpretation of literature seeks to place a literary work in the context of the time and place of its creation. The historical circumstances in which an author works are seen as important contributing factors, and knowledge of these factors is essential to fully understanding the work. A major proponent of this critical method was Edmund Wilson (1895–1972), who, in his lecture "The Historical Interpretation of Literature" (delivered at Princeton University in 1940), asserted that "human arts and institutions [are] to be studied and elucidated as the products of the geographical and climatic conditions in which the people who created them lived, and of the phase of their social development through which they [are] passing at the moment."

Wilson adopted these attitudes from the French historical critic Hippolyte Adolphe Taine (1828–1893), whose method Wilson has described as follows:

The Historical Interpretation of Literature

Taine thought he was a scientist and a mechanist, who was examining works of literature from the same point of view as the chemist's in experimenting with chemical compounds. But the difference between the critic and the chemist is that the critic cannot first combine his elements and then watch to see what they will do: he can only examine phenomena which have already taken place. The procedure that Taine actually follows is to pretend to set the stage for the experiment by describing the moment, the race and the milieu, and then to say: "Such a situation demands such and such a kind of writer."

Wilson was in part reacting against the antihistorical attitudes of the New Criticism. Wilson suggested that while this method can bring interesting connections to light, it nonetheless ignores the fact that literature is centered in history. The New Critic, according to Wilson:

. . . sees, or tries to see, the whole of literature, so far as he is acquainted with it, spread out before him under the aspect of eternity. He then compares the work of different periods and countries, and tries to draw from it general conclusions about what literature ought to be.

Edmund Wilson, 1940

However, in the 1960s, with the increasing acceptance of the writer Marshall McLuhan's ideas on the transformative nature of all media, including written texts as well as moving images, war novels commonly became occasions for authors to question the validity of traditionally realistic prose styles and to experiment with new approaches to fictional records of wartime perceptions. American literature includes a long tradition of deromanticizing the military. In the 1960s authors writing about World War II found their models not in the novels of the 1940s and 1950s but in such precedents as Ambrose Bierce's scathing nineteenth-century

On August 28, 1963, the civil rights leader Martin Luther King, Jr. led a march to the Lincoln Memorial, where he delivered his famous "I Have a Dream" speech.

satires of the Civil War and Dalton Trumbo's horrific tale of a limbless, deaf-mute, and blind war veteran, *Johnny Got His Gun* (1939). Novels such as Joseph Heller's *Catch-22* (1961) and Thomas Pynchon's *Gravity's Rainbow* (1973) emphasize the injustice, horror, and absurdity of war.

Many of the authors of the first wave of World War II novels came to recognize the literary implications of incurable subjectivity and later abandoned the attempt to write purportedly realistic fiction. Norman Mailer and Truman Capote wrote nonfiction in the 1950s until they realized that the same subjectivity that undermines realistic fiction undermines realistic nonfiction as well. In the late 1960s both authors began experimenting with a hybrid form of fictionalized journalism. Among Mailer's early works in this genre was his account of a 1967 antiwar march on the Pentagon, *The Armies of the Night* (1968). More recent war novels, such as Bobbie Ann Mason's *In Country* (1985), have focused on the Vietnam War and its home-front consequences.

While mainstream authors were attempting to draw meaning from their war experiences, African-American authors were engaged in a domestic war of their own, struggling to gain entry into the American literary scene, much as all African Americans were struggling to improve their position in American society. With the publication of his novel *Native Son* (1940), Richard Wright became the first

African-American author to reach a large audience. A grimly detailed depiction of the urban ghetto that shaped the African-American protagonist, Bigger Thomas, who expresses his enraged frustration through murderous violence, this work marked the beginning of a new literature of black protest. Wright drew reactionary objections from alarmed whites, but the controversy only increased book sales. The success of Wright's autobiographical novel, *Black Boy* (1945), also facilitated publication of Ralph Ellison and James Baldwin in the 1950s. The works of a second, more stridently revolutionary generation of African-American authors, including Malcolm X, Eldridge Cleaver, and Amiri Baraka, appeared in the 1960s.

In the 1970s and 1980s the works of African-American women began to receive public validation as bestsellers. Alice Walker's epistolary novel *The Color Purple* (1982) won a National Book Award, and Toni Morrison's novel *Beloved* (1988) won a Pulitzer Prize. Morrison employs a wide range of narrative voices and imaginative resources, drawing technical inspiration from European and American modernist conventions, from the oral vernacular traditions of American slave culture, and from the richly creative literatures of Africa and of South and Central America. Combining these influences, she explores the possibility of free will and self-definition in an era burdened by widespread alienation, fragmented families as well as fragmented psyches, and an absence of ethical consensus. These problems are both complicated and much illuminated by the addition of the female African-American perspective.

During World War II and the tumultuous civil rights movement, regional writing continued to flourish. Eudora Welty, Katherine Anne Porter's protégé, began incorporating myth and symbolism into her fiction and produced some of her finest short stories of the comic and the grotesque during the 1940s and 1950s. *The Heart is a Lonely Hunter* (1940), the first novel by Carson McCullers, another southerner writing about the South, demonstrates her preoccupation with grotesque characters driven to violent actions. Flannery O'Connor, like McCullers a Georgian interested in the grotesque and the violent, began her brief publishing career with short stories in the 1940s, followed by her first novel, *Wise Blood*, in 1952. Her combinations of overheated southern landscapes, Calvinist religion, eccentric humor, and creative brilliance won her a large and loyal readership.

John Cheever also combined religious themes and idiosyncratic humor in his depictions of northeastern America. Claiming suburban New York and New England as his own, he excelled in satirizing social and individual pretensions and in framing particular moments of illumination and folly in the lives of urbanites and commuters. Many of Cheever's stories first appeared in the *New Yorker* magazine, a very influential force in the advancement of the short-story genre during the 1950s and 1960s. Although it published work by a wide variety of artists, such as the luminous and intricate stories by the Russian émigré Vladimir Nabokov, the *New Yorker* favored stories by and about the American upper middle class, such as those of Mary McCarthy and J. D. Salinger.

John Updike, who began working as a writer and critic for the *New Yorker* in 1955, has become one of America's most prolific writers. His eye for visual detail is acute; his fictional observations of contemporary American manners, especially in matters of sex, money, religion, and race, are provocative. Many of his novels deal with the topography of his character's emotions within and outside marriage and with the domestic artifacts of middle-class American life. These issues also figure largely in stories published in the 1980s by authors investigating the uses of "minimalist" narrative techniques, such as Frederick Barthelme, Annie Dillard, and Raymond Carver. Carver deploys a laconic, elliptical style reminiscent of Ernest Hemingway's to portray middle-class characters trapped in dialogues of avoidance and of emotional confrontration. Whereas regional writers focus on a geographically defined culture, Updike and others write of a population united by the common concerns and vocabulary of shared class standing.

In the late 1940s a group of writers claiming to represent "the beat generation" of young Americans traumatized by World War II began producing exuberant and stylistically original works celebrating their escape from the middle class. Their reckless and exhilarating forays into the subterranean life of urban and rural America were recorded most famously in Kerouac's novel *On the Road* (1957). In the 1970s and 1980s Joyce Carol Oates has typically investigated the same subterranean America that attracted the beat poets but found little there to celebrate. Her characters are typically drawn from the lower middle or working classes, and her fiction reveals a fascination with the American propensity for violence. In her novels, short stories, and nonfiction works she traces the undercurrents of brutality in everyday life, especially in male/female relationships.

Only after 1960 did the reading public begin to notice the work of Native Americans. The stories, myth cycles, and novels of N. Scott Momaday (of Kiowa ancestry) and of Leslie Marmon Silko (descended from the Laguna Pueblo tribe) draw their narrative and stylistic strengths from Native-American storytelling traditions. Momaday's novel *House Made of Dawn* (1968), concerning a young Native American's estrangement from his ancestral roots, was quickly followed by *The Way to Rainy Mountain* (1969), a cycle of Kiowa legends. In *Ceremony* (1977) Silko portrays the alienation and repatriation of a Native-American soldier. Her shorter piece "Storyteller" (1981) uses alternating styles and techniques—Native-American myths and songs interspersed with linear and chronological narrative.

Jewish authors, also writing out of a cultural legacy of geographic displacement, found publishers and readers earlier and more easily than did African Americans and Native Americans. Henry Roth published his novel *Call It Sleep* in 1937; novels and short stories by Saul Bellow, Bernard Malamud, and Herbert Gold appeared in the 1950s. Bellow translated Isaac Bashevis Singer's story "Gimpel the Fool" (1957) from Yiddish for the *Partisan Review;* it has echoed in the work of Jewish authors ever since. Bellow's own fiction reveals his close engagement with American life after World War II, with the often tragicomic interplay between the intellectual backgrounds and European culture of his characters, and with the hyperkinetic flow of everyday life in American cities. Malamud, too, wrote about urban communities. In *The Assistant* (1957) he describes the painfully constrained lives of a Jewish grocer and his family in Brooklyn, mingling comedy and pathos in a story of suffering and muted triumphs. A second generation of Jewish authors who began writing after 1960 includes Frederick Busch, Grace Paley, Cynthia Ozick, Philip Roth, and Susan Sontag.

Hispanic literature has become increasingly prominent in the late twentieth century, perhaps because it generally reflects a sensibility that is closely allied to the ethos of the postmodern writer. Marked by a willingness to employ narrative strategies that incorporate structural disjunction with a subjective lyricism, and by a commitment to political change, the work of Hispanic authors has lost its marginal status and has been absorbed by the larger current of postmodernism. The works of Chicano literature began to flourish in the post-World War II era, particularly in New York City and in the barrio areas of urban America. However, it was the work of Luís Valdez, with César Chávez and the farm laborers, in El Teatro Campesino (founded in 1965) that brought widespread public attention to Chicano literature. Valdez's work was so effective that by 1967 a strictly Chicano press was established in Berkeley, California. Quinto Sol Publications promoted the work of contemporary Chicano writers, finally providing prose writers such as Rudolfo Anaya, Denise Chávez, Rolando Hinojosa-Smith, and Tomás Rivera with mainstream attention. Like Valdez these writers mixed street dialect with literary conceits, combined the Spanish language with English, and re-examined the past, creating a multi-voiced, bilingual literature. Out of these seemingly incongruous combinations, a Chicano identity in fiction writing was created.

Paradoxically, just as previously voiceless ethnic groups were entering the American literary canon in the 1940s and 1950s, the international tensions of the cold war produced a malignant atmosphere of political repression in America. Senator Joseph McCarthy's crusade against suspected "card-carrying Communists" in government and in the military (though he never found one) spread to include investigations of private citizens. Those who had sympathized with Socialist reform movements in the 1930s were called to account for their actions. Artists and authors, including Dashiell Hammett, Ring Lardner, and Dalton Trumbo, were summoned to testify before McCarthy's investigating committees; uncooperative witnesses were jailed and/or blacklisted in the theater, television, and film industries. Even writers who had merely associated with suspected Communists were silenced as effectively as if they had been exiled to a Siberian gulag.

One of the casualties in McCarthy's crusade was Hammett, who was actively involved in Communist party activities during the 1930s. His refusal to name his associates resulted in a six-month imprisonment in 1951. Before he quit writing in the 1940s, Hammett introduced the reading public to detective fiction. His followers in this extremely durable literary form borrowed Hammett's technical inspiration but not his Socialist principles. Raymond Chandler and Ross MacDonald worked to elevate the detective novel above the level of pulp fiction. Both were chastized for writing beneath their talents, and both produced sophisticated and articulate theoretical defenses of the genre. Chandler's hero, Philip Marlowe, has beneath his crusty exterior as much in common with a romanticized knight rescuing tawdry gutter damsels as he does with real detectives. Chandler quite self-consciously emphasizes Marlowe's knightly qualities with symbolic and literary allusions; the author's literary refinements of his chosen genre bridged the gap between high culture and low culture.

Writers of contemporary western fiction have inherited a literary tradition in which the harsh dynamics of the ever-threatening wilderness serve as a backdrop for the exploration of the American psyche and its relationship to the frontier. Among those important in establishing the western tradition were Owen Wister, James Fenimore Cooper, Zane Grey, and, more recently, Louis L'Amour. In the intersection of postmodernism and the western literary tradition, current writers fracture traditional western images and motifs to correspond to the fragmented nature of contemporary society. Ken Kesey's *Sometimes A Great Notion* (1971) helped establish this connection between postmodern fiction and the contemporary frontier. Larry McMurtry, author of such western novels as *Horseman, Pass By* (1961), *Leaving Cheyenne* (1963), *The Last Picture Show* (1966), and *Lonesome Dove* (1985), has become the most visible proponent of this trend. Thomas McGuane, Richard Ford, Edward Abbey, and Jim Harrison all create fictions that are closely tied to the frontier terrain, whereas Joan Didion and Kathy Acker deal with the myth in a manner that makes the western a primary genre within the canon of postmodernism.

Since World War II, efforts to dismantle exclusive canonical literary restrictions on fiction have moved unsteadily but irreversibly forward. Categories such as high culture versus low, fiction versus nonfiction, mainstream versus marginal, and politically correct versus criminally indictable are not applied as stringently as they once were. The result has been the creation of an increasingly dynamic, diverse, and inclusive literature.

Richard Wright
(1908–1960)

In 1947 Richard Wright left Manhattan to become a permanent resident of Paris, which remained his home until his death after a heart attack in 1960. He had modeled his first novel, *Lawd Today* (completed in 1938 but published in 1963), on the design of James Joyce's *Ulysses* (1922). In fleeing the constrictions of American society, Wright followed the example set by Joyce, Gertrude Stein, and other expatriots and hoped that his creative powers would thrive outside his native culture. This hope was sadly unrealized; most of Wright's best fiction was written before his exasperated departure. But his early novels and stories, together with his autobiographical and sociological writings, establish him as one of the most influential American writers of the twentieth century. Much of the power of Wright's prose derives from his personal experience of both southern and northern forms of racist suppression and exploitation.

Wright was born in a sharecropper's cabin on a farm in Roxie, Mississippi, in 1908. His father, an illiterate sharecropper, moved the family to Memphis in 1911 and abandoned them in 1913. Ella Wilson Wright, a former schoolteacher reduced to menial labor, could not afford to feed her sons Richard and Alan; hunger became one of Wright's most vivid metaphors in his definitions of the difference between black and white America. When their mother became ill, Richard and Alan were left in an orphanage for two years.

In 1916 Ella Wright took the boys to live with her sister and brother-in-law in Elaine, Arkansas. Soon after they arrived, Wright's uncle was murdered for his property by a group of whites who threatened to kill the rest of the family. The Wrights escaped and wandered between Arkansas and Mississippi until ill health forced Ella Wright to place the boys with relatives in 1919. Richard could not stand the restrictive scrutiny of an overbearing aunt and uncle in Greenwood, Mississippi, and chose instead to live with his grandmother and another aunt in Jackson, Mississippi, where he stayed until 1925.

Denied the opportunity to attend school regularly until he entered the Seventh-Day Adventist School in 1920, Wright was tutored by his mother and his aunt. He was advanced to the sixth grade two weeks after enrolling and proved an excellent student with a gift for writing. In 1924 his short story "The Voodoo of Hell's Half Acre" was published in a Jackson newspaper; in 1925 he was valedictorian of his junior high school class. When school officials asked that he read a valedictory address written by a white administrator, Wright argued until permitted to read his own speech. His formal education was cut short that year when he had to help support his family, but he continued to read widely, borrowing books from the white library with a card loaned to him by a kindly white mentor.

In 1927 Wright moved to the North for reasons similar to those prompting his European self-exile in 1947: to come to terms with the South. He lived in Chicago during the Great Depression and became a director of the Federal Negro Theater of the Federal Writers Project; he also worked at odd jobs and went on relief when unemployed. He continued reading, introducing himself to the work of Feodor Dostoevski, of Sinclair Lewis, and of Sherwood Anderson. Theodore Dreiser's naturalist novels particularly impressed Wright; the blistering cultural critique in Wright's novel *Native Son* (1940) echoes the tenets of Dreiser's social determinism.

Wright first began writing seriously during his years in Chicago. He met other writers by participating in the National Negro Congress, the South Side Writers' Group, and the Chicago John Reed Club, a Communist literary organization. He joined the Communist party in 1933 and contributed revolutionary poems to leftist publications such as the *New Masses*. For a time, Wright's poetry and critical essays seemed politically correct—as long as he wrote poems with titles such as "We of the Streets" (1937) and "Red Leaves of Red Books" (1935). In 1941 he married a devoted party member, Ellen Poplar (his first marriage, to the dancer Rose Dhima Meadman, dissolved in less than a year). But when he began compiling biographical sketches of black party members, his insistence on the singularity of the black proletariat experience was unacceptable to the Chicago branch of the Communist party. Wright left the party in 1944 and remained actively sympathetic to aspects of it, although he became an active anti-Communist in the 1950s and wrote about the inhumanity of Communist methods.

After moving to New York in 1937 Wright co-edited and wrote for the *Daily Worker* and other journals. In *Uncle Tom's Children* (1938, 1940), a publishing sensation, he focuses an outraged eye on the plight of African Americans in the rural South. That collection includes some of his most brilliant work and led to a Guggenheim Fellowship. With the publication of *Native Son* in 1940, Wright created the genre of the African-American protest novel. Twenty years later civil rights protests on behalf of the urban African-American populace would address precisely those inhuman living conditions Wright paints with such brutally realistic clarity in *Native Son*. That novel was a record-breaking bestseller; Orson Welles directed a film version in 1951 with Wright cast in the lead role.

Wright typically instilled his fiction with autobiographical reminiscences, but in the story "Bright and Morning Star" (1940) the devoted mother notably contrasts with Wright's own experience of maternal figures. In *Black Boy: A Record of Childhood and Youth* (1945) he recalls how his mother once punished him by beating him into uncon-

Richard Wright's Native Son *was made into a 1950 motion picture in which Wright starred as Bigger Thomas.*

sciousness. He remarks that "for a long time I was chastened whenever I remembered that my mother had come close to killing me." His aunt and grandmother forced upon him a peculiarly mean-spirited and fanatical form of Seventh Day Adventism; in Wright's last writings in the late 1950s, his rejection of institutionalized religious observance sprung from his emotional conviction of this early period. That autobiography and his second one, *American Hunger* (published posthumously in 1977), were both well received. His experiments with existential fiction in the 1950s were less successful in America than in Europe, where his reputation was strengthened by his association with the circle of the existentialist writers Jean-Paul Sartre and Simone de Beauvoir. American critics were less than kind in reviewing Wright's late writing, but the critic Irving Howe anticipated a 1970s and 1980s resurgence of appreciation for Wright's work when he eulogized Wright in *A World More Attractive* (1963) after Wright's death of a heart attack in 1960: "If such younger Negro novelists as James Baldwin and Ralph Ellison were to move beyond Wright's harsh naturalism and toward more subtle modes of fiction, that was possible only because Wright had been there first, courageous enough to release the full weight of his anger."

Suggested Readings: *Native Son*, 1940. *12 Million Black Voices*, 1941. *Black Boy: A Record of Childhood and Youth*, 1945. *White Man, Listen!*, 1957. *Eight Men*, 1961. *American Hunger*, 1977. M. Fabre, *The Unfinished Quest of Richard Wright*, 1973. *Richard Wright: A Primary Bibliography*, ed. C. T. Davis and M. Fabre, 1982. M. Fabre, *The World of Richard Wright*, 1985. *Modern Critical Views: Richard Wright*, ed. H. Bloom, 1987. K. Kinnamon et al., *A Richard Wright Bibliography: Fifty Years of Criticism and Commentary*, 1988.

Text Used: *Uncle Tom's Children*, 1989.

from   UNCLE TOM'S CHILDREN*

BRIGHT AND MORNING STAR

I

She stood with her black face some six inches from the moist windowpane and wondered when on earth would it ever stop raining. It might keep up like this all week, she thought. She heard rain droning upon the roof and high up in the wet sky her eyes followed the silent rush of a bright shaft of yellow that swung from the airplane beacon in far off Memphis. Momently she could see it cutting through the rainy dark; it would hover a second like a gleaming sword above her head, then vanish. She sighed, troubling, Johnny-Boys been trampin in this slop all day wid no decent shoes on his feet. . . . Through the window she could see the rich black earth sprawling outside in the night. There was more rain than the clay could soak up; pools stood everywhere. She yawned and mumbled: "Rains good n bad. It kin make seeds bus up thu the ground, er it kin bog things down lika watah-soaked coffin." Her hands were folded loosely over her stomach and the hot air of the kitchen traced a filmy vein of sweat on her forehead. From the cook stove came the soft singing of burning wood and now and then a throaty bubble rose from a pot of simmering greens.

"Shucks, Johnny-Boy coulda let somebody else do all tha runnin in the rain. Theres others bettah fixed for it than he is. But, naw! Johnny-boy ain the one t trust nobody t do nothin. Hes gotta do it *all* hissef. . . ."

She glanced at a pile of damp clothes in a zinc tub. Waal, Ah bettah git t work. She turned, lifted a smoothing iron with a thick pad of cloth, touched a spit-wet finger to it with a quick, jerking motion: *smiiitz!* Yeah; its hot! Stooping, she took a blue work-shirt from the tub and shook it out. With a deft twist of her shoulders she caught the iron in her right hand; the fingers of her left hand took a piece of wax from a tin box and a frying sizzle came as she smeared the bottom. She was thinking of nothing now; her hands followed a life-long ritual of toil. Spreading a sleeve, she ran the hot iron to and fro until the wet cloth became stiff. She was deep in the midst of her work when a song rose up out of the far off days of her childhood and broke through half-parted lips:

> *Hes the Lily of the Valley, the Bright n*
> *Mawnin Star*
> *Hes the Fairest of Ten Thousan t ma soul . . .*

A gust of wind dashed rain against the window. Johnny-Boy oughta c mon home n eat his suppah. Aw, Lawd! Itd be fine ef Sug could eat wid us tonight! Itd be like ol times! Mabbe aftah all it wont be long fo he comes back. Tha lettah Ah got from im last week said *Don give up hope*. . . . Yeah; we gotta live in hope. Then both of her sons, Sug and Johnny-Boy, would be back with her.

---

* First published as *Uncle Tom's Children: Four Novellas* in 1938 and enlarged to *Uncle Tom's Children: Five Long Stories* in 1940 with the inclusion of the introductory essay "The Ethics of Living Jim Crow" and "Bright and Morning Star," which was first published in the *New Masses* in 1939. The story's title is from an old African-American hymn.

With an involuntary nervous gesture, she stopped and stood still, listening. But the only sound was the lulling fall of rain. Shucks, ain no usa me ackin this way, she thought. Ever time they gits ready to hol them meetings Ah gits jumpity. Ah been a lil scared ever since Sug went t jail. She heard the clock ticking and looked. Johnny-boys a *hour* late! He sho must be havin a time doin all tha trampin, trampin thu the mud. . . . But her fear was a quiet one; it was more like an intense brooding than a fear; it was a sort of hugging of hated facts so closely that she could feel their grain, like letting cold water run over her hand from a faucet on a winter morning.

She ironed again, faster now, as if she felt the more she engaged her body in work the less she would think. But how could she forget Johnny-Boy out there on those wet fields rounding up white and black Communists for a meeting tomorrow? And that was just what Sug had been doing when the sheriff had caught him, beat him, and tried to make him tell who and where his comrades were. Po Sug! They sho musta beat the boy somethin awful! But, thank Gawd, he didn't talk! He ain no weaklin, Sug ain! Hes been lion-hearted all his life long.

That had happened a year ago. And now each time those meetings came around the old terror surged back. While shoving the iron a cluster of toiling days returned; days of washing and ironing to feed Johnny-Boy and Sug so they could do party work; days of carrying a hundred pounds of white folks' clothes upon her head across fields sometimes wet and sometimes dry. But in those days a hundred pounds was nothing to carry carefully balanced upon her head while stepping by instinct over the corn and cotton rows. The only time it had seemed heavy was when she had heard of Sug's arrest. She had been coming home one morning with a bundle upon her head, her hands swinging idly by her sides, walking slowly with her eyes in front of her, when Bob, Johnny-Boy's pal, had called from across the fields and had come and told her that the sheriff had got Sug. That morning the bundle had become heavier than she could ever remember.

And with each passing week now, though she spoke of it to no one, things were becoming heavier. The tubs of water and the smoothing iron and the bundles of clothes were becoming harder to lift, with her back aching so; and her work was taking longer, all because Sug was gone and she didn't know just when Johnny-Boy would be taken too. To ease the ache of anxiety that was swelling her heart, she hummed, then sang softly:

> *He walks wid me, He talks wid me*
> *He tells me Ahm His own.* . . .

Guiltily, she stopped and smiled. Looks like Ah jus cant seem t fergit them ol songs, no mattah how hard Ah tries. . . . She had learned them when she was a little girl living and working on a farm. Every Monday morning from the corn and cotton fields the slow strains had floated from her mother's lips, lonely and haunting; and later, as the years had filled with gall, she had learned their deep meaning. Long hours of scrubbing floors for a few cents a day had taught her who Jesus was, what a great boon it was to cling to Him, to be like Him and suffer without a mumbling word. She had poured the yearning of her life into the songs, feeling buoyed with a faith beyond this world. The figure of the Man nailed in agony to the Cross, His burial in a cold grave, His transfigured Resurrection, His being breath and clay, God and Man—all had focused her feelings upon an imagery which had swept her life into a wondrous vision.

But as she had grown older, a cold white mountain, the white folks and their laws, had swum into her vision and shattered her songs and their spell of peace. To her that white mountain was temptation, something to lure her from her Lord, a part of the world God had made in order that she might endure it and come through all the stronger, just as Christ had risen with greater glory from the tomb. The days crowded with trouble had enhanced her faith and she had grown to love hardship with a bitter pride; she had obeyed the laws of the white folks with a soft smile of secret knowing.

After her mother had been snatched up to heaven in a chariot of fire, the years had brought her a rough workingman and two black babies, Sug and Johnny-Boy, all three of whom she had wrapped in the charm and magic of her vision. Then she was tested by no less than God; her man died, a trial which she bore with the strength shed by the grace of her vision; finally even the memory of her man faded into the vision itself, leaving her with two black boys growing tall, slowly into manhood.

Then one day grief had come to her heart when Johnny-boy and Sug had walked forth demanding their lives. She had sought to fill their eyes with her vision, but they would have none of it. And she had wept when they began to boast of the strength shed by a new and terrible vision.

But she had loved them, even as she loved them now; bleeding, her heart had followed them. She could have done no less, being an old woman in a strange world. And day by day her sons had ripped from her startled eyes her old vision, and image by image had given her a new one, different, but great and strong enough to fling her into the light of another grace. The wrongs and sufferings of black men had taken the place of Him nailed to the Cross; the meager beginnings of the party had become another Resurrection; and the hate of those who would destroy her new faith had quickened in her a hunger to feel how deeply her new strength went.

"Lawd, Johnny-Boy," she would sometimes say, "Ah jus wan them white folks t try t make me tell *who* is *in* the party n who *ain!* Ah jus wan em t try, Ahll show em somethin they never thought a black woman could have!"

But sometimes like tonight, while lost in the forgetfulness of work, the past and the present would become mixed in her; while toiling under a strange star for a new freedom the old songs would slip from her lips with their beguiling sweetness.

The iron was getting cold. She put more wood into the fire, stood again at the window and watched the yellow blade of light cut through the wet darkness. Johnny-Boy ain here yit . . . Then, before she was aware of it, she was still, listening for sounds. Under the drone of rain she heard the slosh of feet in mud. Tha ain Johnny-Boy. She knew his long, heavy footsteps in a million. She heard feet come on the porch. Some woman. . . . She heard bare knuckles knock three times, then once. Thas some of them comrades! She unbarred the door, cracked it a few inches, and flinched from the cold rush of damp wind.

"Whos tha?"

"Its me!"

"Who?"

"Me, Reva!"

She flung the door open.

"Lawd, chile, c mon in!"

She stepped to one side and a thin, blond-haired white girl ran through the door; as she slid the bolt she heard the girl gasping and shaking her wet clothes. Somethings wrong! Reva wouldna walked a mil t mah house in all this slop fer nothin! That gals stuck onto Johnny-Boy. Ah wondah ef anythin happened t im?

"Git on inter the kitchen, Reva, where its warm."

"Lawd, Ah sho is wet!"

"How yuh reckon yuhd be, in all tha rain?"

"Johnny-Boy ain here *yit?*" asked Reva.

"Naw! N ain no usa yuh worryin bout im. Jus yuh git them shoes off! Yuh wanna ketch yo deatha col?" She stood looking absently. Yeah; its somethin about the party er Johnny-Boy thas gone wrong. Lawd, Ah wondah ef her pa knows how she feels bout Johnny-Boy? "Honey, yuh hadn't oughta come out in sloppy weather like this."

"Ah had t come, An Sue."

She led Reva to the kitchen.

"Git them shoes off n git close t the stove so yuhll git dry!"

"An Sue, Ah got somethin t tell yuh . . ."

The words made her hold her breath. Ah bet its somethin bout Johnny-Boy!

"Whut, honey?"

"The sheriff wuz by our house tonight. He come t see pa."

"Yeah?"

"He done got word from somewheres bout tha meetin tomorrow."

"Is it Johnny-Boy, Reva?"

"Aw, naw, An Sue! Ah ain hearda word bout im. Ain yuh seen im tonight?"

"He ain come home t eat yit."

"Where kin he be?"

"Lawd knows, chile."

"Somebody's gotta tell them comrades that meetings off," said Reva. "The sheriffs got men watchin our house. Ah had t slip out t git here widout em followin me."

"Reva?"

"Hunh?"

"Ahma ol woman n Ah wans yuh t tell me the truth."

"Whut, An Sue?"

"Yuh ain tryin t fool me, is yuh?"

"*Fool* yuh?"

"Bout Johnny-Boy?"

"Lawd, naw, An Sue!"

"Ef theres anythin wrong jus tell me, chile. Ah kin stan it."

She stood by the ironing board, her hands as usual folded loosely over her stomach, watching Reva pull off her water-clogged shoes. She was feeling that Johnny-Boy was already lost to her; she was feeling the pain that would come when she knew it for certain; and she was feeling that she would have to be brave and bear it. She was like a person caught in a swift current of water and knew where the water was sweeping her and did not want to go on but had to go on to the end.

"It ain nothin bout Johnny-Boy, An Sue," said Reva, "But we gotta do somethin er we'll all git inter trouble."

"How the sheriff know about tha meetin?"

"Thas whut pa wants t know."

"Somebody done turned Judas."[1]

"Sho looks like it."

"Ah bet it wuz some of them new ones," she said.

"Its hard t tell," said Reva.

"Lissen, Reva, yuh oughta stay here n git dry, but yuh bettah git back n tell yo pa Johnny-Boy ain here n Ah don know when hes gonna show up. *Some*bodys gotta tell them comrades t stay erway from yo pas house."

She stood with her back to the window, looking at Reva's wide, blue eyes. Po critter! Gotta go back thu all tha slop! Though she felt sorry for Reva, not once did she think that it would not have to be done. Being a woman, Reva was not suspect; she would *have* to go. It was just as natural for Reva to go back through the cold rain as it was for her to iron night and day, or for Sug to be in jail. Right now, Johnny-Boy was out there on those dark fields trying to get home. Lawd, don let em git im tonight! In spite of herself her feelings became torn. She loved her son and, loving him, she loved what he was trying to do. Johnny-Boy was happiest when he was working for the party, and her love for him was for his happiness. She frowned, trying hard to fit something together in her feelings: for her to try to stop Johnny-Boy was to admit that all the toil of years meant nothing; and to let him go meant that sometime or other he would be caught, like Sug. In facing it this way she felt a little stunned, as though she had come suddenly upon a blank wall in the dark. But outside in the rain were people, white and black, whom she had known all her life. Those people depended upon Johnny-Boy, loved him and looked to him as a man and leader. Yeah; hes gotta keep on; he cant stop now. . . . She looked at Reva; she was crying and pulling her shoes back on with reluctant fingers.

"Whut yuh carryin on tha way fer, chile?"

"Yuh done los Sug, now yuh sendin Johnny-Boy . . ."

"Ah got t, honey."

She was glad she could say that. Reva believed in black folks and not for anything in the world would she falter before her. In Reva's trust and acceptance of her she had found her first feelings of humanity; Reva's love was her refuge from shame and degradation. If in the early days of her life the white mountain had driven her back from the earth, then in her last days Reva's love was drawing her toward it, like the beacon that swung through the night outside. She heard Reva sobbing.

"Hush, honey!"

"Mah brothers in jail too! Ma cries ever day . . ."

"Ah know, honey."

She helped Reva with her coat; her fingers felt the scant flesh of the girl's shoulders. She don git ernuff t eat, she thought. She slipped her arms around Reva's waist and held her close for a moment.

"Now, yuh stop that cryin."

"A-a-ah c-c-cant hep it. . . ."

"Everythingll be awright; Johnny-Boyll be back."

"Yuh think so?"

"Sho, chile. Cos he will."

[1] Judas Iscariot, Jesus' betrayer (see Matthew 26).

Neither of them spoke again until they stood in the doorway. Outside they could hear water washing through the ruts of the street.

"Be sho n send Johnny-Boy t tell the folks t stay erway from pas house," said Reva.

"Ahll tell im. Don yuh worry."

"Good-bye!"

"Good-bye!"

Leaning against the door jamb,[2] she shook her head slowly and watched Reva vanish through the falling rain.

II

She was back at her board, ironing, when she heard feet sucking in the mud of the back yard; feet she knew from long years of listening were Johnny-Boy's. But tonight, with all the rain and fear, his coming was like a leaving, was almost more than she could bear. Tears welled to her eyes and she blinked them away. She felt that he was coming so that she could give him up; to see him now was to say good-bye. But it was a good-bye she knew she could never say; they were not that way toward each other. All day long they could sit in the same room and not speak; she was his mother and he was her son. Most of the time a nod or a grunt would carry all the meaning that she wanted to convey to him, or he to her. She did not even turn her head when she heard him come stomping into the kitchen. She heard him pull up a chair, sit, sigh, and draw off his muddy shoes; they fell to the floor with heavy thuds. Soon the kitchen was full of the scent of his drying socks and his burning pipe. Tha boys hongry! She paused and looked at him over her shoulder; he was puffing at his pipe with his head tilted back and his feet propped up on the edge of the stove; his eyelids drooped and his wet clothes steamed from the heat of the fire. Lawd, tha boy gits mo like his pa every day he lives, she mused, her lips breaking in a slow faint smile. Hols tha pipe in his mouth just like his pa usta hol his. Wondah how they woulda got erlong ef his pa hada lived? They oughta liked each other, they so mucha like. She wished there could have been other children besides Sug, so Johnny-Boy would not have to be so much alone. A man needs a woman by his side. . . . She thought of Reva; she liked Reva; the brightest glow her heart had ever known was when she had learned that Reva loved Johnny-Boy. But beyond Reva were cold white faces. Ef theys caught it means *death*. . . . She jerked around when she heard Johnny-Boy's pipe clatter to the floor. She saw him pick it up, smile sheepishly at her, and wag his head.

"Gawd, Ahm sleepy," he mumbled.

She got a pillow from her room and gave it to him.

"Here," she said.

"Hunh," he said, putting the pillow between his head and the back of the chair.

They were silent again. Yes, she would have to tell him to go back out into the cold rain and slop; maybe to get caught; maybe for the last time; she didn't know. But she would let him eat and get dry before telling him that the sheriff knew of the meeting to be held at Lem's tomorrow. And she would make him take a big

---

[2] The side post.

dose of soda before he went out; soda always helped to stave off a cold. She looked at the clock. It was eleven. Theres time yit. Spreading a newspaper on the apron of the stove, she placed a heaping plate of greens upon it, a knife, a fork, a cup of coffee, a slab of cornbread, and a dish of peach cobbler.

"Yo suppahs ready," she said.

"Yeah," he said.

He did not move. She ironed again. Presently, she heard him eating. When she could no longer hear his knife tinkling against the edge of the plate, she knew he was through. It was almost twelve now. She would let him rest a little while longer before she told him. Till one er'clock, mabbe. Hes so tired. . . . She finished her ironing, put away the board, and stacked the clothes in her dresser drawer. She poured herself a cup of black coffee, drew up a chair, sat down and drank.

"Yuh almos dry," she said, not looking around.

"Yeah," he said, turning sharply to her.

The tone of voice in which she had spoken had let him know that more was coming. She drained her cup and waited a moment longer.

"Reva wuz here."

"Yeah?"

"She lef bout a hour ergo."

"Whut she say?"

"She said ol man Lem hada visit from the sheriff today."

"Bout the meetin?"

She saw him stare at the coals glowing red through the crevices of the stove and run his fingers nervously through his hair. She knew he was wondering how the sheriff had found out. In the silence he would ask a wordless question and in the silence she would answer wordlessly. Johnny-Boys too trustin, she thought. Hes trying t make the party big n hes takin in folks fastern he kin git t know em. You cant trust ever white man yuh meet. . . .

"Yuh know, Johnny-Boy, yuh been takin in a lotta them white folks lately . . ."

"Aw, ma!"

"But, Johnny-Boy . . ."

"Please, dont talk t me bout tha now, ma."

"Yuh ain t ol t lissen n learn, son," she said.

"Ah know whut yuh gonna say, ma. N yuh wrong. Yuh cant judge folks just by how yuh feel bout em n by how long yuh done knowed em. Ef we start that we wouldnt have *no*body in the party. When folks pledge they word t be with us, then we gotta take em in. Wes too weak t be choosy."

He rose abruptly, rammed his hands into his pockets, and stood facing the window; she looked at his back in a long silence. She knew his faith; it was deep. He had always said that black men could not fight the rich bosses alone; a man could not fight with every hand against him. But he believes so hard hes blind, she thought. At odd times they had had these arguments before; always she would be pitting her feelings against the hard necessity of his thinking, and always she would lose. She shook her head. Po Johnny-Boy; he don know . . .

"But ain nona our folks tol, Johnny-Boy," she said.

"How yuh know?" he asked. His voice came low and with a tinge of anger. He still faced the window and now and then the yellow blade of light flicked across the sharp outline of his black face.

"Cause Ah know em," she said.

"*Any*body mighta tol," he said.

"It wuznt nona *our* folks," she said again.

She saw his hand sweep in a swift arc of disgust.

"*Our* folks! Ma, who in Gawds name is *our* folks?"

"The folks we wuz born n raised wid, son. The folks we *know!*"

"We cant make the party grow tha way, ma."

"It mighta been Booker," she said.

"Yuh don know."

". . . er Blattberg . . ."

"Fer Chrissakes!"

". . . er any of the fo-five others whut joined las week."

"Ma, yuh jus don wan me t go out tonight," he said.

"Yo ol ma wans yuh t be careful, son."

"Ma, when yuh start doubtin folks in the party, then there ain no end."

"Son, Ah knows ever black man n woman in this parta the country," she said, standing too. "Ah watched em grow up; Ah even heped birth n nurse some of em; Ah knows em *all* from way back. There ain none of em that *coulda* tol! The folks Ah know jus don open they dos n ast death t walk in! Son, it wuz some of them *white* folks! Yuh just mark mah word n wait n see!"

"Why is it gotta be *white* folks?" he asked. "Ef they tol, then theys jus Judases, thas all."

"Son, look at whuts befo yuh."

He shook his head and sighed.

"Ma, Ah done tol yuh a hundred times. Ah cant see white n Ah cant see black," he said. "Ah sees rich men n Ah sees po men."

She picked up his dirty dishes and piled them in a pan. Out of the corners of her eyes she saw him sit and pull on his wet shoes. Hes goin! When she put the last dish away he was standing fully dressed, warming his hands over the stove. Jus a few mo minutes now n hell be gone, like Sug, mabbe. Her throat tightened. This black mans fight takes *ever*thin! Looks like Gawd put us in this world jus t beat us down!

"Keep this, ma," he said.

She saw a crumpled wad of money in his outstretched fingers.

"Naw, yuh keep it. Yuh might need it."

"It ain mine, ma. It berlongs t the party."

"But, Johnny-Boy, yuh might hafta go erway!"

"Ah kin make out."

"Don fergit yosef too much, son."

"Ef Ah don come back theyll need it."

He was looking at her face and she was looking at the money.

"Yuh keep tha," she said slowly. "Ahll give em the money."

"From where?"

"Ah got some."

"Where yuh git it from?"

She sighed.

"Ah been savin a dollah a week fer Sug ever since hes been in jail."

"Lawd, ma!"

She saw the look of puzzled love and wonder in his eyes. Clumsily, he put the money back into his pocket.

"Ahm gone," he said.

"Here; drink this glass of soda watah."

She watched him drink, then put the glass away.

"Waal," he said.

"Take the stuff outta yo pockets!"

She lifted the lid of the stove and he dumped all the papers from his pocket into the fire. She followed him to the door and made him turn round.

"Lawd, yuh tryin to maka revolution n yuh cant even keep yo coat buttoned." Her nimble fingers fastened his collar high around his throat. "There!"

He pulled the brim of his hat low over his eyes. She opened the door and with the suddenness of the cold gust of wind that struck her face, he was gone. She watched the black fields and the rain take him, her eyes burning. When the last faint footstep could no longer be heard, she closed the door, went to her bed, lay down, and pulled the cover over her while fully dressed. Her feelings coursed with the rhythm of the rain: Hes gone! Lawd, Ah *knows* hes gone! Her blood felt cold.

III

She was floating in a grey void somewhere between sleeping and dreaming and then suddenly she was wide awake, hearing and feeling in the same instant the thunder of the door crashing in and a cold wind filling the room. It was pitch black and she stared, resting on her elbows, her mouth open, not breathing, her ears full of the sound of tramping feet and booming voices. She knew at once: They lookin fer im! Then, filled with her will, she was on her feet, rigid, waiting, listening.

"The lamps burnin!"

"Yuh see her?"

"Naw!"

"Look in the kitchen!"

"Gee, this place smells like niggers!"

"Say, somebodys here er been here!"

"Yeah; theres fire in the stove!"

"Mabbe hes been here n gone?"

"Boy, look at these jars of jam!"

"Niggers make good jam!"

"Git some bread!"

"Heres some cornbread!"

"Say, lemme git some!"

"Take it easy! Theres plenty here!"

"Ahma take some of this stuff home!"

"Look, heres a pota greens!"

"N some hot cawffee!"

"Say, yuh guys! C mon! Cut it out! We didn't come here fer a feas!"

She walked slowly down the hall. They lookin fer im, but they ain got im yit! She stopped in the doorway, her gnarled, black hands as always folded over her stomach, but tight now, so tightly the veins bulged. The kitchen was crowded with white men in glistening raincoats. Though the lamp burned, their flashlights still glowed in red fists. Across her floor she saw the muddy tracks of their boots.

"Yuh white folks git outta mah house!"

There was a quick silence; every face turned toward her. She saw a sudden movement, but did not know what it meant until something hot and wet slammed her squarely in the face. She gasped, but did not move. Calmly, she wiped the warm, greasy liquor of greens from her eyes with her left hand. One of the white men had thrown a handful of greens out of the pot at her.

"How they taste, ol bitch?"

"Ah ast yuh t git outta mah house!"

She saw the sheriff detach himself from the crowd and walk toward her.

"Now, Anty . . ."

"White man, don yuh *Anty* me!"

"Yuh ain got the right sperit!"

"Sperit hell! Yuh git these men outta mah house!"

"Yuh ack like yuh don like it!"

"Naw, Ah don like it, n yuh knows dam waal Ah don!"

"What yuh gonna do about it?"

"Ahm telling yuh t git outta mah house!"

"Gittin sassy?"

"Ef telling yuh t git outta mah house is sass, then Ahm sassy!"

Her words came in a tense whisper; but beyond, back of them, she was watching, thinking, judging the men.

"Listen, Anty," the sheriff's voice came soft and low. "Ahm here t hep yuh. How come yuh wanna ack this way?"

"Yuh ain never heped yo *own* sef since yuh been born," she flared. "How kin the likes of yuh hep me?"

One of the white men came forward and stood directly in front of her.

"Lissen, nigger woman, yuh talkin t *white* men!"

"Ah don care who Ahm talkin t!"

"Yuhll wish some day yuh did!"

"Not t the likes of yuh!"

"Yuh need somebody t teach yuh how t be a good nigger!"

"*Yuh* cant teach it t me!"

"Yuh gonna change yo tune."

"Not longs mah bloods warm!"

"Don git smart now!"

"Yuh git outta mah house!"

"Spose we don go?" the sheriff asked.

They were crowded around her. She had not moved since she had taken her place in the doorway. She was thinking only of Johnny-Boy as she stood there giving and taking words; and she knew that they, too, were thinking of Johnny-Boy. She knew they wanted him, and her heart was daring them to take him from her.

"Spose we don go?" the sheriff asked again.

"Twenty of yuh runnin over one ol woman! Now, ain yuh white men glad yuh so brave?"

The sheriff grabbed her arm.

"C mon, now! Yuh don did ernuff sass fer one night. Wheres tha nigger son of yos?"

"Don yuh wished yuh knowed?"

"Yuh wanna git slapped?"

"Ah ain never seen one of yo kind that wuznt too low fer . . ."

The sheriff slapped her straight across her face with his open palm. She fell back against a wall and sank to her knees.

"Is tha whut white men do t nigger women?"

She rose slowly and stood again, not even touching the place that ached from his blow, her hands folded over her stomach.

"Ah ain never seen one of yo kind tha wuznt too low fer . . ."

He slapped her again; she reeled backward several feet and fell on her side.

"Is tha whut we too low t do?"

She stood before him again, dry-eyed, as though she had not been struck. Her lips were numb and her chin was wet with blood.

"Aw, let her go! Its the nigger we wan!" said one.

"Wheres that nigger son of yos?" the sheriff asked.

"Find im," she said.

"By Gawd, ef we hafta find im well kill im!"

"He wont be the only nigger yuh ever killed," she said.

She was consumed with a bitter pride. There was nothing on this earth, she felt then, that they could not do to her but that she could take. She stood on a narrow plot of ground from which she would die before she was pushed. And then it was, while standing there feeling warm blood seeping down her throat, that she gave up Johnny-Boy, gave him up to the white folks. She gave him up because they had come tramping into her heart demanding him, thinking they could get him by beating her, thinking they could scare her into making her tell where he was. She gave him up because she wanted them to know that they could not get what they wanted by bluffing and killing.

"Wheres this meetin gonna be?" the sheriff asked.

"Don yuh wish yuh knowed?"

"Ain there gonna be a meetin?"

"How come yuh astin me?"

"There *is* gonna be a meetin," said the sheriff.

"Is it?"

"Ah gotta great mind t choke it outta yuh!"

"Yuh so smart," she said.

"We ain playing wid yuh!"

"Did Ah say yuh wuz?"

"That nigger son of yos is erroun here somewheres n Ah aim to find im," said the sheriff. "Ef yuh tell us where he is n ef he talks, mabbe hell git off easy. But ef we hafta find im, well kill im! Ef we hafta find im, then yuh git a sheet t put over im in the mawnin, see? Git yuh a sheet, cause hes gonna be dead!"

"He wont be the only nigger yuh ever killed," she said again.

The sheriff walked past her. The others followed. Yuh didnt git whut yuh wanted! she thought exultingly. N yuh ain gonna *never* git it! Hotly, something arched in her to make them feel the intensity of her pride and freedom; her heart groped to turn the bitter hours of her life into words of a kind that would make them feel that she had taken all they had done to her in stride and could still take more. Her faith surged so strongly in her she was all but blinded. She walked behind them to the door, knotting and twisting her fingers. She saw them step to the muddy ground. Each whirl of the yellow beacon revealed glimpses of slanting rain. Her lips moved, then she shouted:

"Yuh didnt git whut yuh wanted! N yuh ain gonna nevah git it!"

The sheriff stopped and turned; his voice came low and hard.

"Now, by Gawd, thas ernuff outta yuh!"

"Ah know when Ah done said ernuff!"

"Aw, naw, yuh don!" he said. "Yuh don know when yuh done said ernuff, but Ahma teach yuh ternight!"

He was up the steps and across the porch with one bound. She backed into the hall, her eyes full on his face.

"Tell me when yuh gonna stop talkin!" he said, swinging his fist.

The blow caught her high on the cheek; her eyes went blank; she fell flat on her face. She felt the hard heel of his wet shoes coming into her temple and stomach.

"Lemme hear yuh talk some mo!"

She wanted to, but could not; pain numbed and choked her. She lay still and somewhere out of the grey void of unconsciousness she heard someone say: *Aw fer chrissakes leave her erlone, its the nigger we wan. . . .*

IV

She never knew how long she had lain huddled in the dark hallway. Her first returning feeling was of a nameless fear crowding the inside of her, then a deep pain spreading from her temple downward over her body. Her ears were filled with the drone of rain and she shuddered from the cold wind blowing through the door. She opened her eyes and at first saw nothing. As if she were imagining it, she knew she was half lying and half sitting in a corner against a wall. With difficulty she twisted her neck and what she saw made her hold her breath—a vast white blur was suspended directly above her. For a moment she could not tell if her fear was from the blur or if the blur was from her fear. Gradually the blur resolved itself into a huge white face that slowly filled her vision. She was stone still, conscious really of the effort to breathe, feeling somehow that she existed only by the mercy of that white face. She had seen it before; its fear had gripped her many times; it had for her the fear of all the white faces she had ever seen in her life. *Sue* . . . As from a great distance, she heard her name being called. She was regaining consciousness now, but the fear was coming with her. She looked into the face of a white man, wanting to scream out for him to go; yet accepting his presence because she felt she had to. Though some remote part of her mind was active, her limbs were powerless. It was as if an invisible knife had split her in two, leaving one half of her lying there helpless, while the other half shrank in dread from a forgotten but familiar enemy. *Sue its me Sue its me* . . . Then all at once the voice came clearly.

"Sue, its me! Its Booker!"

And she heard an answering voice speaking inside of her. Yeah, its Booker . . . The one whut just joined . . . She roused herself, struggling for full consciousness; and as she did so she transferred to the person of Booker the nameless fear she felt. It seemed that Booker towered above her as a challenge to her right to exist upon the earth.

"Yuh awright?"

She did not answer; she started violently to her feet and fell.

"Sue, yuh hurt!"

"Yeah," she breathed.

"Where they hit yuh?"

"Its mah head," she whispered.

She was speaking even though she did not want to; the fear that had hold of her compelled her.

"They beat yuh?"

"Yeah."

"Them bastards! Them Gawddam bastards!"

She heard him saying it over and over; then she felt herself being lifted.

"Naw!" she gasped.

"Ahma take yuh t the kitchen!"

"Put me down!"

"But yuh cant stay here like this!"

She shrank in his arms and pushed her hands against his body; when she was in the kitchen she freed herself, sank into a chair, and held tightly to its back. She looked wonderingly at Booker. There was nothing about him that should frighten her so, but even that did not ease her tension. She saw him go the water bucket, wet his handkerchief, wring it, and offer it to her. Distrustfully, she stared at the damp cloth.

"Here; put this on yo fohead . . ."

"Naw!"

"C mon; itll make yuh feel bettah!"

She hesitated in confusion. What right had she to be afraid when someone was acting as kindly as this toward her? Reluctantly, she leaned forward and pressed the damp cloth to her head. It helped. With each passing minute she was catching hold of herself, yet wondering why she felt as she did.

"Whut happened?"

"Ah don know."

"Yuh feel bettah?"

"Yeah."

"Who all wuz here?"

"Ah don know," she said again.

"Yo head still hurt?"

"Yeah."

"Gee, Ahm sorry."

"Ahm awright," she sighed and buried her face in her hands.

She felt him touch her shoulder.

"Sue, Ah got some bad news fer yuh . . ."

She knew; she stiffened and grew cold. It had happened; she stared dry-eyed, with compressed lips.

"Its mah Johnny-Boy," she said.

"Yeah; Ahm awful sorry t hafta tell yuh this way. But Ah thought yuh oughta know . . ."

Her tension eased and a vacant place opened up inside of her. A voice whispered, Jesus, hep me!

"W-w-where is he?"

"They got im out t Foleys Woods tryin t make him tell who the others is."

"He ain gonna tell," she said, "They jus as waal kill im, cause he ain gonna nevah tell."

"Ah hope he don," said Booker. "But he didnt have a chance t tell the others. They grabbed im jus as he got t the woods."

Then all the horror of it flashed upon her; she saw flung out over the rainy countryside an array of shacks where white and black comrades were sleeping; in the morning they would be rising and going to Lem's; then they would be caught. And that meant terror, prison, and death. The comrades would have to be told; she would have to tell them; she could not entrust Johnny-Boy's work to another, and especially not to Booker as long as she felt toward him as she did. Gripping the bottom of the chair with both hands, she tried to rise; the room blurred and she swayed. She found herself resting in Booker's arms.

"Lemme go!"

"Sue, yuh too weak t walk!"

"Ah gotta tell em!" she said.

"Set down, Sue! Yuh hurt! Yuh sick!"

When seated, she looked at him helplessly.

"Sue, lissen! Johnny-Boys caught. Ahm here. Yuh tell me who they is n Ahll tell em."

She stared at the floor and did not answer. Yes; she was too weak to go. There was no way for her to tramp all those miles through the rain tonight. But should she tell Booker? If only she had somebody like Reva to talk to! She did not want to decide alone; she must make no mistake about this. She felt Booker's fingers pressing on her arm and it was as though the white mountain was pushing her to the edge of a sheer height; she again exclaimed inwardly. Jesus, hep me! Booker's white face was at her side, waiting. Would she be doing right to tell him? Suppose she did not tell and then the comrades were caught? She could not ever forgive herself for doing a thing like that. But maybe she was wrong; maybe her fear was what Johnny-Boy had always called "jus foolishness." She remembered his saying, Ma, we cant make the party grow ef we start doubtin everbody. . . .

"Tell me who they is, Sue, n Ahll tell em. Ah jus joined n Ah don know who they is."

"Ah don know who they is," she said.

"Yuh *gotta* tell me who they is, Sue!"

"Ah tol yuh Ah don know!"

"Yuh *do* know! C mon! Set up n talk!"

"Naw!"

"Yuh wan em all t git *killed?*"

She shook her head and swallowed. Lawd, Ah don believe in this man!

"Lissen, Ahll call the names n yuh tell me which ones is in the party n which ones ain, see?"

"Naw!"

"Please, Sue!"

"Ah don know," she said.

"Sue, yuh ain doin right by em. Johnny-Boy wouldnt wan yuh t be this way. Hes out there holdin up his end. Les hol up ours . . ."

"Lawd, Ah don know . . ."

"Is yuh scared a me cause Ahm *white?* Johnny-Boy ain like tha. Don let all the work we done go fer nothin."

She gave up and bowed her head in her hands.

"Is it Johnson? Tell me, Sue?"

"Yeah," she whispered in horror; a mounting horror of feeling herself being undone.

"Is it Green?"

"Yeah."

"Murphy?"

"Lawd, Ah don know!"

"Yuh gotta tell me, Sue!"

"Mistah Booker, please leave me erlone . . ."

"Is it Murphy?"

She answered yes to the names of Johnny-Boy's comrades; she answered until he asked her no more. Then she thought, How he know the sheriffs men is watchin Lems house? She stood up and held onto her chair, feeling something sure and firm within her.

"How yuh know about Lem?"

"Why . . . How Ah know?"

"Whut yuh doin here this tima night? How yuh know the sheriff got Johnny-Boy?"

"Sue, don yuh believe in me?"

She did not, but she could not answer. She stared at him until her lips hung open; she was searching deep within herself for certainty.

"You meet Reva?" she asked.

"Reva?"

"Yeah, Lems gal?"

"Oh, yeah. Sho, Ah met Reva."

"She tell yuh?"

She asked the question more of herself than of him; she longed to believe.

"Yeah," he said softly. "Ah reckon Ah oughta be goin t tell em now."

"Who?" she asked. "Tell *who?*"

The muscles of her body were stiff as she waited for his answer; she felt as though life depended upon it.

"The comrades," he said.

"Yeah," she sighed.

She did not know when he left; she was not looking or listening. She just suddenly saw the room empty and from her the thing that had made her fearful was gone.

V

For a space of time that seemed to her as long as she had been upon the earth, she sat huddled over the cold stove. One minute she would say to herself, They both gone now; Johnny-Boy n Sug . . . Mabbe Ahll never see em ergin. Then a surge of guilt would blot out her longing. "Lawd, Ah shouldna tol!" she mumbled. "But no man kin be so lowdown as to do a thing like that . . ." Several times she had an impulse to try to tell the comrades herself; she was feeling a little better now. But what good would that do? She had told Booker the names. He jus couldnt be a Judas to po folks like us . . . He *couldnt!*

"An Sue!"

Thas Reva! Her heart leaped with an anxious gladness. She rose without answering and limped down the dark hallway. Through the open door, against the background of rain, she saw Reva's face lit now and then to whiteness by the whirling beams of the beacon. She was about to call, but a thought checked her. Jesus, hep me! Ah gotta tell her bout Johnny-Boy . . . Lawd, Ah cant!

"An Sue, yuh there?"

"C mon in, chile!"

She caught Reva and held her close for a moment without speaking.

"Lawd, Ahm sho glad yuh here," she said at last.

"Ah thought somethin had happened t yuh," said Reva, pulling away. "Ah saw the do open . . . Pa told me to come back n stay wid yuh tonight . . ." Reva paused and started, "W-w-whuts the mattah?"

She was so full of having Reva with her that she did not understand what the question meant.

"Hunh?"

"Yo neck . . ."

"Aw, it ain nothin, chile. C mon in the kitchen."

"But theres blood on yo neck!"

"The sheriff wuz here . . ."

"Them fools! Whut they wanna bother yuh fer? Ah could kill em! So hep me Gawd, Ah could!"

"It ain nothin," she said.

She was wondering how to tell Reva about Johnny-Boy and Booker. Ahll wait a lil while longer, she thought. Now that Reva was here, her fear did not seem as awful as before.

"C mon, lemme fix yo head, An Sue. Yuh hurt."

They went to the kitchen. She sat silent while Reva dressed her scalp. She was feeling better now; in just a little while she would tell Reva. She felt the girl's finger pressing gently upon her head.

"Tha hurt?"

"A lil, chile."

"Yuh po thing."

"It ain nothin."

"Did Johnny-Boy come?"

She hesitated.

"Yeah."

"He done gone t tell the others?"

Reva's voice sounded so clear and confident that it mocked her. Lawd, Ah cant tell this chile . . .

"Yuh tol im, didnt yuh, An Sue?"

"Y-y-yeah . . ."

"Gee! Thas good! Ah tol pa he didnt hafta worry ef Johnny-Boy got the news. Mabbe thingsll come out awright."

"Ah hope . . ."

She could not go on; she had gone as far as she could. For the first time that night she began to cry.

"Hush, An Sue! Yuh awways been brave. Itll be awright!"

"Ain nothin awright, chile. The worls jus too much fer us, Ah reckon."

"Ef yuh cry that way itll make me cry."

She forced herself to stop. Naw; Ah cant carry on this way in fronta Reva . . . Right now she had a deep need for Reva to believe in her. She watched the girl get pine-knots from behind the stove, rekindle the fire, and put on the coffee pot.

"Yuh wan some cawffee?" Reva asked.

"Naw, honey."

"Aw, c mon, An Sue."

"Jusa lil, honey."

"Thas the way to be. Oh, say, Ah fergot," said Reva, measuring out spoonsful of coffee. "Pa tol me t tell yuh t watch out fer tha Booker man. Hes a stool."

She showed not one sign of outward movement or expression, but as the words fell from Reva's lips she went limp inside.

"Pa tol me soon as Ah got back home. He got word from town . . ."

She stopped listening. She felt as though she had been slapped to the extreme outer edge of life, into a cold darkness. She knew now what she had felt when she had looked up out of her fog of pain and had seen Booker. It was the image of all the white folks, and the fear that went with them, that she had seen and felt during her lifetime. And again, for the second time that night, something she had felt had come true. All she could say to herself was, Ah didnt like im! Gawd knows, Ah didnt! Ah tol Johnny-Boy it wuz some of them white folks . . .

"Here; drink yo cawffee . . ."

She took the cup; her fingers trembled, and the steaming liquid spilt onto her dress and leg.

"Ahm sorry, An Sue!"

Her leg was scalded, but the pain did not bother her.

"Its awright," she said.

"Wait; lemme put some lard on tha burn!"

"It don hurt."

"Yuh worried bout somethin."

"Naw, honey."

"Lemme fix yuh so mo cawffee."

"Ah don wan nothin now, Reva."

"Waal, buck up. Don be tha way . . ."

They were silent. She heard Reva drinking. No; she would not tell Reva; Reva was all she had left. But she had to do something, some way, somehow. She was undone too much as it was; and to tell Reva about Booker or Johnny-Boy was more than she was equal to; it would be too coldly shameful. She wanted to be alone and fight this thing out with herself.

"Go t bed, honey. Yuh tired."

"Naw; Ahm awright, An Sue."

She heard the bottom of Reva's empty cup clank against the top of the stove. Ah *got* t make her go t bed! Yes; Booker would tell the names of the comrades to the sheriff. If she could only stop him some way! That was the answer, the point, the star that grew bright in the morning of new hope. Soon, maybe half an hour from now, Booker would reach Foleys Woods. Hes boun t go the long way, cause he don know no short cut, she thought. Ah could wade the creek n beat im there . . . But what would she do after that?

"Reva, honey, go t bed. Ahm awright. Yuh need res."

"Ah ain sleepy, An Sue."

"Ah knows whuts bes fer yuh, chile. Yuh tired n wet."

"Ah wanna stay up wid yuh."

She forced a smile and said:

"Ah don think they gonna hurt Johnny-Boy . . ."

"Fer *real*, An Sue?"

"Sho, honey."

"But Ah wanna wait up wid yuh."

"Thas mah job, honey. Thas whut a mas fer, t wait up fer her chullun."

"Good night, An Sue."

"Good night, honey."

She watched Reva pull up and leave the kitchen; presently she heard the shucks in the mattress whispering, and she knew that Reva had gone to bed. She was alone. Through the cracks of the stove she saw the fire dying to grey ashes; the room was growing cold again. The yellow beacon continued to flit past the window and the rain still drummed. Yes; she was alone; she had done this awful thing alone; she must find some way out, alone. Like touching a festering sore, she put her finger upon that moment when she had shouted her defiance to the sheriff, when she had shouted to feel her strength. She had lost Sug to save others; she had let Johnny-Boy go to save others; and then in a moment of weakness that came from too much strength she had lost all. If she had not shouted to the sheriff, she would have been strong enough to have resisted Booker; she would have been able to tell the comrades herself. Something tightened in her as she remembered and understood the fit of fear she had felt on coming to herself in the dark hallway. A part of her life she thought she had done away with forever had had hold of her then. She had thought the soft, warm past was over; she had thought that it did not mean much when now she sang: *"Hes the Lily of the Valley, the Bright n Mawnin Star"* . . . The days when she had sung that song were the days when she had not hoped for anything on this earth, the days when the cold mountain had driven her into the arms of Jesus. She had thought that Sug and Johnny-Boy had taught her to forget Him, to fix her hope upon the fight of black men for freedom. Through the gradual years she had believed and worked with them, had felt strength shed from the grace of their terrible vision. That grace had been upon her when she had let the sheriff slap her down; it had been upon her when she had risen time and again from the floor and faced him. But she had trapped herself with her own hunger; to water the long, dry thirst of her faith; her pride had made a bargain which her flesh could not keep. Her having told the names of Johnny-Boy's comrades was but an incident in a deeper horror. She stood up and looked at the floor while call and counter-call, loyalty and counter-loyalty struggled in her soul. Mired she was between two abandoned worlds, living, but dying without the strength of the grace that either gave. The clearer she felt it the fuller did something well up from the depths of her for release; the more urgent did she feel the need to fling into her black sky another star, another hope, one more terrible vision to give her the strength to live and act. Softly and restlessly she walked about the kitchen, feeling herself naked against the night, the rain, the world; and shamed whenever the thought of Reva's love crossed her mind. She lifted her empty hands and looked at her writhing fingers. Lawd, whut kin Ah do now? She could still wade the creek and get to Foleys Woods before Booker. And then what? How could she manage to see Johnny-Boy or Booker? Again she heard the sheriff's threatening voice: Git yuh a sheet, cause hes gonna be dead! The sheet! Thas it, the *sheet!* Her whole being leaped with will; the long years of her life bent toward a moment of focus, a point. Ah kin go wid mah sheet! Ahll be doin whut he said! Lawd Gawd in Heaven, Ahma go lika nigger woman wid mah windin sheet t git mah dead son! But then what? She stood straight and smiled grimly; she had in her heart the whole meaning of her life; her entire personality was poised on the brink of a total act. Ah know! Ah *know!* She thought of Johnny-Boy's gun in the dresser drawer. Ahll hide the gun in the sheet n go aftah Johnny-Boys body. . . . She tiptoed to her room, eased out the dresser drawer, and got a sheet. Reva was sleeping; the darkness was filled with her quiet breathing. She groped in the drawer and found the gun. She wound the gun in the sheet and held them both under her apron. Then she stole to the bedside and watched Reva. Lawd, hep her! But mabbe shes bettah off. This had t happen sometime . . . She n Johnny-Boy couldna been together in this here South . . . N Ah couldnt tell her about Booker. Itll come out awright n she wont nevah know. Reva's trust would never be shaken. She caught her breath as the shucks in the mattress rustled dryly; then all was quiet and she breathed easily again. She tiptoed to the door, down the hall, and stood on the porch. Above her the yellow beacon whirled through the rain. She went over the muddy ground, mounted a slope, stopped and looked back at her house. The lamp glowed in her window, and the yellow beacon that swung every few seconds seemed to feed it with light. She turned and started across the fields, holding the gun and sheet tightly, thinking, Po Reva . . . Po critter . . . Shes fas ersleep . . .

VI

For the most part she walked with her eyes half shut, her lips tightly compressed, leaning her body against the wind and the driving rain, feeling the pistol in the sheet sagging cold and heavy in her fingers. Already she was getting wet; it seemed that her feet found every puddle of water that stood between the corn rows.

She came to the edge of the creek and paused, wondering at what point was it low. Taking the sheet from under her apron, she wrapped the gun in it so that her finger could be upon the trigger. Ahll cross here, she thought. At first she did not feel the water; her feet were already wet. But the water grew cold as it came up to her knees; she gasped when it reached her waist. Lawd, this creeks high! When she had passed the middle, she knew that she was out of danger. She came out of the water, climbed a grassy hill, walked on, turned a bend and saw the lights of autos gleaming ahead. Yeah; theys still there! She hurried with her head down. Wondah did Ah beat im here? Lawd, Ah *hope* so! A vivid image of Booker's white face hovered a moment before her eyes and a surging will rose up in her so hard and strong that it vanished. She was among the autos now. From nearby came the hoarse voices of the men.

"Hey, yuh!"

She stopped, nervously clutching the sheet. Two white men with shotguns came toward her.

"Whut in hell yuh doin out here?"

She did not answer.

"Didnt yuh hear somebody speak t yuh?"

"Ahm comin aftah mah son," she said humbly.

"Yo *son?*"

"Yessuh."

"What yo son doin out here?"

"The sheriffs got im."

"Holy Scott! Jim, its the niggers ma!"

"Whut yuh got there?" asked one.

"A sheet."

"A *sheet?*"

"Yessuh."

"Fer whut?"

"The sheriff tol me t bring a sheet t git his body."

"Waal, waal . . ."

"Now, ain tha somethin?"

The white men looked at each other.

"These niggers sho love one ernother," said one.

"N tha ain no lie," said the other.

"Take me t the sheriff," she begged.

"Yuh ain given us *orders,* is yuh?"

"Nawsuh."

"Well take yuh when wes good n ready."

"Yessuh."

"So yuh wan his body?"

"Yessuh."

"Waah, he ain dead yit."

"They gonna kill im," she said.

"Ef he talks they wont."

"He ain gonna talk," she said.

"How yuh know?"

"Cause he ain."

"We got ways of makin niggers talk."

"Yuh ain got no way fer im."

"Yuh thinka lot of that black Red, don yuh?"

"Hes mah son."

"Why don yuh teach im some sense?"

"Hes mah son," she said again.

"Lissen, ol nigger woman, yuh stand there wid yo hair white. Yuh got bettah sense than t believe tha niggers kin make a revolution . . ."

"A black republic," said the other one, laughing.

"Take me t the sheriff," she begged.

"Yuh his ma," said one. "Yuh kin make im talk n tell whose in this thing wid im."

"He ain gonna talk," she said.

"Don yuh wan im t live?"

She did not answer.

"C mon, les take her t Bradley."

They grabbed her arms and she clutched hard at the sheet and gun; they led her toward the crowd in the woods. Her feelings were simple; Booker would not tell; she was there with the gun to see to that. The louder became the voices of the men the deeper became her feeling of wanting to right the mistake she had made; of wanting to fight her way back to solid ground. She would stall for time until Booker showed up. Oh, ef theyll only lemme git close t Johnny-Boy! As they led her near the crowd she saw white faces turning and looking at her and heard a rising clamor of voices.

"Whose tha?"

"A nigger woman!"

"Whut she doin out here?"

"This is his ma!" called one of the men.

"Whut she wans?"

"She brought a sheet t cover his body!"

"He ain dead yit!"

"They tryin t make im talk!"

"But he will be dead soon ef he don open up!"

"Say, look! The niggers ma brought a sheet t cover up his body!"

"Now, ain that sweet?"

"Mabbe she wans t hol a prayer meetin!"

"Did she git a preacher?"

"Say, go git Bradley!"

"O.K.!"

The crowd grew quiet. They looked at her curiously; she felt their cold eyes trying to detect some weakness in her. Humbly, she stood with the sheet covering the gun. She had already accepted all that they could do to her.

The sheriff came.

"So yuh brought yuh sheet, hunh?"

"Yessuh," she whispered.

"Looks like them slaps we gave yuh learned yuh some sense, didnt they?"

She did not answer.

"Yuh don need tha sheet. Yo son ain dead yit," he said, reaching toward her.

She backed away, her eyes wide.

"Naw!"

"Now, lissen, Anty!" he said. "There ain no use in yuh ackin a fool! Go in there n tell tha nigger son of yos t tell us whos in this wid im, see? Ah promise we wont kill im ef he talks. We'll let im git outta town."

"There ain nothin Ah kin tell im," she said.

"Yuh wan us t kill im?"

She did not answer. She saw someone lean toward the sheriff and whisper.

"Bring her erlong," the sheriff said.

They led her to a muddy clearing. The rain streamed down through the ghostly glare of the flashlights. As the men formed a semi-circle she saw Johnny-Boy lying in a trough of mud. He was tied with rope; he lay hunched and one side of his face rested in a pool of black water. His eyes were staring questioningly at her.

"Speak t im," said the sheriff.

If she could only tell him why she was here! But that was impossible; she was close to what she wanted and she stared straight before her with compressed lips.

"Say, nigger!" called the sheriff, kicking Johnny-Boy. "Heres yo ma!"

Johnny-Boy did not move or speak. The sheriff faced her again.

"Lissen, Anty," he said. "Yuh got mo say wid im than anybody. Tell im t talk n hava chance. Whut he wanna pertect the other niggers n white folks fer?"

She slid her finger about the trigger of the gun and looked stonily at the mud.

"Go t him," said the sheriff.

She did not move. Her heart was crying out to answer the amazed question in Johnny-Boy's eyes. But there was no way now.

"Waal, yuhre astin fer it. By Gawd, we gotta way to *make* yuh talk t im," he said, turning away. "Say, Tim, git one of them logs n turn that nigger upside-down n put his legs on it!"

A murmur of assent ran through the crowd. She bit her lips; she knew what that meant.

"Yuh wan yo nigger son crippled?" she heard the sheriff ask.

She did not answer. She saw them roll the log up; they lifted Johnny-Boy and laid him on his face and stomach, then they pulled his legs over the log. His kneecaps rested on the sheer top of the log's back and the toes of his shoes pointed groundward. So absorbed was she in watching that she felt that it was she who was being lifted and made ready for torture.

"Git a crowbar!" said the sheriff.

A tall, lank man got a crowbar from a nearby auto and stood over the log. His jaws worked slowly on a wad of tobacco.

"Now, its up t yuh, Anty," the sheriff said. "Tell the man whut t do!"

She looked into the rain. The sheriff turned.

"Mabbe she think wes playin. Ef she don say nothin, then break em at the kneecaps!"

"O.K., Sheriff!"

She stood waiting for Booker. Her legs felt weak; she wondered if she would be able to wait much longer. Over and over she said to herself, Ef he came now Ahd kill em both!

"She ain saying nothin, Sheriff!"

"Waal, Gawddammit, let im have it!"

The crowbar came down and Johnny-Boy's body lunged in the mud and water. There was a scream. She swayed, holding tight to the gun and sheet.

"Hol im! Git the other leg!"

The crowbar fell again. There was another scream.

"Yuh break em?" asked the sheriff.

The tall man lifted Johnny-Boy's legs and let them drop limply again, dropping rearward from the kneecaps. Johnny-Boy's body lay still. His head had rolled to one side and she could not see his face.

"Jus lika broke sparrow wing," said the man, laughing softly.

Then Johnny-Boy's face turned to her; he screamed.

"Go way, ma! Go way!"

It was the first time she had heard his voice since she had come out to the woods; she all but lost control of herself. She started violently forward, but the sheriff's arm checked her.

"Aw, naw! Yuh had yo chance!" He turned to Johnny-Boy. "She kin go ef yuh talk."

"Mistah, he ain gonna talk," she said.

"Go way, ma!" said Johnny-Boy.

"Shoot im! Don make im suffah so," she begged.

"He'll either talk or he'll never hear yuh ergin." the sheriff said. "Theres other things we kin do t im."

She said nothing.

"Whut yuh come here fer, ma?" Johnny-Boy sobbed.

"Ahm gonna split his eardrums," the sheriff said. "Ef yuh got anythin to say t im yuh bettah say it *now!*"

She closed her eyes. She heard the sheriff's feet sucking in mud. Ah could save im! She opened her eyes; there were shouts of eagerness from the crowd as it pushed in closer.

"Bus em, Sheriff!"

"Fix im so he cant hear!"

"He knows how t do it, too!"

"He busted a Jew boy tha way once!"

She saw the sheriff stoop over Johnny-Boy, place his flat palm over one ear and strike his fist against it with all his might. He placed his palm over the other ear and struck again. Johnny-Boy moaned, his head rolling from side to side, his eyes showing white amazement in a world without sound.

"Yuh wouldnt talk t im when yuh had the chance," said the sheriff. "Try n talk now."

She felt warm tears on her cheeks. She longed to shoot Johnny-Boy and let him go. But if she did that they would take the gun from her, and Booker would tell who the others were. Lawd, hep me! The men were talking loudly now, as though the main business was over. It seemed ages that she stood there watching Johnny-Boy roll and whimper in his world of silence.

"Say, Sheriff, heres somebody lookin fer yuh!"

"Who is it?"

"Ah don know!"

"Bring em in!"

She stiffened and looked around wildly, holding the gun tight. Is tha Booker? Then she held still, feeling that her excitement might betray her. Mabbe Ah kin shoot em both! Mabbe Ah kin shoot *twice!* The sheriff stood in front of her, waiting. The crowd parted and she saw Booker hurrying forward.

"Ah know em all, Sheriff!" he called.

He came full into the muddy clearing where Johnny-Boy lay.

"Yuh mean yuh got the names?"

"Sho! The ol nigger . . ."

She saw his lips hang open and silent when he saw her. She stepped forward and raised the sheet.

"Whut . . ."

She fired, once; then without pausing, she turned, hearing them yell. She aimed at Johnny-Boy, but they had their arms around her, bearing her to the ground, clawing at the sheet in her hand. She glimpsed Booker lying sprawled in the mud, on his face, his hands stretched out before him; then a cluster of yelling men blotted him out. She lay without struggling, looking upward through the rain at the white faces above her. And she was suddenly at peace; they were not a white mountain now; they were not pushing her any longer to the edge of life. Its awright . . .

"She shot Booker!"

"She hada gun in the sheet!"

"She shot im right thu the head!"

"Whut she shoot im fer?"

"Kill the bitch!"

"Ah *thought* somethin wuz wrong bout her!"

"Ah wuz fer givin it t her from the firs!"

"Thas whut yuh git fer treatin a nigger nice!"

"Say, Bookers dead!"

She stopped looking into the white faces, stopped listening. She waited, giving up her life before they took it from her; she had done what she wanted. Ef only Johnny-Boy . . . She looked at him; he lay looking at her with tired eyes. Ef she could only tell im! But he lay already buried in a grave of silence.

"Whut yuh kill im fer, hunh?"

It was the sheriff's voice; she did not answer.

"Mabbe she wuz shootin at yuh, Sheriff?"

"Whut yuh kill im fer?"

She felt the sheriff's foot come into her side; she closed her eyes.

"Yuh black bitch!"

"Let her have it!"

"Yuh reckon she foun out bout Booker?"

"She mighta."

"Jesus Chris, whut yuh dummies *waitin* on!"

"Yeah, kill her!"

"Kill em *both!*"

"Let her know her nigger sons dead firs!"

She turned her head toward Johnny-Boy; he lay looking puzzled in a world beyond the reach of voices. At leas he cant hear, she thought.

"C mon, let im have it!"

She listened to hear what Johnny-Boy could not. They came, two of them, one right behind the other; so close together that they sounded like one shot. She did not look at Johnny-Boy now; she looked at the white faces of the men, hard and wet in the glare of the flashlights.

"Yuh hear tha, nigger woman?"

"Did tha surprise im? Hes in hell now wonderin whut hit im!"

"C mon! Give it t her, Sheriff!"

"Lemme shoot her, Sheriff! It wuz mah pal she shot!"

"Awright, Pete! Thas fair ernuff!"

She gave up as much of her life as she could before they took it from her. But the sound of the shot and the streak of fire that tore its way through her chest forced her to live again, intensely. She had not moved, save for the slight jarring impact of the bullet. She felt the heat of her own blood warming her cold, wet back. She yearned suddenly to talk. "Yuh didnt git whut yuh wanted! N yuh ain gonna nevah git it! Yuh didnt kill me; Ah come here by mahsef . . ." She felt rain falling into her wide-open, dimming eyes and heard faint voices. Her lips moved soundlessly. *Yuh didnt git yuh didnt yuh didnt . . .* Focused and pointed she was, buried in the depths of her star, swallowed in its peace and strength; and not feeling her flesh growing cold, cold as the rain that fell from the invisible sky upon the doomed living and the dead that never dies.

THE END

1937, 1939

Eudora Welty
(1909–   )

Born and raised in Jackson, Mississippi, Eudora Welty's writing is suffused with the scents, colors, and sounds of Mississippi. She is ranked with William Faulkner as one of the most distinctly southern voices to have emerged from the Southern Renaissance. Her observations of her fellow Mississippians are unerring. She is a master of the telling detail that carries the reader along with her into the lives of her characters, into the perfumed beauty parlors and sweltering summer streets where parasoled southern character assassins meet to gossip like dueling butterflies. But while critics admire the true tones of her characters' regional dialect, just as often they praise her transcendence of the limits of regionalism. Her story "Petrified Man" (1941) examines in almost clinical detail the very localized vulgarity Welty observed in and around Jackson. Lee J. Richmond called this story "one of the most pitiless indictments of the venal spirit of modern civilization." Welty's gift for simultaneously evoking the particular and the universal won her a Pulitzer Prize in 1973 for her novel *The Optimist's Daughter* (1972).

Welty has been showered with awards, honors, and fellowships since the 1940s but was not an immediate success early in her career. After attending the Mississippi State College for Women, she transferred to the University of Wisconsin, where she majored in English and graduated in 1929. As the depression economy spiraled, her father urged her to acquire some practical means of supporting herself. To that end she studied advertising at the Columbia University School of Business for a year, but her career did not prosper in New York. She returned to Mississippi in 1931. After her father's death that year, she worked part time for newspapers and radio stations. In 1933 she began working as a publicity agent for the federal Works Progress Administration, traveling throughout Mississippi to write feature stories on the various WPA projects. She was both fascinated and appalled by what she heard in interviews and saw from train windows. However, rather than avert her gaze, she developed her skills as a photographer, recording scenes to study in the evenings. Eventually, she shared her vision of economic disaster: in 1936 her photographs were shown in New York; in 1971 she published *One Time, One Place: Mississippi in the Depression, a Snapshot Album*, and in 1989, *Eudora Welty: Photographs*.

She wrote short stories throughout the 1930s, but none were accepted for publication until 1936, when "The Death of a Traveling Salesman" appeared in the "little" magazine *Manuscript*. Soon after that breakthrough she was discovered and encouraged by Robert Penn Warren and Cleanth Brooks, editors of the *Southern Review*. By 1940 her work had impressed the writer and editor Ford Madox Ford and Katherine Anne Porter, who helped her publish her first collection of stories, *A Curtain of Green* (1941). This collection includes the story "A Worn Path," which won the O. Henry Memorial Contest award in 1942. Welty won the same award in 1943 for the title story of her second collection, *The Wide Net and Other Stories* (1943). She also published a novella, *The Robber Bridegroom*, in 1942. The critical success of these first three books confirmed her place in the national literary scene. She broadened her audience when two of her works were adapted for the stage: in 1956 Jerome Chodorov and Joseph Fields produced a theatrical version of her novella *The Ponder Heart* (1954), and in 1974 *The Robber Bridegroom* was made into a Broadway musical. Both productions were successful, and Welty's reputation continued to grow despite a hiatus in publishing new work, lasting from 1955, when *The Bride of the Innisfallen and Other Stories* appeared, to 1970, when she finally published her longest novel, *Losing Battles*. The action of that novel, set in Tishomingo County, Mississippi, occurs in only two days' time at a family reunion, and flashbacks provide the necessary background information. Welty explains in *Eudora Welty*, "I was trying to describe what the characters' lives were like without benefit of any editorial comment at all, or any interior description. I wanted things shown by speech, by action, and by setting, location."

Although Welty has always been very open and articulate in discussing her experiences and techniques as a creative writer, she has rarely discussed her personal life. Rather than fictionalizing her own biography, Welty attempts to imagine her way into the lives of characters completely unlike herself. At times her characters obtrude themselves upon her, uninvited. As she states in *Eudora Welty*, "Technique springs out of the doing. . . . It's

Eudora Welty reproduced images of the South in her writings and photographs. She shot this picture of Fayette, Mississippi, in the 1930s.

after the fact of writing a story that I realize what it has taught me. . . . Writing fiction, I am interpreting every minute, but always by way of the characters' own words and acts. . . . I am in the characters' minds all the time."

In her essay "Place in Fiction" (1957) Welty explains that place "is the named, identified, concrete, exact and exacting, and therefore credible, gathering-spot of all that has been felt, is about to be experienced." With a painterly eye and a perfectly tuned ear, she captures her experiences of her chosen place in her fiction, making the horrific, the hilarious, and the rapturously beautiful equally credible. She varies her placement of the narrative voice, most devastatingly satirizing her grotesque characters from a distance, and exploring other characters from within. Her story "June Recital" (1947) is a narrative tour de force mingling memories with present perceptions, moving from the point of view of a young boy (hanging upside down from a tree, looking into a window of the house next door) to that of his sister (viewing the same scene from inside her own bedroom window).

Whether Welty writes from inside, outside, or in between her characters, she maintains a disciplined distinction between art and autobiography. Requests for an autobiography discouraged her, as she believed that a writer's work, and not an account of his or her life, should be "everything." Her readers were thus astonished when she published her autobiography, *One Writer's Beginnings*, in 1984. Based upon a series of lectures she gave at Harvard University, the book quickly became a bestseller—the first ever published by Harvard University Press, and a demonstration of Welty's broad appeal within, and outside of, academia.

Suggested Readings: *The Robber Bridegroom,* 1942. *Delta Wedding,* 1946. *The Ponder Heart,* 1954. *Losing Battles,* 1970. *The Optimist's Daughter,* 1972. *One Writer's Beginning,* 1984. *Shenandoah: Special Eudora Welty Issue,* XX, No. 2, (Spring) 1969. J. F. Desmond, ed., *A Still Moment: Essays on the Art of Eudora Welty,* 1978. P. W. Prenshaw, ed., *Eudora Welty: Critical Essays,* 1979. M. Kreyling, *Eudora Welty's Achievement of Order,* 1980.

Text Used: *The Collected Stories of Eudora Welty,* 1980.

PETRIFIED MAN*

"Reach in my purse and git me a cigarette without no powder in it if you kin, Mrs. Fletcher, honey," said Leota to her ten o'clock shampoo-and-set customer. "I don't like no perfumed cigarettes."

Mrs. Fletcher gladly reached over to the lavender shelf under the lavender-framed mirror, shook a hair net loose from the clasp of the patent-leather bag, and slapped her hand down quickly on a powder puff which burst out when the purse was opened.

"Why, look at the peanuts, Leota!" said Mrs. Fletcher in her marvelling voice.

"Honey, them goobers has been in my purse a week if they's been in it a day. Mrs. Pike bought them peanuts."

"Who's Mrs. Pike?" asked Mrs. Fletcher, settling back. Hidden in this den of curling fluid and henna packs, separated by a lavender swingdoor from the other customers, who were being gratified in other booths, she could give her curiosity its freedom. She looked expectantly at the black part in Leota's yellow curls as she bent to light the cigarette.

"Mrs. Pike is this lady from New Orleans," said Leota, puffing, and pressing into Mrs. Fletcher's scalp with strong red-nailed fingers. "A friend, not a customer. You see, like maybe I told you last time, me and Fred and Sal and Joe all had us a fuss, so Sal and Joe up and moved out, so we didn't do a thing but rent out their room. So we rented it to Mrs. Pike. And Mr. Pike." She flicked an ash into the basket of dirty towels. "Mrs. Pike is a very decided blonde. *She* bought me the peanuts."

"She must be cute," said Mrs. Fletcher.

"Honey, 'cute' ain't the word for what she is. I'm tellin' you, Mrs. Pike is attractive. She has her a good time. She's got a sharp eye out, Mrs. Pike has."

She dashed the comb through the air, and paused dramatically as a cloud of Mrs. Fletcher's hennaed hair floated out of the lavender teeth like a small storm-cloud.

"Hair fallin'."

"Aw, Leota."

"Uh-huh, commencin' to fall out," said Leota, combing again, and letting fall another cloud.

"Is it any dandruff in it?" Mrs. Fletcher was frowning, her hair-line eyebrows diving down toward her nose, and her wrinkled, beady-lashed eyelids batting with concentration.

"Nope." She combed again. "Just fallin' out."

* First collected in *A Curtain of Green* (1941).

"Bet it was that last perm'nent you gave me that did it," Mrs. Fletcher said cruelly. "Remember you cooked me fourteen minutes."

"You had fourteen minutes comin' to you," said Leota with finality.

"Bound to be somethin'," persisted Mrs. Fletcher. "Dandruff, dandruff. I couldn't of caught a thing like that from Mr. Fletcher, could I?"

"Well," Leota answered at last, "you know what I heard in here yestiddy, one of Thelma's ladies was settin' over yonder in Thelma's booth gittin' a machineless, and I don't mean to insist or insinuate or anything, Mrs. Fletcher, but Thelma's lady just happ'med to throw out—I forgotten what she was talkin' about at the time—that you was p-r-e-g., and lots of times that'll make your hair do awful funny, fall out and God knows what all. It just ain't our fault, is the way I look at it."

There was a pause. The women stared at each other in the mirror.

"Who was it?" demanded Mrs. Fletcher.

"Honey, I really couldn't say," said Leota, "Not that you look it."

"Where's Thelma? I'll get it out of her," said Mrs. Fletcher.

"Now, honey, I wouldn't go and git mad over a little thing like that," Leota said, combing hastily, as though to hold Mrs. Fletcher down by the hair. "I'm sure it was somebody didn't mean no harm in the world. How far gone are you?"

"Just wait," said Mrs. Fletcher, and shrieked for Thelma, who came in and took a drag from Leota's cigarette.

"Thelma, honey, throw your mind back to yestiddy if you kin," said Leota, drenching Mrs. Fletcher's hair with a thick fluid and catching the overflow in a cold wet towel at her neck.

"Well, I got my lady half wound for a spiral," said Thelma doubtfully.

"This won't take but a minute," said Leota. "Who is it you got in there, old Horse Face? Just cast your mind back and try to remember who your lady was yestiddy who happ'm to mention that my customer was pregnant, that's all. She's dead to know."

Thelma drooped her blood-red lips and looked over Mrs. Fletcher's head into the mirror. "Why, honey, I ain't got the faintest," she breathed. "I really don't recollect the faintest. But I'm sure she meant no harm. I declare, I forgot my hair finally got combed and thought it was a stranger behind me."

"Was it that Mrs. Hutchinson?" Mrs. Fletcher was tensely polite.

"Mrs. Hutchinson? Oh, Mrs. Hutchinson." Thelma batted her eyes. "Naw, precious, she come on Thursday and didn't ev'm mention your name. I doubt if she ev'm knows you're on the way."

"Thelma!" cried Leota staunchly.

"All I know is, whoever it is 'll be sorry some day. Why, I just barely knew it myself!" cried Mrs. Fletcher. "Just let her wait!"

"Why? What're you gonna do to her?"

It was a child's voice, and the women looked down. A little boy was making tents with aluminum wave pinchers on the floor under the sink.

"Billy Boy, hon, mustn't bother nice ladies," Leota smiled. She slapped him brightly and behind her back waved Thelma out of the booth. "Ain't Billy Boy a sight? Only three years old and already just nuts about the beauty-parlor business."

"I never saw him here before," said Mrs. Fletcher, still unmollified.

"He ain't been here before; that's how come," said Leota. "He belongs to Mrs. Pike. She got her a job but it was Fay's Millinery. He oughtn't to try on those ladies' hats, they come down over his eyes like I don't know what. They just git to look ridiculous, that's what, an' of course he's gonna put 'em on: hats. They tole Mrs. Pike they didn't appreciate him hangin' around there. Here, he couldn't hurt a thing."

"Well! I don't like children that much," said Mrs. Fletcher.

"Well!" said Leota, moodily.

"Well! I'm almost tempted not to have this one," said Mrs. Fletcher. "That Mrs. Hutchinson! Just looks straight through you when she sees you on the street and then spits at you behind your back."

"Mr. Fletcher would beat you on the head if you didn't have it now," said Leota reasonably. "After going this far."

Mrs. Fletcher sat up straight. "Mr. Fletcher can't do a thing with me."

"He can't!" Leota winked at herself in the mirror.

"No, siree, he can't. If he so much as raises his voice against me, he knows good and well I'll have one of my sick headaches, and then I'm just not fit to live with. And if I really look that pregnant already—"

"Well, now, honey, I just want you to know—I habm't told any of my ladies and I ain't goin' to tell 'em—even that you're losin' your hair. You just get you one of those Stork-a-Lure dresses and stop worryin'. What people don't know don't hurt nobody, as Mrs. Pike says."

"Did you tell Mrs. Pike?" asked Mrs. Fletcher sulkily.

"Well, Mrs. Fletcher, look, you ain't ever goin' to lay eyes on Mrs. Pike or her lay eyes on you, so what diffunce does it make in the long run?"

"I knew it!" Mrs. Fletcher deliberately nodded her head so as to destroy a ringlet Leota was working on behind her ear. "Mrs. Pike!"

Leota sighed. "I reckon I might as well tell you. It wasn't any more Thelma's lady tole me you was pregnant than a bat."

"Not Mrs. Hutchinson?"

"Naw, Lord! It was Mrs. Pike."

"Mrs. Pike!" Mrs. Fletcher could only sputter and let curling fluid roll into her ear. "How could Mrs. Pike possibly know I was pregnant or otherwise, when she doesn't even know me? The nerve of some people!"

"Well, here's how it was. Remember Sunday?"

"Yes," said Mrs. Fletcher.

"Sunday, Mrs. Pike an' me was all by ourself. Mr. Pike and Fred had gone over to Eagle Lake, sayin' they was goin' to catch 'em some fish, but they didn't a course. So we was settin' in Mrs. Pike's car, it's a 1939 Dodge—"

"1939, eh," said Mrs. Fletcher.

"—An' we was gettin' us a Jax beer apiece—that's the beer that Mrs. Pike says is made right in N.O.,[1] so she won't drink no other kind. So I seen you drive up to the drugstore an' run in for just a secont, leavin' I reckon Mr. Fletcher in the car, an' come runnin' out with looked like a perscription. So I says to Mrs. Pike, just to be makin' talk, 'Right yonder's Mrs. Fletcher, and I reckon that's Mr. Fletcher—she's one of my regular customers,' I says."

"I had on a figured print," said Mrs. Fletcher tentatively.

"You sure did," agreed Leota. "So Mrs. Pike, she give you a good look—she's very observant, a good judge of character, cute as a minute, you know—and she says, 'I bet you another Jax that lady's three months on the way.'"

"What gall!" said Mrs. Fletcher. "Mrs. Pike!"

---

[1] New Orleans.

"Mrs. Pike ain't goin' to bite you," said Leota. "Mrs. Pike is a lovely girl, you'd be crazy about her, Mrs. Fletcher. But she can't sit still a minute. We went to the travellin' freak show yestiddy after work. I got through early—nine o'clock. In the vacant store next door. What, you ain't been?"

"No, I despise freaks," declared Mrs. Fletcher.

"Aw. Well, honey, talkin' about bein' pregnant an' all, you ought to see those twins in a bottle, you really owe it to yourself."

"What twins?" asked Mrs. Fletcher out of the side of her mouth.

"Well, honey, they got these two twins in a bottle, see? Born joined plumb together—dead a course." Leota dropped her voice into a soft lyrical hum. "They was about this long—pardon—must of been full time, all right, wouldn't you say?—an' they had these two heads an' two faces an' four arms an' four legs, all kind of joined *here*. See, this face looked this-a-way, and the other face looked that-a-way, over their shoulder, see. Kinda pathetic."

"Glah!" said Mrs. Fletcher disapprovingly.

"Well, ugly? Honey, I mean to tell you—their parents was first cousins and all like that. Billy Boy, git me a fresh towel from off Teeny's stack—this 'n's wringin' wet—an' quit ticklin' my ankles with that curler. I declare! He don't miss nothin'."

"Me and Mr. Fletcher aren't one speck of kin, or he could never of had me," said Mrs. Fletcher placidly.

"Of course not!" protested Leota. "Neither is me an' Fred, not that we know of. Well, honey, what Mrs. Pike liked was the pygmies. They've got these pygmies down there, too, an' Mrs. Pike was just wild about 'em. You know, the teeniniest men in the universe? Well, honey, they can just rest back on their little bohunkus an' roll around an' you can't hardly tell if they're sittin' or standin'. That'll give you some idea. They're about forty-two years old. Just suppose it was your husband!"

"Well, Mr. Fletcher is five foot nine and one half," said Mrs. Fletcher quickly.

"Fred's five foot ten," said Leota, "but I tell him he's still a shrimp, account of I'm so tall." She made a deep wave over Mrs. Fletcher's other temple with the comb. "Well, these pygmies are a kind of a dark brown, Mrs. Fletcher. Not bad lookin' for what they are, you know."

"I wouldn't care for them," said Mrs. Fletcher. "What does that Mrs. Pike see in them?"

"Aw, I don't know," said Leota. "She's just cute, that's all. But they got this man, this petrified man, that ever'thing ever since he was nine years old, when it goes through his digestion, see, somehow Mrs. Pike says it goes to his joints and has been turning to stone."

"How awful!" said Mrs. Fletcher.

"He's forty-two too. That looks like a bad age."

"Who said so, that Mrs. Pike? I bet she's forty-two," said Mrs. Fletcher.

"Naw," said Leota, "Mrs. Pike's thirty-three, born in January, an Aquarian. He could move his head—like this. A course his head and mind ain't a joint, so to speak, and I guess his stomach ain't, either—not yet, anyways. But see—his food, he eats it, and it goes down, see, and then he digests it"—Leota rose on her toes for an instant—"and it goes out to his joints and before you can say 'Jack Robinson,'[2] it's stone—pure stone. He's turning to stone. How'd you like to be

---

[2] A saying thought to derive from a guest known for leaving as suddenly as he arrived; according to James Orchard Halliwell's *Dictionary of Archaic and Provincial Words* (1847), it appeared in a play: "A warke it ys as easie to be doone / As 'tys to saye *Jacke! robys on.*"

married to a guy like that? All he can do, he can move his head just a quarter of an inch. A course he *looks* just *terrible*."

"I should think he would," said Mrs. Fletcher frostily. "Mr. Fletcher takes bending exercises every night of the world. I make him."

"All Fred does is lay around the house like a rug. I wouldn't be surprised if he woke up some day and couldn't move. The petrified man just sat there moving his quarter of an inch though," said Leota reminiscently.

"Did Mrs. Pike like the petrified man?" asked Mrs. Fletcher.

"Not as much as she did the others," said Leota deprecatingly. "And then she likes a man to be a good dresser, and all that."

"Is Mr. Pike a good dresser?" asked Mrs. Fletcher sceptically.

"Oh, well, yeah," said Leota, "but he's twelve or fourteen years older'n her. She ast Lady Evangeline about him."

"Who's Lady Evangeline?" asked Mrs. Fletcher.

"Well, it's this mind reader they got in the freak show," said Leota. "Was real good. Lady Evangeline is her name, and if I had another dollar I wouldn't do a thing but have my other palm read. She had what Mrs. Pike said was the 'sixth mind' but she had the worst manicure I ever saw on a living person."

"What did she tell Mrs. Pike?" asked Mrs. Fletcher.

"She told her Mr. Pike was as true to her as he could be and besides, would come into some money."

"Humph!" said Mrs. Fletcher. "What does he do?"

"I can't tell," said Leota, "because he don't work. Lady Evangeline didn't tell me enough about my nature or anything. And I would like to go back and find out some more about this boy. Used to go with this boy until he got married to this girl. Oh, shoot, that was about three and a half years ago, when you was still goin' to the Robert E. Lee Beauty Shop in Jackson.[3] He married her for her money. Another fortune-teller tole me that at the time. So I'm not in love with him any more, anyway, besides being married to Fred, but Mrs. Pike thought, just for the hell of it, see, to ask Lady Evangeline was he happy."

"Does Mrs. Pike know everything about you already?" asked Mrs. Fletcher unbelievingly. "Mercy!"

"Oh, yeah, I tole her ever'thing about ever'thing, from now on back to I don't know when—to when I first started goin' out," said Leota. "So I ast Lady Evangeline for one of my questions, was he happily married, and she says, just like she was glad I ask her, 'Honey,' she says, 'naw, he idn't. You write down this day, March 8, 1941,' she says, 'and mock it down: three years from today him and her won't be occupyin' the same bed.' There it is, up on the wall with them other dates—see, Mrs. Fletcher? And she says, 'Child, you ought to be glad you didn't git him, because he's so mercenary.' So I'm glad I married Fred. He sure ain't mercenary, money don't mean a thing to him. But I sure would like to go back and have my other palm read."

"Did Mrs. Pike believe in what the fortune-teller said?" asked Mrs. Fletcher in a superior tone of voice.

"Lord, yes, she's from New Orleans. Ever'body in New Orleans believes ever'thing spooky. One of 'em in New Orleans before it was raided says to Mrs. Pike one summer she was goin' to go from State to State and meet some grey-headed men, and, sure enough, she says she went on a beautician convention up to Chicago. . . ."

---

[3] Jackson, Mississippi.

"Oh!" said Mrs. Fletcher. "Oh, is Mrs. Pike a beautician too?"

"Sure she is," protested Leota. "She's a beautician. I'm goin' to git her in here if I can. Before she married. But it don't leave you. She says sure enough, there was three men who was a very large part of making her trip what it was, and they all three had grey in their hair and they went in six States. Got Christmas cards from 'em. Billy Boy, go see if Thelma's got any dry cotton. Look how Mrs. Fletcher's a-drippin'."

"Where did Mrs. Pike meet Mr. Pike?" asked Mrs. Fletcher primly.

"On another train," said Leota.

"I met Mr. Fletcher, or rather he met me, in a rental library," said Mrs. Fletcher with dignity, as she watched the net come down over her head.

"Honey, me an' Fred, we met in a rumble seat[4] eight months ago and we was practically on what you might call the way to the altar inside of half an hour," said Leota in a guttural voice, and bit a bobby pin open. "Course it don't last. Mrs. Pike says nothin' like that ever lasts."

"Mr. Fletcher and myself are as much in love as the day we married," said Mrs. Fletcher belligerently as Leota stuffed cotton into her ears.

"Mrs. Pike says it don't last," repeated Leota in a louder voice. "Now go git under the dryer. You can turn yourself on, can't you? I'll be back to comb you out. Durin' lunch I promised to give Mrs. Pike a facial. You know—free. Her bein' in the business, so to speak."

"I bet she needs one," said Mrs. Fletcher, letting the swing-door fly back against Leota. "Oh, pardon me."

A week later, on time for her appointment, Mrs. Fletcher sank heavily into Leota's chair after first removing a drugstore rental book, called *Life Is Like That,*[5] from the seat. She stared in a discouraged way into the mirror.

"You can tell it when I'm sitting down, all right," she said.

Leota seemed preoccupied and stood shaking out a lavender cloth. She began to pin it around Mrs. Fletcher's neck in silence.

"I said you sure can tell it when I'm sitting straight on and coming at you this way," Mrs. Fletcher said.

"Why, honey, naw you can't," said Leota gloomily, "Why, I'd never know. If somebody was to come up to me on the street and say, 'Mrs. Fletcher is pregnant!' I'd say, 'Heck, she don't look it to me.'"

"If a certain party hadn't found it out and spread it around, it wouldn't be too late even now," said Mrs. Fletcher frostily, but Leota was almost choking her with the cloth, pinning it so tight, and she couldn't speak clearly. She paddled her hands in the air until Leota wearily loosened her.

"Listen, honey, you're just a virgin compared to Mrs. Montjoy," Leota was going on, still absent-minded. She bent Mrs. Fletcher back in the chair and, sighing, tossed liquid from a teacup onto her head and dug both hands into her scalp. "You know Mrs. Montjoy—her husband's that premature-grey-headed fella?"

"She's in the Trojan Garden Club, is all I know," said Mrs. Fletcher.

"Well, honey," said Leota, but in a weary voice, "she come in here not the week before and not the day before she had her baby—she come in here the very selfsame day, I mean to tell you. Child, we was all plumb scared to death. There

---

[4] In early-model cars, an open seat that can be folded away when not in use.
[5] A book by W. B. Creighton.

she was! Come for her shampoo an' set. Why, Mrs. Fletcher, in an hour an' twenty minutes she was layin' up there in the Babtist Hospital with a seb'm-pound son. It was that close a shave. I declare, if I hadn't been so tired I would of drank up a bottle of gin that night."

"What gall," said Mrs. Fletcher. "I never knew her at all well."

"See, her husband was waitin' outside in the car, and her bags was all packed an' in the back seat, an' she was all ready, 'cept she wanted her shampoo an' set. An' havin' one pain right after another. Her husband kep' comin' in here, scared-like, but couldn't do nothin' with her a course. She yelled bloody murder, too, but she always yelled her head off when I give her a perm'nent."

"She must of been crazy," said Mrs. Fletcher. "How did she look?"

"Shoot!" said Leota.

"Well, I can guess," said Mrs. Fletcher. "Awful."

"Just wanted to look pretty while she was havin' her baby, is all," said Leota airily. "Course, we was glad to give the lady what she was after—that's our motto—but I bet a hour later she wasn't payin' no mind to them little end curls. I bet she wasn't thinkin' about she ought to have on a net. It wouldn't of done her no good if she had."

"No, I don't suppose it would," said Mrs. Fletcher.

"Yeah man! She was a-yellin'. Just like when I give her perm'nent."

"Her husband ought to make her behave. Don't it seem that way to you?" asked Mrs. Fletcher. "He ought to put his foot down."

"Ha," said Leota. "A lot he could do. Maybe some women is soft."

"Oh, you mistake me, I don't mean for her to get soft—far from it! Women have to stand up for themselves, or there's just no telling. But now you take me—I ask Mr. Fletcher's advice now and then, and he appreciates it, especially on something important, like is it time for a permanent—not that I've told him about the baby. He says, 'Why, dear, go ahead!' Just ask their *advice*."

"Huh! If I ever ast Fred's advice we'd be floatin' down the Yazoo River[6] on a houseboat or somethin' by this time," said Leota. "I'm sick of Fred. I told him to go over to Vicksburg."

"Is he going?" demanded Mrs. Fletcher.

"Sure. See, the fortune-teller—I went back and had my other palm read, since we've got to rent the room agin—said my lover was goin' to work in Vicksburg, so I don't know who she could mean, unless she meant Fred. And Fred ain't workin' here—that much is so."

"Is he going to work in Vicksburg?" asked Mrs. Fletcher. "And—"

"Sure. Lady Evangeline said so. Said the future is going to be brighter than the present. He don't want to go, but I ain't gonna put up with nothin' like that. Lays around the house an' bulls—did bull—with that good-for-nothin' Mr. Pike. He says if he goes who'll cook, but I says I never get to eat anyway—not meals. Billy Boy, take Mrs. Grover that *Screen Secrets* and leg it."

Mrs. Fletcher heard stamping feet go out the door.

"Is that that Mrs. Pike's little boy here again?" she asked, sitting up gingerly.

"Yeah, that's still him." Leota stuck out her tongue.

Mrs. Fletcher could hardly believe her eyes. "Well! How's Mrs. Pike, your attractive new friend with the sharp eyes who spreads it around town that perfect strangers are pregnant?" she asked in a sweetened tone.

---

[6] A river in western Mississippi that flows into the Mississippi River at Vicksburg.

"Oh, Mizriz Pike." Leota combed Mrs. Fletcher's hair with heavy strokes.

"You act like you're tired," said Mrs. Fletcher.

"Tired? Feel like its four o'clock in the afternoon already," said Leota. "I ain't told you the awful luck we had, me and Fred? It's the worst thing you ever heard of. Maybe *you* think Mrs. Pike's got sharp eyes. Shoot, there's a limit! Well, you know, we rented out our room to this Mr. and Mrs. Pike from New Orleans when Sal an' Joe Fentress got mad at us 'cause they drank up some home-brew we had in the closet—Sal an' Joe did. So, a week ago Sat'day Mr. and Mrs. Pike moved in. Well, I kinda fixed up the room, you know—put a sofa pillow on the couch and picked some ragged robbins[7] and put in a vase, but they never did say they appreciated it. Anyway, then I put some old magazines on the table."

"I think that was lovely," said Mrs. Fletcher.

"Wait. So, come night 'fore last, Fred and this Mr. Pike, who Fred just took up with, was back from they said they was fishin', bein' as neither one of 'em has got a job to his name, and we was all settin' around in their room. So Mrs. Pike was settin' there, readin' a old *Startling G-Man Tales* that was mine, mind you, I'd bought it myself, and all of a sudden she jumps!—into the air—you'd 'a' thought she'd set on a spider—an' says, 'Canfield'—ain't that silly, that's Mr. Pike—'Canfield, my God A'mighty,' she says, 'honey,' she says, 'we're rich, and you won't have to work.' Not that he turned one hand anyway. Well, me and Fred rushes over to her, and Mr. Pike, too, and there she sets, pointin' her finger at a photo in my copy of *Startling G-Man.* 'See that man?' yells Mrs. Pike. 'Remember him, Canfield?' 'Never forget a face,' says Mr. Pike. 'It's Mr. Petrie, that we stayed with him in the apartment next to ours in Toulouse Street in N.O. for six weeks. Mr. Petrie.' 'Well,' says Mrs. Pike, like she can't hold out one secont longer, 'Mr. Petrie is wanted for five hundred dollars cash, for rapin' four women in California, and I know where he is.'"

"Mercy!" said Mrs. Fletcher. "Where was he?"

At some time Leota had washed her hair and now she yanked her up by the back locks and sat her up.

"Know where he was?"

"I certainly don't," Mrs. Fletcher said. Her scalp hurt all over.

Leota flung a towel around the top of her customer's head. "Nowhere else but in that freak show! I saw him just as plain as Mrs. Pike. *He* was the petrified man!"

"Who would ever have thought that!" cried Mrs. Fletcher sympathetically.

"So Mr. Pike says, 'Well whatta you know about that,' an' he looks real hard at the photo and whistles. And she starts dancin' and singin' about their good luck. She meant our bad luck! I made a point of tellin' that fortune-teller the next time I saw her. I said, 'Listen, that magazine was layin' around the house for a month, and there was the freak show runnin' night an' day, not two steps away from my own beauty parlor, with Mr. Petrie just settin' there waitin'. An' it had to be Mr. and Mrs. Pike, almost perfect strangers.'"

"What gall," said Mrs. Fletcher. She was only sitting there, wrapped in a turban, but she did not mind.

"Fortune-tellers don't care. And Mrs. Pike, she goes around actin' like she thinks she was Mrs. God," said Leota. "So they're goin' to leave tomorrow, Mr.

---

[7] Perennial plants of the pink family, with clusters of pink or red flowers.

and Mrs. Pike. And in the meantime I got to keep that mean, bad little old kid here, gettin' under my feet ever' minute of the day an' talkin' back too."

"Have they gotten the five hundred dollars' reward already?" asked Mrs. Fletcher.

"Well," said Leota, "at first Mr. Pike didn't want to do anything about it. Can you feature that? Said he kinda liked that ole bird and said he was real nice to 'em, lent 'em money or somethin'. But Mrs. Pike simply tole him he could just go to hell, and I can see her point. She says, 'You ain't worked a lick in six months, and here I make five hundred dollars in two seconts, and what thanks do I get for it? You go to hell, Canfield,' she says. So," Leota went on in a despondent voice, "they called up the cops and they caught the ole bird, all right, right there in the freak show where I saw him with my own eyes, thinkin' he was petrified. He's the one. Did it under his real name—Mr. Petrie. Four women in California, all in the month of August. So Mrs. Pike gits five hundred dollars. And my magazine, and right next door to my beauty parlor. I cried all night, but Fred said it wasn't a bit of use and to go to sleep, because the whole thing was just a sort of coincidence—you know: can't do nothin' about it. He says it put him clean out of the notion of goin' to Vicksburg for a few days till we rent out the room agin—no tellin' who we'll git this time."

"But can you imagine anybody knowing this old man, that's raped four women?" persisted Mrs. Fletcher, and she shuddered audibly. "Did Mrs. Pike *speak* to him when she met him in the freak show?"

Leota had begun to comb Mrs. Fletcher's hair. "I says to her, I says, 'I didn't notice you fallin' on his neck when he was the petrified man—don't tell me you didn't recognize your fine friend?' And she says, 'I didn't recognize him with that white powder all over his face. He just looked familiar,' Mrs. Pike says, 'and lots of people look familiar.' But she says that ole petrified man did put her in mind of somebody. She wondered who it was! Kep' her awake, which man she'd ever knew it reminded her of. So when she seen the photo, it all come to her. Like a flash. Mr. Petrie. The way he'd turn his head and look at her when she took him in his breakfast."

"Took him in his breakfast!" shrieked Mrs. Fletcher. "Listen—don't tell me. I'd 'a' felt something."

"Four women. I guess those women didn't have the faintest notion at the time they'd be worth a hundred an' twenty-five bucks apiece some day to Mrs. Pike. We ast her how old the fella was then, an' she says he musta had one foot in the grave, at least. Can you beat it?"

"Not really petrified at all, of course," said Mrs. Fletcher meditatively. She drew herself up. "I'd 'a' felt something," she said proudly.

"Shoot! I did feel somethin'," said Leota. "I tole Fred when I got home I felt so funny. I said, 'Fred, that ole petrified man sure did leave me with a funny feelin'.' He says, 'Funny-haha or funny-peculiar?' and I says, 'Funny-peculiar.'" She pointed her comb into the air emphatically.

"I'll bet you did," said Mrs. Fletcher.

They both heard a crackling noise.

Leota screamed, "Billy Boy! What you doin' in my purse?"

"Aw, I'm just eatin' these ole stale peanuts up," said Billy Boy.

"You come here to me!" screamed Leota, recklessly flinging down the comb, which scattered a whole ashtray full of bobby pins and knocked down a row of Coca-Cola bottles. "This is the last straw!"

"I caught him! I caught him!" giggled Mrs. Fletcher. "I'll hold him on my lap. You bad, bad boy, you! I guess I better learn how to spank little old bad boys," she said.

Leota's eleven o'clock customer pushed open the swing-door upon Leota paddling him heartily with the brush, while he gave angry but belittling screams which penetrated beyond the booth and filled the whole curious beauty parlor. From everywhere ladies began to gather round to watch the paddling. Billy Boy kicked both Leota and Mrs. Fletcher as hard as he could, Mrs. Fletcher with her new fixed smile.

Billy Boy stomped through the group of wild-haired ladies and went out the door, but flung back the words, "If you're so smart, why ain't you rich?"

1941

Ralph Ellison
(1914–   )

Ralph Waldo Ellison was born in Oklahoma City in 1914 to Ida Milsap, a maid, and Lewis Ellison, a contractor and small-business owner. Hoping to raise a literary master, they named their son after Emerson. As a teenager Ellison resolved to become a "latter-day Renaissance man," fully educated in both black and white cultural traditions. With his family's encouragement he combined his studies with odd jobs: doing yard work for the conductor of the Oklahoma City orchestra in exchange for instruction in classical music, absorbing black oral narratives from the informal taletellers (cracker-barrels) lounging about the drug store where he swept floors, practicing jazz idioms while playing in dance bands, and reading voraciously. When he entered Alabama's Tuskegee Institute on a scholarship in 1933, he planned to compose symphonies combining classical, jazz, and blues techniques. Ellison's ongoing commitment to cultural synthesis has shaped his aesthetics and his career.

In 1936 Ellison left Tuskegee to sculpt and compose in New York City. Supplementing his income with more odd jobs—in factories, in a psychiatrist's office, in cafeterias—he continued collecting raw materials that he later crafted into symphonic prose incorporating black folklore, surrealism, existentialism, and Freudian dream analysis. After meeting Langston Hughes and Richard Wright, Ellison abandoned sculpture and musical composition in order to write; however, music has retained a seminal place in his work. Like Hughes, Wright, James Baldwin, and more recently August Wilson, Ellison translates the structures and emotional colors of jazz to his experimental narratives. Ellison has continuously attempted to place himself in the white literary tradition without effacing the nontraditional perceptions of a black writer.

Along with Wright and Hughes, Ellison thought he had found a balance of individual freedom and social cooperation in Marxism during the 1930s, but he never joined the Communist party. After he returned from serving in the merchant marines in World War II, he protested the party's intolerance of his need to articulate the black experience of American history. His explorations of his heritage paradoxically mingle echoes of slave narratives and blues lyrics with allusions to Herman Melville, Nathaniel Hawthorne, T. S. Eliot, James Joyce, and Ernest Hemingway. Throughout his career, Ellison has refused to limit himself to a separate but equal literary canon.

His disenchantment with communism finds expression in his satirical portrait of the party in the novel *Invisible Man* (1952), awarded a National Book Award in 1953. The nameless protagonist welcomes the comforting embrace of a radical political group, the Brotherhood, only to discover that the group is founded upon racist principles. In the novel's last pages the Invisible Man is still struggling to define himself in relation to a hostile society. "Battle Royal," commonly published as a short story, forms the first chapter of *Invisible Man* and suggests an overview of the novel as a whole. Long before he encounters the Brotherhood, the Invisible Man hungers for the approving embrace of his hometown's white leaders, an embrace that proves furiously, grotesquely malevolent. In addition to *Invisible Man*, Ellison has published two volumes of essays, *Shadow and Act* (1964) and *Going to the Territory* (1986) and has taught at Bard College and Rutgers and New York Universities.

Suggested Readings: *Shadow and Act*, 1964. *Going to the Territory*, 1986. J. M. Reilly, ed., *Twentieth Century Interpretations of Invisible Man: A Collection of Essays*, 1970. J. F. Trimmer, *A Casebook on Ralph Ellison's Invisible Man*, 1972. J. Hersey, ed., *Ralph Ellison, A Collection of Critical Essays*, 1974. R. B. Stepto, *From Behind the Veil: A Study of Afro-American Narrative*, 1979. R. G. O'Meally, *The Craft of Ralph Ellison*, 1980. R. F. Dietze, *Ralph Ellison: The Genesis of an Artist*, 1982. H. Bloom, ed., *Modern Critical Views: Ralph Ellison*, 1986. K. W. Benston, *Speaking for You: The Vision of Ralph Ellison*, 1987. R. G. O'Meally, ed., *New Essays on Invisible Man*, 1988.

Text Used: *Invisible Man*, 1953.

from   *INVISIBLE MAN**

CHAPTER I: [BATTLE ROYAL]

It goes a long way back, some twenty years. All my life I had been looking for something, and everywhere I turned someone tried to tell me what it was. I accepted their answers too, though they were often in contradiction and even self-contradictory. I was naïve. I was looking for myself and asking everyone except myself questions which I, and only I, could answer. It took me a long time and much painful boomeranging of my expectations to achieve a realization everyone else appears to have been born with: That I am nobody but myself. But first I had to discover that I am an invisible man!

And yet I am no freak of nature, nor of history. I was in the cards, other things having been equal (or unequal) eighty-five years ago. I am not ashamed of my grandparents for having been slaves. I am only ashamed of myself for having at one time been ashamed. About eighty-five years ago[1] they were told that they were free, united with others of our country in everything pertaining to the common good, and, in everything social, separate like the fingers of the hand. And they believed it. They exulted in it. They stayed in their place, worked hard, and brought up my father to do the same. But my grandfather is the one. He was an

---

* First published in 1947; with the addition of a transitional paragraph at the end, the story became Chapter 1 of *Invisible Man* (1952). The ellipses are Ellison's.
[1] The Emancipation Proclamation was issued in 1863.

odd old guy, my grandfather, and I am told I take after him. It was he who caused the trouble. On his deathbed he called my father to him and said, "Son, after I'm gone I want you to keep up the good fight. I never told you, but our life is a war and I have been a traitor all my born days, a spy in the enemy's country ever since I give up my gun back in the Reconstruction. Live with your head in the lion's mouth. I want you to overcome 'em with yeses, undermine 'em with grins, agree 'em to death and destruction, let 'em swoller you till they vomit or bust wide open." They thought the old man had gone out of his mind. He had been the meekest of men. The younger children were rushed from the room, the shades drawn and the flame of the lamp turned so low that it sputtered on the wick like the old man's breathing. "Learn it to the younguns," he whispered fiercely; then he died.

But my folks were more alarmed over his last words than over his dying. It was as though he had not died at all, his words caused so much anxiety. I was warned emphatically to forget what he had said and, indeed, this is the first time it has been mentioned outside the family circle. It had a tremendous effect upon me, however. I could never be sure of what he meant. Grandfather had been a quiet old man who never made any trouble, yet on his deathbed he had called himself a traitor and a spy, and he had spoken of his meekness as a dangerous activity. It became a constant puzzle which lay unanswered in the back of my mind. And whenever things went well for me I remembered my grandfather and felt guilty and uncomfortable. It was as though I was carrying out his advice in spite of myself. And to make it worse, everyone loved me for it. I was praised by the most lily-white men of the town. I was considered an example of desirable conduct— just as my grandfather had been. And what puzzled me was that the old man had defined it as *treachery*. When I was praised for my conduct I felt a guilt that in some way I was doing something that was really against the wishes of the white folks, that if they had understood they would have desired me to act just the opposite, that I should have been sulky and mean, and that that really would have been what they wanted, even though they were fooled and thought they wanted me to act as I did. It made me afraid that some day they would look upon me as a traitor and I would be lost. Still I was more afraid to act any other way because they didn't like that at all. The old man's words were like a curse. On my graduation day I delivered an oration in which I showed that humility was the secret, indeed, the very essence of progress. (Not that I believed this—how could I, remembering my grandfather?—I only believed that it worked.) It was a great success. Everyone praised me and I was invited to give the speech at a gathering of the town's leading white citizens. It was a triumph for our whole community.

It was in the main ballroom of the leading hotel. When I got there I discovered that it was on the occasion of a smoker, and I was told that since I was to be there anyway I might as well take part in the battle royal to be fought by some of my schoolmates as part of the entertainment. The battle royal came first.

All of the town's big shots were there in their tuxedoes, wolfing down the buffet foods, drinking beer and whiskey and smoking black cigars. It was a large room with a high ceiling. Chairs were arranged in neat rows around three sides of a portable boxing ring. The fourth side was clear, revealing a gleaming space of polished floor. I had some misgivings over the battle royal, by the way. Not from a distaste for fighting, but because I didn't care too much for the other fellows who were to take part. They were tough guys who seemed to have no grandfather's curse worrying their minds. No one could mistake their toughness. And besides, I suspected that fighting a battle royal might detract from the dignity of my speech. In those pre-invisible days I visualized myself as a potential Booker T. Washington.[2] But the other fellows didn't care too much for me either, and there were nine of them. I felt superior to them in my way, and I didn't like the manner in which we were all crowded together into the servants' elevator. Nor did they like my being there. In fact, as the warmly lighted floors flashed past the elevator we had words over the fact that I, by taking part in the fight, had knocked one of their friends out of a night's work.

We were led out of the elevator through a rococo[3] hall into an anteroom and told to get into our fighting togs. Each of us was issued a pair of boxing gloves and ushered out into the big mirrored hall, which we entered looking cautiously about us and whispering, lest we might accidentally be heard above the noise of the room. It was foggy with cigar smoke. And already the whiskey was taking effect. I was shocked to see some of the most important men of the town quite tipsy. They were all there—bankers, lawyers, judges, doctors, fire chiefs, teachers, merchants. Even one of the more fashionable pastors. Something we could not see was going on up front. A clarinet was vibrating sensuously and the men were standing up and moving eagerly forward. We were a small tight group, clustered together, our bare upper bodies touching and shining with anticipatory sweat; while up front the big shots were becoming increasingly excited over something we still could not see. Suddenly I heard the school superintendent, who had told me to come, yell, "Bring up the shines,[4] gentlemen! Bring up the little shines!"

We were rushed up to the front of the ballroom, where it smelled even more strongly of tobacco and whiskey. Then we were pushed into place. I almost wet my pants. A sea of faces, some hostile, some amused, ringed around us, and in the center, facing us, stood a magnificent blonde—stark naked. There was dead silence. I felt a blast of cold air chill me. I tried to back away, but they were behind me and around me. Some of the boys stood with lowered heads, trembling. I felt a wave of irrational guilt and fear. My teeth chattered, my skin turned to goose flesh, my knees knocked. Yet I was strongly attracted and looked in spite of myself. Had the price of looking been blindness, I would have looked. The hair was yellow like that of a circus kewpie doll, the face heavily powdered and rouged, as though to form an abstract mask, the eyes hollow and smeared a cool blue, the color of a baboon's butt. I felt a desire to spit upon her as my eyes brushed slowly over her body. Her breasts were firm and round as the domes of East Indian temples, and I stood so close as to see the fine skin texture and beads of pearly perspiration glistening like dew around the pink and erected buds of her nipples. I wanted at one and the same time to run from the room, to sink through the floor, or go to her and cover her from my eyes and the eyes of the others with my body; to feel the soft thighs, to caress her and destroy her, to love her and murder her, to hide from her, and yet to stroke where below the small American flag tattooed upon her belly her thighs formed a capital V. I had a notion that of all in the room she saw only me with her impersonal eyes.

And then she began to dance, a slow sensuous movement; the smoke of a hundred cigars clinging to her like the thinnest of veils. She seemed like a fair bird-

---

[2] Washington (1856–1915) was a famed African-American educator and botanist and author of the autobiographical *Up From Slavery* (1901).

[3] A graceful, delicate style of architecture, art, and music developed in the early eighteenth century in reaction to the heavy baroque style.

[4] Slang for "Negroes": derogatory, as are "coon" and "Sambo."

girl girdled in veils calling to me from the angry surface of some gray and threatening sea. I was transported. Then I became aware of the clarinet playing and the big shots yelling at us. Some threatened us if we looked and others if we did not. On my right I saw one boy faint. And now a man grabbed a silver pitcher from a table and stepped close as he dashed ice water upon him and stood him up and forced two of us to support him as his head hung and moans issued from his thick bluish lips. Another boy began to plead to go home. He was the largest of the group, wearing dark red fighting trunks much too small to conceal the erection which projected from him as though in answer to the insinuating low-registered moaning of the clarinet. He tried to hide himself with his boxing gloves.

And all the while the blonde continued dancing, smiling faintly at the big shots who watched her with fascination, and faintly smiling at our fear. I noticed a certain merchant who followed her hungrily, his lips loose and drooling. He was a large man who wore diamond studs in a shirtfront which swelled with the ample paunch underneath, and each time the blonde swayed her undulating hips he ran his hand through the thin hair of his bald head and, with his arms upheld, his posture clumsy like that of an intoxicated panda, wound his belly in a slow and obscene grind. This creature was completely hypnotized. The music had quickened. As the dancer flung herself about with a detached expression on her face, the men began reaching out to touch her. I could see their beefy fingers sink into the soft flesh. Some of the others tried to stop them and she began to move around the floor in graceful circles, as they gave chase, slipping and sliding over the polished floor. It was mad. Chairs went crashing, drinks were spilt, as they ran laughing and howling after her. They caught her just as she reached a door, raised her from the floor, and tossed her as college boys are tossed at a hazing, and above her red, fixed-smiling lips I saw the terror and disgust in her eyes, almost like my own terror and that which I saw in some of the other boys. As I watched, they tossed her twice and her soft breasts seemed to flatten against the air and her legs flung wildly as she spun. Some of the more sober ones helped her to escape. And I started off the floor, heading for the anteroom with the rest of the boys.

Some were still crying and in hysteria. But as we tried to leave we were stopped and ordered to get into the ring. There was nothing to do but what we were told. All ten of us climbed under the ropes and allowed ourselves to be blindfolded with broad bands of white cloth. One of the men seemed to feel a bit sympathetic and tried to cheer us up as we stood with our backs against the ropes. Some of us tried to grin. "See that boy over there?" one of the men said. "I want you to run across at the bell and give it to him right in the belly. If you don't get him, I'm going to get you. I don't like his looks." Each of us was told the same. The blindfolds were put on. Yet even then I had been going over my speech. In my mind each word was as bright as flame. I felt the cloth pressed into place, and frowned so that it would be loosened when I relaxed.

But now I felt a sudden fit of blind terror. I was unused to darkness. It was as though I had suddenly found myself in a dark room filled with poisonous cottonmouths.[5] I could hear the bleary voices yelling insistently for the battle royal to begin.

"Get going in there!"

"Let me at that big nigger!"

I strained to pick up the school superintendent's voice, as though to squeeze some security out of that slightly more familiar sound.

---

[5] Water moccasins: poisonous snakes common in the southeastern United States.

"Let me at those black sonsabitches!" someone yelled.

"No, Jackson, no!" another voice yelled. "Here, somebody, help me hold Jack."

"I want to get at that ginger-colored nigger. Tear him limb from limb," the first voice yelled.

I stood against the ropes trembling. For in those days I was what they called ginger-colored, and he sounded as though he might crunch me between his teeth like a crisp ginger cookie.

Quite a struggle was going on. Chairs were being kicked about and I could hear voices grunting as with a terrific effort. I wanted to see, to see more desperately than ever before. But the blindfold was tight as a thick skin-puckering scab and when I raised my gloved hands to push the layers of white aside a voice yelled, "Oh, no you don't, black bastard! Leave that alone!"

"Ring the bell before Jackson kills him a coon!" someone boomed in the sudden silence. And I heard the bell clang and the sound of the feet scuffling forward.

A glove smacked against my head. I pivoted, striking out stiffly as someone went past, and felt the jar ripple along the length of my arm to my shoulder. Then it seemed as though all nine of the boys had turned upon me at once. Blows pounded me from all sides while I struck out as best I could. So many blows landed upon me that I wondered if I were not the only blindfolded fighter in the ring, or if the man called Jackson hadn't succeeded in getting me after all.

Blindfolded, I could no longer control my motions. I had no dignity. I stumbled about like a baby or a drunken man. The smoke had become thicker and with each new blow it seemed to sear and further restrict my lungs. My saliva became like hot bitter glue. A glove connected with my head, filling my mouth with warm blood. It was everywhere. I could not tell if the moisture I felt upon my body was sweat or blood. A blow landed hard against the nape of my neck. I felt myself going over, my head hitting the floor. Streaks of blue light filled the black world behind the blindfold. I lay prone, pretending that I was knocked out, but felt myself seized by hands and yanked to my feet. "Get going, black boy! Mix it up!" My arms were like lead, my head smarting from blows. I managed to feel my way to the ropes and held on, trying to catch my breath. A glove landed in my midsection and I went over again, feeling as though the smoke had become a knife jabbed into my guts. Pushed this way and that by the legs milling around me, I finally pulled erect and discovered that I could see the black, sweat-washed forms weaving in the smoky-blue atmosphere like drunken dancers weaving to the rapid drum-like thuds of blows.

Everyone fought hysterically. It was complete anarchy. Everybody fought everybody else. No group fought together for long. Two, three, four, fought one, then turned to fight each other, were themselves attacked. Blows landed below the belt and in the kidney, with the gloves open as well as closed, and with my eye partly opened now there was not so much terror. I moved carefully, avoiding blows, although not too many to attract attention, fighting from group to group. The boys groped about like blind, cautious crabs crouching to protect their midsections, their heads pulled in short against their shoulders, their arms stretched nervously before them, with their fists testing the smoke-filled air like the knobbed feelers of hypersensitive snails. In one corner I glimpsed a boy violently punching the air and heard him scream in pain as he smashed his hand against a ring post. For a second I saw him bent over holding his hand, then going down as a blow caught his unprotected head. I played one group against the other, slipping in and throwing a punch then stepping out of range while pushing the others into the melee to take the blows blindly aimed at me. The smoke was agonizing and there were no rounds, no bells at three minute intervals to relieve our exhaustion. The room spun round me, a swirl of lights, smoke, sweating bodies surrounded by tense white faces. I bled from both nose and mouth, the blood spattering upon my chest.

The men kept yelling, "Slug him, black boy! Knock his guts out!"

"Uppercut him! Kill him! Kill that big boy!"

Taking a fake fall, I saw a boy going down heavily beside me as though we were felled by a single blow, saw a sneaker-clad foot shoot into his groin as the two who had knocked him down stumbled upon him. I rolled out of range, feeling a twinge of nausea.

The harder we fought the more threatening the men became. And yet, I had begun to worry about my speech again. How would it go? Would they recognize my ability? What would they give me?

I was fighting automatically when suddenly I noticed that one after another of the boys was leaving the ring. I was surprised, filled with panic, as though I had been left alone with an unknown danger. Then I understood. The boys had arranged it among themselves. It was the custom for the two men left in the ring to slug it out for the winner's prize. I discovered this too late. When the bell sounded two men in tuxedoes leaped into the ring and removed the blindfold. I found myself facing Tatlock, the biggest of the gang. I felt sick at my stomach. Hardly had the bell stopped ringing in my ears than it clanged again and I saw him moving swiftly toward me. Thinking of nothing else to do I hit him smash on the nose. He kept coming, bringing the rank sharp violence of stale sweat. His face was a black blank of a face, only his eyes alive—with hate of me and aglow with a feverish terror from what had happened to us all. I became anxious. I wanted to deliver my speech and he came at me as though he meant to beat it out of me. I smashed him again and again, taking his blows as they came. Then on a sudden impulse I struck him lightly and as we clinched, I whispered, "Fake like I knocked you out, you can have the prize."

"I'll break your behind," he whispered hoarsely.

"For *them?*"

"For *me,* sonofabitch!"

They were yelling for us to break it up and Tatlock spun me half around with a blow, and as a joggled camera sweeps in a reeling scene, I saw the howling red faces crouching tense beneath the cloud of blue-gray smoke. For a moment the world wavered, unraveled, flowed, then my head cleared and Tatlock bounced before me. That fluttering shadow before my eyes was his jabbing left hand. Then falling forward, my head against his damp shoulder, I whispered,

"I'll make it five dollars more."

"Go to hell!"

But his muscles relaxed a trifle beneath my pressure and I breathed, "Seven?"

"Give it to your ma," he said, ripping me beneath the heart.

And while I still held him I butted him and moved away. I felt myself bombarded with punches. I fought back with hopeless desperation. I wanted to deliver my speech more than anything else in the world, because I felt that only these men could judge truly my ability, and now this stupid clown was ruining my chances. I began fighting carefully now, moving in to punch him and out again with my greater speed. A lucky blow to his chin and I had him going too—until I heard a loud voice yell, "I got my money on the big boy."

Hearing this, I almost dropped my guard. I was confused: Should I try to win against the voice out there? Would not this go against my speech, and was not this a moment for humility, for nonresistance? A blow to my head as I danced about sent my right eye popping like a jack-in-the-box and settled my dilemma. The room went red as I fell. It was a dream fall, my body languid and fastidious as to where to land, until the floor became impatient and smashed up to meet me. A moment later I came to. An hypnotic voice said FIVE emphatically. And I lay there, hazily watching a dark red spot of my own blood shaping itself into a butterfly, glistening and soaking into the soiled gray world of the canvas.

When the voice drawled TEN I was lifted up and dragged to a chair. I sat dazed. My eye pained and swelled with each throb of my pounding heart and I wondered if now I would be allowed to speak. I was wringing wet, my mouth still bleeding. We were grouped along the wall now. The other boys ignored me as they congratulated Tatlock and speculated as to how much they would be paid. One boy whimpered over his smashed hand. Looking up front, I saw attendants in white jackets rolling the portable ring away and placing a small square rug in the vacant space surrounded by chairs. Perhaps, I thought, I will stand on the rug to deliver my speech.

Then the M.C.[6] called to us, "Come on up here boys and get your money."

We ran forward to where the men laughed and talked in their chairs, waiting. Everyone seemed friendly now.

"There it is on the rug," the man said. I saw the rug covered with coins of all dimensions and a few crumpled bills. But what excited me, scattered here and there, were the gold pieces.

"Boys, it's all yours," the man said. "You get all you grab."

"That's right, Sambo," a blond man said, winking at me confidentially.

I trembled with excitement, forgetting my pain. I would get the gold and the bills, I thought. I would use both hands. I would throw my body against the boys nearest me to block them from the gold.

"Get down around the rug now," the man commanded, "and don't anyone touch it until I give the signal."

"This ought to be good," I heard.

As told, we got around the square rug on our knees. Slowly the man raised his freckled hand as we followed it upward with our eyes.

I heard, "These niggers look like they're about to pray!"

Then, "Ready," the man said. "Go!"

I lunged for a yellow coin lying on the blue design of the carpet, touching it and sending a surprised shriek to join those rising around me. I tried frantically to remove my hand but could not let go. A hot, violent force tore through my body, shaking me like a wet rat. The rug was electrified. The hair bristled up on my head as I shook myself free. My muscles jumped, my nerves jangled, writhed. But I saw that this was not stopping the other boys. Laughing in fear and embarrassment, some were holding back and scooping up the coins knocked off by the painful contortions of the others. The men roared above us as we struggled.

"Pick it up, goddamnit, pick it up!" someone called like a bass-voiced parrot. "Go on, get it!"

I crawled rapidly around the floor, picking up the coins, trying to avoid the coppers and to get greenbacks and the gold. Ignoring the shock by laughing, as I brushed the coins off quickly, I discovered that I could contain the electricity—a contradiction, but it works. Then the men began to push us onto the rug. Laughing embarrassedly, we struggled out of their hands and kept after the coins. We were

[6] Emcee.

all wet and slippery and hard to hold. Suddenly I saw a boy lifted into the air, glistening with sweat like a circus seal, and dropped, his wet back landing flush upon the charged rug, heard him yell and saw him literally dance upon his back, his elbows beating a frenzied tattoo upon the floor, his muscles twitching like the flesh of a horse stung by many flies. When he finally rolled off, his face was gray and no one stopped him when he ran from the floor amid booming laughter.

"Get the money," the M.C. called. "That's good hard American cash!"

And we snatched and grabbed, snatched and grabbed. I was careful not to come too close to the rug now, and when I felt the hot whiskey breath descend upon me like a cloud of foul air I reached out and grabbed the leg of a chair. It was occupied and I held on desperately.

"Leggo, nigger! Leggo!"

The huge face wavered down to mine as he tried to push me free. But my body was slippery and he was too drunk. It was Mr. Colcord, who owned a chain of movie houses and "entertainment palaces." Each time he grabbed me I slipped out of his hands. It became a real struggle. I feared the rug more than I did the drunk, so I held on, surprising myself for a moment by trying to topple *him* upon the rug. It was such an enormous idea that I found myself actually carrying it out. I tried not to be obvious, yet when I grabbed his leg, trying to tumble him out of the chair, he raised up roaring with laughter, and, looking at me with soberness dead in the eye, kicked me viciously in the chest. The chair leg flew out of my hand and I felt myself going and rolled. It was as though I had rolled through a bed of hot coals. It seemed a whole century would pass before I would roll free, a century in which I was seared through the deepest levels of my body to the fearful breath within me and the breath seared and heated to the point of explosion. It'll all be over in a flash, I thought as I rolled clear. It'll all be over in a flash.

But not yet, the men on the other side were waiting, red faces swollen as though from apoplexy as they bent forward in their chairs. Seeing their fingers coming toward me I rolled away as a fumbled football rolls off the receiver's fingertips, back into the coals. That time I luckily sent the rug sliding out of place and heard the coins ringing against the floor and the boys scuffling to pick them up and the M.C. calling, "All right, boys, that's all. Go get dressed and get your money."

I was limp as a dish rag. My back felt as though it had been beaten with wires.

When we had dressed the M.C. came in and gave us each five dollars, except Tatlock, who got ten for being last in the ring. Then he told us to leave. I was not to get a chance to deliver my speech, I thought. I was going out into the dim alley in despair when I was stopped and told to go back. I returned to the ballroom, where the men were pushing back their chairs and gathering in groups to talk.

The M.C. knocked on a table for quiet. "Gentlemen," he said, "we almost forgot an important part of the program. A most serious part, gentlemen. This boy was brought here to deliver a speech which he made at his graduation yesterday . . ."

"Bravo!"

"I'm told that he is the smartest boy we've got out there in Greenwood. I'm told that he knows more big words than a pocket-sized dictionary."

Much applause and laughter.

"So now, gentlemen, I want you to give him your attention."

There was still laughter as I faced them, my mouth dry, my eye throbbing. I began slowly, but evidently my throat was tense, because they began shouting, "Louder! Louder!"

"We of the younger generation extol the wisdom of that great leader and educator," I shouted, "who first spoke these flaming words of wisdom: 'A ship lost at sea for many days suddenly sighted a friendly vessel. From the mast of the unfortunate vessel was seen a signal: "Water, water; we die of thirst!" The answer from the friendly vessel came back: "Cast down your bucket where you are." The captain of the distressed vessel, at last heeding the injunction, cast down his bucket, and it came up full of fresh sparkling water from the mouth of the Amazon River.' And like him I say, and in his words, 'To those of my race who depend upon bettering their condition in a foreign land, or who underestimate the importance of cultivating friendly relations with the Southern white man, who is his next-door neighbor, I would say: "Cast down your bucket where you are"—cast it down in making friends in every manly way of the people of all races by whom we are surrounded . . . '"[7]

I spoke automatically and with such fervor that I did not realize that the men were still talking and laughing until my dry mouth, filling up with blood from the cut, almost strangled me. I coughed, wanting to stop and go to one of the tall brass, sand-filled spittoons to relieve myself, but a few of the men, especially the superintendent, were listening and I was afraid. So I gulped it down, blood, saliva and all, and continued. (What powers of endurance I had during those days! What enthusiasm! What a belief in the rightness of things!) I spoke even louder in spite of the pain. But still they talked and still they laughed, as though deaf with cotton in dirty ears. So I spoke with greater emotional emphasis. I closed my ears and swallowed blood until I was nauseated. The speech seemed a hundred times as long as before, but I could not leave out a single word. All had to be said, each memorized nuance considered, rendered. Nor was that all. Whenever I uttered a word of three or more syllables a group of voices would yell for me to repeat it. I used the phrase "social responsibility" and they yelled:

"What's that word you say, boy?"

"Social responsibility," I said.

"What?"

"Social . . ."

"Louder."

" . . . responsibility."

"More!"

"Respon—"

"Repeat!"

"—sibility."

The room filled with the uproar of laughter until, no doubt, distracted by having to gulp down my blood, I made a mistake and yelled a phrase I had often seen denounced in newspaper editorials, heard debated in private.

"Social . . ."

"What?" they yelled.

" . . . equality."

The laughter hung smokelike in the sudden stillness. I opened my eyes, puzzled. Sounds of displeasure filled the room. The M.C. rushed forward. They shouted hostile phrases at me. But I did not understand.

A small dry mustached man in the front row blared out, "Say that slowly, son!"

---

[7] From Booker T. Washington's famous Atlanta Exposition speech of 1895, known as the Atlanta Compromise; the address is presented in Ch. XIV of *Up From Slavery*.

"What, sir?"

"What you just said!"

"Social responsibility, sir," I said.

"You weren't being smart, were you, boy?" he said, not unkindly.

"No, sir!"

"You sure that about 'equality' was a mistake?"

"Oh, yes, sir," I said. "I was swallowing blood."

"Well, you had better speak more slowly so we can understand. We mean to do right by you, but you've got to know your place at all times. All right, now, go on with your speech."

I was afraid. I wanted to leave but I wanted also to speak and I was afraid they'd snatch me down.

"Thank you, sir," I said, beginning where I had left off, and having them ignore me as before.

Yet when I finished there was a thunderous applause. I was surprised to see the superintendent come forth with a package wrapped in white tissue paper, and, gesturing for quiet, address the men.

"Gentlemen, you see that I did not overpraise this boy. He makes a good speech and some day he'll lead his people in the proper paths. And I don't have to tell you that that is important in these days and times. This is a good, smart boy, and so to encourage him in the right direction, in the name of the Board of Education I wish to present him a prize in the form of this . . . "

He paused, removing the tissue paper and revealing a gleaming calfskin brief case.

" . . . in the form of this first-class article from Shad Whitmore's shop."

"Boy," he said, addressing me, "take this prize and keep it well. Consider it a badge of office. Prize it. Keep developing as you are and some day it will be filled with important papers that will help shape the destiny of your people."

I was so moved that I could hardly express my thanks. A rope of bloody saliva forming a shape like an undiscovered continent drooled upon the leather and I wiped it quickly away. I felt an importance that I had never dreamed.

"Open it and see what's inside," I was told.

My fingers a-tremble, I complied, smelling the fresh leather and finding an official-looking document inside. It was a scholarship to the state college for Negroes. My eyes filled with tears and I ran awkwardly off the floor.

I was overjoyed; I did not even mind when I discovered that the gold pieces I had scrambled for were brass pocket tokens advertising a certain make of automobile.

When I reached home everyone was excited. Next day the neighbors came to congratulate me. I even felt safe from grandfather, whose deathbed curse usually spoiled my triumphs. I stood beneath his photograph with my brief case in hand and smiled triumphantly into his stolid black peasant's face. It was a face that fascinated me. The eyes seemed to follow everywhere I went.

That night I dreamed I was at a circus with him and that he refused to laugh at the clowns no matter what they did. Then later he told me to open my brief case and read what was inside and I did, finding an official envelope stamped with the state seal; and inside the envelope I found another and another, endlessly, and I thought I would fall of weariness. "Them's years," he said. "Now open that one." And I did and in it I found an engraved document containing a short message in letters of gold. "Read it," my grandfather said. "Out loud!"

"To Whom It May Concern," I intoned. "Keep This Nigger-Boy Running."

I awoke with the old man's laughter ringing in my ears.

(It was a dream I was to remember and dream again for many years after. But at that time I had no insight into its meaning. First I had to attend college.)

1947

═CONTEXTS═

The Jewish Immigrant Experience

With the influx of European immigrants to America in the early to middle twentieth century came an influx of literature dealing with the experiences of those immigrants. For Jewish immigrants much of this literature was an attempt to reconcile the harshness of their life in America with the deep spiritual values and traditions of their European homelands. The conditions under which many Jewish immigrants lived are exposed in such works as the posthumously published *How the Other Half Lives* (1919), by the Danish-born journalist Jacob Riis (1849–1914), which examines the problems caused by overcrowding in the tenement districts of early twentieth-century New York City. Many European immigrants settled in urban areas where jobs were plentiful, but the extreme poverty and large numbers of people, combined with the greed of tenement owners, often led to unsanitary, nearly inhuman living conditions.

That European immigrants to America were faced with hostility and insensitivity to their cultural differences as well is also reflected in literature. A major voice in Yiddish literature is the 1978 Nobel Laureate Isaac Bashevis Singer (1904–). After immigrating to the United States in 1935, he began to write stories incorporating Jewish folklore and life in his native Poland. In such stories as "Gimpel The Fool" (1953) Singer establishes the importance in Jewish life of piety and of the individual's relationship with God. In his later stories about Jewish immigrants, Singer points out the problems of maintaining a sense of racial identity and culture. In "The Little Shoemakers" (1954) Abba Shuster chooses to remain in Poland while his sons leave for America. Only the bombing of his village during World War II and the destruction of his family home force his departure to America. The journey is arduous, and along the way Abba loses his prayer shawl and other religious articles. Reaching New Jersey and his sons, he feels alienated until he rediscovers his shoemaking tools. The ability to ply his old trade renews his strength, and when his sons join him, they solidify the bonds of tradition that immigration threatened to break:

The Little Shoemakers

Abba's sons spread sackcloth aprons on their knees and went to work, cutting soles and shaping heels, boring holes and hammering pegs, as in the good old days. . . . In the high spring sky, lofting over the grass and the water, floated clouds in the form of brooms, sailboats, flocks of sheep, herds of elephants. Birds sang, flies buzzed, butterflies fluttered about.

Abba raised his dense eyebrows, and his sad eyes looked around at his heirs, the seven shoemakers. . . . No, praise God, they had not become idolaters in Egypt. They had not forgotten their heritage, nor had they lost themselves among the unworthy.

Isaac Bashevis Singer, 1954

Flannery O'Connor
(1925–1964) ·

To Flannery O'Connor the basis for art was truth, and religion was the truth. Her Catholic views, such as a belief in the Fall, Redemption, and Judgment, infused her two novels and thirty-one short stories with a moral structure and sensibility. She created characters who must face evil as well as grace, the certainty and mystery of which are behind every word she wrote. O'Connor comments in perhaps her most well-known essay, "The Fiction Writer & His Country," found in her volume of critical writing, *Mystery and Manners* (1969), that people always point out to her that life in Georgia is not at all how she depicts it. Nonetheless, her aim was to write "realistic" fiction. She states in another essay that she is "more interested in possibility than in probability." Her moral vision demands that her "real" and "possible" worlds be grounded in truth.

O'Connor's vision is distinguished from that of most other writers by her profound belief in the existence of evil. She complained that most people have a "diluted" sense of evil, without which Redemption would be meaningless. Her characters commit suicide, drown, suffer heart attacks, are gored or shot to death, or have their wooden legs stolen. Seductions backfire, love betrays, and families fail. Violence, she felt, brought her characters back to reality and made them ready to accept their "moment of grace."

This remarkable woman whose considerably small body of work has generated an enormous response—at least twenty-five books and countless articles and dissertations have been written about O'Connor—spent most of her life in Georgia. She was born Mary Flannery O'Connor in 1925 in Savannah. After earning her undergraduate degree at Georgia State College for Women, she attended the University of Iowa, where she earned a master of fine arts degree in 1947. O'Connor's stories and sections from her first novel, *Wise Blood* (1952), then began to appear in magazines. After briefly residing at the writer's colony Yaddo in Saratoga Springs, New York, she moved to New York City in 1949 and to Connecticut later that year. There she lived with the writers Robert and Sally Fitzgerald (who subsequently edited O'Connor's work), writing and helping to look after the children. O'Connor was forced to leave a year later when, at age twenty-five, she was struck with a form of lupus, the same inflammatory disease that claimed her father's life. After a long hospital stay and many blood transfusions, she returned to her mother's home on a farm near Milledgeville, Georgia. Except for short lecture trips and readings, she remained there the rest of her life.

New medication controlled the disease enough so that O'Connor was able to write. *Wise Blood* was published to rather curious critical acclaim. Who was this woman, people wondered, who had written such a disturbing and shocking novel? The story of Hazel Motes, a religious fanatic who wants to convert people to the "Church without Christ," *Wise Blood* nonetheless established O'Connor's literary career. A Kenyon Fellowship followed the novel, the cash award helping with medical costs and allowing her to continue to write. Several subsequent O'Connor stories won O'Henry Prizes, and in 1955 her first short-story collection, *A Good Man Is Hard to Find*, was published. In 1956 she began lecture trips to colleges. The following year she traveled with her mother to Lourdes, France, and then to Rome for an audience with the Pope, although by then she was re-

Flannery O'Connor's mother was once directed to a house billed as easy to find: the only one in town with an "artificial nigger." O'Connor used that phrase, "a terrible symbol of what the South has done to itself," as the basis for "The Artificial Nigger."

stricted to crutches. Her second novel, *The Violent Bear It Away* (1960), is the story of the education of her character Francis Tarwater, first by a religious zealot and then by a scientific rationalist. After O'Connor's death at age thirty-nine in 1964, a second volume of short stories, *Everything That Rises Must Converge* (1965), appeared. Six years later *The Complete Stories of Flannery O'Connor,* which includes the two earlier collections plus twelve additional stories, was published.

Two subsequent collections—one volume of prose written for special occasions and another of selected correspondence—were greeted with as much interest as her stories were. The essays in *Mystery and Manners* explore what O'Connor perceived to be the peculiar problem of the short-story writer: revealing in the action "as much of the mystery of existence as possible." There she writes in plain language about why she writes the way she writes and opens the volume with an essay on peacocks, which she raised in great numbers. *The Habit of Being* (1979), a selection of her letters from 1948 until her death, has gained extraordinary attention. Increasingly restricted by lupus, O'Connor depended heavily on her correspondence for social interaction. Her letters reveal the same searching mind and dark wit that is evident throughout her fiction. In them she comments on her fiction and her faith, wrestling with the profound questions of each.

Her fiction has commonly been termed grotesque, a description she disliked (preferring "realistic" or "literal") but acknowledged as appropriate. She explains in "The Fiction Writer & His Country" that her characters are deliberately distorted and act in unexpected ways because "to the hard of hearing you shout, and for the almost-blind you draw large and startling figures." O'Connor believed that most people are too accustomed to the world's evil to notice it; hence she imagined her audience to be partly deaf and blind.

O'Connor's style is consequently direct, deliberate, and relentless. Critics have long praised her carefully crafted fiction, generally preferring the short stories to the novels. Again and again her writing is called "precise" and "unsentimental." Her keen ear for dialogue and her unsettling humor are deservedly singled out. Although O'Connor's stories tend to elicit discomfort, even shock, they also penetrate the mystery of the "real" and the "possible."

Suggested Readings: *Wise Blood,* 1952. *The Violent Bear It Away,* 1960. *Mystery and Manners: Occasional Prose,* ed. R. Fitzgerald and S. Fitzgerald, 1969. *The Complete Stories of Flannery O'Connor,* 1971. *The Habit of Being,* ed. S. Fitzgerald, 1979. *Conversations With Flannery O'Connor,* ed. R. Magee, 1987. Georgia College, *The Flannery O'Connor Bulletin,* 1972– . M. Stephens, *The Question of Flannery O'Connor,* 1973. D. Walters, *Flannery O'Connor,* 1973. R. Coles, *Flannery O'Connor's South,* 1980. M. Friedman and B. L. Clark, eds., *Critical Essays on Flannery O'Connor,* 1985. H. Bloom, ed., *Flannery O'Connor,* 1986.

Text Used: *Collected Works,* ed. S. Fitzgerald, 1988.

THE ARTIFICIAL NIGGER

Mr. Head awakened to discover that the room was full of moonlight. He sat up and stared at the floor boards—the color of silver—and then at the ticking on his pillow, which might have been brocade, and after a second, he saw half of the moon five feet away in his shaving mirror, paused as if it were waiting for his permission to enter. It rolled forward and cast a dignifying light on everything. The straight chair against the wall looked stiff and attentive as if it were awaiting an order and Mr. Head's trousers, hanging to the back of it, had an almost noble air, like the garment some great man had just flung to his servant; but the face on the moon was a grave one. It gazed across the room and out the window where it floated over the horse stall and appeared to contemplate itself with the look of a young man who sees his old age before him.

Mr. Head could have said to it that age was a choice blessing and that only with years does a man enter into that calm understanding of life that makes him a suitable guide for the young. This, at least, had been his own experience.

He sat up and grasped the iron posts at the foot of his bed and raised himself until he could see the face on the alarm clock which sat on an overturned bucket beside the chair. The hour was two in the morning. The alarm on the clock did not work but he was not dependent on any mechanical means to awaken him. Sixty years had not dulled his responses; his physical reactions, like his moral ones, were guided by his will and strong character, and these could be seen plainly in his features. He had a long tube-like face with a long rounded open jaw and a long depressed nose. His eyes were alert but quiet, and in the miraculous moonlight they had a look of composure and of ancient wisdom as if they belonged to one of the great guides of men. He might have been Vergil summoned in the middle of the night to go to Dante, or better, Raphael, awakened by a blast of God's light to fly to the side of Tobias.[1] The only dark spot in the room was Nelson's pallet,[2] underneath the shadow of the window.

---

[1] Virgil, or Publius Vergilius Maro (70–19 B.C.), the Roman poet who wrote the *Aeneid;* Dante Alighieri (1265–1321), the Italian poet who wrote *The Divine Comedy;* Raffaelo Sanzio (1483–1520), an Italian painter and architect, master of the Italian High Renaissance; Tobit, a Hebrew captive in Ninevah whose story is told in a book of the Apocrypha.

[2] A small bed or pad filled with straw, used on the floor.

Nelson was hunched over on his side, his knees under his chin and his heels under his bottom. His new suit and hat were in the boxes that they had been sent in and these were on the floor at the foot of the pallet where he could get his hands on them as soon as he woke up. The slop jar, out of the shadow and made snow-white in the moonlight, appeared to stand guard over him like a small personal angel. Mr. Head lay back down, feeling entirely confident that he could carry out the moral mission of the coming day. He meant to be up before Nelson and to have the breakfast cooking by the time he awakened. The boy was always irked when Mr. Head was the first up. They would have to leave the house at four to get to the railroad junction by five-thirty. The train was to stop for them at five forty-five and they had to be there on time for this train was stopping merely to accommodate them.

This would be the boy's first trip to the city though he claimed it would be his second because he had been born there. Mr. Head had tried to point out to him that when he was born he didn't have the intelligence to determine his whereabouts but this had made no impression on the child at all and he continued to insist that this was to be his second trip. It would be Mr. Head's third trip. Nelson had said, "I will've already been there twict and I ain't but ten."

Mr. Head had contradicted him.

"If you ain't been there in fifteen years, how you know you'll be able to find your way about?" Nelson had asked. "How you know it hasn't changed some?"

"Have you ever," Mr. Head had asked, "seen me lost?"

Nelson certainly had not but he was a child who was never satisfied until he had given an impudent answer and he replied, "It's nowhere around here to get lost at."

"The day is going to come," Mr. Head prophesied, "when you'll find you ain't as smart as you think you are." He had been thinking about this trip for several months but it was for the most part in moral terms that he conceived it. It was to be a lesson that the boy would never forget. He was to find out from it that he had no cause for pride merely because he had been born in a city. He was to find out that the city is not a great place. Mr. Head meant him to see everything there is to see in a city so that he would be content to stay at home for the rest of his life. He fell asleep thinking how the boy would at last find out that he was not as smart as he thought he was.

He was awakened at three-thirty by the smell of fatback frying and he leaped off his cot. The pallet was empty and the clothes boxes had been thrown open. He put on his trousers and ran into the other room. The boy had a corn pone[3] on cooking and had fried the meat. He was sitting in the half-dark at the table, drinking cold coffee out of a can. He had on his new suit and his new gray hat pulled low over his eyes. It was too big for him but they had ordered it a size large because they expected his head to grow. He didn't say anything but his entire figure suggested satisfaction at having arisen before Mr. Head.

Mr. Head went to the stove and brought the meat to the table in the skillet. "It's no hurry," he said. "You'll get there soon enough and it's no guarantee you'll like it when you do neither," and he sat down across from the boy whose hat teetered back slowly to reveal a fiercely expressionless face, very much the same shape as the old man's. They were grandfather and grandson but they looked enough alike to be brothers and brothers not too far apart in age, for Mr. Head had a youthful

---

[3] Bread or cake in small, oval loaves; of southern origin.

expression by daylight, while the boy's look was ancient, as if he knew everything already and would be pleased to forget it.

Mr. Head had once had a wife and daughter and when the wife died, the daughter ran away and returned after an interval with Nelson. Then one morning, without getting out of bed, she died and left Mr. Head with sole care of the year-old child. He had made the mistake of telling Nelson that he had been born in Atlanta. If he hadn't told him that, Nelson couldn't have insisted that this was going to be his second trip.

"You may not like it a bit," Mr. Head continued. "It'll be full of niggers."

The boy made a face as if he could handle a nigger.

"All right," Mr. Head said. "You ain't ever seen a nigger."

"You wasn't up very early," Nelson said.

"You ain't ever seen a nigger," Mr. Head repeated. "There hasn't been a nigger in this county since we run that one out twelve years ago and that was before you were born." He looked at the boy as if he were daring him to say he had ever seen a Negro.

"How you know I never saw a nigger when I lived there before?" Nelson asked. "I probably saw a lot of niggers."

"If you seen one you didn't know what he was," Mr. Head said, completely exasperated. "A six-month-old child don't know a nigger from anybody else."

"I reckon I'll know a nigger if I see one," the boy said and got up and straightened his slick sharply creased gray hat and went outside to the privy.

They reached the junction some time before the train was due to arrive and stood about two feet from the first set of tracks. Mr. Head carried a paper sack with some biscuits and a can of sardines in it for their lunch. A coarse-looking orange-colored sun coming up behind the east range of mountains was making the sky a dull red behind them, but in front of them it was still gray and they faced a gray transparent moon, hardly stronger than a thumbprint and completely without light. A small tin switch box and a black fuel tank were all there was to mark the place as a junction; the tracks were double and did not converge again until they were hidden behind the bends at either end of the clearing. Trains passing appeared to emerge from a tunnel of trees and, hit for a second by the cold sky, vanish terrified into the woods again. Mr. Head had had to make special arrangements with the ticket agent to have this train stop and he was secretly afraid it would not, in which case, he knew Nelson would say, "I never thought no train was going to stop for you." Under the useless morning moon the tracks looked white and fragile. Both the old man and the child stared ahead as if they were awaiting an apparition.

Then suddenly, before Mr. Head could make up his mind to turn back, there was a deep warning bleat and the train appeared, gliding very slowly, almost silently around the bend of trees about two hundred yards down the track, with one yellow front light shining. Mr. Head was still not certain it would stop and he felt it would make an even bigger idiot of him if it went by slowly. Both he and Nelson, however, were prepared to ignore the train if it passed them.

The engine charged by, filling their noses with the smell of hot metal and then the second coach came to a stop exactly where they were standing. A conductor with the face of an ancient bloated bulldog was on the step as if he expected them, though he did not look as if it mattered one way or the other to him if they got on or not. "To the right," he said.

Their entry took only a fraction of a second and the train was already speeding on as they entered the quiet car. Most of the travelers were still sleeping, some with their heads hanging off the chair arms, some stretched across two seats, and some sprawled out with their feet in the aisle. Mr. Head saw two unoccupied seats and pushed Nelson toward them. "Get in there by the winder," he said in his normal voice which was very loud at this hour of the morning. "Nobody cares if you sit there because it's nobody in it. Sit right there."

"I heard you," the boy muttered. "It's no use in you yelling," and he sat down and turned his head to the glass. There he saw a pale ghost-like face scowling at him beneath the brim of a pale ghost-like hat. His grandfather, looking quickly too, saw a different ghost, pale but grinning, under a black hat.

Mr. Head sat down and settled himself and took out his ticket and started reading aloud everything that was printed on it. People began to stir. Several woke up and stared at him. "Take off your hat," he said to Nelson and took off his own and put it on his knee. He had a small amount of white hair that had turned tobacco-colored over the years and this lay flat across the back of his head. The front of his head was bald and creased. Nelson took off his hat and put it on his knee and they waited for the conductor to come ask for their tickets.

The man across the aisle from them was spread out over two seats, his feet propped on the window and his head jutting into the aisle. He had on a light blue suit and a yellow shirt unbuttoned at the neck. His eyes had just opened and Mr. Head was ready to introduce himself when the conductor came up from behind and growled, "Tickets."

When the conductor had gone, Mr. Head gave Nelson the return half of his ticket and said, "Now put that in your pocket and don't lose it or you'll have to stay in the city."

"Maybe I will," Nelson said as if this were a reasonable suggestion.

Mr. Head ignored him. "First time this boy has ever been on a train," he explained to the man across the aisle, who was sitting up now on the edge of his seat with both feet on the floor.

Nelson jerked his hat on again and turned angrily to the window.

"He's never seen anything before," Mr. Head continued. "Ignorant as the day he was born, but I mean for him to get his fill once and for all."

The boy leaned forward, across his grandfather and toward the stranger. "I was born in the city," he said. "I was born there. This is my second trip." He said it in a high positive voice but the man across the aisle didn't look as if he understood. There were heavy purple circles under his eyes.

Mr. Head reached across the aisle and tapped him on the arm. "The thing to do with a boy," he said sagely, "is to show him all it is to show. Don't hold nothing back."

"Yeah," the man said. He gazed down at his swollen feet and lifted the left one about ten inches from the floor. After a minute he put it down and lifted the other. All through the car people began to get up and move about and yawn and stretch. Separate voices could be heard here and there and then a general hum. Suddenly Mr. Head's serene expression changed. His mouth almost closed and a light, fierce and cautious both, came into his eyes. He was looking down the length of the car. Without turning, he caught Nelson by the arm and pulled him forward. "Look," he said.

A hugh coffee-colored man was coming slowly forward. He had on a light suit and a yellow satin tie with a ruby pin in it. One of his hands rested on his stomach which rode majestically under his buttoned coat, and in the other he held the head of a black walking stick that he picked up and set down with a deliberate outward motion each time he took a step. He was proceeding very slowly, his large brown eyes gazing over the heads of the passengers. He had a small white mustache and white crinkly hair. Behind him there were two young women, both coffee-colored, one in a yellow dress and one in a green. Their progress was kept at the rate of his and they chatted in low throaty voices as they followed him.

Mr. Head's grip was tightening insistently on Nelson's arm. As the procession passed them, the light from a sapphire ring on the brown hand that picked up the cane reflected in Mr. Head's eye, but he did not look up nor did the tremendous man look at him. The group proceeded up the rest of the aisle and out of the car. Mr. Head's grip on Nelson's arm loosened. "What was that?" he asked.

"A man," the boy said and gave him an indignant look as if he were tired of having his intelligence insulted.

"What kind of a man?" Mr. Head persisted, his voice expressionless.

"A fat man," Nelson said. He was beginning to feel that he had better be cautious.

"You don't know what kind?" Mr. Head said in a final tone.

"An old man," the boy said and had a sudden foreboding that he was not going to enjoy the day.

"That was a nigger," Mr. Head said and sat back.

Nelson jumped up on the seat and stood looking backward to the end of the car but the Negro had gone.

"I'd of thought you'd know a nigger since you seen so many when you was in the city on your first visit," Mr. Head continued. "That's his first nigger," he said to the man across the aisle.

The boy slid down into the seat. "You said they were black," he said in an angry voice. "You never said they were tan. How do you expect me to know anything when you don't tell me right?"

"You're just ignorant is all," Mr. Head said and he got up and moved over in the vacant seat by the man across the aisle.

Nelson turned backward again and looked where the Negro had disappeared. He felt that the Negro had deliberately walked down the aisle in order to make a fool of him and he hated him with a fierce raw fresh hate; and also, he understood now why his grandfather disliked them. He looked toward the window and the face there seemed to suggest that he might be inadequate to the day's exactions. He wondered if he would even recognize the city when they came to it.

After he had told several stories, Mr. Head realized that the man he was talking to was asleep and he got up and suggested to Nelson that they walk over the train and see the parts of it. He particularly wanted the boy to see the toilet so they went first to the men's room and examined the plumbing. Mr. Head demonstrated the ice-water cooler as if he had invented it and showed Nelson the bowl with the single spigot where the travelers brushed their teeth. They went through several cars and came to the diner.

This was the most elegant car in the train. It was painted a rich egg-yellow and had a wine-colored carpet on the floor. There were wide windows over the tables and great spaces of the rolling view were caught in miniature in the sides of the coffee pots and in the glasses. Three very black Negroes in white suits and aprons were running up and down the aisle, swinging trays and bowing and bending over the travelers eating breakfast. One of them rushed up to Mr. Head and Nelson and said, holding up two fingers, "Space for two!" but Mr. Head replied in a loud voice, "We eaten before we left!"

The waiter wore large brown spectacles that increased the size of his eye whites. "Stan' aside then please," he said with an airy wave of the arm as if he were brushing aside flies.

Neither Nelson nor Mr. Head moved a fraction of an inch. "Look," Mr. Head said.

The near corner of the diner, containing two tables, was set off from the rest by a saffron-colored curtain. One table was set but empty but at the other, facing them, his back to the drape, sat the tremendous Negro. He was speaking in a soft voice to the two women while he buttered a muffin. He had a heavy sad face and his neck bulged over his white collar on either side. "They rope them off," Mr. Head explained. Then he said, "Let's go see the kitchen," and they walked the length of the diner but the black waiter was coming fast behind them.

"Passengers are not allowed in the kitchen!" he said in a haughty voice. "Passengers are NOT allowed in the kitchen!"

Mr. Head stopped where he was and turned. "And there's good reason for that," he shouted into the Negro's chest, "because the cockroaches would run the passengers out!"

All the travelers laughed and Mr. Head and Nelson walked out, grinning. Mr. Head was known at home for his quick wit and Nelson felt a sudden keen pride in him. He realized the old man would be his only support in the strange place they were approaching. He would be entirely alone in the world if he were ever lost from his grandfather. A terrible excitement shook him and he wanted to take hold of Mr. Head's coat and hold on like a child.

As they went back to their seats they could see through the passing windows that the countryside was becoming speckled with small houses and shacks and that a highway ran alongside the train. Cars sped by on it, very small and fast. Nelson felt that there was less breath in the air than there had been thirty minutes ago. The man across the aisle had left and there was no one near for Mr. Head to hold a conversation with so he looked out the window, through his own reflection, and read aloud the names of the buildings they were passing. "The Dixie Chemical Corp!" he announced. "Southern Maid Flour! Dixie Doors! Southern Belle Cotton Products! Patty's Peanut Butter! Southern Mammy Cane Syrup!"

"Hush up!" Nelson hissed.

All over the car people were beginning to get up and take their luggage off the overhead racks. Women were putting on their coats and hats. The conductor stuck his head in the car and snarled, "Firstopppppmry," and Nelson lunged out of his sitting position, trembling. Mr. Head pushed him down by the shoulder.

"Keep your seat," he said in dignified tones. "The first stop is on the edge of town. The second stop is at the main railroad station." He had come by this knowledge on his first trip when he had got off at the first stop and had had to pay a man fifteen cents to take him into the heart of town. Nelson sat back down, very pale. For the first time in his life, he understood that his grandfather was indispensable to him.

The train stopped and let off a few passengers and glided on as if it had never ceased moving. Outside, behind rows of brown rickety houses, a line of blue buildings stood up, and beyond them a pale rose-gray sky faded away to nothing. The train moved into the railroad yard. Looking down, Nelson saw lines and lines of silver tracks multiplying and criss-crossing. Then before he could start counting them, the face in the window started out at him, gray but distinct, and he looked the other way. The train was in the station. Both he and Mr. Head jumped up and ran to the door. Neither noticed that they had left the paper sack with the lunch in it on the seat.

They walked stiffly through the small station and came out of a heavy door into the squall of traffic. Crowds were hurrying to work. Nelson didn't know where to look. Mr. Head leaned against the side of the building and glared in front of him.

Finally Nelson said, "Well, how do you see what all it is to see?"

Mr. Head didn't answer. Then as if the sight of people passing had given him the clue, he said, "You walk" and started off down the street. Nelson followed, steadying his hat. So many sights and sounds were flooding in on him that for the first block he hardly knew what he was seeing. At the second corner, Mr. Head turned and looked behind him at the station they had left, a putty-colored terminal with a concrete dome on top. He thought that if he could keep the dome always in sight, he would be able to get back in the afternoon to catch the train again.

As they walked along, Nelson began to distinguish details and take note of the store windows, jammed with every kind of equipment—hardware, drygoods, chicken feed, liquor. They passed one that Mr. Head called his particular attention to where you walked in and sat on a chair with your feet upon two rests and let a Negro polish your shoes. They walked slowly and stopped and stood at the entrances so he could see what went on in each place but they did not go into any of them. Mr. Head was determined not to go into any city store because on his first trip here, he had got lost in a large one and had found his way out only after many people had insulted him.

They came in the middle of the next block to a store that had a weighing machine in front of it and they both in turn stepped up on it and put in a penny and received a ticket. Mr. Head's ticket said "You weigh 120 pounds. You are upright and brave and all your friends admire you." He put the ticket in his pocket, surprised that the machine should have got his character correct but his weight wrong, for he had weighed on a grain scale not long before and knew he weighed 110. Nelson's ticket said, "You weigh 98 pounds. You have a great destiny ahead of you but beware of dark women." Nelson did not know any women and he weighed only 68 pounds but Mr. Head pointed out that the machine had probably printed the number upsidedown, meaning the 9 for a 6.

They walked on and at the end of five blocks the dome of the terminal sank out of sight and Mr. Head turned to the left. Nelson could have stood in front of every store window for an hour if there had not been another more interesting one next to it. Suddenly he said, "I was born here!" Mr. Head turned and looked at him with horror. There was a sweaty brightness about his face. "This is where I come from!" he said.

Mr. Head was appalled. He saw the moment had come for drastic action. "Lemme show you one thing you ain't seen yet," he said and took him to the corner where there was a sewer entrance. "Squat down," he said, "and stick your head in there," and he held the back of the boy's coat while he got down and put his head in the sewer. He drew it back quickly, hearing a gurgling in the depths under the sidewalk. Then Mr. Head explained the sewer system, how the entire city was underlined with it, how it contained all the drainage and was full of rats and how a man could slide into it and be sucked along down endless pitchblack tunnels. At any minute any man in the city might be sucked into the sewer and never heard from again. He described it so well that Nelson was for some seconds shaken. He connected the sewer passages with the entrance to hell and understood for the first time how the world was put together in its lower parts. He drew away from the curb.

Then he said, "Yes, but you can stay away from the holes," and his face took on that stubborn look that was so exasperating to his grandfather. "This is where I come from!" he said.

Mr. Head was dismayed but he only muttered, "You'll get your fill," and they walked on. At the end of two more blocks he turned to the left, feeling that he was circling the dome; and he was correct for in a half-hour they passed in front of the railroad station again. At first Nelson did not notice that he was seeing the same stores twice but when they passed the one where you put your feet on the rests while the Negro polished your shoes, he perceived that they were walking in a circle.

"We done been here!" he shouted. "I don't believe you know where you're at!"

"The direction just slipped my mind for a minute," Mr. Head said and they turned down a different street. He still did not intend to let the dome get too far away and after two blocks in their new direction, he turned to the left. This street contained two- and three-story wooden dwellings. Anyone passing on the sidewalk could see into the rooms and Mr. Head, glancing through one window, saw a woman lying on an iron bed, looking out, with a sheet pulled over her. Her knowing expression shook him. A fierce-looking boy on a bicycle came driving down out of nowhere and he had to jump to the side to keep from being hit. "It's nothing to them if they knock you down," he said. "You better keep closer to me."

They walked on for some time on streets like this before he remembered to turn again. The houses they were passing now were all unpainted and the wood in them looked rotten; the street between was narrower. Nelson saw a colored man. Then another. Then another. "Niggers live in these houses," he observed.

"Well come on and we'll go somewheres else," Mr. Head said. "We didn't come to look at niggers," and they turned down another street but they continued to see Negroes everywhere. Nelson's skin began to prickle and they stepped along at a faster pace in order to leave the neighborhood as soon as possible. There were colored men in their undershirts standing in the doors and colored women rocking on the sagging porches. Colored children played in the gutters and stopped what they were doing to look at them. Before long they began to pass rows of stores with colored customers in them but they didn't pause at the entrances of these. Black eyes in black faces were watching them from every direction. "Yes," Mr. Head said, "this is where you were born—right here with all these niggers."

Nelson scowled. "I think you done got us lost," he said.

Mr. Head swung around sharply and looked for the dome. It was nowhere in sight. "I ain't got us lost either," he said. "You're just tired of walking."

"I ain't tired, I'm hungry," Nelson said. "Give me a biscuit."

They discovered then that they had lost the lunch.

"You were the one holding the sack," Nelson said. "I would have kepaholt of it."

"If you want to direct this trip, I'll go on by myself and leave you right here," Mr. Head said and was pleased to see the boy turn white. However, he realized they were lost and drifting farther every minute from the station. He was hungry himself and beginning to be thirsty and since they had been in the colored neighborhood, they had both begun to sweat. Nelson had on his shoes and he was unaccustomed to them. The concrete sidewalks were very hard. They both wanted to find a place to sit down but this was impossible and they kept on walking, the boy muttering under his breath, "First you lost the sack and then you lost the way," and Mr. Head growling from time to time, "Anybody wants to be from this nigger heaven can be from it!"

By now the sun was well forward in the sky. The odor of dinners cooking drifted out to them. The Negroes were all at their doors to see them pass. "Whyn't you ast one of these niggers the way?" Nelson said. "You got us lost."

"This is where you were born," Mr. Head said. "You can ast one yourself if you want to."

Nelson was afraid of the colored men and he didn't want to be laughed at by the colored children. Up ahead he saw a large colored woman leaning in a doorway that opened onto the sidewalk. Her hair stood straight out from her head for about four inches all around and she was resting on bare brown feet that turned pink at the sides. She had on a pink dress that showed her exact shape. As they came abreast of her, she lazily lifted one hand to her head and her fingers disappeared into her hair.

Nelson stopped. He felt his breath drawn up by the woman's dark eyes. "How do you get back to town?" he said in a voice that did not sound like his own.

After a minute she said, "You in town now," in a rich low tone that made Nelson feel as if a cool spray had been turned on him.

"How do you get back to the train?" he said in the same reed-like voice.

"You can catch you a car," she said.

He understood she was making fun of him but he was too paralyzed even to scowl. He stood drinking in every detail of her. His eyes traveled up from her great knees to her forehead and then made a triangular path from the glistening sweat on her neck down and across her tremendous bosom and over her bare arm back to where her fingers lay hidden in her hair. He suddenly wanted her to reach down and pick him up and draw him against her and then he wanted to feel her breath on his face. He wanted to look down and down into her eyes while she held him tighter and tighter. He had never had such a feeling before. He felt as if he were reeling down through a pitchblack tunnel.

"You can go a block down yonder and catch you a car take you to the railroad station, Sugarpie," she said.

Nelson would have collapsed at her feet if Mr. Head had not pulled him roughly away. "You act like you don't have any sense!" the old man growled.

They hurried down the street and Nelson did not look back at the woman. He pushed his hat sharply forward over his face which was already burning with shame. The sneering ghost he had seen in the train window and all the foreboding feelings he had on the way returned to him and he remembered that his ticket from the scale had said to beware of dark women and that his grandfather's had said he was upright and brave. He took hold of the old man's hand, a sign of dependence that he seldom showed.

They headed down the street toward the car tracks where a long yellow rattling trolley was coming. Mr. Head had never boarded a streetcar and he let that one pass. Nelson was silent. From time to time his mouth trembled slightly but his grandfather, occupied with his own problems, paid him no attention. They stood on the corner and neither looked at the Negroes who were passing, going about their business just as if they had been white, except that most of them stopped and eyed Mr. Head and Nelson. It occurred to Mr. Head that since the streetcar ran on tracks, they could simply follow the tracks. He gave Nelson a slight push and explained that they would follow the tracks on into the railroad station, walking, and they set off.

Presently to their great relief they began to see white people again and Nelson sat down on the sidewalk against the wall of a building. "I got to rest myself some," he said. "You lost the sack and the direction. You can just wait on me to rest myself."

"There's the tracks in front of us," Mr. Head said. "All we got to do is keep them in sight and you could have remembered the sack as good as me. This is where you were born. This is your old home town. This is your second trip. You ought to know how to do," and he squatted down and continued in this vein but the boy, easing his burning feet out of his shoes, did not answer.

"And standing there grinning like a chim-pan-zee while a nigger woman gives you directions. Great Gawd!" Mr. Head said.

"I never said I was nothing but born here," the boy said in a shaky voice. "I never said I would or wouldn't like it. I never said I wanted to come. I only said I was born here and I never had nothing to do with that. I want to go home. I never wanted to come in the first place. It was all your big idea. How you know you ain't following the tracks in the wrong direction?"

This last had occurred to Mr. Head too. "All these people are white," he said.

"We ain't passed here before," Nelson said. This was a neighborhood of brick buildings that might have been lived in or might not. A few empty automobiles were parked along the curb and there was an occasional passerby. The heat of the pavement came up through Nelson's thin suit. His eyelids began to droop, and after a few minutes his head tilted forward. His shoulders twitched once or twice and then he fell over on his side and lay sprawled in an exhausted fit of sleep.

Mr. Head watched him silently. He was very tired himself but they could not both sleep at the same time and he could not have slept anyway because he did not know where he was. In a few minutes Nelson would wake up, refreshed by his sleep and very cocky, and would begin complaining that he had lost the sack and the way. You'd have a mighty sorry time if I wasn't here, Mr. Head thought; and then another idea occurred to him. He looked at the sprawled figure for several minutes; presently he stood up. He justified what he was going to do on the grounds that it is sometimes necessary to teach a child a lesson he won't forget, particularly when the child is always reasserting his position with some new impudence. He walked without a sound to the corner about twenty feet away and sat down on a covered garbage can in the alley where he could look out and watch Nelson wake up alone.

The boy was dozing fitfully, half conscious of vague noises and black forms moving up from some dark part of him into the light. His face worked in his sleep and he had pulled his knees up under his chin. The sun shed a dull dry light on the narrow street; everything looked like exactly what it was. After a while Mr. Head, hunched like an old monkey on the garbage can lid, decided that if Nelson didn't wake up soon, he would make a loud noise by bamming his foot against the can. He looked at his watch and discovered that it was two o'clock. Their train left at six and the possibility of missing it was too awful for him to think of. He kicked his foot backwards on the can and a hollow boom reverberated in the alley.

Nelson shot up onto his feet with a shout. He looked where his grandfather should have been and stared. He seemed to whirl several times and then, picking up his feet and throwing his head back, he dashed down the street like a wild maddened pony. Mr. Head jumped off the can and galloped after but the child was almost out of sight. He saw a streak of gray disappearing diagonally a block ahead. He ran as fast as he could, looking both ways down every intersection, but without sight of him again. Then as he passed the third intersection, completely winded, he saw about half a block down the street a scene that stopped him altogether. He crouched behind a trash box to watch and get his bearings.

Nelson was sitting with both legs spread out and by his side lay an elderly woman, screaming. Groceries were scattered about the sidewalk. A crowd of women had already gathered to see justice done and Mr. Head distinctly heard the old woman on the pavement shout, "You've broken my ankle and your daddy'll pay for it! Every nickel! Police! Police!" Several of the women were plucking at Nelson's shoulder but the boy seemed too dazed to get up.

Something forced Mr. Head from behind the trash box and forward, but only at a creeping pace. He had never in his life been accosted by a policeman. The women were milling around Nelson as if they might suddenly all dive on him at once and tear him to pieces, and the old woman continued to scream that her ankle was broken and to call for an officer. Mr. Head came on so slowly that he could have been taking a backward step after each forward one, but when he was about ten feet away, Nelson saw him and sprang. The child caught him around the hips and clung panting against him.

The women all turned on Mr. Head. The injured one sat up and shouted, "You sir! You'll pay every penny of my doctor's bill that your boy caused. He's a juve-nile delinquent! Where is an officer? Somebody take this man's name and address!"

Mr. Head was trying to detach Nelson's fingers from the flesh in the back of his legs. The old man's head had lowered itself into his collar like a turtle's; his eyes were glazed with fear and caution.

"Your boy has broken my ankle!" the old woman shouted. "Police!"

Mr. Head sensed the approach of the policeman from behind. He stared straight ahead at the women who were massed in their fury like a solid wall to block his escape. "This is not my boy," he said. "I never seen him before."

He felt Nelson's fingers fall out of his flesh.

The women dropped back, staring at him with horror, as if they were so repulsed by a man who would deny his own image and likeness that they could not bear to lay hands on him. Mr. Head walked on, through a space they silently cleared, and left Nelson behind. Ahead of him he saw nothing but a hollow tunnel that had once been the street.

The boy remained standing where he was, his neck craned forward and his hands hanging by his sides. His hat was jammed on his head so that there were no longer any creases in it. The injured woman got up and shook her fist at him and the others gave him pitying looks, but he didn't notice any of them. There was no policeman in sight.

In a minute he began to move mechanically, making no effort to catch up with his grandfather but merely following at about twenty paces. They walked on for five blocks in this way. Mr. Head's shoulders were sagging and his neck hung forward at such an angle that it was not visible from behind. He was afraid to turn his head. Finally he cut a short hopeful glance over his shoulder. Twenty feet behind him, he saw two small eyes piercing into his back like pitchfork prongs.

The boy was not of a forgiving nature but this was the first time he had ever had anything to forgive. Mr. Head had never disgraced himself before. After two more blocks, he turned and called over his shoulder in a high desperately gay voice, "Let's us go get us a Co' Cola somewheres!"

Nelson, with a dignity he had never shown before, turned and stood with his back to his grandfather.

Mr. Head began to feel the depth of his denial. His face as they walked on became all hollows and bare ridges. He saw nothing they were passing but he perceived that they had lost the car tracks. There was no dome to be seen anywhere and the afternoon was advancing. He knew that if dark overtook them in the city, they would be beaten and robbed. The speed of God's justice was only what he expected for himself, but he could not stand to think that his sins would be visited upon Nelson and that even now, he was leading the boy to his doom.

They continued to walk on block after block through an endless section of small brick houses until Mr. Head almost fell over a water spigot sticking up about six inches off the edge of a grass plot. He had not had a drink of water since early morning but he felt he did not deserve it now. Then he thought that Nelson would be thirsty and they would both drink and be brought together. He squatted down and put his mouth to the nozzle and turned a cold stream of water into his throat. Then he called out in the high desperate voice, "Come on and getcher some water!"

This time the child stared through him for nearly sixty seconds. Mr. Head got up and walked on as if he had drunk poison. Nelson, though he had not had water since some he had drunk out of a paper cup on the train, passed by the spigot, disdaining to drink where his grandfather had. When Mr. Head realized this, he lost all hope. His face in the waning afternoon light looked ravaged and abandoned. He could feel the boy's steady hate, traveling at an even pace behind him and he knew that (if by some miracle they escaped being murdered in the city) it would continue just that way for the rest of his life. He knew that now he was wandering into a black strange place where nothing was like it had ever been before, a long old age without respect and an end that would be welcome because it would be the end.

As for Nelson, his mind had frozen around his grandfather's treachery as if he were trying to preserve it intact to present at the final judgment. He walked without looking to one side or the other, but every now and then his mouth would twitch and this was when he felt, from some remote place inside himself, a black mysterious form reach up as if it would melt his frozen vision in one hot grasp.

The sun dropped down behind a row of houses and hardly noticing, they passed into an elegant suburban section where mansions were set back from the road by lawns with birdbaths on them. Here everything was entirely deserted. For blocks they didn't pass even a dog. The big white houses were like partially submerged icebergs in the distance. There were no sidewalks, only drives, and these wound around and around in endless ridiculous circles. Nelson made no move to come nearer to Mr. Head. The old man felt that if he saw a sewer entrance he would drop down into it and let himself be carried away; and he could imagine the boy standing by, watching with only a slight interest, while he disappeared.

A loud bark jarred him to attention and he looked up to see a fat man approaching with two bulldogs. He waved both arms like someone shipwrecked on a desert island. "I'm lost!" he called, "I'm lost and can't find my way and me and this boy have got to catch this train and I can't find the station. Oh Gawd I'm lost! Oh hep me Gawd I'm lost!"

The man, who was bald-headed and had on golf knickers, asked him what train he was trying to catch and Mr. Head began to get out his tickets, trembling so violently he could hardly hold them. Nelson had come up to within fifteen feet and stood watching.

"Well," the fat man said, giving him back the tickets, "you won't have time to get back to town to make this but you can catch it at the suburb stop. That's three blocks from here," and he began explaining how to get there.

Mr. Head stared as if he were slowly returning from the dead and when the man had finished and gone off with the dogs jumping at his heels, he turned to Nelson and said breathlessly, "We're going to get home!"

The child was standing about ten feet away, his face bloodless under the gray hat. His eyes were triumphantly cold. There was no light in them, no feeling, no interest. He was merely there, a small figure, waiting. Home was nothing to him.

Mr. Head turned slowly. He felt he knew now what time would be like without seasons and what heat would be like without light and what man would be like without salvation. He didn't care if he never made the train and if it had not been for what suddenly caught his attention, like a cry out of the gathering dusk, he might have forgotten there was a station to go to.

He had not walked five hundred yards down the road when he saw, within reach of him, the plaster figure of a Negro sitting bent over on a low yellow brick fence that curved around a wide lawn. The Negro was about Nelson's size and he was pitched forward at an unsteady angle because the putty that held him to the wall had cracked. One of his eyes was entirely white and he held a piece of brown watermelon.

Mr. Head stood looking at him silently until Nelson stopped at a little distance. Then as the two of them stood there, Mr. Head breathed, "An artificial nigger!"

It was not possible to tell if the artificial Negro were meant to be young or old; he looked too miserable to be either. He was meant to look happy because his mouth was stretched up at the corners but the chipped eye and the angle he was cocked at gave him a wild look of misery instead.

"An artificial nigger!" Nelson repeated in Mr. Head's exact tone.

The two of them stood there with their necks forward at almost the same angle and their shoulders curved in almost exactly the same way and their hands trembling identically in their pockets. Mr. Head looked like an ancient child and Nelson like a miniature old man. They stood gazing at the artificial Negro as if they were faced with some great mystery, some monument to another's victory that brought them together in their common defeat. They could both feel it dissolving their differences like an action of mercy. Mr. Head had never known before what mercy felt like because he had been too good to deserve any, but he felt he knew now. He looked at Nelson and understood that he must say something to the child to show that he was still wise and in the look the boy returned he saw a hungry need for that assurance. Nelson's eyes seemed to implore him to explain once and for all the mystery of existence.

Mr. Head opened his lips to make a lofty statement and heard himself say, "They ain't got enough real ones here. They got to have an artificial one."

After a second, the boy nodded with a strange shivering about his mouth, and said, "Let's go home before we get ourselves lost again."

Their train glided into the suburb stop just as they reached the station and they boarded it together, and ten minutes before it was due to arrive at the junction, they went to the door and stood ready to jump off if it did not stop; but it did, just as the moon, restored to its full splendor, sprang from a cloud and flooded the clearing with light. As they stepped off, the sage grass was shivering gently in shades of silver and the clinkers under their feet glittered with a fresh black light. The treetops, fencing the junction like the protecting walls of a garden, were darker than the sky which was hung with gigantic white clouds illuminated like lanterns.

Mr. Head stood very still and felt the action of mercy touch him again but this time he knew that there were no words in the world that could name it. He understood that it grew out of agony, which is not denied to any man and which is given in strange ways to children. He understood it was all a man could carry into death to give his Maker and he suddenly burned with shame that he had so little of it to take with him. He stood appalled, judging himself with the thoroughness of God, while the action of mercy covered his pride like a flame and consumed it. He had never thought himself a great sinner before but he saw now that his true depravity had been hidden from him lest it cause him despair. He realized that he was forgiven for sins from the beginning of time, when he had conceived in his own heart the sin of Adam,[4] until the present, when he had denied poor Nelson. He saw that no sin was too monstrous for him to claim as his own, and since God loved in proportion as He forgave, he felt ready at that instant to enter Paradise.

Nelson, composing his expression under the shadow of his hat brim, watched him with a mixture of fatigue and suspicion, but as the train glided past them and disappeared like a frightened serpent into the woods, even his face lightened and he muttered, "I'm glad I've went once, but I'll never go back again!"

1955

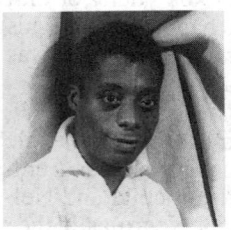

James Baldwin
(1924–1987)

James Baldwin, born in Harlem in 1924, was the illegitimate child of a domestic worker who later married a sternly moralistic storefront preacher. In his first novel, *Go Tell It on the Mountain* (1953), Baldwin drew upon memories of his difficult relationship with his stepfather. Like Baldwin, the protagonist of that novel undergoes a conversion experience as an adolescent and becomes an evangelist. At age fourteen Baldwin converted to the Pentecostal faith and preached weekly until he left home in 1942 to become a railroad worker in New Jersey. In Harlem Baldwin had enjoyed the intellectually nurturing influence of Countee Cullen, the advisor to Baldwin's high school literary club, and had been somewhat sheltered from racism. After two years' exposure to blatant racist abuses in New Jersey, he settled in New York City's Greenwich Village in 1944. There he met other writers who were enthusiastic about his work, including Richard Wright, who helped Baldwin obtain fellowship funding for his early writing efforts.

---

[4] Original Sin, the sin of disobedience (see Genesis 3).

Jazz is a major American cultural contribution. Here, two jazz greats, Charlie "Bird" Parker (on saxophone) and Miles Davis (on trumpet), perform in 1947. The writing styles of authors such as Ralph Ellison and James Baldwin have been influenced by jazz.

African-American writers such as Richard Wright and Chester Himes moved to Europe after World War II. Baldwin left for Paris in 1948 and spent most of his life in Europe and the Middle East, while his books became bestsellers in America. Other African-American writers criticized this self-imposed exile—most notably Eldridge Cleaver, who scathingly and scatologically denounced Baldwin's homosexuality as well as his absence from many 1960s civil rights demonstrations. But Baldwin was not uninvolved in the protest movement: he will be remembered as much for his essays chronicling the civil rights movement—*The Fire Next Time* (1963) and *No Name in the Street* (1972)—as for his fiction. As the radicalism of the 1960s disappointingly sputtered in the early 1970s, Baldwin grew increasingly militant, condoning the violence of the Black Panthers and even, in 1972, accepting Cleaver's viciously personal criticism as a "necessary warning."

Autobiographical elements are common in Baldwin's work. His characters are typically lonely men, some alienated by homosexuality (as in *Giovanni's Room* [1956] and *Just Above My Head* [1979]) as well as by race. He viewed the concepts of "Negro" and "homosexual" as categorical ghettos invented by mainstream culture: "People invent categories to feel safe. White people invented black people to give white people identity." Many of his black characters are entertainers—such as jazz musicians Rufus of *Another Country* (1962) and Sonny of "Sonny's Blues" (1957)—who have taken the invented identity thrust upon them and made it their livelihood. They feel trapped within artificial personae that paradoxically shield them, whether in a theater or a police lineup, as they desperately struggle to anticipate the demands of their audiences. "How," one of Baldwin's narrators asks, "can one be prepared for the spittle in the face, all the tireless ingenuity which goes into the spite and fear of small, unutterably miserable people whose . . . joy, whose safety, is entirely dependent on the humiliation and anguish of others?"

Baldwin's most tragic characters are those who, unable to discard the masks they hope will win the love or at least the tolerance of white society, find themselves estranged from their family and friends. Many of these characters turn to musical forms of communication or, like Baldwin himself, turn their gazes inward—a tendency Eldridge Cleaver considered a form of internal expatriation, a culpably irresponsible elopement with the self. Throughout Baldwin's career he insisted that the artist's private and public responsibilities are inextricably involved; he wanted to be a man who was both honest and a good writer and did not feel he could be one without being the other. By the time of his death in 1987, he had more than accomplished at least the latter goal.

Suggested Readings: *Go Tell It on the Mountain*, 1953. *The Amen Corner*, 1954. *Notes of a Native Son*, 1955. *Giovanni's Room*, 1956. *Nobody Knows My Name*, 1961. *Another Country*, 1962. *The Fire Next Time*, 1963. *The Blues for Mr. Charlie*, 1964. *Tell Me How Long the Train's Been Gone*, 1968. *No Name in the Street*, 1972. *If Beale Street Could Talk*, 1974. *Just Above My Head*, 1979. *The Evidence of Things Not Seen*, 1985. *Jimmy's Blues: Selected Poems*, 1985. *The Price of the Ticket: Collected Nonfiction*, 1985. *Harlem Quartet*, 1987. F. M. Eckman, *The Furious Passage of James Baldwin*, 1966. K. Kinnamon, ed., *James Baldwin: A Collection of Critical Essays*, 1974. H. Bloom, ed., *Modern Critical Views: James Baldwin*, 1986.

Text Used: *Going to Meet the Man*, 1965.

SONNY'S BLUES*

I read about it in the paper, in the subway, on my way to work. I read it, and I couldn't believe it, and I read it again. Then perhaps I just stared at it, at the newsprint spelling out his name, spelling out the story. I stared at it in the swinging lights of the subway car, and in the faces and bodies of the people, and in my own face, trapped in the darkness which roared outside.

It was not to be believed and I kept telling myself that, as I walked from the subway station to the high school. And at the same time I couldn't doubt it. I was scared, scared for Sonny. He became real to me again. A great block of ice got settled in my belly and kept melting there slowly all day long, while I taught my classes algebra. It was a special kind of ice. It kept melting, sending trickles of ice water all up and down my veins, but it never got less. Sometimes it hardened and seemed to expand until I felt my guts were going to come spilling out or that I was going to choke or scream. This would always be at a moment when I was remembering some specific thing Sonny had once said or done.

When he was about as old as the boys in my classes his face had been bright and open, there was a lot of copper in it; and he'd had wonderfully direct brown eyes, and great gentleness and privacy. I wondered what he looked like now. He had been picked up, the evening before, in a raid on an apartment downtown, for peddling and using heroin.

* First published in the *Partisan Review* of summer 1957 and collected in *Going to Meet the Man* (1965).

I couldn't believe it: but what I mean by that is that I couldn't find any room for it anywhere inside me. I had kept it outside me for a long time. I hadn't wanted to know. I had had suspicions, but I didn't name them, I kept putting them away. I told myself that Sonny was wild, but he wasn't crazy. And he'd always been a good boy, he hadn't ever turned hard or evil or disrespectful, the way kids can, so quick, so quick, especially in Harlem. I didn't want to believe that I'd ever see my brother going down, coming to nothing, all that light in his face gone out, in the condition I'd already seen so many others. Yet it had happened and here I was, talking about algebra to a lot of boys who might, every one of them for all I knew, be popping off needles every time they went to the head. Maybe it did more for them than algebra could.

I was sure that the first time Sonny had ever had horse,[1] he couldn't have been much older than these boys were now. These boys, now, were living as we'd been living then, they were growing up with a rush and their heads bumped abruptly against the low ceiling of their actual possibilities. They were filled with rage. All they really knew were two darknesses, the darkness of their lives, which was now closing in on them, and the darkness of the movies, which had blinded them to that other darkness, and in which they now vindictively, dreamed, at once more together than they were at any other time, and more alone.

When the last bell rang, the last class ended, I let out my breath. It seemed I'd been holding it for all that time. My clothes were wet—I may have looked as though I'd been sitting in a steam bath, all dressed up, all afternoon. I sat alone in the classroom a long time. I listened to the boys outside, downstairs, shouting and cursing and laughing. Their laughter struck me for perhaps the first time. It was not the joyous laughter which —God knows why—one associates with children. It was mocking and insular, its intent was to denigrate. It was disenchanted, and in this, also, lay the authority of their curses. Perhaps I was listening to them because I was thinking about my brother and in them I heard my brother. And myself.

One boy was whistling a tune, at once very complicated and very simple, it seemed to be pouring out of him as though he were a bird, and it sounded very cool and moving through all that harsh, bright air, only just holding its own through all those other sounds.

I stood up and walked over to the window and looked down into the courtyard. It was the beginning of the spring and the sap was rising in the boys. A teacher passed through them every now and again, quickly, as though he or she couldn't wait to get out of that courtyard, to get those boys out of their sight and off their minds. I started collecting my stuff. I thought I'd better get home and talk to Isabel.

The courtyard was almost deserted by the time I got downstairs. I saw this boy standing in the shadow of a doorway, looking just like Sonny. I almost called his name. Then I saw that it wasn't Sonny, but somebody we used to know, a boy from around our block. He'd been Sonny's friend. He'd never been mine, having been too young for me, and, anyway, I'd never liked him. And now, even though he was a grown-up man, he still hung around that block, still spent hours on the street corners, was always high and raggy. I used to run into him from time to time and he'd often work around to asking me for a quarter or fifty cents. He always had some real good excuse, too, and I always gave it to him, I don't know why.

[1] Heroin.

But now, abruptly, I hated him. I couldn't stand the way he looked at me, partly like a dog, partly like a cunning child. I wanted to ask him what the hell he was doing in the school courtyard.

He sort of shuffled over to me, and he said, "I see you got the papers. So you already know about it."

"You mean about Sonny? Yes, I already know about it. How come they didn't get you?"

He grinned. It made him repulsive and it also brought to mind what he'd looked like as a kid. "I wasn't there. I stay away from them people."

"Good for you." I offered him a cigarette and I watched him through the smoke. "You come all the way down here just to tell me about Sonny?"

"That's right." He was sort of shaking his head and his eyes looked strange, as though they were about to cross. The bright sun deadened his damp dark brown skin and it made his eyes look yellow and showed up the dirt in his kinked hair. He smelled funky. I moved a little away from him and I said, "Well, thanks. But I already know about it and I got to get home."

"I'll walk you a little ways," he said. We started walking. There were a couple of kids still loitering in the courtyard and one of them said goodnight to me and looked strangely at the boy beside me.

"What're you going to do?" he asked me. "I mean, about Sonny?"

"Look. I haven't seen Sonny for over a year, I'm not sure I'm going to do anything. Anyway, what the hell *can* I do?"

"That's right," he said quickly, "ain't nothing you can do. Can't much help old Sonny no more, I guess."

It was what I was thinking and so it seemed to me he had no right to say it.

"I'm surprised at Sonny, though," he went on—he had a funny way of talking, he looked straight ahead as though he were talking to himself—"I thought Sonny was a smart boy, I thought he was too smart to get hung."

"I guess he thought so too," I said sharply, "and that's how he got hung. And now about you? You're pretty goddamn smart, I bet."

Then he looked directly at me, just for a minute. "I ain't smart," he said. "If I was smart, I'd have reached for a pistol a long time ago."

"Look. Don't tell *me* your sad story, if it was up to me, I'd give you one." Then I felt guilty—guilty, probably, for never having supposed that the poor bastard *had* a story of his own, much less a sad one, and I asked, quickly, "What's going to happen to him now?"

He didn't answer this. He was off by himself some place. "Funny thing," he said, and from his tone we might have been discussing the quickest way to get to Brooklyn, "when I saw the papers this morning, the first thing I asked myself was if I had anything to do with it. I felt sort of responsible."

I began to listen more carefully. The subway station was on the corner, just before us, and I stopped. He stopped, too. We were in front of a bar and he ducked slightly, peering in, but whoever he was looking for didn't seem to be there. The juke box was blasting away with something black and bouncy and I half watched the barmaid as she danced her way from the juke box to her place behind the bar. And I watched her face as she laughingly responded to something someone said to her, still keeping time to the music. When she smiled one saw the little girl, one sensed the doomed, still-struggling woman beneath the battered face of the semi-whore.

"I never *give* Sonny nothing," the boy said finally, "but a long time ago I come to school high and Sonny asked me how it felt." He paused, I couldn't bear to watch him, I watched the barmaid, and I listened to the music which seemed to be causing the pavement to shake. "I told him it felt great." The music stopped, the barmaid paused and watched the juke box until the music began again. "It did."

All this was carrying me some place I didn't want to go. I certainly didn't want to know how it felt. It filled everything, the people, the houses, the music, the dark, quicksilver barmaid, with menace; and this menace was their reality.

"What's going to happen to him now?" I asked again.

"They'll send him away some place and they'll try to cure him." He shook his head. "Maybe he'll even think he's kicked the habit. They they'll let him loose"—he gestured, throwing his cigarette into the gutter. "That's all."

"What do you mean, that's *all?*"

But I knew what he meant.

"I *mean*, that's *all*." He turned his head and looked at me, pulling down the corners of his mouth. "Don't you know what I mean?" he asked, softly.

"How the hell *would* I know what you mean?" I almost whispered it, I don't know why.

"That's right," he said to the air, "how would *he* know what I mean?" He turned toward me again, patient and calm, and yet I somehow felt him shaking, shaking as though he were going to fall apart. I felt that ice in my guts again, the dread I'd felt all afternoon; and again I watched the barmaid, moving about the bar, washing glasses, and singing. "Listen. They'll let him out and then it'll just start all over again. That's what I mean."

"You mean—they'll let him out. And then he'll just start working his way back in again. You mean he'll never kick the habit. Is that what you mean?"

"That's right," he said, cheerfully. "*You* see what I mean."

"Tell me," I said at last, "why does he want to die? He must want to die, he's killing himself, why does he want to die?"

He looked at me in surprise. He licked his lips. "He don't want to die. He wants to live. Don't nobody want to die, ever."

Then I wanted to ask him—too many things. He could not have answered, or if he had, I could not have borne the answers. I started walking. "Well, I guess it's none of my business."

"It's going to be rough on old Sonny," he said. We reached the subway station. "This is your station?" he asked. I nodded. I took one step down. "Damn!" he said, suddenly. I looked up at him. He grinned again. "Damn it if I didn't leave all my money home. You ain't got a dollar on you, have you? Just for a couple of days, is all."

All at once something inside gave and threatened to come pouring out of me. I didn't hate him any more. I felt that in another moment I'd start crying like a child.

"Sure," I said. "Don't sweat." I looked in my wallet and didn't have a dollar, I only had a five. "Here," I said. "That hold you?"

He didn't look at it—he didn't want to look at it. A terrible, closed look came over his face, as though he were keeping the number on the bill a secret from him and me. "Thanks," he said, and now he was dying to see me go. "Don't worry about Sonny. Maybe I'll write him or something."

"Sure," I said. "You do that. So long."

"Be seeing you," he said. I went on down the steps.

And I didn't write Sonny or send him anything for a long time. When I finally did, it was just after my little girl died, he wrote me back a letter which made me feel like a bastard.

Here's what he said:

> Dear brother,
> You don't know how much I needed to hear from you. I wanted to write you many a time but I dug how much I must have hurt you and so I didn't write. But now I feel like a man who's been trying to climb up out of some deep, real deep and funky hole and just saw the sun up there, outside. I got to get outside.
> I can't tell you much about how I got here. I mean I don't know how to tell you. I guess I was afraid of something or I was trying to escape from something and you know I have never been very strong in the head (smile). I'm glad Mama and Daddy are dead and can't see what's happened to their son and I swear if I'd known what I was doing I would never have hurt you so, you and a lot of other fine people who were nice to me and who believed in me.
> I don't want you to think it had anything to do with me being a musician. It's more than that. Or maybe less than that. I can't get anything straight in my head down here and I try not to think about what's going to happen to me when I get outside again. Sometime I think I'm going to flip and *never* get outside and sometime I think I'll come straight back. I tell you one thing, though, I'd rather blow my brains out than go through this again. But that's what they all say, so they tell me. If I tell you when I'm coming to New York and if you could meet me, I sure would appreciate it. Give my love to Isabel and the kids and I was sure sorry to hear about little Gracie. I wish I could be like Mama and say the Lord's will be done, but I don't know it seems to me that trouble is the one thing that never does get stopped and I don't know what good it does to blame it on the Lord. But maybe it does some good if you believe it.
>
> > Your brother,
> > Sonny

Then I kept in constant touch with him and I sent him whatever I could and I went to meet him when he came back to New York. When I saw him many things I thought I had forgotten came flooding back to me. This was because I had begun, finally, to wonder about Sonny, about the life that Sonny lived inside. This life, whatever it was, had made him older and thinner and it had deepened the distant stillness in which he had always moved. He looked very unlike my baby brother. Yet, when he smiled, when we shook hands, the baby brother I'd never known looked out from the depths of his private life, like an animal waiting to be coaxed into the light.

"How you been keeping?" he asked me.

"All right. And you?"

"Just fine." He was smiling all over his face. "It's good to see you again."

"It's good to see you."

The seven years' difference in our ages lay between us like a chasm: I wondered if these years would ever operate between us as a bridge. I was remembering, and it made it hard to catch my breath, that I had been there when he was born; and I had heard the first words he had ever spoken. When he started to walk, he walked from our mother straight to me. I caught him just before he fell when he took the first steps he ever took in this world.

"How's Isabel?"

"Just fine. She's dying to see you."

"And the boys?"

"They're fine, too. They're anxious to see their uncle."

"Oh, come on. You know they don't remember me."

"Are you kidding? Of course they remember you."

He grinned again. We got into a taxi. We had a lot to say to each other, far too much to know how to begin.

As the taxi began to move, I asked, "You still want to go to India?"

He laughed. "You still remember that. Hell, no. This place is Indian enough for me."

"It used to belong to them," I said.

And he laughed again. "They damn sure knew what they were doing when they got rid of it."

Years ago, when he was around fourteen, he'd been all hipped on the idea of going to India. He read books about people sitting on rocks, naked, in all kinds of weather, but mostly bad, naturally, and walking barefoot through hot coals and arriving at wisdom. I used to say that it sounded to me as though they were getting away from wisdom as fast as they could. I think he sort of looked down on me for that.

"Do you mind," he asked, "if we have the driver drive alongside the park? On the west side—I haven't seen the city in so long."

"Of course not," I said. I was afraid that I might sound as though I were humoring him, but I hoped he wouldn't take it that way.

So we drove along, between the green of the park and the stony, lifeless elegance of hotels and apartment buildings, toward the vivid, killing streets of our childhood. These streets hadn't changed, though housing projects jutted up out of them now like rocks in the middle of a boiling sea. Most of the houses in which we had grown up had vanished, as had the stores from which we had stolen, the basements in which we had first tried sex, the rooftops from which we had hurled tin cans and bricks. But houses exactly like the houses of our past yet dominated the landscape, boys exactly like the boys we once had been found themselves smothering in these houses, came down into the streets for light and air and found themselves encircled by disaster. Some escaped the trap, most didn't. Those who got out always left something of themselves behind, as some animals amputate a leg and leave it in the trap. It might be said, perhaps, that I had escaped, after all, I was a school teacher; or that Sonny had, he hadn't lived in Harlem for years. Yet, as the cab moved uptown through streets which seemed, with a rush, to darken with dark people, and as I covertly studied Sonny's face, it came to me that what we both were seeking through our separate cab windows was that part of ourselves which had been left behind. It's always at the hour of trouble and confrontation that the missing member aches.

We hit 110th Street and started rolling up Lenox Avenue.[2] And I'd known this avenue all my life, but it seemed to me again, as it had seemed on the day I'd first heard about Sonny's trouble, filled with a hidden menace which was its very breath of life.

___

[2] In central Manhattan; heading toward Harlem.

"We almost there," said Sonny.

"Almost." We were both too nervous to say anything more.

We live in a housing project. It hasn't been up long. A few days after it was up it seemed uninhabitably new, now, of course, it's already rundown. It looks like a parody of the good, clean, faceless life—God knows the people who live in it do their best to make it a parody. The beat-looking grass lying around isn't enough to make their lives green, the hedges will never hold out the streets, and they know it. The big windows fool no one, they aren't big enough to make space out of no space. They don't bother with the windows, they watch the TV screen instead. The playground is most popular with the children who don't play at jacks, or skip rope, or roller skate, or swing, and they can be found in it after dark. We moved in partly because it's not too far from where I teach, and partly for the kids; but it's really just like the houses in which Sonny and I grew up. The same things happen, they'll have the same things to remember. The moment Sonny and I started into the house I had the feeling that I was simply bringing him back into the danger he had almost died trying to escape.

Sonny has never been talkative. So I don't know why I was sure he'd be dying to talk to me when supper was over the first night. Everything went fine, the oldest boy remembered him, and the youngest boy liked him, and Sonny had remembered to bring something for each of them; and Isabel, who is really much nicer than I am, more open and giving, had gone to a lot of trouble about dinner and was genuinely glad to see him. And she's always been able to tease Sonny in a way that I haven't. It was nice to see her face so vivid again and to hear her laugh and watch her make Sonny laugh. She wasn't, or, anyway, she didn't seem to be, at all uneasy or embarrassed. She chatted as though there were no subject which had to be avoided and she got Sonny past his first, faint stiffness. And thank God she was there, for I was filled with that icy dread again. Everything I did seemed awkward to me, and everything I said sounded freighted with hidden meaning. I was trying to remember everything I'd heard about dope addiction and I couldn't help watching Sonny for signs. I wasn't doing it out of malice. I was trying to find out something about my brother. I was dying to hear him tell me he was safe.

"Safe!" my father grunted, whenever Mama suggested trying to move to a neighborhood which might be safer for children. "Safe, hell! Ain't no place safe for kids, nor nobody."

He always went on like this, but he wasn't, ever, really as bad as he sounded, not even on weekends, when he got drunk. As a matter of fact, he was always on the lookout for "something a little better," but he died before he found it. He died suddenly, during a drunken weekend in the middle of the war, when Sonny was fifteen. He and Sonny hadn't ever got on too well. And this was partly because Sonny was the apple of his father's eye. It was because he loved Sonny so much and was frightened for him, that he was always fighting with him. It doesn't do any good to fight with Sonny. Sonny just moves back, inside himself, where he can't be reached. But the principal reason that they never hit it off is that they were so much alike. Daddy was big and rough and loud-talking, just the opposite of Sonny, but they both had—that same privacy.

Mama tried to tell me something about this, just after Daddy died. I was home on leave from the army.

This was the last time I ever saw my mother alive. Just the same, this picture gets all mixed up in my mind with pictures I had of her when she was younger.

The way I always see her is the way she used to be on a Sunday afternoon, say, when the old folks were talking after the big Sunday dinner. I always see her wearing pale blue. She'd be sitting on the sofa. And my father would be sitting in the easy chair, not far from her. And the living room would be full of church folks and relatives. There they sit, in chairs all around the living room, and the night is creeping up outside, but nobody knows it yet. You can see the darkness growing against the windowpanes and you hear the street noises every now and again, or maybe the jangling beat of a tambourine from one of the churches close by, but it's real quiet in the room. For a moment nobody's talking, but every face looks darkening, like the sky outside. And my mother rocks a little from the waist, and my father's eyes are closed. Everyone is looking at something a child can't see. For a minute they've forgotten the children. Maybe a kid is lying on the rug, half asleep. Maybe somebody's got a kid in his lap and is absent-mindedly stroking the kid's head. Maybe there's a kid, quiet and big-eyed, curled up in a big chair in the corner. The silence, the darkness coming, and the darkness in the faces frightens the child obscurely. He hopes that the hand which strokes his forehead will never stop—will never die. He hopes that there will never come a time when the old folks won't be sitting around the living room, talking about where they've come from, and what they've seen, and what's happened to them and their kinfolk.

But something deep and watchful in the child knows that this is bound to end, is already ending. In a moment someone will get up and turn on the light. Then the old folks will remember the children and they won't talk any more that day. And when light fills the room, the child is filled with darkness. He knows that every time this happens he's moved just a little closer to that darkness outside. The darkness outside is what the old folks have been talking about. It's what they've come from. It's what they endure. The child knows that they won't talk any more because if he knows too much about what's happened to *them,* he'll know too much too soon, about what's going to happen to *him.*

The last time I talked to my mother, I remember I was restless. I wanted to get out and see Isabel. We weren't married then and we had a lot to straighten out between us.

There Mama sat, in black, by the window. She was humming an old church song, *Lord, you brought me from a long ways off.* Sonny was out somewhere. Mama kept watching the streets.

"I don't know," she said, "if I'll ever see you again, after you go off from here. But I hope you'll remember the things I tried to teach you."

"Don't talk like that," I said, and smiled. "You'll be here a long time yet."

She smiled, too, but she said nothing. She was quiet for a long time. And I said, "Mama, don't you worry about nothing. I'll be writing all the time, and you be getting the checks. . . ."

"I want to talk to you about your brother," she said, suddenly. "If anything happens to me he ain't going to have nobody to look out for him."

"Mama," I said, "ain't nothing going to happen to you *or* Sonny. Sonny's all right. He's a good boy and he's got good sense."

"It ain't a question of his being a good boy," Mama said, "nor of his having good sense. It ain't only the bad ones, nor yet the dumb ones that gets sucked under." She stopped, looking at me. "Your Daddy once had a brother," she said, and she smiled in a way that made me feel she was in pain. "You didn't never know that, did you?"

"No," I said, "I never knew that," and I watched her face.

"Oh, yes," she said, "your Daddy had a brother." She looked out of the window again. "I know you never saw your Daddy cry. But *I* did—many a time, through all these years."

I asked her, "What happened to his brother? How come nobody's ever talked about him?"

This was the first time I ever saw my mother look old.

"His brother got killed," she said, "when he was just a little younger than you are now. I knew him. He was a fine boy. He was maybe a little full of the devil, but he didn't mean nobody no harm."

Then she stopped and the room was silent, exactly as it had sometimes been on those Sunday afternoons. Mama kept looking out into the streets.

"He used to have a job in the mill," she said, "and, like all young folks, he just liked to perform on Saturday nights. Saturday nights, him and your father would drift around to different places, go to dances and things like that, or just sit around with people they knew, and your father's brother would sing, he had a fine voice, and play along with himself on his guitar. Well, this particular Saturday night, him and your father was coming home from some place, and they were both a little drunk and there was a moon that night, it was bright like day. Your father's brother was feeling kind of good, and he was whistling to himself, and he had his guitar slung over his shoulder. They was coming down a hill and beneath them was a road that turned off from the highway. Well, your father's brother, being always kind of frisky, decided to run down this hill, and he did, with that guitar banging and clanging behind him, and he ran across the road, and he was making water behind a tree. And your father was sort of amused at him and he was still coming down the hill, kind of slow. Then he heard a car motor and that same minute his brother stepped from behind the tree, into the road, in the moonlight. And he started to cross the road. And your father started to run down the hill, he says he don't know why. This car was full of white men. They was all drunk, and when they seen your father's brother they let out a great whoop and holler and they aimed the car straight at him. They was having fun, they just wanted to scare him, the way they do sometimes, you know. But they was drunk. And I guess the boy, being drunk, too, and scared, kind of lost his head. By the time he jumped it was too late. Your father says he heard his brother scream when the car rolled over him, and he heard the wood of that guitar when it give, and he heard them strings go flying, and he heard them white men shouting, and the car kept on a-going and it ain't stopped till this day. And, time your father got down the hill, his brother weren't nothing but blood and pulp."

Tears were gleaming on my mother's face. There wasn't anything I could say.

"He never mentioned it," she said, "because I never let him mention it before you children. Your Daddy was like a crazy man that night and for many a night thereafter. He says he never in his life seen anything as dark as that road after the lights of that car had gone away. Weren't nothing, weren't nobody on that road, just your Daddy and his brother and that busted guitar. Oh, yes. Your Daddy never did really get right again. Till the day he died he weren't sure but that every white man he saw was the man that killed his brother."

She stopped and took out her handkerchief and dried her eyes and looked at me.

"I ain't telling you all this," she said, "to make you scared or bitter or to make you hate nobody. I'm telling you this because you got a brother. And the world ain't changed."

I guess I didn't want to believe this. I guess she saw this in my face. She turned away from me, toward the window again, searching those streets.

"But I praise my Redeemer," she said at last, "that He called your Daddy home before me. I ain't saying it to throw no flowers at myself, but, I declare, it keeps me from feeling too cast down to know I helped your father get safely through this world. Your father always acted like he was the roughest, strongest man on earth. And everybody took him to be like that. But if he hadn't had *me* there—to see his tears!"

She was crying again. Still, I couldn't move. I said, "Lord, Lord, Mama, I didn't know it was like that."

"Oh, honey," she said, "there's a lot that you don't know. But you are going to find it out." She stood up from the window and came over to me. "You got to hold on to your brother," she said, "and don't let him fall, no matter what it looks like is happening to him and no matter how evil you gets with him. You going to be evil with him many a time. But don't you forget what I told you, you hear?"

"I won't forget," I said. "Don't you worry, I won't forget. I won't let nothing happen to Sonny."

My mother smiled as though she were amused at something she saw in my face. Then, "You may not be able to stop nothing from happening. But you got to let him know you's *there*."

Two days later I was married, and then I was gone. And I had a lot of things on my mind and I pretty well forgot my promise to Mama until I got shipped home on a special furlough for her funeral.

And, after the funeral, with just Sonny and me alone in the empty kitchen, I tried to find out something about him.

"What do you want to do?" I asked him.

"I'm going to be a musician," he said.

For he had graduated, in the time I had been away, from dancing to the juke box to finding out who was playing what, and what they were doing with it, and he had bought himself a set of drums.

"You mean, you want to be a drummer?" I somehow had the feeling that being a drummer might be all right for other people but not for my brother Sonny.

"I don't think," he said, looking at me very gravely, "that I'll ever be a good drummer. But I think I can play a piano."

I frowned. I'd never played the role of the older brother quite so seriously before, had scarcely ever, in fact, *asked* Sonny a damn thing. I sensed myself in the presence of something I didn't really know how to handle, didn't understand. So I made my frown a little deeper as I asked: "What kind of musician do you want to be?"

He grinned. "How many kinds do you think there are?"

"Be *serious*," I said.

He laughed, throwing his head back, and then looked at me. "I *am* serious."

"Well, then, for Christ's sake, stop kidding around and answer a serious question. I mean, do you want to be a concert pianist, you want to play classical music and all that, or—or what?" Long before I finished he was laughing again. "For Christ's *sake*, Sonny!"

He sobered, but with difficulty. "I'm sorry. But you sound so—*scared!*" and he was off again.

"Well, you may think it's funny now, baby, but it's not going to be so funny when you have to make your living at it, let me tell you *that*." I was furious because I knew he was laughing at me and I didn't know why.

"No," he said, very sober now, and afraid, perhaps, that he'd hurt me, "I don't want to be a classical pianist. That isn't what interests me. I mean"—he paused, looking hard at me, as though his eyes would help me to understand, and then gestured helplessly, as though perhaps his hand would help—"I mean, I'll have a lot of studying to do, and I'll have to study *everything*, but, I mean, I want to play *with*—jazz musicians." He stopped. "I want to play jazz," he said.

Well, the word had never before sounded as heavy, as real, as it sounded that afternoon in Sonny's mouth. I just looked at him and I was probably frowning a real frown by this time. I simply couldn't see why on earth he'd want to spend his time hanging around nightclubs, clowning around on bandstands, while people pushed each other around a dance floor. It seemed—beneath him, somehow. I had never though about it before, had never been forced to, but I suppose I had always put jazz musicians in a class with what Daddy called "good-time people."

"Are you *serious*?"

"Hell, *yes*, I'm serious."

He looked more helpless than ever, and annoyed, and deeply hurt.

I suggested, helpfully: "You mean—like Louis Armstrong?"[3]

His face closed as though I'd struck him. "No. I'm not talking about none of that old-time, down home crap."

"Well, look, Sonny, I'm sorry, don't get mad. I just don't altogether get it, that's all. Name somebody—you know, a jazz musician you admire."

"Bird."

"Who?"

"Bird! Charlie Parker![4] Don't they teach you nothing in the goddamn army?"

I lit a cigarette. I was surprised and then a little amused to discover that I was trembling. "I've been out of touch," I said. "You'll have to be patient with me. Now. Who's this Parker character?"

"He's just one of the greatest jazz musicians alive," said Sonny, sullenly, his hands in his pockets, his back to me. "Maybe *the* greatest," he added, bitterly, "that's probably why *you* never heard of him."

"All right," I said, "I'm ignorant. I'm sorry. I'll go out and buy all the cat's records right away, all right?"

"It don't," said Sonny, with dignity, "make any difference to me. I don't care what you listen to. Don't do me no favors."

I was beginning to realize that I'd never seen him so upset before. With another part of my mind I was thinking that this would probably turn out to be one of those things kids go through and that I shouldn't make it seem important by pushing it too hard. Still, I didn't think it would do any harm to ask: "Doesn't all this take a lot of time? Can you make a living at it?"

He turned back to me and half leaned, half sat, on the kitchen table. "Everything takes time," he said, "and—well, yes, sure, I can make a living at it. But what I don't seem to be able to make you understand is that it's the only thing I want to do."

[3] Armstrong (1900–1971), called Satchmo, was a jazz trumpet virtuoso who invented the "scat" singing style.

[4] Charles Christopher Parker, Jr. (1920–1955), or Bird; a great jazz saxophonist who promoted bebop.

"Well, Sonny," I said, gently, "you know people can't always do exactly what they *want* to do—"

"*No,* I don't know that," said Sonny, surprising me. "I think people *ought* to do what they want to do, what else are they alive for?"

"You getting to be a big boy," I said desperately, "it's time you started thinking about your future."

"I'm thinking about my future," said Sonny, grimly. "I think about it all the time."

I gave up. I decided, if he didn't change his mind, that we could always talk about it later. "In the meantime," I said, "you got to finish school." We had already decided that he'd have to move in with Isabel and her folks. I knew this wasn't the ideal arrangement because Isabel's folks are inclined to be dicty[5] and they hadn't especially wanted Isabel to marry me. But I didn't know what else to do. "And we have to get you fixed up at Isabel's."

There was a long silence. He moved from the kitchen table to the window. "That's a terrible idea. You know it yourself."

"Do you have a *better* idea?"

He just walked up and down the kitchen for a minute. He was as tall as I was. He had started to shave. I suddenly had the feeling that I didn't know him at all.

He stopped at the kitchen table and picked up my cigarettes. Looking at me with a kind of mocking, amused defiance, he put one between his lips. "You mind?"

"You smoking already?"

He lit the cigarette and nodded, watching me through the smoke. "I just wanted to see if I'd have the courage to smoke in front of you." He grinned and blew a great cloud of smoke to the ceiling. "It was easy." He looked at my face. "Come on, now. I bet you was smoking at my age, tell the truth."

I didn't say anything but the truth was on my face, and he laughed. But now there was something very strained in his laugh. "Sure. And I bet that ain't all you was doing."

He was frightening me a little. "Cut the crap," I said. "We already decided that you was going to go and live at Isabel's. Now what's got into you all of a sudden?"

"*You* decided it," he pointed out. "*I* didn't decide nothing." He stopped in front of me, leaning against the stove, arms loosely folded. "Look, brother. I don't want to stay in Harlem no more, I really don't." He was very earnest. He looked at me, then over toward the kitchen window. There was something in his eyes I'd never seen before, some thoughtfulness, some worry all his own. He rubbed the muscle of one arm. "It's time I was getting out of here."

"Where do you want to *go,* Sonny?"

"I want to join the army. Or the navy, I don't care. If I say I'm old enough, they'll believe me."

Then I got mad. It was because I was so scared. "You must be crazy. You goddamn fool, what the hell do you want to go and join the *army* for?"

"I just told you. To get out of Harlem."

"Sonny, you haven't even finished *school.* And if your really want to be a musician, how do you expect to study if you're in the *army?*"

[5] Snobby.

He looked at me, trapped, and in anguish. "There's ways. I might be able to work out some kind of deal. Anyway, I'll have the G.I. Bill when I come out."

"*If* you come out." We stared at each other. "Sonny, please. Be reasonable. I know the setup is far from perfect. But we got to do the best we can."

"I ain't learning nothing in school," he said. "Even when I go." He turned away from me and opened the window and threw his cigarette out into the narrow alley. I watched his back. "At least, I ain't learning nothing you'd want me to learn." He slammed the window so hard I thought the glass would fly out, and turned back to me. "And I'm sick of the stink of these garbage cans!"

"Sonny," I said, "I know how you feel. But if you don't finish school now, you're going to be sorry later that you didn't." I grabbed him by the shoulders. "And you only got another year. It ain't so bad. And I'll come back and I swear I'll help you do *whatever* you want to do. Just try to put up with it till I come back. Will you please do that? For me?"

He didn't answer and he wouldn't look at me.

"Sonny. You hear me?"

He pulled away. "I hear you. But you never hear anything *I* say."

I didn't know what to say to that. He looked out of the window and then back at me. "OK," he said, and sighed. "I'll try."

Then I said, trying to cheer him up a little, "They got a piano at Isabel's. You can practice on it."

And as a matter of fact, it did cheer him up for a minute. "That's right," he said to himself. "I forgot that." His face relaxed a little. But the worry, the thoughtfulness, played on it still, the way shadows play on a face which is staring into the fire.

But I thought I'd never hear the end of that piano. At first, Isabel would write me, saying how nice it was that Sonny was so serious about his music and how, as soon as he came in from school, or wherever he had been when he was supposed to be at school, he went straight to that piano and stayed there until suppertime. And, after supper, he went back to that piano and stayed there until everybody went to bed. He was at the piano all day Saturday and all day Sunday. Then he bought a record player and started playing records. He'd play one record over and over again, all day long sometimes, and he'd improvise along with it on the piano. Or he'd play one section of the record, one chord, one change, one progression, then he'd do it on the piano. Then back to the record. Then back to the piano.

Well, I really don't know how they stood it. Isabel finally confessed that it wasn't like living with a person at all, it was like living with sound. And the sound didn't make any sense to her, didn't make any sense to any of them—naturally. They began, in a way, to be afflicted by this presence that was living in their home. It was as though Sonny were some sort of god, or monster. He moved in an atmosphere which wasn't like theirs at all. They fed him and he ate, he washed himself, he walked in and out of their door; he certainly wasn't nasty or unpleasant or rude, Sonny isn't any of those things; but it was as though he were all wrapped up in some cloud, some fire, some vision all his own; and there wasn't any way to reach him.

At the same time, he wasn't really a man yet, he was still a child, and they had to watch out for him in all kinds of ways. They certainly couldn't throw him out. Neither did they dare to make a great scene about that piano because even they dimly sensed, as I sensed, from so many thousands of miles away, that Sonny was at that piano playing for his life.

But he hadn't been going to school. One day a letter came from the school board and Isabel's mother got it—there had, apparently, been other letters but Sonny had torn them up. This day, when Sonny came in, Isabel's mother showed him the letter and asked where he'd been spending his time. And she finally got it out of him that he'd been down in Greenwich Village, with musicians and other characters, in a white girl's apartment. And this scared her and she started to scream at him and what came up, once she began—though she denies it to this day—was what sacrifices they were making to give Sonny a decent home and how little he appreciated it.

Sonny didn't play the piano that day. By evening, Isabel's mother had calmed down but then there was the old man to deal with, and Isabel herself. Isabel says she did her best to be calm but she broke down and started crying. She says she just watched Sonny's face. She could tell, by watching him, what was happening with him. And what was happening was that they penetrated his cloud, they had reached him. Even if their fingers had been a thousand times more gentle than human fingers ever are, he could hardly help feeling that they had stripped him naked and were spitting on that nakedness. For he also had to see that his presence, that music, which was life or death to him, had been torture for them and that they had endured it, not at all for his sake, but only for mine. And Sonny couldn't take that. He can take it a little better today than he could then but he's still not very good at it and, frankly, I don't know anybody who is.

The silence of the next few days must have been louder than the sound of all the music ever played since time began. One morning, before she went to work, Isabel was in his room for something and she suddenly realized that all of his records were gone. And she knew for certain that he was gone. And he was. He went as far as the navy would carry him. He finally sent me a postcard from some place in Greece and that was the first I knew that Sonny was still alive. I didn't see him any more until we were both back in New York and the war had long been over.

He was a man by then, of course, but I wasn't willing to see it. He came by the house from time to time, but we fought almost every time we met. I didn't like the way he carried himself, loose and dreamlike all the time, and I didn't like his friends, and his music seemed to be merely an excuse for the life he led. It sounded just that weird and disordered.

Then we had a fight, a pretty awful fight, and I didn't see him for months. By and by I looked him up, where he was living, in a furnished room in the Village, and I tried to make it up. But there were lots of people in the room and Sonny just lay on his bed, and he wouldn't come downstairs with me, and he treated these other people as though they were his family and I weren't. So I got mad and then he got mad, and then I told him that he might just as well be dead as live the way he was living. Then he stood up and he told me not to worry about him any more in life, that he *was* dead as far as I was concerned. Then he pushed me to the door and the other people looked on as though nothing were happening, and he slammed the door behind me. I stood in the hallway, staring at the door. I heard somebody laugh in the room and then the tears came to my eyes. I started down the steps, whistling to keep from crying, I kept whistling to myself, *You going to need me, baby, one of these cold, rainy days.*

I read about Sonny's trouble in the spring. Little Grace died in the fall. She was a beautiful little girl. But she only lived a little over two years. She died of polio and she suffered. She had a slight fever for a couple of days, but it didn't seem like anything and we just kept her in bed. And we would certainly have called the doctor, but the fever dropped, she seemed to be all right. So we thought it had just been a cold. Then, one day, she was up, playing, Isabel was in the kitchen fixing lunch for the two boys when they'd come in from school, and she heard Grace fall down in the living room. When you have a lot of children you don't always start running when one of them falls, unless they start screaming or something. And, this time, Grace was quiet. Yet, Isabel says that when she heard that *thump* and then that silence, something happened in her to make her afraid. And she ran to the living room and there was little Grace on the floor, all twisted up, and the reason she hadn't screamed was that she couldn't get her breath. And when she did scream, it was the worst sound, Isabel says, that she'd ever heard in all her life, and she still hears it sometimes in her dreams. Isabel will sometimes wake me up with a low, moaning, strangled sound and I have to be quick to awaken her and hold her to me and where Isabel is weeping against me seems a mortal wound.

I think I may have written Sonny the very day that little Grace was buried. I was sitting in the living room in the dark, by myself, and I suddenly thought of Sonny. My trouble made his real.

One Saturday afternoon, when Sonny had been living with us, or, anyway, been in our house, for nearly two weeks, I found myself wandering aimlessly about the living room, drinking from a can of beer, and trying to work up the courage to search Sonny's room. He was out, he was usually out whenever I was home, and Isabel had taken the children to see their grandparents. Suddenly I was standing still in front of the living room window, watching Seventh Avenue. The idea of searching Sonny's room made me still. I scarcely dared to admit to myself what I'd be searching for. I didn't know what I'd do if I found it. Or if I didn't.

On the sidewalk across from me, near the entrance to a barbecue joint, some people were holding an old-fashioned revival meeting. The barbecue cook, wearing a dirty white apron, his conked[6] hair reddish and metallic in the pale sun, and a cigarette between his lips, stood in the doorway, watching them. Kids and older people paused in their errands and stood there, along with some older men and a couple of very tough-looking women who watched everything that happened on the avenue, as though they owned it, or were maybe owned by it. Well, they were watching this, too. The revival was being carried on by three sisters in black, and a brother. All they had were their voices and their Bibles and a tambourine. The brother was testifying and while he testified two of the sisters stood together, seeming to say, amen, and the third sister walked around with the tambourine outstretched and a couple of people dropped coins into it. Then the brother's testimony ended and the sister who had been taking up the collection dumped the coins into her palm and transferred them to the pocket of her long black robe. Then she raised both hands, striking the tambourine against the air, and then against one hand, and she started to sing. And the two other sisters and the brother joined in.

It was strange, suddenly, to watch, though I had been seeing these street meetings all my life. So, of course, had everybody else down there. Yet, they paused and watched and listened and I stood still at the window. *"Tis the old ship of Zion,"* they sang, and the sister with the tambourine kept a steady, jangling beat, *"it has rescued many a thousand!"* Not a soul under the sound of their voices was

---

[6] Chemically straightened and smoothed down.

hearing this song for the first time, not one of them had been rescued. Nor had they seen much in the way of rescue work being done around them. Neither did they especially believe in the holiness of the three sisters and the brother, they knew too much about them, knew where they lived, and how. The woman with the tambourine, whose voice dominated the air, whose face was bright with joy, was divided by very little from the woman who stood watching her, a cigarette between her heavy, chapped lips, her hair a cuckoo's nest, her face scarred and swollen from many beatings, and her black eyes glittering like coal. Perhaps they both knew this, which was why, when, as rarely, they addressed each other, they addressed each other as Sister. As the singing filled the air the watching, listening faces underwent a change, the eyes focusing on something within; the music seemed to soothe a poison out of them; and time seemed, nearly, to fall away from the sullen, belligerent, battered faces, as though they were fleeing back to their first condition, while dreaming of their last. The barbecue cook half shook his head and smiled, and dropped his cigarette and disappeared into his joint. A man fumbled in his pockets for change and stood holding it in his hand impatiently, as though he had just remembered a pressing appointment further up the avenue. He looked furious. Then I saw Sonny, standing on the edge of the crowd. He was carrying a wide, flat notebook with a green cover, and it made him look, from where I was standing, almost like a schoolboy. The coppery sun brought out the copper in his skin, he was very faintly smiling, standing very still. Then the singing stopped, the tambourine turned into a collection plate again. The furious man dropped in his coins and vanished, so did a couple of the women, and Sonny dropped some change in the plate, looking directly at the woman with a little smile. He started across the avenue, toward the house. He has a slow, loping walk, something like the way Harlem hipsters walk, only he's imposed on this his own half-beat. I had never really noticed it before.

I stayed at the window, both relieved and apprehensive. As Sonny disappeared from my sight, they began singing again. And they were still singing when his key turned in the lock.

"Hey," he said.

"Hey, yourself. You want some beer?"

"No. Well, maybe." But he came up to the window and stood beside me, looking out. "What a warm voice," he said.

They were singing *If I could only hear my mother pray again!*

"Yes," I said, "and she can sure beat that tambourine."

"But what a terrible song," he said, and laughed. He dropped his notebook on the sofa and disappeared into the kitchen. "Where's Isabel and the kids?"

"I think they went to see their grandparents. You hungry?"

"No." He came back into the living room with his can of beer. "You want to come some place with me tonight?"

I sensed, I don't know how, that I couldn't possibly say no. "Sure. Where?"

He sat down on the sofa and picked up his notebook and started leafing through it. "I'm going to sit in with some fellows in a joint in the Village."

"You mean, you're going to play, tonight?"

"That's right." He took a swallow of his beer and moved back to the window. He gave me a sidelong look. "If you can stand it."

"I'll try," I said.

He smiled to himself and we both watched as the meeting across the way broke up. The three sisters and the brother, heads bowed, were singing *God be with you till we meet again.* The faces around them were very quiet. Then the song ended. The small crowd dispersed. We watched the three women and the lone man walk slowly up the avenue.

"When she was singing before," said Sonny, abruptly, "her voice reminded me for a minute of what heroin feels like sometimes—when it's in your veins. It makes you feel sort of warm and cool at the same time. And distant. And—and sure." He sipped his beer, very deliberately not looking at me. I watched his face. "It makes you feel—in control. Sometimes you've got to have that feeling."

"Do you?" I sat slowly in the easy chair.

"Sometimes." He went to the sofa and picked up his notebook again. "Some people do."

"In order," I asked, "to play?" And my voice was very ugly, full of contempt and anger.

"Well"—he looked at me with great, troubled eyes, as though, in fact, he hoped his eyes would tell me things he could never otherwise say—"they *think* so. And *if* they think so—!"

"And what do *you* think?" I asked.

He sat on the sofa and put his can of beer on the floor. "I don't know," he said, and I couldn't be sure if he were answering my question or pursuing his thoughts. His face didn't tell me. "It's not so much to *play.* It's to *stand* it, to be able to make it at all. On any level." He frowned and smiled: "In order to keep from shaking to pieces."

"But these friends of yours," I said, "they seem to shake themselves to pieces pretty goddamn fast."

"Maybe." He played with the notebook. And something told me that I should curb my tongue, that Sonny was doing his best to talk, that I should listen. "But of course you only know the ones that've gone to pieces. Some don't—or at least they haven't *yet* and that's just about all *any* of us can say." He paused. "And then there are some who just live, really, in hell, and they know it and they see what's happening and they go right on. I don't know." He sighed, dropped the notebook, folded his arms. "Some guys, you can tell from the way they play, they on something *all* the time. And you can see that, well, it makes something real for them. But of course," he picked up his beer from the floor and sipped it and put the can down again, "they *want* to, too, you've got to see that. Even some of them that say they don't—*some,* not all."

"And what about you?" I asked—I couldn't help it. "What about you? Do *you* want to?"

He stood up and walked to the window and remained silent for a long time. Then he sighed. "Me," he said. Then: "While I was downstairs before, on my way here, listening to that woman sing, it struck me all of a sudden how much suffering she must have had to go through—to sing like that. It's *repulsive* to think you have to suffer that much."

I said: "But there's no way not to suffer—is there, Sonny?"

"I believe not," he said and smiled, "but that's never stopped anyone from trying." He looked at me. "Has it?" I realized, with this mocking look, that there stood between us, forever, beyond the power of time or forgiveness, the fact that I had held silence—so long!—when he had needed human speech to help him. He turned back to the window. "No, there's no way not to suffer. But you try all kinds of ways to keep from drowning in it, to keep on top of it, and to make it seem—well, like *you.* Like you did something, all right, and now you're suffering for it. You know?" I said nothing. "Well you know," he said, impatiently, "why *do* people suffer? Maybe it's better to do something to give it a reason, *any* reason."

" But we just agreed," I said, "that there's no way not to suffer. Isn't it better, then, just to—take it?"

"But nobody just takes it," Sonny cried, "that's what I'm telling you! *Everybody* tries not to. You're just hung up on the *way* some people try—it's not *your* way!"

The hair on my face began to itch, my face felt wet. "That's not true," I said, "that's not true. I don't give a damn what other people do, I don't even care how they suffer. I just care how *you* suffer." And he looked at me. "Please believe me," I said, "I don't want to see you—die—trying not to suffer."

"I won't," he said, flatly, "die trying not to suffer. At least, not any faster than anybody else."

"But there's no need," I said, trying to laugh, "is there? in killing yourself."

I wanted to say more, but I couldn't. I wanted to talk about will power and how life could be—well, beautiful. I wanted to say that it was all within; but was it? or, rather, wasn't that exactly the trouble? And I wanted to promise that I would never fail him again. But it would all have sounded—empty words and lies.

So I made the promise to myself and prayed that I would keep it.

"It's terrible sometimes, inside," he said, "that's what's the trouble. You walk these streets, black and funky and cold, and there's not really a living ass to talk to, and there's nothing shaking, and there's no way of getting it out—that storm inside. You can't talk it and can't make love with it, and when you finally try to get with it and play it, you realize *nobody's* listening. So *you've* got to listen. You got to find a way to listen."

And then he walked away from the window and sat on the sofa again, as though all the wind had suddenly been knocked out of him. "Sometimes you'll do *anything* to play, even cut your mother's throat." He laughed and looked at me. "Or your brother's." Then he sobered. "Or your own." Then: "Don't worry. I'm all right now and I think I'll *be* all right. But I can't forget—where I've been. I don't mean just the physical place I've been, I mean where I've *been*. And *what* I've been."

"What have you been, Sonny?" I asked.

He smiled—but sat sideways on the sofa, his elbow resting on the back, his fingers playing with his mouth and chin, not looking at me. "I've been something I didn't recognize, didn't know I could be. Didn't know anybody could be." He stopped, looking inward, looking helplessly young, looking old. "I'm not talking about it now because I feel *guilty* or anything like that—maybe it would be better if I did, I don't know. Anyway, I can't really talk about it. Not to you, not to anybody," and now he turned and faced me. "Sometimes, you know, and it was actually when I was most *out* of the world, I felt that I was in it, that I was *with* it, really, and I could play or I didn't really have to *play*, it just came out of me, it was there. And I don't know how I played, thinking about it now, but I know I did awful things, those times, sometimes, to people. Or it wasn't that I *did* anything to them—it was that they weren't real." He picked up the beer can; it was empty; he rolled it between his palms: "And other times—well, I needed a fix, I needed to find a place to lean, I needed to clear a space to *listen*—and I couldn't find it, and I—went crazy, I did terrible things to *me*, I was terrible *for* me." He began pressing the beer can between his hands, I watched the metal begin to give.

It glittered, as he played with it, like a knife, and I was afraid he would cut himself, but I said nothing. "Oh well. I can never tell you. I was all by myself at the bottom of something, stinking and sweating and crying and shaking, and I smelled it, you know? *my* stink, and I thought I'd die if I couldn't get away from it and yet, all the same, I knew that everything I was doing was just locking me in with it. And I didn't know," he paused, still flattening the beer can, "I didn't know, I still *don't* know, something kept telling me that maybe it was good to smell your own stink, but I didn't think that *that* was what I'd been trying to do—and—who can stand it?" and he abruptly dropped the ruined beer can, looking at me with a small, still smile, and then rose, walking to the window as though it were the lodestone rock. I watched his face, he watched the avenue. "I couldn't tell you when Mama died—but the reason I wanted to leave Harlem so bad was to get away from drugs. And then, when I ran away, that's what I was running from—really. When I came back, nothing had changed, *I* hadn't changed, I was just—older." And he stopped, drumming with his fingers on the windowpane. The sun had vanished, soon darkness would fall. I watched his face. "It can come again," he said, almost as though speaking to himself. Then he turned to me. "It can come again," he repeated. "I just want you to know that."

"All right," I said, at last. "So it can come again. All right."

He smiled, but the smile was sorrowful. "I had to try to tell you," he said.

"Yes," I said, "I understand that."

"You're my brother," he said, looking straight at me, and not smiling at all.

"Yes," I repeated, "yes. I understand that."

He turned back to the window, looking out. "All that hatred down there," he said, "all that hatred and misery and love. It's a wonder it doesn't blow the avenue apart."

We went to the only nightclub on a short, dark street, downtown. We squeezed through the narrow, chattering, jampacked bar to the entrance of the big room, where the bandstand was. And we stood there for a moment, for the lights were very dim in this room and we couldn't see. Then, "Hello, boy," said a voice and an enormous black man, much older than Sonny or myself, erupted out of all that atmospheric lighting and put an arm around Sonny's shoulder. "I been sitting right here," he said, "waiting for you."

He had a big voice, too, and heads in the darkness turned toward us.

Sonny grinned and pulled a little away, and said, "Creole, this is my brother. I told you about him."

Creole shook my hand. "I'm glad to meet you, son," he said, and it was clear that he was glad to meet me *there*, for Sonny's sake. And he smiled, "You got a real musician in *your* family," and he took his arm from Sonny's shoulder and slapped him, lightly, affectionately, with the back of his hand.

"Well. Now I've heard it all," said a voice behind us. This was another musician, and a friend of Sonny's, a coal-black, cheerful-looking man, built close to the ground. He immediately began confiding to me, at the top of his lungs, the most terrible things about Sonny, his teeth gleaming like a lighthouse and his laugh coming up out of him like the beginning of an earthquake. And it turned out that everyone at the bar knew Sonny, or almost everyone; some were musicians, working there, or nearby, or not working, some were simply hangers-on, and some were there to hear Sonny play. I was introduced to all of them and they were all very polite to me. Yet, it was clear that, for them, I was only Sonny's brother.

Here, I was in Sonny's world. Or, rather: his kingdom. Here, it was not even a question that his veins bore royal blood.

They were going to play soon and Creole installed me, by myself, at a table in a dark corner. Then I watched them, Creole, and the little black man, and Sonny, and the others, while they horsed around, standing just below the bandstand. The light from the bandstand spilled just a little short of them and, watching them laughing and gesturing and moving about, I had the feeling that they, nevertheless, were being most careful not to step into that circle of light too suddenly: that if they moved into the light too suddenly, without thinking, they would perish in flame. Then, while I watched, one of them, the small, black man, moved into the light and crossed the bandstand and started fooling around with his drums. Then—being funny and being, also, extremely ceremonious—Creole took Sonny by the arm and led him to the piano. A woman's voice called Sonny's name and a few hands started clapping. And Sonny, also being funny and being ceremonious, and so touched, I think, that he could have cried, but neither hiding it nor showing it, riding it like a man, grinned, and put both hands to his heart and bowed from the waist.

Creole then went to the bass fiddle and a lean, very bright-skinned brown man jumped up on the bandstand and picked up his horn. So there they were, and the atmosphere on the bandstand and in the room began to change and tighten. Someone stepped up to the microphone and announced them. Then there were all kinds of murmurs. Some people at the bar shushed others. The waitress ran around, frantically getting in the last orders, guys and chicks got closer to each other, and the lights on the bandstand, on the quartet, turned to a kind of indigo. Then they all looked different there. Creole looked about him for the last time, as though he were making certain that all his chickens were in the coop, and then he—jumped and struck the fiddle. And there they were.

All I know about music is that not many people ever really hear it. And even then, on the rare occasions when something opens within, and the music enters, what we mainly hear, or hear corroborated, are personal, private, vanishing evocations. But the man who creates the music is hearing something else, is dealing with the roar rising from the void and imposing order on it as it hits the air. What is evoked in him, then, is of another order, more terrible because it has no words, and triumphant, too, for that same reason. And his triumph, when he triumphs, is ours. I just watched Sonny's face. His face was troubled, he was working hard, but he wasn't with it. And I had the feeling that, in a way, everyone on the bandstand was waiting for him, both waiting for him and pushing him along. But as I began to watch Creole, I realized that it was Creole who held them all back. He had them on a short rein. Up there, keeping the beat with his whole body, wailing on the fiddle, with his eyes half closed, he was listening to everything, but he was listening to Sonny. He was having a dialogue with Sonny. He wanted Sonny to leave the shoreline and strike out for the deep water. He was Sonny's witness that deep water and drowning were not the same thing—he had been there, and he knew. And he wanted Sonny to know. He was waiting for Sonny to do the things on the keys which would let Creole know that Sonny was in the water.

And, while Creole listened, Sonny moved, deep within, exactly like someone in torment. I had never before thought of how awful the relationship must be between the musician and his instrument. He has to fill it, this instrument, with the breath of life, his own. He has to make it do what he wants it to do. And a piano is just a piano. It's made out of so much wood and wires and little hammers and big ones, and ivory. While there's only so much you can do with it, the only way to find this out is to try; to try and make it do everything.

And Sonny hadn't been near a piano for over a year. And he wasn't on much better terms with his life, not the life that stretched before him now. He and the piano stammered, started one way, got scared, stopped; started another way, panicked, marked time, started again; then seemed to have found a direction, panicked again, got stuck. And the face I saw on Sonny I'd never seen before. Everything had been burned out of it, and, at the same time, things usually hidden were being burned in, by the fire and fury of the battle which was occurring in him up there.

Yet, watching Creole's face as they neared the end of the first set, I had the feeling that something had happened, something I hadn't heard. Then they finished, there was scattered applause, and then, without an instant's warning, Creole started into something else, it was almost sardonic, it was *Am I Blue.*[7] And, as though he commanded, Sonny began to play. Something began to happen. And Creole let out the reins. The dry, low, black man said something awful on the drums, Creole answered, and the drums talked back. Then the horn insisted, sweet and high, slightly detached perhaps, and Creole listened, commenting now and then, dry, and driving, beautiful and calm and old. Then they all came together again, and Sonny was part of the family again. I could tell this from his face. He seemed to have found, right there beneath his fingers, a damn brand-new piano. It seemed that he couldn't get over it. Then, for awhile, just being happy with Sonny, they seemed to be agreeing with him that brand-new pianos certainly were a gas.

Then Creole stepped forward to remind them that what they were playing was the blues. He hit something in all of them, he hit something in me, myself, and the music tightened and deepened, apprehension began to beat the air. Creole began to tell us what the blues were all about. They were not about anything very new. He and his boys up there were keeping it new, at the risk of ruin, destruction, madness, and death, in order to find new ways to make us listen. For, while the tale of how we suffer, and how we are delighted, and how we may triumph is never new, it always must be heard. There isn't any other tale to tell, it's the only light we've got in all this darkness.

And this tale, according to that face, that body, those strong hands on those strings, has another aspect in every country, and a new depth in every generation. Listen, Creole seemed to be saying, listen. Now these are Sonny's blues. He made the little black man on the drums know it, and the bright, brown man on the horn. Creole wasn't trying any longer to get Sonny in the water. He was wishing him Godspeed. Then he stepped back, very slowly, filling the air with the immense suggestion that Sonny speak for himself.

Then they all gathered around Sonny and Sonny played. Every now and again one of them seemed to say, amen. Sonny's fingers filled the air with life, his life. But that life contained so many others. And Sonny went all the way back, he really began with the spare, flat statement of the opening phrase of the song. Then he began to make it his. It was very beautiful because it wasn't hurried and it was no longer a lament. I seemed to hear with what burning he had made it his, with what burning we had yet to make it ours, how we could cease lamenting. Freedom lurked around us and I understood, at last, that he could help us to be free if we would listen, that he would never be free until we did. Yet, there was no battle in

[7] A 1929 song by Grant Clarke and Harry Akst.

his face now. I heard what he had gone through, and would continue to go through until he came to rest in earth. He had made it his: that long line, of which we knew only Mama and Daddy. And he was giving it back, as everything must be given back, so that, passing through death, it can live forever. I saw my mother's face again, and felt, for the first time, how the stones of the road she had walked on must have bruised her feet. I saw the moonlit road where my father's brother died. And it brought something else back to me, and carried me past it, I saw my little girl again and felt Isabel's tears again, and I felt my own tears begin to rise. And I was yet aware that this was only a moment, that the world waited outside, as hungry as a tiger, and that trouble stretched above us, longer than the sky.

Then it was over. Creole and Sonny let out their breath, both soaking wet, and grinning. There was a lot of applause and some of it was real. In the dark, the girl came by and I asked her to take drinks to the bandstand. There was a long pause, while they talked up there in the indigo light and after awhile I saw the girl put a Scotch and milk on top of the piano for Sonny. He didn't seem to notice it, but just before they started playing again, he sipped from it and looked toward me, and nodded. Then he put it back on top of the piano. For me, then, as they began to play again, it glowed and shook above my brother's head like the very cup of trembling.[8]

1957

Toni Morrison
(1931–   )

Toni Morrison contends that writing " . . . should have something in it that enlightens; something in it that opens the door and points the way. Something in it that suggests what the conflicts are, what the problems are. But it need not solve those problems because it is not a case study, it is not a recipe" (*Black Women Writers*, Mari Evans, 1984). True to her word, she does not hand her readers answers but envelops them in a cultural richness in which growth and transformation are possible, even when painful.

Born Chloe Anthony Wofford in 1931, she grew up in Lorain, Ohio. The setting of four of her five novels, the Midwest has offered her a way out of the settings stereotypical of African Americans. After completing her undergraduate studies at Howard University in 1953, Wofford attended Cornell University, where she earned an M.A. in 1955. Since then she has taught at such distinguished institutions as Howard and Princeton University. During her second stay at Howard, she married Harold Morrison, an architect; they have since divorced. As a senior editor at a leading publisher in New York City, Morrison promoted the work of other African-American writers, including the novelists Toni Cade Bambara and Gayl Jones.

As Morrison notes in *Conversations With American Writers* (Charles Ruas, 1984), she wrote her first novel, *The Bluest Eye* (1970), because she "wanted to read it." Her novels

---

[8] "Thou hast drunken the dregs of the cup of trembling," from Isaiah 51:17.

explore the tremendous power and danger inherent in growing up black and female in America. *Sula* (1973), the story of the friendship of two African-American girls, was nominated for a National Book Award. Her third novel, *Song of Solomon* (1977), won the National Book Critics' Circle Award, and *Tar Baby* (1981), which examines the complex relationship of race, gender, and class as played out on a Caribbean island, was also well received. *Beloved* (1987), winner of the Pulitzer Prize for fiction, takes place in Ohio during Reconstruction and concerns the lives of newly freed African Americans who are literally haunted by the legacy of slavery.

When Robert Smith promises to "fly from Mercy" on the opening page of *Song of Solomon*, it is but the first of the novel's many allusions to an empowering African-American folktale as old as the African presence in the Americas. Wherever Africans were transported into slavery there are stories of slaves who returned to Africa. This "old folks' lie" is one of the keys to the past that animates the quest of the novel's hero, Macon Dead, to reclaim a heritage far more precious than the gold he sets off to find. Like all Morrison's novels, *Song of Solomon* asserts the life-giving qualities of African-American folk culture, which is under siege not only from the old enemies of poverty and racism, but from modern materialism as well.

Morrison's elegant prose and vivid imagery define a style that counters reductive conceptions of African-American language, like those of Mark Twain and Joel Chandler Harris, based primarily on transcribing dialect pronunciation. She seeks the true African-American voice, "its syntax, its metaphors, and its music." In *Song of Solomon* Macon Dead wishes for an ancestor "whose name was not a joke," but in jokes such as the ironic renaming of "Not Doctor Street" and "No Mercy Hospital," history and identity are preserved through passionate uses of language. The name "Macon Dead" itself is in one sense a cruel reminder of the careless power of whites to define African Americans, but as passed down from father to son it also testifies to the persistence of African-American identity.

Suggested Readings: *The Bluest Eye*, 1970. *Sula*, 1973. *Tar Baby*, 1981. *Beloved*, 1987. R. Stepto, "Intimate Things in Place: A Conversation With Toni Morrison," in *Massachusetts Review*, 18, 1977. J. Bakerman, "The Seams Can't Show," in *Black American Literature Forum*, 12, 1978. B. Parker, "Complexity: Toni Morrison's Women: An Interview Essay," in *Sturdy Black Bridges: Visions of Black Women in Literature*, eds. R. Bell, B. Parker, and B. Guy-Sheftall, 1979. J. Bakerman, "Failures of Love: Female Initiation in the Novels of Toni Morrison," in *American Literature*, 52:4, 1981. S. Willis, "Eruptions of Funk: Historicizing Toni Morrison," in *Black American Literature Forum*, 16:1, 1982. M. Evans, ed., *Women Writers (1950–1980)*, 1984. S. Willis, " 'The Sweet Life' in Toni Morrison's Fiction," in *American Literature*, 56:2, 1984. N. Y. McKay, ed., *Critical Essays on Toni Morrison*, 1988.

Text Used: *Song of Solomon*, 1977.

from SONG OF SOLOMON*

CHAPTER 1

The North Carolina Mutual Life Insurance[1] agent promised to fly from Mercy to the other side of Lake Superior at three o'clock. Two days before the event was to take place he tacked a note on the door of his little yellow house:

---

* Named for the biblical book consisting of the dramatic, lyrical love poem attributed to Solomon, a wise king of Israel.

[1] An African-American insurance company that catered exclusively to African Americans.

At 3:00 P. M. on Wednesday the 18th of February, 1931, I will take off from Mercy and fly away on my own wings. Please forgive me. I loved you all.

(signed) Robert Smith,
Ins. agent

Mr. Smith didn't draw as big a crowd as Lindbergh[2] had four years earlier—not more than forty or fifty people showed up—because it was already eleven o'clock in the morning, on the very Wednesday he had chosen for his flight, before anybody read the note. At that time of day, during the middle of the week, word-of-mouth news just lumbered along. Children were in school; men were at work; and most of the women were fastening their corsets and getting ready to go see what tails or entrails the butcher might be giving away. Only the unemployed, the self-employed, and the very young were available—deliberately available because they'd heard about it, or accidentally available because they happened to be walking at that exact moment in the shore end of Not Doctor Street, a name the post office did not recognize. Town maps registered the street as Mains Avenue, but the only colored doctor in the city had lived and died on that street, and when he moved there in 1896 his patients took to calling the street, which none of them lived in or near, Doctor Street. Later, when other Negroes moved there, and when the postal service became a popular means of transferring messages among them, envelopes from Louisiana, Virginia, Alabama, and Georgia began to arrive addressed to people at house numbers on Doctor Street. The post office workers returned these envelopes or passed them on to the Dead Letter Office. Then in 1918, when colored men were being drafted, a few gave their address at the recruitment office as Doctor Street. In that way, the name acquired a quasi-official status. But not for long. Some of the city legislators, whose concern for appropriate names and the maintenance of the city's landmarks was the principal part of their political life, saw to it that "Doctor Street" was never used in any official capacity. And since they knew that only Southside residents kept it up, they had notices posted in the stores, barbershops, and restaurants in that part of the city saying that the avenue running northerly and southerly from Shore Road fronting the lake to the junction of routes 6 and 2 leading to Pennsylvania, and also running parallel to and between Rutherford Avenue and Broadway, had always been and would always be known as Mains Avenue and not Doctor Street.

It was a genuinely clarifying public notice because it gave Southside residents a way to keep their memories alive and please the city legislators as well. They called it Not Doctor Street, and were inclined to call the charity hospital at its northern end No Mercy Hospital since it was 1931, on the day following Mr. Smith's leap from its cupola, before the first colored expectant mother was allowed to give birth inside its wards and not on its steps. The reason for the hospital's generosity to that particular woman was not the fact that she was the only child of this Negro doctor, for during his entire professional life he had never been granted hospital privileges and only two of his patients were ever admitted to Mercy, both white. Besides, the doctor had been dead a long time by 1931. It must have been Mr. Smith's leap from the roof over their heads that made them admit her. In any case, whether or not the little insurance agent's conviction that he could fly contributed to the place of her delivery, it certainly contributed to its time.

---

[2] Charles A. Lindbergh (1908–1981), the aviator who earned instant fame by making the first non-stop solo flight across the Atlantic Ocean, from New York to Paris, in 1927.

When the dead doctor's daughter saw Mr. Smith emerge as promptly as he had promised from behind the cupola, his wide blue silk wings curved forward around his chest, she dropped her covered peck basket,[3] spilling red velvet rose petals. The wind blew them about, up, down, and into small mounds of snow. Her half-grown daughters scrambled about trying to catch them, while their mother moaned and held the underside of her stomach. The rose-petal scramble got a lot of attention, but the pregnant lady's moans did not. Everyone knew the girls had spent hour after hour tracing, cutting, and stitching the costly velvet, and that Gerhardt's Department Store would be quick to reject any that were soiled.

It was nice and gay there for a while. The men joined in trying to collect the scraps before the snow soaked through them—snatching them from a gust of wind or plucking them delicately from the snow. And the very young children couldn't make up their minds whether to watch the man circled in blue on the roof or the bits of red flashing around on the ground. Their dilemma was solved when a woman suddenly burst into song. The singer, standing at the back of the crowd, was as poorly dressed as the doctor's daughter was well dressed. The latter had on a neat gray coat with the traditional pregnant-woman bow at her navel, a black cloche,[4] and a pair of four-button ladies' galoshes. The singing woman wore a knitted navy cap pulled far down over her forehead. She had wrapped herself up in an old quilt instead of a winter coat. Her head cocked to one side, her eyes fixed on Mr. Robert Smith, she sang in a powerful contralto:

> O Sugarman done fly away
> Sugarman done gone
> Sugarman cut across the sky
> Sugarman gone home. . . .

A few of the half a hundred or so people gathered there nudged each other and sniggered. Others listened as though it were the helpful and defining piano music in a silent movie. They stood this way for some time, none of them crying out to Mr. Smith, all of them preoccupied with one or the other of the minor events about them, until the hospital people came.

They had been watching from the windows—at first with mild curiosity, then, as the crowd seemed to swell to the very walls of the hospital, they watched with apprehension. They wondered if one of those things that racial-uplift groups were always organizing was taking place. But when they saw neither placards nor speakers, they ventured outside into the cold: white-coated surgeons, dark-jacketed business and personnel clerks, and three nurses in starched jumpers.

The sight of Mr. Smith and his wide blue wings transfixed them for a few seconds, as did the woman's singing and the roses strewn about. Some of them thought briefly that this was probably some form of worship. Philadelphia, where Father Divine[5] reigned, wasn't all that far away. Perhaps the young girls holding baskets of flowers were two of his virgins. But the laughter of a gold-toothed man brought them back to their senses. They stopped daydreaming and swiftly got down to business, giving orders. Their shouts and bustling caused great confusion

---

[3] A basket with the capacity of one peck, or eight quarts.   [4] A closefitting women's hat.
[5] George Baker (1877–1965), an African-American religious leader who founded the Peace Mission (1919), a communal religious society.

where before there had been only a few men and some girls playing with pieces of velvet and a woman singing.

One of the nurses, hoping to bring some efficiency into the disorder, searched the faces around her until she saw a stout woman who looked as though she might move the earth if she wanted to.

"You," she said, moving toward the stout woman. "Are these your children?"

The stout woman turned her head slowly, her eyebrows lifted at the carelessness of the address. Then, seeing where the voice came from, she lowered her brows and veiled her eyes.

"Ma'am?"

"Send one around-back to the emergency office. Tell him to tell the guard to get over here quick. That boy there can go. That one." She pointed to a cat-eyed boy about five or six years old.

The stout woman slid her eyes down the nurse's finger and looked at the child she was pointing to.

"Guitar, ma'am."

"What?"

"Guitar."

The nurse gazed at the stout woman as though she had spoken Welsh. Then she closed her mouth, looked again at the cat-eyed boy, and lacing her fingers, spoke her next words very slowly to him.

"Listen. Go around to the back of the hospital to the guard's office. It will say 'Emergency Admissions' on the door. A-D-M-I-S-I-O-N-S. But the guard will be there. Tell him to get over here—on the double. Move now. Move!" She unlaced her fingers and made scooping motions with her hands, the palms pushing against the wintry air.

A man in a brown suit came toward her, puffing little white clouds of breath. "Fire truck's on its way. Get back inside. You'll freeze to death."

The nurse nodded.

"You left out a *s,* ma'am," the boy said. The North was new to him and he had just begun to learn he could speak up to white people. But she'd already gone, rubbing her arms against the cold.

"Granny, she left out a *s.*"

"And a 'please.'"

"You reckon he'll jump?"

"A nutwagon do anything."

"Who is he?"

"Collects insurance. A nutwagon."

"Who is that lady singing?"

"That, baby, is the very last thing in pea-time." But she smiled when she looked at the singing woman, so the cat-eyed boy listened to the musical performance with at least as much interest as he devoted to the man flapping his wings on top of the hospital.

The crowd was beginning to be a little nervous now that the law was being called in. They each knew Mr. Smith. He came to their houses twice a month to collect one dollar and sixty-eight cents and write down on a little yellow card both the date and their eighty-four cents a week payment. They were always half a month or so behind, and talked endlessly to him about paying ahead—after they had a preliminary discussion about what he was doing back so soon anyway.

"You back in here already? Look like I just got rid of you."

"I'm tired of seeing your face. Really tired."

"I knew it. Soon's I get two dimes back to back, here you come. More regular than the reaper. Do Hoover[6] know about you?"

They kidded him, abused him, told their children to tell him they were out sick or gone to Pittsburgh. But they held on to those little yellow cards as though they meant something—laid them gently in the shoe box along with the rent receipts, marriage licenses, and expired factory identification badges. Mr. Smith smiled through it all, managing to keep his eyes focused almost the whole time on his customers' feet. He wore a business suit for his work, but his house was not better than theirs. He never had a woman that any of them knew about and said nothing in church but an occasional "Amen." He never beat anybody up and he wasn't seen after dark, so they thought he was probably a nice man. But he was heavily associated with illness and death, neither of which was distinguishable from the brown picture of the North Carolina Mutual Life Building on the back of their yellow cards. Jumping from the roof on Mercy was the most interesting thing he had done. None of them had suspected he had it in him. Just goes to show, they murmured to each other, you never really do know about people.

The singing woman quieted down and, humming the tune, walked through the crowd toward the rose-petal lady, who was still cradling her stomach.

"You should make yourself warm," she whispered to her, touching her lightly on the elbow. "A little bird'll be here with the morning."

"Oh?" said the rose-petal lady. "Tomorrow morning?"

"That's the only morning coming."

"It can't be," the rose-petal lady said. "It's too soon."

"No it ain't. Right on time."

The women were looking deep into each other's eyes when a loud roar went up from the crowd—a kind of wavy *oo* sound. Mr. Smith had lost his balance for a second, and was trying gallantly to hold on to a triangle of wood that jutted from the cupola. Immediately the singing woman began again:

> O Sugarman done fly
> O Sugarman done gone . . .

Downtown the firemen pulled on their greatcoats, but when they arrived at Mercy, Mr. Smith had seen the rose petals, heard the music, and leaped on into the air.

The next day a colored baby was born inside Mercy for the first time. Mr. Smith's blue silk wings must have left their mark, because when the little boy discovered, at four, the same thing Mr. Smith had learned earlier—that only birds and airplanes could fly—he lost all interest in himself. To have to live without that single gift saddened him and left his imagination so bereft that he appeared dull even to the women who did not hate his mother. The ones who did, who accepted her invitations to tea and envied the doctor's big dark house of twelve rooms and the green sedan, called him "peculiar." The others, who knew that the house was more prison than palace, and that the Dodge sedan was for Sunday drives only, felt sorry for Ruth Foster and her dry daughters, and called her son "deep." Even mysterious.

[6] J. Edgar Hoover (1895–1972), director of the FBI from 1924 to 1972.

"Did he come with a caul?"

"You should have dried it and made him some tea from it to drink. If you don't he'll see ghosts."

"You believe that?"

"I don't, but that's what the old people say."

"Well, he's a deep one anyway. Look at his eyes."

And they pried pieces of baked-too-fast sunshine cake from the roofs of their mouths and looked once more into the boy's eyes. He met their gaze as best he could until, after a pleading glance toward his mother, he was allowed to leave the room.

It took some planning to walk out of the parlor, his back washed with the hum of their voices, open the heavy double doors leading to the dining room, slip up the stairs past all those bedrooms, and not arouse the attention of Lena and Corinthians sitting like big baby dolls before a table heaped with scraps of red velvet. His sisters made roses in the afternoon. Bright, lifeless roses that lay in peck baskets for months until the specialty buyer at Gerhardt's sent Freddie the janitor over to tell the girls that they could use another gross. If he did manage to slip by his sisters and avoid their casual malice, he knelt in his room at the window sill and wondered again and again why he had to stay level on the ground. The quiet that suffused the doctor's house then, broken only by the murmur of the women eating sunshine cake, was only that: quiet. It was not peaceful, for it was preceded by and would soon be termintaed by the presence of Macon Dead.

Solid, rumbling, likely to erupt without prior notice, Macon kept each member of his family awkward with fear. His hatred of his wife glittered and sparked in every word he spoke to her. The disappointment he felt in his daughters sifted down on them like ash, dulling their buttery complexions and choking the lilt out of what should have been girlish voices. Under the frozen heat of his glance they tripped over doorsills and dropped the salt cellar into the yolks of their poached eggs. The way he mangled their grace, wit, and self-esteem was the single excitement of their days. Without the tension and drama he ignited, they might not have known what to do with themselves. In his absence his daughters bent their necks over blood-red squares of velvet and waited eagerly for any hint of him, and his wife, Ruth, began her days stunned into stillness by her husband's contempt and ended them wholly animated by it.

When she closed the door behind her afternoon guests, and let the quiet smile die from her lips, she began the preparation of food her husband found impossible to eat. She did not try to make her meals nauseating; she simply didn't know how not to. She would notice that the sunshine cake was too haggled to put before him and decide on a rennet[7] dessert. But the grinding of the veal and beef for a meat loaf took so long she not only forgot the pork, settling for bacon drippings poured over the meat, she had no time to make a dessert at all. Hurriedly, then, she began to set the table. As she unfolded the white linen and let it billow over the fine mahogany table, she would look once more at the large water mark. She never set the table or passed through the dining room without looking at it. Like a lighthouse keeper drawn to his window to gaze once again at the sea, or a prisoner automatically searching out the sun as he steps into the yard for his hour of exercise, Ruth looked for the water mark several times during the day. She knew it was there, would always be there, but she needed to confirm its presence. Like the

---

[7] A junket, or custardlike dessert made from curdled milk.

keeper of the lighthouse and the prisoner, she regarded it as a mooring, a check-point, some stable visual object that assured her that the world was still there; that this was life and not a dream. That she was alive somewhere, inside, which she acknowledged to be true only because a thing she knew intimately was out there, outside herself.

Even in the cave of sleep, without dreaming of it or thinking of it all, she felt its presence. Oh, she talked endlessly to her daughters and her guests about how to get rid of it—what might hide this single flaw on the splendid wood: Vaseline, tobacco juice, iodine, sanding followed by linseed oil. She had tried them all. But her glance was nutritious; the spot became, if anything, more pronounced as the years passed.

The cloudy gray circle identified the place where the bowl filled every day during the doctor's life with fresh flowers had stood. Every day. And when there were no flowers, it held a leaf arrangement, a gathering of twigs, and berries, pussy willow, Scotch pine. . . . But always something to grace the dinner table in the evening.

It was for her father a touch that distinguished his own family from the people among whom they lived. For Ruth it was the summation of the affectionate elegance with which she believed her childhood had been surrounded. When Macon married her and moved into Doctor's house, she kept up the centerpiece-arranging. Then came the time she walked down to the shore through the roughest part of the city to get some driftwood. She had seen an arrangement of driftwood and dried seaweed in the homemakers section of the newspaper. It was a damp November day, and Doctor was paralyzed even then and taking liquid food in his bedroom. The wind had lifted her skirt from around her ankles and cut through her laced shoes. She'd had to rub her feet down with warm olive oil when she got back. At dinner, where just the two of them sat, she turned toward her husband and asked him how he liked the centerpiece. "Most people overlook things like that. They see it, but they don't see anything beautiful in it. They don't see that nature has already made it as perfect as it can be. Look at it from the side. It is pretty, isn't it?"

Her husband looked at the driftwood with its lacy beige seaweed, and without moving his head, said, "Your chicken is red at the bone. And there is probably a potato dish that is supposed to have lumps in it. Mashed ain't the dish."

Ruth let the seaweed disintegrate, and later, when its veins and stems dropped and curled into brown scabs on the table, she removed the bowl and brushed away the scabs. But the water mark, hidden by the bowl all these years, was exposed. And once exposed, it behaved as though it were itself a plant and flourished into a huge suede-gray flower that throbbed like fever, and sighed like the shift of sand dunes. But it could also be still. Patient, restful, and still.

But there was nothing you could do with a mooring—except acknowledge it, use it for the verification of some idea you wanted to keep alive. Something else is needed to get from sunup to sundown: a balm, a gentle touch or nuzzling of some sort. So Ruth rose up and out of her guileless inefficiency to claim her bit of balm right after the preparation of dinner and just before the return of her husband from his office. It was one of her two secret indulgences—the one that involved her son—and part of the pleasure it gave her came from the room in which she did it. A damp greenness lived there, made by the evergreen that pressed against the window and filtered the light. It was just a little room that Doctor had called a study, and aside from a sewing machine that stood in the corner along with a dress form, there was only a rocker and tiny footstool. She sat in this room holding her son on her lap, staring at his closed eyelids and listening to the sound of his sucking. Staring not so much from maternal joy as from a wish to avoid seeing his legs dangling almost to the floor.

In late afternoon, before her husband closed his office and came home, she called her son to her. When he came into the little room she unbuttoned her blouse and smiled. He was too young to be dazzled by her nipples, but he was old enough to be bored by the flat taste of mother's milk, so he came reluctantly, as to a chore, and lay as he had at least once each day of his life in his mother's arms, and tried to pull the thin faintly sweet milk from her flesh without hurting her with his teeth.

She felt him. His restraint, his courtesy, his indifference, all of which pushed her into fantasy. She had the distinct impression that his lips were pulling from her a thread of light. It was though she were a cauldron issuing spinning gold. Like the miller's daughter—the one who sat at night in a straw-filled room, thrilled with the secret power Rumpelstiltskin had given her: to see golden thread stream from her very own shuttle. And that was the other part of her pleasure, a pleasure she hated to give up. So when Freddie the janitor, who liked to pretend he was a friend of the family and not just their flunky as well as their tenant, brought his rent to the doctor's house late one day and looked in the window past the evergreen, the terror sprang to Ruth's eyes came from the quick realization that she was to lose fully half of what made her daily life bearable. Freddie, however, interpreted her look as simple shame, but that didn't stop him from grinning.

"Have mercy. I be damn."

He fought the evergreen for a better look, hampered more by his laughter than by the branches. Ruth jumped up as quickly as she could and covered her breast, dropping her son on the floor and confirming for him what he had begun to suspect—that these afternoons were strange and wrong.

Before either mother or son could speak, rearrange themselves properly, or even exchange looks, Freddie had run around the house, climbed the porch steps, and was calling them between gulps of laughter.

"Miss Rufie. Miss Rufie. Where you? Where you all at?" He opened the door to the green room as though it were his now.

"I be damn, Miss Rufie. When the last time I seen that? I don't even know the last time I seen that. I mean, ain't nothing wrong with it. I mean, old folks swear by it. It's just, you know, you don't see it up here much. . . . " But his eyes were on the boy. Appreciative eyes that communicated some complicity she was excluded from. Freddie looked the boy up and down, taking in the steady but secretive eyes and the startling contrast between Ruth's lemony skin and the boy's black skin. "Used to be a lot of womenfolk nurse they kids a long time down South. Lot of 'em. But you don't see it much no more. I knew a family—the mother wasn't too quick, though—nursed hers till the boy, I reckon, was near 'bout thirteen. But that's a bit much, ain't it?" All the time he chattered, he rubbed his chin and looked at the boy. Finally he stopped, and gave a long low chuckle. He'd found the phrase he'd been searching for. "A milkman. That's what you got here, Miss Rufie. A natural milkman if ever I seen one. Look out, womens. Here he come. Huh!"

Freddie carried his discovery not only into the homes of Ruth's neighborhood, but to Southside, where he lived and where Macon Dead owned rent houses. So Ruth kept close to home and had no afternoon guests for the better part of two months, to keep from hearing that her son had been rechristened with a name he was never able to shake and that did nothing to improve either one's relationship with his father.

Macon Dead never knew how it came about—how his only son acquired the nickname that stuck in spite of his own refusal to use it or acknowledge it. It was a matter that concerned him a good deal, for the giving of names in his family was always surrounded by what he believed to be monumental foolishness. No one mentioned to him the incident out of which the nickname grew because he was a difficult man to approach—a hard man, with a manner so cool it discouraged casual or spontaneous conversation. Only Freddie the janitor took liberties with Macon Dead, liberties he purchased with the services he rendered, and Freddie was the last person on earth to tell him. So Macon Dead neither heard of nor visualized Ruth's sudden terror, her awkward jump from the rocking chair, the boy's fall broken by the tiny footstool, or Freddie's amused, admiring summation of the situation.

Without knowing any of the details, however, he guessed, with the accuracy of a mind sharpened by hatred, that the name he heard schoolchildren call his son, the name he overheard the ragman use when he paid the boy three cents for a bundle of old clothes—he guessed that this name was not clean. Milkman. It certainly didn't sound like the honest job of a dairyman, or bring to his mind cold bright cans standing on the back porch, glittering like captains on guard. It sounded dirty, intimate, and hot. He knew that wherever the name came from, it had something to do with his wife and was, like the emotion he always felt when thinking of her, coated with disgust.

This disgust and the uneasiness with which he regarded his son affected everything he did in that city. If he could have felt sad, simply sad, it would have relieved him. Fifteen years of regret at not having a son had become the bitterness of finally having one in the most revolting circumstances.

There had been a time when he had a head full of hair and when Ruth wore lovely complicated underwear that deliberately took a long time to undo. When all of his foreplay was untying, unclasping, unbuckling the snaps and strings of what must have been the most beautiful, the most delicate, the whitest and softest underwear on earth. Each eye of her corset he toyed with (and there were forty—twenty on each side); each grosgrain ribbon that threaded its pale-blue way through the snowy top of her bodice he unlaced. He not only undid the blue bow; he pulled it all the way out of the hem, so she had to rethread it afterward with a safety pin. The elastic bands that connected her perspiration shields to her slip he unsnapped and snapped again, teasing her and himself with the sound of the snaps and the thrill of his fingertips on her shoulders. They never spoke during these undressings. But they giggled occasionally, and as when children play "doctor," undresssing of course was the best part.

When Ruth was naked and lying there moist and crumbly as unbleached sugar, he bent to unlace her shoes. That was the final delight, for once he had undressed her feet, he peeled her stockings down over her ankles and toes, he entered her and ejaculated quickly. She liked it that way. So did he. And in almost twenty years during which he had not laid eyes on her naked feet, he missed only the underwear.

Once he believed that the sight of her mouth on the dead man's fingers would be the thing he would remember always. He was wrong. Little by little he remembered fewer and fewer of the details, until finally he had to imagine them, even fabricate them, guess what they must have been. The image left him, but the odiousness never did. For the nourishment of his outrage he depended on the memory of her underwear; those round, innocent corset eyes now lost to him forever.

So if the people were calling his son Milkman, and if she was lowering her eyelids and dabbing at the sweat on her top lip when she heard it, there was definitely some filthy connection and it did not matter at all to Macon Dead whether anyone gave him the details or not.

And they didn't. Nobody dared enough and cared enough to tell him. The ones who cared enough, Lena and Corinthians, the living proof of those years of undressing his wife, did not dare. And the one person who dared to but didn't care to was the one person in the world he hated more than his wife in spite of the fact that she was his sister. He had not crossed the tracks to see her since his son was born and he had no intention of renewing their relationship now.

Macon Dead dug in his pocket for his keys, and curled his fingers around them, letting their bunchy solidity calm him. They were the keys to all the doors of his houses (only four true houses; the rest were really shacks), and he fondled them from time to time as he walked down Not Doctor Street to his office. At least he thought of it as his office, had even painted the word OFFICE on the door. But the plate-glass window contradicted him. In peeling gold letters arranged in a semicircle, his business establishment was declared to be Sonny's Shop. Scraping the previous owner's name off was hardly worth the trouble since he couldn't scrape it from anybody's mind. His storefront office was never called anything but Sonny's Shop, although nobody now could remember thirty years back, when, presumably, Sonny did something or other there.

He walked there now—strutted is the better word, for he had a high behind and an athlete's stride—thinking of names. Surely, he thought, he and his sister had some ancestor, some lithe young man with onyx skin and legs as straight as cane stalks, who had a name that was real. A name given to him at birth with love and seriousness. A name that was not a joke, nor a disguise, nor a brand name. But who this lithe young man was, and where his cane-stalk legs carried him from or to, could never be known. No. Nor his name. His own parents, in some mood of perverseness of resignation, had agreed to abide by a naming done to them by somebody who couldn't have cared less. Agreed to take and pass on to all their issue this heavy name scrawled in perfect thoughtlessness by a drunken Yankee in the Union Army. A literal slip of the pen handed to his father on a piece of paper and which he handed on to his only son, and his son likewise handed on to his; Macon Dead who begat a second Macon Dead who married Ruth Foster (Dead) and begat Magdalene called Lena Dead and First Corinthians Dead and (when he least expected it) another Macon Dead, now known to the part of the world that mattered as Milkman Dead. And as if that were not enough, a sister named Pilate Dead, who would never mention to her brother the circumstances of the details of this foolish misnaming of his son because the whole thing would have delighted her. She would savor it, maybe fold it too in a brass box and hang it from her other ear.

He had cooperated as a young father with the blind selection of names from the Bible for every child other than the first male. And abided by whatever the finger pointed to, for he knew every configuration of the naming of his sister. How his father, confused and melancholy over his wife's death in childbirth, had thumbed through the Bible, and since he could not read a word, chose a group of letters that seemed to him strong and handsome; saw in them a large figure that looked like a tree hanging in some princely but protective way over a row of smaller trees. How he had copied the group of letters out on a piece of brown paper; copied, as illiterate people do, every curlicue, arch, and bend in the letters, and presented it to the midwife.

"That's the baby's name."

"You want this for the baby's name?"

"I want that for the baby's name. Say it."

"You can't name the baby this."

"Say it."

"It's a man's name."

"Say it."

"Pilate."

"What?"

"Pilate. You wrote down Pilate."

"Like a riverboat pilot?"

"No. Not like no riverboat pilot. Like a Christ-killing Pilate.[8] You can't get much worse than that for a name. And a baby girl at that."

"That's where my finger went down at."

"Well, your brain ain't got to follow it. You don't want to give this motherless child the name of the man that killed Jesus, do you?"

"I asked Jesus to save my wife."

"Careful, Macon."

"I asked him all night long."

"He give you your baby."

"Yes. He did. Baby name Pilate."

"Jesus, have mercy."

"Where you going with that piece of paper?"

"It's going back where it came from. Right in the Devil's flames."

"Give it here. It come from the Bible. It stays in the Bible."

And it did stay there, until the baby girl turned twelve and took it out, folded it up into a tiny knot and put it in a little brass box, and strung the entire contraption through her left earlobe. Fluky about her own name at twelve, how much more fluky she'd become since then Macon could only guess. But he knew for certain that she would treat the naming of the third Macon Dead with the same respect and awe she had treated the boy's birth.

Macon Dead remembered when his son was born, how she seemed to be more interested in this first nephew of hers than she was in her own daughter, and even that daughter's daughter. Long after Ruth was up and about, as capable as she ever would be—and that wasn't much—of running the house again, Pilate continued to visit, her shoelaces undone, a knitted cap pulled down over her forehead, bringing her foolish earring and sickening smell into the kitchen. He had not seen her since he was sixteen years old, until a year before the birth of his son, when she appeared in his city. Now she was acting like an in-law, like an aunt, dabbling at helping Ruth and the girls, but having no interest in or knowledge of decent housekeeping, she got in the way. Finally she just sat in a chair near the crib,

---

[8] Pontius Pilate (1st century A. D.), the Roman official who tried Jesus and condemned him to crucifixion.

singing to the baby. That wasn't so bad, but what Macon Dead remembered most was the expression on her face. Surprise, it looked like, and eagerness. But so intense it made him uneasy. Or perhaps it was more than that. Perhaps it was seeing her all those years after they had separated outside that cave, and remembering his anger and her betrayal. How far down she had slid since then. She had cut the last thread of propriety. At one time she had been the dearest thing in the world to him. Now she was odd, murky, and worst of all, unkempt. A regular source of embarrassment, if he would allow it. But he would not allow it.

Finally he had told her not to come again until she could show some respect for herself. Could get a real job instead of running a wine house.

"Why can't you dress like a woman?" He was standing by the stove. "What's that sailor's cap doing on your head? Don't you have stockings? What are you trying to make me look like in this town?" He trembled with the thought of the white men in the bank—the men who helped him buy and mortgage houses—discovering that this raggedy bootlegger was his sister. That the propertied Negro who handled his business so well and who lived in the big house on Not Doctor Street had a sister who had a daughter but no husband, and that daughter had a daughter but no husband. A collection of lunatics who made wine and sang in the streets "like common street women! Just like common street women!"

Pilate had sat there listening to him, her wondering eyes resting on his face. Then she said, "I been worried sick about you too, Macon."

Exasperated, he had gone to the kitchen door. "Go 'head, Pilate. Go on now. I'm on the thin side of evil and trying not to break through."

Pilate stood up, wrapped her quilt around her, and with a last fond look at the baby, left through the kitchen door. She never came back.

When Macon Dead got to the front door of his office he saw a stout woman and two young boys standing a few feet away. Macon unlocked his door, walked over to his desk, and settled himself behind it. As he was thumbing through his accounts book, the stout woman entered, alone.

"Afternoon Mr. Dead, sir. I'm Mrs. Bains. Live over at number three on Fifteenth Street."

Macon Dead remembered—not the woman, but the circumstances at number three. His tenant's grandmother or aunt or something had moved in there and the rent was long overdue.

"Yes, Mrs. Bains, You got something for me?"

"Well, that's what I come to talk to you about. You know Cency left all them babies with me. And my relief check ain't no more'n it take to keep a well-grown yard dog alive—half alive, I should say."

"Your rent is four dollars a month, Mrs. Bains. You two months behind already."

"I do know that, Mr. Dead, sir, but babies can't make it with nothing to put in they stomach."

Their voices were low, polite, without any hint of conflict.

"Can they make it in the street, Mrs. Bains? That's where they gonna be if you don't figure out some way to get me my money."

"No sir. They can't make it in the street. We need both, I reckon. Same as yours does."

"Then you better rustle it up, Mrs. Bains. You got till"—he swiveled around to consult the calendar on the wall—"till Saturday coming. Saturday, Mrs. Bains. Not Sunday. Not Monday. Saturday."

If she had been younger and had more juice, the glitter in her eyes would have washed down onto her cheeks. Now, at her time of life, it simply gleamed. She pressed the flat of her hand on Macon Dead's desk and, holding the gleam steady in her eyes, pushed herself up from the chair. She turned her head a little to look out the plate-glass window; and then back at him.

"What's it gonna profit you, Mr. Dead, sir, to put me and them children out?"

"Saturday, Mrs. Bains."

Lowering her head, Mrs. Bains whispered something and walked slowly and heavily from the office. As she closed the door to Sonny's Shop, her grandchildren moved out of the sunlight into the shadow where she stood.

"What he say, Granny?"

Mrs. Bains put a hand on the taller boy's hair and fingered it lightly, absently searching with her nails for tetter spots.[9]

"He must've told her no," said the other boy.

"Do we got to move?" The tall boy tossed his head free of her fingers and looked at her sideways. His cat eyes were gashes of gold.

Mrs. Bains let her hand fall to her side. "A nigger in business is a terrible thing to see. A terrible, terrible thing to see."

The boys looked at each other and back at their grandmother. Their lips were parted as though they had heard something important.

When Mrs. Bains closed the door, Macon Dead went back to the pages of his accounts book, running his fingertips over the figures and thinking with the unoccupied part of his mind about the first time he called on Ruth Foster's father. He had only two keys in his pocket then, and if he had let people like the woman who just left have their way, he wouldn't have had any keys at all. It was because of those keys that he could dare walk over to that part of Not Doctor Street (it was still Doctor Street then) and approach the most important Negro in the city. To lift the lion's paw knocker, to entertain thoughts of marrying the doctor's daughter was possible because each key represented a house which he owned at the time. Without those keys he would have floated away at the doctor's first word: "Yes?" Or he would have melted like new wax under the heat of that pale eye. Instead he was able to say that he had been introduced to his daughter, Miss Ruth Foster, and would appreciate having the doctor's permission to keep her company now and then. That his intentions were honorable and that he himself was certainly worthy of the doctor's consideration as a gentleman friend for Miss Foster since, at twenty-five, he was already a colored man of property.

"I don't know anything about you," the doctor said, "other than your name, which I don't like, but I will abide by my daughter's preference."

In fact the doctor knew a good deal about him and was more grateful to this tall young man than he ever allowed himself to show. Fond as he was of his only child, useful as she was in his house since his wife had died, lately he had begun to chafe under her devotion. Her steady beam of love was unsettling, and she had never dropped those expressions of affection that had been so lovable in her childhood. The good-night kiss was itself a masterpiece of slow-wittedness on her part and discomfort on his. At sixteen, she still insisted on having him come to her at night, sit on her bed, exchange a few pleasantries, and plant a kiss on her lips. Perhaps it was the loud silence of his dead wife, perhaps it was Ruth's disturbing resemblance to her mother. More probably it was the ecstasy that always seemed

---

[9] Evidence of a skin disease such as eczema.

to be shining in Ruth's face when he bent to kiss her—an ecstasy he felt inappropriate to the occasion.

None of that, of course, did he describe to the young man who came to call. Which is why Macon Dead still believed the magic had lain in the two keys.

In the middle of his reverie, Macon was interrupted by rapid tapping on the window. He looked up, saw Freddie peeping through the gold lettering, and nodded for him to enter. A gold-toothed bantamweight, Freddie was as much of a town crier as Southside had. It was this same rapid tapping on the windowpane, the same flash-of-gold smile that had preceded his now-famous scream to Macon: "Mr. Smith went splat!" It was obvious to Macon that Freddie now had news of another calamity.

"Porter gone crazy drunk again! Got his shotgun!"

"Who's he out for?" Macon began closing books and opening desk drawers. Porter was a tenant and tomorrow was collection day.

"Ain't out for nobody in particular. Just perched himself up in the attic window and commenced to waving a shotgun. Say he gotta kill him somebody before morning."

"He go to work today?"

"Yep. Caught the eagle too."

"Drunk it all up?"

"Not all of it. He only got one bottle, and he still got a fist fulla money."

"Who's crazy enough to sell him any liquor?"

Freddie showed a few gold teeth but said nothing, so Macon knew it was Pilate. He locked all his drawers save one—the one he unlocked and took a small .32 from.

"Police warn every bootlegger in the county, and he still gets it somehow." Macon went on with the charade, pretending he didn't know his sister was the one Porter and anybody else—adult, child, or beast—could buy wine from. He thought for the hundredth time that she needed to be in jail and that he would be willing to put her there if he could be sure she wouldn't loudmouth him and make him seem trashy in the eyes of the law—and the banks.

"You know how to use that thing, Mr. Dead, sir?"

"I know how."

"Porter's crazy when he drunk."

"I know what he is."

"How you aiming to get him down?"

"I ain't aiming to get him down. I'm aiming to get my money down. He can go on and die up there if he wants to. But if he don't toss me my rent, I'm going to blow him out of that window."

Freddie's giggle was soft, but his teeth strengthened its impact. A born flunky, he loved gossip and the telling of it. He was the ear that heard every murmur of complaint, every namecalling; and his was the eye that saw everything: the secret loving glances, the fights, the new dresses.

Macon knew Freddie as a fool and a liar, but a reliable liar. He was always right about his facts and always wrong about the motives that produced the facts. Just as now he was right about Porter having a shotgun, being in the attic window, and being drunk. But Porter was not waiting to kill somebody, meaning anybody, before morning. In fact he was very specific about whom he wanted to kill—himself. However, he did have a precondition which he shouted down, loud and clear, from the attic. "I want to fuck! Send me up somebody to fuck! Hear me? Send me up somebody, I tell ya, or I'ma blow my brains out!"

As Macon and Freddie approached the yard, the women from the rooming house were hollering answers to Porter's plea.

"What kinda bargain is that?"

"Kill yourself first and then we'll send you somebody."

"Do it have to be a woman?"

"Do it got to be human?"

"Do it got to be alive?"

"Can it be a piece of liver?"

"Put that thing down and throw me my goddam money!" Macon's voice cut through the women's fun. "Float those dollars down here, nigger, then blow yourself up!"

Porter turned and aimed his shotgun at Macon.

"If you pull that trigger," shouted Macon, "you better not miss. If you take a shot you better make sure I'm dead, cause if you don't I'm gonna shoot your balls up in your throat!" He pulled out his own weapon. "Now get the hell outta that window!"

Porter hesistated for only a second, before turning the barrel of the shotgun toward himself—or trying to. Its length made it difficult; his drunkenness made it impossible. Struggling to get the right angle, he was suddenly distracted. He leaned his shotgun on the window sill, pulled out his penis and in a high arc, peed over the heads of the women, making them scream and run in a panic that the shotgun had not been able to create. Macon rubbed the back of his head while Freddie bent double with laughter.

For more than an hour Porter held them at bay: cowering, screaming, threatening, urinating, and interspersing all of it with pleas for a woman.

He would cry great shoulder-heaving sobs, followed by more screams.

"I love ya! I love ya all. Don't act like that. You women. Stop it. Don't act like that. Don't you see I love ya? I'd die for ya, kill for ya. I'm saying I love ya. I'm telling ya. Oh, God have mercy. What I'm gonna do? What in this fuckin world am I gonna dooooo?"

Tears streamed down his face and he cradled the barrel of the shotgun in his arms as though it were the woman he had been begging for, searching for, all his life. "Gimme hate, Lord," he whimpered. "I'll take hate any day. But don't give me love. I can't take no more love, Lord. I can't carry it. Just like Mr. Smith. He couldn't carry it. It's too heavy. Jesus, *you* know. You know all about it. Ain't it heavy? Jesus? Ain't love heavy? Don't you see, Lord? You own son couldn't carry it. If it killed Him, what You think it's gonna do to me? Huh? Huh?" He was getting angry again.

"Come down outta there, nigger!" Macon's voice was still loud, but it was getting weary.

"An you, you baby-dicked baboon"—he tried to point at Macon—"you the worst. You need killin, you really *need* killin. You know why? Well, I'm gonna tell you why. I *know* why. Everybody . . . "

Porter slumped down in the window, muttering, "Everybody know why," and fell fast asleep. As he sank deeper into it, the shotgun slipped from his hand, rattled down the roof, and hit the ground with a loud explosion. The shot zipped past a by-stander's shoe and blew a hole in the tire of a stripped Dodge parked in the road.

"Go get my money," Macon said.

"Me?" Freddie asked. "Suppose he . . . "

"Go get me my money."

Porter was snoring. Through the blast of the gun and the picking of his pocket he slept like a baby.

When Macon walked out of the yard, the sun had disappeared behind the bread company. Tired, irritable, he walked down Fifteenth Street, glancing up as he passed one of his other houses, its silhouette melting in the light that trembled between dusk and twilight. Scattered here and there, his houses stretched up beyond him like squat ghosts with hooded eyes. He didn't like to look at them in this light. During the day they were reassuring to see; now they did not seem to belong to him at all—in fact he felt as though the houses were in league with one another to make him feel like the outsider, the propertyless, landless wanderer. It was this feeling of loneliness that made him decide to take a shortcut back to Not Doctor Street, even though to do so would lead him past his sister's house. In the gathering darkness, he was sure his passing would be unnoticed by her. He crossed a yard and followed a fence that led into Darling Street where Pilate lived in a narrow single-story house whose basement seemed to be rising from rather than settling into the ground. She had no electricity because she would not pay for the service. Nor for gas. At night she and her daughter lit the house with candles and kerosene lamps; they warmed themselves and cooked with wood and coal, pumped kitchen water into a dry sink through a pipeline from a well and lived pretty much as though progress was a word that meant walking a little farther on down the road.

Her house sat eighty feet from the sidewalk and was backed by four huge pine trees, from which she got the needles she stuck into her mattress. Seeing the pine trees started him thinking about her mouth; how she loved, as a girl, to chew pine needles and as a result smelled even then like a forest. For a dozen years she had been like his own child. After their mother died, she had come struggling out of the womb without help from throbbing muscles or the pressure of swift womb water. As a result, for all the years he knew her, her stomach was as smooth and sturdy as her back, at no place interrupted by a navel. It was the absence of a navel that convinced people that she had not come into this world through normal channels; had never lain, floated, or grown in some warm and liquid place connected by a tissue-thin tube to a reliable source of human nourishment. Macon knew otherwise, because he was there and had seen the eyes of the midwife as his mother's legs collapsed. And heard as well her shouts when the baby, who they had believed was dead also, inched its way headfirst out of a still, silent, and indifferent cave of flesh, dragging her own cord and her own afterbirth behind her. But the rest was true. Once the new baby's lifeline was cut, the cord stump shriveled, fell off, and left no trace of having ever existed, which, as a young boy taking care of his baby sister, he thought no more strange than a bald head. He was seventeen years old, irreparably separated from her and already pressing forward in his drive for wealth, when he learned that there was probably not another stomach like hers on earth.

Now, nearing her yard, he trusted that the dark would keep anyone in her house from seeing him. He did not even look to his left as he walked by it. But then he heard the music. They were singing. All of them. Pilate, Reba, and Reba's daughter, Hagar. There was no one on the street that he could see; people were at supper, licking their fingers, blowing into saucers of coffee, and no doubt chattering about Porter's escapade and Macon's fearless confrontation of the wild man in the attic. There were no street lights in this part of town; only the moon directed the way of a pedestrian. Macon walked on, resisting as best he could the sound of the voices that followed him. He was rapidly approaching a part of the road where the music could not follow, when he saw, like a scene on the back of a postcard, a picture of where he was headed—his own home; his wife's narrow unyielding back; his daughters, boiled dry from years of yearning; his son, to whom he could speak only if his words held some command or—criticism. "Hello, Daddy." "Hello, son, tuck your shirt in." "I found a dead bird, Daddy." "Don't bring that mess in this house. . . ." There was no music there, and tonight he wanted just a bit of music—from the person who had been his first caring for.

He turned back and walked slowly toward Pilate's house. They were singing some melody that Pilate was leading. A phrase that the other two were taking up and building on. Her powerful contralto, Reba's piercing soprano in counterpoint, and the soft voice of the girl, Hagar, who must be about ten or eleven now, pulled him like a carpet tack under the influence of a magnet.

Surrendering to the sound, Macon moved closer. He wanted no conversation, no witness, only to listen and perhaps to see the three of them, the source of that music that made him think of fields and wild turkey and calico. Treading as lightly as he could, he crept up to the side window where the candlelight flickered lowest, and peeped in. Reba was cutting her toenails with a kitchen knife or a switchblade, her long neck bent almost to her knees. The girl, Hagar, was braiding her hair, while Pilate, whose face he could not see because her back was to the window, was stirring something in a pot. Wine pulp, perhaps. Macon knew it was not food she was stirring, for she and her daughters ate like children. Whatever they had a taste for. No meal was ever planned or balanced or served. Nor was there any gathering at the table. Pilate might bake hot bread and each one of them would eat it with butter whenever she felt like it. Or there might be grapes, left over from the winemaking, or peaches for days on end. If one of them bought a gallon of milk they drank it until it was gone. If another got a half bushel of tomatoes or a dozen ears of corn, they ate them until they were gone too. They ate what they had or came across or had a craving for. Profits from their wine-selling evaporated like sea water in a hot wind—going for junk jewelry for Hagar, Reba's gifts to men, and he didn't know what all.

Near the window, hidden by the dark, he felt the irritability of the day drain from him and relished the effortless beauty of the women singing in the candlelight. Reba's soft profile, Hagar's hands moving, moving in her heavy hair, and Pilate. He knew her face better than he knew his own. Singing now, her face would be a mask; all emotion and passion would have left her features and entered her voice. But he knew that when she was neither singing nor talking, her face was animated by her constantly moving lips. She chewed things. As a baby, as a very young girl, she kept things in her mouth—straw from brooms, gristle, buttons, seeds, leaves, string, and her favorite, when he could find some for her, rubber bands and India rubber erasers. Her lips were alive with small movements. If you were close to her, you wondered if she was about to smile or was she merely shifting a straw from the baseline of her gums to her tongue. Perhaps she was dislodging a curl of rubber band from inside her cheek, or was she really smiling? From a distance she appeared to be whispering to herself, when she was only nibbling or splitting tiny seeds with her front teeth. Her lips were darker than her skin, wine-stained, blueberry-dyed, so her face had a cosmetic look—as though she had applied a very dark lipstick neatly and blotted away its shine on a scrap of newspaper.

As Macon felt himself softening under the weight of memory and music, the song died down. The air was quiet and yet Macon Dead could not leave. He liked looking at them freely this way. They didn't move. They simply stopped singing and Reba went on paring her toenails, Hagar threaded and unthreaded her hair, and Pilate swayed like a willow over her stirring.

1977

Philip Roth
(1933–   )

Like Quentin Compson in William Faulkner's *Absalom, Absalom!* (1936), Philip Roth has often had to defend his relationship to his heritage. His short-story collection *Goodbye, Columbus* (1959), which includes "Defender of the Faith," won a National Book Award but opened a floodgate of criticism about Roth's portrayal of his lower middle-class Jewish roots in Newark, New Jersey. Roth was born in Newark in 1933 and studied at the Newark campus of Rutgers University from 1950 to 1951. He completed his undergraduate work at Bucknell University in 1954. After receiving an M. A. in English from the University of Chicago in 1955, he joined the army but was discharged after suffering a back injury in basic training. Roth continued graduate studies at Chicago until 1957.

Roth's first two novels, *Letting Go* (1962) and *When She Was Good* (1967), demonstrate his ability to extend beyond the somewhat narrow range of *Goodbye, Columbus*. The novels explore Jewish-Gentile relations and examine love, family, sex, and marriage in university and midwestern settings. With *Portnoy's Complaint* (1969) Roth returned to his New Jersey boyhood to recall old radio shows, softball games, and lusting after girls; the narrative's sometimes crude humor and scenes of masturbation earned Roth widespread notoriety as the author of a "dirty" book. It was followed by *Our Gang* (1970), *The Breast* (1971), and *The Great American Novel* (1973)—three uneven works struggling to get out from under their initial conceits of social and political fantasy. But with *My Life as a Man* (1974) and *The Professor of Desire* (1977), Roth returned to the kind of social analysis and examination of relationships between individuals and their cultures that moves beyond what it means to be a Jew in America to explore more universal forms of discontent and dislocation.

Throughout Roth's career his endless self-examination has threatened to turn into self-absorption and parody, and yet his novels consistently transform private reflection into public revelation. His ironic humor and ruthless social scrutiny have often been perceived as the pursuit of a cheap joke in the creation of ethnic caricatures. But Roth's later work, particularly *Zuckerman Bound* (1985) and *The Counterlife* (1986), has transcended this criticism to fulfill the promise of his early work. In *Zuckerman Bound*, consisting of the novels *The Ghost Writer* (1979), *Zuckerman Unbound* (1981), and *The Anatomy Lesson* (1983) and the story "The Prague Orgy," Roth charts the ways in which the works of Nathan Zuckerman intersect the lives of his family, literary fathers, and an odd assortment

Philip Roth's Goodbye, Columbus *was made into a 1969 motion picture starring Ali McGraw and Richard Benjamin.*

of characters—from a woman Zuckerman imagines is Anne Frank to an alter ego modeled after a 1950s quiz-show champion. *Portnoy's Complaint,* now called *Carnovsky,* haunts these works and their author nearly as persistently as do questions of Judaism and of the boundaries between fiction and reality. In the novel *The Counterlife* (1986) Roth turns these questions into a powerful narrative technique, as Zuckerman and his brother, Henry, suffer from impotence brought on by medication. The story ends with Zuckerman's lover writing a letter to say that she is "leaving the novel before anything dreadful happens." Here, questions of Judaism intersect with questions of Zionism, and the relationships between self and culture stretch from America to England and Israel.

Roth has been a faculty member at such colleges as the University of Iowa, Princeton University (as writer in residence), and the University of Pennsylvania. His wife since 1959, Margaret Martinson, died in 1968. Roth has isolated himself from the literary community, maintaining residences in Connecticut and London with the British actress Claire Bloom; the couple married in 1990. And while isolated he continues to write; his *Deceptions* (1990) and *Patrimony* (1991) are both semi-autobiographical novels.

Suggested Readings: *When She Was Good,* 1967. *Portnoy's Complaint,* 1969. *Our Gang,* 1970. *The Great American Novel,* 1973. *My Life As a Man,* 1974. *Reading Myself and Others,* 1975. *The Professor of Desire,* 1977. *Zuckerman Bound,* 1985. *The Counterlife,* 1986. *The Facts: A Novelist's*

Autobiography, 1988. A. Kazin, *Contemporaries*, 1962. A. Guttman, *The Jewish Writer in America*, 1971. T. Tanner, *City of Words: American Fiction 1950–1970*, 1971. R. Wisse, *The Schlemiel as Modern Hero*, 1971. I. Howe, "Philip Roth Reconsidered," in *Commentary*, 54, (December) 1972. B. F. Rodgers, *Philip Roth*, 1978. H. Lee, *Philip Roth*, 1982. G. J. Searles, *The Fiction of John Updike and Philip Roth*, 1985.

Text Used: *Goodbye, Columbus*, 1959.

from   *GOODBYE, COLUMBUS*

DEFENDER OF THE FAITH*

In May of 1945, only a few weeks after the fighting had ended in Europe,[1] I was rotated back to the States, where I spent the remainder of the war with a training company at Camp Crowder, Missouri. Along with the rest of the Ninth Army, I had been racing across Germany so swiftly during the late winter and spring that when I boarded the plane, I couldn't believe its destination lay to the west. My mind might inform me otherwise, but there was the inertia of the spirit that told me we were flying to a new front, where we would disembark and continue our push eastward—eastward until we'd circled the globe, marching through villages along whose twisting, cobbled streets crowds of the enemy would watch us take possession of what, up till then, they'd considered their own. I had changed enough in two years not to mind the trembling of the old people, the crying of the very young, the uncertainty and fear in the eyes of the once arrogant. I had been fortunate enough to develop an infantryman's heart, which, like his feet, at first aches and swells but finally grows horny enough for him to travel the weirdest paths without feeling a thing.

Captain Paul Barrett was my C. O. in Camp Crowder. The day I reported for duty, he came out of his office to shake my hand. He was short, gruff, and fiery, and—indoors or out—he wore his polished helmet liner pulled down to his little eyes. In Europe, he had received a battlefield commission and a serious chest wound, and he'd been returned to the States only a few months before. He spoke easily to me, and at the evening formation he introduced me to the troops. "Gentlemen," he said, "Sergeant Thurston, as you know, is no longer with this company. Your new first sergeant is Sergeant Nathan Marx, here. He is a veteran of the European theater, and consequently will expect to find a company of soldiers here, and not a company of *boys*."

I sat up late in the orderly room that evening, trying half-heartedly to solve the riddle of duty rosters, personnel forms, and morning reports. The Charge of Quarters[2] slept with his mouth open on a mattress on the floor. A trainee stood reading the next day's duty roster, which was posted on the bulletin board just inside the screen door. It was a warm evening, and I could hear radios playing dance music over in the barracks. The trainee, who had been staring at me whenever he thought I wouldn't notice, finally took a step in my direction.

---

* First published in the *New Yorker* in 1959 and collected in *Goodbye, Columbus* later that year.
[1] World War II ended in Europe when Germany surrendered on May 7, 1945; it ended in the Pacific when Japan surrendered on September 2, 1945.
[2] The noncommissioned officer in charge of the barracks on weekends and at night; C. Q.

"Hey, Sarge—we having a G. I. party tomorrow night?" he asked. A G. I. party is a barracks cleaning.

"You usually have them on Friday nights?" I asked him.

"Yes," he said, and then he added, mysteriously, "that's the whole thing."

"Then you'll have a G. I. party."

He turned away, and I heard him mumbling. His shoulders were moving, and I wondered if he was crying.

"What's your name, soldier?" I asked.

He turned, not crying at all. Instead, his green-speckled eyes, long and narrow, flashed like fish in the sun. He walked over to me and sat on the edge of my desk. He reached out a hand. "Sheldon," he said.

"Stand on your feet, Sheldon."

Getting off the desk, he said, "Sheldon Grossbart." He smiled at the familiarity into which he'd led me.

"You against cleaning the barracks Friday night, Grossbart?" I said. "Maybe we shouldn't have G. I. parties. Maybe we should get a maid." My tone startled me. I felt I sounded like every top sergeant I had ever known.

"No, Sergeant." He grew serious, but with a seriousness that seemed to be only the stifling of a smile. "It's just—G. I. parties on Friday night, of all nights."

He slipped up onto the corner of the desk again—not quite sitting, but not quite standing, either. He looked at me with those speckled eyes flashing, and then made a gesture with his hand. It was very slight—no more than a movement back and forth of the wrist—and yet it managed to exclude from our affairs everything else in the orderly room, to make the two of us the center of the world. It seemed, in fact, to exclude everything even about the two of us except our hearts.

"Sergeant Thurston was one thing," he whispered, glancing at the sleeping C. Q., "but we thought that with you here things might be a little different."

"We?"

"The Jewish personnel."

"Why?" I asked, harshly. "What's on your mind?" Whether I was still angry at the "Sheldon" business, or now at something else, I hadn't time to tell, but clearly I was angry.

"We thought you—Marx, you know, like Karl Marx. The Marx Brothers. Those guys are all—M-a-r-x. Isn't that how *you* spell it, Sergeant?"

"M-a-r-x."

"Fishbein said—" He stopped. "What I mean to say, Sergeant—" His face and neck were red, and his mouth moved but no words came out. In a moment, he raised himself to attention, gazing down at me. It was as though he had suddenly decided he could expect no more sympathy from me than from Thurston, the reason being that I was of Thurston's faith, and not his. The young man had managed to confuse himself as to what my faith really was, but I felt no desire to straighten him out. Very simply, I didn't like him.

When I did nothing but return his gaze, he spoke, in an altered tone. "You see, Sergeant," he explained to me, "Friday nights, Jews are supposed to go to services."

"Did Sergeant Thurston tell you you couldn't go to them when there was a G. I. party?"

"No."

"Did he say you had to stay and scrub the floors?"

"No, Sergeant."

"Did the Captain say you had to stay and scrub the floors?"

"That isn't it, Sergeant. It's the other guys in the barracks." He leaned toward me. "They think we're goofing off. But we're not. That's when Jews go to services, Friday night. We have to."

"Then go."

"But the other guys make accusations. They have no right."

"That's not the Army's problem, Grossbart. It's a personal problem you'll have to work out yourself."

"But it's un*fair*."

I got up to leave. "There's nothing I can do about it," I said.

Grossbart stiffened and stood infront of me. "But this is a matter of *religion,* sir."

"Sergeant," I said.

"I mean 'Sergeant,'" he said, almost snarling.

"Look, go see the chaplain. You want to see Captain Barrett, I'll arrange an appointment."

"No, no. I don't want to make trouble, Sergeant. That's the first thing they throw up to you. I just want my rights!"

"Damn it, Grossbart, stop whining. You have your rights. You can stay and scrub floors or you can go to shul[3]—"

The smile swam in again. Spittle gleamed at the corners of his mouth. "You mean church, Sergeant."

"I mean shul, Grossbart!"

I walked past him and went outside. Near me, I heard the scrunching of a guard's boots on gravel. Beyond the lighted windows of the barracks, young men in T shirts and fatigue pants were sitting on their bunks, polishing their rifles. Suddenly there was a light rustling behind me. I turned and saw Grossbart's dark frame fleeing back to the barracks, racing to tell his Jewish friends that they were right—that, like Karl and Harpo,[4] I was one of them.

The next morning, while chatting with Captain Barrett, I recounted the incident of the previous evening. Somehow, in the telling, it must have seemed to the Captain that I was not so much explaining Grossbart's position as defending it. "Marx, I'd fight side by side with a nigger if the fella proved to me he was a man. I pride myself," he said, looking out the window, "that I've got an open mind. Consequently, Sergeant, nobody gets special treatment here, for the good *or* the bad. All a man's got to do is prove himself. A man fires well on the range, I give him a weekend pass. He scores high in P. T.,[5] he gets a weekend pass. He *earns* it." He turned from the window and pointed a finger at me. "You're a Jewish fella, am I right, Marx?"

"Yes, sir."

"And I admire you. I admire you because of the ribbons on your chest. I judge a man by what he shows me on the field of battle, Sergeant. It's what he's got *here,*" he said, and then, though I expected he would point to his heart, he jerked a thumb toward the buttons straining to hold his blouse across his belly. "Guts," he said.

"O. K., sir. I only wanted to pass on to you how the men felt."

---

[3] "Synagogue" (Yiddish).   [4] Harpo Marx (1893–1964), the silent Marx brother.
[5] Physical training.

"Mr. Marx, you're going to be old before your time if you worry about how the men feel. Leave that stuff to the chaplain—that's his business, not yours. Let's us train these fellas to shoot straight. If the Jewish personnel feels the other men are accusing them of goldbricking—well, I just don't know. Seems awful funny that suddenly the Lord is calling so loud in Private Grossman's ear he's just got to run to church."

"Synagogue," I said.

"Synagogue is right, Sergeant. I'll write that down for handy reference. Thank you for stopping by."

That evening, a few minutes before the company gathered outside the orderly room for the chow formation, I called the C. Q., Corporal Robert LaHill, in to see me. LaHill was a dark, burly fellow whose hair curled out of his clothes wherever it could. He had a glaze in his eyes that made one think of caves and dinosaurs. "LaHill," I said, "when you take the formation, remind the men that they're free to attend church services *whenever* they are held, provided they report to the orderly room before they leave the area."

LaHill scratched his wrist, but gave no indicaton that he'd heard or understood.

"LaHill," I said, "*church*. You remember? Church, priest, Mass, confession."

He curled one lip into a kind of smile; I took it for a signal that for a second he had flickered back up into the human race.

"Jewish personnel who want to attend services this evening are to fall out in front of the orderly room at 1900," I said. Then, as an afterthought, I added, "By order of Captain Barrett."

A little while later, as the day's last light—softer than any I had seen that year—began to drop over Camp Crowder, I heard LaHill's thick, inflectionless voice outside my window: "Give me your ears, troopers. Toppie says for me to tell you that at 1900 hours all Jewish personnel is to fall out in front, here, if they want to attend the Jewish Mass."

At seven o'clock, I looked out the orderly-room window and saw three soldiers in starched khakis standing on the dusty quadrangle. They looked at their watches and fidgeted while they whispered back and forth. It was getting dimmer, and, alone on the otherwise deserted field, they looked tiny. When I opened the door, I heard the noises of the G. I. party coming from the surrounding barracks—bunks being pushed to the walls, faucets pounding water into buckets, brooms whisking at the wooden floors, cleaning the dirt away for Saturday's inspection. Big puffs of cloth moved round and round on the windowpanes. I walked outside, and the moment my foot hit the ground I thought I heard Grossbart call to the others, "'Ten-*hut!*" Or maybe, when they all three jumped to attention, I imagined I heard the command.

Grossbart stepped forward. "Thank you, sir," he said.

"'Sergeant,' Grossbart," I reminded him. "You call officers 'sir.' I'm not an officer. You've been in the Army three weeks—you know that."

He turned his palms out at his sides to indicate that, in truth, he and I lived beyond convention. "Thank you, anyway," he said.

"Yes," a tall boy behind him said. "Thanks a lot."

And the third boy whispered, "Thank you," but his mouth barely fluttered, so that he did not alter by more than a lip's movement his posture of attention.

"For what?" I asked.

Grossbart snorted happily. "For the announcement. The Corporal's announcement. It helped. It made it—"

"Fancier." The tall boy finished Grossbart's sentence.

Grossbart smiled. "He means formal, sir. Public," he said to me. "Now it won't seem as though we're just taking off—goldbricking because the work has begun."

"It was by order of Captain Barrett," I said.

"Aaah, but you pull a little weight," Grossbart said. "So we thank you." Then he turned to his companions. "Sergeant Marx, I want you to meet Larry Fishbein."

The tall boy stepped forward and extended his hand. I shook it. "You from New York?" he asked.

"Yes."

"Me, too." He had a cadaverous face that collapsed inward from his cheekbone to his jaw, and when he smiled—as he did at the news of our communal attachment—revealed a mouthful of bad teeth. He was blinking his eyes a good deal, as though he were fighting back tears. "What borough?" he asked.

I turned to Grossbart. "It's five after seven. What time are services?"

"Shul," he said, smiling, "is in ten minutes. I want you to meet Mickey Halpern. This is Nathan Marx, our sergeant."

The third boy hopped forward. "Private Michael Halpern." He saluted.

"Salute officers, Halpern," I said. The boy dropped his hand, and, on its way down, in his nervousness, checked to see if his shirt pockets were buttoned.

"Shall I march them over, sir?" Grossbart asked. "Or are you coming along?"

From behind Grossbart, Fishbein piped up. "Afterward, they're having refreshments. A ladies' auxiliary from St. Louis, the rabbi told us last week."

"The chaplain," Halpern whispered.

"You're welcome to come along," Grossbart said.

To avoid his plea, I looked away, and saw, in the windows of the barracks, a cloud of faces staring out at the four of us. "Hurry along, Grossbart," I said.

"O. K., then," he said. He turned to the others. "Double time, *march!*"

They started off, but ten feet away Grossbart spun around and, running backward, called to me, "Good *shabbus,*[6] sir!" And then the three of them were swallowed into the alien Missouri dusk.

Even after they had disappeared over the parade ground, whose green was now a deep blue, I could hear Grossbart singing the double-time cadence, and as it grew dimmer and dimmer, it suddenly touched a deep memory—as did the slant of the light—and I was remembering the shrill sounds of the Bronx playground where, years ago, beside the Grand Concourse,[7] I had played on long spring evenings such as this. It was a pleasant memory for a young man so far from peace and home, and it brought so many recollections with it that I began to grow exceedingly tender about myself. In fact, I indulged myself in a reverie so strong that I felt as though a hand were reaching down inside me. It had to reach so very far to touch me! It had to reach past those days in the forests of Belgium, and past the dying I'd refused to weep over; past the nights in German farmhouses whose books we'd burned to warm us; past endless stretches when I had shut off all softness I might feel for my fellows, and had managed even to deny myself the posture of a conqueror—the swagger that I, as a Jew, might well have worn as my boots whacked against the rubble of Wesel, Münster, and Braunschweig.

---

[6] "Sabbath" (Yiddish).

[7] A boulevard in the Bronx; the surrounding neighborhood was then mainly middle-class Jewish.

But now one night noise, one rumor of home and time past, and memory plunged down through all I had anesthetized, and came to what I suddenly remembered was myself. So it was not altogether curious that, in search of more of me, I found myself following Grossbart's tracks to Chapel No. 3, where the Jewish services were being held.

I took a seat in the last row, which was empty. Two rows in front of me sat Grossbart, Fishbein, and Halpern, holding little white Dixie cups. Each row of seats was raised higher than the one in front of it, and I could see clearly what was going on. Fishbein was pouring the contents of his cup into Grossbart's, and Grossbart looked mirthful as the liquid made a purple arc between Fishbein's hand and his. In the glaring yellow light, I saw the chaplain standing on the platform at the front; he was chanting the first line of the responsive reading. Grossbart's prayer book remained closed on his lap; he was swishing the cup around. Only Halpern responded to the chant by praying. The fingers of his right hand were spread wide across the cover of his open book. His cap was pulled down low onto his brow, which made it round, like a yarmulke.[8] From time to time, Grossbart wet his lips at the cup's edge; Fishbein, his long yellow face a dying light bulb, looked from here to there, craning forward to catch sight of the faces down the row, then of those in front of him, then behind. He saw me, and his eyelids beat a tattoo. His elbow slid into Grossbart's side, his neck inclined toward his friend, he whispered something, and then, when the congregation next responded to the chant, Grossbart's voice was among the others. Fishbein looked into his book now, too; his lips, however, didn't move.

Finally, it was time to drink the wine. The chaplain smiled down at them as Grossbart swigged his in one long gulp, Halpern sipped, meditating, and Fishbein faked devotion with an empty cup. "As I look down amongst the congregation"— the chaplain grinned at the word—"this night, I see many new faces, and I want to welcome you to Friday-night services here at Camp Crowder. I am Major Leo Ben Ezra, your chaplain." Though an American, the chaplain spoke deliberately— syllable by syllable, almost—as though to communicate, above all, with the lip readers in his audience. "I have only a few words to say before we adjourn to the refreshment room, where the kind ladies of the Temple Sinai, St. Louis, Missouri, have a nice setting for you."

Applause and whistling broke out. After another momentary grin, the chaplain raised his hands, palms out, his eyes flicking upward a moment, as if to remind the troops where they were and Who Else might be in attendance. In the sudden silence that followed I thought I heard Grossbart cackle, "Let the goyim[9] clean the floors!" Were those the words? I wasn't sure, but Fishbein, grinning, nudged Halpern. Halpern looked dumbly at him, then went back to his prayer book, which had been occupying him all through the rabbi's talk. One hand tugged at the black kinky hair that stuck out under his cap. His lips moved.

The rabbi continued. "It is about the food that I want to speak to you for a moment. I know, I know, I know," he intoned, wearily, "how in the mouths of most of you the *trafe*[10] food tastes like ashes. I know how you gag, some of you, and how your parents suffer to think of their children eating foods unclean and offensive to the palate. What can I tell you? I can only say, close your eyes and swallow as best you can. Eat what you must to live, and throw away the rest. I

---

[8] "Skullcap" (Yiddish).   [9] "Gentiles" (Yiddish); the singular is "*goy*."
[10] "Nonkosher" (Yiddish).

wish I could help more. For those of you who find this impossible, may I ask that you try and try, but then come to see me in private. If your revulsion is so great, we will have to seek aid from those higher up.'"

A round of chatter rose and subsided. Then everyone sang "Ain Kelohainu";[11] after all those years, I discovered I still knew the words. Then, suddenly, the service over, Grossbart was upon me. "Higher up? He means the General?"

"Hey, Shelly," Fishbein said, "he means God." He smacked his face and looked at Halpern. "How high can you go!"

"Sh-h-h!" Grossbart said. "What do you think, Sergeant?"

"I don't know," I said. "You better ask the chaplain."

"I'm going to. I'm making an appointment to see him in private. So is Mickey."

Halpern shook his head. "No, no, Sheldon—"

"You have rights, Mickey," Grossbart said. "They can't push us around."

"It's O. K.," said Halpern. "It bothers my mother, not me."

Grossbart looked at me. "Yesterday he threw up. From the hash. It was all ham and God knows what else."

"I have a cold—that was why," Halpern said. He pushed his yarmulke back into a cap.

"What about you, Fishbein?" I asked. "You kosher, too?"

He flushed. "A little. But I'll let it ride. I have a very strong stomach, and I don't eat a lot anyway." I continued to look at him, and he held up his wrist to reinforce what he'd just said; his watch strap was tightened to the last hole, and he pointed that out to me.

"But services are important to you?" I asked him.

He looked at Grossbart. "Sure, sir."

"'Sergeant.'"

"Not so much at home," said Grossbart, stepping between us, "but away from home it gives one a sense of his Jewishness."

"We have to stick together," Fishbein said.

I started to walk toward the door; Halpern stepped back to make way for me.

"That's what happened in Germany," Grossbart was saying, loud enough for me to hear. "They didn't stick together. They let themselves get pushed around."

I turned. "Look, Grossbart. This is the Army, not summer camp."

He smiled. "So?"

Halpern tried to sneak off, but Grossbart held his arm.

"Grossbart, how old are you?" I asked.

"Nineteen."

"And you?" I said to Fishbein.

"The same. The same month, even."

"And what about him?" I pointed to Halpern, who had by now made it safely to the door.

"Eighteen," Grossbart whispered. "But like he can't tie his shoes or brush his teeth himself. I feel sorry for him."

"I feel sorry for all of us, Grossbart," I said, "but just act like a man. Just don't overdo it."

"Overdo what, sir?"

"The 'sir' business, for one thing. Don't overdo that," I said.

<hr>

[11] "None Like Our God" (Hebrew).

I left him standing there. I passed by Halpern, but he did not look at me. Then I was outside, but, behind, I heard Grossbart call, "Hey, Mickey, my *leben*,[12] come on back. Refreshments!"

"*Leben!*" My grandmother's word for me!

One morning a week later, while I was working at my desk, Captain Barrett shouted for me to come into his office. When I entered, he had his helmet liner squashed down so far on his head that I couldn't even see his eyes. He was on the phone, and when he spoke to me, he cupped one hand over the mouthpiece. "Who the hell is Grossbart?"

"Third platoon, Captain," I said. "A trainee."

"What's all this stink about food? His mother called a goddam congressman about the food." He uncovered the mouthpiece and slid his helmet up until I could see his bottom eyelashes. "Yes, sir," he said into the phone. "Yes, sir. I'm still here, sir. I'm asking Marx, here, right now—"

He covered the mouthpiece again and turned his head back toward me. "Lightfoot Harry's on the phone," he said, between his teeth. "This congressman calls General Lyman, who calls Colonel Sousa, who calls the Major, who calls me. They're just dying to stick this thing on me. Whatsa matter?" He shook the phone at me. "I don't feed the troops? What the hell is this?"

"Sir, Grossbart is strange—" Barrett greeted that with a mockingly indulgent smile. I altered my approach. "Captain, he's a very othodox Jew, and so he's only allowed to eat certain foods."

"He throws up, the congressman said. Every time he eats something, his mother says, he throws up!"

"He's accustomed to observing the dietary laws, Captain."

"So why's his old lady have to call the White House?"

"Jewish parents, sir—they're apt to be more protective than you expect. I mean, Jews have a very close family life. A boy goes away from home, sometimes the mother is liable to get very upset. Probably the boy mentioned something in a letter, and his mother misinterpreted."

"I'd like to punch him one right in the mouth," the Captain said. "There's a goddam war on, and he wants a silver platter!"

"I don't think the boy's to blame, sir. I'm sure we can straighten it out by just asking him. Jewish parents worry—"

"*All* parents worry, for Christ's sake. But they don't get on their high horse and start pulling strings—"

I interrupted, my voice higher, tighter than before. "The home life, Captain, is very important—but you're right, it may sometimes get out of hand. It's a very wonderful thing, Captain, but because it's so close, this kind of thing . . . "

He didn't listen any longer to my attempt to present both myself and Lightfoot Harry with an explanation for the letter. He turned back to the phone. "Sir?" he said. "Sir—Marx, here, tells me Jews have a tendency to be pushy. He says he thinks we can settle it right here in the company. . . . Yes, sir. . . . I *will* call back, sir, soon as I can." He hung up. "Where are the men, Sergeant?"

"On the range."

With a whack on the top of his helmet, he crushed it down over his eyes again, and charged out of his chair. "We're going for a ride," he said.

---

[12] "Life" (Yiddish): a term of great affection.

The Captain drove, and I sat beside him. It was a hot spring day, and under my newly starched fatigues I felt as though my armpits were melting down onto my sides and chest. The roads were dry, and by the time we reached the firing range, my teeth felt gritty with dust, though my mouth had been shut the whole trip. The Captain slammed the brakes on and told me to get the hell out and find Grossbart.

I found him on his belly, firing wildly at the five-hundred-feet target. Waiting their turns behind him were Halpern and Fishbein. Fishbein, wearing a pair of steel-rimmed G. I. glasses I hadn't seen on him before, had the appearance of an old peddler who would gladly have sold you his rifle and the cartridges that were slung all over him. I stood back by the ammo boxes, waiting for Grossbart to finish spraying the distant targets. Fishbein straggled back to stand near me.

"Hello, Sergeant Marx," he said.

"How are you?" I mumbled.

"Fine, thank you. Sheldon's really a good shot."

"I didn't notice."

"I'm not so good, but I think I'm getting the hang of it now. Sergeant, I don't mean to, you know, ask what I shouldn't—" The boy stopped. He was trying to speak intimately, but the noise of the shooting forced him to shout at me.

"What is it?" I asked. Down the range, I saw Captain Barrett standing up in the jeep, scanning the line for me and Grossbart.

"My parents keep asking and asking where we're going," Fishbein said. "Everybody says the Pacific. I don't care, but my parents— If I could relieve their minds, I think I could concentrate more on my shooting."

"I don't know where, Fishbein. Try to concentrate anyway."

"Sheldon says you might be able to find out."

"I don't know a thing, Fishbein. You just take it easy, and don't let Sheldon—"

"*I'm* taking it easy, Sergeant. It's at home—"

Grossbart had finished on the line, and was dusting his fatigues with one hand. I called to him. "Grossbart, the Captain wants to see you."

He came toward us. His eyes blazed and twinkled. "Hi!"

"Don't point that goddam rifle!" I said.

"I wouldn't shoot you, Sarge." He gave me a smile as wide as a pumpkin, and turned the barrel aside.

"Damn you, Grossbart, this is no joke! Follow me."

I walked ahead of him, and had the awful suspicion that, behind me, Grossbart was *marching,* his rifle on his shoulder, as though he were a one-man detachment. At the jeep, he gave the Captain a rifle salute. "Private Sheldon Grossbart, sir."

"At ease, Grossman." The Captain sat down, slid over into the empty seat, and, crooking a finger, invited Grossbart closer.

"Bart, sir. Sheldon Gross*bart*. It's a common error." Grossbart nodded at me; *I* understood, he indicated. I looked away just as the mess truck pulled up to the range, disgorging a half-dozen K. P.s with rolled-up sleeves. The mess sergeant screamed at them while they set up the chow-line equipment.

"Grossbart, your mama wrote some congressman that we don't feed you right. Do you know that?" the Captain said.

"It was my father, sir. He wrote to Representative Franconi that my religion forbids me to eat certain foods."

"What religion is that, Grossbart?"

"Jewish."

"'Jewish, *sir,*'" I said to Grossbart.

"Excuse me, sir. Jewish, sir."

"What have you been living on?" the Captain asked. You've been in the Army a month already. You don't look to me like you're falling to pieces."

"I eat because I have to, sir. But Sergeant Marx will testify to the fact that I don't eat one mouthful more than I need to in order to survive."

"Is that so, Marx?" Barrett asked.

"I've never seen Grossbart eat, sir," I said.

"But you heard the rabbi," Grossbart said. "He told us what to do, and I listened."

The Captain looked at me. "Well, Marx?"

"I still don't know what he eats and doesn't eat, sir."

Grossbart raised his arms to plead with me, and it looked for a moment as though he were going to hand me his weapon to hold. "But, Sergeant—"

"Look, Grossbart, just answer the Captain's questions," I said sharply.

Barrett smiled at me, and I resented it. "All right, Grossbart," he said. "What is it you want? The little piece of paper? You want out?"

"No, sir. Only to be allowed to live as a Jew. And for the others, too."

"What others?"

"Fishbein, sir, and Halpern."

"They don't like the way we serve, either?"

"Halpern throws up, sir. I've seen it."

"I thought *you* throw up."

"Just once, sir. I didn't know the sausage was sausage."

"We'll give menus, Grossbart. We'll show training films about the food, so you can identify when we're trying to poison you."

Grossbart did not answer. The men had been organized into two long chow lines. At the tail end of one, I spotted Fishbein—or, rather, his glasses spotted me. They winked sunlight back at me. Halpern stood next to him, patting the inside of his collar with a khaki handkerchief. They moved with the line as it began to edge up toward the food. The mess sergeant was still screaming at the K. P.s For a moment, I was actually terrified by the thought that somehow the mess sergeant was going to become involved in Grossbart's problem.

"Marx," the Captain said, "you're a Jewish fella—am I right?"

I played straight man. "Yes, sir."

"How long you been in the Army? Tell this boy."

"Three years and two months."

"A year in combat, Grossbart. Twelve goddam months in combat all through Europe. I admire this man." The Captain snapped a wrist against my chest. "Do you hear him peeping about the food? Do you? I want an answer, Grossbart. Yes or no."

"No, sir."

"And why not? He's a Jewish fella."

"Some things are more important to some Jews than other things to other Jews."

Barrett blew up. "Look, Grossbart. Marx, here, is a good man—a goddam hero. When you were in high school, Sergeant Marx was killing Germans. Who does more for the Jews—you, by throwing up over a lousy piece of sausage, a piece of first-cut meat, or Marx, by killing those Nazi bastards? If I was a Jew, Grossbart, I'd kiss this man's feet. He's a goddam hero, and *he* eats what we give him. Why do you have to cause trouble is what I want to know! What is it you're buckin' for—a discharge?"

"No, sir."

"I'm talking to a wall! Sergeant, get him out of my way." Barrett swung himself back into the driver's seat. "I'm going to see the chaplain." The engine roared, the jeep spun around in a whirl of dust, and the Captain was headed back to camp.

For a moment, Grossbart and I stood side by side, watching the jeep. Then he looked at me and said, "I don't want to start trouble. That's the first thing they toss up to us."

When he spoke, I saw that his teeth were white and straight, and the sight of them suddenly made me understand that Grossbart actually did have parents—that once upon a time someone had taken little Sheldon to the dentist. He was their son. Despite all the talk about his parents, it was hard to believe in Grossbart as a child, an heir—as related by blood to anyone, mother, father, or, above all, to me. This realization led me to another.

"What does your father do, Grossbart?" I asked as we started to walk back toward the chow line.

"He's a tailor."

"An American?"

"Now, yes. A son in the Army," he said, jokingly.

"And your mother?" I asked.

He winked. "A *ballabusta*.[13] She practically sleeps with a dustcloth in her hand."

"She's also an immigrant?"

"All she talks is Yiddish, still."

"And your father, too?"

"A little English. 'Clean,' 'Press,' 'Take the pants in.' That's the extent of it. But they're good to me."

"Then, Grossbart—" I reached out and stopped him. He turned toward me, and when our eyes met, his seemed to jump back, to shiver in their sockets. "Grossbart—you were the one who wrote that letter, weren't you?"

It took only a second or two for his eyes to flash happy again. "Yes." He walked on, and I kept pace. "It's what my father *would* have written if he had known how. It was his name, though. *He* signed it. He even mailed it. I sent it home. For the New York postmark."

I was astonished, and he saw it. With complete seriousness, he thrust his right arm in front of me. "Blood is blood, Sergeant," he said, pinching the blue vein in his wrist.

"What the hell *are* you trying to do, Grossbart?" I asked. "I've seen you eat. Do you know that? I told the Captain I don't know what you eat, but I've seen you eat like a hound at chow."

"We work hard, Sergeant. We're in training. For a furnace to work, you've got to feed it coal."

"Why did you say in the letter that you threw up all the time?"

"I was really talking about Mickey there. I was talking *for* him. He would never write, Sergeant, though I pleaded with him. He'll waste away to nothing if I don't help. Sergeant, I used my name—my father's name—but it's Mickey, and Fishbein, too, I'm watching out for."

"You're a regular Messiah, aren't you?"

We were at the chow line now.

---

[13] "Good housekeeper" (Yiddish).

"That's a good one, Sergeant," he said, smiling. "But who knows? Who can tell? Maybe you're the Messiah—a little bit. What Mickey says is the Messiah is a collective idea. He went to Yeshiva,[14] Mickey, for a while. He says *together* we're the Messiah. Me a little bit, you a little bit. You should hear that kid talk, Sergeant, when he gets going."

"Me a little bit, you a little bit," I said. "You'd like to believe that, wouldn't you, Grossbart? That would make everything so clean for you."

"It doesn't seem too bad a thing to believe, Sergeant. It only means we should all *give* a little, is all."

I walked off to eat my rations with the other noncoms.

Two days later, a letter addressed to Captain Barrett passed over my desk. It had come through the chain of command—from the office of Congressman Franconi, where it had been received, to General Lyman, to Colonel Sousa, to Major Lamont, now to Captain Barrett. I read it over twice. It was dated May 14, the day Barrett had spoken with Grossbart on the rifle range.

> *Dear Congressman:*
>
> First let me thank you for your interest in behalf of my son, Private Sheldon Grossbart. Fortunately, I was able to speak with Sheldon on the phone the other night, and I think I've been able to solve our problem. He is, as I mentioned in my last letter, a very religious boy, and it was only with the greatest difficulty that I could persuade him that the religious thing to do—what God Himself would want Sheldon to do—would be to suffer the pangs of religious remorse for the good of his country and all mankind. It took some doing, Congressman, but finally he saw the light. In fact, what he said (and I wrote down the words on a scratch pad so as never to forget), what he said was "I guess you're right, Dad. So many millions of my fellow-Jews gave up their lives to the enemy, the least I can do is live for a while minus a bit of my heritage so as to help end this struggle and regain for all the children of God dignity and humanity." That, Congressman, would make any father proud.
>
> By the way, Sheldon wanted me to know—and to pass on to you—the name of a soldier who helped him reach this decision: SERGEANT NATHAN MARX. Sergeant Marx is a combat veteran who is Sheldon's first sergeant. This man has helped Sheldon over some of the first hurdles he's had to face in the Army, and is in part responsible for Sheldon's changing his mind about the dietary laws. I know Sheldon would appreciate any recognition Marx could receive.
>
> Thank you and good luck. I look forward to seeing your name on the next election ballot.
>
> > *Respectfully,*
> > *Samuel E. Grossbart*

Attached to the Grossbart communiqué was another, addressed to General Marshall Lyman, the post commander, and signed by Representative Charles E. Franconi, of the House of Representatives. The communiqué informed General Lyman that Sergeant Nathan Marx was a credit to the U. S. Army and the Jewish people.

What was Grossbart's motive in recanting? Did he feel he'd gone too far? Was

[14] A Jewish seminary.

the letter a strategic retreat—a crafty attempt to strengthen what he considered our alliance? Or had he actually changed his mind, via an imaginary dialogue between Grossbart *pére* and Grossbart *fils?* I was puzzled, but only for a few days—that is, only until I realized that, whatever his reasons, he had actually decided to disappear from my life; he was going to allow himself to become just another trainee. I saw him at inspection, but he never winked; at chow formations, but he never flashed me a sign. On Sundays, with the other trainees, he would sit around watching the noncoms' softball team, for which I pitched, but not once did he speak an unnecessary word to me. Fishbein and Halpern retreated, too—at Grossbart's command, I was sure. Apparently he had seen that wisdom lay in turning back before he plunged over into the ugliness of privilege undeserved. Our separation allowed me to forgive him our past encounters, and, finally, to admire him for his good sense.

Meanwhile, free of Grossbart, I grew used to my job and my administrative tasks. I stepped on a scale one day, and discovered I had truly become a noncombatant; I had gained seven pounds. I found patience to get past the first three pages of a book. I thought about the future more and more, and wrote letters to girls I'd known before the war. I even got a few answers. I sent away to Columbia for a Law School catalogue. I continued to follow the war in the Pacific, but it was not my war. I thought I could see the end, and sometimes, at night, I dreamed that I was walking on the streets of Manhattan—Broadway, Third Avenue, 116th Street, where I had lived the three years I attended Columbia. I curled myself around these dreams and I began to be happy.

And then, one Saturday, when everybody was away and I was alone in the orderly room reading a month-old copy of the *Sporting News,* Grossbart reappeared.

"You a baseball fan, Sergeant?"

I looked up. "How are you?"

"Fine," Grossbart said. "They're making a soldier out of me."

"How are Fishbein and Halpern?"

"Coming along," he said. "We've got no training this afternoon. They're at the movies."

"How come you're not with them?"

"I wanted to come over and say hello."

He smiled—a shy, regular-guy smile, as though he and I well knew that our friendship drew its sustenance from unexpected visits, remembered birthdays, and borrowed lawnmowers. At first it offended me, and then the feeling was swallowed by the general uneasiness I felt at the thought that everyone on the post was locked away in a dark movie theater and I was here alone with Grossbart. I folded up my paper.

"Sergeant," he said, "I'd like to ask a favor. It is a favor, and I'm making no bones about it."

He stopped, allowing me to refuse him a hearing—which, of course, forced me into a courtesy I did not intend. "Go ahead."

"Well, actually it's two favors."

I said nothing.

"The first one's about these rumors. Everybody says we're going to the Pacific."

"As I told your friend Fishbein, I don't know." I said. "You'll just have to wait to find out. Like everybody else."

"You think there's a chance of any of us going East?"

"Germany?" I said. "Maybe."

"I meant New York."

"I don't think so, Grossbart. Offhand."

"Thanks for the information, Sergeant," he said.

"It's not information, Grossbart. Just what I surmise."

"It certainly would be good to be near home. My parents—you know." He took a step toward the door and then turned back. "Oh, the other thing. May I ask the other?"

"What is it?"

"The other thing is—I've got relatives in St. Louis, and they say they'll give me a whole Passover dinner if I can get down there. God, Sergeant, that'd mean an awful lot to me."

I stood up. "No passes during basic, Grossbart."

"But we're off from now till Monday morning, Sergeant. I could leave the post and no one would even know."

"I'd know. You'd know."

"But that's all. Just the two of us. Last night, I called my aunt, and you should have heard her. 'Come—come,' she said. 'I got gefilte fish, *chrain*[15]—the works!' Just a day, Sergeant. I'd take the blame if anything happened."

"The Captain isn't here to sign a pass."

"You could sign."

"Look, Grossbart—"

"Sergeant, for two months, practically, I've been eating *trafe* till I want to die."

"I thought you'd made up your mind to live with it. To be minus a little bit of heritage."

He pointed a finger at me. "You!" he said. "That wasn't for you to read."

"I read it. So what?"

"That letter was addressed to a congressman."

"Grossbart, don't feed me any baloney. You *wanted* me to read it."

"Why are you persecuting me, Sergeant?"

"Are you kidding!"

"I've run into this before," he said, "but never from my own!"

"Get out of here, Grossbart! Get the hell out of my sight!"

He did not move. "Ashamed, that's what you are," he said. "So you take it out on the rest of us. They say Hitler himself was half a Jew. Hearing you, I wouldn't doubt it."

"What are you trying to do with me, Grossbart?" I asked him. "What are you after? You want me to give you special privileges, to change the food, to find out about your orders, to give you weekend passes."

"You even talk like a goy!" Grossbart shook his fist. "Is this just a weekend pass I'm asking for? Is a Seder[16] sacred or not?"

Seder! It suddenly occurred to me that Passover had been celebrated weeks before. I said so.

"That's right," he replied. "Who says no? A month ago—and I was in the field eating hash! And now all I ask is a simple favor. A Jewish boy I thought would

---

[15] "Horseradish" (Yiddish).

[16] A ceremonial dinner during Passover, a holiday commemorating the Israelites' escape from bondage in Egypt.

understand. My aunt's willing to go out of her way—to make a Seder a month later. . . . " He turned to go, mumbling.

"Come back here!" I called. He stopped and looked at me. "Grossbart, why can't you be like the rest? Why do you have to stick out like a sore thumb?"

"Because I'm a Jew, Sergeant. I *am* different. Better, maybe not. But different."

"This is a war, Grossbart. For the time being *be* the same."

"I refuse."

"What?"

"I refuse. I can't stop being me, that's all there is to it." Tears came to his eyes. "It's a hard thing to be a Jew. But now I understand what Mickey says—it's a harder thing to stay one." He raised a hand sadly toward me. "Look at *you*."

"Stop crying!"

"Stop this, stop that, stop the other thing! *You* stop, Sergeant. Stop closing your heart to your own!" And, wiping his face with his sleeve, he ran out the door. "The least we can do for one another—the least . . . "

An hour later, looking out of the window, I saw Grossbart headed across the field. He wore a pair of starched khakis and carried a little leather ditty bag. I went out into the heat of the day. It was quiet; not a soul was in sight except, over by the mess hall, four K. P.s sitting around a pan, sloped forward from their waists, gabbing and peeling potatoes in the sun.

"Grossbart!" I called.

He looked toward me and continued walking.

"Grossbart, get over here!"

He turned and came across the field. Finally, he stood before me.

"Where are you going?" I asked.

"St. Louis. I don't care."

"You'll get caught without a pass."

"So I'll get caught without a pass."

"You'll go to the stockade."

"I'm *in* the stockade." He made an about-face and headed off.

I let him go only a step or two. "Come back here," I said, and he followed me into the office, where I typed out a pass and signed the Captain's name, and my own initials after it.

He took the pass and then, a moment later, reached out and grabbed my hand. "Sergeant, you don't know how much this means to me."

"O. K., " I said. "Don't get in any trouble."

"I wish I could show you how much this means to me."

"Don't do me any favors. Don't write any more congressmen for citations."

He smiled. "You're right. I won't. But let me do something."

"Bring me a piece of that gefilte fish. Just get out of here."

"I will!" he said. "With a slice of carrot and a little horseradish. I won't forget."

"All right. Just show your pass at the gate. And don't tell *anybody*."

"I won't. It's a month late, but a good Yom Tov[17] to you."

"Good Yom Tov, Grossbart," I said.

"You're a good Jew, Sergeant. You like to think you have a hard heart, but underneath you're a fine, decent man. I mean that."

---

[17] "Praise the day" (Yiddish): good holiday.

Those last three words touched me more than any words from Grossbart's mouth had the right to. "All right, Grossbart," I said. "Now call me 'sir,' and get the hell out of here."

He ran out the door and was gone. I felt very pleased with myself; it was a great relief to stop fighting Grossbart, and it had cost me nothing. Barrett would never find out, and if he did, I could manage to invent some excuse. For a while, I sat at my desk, comfortable in my decision. Then the screen door flew back and Grossbart burst in again. "Sergeant!" he said. Behind him I saw Fishbein and Halpern, both in starched khakis, both carrying ditty bags like Grossbart's.

"Sergeant, I caught Mickey and Larry coming out of the movies. I almost missed them."

"Grossbart—did I say tell no one?" I said.

"But my aunt said I could bring friends. That I should, in fact."

"*I'm* the Sergeant, Grossbart—not your aunt!"

Grossbart looked at me in disbelief. He pulled Halpern up by his sleeve. "Mickey, tell the Sergeant what this would mean to you."

Halpern looked at me and, shrugging, said. "A lot."

Fishbein stepped forward without prompting. "This would mean a great deal to me and my parents, Sergeant Marx."

"No!" I shouted.

Grossbart was shaking his head. "Sergeant, I could see you denying me, but how you can deny Mickey, a Yeshiva boy—that's beyond me."

"I'm not denying Mickey anything," I said. "You just pushed a little too hard, Grossbart. *You* denied him."

"I'll give him my pass, then," Grossbart said. "I'll give him my aunt's address and a little note. At least let him go."

In a second, he had crammed the pass into Halpern's pants pocket. Halpern looked at me, and so did Fishbein. Grossbart was at the door, pushing it open. "Mickey, bring me a piece of gefilte fish, at least," he said, and then he was outside again.

The three of us looked at one another, and then I said, "Halpern, hand that pass over."

He took it from his pocket and gave it to me. Fishbein had now moved to the doorway, where he lingered. He stood there for a moment with his mouth slightly open, and then he pointed to himself. "And me?" he asked.

His utter ridiculousness exhausted me. I slumped down in my seat and felt pulses knocking at the back of my eyes. "Fishbein," I said, "you understand I'm not trying to deny you anything, don't you? If it was my Army, I'd serve gefilte fish in the mess hall. I'd sell *kugel* in the PX,[18] honest to God."

Halpern smiled.

"You understand, don't you Halpern?"

"Yes, Sergeant."

"And you, Fishbein? I don't want enemies. I'm just like you—I want to serve my time and go home. I miss the same things you miss."

"Then, Sergeant," Fishbein said, "why don't you come, too?"

"Where?"

---

[18] Baked noodle or potato pudding in the post exchange, or the military-run store.

"To St. Louis. To Shelly's aunt. We'll have a regular Seder. Play hide-the matzoh."[19] He gave me a broad, black-toothed smile.

I saw Grossbart again, on the other side of the screen.

"Pst!" He waved a piece of paper. "Mickey, here's the address. Tell her I couldn't get away."

Halpern did not move. He looked at me, and I saw the shrug moving up his arms into his shoulders again. I took the cover off my typewriter and made out passes for him and Fishbein. "Go," I said. "The three of you."

I thought Halpern was going to kiss my hand.

That afternoon, in a bar in Joplin, I drank beer and listened with half an ear to the Cardinal game. I tried to look squarely at what I'd become involved in, and began to wonder if perhaps the struggle with Grossbart wasn't as much my fault as his. What was I that I had to *muster* generous feelings? Who was I to have been feeling so grudging, so tight-hearted? After all, I wasn't being asked to move the world. Had I a right, then, or a reason, to clamp down on Grossbart, when that meant clamping down on Halpern, too? And Fishbein—that ugly, agreeable soul? Out of the many recollections of my childhood that had tumbled over me these past few days I heard my grandmother's voice: "What are you making a *tsimmes?*"[20] It was what she would ask my mother when, say, I had cut myself while doing something I shouldn't have done, and her daughter was busy bawling me out. I needed a hug and a kiss, and my mother would moralize. But my grandmother knew—mercy overrides justice. I should have known it, too. Who was Nathan Marx to be such a penny pincher with kindness? Surely, I thought, the Messiah himself—if He should ever come—won't niggle over nickels and dimes. God willing, he'll hug and kiss.

The next day, while I was playing softball over on the parade ground, I decided to ask Bob Wright, who was non-com in charge of Classification and Assignment, where he thought our trainees would be sent when their cycle ended, in two weeks. I asked casually, between innings, and he said, "They're pushing them all into the Pacific. Shulman cut the orders on your boys the other day."

The news shocked me, as though I were the father of Halpern, Fishbein, and Grossbart.

That night, I was just sliding into sleep when someone tapped on my door. "Who is it?" I asked.

"Sheldon."

He opened the door and came in. For a moment, I felt his presence without being able to see him. "How was it?" I asked.

He popped into sight in the near-darkness before me. "Great, Sergeant." Then he was sitting on the edge of the bed. I sat up.

"How about you?" he asked. "Have a nice weekend?"

"Yes."

"The others went to sleep." He took a deep, paternal breath. We sat silent for a while, and a homey feeling invaded my ugly little cubicle; the door was locked, the cat was out, the children were safely in bed.

---

[19] Unleavened bread; a Seder ritual involves hiding a piece of matzoh and sending the children to find it.
[20] A carrot stew; also, a fuss (Yiddish).

"Sergeant, can I tell you something? Personal?"

I did not answer, and he seemed to know why. "Not about me. About Mickey. Sergeant, I never felt for anybody like I feel for him. Last night I heard Mickey in the bed next to me. He was crying so, it could have broken you heart. Real sobs."

"I'm sorry to hear that."

"I had to talk to him to stop him. He held my head, Sergeant—he wouldn't let it go. He was almost hysterical. He kept saying if he only knew where we were going. Even if he knew it *was* the Pacific, that would be better than nothing. Just to know."

Long ago, someone had taught Grossbart the sad rule that only lies can get the truth. Not that I couldn't believe in the fact of Halpern's crying; his eyes *always* seemed red-rimmed. But, fact or not, it became a lie when Grossbart uttered it. He was entirely strategic. But then—it came with the force of indictment—so was I! There are strategies of aggression, but there are strategies of retreat as well. And so, recognizing that I myself had not been without craft and guile, I told him what I knew. "It is the Pacific."

He let out a small gasp, which was not a lie. "I'll tell him. I wish it was otherwise."

"So do I."

He jumped on my words. "You mean you think you could do something? A change, maybe?"

"No, I couldn't do a thing."

"Don't you know anybody over at C. and A.?"

"Grossbart, there's nothing I can do," I said. "If your orders are for the Pacific, then it's the Pacific."

"But Mickey—"

"Mickey, you, me—everybody, Grossbart. There's nothing to be done. Maybe the war'll end before you go. Pray for a miracle."

"But—"

"Good night, Grossbart." I settled back, and was relieved to feel the springs unbend as Grossbart rose to leave. I could see him clearly now; his jaw had dropped, and he looked like a dazed prizefighter. I noticed for the first time a little paper bag in his hand.

"Grossbart." I smiled. "My gift?"

"Oh, yes, Sergeant. Here—from all of us." He handed me the bag. "It's egg roll."

"Egg roll?" I accepted the bag and felt a damp grease spot on the bottom. I opened it, sure that Grossbart was joking.

"We thought you'd probably like it. You know—Chinese egg roll. We thought you'd probably have a taste for—"

"Your aunt served egg roll?"

"She wasn't home."

"Grossbart, she invited you. You told me she invited you and your friends."

"I know," he said. "I just reread the letter. *Next* week."

I got out of bed and walked to the window. "Grossbart," I said. But I was not calling to him.

"What?"

"What are you, Grossbart? Honest to God, what are you?"

I think it was the first time I'd asked him a question for which he didn't have an immediate answer.

"How can you do this to people?" I went on.

"Sergeant, the day away did us all a world of good. Fishbein, you should see him, he *loves* Chinese food."

"But the Seder," I said.

"We took second best, Sergeant."

Rage came charging at me. I didn't sidestep. "Grossbart, you're a liar!" I said. "You're a schemer and a crook. You've got no respect for anything. Nothing at all. Not for me, for the truth—not even for poor Halpern! You use us all—"

"Sergeant, Sergeant, I feel for Mickey. Honest to God, I do. I *love* Mickey. I try—"

"You try! You feel!" I lurched toward him and grabbed his shirt front. I shook him furiously. "Grossbart, get out! Get out and stay the hell away from me. Because if I see you, I'll make your life miserable. *You understand that?*"

"Yes."

I let him free, and when he walked from the room, I wanted to spit on the floor where he had stood. I couldn't stop the fury. It engulfed me, owned me, till it seemed I could only rid myself of it with tears or an act of violence. I snatched from the bed the bag Grossbart had given me and, with all my strength, threw it out the window. And the next morning, as the men policed the area around the barracks, I heard a great cry go up from one of the trainees, who had been anticipating only his morning handful of cigarette butts and candy wrappers. "Egg roll!" he shouted. "Holy Christ, Chinese goddam egg roll!"

A week later, when I read the orders that had come down from C. and A., I couldn't believe my eyes. Every single trainee was to be shipped to Camp Stoneman, California, and from there to the Pacific—every trainee but one. Private Sheldon Grossbart. He was to be sent to Fort Monmouth, New Jersey. I read the mimeographed sheet several times. Dee, Farrell, Fishbein, Fuselli, Fylypowycz, Glinicki, Gromke, Gucwa, Halpern, Hardy, Helbrandt, right down to Anton Zygadlo—all were to be headed West before the month was out. All except Grossbart. He had pulled a string, and I wasn't it.

I lifted the phone and called C. and A.

The voice on the other end said smartly, "Corporal Shulman, sir."

"Let me speak to Sergeant Wright."

"Who is this calling, sir?"

"Sergeant Marx."

And to my surprise, the voice said, *"Oh!"* Then, "Just a minute, Sergeant."

Shulman's *"Oh!"* stayed with me while I waited for Wright to come to the phone. Why *"Oh!"* Who was Shulman? And then, so simply, I knew I'd discovered the string that Grossbart had pulled. In fact, I could hear Grossbart the day he'd discovered Shulman in the PX, or in the bowling alley, or maybe even at services. "Glad to meet you. Where you from? Bronx? Me, too. Do you know So-and-So? And So-and-So? Me, too! You work at C. and A.? Really? Hey, how's chances of getting East? Could you do something? Change something? Swindle, cheat, lie? We gotta help each other, you know. If the Jews in Germany . . ."

Bob Wright answered the phone. "How are you, Nate? How's the pitching arm?"

"Good. Bob, I wonder if you could do me a favor." I heard clearly my own words, and they so reminded me of Grossbart that I dropped more easily than I could have imagined into what I had planned. "This may sound crazy, Bob, but I got a kid here on order to Monmouth who wants them changed. He had a brother killed in Europe, and he's hot to go to the Pacific. Says he'd feel like a coward if he wound up Stateside. I don't know, Bob—can anything be done? Put somebody else in the Monmouth slot?"

"Who?" he asked cagily.

"Anybody. First guy in the alphabet. I don't care. The kid just asked if something could be done."

"What's his name?"

"Grossbart, Sheldon."

Wright didn't answer.

"Yeah," I said. "He's a Jewish kid, so he thought I could help him out. You know."

"I guess I can do something," he finally said. "The Major hasn't been around here for weeks. Temporary duty to the golf course. I'll try, Nate, that's all I can say."

"I'd appreciate it, Bob. See you Sunday." And I hung up, perspiring.

"The following day, the corrected orders appeared: Fishbein, Fuselli, Fyly-powycz, Glinicki, Gromke, Grossbart, Gucwa, Halpern, Hardy . . . Lucky Private Harley Alton was to go to Fort Monmouth, New Jersey, where, for some reason or other, they wanted an enlisted man with infantry training.

After chow that night, I stopped back at the orderly room to straighten out the guard-duty roster. Grossbart was waiting for me. He spoke first.

"You son of a bitch!"

I sat down at my desk, and while he glared at me, I began to make the necessary alterations in the duty roster.

"What do you have against me?" he cried. "Against my family? Would it kill you for me to be near my father, God knows how many months he has left to him?"

"Why so?"

"His heart," Grossbart said. "He hasn't had enough troubles in a lifetime, you've got to add to them. I curse the day I ever met you, Marx! Shulman told me what happened over there. There's no limit to your anti-Semitism, is there? The damage you've done here isn't enough. You have to make a special phone call! You really want me dead!"

I made the last few notations in the duty roster and got up to leave. "Good night, Grossbart."

"You owe me an explanation!" He stood in my path.

"Sheldon, you're the one who owes explanations."

He scowled, "To *you?*"

"To me, I think so—yes. Mostly to Fishbein and Halpern."

"That's right, twist things around. I owe nobody nothing, I've done all I could do for them. Now I think I've got the right to watch out for myself."

"For each other we have to learn to watch out, Sheldon. You told me yourself."

"You call this watching out for me—what you did?"

"No. For all of us."

I pushed him aside and started for the door. I heard his furious breathing behind me, and it sounded like steam rushing from an engine of terrible strength.

"*You'll* be all right," I said from the door. And, I thought, so would Fishbein and Halpern be all right, even in the Pacific, if only Grossbart continued to see—

in the obsequiousness of the one, the soft spirituality of the other—some profit for himself.

I stood outside the orderly room, and I heard Grossbart weeping behind me. Over in the barracks, in the lighted windows, I could see the boys in their T shirts sitting on their bunks talking about their orders, as they'd been doing for the past two days. With a kind of quiet nervousness, they polished shoes, shined belt buckles, squared away underwear, trying as best they could to accept their fate. Behind me, Grossbart swallowed hard, accepting his. And then, resisting with all my will an impulse to turn and seek pardon for my vindictiveness, I accepted my own.

1959

=CONTEXTS=

Interpretation

In the essay "Against Interpretation" (1964) Susan Sontag (1933–   ) reacts against elitism and sexism in modern literary criticism by suggesting new, more socially enlightened methods of interpretation. She sees the traditional forms of hermenutics, or literary interpretation, as acts of violence against works of literature, as attempts to impose the will of the critic on the meaning of the work of art:

Against Interpretation

The modern style of interpretation excavates, and as it excavates, destroys; it digs "behind" the text, to find a sub-text which is the true one. The most celebrated and influential modern doctrines, those of Marx and Freud, actually amount to elaborate systems of hermeneutics, aggressive and impious theories of interpretation. . . . Today is such a time, when the project of interpretation is largely reactionary, stifling. Like the fumes of the automobile and of heavy industry which befoul the urban atmosphere, the effusion of interpretations of art today poisons our sensibilities. In a culture whose already classical dilemma is the hypertrophy of the intellect at the expense of energy and sensual capability, interpretation is the revenge of the intellect upon art.

In place of the "brutality" of literary interpretation Sontag postulates a more "sensuous" approach to art and literature:

What is important now is to recover our senses. We must learn to *see* more, to *hear* more, to *feel* more.

Our task is not to find the maximum amount of content in a work of art, much less to squeeze more content out of the work than is already there. Our task is to cut back content so that we can see the thing at all.

In place of a hermeneutics we need an erotics of art.

Susan Sontag, 1964

N. Scott Momaday
(1934–   )

Navarre Scott Momaday was born in 1934 in Kiowa Indian country in southwestern Oklahoma. His parents, both teachers, raised him in Native-American and non-Native-American communities in Oklahoma, in Arizona, and in New Mexico, including Jemez Pueblo, New Mexico. Momaday earned a B.A. from the University of New Mexico in 1958, an M.A. from Stanford University in 1960, and a Ph.D. from Stanford in 1963. During the 1960s he received a Guggenheim Fellowship to study New England poets and edited *The Complete Poems of Frederick Goddard Tuckerman* (1965). In 1968 Momaday's Pulitzer Prize-winning novel, *House Made of Dawn*, was published. Abel, the protagonist, comes from Jemez Pueblo. He experiences a homeland obscured by a vague ancestry and painful encounters with World War II and with post war Los Angeles. He returns to Jemez, filled with harsh memories but also with hints of a renewed sense of place and of the power of sacred words.

The narrative *The Way to Rainy Mountain* (1969) grew out of *The Journey of Tai-me* (1967), Momaday's collection of Kiowa and family stories. *Rainy Mountain* celebrates the tribe's story in myth, history, and personal memory. Momaday knows that the golden years of the Kiowa culture—the Sun Dance, the buffalo herds, the glorious horsemen— are gone forever. And yet, his commitment to memories of oral traditions and to the power of imagination enables him to make the past a vital part of the present and to fix it at the center of a complex chronology of myth, fact, and recollection. In *Rainy Mountain* Momaday preserves the timeless moments of the Kiowas in a three-voice narrative. Each of its twenty-four sections contains a story, a history, and a lyric remembrance, each set in a different typeface.

Momaday is able to preserve these moments successfully because of his reverence for the power of language—a reverence he fears is declining in the modern "white" world. For Momaday, as he explains in *Rainy Mountain*, "a word has power in and of itself. It comes from nothing into sound and meaning; it gives origin to all things. By means of words can a man deal with the world on equal terms. And the word is sacred."

Momaday has traveled throughout the world lecturing and reading from his works. He has taught at the University of California at Berkeley, Stanford University, and the University of Arizona as well as in Germany and the Soviet Union. An autobiography of his early years, *The Names*, was published in a complex memoir form in 1976. He based his second novel, *The Ancient Child* (1989), on a Kiowa story about a man transformed into a bear. And Momaday has written two books of poetry, *Angle of Geese* (1974) and *The Gourd Dancer* (1976). Like his father, Al Momaday, he is also an artist, and his paintings and drawings have been displayed in Germany and Switzerland.

Suggested Readings: *The Journey of Tai-me,* 1967. *House Made of Dawn,* 1968. *Colorado: Summer, Fall, Winter, Spring,* 1973. *Angle of Geese,* 1974. *The Gourd Dancer,* 1976. *The Names: A Memoir,* 1976. *The Ancient Child,* 1989. M. S. Trimble, *N. Scott Momaday,* 1973. H. A. Baker, Jr., ed., *Three American Literatures: Essays in Chicano, Native American, Asian-American Literature for Teachers of American Literature,* 1982. A. R. Velie, *Four American Indian Literary Masters,* 1982. M. Schubnell, *N. Scott Momaday,* 1985. K. M. Roemer, ed., *Approaches to Teaching Momaday's The Way to Rainy Mountain,* 1988.

Text Used: *The Way to Rainy Mountain,* 1969.

America's first literary expressions appear in ancient cave paintings by Native Americans of the Southwest. N. Scott Momaday retains the tradition of the visual narrative in The Way to Rainy Mountain *with this drawing of a buffalo hunter by his father, Al Momaday.*

THE WAY TO RAINY MOUNTAIN*

HEADWATERS

Noon in the intermountain plain:
There is scant telling of the marsh—
A log, hollow and weather-stained,
An insect at the mouth, and moss—
Yet waters against the roots,

---

* In the Wichita Mountain Range of southwestern Oklahoma. The narrative's introduction first appeared in *The Reporter* on January 26, 1967. Momaday's note: "I wish to acknowledge my own book, *The Journey of Tai-me,* which is in a special sense the archetype of the present volume."

Stand brimming to the stalks. What moves?
What moves on this archaic force
Was wild and welling at the source.

PROLOGUE

The journey began one day long ago on the edge of the northern Plains. It was carried on over a course of many generations and many hundreds of miles. In the end there were many things to remember, to dwell upon and talk about.

"You know, everything had to begin. . . . " For the Kiowas[1] the beginning was a struggle for existence in the bleak northern mountains. It was there, they say, that they entered the world through a hollow log. The end, too, was a struggle, and it was lost. The young Plains culture of the Kiowas withered and died like grass that is burned in the prairie wind. There came a day like destiny; in every direction, as far as the eye could see, carrion lay out in the land. The buffalo was the animal representation of the sun, the essential and sacrificial victim of the Sun Dance. When the wild herds were destroyed, so too was the will of the Kiowa people; there was nothing to sustain them in spirit. But these are idle recollections, the mean and ordinary agonies of human history. The interim was a time of great adventure and nobility and fulfillment.

Tai-me came to the Kiowas in a vision born of suffering and despair. "Take me with you," Tai-me said, "and I will give you whatever you want." And it was so. The great adventure of the Kiowas was a going forth into the heart of the continent. They began a long migration from the headwaters of the Yellowstone River eastward to the Black Hills and south to the Wichita Mountains.[2] Along the way they acquired horses, the religion of the Plains, a love and possession of the open land. Their nomadic soul was set free. In alliance with the Comanches they held dominion in the southern Plains for a hundred years. In the course of that long migration they had come of age as a people. They had conceived a good idea of themselves; they had dared to imagine and determine who they were.

In one sense, then, the way to Rainy Mountain is preeminently the history of an idea, man's idea of himself, and it has old and essential being in language. The verbal tradition by which it has been preserved has suffered a deterioration in time. What remains is fragmentary: mythology, legend, lore, and hearsay—and of course the idea itself, as crucial and completed as it ever was. That is the miracle.

The journey herein recalled continues to be made anew each time the miracle comes to mind, for that is peculiarly the right and responsibility of the imagination. It is a whole journey, intricate with motion and meaning; and it is made with the whole memory, that experience of the mind which is legendary as well as historical, personal as well as cultural. And the journey is an evocation of three things in particular: a landscape that is incomparable, a time that is gone forever, and the human spirit, which endures. The imaginative experience and the historical express equally the traditions of man's reality. Finally, then, the journey recalled is among other things the revelation of one way in which these traditions are conceived, developed, and interfused in the human mind. There are on the way to

---

[1] The tribes mentioned throughout are those of the Plains Indians.

[2] A river flowing through Wyoming and Montana; mountains in South Dakota; a mountain range in Oklahoma.

Rainy Mountain many landmarks, many journeys in the one. From the beginning the migration of the Kiowas was an expression of the human spirit, and that expression is most truly made in terms of wonder and delight: "There were many people, and oh, it was beautiful. That was the beginning of the Sun Dance.[3] It was all for Tai-me, you know, and it was a long time ago."

INTRODUCTION

A single knoll rises out of the plain in Oklahoma, north and west of the Wichita Range. For my people, the Kiowas, it is an old landmark, and they gave it the name Rainy Mountain. The hardest weather in the world is there. Winter brings blizzards, hot tornadic winds arise in the spring, and in summer the prairie is an anvil's edge. The grass turns brittle and brown, and it cracks beneath your feet. There are green belts along the rivers and creeks, linear groves of hickory and pecan, willow and witch hazel. At a distance in July or August the steaming foliage seems almost to writhe in fire. Great green and yellow grasshoppers are everywhere in the tall grass, popping up like corn to sting the flesh, and tortoises crawl about on the red earth, going nowhere in the plenty of time. Loneliness is an aspect of the land. All things in the plain are isolate; there is no confusion of objects in the eye, but *one* hill or *one* tree or *one* man. To look upon that landscape in the early morning, with the sun at your back, is to lose the sense of proportion. Your imagination comes to life, and this, you think, is where Creation was begun.

I returned to Rainy Mountain in July. My grandmother had died in the spring, and I wanted to be at her grave. She had lived to be very old and at last infirm. Her only living daughter was with her when she died, and I was told that in death her face was that of a child.

I like to think of her as a child. When she was born, the Kiowas were living that last great moment of their history. For more than a hundred years they had controlled the open range from the Smoky Hill River to the Red, from the headwaters of the Canadian to the fork of the Arkansas and Cimarron.[4] In alliance with the Comanches, they had ruled the whole of the southern Plains. War was their sacred business, and they were among the finest horsemen the world has ever known. But warfare for the Kiowas was preeminently a matter of disposition rather than of survival, and they never understood the grim, unrelenting advance of the U.S. Cavalry. When at last, divided and ill-provisioned, they were driven onto the Staked Plains[5] in the cold rains of autumn, they fell into panic. In Palo Duro Canyon[6] they abandoned their crucial stores to pillage and had nothing then but their lives. In order to save themselves, they surrendered to the soldiers at Fort Sill[7] and were imprisoned in the old stone corral that now stands as a military museum. My grandmother was spared the humiliation of those high gray walls by

---

[3] A sacred ceremony of the Plains Indians, lasting eight days.

[4] From central Kansas to the Red River of the North, which crosses the Canadian border between North Dakota and Minnesota; to the fork of the Arkansas River (which flows through Oklahoma, Arkansas, and Mississippi) and the Cimarron River (which flows through New Mexico, Oklahoma, and Arkansas) at eastern Oklahoma.

[5] A large plateau extending over parts of New Mexico, Texas, and Oklahoma.

[6] A canyon in Texas.   [7] A military reserve outside Lawton, Oklahoma.

eight or ten years, but she must have known from birth the affliction of defeat, the dark brooding of old warriors.

Her name was Aho, and she belonged to the last culture to evolve in North America. Her forebears came down from the high country in western Montana nearly three centuries ago. They were a mountain people, a mysterious tribe of hunters whose language has never been positively classified in any major group. In the late seventeenth century they began a long migration to the south and east. It was a journey toward the dawn, and it led to a golden age. Along the way the Kiowas were befriended by the Crows, who gave them the culture and religion of the Plains. They acquired horses, and their ancient nomadic spirit was suddenly free of the ground. They acquired Tai-me, the sacred Sun Dance doll, from that moment the object and symbol of their worship, and so shared in the divinity of the sun. Not least, they acquired the sense of destiny, therefore courage and pride. When they entered upon the southern Plains they had been transformed. No longer were they slaves to the simple necessity of survival; they were a lordly and dangerous society of fighters and thieves, hunters and priests of the sun. According to their origin myth, they entered the world through a hollow log. From one point of view, their migration was the fruit of an old prophecy, for indeed they emerged from a sunless world.

Although my grandmother lived out her long life in the shadow of Rainy Mountain, the immense landscape of the continental interior lay like memory in her blood. She could tell of the Crows, whom she had never seen, and of the Black Hills, where she had never been. I wanted to see in reality what she had seen more perfectly in the mind's eye, and traveled fifteen hundred miles to begin my pilgrimage.

Yellowstone, it seemed to me, was the top of the world, a region of deep lakes and dark timber, canyons and waterfalls. But, beautiful as it is, one might have the sense of confinement there. The skyline in all directions is close at hand, the high wall of the woods and deep cleavages of shade. There is a perfect freedom in the mountains, but it belongs to the eagle and the elk, the badger and the bear. The Kiowas reckoned their stature by the distance they could see, and they were bent and blind in the wilderness.

Descending eastward, the highland meadows are a stairway to the plain. In July the inland slope of the Rockies is luxuriant with flax and buckwheat, stonecrop and larkspur. The earth unfolds and the limit of the land recedes. Clusters of trees, and animals grazing far in the distance, cause the vision to reach away and wonder to build upon the mind. The sun follows a longer course in the day, and the sky is immense beyond all comparison. The great billowing clouds that sail upon it are shadows that move upon the grain like water, dividing light. Farther down, in the land of the Crows and Blackfeet, the plain is yellow. Sweet clover takes hold of the hills and bends upon itself to cover and seal the soil. There the Kiowas paused on their way; they had come to the place where they must change their lives. The sun is at home on the plains. Precisely there does it have the certain character of a god. When the Kiowas came to the land of the Crows, they could see the dark lees of the hills at dawn across the Bighorn River,[8] the profusion of light on the grain shelves, the oldest deity ranging after the solstices. Not yet would they veer southward to the caldron of the land that lay below; they must wean their blood from

---

[8] A river flowing from Wyoming through Montana.

the northern winter and hold the mountains a while longer in their view. They bore Tai-me in procession to the east.

A dark mist lay over the Black Hills, and the land was like iron. At the top of a ridge I caught sight of Devil's Tower[9] upthrust against the gray sky as if in the birth of time the core of the earth had broken through its crust and the motion of the world was begun. There are things in nature that engender an awful quiet in the heart of man; Devil's Tower is one of them. Two centuries ago, because they could not do otherwise, the Kiowas made a legend at the base of the rock. My grandmother said:

> *Eight children were there at play, seven sisters and their brother. Suddenly the boy was struck dumb; he trembled and began to run upon his hands and feet. His fingers became claws, and his body was covered with fur. Directly there was a bear where the boy had been. The sisters were terrified; they ran, and the bear after them. They came to the stump of a great tree, and the tree spoke to them. It bade them climb upon it, and as they did so it began to rise into the air. The bear came to kill them, but they were just beyond its reach. It reared against the tree and scored the bark all around with its claws. The seven sisters were borne into the sky, and they became the stars of the Big Dipper.[10]*

From that moment, and so long as the legend lives, the Kiowas have kinsmen in the night sky. Whatever they were in the mountains, they could be no more. However tenuous their well-being, however much they had suffered and would suffer again, they had found a way out of the wilderness.

My grandmother had a reverence for the sun, a holy regard that now is all but gone out of mankind. There was a wariness in her, and an ancient awe. She was a Christian in her later years, but she had come a long way about, and she never forgot her birthright. As a child she had been to the Sun Dances; she had taken part in those annual rites, and by them she had learned the restoration of her people in the presence of Tai-me. She was about seven when the last Kiowa Sun Dance was held in 1887 on the Washita River[11] above Rainy Mountain Creek. The buffalo were gone. In order to consummate the ancient sacrifice—to impale the head of a buffalo bull upon the medicine tree—a delegation of old men journeyed into Texas, there to beg and barter for an animal from the Goodnight herd. She was ten when the Kiowas came together for the last time as a living Sun Dance culture. They could find no buffalo; they had to hang an old hide from the sacred tree. Before the dance could begin, a company of soldiers rode out from Fort Sill under orders to disperse the tribe. Forbidden without cause the essential act of their faith, having seen the wild herds slaughtered and left to rot upon the ground, the Kiowas backed away forever from the medicine tree. That was July 20, 1890, at the great bend of the Washita. My grandmother was there. Without bitterness, and for as long as she lived, she bore a vision of deicide.

Now that I can have her only in memory, I see my grandmother in the several postures that were peculiar to her: standing at the wood stove on a winter morning and turning meat in a great iron skillet; sitting at the south window, bent above her

---

[9] An 865-foot-high rock tower of volcanic origin in the Black Hills of Wyoming; established as a national monument in 1906.

[10] The seven principal stars of the constellation Ursa Major, arranged in a form resembling a dipper.

[11] A river in Oklahoma.

beadwork, and afterwards, when her vision failed, looking down for a long time into the folds of her hands; going out upon a cane, very slowly as she did when the weight of age came upon her; praying. I remember her most often at prayer. She made long, rambling prayers out of suffering and hope, having seen many things. I was never sure that I had the right to hear, so exclusive were they of all mere custom and company. The last time I saw her she prayed standing by the side of her bed at night, naked to the waist, the light of a kerosene lamp moving upon her dark skin. Her long, black hair, always drawn and braided in the day, lay upon her shoulders and against her breasts like a shawl. I do not speak Kiowa, and I never understood her prayers, but there was something inherently sad in the sound, some merest hesitation upon the syllables of sorrow. She began in a high and descending pitch, exhausting her breath to silence; then again and again—and always the same intensity of effort, of something that is, and is not, like urgency in the human voice. Transported so in the dancing light among the shadows of her room, she seemed beyond the reach of time. But that was illusion; I think I knew then that I should not see her again.

Houses are like sentinels in the plain, old keepers of the weather watch. There, in a very little while, wood takes on the appearance of great age. All colors wear soon away in the wind and rain, and then the wood is burned gray and the grain appears and the nails turn red with rust. The windowpanes are black and opaque; you imagine there is nothing within, and indeed there are many ghosts, bones given up to the land. They stand here and there against the sky, and you approach them for a longer time than you expect. They belong in the distance; it is their domain.

Once there was a lot of sound in my grandmother's house, a lot of coming and going, feasting and talk. The summers there were full of excitement and reunion. The Kiowas are a summer people; they abide the cold and keep to themselves, but when the season turns and the land becomes warm and vital they cannot hold still; an old love of going returns upon them. The aged visitors who came to my grandmother's house when I was a child were made of lean and leather, and they bore themselves upright. They wore great black hats and bright ample shirts that shook in the wind. They rubbed fat upon their hair and wound their braids with strips of colored cloth. Some of them painted their faces and carried the scars of old and cherished enmities. They were an old council of warlords, come to remind and be reminded of who they were. Their wives and daughters served them well. The women might indulge themselves; gossip was at once the mark and compensation of their servitude. They made loud and elaborate talk among themselves, full of jest and gesture, fright and false alarm. They went abroad in fringed and flowered shawls, bright beadwork and German silver. They were at home in the kitchen, and they prepared meals that were banquets.

There were frequent prayer meetings, and great nocturnal feasts. When I was a child I played with my cousins outside, where the lamplight fell upon the ground and the singing of the old people rose up around us and carried away into the darkness. There were a lot of good things to eat, a lot of laughter and surprise. And afterwards, when the quiet returned, I lay down with my grandmother and could hear the frogs away by the river and feel the motion of the air.

Now there is a funeral silence in the rooms, the endless wake of some final word. The walls have closed in upon my grandmother's house. When I returned to it in mourning, I saw for the first time in my life how small it was. It was late at night, and there was a white moon, nearly full. I sat for a long time on the stone steps by the kitchen door. From there I could see out across the land; I could see the long row of trees by the creek, the low light upon the rolling plains, and the stars of the Big Dipper. Once I looked at the moon and caught sight of a strange thing. A cricket had perched upon the handrail, only a few inches away from me. My line of vision was such that the creature filled the moon like a fossil. It had gone there, I thought, to live and die, for there, of all places, was its small definition made whole and eternal. A warm wind rose up and purled like the longing within me.

The next morning I awoke at dawn and went out on the dirt road to Rainy Mountain. It was already hot, and the grasshoppers began to fill the air. Still, it was early in the morning, and the birds sang out of the shadows. The long yellow grass on the mountain shone in the bright light, and a scissortail hied above the land. There, where it ought to be, at the end of a long and legendary way, was my grandmother's grave. Here and there on the dark stones were ancestral names. Looking back once, I saw the mountain and came away.

THE SETTING OUT

I

You know, everything had to begin, and this is how it was: the Kiowas came one by one into the world through a hollow log. They were many more than now, but not all of them got out. There was a woman whose body was swollen up with child, and she got stuck in the log. After that, no one could get through, and that is why the Kiowas are a small tribe in number. They looked all around and saw the world. It made them glad to see so many things. They called themselves *Kwuda*, "coming out."

They called themselves *Kwuda* and later *Tepda*, both of which mean "coming out." And later still they took the name *Gaigwu*, a name which can be taken to indicate something of which the two halves differ from each other in appearance. It was once a custom among Kiowa warriors that they cut their hair on the right side of the head only and on a line level with the lobe of the ear, while on the left they let the hair grow long and wore it in a thick braid wrapped in otter skin. "Kiowa" is indicated in sign language by holding the hand palm up and slightly cupped to the right side of the head and rotating it back and forth from the wrist. "Kiowa" is thought to derive from the softened Comanche form of *Gaigwu*.

I remember coming out upon the northern Great Plains in the late spring. There were meadows of blue and yellow wildflowers on the slopes, and I could see the still, sunlit plain below, reaching away out of sight. At first there is no discrimination in the eye, nothing but the land itself, whole and impenetrable. But then smallest things begin to stand out of the depths—herds and rivers and groves—and each of these has perfect being in terms of distance and of silence and of age. Yes, I thought, now I see the earth as it really is; never again will I see things as I saw them yesterday or the day before.

II

They were going along, and some were hunting, An antelope was killed and quartered in the meadow. Well, one of the big chiefs came up and took the udders of that animal for himself, but another big chief wanted those udders also, and there was a great quarrel between them. Then, in anger, one of these chiefs gathered all of his followers together and went away. They are called *Azatanhop*, "the udder-angry travelers off." No one knows where they went or what happened to them.

This is one of the oldest memories of the tribe. There have been reports of a people in the Northwest who speak a language that is similar to Kiowa.
    In the winter of 1848–49, the buffalo ranged away from easy reach, and food was scarce. There was an antelope drive in the vicinity of Bent's Fort, Colorado. According to ancient custom, antelope medicine was made, and the Kiowas set out on foot and on horseback—men, women, and children—after game. They formed a great circle, inclosing a large area of the plain, and began to converge upon the center. By this means antelope and other animals were trapped and killed, often with clubs and even with the bare hands. By necessity were the Kiowas reminded of their ancient ways.

One morning on the high plains of Wyoming I saw several pronghorns in the distance. They were moving very slowly at an angle away from me, and they were almost invisible in the tall brown and yellow grass. They ambled along in their own wilderness dimension of time, as if no notion of flight could ever come upon them. But I remembered once having seen a frightened buck on the run, how the white rosette of its rump seemed to hang for the smallest fraction of time at the top of each frantic bound—like a succession of sunbursts against the purple hills.

III

Before there were horses the Kiowas had need of dogs. That was a long time ago, when dogs could talk. There was a man who lived alone; he had been thrown away, and he made his camp here and there on the high ground. Now it was dangerous to be alone, for there were enemies all around. The man spent his arrows hunting food. He had one arrow left, and he shot a bear; but the bear was only wounded and it ran away. The man wondered what to do. Then a dog came up to him and said that many enemies were coming; they were close by and all around. The man could think of no way to save himself. But the dog said: "You know, I have puppies. They are young and weak and they have nothing to eat. If you will take care of my puppies, I will show you how to get away." The dog led the man here and there, around and around, and they came to safety.

A hundred years ago the Comanche Ten Bears remarked upon the great number of horses which the Kiowas owned. "When we first knew you," he said, "you had nothing but dogs and sleds." It was so; the dog is primordial. Perhaps it was dreamed into being.
    The principal warrior society of the Kiowas was the Ka-itsenko, "Real Dogs," and it was made up of ten men only, the ten most brave. Each of these men wore a long ceremonial sash and carried a sacred arrow. In time of battle he must by

means of this arrow impale the end of his sash to the earth and stand his ground to the death. Tradition has it that the founder of the Ka-itsenko had a dream in which he saw a band of warriors, outfitted after the fashion of the society, being led by a dog. The dog sang the song of the Ka-itsenko, then said to the dreamer: "You are a dog; make a noise like a dog and sing a dog song."

There were always dogs about my grandmother's house. Some of them were nameless and lived a life of their own. They belonged there in a sense that the word "ownership" does not include. The old people paid them scarcely any attention, but they should have been sad, I think, to see them go.

IV

They lived at first in the mountains. They did not yet know of Tai-me, but this is what they knew: There was a man and his wife. They had a beautiful child, a little girl whom they would not allow to go out of their sight. But one day a friend of the family came and asked if she might take the child outside to play. The mother guessed that would be all right, but she told the friend to leave the child in its cradle and to place the cradle in a tree. While the child was in the tree, a redbird came among the branches. It was not like any bird that you have seen; it was very beautiful, and it did not fly away. It kept still upon a limb, close to the child. After a while the child got out of its cradle and began to climb after the redbird. And at the same time the tree began to grow taller, and the child was borne up into the sky. She was then a woman, and she found herself in a strange place. Instead of a redbird, there was a young man standing before her. The man spoke to her and said: "I have been watching you for a long time, and I knew that I would find a way to bring you here. I have brought you here to be my wife." The woman looked all around; she saw that he was the only living man there. She saw that he was the sun.

There the land itself ascends into the sky. These mountains lie at the top of the continent, and they cast a long rain shadow on the sea of grasses to the east. They arise out of the last North American wilderness, and they have wilderness names: Wasatch, Bitterroot, Bighorn, Wind River.[12]

I have walked in a mountain meadow bright with Indian paintbrush, lupine, and wild buckwheat, and I have seen high in the branches of a lodgepole pine the male pine grosbeak, round and rose-colored, its dark, striped wings nearly invisible in the soft, mottled light. And the uppermost branches of the tree seemed very slowly to ride across the blue sky.

V

After that the woman grew lonely. She thought about her people, and she wondered how they were getting on. One day she had a quarrel with the sun, and the

---

[12] A mountain range extending through parts of Idaho and Utah; a Rocky Mountain range on the Idaho-Montana boundary; mountains in northern Wyoming; a mountain range in central Wyoming.

sun went away. In her anger she dug up the root of a bush which the sun had warned her never to go near. A piece of earth fell from the root, and she could see her people far below. By that time she had given birth; she had a child—a boy by the sun. She made a rope out of sinew and took her child upon her back; she climbed down upon the rope, but when she came to the end, her people were still a long way off, and there she waited with her child on her back. It was evening; the sun came home and found his woman gone. At once he thought of the bush and went to the place where it had grown. There he saw the woman and the child, hanging by the rope half way down to the earth. He was very angry, and he took up a ring, a gaming wheel, in his hand. He told the ring to follow the rope and strike the woman dead. Then he threw the ring and it did what he told it to do; it struck the woman and killed her, and then the sun's child was all alone.

The plant is said to have been the *pomme blanche,* or *pomme de prairie,* of the voyageurs, whose chronicles refer time and again to its use by the Indians. It grows on the high plains and has a farinaceous root that is turnip-like in taste and in shape. This root is a healthful food, and attempts have been made to cultivate the plant as a substitute for the potato.

The anthropologist Mooney[13] wrote in 1896: "Unlike the neighboring Cheyenne and Arapaho, who yet remember that they once lived east of the Missouri and cultivated corn, the Kiowa have no tradition of ever having been an agriculture people or anything but a tribe of hunters."

Even now they are meateaters; I think it is not in them to be farmers. My grandfather, Mammedaty, worked hard to make wheat and cotton grow on his land, but it came to very little in the end. Once when I was a small boy I went across the creek to the house where the old woman Keahdinekeah lived. Some men and boys came in from the pasture, where a calf had just been killed and butchered. One of the boys held the calf's liver—still warm and wet with life—in his hand, eating of it with great relish. I have heard that the old hunters of the Plains prized the raw liver and tongue of the buffalo above all other delicacies.

VI

The sun's child was big enough to walk around on the earth, and he saw a camp nearby. He made his way to it and saw that a great spider—that which is called a grandmother—lived there. The spider spoke to the sun's child, and the child was afraid. The grandmother was full of resentment; she was jealous, you see, for the child had not yet been weaned from its mother's breasts. She wondered whether the child were a boy or a girl, and therefore she made two things, a pretty ball and a bow and arrows. These things she left alone with the child all the next day. When she returned, she saw that the ball was full of arrows, and she knew then that the child was a boy and that he would be hard to raise. Time and again the grandmother tried to capture the boy, but he always ran away. Then one day she made a snare out of rope. The boy was caught up in the snare, and he cried and cried, but the grandmother sang to him and at last he fell asleep.

---

[13] James A. Mooney (1861–1921), an ethnologist, in *The Ghost Dance Religion and the Sioux Outbreak of 1890* (1896).

Go to sleep and do not cry.
Your mother is dead, and still you feed
   upon her breasts.
Oo-oo-la-la-la-la, oo-oo.

In the autumn of 1874, the Kiowas were driven southward towards the Staked
Plains. Columns of troops were converging upon them from all sides, and they
were bone-weary and afraid. They camped on Elk Creek,[14] and the next day it
began to rain. It rained hard all that day, and the Kiowas waited on horseback for
the weather to clear. Then, as evening came on, the earth was suddenly crawling
with spiders, great black tarantulas, swarming on the flood.

*I know of spiders. There are dirt roads in the Plains. You see them, and you
wonder where and how far they go. They seem very old and untraveled, as if they
all led away to deserted houses. But creatures cross these roads: dung beetles and
grasshoppers, sidewinders and tortoises. Now and then there comes a tarantula,
at evening, always larger than you imagine, dull and dark brown, covered with
long, dusty hairs. There is something crochety about them; they stop and go and
angle away.*

VII

The years went by, and the boy still had the ring which killed his mother. The
grandmother spider told him never to throw the ring into the sky, but one day he
threw it up, and it fell squarely on top of his head and cut him in two. He looked
around, and there was another boy, just like himself, his twin. The two of them
laughed and laughed, and then they went to the grandmother spider. She nearly
cried aloud when she saw them, for it had been hard enough to raise the one. Even
so, she cared for them well and made them fine clothes to wear.

Mammedaty owned horses. And he could remember that it was essentially good to
own horses, that it was hard to be without horses. There was a day: Mammedaty
got down from a horse for the last time. Of all the tribes of the Plains, the Kiowas
owned the greatest number of horses per person.

*On summer afternoons, I went swimming in the Washita River. The current was
slow, and the warm, brown water seemed to be standing still. It was a secret
place. There in the deep shade, inclosed in the dense, overhanging growth of the
banks, my mind fixed on the wings of a dragonfly or the flitting motion of a water
strider, the great open land beyond was all but impossible to imagine. But it was
there, a stone's throw away. Once, from the limb of a tree, I saw myself in the
brown water; then a frog leaped from the bank, breaking the image apart.*

VIII

Now each of the twins had a ring, and the grandmother spider told them never to
throw the rings into the sky. But one day they threw them up into the high wind.

---

[14] In western Oklahoma, just west of the Wichita Mountains.

The rings rolled over a hill, and the twins ran after them. They ran beyond the top of the hill and fell down into the mouth of a cave. There lived a giant and his wife. The giant had killed a lot of people in the past by building fires and filling the cave with smoke, so that the people could not breathe. Then the twins remembered something that the grandmother spider had told them: "If ever you get caught in the cave, say to yourselves the word *thain-mom*, 'above my eyes.'" When the giant began to set fires around, the twins repeated the word *thain-mom* over and over to themselves, and the smoke remained above their eyes. When the giant had made three great clouds of smoke, his wife saw that the twins sat without coughing or crying, and she became frightened. "Let them go," she said, "or something bad will happen to us." The twins took up their rings and returned to the grandmother spider. She was glad to see them.

A word has power in and of itself. It comes from nothing into sound and meaning; it gives origin to all things. By means of words can a man deal with the world on equal terms. And the word is sacred. A man's name is his own; he can keep it or give it away as he likes. Until recent times, the Kiowas would not speak the name of a dead man. To do so would have been disrespectful and dishonest. The dead take their names with them out of the world.

When Aho saw or heard or thought of something bad, she said the word zei-dl-bei, *"frightful." It was the one word with which she confronted evil and the incomprehensible. I liked her to say it, for she screwed up her face in a wonderful look of displeasure and clicked her tongue. It was not an exclamation so much, I think, as it was a warding off, an exertion of language upon ignorance and disorder.*

IX

The next thing that happened to the twins was this: They killed a great snake which they found in their tipi. When they told the grandmother spider what they had done, she cried and cried. They had killed their grandfather, she said. And after that the grandmother spider died. The twins wrapped her in a hide and covered her with leaves by the water. The twins lived on for a long time, and they were greatly honored among the Kiowas.

In another and perhaps older version of the story, it is a porcupine and not a redbird that is the representation of the sun. In that version, too, one of the twins is said to have walked into the waters of a lake and disappeared forever, while the other at last transformed himself into ten portions of "medicine," thereby giving of his own body in eucharistic form to the Kiowas. The ten bundles of the talyi-da-i, "boy medicine" are, like Tai-me, chief objects of religious veneration.

When he was a boy, my father went with his grandmother, Keahdinekeah, to the shrine of one of the talyi-da-i. The old woman made an offering of bright cloth, and she prayed. The shrine was a small, specially-made tipi; inside, suspended from the lashing of the poles, was the medicine itself. My father knew that it was very powerful, and the very sight of it filled him with wonder and regard. The holiness of such a thing can be imparted to the human spirit, I believe, for I remember that it shone in the sightless eyes of Keahdinekeah. Once I was taken to see her at the old house on the other side of Rainy Mountain Creek. The room was dark, and her old age filled it like a substance. She was white-haired and blind, and, in that strange reversion that comes upon the very old, her skin was as soft as the skin of a baby. I remember the sound of her glad weeping and the water-like touch of her hand.

X

Long ago there were bad times. The Kiowas were hungry and there was no food. There was a man who heard his children cry from hunger, and he went out to look for food. He walked four days and became very weak. On the fourth day he came to a great canyon. Suddenly there was thunder and lightning. A voice spoke to him and said, "Why are you following me? What do you want?" The man was afraid. The thing standing before him had the feet of a deer, and its body was covered with feathers. The man answered that the Kiowas were hungry. "Take me with you," the voice said, "and I will give you whatever you want." From that day Tai-me has belonged to the Kiowas.

The great central figure of the *kado*, or Sun Dance, ceremony is the *taime*. This is a small image, less than 2 feet in length, representing a human figure dressed in a robe of white feathers, with a headdress consisting of a single upright feather and pendants of ermine skin, with numerous strands of blue beads around its neck, and painted upon the face, breast, and back with designs symbolic of the sun and moon. The image itself is of dark-green stone, in form rudely resembling a human head and bust, probably shaped by art like the stone fetishes of the Pueblo tribes. It is preserved in a rawhide box in charge of the hereditary keeper, and is never under any circumstances exposed to view except at the annual Sun Dance, when it is fastened to a short upright stick planted within the medicine lodge, near the western side. It was last exposed in 1888.—Mooney

Once I went with my father and grandmother to see the Tai-me bundle. It was suspended by means of a strip of ticking from the fork of a small ceremonial tree. I made an offering of bright red cloth, and my grandmother prayed aloud. It seemed a long time we were there. I had never come into the presence of Tai-me before—nor have I since. There was a great holiness all about in the room, as if an old person had died there or a child had been born.

XI

A long time ago there were two brothers. It was winter, and the buffalo had wandered far away. Food was very scarce. The two brothers were hungry, and they wondered what to do. One of them got up in the early morning and went out, and he found a lot of fresh meat there on the ground in front of the tipi. He was very happy, and he called his brother outside. "Look," he said. "Something very good has happened, and we have plenty of food." But his brother was afraid and said: "This is too strange a thing. I believe that we had better not eat that meat." But the first brother scolded him and said that he was foolish. Then he went ahead and ate of the meat all by himself. In a little while something awful happened to him; he began to change. When it was all over, he was no longer a man; he was some kind of water beast with little short legs and a long, heavy tail. Then he spoke to his brother and said: "You were right, and you must not eat of that meat. Now I must go and live in the water, but we are brothers, and you ought to come and see me now and then." After that the man went down to the water's edge, sometimes, and called his brother out. He told him how things were with the Kiowas.

During the peyote[15] ritual a fire is kept burning in the center of the tipi, inclosed within a crescent-shaped altar. On top of the altar there is a single, sacred peyote. After the chief priest utters the opening prayer, four peyotes are given to each celebrant, who eats them one after another. Then, in turn, each man sings four sacred songs, and all the while there is the sound of the rattle and the drum—and the fitful, many-colored glare of the fire. The songs go on all through the night, broken only by intervals of prayer, additional distributions of peyote, and, at midnight, a peculiar baptismal ceremony.

Mammedaty was a peyote man, and he was therefore distinguished by these things: a necklace of beans, a beaded staff and rattle, an eagle-bone whistle, and a fan made from the feathers of a water bird. He saw things that other men do not see. Once a heavy rain caused the Washita River to overflow and Rainy Mountain Creek to swell and "back up." Mammedaty went to the creek, near the crossing, to swim. And while he was there, the water began strangely to move against him, slowly at first, then fast, in high, hard waves. There was some awful commotion beneath the surface, and Mammedaty got out of the water and ran away. Later he went back to that place. There was a wide swath in the brush of the bank and the tracks of a huge animal, leading down to the water's edge.

The Going On

XII

An old man there was who lived with his wife and child. One night the woman was pounding meat, and her little son wanted to taste it. She gave him a ball of meat and he went outside to eat it. Then he returned and wanted more. She gave him another ball of meat, and again he went outside. A third time he came and asked for meat. The old man began to be afraid. He told his wife to give the child a large ball of meat and to act as if these things were all right. When the little boy came in again, there was an enemy with him. The enemy said: "There are many of us and we are all around. We came to kill you, but your son has given me food. If you will feed us all, we will not harm you." But the old man did not believe his enemy, and while his wife cooked fat upon the fire he crept out and led their horses upstream. When he was well away, he called out in the voice of a bird. Then the woman knew that it was time to go. She set fire to the fat and threw it all around upon the enemies, who were sitting there; then she took up the little boy in her arms and ran upstream. That is how the old man and the woman and their

[15] A stimulant drug derived from buttonlike tops of the mescal cactus, chewed by some Mexican Indians and Native Americans during religious ceremonies.

child got away. From a safe distance they could see the fire and hear the screams of their enemies.

In the winter of 1872–73, a fine heraldic tipi was accidentally destroyed by fire. Known as the *Do-giagya guat,* "tipi with battle pictures," it was ornamented with fine pictures of fighting men and arms on one side and wide, horizontal bands of black and yellow on the other. The *Do-giagya guat* belonged to the family of the great chief Dohasan and occupied the second place in the tribal circle on ceremonial occasions.

There are meadowlarks and quail in the open land. One day late in the afternoon I walked about among the headstones at Rainy Mountain Cemetery. The shadows were very long; there was a deep blush on the sky, and the dark red earth seemed to glow with the setting sun. For a few moments, at that particular time of the day, there is deep silence. Nothing moves, and it does not occur to you to make any sound. Something is going on there in the shadows. Everything has slowed to a stop in order that the sun might take leave of the land. And then there is the sudden, piercing call of a bobwhite. The whole world is startled by it.

XIII

If an arrow is well made, it will have tooth marks upon it. That is how you know. The Kiowas made fine arrows and straightened them in their teeth. Then they drew them to the bow to see if they were straight. Once there was a man and his wife. They were alone at night in their tipi. By the light of the fire the man was making arrows. After a while he caught sight of something. There was a small opening in the tipi where two hides were sewn together. Someone was there on the outside, looking in. The man went on with his work, but he said to his wife: "Someone is standing outside. Do not be afraid. Let us talk easily, as of ordinary things." He took up an arrow and straightened it in his teeth; then, as it was right for him to do, he drew it to the bow and took aim, first in this direction and then in that. And all the while he was talking, as if to his wife. But this is how he spoke: "I know that you are there on the outside, for I can feel your eyes upon me. If you are a Kiowa, you will understand what I am saying, and you will speak your name." But there was no answer, and the man went on in the same way, pointing the arrow all around. At last his aim fell upon the place where his enemy stood, and he let go of the string. The arrow went straight to the enemy's heart.

The old men were the best arrowmakers, for they could bring time and patience to their craft. The young men—the fighters and hunters—were willing to pay a high price for arrows that were well made.

When my father was a boy, an old man used to come to Mammedaty's house and pay his respects. He was a lean old man in braids and was impressive in his age and bearing. His name was Cheney, and he was an arrowmaker. Every morning, my father tells me, Cheney would paint his wrinkled face, go out, and pray aloud to the rising sun. In my mind I can see that man as if he were there now. I like to watch him as he makes his prayer. I know where he stands and where his voice

*goes on the rolling grasses and where the sun comes up on the land. There, at
dawn, you can feel the silence. It is cold and clear and deep like water. It takes
hold of you and will not let you go.*

XIV

The Kiowa language is hard to understand, but, you know, the storm spirit understands it. This is how it was: Long ago the Kiowas decided to make a horse; they
decided to make it out of clay, and so they began to shape the clay with their
hands. Well, the horse began to be. But it was a terrible, terrible thing. It began to
writhe, slowly at first, then faster and faster until there was a great commotion
everywhere. The wind grew up and carried everything away; great trees were
uprooted, and even the buffalo were thrown up into the sky. The Kiowas were
afraid of that awful thing, and they went running about, talking to it. And at last it
was calm. Even now, when they see the storm clouds gathering, the Kiowas know
what it is: that a strange wild animal roams on the sky. It has the head of a horse
and the tail of a great fish. Lightning comes from its mouth, and the tail, whipping
and thrashing on the air, makes the high, hot wind of the tornado. But they speak
to it, saying "Pass over me." They are not afraid of *Man-ka-ih,* for it understands
their language.

At times the plains are bright and calm and quiet; at times they are black with the
sudden violence of weather. Always there are winds.

*A few feet from the southwest corner of my grandmother's house, there is a storm
cellar. It will be there, I think, when the house and the arbor and the barn have
disappeared. There are many of those crude shelters in that part of the world.
They conform to the shape of the land and are scarcely remarkable: low earthen
mounds with heavy wooden trapdoors that appear to open upon the underworld. I
have seen the wind drive the rain so hard that a grown man could not open the
door against it, and once, descending into that place, I saw the whole land at
night become visible and blue and phosphorescent in the flash of lightning.*

XV

Quoetotai was a good-looking young man and a great warrior besides. One of
Many Bears' wives fell in love with him, and they carried on. After that, Quoetotai went out one day. As he was crossing the river, Many Bears came out of a
hiding place on the bank and shot him with an arrow; then he ran away. Quoetotai
went back to the camp and someone pulled the arrow out of him. He was very
sick, and he had lost a lot of blood. The medicine man worked over him for a long
time, and the next day Quoetotai was all right. You know, he made up his mind to
take Many Bears' wife away. After that, some of the men wanted to raid in Mexico. It was the custom to have a dance on the night before the men went away.
There was a lot of singing, and now and then someone got up to say brave things.
Many Bears' wife got up and called attention to herself. She said: "All of you,
listen to my song. Something will happen tonight." Then she sang, and, you
know, the old people still remember her song.

I am going to leave my belongings,
I am going to leave my home.
Again I say it, I am going to leave my son.

Quoetotai took that woman away, and they roamed with the Comanches for fifteen years. When at last they returned to their own people, Many Bears was the first man to welcome them. "Quoetotai," he said, "from this time on you and I will be brothers. Now I give you six horses."

The artist George Catlin[16] traveled among the Kiowas in 1834. He observes that they are superior to the Comanches and Wichitas in appearance. They are tall and straight, relaxed and graceful. They have fine, classical features, and in this respect they resemble more closely the tribes of the north than those of the south.

Catlin's portrait of Kotsatoah is the striking figure of a man, tall and lean, yet powerful and fully developed. He is lithe, and he knows beyond any doubt of his great strength and vigor. He stands perfectly at ease, the long drape of his robe flowing with the lines of his body. His left hand rests upon his shield and holds a bow and arrows. His head is set firmly, and there is a look of bemused and infinite tolerance in his eyes. He is said to have been nearly seven feet tall and able to run down and kill a buffalo on foot. I should like to have seen that man, as Catlin saw him, walking toward me, or away in the distance, perhaps, alone and against the sky.

XVI

There was a strange thing, a buffalo with horns of steel. One day a man came upon it in the plain, just there where once upon a time four trees stood close together. The man and the buffalo began to fight. The man's hunting horse was killed right away, and the man climbed one of the trees. The great bull lowered its head and began to strike the tree with its black metal horns, and soon the tree fell. But the man was quick, and he leaped to the safety of the second tree. Again the bull struck with its unnatural horns, and the tree soon splintered and fell. The man leaped to the third tree and all the while he shot arrows at the beast; but the arrows glanced away like sparks from its dark hide. At last there remained only one tree and the man had only one arrow. He believed then that he would surely die. But something spoke to him and said: "Each time the buffalo prepares to charge, it spreads its cloven hooves and strikes the ground. Only there in the cleft of the hoof is it vulnerable; it is there you must aim." The buffalo went away and turned, spreading its hooves, and the man drew the arrow to his bow. His aim was true and the arrow struck deep into the soft flesh of the hoof. The great bull shuddered and fell, and its steel horns flashed once in the sun.

Forty years ago the townspeople of Carnegie, Oklahoma, gathered about two old Kiowa men who were mounted on work horses and armed with bows and arrows. Someone had got a buffalo, a poor broken beast in which there was no trace left of

---

[16] Catlin (1796–1872) was an author and painter who depicted Plains Indians.

the wild strain. The old men waited silently amid the laughter and talk; then, at a signal, the buffalo was let go. It balked at first, more confused, perhaps, than afraid, and the horses had to be urged and then brought up short. The people shouted, and at last the buffalo wheeled and ran. The old men gave chase, and in the distance they were lost to view in a great, red cloud of dust. But they ran that animal down and killed it with arrows.

One morning my father and I walked in Medicine Park, on the edge of a small herd of buffalo. It was late in the spring, and many of the cows had newborn calves. Nearby a calf lay in the tall grass; it was red-orange in color, delicately beautiful with new life. We approached, but suddenly the cow was there in our way, her great dark head low and fearful-looking. Then she came at us, and we turned and ran as hard as we could. She gave up after a short run, and I think we had not been in any real danger. But the spring morning was deep and beautiful and our hearts were beating fast and we knew just then what it was to be alive.

XVII

Bad women are thrown away. Once there was a handsome young man. He was wild and reckless, and the chief talked to the wind about him. After that, the man went hunting. A great whirlwind passed by, and he was blind. The Kiowas have no need of a blind man; they left him alone with his wife and child. The winter was coming on and food was scarce. In four days the man's wife grew tired of caring for him. A herd of buffalo came near, and the man knew the sound. He asked his wife to hand him a bow and an arrow. "You must tell me," he said, "when the buffalo are directly in front of me." And in that way he killed a bull, but his wife said that he had missed. He asked for another arrow and killed another bull, but again his wife said that he had missed. Now the man was a hunter, and he knew the sound an arrow makes when it strikes home, but he said nothing. Then his wife helped herself to the meat and ran away with her child. The man was blind; he ate grass and kept himself alive. In seven days a band of Kiowas found him and took him to their camp. There in the firelight a woman was telling a story. She told of how her husband had been killed by enemy warriors. The blind man listened, and he knew her voice. That was a bad woman. At sunrise they threw her away.

In the Kiowa calendars[17] there is graphic proof that the lives of women were hard, whether they were "bad women" or not. Only the captives, who were slaves, held lower status. During the Sun Dance of 1843, a man stabbed his wife in the breast because she accepted Chief Dohasan's invitation to ride with him in the ceremonial procession. And in the winter of 1851–52, Big Bow stole the wife of a man who was away on a raiding expedition. He brought her to his father's camp and made her wait outside in the bitter cold while he went in to collect his things. But his father knew what was going on, and he held Big Bow and would not let him go. The woman was made to wait in the snow until her feet were frozen.

---

[17] Pictorial calendars of Kiowa history, as seen in Mooney's *Calendar History of the Kiowa Indians* (1898).

*Mammedaty's grandmother, Kau-au-ointy, was a Mexican captive, taken from
her homeland when she was a child of eight or ten years. I never knew her, but I
have been to her grave at Rainy Mountain.*

KAU-AU-OINTY
BORN 1834
DIED 1929
AT REST

*She raised a lot of eyebrows, they say, for she would not play the part of a Kiowa
woman. From slavery she rose up to become a figure in the tribe. She owned a
great herd of cattle, and she could ride as well as any man. She had blue eyes.*

XVIII

You know, the Kiowas are a summer people. Once upon a time a group of young
men sat down in a circle and spoke of mighty things. This is what they said:
"When the fall of the year comes around, where does the summer go? Where does
it live?" They decided to follow the sun southward to its home, and so they set out
on horseback. They rode for days and weeks and months, farther to the south than
any Kiowa had ever gone before, and they saw many strange and wonderful
things. At last they came to the place where they saw the strangest thing of all.
Night was coming on, and they were very tired of riding; they made camp in a
great thicket. All but one of them went right to sleep. He was a good hunter, and
he could see well in the moonlight. He caught sight of something: men were all
about in the trees, moving silently from limb to limb. They darted across the face
of the full moon, and he saw that they were small and had tails! He could not
believe his eyes, but the next morning he told the others of what he had seen.
They only laughed at him and told him not to eat such a large supper again. But
later, as they were breaking camp, a certain feeling came over them all at once:
they felt that they were being watched. And when they looked up, the small men
with tails began to race about in the limbs overhead. That is when the Kiowas
turned around and came away; they had had quite enough of that place. They had
found the sun's home after all, they reasoned, and they were hungry for the good
buffalo meat of their homeland.

It is unnecessary to dilate on the revolution made in the life of the Indian by the
possession of the horse. Without it he was a half-starved skulker in the timber,
creeping up on foot toward the unwary deer or building a brush corral with infinite
labor to surround a herd of antelope, and seldom venturing more than a few days'
journey from home. With the horse he was transformed into the daring buffalo
hunter, able to procure in a single day enough food to supply his family for a year,
leaving him free then to sweep the plains with his war parties along a range of a
thousand miles.—Mooney

*Some of my earliest memories are of the summers on Rainy Mountain Creek, when
we lived in the arbor, on the north side of my grandmother's house. From there
you could see downhill to the pecan grove, the dense, dark growth along the
water, and beyond, the long sweep of the earth itself, curving out on the sky. The
arbor was open on all sides to the light and the air and the sounds of the land.*

*You could see far and wide even at night, by the light of the moon; there was
nothing to stand in your way. And when the season turned and it was necessary to
move back into the house, there was a sense of confinement and depression for a
time. Now and then in winter, when I passed by the arbor on my way to draw
water at the well, I looked inside and thought of the summer. The hard dirt floor
was dark red in color—the color of pipestone.*

THE CLOSING IN

XIX

On a raid against the Utes, one of two brothers was captured. The other, alone and
of his own will, stole into the Ute camp and tried to set his brother free, but he too
was captured. The chief of the Utes had respect for the man's bravery, and he
made a bargain with him. If he could carry his brother on his back and walk upon
a row of greased buffalo heads without falling to the ground, both brothers would
be given horses and allowed to return in safety to their home. The man bore his
brother on his back and walked upon the heads of the buffalo and kept his footing.
The Ute chief was true to his word, and the brothers returned to their own people
on horseback.

After the fight at Palo Duro Canyon, the Kiowas came in, a few at a time, to
surrender at Fort Sill. Their horses and weapons were confiscated, and they were
imprisoned. In a field just west of the post, the Indian ponies were destroyed.
Nearly *800* horses were killed outright; two thousand more were sold, stolen,
given away.

SUMMER 1879

Tsen-pia Kado, "Horse-eating sun dance." It is indicated on the Set-tan
calendar by the figure of a horse's head above the medicine lodge. This dance was
held on Elm Fork of Red River, and was so called because the buffalo had now
become so scarce that the Kiowa, who had gone on their regular hunt the
preceding winter, had found so few that they were obliged to kill and eat their
ponies during the summer to save themselves from starving. This may be recorded
as the date of the disappearance of the buffalo from the Kiowa country.
Thenceforth the appearance of even a single animal was a rare event.—Mooney

*In New Mexico the land is made of many colors. When I was a boy I rode out over
the red and yellow and purple earth to the west of Jemez Pueblo. My horse was a
small red roan, fast and easy-riding. I rode among the dunes, along the bases of
mesas and cliffs, into canyons and arroyos. I came to know that country, not in
the way a traveler knows the landmarks he sees in the distance, but more truly and
intimately, in every season, from a thousand points of view. I know the living
motion of a horse and the sound of hooves. I know what it is, on a hot day in
August or September, to ride into a bank of cold, fresh rain.*

XX

Once there was a man who owned a fine hunting horse. It was black and fast and afraid of nothing. When it was turned upon an enemy it charged in a straight line and struck at full speed; the man need have no hand upon the rein. But, you know, that man knew fear. Once during a charge he turned that animal from its course. That was a bad thing. The hunting horse died of shame.

In 1861 a Sun Dance was held near the Arkansas River in Kansas. As an offering to Tai-me, a spotted horse was left tied to a pole in the medicine lodge, where it starved to death. Later in that year an epidemic of smallpox broke out in the tribe, and the old man Gaapiatan sacrificed one of his best horses, a fine black-eared animal, that he and his family might be spared.

I like to think of old man Gaapiatan and his horse. I think I know how much he loved that animal; I think I know what was going on in his mind: If you will give me my life and the lives of my family, I will give you the life of this black-eared horse.

XXI

Mammedaty was the grandson of Guipahgo, and he was well-known on that account. Now and then Mammedaty drove a team and wagon out over the plain. Once, in the early morning, he was on the way to Rainy Mountain. It was summer and the grass was high and meadowlarks were calling all around. You know, the top of the plain is smooth and you can see a long way. There was nothing but the early morning and the land around. Then Mammedaty heard something. Someone whistled to him. He looked up and saw the head of a little boy nearby above the grass. He stopped the horses and got down from the wagon and went to see who was there. There was no one; there was nothing there. He looked for a long time, but there was nothing there.

There is a single photograph of Mammedaty. He is looking past the camera and a little to one side. In his face there is calm and good will, strength and intelligence. His hair is drawn close to the scalp, and his braids are long and wrapped with fur. He wears a kilt, fringed leggings, and beaded moccasins. In his right hand there is a peyote fan. A family characteristic: the veins stand out in his hands, and his hands are small and rather long.

Mammedaty saw four things that were truly remarkable. This head of the child was one, and the tracks of the water beast another. Once, when he walked near the pecan grove, he saw three small alligators on a log. No one had ever seen them before and no one ever saw them again. Finally, there was this: something had always bothered Mammedaty, a small aggravation that was never quite out of mind, like a name on the tip of the tongue. He had always wondered how it is that the mound of earth which a mole makes around the opening of its burrow is so fine. It is nearly as fine as powder, and it seems almost to have been sifted. One day Mammedaty was sitting quietly when a mole came out of the earth. Its cheeks were puffed out as if it had been a squirrel packing nuts. It looked all around for a moment, then blew the fine dark earth out of its mouth. And this it did again and again, until there was a ring of black, powdery earth on the ground. That was a strange and meaningful thing to see. It meant that Mammedaty had got possession of a powerful medicine.

XXII

Mammedaty was the grandson of Guipahgo, and he got on well most of the time. But, you know, one time he lost his temper. This is how it was: There were several horses in a pasture, and Mammedaty wanted to get them out. A fence ran all the way around and there was just one gate. There was a lot of ground inside. He could not get those horses out. One of them led the others; every time they were driven up to the gate, that one wheeled and ran as fast as it could to the other side. Well, that went on for a long time, and Mammedaty burned up. He ran to the house and got his bow and arrows. The horses were running in single file, and he shot at the one that was causing all the trouble. He missed, though, and the arrow went deep into the neck of the second horse.

In the winter of 1852–53, a Pawnee boy who had been held as a captive among the Kiowas succeeded in running away. He took with him an especially fine hunting horse, known far and wide as *Guadal-tseyu*, "Little Red." That was the most important event of the winter. The loss of that horse was a hard thing to bear.

Years ago there was a box of bones in the barn, and I used to go there to look at them. Later someone stole them, I believe. They were the bones of a horse which Mammedaty called by the name "Little Red." It was a small bay, nothing much to look at, I have heard, but it was the fastest runner in that whole corner of the world. White men and Indians alike came from far and near to match their best animals against it, but it never lost a race. I have often thought about that red horse. There have been times when I thought I understood how it was that a man might be moved to preserve the bones of a horse—and another to steal them away.

XXIII

Aho remembered something, a strange thing. This is how it was: You know, the Tai-me bundle is not very big, but it is full of power. Once Aho went to see the Tai-me keeper's wife. The two of them were sitting together, passing the time of day, when they heard an awful noise, as if a tree or some other very heavy object had fallen down. It frightened them, and they went to see what on earth it was. It was Tai-me—Tai me- had fallen to the floor. No one knows how it was that Tai-me fell; nothing caused it, as far as anyone could see.

For a time Mammedaty wore one of the grandmother bundles. This he did for his mother Keahdinekeah; he wore it on a string tied around his neck. Aho remembered this: that if anyone who wore a medicine bundle failed to show it the proper respect, it grew extremely heavy around his neck.

There was a great iron kettle which stood outside of my grandmother's house next to the south porch. It was huge and immovable, or so I thought when I was a child; I could not imagine that anyone had strength enough to lift it up. I don't know where it came from; it was always there. It rang like a bell when you struck it, and with the tips of your fingers you could feel the black metal sing for a long time afterward. It was used to catch the rainwater with which we washed our hair.

XXIV

East of my grandmother's house, south of the pecan grove, there is buried a woman in a beautiful dress. Mammedaty used to know where she is buried, but now no one knows. If you stand on the front porch of the house and look eastward towards Carnegie, you know that the woman is buried somewhere within the range of your vision. But her grave is unmarked. She was buried in a cabinet, and she wore a beautiful dress. How beautiful it was! It was one of those fine buckskin dresses, and it was decorated with elk's teeth and beadwork. That dress is still there, under the ground.

Aho's high moccasins are made of softest, cream-colored skins. On each instep there is a bright disc of beadwork—an eight-pointed star, red and pale blue on a white field—and there are bands of beadwork at the soles and ankles. The flaps of the leggings are wide and richly ornamented with blue and red and green and white and lavender beads.

East of my grandmother's house the sun rises out of the plain. Once in his life a man ought to concentrate his mind upon the remembered earth, I believe. He ought to give himself up to a particular landscape in his experience, to look at it from as many angles as he can, to wonder about it, to dwell upon it. He ought to imagine that he touches it with his hands at every season and listens to the sounds that are made upon it. He ought to imagine the creatures there and all the faintest motions of the wind. He ought to recollect the glare of noon and all the colors of the dawn and dusk.

EPILOGUE

During the first hours after midnight on the morning of November 13, 1833, it seemed that the world was coming to an end. Suddenly the stillness of the night was broken; there were brilliant flashes of light in the sky, light of such intensity that people were awakened by it. With the speed and density of a driving rain, stars were falling in the universe. Some were brighter than Venus; one was said to be as large as the moon.

That most brilliant shower of Leonid[18] meteors has a special place in the memory of the Kiowa people. It is among the earliest entries in the Kiowa calendars, and it marks the beginning as it were of the historical period in the tribal mind. In the preceding year Tai-me had been stolen by a band of Osages, and although it

---

[18] One of the shooting stars constituting the meteor shower that occurs around November 15, appearing to radiate from the constellation Leo.

was later returned, the loss was an almost unimaginable tragedy; and in 1837 the Kiowas made the first of their treaties with the United States. The falling stars seemed to image the sudden and violent disintegration of an old order.

But indeed the golden age of the Kiowas had been short-lived, ninety or a hundred years, say, from about 1740. The culture would persist for a while in decline, until about 1875, but then it would be gone, and there would be very little material evidence that it had ever been. Yet it is within the reach of memory still, though tenuously now, and moreover it is even defined in a remarkaby rich and living verbal tradition which demands to be preserved for its own sake. The living memory and the verbal tradition which transcends it were brought together for me once and for all in the person of Ko-sahn.

A hundred-year-old woman came to my grandmother's house one afternoon in July. Aho was dead; Mammedaty had died before I was born. There were very few Kiowas left who could remember the Sun Dances; Ko-sahn was one of them; she was a grown woman when my grandparents came into the world. Her body was twisted and her face deeply lined with age. Her thin white hair was held in place by a cap of black netting, though she wore braids as well, and she had but one eye. She was dressed in the manner of a Kiowa matron, a dark, full-cut dress that reached nearly to the ankles, full, flowing sleeves, and a wide, apron-like sash. She sat on a bench in the arbor so concentrated in her great age that she seemed extraordinarily small. She was quiet for a time—she might almost have been asleep—and then she began to speak and to sing. She spoke of many things, and once she spoke of the Sun Dance:

My sisters and I were very young; that was a long time ago. Early one morning they came to wake us up. They had brought a great buffalo in from the plain. Everyone went out to see and to pray. We heard a great many voices. One man said that the lodge was almost ready. We were told to go there, and someone gave me a piece of cloth. It was very beautiful. Then I asked what I ought to do with it, and they said that I must tie it to the Tai-me tree. There were other pieces of cloth on the tree, and so I put mine there as well.
When the lodge frame was finished, a woman—sometimes a man—began to sing. It was like this:

> *Everything is ready.*
> *Now the four societies must go out.*
> *They must go out and get the leaves,*
> > *the branches for the lodge.*

And when the branches were tied in place, again there was singing:

> *Let the boys go out.*
> *Come on, boys, now we must get the earth.*

The boys began to shout. Now they were not just ordinary boys, not all of them; they were those for whom prayers had been made, and they were dressed in different ways. There was an old, old woman. She had something on her back. The boys went out to see. The old woman had a bag full of earth on her back. It was a certain kind of sandy earth. That is what they must have in the lodge. The dancers must dance upon the sandy earth. The old woman held a digging tool in her hand. She turned towards the south and pointed with her lips. It was like a kiss, and she began to sing:

> *We have brought the earth.*
> *Now it is time to play;*
> *As old as I am, I still have the feeling of play.*

That was the beginning of the Sun Dance. The dancers treated themselves with buffalo medicine, and slowly they began to take their steps . . . And all the people were around, and they wore splendid things—beautiful buckskin and beads. The chiefs wore necklaces, and their pendants shone like the sun. There were many people, and oh, it was beautiful! That was the beginning of the Sun Dance. It was all for Tai-me, you know, and it was a long time ago.

It was—all of this and more—a quest, a going forth upon the way to Rainy Mountain. Probably Ko-sahn too is dead now. At times, in the quiet of evening, I think she must have wondered, dreaming, who she was. Was she become in her sleep that old purveyor of the sacred earth, perhaps, that ancient one who, old as she was, still had the feeling of play? And in her mind, at times, did she see the falling stars?

RAINY MOUNTAIN CEMETERY

Most is your name the name of this dark stone.
Deranged in death, the mind to be inheres
Forever in the nominal unknown,
The wake of nothing audible he hears
Who listens here and now to hear your name.

The early sun, red as a hunter's moon,
Runs in the plain. The mountain burns and shines;
And silence is the long approach of noon
Upon the shadow that your name defines—
And death this cold, black density of stone.

1967–1968, 1969

Joyce Carol Oates
(1938–   )

Born in the town of Lockport, New York, in 1938, Joyce Carol Oates was raised Roman Catholic in a working-class family. She received her early education in a rural one-room schoolhouse and went on to graduate as class valedictorian from Syracuse University in 1960. Oates earned an M.A. in English from the University of Wisconsin in 1961 and began an academic career that has included teaching positions at the University of Detroit, the University of Windsor, Ontario, and New York University, and in 1978 she became a member of the creative writing department of Princeton University. One of the most prolific and celebrated writers in America today, Oates has contributed novels, short stories, plays, volumes of poetry, books of critical essays, and scholarly studies as well as the book-length essay *On Boxing* (1987). Oates's first published story, "In the Old World," won the college fiction prize offered by *Mademoiselle* magazine in 1959, and she has since won such honors as the Rosenthal Foundation Award, a National Book Award (for the novel *them* [1969]), a Guggenheim Fellowship, the Rea Award for short stories, and the O. Henry Prize for Continuing Achievement.

In its various forms Oates's fiction offers a vision of contemporary America, ranging from portraits of suburban affluent society to experimental Gothic romances. But her intention is always to locate a moral center among even the most grotesque and violent occurrences. Beginning with her first novel, *With Shuddering Fall* (1964), and continuing through her most recent work, Oates commonly uses the shock of the macabre to recreate the mental equivalent of her characters' experiences within the mind of the reader. To Oates art is didactic—illustrative, moral, educational. This instruction is typically achieved through the accumulated detail of her rich, imaginary worlds and the cathartic release that accompanies the often unsettling violence of her plots. Another thread that runs throughout Oates's work is the exploration of social and economic histories as revealed through personal narratives. From her early trilogy of novels—*A Garden of Earthly Delights* (1967), *Expensive People* (1968), and *them* (1969)—to *The Assignation* (1988) and *Because It Is Bitter and Because It Is My Heart* (1990), Oates has combined a keen, naturalistic attention to minute particulars with a fascination for psychological drama to create a social history that defies easy categorization, providing imaginative insight into the problems of "ordinary people." Equally at home in the fantasy world of *Bellefleur* (1980), the mythical/historical realm of *Angel of Light* (1981), and the gritty realism of *You Must Remember This* (1987), Oates's distinctive moral vision remains the one constant throughout her wide variety of formal and generic experiments.

Suggested Readings: *Marya: A Sweeping Flood and Other Stories*, 1966. *A Garden of Earthly Delights*, 1967. *them*, 1969. *The Goddess and Other Women*, 1974. *The Assassins*, 1975. *Bellefleur*, 1980. *Angel of Light*, 1981. *Contraries*, 1981. *The Profane Art: Essays and Reviews*, 1983. *Mysteries of Winterthurn*, 1985. *Raven's Wing*, 1986. *You Must Remember This*, 1987. *The Assignation*, 1988. *Woman Writer: Occasions and Opportunities*, 1988. *The Time Traveler: Poems 1983–1989*, 1989. M. K. Grant, *The Tragic Vision of Joyce Carol Oates*, 1978. J. V. Creighton, *Joyce Carol Oates*, 1979. L. W. Wagner, ed., *Critical Essays on Joyce Carol Oates*, 1979. K. Bastion, *Joyce Carol Oates's Short Stories: Between Tradition and Innovation*, 1983. G. Johnson, *Understanding Joyce Carol Oates*, 1987.

Text Used: *The Wheel of Love and Other Stories*, 1970.

WHERE ARE YOU GOING, WHERE HAVE YOU BEEN?*

For Bob Dylan

Her name was Connie. She was fifteen and she had a quick, nervous giggling habit of craning her neck to glance into mirrors or checking other people's faces to make sure her own was all right. Her mother, who noticed everything and knew everything and who hadn't much reason any longer to look at her own face, always scolded Connie about it. "Stop gawking at yourself. Who are you? You think you're so pretty?" she would say. Connie would raise her eyebrows at these

---

* First published in *Epoch* in autumn 1966 and later collected in *The Wheel of Love and Other Stories* (1970).

familiar old complaints and look right through her mother, into a shadowy vision of herself as she was right at that moment: she knew she was pretty and that was everything. Her mother had been pretty once too, if you could believe those old snapshots in the album, but now her looks were gone and that was why she was always after Connie.

"Why don't you keep your room clean like your sister? How've you got your hair fixed—what the hell stinks? Hair spray? You don't see your sister using that junk."

Her sister June was twenty-four and still lived at home. She was a secretary in the high school Connie attended, and if that wasn't bad enough—with her in the same building—she was so plain and chunky and steady that Connie had to hear her praised all the time by her mother and her mother's sisters. June did this, June did that, she saved money and helped clean the house and cooked and Connie couldn't do a thing, her mind was all filled with trashy daydreams. Their father was away at work most of the time and when he came home he wanted supper and he read the newspaper at supper and after supper he went to bed. He didn't bother talking much to them, but around his bent head Connie's mother kept picking at her until Connie wished her mother was dead and she herself was dead and it was all over. "She makes me want to throw up sometimes," she complained to her friends. She had a high, breathless, amused voice that made everything she said sound a little forced, whether it was sincere or not.

There was one good thing: June went places with girl friends of hers, girls who were just as plain and steady as she, and so when Connie wanted to do that her mother had no objections. The father of Connie's best girl friend drove the girls the three miles to town and left them at a shopping plaza so they could walk through the stores or go to a movie, and when he came to pick them up again at eleven he never bothered to ask what they had done.

They must have been familiar sights, walking around the shopping plaza in their shorts and flat ballerina slippers that always scuffed the sidewalk, with charm bracelets jingling on their thin wrists; they would lean together to whisper and laugh secretly if someone passed who amused or interested them. Connie had long dark blond hair that drew anyone's eye to it, and she wore part of it pulled up on her head and puffed out and the rest of it she let fall down her back. She wore a pull-over jersey blouse that looked one way when she was at home and another way when she was away from home. Everything about her had two sides to it, one for home and one for anywhere that was not home: her walk, which could be childlike and bobbing, or languid enough to make anyone think she was hearing music in her head; her mouth, which was pale and smirking most of the time, but bright and pink on these evenings out; her laugh, which was cynical and drawling at home—"Ha, ha, very funny,"—but high-pitched and nervous anywhere else, like the jingling of the charms on her bracelet.

Sometimes they did go shopping or to a movie, but sometimes they went across the highway, ducking fast across the busy road, to a drive-in restaurant where older kids hung out. The restaurant was shaped like a big bottle, though squatter than a real bottle, and on its cap was a revolving figure of a grinning boy holding a hamburger aloft. One night in midsummer they ran across, breathless with daring, and right away someone leaned out a car window and invited them over, but it was just a boy from high school they didn't like. It made them feel good to be able to ignore him. They went up through the maze of parked and cruising cars to the bright-lit, fly-infested restaurant, their faces pleased and expectant as if they were entering a sacred building that loomed up out of the night to give them what haven and blessing they yearned for. They sat at the counter and crossed their legs at the ankles, their thin shoulders rigid with excitement, and listened to the music that made everything so good: the music was always in the background, like music at a church service; it was something to depend upon.

A boy named Eddie came in to talk with them. He sat backwards on his stool, turning himself jerkily around in semicircles and then stopping and turning back again, and after a while he asked Connie if she would like something to eat. She said she would and so she tapped her friend's arm on her way out—her friend pulled her face up into a brave, droll look—and Connie said she would meet her at eleven, across the way. "I just hate to leave her like that," Connie said earnestly, but the boy said that she wouldn't be alone for long. So they went out to his car, and on the way Connie couldn't help but let her eyes wander over the windshields and faces all around her, her face gleaming with a joy that had nothing to do with Eddie or even this place; it might have been the music. She drew her shoulders up and sucked in her breath with the pure pleasure of being alive, and just at that moment she happened to glance at a face just a few feet from hers. It was a boy with shaggy black hair, in a convertible jalopy painted gold. He stared at her and then his lips widened into a grin. Connie slit her eyes at him and turned away, but she couldn't help glancing back and there he was, still watching her. He wagged a finger and laughed and said, "Gonna get you, baby," and Connie turned away again without Eddie noticing anything.

She spent three hours with him, at the restaurant where they ate hamburgers and drank Cokes in wax cups that were always sweating, and then down an alley a mile or so away, and when he left her off at five to eleven only the movie house was still open at the plaza. Her girl friend was there, talking with a boy. When Connie came up, the two girls smiled at each other and Connie said, "How was the movie?" and the girl said, "*You* should know." They rode off with the girl's father, sleepy and pleased, and Connie couldn't help but look back at the darkened shopping plaza with its big empty parking lot and its signs that were faded and ghostly now, and over at the drive-in restaurant where cars were still circling tirelessly. She couldn't hear the music at this distance.

Next morning June asked her how the movie was and Connie said, "So-so."

She and that girl and occasionally another girl went out several times a week, and the rest of the time Connie spent around the house—it was summer vacation—getting in her mother's way and thinking, dreaming about the boys she met. But all the boys fell back and dissolved into a single face that was not even a face but an idea, a feeling, mixed up with the urgent insistent pounding of the music and the humid night air of July. Connie's mother kept dragging her back to the daylight by finding things for her to do or saying suddenly, "What's this about the Pettinger girl?"

And Connie would say nervously, "Oh, her. That dope." She always drew thick clear lines between herself and such girls, and her mother was simple and kind enough to believe it. Her mother was so simple, Connie thought, that it was maybe cruel to fool her so much. Her mother went scuffling around the house in old bedroom slippers and complained over the telephone to one sister about the other, then the other called up and the two of them complained about the third one. If June's name was mentioned her mother's tone was approving, and if Connie's name was mentioned it was disapproving. This did not really mean she disliked Connie, and actually Connie thought that her mother preferred her to June just because she was prettier, but the two of them kept up a pretense of exasperation, a sense that they were tugging and struggling over something of little value to either of them. Sometimes, over coffee, they were almost friends, but something would come up—some vexation that was like a fly buzzing suddenly around their heads—and their faces went hard with contempt.

One Sunday Connie got up at eleven—none of them bothered with church—and washed her hair so that it could dry all day long in the sun. Her parents and sister were going to a barbecue at an aunt's house and Connie said no, she wasn't interested, rolling her eyes to let her mother know just what she thought of it. "Stay home alone then," her mother said sharply. Connie sat out back in a lawn chair and watched them drive away, her father quiet and bald, hunched around so that he could back the car out, her mother with a look that was still angry and not at all softened through the windshield, and in the back seat poor old June, all dressed up as if she didn't know what a barbecue was, with all the running yelling kids and the flies. Connie sat with her eyes closed in the sun, dreaming and dazed with the warmth about her as if this were a kind of love, the caresses of love, and her mind slipped over onto thoughts of the boy she had been with the night before and how nice he had been, how sweet it always was, not the way someone like June would suppose but sweet, gentle, the way it was in movies and promised in songs; and when she opened her eyes she hardly knew where she was, the back yard ran off into weeds and a fence-like line of trees and behind it the sky was perfectly blue and still. The asbestos "ranch house" that was now three years old startled her—it looked small. She shook her head as if to get awake.

It was too hot. She went inside the house and turned on the radio to drown out the quiet. She sat on the edge of her bed, barefoot, and listened for an hour and a half to a program called XYZ Sunday Jamboree, record after record of hard, fast, shrieking songs she sang along with, interspersed by exclamations from "Bobby King": "An' look here, you girls at Napolean's—Son and Charley want you to pay real close attention to this song coming up!"

And Connie paid close attention herself, bathed in a glow of slow-pulsed joy that seemed to rise mysteriously out of the music itself and lay languidly about the airless little room, breathed in and breathed out with each gentle rise and fall of her chest.

After a while she heard a car coming up the drive. She sat up at once, startled, because it couldn't be her father so soon. The gravel kept crunching all the way in from the road—the driveway was long—and Connie ran to the window. It was a car she didn't know. It was an open jalopy, painted a bright gold that caught the sunlight opaquely. Her heart began to pound and her fingers snatched at her hair, checking it, and she whispered, "Christ. Christ," wondering how bad she looked. The car came to a stop at the side door and then the horn sounded four short taps, as if this were a signal Connie knew.

She went into the kitchen and approached the door slowly, then hung out the screen door, her bare toes curling down off the step. There were two boys in the car and now she recognized the driver: he had shaggy, shabby black hair that looked crazy as a wig and he was grinning at her.

"I ain't late, am I?" he said.

"Who the hell do you think you are?" Connie said.

"Toldja I'd be out, didn't I?"

"I don't even know who you are."

She spoke sullenly, careful to show no interest or pleasure, and he spoke in a fast, bright monotone. Connie looked past him to the other boy, taking her time. He had fair brown hair, with a lock that fell onto his forehead. His sideburns gave him a fierce, embarrassed look, but so far he hadn't even bothered to glance at her. Both boys wore sunglasses. The driver's glasses were metallic and mirrored everything in miniature.

"You wanta come for a ride?" he said.

Connie smirked and let her hair fall loose over one shoulder.

"Don'tcha like my car? New paint job," he said. "Hey."

"What?"

"You're cute."

She pretended to fidget, chasing flies away from the door.

"Don'tcha believe me, or what?" he said.

"Look, I don't even know who you are," Connie said in disgust.

"Hey, Ellie's got a radio, see. Mine broke down." He lifted his friend's arm and showed her the little transistor radio the boy was holding, <u>and now Connie began to hear the music</u>. It was the same program that was playing inside the house.

"Bobby King?" she said.

"I listen to him all the time. I think he's great."

"He's kind of great," Connie said reluctantly.

"Listen, that guy's *great*. He knows where the action is."

Connie blushed a little, because the glasses made it impossible for her to see just what this boy was looking at. She couldn't decide if she liked him or if he was just a jerk, and so she dawdled in the doorway and wouldn't come down or go back inside. She said, "What's all that stuff painted on your car?"

"Can'tcha read it?" He opened the door very carefully, as if he were afraid it might fall off. He slid out just as carefully, planting his feet firmly on the ground, the tiny metallic world in his glasses slowing down like gelatine hardening, and in the midst of it Connie's bright green blouse. "This here is my name, to begin with," he said. ARNOLD FRIEND was written in tarlike black letters on the side, with a drawing of a round, grinning face that reminded Connie of a pumpkin, except it wore sunglasses. "I wanta introduce myself, I'm Arnold Friend and that's my real name and I'm gonna be your friend, honey, and inside the car's Ellie Oscar, he's kinda shy." Ellie brought his transistor radio up to his shoulder and balanced it there. "Now, these numbers are a secret code, honey," Arnold Friend explained. He read off the numbers 33, 19, 17 and raised his eyebrows at her to see what she thought of that, but she didn't think much of it. The left rear fender had been smashed and around it was written, on the gleaming gold background: DONE BY CRAZY WOMAN DRIVER. Connie had to laugh at that. Arnold Friend was pleased at her laughter and looked up at her. "Around the other side's a lot more—you wanta come and see them?"

"No."

"Why not?"

"Why should I?"

"Don'tcha wanta see what's on the car? Don'tcha wanta go for a ride?"

"I don't know."

"Why not?"

"I got things to do."

"Like what?"

"Thighs."

He laughed as if she had said something funny. He slapped his thighs. He was standing in a strange way, leaning back against the car as if he were balancing himself. He wasn't tall, only an inch or so taller than she would be if she came down to him. Connie liked the way he was dressed, which was the way all of them dressed: tight faded jeans stuffed into black, scuffed boots, a belt that pulled his waist in and showed how lean he was, and a white pull-over shirt that was a little soiled and showed the hard small muscles of his arms and shoulders. He looked as if he probably did hard work, lifting and carrying things. Even his neck looked muscular. And his face was a familiar face, somehow: the jaw and chin and cheeks slightly darkened because he hadn't shaved for a day or two, and the nose long and hawklike, sniffing as if she were a treat he was going to gobble up and it was all a joke.

"Connie, you ain't telling the truth. This is your day set aside for a ride with me and you know it," he said, still laughing. The way he straightened and recovered from his fit of laughing showed that it had been all fake.

"How do you know what my name is?" she said suspiciously.

"It's Connie."

"Maybe and maybe not."

"I know my Connie," he said, wagging his finger. Now she remembered him even better, back at the restaurant, and her cheeks warmed at the thought of how she had sucked in her breath just at the moment she passed him—how she must have looked to him. And he had remembered her. "Ellie and I come out here especially for you," he said. "Ellie can sit in back. How about it?"

"Where?"

"Where what?"

"Where're we going?"

He looked at her. He took off the sunglasses and she saw how pale the skin around his eyes was, like holes that were not in shadow but instead in light. His eyes were like chips of broken glass that catch the light in an amiable way. He smiled. It was as if the idea of going for a ride somewhere, to someplace, was a new idea to him.

"Just for a ride, Connie sweetheart."

"I never said my name was Connie," she said.

"But I know what it is. I know your name and all about you, lots of things," Arnold Friend said. He had not moved yet but stood still leaning back against the side of his jalopy. "I took a special interest in you, such a pretty girl, and found out all about you—like I know your parents and sister are gone somewheres and I know where and how long they're going to be gone, and I know who you were with last night, and your best girl friend's name is Betty. Right?"

He spoke in a simple lilting voice, exactly as if were reciting the words to a song. His smile assured her that everything was fine. In the car Ellie turned up the volume on his radio and did not bother to look around at them.

"Ellie can sit in the back seat," Arnold Friend said. He indicated his friend with a casual jerk of his chin, as if Ellie did not count and she should not bother with him.

"How'd you find out all that stuff?" Connie said.

"Listen: Betty Schultz and Tony Fitch and Jimmy Pettinger and Nancy Pettinger," he said in a chant. "Raymond Stanley and Bob Hutter—"

"Do you know all those kids?"

"I know everybody."

"Look, you're kidding. You're not from around here."

"Sure."

"But—how come we never saw you before?"

"Sure you saw me before," he said. He looked down at his boots, as if he were a little offended. "You just don't remember."

"I guess I'd remember you," Connie said.

"Yeah?" He looked up at this, beaming. He was pleased. He began to mark time with the music from Ellie's radio, tapping his fists lightly together. Connie looked away from his smile to the car, which was painted so bright it almost hurt her eyes to look at it. She looked at that name, ARNOLD FRIEND. And up at the front fender was an expression that was familiar—MAN THE FLYING SAUCERS. It was an expression kids had used the year before but didn't use this year. She looked at it for a while as if the words meant something to her that she did not yet know.

"What're you thinking about? Huh?" Arnold Friend demanded. "Not worried about your hair blowing around in the car, are you?"

"No."

"Think I maybe can't drive good?"

"How do I know?"

"You're a hard girl to handle. How come?" he said. "Don't you know I'm your friend? Didn't you see me put my sign in the air when you walked by?"

"What sign?"

"My sign." And he drew an X in the air, leaning out toward her. They were maybe ten feet apart. After his hand fell back to his side the X was still in the air, almost visible. Connie let the screen door close and stood perfectly still inside it, listening to the music from her radio and the boy's blend together. She stared at Arnold Friend. He stood there so stiffly relaxed, pretending to be relaxed, with one hand idly on the door handle as if he were keeping himself up that way and had no intention of ever moving again. She recognized most things about him, the tight jeans that showed his thighs and buttocks and the greasy leather boots and the tight shirt, and even that slippery friendly smile of his, that sleepy dreamy smile that all the boys used to get across ideas they didn't want to put into words. She recognized all this and also the singsong way he talked, slightly mocking, kidding, but serious and a little melancholy, and she recognized the way he tapped one fist against the other in homage to the perpetual music behind him. But all these things did not come together.

She said suddenly, "Hey, how old are you?"

His smile faded. She could see then that he wasn't a kid, he was much older—thirty, maybe more. At this knowledge her heart began to pound faster.

"That's a crazy thing to ask. Can'tcha see I'm your own age?"

"Like hell you are."

"Or maybe a coupla years older. I'm eighteen."

"Eighteen?" she said doubtfully.

He grinned to reassure her and lines appeared at the corners of his mouth. His teeth were big and white. He grinned so broadly his eyes became slits and she saw how thick the lashes were, thick and black as if painted with a black tarlike material. Then, abruptly, he seemed to become embarrassed and looked over his shoulder at Ellie. "*Him,* he's crazy," he said. "Ain't he a riot? He's a nut, a real character." Ellie was still listening to the music. His sunglasses told nothing about what he was thinking. He wore a bright orange shirt unbuttoned halfway to show his chest, which was a pale, bluish chest and not muscular like Arnold Friend's. His shirt collar was turned up all around and the very tips of the collar pointed out past his chin as if they were protecting him. He was pressing the transistor radio up against his ear and sat there in a kind of daze, right in the sun.

"He's kinda strange," Connie said.

"Hey, she says you're kinda strange! Kinda strange!" Arnold Friend cried. He pounded on the car to get Ellie's attention. Ellie turned for the first time and Connie saw with shock that he wasn't a kid either—he had a fair, hairless face, cheeks reddened slightly as if the veins grew too close to the surface of his skin, the face of a forty-year-old baby. Connie felt a wave of dizziness rise in her at this sight and she stared at him as if waiting for something to change the shock of the moment, make it all right again. Ellie's lips kept shaping words, mumbling along with the words blasting in his ear.

"Maybe you two better go away," Connie said faintly.

"What? How come?" Arnold Friend cried. "We come out here to take you for a ride. It's Sunday." He had the voice of the man on the radio now. It was the same voice, Connie thought. "Don'tcha know it's Sunday all day? And honey, no matter who you were with last night, today you're with Arnold Friend and don't you forget it! Maybe you better step out here," he said, and this last was in a different voice. It was a little flatter, as if the heat was finally getting to him.

"No. I got things to do."

"Hey."

"You two better leave."

"We ain't leaving until you come with us."

"Like hell I am—"

"Connie, don't fool around with me. I mean—I mean, don't fool *around*," he said, shaking his head. He laughed incredulously. He placed his sunglasses on top of his head, carefully, as if he were indeed wearing a wig, and brought the stems down behind his ears. Connie stared at him, another wave of dizziness and fear rising in her so that for a moment he wasn't even in focus but was just a blur standing there against his gold car, and she had the idea that he had driven up the driveway all right but had come from nowhere before that and belonged nowhere and that everything about him and even about the music that was so familiar to her was only half real.

"If my father comes and sees you—"

"He ain't coming. He's at a barbecue."

"How do you know that?"

"Aunt Tillie's. Right now they're—uh—they're drinking. Sitting around," he said vaguely, squinting as if he were staring all the way to town and over to Aunt Tillie's back yard. Then the vision seemed to get clear and he nodded energetically. "Yeah. Sitting around. There's your sister in a blue dress, huh? And high heels, the poor sad bitch—nothing like you, sweetheart! And your mother's helping some fat woman with the corn, they're cleaning the corn—husking the corn—"

"What fat woman?" Connie cried.

"How do I know what fat woman, I don't know every goddamn fat woman in the world!" Arnold Friend laughed.

"Oh, that's Mrs. Hornsby. . . . Who invited her?" Connie said. She felt a little lightheaded. Her breath was coming quickly.

"She's too fat. I don't like them fat. I like them the way you are, honey," he said, smiling sleepily at her. They stared at each other for a while through the screen door. He said softly, "Now what you're going to do is this: you're going to come out that door. You're going to sit up front with me and Ellie's going to sit in the back, the hell with Ellie, right? This isn't Ellie's date. You're my date. I'm your lover, honey."

"What? You're crazy—"

"Yes, I'm your lover. You don't know what that is but you will," he said. "I know that too. I know all about you. But look: it's real nice and you couldn't ask for nobody better than me, or more polite. I always keep my word. I'll tell you how it is, I'm always nice at first, the first time. I'll hold you so tight you won't think you have to try to get away or pretend anything because you'll know you can't. And I'll come inside you where it's all secret and you'll give in to me and you'll love me—"

"Shut-up! You're crazy!" Connie said. She backed away from the door. She put her hands up against her ears as if she'd heard something terrible, something not meant for her. "People don't talk like that, you're crazy," she muttered. Her heart was almost too big now for her chest and its pumping made sweat break out all over her. She looked out to see Arnold Friend pause and then take a step toward the porch, lurching. He almost fell. But, like clever drunken man, he managed to catch his balance. He wobbled in his high boots and grabbed hold of one of the porch posts.

"Honey?" he said. "You still listening?"

"Get the hell out of here!"

"Be nice, honey. Listen."

"I'm going to call the police—"

He wobbled again and out of the side of his mouth came a fast spat curse, an aside not meant for her to hear. But even this "Christ!" sounded forced. Then he began to smile again. She watched this smile come, awkward as if he were smiling from inside a mask. His whole face was a mask, she thought wildly, tanned down to his throat but then running out as if he had plastered make-up on his face but had forgotten about his throat.

"Honey—? Listen, here's how it is. I always tell the truth and I promise you this: I ain't coming in that house after you."

"You better not! I'm going to call the police if you—if you don't—"

"Honey," he said, talking right through her voice, "honey, I'm not coming in there but you are coming out here. You know why?"

She was panting. The kitchen looked like a place she had never seen before, some room she had run inside but that wasn't good enough, wasn't going to help her. The kitchen window had never had a curtain, after three years, and there were dishes in the sink for her to do—probably—and if you ran your hand across the table you'd probably feel something sticky there.

"You listening, honey? Hey?"

"—going to call the police—"

"Soon as you touch the phone I don't need to keep my promise and can come inside. You won't want that."

She rushed forward and tried to lock the door. Her fingers were shaking. "But why lock it," Arnold Friend said gently, talking right into her face. "It's just a screen door. It's just nothing." One of his boots was at a strange angle, as if his foot wasn't in it. It pointed out to the left, bent at the ankle. "I mean, anybody can break through a screen door and glass and wood and iron or anything else if he needs to, anybody at all, and specially Arnold Friend. If the place got lit up with a fire, honey, you'd come runnin' out into my arms, right into my arms an' safe at home—like you knew I was your lover and'd stopped fooling around. I don't mind a nice shy girl but I don't like no fooling around." Part of those words were spoken with a slight rhythmic lilt, and Connie somehow recognized them—the echo of a song from last year, about a girl rushing into her boy friend's arms and coming home again—

Connie stood barefoot on the linoleum floor, staring at him. "What do you want?" she whispered.

"I want you," he said.

"What?"

"Seen you that night and thought, that's the one, yes sir. I never needed to look anymore."

"But my father's coming back. He's coming to get me. I had to wash my hair first—" She spoke in a dry, rapid voice, hardly raising it for him to hear.

"No, your daddy is not coming and yes, you had to wash your hair and you washed it for me. It's nice and shining and all for me. I thank you sweetheart," he said with a mock bow, but again he almost lost his balance. He had to bend and adjust his boots. Evidently his feet did not go all the way down; the boots must have been stuffed with something so that he would seem taller. Connie stared out at him and behind him at Ellie in the car, who seemed to be looking off toward Connie's right, into nothing. This Ellie said, pulling the words out of the air one after another as if he were just discovering them, "You want me to pull out the phone?"

"Shut your mouth and keep it shut," Arnold Friend said, his face red from bending over or maybe from embarrassment because Connie had seen his boots. "This ain't none of your business."

"What—what are you doing? What do you want?" Connie said. "If I call the police they'll get you, they'll arrest you—"

"Promise was not to come in unless you touch that phone, and I'll keep that promise," he said. He resumed his erect position and tried to force his shoulders back. He sounded like a hero in a movie, declaring something important. But he spoke too loudly and it was as if he were speaking to someone behind Connie. "I ain't made plans for coming in that house where I don't belong but just for you to come out to me, the way you should. Don't you know who I am?"

"You're crazy," she whispered. She backed away from the door but did not want to go into another part of the house, as if this would give him permission to come through the door. "What do you . . . you're crazy, you. . . . "

"Huh? What're you saying, honey?"

Her eyes darted everywhere in the kitchen. She could not remember what it was, this room.

"This is how it is, honey: you come out and we'll drive away, have a nice ride. But if you don't come out we're gonna wait till your people come home and then they're all going to get it."

"You want that telephone pulled out?" Ellie said. He held the radio away from his ear and grimaced, as if without the radio the air was too much for him.

"I toldja shut up, Ellie," Arnold Friend said, "you're deaf, get a hearing aid, right? Fix yourself up. This little girl's no trouble and's gonna be nice to me, so Ellie keep to yourself, this ain't your date—right? Don't hem in on me, don't hog, don't crush, don't bird dog, don't trail me," he said in a rapid, meaningless voice, as if he were running through all the expressions he'd learned but was no longer sure which of them was in style, then rushing on to new ones, making them up with his eyes closed. "Don't crawl under my fence, don't squeeze in my chipmunk hole, don't sniff my glue, suck my popsicle, keep your own greasy fingers on yourself!" He shaded his eyes and peered in at Connie, who was backed against the kitchen table. "Don't mind him, honey, he's just a creep. He's a dope. Right? I'm the boy for you and like I said, you come out here nice like a lady and give me your hand, and nobody else gets hurt, I mean, your nice old bald-headed daddy and your mummy and your sister in her high heels. Because listen: why bring them in this?"

"Leave me alone," Connie whispered.

"Hey, you know that old woman down the road, the one with the chickens and stuff—you know her?"

"She's dead!"

"Dead? What? You know her?" Arnold Friend said.

"She's dead—"

"Don't you like her?"

"She's dead—she's—she isn't here any more—"

"But don't you like her, I mean, you got something against her? Some grudge or something?" Then his voice dipped as if he were conscious of a rudeness. He touched the sunglasses perched up on top of his head as if to make sure they were still there. "Now, you be a good girl."

"What are you going to do?"

"Just two things, or maybe three," Arnold Friend said. "But I promise it won't last long and you'll like me the way you get to like people you're close to. You will. It's all over for you here, so come on out. You don't want your people in any trouble, do you?"

She turned and bumped against a chair or something, hurting her leg, but she ran into the back room and picked up the telephone. Something roared in her ear, a tiny roaring, and she was so sick with fear that she could do nothing but listen to it—the telephone was clammy and very heavy and her fingers groped down to the dial but were too weak to touch it. She began to scream into the phone, into the roaring. She cried out, she cried for her mother, she felt her breath start jerking back and forth in her lungs as if it were something Arnold Friend was stabbing her with again and again with no tenderness. A noisy sorrowful wailing rose all about her and she was locked inside it the way she was locked inside this house.

After a while she could hear again. She was sitting on the floor with her wet back against the wall.

Arnold Friend was saying from the door, "That's a good girl. Put the phone back."

She kicked the phone away from her.

"No, honey. Pick it up. Put it back right."

She picked it up and put it back. The dial tone stopped.

"That's a good girl. Now, you come outside."

She was hollow with what had been fear but what was now just an emptiness. All that screaming had blasted it out of her. She sat, one leg cramped under her, and deep inside her brain was something like a pinpoint of light that kept going and would not let her relax. She thought, I'm not going to see my mother again. She thought, I'm not going to sleep in my bed again. Her bright green blouse was all wet.

Arnold Friend said, in a gentle-loud voice that was like a stage voice, "The place where you came from ain't there any more, and where you had in mind to go is cancelled out. This place you are now—inside your daddy's house—is nothing but a cardboard box I can knock down any time. You know that and always did know it. You hear me?"

She thought, I have got to think. I have got to know what to do.

"We'll go out to a nice field, out in the country here where it smells so nice and it's sunny," Arnold Friend said. "I'll have my arms tight around you so you won't need to try to get away and I'll show you what love is like, what it does. The hell with this house! It looks solid all right," he said. He ran a fingernail down the screen and the noise did not make Connie shiver, as it would have the day before. "Now, put your hand on your heart, honey. Feel that? That feels solid too but we know better. Be nice to me, be sweet like you can because what else is there for a girl like you but to be sweet and pretty and give in?—and get away before her people come back?"

She felt her pounding heart. Her hand seemed to enclose it. She thought for the first time in her life that it was nothing that was hers, that belonged to her, but just a pounding, living thing inside this body that wasn't really hers either.

"You don't want them to get hurt," Arnold Friend went on. "Now, get up, honey. Get up all by yourself."

She stood.

"Now, turn this way. That's right. Come over here to me.—Ellie, put that away, didn't I tell you? You dope. You miserable creepy dope," Arnold Friend said. His words were not angry but only part of an incantation. The incantation was kindly. "Now, come out through the kitchen to me, honey, and let's see a smile, try it, you're a brave, sweet little girl and now they're eating corn and hot dogs cooked to bursting over an outdoor fire, and they don't know one thing about you and never did and honey, you're better than them because not a one of them would have done this for you."

Connie felt the linoleum under her feet; it was cool. She brushed her hair back out of her eyes. Arnold Friend let go of the post tentatively and opened his arms for her, his elbows pointing in toward each other and his wrists limp, to show that this was an embarrassed embrace and a little mocking, he didn't want to make her self-conscious.

1966

Alice Walker

(1944–   )

In a 1970 interview in *Library Journal*, Alice Walker described her writing about the relationship between forms of racism and the African-American family structure: "I was curious to know why people in families (specifically black families) are often cruel to each other and how much of this cruelty is caused by outside forces such as various social injustices, segregation, unemployment, etc." This fascination with violence and family gives Walker's work an added urgency in that forms of art—from quilting and sewing to the act of writing itself—become her characters' only means of finding spirituality and continuity in a deeply divided culture. As she writes in the essay "In Search of Our Mother's Gardens" (1983) of her mother's love of gardening, "her face, as she prepares the Art that is her gift, is a legacy of respect she leaves to me, for all that illuminates and cherishes life. She has handed down respect for the possibilities—and the will to grasp them."

Walker's own possibilities must have seemed particularly limited: born in 1944, she was the eighth and youngest child of Minnie Lou Grant and Willie Lee Walker, sharecroppers in Eatonton, Georgia. When Walker was eight, one of her brothers shot her with a BB gun, leaving her blind in one eye and feeling ugly and outcast, until the eye was healed in an operation when she was fourteen. Walker found her own ways to heal her spirit, writing poetry and keeping a private notebook as well as discovering an alternative world in the books her teachers lent her. She was awarded a "rehabilitation scholarship" from Georgia and attended Spelman College in Atlanta and Sarah Lawrence College in Bronxville, New York, in the 1960s during the height of the civil rights movement—a frightening but vital time that Walker celebrates in her early poems, her short stories, and her second novel, *Meridian* (1976). While at Sarah Lawrence, Walker became pregnant and grew increasingly suicidal, finding herself, as she said in an interview, "at the mercy of everything, including my body." Her rescue came in the release she found in her writing and in the community of women, from writers such as Virginia Woolf and Zora Neale Hurston to friends such as Muriel Rukeyser, a poet who shared Walker's horror at the restrictions that limited the lives of all women. Shortly after her graduation from Sarah Lawrence in 1965, Walker began to publish stories and poems. Marrying the civil rights attorney Melvyn Leventhal in 1967, she was faced with a new challenge: the harrassment she and her husband endured as an interracial couple in their new home, Mississippi.

Delineating the effects of racial and sexual restrictions led Walker to write what she has termed "womanist" works. Such works focus on the shared dangers of racism and sexism in the hope of going beyond the boundaries imposed on literature termed "feminist" or "African American" and of expressing the plight of a larger, more international community. From her first novel, *The Third Life of Grange Copeland* (1970), to her collections of short stories and poems, to her most recent successes—*The Color Purple* (1982), which won a Pulitzer Prize and an American Book Award, and the counter-myth *The Temple of My Familiar* (1989)—Walker's work explores the racial and sexual violence that combine to destroy the sense of self and traces networks of matriarchal and familial love, even self-love, that restore a sense of identity. Walker has also sought to restore and reshape our sense of a literary heritage, writing the biography *Langston Hughes, American Poet* (1974) and editing an anthology of Zora Neale Hurston's works, *I Love Myself When I Am Laughing* (1979). Remaining an active supporter for civil rights and speaking for such causes as the Woman's Party for Survival against nuclear weapons, Walker told an audience in 1982 that "only justice can stop a curse," and her writing actively seeks those forms of justice that can defeat the destructive curses of our society.

Suggested Readings: *The Third Life of Grange Copeland*, 1970. *Revolutionary Petunias & Other Poems*, 1973. *Meridian*, 1976. *The Color Purple*, 1982. *You Can't Keep a Good Woman Down*, 1982. *In Search of Our Mother's Gardens: Womanist Prose*, 1983. *Horses Make a Landscape Look More Beautiful: Poems*, 1986. *To Hell With Dying*, 1988. *The Temple of My Familiar*, 1989. T. Harris, "Folklore in the Fiction of Alice Walker," in *Black American Literature Forum*, 11, 1977. C. J. Fantenot, "Alice Walker, 'The Diary of an African Nun' and Du Bois' Double Consciousness," in *Sturdy Black Bridges: Visions of Black Women in Literature*, eds. R. Bell, B. Parker, and B. G. Sheftall, 1979. M. H. Washington, "An Essay on Alice Walker," in *Sturdy Black Bridges: Visions of Black Women in Literature*, eds. R. Bell, B. Parker, and B. G. Sheftall, 1979. D. McDowell, "The

Self in Bloom: Alice Walker's *Meridian*," in *College Language Association Journal*, 24, 1981. T. Harris, "Tiptoeing Through Taboo: Incest in 'The Child Who Favored Daughter,'" in *Modern Fiction Studies*, 28, (Autumn) 1982. B. Christian, "Alice Walker," in *Black Women Writers (1950–1980)*, ed. M. Evans, 1984.

Text Used: *In Love & Trouble: Stories of Black Women*, 1973.

EVERYDAY USE

for your grandmama

I will wait for her in the yard that Maggie and I made so clean and wavy yesterday afternoon. A yard like this is more comfortable than most people know. It is not just a yard. It is like an extended living room. When the hard clay is swept clean as a floor and the fine sand around the edges lined with tiny, irregular grooves, anyone can come and sit and look up into the elm tree and wait for the breezes that never come inside the house.

Maggie will be nervous until after her sister goes: she will stand hopelessly in corners, homely and ashamed of the burn scars down her arms and legs, eying her sister with a mixture of envy and awe. She thinks her sister has held life always in the palm of one hand, that "no" is a word the world never learned to say to her.

You've no doubt seen those TV shows[1] where the child who has "made it" is confronted, as a surprise, by her own mother and father, tottering in weakly from backstage. (A pleasant surprise, of course: What would they do if parent and child came on the show only to curse out and insult each other?) On TV mother and child embrace and smile into each other's faces. Sometimes the mother and father weep, the child wraps them in her arms and leans across the table to tell how she would not have made it without their help. I have seen these programs.

Sometimes I dream a dream in which Dee and I are suddenly brought together on a TV program of this sort. Out of a dark and soft-seated limousine I am ushered into a bright room filled with many people. There I meet a smiling, gray, sporty man like Johnny Carson who shakes my hand and tells me what a fine girl I have. Then we are on the stage and Dee is embracing me with tears in her eyes. She pins on my dress a large orchid, even though she has told me once that she thinks orchids are tacky flowers.

In real life I am a large, big-boned woman with rough, man-working hands. In the winter I wear flannel nightgowns to bed and overalls during the day. I can kill and clean a hog as mercilessly as a man. My fat keeps me hot in zero weather. I can work outside all day, breaking ice to get water for washing; I can eat pork liver cooked over the open fire minutes after it comes steaming from the hog. One winter I knocked a bull calf straight in the brain between the eyes with a sledge hammer and had the meat hung up to chill before nightfall. But of course all this does not show on television. I am the way my daughter would want me to be: a hundred pounds lighter, my skin like an uncooked barley pancake. My hair glis-

---

[1] *This Is Your Life*, hosted by Ralph Edwards, reunited friends, relatives, and people who influenced the guest star; it ran from 1952 to 1961 and 1970 to 1973.

tens in the hot bright lights. Johnny Carson has much to do to keep up with my quick and witty tongue.

But that is a mistake. I know even before I wake up. Who ever knew a Johnson with a quick tongue? Who can even imagine me looking a strange white man in the eye? It seems to me I have talked to them always with one foot raised in flight, with my head turned in whichever way is farthest from them. Dee, though. She would always look anyone in the eye. Hesitation was no part of her nature.

"How do I look, Mama?" Maggie says, showing just enough of her thin body enveloped in pink skirt and red blouse for me to know she's there, almost hidden by the door.

"Come out into the yard," I say.

Have you ever seen a lame animal, perhaps a dog run over by some careless person rich enough to own a car, sidle up to someone who is ignorant enough to be kind to him? That is the way my Maggie walks. She has been like this, chin on chest, eyes on ground, feet in shuffle, ever since the fire that burned the other house to the ground.

Dee is lighter than Maggie, with nicer hair and a fuller figure. She's a woman now, though sometimes I forget. How long ago was it that the other house burned? Ten, twelve years? Sometimes I can still hear the flames and feel Maggie's arms sticking to me, her hair smoking and her dress falling off her in little black papery flakes. Her eyes seemed stretched open, blazed open by the flames reflected in them. And Dee. I see her standing off under the sweet gum tree she used to dig gum out of; a look of concentration on her face as she watched the last dingy gray board of the house fall in toward the red-hot brick chimney. Why don't you do a dance around the ashes? I'd wanted to ask her. She had hated the house that much.

I used to think she hated Maggie, too. But that was before we raised the money, the church and me, to send her to Augusta[2] to school. She used to read to us without pity; forcing words, lies, other folks' habits, whole lives upon us two, sitting trapped and ignorant underneath her voice. She washed us in a river of make-believe, burned us with a lot of knowledge we didn't necessarily need to know. Pressed us to her with the serious way she read, to shove us away at just the moment, like dimwits, we seemed about to understand.

Dee wanted nice things. A yellow organdy dress to wear to her graduation from high school; black pumps to match a green suit she'd made from an old suit somebody gave me. She was determined to stare down any disaster in her efforts. Her eyelids would not flicker for minutes at a time. Often I fought off the temptation to shake her. At sixteen she had a style of her own: and knew what style was.

I never had an education myself. After second grade the school was closed down. Don't ask me why: in 1927 colored asked fewer questions than they do now. Sometimes Maggie reads to me. She stumbles along good-naturedly but can't see well. She knows she is not bright. Like good looks and money, quickness passed her by. She will marry John Thomas (who has mossy teeth in an earnest face) and then I'll be free to sit here and I guess just sing church songs to myself. Although I never was a good singer. Never could carry a tune. I was always better at a man's job. I used to love to milk till I was hooked[3] in the side in

---

[2] Augusta, Georgia, where Paine College is located.   [3] Kicked.

'49. Cows are soothing and slow and don't bother you, unless you try to milk them the wrong way.

I have deliberately turned my back on the house. It is three rooms, just like the one that burned, except the roof is tin; they don't make shingle roofs any more. There are no real windows, just some holes cut in the sides, like the portholes in a ship, but not round and not square, with rawhide holding the shutters up on the outside. This house is in a pasture, too, like the other one. No doubt when Dee sees it she will want to tear it down. She wrote me once that no matter where we "choose" to live, she will manage to come see us. But she will never bring her friends. Maggie and I thought about this and Maggie asked me, "Mama, when did Dee ever *have* any friends?"

She had a few. Furtive boys in pink shirts hanging about on washday after school. Nervous girls who never laughed. Impressed with her they worshiped the well-turned phrase, the cute shape, the scalding humor that erupted like bubbles in lye. She read to them.

When she was courting Jimmy T she didn't have much time to pay to us, but turned all her faultfinding power on him. He *flew* to marry a cheap city girl from a family of ignorant flashy people. She hardly had time to recompose herself.

When she comes I will meet—but there they are!

Maggie attempts to make a dash for the house, in her shuffling way, but I stay her with my hand. "Come back here," I say. And she stops and tries to dig a well in the sand with her toe.

It is hard to see them clearly through the strong sun. But even the first glimpse of leg out of the car tells me it is Dee. Her feet were always neat-looking, as if God himself had shaped them with a certain style. From the other side of the car comes a short, stocky man. Hair is all over his head a foot long and hanging from his chin like a kinky mule tail. I hear Maggie suck in her breath. "Uhnnnh," is what it sounds like. Like when you see the wriggling end of a snake just in front of your foot on the road. "Uhnnnh."

Dee next. A dress down to the ground, in this hot weather. A dress so loud it hurts my eyes. There are yellows and oranges enough to throw back the light of the sun. I feel my whole face warming from the heat waves it throws out. Earrings gold, too, and hanging down to her shoulders. Bracelets dangling and making noises when she moves her arm up to shake the folds of the dress out of her armpits. The dress is loose and flows, and as she walks closer, I like it. I hear Maggie go "Uhnnnh" again. It is her sister's hair. It stands straight up like the wool on a sheep. It is black as night and around the edges are two long pigtails that rope about like small lizards disappearing behind her ears.

"Wa-su-zo-Tean-o!"[4] she says, coming on in that gliding way the dress makes her move. The short stocky fellow with the hair to his navel is all grinning and he follows up with "Asalamalakim,[5] my mother and sister!" He moves to hug Maggie but she falls back, right up against the back of my chair. I feel her trembling there and when I look up I see the perspiration falling off her chin.

"Don't get up," says Dee. Since I am stout it takes something of a push. You can see me trying to move a second or two before I make it. She turns, showing white heels through her sandals, and goes back to the car. Out she peeks next with a Polaroid. She stoops down quickly and lines up picture after picture of me sitting

---

[4] A Swahili greeting, used by Black Muslims.   [5] "Peace be with you" (Arabic).

there in front of the house with Maggie cowering behind me. She never takes a shot without making sure the house is included. When a cow comes nibbling around the edge of the yard she snaps it and me and Maggie *and* the house. Then she puts the Polaroid in the back seat of the car, and comes up and kisses me on the forehead.

Meanwhile Asalamalakim is going through motions with Maggie's hand. Maggie's hand is as limp as a fish, and probably as cold, despite the sweat, and she keeps trying to pull it back. It looks like Asalamalakim wants to shake hands but wants to do it fancy. Or maybe he don't know how people shake hands. Anyhow, he soon gives up on Maggie.

"Well," I say. "Dee."

"No, Mama," she says. "Not 'Dee,' Wangero Leewanika Kemanjo!"

"What happened to 'Dee'?" I wanted to know.

"She's dead," Wangero said. "I couldn't bear it any longer, being named after the people who oppress me."

"You know as well as me you was named after your aunt Dicie," I said. Dicie is my sister. She named Dee. We called her "Big Dee" after Dee was born.

"But who was *she* named after?" asked Wangero.

"I guess after Grandma Dee," I said.

"And who was she named after?" asked Wangero.

"Her mother," I said, and saw Wangero was getting tired. "That's about as far back as I can trace it," I said. Though, in fact, I probably could have carried it back beyond the Civil War through the branches.

"Well," said Asalamalakim, "there you are."

"Uhnnnh," I heard Maggie say.

"There I was not," I said, "before 'Dicie' cropped up in our family, so why should I try to trace it that far back?"

He just stood there grinning, looking down on me like somebody inspecting a Model A car.[6] Every once in a while he and Wangero sent eye signals over my head.

"How do you pronounce this name?" I asked.

"You don't have to call me by it if you don't want to," said Wangero.

"Why shouldn't I?" I asked. "If that's what you want us to call you, we'll call you."

"I know it might sound awkward at first," said Wangero.

"I'll get used to it," I said. "Ream it out again."

Well, soon we got the name out of the way. Asalamalakim had a name twice as long and three times as hard. After I tripped over it two or three times he told me to just call him Hakim-a-barber. I wanted to ask him was he a barber, but I didn't really think he was, so I didn't ask.

"You must belong to those beef-cattle peoples down the road," I said. They said "Asalamalakim" when they met you, too, but they didn't shake hands. Always too busy: feeding the cattle, fixing the fences, putting up salt-lick shelters,[7] throwing down hay. When the white folks poisoned some of the herd the men stayed up all night with rifles in their hands. I walked a mile and a half just to see the sight.

---

[6] A low-priced, durable car introduced by the Ford Motor Company in 1927; it replaced the Model T.
[7] Shelters to keep salt blocks, given to cattle in hot weather, from dissolving in rain.

Hakim-a-barber said, "I accept some of their doctrines, but farming and raising cattle is not my style." (They didn't tell me, and I didn't ask, whether Wangero (Dee) had really gone and married him.)

We sat down to eat and right away he said he didn't eat collards and pork was unclean. Wangero, though, went on through the chitlins and corn bread, the greens and everything else. She talked a blue streak over the sweet potatoes. Everything delighted her. Even the fact that we still used the benches her daddy made for the table when we couldn't afford to buy chairs.

"Oh, Mama!" she cried. Then turned to Hakim-a-barber. "I never knew how lovely these benches are. You can feel the rump prints," she said, running her hands underneath her and along the bench. Then she gave a sigh and her hand closed over Grandma Dee's butter dish. "That's it!" she said. "I knew there was something I wanted to ask you if I could have." She jumped up from the table and went over in the corner where the churn stood, the milk in it clabber[8] by now. She looked at the churn and looked at it.

"This churn top is what I need," she said. "Didn't Uncle Buddy whittle it out of a tree you all used to have?"

"Yes," I said.

"Uh huh," she said happily. "And I want the dasher, too."

"Uncle Buddy whittle that, too?" asked the barber.

Dee (Wangero) looked up at me.

"Aunt Dee's first husband whittled the dash," said Maggie so low you almost couldn't hear her. "His name was Henry, but they called him Stash."

"Maggie's brain is like an elephant's," Wangero said, laughing. "I can use the churn top as a centerpiece for the alcove table," she said, sliding a plate over the churn, "and I'll think of something artistic to do with the dasher."[9]

When she finished wrapping the dasher the handle stuck out. I took it for a moment in my hands. You didn't even have to look close to see where hands pushing the dasher up and down to make butter had left a kind of sink in the wood. In fact, there were a lot of small sinks; you could see where thumbs and fingers had sunk into the wood. It was beautiful light yellow wood, from a tree that grew in the yard where Big Dee and Stash had lived.

After dinner Dee (Wangero) went to the trunk at the foot of my bed and started rifling through it. Maggie hung back in the kitchen over the dishpan. Out came Wangero with two quilts. They had been pieced by Grandma Dee and then Big Dee and me had hung them on the quilt frames on the front porch and quilted them. One was in the Lone Star pattern. The other was Walk Around the Mountain. In both of them were scraps of dresses Grandma Dee had worn fifty and more years ago. Bits and pieces of Grandpa Jarrell's Paisley shirts. And one teeny faded blue piece, about the size of a penny matchbox, that was from Great Grandpa Ezra's uniform that he wore in the Civil War.

"Mama," Wangero said sweet as a bird. "Can I have these old quilts?"

I heard something fall in the kitchen, and a minute later the kitchen door slammed.

"Why don't you take one or two of the others?" I asked. "These old things was just done by me and Big Dee from some tops your grandma pieced before she died."

---

[8] Sour, curdled.   [9] The part of the churn that agitates.

"No," said Wangero. "I don't want those. They are stitched around the borders by machine."

"That'll make them last better," I said.

"That's not the point," said Wangero. "These are all pieces of dresses Grandma used to wear. She did all this stitching by hand. Imagine!" She held the quilts securely in her arms, stroking them.

"Some of the pieces, like those lavender ones, come from old clothes her mother handed down to her," I said, moving up to touch the quilts. Dee (Wangero) moved back just enough so that I couldn't reach the quilts. They already belonged to her.

"Imagine!" she breathed again, clutching them closely to her bosom.

"The truth is," I said, "I promised to give them quilts to Maggie, for when she marries John Thomas."

She gasped like a bee had stung her.

"Maggie can't appreciate these quilts!" she said. "She'd probably be backward enough to put them to everyday use."

"I reckon she would," I said. "God knows I been saving 'em for long enough with nobody using 'em. I hope she will!" I didn't want to bring up how I had offered Dee (Wangero) a quilt when she went away to college. Then she had told me they were old-fashioned, out of style.

"But they're *priceless!*" she was saying now, furiously; for she has a temper. "Maggie would put them on the bed and in five years they'd be in rags. Less than that!"

"She can always make some more," I said. "Maggie knows how to quilt."

Dee (Wangero) looked at me with hatred. "You just will not understand. The point is these quilts, *these* quilts!"

"Well," I said, stumped. "What would *you* do with them?"

"Hang them," she said. As if that was the only thing you *could* do with quilts.

Maggie by now was standing in the door. I could almost hear the sound her feet made as they scraped over each other.

"She can have them, Mama," she said, like somebody used to never winning anything, or having anything reserved for her. "I can 'member Grandma Dee without the quilts."

I looked at her hard. She had filled her bottom lip with checkerberry[10] snuff and it gave her face a kind of dopey, hangdog look. It was Grandma Dee and Big Dee who taught her how to quilt herself. She stood there with her scarred hands hidden in the folds of her skirt. She looked at her sister with something like fear but she wasn't mad at her. This was Maggie's portion. This was the way she knew God to work.

When I looked at her like that something hit me in the top of my head and ran down to the soles of my feet. Just like when I'm in church and the spirit of God touches me and I get happy and shout. I did something I never had done before: hugged Maggie to me, then dragged her on into the room, snatched the quilts out of Miss Wangero's hands and dumped them into Maggie's lap. Maggie just sat there on my bed with her mouth open.

"Take one or two of the others," I said to Dee.

But she turned without a word and went out to Hakim-a-barber.

"You just don't understand," she said, as Maggie and I came out to the car.

---

[10] From the wintergreen bush.

"What don't I understand?" I wanted to know.

"Your heritage," she said. And then she turned to Maggie, kissed her, and said, "You ought to try to make something of yourself, too, Maggie. It's really a new day for us. But from the way you and Mama still live you'd never know it."

She put on some sunglasses that hid everything above the tip of her nose and her chin.

Maggie smiled; maybe at the sunglasses. But a real smile, not scared. After we watched the car dust settle I asked Maggie to bring me a dip of snuff. And then the two of us sat there just enjoying, until it was time to go in the house and go to bed.

1973

Leslie Marmon Silko
(1948–   )

Leslie Marmon was raised in the Native-American settlement of Laguna Pueblo, New Mexico, near Albuquerque, where she was born in 1948. She has sought to capture in her work the stories and traditions that bind a people into a community. Of mixed Native-American, Mexican, and Caucasian origin, she attended Bureau of Indian Affairs Schools and married John Silko, an attorney. In 1969 she graduated *magna cum laude* from the University of New Mexico. Silko spent more than a year in law school before she decided to obtain a graduate degree in English and to pursue a career as a writer. She has taught at Navajo Community College in Arizona, and the universities of Washington and New Mexico. She is the recipient of a National Endowment for the Humanities Award and a Mac-Arthur Foundation Fellowship. Now divorced from her husband, Silko is the mother of two sons.

Silko published a volume of poetry, *Laguna Woman,* in 1974 but first came to national attention when her short story "Lullaby" was included in *The Best Short Stories of 1975.* Typical of her fiction, "Lullaby" mixes prose and poetry, traditional Navajo myth, and the all-too-real modern conditions of Native Americans. The story explores the ways in which a community and its attendant legends can empower the dispossessed. In the narrative *Ceremony* (1977) her protagonist, Tayo, escapes madness and death through a healing ceremony taught to him by an old medicine man and a young Laguna woman. Tayo, a half-breed Laguna Indian, returns home from World War II shattered by his experience as a Japanese prisoner of war and alienated from his family and from the white world of his soldiering. Only by embracing the traditional widsom of his tribe and learning to live with "great patience and love" does Tayo come to feel himself at one with the elements of his world and with the members of his tribe.

Storyteller (1981) combines narrative with verse and includes twenty-six photographs from Silko's father's and grandfather's lifetime collections. As Silko explains in the book, the photographs are "part of many of the stories, and . . . many of the stories can be traced in the photographs." Mixing traditional legends with stories of modern Native Americans, *Storyteller* charts the movement of stories and storytelling across generations and among Native-American and Anglo cultures. The book juxtaposes the myths of Corn

Woman and Buffalo Man with the history of Silko's Grandpa Hank. As always, the strength of Silko's communities is found in the power of her stories.

Suggested Readings: *Laguna Woman*, 1974. *Ceremony*, 1977. *The Delicacy and Strength of Lace*, ed. A. Wright, 1986. E. Bicksilver, "Traditionalism vs. Modernity: Leslie Silko on American Indian Women," in *Southwest Review*, 64:2, 1979. A. L. Ruoff, "Ritual and Renewal: Keres Traditions in the Short Fiction of Leslie Silko," in *MELUS*, 5, 1979. D. Fisher, "Stories and Their Tellers—A Conversation With Leslie Marmon Silko," in *The Third Woman: Minority Women Writers of the United States*, 1980. P. Seyersted, *Leslie Marmon Silko*, 1980. J. Ruppert, "Story Telling: The Fiction of Leslie Silko," in *The Journal of Ethnic Studies*, 9:1, 1981.

Text Used: *Storyteller*, 1981.

STORYTELLER

Every day the sun came up a little lower on the horizon, moving more slowly until one day she got excited and started calling the jailer. She realized she had been sitting there for many hours, yet the sun had not moved from the center of the sky. The color of the sky had not been good lately; it had been pale blue, almost white, even when there were no clouds. She told herself it wasn't a good sign for the sky to be indistinguishable from the river ice, frozen solid and white against the earth. The tundra rose up behind the river but all the boundaries between the river and hills and sky were lost in the density of the pale ice.

She yelled again, this time some English words which came randomly into her mouth, probably swear words she'd heard from the oil drilling crews last winter. The jailer was an Eskimo, but he would not speak Yupik[1] to her. She had watched people in other cells, when they spoke to him in Yupik he ignored them until they spoke English.

He came and stared at her. She didn't know if he understood what she was telling him until he glanced behind her at the small high window. He looked at the sun, and turned and walked away. She could hear the buckles on his heavy snowmobile boots jingle as he walked to the front ot the building.

It was like the other buildings that white people, the Gussucks, brought with them: BIA[2] and school buildings, portable buildings that arrived sliced in halves, on barges coming up the river. Squares of metal panelling bulged out with the layers of insulation stuffed inside. She had asked once what it was and someone told her it was to keep out the cold. She had not laughed then, but she did now. She walked over to the small double-pane window and she laughed out loud. They thought they could keep out the cold with stringy yellow wadding. Look at the sun. It wasn't moving; it was frozen, caught in the middle of the sky. Look at the sky, solid as the river with ice which had trapped the sun. It had not moved for a long time; in a few more hours it would be weak, and heavy frost would begin to appear on the edges and spread across the face of the sun like a mask. Its light was pale yellow, worn thin by the winter.

She could see people walking down the snow-packed roads, their breath steaming out from their parka hoods, faces hidden and protected by deep ruffs of fur.

[1] An Eskimo-Aleut language used throughout arctic America from western Alaska to Greenland.
[2] The Bureau of Indian Affairs.

There were no cars or snowmobiles that day; the cold had silenced their machines. The metal froze; it split and shattered. Oil hardened and moving parts jammed solidly. She had seen it happen to their big yellow machines and the giant drill last winter when they came to drill their test holes. The cold stopped them, and they were helpless against it.

Her village was many miles upriver from this town, but in her mind she could see it clearly. Their house was not near the village houses. It stood alone on the bank upriver from the village. Snow had drifted to the eaves of the roof on the north side, but on the west side, by the door, the path was almost clear. She had nailed scraps of red tin over the logs last summer. She had done it for the bright red color, not for added warmth the way the village people had done. This final winter had been coming even then; there had been signs of its approach for many years.

She went because she was curious about the big school where the Government sent all the other girls and boys. She had not played much with the village children while she was growing up because they were afraid of the old man, and they ran when her grandmother came. She went because she was tired of being alone with the old woman whose body had been stiffening for as long as the girl could remember. Her knees and knuckles were swollen grotesquely, and the pain had squeezed the brown skin of her face tight against the bones; it left her eyes hard like river stone. The girl asked once what it was that did this to her body, and the old woman had raised up from sewing a sealskin boot, and stared at her.

"The joints," the old woman said in a low voice, whispering like wind across the roof, "the joints are swollen with anger."

Sometimes she did not answer and only stared at the girl. Each year she spoke less and less, but the old man talked more—all night sometimes, not to anyone but himself; in a soft deliberate voice, he told stories, moving his smooth brown hands above the blankets. He had not fished or hunted with the other men for many years, although he was not crippled or sick. He stayed in his bed, smelling like dry fish and urine, telling stories all winter; and when warm weather came, he went to his place on the river bank. He sat with a willow stick, poking at the smoldering moss he burned against the insects while he continued with the stories.

The trouble was that she had not recognized the warnings in time. She did not see what the Gussuck school would do to her until she walked into the dormitory and realized that the old man had not been lying about the place. She thought he had been trying to scare her as he used to when she was very small and her grandmother was outside cutting up fish. She hadn't believed what he told her about the school because she knew he wanted to keep her there in the log house with him. She knew what he wanted.

The dormitory matron pulled down her underpants and whipped her with a leather belt because she refused to speak English.

"Those backwards village people," the matron said, because she was an Eskimo who had worked for the BIA a long time, "they kept this one until she was too big to learn." The other girls whispered in English. They knew how to work the showers, and they washed and curled their hair at night. They ate Gussuck food. She lay on her bed and imagined what her grandmother might be sewing, and what the old man was eating in his bed. When summer came, they sent her home.

The way her grandmother had hugged her before she left for school had been a warning too, because the old woman had not hugged or touched her for many years. Not like the old man, whose hands were always hunting, like ravens circling lazily in the sky, ready to touch her. She was not surprised when the priest and the old man met her at the landing strip, to say that the old lady was gone. The priest asked her where she would like to stay. He referred to the old man as her grandfather, but she did not bother to correct him. She had already been thinking about it; if she went with the priest, he would send her away to a school. But the old man was different. She knew he wouldn't send her back to school. She knew he wanted to keep her.

He told her one time, that she would get too old for him faster than he got too old for her; but again she had not believed him because sometimes he lied. He had lied about what he would do with her if she came into his bed. But as the years passed, she realized what he said was true. She was restless and strong. She had no patience with the old man who had never changed his slow smooth motions under the blankets.

The old man was in his bed for the winter; he did not leave it except to use the slop bucket in the corner. He was dozing with his mouth open slightly; his lips quivered and sometimes they moved like he was telling a story even while he dreamed. She pulled on the sealskin boots, the mukluks with the bright red flannel linings her grandmother had sewn for her, and she tied the braided red yarn tassels around her ankles over the gray wool pants. She zipped the wolfskin parka. Her grandmother had worn it for many years, but the old man said that before she died, she instructed him to bury her in an old black sweater, and to give the parka to the girl. The wolf pelts were creamy colored and silver, almost white in some places, and when the old lady had walked across the tundra in the winter, she was invisible in the snow.

She walked toward the village, breaking her own path through the deep snow. A team of sled dogs tied outside a house at the edge of the village leaped against their chains to bark at her. She kept walking, watching the dusky sky for the first evening stars. It was warm and the dogs were alert. When it got cold again, the dogs would lie curled and still, too drowsy from the cold to bark or pull at the chains. She laughed loudly because it made them howl and snarl. Once the old man had seen her tease the dogs and he shook his head. "So that's the kind of woman you are," he said, "in the wintertime the two of us are no different from those dogs. We wait in the cold for someone to bring us a few dry fish."

She laughed out loud again, and kept walking. She was thinking about the Gussuck oil drillers. They were strange; they watched her when she walked near their machines. She wondered what they looked like underneath their quilted goosedown trousers; she wanted to know how they moved. They would be something different from the old man.

The old man screamed at her. He shook her shoulders so violently that her head bumped against the log wall. "I smelled it!" he yelled, "as soon as I woke up! I am sure of it now. You can't fool me!" His thin legs were shaking inside the baggy wool trousers; he stumbled over her boots in his bare feet. His toenails were long and yellow like bird claws; she had seen a gray crane last summer fighting another in the shallow water on the edge of the river. She laughed out loud and pulled her shoulder out of his grip. He stood in front of her. He was breathing hard and shaking; he looked weak. He would probably die next winter.

"I'm warning you," he said, "I'm warning you." He crawled back into his bunk then, and reached under the old soiled feather pillow for a piece of dry fish. He lay back on the pillow, staring at the ceiling and chewed dry stips of salmon. "I don't know what the old woman told you," he said, "but there will be trouble." He looked over to see if she was listening. His face suddenly relaxed into a smile, his dark slanty eyes were lost in wrinkles of brown skin. "I could tell you, but you are too good for warnings now. I can smell what you did all night with the Gussucks."

She did not understand why they came there, because the village was small and so far upriver that even some Eskimos who had been away to school did not want to come back. They stayed downriver in the town. They said the village was too quiet. They were used to the town where the boarding school was located, with electric lights and running water. After all those years away at school, they had forgotten how to set nets in the river and where to hunt seals in the fall. When she asked the old man why the Gussucks bothered to come to the village, his narrow eyes got bright with excitement.

"They only come when there is something to steal. The fur animals are too difficult for them to get now, and the seals and fish are hard to find. Now they come for oil deep in the earth. But this is the last time for them." His breathing was wheezy and fast; his hands gestured in the sky. "It is approaching. As it comes, ice will push across the sky." His eyes were open wide and he stared at the low ceiling rafters for hours without blinking. She remembered all this clearly because he began the story that day, the story he told from that time on. It began with a giant bear which he described muscle by muscle, from the curve of the ivory claws to the whorls of hair at the top of the massive skull. And for eight days he did not sleep, but talked continuously of the giant bear whose color was pale blue glacier ice.

The snow was dirty and worn down in a path to the door. On either side of the path, the snow was higher than her head. In front of the door there were jagged yellow stains melted into the snow where men had urinated. She stopped in the entry way and kicked the snow off her boots. The room was dim; a kerosene lantern by the cash register was burning low. The long wooden shelves were jammed with cans of beans and potted meats. On the bottom shelf a jar of mayonnaise was broken open, leaking oily white clots on the floor. There was no one in the room except the yellowish dog sleeping in front of the long glass display case. A reflection made it appear to be lying on the knives and ammunition inside the case. Gussucks kept dogs inside their houses with them; they did not seem to mind the odors which seeped out of the dogs. "They tell us we are dirty for the food we eat—raw fish and fermented meat. But we do not live with dogs," the old man once said. She heard voices in the back room, and the sound of bottles set down hard on the tables.

They were always confident. The first year they waited for the ice to break up on the river, and then they brought their big yellow machines up river on barges. They planned to drill their test holes during the summer to avoid the freezing. But the imprints and graves of their machines were still there, on the edge of the tundra above the river, where the summer mud had swallowed them before they ever left sight of the river. The village people had gathered to watch the white men, and to laugh as they drove the giant machines, one by one, off the steel ramp into the bogs; as if sheer numbers of vehicles would somehow make the tundra solid. But the old man said they behaved like desperate people, and they would come back again. When the tundra was frozen solid, they returned.

Village women did not even look through the door to the back room. The priest had warned them. The storeman was watching her because he didn't let Eskimos or Indians sit down at the tables in the back room. But she knew he couldn't throw her out if one of the Gussuck customers invited her to sit with him. She walked across the room. They stared at her, but she had the feeling she was walking for someone else, not herself, so their eyes did not matter. The red-haired man pulled out a chair and motioned for her to sit down. She looked back at the storeman while the red-haired man poured her a glass of red sweet wine. She wanted to laugh at the storeman the way she laughed at the dogs, straining against the chains, howling at her.

The red-haired man kept talking to the other Gussucks sitting around the table, but he slid one hand off the top of the table to her thighs. She looked over at the storeman to see if he was still watching her. She laughed out loud at him and the red-haired man stopped talking and turned to her. He asked if she wanted to go. She nodded and stood up.

Someone in the village had been telling him things about her, he said as they walked down the road to his trailer. She understood that much of what he was saying, but the rest she did not hear. The whine of the big generators at the construction camp sucked away the sound of his words. But English was of no concern to her anymore, and neither was anything the Christians in the village might say about her or the old man. She smiled at the effect of the subzero air on the electric lights around the trailers; they did not shine. They left only flat yellow holes in the darkness.

It took him a long time to get ready, even after she had undressed for him. She waited in the bed with the blankets pulled close, watching him. He adjusted the thermostat and lit candles in the room, turning out the electric lights. He searched through a stack of record albums until he found the right one. She was not sure about the last thing he did: he taped something on the wall behind the bed where he could see it while he lay on top of her. He was shriveled and white from the cold; he pushed against her body for warmth. He guided her hands to his thighs; he was shivering.

She had returned a last time because she wanted to know what it was he stuck on the wall above the bed. After he finished each time, he reached up and pulled it loose, folding it carefully so that she could not see it. But this time she was ready; she waited for his fast breathing and sudden collapse on top of her. She slid out from under him and stood up beside the bed. She looked at the picture while she got dressed. He did not raise his face from the pillow, and she thought she heard teeth rattling together as she left the room.

She heard the old man move when she came in. After the Gussuck's trailer, the log house felt cool. It smelled like dry fish and cured meat. The room was dark except for the blinking yellow flame in the mica[3] window of the oil stove. She

---

[3] A mineral that crystallizes into thin, transparent sheets.

squatted in front of the stove and watched the flames for a long time before she walked to the bed where her grandmother had slept. The bed was covered with a mound of rags and fur scraps the old woman had saved. She reached into the mound until she felt something cold and solid wrapped in a wool blanket. She pushed her fingers around it until she felt smooth stone. Long ago, before the Gussucks came, they had burned whale oil in the big stone lamp which made light and heat as well. The old woman had saved everything they would need when the time came.

In the morning, the old man pulled a piece of dry caribou meat from under the blankets and offered it to her. While she was gone, men from the village had brought a bundle of dry meat. She chewed it slowly, thinking about the way they still came from the village to take care of the old man and his stories. But she had a story now, about the red-haired Gussuck. The old man knew what she was thinking, and his smile made his face seem more round than it was.

"Well," he said, "what was it?"

"A woman with a big dog on top of her."

He laughed softly to himself and walked over to the water barrel. He dipped the tin cup into the water.

"It doesn't surprise me," he said.

"Grandma," she said, "there was something red in the grass that morning. I remember." She had not asked about her parents before. The old woman stopped splitting the fish bellies open for the willow drying racks. Her jaw muscles pulled so tightly against her skull, the girl thought the old woman would not be able to speak.

"They bought a tin can full of it from the storeman. Late at night. He told them it was alcohol safe to drink. They traded a rifle for it." The old woman's voice sounded like each word stole strength from her. "It made no difference about the rifle. That year the Gussuck boats had come, firing big guns at the walrus and seals. There was nothing left to hunt after that anyway. So," the old lady said, in a low soft voice the girl had not heard for a long time, "I didn't say anything to them when they left that night."

"Right over there," she said, pointing at the fallen poles, half buried in the river sand and tall grass, "in the summer shelter. The sun was high half the night then. Early in the morning when it was still low, the policeman came around. I told the interpreter to tell him that the storeman had poisoned them." She made outlines in the air in front of her, showing how their bodies lay twisted on the sand; telling the story was like laboring to walk through deep snow; sweat shone in the white hair around her forehead. "I told the priest too, after he came. I told him the storeman lied." She turned away from the girl. She held her mouth even tighter, set solidly, not in sorrow or anger, but against the pain, which was all that remained. "I never believed," she said, "not much anyway. I wasn't surprised when the priest did nothing."

The wind came off the river and folded the tall grass into itself like river waves. She could feel the silence the story left, and she wanted to have the old woman go on.

"I heard sounds that night, grandma. Sounds like someone was singing. It was light outside. I could see something red on the ground." The old woman did not answer her; she moved to the tub full of fish on the ground beside the workbench.

She stabbed her knife into the belly of a whitefish and lifted it onto the bench. "The Gussuck storeman left the village right after that," the old woman said as she pulled the entrails from the fish, "otherwise, I could tell you more." The old woman's voice flowed with the wind blowing off the river; they never spoke of it again.

When the willows got their leaves and the grass grew tall along the river banks and around the sloughs, she walked early in the morning. While the sun was still low on the horizon, she listened to the wind off the river; its sound was like the voice that day long ago. In the distance, she could hear the engines of the machinery the oil drillers had left the winter before, but she did not go near the village or the store. The sun never left the sky and the summer became the same long day, with only the winds to fan the sun into brightness or allow it to slip into twilight.

She sat beside the old man at his place on the river bank. She poked the smoky fire for him, and felt herself growing wide and thin in the sun as if she had been split from belly to throat and strung on the willow pole in preparation for the winter to come. The old man did not speak anymore. When men from the village brought him fresh fish he hid them deep in the river grass where it was cool. After he went inside, she split the fish open and spread them to dry on the willow frame the way the old woman had done. Inside, he dozed and talked to himself. He had talked all winter, softly and incessantly, about the giant polar bear stalking a lone hunter across Bering Sea ice. After all the months the old man had been telling the story, the bear was within a hundred feet of the man; but the ice fog had closed in on them now and the man could only smell the sharp ammonia odor of the bear, and hear the edge of the snow crust crack under the giant paws.

One night she listened to the old man tell the story all night in his sleep, describing each crystal of ice and the slightly different sounds they made under each paw; first the left and then the right paw, then the hind feet. Her grandmother was there suddenly, a shadow around the stove. She spoke in her low wind voice and the girl was afraid to sit up to hear more clearly. Maybe what she said had been to the old man because he stopped telling the story and began to snore softly the way he had long ago when the old woman had scolded him for telling his stories while others in the house were trying to sleep. But the last words she heard clearly: "It will take a long time, but the story must be told. There must not be any lies." She pulled the blankets up around her chin, slowly, so that her movements would not be seen. She thought her grandmother was talking about the old man's bear story; she did not know about the other story then.

She left the old man wheezing and snoring in his bed. She walked through river grass glistening with frost; the bright green summer color was already fading. She watched the sun move across the sky, already lower on the horizon, already moving away from the village. She stopped by the fallen poles of the summer shelter where her parents had died. Frost glittered on the river sand too; in a few more weeks there would be snow. The predawn light would be the color of an old woman. An old woman sky full of snow. There had been something red lying on the ground the morning they died. She looked for it again, pushing aside the grass with her foot. She knelt in the sand and looked under the fallen structure for some trace of it. When she found it, she would know what the old woman had never told her. She squatted down close to the gray poles and leaned her back against them. The wind made her shiver.

The summer rain had washed the mud from between the logs; the sod blocks stacked as high as her belly next to the log walls had lost their square-cut shape and had grown into soft mounds of tundra moss and stiff-bladed grass bending with clusters of seed bristles. She looked at the northwest, in the direction of the Bering Sea. The cold would come down from there to find narrow slits in the mud, rainwater holes in the outer layer of sod which protected the log house. The dark green tundra stretched away flat and continuous. Somewhere the sea and the land met; she knew by their dark green colors there were no boundaries between them. That was how the cold would come: when the boundaries were gone the polar ice would range across the land into the sky. She watched the horizon for a long time. She would stand in that place on the north side of the house and she would keep watch on the northwest horizon, and eventually she would see it come. She would watch for its approach in the stars, and hear it come with the wind. These preparations were unfamiliar, but gradually she recognized them as she did her own footprints in the snow.

She emptied the slop jar beside his bed twice a day and kept the barrel full of water melted from river ice. He did not recognize her anymore, and when he spoke to her, he called her by her grandmother's name and talked about people and events from long ago, before he went back to telling the story. The giant bear was creeping across the new snow on its belly, close enough now that the man could hear the rasp of its breathing. On and on in a soft singing voice, the old man caressed the story, repeating the words again and again like gentle strokes.

The sky was gray like a river crane's egg; its density curved into the thin crust of frost already covering the land. She looked at the bright red color of the tin against the ground and the sky and she told the village men to bring the pieces for the old man and her. To drill the test holes in the tundra, the Gussucks had used hundreds of barrels of fuel. The village people split open the empty barrels that were abandoned on the river bank, and pounded the red tin into flat sheets. The village people were using the strips of tin to mend walls and roofs for winter. But she nailed it on the log walls for its color. When she finished, she walked away with the hammer in her hand, not turning around until she was far away, on the ridge above the river banks, and then she looked back. She felt a chill when she saw how the sky and the land were already losing their boundaries, already becoming lost in each other. But the red tin penetrated the thick white color of earth and sky; it defined the boundaries like a wound revealing the ribs and heart of a great caribou about to bolt and be lost to the hunter forever. That night the wind howled and when she scratched a hole through the heavy frost on the inside of the window, she could see nothing but the impenetrable white; whether it was blowing snow or snow that had drifted as high as the house, she did not know.

It had come down suddenly, and she stood with her back to the wind looking at the river, its smoky water clotted with ice. The wind had blown the snow over the frozen river, hiding thin blue streaks where fast water ran under ice translucent and fragile as memory. But she could see shadows of boundaries, outlines of paths which were slender branches of solidity reaching out from the earth. She spent days walking on the river, watching the colors of ice that would safely hold her, kicking the heel of her boot into the snow crust, listening for a solid sound. When she could feel the paths through the soles of her feet, she went to the middle of the river where the fast gray water churned under a thin pane of ice. She looked back.

On the river bank in the distance she could see the red tin nailed to the log house, something not swallowed up by the heavy white belly of the sky or caught in the folds of the frozen earth. It was time.

The wolverine fur around the hood of her parka was white with the frost from her breathing. The warmth inside the store melted it, and she felt tiny drops of water on her face. The storeman came in from the back room. She unzipped the parka and stood by the oil stove. She didn't look at him, but stared instead at the yellowish dog, covered with scabs of matted hair, sleeping in front of the stove. She thought of the Gussuck's picture, taped on the wall above the bed and she laughed out loud. The sound of her laughter was piercing; the yellow dog jumped to its feet and the hair bristled down its back. The storeman was watching her. She wanted to laugh again because he didn't know about the ice. He did not know that it was prowling the earth, or that it had already pushed its way into the sky to seize the sun. She sat down in the chair by the stove and shook her long hair loose. He was like a dog tied up all winter, watching while the others got fed. He remembered how she had gone with the oil drillers, and his blue eyes moved like flies crawling over her body. He held his thin pale lips like he wanted to spit on her. He hated the people because they had something of value, the old man said, something which the Gussucks could never have. They thought they could take it, suck it out of the earth or cut it from the mountains; but they were fools.

There was a matted hunk of dog hair on the floor by her foot. She thought of the yellow insulation coming unstuffed: their defense against the freezing going to pieces as it advanced on them. The ice was crouching on the northwest horizon like the old man's bear. She laughed out loud again. The sun would be down now; it was time.

The first time he spoke to her, she did not hear what he said, so she did not answer or even look up at him. He spoke to her again but his words were only noises coming from his pale mouth, trembling now as his anger began to unravel. He jerked her up and the chair fell over behind her. His arms were shaking and she could feel his hands tense up, pulling the edges of the parka tighter. He raised his fist to hit her, his thin body quivering with rage; but the fist collapsed with the desire he had for the valuable things, which, the old man had rightly said, was the only reason they came. She could hear his heart pounding as he held her close and arched his hips against her, groaning and breathing in spasms. She twisted away from him and ducked under his arms.

She ran with a mitten over her mouth, breathing through the fur to protect her lungs from the freezing air. She could hear him running behind her, his heavy breathing, the occasional sound of metal jingling against metal. But he ran without his parka or mittens, breathing the frozen air; its fire squeezed the lungs against the ribs and it was enough that he could not catch her near his store. On the river bank he realized how far he was from his stove, and the wads of yellow stuffing that held off the cold. But the girl was not able to run very fast through the deep drifts at the edge of the river. The twilight was luminous and he could still see clearly for a long distance; he knew he could catch her so he kept running.

When she neared the middle of the river she looked over her shoulder. He was not following her tracks; he went straight across the ice, running the shortest distance to reach her. He was close then; his face was twisted and scarlet from the exertion and the cold. There was satisfaction in his eyes; he was sure he could outrun her.

She was familiar with the river, down to the instant ice flexed into hairline fractures, and the cracking bone-sliver sounds gathered momentum with the opening ice until the churning gray water was set free. She stopped and turned to the sound of the river and the rattle of swirling ice fragments where he fell through. She pulled off a mitten and zipped the parka to her throat. She was conscious then of her own rapid breathing.

She moved slowly, kicking the ice ahead with the heel of her boot, feeling for sinews of ice to hold her. She looked ahead and all around herself; in the twilight, the dense white sky had merged into the flat snow-covered tundra. In the frantic running she had lost her place on the river. She stood still. The east bank of the river was lost in the sky; the boundaries had been swallowed by the freezing white. But then, in the distance, she saw something red, and suddenly it was as she had remembered all those years.

She sat on her bed and while she waited, she listened to the old man. The hunter had found a small jagged knoll on the ice. He pulled his beaver fur cap off his head; the fur inside it steamed with his body heat and sweat. He left it upside down on the ice for the great bear to stalk, and he waited downwind on top of the ice knoll; he was holding the jade knife.

She thought she could see the end of his story in the way he wheezed out the words; but still he reached into his cache of dry fish and dribbled water into his mouth from the tin cup. All night she listened to him describe each breath the man took, each motion of the bear's head as it tried to catch the sound of the man's breathing, and tested the wind for his scent.

The state trooper asked her questions, and the woman who cleaned house for the priest translated them into Yupik. They wanted to know what happened to the storeman, the Gussuck who had been seen running after her down the road onto the river late last evening. He had not come back, and the Gussuck boss in Anchorage was concerned about him. She did not answer for a long time because the old man suddenly sat up in his bed and began to talk excitedly, looking at all of them—the trooper in his dark glasses and the housekeeper in her corduroy parka. He kept saying, "The story! The story! Eh-ya! The great bear! The hunter!"

They asked her again, what happened to the man from the Northern Commercial store. "He lied to them. He told them it was safe to drink. But I will not lie." She stood up and put on the gray wolfskin parka. "I killed him," she said, "but I don't lie."

The attorney came back again, and the jailer slid open the steel doors and opened the cell to let him in. He motioned for the jailer to stay to translate for him. She laughed when she saw how the jailer would be forced by this Gussuck to speak Yupik to her. She liked the Gussuck attorney for that, and for the thinning hair on his head. He was very tall, and she liked to think about the exposure of his head to the freezing; she wondered if he would feel the ice descending from the sky before the others did. He wanted to know why she told the state trooper she had killed the storeman. Some village children had seen it happen, he said, and it was an accident. "That's all you have to say to the judge: it was an accident." He kept repeating it over and over again to her, slowly in a loud but gentle voice: "It was an accident. He was running after you and he fell through the ice. That's all you have to say in court. That's all. And they will let you go home. Back to your village." The jailer translated the words sullenly, staring down at the floor. She shook her head. "I will not change the story, not even to escape this place and go home. I intended that he die. The story must be told as it is." The attorney exhaled loudly; his eyes looked tired. "Tell her that she could not have killed him that way. He was a white man. He ran after her without a parka or mittens. She could not have planned that." He paused and turned toward the cell door. "Tell her I will do all I can for her. I will explain to the judge that her mind is confused." She laughed out loud when the jailer translated what the attorney said. The Gussucks did not understand the story; they could not see the way it must be told, year after year as the old man had done, without lapse or silence.

She looked out the window at the frozen white sky. The sun had finally broken loose from the ice but it moved like a wounded caribou running on strength which only dying animals find, leaping and running on bullet-shattered lungs. Its light was weak and pale; it pushed dimly through the clouds. She turned and faced the Gussuck attorney.

"It began a long time ago," she intoned steadily, "in the summertime. Early in the morning, I remember, something red in the tall river grass. . . . "

The day after the old man died, men from the village came. She was sitting on the edge of her bed, across from the woman the trooper hired to watch her. They came into the room slowly and listened to her. At the foot of her bed they left a king salmon that had been slit open wide and dried last summer. But she did not pause or hesitate; she went on with the story, and she never stopped, not even when the woman got up to close the door behind the village men.

The old man would not change the story even when he knew the end was approaching. Lies could not stop what was coming. He thrashed around on the bed, pulling the blankets loose, knocking bundles of dried fish and meat on the floor. The hunter had been on the ice for many hours. The freezing winds on the ice knoll had numbed his hands in the mittens, and the cold had exhausted him. He felt a single muscle tremor in his hand that he could not stop, and the jade knife fell; it shattered on the ice, and the blue glacier bear turned slowly to face him.

1981

Writing About Literature

To read literature is to enter a conversation—a dialogue, really—with the author and other readers, to respond to their interpretations of the human situation with comments of your own. Writing about great literature may at first be intimidating—you may think "I can't say anything *new* about Mark Twain" or "I don't know as much about Black America as James Baldwin does." But if literature *doesn't* provoke you to respond, then the author hasn't done the job.

To provoke a response is why your instructor asks you to write about the works you read: to make you think, to make you take part in the conversation, even if your thoughts, discoveries, and "lines" in the dialogue have all been uttered before. You, too, have a right to take part in the ongoing discussion about American literature and to convey your response to your readers.

The nature of that response will vary from reader to reader and from situation to situation. You may react to a work differently in a short-answer exam question than you would in a ten-page paper, or differently if you particularly like a work than if you are particularly offended by it. Some readers are fascinated by works about the areas where they grew up, whereas others prefer the lure of faraway places and exotic situations. But all readers will create their interpretations based on several similar principles: the nature of their own readers, the kind of response for which they are asked, and the angle of their approach.

In literature classes you may be asked to construct your interpretation of a particular text, based only on the materials in this book and on your class discussions. Or your instructor may send you to outside sources to give you other perspectives as a way of shaping your response. We will discuss the procedures and pitfalls of both methods. But first we need to make some important observations about reading literature.

READING LITERATURE TO WRITE ABOUT IT

You can read a work of literature in two ways: *precritically* and *critically*. A *precritical reading* is a surface reading: you read to find out what goes on where, what happens, who says what about whatever. You do not look very deeply; you just go from the first line to the last. The dangers of such reading to writing about the work are many: you can write only about the obvious things. You can recount the plot and explain the obvious symbols and devices the author uses, but not in any great depth. The only audiences interested in this kind of writing are people who have not read the work—and your instructor does not fit into this group. A surface reading alone generally guarantees a disastrous paper.

A *critical reading* involves slow, careful, close reading and *rereading* of the text. You read "between the lines," trying to figure out what is really going on, what the author expects of you. You should take notes; ask questions; jot down your ideas, responses, perplexities. This careful process of reading and rereading will help you unfold a text's possibilities. You will write about *how* things happen in the work; you can assume that your readers already know what happens in the work and are interested in exploring beneath the surface with you.

FINDING A SUBJECT: THINKING ABOUT YOUR READERS

You need to remember a special factor of taking part in the conversation about literature: the readers with whom you are conversing. You must consciously imagine *someone* reading your paper. Generally, your reader will be your instructor, who will have special expectations regarding your response. Your instructor will want to see how clear an understanding of the work you have developed, how well you can express your response, and how strong a case you can make. The instructor typically does not want you to recount the plot in great detail: he or she has also read the work! (Think of conversations you have had in which someone repeated a story everyone else in the group already knew well. How interested were you in hearing that story?)

You do not want your readers to say "So what?" about your paper. You do not want to bore them with vague, uninteresting statements. A thesis like "There are many references to homemade items in 'Everyday Use'" will probably elicit the "so what?" response; who cares? But saying "Alice Walker uses domestic objects to emphasize values that readers might not consider otherwise" makes readers say "Really? Tell me how." That is the response you want.

USING ONLY A PRIMARY SOURCE

When you start to write about a work of literature, first ask yourself "What in this work might catch my readers' interest?" Some elements are so obvious that most readers understand their use the first time they read a work; these probably are not good elements to discuss. Go back to the notes you made in your critical reading. Look for an element that you had to think about for a while before you really understood it. Chances are that such an element will lead you to an interesting paper. These interesting elements tend to fall into three categories—*construction, language,* and *context*—within which you can usually find an angle of attack for your paper.

Writing About Construction

If you are writing about a work without referring to secondary sources such as journal articles or critical books, the work's construction is one of the best places to start: its plot (what happens), setting (when and where it happens), and its characters (to whom it happens, or who makes it happen). Each of these building blocks contributes to the overall structure of the work. The following list of questions can help you think about these elements. Not all the questions will apply to all works, but some will certainly apply to the work you are studying.

Plot. Does the work have a plot? (Some poems, for instance, do not.) What is the sequence of events? Did the author put them in chronological order or not, and why? Are key events omitted or just hinted at and why? Does the work have a particular pace or rhythm? Does the action seem to speed up or slow down? Where does the action happen, and why? Does the story seem to reach a climax, and where does that occur?

Setting. When and where does the work take place? In what ways would the work be different if it took place somewhere else? Does the choice of setting influence the action in different ways? (For instance, if the work were set upon a ship rather than in a large city, what would have to be left out of the plot?) How are the people and events in the work influenced by the setting?

Characters. Who are they? Do they actually appear in the work? (For instance, Miss Emily's father and fianceé are dead before William Faulkner's "A Rose for Emily" begins.) What sorts of elements in the work tell us about the characters: what they do, what they say, how they dress, what other people say about them, etc.? Who tells us about these characters: themselves, other characters, a narrator? Do the characters seem real (traditionally called "round" characters), or do they seem more like cartoon stereotypes ("flat" characters)?

Writing About Language

Few words in a work of literature are there accidentally; authors choose each word for precise reasons. Paying attention to what things are called, how they are described, and what those words bring to mind may lead to interesting angles for your "conversation" about the work. Here are some suggestions you can use to focus your attention on literary language.

Metaphor is a general term for language that has enriched meanings and a specific term for literary comparison. In general, metaphoric language is loaded with multiple meanings and connotations. In particular, a metaphor is an equation of two unlike objects:

> My life had stood — a Loaded Gun —
> In Corners —   (Emily Dickinson)

In this equation, the abstract concept "life" suddenly becomes the physical object "a Loaded Gun—In Corners." The comparison surprises us: women do not typically compare themselves to "masculine" items such as guns or see themselves as weapons to guard their homes and loved ones. Dickinson challenges her readers to see the implications of this comparison. The more oblique and nonstereotyped the comparison of objects being equated, the better—the deeper readers must explore to see the ramifications, and the richer the possibilities for writing.

Simile is a type of metaphorical language that compares two unrelated concepts, using the words "like" or "as" to emphasize the relationships. Unlike metaphor, which says one thing *is* another, simile suggests comparisons less forcefully:

> Like travelers with exotic destinations on their minds, the graduates were remarkably forgetful.   (Maya Angelou)

This example compares eighth-graders contemplating high school to travelers about to undertake some extraordinary journey; a little humor is implied in the comparison. Examining similes allows you to write about some of the most subtle effects an author creates.

Symbols are images that have literal as well as deeper meanings. By recognizing a symbol, readers can understand some of a work's deep implications. Some symbols have generalized meanings: a cross calls up Christian images; the American flag, patriotic images; a pillared mansion, images of the South and the Civil War. Other symbols have particular meanings in the work where they appear: Faith's pink hair ribbons in Nathaniel Hawthorne's "Young Goodman Brown," the quilts in "Everyday Use," the Mississippi River in Mark Twain's *Huckleberry Finn*. Writing about a symbol or set of symbols allows you to show your readers another level of meaning in the works you examine.

Tone is the author's attitude to the people and events described in a work: comic, ironic, satiric, sentimental, and so forth. Many things contribute to tone, including the narrator's point of view, the way things are described (for instance, journalistically, overstatedly, understatedly), the reactions of other characters in the work, and the types of sentences and vocabulary the author uses. Tone is sometimes hard to pin down, but writing about it is typically rewarding for both you and your readers because it requires you to look at how many elements work together to create an overall effect.

Writing About Context

Literature does not just happen in a vacuum. Writers are part of their times and part of literary history. When they create a work of literature, they draw on what they know of their own and of past times, the ideas and controversies that were important in their world, as well as the many things they have read. Examining one of these elements may give you an angle from which to approach your paper.

The writer's biography can play an important part in your discussion. The headnotes and introductions in this anthology may help you to understand what a writer has experienced in creating a particular work; for instance, knowing about

Anne Bradstreet's family tragedies may give you insight into some of her poems, and knowing about life in New Orleans can help you better understand Kate Chopin's stories. Knowing about Whitman's service as a nurse to wounded Civil War soldiers and his devotion to Abraham Lincoln lets you see new depths in "When Lilacs Last in the Dooryard Bloom'd." Knowing about Adrienne Rich's involvement in feminism helps you interpret "Snapshots of a Daughter-in-Law." Be careful, though, not to force correspondences: an author cannot control history but *does* control how history enters a particular work. The fickle women in Ernest Hemingway's war novels are not the actual nurse who jilted him, though that experience probably contributed to his development of those female characters.

Political and philosophical movements also contribute greatly to works. The introductions and nonfiction prose selections in this anthology show you how much literature is influenced by the ideas to which authors are exposed. Benjamin Franklin, Thomas Jefferson, John Adams, Thomas Paine, Alexander Hamilton, and James Madison, for instance, wrote in an era when revolution, democracy, and representative government were being widely discussed. Middle nineteenth-century writers were heavily influenced by the emancipation and women's rights movements. Late twentieth-century writers react to the civil rights movement, feminism, and the Vietnam War. A literary work interpreted in light of these movements can yield an interesting paper.

Allusion allows a writer to connect his or her work to other works of literature. In "The Jolly Corner" when Henry James refers to Penelope and Ulysses, James is suggesting that readers connect the long separation of his heroine and protagonist with those figures from Homer's *Odyssey*. In "The Jacob's Ladder" Denise Lever-tov is referring to a familiar episode in the Old Testament. The challenge in writing about allusions is for you to show readers *how* thinking about these suggested comparisons expands your understanding of the work in which they occur.

USING SECONDARY SOURCES

When your instructor asks you to use secondary sources, such as books and journal articles to help you write about literature, you are *not* being asked to summarize what everyone else thinks about a work, but to support *your* interpretation of a work with what other people have written. You are like a lawyer presenting a case: you make the arguments to the jury and call witnesses (the secondary sources) to provide evidence for your case. You have three tasks when you use secondary sources in writing a paper. First, you must find an angle of attack, just as you do when you write from a primary source only. Second, you must find supporting evidence in the works of other writers. And third, you must present that supporting evidence in correct fashion. We have already reviewed the first task, so let us look at what the other two involve.

Finding Secondary Sources

Libraries are full of secondary sources: biographies, collections of letters and diaries, critical interpretations, collections, and the like. You may wish to begin by looking in the card catalog and scanning the shelves for books that may apply. Skim the introductions, conclusions, tables of contents, and indexes to see if the work you are studying is covered in those books. You can use reference books and computer sources such as *Book Review Digest* or the *MLA International Bibliography* to find articles and reviews. (You can also check the suggested readings and texts used in this anthology). The sources you choose will depend on the author you are studying and your angle of approach.

Citing Sources in Your Paper

Every discipline has its own conventions for format and citing secondary sources. In literature those conventions are established by the Modern Language Association and set out in two books: the *MLA Handbook for Writers of Research Papers* (1988) and *the MLA Style Manual* (1985). These books cover in great detail the fine points we will summarize here; your instructor or reference librarian can help you find the books if you have questions not answered here.

Paper Format

In general, put your name and identification number, instructor's name, course name, and date in the top left corner of the first page, with a one-inch margin all around. Doublespace down and input the title, underlining only the names of complete works (see below). Put your last name and the page number in the upper right corner of every page after the first, and staple or clip the pages together firmly in the upper left corner. *Doublespace* the entire paper, including quotations and your list of Works Cited. Do not use a separate cover page or folder unless your instructor calls for it.

Working Quotations Into Your Text

Cite sources within your text through parenthetical references to sources you quote, paraphrase, or summarize. If the material you quote, paraphrase, or summarize takes up less than four typed lines, place a page reference in parentheses *after* the quotation marks and *before* the next major punctuation mark:

```
M. Wynn Thomas calls this lecture "astonishing" (243).
```

OR:

```
Richard F. Adams has found seven of the traditional seventeen

elements of pastoral elegy in "When Lilacs Last in the

Dooryard Bloom'd" (479-487).
```

(The end punctuation goes inside the quotation marks only when the line ends with a question mark or exclamation point, or when there is no parenthetical reference.) Drama is cited by act, scene, and line number rather than page number: (3.1.74). When making a first reference to a text not named in your introduction to the quote, briefly identify it with the parenthetical page reference: (Wright 564) or ("Lilacs" 23).

If a direct quote consists of more than four typed lines of prose or dialogue or more than two typed lines of poetry, end the introductory material with whatever punctuation mark is appropriate (or none, if none is required). Then doublespace, indent ten spaces from the left margin, and doublespace the long quotation (with no opening quotation marks, unless they appear in the original text). End the quote with the punctuation the original text uses, move two spaces to the right, and put the quote's page numbers in parentheses. No punctuation follows the parentheses. Then doublespace and return to your text. If continuing the same paragraph, return to the left margin; if starting a new paragraph, indent the usual five spaces.

Fine Points. If the original text has unusual spelling, punctuation, capitalization, or spacing, do your best to reproduce it on your page. If you begin quoting from poetry in the middle of a line, indent that line the number of spaces missing to indicate this positioning. Underline only the titles of complete works (such as novels, plays, long poems, and collections); names of newspapers, journals, magazines, movies, TV programs, records, and works of art; and unfamiliar foreign words and phrases. Use quotation marks around the titles of poems, articles in journals or magazines, and essays, introductions, forewords, and the like not published separately. (Follow these rules in the text, your title, and your list of Works Cited.)

If you leave words or sentences out of a quotation in your paper, use ellipsis marks, the spaced sets of three or four dots, to show readers where you have trimmed the original text. Three spaced dots indicate words or phrases are omitted; four spaced dots indicate that the omission includes the end of one or more sentences. (Omissions of one or more paragraphs may be indicated by three spaced asterisks.) If you need to tailor a quote to match your sentence grammar, include your alterations in square brackets to show your editorial changes. If there is a mistake, such as a typographical error, in your source, copy the mistake exactly and follow it with the Latin term "*sic*" in square brackets to tell your readers you recognize the mistake. To call attention to particular words, underline them to italicize them. (If you underline words in a direct quote, add the phrase *emphasis mine* to the cited page numbers to point out the change.)

Citing Sources at the End of Your Text

A bibliography, called a list of Works Cited, starts on a new page following your paper, with the title *Works Cited* centered one inch from the top of the page. Works you quoted, summarized, or paraphrased in your essay are listed here in alphabetical order by author. If a source has no author, list it alphabetically by the first word of its title (excepting "a," "an," and "the").

In accordance with recently adopted MLA guidelines, for every work cited give (1) the author's name (if applicable), last name first; (2) the full title (underlined or in quotations; use single quotation marks for a quotation within a quotation), followed by the edition number, if any; (3) the source in which the work appears (if appropriate), underlined; (4) the city (and state, if the city is not well known) of publication, followed by a colon; (5) the publisher (abbreviating "University" to "U" and "Press" to "P"), followed by a comma; and (6) the year or years published. For sources that appear in other bound volumes (such as articles in a journal or essays in a collection), include (7) the beginning and ending page numbers. Each of these seven elements, except for the place of publication and publisher, is separated from the others by a period and two spaces. Begin each reference at the left margin and indent continuation lines five spaces.

Works Cited entries can take hundreds of forms. Here are examples of the most common; you can find examples of other forms in the *MLA Handbook*.

A Book

Thomas, M. Wynn. The Lunar Light of Whitman's Poetry. Cambridge:

   Harvard UP, 1987.

A Literary Work in a Book

Adams, Richard P. " 'Lilacs' as Pastoral Elegy." Critics on

   Walt Whitman: Readings in Literary Criticism. Ed. Richard

   H. Rupp. Coral Gables: U Miami P, 1972. 69-76.

An Edited Text

This form draws attention to the author:

Whitman, Walt. "When Lilacs Last in the Dooryard Bloom'd."

   Leaves of Grass: A Textual Variorum of the Printed Poems.

   Ed. Sculley Bradley, Harold W. Blodgett, Arthur Golden, and

   William White. New York: New York UP, 1980. 2:529-539.

This form draws attention to the editors:

Bradley, Sculley, Harold W. Blodgett, Arthur Golden, and William

   White, eds. "When Lilacs Last in the Dooryard Bloom'd."

   By Walt Whitman. Leaves of Grass: A Textual Variorum of

   the Printed Poems. New York: New York UP, 1980. 2:529-539.

An Article Appearing in a Journal

Wright, George T. "The Lyric Present: Simple Present Verbs in

   English Poems." PMLA 89 (1974): 563-579.

A Book Review

Kakutani, Michiko. Rev. of Sweet Desserts, by Lucy Ellmann.

   New York Times 6 June 1989: B6.

Avoiding Plagiarism

Plagiarism is one of the worst of scholarly crimes. When you plagiarize, you present another writer's thoughts or words or concepts as if they were yours. Plagiarism not only denies writers true credit for their work, but it blurs the distinctions between your own arguments and the supporting evidence. You can suffer many penalties for plagiarism: an "F" on the paper or in the course, probation, suspension, even expulsion. It is important to indicate which ideas in your paper are yours and which come from your sources, in order to avoid committing this serious offense.

To avoid plagiarism, follow four simple rules. One, *keep accurate notes*. When making notes from a book or journal, use quotations marks to indicate words you have copied directly from your sources. Use underlining or highlighting pen to indicate information and ideas you have paraphrased or summarized. Anything that comes from your source must be documented in your paper.

Two, *provide an introduction* to all source material you use in your paper. This attribution can be as simple as "According to Gay Wilson Allen," "Feidelson argues that," or "Critics such as Allen (1970) and Thomas (1987) suggest." By introducing your sources, you signal to your reader that secondary material follows; you are providing expert evidence to back up your contentions, showing your audience that other readers agree with your interpretations. Attributions make your paper seem better integrated, not just a collection of notecards and photocopies cut and pasted together to form an essay.

Three, *include parenthetical references* to the sources of your evidence. These page or line references tell your readers specifically where you got your evidence, so that they can find it easily if they become interested in further exploring your topic. The sample student paper below shows you several skillful ways of incorporating these references to give the information without interrupting the prose.

Four, *provide a list of Works Cited*. This bibliography helps the interested reader find the sources of your evidence. It also provides continuity to the "conversation" by showing where in the discussion of a particular work you place yourself in that conversation. If you provide all four of these elements, you should produce a carefully documented paper that lets your readers easily see what your arguments are and how the evidence in secondary sources supports your positions.

Sample Student Paper

On the following pages you will find a sample student paper based on a student's reading of Whitman's poem "When Lilacs Last in the Dooryard Bloom'd." We point out her thesis and supporting arguments to show how she constructed her paper; we also provide annotations to show you some of the technical aspects of presentation. Following the paper is a paragraph from another paper on "Lilacs," this one using secondary sources to support the argument. These examples should help you see how a written response to literature is assembled.

1   Susanna Jones (8583432)

       Dr. Tarvers

       Principles of Literary Study

       October 14, 19--

                    A Time to Mourn

            Funerals and memorial services are for the living,

       the cliché goes. They are an organized way to express

       grief and put it behind us, a way to stop thinking

       about the past ("Remember when . . .?") and the future

       ("She could have been . . . .") and return to the

2   present in which we must live. In "When Lilacs Last

       in the Dooryard Bloom'd," Walt Whitman conducts such

       a memorial service, forcing both himself and his

       readers to cease grieving for Abraham Lincoln and to

       move toward a future worthy of Lincoln's efforts, as

       a way of keeping Lincoln's memory perpetually present.

       Whitman reinforces this determination to leave the past

3   behind by repeatedly manipulating verb tenses through-

       out the poem.

1. Leave one-inch margins all around.
2. Titles of works not published are placed separately in quotation marks.
3. Thesis of the student's paper.

Jones 2   **4**

The poem begins in the sad past of 1865, when

lilacs "bloom'd," Venus "droop'd," and the narrator

"mourn'd" for the fallen president ("Lilacs" 1-3).   **5, 6**

Immediately Whitman uses tense to force his readers to

7 leave the past behind by reminding us that "Ever-

returning spring" brings a "trinity sure" to mind: the

lilac, the star, and the memory of Lincoln. Moreover,

like the Holy Trinity of Christian symbolism, this

trinity exists in the present, always the same, always

true, always with us. The symbol representing the truth

is described in the present tense: ". . . near the   **8**

white-wash'd palings, / <u>Stands</u> the lilac-bush" (12-13;   **9**

10 emphasis mine). And, in affirmation of the present,

the narrator tells us that "a sprig with its flower

I break" (17) at the same time that the hidden hermit

thrush "sings by himself a song" (22). In choosing

the present tense to describe these eternal symbols,

Whitman reminds us that truth and love are timeless.

4. From page 2 on, put your last name and the page number in the right corner, one-half inch from the top.

5. Use a short title for the first citation of the work.

6. Indicate line numbers without using the abbreviation *ll*.

7. One of the student's supporting arguments.

8. Ellipsis marks show the omission of words.

9. Poetry quotes of fewer than three lines are run into the text, separated by a slash with one space on either side.

10. "Emphasis mine" shows that underlining was added by the student.

Jones 3

The lilac and birdsong prompt the narrator to
remember Lincoln's funeral procession, with a grief
so real that past events seem to become real in the
present. Amid positive images of birth-budding
violets, sprouting grain, and blooming trees, "night
and day journeys a coffin" (32). The narrator's
present-tense report makes this stark contrast   }   7
seem as if he had just now observed it: the coffin
"passes," it "journey[s]," and he "give[s]" it the   11
spray of lilac (Stanza 6). His memory keeps these
past actions alive.

Again the narrator gathers his composure and
forces his attention back to the present by choosing
the present tense. He assures us that he does not
mourn for Lincoln alone but for everyone who has died
in the past: "Blossoms and branches green to all coffins
I bring" (47); ". . . I cover you with roses and early
lilies, / ... I break the sprigs from the bushes"
(50, 52). But his grasp on the present is still weak,
and his memories again draw him back, as he turns to
address the evening star: "Now I know what you must

11. The student's editorial changes for smooth grammar are enclosed in brackets.

Jones 4

have meant as a month since I walk'd" (56). He tells

the thrush "I hear, I come presently . . ." (68), "But

a moment I linger, for the lustrous star has detain'd

me" (69). Memories of the fallen president, "the dead

one there I loved" (71), make the future without

Lincoln seem overwhelming; the poet shifts into the

future tense as he wrestles with the impossibility of

finding a suitable way to mourn his lost leader

(Stanza 10).

Whitman's solution to this dilemma is to escape

out of time entirely. He poses the question "how

shall I warble for the dead one there I loved?" (71)   7

and answers in phrases without verb tense—fragments

that use present participles to construct a timeless

picture of the vital, growing America that was Lincoln's

dream and will be his best monument: "growing spring

and farms and homes," "the fresh sweet herbage under

foot," and, above all,

12

> the city at hand with dwellings so
>
> dense, and stacks of chimneys,
>
> And all the scenes of life and the workshops,
>
> and the workmen homeward returning. . . .

12. Poetry quotes of three lines or more are treated as excerpts, indented ten spaces, and doublespaced. Extra indention of the first line shows that this quote begins in mid-line. Turnovers (continuation lines) are also indented.

Jones 5

The varied and ample land, the South and the

North in the light, Ohio's shores and

flashing Missouri . . . .

The miracle spreading bathing all, the

fulfill'd noon,

The coming eve delicious, the welcome night

and the stars,

Over my cities shining all, enveloping man

and land. (87-98)   13

7   To celebrate this escape out of time, the poet

returns to the present tense and encourages the thrush

to sing on. The thrush's carol uses present tense to

remind us that death is always with us, just as are

life and joy, the objects of human curiosity, day and

night. But the song's calm acceptance of death sends

Whitman's memory back to the past one last time, to a

month before Lincoln's death and a night when Whitman

found himself at the edge of a marsh, listening to

another thrush, smelling lilacs, and watching the

evening star. That night Whitman had thought the

thrush "sang the carol of death, and a verse for him I

love" (128) in memory of the soldiers who died during

the Civil War--the men whom Whitman had nursed and whose

sufferings he describes so graphically (171-184).   14

13. Line reference numbers follow the punctuation in the last line of the excerpt.
14. Reference to summarized material.

Jones 6

This memory, underscored by the thrush's song,
"sadly sinking and fainting . . . and yet again
bursting with joy" (190), is transformed, just as
Whitman would later claim Lincoln's death had been,
into one of "those climax moments on the stage of
universal Time . . . suddenly ringing down the curtain"

15 (<u>Prose</u> 2:508). At last, through the agency of the
thrush's carol, Whitman passes from the grief of the
past into the determination of the present and future: **7**

> As that powerful psalm in the night I <u>heard</u>
>   from recesses,
> Passing, I <u>leave</u> thee lilac with heart-shaped
>   leaves,
> I <u>leave</u> thee there in the dooryard, blooming,
>   returning with spring. (192-194, emphasis
>   mine)   **10**

His grief has been mastered. From here on, he will
live and write about Lincoln in the present tense, and,
in doing so, will keep the memories of Lincoln, his
fallen soldiers, the lilac, the star, and the thrush
ever alive, ever well, ever present. The funeral is
over; life can go on.

15. Reference to another work by Whitman; the reference indicates Volume 2,
followed by a colon and the page number.

Jones 7   **16**

Works Cited

Whitman, Walt. "When Lilacs Last in the Dooryard

Bloom'd." American Literature: A Prentice Hall

Anthology. Ed. Emory Elliott, Linda Kerber,

A. Walton Litz, and Terence Martin. Englewood

Cliffs: Prentice Hall, 1991. 1:2014-2020.

——————. "The Death of Abraham Lincoln." Prose   **17**

Works. Ed. Floyd Stovall. New York: New York U,

1963-1964. 2:497-509.

Sample Paragraph From a Paper With Secondary Sources

Although critics such as Feidelson (1956), Adams

(1957), Allen (1970), and Thomas (1987) have explored   **18**

the classical elements of mourning in this poem, few

other than George T. Wright have given weight to the

Christian religious imagery Whitman incorporates into

his elegy. This incorporation is subtle, handled mostly

through vocabulary and grammar. Every action is consid-

ered carefully, performed deliberately, and reinforced

by the poet's choice of the present tense, as in a

religious service. Wright (1974) calls this tense the   **19**

16. The Works Cited list begins on a new page.

17. Reference to a second work by the same author is indicated by typing ten
hyphens followed by a period.

18. Attribution to secondary sources: author's last name and date.

19. First reference to an article: author's last name and date.

"lyric present," and notes that it "characteristically
convey[s] a sense of elevation and, often, of solemnity
which seems appropriate to visionary experience." Citing
Whitman's "here, coffin, that slowly passes, / I <u>give</u> you
my sprig of lilac" (emphasis his), Wright argues that the
poet is acting as if he were the minister conducting
Lincoln's funeral (568). This impression is reinforced
by Whitman's references to the "trinity" of symbols and
by his descriptions of dirges, processions, chants,
miracles, souls, and powerful psalms in the poem.

20. Shows that the emphasis was added by the source, not the student.

21. Placing the parenthetical reference at the end of several sentences with attribution shows that everything between the first attribution and this reference comes from the same source.

Glossary

Allegory: a narrative in which the persons, things, concepts, or events signify a hidden or symbolic meaning; an extension of **metaphor**.

Alliteration: the repetition of a (generally initial) consonant sound within a line or phrase.

Allusion: an explicit or indirect reference in a work to something outside the work itself.

Apron: in theater, the part of the stage in front of the **proscenium arch**.

Archetype: themes, images, character types, or narrative designs that seem to be identifiable in a wide array of literature as well as in myths and dreams. Examples of archetypes are death and rebirth and Paradise versus Hell.

Assonance: the repetition of a vowel sound within a line, stanza, or sentence.

Ballad: a narrative poem, originally of folk origin and meant to be sung, that tends to focus upon a climactic episode and is told without comment.

Beat poetics: an often impassioned poetry of the 1950s and 1960s distinguished by its celebration of freedom, rejection of social mores, and frequent use of colloquial language, as exemplified by the work of such poets as Allen Ginsberg, Lawrence Ferlinghetti, and Leonard Cohen. "Beat" suggests the beat of the bongo drum, which often accompanied readings of beat poetry, as well as "beatniks," with whom the beat poets were associated.

Bildungsroman: a German term for a novel of development, which recounts a protagonist's life experience and typically involves a crisis of conscience.

Blank verse: lines of unrhymed iambic pentameter (see **meter**) in verse paragraphs rather than stanzas.

Burlesque: a form of satire that attempts to ridicule a serious literary work by means of an amusing imitation. Two classes of burlesque are *parody,* which imitates the serious materials and style of a work and applies them to a lowly subject, and *travesty,* which mocks a work by treating its lofty subject in a jocular and undignified manner.

Canto: a major division of a long poem; originally a singing or chanting section of a poem.

Closed form: a form of poetry in which the thought and grammar are complete within a couplet.

Dénouement: a French term for the final outcome or unraveling of a plot.

Deus ex machina: a Latin term (meaning "god from a machine") for any unlikely plot contrivance.

Didactic: intended to be instructive, educational, or moralistic.

Dramatic irony: an ironic situation in which a reader or the audience is aware of things of which a character is not, or in which a character's speech and actions reveal that character to differ from his or her self-image.

Elegy: a poem lamenting the death of a particular person, or a meditative poem concerning mortality.

Epic: a long narrative poem of elevated diction, typically recounting history, legend, or the deeds of a national hero.

Epistolary: written in, or conducted by, letters.

Foot: the basic metrical unit in poetry, generally containing one stressed syllable and one or two unstressed syllables.

Free verse: poetry free of traditional metrical, rhyming, and stanzaic patterns, although not necessarily free of a patterning device such as **alliteration** or a visual repetition of line length.

Genre: a French term for a literary form, such as **epic** poem, captivity narrative, or western novel.

Heroic couplet: a rhyming couplet of lines of ten syllables, so called because it was originally used for heroic, or epic poetry.

Homiletic: like a homily, or sermon.

Hudibrastic: in the style of Samuel Butler's *Hudibras* (1663–1678), a **mock-epic** satirical poem that ridiculed the Puritans.

Hyperbole: an overstatement or exaggeration.

Idiom: the language or dialect of a group or class, or a language unit of a group or class that differs from the norm in syntax or meaning.

Imagism: a poetic movement that flourished in England and America between about 1909 and 1917 as a reaction to **romanticism** and called for poetry that renders the poet's response to a visual object or scene as exactly and tersely as possible without abstraction. Influenced by T. E. Hulme's aesthetic philosophy and by the Japanese haiku, the movement's leaders included Ezra Pound, Amy Lowell, and Hilda Doolittle.

Irony: an expression in which the intended meaning is different from, or opposite to, the literal meaning.

"Little" magazine: a literary magazine, commonly avant-garde, with a small readership and generally a small page size.

Local color: writing that emphasizes the setting, dialect, ways of thinking and feeling, dress, and custom characteristic of a specific region; used most often in connection with the local-color movement in American literature from 1870 to 1890.

Lyric poetry: originally, ancient Greek poetry accompanied by a lyre; now, a relatively short nonnarrative poem expressing the poet's thoughts or feelings.

Masque: a short, elaborately staged court drama with actors and dancers usually masked.

Melodrama: a form of drama, especially popular in the nineteenth century, full of tragic elements but with a happy ending; the characters are flat types: the hero and heroine epitomize virtue, and the villain is Satan incarnate.

Metaphor: a figure of speech in which one thing is equated to another, normally unrelated thing, without the use of a word of comparison, such as "like" or "as"; for example, "Her wrinkles are love's graves."

Meter: a measure of poetic rhythm, determined by the type and number of **feet** in a **poetic line.** The four standard meters of verse in English are *iambic* (an unstressed syllable followed by a stressed), *anapestic* (two unstressed syllables followed by a stressed), *trochaic* (a stressed syllable followed by an unstressed), and *dactylic* (a stressed syllable followed by two unstressed). The number of feet in a line determines the type of verse: trimeter for a line with three feet, tetrameter for four feet, pentameter for five feet, and so on.

Metonymy: a figure of speech in which a closely related term is substituted for what is actually meant: for example, "the White House denies any wrongdoing" for "the president denies any wrongdoing."

Mock epic: a poem in **epic** form and manner, ludicrously elevating some trivial subject to epic grandeur (also known as mock heroic).

Modernism: a trend in literature of the first half of the twentieth century toward radical experimentation, such as the use of **stream-of-consciousness** narration and of **myth** as a structural principle. Cultural relativism, discontinuity, and alienation are the driving forces behind much modernist literature, which was promoted by such writers as T. S. Eliot, Ezra Pound, James Joyce, Virginia Woolf, and William Faulkner.

Motif: a frequently recurring literary element, such as a word, an image, or a symbol. A *leitmotif* is a recurrent element in a single work or in the work of a single author.

Myth: an ancient story dealing with fabulous deeds of gods or heroes, or an imaginary world in which fictitious characters and events are faithful to moral, philosophical, and/or aesthetic "truths" rather than to scientific truths.

Naturalism: a literary philosophy by which human beings are seen as part of the natural order, unconnected to a spiritual world outside nature, and as such are victims of blind external or biological forces. It evolved in the nineteenth century from **realism** and was influenced by the evolutionary principles of Charles Darwin and by scientific determinism.

Neoclassicism: an artistic and literary movement that began around 1660 in France and lasted until the age of **romanticism,** at the end of the eighteenth century. Neoclassicist writers, such as John Dryden and Alexander Pope, are distinguished by their interest in order, decorum, dialectical reasoning, and a return to classical aesthetic principles.

New Criticism: a methodology for interpreting literature, made popular in America by the work of Cleanth Brooks and Robert Penn Warren, which predominated in the 1940s and 1950s. New Critics are concerned with the autonomous nature of a text and with the interplay of meaning and structure rather than with biographical or historical considerations.

Ode: a serious poem on an exalted subject, generally in an elevated style.

Onomatopoeia: words that sound like their meaning, such as "buzz," "bark," and "hiss." Sound patterns that reinforce meaning over one or more lines may also be onomatopoeic.

Open form: a form of poetry in which the sense of the second line of a couplet is completed in the next couplet.

Organic form: the way in which structure may seem to develop inherently within a text as it unifies and stabilizes the work as a whole.

Oxymoron: the juxtaposition of terms or ideas that are literally contradictory, such as "living death," "howling stillness."

Paradox: a statement that seems self-contradictory but is somehow true.

Persona: a Latin term for "mask"; the projected speaker or narrator of a text, a mask for the author.

Personification: the attribution of human qualities to nature, animals, or objects.

Picaresque: a type of fiction, generally satiric, that deals with the adventures of a roguish hero.

Poetic line: a structural unit of measurement in verse; unlike a line of prose, a poetic line need not make sense as a unit. In *metrical verse,* the length of a line is determined by the number of **feet** it contains and by the **meter** used; in *accentual verse,* by the number of accented syllables; in *syllabic verse,* by a syllable count; and in **free verse,** by units of conversational rhythm, of syntax, of breath, or of thought, or by rhetorical units.

Point of view: the perspective through which a literary work is given. With a *first-person* point of view, the narrator identifies himself or herself as "I" and is commonly the main character. With a *third-person* point of view, the narrator is outside the story and refers to characters as "he," "she," and "they." With an *omniscient* point of view, the third-person narrator knows all, can be everywhere, and can enter characters' minds.

Postmodernism: a literary and artistic philosophy that rejects all formal constraints, following the **modernism** of the early twentieth century. The postmodern artist tends to accept the world as fragmented and incoherent and to represent those characteristics in art, typically in a comic and self-reflexive style.

Proscenium arch: an arch over the front of a stage. The arch, from which a curtain typically is hung, separates the audience from the action.

Prosody: the analysis of versification, including description of **meters** and of **stanzaic forms.**

Quatrain: a stanza consisting of four lines with some pattern of rhyme; it is the most common **stanzaic form** in English.

Realism: a nineteenth-century literary philosophy that attempted to represent "real life" faithfully as the common reader might know it, partly in reaction to **romanticism.** Realism also refers to a recurrent style of writing typified by the nineteenth-century realists.

Romanticism: a wide-ranging artistic and literary movement inspired politically, by the revolutions in America and in France, and intellectually, as a reaction to the Enlightenment. Romantic works are known for their rejection of classical models, the privileging of individual experience, the celebration of imagination, and a marked interest in the artist as a hero and prophet aspiring beyond human limitation.

Satire: literature that ridicules social institutions or vices and follies.

Sestina: a complicated verse form, invented by twelfth-century French troubadours, that consists of six stanzas of six lines each and a concluding tercet, or grouping of three lines. The terminal words of the first stanza are repeated as terminal words in the succeeding stanzas, as in the tercets, in a strict but varying order.

Socratic irony: an ironic situation in which a character feigns ignorance and a desire to be enlightened by opinions that turn out to be erroneous.

Soliloquy: in drama, a speech given by a character generally alone on stage, expressing thoughts aloud.

Sonnet: a poem of fourteen lines in *iambic pentameter* (see **meter**) with a rhyme scheme.

Stanzaic form: in poetry, a structure consisting of stanzas (groupings of verse/lines), generally marked by a recurrent rhyme scheme. Typical stanzaic forms are the *couplet,* a pair of rhymed lines; the *tercet,* or *triplet,* three lines with a single rhyme; and the **quatrain,** a four-line stanza.

Stream of consciousness: a narrative technique that attempts to reproduce the uninterrupted flow of a character's mental processes; ideas and sense impressions may intermingle without logical progression.

Synecdoche: a figure of speech in which a part is substituted for the whole, or vice-versa, such as "wheels" for "car" or "copper" for "penny."

Synesthesia: the description of one type of sensory experience in terms of another: for example, sound might be described in terms of color, as in "the trumpet's red blare."

Tone: the author's attitude—playful, serious, somber, ironic, and so on—revealed through language, atmosphere, and mood.

Transcendentalism: in American literature, a nonsystematic nineteenth-century philosophy that holds that all of creation is spiritual in nature and is best known through the intuitive rather than the rational mind. Largely developed by Ralph Waldo Emerson and derived from the work of Immanuel Kant and of Thomas Carlyle, among others, it was seen by many as a threat to traditional Christianity because of its pantheistic strain.

Unity: the sense that the aspects of a play form a unified entity: the *"three unities,"* as defined by Aristotle, are *unity of time* (the play's action occurring in one day), *unity of place* (in one setting), and *unity of action* (in an orderly manner leading toward the plot's resolution).

Vorticism: an artistic movement, begun in the early twentieth century, that relates art forms to the machine and to modern industrial civilization. Regarding lifelike representation as unnecessary, it insists upon an imaginative reconstruction of nature in mechanistic designs, aligning it with cubism and futurism.

Acknowledgments

Paula Gunn Allen. "C'Koy'u, Old Woman," "Pocahontas to Her English Husband, John Rolfe," "Coyote Jungle," "Weed," "Myth/Telling—Dream/Showing" from *Skins and Bones* by Paula Gunn Allen. West End Press, Inc., 1988.

John Ashbery. "Some Trees," "The Painter," "Rivers and Mountains," "Farm Implements and Rutabagas in a Landscape," "Wet Casements," "My Erotic Double," from *Selected Poems* by John Ashbery. Copyright © 1985 by John Ashbery. "Frost" from *April Galleons* by John Ashbery. Copyright © 1984, 1985, 1986, 1987 by John Ashbery. Reprinted by permission of the publisher, Viking Penguin, a division of Penguin Books USA Inc.

James Baldwin. "Sonny's Blues" from *Going to Meet the Man* by James Baldwin. Copyright © 1957 by James Baldwin. Used by permission of Doubleday, a division of Bantam, Doubleday, Dell Publishing Group, Inc.

Amiri Baraka. "I Substitute for the Dead Lecturer" and "Political Poem" from *The Dead Lecturer* by Amiri Baraka. Copyright © 1964 by Amiri Baraka. Reprinted by permission of Sterling Lord Literistic, Inc. "Legacy" from *Black Magic: 1961–1967* by Amiri Baraka. Copyright © 1969 by Amiri Baraka. Reprinted by permission of Sterling Lord Literistic, Inc. "A Poem for Black Hearts" and "Preface to a Twenty Volume Suicide Note" from *Selected Poetry of Amiri Baraka/LeRoi Jones* by Amiri Baraka. Copyright © 1979 by Amiri Baraka. Reprinted by permission of William Morrow & Co., Inc.

Joel Barlow. "Advice to a Raven in Russia" is reprinted with the permission of the Henry E. Huntington Library, 1938.

John Berryman. "The Ball Poem" and "The Song of the Tortured Girl" from *Short Poems* by John Berryman. Copyright 1948 by John Berryman. Renewal copyright © 1972 by Kate Berryman. Poems 1, 14, 18, 29, 40, 76, 77, 127, 153, 157, 187, 366 from *The Dream Songs* by John Berryman. Copyright © 1959, 1962, 1963, 1964, 1965, 1966, 1967, 1968 by John Berryman. All reprinted by permission of Farrar, Straus & Giroux, Inc.

Elizabeth Bishop. "The Map," "The Imaginary Iceberg," "The Bight," "Questions of Travel," "Poem," "In the Waiting Room," "The Moose" from *The Complete Poems, 1927–1979* by Elizabeth Bishop. Copyright 1935, 1936, 1949, © 1956, 1963, 1964, 1971, 1972, 1976, 1978 by Elizabeth Bishop. Copyright © 1979, 1983 by Alice Helen Methfessel. Reprinted by permission of Farrar, Straus & Giroux, Inc.

Louise Bogan. "Sonnet," "Single Sonnet," "Italian Morning," "Evening in the Sanitarium," "Night" from *The Blue Estuaries* by Louise Bogan. Copyright 1923, 1929, 1930, 1931, 1933, 1934, 1935, 1936, 1937, 1938, 1941, 1949, 1951, 1952, 1954, © 1957, 1958, 1962, 1963, 1964, 1965, 1966, 1967, 1968 by Louise Bogan. Reprinted by permission of Farrar, Straus & Giroux, Inc.

William Bradford. From *Of Plymouth Plantation* by William Bradford, edited by Samuel Eliot Morison. Copyright 1952 by Samuel Eliot Morison and renewed © 1980 by Emily M. Beck. Reprinted by permission of Alfred A. Knopf, Inc.

Anne Bradstreet. Reprinted by permission of the publishers from *Works of Anne Bradstreet,* edited by Jeannine Hensely, Cambridge, Mass.: Harvard University Press, Copyright © 1967 by the President and Fellows of Harvard College. All rights reserved.

Gwendolyn Brooks. "The Mother," "A Song in the Front Yard," "The Bean Eaters," "We Real Cool" from *Blacks* by Gwendolyn Brooks, published by The David Company, Chicago. Copyright © 1987 by The David Company.

Charles Brockden Brown. From *Wieland and "Memoirs of Carwin"* by Charles Brockden Brown. Edited by Sydney J. Krause and S. W. Reid. C.S.E. Edition. The Kent State University Press, 1977.

William Byrd, II. Reprinted by permission of the publishers from *The Prose of William Byrd of Westover,* edited by Louis B. Wright, Cambridge, Mass.: The Belknap Press of Harvard University Press, Copyright © 1966 by the President and Fellows of Harvard College.

Lydia Maria Child. From *The American Frugal Housewife* by Lydia Maria Child. Reprinted by permission of Alice M, Geffen, 1972.

Hart Crane. "My Grandmother's Love Letters," "Chaplinesque," "At Melville's Tomb," "Voyages," "To Brooklyn Bridge," "The Broken Tower" reprinted from *The Poems of Hart Crane,* edited by Marc Simon, by permission of Liveright Publishing Corporation. Copyright © 1986 by Marc Simon.

Stephen Crane. From *The Works of Stephen Crane,* edited by Fredson Bowers and published by the University Press of Virginia: "The Open Boat" and "The Bride Comes to Yellow Sky" in *Tales of Adventure,* Vol. V, 1970. "Stephen Crane's Own Story" in *Reports of War,* Vol. IX, No. 17, 1971. Poems 1, 19, and 24 in *The Black Riders and Other Lines,* Vol. X, 1975. Poems 69 and 89 in *War Is Kind,* Vol. X, 1975.

Countee Cullen. "Heritage" (excerpts) from *On These I Stand* by Countee Cullen. Copyright 1925 by Harper & Brothers; copyright renewed 1953 by Ida M. Cullen. Reprinted by permission of GRM Associates, Inc., Agents for the Estate of Ida M. Cullen.

Emily Dickinson. "Title divine—is mine" from *Life and Letters of Emily Dickinson,* edited by Martha D. Bianchi. Copyright 1924 by Martha Dickinson Bianchi. Copyright renewed 1952 by Alfred Leete Hampson. Reprinted by permission of Houghton Mifflin Company. Poems 285, 293, 341, 657, 725, 754 from *The Complete Poems of Emily Dickinson,* edited by Thomas H. Johnson. Copyright 1929 by Martha Dickinson Bianchi. Copyright © renewed 1957 by Mary L. Hampson. Reprinted by permission of Little, Brown and Company. All other poems reprinted by permission of the publishers and Trustees of Amherst College from *The Poems of Emily Dickinson,* edited by Thomas H. Johnson, Cambridge Mass.: The Belknap Press of Harvard University Press, Copyright 1951, © 1955, 1979, 1983 by the President and Fellows of Harvard College.

Hilda Doolittle (H.D.). "Pear Tree," "Helen," "If You Take the Moon in Your Hands," "The Mysteries Remain," from *H. D.: The Collected Poems, 1912–1944.* Copyright © 1982 by The Estate of Hilda Doolittle. Reprinted by permission of New Directions Publishing Corporation.

Theodore Dreiser. "The Second Choice" from *Free and Other Stories* by Theodore Dreiser, 1918. Reprinted by permission of the Dreiser Trust.

T. S. Eliot. "The Love Song of J. Alfred Prufrock," "Cousin Nancy," "Sweeney Among the Nightingales," "The Waste Land," from *Collected Poems 1909–1962* by T. S. Eliot. Copyright 1936 by Harcourt Brace Jovanovich, Inc. Copyright © 1964, 1963 by T. S. Eliot. Reprinted by permission of the publisher. Reprinted by permission of Faber and Faber Ltd. "East Coker" from *Four Quartets* by T. S. Eliot. Copyright 1943 by T. S. Eliot and renewed © 1971 by Esme Valerie Eliot. Reprinted by permission of Harcourt Brace Jovanovich, Inc. Reprinted by permission of Faber and Faber Ltd.

Ralph Ellison. From *Invisible Man* by Ralph Ellison. Copyright 1952 by Ralph Ellison. Reprinted by permission of Random House, Inc.

Ralph Waldo Emerson. "Nature," "The American Scholar," "Self-Reliance" and "The Poet" are reprinted by permission of the publishers from *The Collected Works of Ralph Waldo Emerson,* edited by Alfred R. Ferguson; Vol. I, Introduction and Notes by Robert E. Spiller; Vols. II & III, Introduction and Notes by Joseph Slater; Cambridge, Mass.: The Belknap Press of Harvard University Press, copyright © 1971, 1979, 1983 by the President and Fellows of Harvard College. Diary entry On Hawthorne (May 24, 1864) is reprinted by permission of the publishers from *The Journals and Miscellaneous Notebooks of Ralph Waldo Emerson,* Vol. XV, Allardt and Hill, eds.; Cambridge, Mass.: The Belknap Press of Harvard University Press, copyright © 1982 by the President and Fellows of Harvard College. Letter to Walt Whitman (1855) is reprinted by permission of New York University Press from *Walt Whitman: Leaves of Grass,* Reader's Comprehensive Edition, edited by Harold W. Blodgett and Sculley Bradley. Copyright © 1965 by New York University.

William Faulkner. "A Rose for Emily" and "That Evening Sun" from *Collected Stories of William Faulkner.* Copyright 1950 by Random House, Inc. Reprinted by permission of Random House, Inc.

The Federalist. Reprinted by permission of the publishers from *The Federalist* by Alexander Hamilton, James Madison and John Jay, edited by Benjamin Hitch Wright, Cambridge, Mass.: The Belknap Press of Harvard University Press, Copyright © 1961 by the President and Fellows of Harvard College.

Fannie Fern. From *Ruth Hall and Other Writings* by Fanny Fern, edited by Joyce W. Warren. Copyright © 1986 by Rutgers, The State University. Reprinted by permission of Rutgers University Press.

F. Scott Fitzgerald. "Babylon Revisited" from *Taps at Reveille* by F. Scott Fitzgerald. Copyright 1931 by The Curtis Publishing Company; renewal copyright © 1959 by Frances Scott Fitzgerald Lanahan. Reprinted with permission of Charles Scribner's Sons, an imprint of Macmillan Publishing Company.

Benjamin Franklin. Texts from *The Autobiography of Benjamin Franklin,* pages 43–79, 148–60, copyright © 1964 by the American Philosophical Society and Yale University. All rights reserved. From *The Papers of Benjamin Franklin,* copyright © 1963 by the American Philosophical Society and Yale University. All rights reserved.

Philip Freneau. "The Wild Honeysuckle," "The Indian Burying Ground," "To an Author," "On the Religion of Nature" from *Poems of Philip Freneau,* edited by Harry Hayden Clark. New York: Hafner Press, 1960. "To Sir Toby" from *The Poems of Philip Freneau,* Vol. II, edited by Fred Lewis Pattee. New York: Russell & Russell, 1963.

Robert Frost. "The Pasture," "Mowing," "Home Burial," "After Apple-Picking," "The Wood-Pile," "The Oven Bird," "Birches," " 'Out, Out—'," "Stopping by Woods on a Snowy Evening," "Once by the Pacific," "Acquainted With the Night," "Design," "The Silken Tent," "Come In," "Never Again Would Birds' Song Be the Same," "Directive" from *The Poetry of Robert Frost,* edited by Edward Connery Lathem. Copyright 1916, 1923, 1928, 1930, 1934, 1939, 1947, © 1967, 1969 by Holt, Rinehart & Winston. Copyright 1936, 1942, 1944, 1951 © 1956, 1958, 1962 by Robert Frost. Copyright © 1964, 1967, 1970, 1975 by Lesley Frost Ballantine. Reprinted by permission of Henry Holt and Company, Inc.

Allen Ginsberg. "Howl," "A Supermarket in California," "America," "Ode to Failure" from *Collected Poems 1947–1980* by Allen Ginsberg. Copyright © 1955, 1956, 1959, 1984 by Allen Ginsberg. Reprinted by permission of Harper & Row, Publishers, Inc.

Louise Glück. "Cottonmouth Country" from *Firstborn* by Louise Glück, first published by The Ecco Press in 1983. Copyright © 1968 by Louise Glück. "The Drowned Children" and "Palais des Arts" from *Descending Figure* by Louise Glück, first published by The Ecco Press in 1980. Copyright © 1976, 1977, 1978, 1979, 1980 by Louise Glück. "Elms," "Horse," "Mythic Fragment" from *The Triumph of Achilles* by Louise Glück, first published by The Ecco Press in 1985. Copyright © 1985 by Louise Glück. All reprinted by permission.

Frances E. W. Harper. From *Complete Poems of Frances E. W. Harper,* edited by Maryemma Graham. Copyright © 1988 by Oxford University Press, Inc. Reprinted by permission.

Nathaniel Hawthorne. Copyright © 1965, 1972, 1974 by The Ohio State University Press.

Ernest Hemingway. "Big Two-Hearted River" from *In Our Time* by Ernest Hemingway. Copyright 1925 by Charles Scribner's Sons, renewal copyright 1953 by Ernest Hemingway. Reprinted with permission of Charles Scribner's Sons, an imprint of Macmillan Publishing Company.

Langston Hughes. "The Negro Speaks of Rivers" and "The Weary Blues" from *Selected Poems of Langston Hughes.* Copyright 1926 by Alfred A. Knopf, Inc. and renewed 1954 by Langston Hughes. Reprinted by permission of Alfred A. Knopf, Inc. "Dream Boogie" and "Theme for English B" from *Selected Poems of Langston Hughes.* Copyright 1951 by Langston Hughes. Copyright renewed © 1979 by George Houston Bass. Reprinted by permission of Harold Ober Associates Inc. "Harlem" from *The Panther and the Lash* by Langston Hughes. Copyright 1951 by Langston Hughes. Reprinted by permission of Alfred A. Knopf, Inc.

Zora Neale Hurston. "How It Feels to Be Colored Me" from *I Love Myself—A Zora Neale Hurston Reader* edited by Alice Walker. Reprinted with permission of Clifford Hurston, 1985.

Washington Irving. "The Author's Account of Himself" and "Rip Van Winkle" from *The Sketch-Book* by Washington Irving. Copyright © 1978 and reprinted with the permission of Twayne Publishers, a division of G. K. Hall & Co., Boston.

Harriet Jacobs. From *Incidents in the Life of a Slave Girl* by Harriet Jacobs, edited by Valerie Smith. The Schomburg Library of Nineteenth-Century Black Women Writers, copyright © 1988 by Oxford University Press, Inc. Reprinted by permission.

Randall Jarrell. "The Death of the Ball Turret Gunner" and "90 North" from *The Complete Poems* by Randall Jarrell. Copyright 1941, 1945 and renewal copyright © 1968, 1972 by Mrs. Randall Jarrell. Reprinted by permission of Farrar, Straus & Giroux, Inc. "Bats" from *The Bat-Poet* by Randall Jarrell. Copyright © 1963, 1964 by Macmillan Publishing Company. Reprinted with permission of Macmillan Publishing Company. "The Woman at the Washington Zoo" reprinted by permission of Mary Jarrell for the Estate of Randall Jarrell, 1969.

Thomas Jefferson. From *Notes on the State of Virginia,* edited by William Peden. Copyright © 1955 The University of North Carolina Press. Reprinted by permission.

Martin Luther King, Jr. From *I Have a Dream . . . The Life and Times of Martin Luther King, Jr.,* by Lenwood G. Davis. Copyright © 1969 by Lenwood G. Davis.

Denise Levertov. "The Jacob's Ladder" and "The Ache of Marriage" from *Poems 1960–1967* by Denise Levertov. Copyright © 1961, 1964 by Denise Levertov Goodman. "O Taste and See" from *O Taste and See* by Denise Levertov. Copyright © 1964 by Denise Levertov Goodman. Reprinted by permission of New Directions Publishing Corporation.

Robert Lowell. "My Last Afternoon With Uncle Devereux Winslow," "The Neo-Classical Urn," "For the Union Dead," "Reading Myself" from *Selected Poems* by Robert Lowell. Copyright 1944, 1946, 1947, 1950, 1951, © 1956, 1960, 1961, 1962, 1963, 1964, 1965, 1966, 1967, 1968, 1969,

1970, 1973, 1976 by Robert Lowell. Renewal copyright © 1972, 1974, 1975 by Robert Lowell. Reprinted by permission of Farrar, Straus & Giroux, Inc. "The Quaker Graveyard in Nantucket" and "Mr. Edwards and the Spider" from *Lord Weary's Castle* by Robert Lowell. Copyright 1946 and renewed © 1974 by Robert Lowell. Reprinted by permission of Harcourt Brace Jovanovich, Inc. "Epilogue" from *Day by Day* by Robert Lowell. Copyright © 1977 by Robert Lowell. Reprinted by permission of Farrar, Straus & Giroux, Inc.

Cotton Mather. Reprinted by permission of the publishers from *Bonifacius: An Essay Upon The Good* edited by David Levin, Cambridge, Mass.: The Belknap Press of Harvard University Press. Copyright © 1966 by the President and Fellows of Harvard College.

James Merrill. "Charles on Fire" from *Nights and Days* by James Merrill. Copyright © 1960, 1961, 1962, 1963, 1964, 1965, 1966 by James Merrill. Reprinted with permission of Atheneum Publishers, an imprint of Macmillan Publishing Company. "Farewell Performance" from *The Inner Room* by James Merrill. Copyright © 1988 by James Merrill. Reprinted by permission of Alfred A. Knopf, Inc.

W. S. Merwin. "One-Eye" and "The Drunk in the Furnace" from *The Drunk in the Furnace.* "The Animals" and "For the Anniversary of My Death" from *The Lice.* Copyright 1952, © 1956, 1957, 1958, 1959, 1960, 1963, 1967 by W. S. Merwin. Reprinted by permission of Georges Borchardt, Inc. and the author. "The Judgment of Paris" from *The Carrier of Ladders* by W. S. Merwin. Reprinted with permission of Atheneum Publishers, an imprint of Macmillan Publishing Company. Copyright © 1970 by W. S. Merwin. Originally appeared in *The New Yorker.* "Thanks" from *The Rain in the Trees* by W. S. Merwin. Copyright © 1988 by W. S. Merwin. Reprinted by permission of Alfred A. Knopf, Inc. "Flies" from *Writings to an Unfinished Accompaniment* by W. S. Merwin. Copyright © 1969, 1970, 1971, 1972, 1973 by W. S. Merwin. Reprinted with permission of Atheneum Publishers, an imprint of Macmillan Publishing Company.

N. Scott Momaday. *The Way to Rainy Mountain,* Copyright © 1969, The University of New Mexico Press. Reprinted with permission.

Marianne Moore. From *Collected Poems* by Marianne Moore: "Nine Nectarines," "When I Buy Pictures," "Poetry" Copyright 1935 by Marianne Moore, renewed © 1963 by Marianne Moore and T. S. Eliot. "What Are Years?" Copyright 1941 and renewed © 1969 by Marianne Moore. Reprinted with permission of Macmillan Publishing Company. "The Steeple-Jack," "A Jelly-Fish," and "Baseball and Writing" from *Complete Poems of Marianne Moore"* Copyright © 1959 and 1961 by Marianne Moore. Reprinted by permission of the publisher, Viking Penguin, a division of Penguin Books USA Inc.

Samuel Eliot Morison. From *The European Discovery of America: The Southern Voyages 1492– 1616* by Samuel Eliot Morison, Copyright © 1974 by Samuel Eliot Morison. Reprinted by permission of Oxford University Press, Inc.

Toni Morrison. From *Song of Solomon* by Toni Morrison. Copyright © 1977 by Toni Morrison. Reprinted by permission of Alfred A. Knopf, Inc.

Joyce Carol Oates. "Where Are You Going, Where Have You Been?" from *Wheel of Love and Other Stories* by Joyce Carol Oates. Copyright © 1965 by Joyce Carol Oates. Reprinted by permission of John Hawkins & Associates, Inc.

Flannery O'Connor. "The Artificial Nigger" from *A Good Man Is Hard to Find and Other Stories* by Flannery O'Connor. Copyright 1955 by Flannery O'Connor and renewed © 1983 by Regina O'Connor. Reprinted by permission of Harcourt Brace Jovanovich, Inc.

Eugene O'Neill. *Desire Under the Elms* from *The Plays of Eugene O'Neill.* Copyright 1924 and renewed 1952 by Eugene O'Neill. Reprinted by permission of Random House, Inc.

Simon J. Ortiz. "Grief" and "The Sky Is Brilliant" from *From Sand Creek* by Simon J. Ortiz. Copyright © 1981 by Simon J. Ortiz. Used by permission of the publisher, Thunder's Mouth Press. "Dry Root in a Wash," "A Story of How a Wall Stands," "Wind and Glacier Voices," "The Creation According to Coyote" from *Going for the Rain* by Simon J. Ortiz. Copyright © 1976 by Simon J. Ortiz. Reprinted by permission of the author.

Thomas Paine. From *The Writings of Thomas Paine,* collected and edited by Moncure Daniel Conway, Vol. IV, 1967. Reprinted by permission of AMS Press, Inc.

Sylvia Plath. "Tulips," "Lady Lazarus," "The Bee Meeting," "Ariel," "Daddy," "Nick and the Candlestick," "Edge" from *The Collected Poems of Sylvia Plath,* edited by Ted Hughes. Copyright © 1962, 1963, 1965, 1966 by Ted Hughes. Reprinted by permission of Harper & Row, Publishers, Inc. Published by Faber and Faber, London. Copyright © Ted Hughes 1965, 1981. By permission of Olwyn Hughes.

Katherine Anne Porter. "Flowering Judas" from *Flowering Judas and Other Stories* by Katherine Ann Porter. Copyright 1930 and renewed © 1958 by Katherine Ann Porter. Reprinted by permission of Harcourt Brace Jovanovich, Inc.

Ezra Pound. From *Personae* by Ezra Pound. Copyright 1926 by Ezra Pound. Reprinted by permission of New Directions Publishing Corporation.

John Crowe Ransom. "Vision by Sweetwater" from *Selected Poems*, Third Edition, Revised and Enlarged by John Crowe Ransom. Copyright 1927 by Alfred A. Knopf, Inc. and renewed 1955 by John Crowe Ransom. Reprinted by permission of the publisher.

Adrienne Rich. "Living in Sin," "Snapshots of a Daughter-in-Law," "Face to Face," "Orion," "A Valediction Forbidding Mourning," "From a Survivor," are reprinted from *The Fact of a Doorframe, Poems Selected and New, 1950–1984*, by Adrienne Rich, by permission of W. W. Norton & Company, Inc. Copyright © 1984 by Adrienne Rich. Copyright © 1975, 1978 by W.W. Norton & Company, Inc. Copyright © 1981 by Adrienne Rich. "In Memoriam: D.K." is reprinted from *Time's Power, Poems 1985–1988*, by Adrienne Rich, by permission of W. W. Norton & Company, Inc. Copyright © 1989 by Adrienne Rich.

Theodore Roethke. From *The Collected Poems of Theodore Roethke:* "The Lost Son," "The Waking," "I Knew a Woman" Copyright 1947, 1953, 1954 by Theodore Roethke. "Root Cellar" Copyright 1943 by Modern Poetry Association, Inc. "My Papa's Waltz" Copyright 1942 by Hearst Magazines, Inc. "In a Dark Time" Copyright © 1960 by Beatrice Roethke, Administratrix of the Estate of Theodore Roethke. All poems used by permission of Doubleday, a division of Bantam, Doubleday, Dell Publishing Group, Inc.

Philip Roth. From *Goodbye Columbus* by Philip Roth. Copyright © 1959 by Philip Roth. Reprinted by permission of Houghton Mifflin Company.

Susanna Haswell Rowson. From *Charlotte Temple* by Susanna Rowson, edited by Cathy N. Davidson. Copyright © 1987 by Cathy N. Davidson. Reprinted by permission of Oxford University Press, Inc.

Louis Ruchames. From *The Abolitionists* by Louis Ruchames. Copyright © 1963 by Louis Ruchames. Reprinted by permission of The Putnam Publishing Group.

Anne Sexton. "Her Kind," from *To Bedlam and Part Way Back* by Anne Sexton. Copyright © 1960 by Anne Sexton. "All My Pretty Ones" and "The Truth the Dead Know" from *All My Pretty Ones* by Anne Sexton. Copyright © 1962 by Anne Sexton. "Us" from *Love Poems* by Anne Sexton. Copyright © 1967, 1968, 1969 by Anne Sexton. All reprinted by permission of Houghton Mifflin Company.

Leslie Marmon Silko. From *Storyteller* by Leslie Marmon Silko. Copyright © 1981 by Leslie Marmon Silko. Reprinted by permission of Seaver Books, New York, New York.

Susan Sontag. Excerpts from *Against Interpretation* by Susan Sontag. Copyright © 1966 by Susan Sontag. Reprinted by permission of Farrar, Straus & Giroux, Inc.

William Stafford. From *Stories That Could Be True* by William Stafford: "Traveling Through the Dark," "Accountability," "The Farm on the Great Plains," "At the Bomb Testing Sight," "The Epitaph Ending in And" copyright © 1960, 1965, 1973, 1976, 1977 by William Stafford. "After Arguing Against the Contention . . . " from *A Glass Face in the Rain* by William Stafford, copyright © 1978 by William Stafford. "An Oregon Message" from *An Oregon Message* by William Stafford, copyright © 1987 by William Stafford. All reprinted by permission of Harper & Row, Publisher, Inc.

Wallace Stevens. Reprinted from *The Collected Poems of Wallace Stevens* by permission of Alfred A. Knopf, Inc. "Sunday Morning," "Thirteen Ways of Looking at a Blackbird," "Nuances of a Theme by Williams," "Anecdote of the Jar," "The Snow Man," "Tea at the Palaz of Hoon," "The Emperor of Ice-Cream" copyright 1923 & renewed 1951 by Wallace Stevens. "The Idea of Order at Key West," "Anglais Mort à Florence," copyright 1936 by Wallace Stevens & renewed 1964 by Holly Stevens. "Of Hartford in a Purple Light" and "Asides on the Oboe" copyright 1942 by Wallace Stevens. "So-and-So Reclining on Her Couch" copyright 1954 by Wallace Stevens. "Angel Surrounded by Paysans" copyright 1950 by Wallace Stevens. "To an Old Philosopher in Rome" copyright 1952 by Wallace Stevens. "The Course of a Particular" and "Of Mere Being" copyright © 1957 by Elsie Stevens and Holly Stevens.

Edward Taylor. From *Poems of Edward Taylor*, edited by Donald E. Stanford. Copyright © 1960 by Donald E. Stanford, renewed 1988. Reprinted by permission.

Henry David Thoreau. "Resistance to Civil Government" from *Writings of Henry D. Thoreau: Reform Papers*. Copyright © 1973 Princeton University Press. Reprinted with permission of Princeton University Press. "Economy"; "Where I Lived . . . "; "Brute Neighbors"; "Spring"; "Conclusion" from *Walden: Writings of Henry D. Thoreau*. Copyright © 1971, 1989 Princeton University Press. Reprinted with permission of Princeton University Press.

Thomas Bangs Thorpe. "The Big Bear of Arkansas" from *Humor of the Old Southwest*, edited by Hennig Cohen and William B. Dillingham. Copyright © 1964, 1975, The University of Georgia Press.

Alice Walker. "Everyday Use" from *In Love & Trouble* by Alice Walker. Copyright © 1973 by Alice Walker. Reprinted by permission of Harcourt Brace Jovanovich, Inc.

Eudora Welty. "Petrified Man" from *A Curtain of Green and Other Stories* by Eudora Welty. Copyright 1939 and renewed © 1967 by Eudora Welty. Reprinted by permission of Harcourt Brace Jovanovich, Inc.

Phillis Wheatley. From *The Poems of Phillis Wheatley:* Revised and Enlarged Edition, edited by Julian D. Mason. Copyright © 1989 The University of North Carolina Press. Reprinted by permission.

Walt Whitman. Reprinted by permission of New York University Press from *Walt Whitman: Leaves of Grass,* Reader's Comprehensive Edition, edited by Harold W. Blodgett and Sculley Bradley. Copyright © 1965 by New York University.

Richard Wilbur. "Love Calls Us to the Things of This World" from *Things of This World* by Richard Wilbur. Copyright © 1956 and renewed 1984 by Richard Wilbur. "For Dudley" from *Walking to Sleep* by Richard Wilbur. Copyright © 1969 by Richard Wilbur. "The Writer" and "To the Etruscan Poets" from *The Mind Reader* by Richard Wilbur. Copyright © 1971, 1975 by Richard Wilbur. "Lying" from *New and Collected Poems* by Richard Wilbur. Copyright © 1987 by Richard Wilbur. All reprinted by permission of Harcourt Brace Jovanovich, Inc.

Tennessee Williams. *The Glass Menagerie* by Tennessee Williams. Copyright 1945 by Tennessee Williams and Edwina D. Williams and renewed © 1973 by Tennessee Williams. Reprinted by permission of Random House, Inc.

William Carlos Williams. "Tract," "El Hombre" "Portrait of a Lady," "Overture to a Dance of Locomotives," "Spring and All," "The Red Wheelbarrow," "The Wildflower," "The Attic Which Is Desire," "This Is Just to Say," "The Locust Tree in Flower" (2 versions), "The Yachts," "Fine Work With Pitch and Copper," "The Late Singer" from *Collected Poems Volume I, 1909–1939* by William Carlos Williams. Copyright 1938 by New Directions Corporation. Reprinted by permission. "Landscape With the Fall of Icarus" from *Collected Poems Volume II, 1939–1962* by William Carlos Williams. Copyright 1944, 1948, © 1962 by William Carlos Williams. Reprinted by permission of New Directions Publishing Corporation.

Edmund Wilson. Excerpts from *The Triple Thinkers* by Edmund Wilson. Copyright 1938, 1948 by Edmund Wilson. Renewal copyright © 1956, 1971 by Edmund Wilson and © 1976 by Elena Wilson. Reprinted by permission of Farrar, Straus and Giroux, Inc.

Richard Wright. From *Uncle Tom's Children* by Richard Wright. Copyright 1936 by Richard Wright, renewed © 1964 by Ellen Wright. Reprinted by permission of Harper & Row, Publishers, Inc.

PHOTO ILLUSTRATIONS

American Antiquarian Society, Worcester, Mass.: p. 258. Amistad Research Center Collection: p. 1545. AP/Wide World Photos: pp. 1473, 1528, 1646, 2009. Courtesy of The Art Institute of Chicago, Helen Birch Bartlett Memorial Collection: p. 1440. Association of American Railroads, Washington, D.C.: p. 620. The Berkshire Museum: p. 440. Brian J. Berman: p. 2113. The Bettman Archive: pp. 133, 311, 497, 1008, 1105, 1146, 1302, 1370, 1423, 1458, 1486, 1487, 1539, 1553, 1555, 1584, 1590, 1613, 1623, 1646, 1668, 1742, 1744, 1804, 1805, 1838, 1884, 1916, 2025. Boston Athenaeum: p. 936. Courtesy of the British Museum: pp. 15, 247. Brown University Library: p. 373. Courtesy of the Chicago Historical Society: p. 1000. Nancy Crampton: pp. 1897, 1906, 1985. Culver Pictures: pp. 1289, 1497. Field Museum of National History: p. 209. Ewing Galloway, N.Y.: p. 443. Giraudon/Art Resource: p. 1500. Eugene Gordon: p. 1691. The Historical Society of Pennsylvania: p. 160. By permission of the Houghton Library, Harvard University: p. 629. The Henry E. Huntington Library and Art Gallery: pp. 55, 1438. Independence National Historic Park, Philadelphia: p. 317. Thomas Jefferson Memorial Foundation: p. 213. The Jones Library, Incorporated, Amherst, Mass.: p. 1106. Paul Briol/Kenyon College: p. 1791. Photo © Lamson, Portland: p. 959. Library of Congress: pp. 52, 100, 132, 271, 495, 627, 735, 833, 845, 856, 989, 996, 1001, 1167, 1179, 1612, 1641, 1642, 1840, 1959, 2024. Lilly Library, Indiana University: p. 375. Robert Capa/Magnum Photos: p. 1670; Elliott Erwitt/Magnum Photos: pp. 1697, 2065; Burt Glinn/Magnum Photos: p. 1794. Courtesy of Masco Corporation: p. 1143. Massachusetts Historical Society: p. 344. Rollie McKenna: pp. 1859, 1865, 1917. Photo by Barbara McKenzie, University of Georgia Press, Athens, Ga. Reproduced with permission: p. 2010. Gerard Melanga: p. 1949. Metropolitan Arts

Commission, Portland, Oregon: p. 1943. The Metropolitan Museum of Art, Bequest of Gertrude Stein, 1946: p. 1591. Mississippi Department of Archives and History, Eudora Welty Collection: p. 1987. Missouri Historical Society: pp. 1268, 1270. Moorland-Spingarn Research Center, Howard University: p. 983. Courtesy of Mount Holyoke College: p. 592. Movie Still Archives: pp. 1961, 2066. © Maria Mulas: p. 2047. Museum of the City of New York: pp. 1005, 1138. NASA: p. 1693. National Archives: pp. 1409, 1415, 1955. National Gallery of Art, Washington, D.C.: pp. 346, 1905. National Portrait Gallery, Smithsonian Institution: pp. 345, 733, 1182, 1477. Nebraska State Historical Society: p. 1585. New England Mutual Life Insurance Company, Boston: p. 46. New-York Historical Society, New York City: pp. 216, 258, 921, 960 (Gift of Miss Eliza Alice Hoovenden, great-niece of the artist). New York State Historical Association, Cooperstown: p. 364. New York Public Library: pp. 7, 22, 24, 25, 44, 77, 119, 157, 231, 232, 246, 259, 281, 282, 309, 320, 334, 430, 584, 593, 594, 623, 946, 1277, 1305, 1648, 1702. The Perry Pictures, Boston Edition: p. 954. Philadelphia Museum of Art, Louise and Walter Arensberg Collection: p. 1417. Roger-Viollet, Paris: p. 1148. Photo by Sarony, New York: p. 953. Smith College Library, Rare Book Room: p. 1918. Sterling Memorial Library, Yale University: p. 1371. A. J. Telfer, Cooperstown, New York: p. 362. Courtesy of University of New Mexico Press: p. 2089. Courtesy of Worcester Art Museum: p. 319. Collection of Mr. and Mrs. William Carlos Williams, Rutherford, N.J.: p. 1459. Yale University Art Gallery: p. 203.

Index